The Official NFL Encyclopedia of Pro Football

A National Football League Book

Prepared by the Creative Services Division,
National Football League Properties, Inc.

Edited, Written, and Compiled by
Bill Barron,
Tom Bennett,
David Boss,
Jim Campbell,
Larry Eldridge, Jr.,
Chuck Garrity, Jr.,
Jack Hand,
Jim Natal,
Beau Riffenburgh,
Seymour Siwoff,
Rick Smith,
and John Wiebusch

Designed by
Nancy Evans,
Glen Iwasaki,
and David Johnston

Production Coordinated by
Jere Wright

The Official NFL Encyclopedia of Pro Football

NAL BOOKS

NEW AMERICAN LIBRARY

TIMES MIRROR

NEW YORK AND SCARBOROUGH, ONTARIO

A National Football League Book

Prepared by National Football League Properties, Inc., Creative Services Division.

"A Diagram History of Football"
From the book *The Pro Style* by Tom Bennett. Copyright 1976 by National Football League Properties, Inc. Published by Prentice-Hall, Inc., Englewood Cliffs, New Jersey.

Library of Congress Catalog Card Number: 82-81659
ISBN 0-453-00431-8

NAL BOOKS TRADEMARK REG. U.S. PAT. OFF. AND FOREIGN COUNTRIES
REGISTERED TRADEMARK—MARCA REGISTRADA
HECHO EN CRAWFORDSVILLE, INDIANA, Y WILLARD, OHIO, U.S.A.

SIGNET, SIGNET CLASSICS, MENTOR, PLUME, MERIDIAN, and NAL BOOKS are published *in the United States* by The New American Library, Inc., 1633 Broadway, New York, New York 10019; *in Canada* by The New American Library of Canada Limited, 81 Mack Avenue, Scarborough, Ontario M1L 1M8.

First Printing, September, 1982
1 2 3 4 5 6 7 8 9
PRINTED IN THE UNITED STATES OF AMERICA

CONTENTS

Introduction 7
ROOTS OF PRO FOOTBALL 9
    The history of the sport before the formation
    of the National Football League in 1920.
SEVEN DECADES OF THE NFL 17
    The chronological history of the league and
    the annual standings and statistical leaders
    of pro football.
THE RECORD HOLDERS 65
    Color photographs of some of the men
    whose names and NFL accomplishments
    will go down in history.
THE GROWTH OF PRO FOOTBALL/EXTINCT
TEAMS, EXTINCT LEAGUES 103
    NFL teams and rival professional leagues
    that failed, including maps tracing the geo-
    graphical spread of the game.
TEAMS OF THE NFL 125
    Chronological history, annual won-lost
    record, coaching history, first player selected,
    and all-time player roster for each NFL team.
    Atlanta Falcons 126
    Baltimore Colts 130
    Buffalo Bills 136
    Chicago Bears 141
    Cincinnati Bengals. 150
    Cleveland Browns 154
    Dallas Cowboys. 160
    Denver Broncos. 165
    Detroit Lions 170
    Green Bay Packers 179
    Houston Oilers. 189
    Kansas City Chiefs 194
    Los Angeles Rams. 199
    Miami Dolphins. 207
    Minnesota Vikings. 212
    New England Patriots 217
    New Orleans Saints 222
    New York Giants 226
    New York Jets 236
    Oakland Raiders 241
    Philadelphia Eagles 246
    Pittsburgh Steelers. 255
    St. Louis Cardinals 264
    San Diego Chargers. 273
    San Francisco 49ers. 278
    Seattle Seahawks. 284
    Tampa Bay Buccaneers 287
    Washington Redskins. 290

ALL-TIME TEAM VS. TEAM. 299
THE SUPER BOWL 321
CHAMPIONSHIP GAMES 355
DIVISIONAL PLAYOFF GAMES. 381
WILD CARD GAMES 395
PRO BOWL GAMES 399
    Pro Bowl selections 408
CHICAGO ALL-STAR GAMES 415
ALL-PROS 425
    All-pro squads of the decades 433
THE HALL OF FAME 437
    Hall of Fame classes and presenters 466
ALL-TIME RECORDS 467
THE DRAFT 499
A DIAGRAM HISTORY OF PRO
    FOOTBALL. 505
PRO FOOTBALL LANGUAGE. 515
STADIUMS OF PRO FOOTBALL 521
RULES OF THE GAME 533
    Digest of the rules; major rules changes
    in NFL history; the tools of NFL officials;
    official signals; penalties.
A HISTORY OF FOOTBALL EQUIPMENT 551
Acknowledgments . . . ; 560
Photography credits 560

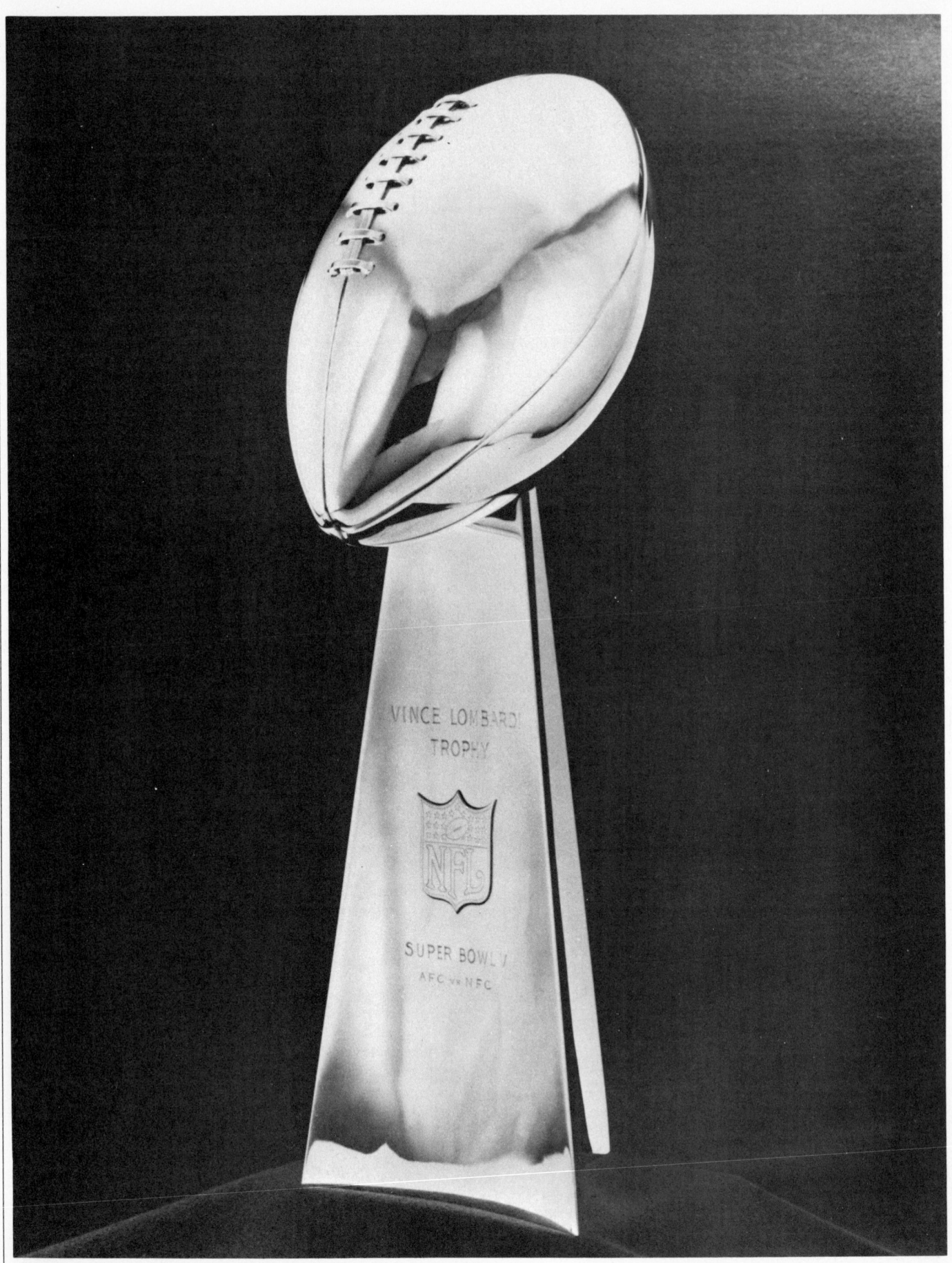

The Vince Lombardi Trophy, which is emblematic of the Super Bowl championship.

INTRODUCTION

A dedicated, modest, and rather mysterious researcher in Pittsburgh walked into the office of Daniel M. Rooney of the Pittsburgh Steelers several years ago and handed him a 49-page paper on early pro football in Pennsylvania. Rooney greeted him and studied the paper briefly. The two of them talked for a few moments and then the visitor departed. Rooney read further in the report and began to see that it had great value. The manuscript was, however, unsigned. Rooney frantically searched his memory; what was the visitor's name? It was, as best he could recall, Nelson Ross. He tried to track down Ross, even enlisting the help of the Pittsburgh newspapers. Finally he turned the manuscript over to the NFL office in New York City. After the construction of the Pro Football Hall of Fame in Canton, Ohio, in 1963, the Ross paper was sent there and filed away.

Accompanying the paper was a yellowing expense sheet prepared by O. D. Thompson, manager of the Allegheny Athletic Association in Pittsburgh in 1892. The expenses included the following: "Game performance bonus to W. Heffelfinger for playing (cash) $500.00." This expense sheet was put on display in the Hall of Fame. Inexplicably, it was displayed for years immediately next to a cubicle of photos of John Brallier of the Latrobe, Pennsylvania, Y.M.C.A. team of 1896. The display hailed Brallier as the first professional football player in history. William (Pudge) Heffelfinger, however, antedated Brallier by four years.

Ross's paper was "rediscovered." A determined effort was made to study its findings and put them in perspective. At the same time, a second researcher, Thomas Jable of William Paterson College in New Jersey, presented a paper to the annual convention of the American Association of Health, Physical Education, and Recreation in 1976 corroborating Ross's findings, largely through the study of old newspapers in Pittsburgh. Jable's report added new details to the account of Heffelfinger and the Allegheny Athletic Association.

The works of Ross, Jable, and an expert on early pro football in Ohio, Milton Roberts, are collected here for the first time in any pro football work of history, in the chapter entitled "Roots of Pro Football" (pages 9-16). Disciplined, determined to get to the heart of this subject, possessed of a wit that can be seen around the rough edges of his writing, and yet so modest that he did not even type his name on his manuscript, the mysterious Nelson Ross has left pro football an important document.

The presentation of Ross's research is one bit of evidence that *The Official NFL Encyclopedia of Pro Football* is a major effort to produce the most comprehensive and entertaining history of pro football ever done. Admittedly, this book, which has been revised and up-dated from its last publishing in 1977, has had an advantage—the source, subject, and creator are the same. This is the NFL's book about itself. It has been produced, however, with objectivity and with an eye for what is enjoyable to the reader and useful to the researcher.

Pro football is the greatest success story in American sport. Because of its stability and its relative youth, therefore, it may be assumed that producing a history of it is an easy thing to do. It is not. Ross's material and additional research into the early Pennsylvania and Ohio period opens up a whole new era, and uncovers numerous teams to study and classify.

Practically every pro football fan is familiar with the American Football League that began in 1960. How many are informed, however, about the AFLs of 1926, 1936-37, and 1940-41? Each of them failed and added to the profusion of franchises, teams, coaches, and players. So did the All-America Football Conference in 1946-49 and the World Football League of 1974-75.

Twelve current NFL teams played in another city, had another name, or started in the AAFC. The Decatur Staleys became the Chicago Staleys in 1921 and the Chicago Bears in 1922. The Boston Braves became the Boston Redskins in 1933 and the Washington Redskins in 1937. The Pittsburgh Pirates became the Pittsburgh Steelers in 1941. The Portsmouth Spartans became the Detroit Lions in 1934. The Cleveland Rams became the Los Angeles Rams in 1946. The Baltimore Colts, Cleveland Browns, and San Francisco 49ers moved from the AAFC to the NFL in 1950, but the Colts folded in one year's time. An entirely different Colts' team reappeared in 1953.

The Chicago Cardinals became the St. Louis Cardinals in 1960. The Los Angeles Chargers became the San Diego Chargers in 1961. The Dallas Texans became the Kansas City Chiefs and the New York Titans became the New York Jets in 1963. The Boston Patriots became the New England Patriots in 1971.

The appropriate nickname appears in this book anytime a New York team is mentioned because of the many teams that have played in that city—the Crescents, Knickerbockers, Giants, Yankees, Americans, Bulldogs, Yanks, Titans, Jets, and Stars.

There has been a tendency for cities to reinstate the nicknames of failed franchises. Even though a team may not succeed, it was the pioneer of pro football in a city and the citizens seemingly want to perpetuate that name. Examples are the nicknames "Baltimore Colts," "Buffalo Bills," and "Cincinnati Bengals." In each case, there was a team in the city by that name before the advent of the present team. Nelson Ross also proved there was a team called the "Pittsburgh Steelers" in 1902.

Philadelphia and Pittsburgh merged in 1943, when World War II made the going rough for pro football teams, and became a club named the "Steagles." When Pittsburgh and the Chicago Cardinals merged a year later, they became the less outlandish but functional "Card-Pitt." The wins, losses, and ties of these aberrations have gone into the record of each of their member teams.

In the contemporary method of figuring pro football percentages, ties count as a half game won and a half game lost; that has been the rule since 1972. Every compilation done since then has been done by that rule. Thus, the all-time totals for teams in this history are figured that way, whereas, year-by-year percentages before 1972 are not.

"Modern" is the most relative of terms. Periodic references in football histories to "modern-day football" may only define the period of the writer's consciousness of the sport. So-called "firsts" may not be firsts at all. The Chicago Bears did not "invent" the T-formation and man-in-motion in 1940; both were part of the game of football at the turn of the century. Marion Motley, Bill Willis, and Kenny Washington did not "break the color line" in football in 1946; there were black players in the sport as early as 1904. Dan Reeves and Tony Morabito did not "open the west coast to professional sports"; a football team called the Los Angeles Bulldogs made a transcontinental road trip in 1937, had an unbeaten record, and won the American Football League championship. The careless delineation of "firsts" and the setting up of a period of "modern-day football" in which all those "firsts" took place are two mistakes this publication has avoided.

Similarly, the Pro Bowl did not begin with Otto Graham's great performance for the American Conference in 1951. It began 12 years earlier, in the same city and with the same partners in sponsorship, the NFL and the *Los Angeles Times*. Five games were played before World War II. This book is the first ever to publish lineups, line scores, and scoring summaries of every Pro Bowl game, and a table of all-time selections for the game. The section begins on page 399.

Another famous football event, the Chicago All-Star Game, which is the subject of an entire chapter (pages 415-423), was canceled in 1976. It is now an extinct species but a complete history of it is preserved in this *Encyclopedia*.

The all-pro teams listed in the book (pages 425-436) are the teams considered to have been official each year.

The all-time records (pages 467-498) include AFL records from 1960-69. The AFL is the only league to succeed in merging fully with the NFL and having its statistical feats entered for consideration along with those of the NFL as all-time professional football records. Another league, the All-America Football Conference of 1946-49, had famous players who later became stars in the NFL after the limited merger in 1950, but AAFC achievements were not accepted for the all-time records.

A variety of categories were used in the past to determine the individual passing leader each season. Since 1973, quarterbacks have been rated, based on performance standards established for completion percentage, interception percentage, touchdown percentage, and average gain. Passers are allocated points according to how their marks compare with those standards, and the points are then converted to a scale roughly approximating 100.0.

Punting statistics began in 1939, interceptions in 1940, and punt and kickoff returns in 1941.

There are four position designations in pro football that were first used in the 1960-69 AFL and gained acceptance in the NFL (approximately 1966). They are running back instead of halfback and fullback; wide receiver and tight end instead of end; and cornerback instead of defensive halfback.

The emergence of the 3-4 defense in the 1970s brought about the position designation of nose tackle (or middle guard). There are four linebackers in the 3-4—two outside (left and right) and two inside (left and right).

NFL history is a rich and lively subject that is chronicled as never before in *The Official NFL Encyclopedia of Pro Football*. This is a complete reference book that will provide you with countless hours of informative and entertaining reading.

I recommend it to you highly.

Pete Rozelle
Commissioner, National Football League

Roots of
Pro Football

The game we call "football" is indigenous to North America. It is about 100 years old. It did not have one inventor; rather, it developed gradually from soccer to rugby to "rugby football" to football. Why? Because these games were fun and people kept tinkering with them and improving them so they would be even more fun. At last football emerged, but then another quarter-century or more passed before it began to look anything like what we would recognize as the game today. Many rules changes were made and football became the biggest college sport. Athletic clubs and imitative town teams took it up. At the end of this long chain of events, professional football arrived, perhaps in 1892. It was centered in Pennsylvania and then it spread to Ohio. There the league that eventually became known as the "National Football League" was formed in 1920. It was a curious and novel little organization then but it went on to great success. How that happened cannot be fully understood without returning to the tumultuous years of the growth of this American game, to trace the roots of pro football.

I. GROWTH OF COLLEGE FOOTBALL

American football comes from English soccer and rugby. Soccer is called football on other continents; it is the most popular game in the world. Rugby is also played practically everywhere, the by-product of British imperialism. American football is the cousin of these games and they all involve, in one way or another, the kicking of some object up and down a field. This has been a natural thing for humans to make a game of as long as the species has had feet. The kicking games of primitive tribes, *harpaston* in the Greek city-state of Sparta, *calcio* in ancient Rome, and the varieties of soccer that have been played for perhaps 2,000 years, according to Allison Danzig, can be considered ancestors of football. The ball used in those games might have been leather filled with sawdust, the bladder of some slaughtered animal, or the skull of an adversary slain in battle.

Soccer football was played in the American colonies, according to John Allen Krout in *Annals of American Sport*. "Here and there in the records of colonial days," he wrote, "one catches glimpses of boys and young men, occasionally young women, playing a game known as football. It might more accurately have been called handball, for throwing and passing the inflated bladder or sawdust-filled leather seems to have been more important than kicking it. In the latter part of the eighteenth century this haphazard game assumed a place with fisticuffs, wrestling matches, and drinking bouts, enjoyed by undergraduates, as a means of relief from the severe mental discipline of college life."

Two important steps in the evolution of football then occurred in the mother country of England. First, rugby was invented. A student at the Rugby School named William Webb Ellis picked up the ball and ran with it during a soccer football game in 1823. The rules forbade advancing the ball any way except kicking it, and the other players in the game were outraged at Ellis for breaking the rules. His innovation, however, became the basis for a new game, one that would influence American football greatly because the runner could carry the ball and not just kick it. Ellis also became the subject of countless stirring juvenile stories about bold young men unafraid to go against the mainstream of opinion, to be nonconformists. A photograph of the plaque at Rugby College commemorating Ellis's achievement is virtually a requisite in any football history. Of Ellis's later life, Krout wrote that the inventor of rugby "became a London clergyman and rector of St. Clement Dane's in the Strand."

The second thing that happened in England was the formation of the London Football Association in

1862. It was organized by the proponents of the kicking game. They drew up rules forbidding the carrying of the ball. From then on their game was called association football or soccer. But that was not their largest contribution to American football. More importantly, they wrote rules that independent-minded Americans would overhaul and rewrite to create their own rules. And by having a rules convention the British established a rite of the sport, a tradition as much a part of it as bringing the uniforms out of storage for the first practice each year and blowing up the footballs.

There was high school soccer football before there was college soccer football. Boston secondary schools were playing games against each other on the Common as early as 1860, according to Allison Danzig in *The History of American Football*. Gerritt Smith Miller, a student at the Dixwell School from Peterboro, New York, organized the Oneida Football Club of Boston, "the first definite and formal football organization in the United States," in 1862.

College football began November 6, 1869. Rutgers and Princeton both had soccer football teams and they were close to each other, so they played a game. It vaguely resembled what we know as football today. Each team had 25 players, the ball was advanced by kicking it or butting it with the head, and there were goal posts that were 25 yards apart. These were modified London Football Association rules. The first team to make six goals won, and Rutgers triumphed six goals to four.

Yale and Columbia also had soccer football teams. Princeton and Yale formed football associations for games between classes. Harvard, however, played a different game, one more like rugby, called the "Boston Game." Canada then made the next and one of the most important contributions of all to the evolution of football. McGill University in Montreal played rugby; the sport had probably been brought to Canada by the British army. McGill played three games against Harvard in 1874, two at Cambridge and one at Montreal. As a result of these games Harvard took up rugby completely instead of soccer. The rugby principles of running with the ball and tackling had a foot in the door of American football.

It seemed as if everyone had different rules, and the sport was in a state of confusion. Then came the Massasoit convention of 1876 at which the first rules for American football were written. That same year the imposing figure of the man who would become the father of the game as we know it today, Walter Camp of Yale, appeared on the stage of football.

In a football game today, the ball does not pass back and forth at random but instead is held by each team for at least four downs. Each has to make a given number of yards, 10, in those four downs or lose the ball. Each has 11 players on the field. The principal handler of the ball is the "quarterback." The center snaps the ball to him. Walter Camp is responsible for all these innovations. Parke Davis, the Plutarch of early college football, wrote that, "What Washington was to his country, Camp was to American football—the friend, the founder, and the father."

A Yale athlete and coach, Camp was so heroic and romantic a figure, so chivalrous, so simon-pure of motive and deed, that he was said to have been the model for the fictional character "Frank Merriwell of Yale" on which a whole generation of American boys were weaned.

Camp was so respected as a football authority that, while he wore the hat of magazine writer, he alone was archbishop at the annual coronation in *Collier's Weekly* of the knights of the gridiron, the All-Americas.

He ruled over the first college football juggernaut, Yale, before 1910. And he created the Daily Dozen exercise program for a feeble and flabby American

public. He was aristocratic, a *bon vivant* and raconteur who was a celebrity and living legend everywhere he went.

When Walter Camp entered Yale in 1876, he was the product of one of the correct New Haven families and of the exclusive Hopkins Grammar School. He learned the variety of football then being played at Yale from Gene Baker, the captain of the team. Baker was Yale's delegate to the convention at the Massasoit House, a hotel, in Springfield, Massachusetts. Playing rules were adopted there and an intercollegiate association was formed; it was the forerunner of the National Collegiate Athletic Association. The rules it adopted resembled those of rugby and it was called rugby football.

Camp played halfback in rugby football. He was a brilliant runner and kicker, a dashing figure with a flowing mustache and long hair held in place by a headband; in actuality he looked very much like many young men a century later. With Camp making drop-kicks or picking up the ball and darting through the entire opposing team, Yale won 25, lost 1, and tied 6 in six years of intercollegiate play. At last, in a move aimed directly at him, the annual rules convention limited eligibility to five years. By then, Camp was in the Yale Medical School, and captain of the football team for the third time. He left medical school just one year short of his degree. He gave as his reason the fact that he could not stand the sight of blood, but it really may have been because he could no longer captain the Yale team and also compete, as he had, in baseball, track (he is credited by some with having been the first to run the hurdles and not jump each of them), tennis, and gymnastics.

The most remarkable fact of Camp's student days, however, is that he represented his university at the annual rules convention as a sophomore, in 1877. At that point, the game was one in which the ball was put down on the field with both teams clustering around it and all of them kicking at the ball and trying to drive it free. Someone finally would succeed in picking it up and starting off on a run. Then he probably would meet opposition and kick the ball away or make a lateral or backward pass. But he also may have been knocked to the turf before doing any of these things.

In 1880, Camp had an idea to give one side undisputed possession of the ball until that side, of its own volition, gave the ball up. This was passed by the rules convention, and Camp had invented scrimmage. In the same year, he convinced his colleagues that a team should number 11, not 15, players. Further, the person receiving the ball from a "snapback," later called a center, should be called the "quarterback." Snaps were first made with the foot. Later, players were allowed to guide the ball with a hand. Finally they came to center entirely with the hands.

Having created the position of quarterback, Camp, as Yale captain, then became the first to have his quarterback call signals. For example, the quarterback would say, "Play up sharp, Charlie!" if a kick was about to be made.

But Camp's conviction that the chivalrous Ivy Leaguers would gladly give up the ball when they could not gain ground during scrimmage was ill-founded. The "block game" resulted; one team kept the ball the whole first half and the other the whole second half. This led Camp to suggest—and the convention pass—a rule requiring a team to make five yards in three downs; it was increased later to 10 yards in four downs.

There always are ready opportunities for the well-born and the former football star; Camp was both. After leaving medical school he took a position with his uncle's business, the New Haven Clock Company. He also kept his affiliation with Yale; indeed, he would soon dominate its athletic department. And he would continue to be a member of one committee of football rulesmakers or another until the day he died.

Camp never was a paid coach nor did he ever assume the title. Instead, a series of coaches drew their authority from him. And he held the purse strings of the fund made from Yale Field gate receipts.

Tad Jones, who had been a Camp player and was later Yale's coach, explained that, "Camp coached through the coaches. He seldom took an active part on the field. ... He had no more authoritative position than treasurer of the Yale Field Association, but his advice had authority because it was good advice. The practice then was to have the former year's captain return as head coach, and Camp, by serving every year as adviser, gave unity and continuity to these shifting assistants."

Coach, captain, and quarterback met with Camp on Sunday afternoons in the library of his home on Gill Street in New Haven to discuss the mistakes of the previous day's game and plan the tactics of the coming game. Yale prospered, regularly beating the other members of the Big Three, Harvard and Princeton.

In 1888 Camp proposed—and the convention passed—a rule permitting tackling as low as the knees. Its effect on football was stupefying. Runners who were tackled that way went down to stay. The savage mass play era dawned. Offenses contracted and bunched themselves around the runner. The dangerous "wedge" appeared. Lorin Deland of Harvard created the even more dangerous flying wedge. Camp and Yale fostered the shoving wedge. Play became brutal, fights proliferated, and there were deaths on the gridiron.

A public outcry arose. The mass play era split intercollegiate football, led to the White House conference of 1905 and the subsequent formation of the NCAA.

President Theodore Roosevelt called representatives of Yale, Harvard, and Princeton to the White House, according to Allison Danzig, and told them to clean up football. "Brutality and foul play should receive the same summary punishment given to a man who cheats at cards."

The President could provide moral leadership but the real reform of football occurred in the nuts-and-bolts work of the rules committees. There were two meetings in December, 1905 and as a result of them an old and new committee combined themselves and the Intercollegiate Athletic Association was formed. The name was changed to National Collegiate Athletic Association later.

Camp headed the old committee, Captain Palmer Pierce of West Point the new, and they sat down together for the first time in January, 1906. They legalized the forward pass. More reforms were made in succeeding years. But the game of football had been defined by Camp and his associates and it was this game that the National Football League adopted in 1920 and did not change for more than a decade.

II. PREHISTORIC PRO FOOTBALL

Sports took root in America after the Civil War. People fled the factories and went outdoors to ride bicycles and play golf and other sports. One of the most important aspects of this movement was the advent of the athletic club. The first was the New York Athletic Club in 1868, according to sports historian John R. Betts. Virtually every other city acquired one after that. These clubs sponsored teams in a great variety of sports. They gave tremendous impetus to competition in all of them. And they probably started pro football.

The photographs are still with us today, legions of them in seemingly endless supply, with players reclining somber-faced in their uniforms in front of pastoral studio backdrops, a melon-shaped football at

their feet with lettering such as "Johnstown A.C. 1891" on them. It is astonishing how many team pictures remain. Clearly, club football teams were everywhere. Were they all, every club and every player, amateurs? Probably not.

One of their number, William (Pudge) Heffelfinger of the Allegheny Athletic Association of Pittsburgh, received what history records as the first payment to play football in 1892. But he was the most famous player of his day; others more obscure than Heffelfinger may have received payments earlier than he did. And it is known that some athletic clubs bent the rules and awarded their players in ways that carried the clubs to the brink of professionalism—and perhaps beyond.

Baseball had gone professional with the formation of the American Association in 1871 and the new Amateur Athletic Union was determined to stop this "evil" from spreading to other sports, and rid them all of the "tramp athlete," the opportunist who moved about and sold his services to college or athletic club. He was the bane of the athletic world and the AAU gained much support. It grew into an organization with great power. Each year it held a sports carnival in New York City where athletes could compete for national championships in their respective sports.

But the AAU inadvertently helped bring about the rise of pro football. In 1889, six athletic clubs in the East decided to copy the parent AAU and form their own union, or league. They were the Baltimore Athletic Club, the Boston Athletic Association, the New York Athletic Club, the New York Crescents Athletic Club, the New York Manhattans, and the Orange, New Jersey, Athletic Club. They played for the "amateur title of America" each year for over a decade. There was now a league of amateur teams. The next step was to begin talking about going professional.

The AAU moved against what it believed to be professionalism on two fronts in 1890. The San Francisco Olympic Athletic Club was accused by a rival of obtaining jobs for its players in order to get them to jump to the Olympic Club. The AAU decreed, however, that while San Francisco's action was not to be commended, it was not actually professionalism, only a "semi" form of it; the Olympic Club got off with a reprimand and the term "semipro" was born.

In New Jersey, the Orange Athletic Club awarded trophies or watches to its best players at the end of each season. Accusations were made against Orange but apparently this was the practice of several clubs in the New York City area. According to Dr. Harry March, the recipient of the gift could then be seen "threading his way to some well-known pawnbroker where the watch was placed in hock, the usual sum received thereby being a sawbuck—twenty smackers. Then the player, still strictly amateur, somehow ran across the man who managed those amateur games and sold him the pawn ticket for another twenty dollars. By some special sense of divination, second sightedness or mental telepathy, the promoter found himself urged towards the same pawn shop and under an irresistable impulse, retrieved the pawned watch, paying a small interest and twenty dollars. Then, after the next game, the player received as his trophy the same gold watch, which then went through the same identical loaning experience."

The AAU ruled that clubs could no longer award trophies; they had to limit their gifts to banners costing 25 cents apiece. But the big athletic clubs continued to find ways to get around the rules. One way was to hand out travel expenses equal to double the amount of the fare. There obviously were "professional" players on athletic clubs in other cities before a celebrated "ringer" named Pudge Heffelfinger was paid $500 under the table by a club in Pittsburgh and started the recorded history of pro football.

III. THE PENNSYLVANIA PERIOD

Pennsylvania is an historic state. It was one of the 13 original colonies. The Articles of Confederation, Declaration of Independence, and Constitution were signed there. General George Washington and his troops encamped there at Valley Forge in 1777. Later, the Civil War reached its turning point when a Confederate army led by General Robert E. Lee advanced as far north as Gettysburg—and met defeat.

Much westward expansion moved across Pennsylvania's breadth. In the west, the Allegheny and Monongahela rivers meet in Pittsburgh and form the mighty Ohio River. This great waterway was the gateway to the West for American settlers for 200 years.

Similarly, the game of football moved toward becoming a professional game westward from colleges such as Yale, Princeton, Rutgers, and Harvard, across Pennsylvania to Pittsburgh where, through the phenomenon of the athletic club, the first known pro football was played. Pro football then moved directly westward into Ohio, into towns such as Akron, Canton, and Massillon. And they and others formed what became the NFL.

Pittsburgh's first athletic clubs were the Allegheny Athletic Association and the Pittsburgh Athletic Club. Such clubs emerged after the Civil War, according to researcher Thomas Jable, as an antidote to Victorianism. American men could through competitive athletics at their clubs "countermand the Victorian principles of delicacy and refinement." Football, aggressive and sometimes violent, served this need especially well; it "represented a significant triumph of robust manliness over tender and fragile femininity." Membership in an athletic club also meant prestige and an opportunity to identify vicariously with the big names in college football.

Anyone who has ever arrived at a city park all set for a good, hard-fought touch football game, only to see that the opposition has brought along a few surprise players all of whom are better and more experienced than anyone else there, is familiar with the term "ringer." And ringers hired by the Allegheny Athletic Association of Pittsburgh in 1892 were the first pro football players.

In Jable's words, "As competition increased in intensity and winning became important, the athletic club turned to the established athlete from the outside ... In hiring the gifted player or professional, the athletic club shattered the amateur ideal upon which it was founded, that is, participation for the sheer love of the game. Victory meant fame, glory, and increased income for the athletic club. Big money was made by individual members who wagered heavily on their club's eleven. From this atmosphere at the athletic club, professionalism crept into football as the Allegheny Athletic Association and the Pittsburgh Athletic Club vied for notoriety, prestige, and profits."

The Allegheny Athletic Association was organized by two Pittsburgh businessmen, John Moorehead and O.D. Thompson, who were graduates of Yale and who had played football there. The club was called "A.A.A.," the "A.A.A.'s," "Three A's," and as it edged nearer professionalism, sometimes "Four A's" with a tongue-in-cheek extra "A" for "amateur." It had the first club football team in Pittsburgh in about 1890.

The Pittsburgh Athletic Club was located in the city's East End. Its gym was the largest and best in western Pennsylvania; for that reason the team was sometimes called the "Gyms." The Pittsburgh Athletic Club was older than the A.A.A. It formed a football team in 1891 because it felt the A.A.A. team was getting more than its share of publicity in the Pittsburgh newspapers.

Professor William Kirschner was the physical director of the P.A.C. and became its star football player. Researcher Nelson Ross writes that Kirschner "had little football experience, but he possessed tremendous strength and size and learned quickly." And he was probably a semi-professional.

"Professor Kirschner received a regular salary for teaching his gym classes," Ross writes. "It was noted, however, that during the football season his 'teaching' salary went up considerably. It was denied that this had any connection with his playing on the P.A.C. football team, but rivals noted that while his salary doubled his classes were only half their normal size during the football season. Pittsburgh papers were at times critical of Kirschner's status but no one accused him outright."

P.A.C. challenged A.A.A. to a game. A.A.A. ignored the challenge. The feud grew hotter when A.A.A. lured away four of P.A.C.'s best players. At last a game was scheduled for Columbus Day, October 21, 1892 at the P.A.C. field in Pittsburgh's East Liberty section. More than 3,000 spectators flocked to the grounds, Jable wrote, "in drags, tallyhos, dog carts, street cars, and railroad cars. They filled the seating accommodations at P.A.C. Park to more than capacity. Hundreds more packed the surrounding buildings from the first floor to the roof, viewing the game at no expense. More spectators would have been in attendance had not the lengthy Columbus Day parade prevented a number of street cars and other public conveyances from reaching East Liberty. The fashionable crowd was evenly split between the two teams, though each faction was easily distinguishable by the colors it wore. P.A.C. rooters wore red and white ribbons, while the A.A.A. followers donned blue and white colors."

The game ended in a 6–6 tie. Dr. George Proctor, a physician, scored the only goal for P.A.C. and Norman McClintock of Yale, playing for A.A.A., scored its goal. The same players also kicked their teams' goals; a touchdown counted four points and a successful place kick counted two. The teams divided $1,200 in gate receipts and as a result of the great interest in the game each club processed about 100 new members during the weeks that followed.

The news that P.A.C. had played a ringer, however, stirred new hostilities. A.C. Read, captain of the Pennsylvania State College team and a shotputter, had played for P.A.C. under the name of "Stayer." The P.A.C. captain had misled A.A.A., saying "Stayer" was an old friend he had met him on the street and invited him to play in the game. A.A.A. was incensed to learn that "Stayer" was actually the Penn State captain, and as A.A.A. plotted how to get even, a famous Yale All-America who was then in faraway Chicago loomed in the future of Pittsburgh football.

William Walter (Pudge) Heffelfinger played guard for Yale in 1888–1891. Walter Camp was his mentor and Amos Alonzo Stagg his teammate. Heffelfinger made the first All-America team ever selected, in 1889. He also made the team for two more years and has been one of the guards on virtually every all-time All-America team selected anywhere since. In 1892, his Yale days behind him, he was working in a nondescript railroad office job in Omaha, Nebraska, when he grew bored and asked for a leave of absence in order to join a Chicago amateur club called the Chicago A.A. on an Eastern tour in which it would play teams in Cleveland, Rochester, Princeton, Philadelphia, Cambridge, and Brooklyn. The Chicago A.A. was a controversial member of the AAU. Its playing manager, Billy Crawford, was paying ample expenses to players and enraging the AAU with talk of a "professional football league" in cities such as Chicago, Detroit, Cleveland, Pittsburgh, and New York; he was a man 28 years ahead of his time.

The Chicago A.A.'s tour was not scheduled to stop

in Pittsburgh, but it was the talk of the athletic clubs there, and when the tour reached Cleveland two members of the Pittsburgh Athletic Club were in the stands to watch the game. "Both cheered wildly," wrote Ross, "when the magnificent Heffelfinger hit the Cleveland fullback so hard that he fumbled the ball, with William grabbing it and streaking with incredible speed for a man so large, over the Cleveland goal line."

The big rematch in Pittsburgh between the P.A.C. and A.A.A. was a few weeks away. The people of Pittsburgh were shocked to read in the *Press* of October 30 that P.A.C. was rumored to be offering $250 each to Heffelfinger and another Chicago A.A. player, Knowlton (Snake) Ames, to play against A.A.A. The rumors persisted as the game drew nearer.

Many years have gone by since that fateful game, and as time has passed football teams have learned to squash rumors that they are close to signing a player to a contract. Negotiations can always go sour at the last minute and the team is left with nothing except an unsigned contract and a credibility gap. This postulate of present-day football was not there for the Pittsburgh Athletic Club to follow in 1892. And when the arch-rivals of club football lined up against each other at Recreation Park on Pittsburgh's North Side November 13, Heffelfinger was there all right, but not with P.A.C. He was in the colors of the hated A.A.A. So were his former Chicago A.A. teammates Ed Malley, a shotputter from Detroit, and Ben (Sport) Donnelly, former Princeton star; Snake Ames had decided to forego the game rather than risk his amateur status.

It was a cold day and there was snow on the ground. A crowd of about 3,000 watched as the Pittsburgh Athletic Club angrily protested the presence of A.A.A. ringers. All bets were off, P.A.C. declared. It offered to play a scrub game. While the crowd grew restive, the substitutes of each team began to play while the regulars argued. O.D. Thompson, the manager of A.A.A., pointed out that P.A.C. planned to play A.C. Read, "Stayer" in the first game, this time under his real name, and P.A.C. also had Clarence Lomax of Cornell and Simon Martin of the Steelton, Pennsylvania Athletic Club in its lineup. The arguments continued until the two teams at last agreed to play an "exhibition" game with all bets canceled. They settled on two 30-minute halves. A.A.A. won 4–0. Heffelfinger picked up a fumble by one of his teammates, ran around end, and went 25 yards for a touchdown. Ed Malley missed the place-kick for goal. The bickering before the game had delayed it and darkness now ended it 18 minutes into the second half.

Heffelfinger demonstrated a vicious method for breaking P.A.C.'s wedge. "...When P.A.C. wedged down the field, he ran and jumped at it with full speed, bringing his knees against the mass. The wedge didn't last long."

The P.A.C. captain, Charley Aull, left the game with a badly injured back. His brother, Burt, retired after receiving "a fierce blow to the head." Sport Donnelly received "a terrific smash in the eye."

After the game Heffelfinger was paid $500 for playing and $25 for expenses, Malley and Donnelly $25 for travel. Heffelfinger was thus the first professional football player on record. Gross receipts totaled $1,683. After Heffelfinger's fee, a visitors' guarantee of $428, and miscellaneous expenses, the A.A.A. made a profit of $621.

A furor over professionalism raged for weeks in Pittsburgh's newspapers. O.D. Thompson, A.A.A. manager, a skillful lawyer, and the man primarily responsible for making Heffelfinger a professional, left town. He went to New York to defend A.A.A. track stars named E.V. Pant and J.B. McKennan

against AAU charges that *they* were professionals.

A guard and assistant manager on the football team named Billy Kountz was left to fend off the questions the press was asking about pros on the A.A.A. Thompson returned too late for a rubber match to be played against P.A.C. Heffelfinger and Malley left Pittsburgh but Sport Donnelly stayed and one week after the P.A.C. game played for A.A.A. against Washington and Jefferson College; he was paid $250 and thus became the second known pro football player in history. The next year three players named Rafferty, Van Cleve, and Wright (their first names are not known) became the third, fourth, and fifth when they received contracts to play for A.A.A. for $50 a game—the first pro football contracts in history. The athletic clubs threw caution and their AAU affiliation to the wind and ended forever the pretense that they were "amateur." Allegheny Athletic Association was barred permanently from the AAU in 1895. Many of its members resigned. The others, who openly admitted their professionalism, imported Heffelfinger, Donnelly, and other members of the touring Chicago A.A. and other well-known football players such as Tom (Doggie) Trenchard and Langdon (Biffy) Lea of Princeton. They played back-to-back games in 1896 against P.A.C. and the new Pittsburgh Duquesnes, November 10 and 11, and won both games, 18–0 and 12–0. Heffelfinger and the other imports apparently were paid a staggering $100 a game. The players who had been together in 1892 enjoyed their reunion and held marathon beer drinking sessions talking over old times. A.A.A. finished the season playing a barnstorming tour against amateur teams in western Pennsylvania, West Virginia, and Ohio. But the payroll for the back-to-back games in November had bankrupted the club. By 1897, "for all practical purposes, it ceased to exist as a functioning year-round club," Ross wrote. "Professionalism and its opponents had dealt it a death blow." There was one more uneventful season before the club broke up when its most patriotic members left to fight in the Spanish-American War. When they returned there were high-priced bidding contests as they sold their services to the Duquesnes or P.A.C. What was left of A.A.A. sponsored an amateur team made up of Western Pennsylvania Theological Seminary students, a team that must have been quite different in character from the rollicking Alleghenies of earlier years.

America's first known pro football team had come and gone. It was, however, just the beginning for Pittsburgh's early adventures in the sport. There followed a calamitous period in which a wealthy Pittsburgh man named W.C. Temple became the first known club owner in pro football history; he was joined in that capacity by two of the city's foremost steel tycoons, one of whom later became the president of U.S. Steel; open football professionalism spread to the clubs of the small towns in the surrounding coal region; pro football appeared in other states; and a "World Series" was played indoors at Madison Square Garden in New York City in both 1902 and 1903, antedating—and giving rise to—the same event in the game of professional baseball.

Wealthy men who donate their means to help others can count on never being forgotten. William Chase Temple was an industrialist who donated the "Temple Cup," a portentous silver trophy, to the winner of a playoff between the first-place and second-place finishers in the National League of Professional Baseball Clubs between 1894 and 1897 (there was no American League in baseball until 1901). Temple also gave a cup to the winner of the football "Challenge Cup" competition among Pittsburgh's three athletic club football teams. The newest of them was the Duquesne Country and Athletic Club, or Pittsburgh Duquesnes. This team ran up a

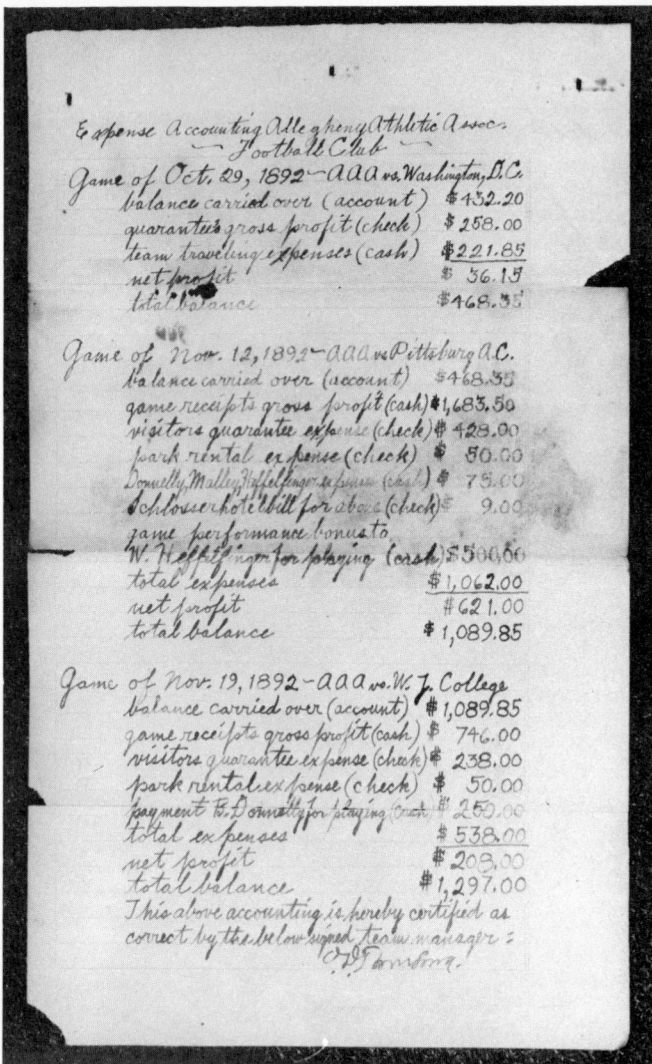

William (Pudge) Heffelfinger (left) and the Allegheny Athletic Association expense sheet proving he was a professional football player in 1892.

huge payroll in signing players returning from the Spanish-American War. In 1899, it found itself in the unique position, according to Ross, of having every player on the team salaried and its payroll considerable. It looked to the wealthy Temple for help. He bought the football team from the athletic club and thus became pro football's first individual owner.

William E. Corey and A. C. Dinkey were next. They were Pittsburgh steel barons and friends of Temple. They formed teams to play his Duquesnes. But while he had a big-city team theirs were located in the grimy steel mill towns of Braddock and Homestead east of the city. Interest in club football ran high there among the miners and mill laborers who dug the ore and worked the blast furnaces. Corey's team was the Braddock Carnegies, the original club team having been named earlier for steel magnate Andrew Carnegie; Dinkey's was the Homestead Library and Athletic Club, or Athletics, or, later, Homestead Steelers.

Corey was a generous, kindly man whose team was made up mostly of steelworkers; it had only a few token college products. The steelworkers got a football bonus in addition to their regular salaries and were excused from work in the mills during football season.

Dinkey, in contrast, went after the big college All-Americas. He also raided Temple's Duquesnes for players. With such high-priced talent, Dinkey won the "world's championship," which actually meant the championship of the athletic clubs in and around Pittsburgh, in 1900 and 1901.

Friendships among wealthy men often are tested by sports competition. Temple was outraged by Dinkey's actions. Temple and owner Barney Dreyfuss of the baseball Pittsburgh Pirates—a name gained through pirating the players of other teams—formed a new football club called the Pittsburgh Professionals, or Pros. For the first time a team openly admitted it was professional. It immediately began raiding back the players Dinkey had stolen. And to stir interest and support, Temple and Dreyfuss decided to use their contacts in baseball and get an intra-state rivalry going with Philadelphia.

There is still one team in American sports whose name goes all the way back to the era of athletic clubs and their preeminence. It is the Oakland Athletics. This baseball team, which a famous manager named Connie Mack led for a half-century, played in Philadelphia until 1954, in Kansas City until 1968, and is now in Oakland.

In 1902, Mack's team was American League champion. He and Ben Shibe, the owner, then decided to field a football team, too. So did the rival Philadelphia Nationals or Phillies of the National League. During the 1902 season, the Athletics, Phillies, and the Pittsburgh team that was known that year either as the Pros or the Stars played games against each other. Mack's team was 11–2–1 in all games for the season, according to researcher Milt Roberts; 2–1 against the Phillies and 1–1–1 against Pittsburgh.

Pitcher Rube Waddell played on Mack's football team some of the time. In one of the three games against Pittsburgh, pitcher Christy Mathewson played fullback for Pittsburgh. Because of the presence of these famous baseball personages, the one-year foray of Mack into football is given perhaps more importance than it deserves in some histories. Nevertheless, he could rightfully claim the pro football championship of 1902.

Philadelphia defeated Pittsburgh 11–0 in midseason. They met again Thanksgiving Day, November 27, at Exposition Park in Pittsburgh. The crowd was not as large as expected because there was also a college game between Pittsburgh and Washington and Jefferson being played that day. Mack, the Athletics' manager, was concerned that the gate receipts were going to be too small and refused to put his team on the field unless he was paid his $3,000 guarantee in advance. Arguments followed and the crowd grew restive. William Corey, owner of the Homestead Steelers, was sitting in the stands; his enlightened methods of operation as a club owner, in which he employed his steelworkers as players instead of big-name stars, no doubt explained why he was merely a spectator at this championship game. He, too, was anxious for the game to begin.

"He went down to the cluster of debators on the field," Ross wrote. " 'What's the delay?' he asked.

When told by Mr. Mack that the Athletics wanted their $3,000 guarantee in advance, he snorted, wrote out a check for $3,000 and said, 'Let's get the game started.' Handing the check to Mack, he turned and walked away. Mack wasn't so sure about taking checks from strangers, but when he was informed Mr. Corey carried almost as much weight as Andrew Carnegie himself, his mouth dropped open and the game commenced."

It ended in a 0–0 tie but it was such a hard-fought, exhausting game that spectator Corey got his money's worth, according to Ross. Pittsburgh won a third game the following Saturday by the score of 11–0, which must have pleased Corey. Apparently that was Connie Mack's last trip to Pittsburgh with his football team.

The first "world series" was played in football, not baseball. Furthermore, football was played indoors more than half a century before the Astrodome, Louisiana Superdome, Silverdome, Kingdome and every other arena in which pro football was later played under a roof. Pro football was growing in popularity not only in Pennsylvania in 1902, but in other states as well. The New York Knickerbockers, a football team about which little else is known, was impressed with the interest shown in the Philadelphia-Pittsburgh games and conceived the idea of a world series. It was actually to be a four-team tournament, and a promoter named Tom O'Rourke arranged for it to be held in Madison Square Garden, the original Garden at Madison Avenue and Twenty-Sixth Street in New York City.

There was one world series in 1902 and another in 1903. The first was played between the Knickerbockers, the Philadelphia Athletics, the Watertown, New York, Red and Blacks, and the Syracuse, New York, Athletic Club. Syracuse won. Glenn (Pop) Warner, later a famous coach of the Carlisle Indian School, Stanford, and other college teams, played center for Syracuse in the first World Series.

The second was in 1903 and included Philadelphia, Watertown, the Orange, New Jersey, Athletic Club, and the Franklin, Pennsylvania, Athletic Club, which had lured away many of the best players from Pittsburgh with high salaries. Franklin defeated every other team and won the tournament.

World series were important events and, according to Dr. Harry March in *Pro Football's Ups and Downs,* "Frank Hinkey, former Yale end, and Big Bill Edwards officiated the night football games at Madison Square Garden in evening dress—tuxedos, top hats, white gloves, and patent leather shoes.

"In the very last play of the Franklin-Watertown game, with the contest safely in the bag, the Franklin backfield huddled and agreed to run over Frank Hinkey, dress suit and all. They did, soiling him effectively and emphatically. He took it good-naturedly and the Franklin management paid his cleaning and pressing bill."

Football's world series did not become a lasting event but baseball adopted the idea and, in its first series, Boston of the American League defeated Dreyfuss's Pittsburgh team of the National League in 1903, five games to three. There was no series in 1904 but it was resumed in 1905 and there has been one ever since.

There was professional football in other Pennsylvania cities. Lawson Fiscus, celebrated Princeton player, apparently got $20 a game in 1894 to play for the Greensburg, Pennsylvania, Athletic Association. John Brallier, quarterback at Indiana, Pennsylvania, State College in 1895, accepted $10 and "cakes"—expenses—to play for the Latrobe, Pennsylvania, Athletic Club.

Brallier later became a dentist in Latrobe. He corresponded with Dr. Henry March, the New York Giants' doctor and a dabbler in pro football. Brallier

wrote that he had been the first professional football player in history in 1895 with Latrobe. March published Brallier's claim in his 1934 book, the rambling, often misinformed *Pro Football's Ups and Downs.* Brallier became a figure of history. The game in which he had played for the first time for Latrobe was called the first pro game in history. The myth grew; the Pro Football Hall of Fame was almost located in Latrobe instead of the city of the founding of the NFL, Canton, Ohio. It was not until 1971 that Nelson Ross's research and an actual expense sheet of the Allegheny Athletic Association showing it paid Pudge Heffelfinger $500 in 1892 proved that Heffelfinger, not Brallier, was the first known pro.

Other pro football teams not in Pittsburgh included the Olympic Athletic Club of McKeesport, Jeanette Athletic Association, Pitcairn Quakers, Conshohocken Pros, Coaldale Big Green, and Pottsville All-Service.

Pro football declined in Pittsburgh after 1903. The Alleghenies had faded from view. The Duquesne Country and Athletic Club had been absorbed by the Pros or Stars and they in turn by the Franklin team that won the second world series. The Mill teams at Braddock and Homestead disappeared when their owners, Corey and Dinkey, lost interest; Corey, one of the first three club owners in pro football, became president of United States Steel in August, 1903 and held that position until 1911.

Several players from the Pittsburgh Athletic Club were hired by the Massillon, Ohio, Tigers. That made Massillon a professional team. More Ohio towns followed suit and hired pro players from Pennsylvania. The Pennsylvania period of early pro football history ended and the Ohio period began.

Pennsylvania had both the big-city athletic clubs and the small town teams. Arguments continue today over which contributed the most to the game. The sport is young enough that octogenarians who remember club or town football in Pennsylvania still totter into the Hall of Fame occasionally and argue long and hard for the contributions of one or the other. The stories they tell of pro football in Pennsylvania at the turn of the century are rich and colorful.

IV. THE OHIO PERIOD

Athletic clubs and their "ringers" ushered in pro football. It "came out of the closet" in Pennsylvania when teams there openly declared themselves pros. And it grew into a league in Ohio. This was one of the most important steps in American sports history.

That it happened where it did was no accident. Ohio is steeped in history and its strategic location between Lake Erie and the Ohio River in the path of westward expansion has made it the setting for countless historical events.

George Rogers Clark defeated the Indians in the French and Indian War in Ohio in 1780. Commodore Oliver H. Perry defeated the British in the War of 1812 off Put-in-Bay, Ohio, and sent his famous message, "We have met the enemy and he is ours." Settlers moved west along Ohio's National Road or went by water along the Ohio on barges, flatboats, or steamers. Some of the settlers rooted themselves in Ohio and became its farmers or its steel, coal, oil, and rubber barons and made the state one of the industrial centers of America. Army notables Ulysses S. Grant, William Tecumseh Sherman, and George Armstrong Custer were born in Ohio.

Ohio had seven presidents between 1876 and 1920: Grant, Rutherford B. Hayes, James A. Garfield, Benjamin Harrison, William McKinley, William Howard Taft, and Warren G. Harding. Both candidates in the presidential election of 1920 were Ohioans, Harding and Governor James M. Cox.

John D. Rockefeller and his associates formed the Standard Oil Company and cornered the oil markets

of the U.S. from their base in Cleveland. Wilbur and Orville Wright, Dayton bicycle repair shop mechanics, were the first to achieve flight in 1903 at Kitty Hawk, North Carolina. Annie Oakley of Darke County, Ohio, was traveling with Buffalo Bill's Wild West Show.

The purpose of this exterior history is an obvious one; it is to show that the advent of professional football in Ohio was not an isolated event in a remote place. The game grew up in prosperous, growing cities; the population of rubber capital Akron was 69,067 in 1910 and Canton's was 50,217. And these cities were in the eye of the press and public. McKinley and Harding both ran their presidential campaigns from their front porches, McKinley in Canton and Harding in Marion, and they kept their homes in those Ohio cities while they were president.

In this setting, pro football arrived. Predictably, it had its roots in athletic club teams. According to Nelson Ross, there were club teams in Dayton in 1889, Cleveland in 1890, Cincinnati in 1891, Akron in 1894, and Canton and Youngstown in 1895. Other club teams appeared in Alliance, Byesville, Columbus, Lorain, Marion, Newark, Sandusky, Salem, Shelby, and Toledo. There was a state champion proclaimed every year after 1896, according to Ross.

"But in 1903 a new team appeared on the horizon named the Massillon Tigers. That town had never had an independent football team before, but organized one for the '03 season, defeated amateur Canton in the first of many blood battles between them, and then promptly challenged defending and unscored-on state champion East Akron A.A. in a game for the amateur title of Ohio."

Massillon imported professionals from the Pittsburgh Athletic Club, won the game 12–0, and professionalism had invaded Ohio football.

Within one year, the state had at least eight pro teams and in 1904 there was an abortive attempt to form a league and end cutthroat bidding for players. It

Herman Kerchoffe, stolen from Massillon in 1906.

The Nesser family of Columbus, Ohio, which gave six sons to pro football.

became the second known discussion of a pro league, the first having been by Billy Crawford of the Chicago Athletic Association in 1892. Ohio's attempts to form a league in 1904 never amounted to anything, either, and the all-out scrambling for players continued.

There were three periods of pre-1920 pro football in Ohio. The first extended from the importation of the first pros by Massillon in 1903 until 1906, when scandal in a game between Canton and Massillon rocked the sport, shamed the participants, and caused interest in the sport to decline; the 1907–1914 era, which historian Milton Roberts calls "the unglamorous years" of early Ohio pro football; and the period of 1915-19, when Canton signed Jim Thorpe, former Carlisle Indian Industrial School star and the hero of the 1912 Olympics. Thorpe had his greatest years in that period.

Canton also was the site of the organizational meeting of the league in 1920. But the other cities and teams of Ohio pro football had their appeal, too.

Eddie Stewart, the city editor of the *Massillon Independent*, and Charles (Cy) Rigler were prominent managers of the football team in Massillon. It got the name "Tigers" when Stewart bought a supply of jerseys with striped sleeves, in the style of Princeton University, at a cut rate from a sporting goods store. Massillon was state champion in 1904, 1905, and 1906. It suffered a stinging defeat at the hands of Canton in 1911, dropped out of football for a while, and returned in 1916.

A.A. (Buzz) Wesbacker, who was a high school coach in Greensburg, Pennsylvania in 1917, also played for the Massillon Tigers. "The pro games were always on Sunday," he recalled, "and each team would get together Sunday morning with the coach, who would map out the plays and signals. We would practice for an hour, and that was it. If the coach liked the way you played in the actual game, you were signed up for the following week.

"I got fifty dollars a game and expenses. The crowds were mostly rubber, steel, and factory workers. The games were played on baseball fields with stands on one side and a rope stretched on the other; that was standing room only, where most of the betting took place. The bets were placed on the ground, just inside the rope, anchored with a rock, never to be touched until the game ended. At times some young punk would try his luck at getting the loot, only to be warned with a big juicy spit of tobacco near his feet. It certainly was effective."

Akron was such a hotbed of football that in the days of amateur teams it had not one but two of them. When East Akron lost the 12–0 game to Massillon in 1903, the first known game west of Pennsylvania to have involved professionalism, Akron pretended to disdain the hiring of pros for a while. By the end of 1904, however, according to Ross, it was one of the cities pushing the hardest in the ill-fated attempt to organize a pro league that year.

The Akron Indians, state champions in 1909, were a team of players from Southeast Akron who had played football together since they were boys. They lost the championship in 1910, however, to the Shelby Blues, who were led by George (Peggy) Parrott, a former star player for Case Western College in Cleveland. By 1913, however, Parrott had switched his allegiance to Akron; he led that team to a victory over Shelby. Parrott became a celebrated player-manager who was a lively promoter of the game and recruiter of talent. He enjoyed beating the rival Canton Bulldogs. In 1914, he imported the entire left side of Norte Dame's 1913 line, including end Knute Rockne, later the Notre Dame coach, and Akron beat Canton 21–0 and was named the state champion.

The players for the Columbus Panhandles were, in their regular jobs, mechanics for the Panhandle Division of the Pennsylvania Railroad. "They had free transportation and so they were an inexpensive team to play," Dr. Harry March wrote. "The boys worked in the shop until four o'clock Saturday afternoon, got their suppers at home, grabbed the rattlers [trains] to any point within twelve hours' ride of Columbus, played the Sunday game, took another train to Columbus, and punched the time clock at seven Monday morning."

Joe Carr organized the Panhandles in 1904 when he was assistant sports editor of the *Ohio State Journal* in Columbus. Carr's sports involvement grew and he became the manager of the minor league baseball team in Columbus and a professional basketball team. He later became president of the National Football League from 1921 until his death in 1939.

Katherine and Theodore Nesser, German immigrants who lived in Columbus, had six sons and all of them became professional football players for the Columbus Panhandles. They were Al, Frank, Fred, John, Phil, and Ted. It was the only time in history that six members of the same family played pro football.

The Dover Canals got their name because Dover was a port on the Ohio and Erie Canals. The Elyria Athletics represented Elyria, named for the Ely family that founded the town. Elyria came out of nowhere and shocked Canton to win the Ohio championship in 1912. The Shelby Blues had the first known black professional football player, Charles Follis, in 1904.

No other Ohio team, however, made as much history or contributed as much to professional football before 1920 as the Canton Bulldogs. They turned pro in 1905. Outsiders were imported with the express purpose of beating the arch-rival Massillon Tigers, seven miles to the west, and taking the Stark County and Ohio professional championships. The ringers didn't help, however; Massillon went undefeated, beat Canton 14-4, and won the state championship again. More Canton-Massillon battles, and an eventful 1906 football season, loomed ahead.

In 1906, Peggy Parrott joined Massillon. Canton's playing coach, Bill Laub, was injured and did not return. He was replaced by Blondy Wallace, who would become a figure of notoriety almost unparalleled among all pro football coaches. Wallace, according to Dr. Harry March, "knew where to get the right men, how to condition them, and how to build up an attack and defense, but he never won their confidence in his integrity and honesty."

Wallace raided Massillon's team and landed four of its players—Clark Schrontz, Jack Lang, Jack Hayden, and Herman Kerchoffe. It was the year that the rules committee of Walter Camp and his associates legalized the forward pass, and Wallace took the Canton Bulldogs to Pennsylvania State College to learn the new maneuver from the coach there.

Canton and Massillon played a two-game series in 1906. The games were eagerly awaited in the neighboring cities and even far outside their realm of Stark County and Ohio. Grantland Rice, the most eminent of sportswriters, wrote grandly before the first game: "There have been a few football games before. Yale has faced Princeton, Harvard has tackled Penn, and Michigan and Chicago have met in one or two steamy affairs. But these were not the Real Product when measured by the football standard set by the warring factions of Stark County, Ohio, now posing in the football limelight."

He even penned these lines of verse about the game:

In days of old when Knights were bold,
And barons held their sway—
The atmosphere was rife, I hear,
With war cries day by day.
From morn to night, they'd scrap and fight
With battle ax and mace—
While seas of blood poured like a flood
About the market place.
But no fight ever fought beneath the shining sun
Will be like that when Canton's team lines up
with Massillon.

The two titans of pro football squared off for the first time at the Tigers' field on the grounds of the Ohio state asylum in Massillon. A big crowd watched. Some stood atop a trolley car stopped on the tracks nearby, others along the top of the rickety wooden fence that surrounded the field. Massillon won 10–5. The second game was at Canton two weeks later and the Tigers won again 13–6.

Controversy swelled around both games. "Canton players had been drawing very little money from Wallace," March wrote, "letting him keep their funds for fear a big poker game or other luxuries would lead them to extravagance. They had asked him to bet the money on the first game with Massillon.

"When the game resulted in a Massillon victory he told the fellows he had bet it on the second game."

Wallace's troubles had just begun. The *Massillon Independent* accused him of having tried to throw the second game by influencing the Massillon players and, failing that, persuaded a Canton player to throw it. "When accused by his teammates," March wrote, "this player said he had simply obeyed orders as he was accustomed to do. At any rate he left town hurriedly, on the first train, in his playing togs—his belongings following later—maybe."

A Canton fan who lost heavily on the second game confronted the Bulldogs' players at the Courtland Hotel bar in Canton. Angry words were exchanged. Punches were thrown, and soon a brawl was in progress. The crowd surged through a plate glass window and out into Court Street, where police arrived and broke it up with their night sticks.

Blondy Wallace sued the *Massillon Independent* for libel. The suit was thrown out of court.

Shamed, Canton quit pro football. Its "big team" (there were neighborhood teams that sprang up periodically) apparently did not return for five years, until 1911. In 1912, a 21-year-old clerk at the Canton gas company named Jack Cusack became the secretary-treasurer of the team. Cusack had good business sense, organized well, and was a hard worker. During the next few years he would bring about one organizational triumph after another in behalf of the Canton Bulldogs, climaxed by signing Jim Thorpe. Then Cusack would leave the city forever, and perhaps also leave behind a chance at ever gaining a niche in the Hall of Fame for his contributions to early pro football.

Cusack accepted the job of secretary-treasurer in 1912 as a favor to Roscoe Oberlin, who owned the team. H.H. Halter was manager and resented the intrusion of a man as young as Cusack. Halter was having trouble negotiating a contract for games with Peggy Parrott and the Akron Indians; Parrott felt Akron was a bigger drawing card than Canton and therefore did not have to divide the gate receipts evenly with the Bulldogs. Cusack entered the negotiations and, after five hours of dealing with Parrott, came away with the half-and-half arrangement. Halter was ousted as manager.

The team took the name "Professionals," to make fans forget the tainted past of the Bulldogs. It moved out to lease a new field, League Park. Cusack was made a full partner with Oberlin. They added 1,500 seats to the park in 1913 and sold season tickets for the first time in 1914. Cusack quit his job at the gas company to work full-time for the team. There were hard times as Cusack struggled to make a profit. He found a financial angel in J. J. Frey of the Home Brewing Company, who opened a $10,000 line of credit for the team at the Canton Bank. But Cusack's troubles continued. Center Harry Turner died of injuries he received in a game in 1914; Canton played out the season amid protests and before small crowds.

Jim Thorpe came to Canton in November, 1915. Cusack signed him for $250 a game just before the first game of the season against Massillon. Thorpe was the world's most celebrated athlete. A Sac and Fox Indian from Oklahoma, he had been a sensational halfback and All-America for the Carlisle Indian Industrial School in Carlisle, Pennsylvania, coached by Glenn (Pop) Warner. In 1912, he won the decathlon and pentathlon for the United States in the fifth modern Olympiad at Stockholm, Sweden. "Sir, you are the greatest athlete in the world," King Gustav V of Sweden told Thorpe as he presented him his medals. But heartbreaking sadness followed for Thorpe; his Olympic medals were taken from him when it was learned that he had played semipro baseball in Rocky Mount, North Carolina, for $25 a game in 1911 during the summer months while a student at Carlisle; unlike countless other college athletes who did the same thing, he had not played the professional sport under an assumed name. He was disgraced. When Jack Cusack signed him for Canton, Thorpe was the veteran of one season of pro football with Pine Village, Indiana, in 1913, was a reserve outfielder with the New York Giants during the summer months, and was employed in the fall months as backfield coach for the University of Indiana.

His one season with Pine Village had been insignificant; he now found in the Canton Bulldogs the right supporting cast to become a sensational professional player. Cusack also signed other notables from college football that year such as Hube Wagner of Pittsburgh, Bill Gardner of Carlisle, Earle (Greasy) Neale, the coach at West Virginia Wesleyan, and his line coach, John Kellison. Neale and Kellison played as pros under aliases.

Cusack's friends warned him he had made a terrible mistake in signing Thorpe for so much money. The Bulldogs, however, played before 6,000 fans at Massillon, losing 16–0. Thorpe is supposed to have slipped on the wet field on the way to two touchdowns. There were 8,000 fans for the second game at League Park in Canton. So many fans clamored to get into the park for the second meeting of the two teams that the Bulldogs sold standing-room-only tickets in the end zones and the two teams agreed on the ground rule that any player crossing the goal line into the crowd must be in possession of the ball when he emerged from it.

Thorpe dropkicked two field goals and Canton led 6–0. Three quarters went by and the Bulldogs were on the verge of a great victory. Massillon's passing attack began working, however, and an end named Briggs caught a pass on the 15-yard line and raced across the end zone, disappearing into the surging crowd. Gideon (Charley) Smith, the first black player on the Canton team, followed Briggs in mad pursuit into the crowd. There, out of sight, a Canton trolley-car conductor kicked the ball out of Briggs's hands and into the arms of Smith, who emerged from the sea of humanity onto the playing field, the ball in his hands. It was a touchback and Canton's victory was preserved.

Massillon fans streamed onto the field in protest. The officials called the game. Massillon demanded that the officials settle the matter by making a statement about the referee's decision awarding the touchback. The officials agreed but only if it could be placed in a sealed envelope and opened by the manager of the Massillon team at 30 minutes after midnight at the Courtland Hotel that night.

A tense crowd divided equally among Canton and Massillon supporters was on hand at 12:30 A.M. as the envelope with the statement was opened. It was read aloud and Canton's victory was upheld. Years later, the conductor whose kicking game equaled Thorpe's that day confessed to his crime while riding a streetcar through Canton with Jack Cusack.

The next season, 1916, was the best of all for Canton and Thorpe. "The 1916 Bulldogs," Cusack wrote in the 1960s, "were one of the greatest teams ever assembled, one I would match against any team in professional football today if they played under the rules and with the same ball in vogue at that time."

Thorpe missed the first two games because he was playing baseball for the Giants; Canton defeated Altoona, Pennsylvania, 23–0 and Pitcairn, Pa., 7–0. In his first game with the team, the Bulldogs swamped a team called the Buffalo All-Stars 77–0. The New York All-Stars fell 67–0. Canton then won a tough game against the Columbus Panhandles, who had five Nesser brothers in the lineup, by the score of 12–0; Cusack says in his memoirs that Thorpe made an 85-yard punt that day.

Canton defeated Peggy Parrott and the Cleveland Indians twice, 27–0 and 14–7. Thorpe made a 71-yard punt return in the first game and won the second on a touchdown run around end. Youngstown fell to Canton 13–0. The first game of the year against Massillon ended in a 0–0 tie when Thorpe left the game after the first quarter with a foot injury. For the second, Cusack signed Carlisle star Pete Calac and he and Thorpe led Canton to a 24–0 shutout of the Tigers. The season ended with Canton the professional champion of the world, winner of 10 straight games; its defense had allowed only seven points all season.

Early pro football in Pittsburgh had suffered when some of its players left the game to fight in the Spanish-American War in 1897. In 1917, 20 years later, Cusack and other pro managers in Ohio lost some of their best players to World War I. The Bulldogs still fielded another strong team, however, and played two stirring games against Massillon. Charlie Brickley, former Harvard All-America and a dropkicker of renown, now led Massillon. He imported "an entire Army Ambulance Corps team from Allentown, Pennsylvania" to play against Canton but the Bulldogs won the first game of the year between the two teams 14–3. In the second game, Thorpe and Stan Cofall, a former Notre Dame star now with Massillon, waged a dropkicking duel that Thorpe lost; Cofall's two field goals won the game for Massillon 6–0. Thorpe was later named the first president and Cofall the vice-president of the American Professional Football Association, forerunner of the NFL.

Cusack's strange and ill-timed departure from the Bulldogs followed. Apparently because of the war and the difficulties football managers were having in signing players, Cusack left the Bulldogs and went to Oklahoma to become an oil-field wildcatter. He caught malaria in Arkansas in 1921.

He eventually returned to Canton to recover from his illness and soon thereafter went to Cleveland where he became Jim Thorpe's personal business manager; Thorpe now played for the Cleveland Indians. Cusack visited Canton often but he never lived there again.

It remained for an automobile dealer named Ralph Hay to take over Cusack's Canton Bulldogs interests. It was Hay who was the owner of record when Canton was the site of the organizational meeting of the league that would become the NFL, in 1920. Every history of the sport, definitive or superficial, identifies Hay's Hupmobile agency showroom in Canton as the meeting site. He captured a permanent place in pro football history.

Cusack, in contrast, lived out his days in the oil business in Texas and Oklahoma. He was well off but he did not become a rich man. He enjoyed coming back to Canton and was prominent there even in the years after the completion of the Hall of Fame shrine in 1963. An old man, he could be seen at a gathering of one kind or another, standing quietly off to himself, alone in his thoughts of Jim Thorpe and the Bulldogs and the years when pro football grew up in Ohio. He died at 84 in 1974.

Seven Decades of the NFL

1920 There had been professional football in the United States for at least 28 years, since Pudge Heffelfinger played for Allegheny Athletic Association in Pittsburgh for $500 in 1892. The sport, however, was in a state of confusion. Teams were loosely organized and players moved freely from one to another. There was no control of the competitive bidding among teams for the best college football players. Pro football was operated poorly and governed hardly at all. A league in which all the member teams would follow the same rules of operation clearly seemed the answer and there had been talk of forming such a league as early as 1892, when the era of athletic clubs and their semi-professional teams were at their peak. A serious attempt at organization failed in Ohio in 1904.

A second attempt to form a league was now under way. A meeting was held among interested teams in August. A second meeting was held September 17, 1920 in Canton, Ohio. This city was prominent in professional football because of the rivalry that had gone on for many years between the Canton Bulldogs, for whom the famous athlete Jim Thorpe played, and the Massillon, Ohio, Tigers, whose home city was located seven miles west of Canton.

The teams that were represented at the meeting were from five states. A.F. Ranney, co-owner of the Akron, Ohio, Professionals, was elected the secretary of the group. He was faithful in recording in the minutes of the meeting the full names of the Ohio teams with which he was familiar. He was not as careful in recording for posterity the names of the other teams that were represented.

Attending were the Akron Pros; Canton Bulldogs; Cleveland, Ohio, Indians; Dayton, Ohio, Triangles; Decatur, Illinois, Staleys Athletic Club, or Staleys; Hammond, Indiana, Pros; Massillon Tigers; Muncie, Indiana, Flyers; Racine (a Chicago street) Cardinals; Rochester, New York, Jeffersons; Rock Island, Illinois, Independents; and "Wisconsin."

It was named the American Professional Football Association. Capitalizing on his fame, Thorpe was named league president. Stan Cofall of Massillon was elected vice-president and Ranney secretary-treasurer. A membership fee of $100 per team was arrived at to give an appearance of respectability; no team ever paid it. Each team agreed to print the words, "Member of American Professional Football Association" on its stationery.

"Mr. Marshall of the Brunswick-Balke Connender Company, Tire Division, presented a silver loving cup to be given the team awarded the championship by the Association. Any team winning the cup three times should be adjudged the owner.

"It was moved and seconded that a vote of thanks be extended by the Secretary to Mr. Marshall.

"The meeting was adjourned."

The owner-manager of the Canton Bulldogs was named Ralph Hay. He operated a Hupmobile automobile dealership and the meeting was held in his showroom. There were not enough chairs in the room and some of the persons present had to sit on the running boards and fenders of the automobiles.

The Buffalo, New York, All-Americans; Chicago Tigers; Columbus, Ohio, Panhandles; and Detroit Heralds joined the league later.

Professional teams had good years and bad. When they were winning, they could draw crowds and prosper; when they were losing, they suffered through hard times and dropped out of the competition. The Massillon Tigers were going through losing seasons at the time of the formation of the league, and so were the Muncie Flyers, and they did not field teams in 1920.

There were professional teams that attended APFA and, later, NFL meetings held at Atlantic City each

Jim Thorpe of the Canton Bulldogs; he also played for seven other NFL teams.

season, keeping their membership and paying dues but staying out of the competition until their chances for success improved.

The league was loosely organized. Teams played as many non-members as they did member teams. There were either no standings kept by anyone in the league or they were kept and have since been lost.

The typical stadium of the league was a minor league baseball park or an open field with circus bleachers seating some fans and others standing along the sidelines, separated from the action by a rope.

Akron, Buffalo, and Canton all claimed the championship and a hastily arranged series of games failed to decide the issue. One of the special games between the Canton Bulldogs and Buffalo All-Americans was played at the Polo Grounds in New York City. It "was the first real game between representative teams ever played in the metropolis and attracted over 15,000 paid admissions," Dr. Harry March wrote in *Pro Football's Ups and Downs*. "Buffalo won, 7 to 3, with Youngstrom blocking one of Thorpe's punts and falling on the ball for a touchdown. Thorpe kicked one field goal in three attempts. The New York newspapers said he was slowing down greatly."

The first recorded player deal occurred when Bob Nash, a tackle and end for Akron, was sold to Buffalo for $300 and five percent of the gate receipts.

1921 Professional football operators decided they needed more experienced leadership. Joe Carr, a

Columbus, Ohio, sportswriter, manager of the Columbus Panhandles, minor league baseball executive, and pioneer in professional basketball, was named president of the American Professional Football Association at a meeting in Akron April 30. Carr established the league office in Columbus. Carl Storck of the Dayton Triangles was named secretary-treasurer of the league.

The Chicago Tigers, beaten by the Cardinals in a 1920 game for the "rights" to Chicago, dropped out and so did Hammond. Green Bay, which was sponsored by the Acme Packing Company and coached by Earl (Curly) Lambeau, and the Cincinnati Celts joined to leave the membership at 13 franchises.

Jim Thorpe left the Canton Bulldogs and he and Joe Guyon, another famous Indian player who had attended the Carlisle Indian Industrial School, joined Cleveland.

Five teams who dropped out of the league early in the season had their records stricken, unfairly or not, from the league standings. They were Evansville, Indiana; Hammond, Indiana; Louisville, Kentucky; Minneapolis, Minnesota; and Muncie, Indiana.

A. E. Staley was the owner of the starch company in Decatur, Illinois that sponsored the Staleys Athletic Club. His business was not doing very well so he turned the football team over to its player-coach, George Halas. Halas was permitted to move the team to Chicago and Cubs' Park (renamed Wrigley Field when it was enlarged in 1926) if he would keep the name "Staleys" one more year. Dutch Sternaman, one of the Staleys' players, became Halas's partner in the ownership of the team. The two of them, along with Guy Chamberlin and George Trafton, were the nucleus of the relocated team.

The Staleys claimed the league championship with a 10–1–1 record, followed by Buffalo's 9–1–2. Buffalo objected, saying Chicago included nonleague games in its record, but president Joe Carr ruled in favor of the Staleys.

1921 STANDINGS	W	L	T	Pct.
Chicago Staleys	10	1	1	.909
Buffalo All-Americans	9	1	2	.900
Akron Pros	7	2	1	.778
Green Bay Packers	6	2	2	.750
Canton Bulldogs	4	3	3	.571
Dayton Triangles	4	3	1	.571
Rock Island Independents	5	4	1	.556
Racine Cardinals	2	3	2	.400
Cleveland Indians	2	6	0	.250
Rochester Jeffersons	2	6	0	.250
Detroit Heralds	1	7	1	.125
Columbus Panhandles	0	6	0	.000
Cincinnati Celts	0	8	0	.000

1922 The name of the league was changed to "National Football League." The Chicago Staleys became the Chicago Bears. The league grew to 18 teams. It disciplined the Green Bay Packers, who had been using college players under assumed names, and dismissed them from the league, but the Packers returned, bought back their franchise, and were restored to the good graces of the league.

The league's first powerhouse team, the Canton Bulldogs coached by Guy Chamberlin, emerged. Chamberlin left the Staleys/Bears and became coach in Canton. He was in the lineup and so were two great tackles, Wilbur (Pete) Henry and Link Lyman. The Bulldogs had a 10–0–2 record, starting a string of games in which they would win 21, lose 0, and tie 3 and capture three consecutive NFL championships.

Thorpe, once Canton's greatest star, moved to another team. He and other Indian players formed a team called the Oorang Indians, who were sponsored by a man named Walter Lingo who owned the Oorang Kennels; Oorang is a strain of Airedale. The kennel was in LaRue, Ohio, but the games were played in Marion, the hometown of Warren Harding, then President of the United States. Guyon was one of Thorpe's teammates.

Halas's Chicago team took the name "Bears" because he was a fan of the Cubs baseball team with which he shared the stadium. The Bears paid the Rock Island, Illinois, Independents $100 for Ed Healey, a great tackle. Chicago had a 9–3 record, finished second in the league to Canton, and co-owners Halas and Sternaman made a profit of $1,476.92.

Carr, the president of the league, decided to make an example of the Packers and prevent other teams from using college players under assumed names. Green Bay's franchise was revoked and a $50 fee returned to the Acme Packing Company. Curly Lambeau, player-coach of the team, used $50 of his own money to buy back the franchise. A friend named Don Murphy sold his car so Lambeau would have train fare to the league meeting. There, Lambeau promised to obey the rules and the Green Bay franchise was awarded to him. Murphy, Lambeau's friend, was allowed to start the opening game of the season for Green Bay and play one minute of pro football in exchange for his financial help.

The Packers were plagued by bad weather and low attendance. Merchants of Green Bay raised $2,500 and loaned it to the team, and a public non-profit corporation was set up to operate it, with Lambeau as manager and coach.

Cincinnati, Cleveland, and Detroit left the league.

The 1920 Decatur Staleys; George Halas is in the center, front row.

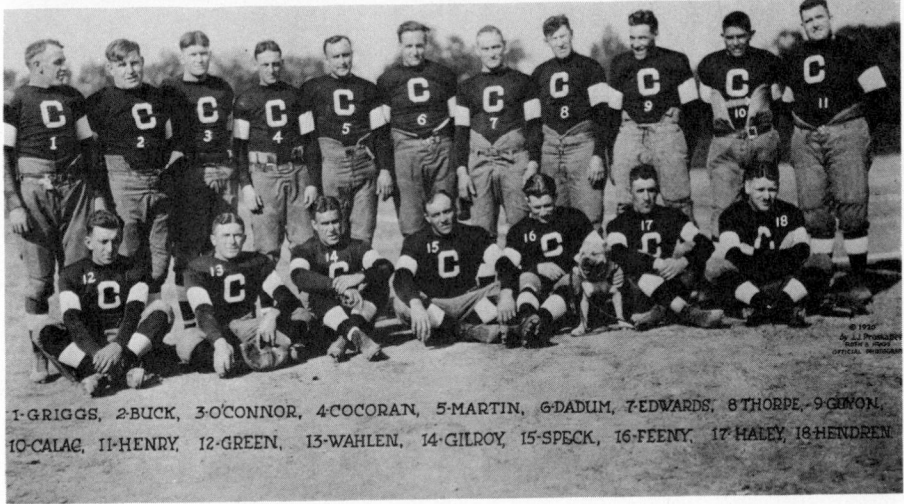

1-GRIGGS, 2-BUCK, 3-O'CONNOR, 4-COCORAN, 5-MARTIN, 6-DADUM, 7-EDWARDS, 8-THORPE, 9-GUYON, 10-CALAC, 11-HENRY, 12-GREEN, 13-WAHLEN, 14-GILROY, 15-SPECK, 16-FEENY, 17-HALEY, 18-HENDREN

The 1920 Canton Bulldogs; Thorpe is fourth from right, second row.

The 1921 Acme Packers, Green Bay; Earl (Curly) Lambeau stands in center, front row.

The 1925 Chicago Cardinals.

Hagemeister Brewery Park, Green Bay, Wisconsin.

Evansville, Indiana; Hammond, Indiana; Louisville, Kentucky; Milwaukee; Minneapolis; Racine, Wisconsin; and Toledo, Ohio were new or returning franchises.

1922 STANDINGS	W	L	T	Pct.
Canton Bulldogs	10	0	2	1.000
Chicago Bears	9	3	0	.750
Chicago Cardinals	8	3	0	.727
Toledo Maroons	5	2	2	.714
Rock Island Independents	4	2	1	.667
Dayton Triangles	4	3	1	.571
Green Bay Packers	4	3	3	.571
Racine Legion	5	4	1	.556
Akron Pros	3	4	2	.429
Buffalo All-Americans	3	4	1	.429
Milwaukee Badgers	2	4	3	.333
Oorang Indians (Marion)	2	6	0	.250
Minneapolis Marines	1	3	0	.250
Evansville Crimson Giants	0	2	0	.000
Louisville Brecks	0	3	0	.000
Rochester Jeffersons	0	3	1	.000
Hammond Pros	0	4	1	.000
Columbus Panhandles	0	7	0	.000

1923 Canton went undefeated again—it was tied once—and the Chicago Bears were runners-up again. The league grew to 20 teams but it did not regulate the schedule of each member team; some played as many as 12 games against member teams, others as few as 2. The Cleveland Indians returned to the league, the Duluth, Minnesota, Kelleys appeared for the first time, and Evansville, Indiana, left the league for good.

Jim Thorpe began the season as player-coach of the Oorang Indians but they folded with a 1–10 record and Thorpe joined the Toledo Maroons.

Player-coach George Halas of Chicago recovered a fumble by Thorpe in a game against Oorang and ran 98 yards for a touchdown. "I could feel Thorpe breathing down my neck all the way," Halas said.

John (Paddy) Driscoll was the star player of the rival Cardinals in Chicago. He scored four touchdowns and the Cardinals had nine in all against the Rochester Jeffersons October 7. These statistics were left to history but the score of the game was not.

1923 STANDINGS	W	L	T	Pct.
Canton Bulldogs	11	0	1	1.000
Chicago Bears	9	2	1	.818
Green Bay Packers	7	2	1	.778
Milwaukee Badgers	7	2	3	.778
Cleveland Indians	3	1	3	.750
Chicago Cardinals	8	4	0	.667
Duluth Kelleys	4	3	0	.571
Buffalo All-Americans	5	4	3	.556
Columbus Tigers	5	4	1	.556
Racine Legion	4	4	2	.500
Toledo Maroons	2	3	2	.400
Rock Island Independents	2	3	3	.400
Minneapolis Marines	2	5	2	.286
St. Louis All-Stars	1	4	2	.200
Hammond Pros	1	5	1	.167
Dayton Triangles	1	6	1	.143
Akron Indians	1	6	0	.143
Oorang Indians (Marion)	1	10	0	.091
Rochester Jeffersons	0	2	0	.000
Louisville Brecks	0	3	0	.000

1924 At the height of their success, the Canton Bulldogs moved their francise to another city. Their payroll was rising and needed larger crowds and more income. Player-coach Guy Chamberlin and most of the players that had starred for Canton moved 55 miles north to the larger city of Cleveland, where they became the Cleveland Bulldogs. Star tackle Pete Henry did not make the move with his teammates; instead, he joined the Pottsville, Pennsylvania, Maroons, a pro team not then in the NFL.

Philadelphia was represented in the league for the first time by the Frankford Yellowjackets; Frankford is a suburb of Philadelphia. The Yellowjackets had been playing pro football for five or six years when they applied for and gained membership in the league. Blue laws in Pennsylvania prevented them from playing their home games on Sunday but it was common for them to play a home game on Saturday and a road game somewhere else the very next day.

The Kansas City Cowboys were another new team that played all its games on the road. The Cowboys had Steve Owen at tackle.

Cleveland and Frankford scheduled weak opponents late in the season so they could fatten their won-lost records. President Joe Carr, however, later ruled all games played after November 30 invalid. Cleveland and player-coach Chamberlin won its third straight league championship with a 7–1–1 record and an .875 percentage. The Chicago Bears lost their first game of the season but then came back to finish in second place. Frankford had 11 victories, a large number due to its frequent practice of playing back-to-back games on Saturday and Sunday, but its .846 percentage was only good for third place.

1924 STANDINGS	W	L	T	Pct.
Cleveland Bulldogs	7	1	1	.875
Chicago Bears	6	1	4	.857
Frankford Yellowjackets	11	2	1	.846
Duluth Kelleys	5	1	0	.833
Rock Island Independents	6	2	2	.750
Green Bay Packers	8	4	0	.667
Buffalo Bisons	6	4	0	.600
Racine Legion	4	3	3	.571
Chicago Cardinals	5	4	1	.556
Columbus Tigers	4	4	0	.500
Hammond Pros	2	2	1	.500
Milwaukee Badgers	5	8	0	.385
Dayton Triangles	2	7	0	.222
Kansas City Cowboys	2	7	0	.222
Akron Indians	1	6	0	.143
Kenosha Maroons	0	5	1	.000
Minneapolis Marines	0	6	0	.000
Rochester Jeffersons	0	7	0	.000

1925 The most momentous season in the NFL's brief history proceeded through a series of tumultuous events ending in a dispute between two teams for the league championship.

Red Grange of Illinois, "the Galloping Ghost," the most celebrated player in the history of college football, entered pro football and immeasurably changed it for the better. C. C. (Cash and Carry) Pyle, a promotion-minded individual who operated a movie theater in Champaign, Illinois, became Grange's manager. The University of Illinois season ended in mid-November, 1925. Grange signed a contract to play for the Chicago Bears immediately; there was no rule at the time preventing college players from doing so.

The Bears played their traditional Thanksgiving Day game against the rival Chicago Cardinals and, with Grange in the lineup, drew a crowd of 38,000 fans. Grange was spectacular on punt returns but Paddy Driscoll, the Cardinals' star, punted the ball away from Grange for the entire game and as a result was booed by the fans who wanted to see Grange make a long runback.

An unprecedented barnstorming tour then began in which the Bears played seven games in 11 days in St. Louis, Philadelphia, New York City, and then cities in the South and on the West Coast. Large crowds turned out everywhere to see Grange play. Newspapers followed the tour with great interest. College football had been popular for years while the "professionalism" of the sport had been looked on with disfavor. The Grange Tour, as it was called, helped dispel these prejudices and gained countless new fans for pro football.

New York City entered the NFL. Tim Mara, a bookmaker, and Billy Gibson, the manager of boxer Gene Tunney, were awarded a franchise for either $500 or $2,500; histories differ on the amount. Their team was named the football Giants and played at the Polo Grounds. They were losing money until the Grange Tour arrived. A crowd of over 70,000 people watched Grange and the Bears play against the Giants. This game ensured the future of the Giants

John (Paddy) Driscoll.

Red Grange, left, and C.C. (Cash and Carry) Pyle.

Joe F. Carr, NFL president.

and an all-important NFL franchise in the city.

Three more important franchises joined the league. They were the Detroit Panthers, who were coached by Jimmy Conzelman; the Pottsville, Pennsylvania, Maroons; and the Providence, Rhode Island, Steamroller. There was a new team in Canton, Ohio, again called the Bulldogs.

Guy Chamberlin, winner of three consecutive league championships, became the player-coach of the Frankford Yellowjackets.

The Pottsville Maroons had great success their first year in the league. They defeated the Chicago Cardinals 21–7 for what they thought was the championship of the NFL. One week later, however, the Maroons played the "Notre Dame All-Stars," a team of former players for the university, including the famous Four Horsemen backfield of Jim Crowley, Elmer Layden, Don Miller, and Harry Stuhldreher. The game was played in Philadelphia. Player-coach Chamberlin of the Frankford Yellowjackets protested, saying his team's "territorial rights" had been impinged upon.

President Joe Carr upheld the protest, canceled the Pottsville franchise, and ordered the Cardinals to play two more games. They did, defeating Hammond, Indiana and Milwaukee. Hammond had an 1–4 and Milwaukee an 0–6 record. The Cardinals now had a better record than Pottsville and were proclaimed NFL champions.

It was then learned that the Milwaukee team had used four high school players in its game against the Cardinals. Carr suspended Milwaukee's manager, Arthur Folz, "for life."

The Green Bay Packers left a ramshackle structure called Hegemeister Brewery Park and moved into City Stadium, a 6,000-seat park with wooden stands and fences that may have been the first stadium in the NFL built expressly for football.

1925 STANDINGS	W	L	T	Pct.
Chicago Cardinals	11	2	1	.846
Pottsville Maroons	10	2	0	.833
Detroit Panthers	8	2	2	.800
New York Giants	8	4	0	.667
Akron Indians	4	2	2	.667
Frankford Yellowjackets	13	7	0	.650
Chicago Bears	9	5	3	.643
Rock Island Independents	5	3	3	.625
Green Bay Packers	8	5	0	.615
Providence Steamroller	6	5	1	.545
Canton Bulldogs	4	4	0	.500
Cleveland Bulldogs	5	8	1	.385
Kansas City Cowboys	2	5	1	.286
Hammond Pros	1	3	0	.250
Buffalo Bisons	1	6	2	.143
Duluth Kelleys	0	3	0	.000
Rochester Jeffersons	0	6	1	.000
Milwaukee Badgers	0	6	0	.000
Dayton Triangles	0	7	1	.000
Columbus Tigers	0	9	0	.000

1926 Red Grange's manager, C. C. (Cash and Carry) Pyle, told the Chicago Bears Grange would not play for them in 1926 unless he was paid a five-figure salary and was given one-third ownership of the team. The Bears refused and lost the services of Grange. Pyle leased Yankee Stadium in New York City, petitioned for an NFL franchise and was refused, and therefore decided to start his own league. It was named the American Football League.

Grange was the figure around which this league was built. He played for Pyle's team, the New York Yankees. The other teams in the league were the Boston Bulldogs, Brooklyn Horsemen, Chicago Bulls, Cleveland Panthers, Newark Bears, Philadelphia Quakers, and a road team called the Los Angeles Wildcats. The Rock Island, Illinois, Independents left the NFL and joined the AFL. These teams played before small crowds and the league folded up after one season. Its champion, the Philadelphia Quakers, played a postseason game against the New York Giants of the NFL and lost 31–0.

Red Grange of the New York Yankees against the Los Angeles Wildcats at Yankee Stadium, 1926, the first AFL.

The NFL allowed its membership to grow to 22 teams to frustrate the AFL. The league was in a confused state in which the names of teams and their true identities differed. The Los Angeles Buccaneers and the Louisville Colonels actually were road teams based in Chicago. Los Angeles was a growing center of pro football interest because of the enthusiastic crowd that had watched Red Grange play there on his tour in 1925, but the 1926 Buccaneers of the NFL and the Wildcats of the AFL never actually played a game in the city which they supposedly represented.

Paddy Driscoll of the Cardinals was sold to the rival Bears and they gave him a good contract, ensuring that he did not sign with the AFL. Ole Haugsrud, the operator of a team in Duluth, Minnesota, gained an NFL franchise and signed Ernie Nevers, the star fullback of Glenn (Pop) Warner's team at Stanford University. The NFL thus acquired a gate attraction to rival Grange of the AFL.

Haugsrud's team was called the Duluth Eskimos. They played two games at home while the weather in their city still permitted it, and then completed the season on the road. They played 29 league or exhibition games. There were only 13 players and sportswriter Grantland Rice named them "the Iron Men of the North."

Jim Thorpe rejoined Canton and played another season for the Bulldogs. Steve Owen moved from the Kansas City Cowboys to the New York Giants.

The Frankford Yellowjackets, led by player-coach Guy Chamberlin, won the championship. They defeated Chicago in a game that broke a 10-game winning streak for the Bears. Chamberlin broke through and blocked a field goal attempt by Driscoll.

Chicago finished second in the league and Pottsville third.

The NFL had been severely criticized for signing Grange immediately after his last college game. Coexistence with college football was assured when Halas of the Bears pushed through an NFL rule prohibiting any team from having in its lineup a player whose college class had not graduated.

1926 STANDINGS	W	L	T	Pct.
Frankford Yellowjackets	14	1	1	.933
Chicago Bears	12	1	3	.923
Pottsville Maroons	10	2	1	.833
Kansas City Cowboys	8	3	1	.727
Green Bay Packers	7	3	3	.700
Los Angeles Buccaneers	6	3	1	.667
New York Giants	8	4	1	.667
Duluth Eskimos	6	5	2	.545
Buffalo Rangers	4	4	2	.500
Chicago Cardinals	5	6	1	.455
Providence Steamroller	5	7	0	.417
Detroit Panthers	4	6	2	.400
Hartford Blues	3	7	0	.300
Brooklyn Lions	3	8	0	.273
Milwaukee Badgers	2	7	0	.222
Akron Indians	1	4	3	.200
Dayton Triangles	1	4	1	.200
Racine Legion	1	4	0	.200
Columbus Tigers	1	6	0	.143
Canton Bulldogs	1	9	3	.100
Hammond Pros	0	4	0	.000
Louisville Colonels	0	4	0	.000

1927 Professional football entered a depression. It went from 31 teams and two leagues to 12 teams and one league. Pyle's New York Yankees moved to the NFL; no other AFL team survived. The traveling Los Angeles Buccaneers and Kansas City Cowboys went out of business. And three midwest franchises that had been the foundation for the league in its earlier years—the Akron Indians, Canton Bulldogs, and Columbus Panhandles—vanished. They never appeared in the league membership again.

Grange was still with the Yankees but he suffered a knee injury in the third game of the season. His days as a feared runner were over. George (Wildcat) Wilson of the defunct Los Angeles Wildcats joined the Providence Steamroller. Jimmy Conzelman left

Al Nesser, seated at left; Steve Owen, seated at right; and other 1926 New York Giants.

Ernie Nevers.

Guy Chamberlin.

Earl (Dutch) Clark at Colorado College.

Cliff Battles.

Clarke Hinkle.

1931 Professional football shrank to 10 teams. Green Bay won its third consecutive NFL championship with Arnie Herber passing to Johnny Blood (Mc-Nally) and Verne Lewellen. The Portsmouth Spartans became a big winner behind rookie tailback Earl (Dutch) Clark of Colorado College. George (Potsy) Clark (who was not related to Dutch Clark) coached the Spartans. Green Bay was 12–2–0 and Portsmouth 11–3–0; there was apparently supposed to be a game between them for the championship but it was never played.

The player limit for NFL teams was 20 but the Packers would sometimes play an entire game with only 12 or 13 men.

The playing career of Al Nesser, last of the Nesser brothers in the NFL, ended when his team, the Cleveland Indians, disbanded.

Steve Owen and Benny Friedman became co-coaches of the New York Giants after LeRoy Andrews quit in midseason.

Joe Carr, president of the NFL, fined the Chicago Bears, Green Bay Packers, and Portsmouth Spartans $1,000 each for using players whose college classes had not graduated.

1931 STANDINGS	W	L	T	Pct.
Green Bay Packers	12	2	0	.857
Portsmouth Spartans	11	3	0	.786
Chicago Bears	8	5	0	.667
Chicago Cardinals	5	4	0	.556
New York Giants	7	6	1	.500
Providence Steamroller	4	4	3	.500
Stapleton Stapes	4	6	1	.400
Cleveland Indians	2	8	0	.200
Brooklyn Dodgers	2	12	0	.143
Frankford Yellowjackets	1	6	1	.143

1932 In the depths of the depression, the National Football League's membership fell to eight teams, the smallest in its history, and it hung on gamely, hoping things would improve.

This was the miniature league of 1932: Chicago's teams, the Bears and Cardinals; the New York Giants, Brooklyn Dodgers, and Stapleton Stapes in New York; the Boston Braves; the Green Bay Packers; and the Portsmouth Spartans. The Braves, the only new team, played at Braves Field, and were owned by George Preston Marshall, owner of a chain of laundries in Washington, D.C. Cliff Battles, a Braves' rookie, led the league in rushing with 576 yards. Glen (Turk) Edwards, a tackle, was another impressive rookie for Boston.

Battles's rushing figure is known because the league kept rudimentary individual statistics for the first time. Joe Carr, the league president, maintained his offices in Columbus, Ohio, even though most of the NFL's teams were in Chicago and New York. Carr was also the operator of the minor league baseball team in Columbus. Carl Storck, secretary-treasurer of the league, had a full-time job as the supervisor of shock absorbers production for General Motors in Dayton, Ohio.

The shortcomings of the style of pro football in 1932 cost the Green Bay Packers a fourth consecutive NFL championship and led to a playoff game that changed the sport as profoundly as any in its history.

Green Bay added rookie fullback Clarke Hinkle to its array of stars and ran up a 10–1–1 record with two weeks left to play in the season. However, the Packers then lost back-to-back games to Portsmouth and the Chicago Bears. Green Bay's 10–3–1 record

gave it a percentage of .769. The Bears' offense sputtered and the team compiled the outlandish total of six ties; its record was 6–1–6 for a percentage of .857. Portsmouth, 6–1–4, also had an .857 percentage. Both were better than Green Bay's; the tie games did not count in the winning percentage at all. The Packers were shunted to third place and a postseason playoff was arranged between the Bears and Spartans.

The Bears' victory over Green Bay in the last game of the season was played in the snow at Wrigley Field. The playoff game was scheduled for the same site but Chicago's weather grew worse. George Halas, owner of the Bears' team, decided to move the game indoors to Chicago Stadium.

There was a layer of dirt on the arena floor, left over from a circus. There was room for only an 80-yard field. It came right up to the walls, so each team agreed to move the goal posts from the end line to the goal line and create inbounds lines; each time the ball was carried outside them it would, for safety's sake, be returned to those lines for the start of the next play.

A crowd of 11,198 saw the game. Portsmouth was without its star, Earl (Dutch) Clark, who had already left the team for his off-season job as basketball coach at Colorado College.

The two teams played for three quarters without a score until Dick Nesbitt of the Bears intercepted a pass by Leroy (Ace) Gutowsky of Portsmouth at the Spartans' 7-yard line. Chicago fullback Bronko Nagurski made six yards, then was stopped for no gain twice. On fourth down and goal, quarterback Carl Brumbaugh handed off to Nagurski, who faked a plunge into the line, backed up two steps, and passed

Chicago Stadium, 1932 indoor playoff, Chicago Bears vs. Portsmouth Spartans.

to Red Grange in the end zone for a touchdown.

The rules of football stated that passes had to be thrown from at least five yards behind the line of scrimmage. Angry coach George (Potsy) Clark of Portsmouth screamed that Nagurski's pass to George broke this rule. His words fell on deaf ears. Chicago added a safety and won 9-0.

1932 STANDINGS

	W	L	T	Pct.
Chicago Bears	6	1	6	.857
Portsmouth Spartans	6	1	4	.857
Green Bay Packers	10	3	1	.769
Boston Braves	4	4	2	.500
New York Giants	4	6	2	.400
Brooklyn Dodgers	3	9	0	.250
Chicago Cardinals	2	6	2	.250
Stapleton Stapes	2	7	3	.222

1933 The NFL made a significant change in the rules of football for the first time and began to independently develop rules serving its needs and the style of play it preferred. As a result of the successful use of inbounds lines or hashmarks in the Chicago Stadium indoor playoff of 1932, the NFL passed a rule that the ball would be moved in 10 yards to inbounds lines whenever it was in play within five yards of the sidelines. The goal posts were moved from the end lines to the goal lines to help field goal kickers, increase scoring, and reduce the number of tie games.

The league had 10 members and at the suggestion of George Preston Marshall of Boston it was divided into two five-team divisions, the winners of each to meet at the end of the season in a championship game, a parallel to baseball's World Series. Thus division play in football and the NFL championship were born.

Philadelphia returned to the NFL, and Pittsburgh, site of the first known pro football in the United States in 1892, joined the league. The Frankford Yellowjackets' franchise that had been inactive for a year was declared forfeited and the Philadelphia territory was awarded to Bert Bell and Lud Wray, who named their team the "Eagles" and adopted the symbol, an eagle, of the National Recovery Administration of the "New Deal" of President Franklin D. Roosevelt for the nation's recovery from the depression. A franchise for Pittsburgh was awarded to Art Rooney and he named it "Pirates"; that was also the name of the baseball team that played at Forbes Field.

Boston changed its name from Braves to "Redskins."

George Halas bought out his partner, Ed (Dutch) Sternaman, and became sole owner of the Chicago Bears.

The Stapleton Stapes disbanded. The Cincinnati Reds joined the league.

Harry Newman, New York Giants' rookie from Michigan, completed 11 touchdown passes. John (Shipwreck) Kelly, co-owner of the Brooklyn Dodgers, led the league in pass receiving with 22 catches, the last time a back led the league in that statistic for 41 years. Ken Strong left the defunct Stapes, joined the New York Giants, and tied for the league scoring championship with Portsmouth's Glenn Presnell; each scored 64 points.

Earl (Dutch) Clark decided to remain at his job as coach at Colorado College and did not play for the Portsmouth Spartans.

The New York Giants became the first Eastern Division champion and the Chicago Bears the first Western Division champion. They played the first NFL championship game in history at Wrigley Field in Chicago December 17. The Bears won 23-21 on a touchdown in the fourth quarter when Bronko Nagurski threw a pass to Bill Hewitt, who lateraled the ball to Bill Karr, who scored.

1933 STANDINGS

Eastern Division	W	L	T	Pct.	Pts.	OP
N.Y. Giants	11	3	0	.786	244	101
Brooklyn Dodgers	5	4	1	.556	93	54
Boston Redskins	5	5	2	.500	103	97
Philadelphia	3	5	1	.375	77	158
Pittsburgh	3	6	2	.333	67	208
Western Division	W	L	T	Pct.	Pts.	OP
Chicago Bears	10	2	1	.833	133	82
Portsmouth Spartans	6	5	0	.545	128	87
Green Bay	5	7	1	.423	170	107
Cincinnati Reds	3	6	1	.333	38	110
Chicago Cardinals	1	9	1	.100	52	101

NFL championship: Chicago Bears 23, N.Y. Giants 21

LEADING RUSHERS	Att.	Yards	Avg.	TD
Jim Musick, Boston	173	809	4.7	5
Cliff Battles, Boston	146	737	5.0	3
Bronko Nagurski, Chicago Bears	128	533	4.2	1
Glenn Presnell, Portsmouth	118	522	4.5	6
Swede Hanson, Philadelphia	133	494	3.7	3

LEADING PASSERS	Att.	Comp.	Yards	TD	Int.
Harry Newman, N.Y. Giants	136	53	973	11	17
Glenn Presnell, Portsmouth	125	47	774	10	12
Arnie Herber, Green Bay	126	50	656	4	12
Benny Friedman, Brooklyn	80	42	597	5	7
Chris Cagle, Brooklyn	74	31	385	2	9

LEADING RECEIVERS	No.	Yards	Avg.	TD
John (Shipwreck) Kelly, Brooklyn	22	246	11.2	3
Bill Hewitt, Chicago Bears	16	274	17.1	2
Roger Grove, Green Bay	15	217	14.5	0
Ray Tesser, Pittsburgh	14	274	19.6	0
Lavern Dilweg, Green Bay	14	225	17.3	0
Paul Moss, Pittsburgh	13	383	29.5	2
Les Peterson, Brooklyn	13	170	13.1	0

Mel Hein (7) and Ray Flaherty of the New York Giants tackling Bronko Nagurski of the Chicago Bears, 1934 championship, the "Sneakers Game."

1934 Professional football gained new prestige and there was more press and fan interest in it when the Chicago Bears, NFL champions, were matched against the best, most famous college players in the first Chicago All-Star Game. The *Chicago Tribune* sponsored the game and the college all-stars were selected in a poll of 105 newspapers throughout the country. Noble Kizer of Purdue accepted the job of coaching the all-stars despite the fact that some of his associates urged him not to coach a game against professionals. The game was a scoreless tie and there were only nine first downs but there was a huge crowd of 79,432 fans to see the game at Soldier Field on the lakefront in Chicago.

The NFL committed itself to a more wide-open game with more forward passes when it passed a rule permitting them to be thrown anywhere behind the line of scrimmage, a decision growing out of the controversial pass by Bronko Nagurski in the 1932 indoor playoff game.

G. A. (Dick) Richards bought the Portsmouth Spartans and moved them to Detroit, to play their games at University of Detroit Stadium and take the name "Lions." Dutch Clark ended his one-year retirement and rejoined the team.

The Cincinnati Reds lost eight straight games and the franchise and some of the players moved to St. Louis. The team played three games, losing two of them, as the St. Louis Gunners.

Beattie Feathers, rookie halfback for the Chicago Bears, followed the blocking of fullback Bronko Nagurski and became the first professional runner in history to gain 1,000 yards in a season when he gained 1,004. "Did you ever see a fellow run so fast and so low as that Feathers?" Jack McEwan of Brooklyn asked after the Bears defeated the Dodgers 21–7 at Ebbets Field. "He's a sweetheart of a football player and he certainly beat us today."

Chicago won 13 straight games, and the new Detroit Lions team, which had a tremendous defensive record, scoring seven consecutive shutouts, had to settle for second place in the Western Division behind Chicago. The two division rivals met in the first Thanksgiving Day game in Detroit, starting a pro football tradition there, and Chicago won 19–16. It was the first NFL game broadcast nationally; Graham McNamee was the announcer for NBC Radio.

The Bears had played in the first Chicago All-Star Game, given the league its first 1,000-yard rusher, won 13 straight games, and had one of their games broadcast nationally on radio. They appeared to be an unbeatable team as they faced the Eastern Division champion New York Giants for the NFL championship. It was an extremely cold day at the Polo Grounds in New York City and the field was icy and slick. Some of the Giants' players put on basketball shoes or sneakers at halftime to gain better footing and defeated the Bears 30-13 for the championship. The game was dubbed the "Sneakers Game." The winning share for the Giants' players was $621.

Red Grange retired from professional football at the age of 30.

1934 STANDINGS

Eastern Division	W	L	T	Pct.	Pts.	OP
N.Y. Giants	8	5	0	.615	147	107
Boston Redskins	6	6	0	.500	107	94
Brooklyn Dodgers	4	7	0	.364	61	153
Philadelphia	4	7	0	.364	127	85
Pittsburgh	2	10	0	.167	51	206
Western Division	W	L	T	Pct.	Pts.	OP
Chicago Bears	13	0	0	1.000	286	86
Detroit	10	3	0	.769	238	59
Green Bay	7	6	0	.538	156	112
Chicago Cardinals	5	6	0	.455	80	84
St. Louis Gunners	1	2	0	.333	27	61
Cincinnati Reds	0	8	0	.000	10	243

NFL championship: N.Y. Giants 30, Chicago Bears 13

LEADING RUSHERS

	Att.	Yards	Avg.	TD
Beattie Feathers, Chicago Bears	101	1,004	9.9	8
Swede Hanson, Philadelphia	147	805	5.5	7
Dutch Clark, Detroit	122	763	6.3	8
Bronko Nagurski, Chicago Bears	123	586	4.8	7
Warren Heller, Pittsburgh	132	528	4.0	1

LEADING PASSERS

	Att.	Comp.	Yards	TD	Int.
Arnie Herber, Green Bay	115	42	799	8	12
Harry Newman, N.Y. Giants	91	35	366	1	5
Warren Heller, Pittsburgh	112	31	511	2	15
Dutch Clark, Detroit	49	23	383	0	3
Ed Matesic, Philadelphia	60	20	272	3	5

LEADING RECEIVERS

	No.	Yards	Avg.	TD
Joe Carter, Philadelphia	16	238	14.9	4
Red Badgro, N.Y. Giants	16	206	12.9	1
Ben Smith, Pittsburgh	12	190	15.8	0
Charley Malone, Boston	11	121	11.0	2
Joe Skladany, Pittsburgh	10	222	22.2	2

1935 The Reds-Gunners franchise that had played in two cities did not return and professional football was reduced to nine teams again.

Alarmed by the domination of the league by the Chicago Bears and New York Giants, Bert Bell of Philadelphia proposed in May that the NFL teams draft college players, with the team that finished last in the standings having the first choice in each round of the draft. The proposal was accepted and the first draft was scheduled for 1936.

End Don Hutson of the University of Alabama joined the Green Bay Packers and made a feared passing combination with tailback Arnie Herber.

The inbounds lines or hashmarks established at 10 yards in 1933 were moved nearer the center of the field, 15 yards from each side line.

Detroit ousted the Chicago Bears as Western Division champions and, led by Earl (Dutch) Clark and Leroy (Ace) Gutowsky, defeated the New York Giants 26-7 in the NFL championship game on a raw, snowy day at the University of Detroit Stadium before a sparse crowd of 15,000 fans. Raymond (Buddy) Parker, a rookie back for the Lions, scored his team's final touchdown. The victory gave Detroit the football and baseball championships of 1935; the baseball Tigers had won their first World Series earlier.

Five members of the 1934 St. Louis Gunners, one of whom disdained a helmet.

1935 STANDINGS

Eastern Division	W	L	T	Pct.	Pts.	OP
N. Y. Giants	9	3	0	.750	180	96
Brooklyn Dodgers	5	6	1	.455	90	141
Pittsburgh	4	8	0	.333	100	209
Boston Redskins	2	8	1	.200	65	123
Philadelphia	2	9	0	.182	60	179
Western Division	**W**	**L**	**T**	**Pct.**	**Pts.**	**OP**
Detroit	7	3	2	.700	191	111
Green Bay	8	4	0	.667	181	96
Chicago Bears	6	4	2	.600	192	106
Chicago Cardinals	6	4	2	.600	99	97

NFL championship: Detroit 26, N.Y. Giants 7
One game between Boston and Philadelphia was canceled.

LEADING RUSHERS	Att.	Yards	Avg.	TD	
Doug Russell, Chicago Cardinals	140	499	3.6	0	
Ernie Caddel, Detroit	87	450	5.2	6	
King Richards, N.Y. Giants	149	449	3.0	4	
Dutch Clark, Detroit	120	412	3.4	4	
Bill Shepherd, Boston-Detroit	143	425	3.0	4	
LEADING PASSERS	**Att.**	**Comp.**	**Yards**	**TD**	**Int.**
Ed Danowski, N.Y. Giants	113	57	794	10	9
Arnie Herber, Green Bay	109	40	729	8	14
Bob Monnett, Green Bay	65	31	354	2	5
Phil Sarboe, Chicago Cardinals	67	31	368	0	10
Bill Shepherd, Boston-Detroit	64	28	417	2	14
John Gildea, Pittsburgh	105	28	529	2	20
LEADING RECEIVERS	**No.**	**Yards**	**Avg.**	**TD**	
Ted Goodwin, N.Y. Giants	26	432	16.6	4	
J. Blood (McNally), Green Bay	25	404	16.2	3	
Bill Smith, Chicago Cardinals	24	318	13.3	2	
Charley Malone, Boston	22	433	19.7	2	
Luke Johnsos, Chicago Bears	19	298	15.7	4	

1936 There were no franchise shifts for the first time since the formation of the NFL. It also was the first year in which all member teams played the same number of games.

The player limit was increased to 25.

The Philadelphia Eagles of Bert Bell finished last with a 2–9 record, so the man who had proposed the draft now made the first choice in the first draft. Philadelphia chose Jay Berwanger, All-America halfback of the University of Chicago. The Eagles, however, traded the negotiation rights to him to the Chicago Bears in exchange for tackle Art Buss. Berwanger never agreed to terms with the Bears and never played pro football. The Bears, however, made exceptional choices when they took tackle Joe Stydahar of West Virginia and guard Danny Fortmann of Colgate.

A rival league was formed and it became the second organization to call itself the American Football League. The Boston Shamrocks were its champion and the other teams were the Brooklyn Tigers, Cleveland Rams, New York Yankees, Pittsburgh Ameri-

Jay Berwanger of the University of Chicago, first draft choice, 1936.

Sammy Baugh of Washington passing against the Chicago Bears, 1937 championship.

Johnny Blood (McNally), Byron (Whizzer) White, and Art Rooney, left to right, 1938 Pittsburgh Pirates.

cans, and Rochester Tigers. It was the "second AFL."

Green Bay had Arnie Herber and Clarke Hinkle in its backfield and Don Hutson at end. Hutson scored eight touchdowns and the Packers easily won the Western Division. The Boston Redskins emerged as a strong team and captured the Eastern Division championship.

There were only 5,000 fans at Fenway Park in Boston when the Redskins defeated Pittsburgh to win the division title. An angry George Preston Marshall, owner of the Boston team, moved the championship game with Green Bay to the Polo Grounds in New York. A crowd of 29,545 attended as Herber and Hutson led Green Bay to a 21–6 victory over Marshall's Redskins.

1936 STANDINGS

Eastern Division	W	L	T	Pct.	Pts.	OP
Boston Redskins	7	5	0	.583	149	110
Pittsburgh	6	6	0	.500	98	187
N.Y. Giants	5	6	1	.455	115	163
Brooklyn Dodgers	3	8	1	.273	92	161
Philadelphia	1	11	0	.083	51	206
Western Division	**W**	**L**	**T**	**Pct.**	**Pts.**	**OP**
Green Bay	10	1	1	.909	248	118
Chicago Bears	9	3	0	.750	222	94
Detroit	8	4	0	.667	235	102
Chicago Cardinals	3	8	1	.273	74	143

NFL championship: Green Bay 21, Boston 6

LEADING RUSHERS	Att.	Yards	Avg.	TD
Tuffy Leemans, N.Y. Giants	206	830	4.0	2
Ace Gutowsky, Detroit	191	827	4.3	6
Dutch Clark, Detroit	123	628	5.1	7
Cliff Battles, Boston	176	614	3.5	5
G.Grosvenor, Chi. Bears-Cardinals	170	612	3.6	4

LEADING PASSERS	Att.	Comp.	Yards	TD	Int.
Arnie Herber, Green Bay	173	77	1,239	11	13
Ed Matesic, Pittsburgh	138	64	850	5	16
Phil Sarboe, Chi. Card.-Brooklyn	114	47	680	3	13
Ed Danowski, N.Y. Giants	104	47	515	6	10
Dutch Clark, Detroit	71	38	467	4	6

LEADING RECEIVERS	No.	Yards	Avg.	TD
Don Hutson, Green Bay	34	536	15.8	8
Bill Smith, Chicago Cardinals	20	414	20.7	1
Ernie Caddel, Detroit	19	150	7.9	1
Wayne Millner, Boston	18	211	11.7	0
Eggs Manske, Philadelphia	17	325	19.1	0

1937 George Preston Marshall moved the Redskins from Boston to his hometown of Washington, D.C. Griffith Stadium was leased for the Redskins' games. Washington signed All-America quarterback (tailback) Sammy Baugh of Texas Christian University to a contract for $8,000.

The nation's capital embraced the exciting Redskins. A Friday night game against the New York Giants was moved up to Thursday night so it would not conflict with one of President Franklin D. Roosevelt's "fireside chats" on the radio. The Redskins played the Giants in another game in New York and 12,000 fans accompanied them on the trip.

There had been a Cleveland Rams team in the 1936 season of the second American Football League. A new team called the Cleveland Rams, which had no relationship to the former team other than it had the same name, was formed by Homer Marshman and joined the NFL. The league once more had 10 teams.

Dutch Clark became the coach of the Detroit Lions and Johnny Blood (McNally) the coach of the Pittsburgh Pirates.

Philadelphia made the first draft choice again, selecting back Sam Francis of Nebraska but trading the rights to him to the Chicago Bears.

Tailback Clarence (Ace) Parker was a rookie star for the Brooklyn Dodgers. Rookies Pat Coffee and Gaynell Tinsley of Louisiana State University combined on a 97-yard touchdown pass while playing for the Chicago Cardinals against the Bears.

The Los Angeles Bulldogs had an 8–0 record in the American Football League, which then folded. The other 1937 teams were the Boston Shamrocks, Cincinnati Bengals, New York Yankees, Pittsburgh Americans, and Rochester Tigers.

Baugh was the NFL's leading passer and the Redskins won six of their last seven games enroute to the Eastern Division championship. They met the Western champions, the Chicago Bears, on a frigid day at Griffith Stadium in Washington. Despite the bitter cold, Baugh had a sensational passing game in which he completed 18 of 33 for an unprecedented 335 yards. The Redskins were the NFL champions, 28–21.

Bronko Nagurski of the Chicago Bears retired from football.

1937 STANDINGS

Eastern Division	W	L	T	Pct.	Pts.	OP
Washington	8	3	0	.727	195	120
N.Y. Giants	6	3	2	.667	128	109
Pittsburgh	4	7	0	.364	122	145
Brooklyn Dodgers	3	7	1	.300	82	174
Philadelphia	2	8	1	.200	86	177
Western Division	**W**	**L**	**T**	**Pct.**	**Pts.**	**OP**
Chicago Bears	9	1	1	.900	201	100
Green Bay	7	4	0	.636	220	122
Detroit	7	4	0	.636	180	105
Chicago Cardinals	5	5	1	.500	135	165
Cleveland	1	10	0	.091	75	207

NFL championship: Washington 28, Chicago Bears 21

LEADING RUSHERS	Att.	Yards	Avg.	TD
Cliff Battles, Washington	216	874	4.0	5
Clarke Hinkle, Green Bay	129	552	4.3	5
John Karcis, Pittsburgh	128	511	4.0	3
Dutch Clark, Detroit	96	468	4.9	5
G. Grosvenor, Chicago Cardinals	137	461	3.4	2

LEADING PASSERS	Att.	Comp.	Yards	TD	Int.
Sammy Baugh, Washington	171	81	1,127	8	14
Ed Danowski, N.Y. Giants	134	66	814	8	5
Pat Coffee, Chicago Cardinals	119	52	804	5	11
Arnie Herber, Green Bay	104	47	676	7	10
Dave Smukler, Philadelphia	118	42	432	6	14

LEADING RECEIVERS	No.	Yards	Avg.	TD
Don Hutson, Green Bay	41	552	13.5	7
Gaynell Tinsley, Chicago Cardinals	36	675	18.8	5
Charley Malone, Washington	28	419	15.0	4
Jeff Barrett, Brooklyn	20	461	23.1	3
Bill Hewitt, Philadelphia	16	197	12.3	5

1938 Baugh of the Redskins had gotten rough treatment at times during his rookie season and, as a result, the rules were changed. A new rule called for a 15-yard penalty for roughing the passer after the ball had left his hand. The player limit increased to 30.

Hugh (Shorty) Ray, a Chicago school teacher, coach, and supervisor of football officials, became a technical advisor to the NFL on rules, at the suggestion of owner George Halas of the Chicago Bears.

Corbett Davis, back from Indiana, was the first choice in the NFL draft. He was the selection of the Cleveland Rams, who had finished 1–10. Sid Luckman was a rookie with the Chicago Bears, Ward Cuff with the New York Giants, Frank (Bruiser) Kinard with the Brooklyn Dodgers, and Alex Wojciechowicz with the Detroit Lions. Pittsburgh shocked the other teams when owner Art Rooney gave a $15,800 contract to All-America Byron (Whizzer) White of Colorado to play for the Pirates. White had a storied career in college, scoring 34 points in his last game at Colorado. He became the NFL's leading rusher with 567 yards as a rookie, but the Pirates won only two games and finished last in the Eastern Division.

The New York Giants captured the East, defeating the Redskins 36–0 on the last day of the season. Green Bay won the Western Division; Detroit was second. The Giants defeated Green Bay 23–17 in the NFL championship before a record crowd of 48,120 at the Polo Grounds.

George Preston Marshall of the Redskins had met in Los Angeles during the summer with two notable sports figures to discuss a pet idea of his. He wanted an annual all-star game between the league champions and a team of all-stars. He sold the idea to sports editor Bill Henry of the *Los Angeles Times* and promoter Tom Gallery. The game was to be called the "Pro Bowl."

Don Hutson, left, and Arnie Herber, Green Bay Packers.

Bronko Nagurski.

Cover of sheet music for Bears fight song.

1938 STANDINGS

Eastern Division	W	L	T	Pct.	Pts.	OP
N.Y. Giants	8	2	1	.800	194	79
Washington	6	3	2	.667	148	154
Brooklyn Dodgers	4	4	3	.500	131	161
Philadelphia	5	6	0	.455	154	164
Pittsburgh	2	9	0	.182	79	169
Western Division	W	L	T	Pct.	Pts.	OP
Green Bay	8	3	0	.727	223	118
Detroit	7	4	0	.636	119	108
Chicago Bears	6	5	0	.545	194	148
Cleveland	4	7	0	.364	131	215
Chicago Cardinals	2	9	0	.182	111	168

NFL championship: N.Y. Giants 23, Green Bay 17

LEADING RUSHERS	Att.	Yards	Avg.	TD
Byron (Whizzer) White, Pittsburgh	152	567	3.7	4
Tuffy Leemans, N.Y. Giants	121	463	3.8	4
Bill Shepherd, Detroit	100	455	4.6	3
Cecil Isbell, Green Bay	85	445	5.2	2
Ace Gutowsky, Detroit	131	444	3.4	2

LEADING PASSERS	Att.	Comp.	Yards	TD	Int.
Ed Danowski, N.Y. Giants	129	70	848	7	8
Ace Parker, Brooklyn	148	63	865	5	7
Sammy Baugh, Washington	128	63	853	6	11
John Robbins, Chi. Cardinals	97	52	577	2	9
Bernie Masterson, Chi. Bears	112	46	848	7	9

LEADING RECEIVERS	No.	Yards	Avg.	TD
Gaynell Tinsley, Chicago Cardinals	41	516	12.6	1
Don Hutson, Green Bay	32	548	17.1	9
Joe Carter, Philadelphia	27	386	14.3	7
Charley Malone, Washington	24	257	10.7	1
Jim Benton, Cleveland	21	418	19.9	5

1939 The first Pro Bowl game was played at Wrigley Field in Los Angeles January 15. The champion New York Giants defeated the "Pro All-Stars" 13–10 before a crowd of 20,000.

Joe F. Carr, president of the National Football League since 1921, died May 20. Secretary-treasurer Carl Storck was named to succeed Carr as acting president.

An NFL game was televised for the first time when the National Broadcasting Company took a camera to Ebbets Field in Brooklyn October 22 and beamed the game between the Dodgers and the Pittsburgh Pirates back to the studios of the network and to the handful of sets then in New York.

Sid Luckman replaced Bernie Masterson as the starting quarterback for the Chicago Bears. They played the T-formation with man-in-motion while other clubs played long-snap formations such as the so-called "A" formation and double and single wing. Clark Shaughnessy of the University of Chicago was assisting George Halas and his Bears' coaching staff in developing new plays. Luckman became the smart leader and good ball-handler Halas needed to run the system, which was becoming more and more complex and radical. Bill Osmanski, the Bears' rookie fullback from Holy Cross, led the league in rushing with 699 yards.

New York and Washington were strong again and owner Marshall of the Redskins led both a parade of some 12,000 fans from Washington and the Redskins' Band up Broadway on the way to the Polo Grounds at 151st Street for the final game of the regular season. Sportswriter Bill Corum wrote later that, "At the head of a 150-piece brass band and 12,000 fans, George Preston Marshall slipped unobtrusively into New York today."

New York won the game, however, 9–7 and Marshall was angry afterwards, yelling "foul" over a call by referee Bill Halloran that a Redskins' field goal attempt by Torrance (Bo) Russell was no good.

The Giants were Eastern champions. They went to Wisconsin to meet the Western Division champion Green Bay Packers. There was limited seating in City Stadium in Green Bay, so the game was moved to the Wisconsin State Fair Park in Milwaukee and the ticket price increased to $4.40. A crowd of 32,279 watched as coach Earl (Curly) Lambeau gained revenge for the previous year's defeat with a 27–0 triumph for the NFL championship.

League attendance set a record. It was 1,071,200.

Davey O'Brien, Philadelphia Eagles.

Elmer Layden, NFL commissioner.

Art Rooney, left, and Bert Bell, Pittsburgh Pirates.

1939 STANDINGS

Eastern Division	W	L	T	Pct.	Pts.	OP
N.Y. Giants	9	1	1	.900	168	85
Washington	8	2	1	.800	242	94
Brooklyn Dodgers	4	6	1	.400	108	219
Philadelphia	1	9	1	.100	105	200
Pittsburgh	1	9	1	.100	114	216
Western Division	W	L	T	Pct.	Pts.	OP
Green Bay	9	2	0	.818	233	153
Chicago Bears	8	3	0	.727	298	157
Detroit	6	5	0	.545	145	150
Cleveland	5	5	1	.500	195	164
Chicago Cardinals	1	10	0	.091	84	254

NFL championship: Green Bay 27, N.Y. Giants 0

LEADING RUSHERS	Att.	Yards	Avg.	TD
Bill Osmanski, Chicago Bears	121	699	5.8	7
Andy Farkas, Washington	139	547	3.9	5
Joe Maniaci, Chicago Bears	77	544	7.1	4
Pug Manders, Brooklyn	114	482	4.2	2
Parker Hall, Cleveland	120	458	3.8	2

LEADING PASSERS	Att.	Comp.	Yards	TD	Int.
Parker Hall, Cleveland	208	106	1,227	9	13
Davey O'Brien, Philadelphia	201	99	1,324	6	17
Ace Parker, Brooklyn	157	72	977	4	13
Arnie Herber, Green Bay	139	57	1,107	8	9
Frank Filchock, Washington	89	55	1,094	11	7

LEADING RECEIVERS	No.	Yards	Avg.	TD
Don Hutson, Green Bay	34	846	24.9	6
Perry Schwartz, Brooklyn	33	550	16.7	3
Vic Spadaccini, Cleveland	32	292	9.1	1
Red Ramsey, Philadelphia	31	359	11.6	1
Jim Benton, Cleveland	27	388	14.4	7

1940 Art Rooney left professional football, selling the Pittsburgh Pirates to Alexis Thompson. George Richards sold the Detroit Lions to Fred Mandel after the Lions were fined $5,000 by NFL president Carl Storck; the Lions had tampered with Clyde (Bulldog) Turner of Hardin-Simmons College after he had been drafted by the Chicago Bears.

Dr. John Bain (Jock) Sutherland, the former coach of national championship teams at the University of Pittsburgh, moved into pro football as coach of the Brooklyn Dodgers. Jimmy Conzelman took over as coach of the Chicago Cardinals.

Turner, back George McAfee, end Ken Kavanaugh, and linemen Ed Kolman and Lee Artoe joined the powerful Chicago Bears.

For the third time, a rival league appeared to challenge the NFL. Just as the earlier rival leagues had done, this one took the name "American Football League." The Columbus Bullies won its championship with an 8-1-1 record and the other teams were the Boston Bears, Buffalo Indians, Cincinnati Bengals, Milwaukee Chiefs, and New York Yankees.

Byron (Whizzer) White had been in England for studies as a Rhodes scholar. He returned to pro football, this time with the Detroit Lions, and again led the league in rushing, gaining 514 yards. Quarterback Davey O'Brien of the Philadelphia Eagles threw 60 passes in one game. End Don Looney of the Eagles caught 58 passes for the season.

The Chicago Bears won the Western Division, the Washington Redskins the Eastern Division. Chicago lost only three games, one of them to the Redskins by the score of 7–3; there was a disputed play late in the game in which the Bears demanded a pass interference call and were denied. George Preston Marshall of the Redskins later called the Bears "crybabies." The NFL championship game between the two teams was to be in Washington.

Clark Shaughnessy, who had become coach of Stanford University in Palo Alto, California, and won 10 straight games using the T-formation with man-in-motion, rejoined the Bears for their preparations. He studied film of the 7–3 game and saw that the Redskins had a predictable defense. They stayed in a five-three and always shifted their linebackers toward the man-in-motion. He and the Bears' coaches saw that it was an easy defense to exploit. Counter plays were put in the game plan to send Bears' runners away from the movement of the linebackers. The Bears would control the ball, it was decided, and keep it away from Washington's great passer, Sammy Baugh. Shaughnessy also wrote new terminology for Bears' play-calling that made the team's blocking more efficient.

Fullback Bill Osmanski ran 68 yards for a touchdown on the second play of the game. It was not a counter play. Rather, it was to the same side as the man-in-motion, George McAfee, and Osmanski started off left guard but then cut outside. End George Wilson made a great block clearing the last Redskins' defender out of the way downfield.

Chicago's offense continued to work efficiently and mow down the Redskins. Baugh and other Washington tailbacks threw careless passes that the Bears returned for touchdowns. When it was over, the Bears had won the NFL championship by the astounding score of 73–0, the most one-sided of all title games and one of the most celebrated victories in football history.

The championship game was the first ever carried on network radio. Red Barber broadcast it to 120 stations of the Mutual Broadcasting System, which paid $2,500 for the rights to the game.

1940 STANDINGS

Eastern Division	W	L	T	Pct.	Pts.	OP
Washington	9	2	0	.818	245	142
Brooklyn Dodgers	8	3	0	.727	186	120
N.Y. Giants	6	4	1	.600	131	133
Pittsburgh	2	7	2	.222	60	178
Philadelphia	1	10	0	.091	111	211
Western Division	W	L	T	Pct.	Pts.	OP
Chicago Bears	8	3	0	.727	238	152
Green Bay	6	4	1	.600	238	155
Detroit	5	5	1	.500	138	153
Cleveland	4	6	1	.400	171	191
Chicago Cardinals	2	7	2	.273	139	222

NFL championship: Chicago Bears 73 Washington 0

LEADING RUSHERS	Att.	Yards	Avg.	TD
Byron (Whizzer) White, Detroit	146	514	3.5	5
Johnny Drake, Cleveland	134	480	3.6	9
Tuffy Leemans, N.Y. Giants	132	474	3.6	1
Banks McFadden, Brooklyn	65	411	6.3	1
Dick Todd, Washington	76	408	5.4	4

LEADING PASSERS	Att.	Comp.	Yards	TD	Int.
Sammy Baugh, Washington	177	111	1,367	12	10
Davey O'Brien, Philadelphia	277	124	1,290	5	17
Cecil Isbell, Green Bay	150	68	1,037	9	12
Sid Luckman, Chicago Bears	105	48	941	4	9
Ace Parker, Brooklyn	111	49	817	10	7

LEADING RECEIVERS	No.	Yards	Avg.	TD
Don Looney, Philadelphia	58	707	12.1	4
Don Hutson, Green Bay	45	664	14.7	7
Jimmy Johnston, Washington	29	350	12.1	3
Jim Benton, Cleveland Rams	22	351	15.9	3
Vic Spadaccini, Cleveland Rams	22	276	12.5	2

1941 Elmer Layden, head coach and athletic director at the University of Notre Dame, and one of that university's famous "Four Horsemen" backfield of the 1920s, was named the first commissioner of the National Football League March 1. The title of "president" was discarded. Layden established the NFL office in Chicago. Carl Storck, acting president of the league since the death of Joe Carr in 1939, resigned.

Art Rooney returned to pro football, buying half-interest in the Philadelphia Eagles. He and Bert Bell were co-owners of the Eagles. They swapped them to Alexis Thompson in exchange for the Pittsburgh Steelers.

Homer Marshman sold the Cleveland Rams to Dan Reeves and Fred Levy, Jr.

The league by-laws were revised to provide for playoffs in case there were ties in division races, and sudden death overtime in case a playoff game was tied after four quarters.

An official *Record Manual* was published by the NFL for the first time. It replaced the pro football guides that had been published by the Spalding sporting goods company in the 1930s.

The third American Football League folded.

Earle (Greasy) Neale became the head coach and Tommy Thompson the quarterback of the Philadel-

Sid Luckman, hooded, and George Halas during the 1940 championship game.

Byron (Whizzer) White of Detroit, the NFL's leading rusher in 1940.

Quarterback Baugh of the Redskins was now accustomed to the team's new T-formation.

Washington met the Cleveland Rams in the title game at Municipal Stadium in Cleveland on a frigid day when the temperature was six degrees. Baugh threw a pass from his own end zone in the first quarter. The pass hit the goal post and it was ruled a safety and two points for Cleveland. Waterfield threw a touchdown pass to Benton and the extra point was good, giving the Rams a 9–7 lead. Cleveland went on to win 15–14.

1945 STANDINGS

Eastern Division	W	L	T	Pct.	Pts.	OP
Washington	8	2	0	.800	209	121
Philadelphia	7	3	0	.700	272	133
N.Y. Giants	3	6	1	.333	179	198
Boston Yanks	3	6	1	.333	123	211
Pittsburgh	2	8	0	.200	79	220
Western Division	W	L	T	Pct.	Pts.	OP
Cleveland	9	1	0	.900	244	136
Detroit	7	3	0	.700	195	194
Green Bay	6	4	0	.600	258	173
Chicago Bears	3	7	0	.300	192	235
Chicago Cardinals	1	9	0	.100	98	228

NFL championship: Cleveland 15, Washington 14

LEADING RUSHERS	Att.	Yards	Avg.	Long	TD
Steve Van Buren, Philadelphia	143	832	5.8	69	15
Frank Akins, Washington	147	797	5.4	45	6
Henry Margarita, Chicago Bears	112	497	4.4	38	3
Fred Gehrke, Cleveland Rams	74	467	6.3	72	7
Fred Gillette, Cleveland Rams	63	390	6.1	52	1

LEADING PASSERS	Att.	Comp.	Yards	TD	Int.
Sammy Baugh, Washington	182	128	1,669	11	4
Sid Luckman, Chicago Bears	217	117	1,725	14	10
Bob Waterfield, Cleveland Rams	171	88	1,609	14	16
Leroy Zimmerman, Philadelphia	132	67	991	9	8
Paul Christman, Chi. Cardinals	219	89	1,147	5	12

LEADING RECEIVERS	No.	Yards	Avg.	Long	TD
Don Hutson, Green Bay	47	834	17.7	75	9
Jim Benton, Cleveland Rams	45	1,067	23.7	84	8
Steve Bagarus, Washington	35	623	17.8	70	5
George Wilson, Chicago Bears	28	259	9.2	18	3
John Greene, Detroit	26	550	21.1	63	4

1946 The NFL had waited for years for the return of peace and prosperity. It arrived at last, but when it did it had to be shared with a rival organization called the All-America Football Conference. Founded by sports editor Arch Ward of the *Chicago Tribune,* it began play in Brooklyn, Buffalo, Chicago, Cleveland, Los Angeles, Miami, New York, and San Francisco.

The NFL champion Cleveland Rams had been trying to gain league approval to move to Los Angeles. It was refused at first, and then the league relented and the team made its move. The NFL became a coast-to-coast league for the first time.

There was direct competition between NFL and AAFC teams in three cities. The New York Giants were in competition with the Brooklyn Dodgers and New York Yankees of the AAFC. The Chicago Bears and Cardinals had competition from the Chicago Rockets of the AAFC. And the new Los Angeles Rams were in competition with the Los Angeles Dons of the AAFC.

The contract of NFL Commissioner Elmer Layden was not renewed, and Bert Bell, co-owner of the Pittsburgh Steelers, was named to replace him. Bell won a three-year contract and accepted the job of leading the league against its rival, the AAFC. He moved the NFL headquarters from Chicago to Philadelphia.

The rule that cost the Washington Redskins a safety in the 1945 championship game was changed so that a forward pass hitting the goal posts was now an incomplete pass. Free substitution was being debated hotly, especially in college football, and the NFL restricted its rule, limiting substitutions to three men at a time.

The Los Angeles Rams averaged 38,700 fans in Memorial Coliseum. They added backs Tom Harmon and Kenny Washington to their lineup but failed to repeat as champions. The Chicago Bears won the Western Division, recapturing the glory they had

Bert Bell.

Dan Reeves.

Bill Dudley.

known before World War II. They had a backfield of Sid Luckman at quarterback, Hugh Gallarneau and Dante Magnani at halfbacks, and Bill Osmanski at fullback.

Frank Filchock, acquired from Washington, led the New York Giants to the Eastern championship. Philadelphia finished third for the third consecutive year. The Chicago Cardinals, coached by Jimmy Conzelman, were growing stronger and had Paul Christman, Marshall Goldberg, and Pat Harder in their backfield.

Dr. John Bain (Jock) Sutherland, who had coached great college teams at the University of Pittsburgh, returned from military service and became coach of the Pittsburgh Steelers. Tailback Bill Dudley of the Steelers had a great season, leading the league in scoring and winning the most valuable player award. But Dudley and Sutherland feuded and the Steelers remained unsuccessful.

There were reports of a betting scandal on the eve of the championship game in New York between the Giants and the Chicago Bears. The Giants' Filchock and Merle Hapes were questioned about an attempt by a New York man to fix the game. Hapes was suspended for failing to report the contact, but Filchock was permitted to play the game. He played well but Chicago won 24–14. Luckman ran 19 yards on a keeper play for the decisive touchdown. A title game record crowd of 58,346 watched.

The league was in competition with a rival organization and a number of its players had jumped to the other league. The NFL nevertheless set an attendance record of 1,732,135, an average of 31,494 a game.

Don Hutson of the Green Bay Packers retired from pro football.

1946 STANDINGS

Eastern Division	W	L	T	Pct.	Pts.	OP
N.Y. Giants	7	3	1	.700	236	162
Philadelphia	6	5	0	.545	231	220
Washington	5	5	1	.500	171	191
Pittsburgh	5	5	1	.500	136	117
Boston Yanks	2	8	1	.200	189	273
Western Division	W	L	T	Pct.	Pts.	OP
Chicago Bears	8	2	1	.800	289	193
Los Angeles	6	4	1	.600	277	257
Chicago Cardinals	6	5	0	.545	260	198
Green Bay	6	5	0	.545	148	158
Detroit	1	10	0	.091	142	310

NFL championship: Chicago Bears 24, N.Y. Giants 14

LEADING RUSHERS	Att.	Yards	Avg.	Long	TD
Bill Dudley, Pittsburgh	146	604	4.1	41	3
Pat Harder, Chicago Cardinals	106	545	5.1	55	4
Steve Van Buren, Philadelphia	116	529	4.6	58	5
Hugh Gallarneau, Chicago Bears	112	476	4.2	52	7
Tony Canadeo, Green Bay	122	476	3.9	27	0

LEADING PASSERS	Att.	Comp.	Yards	TD	Int.
Bob Waterfield, Los Angeles	251	127	1,747	18	17
Sid Luckman, Chicago Bears	229	110	1,826	17	16
Paul Governali, Boston	192	83	1,293	13	10
Paul Christman, Chi. Cardinals	229	100	1,656	13	18
Sammy Baugh, Washington	161	87	1,163	8	17

LEADING RECEIVERS	No.	Yards	Avg.	Long	TD
Jim Benton, Los Angeles	63	981	15.5	57	6
Harold Crisler, Boston Yanks	32	385	12.0	62	5
Steve Bagarus, Washington	31	438	14.1	51	3
Jack Ferrante, Philadelphia	28	451	16.1	48	4
Bill Dewell, Chicago Cardinals	27	643	23.8	82	7
Mal Kutner, Chicago Cardinals	27	634	23.5	63	5

1947 Charles W. Bidwill, owner of the Chicago Cardinals, won a bidding war with the New York Yankees of the All-America Football Conference and signed star halfback Charley Trippi of the University of Georgia. It gave the NFL a decisive victory over the AAFC.

A "bonus" draft choice was made for the first time. One team a year would get a special bonus choice before the first round began. The Chicago Bears won rights to the first "bonus" and chose back Bob Fenimore of Oklahoma A&M but he lasted only one season with them.

Sudden death was adopted for championship games. A fifth official, the back judge, was added.

The player limit was increased to 35 for the first three games and 34 for the rest of the season.

Jock Sutherland, coach of the Pittsburgh Steelers, traded star tailback Bill Dudley to the Detroit Lions and installed Johnny Clement as the Steelers' tailback.

Illness took the life of Charles Bidwill, owner of the Chicago Cardinals. Bidwill's wife and sons retained ownership of the team that became the strongest in the league. The Cardinals had what was called a "dream backfield" made up of Trippi, Elmer Angsman, Paul Christman, and Pat Harder. They defeated the Bears 30–21 in a climactic game that gave the Cardinals the division championship. Harder scored 102 points to lead the league.

The Cardinals had won a title at last after years as an also-ran. The same thing happened in the Eastern Division, where the Philadelphia Eagles of coach Earle (Greasy) Neale were developing into a powerful team. Left halfback Steve Van Buren gained 1,008 yards rushing, becoming the first 1,000-yard rusher in the NFL since 1934.

A "day" was held for Redskins' star Sammy Baugh at Griffith Stadium in Washington and he responded by throwing six touchdown passes as the Redskins beat the New York Giants.

Philadelphia had a feared offense in which Van Buren went off the right side time after time on power plays from the T-formation. The Eagles tied for the division championship with a Pittsburgh Steelers' team coached by Sutherland and still playing the single-wing formation. They met in a playoff and Philadelphia won 21–0.

The Western champions, the Cardinals, changed from their usual passing attack to a running game and made 282 yards on the ground in the championship game against the Eagles. The running of Chicago's Trippi and Angsman offset the passing of Philadelphia's Tommy Thompson and the Cardinals won the NFL championship 28–21.

1947 STANDINGS

Eastern Division	W	L	T	Pct.	Pts.	OP
Philadelphia	8	4	0	.667	308	242
Pittsburgh	8	4	0	.667	240	259
Boston Yanks	4	7	1	.364	168	256
Washington	4	8	0	.333	295	367
N.Y. Giants	2	8	2	.200	190	309
Western Division	**W**	**L**	**T**	**Pct.**	**Pts.**	**OP**
Chicago Cardinals.....	9	3	0	.750	306	231
Chicago Bears	8	4	0	.667	363	241
Green Bay	6	5	1	.545	274	210
Los Angeles	6	6	0	.500	259	214
Detroit	3	9	0	.250	231	305

Eastern Division playoff: Philadelphia 21, Pittsburgh 0
NFL championship: Chicago Cardinals 28, Philadelphia 21

LEADING RUSHERS	Att.	Yards	Avg.	Long	TD
Steve Van Buren, Philadelphia	217	1,008	4.6	45	14
J. (Zero) Clement, Pittsburgh	129	670	5.2	43	4
Tony Canadeo, Green Bay	103	464	4.5	35	2
Kenny Washington, Los Angeles	60	444	7.4	92	5
Walt Schlinkman, Green Bay	115	439	3.8	20	2

LEADING PASSERS	Att.	Comp.	Yards	TD	Int.
Sammy Baugh, Washington	354	210	2,938	25	15
Tommy Thompson, Philadelphia	201	106	1,680	16	15
Sid Luckman, Chicago Bears	323	176	2,712	24	31
Jack Jacobs, Green Bay	242	108	1,615	16	17
Paul Christman, Chi. Cardinals	301	138	2,191	17	22

LEADING RECEIVERS	No.	Yards	Avg.	Long	TD
Jim Keane, Chicago Bears	64	910	14.2	50	10
Bob Nussbaumer, Washington	47	597	12.7	55	4
Mal Kutner, Chicago Cardinals	43	944	21.9	70	7
Nolan Luhn, Green Bay	42	696	16.5	44	7
Bill Dewell, Chicago Cardinals	42	576	13.7	46	4

1948 The National Football League and All-America Football Conference were at war for players. Their clubs were strained to their financial limits as they vied to sign stars. Washington had the "bonus" choice in the NFL and used it to draft tailback Harry Gilmer of Alabama, who was supposed to be the eventual successor to Sammy Baugh as quarterback of the Redskins. George Preston Marshall, owner of the Redskins, now had both Baugh and Gilmer and so he

Sid Luckman, George McAfee, Ray (Scooter) McLean of the Bears, left to right, after 1946 title game.

Bill, left, and Charles Bidwill, right, with Chicago Cardinals coach Jimmy Conzelman, about 1947.

Pat Harder, Chicago Cardinals, vs. Los Angeles Rams, 1949.

Steve Van Buren, Philadelphia Eagles, vs. Washington Redskins, about 1949.

sold the rights to Charlie Conerly of Mississippi to the New York Giants. The Giants finally signed Conerly after a fight with the Brooklyn Dodgers of the AAFC and Dodgers' owner Branch Rickey.

The Detroit Lions drafted Y. A. Tittle of Louisiana State but he signed with the Baltimore Colts of the AAFC.

Baugh was nearing the end of his Redskins' career, and so was another NFL quarterbacking great, Sid Luckman of the Chicago Bears. Owner George Halas of the Bears signed both Bobby Layne of Texas and Johnny Lujack of Notre Dame. Layne had been drafted by Pittsburgh but didn't want to play the single-wing formation of John Michelosen, who had taken over the Steelers after the death of Jock Sutherland. Layne asked to be traded to Chicago.

Prominent rookies included tackle George Connor with the Chicago Bears, safety Emlen Tunnell with the New York Giants, and end Tom Fears with the Los Angeles Rams. Fears caught 51 passes to lead the league.

Fred Mandel sold the Detroit Lions to a syndicate headed by D. Lyle Fife.

Halfback Fred Gehrke of the Los Angeles Rams, who had studied art in college at Utah, painted horns on the leather helmets of the Rams, the first helmet emblems in pro football.

Each division champion repeated. Tommy Thompson threw 25 touchdown passes and Steve Van Buren gained 945 yards as the Philadelphia Eagles had a 9–2–1 record in the East. Pat Harder scored 110 points and the Chicago Cardinals ran up an 11–1 record.

A blizzard blanketed the field at Shibe Park in Philadelphia before the Eagles and Cardinals met in the championship game. The yard lines were obliterated, making the job of referee Ron Gibbs and his crew extremely difficult. The teams struggled for three quarters without any points until tackle Frank (Bucko) Kilroy of the Eagles recovered a Cardinals' fumble at the Chicago 17-yard line. Van Buren later scored from the 5 and the Eagles won 7–0.

1948 STANDINGS

Eastern Division	W	L	T	Pct.	Pts.	OP
Philadelphia	9	2	1	.818	376	156
Washington	7	5	0	.583	291	287
N.Y. Giants	4	8	0	.333	297	388
Pittsburgh	4	8	0	.333	200	243
Boston Yanks	3	9	0	.250	174	372
Western Division	**W**	**L**	**T**	**Pct.**	**Pts.**	**OP**
Chicago Cardinals	11	1	0	.917	395	226
Chicago Bears	10	2	0	.833	375	151
Los Angeles	6	5	1	.545	327	269
Green Bay	3	9	0	.250	154	290
Detroit	2	10	0	.167	200	407

NFL championship: Philadelphia 7, Chicago Cardinals 0

LEADING RUSHERS	Att.	Yards	Avg.	Long	TD
Steve Van Buren, Philadelphia	201	945	4.7	29	10
Charley Trippi, Chi. Cardinals	128	690	5.4	50	6
Elmer Angsman, Chi. Cardinals	131	638	4.9	72	8
Warren Wilson, Detroit	157	612	3.9	38	2
Tony Canadeo, Green Bay	123	589	4.8	49	4

LEADING PASSERS	Att.	Comp.	Yards	TD	Int.
Tommy Thompson, Philadelphia	246	141	1,965	25	11
Jim Hardy, Los Angeles	211	112	1,390	14	7
Charlie Conerly, N.Y. Giants	299	162	2.175	22	13
Sammy Baugh, Washington	315	185	2,599	22	23
Ray Mallouf, Chicago Cardinals	143	73	1,160	13	6

LEADING RECEIVERS	No.	Yards	Avg.	Long	TD
Tom Fears, Los Angeles	51	698	13.7	80	4
Pete Pihos, Philadelphia	46	766	16.7	48	11
Mal Kutner, Chicago Cardinals	41	943	23.0	71	14
Val Jansante, Pittsburgh	39	623	16.0	66	3
Bill Swiacki, N.Y. Giants	39	550	14.1	65	10

1949 The attrition of the NFL-AAFC war was felt by every team. The champion Philadelphia Eagles, at the peak of their greatness, lost money and were sold by Alexis Thompson to a syndicate headed by James P. Clark. The Green Bay Packers were in financial straits, having been hit the hardest of any NFL team in the bidding war with the AAFC to sign players. The Boston Yanks quit that city and moved to New York,

Tony Canadeo, Green Bay Packers.

Joe Golding, New York Bulldogs, vs. Washington, 1949.

became the "Bulldogs," and played home games at the Polo Grounds when the Giants were on the road.

The Chicago Rockets of the All-American Football Conference had new ownership and changed their name to "Hornets." The AAFC Brooklyn Dodgers merged with the New York Yankees. There had been talks between the two leagues about a possible merger ending the pro football war and these discussions continued.

Elroy (Crazylegs) Hirsch joined the Los Angeles Rams from the AAFC Chicago Rockets and he and ends Tom Fears and Bob Shaw became a great passing combination with quarterbacks Bob Waterfield and Norm Van Brocklin, a rookie from Oregon. George Blanda was a rookie with the Chicago Bears and Chuck Bednarik with the Philadelphia Eagles.

The league had two 1,000-yard rushers for the first time. Steve Van Buren gained 1,146 for Philadelphia and Tony Canadeo 1,052 for Green Bay.

In addition to Van Buren, Philadelphia also had Bosh Pritchard at halfback and quarterback Tommy Thompson passing to ends Pete Pihos and Jack Ferrante. The Eagles raced to an 11–1 record.

Los Angeles, coached by Clark Shaughnessy, won the Western Division. Fears caught 77 passes.

Peace came to pro football December 9. Bert Bell, the NFL commissioner, announced a merger agreement in which three teams of the AAFC—the Cleveland Browns, San Francisco 49ers, and Baltimore Colts—would join the NFL in 1950.

Los Angeles Memorial Coliseum was the site for the championship game between the Rams and the Philadelphia Eagles. Heavy rain drenched the field

and there were only 22,945 fans in attendance as Van Buren gained 196 yards on 31 carries, leading the Eagles to a 14–0 victory and their second straight NFL championship.

Earl (Curly) Lambeau, Green Bay's head coach since 1921, left the Packers.

1949 STANDINGS

Eastern Division	W	L	T	Pct.	Pts.	OP
Philadelphia	11	1	0	.917	364	134
Pittsburgh	6	5	1	.545	224	214
N.Y. Giants	6	6	0	.500	287	298
Washington	4	7	1	.364	268	339
N.Y. Bulldogs	1	10	1	.091	153	368
Western Division	**W**	**L**	**T**	**Pct.**	**Pts.**	**OP**
Los Angeles	8	2	2	.800	360	239
Chicago Bears	9	3	0	.750	332	218
Chicago Cardinals	6	5	1	.545	360	301
Detroit	4	8	0	.333	237	259
Green Bay	2	10	0	.167	114	329

NFL championship: Philadelphia 14, Los Angeles 0

LEADING RUSHERS	Att.	Yards	Avg.	Long	TD
Steve Van Buren, Philadelphia	263	1,146	4.4	41	11
Tony Canadeo, Green Bay	208	1,052	5.1	54	4
Elmer Angsman, Chi. Cardinals	125	674	5.4	82	6
Gene Roberts, N.Y. Giants	152	634	4.2	63	9
Jerry Nuzum, Pittsburgh	139	611	4.4	64	5
LEADING PASSERS	**Att.**	**Comp.**	**Yards**	**TD**	**Int.**
Sammy Baugh, Washington	255	145	1,903	18	14
Johnny Lujack, Chicago Bears	312	162	2,658	23	22
Tommy Thompson, Philadelphia	214	116	1,727	16	11
Bob Waterfield, Los Angeles	296	154	2,168	17	24
Charlie Conerly, N.Y. Giants	305	152	2,138	17	20
LEADING RECEIVERS	**No.**	**Yards**	**Avg.**	**Long**	**TD**
Tom Fears, Los Angeles	77	1,013	13.2	51	9
Bob Mann, Detroit	66	1,014	15.4	64	4
Bill Chipley, N.Y. Bulldogs	57	631	11.1	69	2
Jim Keane, Chicago Bears	47	696	14.8	39	6
Bill Swiacki, N.Y. Giants	47	652	13.9	42	4

1950 The complicated terms were worked out for the assimilation of three new teams into the league. "Divisions" were scrapped and replaced by the "American Conference" and "National Conference." The Cleveland Browns entered the American and the Baltimore Colts and San Francisco 49ers went into the National. The team that had been the New York Bulldogs became the New York Yanks and it divided the players of the former AAFC Yankees with the New York Giants. A special allocation draft was held allowing the 13 teams to draft the remaining AAFC players, with Baltimore being granted special consideration with 15 choices compared to 10 for the other teams.

For the first time in history, an NFL team, the Los Angeles Rams, contracted to have all its games televised. The arrangement covered both home and away games and the sponsor agreed to make up the difference in home game income if it was lower than it had been the season before. Attendance fell and the cost to the sponsor was $307,000. The Washington Redskins followed the Rams in arranging to televise their games; other teams made deals to put selected games on television.

Unlimited free substitution was restored in the NFL and the way opened for the era of two platoons and specialization in pro football.

An exceptional number of talented players entered the league. Defensive tackle Arnie Weinmeister and defensive backs Tom Landry, Otto Schnellbacher, and Harmon Rowe joined the New York Giants from the defunct AAFC Yankees. The Cleveland Browns' array of stars such as quarterback Otto Graham, backs

Norm Van Brocklin of Los Angeles passes against Detroit in 1953; Jim Cain, 88, and Thurman McGraw, 73, rush for the Lions.

Marion Motley and Dub Jones, ends Dante Lavelli and Mac Speedie, and linemen Lou Groza and Bill Willis moved into the NFL, and so did San Francisco stars such as quarterback Frankie Albert and halfback Joe Perry, and quarterback Y.A. Tittle of the Baltimore Colts.

The NFL draft yielded tackle Art Donovan for Baltimore; end Leon Hart and back Doak Walker for Detroit (Walker had actually been drafted in 1949 but did not join Detroit until 1950); quarterback Tobin Rote for Green Bay; tackle Ernie Stautner for Pittsburgh; tackle Leo Nomellini and end Gordy Soltau for San Francisco; and halfback Charlie (Choo Choo) Justice and quarterback Eddie LeBaron for Washington.

Commissioner Bert Bell set up a first-weekend test of strength between the NFL and AAFC when he scheduled the champion Philadelphia Eagles against the four-time AAFC champion Cleveland Browns on Saturday night before the regular opening day of the season. Cleveland won 35-10 before 71,237 fans. The Browns, coached by Paul Brown, went on to compile a 10-2 regular season record. The New York Giants beat them 6-0 and 17-13, throwing an Umbrella defense over the Browns' passing attack of Graham to Lavelli, Speedie, and Jones.

Motley of the Browns won the league rushing championship with 810 yards. Tom Fears of the Los Angeles Rams had a great season, catching 84 passes. Rookie Walker of the Lions—who also place-kicked—scored 128 points in the 12-game season.

For the first time ever, there were deadlocks in each conference, or division, and playoffs were necessary in each. Cleveland gained revenge against the New York Giants, winning their American Conference playoff 8–3 on two field goals by Groza and a safety. Los Angeles defeated the Chicago Bears 24–14 in the National Conference playoff.

The Browns edged the Rams 30–28 on a 16-yard field goal by Groza with 28 seconds to play at Cleveland Municipal Stadium in one of the most exciting title games ever played.

1950 STANDINGS

American Conference	W	L	T	Pct.	Pts.	OP
Cleveland	10	2	0	.833	310	144
N.Y. Giants	10	2	0	.833	268	150
Philadelphia	6	6	0	.500	254	141
Pittsburgh	6	6	0	.500	180	195
Chicago Cardinals	5	7	0	.417	233	287
Washington	3	9	0	.250	232	326
National Conference	**W**	**L**	**T**	**Pct.**	**Pts.**	**OP**
Los Angeles	9	3	0	.750	466	309
Chicago Bears	9	3	0	.750	279	207
N.Y. Yanks	7	5	0	.583	366	367
Detroit	6	6	0	.500	321	285
Green Bay	3	9	0	.250	244	406
San Francisco	3	9	0	.250	213	300
Baltimore	1	11	0	.083	213	462

American Conference playoff: Cleveland 8, N.Y. Giants 3
National Conference playoff: Los Angeles 24, Chicago Bears 14
NFL championship: Cleveland 30, Los Angeles 28

LEADING RUSHERS	Att.	Yards	Avg.	Long	TD
Marion Motley, Cleveland	140	810	5.8	69	3
Frank Ziegler, Philadelphia	172	733	4.3	52	1
Joe Geri, Pittsburgh	188	705	3.8	47	2
Eddie Price, N.Y. Giants	126	703	5.6	74	4
Joe Perry, San Francisco	124	647	5.2	78	5

LEADING PASSERS	Att.	Comp.	Yards	TD	Int.
Norm Van Brocklin, Los Angeles	233	127	2,061	18	14
Otto Graham, Cleveland	253	137	1,943	14	20
Joe Geri, Pittsburgh	113	41	866	6	15
George Ratterman, N.Y. Yanks	294	140	2,251	22	24
Charlie Conerly, N.Y. Giants	132	56	1,000	8	7

LEADING RECEIVERS	No.	Yards	Avg.	Long	TD
Tom Fears, Los Angeles	84	1,116	13.3	53	7
Dan Edwards, N.Y. Yanks	52	775	14.9	82	6
Cloyce Box, Detroit	50	1,009	20.2	82	11
Paul Salata, Baltimore	50	618	12.4	57	4
Bob Shaw, Chicago Cardinals	48	971	20.2	65	12

1951 The Pro Bowl game, dormant since 1942, was revived under a new format in which the all-stars of each conference would be matched against each

other. The game would be played in Los Angeles at the Memorial Coliseum each year after the championship game, and would be sponsored by the *Los Angeles Times.* Otto Graham, quarterback of the 1950 champion Cleveland Browns, completed 19 of 27 passes for 252 yards and a touchdown, and ran for two touchdowns, to lead the American Conference to a 28–27 victory over the National Conference in the first Pro Bowl game with this new format. It was one of the most exciting all-star games, with Graham's quarterback rivals, teammates Bob Waterfield and Norm Van Brocklin of Los Angeles, combining for 21 completions in 44 pass attempts for 294 yards and three touchdowns.

The Baltimore Colts' franchise that had come into the NFL from the All-America Football Conference died after one season. Abraham Watner, its owner, turned the franchise and player contracts back to the NFL for $50,000. Baltimore's former pro players were made available for drafting at the same time as college players January 18. Four former Colts were among the 13 players selected in the first round—quarterback Y. A. Tittle by San Francisco, back Billy Stone by the Chicago Bears, back Jim Spavital by the New York Giants, and back Chet Mutryn by Philadelphia.

Tailback Kyle Rote of Southern Methodist was the "bonus" choice in the draft. He was selected by the New York Giants, who converted him into a halfback or flanker back.

The Los Angeles Rams had their greatest season. They had two fine quarterbacks in Bob Waterfield and Norm Van Brocklin, who shared the position, and

ends Tom Fears and Bob Boyd and flanker back Elroy (Crazylegs) Hirsch as pass targets. The starting backfield of big, fast Dan Towler, Dick Hoerner, and Paul (Tank) Younger was nicknamed the "Bull Elephant Backfield." The "pony backs" were in reserve. They were Glenn Davis, Volney (Skeet) Quinlan, and Verda (Vitamin T.) Smith.

Van Brocklin had an NFL record 554 yards passing in a game against the New York Yanks. Waterfield, however, ended the season as the NFL's leading passer. Waterfield also was the Rams' placekicker and Van Brocklin the punter. Hirsch caught 66 passes for a record 1,495 yards and 17 touchdowns.

The Rams' attendance went up as they reversed their television policy and aired only road games.

They were a high-scoring team but the Rams had to fight to win their conference championship. The Detroit Lions had Raymond (Buddy) Parker as coach and players such as quarterback Bobby Layne, fullback Pat Harder, and halfbacks Bob Hoernschemeyer and Doak Walker. Detroit beat Los Angeles in a key game one week before the end of the season and took over first place. The Lions then lost their final game to San Francisco while the Rams defeated Green Bay and captured the National Conference title.

The Cleveland Browns were the strongest team in the American Conference. Dub Jones, the Browns' all-around halfback, scored six touchdowns in one game against the Chicago Bears, tying an NFL record set by Ernie Nevers in 1929. Cleveland lost its opening game to San Francisco and then roared back, winning 11 straight.

The championship game was televised coast-to-

Otto Graham goes over for a one-yard touchdown in the 1951 Pro Bowl Game.

Jerry Williams returns a punt as a teammate leg-whips Pat Canamella of the Dallas Texans, 1952.

Autograph seekers surround Sammy Baugh after his last game for Washington, 1952.

Chick Jagade scores Cleveland's only touchdown in its 17–7 loss to Detroit in 1952 title game.

coast for the first time. It was on the DuMont network, which paid $75,000 for the rights to it. The Rams defeated the Browns 24–17 in an exciting game before 57,522 at Los Angeles Memorial Coliseum. Alternate quarterback Van Brocklin and Fears combined for a 73-yard touchdown pass in the final quarter to win the game. The winning and losing shares set records, $2,108 for each member of the Rams' team and $1,483 for each member of the Browns.

1951 STANDINGS

American Conference	W	L	T	Pct.	Pts.	OP
Cleveland	11	1	0	.917	331	152
N.Y. Giants	9	2	1	.818	254	161
Washington	5	7	0	.417	183	296
Pittsburgh	4	7	1	.364	183	235
Philadelphia	4	8	0	.333	234	264
Chicago Cardinals	3	9	0	.250	210	287
National Conference	**W**	**L**	**T**	**Pct.**	**Pts.**	**OP**
Los Angeles	8	4	0	.667	392	261
Detroit	7	4	1	.636	336	259
San Francisco	7	4	1	.636	255	205
Chicago Bears	7	5	0	.583	286	282
Green Bay	3	9	0	.250	254	375
N.Y. Yanks	1	9	2	.100	241	382

NFL championship: Los Angeles 24, Cleveland 17

LEADING RUSHERS	Att.	Yards	Avg.	Long	TD
Eddie Price, N.Y. Giants	271	971	3.6	80t	7
Rob Goode, Washington	208	951	4.6	33	9
Dan Towler, Los Angeles	126	854	6.8	79t	6
Bob Hoernschemeyer, Detroit	132	678	5.1	85t	2
Joe Perry, San Francisco	136	677	5.0	58t	3

LEADING PASSERS	Att.	Comp.	Yards	TD	Int.
Bob Waterfield, Los Angeles	176	88	1,566	13	10
Norm Van Brocklin, Los Angeles	194	100	1,725	13	11
Otto Graham, Cleveland	265	147	2,205	17	16
Steve Romanik, Chicago Bears	101	43	791	3	9
Bob Celeri, N.Y. Yanks	238	102	1,797	12	15
Johnny Lujack, Chicago Bears	176	85	1,295	8	8

LEADING RECEIVERS	No.	Yards	Avg.	Long	TD
Elroy Hirsch, Los Angeles	66	1,495	22.7	91t	17
Gordy Soltau, San Francisco	59	826	14.0	48t	7
Fran Polsfoot, Chi. Cardinals	57	796	14.0	80t	4
Bob Mann, Green Bay	50	696	13.9	52	8
Dante Lavelli, Cleveland	43	586	13.6	47	6

1952 Ted Collins, owner of the New York Yanks' franchise, decided to give up trying to field a successful NFL team after eight years. He sold the Yanks to the NFL who in turn sold it to a Texas group. It moved to Dallas as the "Texans," the first NFL franchise in that state.

Collins had operated the team since 1944 as the Boston Yanks, New York Bulldogs, and New York Yanks during eight futile seasons.

One of the best groups of rookie players in history entered the NFL. It included the "bonus" draft choice, quarterback Bill Wade of Los Angeles; halfback Frank Gifford of the New York Giants, linebacker Bill George of the Chicago Bears, defensive end Gino Marchetti of the Dallas Texans, back Ollie Matson of the Chicago Cardinals, back Hugh McElhenny of San Francisco, and back Ed Modzelewski of Pittsburgh. Marchetti and Matson were from the same college, San Francisco.

Joe Bach replaced John Michelosen as coach at Pittsburgh and the Steelers abandoned the single-wing for the T-formation, the last professional team to do so.

The Dallas franchise drew small crowds and midway through the season became a traveling road team based at Hershey, Pennsylvania. It won a game Thanksgiving Day against the Chicago Bears at Akron, Ohio before 3,000 fans. The "Texans" lost 11 other games and went out of business. It was the last time an NFL team failed.

Bob Waterfield of the Los Angeles Rams led one of the most spectacular comebacks in the history of the league when he rallied the Rams from a 28–6 deficit with 12 minutes to play and they beat the Green Bay Packers 30–28.

Detroit lost two of its first three games but then stormed back to finish in a tie with Los Angeles for the National Conference championship. They met in a playoff and Pat Harder scored 19 points to lead Detroit to a 31–21 victory.

Cleveland lost four games but still won the American Conference title and the first NFL championship game between two growing rivals, the Lions and Browns, followed. Detroit won 17–7 and claimed its first NFL championship in 17 years. Raymond (Buddy) Parker, coach of the Lions, had been their quarterback when they won the championship the last time in 1935.

Two of the greatest NFL players in history, Sammy Baugh of the Washington Redskins and Steve Van Buren of the Philadelphia Eagles, retired.

J. R. Boone makes a catch for Green Bay; Bert Rechichar and Don Shula defend for Baltimore.

1952 STANDINGS

American Conference	W	L	T	Pct.	Pts.	OP
Cleveland	8	4	0	.667	310	213
N.Y. Giants	7	5	0	.583	234	231
Philadelphia	7	5	0	.583	252	271
Pittsburgh	5	7	0	.417	300	273
Chicago Cardinals	4	8	0	.333	172	221
Washington	4	8	0	.333	240	287
National Conference	**W**	**L**	**T**	**Pct.**	**Pts.**	**OP**
Detroit	9	3	0	.750	344	192
Los Angeles	9	3	0	.750	349	234
San Francisco	7	5	0	.583	285	221
Green Bay	6	6	0	.500	295	312
Chicago Bears	5	7	0	.417	245	326
Dallas Texans	1	11	0	.083	182	427

National Conference playoff: Detroit 31, Los Angeles 21
NFL championship: Detroit 17, Cleveland 7

LEADING RUSHERS	Att.	Yards	Avg.	Long	TD
Dan Towler, Los Angeles	156	894	5.7	44t	10
Eddie Price, N.Y. Giants	183	748	4.1	75t	5
Joe Perry, San Francisco	158	725	4.6	78t	8
Hugh McElhenny, San Francisco	98	684	7.0	89t	6
Bob Hoernschemeyer, Detroit	106	457	4.3	41	4

LEADING PASSERS	Att.	Comp.	Yards	TD	Int.
Norm Van Brocklin, Los Angeles	205	113	1,736	14	17
Tobin Rote, Green Bay	157	82	1,268	13	8
Babe Parilli, Green Bay	177	77	1,416	13	17
Otto Graham, Cleveland	364	181	2,816	20	24
Frankie Albert, San Francisco	129	71	964	8	10

LEADING RECEIVERS	No.	Yards	Avg.	Long	TD
Mac Speedie, Cleveland	62	911	14.7	50	5
Harry (Bud) Grant, Philadelphia	56	997	17.8	84t	7
Elbie Nickel, Pittsburgh	55	884	16.1	54t	9
Gordie Soltau, San Francisco	55	774	14.1	49t	7
Don Stonesifer, Chi. Cardinals	54	617	11.4	26	0

1953 Baltimore rejoined the NFL. Commissioner Bert Bell awarded the holdings of the defunct Dallas Texans' franchise to a group headed by Carroll Rosenbloom, which formed a new team called the "Colts"; that was also the name of the former team in Baltimore that had died after the 1950 season.

The NFL won an important court victory when Bell's policy of blacking out television of home games was upheld by Judge Allan K. Grim of the United States District Court for the Eastern District of Philadelphia.

The names of the American and National Conferences were changed to "Eastern Conference" and "Western Conference."

Mickey McBride, founder of the Cleveland Browns, sold them to a group headed by Dave R. Jones.

The league had another fine collection of rookies. Roosevelt Brown, Jack Stroud, and Ray Wietecha joined the New York Giants; Joe Schmidt joined the Detroit Lions, Jim Ringo the Green Bay Packers, Doug Atkins the Chicago Bears, Bob St. Clair the San Francisco 49ers, and Gene (Big Daddy) Lipscomb, who had not played college football, was in his first year with the Los Angeles Rams.

Lou Groza of the Cleveland Browns kicked a record 23 field goals. Joe Perry of San Francisco gained 1,018 yards rushing and won a bonus of $5,090, $5 for every yard he gained. Harry (Bud) Grant, an end for the Philadelphia Eagles, left them to sign a contract with the Canadian Football League and his successor at his position, Pete Pihos, led the NFL with 63 pass receptions.

The Detroit Lions won the Western Conference.

Joe Perry of the 49ers wearing the face mask that protected his broken jaw in 1953.

Otto Graham scores one of six touchdowns he accounted for in 56–10 victory, in 1954 championship.

Alan Ameche, leading rusher as a rookie in 1955, carries the ball against San Francisco.

Their Great Lakes rival, the Cleveland Browns, appeared on their way to a perfect season but lost their last game and finished 11-1. The Browns still won the Eastern Division easily. In the championship game, quarterback Bobby Layne of the Lions brought them from behind in the closing minutes and threw the winning touchdown pass to end Jim Doran for a 17–16 victory.

Steve Owen of the New York Giants suffered through a long season and one of his losses was a 62–14 drubbing at the hands of the Browns. He departed the Giants after 23 years as their head coach. Bob Waterfield of the Los Angeles Rams and Clyde (Bulldog) Turner of the Chicago Bears retired.

Jim Thorpe, former great player and president of the American Professional Football Association, forerunner of the NFL, died at Lomita, California, March 28.

1953 STANDINGS

Eastern Conference	W	L	T	Pct.	Pts.	OP
Cleveland	11	1	0	.917	348	162
Philadelphia	7	4	1	.636	352	215
Washington	6	5	1	.545	208	215
Pittsburgh	6	6	0	.500	211	263
N.Y. Giants	3	9	0	.250	179	277
Chicago Cardinals	1	10	1	.091	190	337
Western Conference	**W**	**L**	**T**	**Pct.**	**Pts.**	**OP**
Detroit	10	2	0	.833	271	205
San Francisco	9	3	0	.750	372	237
Los Angeles	8	3	1	.727	366	236
Chicago Bears	3	8	1	.273	218	262
Baltimore	3	9	0	.250	182	350
Green Bay	2	9	1	.182	200	338

NFL championship: Detroit 17, Cleveland 16

LEADING RUSHERS	Att.	Yards	Avg.	Long	TD
Joe Perry, San Francisco	192	1,018	5.3	51t	10
Dan Towler, Los Angeles	152	879	5.8	73t	7
Skeet Quinlan, Los Angeles	97	705	7.3	74t	4
Charley Justice, Washington	115	616	5.4	43	2
Fran Rogel, Pittsburgh	137	527	3.8	58	2
John Huzvar, Baltimore	119	515	4.3	36	4

LEADING PASSERS	Att.	Comp.	Yards	TD	Int.
Otto Graham, Cleveland	258	167	2,722	11	9
Norm Van Brocklin, Los Angeles	286	156	2,393	19	14
Y.A. Tittle, San Francisco	259	149	2,121	20	16
Bobby Thomason, Philadelphia	304	162	2,462	21	20
Bobby Layne, Detroit	273	125	2,088	16	21
John Scarbath, Washington	129	45	862	9	12

LEADING RECEIVERS	No.	Yards	Avg.	Long	TD
Pete Pihos, Philadelphia	63	1,049	16.7	59	10
Elbie Nickel, Pittsburgh	62	743	12.0	40	4
Elroy Hirsch, Los Angeles	61	941	15.4	70	4
Don Stonesifer, Chi. Cardinals	56	684	12.2	46	2
Jim Dooley, Chicago Bears	53	841	15.9	72	4
Billy Wilson, San Francisco	51	840	16.5	61	10

1954 Commissioner Bert Bell was given a new 12-year contract by the NFL and two of its teams made significant coaching moves. The New York Giants named Jim Lee Howell head coach. He hired Vince Lombardi as offensive coach and had Tom Landry as player-coach of his defensive team. The Baltimore Colts hired Weeb Ewbank, an assistant to Paul Brown at Cleveland, as head coach.

Brown of the Browns was concerned that his quarterback, Otto Graham, was near retirement and drafted Bobby Garrett of Stanford as the NFL "bonus" choice. Garrett's availability became uncertain because of military commitments, however, and Brown traded him to Green Bay for Babe Parilli. Parilli himself was in the army but was due to return to pro football in two years.

Canadian Football League teams were raiding NFL teams and signed quarterback Eddie LeBaron and defensive end Gene Brito of the Washington Redskins.

Quarterback Adrian Burk of the Philadelphia Eagles threw seven touchdown passes in one game against Washington, tying the record set by Sid Luckman in 1943.

Joe Perry of the San Francisco 49ers became the first back in league history to gain 1,000 yards rushing in consecutive seasons. He led the league with 1,049.

Cleveland and Detroit were headed for their third straight meeting in the championship game. The

Browns again started slowly, losing two of their first three games before winning eight in a row. A game with the Lions, postponed because of a conflict with the Cleveland Indians' baseball World Series against the New York Giants, was rescheduled for December 19, a week after the other clubs finished their season. Detroit won 14–10 in a blizzard.

Raymond (Buddy) Parker of Detroit was gaining a reputation as one who held a jinx over his coaching rival, Brown of Cleveland. Parker had his alter ego, Bobby Layne, at quarterback. Giant tackle Les Bingaman anchored Detroit's five-man line on defense. Safety Jack Christiansen led a superb secondary nicknamed "Chris's Crew."

It was an exceptional team but it was not the equal of the Browns in the 1954 title game. Graham, playing what he said was his last game at quarterback for Cleveland, made it one of his greatest ever when he threw three touchdown passes and scored three times himself as the Browns routed the Lions 56–10.

1954 STANDINGS

Eastern Conference	W	L	T	Pct.	Pts.	OP
Cleveland	9	3	0	.750	336	162
Philadelphia	7	4	1	.625	284	230
N.Y. Giants	7	5	0	.583	293	184
Pittsburgh	5	7	0	.417	219	263
Washington	3	9	0	.250	207	432
Chicago Cardinals	2	10	0	.167	183	347
Western Conference	**W**	**L**	**T**	**Pct.**	**Pts.**	**OP**
Detroit	9	2	1	.818	337	189
Chicago Bears	8	4	0	.667	301	279
San Francisco	7	4	1	.636	313	251
Los Angeles	6	5	1	.545	314	285
Green Bay	4	8	0	.333	234	251
Baltimore	3	9	0	.250	131	279

NFL championship: Cleveland 56, Detroit 10

LEADING RUSHERS	Att.	Yards	Avg.	Long	TD
Joe Perry, San Francisco	173	1,049	6.1	58	8
J. Henry Johnson, San Francisco	129	681	5.3	38t	9
Tank Younger, Los Angeles	91	610	6.7	75t	8
Dan Towler, Los Angeles	149	599	4.0	24	11
Maurice Bassett, Cleveland	144	588	4.1	22	6
Eddie Price, N.Y. Giants	135	555	4.1	47	2

LEADING PASSERS	Att.	Comp.	Yards	TD	Int.
Norm Van Brocklin, Los Angeles	260	139	2,637	13	21
Otto Graham, Cleveland	240	142	2,092	11	17
Zeke Bratkowski, Chicago Bears	130	67	1,087	8	17
Tom Dublinski, Detroit	138	77	1,073	8	7
Bob Clatterbuck, N.Y. Giants	101	50	781	6	7

LEADING RECEIVERS	No.	Yards	Avg.	Long	TD
Pete Pihos, Philadelphia	60	872	14.5	34	10
Billy Wilson, San Francisco	60	830	13.8	43	5
Bob Boyd, Los Angeles	53	1,212	22.9	80t	6
Bill Howton, Green Bay	52	768	14.8	59	2
Dante Lavelli, Cleveland	47	802	17.1	64	7

1955 The Washington expatriates, LeBaron and Brito, returned from the Canadian Football League and rejoined the Redskins. Paul Brown, the Cleveland Browns' coach, talked his quarterback, Otto Graham, out of retirement. Semipro quarterback Johnny Unitas tried out with the Pittsburgh Steelers but was rejected; Walt Kiesling, the Steelers' coach, chose quarterbacks Jim Finks and Ted Marchibroda over Unitas. The Baltimore Colts made an 80-cent telephone call to the rejected quarterback, and signed him as a free agent.

George Halas announced he was coaching his last season for the Chicago Bears. And Sid Gillman, a little-known college coach at Cincinnati, took over as head coach of the Los Angeles Rams.

Ball carriers in pro football could continue to advance the ball, even by crawling along the ground, until they were stopped. In contrast, runners in college and high school football were downed and the play blown dead as soon as anything other than their feet touched the ground. The professional rule led to a brand of rough-and-tumble football. There were charges of "dirty play." As a result, the rules were changed so that the ball would be declared dead immediately if a player touched the ground with any part of his body, except his hands or feet, while in the grasp of an opponent "and irrespective of the grasp

Jim Thorpe in his later years.

Adrian Burk.

Rookie coach Sid Gillman of Los Angeles, 1955.

being broken." It was called the NFL's "dead ball rule."

The league's sudden death overtime rule was used for the first time in a preseason game at Portland, Oregon. The promoter of the game there between the Los Angeles Rams and New York Giants convinced them to play under the rule of sudden death, and also an oddball system of numbering the field yard lines from 1 to 100. To the dismay of both coaches, Sid Gillman of the Rams and Jim Lee Howell of the Giants, the game was tied 17–17 after four quarters and an overtime period was necessary. The Rams scored three minutes later on a two-yard run by Paul (Tank) Younger and won 23–17.

Graham started slowly for Cleveland but hit his stride and led the league in passing. The Browns were strengthened by the acquisition of Ed Modzelewski from Pittsburgh and Fred (Curly) Morrison from the Chicago Bears to carry the ball, and Darrell (Pete) Brewster and Ray Renfro joined Dante Lavelli as targets for Graham's accurate passes. Cleveland won its sixth straight NFL division championship and tenth title in a row counting its four years in the All-America Football Conference.

Detroit did not do as well. It went into a tailspin after middle guard Les Bingaman retired and quarterback Bobby Layne strained his shoulder while lassoing a calf in the offseason in Texas. The Lions struggled to a 3-9 record and finished last in the Western Conference.

Rookie coach Gillman of Los Angeles lost twice to the Chicago Bears but still won the West in his first season. The Bears' attempts to win a title for Halas in his last season failed when the crosstown Chicago Cardinals crushed them 53–14.

The Los Angeles Memorial Coliseum, where the Rams and Browns had played their classic 1951 championship, was the scene once more for the title game. Graham of Cleveland, as he had the year before against Detroit, was once more playing what he said was his last game of professional football. He dominated the Rams, running for two touchdowns and passing for two others to swamp Los Angeles 38–14 before a championship game record crowd of 85,693.

The National Broadcasting Company replaced the DuMont network as the network carrying the title game, for which it paid a rights fee of $100,000.

1955 STANDINGS

Eastern Conference	W	L	T	Pct.	Pts.	OP
Cleveland	9	2	1	.818	349	218
Washington	8	4	0	.667	246	222
N.Y. Giants	6	5	1	.545	267	223
Chicago Cardinals	4	7	1	.364	224	252
Philadelphia	4	7	1	.364	248	231
Pittsburgh	4	8	0	.333	195	285
Western Conference	**W**	**L**	**T**	**Pct.**	**Pts.**	**OP**
Los Angeles	8	3	1	.727	260	231
Chicago Bears	8	4	0	.667	294	251
Green Bay	6	6	0	.500	258	276
Baltimore	5	6	1	.455	214	239
San Francisco	4	8	0	.333	216	298
Detroit	3	9	0	.250	230	275

NFL championship: Cleveland 38, Los Angeles 14

LEADING RUSHERS	Att.	Yards	Avg.	Long	TD
Alan Ameche, Baltimore	213	961	4.5	79t	9
Howie Ferguson, Green Bay	192	859	4.5	57	4
F. (Curley) Morrison, Cleveland	156	824	5.3	56	3
Ron Waller, Los Angeles	151	716	4.7	55t	7
Joe Perry, San Francisco	156	701	4.5	42	2

LEADING PASSERS	Att.	Comp.	Yards	TD	Int.
Otto Graham, Cleveland	185	98	1,721	15	8
Ed Brown, Chicago Bears	164	85	1,307	9	10
Bobby Thomason, Philadelphia	171	88	1,337	10	7
Y.A. Tittle, San Francisco	287	147	2,185	17	28
Eddie LeBaron, Washington	178	79	1,270	9	9

LEADING RECEIVERS	No.	Yards	Avg.	Long	TD
Pete Pihos, Philadelphia	62	864	13.9	40t	7
Billy Wilson, San Francisco	53	831	15.7	72t	7
Billy Howton, Green Bay	44	697	15.8	60	5
Dave Middleton, Detroit	44	663	15.1	77t	3
Tom Fears, Los Angeles	44	569	12.9	31	2
Lew Carpenter, Detroit	44	312	7.1	34t	2

Ollie Matson, Chicago Cardinals, 1955.

Bill Wade, Los Angeles Rams.

1956 The year began with Jack Christensen of Detroit and the Western Conference returning the opening kickoff of the Pro Bowl game 103 yards for a touchdown, and Ollie Matson of the Chicago Cardinals and the Eastern Conference returning the second half kickoff 91 yards for a touchdown. There were two more exciting returns when the 1956 season began. Al Carmichael of the Green Bay Packers went 106 yards with a kickoff against the Chicago Bears October 7, the longest play in pro football history, and the very next week the brilliant Matson raced 105 yards with a kickoff return against the Washington Redskins. In the same game, Frank Bernardi of the Cardinals returned a punt 95 yards.

The CBS television network became the first to broadcast some NFL regular season games to selected television markets across the nation.

The rules were changed so that it was illegal to grab an opponent's face mask. "Loudspeaker coaching" from the sideline was prohibited. A brown ball with white stripes, not a white ball with black stripes, was ordered for use in night games. And the language of the "dead ball rule" was improved; the ball was now dead immediately when the runner was contacted by a defensive player and touched the ground with any part of his body except his hands or feet.

Frankie Albert, former quarterback of the San Francisco 49ers, took over as their head coach. There were several notable rookies such as back J. C.

Caroline of the Chicago Bears, back Howard (Hopalong) Cassady of the Detroit Lions, tackles Forrest Gregg and Bob Skoronski of the Green Bay Packers; quarterback Earl Morrall of San Francisco, and back Lenny Moore of the Baltimore Colts.

The championship teams of 1955, the Cleveland Browns and Los Angeles Rams, went from greatness to mediocrity. Otto Graham made good his retirement from pro football and the Browns tried unsuccessfully to replace him with Tommy O'Connell, Babe Parilli, and George Ratterman, finishing with their first losing season and failing to capture a divisional championship for the first time in club history.

Los Angeles plunged to last place in the Western Conference. Sid Gillman, the Rams' coach, vacillated between Norm Van Brocklin and Bill Wade at quarterback and had trouble replacing defensive linemen Andy Robustelli, who had been traded to the New York Giants, and Gene (Big Daddy) Lipscomb, who had been waived to the Baltimore Colts.

The season belonged, instead, to the New York Giants and Chicago Bears. The Giants moved from the Polo Grounds to Yankee Stadium. Trades brought them Robustelli and defensive back Ed Hughes from the Rams and defensive tackle Dick Modzelewski from the Pittsburgh Steelers. Kicker Don Chandler, linebacker Sam Huff, and defensive end Jim Katcavage were Giants' rookies. Frank Gifford, Kyle Rote, Mel Triplett, and Alex Webster were in the Giants'

backfield to run the ball and catch passes. And Jim Lee Howell had a novel system in which he would start Don Heinrich at quarterback to probe the defense and determine how it was playing, and then send in Charlie Conerly to play the rest of the game.

Paddy Driscoll, a former teammate and a longtime friend and coaching associate of George Halas, replaced him as coach of the Bears. They were humiliated 42–10 early in the season by the revived Detroit Lions, but came back to capture the conference championship by beating Detroit 38–21 in the final week of the season. The second game was marred by controversy when defensive end Ed Meadows hit Lions' quarterback Bobby Layne and put him out of action.

Ed Brown established himself as Chicago's quarterback and led the league in passing. His exciting receiver, Harlon Hill, caught 47 passes. Fullback Rick Casares gained 1,126 yards rushing.

Johnny Unitas took over as quarterback of the Baltimore Colts after George Shaw suffered a broken leg.

The Giants and Bears met for the championship at Yankee Stadium. Clark Shaughnessy, the Bears' offensive coach, changed to an entirely different game plan the day of the game. New York got a quick touchdown when Gene Filipski returned the opening kickoff 58 yards and Triplett scored on a 17-yard run moments later. The Giants went on to rout the Bears 47–7.

1956 STANDINGS

Eastern Conference	W	L	T	Pct.	Pts.	OP
N.Y. Giants	8	3	1	.727	264	197
Chicago Cardinals	7	5	0	.583	240	182
Washington	6	6	0	.500	183	225
Cleveland	5	7	0	.417	167	177
Pittsburgh	5	7	0	.417	217	250
Philadelphia	3	8	1	.273	143	215
Western Conference	**W**	**L**	**T**	**Pct.**	**Pts.**	**OP**
Chicago Bears	9	2	1	.818	363	246
Detroit	9	3	0	.750	300	188
San Francisco	5	6	1	.455	233	284
Baltimore	5	7	0	.417	270	322
Green Bay	4	8	0	.333	264	342
Los Angeles	4	8	0	.333	291	307

NFL championship: N.Y. Giants 47, Chicago Bears 7

LEADING RUSHERS

	Att.	Yards	Avg.	Long	TD
Rick Casares, Chicago Bears	234	1,126	4.8	68t	12
Ollie Matson, Chicago Cardinals	192	924	4.8	79t	5
Hugh McElhenny, San Francisco	185	916	5.0	86t	8
Alan Ameche, Baltimore	178	858	4.8	43	8
Frank Gifford, N.Y. Giants	159	819	5.2	69	5

LEADING PASSERS

	Att.	Comp.	Yards	TD	Int.
Ed Brown, Chicago Bears	168	96	1,667	11	12
Bill Wade, Los Angeles	178	91	1,461	10	13
Bobby Layne, Detroit	244	129	1,909	9	17
Norm Van Brocklin, Los Angeles	124	68	966	7	12
Lamar McHan, Chi. Cardinals	152	72	1,159	10	8

LEADING RECEIVERS

	No.	Yards	Avg.	Long	TD
Billy Wilson, San Francisco	60	889	14.8	77t	5
Billy Howton, Green Bay	55	1,188	21.6	66t	12
Frank Gifford, N.Y. Giants	51	603	11.8	48	4
Harlon Hill, Chicago Bears	47	1,128	24.0	79t	11
Jim Mutscheller, Baltimore	44	715	16.3	53t	6

1957 Raymond (Buddy) Parker, coach of the Detroit Lions, shocked the team, the city, and all pro football when he resigned while at the podium addressing a "Meet the Lions" banquet at a Detroit hotel before the season. He moved to the Pittsburgh Steelers as head coach and was replaced in Detroit by his former assistant, George Wilson.

Pete Rozelle was named general manager of the Los Angeles Rams.

The Pittsburgh Steelers and Cleveland Browns each had had 5–7 records and were tied for the fourth draft pick. A coin flip was held to break the tie and Pittsburgh won. It selected quarterback Len Dawson of Purdue and Cleveland took fullback Jim Brown of Syracuse. Dawson became a substitute with the Steelers; they traded with the San Francisco 49ers to get Earl Morrall as their starting quarterback. Brown, however, became a sensation with Cleveland.

Other notable first-year players included halfback Jon Arnett of Los Angeles, quarterback John Brodie of San Francisco, "bonus" draft choice halfback Paul Hornung and end Ron Kramer of Green Bay, quarterback Sonny Jurgensen and flanker Tommy McDonald of Philadelphia, and guard-tackle Jim Parker of Baltimore.

Cleveland ascended to the championship of the Eastern Conference again with Tommy O'Connell playing quarterback and Brown leading the league with 942 yards rushing and setting an NFL record with 237 yards in one game against the Los Angeles Rams.

The coaching change in Detroit did not affect the Lions adversely. They battled with the San Francisco 49ers for the Western Conference title. George Wilson, Detroit's new coach, used Bobby Layne and Tobin Rote in a two-quarterback system. Fullback John Henry Johnson was the major offensive weapon for the Lions. Layne suffered a broken ankle late in the season and Rote had the quarterback job to himself.

San Francisco went through one of the most momentous seasons any NFL team ever had. The 49ers had Hugh McElhenny and Joe Perry in the backfield with quarterback Y. A. Tittle, who had a sensational new passing target in end R. C. Owens. Owens stood 6 foot 5 inches. Tittle threw "alley-oop" passes high in the air and Owens leaped above smaller defensive backs to make the catches.

Tony Morabito, founder and co-owner of the 49ers,

Yankee Stadium, the Giants' new home in 1956.

Anthony J. (Tony) Morabito.

Raymond (Buddy) Parker.

Rookie Paul Hornung of Green Bay, 1957; 45 is New York's Emlen Tunnell.

Tobin Rote during Detroit's amazing playoff game comeback against San Francisco in 1957.

suffered a heart attack and died during their game at Kezar Stadium against the Chicago Bears, October 28.

The 49ers were a big gate attraction everywhere they played and an NFL record crowd of 102,368 watched them play the Rams at Los Angeles Memorial Coliseum, November 10.

Detroit and San Francisco tied for the Western Conference lead and the Lions won an amazing playoff victory, coming from behind for a 31–27 victory after trailing 27–7 in the third quarter.

Detroit then met Cleveland for the NFL title and, with quarterback Tobin Rote throwing four touchdown passes and running for another, smashed the Browns 59–14. It was the worst defeat Cleveland ever suffered and avenged the Lions' one-sided loss to the Browns in the 1954 title game.

1957 STANDINGS

Eastern Conference	W	L	T	Pct.	Pts.	OP
Cleveland	9	2	1	.818	269	172
N.Y. Giants	7	5	0	.583	254	211
Pittsburgh	6	6	0	.500	161	178
Washington	5	6	1	.455	251	230
Philadelphia	4	8	0	.333	173	230
Chicago Cardinals	3	9	0	.250	200	299
Western Conference	**W**	**L**	**T**	**Pct.**	**Pts.**	**OP**
Detroit	8	4	0	.667	251	231
San Francisco	8	4	0	.667	260	264
Baltimore	7	5	0	.583	303	235
Los Angeles	6	6	0	.500	307	278
Chicago Bears	5	7	0	.417	203	211
Green Bay	3	9	0	.250	218	311

Western Conference playoff: Detroit 31, San Francisco 27
NFL championship: Detroit 59, Cleveland 14

LEADING RUSHERS	Att.	Yards	Avg.	Long	TD
Jim Brown, Cleveland	202	942	4.7	69t	9
Rick Casares, Chicago Bears	204	700	3.4	25t	6
Don Bosseler, Washington	167	673	4.0	28	7
John Henry Johnson, Detroit	129	621	4.8	62	5
Tommy Wilson, Los Angeles	127	616	4.9	46	3

LEADING PASSERS	Att.	Comp.	Yards	TD	Int.
Tommy O'Connell, Cleveland	110	63	1,229	9	8
Eddie LeBaron, Washington	167	99	1,508	11	10
Johnny Unitas, Baltimore	301	172	2,550	24	17
Norm Van Brocklin, Los Angeles	265	132	2,105	20	21
Lamar McHan, Chi. Cardinals	200	87	1,568	10	15

LEADING RECEIVERS	No.	Yards	Avg.	Long	TD
Billy Wilson, San Francisco	52	757	14.6	40	6
Raymond Berry, Baltimore	47	800	17.0	67t	6
Jack McClairen, Pittsburgh	46	630	13.7	48t	2
Frank Gifford, N.Y. Giants	41	588	14.3	63	4
Lenny Moore, Baltimore	40	687	17.2	82t	7

1958 George Halas reinstated himself as head coach of the Chicago Bears. It was the third time he had come back to coach, the others having been in 1933 and 1946.

Raymond (Buddy) Parker, coach of the Pittsburgh Steelers, traded quarterback Earl Morrall to the Detroit Lions in exchange for Bobby Layne, the quarterback of the Lions' great teams when Parker was their coach.

Lawrence (Buck) Shaw was named coach of the Philadelphia Eagles and they made a trade with the Los Angeles Rams, landing quarterback Norm Van Brocklin.

Quarterback King Hill was selected by the Chicago Cardinals and became the last "bonus" draft choice. The practice was then abolished.

Quarterbacks were in the news but none more than Johnny Unitas of the Baltimore Colts. A collapsed lung and three broken ribs kept him out of two games but when he returned he threw a 58-yard touchdown pass to halfback Lenny Moore on the first play against the Green Bay Packers. Baltimore beat the Chicago Bears 17–0 in an important game in November; it was the first time the Bears had been shut out since 1946. Halas had to settle for a tie with Los Angeles for second place behind Baltimore in his first year back as Bears' coach.

The Green Bay Packers lost 10 games and finished last in the Western Conference despite having players such as linebackers Dan Currie and Ray Nitschke,

Lawrence (Buck) Shaw.

Johnny Unitas.

center Jim Ringo, and backs Paul Hornung and Jim Taylor.

The New York Giants captured the Eastern Conference after a bitter fight with the Cleveland Browns. Jim Brown of the Browns broke Steve Van Buren's NFL rushing record with 1,527 yards and led the league in scoring with 18 touchdowns and 108 points. He also had a good running mate when Bobby Mitchell joined him in the Browns' backfield.

The Giants got into a playoff against Cleveland by beating the Browns 13-10 in the last week of the season. Pat Summerall of New York kicked a 49-yard field goal in the snow for the victory. In the playoff game, the Giants held Jim Brown to eight yards and the entire Browns' offense to 86 and won 10–0.

Baltimore and New York met for the championship at Yankee Stadium. The Giants rallied from a 14–3 halftime deficit for a 17–14 lead only to have Unitas of the Colts complete pass after pass to end Raymond Berry, setting up a tying 20-yard field goal by Steve Myhra with 7 seconds to play. They entered sudden death, the first time in history a title game had gone into overtime. New York had the ball first but had to punt and the Colts went all the way. A second down pass from Unitas to end Jim Mutscheller set up a one-yard plunge by fullback Alan Ameche, winning it for Baltimore 23–17.

A dramatic sudden death championship game on national television captured the imagination of millions. Tex Maule's story on the game for *Sports Illustrated* in its January 5, 1959 issue was headlined, "The Best Football Game Ever Played."

NBC's live telecast of the game, with Chuck Thompson of Baltimore doing the play-by-play, reached an estimated 10,820,000 homes in America. It was not shown in the largest market, however; New York City was blacked out. New Yorkers also could not read about it because the city was in the midst of a newspaper strike.

1958 STANDINGS

Eastern Conference	W	L	T	Pct.	Pts.	OP
Cleveland	9	3	0	.750	302	217
N.Y. Giants	9	3	0	.750	246	183
Pittsburgh	7	4	1	.636	261	230
Washington	4	7	1	.364	214	268
Chicago Cardinals	2	9	1	.182	261	356
Philadelphia	2	9	1	.182	235	306
Western Conference	W	L	T	Pct.	Pts.	OP
Baltimore	9	3	0	.750	381	203
Chicago Bears	8	4	0	.667	298	230
Los Angeles	8	4	0	.667	344	278
San Francisco	6	6	0	.500	257	324
Detroit	4	7	1	.364	261	276
Green Bay	1	10	1	.091	193	382

Eastern Conference playoff: N.Y. Giants 10, Cleveland 0
NFL championship: Baltimore 23, N.Y. Giants 17, sudden death overtime

LEADING RUSHERS	Att.	Yards	Avg.	Long	TD
Jim Brown, Cleveland	257	1,527	5.9	65t	17
Alan Ameche, Baltimore	171	791	4.6	28	8
Joe Perry, San Francisco	125	758	6.1	73t	4
Tom Tracy, Pittsburgh	169	714	4.2	64	5
Jon Arnett, Los Angeles	133	683	5.1	57	4

LEADING PASSERS	Att.	Comp.	Yards	TD	Int.
Eddie LeBaron, Washington	145	79	1,365	11	10
Milt Plum, Cleveland	189	102	1,619	11	11
Bobby Layne, Pittsburgh	294	145	2,510	14	12
Bill Wade, Los Angeles	341	181	2,875	18	22
Johnny Unitas, Baltimore	263	136	2,007	19	7

LEADING RECEIVERS	No.	Yards	Avg.	Long	TD
Raymond Berry, Baltimore	56	794	14.2	54	9
Pete Retzlaff, Philadelphia	56	766	13.7	49	2
Del Shofner, Los Angeles	51	1,097	21.5	92t	8
Lenny Moore, Baltimore	50	938	18.5	77t	7
Clyde Conner, San Francisco	49	512	10.4	26	5

1959 Vince Lombardi, offensive coach of the New York Giants, was named head coach of the Green Bay Packers.

Tim Mara, cofounder of the Giants, died at the age of 71, February 17.

Randy Duncan, number-one draft choice of Green Bay and the entire NFL, did not sign with the Packers and joined the Canadian Football League.

General manager Pete Rozelle of the Los Angeles Rams traded eight players and a draft choice—the rights to nine players—to the Chicago Cardinals in exchange for running back Ollie Matson.

Lamar Hunt, a Dallas, Texas businessman who had been unsuccessful in attempts to buy the Chicago Cardinals' franchise, announced his intentions to form a second professional football league. He found interested parties for franchises and the first meeting of the league was held at the Conrad Hilton Hotel in Chicago, August 14. The representatives and their cities were: Hunt, Dallas; Bob Howsam, Denver; K. S. (Bud) Adams, Houston; Barron Hilton, Los Angeles; Max Winter and William Boyer, Minneapolis-St. Paul; and Harry Wismer, New York City. They made plans to begin league play in 1960. Eight days later at another meeting in Dallas, they announced that the league would be called the "American Football League."

Buffalo became the seventh AFL team, October 28, and Boston the eighth, November 22. Buffalo was represented by Ralph C. Wilson and Boston by a syndicate headed by William H. Sullivan.

The AFL held a draft rivaling that of the NFL and named former flying ace and South Dakota governor Joe Foss its commissioner.

NFL commissioner Bert Bell died of a heart attack while attending a Philadelphia Eagles' game at Franklin Field, October 11. Austin Gunsel, the league treasurer, was named interim president.

Baltimore's passing combination of Johnny Unitas and Raymond Berry had a great year as the Colts won the Western Conference championship again. Unitas

A fan exults as Pat Summerall's kick gives the Giants 13-10 victory over Cleveland, 1958.

Jim Brown.

Lamar Hunt.

Charlie Conerly of the New York Giants, the NFL's leading passer in 1959.

threw 32 touchdown passes and Berry had 66 receptions.

Green Bay was the West's most improved team. New coach Lombardi established Bart Starr as his quarterback and Paul Hornung as his left halfback. Hornung led the NFL in scoring with 94 points as a runner and kicker.

Quarterback Charlie Conerly led the New York Giants to another Eastern Conference championship. They beat the Cleveland Browns 10-6 and 48-7. Cleveland's Jim Brown had another season over 1,000 yards with 1,329.

Baltimore again defeated the Giants in the NFL title game. New York led 9-7 going into the last quarter but Unitas and Lenny Moore were the principal figures as the Colts put together a 24-point fourth period and Baltimore won 31-16, claiming its second straight championship.

1959 STANDINGS

Eastern Conference	W	L	T	Pct.	Pts.	OP
N.Y. Giants	10	2	0	.833	284	170
Cleveland	7	5	0	.583	270	214
Philadelphia	7	5	0	.583	268	278
Pittsburgh	6	5	1	.545	257	216
Washington	3	9	0	.250	185	350
Chicago Cardinals	2	10	0	.167	234	324
Western Conference	**W**	**L**	**T**	**Pct.**	**Pts.**	**OP**
Baltimore	9	3	0	.750	374	251
Chicago Bears	8	4	0	.667	252	196
Green Bay	7	5	0	.583	248	246
San Francisco	7	5	0	.583	255	237
Detroit	3	8	1	.273	203	275
Los Angeles	2	10	0	.167	242	315

LEADING RUSHERS	Att.	Yards	Avg.	Long	TD
Jim Brown, Cleveland	290	1,329	4.6	70t	14
J.D. Smith, San Francisco	207	1,036	5.0	73t	10
Ollie Matson, Los Angeles	161	863	5.4	50	6
Tom Tracy, Pittsburgh	199	794	4.0	51	3
Bobby Mitchell, Cleveland	131	743	5.7	90t	5

LEADING PASSERS	Att.	Comp.	Yards	TD	Int.
Charlie Conerly, N.Y. Giants	194	113	1,706	14	4
Earl Morrall, Detroit	137	65	1,102	5	6
Johnny Unitas, Baltimore	367	193	2,899	32	14
Norm Van Brocklin, Philadelphia	340	191	2,617	16	14
Bill Wade, Los Angeles	261	153	2,001	12	17

LEADING RECEIVERS	No.	Yards	Avg.	Long	TD
Raymond Berry, Baltimore	66	959	14.5	55t	14
Del Shofner, Los Angeles	47	936	19.9	72t	7
Lenny Moore, Baltimore	47	846	18.0	72	6
Tommy McDonald, Philadelphia	47	846	18.0	71	10
Jim Mutscheller, Baltimore	44	699	15.9	40t	8
Billy Wilson, San Francisco	44	540	12.3	57t	4

1960 Pete Rozelle was elected commissioner of the NFL. The Chicago Cardinals, one of the most eminent and longstanding NFL teams, left their original city and moved to St. Louis. Two new teams were born. The Dallas Cowboys were formed to begin play in the NFL in 1960 and would be in direct competition in the Texas city with the Dallas Texans of the American Football League. Tex Schramm was named the Cowboys' general manager and Tom Landry their head coach. The Minnesota Vikings became the second new team; they were to begin competition in 1961.

Lamar Hunt, founder of the AFL, was elected its president for 1960. The league's Minneapolis-St. Paul franchise withdrew and Oakland became the eighth AFL team. They were owned by an eight-man syndicate headed by Y. C. (Chet) Soda and acquired their first players by drafting from the rosters of the seven other clubs. The league signed a contract with ABC for its games to be televised. It split into divisions with Boston, Buffalo, Houston, and New York in the East and Dallas, Denver, Los Angeles, and Oakland in the West. Rules were adopted allowing for a one- or two-point conversion attempt after touchdowns; one point could be made by kicking and two points by running or passing successfully for the extra point. The players' names were added to the backs of their jerseys.

Pete Rozelle.

Joe Foss.

In the first player dispute between the leagues, a Los Angeles court declared invalid the contract half-back Billy Cannon had with the Rams and freed him to play for Houston of the AFL. Quarterback Don Meredith of Southern Methodist, sought by both Dallas teams, settled on the Cowboys.

The Boston Patriots defeated the Buffalo Bills 28-7 at Buffalo in the first AFL preseason game before 16,000, July 30, and the Denver Broncos defeated Boston 13-10 at Boston in the first AFL regular season game before 21,597, September 9.

The Houston Oilers, coached by Lou Rymkus and quarterbacked by George Blanda, compiled a 10-4 record and won the Eastern Division. The Los Angeles Chargers, coached by the former boss of the NFL Rams, Sid Gillman, also had a 10-4 record and captured the Western championship. Blanda threw three touchdown passes as Houston defeated Los Angeles 24-16 in the first AFL Championship Game.

Vince Lombardi won his first division championship as coach of the Green Bay Packers. They won a title for the first time since 1944. Halfback Paul Hornung had a sensational season, scoring 176 points on 15 touchdowns, 15 field goals, and 41 extra points in a 12-game regular season.

The Philadelphia Eagles, coached by Lawrence (Buck) Shaw and led by quarterback Norm Van Brocklin and center and linebacker Chuck Bednarik, took over from their rivals, the New York Giants, as Eastern champions.

Three NFL runners had over 1,000 yards. They were Jim Brown of Cleveland, Jim Taylor of Green Bay, and John David Crow of St. Louis.

The new Dallas Cowboys finished with an 0-11-1 record.

The San Francisco 49ers adopted a Shotgun offense for their last five games and won four of them.

Bednarik went both ways, playing 60 minutes of offense and defense, during five games for Philadelphia. He accomplished the same feat in the Eagles' championship game against Green Bay. It was one of the most hard-fought title games ever and Philadelphia won 17-13. Time ran out after Bednarik tackled the Packers' Taylor at the Eagles' 9-yard line. Shaw, the coach, and Van Brocklin, the quarterback, announced their retirements.

The Detroit Lions won the first "Bert Bell Benefit Bowl" or "Playoff Bowl," defeating the Cleveland Browns 17-16.

The NFL attendance for the 1960 season was 3,128,296 for 78 games and the AFL's was 926,156 for 56 games.

Ted Dean follows a block by Bobby Walston in the 1960 NFL Championship Game.

1960 AFL STANDINGS

Eastern Division	W	L	T	Pct.	Pts.	OP
Houston	10	4	0	.714	379	285
N.Y. Titans	7	7	0	.500	382	399
Buffalo	5	8	1	.358	296	303
Boston Patriots	5	9	0	.357	286	349

Western Division	W	L	T	Pct.	Pts.	OP
Los Angeles Chargers	10	4	0	.714	373	336
Dallas Texans	8	6	0	.571	362	253
Oakland	6	8	0	.429	319	388
Denver	4	9	1	.308	309	393

AFL championship: Houston 24, Los Angeles Chargers 16

LEADING RUSHERS	Att.	Yards	Avg.	Long	TD
Abner Haynes, Dallas Texans	156	875	5.6	57	9
Paul Lowe, Los Angeles Chargers	136	855	6.3	69	9
Billy Cannon, Houston	152	644	4.2	60	1
Dave Smith, Houston	154	643	4.2	65	5
Tony Teresa, Oakland	139	608	4.4	83	6

LEADING PASSERS	Att.	Comp.	Yards	TD	Int.
Jack Kemp, Los Angeles Chargers	406	211	3,018	20	25
Al Dorow, N.Y. Titans	396	201	2,748	26	26
Frank Tripucka, Denver	478	248	3,038	24	34
E. (Butch) Songin, Boston	392	187	2,476	22	15
Cotton Davidson, Dallas Texans	379	179	2,474	15	16

LEADING RECEIVERS	No.	Yards	Avg.	Long	TD
Lionel Taylor, Denver	92	1,235	13.4	80	12
Bill Groman, Houston	72	1,473	20.5	92	12
Don Maynard, N.Y. Titans	72	1,265	17.6	65	6
Art Powell, N.Y. Titans	69	1,167	16.9	76	14
Abner Haynes, Dallas Texans	55	576	10.5	34	3

1960 NFL STANDINGS

Eastern Conference	W	L	T	Pct.	Pts.	OP
Philadelphia	10	2	0	.833	321	246
Cleveland	8	3	1	.727	362	217
N.Y. Giants	6	4	2	.600	271	261
St. Louis	6	5	1	.545	288	230
Pittsburgh	5	6	1	.455	240	275
Washington	1	9	2	.100	178	309

Western Conference	W	L	T	Pct.	Pts.	OP
Green Bay	8	4	0	.667	332	209
Detroit	7	5	0	.583	239	212
San Francisco	7	5	0	.583	208	205
Baltimore	6	6	0	.500	288	234
Chicago Bears	5	6	1	.455	194	299
Los Angeles Rams	4	7	1	.364	265	297
Dallas Cowboys	0	11	1	.000	177	369

NFL championship: Philadelphia 17, Green Bay 13

LEADING RUSHERS	Att.	Yards	Avg.	Long	TD
Jim Brown, Cleveland	215	1,257	5.8	71t	9
Jim Taylor, Green Bay	230	1,101	4.8	32	11
John David Crow, St. Louis	183	1,071	5.9	57	6
Nick Pietrosante, Detroit	161	872	5.4	57	8
J.D. Smith, San Francisco	174	780	4.5	41	5

LEADING PASSERS	Att.	Comp.	Yards	TD	Int.
Milt Plum, Cleveland	250	151	2,297	21	5
Norm Van Brocklin, Philadelphia	284	153	2,471	24	17
Johnny Unitas, Baltimore	378	190	3,099	25	24
Bill Wade, Los Angeles	182	106	1,294	12	11
Bobby Layne, Pittsburgh	209	103	1,814	13	17

LEADING RECEIVERS	No.	Yards	Avg.	Long	TD
Raymond Berry, Baltimore	74	1,298	17.5	70t	10
Sonny Randle, St. Louis	62	893	14.4	57t	15
Jim (Red) Phillips, Los Angeles	52	883	17.0	61t	8
Jim Gibbons, Detroit	51	604	11.8	65t	2
Pete Retzlaff, Philadelphia	46	826	18.0	57t	5

1961 Commissioner Rozelle signed a two-year contract awarding NBC radio and television rights to the NFL Championship Game for $615,000 annually. Congress then passed a bill legalizing single network television contracts by professional sports leagues.

Van Brocklin, quarterback of the champion Philadelphia Eagles, was named head coach of the new Minnesota Vikings. His former understudy, Sonny Jurgensen, took over at quarterback for the Eagles. Y. A. Tittle, one of four quarterbacks on the roster of the San Francisco 49ers, was traded to the New York Giants because rookie Billy Kilmer and veterans John Brodie and Bobby Waters were better suited for the needs of the 49ers' new Shotgun offense. The Tittle trade was just one of several made by New York. It also acquired defensive back Erich Barnes from the Chicago Bears and ends Del Shofner from the Los Angeles Rams and Joe Walton from the Washington Redskins.

The Redskins moved from Griffith Stadium to the new District of Columbia Stadium.

The first American Football League franchise shift occurred when the Los Angeles Chargers were moved and became the San Diego Chargers. Ed McGah, Wayne Valley, and Robert Osborne bought out their partners in the ownership of the Oakland Raiders; McGah was named Raiders' president. Bob and Lee Howsam sold the Denver Broncos to a group headed by Calvin Kunz.

Art Modell bought controlling interest in the Cleveland Browns.

Three original AFL coaches departed during the season. Wally Lemm replaced Lou Rymkus at Houston, Mike Holovak replaced Lou Saban at Boston, and Marty Feldman replaced Eddie Erdelatz at Oakland.

End Willard Dewveall of the Chicago Bears played out his option and joined Houston of the AFL, the first player to voluntarily move from one league to the other.

The Chargers, playing in a new city, won the Western Division title again and the Oilers repeated as Eastern champions. San Diego had two giant rookie linemen in Earl Faison and Ernie Ladd, and won its first 11 games in a row. Houston's Blanda completed seven touchdown passes in one game.

Lionel Taylor of the Denver Broncos caught a pro football record 100 passes.

Houston defeated San Diego 10-3 for its second straight AFL title.

The Green Bay Packers of Vince Lombardi ruled the NFL. Halfback Paul Hornung led the league in scoring for the third year in a row despite the fact that it was the time of the Berlin crisis and he was on active duty in the army reserve, stationed at Fort Riley, Kansas; he had to travel back and forth each weekend from Fort Riley to the Packers' games. He scored 33 points in one game against Baltimore.

San Francisco's Shotgun offense was the talk of the league. Coach Red Hickey alternated Brodie, Kilmer, and Waters at quarterback in the unusual formation in which they took the snap from center seven to nine yards back and then ran, passed, or handed off. The 49ers ran up a 4-1 record until the Chicago Bears stopped them 31-0, playing middle linebacker Bill George at middle guard, where he befuddled the 49ers' center and put pressure on their passers. San Francisco went back to an ordinary pro formation after that.

Detroit won six games on the road but only two at home. The new Minnesota Vikings had a respectable 3-11 record and their rookie quarterback, Fran Tarkenton, starred as they won their first regular season game 37-13 over the Chicago Bears. Tarkenton passed for four touchdowns and ran for a fifth.

Tittle, the new leader of the New York Giants, had 17 touchdown passes as they won the Eastern Conference. Sonny Jurgensen of Philadelphia set an NFL

record by passing for 3,723 yards, but the Eagles lost both their games against New York. Jim Brown of Cleveland led the NFL in rushing for the fifth straight time and tied his own single-game mark with 237 yards against Philadelphia.

Hornung set a championship record when he scored 19 points to lead the Green Bay Packers to their first NFL championship since 1944 and first under Lombardi 37-0 over the New York Giants in the title game, December 31.

1961 AFL STANDINGS

Eastern Division	W	L	T	Pct.	Pts.	OP
Houston	10	3	1	.769	513	242
Boston Patriots	9	4	1	.692	413	313
N.Y. Titans	7	7	0	.500	301	390
Buffalo	6	8	0	.429	294	342
Western Division	**W**	**L**	**T**	**Pct.**	**Pts.**	**OP**
San Diego	12	2	0	.857	396	219
Dallas Texans	6	8	0	.429	334	343
Denver	3	11	0	.214	251	432
Oakland	2	12	0	.143	237	458

AFL championship: Houston 10, San Diego 3

LEADING RUSHERS	Att.	Yards	Avg.	Long	TD
Billy Cannon, Houston	200	948	4.7	61	6
Bill Mathis, N.Y. Titans	202	846	4.2	30	7
Abner Haynes, Dallas Texans	179	841	4.7	59	9
Paul Lowe, San Diego	175	767	4.4	87	9
Charlie Tolar, Houston	157	577	3.7	28	4

LEADING PASSERS	Att.	Comp.	Yards	TD	Int.
George Blanda, Houston	362	187	3,330	36	22
Tom Flores, Oakland	366	190	2,176	15	19
Jack Kemp, San Diego	364	165	2,686	15	22
Al Dorow, N.Y. Titans	438	197	2,651	19	30
Babe Parilli, Boston	198	104	1,314	13	9

LEADING RECEIVERS	No.	Yards	Avg.	Long	TD
Lionel Taylor, Denver	100	1,176	11.8	52	4
Charley Hennigan, Houston	82	1,756	21.3	80	12
Art Powell, N.Y. Titans	71	881	12.4	48	5
Dave Kocourek, San Diego	55	1,055	19.2	76	4
Chris Burford, Dallas	51	850	16.7	54	4

1961 NFL STANDINGS

Eastern Conference	W	L	T	Pct.	Pts.	OP
N.Y. Giants	10	3	1	.769	368	220
Philadelphia	10	4	0	.714	361	297
Cleveland	8	5	1	.615	319	270
St. Louis	7	7	0	.500	279	267
Pittsburgh	6	8	0	.429	295	287
Dallas Cowboys	4	9	1	.308	236	380
Washington	1	12	1	.077	174	392
Western Conference	**W**	**L**	**T**	**Pct.**	**Pts.**	**OP**
Green Bay	11	3	0	.786	391	223
Detroit	8	5	1	.615	270	258
Baltimore	8	6	0	.571	302	307
Chicago Bears	8	6	0	.571	326	302
San Francisco	7	6	1	.538	346	272
Los Angeles	4	10	0	.286	263	333
Minnesota	3	11	0	.214	285	407

NFL championship: Green Bay 37, N.Y. Giants 0

LEADING RUSHERS	Att.	Yards	Avg.	Long	TD
Jim Brown, Cleveland	305	1,408	4.6	38	8
Jim Taylor, Green Bay	243	1,307	5.4	53	15
Alex Webster, N.Y. Giants	196	928	4.7	59	2
Nick Pietrosante, Detroit	201	841	4.2	42	5
J.D. Smith, San Francisco	167	823	4.9	33	8

LEADING PASSERS	Att.	Comp.	Yards	TD	Int.
Milt Plum, Cleveland	302	177	2,416	18	10
Sonny Jurgensen, Philadelphia	416	235	3,723	32	24
Bart Starr, Green Bay	295	172	2,418	16	16
John Brodie, San Francisco	283	155	2,588	14	12
Bill Wade, Chicago	250	139	2,258	22	13

LEADING RECEIVERS	No.	Yards	Avg.	Long	TD
Jim (Red) Phillips, Los Angeles	78	1,092	14.0	69t	5
Raymond Berry, Baltimore	75	873	11.6	44	0
Del Shofner, N.Y. Giants	68	1,125	16.5	46t	11
Tommy McDonald, Philadelphia	64	1,144	17.9	66	13
Mike Ditka, Chicago	56	1,076	19.2	76t	12
Billy Howton, Dallas	56	785	14.0	53	4

1962 Pete Rozelle of the NFL and Joe Foss of the AFL each were given new five-year contracts.

Dan Reeves bought out his partners and took complete control of the Los Angeles Rams. There was an unusual coaching change when Wally Lemm left the Houston Oilers of the AFL after winning a championship and moved to the St. Louis Cardinals. Frank (Pop) Ivy, coach of the Cardinals, moved to the Oilers. Jack Kemp, a quarterback for the San Diego Chargers, was put on waivers and picked up by the Buffalo Bills. A strong contingent of NFL rookies included quarterback Roman Gabriel and defensive tackle Merlin Olsen of Los Angeles and end Gary Collins of Cleveland. Two old pros, quarterback Bobby Layne of Pittsburgh and linebacker Chuck Bednarik of Philadelphia, retired.

There was intense competition between the two leagues for college players. The NFL signed most of the big-name players and also won a court victory after a two-and-a-half-year battle when a U.S. District judge ruled against the AFL's charges of monopoly and conspiracy in expansion, television, and signings.

Len Dawson requested and was granted his release from the Cleveland Browns. He signed with the Dallas Texans and was reunited with his former Purdue coach, Hank Stram.

The NFL entered into a single network agreement with CBS for telecasting of all regular season games for $4,650,000 annually.

The rules were changed, making it illegal to grab another player's face mask.

The AFL voted to make the scoreboard clock the official timer of the game.

Art Modell.

Jack Kemp.

Dan Reeves.

Paul Hornung throws a halfback option pass in the 1961 NFL Championship Game despite the defensive efforts of Andy Robustelli.

Ivy, the new Oilers' coach, became the third to guide them to a division championship and had an 11-3 record. The Dallas Texans captured the West behind coach Hank Stram.

Cookie Gilchrist, who had been playing in the Canadian Football league, came into the AFL as a rookie with Buffalo and led the league in rushing with 1,096 yards.

The Texans defeated the Oilers 20-17 for the AFL championship in the longest pro game ever played up to that point. It went into a second quarter of sudden death overtime, 77 minutes and 54 seconds, before Tommy Brooker of Dallas kicked a 25-yard field goal to win it.

Green Bay withstood a challenge from Detroit to once again win the NFL's Western Conference. The Packers prevailed even though the Lions upset them 26-14 on Thanksgiving Day, sacking quarterback Bart Starr for 110 yards in losses. Starr survived and led the NFL in passing. Fullback Jim Taylor had his greatest season, gaining 1,474 yards to oust Jim Brown of Cleveland as the league rushing leader. Taylor also led the league with 19 touchdowns.

Quarterback Y.A. Tittle of the New York Giants passed for seven touchdowns and 505 yards against Washington, October 28.

Sam Huff, the Giants' middle linebacker, waged a fierce personal duel with the Packers' Taylor as the two teams played for the NFL championship. It was bitter cold and the wind was blowing 40 miles an hour at Yankee Stadium in New York. Taylor gained 85 yards and his teammate Jerry Kramer kicked three field goals as the Packers won their second consecutive NFL title, 16-7.

1962 AFL STANDINGS

Eastern Division	W	L	T	Pct.	Pts.	OP
Houston	11	3	0	.786	387	270
Boston Patriots	9	4	1	.692	346	295
Buffalo	7	6	1	.538	309	272
N.Y. Titans	5	9	0	.357	278	423
Western Division	W	L	T	Pct.	Pts.	OP
Dallas Texans	11	3	0	.786	389	233
Denver	7	7	0	.500	353	334
San Diego	4	10	0	.286	314	392
Oakland	1	13	0	.071	213	370

AFL championship: Dallas Texans 20, Houston 17, sudden death overtime

LEADING RUSHERS	Att.	Yards	Avg.	Long	TD
Cookie Gilchrist, Buffalo	214	1,096	5.1	44	13
Abner Haynes, Dallas Texans	221	1,049	4.7	71	13
Charlie Tolar, Houston	244	1,012	4.1	25	7
Clem Daniels, Oakland	161	766	4.7	72	7
Curtis McClinton, Dallas Texans	111	604	5.4	69	2

LEADING PASSERS	Att.	Comp.	Yards	TD	Int.
Len Dawson, Dallas Texans	310	189	2,759	29	17
Babe Parilli, Boston	253	140	1,988	18	8
Frank Tripucka, Denver	440	240	2,917	17	25
George Blanda, Houston	418	197	2,810	27	42
Johnny Green, N.Y. Titans	258	128	1,741	10	18

LEADING RECEIVERS	No.	Yards	Avg.	Long	TD
Lionel Taylor, Denver	77	908	11.7	45	4
Art Powell, N.Y. Titans	64	1,130	17.6	80	8
Dick Christy, N.Y. Titans	62	538	8.6	41	3
Richard (Bo) Dickinson, Denver	60	554	9.2	33	4
Don Maynard, N.Y. Titans	56	1,041	18.5	86	8

1962 NFL STANDINGS

Eastern Conference	W	L	T	Pct.	Pts.	OP
N.Y. Giants	12	2	0	.857	398	283
Pittsburgh	9	5	0	.643	312	363
Cleveland	7	6	1	.538	291	257
Washington	5	7	2	.417	305	376
Dallas Cowboys	5	8	1	.385	398	402
St. Louis	4	9	1	.308	287	361
Philadelphia	3	10	1	.231	282	356
Western Conference	W	L	T	Pct.	Pts.	OP
Green Bay	13	1	0	.929	415	148
Detroit	11	3	0	.786	315	177
Chicago	9	5	0	.643	321	287
Baltimore	7	7	0	.500	293	288
San Francisco	6	8	0	.429	282	331
Minnesota	2	11	1	.154	254	410
Los Angeles	1	12	1	.077	220	334

NFL championship: Green Bay 16, N.Y. Giants 7

Jim Taylor.

Y. A. Tittle.

Pro Football Hall of Fame, Canton, Ohio.

LEADING RUSHERS	Att.	Yards	Avg.	Long	TD
Jim Taylor, Green Bay	272	1,474	5.4	51	19
John Henry Johnson, Pittsburgh	251	1,141	4.5	40	7
Dick Bass, Los Angeles	196	1,033	5.3	57	6
Jim Brown, Cleveland	230	996	4.3	31	13
Don Perkins, Dallas	222	945	4.3	35	7

LEADING PASSERS	Att.	Comp.	Yards	TD	Int.
Bart Starr, Green Bay	285	178	2,438	12	9
Y.A. Tittle, N.Y. Giants	375	200	3,224	33	20
Eddie LeBaron, Dallas	166	95	1,436	16	9
Frank Ryan, Cleveland	194	112	1,541	10	7
Sonny Jurgensen, Philadelphia	366	196	3,261	22	26

LEADING RECEIVERS	No.	Yards	Avg.	Long	TD
Bobby Mitchell, Washington	72	1,384	19.2	81t	11
Sonny Randle, St. Louis	63	1,158	18.4	86t	7
Bobby Joe Conrad, St. Louis	62	954	15.4	72t	4
Jim (Red) Phillips, Los Angeles	60	875	14.6	65t	5
Tommy McDonald, Philadelphia	58	1,146	19.8	60t	10
Mike Ditka, Chicago	58	904	15.6	69t	5
Johnny Morris, Chicago	58	889	15.3	73t	5

1963 Commissioner Pete Rozelle indefinitely suspended Paul Hornung of Green Bay and Alex Karras of Detroit for placing bets on their own teams and also fined five other Detroit players $2,000 each for betting on games in which they did not participate. The Detroit Lions Football Company was fined $2,000 on each of two counts for failure to report information promptly and for lack of proper sideline supervision.

The competition between the NFL Cowboys and AFL Texans for Dallas football fans ended with the Texans moving to Kansas City and becoming the Chiefs. The struggling New York franchise of the AFL, the Titans, was taken over by the league from owner Harry Wismer and then passed to the control of a group headed by W.A. (Sonny) Werblin, who changed their name to the Jets. The Boston Patriots moved their games from Boston University Field to larger Fenway Park. The Jets and Oakland Raiders, losers of 19 straight games at one point, were allowed to select players from other franchises in hopes of giving the league more competitive balance.

Paul Brown, coach of the Cleveland Browns since their inception, was fired. Don Shula became coach of the Baltimore Colts and Weeb Ewbank coach of the New York Jets. Linebackers Lee Roy Jordan of Dallas and Dave Robinson of Green Bay were notable rookies in the NFL and defensive tackle Buck Buchanan and guard Ed Budde started their careers with the Kansas City Chiefs.

The Pro Football Hall of Fame was dedicated at Canton, Ohio, the city in which the league that became the NFL was organized in 1920. Seventeen charter members were inducted.

San Diego won the AFL Western Division title again, but only after a struggle with Oakland. The Raiders, coached by former Chargers assistant Al Davis, won their last eight games and finished second with a 10-4 record.

Clem Daniels of Oakland led the league with 1,099 yards rushing and Cookie Gilchrist of Buffalo set a professional record with 243 yards rushing in a game against the New York Jets.

The Boston Patriots and Buffalo Bills finished in a tie for the Eastern Division title and the Patriots won a playoff 26-8 on a snow-covered field at Buffalo.

San Diego crushed Boston 51-10 in the Championship Game behind 206 yards rushing and 329 combined net yards by halfback Keith Lincoln.

The Chicago Bears, coached by George Halas, denied the Green Bay Packers another NFL championship. The Bears had a solid defense led by linebackers Joe Fortunato, Bill George, and Larry Morris and won the Western Conference. Green Bay stayed close behind losing quarterback Bart Starr with a broken hand. Los Angeles had a massive defensive line called the Fearsome Foursome, made up of ends David (Deacon) Jones and Lamar Lundy and tackles Roosevelt Grier and Merlin Olsen.

Y. A. Tittle of the New York Giants had another

George Halas watches the final seconds tick off in the Bears' 1963 NFL Championship Game win over the New York Giants.

brilliant season, throwing 36 touchdown passes, and the Giants won their third straight Eastern Conference championship. Jim Brown, the Cleveland Browns' great fullback, thrived under a new coach, Blanton Collier, and had his most productive season with 1,863 yards and games of 232 against Dallas and 223 against Philadelphia on the way to his sixth title in seven years.

The domination of the Western Conference in the title game continued. The Chicago Bears stopped the Giants 14-10, intercepting five passes by Tittle, who twisted a knee in the second quarter but nevertheless played the second half in a losing effort.

1963 AFL STANDINGS

Eastern Division	W	L	T	Pct.	Pts.	OP
Boston Patriots	7	6	1	.538	317	257
Buffalo	7	6	1	.538	304	291
Houston	6	8	0	.429	302	372
N.Y. Jets	5	8	1	.385	249	399

Western Division	W	L	T	Pct.	Pts.	OP
San Diego	11	3	0	.786	399	256
Oakland	10	4	0	.714	363	288
Kansas City	5	7	2	.417	347	263
Denver	2	11	1	.154	301	473

Eastern Division playoff: Boston 26, Buffalo 8
AFL championship: San Diego 51, Boston 10

LEADING RUSHERS	Att.	Yards	Avg.	Long	TD
Clem Daniels, Oakland	215	1,099	5.1	74	3
Paul Lowe, San Diego	177	1,010	5.7	66	8
Cookie Gilchrist, Buffalo	232	979	4.2	32	12
Keith Lincoln, San Diego	128	826	6.4	76	5
Larry Garron, Boston	179	750	4.1	47	2

LEADING PASSERS	Att.	Comp.	Yards	TD	Int.
Tobin Rote, San Diego	286	170	2,510	20	17
Tom Flores, Oakland	247	113	2,101	20	13
Jack Kemp, Buffalo	384	194	2,914	13	20
Len Dawson, Kansas City	352	190	2,389	26	19
George Blanda, Houston	423	224	3,003	24	25

LEADING RECEIVERS	No.	Yards	Avg.	Long	TD
Lionel Taylor, Denver	78	1,101	14.1	72	10
Art Powell, Oakland	73	1,304	17.8	85	16
Robert (Bake) Turner, N.Y. Jets	71	1,007	14.1	53	6
Bill Miller, Buffalo	69	860	12.4	36	3
Chris Burford, Kansas City	68	824	12.1	69	9

Keith Lincoln.

1963 NFL STANDINGS

Eastern Conference	W	L	T	Pct.	Pts.	OP
N.Y. Giants	11	3	0	.786	448	280
Cleveland	10	4	0	.714	343	262
St. Louis	9	5	0	.643	341	283
Pittsburgh	7	4	3	.636	321	295
Dallas	4	10	0	.286	305	378
Washington	3	11	0	.214	279	398
Philadelphia	2	10	2	.167	242	381

Western Conference	W	L	T	Pct.	Pts.	OP
Chicago	11	1	2	.917	301	144
Green Bay	11	2	1	.846	369	206
Baltimore	8	6	0	.571	316	285
Detroit	5	8	1	.385	326	265
Minnesota	5	8	1	.385	309	390
Los Angeles	5	9	0	.357	210	350
San Francisco	2	12	0	.143	198	391

NFL championship: Chicago 14, N.Y. Giants 10

LEADING RUSHERS	Att.	Yards	Avg.	Long	TD
Jim Brown, Cleveland	291	1,863	6.4	80t	12
Jim Taylor, Green Bay	248	1,018	4.1	40t	9
Timmy Brown, Philadelphia	192	841	4.4	34	6
John Henry Johnson, Pittsburgh	186	773	4.2	48	4
Tommy Mason, Minnesota	166	763	4.6	70t	7

LEADING PASSERS	Att.	Comp.	Yards	TD	Int.
Y.A. Tittle, N.Y. Giants	367	221	3,145	36	14
Johnny Unitas, Baltimore	410	237	3,481	20	12
Earl Morrall, Detroit	328	174	2,621	24	14
Frank Ryan, Cleveland	256	135	2,026	25	13
Charley Johnson, St. Louis	423	222	3,280	28	21

LEADING RECEIVERS	No.	Yards	Avg.	Long	TD
Bobby Joe Conrad, St. Louis	73	967	13.2	48	10
Bobby Mitchell, Washington	69	1,436	20.8	99t	7
Terry Barr, Detroit	66	1,086	16.5	75t	13
Del Shofner, N.Y. Giants	64	1,181	18.5	70t	9
Buddy Dial, Pittsburgh	60	1,295	21.6	83t	9

1964 The NFL signed a new contract with CBS television for a total of $14.1 million for the rights to regular season games for the next two years. Each NFL club would receive more than $1 million a year. In addition, CBS acquired the rights to the 1964 and 1965 NFL Championship Games for $1.8 million each.

The AFL signed a new five year, $36 million television contract with NBC. The deal assured each

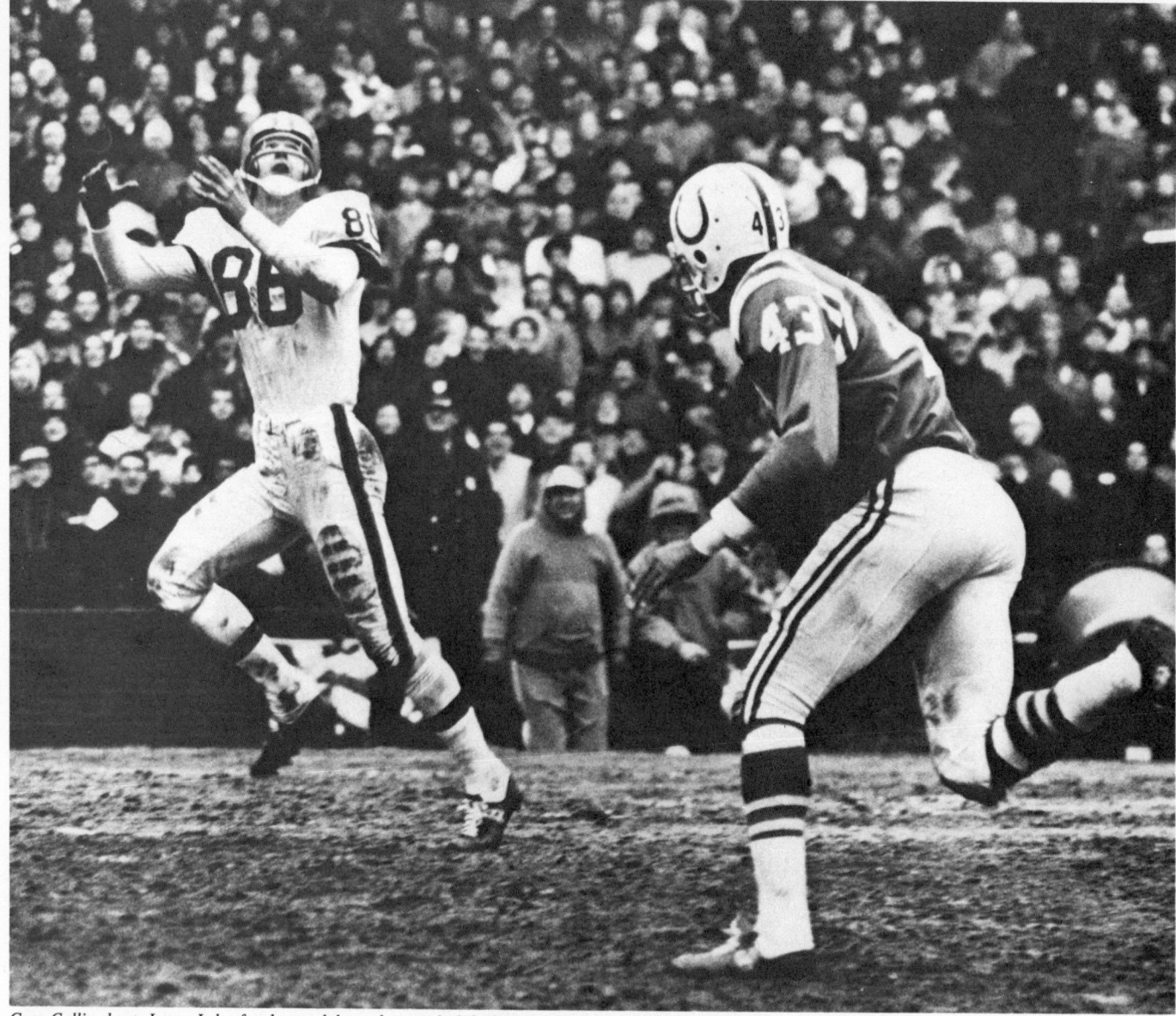

Gary Collins beats Lenny Lyles for the touchdown that sparked the Browns' 27-0 win in the 1964 NFL Championship Game.

team approximately $900,000 a year from television rights.

Jerry Wolman, the new owner of the Philadelphia Eagles, hired Joe Kuharich as head coach. Kuharich shook up the Eagles, trading quarterback Sonny Jurgensen to Washington for quarterback Norm Snead and also dealing with Green Bay for center Jim Ringo and Detroit for halfback Ollie Matson.

The New York Giants traded linebacker Sam Huff to Washington and defensive tackle Ed Modzelewski to Cleveland.

In addition to Jurgensen and Huff, the Redskins also acquired rookie halfback Charley Taylor.

The Chicago Bears suffered a stunning loss when halfback Willie Galimore and end John Farrington were killed in an auto crash near the Bears' training camp at Rensselaer, Indiana.

Soccer player Pete Gogolak of Cornell University became the first soccer-style kicker in pro football, signing a contract with the Buffalo Bills of the AFL.

The New York Jets moved from the shabby Polo Grounds to new Shea Stadium in Flushing Meadows.

Gogolak had 19 field goals but was overshadowed by Gino Cappelletti of Boston, who had 25, along with 38 extra points and seven touchdowns as a pass receiver to lead the league in scoring with 155 points. New York managed no better than third in the Eastern Division but set a club attendance record of 298,972 in its new stadium, despite having to play some home games on Saturday nights to avoid conflict with the baseball Mets. Buffalo captured the Eastern title by beating Boston 24-14 on the last day of the season at snow-covered Fenway Park in a near-blizzard.

The AFL's reputation for wide-open football grew as San Diego's Lance Alworth became perhaps the best wide receiver in the game, and as Houston quarterback George Blanda attempted 505 passes for the season, including 68 in one game against Buffalo that the Oilers lost 24-10. Charley Hennigan caught 101 of Blanda's passes, breaking the single-season record set by Lionel Taylor of Denver in 1961.

San Diego won the West behind the pass catching of Alworth, the passing of John Hadl, the running of Keith Lincoln and Paul Lowe, and a solid defense. Kansas City embarrassed the Chargers late in the season, however, beating them 49-6.

In the championship game, Cookie Gilchrist of Buffalo gained 144 yards rushing on a foggy day at War Memorial Stadium in Buffalo and the Bills defeated the Chargers 20-7.

Blanton Collier, the Cleveland coach, continued to build a powerful team. Fullback Jim Brown led the league in rushing for the seventh time in eight years and boosted his career touchdown total to 105. Frank Ryan was the Browns' quarterback and he had Gary Collins at flanker and first-round draft choice Paul Warfield at split end. Warfield caught 52 passes and the Browns held off a challenge from the St. Louis Cardinals to win the Eastern Conference. The Giants, perennial powers in the East, fell to last place.

The same fate befell the Chicago Bears, defending Western champions. Shaken by the tragic accident during their training camp period, they dropped to sixth place despite end Johnny Morris's 93 pass receptions.

Paul Hornung of Green Bay, suspended the previous season, rejoined the Packers. Quarterback Bart Starr led the league's passers and fullback Jim Taylor had his fifth season with over 1,000 yards. Minnesota became a contending team in only its fourth season, tying the Packers for second place in the West behind 22 touchdown passes by Fran Tarkenton. Alex Karras, who like Hornung had been suspended, rejoined Detroit.

The Baltimore Colts were the Western champions and had the best record in the NFL, 12-2. Quarterback Johnny Unitas guided the Colts' attack that included halfback-flanker Lenny Moore, who scored an NFL record 20 touchdowns.

Baltimore was favored in the title game against the surprising Eastern champions, the Cleveland Browns. Cleveland, however, pulled off one of the biggest upsets in the game's history. Ryan threw three touchdown passes to Collins and Cleveland won 27-0 before 79,544 at Cleveland Stadium. The winning and losing shares were records, $8,052 for each member of the Browns and $5,571 for each member of the Colts.

Y.A. Tittle and Andy Robustelli, two of the greatest players in New York Giants' history, retired from pro football.

1964 AFL STANDINGS

Eastern Division	W	L	T	Pct.	Pts.	OP
Buffalo	12	2	0	.857	400	242
Boston Patriots	10	3	1	.769	365	297
N.Y. Jets	5	8	1	.385	278	315
Houston	4	10	0	.286	310	355

Western Division	W	L	T	Pct.	Pts.	OP
San Diego	8	5	1	.615	341	300
Kansas City	7	7	0	.500	366	306
Oakland	5	7	2	.417	303	350
Denver	2	11	1	.154	240	438

AFL championship: Buffalo 20, San Diego 7

LEADING RUSHERS	Att.	Yards	Avg.	Long	TD
Cookie Gilchrist, Buffalo	230	981	4.3	67	6
Matt Snell, N.Y. Jets	215	948	4.4	42	5
Clem Daniels, Oakland	173	824	4.8	42	2
Sid Blanks, Houston	145	756	5.2	91	6
Abner Haynes, Kansas City	139	697	5.0	80	4

LEADING PASSERS	Att.	Comp.	Yards	TD	Int.
Len Dawson, Kansas City	354	199	2,879	30	18
Babe Parilli, Boston	473	228	3,465	31	27
George Blanda, Houston	505	262	3,287	17	27
John Hadl, San Diego	274	147	2,157	18	15
Cotton Davidson, Oakland	320	155	2,497	21	19

LEADING RECEIVERS	No.	Yards	Avg.	Long	TD
Charley Hennigan, Houston	101	1,546	15.3	53	8
Art Powell, Oakland	76	1,361	17.9	77	11
Lionel Taylor, Denver	76	873	11.5	57	7
Frank Jackson, Kansas City	62	943	15.2	72	9
Lance Alworth, San Diego	61	1,235	20.2	82	13

1964 NFL STANDINGS

Eastern Conference	W	L	T	Pct.	Pts.	OP
Cleveland	10	3	1	.769	415	293
St. Louis	9	3	2	.750	357	331
Philadelphia	6	8	0	.429	312	313
Washington	6	8	0	.429	307	305
Dallas	5	8	1	.385	250	289
Pittsburgh	5	9	0	.357	253	315
N.Y. Giants	2	10	2	.167	241	399

Western Conference	W	L	T	Pct.	Pts.	OP
Baltimore	12	2	0	.857	428	225
Green Bay	8	5	1	.615	342	245
Minnesota	8	5	1	.615	355	296
Detroit	7	5	2	.583	280	260
Los Angeles	5	7	2	.417	283	339
Chicago	5	9	0	.357	260	379
San Francisco	4	10	0	.286	236	330

NFL championship: Cleveland 27, Baltimore 0

LEADING RUSHERS	Att.	Yards	Avg.	Long	TD
Jim Brown, Cleveland	280	1,446	5.2	71	7
Jim Taylor, Green Bay	235	1,169	5.0	84t	12
John Henry Johnson, Pittsburgh	235	1,048	4.5	45t	7
Bill Brown, Minnesota	226	866	3.8	48	7
Don Perkins, Dallas	174	768	4.4	59	6

LEADING PASSERS	Att.	Comp.	Yards	TD	Int.
Bart Starr, Green Bay	272	163	2,144	15	4
Fran Tarkenton, Minnesota	306	171	2,506	22	11
Sonny Jurgensen, Washington	385	207	2,934	24	13
Johnny Unitas, Baltimore	305	158	2,824	19	6
Milt Plum, Detroit	287	154	2,241	18	15

LEADING RECEIVERS	No.	Yards	Avg.	Long	TD
Johnny Morris, Chicago	93	1,200	12.9	63t	10
Mike Ditka, Chicago	75	897	12.0	34	5
Frank Clarke, Dallas	65	973	15.0	49	5
Bobby Joe Conrad, St. Louis	61	780	12.8	53	6
Bobby Mitchell, Washington	60	904	15.1	60	10

1965 Sonny Werblin signed quarterback Joe Namath of Alabama to a record contract reported to be $400,000 a year. He was the most talked-about member of an exceptional class of rookies that also includ-

ed halfback Gale Sayers and linebacker Dick Butkus of the Chicago Bears, end Bob Hayes of the Dallas Cowboys, end Fred Biletnikoff of the Oakland Raiders, and fullback Ken Willard of the San Francisco 49ers.

Cookie Gilchrist was traded from the Buffalo Bills to the Denver Broncos.

Raymond (Buddy) Parker quit as coach of the Pittsburgh Steelers.

CBS signed a new television contract with the NFL calling for $18.8 million a year, plus $2 milion for the championship game. The network also received permission to telecast three night games in prime time and also to modify the blackout so that one game could be seen in a city when the club was home.

Each league decided to expand. The NFL added Atlanta and the AFL added Miami, both for 1966.

NFL rules were changed increasing the number of officials for each game from five to six; the sixth official was called the "line judge." Officials' penalty flags were changed in color from white to bright gold.

The Houston Oilers, who had been playing their home games at Jeppesen Stadium, a 38,000-seat high school facility, announced they would not play in the new Astrodome because of "an unrealistic lease agreement" and signed a five-year lease for the use of 70,000-seat Rice Stadium.

Buffalo and San Diego repeated as champions of their divisions in the AFL. Namath, New York's new

quarterback, took over as starter and threw 18 touchdown passes, 14 of them to wide receiver Don Maynard.

Buffalo won the title game for the second year in a row, shutting out San Diego 23-0.

Jim Brown's ninth season for Cleveland was another great one but the Browns got a challenge from the Dallas Cowboys in the Eastern Conference for the first time. Dallas reached .500 with a 7-7 record. Quarterback Don Meredith threw 22 touchdown passes and brilliant rookie split end Bob Hayes caught 46 for 1,003 yards, a sensational 21.8-yard average per catch, and 12 touchdowns.

Chicago finished third in the Western Conference but halfback Gale Sayers was almost unstoppable. He scored six touchdowns in one game against San Francisco and had a record 22 for the year.

Norm Van Brocklin quit as coach of the Vikings in midseason, then changed his mind and returned a few days later.

Green Bay and Baltimore were the conference's best teams but wound up deadlocked. The Packers missed a chance to clinch the title when they were tied by the 49ers on the last day of the season. The Colts went through a difficult season, losing quarterback Johnny Unitas with a knee injury and his replacement, Gary Cuozzo, with a shoulder separation. Halfback Tom Matte, who had played quarterback in college at Ohio State, took over the position for Baltimore and, reading his plays off a wristband, led the Colts to a victory over Los Ange-

Joe Namath prepares to hand off in first game as a pro, 1965.

Tex Schramm.

Al Davis.

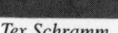

Jim Brown barges forward for yardage in his last NFL game, the 1966 Pro Bowl.

les. That set up a playoff against the Packers at Green Bay. Matte was the makeshift quarterback for the Colts and the Packers' starter, Bart Starr, was injured early in the game and replaced by Zeke Bratkowski. The Colts argued unsuccessfully that a field goal by Chandler that tied the game 10-10 in the fourth quarter was wide of the goal posts. The teams played 13 minutes and 39 seconds of sudden death overtime before a field goal by Don Chandler won the game 13-10 for Green Bay.

Wintry Green Bay was the site of the title game between the Packers and Browns. A morning storm made roads nearly impassable, delayed the arrival of the Browns, and sent a work crew using shovels and snow plows into action. Playing on the muddy turf, the Packers used their ball-control game, with Hornung gaining 105 yards and Taylor 96, while Brown was held to 50 in a 23-12 Green Bay victory, its third NFL championship under coach Vince Lombardi.

Except for the Pro Bowl it was the last game for Cleveland's Brown. He left behind a career total of 12,312 yards rushing, seven 1,000-yard seasons, 58 100-yard games, four 200-yard games, a career average of 5.2 yards per rush, and 126 touchdowns.

Brown ended his career appropriately in the Pro Bowl, scoring three touchdowns and winning the outstanding back award in the East's 36-7 victory.

After the season, the AFL All-Star game ran into trouble in New Orleans when some players charged they were racially discriminated against. The game was shifted to Houston.

Two men who played important roles in NFL history died. They were Earl (Curly) Lambeau, founder and former coach of the Green Bay Packers, and Jack Mara, co-owner of the New York Giants.

1965 AFL STANDINGS

Eastern Division	W	L	T	Pct.	Pts.	OP
Buffalo	10	3	1	.769	313	226
N.Y. Jets	5	8	1	.385	285	303
Boston Patriots	4	8	2	.333	244	302
Houston	4	10	0	.286	298	429
Western Division	W	L	T	Pct.	Pts.	OP
San Diego	9	2	3	.818	340	227
Oakland	8	5	1	.615	298	239
Kansas City	7	5	2	.583	322	285
Denver	4	10	0	.286	303	392

AFL championship: Buffalo 23, San Diego 0

LEADING RUSHERS	Att.	Yards	Avg.	Long	TD
Paul Lowe, San Diego	222	1,121	5.0	59	7
Cookie Gilchrist, Denver	252	954	3.8	44	6
Clem Daniels, Oakland	219	884	4.0	57	5
Matt Snell, N.Y. Jets	169	763	4.5	44	4
Curtis McClinton, Kansas City	175	661	3.8	48	6

LEADING PASSERS	Att.	Comp.	Yards	TD	Int.
John Hadl, San Diego	348	174	2,798	20	21
Len Dawson, Kansas City	305	163	2,262	21	14
Joe Namath, N.Y. Jets	340	164	2,220	18	15
Jack Kemp, Buffalo	391	179	2,368	10	18
George Blanda, Houston	442	186	2,542	20	30

LEADING RECEIVERS	No.	Yards	Avg.	Long	TD
Lionel Taylor, Denver	85	1,131	13.3	63	6
Lance Alworth, San Diego	69	1,602	23.2	85	14
Don Maynard, N.Y. Jets	68	1,218	17.9	56	14
Ode Burrell, Houston	55	650	11.8	52	4
Art Powell, Oakland	52	800	15.4	66	12

1965 NFL STANDINGS

Eastern Conference	W	L	T	Pct.	Pts.	OP
Cleveland	11	3	0	.786	363	325
Dallas	7	7	0	.500	325	280
N.Y. Giants	7	7	0	.500	270	338
Washington	6	8	0	.429	257	301
Philadelphia	5	9	0	.357	363	359
St. Louis	5	9	0	.357	296	309
Pittsburgh	2	12	0	.143	202	397
Western Conference	W	L	T	Pct.	Pts.	OP
Baltimore	10	3	1	.769	389	284
Green Bay	10	3	1	.769	316	224
Chicago	9	5	0	.643	409	275
San Francisco	7	6	1	.538	421	402
Minnesota	7	7	0	.500	383	403
Detroit	6	7	1	.462	257	295
Los Angeles	4	10	0	.286	269	328

Western Conference playoff: Green Bay 13, Baltimore 10, sudden death overtime

NFL championship: Green Bay 23, Cleveland 12

Pete Rozelle awards Vince Lombardi of Green Bay the trophy for winning the first AFL-NFL World Championship Game.

LEADING RUSHERS	Att.	Yards	Avg.	Long	TD	
Jim Brown, Cleveland	289	1,544	5.3	67	17	
Gale Sayers, Chicago	166	867	5.2	61t	14	
Timmy Brown, Philadelphia	158	861	5.4	54t	6	
Ken Willard, San Francisco	189	778	4.1	32	5	
Jim Taylor, Green Bay	207	734	3.5	35	4	
LEADING PASSERS	Att.	Comp.	Yards	TD	Int.	
Rudy Bukich, Chicago	312	176	2,641	20	9	
Johnny Unitas, Baltimore	282	164	2,530	23	12	
John Brodie, San Francisco	391	242	3,112	30	16	
Bart Starr, Green Bay	251	140	2,055	16	9	
Earl Morrall, N.Y. Giants	302	155	2,446	22	12	
LEADING RECEIVERS	No.	Yards	Avg.	Long	TD	
Dave Parks, San Francisco	80	1,344	16.8	53t	12	
Tommy McDonald, Los Angeles	67	1,036	15.5	51	9	
Pete Retzlaff, Philadelphia	66	1,190	18.0	78	10	
Bobby Mitchell, Washington	60	867	14.5	80t	6	
Bernie Casey, San Francisco	59	765	13.0	59t	8	

1966 The war between the leagues reached a peak. They spent a combined total of $7 million to sign 1966 draft choices. The Green Bay Packers spent $1 million for running backs Donny Anderson of Texas Tech and Jim Grabowski of Illinois.

The NFL signed 75 percent of its 232 draftees, and the AFL 46 percent of its 181. Of 111 common draft choices, 79 went with the NFL, 28 with the AFL, and four went unsigned.

Joe Foss, Commissioner of the AFL since its in-ception, resigned in April and was replaced by Al Davis, coach of the Oakland Raiders. Lamar Hunt of the Kansas City Chiefs and Tex Schramm of the Dallas Cowboys held secret talks about a possible merger of the two leagues. Kicker Pete Gogolak, who had played out his option with the Buffalo Bills and become a free agent, was signed by the New York Giants. As a result, AFL clubs retaliated by signing such established NFL stars as John Brodie, Mike Ditka, and Roman Gabriel.

It came as a complete surprise when NFL Commissioner Pete Rozelle announced a merger of the NFL and AFL June 8. The leagues agreed that their champions would meet in a World Championship Game starting after the 1966 season. There would be a common draft of players and preseason games between the teams of each league starting in 1967. The new league would expand to 26 teams by 1968 and would continue to play separate schedules until 1970, when they would combine in one league with Rozelle as Commissioner.

Congress approved the pro football merger, October 21.

The Atlanta Falcons became the fifteenth NFL team and were placed in the Eastern Conference for purposes of the standings but were given a round-robin schedule in which they met every other league team in 1966.

Another southern city, New Orleans, was accepted as the sixteenth NFL team, to begin play in 1967. A reorganization plan was made in which the league would be split into four divisions of four teams starting in 1967.

Assistant coach George Allen left the Bears and became head coach of the Los Angeles Rams after a bitter court fight with Bears' owner George Halas, who finally withdrew his suit in opposition to Los Angeles's hiring of Allen.

The Raiders moved into the new Oakland-Alameda County Coliseum.

Goal posts offset from the goal line were installed in NFL stadiums, and their uprights were raised to a minimum 20 feet above the crossbar.

The Kansas City Chiefs were coached by Hank Stram and quarterbacked by Len Dawson. They beat the Buffalo Bills 31-7 in the AFL Championship Game.

The Dallas Cowboys, who had been rivals in their city in the early sixties with the Texans, narrowly missed winning the NFL championship and joining them in the first World Championship Game. Dallas captured the Eastern Conference championship in its seventh season, becoming the first expansion team in history to win a division or conference title. The Cowboys, however, lost a thrilling NFL Championship Game to Green Bay. Dallas rallied in the final minutes and had the ball on the Packers' 2-yard line when quarterback Don Meredith rolled out and was hit by linebacker Dave Robinson. He got off the pass but it was intercepted in the end zone by safety Tom Brown. The Packers of Vince Lombardi had won 34-27 and gained the right to represent their league in its first confrontation with the AFL.

Gino Marchetti of the Baltimore Colts and Ollie Matson of the Philadelphia Eagles retired.

1966 AFL STANDINGS

Eastern Division	W	L	T	Pct.	Pts.	OP
Buffalo	9	4	1	.692	358	255
Boston Patriots	8	4	2	.667	315	283
N.Y. Jets.	6	6	2	.500	322	312
Houston	3	11	0	.214	335	396
Miami	3	11	0	.214	213	362

Western Division	W	L	T	Pct.	Pts.	OP
Kansas City.	11	2	1	.846	448	276
Oakland.	8	5	1	.615	315	288
San Diego	7	6	1	.538	335	284
Denver.	4	10	0	.286	196	381

AFL championship: Kansas City 31, Buffalo 7

LEADING RUSHERS	Att.	Yards	Avg.	Long	TD
Jim Nance, Boston	299	1,458	4.9	65	11
Mike Garrett, Kansas City	147	801	5.4	77	6
Clem Daniels, Oakland	204	801	3.9	64	7
Bobby Burnett, Buffalo	187	766	4.1	32	4
Wray Carlton, Buffalo	156	696	4.5	23	6

LEADING PASSERS	Att.	Comp.	Yards	TD	Int.
Len Dawson, Kansas City	284	159	2,527	26	10
John Hadl, San Diego	375	200	2,846	23	14
Tom Flores, Oakland	306	151	2,638	24	14
Joe Namath, N.Y. Jets	471	232	3,379	19	27
Babe Parilli, Boston	382	181	2,721	20	20

LEADING RECEIVERS	No.	Yards	Avg.	Long	TD
Lance Alworth, San Diego	73	1,383	18.9	78	13
George Sauer, N.Y. Jets	63	1,079	17.0	77	5
Otis Taylor, Kansas City	58	1,297	22.4	89	8
Chris Burford, Kansas City	58	758	13.1	38	8
Willie Frazier, Houston	57	1,129	19.8	79	12

1966 NFL STANDINGS

Eastern Conference	W	L	T	Pct.	Pts.	OP
Dallas.	10	3	1	.769	445	239
Cleveland	9	5	0	.643	403	259
Philadelphia	9	5	0	.643	326	340
St. Louis.	8	5	1	.615	264	265
Washington	7	7	0	.500	351	355
Pittsburgh	5	8	1	.385	316	347
Atlanta	3	11	0	.214	204	437
N.Y. Giants	1	12	1	.077	263	501

Western Conference	W	L	T	Pct.	Pts.	OP
Green Bay.	12	2	0	.857	335	163
Baltimore.	9	5	0	.643	314	226
Los Angeles	8	6	0	.571	289	212
San Francisco.	6	6	2	.500	320	325
Chicago.	5	7	2	.417	234	272
Detroit	4	9	1	.308	206	317
Minnesota	4	9	1	.308	292	304

NFL championship: Green Bay 34, Dallas 27
Super Bowl I: Green Bay (NFL) 35, Kansas City (AFL) 10

LEADING RUSHERS	Att.	Yards	Avg.	Long	TD
Gale Sayers, Chicago	229	1,231	5.4	58t	8
Leroy Kelly, Cleveland	209	1,141	5.5	70t	15
Dick Bass, Los Angeles	248	1,090	4.4	50	8
Bill Brown, Minnesota	251	829	3.3	33t	6
Ken Willard, San Francisco	191	763	4.0	49	5

LEADING PASSERS	Att.	Comp.	Yards	TD	Int.
Bart Starr, Green Bay	251	156	2,257	14	3
Sonny Jurgensen, Washington	436	252	3,209	28	19
Frank Ryan, Cleveland	382	200	2,974	29	14
Don Meredith, Dallas	344	177	2,805	24	12
Johnny Unitas, Baltimore	348	195	2,748	22	24

LEADING RECEIVERS	No.	Yards	Avg.	Long	TD
Charley Taylor, Washington	72	1,119	15.5	86t	12
Pat Studstill, Detroit	67	1,266	18.9	99t	5
Dave Parks, San Francisco	66	974	14.8	65t	5
Bob Hayes, Dallas	64	1,232	19.3	95t	13
Tom Moore, Los Angeles	60	433	7.2	30t	3

1967 The Los Angeles Memorial Coliseum was the site for the first World Championship Game; the name "Super Bowl" was not yet official for the

Charlie Mitchell (27) and the Broncos beat the Lions 13-7 in 1967, giving the AFL its first win over the NFL.

event. Both the CBS and NBC television networks broadcast the game, and it was not a sellout; a crowd of 63,035 attended. Green Bay held a 14-10 lead at the half and broke the game open in the second half when Willie Wood ran 50 yards with an interception to set up a touchdown by Elijah Pitts. Quarterback Bart Starr threw two touchdown passes to Max McGee and the Packers won 35-10.

The NFL had four divisions for the first time. Its 16 teams were divided into the Century and Capitol divisions of the Eastern Conference and the Central and Coastal divisions of the Western Conference. New Orleans began play with Tom Fears as its head coach. Cincinnati came into pro football as the tenth AFL team, to begin competition in 1968.

The first combined AFL-NFL draft was held March 14. The Baltimore Colts traded with New Orleans for the first pick and chose defensive end Bubba Smith of Michigan State. Bob Griese of the Miami Dolphins and Gene Upshaw of the Oakland Raiders were other notable rookies.

Coach Norm Van Brocklin and quarterback Fran Tarkenton of the Minnesota Vikings had a falling out. Van Brocklin quit as coach and was replaced by Bud Grant. Tarkenton was traded to the New York Giants.

The San Diego Chargers moved into the new San Diego Stadium.

An NFL team lost to an AFL team for the first time when the Denver Broncos beat the Detroit Lions 13-7 August 5 in a preseason game.

Quarterback Daryle Lamonica led the Oakland Raiders to a 13-1 record and the AFL West title. George Blanda, 39 years old, signed as a free agent

after being released by Houston, became the Raiders' kicker and Lamonica's backup at quarterback. Houston took the Eastern title despite a great year by quarterback Joe Namath for the New York Jets. He had 4,007 yards and 26 touchdowns passing.

Oakland whipped Houston 40-7 in the championship game.

Green Bay won the NFL Central Division with rookie Travis Williams setting a record by running back four kickoffs for touchdowns. The Packers beat Coastal Division winner Los Angeles 28-7 for the Western Conference title.

Jim Taylor, former Packers' star, ended his career playing part-time for the New Orleans Saints.

Dallas won the Capitol and Cleveland the Century Division. Sonny Jurgensen of Washington completed 288 passes for 3,747 yards, and Jim Bakken of St. Louis kicked seven field goals in one game against Pittsburgh. In the Eastern Conference title game, the Cowboys won a one-sided 52-14 victory over Cleveland.

Lambeau Field in Green Bay was the site for the title game. The weather in Green Bay was Arctic. The day before the game, Vince Lombardi showed the press the electric wiring under the turf which he, he said, would guarantee an unfrozen field when the Packers and Cowboys played the next day.

The field did freeze, however. The temperature was 13 degrees below zero and the wind chill 40 below. Green Bay and Dallas played what many consider the most dramatic title game in league history. The Packers won 21-17 with 13 seconds to play, they scored when quarterback Bart Starr went over on a one-yard sneak behind a tremendous block by guard Jerry Kramer on Dallas defensive tackle Jethro Pugh. Later, Lombardi said he had passed up an almost sure field goal in favor of the sneak for the touchdown because, ''I couldn't see going for a tie and making all those people in the stands suffer through sudden death in this weather.''

George Halas, 73, retired for the fourth and last time as head coach of the team he owned, the Chicago Bears.

End Raymond Berry and guard Jim Parker of the Baltimore Colts, kicker Lou Groza of the Cleveland Browns (for the second time), and center Jim Ringo of Philadelphia were notable players who retired from football.

1967 AFL STANDINGS

Eastern Division	W	L	T	Pct.	Pts.	OP
Houston	9	4	1	.692	258	199
N.Y. Jets	8	5	1	.615	371	329
Buffalo	4	10	0	.286	237	285
Miami	4	10	0	.286	219	407
Boston Patriots	3	10	1	.231	280	389
Western Division	W	L	T	Pct.	Pts.	OP
Oakland	13	1	0	.929	468	233
Kansas City	9	5	0	.643	408	254
San Diego	8	5	1	.615	360	352
Denver	3	11	0	.214	256	409

AFL championship: Oakland 40, Houston 7

LEADING RUSHERS	Att.	Yards	Avg.	Long	TD
Jim Nance, Boston	269	1,216	4.5	53	7
Hoyle Granger, Houston	238	1,194	5.1	67	6
Mike Garrett, Kansas City	236	1,087	4.6	58	9
Dickie Post, San Diego	161	663	4.1	67t	7
Brad Hubbert, San Diego	116	643	5.5	80t	2

LEADING PASSERS	Att.	Comp.	Yards	TD	Int.
Daryle Lamonica, Oakland	425	220	3,228	30	20
Len Dawson, Kansas City	357	206	2,651	24	17
Joe Namath, N.Y. Jets	491	258	4,007	26	28
John Hadl, San Diego	427	217	3,365	24	22
Bob Griese, Miami	331	166	2,005	15	18

LEADING RECEIVERS	No.	Yards	Avg.	Long	TD
George Sauer, N.Y. Jets	75	1,189	15.9	61t	6
Don Maynard, N.Y. Jets	71	1,434	20.2	75t	10
Jack Clancy, Miami	67	868	13.0	44t	2
Otis Taylor, Kansas City	59	958	16.2	71t	11
Hewritt Dixon, Oakland	59	563	9.5	48	2

1967 NFL STANDINGS
EASTERN CONFERENCE

Capitol Division	W	L	T	Pct.	Pts.	OP
Dallas	9	5	0	.643	342	268
Philadelphia	6	7	1	.462	351	409
Washington	5	6	3	.455	347	353
New Orleans	3	11	0	.214	233	379
Century Division	W	L	T	Pct.	Pts.	OP
Cleveland	9	5	0	.643	334	297
N.Y. Giants	7	7	0	.500	369	379
St. Louis	6	7	1	.462	333	356
Pittsburgh	4	9	1	.308	281	320

WESTERN CONFERENCE

Coastal Division	W	L	T	Pct.	Pts.	OP
Los Angeles	11	1	2	.917	398	196
Baltimore	11	1	2	.917	394	198
San Francisco	7	7	0	.500	273	337
Atlanta	1	12	1	.077	175	422
Central Division	W	L	T	Pct.	Pts.	OP
Green Bay	9	4	1	.692	332	209
Chicago	7	6	1	.538	239	218
Detroit	5	7	2	.417	260	259
Minnesota	3	8	3	.273	233	294

Conference championships: Dallas 52, Cleveland 14; Green Bay 28, Los Angeles 7
NFL championship: Green Bay 21, Dallas 17
Super Bowl II: Green Bay (NFL) 33, Oakland (AFL) 14

LEADING RUSHERS	Att.	Yards	Avg.	Long	TD
Leroy Kelly, Cleveland	235	1,205	5.1	42t	11
Dave Osborn, Minnesota	215	972	4.5	73	2
Gale Sayers, Chicago	186	880	4.7	70	7
Johnny Roland, St. Louis	234	876	3.7	70	10
Mel Farr, Detroit	206	860	4.2	57	3

LEADING PASSERS	Att.	Comp.	Yards	TD	Int.
Sonny Jurgensen, Washington	508	288	3,747	31	16
Johnny Unitas, Baltimore	436	255	3,428	20	16
Fran Tarkenton, N.Y. Giants	377	204	3,088	29	19
Roman Gabriel, Los Angeles	371	196	2,779	25	13
Norm Snead, Philadelphia	434	240	3,399	29	24

LEADING RECEIVERS	No.	Yards	Avg.	Long	TD
Charley Taylor, Washington	70	990	14.1	86t	9
Jerry Smith, Washington	67	849	12.7	43	12
Willie Richardson, Baltimore	63	860	13.7	31t	8
Bobby Mitchell, Washington	60	866	14.4	65t	6
Ben Hawkins, Philadelphia	59	1,265	21.4	87t	10

Bart Starr rolls away from Dallas defensive tackle Willie Townes in the 1967 NFL Championship Game.

1968 The temperature was 65, 78 degrees higher than it had been two weeks earlier in Green Bay, when the Packers beat Oakland 33-14 at the Orange Bowl in Miami in the second World Championship Game. Don Chandler kicked four field goals for the Packers and Starr directed an offensive attack that ran up 325 yards against the Raiders.

It was Lombardi's second consecutive world championship coming on the heels of his third straight NFL championship. He stunned the football world by announcing his retirement as Packers' head coach. Assistant coach Phil Bengtson would replace him and he would remain as general manager.

Sonny Werblin sold his interest in the New York Jets to four partners and one of them, Don Lillis, became the acting head of the corporation. Lillis died two months later and Phil Iselin was named Jets' president.

The Houston Oilers left Rice Stadium and began playing their games in the Astrodome.

The AFL reached an agreement with its players association for a pension increase but a prolonged dispute between NFL owners and the NFL Players Association turned into a strike in July. It was settled a few days before training camps opened.

Paul Brown returned to pro football as part-owner and head coach of the expansion team in Cincinnati, the Bengals.

The New York Jets easily won the AFL East behind a strong passing attack, Joe Namath throwing to George Sauer and Don Maynard. New York also had strong running with Matt Snell, Emerson Boozer, and Bill Mathis.

The Jets were in a tense game with the Oakland Raiders at Oakland. New York led 32-29 with one minute, five seconds to play when NBC television switched from the game to begin the movie, *Heidi*. The network's switchboard lit up with angry protests while the Raiders came back with two late touchdowns to win what was dubbed the "Heidi Game" 43-32.

Oakland and Kansas City tied for first place in the Western Division with 12-2 records. The Raiders won an overwhelming playoff victory 41-6 as Daryle Lamonica bombed the Chiefs with five touchdown passes.

The Jets won the East and met the surging Raiders for the AFL championship. Namath outpassed Lamonica, throwing for three touchdowns, and the Jets won 27-23.

Earl Morrall, acquired from the New York Giants, took over as quarterback of the Baltimore Colts when Johnny Unitas went out with an elbow injury. Morrall had a sensational 26-touchdown season and the Colts, coached by Don Shula, lost only to Cleveland 30-20 while compiling a 13-1 record, one of the best in NFL history. Baltimore won the Coastal Division easily. Minnesota had an excellent front four in ends Carl Eller and Jim Marshall and tackles Alan Page and Gary Larsen, called the Purple People Eaters, that won the Central, its first division title. The Colts won a playoff from the Vikings 24-14 for the Western Conference championship.

There was an important quarterback switch in the Eastern Conference, too. Bill Nelsen replaced Frank Ryan as leader of the Cleveland Browns and led them to the Century Division title and then a 31-20 victory over Capitol Division winner Dallas for the Eastern title. Leroy Kelly scored two touchdowns for Cleveland in its victory over Dallas.

The Browns met their match in the NFL title game, however. Baltimore swamped them 34-0 with

Bill Mathis escorts Matt Snell in Super Bowl III. Snell ran for a then-Super Bowl record 121 yards and scored the Jets' only touchdown in their 16-7 victory.

The Record Holders

Franco Harris (page 65) proved to be both durable and productive in the NFL. During his first 10 seasons (Pittsburgh since 1972), Harris carried the ball a total of 2,462 times for the Steelers to set the record for most career rushing attempts. In 1981, he became the third NFL running back to rush for more than 10,000 yards in a career.

Two other legendary examples of endurance were provided by Jim Marshall (opposite page) and George Blanda (right). During his 20-year career, Marshall (Cleveland 1960, Minnesota 1961-1979) played in an NFL record 282 consecutive games. The reliable defensive end acutally *started* every game in his 19 seasons with the Vikings. Blanda's memorable career as a quarterback and placekicker spanned 26 years (an NFL high) with four teams: the Chicago Bears 1949, 1950-58; Baltimore 1950; Houston 1960-66; and Oakland 1967-1975. He is the NFL's all-time leading scorer with 2,002 points, and holds the league's career records for most extra points (943) and most field goals (335).

Fran Tarkenton (opposite page) earned fame as a scrambling quarterback during his 18 NFL seasons (Minnesota 1961-1966, 1972-78; New York Giants 1967-1971). But when Tarkenton retired in 1978 he also had accumulated a staggering total of 47,003 yards passing—an all-time NFL high. One of only two quarterbacks to surpass the 40,000-yard mark (Johnny Unitas, with 40,239, is the other), Tarkenton also set NFL career records for most passing attempts (6,467), completions (3,686), and touchdowns (342).

Don Maynard (left) also compiled an impressive statistical portfolio during a 15-year career (New York Giants 1958, New York Jets 1960-1972, St. Louis 1973). In addition to ranking second on the all-time career reception list with 633 catches (behind Charley Taylor's record total of 649), Maynard set NFL standards for most yards receiving in a career (11,834) and most games with 100 or more yards receiving (50). He also caught 88 touchdown passes, second only to Don Hutson's NFL record of 99.

As the new age of passing dawned in the NFL in the late 1970s, quarterback Dan Fouts (San Diego since 1973) began his own personal assault on the NFL record book. In 1979, Fouts (left) became the second quarterback in NFL history to pass for more than 4,000 yards (4,082). The following season he improved on that mark by passing for 4,715 yards. In 1981, he pushed the record still higher by throwing for 4,802 yards, while also setting new single-season marks for most passing attempts (609) and completions (360).

    In both 1980, when Fouts set another record for most 300-yard games in a season (8), and 1981, his most frequent target was Kellen Winslow (San Diego since 1979). Winslow (above) led the NFL in receptions in 1980 with 89, which set a record for most catches by a tight end. In 1981, Winslow caught 88 passes, and tied an NFL single-game record by catching five touchdown passes (from Fouts) in a victory against Oakland.

The most accurate passing performance in an NFL game occurred on November 10, 1974, when quarterback Ken Anderson (right, in action in 1981) connected on 20 of his 22 passes for a completion percentage of 90.91. Anderson (Cincinnati since 1971), who led the NFL in passing in 1974, 1975, and 1981, also set the Super Bowl passing accuracy record in Game XVI against San Francisco by completing 25 of 34 passes, a percentage of 73.5.

The legacy established by running back Jim Brown (Cleveland 1957-1965) is reflected by the number of career rushing records he achieved. In addition to rushing for 12,312 yards to become the NFL's all-time leading rusher, Brown (opposite) set career NFL records for most touchdowns rushing (106), highest rushing average (5.22), most 100-yard rushing games (58), most 1,000-yard seasons (7), and most seasons as the NFL's leading rusher (8).

Only one year after winning the Heisman Trophy and leading the NCAA in rushing at the University of South Carolina, George Rogers (New Orleans since 1981), the NFL's number-one draft pick in 1981, led the league in rushing with 1,674 yards. In the process Rogers (above) broke the NFL's rookie rushing record and set a new record for most rushing attempts in a season with 378 (Earl Campbell held the previous record with 373).

On November 20, 1977, running back Walter Payton (Chicago since 1975) entered his name in the NFL record book with the single greatest rushing day in the history of the league. In a 10-7 victory over Minnesota, Payton (pictured right in a game against Tampa Bay in 1978) gained 275 yards on 40 attempts to break the record of 273 set just one year earlier by O.J. Simpson.

The distinguished career of linebacker Ted Hendricks (left, about to sack Denver quarterback Craig Morton) has been decorated by many postseason honors. In addition to his status as perhaps the greatest kick blocker in NFL history, Hendricks (Baltimore 1969-1973, Green Bay 1974, Oakland since 1975) also holds the NFL record for most safeties in a career with four.

Safety Ken Houston (above) intercepted 49 passes in his 14-year career (Houston 1967-1972, Washington 1973-1980). He returned nine of his interceptions for touchdowns to set an NFL career record. In 1971 Houston also set the NFL single-season record for interception returns for touchdowns with four. That record was tied a year later by Jim Kearney of Kansas City.

The record for most punt return yards in a career is held by Rick Upchurch (Denver since 1975). Upchurch significantly helped build his career total of 2,714 yards on punt returns in 1977 when he totaled 653—just 2 yards shy of Neal Colzie's NFL single-season record of 655. The previous season Upchurch returned four punts for touchdowns to tie an NFL record originally set in 1951 by Jack Christiansen.

an offensive barrage that included three touchdowns by Tom Matte.

1968 AFL STANDINGS

Eastern Division	W	L	T	Pct.	Pts.	OP
N.Y. Jets	11	3	0	.786	419	280
Houston	7	7	0	.500	303	248
Miami	5	8	1	.385	276	355
Boston Patriots	4	10	0	.286	229	406
Buffalo	1	12	1	.077	199	367

Western Division	W	L	T	Pct.	Pts.	OP
Kansas City	12	2	0	.857	371	170
Oakland	12	2	0	.857	453	233
San Diego	9	5	0	.643	382	310
Denver	5	9	0	.357	255	404
Cincinnati	3	11	0	.214	215	329

Western Division playoff: Oakland 41, Kansas City 6
AFL championship: N.Y. Jets 27, Oakland 23

LEADING RUSHERS	Att.	Yards	Avg.	Long	TD
Paul Robinson, Cincinnati	238	1,023	4.3	87t	8
Robert Holmes, Kansas City	174	866	5.0	76t	7
Hewritt Dixon, Oakland	206	865	4.2	28	2
Hoyle Granger, Houston	202	848	4.2	47t	7
Dickie Post, San Diego	151	758	5.0	62t	3

LEADING PASSERS	Att.	Comp.	Yards	TD	Int.
Len Dawson, Kansas City	224	131	2,019	17	9
Daryle Lamonica, Oakland	416	206	3,245	25	15
Joe Namath, N.Y. Jets	380	187	3,147	15	17
Bob Griese, Miami	355	186	2,473	21	16
John Hadl, San Diego	440	208	3,473	27	32

LEADING RECEIVERS	No.	Yards	Avg.	Long	TD
Lance Alworth, San Diego	68	1,312	19.3	80t	10
George Sauer, N.Y. Jets	66	1,141	17.3	43	3
Fred Biletnikoff, Oakland	61	1,037	17.0	82	6
Karl Noonan, Miami	58	760	13.1	50t	11
Don Maynard, N.Y. Jets	57	1,297	22.8	87t	10

1968 NFL STANDINGS
EASTERN CONFERENCE

Capitol Division	W	L	T	Pct.	Pts.	OP
Dallas	12	2	0	.857	431	186
N.Y. Giants	7	7	0	.500	294	325
Washington	5	9	0	.357	249	358
Philadelphia	2	12	0	.143	202	351

Century Division	W	L	T	Pct.	Pts.	OP
Cleveland	10	4	0	.714	394	273
St. Louis	9	4	1	.692	325	289
New Orleans	4	9	1	.308	246	327
Pittsburgh	2	11	1	.154	244	397

WESTERN CONFERENCE

Coastal Division	W	L	T	Pct.	Pts.	OP
Baltimore	13	1	0	.929	402	144
Los Angeles	10	3	1	.769	312	200
San Francisco	7	6	1	.538	303	310
Atlanta	2	12	0	.143	170	389

Central Division	W	L	T	Pct.	Pts.	OP
Minnesota	8	6	0	.571	282	242
Chicago	7	7	0	.500	250	333
Green Bay	6	7	1	.462	281	227
Detroit	4	8	2	.333	207	241

Conference championships: Cleveland 31, Dallas 20; Baltimore 24, Minnesota 14
NFL championship: Baltimore 34, Cleveland 0
Super Bowl III: N.Y. Jets (AFL) 16, Baltimore (NFL) 7

LEADING RUSHERS	Att.	Yards	Avg.	Long	TD
Leroy Kelly, Cleveland	248	1,239	5.0	65	16
Ken Willard, San Francisco	227	967	4.3	69t	7
Tom Woodeshick, Philadelphia	217	947	4.4	54t	3
Dick Hoak, Pittsburgh	175	858	4.9	77t	3
Gale Sayers, Chicago	138	856	6.2	63	2

LEADING PASSERS	Att.	Comp.	Yards	TD	Int.
Earl Morrall, Baltimore	317	182	2,909	26	17
Don Meredith, Dallas	309	171	2,500	21	12
John Brodie, San Francisco	404	234	3,020	22	21
Bart Starr, Green Bay	171	109	1,617	15	8
Fran Tarkenton, N.Y. Giants	337	182	2,555	21	12

LEADING RECEIVERS	No.	Yards	Avg.	Long	TD
Clifton McNeil, San Francisco	71	994	14.0	65t	7
Roy Jefferson, Pittsburgh	58	1,074	18.5	62	11
Lance Rentzel, Dallas	54	1,009	18.7	65t	6
Dan Abramowicz, New Orleans	54	890	16.5	47t	7
Bob Hayes, Dallas	53	909	17.2	54t	10

1969 "Super Bowl" was now the official name for what had been called the World Championship Game, and the Colts, 15-1 in regular and postseason games, were solid favorites as they faced the AFL champion Jets at Miami. Three days before the game, however, Namath of the Jets was attending a sports dinner when he predicted, "We are going to win on Sunday, I guarantee you."

Namath made his boast reality when he completed 17 of 28 passes, sent Matt Snell rushing for 121

Paul Brown.

Earl Morrall.

Joe Kapp.

yards, and the Jets won 16-7 to become the first AFL team to win a Super Bowl.

George Allen, fired as coach of the Los Angeles Rams by owner Dan Reeves, was rehired after his players protested the firing. Vince Lombardi left the general managership of the Green Bay Packers and became part-owner, executive vice-president, and head coach of the Washington Redskins. John Madden became head coach of the Oakland Raiders and Chuck Noll head coach of the Pittsburgh Steelers.

O. J. Simpson of USC, winner of the Heisman Trophy, was the first choice in the draft, by the Buffalo Bills.

Commissioner Pete Rozelle announced a new television contract with the ABC network for 13 regular season Monday night games in prime time during 1970, 1971, and 1972.

It was necessary to thrash out the format under which the 26 teams would compete once they were all one league starting in 1970. The owners alternately argued, dozed, agreed, ate, and eventually compromised in a marathon 35-hour, 45-minute realignment meeting in May. As a result of the meeting, the Baltimore Colts, Cleveland Browns, and Pittsburgh Steelers joined the 10 AFL teams in a new 13-team American Football Conference and the remaining 13 teams from the 16-club NFL became the National Football Conference. There would also be a "wild card" or best second-place team in each conference going into the playoffs each year. All this was to become effective the next year.

For 1969 only, the AFL played under a format in which the second-place team in each division would play the champion of the other division.

New York and Houston in the East and Oakland and Kansas City in the West were the best teams in the AFL again as it went through its last season with the identity it had had since 1960.

Quarterback Daryle Lamonica threw 34 touchdown passes. Kicker Jan Stenerud of Kansas City had 16 consecutive field goals. Wide receiver Lance Alworth of San Diego completed a string in which he caught at least one pass in 96 consecutive games.

Sid Gillman, coach of the Chargers since their inception, was forced to step down after nine games because of ulcers and was succeeded by assistant coach Charlie Waller.

Kansas City, second place in the West, unseated the defending champion Jets 13-6 in one hard-fought AFL playoff, while Oakland had no trouble in the other, routing Houston 56-7 behind six touchdown passes by Lamonica.

Kansas City won the AFL title game, stopping Oakland 17-7. Lamonica was injured and 42-year-old George Blanda took over in a losing effort. The Chiefs and their coach, Hank Stram, advanced to the Super Bowl and a chance to avenge their loss in the first world championship game four seasons before.

Los Angeles, behind Allen, ousted Baltimore as Coastal Division winner in the NFL. Minnesota again won the Central, Dallas the Capitol, and Cleveland the Century.

Washington came in second in the Capitol and had its best record, 7-5-2, since 1955 under its new coach, Lombardi.

Quarterback Bill Nelsen led Cleveland to a rousing victory over Dallas, 38-14, for the Eastern Conference title. Joe Kapp, unorthodox leader of the Vikings, led them from a 17-7 deficit to a 23-20 victory over Los Angeles to claim the Western Conference championship.

In the NFL title game, Kapp threw a touchdown pass and scored once as Minnesota defeated Cleveland 27-7.

Owner George Preston Marshall of the Washington Redskins died at 72.

Vince Lombardi's funeral, St. Patrick's Cathedral, New York City, 1970.

Don Shula.

Brian Piccolo.

1970 Minnesota met Kansas City in Super Bowl IV at New Orleans. The Vikings were favored but Mike Garrett and Otis Taylor scored touchdowns and Jan Stenerud kicked three field goals, giving the Chiefs a 23-7 victory. Losers in the first Super Bowl, Kansas City won the last such game played between the champions of the two leagues before their reorganization.

The merger agreement of 1966 was implemented, and the 26 teams of pro football were realigned into the American and National Football Conferences and began playing interleague regular season games.

New Orleans's Tom Dempsey kicks an NFL record 63-yard field goal to defeat the Detroit Lions 19-17, 1970.

The AFC was made up of the Baltimore Colts, Boston Patriots, Buffalo Bills, Miami Dolphins, and New York Jets in the Eastern Division; the Cincinnati Bengals, Cleveland Browns, Houston Oilers, and Pittsburgh Steelers in the Central Division; and the Denver Broncos, Kansas City Chiefs, Oakland Raiders, and San Diego Chargers in the Western Division.

The NFC realignment was not arrived at until months of discussion and, finally, one of the five plans submitted by Commissioner Pete Rozelle was drawn in a lottery. The new NFC was made up of the Dallas Cowboys, New York Giants, Philadelphia Eagles, St. Louis Cardinals, and Washington Redskins in the Eastern Division; the Chicago Bears, Detroit Lions, Green Bay Packers, and Minnesota Vikings in the Central Division; and the Atlanta Falcons, Los Angeles Rams, New Orleans Saints, and San Francisco 49ers in the Western Division.

Each team was to play home-and-home with each other team in its division, three or five games with other teams of its own conference, and three interconference games. Because of the odd number of clubs in each Conference, one would play four intersectional games.

Rozelle had to settle charges of tampering by the Miami Dolphins in their efforts to lure coach Don Shula from Baltimore. Shula was permitted to make

the move but Miami was assessed a number-one draft choice in 1971. Don McCafferty replaced Shula as coach of the Colts.

Vince Lombardi, former coach of the Green Bay Packers and Washington Redskins, and Brian Piccolo, former running back for the Chicago Bears, died of cancer.

Jimmy Conzelman, who had been a prominent figure in the early days of pro football and who is a member of the Pro Football Hall of Fame, died.

The Cincinnati Bengals moved into new 56,200-seat Riverfront Stadium and the Pittsburgh Steelers into new 50,350-seat Three Rivers Stadium.

Monday night football became a TV success as ABC began the first of a three-year contract.

There was the possibility of a strike by NFL players until early August. A new four-year agreement was signed between the owners and the NFL Players' Association.

The rules were changed requiring players' names on the backs of their jerseys, as they had been in the AFL, and making the stadium clock the official timer of the game, as had been the case in the AFL.

George Blanda, playing his twenty-first year of pro ball at the age of 43, engineered a series of dramatic finishes for Oakland. Blanda, backup to Daryle Lamonica as well as the Raiders' kicker, did this in a five-week span: threw two touchdown passes

against Pittsburgh; kicked a 48-yard field goal with three seconds to go, tying Kansas City 17-17; kicked a 52-yard field goal with three seconds to play to beat Cleveland 23-20, drove the Raiders to a winning touchdown against Denver 24-19, and beat San Diego 20-17 on another field goal with four seconds left.

Tom Dempsey of New Orleans set an NFL field goal distance record of 63 yards on the game's last play to defeat Detroit 19-17, November 8.

Gale Sayers of the Chicago Bears underwent surgery for a knee injury in midseason and never again regained his form. The New York Jets were handicapped by Joe Namath's broken wrist and Matt Snell's injured Achilles tendon. Minnesota quarterback Joe Kapp went to Boston, where he reported late and threw only three touchdown passes and was intercepted 17 times.

McCafferty's Colts won the AFC East at 11-2-1 and runner-up Miami's 10-4 record put the Dolphins into the playoffs as the wild card team. Paul Brown's expansion team in Cincinnati won the AFC Central in its third season with an 8-6 record. Oakland's 8-4-2 beat Kansas City's 7-5-2 in the AFC West.

Dallas (10-4) beat out the New York Giants (9-5) in the NFC East with the help of rookie running back Duane Thomas. Quarterback John Brodie led the San Francisco 49ers to the Western title at 10-3-1. De-

Rookie Duane Thomas eludes Skip Vanderbundt (52) and Roland Lakes on his way to a 143-yard day as the Cowboys defeat the 49ers for the NFC championship, 1970.

fense and Fred Cox's field goals were major factors in Minnesota's 12-2 winning record in the NFC Central, where runner-up Detroit (10-4) was the wild card qualifier.

In the AFC playoffs, Baltimore blanked Cincinnati 17-0 and Oakland defeated Miami 21-14 in the first round. Dallas beat Detroit 5-0 on a field goal and safety and the 49ers surprised the Vikings at Minnesota 17-14 in the other NFC playoff.

Baltimore defeated Oakland 27-17 in the AFC Championship Game. Duane Thomas gained 143 yards and Walt Garrison 71 in Dallas's 17-10 NFC Championship Game win over San Francisco.

The NFC won the competition with the AFC in the first season they played interconference games. There were 40 such games and the NFC won 27, the AFC 12, and there was one tie.

1970 AFC STANDINGS

Eastern Division	W	L	T	Pct.	Pts.	OP
Baltimore	11	2	1	.846	321	234
Miami*	10	4	0	.714	297	228
N.Y. Jets	4	10	0	.286	255	286
Buffalo	3	10	1	.231	204	337
Boston Patriots	2	12	0	.143	149	361

Central Division	W	L	T	Pct.	Pts.	OP
Cincinnati	8	6	0	.571	312	255
Cleveland	7	7	0	.500	286	265
Pittsburgh	5	9	0	.357	210	272
Houston	3	10	1	.231	217	352

Western Division	W	L	T	Pct.	Pts.	OP
Oakland	8	4	2	.667	300	293
Kansas City	7	5	2	.583	272	244
San Diego	5	6	3	.455	282	278
Denver	5	8	1	.385	253	264

Wild Card qualifier for playoffs
Divisional playoffs: Baltimore 17, Cincinnati 0;
Oakland 21, Miami 14
AFC championship: Baltimore 27, Oakland 17

LEADING RUSHERS	Att.	Yards	Avg.	Long	TD
Floyd Little, Denver	209	901	4.3	80t	3
Larry Csonka, Miami	193	874	4.5	53	6
Hewritt Dixon, Oakland	197	861	4.4	39t	1
Ed Podolak, Kansas City	168	749	4.5	65t	3
John (Frenchy) Fuqua, Pittsburgh	138	691	5.0	85t	7

LEADING PASSERS	Att.	Comp.	Yards	TD	Int.
Daryle Lamonica, Oakland	356	179	2,516	22	15
John Hadl, San Diego	327	162	2,388	22	15
Len Dawson, Kansas City	262	141	1,876	13	14
Bob Griese, Miami	245	142	2,019	12	17
Dennis Shaw, Buffalo	321	178	2,507	10	20

LEADING RECEIVERS	No.	Yards	Avg.	Long	TD
Marlin Briscoe, Buffalo	57	1,036	18.2	48	8
Eddie Hinton, Baltimore	47	733	15.6	40	5
Al Denson, Denver	47	646	13.7	42	2
Alvin Reed, Houston	47	604	12.9	34	2
Fred Biletnikoff, Oakland	45	768	17.1	51	7

1970 NFC STANDINGS

Eastern Division	W	L	T	Pct.	Pts.	OP
Dallas	10	4	0	.714	299	221
N.Y. Giants	9	5	0	.643	301	270
St. Louis	8	5	1	.615	325	228
Washington	6	8	0	.429	297	314
Philadelphia	3	10	1	.231	241	332

Central Division	W	L	T	Pct.	Pts.	OP
Minnesota	12	2	0	.857	335	143
Detroit*	10	4	0	.714	347	202
Chicago	6	8	0	.429	256	261
Green Bay	6	8	0	.429	196	293

Western Division	W	L	T	Pct.	Pts.	OP
San Francisco	10	3	1	.769	352	267
Los Angeles	9	4	1	.692	325	202
Atlanta	4	8	2	.333	206	261
New Orleans	2	11	1	.154	172	347

Wild Card qualifier for playoffs
Divisional playoffs: Dallas 5, Detroit 0;
San Francisco 17, Minnesota 14
NFC championship: Dallas 17, San Francisco 10
Super Bowl V: Baltimore (AFC) 16, Dallas (NFC) 13

LEADING RUSHERS	Att.	Yards	Avg.	Long	TD
Larry Brown, Washington	237	1,125	4.7	75t	5
Ron Johnson, N.Y. Giants	263	1,027	3.9	68t	8
MacArthur Lane, St. Louis	206	977	4.7	75	11
Donny Anderson, Green Bay	222	853	3.8	54	5
Duane Thomas, Dallas	151	803	5.3	47t	5

LEADING PASSERS	Att.	Comp.	Yards	TD	Int.
John Brodie, San Francisco	378	223	2,941	24	10
Sonny Jurgensen, Washington	337	202	2,354	23	10
Fran Tarkenton, N.Y. Giants	389	219	2,777	19	12
Bob Berry, Atlanta	269	156	1,806	16	13
Craig Morton, Dallas	207	102	1,819	15	7

LEADING RECEIVERS	No.	Yards	Avg.	Long	TD
Dick Gordon, Chicago	71	1,026	14.5	69t	13
Dan Abramowicz, New Orleans	55	906	16.5	48	5
Gene Washington, San Francisco	53	1,100	20.8	79t	12
Jack Snow, Los Angeles	51	859	16.8	71	7
Clifton McNeil, N.Y. Giants	50	764	15.3	59	4
Lee Bougess, Philadelphia	50	401	8.0	34	1

1971 Super Bowl V was a battle of turnovers at the Orange Bowl. The Colts gave up three interceptions and three fumbles and the Cowboys had three passes intercepted and lost a fumble. Jim O'Brien's 32-yard field goal with five seconds to play won it for the Colts 16-13. Earl Morrall led Baltimore to victory after Johnny Unitas suffered damaged ribs.

The NFC won the first AFC-NFC Pro Bowl 27-6 as Mel Renfro of the Dallas Cowboys returned punts 82 and 56 yards for touchdowns. The game was played in Los Angeles.

Five teams switched to new stadiums. The Dallas Cowboys left the Cotton Bowl, their home since 1960, to open the new 65,101-seat Texas Stadium at Irving, Texas, another suburban location. The Philadelphia Eagles occupied 66,052-seat Veterans Stadium and the San Francisco 49ers switched from Kezar Stadium to 61,246-seat Candlestick Park. The Chicago Bears, who had played at Wrigley Field (originally Cubs' Park) since they had moved from Decatur, Illinois, in 1921, moved into Soldier Field. The huge stadium's seating capacity was reduced to 55,049.

The Boston Patriots had wandered from Boston University, to Fenway Park, to Boston College, and Harvard Stadium. They finally got their own stadium in Foxboro, Massachusetts, when the 61,275-seat Schaefer Stadium was opened. The team then changed its name to the New England Patriots.

George Allen, insisting "the future is now," took over the Washington Redskins and made a series of trades that brought defensive tackle Diron Talbert, linebackers Myron Pottios and Jack Pardee, and a host of other former Los Angeles Rams to Washington in return mainly for future draft choices.

The San Diego Chargers brought back Sid Gillman, who lasted until midseason, when general manager Harland Svare took over as coach. Lou Saban quit as coach of the Denver Broncos after nine games and assistant Jerry Smith took over.

Three college quarterbacks were selected one, two, three in the draft. All of them became starters. Stanford's Jim Plunkett was number one for the Patriots, throwing 19 touchdown passes. Santa Clara's Dan Pastorini took over at Houston. Mississippi's Archie Manning started strong with the Saints but injuries made him a part-time performer.

The number-one draft choice the Balitmore Colts had been awarded from Miami in exchange for coach Don Shula was used to draft running back Don McCauley of North Carolina.

Five players rushed for 1,000 yards or more. John Brockington of Green Bay led the NFC as a rookie with 1,105 and Denver's Floyd Little topped the AFC with 1,133. Larry Csonka of Miami had 1,051, Steve Owens of Detroit had 1,035, and Willie Ellison of the Rams 1,000, including an NFL record 247-yard day against New Orleans.

George Blanda, Oakland's veteran kicker, moved into first place on the all-time scoring list with 1,647 points, topping Lou Groza, and Bob Tucker of the New York Giants became the first tight end to lead a conference in receiving with 59 in the NFC.

Allen coached the Redskins into the NFC playoffs as the wild card team with a 9-4-1 record. It was the first time Washington reached the playoffs since 1945. Dallas won the Eastern Division.

San Francisco won the Western Division championship again, and Minnesota won the Central.

Cleveland overcame a midseason slump and won the AFC Central with a 9-5 record in Nick Skorich's first year as coach. Kansas City's 10-3-1 topped Oakland's 8-4-2 in the AFC West.

Miami won 10 games and captured the AFC Eastern Division. Baltimore was the runner-up and wild card team.

In a divisional playoff, the Dolphins edged Kansas

Willie Ellison sets a then NFL record, gaining 247 yards against New Orleans, 1971.

Garo Yepremian kicks a 37-yard field goal to defeat Kansas City 27-24 in the longest NFL game ever, 1971.

City 27-24 in the longest game ever played when Garo Yepremian kicked a 37-yard field goal after 22 minutes and 40 seconds of overtime on Christmas afternoon. Jan Stenerud of the Chiefs missed a 31-yard field goal try with 35 seconds left in regulation time. Baltimore beat Cleveland 20-3 in the other playoff.

San Francisco defeated Washington 24-20 in a divisional playoff. Dallas won the other first-round playoff 20-12 over Minnesota.

In the AFC Championship Game, safety Dick Anderson of Miami intercepted three passes by Johnny Unitas, and Miami defeated Baltimore 21-0.

Dallas went ahead quickly and outlasted San Francisco 14-3 in the NFC Championship Game.

1971 AFC STANDINGS

Eastern Division	W	L	T	Pct.	Pts.	OP
Miami	10	3	1	.769	315	174
Baltimore*	10	4	0	.714	313	140
New England	6	8	0	.429	238	325
N.Y. Jets	6	8	0	.429	212	299
Buffalo	1	13	0	.071	184	394
Central Division	W	L	T	Pct.	Pts.	OP
Cleveland	9	5	0	.643	285	273
Pittsburgh	6	8	0	.429	246	292
Houston	4	9	1	.308	251	330
Cincinnati	4	10	0	.286	284	265
Western Division	W	L	T	Pct.	Pts.	OP
Kansas City	10	3	1	.769	302	208
Oakland	8	4	2	.667	344	278
San Diego	6	8	0	.429	311	341
Denver	4	9	1	.308	203	275

*Wild Card qualifier for playoffs
Divisional playoffs: Miami 27, Kansas City 24, sudden death overtime
Baltimore 20, Cleveland 3
AFC championship: Miami 21, Baltimore 0

LEADING RUSHERS	Att.	Yards	Avg.	Long	TD
Floyd Litte, Denver	284	1,133	4.0	40	6
Larry Csonka, Miami	195	1,051	5.4	28	7
Marv Hubbard, Oakland	181	867	4.8	20	5
Leroy Kelly, Cleveland	234	865	3.7	35	10
Carl Garrett, New England	181	784	4.3	38	1

LEADING PASSERS	Att.	Comp.	Yards	TD	Int.
Bob Griese, Miami	263	145	2,089	19	9
Len Dawson, Kansas City	301	167	2,504	15	13
Virgil Carter, Cincinnati	222	138	1,624	10	7
John Hadl, San Diego	431	233	3,075	21	25
Bill Nelsen, Cleveland	325	174	2,319	13	23

LEADING RECEIVERS	No.	Yards	Avg.	Long	TD
Fred Biletnikoff, Oakland	61	929	15.2	49	9
Otis Taylor, Kansas City	57	1,110	19.5	82	7
Randy Vataha, New England	51	872	17.1	88t	9
Ron Shanklin, Pittsburgh	49	652	13.3	42	6
John (Frenchy) Fuqua, Pittsburgh	49	427	8.7	40t	1

1971 NFC STANDINGS

Eastern Division	W	L	T	Pct.	Pts.	OP
Dallas	11	3	0	.786	406	222
Washington*	9	4	1	.692	276	190
Philadelphia	6	7	1	.462	221	302
St. Louis	4	9	1	.308	231	279
N.Y. Giants	4	10	0	.286	228	362
Central Division	W	L	T	Pct.	Pts.	OP
Minnesota	11	3	0	.786	245	139
Detroit	7	6	1	.538	341	286
Chicago	6	8	0	.429	185	276
Green Bay	4	8	2	.333	274	298
Western Division	W	L	T	Pct.	Pts.	OP
San Francisco	9	5	0	.643	300	216
Los Angeles	8	5	1	.615	313	260
Atlanta	7	6	1	.538	274	277
New Orleans	4	8	2	.333	266	347

*Wild Card qualifier for playoffs
Divisional playoffs: Dallas 20, Minnesota 12; San Francisco 24, Washington 20
NFC championship: Dallas 14, San Francisco 3
Super Bowl VI: Dallas (NFC) 24, Miami (AFC) 3

LEADING RUSHERS	Att.	Yards	Avg.	Long	TD
John Brockington, Green Bay	216	1,105	5.1	52t	4
Steve Owens, Detroit	246	1,035	4.2	23	8
Willie Ellison, Los Angeles	211	1,000	4.7	80t	4
Larry Brown, Washington	253	948	3.7	34	4
Ken Willard, San Francisco	216	855	4.0	49	4

LEADING PASSERS	Att.	Comp.	Yards	TD	Int.
Roger Staubach, Dallas	211	126	1,882	15	4
Greg Landry, Detroit	261	136	2,237	16	13
Billy Kilmer, Washington	306	166	2,221	13	13
Bob Berry, Atlanta	226	136	2,005	11	16
Roman Gabriel, Los Angeles	352	180	2,238	17	10

LEADING RECEIVERS	No.	Yards	Avg.	Long	TD
Bob Tucker, N.Y. Giants	59	971	16.4	63t	4
Ted Kwalick, San Francisco	52	664	12.8	42t	5
Harold Jackson, Philadelphia	47	716	15.2	69t	3
Roy Jefferson, Washington	47	701	14.9	70t	4
Gene Washington, San Francisco	46	884	19.2	71t	4
George Farmer, Chicago	46	737	16.0	64	5

1972 The NFC won the Super Bowl when Dallas beat Miami 24-3.

Three teams had management changes. Robert Irsay bought the Los Angeles Rams from the estate of the late Dan Reeves, and traded the franchise with Carroll Rosenbloom, owner of the Baltimore Colts. Isray wound up as owner of the Colts and Rosenbloom took control of the Rams. William Bidwill became the sole owner of the St. Louis Cardinals, buying out his brother, Charles (Stormy) Bidwill. Kansas City moved into 78,907-seat Arrowhead Stadium.

In hopes of increasing scoring and countering the zone defense, the owners adopted a new rule to move in the hashmarks or inbound lines from 20 yards to 23 yards, 1 foot, 9 inches, leaving only 18 feet, 6 inches, the width of the goal post crossbar, in the middle of the field.

A series of trades involved "big name" players in the league. Quarterback Fran Tarkenton, traded to the Giants by the Vikings in early 1967, went back to Minnesota in a swap that sent receiver Bob Grim and draft choices to New York. Running back Duane Thomas was shipped to San Diego by Dallas, and defensive end Fred Dryer went from the Giants to the Rams via the Patriots. Denver dealt with Houston to get quarterback Charley Johnson.

Jack Tatum of Oakland erased a 49-year-old record when he ran 104 yards with a recovered fumble, beating the old mark of 98 by George Halas of the Bears against the Oorang Indians of Marion, Ohio, in 1923.

The running backs responded to the rules changes with a record 10 players rushing for 1,000 yards or more. O.J. Simpson found the offensive style of the Buffalo Bills' new coach Lou Saban just what he wanted and led the league with 1,251 yards. Larry Brown of Washington led the NFC with 1,216. Ron Johnson of the Giants had 1,182, Calvin Hill of Dallas 1,036, and John Brockington of Green Bay 1,027 in the NFC, and Larry Csonka of Miami 1,117, Marv Hubbard of Oakland 1,100, rookie Franco Harris of Pittsburgh 1,055, Mike Garrett of San Diego 1,031, and Eugene (Mercury) Morris of Miami 1,000 in the AFC. Morris made it when the league found an error in scoring in which Morris had been charged with a nine-yard loss that should have been listed as a fumble by Earl Morrall. Dave Hampton of Atlanta made it to 1,001 yards in the last game but was thrown for a six-yard loss and finished at 995 yards.

Don Maynard of the New York Jets topped the all-time pass receivers with 632 receptions, one more than the retired Raymond Berry. Bobby Douglass of the Bears ran for 968 yards, a record for a quarterback, and led the Bears in rushing. Chester Marcol's 33 field goals for Green Bay were the most since Jim Turner kicked a record 34 for the Jets in 1968.

Coach Don Shula's Dolphins breezed to a 14-0 record, seven full games ahead of the runner-up Jets (7-7) in the AFC East. Oakland regained control of the AFC West at 10-3-1 after a one-year lapse. Chuck Noll brought Pittsburgh its first division title at 11-3

Bobby Douglass.

Mike Garrett.

Don Maynard.

in the AFC Central and runner-up Cleveland (10-4) qualified as the wild card team.

Washington shaded Dallas in the NFC East with both qualifying for the playoffs. Green Bay won the NFC Central and San Francisco made it three in a row in the NFC West at 8-5-1.

Miami had to come from behind to beat Cleveland 20-14 in its first playoff game and Pittsburgh had to come up with a near-miraculous play to defeat Oakland 13-7. Terry Bradshaw threw a desperation pass on fourth and 10 with 22 seconds to play and the Raiders winning 7-6. The ball, intended for John (Frenchy) Fuqua, bounced off Oakland safety Jack Tatum and was caught by Franco Harris just off his shoe tops. Harris ran 60 yards for the winning touchdown.

In the NFC divisional playoffs, Roger Staubach threw two touchdown passes in 38 seconds as Dallas rallied to beat the 49ers 30-28, and Washington defeated Green Bay 16-3.

Miami beat Pittsburgh 21-17 for the AFC championship and Washington advanced to the Super Bowl with a 26-3 victory over the Cowboys on four field goals by Curt Knight and two touchdown passes by Billy Kilmer, playing for the injured Sonny Jurgensen.

Jack Tatum goes 104 yards with a fumble recovery, an NFL record, 1972.

1972 AFC STANDINGS

Eastern Division	W	L	T	Pct.	Pts.	OP
Miami	14	0	0	1.000	385	171
N.Y. Jets	7	7	0	.500	367	324
Baltimore	5	9	0	.429	235	252
Buffalo	4	9	1	.321	257	377
New England	3	11	0	.214	192	446
Central Division	W	L	T	Pct.	Pts.	OP
Pittsburgh	11	3	0	.786	343	175
Cleveland*	10	4	0	.714	268	249
Cincinnati	8	6	0	.571	299	229
Houston	1	13	0	.071	164	380
Western Division	W	L	T	Pct.	Pts.	OP
Oakland	10	3	1	.750	365	248
Kansas City	8	6	0	.571	287	254
Denver	5	9	0	.357	325	350
San Diego	4	9	1	.321	264	344

Wild Card qualifier for playoffs
Divisional playoffs: Pittsburgh 13, Oakland 7;
　　　　　　　　　Miami 20, Cleveland 14
AFC championship: Miami 21, Pittsburgh 17

LEADING RUSHERS

	Att.	Yards	Avg.	Long	TD
O. J. Simpson, Buffalo	292	1,251	4.3	94t	6
Larry Csonka, Miami	213	1,117	5.2	45	6
Marv Hubbard, Oakland	219	1,100	5.0	39	4
Franco Harris, Pittsburgh	188	1,055	5.6	75t	10
Mike Garrett, San Diego	272	1,031	3.8	41t	6

LEADING PASSERS

	Att.	Comp.	Yards	TD	Int.
Earl Morrall, Miami	150	83	1,360	11	7
Daryle Lamonica, Oakland	281	149	1,998	18	12
Charley Johnson, Denver	238	132	1,783	14	14
Johnny Unitas, Baltimore	157	88	1,111	4	6
Ken Anderson, Cincinnati	301	171	1,918	7	7

LEADING RECEIVERS

	No.	Yards	Avg.	Long	TD
Fred Biletnikoff, Oakland	58	802	13.8	39t	7
Otis Taylor, Kansas City	57	821	14.4	44	6
Chip Myers, Cincinnati	57	792	13.9	42	3
J. D. Hill, Buffalo	52	754	14.5	58t	5
Gary Garrison, San Diego	52	744	14.3	52t	7

1972 NFC STANDINGS

Eastern Division	W	L	T	Pct.	Pts.	OP
Washington	11	3	0	.786	336	218
Dallas*	10	4	0	.714	319	240
N.Y. Giants	8	6	0	.571	331	247
St. Louis	4	9	1	.321	193	303
Philadelphia	2	11	1	.179	145	352
Central Division	W	L	T	Pct.	Pts.	OP
Green Bay	10	4	0	.714	304	226
Detroit	8	5	1	.607	339	290
Minnesota	7	7	0	.500	301	252
Chicago	4	9	1	.321	225	275
Western Division	W	L	T	Pct.	Pts.	OP
San Francisco	8	5	1	.607	353	249
Atlanta	7	7	0	.500	269	274
Los Angeles	6	7	1	.464	291	286
New Orleans	2	11	1	.179	215	361

Wild Card qualifier for playoffs
Divisional playoffs: Dallas 30, San Francisco 28;
　　　　　　　　　Washington 16, Green Bay 3
NFC championship: Washington 26, Dallas 3
Super Bowl VII: Miami (AFC) 14, Washington (NFC) 7

The Immaculate Reception: Franco Harris on his way to the winning touchdown, 1972.

Behind the blocking of Joe DeLamielleure (68), O. J. Simpson breaks the 2,000-yard mark in one season, 1973.

LEADING RUSHERS	Att.	Yards	Avg.	Long	TD
Larry Brown, Washington	285	1,216	4.3	38t	8
Ron Johnson, N.Y. Giants	298	1,182	4.0	35t	9
Calvin Hill, Dallas	245	1,036	4.2	26	6
John Brockington, Green Bay	274	1,027	3.7	30t	8
Dave Hampton, Atlanta	230	995	4.3	56t	6

LEADING PASSERS	Att.	Comp.	Yards	TD	Int.
Norm Snead, N.Y. Giants	325	196	2,307	17	12
Bob Berry, Atlanta	277	154	2,158	13	12
Fran Tarkenton, Minnesota	378	215	2,651	18	13
Bill Kilmer, Washington	225	120	1,648	19	11
Steve Spurrier, San Francisco	269	147	1,983	18	16

LEADING RECEIVERS	No.	Yards	Avg.	Long	TD
Harold Jackson, Philadelphia	62	1,048	16.9	77t	4
Bob Tucker, N.Y. Giants	55	764	13.9	39	4
Art Malone, Atlanta	50	585	11.7	57t	2
Charley Taylor, Washington	49	673	13.7	70t	7
John Gilliam, Minnesota	47	1,035	22.0	66t	7
Bob Newland, New Orleans	47	579	12.3	42t	2

1973 The Miami Dolphins made NFL history when they went through an entire season without defeat, climaxing their 17-0 season with a 14-7 victory over Washington in Super Bowl VII before a record crowd of 90,182 at the Los Angeles Coliseum. No team ever had gone all the way without a defeat or a tie.

The Dolphins ended their perfect season by shutting out the Redskins until Garo Yepremian, trying to salvage something from an abortive field goal try,

attempted to pass and fumbled. Mike Bass grabbed the ball and ran 49 yards for the lone Washington score with 2:07 to play.

Running back Gale Sayers of Chicago, quarterback Bart Starr of Green Bay, and safety Larry Wilson of St. Louis retired.

Congress passed a three-year bill that lifted the hometown TV blackouts on games sold out 72 before kickoff. The NFL opposed the legislation as a threat to the sale of season tickets and the first step toward a television studio-type game with empty seats at the stadiums.

The league formed NFL Charities, a nonprofit foundation that would receive its revenue from licensing league and club trademarks, to meet educational and charitable needs and provide economic support for former players.

Chuck Knox became coach of the Los Angeles Rams. General manager Sid Gillman took over as head coach of the Houston Oilers during the season.

The Rams traded for quarterback John Hadl from San Diego and wide receiver Harold Jackson from Philadelphia and sent quarterback Roman Gabriel off to the Eagles. San Diego purchased the contract of Baltimore quarterback Johnny Unitas.

The New York Giants were forced to move out of Yankee Stadium, their home since 1956, due to stadium renovations, and played their last five games at the Yale Bowl in New Haven, Connecticut. Buffalo opened 80,020-seat Rich Stadium at suburban Orchard Park, New York.

An expansion committee, headed by Dan Rooney of Pittsburgh, was formed to explore future expansion.

The World Football League was formed in a meeting in Los Angeles in October and announced its plans to begin play in 1974.

Miami's bid for a second straight perfect season ended early. The Dolphins won their opener 21-13 over San Francisco for 18 straight, tying the record set by the 1933-34 Chicago Bears and equaled by the 1941-42 Bears. However, the Dolphins were tripped up by the Raiders 12-7 in their second game, which was played in Berkeley on September 23.

O.J. Simpson of the Buffalo Bills broke the single-season rushing record with 2,003 yards. He had a record 250 yards against New England opening day. He passed midseason with 1,000 yards, the goal of most outstanding runners for a full season. At the end he had set records for most rushing attempts (332), most 100-yard games in a season (11), and most 200-yard games in a season (3).

John Brockington of Green Bay also put his name in the record book as the only man to gain over 1,000 yards in each of his first three pro seasons. He gained 1,144 yards. Other 1,000-yard runners of the season were Calvin Hill of Dallas with 1,142, rookie Lawrence McCutcheon of Los Angeles with 1,097, and Larry Csonka of Miami with 1,003.

The Dolphins lost only one more game on the way to a 12-2 record and a third straight title in the AFC East with Bob Griese doing the passing, a three-pronged running attack of Csonka, Mercury Morris, and Jim Kiick, and the "No Name Defense," so-called because of its lack of individual recognition.

Ken Anderson and Essex Johnson, aided by rookies Charles (Boobie) Clark and Isaac Curtis, brought Cincinnati the AFC Central title at 10-4, winning the division despite Pittsburgh's matching 10-4 because the Bengals had a better record in intraconference games. The Steelers qualified for the playoffs as the wild card team. Oakland took the West at 9-4-1 by beating runner-up Denver (7-5-2) in the final game 21-7.

Dallas (10-4) and George Allen's "Over the Hill Gang" at Washington (10-4) ruled the NFC East, with Dallas winning the division on an edge in total points for the two games the clubs split. Washington got the NFC wild card spot.

Rookie Chuck Foreman teamed with Fran Tarkenton to help the Vikings to the NFC West title with a 12-2 record. The Los Angeles Rams' 12-2 mark under new coach Chuck Knox ended three years of domination by the 49ers in the NFC West.

In the AFC playoffs Miami disposed of Cincinnati 34-16 and Oakland got even with Pittsburgh 33-14. Minnesota ousted Washington 27-20 and Roger Staubach's 83-yard pass to Drew Pearson helped Dallas beat Los Angeles 27-16 in the NFC playoffs.

The Dolphins won the AFC championship by defeating Oakland 27-10 on 117 yards and three touchdowns by Larry Csonka. The Vikings ran over the Cowboys 27-10 for the NFC title.

1973 AFC STANDINGS

Eastern Division

	W	L	T	Pct.	Pts.	OP
Miami	12	2	0	.857	343	150
Buffalo	9	5	0	.643	259	230
New England	5	9	0	.357	258	300
Baltimore	4	10	0	.286	226	341
N.Y. Jets	4	10	0	.286	240	306

Central Division

	W	L	T	Pct.	Pts.	OP
Cincinnati	10	4	0	.714	286	231
Pittsburgh*	10	4	0	.714	347	210
Cleveland	7	5	2	.571	234	255
Houston	1	13	0	.071	199	447

Western Division

	W	L	T	Pct.	Pts.	OP
Oakland	9	4	1	.679	292	175
Denver	7	5	2	.571	354	296
Kansas City	7	5	2	.571	231	192
San Diego	2	11	1	.179	188	386

*Wild Card qualifier for playoffs
Divisional playoffs: Oakland 33, Pittsburgh 14;
Miami 34, Cincinnati 16
AFC championship: Miami 27, Oakland 10

LEADING RUSHERS

	Att.	Yards	Avg.	Long	TD
O.J. Simpson, Buffalo	332	2,003	6.0	80t	12
Larry Csonka, Miami	219	1,003	4.6	25	5
Essex Johnson, Cincinnati	195	997	5.1	46	4
Boobie Clark, Cincinnati	254	988	3.9	26	8
Floyd Little, Denver	256	979	3.8	47	12

LEADING PASSERS

	Att.	Comp.	Yards	TD	Int.
Ken Stabler, Oakland	260	163	1,997	14	10
Bob Griese, Miami	218	116	1,422	17	8
Ken Anderson, Cincinnati	329	179	2,428	18	12
Charley Johnson, Denver	346	184	2,465	20	17
Al Woodall, N.Y. Jets	201	101	1,228	9	8

LEADING RECEIVERS

	No.	Yards	Avg.	Long	TD
Fred Willis, Houston	57	371	6.5	50	1
Ed Podolak, Kansas City	55	445	8.1	25	0
Reggie Rucker, New England	53	743	14.0	64	3
Fred Biletnikoff, Oakland	48	660	13.8	32	4
Isaac Curtis, Cincinnati	45	843	18.7	77t	9
Mike Siani, Oakland	45	742	16.5	80t	3
Boobie Clark, Cincinnati	45	347	7.7	39	0

1973 NFC STANDINGS

Eastern Division

	W	L	T	Pct.	Pts.	OP
Dallas	10	4	0	.714	382	203
Washington*	10	4	0	.714	325	198
Philadelphia	5	8	1	.393	310	393
St. Louis	4	9	1	.321	286	365
N.Y. Giants	2	11	1	.179	226	362

Central Division

	W	L	T	Pct.	Pts.	OP
Minnesota	12	2	0	.857	296	168
Detroit	6	7	1	.464	271	247
Green Bay	5	7	2	.429	202	259
Chicago	3	11	0	.214	195	334

Western Division

	W	L	T	Pct.	Pts.	OP
Los Angeles	12	2	0	.857	388	178
Atlanta	9	5	0	.643	318	224
New Orleans	5	9	0	.357	163	312
San Francisco	5	9	0	.357	262	319

*Wild Card qualifier for playoffs
Divisional playoffs: Minnesota 27, Washington 20;
Dallas 27, Los Angeles 16
NFC championship: Minnesota 27, Dallas 10
Super Bowl VIII: Miami (AFC) 24, Minnesota (NFC) 7

LEADING RUSHERS

	Att.	Yards	Avg.	Long	TD
John Brockington, Green Bay	265	1,144	4.3	53	3
Calvin Hill, Dallas	273	1,142	4.2	21	6
Lawrence McCutcheon, Los Angeles	210	1,097	5.2	37	2
Dave Hampton, Atlanta	263	997	3.8	25	4
Tom Sullivan, Philadelphia	217	968	4.5	37	4

LEADING PASSERS

	Att.	Comp.	Yards	TD	Int.
Roger Staubach, Dallas	286	179	2,428	23	15
Fran Tarkenton, Minnesota	274	169	2,113	15	7
John Hadl, Los Angeles	258	135	2,008	22	11
Roman Gabriel, Philadelphia	460	270	3,219	23	12
Bill Kilmer, Washington	227	122	1,656	14	9

LEADING RECEIVERS

	No.	Yards	Avg.	Long	TD
Harold Carmichael, Philadelphia	67	1,116	16.7	73	9
Charley Taylor, Washington	59	801	13.6	53	7
Charles Young, Philadelphia	55	854	15.5	80t	6
Bob Tucker, N.Y. Giants	50	681	13.6	33	5
Tom Sullivan, Philadelphia	50	322	6.4	29	1

1974 The Dolphins joined the Green Bay Packers as two-time Super Bowl winners by beating the Vikings 24-7 with Csonka rushing for a record 145 yards at Rice Stadium in Houston.

Significant rules changes were made. Sudden death overtime was adopted for all preseason and regular season games. The goal posts were moved back to the end line and kickoffs were to be made from the 35, not the 40. Missed field goals outside the 20 were to go back to the line of scrimmage instead of being called touchbacks. Only two outside men of the kicking team were allowed downfield before the ball was punted. Defensive players were allowed to "chuck" or bump a pass receiver only once, and rolling blocks on wide receivers were made illegal. The holding penalty was reduced to 10 yards and receivers were prohibited from making "crackback" blocks below the waist.

The Toronto Northmen of the World Football League made news in March when they announced that Larry Csonka, Paul Warfield, and Jim Kiick of the NFL champion Miami Dolphins would play out their options in 1974 and join the Northmen in 1975 in a reported three-year $3 million deal.

The NFL decided to expand to 28 clubs by adding Tampa Bay and Seattle to begin play in 1976. Commissioner Rozelle was voted a new 10-year contract and a 47-man player limit was adopted.

Weeb Ewbank, coach of the New York Jets, retired and was replaced by his son-in-law, assistant coach Charley Winner.

Coach Don McCafferty of the Detroit Lions died of a heart attack during the preseason and was re-

John Hadl, 1973.

Weeb Ewbank, on his retirement from coaching, is honored in Baltimore, 1974.　　*Otis Armstrong, the NFL's leading rusher, 1974.*

placed by Rick Forzano.

Los Angeles traded quarterback John Hadl to Green Bay for draft choices. Dallas shipped quarterback Craig Morton to the New York Giants, who sent Norm Snead to San Francisco. Johnny Unitas retired after 18 years. Defensive tackle Curley Culp moved from Kansas City to Houston, where he became the key as the nose tackle in a three-man defensive line.

Owners and players were unable to agree on a new collective bargaining agreement as the old four-year pact expired. Rookies came to training camp but the veterans stayed out, many of them carrying picket signs. The annual Chicago All-Star Game was canceled. The veterans reported under provisions of a 14-day cooling off period and the strike ended August 28 in time for the final preseason games, most of which were played with rookie teams.

The results of the rules changes were a considerable increase in touchdowns, fewer field goals, fewer fair catch signals, and longer punt and kickoff returns.

The Pittsburgh Steelers won the AFC Central Division. Miami won the Eastern and Oakland the Western Division.

Coach Don Coryell put the St. Louis Cardinals in the playoffs for the first time since they left Chicago in 1960 by winning the NFC East. St. Louis and Washington finished 10-4 but the Cardinals beat the Redskins twice to win the division while the Redskins became the wild card entry. The Minnesota Vikings and Los Angeles Rams easily won the Central and Western Divisions in the NFC.

Otis Armstrong of Denver led the league's rushers

with 1,407 yards and rookie Don Woods of San Diego set a record for a first-year man with 1,162. Other 1,000-yard rushers were O.J. Simpson of Buffalo with 1,125, Lawrence McCutcheon of Los Angeles with 1,109, and Franco Harris of Pittsburgh with 1,006.

Cincinnati quarterback Ken Anderson set a record when he completed 16 consecutive passes against Baltimore, but Bert Jones of Baltimore broke it a month later with 17 straight against the New York Jets.

Lydell Mitchell of Baltimore set a record for a running back with a league-leading 72 pass receptions.

The WFL staggered through its first year, starting with eight teams and ending with five. Padded attendance figures, missed payrolls, and shifting franchises left the league's future in doubt. The Toronto Northmen were forced from Canada, moved to Memphis, and became the Southmen. The New York Stars moved to Charlotte, North Carolina, in midseason. The Chicago, Detroit, and Jacksonville franchises folded.

The Miami Dolphins' reign in the NFL ended when they were beaten by Oakland 28-26 on a sensational catch by Clarence Davis of Ken Stabler's pass with 26 seconds to play in the AFC Divisional Play-off Game. Pittsburgh beat Buffalo in the other AFC playoff. In the NFC, Minnesota defeated St. Louis 30-14 and Los Angeles won over Washington 19-10.

Pittsburgh reached the Super Bowl for the first time by defeating Oakland 24-13 in the AFC Championship Game and Minnesota returned to the game for the third time by handing Los Angeles a 14-10

defeat for the NFC title.

1974 AFC STANDINGS

Eastern Division	W	L	T	Pct.	Pts.	OP
Miami	11	3	0	.786	327	216
Buffalo*	9	5	0	.643	264	244
New England	7	7	0	.500	348	289
N.Y. Jets	7	7	0	.500	279	300
Baltimore	2	12	0	.143	190	329
Central Division	**W**	**L**	**T**	**Pct.**	**Pts.**	**OP**
Pittsburgh	10	3	1	.750	305	189
Cincinnati	7	7	0	.500	283	259
Houston	7	7	0	.500	236	282
Cleveland	4	10	0	.286	251	344
Western Division	**W**	**L**	**T**	**Pct.**	**Pts.**	**OP**
Oakland	12	2	0	.857	355	228
Denver	7	6	1	.536	302	294
Kansas City	5	9	0	.357	233	293
San Diego	5	9	0	.357	212	285

*Wild Card qualifier for playoffs
Divisional playoffs: Oakland 28, Miami 26;
Pittsburgh 32, Buffalo 14
AFC championship: Pittsburgh 24, Oakland 13

LEADING RUSHERS	Att.	Yards	Avg.	Long	TD
Otis Armstrong, Denver	263	1,407	5.3	43	9
Don Woods, San Diego	227	1,162	5.1	56t	7
O. J. Simpson, Buffalo	270	1,125	4.2	41t	3
Franco Harris, Pittsburgh	208	1,006	4.8	54	5
Marv Hubbard, Oakland	188	865	4.6	32	4

LEADING PASSERS	Att.	Comp.	Yards	TD	Int.
Ken Anderson, Cincinnati	328	213	2,667	18	10
Ken Stabler, Oakland	310	178	2,469	26	12
Charley Johnson, Denver	244	136	1,969	13	9
Bob Griese, Miami	253	152	1,968	16	15
Dan Pastorini, Houston	247	140	1,571	10	10

LEADING RECEIVERS	No.	Yards	Avg.	Long	TD
Lydell Mitchell, Baltimore	72	544	7.6	24	2
Cliff Branch, Oakland	60	1,092	18.2	67t	13
Ed Podolak, Kansas City	43	306	7.1	26	1
Riley Odoms, Denver	42	639	15.2	41	6
Fred Biletnikoff, Oakland	42	593	14.1	46	7

1974 NFC STANDINGS

Eastern Division	W	L	T	Pct.	Pts.	OP
St. Louis	10	4	0	.714	285	218
Washington*	10	4	0	.714	320	196
Dallas	8	6	0	.571	297	235
Philadelphia	7	7	0	.500	242	217
N.Y. Giants	2	12	0	.143	195	299
Central Division	W	L	T	Pct.	Pts.	OP
Minnesota	10	4	0	.714	310	195
Detroit	7	7	0	.500	256	270
Green Bay	6	8	0	.429	210	206
Chicago	4	10	0	.286	152	279
Western Division	W	L	T	Pct.	Pts.	OP
Los Angeles	10	4	0	.714	263	181
San Francisco	6	8	0	.429	226	236
New Orleans	5	9	0	.357	166	263
Atlanta	3	11	0	.214	111	271

*Wild Card qualifier for playoffs
Divisional playoffs: Minnesota 30, St. Louis 14;
Los Angeles 19, Washington 10
NFC championship: Minnesota 14, Los Angeles 10
Super Bowl IX: Pittsburgh (AFC) 16, Minnesota (NFC) 6

LEADING RUSHERS	Att.	Yards	Avg.	Long	TD
Lawrence McCutcheon, Los Angeles	236	1,109	4.7	23t	3
John Brockington, Green Bay	266	883	3.3	33	5
Calvin Hill, Dallas	185	844	4.6	27	7
Chuck Foreman, Minnesota	199	777	3.9	32	9
Tom Sullivan, Philadelphia	244	760	3.1	28t	11

LEADING PASSERS	Att.	Comp.	Yards	TD	Int.
Sonny Jurgensen, Washington	167	107	1,185	11	5
James Harris, Los Angeles	198	106	1,544	11	6
Billy Kilmer, Washington	234	137	1,632	10	6
Fran Tarkenton, Minnesota	351	199	2,598	17	12
Jim Hart, St. Louis	388	200	2,411	20	8

LEADING RECEIVERS	No.	Yards	Avg.	Long	TD
Charles Young, Philadelphia	63	696	11.0	29	3
Drew Pearson, Dallas	62	1,087	17.5	50t	2
Harold Carmichael, Philadelphia	56	649	11.6	39	8
Ron Jessie, Detroit	54	761	14.1	46	3
Charley Taylor, Washington	54	738	13.7	51	5

1975 Owner Art Rooney finally came up with a winner in Pittsburgh after 42 years. Chuck Noll's Steelers went all the way to a Super Bowl championship. Running back Franco Harris broke a record with 158 yards rushing in the Steelers' 16-6 victory over the Vikings in Super Bowl IX at Tulane Stadium in New Orleans.

Sonny Jurgensen of the Washington Redskins and Jim Otto of the Oakland Raiders retired.

An interpretation of the rules made oversized huddles and "lingering on the field" illegal. The owners established a 43-man player limit and did away with taxi squads.

The playoff format was changed to reward the teams with the highest won-lost percentages by making them the hosts for the divisional playoffs. The ultimate survivors with the best records would host the championship games.

Legal problems plagued the owners. A court decision declaring the compensation rule, commonly known as the Rozelle Rule, illegal, was appealed.

A one-game strike during the preseason schedule preceded another year without an agreement between the NFL and the Players Association. The New England Patriots refused to play a preseason game with the Jets but all five striking teams agreed to open the regular season despite rejection of a contract offer by the NFL Management Council.

The New Orleans Saints left Tulane Stadium, their home since 1967, and moved into the 72,000-seat Louisiana Superdome. The Detroit Lions left Tiger Stadium, where they had played since 1937, and moved to the new suburban Pontiac Metropolitan Stadium in Pontiac, Michigan.

The Superdome was built on a 53-acre tract in downtown New Orleans and its huge dome rose 273 feet above the ground. It was equipped with five giant television screens to add to the fans' enjoyment of the games.

An unusual feature of the Pontiac stadium was its roof, a tent of Teflon-coated fiberglass fabric fitting over the top, held up by steel cables, and inflated by compressed air.

Clarence Davis pulls in the winning touchdown against Miami in the 1974 playoffs.

Chuck Foreman, the NFC's leading receiver and number-two rusher in 1975.

The reorganized World Football League under new president Chris Hemmeter ended its operation in the twelfth week of its second season, putting 380 players out of work.

Last in the Eastern Division at 2-12 in 1974, Baltimore started with a 1-4 record under new coach Ted Marchibroda, then ran off nine straight victories. The Colts beat Miami twice, 33-17 and 10-7 on a 31-yard field goal by Toni Linhart after 12:44 of sudden death overtime. Their success in those two games was the difference in the AFC East because Miami also was 10-4.

Chuck Noll's Steelers lost their second game of the season to Buffalo, then went on an 11-game win streak before bowing to Los Angeles in the final game for a 12-2 season. Until the Rams game, the Steelers had won 10 in a row on the road and were 9-0 against the NFC since 1972. Despite the streaks, the Steelers had tough competition in the AFC Central with runner-up and wild card Cincinnati 11-3 and Houston 10-4. The Oilers lost two each to the Steelers and Bengals.

Oakland ran away with the AFC West for its fourth straight division title and eighth in nine years.

St. Louis, Minnesota, and Los Angeles won the NFC division races.

Quarterback Fran Tarkenton of the Minnesota Vikings finished the season with all-time records for most touchdown passes in a career (291), most completions (2,931), and most attempts (5,225), all held previously by the retired Johnny Unitas.

George Blanda, 49, played his final season for Oakland and left a list of records including most active seasons (26), most games played (340), most consecutive games played (224), most points scored (2,002), most field goals (335), and most points after touchdown (943). Charley Taylor, Washington's wide receiver, bested Don Maynard's record with a lifetime total of 635 receptions, an all-time high for pro football.

The NFL had eight 1,000-yard runners, led by O.J. Simpson of Buffalo with 1,817, third best in league history.

Simpson and Chuck Foreman engaged in a tight battle for the 1975 scoring title. Simpson won with 23 touchdowns, a record, and 138 points to Foreman's 132 on 22 touchdowns, tying the previous record set by Gale Sayers as a rookie in 1965.

The Colts' string was snapped by Pittsburgh 28-10 in the first playoff game, one in which quarterback Bert Jones was injured. Oakland held on against a Cincinnati closing rush for a 31-28 victory in the other divisional playoff.

Despite Tarkenton's 25 touchdown passes and Foreman's 22 touchdowns and 1,070 yards, Minnesota couldn't make it to Super Bowl X. The Vikings were eliminated in the first round by Dallas, the wild card team whose 10-4 record was second to St. Louis's 11-3 in the NFC East. A last-minute 50-yard pass from Roger Staubach to Drew Pearson that was disputed by the Vikings gave Dallas a 17-14 playoff win. Los Angeles romped in the NFC West at 12-2

and defeated St. Louis 35-23 behind reserve quarterback Ron Jaworski.

Pittsburgh outlasted the Raiders 16-10 on an icy field at Pittsburgh for the AFC championship when Jack Lambert recovered three fumbles. The Raiders had reached the Steelers' 15 when time ran out.

Dallas became the first wild card team to reach the Super Bowl (although second-place Kansas City of the AFC West in 1969 had won Super Bowl IV before the wild card system) when the Cowboys shocked the Rams 37-7 on four touchdown passes by Roger Staubach, three to Preston Pearson, to win the NFC title.

1975 AFC STANDINGS

Eastern Division	W	L	T	Pct.	Pts.	OP
Baltimore	10	4	0	.714	395	269
Miami	10	4	0	.714	357	222
Buffalo	8	6	0	.571	420	355
New England	3	11	0	.214	258	358
N.Y. Jets	3	11	0	.214	258	433
Central Division	W	L	T	Pct.	Pts.	OP
Pittsburgh	12	2	0	.857	373	162
Cincinnati*	11	3	0	.786	340	246
Houston	10	4	0	.714	293	226
Cleveland	3	11	0	.214	218	372
Western Division	W	L	T	Pct.	Pts.	OP
Oakland	11	3	0	.786	375	255
Denver	6	8	0	.429	254	307
Kansas City	5	9	0	.357	282	341
San Diego	2	12	0	.143	189	345

*Wild Card qualifier for playoffs
Divisional playoffs: Pittsburgh 28, Baltimore 10;
Oakland 31, Cincinnati 28
AFC championship: Pittsburgh 16, Oakland 10

LEADING RUSHERS	Att.	Yards	Avg.	Long	TD
O. J. Simpson, Buffalo	329	1,817	5.5	88t	16
Franco Harris, Pittsburgh	262	1,246	4.8	36	10
Lydell Mitchell, Baltimore	289	1,193	4.1	70t	11
Greg Pruitt, Cleveland	217	1,067	4.9	50	8
John Riggins, N.Y. Jets	238	1,005	4.2	42	8

LEADING PASSERS	Att.	Comp.	Yards	TD	Int.
Ken Anderson, Cincinnati	377	228	3,169	21	11
Len Dawson, Kansas City	140	93	1,095	5	4
Bert Jones, Baltimore	344	203	2,483	18	8
Terry Bradshaw, Pittsburgh	286	165	2,055	18	9
Bob Griese, Miami	191	118	1,693	14	13

LEADING RECEIVERS	No.	Yards	Avg.	Long	TD
Reggie Rucker, Cleveland	60	770	12.8	40t	3
Lydell Mitchell, Baltimore	60	544	9.1	35t	4
Bob Chandler, Buffalo	55	746	13.6	35	6
Ken Burrough, Houston	53	1,063	20.1	77t	8
Clifford Branch, Oakland	51	893	17.5	53	9

1975 NFC STANDINGS

Eastern Division	W	L	T	Pct.	Pts.	OP
St. Louis	11	3	0	.786	356	276
Dallas*	10	4	0	.714	350	268
Washington	8	6	0	.571	325	276
N.Y. Giants	5	9	0	.357	216	306
Philadelphia	4	10	0	.286	225	302
Central Division	W	L	T	Pct.	Pts.	OP
Minnesota	12	2	0	.857	377	180
Detroit	7	7	0	.500	245	262
Chicago	4	10	0	.286	191	379
Green Bay	4	10	0	.286	226	285
Western Division	W	L	T	Pct.	Pts.	OP
Los Angeles	12	2	0	.857	312	135
San Francisco	5	9	0	.357	255	286
Atlanta	4	10	0	.286	240	289
New Orleans	2	12	0	.143	165	360

*Wild Card qualifier for playoffs
Divisional playoffs: Los Angeles 35, St. Louis 23;
Dallas 17, Minnesota 14
NFC championship: Dallas 37, Los Angeles 7
Super Bowl X: Pittsburgh (AFC) 21, Dallas (NFC) 17

LEADING RUSHERS	Att.	Yards	Avg.	Long	TD
Jim Otis, St. Louis	269	1,076	4.0	30	5
Chuck Foreman, Minnesota	280	1,070	3.8	31t	13
Dave Hampton, Atlanta	250	1,002	4.0	22	5
Robert Newhouse, Dallas	209	930	4.4	29	2
Mike Thomas, Washington	235	919	3.9	34	4

LEADING PASSERS	Att.	Comp.	Yards	TD	Int.
Fran Tarkenton, Minnesota	425	273	2,994	25	13
Roger Staubach, Dallas	348	198	2,666	17	16
Billy Kilmer, Washington	346	178	2,440	23	16
James Harris, Los Angeles	285	157	2,148	14	15
Norm Snead, San Francisco	189	108	1,337	9	10

LEADING RECEIVERS	No.	Yards	Avg.	Long	TD
Chuck Foreman, Minnesota	73	791	9.5	33	9
Ken Payne, Green Bay	58	766	13.2	54	0
Ed Marinaro, Minnesota	54	462	8.6	25	3
Charley Taylor, Washington	53	744	14.0	64	6
John Gilliam, Minnesota	50	777	15.5	46	7

Mel Blount takes a pass away from Isaac Curtis of Cincinnati, 1975.

1976 Terry Bradshaw's 64-yard pass to Lynn Swann helped the Steelers win their second straight Super Bowl at Miami 21-17 over the Cowboys who rallied and threatened again until Glen Edwards made an interception in the end zone on the final play.

The NFL expanded to 28 teams with the addition of the Seattle Seahawks and the Tampa Bay Buccaneers for the 1976 season. The Seahawks moved into the new 65,000-seat Kingdome and the Buccaneers took over Tampa Stadium, expanded to a capacity of 71,400. The New York Giants, who had been forced to play their home games in Yale Bowl and Shea Stadium since 1973, settled into Giants Stadium with its 76,500 seats in East Rutherford, New Jersey.

Legal complicatons involving the process of allocating veteran players to Seattle and Tampa Bay delayed the process until March 30-31 with a resultant delay of the college draft until April 8-9.

Tampa Bay had the first draft pick after winning a coin toss with Seattle and selected Oklahoma's Lee Roy Selmon, a defensive lineman.

There were several trades. New England sent Jim Plunkett to San Francisco and decided to rely on young Steve Grogan, a second-year quarterback. Green Bay shipped veteran quarterback John Hadl to Houston for quarterback Lynn Dickey, who had been a reserve behind Dan Pastorini. San Francisco traded Steve Spurrier to Tampa Bay for Willie McGee, Bruce Elia, and a draft choice.

The NFL operated without an agreement with the Players Association for the third consecutive year although there were several meetings between the two groups. A court decision found the then draft system in violation of the law in the absence of collective bargaining.

Thirty-second clocks were installed to make everyone aware of the time remaining between the ready-to-play signal and the snap of the ball. The 43-man player limit was continued.

Paul Brown stepped down at Cincinnati after coaching high school, college, military, and professional teams for 41 years. He picked a long-time assistant, Bill Johnson, as his successor and remained as general manager of the Bengals.

O.J. Simpson sought a trade to the Los Angeles Rams, and did not re-sign with the Buffalo Bills until just before their opening game.

Free agents Calvin Hill, Jean Fugett and John Riggins wound up with Washington, Larry Csonka with the Giants, Paul Warfield with Cleveland, and John Gilliam with Atlanta.

A record 12 backs rushed for 1,000 or more yards, topped by Simpson, who wound up with 1,503 yards, including an NFL single-game record of 273 yards against Detroit Thanksgiving Day. Walter Payton of the Bears had a sensational year, losing the league title on the final day as he wound up with 1,390.

Tarkenton moved past Johnny Unitas in career total passing yardage with 41,801 yards while increasing his other records to 308 touchdown passes, 5,637 attempts, and 3,186 completions. Jim Marshall of the Vikings extended his streak of consecutive games to 236, passing the retired George Blanda. Ken Stabler's .667 completion percentage was the best since Sammy Baugh in 1945. Ken Anderson of Cincinnati became the top active passer in the point rating system, but he lost the 1976 AFC title to Stabler after winning two in a row.

Baltimore repeated in the AFC East, although New England also matched the 11-3 record. The Colts took the division on a better intradivision record, 7-1 to 6-2. The Patriots made the playoffs for the first time since the merger as the wild card entry.

Pittsburgh came back after losing four of its first five, including blowing a 28-14 lead at Oakland in the final three minutes of the season's first game. The

Louis Carter is stopped for a short gain in the first game between Seattle and Tampa Bay, 1976.

Steelers swept their last nine, five by shutouts, matching front-running Cincinnati's 10-4 record in the AFC Central. The Steelers advanced to the playoffs since they had beaten the Bengals twice.

Oakland won the AFC West with a 10-game win streak despite injuries to the defensive unit that forced coach John Madden to use a three-man line.

In the NFC, Dallas won the Eastern Division, Minnesota the Central, and Los Angeles the Western. Washington, counted out several times, made the playoffs as the wild card team at 10-4 by beating Dallas in the final game.

Pittsburgh rolled over Baltimore 40-14 in the AFC Divisional Playoffs while Oakland won a 24-21 victory over New England, which suffered a costly roughing-the-passer call on the Raiders' game-winning drive in the final minute.

Brent McClanahan and Foreman each rushed for more than 100 yards in Minnesota's first-round win over Washington 35-20, while Los Angeles edged Dallas 14-12 in the NFC Divisional Playoffs.

Pittsburgh's hopes for a possible third Super Bowl ended in the AFC Championship Game at Oakland. The Steelers lost 24-7 as both regular running backs, Franco Harris and Rocky Bleier, were out with injuries.

Minnesota shocked Los Angeles for the NFC championship as Bobby Bryant scooped up a blocked field-goal try and ran 90 yards for a touchdown that started them on the way to a 24-13 win.

Defensive tackle Merlin Olsen of the Los Angeles Rams retired.

1976 AFC STANDINGS

Eastern Division	W	L	T	Pct.	Pts.	OP
Baltimore	11	3	0	.786	417	246
New England*	11	3	0	.786	376	236
Miami	6	8	0	.429	263	264
N.Y. Jets	3	11	0	.214	169	383
Buffalo	2	12	0	.143	245	363
Central Division	W	L	T	Pct.	Pts.	OP
Pittsburgh	10	4	0	.714	342	138
Cincinnati	10	4	0	.714	335	210
Cleveland	9	5	0	.643	267	287
Houston	5	9	0	.357	222	273
Western Division	W	L	T	Pct.	Pts.	OP
Oakland	13	1	0	.929	350	237
Denver	9	5	0	.643	315	206
San Diego	6	8	0	.429	248	285
Kansas City	5	9	0	.357	290	376
Tampa Bay	0	14	0	.000	125	412

*Wild Card qualifier for playoffs
Divisional playoffs: Oakland 24, New England 21;
Pittsburgh 40, Baltimore 14
AFC championship: Oakland 24, Pittsburgh 7

LEADING RUSHERS	Att.	Yards	Avg.	Long	TD
O. J. Simpson, Buffalo	290	1,503	5.2	75t	8
Lydell Mitchell, Baltimore	289	1,200	4.2	43	5
Franco Harris, Pittsburgh	289	1,128	3.9	30	14
Rocky Bleier, Pittsburgh	220	1,036	4.7	28	5
Mark van Eeghen, Oakland	233	1,012	4.3	21	3

LEADING PASSERS	Att.	Comp.	Yards	TD	Int.
Ken Stabler, Oakland	291	194	2,737	27	17
Bert Jones, Baltimore	343	207	3,104	24	9
Joe Ferguson, Buffalo	151	74	1,086	9	1
Bob Griese, Miami	272	162	2,097	11	12
Mike Livingston, Kansas City	338	189	2,682	12	13

LEADING RECEIVERS	No.	Yards	Avg.	Long	TD
MacArthur Lane, Kansas City	66	686	10.4	44	1
Bob Chandler, Buffalo	61	824	13.5	58t	10
Lydell Mitchell, Baltimore	60	555	9.3	40t	3
Dave Casper, Oakland	53	691	13.0	30t	10
Ken Burrough, Houston	51	932	18.3	69t	7

1976 NFC STANDINGS

Eastern Division	W	L	T	Pct.	Pts.	OP
Dallas	11	3	0	.786	296	194
Washington*	10	4	0	.714	291	217
St. Louis	10	4	0	.714	309	267
Philadelphia	4	10	0	.286	165	286
N.Y. Giants	3	11	0	.214	170	250

Central Division	W	L	T	Pct.	Pts.	OP
Minnesota	11	2	1	.821	305	176
Chicago	7	7	0	.500	253	216
Detroit	6	8	0	.429	262	220
Green Bay	5	9	0	.357	218	299

Western Division	W	L	T	Pct.	Pts.	OP
Los Angeles	10	3	1	.750	351	190
San Francisco	8	6	0	.571	270	190
Atlanta	4	10	0	.286	172	312
New Orleans	4	10	0	.286	253	346
Seattle	2	12	0	.143	229	429

*Wild Card qualifiers for playoffs
Divisional playoffs: Minnesota 35, Washington 20;
Los Angeles 14, Dallas 12
NFC championship: Minnesota 24, Los Angeles 13
Super Bowl XI: Oakland (AFC) 32, Minnesota (NFC) 14

LEADING RUSHERS

	Att.	Yards	Avg.	Long	TD
Walter Payton, Chicago	311	1,390	4.5	60	13
Delvin Williams, San Francisco	248	1,203	4.9	80t	7
Lawrence McCutcheon, Los Angeles	291	1,168	4.0	40	9
Chuck Foreman, Minnesota	278	1,155	4.2	46	13
Mike Thomas, Washington	254	1,101	4.3	28	5

LEADING PASSERS

	Att.	Comp.	Yards	TD	Int.
James Harris, Los Angeles	158	91	1,460	8	6
Greg Landry, Detroit	291	168	2,191	17	8
Fran Tarkenton, Minnesota	412	255	2,961	17	8
Jim Hart, St. Louis	388	218	2,946	18	13
Roger Staubach, Dallas	369	208	2,715	14	11

LEADING RECEIVERS

	No.	Yards	Avg.	Long	TD
Drew Pearson, Dallas	58	806	13.9	40t	6
Chuck Foreman, Minnesota	55	567	10.3	41t	1
Steve Largent, Seattle	54	705	13.1	45	4
Tony Galbreath, New Orleans	54	420	7.8	35	1
Ahmad Rashad, Minnesota	53	671	12.7	47	3

1977 The Oakland Raiders, who had lost six AFC Championship Games since being in their last Super Bowl, got over the championship hurdle with a 32-14 rout of Minnesota in Super Bowl XI on January 9, at the Rose Bowl in Pasadena. Clarence Davis rushed for 137 yards to lead Oakland to a Super Bowl record 429 yards total offense.

The National Football League Players Association and the National Football League Management Council ratified a collective bargaining agreement extending until July 15, 1982, covering five football seasons while continuing the pension plan—including the years 1974, 1975, and 1976—with contributions totaling more than $55 million. Total cost of the agreement was estimated at $107 million. The agreement called for a college draft at least through 1986, contained a no-strike, no-suit clause, established a 45-man player limit, reduced pension vesting to four years, and provided for increases in minimum salaries and preseason and postseason play, improved insurance, medical, and dental benefits, and modified previous practices in player movement and control. The agreement reaffirmed the NFL Commissioner's disciplinary authority. Additionally, the agreement called for the NFL member clubs to make payments totaling $16 million over the next 10 years to settle various legal disputes.

Rule changes were adopted to open up the passing game and to cut down on injuries. Defenders were permitted to make contact with eligible receivers only once, the head slap was outlawed, and wide receivers were prohibited from clipping, even in the legal clipping zone.

Tampa Bay was permanently aligned in the NFC Central Division and Seattle in the AFC Western Division.

Tampa Bay had the first draft choice and selected USC tailback Ricky Bell. Dallas traded with Seattle for the number-two pick and drafted running back Tony Dorsett, the Heisman Trophy winner from Pittsburgh.

There were two major trades involving quarterbacks. Denver sent starting quarterback Steve Ramsey to the New York Giants for veteran Craig Morton, and Los Angeles sent backup quarterback Ron Jaworski to Philadelphia for the rights to tight end Charle Young.

Three former all-pros died: Hall of Famer Joe Stydahar; Cal Hubbard, the only person in both the Pro Football and Baseball Hall of Fames; and former Eagles quarterback Davey O'Brien.

A number of long-time all-pros retired, including Tommy Nobis of Atlanta, Lee Roy Jordan of Dallas, Nick Buoniconti of Miami, Ed Budde of Kansas City, and Earl Morrall, who had played 21 years with six clubs, quarterbacking two of them (Baltimore and Miami) to the Super Bowl.

John Madden gets a super ride after the Raiders defeat the Vikings in Super Bowl XI.

Red Miller took over for John Ralston as head coach at Denver. In his first year he led the Broncos to the Super Bowl. The Falcons started building for the future with the replacement of interim coach Pat Peppler by Leeman Bennett, who came from an assistant's job with the Los Angeles Rams. Walt Michaels was named as the new head coach of the New York Jets.

Before the season began, Edward J. DeBartolo, Jr. bought the San Francisco 49ers, and replaced coach Monte Clark with Ken Meyer.

The NFL had nine 1,000-yard runners, led by Walter Payton of Chicago with 1,852—the third highest total ever—on a record 339 carries. Payton also broke the all-time record for yards in one game when he ran for 275 against Minnesota.

Although an injury prevented him from rushing for 1,000 yards for the sixth consecutive season, O. J. Simpson joined Jimmy Brown as the only player in history to run for 10,000 yards in a career. Fred Cox of the Minnesota Vikings, passed Lou Groza to become the second-highest scorer in league history behind George Blanda. On December 4, Kansas City and Cincinnati played in the 5,000th game in NFL history.

The Denver Broncos made the playoffs for the first time in the history of the franchise by winning the AFC Western Division with a 12-2 record. Runner-up Oakland was the wild card qualifier with an 11-3 record, the second best mark in the AFC.

Baltimore won in the AFC East for the third consecutive year, with a 10-4 record. Miami had the same record but the Colts took the division on the basis of a better record within the conference, 9-3 to 8-4 for the Dolphins.

Pittsburgh made the playoffs for the sixth year in a row.

In the NFC, Dallas won its first eight games on the way to a 12-2 record, Los Angeles was the only team in the West to have a winning record, and Minnesota and Chicago had the same record in the Central, 9-5. The Vikings won the title on the basis of more victories in games against common opponents. The Bears qualified for the playoffs as a wild card team.

Oakland defeated Baltimore 37-31 after 15:43 of overtime in the third-longest game in NFL history, and Denver topped Pittsburgh 34-21 in the AFC Divisional Playoffs.

In the NFC, Minnesota beat Los Angeles 14-7 in a downpour in Los Angeles, and Dallas defeated Chicago 37-7.

Oakland's hopes for a second-consecutive Super Bowl were ended by Denver's combination of Craig Morton and Haven Moses, who connected for two touchdowns in a 20-17 Broncos victory.

Dallas qualified for a record fourth Super Bowl on the strength of its defense, which shut down Minnesota 23-6.

1977 AFC STANDINGS

Eastern Division	W	L	T	Pct.	Pts.	OP
Baltimore	10	4	0	.714	295	211
Miami	10	4	0	.714	313	197
New England	9	5	0	.643	278	217
N.Y. Jets	3	11	0	.214	191	300
Buffalo	3	11	0	.214	160	313

Central Division	W	L	T	Pct.	Pts.	OP
Pittsburgh	9	5	0	.643	283	243
Houston	8	6	0	.571	299	230
Cincinnati	8	6	0	.571	238	235
Cleveland	6	8	0	.429	269	267

Western Division	W	L	T	Pct.	Pts.	OP
Denver	12	2	0	.857	274	148
Oakland*	11	3	0	.786	351	230
San Diego	7	7	0	.500	222	205
Seattle	5	9	0	.357	282	373
Kansas City	2	12	0	.143	225	349

*Wild Card qualifier for playoffs
Divisional playoffs: Denver 34, Pittsburgh 21;
Oakland 37, Baltimore 31,
sudden death overtime
AFC championship: Denver 20, Oakland 17

LEADING RUSHERS	Att.	Yards	Avg.	Long	TD
Mark van Eeghen, Oakland	324	1,273	3.9	27	7
Franco Harris, Pittsburgh	300	1,162	3.9	61t	11
Lydell Mitchell, Baltimore	301	1,159	3.9	64t	3
Greg Pruitt, Cleveland	236	1,086	4.6	78t	3
Sam Cunningham, New England	270	1,015	3.8	31t	4

LEADING PASSERS	Att.	Comp.	Yards	TD	Int.
Bob Griese, Miami	307	180	2,252	22	13
Craig Morton, Denver	254	131	1,929	14	8
Bert Jones, Baltimore	393	224	2,686	17	11
Ken Stabler, Oakland	294	169	2,176	20	20
Terry Bradshaw, Pittsburgh	314	162	2,523	17	19

LEADING RECEIVERS	No.	Yards	Avg.	Long	TD
Lydell Mitchell, Baltimore	71	620	8.7	38	4
Bob Chandler, Buffalo	60	745	12.4	31	4
Clark Gaines, New York Jets	55	469	8.5	31	1
Nat Moore, Miami	52	765	14.7	73t	12
Don McCauley, Baltimore	51	495	9.7	34t	2

1977 NFC STANDINGS

Eastern Division	W	L	T	Pct.	Pts.	OP
Dallas	12	2	0	.857	345	212
Washington	9	5	0	.643	196	189
St. Louis	7	7	0	.500	272	287
Philadelphia	5	9	0	.357	220	207
N.Y. Giants	5	9	0	.357	181	265
Central Division	**W**	**L**	**T**	**Pct.**	**Pts.**	**OP**
Minnesota	9	5	0	.643	231	227
Chicago*	9	5	0	.643	255	253
Detroit	6	8	0	.429	183	252
Green Bay	4	10	0	.286	134	219
Tampa Bay	2	12	0	.143	103	223
Western Division	**W**	**L**	**T**	**Pct.**	**Pts.**	**OP**
Los Angeles	10	4	0	.714	302	146
Atlanta	7	7	0	.500	179	129
San Francisco	5	9	0	.357	220	260
New Orleans	3	11	0	.214	232	336

*Wild Card qualifier for playoffs
Divisional playoffs: Dallas 37, Chicago 7;
Minnesota 14, Los Angeles 7
NFC championship: Dallas 23, Minnesota 6
Super Bowl XII: Dallas (NFC) 27, Denver (AFC) 10

LEADING RUSHERS	Att.	Yards	Avg.	Long	TD
Walter Payton, Chicago	339	1,852	5.5	73	14
Lawrence McCutcheon, Los Angeles	294	1,238	4.2	48	7
Chuck Foreman, Minnesota	270	1,112	4.1	51	6
Tony Dorsett, Dallas	208	1,007	4.8	84t	12
Delvin Williams, San Francisco	268	931	3.5	40	7

LEADING PASSERS	Att.	Comp.	Yards	TD	Int.
Roger Staubach, Dallas	361	210	2,620	18	9
Pat Haden, Los Angeles	216	122	1,551	11	6
Fran Tarkenton, Minnesota	258	155	1,734	9	14
Greg Landry, Detroit	240	135	1,359	6	7
Archie Manning, New Orleans	205	113	1,284	8	9

LEADING RECEIVERS	No.	Yards	Avg.	Long	TD
Ahmad Rashad, Minnesota	51	681	13.4	48t	2
James Scott, Chicago	50	809	16.2	72t	3
Drew Pearson, Dallas	48	870	18.1	67	2
Harold Jackson, Los Angeles	48	666	13.9	58	6
Harold Carmichael, Philadelphia	46	665	14.5	50t	7

1978 The Dallas Cowboys evened their Super Bowl record at 2-2 on January 15 with a 27-10 victory over the Denver Broncos in the Louisiana Superdome in New Orleans in Super Bowl XII. The Dallas defense dominated the game, forcing eight turnovers, holding the Broncos to only 156 yards, and allowing Denver to keep the ball just 21 minutes. The game was the first Super Bowl to be played indoors, and was viewed by over 102 million people, making it the most watched sports event in television history.

The Los Angeles Rams announced their intention to move from the Los Angeles Coliseum to Anaheim Stadium following the 1979 season. The Los Angeles Coliseum Commission filed an antitrust suit in federal court challenging NFL principles requiring league approval of transfers of team locations.

The NFL continued a trend toward opening up the offensive game. Rule changes permitted a defender to maintain contact with a receiver within five yards of the line of scrimmage, but restricted contact beyond that point. The pass-blocking rule was interpreted to permit the extending of arms and open hands.

There were a number of increases in the league. A seventh official, the side judge, was added to the game officiating crew; active team rosters were increased to 45 players; and the number of regular-sea-

Jim Youngblood moves up to stop Chuck Foreman in a 1977 NFC playoff game.

Rookie Earl Campbell, the NFL's leading rusher, 1978.

son games was increased from 14 to 16, with the number of preseason games dropped to four.

Wild card teams were added to the playoffs in both conferences. The first week following the regular season would match wild card teams in both conferences.

The league signed a new television contract worth over $5 million to each club. The contract included provisions for prime-time games on Thursday and Sunday nights.

Tampa Bay traded the first draft choice to Houston for tight end Jimmie Giles and the Oilers' first- and second-round draft choices in 1978 and third- and fifth-round choices in 1979. The Oilers drafted Heisman Trophy winner Earl Campbell, a running back from the University of Texas.

There were three other major trades. Buffalo granted O. J. Simpson's request and traded him to San Francisco for five draft choices. Three weeks later the 49ers traded their running back Delvin Williams to Miami for Vern Roberson, Freddie Solomon, and two draft picks. Washington obtained defensive back Lemar Parrish and defensive end Coy Bacon from Cincinnati for a first-round choice.

Coaches moved almost as frequently as players. There were 10 new head coaches at the beginning of the season, including Chuck Knox at Buffalo; George Allen, who had moved to Los Angeles to take Knox's old position; Jack Pardee, who moved from Chicago to Washington; Neill Armstrong, a Minnesota assistant who replaced Pardee; Bud Wilkinson, legendary coach of the Oklahoma Sooners, at St. Louis, replacing Don Coryell; Sam Rutigliano, who took over at Cleveland and Marv Levy was named new head coach at Kansas City. During the preseason, Allen was fired and replaced by offensive coordinator Ray Malavasi. San Diego coach Tommy Prothro resigned in the middle of the season and was replaced by Coryell. Homer Rice took over for Bill Johnson at Cincinnati after five games.

With one game left in the 1978 season, Chuck Fairbanks quit his position as New England head coach and general manager to take the head coaching position at the University of Colorado. Successful Oakland Raiders head coach John Madden retired at the end of the season due to a severe ulcer condition.

Some long-time players retired as well. Fred Cox, John Hadl, Joe Namath, Mel Renfro, Jackie Smith, Paul Warfield, and all-time receiving leader Charley Taylor all called it quits after long careers.

Two Hall of Famers died during the year—quarterback Earl (Dutch) Clark and tackle Ed Healey.

The NFL had 11 backs who rushed for 1,000 or more yards, topped by Houston's Campbell, whose 1,450 yards were the most ever by a rookie. Walter Payton of Chicago was a close second with 1,395.

Rickey Young of Minnesota caught 88 passes, an all-time record for a running back. And his quarterback, Fran Tarkenton, increased his own career passing records by throwing a record number of passes (572) and completions (345). In addition he threw 25 touchdowns and 32 interceptions.

In the AFC Central, Pittsburgh won its first seven games en route to a 14-2 record, the best in the league. Houston went 10-6 and earned one of the two wild card spots.

New England and Miami each finished with 11-5 records. The Patriots were crowned the AFC East champion and the Dolphins the second wild card team.

In the West, Denver won seven of eight games in the division to edge out Oakland, Seattle, and San Diego by a game.

Dallas and Los Angeles ended with the best records (12-4) in the NFC, with their runners-up, Philadelphia and Atlanta, (both 9-7) gaining the wild card

spots. In the Central Division, Minnesota won despite an 8-7-1 record, the poorest ever to win a title in the NFL.

In the wild card games, Atlanta edged Philadelphia 14-13 and Houston surprised Miami 17-9.

The AFC Divisional Playoffs were one-sided games. Pittsburgh totally shut down Denver 33-10. Houston caught New England flat—perhaps from the announcement that their coach had quit—and won 31-14.

Dallas and Los Angeles were dominant in the NFC playoffs. The Cowboys came from behind with substitute quarterback Danny White to defeat Atlanta 27-20, and the Rams broke open a close game at the half to defeat Minnesota 34-10.

The Cowboys earned the right to their second-consecutive Super Bowl, and a record fifth overall, with 28 points in the second half of a 28-0 win over the Rams in the NFC Championship Game.

Pittsburgh dominated the Oilers on a frozen field to win 34-5 in the AFC Championship Game, setting the stage for the first Super Bowl rematch.

1978 AFC STANDINGS

Eastern Division	W	L	T	Pct.	Pts.	OP
New England	11	5	0	.688	358	286
Miami*	11	5	0	.688	372	254
N.Y. Jets	8	8	0	.500	359	364
Buffalo	5	11	0	.313	302	354
Baltimore	5	11	0	.313	239	421
Central Division	W	L	T	Pct.	Pts.	OP
Pittsburgh	14	2	0	.875	356	195
Houston*	10	6	0	.625	283	298
Cleveland	8	8	0	.500	334	356
Cincinnati	4	12	0	.250	252	284
Western Division	W	L	T	Pct.	Pts.	OP
Denver	10	6	0	.625	282	198
Oakland	9	7	0	.563	311	283
Seattle	9	7	0	.563	345	358
San Diego	9	7	0	.563	355	309
Kansas City	4	12	0	.250	243	327

*Wild Card qualifier for playoffs
Wild card game: Houston 17, Miami 9
Divisional playoffs: Pittsburgh 33, Denver 10;
Houston 31, New England 14
AFC championship: Pittsburgh 34, Houston 5

LEADING RUSHERS	Att.	Yards	Avg.	Long	TD
Earl Campbell, Houston	302	1,450	4.8	81t	13
Delvin Williams, Miami	272	1,258	4.6	58	8
Franco Harris, Pittsburgh	310	1,082	3.5	37	8
Mark van Eeghen, Oakland	270	1,080	4.0	34	9
Terry Miller, Buffalo	238	1,060	4.5	60t	7

LEADING PASSERS	Att.	Comp.	Yards	TD	Int.
Terry Bradshaw, Pittsburgh	368	207	2,915	28	20
Dan Fouts, San Diego	381	224	2,999	24	20
Bob Griese, Miami	235	148	1,791	11	11
Brian Sipe, Cleveland	399	222	2,906	21	15
Craig Morton, Denver	267	146	1,802	11	8

LEADING RECEIVERS	No.	Yards	Avg.	Long	TD
Steve Largent, Seattle	71	1,168	16.5	57t	8
Dave Casper, Oakland	62	852	13.7	44	9
Lynn Swann, Pittsburgh	61	880	14.4	62	11
Lydell Mitchell, San Diego	57	500	8.8	55t	2
John Jefferson, San Diego	56	1,001	17.9	46t	13

1978 NFC STANDINGS

Eastern Division	W	L	T	Pct.	Pts.	OP
Dallas	12	4	0	.750	384	208
Philadelphia*	9	7	0	.563	270	250
Washington	8	8	0	.500	273	283
St. Louis	6	10	0	.375	248	296
N.Y. Giants	6	10	0	.375	264	298
Central Division	W	L	T	Pct.	Pts.	OP
Minnesota	8	7	1	.531	294	306
Green Bay	8	7	1	.531	249	269
Detroit	7	9	0	.438	290	300
Chicago	7	9	0	.438	253	274
Tampa Bay	5	11	0	.313	241	259
Western Division	W	L	T	Pct.	Pts.	OP
Los Angeles	12	4	0	.750	316	245
Atlanta*	9	7	0	.563	240	290
New Orleans	7	9	0	.438	281	298
San Francisco	2	14	0	.125	219	350

*Wild Card qualifier for playoffs
Wild card game: Atlanta 14, Philadelphia 13
Divisional playoffs: Dallas 27, Atlanta 20;
Los Angeles 34, Minnesota 10
NFC championship: Dallas 28, Los Angeles 0
Super Bowl XIII: Pittsburgh (AFC) 35, Dallas (NFC) 31

LEADING RUSHERS	Att.	Yards	Avg.	Long	TD
Walter Payton, Chicago	333	1,395	4.2	76	11
Tony Dorsett, Dallas	290	1,325	4.6	63	7
Wilbert Montgomery, Philadelphia	259	1,220	4.7	47	9
Terdell Middleton, Green Bay	284	1,116	3.9	76t	11
John Riggins, Washington	248	1,014	4.1	31	5

LEADING PASSERS	Att.	Comp.	Yards	TD	Int.
Roger Staubach, Dallas	413	231	3,190	25	16
Archie Manning, New Orleans	471	291	3,416	17	16
Gary Danielson, Detroit	351	199	2,294	18	17
Fran Tarkenton, Minnesota	572	345	3,468	25	32
Ron Jaworski, Philadelphia	398	206	2,487	16	16

LEADING RECEIVERS	No.	Yards	Avg.	Long	TD
Rickey Young, Minnesota	88	704	8.0	48	5
Tony Galbreath, New Orleans	74	582	7.9	35	2
Ahmad Rashad, Minnesota	66	769	11.7	58t	8
Pat Tilley, St. Louis	62	900	14.5	43	3
Chuck Foreman, Minnesota	61	396	6.5	20	2

1979 Pittsburgh, behind Terry Bradshaw's four touchdown passes, defeated Dallas 35-31 in Super Bowl XIII to become the first team to win three Super Bowls. Playing in front of a sellout crowd in Miami's Orange Bowl and the largest audience ever to watch a televised event (35,090,000 homes), the Steelers built up a big lead and then held off the Cowboys' late surges.

The NFL's rule changes emphasized additional player safety. The changes prohibited players on the receiving team from blocking below the waist during kickoffs, punts, and field goal attempts; prohibited the wearing of torn or altered equipment and exposed pads that could be hazardous; extended the zone in which there could be no crackback blocks; and instructed officials quickly to whistle a play dead when a quarterback was clearly in the grasp of a tackler.

The teams also were permitted to activate 3 players from the injured reserved list after the final cutdown to 45 players, providing certain stipulations were met.

Charlie Waters intercepts a pass to set up the first Dallas touchdown in the 1978 NFC Championship Game.

The 1980 AFC-NFC Pro Bowl Game was awarded to Honolulu, Hawaii, marking the first time in the 30-year history of the game that it would be played in a non-NFL city.

Carroll Rosenbloom, the owner and the president of the Los Angeles Rams, drowned off the coast of Florida in the spring. His widow, Georgia, took over the operation of the club.

There were three other notable deaths during the year: Hall of Famers Alphonse (Tuffy) Leemans and Ken Strong, and St. Louis Cardinals tight end J. V. Cain. Cain had a heart attack in training camp in the summer, collapsing on the practice field.

Several veteran all-pros retired. Guard Tom Mack of the Rams, defensive tackle Jethro Pugh of the Cowboys, and quarterback Fran Tarkenton and center Mick Tingelhoff of the Vikings called it quits after distinguished careers. Tarkenton, who had quarterbacked the Vikings and the New York Giants for 18 years, retired with NFL career records for most pass attempts (6,467), completions (3,686), yards (47,003), and touchdown passes (342).

Four new head coaches came into the league, two in each conference. In the AFC, Ron Erhardt was named Chuck Fairbanks's successor at New England, and Tom Flores replaced retired John Madden at Oakland. In the NFC, Bill Walsh returned to pro football from Stanford University to become the head coach at San Francisco, and Ray Perkins took over for John McVay as head coach of the New York Giants.

There were several noteworthy trades. Quarterback Greg Landry was traded from Detroit to Baltimore for draft choices; Los Angeles traded linebacker Isiah Robertson to Buffalo for draft choices; and running back Mike Thomas went from Washington to San Diego in exchange for a draft choice. Cleveland traded its first-round draft choice to San Diego for the Chargers' first- and second-round choices. San Diego subsequently chose tight end Kellen Winslow, while the Browns drafted wide receiver Willis Adams and tackle Sam Claphan.

Buffalo made Ohio State All-America Tom Cousineau the first pick of the draft, but the rookie linebacker signed with Montreal of the Canadian Football League.

The NFC had nine backs who rushed for over 1,000 yards, and the AFC only three. The best of all was Earl Campbell of the Oilers, who led the league in rushing for the second year in a row, with 1,697 yards. Close behind were Walter Payton of Chicago (1,610) and rookie Ottis Anderson of St. Louis (1,605).

Dan Fouts of the Chargers broke Joe Namath's 12-year-old record for passing yardage in a season by throwing for 4,082 yards, and unheralded Steve DeBerg of San Francisco set an all-time record with 347 completions.

Harold Carmichael broke the all-time record for most consecutive games with at least one pass reception, finishing the season with a streak of 112 games. Paul Krause surpassed Emlen Tunnell as the NFL's leading career interceptor, raising his total to 81. Jim Marshall of the Vikings became the first defensive player in league history to play for 20 years, and ran his consecutive game streak to a record 282 games.

Pittsburgh won its sixth straight AFC Central title with a 12-4 record, the best in football, but just edged out the improved Oilers. After losing to Pittsburgh 38-7 early in the season, Houston defeated the Steelers 20-17 at the end of the year to finish 11-5.

San Diego's record-breaking passing attack propelled it to the AFC West title, with runner-up Denver earning a wild card spot.

A collapse by New England late in the year allowed Miami to win the AFC East by one game with

Tom Mack.

Dan Fouts.

Vernon Perry picks off one of his four interceptions in the 1979 AFC Divisional Playoff Game.

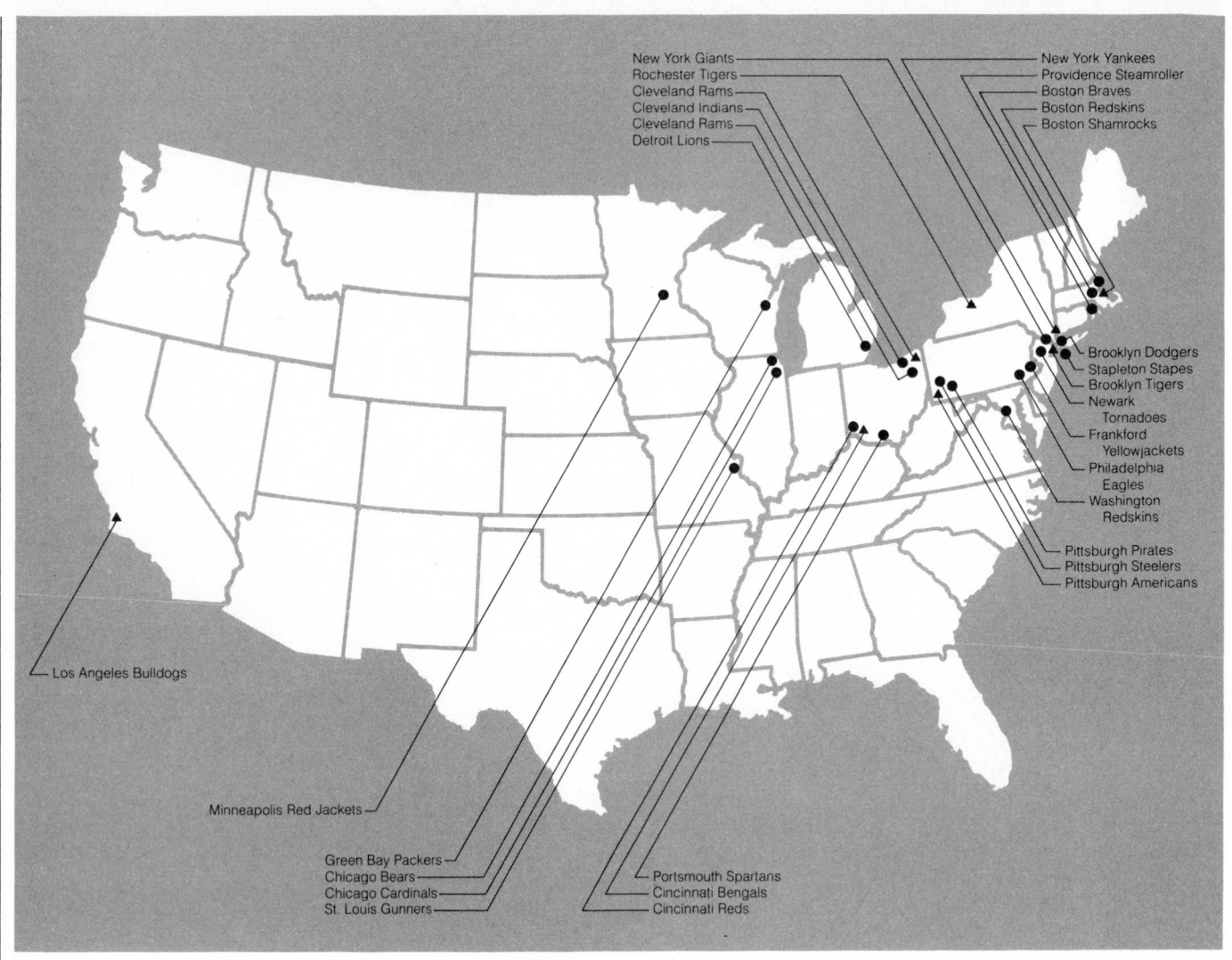

New York Giants
Rochester Tigers
Cleveland Rams
Cleveland Indians
Cleveland Rams
Detroit Lions

New York Yankees
Providence Steamroller
Boston Braves
Boston Redskins
Boston Shamrocks

Brooklyn Dodgers
Stapleton Stapes
Brooklyn Tigers
Newark Tornadoes
Frankford Yellowjackets
Philadelphia Eagles
Washington Redskins

Pittsburgh Pirates
Pittsburgh Steelers
Pittsburgh Americans

Los Angeles Bulldogs

Minneapolis Red Jackets

Green Bay Packers
Chicago Bears
Chicago Cardinals
St. Louis Gunners

Portsmouth Spartans
Cincinnati Bengals
Cincinnati Reds

1930s

● NATIONAL FOOTBALL LEAGUE

Brooklyn Dodgers
Chicago Bears
Chicago Cardinals
Frankford Yellowjackets
Green Bay Packers
Minneapolis Red Jackets
New York Giants
Newark Tornadoes
Portsmouth Spartans
Providence Steamroller
Stapleton Stapes
Cleveland Indians
Boston Braves
Boston Redskins
Cincinnati Reds
Philadelphia Eagles
Pittsburgh Pirates
Detroit Lions
St. Louis Gunners
Cleveland Rams
Washington Redskins
Pittsburgh Steelers

▲ AMERICAN FOOTBALL LEAGUE, 1936-37

Boston Shamrocks
Brooklyn Tigers
Cleveland Rams
New York Yankees
Pittsburgh Americans
Rochester Tigers
Cincinnati Bengals
Los Angeles Bulldogs

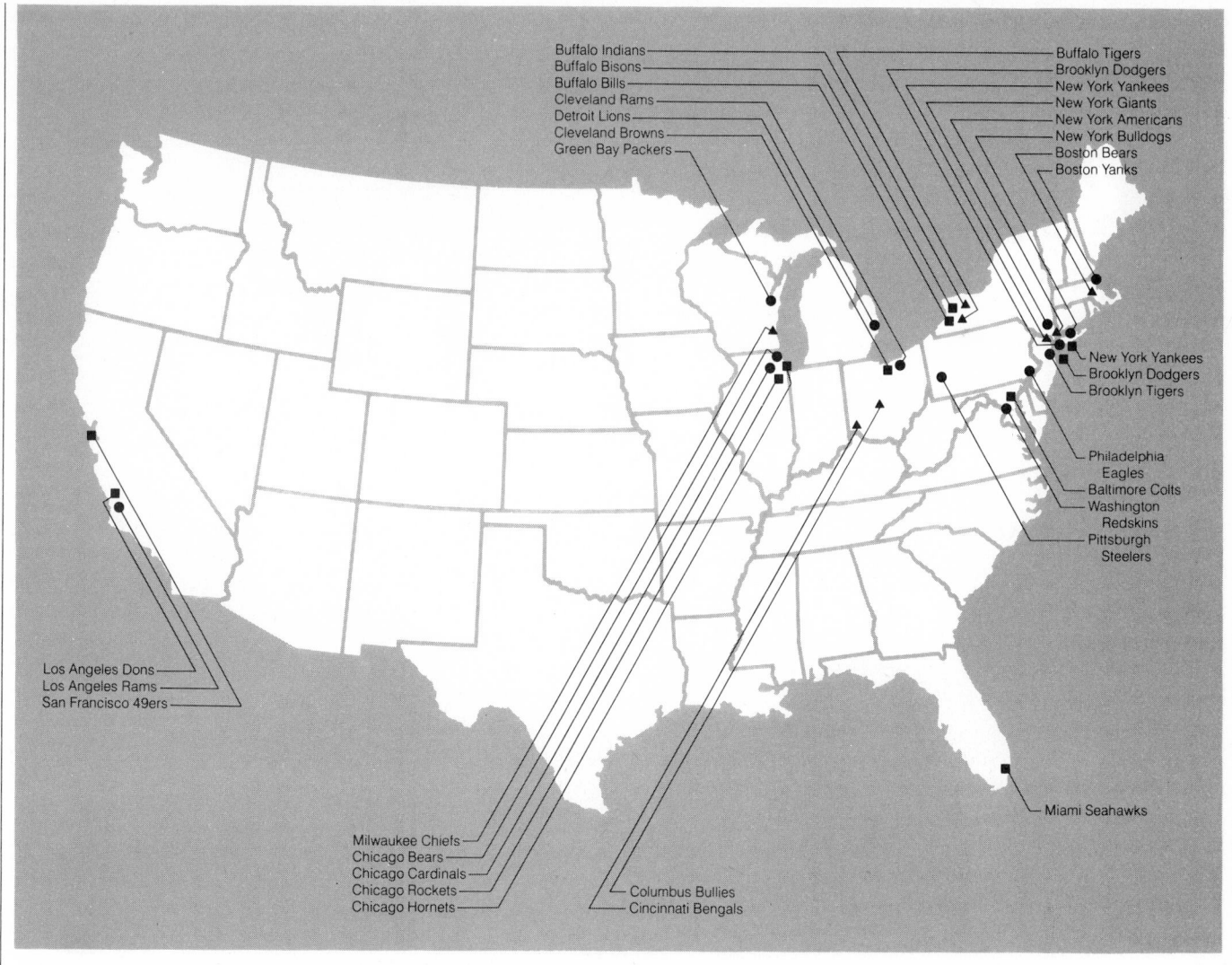

Buffalo Indians
Buffalo Bisons
Buffalo Bills
Cleveland Rams
Detroit Lions
Cleveland Browns
Green Bay Packers

Buffalo Tigers
Brooklyn Dodgers
New York Yankees
New York Giants
New York Americans
New York Bulldogs
Boston Bears
Boston Yanks

New York Yankees
Brooklyn Dodgers
Brooklyn Tigers

Philadelphia Eagles
Baltimore Colts
Washington Redskins
Pittsburgh Steelers

Miami Seahawks

Los Angeles Dons
Los Angeles Rams
San Francisco 49ers

Milwaukee Chiefs
Chicago Bears
Chicago Cardinals
Chicago Rockets
Chicago Hornets

Columbus Bullies
Cincinnati Bengals

1940s

● NATIONAL FOOTBALL LEAGUE

Brooklyn Dodgers
Chicago Bears
Chicago Cardinals
Cleveland Rams
Detroit Lions
Green Bay Packers
New York Giants
Philadelphia Eagles
Pittsburgh Steelers
Washington Redskins
Boston Yanks
Brooklyn Tigers
Los Angeles Rams
New York Bulldogs
Philadelphia-Pittsburgh merger, 1943
Chi. Cardinals-Pittsburgh merger, 1944

▲ AMERICAN FOOTBALL LEAGUE, 1940-41

Boston Bears
Buffalo Indians 1940
Cincinnati Bengals
Columbus Bullies
Milwaukee Chiefs
New York Yankees
Buffalo Tigers 1941
New York Americans 1941

■ ALL-AMERICA FOOTBALL CONFERENCE, 1946-49

Brooklyn Dodgers 1946-48
Buffalo Bisons 1946
Chicago Rockets 1946-48
Cleveland Browns
Los Angeles Dons
Miami Seahawks 1946
New York Yankees 1946-48
San Francisco 49ers
Baltimore Colts 1947-49
Buffalo Bills 1947-49
Chicago Hornets 1949
Brooklyn-New York Yankees merger, 1949

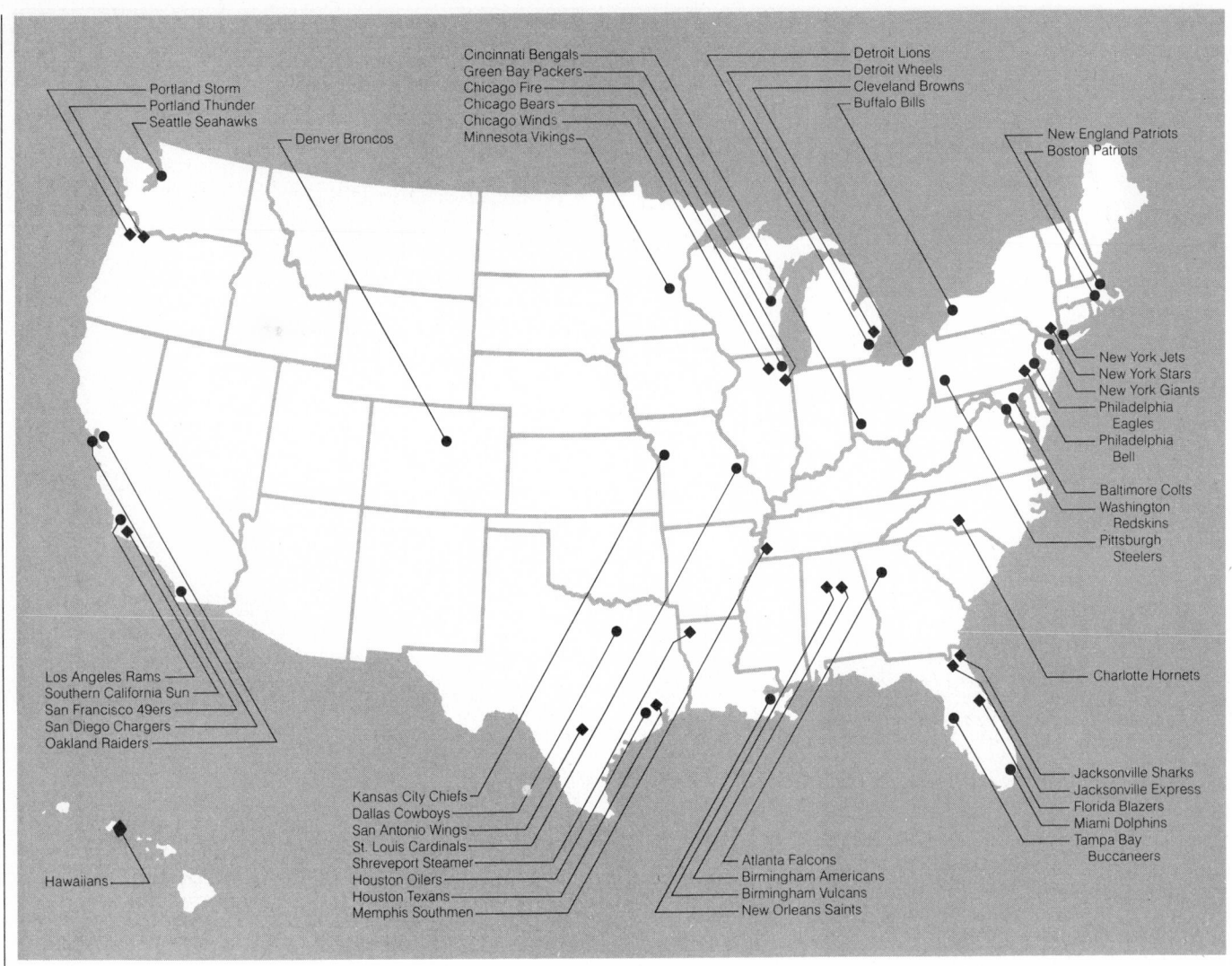

Portland Storm
Portland Thunder
Seattle Seahawks

Denver Broncos

Cincinnati Bengals
Green Bay Packers
Chicago Fire
Chicago Bears
Chicago Winds
Minnesota Vikings

Detroit Lions
Detroit Wheels
Cleveland Browns
Buffalo Bills

New England Patriots
Boston Patriots

New York Jets
New York Stars
New York Giants
Philadelphia Eagles
Philadelphia Bell

Baltimore Colts
Washington Redskins
Pittsburgh Steelers

Charlotte Hornets

Los Angeles Rams
Southern California Sun
San Francisco 49ers
San Diego Chargers
Oakland Raiders

Hawaiians

Kansas City Chiefs
Dallas Cowboys
San Antonio Wings
St. Louis Cardinals
Shreveport Steamer
Houston Oilers
Houston Texans
Memphis Southmen

Atlanta Falcons
Birmingham Americans
Birmingham Vulcans
New Orleans Saints

Jacksonville Sharks
Jacksonville Express
Florida Blazers
Miami Dolphins
Tampa Bay Buccaneers

1970s-1980s

● NATIONAL FOOTBALL LEAGUE

Atlanta Falcons
Baltimore Colts
Boston Patriots
Buffalo Bills
Chicago Bears
Cincinnati Bengals
Cleveland Browns
Dallas Cowboys
Denver Broncos
Detroit Lions
Green Bay Packers
Houston Oilers
Kansas City Chiefs
Los Angeles Rams
Miami Dolphins
Minnesota Vikings
New England Patriots
New Orleans Saints
New York Giants
New York Jets
Oakland Raiders
Philadelphia Eagles
Pittsburgh Steelers
St. Louis Cardinals
San Diego Chargers
San Francisco 49ers

Seattle Seahawks
Tampa Bay Buccaneers
Washington Redskins

◆ WORLD FOOTBALL LEAGUE, 1974-75

Birmingham Americans 1974
Birmingham Vulcans 1975
New York Stars 1974
Charlotte Hornets
Chicago Fire 1974
Chicago Winds 1975
Detroit Wheels 1974
Florida Blazers 1974
Hawaiians
Houston Texans 1974
Jacksonville Express
Jacksonville Sharks 1974
Memphis Southmen (Grizzlies)
Philadelphia Bell
Portland Storm 1974
Portland Thunder 1975
San Antonio Wings
Shreveport Steamer
Southern California Sun

EXTINCT TEAMS

The Green Bay Packers are a good model to help fully understand the roots of the National Football League. With a population of 85,000, the city of Green Bay is by far the smallest in the NFL. The Packers, it is often quipped, are the last-remaining "town team." At one time, the entire league was made up of what essentially were town teams.

The league had its origins in midwestern locales such as Green Bay, primarily in industrial cities of Ohio, Indiana, and Illinois. Of the 12 teams attending the NFL organizational meeting on September 17, 1920 at Canton, Ohio, in the Jordan and Hupmobile auto showroom of Ralph Hay, only two are in existence today. The Decatur, Illinois, Staleys are now the Chicago Bears, and the Racine Cardinals of Chicago have been located in St. Louis since 1960.

Gradually, as the league matured, the smaller midwestern franchises began to be replaced by teams from the more urban areas of the northeastern section of the county. The shifting of franchises was not always as clear cut as the relatively recent changes in locale, such as the Cardinals moving from Chicago to St. Louis, or the Dallas Texans becoming the Kansas City Chiefs in 1963. It was more of a case of one franchise folding and finding someone else to field a team in that city or another city where the pro game was popular.

In the so-called "rag days" (because of the finances and uniform conditions of many early teams) of pro football, the NFL's membership fluctuated from a high of 22 teams in 1926 to a low of 8 teams in 1932.

Several teams, now defunct, were in existence long enough to play a significant role in the shaping of the NFL. The majority of the teams that have disappeared, though, played only a season or so.

The Brooklyn Dodgers, who, like their baseball counterparts, played at Flatbush's Ebbets Field, were league members from 1930-1943. In 1944, the franchise changed its name to the Tigers. The following season, the last played under the manpower shortage of World War II, Brooklyn merged with the one-year-old Boston Yanks.

Three members of the Dodgers earned eventual enshrinement in the Pro Football Hall of Fame: end Morris (Red) Badgro, tackle Frank (Bruiser) Kinard, and halfback Clarence (Ace) Parker.

It was while Kinard and Parker played for the Dodgers that they scored several upsets over the Giants, and came within a game of winning Eastern Division titles in 1940 and 1941. During those years, the team was coached by Dr. John Bain (Jock) Sutherland, who became available to the pros after the University of Pittsburgh de-emphasized football because of "too much" success in the mid and late 1930s.

Other players of note throughout the Dodgers' history included Boyd Brumbaugh, Chris Cagle, Merlyn Condit, Beattie Feathers, Benny Friedman, Herman Hickman, John (Bull) Karcis, Ralph Kercheval, Bill Lee, Roy (Father) Lumpkin, Clarence (Pug) Manders, Paul Riblett, Perry Schwartz, Ralph Sivell, and John (Stumpy) Thomason.

To show how complicated finding one's NFL roots can be, take the case of the Dayton Triangles, one of the founding NFL teams in 1920 who exist today as the Baltimore Colts.

The 1929 Dayton Triangles became the 1930 Brooklyn Dodgers, who became the 1944 Brooklyn Tigers, who merged with the 1945 Boston Yanks, who became the 1949 New York Bulldogs, who became the 1950 New York Yanks (and were joined by many key players from the floundering Baltimore

Perry Schwartz of the Brooklyn Dodgers drives for a first down against Washington, 1941.

Colts in 1951), who became the 1952 Dallas Texans, who eventually became the re-born Colts in 1953.

It was the takeover of the Dayton franchise by Brooklyn in 1930 that signaled the move of NFL teams to metropolitan centers. The Triangles also were the first NFL team to sign Hawaiians. The University of Dayton enrolled students from Hawaii during the first part of the century, Walter (Sneeze) Achiu and Sam Hippa being the most notable Island players to go to the pros.

Other Triangles players included Francis Bacon, John Becker, Bill Belanich, Al Graham, Russ Hathaway, Ken Huffine, George Kinderdine, Lou Partlow, Dave Reese, Eddie Sauer, and Walter (Tillie) Voss.

The Colts, eventual heirs to the Dayton legacy, had parallel roots in Baltimore of the All-America Football Conference. They were one of three teams admitted to the NFL as part of the merger agreement between the AAFC and NFL in 1950.

After a 1-11-0 inaugural season in the NFL, the franchise disbanded. Several of the key players joined the New York Yanks for the 1951 season.

The Yanks, who had their own troubles in 1950, folded after the 1951 season.

Dallas was granted a franchise in 1952. The Texans included many of the players from the 1951 Yanks. This team had very little success, and, after four home games that did not draw well, the franchise was turned over to the league. The team was quartered in Hershey, Pennsylvania, and played the rest of its schedule on the road.

Baltimore then re-applied for an NFL franchise. A civic effort resulted in pledges and sales of 15,000 season tickets, and the league granted Baltimore the franchise for 1953.

Prominent players from the Boston Yanks, Baltimore Colts, New York Bulldogs, New York Yanks, and Dallas Texans who do not appear on other teams' rosters included Bruce Alford, Pat Cannamela, Bob Celeri, Bill Chipley, Ken Cooper, Frank (Boley) Dancewicz, Bob Davis, Don Deeks, Joe Domnanovich, Joe Golding, Bob Hazelhurst, Harvey Johnson, Eddie King, Vito Kissell, Lou Kusserow, Hank Lauricella, Pete Layden, Bob Livingston, Jim Magee, Vaughn Mancha, Darrell

Meisenheimer, Chet Mutryn, Johnny North, Jim Owens, John Petitbon, Rudy Romboli, Martin Ruby, Jack Russell, Orban (Spec) Sanders, Joe Sebastean-ski, Nick Scollard, George Sergienko, Jim Spavital, Ken Steinmetz, Art Tait, Sam Tamburo, Jim Tyree, Carroll Vogelaar, Art Weiner, and John Wozniak.

Several early NFL championships were won by defunct teams. Perhaps the best known of these was the Canton, Ohio, Bulldogs. The Bulldogs, one of the first pro football powers, were led by Jim Thorpe in their pre-NFL years. Thorpe had been brought to the Bulldogs from the Pine Village, Indiana, team in 1915 by Jack Cusack, a Canton businessman. It was Thorpe, who earned $500 a game, and a nucleus of players from the pre-World War I days who made the Canton team a force in the first years of the NFL. Thorpe served as the first league president while playing in 1920, although he was voted the position to some degree to capitalize on his Olympic success and subsequent major league baseball and All-America football reputation.

Canton, along with the Akron, Ohio, Professionals, the Buffalo All-Americans, and the Decatur, Illinois, Staleys, claimed at least a share of the 1920 NFL championship. Despite hastily-arranged playoff games, no clear winner emerged, and to this day the NFL does not officially recognize a titlist for the first season, nor does it list formal standings.

Thorpe, who left Canton for Cleveland in 1921, was not the only quality player on the first Bulldogs team. Future Pro Football Hall of Famers Wilbur (Pete) Henry and Joe Guyon were on the roster. Other outstanding players included Howard (Cub) Buck, Pete Calac, John Kellison, George (Bull) Lowe, Roy (Ike) Martin, and Lou Smythe.

In other seasons, Canton's roster included Rudy Comstock, Wallace (Doc) Elliott, Gil Falcon, Cecil (Tex) Griggs, Roy (Link) Lyman, Robert (Duke) Osborn, Harry Robb, Ben Roderick, and Norb Sacksteder.

There was much movement on the part of players and teams in the pioneer days. This movement, as well as the use of college players playing under assumed names, was summed up best by Hall of Fame coach Earle (Greasy) Neale. Neale, himself an early nomad, said, "I recall playing end across from Knute

Rockne [Notre Dame's famed coach] on six different Sundays, with six different teams, with Rock using six different names."

Canton, coached by Guy Chamberlin (another member of the Pro Football Hall of Fame), won league championships in 1922 and 1923. When the team and Chamberlin moved to Cleveland in 1924, they again were league champions.

Another Canton team called the Bulldogs played in the NFL in 1925 and 1926. Many of the 1926 Canton players returned from the team that had moved to Cleveland. But the Bulldogs had lost their bite; 1926 was the last year for Canton in the NFL.

Thorpe, with help from former Carlisle and Canton teammate Guyon, formed an interesting early NFL entry in 1922.

The team was sponsored by the Oorang Airedale Kennels in Larue, Ohio, and played in nearby Marion as the Oorang Indians. Thorpe collected many native Americans for the team including Reggie Attache, Arrowhead, Big Bear, Black Bear, Leon Boutwell, Buffalo, Deadeye, Xavier Downwind, Eagle Feather, Gray Horse, Laughing Gas, Joe Little Twig, Lone Wolf, Bemus Pierce, Red Fang, Red Fox, Running Deer, Tom St. Germaine, Stillwell Sanooke, Baptiste Thunder, Tomahawk, Woodchuck Welmus, Bill Winneshek, and Wrinkle Meat.

The team featured authentic Indian costumes for pregame and halftime shows, during which the players performed a variety of tribal dances. Never very successful on the playing field, the Indians folded after the 1923 season.

The Akron team, which claimed a piece of the disputed 1920 title, made history by having Fritz Pollard as its coach. Although it was hardly noted at the time, Pollard was the first black to coach an NFL team. Only in later years was much made of the fact and an effort made to ascertain the role Pollard played in the handling of the team.

During Akron's NFL tenure (1920-26), Paul (Scotty) Bierce, Charley Copley, Jim Flower, Al Nesser, Paul Robeson (another black pioneer who was later noted as an actor and singer), Dick Stahlman, Elgin Tobin, and Milt Wilson were some of the more prominent players.

In 1925, Pottsville, Pennsylvania, entered a team in the NFL. With outside help from Frank Bucher, Russ Hathaway, Duke Osborn, Eddie Sauer, Herb and Russ Stein, to augment a nucleus of players from the state's anthracite coal region, the Maroons won the league championship—and then lost it.

The area players included Charlie Berry, Harry Dayhoff, Howard (Fungy) Lebengood, Tony Latone, Frankie Racis, and Dick Rauch.

The lost or "stolen" championship, as it is still termed by local residents, has long been a matter of controversy. Pottsville beat the Chicago Cardinals 27-7 in a game that made them champions of the league. But they defied president Joe Carr's orders not to play a game a week later against an all-star team of former Notre Dame stars (including the Four Horsemen), and were stripped of the title by Carr.

Pottsville challenged for the league championship again in 1926, finishing second, but the team was gone by 1929. Some of the players went to a new Boston Bulldogs franchise for the 1929 season.

The Boston team was active only one season (1929), and was not connected with the franchise formed in 1932 known as the Braves, which eventually became the Washington Redskins.

Players from Pottsville and Boston (1929) included Johnny Blood (McNally), William (Hoot) Flanagan, Walter French, Pete Henry, George Kenneally, Walt Kiesling, Gibby Welsh, and Frank (Yank) Youngfleish.

Under Guy Chamberlin, the Frankford Yellow-

jackets, who represented a section of Philadelphia, won the 1926 NFL championship.

Because of the state's "blue laws," which prevented professional sports on Sundays in Pennsylvania, the Yellowjackets played Saturdays at home and often took an overnight train to play an out of state opponent the next day. Frankford entered the league in 1924 and played through 1931.

Standouts on the championship team, the fourth coached by Chamberlin in a five-year period, included Russ (Bull) Behman, Johnny Budd, Woodie (Doc) Bruder, Rae Crowther, Ernie (Tex) Hamer, Henry (Two Bits) Homan, Ben Jones, Dale (Hap) Moran, Houston Stockton, and Adolph (Swede) Youngstrom. Other prominent players from other years included Nate Barragar, Earl Britton, Wally Diehl, Eddie Halicki, Herb Joesting, Tom (Pottsville) Jones, Ken Mercer, Ray Richards, and Ed Weir.

The Steamroller of Providence, Rhode Island, is another team no longer in existence that won an NFL championship. Jimmy Conzelman, an early player and coach, led the team to the 1928 title. He later coached the Chicago Cardinals to division and league championships. Players included Bill Cronin, Tony Golembeski, Grady Jackson, Joe Koslowski, Olaf (Curly) Oden, Orland Smith, Art (Pop) Williams, and George (Wildcat) Wilson. The team was a league member from 1925 through 1931.

Buffalo had an NFL franchise from 1920-27 and in 1929. During the first years the team was known as the All-Americans. The 1924 and 1925 squads were called the Bisons, and the 1926 team was nicknamed the Rangers. The Bisons was the adopted name for the 1927 and 1929 seasons.

The 1920 team claimed at least a share of the league title and the All-Americans placed second in the league in 1921.

Players included Ben Lee Boynton, Bill Brace, Rudy (Swede) Hagberg, Tommy Hughitt, Jim Laird, Barney Lepper, Frank Morrissey, Bob (Nasty) Nash, Elmer Oliphant, Johnny Scott, and Pat Smith.

In 1926, All-America fullback Ernie Nevers of Stanford was second only to Red Grange as a publicized college player. So when coach Ole Haugsrud signed Nevers for the newly-formed Duluth Eskimos, it was big news.

The Eskimos were known as "The Ironmen of the North." They had a roster of about 15 players, and most of them played the full 60 minutes each game. After two early season home games, the Eskimos donned their unique white mackinaws, which advertised Nevers and the team on the back, and played a long succession of away games. During the 29-game 1926 season, Nevers played all but 26 minutes—missing most of that time in one game.

The Eskimos, thanks mainly to Nevers's Hall of Fame career, remain part of NFL folklore despite only two seasons in the league.

Prior to the Eskimos, the Duluth Kelleys held an NFL franchise from 1923-25.

Three members of the Pro Football Hall of Fame were Eskimos, Nevers, Walt Kiesling, and Johnny Blood (McNally). Other players included Jim Manion, Russ Method, Clem Neacy, the Rooney Brothers (Bill, Cobb, and Joe), Dewey Scanlon, and Jack Underwood.

Several of the NFL's charter teams existed for a short time only. The shortest duration belongs to Massillon, Ohio, the bitter rival of neighboring Canton. Massillon was given a franchise at the league's organizational meeting, but never fielded a team.

Chicago, although not represented at the 1920 meeting, had a franchise named the Tigers in the league's first year. Paul (Shorty) Des Jardien coached the team to a 1-5-1 record in its only season.

Cleveland was a charter NFL team known as the Tigers (no relation, except nickname, to the Chicago Tigers of the same season). When Jim Thorpe left Canton and joined Cleveland in 1921, the team nickname changed to the Indians. The team disbanded in 1923, but returned as the Bulldogs in 1924 and 1925. It was the 1924 team (with most of the players coming from Canton) that Guy Chamberlin coached to an NFL title. In 1926 the team again disbanded, with many of the players returning to Canton.

The Bulldogs (Cleveland) re-entered the league in 1927. Cleveland had no NFL franchise from 1928 until 1937, with the exception of the Indians in 1931.

Chamberlin, as a player-coach in 1924, surrounded himself with talent. Players included Scotty Bierce, Doc Elliott, Ben Jones, Link Lyman, Duke Osborn, and Walcott (Wooky) Roberts.

On the roster in other years were Hal Broda, Al Cornsweet, Hank Critchfield, Benny Friedman, Milt Ghee, Stan Keck, Claude (Tiny) Thornhill, and Ralph Vince.

The Columbus, Ohio, Panhandles were one of the legendary teams of the pioneering days of pro football. Although they were a charter franchise, they were a power for years before the NFL was organized.

The team name came from the fact that many of the players were employed in the repair shops of the Pennsylvania Railroad's Panhandle Division, which was located in Columbus. Because of their affiliation with the railroad, the players had rail passes and could ride without charge to distant games. For that reason, the Panhandles played mostly away games.

The nucleus of the team were the six Nesser brothers: Al (who played five seasons, and then another five with various NFL teams), Frank, Fred, John, Phil, and Ted.

In truth, most of the Nessers—and thus the team—were past their playing prime by the time they joined the NFL in 1920. Ted was 47 and Phil was 39.

Columbus fielded teams through 1926. The nickname changed to the Tigers in 1923. Besides the Nessers, players included Ray Eichenlaub, Paul Goebel, Andy Nemecek, Bob (Goldie) Rapp, and Lee Snoots.

Joe Carr, who was the league president in 1921, first became involved with pro football through the Panhandles prior to their joining the NFL. Carr served as NFL president until his death in 1939 and became a charter member of the Pro Football Hall of Fame.

The Detroit Heralds lasted only the charter season, as such, but put another team on the field after changing their name to the Panthers in 1921. The franchise was inactive from 1922-24, but returned in 1925 with Jimmy Conzelman as coach to finish 8-2-2.

After a mediocre 1926 season, the team disbanded until 1928, when they returned as the Wolverines. Benny Friedman paced that team to a third-place finish.

Detroit did not have an NFL franchise after 1928 until the Portsmouth, Ohio, Spartans were moved there for the 1934 season.

Notable players from the early Detroit teams included Carl Bacchus, John Barrett, Joe (Dinger) Doane, Elvin (Tiny) Feather, Al Hadden, Clarence (Steamer) Horning, and Rex Thomas.

Another charter team, the Hammond, Indiana, Pros won only five league games, but remained in the NFL for seven seasons.

Fritz Pollard served as head coach during the 1923 and 1924 seasons. Jay (Inky) Williams, one of the few early black players, was a mainstay for the Pros from 1922-26.

Other players included Dunc Annan, Sol Butler,

Frank Rydzewski, Len Sachs, and Rube Ursella.

The Muncie, Indiana, Flyers also were a charter NFL team, although they only played (and lost) one official game in 1920. After an 0-2-0 season in 1921, the team disbanded. One Flyers' player was Wilfrid Smith, later a sports editor of the *Chicago Tribune* and an NFL official.

Other players included Severin (Coonie) Checkaye, Chuck Helvie, Ken Huffine, and Pete Stone.

The Rochester, New York, Jeffersons, a charter team, too, played through the 1925 season.

The team, coached mainly by Leo Lyons, seldom won. Players included Oscar (Ockie) Anderson, Joe Bachmaier, Howard Berry, Ben Lee Boynton, John Dooley, Darby Lowery, Frank Matteo, Hank Smith and Ray Witter.

The Rock Island, Illinois, Independents played through the first six years of the NFL. Bobby (Rube) Marshall, an end, was one notable player. A black from the University of Minnesota, Marshall was 40 years old when he played the 1920 season.

Other players included Fred Chicken, Pat (Buck) Gavin, Ed Healey, Roddy Lamb, Sid Nichols, Eddie Novack, Fred (Duke) Slater, and Arnie Wyman.

Many early non-charter teams also came and went.

The Cincinnati Celts played only the 1921 season. They were coached by Bill Doherty, who also played center. Other players included Dave Dasstling, Guy Early, and Earl Hauser.

The Evansville, Indiana, Crimson Giants played the 1921 and 1922 seasons in the NFL.

Players included Bourbon Bondurant, Frank Fausch, Menzies Lindsey, Bob Slyker, and Travis Williams.

The Hartford, Connecticut, Blues played only the 1926 season. Players included Dilly Dally, Hec Garvey, Denny Gildea, Jim Manning, and Elbert (Mule) Werwaiss.

The Kansas City Cowboys became the league's western-most team when they joined the NFL in 1924. The Cowboys were the team with which Pro Football Hall of Fame coach Steve Owen first played professionally. The Cowboys played their last season in 1926 after placing fourth in a 22-team league. Leroy Andrews coached the Cowboys. Later, along with Owen, Andrews went to the New York Giants, where he became head coach. Players of note were Elbert Bloodgood, Chuck Corgan, Charlie Hill, Bill Owen, Milt Rhenquist, and Phil White.

Kenosha, Wisconsin, had an NFL franchise for one season—the Maroons in 1924.

Players included Irv Carlson, Walter (Pard) Pearce, George Seasholtz, Dick Stahlman, and Dick Vick.

In 1926 the National Football League attempted to become truly national. A franchise representing Los Angeles, the Buccaneers, was placed in the league. But it was strictly a traveling team, never hosting games on the West Coast. They disbanded after their initial season.

Several of their key players had outstanding college reputations from West Coast schools. Talma (Tut) Imlay (USC) and Harold (Brick) Muller (California) coached and played. Other players included Julian Ash (Oregon State), Ben Bangs (Washington State), Elmo (Tuffy) Maul (St. Mary's), Pete Schaffnit (California), and Al Yount (California).

The Louisville, Kentucky, Brecks lost all six of their league games during the two seasons they were in the NFL, 1922 and 1923. The team disbanded in 1924, and although Louisville was represented in the NFL in 1926, use of that city name was somewhat misleading.

Known as the Colonels, the 1926 team was actually based in Chicago, but played only away games—

The 1933 Cincinnati Reds turn out for passing practice: number 30 at right is Gil Lefebvre.

again without much success. They were 0-4-0.

Louisville players included Bob Karch, Jim Kendricks, and Gaylord (Pete) Stinchcomb.

With the exception of the 1923 team, which placed fourth in a 20-team league, the Milwaukee, Wisconsin, Badgers had only moderate success during their five years in the NFL, 1922-1926.

Fritz Pollard coached the team in 1922, and had Paul Robeson under contract. Duke Slater, also a black pioneer, played on the 1926 team.

Jimmy Conzelman coached the 1923 and 1924 squads. Notable players included Joe Alexander, Johnny Blood (McNally), LaVerne Dilweg, Joe (Red) Dunn, Alvin (Bo) McMillan, Henry (Heinie) Miller, Romanus (Peaches) Nadolney, Clem Neacy, Al Pierotti, Earl Potteiger, and Evar Swanson.

Minneapolis twice had entries in the NFL. The Marines played 1921-24 and the Red Jackets were league members in 1929 and 1930.

Herb Joesting, an All-America at the University of Minnesota in 1926 and 1927, coached the 1929 team and played on the 1930 team.

Other Marines/Red Jackets included Nate Barragar, Hal Erickson, Mal Nydall, Orrin Pape, Lee Wilson, and Sam Young.

The New York Yankees are of interest because of Red Grange's affiliation with them. Grange, who barnstormed with the Chicago Bears in late 1925 and early 1926, decided to form his own rival pro league with help from his manager Charles C. (Cash and Carry) Pyle.

Grange's American Football League lasted for only the 1926 season. Nevertheless, Grange was given an NFL franchise in New York, the Yankees, for the next season. After he was forced to miss the 1928 season because of a knee injury, the Yankees disbanded. Grange returned to the Bears in 1929.

Prominent Yankees included Roy (Bullet) Baker, Francis (Jug) Earpe, Ray Flaherty, August (Mike) Michalske, John (Bo) Molenda, Les Stephens, and Eddie Tryon.

A team called the Tornadoes played two seasons in the NFL—from Orange, New Jersey, in 1929 and from Newark in 1930.

Racine, Wisconsin's, membership in the NFL spanned four seasons, 1922-24 and 1926. The first entries were known as the Legion. The 1926 team was called the Tornadoes.

The teams consistently finished in the middle of the pack. Players include Wallace (Shorty) Barr, Roman (Kibo) Brumm, Al Elliott, Hank Gillo, Dick Halladay, George Hartong, Fred Johnson, Jake Minton, Johnny Mohardt, and Milt Romney.

St. Louis had a franchise in 1923 named the All-Stars. The team finished its only season with a 1-4-2 record.

Ollie Kraehe was player-coach. Players included Leroy Andrews, Al Casey, and Truman (Bud) Weller.

St. Louis next appeared in the NFL in 1934, when it merged with the Cincinnati Reds late in the season. Cincinnati fielded a team in 1933, which finished 3-6-1. After an 0-8-0 start the next year, the merger was arranged, and the combined Cincinnati/St. Louis team, which played under the name Gunners, won one of the last three games.

The most notable player of this combination was little (5 foot 6 inch, 157 pound) Gil LeFebvre, whose 98-yard punt return is still an NFL record—although it has since been tied twice.

Other players included Jim Bausch, Les Caywood, Myers (Algy) Clark, Les Corzine, Fait (Chief) Elkins, Benny LaPresta, Hilary (Biff) Lee, Jim Mooney, Lew Pope, Sigmund (Sandy) Sandberg, and Blake Workman.

The Staten Island Stapletons fielded teams in 1929, 1930, and 1931 before giving up their franchise. Players included Ken Strong, who eventually entered the Pro Football Hall of Fame after playing 1929 with the Stapes and many years with the New York Football Giants, Joe Demmy (Demyanovich), Tom Leary, Jim (Bing) Miller, Sammy Stein, Cy Williams, and Doug Wycoff.

The Toledo, Ohio, Maroons entered the NFL in 1922. They finished fourth in an 18-team league. After a 2-3-2 record in 1923, the team disbanded.

Players included Dunc Annan, Gil Falcon, Casimir (Hippo) Gozdowski, Cy (Truck) Myers, Tom (Tip) O'Neil, Jim (Red) Roberts, brothers Herb and Russ Stein, and Grady (Rat) Watson.

THE THREE EARLY AFLs

There have been four American Football Leagues—in 1926, 1936-37, 1940-41, and 1960-69. Each entered into competition with the NFL seeking parity with it as an entity of American sport. The fourth succeeded and is now the American Football Conference. The first three failed and are all but forgotten.

Timothy J. Mara purchased an NFL franchise for New York City in 1925. The Giants' games at the Polo Grounds drew small crowds and the team was losing money until the arrival of Red Grange. The great Illinois halfback, the "Galloping Ghost," finished his college career in mid-November, 1925, and within 10 days had signed a contract with the Chicago Bears and played in their then traditional Thanksgiving day game against the Cardinals. A record crowd of 38,000 watched at Wrigley Field. Then the Bears left on a barnstorming tour that would inestimably benefit pro football. When Grange played in the Polo Grounds in New York, 70,000 attended. It made Mara see the potential of pro football.

Grange's personal manager, C. C. (Cash and Carry) Pyle, informed the Bears that Grange would not play for them in 1926 unless he was given a five-figure salary and one-third ownership of the team. George Halas and Dutch Sternaman, owners of the team, refused.

So Pyle went to New York, the site of Grange's conquests the year before, and leased Yankee Stadium from the baseball team. He then petitioned the NFL for a franchise.

Mara, whose Giants played just across the Harlem River at the Polo Grounds, would not agree to that. But he and the other NFL owners did agree that a second franchise could be located in New York City provided it was at Ebbets Field in Brooklyn. This compromise was rejected by Pyle, who wanted an NFL team at Yankee Stadium. If he did not get it, he said, he would start his own league, which he did.

The AFL of 1926 was built around Grange and the Yankees. The other teams were the Boston Bulldogs, Brooklyn Horsemen, Chicago Bulls, Cleveland Panthers, Newark Bears, Philadelphia Quakers, and a road team listed as the Los Angeles Wildcats. In addition, the Rock Island, Illinois, Independents left the NFL to join the AFL. Politician and former Princeton athlete Bill Edwards was hired by Pyle to be commissioner of the AFL at a salary of $25,000, 10 times the $2,500 salary paid NFL commissioner Joe Carr. But it is believed that Edwards and AFL coaches and players never received their salaries in full.

New York Giants' coach Bob Folwell left to join the Philadelphia Quakers and so did the Giants' star tackle, Century Milstead. Al Nesser played for a time with the Cleveland Panthers. Mike Michalske played for the Yankees and Ray Flaherty for the Los Angeles Wildcats; both were NFL stars later with the Packers and Giants, respectively. Joey Sternaman, brother of the Bears' co-owner, formed the Chicago Bulls, who leased Comiskey Park, forcing the NFL Cardinals to move to smaller Normal Park.

Support of the AFL was minimal outside New York City. Rock Island dropped out. Newark's team disbanded and its players sued for their salaries. The Brooklyn Horsemen merged with the NFL Brooklyn Lions. Only the Yankees, Quakers, and the traveling Wildcats remained in business at season's end.

Mara of the Giants, who had suffered losses in the war with the AFL, wanted one more crack at it and challenged Pyle's Yankees to a game. Pyle agreed to it at first, then backed down. Mara turned to the Quakers, champions of the AFL. The Quakers, anxious to make a few extra dollars, agreed.

The New York Yankees' Red Grange (77) gets loose for a 55-yard touchdown against Boston, 1926.

The first AFL thus achieved in one year what other challengers to the NFL would not in the years ahead—an interleague playoff. The game the Quakers and Giants played December 12, 1926 has been called "the first Super Bowl." But the fact remains that the Giants had finished seventh in the NFL that year.

Bad weather engulfed the Polo Grounds on the day of the game and snow obliterated the yard lines. Only 5,000 persons watched as the Quakers managed only one first down and the Giants won 31-0.

As a lone concession to the AFL, the NFL extended membership to the Yankees the following season and they remained in the league for two more years until they went out of business.

1926 AFL STANDINGS	W	L	T	Pct.
Philadelphia Quakers	7	2	0	.778
New York Yankees	9	5	0	.643
Cleveland Panthers	3	2	0	.600
Los Angeles Wildcats	6	6	2	.500
Chicago Bulls	5	6	3	.455
Boston Bulldogs	2	4	0	.333
Rock Island Independents	2	5	1	.286
Brooklyn Horsemen	1	3	0	.250
Newark Bears	0	4	2	.000

Ten years after the demise of the first AFL, another rival league appeared having the same name. It lasted two years and it never had more than six teams as members. The Boston Shamrocks, New York Yankees, Pittsburgh Americans, and Rochester Tigers operated both seasons, 1936 and 1937. The Brooklyn Tigers and Cleveland Rams played only in 1936. And the Cincinnati Bengals and Los Angeles Bulldogs were part of the league only in 1937. Boston won the championship in 1936 and Los Angeles was the undefeated champion in 1937.

The second AFL had a team in Yankee Stadium called the Yankees. This was an obligatory feature of every rival league to operate in the years before the Giants quit the Polo Grounds and moved to Yankee Stadium themselves in 1956.

An AFL team called the Brooklyn Tigers set up shop at Ebbets Field to play home games while the Dodgers were on the road. Dodgers' owner Dan Topping objected strongly to the arrangement. Dr. Harry March, former team physician of the Giants, close friend of Tim Mara's, and author of a 1934 book

titled *Pro Football's Ups and Downs,* virtually the only history of the game written before 1940, was the AFL's president. March gave a curious explanation of the Brooklyn arrangement to the newspapers, saying that "continuous football at Ebbets Field . . . would work toward the benefit of both clubs, keeping football interest at a high pitch."

Mike Palm became coach of the Brooklyn Tigers. He gathered them in the Catskills for preseason practice. A New York newspaper wrote, "The home opening of the Brooklyn Tigers, a mysterious group of athletes sequestered, under the wing of Mr. Palm, somewhere around Bear Mountain at the moment, is slated for Oct. 15. It will be a night game against Cleveland."

It was this very league that made the second abortive attempt to establish pro football in Cincinnati. This time the name "Bengals" was adopted, and, while the pros failed again to take hold in the Ohio city, the nickname would reappear with another team—and one that would survive—32 years later.

The second AFL was the first league to have a Los Angeles franchise that did not play every game on the road. The hugely successful 1937 Bulldogs played two of their eight games at home at Gilmore Stadium in Los Angeles.

And in 1936 two teams from this league played the first pro game in a then insignificant arena in Miami that would grow into the Orange Bowl. Hank Soar scored two touchdowns to lead the Boston Shamrocks to a 14-6 victory over the New York Yankees. The Grange tour had stopped in Miami in 1925 during the Florida land boom, when the Bears and their opponents played in a ramshackle stadium that was thrown up overnight for the occasion and torn down the following day. This AFL game of 1936, then, played an important role in the history of a later and more permanent stadium. As sports editor Dinty Dennis of the *Miami Herald* wrote, "The game was the football 'swan song' for the wooden sports arena, E. E. Seiler, stadium manager [Ernie Seiler, later the empresario of breathtaking Orange Bowl shows], announcing the wrecking crews would go to work early this week to demolish the inadequate stands and make way for the new concrete Orange Bowl stadium."

Tom Harmon, 1940 Heisman Trophy winner, makes his pro debut, 1941, for the New York Americans.

Notable players were part of the second AFL. There were three well known former New York Giants in the league. Ken Strong played for the Yankees, Harry Newman for Brooklyn and Rochester, and Morris (Red) Badgro was player-coach of Rochester in 1936. Sid Gillman, later a famous coach and general manager, played end for the 1936 Cleveland Rams.

Difficulty struck the Yankees' franchise when, after an estimated 26,000 fans had already arrived for a game against the Pittsburgh Americans, vandals cut the wires lighting the outside of Yankee Stadium. According to a newspaper report, "With no lights available, ticket sellers could not operate and the drastic act of closing all gates was the only alternative as a milling throng assailed two police emergency squads which were rushed to the gates."

No such problems beset the champion Boston Shamrocks. A Boston paper wrote of "the customary scant crowd at Fenway Park" for a Shamrocks' game. A championship game was scheduled at Cleveland, but the Boston players refused to go because they were owed pay for past games. Boston was the league champion, anyway, because it had the best won-lost record.

1936 AFL STANDINGS	W	L	T	Pct.
Boston Shamrocks	8	3	0	.727
Cleveland Rams	5	2	2	.714
New York Yankees	5	3	2	.625
Pittsburgh Americans	3	2	1	.600
Rochester Tigers	1	6	0	.143
Brooklyn Tigers	0	6	1	.000

The AFL of 1937 had the first genuine Los Angeles franchise, the first to actually operate in that city. It was hoped, as a press release distributed with the schedule explained, that "the powerful Los Angeles club will provide the intersectional tang which has done so much to inspirit collegiate football....

"The Los Angeles club will come East and remain here to complete its away-from-home schedule, then return to its own gridiron to meet successive waves of league invasion."

In another attempt to stimulate public interest, the league announced that "Jack Dempsey, former heavyweight champion; Bing Crosby, screen and radio star; and Abraham Dreier, New York hotel owner, will serve as an advisory board."

The Los Angeles Bulldogs had operated as an independent team the year before they joined the AFL and reportedly defeated three NFL teams in exhibition games. They had a former USC tailback named Bill Howard, another runner of note named Ed (Crazylegs) Stark, and a barefooted punter named Bob Miller. They strengthened themselves with new players for 1937 and even tried unsuccessfully to arrange a film contract for Sammy Baugh of TCU to convince him to sign a contract with them; he signed with the Washington Redskins of the NFL instead.

Gus Henderson was the coach of the Bulldogs. He had been head coach at USC for six years and at the University of Tulsa for 11. He employed spread formations, something he called the "Befuddle Huddle," and details of coaching more often credited to coaches such as Paul Brown. They were described in a Rochester newspaper: "There is a set time for arising in the morning. Only special foods are allowed at the training table—at home and on the road. The players always travel in one group and never are allowed to separate without special permission from Coach Henderson."

The Bulldogs gained the distinction of being the only pro team ever to play out the entire period of its membership in a league without being defeated. They won every game on their eastern swing and then defeated the teams that came to California to play them. The league folded with the Bulldogs as its last

champions.

Los Angeles was left with a championship in 1937—and no team. But the second American Football League had given birth to a team in Cleveland called the Rams, which under new management applied for and gained NFL membership in 1937. Nine years later, it was this Rams team that left Ohio and moved west to Los Angeles.

1937 AFL STANDINGS	W	L	T	Pct.
Los Angeles Bulldogs	8	0	0	1.000
Rochester Tigers	3	3	1	.500
New York Yankees	2	3	1	.400
Cincinnati Bengals	2	3	2	.400
Boston Shamrocks	2	5	0	.286
Pittsburgh Americans	0	3	0	.000

Of all the rival leagues in history, six have been accorded major league status. Of those six, none was smaller, more poorly timed, or appears to have had less meaning than the third American Football League, which operated in 1940-41.

Organized at a meeting in Buffalo, it immediately faced a challenge over its right to call itself the "American Football League" because there was another group by that name, which had formerly been known as the Mid-West Professional Football League.

That crisis passed and the new AFL set up headquarters in Columbus, Ohio, the same city in which the NFL headquarters had been located since its inception. W. D. Griffith, former publicity director of Ohio State University, became president of the new AFL. And the Columbus Bullies won the league championship in both seasons the league operated.

The Milwaukee Chiefs, who had been denied an NFL franchise because the NFL said the Green Bay Packers had "territorial rights" to Milwaukee, joined the AFL. The league gave birth to another team called the New York Yankees, another called the Cincinnati Bengals, and new teams in Boston, the Bears, and in Buffalo, the Indians.

1940 AFL STANDINGS	W	L	T	Pct.
Columbus Bullies	8	1	1	.889
Milwaukee Chiefs	7	2	0	.777
Boston Bears	5	4	1	.556
New York Yankees	4	5	0	.445
Buffalo Indians	2	8	0	.200
Cincinnati Bengals	1	7	0	.125

The New York Yankees changed their name to the Americans for the 1941 season. The third AFL failed to sign many big-name players but former college stars John Kimbrough of Texas A&M and Tom Harmon of Michigan made their pro football debuts with the Americans October 19, 1941 in a 7-7 tie with the Columbus Bullies. Kimbrough made the all-league team even though he only played half the season.

Center Lee Mulleneaux of the Columbus Bullies had previously played with six different NFL teams and with the Cincinnati Bengals of the second AFL.

A game in Cincinnati was forfeited because the Bengals did not have enough players. The AFL's personnel troubles continued as Harmon and other players enlisted in the armed forces. Kimbrough was in Los Angeles making a movie when the plans were being laid for another season in 1942. As a Hall of Fame press release in later years explained, "World War II was undoubtedly the major reason why AFL number three met with failure, but there was nothing in its two-year existence to indicate any other eventual outcome."

1941 AFL STANDINGS	W	L	T	Pct.
Columbus Bullies	5	1	2	.833
New York Americans	5	2	1	.714
Milwaukee Chiefs	4	3	1	.571
Buffalo Indians	2	6	0	.250
Cincinnati Bengals	1	5	2	.167

THE AAFC

The All-America Football Conference of 1946-49 had a greater influence on professional football, reached more people, and made more inroads on the strength of the National Football League than any other rival league in history now defunct.

The AAFC produced the Baltimore Colts, Cleveland Browns, and San Francisco 49ers. It produced a host of players who went on to star in the NFL such as Otto Graham, Elroy (Crazylegs) Hirsch, Joe Perry, and Y.A. Tittle. It placed the first permanent franchise in California, the 49ers (they and the Los Angeles Dons were in business by those names before the Rams arrived from Cleveland).

The AAFC was the first league to play a 14-game regular season schedule; its teams played that many games in each of its first three years. It was the first to travel by air; it made charter arrangements with airlines while the NFL still rode trains. The AAFC occupied three big stadiums that no NFL team then used—Municipal Stadium in Cleveland, Memorial Coliseum in Los Angeles (which the Dons shared with the new Los Angeles Rams), and Yankee Stadium in New York—and with occasional big crowds in them the AAFC actually had a greater average attendance in the four years of its existence than the NFL—38,319 to 27,602.

Blacks had been part of pro football since the twenties, but they gained increased stature in the game through the play of AAFC stars such as Marion Motley and Bill Willis of Cleveland, Len Ford of Los Angeles, Buddy Young of the New York Yankees, and Joe Perry of San Francisco.

The new league also had a woman executive, vice-president Eleanor Gehrig, wife of the late baseball player Lou Gehrig.

The AAFC probably spawned the widespread use of zone defenses in pro football. It willingly hired college coaches and they had been teaching that kind of pass defense for years while man-for-man was the style in the NFL.

Finally, the AAFC hurt the NFL, signed many of its players, succeeded in getting college stars the NFL wanted, drained away fans and interest, and fought hard for its survival. It gave players an alternative, and NFL teams were forced to pay higher salaries. Those teams that did not became losers. That was how the AAFC, more than anything else, influenced professional football.

World War II weakened the NFL. The Cleveland Rams dropped out of the league one year. Pittsburgh merged its team with Philadelphia one season and with the Chicago Cardinals the next. Players were at such a premium that Bronko Nagurski, who had not worn a football uniform since 1937, rejoined the Chicago Bears and played for them in the 1943 championship game against Washington.

But there was a feeling that there would be prosperity as never before once the war ended. There was so much prosperity, in fact, that a second pro league seemed possible to many visionaries and there were men willing to finance it. Mickey McBride, owner of a taxicab company in Cleveland, had attempted unsuccessfully to buy the Rams. Oilman James F. Brueil, representing Buffalo, had deposited $25,000 with the NFL for a franchise. Anthony Morabito, owner of a lumber business in San Francisco, had been trying to arrange an NFL franchise for that city since 1940. Actor Don Ameche had asked his friend, sports editor Arch Ward of the Chicago Tribune, to help him get a team in the NFL.

The climate for sports seemed especially good in Chicago. The major commissioners of sport, Elmer Layden of football and Judge Kenesaw Mountain Landis of baseball, both had their offices there in the early forties. It was in Chicago that the great Bears' teams before the war had first played their T-formation with man-in-motion and in 1940 stunned the nation by winning the NFL Championship Game 73-0. And it was there that Ward, a canny newspaperman, had organized the baseball all-star game and football Chicago All-Star Game and established himself as a man with clout in the world of sport.

Ward's influence at his newspaper was considerable. The promotions he created convinced advertisers of the power of the Tribune. This won him the confidence of his publisher, Colonel Robert McCormick, and it was Ward who often represented the paper at Associated Press publishers' conventions.

Ward was considered a possibility for the commissionership of the National Football League in 1940. He turned it down. His name came up again in 1941 and he again refused it. But he recommended Elmer Layden, coach and athletic director at Notre Dame, and Layden was hired by the NFL.

Ward still did business with the NFL each year as the director of the Chicago All-Star Game between college players and the NFL champion. He wanted pro football to expand. He wanted to see an annual "world series of football." And he was frustrated that he could not get the NFL to admit his friend, Ameche, as a club owner. For all these reasons, Ward decided to organize a new pro football league that would begin its operations as soon as World War II ended.

Two other groups, the Trans-America League and the United States Football League, also planned to begin play once the war ended. But they faded from view as the AAFC began to gain momentum. The first meeting of the league was held in St. Louis in June, 1944. People representing Buffalo, Chicago, Cleveland, Los Angeles, New York, and San Francisco were present. Miami entered the league a year later. The New York investor withdrew and each AAFC team paid $75,000, and promised $25,000 from its gate receipts, to Dan Topping to move his Brooklyn Dodgers' team from the NFL to the new league. He purchased controlling interest in the baseball Yankees and his football team became the New York Yankees. A new franchise in Brooklyn secured Ebbets Field and took the name Dodgers.

The league chose to name itself "All-America Football Conference" because "All-America" was a popular sports term and it reflected the fact that the league stretched from border to border. Jim Crowley became its commissioner. He had been a member—along with NFL commissioner Layden—of the 1924 Notre Dame backfield that sportswriter Grantland Rice named the "Four Horsemen of Notre Dame."

Layden was present at the Chicago Tribune's annual pregame smoker the night before the All-Star Game in August, 1945. He learned that Ward was going to use the occasion to make an announcement about the All-America Football Conference. Layden decided to issue a statement about it through his press agent, George Strickler. Layden recalled later, "I reminded George that over the years there had always been talk about new professional leagues sprouting up and that as far as I was concerned the All-America Conference should 'first get a ball, then make a schedule, and then play a game.'"

The statement would be flung at Layden in print for the next four years. It is the thing that is most remembered from his commissionership, that (as expedient historians have simplified it) he said of the AAFC, "Tell them to get a football first."

Gerald Smith, vice-president of the Street & Smith publishing house that put out a popular annual football magazine, was one of the owners of the Brooklyn team. It hired Dr. Mal Stevens, an orthopedic surgeon, as coach and rented Ebbets Field.

Brueil, the oilman, owned the Buffalo team, called the "Bisons." He hired Sam Cordovano, who was replaced by Lowell (Red) Dawson as coach before the season began, and rented Memorial Stadium.

John L. Keeshin, owner of a race track, headed the Chicago Rockets. He said their name was "inspired by the new speed age in which rocket travel, even to the moon, is predicted." Dick Hanley was hired as Rockets' coach and Soldier Field was secured for the team's games.

McBride, owner of a Cleveland cab company, became president of the team he later named the Browns. Seeking a coach, he asked John Dietrich of the Cleveland Press, "Who is the best football coach in America?"

Dietrich replied, "Paul Brown." McBride hired the former Ohio high school and Ohio State University coach. And the Browns' owner rented 80,000-seat Municipal Stadium although the Cleveland Rams, who had now departed for Los Angeles, had played their regular season games in smaller League Park since 1942.

There were now two pro football teams in Los Angeles, where there had been none. Each scheduled its games at Memorial Coliseum. The AAFC Dons, owned by Ameche, Ben Lindheimer, and others, hired Dudley DeGroot as coach.

Miami Seahawks owner Harvey Hester hired Jack Meagher as coach and secured Orange Bowl Stadium. New York Yankees' owner Topping hired Ray Flaherty to coach his team at Yankee Stadium. And Morabito, founder of the San Francisco 49ers, named Lawrence (Buck) Shaw his coach and rented Kezar Stadium.

The AAFC teams had no trouble finding players. There were scores of them leaving military service or coming out of college football. Brooklyn signed tackle Martin Ruby of Texas A&M, captain of the 1946 College All-Stars, and Glenn Dobbs of Tulsa. Buffalo got Steve Juzwik of Notre Dame. Chicago's coach, Hanley, its most celebrated player, Elroy (Crazylegs) Hirsch, and many of its other players had been together on the team at El Toro Marine Air Base in California and were signed by the Rockets as a group. As a result, it was predicted that the Rockets would be the best team in the league.

One-hundred former NFL players eventually signed with AAFC teams. Cleveland signed Chet Adams of the Rams, saying his contract was with the Cleveland, not the Los Angeles, Rams. A court upheld the Browns' claim to Adams. Cleveland also signed Otto Graham of Northwestern.

Los Angeles lured all-pro tackle Lee Artoe away from the Chicago Bears and won a legal dispute honoring the contract it had signed with Angelo Bertelli of Notre Dame, winner of the Heisman Trophy. Miami got Hampton Pool of the Chicago Bears.

Orban (Spec) Sanders had been only a substitute at the University of Texas before World War II, but the New York Yankees, recognizing his potential, signed him to a three-year contract promising him $6,000, $17,000, and $25,000. New York also signed 1944 NFL most valuable player Frank Sinkwich of Detroit. "There is a strong possibility that this may form the basis of a little fight," said coach Gus Dorais of Detroit, but the Yankees kept Sinkwich. The New York team also received one player from each of the other teams in the league, an indemnity in addition to the $75,000 each team paid owner Topping to move to the AAFC.

San Francisco landed Norm Standlee, who had been a star for the Chicago Bears before the war, and Frankie Albert of Stanford.

Orban (Spec) Sanders of the AAFC New York Yankees, 1946. Earl Audet (42) of Los Angeles closes in.

Forty of the 66 College All-Stars signed with the AAFC. Chicago, Los Angeles, the New York Yankees, and San Francisco were heavily stocked with former service players.

There were enough players, commissioner Crowley said, "for a dozen leagues." The AAFC did not hold a draft its first year and the NFL held its draft in secret to avoid giving the AAFC a ready list of players to seek out and attempt to sign.

The Washington Redskins appeared to be the NFL team hardest hit by the AAFC signings. They lost their pre-war coach, Flaherty, to the New York Yankees; their 1945 coach, DeGroot, to Los Angeles; and a dozen of their players to various teams in the AAFC. They had been Eastern Divisions champions in 1945 but they did not win another championship of any kind for the next quarter of a century.

The AAFC's adoption of air travel was not so much an achievement as it was a necessity. No other league in any sport had ever attempted to play weekly games in cities as farflung as Los Angeles, San Francisco, and Miami. The charter contract with United Air Lines to carry AAFC clubs in DC-4 planes was called the largest such contract in history. ("The whole league is gonna fly!" said one smiling fan to another in the *Flyin' Dodgers* comic book.) And although there no doubt were suitable training camp sites nearby, the Dodgers trained in Bend, Oregon, the Chicago Rockets in Santa Rosa, California, and the Miami Seahawks in North Carolina.

The league schedule was a demanding one not only because of the unprecedented cross-country flights it entailed but also because it was a crazy quilt in which some teams played Sunday, others Friday night, and others at night in the middle of the week.

The Cleveland Browns won their first six games by a total score of 149-20. A crowd of 60,135 watched their regular season opener, when they crushed Miami 44-0. The crowd was a professional football record. It was broken weeks later in Cleve-

land when 71,134 watched a 31-14 victory over Los Angeles. Graham, the Browns' quarterback, led an attack that featured fullback Marion Motley and ends Dante Lavelli and Mac Speedie. The Browns won 12 of their 14 games and the league championship. Owner McBride promoted the team on his taxicabs, on billboards, and in radio advertising. He formed an all-girl band called the Musical Majorettes, who performed at halftime. The team drew 400,000 fans and made $200,000 in profits. Brown, who had signed as coach for a $25,000 salary and 15 percent of the profits, made $55,000 for the year.

Brooklyn won only three games, but tailback Glenn Dobbs was a sensational performer, leading the league in passing and punting. He was named the AAFC's most valuable player.

In the Dodgers' opening game, Dobbs came out of the game with a chipped bone in his hand. His coach, surgeon Dr. Mal Stevens, applied a flexible splint to the hand. Dobbs then went back in and led the Dodgers to a 28-14 victory.

Troubles struck the Miami Seahawks and Chicago Rockets. The Seahawks played home games on Monday nights. They did not have a very good team, and, although they were in Miami, they became the first pro team to be rained out twice in one season. The largest crowd of the season at their games was 9,700 and the smallest was 2,250. Their coach, Jack Meagher, resigned after six games and Hamp Pool was player-coach for the rest of the season. After the season, the AAFC paid $61,000 in salaries owed to Seahawks players, $19,000 owed to United Air Lines, and expelled the Seahawks from the league. Harvey Hester, the team's president, lost his life's savings of $51,000.

Instead of becoming one of the league's best teams as expected, the Chicago Rockets became one of its worst. Hanley, the coach, could not exert the discipline he had practiced as a Marine colonel and coach of many of the same players at El Toro Marine Air

Base. Early in the Rockets' season, the players demanded that Hanley be fired and he was replaced by a committee of players—Bob Dove, Ned Matthews, and Willie Wilkin. Hanley's former assistants, Pat Boland and Ernie Nevers, were left in limbo as the players' committee remained in charge for two games and in fact won both of them. The *Chicago Tribune* covered a practice in which Nevers passed the time by stripping to the waist and taking a sun bath. After two games, the team was placed in the hands of Boland and Nevers and it finished in last place.

Stevens, the Brooklyn surgeon and coach, resigned after seven games and was replaced by co-coaches Cliff Battles and Tom Scott.

The all-league team was made up of ends Alyn Beals of San Francisco and Lavelli of Cleveland; tackles Martin Ruby of Brooklyn and Frank (Bruiser) Kinard of the New York Yankees; guards Bruno Banducci of San Francisco and Bill Willis of Cleveland; center Bob Nelson of Los Angeles; quarterback Graham of Cleveland; halfbacks Dobbs of Brooklyn and Sanders of the New York Yankees; and fullback Motley of Cleveland.

Noting that costs were high, commissioner Crowley wrote in a magazine article that pro salaries had increased 100 to 200 percent. "Should the two leagues ever agree on a common draft and a hands-off policy, the figures will drop somewhat," he wrote. "But they will never go back to the days when a good lineman played for only $100 to $150 a game."

The minutes of a league meeting in San Francisco said that there was a "resolution of thanks and tribute to Mr. Ward drawn up—it was the first meeting he did not attend."

1946 AAFC STANDINGS

Eastern Division	W	L	T	Pct.	Pts.	OP
New York Yankees	10	3	1	.769	270	192
Brooklyn Dodgers	3	10	1	.231	226	339
Buffalo Bisons	3	10	1	.231	249	370
Miami Seahawks	3	11	0	.154	167	378

Western Division	W	L	T	Pct.	Pts.	OP
Cleveland Browns	12	2	0	.857	423	137
San Francisco 49ers	9	5	0	.643	307	189
Los Angeles Dons	7	5	2	.583	305	290
Chicago Rockets	5	6	3	.455	263	315

AAFC championship: Cleveland 14, New York 9

LEADING RUSHERS	Att.	Yards	Avg.	TD
Spec Sanders, New York	140	709	5.1	6
Norm Standlee, San Francisco	134	651	4.9	2
Vic Kulbitski, Buffalo	97	605	6.2	2
Marion Motley, Cleveland	73	601	8.2	5
Edgar Jones, Cleveland	77	539	7.0	4

LEADING PASSERS	Att.	Comp.	Yards	TD	Int.
Glenn Dobbs, Brooklyn	269	135	1,886	13	15
Otto Graham, Cleveland	174	95	1,834	17	5
Charlie O'Rourke, Los Angeles	182	105	1,250	12	14
Frankie Albert, San Francisco	197	104	1,404	14	14
Bob Hoernschemeyer, Chicago	193	95	1,266	14	14

LEADING RECEIVERS	No.	Yards	Avg.	TD
Dante Lavelli, Cleveland	40	843	21.1	8
Alyn Beals, San Francisco	40	586	14.7	10
Saxon Judd, Brooklyn	34	443	13.0	4
Ed King, Buffalo	30	466	15.5	6
Elroy Hirsch, Chicago	27	347	12.9	3

The failure of the Seahawks and the uncertain launching of the Rockets had embarrassed the All-America Football Conference. In 1947 there were more administrative changes, coaching changes, and symptoms of an illness that could be fatal—imbalance, a widening gulf between the league's haves and its have-nots.

But 1947 was, nevertheless, the greatest year in the brief history of the AAFC. Cleveland won the championship again and appeared more unbeatable than ever. And the league's teams in New York City and Los Angeles were exciting ones that won more games and attracted more fans than their NFL rivals.

There was no larger manifestation of faith in the league's future than that made by its commissioner,

Jim Crowley, who turned his back on the security of his five-year contract, resigned, and headed a group that purchased the struggling Rockets. In addition, Crowley became their coach.

There was another manifestation of faith in the league in New York. Larry MacPhail and Del Webb, co-owners with Dan Topping of the baseball Yankees, bought into his football team.

Crowley was replaced as commissioner by Admiral Jonas J. Ingram, former commander of the Atlantic fleet. He hired as his deputy Admiral O. O. (Scrappy) Kessing. These years were the period of the most intense participation in pro football by admirals; the Washington Redskins of the NFL were coached, with mixed success, by Admiral John (Billich) Whelchel in 1949.

AAFC commissioner Ingram moved the league offices to New York. Its address was: Empire State Building, New York 1, New York. The AAFC made a new charter agreement with Howard Hughes's Trans World Airlines and announced a more sensible schedule in which games were confined to Friday nights and Sunday afternoons, except that there would be two Thanksgiving Day games. The New York Yankees got a break in the schedule in that they would play Los Angeles and San Francisco on successive dates whereas all other clubs had to cross the Rockies twice; the Los Angeles Dons would have to fly to the East Coast three times.

Representatives seeking a franchise in Baltimore had attended early meetings of the AAFC in 1944 and 1945, but had been unable at first to rent a stadium for their games and missed being charter members of the league. Baltimore now entered the AAFC as its eighth city, replacing Miami. Robert H. Rodenberg was the principal owner of the Baltimore team, the Colts, and he hired Cecil Isbell to coach the team at Municipal Stadium.

The Bisons changed their name to the Bills.

National attention was focused on the San Francisco 49ers when owner Tony Morabito drafted Glenn Davis of Army and also traded for the rights to Davis's famous partner in Army's "Mr. Inside and Mr. Outside" backfield, Felix (Doc) Blanchard. Morabito wanted them to delay their 90-day furlough following their graduation from West Point and join the 49ers. There was a great national controversy about whether these men should pursue their army careers or sign professional football contracts. The War Department at last ordered them to abide by existing policy. Davis later played for the Los Angeles Rams, but Blanchard became a career Air Force officer.

Buddy Young of Illinois and George Ratterman of Notre Dame led the College All-Stars to a 16-0 victory over the Chicago Bears and then Young signed a contract with the New York Yankees and Ratterman with the Buffalo Bills.

The powerful Browns were the focus of widespread interest. When they opened their 1947 season by routing Buffalo 30-14, they were watched by the entire coaching staff of the Chicago Bears.

The most sensational AAFC trade occurred when the Dodgers sent most valuable player Glenn Dobbs to Los Angeles, which sent Angelo Bertelli to Chicago, which sent Bob (Hunchy) Hoernschemeyer to Brooklyn. Dodgers' coach Cliff Battles wanted Hoernschemeyer for his quarterback and the Dons wanted an exciting back to compete for attention in Los Angeles with the Rams' Bob Waterfield.

Dobbs made the Los Angeles Dons an exciting team that played before 304,177 fans, including a professional record crowd of 82,576 that watched the Dons lose to the New York Yankees 30-14 September 12 at the Los Angeles Coliseum.

John Strzykalski of San Francisco gained 906 yards. Otto Graham of Cleveland completed over 60

Arch Ward, founder of the AAFC.

percent of his passes and teammate Mac Speedie caught 67 passes. But by far the most sensational player of the year was single-wing tailback Spec Sanders of the New York Yankees. He rushed for 1,432 yards, a figure that would rank as one of the 10 best in history if the AAFC statistics had been accepted for the all-time pro football records. He also passed for 1,442 yards, gained 250 yards rushing in one game against Chicago October 24, had 450 yards of total offense November 9 against San Francisco, punted for a 42.1-yard average, and scored 19 touchdowns.

The AAFC game that is remembered more than any other was played November 23, 1947 at Yankee Stadium. The Yankees (9-2) took the field against the Browns (10-1) before a crowd of 70,060. The Yankees stunned the Browns by going ahead 28-0 in the first half, but Graham brought the Browns from behind in a stirring comeback that was climaxed when Lou Saban, who was playing in place of the injured Lou Groza, kicked the tying extra point and the game ended 28-28. The same two teams played three weeks later for the AAFC championship and Cleveland won 14-3.

Cleveland, New York, Buffalo, San Francisco, and Los Angeles all were winners, but Brooklyn, Baltimore, and the Chicago Rockets all had dismal records.

Graham was named most valuable player and the all-league team for 1947 was: ends Lavelli and Speedie of Cleveland; tackles Nate Johnson of the New York Yankees and Lou Rymkus of Cleveland; guards Bruno Banducci of San Francisco and Bill Willis of Cleveland; center Bob Nelson of Los Angeles; quarterback Graham; halfbacks Chet Mutryn of Buffalo and Sanders of the New York Yankees; and fullback Marion Motley of Cleveland.

1947 AAFC STANDINGS

Eastern Division	W	L	T	Pct.	Pts.	OP
New York Yankees	11	2	1	.846	378	239
Buffalo Bills	8	4	2	.667	320	288
Brooklyn Dodgers	3	10	1	.231	181	340
Baltimore Colts	2	11	1	.154	167	377
Western Division	**W**	**L**	**T**	**Pct.**	**Pts.**	**OP**
Cleveland Browns	12	1	1	.923	410	185
San Francisco 49ers . . .	8	4	2	.667	327	264
Los Angeles Dons	7	7	0	.500	328	256
Chicago Rockets	1	13	0	.071	263	425

AAFC championship: Cleveland 14, New York 3.

Paul Brown, Cleveland Browns.

LEADING RUSHERS	Att.	Yards	Avg.	TD
Spec Sanders, New York	231	1,432	6.2	18
John Strzykalski, San Francisco	143	906	6.3	5
Marion Motley, Cleveland	146	889	6.0	8
Chet Mutryn, Buffalo	140	868	6.2	9
Buddy Young, New York	116	712	6.1	3

LEADING PASSERS	Att.	Comp.	Yards	TD	Int.
Otto Graham, Cleveland	269	163	2,753	25	11
Bud Schwenk, Baltimore	327	168	2,236	13	20
Frankie Albert, San Francisco	242	128	1,692	18	15
George Ratterman, Buffalo	244	124	1,840	22	20
Spec Sanders, New York	171	93	1,442	14	17

LEADING RECEIVERS	No.	Yards	Avg.	TD
Mac Speedie, Cleveland	67	1,146	17.1	6
Dante Lavelli, Cleveland	49	799	16.3	9
Alyn Beals, San Francisco	47	655	13.9	10
Lamar Davis, Baltimore	46	515	11.2	2
Billy Hillenbrand, Baltimore	39	702	18.0	7

The member teams of the AAFC began to see by 1948 that the optimistic predictions they had made earlier for their attendance, income, and success in competing against the National Football League were not being realized. The outlook grew dimmer and dimmer for the league's weak teams. Wholesale ownership and coaching changes began, the commissioner made a novel and unsuccessful attempt to balance competition in the league, and for the first time there were public overtures made to the NFL for a merger.

New ownership headed by Robert C. Embry took over the Baltimore Colts. Branch Rickey, who ran baseball's Brooklyn Dodgers and Ebbets Field, took control of the struggling Dodgers football team. R. Edward Garn headed a Chicago civic group that purchased the Rockets.

The new coaches were Carl Voyles at Brooklyn, Ed McKeever at Chicago, Jimmy Phelan at Los Angeles, and Norman (Red) Strader for the New York Yankees in midseason.

AAFC commissioner Ingram ordered the strongest teams in the league to distribute some of their players to the weakest clubs in order to create more balance. The Yankees were the only team to abide by both the letter and the spirit of the directive. They apparently were even more generous than they needed to be and, with many of their best players scattered to other cities, dropped to a 6-8 record in 1948. New York never had a strong AAFC team again. The Browns, complying with Ingram's order, gave rookie quarterback Y. A. Tittle outright to the Baltimore Colts.

When committees from the two leagues met in December and issued a joint statement about their willingness to end the war, it was the first time the NFL officially recognized that the AAFC existed. In the talks, the NFL offered to take in Cleveland and San Francisco and let Lindheimer of the Dons' owning group buy into the Los Angeles Rams. An AAFC concession came when Topping of the Yankees offered to cease operations and be satisfied to collect rent from another team for Yankee Stadium. The discussions ended, however, when the NFL adamantly refused to admit any teams other than the Browns and 49ers. The AAFC decided to prolong the struggle another year.

The league's two best teams were together in the same division. Cleveland went through an entire season without losing a game for the first time, and San Francisco was 12-2. When they met in a regular season game at Cleveland, 82,769 were present. Quarterback Otto Graham of Cleveland passed for 25 touchdowns for the season and Frankie Albert of San Francisco had 29. In addition, the 49ers had a team rushing average of 6.1 yards per carry.

The Browns defeated the Yankees in New York on a Sunday, the Dons in Los Angeles the following Thursday (Thanksgiving Day), and the 49ers 31-28 in San Francisco three days later on Sunday—three victories in eight days.

Tailback Glenn Dobbs of Los Angeles passed for 405 yards in a game against the 49ers, but also threw seven interceptions that day and the Dons lost. Rookie quarterback Y. A. Tittle of the Baltimore Colts had 346 yards passing on just 11 completions, a 31.5 average per completion, in a game against the New York Yankees.

Two teams with .500 records, Baltimore and Buffalo, played off for the Eastern Division championship and the winner, Buffalo, lost the AAFC Championship Game to Cleveland 49-7.

Graham and Albert were named co-most valuable players. The all-league team was made up of ends Alyn Beals of San Francisco and Mac Speedie of Cleveland; tackles Bob Reinhard of Los Angeles and Lou Rymkus of Cleveland; guards Dick Barwegan of Baltimore and Bill Willis of Cleveland; center Bob Nelson of Los Angeles; quarterback Graham; halfbacks Chet Mutryn of Buffalo and John Strzykalski of San Francisco; and fullback Marion Motley of Cleveland.

1948 AAFC STANDINGS

Eastern Division	W	L	T	Pct.	Pts.	OP
Buffalo Bills	7	7	0	.500	360	358
Baltimore Colts	7	7	0	.500	333	327
New York Yankees	6	8	0	.429	265	301
Brooklyn Dodgers	2	12	0	.143	253	387
Western Division	**W**	**L**	**T**	**Pct.**	**Pts.**	**OP**
Cleveland Browns	14	0	0	1.000	389	190
San Francisco 49ers	12	2	0	.857	495	248
Los Angeles Dons	7	7	0	.500	258	305
Chicago Rockets	1	13	0	.071	202	439

Eastern Division playoff: Buffalo 28, Baltimore 17
AAFC championship: Cleveland 49, Buffalo 7

LEADING RUSHERS	Att.	Yards	Avg.	TD
Marion Motley, Cleveland	157	964	6.2	5
John Strzykalski, San Francisco	141	915	6.5	4
Chet Mutryn, Buffalo	147	823	5.6	10
Spec Sanders, N.Y. Yankees	169	759	4.5	9
Lou Tomasetti, Buffalo	134	716	5.3	7

LEADING PASSERS	Att.	Comp.	Yards	TD	Int.
Otto Graham, Cleveland	333	173	2,713	25	15
Glenn Dobbs, Los Angeles	369	185	2,403	21	20
Y. A. Tittle, Baltimore	289	161	2,522	16	9
George Ratterman, Buffalo	335	168	2,577	16	22
Frankie Albert, San Francisco	246	154	1,990	29	10

LEADING RECEIVERS	No.	Yards	Avg.	TD
Mac Speedie, Cleveland	58	816	14.1	4
Al Baldwin, Buffalo	54	916	17.0	8
Billy Hillenbrand, Baltimore	50	970	19.4	6
Dolly King, Chicago	50	647	12.9	7
Alyn Beals, San Francisco	45	591	13.1	14

The All-America Football Conference was always fully covered in the pages of the *Chicago Tribune*.

"Special Delivery" Jones, Los Angeles Dons, against Cleveland, 1947.

Buffalo's Steve Juzwik (88) eludes Los Angeles's John Kimbrough (77) at the Los Angeles Coliseum, 1947.

Paul Patterson, Chicago Hornets, 1949.

Arch Ward was the sports editor of the paper and the founder of the league. He was also the director of the Chicago All-Star Game, which matched the NFL champion and the College All-Stars. In 1949 all three came together in a critical issue with Ward at its vortex.

He promised the AAFC he would get its champion into the all-star game. The contract with the NFL was up and Ward told NFL owners he wasn't going to renew. Suddenly, however, Ward reversed himself and signed a new contract with the NFL, shutting out the AAFC.

A gleeful NFL celebrated and some people concluded in print that Ward had lacked faith in the ability of the AAFC to keep the all-star game alive. But Ward had actually suffered a rare defeat at his newspaper. The NFL owners had gone over his head. Warned by publicity director and former *Tribune* sportswriter George Strickler of Ward's influence with Col. McCormick, the publisher, the NFL went instead to managing editor J. Loy Maloney, who put the question before the paper's board of directors. The board renewed the NFL's contract.

Crushed, the AAFC staggered on. The Brooklyn Dodgers, "Branch Rickey's white elephant," merged with the New York Yankees. The Baltimore Colts acquired their third president in three years, Walter S. Driskill. James C. Thompson and others purchased the struggling Chicago Rockets and renamed them the Hornets.

Lindheimer of the Dons, who apparently aided other clubs as well with outright payments, traded back Herman Wedemeyer to Baltimore and when the Colts said they could not handle his $12,000 contract, Lindheimer agreed to pay half of it.

The league's attendance dropped 30 percent from the previous year. Coaching shuffles were everywhere. Owner Driskill replaced Cecil Isbell as coach at Baltimore after four games; Driskill's record was 1-7. Clem Crowe became coach at Buffalo. Ray Flaherty, former Yankees coach, took over the Chicago Rockets. Of all AAFC coaches, only Paul Brown of Cleveland and Lawrence (Buck) Shaw of San Francisco coached their teams throughout the league's four-year existence.

Admiral Jonas Ingram resigned as commissioner and another nautical commissioner and Ingram's former deputy, O. O. (Scrappy) Kessing, took over. He said, "Our league is not dead, not dying, and not going to die."

It died in December, 1949. The merger was instigated by Horace Stoneham, owner of the baseball Giants and the Polo Grounds, where the football Giants played and which was one of the stadiums suffering from the malaise of the pro football war. Stoneham arranged a meeting between George Weiss of the baseball and football Yankees and Bert Bell, Commissioner of the NFL, in New York City. Out of this came a meeting between Bell and J. Arthur Friedlund, a lawyer who represented the All-America Football Conference. "They talked for a while there in New York and then came to Philadelphia [to Bell's office] two days ago," the *New York Mirror* reported. "Three days of round-the-clock conferences came to an end shortly after noon today and the two men, tired but jubilant, summoned reporters to break the news."

The Cleveland Browns, "the one prize the National League wants," Gordon Cobbledick wrote in the *Cleveland Plain-Dealer*, joined the NFL.

So did the San Francisco 49ers, because they were an exciting winning team and because NFL teams on the East Coast could go west and play both Los Angeles and San Francisco for the same amount of plane fare, and receive two cash guarantees from gate receipts.

The Baltimore Colts won only one game in 1949 but they came into the NFL, too. Owner George Preston Marshall of the Washington Redskins, who had been a fiery opponent of the AAFC, became convinced that Baltimore could become a strong rival—and one with little travel costs—for the Redskins. The *New York Times* reported, "It was Marshall's willingness to let the Baltimore Colts into the NFL which reportedly dissolved the four-year feud ... Marshall revealed he had cleared the way for Baltimore's admission by waiving his territorial rights for a 'nominal fee.' [The 'nominal fee' was $150,000.]

"Puffing on an Indian peace pipe for the benefit of photographers, Marshall called league Commissioner Bert Bell in Philadelphia to try to clear up some points about the armistice.

" 'Hello, peace pipe,' he greeted Bell. 'What league am I supposed to be in?' "

The Redskins were placed in the new American Conference of the NFL.

James F. Breuil, owner of the Buffalo Bills, received a 25 percent interest in the Cleveland Browns and the Browns were awarded three Bills' players —Rex Bumgardner, John Kissell, and Abe Gibron.

Six Brooklyn-New York Yankees players were awarded to the New York Giants, including Tom Landry, Otto Schnellbacher, Harmon Rowe, and Arnie Weinmeister. Some called it "the greatest input of talent in the Giants' history."

Ted Collins, owner of the NFL New York Bulldogs, was given a 10-year lease on Yankee Stadium.

He had moved his team from Boston to New York, expecting the AAFC to fold earlier, and when it did not he had had to share Horace Stoneham's Polo Grounds with the New York Giants.

Collins's team took the name New York Yanks and acquired the star backs of the old AAFC Yankees, Spec Sanders and Buddy Young. In other notable player shifts, end Len Ford of the Dons joined Cleveland and back Bob (Hunchy) Hoernschemeyer of the Yankees joined the Detroit Lions.

The interests of the Chicago Hornets were purchased by the league and the franchise was disbanded.

The merger agreement was announced the day before the Browns and 49ers were to play for the last championship, December 11, 1949. Only 22,000 fans watched as Cleveland won 21-7. The Browns then agreed to play a team of AAFC all-stars in Houston. Only a small crowd attended and the all-stars won 12-7.

The AAFC never named a most valuable player for 1949. The all-star team was made up of ends Alyn Beals of San Francisco and Mac Speedie of Cleveland; tackles Bob Reinhard of Los Angeles and Arnie Weinmeister of Brooklyn-New York; guards Dick Barwegan of Baltimore and Visco Grgich of San Francisco; center (an accommodation because he actually played linebacker) Lou Saban of Cleveland; quarterback Otto Graham of Cleveland; halfbacks Frankie Albert of San Francisco (an accommodation because he actually played quarterback) and Chet Mutryn of Buffalo; and fullback Joe Perry of San

Dick Barwegan of the Baltimore Colts, against Los Angeles, 1949.

Francisco.

The AAFC's all-time statistical champions were Marion Motley of Cleveland, rushing, 3,024 yards; Graham, passing, 592 completions, 10,085 yards, and 86 touchdowns; Speedie, receiving, 211; and Beals, scoring, 46 touchdowns and two extra points for a total of 278 points.

For a period of about two months after the merger, the NFL in its press releases and in newspaper articles was called the "National-American Football League." That ended in March and the name National Football League was restored.

Many reasons have been given why the AAFC failed. The Cleveland Browns had a 51-4-3 record and were too good for the rest of the league. If Cleveland and New York had been in the same division, there would have been a tighter race in the East and strong competition in the West between Los Angeles and San Francisco.

The AAFC was in direct competition with the NFL in New York, Chicago, and Los Angeles. During 1946-49, there were three teams in Chicago—the Bears, Cardinals, and Hornets-Rockets.

Former player Buddy Young says, "The weakness of the AAFC was in overall coaching and player depth. Some of the coaches had never been associated with pro football and didn't realize the necessity of having more than eleven or fifteen good players. In college, you could get by that way but in the pros you must have depth."

In a master stroke, NFL Commissioner Bell scheduled the AAFC champion Browns against the NFL champion Philadelphia Eagles on a Saturday night of the 1950 season, before the rest of the league's teams opened the following day. Cleveland won 35-10, lost only two games the entire season, and won the league championship.

1949 AFC STANDINGS	W	L	T	Pct.	Pts.	OP
Cleveland Browns	9	1	2	.900	339	171
San Francisco 49ers	9	3	0	.750	416	227
Brooklyn-N.Y. Yankees	8	4	0	.667	196	206
Buffalo Bills	5	5	2	.500	236	256
Chicago Hornets	4	8	0	.333	179	268
Los Angeles Dons	4	8	0	.333	253	322
Baltimore Colts	1	11	0	.083	172	341

Playoff: Cleveland 31, Buffalo 21
Playoff: San Francisco 17, Brooklyn-New York 7
Championship: Cleveland 21, San Francisco 7

LEADING RUSHERS	Att.	Yards	Avg.	TD
Joe Perry, San Francisco	115	783	6.8	8
Chet Mutryn, Buffalo	131	696	5.3	5
Marion Motley, Cleveland	113	570	5.0	8
Ollie Cline, Buffalo	125	518	4.1	3
Buddy Young, Brooklyn-New York	76	495	6.5	5

LEADING PASSERS	Att.	Comp.	Yards	TD
Otto Graham, Cleveland	285	161	2,785	19
Y. A. Tittle, Baltimore	289	148	2,209	14
George Ratterman, Buffalo	252	146	1,777	14
Frankie Albert, San Francisco	260	129	1,862	27
Bob Hoernschemeyer, Chicago	167	69	1,063	6

LEADING RECEIVERS	No.	Yards	Avg.	TD
Mac Speedie, Cleveland	62	1,028	16.6	7
Al Baldwin, Buffalo	53	719	13.6	7
Alyn Beals, San Francisco	44	678	15.4	12
Dan Edwards, Chicago	42	573	13.6	3
Lamar Davis, Baltimore	38	548	14.4	1

Len Ford, Los Angeles Dons, 1949.

THE WFL

The overwhelming success of the American Football League of 1960-69 set off an era of expansion in sport. By merging with the NFL, the AFL increased professional football to 26 teams. Baseball grew to 24. Rival basketball and hockey leagues, the American Basketball Association and World Hockey Association, appeared.

The latter creations were the work of Dennis Murphy, a southern California public relations man, and Gary L. Davidson and Donald J. Regan, lawyers who had an office across the hall from Murphy in a building in Newport Beach. Davidson became the first president of each league, the ABA in 1967 and the WHA in 1971.

He resigned the presidency of the hockey league in October, 1973 and began laying plans for a third creation, the World Football League. He took the title of commissioner and pursued buyers for franchises in the league. It was announced that the league "would eventually encompass the entire world."

Its first meeting took place in Los Angeles in January, 1974. Twelve franchises existed at the time or grew from that meeting. Their locations, their names, and their ownership changed often. Sometimes the owners were from the enfranchised cities and sometimes they were not.

The Birmingham Americans franchise was headed by Bill Putnam, a former Navy underwater demolition expert, vice-president of the J. P. Morgan Company in New York City, executive vice-president of Jack Kent Cooke Enterprises, owner of the Philadelphia Flyers of the National Hockey League, and president of the group controlling the Atlanta Hawks of the National Basketball Association and Atlanta Flames of the NHL. A former secretary named Carol Tygart Stallworth became part-owner and president of the Americans. Jack Gotta was hired as coach and the team arranged to play at Legion Field in Birmingham.

Nick Mileti, part-owner of baseball's Cleveland Indians, basketball's Cleveland Cavaliers, and hockey's Cleveland Crusaders, purchased a franchise he in turn sold to Tom Origer, an owner of apartment buildings in Chicago. This franchise became the Chicago Fire. Origer was the first owner to sign a player, wide receiver Jim Seymour. He named Jim Spavital his coach and secured Soldier Field for the Fire's games.

The Detroit Wheels became the property of a large groups of investors headed by Louis R. Lee, a 28-year-old Detroit lawyer and a former University of Michigan football player. The team's identity as a Detroit franchise was strained when it arranged to play at Rynearson Stadium on the campus of Eastern Michigan University, 37 miles away in Ypsilanti. Dan Boisture became the Wheels' coach.

The Florida Blazers had origins elsewhere. E. Joseph Wheeler, owner of a marine biology and engineering company, purchased a franchise he named variously as the Washington Capitals, the Washington-Baltimore Ambassadors, and the Washington Ambassadors. He was unable to lease RFK Stadium in Washington and moved the team to Norfolk, Virginia, in April. In May, he sold the team to a group headed by Rommie L. Loudd, which moved it to Orlando and named it the Florida Blazers. Jack Pardee had already been named coach of the team, which rented the Tangerine Bowl Stadium. Loudd had been an All-Pacific Coast end at UCLA in 1954 and 1955 and played with the Los Angeles Chargers and Boston Patriots of the AFL from 1960-62. He also scouted and coached for Boston.

A franchise that became The Hawaiians, in Honolulu, was originally started by Danny Rogers, manager of a sales firm and a former basketball coach. Chris B. Hemmeter, developer of restaurants and building projects in Hawaii, and Sam D. Battistone, the president of Invest West, which owned Sambo's restaurants, became owners of the Hawaiians. Mike Giddings was hired as their coach, and Honolulu Stadium the site of their home games.

Steve Arnold, a San Franciscan who once was the player agent of Jim Brown of the Cleveland Browns, owned a franchise the WFL first intended for Memphis but which became the Houston Texans. The Astrodome was rented and Jim Garrett became Texans' coach.

Fran Monaco, operator of medical laboratories and co-owner of a restaurant in Deland, Florida, with former Chicago Bears middle linebacker Dick Butkus, became the owner of the Jacksonville Sharks. He named his wife, Douglas, as the vice-president and they hired Bud Asher, the coach of New Smyrna Beach, Florida, High School to coach the Sharks. It was to play its games at the Gator Bowl Stadium.

The franchise of John Bassett, Jr., was originally the Toronto, Ontario, Northmen, but it became the Memphis, Tennessee, Southmen. Bassett, a millionaire Canadian, had interests in a television station, a newspaper, a film company, and Toronto's Canadian Football League team and World Hockey Association team. But he had to move his WFL team because of opposition from the CFL, which enlisted the Canadian minister of health and welfare in its cause. Memphis investors joining Bassett in the team's ownership included entertainers Charlie Rich and Isaac Hayes. John McVay was named coach of the Southmen and they rented Memphis Memorial Stadium.

The New York Stars had an active period of development. Howard Baldwin, 31-year-old president of the New England Whalers of the World Hockey Association, originally intended to form a team in Boston that was first called the Bulldogs, then the Bulls. It signed a player, wide receiver George Sauer, and hired a coach, Babe Parilli, while it was still the Bulldogs. Baldwin, however, could not find financial backing. Robert J. Schmertz, land developer and owner of the Boston Celtics of basketball, emerged as the Bulldogs' principal owner and moved them to New York, where they became the Stars. The site they preferred, Yankee Stadium, was undergoing renovation and the Stars found themselves at a serious disadvantage when they had to settle for aging Downing Stadium on Randall's Island.

The city of Philadelphia was represented at the first meeting of the WFL by Ken Bogdanoff, who had once been a lifeguard at an apartment complex in Philadelphia where future Birmingham owner Bill Putnam lived while he was owner of the Flyers hockey team. The two often talked sports at poolside. Bogdanoff later worked as assistant ticket manager of the Flyers, but he was unemployed at the time of the WFL meeting. With money borrowed from relatives, he and a partner raised $50,000 to make a down payment on a WFL franchise priced by Davidson at $400,000. The partner dropped out with his $25,000, however, and so did Bogdanoff on the morning of the organizational meeting. But at the request of the founders, he stayed to answer the roll call for Philadelphia. Control of the team was later passed to John B. Kelly, Jr., wealthy sportsman and Philadelphia city councilman, and then to attorney John Bosacco. The team, which was called the Bell, rented JFK Stadium and named Ron Waller as its coach.

Grant Gelker, an Orange County, California, businessman, founder of the Saddleback Inn chain of hotels and motels, and a friend of Davidson, headed a franchise originally intended for New York City but which finally was placed in Portland and became the Storm. Dick Coury became its coach and it leased Civic Stadium.

Larry G. Hatfield was, with Davidson, a member of the Balboa Bay Club at Newport Beach, California. Hatfield had become wealthy operating a computer and graphics company in Jackson, Mississippi, and then a trucking company in southern California. He formed the Southern California Sun. Al Lapin, head of the parent company of International House of Pancakes and Orange Julius chains, was also a Sun backer. The southern California team rented Anaheim Stadium and hired Tom Fears as coach.

Franchises in Tokyo and Mexico City were discussed but did not materialize.

The league held a draft of players and arranged a novel schedule in which each team would begin its season in July while the NFL teams were still in training camps, and the majority of the WFL's games would be played Wednesday nights. Each team would play 20 games and there would be no preseason. A contract was made with the independent TVS Television Network for one WFL game a week to be played Thursday night and shown on prime-time television. Never had pro football been played and televised nationally in midweek.

Making a schedule proved a difficult task. Hawaii adamantly insisted on Sunday games, saying midweek football would not go over in Honolulu. Detroit could not play a home game in a week when Eastern Michigan had a home game. Toronto moved to Memphis, and Washington moved to Virginia, then Florida. The problems were overcome, however, and a schedule was announced in May.

The schedule was not the WFL's only novelty. The league's singular instead of plural nicknames began with the Fire in Chicago; the Bell, Storm, and Sun followed. Changes in pro football rules were announced. The WFL voted to kick off from the 30-yard line instead of the 40; to move the goal posts from the goal lines to the end lines; to move in hashmarks; to ban fair catches of punts; to allow men in motion toward the line of scrimmage before the snap; to play a fifth quarter in the event of a tie; to require receivers to have only one foot inbounds to make a legal catch; to prohibit bump-and-run against receivers once they're three yards past the line of scrimmage; to bring the ball back to the line of scrimmage instead of the 20-yard line after field goals missed from outside the 20 and fourth down passes incomplete inside the 20; and to count touchdowns as seven instead of six points and have an "action point" counting one point, to be made after a touchdown by either running or passing, not kicking. The WFL decided to use an invention called a "Dickerrod" instead of the orthodox chain unit for measuring down yardage. And the league at first intended to use a football with swirls painted on it, similar to the red, white, and blue basketball used in the American Basketball Association that Davidson once headed. It dropped the colored ball idea, however.

Despite its novelties, skepticism about the WFL prevailed until March 31, 1974 when owner John Bassett, Jr., of the team then known as the Toronto Northmen announced he had signed Larry Csonka, Jim Kiick, and Paul Warfield of the two-time Super Bowl champion Miami Dolphins to three-year contracts starting with the 1975 football season, a year away. What was described as a $3 million package for the three of them had iron-clad guarantees they would get the money whatever happened to the league.

Other signings followed. Bill Bergey of Cincinnati with the Florida Blazers; John Gilliam of Minnesota, Calvin Hill of Dallas, and Ted Kwalick of San Fran-

Gary Davidson, World Football League.

cisco with the Hawaiians; and Curley Culp of Kansas City and Daryle Lamonica of Oakland with the Southern California Sun. By June 4, WFL teams claimed the signings of 59 NFL players who were playing out their options and would be ready to join the WFL, most of them in 1975. The NFL was stunned and the Dallas Cowboys obtained a restraining order blocking the signing of other Cowboys' players.

Big crowds were reported at opening games of the WFL in mid-July. There was a revelation from Philadelphia, however, that dealt the league a heavy blow. The Bell had announced an attendance of 55,534 for its opening game against Portland and 64,719 for a game 15 days later against the New York Stars. But an official of the team admitted the figures were inflated. He disclosed that for tax purposes the team had actually reported having sold 13,800 tickets for the first game and 6,200 for the second; the rest of the tickets had been given away. Credibility of the league suffered from this news.

Four teams—one-third of the league—fell on hard times two months into the season. The league took over the operations of the Detroit Wheels and Jacksonville Sharks, and then both teams folded. The Houston Texans were moved to Shreveport, Louisiana, and became the Steamer, and the New York Stars moved to Charlotte, North Carolina, and became the Hornets.

Detroit's former general manager had asserted in his team's media book that the Wheels "could make an honest, qualified run at the WFL title in our first year." It did not, losing its first 10 games and drawing no crowd larger than 10,631. The owners of the team reportedly borrowed $265,000 from the league. Troubles continued. According to the *Washington Post,* the Wheels' trainer had to borrow athletic tape from other teams, the players had to bring their own towels, and the coach could not afford to have the games filmed. The team went bankrupt and listed debts of $2.5 million.

In Jacksonville, the owner reportedly borrowed $27,000 from his coach, Asher, and then fired him. Charlie Tate was named the new coach. Players went unpaid for several weeks and Commissioner Davidson visited them when they played in Southern California and handed out an estimated $65,000 in paychecks. The franchise was surrendered to the league October 8.

Difficulty in meeting the Astrodome rent contributed to the relocation of the Texans to Shreveport. In New York, the Stars averaged only 8,000 fans for six home games. On opening night, the keys to the ticket

Chris Hemmeter.

Anthony Davis, the WFL's leading rusher in 1975.

booths at Downing Stadium could not be located and the booths were broken open so tickets could be sold. Traffic in and out of the island stadium jammed often. Relocated in Charlotte, North Carolina, the team was taken over by a group led by Upton Bell, son of former NFL Commissioner Bert Bell and former general manager of the New England Patriots. Difficulties continued and in November the operator of a cleaning service, J. Rodney Ryan, filed suit against the team for money he was owed, and immediately after a game the Hornets had to surrender their jerseys, pants, and other equipment to sheriff's deputies bearing writs impounding the equipment.

Davidson resigned the commissionership October 29. Owners Origer of the Chicago Fire and Bassett of the Memphis Southmen were said to have urged his resignation. Origer, who said he had lost $750,000 to $800,000, apparently threatened to fold his team if Davidson did not quit. A month later, Hemmeter of Hawaii was named the new commissioner.

The WFL playoff structure went through several changes in which the field grew from four teams to six to eight, the latter only one less than the league membership. The playoff field was then reduced to three, then increased again to six. In the playoffs, Southern California Sun players Booker Brown, Kermit Johnson, and James McAlister did not play following a dispute and the Sun lost in the first round.

The "World Bowl" for the WFL championship December 5 at Birmingham matched two teams that reflected the league's troubles. The Birmingham Americans were supposed to have missed five payrolls in a row, the Florida Blazers fifteen. The Americans were hounded by creditors. Their players threatened to boycott the game and then changed their minds and agreed to play.

Florida was a sentimental favorite, *Sports Illustrated* wrote, "because of its greater deprivation." The team was under the operation of the league. A sale to a new owner had fallen through when, according to newspaper reports, it was learned the buyer was a convicted felon. Coach Jack Pardee and his assistants were providing the team with toilet paper for the locker room.

Alternate quarterbacks George Mira and Matthew Reed led the Americans to a narrow 22-21 victory for the championship. Mira was named the game's most valuable player. When it ended, a Florida player snatched the game ball and dashed away but Birmingham players caught up with him under the stands and, after a tussle, reclaimed the football.

The Americans' uniforms were repossessed after

the game by sheriff's deputies. The equipment was later sold as souvenirs by a sporting goods store.

Quarterback Tony Adams of Southern California and running backs J. J. Jennings of Memphis and Tommy Reamon of Florida were named tri-most valuable players in the league. Reamon reportedly did not receive any salary from the Blazers all season.

1974 WFL STANDINGS

Eastern Division	W	L	T	Pct.	Pts.	OP
Florida Blazers	14	6	0	.700	419	280
N.Y. Stars-Char. Hornets	10	10	0	.500	467	350
Philadelphia Bell	9	11	0	.421	493	413
Jacksonville Sharks	4	10	0	.286	258	358
Central Division	**W**	**L**	**T**	**Pct.**	**Pts.**	**OP**
Memphis Southmen	17	3	0	.850	629	365
Birmingham Americans .	15	5	0	.750	503	394
Chicago Fire	7	13	0	.368	446	622
Detroit Wheels	1	13	0	.071	209	358
Western Division	**W**	**L**	**T**	**Pct.**	**Pts.**	**OP**
Southern California Sun	13	7	0	.650	486	441
Hawaiians	9	11	0	.450	413	425
Portland Storm	7	12	1	.375	264	426
Hou. Tex.-Shrev. Steamer	7	12	1	.375	240	415

First round playoffs: Florida 18, Philadelphia 3;
Hawaiians 34, Southern California 14
Semifinals: Florida, 18, Memphis 15;
Birmingham 22, Hawaiians 19
"World Bowl": Birmingham 22, Florida 21

LEADING RUSHERS	Att.	Yards	Avg.	Long	TD
Tommy Reamon, Florida	386	1,576	4.1	55	11
J. J. Jennings, Memphis	322	1,524	4.7	21	11
Jim Nance, Houston-Shrev.	300	1,240	4.1	27	8
John Land, Philadelphia	243	1,136	4.7	46	8
Rufus Ferguson, Portland	260	1,086	4.2	74	6
LEADING PASSERS	**Att.**	**Comp.**	**Yards**	**TD**	**Int.**
Tony Adams, So. California	510	276	3,905	23	18
Jim (King) Corcoran, Philadelphia	545	280	3,631	31	24
Bob Davis, Florida	413	232	2,977	21	23
Virgil Carter, Chicago	358	195	2,629	27	16
John Huarte, Memphis	296	154	2,416	24	16
LEADING RECEIVERS	**No.**	**Yards**	**Avg.**	**Long**	**TD**
Tim Delaney, Hawaiians	89	1,232	13.8	42	8
Rick Eber, Houston-Shreveport	66	771	11.7	63	5
James McAlister, So. California	65	772	11.9	70	4
Dennis Homan, Birmingham	61	930	15.3	73	8
Alfred Jenkins, Birmingham	60	1,326	22.1	95	12
Ed Marshall, Memphis	60	1,159	19.3	56	19

The World Football League returned in 1975 saying it was a different organization altogether; it was now the New World Football League. All the debts from the first year would be paid, but no deadline was given. The statistics and records that had been made by the teams the first year appeared in the press manual "as a service to the media who may be interested in the continuity of such records."

"It should be noted, however, that last year's teams played for what is now legally known as the Football Creditor's Payment Plan, Inc., formerly known as

the World Football League, and now in Chapter Eleven reorganizational proceedings. This year's World Football League is a completely separate and distinctive league, even though some players and franchise locations are the same as the 'old' World Football League of 1974."

Ten teams were in fact in the same place. Every franchise except the hapless Detroit Wheels was resurrected. Everyone but three had new leadership; John Bassett, Jr., still controlled the Memphis franchise, John Bosacco still owned the Philadelphia Bell, and Upton Bell still led a group controlling the Charlotte team.

The Florida Blazers were moved to Texas to become the San Antonio Wings. Birmingham was now the Vulcans, Chicago the Winds, Jacksonville the Express, and Portland the Thunder. Sometimes Memphis was called the Southmen and sometimes it was called the Grizzlies.

Each ownership group was forbidden to sell for three years, and ordered to escrow $545,000 and make a $75,000 payment to league headquarters, which were relocated in New York. Each team was to adopt an austere budget and face inspection of its books every two weeks. Padding of attendance figures was strictly forbidden.

Hemmeter, the new commissioner, announced a profit-sharing concept that became known as the Hemmeter Plan. It called for players to share in the net income with their owners; if there was no income, the players would get the minimum salary, $500 a game for 20 games. The Hemmeter Plan did not affect the large contracts such as the ones made between John Bassett, Jr., and Larry Csonka, Jim Kiick, and Paul Warfield.

Two of a team's games would be exhibitions, for which players would get $200 a game. There would be no training camp pay.

The WFL schedule for 1975 called for Saturday night, not Wednesday night games, and had an oddity in that, because of a stadium conflict, there would be a regular season game between Charlotte and San Antonio during the exhibition part of the schedule. TVS did not renew its contract to televise WFL games. An experiment in which linebackers wore red pants, running backs green pants, receivers orange pants, defensive backs yellow pants, offensive linemen white pants, and defensive linemen black pants in exhibition games was roundly criticized and abandoned. The Dickerrod was dropped. And the league decided that for economy reasons only one game official, the referee, would travel; the other officials would be provided locally.

Bubba Bean

Bob Berry

Greg Brezina

Ray Brown

Ken Burrow

Jim Butler

Junior Coffey

Despite 300 points by the offense, the "Grits Blitz" defense broke down, allowing 388 points. After winning their first two games, the Falcons lost 9 of the next 11 and finished 6-10.

1980 Tight end Junior Miller and linebacker Buddy Curry both turned out to be promising draft picks. When the season began, the Falcons started slowly, posting a 3-3 record after six weeks. But with Bartkowski setting team passing records, the Falcons set a club record with a nine-game winning streak. On October 19, Bartkowski threw four touchdown passes against the Saints, and three weeks later he passed for a team-record 378 yards against St. Louis. The key victory in the streak occurred on October 26 against Los Angeles, when Bartkowski overcame a third-and-38 to throw a game-winning, 54-yard touchdown pass to Alfred Jackson in the waning moments of the game. Despite a return loss to the Rams in the regular season finale, the Falcons won their first NFC West title with a 12-4 record. Bartkowski passed for 3,544 yards and 31 touchdowns, with Alfred Jenkins catching passes for 1,025 yards.

1981 The Falcons dominated the first three quarters of their divisional playoff game with Dallas on January 4, but lost 30-27 when the Cowboys erupted for 20 points in the final period. On February 1, six Falcons played in the Pro Bowl, led by Bartkowski, who passed for a game-record 173 yards and a 55-yard touchdown to Jenkins. The 1981 season began in awesome fashion, as the Falcons crushed New Orleans, Green Bay, and San Francisco behind seven touchdown passes by Bartkowski. But having suffered some key injuries, Atlanta lost three in a row, falling to 6-6 late in the season. A 31-27 victory over Houston on November 29 boosted the Falcons' playoff chances, but they lost the last three games of the year to finish 7-9. Despite the losing record, the Falcons led the NFC in scoring with 426 points; the team's weak point was the defense, which allowed 355 points. Bartkowski threw 30 touchdown passes, while Jenkins led the league with 1,358 yards receiving and 13 touchdown catches. Andrews had his third straight 1,000 yard rushing season (1,301) and set a team record by catching 81 passes.

MEMBERS OF HALL OF FAME:
None

FALCONS RECORD, 1966-81

Year	Won	Lost	Tied	Pct.	Pts.	OP
1966	3	11	0	.214	204	437
1967	1	12	1	.077	175	422
1968	2	12	0	.143	170	389
1969	6	8	0	.429	276	268
1970	4	8	2	.333	206	261
1971	7	6	1	.538	274	277
1972	7	7	0	.500	269	274
1973	9	5	0	.643	318	224
1974	3	11	0	.214	111	271
1975	4	10	0	.286	240	289
1976	4	10	0	.286	172	312
1977	7	7	0	.500	179	129
1978*	9	7	0	.563	240	290
1979	6	10	0	.375	300	388
1980§	12	4	0	.750	405	272
1981	7	9	0	.438	426	355
16 Years	**91**	**137**	**4**	**401**	**3,965**	**4,858**

*NFC Wild Card Qualifier for Playoffs
§NFC Western Division Champion

RECORD HOLDERS

Rushing (Yards)	William Andrews, 1980	1,308
Passing (Pct.)	Bob Berry, 1971	60.2
Passing (Yards)	Steve Bartkowski, 1981	3,829
Passing (TDs)	Steve Bartkowski, 1980	31
Receiving (No.)	William Andrews, 1981	81
Receiving (Yards)	Alfred Jenkins, 1981	1,358
Interceptions (No.)	Rolland Lawrence, 1975	9
Punting (Avg.)	Billy Lothridge, 1968	44.3
Punt Ret. (Avg.)	Gerald Tinker, 1974	13.9
Kickoff Ret. (Avg.)	Dennis Pearson, 1978	26.7
Touchdowns (Total)	Alfred Jenkins, 1981	13
Field Goals Made	Nick Mike-Mayer, 1973	26
Points (No.)	Mick Luckhurst, 1981	114

COACHING HISTORY

1966-68	Norb Hecker*	4-26-1
1968-74	Norm Van Brocklin**	37-49-3
1974-76	Marion Campbell***	6-19-0
1976	Pat Peppler	3- 6-0
1977-81	Leeman Bennett	41-37-0

*Replaced after three games in 1968
**Replaced after eight games in 1974
***Replaced after five games in 1976

FIRST PLAYER SELECTED

1966	Tommy Nobis, LB, Texas
1967	Leo Carroll, DE (2), San Diego State
1968	Claude Humphrey, DE, Tennessee State
1969	George Kunz, T, Notre Dame
1970	John Small, LB, Citadel
1971	Joe Profit, RB, Northeast Louisiana
1972	Clarence Ellis, DB, Notre Dame
1973	Greg Marx, DT (2), Notre Dame
1974	Gerald Tinker, WR (2), Kent State
1975	Steve Bartkowski, QB, California
1976	Bubba Bean, RB, Texas A&M
1977	Warren Bryant, T, Kentucky
1978	Mike Kenn, T, Michigan
1979	Don Smith, DE, Miami
1980	Junior Miller, TE, Nebraska
1981	Bobby Butler, CB, Florida State
1982	Gerald Riggs, RB, Arizona State

ATLANTA FALCONS, 1966-81

Absher, Dick, LB, Maryland		1967-68
Acks, Ron, LB, Illinois		1968-71
Adams, Bob, TE, Pacific		1976
Adams, Brent, T, Tennessee-Chattanooga		1975-78
Allen, Grady, LB, Texas A&M		1969-72
Anderson, Anthony, RB, Temple		1980
Anderson, Taz, TE, Georgia Tech		1966-67
Andrews, William, RB, Auburn		1979-81
Auer, Joe, RB, Georgia Tech		1968

B

Bailey, Jim, DT, Kansas		1976-78
Bailey, Larry, DT, Pacific		1974
Barnes, Gary, WR, Clemson		1966-67
Bartkowski, Steve, QB, California		1975-81
Bean, Bubba, RB, Texas A&M		1976, 1978-79
Bebout, Nick, T, Wyoming		1973-75
Bell, Bill, K, Kansas		1971-72
Belton, Willie, RB, Maryland-Eastern Shore		1971-72
Benson, Duane, LB, Hamline		1972-73
Berry, Bob, QB, Oregon		1968-72
Bleick, Tom, S, Georgia Tech		1967
Bosley, Bruce, G, West Virginia		1969
Bowling, Andy, LB, Virginia Tech		1967
Bramlett, John, LB, Memphis State		1971
Breitenstein, Bob, G-T, Tulsa		1969-70
Brett, Walt, G, Montana		1976
Brezina, Greg, LB, Houston		1968-69, 1971-79
Brooks, Jonathan, LB, Clemson		1980
Brown, Ray, S, West Texas State		1971-78
Brunson, Mike, WR-RB, Arizona State		1970
Bryant, Charles, RB, Allen		1969
Bryant, Warren, T, Kentucky		1978-81
Bruke, Vern, WR, Oregon State		1966
Burrow, Ken, WR, San Diego State		1971-75
Burson, Jimmy, CB-S, Auburn		1968

Butler, Bobby, CB, Florida State		1981
Butler, Jim, RB, Edward Waters		1968-71
Byas, Rick, DB, Wayne State		1974-80

C

Cabral, Brian, LB, Colorado		1979
Cahill, Dave, DT, Northern Arizona		1969
Cain, Lynn, RB, USC		1979-81
Calland, Lee, CB, Louisville		1966-68
Campbell, Sonny, RB, Northern Arizona		1970-71
Cash, Rick, DE, Northeast Missouri		1968
Cavness, Grady, CB, Texas-El Paso		1970
Cerne, Joe, C, Northwestern		1968
Chesson, Wes, WR, Duke		1971-73
Childs, Henry, TE, Kansas State		1974
Claridge, Dennis, QB, Nebraska		1966
Coffey, Junior, RB, Washington		1966-67, 1969
Cogdill, Gail, WR, Washington State		1969-70
Coia, Angelo, WR, USC		1966
Collins, Sonny, RB, Kentucky		1976
Condren, Glen, DT, Oklahoma		1969-72
Cook, Ed, G, Notre Dame		1966-67
Cope, Jim, LB, Ohio		1976
Cordill, Ollie, WR, Memphis State		1968
Correal, Chuck, C, Penn. State		1979-80
Cottrell, Ted, LB, Delaware Valley		1969-70
Crowe, Larry, DB, Texas Southern		1975
Curry, Buddy, LB, North Carolina		1980-81

D

Dabney, Carlton, DT, Morgan State		1968
Davis, Brad, RB, Louisiana State		1975
Davis, Paul, LB, North Carolina		1981
Daykin, Tony, LB, Georgia Tech		1979-81
Dodd, Al, WR, Northwestern Louisiana		1973-74
Donohoe, Mike, TE, San Francisco		1968, 1970-71
Duich, Steve, G, San Diego State		1968
Dunaway, Dave, WR, Duke		1968
Dunn, Perry Lee, RB, Mississippi		1966-68

E

East, Ron, DT, Montana State		1976
Easterling, Ray, S, Richmond		1972-79
Eber, Rick, WR, Tulsa		1968
Eley, Monroe, RB, Arizona State		1975, 1977-78
Ellis, Clarence, CB, Notre Dame		1972-74
Enderle, Dick, G, Minnesota		1969-71
Esposito, Mike, RB, Boston College		1976-79
Etter, Bob, K, Georgia		1968-69

F

Farmer, Karl, WR, Pittsburgh		1976-77
Faumuina, Wilson, DT, San Jose State		1977-81
Ferguson, Jim, C, USC		1969
Fields, Edgar, DT, Texas A&M		1977-81
Fitzgerald, Mickey, RB, Virginia Tech		1981
Fitzgerald, Mike, CB-S, Iowa State		1967
Flatley, Paul, WR, Northwestern		1968-69
Fortner, Larry, QB, Miami, Ohio		1980
Francis, Wallace, WR, Arkansas-Pine Bluff		1975-81
Franklin, George, RB, Texas A&I		1978
Freeman, Mike, CB-S, Fresno State		1968-70
Fritsch, Ted, C, St. Norbert		1972-74

G

Gaison, Blane, DB, Hawaii		1981
Gallagher, Frank, G, North Carolina		1973
Garcia, Jim, DE, Purdue		1968
George, Steve, DT, Houston		1976
Geredine, Thomas, WR, Northeast Missouri State		1973-74
Germany, Willie, S, Morgan State		1972
Gilbert, Lewis, TE, Florida		1978-79
Gilliam, John, WR, South Carolina State		1976
Gipson, Paul, RB, Houston		1969-70
Glass, Glenn, WR, Tennessee		1966
Glazebrook, Bob, DB, Fresno State		1978-81
Goodwin, Doug, RB, Maryland-Eastern Shore		1968
Gotshalk, Len, T, Humboldt State		1972-76
Grimm, Dan, G-C, Colorado		1966-68

H

Halverson, Dean, LB, Washington		1970

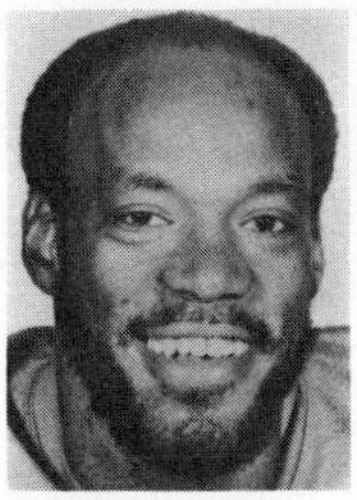
Dave Hampton

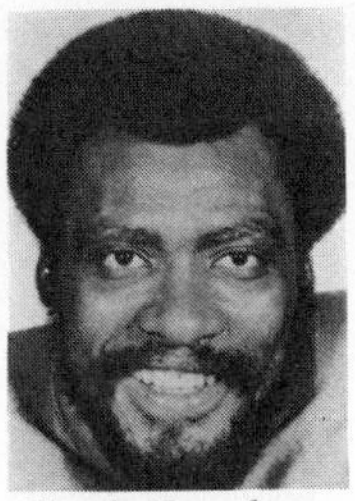
Claude Humphrey

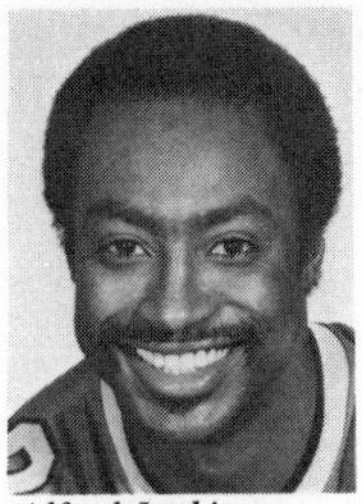
Alfred Jenkins

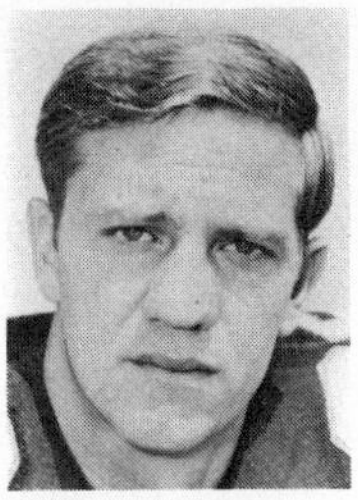
Billy Lothridge

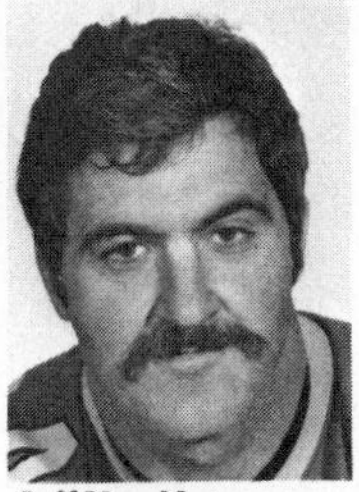
Jeff Van Note

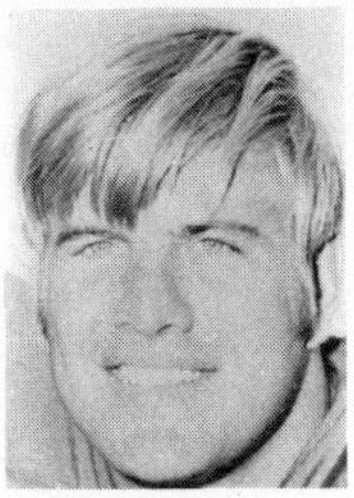
Harmon Wages

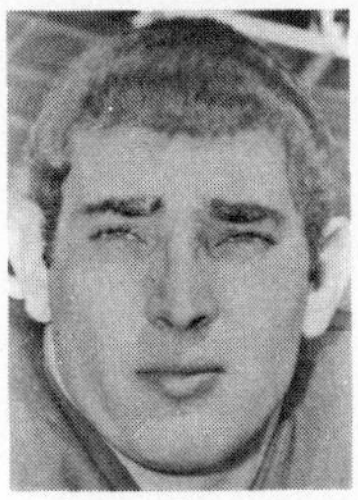
John Zook

Hampton, Dave, RB, Wyoming 1972-76
Hansen, Don, LB, Illinois 1969-75
Harmon, Tom, G, Gustavus Adolphus 1967
Harris, Bill, RB, Colorado 1968
Hart, Leo, QB, Duke 1971
Havig, Dennis, G, Colorado 1972-75
Hawkins, Alex, WR, South Carolina 1966-67
Hayes, Tom, CB, San Diego State 1971-75
Heck, Ralph, LB, Colorado 1966-68
Herman, Chuck, G, Arkansas 1980
Herron, Mack, RB, Kansas State 1975
Hettema, Dave, T, New Mexico 1970
Hilton, Roy, DE, Jackson State 1975
Holmes, Rudy, DE, Drake 1974
Howell, Pat, G, USC 1979-81
Hudlow, Floyd, CB-S, Arizona 1967-68
Hughes, Bob, DE, Jackson State 1967, 1969
Humphrey, Claude, DE, Tennessee State . . . 1968-74, 1976-78
Hunter, Scott, QB, Alabama 1976-78
Hutchinson, Tom, WR, Kentucky 1966

J

Jackson, Alfred, WR, Texas 1978-81
Jackson, Ernie, CB, Duke 1978
Jackson, Larron, G, Missouri 1975-76
James, John, P, Florida 1972-81
Jarvis, Ray, WR, Norfolk State 1971-72
Jenke, Noel, LB, Minnesota 1972
Jenkins, Alfred, WR, Morris Brown 1975-81
Jobko, Bill, LB, Ohio State 1966
Johnson, Kenny, DB, Mississippi State 1980-81
Johnson, Randy, QB, Texas A&I 1966-70
Johnson, Rudy, RB, Nebraska 1966
Jones, Bob, WR, San Diego State 1969
Jones, Bob, DB, Virginia Union 1975-76
Jones, Earl, DB, Norfolk State 1980-81
Jones, Jerry, DT, Bowling Green 1966
Jones, June, QB, Portland State 1977-79, 1981

K

Kay, Rick, LB, Colorado 1977
Kendrick, Vince, RB, Florida 1974
Kenn, Mike, T, Michigan 1978-81
Kindle, Gregg, G, Tennessee State 1976
Kirouac, Lou, G-K, Boston College 1966-67
Koeper, Rich, T, Oregon State 1966
Kuechenberg, Rudy, LB, Indiana 1971
Kunz, George, T, Notre Dame 1969-74
Kupp, Jake, G, Washington 1967
Kuykendall, Fulton, LB, UCLA 1975-81

L

Lamb, Ron, RB, South Carolina 1972
Laughlin, Jim, LB, Ohio State 1980-81
Lavan, Al, S, Colorado State 1969-70
Lawrence, Kent, WR, Georgia 1970
Lawrence, Rolland, DB, Tabor 1973-80
Ledbetter, Monte, WR, Northwestern Louisiana 1969
Lee, Bob, WR, Minnesota 1969
Lee, Bob, QB, Pacific 1973-74
Lee, Dwight, RB, Michigan State 1968
Lemmerman, Bruce, QB, Cal State-Northridge 1968-69
Lens, Greg, DT, Trinity, Texas 1970-71
Lewis, Mike, DT, Arkansas-Pine Bluff 1971-79
Linden, Errol, T, Houston 1966-68
Long, Bob, WR, Wichita State 1968
Lothridge, Billy, P-S, Georgia Tech 1966-71
Luckhurst, Mick, K, California 1981

M

Mabra, Ron, DB, Howard U. 1975-76
Mack, Red, WR, Notre Dame 1966
Mallory, John, S, West Virginia 1969-71
Malone, Art, RB, Arizona State 1970-74
Mankins, Jim, RB, Florida State 1967
Manning, Roosevelt, T, Northeastern Oklahoma 1972-75
Marchlewski, Frank, C, Minnesota 1966-68
Marshall, Randy, DE, Linfield 1970-71
Marshall, Rich, DT, Stephen F. Austin 1966
Martin, Billy, TE, Georgia Tech 1966-67
Marx, Greg, DT, Notre Dame 1973
Matlock, John, C, Miami 1970-71
Matthews, Henry, RB, Michigan State 1973
Maurer, Andy, G, Oregon 1970-73
Mayberry, James, RB, Colorado 1979-81
Mazzetti, Tim, K, Pennsylvania 1978-80
McCarthy, Brendan, RB, Boston College 1968
McCartney, Ron, LB, Tennessee 1977-79
McCauley, Tom, S-WR, Wisconsin 1969-71
McClain, Dewey, LB, East Central Oklahoma 1976-80
McCrary, Gregg, TE, Clark 1975, 1977
McDermott, Gary, RB, Tulsa 1969
McDonald, Tommy, WR, Oklahoma 1967
McGee, Molly, RB, Rhode Island 1974
McInnis, Hugh, TE, Southern Mississippi 1966
McIntyre, Secedrick, RB, Auburn 1977
McKinnely, Phil, T, UCLA 1976-80
McQuilken, Kim, QB, Lehigh 1974-77
Merrow, Jeff, DE, West Virginia 1975-81
Mialik, Larry, TE, Wisconsin 1972-74
Mike-Mayer, Nick, K, Temple 1973-77
Mikeska, Russ, TE, Texas A&M 1979-81
Miller, Jim, G, Iowa 1971-72, 1974
Miller, Junior, TE, Nebraska 1980-81
Mitchell, Ken, LB, Nevada-Las Vegas 1973-74
Mitchell, Jim, TE, Prairie View 1969-79
Montgomery, Marv, T, USC 1978
Moore, Tom, RB, Vanderbilt 1967
Moriarty, Tom, S, Bowling Green 1977-79, 1981
Moroski, Mike, QB, California-Davis 1979-81
Morris, Larry, LB, Georgia Tech 1966
Murphy, Robert, S, Ohio State 1981
Musser, Neal, LB, North Carolina State 1981

N

Neal, Louis, WR, Prairie View 1973-74
Nobis, Tommy, LB, Texas 1966-76
Nofsinger, Terry, QB, Utah 1967
Norton, Jim, DT-DE, Washington 1967-68

O

Ogden, Ray, TE, Alabama 1967-68
Ortega, Ralph, LB, Florida 1975-78

P

Palmer, Dick, LB, Kentucky 1974
Patton, Ricky, RB, Jackson State 1978
Pearson, Dennis, WR, San Diego State 1978-79
Pennywell, Robert, LB, Grambling 1977-80
Piper, Scott, WR, Arizona 1976
Plummer, Tony, S, Pacific 1971-73
Poage, Ray, TE, Texas 1971
Pridemore, Tom, S, West Virginia 1978-81
Pritchett, Billy Ray, RB, West Texas State 1976-77
Profit, Joe, RB, Northeastern Louisiana State 1971-73

R

Rassas, Nick, S, Notre Dame 1966-68
Ray, Eddie, RB, Louisiana State 1972-74
Reaves, Ken, CB, Norfolk State 1966-73
Rector, Ron, RB, Northwestern 1966-67
Redmond, Rudy, CB, Pacific 1969-71
Reed, Frank, DB, Washington 1976-80
Reed, Oscar, RB, Colorado State 1975
Reese, Guy, DT, Southern Methodist 1966
Richards, Bobby, DE, Louisiana State 1966-67
Richardson, Al, LB, Georgia Tech 1980-81
Richardson, Jerry, CB-S, West Texas State 1966-67
Ridlehuber, Preston, RB, Georgia 1966
Riggle, Bob, S, Penn State 1966-67
Roberts, Gary, G, Purdue 1970
Roberts, Guy, LB, Maryland 1976
Robinson, Bo, RB, West Texas State 1981
Rubke, Karl, DT-C, USC 1966-67
Rushing, Marion, LB, Southern Illinois 1966-68
Russ, Carl, LB, Michigan 1975
Ryckman, Billy, WR, Louisiana Tech 1977-79
Ryczek, Paul, C, Virginia 1974-79

S

Sabatino, Bill, DT, Colorado 1969
Sandeman, Bill, T, Pacific 1967-73
Sanders, Bob, LB, North Texas State 1967
Sanders, Eric, T, Nevada-Reno 1981
Scales, Charlie, RB, Indiana 1966
Schmidt, Roy, G-T, Long Beach State 1969
Scott, Dave, T, Kansas 1976-81
Scully, John, C, Notre Dame 1981
Shay, Jerry, DT, Purdue 1968-69
Shears, Larry, CB, Lincoln, Missouri 1971
Sherlag, Bob, WR, Memphis State 1966
Shiner, Dick, QB, Maryland 1971, 1973
Sidle, Jimmy, TE-RB, Auburn 1966
Sieminski, Chuck, DT, Penn State 1966-67
Silvestri, Carl, CB-S, Wisconsin 1966
Simmons, Jerry, WR, Bethune-Cookman 1967-69
Simon, Jim, G-T, Miami 1966-68
Sloan, Steve, QB, Alabama 1966-67
Small, John, DT, Citadel 1970-72
Smith, Don, DE, Miami 1979-81
Smith, Mike, WR, Grambling 1980
Smith, Ralph, TE, Mississippi 1969
Smith, Reggie, WR, North Carolina Central 1980-81
Smith, Ron, CB-WR, Wisconsin 1966-67
Smith, Royce, G, Georgia 1974-76
Snider, Malcolm, G, Stanford 1969-71
Snyder, Todd, WR, Ohio U. 1970-72
Sobocinski, Phil, C, Wisconsin 1968
Spiller, Phil, S, Cal State-Los Angeles 1968
Spiva, Andy, LB, Tennessee 1977
Stanback, Haskel, RB, Tennessee 1974-79
Stanciel, Jeff, RB, Mississippi Valley 1969
Steinfort, Fred, K, Boston College 1977-78
Stewart, Steve, LB, Minnesota 1978
Strahan, Art, DT, Texas Southern 1968
Strong, Ray, RB, Nevada-Las Vegas 1978-81
Suchy, Larry, CB, Mississippi College 1968
Sullivan, Jim, DE, Lincoln, Missouri 1970
Sullivan, Pat, QB, Auburn 1972-75
Szczecko, Joe, DT, Northwestern 1966-68

T

Talbert, Don, T, Texas 1966-68
Teague, Matthew, DE, Prairie View 1981
Ten Napel, Garth, LB, Texas A&M 1978
Thielemann, R.C., G-C, Arkansas 1977-81
Thompson, Woody, RB, Miami 1975-77
Tilleman, Mike, DT, Montana 1973-76
Tinker, Gerald, WR, Kent State 1974-75
Tolleson, Tommy, WR, Alabama 1966
Traynham, Wade, K, Frederick 1966-67

V

Van Note, Jeff, C, Kentucky 1969-81
Vinyard, Kenny, K, Texas Tech 1970

W

Wages, Harmon, RB, Florida 1968-71, 1973
Walker, Chuck, DT, Duke 1972-75
Walker, Cleo, LB, Louisville 1971
Warwick, Lonnie, LB, Tennessee Tech 1973-74
Washington, Joe, RB, Illinois State 1973
Waskiewicz, Jim, C, Wichita State 1969
Weatherford, Jim, S, Tennessee 1969
Weatherley, Jim, C, No college 1976
Wheelwright, Ernie, RB, Southern Illinois 1966-67
White, Lyman, LB, Louisiana State 1981
Whitlow, Bob, C, Arizona 1966
Williams, Joel, LB, Wisconsin-LaCrosse 1979-81
Williams, Sam, DE, Michigan State 1966-67
Wilson, Jim, C, Georgia 1967
Windauer, Bill, DT, Iowa 1976
Winkler, Randy, G, Tarleton State 1968
Woerner, Scott, DB, Georgia 1981
Wolski, Bill, RB, Notre Dame 1966
Wood, Bo, DE, North Carolina 1967
Wright, James, TE, Texas Christian 1978-79
Wright, John, WR, Illinois 1968
Wright, Nate, S, San Diego State 1969

Y

Yeates, Jeff, DT, Boston College 1976-81

Z

Zele, Mike, DT, Kent State 1979-81
Zook, John, DE, Kansas 1969-75

BALTIMORE COLTS

1952 A team called the Baltimore Colts had played in the All-America Football Conference from 1946-49 and in the National Football League in 1950, but that franchise folded. NFL Commissioner Bert Bell, facing a suit by Baltimore stockholders for reinstatement of a franchise in the city, turned over the defunct Dallas Texans team, which had won just one game that season, December 3. But Bell insisted that Baltimore sell 15,000 season tickets before he would grant the franchise. That goal was met by the end of December. There was no club ownership or organization.

1953 By the time the campaign ended, $300,000 was in the bank and Bell found an owner, Carroll D. Rosenbloom, a business executive who had played in the backfield for Bell when Bell was coaching at the University of Pennsylvania in 1927. At Bell's suggestion, Rosenbloom hired Donald S. Kellett, a television executive who had been a coach and star athlete at Penn, as general manager, January 23. Keith Molesworth was named coach at the same time. Rosenbloom took 51 percent of the stock and distributed the rest among William F. Hilgenberg, Zanvyl Krieger, Tom Mullan, Sr., and R. Bruce Livie. The team set up training facilities at Western Maryland College in Westminister. The team nickname, "Colts," was taken from the extinct Baltimore team. The Colts were placed in the NFL's Western Conference. The team colors were blue, silver, and white. It had notable players it had inherited from the Texans such as tackle Art Donovan, defensive end Gino Marchetti, and back Claude (Buddy) Young. The Colts stunned the Chicago Bears 13-9 in their first game, September 27. The team won three of its first five games, but then lost its last seven. Home crowds averaged 28,000.

1954 Molesworth was shifted to chief talent scout as the Colts prepared to start play in Baltimore's new Memorial Stadium. Rosenbloom and Kellett tried to get Cleveland assistant Blanton Collier as their head coach but settled instead on Browns' aide Wilbur C. (Weeb) Ewbank, May, 1954. The Colts won only three games under Ewbank, but he told Rosenbloom he would produce a champion within five years.

1955 Molesworth's scouting system began to pay off. Twelve rookies made the team, including quarterback George Shaw, fullback Alan Ameche, halfback L. G. Dupre, tackles Jack Patera and George Preas, and center Dick Szymanski. All became regulars. The team won five games and was fourth in the Western Conference.

1956 Four more important additions were made. Gene (Big Daddy) Lipscomb was picked up on waivers from Los Angeles. Lenny Moore was a first-round draft choice from Penn State. Billy Vessels, drafted first in 1953, joined the club after playing three seasons in Canada. And a lanky, bony-faced young man who had had a tryout with the Pittsburgh Steelers in 1955 responded to an 80-cent phone call from Kellett and joined the team to understudy Shaw. His name was Johnny Unitas. Shaw injured his knee during the season. The Colts tried to pry Gary Kerkorian away from law school to replace him. Kerkorian finally came but by that time the quarterback was Unitas. The season was erratic. Late in the year the team lost three games in a row and Ewbank's job was reported to be in jeopardy. But in the last game, Unitas threw a 53-yard scoring pass to beat Washington 19-17, December 23. Ewbank kept his job.

1957 Rosenbloom was named the team's president, February 4. Most of the personnel who would carry the Colts to the heights were assembled. Ends Ray-

Quarterback Johnny Unitas fakes in the 1959 NFL Championship Game against the Giants.

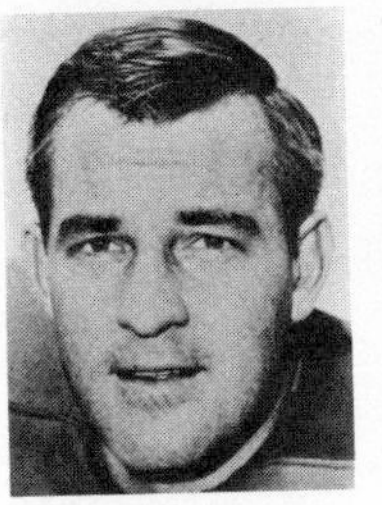

Jerry Hill

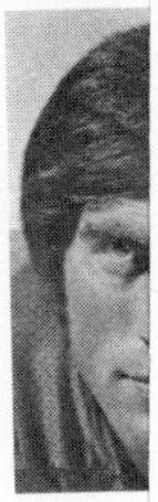

David L

Mayne, Lew, B, Texas. . . . .
Mayo, Ron, TE, Morgan State . . . .
Mazzanti, Gino, B, Arkansas . . . .
McCall, Reese, TE, Auburn. . . . .
McCauley, Don, RB, North Carolina. . .
McCormick, Len, C, Baylor. . . . .
McHan, Lamar, QB, Arkansas . . . .
McMillan, Chuck, B, John Carroll . . . .
McMillan, Randy, RB, Pittsburgh . . . . .
McPhail, Buck, RB, Oklahoma . . . .
Mellus, John, T, Villanova . . . .
Memmelaar, Dale, G, Wyoming . . . . .
Mendenhall, Ken, C, Oklahoma . . . . .
Mertes, Bus, B, Iowa . . . .
Meyer, Gil, E, Wake Forest . . . .
Michaels, Lou, DE, K, Kentucky . . . . .
Mike-Mayer, Steve, K, Maryland . . . . .
Mildren, Jack, S, Oklahoma . . . .
Miller, Fred, DT, Louisiana State . . . . .
Mioduszewski, Ed, B, William & Mary
Mitchell, Lydell, RB, Penn State . . . . .
Mitchell, Tom, TE, Bucknell . . . .
Mobley, Ruby, B, Hardin-Simmons . .
Mooney, Ed, LB, Texas Tech . . . .
Moore, Henry, B, Arkansas . . . .
Moore, Jimmy, G, Ohio State . . . .
Moore, Lenny, RB, Penn State . . . . .
Morrall, Earl, QB, Michigan State . . .
Morrison, Don, OT, Texas-Arlington .
Mosier, John, TE, Kansas . . . .
Moss, Roland, RB, TE, Toledo . . . . .
Mumphord, Lloyd, CB, Texas Southe
Munsey, Nelson, CB, Wyoming. . . . .
Murray, Earl, G, Purdue . . . .
Mutryn, Chet, B, Xavier . . . .
Mutscheller, Jim, E, Notre Dame . . .
Myers, Bob, T, Ohio State . . . .
Myhra, Steve, LB, K, North Dakota .

N

Neal, Dan, C, Kentucky . . . .
Nelson, Andy, DB, Memphis State . .
Nelson, Bob, C, Baylor . . . .
Nelson, Dennis, T, Illinois State . . .
Nemeth, Steve, B, Notre Dame . . .
Nettles, Doug, CB, Vanderbilt. . . . .
Newsome, Billy, DE, Grambling . . .
Nichols, Robbie, LB, Tulsa . . . .
Nolander, Don, C, Minnesota . . . . .
North, John, E, Vanderbilt . . . .
Nottingham, Don, RB, Kent State. .
Novak, Ken, DT, Purdue. . . . .
Nowaskey, Bob, DE, George Washi
Nowatzke, Tom, RB, Indiana. . . . . .
Nutter, Buzz, C, VPI . . . .
Nyers, Dick, B, Indiana Central . . .

O

O'Brien, Jim, K, WR, Cincinnati . .
O'Dell, Stu, LB, Indiana. . . . .
Oldham, Ray, S, Middle Tennessee
Olds, Bill, RB, Nebraska . . . .
O'Neal, Calvin, LB, Michigan . . . .
Orduna, Joe, RB, Nebraska . . . . .
Oristaglio, Bob, E, Pennsylvania .
O'Rourke, Charles, B, Boston Coll
Orr, Jimmy, E, Georgia . . . .
Orvis, Herb, DT, Colorado . . . . . .
Owens, Jim, E, Oklahoma . . . .
Owens, Luke, T, Kent State . . . . .
Owens, R. C., E, College of Idaho
Ozdowski, Mike, DE, Virginia . . . .

P

Page, Paul, B, Southern Methodis
Parker, Jim, T, G, Ohio State . . . .
Patera, Jack, LB, Oregon . . . . . .
Pear, Dave, DT, Washington . . . .
Pearson, Preston, RB, Illinois . . .
Pellington, Bill, LB, Rutgers . . . .
Pepper, Gene, G, Missouri . . . . .
Perina, Bob, B, Princeton . . . . . .

mond Berry and Jim Mutscheller joined Unitas, Ameche, Moore, and Dupre. The linemen included Art Donovan, Lipscomb, Marchetti, Don Joyce, and rookie Jim Parker. Patera, Don Shinnick, and Doug Eggers were capable linebackers. Rookies Milt Davis and Andy Nelson joined veterans Carl Taseff and Bert Rechichar in the secondary. An injury to Taseff seriously weakened the pass defense, but with two games to play the Colts were tied with San Francisco and Detroit for the Western Conference lead. Then they lost to the 49ers (17-13), December 8, and the Rams (37-21), December 15.

1958 Linebacker Leo Sanford and tackle Ray Krouse joined the team in trades and three rookies—halfback Lenny Lyles and defensive backs Ray Brown and Johnny Sample—made the team. The Colts won their first six games. The sixth was a 56-0 rout of the Packers but Unitas suffered fractured ribs and a punctured lung, November 2. Although Shaw played well in relief, Baltimore lost to New York 24-21. The defense was instrumental in a 17-0 win over the Bears, November 16. Unitas wore a special harness to protect his ribs and came back the next week. He threw a 58-yard pass to Moore on the first play from scrimmage and Baltimore romped over the Rams 34-7, November 23. By the end of the tenth game, and before they had to make what had become a "jinx" trip to the West Coast, the Colts had clinched their first division championship. New York won an Eastern Division playoff from Cleveland to advance to the championship game. Baltimore led the Giants 14-3 at halftime. In the third quarter, the Colts threatened to break the game open, marching to the Giants' 1-yard line. But the New York defense held. It was the Giants' turn—for two touchdowns and a 17-14 lead with two minutes to play. Baltimore was on its own 14. Unitas hit Berry on three short passes and, with seven seconds left, Steve Myhra kicked a 20-yard field goal that sent the game into sudden death overtime, the first ever in league play. The Giants got the ball first but had to punt. Baltimore took over on its 21. Unitas put together a brilliant drive. Finally, from the Giants' 8, he threw to Mutscheller for seven yards. Then Ameche ran through a gaping hole for the winning touchdown and a 23-17 victory, December 28. The Colts were greeted by 30,000 people at the airport.

1959 The Colts had a 4-3 record after losing to Washington 27-24, November 8. Baltimore regrouped in the last five games, however, scoring 28, 45, 35, 34, and 45 points in consecutive victories. In the final game, the Colts scored 21 points in the fourth quarter to come from behind to defeat Los Angeles 45-26 in the Los Angeles Coliseum, December 12. In the championship game, played before 57,545 in Baltimore, Unitas combined with Moore on a first-half touchdown but New York led 9-7 in the third quarter. After that it was all Colts, however. Unitas ran for a touchdown. Two interceptions by Sample and one by Andy Nelson set up three more scores as Baltimore won 31-16, December 27.

1960 Some of the championship edge was gone. The superb defensive unit was growing slower with age. Unitas suffered a fractured vertebrae high in his back early in the season, and, while he could still throw well enough, he was forbidden to run. So teams mounted an all-out rush against him. Ameche was benched. And the team's three top receivers—Berry, Moore, and Mutscheller—all were hurt. Baltimore came into the stretch with a 6-2 record, but lost four in a row and finished fourth. Unitas's 47-game touchdown passing streak was stopped by Los Angeles, December 11. But he set an NFL record with 3,099 yards passing.

1961 Running back Joe Perry was acquired in a trade with San Francisco. A jammed finger on his throwing hand slowed Unitas for much of the season. The highlight of a sporadic Colts' year was a 45-21 victory over eventual NFL champion Green Bay in Baltimore, November 5. The Colts finished with four victories in five games to tie for third place. Perry rushed for 675 yards.

1962 The Colts lost two close games to the Packers, 17-6, October 28, and 17-13, November 18, and had to win their last two games to finish 7-7. Unitas had an injury-free season, but his pass protection was suspect. Moore missed six games with a cracked kneecap. Perry gained only 359 yards.

1963 Rosenbloom changed coaches, signing a former Colts' defensive back, Don Shula, to replace Weeb Ewbank, January 8. Shula, who had been a defensive coach with the Detroit Lions, was only 33, but Rosenbloom said, "Football is a young man's game." Two Baltimore playing greats, defensive end Gino Marchetti and linebacker Bill Pellington, became player-coaches. Three other men who had helped the Colts to their 1958 and 1959 titles—Charley Winner, Don McCafferty, and John Sandusky—were retained on the coaching staff. A good nucleus was back in Unitas, Berry, Parker, Moore, Marchetti, and leading receiver Jimmy Orr, and the Colts looked more to youth than they had in years, with such rookies as tight end John Mackey, fullback Jerry Hill, tackles Bob Vogel and Fred Miller, and safety Jerry Logan. The team got off to a stumbling, injury-marred start but finished with five victories in its last six games and placed third.

1964 Rosenbloom purchased all remaining stock to gain full ownership, January 20. After an opening loss, the Colts won 11 games in a row, clinching their third Western Conference title by beating the Rams 24-7 in Los Angeles behind a strong defense, November 22. Baltimore scored a team high 428 points. Moore scored a then NFL record 20 touchdowns. Berry increased his then NFL career receiving total to 506. The defense forced opponents into 41 turnovers. The season was a huge success except for the NFL Championship Game with Cleveland, December 27. Neither team scored in the first half, but the Browns got 17 points in the third quarter behind Frank Ryan and Jim Brown and went on to win 27-0.

1965 Marchetti and Pellington retired as players. But the Colts still were a young team and players such as Dennis Gaubatz and Steve Stonebreaker filled in well. The Colts raced to a 9-1-1 record, and held first place in the Western Division. Then Unitas injured his back and number-two quarterback Gary Cuozzo suffered a shoulder separation. Shula had to make running back Tom Matte his quarterback. Matte responded with a dramatic performance that led the Colts past the Rams 20-17. He led the game's ball carriers with 99 yards, set up the deciding field goal, and handled the ball flawlessly. That victory got Baltimore into a Western Conference playoff with Green Bay. The undermanned Colts played courageously, taking the Packers into sudden death, but they were beaten 13-10 by a Don Chandler field goal, December 26.

1966 The Colts defeated the Cowboys 35-3 in the Playoff Bowl, January 9. Baltimore won seven of its first nine games. Unitas injured his shoulder and the team collapsed in the stretch run. The Colts continued to have trouble with the Packers—Vince Lombardi maintaining a seeming jinx over Shula—and two more losses to Green Bay (in five seasons Baltimore's record against the Packers was 2-9) helped consign the Colts to second place, three games behind Green Bay.

1967 The Colts won 20-14 over Philadelphia in the Playoff Bowl, January 8. Shula and newly named general manager Joe Campanella were made vice presidents, January 23. Campanella died, February 15. Publicity director Harry Hulmes was selected to become general manager. The top draft choices were defensive lineman Bubba Smith and safetyman Rick Volk. Under an NFL realignment, the Colts were moved into the Coastal Division. In a match of unbeaten Coastal Division teams, the Colts and Rams battled to a 24-24 tie in Baltimore, October 15. It all came down to a rematch in Los Angeles in the final game of the season, December 17. Baltimore had an 11-0-2 record; Los Angeles was 10-1-2. The winner would advance to the playoffs. Rams quarterback Roman Gabriel threw touchdown passes to Jack Snow, Bernie Casey, and Billy Truax, hitting 18 of 22 passes for 257 yards as the Rams won 34-10. Baltimore finished with an 11-1-2 record and its defense allowed a club low of 198 points, but the Colts did not make the playoffs because of the loss to the Rams who were also 11-1-2. Shula was named NFL co-coach of the year with Los Angeles's George Allen.

1968 Art Donovan became the first Colt to be enshrined in the Pro Football Hall of Fame, August 3. The Colts began the season by winning five games, before losing 30-20 to Cleveland, October 20. The Colts then put together an eight-game winning streak, highlighted by two victories over Los Angeles and one over Green Bay. Baltimore ran its win-

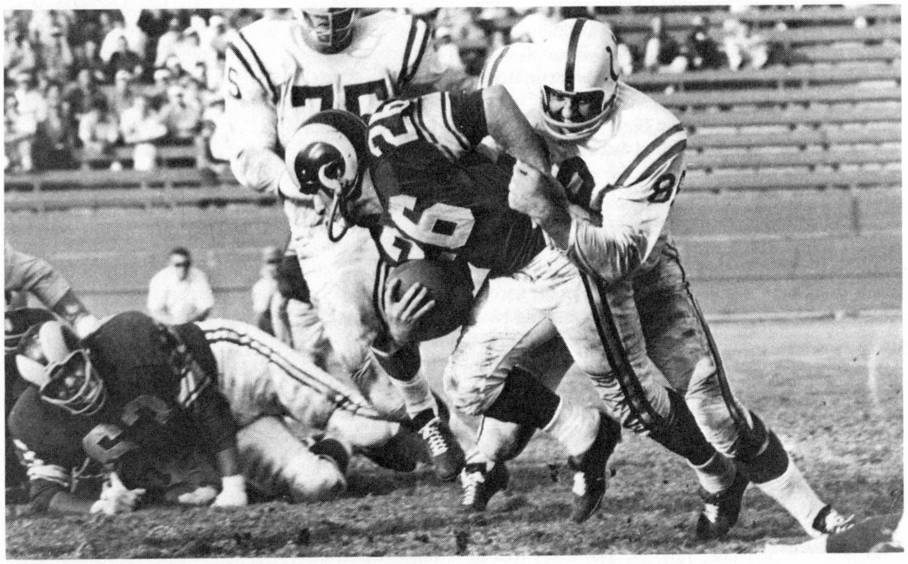

Gino Marchetti wraps up the Rams' Jon Arnett, 1960.

Alan Ameche

Carr, Roger, WR, Louisiana Tech
Case, Ernie, B, UCLA . . . .
Castiglia, Jim, B, Georgetown .
Celotto, Mario, LB, USC . . . . .
Cheatham, Ernie, T, Loyola, Cal
Cherry, Stan, LB, Morgan State
Chester, Raymond, TE, Morgan
Cheyunski, Jim, LB, Syracuse .
Chorovich, Dick, T, Miami, Ohio
Clemens, Bob, B, Pittsburgh . .
Cogdill, Gail, E, Washington Sta
Cole, Terry, RB, Indiana . . . . .
Collett, Elmer, G, San Francisco
Coleman, Herb, C, Notre Dame
Collins, Albin (Rip), B, Louisian
Colo, Don, T, Brown . . . . . .
Colteryahn, Lloyd, E, Maryland
Colvin, Jim, T, Houston. . . . . .
Conjar, Larry, B, Notre Dame .
Cook, Fred, DE, Southern Miss
Cooke, Ed, E, Maryland. . . . . .
Cooper, Ken, C, Vanderbilt . . .
Corley, Elbert, C, Mississippi S
Coutre, Larry, B, Notre Dame .
Cowan, Bob, C, Indiana . . . . .
Craddock, Nate, RB, Parsons .
Crisler, Hal, E, San Jose State
Cuozzo, Gary, QB, Virginia . . .
Cure, Armand, B, Rhode Island
Curry, Bill, C, Georgia Tech . . .
Curtis, Mike, LB, Duke . . . . . .
Curtis, Tom, DB, Michigan. . . .

Davidson, Cotton, QB, Baylor.
Davis, Lamar, E, Georgia. . . . .
Davis, Milt, DB, UCLA . . . . . .
Davis, Norman, G, Grambling
Davis, Ted, LB, Georgia Tech
DeCarlo, Art, E, Georgia . . . .
DelBello, Jack, B, Miami . . . .
Dellerba, Spiro, B, Ohio State
DeRoo, Brian, WR, Redlands
Dickel, Dan, LB, Iowa. . . . . .
Dickey, Curtis, RB, Texas A&M
Diehl, John, T, Virginia . . . . . .
Dilts, Bucky, P, Georgia . . . . .
Dixon, Zachary, RB, Temple .
Domres, Marty, QB, Columbia
Donaldson, Ray, C, Georgia .
Donovan, Art, DT, Boston Col
Doughty, Glenn, WR, Michiga
Drougas, Tom, T, Oregon. . . .
Dudish, Andy, B, Georgia . . .
Duncan, James, DB, Marylan
Dunlap, Len, DB, North Texas
Dunn, Perry Lee, RB, Mississ
Dupre, L. G., RB, Baylor . . . .
Dutton, John, DE, Nebraska

Ecklund, Brad, C, Oregon. . .
Edmunds, Randy, LB, Georg
Edwards, Dan, E, Georgia. .
Eggers, Doug, LB, South Da
Ehrmann, Joe, DT, Syracuse
Embree, Mel, E, Pepperdine
Enke, Fred, QB, Arizona . . .

Faunce, Everett, B, Minneso
Feagin, Wiley, G, Houston . .
Feamster, Tom, T, Florida Sta
Federspiel, Joe, LB, Kentuck
Felts, Bob, B, Florida A&M .
Fernandes, Ron, DE, Easter
Fields, Greg, DE, Grambling
Filchock, Frank, B, Indiana .
Finnin, Tom, DT, Detroit . . . .
Fletcher, Oliver, E, USC . . . .
Flowers, Bernie, E, Purdue .
Flowers, Dick, B, Northwest

O.J. Simpson breaks through the Kansas City defense on his way to an NFL season record 2,003 yards, 1973.

BUFFALO BILLS

1959 Ralph C. Wilson, a minority stockholder of the Detroit Lions who long had sought a team of his own, was granted an American Football League franchise for Buffalo. Wilson put up a $100,000 performance bond and signed a lease on War Memorial Stadium. The city voted to increase the seating capacity in the stadium by 14,000, from 22,500 to 36,500. Wilson named the team the "Bills." Richie Lucas, an All-America quarterback from Penn State, was the team's first draft choice. Garrard (Buster) Ramsey was named head coach. Dick Gallagher, an assistant coach and director of player personnel with the Cleveland Browns, was selected as general manager.

1960 Lucas signed with the Bills. The club opened its first training camp in East Aurora, New York. On the day before the first preseason game with Boston more than 100,000 Buffalo residents turned out on Main Street to greet the team in a welcome home parade. The Bills were beaten 28-7 by Lou Saban's Patriots in the AFL's first game at War Memorial Stadium. In the first league game, the New York Titans defeated Buffalo 27-3. The Bills recorded their first victory, shutting out Boston 13-0, September 23. The team averaged just 16,000 people at home the first year.

1961 Denver ruined the Bills' home opener at War Memorial Stadium with a 22-10 victory. Lou Saban was replaced by Mike Holovak in Boston, and immediately was hired as Buffalo's new director of player personnel, amid rumors he would be the Bills' next head coach. A 28-10 loss to San Diego concluded a disappointing Buffalo season with a 6-8 record.

1962 The rumors proved true. Ramsey was fired and Saban hired as head coach. The Bills signed a 6-foot 2-inch, 243-pound former Canadian Football League running back, Cookie Gilchrist. Quarterback Jack Kemp was claimed for the $100 waiver price from San Diego in a surprising deal. Houston ruined Saban's debut, beating the Bills 28-23. But Buffalo finished with seven wins and a tie in the last nine games. Gilchrist gained 1,099 yards, becoming the AFL's first 1,000-yard runner.

1963 The Bills signed their first two "name" players, Dave Behrman, a center from Michigan State, and Jim Dunaway, a tackle from Mississippi. They also signed quarterback Daryle Lamonica of Notre Dame. The club moved its training camp to suburban Blasdell, New York. Gilchrist set an all-time pro rushing record, gaining 243 yards and scoring five touchdowns in a 45-14 victory over the New York Jets. Buffalo lost 26-8 to Boston in an Eastern Division playoff game in 24-degree weather.

1964 The home opener proved a sign of things to come. The Bills defeated Kansas City 34-17. Before a crowd of 61,929, Buffalo won its ninth in a row, defeating the Jets 20-7 at Shea Stadium. The Eastern Division title was secured with a 24-14 victory over Boston in snow at Fenway Park, December 20. Before a standing-room-only crowd of 40,242 at War Memorial Stadium, the Bills won the AFL championship 20-7 over San Diego, December 27. Jack Kemp, the Chargers' former quarterback, completed 10 passes in the game and scored the Bills' final touchdown.

1965 Gilchrist, who had demanded extra money after the team won the championship in December, was traded to Denver for fullback Billy Joe in a deal that created controversy. In his three years with the Bills, Gilchrist had run for 3,058 yards and scored 35 touchdowns. Before a capacity crowd of 45,502, the defending AFL champions beat Boston 24-7 in the

season opener. A 29-18 victory over Houston in Rice Stadium clinched the Bills' second straight Eastern Division title, December 5. Buffalo's brilliant defense shut down the Chargers in San Diego and the Bills won their second consecutive AFL championship 23-0, December 26.

1966 In a shocking move, Saban announced he was resigning to accept a position as the head coach at the University of Maryland. Joe Collier, an assistant coach, was named head coach. The AFL all-stars defeated the Bills 30-19 in the league all-star game, January 15. Fullback Billy Joe was among four players claimed by Miami in the league's expansion draft. Collier's regular season head coaching debut was unsuccessful. San Diego beat the Bills 27-7, September 4. Buffalo rallied to have another good season and defeated Denver in the last game of the year to win a third straight Eastern Division championship. Bobby Burnett, running back from Arkansas, was named rookie of the year.

1967 Kansas City ended the Bills' hold on the AFL championship, winning 31-7 in Buffalo before 42,080 at War Memorial Stadium, January 1. Daryle Lamonica was sent to Oakland for quarterback Tom Flores and wide receiver Art Powell. Playing a National Football League opponent for the first time in the preseason, the Bills lost to Detroit 19-17 before 43,503 in Buffalo.

1968 Quarterback Kemp was injured and lost for the season. Former Bill Daryle Lamonica came to town and helped Oakland beat Buffalo 48-6. Collier was fired and replaced by Harvey Johnson, the team's director of player personnel. Bob Celeri and Marvin Bass were added to the coaching staff and Jerry Smith resigned. Flanker Elbert Dubenion, the last of the original Bills, retired as a player and joined the team's scouting department.

1969 John Rauch resigned as Oakland head coach and agreed to a four-year contract to coach the Bills. In the most significant draft in the history of the franchise, O.J. Simpson was selected as the first choice. Four months of intense negotiations followed with the Heisman Trophy winner from USC and his agent. A month after training camp opened, O.J. signed a long-term contract with the Bills and reported for duty, August 9. Rauch got his first victory as a Buffalo coach, beating Denver 41-28, September 28 after losing two.

1970 In the first season of interleague play, the Bills began to show promise for the future. Dennis Shaw completed 178 of 321 passes for 2,507 yards and 10 touchdowns and was NFL rookie of the year in all polls. Marlin Briscoe was the AFC's top receiver with 57 catches. The roster contained several other highly regarded players, such as cornerback Robert James and Haven Moses, another speedy pass catcher. But through it all, there was concern about O.J. Simpson, who had been something of a disappointment in his first two years. Some felt he simply wasn't as good as advertised. Others contended it was impossible to run on a team that couldn't block. Still more wondered why Rauch didn't find ways to get him the ball more often.

1971 J.D. Hill, a receiver from Arizona State, was the club's first draft choice. Early in training camp, Rauch resigned. Harvey Johnson once again was named interim coach. The Bills defeated New England 27-20, November 28. It was significant because it was their first—and only—regular season victory of the year. Lou Saban returned from his six-year exile to become "vice president in charge of football" and head coach, December 23.

1972 Convinced the Bills had to be built from the bottom up, Saban began by fortifying the trenches. His first pick—and the number-one choice in the NFL draft—was Walt Patulski, 6-foot 6-inch,

259-pound Notre Dame defensive end. His second pick was guard Reggie McKenzie, the All-America blocker from Michigan. Just before the season opened, he obtained tackle Dave Foley on waivers from the Jets. Two other defensive linemen, Don Croft from Baltimore and Jerry Patton from Minnesota, were added. All were starters almost immediately. In April, ground was broken for the club's new 80,000-seat stadium in Orchard Park, New York. Saban won his first regular season game since returning, beating San Francisco 27-20, September 24. Getting the ball much more often, O.J. Simpson started to live up to his reputation. He had his first 1,000-yard season and was named the AFC's player of the year by United Press International.

1973 Simpson was named the most valuable player in the Pro Bowl. Teammates Robert James and J.D. Hill joined him in the game. Continuing his search for capable linemen, Saban made Michigan tackle Paul Seymour and Michigan State guard Joe DeLamielleure his first two selections in the draft. The Bills' season ticket sale for their first year in Orchard Park passed 46,206, the listed capacity of old War Memorial Stadium. A sellout crowd of 80,020 watched the first game in Orchard Park, a preseason game won by the Washington Redskins 37-21. O.J. Simpson set a single-game NFL record of 250 yards in Buffalo's 31-13 opening game win over New England in Foxboro. The Bills made their Monday night television debut, beating Kansas City 23-14 with Simpson going over 1,000 yards for the season, October 29. In a dramatic final game at Shea Stadium, Simpson ran for 200 yards and finished with 2,003 for the season, breaking Jim Brown's 10-year-old rushing record. The Bills became the first team in league history to run for more than 3,000 yards.

1974 The Bills participated in the Hall of Fame game in Canton, Ohio, losing to St. Louis 21-13. In the season opener, Buffalo edged Oakland 21-20 in the final minute. A 29-28 victory over New England was the Bills' sixth consecutive victory and gave them possession of first place in the AFC Eastern Division, November 3. A 6-0 shutout of Baltimore was their ninth win of the season and first shutout since 1965. O.J. Simpson went over 1,000 yards for the season in that game, the third consecutive year he surpassed that mark. Miami defeated Cincinnati, assuring the Bills their first appearance in a postseason playoff since 1966, December 12. Pittsburgh beat the Bills 32-14 in the first round in Pittsburgh, December 22.

1975 In the season opener, Buffalo warmed up its potent offense to bombard the New York Jets 42-14. In their first Monday night television loss, the Bills dropped a 17-14 decision to the New York Giants. O.J. Simpson went over 1,000 yards for the season, this time clearing that figure in a 24-23 win over the New York Jets, November 2. In the final game of the season, Simpson scored his twenty-third touchdown, setting another NFL record.

1976 The lingering story of the summer was O.J. Simpson's insistence on a trade to Los Angeles. On the day before the season opened, Simpson traveled to New York and signed a three-year contract estimated at $2 million-plus to play in Buffalo. After three losses in the first five games, Lou Saban resigned "in the best interests of the team," he said. Jim Ringo, the offensive line coach and former all-pro center with Vince Lombardi's Green Bay Packers, was signed as the new coach. Two games later, the new coach lost his quarterback. Joe Ferguson suffered some broken bones in his back and was out for the season. The Bills never recovered and did not win a game under Ringo. Simpson started slowly, gaining only 105 yards in the first three games, but he finished with 1,503 to lead the league.

Joe Ferguson passes behind excellent protection in a victory against Chicago, 1974.

BILLS RECORD, 1960-81

Year	Won	Lost	Tied	Pct.	Pts.	OP
1960.......	5	8	1	.385	296	303
1961.......	6	8	0	.429	294	342
1962.......	7	6	1	.538	309	272
1963.......	7	6	1	.538	304	291
1964‡.......	12	2	0	.857	400	242
1965‡.......	10	3	1	.769	313	226
1966§.......	9	4	1	.692	358	255
1967.......	4	10	0	.286	237	285
1968.......	1	12	1	.077	199	367
1969.......	4	10	0	.286	230	359
1970.......	3	10	1	.231	204	337
1971.......	1	13	0	.071	184	394
1972.......	4	9	1	.321	257	377
1973.......	9	5	0	.643	259	230
1974*.......	9	5	0	.643	264	244
1975.......	8	6	0	.571	420	355
1976.......	2	12	0	.143	245	363
1977.......	3	11	0	.214	160	313
1978.......	5	11	0	.313	302	354
1979.......	7	9	0	.438	268	279
1980†.......	11	5	0	.688	320	260
1981*.......	10	6	0	.625	311	276
22 Years.....	137	171	8	.446	6,134	6,724

‡*AFL Champion*
§*AFL Eastern Division Champion*
**AFC Wild Card Qualifier for Playoffs*
†*AFC Eastern Division Champion*

RECORD HOLDERS

Rushing (Yards)	O. J. Simpson, 1973	2,003
Passing (Pct.)	Joe Ferguson, 1980	57.2
Passing (Yards)	Joe Ferguson, 1981	3,652
Passing (TDs)	Joe Ferguson, 1975	25
Receiving (No.)	Frank Lewis, 1981	70
Receiving (Yards)	Frank Lewis, 1981	1,244
Interceptions (No.)	Billy Atkins, 1961, and	
	Tom Janik, 1967	10
Punting (Avg.)	Billy Atkins, 1961	44.5
Punt Ret. (Avg.)	Keith Moody, 1977	13.1
Kickoff Ret. (Avg.)	Ed Rutkowski, 1963	30.2
Touchdowns (Total)	O. J. Simpson, 1975	23
Field Goals Made	Pete Gogolak, 1964	28
Points (No.)	O. J. Simpson, 1975	138

COACHING HISTORY

1960-61	Garrard (Buster) Ramsey	11-16-1
1962-65	Lou Saban	36-17-3
1966-68	Joel Collier*	13-16-1
1968	Harvey Johnson	1-10-1
1969-70	John Rauch	7-20-1
1971	Harvey Johnson	1-13-0
1972-76	Lou Saban**	32-28-1
1976-77	Jim Ringo	3-20-0
1978-81	Chuck Knox	33-31-0

**Replaced after two games in 1968*
***Resigned after five games in 1976*

FIRST PLAYER SELECTED

1960	Richie Lucas, QB, Penn State
1961	Ken Rice, T, Auburn
1962	Ernie Davis, RB, Syracuse
1963	Dave Behrman, C, Michigan State
1964	Carl Eller, DE, Minnesota
1965	Jim Davidson, T, Ohio State
1966	Mike Dennis, RB, Mississippi
1967	John Pitts, S, Arizona State
1968	Haven Moses, WR, San Diego State
1969	O. J. Simpson, RB, USC
1970	Al Cowlings, DE, USC
1971	J. D. Hill, WR, Arizona State
1972	Walt Patulski, DE, Notre Dame
1973	Paul Seymour, T, Michigan
1974	Reuben Gant, TE, Oklahoma State
1975	Tom Ruud, LB, Nebraska
1976	Mario Clark, DB, Oregon
1977	Phil Dokes (2), DT, Oklahoma State
1978	Terry Miller, RB, Oklahoma State
1979	Tom Cousineau, LB, Ohio State
1980	Jim Ritcher, C, North Carolina State
1981	Booker Moore, RB, Penn State
1982	Perry Tuttle, WR, Clemson

BUFFALO BILLS, 1960-81

Abramowicz, Dan, WR, Xavier 1974-75
Abruzzese, Ray, DB, Alabama 1962-64
Adams, Bill, G, Holy Cross................1972, 1973-78
Alexander, Glenn, WR, Grambling..................1970
Alford, Bruce, K, Texas Christian 1968-69
Allen, Doug, LB, Penn State 1974-75
Allen, Jackie, DB, Baylor 1970-71
Alvers, Steve, TE, Miami 1981
Anderson, Max, RB, Arizona State..............1968-70
Anderson, Tim, DB, Ohio State 1976

1977 Seven games into the season a knee injury did what NFL defenses hadn't been able to do—stop O. J. Simpson. After rushing for more than 7,500 yards in the previous five seasons, Simpson missed the last half of the season and finished the year with only 557. The Bills won only once with Simpson and twice without him, and head coach Jim Ringo was dismissed at the end of the 3-11 season. Ferguson was one of the bright spots, leading the NFL in passing yardage (2,803).

1978 Buffalo hired former Rams head coach Chuck Knox as head football coach and vice president in charge of football operations on January 12. Two months later, the Bills obtained a number of high draft choices for Simpson in a trade with San Francisco. To replace Simpson, Knox drafted running back Terry Miller, the Heisman Trophy runner-up from Oklahoma State. Miller led the Bills with 1,060 yards, including 97 in Knox's first victory at Buffalo, a 24-17 win over Baltimore on September 24. The Bills finished 5-11, but 7 of those losses were by a touchdown or less.

1979 The Bills' main concern was to shore up a weak defense. They were successful, giving up 75 fewer points than the season before. The leaders of the defense were rookie nose tackle Fred Smerlas, linebacker Jim Haslett, who was named defensive rookie of the year, and former Rams linebacker Isiah Robertson. The Bills used the first pick of the 1979 NFL draft on former Ohio State linebacker Tom Cousineau, but he signed with Montreal of the Canadian Football League. The defense continued to improve, but the Bills stalled late in the season due to an inconsistent offense that scored 21 touchdowns in five early games but only 9 the rest of the season. In fact, the offense did not score a touchdown the last three games of the year, all losses. Ferguson threw for a

Bills' record 3,572 yards. Against the Jets on September 23, he hit NFL offensive rookie of the year Jerry Butler with 10 passes for 255 yards.

1980 Knox continued to build up the defense, obtaining linebacker Phil Villapiano from the Raiders and safety Bill Simpson from the Rams. The biggest draft choice was running back Joe Cribbs from Auburn, who ran for 1,185 yards, caught 52 passes, and earned rookie of the year honors. With some needed spark offensively and a defense that gave up the fewest yards in the NFL, the Bills went on to win their first division title since 1966. A 26-24 victory over San Diego on October 5 gave Buffalo a 5-0 record, the best in pro football, and the division lead. An 18-13 win over San Francisco on December 21 clinched the AFC East title.

1981 The Bills lost to San Diego 20-14 when Dan Fouts threw a 50-yard touchdown pass to Ron Smith with two minutes left in the 1980 AFC Divisional Playoff Game on January 3. Led by Cribbs, who again ran for over 1,000 yards and also caught seven touchdown passes, Buffalo engaged in a season-long race with Miami and the New York Jets for the 1981 AFC East crown. On December 19, the Dolphins defeated the Bills 16-6 in the final game of the season to win the title. The loss dropped Buffalo to third behind the New York Jets, but all three teams made the playoffs. On December 26, the Bills took a 24-0 lead in the wild card game at Shea Stadium and then used a goal-line interception by Bill Simpson in the last minute to hold off the Jets, 31-27.

1982 Trailing by a touchdown in the 1981 AFC Divisional Playoff Game on January 3, the Bills picked up a first down at the Cincinnati 14. But a delay of game penalty forced them to replay the down. They didn't make the first down the second time, and Cincinnati ran out the clock and won 28-21.

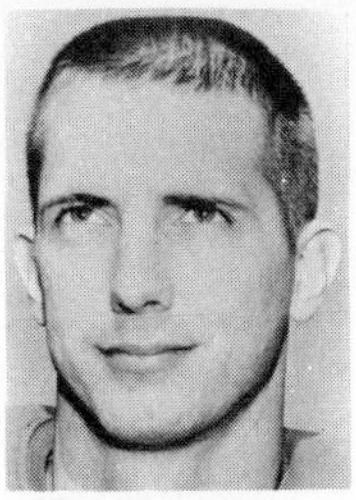
Bobby Burnett

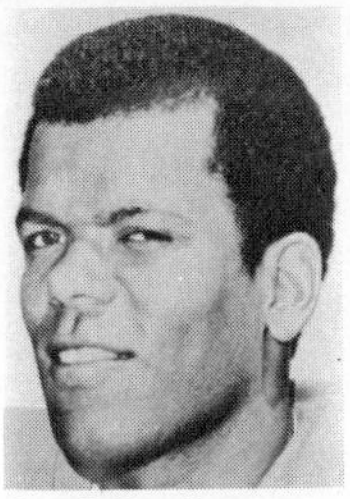
Butch Byrd

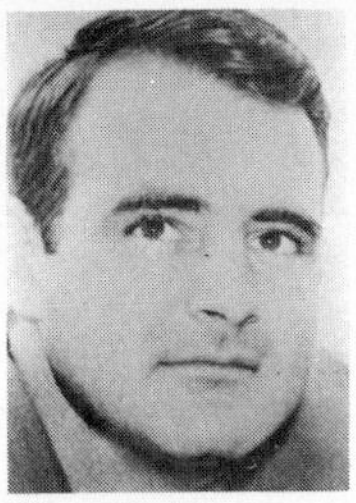
Wray Carlton

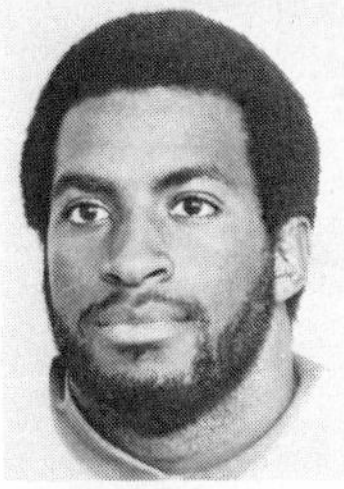
Joe Cribbs

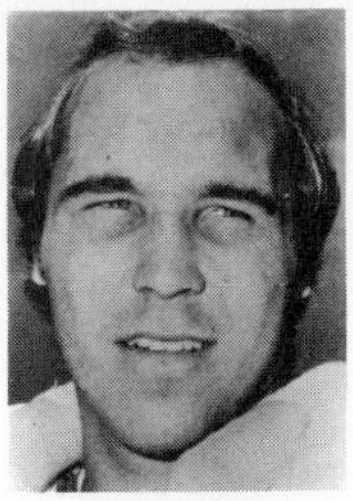
Joe DeLamielleure

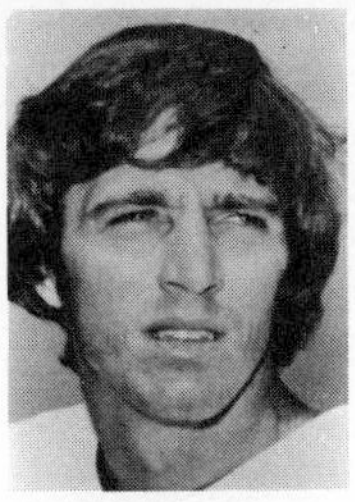
Joe Ferguson

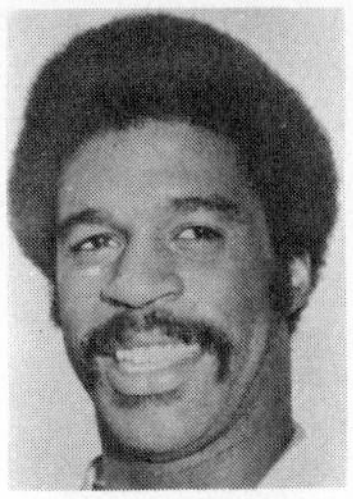
Tony Greene

Andrews, AL, LB, New Mexico State ... 1970-71
Atkins, Billy, DB, Auburn ... 1960-63
Auer, Joe, HB, Georgia Tech ... 1964-65

B

Bailey, Bill, FB, Cincinnati ... 1967
Baker, Art, FB, Syracuse ... 1961-62
Baker, Mel, WR, Texas Southern ... 1977
Barber, Stew, T, Penn State ... 1961-69
Barnett, Buster, TE, Jackson State ... 1981
Barrett, Robert, E, Baldwin-Wallace ... 1960
Bass, Glenn, E, East Carolina ... 1961-66
Bateman, Marv, P, Utah ... 1974-77
Beamer, Tim, S, J. C. Smith ... 1971
Beard, Tom, C, Michigan State ... 1972
Becker, Doug, LB, Notre Dame ... 1978
Behrman, Dave, C, Michigan State ... 1963, 1965
Bemiller, Al, C, Syracuse ... 1961-69
Besana, Fred, QB, California ... 1977
Bess, Rufus, CB, South Carolina State ... 1980-81
Bivins, Charley, HB, Morris Brown ... 1967
Blazer, Phil, G, North Carolina ... 1960
Bohling, Dewey, RB, Hardin-Simmons ... 1961
Borchardt, Jon, T, Montana State ... 1979-81
Borden, Nate, E, Indiana ... 1962
Brammer, Mark, TE, Michigan State ... 1980-81
Braxton, Hezekiah, HB, Virginia Union ... 1963
Braxton, Jim, RB, West Virginia ... 1971-78
Briscoe, Marlin, WR, Omaha ... 1969-71
Brodhead, Bob, QB, Duke ... 1960
Brooks, Clifford, DB, Tennessee State ... 1976
Brown, Charley, S, Syracuse ... 1968
Brown, Curtis, RB, Missouri ... 1977-81
Brown, Fred, HB, Georgia ... 1961-63
Brubaker, Dick, E, Ohio State ... 1960
Bugenhagen, Gary, T, Syracuse ... 1967
Burnett, Bobby, HB, Arkansas ... 1966-67
Butler, Jerry, WR, Clemson ... 1979-81
Buziniski, Berie, LB, Holy Cross ... 1960
Byrd, George (Butch), CB, Boston University ... 1964-70

C

Cahill, Bill, S, Washington ... 1973-74
Calhoun, Don, RB, Kansas State ... 1974-75
Cannavino, Joe, DB, Ohio State ... 1962
Cappadonna, Bob, RB, Northeastern ... 1968
Carlton, Wray, FB, Duke ... 1960-67
Carr, Levert, T, North Central State ... 1970-71
Carwell, Larry, S, Iowa State ... 1973
Cater, Greg, P, Tennessee-Chattanooga ... 1980-81
Celotto, Mario, LB, USC ... 1978
Chamberlain, Dan, E, Sacramento State ... 1960-61
Chandler, Bob, WR, USC ... 1971-79
Chandler, Edgar, LB, Georgia ... 1968-72
Chapple, Dave, P, California-Santa Barbara ... 1971
Charon, Carl, DB, Michigan State ... 1962-63
Cheek, Richard, G, Auburn ... 1970
Chelf, Don, G, Iowa ... 1960-61
Cheyunski, Jim, LB, Syracuse ... 1973-74
Christiansen, Bob, TE, UCLA ... 1972
Clark, Mario, DB, Oregon ... 1976-81
Clark, Mike, K, Texas A&M ... 1972
Clarke, Hagood, DB, Florida ... 1964-68
Cole, Linzy, WR, Texas Christian ... 1972
Coleman, Fred, TE, Northeastern Louisiana ... 1976
Collier, Mike, RB, Morgan State ... 1977-79
Collins, Greg, LB, Notre Dame ... 1977
Collins, Jerald, LB, Western Michigan ... 1969-71
Cornell, Robert (Bo), LB, Washington ... 1973-77
Cornish, Frank, DT, Alcorn State ... 1972
Costa, Dave, DT, Utah ... 1966, 1974
Costa, Paul, TE-T, Notre Dame ... 1965-72
Cowlings, Al, DE, USC ... 1970-72
Craig, Neal, S, Fisk ... 1974
Craig, Reggie, WR, Arkansas ... 1977
Crawford, Hilton, S, Grambling ... 1969
Cribbs, Joe, RB, Auburn ... 1980-81
Crockett, Bobby, WR, Arkansas ... 1966, 1968-69
Crockett, Monte, E, New Mexico Highlands ... 1960-62
Croft, Don, DT, Texas-El Paso ... 1972, 1974-75
Crotty, Jim, DB, Notre Dame ... 1961-62
Crow, Wayne, HB, California ... 1962-63
Croyle, Phil, LB, California ... 1973
Cudzik, Walt, C, Purdue ... 1964
Cunningham, Dick, T, Arkansas ... 1967-68, 1970-72
Curchin, Jeff, G, Florida State ... 1972

D

Darragh, Dan, QB, William & Mary ... 1968-70
Day, Tom, DE, North Carolina A&T ... 1961-66, 1968
DeLamielleure, Joe, G, Michigan State ... 1973-79
Delucca, Gerry, T, Middle Tennessee State ... 1962-63
Dempsey, Tom, K, Palomar Junior College ... 1978-79
Denney, Austin, TE, Tennessee ... 1970-71
Desutter, Wayne, T, Western Illinois ... 1966
Devleiger, Chuck, DT, Memphis State ... 1969
Devlin, Joe, T, Iowa ... 1976-81
Discenzo, Tony, T, Michigan State ... 1960
Dittrich, John, G, Wisconsin ... 1961
Dobbins, Oliver, DB, Morgan State ... 1964
Dobler, Conrad, G, Wyoming ... 1980-81
Dokes, Phil, DE, Oklahoma State ... 1977-78
Donaldson, Gene, RB, Purdue ... 1967
Dorow, Al, QB, Michigan State ... 1962
Drungo, Elbert, T, Tennessee State ... 1978
Dubenion, Elbert, WR, Bluffton ... 1960-68
Dunaway, Jim, DT, Mississippi ... 1963-71
Dunstan, Bill, DT, Utah State ... 1977

E

Edgerson, Booker, CB, Western Illinois ... 1962-69
Edwards, Earl, DE, Wichita State ... 1973-75
Edwards, Emmett, WR, Kansas ... 1976
Ehlers, Tom, LB, Kentucky ... 1978
Enyart, Bill, RB, Oregon State ... 1969-70

F

Farley, Dale, LB, West Virginia ... 1972-73
Felton, Ralph, LB, Maryland ... 1961-62
Fergerson, Duke, WR, San Diego State ... 1980
Ferguson, Charley, TE, Tennessee State ... 1963, 1965-66, 1969
Ferguson, Joe, QB, Arkansas ... 1973-81
Flint, George, G, Arizona State ... 1962-65, 1968-69
Flores, Tom, QB, Pacific ... 1967-69
Foley, Dave, T, Ohio State ... 1972-77
Ford, Charley, DB, Houston ... 1975
Ford, Fred, RB, Cal Poly-San Luis Obispo ... 1960
Forsberg, Fred, LB, Washington ... 1973
Fowler, Wayne, C, Richmond ... 1970
Fowler, Willmer, RB, Northwestern ... 1960-61
Francis, Wallace, WR, Arkansas-Pine Bluff ... 1973-74
Franckowiak, Mike, TE, Central Michigan ... 1977-78
Franklin, Byron, WR, Auburn ... 1981
Frantz, Jack, C, California ... 1968
Frazier, Wayne, C, Auburn ... 1967
Freeman, Steve, DB, Mississippi State ... 1975-81
Fulton, Dan, WR, Nebraska-Omaha ... 1979
Fulton, Ed, G, Maryland ... 1979

G

Gaddis, Bob, WR, Mississippi Valley ... 1976
Gant, Reuben, TE, Oklahoma State ... 1974-80
Gantt, Jerome, T, North Carolina Central ... 1970
Garror, Leon, S, Alcorn State ... 1972-73
Gibson, Reuben, RB, Memphis State ... 1977
Gilchrist, Cookie, FB, No college ... 1962-64
Gladieux, Bob, RB, Notre Dame ... 1970
Glosson, Clyde, WR, Texas-El Paso ... 1970
Gogolak, Pete, K, Cornell ... 1964-65
Goode, Irv, G, Kentucky ... 1972
Goodwin, Doug, FB, Maryland State ... 1966
Grabosky, Gene, T, Syracuse ... 1960
Graham, Tom, LB, Oregon ... 1978
Grant, Wes, DE, UCLA ... 1971
Grant, Will, C, Kentucky ... 1978-81
Grate, Willie, TE, South Carolina State ... 1969-70
Green, Donnie, T, Purdue ... 1971-76
Green, John, QB, Tennessee-Chattanooga ... 1960-61
Green, Van, DB, Shaw ... 1976
Greene, Doug, DB, Texas A&I ... 1979-80
Greene, Tony, CB, Maryland ... 1971-79
Gregory, Ben, RB, Nebraska ... 1968
Groman, Bill, E, Heidelberg ... 1964-65
Guidry, Paul, LB, McNeese State ... 1966-72
Guthrie, Grant, K, Florida State ... 1970-71

H

Hagen, Halvor, T, Weber State ... 1973-75
Hardison, Dee, DE-OT, North Carolina ... 1978-80
Harper, Darrell, HB, Michigan ... 1960
Harris, Jim, QB, Grambling ... 1969-71
Harrison, Dwight, DB, Texas A&I ... 1972-77
Hart, Dick, G, No college ... 1972
Hart, Leo, QB, Duke ... 1972-73
Harvey, Waddey, DT, Virginia Tech ... 1969-70
Haslerig, Clint, RB, Michigan ... 1974-75
Haslett, Jim, LB, Indiana, Pennsylvania ... 1979-81
Hayman, Gary, RB, Penn State ... 1974-75
Healy, Don, T, Maryland ... 1962
Heath, Clayton, RB, Wake Forest ... 1976
Henley, Carey, HB, Chattanooga ... 1962
Hergert, Joe, HB, Florida ... 1960-61
Hews, Bob, T, Princeton ... 1971
Higgins, Tom, LB, North Carolina State ... 1979
Hill, Ike, CB, Catawba ... 1970-71
Hill, J. D., WR, Arizona State ... 1971-75
Hoisington, Al, E, Pasadena C.C. ... 1960
Holland, John, WR, Tennessee State ... 1975-77
Holmes, Mike, WR, Texas Southern ... 1976
Hooks, Roland, RB, North Carolina State ... 1976-81
Hudlow, Floyd, DB, Arizona ... 1965
Hudson, Dick, T, Memphis State ... 1963-67
Humiston, Mike, LB, Weber State ... 1981
Humm, David, QB, Nebraska ... 1980
Hunter, Scott, QB, Alabama ... 1974
Hurston, Chuck, DE, Auburn ... 1971
Hutchinson, Scott, DE, Florida ... 1978-80

I

Irvin, Darrell, DE, Oklahoma ... 1980-81

J

Jackson, Randy, RB, Wichita State ... 1972
Jackson, Rusty, P, Louisiana State ... 1978-79
Jackunas, Frank, C, Detroit ... 1962
Jacobs, Harry, LB, Bradley ... 1963-69
Jakowenko, George, K, Syracuse ... 1976
James, Bob, CB, Fisk ... 1969-74
Janik, Tom, S, Texas A&I ... 1965-68
Jarvis, Bruce, C, Washington ... 1971-74
Jarvis, Ray, WR, Norfolk State ... 1973
Jenkins, Ed, RB, Holy Cross ... 1974
Jessie, Ron, WR, Kansas ... 1980-81
Jilek, Dan, LB, Michigan ... 1976-79
Joe, Billy, FB, Villanova ... 1965
Johnson, Dennis, DT, Delaware ... 1978
Johnson, Dennis, FB, Mississippi State ... 1978-79
Johnson, Jack, RB, Miami ... 1960-61
Johnson, Ken, QB, Colorado ... 1977
Johnson, Ken, DE, Knoxville ... 1979-81
Johnson, Mark, LB, Missouri ... 1975-76
Jones, Doug, DB, Cal State-Northridge ... 1975-78
Jones, Ed, DB, Rutgers ... 1975
Jones, Greg, RB, UCLA ... 1970-71
Jones, Ken, DE, Arkansas State ... 1976-81
Jones, Spike, P, Georgia ... 1971-74
Jones, Steve, RB, Duke ... 1973-74
Jones, Willie, HB, Purdue ... 1962

K

Kadish, Mike, DT, Notre Dame ... 1973-81
Kalsu, Bob, G, Oklahoma ... 1968
Kampa, Bob, DT, California ... 1973-74
Keating, Chris, LB, Maine ... 1979-81
Keating, Tom, DT, Michigan ... 1964-65
Kellerman, Ernie, S, Miami, Ohio ... 1973
Kemp, Jack, QB, Occidental ... 1962-67, 1969
Kern, Rex, S, Ohio State ... 1974
Kimbrough, John, WR, St. Cloud State ... 1977
Kinard, Billy, DB, Mississippi ... 1960
Kindig, Howard, C, DE, Cal State-Los Angeles ... 1967-71
King, Charley, CB, Purdue ... 1966-67
King, Tony, DB, Findlay ... 1967
Kingrea, Rick, LB, Tulane ... 1973
Kinney, Jeff, RB, Nebraska ... 1976
Kochman, Roger, HB, Penn State ... 1963

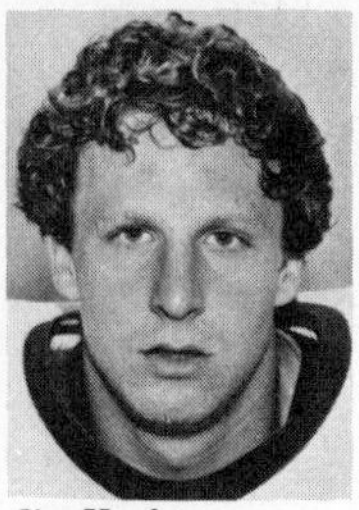
Jim Haslett

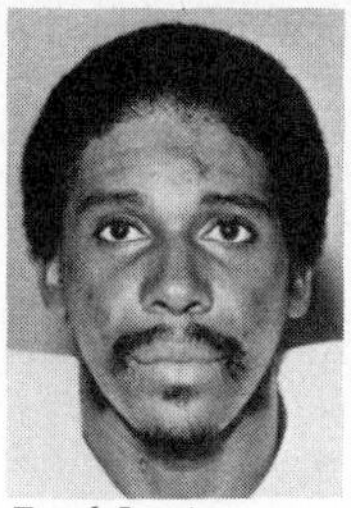
Frank Lewis

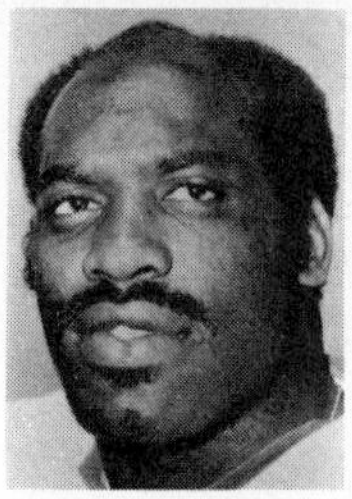
Reggie McKenzie

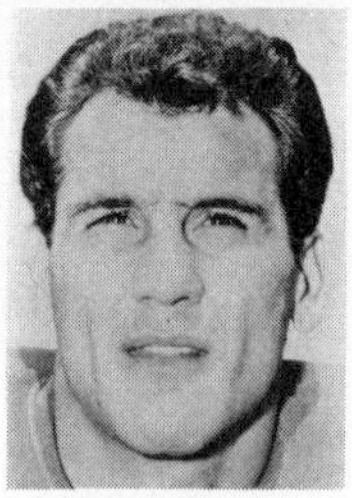
George Saimes

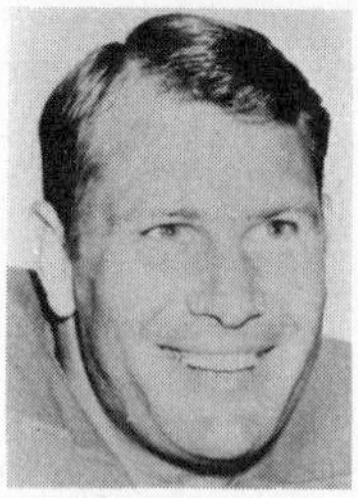
Tom Sestak

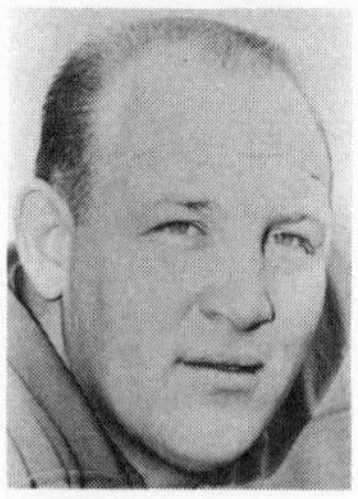
Billy Shaw

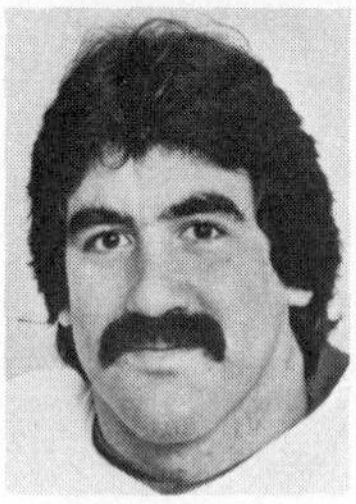
Fred Smerlas

Koy, Ted, LB-TE, Texas 1971-74
Krakau, Merv, LB, Iowa State 1973-78
Kruse, Bob, G, Wayne State 1969
Kulbacki, Joe, HB, Purdue 1960
Kush, Rod, S, Nebraska-Omaha 1980-81

L

Lamonica, Daryle, QB, Notre Dame 1963-66
Laraway, Jack, LB, Purdue 1960
Laskey, Bill, LB, Michigan 1965
Laster, Art, T, Maryland State 1970
Lawson, Jerome, CB, Utah 1968
Leaks, Roosevelt, RB, Texas 1980-81
Ledbetter, Monte, WR, Northwestern Louisiana 1967-69
Lee, Ken, LB, Washington 1972
LeMoine, Jim, G, Utah State 1967
Leo, Chuck, G, Indiana 1963
Letner, Bob, LB, Tennessee 1961
Levenseller, Mike, WR, Washington State 1978
Lewis, Frank, WR, Grambling 1978-81
Lewis, Harold, HB, Houston 1960
Lewis, Richard, LB, Portland State 1973-74
Leypoldt, John, K, No college 1971-76
Lincoln, Keith, HB, Washington State 1967-68
Little, John, DT, Oklahoma State 1977
Lloyd, Jeff, DT, West Texas State 1976
Long, Carson, K, Pittsburgh 1977
Louderback, Tom, LB, San Jose State 1962
Loukas, Angelo. G, Northwestern 1969
Lucas, Richie, QB-RB, Penn State 1960-61
Lusteg, Booth, K, Connecticut 1966
Lyman, Jeff, LB, Brigham Young 1972
Lynch, Tom, G, Boston College 1981

M

Maguire, Paul, LB-K, Citadel 1964-70
Majors, Bill, DB, Tennessee 1961
Manucci, Dan, QB, Kansas State 1979-80
Marangi, Gary, QB, Boston College 1974-76
Marchlewski, Frank, C, Minnesota 1970
Masters, Billy, TE, Louisiana State 1967-69
Matlock, John, C, Miami 1972
Matsos, Archie, LB, Michigan State 1960-62
Matuszak, Marv, LB, Tulsa 1962-63
Mays, David, QB, Texas Southern 1978
McBath, Mike, DE, Penn State 1968-72
McCabe, Richie, DB, Pittsburgh 1960-61
McCaffrey, Mike, LB, California 1970
McConnell, Brian, LB, Michigan State 1973
McCrumbly, John, LB, Texas A&M 1975
McCutcheon, Lawrence, RB, Colorado State 1981
McDermott, Gary, RB, Tulsa 1968
McDole, Ron, DE, Nebraska 1963-70
McDonald, Don, DB, Houston 1961
McFarland, Jim, TE, Nebraska 1970
McGrew, Dan, C, Purdue 1960
McKenzie, Reggie, G, Michigan 1972-81
McKinley, Bill, LB, Arizona 1971
McKinney, Royce, DB, Kentucky State 1975
McLanahan, Randy, LB, Southwestern Louisiana 1978
McMillan, Eddie, CB, Florida State 1978
McMurtry, Chuck, DT, Whittier 1960-61
Means, Dave, DE, Southeast Missouri State 1974
Mercer, Mike, K, Northern Arizona 1967-68
Meredith, Dudley, DE, Lamar U. 1964-68
Meyer, Ed, T, West Texas State 1960
Mike-Mayer, Nick, K, Temple 1979-81
Miller, Bill, E, Miami 1963
Miller, Terry, RB, Oklahoma State 1978-80
Mills. Sullivan, E-DB, Wichita State 1965-66
Minter, Tom, HB, Baylor 1962
Mitchell, Charley, RB, Washington 1968
Montler, Mike, C, Colorado 1973-76
Moody, Keith, DB, Syracuse 1976-79
Moore, Leroy, DE, Fort Valley State 1960, 1962-63
Morton, Greg, DE, Michigan 1977
Moses, Haven, WR, San Diego State 1968-72
Mosley, Wayne, RB, Alabama A&M 1974
Moss, Roland, RB, Toledo 1970
Muelhaupt, Ed, G, Iowa State 1960-61
Munson, Bill, QB, Utah State 1978-79
Murdock, Jesse, FB, California Western 1963

N

Nelson, Bob, LB, Nebraska 1975-77
Nelson, Shane, LB, Baylor 1977-81
Nighswander, Nick, C, Morehead State 1974
Nixon, Jeff, DB, Richmond 1979-81
Nunamaker, Julian, DE, Tennessee-Martin 1969-70

O

O'Connell, Tom, QB, Illinois 1960-61
O'Donnell, Joe, G, Michigan 1964-71
O'Donoghue, Neil, K, Auburn 1977
Ogas, Dave, LB, San Diego State 1969
Okoniewski, Steve, DT, Montana 1972-73
Oliver, Frank, DB, Kentucky State 1975
Olson, Harold, T, Clemson 1960-62

P

Palmer, Dick, LB, Kentucky 1972
Palumbo, Sam, C, Notre Dame 1960
Parker, Ervin, LB, South Carolina State 1980-81
Parker, Willie, C, North Texas State 1973-79
Pate, Lloyd, RB, Cincinnati 1970
Paterra, Herb, LB, Michigan State 1963
Patrick, Wayne, RB, Louisville 1968-72
Patton, Bob, C, Delaware 1976
Patton, Jerry, DT, Nebraska 1972-73
Patulski, Walt, DE, Notre Dame 1972-75
Penchion, Robert, G, Alcorn State 1972-73
Petrich, Bob, DE, West Texas State 1967
Pharr, Tommy, S, Mississippi State 1970
Piccone, Lou, WR, West Liberty State 1977-81
Pitts, John, S, Arizona State 1967-73
Ply, Bobby, DB, Baylor 1967
Powell, Art, E, San Jose State 1967
Powell, Darnell, RB, Tennessee-Chattanooga 1976
Powell, Steve, RB, Northeast Missouri State 1978-79
Prudhomme, Remi, C, Louisiana State 1966-67, 1972

R

Rabb, Warren, QB, Louisiana State 1961-62
Randolph, Al, S, Iowa 1974
Rashad, Ahmad, WR, Oregon 1974
Ray, Eddie, RB, Louisiana State 1976
Reeves, Roy, WR, South Carolina 1969
Reid, Andy, RB, Georgia 1976
Reilly, Jim, G, Notre Dame 1970-71
Remmert, Dennis, T, Iowa State 1960
Reynolds, M. C. (Mack), QB, Louisiana State 1961
Ricardo, Benny, K, San Diego State 1976
Rice, Ken, T, Auburn 1961, 1963
Richards, Perry, E, Detroit 1961
Richardson, Pete, CB, Dayton 1969-71
Richey, Mike, T, North Carolina 1969
Riddick, Robb, RB, Millersville State 1981
Ridlehuber, Preston, RB, Georgia 1969
Rissmiller, Ray, T, Georgia 1968
Ritcher, Jim, C, North Carolina State 1980-81
Rivera, Hank, DB, Oregon State 1963
Roberson, Bo, E, Cornell 1965
Robertson, Isiah, LB. Southern U. 1979-81
Robinson, Matt, QB, Georgia 1981
Romes, Charles, DB, North Carolina Central 1977-81
Rosdahl, Harrison, DE, Penn State 1964
Ross, Louis, DE, South Carolina State 1971-72
Ross, Willie, FB, Nebraska 1964
Russell, Ben, QB, Louisville 1968
Rutkowski, Charles, E, Ripon 1960
Rutkowski, Ed, QB-WR, Notre Dame 1963-68
Ruud, Tom, LB, Nebraska 1975-77
Rychlec, Tom, E, American International 1960-62

S

Saidock, Tom, DT, Michigan State 1962
Saimes, George, S, Michigan State 1963-69
Sanford, Lucius, LB, Georgia Tech 1978-81
Saunders, John, S, Toledo 1972
Schaffer, Joe, HB, Tennessee 1960
Schmidt, Bob, C, Minnesota 1966-67
Schmidt, Henry, DT, USC 1965
Schnarr, Steve, RB, Otterbein 1975
Schottenheimer, Marty, LB, Pittsburgh 1965-68
Scott, John, T, Ohio State 1960-61
Sedlock, Bob, DT, Georgia 1960
Selfridge, Andy, LB, Virginia 1972
Sestak, Tom, DT, McNeese State 1962-68
Seymour, Paul, TE, Michigan 1973-77
Shaw, Billy, G, Georgia Tech 1961-69
Shaw, Dennis, QB, San Diego State 1970-73
Sherman, Tom, QB, Penn State 1969
Shipp, Joe, TE, USC 1979
Shockley, Bill, HB, West Chester State 1961
Simpson, Bill, S, Michigan State 1980-81
Simpson, O. J., RB, USC 1969-77
Skorupan, John, LB, Penn State 1973-77
Smerlas, Fred, NT, Boston College 1979-81
Smith, Allen, HB, Fort Valley State 1966-67
Smith, Bobby, HB, North Texas State 1964-65
Smith, Carl, FB, Tennessee 1960
Smith, Marty, DT, Louisville 1976
Smith, Tody, DE, USC 1976
Snowden, Cal, DE, Indiana 1971
Sorey, Jim, DT, Texas Southern 1960-62
Spikes, Jack, RB, Texas Christian 1966-67
Stephenson, Kay, QB, Florida 1968
Stone, Don, RB, Arkansas 1965
Stone, Ken, S, Vanderbilt 1973
Stratton, Mike, LB, Tennessee 1962-72
Switzer, Marvin, DB, Kansas State 1978
Sykes, Gene, DB, Louisiana State 1963-65

T

Taliaferro, Mike, QB, Illinois 1972
Taseff, Carl, DB, John Carrol 1962
Tatarek, Bob, DT, Miami 1968-72
Thomas, Ike, DB, Bishop 1975
Thornton, Bubba, WR, Texas Christian 1969
Toomay, Pat, DE, Vanderbilt 1975
Torczon, Laverne, DE, Nebraska 1960-62
Tracey, John, LB, Texas A&M 1962-67
Trapp, Richard, WR, Florida 1968
Tyler, Maurice, S, Morgan State 1972

V

Valdez, Vernon, DB, San Diego University 1961
Vanvalkenburg, Pete, RB, Brigham Young 1973
Villapiano, Phil, LB, Bowling Green 1980-81
Vogler, Tim, C, Ohio State 1979-81

W

Wagstaff, Jim, DB, Idaho State 1960-61
Walker, Donnie, DB, Central State, Ohio 1973-74
Walton, Larry, WR, Arizona State 1978
Warlick, Ernie, E, North Carolina Central 1962-65
Warner, Charley, DB, Prairie View 1964-66
Washington, Dave, LB, Alcorn State 1972-74
Washington, Vic, RB, Wyoming 1975-76
Watkins, Larry, RB, Alcorn State 1973-74
Wegert, Ted, RB, No college 1960
West, Willie, DB, Oregon 1962-63
Wheeler, Manch, QB, Maine 1962
White, Jan, TE, Ohio State 1971-72
White, Sherman, DE, California 1976-81
Williams, Ben, DE, Mississippi 1976-81
Williams, Chris, CB, Louisiana State 1981
Willis, Len, WR, Ohio State 1977-79
Wilson, Mike, G, Dayton 1971
Winans, Jeff, DT, USC 1973, 1975
Winfrey, Stan, RB, Arkansas State 1977
Wolff, Wayne, G, Wake Forest 1961
Word, Roscoe, DB, Jackson State 1976
Wyatt, Alvin, DB, Bethune-Cookman 1971-73
Wyche, Sam, QB, Furman 1976

Y

Yaccino, John, DB, Pittsburgh 1962
Yeates, Jeff, DT, Boston College 1974-76
Yoho, Mack, DE, Miami, Ohio 1960-63
Young, Willie, T, Alcorn State 1971
Youngelman, Sid, T, Alabama 1962-63

Z

Zecher, Rich, DT, Utah State 1967
Zelencik, Connie, C, Purdue 1977

CHICAGO BEARS

1920 A. E. Staley, who owned the Staley Starch Company in Decatur, Illinois, hired 25-year-old George Halas to work in his plant, play on his semi-pro baseball team, and organize a company football team. Staley promised Halas enough of a budget to attract top ballplayers, and he also agreed to let them practice on company time. Halas signed end Guy Chamberlin, halfback Jimmy Conzelman, halfback Ed (Dutch) Sternaman, center George Trafton, and quarterback Charley Dressen. Halas himself played end. Halas contacted Ralph Hay about playing the Canton Bulldogs, whom Hay managed. Hay told Halas of a plan to organize professional football. Representatives of the Staleys, Bulldogs, and nine other teams met in a preliminary meeting, August 20. The group formally organized itself as the American Professional Football Association, September 17. The league was loosely organized. There were either no standings kept, or they have been lost. The Staleys finished with a 10-1-2 record. They claimed a share of the championship on the grounds that they had held the other claimant, the undefeated Akron, Ohio, Pros to a scoreless tie in their only meeting. The Staleys had many odd formations in their small notebook of plays, but Halas's favorite was the T-formation. He had played it under coach Bob Zuppke at Illinois. Decatur was one of the few teams to show a profit in the first year of operation. Each member of the squad received $1,900 for his season's work.

1921 A business recession after the 1920 season cut into Staley's starch profits, and he was forced to withdraw sponsorship of his football team. He suggested to Halas that he take over the team. Halas agreed and decided to move the team to Chicago. For $5,000, he further agreed to call the team the "Chicago Staleys" for one year. Halas secured permission for the move from Chris O'Brien, owner of the Racine Cardinals, who held the territorial rights to the city of Chicago. Halas made his former Illinois classmate Dutch Sternaman half-owner of the team instead of paying him a salary. Halas and Sternaman signed a lease with William Veeck, Sr., owner of the Chicago Cubs, to play at Cub Park in exchange for 15 percent of each game's gross. They signed Guy Chamberlin and George Trafton from the old Staleys team. The Staleys won the APFA championship with a 10-1-1 record. Second-place Buffalo (9-1-2) protested that Chicago's record included nonleague games, but league president Joe Carr ruled in favor of Chicago.

1922 At Halas's suggestion the league rechristened itself the National Football League. Halas renamed his team the Chicago Bears, January 28. His agreement with Staley had expired, and he thought some nickname association with the Cubs would be appropriate. Halas engineered Chicago's first trade, November 27. Impressed after he was unable to block Rock Island's great end Ed Healey, Halas paid the Independents $100 for Healey's contract. The Bears lost two games to the Chicago Cardinals, 6-0 and 9-0, in which all the scoring came on John (Paddy) Driscoll's field goals. The Bears finished second behind Canton with a 9-3 record. Halas and Sternaman turned a profit; they made $1,476.92 for the season.

1923 Halas scooped up a fumble by Jim Thorpe of the Oorang Indians at the Bears' 2-yard line and raced a record 98 yards to a touchdown, November 4. The Bears finished second behind Canton once again. Chicago went 9-2-1, while Canton was undefeated at 11-0-1.

1924 The Bears lost to Green Bay in the opening game of the season, but did not lose again. They fin-

Hall of Fame halfback Red Grange, 1932.

ished with a 6-1-4 record, which was good enough for second place behind the Cleveland Bulldogs. Halas and Sternaman split $20,000 profit at the end of the season.

1925 Halas signed Red Grange, who had finished his collegiate career with the University of Illinois one day earlier, November 22. In return for a significant share of the gate, Grange, through his agent, C.C. Pyle, agreed to play the rest of the season with the Bears, including a 19-game postseason barnstorming tour. On November 26, 36,000 people showed up for Grange's first game, but he gained only 36 yards in a 0-0 tie with the Cardinals. Nonetheless, Grange proved he was the first strong gate attraction in the

NFL. Over 73,000 New Yorkers watched as Grange and the Bears defeated the Giants at the Polo Grounds 19-7, December 6. The Bears played the Los Angeles Tigers before 75,000 at the Los Angeles Coliseum, January 16. The Bears beat the Washington All-Stars in Seattle 34-0, to end the tour, January 31. The tour netted Pyle and Grange $100,000 each. The Bears had a 13-5-1 record on the tour.

1926 Cubs Park was renamed Wrigley Field. Pyle asked the Bears for a five-figure salary and one-third ownership of the Bears for Grange. Halas refused, and Pyle started the American Football League, putting Grange with the New York Yankees. That left Chicago without a running star or a drawing card.

The problem was solved when Halas acquired Paddy Driscoll from the financially depressed Cardinals for $3,500. The Bears, the Pottsville, Pennsylvania, Maroons, and the Frankford, Pennsylvania, Yellow-jackets all fought for the league championship. Chicago was in contention until late in the season, when it played Frankford. Former Bear Guy Chamberlin was the Yellowjackets' player-coach, and he blocked Driscoll's extra point attempt to give his team a 7-6 win. Frankford ended the season with a 14-1-1 record. The Bears were second at 12-1-3.

1927 The champion Giants beat Chicago in a key game. Joe Guyon sent George Halas out of the game with broken ribs on a play on which Halas also was called for clipping. The Bears dropped to third place with a 9-3-2 record.

1928 Friction between the owners caused some problems on the Bears. Both Halas and Sternaman wanted to run the offense. Chicago finished fifth with a 7-5-1 record.

1929 Red Grange came out of retirement to play for the Bears. A knee injury affected his once peerless maneuverability, but he was still a sound, all-purpose back. They were 4-1-1 in their first six games, but lost seven of their last eight, to finish with their first losing season.

1930 Halas stepped down as coach and retired as a player. He and Sternaman compromised their disagreements by hiring former Illinois assistant Ralph Jones, who was the head coach at Lake Forest Academy, Illinois. Jones promised Halas and Sternaman a championship in three years. He changed the Bears' T-formation. He moved the ends wide, spaced the halfbacks wider, and made one of the halfbacks a man-in-motion. He could become a third end and run downfield for a pass; turn and crackback block the defensive end; or cross up the defense by going in motion in one direction several plays and then begin going in the opposite direction. This spiced up the ancient, plodding T-formation. Driscoll retired and George Trafton was not invited back. Trafton ignored the message, however. He reported and won back the center's job with outstanding preseason play. The Bears signed 6-foot 2-inch, 230-pound fullback Bronko Nagurski from the University of Minnesota. Carl Brumbaugh, a rookie from the University of Florida, became the Bears' quarterback. Right after the completion of the college season, Halas signed Notre Dame fullback Joe Savoldi. NFL President Carr fined the Bears $1,000 for signing a collegian before his class had graduated. Ironically, Savoldi lasted only four games; the competition with Nagurski was too great. The Bears moved into third place with a 9-4-1 record.

1931 The Bears gained a top halfback when they signed Keith Molesworth, who could run, pass, return kicks, and back up Brumbaugh. The Bears finished in third place again. The league announced its first official all-pro team. Red Grange was the only Bears' player to make it.

1932 The Bears signed end Bill Hewitt from Michigan. A veteran from the 1929 club, Joe Kopcha, returned from retirement to play guard. In the last game of the season, the Bears beat the Green Bay Packers 9-0 on a 14-yard field goal by Paul (Tiny) Engebretsen and a 56-yard run by Nagurski. That gave Chicago a 7-1-6 record and forced a playoff between the Bears and the Portsmouth, Ohio, Spartans which was held in Chicago, December 18. Below-zero temperatures forced Halas to move the game indoors to Chicago Stadium. The field was only 80 yards long, and it was surrounded by a solid fence only a few feet from the side and end lines. The Bears won 9-0 when Nagurski took a fourth down handoff near the goal line but stopped suddenly, backed up, and lobbed a pass to Grange, who was all alone in the end zone. Ralph Jones had kept his promise to deliver a championship within three years. The Bears' Nagurski, end Luke Johnsos, and guard Jules Carlson were named to the all-pro team. The Bears, however, lost $18,000 for the year. As a result, Sternaman

Members of the Chicago Bears hold owner-coach George Halas aloft after their 73-0 victory over the Washington Redskins in the 1940 NFL Championship Game.

wanted out; he sold his half of the team to Halas for $38,000. Halas had to borrow the money, $5,000 of which came from businessman Charles Bidwill.

1933 The league aligned itself into Eastern and Western divisions; the Bears were named one of the five Western teams. Ralph Jones resigned as coach. Halas returned to the sidelines as his replacement. The Bears had their first out-of-town training camp, at Notre Dame. Tackle Link Lyman ended a one-year retirement. Three promising rookies joined the club —fullback-kicker Jack Manders from Minnesota, 260-pound tackle George Musso from Millikin College, and end Bill Karr from West Virginia. The Bears won the Western Division title with a 10-2-1 record. In the NFL's first championship game, 26,000 people watched at Wrigley Field as Jack Manders kicked three field goals and two extra points and the Bears defeated the New York Giants 23-21. The winning points were scored when Nagurski lobbed a short pass to Hewitt, who lateraled to Karr, who scored a 36-yard touchdown.

1934 The Bears held training camp at Lane Tech High School in Chicago. They played the best college players in the first Chicago All-Star game, before 79,432 at Soldier Field, August 31. The game ended in a scoreless tie. Chicago signed rookie halfback Beattie Feathers of Tennessee. The Bears won all 13 league contests. Feathers became the first pro back to gain 1,000 yards, totaling 1,004 yards. He also set an NFL record by averaging 9.94 yards per carry. Nagurski's blocks helped clear the way for him. The Bears met the Giants in the Polo Grounds for the NFL championship, December 9. The day was cold, and the field was frozen. The Bears led 13-3 after three quarters. But some of the Giants' players switched to tennis shoes and gained better traction. New York scored 27 points in the final period and won 30-13. The Bears dominated the all-pro selections. Feathers, Nagurski, Hewitt, and Kopcha made first-team; Lyman and center Eddie Kawal made the second team. Red Grange, who had been a reserve during the season, retired.

1935 The Bears switched their training camp to St. Johns Military Academy in Delafield, Wisconsin. Brumbaugh and Lyman retired before the season. Nagurski was out most of the year with a hip injury. Feathers was hurt off and on all season. The Bears struggled to a 6-4-2 record. Karr, Musso, and Kopcha made the all-pro team.

1936 The NFL held its first draft of college seniors. On the advice of West Virginians Karr and Brumbaugh, Halas took lineman Joe Stydahar from that school on the first round. He also picked halfback Ray Nolting in a later round. On the ninth round he chose guard Danny Fortmann. The Bears obtained the rights from Philadelphia for the NFL's very first draft pick, Jay Berwanger, but the University of Chicago star chose not to play professional football. Stydahar and Fortmann became starters. Nagurski came back strong from his injuries. Manders led the league in field goals for the third year. Hewitt, who refused to wear a helmet when he played, was named all-pro for the third time. The Bears finished second with a 9-3-0 record.

1937 Two outstanding newcomers, end George Wilson, and former Eagles' end Edgar (Eggs) Manske made the squad. Stydahar, Musso, Fortmann, and Frank Bausch were named to the all-pro team. The Bears coasted to the Western Division title. In the NFL championship before 15,870 people at Wrigley Field, the Bears lost 28-21 to the Washington Redskins as Sammy Baugh completed 17 of 34 passes for 347 yards in near zero weather. Each Chicago player received $127.78 as his share of the championship purse. Nagurski retired.

1938 Feathers was traded to Brooklyn, and Keith

Molesworth quit to coach at the U.S. Naval Academy. At mid-year, Halas purchased fullback Joe Maniaci from the Brooklyn Dodgers. The Bears finished with their poorest record since 1929, 6-5-0.

1939 The Bears' T-formation was growing more complex each year. New plays were drawn for it constantly by Halas and his assistants and voluntary assistant Clark Shaughnessy, head coach of the University of Chicago. The offense acquired a complicated play-calling system. It also put emphasis on a quarterback who was a good ball handler. The Bears drafted tailback Sid Luckman of Columbia on the first round, intending to develop him into a T-quarterback who could absorb the system and run the plays. They also drafted fullback Bill Osmanski of Holy Cross. Luckman spent his rookie season playing left halfback and Osmanski led the league in rushing with 699 yards. Chicago moved up to second in the Western Division with an 8-3 record.

1940 The Bears obtained Duke halfback George McAfee, who had been drafted by the Philadelphia Eagles in the first round, in exchange for three players. The Bears also drafted center Clyde (Bulldog) Turner from Hardin-Simmons; Lee Artoe, a tackle from California; Ed Kolman, a tackle from Temple; end Ken Kavanaugh from Louisiana State; and halfback Ray (Scooter) McLean from St. Anselms in New Hampshire. Bernie Masterson retired and Luckman became the starting quarterback. McAfee ran 93 yards for a touchdown against the Green Bay Packers on the first kickoff he fielded in league competition. The Bears won the Western Division title with an 8-3 record. They faced the Redskins in Washington, D.C., for the NFL championship, December 8. Ten different Bears scored touchdowns as Chicago smashed Washington 73-0. Chicago's defense intercepted eight passes and allowed only 22 yards rushing. The Bears got $873 per man as their championship share.

1941 The Bears drafted backs Norm Standlee and Hugh Gallarneau from Stanford's 1940 Rose Bowl team. They alternated with Osmanski and McAfee in a backfield that rushed for more than 1,500 yards. McAfee led the league in average yards per carry at 7.3. The Bears averaged over 36 points a game on their way to tying Green Bay for the Western Division title. Both teams had 10-1-0 records, and they met in a playoff at Wrigley Field, before 43,425, December 14. Gallarneau returned a punt 81 yards for a touchdown in the first quarter, and the Bears went on to win 33-14. A crowd of 13,341 showed up at Wrigley Field to watch the Bears play the Giants for the NFL championship, December 21. Standlee scored two touchdowns and McAfee and Kavanaugh one each as the Bears won 37-9.

1942 McAfee and Standlee went into the service. Halas was down to his fourth-string fullback, Gary Famiglietti. Stydahar was inducted into the army toward the end of the year. Halas himself joined the navy, December 13. He was replaced by assistants Hunk Anderson and Luke Johnsos. The Bears posted an 11-0-0 season record. They faced the Redskins in Washington for the NFL title. Artoe picked up a fumble and ran 50 yards for a Chicago score in the second period. But a touchdown pass by Baugh and some fine running by Andy Farkas gave Washington a 14-6 victory.

1943 Bronko Nagurski, 35, came out of retirement to play tackle for the Bears. Luckman became the first professional quarterback to pass for over 400 yards in a game as he threw for 433 yards and seven touchdowns in a 56-7 win over the New York Giants, November 14. The Bears had 702 yards in total offense against New York. Chicago won the division with an 8-1-1 record and hosted the championship game against the Washington Redskins before

34,320 in Wrigley Field. Luckman threw five touchdown passes, and Nagurski scored his last NFL touchdown as the Bears won 41-21. Nagurski retired for the second and last time.

1944 Chicago set up training facilities at St. Joseph's College in Rensselaer, Indiana. Luckman was called into the merchant marine service and was available to the team only on weekends. His understudy was 35-year-old Gene Ronzani. The Bears lost their first two games, to Green Bay and Cleveland, and never caught the Packers. They finished second with a 6-3-1 record.

1945 The war-depleted Bears lost seven of their first eight games. Halas came back from the navy, November 22. Kavanaugh, Stydahar, McAfee, and Gallarneau all came back before the season ended. McAfee returned for the next-to-the-last game of the season. He made Halas promise to use him sparingly. Halas put him in for only 12 minutes, and in that time McAfee scored three touchdowns. The Bears won their last two games and finished fourth with a 3-7-0 record.

1946 Prewar stars McAfee, Osmanski, Gallarneau, Luckman, Turner, and Wilson were back. The Bears had an 8-2-1 record and won the Western Division title. In the championship game in New York, the Bears defeated the New York Giants 24-14. Luckman ran a quarterback keeper 19 yards for a fourth-quarter touchdown that broke a 14-14 tie.

1947 Chicago lost its first two games, including one to the crosstown rival Cardinals 31-7. But they won eight of their next nine contests and went into a game against the Cardinals in the final week of the season tied with the Cardinals at 8-3. The Cardinals scored on the first play of the game and went on to win 30-21. Luckman, Ken Kavanaugh, and tackle Fred Davis were named to the all-pro team.

1948 The Bears drafted Texas quarterback Bobby Layne in the first round. Halas outbid the All-America Football Conference to sign Layne with a $22,500 contract, including a $10,000 bonus for signing. Other promising rookies also came high. Notre Dame quarterback Johnny Lujack signed for $18,000, and Notre Dame tackle George Connor got a no-cut contract. Connor became an immediate starter. Lujack started on defense. Layne was a reserve. The Bears ended with a 10-2-0 record, but lost the Western Division title to the Cardinals on the last day of the season when the Cardinals beat them 24-21.

1949 Just before the season started, Halas sold Layne to the New York Bulldogs. Luckman contracted a thyroid condition which kept him out most of the season, and Johnny Lujack became the starting quarterback. Lujack set an NFL passing record by throwing for 468 yards against the Cardinals, December 11. Lujack threw six touchdown passes in the 52-21 victory over the Cardinals. The Bears finished at 9-3, one game behind the Rams, who were 8-2-2. Guard Ray Bray was named to the all-pro team.

1950 The All-America Football Conference folded, and the NFL absorbed three of its teams and restructured into two conferences, the National and the American. The Bears became one of seven teams in the National Conference. The Bears had a 9-3 record, tying the Rams for the National Conference lead. The two teams played off in the Los Angeles Coliseum with the Rams' Tom Fears catching three touchdown passes in Los Angeles's 24-14 victory over Chicago, December 17.

1951 Quarterback Sid Luckman, halfback George McAfee, and end Ken Kavanaugh all retired. Going into the final week of the season, the Lions led the Bears and the Rams by a half game. But Los Angeles routed Green Bay 42-14 while the Bears were being surprised 24-14 by the crosstown Cardinals.

1952 The Bears drafted end-defensive back Jim Dooley from Georgia in the first round. In later rounds, they got end Bill McColl from Stanford and linebacker Bill George from Wake Forest. Johnny Lujack retired to assist Frank Leahy at Notre Dame. Three young quarterbacks competed for his job: George Blanda, Steve Romanik, and Bob Williams. The Bears dropped to fifth place at 5-7-0, the first time since 1945 that they fell below .500.

1953 Bulldog Turner, the last of the 1940-41 championship players, retired. In the tenth week of the season, the Bears beat Los Angeles 24-21, a victory that knocked the Rams out of title contention. Still, the Bears struggled to a 3-8-1 season.

1954 Chicago drafted quarterback Zeke Bratkowski from Georgia in the first round. In a low round, the Bears also got end Harlon Hill from Florence State Teachers College in Alabama. Halas traded for fullback Harry (Chick) Jagade, formerly of Cleveland. Bratkowski alternated with Blanda at quarterback, and between them they threw for over 3,000 yards. Hill gained over 1,000 yards on 45 receptions. Two rookies, Stan Jones and Larry Strickland, became starters in the offensive line. George Connor was lost for the year with an injury. The Bears won their last four games, ending the season with a 28-24 victory over the National Conference champion Lions. Chicago had an 8-4 record for the year.

1955 Halas announced he would retire in favor of a younger coach after the 1955 season. Rookie running backs Rick Casares and Bobby Watkins became starters. Both averaged over five yards a carry. Bratkowski went into the service, and second-year quarterback Ed Brown took over the position. Hill caught 42 passes. The Bears lost their first three games, then they won six in a row before suffering a 53-14 upset by the Cardinals. The loss knocked the Bears (8-4-1) out of a conference title, as the Rams (8-3-1) finished a half game in front.

1956 True to his promise, Halas gave way to a younger man. Long-time assistant Paddy Driscoll, who was two years younger than Halas, became the new head coach. George Connor retired. The Bears lost their first game to Baltimore 28-21, then won or tied the next eight. In a rematch with the Colts, Chicago won 58-27. In the tenth game, the Bears lost 42-10 to Detroit. Going into the final game, again against Detroit, the Bears were 8-2-1, while the Lions were 9-2. Chicago won the rematch 38-21 and with it the National Conference title. Hill ended the year with 47 catches. Casares rushed 234 times for 1,126 yards. Brown completed 57 percent of his passes. The NFL Championship Game was played against the Giants on an icy field in Yankee Stadium. The Giants wore tennis shoes for improved traction, and won 47-7.

1957 Bratkowski returned from the service. The Bears drafted running back Willie Galimore. They lost to Green Bay, Baltimore, and San Francisco in their first three starts. The defense actually allowed fewer points than it had in the 1956 championship season, but the Bears finished at 5-7-0.

1958 Halas returned as head coach. The Bears were in a title race most of the year. Eventual winner Baltimore beat them twice, and their only other losses were to Los Angeles and Pittsburgh. The Bears and Rams drew 90,833 to a game in the Los Angeles Coliseum. Chicago finished second, one game behind the Colts at 8-4.

1959 Chicago lost four of its first five games, then won seven in a row. On the last Sunday of the season, the Bears were tied with San Francisco for second place at 7-4. Baltimore was on top with an 8-3 record. San Francisco lost to Green Bay 36-14, and Chicago beat Detroit 25-14. But Baltimore outscored Los Angeles 45-26 to clinch the National Conference title.

Walter Payton follows a block by Robin Earl in a game against Kansas City, 1977.

1960 The Bears were one-half game out of first place in mid-November with a 5-3-1 record. But then they lost to the Packers 41-13, the Browns 42-0, and the Lions 36-0. They finished fifth with a 5-6-1 record. It was only the sixth time the Bears were under .500 since 1920.

1961 Fire destroyed the Bears' offices, and they moved to new ones at 173 West Madison Street. In the first round of the draft, Chicago picked Mike Ditka from Pittsburgh. Halas obtained veteran quarterback Billy Wade from the Rams. The Bears dismantled the 49ers' Shotgun offense 31-0, October 22. Chicago yielded only six first downs and 132 yards to the previously unstoppable offense. Green Bay jumped off to a 28-7 lead over the Bears, then held off a Chicago comeback for a 31-28 victory, November 12. The Bears ended the season tied for third place at 8-6. Ditka caught 56 passes for 1,076 yards on the season. Wade passed for 2,258 yards and 22 touchdowns.

1962 Injuries sidelined running backs Casares and Galimore. Rookie Ronnie Bull from Baylor won rookie of the year honors at halfback. Wade set two team records by passing for 3,172 yards and by completing 225 passes. Both marks were previously held by Sid Luckman. Ditka and fifth-year receiver Johnny Morris caught 58 passes each. Chicago had a 9-5 record, third best in the Western Conference behind Green Bay (13-1) and Detroit (11-3).

1963 Assistant coach George Allen installed a zone defense, and suddenly the Bears had the strongest defense in the NFL. Chicago won its first five games before losing to San Francisco. The Bears defeated Green Bay twice, 10-3 and 26-7. Chicago won the Western Conference with an 11-1-2 record, one-half

game ahead of the Packers, 11-2-1. The Bears' defense allowed an average of only 10.1 points a game. Ditka caught 59 passes, Morris 47. The NFL Championship Game was played in eight-degree weather before 45,801 at Wrigley Field against the New York Giants, December 29. Chicago intercepted five Y. A. Tittle passes, Wade scored two touchdowns, and the Bears won 14-10. The winning share was $5,899 a player. It was Chicago's first NFL championship since 1946.

1964 Running back Willie Galimore and end John Farrington were killed in an automobile accident during training camp. Injuries handicapped the Bears' defense, and one of the early season embarrassments was a 52-0 loss to Baltimore. Ends Doug Atkins and Ed O'Bradovich missed most of the season with injuries. Linebacker Bill George played the early season with a hamstring injury and missed the last six games with a bad knee. Halas switched from Wade to Rudy Bukich at quarterback. Morris set a league record by catching 93 passes for 1,200 yards. Ditka added 75 for 897 yards. Chicago finished sixth with a 5-9 record.

1965 Linebacker Dick Butkus from Illinois and running back Gale Sayers from Kansas both were drafted on the first round. Sayers scored six touchdowns against the 49ers in a 61-20 Chicago win that avenged an earlier 52-24 loss to San Francisco. The Bears finished third in the Western Conference with a 9-5 record. Sayers set an NFL record by scoring 22 touchdowns. He and Butkus both were all-pro after their first seasons.

1966 Assistant coach George Allen resigned to become head coach of the Rams. Morris was out for most of the year with an injured knee and caught only five passes. Sayers had another record-setting year, gaining a combined 2,440 yards. He led the NFL in rushing with 1,231 yards, caught 34 passes, and led the league in kickoff returns. Chicago finished fifth with a 5-7-2 record.

1967 The NFL expanded to 16 teams. The Eastern and Western Conferences were subdivided into two four-team divisions each. Chicago was put into the Central Division of the Western Conference, with Detroit, Green Bay, and Minnesota. Halas traded Ditka to Philadelphia for quarterback Jack Concannon. After a slow start, the Bears finished with a 5-1-1 record in their last seven games, to place second behind the Packers at 7-6-1. Sayers had over 1,600 combined yards.

1968 Halas, 73, retired as head coach of the Bears, May 27. After 40 seasons of pro coaching his record was 320 wins, 147 defeats, and 30 ties. Jim Dooley, a player or coach with the Bears since 1952, was named head coach, May 28. The Bears lost their first two games before beating the Vikings. In the Minnesota game, Concannon fractured a collarbone, and his backup, Rudy Bukich, separated a shoulder. Virgil Carter, third-string quarterback, led the Bears to four straight wins at midyear. The last game of that four was against San Francisco. In it, 49ers defensive back Kermit Alexander tackled Sayers low, and the impact tore ligaments and cartilage in Sayers's right knee, putting him out for the year. Carter broke his ankle a week later, against Atlanta. The Bears lost three of their last five games and finished second behind the Vikings at 7-7.

1969 Sayers came back from knee surgery to lead the league in rushing with 1,032 yards. Concannon, Carter, and rookie Bobby Douglass alternated at quarterback. The defense allowed an average of 24.2 points a game. Chicago dropped into last place with a 1-13 record, their poorest in 50 years of play in the NFL.

1970 Halas, 75, was elected president of the National Football Conference, March 19. Halfback Brian Piccolo, 26, died of cancer, June 16. Sayers hurt his right knee in preseason. Douglass was made the starting quarterback in late season. In his first start, he threw four touchdown passes as the Bears beat Buffalo. But late in that game Douglass broke his wrist, sidelining him for the year. Sayers had to undergo knee surgery again in October. Rookie Cecil Turner returned four kickoffs for touchdowns tying the single-season NFL record. The Bears whipped Green Bay 35-17 in their last game in Wrigley Field, December 13. They finished third with a 6-8-0 record.

1971 The Bears moved into Soldier Field. Chicago won five out of its first seven games. Then both the first- and second-string quarterbacks, Kent Nix and Jack Concannon, got hurt. Douglass took over, but the Bears lost six of the last seven games. Sayers's bad knee kept him immobilized most of the year; he carried the ball only 13 times for 38 yards. Butkus was a unanimous all-pro. Dooley, whose four-year record was 20-36, was dismissed as coach.

1972 Abe Gibron, former Bears player and assistant coach since 1965, was named head coach, January 27. Sayers retired before the season began. Douglass was given the starting quarterback spot again. He completed only 38 percent of his passes, last in the NFL in that category, but he gained a quarterback rushing record of 968 yards. The Bears led the NFC in rushing yardage. Chicago played .500 football the first half of the season, then dropped six of its last seven games to finish last in the NFC Central with a 4-9-1 record.

1973 The Bears drafted tackle Wally Chambers from Eastern Kentucky on the first round. Gibron kept Douglass at quarterback until midseason; rookie

Gary Huff from Florida State was given the job, November 18. Huff threw four interceptions in his debut as the Lions beat the Bears 30-7. The Bears finished last again in the NFC Central at 3-11-0. Middle linebacker Butkus retired.

1974 The Bears drafted linebacker Waymond Bryant from Tennessee State in the first round. Chicago named a non-Bear, Jim Finks, to run their operation. Finks was named executive vice president, general manager, and chief operating officer. The Bears finished last for the third year in a row with a 4-10 record. After the last game, Abe Gibron, who compiled a three-year record of 11-30-1, was fired, December 17. Jack Pardee, former NFL linebacker, was named head coach December 31.

1975 Chicago took Walter Payton, a running back from Jackson State, on the first round of the draft. The Bears opened their new training facility at Lake Forest Academy in Lake Forest, Illinois, May 1. A 26-yard field goal by Bob Thomas gave Pardee his first NFL coaching win, 15-13 over Philadelphia, September 28. Bob Avellini, a rookie from Maryland, became the starting quarterback. Payton gained a combined total of 300 yards in a 42-17 victory over the Saints, December 21. For the season, the Bears defense allowed 379 points, most in the NFC. Chicago waived, traded, or released 76 players under contract to them in 1975. Chicago ended the season with a 4-10 record, its seventh consecutive losing year.

1976 The Bears moved their executive offices to 55 East Jackson Street. Payton rushed for 148 yards in Chicago's 19-12 surprise of San Francisco, September 19. Chicago upset eventual NFC champion Minnesota 14-13, October 31. Payton became the NFL's first rusher of the year to go over 1,000 yards, November 14. His 109 yards in 18 carries in a 24-13 victory over Green Bay gave him 1,008 yards, along with 12 touchdowns. Payton set a Bears' rushing record and led the NFC with 1,390 yards, finishing second only to O.J. Simpson's 1,503 yards in the NFL. The Bears had a 7-7 record, their best since 1968 and good for a second-place finish behind Minnesota.

1977 Former running back Gale Sayers was inducted into the Pro Football Hall of Fame in the offseason, and quarterback Mike Phipps was obtained from Cleveland shortly before the season started. Payton got the Bears off to a fast start with 160 yards rushing in a season-opening 30-20 victory over Detroit, but the team stumbled to a 3-5 start. The Bears appeared to be in total disarray following a 47-0 defeat to Houston, but the season was turned around when the Bears overcame a 17-0 deficit to defeat Kansas City 28-27 on November 13. A week later Payton rushed for 275 yards against Minnesota to establish an NFL single-game rushing record. The Bears carried a five-game winning streak into the final game, needing only a victory over the New York Giants to lock up a wild card spot in the playoffs. Despite bad game conditions, the Bears pulled out that game when Bob Thomas kicked a 28-yard field goal with only nine seconds left in overtime. But the magic ended for Chicago on December 26, when the Bears were routed by Dallas 37-7 in the first round of the playoffs. Payton finished the season with a league-leading 1,852 yards rushing, a Bears record.

1978 With a three-year coaching record of 20-22, Jack Pardee resigned on January 19 to accept the head coaching position with Washington. Neill Armstrong, the Minnesota Vikings' defensive coordinator, replaced Pardee on February 16. One of the mainstays of the Bears' defensive line, Wally Chambers, was traded to Tampa Bay for a draft choice, and the Bears acquired defensive end Tommy Hart from San Francisco. Chicago opened the season with three victories, but then dropped eight games in a row to

fall out of playoff contention. After 10 weeks, Phipps replaced Avellini as the starting quarterback. Four victories in the last six games improved the Bears' record to 7-9. On October 12, former all-pro defensive tackle Alan Page was acquired by the Bears from the Vikings, and he proceeded to lead the team in sacks with 11½. Payton rushed for 1,395 yards and was named all-pro for the third consecutive year.

1979 Another Chicago great, linebacker Dick Butkus, was inducted into the Pro Football Hall of Fame. On September 3, the club moved into Halas Hall, a $1.6 million headquarters on the Lake Forest College campus. The Bears began the season by defeating divisional foes Green Bay and Minnesota. On September 16 they lost to the Cowboys 24-20, despite 134 yards rushing by Payton, who supplanted Rick Casares as the club's all-time rushing leader. A sputtering offense cost the Bears losses in four of the next five games; even more costly was the loss of quarterback Vince Evans for the season with a staph infection after he made only three starts. But Phipps, who replaced Avellini after three games, guided the Bears to seven victories in the last eight games, and they secured a wild card playoff position with a 10-6 record. The euphoria over the season-ending 42-6 rout of St. Louis was tempered by the sudden death of club president George Halas, Jr., who was stricken with a heart attack. On December 23, the Bears' season ended with a 27-17 loss to Philadelphia in the wild card game, a contest Chicago led at halftime 17-0.

1980 George S. Halas, the chairman of the board, assumed the role of club president. Fully recovered from his illness, Evans became the Bears' starting quarterback after the team began the season with a 2-4 record. Under their new quarterback, the Bears played .500 football and finished the season 7-9, including a 61-7 victory over the Packers on December 7. Payton raised his combined yardage total to over 10,000 yards, breaking Sayers's team total.

1981 In an effort to improve the offense, Armstrong hired assistants Ted Marchibroda and Dick Stanfel, but the team suffered a blow before the season even started when wide receiver James Scott signed with Montreal of the Canadian Football League. The Bears lost six of their first seven games, but on October 25 they upset San Diego 20-17 in overtime. Three consecutive victories over Minnesota, Oakland, and Denver at the end of the season produced a final 6-10 record that included a 4-0 mark against AFC West teams. In his first full season as a starter, Evans passed for 2,354 yards. After three and a half years with the club, and 15 in the League, Page retired at the end of the season.

1982 In January, Armstrong was released as head coach. Several weeks later former Bears tight end Mike Ditka was named his successor.

MEMBERS OF HALL OF FAME:
Doug Atkins, George Blanda, Dick Butkus, Guy Chamberlin, George Connor, John (Paddy) Driscoll, Danny Fortmann, Bill George, Red Grange, George Halas, Ed Healey, Bill Hewitt, Walt Kiesling, Bobby Layne, Sid Luckman, Roy (Link) Lyman, George McAfee, George Musso, Bronko Nagurski, Gale Sayers, Joe Stydahar, George Trafton, Clyde (Bulldog) Turner.

BEARS RECORD, 1920-81

Year	Won	Lost	Tied	Pct.	Pts.	OP
Decatur Staleys						
1920........	10	1	1	.909		
Chicago Staleys						
1921‡........	10	1	1	.909		
Chicago Bears						
1922........	9	3	0	.750		
1923........	9	2	1	.818		
1924........	6	1	4	.857		
1925........	9	5	3	.643		
1926........	12	1	3	.923		
1927........	9	3	2	.750		
1928........	7	5	1	.583		
1929........	4	8	2	.333		
1930........	9	4	1	.692		

H. (Hunk) Anderson   Doug Atkins   Ray Bray   Ed Brown   Doug Buffone   Ronnie Bull   Jim Cadile

Year	Won	Lost	Tied	Pct.	Pts.	OP
1931......	8	4	0	.667		
1932‡.....	7	1	6	.875		
1933‡......	10	2	1	.833	133	82
1934§......	13	0	0	1.000	286	86
1935.......	6	4	2	.600	192	106
1936.......	9	3	0	.750	222	94
1937§......	9	1	1	.900	201	100
1938.......	6	5	0	.545	194	148
1939.......	8	3	0	.727	298	157
1940‡......	8	3	0	.727	238	152
1941‡......	10	1	0	.909	396	147
1942§......	11	0	0	1.000	376	84
1943‡......	8	1	1	.889	303	157
1944.......	6	3	1	.667	258	172
1945.......	3	7	0	.300	192	235
1946‡......	8	2	1	.800	289	193
1947.......	8	4	0	.667	363	241
1948.......	10	2	0	.833	375	151
1949.......	9	3	0	.750	332	218
1950.......	9	3	0	.750	279	207
1951.......	7	5	0	.583	286	282
1952.......	5	7	0	.417	245	326
1953.......	3	8	1	.273	218	262
1954.......	8	4	0	.667	301	279
1955.......	8	4	0	.667	294	251
1956†......	9	2	1	.818	363	246
1957.......	5	7	0	.417	203	211
1958.......	8	4	0	.667	298	230
1959.......	8	4	0	.667	252	196
1960.......	5	6	1	.455	194	299
1961.......	8	6	0	.571	326	302
1962.......	9	5	0	.643	321	287
1963‡......	11	1	2	.917	301	144
1964.......	5	9	0	.357	260	379
1965.......	9	5	0	.643	409	275
1966.......	5	7	2	.417	234	272
1967.......	7	6	1	.538	239	218
1968.......	7	7	0	.500	.250	333
1969.......	1	13	0	.071	210	339
1970.......	6	8	0	.429	256	261
1971.......	6	8	0	.429	185	276
1972.......	4	9	1	.321	225	275
1973.......	3	11	0	.214	195	334
1974.......	4	10	0	.286	152	279
1975.......	4	10	0	.286	191	379
1976.......	7	7	0	.500	253	216
1977*......	9	5	0	.643	255	253
1978.......	7	9	0	.438	253	274
1979*......	10	6	0	.625	306	249
1980.......	7	9	0	.438	304	264
1981.......	6	10	0	.375	253	324
62 Years.....	461	298	41	.602		

‡NFL Champion
§NFL Western Division Champion
†NFL Western Conference Champion
*NFC Wild Card Qualifier for Playoffs

RECORD HOLDERS

Rushing (Yards)	Walter Payton, 1977	1,852
Passing (Pct.)	Rudy Bukich, 1964	61.9
Passing (Yards)	Bill Wade, 1962	3,172
Passing (TDs)	Sid Luckman, 1943	28
Receiving (No.)	Johnny Morris, 1964	93
Receiving (Yards)	Johnny Morris, 1964	1,200
Interceptions (No.)	Roosevelt Taylor, 1963	9
Punting (Avg.)	Bobby Joe Green, 1963	46.5
Punt Ret. (Avg.)	Harry Clark, 1943	15.8
Kickoff Ret. (Avg.)	Gale Sayers, 1967	37.7
Touchdowns (Total)	Gale Sayers, 1965	22
Field Goals Made	Mac Percival, 1968	25
Points (No.)	Gale Sayers, 1965	132

COACHING HISTORY

1920-29	George Halas	85-30-18
1930-32	Ralph Jones	24- 9- 7
1933-42	George Halas*	85-22- 4
1942-45	Hunk Anderson, Luke Johnsos**	22-11- 2
1946-55	George Halas	75-42- 2
1956-57	John (Paddy) Driscoll	14- 9- 1
1958-67	George Halas	75-53- 6
1968-71	Jim Dooley	20-36- 0
1972-74	Abe Gibron	11-30- 1
1975-77	Jack Pardee	20-22- 0
1978-81	Neill Armstrong	30-34- 0

*Resigned after six games in 1942 to enter U.S. Navy
**Co-coaches

FIRST PLAYER SELECTED

1936	Joe Stydahar, T, West Virginia	
1937	Les McDonald, E, Nebraska	
1938	Joe Gray, B, Oregon State	
1939	Sid Luckman, B, Columbia	
1940	Clyde (Bulldog) Turner, C, Hardin-Simmons	
1941	Tom Harmon, B, Michigan	
1942	Frankie Albert, B, Stanford	
1943	Bob Steuber, B, Missouri	
1944	Ray Evans, B, Kansas	
1945	Don Lund, B, Michigan	
1946	Johnny Lujack, B, Notre Dame	
1947	Bob Fenimore, B, Oklahoma A&M	
1948	Bobby Layne, B, Texas	
1949	Dick Harris, C, Texas	
1950	Chuck Hunsinger, B, Florida	
1951	Bob Williams, B, Notre Dame	
1952	Jim Dooley, B, Miami	
1953	Billy Anderson, B, Compton (Calif.) JC	
1954	Stan Wallace, B, Illinois	
1955	Ron Drzewiecki, B, Marquette	
1956	Menan (Tex) Schriewer, E, Texas	
1957	Earl Leggett, T, Louisiana State	
1958	Chuck Howley, G, West Virginia	
1959	Don Clark, B, Ohio State	
1960	Roger Davis, G, Syracuse	
1961	Mike Ditka, E, Pittsburgh	
1962	Ron Bull, RB, Baylor	
1963	Dave Behrman, C, Michigan State	
1964	Dick Evey, DT, Tennessee	
1965	Dick Butkus, LB, Illinois	
1966	George Rice, DT, Louisiana State	
1967	Loyd Phillips, DE, Arkansas	
1968	Mike Hull, RB, USC	
1969	Rufus Mayes, T, Ohio State	
1970	George Farmer, WR (3), UCLA	
1971	Joe Moore, RB, Missouri	
1972	Lionel Antoine, T, Southern Illinois	
1973	Wally Chambers, DE, Eastern Kentucky	
1974	Waymond Bryant, LB, Tennessee State	
1975	Walter Payton, RB, Jackson State	
1976	Dennis Lick, T, Wisconsin	
1977	Ted Albrecht, T, California	
1978	Brad Shearer, DT (3), Texas	
1979	Dan Hampton, DT, Arkansas	
1980	Otis Wilson, LB, Louisville	
1981	Keith Van Horne, T, USC	
1982	Jim McMahon, QB, Brigham Young	

DECATUR STALEYS, 1920;
CHICAGO STALEYS, 1921;
CHICAGO BEARS, 1922-81

Abbey, Joe, E, North Texas State	1948-49
Adamle, Mike, RB, Northwestern	1975-76
Adams, John, B, Cal State-Los Angeles	1959-62
Adkins, Roy, G, Millikin	1920-21
Akin, Len, G, Baylor	1942
Albrecht, Ted, T, California	1977-81
Allen, Duane, E, Santa Ana Junior College	1966-67
Allen, Eddie, FB, Pennsylvania	1947
Allman, Bob, E, Michigan State	1936
Amsler, Marty, DE, Evansville	1967, 1969
Anderson, Art, T, Idaho	1961-62
Anderson, Eddie, E, Notre Dame	1923
Anderson, Henry, G, Northwestern	1931
Anderson, Hunk, G, Notre Dame	1922-26
Anderson, Marcus, WR, Tulane	1981
Anderson, Ralph, E, Cal State-Los Angeles	1958
Anderson, Billy, WR, Compton	1953-54
Antoine, Lionel, T, Southern Illinois	1972-76, 1978
Apolskis, Chuck, E, DePaul	1938-39
Ardizzone, Tony, C, Northwestern	1979
Arnett, Jon, RB, USC	1964-66
Artoe, Lee, T, California	1940-42, 1945
Ashburn, Cliff, T, Nebraska	1930
Asher, Bob, T, Vanderbilt	1972-75
Ashmore, M. Roger, T, Gonzaga	1927

A

Aspatore, Ed, T, Marquette	1934
Atkins, Doug, E, Tennessee	1955-66
Autrey, Billy, C, Stephen F. Austin	1953
Avellini, Bob, QB, Maryland	1975-81
Aveni, John, E, Indiana	1959-60

B

Babartsky, Al, T, Fordham	1943-45
Babinecz, John, LB, Villanova	1975
Badaczewski, John, G, Western Reserve	1953
Baisi, Al, G, West Virginia	1940-41, 1946
Barker, Dick, G, Iowa State	1921
Barnes, Erich, DB, Purdue	1958-60
Barnes, Gary, E, Clemson	1964
Barnes, Joe, RB, Texas Tech	1974
Barnett, Steve, T, Oregon	1963
Barwegan, Dick, G, Purdue	1950-52
Baschnagel, Brian, WR-KR, Ohio State	1976-81
Bassi, Dick, G, Santa Clara	1938-39
Battles, Bill, E, Brown	1939
Bauman, Alf, T, Northwestern	1948-50
Bausch, Frank, C, Kansas	1937-40
Baynham, Craig, RB, Georgia Tech	1970
Becker, Dave, S, Iowa	1980-81
Becker, Doug, LB, Notre Dame	1978
Becker, Wayland, E, Marquette	1934
Bell, Kay, T, Washington State	1937
Bell, Todd, DB, Ohio State	1981
Benton, Jim, E, Arkansas	1943
Bergerson, Gill, G, Oregon State	1932-33
Berry, Connie Mack, E, North Carolina State	1942-46
Berry, Royce, DE, Houston	1976
Best, Art, RB, Kent State	1977-78
Bettis, Tom, LB, Purdue	1963
Bettridge, John, B, Ohio State	1937
Bingham, Don, B, Sul Ross State	1956
Bishop, Bill, T, North Texas State	1952-60
Bishop, Don, E, Los Angeles CC	1959
Bivins, Charley, B, Morris Brown	1960-66
Bjork, Del, T, Oregon	1937-38
Blackburn, J. A., T, No college	1923
Blacklock, Hugh, T, Michigan State	1920-25
Blackman, Lennon, B, Tulsa	1930
Blanda, George, QB, Kentucky	1949-58
Boden, Lynn, G, South Dakota State	1979
Bolan, George, FB, Purdue	1921-24
Bonderant, J. Bourbon, C, DePauw	1922
Boone, J. R., B, Tulsa	1948-51
Brackett, M. L., T, Auburn	1956-57
Bradley, Chuck, TE, Oregon	1977
Bradley, Ed, G, Wake Forest	1950, 1952
Braidwood, Chuck, E, Tennessee-Chattanooga	1932
Bramhall, Art, B, DePaul	1931
Bratkowski, Zeke, QB, Georgia	1954, 1957-60
Bray, Ray, G, Western Michigan	1939-42, 1946-51
Brink, Larry, E, Northern Illinois	1954
Britton, Earl, B, Illinois	1925
Brockman, Ed, B, Oklahoma	1930
Brown, Charley, DB, Syracuse	1966-67
Brown, Ed, QB, San Francisco	1954-61
Brown, Bill, B, Illinois	1961
Bruer, Bob, TE, Mankato State	1976
Brumbaugh, Carl, QB, Florida	1930-34, 1936, 1938
Brupbacher, Ross, LB, Texas A&M	1970-72, 1976
Bryan, Johnny, B, Chicago	1923-26
Bryant, Waymond, LB, Tennessee	1974-77
Buck, Art, B, John Carroll	1941
Buckler, Bill, G, Alabama	1926-28, 1931-33
Buffone, Doug, LB, Louisville	1966-79
Buivid, Ray, QB-HB, Marquette	1937-38
Bukich, Rudy, QB, USC	1958-59, 1962-68
Bull, Ronnie, B, Baylor	1962-70
Burdick, Lloyd, T, Illinois	1931-32
Burgeis, Glenn, T, Tulsa	1945
Burks, Randy, WR, Southeast Oklahoma State	1976
Burman, George, T, Northwestern	1964
Burnell, Max, B, Notre Dame	1944
Buss, Art, T, Michigan State	1934-35
Bussey, Young, QB, Louisiana State	1940-41
Butkus, Dick, LB, Illinois	1965-73
Butler, Gary, TE, Rice	1975
Buzin, Rich, T, Penn State	1972

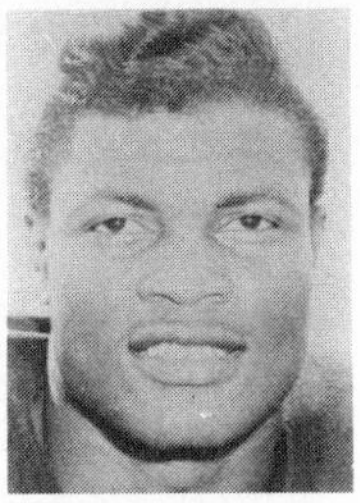

J.C. Caroline

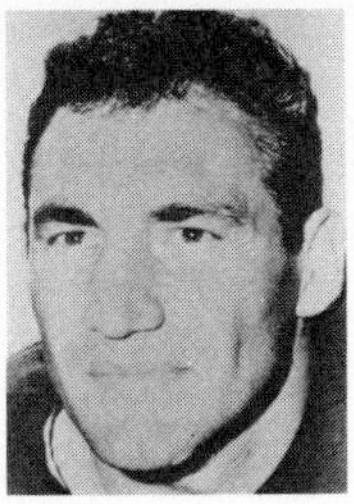

Rick Casares

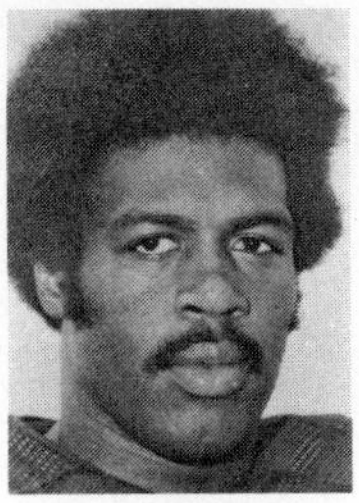

Wally Chambers

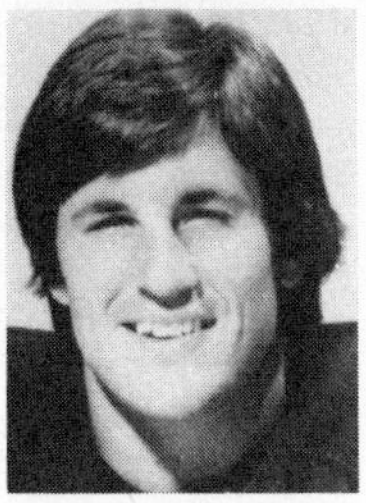

Gary Fencik

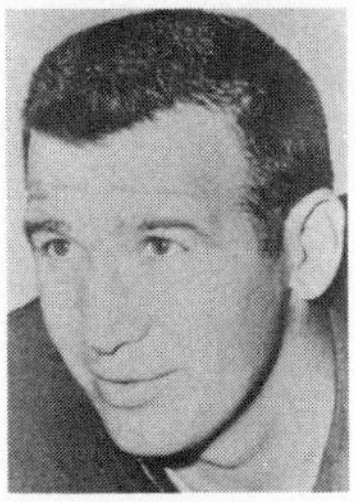

Joe Fortunato

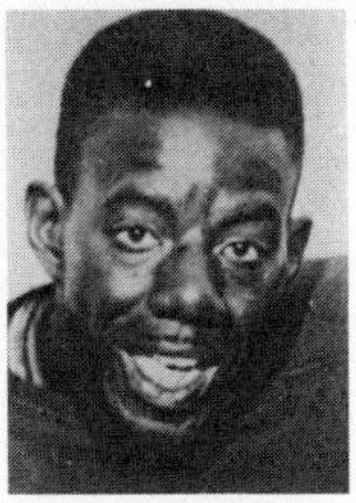

Willie Galimore

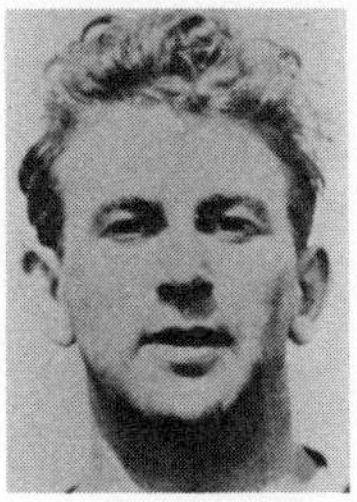

Hugh Gallarneau

C

- Cabral, Brian, LB, Colorado ... 1981
- Cadile, Jim, G, San Jose State ... 1962-72
- Caffey, Lee Roy, LB, Texas A&M ... 1970
- Calland, Lee, CB, Louisville ... 1969
- Campana, Al, B, Youngstown ... 1950-53
- Campbell, Gary, LB, Colorado ... 1977-81
- Campbell, Leon, RB, Arkansas ... 1952-54
- Canady, Jim, B, Texas ... 1948-49
- Carey, Bob, E, Michigan State ... 1958
- Carl, Harland, B, Wisconsin ... 1956
- Carlson, Jules (Zuck), G, Oregon State ... 1929-36
- Caroline, J. C., B, Illinois ... 1956-65
- Carter, Virgil, QB, Brigham Young ... 1968-69, 1976
- Casares, Rick, RB, Florida ... 1955-64
- Casey, Tim, LB, Oregon ... 1969
- Castete, Jesse, B, McNeese State ... 1956
- Chamberlin, Guy, E, Nebraska ... 1920-21
- Chambers, Wally, DT, Eastern Kentucky ... 1973-77
- Chesney, Chet, C, DePaul ... 1939-40
- Childs, Clarence, DB, Florida A&M ... 1968
- Cifers, Ed, E, Tennessee ... 1947-48
- Clark, Gail, LB, Michigan State ... 1973
- Clark, Harry, B, West Virginia ... 1940-43
- Clark, Herman, G, Oregon State ... 1952, 1954-57
- Clark, Phil, DB, Northwestern ... 1970
- Clarkson, Stu, G, Texas A&I ... 1942, 1946-51
- Clemons, Craig, S, Iowa ... 1972-77
- Coady, Rich, C-E, Memphis State ... 1970-74
- Cobb, Mike, TE, Michigan State ... 1978-81
- Cody, Ed, B, Purdue ... 1949-50
- Coia, Angelo, B, USC ... 1960-63
- Cole, Emerson, B, Toledo ... 1952
- Cole, Linzy, WR, Texas Christian ... 1970
- Concannon, Jack, QB, Boston College ... 1967-71
- Conkright, Bill, C, Oklahoma ... 1937-38
- Connor, George, T, Notre Dame ... 1948-55
- Conzelman, Jimmy, QB, Washington, Missouri ... 1920
- Cooke, Ed, E, Maryland ... 1958
- Copeland, Ron, WR, UCLA ... 1969
- Corbett, George, B, Millikin ... 1932-38
- Cornish, Frank, DT, Grambling ... 1966-70
- Corzine, Les, B, Davis & Elkins ... 1938
- Cotton, Craig, TE, Youngstown ... 1973
- Cowan, Les, T, McMurry ... 1951
- Crawford, Fred, T, Duke ... 1934-35
- Crawford, Walt, G, Illinois ... 1925
- Croft, Abe, E, Southern Methodist ... 1944-45
- Croftcheck, Don, G, Indiana ... 1967
- Cross, Bobby, T, Stephen F. Austin ... 1952-53
- Culver, Al, T, Notre Dame ... 1932
- Cunningham, Harold, E, Ohio State ... 1929
- Curchin, Jeff, T, Florida State ... 1970-71

D

- Daffer, Ted, E, Tennessee ... 1954
- Damore, John, C, Northwestern ... 1957, 1959
- Daniell, Jim, T, Ohio State ... 1945
- Daniels, Dick, S, Pacific, Oregon ... 1969-70
- Davis, Art, T, Alabama State ... 1953
- Davis, Fred, T, Alabama ... 1946-51
- Davis, Harper, HB, Mississippi State ... 1950
- Davis, John, DB, Missouri ... 1970
- Davis, Roger, G, Syracuse ... 1960-63
- Dean, Fred, G, Texas Southern ... 1977
- DeCorrevont, Bill, B, Northwestern ... 1948-49
- DeLong, Steve, DE, Tennessee ... 1972
- Deloplaine, Jack, RB, Salem, West Virginia ... 1979
- Dempsey, Frank, G, Florida ... 1950-53
- Denney, Austin, E, Tennessee ... 1967-69
- Devlin, Chris, LB, Penn State ... 1978
- Dewveall, Willard, E, Southern Methodist ... 1959-60
- Digris, Bernie, T, Holy Cross ... 1943
- Dimancheff, Babe, B, Purdue ... 1952
- Ditka, Mike, TE, Pittsburgh ... 1961-66
- Dodd, Al, DB, Northwestern Louisiana ... 1967
- Doehring, John (Bull), B, No college ... 1932-34, 1936-37
- Donchez, Tom, RB, Penn State ... 1975
- Dooley, Jim, E, Miami ... 1952-54, 1956-57, 1959-62
- Dottley, John, B, Mississippi ... 1951-53
- Douglas, Merrill, B, Utah ... 1958-60
- Douglass, Bobby, QB, Kansas ... 1969-75
- Douthitt, Earl, S, Iowa ... 1975
- Dreher, Fred, E, Denver ... 1938
- Dressen, Charlie, QB, No college ... 1920
- Drews, Ted, E, Princeton ... 1928
- Dreyer, Wally, B, Wisconsin ... 1949
- Driscoll, Paddy, HB, Northwestern ... 1920, 1926-29
- Drulis, Chuck, G, Temple ... 1942, 1945-49
- Drury, Lyle, E, St. Louis ... 1930-31
- Drzewiecki, Ron, B, Marquette ... 1955, 1957
- Dugger, Jack, E, Ohio State ... 1949
- Dunlap, Bob, QB, Oklahoma ... 1935

E

- Earl, Robin, RB, Washington ... 1977-81
- Ecker, Ed, T, John Carroll ... 1947
- Edwards, Cid, RB, Tennessee State ... 1975
- Ellis, Allen, CB, UCLA ... 1973-77, 1979-80
- Elnes, Leland, QB, Bradley ... 1929
- Ely, Harold, G, Iowa ... 1932
- Ely, Larry, LB, Iowa ... 1975
- Engebretsen, Paul, G, Northwestern ... 1932
- Englund, Harry, E, No college ... 1920-22, 1924
- Erickson, Harold, HB, Washington & Jefferson ... 1925
- Evans, Earl, T, Harvard ... 1926-29
- Evans, Fred, B, Notre Dame ... 1948
- Evans, Vince, QB-KR, USC ... 1977-81
- Evey, Dick, T, Tennessee ... 1964-69

F

- Falkenberg, Herb, B, Trinity ... 1951
- Famiglietti, Gary, FB, Boston University ... 1938-45
- Fanning, Stan, T, Idaho ... 1960-62
- Farmer, George, WR, UCLA ... 1970-75
- Farrington, John, E, Prairie View ... 1960-63
- Farris, Tom, QB, Wisconsin ... 1946-47
- Feathers, Beattie, B, Tennessee ... 1934-37
- Febel, Fritz, G, Purdue ... 1935
- Federovich, John, T, Davis & Elkins ... 1941, 1946
- Feichtinger, Andy, E, No college ... 1920-21
- Fenick, Gary, S, Yale ... 1976-81
- Fenimore, Bob, HB, Oklahoma State ... 1947
- Ferguson, J. B., T, No college ... 1932
- Ferguson, Jim. C-LB, USC ... 1969
- Fetz, Gus, B, No college ... 1923
- Figner, George, B, Colorado ... 1953
- Fisher, Bob, TE, Southern Methodist ... 1980-81
- Fisher, Jeff, CB, USC ... 1981
- Flaherty, Pat, E, Princeton ... 1923
- Flanagan, Dick, G, Ohio State ... 1948-49
- Flanagan, Latham, E, Carnegie Tech ... 1931
- Fleckenstein, Bill, G, Iowa ... 1925-30
- Floyd, Bobby Jack, B, Texas Christian ... 1953
- Ford, Charlie, CB, Houston ... 1971-73
- Fordham, Jim, B, Georgia ... 1944-45
- Forrest, Tom, G, Cincinnati ... 1974
- Forte, Aldo, G, Montana ... 1939-41, 1946
- Fortmann, Dan, G, Colgate ... 1936-43
- Fortunato, Joe, LB, Mississippi State ... 1955-66
- Francis, Sam, FB, Nebraska ... 1937-38
- Franklin, Paul, E, Franklin ... 1930-33
- Frazier, Leslie, DB, Alcorn State ... 1981
- Frump, Milton, G, Ohio Wesleyan ... 1930

G

- Gagnon, Dave, RB, Ferris State ... 1974
- Gaines, Wentford, CB, Cincinnati ... 1978-80
- Galimore, Willie, B, Florida A&M ... 1957-63
- Gallagher, Dave, DE, Michigan ... 1974
- Gallarneau, Hugh, B, Stanford ... 1941-42, 1945-47
- Garrett, Carl, RB, New Mexico Highlands ... 1973-74
- Garrett, Thurman, C, Oklahoma State ... 1947-48
- Garrett, W. D., T, Mississippi State ... 1950
- Garvey, Ed, B, Notre Dame ... 1925
- Garvey, Hec, E, Notre Dame ... 1922-25
- Gentry, Curtiss, DB, Maryland-Eastern Shore ... 1966-68
- George, Bill, LB, Wake Forest ... 1952-65
- Gepford, Sid, B, Millikin & Bethany ... 1920
- Gersbach, Carl, LB, West Chester State ... 1975
- Geyer, Bill, B, Colgate ... 1942-43, 1946
- Gibron, Abe, G, Purdue ... 1958-59
- Gilbert, Kline, T, Mississippi ... 1953-57
- Gilliam, John, WR, South Carolina State ... 1977
- Glenn, Bill, QB, Eastern Illinois ... 1944
- Glueck, Larry, B, Villanova ... 1963-65
- Goebel, Paul, E, Michigan ... 1925
- Goodnight, Owen, B, Hardin-Simmons ... 1946
- Gordon, Dick, WR, Michigan State ... 1965-71
- Gordon, Lou, T, Illinois ... 1938
- Gorgal, Ken, HB, Purdue ... 1955-56
- Grabowski, Jim, RB, Illinois ... 1971
- Graham, Conrad, DB, Tennessee ... 1973
- Grandberry, Ken, RB, Washington State ... 1974
- Grange, Garland, E, Illinois ... 1929-31
- Grange, Red, B, Illinois ... 1925, 1929-34
- Green, Bobby Joe, P, Florida ... 1962-73
- Greenwood, Glenn, B, Iowa ... 1924
- Grim, Bob, WR, Oregon State ... 1975
- Grosvenor, George, B, Colorado ... 1935-36
- Grygo, Al, B, South Carolina ... 1944-45
- Gudauskas, Pete, G, Murray State ... 1943-45
- Gulyanics, George, B, Ellisville JC ... 1947-52
- Gunn, Jimmy, LB, USC ... 1970-75
- Gunner, Harry, DE, Oregon State ... 1970

H

- Haddon, Al, B, Washington & Jefferson ... 1928
- Haines, Kris, WR, Notre Dame ... 1979-81
- Halas, George, E, Illinois ... 1920-29
- Hale, Dave, DE, Ottawa, Kansas ... 1969-71
- Haluska, Jim, B, Wisconsin ... 1956
- Hamity, Lewis, B, Chicago ... 1941
- Hamlin, Gene, C, Western Michigan ... 1971
- Hammond, Henry, E, Southwestern, Memphis ... 1937
- Hampton, Dan, DE, Arkansas ... 1979-81
- Hanke, Carl, G, Minnesota ... 1922
- Hanny, Frank, E, Indiana ... 1923-27
- Hansen, Cliff, B, Luther ... 1933
- Hansen, Wayne, C, Texas Western ... 1950-58
- Hardy, Cliff, CB, Michigan State ... 1971
- Harley, Chic, RB, Ohio State ... 1921
- Harper, Roland, RB, Louisiana Tech ... 1975-78, 1980-81
- Harris, Al, DE, Arizona State ... 1979-81
- Harris, Richard, DE, Grambling ... 1974-75
- Harrison, Jim, RB, Missouri ... 1971-74
- Hart, Tommy, DE, Morris Brown ... 1978-79
- Hartenstine, Mike, DE, Penn State ... 1975-81
- Hartman, Fred, T, Rice ... 1947
- Haselrig, Clint, WR, Michigan ... 1974
- Hatley, John, G, Sul Ross State ... 1953
- Hazelton, Major, DB, Florida A&M ... 1968-69
- Healey, Ed, T, Dartmouth ... 1922-27
- Healy, Don, G, Maryland ... 1958-59
- Hearden, Tom, B, Notre Dame ... 1929
- Heileman, Charles, E, Iowa State ... 1939
- Helwig, John, G, Notre Dame ... 1953-56
- Hempel, Bill, T, Carroll ... 1942
- Henderson, Reuben, CB, San Diego State ... 1981
- Hensley, Dick, E, Kentucky ... 1953
- Herron, Bruce, LB, New Mexico ... 1978-81
- Hester, Jim, TE, North Dakota ... 1970
- Hewitt, Bill, E, Michigan ... 1932-36
- Hibbs, Jesse, T, USC ... 1931
- Hicks, Tom, LB, Illinois ... 1976-80
- High, Lennie, B, No college ... 1920
- Hilgenberg, Jay, C, Iowa ... 1981
- Hill, Harlon, E, Florence State ... 1954-61
- Hill, Ike, WR, Catawba ... 1973-74
- Hoban, Mike, G, Michigan ... 1974
- Hobscheid, Fred, G, Chicago ... 1927
- Hodgins, Norm, S, Louisiana State ... 1974
- Hoffman, Jack, E, Xavier ... 1952, 1955-58
- Hoffman, John, E, Arkansas ... 1949-56
- Hoffman, John, DE, Hawaii ... 1971
- Hoke, Jonathan, CB, Ball State ... 1980
- Holloway, Glen, G, North Texas State ... 1970-73
- Holman, Willie, DE, South Dakota State ... 1968-73
- Holmer, Walter, B, Northwestern ... 1929-30
- Holovak, Mike, B, Boston College ... 1947-48
- Hoptowit, Al, T, Washington State ... 1942-45
- Horton, Larry, DT, Iowa ... 1972-73
- Howley, Charles, C, West Virginia ... 1958-59
- Hrivnak, Gary, DT, Purdue ... 1973-75

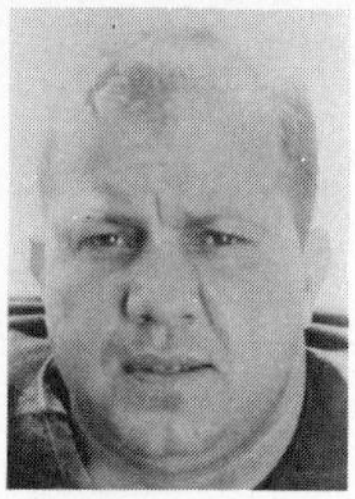

Abe Gibron

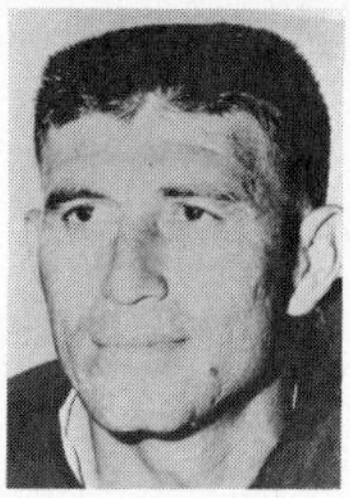

Harlon Hill

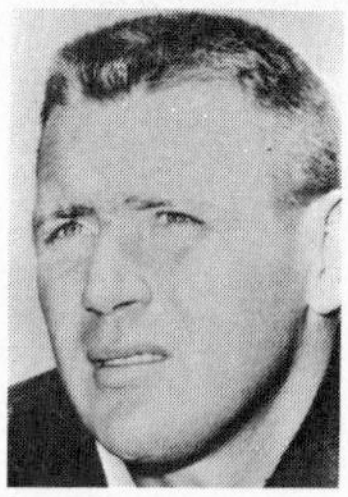

Stan Jones

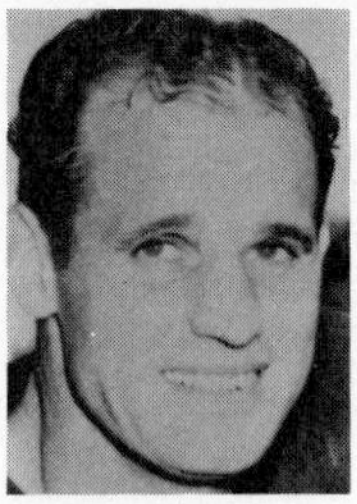

Ken Kavanaugh

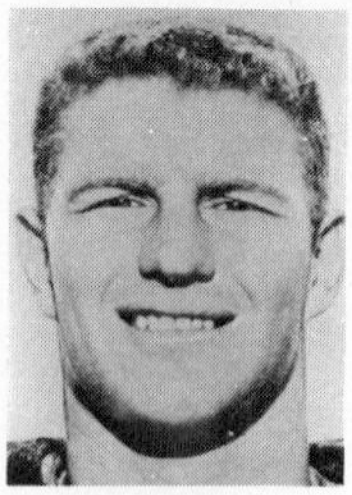

Bill McColl

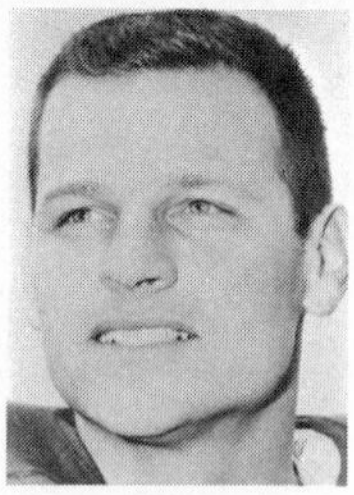

Johnny Morris

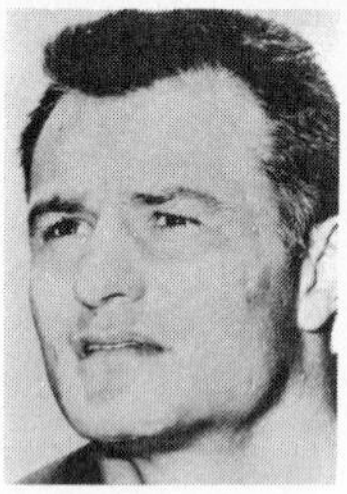

Larry Morris

Huarte, John, QB, Notre Dame 1972
Huff, Gary, QB, Florida State........ 1973-76
Huffine, Ken, B, Purdue........ 1921
Hugasian, Harry, HB, Stanford........ 1955
Hughes, Bernie, C, Oregon 1941
Hughes, Billy, C, Texas 1940-41
Hull, Mike, RB, USC........ 1968-70
Hultz, Don, DT, Southern Mississippi 1974
Hunsinger, Chuck, B, Florida 1950-52
Hunt, Jackie, B, Marshall 1945
Hurst, Bill, G, Oregon........ 1924
Hyland, Bob, C, Boston College 1970

I

Ingwerson, Burt, G, Illinois 1920-21
Ippolito, Tony, G, Purdue........ 1943

J

Jackson, Bobby, B, Alabama 1961
Jackson, Noah, G, Tampa........ 1975-81
Jackson, Randy, T, Florida........ 1967-74
Jagade, Chick, B, Indiana........ 1954-55
James, Dan, T, Ohio........ 1967
Janet, Ernie, G, Washington 1972-74
Jarmoluk, Mike, T, Temple 1946-47
Jecha, Ralph, G, Northwestern 1955
Jencks, Bob, E, Miami, Ohio........ 1963-64
Jensvold, Leo, B, Iowa........ 1931
Jeter, Bob, CB, Iowa........ 1971-73
Jeter, Perry, RB, Cal Poly-San Luis Obispo........ 1956
Jewett, Bob, E, Michigan State 1958
Jiggetts, Dan, T, Harvard........ 1976-81
Joesting, Herb, B, Minnesota 1931-32
Johnson, Al, B, Kentucky 1938
Johnson, Bill, G, Southern Methodist 1947
Johnson, Greg, DT, Florida State........ 1977
Johnson, Jack, B, Miami........ 1957
Johnson, John, T, Indiana 1963-68
Johnson, Leo, B, Millikin 1920
Johnson, O. G., B, No college 1924
Johnson, Pete, B, Virginia Military 1959
Johnsos, Luke, E, Northwestern 1929-36, 1938
Jones, Bob, E, San Diego State 1967-69
Jones, Edgar (Special Delivery), B, Pittsburgh 1945
Jones, Jerry, G, Notre Dame........ 1920-21
Jones, Jimmy, E, Wisconsin 1965-67
Jones, Stan, T, Maryland 1954-65
Juenger, Dave, WR, Ohio U........ 1973

K

Karr, Bill, E, West Virginia........ 1933-38
Karras, Ted, G, Indiana 1960-64
Karwales, Jack, E, Michigan........ 1946-47
Kassel, Chuck, E, Illinois........ 1927
Kavanaugh, Ken, E, Louisiana State........ 1940-41, 1945-50
Kawal, Ed, C, Illinois........ 1931, 1934-36
Keane, Jim, E, Iowa 1946-51
Keefe, Jerry, G, Notre Dame........ 1920
Kelly, Elmo, E, Wichita State........ 1944
Kelly, Jim, TE, Tennessee State 1974
Kendrick, Jim, T, Texas A&M 1924
Keriasotis, Nick, G, St. Ambrose........ 1942, 1945
Kiesling, Walt, G, St. Thomas, Minnesota........ 1934
Kilcullen, Bob, T, Texas Tech 1957-58, 1960-66
Kilgore, Jon, P, Auburn 1968
Kindt, Don, B, Wisconsin........ 1947-55
King, Ralph, T, Chicago........ 1925
Kinney, Steve, T, Utah State 1973-74
Kirk, Ken, C, Mississippi 1960-61
Kissell, Adolph, B, Boston College 1942
Klawitter, Dick, C, South Dakota State 1956
Klein, Dick, T, Iowa........ 1958-59
Knop, Oscar, B, Illinois 1923-28
Knox, Bill, DB, Purdue 1974-76
Knox, Ron, QB, UCLA 1957
Koehler, Bob, B, Northwestern 1920
Kolman, Ed, T, Temple........ 1940-42, 1946-47
Konovsky, Bob, G, Wisconsin........ 1960
Kopcha, Joe, G, Tennessee-Chattanooga........ 1929, 1932-35
Kortas, Ken, T, Louisville........ 1969
Kosins, Gary, RB, Dayton 1972-74
Kreamcheck, John, T, William & Mary........ 1953-55
Kreitling, Rich, E, Illinois 1964
Kriewald, Doug, G, West Texas State 1967-68
Kuechenberg, Rudy, LB, Indiana........ 1967-69
Kunz, Lee, LB, Nebraska........ 1979-81
Kurek, Ralph, B, Wisconsin........ 1965-70

L

LaFleur, Joe, B, Marquette 1922-24
LaForest, Bill, B, No college........ 1920
Lahar, Hal, G, Oklahoma........ 1941
Lamb, Walt, E, Oklahoma 1946
Lanum, Jake, B, Illinois 1920-24
Larson, Fred, C, Notre Dame 1922
Latta, Greg, TE, Morgan State 1975-80
Lawler, Allen, B, Texas........ 1948
Lawson, Roger, RB, Western Michigan........ 1972-73
Layne, Bobby, QB, Texas 1948
Leclerc, Roger, LB, Trinity 1960-66
Lee, Buddy, QB, Louisiana State........ 1971
Lee, Herman, T, Florida A&M 1958-66
Leeuwenburg, Rich, T, Stanford........ 1965
Leggett, Earl, T, Louisiana State 1957-60, 1962-65
Lemon, Cliff, T, Centre........ 1926
Leonard, Jim, T, Colgate 1924
Lesane, Jimmy, B, Virginia........ 1952, 1954
Lick, Dennis, T, Wisconsin........ 1976-81
Line, Bill, DT, Southern Methodist 1972
Lintzenich, Joe, B, St. Louis 1930-31
Lipscomb, Paul, T, Tennessee 1954
Livers, Virgil, CB-KR, Western Kentucky........ 1975-79
Livingston, Andy, B, Phoenix JC 1964-65, 1967-68
Logan, Jim, G, Indiana 1943
Long, Harvey, T, Detroit........ 1929
Long, Johnny, QB, Colgate........ 1944-45
Lowe, Lloyd, B, North Texas State 1953-54
Luckman, Sid, QB, Columbia 1939-50
Lujack, Johnny, QB, Notre Dame........ 1948-51
Lusby, Vaughn, CB, Arkansas 1980
Lyle, Garry, CB, George Washington........ 1968-74
Lyman, Link, T, Nebraska........ 1926-28, 1930-31, 1933-34
Lyon, George, T, Kansas State........ 1931

M

MacLeod, Bob, B, Dartmouth........ 1939
MacWherter, Kile, B, Bethany........ 1920
Macon, Ed, B, Pacific........ 1952-53
Magnani, Dante, B, St. Mary's, Cal........ 1943, 1946, 1949
Maillard, Ralph, T, Creighton 1929
Malone, Charlie, E, Texas A&M 1933
Manders, Jack, B, Minnesota 1933-40
Maniaci, Joe, B, Fordham 1938-41
Manning, Pete, E, Wake Forest........ 1960-61
Manske, Eggs, E, Northwestern........ 1937-40
Marconi, Joe, B, West Virginia 1962-66
Margarita, Bob, B, Brown 1944-46
Margerum, Ken, WR, Stanford 1981
Martin, Bill, E, Georgia Tech 1964
Martin, Billy, B, Minnesota........ 1962-64
Martin, Dave, LB, Notre Dame........ 1969
Martin, Frank, B, Alabama 1941
Martinovich, Phil, G, Pacific 1940
Maslowski, Matt, WR, San Diego U. 1972
Mass, Wayne, T, Clemson 1968-70
Masters, Bob, B, Baylor........ 1943-44
Masterson, Bernie, QB, Nebraska........ 1934-40
Masterson, Forest, C, Iowa 1945
Mastrogany, Gus, E, Iowa 1931
Matheson, Jack, E, Western Michigan 1947
Mattson, Riley, T, Oregon 1965
Matuza, Al, C, Georgetown........ 1941-43
May, Chester, G, No college........ 1920
May, Walt, G, No college........ 1920
Mayes, Rufus, T, Ohio State 1969
Maznicki, Frank, B, Boston College 1942, 1946
McAfee, George, HB, Duke 1940-41, 1945-50
McClendon, Willie, RB, Georgia........ 1979-81
McColl, Bill, E, Stanford........ 1952-59
McDonald, Les, E, Nebraska 1937-39
McElwain, Bill, B, Northwestern 1925
McEnulty, Doug, B, Wichita State........ 1943-44
McGee, Tony, DE, Bishop College........ 1971-73
McKinney, Bill, LB, West Texas State........ 1972
McLean, Ray (Scooter), B, St. Anselms 1940-47
McMichael, Steve, DT, Texas 1981
McMillen, Jim, G, Illinois........ 1924-28
McMullen, Dan, G, Nebraska........ 1930-31
McPherson, Forrest, G, Nebraska........ 1935
McRae, Bennie, B, Michigan 1962-70
McRae, Franklin, DT, Tennessee State 1967
Meadows, Ed, E, Duke 1954, 1956-57
Mellekas, John, T, Arizona 1956, 1958-61
Merkel, Monte, G, Kansas........ 1943
Merrill, Mark, LB, Minnesota........ 1979
Meyers, Jerry, DE-DT, Northern Illinois 1976-79
Michaels, Eddie, G, Villanova........ 1935
Mihal, Joe, T, Purdue 1940-41
Miller, Charles (Ookie), C, Purdue 1932-36
Miller, Milford, T, Chadron State 1935
Milner, Bill, G, Duke 1947-49
Minini, Frank, HB, San Jose State 1947-49
Mintum, Jack, C, No college........ 1921-22
Mitchell, Charley, B, Tulsa........ 1945
Mohardt, John, B, Notre Dame........ 1925
Molesworth, Keith, B, Monmouth 1931-37
Montgomery, Randy, CB, Weber State 1974
Montgomery, Ross, B, Texas Christian 1969-70
Mooney, Jim, E, Georgetown 1935
Mooney, Tipp, B, Abilene Christian 1944-45
Moore, Albert, QB, Northwestern........ 1932
Moore, Jerry, S, Arkansas 1971-72
Moore, Joe, RB, Missouri........ 1971, 1973
Moore, McNeil, B, Sam Houston State........ 1954, 1956-57
Moore, Rocco, G, Western Michigan 1980
Moorehead, Emery, WR-KR, Colorado 1981
Morgan, Mike, RB, Wisconsin........ 1978
Morris, Francis, B, Boston U. 1942
Morris, Johnny, WR, U.C. Santa Barbara 1958-67
Morris, Jon, C, Holy Cross 1978
Morris, Larry, LB, Georgia Tech 1959-65
Morrison, Fred (Curley), B, Ohio State 1950-53
Morton, John, E, Purdue 1945
Moser, Robert, C, Pacific........ 1951-53
Mosley, Henry, B, Morris Brown 1955
Mucha, Rudy, G, Washington........ 1945-46
Muckensturm, Jerry, LB, Arkansas State 1976-80
Mudd, Howard, G, Hillsdale 1969-70
Mullen, Verne, E, Illinois........ 1924-26
Mullins, Don, B, Houston........ 1961-62
Mullins, Noah, B, Kentucky........ 1946-48
Mundee, Fred, C, Notre Dame........ 1943-45
Murray, Dick, T, Marquette 1924
Murry, Don, T, Wisconsin........ 1925-32
Musso, George, G, Millikin 1933-44
Musso, Johnny, RB, Alabama........ 1975-77
Myers, Denny, T, Iowa 1931

N

Nagurski, Bronko, B, Minnesota 1930-37, 1943
Neacy, Clem, E, Colgate........ 1927
Neal, Dan, C, Kentucky........ 1975-81
Neal, Ed, G, Louisiana State........ 1951
Neck, Tommy, B, Louisiana State........ 1962
Negus, Fred, C, Wisconsin........ 1950
Neidert, John, LB, Louisville........ 1970
Nelson, Everett, T, Illinois 1929
Nesbitt, Dick, B, Drake 1930-33
Newsome, Billy, DE, Grambling........ 1977
Newton, Bob, G, Nebraska........ 1971-75
Nickla, Ed, G, Maryland 1959
Nielsen, Hans, K, Michigan State 1981
Nix, Kent, QB, Texas Christian 1970-71
Nolting, Ray, HB, Cincinnati 1936-43
Norberg, Hank, E, Stanford........ 1948
Nordquist, Mark, G-C, Pacific........ 1975-76
Nori, Reino, B, DeKalb........ 1938
Norman, Dick, QB, Stanford 1961
Nowaskey, Bob, E, George Washington 1940-42

O

O'Bradovich, Ed, E, Illinois 1962-71
O'Connell, J. F., C, Penn State 1924
O'Connell, Tom, QB, Illinois 1953
Oech, Verne, G, Minnesota........ 1936
Oelerich, John, B, St. Ambrose 1938

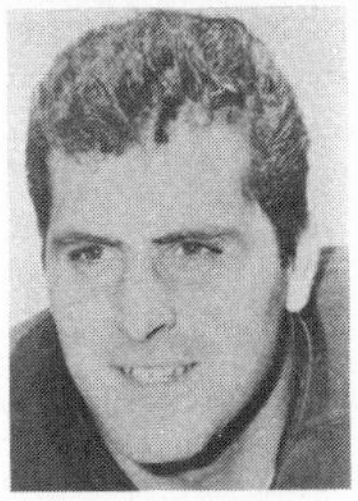
Ed O'Bradovich

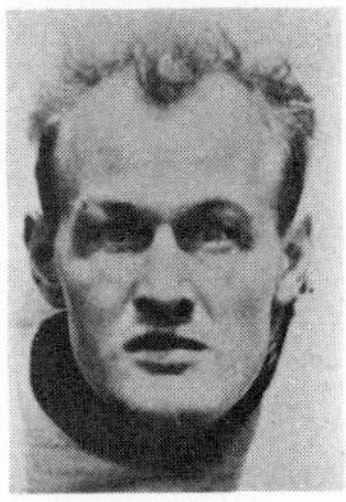
Bill Osmanski

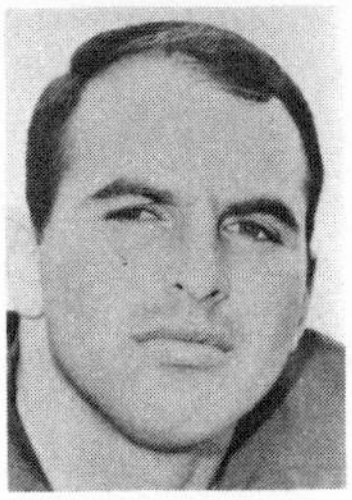
Brian Piccolo

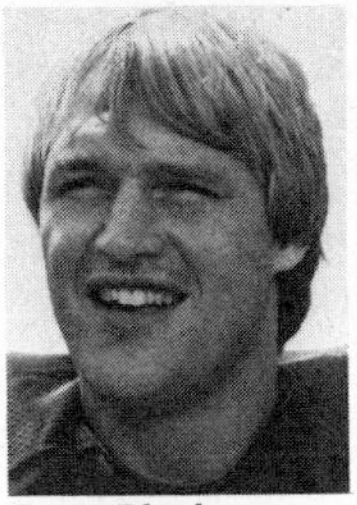
Doug Plank

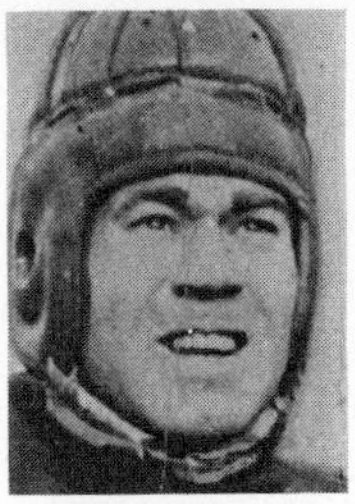
Joe Sternaman

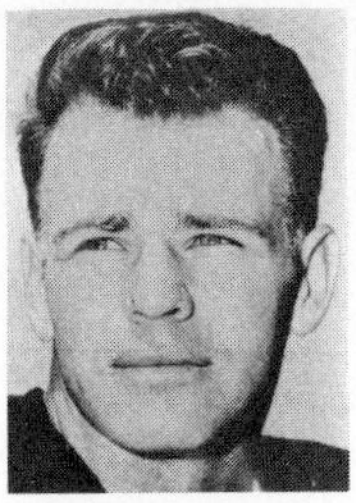
Billy Wade

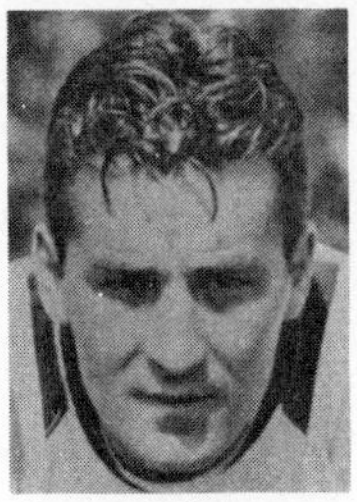
George Wilson

Ogden, Ray, TE, Alabama ... 1969-71
O'Quinn, John (Red), E, Wake Forest ... 1950-51
O'Rourke, Charley, QB, Boston College ... 1942
Osborne, Jim, DT, Southern U. ... 1972-81
Osmanski, Bill, B, Holy Cross ... 1939-43, 1946-47
Osmanski, Joe, B, Holy Cross ... 1946-49

P

Pagac, Fred, TE, Ohio State ... 1974
Page, Alan, DT, Notre Dame ... 1978-81
Parsons, Bob, P-TE, Penn State ... 1972-81
Patterson, Billy, QB, Baylor ... 1939
Pauley, Frank, T, Washington & Jefferson ... 1930
Payton, Walter, RB, Jackson State ... 1975-81
Pearce, Walter (Pard), QB, Pennsylvania ... 1920-22
Pearson, Bert, C, Kansas State ... 1929-34
Pederson, Jim, B, Augsburg ... 1932
Peiffer, Dan, C, Southeast Missouri State ... 1975-77
Percival, Mac, K, Texas Tech ... 1967-73
Perez, Pete, G, Illinois ... 1945
Perina, Bob, B, Princeton ... 1949
Perini, Pete, B, Ohio State ... 1954-55
Perkins, Don, B, Plattesville State ... 1945-46
Perrin, Lonnie, B, Illinois ... 1979
Petitbon, Richie, S, Tulane ... 1959-68
Petty, John, B, Purdue ... 1942
Petty, Ross, G, Illinois ... 1920
Phillips, Loyd, DE, Arkansas ... 1967-69
Phipps, Mike, QB. Purdue ... 1977-81
Piccolo, Brian, RB, Wake Forest ... 1966-69
Pickens, Bob, T, Nebraska ... 1967-69
Pifferini, Bob, LB, UCLA ... 1972-75
Pinder, Cyril, RB, Illinois ... 1971-72
Plank, Doug, S, Ohio State ... 1975-81
Plasman, Dick, E, Vanderbilt ... 1937-41, 1944
Podmajersky, Paul, G, Illinois ... 1944
Polisky, John, G, Notre Dame ... 1929
Pollock, Bill, HB, Widener ... 1935-36
Pool, Hampton, E, Stanford ... 1940-43
Preston, Pat, G, Wake Forest ... 1946-49
Pride, Dan, LB, Jackson State ... 1968-69
Proctor, Rex, B, Rice ... 1953
Purnell, Jim, LB, Wisconsin ... 1964, 1966-68
Pyle, Mike, C, Yale ... 1961-69

R

Rabold, Mike, G, Indiana ... 1964-67
Rakestraw, Larry, QB, Georgia ... 1964, 1966-68
Ramsey, Frank, G, Oregon State ... 1945
Rather, Bo, WR, Michigan ... 1974-78
Reader, Russ, B, Michigan State ... 1947
Reese, Lloyd, B, Tennessee ... 1946
Reilly, Mike, LB, Iowa ... 1964-68
Rentner, Pug, B, Northwestern ... 1937
Reppond, Mike, WR, Arkansas ... 1973
Rice, Andy, DT, Texas Southern ... 1972-73
Richards, Golden, WR, Hawaii ... 1978-79
Richards, Ray, T, Nebraska ... 1933, 1935
Richman, Harry, G, Illinois ... 1929
Rivera, Steve, WR, California ... 1977
Rives, Don, LB, Texas Tech ... 1973-78
Roberts, Tom, G, DePaul ... 1944-45
Roberts, Willie, CB, Houston ... 1973
Roder, Mirro, K, No college ... 1973-74
Roehnelt, Bill, G, Bradley ... 1958-59
Rogers, Mel, LB, Florida A&M ... 1977
Roggeman, Tom, G, Purdue ... 1956-57
Romanik, Steve, QB, Villanova ... 1950-53
Romney, Milt, QB, Chicago ... 1924-28
Ronzani, Gene, QB, Marquette ... 1933-38, 1944-45
Rosequist, Ted, T, Ohio State ... 1934-36
Roveto, John, K, Southwestern Louisiana ... 1981
Rowden, Larry, LB, Houston ... 1971
Rowland, Brad, B, McMurry ... 1951
Rowland, Justin, B, Texas Christian ... 1960
Rupp, Nelson, QB, Denison ... 1921
Russell, Reg, E, Northwestern ... 1928
Ryan, John, T, Detroit ... 1929
Ryan, Rocky, E, Illinois ... 1958
Rydalch, Ron, DT, Utah ... 1975-80
Rydzewski, Frank, C, Notre Dame ... 1923
Rykovich, Julie, B, Illinois ... 1949-51

S

Sacrinty, Nick, QB, Wake Forest ... 1947
Sanderson, Reggie, RB, Stanford ... 1973
Savoldi, Joe, B, Notre Dame ... 1930
Sayers, Gale, RB, Kansas ... 1965-71
Schiechi, John, C, Santa Clara ... 1945-46
Schmidt, Terry, S, Ball State ... 1976-81
Schreiber, Larry, RB, Tennessee Tech ... 1976
Schroeder, Gene, E, Virginia ... 1951-52, 1954-57
Schubert, Steve, WR-KR, Massachusetts ... 1975-79
Schuette, Paul, G, Wisconsin ... 1930-32
Schweda, Brian, DE, Kansas ... 1966
Schweidler, Dick, B, St. Louis ... 1938-39, 1946
Scott, James, WR, Henderson JC ... 1976-80
Scott, Ralph, T, Wisconsin ... 1921-25
Seals, George, G, Missouri ... 1965-71
Seibering, Gerald, B, Drake ... 1932
Senn, Bill, B, Knox ... 1926-31
Serini, Washington, G, Kentucky ... 1948-51
Sevy, Jeff, T-DE, California ... 1975-78
Seymour, Jim, WR, Notre Dame ... 1970-72
Shank, Henry, HB, No college ... 1920
Shanklin, Ron, WR, North Texas State ... 1975-76
Shaw, Glenn, HB, Kentucky ... 1960
Shearer, Brad, DT, Texas ... 1978, 1980-81
Shellog, Alec, T, Notre Dame ... 1939
Sherman, Saul, QB, Chicago ... 1939-40
Shipkey, Jerry, FB, UCLA ... 1953
Shoemake, Hub, G, Illinois ... 1920-21
Shy, Don, RB, San Diego State ... 1970-72
Siegal, John, E, Columbia ... 1939-43
Sigillo, Dom, T, Xavier ... 1943-44
Sigmund, Art, G, No college ... 1923
Simmons, Jerry, WR, Bethune-Cookman ... 1969
Singletary, Mike, LB, Baylor ... 1981
Sisk, John, B, Marquette ... 1932-36
Sisk, John Jr., B, Miami ... 1964
Skibinski, John, RB, Purdue ... 1978-81
Smeja, Rudy, E, Michigan ... 1944-45
Smith, Clarence, E, Georgia ... 1942
Smith, Gene, G, Georgia Tech ... 1930
Smith, Allen, E, Mississippi ... 1947-48
Smith, J. D., B, North Carolina A&T ... 1956
Smith, James (Jet Stream), B, Compton JC ... 1961
Smith, Ray Gene, B, Midwestern ... 1954-57
Smith, Ron, S, Wisconsin ... 1965, 1970-72
Smith, Russ, T, Illinois ... 1921, 1922, 1925
Snyder, Bob, QB, Ohio U ... 1939-41, 1943
Sorey, Revie, G, Illinois ... 1975-81
Spivey, Mike, CB, Colorado ... 1977-79
Sprinkle, Ed, E, Hardin-Simmons ... 1944-55
Stahlman, Dick, T, DePaul ... 1933
Staley, Bill, DT, Utah State ... 1970-72
Standlee, Norm, B, Stanford ... 1941
Stautberg, Jerry, G, Cincinnati ... 1951
Steinbach, Larry, G, St. Thomas ... 1930-31
Steinkemper, Bill, T, Notre Dame ... 1943
Stenn, Paul, G, Villanova ... 1948-51
Sternaman, Edward (Dutch), B, Illinois ... 1920-27
Sternaman, Joey, QB, Illinois ... 1922-25, 1927-30
Steuber, Bob, HB, Missouri ... 1942-43
Stickel, Walt, T, Pennsylvania ... 1946-49
Stillwell, Roger, DE-DT, Stanford ... 1975-77
Stinchcomb, Pete, QB, Ohio State ... 1921-22
Stoepel, Terry, G, Tulsa ... 1967
Stolfa, Anton, B, Luther ... 1939
Stone, Billy, B, Bradley ... 1951-54
Strickland, Larry, C, North Texas State ... 1954-59
Sturtridge, Dick, HB, DePaul ... 1928-29
Stydahar, Joe, T, West Virginia ... 1936-42, 1945-46
Suhey, Matt, RB, Penn State ... 1980-81
Sullivan, Frank, C, Loyola (La.) ... 1935-39
Sumner, Charlie, B, William & Mary ... 1955, 1958-60
Sweeney, Jake, T, Cincinnati ... 1944
Swisher, Bobby, B, Northwestern ... 1938-41, 1945
Szymanski, Frank, C, Notre Dame ... 1949

T

Tabor, Paul, C, Oklahoma ... 1980
Tackwell, Cookie, E, Kansas State ... 1931-33
Taft, Merrill, B, Wisconsin ... 1924
Taylor, Clifton, RB, Memphis State ... 1974
Taylor, John (Tarzan), G, Ohio State ... 1920-21
Taylor, Joe, DB, North Carolina A&T ... 1967-74
Taylor, Lionel, WR, New Mexico Highlands ... 1959
Taylor, Roosevelt, DB, Grambling ... 1961-69
Thomas, Bob, K, Notre Dame ... 1975-81
Thomas, Earl, WR, Houston ... 1971-73
Thompson, Russ, T, Nebraska ... 1936-39
Thrower, Willie, QB, Michigan State ... 1953
Tom, Mel, DE, San Jose State ... 1973-75
Torrance, Jack, T, Louisiana Tech ... 1939-40
Trafton, George, C, Notre Dame ... 1920-32
Trost, Milt, T, Marquette ... 1935-39
Tucker, Bill, RB, Tennessee State ... 1971
Turner, Cecil, WR, Cal Poly-San Luis Obispo ... 1968-73
Turner, Clyde (Bulldog), C, Hardin-Simmons ... 1940-52

U

Ulmer, Mike, CB, Doane ... 1980
Usher, Lou, T, Syracuse ... 1921, 1923

V

Vactor, Ted, CB, Nebraska ... 1975
Vallez, Emilo, TE, New Mexico ... 1968-69
Van Horne, Keith, T, USC ... 1981
Van Valkenburg, Pete, RB, Brigham Young ... 1974
Veach, Walter, B, No college ... 1920
Venturelli, Fred, T, No college ... 1948
Vick, Ernie, C, Michigan ... 1927-28
Vick, Dick, QB, Washington & Jefferson ... 1925
Vodicka, Joe, HB, Lewis Institute ... 1943, 1945
Voss, Walter (Tillie), E, Detroit ... 1927-28
Vucinich, Milt, G, Stanford ... 1945

W

Wade, Bill, QB, Vanderbilt ... 1961-66
Wade, Charles, WR, Tennessee State ... 1974
Wager, Clint, E, St. Mary's, Minnesota ... 1941-42
Wallace, Bob, E, Texas-El Paso ... 1968-72
Wallace, Stan, B, Illinois ... 1954, 1956-58
Walquist, Laurie, QB, Illinois ... 1922-31
Walterscheid, Lennie, S-KR, Southern Utah State ... 1977-81
Ward, John, C-G, Oklahoma State ... 1976
Washington, Harry, WR, Colorado State ... 1979
Watkins, Bobby, B, Ohio State ... 1955-57
Watts, Rickey, WR, Tulsa ... 1979-81
Weatherly, Gerald (Bones), C, Rice ... 1950, 1952-54
Wetoska, Bob, T, Notre Dame ... 1960-69
Wetzel, Damon, HB, Ohio State ... 1935
Wheeler, Ted, G, West Texas State ... 1970
Wheeler, Wayne, WR, Alabama ... 1974
White, Roy, B, Valparaiso ... 1924-25, 1927-29
White, Wilford (Whizzer), B, Arizona State ... 1951-52
Whitman, S. J., B, Tulsa ... 1953-54
Whitsell, Dave, DB, Indiana ... 1961-66
Whittenton, Jesse, HB, Texas Western ... 1958
Wightkin, Bill, DE, Notre Dame ... 1950-57
Williams, Bob, QB, Notre Dame ... 1951-52, 1955
Williams, Brooks, TE, North Carolina ... 1981
Williams, Broughton, T, Florida ... 1947
Williams, Dave, RB, Colorado ... 1979-81
Williams, Fred, T, Arkansas ... 1952-63
Williams, Perry, RB, Purdue ... 1974
Wilson, George, E, Northwestern ... 1937-46
Wilson, Nemiah, CB, Grambling ... 1975
Wilson, Otis, LB, Louisville ... 1980-81
Wright, Steve, T, Alabama ... 1971
Wynne, Elmer, FB, Notre Dame ... 1928

Y

Youmans, Maury, T, Syracuse ... 1960-62
Young, Adrian, LB, USC ... 1973
Young, Randolph, T, Millikin ... 1920
Youngblood, George, S, Cal State-Los Angeles ... 1969
Yourist, Abe, E, No college ... 1923

Z

Zanders, Emanual, G, Jackson State ... 1981
Zarnas, Gust, G, Ohio State ... 1938
Zeller, Joe, G, Indiana ... 1933-38
Zizak, Vince, G, Villanova ... 1934
Zorich, George, G, Northwestern ... 1944-45
Zucco, Vic, B, Michigan State ... 1957-60

CINCINNATI BENGALS

1965 Paul Brown was living comfortably in La Jolla, California, reflecting on his 17 seasons as head coach of the Cleveland Browns. He had left the Browns following the 1962 season with a record of 158 victories, 48 losses, and 8 ties, seven conference titles, and three NFL championships. Brown had the urge to get back into football but he wasn't sure where he wanted to be. His son, Mike, did a study on pro football expansion and recommended Cincinnati as a potential site. Brown met with Governor James Rhodes and the two agreed the state could accommodate a second pro football team.

1966 Fearful the Reds' baseball team would leave town and feeling pressure from local businessmen pushing for a pro football franchise, Cincinnati's City Council approved the construction of Riverfront Stadium, December 15. The stadium was granted a 48-acre downtown site, bounded by Second Street and the Ohio River.

1967 Brown's group was awarded an AFL expansion franchise, September 27. "I feel as if I'm breathing again," Brown said. Brown hired Al LoCasale as director of player personnel. Brown called the team the Bengals, the name of the previous Cincinnati AFL franchises in 1927, 1930, and 1931. The Bengals acquired their first player, trading two draft choices to Miami for quarterback John Stofa, December 26.

1968 The Bengals were awarded 40 veteran players in the allocation draft. Brown's AFL rivals were not particularly generous. As UPI reported: "The owners made sure that Brown doesn't start another dynasty too soon." Cincinnati fared better in the college draft, selecting Tennessee center Bob Johnson on its first pick. Other quality draftees included running backs Jess Phillips and Essex Johnson, tight end Bob Trumpy, linebacker Al Beauchamp, and tackle Howard Fest. The Bengals lost their first preseason game 38-14 to Kansas City before 21,682 fans at Nippert Stadium. They went the entire first half without a first down. The Bengals played respectably during the regular season, upsetting Denver 24-10 and Buffalo 34-23 in their first two home games. Paul Robinson won the AFL rushing title with 1,023 yards and was named AFL rookie of the year.

1969 Brown selected quarterback Greg Cook of the University of Cincinnati in the first round of the draft, January 28. The same draft produced middle linebacker Bill Bergey, defensive end Royce Berry, cornerback Ken Riley, and wide receiver Speedy Thomas. Other AFL teams stopped referring to them as "the Baby Bengals" when they beat Miami 27-21 in the opener, September 14. It was Brown's three-hundredth coaching victory and an impressive debut for German-born Horst Muhlmann, who kicked two field goals out of Nippert Stadium. The following week, Cook passed for three touchdowns and ran for another as Cincinnati surprised San Diego 34-20. Then the Bengals defeated Kansas City 24-19 to stretch their record to 3-0. However, Cook suffered a serious arm injury when he was hit by Willie Lanier and sat out the next four games. The Bengals lost all four games. Cook returned to spark a 31-17 win over Oakland and a 31-31 tie with Houston. Against the Oilers, Cook passed for four touchdowns. Brown was named AFL coach of the year. Bergey was honored as AFL defensive rookie of the year. Cook won the AFL passing championship.

1970 The season opened gloomily as Cook's arm went dead at the Wilmington College training camp. Brown put Cook on the injured list and enlisted Virgil Carter, a Chicago Bears' and Buffalo Bills' cast-off, to play quarterback. The Bengals beat Oakland in the opener 31-21 but lost the next six, falling to last place in the Central Division. Carter ended the skid, throwing three touchdown passes in a 43-14 rout of Buffalo, November 8. The following week, the biggest sports crowd in Cincinnati history (60,007) jammed the new Riverfront Stadium to watch Brown upset his old Cleveland team 14-10. Key players in the win were rookie defensive tackles Mike Reid and Ron Carpenter. The Bengals staged a remarkable comeback, sweeping their last seven games to win the Central Division with an 8-6 record. They clinched their first division title with a 45-7 win over Boston before 60,157 fans at Riverfront Stadium, December 20. The inexperienced Bengals were no match for Baltimore in their AFC playoff game as the Colts dominated 17-0.

1971 The Bengals fared well in the draft, adding quarterback Ken Anderson and tackle Vernon Holland. The Bengals looked invincible as they rolled through a 5-0-1 preseason and manhandled Philadelphia 37-14 in the league opener. Carter passed for 273 yards and three touchdowns against the Eagles. Reid sacked Philadelphia passer Pete Liske five times. The season disintegrated rapidly, however, as the Bengals lost their next seven games. The most damaging setback was a 20-17 loss in Green Bay in which Carter and safety Ken Dyer were injured. Dyer snapped a vertebra in his neck, and it was a year before he regained the use of his arms and legs. A 10-6 loss in Houston was the most humiliating game in Cincinnati's brief history. The Oilers scored on a 48-yard interception return on which no Bengals player gave chase. "I am embarrassed," an angry Brown said. "I just hope we never go through another season like this."

1972 Brown went for defensive help in the college draft, February 1. In order, Brown selected end Sherman White, safety Tommy Casanova, linebacker Jim LeClair, and cornerback Bernard Jackson. Anderson, rapidly gaining maturity, unseated Carter as Cincinnati's number-one quarterback. The season unfolded in three separate stages: the start—four wins in five games; the midseason slump—four losses in five games; and the finish—winning three of their last four. But they couldn't catch Cleveland for the AFC wild card berth. Chip Myers set a club record with 57 pass receptions.

1973 Brown went shopping for offense in the draft

Quarterback Ken Anderson rolls out in a victory over Los Angeles, 1981.

and came away with another splendid haul. Brown selected wide receiver Isaac Curtis (first round) and runners Charles (Boobie) Clark (thirteenth) and Lenvil Elliott (tenth). Those additions, combined with the rapid development of Anderson at quarterback, gave Cincinnati game-breaking potential. It took a while for the new players to blend as the Bengals went 4-4. They swept their last six games and won their second Central Division championship. Cincinnati lost to Miami 34-16 in the AFC playoffs at Miami, December 23. The Dolphins rushed for 241 yards and opened a 21-3 lead early in the second quarter. Neal Craig's interception return and two Muhlmann field goals cut it to 21-16 at halftime but the Bengals wilted in the third quarter. Clark, who finished the year with 988 yards rushing and 45 pass receptions, was named AFC rookie of the year. Veteran Essex Johnson led Cincinnati with a career-high 997 yards rushing. Curtis caught 45 passes.

1974 Cincinnati traded Bergey to Philadelphia for two first-round draft choices and a third-round pick in 1977. LeClair, an aggressive three-year veteran from North Dakota, replaced Bergey at middle linebacker. The Bengals won four of their first five games to lead the Central Division but couldn't keep pace with Super Bowl-bound Pittsburgh. Brown derived some consolation from his first season series sweep of Cleveland. Curtis caught five passes for 117 yards and a touchdown in the Bengals' 33-7 win over the Browns in the opener, September 15. Four weeks later, Anderson threw three more scoring passes as Cincinnati beat the Browns 34-24. Anderson threw four touchdown passes in a 33-6 rout of Kansas City, November 24. Anderson won the NFL passing championship, completing a club record 64.9 percent of his attempts. Cornerback Lemar Parrish led the NFL in punt returns, including a 90-yard touchdown against Washington, October 6.

1975 The Bengals launched their season by winning the first six games. LeClair preserved a 21-19 victory over Houston, making all four tackles in a goal line stand. Anderson handled the scoring, throwing three touchdown passes. Rookie Marvin Cobb raced 52 yards with his first pro interception to give Cincinnati a 14-10 win over Oakland. The Bengals won their eighth game in nine starts against Buffalo, 33-24, as Anderson completed 30 of 46 passes for 447 yards and two touchdowns, November 17. The yardage was the tenth highest one-game total in NFL history. Anderson missed a game with an injury, but reserve quarterback John Reaves led the Bengals to a 23-19 win over Houston, November 30. Cincinnati scored 27 points in the first quarter to crush San Diego 47-14 and finish with its best regular season record, 11-3. The Bengals qualified as the wild card team for the AFC playoffs but their losing postseason record continued with a 31-28 loss to Oakland, December 28. They fell behind 31-14, then stormed back on Anderson's two fourth-quarter touchdown passes. Anderson won his second NFL passing championship. A serious blow was the loss of defensive tackle Mike Reid, who retired at 26 to pursue a career in music.

1976 Paul Brown announced his retirement after 41 seasons of coaching, January 1. Brown named Bill Johnson, his long-time line coach, to succeed him. Brown continued to serve as the club's general manager, vice president, and owner. The Bengals upgraded their roster, acquiring defensive end Coy Bacon in a trade with San Diego and drafting several top rookies, including halfback Archie Griffin, the two-time Heisman Trophy winner from Ohio State. Other standout rookies included wide receiver Billy Brooks of Oklahoma and kicker Chris Bahr of Penn State. As always, the Bengals set a fast pace in the Central Division, winning 9 of their first 11 games. Anderson had his best game in a 45-21 win over

Tommy Casanova returns a punt for a touchdown against Denver, 1972.

Fullback Pete Johnson plows for a gain in a victory against San Diego, 1981.

Bill Bergey

Virgil Carter

Boobie Clark

Greg Cook

Archie Griffin

Vernon Holland

Bob Johnson

Cleveland, throwing for four touchdowns. Griffin, who became a starter as a rookie, rushed for 139 yards and scored on a 77-yard run as Cincinnati rallied to beat Kansas City 27-24. The season came down to two games against Pittsburgh and Oakland and the Bengals lost both—7-3 to the Steelers, November 28, and 35-20 to Oakland, December 6. Those defeats not only cost Cincinnati the Central Division title but the AFC wild card spot as well. Cornerback Ken Riley led the AFC with nine interceptions.

1977 Cincinnati drafted defensive tackles Eddie Edwards and Wilson Whitley, and tight end Mike Cobb in the first round of the draft on May 2. The Bengals started slowly, winning only two of their first six games. Then they turned their season around, going 6-1 and getting back into playoff contention. The last victory in that streak was 17-10 over the Steelers on December 10, a game that the Bengals won with 10 points in 18 seconds. Needing a win in Houston in the final game of the season to clinch the division, the Bengals were defeated by the Oilers 21-16, as Billy (White Shoes) Johnson ran for 263 all-purpose (rushing, receiving, and returns) yards.

1978 Cincinnati used its two first-round draft choices to select Lombardi Trophy winner Ross Browner, a defensive tackle from Notre Dame, and Washington center Blair Bush. Preseason injuries to Anderson kept him out for more than a month, and the Bengals lost their first eight games, at one point scoring only three points in a three-game span. After five losses, Bill Johnson resigned as head coach on October 2 and was replaced by Homer Rice. On October 29, Anderson was back into the lineup to throw bombs of 45 and 57 yards to lead Cincinnati to its first victory, 28-13 over Houston. The Bengals then lost four in a row, but closed with consecutive victories over Atlanta (37-7), Los Angeles (20-19), and Cleveland (48-16).

1979 After the fast finish the season before, Cincinnati expected big things, but got a repeat of the previous season's 4-12 record. The Bengals defeated two playoff-bound teams, Philadelphia and the Super Bowl champion Steelers. The defense gave up more points than any other NFL team, including 51 to Buffalo, 42 to Houston, and 38 to Dallas and Baltimore. Despite a 16-12 victory over Cleveland in the season finale on December 16, Rice was fined. Former Cleveland Browns coach Forrest Gregg was named head coach on December 28.

1980 Having already built a strong defensive line through the draft, the Bengals dramatically improved their offensive line with the addition of number-one pick Anthony Munoz of USC on April 29. The Bengals' season got off to a bad start when Anderson was injured in preseason. Although he started 12 games, Anderson completed only 2 because of injuries and was limited to six touchdown passes all year. Despite two early victories over Pittsburgh, the Bengals entered the last month of the season with a 3-9 record. Consecutive victories over Kansas City, Baltimore, Chicago, and Cleveland brought the Bengals' final record to 6-10.

1981 The Bengals unveiled their new uniforms with

tiger-striped helmets, jerseys, and pants on April 9. Three weeks later, in the second round of the draft, Cincinnati picked wide receiver Cris Collinsworth of Florida. The Bengals started off fast, winning their first two games. At midseason they still led the AFC Central with a 5-3 record, and they increased their lead thereafter, finishing the last half of the season 7-1, the only loss being to San Francisco. On December 6, Anderson threw two touchdown passes and the Bengals clinched the Central Division with a 17-10 victory over the Steelers. Anderson led the NFL in passing with a 98.5 rating.

1982 In the 1981 AFC Divisional Playoff Game against Buffalo on January 3, the Bengals jumped out to a 14-0 lead. Every time the Bills came back, the Bengals would score again and won 28-21. Playing in their first AFC Championship Game ever, the Bengals

Wide receiver Cris Collinsworth, 1981.

defeated the San Diego Chargers 27-7 on a day in which the weather gained as much attention as the teams. The temperature was nine degrees below zero at game time, with a wind-chill factor of minus 59, as the Bengals—and the cold—shut down the Chargers' passing attack. In Super Bowl XVI on January 24, the Bengals were trailing the 49ers 20-0 by halftime. A second-half rally couldn't make up the deficit, and the 49ers won 26-21.

MEMBERS OF HALL OF FAME:
Paul Brown

BENGALS RECORD, 1968-81

Year	Won	Lost	Tied	Pct.	Pts.	OP
1968	3	11	0	.214	215	329
1969	4	9	1	.308	280	367
1970§	8	6	0	.571	312	255
1971	4	10	0	.286	284	265
1972	8	6	0	.571	299	229
1973§	10	4	0	.714	286	231
1974	7	7	0	.500	283	259
1975*	11	3	0	.786	340	246
1976	10	4	0	.714	335	210
1977	8	6	0	.571	238	235
1978	4	12	0	.250	252	284
1979	4	12	0	.250	337	421
1980	6	10	0	.375	244	312
1981‡	12	4	0	.750	421	304
14 Years	99	104	1	.488	4,126	3,947

§AFC Central Division Champion
*AFC Wild Card Qualifier for Playoffs
‡AFC Champion

RECORD HOLDERS

Rushing (Yards)	Pete Johnson, 1981	1,077
Passing (Pct.)	Ken Anderson, 1974	64.9
Passing (Yards)	Ken Anderson, 1981	3,754
Passing (TDs)	Ken Anderson, 1981	29
Receiving (No.)	Dan Ross, 1981	71
Receiving (Yards)	Cris Collinsworth, 1981	1,009
Interceptions (No.)	Ken Riley, 1976	9
Punting (Avg.)	Dave Lewis, 1970	46.2
Punt Ret. (Avg.)	Lemar Parrish, 1975	18.8
Kickoff Ret. (Avg.)	Lemar Parrish, 1970	30.1
Touchdowns (Total)	Pete Johnson, 1981	16
Field Goals Made	Horst Muhlmann, 1972	27
Points (No.)	Jim Breech, 1981	115

COACHING HISTORY

1968-75	Paul Brown	55-56- 1
1976-78	Bill Johnson*	18-15
1978-79	Homer Rice	8-19- 0
1980-81	Forrest Gregg	18-14- 0

*Replaced after five games in 1978

FIRST PLAYER SELECTED

1968	Bob Johnson, C, Tennessee
1969	Greg Cook, QB, Cincinnati
1970	Mike Reid, DT, Penn State
1971	Vernon Holland, T, Tennessee State
1972	Sherman White, DE, California
1973	Isaac Curtis, WR, San Diego State
1974	Bill Kollar, DT, Montana State
1975	Glenn Cameron, LB, Florida
1976	Billy Brooks, WR, Oklahoma
1977	Eddie Edwards, DT, Miami, Fla.
1978	Ross Browner, DE, Notre Dame
1979	Jack Thompson, QB, Washington State
1980	Anthony Munoz, T, USC
1981	David Verser, WR, Kansas
1982	Glen Collins, DE, Mississippi State

CINCINNATI BENGALS, 1968-81

Adams, Doug, LB, Ohio State	1971-74
Alexander, Charles, RB, Louisiana State	1979-81
Alexis, Alton, WR, Tulane	1980
Amsler, Marty, DE, Evansville	1970
Anderson, Ken, QB, Augustana, Illinois	1971-81
Anderson, Jerry, S, Oklahoma	1977
Archer, Dan, T, Oregon	1968
Avery, Ken, LB, Southern Mississippi	1969-74

B

Baccaglio, Martin, DE, San Jose State	1968-70
Bacon, Coy, DE, Jackson State	1976-78
Bahr, Chris, K, Penn State	1976-79
Banks, Estes, RB, Colorado	1968
Bass, Don, TE, Houston	1978-81
Beauchamp, Al, LB, Southern U.	1969-75
Bergey, Bill, LB, Arkansas State	1969-73
Berry, Royce, DE, Houston	1969-75
Blackwood, Lyle, S, Texas Christian	1973-75
Brabham, Danny, LB, Arkansas	1968
Breech, Jim, K, California	1980-81
Breeden, Louis, CB, North Carolina Central	1978-81
Bright, Greg, DB, Morehead State	1980-81
Brooks, Billy, WR, Oklahoma	1976-79
Brown, Bob, DT, Arkansas AM&N	1975-76
Browner, Jim, S, Notre Dame	1979
Browner, Ross, DE, Notre Dame	1978-81
Buchanan, Tim, LB, Hawaii	1969
Buie, Drew, WR, Catawba	1972
Bujnoch, Glenn, G, Texas A&M	1976-81
Buncom, Frank, LB, USC	1968

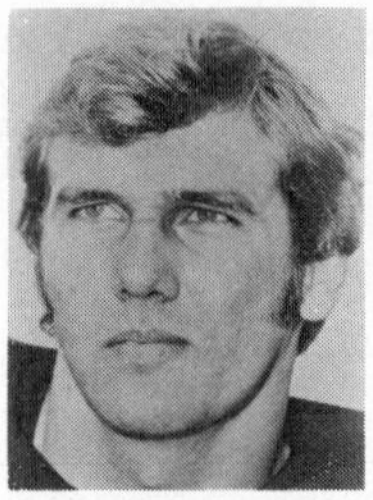
Jim LeClair

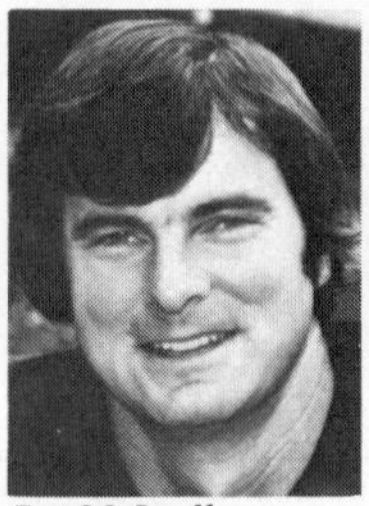
Pat McInally

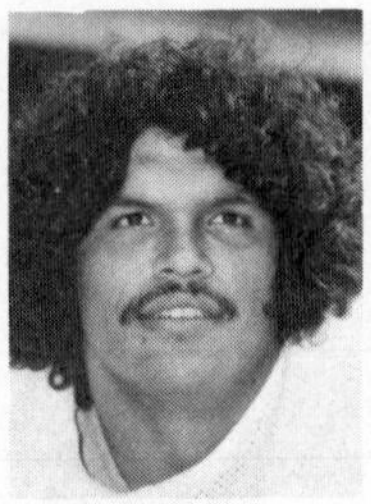
Anthony Munoz

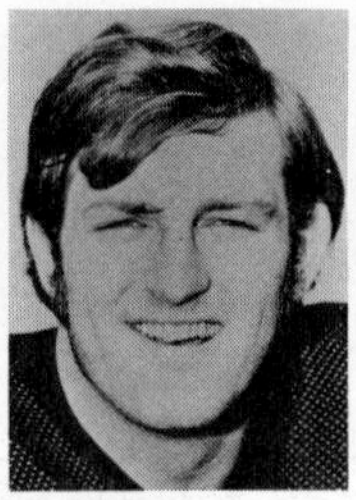
Mike Reid

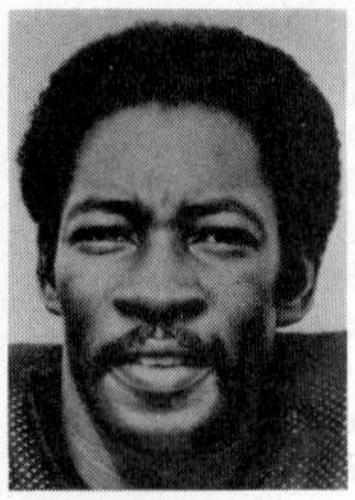
Ken Riley

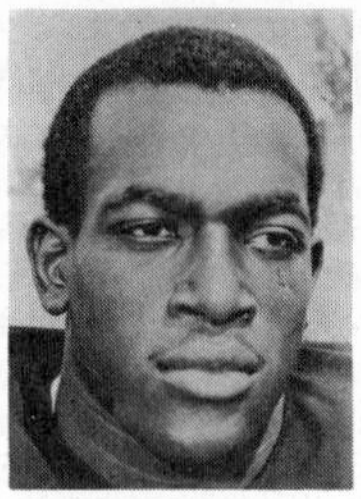
Paul Robinson

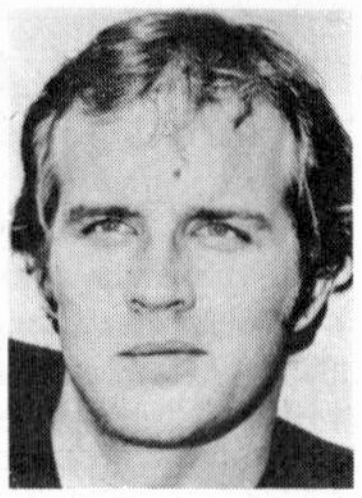
Bob Trumpy

Burk, Scott, S, Oklahoma State 1979
Burley, Gary, DE, Pittsburgh 1976-81
Bush, Blair, C, Washington 1978-81

C

Cameron, Glenn, LB, Florida 1975-81
Canale, Justin, G, Mississippi State 1969
Carpenter, Ron, DE, North Carolina State 1969-76
Carter, Virgil, QB, Brigham Young 1970-73
Casanova, Tom, S, Louisiana State 1972-77
Chandler, Al, TE, Oklahoma 1973-74
Chapman, Clarence, CB, Eastern Michigan 1980-81
Chomyszak, Steve, DT, Syracuse 1968-73
Clark, Boobie, RB, Bethune-Cookman 1973-78
Clark, Wayne, QB, U.S. International 1974
Cobb, Marvin, CB-S, USC 1975-79
Cobb, Mike, TE, Michigan State 1977
Coleman, Al, S, Tennessee State 1969-71
Collinsworth, Cris, WR, Florida 1981
Conley, Steve, RB, Kansas 1972
Cook Greg, QB, Cincinnati 1969-74
Corbett, Jim, TE, Pittsburgh 1977-80
Cornish, Frank, DT, Grambling 1970
Coslet, Bruce, TE, Pacific 1969-76
Cotton, Barney, G, Nebraska 1979
Cousino, Brad, LB, Miami, Ohio 1975
Crabtree, Eric, WR, Pittsburgh 1969-71
Craig, Neal, S, Fisk 1971-73
Curtis, Isaac, WR, San Diego State 1973-81

D

Davis, Charlie, RB, Colorado 1974
Davis, Oliver, S, Tennessee State 1981
Davis, Ricky, S, Alabama 1975
Davis, Tony, RB, Nebraska 1976-78
DeLeone, Tom, G-C, Ohio State 1972-73
Dennis, Guy, G, Florida 1969-72
DePaso, Tom, LB, Penn State 1978
Devlin, Chris, LB, Penn State 1975-78
Dinkel, Tom, LB, Kansas 1978-81
Donahue, Mark, G, Michigan 1978-79
Dressler, Doug, RB, Chico State 1970-74
Dunn, Paul, RB-WR, U.S. International 1970
Durko, Sandy, S, USC 1970-71
Dyer, Ken, S, Arizona State 1969-71

E

Edwards, Eddie, DB, Miami 1977-81
Elliott, Lenvil, RB, Northeast Missouri State 1973-78
Ely, Larry, LB, Iowa 1970-71
Elzey, Paul, LB, Toldeo 1968
Erickson, Bernard, LB, Abilene Christian 1968
Ernst, Mike, QB, Cal State-Fullerton 1973-74

F

Fairchild, Greg, G, Tulsa 1976-77
Fest, Howard, G-T, Texas 1968-75
Frazier, Curt, CB, Fresno State 1968
Frazier, Guy, LB, Wyoming 1981
Fritts, Stan, RB, North Carolina State 1975-76

G

Gehrke, Jack, WR, Utah 1969-70
George, Tim, WR, Carson-Newman 1973
Glass, Billy, G, Baylor 1980
Graham, Ken, S, Washington State 1970
Graves, White, S, Louisiana State 1968
Green, Dave, P-PK, Ohio U. 1974-75
Griffin, Archie, RB, Ohio State 1976-81
Griffin, Jim, DE, Grambling 1968-69
Griffin, Ray, CB-KR, Ohio State 1978-81
Guillory, John, S, Stanford 1969-70
Gunner, Harry, DE, Oregon 1968-69

H

Haffner, Mike, WR, UCLA 1971
Hargrove, Jim, RB, Wake Forest 1981
Harmon, Ed, LB, Louisville 1969
Harris, Bo, LB, Louisiana State 1975-81
Harris, M. L., TE, Kansas State 1980-81
Headrick, Sherrill, LB, Texas Christian 1968
Heath, Jo Jo, KR-DB, Pittsburgh 1980
Henson, Champ, RB, Ohio State 1975
Herock, Ken, TE, West Virginia 1968
Hertel, Rob, QB, USC 1978
Hibler, Mike, LB, Stanford 1968
Hicks, Bryan, DB, McNeese State 1980-81
Holden, Steve, WR, Arizona State 1977
Holland, Vernon, T, Tennessee State 1971-79
Horn, Rod, NT, Nebraska 1981
Hunt, Bobby, S, Auburn 1968-69
Hunt, Ron, T, Oregon 1976-78

J

Jackson, Bernard, S-CB, Washington State 1972-76
Jauron, Dick, S, Yale 1978-80
Johnson, Bob, C, Tennessee 1968-79
Johnson, Essex, RB, Grambling 1968-75
Johnson, Jim, CB, South Carolina State 1968-69
Johnson, Ken, DT, Indiana 1971-77
Johnson, Pete, RB, Ohio State 1977-81
Johnson, Walter, DT, Cal State-Los Angeles 1977
Joiner, Charlie, WR, Grambling 1972-75
Jolitz, Evan, LB, Cincinnati 1974
Jones, Bob, S, Virginia Union 1973
Jones, Willie Lee, DT-DE, Kansas State 1968-71

K

Kearney, Tim, LB, Northern Michigan 1972-74
Keeling, Rex, P, Samford 1968
Kellerman, Ernie, S, Miami, Ohio 1973
Kelly, Bob, T, New Mexico State 1968
Kelly, Mike, TE, Davidson 1970-72
Kemp, Bobby, S, Cal State-Fullerton 1981
Kindricks, Bill, DT, Alabama A&M 1968
King, Charley, S, Purdue 1968-69
Koegel, Vic, LB, Ohio State 1974
Kollar, Bill, DT, Montana State 1974-76
Kreider, Steve, WR, Lehigh 1979-81
Krevis, Al, T, Boston College 1975
Kurnick, Howie, LB, Cincinnati 1979

L

Lamb, Ron, RB, South Carolina 1968-71
Lapham, Dave, G, Syracuse 1974-81
Law, Dennis, KR-WR, East Tennessee State 1978
Lawson, Steve, G, Kansas 1971-72
LeClair, Jim, LB, North Dakota 1972-81
Levenseller, Mike, WR, Washington State 1979-80
Lewis, Dave, P-QB, Stanford 1970-73
Livingston, Dale, P-K, Western Michigan 1968-69
Lusby, Vaughn, KR-CB, Arkansas 1979

M

Maddox, Bob, DE, Frostburg State 1974
Marshall, Ed, WR, Cameron 1971
Matlock, John, C, Miami 1968
Matson, Pat, G, Oregon 1968-74
Mayes, Rufus, T, Ohio State 1970-78
McClure, Wayne, LB, Mississippi 1968, 1970
McDaniel, John, WR, Lincoln 1974-77
McInally, Pat, P-WR, Harvard 1976-81
McVea, Warren, WR, Houston 1968
Middendorf, Dave, G, Washington State 1968-69
Mitchell, Mack, DE, Houston 1979
Montoya, Max, G-T, UCLA 1979-81
Moore, Blake, C, Wooster 1980-81
Moore, Maulty, DT, Bethune-Cookman 1975
Morgan, Melvin, CB, Mississippi Valley 1976-78
Morrison, Reece, RB, Southwestern Texas State 1972-73
Muhlmann, Horst, K, No college 1969-74
Munoz, Anthony, T, USC 1980-81
Myers, Chip, WR, Northwestern Oklahoma 1969-76

N

Niedert, John, LB, Louisville 1968
Novak, Jack, TE, Wisconsin 1975

O

Oates, Brad, T, Brigham Young 1981
Obrovac, Mike, T, Bowling Green 1981

P

Park, Ernie, T, McMurray 1969
Parrish, Lemar, CB, Lincoln, Missouri 1970-78
Peacock, Elvis, RB, Oklahoma 1981
Perreault, Pete, G, Boston U. 1968
Perry, Scott, CB, Williams 1976-79
Peterson, Bill, LB, San Jose State 1968-72
Phillips, Jess, RB, Michigan State 1968-72
Phillips, Ray, LB, Nebraska 1977-78
Poole, Nathan, RB, Louisville 1979-80
Powers, Warren, S, Nebraska 1968
Pritchard, Ron, LB, Arizona State 1972-77
Pureifory, Dave, DT, Eastern Michigan 1978

R

Randall, Dennis, DE, Oklahoma State 1968
Randolph, Al, CB, Iowa 1972
Razzano, Rick, LB, Virginia Tech 1980-81
Reaves, John, QB, Florida 1975-78
Reid, Mike, DT, Penn State 1970-74
Rice, Andy, DT, Texas Southern 1968-69
Riley, Ken, CB, Florida A&M 1969-81
Robinson, Paul, RB, Arizona 1968-72
Roman, Nick, DE, Ohio State 1970-72
Ross, Dan, TE, Northeastern 1979-81
Ruud, Tom, LB, Nebraska 1978-79

S

Saffold, Saint, WR, San Jose State 1968
St. Clair, Mike, DE, Grambling 1980-81
Sawyer, Ken, S, Syracuse 1974
Schonert, Turk, QB, Stanford 1980-81
Schuh, Jeff, LB, Minnesota 1981
Scott, Bill, CB, Idaho 1968
Shelby, Willie, KR-RB, Alabama 1976-77
Sherman, Rod, WR, Idaho 1968
Shinners, John, G, Xavier, Ohio 1972-77
Simmons, John, CB, Southern Methodist 1981
Simpkins, Ron, LB, Michigan 1980
Smiley, Tom, RB, Lamar Tech 1968
Smith, Fletcher, CB-S, Tennessee State 1968-71
Smith, Tommie, WR, San Jose State 1969
Spiller, Phil, S, Cal State-Los Angeles 1968
Staley, Bill, DT, Utah State 1968-69
Stofa, John, QB, Buffalo 1968-69
Suggs, Shafer, S, Ball State 1980
Sunter, Ian, PK, No college 1980
Swanson, Terry, P, Massachusetts 1968-69

T

Thomas, Lee, DE, Jackson State 1973
Thomas, Speedy, WR, Utah 1969-72
Thompson, Jack, QB, Washington State 1979-81
Trumpy, Bob, TE, Utah 1968-77
Turner, Clem, RB, Cincinnati 1969
Turner, Dave, RB, San Diego State 1978-80

V

Verser, David, WR-KR, Kansas 1981
Vincent, Ted, DT, Syracuse 1978
Vitiello, Sandro, K, Massachusetts 1980

W

Walker, Rick, TE, UCLA 1977-79
Walters, Stan, T, Syracuse 1972-74
Warren, Dewey, QB, Tennessee 1968
Washington, Ted, RB, San Diego State 1968
Watson, Pete, RB-TE, Tufts 1972
Wells, Mike, QB, Illinois 1977
White, Andre, TE, Florida A&M 1968
White, Mike, DT, Albany State 1969
White, Sherman, DE, California 1972-75
Whitley, Wilson, DT, Houston 1977-81
Whitten, Bobby, T, Kansas 1981
Williams, Jim, CB, Alcorn State 1968
Williams, Monk, WR, Arkansas-Pine Bluff 1968
Williams, Reggie, LB, Dartmouth 1976-81
Willis, Fred, RB, Boston College 1971-72
Wilson, Joe, RB, Holy Cross 1973
Wilson, Mike, T, Dayton 1969-70
Wilson, Mike, T, Georgia 1979-81
Wright, Ernie, T, Ohio State 1968-71
Wyche, Sam, QB, Furman 1968-70

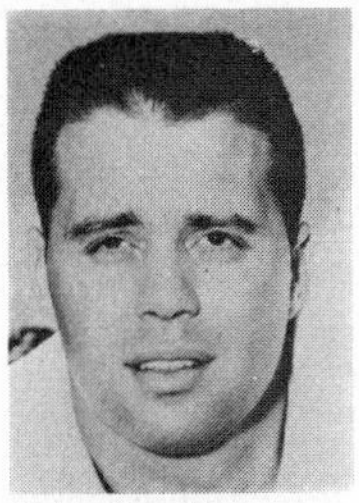
John Gordy

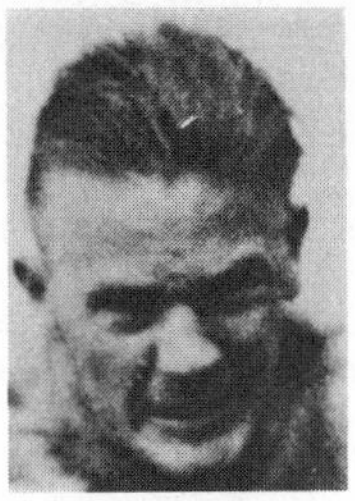
L. (Ace) Gutowsky

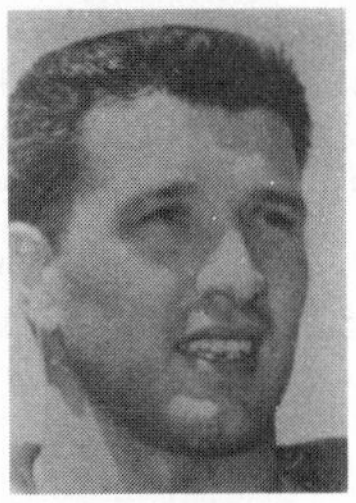
Leon Hart

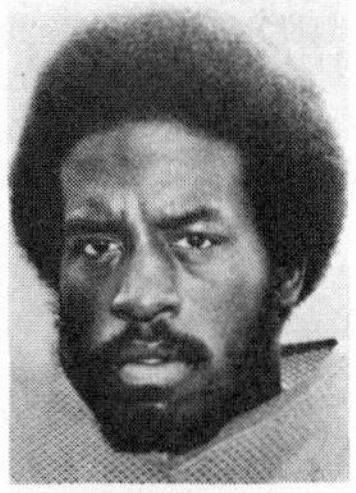
David Hill

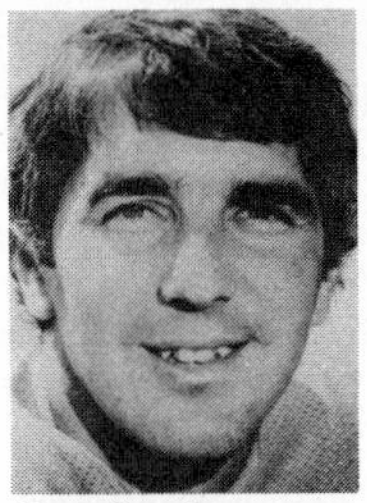
Greg Landry

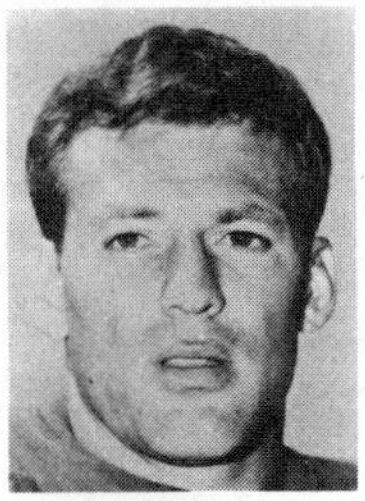
Dick LeBeau

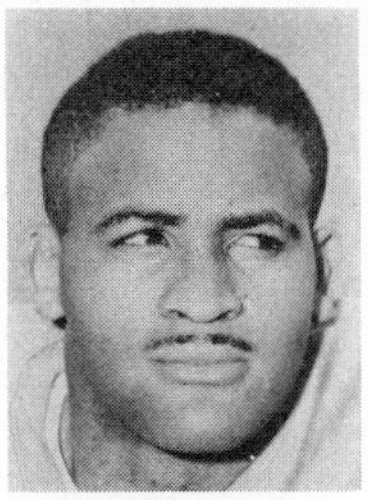
Dan Lewis

Chase, Ben, G, Navy ... 1947
Christensen, Frank, B, Utah ... 1934-37
Christensen, George, T, Oregon ... 1931-38
Christiansen, Jack, DB, Colorado State ... 1951-58
Cifelli, Gus, T, Notre Dame ... 1951-53
Cifers, Bob, B, Tennessee ... 1944-46
Clark, Al, DB, Eastern Michigan ... 1971
Clark, Dutch, B, Colorado College ... 1931-32, 1934-38
Clark, Ernie, LB, Michigan State ... 1963-67
Clark, Wayne, E, Utah ... 1944-45
Clemons, Ray, G, Central Oklahoma State ... 1939
Cline, Ollie, B, Ohio State ... 1950-53
Clowes, John, T, William & Mary ... 1951
Cobb, Garry, LB, USC ... 1979-81
Cody, Bill, LB, Auburn ... 1966
Cogdill, Gail, WR, Washington State ... 1960-68
Cole, Eddie, LB, Mississippi ... 1979-80
Colella, Tommy, B, Canisius ... 1941-43
Compton, Dick, WR, McMurry ... 1962-64
Concannon, Jack, QB, Boston College ... 1975
Conlee, Gerry, C, St. Mary's, Cal ... 1943
Cook, Gene, E, Toledo ... 1959
Cook, Ted, E, Alabama ... 1947
Cooke, Bill, DT, Massachusetts ... 1978
Cooper, Hal, B, Detroit ... 1937
Corgan, Mike, B, Notre Dame ... 1943
Cotton, Craig, TE, Youngstown State ... 1969-72
Cottrell, Bill, T, Delaware Valley ... 1967-70
Crabtree, Clem, T, Wake Forest ... 1940-41
Creekmur, Lou, T, William & Mary ... 1950-59
Cremer, Ted, E, Auburn ... 1946-48
Croft, Don, DT, Texas-El Paso ... 1976
Cronin, Gene, DE, Pacific ... 1956-59
Crosby, Ron, LB, Penn State ... 1977
Crosswhite, Leon, RB, Oklahoma ... 1973-74
Culp, Curley, DT, Arizona State ... 1980-81
Cunningham, Leon, C, South Carolina ... 1955

D

D'Alonzo, Pete, B, Villanova ... 1951-52
Danielson, Gary, QB, Purdue ... 1976-78, 1980-81
David, Jim, DB, Colorado State ... 1952-59
Davis, Ben, DB, Defiance ... 1974-76
Davis, Glenn, E, Ohio State ... 1960-61
Davis, Milt, DB, UCLA ... 1956
Dawley, Fred, B, Michigan ... 1944
Daykin, Tony, LB, Georgia Tech ... 1977-78
DeCorrevont, Bill, B, Northwestern ... 1946
DeFruiter, Bob, DB, Nebraska ... 1947
Delaney, Jeff, S, Pittsburgh ... 1981
DeMarco, Mario, G, Miami ... 1949
Dennis, Guy, G, Florida ... 1973-75
DePoyster, Jerry, K, Wyoming ... 1968
DeShane, Chuck, B, Alabama ... 1945-49
Dibble, Dorne, E, Michigan State ... 1951, 1953-57
Dickel, Dan, LB, Iowa ... 1978
Diehl, Dave, E, Michigan State ... 1939-40, 1944-45
Dieterich, Chris, T, North Carolina State ... 1980-81
Doll, Don, DB, USC ... 1949-52
Doran, Jim, E, Iowa State ... 1951-59
D'Orazio, Joe, T, Ithaca ... 1944
Dorney, Keith, T, Penn State ... 1979-81
Dove, Bob, E-G, Notre Dame ... 1953-54
Dublinski, Tom, QB, Utah ... 1952-54
Dubzinski, Walt, G, Boston College ... 1941
Dudish, Andy, C, Georgia ... 1948
Dudley, Bill, B, Virginia ... 1947-49
Dugger, Jack, E, Ohio State ... 1947-48
Duncan, James, E, Wake Forest ... 1950
Duncan, Rick, P, East Montana State ... 1969
Dunlap, Leonard, DB, North Texas State ... 1975

E

Earon, Blaine, E, Duke ... 1952-53
Ebding, Harry, E, St. Mary's, Cal ... 1931-37
Eddy, Nick, RB, Notre Dame ... 1968-70, 1972
Ehrmann, Joe, DT, Syracuse ... 1981
Eiden, Ed, B, Scranton ... 1944
Elam, Cleveland, DT, Tennessee State ... 1979
Elias, Homer, G, Tennessee State ... 1978-81
Ellis, Ken, CB, Southern U. ... 1979
Ellis, Larry, B, Syracuse ... 1948
Emerick, Bob, T, Miami, Ohio ... 1934
Emerson, Grover (Ox), G, Texas ... 1931-37
Engebretson, Paul, T, Northwestern ... 1934
English, Doug, DT, Texas ... 1975-79, 1981
Enke, Fred, QB, Arizona ... 1948-51
Evans, Murray, B, Hardin-Simmons ... 1942-43
Evey, Dick, DT, Tennessee ... 1971

F

Fantetti, Ken, LB, Wyoming ... 1979-81
Farkas, Andy, B, Detroit ... 1945
Farmer, George, WR, UCLA ... 1975
Farr, Mel, RB, UCLA ... 1967-73
Farr, Miller, DB, Wichita State ... 1973
Feldhaus, Bill, T, Cincinnati ... 1937-40
Felts, Bob, HB, Florida A&M ... 1965-67
Fena, Tom, G, Colorado ... 1937
Fenenbock, Chuck, B, UCLA ... 1943-45
Ferguson, Larry, B, Iowa ... 1963
Fichman, Leon, T, Alabama ... 1946-47
Fields, Edgar, DT, Texas A&M ... 1981
Fifer, Bill, T, West Texas State ... 1978
Fisk, Bill, E, USC ... 1940-43
Flanagan, Ed, C, Purdue ... 1965-74
Flanagan, Dick, LB, Ohio State ... 1950-52
Forte, Aldo, G, Montana ... 1946
Fowler, Amos, G, Southern Mississippi ... 1978-81
Franklin, Dennis, WR, Michigan ... 1975-76
Franks, Dennis, C, Michigan ... 1979
Freitas, Rockne, T, Oregon State ... 1968-77
French, Barry, G, Purdue ... 1951
Friede, Mike, WR, Indiana ... 1980
Frohbose, Bill, DB, Miami ... 1974
Frutig, Ed, E, Michigan ... 1945-46
Fucci, Dom, B, Kentucky ... 1955
Furness, Steve, DT, Rhode Island ... 1981
Furst, Tony, T, Dayton ... 1940-41, 1944

G

Gagnon, Roy, G, Oregon ... 1935
Gaines, Lawrence, FB, Wyoming ... 1976-79
Gallagher, Dave, DT, Michigan ... 1978-79
Gallagher, Frank, G, North Carolina ... 1967-72
Gambrell, Billy, WR, South Carolina ... 1968
Gandee, Sherwin (Sonny), E, Ohio State ... 1952-57
Gatski, Frank, C, Marshall ... 1957
Gaubatz, Dennis, LB, Louisiana State ... 1963-64
Gay, Bill, DE, USC ... 1978-81
Gedman, Gene, B, Indiana ... 1953, 1956-58
George, Ray, T, USC ... 1939
Geremsky, Thad, E, Pittsburgh ... 1951
Germany, Willie, S, Morgan State ... 1973
Gibbons, Jim, E, Iowa ... 1958-68
Gibbs, Sonny, QB, TCU ... 1964
Gill, Sloko, G, Youngstown State ... 1942
Gillette, Jim, B, Virginia ... 1948
Gilmer, Harry, QB, Alabama ... 1955-56
Ginn, Tommie, G-C, Arkansas ... 1980-81
Gipson, Paul, RB, Houston ... 1971
Girard, Earl (Jug), B, Wisconsin ... 1952-56
Glass, Bill, DE, Baylor ... 1958-61
Goich, Dan, DE, California ... 1969-70
Goldman, Sam, E, Howard ... 1949
Golsteyn, Jerry, QB, Northern Illinois ... 1979
Gonzaga, John, T, No college ... 1961-65
Goodman, Henry, T, West Virginia ... 1942
Goovert, Ron, LB, Michigan State ... 1967
Gordon, John, DT, Hawaii ... 1972
Gordy, John, G, Tennessee ... 1957, 1959-67
Gore, Gordon, B, Southwest Oklahoma Teachers ... 1939
Graham, Al, G, No college ... 1930
Graham, Les, G, Tulsa ... 1938
Gray, Dan, DE, Rutgers ... 1978-79
Gray, Hector, DB, Florida State ... 1981
Green, Curtis, DE-DT, Alabama State ... 1981
Green, Donnie, T, Purdue ... 1978
Greene, John, E, Michigan ... 1944-50
Greer, Albert, E, Jackson State ... 1963
Grefe, Ted, E, Notre Dame ... 1945
Grigonis, Frank, B, Chattanooga ... 1942
Grimes, George, B, Virginia ... 1948
Groomes, Mel, B, Indiana ... 1948-49
Grossman, Rex, B, Indiana ... 1950
Grottkau, Bob, G, Oregon ... 1959-60
Gutowsky, Leroy (Ace), B, Oklahoma City U. ... 1932-38

H

Hackenbruck, Johnny, T, Oregon State ... 1940
Hackney, Elmer, B, Kansas State ... 1942-46
Hafen, Bernie, E, Utah ... 1949-50
Haggerty, Mike, T, Miami ... 1973
Hall, Alvin, DB, Miami, Ohio ... 1981
Hall, John, B, Texas Christian ... 1942
Hall, Tom, E, Minnesota ... 1962-63
Hamilton, Ray, E, Arkansas ... 1939
Hamlin, Gene, C, Western Michigan ... 1972
Hand, Larry, DE, Appalachian State ... 1964-77
Hanneman, Chuck, E, Michigan Normal ... 1937-41
Hansen, Dale, T, Michigan State ... 1944, 1948-49
Harder, Pat, B-K, Wisconsin ... 1951-53
Harding, Roger C., California ... 1948
Hardy, Jim, QB, USC ... 1952
Harrell, James, LB, Florida ... 1979-81
Harrison, Granville, E, Mississippi State ... 1942
Hart, Leon, E, Notre Dame ... 1950-57
Haverdick, Dave, DE, Morehead State ... 1970
Hekkers, George, T, Wisconsin ... 1947-49
Held, Paul, B, San Jose State ... 1955
Helms, Jack, E, Georgia Tech ... 1946
Henderson, John, E, Michigan ... 1965-67
Hennigan, Mike, LB, Tennessee Tech ... 1973-75
Hertwig, Craig, T, Georgia ... 1975-77
Heywood, Ralph, E, USC ... 1947
Hickman, Donnie, G, USC ... 1978
Hicks, R. W., C, Humboldt State ... 1975
Hightower, Ben, E, Sam Houston State ... 1943
Hilgenberg, Wally, LB, Iowa ... 1964-66
Hill, David, TE, Texas A&I ... 1976-81
Hill, Harlon, WR, Florence State ... 1962
Hill, J. D., WR, Arizona State ... 1976-78
Hill, Jim, B, Tennessee ... 1951-52
Hill, Jimmy, DB, Sam Houston State ... 1965
Hillman, Bill, B, Tennessee ... 1947
Hilton, John, TE, Richmond ... 1972-73
Hinchman, Hubert, B, Butler ... 1934
Hipple, Eric, QB, Utah State ... 1980-81
Hoernschmeyer, Bob, B, Indiana ... 1950-55
Hogland, Doug, G, Oregon State ... 1958
Holland, Vernon, T, Tennessee State ... 1980
Hollar, John, B, Appalachian State ... 1949
Hooks, Jim, RB, Central State, Oklahoma ... 1973-76
Hoopes, Mitch, P, Arizona ... 1977
Hopp, Harry, B, Nebraska ... 1941-43
Howard, Billy, DT, Alcorn State ... 1974-76
Howard, Bill, B, USC ... 1939
Hubbard, Marv, RB, Colgate ... 1977
Huffman, Vern, B, Indiana ... 1937-38
Hughes, Chuck, WR, Texas-El Paso ... 1970-71
Hunter, James, Grambling ... 1976-81
Hunter, Scott, QB, Alabama ... 1979
Hupke, Tom, G, Alabama ... 1934-37
Hutchison, Elvin, B, Whittier ... 1939

I

Isselhardt, Ralph, G, Franklin ... 1937
Ivory, Bob, G, Detroit ... 1947
Izo, George, QB, Notre Dame ... 1965

J

Jackson, Ernie, DB, Jackson State ... 1979
Jarvis, Ray, WR, Norfolk State ... 1974-78
Jaszewski, Floyd, T, Minnesota ... 1950-51
Jauron, Dick, DB, Yale ... 1973-77
Jefferson, Bill, B, Mississippi State ... 1941
Jenkins, Leon, DB, West Virginia ... 1972
Jenkins, Walt, E, Wayne State ... 1955
Jessie, Ron, WR, Kansas State ... 1971-74
Jett, John, E, Wake Forest ... 1941
Johnson, Jack, T, Utah ... 1934-40
Johnson, John Henry, B, Arizona State ... 1957-59
Johnson, Levi, CB, Texas A&I ... 1973-77
Jolley, Gordon, T, Utah ... 1972-75
Jones, Doug, DB, Cal State-Northridge ... 1979
Jones, Elmer, G, Wake Forest ... 1947-48

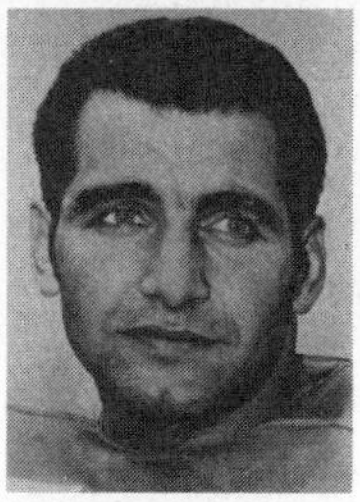

Mike Lucci

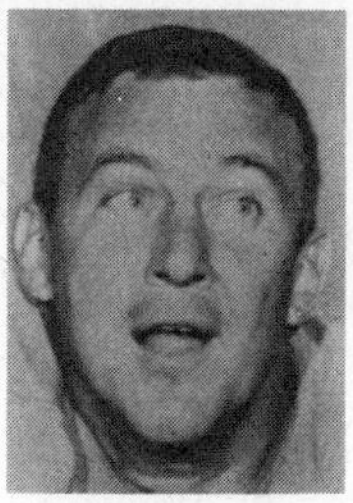

Darris McCord

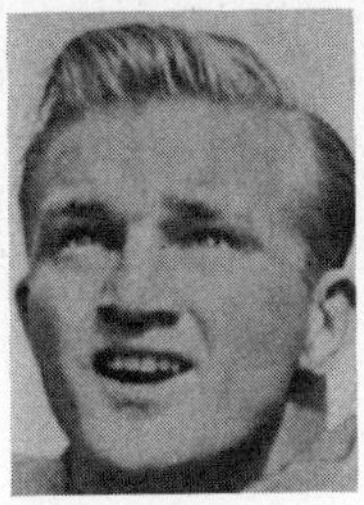

Jim Martin

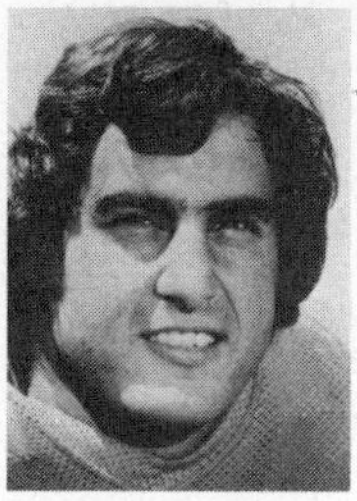

Paul Naumoff

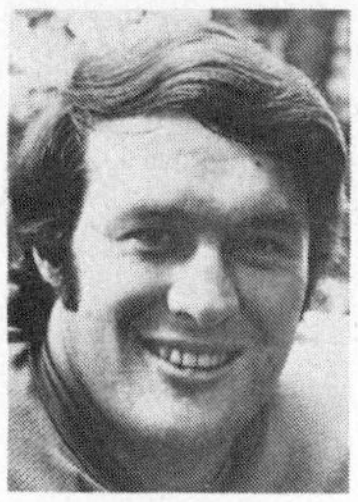

Steve Owens

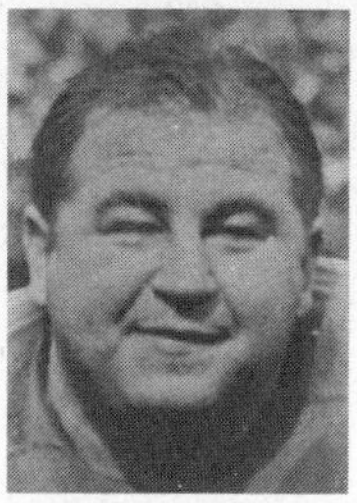

Bill Radovich

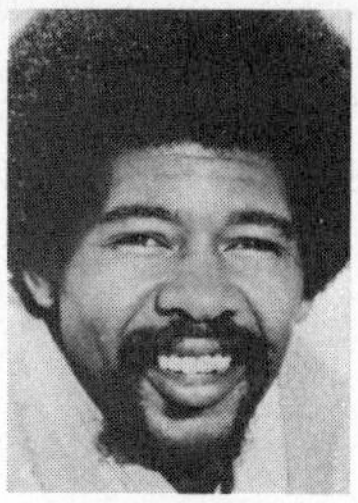

Charlie Sanders

Jones, Jim (Casey), B, Union, Tennessee ... 1946
Jones, Jimmie, RB, UCLA ... 1974
Jones, Ralph, E, Alabama ... 1946
Junker, Steve, E, Xavier ... 1957, 1959-60
Jurkiewicz, Walt, C, Indiana ... 1946

K

Kamanu, Lew, DE, Weber State ... 1967-68
Kane, Rick, RB, San Jose State ... 1977-81
Kaporch, Al, T, St. Bonaventure ... 1943-45
Karilivacz, Carl, DB, Syracuse ... 1953-57
Karras, Alex, DT, Iowa ... 1958-62, 1964-70
Karras, Ted, G, Indiana ... 1965
Karstens, George, C, Indiana ... 1949
Kaska, Tony, B, Illinois Wesleyan ... 1935
Kearney, Jim, DB, Prairie View ... 1965-66
Keene, Bob, B, Detroit ... 1943-45
Kennedy, Bill, E, Michigan State ... 1942, 1944
Kent, Greg, DT, Utah ... 1968
Kercher, Dick, B, Tulsa ... 1954
Ketzko, Alex, T, Michigan State ... 1943
King, Horace, RB, Georgia ... 1975-81
Kipp, Jim, T, Montana State ... 1942
Kizzire, Lee, B, Wyoming ... 1937
Klewicki, Ed, E, Michigan State ... 1935-38
Kmetovic, Pete, B, Stanford ... 1947
Knorr, Larry, C, Dayton ... 1942-45
Knox, Sam, G, New Hampshire ... 1934-36
Komlo, Jeff, QB, Delaware ... 1979-81
Kopay, Dave, RB, Washington ... 1968
Kopcha, Joe, G, Chattanooga ... 1936
Kostiuk, Mike, T, Detroit ... 1945
Kowalkowski, Bob, G, Virginia ... 1966-76
Krall, Gerry, B, Ohio State ... 1950
Kramer, Ron, E, Michigan ... 1965-67
Kring, Frank, B, Texas Christian ... 1945
Krol, Joe, B, West Ontario ... 1945
Krouse, Ray, T, Maryland ... 1956-57
Kuczinski, Bert, E, Pennsylvania ... 1943

L

LaLonde, Roger, DT, Muskingum ... 1964
Landry, Greg, QB, Massachusetts ... 1968-78
Lane, Dick (Night Train), CB, Scottsbluff JC ... 1960-65
LaRose, Dan, T, Missouri ... 1961-63
Lary, Yale, DB-P, Texas A&M ... 1952-53, 1956-64
Larson, Bill, TE, Colorado State ... 1977
Laslavic, Jim, LB, Penn State ... 1973-77
Lawless, Burton, G, Florida ... 1980
Lay, Russ, B, Michigan State ... 1934
Layne, Bobby, QB-K, Texas ... 1950-58
Lear, Les, G, Manitoba ... 1947
LeBeau, Dick, DB, Ohio State ... 1959-72
Lee, Larry, G, UCLA ... 1981
Lee, Ken, LB, Washington ... 1971
Lee, Monte, LB, Texas ... 1963-64
LeForce, Clyde, QB, Tulsa ... 1947-49
Leonard, Tony, CB, Virginia Union ... 1978-79
Lewis, Dan, B, Wisconsin ... 1958-64
Lewis, Eddie, CB, Kansas ... 1979
Liles, Alva, DT, Boise State ... 1980
Liles, Elvin (Sonny), G, Oklahoma State ... 1943-45
Lindon, Luther, T, Kentucky ... 1944-45
Lininger, Ray, C, Ohio State ... 1950-51
Lio, Augie, G, Georgetown ... 1941-43
Lloyd, Dave, C, Georgia ... 1962
Lomakoski, John, T, Western Michigan ... 1962
Long, Ken, G, Purdue ... 1976
Long, Bob, E, UCLA ... 1955-59
Looney, Joe Don, RB, Oklahoma ... 1965-66
Lowe, Gary, B, Michigan State ... 1957-64
Lowther, Russ, B, Detroit ... 1944
Lucci, Mike, LB, Tennessee ... 1965-73
Luce, Derrel, LB, Baylor ... 1980
Lumpkin, Roy (Father), B, Georgia Tech ... 1930-34
Lusk, Bob, C, William & Mary ... 1956

M

Mackenroth, Jack, C, North Dakota ... 1938
Madarik, Elmer (Tippy), B, Detroit ... 1945-47
Maggiolo, Chick, B, Illinois ... 1949
Magnani, Dante, B, St. Mary's, Cal. ... 1950
Maher, Bruce, DB, Detroit ... 1960-67
Mains, Gil, T, Murray State ... 1954-61
Malinchak, Bill, E, Indiana ... 1966-69
Mann, Errol, K, North Dakota ... 1969-76
Mann, Bob, E, Michigan ... 1948-49
Manzo, Joe, T, Boston College ... 1945
Margucci, Joe, B, USC ... 1947-48
Markovich, Mark, G, Penn State ... 1976-77
Maronic, Stephen, T, North Carolina ... 1939-40
Marsh, Amos, B, Oregon State ... 1965-67
Martin, Jim, LB-K, Notre Dame ... 1951-61
Martin, Robbie, WR-KR, Cal Poly-San Luis Obispo ... 1981
Martinovich, Phil, G, Pacific ... 1939
Matheson, Jack, E, Western Michigan ... 1943-46
Matheson, Riley, G, Texas Western ... 1943
Mathews, Ned, B, UCLA ... 1941-43
Mathewson, Morley, E, California ... 1941
Matisi, Tony, T, Pittsburgh ... 1938-39
Matson, Ollie, RB, San Francisco ... 1963
Mattiford, John, G, Marshall ... 1941
Maves, Earl, B, Wisconsin ... 1948
Maxwell, Bruce, RB, Arkansas ... 1970
Mazza, Vince, E, No college ... 1945-46
Mazzanti, Jerry, DE, Arkansas ... 1966
McCambridge, John, DE, Northwestern ... 1967
McClung, Willie, T, Florida A&M ... 1960-61
McCord, Darris, DE, Tennessee ... 1955-67
McCoy, Joel, B, Alabama ... 1946
McCoy, Mike, DT, Notre Dame ... 1980
McCray, Prentice, DB, Arizona State ... 1980
McCullouch, Earl, WR, USC ... 1968-73
McDermott, Lloyd, T, Kentucky ... 1950
McDonald, Jim, B, Ohio State ... 1938-39
McElhenny, Hugh, RB, Washington ... 1964
McGee, Willie, WR, Alcorn State ... 1978
McGraw, Mike, LB, Wyoming ... 1977
McGraw, Thurman, T, Colorado State ... 1950-54
McIhenny, Don, B, Southern Methodist ... 1956
McInnis, Hugh, E, Mississippi Southern ... 1964
McKalip, Bill, E, Oregon State ... 1931-32, 1934, 1936
McLenna, Bruce, B, Hillsdale ... 1966
McMakin, John, TE, Clemson ... 1975
McWilliams, Bill, B, Jordan ... 1934
Melinkovich, Mike, DE, Gray Harbour JC, Washington ... 1967
Mello, Jim, B, Notre Dame ... 1949
Mendenhall, John, DT, Grambling ... 1980
Mesak, Dick, T, St. Mary's, Cal. ... 1945
Messner, Max, LB, Cincinnati ... 1960-63
Middleton, Dave, E, Auburn ... 1955-60
Mike-Mayer, Steve, K, Maryland ... 1977
Miketa, Andy, C, North Carolina ... 1954-55
Miklich, Bill, B, Idaho ... 1948
Milano, Arch, E, St. Francis ... 1945
Miller, Bob, T, Virginia ... 1952-58
Miller, Terry, LB, Illinois ... 1970
Mills, Dick, G, Pittsburgh ... 1961-62
Mitchell, Granville, E, Davis-Elkins ... 1931-35
Mitchell, Jim, DE, Virginia State ... 1970-77
Mitchell, Melvin, C, Tennessee State ... 1977
Mitrick, Frank, T, Oglethorpe ... 1945
Mohring, John, LB, C. W. Post ... 1980
Momsen, Bob, G, Ohio State ... 1951
Monahan, Regis, B, Ohio State ... 1935-38
Montgomery, Jim, T, Texas A&M ... 1946
Montler, Mike, C, Colorado ... 1978
Mooney, Ed, LB, Texas Tech ... 1968-71
Moore, Denis, T, USC ... 1967-69
Moore, Paul, B, Presbyterian ... 1940-41
Moore, Bill, B, Loyola, La. ... 1939
Morlock, Jack, B, Marshall ... 1940
Morrall, Earl, QB, Michigan State ... 1958-64
Morris, Glenn, E, Colorado State ... 1940
Morris, Jon, C, Holy Cross ... 1975-77
Morrison, Don, T, Texas-Arlington ... 1979
Morse, Butch, E, Oregon ... 1935-38, 1940
Moscrip, Jim (Monk), E, Stanford ... 1938-39
Mote, Kelly, E, Duke ... 1947-49
Mugg, Garvin, T, North Texas State ... 1945
Munson, Bill, QB, Utah State ... 1968-76
Murakowski, Art, B, Northwestern ... 1951
Murray, Ed, K, Tulane ... 1980-81
Myers, Tom, QB, Northwestern ... 1965-66

N

Nardi, Dick, B, Ohio State ... 1938
Naumoff, Paul, LB, Tennessee ... 1967-78
Nelson, Reed, C, Brigham Young ... 1947
Nelson, Bob, C, Baylor ... 1941, 1945
Nichols, Mark, WR, San Jose State ... 1981
Ninowski, Jim, QB, Michigan State ... 1960-61
Niziolek, Bob, TE, Colorado ... 1981
Noppenberg, John, B, Miami ... 1941
Nori, Reino, B, Northern Illinois ... 1937
Norris, Ulysses, TE, Georgia ... 1979-81
Nott, Doug, B, Detroit ... 1935
Nowatzke, Tom, RB, Indiana ... 1965-69

O

Oates, Brad, T, Brigham Young ... 1978
Obee, Dunc, C, Dayton ... 1941
O'Brien, Jim, WR, Cincinnati ... 1973
O'Brien, Bill, B, No college ... 1947
Odle, Phil, E, Brigham Young ... 1968-70
Ogle, Rick, LB, Colorado ... 1972
Oldham, Ray, DB, Middle Tennessee State ... 1980-81
Olenski, Mitchell, T, Alabama ... 1947
Olszewski, Johnny, RB, California ... 1961
O'Neil, Ed, LB, Penn State ... 1974-79
O'Neil, Bill, B, Detroit ... 1935
Opalewski, Ed, T, Michigan Normal ... 1943-44
Orvis, Herb, DT, Colorado ... 1972-77
Owens, Steve, RB, Oklahoma ... 1970-74

P

Panciera, Don, B, San Francisco ... 1950
Panelli, John, B, Notre Dame ... 1949-50
Paolucci, Ben, T, Wayne State ... 1959
Parker, Raymond (Buddy), B, Centenary ... 1935-36
Parker, Willie, C, North Texas State ... 1980
Parkin, Dave, DB, Utah State ... 1979
Parson, Ray, T, Minnesota ... 1971
Parsons, Lloyd, B, Gustavus Adolphus ... 1941
Patt, Maurice, E, Carnegie Tech ... 1938
Patterson, Don, DB, Georgia Tech ... 1979
Pavelec, Ted, G, Detroit ... 1941-43
Payton, Eddie, RB, Jackson State ... 1977
Pearson, Lindell, B, Oklahoma ... 1950-52
Perry, Gerry, T, California ... 1954, 1956-59
Pesuit, Wally, C, Kentucky ... 1979-80
Peters, Floyd, T, San Francisco State ... 1963
Peterson, Ken (Ike), B, Gonzaga ... 1936
Picard, Bob, WR, Eastern Washington ... 1976
Pickard, Bob, WR, Xavier ... 1974
Piepul, Milt, B, Notre Dame ... 1941
Pierson, Reggie, Oklahoma State ... 1976
Pietrosante, Nick, RE, Notre Dame ... 1959-65
Pifferini, Bob, C, San Jose State ... 1949
Pingel, Johnny, B, Michigan State ... 1939
Pinkney, Reggie, S, East Carolina ... 1977-78
Plum, Milt, QB, Penn State ... 1962-67
Polansky, John, B, Wake Forest ... 1942
Poole, Oliver, E, Mississippi ... 1949
Porter, Tracy, WR, Louisiana State ... 1981
Potts, Charles, DB, Purdue ... 1972
Prchlik, John, T, Yale ... 1949-53
Pregulman, Merv, G, Michigan ... 1947-48
Prescott, Harold (Ace), E, Hardin-Simmons ... 1949
Presnell, Glenn, B, Nebraska ... 1934-36
Price, Cotton, B, Texas A&M ... 1940-41, 1945
Price, Ernie, DT, Texas A&I ... 1973-78
Pringle, Alan, K, Rice ... 1975
Pureifory, Dave, DE, Eastern Michigan ... 1978-81

Q

Quinlan, Billy, DE, Michigan State ... 1964

R

Rabb, Warren, QB, Louisiana State ... 1960
Rabold, Mike, G, Indiana ... 1959
Radovich, Bill, G, USC ... 1938-41, 1945
Randolph, Al, DB, Iowa ... 1972
Randolph, Clare, C, Indiana ... 1931-36
Ranspot, Keith, E, Southern Methodist ... 1942
Rasley, Rocky, G, Oregon State ... 1969-73
Rasmussen, Wayne, DB, South Dakota State ... 1964-73
Reckmack, Ray, B, Syracuse ... 1937

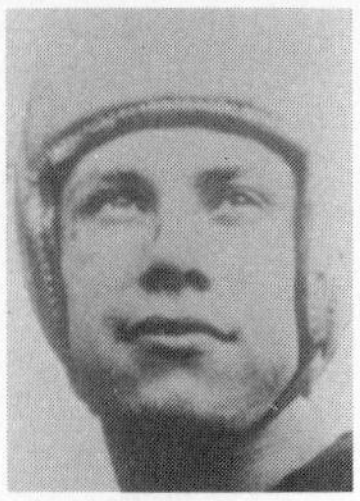
Frank Sinkwich

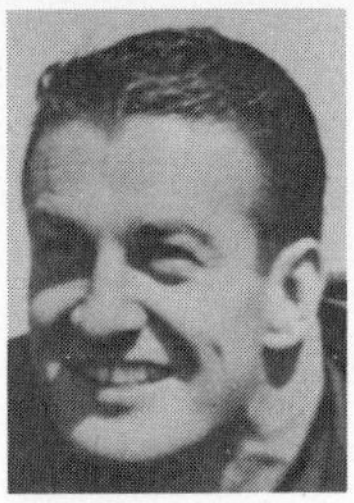
Dick Stanfel

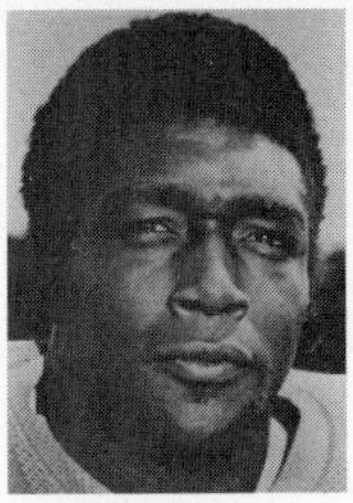
Altie Taylor

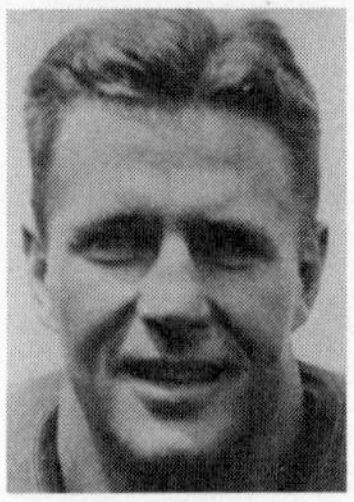
Doak Walker

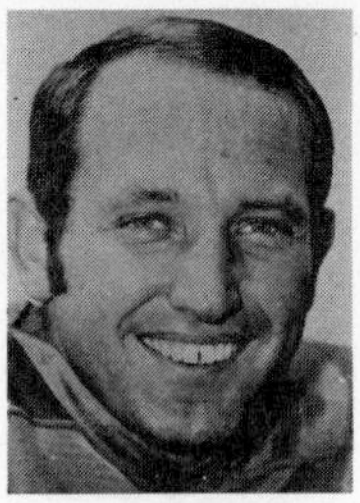
Wayne Walker

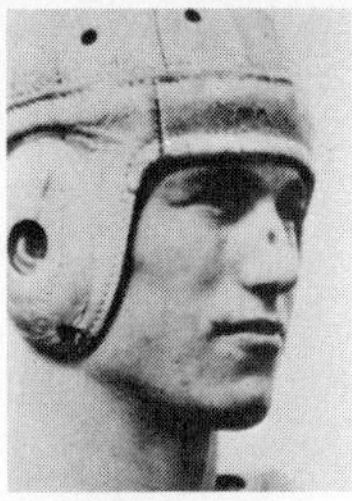
B. (Whizzer) White

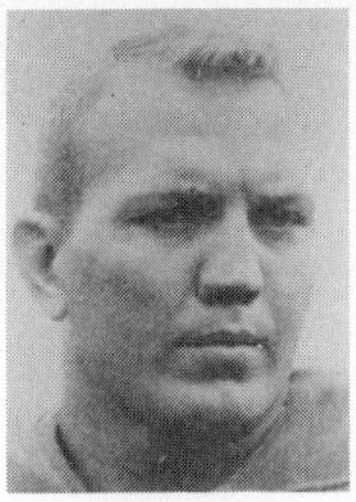
Sam Williams

Redmond, Rudy, DB, Pacific. 1972-73
Reeberg, Lucien, T, Hampton Institute 1963
Reed, Joe, QB, Mississippi State. 1975-79
Reese, Lloyd, B, Tennessee 1947
Reichow, Jerry, WR, Iowa. 1956-59
Rexer, Freeman, E, Tulane. 1944
Reynolds, Bob, T, Stanford 1937-38
Rhodes, Bruce, DB, San Francisco State. 1978
Ricardo, Benny, K, San Diego State 1976-79
Ricca, Jim, T, Georgetown 1955
Rich, Randy, DB, New Mexico 1977
Richards, Perry, E, Detroit. 1958
Richards, Ray, G, Nebraska 1934
Richins, Aldo, B, Utah 1935
Rifenberg, Dick, E, Michigan 1950
Riley, Lee, B, Detroit. 1955
Ritchart, Del, C, Colorado 1936-37
Robb, Joe, DE, Texas Christian 1968-71
Robertson, Lake, E, Mississippi. 1945
Robinson, Bo, RB, West Texas State 1979
Robinson, John, DB, Tennessee State 1966-67
Rockenbach, Lyle, G, Michigan State. 1943
Rogas, Dan, G, Tulane. 1951
Rogers, Bill, T, Villanova 1938-40, 1944
Roskie, Ken, B, South Carolina 1948
Rosteck, Ernie, C, No college. 1943-44
Rote, Tobin, QB, Rice 1957-59
Rothwell, Fred, C, Kansas State. 1974
Rouse, Stillman, E, Missouri 1940
Roussos, Mike, T, Pittsburgh. 1949
Rowe, Bob, B, Colgate 1934
Rubino, Tony, G, Wake Forest 1943-46
Rush, Jerry, DT, Michigan State 1965-71
Russas, Al, T, Tennessee. 1949
Russell, Ken, T, Bowling Green 1957-59
Ryan, Dave, B, Hardin-Simmons 1945-46
Ryan, Kent (Rip), B, Utah State 1938-40
Rychlec, Tom, E, American International 1958
Ryder, Nick, B, Miami. 1963-64

S

Salsbury, Jim, G, UCLA. 1955-56
Sanchez, John, T, San Francisco. 1947
Sanders, Charlie, TE, Minnesota 1968-77
Sanders, Daryl, T, Ohio State 1963-66
Sanders, Ken, DE, Howard Payne 1972-79
Sandifer, Dan, B, Louisiana State. 1950
Sanzotta, Mickey, B, Western Reserve. 1942, 1946
Sarratt, Charley, B, Oklahoma 1948
Sarringhaus, Paul, B, Ohio State 1948
Sartori, Larry, G, Fordham 1942, 1945
Saul, Bill, LB, Penn State. 1970
Schibanoff, Alex, T, Franklin & Marshall 1942-43
Schiechi, John, C, Santa Clara. 1942
Schmidt, Joe, LB, Pittsburgh 1953-65
Schmiesing, Joe, DT, New Mexico State 1972
Schneller, John, E, Wisconsin. 1933-36
Scholtz, Bob, C, Notre Dame 1960-64
Schottel, Ivan, B, Northwest Missouri State 1946, 1948
Schroll, Bill, B, Louisiana State. 1950
Scott, Clyde (Smackover), B, Arkansas 1952
Scott, Fred, WR, Amherst 1978-81
Scott, Perry, E, Muhlenberg 1942
Self, Clarence, B, Wisconsin. 1950-51
Seltzer, Harry, B, Morris-Harvey 1942
Sewell, Harley, G, Texas. 1953-62
Shepherd, Bill, B, Western Maryland. 1935-40
Shoals, Roger, T, Maryland 1965-70
Siegert, Wayne, T, Illinois 1951
Sieminski, Chuck, DT, Penn State 1968
Sigillo, Dom, T, Xavier 1945
Simmons, Davie, LB, North Carolina. 1980
Simmons, Jack, C, Detroit. 1949-50
Simon, Jim, G-T, Miami 1963-65
Simonson, Dave, T, Minnesota 1977
Sims, Billy, RB, Oklahoma 1980-81
Sinkwich, Frank, B, Georgia 1943-44
Sirochman, George, G, Duquesne 1944
Skladany, Tom, P, Ohio State. 1978-81
Slaby, Lou, LB, Pittsburgh. 1966
Sloan, Dwight, B, Arkansas. 1939-40
Small, John, DT, Citadel. 1973-74
Smith, Bobby, DB, UCLA. 1965-66
Smith, Harry, T, USC. 1940
Smith, J. D., T, Rice 1964-66
Smith, Bob, DB, Iowa. 1949-54
Smith, Bob L., B, Texas A&M 1953-54
Smith, Wayne, DB, Purdue 1980-81
Sneddon, Bob, B, St. Mary's, Cal. 1945
Soboleski, Joe, T, Michigan 1950
Sokolosky, John, C, Wayne State. 1978
Souders, Cecil (Cy), E, Ohio State. 1947-49
Spangler, Gene, B, Tulsa. 1946
Speelman, Harry, T, Michigan State. 1940
Spencer, Ollie, T, Kansas. 1953, 1956, 1959-61
Speth, George, T, Murray State 1942
Stacco, Edward, T, Colgate 1947
Stacy, Jim (Red), T, Oklahoma 1935-37
Staggers, Jon, WR, Missouri. 1975
Stanfel, Dick, G, San Francisco 1952-55
Steen, Jim, T, Syracuse 1935-36
Steffen, Jim, B, UCLA 1959-60
Stewart, Jim, DB, Tulsa 1979
Stits, Bill, B, UCLA 1954-56
Stokes, Lee (Dixie), C, Centenary 1937-39
Stovall, Dick, C, Abilene Christian 1947-48
Stringfellow, Joe, E, Southern Mississippi 1942
Stuart, Roy, T, Tulsa 1943
Studstill, Pat, WR-P, Houston 1961-67
Sucic, Steve, B, Illinois. 1947-48
Sugar, Leo, E, Purdue 1962
Sumler, Tony, DB, Wichita State 1978
Summerall, Pat, E, Arkansas. 1952
Summers, Wilbur, P, Louisville 1977
Sunter, Ian, K, No college 1976
Swain, Bill, LB, Oregon 1968-69
Sweetan, Karl, QB, Wake Forest. 1966-67
Swiacki, Bill, E, Columbia 1951-52
Swider, Larry, P, Pittsburgh 1979
Szakash, Paul (Socko), B, Montana. 1938-42
Szymanski, Frank, C, Notre Dame 1945-47

T

Tassos, Damon, G, Texas A&M. 1945-46
Tatarek, Bob, DT, Miami, Ohio 1972
Tautolo, Terry, LB, UCLA 1981
Taylor, Altie, RB, Utah State. 1969-76
Teal, Jim, LB, Purdue. 1973
Tearry, Larry, C, Wake Forest. 1978-79
Ten Napel, Garth, LB, Texas A&M 1976-77
Terry, Nat, DB, Florida State 1978
Thomas, Cal, G, Tulsa 1939-40
Thomas, Russ, T, Ohio State. 1946-49
Thomason, Joe, B, Texas A&M. 1945
Thompson, Bobby, RB, Oklahoma. 1975-76
Thompson, Bobby, DB, Arizona 1964-68
Thompson, Dave, C, Clemson 1971-73
Thompson, Jesse, WR, California 1978-80
Thompson, Leonard, WR, Oklahoma State. 1975-81
Thompson, Vince, RB, Villanova 1981
Thrower, Jim, DB, East Texas State 1973-75
Thuerk, Owen, E, St. Joseph, Indiana. 1941
Todd, Jim, HB, Ball State. 1966
Tomasetti, Louis, B, Bucknell 1941
Tonelli, Amerigo (Tony), C, USC. 1939
Topor, Ted, LB, Michigan. 1955
Torgeson, LaVern, C, Washington State 1951-54
Tracy, Tom, B, Tennessee 1956-57
Treadway, John, T, Hardin-Simmons 1949
Trebotich, Ivan (Buzz), B, St. Mary's, Cal. 1944-45
Tressa, Tom, G, Davis-Elkins. 1942
Triplett, Bill, RB, Miami, Ohio. 1968-72
Triplett, Wally, B, Penn State 1949-50
Tripson, John, T, Mississippi State. 1941
Tripucka, Frank, QB, Notre Dame 1949
Tsoutsouvas, Sam, C, Oregon State 1940
Tuinei, Tom, DT, Hawaii 1980
Tully, Darrell, B, East Texas Teachers 1939
Turner, Hal, E, Tennessee State 1954
Turnure, Tom, C, Washington 1980-81
Tyler, Maurice, DB, Morgan State. 1976

U

Uremovich, Emil, T, Indiana 1940-42, 1945-46

V

Van Horn, Doug, G, Ohio State. 1966
Van Tone, Art, B, Southern Mississippi 1943-45
Vanzo, Fred, B, Northwestern. 1938-41
Vargo, Larry, E, Detroit. 1963
Vaughn, Charles (Pug), B, Tennessee. 1935
Vaughn, Tom, DB, Iowa State 1965-71
Vezmar, Walt, T, Michigan State 1946-47

W

Wagner, Sid, G, Michigan State 1936-38
Walker, Doak, B, Southern Methodist 1950-55
Walker, Wayne, LB-K, Idaho 1958-72
Walker, Willie, B, Tennessee State. 1966
Walters, Rod, G, Iowa 1980
Walton, Chuck, G, Iowa State. 1967-74
Walton, Larry, WR, Arizona State 1969-76
Ward, Elmer, C, Utah State 1935-36
Ward, Paul, T, Whitworth 1961-62
Ward, Bill, G, Washington State 1947-49
Washington, Dave, LB, Alcorn State 1978-79
Washington, Gene, WR, Stanford. 1979
Watkins, Larry, RB, Alcorn State. 1969
Watkins, Tom, B, Iowa State 1962-67
Watson, Joe, C, Rice 1950
Watt, Joe, B, Syracuse. 1947-48
Weatherall, Jim, T, Oklahoma 1959-60
Weaver, Charlie, LB, USC 1971-81
Weaver, Herman, P, Tennessee. 1970-76
Webb, Ken, B, Presbyterian 1958-62
Weber, Dick, B, St. Louis. 1945
Weger, Mike, DB, Bowling Green. 1967-75
Weiss, Howie, B, Wisconsin 1939-40
Weithe, John, G, Xavier 1939-42
Welch, Jim, RB, Southern Methodist. 1968
Wells, Warren, E, Texas Southern. 1964
West, Charlie, DB, Texas-El Paso. 1974-77
Westfall, Bob, B, Michigan 1944-47
Wetterlund, Chet, B, Illinois Wesleyan. 1942
White, Byron (Whizzer), B, Colorado 1940-41
White, Daryl, G, Nebraska. 1974
White, Stan, LB, Ohio State. 1980-81
White, Wilbur, HB, Colorado State 1936
Whited, Mike, T, Pacific 1980
Whitlow, Bob, G-C, Arizona. 1961-65
Whitsell, Dave, DB, Indiana 1958-60
Wiatrak, John, C, Washington. 1939
Wickert, Tom, T, Washington State. 1977
Wickett, Lloyd, T, Oregon State. 1943, 1946
Wiese, Bob, B, Michigan. 1947-48
Williams, Bobby, DB, Central State, Oklahoma 1969-71
Williams, Ray, WR, Washington State 1980
Williams, Rex, C, Texas Tech 1945
Williams, Sam, DE, Michigan State 1960-65
Williams, Walt, DB, New Mexico State. 1977-80
Wilson, Camp, B, Tulsa 1946-49
Winkler, Randy, T, Tarleton State. 1967
Winslow, Bob, E, USC 1940
Wojciechowicz, Alex, C, Fordham 1938-46
Woit, Dick, B, Arkansas State. 1955
Womack, Bruce, G, West Texas State. 1951
Woodcock, John, DT, Hawaii 1976-80
Woods, Larry, DT, Tennessee State 1971-72
Woods, Robert, WR, Grambling. 1979
Wright, John, WR, Illinois. 1969
Wyatt, Doug, DB, Tulsa 1973-74
Wyche, Sam, QB, Furman. 1974

Y

Yarbrough, Jim, T, Florida 1969-77
Yepremian, Garo, K, No college. 1966-67
Young, Adrian, LB, USC 1972
Yowarsky, Walt, E, Kentucky 1955

Z

Zatkoff, Roger, G, Michigan 1957-58
Zawadzkas, Jerry, E, Columbia 1967
Zimmerman, Leroy, B, San Jose State 1947
Zofko, Mickey, RB, Auburn 1971-74
Zuzzio, Tony, G, Muhlenberg 1942

GREEN BAY PACKERS

1919 Earl (Curly) Lambeau, home from school at Notre Dame, went to work for the Indian Packing Company in Green Bay and talked his employer into spending $500 on equipment to back a football team.
1921 After two years of successful operation as an independent team playing clubs from Wisconsin and Upper Michigan, the team joined the American Professional Football Association, predecessor to the National Football League. The franchise was awarded to John Clair of the Acme Packing Company, successor to the Indian Packing Company, August 27, 1921. Green Bay played its home games at Hagemeister Brewery Park with bleachers on one side to seat about 200 people and a portable canvas fence to discourage nonpaying customers. Lambeau was coach, star halfback, passer, general manager, and publicity man. Howard (Cub) Buck, a 287-pound tackle from Wisconsin who had spent 1920 with the Canton Bulldogs, joined the new team; Buck also did the punting and extra point and field goal kicking. Lambeau surrounded himself with Wisconsin players and signed a couple of his old Notre Dame buddies, Norm Barry and Grover Malone, to work with him in the backfield. Playing a rather fluid schedule that included teams such as the Evansville, Indiana, Crimson Giants, Rock Island, Illinois, Independents, Chicago Staleys, and Chicago Cardinals, the Packers finished fourth in the 13-team league with a 6-2-2 record.
1922 John Clair was ordered to surrender the Packers' franchise to the league on charges of playing collegians who were still enrolled in college, January 28. A $1,000 bond was required from all clubs thereafter to guard against such violations. When Lambeau learned the NFL planned a midsummer meeting, he made plans to rescue the Packers' franchise. With the $50 franchise fee in his pocket but lacking the means of traveling to the NFL meeting at Canton, Ohio, Lambeau asked a friend for help. The friend, Don Murphy, sold his Marmon Roadster automobile for $1,500 and accompanied Lambeau to Canton on the promise that Murphy would open the season in the Packers' lineup. Lambeau was awarded the franchise. Murphy played one minute of the opening game with Duluth. The Packers signed Francis (Jug) Earp and Howard (Whitey) Woodin and quarterback Charlie Mathys, who had played for the Hammond, Indiana, Pros. The weather turned against the Packers and it rained at almost every home game. The club bought "rain insurance" for an early season game, calling for .10 of an inch of rain to meet the visiting guarantee. It rained only .09 and the insurance company wouldn't pay off. When it poured on a late November Sunday before a game with the Columbus, Ohio, Panhandles, the insurance had expired and Lambeau was ready to give up. Only the intervention of Andrew Turnbull, publisher of the Green Bay *Press-Gazette,* saved the franchise. Turnbull told Lambeau to play the game and he'd help work out the problems. The Packers finished the season $2,500 in the red.
1923 Civic pride in the community of about 30,000, combined with a love of football, brought solid financial backing to the Packers in 1923. Publisher Turnbull organized a group known as the "Hungry Five," who canceled the debt and started a campaign for civic support. The members were Turnbull; Lambeau; Lee Joannes, a grocery man; Dr. W. Webber Kelly, a physician; and Gerald Clifford, an attorney. At a meeting of 400 citizens at the local Elks club, the team was reorganized as the Green Bay Football Corporation. Stock was sold at $5 a share and every

Don Hutson makes a long reception over Howard Livingston of the New York Giants, 1944.

person who bought five shares was assured a season ticket. Fifty leading citizens pledged to put up $100 each if the club needed additional money. Hagemeister Park was to be the site of a new high school, so the Packers moved to the outskirts of town to play in the new baseball park known as Bellevue Park. The Chicago Bears came to town for the first time and 5,000 people stormed the park to see the visitors from the big city score a 3-0 win. The Packers split a pair of games with the Racine, Wisconsin, Legion for the championship of Wisconsin but never did play the Canton Bulldogs, who went unbeaten at 11-0-1. Green Bay improved its record to 7-2-1 and finished third in the 20-team NFL.
1924 Vern Lewellen of Nebraska, one of the greatest punters of the era, joined the Packers and fit into the regular backfield with Oscar Hendrian, Mathys, and Lambeau. Green Bay beat the Bears for the first time in a bitterly fought opening game, 5-0. The Packers shut out the Kansas City Cowboys, the Milwaukee Badgers, and the Minneapolis Marines in succession and followed with a 6-3 victory over Racine on a sensational catch of a 45-yard pass by Lambeau to Walter (Tillie) Voss. However, the Packers lost a rematch with the Bears 3-0 in Chicago in a game in which Voss and the Bears' Frank Hanny were ejected for fighting, and also bowed to Racine 7-0 in their second game. The club was doing well at the gate and showed promise with an 8-4 record, good for sixth place among the 18 NFL teams.
1925 Green Bay opened City Stadium barely in time to start the season. The stadium, with stands on each side of the field between the 30-yard lines, had a ca-

pacity of 6,000. The bright promise of opening day, when a crowd of 6,000 packed into new City Stadium to watch the Packers beat the Bears 14-10, faded as the Packers ran into trouble in late season and dropped three in a row to the Bears, Pottsville, Pennsylvania, Maroons, and Frankford, Pennsylvania, Yellowjackets. Green Bay and the rest of the 20-team NFL were overshadowed by a college player in 1925, the final year of Red Grange's career at the University of Illinois. Unfortunately for the Packers' treasury, they had already finished their season series with the Bears before Grange turned professional and started off on his whirlwind tour with the Bears that attracted record crowds at nearly every stop. Green Bay finished with an 8-5 record.
1926 Red Grange organized a rival American Football League after his bid for an NFL franchise was turned down. The NFL countered by expanding into an unwieldy 22-team circuit, and getting Ernie Nevers of Stanford for the Duluth Eskimos. Nevers came to Green Bay with the Duluth Eskimos and the Packers played them to a scoreless tie. The Packers finished fifth at 7-3-3, but the three defeats were by a total of only 17 points.
1927 Lambeau was putting in less time as a halfback and more time as a coach and general manager. Joe (Red) Dunn, the former Marquette quarterback who had been playing with Milwaukee and the Chicago Cardinals, arrived to take over at quarterback. Another top acquisition was Lavern Dilweg, a talented end from Marquette who also played with Milwaukee while finishing law school. Another 1927 addition was center Bernard (Boob) Darling. With the

help of this new talent the Packers finished second with a 7-2-1 record behind the 11-1-1 of the New York Giants, a team they never played.

1928 Although Green Bay tied the champion Providence, Rhode Island, Steamroller 7-7 in late season, two defeats by the Frankford Yellowjackets doomed their title hopes. The Packers played the New York Giants for the first time, losing 6-0 at Milwaukee but winning 7-0 at the Polo Grounds. During the season Lambeau picked up fullback John (Bo) Molenda from the New York Yankees. The Packers won their final game from the Bears 6-0 at Cub Park in Chicago on a 48-yard pass from Dunn to end Dick O'Donnell. Green Bay finished fourth. There was an unusual off-the-field competition when two players ran for the office of district attorney of Brown County. Lewellen won in the Republican primary and Dilweg lost in the Democratic primary. Lewellen won the general election and served until 1930.

1929 Lambeau made three master moves during the offseason after discovering that three players—Johnny Blood (McNally), Cal Hubbard, and Mike Michalske—were unhappy with their teams. Blood, a free spirit, had sliced a wide path through Milwaukee, Duluth, and Pottsville and was anxious to move on. Hubbard had seen enough of New York in two years with the Giants. Michalske had played a year with the AFL New York Yankees and two with the NFL Yankees. It was the first unbeaten team in the NFL since the Canton Bulldogs of 1922 (10-0-2) and 1923 (11-0-1). Many of the players on the 18-man squad played 60 minutes in all games. When injury forced a substitution in a game with the Giants, center Earp said, "Oh, how we hated to see a sub come in." When the Packers returned home after defeating the Bears 25-0 in the final game, a crowd of 20,000 surged onto the tracks and forced the train to halt. The Packers allowed only 24 points in 13 games.

1930 Lambeau retired as a player to devote all his time to coaching. Determined to improve the team, Lambeau brought in a new quarterback, Arnie Herber, a hometown boy who had played at Wisconsin and tiny Regis College in Denver, Colorado. After beating Oshkosh, Wisconsin, in an exhibition opener, the Packers ran their three-year string to 22 games without defeat, beating the Bears and Minneapolis twice and the Cardinals, Giants, Frankford, and Portsmouth once each. Their record string finally was broken by the Cardinals 13-6 in a rematch at Comiskey Park. Ernie Nevers, who had moved to the Cardinals, scored one touchdown, passed for another, and outkicked both Lewellen and Blood. A 13-6 loss to the Giants in the Polo Grounds threatened the Packers' plans for a second straight title but they rallied to beat Frankford and the Stapleton Stapes. Despite a 21-0 defeat by the Bears, a 6-6 tie in the last game at Portsmouth, Ohio, enabled Green Bay at 10-3-1 to edge the Giants' 13-4-0 by .004 percentage points, .769 to .765 (ties were disregarded in the standings). The two championships in a row touched off another rousing welcome home after a riotous trip by bus and train during which Blood crawled atop the train and rode home with the engineer and fireman.

1931 Lambeau picked up another excellent runner in Henry (Hank) Bruder of Northwestern. Starting with a 26-0 victory over the new Cleveland Indians, the Packers burst out of the starting gate and raced to nine straight wins. The streak ended against the Chicago Cardinals when Nevers staged another spectac-ular performance in a 21-13 win, November 15. Green Bay headed east and defeated the Giants, the Providence Steamroller, and the Brooklyn Dodgers, and won an unprecedented third straight championship despite a 7-6 defeat by the Bears in the final game. The Packers' 12-2 record was one game better than the Portsmouth Spartans' 11-3. Although the Spartans, who never met the Packers, complained bitterly that a game had been tentatively scheduled, the game was never played. Four Green Bay players—end Dilweg, tackle Hubbard, guard Michalske, and halfback Blood—were named to the first all-pro team. Tackle Dick Stahlman, quarterback Dunn, and fullback Molenda were on the second team.

1932 The best rookie to join the team was Clarke Hinkle, a fullback and leading scorer in the nation at Bucknell. The game that killed Green Bay's hopes for a fourth consecutive title was a 19-0 defeat by the Spartans at Portsmouth, Ohio, December 5. Then the Packers lost 9-0 to the Bears the following Sunday. The Packers won 10 games, more than any other club in the eight-team league. Because ties did not count, the Bears' 7-1-6 record gave them an .875 percentage to the Packers' 10-3-1 for .769. Actually the Bears and Portsmouth tied, and Chicago won an indoor playoff game at the Chicago Stadium. Quarterback Herber made the all-pro team along with Hubbard and Barragar. The first official league statistics showed Herber led the passers by completing 37 of 101 for 639 yards and nine touchdowns. At the end of the 1932 season the Packers were invited to play two games in Honolulu where they scored victories before sellout crowds. On the way home they stopped off in San Francisco to play Ernie Nevers's Pacific Coast All-Americans at Kezar Stadium, a charity game for the Knights of Columbus.

1933 A fan fell out of the temporary wooden bleachers at City Stadium and sued for $5,000 and the two firms carrying the Packers' insurance failed. The team went into receivership and once again the "Hungry Five" had to be called on to save the franchise, cutting front office expenses and player personnel. Top rookie was Charles (Buckets) Goldenberg, a blocking back-linebacker from Wisconsin. Hinkle teamed with Bob Monnett, a rookie halfback from Michigan State, behind Herber. Competing in the five-club Western Division of the newly-divided NFL, the Packers dropped four of their last five and finished third at 5-7-1. After the season Lee Joannes, president of the club from 1930 to 1947, invited 25 businessmen to a special meeting to start a fund-raising campaign. Housewives, high school students, firemen, policemen, and other citizens chipped in for a $15,000 "save the Packers" fund. The club was incorporated by Dilweg, nearing the end of his career as an end, with 600 shares of common stock having no par value and a requirement that any profits be donated to the local American Legion post or other veterans' organization with no dividend or profit for the stockholders.

1934 With a new, sound financial base, the Packers were able to return their attention to the playing field where new opportunities for a passer like Herber had been opened up by the rules changes permitting forward passes anywhere behind the line of scrimmage. Fullback Hinkle was beginning to show the form of his college days. Herber led the league's passers for the second time in three seasons and the Packers started on the way back with a third-place 7-6 record in a division dominated by the 13-0 Bears. Seating capacity at City Stadium was increased to 15,000.

1935 Don Hutson signed with Green Bay after having been pursued by both the Packers and Brooklyn Dodgers following a brilliant career at Alabama. The nimble sprinter played with the College All-Stars in the Chicago All-Star Game against the Bears and saw brief action as a sub in the Packers' opener. By the time the club was ready for its second game, Hutson was ready to start. On the first play Herber sent Blood down the right sideline and threw to Hutson up the middle for a stunning 83-yard touchdown play. Blood, returning after a year in Pittsburgh, was used primarily as a receiver. Although Hutson's catches beat the Bears twice, 7-0 and 17-14, the Packers lost three to the Cardinals and split with Detroit, the Western Division champion at 7-3 to the Packers' 8-4. The arrival of Hutson, who led the league with seven touchdowns while catching 18 passes for 420 yards, an average of 23.3 yards, and the second-place finish filled the stands with paying customers. After the season the Packers made another trip to San Francisco for a charity game with the Pacific All-Stars.

1936 The first college draft produced guard Russ Letlow. Green Bay picked seventh, or third-from-last, because its 1935 won-lost record was third best in the league. The Packers absorbed their worst beating, 30-3 at the hands of the Bears in the second game of the season, but didn't lose again, squaring matters with the Bears later 21-10. Defeats by the Lions and Cardinals in their last two games cost the Bears their chance of catching Green Bay. For the first time since the NFL split into two divisions in 1933 the Packers won the championship, taking the Western Division with a 10-1-1 record and then defeating the Boston Redskins 21-6 in a game played at New York's Polo Grounds because of poor attendance for the Redskins in Boston. Hutson led the league with a record 34 pass receptions and Herber topped the passers for the third time by throwing for 1,239 yards and 11 touchdowns. In addition, other main components in the offense were backs Hinkle, George Sauer, Bob Monnett, and Milt Gantenbein.

1937 The success of 1936 was short-lived. The Packers not only lost the Chicago All-Star Game 6-0 to the collegians, who were led by Sammy Baugh, but also dropped their first two regular season games, bowing to both the Cardinals and Bears at City Stadium. They recovered in a seven-game winning streak, only to lose their last two games to the Giants and Redskins on the road, finishing at 7-4, one game behind the Bears. Herber was slowed by a hip injury and extra weight but he still could throw and Hutson broke his own record with 41 receptions and seven touchdowns. The bulk of the running was done by Hinkle and rookie Eddie Jankowski, a first-round pick from Wisconsin. It was the last year for Michalske and Lon Evans. Green Bay probably made its best first-round draft pick when Lambeau selected quarterback Cecil Isbell of Purdue, December 11. The Packers also picked up back Andy Uram of Minnesota on the fourth round.

1938 Lambeau played Herber and Isbell in the same backfield and both took turns throwing to Hutson. Hinkle scored enough points on runs, pass receptions, conversions, and field goals to lead the league with 58 points. After clinching the Western Division title November 21, the Packers had to wait until December 12 to play the Giants for the league championship. Green Bay lost 23-17 in the title game with a limping Hutson seeing only part-time action because of a knee injury.

1939 Green Bay played a unique doubleheader with the Pittsburgh Steelers with 10-minute exhibition quarters. The Packers tied the first game and won the second 17-0 in a program that lasted from 7:30 P.M. to 11 P.M. Then the Packers went south to Dallas for an exhibition game with the Southwest College All-Stars at the Cotton Bowl, beating a team led by Davey O'Brien and Ki Aldrich 31-20. The busy preseason didn't seem to bother the Packers, although they lost their third game in an upset by the

Cleveland Rams. Uram set a record with a 97-yard touchdown run against the Cardinals, October 8. The Packers straightened out and won seven of their last eight, beating out the Bears to win the Western Division for the second year in a row. Lambeau gave Hutson some relief on defense, switching him to safety while moving Larry Craig, a rookie from South Carolina, to defensive end and blocking back. The championship game with the Giants was shifted to the State Fair Park in Milwaukee, where 32,279 watched Herber, Isbell, and Hutson take the Giants apart 27-0 for their fifth NFL title.

1940 Charley Brock, drafted out of Nebraska in 1939, took over at center and also played in the defensive backfield. Green Bay barely hung on 27-20 when passer Davey O'Brien of the Eagles threw 40 passes in the opening game at City Stadium. Then the Bears came in and won 41-10. "People are beginning to talk," warned Lambeau as he drove his Packers through heavy practice sessions. They responded by beating the Cardinals, but lost to Detroit, the New York Giants, and the Chicago Bears again for a second-place 6-4-1 finish. Although Isbell still kept his left arm taped to his side because of a shoulder separation in a college game, he did most of the passing. Hutson led the league in scoring with 57 points and also was first with six interceptions from his new defensive safety position. Hinkle's nine field goals were only one short of the record.

1941 Tony Canadeo, a rookie from Gonzaga, joined Hinkle and Uram in the backfield and Isbell did all the passing because Herber retired as the result of a leg injury. The formidable Bears, now known as the Monsters of the Midway and featuring Sid Luckman, George McAfee, and Bill Osmanski, held on to beat the Packers 25-17 in their first meeting at Green Bay, but the second game at Wrigley Field resulted in a 16-14 victory for the Packers. Green Bay swept its last eight games, including a rematch with the Bears, and wound up tied with Chicago (10-1) for the Western Division title. The Bears struck for 24 points in the second quarter of the playoff game at Chicago to go into a title game with the Giants. Hutson set records with 95 points and 58 pass receptions, Hinkle led with six field goals and Isbell was the NFL's top passer with 1,479 yards and 15 touchdowns.

1942 There was no stopping Hutson as he won his fifth pass-catching championship. There had been few more spectacular seasons by an individual in the history of the league. Huston scored 138 points by catching 17 touchdown passes from Isbell and Canadeo, kicking a field goal and 33 extra points. His 74 receptions for 1,211 yards set additional marks and Isbell's totals of 2,021 yards passing and 24 touchdowns were records. Ted Fritsch, a rookie from little Stevens Point College in Wisconsin, found a job in the backfield, helping to fill the gap left by the retirement of Hinkle. The Packers once again finished behind the unbeaten Bears (11-0) with an 8-2-1 record. Both defeats were to the Chicago Bears, 44-28 and 38-7. Isbell surprised Packers' fans by retiring after the season to return to his alma mater, Purdue, as an assistant coach. He explained, "I hadn't been up long when I saw Lambeau tell players like Herber, Gantenbein, and Bruder they were all done. I vowed I'd quit before they came around to tell me."

1943 Canadeo became the regular passer, backed by Irv Comp and Lou Brock. The Packers played a 21-21 tie with the Bears on opening day but a 33-7 loss to Washington and a 21-7 defeat by the Bears cost them any chance at first place and they finished fourth. Hutson led again in scoring and receiving and tied for the field goal leadership with three. Hutson even threw a touchdown pass.

1944 Green Bay, playing with veterans, servicemen on leave, and untried youngsters, opened with a six-game win streak before running into a 21-0 shutout by the Bears. They were blanked again 24-0 in New York but finished 8-2 to 6-3-1 for Chicago and Detroit in the west. The Packers went to New York and won their sixth league title, and first since 1939, by beating the Giants 14-7 in the Polo Grounds on two scores by Fritsch. Each Packers player took home $1,149, a record winning share, thanks to a crowd of 46,016. Herber, who had been with the Packers from 1930 to 1940, was the Giants' passer. Hutson still was available to catch 58 passes and 9 of the 12 touchdown passes thrown by Comp, and also to kick extra points for a leading total of 85 points.

1945 Hutson had been talking of retiring for years but Lambeau talked him into staying on as a player-coach for 1945. Hutson caught four touchdown passes and kicked five extra points for 29 points in the second quarter of a game against Detroit in which the Packers also set a record with 41 points in the same quarter en route to a 57-21 victory, October 7. Despite a strong start, the Packers' defense yielded 180 points and they lost four games, dropping to third place in the Western Division behind both the winning Cleveland Rams and the Lions. After winning his eighth pass receiving title, a league record, with 47 receptions, Hutson retired after 11 seasons. He had caught at least one pass in 95 consecutive games.

1946 World War II was over and talent began flowing back to NFL clubs, but the retirement of Hutson left a void in the Packers' offense. The Bears and the newly located Los Angeles Rams each beat Green Bay twice and the Packers also lost to the Chicago Cardinals for a 6-5 finish and third place. Without Hutson the passing game was hurt and the Packers tried to get by on the running of Canadeo, Fritsch, and Walt Schlinkman, a first-round draft choice from Texas Tech. The offense was sluggish, scoring only 148 points in 11 games. Fritsch accounted for most of the scoring. He led the league with 100 points on 10 touchdowns, 9 field goals, and 13 extra points. Roy McKay's 42.7-yard average enabled him to top the punters for the second straight year.

1947 Coach-general manager Lambeau was running into trouble from the front office. Some executive committee members criticized his decision to buy Rockwood Lodge, a training base 15 miles north of Green Bay, for $25,000. The club also bought land and cottages for the coaching staff and their wives to live in during preseason training. An organization of sub-committees on different aspects of club operation was put into operation. Jack Jacobs of Oklahoma became the new quarterback and led the league in punting. The Packers finished third at 6-5 but four of the five defeats were by a total of only nine points.

1948 The war with the rival All-America Football Conference was beginning to hurt the NFL, particularly teams such as the Packers that had limited resources to engage in bidding contests for players. Green Bay had lost first-round draft choices Johnny (Strike) Strzykalski and Ernie Case to the AAFC in 1946 and 1947 but signed Earl (Jug) Girard when he came out of Wisconsin in 1948. Lambeau fined the entire squad a half week's salary after a 17-7 loss to the Chicago Cardinals and didn't relent after a 16-0 win over the Rams the following Sunday. For the first time since 1933 the team finished under .500, losing seven in a row for a 3-9 record. The running of Canadeo and Schlinkman provided the only bright spots.

1949 The Bears shut out the Packers on opening day 17-0 and the Rams bombed them 48-7 the following week. Green Bay beat only the New York Bulldogs and the Lions en route to a last-place 2-10 season, their poorest in history. Attendance dropped with a last-place club and financial problems mounted. Matters became so desperate in late season that an intrasquad game was played and oldtimers such as Verne Lewellen, Arnie Herber, and Johnny Blood (McNally) gave demonstrations to raise $50,000. Canadeo became the first Packer and the third player in NFL history to gain 1,000 yards with 1,052. But Girard and rookie Stan Heath, the number-one draft choice, threw more interceptions than touchdown passes.

1950 Lambeau, founder of the franchise, resigned under fire after a dispute with the citizen organization that ran the club, February 1. Lambeau criticized the system of operation by committee and was rebuffed in an effort to add Don Hutson to the executive committee. Adding to the problems, the Rockwood Lodge burned, January 24. New stock certificates were sold and more than $125,000 was raised. The committee hired Gene Ronzani, a former halfback with the Bears, to become the new head coach. Clayton Tonnemaker, a center, was the number-one draft pick and the Packers got halfback Billy Grimes from the old Los Angeles Dons' roster in the special draft of former AAFC players. Tobin Rote, a draft choice from Rice, shared the quarterback job with Paul Christman, who was released by the Chicago Cardinals. Green Bay improved to 3-9, enough to get out of the cellar but still far out of contention.

1951 The Packers continued a modest improvement under Ronzani, winning three of their first five games before going into a seven-game tailspin that left them at 3-9 in fifth place in the newly named National Conference. Green Bay lost to the New York Yankees 31-28, the only game the Yanks won. Rote passed for 15 touchdowns and led the Packers with 523 yards rushing. Running back Fred Cone, drafted out of Clemson, proved to be an excellent kicker but only a fair runner. Rote was backed up by Bobby Thomason. The defense gave up 375 points, an average of over 31 a game.

1952 The draft brought in such players as Babe Parilli, quarterback from Kentucky, Billy Howton, an end from Rice, and Dave Hanner, a tackle from Arkansas, and the Packers' fortunes turned upward. Ronzani had the Packers in the thick of the race most of the way and was 6-3 with three games to go. One of the early season successes was a 35-20 win over Washington, coached by Lambeau. However, they lost the last three to Detroit, Los Angeles, and San Francisco and finished fourth behind those three teams. Parilli shared the quarterback job with Rote. Howton set a record of 13 touchdown passes in his rookie season while catching 53 for 1,231 yards, another NFL record.

1953 Among the rookies were Syracuse center Jim Ringo and linebacker Bill Forester of Southern Methodist. The Ronzani regime ended in late season when the coach resigned with two games to play at the request of the executive committee. Hugh Devore and Ray (Scooter) McLean, two assistants, finished up. The Packers' only victories in a 2-9-1 season were over the league's new entry, Baltimore.

1954 The 13-man executive committee realized a major change was in order, so they made Verne Lewellen, the punter and halfback of the 1924-1932 period, general manager, and hired Lisle Blackbourn, coach at Marquette University, to succeed Ronzani. The Packers were competitive for the first half at 3-3. But they lost five of their last six, including two tight games against the eventual champion Lions, 21-17 and 28-24, and finished 4-8, barely ahead of the last place Colts. The offense consisted largely of Rote's 14 touchdown passes and his eight scores by rushing. Veryl Switzer, a rookie from Kansas State, led the league in punt returns with a 12.8-yard average and another rookie, Max McGee of Tulane, caught 36 passes and averaged 41.7 yards punting.

1955 The Packers won five of six home games, but lost five of six road games and settled for 6-6 and third place in the Western Conference, their best season since 1947. Howard Ferguson became a solid fullback threat and Rote threw 17 touchdown passes, most of them to Howton and rookie Gary Knafelc of Colorado. Cone kicked 17 field goals. Parilli, McGee, and Art Hunter were in the military service. Attendance increased to 153,241 with City Stadium now at a capacity of more than 20,000. A home game at Milwaukee County Stadium drew a Wisconsin pro record of 40,199.

1956 The Packers were unbeaten in the preseason, including a win over the defending champion Browns. The Packers had an odd schedule that gave the team a bye on opening day. They lost their first two and were 2-5 before they staged a mild rally in midseason by beating the Lions and Cardinals. Defeats by the Rams and 49ers on the road left them in fifth place at 4-8. Tackles Forrest Gregg and Bob Skoronski were rookies. Injuries slowed Ferguson, and Rote's talk of retirement gave rookie quarterback Bart Starr a chance to see limited action. Al Carmichael set an NFL record by returning a Bears' kickoff 106 yards for a touchdown, October 7. It was the Packers last season in City Stadium.

1957 Paul Hornung, Notre Dame's "golden boy," was the Packers' special bonus pick in the draft and quickly became the center of controversy. Coach Blackbourn tried him at quarterback, decided he didn't have the arm for the job, and then shifted him to fullback, where he gained only 319 yards. Tight end Ron Kramer of Michigan and safety John Symank of Florida also were chosen in the draft. Rote was traded to Detroit for four players, including halfback Don McIlhenny and tackle Norm Masters. The new City Stadium, a $1 million structure seating 32,150, was dedicated, September 29. The Packers

beat the Bears 21-17. Unfortunately for Blackbourn, the club won only two more games the rest of the year. Blackbourn was fired with one more year to go on his contract.

1958 The executive committee named assistant coach Ray (Scooter) McLean head coach. McLean had a nice guy image and the players quickly took advantage of it. The result was a 1-10-0 record, the poorest in Green Bay history. The lone victory, 38-35 over Philadelphia, almost got away when the Packers frittered away most of a 38-7 lead. Starr and Parilli shared the quarterback job and the backfield included Hornung and rookie Jim Taylor from Lousiana State. Rookie guard Jerry Kramer from Idaho was in the offensive line and Ray Nitschke of Illinois at linebacker.

1959 Green Bay's executive committee hired Vince Lombardi, an assistant coach with the New York Giants, as head coach and general manager, January 28. "Let's get one thing straight," said Lombardi his first day on the job. "I'm in complete command here." Lombardi spent the winter looking at the films of the 1958 Packers and was convinced he had the basis of a contender. He selected Colorado quarterback Boyd Dowler in the draft, traded with Cleveland for defensive end Bill Quinlan and defensive tackle Henry Jordan, acquired safety Emlen Tunnell from the Giants to help the defensive backfield, and picked up guard Fred (Fuzzy) Thurston from Baltimore. One of Lombardi's first decisions was to shift Hornung to halfback. Lamar McHan, acquired from the Chicago Cardinals, started at quarterback. When the Packers beat the Bears opening day the players carried Lombardi off the field on their shoulders. Two more victories followed. Then came five straight defeats—two to the world champion Colts and one to the Giants. Lombardi switched to Bart Starr at quarterback when McHan was injured and the Pack-

ers swept their last four for a 7-5 record, their best since 1945, and a third-place tie with the 49ers. Hornung scored 94 points kicking and running to lead the NFL.

1960 Lombardi drafted Tom Moore from Vanderbilt, traded with Cleveland for defensive end Willie Davis, and signed free agent Willie Wood as a safety. The Packers had a tough fight in the Western Conference. They wrapped it up by winning their last three on the road, clinching the Western title with a 35-21 victory at Los Angeles where Starr threw a 91-yard touchdown pass to Dowler, who had been converted to flanker. The Packers came up short in the championship game at Philadelphia's Franklin Field, where Norm Van Brocklin led the Eagles to a 17-13 victory. Chuck Bednarik tackled Taylor on the Eagles' 9-yard line at the final gun. Starr again took over from McHan, Taylor rushed for 1,101 yards, and Hornung scored a record 176 points.

1961 Hornung, Dowler, and Nitschke fitted in as many games as possible on weekend leaves from military camps and 42-year-old Ben Agajanian was hired to do the kicking when Hornung was away. Herb Adderley of Michigan State worked as a rookie cornerback. In a regular season game against Baltimore, Hornung had four touchdowns, a field goal, and six extra points for 33 points. The Packers clinched the Western Conference by defeating the Giants at Milwaukee 20-17 and became the league champions by again beating the Giants 37-0 as Hornung scored 19 points, December 31. Hornung led the NFL in scoring again, with 146 points and Taylor gained 1,307 yards, second to Cleveland's Jim Brown. Starr hit Dowler, McGee, and Kramer with most of his 16 touchdown passes.

1962 Lombardi made very few changes. Earl Gros, the top draft choice from Louisiana State, was a part-time performer behind Taylor, Hornung, Moore,

Jim Taylor takes a handoff from Bart Starr and follows the blocking of center Jim Ringo (51) and guard Jerry Kramer (64) in the 1962 NFL Championship Game.

and Elijah Pitts in the backfield that had perfected the run to daylight formula of its coach. The Packers' 10-game win streak was broken on Thanksgiving Day in Detroit when Alex Karras led an assault on Starr for a 26-14 Lions' victory. The Packers won the rest and finished at 13-1 before adding a second straight league championship. When Hornung was injured in midseason, Jerry Kramer took over the kicking duties and booted three field goals in a 16-7 victory over the Giants in the title game played in 20-degree weather with 40-mile-per-hour wind gusts at Yankee Stadium. Taylor's 1,474 yards led the league, the only time in Jim Brown's career at Cleveland that he failed to win the rushing championship. The Packers' fullback scored a record 19 touchdowns by rushing. Starr showed the way in passing with 2,440 yards and Wood was first with nine interceptions. Four former Packers—Lambeau, Hutson, Blood, and Hubbard—were among the 17 charter members of the new Pro Football Hall of Fame at Canton, Ohio.

1963 NFL Commissioner Pete Rozelle suspended Hornung indefinitely for betting on his own team and other NFL teams, April 17. Alex Karras of Detroit also was suspended for the same violations. Moore and Pitts filled in for Hornung. Kramer took over the placekicking job again. The Packers lost their opener to the Bears 10-3, then were battered by the Bears in a 26-7 rematch after winning eight straight. By the time of the second game against the Bears, Starr was out of action with a broken hand and Zeke Bratkowski filled in. Another Thanksgiving Day visit to Detroit resulted in a 13-13 tie and the loss of Nitschke with a broken arm. Although Taylor ran for 1,018 yards, the Packers finished a half game behind the Bears, 11-1-2 to 11-2-1, and had to settle for a 40-23 Playoff Bowl victory over Cleveland in a match of runner-up teams.

1964 Hornung came back to play when his suspension was lifted after one season, but he seemed to have lost his ability to kick under pressure. A missed extra point cost the Packers their first game with Baltimore, and another missed point and five missed field goals by Hornung accounted for a second 24-21 loss to the Colts. Jerry Kramer missed most of the season due to abdominal surgery and Jim Ringo was traded to Philadelphia. Taylor gained more than 1,000 yards for the fifth straight year with 1,169. Hornung contributed 415. Starr led the league in passing and the defense allowed only 227 yards a game. An 8-5-1 finish left the Packers far behind the champion Colts' 12-2 and they suffered another jolt by losing the Playoff Bowl game to St. Louis 24-17.

1965 After the kicking failures of 1964, Lombardi brought in Don Chandler from the Giants to handle both the punting and field goal work. He also acquired Carroll Dale, a receiver, from the Rams for Dan Currie and traded tight end Ron Kramer to Detroit. Dave Robinson had fit into the linebacking corps and Marv Fleming was the new tight end. The Packers trailed the Steelers 9-7 at halftime of their opening game but scored 34 in the second half for a 41-9 victory and started a six-game winning streak that included a 20-17 win over the Colts in which Hornung, Taylor, and Starr were hurt. They beat the Colts again 42-27 on a foggy December day, with Hornung scoring five touchdowns, and appeared to have the title wrapped up. However, a tie with San Francisco in the final game set up a playoff with Baltimore. Starr was injured early in the playoff game that Chandler's disputed field goal sent into overtime, December 19. Another Chandler field goal won for Green Bay in 13:39 of sudden death. During the 1964 and 1965 seasons Starr had a string of 294 consecutive passes without an interception.

1966 The injury-ridden Packers pulled themselves

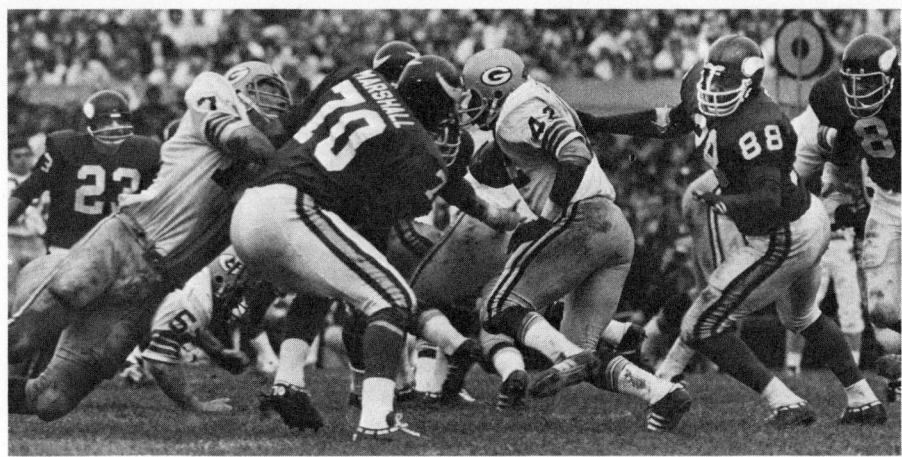

John Brockington challenges the Vikings' Jim Marshall (70), Alan Page (88), and Carl Eller (81), 1973.

together to ruin Jim Brown's last game by beating the Browns for the championship in the snow at newly-renamed Lambeau Field in Green Bay, January 2. The champion Packers signed running backs Donny Anderson of Texas Tech and Jim Grabowski of Illinois, reportedly for $750,000 and $250,000, respectively. The Gold Dust Twins were given backup roles behind Taylor, Pitts, and Hornung. The Packers lost only to the 49ers and Vikings by a total of four points en route to a second Western Conference title at 12-2.

1967 Dallas had won the Eastern Conference for the first time and 74,152 turned out in the Cotton Bowl to watch the Cowboys and Packers play for the title, January 2. Green Bay opened with a 34-20 lead but barely survived a Dallas comeback. With the score 34-27, Dave Robinson pressured Don Meredith into a pass that was intercepted by the Packers' Tom Brown in the end zone. The first Super Bowl, pitting the champions of the NFL and AFL, was played at the Los Angeles Memorial Coliseum as a result of the merger agreement of June 8, 1966. Green Bay beat Kansas City 35-10 on two touchdown passes from Starr to McGee and a key interception by Wood, although the Chiefs trailed only 14-10 at the half. Taylor, who had played out his option, signed with the new New Orleans team, where he was joined by Hornung, who went to the Saints in the expansion draft. No club had won three NFL championships in a row since the Packers of 1929-1931. Injuries sidelined Pitts and Grabowski, and Lombardi seldom had the same backfield combination. He used Anderson and Travis Williams, the sensational kickoff returner, with Ben Wilson and Chuck Mercein, who had been cut by the Giants. Starr missed three games, so Bratkowski and rookie Don Horn saw action. In a game against Cleveland, Green Bay scored a record 35 points in the first quarter, November 12. It was the first year of the new four-division setup in the NFL. After winning the four-team Central Division at 9-4-1, the Packers defeated the Rams 28-7 to win the Western Conference. Then came the NFL Championship Game with Dallas in 13-degree below zero arctic climate at Green Bay, December 31. The Packers won the Ice Game 21-17 on Starr's third down, one-yard quarterback sneak behind Jerry Kramer's block on Jethro Pugh with 13 seconds to play.

1968 Super Bowl II was almost an anticlimax in the 68-degree heat of Miami's Orange Bowl. The Packers whipped Oakland of the AFL 33-14. Two weeks after his second Super Bowl triumph, Lombardi shocked the football world by announcing his retirement as coach. He remained at Green Bay as general manager and named Phil Bengtson, his long-time assistant, as his successor. Thurston, McGee, and Chandler retired. Starr's arm bothered him and he

spent half the year on the bench watching Bratowski play. The Packers desperately tried Mike Mercer, Errol Mann, Kramer, and Mercein as kickers. Fuzzy Thurston's job at guard was taken by Gale Gillingham. Minnesota, on the way to its first of four straight divisional titles, beat the Packers twice. Green Bay finished with a 6-7-1 record.

1969 Lombardi left the Packers to become a part-owner, vice president, general manager, and coach of the Washington Redskins, February 5. Bengtson was given the additional job of Packers' general manager. It was a time of change at Green Bay. Jerry Kramer and Skoronski retired, tackle Ron Kostelnik went to Baltimore, and defensive back Tom Brown to Washington. Williams became the top rusher and rookie Dave Hampton outgained Anderson and Grabowski. Shoulder trouble forced Starr out of the last four games and Horn threw 11 touchdown passes. Both Mercer and Booth Lusteg were inconsistent kickers. The Packers (5-2) were in the race at the halfway mark, but lost four of their next five.

1970 Tackle Henry Jordan, defensive end Willie Davis, and flanker Boyd Dowler retired. The Packers traded Herb Adderley to Dallas, Marv Fleming to Miami, and Elijah Pitts, Bob Hyland, and Lee Roy Caffey to Chicago. Vince Lombardi died of cancer, September 3. The Packers were shut out by the Lions on opening day, their first blank since 1958, and their first at home since 1949. Starr was ailing and Dave Robinson tore an Achilles tendon. Anderson led the team in both rushing yardage and pass receptions. When the club lost six of its last eight, finishing with another 20-0 shutout by the Lions, Bengtson resigned. The 6-8 record tied for last in the NFC Central Division in the first year of the realigned NFL.

1971 Determined to make a complete break with the past, the Packers went into the college ranks to get a successor to Bengtson and signed Dan Devine of Missouri as head coach and general manager. Gregg moved to Dallas to wind up his career and linebacker Nitschke, one of the last holdovers from the Lombardi days, was benched. On opening day, coach Devine was run over on the sidelines by the New York Giants' Bob Hyland and suffered a broken leg while his team was losing to the Giants in a wild 42-40 game. One of the highlights of the year was a 100-yard run by Ken Ellis with a missed field goal against the Giants, September 19. Devine coached the rest of the year on crutches, watching a porous defense nullify the outstanding play of John Brockington, the top draft choice, who gained 1,105 yards. Starr threw only 45 passes and Scott Hunter, a rookie from Alabama, had 17 passes intercepted. The Packers finished last again with a 4-8-2 record.

1972 Coach Devine traded running back Anderson

to the St. Louis Cardinals for MacArthur Lane. The pairing of Lane and Brockington proved effective, with Brockington gaining 1,027 yards and Lane 821. Starr retired as a player but remained as an assistant coach to call the plays for Hunter, whose favorite targets were Brockington and Lane. Wood also retired, but the new deep combination of Ken Ellis, Jim Hill, Al Matthews, and Willie Buchanon, the number-one draft choice, was a strong one. Kicker Chester Marcol, the team's third draft choice, led the league in scoring by hitting 33 of 48 field goal attempts and 29 straight extra points for 128 points. The Packers won six of their last seven games and took their first division title since 1967 but lost 16-3 to Washington in the first round of the playoffs.

1973 The club was 2-1-1 after four games but won only one of the next seven and settled into third place at 5-7-2. Brockington had his third straight year of more than 1,000 yards as he gained 1,144 and led the NFC. Lane gained 528 yards but the passing game was not productive. Jerry Tagge, Hunter, and Jim Del Gaizo all were erratic and the bumper stickers proclaiming "The Pack is Back" were out of style.

1974 Devine definitely was on the spot in his fourth year on the job. When Tagge floundered, Devine made a midseason deal with the Rams for 34-year-old quarterback John Hadl. The Packers gave up their first three draft choices for 1975 and their first two for 1976 in the deal. Marcol kicked four field goals in a 21-19 win over Detroit and four more in a 19-7 win at Minnesota. Steve Odom raced 95 yards with a punt return against the Bears, November 10. The club was in the division race until it nosedived into a three-game losing streak to end the year at 6-8 in third place. Marcol led the league with 94 points on 25 field goals in 39 attempts and 18 consecutive extra points. Devine resigned and moved back to the college game at Notre Dame.

1975 Bart Starr was given the job of trying to lead the Packers back to their former status. His only coaching experience had been one year as an assistant coach to Devine in 1972. Hadl didn't fit into Starr's style of play. The veteran put the ball in the air 353 times and completed 191 for 54.1 percent but only six went for touchdowns and 21 were intercepted. Brockington had his poorest season, dropping to 434 yards. Willard Harrell contributed 359 yards and caught 34 passes. Ken Payne had 12 receptions against Denver, September 29, and led the club with 58 for 766 yards, second best in the NFC. Marcol missed the entire season with a torn leg muscle and was replaced by Joe Danelo of Washington State. Green Bay lost its first four and eight of its first nine, but won three of the last five for a 4-10 record.

1976 Starr traded Hadl to Houston for quarterback Lynn Dickey in a deal that also cost Green Bay cornerback Ken Ellis and a fourth-round draft choice. It took Dickey time to get started after a long wait on the Houston bench but he was coming on when he suffered a shoulder separation in the first Chicago game, November 14. He was lost for the year. Carlos Brown and Randy Johnson finished up and the club lost four of its last five en route to a 5-9 finish and last place in the NFC Central Division.

1977 Former all-pro guard Gale Gillingham, the last player from the Lombardi era, retired before the season. The club opened with a 24-20 victory over New Orleans, but then staggered to nine losses in the next 10 weeks. Quarterback Lynn Dickey was lost for the season when he broke his leg on the last play of a 24-6 loss to Los Angeles on November 13. Rookie David Whitehurst replaced him, starting the final five games. He guided the club to two victories in its last three games. Despite the 4-10 record, the defense allowed just 219 points—its best year since 1974. However, the offense was held to 16 points or less in

every game after the opener. Dickey and wide receiver Steve Odom connected on the longest touchdown pass of the year—a 95-yard play against Minnesota on October 2.

1978 James Lofton, a wide receiver from Stanford, was the team's first draft choice. Whitehurst retained the starting quarterback job with Dickey still recovering from his broken leg. The rejuvenated offense sparked the Packers to a 6-1 start and first place in the NFC Central. Included in the fast start were a 28-17 victory over the Saints, in which Whitehurst and Lofton connected on three touchdown passes, and a 45-28 win over Seattle, which featured four rushing touchdowns by Terdell Middleton. Despite a six-week slump that produced only one victory and one tie, Green Bay moved within one victory of clinching the division with a 17-7 win over Tampa Bay on December 3. But the Packers lost back-to-back games to Chicago and Los Angeles, and Minnesota won the NFC Central with a better head-to-head record against Green Bay. Middleton became only the fourth Packers player to rush for over 1,000 yards in a season, finishing with 1,116. Second-year defensive tackle Ezra Johnson finished with 20½ sacks.

1979 Green Bay drafted two running backs, Eddie Lee Ivery of Georgia Tech and Steve Atkins of Maryland. With the offense performing erratically and the defense hampered by injuries, the club plunged to a 5-11 record. But the season included two memorable victories. In a Monday night game on October 1, the 1,000th game in Green Bay's history, the Packers upset heavily-favored New England 27-14. The defense sparked the victory with five interceptions and five sacks. On November 11, Green Bay ended a five-year drought against Minnesota with a 19-7 victory at Milwaukee County Stadium. Dickey played the second half against Philadelphia on November 25, his first extended appreareance in two years. Although he completed 14 of 22 passes for 144 yards, the Packers lost 21-10.

1980 Defensive tackle Bruce Clark of Penn State was the Packers' top draft choice, but he signed with Toronto of the Canadian Football League. Kicker Chester Marcol became the unlikely running star in the season opener when he scooped up his own blocked field goal attempt in overtime and ran for a 25-yard touchdown in a 12-6 victory over Chicago. The Packers then lost three straight games by big margins. Dickey, still rebounding from the inactivity of two previous seasons, regained his passing touch and directed a 14-9 victory over Cincinnati. In a tie with Tampa Bay on October 12, Dickey set Packers single-game passing records for attempts (51), completions (35), and yards (418). He also set season records with 478 attempts, 278 completions, and 3,529 yards. Dickey's favorite receiver was Lofton, who caught 71 passes for 1,226 yards. Lofton displayed his versatility when he filled in as a defensive back in a 23-16 victory over San Francisco on November 9. Two weeks later, Ivery and Gerry Ellis rushed for 246 yards, and the Packers defeated Minnesota 25-13, their first seasonal sweep of the Vikings since 1965. But the club still finished 5-10-1 for the year.

1981 The Packers opened with a 16-9 victory over Chicago, but lost Eddie Lee Ivery for the season with a knee injury. A week later the Packers lost to Atlanta 31-17 despite Lofton's eight catches for 179 yards. The slumping Packers reached the midseason mark with a 2-6 record. One high point in the first half of the season was the acquisition of wide receiver John Jefferson from San Diego for draft choices and Aundra Thompson. In his first start with the Packers, Jefferson caught seven passes for 121 yards in a loss to Minnesota. While Dickey sat out with a back injury, Whitehurst made his first start in nearly two years, on November 1, and passed for 205 yards and three

touchdowns in a 34-24 victory over Seattle. That win ignited the Packers, who won five of their next six games, the last three with Dickey back in the lineup. With a playoff berth riding on the final game of the season, the Packers lost to the New York Jets 28-3, to finish 8-8.

MEMBERS OF HALL OF FAME:
Herb Adderley, Johnny Blood (McNally), Tony Canadeo, Willie Davis, Forrest Gregg, Arnie Herber, Clarke Hinkle, Cal Hubbard, Don Hutson, Walt Kiesling, Earl (Curly) Lambeau, Vince Lombardi, Mike Michalske, Ray Nitschke, Jim Ringo, Bart Starr, Jim Taylor, Emlen Tunnell

PACKERS RECORD, 1921-81

Year	Won	Lost	Tied	Pct.	Pts.	OP
1921	6	2	2	.750		
1922	4	3	3	.571		
1923	7	2	1	.778		
1924	8	4	0	.667		
1925	8	5	0	.615		
1926	7	3	3	.700		
1927	7	2	1	.778		
1928	6	4	3	.600		
1929‡	12	0	1	1.000		
1930‡	10	3	1	.769		
1931‡	12	2	0	.857		
1932	10	3	1	.769		
1933	5	7	1	.417	170	107
1934	7	6	0	.538	156	112
1935	8	4	0	.667	181	96
1936‡	10	1	1	.909	248	118
1937	7	4	0	.636	220	122
1938§	8	3	0	.727	223	118
1939‡	9	2	0	.818	233	153
1940	6	4	1	.600	238	155
1941	10	1	0	.909	258	120
1942	8	2	1	.800	300	215
1943	7	2	1	.778	264	172
1944‡	8	2	0	.800	238	141
1945	6	4	0	.600	258	173
1946	6	5	0	.545	148	158
1947	6	5	1	.545	274	210
1948	3	9	0	.250	154	290
1949	2	10	0	.167	114	329
1950	3	9	0	.250	244	406
1951	3	9	0	.250	254	375
1952	6	6	0	.500	295	312
1953	2	9	1	.182	200	338
1954	4	8	0	.333	234	251
1955	6	6	0	.500	258	276
1956	4	8	0	.333	264	342
1957	3	9	0	.250	218	311
1958	1	10	1	.091	193	382
1959	7	5	0	.583	248	246
1960§	8	4	0	.667	332	209
1961‡	11	3	0	.786	391	223
1962‡	13	1	0	.929	415	148
1963	11	2	1	.846	369	206
1964	8	5	1	.615	342	245
1965‡	10	3	1	.769	316	224
1966*	12	2	0	.857	335	163
1967*	9	4	1	.692	332	209
1968	6	7	1	.462	281	227
1969	8	6	0	.571	269	221
1970	6	8	0	.429	196	293
1971	4	8	2	.333	274	298
1972†	10	4	0	.714	304	226
1973	5	7	2	.429	202	259
1974	6	8	0	.429	210	206
1975	4	10	0	.286	226	285
1976	5	9	0	.357	218	299
1977	4	10	0	.286	134	219
1978	8	7	1	.531	249	269
1979	5	11	0	.313	246	316
1980	5	10	1	.344	231	371
1981	8	8	0	.500	324	361
61 Years	418	320	35	.563		

RECORD HOLDERS

Rushing (Yards)	Jim Taylor, 1962	1,474
Passing (Pct.)	Bart Starr, 1968	63.7
Passing (Yards)	Lynn Dickey, 1980	3,529
Passing (TDs)	Cecil Isbell, 1942	24
Receiving (No.)	Don Hutson, 1942	74
Receiving (Yards)	James Lofton, 1981	1,294
Interceptions (No.)	Irv Comp, 1942	10
Punting (Avg.)	Jerry Norton, 1963	44.7
Punt Ret. (Avg.)	Bill Grimes, 1950	19.1
Kickoff Ret. (Avg.)	Travis Williams, 1967	41.1
Touchdowns (Total)	Jim Taylor, 1962	19
Field Goals Made	Chester Marcol, 1972	33
Points (No.)	Paul Hornung, 1960	176

‡*NFL Champion*
§*NFL Western Conference Champion*
**Super Bowl Champion*
†*NFC Central Division Champion*

Lionel Aldridge

Donny Anderson

Tom Bettis

Charley Brock

Lee Roy Caffey

Don Chandler

Fred Cone

COACHING HISTORY

1921-49	Earl (Curly) Lambeau	213-104-22
1950-53	Gene Ronzani	14- 33- 1
1954-57	Lisle Blackbourn	17- 31- 0
1958	Ray (Scooter) McLean	1- 10- 1
1959-67	Vince Lombardi	89- 29- 4
1968-70	Phil Bengtson	20- 21- 1
1971-74	Dan Devine	25- 27- 4
1975-81	Bart Starr	39- 65- 2

FIRST PLAYER SELECTED

1936	Russ Letlow, G, San Francisco
1937	Ed Jankowski, B, Wisconsin
1938	Cecil Isbell, B, Purdue
1939	Larry Buhler, B, Minnesota
1940	Hal Van Every, B, Marquette
1941	George Paskvan, B, Wisconsin
1942	Urban Odson, T, Minnesota
1943	Dick Wildung, T, Minnesota
1944	Merv Pregulman, G, Michigan
1945	Walt Schlinkman, G, Texas Tech
1946	Johnny (Strike) Strzykalski, B, Marquette
1947	Ernie Case, B, UCLA
1948	Earl (Jug) Girard, B, Wisconsin
1949	Stan Heath, B, Nevada
1950	Clayton Tonnemaker, C, Minnesota
1951	Bob Gain, T, Kentucky
1952	Babe Parilli, QB, Kentucky
1953	Al Carmichael, B, USC
1954	Art Hunter, T, Notre Dame
1955	Tom Bettis, G, Purdue
1956	Jack Losch, B, Miami
1957	Paul Hornung, B, Notre Dame
1958	Dan Currie, C, Michigan State
1959	Randy Duncan, B, Iowa
1960	Tom Moore, RB, Vanderbilt
1961	Herb Adderley, CB, Michigan State
1962	Earl Gros, RB, Louisiana State
1963	Dave Robinson, LB, Penn State
1964	Lloyd Voss, DT, Nebraska
1965	Donny Anderson, RB, Texas Tech
1966	Gale Gillingham, G, Minnesota
1967	Bob Hyland, C, Boston College
1968	Fred Carr, LB, Texas-El Paso
1969	Rich Moore, DT, Villanova
1970	Mike McCoy, DT, Notre Dame
1971	John Brockington, RB, Ohio State
1972	Willie Buchanon, CB, San Diego State
1973	Barry Smith, WR, Florida State
1974	Barty Smith, RB, Richmond
1975	Bill Bain, G (2), USC
1976	Mark Koncar, T, Colorado
1977	Mike Butler, DE, Kansas
1978	James Lofton, WR, Stanford
1979	Eddie Lee Ivery, RB, Georgia Tech
1980	Bruce Clark, DT, Penn State
1981	Rich Campbell, QB, California
1982	Ron Hallstrom, T, Iowa

GREEN BAY PACKERS, 1921-81

Aberson, Cliff, B, No college . . . 1946
Abrams, Nate, E, No college . . . 1921
Abramson, George, T, Minnesota . . . 1925
Acks, Ron, LB, Arizona State . . . 1974-76
Adams, Chet, T, Ohio U. . . . 1943
Adderley, Herb, DB, Michigan State . . . 1961-69
Adkins, Bob, B, Marshall . . . 1940-41, 45
Afflis, Dick, G, Nevada-Reno . . . 1951-54
Agajanian, Ben, K, New Mexico . . . 1961
Albrecht, Art, T, Wisconsin . . . 1941
Aldridge, Ben, B, Oklahoma State . . . 1953
Aldridge, Lionel, DE, Utah State . . . 1963-71
Allerman, Kurt, LB, Penn State . . . 1980-81
Amsler, Marty, DE, Evansville . . . 1970
Amundsen, Norm, G, Wisconsin . . . 1957
Anderson, Bill, E, Tennessee . . . 1965-66
Anderson, Donny, RB-P, Texas Tech . . . 1966-71
Anderson, John, LB, Michigan . . . 1978-81
Anderson, Vickey Ray, RB, Oklahoma . . . 1980
Ane, Charlie, C, Michigan State . . . 1981
Apsit, Marger, B, USC . . . 1932
Ashmore, Roger, T, Gonzaga . . . 1928-29
Askson, Burt, TE, Texas Southern . . . 1975-77
Atkins, Steve, RB, Maryland . . . 1979-81
Austin, Hise, DB, Prairie View . . . 1973
Aydelette, Buddy, G, Alabama . . . 1980

B

Bailey, Byron, B, Washington State . . . 1953
Bain, Bill, T, USC . . . 1975
Baker, Frank, E, Northwestern . . . 1931
Baker, Roy (Bullet), B, USC . . . 1928-29
Balaz, Frank, B, Iowa . . . 1939-41
Baldwin, Al, E, Arkansas . . . 1950
Banet, Herb, B, Manchester . . . 1937
Barber, Bob, DE, Grambling . . . 1976-79
Barnes, Emery, E, Oregon . . . 1956
Barnes, Gary, E, Clemson . . . 1962-63
Barnett, Solon, T, Baylor . . . 1945-46
Barragar, Nate, C, USC . . . 1931-35
Barrett, Jan, E, Fresno State . . . 1963
Barry, Al, G, USC . . . 1954-57
Barry, Norm, B, Notre Dame . . . 1921
Barton, Don, B, Texas . . . 1953
Barzilauskas, Carl, DT, Indiana . . . 1978-79
Basing, Myrt, B, Lawrence . . . 1923-27
Basinger, Mike, OL, California-Riverside . . . 1974
Baxter, Lloyd, T, Southern Methodist . . . 1948
Beasley, John, B, South Dakota . . . 1924
Beck, Ken, T, Texas A&M . . . 1959-60
Becker, Wayland, E, Marquette . . . 1936-38
Beekley, Bruce, LB, Oregon . . . 1980
Bell, Ed, G, Indiana . . . 1947-49
Bennett, Earl, G, Hardin-Simmons . . . 1946
Berezney, Paul, T, Fordham . . . 1942-44
Berrang, Ed, E, Villanova . . . 1952
Berry, Connie Mack, E, North Carolina State . . . 1940
Bettencourt, Larry, C, St. Mary's, Cal. . . . 1933
Bettis, Tom, LB, Purdue . . . 1955-61
Beverly, David, P, Auburn . . . 1975-80
Bilda, Dick, D, Marquette . . . 1944
Biolo, John, G, Lake Forest . . . 1939
Birney, Tom, K, Michigan State . . . 1979-80
Blaine, Ed, G, Missouri . . . 1962
Blood (McNally), Johnny, B, St. John's, Minn. 1929-33, 1935-36
Bloodgood, Elbert, B, Nebraska . . . 1930
Boedeker, Bill, B, DePaul . . . 1950
Boerio, Chuck, LB, Illinois . . . 1952
Bookout, Billy, B, Austin . . . 1955-56
Boone, J. R., B, Tulsa . . . 1953
Borak, Anthony, E, Creighton . . . 1938
Borden, Nate, E, Indiana . . . 1955-59
Bowdoin, Jim, G, Alabama . . . 1928-31
Bowman, Ken, C, Wisconsin . . . 1964-73
Boyd, Elmo, WR, Eastern Kentucky . . . 1978
Brackins, Charlie, B, Prairie View . . . 1955
Bradley, Dave, G, Penn State . . . 1969-71
Braggs, Byron, DT, Alabama . . . 1981
Branstetter, Kent, G-T, Houston . . . 1973
Bratkowski, Zeke, QB, Georgia . . . 1963-68, 1971
Bray, Ray, G, Western Michigan . . . 1952
Breen, Gene, LB, Virginia Tech . . . 1964
Brennan, Jack, G, Michigan . . . 1939
Brock, Charley, C, Nebraska . . . 1939-47
Brock, Lou, B, Purdue . . . 1940-45
Brockington, John, RB, Ohio State . . . 1971-77
Broussard, Steve, P, Southern Mississippi . . . 1975
Brown, Aaron, DE, Minnesota . . . 1973-74
Brown, Allen, E, Mississippi . . . 1966-67
Brown, Bill, G, Arkansas . . . 1953-56
Brown, Bob, DT, Arkansas-Pine Bluff . . . 1966-73
Brown, Carlos, QB, Pacific . . . 1975-76
Brown, Ken, C, New Mexico . . . 1980
Brown, Tim, B, Ball State . . . 1959
Brown, Tom, HB, Maryland . . . 1964-68
Bruder, Hank, B, Northwestern . . . 1931-39
Bucchianeri, Mike, G, Indiana . . . 1941, 1944-45
Buchanon, Willie, DB, San Diego State . . . 1972-78
Buck, Cub, T, Wisconsin . . . 1921-25
Buhler, Larry, B, Minnesota . . . 1939-41
Buland, Walt, T, No college . . . 1924
Bullough, Hank, G, Michigan State . . . 1955, 1958
Bultman, Art, C, Marquette . . . 1932-34
Burris, Paul (Buddy), G, Oklahoma . . . 1949-51
Burrow, Jim, DB, Nebraska . . . 1976
Butler, Frank, C, Michigan State . . . 1934-36, 1938
Butler, Bill, B, Chattanooga . . . 1959
Butler, Mike, DE, Kansas . . . 1977-81

C

Cabral, Brian, LB, Colorado . . . 1980
Caffey, Lee Roy, LB, Texas A&M . . . 1964-69
Cahoon, Ivan (Tiny), T, Gonzaga . . . 1926-29
Campbell, Rich, QB, California . . . 1981
Canadeo, Tony, B, Gonzaga . . . 1941-43, 1946-52
Cannava, Al, B, Boston College . . . 1950
Capp, Dick, LB, Boston College . . . 1967
Capuzzi, Jim, B, Cincinnati . . . 1955-56
Carey, Joe, G, No college . . . 1921
Carlson, Dean, QB, Iowa State . . . 1974
Carlson, Irv, G, St. John's . . . 1926
Carmichael, Al, B, USC . . . 1953-58
Carpenter, Lew, B, Arkansas . . . 1959-63
Carr, Fred, LB, Texas-El Paso . . . 1968-77
Carroll, Leo, DE, San Diego U. . . . 1968
Carter, Jim, LB, Minnesota . . . 1970-78
Carter, Joe, E, Southern Methodist . . . 1942
Carter, Mike, WR, Sacramento State . . . 1970-71
Casper, Charley, B, Texas Christian . . . 1934
Cassidy, Ron, WR, Utah State . . . 1979-81
Chandler, Don, K, Florida . . . 1965-67
Chesley, Francis, LB, Wyoming . . . 1978
Cheyunski, Jim, LB, Syracuse . . . 1977
Christman, Paul, QB, Missouri . . . 1950
Cifelli, Gus, T, Notre Dame . . . 1953
Cifers, Bob, B, Tennessee . . . 1949
Clancy, Jack, WR, Michigan . . . 1970
Claridge, Dennis, QB, Nebraska . . . 1964-65
Clemens, Cal, B, USC . . . 1936
Clemens, Bob, B, Georgia . . . 1955
Clemens, Ray, G, St. Mary's, Cal. . . . 1947
Cloud, Jack, B, William & Mary . . . 1950-51
Cody, Ed, B, Purdue . . . 1947-48
Coffey, Junior, RB, Washington . . . 1965
Coffman, Paul, TE, Kansas State . . . 1978-81
Collins, Al, B, Louisiana State . . . 1951
Comp, Irv, B, St. Benedict's, Kansas . . . 1943-49
Comstock, Rudy, G, Georgetown . . . 1931-33
Concannon, Jack, QB, Boston College . . . 1974
Conway, David, K, Texas . . . 1971
Cone, Fred, B, Clemson . . . 1951-57
Cook, Jim, G, Wisconsin . . . 1921
Cook, Ted, E, Alabama . . . 1948-50
Cooke, Bill, DE, Massachusetts . . . 1975
Cooney, Mark, DE, Colorado . . . 1974
Coughlin, Frank, B, Notre Dame . . . 1921
Coutre, Larry, B, Notre Dame . . . 1950, 1953
Craig, Larry, B, South Carolina . . . 1939-49
Cremer, Ted, E, Auburn . . . 1948
Crenshaw, Leon, DT, Tuskegee . . . 1968
Crimmins, Bernie, G, Notre Dame . . . 1945
Croft, Milburn, T, Ripon . . . 1942-47
Cronin, Tom, B, Marquette . . . 1922
Crowley, Jim, B, Notre Dame . . . 1925
Crutcher, Tommy, LB, Texas Christian . . . 1964-67, 1971-72
Cuff, Ward, B-K, Marquette . . . 1947
Culbreath, Jim, RB, Oklahoma . . . 1977-79
Culver, Al, T, Notre Dame . . . 1932
Cumby, George, LB, Oklahoma . . . 1980-81
Currie, Dan, LB, Michigan State . . . 1958-64
Curry, Bill, LB, Georgia Tech . . . 1965-66
Cvercko, Andy, G, Northwestern . . . 1960
Cyre, Hector, T, Gonzaga . . . 1926-27

D

Dahms, Tom, T, San Diego State . . . 1955
Dale, Carroll, D, Virginia Tech . . . 1965-72
Danelo, Joe, K, Washington State . . . 1975
Daniell, Averell, T, Pittsburgh . . . 1937
Danjean, Ernie, G, Auburn . . . 1957
Darling, Bernie, C, Beloit . . . 1927-31
Davenport, Bill, B, Hardin-Simmons . . . 1931
Davidson, Ben, T, Washington . . . 1961
Davis, Dave, WR, Tennessee A&I . . . 1971-72
Davis, Harper, B, Mississippi State . . . 1951
Davis, Paul, G, Marquette . . . 1922

Lynn Dickey

LaVern Dilweg

Boyd Dowler

Ted Fritsch

Gale Gillingham

Charles Goldenberg

Dave Hanner

Davis, Ralph, G, Wisconsin 1947-48
Davis, Willie, E, Grambling 1960-69
Dawson, Gib, B, Texas 1953
Deeks, Don, T, Washington 1948
Dees, Bob, T, Southwest Missouri State 1952
Del Gaizo, Jim, QB, Tampa 1973
DeLisle, Jim, DT, Wisconsin 1971
Deschaine, Dick, E, No college 1955-57
Dickey, Lynn, QB, Kansas State 1976-81
Dillon, Bobby, B, Texas 1952-59
Dilweg, LaVern, E, Marquette 1927-34
Dimler, Rich, T, USC 1980
DiPierro, Ray, G, Ohio State 1950-51
Disend, Leo, T, Albright 1940
Dittrich, John, G, Wisconsin 1959
Doncarlos, J., C, Drake 1931
Donohoe, Mike, TE, San Francisco 1973-74
Douglas, George, C, Marquette 1921
Douglass, Bobby, QB, Kansas 1978-81
Douglass, Mike, LB, San Diego State 1978-81
Dowden, Steve, T, Baylor 1952
Dowler, Boyd, E, Colorado 1959-69
Dowling, Brian, QB, Yale 1977
Dreyer, Wally, B, Wisconsin 1950-51
Drulis, Al, G, Temple 1950
Duford, Wilfred, B, Marquette 1924
Duhart, Paul, B, Florida 1944
Dumoe, Bill, E, Beloit 1921
Dunaway, Dave, E, Duke 1968
Duncan, Ken, P-WR, Tulsa 1971
Dunn, Red, B, Marquette 1927-31
Dunningan, Walt, E, Minnesota 1922

E

Earhart, Ralph, B, Texas Tech 1948-49
Earpe, Jug, C, Monmouth 1922-32
Eason, Roger, T, Oklahoma 1949
Ecker, Ed, T, John Carroll 1950-51
Edwards, Earl, DT, Wichita State 1979
Elliott, Burton, B, Marquette 1921
Elliott, Carlton, E, Virginia 1951-54
Ellis, Gerry, RB, Missouri 1980-81
Ellis, Ken, DB, Southern U. 1970-75
Enderle, Dick, G, Minnesota 1976
Engebretsen, Paul (Tiny), G, Northwestern 1934-41
Engelmann, Wuert, B, South Dakota State 1930-33
Enright, Rex, B, Notre Dame 1926-27
Erickson, Harry, B, Washington & Jefferson 1923
Estes, Roy, B, Georgia 1928
Ethridge, Joe, T, Southern Methodist 1949
Evans, Jack, B, California 1929
Evans, Lon, G, Texas Christian 1933-37
Evans, Dick, E, Iowa 1940, 1943

F

Falkenstein, Tony, B, St. Mary's, Cal. 1943
Fanucci, Mike, DE, Arizona State 1974
Faverty, Hal, C, Wisconsin 1952
Faye, Allen, E, Marquette 1922
Feathers, Beattie, B, Tennessee 1940
Felker, Art, E, Marquette 1951
Ferguson, Howie, B, No college 1953-58
Ferry, Lou, T, Villanova 1949
Finely, Jim, G, Michigan State 1942
Finnin, Tom, T, Detroit 1957
Fitzgibbon, Paul, B, Creighton 1930-32
Flaherty, Dick, E, Marquette 1926-27
Flanigan, Jim, LB, Pittsburgh 1967-70
Fleming, Marv, E, Utah 1963-69
Flowers, Bob, C, Texas Tech 1942-48
Floyd, Bobby Jack, B, Texas Christian 1952, 1954
Folkins, Lee, E, Washington 1961
Ford, Len, E, Michigan 1958
Forester, Bill, LB, Southern Methodist 1953-63
Forte, Aldo, G, Montana 1947
Forte, Bob, B, Arkansas 1946-53
Francis, Joe, B, Oregon State 1958-59
Frankowski, Ray, G, Washington 1945
Franta, Herb, T, St. Thomas 1930
Freeman, Bobby, B, Auburn 1959
Fries, Sherwood, G, Colorado State 1943
Fritsch, Ted, B-K, Wisconsin-Stevens Point 1942-50
Frutig, Ed, E, Michigan 1941, 1945

G

Gantenbein, Milt, E, Wisconsin 1931-40
Gardella, August, B, Holy Cross 1922
Gardner, Milt (Moose), G, Wisconsin 1922-26
Garrett, Bobby, B, Stanford 1954
Garrett, Len, TE, New Mexico Highlands 1971-72
Gassert, Ron, T, Virginia 1962
Gatewood, Les, B, Baylor 1946-47
Gavin, Fritz (Buck), E, Marquette 1921, 1923
Gaydos, Kent, WR, Florida State 1975
Gibson, Paul, WR, Texas-El Paso 1972
Gillette, Jim, B, Virginia 1947
Gillingham, Gale, G, Minnesota 1966-74, 1976
Girard, Jug, B, Wisconsin 1948-51
Glass, Leland, WR, Oregon 1972-73
Glick, Eddie, B, Marquette 1921-22
Gofourth, Derrel, C, Oklahoma State 1977-81
Goldenberg, Charles (Buckets), G, Wisconsin 1933-45
Goodman, Les, RB, Yankton 1973-74
Goodnight, Clyde, E, Tulsa 1945-49
Gordon, Lou, T, Illinois 1936-37
Gorgal, Ken, B, Purdue 1956
Grabowski, Jim, B, Illinois 1966-70
Gray, Jack, E, Princeton 1923
Gray, Johnnie, S, Cal State-Fullerton 1975-81
Green, Jessie, WR, Tulsa 1976
Greeney, Norm, G, Notre Dame 1933
Greenfield, Tom, C, Arizona 1939-41
Gregg, Forrest, T, Southern Methodist 1956, 1958-70
Gremminger, Hank, B, Baylor 1956-65
Griffen, Harold, C, Iowa 1928
Grimes, Billy, B, Oklahoma State 1950-52
Grimm, Dan, G, Colorado 1963-65
Gros, Earl, B, Louisiana State 1962-63
Grove, Roger, B, Michigan State 1931-35
Gudauskas, Pete, G, Murray State 1942, 1945
Gudie, Walter, G, Wisconsin 1943-44
Gueno, Jim, LB, Tulane 1976-80

H

Hackbart, Dale, B, Wisconsin 1960
Hadl, John, QB, Kansas 1974-75
Hall, Charlie, DB, Pittsburgh 1971-76
Hampton, Dave, RB, Wyoming 1970-71
Hanner, Dave, T, Arkansas 1952-64
Hanny, Frank (Duke), T, Indiana 1930
Hansen, Don, LB, Illinois 1976-77
Hanson, Roy, B, Marquette 1923
Harden, Leon, DS, Texas-El Paso 1970
Harding, Roger, C, California 1949
Hardy, Kevin, DT, Notre Dame 1970
Harrell, Willard, RB, Pacific 1975-77
Harris, John, B, Minnesota 1930
Harris, Leotis, G, Arkansas 1978-81
Harrison, Reggie, RB, Cincinnati 1978
Hart, Doug, DB, Arlington State 1964-71
Hartwig, Keith, WR, Arizona 1977
Harvey, Maurice, S, Ball State 1981
Hathcock, Dave, B, Memphis State 1966
Havig, Dennis, G, Colorado 1977
Haycraft, Ken, E, Minnesota 1930
Hayes, Norb, E, Marquette 1923
Hayhoe, Bill, T, USC 1969-74
Hays, Dave, E, Notre Dame 1921-22
Hays, George, E, St. Bonaventure 1953
Hearden, Les, B, St. Ambrose 1924
Hearden, Tom, B, Notre Dame 1927-28
Heath, Stan, B, Nevada-Reno 1949
Hefner, Larry, LB, Clemson 1972-75
Held, Paul, QB, San Diego State 1955
Helluin, Jerry, T, Tulane 1954-57
Hendrian, Warren (Dutch), B, Pittsburgh 1924
Hendricks, Ted, LB, Miami 1974
Henry, Urban, T, Georgia Tech 1963
Herber, Arnie, B, Regis 1931-41
Hickman, Larry, B, Baylor 1960
Highsmith, Don, RB, Michigan State 1973
Hill, Don, B, Stanford 1929
Hill, Jim, DB, Texas A&I 1972-74
Hilton, John, TE, Richmond 1970
Himes, Dick, T, Ohio State 1968-77
Hinkle, Clarke, B-K, Bucknell 1932-41
Hinte, Tex, E, Pittsburgh 1941
Holler, Ed, LB, South Carolina 1963
Hood, Estus, DB, Illinois State 1978-81
Horn, Don, QB, San Diego State 1967-70
Hornung, Paul, RB-K, Notre Dame 1957-62, 1964-66
Howard, Lynn (Tubby), B, Indiana 1921-22
Howell, John, B, Nebraska 1938
Howton, Billy, E, Rice 1952-58
Hubbard, Cal, T, Geneva 1929-35
Huckleby, Harlan, RB, Michigan 1980-81
Hudson, Bob, RB, NE Oklahoma State 1972
Hull, Tom, LB, Penn State 1975
Hunt, Ervin, DB, Fresno State 1970
Hunt, Kevin, T, Doane 1972
Hunt, Michael, LB, Minnesota 1978-80
Hunt, Sam, LB, Stephen F. Austin 1980
Hunter, Art, C, Notre Dame 1954
Hunter, Scott, QB, Alabama 1971-73
Hutson, Don, E-K, Alabama 1935-45
Hyland, Bob, C, Boston College 1967-69, 1976

I

Iman, Ken, C, Southeast Missouri 1960-63
Ingalls, Bob, C, Michigan 1942
Isbell, Cecil, B, Purdue 1938-42
Ivery, Eddie Lee, B, Georgia Tech 1979-81

J

Jackson, Mel, G, USC 1976-80
Jacobs, Allen, B, Utah 1965
Jacobs, Jack, B-P, Oklahoma 1947-49
Jacunski, Harry, E, Fordham 1939-44
James, Claudis, WR, Jackson State 1967-69
Jankowski, Eddie, B, Wisconsin 1937-41
Jansante, Val, E, Duquesne 1951
Jean, Walter, G, Bethany (Kansas) 1925-26
Jefferson, John, WR, Arizona State 1981
Jenison, Ray, T, South Dakota State 1931
Jenke, Noel, LB, Minnesota 1973-74
Jennings, Jim, E, Missouri 1955
Jensen, Jim, RB, Iowa 1981
Jeter, Bob, DB, Iowa 1963-70
Johnson, Bill, E, Minnesota 1941
Johnson, Charles, DT, Maryland 1979-80
Johnson, Danny, LB, Tennessee State 1978
Johnson, Ezra, DE, Morris Brown 1977-81
Johnson, Glenn, T, Arizona State 1949
Johnson, Howard (Smiley), G, Georgia 1940-41
Johnson, Joe, B, Boston College 1954-58
Johnson, Marv, B, San Jose State 1952-53
Johnson, Randy, QB, Texas A&I 1976
Johnson, Sammy Lee, B, North Carolina 1979
Johnson, Tom, T, Michigan 1952
Johnston, Chester (Swede), B, Marquette 1934-39
Johnstone, Art, B, Lawrence 1931
Jolly, Mike, S, Michigan 1980
Jones, Bob, G, Indiana 1934
Jones, Bruce, G, Alabama 1927-28
Jones, Ron, TE, Texas-El Paso 1969
Jones, Terry, DT, Alabama 1978-81
Jones, Tom (Pottsville), G, Bucknell 1938
Jordan, Henry, T, Virginia 1959-69
Jorgenson, Carl, T, St. Mary's, Cal. 1934

K

Kahler, Bob, B, Nebraska 1941-44
Kahler, Royal, T, Nebraska 1942
Katalinas, Leo, T, Catholic U. 1938
Keane, Jim, E, Iowa 1952
Keefe, Emmett, T, Notre Dame 1921
Kekeris, Jim, T, Missouri 1948
Kell, Paul, T, Notre Dame 1939-40
Kelley, Bill, E, Texas Tech 1949
Kenyon, Crowell, G, Ripon 1923
Kercher, Bob, E, Georgetown 1944
Kern, Bill, T, Pittsburgh 1929-30
Keuper, Ken, B, Georgia 1945-47
Kiesling, Walt, T, St. Thomas 1935-36
Kilbourne, Warren, T, Michigan 1939
Kimball, Bob, WR, Oklahoma 1979-80

Henry Jordan

Jerry Kramer

Ron Kramer

Verne Lewellen

Max McGee

Elijah Pitts

Buford (Baby) Ray

Kimmel, J. D., T, Houston ... 1958
Kinard, Billy, B, Mississippi ... 1957-58
King, Don, T, Kentucky ... 1956
Kirby, John, B, USC ... 1949
Kitson, Syd, G, Wake Forest ... 1980-81
Klaus, Fee, C, No college ... 1921
Kliebhan, Roger, B, Milwaukee Teachers ... 1921
Knafelc, Gary, E, Colorado ... 1954-62
Knutson, Gene, E, Michigan ... 1954-56
Knutson, Steve, T, USC ... 1976-77
Koch, Greg, T, Arkansas ... 1977-81
Koncar, Mark, T, Colorado ... 1976-81
Kopay, Dave, B, Washington ... 1972
Kostelnik, Ron, T, Cincinnati ... 1961-68
Kotal, Eddie, B, Lawrence ... 1925-29
Kovatch, John, E, Notre Dame ... 1947
Kowalkowski, Bob, G, Virginia ... 1977
Kramer, Jerry, G-K, Idaho ... 1958-68
Kramer, Ron, E, Michigan ... 1957, 1959-64
Kranz, Ken, B, Milwaukee Teachers ... 1949
Krause, Larry, RB, St. Norbert ... 1970-74
Kresky, Joe, G, Wisconsin ... 1930
Kroll, Bob, DB, Northern Michigan ... 1972-73
Kuechenberg, Rudy, LB, Indiana ... 1970
Kuick, Stan, G, Beloit ... 1926
Kurth, Joe, T, Notre Dame ... 1933-34
Kuusisto, Bill, G, Minnesota ... 1941-46

L

Laabs, Kermit, B, Beloit ... 1929
Ladrow, Wally, B, No college ... 1921
Lally, Bob, LB, Cornell ... 1976
Lambeau, Curly, B, Notre Dame ... 1921-30
Lammons, Pete, TE, Texas ... 1972
Lande, Cliff, E, Carroll ... 1921
Landers, Walt, RB, Clark College ... 1978-79
Lane, MacArthur, RB, Utah State ... 1972-74
Lankas, Jim, B, St. Mary's, Cal. ... 1943
Larson, Bill, TE, Colorado State ... 1980
Larson, Fred, C, Notre Dame ... 1925
Lathrop, Kit, DT, Arizona State ... 1979-80
Lauer, Hal, B, Detroit ... 1922
Lauer, Larry, C, Alabama ... 1956-57
Lawrence, Jim, B, Texas Christian ... 1939
Laws, Joe, B, Iowa ... 1934-45
Leaper, Wes, E, Wisconsin ... 1921, 1923
Lee, Bill, T, Alabama ... 1937-42, 1946
Lee, Mark, DB, Washington ... 1980-81
Leigh, Charlie, RB, No college ... 1974
LeJeune, Walt, G, Bethany (Kansas) ... 1925-26
Lester, Darrell, C, Texas Christian ... 1937-38
Letlow, Russ, G, San Francisco ... 1936-42, 1946
Lewellen, Verne, B, Nebraska ... 1924-32
Lewis, Cliff, LB, Southern Mississippi ... 1981
Lewis, Gary, TE, Texas-Arlington ... 1981
Lewis, Mike, DT, Arkansas-Pine Bluff ... 1980
Lidberg, Carl (Cully), B, Minnesota ... 1926-30
Lipscomb, Paul, T, Tennessee ... 1945-49
Livingston, Dale, K, Western Michigan ... 1970
Lofton, James, WR, Stanford ... 1978-81
Logan, Dick, T, Ohio State ... 1952-53
Lollar, George, B, Howard ... 1928
Long, Bob, E, Wichita State ... 1964-67
Loomis, Ace, B, Wisconsin-La Crosse ... 1951-53
Losch, Jack, B, Miami ... 1956
Lucky, Bill, T, Baylor ... 1955
Ludtke, Norm, G, Carroll, Wisconsin ... 1924
Lueck, Bill, G, Arizona ... 1968-74
Luhn, Nolan, E, Tulsa ... 1945-49
Luke, Steve, S, Ohio State ... 1975-80
Lusteg, Booth, K, Connecticut ... 1969-70
Lyle, Dewey, E, Minnesota ... 1922-23
Lyman, Del, T, UCLA ... 1941

M

MacAuliffe, John, B, Beloit ... 1926
MacLeod, Tom, LB, Minnesota ... 1973
Mack, Bill (Red), E, Notre Dame ... 1966
Maddox, George (Buster), T, Kansas State ... 1935
Malone, Grover, B, Notre Dame ... 1921
Manley, Leon, G, Oklahoma ... 1950-51
Mann, Bob, E, Michigan ... 1950-54
Mann, Erroll, K, North Dakota ... 1968, 1976
Marcol, Chester, K, Hillsdale ... 1972-80
Marks, Larry, B, Indiana ... 1928
Marshall, Rich, T, Stephen F. Austin ... 1965
Martell, Herm, E, No college ... 1921
Martinkovic, John, E, Xavier ... 1951-56
Mason, Dave, S, Nebraska ... 1974
Mason, Joel, E, Western Michigan ... 1941-45
Massey, Carlton, E, Texas ... 1957-58
Masters, Norm, T, Michigan State ... 1957-64
Mathys, Charley, B, Indiana ... 1922-26
Matson, Pat, G, Oregon ... 1975
Matthews, Al, CB, Texas A&I ... 1970-75
Mattos, Harry, B, St. Mary's, Cal. ... 1936
Matuszak, Marv, LB, Tulsa ... 1958
Mayer, Frank, G, Notre Dame ... 1927
McBride, Ron, RB, Missouri ... 1973
McCaffrey, Bob, C, USC ... 1975
McCarren, Larry, C, Illinois ... 1973-81
McCoy, Mike, CB, Colorado ... 1976-81
McCoy, Mike, DT, Notre Dame ... 1970-76
McCrary, Hurdis, B, Georgia ... 1929-33
McDougal, Bob, B, Miami ... 1947
McDowell, John, G, St. John's, Minn. ... 1964
McGaw, Walter, G, Beloit ... 1926
McGeary, Clink, T, North Dakota State ... 1950
McGee, Max, E, Tulane ... 1954, 1957-67
McGeorge, Rich, TE, Elon ... 1970-78
McHan, Lamar, B, Arkansas ... 1959-60
McIlhenny, Don, B, Southern Methodist ... 1957-59
McKay, Roy, B, Texas ... 1944-47
McLaughlin, Joe, LB, Massachusetts ... 1979
McLaughlin, Lee, G, Virginia ... 1941
McLean, Ray, B, No college ... 1921
McMath, Herb, DT, Morningside ... 1977
McMillan, Ernie, T, Illinois ... 1975
McPartland, Bill, T, Texas ... 1947
McPherson, Forrest (Amy), T, Nebraska ... 1943-45
Meilinger, Steve, E, Kentucky ... 1958-60
Mendenhall, Ken, C, Oklahoma ... 1970
Mercein, Chuck, B, Yale ... 1967-69
Mercer, Mike, K, Northern Arizona ... 1968-69
Merrill, Casey, DE, California-Davis ... 1979-81
Mestnik, Frank, B, Marquette ... 1963
Michaels, Lou, K, Kentucky ... 1971
Michaels, Walt, G, Washington & Lee ... 1951
Michalske, Mike, G, Penn State ... 1929-35, 1937
Middleton, Terdell, RB, Memphis State ... 1977-81
Midler, Lou, G, Minnesota ... 1940
Mihajlovich, Lou, B, Indiana ... 1954
Miketinac, Nick, G, St. Norbert ... 1937
Milan, Don, QB, Cal Poly-San Luis Obispo ... 1975
Miller, Charles, C, Purdue ... 1938
Miller, Don, B, Southern Methodist ... 1954
Miller, Don, B, Wisconsin ... 1941-42
Miller, Johnny, T, Boston College ... 1960
Miller, Mark, QB, Bowling Green ... 1980
Miller, Paul, B, South Dakota ... 1936-38
Miller, Tom, E, Hampton-Sydney ... 1946
Mills, Tom, B, Penn State ... 1922-23
Milton, Tom, E, Lake Forest ... 1924
Minick, Paul, G, Iowa ... 1928-29
Mitchell, Charlie, B, Tulsa ... 1946
Moje, Dick, E, Loyola, Cal. ... 1951
Molenda, Bo, B, Michigan ... 1929-32
Monnett, Bobby, B, Michigan State ... 1933-38
Monroe, Henry, DB, Mississippi State ... 1979
Moore, Al, E, Texas A&M ... 1939
Moore, Rich, DT, Villanova ... 1969-70
Moore, Tom, B, Vanderbilt ... 1960-65
Moresco, Tim, DB, Syracuse ... 1977
Moselle, Dom, B, Wisconsin-Superior ... 1951-52
Mosley, Russ, B, Alabama ... 1945-46
Moss, Perry, QB, Illinois ... 1948
Mott, Norm, B, Georgia ... 1933
Mulleneaux, Carl, E, Utah State ... 1938-41, 1945-46
Mulleneaux, Lee, T, Arizona State ... 1938
Murphy, Mark, S, West Liberty ... 1980-81
Murray, Dick, T, Marquette ... 1921-24

N

Nadolney, Romanus (Peaches), G, Notre Dame ... 1922
Nash, Tom, E, Georgia ... 1928-32
Neal, Ed, G, Tulane ... 1945-51
Nichols, Ham, G, Rice ... 1951
Niemann, Walt, C, Michigan ... 1922-24
Nitschke, Ray, LB, Illinois ... 1958-72
Nix, Doyle, B, Southern Methodist ... 1955
Nixon, Fred, WR, Oklahoma ... 1980-81
Nogard, Al, E, Stanford ... 1934
Norton, Jerry, DB, Southern Methodist ... 1963-64
Norton, Marty, B, Carleton ... 1925-28
Nussbaumer, Bob, B, Michigan ... 1946
Nuzum, Rick, C, Kentucky ... 1978-79
Nystrom, Lee, OT, Macalester ... 1973-74

O

Oakes, Bill, T, Haskell ... 1921
Oates, Brad, T, Brigham Young ... 1981
Oats, Carleton, DT, Florida A&M ... 1973
O'Boyle, Harry, B, Notre Dame ... 1928-29, 1932
O'Connor, Bob, T, Stanford ... 1935
O'Donahue, Pat, E, Wisconsin ... 1955
O'Donnell, Dick, E, Minnesota ... 1924-30
Odom, Steve, WR, Utah ... 1974-79
Odson, Urban, T, Minnesota ... 1946-49
Ohlgren, Earl, E, Minnesota ... 1942
Okoniewski, Steve, DT, Montana ... 1974-75
Olsen, Ralph, E, Utah ... 1949
Olsonoski, Larry, G, Minnesota ... 1948-49
O'Malley, Tom, QB, Cincinnati ... 1950
O'Malley, Jack, T, USC ... 1970
O'Neil, Ed, LB, Penn State ... 1980
Orlich, Dan, E, Nevada-Reno ... 1949-51
Osborn, Dave, RB, North Dakota ... 1976
Owens, Henry, G, Lake Forest ... 1922

P

Palumbo, Sam, G, Notre Dame ... 1957
Pannell, Ernie, T, Texas A&M ... 1941-42, 1945
Pape, Orrin, B, Iowa ... 1930
Papit, Johnny, B, Virginia ... 1953
Parilli, Vito (Babe), QB, Kentucky ... 1952-53, 1956-58
Paskvan, George, B, Wisconsin ... 1941
Pass, Randy, LB, Georgia Tech ... 1978
Patrick, Frank, QB, Nebraska ... 1970-72
Patton, Ricky, RB, Jackson State ... 1979
Paulekas, Tony, C, Washington & Jefferson ... 1936
Payne, Ken, WR, Langston, Oklahoma ... 1974-77
Pearson, Lindell, B, Oklahoma ... 1952
Peay, Francis, T, Missouri ... 1968-72
Pelfrey, Ray, E, Eastern Kentucky State ... 1951-52
Perkins, Don, B, Wisconsin-Platteville ... 1943-45
Perko, Tom, LB, Pittsburgh ... 1976
Perry, Claude, T, Alabama ... 1927-35
Pesonen, Dick, B, Minnesota-Duluth ... 1960
Peterson, Les, E, Texas ... 1932-35
Peterson, Phil, B, Wisconsin ... 1932
Peterson, Ray, B, San Francisco ... 1937
Petitbon, John, B, Notre Dame ... 1957
Petway, David, S, Northern Illinois ... 1981
Pisarkiewicz, Steve, QB, Missouri ... 1980
Pitts, Elijah, B, Philander Smith ... 1961-69, 1971
Pope, Bucky, WR, Catawba ... 1968
Powers, Sam, G, Northern Michigan ... 1921
Prather, Guy, LB, Grambling ... 1981
Pregulman, Merv, G, Michigan ... 1946
Prescott, Ace, E, Hardin-Simmons ... 1946
Priatko, Bill, G, Pittsburgh ... 1957
Pritko, Steve, E, Villanova ... 1949-50
Provo, Fred, B, Washington ... 1948
Psaltis, Jim, DB, USC ... 1954
Purdy, Pid, B, Beloit ... 1926-27
Pureifory, Dave, DT, Eastern Michigan ... 1972-77
Purnell, Frank, B, Alcorn State ... 1957
Putman, Earl, C, Arizona State ... 1957

Q

Quatse, Jess, T, Pittsburgh ... 1933
Quinlan, Billy, E, Michigan State ... 1959-62

R

Radick, Ken, E, Marquette ... 1930-31
Randolph, Al, DB, Iowa ... 1971

Dave Robinson

Tobin Rote

Bob Skoronski

Fuzzy Thurston

Jesse Whittenton

Willie Wood

Roger Zatkoff

Randolph, Terry, DB, American International 1977
Ranspot, Keith, E, Southern Methodist 1942
Ray, Buford (Baby), T, Vanderbilt 1938-48
Regnier, Pete, B, Minnesota 1922
Reichardt, Bill, B, Iowa 1952
Reid, Floyd (Breezy), B, Georgia 1950-56
Rhodemyre, Jay, C, Kentucky 1948-52
Riddick, Ray, E, Fordham 1940-42, 1946
Ringo, Jim, C, Syracuse 1953-63
Roach, John, QB, Southern Methodist 1961-63
Roberts, Bill, B, Dartmouth 1956
Robinson, Bill, B, Lincoln 1952
Robinson, Dave, LB, Penn State 1963-72
Roche, Alden, DT, Southern U. 1971-76
Rohrig, Herman, B, Nebraska 1941, 1946-47
Roller, Dave, DT, Kentucky 1975-78
Romine, Al, E, Florence State 1955, 1958
Rosatti, Roman (Rosey), T, Michigan 1924, 1926-27
Rose, Al, E, Texas 1932-36
Rose, Bob, C, Ripon 1926
Rosenow, Gus, B, Wisconsin 1921
Roskie, Ken, B, South Carolina 1948
Rote, Tobin, QB, Rice 1950-56
Rowser, John, DB, Michigan 1967-69
Rudzinski, Paul, LB, Michigan State 1978-80
Ruetz, Howie, T, Loras 1951-53
Rule, Gordon, DB, Dartmouth 1968-69
Rush, Clive, E, Miami, Ohio 1953
Ruzich, Steve, G, Ohio State 1952-54

S

Salsbury, Jim, G, UCLA 1957-58
Sample, Chuck, B, Toledo 1942, 1945
Sampson, Howard, DB, Arkansas 1978-79
Sandifer, Dan, B, Louisiana State 1952-53
Sandusky, John, T, Villanova 1956
Sarafiny, Al, C, St. Edward 1933
Sauer, George, B, Nebraska 1935-37
Saunders, Russ, B, USC 1931
Scales, Hurles, DB, North Texas State 1975
Schammel, Fran, G, Iowa 1937
Scherer, Bernie, E, Nebraska 1936-38
Schlinkman, Walt, B, Texas Tech 1946-50
Schmaehl, Art, B, No college 1921
Schmidt, George, C, Lewis 1952-53
Schmitt, John, C, Hofstra 1974
Schneidman, Herm, B, Iowa 1935-39
Schoemann, Roy, C, Marquette 1938
Schroll, Chuck, B, Louisiana State 1951
Schuette, Carl, B, Marquette 1950-51
Schuh, Harry, T, Memphis State 1974
Schultz, Charlie, T, Minnesota 1939-41
Schwammel, Ade, T, Oregon State 1934-37, 1943-44
Scott, Randy, LB, Alabama 1981
Secord, Joe, C, No college 1922
Seeman, George, E, Nebraska 1940
Seibold, Champ, T, Wisconsin 1934-41
Self, Clarence, B, Wisconsin 1952, 1954-55
Serini, Washington, G, Kentucky 1952
Shanley, Jim, B, Oregon 1958
Shelley, Dexter, B, Texas 1932-33
Shirley, Fred, T, Nebraska 1940
Simmons, Davie, LB, North Carolina 1979-80
Simpson, Nate, RB, Tennessee State 1977-79
Skeate, Gil, B, Gonzaga 1927
Skibinski, Joe, G, Purdue 1955-56
Skinner, Gerald, T, Arkansas 1978
Skoglund, Bob, E, Notre Dame 1947
Skoronski, Bob, T, Indiana 1956, 1959-68
Sleight, Elmer (Red), T, Purdue 1930-31
Smith, Barry, WR, Florida State 1973-75
Smith, Barty, RB, Richmond 1974-80
Smith, Ben, E, Alabama 1933
Smith, Blane, G, Purdue 1977
Smith, Bruce, B, Minnesota 1945-48
Smith, Donnell, DE, Southern U. 1971
Smith, Earl, T, Ripon 1922
Smith, Ed, B, New York U. 1937
Smith, Ernie, T, USC 1935-37, 1939
Smith, Jerry, G, Wisconsin 1956
Smith, Ollie, WR, Tennessee State 1976-77
Smith, Oscar, B, Texas-El Paso 1948-49
Smith, Perry, DB, Colorado State 1973-76
Smith, Rex, E, Wisconsin-Lacrosse 1922
Smith, Richard (Red), G, Notre Dame 1927-29
Smith, Warren, C, Carleton 1921
Snelling, Ken, B, UCLA 1945
Snider, Malcolm, G, Stanford 1972-74
Sorenson, Glen, G, Utah State 1943-45
Sparlis, Al, G, UCLA 1946
Spencer, Joe, T, Oklahoma State 1950-51
Spencer, Ollie, T, Kansas 1957-58
Spilis, John, WR, Northern Illinois 1969-71
Spinks, Jack, G, Alcorn State 1955-56
Sproul, Dennis, QB, Arizona State 1978
Stachowicz, Ray, P, Michigan State 1981
Staggers, Jon, WR, Missouri 1972-74
Stahlman, Dick, E, Chicago 1931-32
Stansauk, Don, T, Denver 1950-51
Starch, Ken, RB, Wisconsin 1976
Staroba, Paul, WR, Michigan 1973
Starr, Bart, QB, Alabama 1956-71
Starret, Ben, B, St. Mary's, Cal. 1942-45
Steen, Frank, E, Rice 1939
Steiner, Rebel, E, Alabama 1950-51
Stenerud, Jan, K, Montana State 1980-81
Stephenson, Dave (Trapper), G, West Virginia 1951-55
Stevens, Bill, QB, Texas-El Paso 1968-69
Stewart, Steve, LB, Minnesota 1979
Stokes, Tim, T, Oregon 1978-81
Stonebraker, John, E, USC 1942
Sturgeon, Lyle, T, North Dakota State 1937
Sullivan, Walter, B, Beloit 1921
Summerhays, Bob, B, Utah 1949-51
Svendsen, Earl (Bud), C, Minnesota 1937-40
Svendsen, George, C, Minnesota 1935-37, 1939-41
Swanke, Karl, T-C, Boston College 1980-81
Switzer, Veryl, B, Kansas State 1954-55
Symank, John, B, Florida 1957-62
Szafaryn, Len, T, North Carolina 1950, 1953-56

T

Tagge, Jerry, QB, Nebraska 1972-74
Tassos, Damon, G, Texas A&M 1947-49
Taugher, Claude, B, Marquette 1922
Taylor, Cliff, RB, Memphis State 1976
Taylor, Jim, B, Louisiana State 1958-66
Temp, Jim, E, Wisconsin 1957-60
Tenner, Bob, E, Minnesota 1935
Teteak, Deral, G, Wisconsin 1952-56
Thomas, Ike, CB, Bishop College 1972-73
Thomason, Bobby, B, Virginia Military 1951
Thompson, Arland, G, Baylor 1981
Thompson, Aundra, WR, East Texas State 1977-81
Thompson, Clarence (Tuffy), B, Minnesota 1939
Thompson, John, TE, Utah State 1979-81
Thurston, Fred (Fuzzy), G, Valparaiso 1959-67
Timberlake, George, C, USC 1955
Tinker, Gerald, WR, Kent State 1975
Tinsley, Pete, G, Georgia 1938-45
Toburen, Nelson, LB, Wichita State 1961-62
Tollefson, Chuck, G, Iowa 1944-46
Toner, Tom, LB, Idaho State 1973-77
Tonnemaker, Clayton, C, Minnesota 1950, 1953-54
Torkelson, Eric, RB, Connecticut 1974-81
Troup, Bill, QB, South Carolina 1980
Tullis, Walter, WR, Delaware State 1978-79
Tunnell, Emlen, B, Iowa 1959-61
Turner, Richard, DT, Oklahoma 1981
Turner, Wylie, DB, Angelo State 1979-80
Tuttle, Dick, E, Minnesota 1927
Twedell, Frank, G, Minnesota 1939

U

Uram, Andy, B, Minnesota 1938-43
Urban, Alex, E, South Carolina 1941, 1944-45
Usher, Eddie, Ed, B, Michigan 1922-24

V

Vairo, Dominic, E, Notre Dame 1935
Vandersea, Phil, B-LB, Massachusetts 1966, 1968-70
Van Dyke, Bruce, G, Missouri 1974-76
Van Every, Hal, B, Minnesota 1940-41
Vanoy, Vernon, DT, Kansas 1972
Van Sickle, Clyde, C, Arkansas 1932-33
Vant Hull, Fred, G, Minnesota 1942
Van Valkenburg, Pete, RB, Brigham Young 1974
Vataha, Randy, WR, Stanford 1977
Vereen, Carl, T, Georgia Tech 1957
Vegara, George, E, Notre Dame 1925
Vogds, Evan, G, Wisconsin 1948-49
Voss, Lloyd, T, Nebraska 1964-65
Voss, Walter (Tillie), E, Detroit 1924

W

Wagner, Buff, B, Northern Michigan 1921
Wagner, Steve, DB, Wisconsin 1976-79
Walker, Cleo, C-LB, Louisville 1970
Walker, Malcolm, C, Rice 1970
Walker, Randy, P, Northwestern Louisiana 1974
Walker, Val Joe, B, Southern Methodist 1953-56
Walsh, Ward, RB, Colorado 1972
Weatherwax, Jim, T, Cal State-Los Angeles 1966-69
Weaver, Gary, LB, Fresno State 1975-79
Webber, Howard (Dutch), E, Kansas State 1928
Webster, Tim, K, Arkansas 1971
Wehba, Ray, E, USC 1944
Weisgerber, Dick, B, Willamette 1938-40, 1942
Wellman, Mike, C, Kansas 1979-80
Wells, Don, E, Georgia 1946-49
Wells, Terry, RB, Southern Mississippi 1975
West, Pat, B, USC 1948
Wheeler, Lyle, E, Ripon 1921-23
Whitaker, Bill, DB, Missouri 1981
White, Gene, B, Georgia 1954
Whitehurst, David, QB, Furman 1977-81
Whittenton, Jess, B, Texas Western 1958-64
Widby, Ron, P, Tennessee 1972
Wildung, Dick, T, Minnesota 1946-51, 1953
Wilkins, Ted, E, Indiana 1925
Williams, A. D., E, Pacific 1959
Williams, Clarence, DE, Prairie View 1970-77
Williams, Delvin, RB, Kansas 1981
Williams, Dick, B, Wisconsin 1921
Williams, Howie, B, Howard 1962-63
Williams, Perry, RB, Purdue 1969-73
Williams, Travis, RB-KR, Arizona State 1967-70
Wilson, Ben, FB, USC 1967
Wilson, Faye (Mule), B, Texas A&M 1931
Wilson, Gene, E, Southern Methodist 1947-48
Wilson, John, B, Dubuque 1939
Wilson, Milt, T, Wisconsin Teachers 1921
Wimberly, Abner, E, Louisiana State 1950-52
Wingo, Rich, LB, Alabama 1979-81
Winkler, Francis, DE, Memphis State 1968-69
Winkler, Randy, G, Tarleton State 1971
Winslow, Paul, E, North Carolina College 1960
Winters, Arnie, T, No college 1941
Winther, Wimpy, C, Mississippi 1971
Withrow, Cal, C, Kentucky 1971-73
Witte, Earl, B, Gustavus Adolphus 1934
Wizbicki, Alex, B, Holy Cross 1950
Wood, Willie, DB, USC 1960-71
Woodin, Whitey, G, Marquette 1922-30
Wortman, Keith, G, Nebraska 1972-75
Wright, Steve, T, Alabama 1964-66
Wunsch, Harry, G, Notre Dame 1934

Y

Young, Bill, G, Ohio State 1929
Young, Glenn, B, Purdue 1956-57
Young Paul, C, Oklahoma 1933
Young, Steve, T, Colorado 1979

Z

Zarnas, Gust, G, Ohio State 1939-40
Zatkoff, Roger, LB, Michigan 1953-56
Zeller, Joe, G, Indiana 1932
Zimmerman, Don, WR, Northeastern Louisiana 1976
Zoll, Carl, G, No college 1921-22
Zoll, Dick, G, Indiana 1939
Zoll, Marty, G, No college 1921
Zuidmulder, Dave, B, St. Ambrose 1929-31
Zupek, Al, E, Lawrence 1946
Zuver, Merle, C, Nebraska 1930

HOUSTON OILERS

1959 K.S. (Bud) Adams, Jr., an oilman, announced Houston's entry into the American Football League, joining five other franchises—Dallas, Denver, Los Angeles, Minneapolis-St. Paul, and New York. The AFL was to begin play in 1960. The name "Oilers" was selected for the team by Adams "for sentimental and social reasons." John Breen was hired as Oilers' player personnel director. Rice University refused to allow professional football the use of its 70,000-seat stadium; it had been Adams's first choice. In the first AFL player draft, the Oilers made Billy Cannon, All-America halfback and Heisman Trophy winner from Louisiana State University, their first choice.

1960 The Oilers signed Cannon. A week later, however, they had to file suit to establish the validity of the contract because Cannon also signed with the Los Angeles Rams of the National Football League. Cannon then announced he wanted to play in Texas and the court eventually ruled he was free to join Houston. Lou Rymkus was named the Oilers' head coach and hired Wally Lemm to handle his defensive backfield. John Breen, searching for an experienced quarterback, decided on George Blanda, formerly of the Chicago Bears, and lured him out of a one-year retirement. "While he is not the greatest quarterback in the world in some departments, he really knows how to take a defense apart," said Breen. Adams leased Jeppesen Stadium, a high school facility, and spent $200,000 renovating it and increasing the seating capacity from 22,000 to 36,000. The team opened its first training camp at the University of Houston. The Oilers lost their first preseason game 27-10 to Dallas, but came back to beat Denver 42-3 before 18,500 in the home opener at Jeppesen. The Oilers went 10-4, scored 379 points, and clinched the AFL's Eastern Division title by beating Buffalo 31-23 in Houston.

1961 The Oilers won the first AFL championship 24-16 over the Los Angeles Chargers before 32,000 at Jeppesen Stadium, January 1. Cannon was named the game's most valuable player and Blanda completed 16 of 32 passes for 301 yards and three touchdowns. The winning players' share in the game was $1,016.42. Tight end Willard Dewveall, a former Southern Methodist University star, became the first player to jump leagues, playing out his option with the Chicago Bears and signing with Houston. Harris County voters passed a $22 million bond issue to finance a new domed stadium designated to be the home of the Oilers. Adams announced the team would train in Honolulu. Don Suman was named the club's new vice president and general manager. Lemm resigned as an assistant and entered private business. Six months later, after just one victory in the Oilers' first five starts, Lemm was rehired to replace Rymkus as head coach. The Oilers ran off 10 victories in a row, became the first pro team in history to score more than 500 points in a season, and won the AFL title for the second year in a row 10-3 over the new San Diego Chargers in California.

1962 Lemm resigned to become head coach of the St. Louis Cardinals of the NFL. Frank (Pop) Ivy was signed by Adams as his third head coach in three years. The owner also moved the training camp to Ellington Air Force Base, Texas. Blanda and running back Charlie Tolar both enjoyed big seasons. Blanda completed six touchdown passes in a 56-17 victory over the New York Titans, and Tolar finished with 1,012 yards. The Oilers went 11-3 and won their third consecutive Eastern Division title, crushing the Titans 44-10. But in the AFL title game, Houston lost for the first time, although it took an historic six-quarter, double-overtime 20-17 win by the

Billy Cannon makes a gain on the way to leading the AFL in rushing, 1961.

Dallas Texans to do it.

1963 Ivy signed a new two-year contract as head coach and general manager. The Oilers also outbid the NFL competition for their top draft choice, Danny Brabham, a linebacker from Arkansas. The Oilers trained at Colorado Springs, Colorado. The season started with a 24-13 loss to Oakland and got worse. The club suffered its first losing record, finishing 6-8, then tried to make up for it by drafting Texas All-America tackle Scott Appleton number one and signing Baylor quarterback Don Trull, the top future pick in a previous draft.

1964 The Oilers signed number-one draft choice Scott Appleton. The club began construction of a new training facility in Houston. Sammy Baugh was named backfield coach. Less than a month later, June 2, Adams relieved Ivy as head coach, replacing him with Baugh and naming Carroll Martin the new general manager. Cannon, once the club's most distinguished player, was traded to Oakland for three little-known players, Bob Jackson, Sonny Bishop,

and Dobie Craig. A 4-10 season ended with the final pro game in Jeppesen Stadium, a 34-15 Oilers' victory over Denver. Charley Hennigan, all-AFL wide receiver, established a professional record in that game, catching his one hundred and first pass. In still another coaching change, Baugh was relieved as head coach but stayed on to assist his successor, Hugh (Bones) Taylor. Rymkus also rejoined the staff as offensive line coach.

1965 The club announced it would not play in the Astrodome, Houston's new domed stadium, because of "an unrealistic lease agreement." A five-year lease was completed with Rice University for its 70,000-seat stadium. The Houston contract of tackle Ralph Neely was declared invalid by an Oklahoma City Federal Court after the University of Oklahoma All-America had signed with both the Oilers and the NFL Dallas Cowboys. The club made Tommy Nobis, All-America linebacker from Texas, its number-one draft choice, but eventually lost him to Atlanta. The Oilers finished their second straight 4-10 season with a 42-14 loss to Boston.

1966 Bud Adams appointed Don Klosterman the club's new executive vice president and general manager. Shortly afterward, it was announced the Hugh Taylor's contract was not renewed and that Wally Lemm was back as head coach again. Ernie Ladd, the Chargers' giant tackle, was signed by the Oilers. The league ruled that Willie Frazier and Pete Jaquess be awarded to San Diego as compensation. The Oilers finished 3-11, worst record in their history.

1967 In the first common draft involving the two leagues, the Oilers chose George Webster, the Michigan State All-America linebacker, number one. A month later, they signed him. Two of the stars of the early years in Houston, George Blanda and Charley Hennigan, were let go. Blanda was released, while Hennigan was traded to San Diego. The club announced still another new training camp site, this time at Schreiner Institute in Kerrville, Texas. The Oilers became the first team to go from the cellar to the division championship in one season, going 9-4-1 with 15 rookies on the squad to qualify for the AFL Championship Game.

1968 The Oakland Raiders ruined the New Year's celebrations in Texas, routing the Oilers 40-7 in the AFL championship game, January 1. Adams announced the team would move into the new Astrodome, after all, beginning with the 1968 season. The contract with Rice would be settled. After the players and owners settled their own controversial strike, the Oilers opened in the Astrodome by defeating Washington 9-3. The regular season started in the Dome, too, with Houston losing to Kansas City 26-21. Although 11 Oilers were named to various all-star teams, the club finished the season with a 7-7 record.

1969 George Webster was one of four AFL players named to the first combined all-pro team. Jim Norton, last of the original Oilers, retired and the club retired his jersey, number 43. Despite an up-and-down, 6-6-2 record, the team squeezed into the playoffs under the new wild card system, but lost to Oakland 56-7 as quarterback Daryle Lamonica threw six touchdown passes.

1970 Don Klosterman resigned as general manager to accept the same position with the Baltimore Colts. Quarterback Pete Beathard and cornerback Miller Farr were traded to St. Louis for quarterback Charley Johnson and cornerback Bob Atkins. Club veterans joined the NFL Players Association strike and were barred from training camp, June 30. The strike ended and the veterans reported August 3. In one of the most emotional games in the history of the franchise, the Oilers defeated the Dallas Cowboys for the first time, 37-21 in a preseason game. Lemm announced late in the season he would retire when it was over. The Oilers finished with a 3-10-1 record, losing 52-10 to Dallas in the final game. Doug Wilkerson, the club's top draft pick, was traded to San Diego for tight end Willie Frazier.

1971 Ed Hughes, backfield coach for the San Francisco 49ers, was named the sixth coach in Oilers' history. He was signed to a five-year contract. In a draft known for its quality quarterbacks, Houston selected Dan Pastorini of Santa Clara on the first round and Kansas State's Lynn Dickey on round three. Bob Brodhead was announced as the team's new general manager. He resigned after only one month on the job. John Breen, the first pro football employee ever hired by Bud Adams, was given back his old job as general manager. Before the season was over, offensive line coach Ernie Zwahlen and offensive backfield coach Walt Schlinkman were fired. Shortly thereafter, Bud Adams reported Hughes's five-year contract had been terminated by mutual settlement. Rice University coach Bill Peterson was signed to replace him.

1972 Bud Adams campaigned for and won the Super Bowl VIII (1974) game for the city of Houston. Quarterback Charley Johnson was traded to Denver for an undisclosed draft choice. Second-year quarterback Dickey injured his hip in an exhibition game and was out for the season. In October, linebacker Ron Pritchard and wide receiver Charlie Joiner were traded to Cincinnati for running backs Paul Robinson and Fred Willis. In still another deal, former all-pro linebacker George Webster was traded to Pittsburgh for wide receiver Dave Smith. Houston finished 1-13.

1973 The Oilers made John Matuszak, a 6-foot 7-inch, 282-pound defensive end from Tampa, the first selection in the entire NFL draft. Veteran coach and front office executive Sid Gillman was announced as the new executive vice president and general manager, replacing John Breen, who retired. All-pro safety Ken Houston and a draft choice were shipped to Washington in return for five Redskins players. After Peterson's two-year record reached 1-18, he was fired and Gillman assumed a dual role of coach and general manager. The Oilers finished their second straight 1-13 season with a 27-14 loss to Cincinnati.

1974 Sid Gillman announced his decision to stay at least one more season as coach and general manager. O.A. (Bum) Phillips was hired as the club's new defensive coordinator. The Oilers moved their training camp to Sam Houston State College in Huntsville, Texas. Running back Vic Washington was acquired from San Francisco for a first-round draft choice in 1976 and a third-round pick in 1977. Matuszak attempted to jump his contract to sign with Houston of the World Football League. He eventually was put on the Oilers' inactive list and was traded, along with a number-three draft choice, to Kansas City for defensive tackle Curley Culp and a number-one draft pick. Culp became an immediate force in Houston's new three-four defensive alignment and the Oilers won four in a row and jump six of their last eight to finish 7-7, their best record since 1969.

1975 Phillips was named head coach by Gillman, who said he would remain as general manager, January 25. A few weeks later, Gillman had to give up that job, too. The decision was announced by mutual consent of Gillman and Adams. Phillips was given the added duties of general manager. The Oilers started fast with five wins in their first six starts, including their first ever over an NFC team, 13-10 against Washington. Pittsburgh stopped the streak 24-17 on November 10, but the Oilers came back to beat Miami 20-19 as Billy (White Shoes) Johnson tied an NFL record for touchdowns in one season on kick returns. He had three on punts and one on a kickoff, including 83 yards with a punt in the victory over the Dolphins. The club finished the season with a 10-4 record, setting a new Houston home attendance record (48,000 average) in seven home games, but missed the playoffs.

1976 Johnson was named the most valuable player in the Pro Bowl game in New Orleans after setting a record for kick returns and sprinting 90 yards for one touchdown. After four wins in the first five games, the Oilers suffered a series of injuries and lost six in a row. They staggered home with a 5-9 record.

1977 The Oilers got off to a strong start and, after a 27-10 victory over the Steelers on October 9, led the AFC Central Division. Pastorini was injured in the Pittsburgh game, and the Oilers had to go with veteran John Hadl. By the time Pastorini had fully recovered, Houston had dropped three straight. Celebrating Pastorini's return, the Oilers blasted Chicago 47-0 on November 6, and then won four of their last five to finish 8-6 for the season.

1978 The Oilers obtained the player they thought would lead them to the top by trading tight end Jimmie Giles and four draft choices to Tampa Bay for the right to make the number-one draft pick, which they used for Heisman Trophy-winning running back Earl Campbell. The Oilers also acquired Pro Bowl tackle Leon Gray from New England. Houston also drafted quarterback Gifford Nielsen and wide receiver Mike Renfro. On October 23, the Oilers defeated the Steelers 24-17 for their first victory ever in a Monday night game. Four weeks later, the Oilers won again on Monday night, 35-30 over Miami, as Campbell ran for 199 yards and four touchdowns. Houston clinched a wild card berth in the playoffs on December 10 with a 17-12 victory over New Orleans. The wild card game was a rematch of the earlier Monday night game with Miami, and the Oilers again defeated the Dolphins, 17-9, behind a 20-for-29 passing performance by Pastorini. On December 31, Pastorini did it again, leading the Oilers to a 31-14 victory over New England, which had just lost head coach Chuck Fairbanks.

1979 Houston's Cinderella season came to a close on January 7, as the Steelers scored 17 points in a two-minute span and won the AFC Championship Game 34-5. The Oilers were put into a hole early in their 1979 quest for the division championship: Pittsburgh defeated them 38-7 on September 9. But Houston won 9 of its next 11 games to carry a 10-3 record into December. Despite a 20-17 Monday night victory over Pittsburgh on December 10, the Oilers again finished second to the Steelers, with an 11-5 record. Campbell tied NFL records by rushing for 100 or more yards 11 times in the season, 7 in succession, and by scoring 19 rushing touchdowns. In the first playoff game in Houston since 1961, the Oilers overcame injuries to Campbell and Pastorini to defeat Denver 13-7 on December 23 in the wild card game. Again without Campbell and Pastorini, the Oilers shut down the NFL's best passing attack with four interceptions by Vernon Perry in a 17-14 win over San Diego in the divisional playoffs.

George Webster closes in for a sack, 1968.

1980 In a rematch of the 1978 AFC Championship Game, the Oilers lost 27-13 to the Steelers on January 6. The Oilers traded Pastorini for Oakland quarterback Ken Stabler on May 15. Houston started the 1980 season 3-3, including a 31-17 loss to Pittsburgh in the opener, but on October 14 they turned their year around by obtaining tight end Dave Casper from Oakland for three draft choices. Utilizing a two-tight-end offense, the Oilers went 8-2 and defeated the Steelers 6-0 on December 4. Campbell gained 1,934 yards rushing, the second highest total in NFL history. Despite having the same record as the Browns, the Oilers qualified for the playoffs as an AFC wild card team. In the first round of the playoffs the Raiders shut down Stabler and Campbell and won 27-7 on December 28. It was the third consecutive year that the Oilers had been defeated by the eventual Super Bowl champs. Three days later, Phillips was relieved as head coach.

1981 On January 2, former defensive coordinator Ed Biles was named head coach and Ladd K. Herzeg became executive vice president-general manager. Biles discarded Phillips's two-tight-end system and put Rob Carpenter in the backfield with Campbell. After a slow start, Biles returned blocking back Tim Wilson as Campbell's backfield mate and Campbell responded with 182 yards against the Bengals and 186 against Seattle. Carpenter was traded to the New York Giants. Campbell didn't run for 100 yards in any other game the rest of the season and the Oilers finished 7-9. Late in the season, Biles replaced Stabler with Nielsen. Campbell, who finished the season with 1,376 yards, led the AFC in rushing for the fourth straight year. He made the AFC Pro Bowl team along with linebacker Robert Brazile, tackle Leon Gray, and kick returner Carl Roaches.

MEMBERS OF HALL OF FAME:
George Blanda

OILERS RECORD, 1960-81

Year	Won	Lost	Tied	Pct.	Pts.	OP
1960‡	10	4	0	.714	379	285
1961‡	10	3	1	.769	513	242
1962§	11	3	0	.786	387	270
1963	6	8	0	.429	302	372
1964	4	10	0	.286	310	355
1965	4	10	0	.286	298	429
1966	3	11	0	.214	335	396
1967§	9	4	1	.692	258	199
1968	7	7	0	.500	303	248
1969	6	6	2	.500	278	279
1970	3	10	1	.231	217	352
1971	4	9	1	.308	251	330
1972	1	13	0	.071	164	380
1973	1	13	0	.071	199	447
1974	7	7	0	.500	236	282
1975	10	4	0	.714	293	226
1976	5	9	0	.357	222	273
1977	8	6	0	.571	299	230
1978*	10	6	0	.625	283	298
1979*	11	5	0	.688	362	331
1980*	11	5	0	.688	295	251
1981	7	9	0	.438	281	355
22 Years	148	162	6	.478	6,465	6,830

‡*AFL Champion*
§*AFL Eastern Division Champion*
AFC Wild Card Qualifier for Playoffs

RECORD HOLDERS

Rushing (Yards)	Earl Campbell, 1980	1,934
Passing (Pct.)	Ken Stabler, 1980	64.1
Passing (Yards)	George Blanda, 1961	3,330
Passing (TDs)	George Blanda, 1961	36
Receiving (No.)	Charley Hennigan, 1964	101
Receiving (Yards)	Charley Hennigan, 1961	1,746
Interceptions (No.)	Fred Glick, 1963	12
	Mike Reinfeldt, 1979	12
Punting (Avg.)	Jim Norton, 1965	44.2
Punt Ret. (Avg.)	Billy Johnson, 1977	15.4
Kickoff Ret. (Avg.)	Ken Hall, 1960	31.3
Touchdowns (Total)	Earl Campbell, 1979	19
Field Goals Made	Toni Fritsch, 1979	21
Points (No.)	George Blanda, 1960	115

COACHING HISTORY

1960-61	Lou Rymkus*		11- 7-1
1961	Wally Lemm		9- 0-0
1962-63	Frank (Pop) Ivy		17-11-0
1964	Sammy Baugh		4-10-0
1965	Hugh (Bones) Taylor		4-10-0
1966-70	Wally Lemm		28-38-4
1971	Ed Hughes		4- 9-1
1972-73	Bill Peterson**		1-18-0
1973-74	Sid Gillman		8-15-0
1975-80	O. A. (Bum) Phillips		55-35-0
1981	Ed Biles		7- 9-0

Replaced after five games in 1961
**Replaced after five games in 1973*

FIRST PLAYER SELECTED

1960	Billy Cannon, RB, Louisiana State	
1961	Mike Ditka, E, Pittsburgh	
1962	Ray Jacobs, DT, Howard Payne	
1963	Danny Brabham, LB, Arkansas	
1964	Scott Appleton, DT, Texas	
1965	Lawrence Elkins, WR, Baylor	
1966	Tommy Nobis, LB, Texas	
1967	George Webster, LB, Michigan State	
1968	Mac Haik, WR (2), Mississippi	
1969	Ron Pritchard, LB, Arizona State	
1970	Doug Wilkerson, G, North Carolina Central	
1971	Dan Pastorini, QB, Santa Clara	
1972	Greg Sampson, DE, Stanford	
1973	John Matuszak, DE, Tampa	
1974	Steve Manstedt, LB (4), Nebraska	
1975	Robert Brazile, LB, Jackson State	
1976	Mike Barber, TE (2), Louisiana Tech	
1977	Morris Towns, T, Missouri	
1978	Earl Campbell, RB, Texas	
1979	Mike Stensrud, DE (2), Iowa State	
1980	Angelo Fields, T (2), Michigan State	
1981	Michael Holston, WR (3), Morgan State	
1982	Mike Munchak, G, Penn State	

Earl Campbell picks up yardage against Tampa Bay en route to his third consecutive rushing title, 1980.

HOUSTON OILERS, 1960-81

Aldridge, Allen, DE, Prairie View	1971-72
Alexander, Willie, CB, Alcorn State	1971-79
Allen, Dalva, DE, Houston	1960-61
Allen, George, DT, West Texas State	1966-67
Alston, Mack, TE, Maryland-Eastern Shore	1973-76
Amundson, George, RB, Iowa State	1973-74
Anderson, Billy Guy, QB, Tulsa	1967
Appleton, Scott, DT, Texas	1964-66
Armstrong, Adger, RB, Texas A&M	1980-81
Atchason, Jack, TE, Western Illinois	1960
Atkins, Bob, CB, Grambling	1970-75
Autry, Hank, C, Southern Mississippi	1969-70

B

Babb, Gene, LB, Stephen F. Austin	1962-63
Bailey, Harold, WR, Oklahoma State	1981
Baker, Jesse, DT, Jacksonville State	1979-81
Baker, Johnny, LB, Mississippi State	1963-66
Baker, Ed, QB, Lafayette	1972
Baker, Melvin, WR, Texas Southern	1972
Banfield, Tony, CB, Oklahoma State	1960-65
Barber, Mike, Louisiana Tech	1976-81
Barnes, Pete, LB, Southern U.	1967-68
Bass, Glenn, WR, East Carolina	1967-68
Baumgartner, Steve, DE, Purdue	1977-79
Beams, Byron, DT, Notre Dame	1961
Beathard, Pete, QB, USC	1967-69
Beck, Braden, K, Stanford	1971
Beirne, Jim, WR, Purdue	1968-73, 1975-76
Belotti, George, C, USC	1960-61
Benson, Duane, LB, Hamline	1974-76
Bergey, Bruce, DT, UCLA	1971
Bethea, Elvin, DE, North Carolina A&T	1968-81

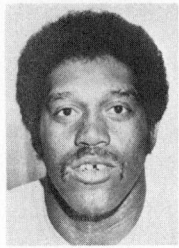
Elvin Bethea

Gregg Bingham

Robert Brazile

Ken Burrough

Don Floyd

Fred Glick

Hoyle Granger

Beverly, David, P, Auburn 1974
Billings ey, Ron, DT, Wyoming. 1971-72
Bingham, Gregg, LB, Purdue 1973-81
Bishop, Sonny, G, Fresno State 1964-69
Blahak, Joe, S, Nebraska 1973
Blanda, George, QB-K, Kentucky 1960-66
Blanks, Sid, RB, Texas A&I 1964-68
Botchan, Ron, LB, Occidental 1961
Boyette, Garland, LB, Grambling. 1966-72
Brabham, Danny, LB, Arkansas 1963-67
Bradshaw, Craig, QB, Utah State 1980
Brazile, Robert, LB, Jackson State. 1975-81
Brezina, Bobby, RB, Houston 1963
Broadnax, Jerry, TE, Southern U. 1974
Brooks, Billy, WR, Oklahoma 1981
Brooks, Leo, DT, Texas. 1970-72
Brown, Don, RB, Houston 1960
Burke, Ed, G, Notre Dame 1964
Burrell, Ode, RB, Mississippi State 1964-69
Burrough, Ken, WR, Texas Southern 1971-81
Burton, Al, DE, Bethune-Cookman 1976
Butler, Jim, TE, Tulsa 1972
Butler, Skip, K, Texas-Arlington 1972-76

C

Campbell, Earl, RB, Texas. 1978-81
Campbell, Woody, RB, Northwestern 1967-71
Cannon, Billy, RB, Louisiana State 1960-63
Carpenter, Rob, RB, Miami, Ohio 1977-81
Carr, Levert, T, North Central State. 1972-73
Carrell, John, LB, Texas Tech 1966
Carrington, Ed, TE, Virginia 1969
Carroll, Ronnie, G, Sam Houston State 1974-75
Carson, Johnny, TE, Georgia 1960
Carter, David, G-C, Western Kentucky 1977-81
Carwell, Larry, CB, Iowa State 1967-68
Casper, Dave, TE, Notre Dame 1980-81
Caster, Rich, WR, Jackson State 1978-80
Caveness, Ron, LB, Arkansas 1966-68
Chancelor, Ken, C, Houston 1964
Charles, John, S, Purdue 1971-74
Cheek, Richard, G, Auburn. 1972
Cheeks, B. W., RB, Texas Southern 1965
Cindrich, Ralph, LB, Pittsburgh 1973-75
Clark, Boobie, RB, Bethune-Cookman 1979-80
Cline, Doug, LB, Clemson 1960-66
Cochrane, Kelly, QB, Miami 1972
Cole, Linzy, WR, Texas Christian 1971
Coleman, Ronnie, RB, Alabama A&M 1974-81
Compton, Dick, WR, McMurray 1965
Corker, John, LB, Oklahoma State 1980-81
Cotney, Mark, S, Cameron State 1975
Cowlings, Al, LB, USC 1973-74
Craig, Dobie, WR, Howard Payne 1964
Croyle, Phil, LB, California. 1971-73
Culp, Curley, G, Arizona State 1974-80
Culpepper, Ed, DT, Alabama 1962-63
Cunningham, Dick, LB, Arkansas 1973
Currier, Bill, DB, South Carolina 1977-79
Curry, Bill, C, Georgia Tech. 1973
Cutsinger, Gary, DE, Oklahoma State 1962-68

D

Darby, Al, WR, Florida 1976
Davidson, Greg, C, North Texas State. 1980-81
Davidson, Pete, WR, Citadel. 1960
Davis, Bob, QB, Virginia 1967-69
Davis, Donnie, TE, Southern U. 1970
Davis, Marvin, LB, Southern U. 1974
Dawkins, Joe, RB, Wisconsin. 1970-71, 1976
Dawson, Rhett, WR, Florida State 1972
Dean, Jimmy, DE, Texas A&M 1978
Dempsey, Tom, K, Palomar JC 1977
Dewveall, Willard, TE, Southern Methodist 1961-64
Dickey, Lynn, QB, Kansas State 1971-75
Dickenson, Bo, RB, Southern Mississippi. 1963
Dirden, Johnnie, WR, Sam Houston 1978
Domres, Tom, DT, Wisconsin 1968-71
Dorris, Andy, DE, New Mexico State 1977-81
Douglas, John, CB, Texas Southern 1969-70
Drungo, Elbert, T, Tennessee State 1969-77
Dukes, Mike, LB, Clemson 1960-63

Duncan, Brian, RB, Southern Methodist. 1978
Duniven, Tom, QB, Texas Tech 1977-78

E

Eaglin, Larry, CB, Stephen F. Austin 1973
Edwards, Emmett, WR, Kansas 1975
Elkins, Lawrence, WR, Baylor 1965-68
Ellender, Richard, WR, McNeese State 1979
Evans, Norm, T, Texas Christian 1965
Evans, Robert, E, Texas A&M 1965
Eyre, Nick, T, Brigham Young 1981

Charley Hennigan, the Oilers' leading receiver, 1961.

F

Fairley, Leonard, S, Alcorn, State. 1974
Farr, Miller, CB, Wichita State 1967-69
Fanning, Stan, DE, Idaho 1968
Fanucci, Mike, DE, Arizona State 1973
Faulkner, Staley, T, Texas. 1964
Ferguson, Gene, T, Norfolk State 1971-72
Fields, Angelo, T, Michigan State. 1980-81
Fisher, Ed, G, Arizona State 1974-81
Floyd, Don, DE, Texas Christian 1960-68
Foote, James, QB, Delaware Valley 1974-76
Foster, Eddie, WR, Houston 1977-78

Fowler, Jerry, G, Northwestern Louisiana 1964
Frazier, Charley, WR, Texas Southern 1962-68
Frazier, Wayne, C, Auburn. 1965
Frazier, Willie, TE, Arkansas-Pine Bluff ... 1964-65, 1971, 1975
Freelon, Solomon, G, Grambling 1972-74
Frey, Dick, G, Texas A&M 1961
Fritsch, Toni, K, No college 1977-81
Frongillo, John, C, Baylor 1962-66
Funchess, Tommy, T, Jackson State 1971-73

G

Garrison, Gary, WR, San Diego State 1977
Gerela, Roy, K, New Mexico State 1969-70
Germany, Willie, S, Morgan State 1975
Giles, Jimmie, TE, Alcorn State 1977
Glick, Freddy, S, Colorado State 1961-66
Goode, Tom, C, Mississippi State 1962-65
Goodman, Brian, G, UCLA 1973-74
Gordon, Bobby, S, Tennessee 1960
Granger, Hoyle, RB, Mississippi State 1966-70, 1972
Grant, Wes, DT, UCLA 1973
Gray, Ken, G, Howard Payne 1970
Gray, Leon, T, Jackson State 1979-81
Greaves, Gary, DE, Miami 1960
Green, Dave, P, Ohio U. 1973
Gresham, Bob, RB, West Virginia 1973-74
Groman, Bill, WR, Heidelberg 1960-62, 1966
Groth, Jeff, WR, Bowling Green 1979-80
Gruneisen, Sam, C, Villanova. 1973
Guidry, Paul, LB, McNeese State 1973
Guy, Buzz, G, Duke 1961
Guzik, John, LB, Pittsburgh 1961

H

Hadl, John, QB, Kansas 1976-77
Haik, Mac, WR, Mississippi 1968-71
Hall, Ken, RB, Texas A&M 1960-61
Hardeman, Don, RB, Texas A&I 1975-77
Harris, Larry, G, Oklahoma State 1978
Hartwig, Carter, DB, USC 1979-81
Harvey, Claude, LB, Prairie View 1970-71
Harvey, Jim, G, Mississippi. 1972
Havig, Dennis, G, Colorado 1976
Hawkins, Nat, WR, Nevada-Las Vegas 1975
Hayes, Jim, DT, Jackson State 1965-66
Hayman, Conway, G, Delaware 1975-80
Haymond, Alvin, S-KR, Southern U. 1973
Helluin, Jerry, DT, Tulane 1960
Henderson, Thomas, LB, Langston, Oklahoma. 1980
Hennigan, Charley, WR, Northwestern Louisiana ... 1960-66
Herchman, Bill, DT, Texas Tech 1962
Hicks, W. K., CB, Texas Southern. 1964-69
Highsmith, Walt, T, Florida A&M 1972
Hines, Glen Ray, T, Arkansas 1966-70
Hinton, Eddie, WR, Oklahoma 1973
Hoaglin, Fred, C, Pittsburgh 1974-75
Hoffman, Dalton, RB, Baylor. 1964
Holigan, Henry, RB, Bishop, Texas 1963
Holmes, Pat, DE, Texas Tech 1966-72
Holmes, Robert, RB, Southern U. 1971-72, 1975
Holston, Michael, WR, Morgan State. 1981
Hopkins, Andy, RB, Stephen F. Austin 1971
Hopkins, Roy, RB, Texas Southern 1967-71
Houston, Ken, S, Prairie View 1967-72
Humphrey, Buddy, QB, Baylor 1966
Hunt, Calvin, C, Baylor. 1972-73
Hunt, Daryl, LB, Oklahoma 1979-81
Hunt, Kevin, T, Doane, Nebraska 1973-77
Husmann, Ed, DT, Nebraska 1961-65

J

Jackson, Bobby, RB, New Mexico State. 1964
Jacobs, Ray, DT, Howard Payne 1963
Jamison, Al, T, Colgate 1960-62
Jancik, Bobby, S, Lamar U. 1962-67
Jaquess, Pete, CB, Eastern New Mexico 1964-65
Jefferson, Charles, CB, McNeese State 1979
Jenkins, Al, G, Tulsa 1973
Johns, Pete, S, Tulane 1967-69
Johnson, Al, S, Cincinnati 1972-78
Johnson, Benny, CB, J. C. Smith 1970-73
Johnson, Billy (White Shoes), WR-KR, Widener. 1974-80

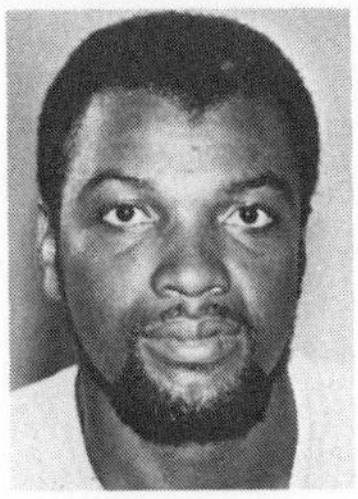
Leon Gray

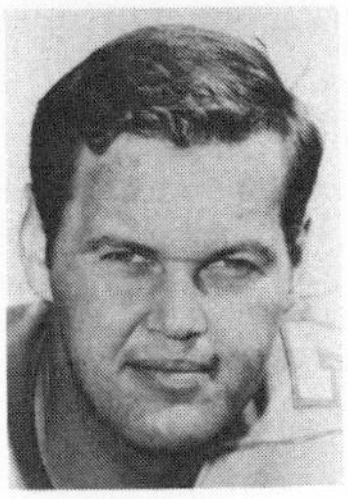
Pat Holmes

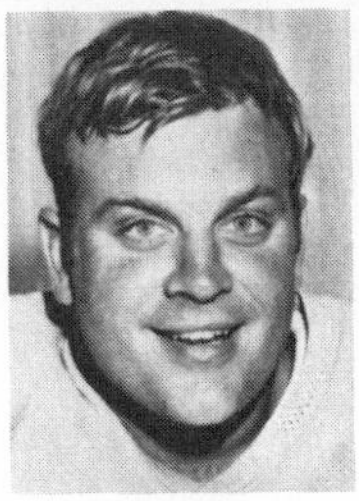
Carl Mauck

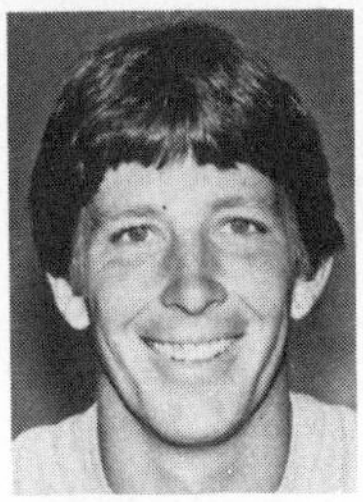
Gifford Nielsen

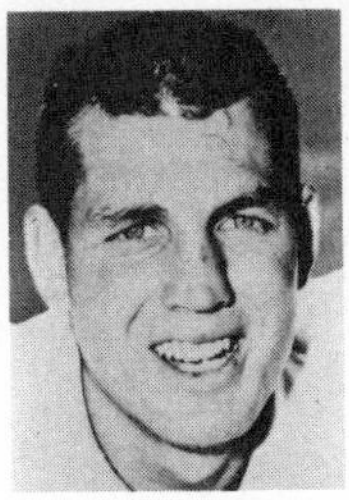
Jim Norton

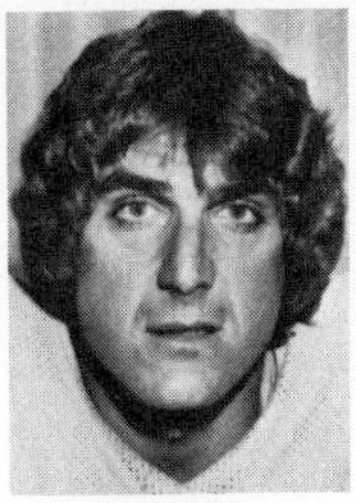
Dan Pastorini

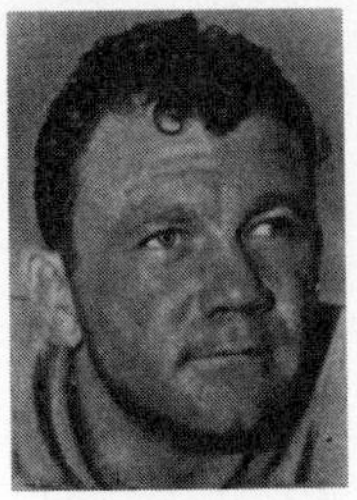
Charley Tolar

Johnson, Charley, QB, New Mexico State 1970-71
Johnson, John Henry, RB, Arizona State 1966
Johnson, Rich, RB, Illinois 1969
Johnston, Mark, CB, Northwestern 1960-63
Joiner, Charlie, WR, Grambling 1969-72
Jolley, Lewis, RB, North Carolina 1972-73
Jones, Gene, CB, Rice 1961
Jones, Harris, G, J. C. Smith 1973-74
Jones, Spike, P, Georgia 1970
Jones, Willie, DE, Kansas State 1967

K

Kay, Bill, DB, Purdue 1981
Kelly, Bob, DT, New Mexico State 1961-63
Kendall, Chuck, S, UCLA 1960
Kennard, Ken, NT-DT, Angelo State 1977-81
Kerbow, Randy, WR, Rice 1963-64
Kinderman, Keith, RB, Florida State 1965
Kiner, Steve, LB, Tennessee 1974-78
King, Claude, RB, Houston 1961
King, Kenny, RB, Oklahoma 1979
Kinney, George, DE, Wylie 1965
Kirk, Ernest, DE, Howard Payne 1977
Klotz, Jack, T, Widener 1964
Knoff, Kurt, DB, Kansas 1977-78

L

Ladd, Ernie, DT, Grambling 1966
Lanphear, Dan, DE, Wisconsin 1960-62
Laraway, Jack, LB, Purdue 1961
Lee, Jacky, QB, Cincinnati 1960-63, 1966-67
Ledbetter, Monte, WR, Northwestern Louisiana 1967
LeMoine, Jim, G, Utah State 1968-69
LeVias, Jerry, WR, Southern Methodist 1969-70
Lewis, Jess, LB, Oregon State 1970
Lewis, Richard, LB, Portland State 1972
Little, John, DT, Oklahoma State 1975-76
Lou, Ron, C, Arizona State 1972-73; 1976
Lumpkin, Ron, CB, Arizona State 1975

M

Majors, Joe, DB, Florida State 1960
Maples, Bobby, C, Baylor 1965-70
Marcol, Chester, K, Hillsdale 1980
Marcontell, Ed, G, Lamar U. 1967
Marshall, Rich, DT, Stephen F. Austin 1967-68
Matuszak, John, DT, Tampa 1973
Mauck, Carl, C, Southern Illinois 1975-81
Maxwell, Tommy, S, Texas A&M 1974
Mayes, Ben, DT, Drake 1969
Mayo, Ron, TE, Morgan State 1973
McCanless, Jim, G, Clemson 1960
McCollum, Bubba, DT, Kentucky 1974
McConnell, Brian, LB, Michigan State 1973
McDaniel, Ed (Wahoo), LB, Oklahoma 1960
McDole, Ron, DE, Nebraska 1962
McFadin, Bud, DT, Texas 1964-65
McLeod, Bob, TE, Abilene Christian 1961-65
McNeil, Clifton, WR, Grambling 1973
Meredith, Dudley, DT, Lamar U. 1963, 1968
Merkens, Guido, WR-S, Sam Houston State 1978-80
Meyer, John, LB, Notre Dame 1966-67
Michael, Rich, T, Ohio State 1960-63, 1965-66
Miller, Bill, DT, New Mexico Highlands 1962
Miller, Ralph, G, Alabama State 1972-73
Milstead, Charley, QB, Texas A&M 1960-61
Mitchell, Leroy, CB, Texas Southern 1969-70
Montgomery, Mike, WR, Kansas State 1974
Moore, Zeke, CB, Lincoln 1967-77
Morris, Dennit, LB, Oklahoma 1960-61
Morrison, Ron, T, New Mexico 1960
Moseley, Mark, K, Stephen F. Austin 1971-72
Murdock, Guy, C, Michigan 1972
Murphy, Mike, LB, Southwest Missouri State 1979
Musgrove, Spain, T, Utah State 1970

N

Naponic, Bob, QB, Illinois 1970
Nelson, Benny, S, Alabama 1964
Nery, Ron, DE, Kansas State 1963
Nicholson, Oliver, LB, Texas Southern 1975
Nielsen, Gifford, QB, Brigham Young 1978-81
Nix, Kent, QB, Texas Christian 1972
Norton, Jim, S, Idaho 1960-68

O

Odom, Sammy, LB, Northwestern Louisiana 1964
Olerich, Dave, LB, San Francisco 1971
Onesti, Larry, LB, Northwestern 1962-65
Owens, Joe, DE, Alcorn State 1976

P

Parker, Willie, DT, Arkansas-Pine Bluff 1967-70
Parks, Billy, WR, Long Beach State 1973-75
Parks, Dave, WR, Texas Tech 1973
Parrish, Bernie, CB, Florida 1966
Parsley, Cliff, P, Oklahoma State 1977-81
Pastorini, Dan, QB-P, Santa Clara 1971-79
Peacock, Johnny, S, Houston 1969-70
Perkins, Willis, G, Texas Southern 1961-63
Perlo, Phil, G, Maryland 1960
Perry, Vernon, S, Jackson State 1979-81
Pitts, Hugh, C, Texas Christian 1960
Poole, Bob, TE, Clemson 1966-67
Poole, Larry, RB, Kent State 1978
Post, Dickie, RB, Houston 1971
Pritchard, Ron, LB, Arizona State 1969-72

Q

Queen, Jeff, TE, Morgan State 1974
Quinn, Steve, C, Notre Dame 1968

R

Randall, Tom, G, Iowa State 1979
Reaves, John, QB, Florida 1981
Reed, Alvin, TE, Prairie View 1967-72
Reed, Leo, G, Colorado State 1961
Regner, Tom, G, Notre Dame 1967-72
Reihner, George, G, Penn State 1977-79
Reinfeldt, Mike, S, Wisconsin-Milwaukee 1976-81
Renfro, Mike, WR, Texas Christian 1978-81
Rhome, Jerry, QB, Tulsa 1970
Rice, Andy, DT, Texas Southern 1967
Rice, Floyd, LB, Alcorn State 1971-73
Rice, George, DT, Louisiana State 1966-70
Richardson, Mike, RB, Southern Methodist 1969-71
Rieves, Charles, LB, Houston 1964
Riley, Avon, LB, UCLA 1981
Roaches, Carl, WR-KR, Texas A&M 1980-81
Roberts, Guy, LB, Maryland 1972-75
Robertson, Bob, T, Illinois 1968
Robinson, Paul, RB, Arizona 1972-73
Rodgers, Willie, RB, Kentucky State 1972-75
Rossovich, Tim, LB, USC 1976
Rucker, Conrad, TE, Southern U. 1978-79
Rudolph, Council, DE, Kentucky State 1972
Rushing, Marion, LB, Southern Illinois 1968

S

Sampson, Greg, T, Stanford 1972-78
Saul, Ron, G, Michigan State 1970-75
Sawyer, John, TE, Southern Mississippi 1975-76
Schmidt, Bob, C, Minnesota 1961-63
Schuhmacher, John, G, USC 1978-81
Severson, Jeff, S, Long Beach State 1973-74
Shirkey, George, DT, Stephen F. Austin 1960-61
Simerson, John, G, Purdue 1960
Simon, Bobby, G, Grambling 1976
Simonsen, Todd, T, South Dakota State 1976
Skaugstad, Daryle, NT, California 1981
Sledge, Leroy, RB, Bakersfield JC 1971
Smiley, Tom, RB, Lamar U. 1970
Smith, Bob, S, Miami, Ohio 1968
Smith, Bubba, DE, Michigan State 1975-76
Smith, Dave, RB, Ripon 1960-64
Smith, Dave, WR, Indiana, Pennsylvania 1972
Smith, Sid, C, USC 1974
Smith, Tim, WR, Nebraska 1980-81
Smith, Tody, DE, USC 1973-76
Sowells, Rich, DB, Alcorn State 1977
Spence, Julian, S, Sam Houston State 1960-61
Spikes, Jack, RB, Texas Christian 1965
Stabler, Ken, QB, Alabama 1980-81
Stemrick, Greg, CB, Colorado State 1975-81
Stensrud, Mike, DE, Iowa State 1979-81
Stith, Carel, DT, Nebraska 1967-69
Stoepel, Terry, T, Tulsa 1970
Stone, Donnie, RB, Arkansas 1966
Slotter, Rich, LB, Houston 1968
Strahan, Art, DE, Texas Southern 1965
Stringer, Art, LB, Ball State 1977-81
Sturm, Jerry, C, Illinois 1971
Suci, Bob, S, Michigan State 1962
Suggs, Walt, T, Mississippi State 1962-71
Sutton, Mickey, S, Auburn 1966
Swatland, Dick, G, Notre Dame 1968

T

Talamini, Bob, G, Kentucky 1960-67
Tatum, Jack, S, Ohio State 1980
Taylor, Altie, RB, Utah State 1976
Taylor, Lionel, WR, New Mexico Highlands 1967-68
Thomas, Bill, RB, Boston College 1973
Thomas, Earl, WR, Houston 1976
Thomas, Lee, DE, Jackson State 1975
Thomaselli, Rich, RB, West Virginia Wesleyan 1981
Thompson, Ted, LB, Southern Methodist 1975-81
Tilleman, Mike, DT, Montana 1971-72
Tobin, Bill, RB, Missouri 1963
Tolar, Charley, RB, Northwestern Louisiana 1960-66
Tolbert, Jim, CB, Lincoln 1972
Towns, Morris, G-T, Missouri 1977-81
Trammell, Allen, S, Florida 1966
Trask, Orville, DT, Rice 1960-61
Trull, Don, QB, Baylor 1964-69
Tullis, Willie, QB-KR, Troy State 1981

U

Underwood, Olen, LB, Texas 1966-70

V

Vanoy, Vernon, DT, Kansas 1973
Vittz, Theo, CB, USC 1966
Voight, Mike, RB, North Carolina 1977

W

Wainscott, Loyd, LB, Texas 1969-70
Walker, Wayne, K, Northwestern Louisiana 1968
Wallner, Fred, G, Notre Dame 1960
Walsh, Ward, RB, Colorado 1971-72
Walton, Sam, T, East Texas State 1971
Washington, Ted, LB, Mississippi Valley 1973-81
Washington, Vic, RB, Wyoming 1974
Watson, Ed, LB, Grambling 1969
Webster, George, LB, Michigan State 1967-72
Wegener, Bucky, DT, Missouri 1962-63
Weger, Mike, S, Bowling Green 1976-77
Weir, Sammy, WR, Arkansas State 1965
Wells, Robert, T, J. C. Smith 1972
Wells, Terry, RB, Southern Mississippi 1974
Wharton, Hogan, G, Houston 1960-63
White, Bob, RB, Ohio State 1960
White, Jim, DE, Colorado State 1974-75
White, John, TE, Texas Southern 1960-61
Whittington, C. L., S, Prairie View 1974-78
Wilkerson, Doug, G, North Carolina Central 1970
Williams, Maxie, G, Southeastern Louisiana 1965
Williams, Sam, CB, New Mexico Highlands 1976
Willis, Fred, RB, Boston College 1972-77
Wilson, J. C., CB, Pittsburgh 1978-81
Wilson, Tim, RB, Maryland 1977-81
Wisener, Gary, CB, Baylor 1961
Witcher, Al, S, Baylor 1960
Wittenborn, John, G, Southeast Missouri State 1964-68
Woods, Glenn, DT, Prairie View 1969
Woods, Robert, WR, Grambling 1978
Wright, Elmo, WR, Houston 1975
Wyatt, Alvin, CB, Bethune-Cookman 1973

Y

Yeats, James, TE, Florida 1960
Young, Bob, G, Howard Payne 1971, 1980
Young, James, DE, Texas Southern 1977-79

Z

Zaeske, Paul, WR, North Park College 1969-70

KANSAS CITY CHIEFS

1959 Unsuccessful in his attempts to acquire a National Football League franchise for Dallas, millionaire Lamar Hunt founded and organized the American Football League with six original cities —New York, Houston, Denver, Los Angeles, Minneapolis, and Hunt's home, Dallas. Buffalo and Boston were added and Oakland replaced Minneapolis. "Before there was a player, coach, or general manager in the league, there was Lamar Hunt," was the way Boston's Billy Sullivan put it. "Hunt was the cornerstone, the integrity of the league. Without him, there would have been no AFL." Not long after the Dallas Texans went into business, the National Football League announced it would establish a club in Dallas to compete with the new league. The other Dallas franchise was awarded to Clint Murchison, Jr. and Bedford Wynne, both oil millionaires. Hunt hired an unknown assistant at the University of Miami named Hank Stram as his head coach. A self-styled disciplinarian, Stram was a short barrel-chested man who said, "Show me a good loser, and I'll show you a loser—period."

1960 For their inaugural season in the Cotton Bowl, the Texans had a strong home-state identity. The quarterback was Frank (Cotton) Davidson, an All-America from Baylor. Fullback Jack Spikes had been an outstanding player at Texas Christian, and Abner Haynes had played at North Texas State. After winning five straight preseason games, the Texans drew 51,000 people for the final preseason game against Houston, a 42-3 victory. Haynes led the new league in rushing with 875 yards and touchdowns with nine. The Texans had a flashy, high-scoring club, and only three close losses kept them from challenging for the division championship. A variety of promotional ploys helped the Texans average 24,500 for their home games, highest in the new league.

1961 E.J. Holub, the Texas Tech All-America center described as "the best football player in America" by many scouts, was drafted first by both Dallas teams. Hunt, the Texans' owner, considered it a major victory when Holub decided to play for his club. Hunt also signed three more quality rookies, Southern Methodist's Jerry Mays, Michigan State's Fred Arbanas, and Ohio State's Jim Tyrer. The revitalized Texans won four of their five preseason games and three of their first four in the regular season. But during that period, Spikes was injured, and his absence from the running attack put even more pressure on Davidson's already erratic passing. The team fell into a six-game losing streak, then rallied to win three of its last four and finished second in the Western Division at 6-8.

1962 Don Klosterman was named the club's player personnel director. Stram made his most important acquisition when he invited Len Dawson, a quarterback he once coached at Purdue, to join Dallas. Dawson had been cut by the Cleveland Browns of the NFL, but he moved in to star for the Texans. Another key addition was Curtis McClinton, a 6-foot 3-inch, 227-pound running back who had enough speed to run the high hurdles at Kansas. With Dawson directing Haynes and McClinton, the Texans clinched the Western Division championship in November. They finished with an 11-3 record. Arbanas, fully recovered from the back injury that had kept him out of the 1961 season, was instrumental in the Texans' turnabout both as a receiver and an excellent blocker. His contribution to the ground game helped Haynes to his greatest year, which included 1,049 yards and a record 13 touchdowns rushing. AFL writers voted Dawson, who threw 29 touchdown passes, player of the year, McClinton rookie of the year, and Stram coach of the year. Dallas won the AFL championship in the second overtime period when Tommy Brooker kicked a 25-yard field goal to make the final score 20-17 over Houston, December 23.

1963 H. Roe Bartle, the mayor of Kansas City, invited Hunt to move his team to Missouri. Bartle promised to enlarge Kansas City's Municipal Stadium and guaranteed Hunt three times as many season ticket sales as the Texans had in Dallas. Impressed with the inducements and the fact the nearest pro football rival was 250 miles away, Hunt announced he was shifting the franchise to Kansas City and renaming it the Chiefs, May 14. Rookie Stone Johnson suffered a fatal injury in a preseason game. Kansas City opened the regular season with a 59-7 victory over Denver, but the new-look Chiefs managed only one win and two ties in their next nine games. Guard Ed Budde, defensive tackle Buck Buchanan, and linebacker Bobby Bell were rookies who became starters.

1964 Ten regulars were hurt at one time or another during the season. Curtis McClinton broke a hand in training camp. It bothered him all year. E.J. Holub tore a knee and missed the last five games. Johnny Robinson, the outstanding defensive back, suffered a rib injury in November and was out for the season. Arbanas, the tight end, was mugged on a Kansas City street and blinded in his left eye. Burdened with such ill fortune, the Chiefs played erratically. They beat the Chargers 49-6 and the Jets 24-7, but they lost to Denver 33-27. Attendance was as disappointing as the final 7-7 record. Seven home games at Municipal Stadium drew only 126,881, and when AFL owners' meetings were held, there was discussion about the Chiefs' future in Kansas City.

1965 Gale Sayers, the spectacular breakaway runner from Kansas, was the club's number-one draft choice. But the Chicago Bears also made him their first selection and finally won him in a bidding duel. Otis Taylor, a wide receiver from Prairie View, joined the team. Haynes was traded to Denver for linebacker Jim Fraser and cash. Mack Lee Hill, a virtually unknown free agent running back signed in 1964, muscled his way into the regular lineup. In a relatively routine knee surgery late in the season, Hill died on the operating table. The Chiefs finished 7-5-2; three of the losses were by three points or less.

1966 Running back Mike Garrett, the Heisman Trophy winner from USC, was drafted in the twentieth round. Garrett also was drafted by his hometown Los Angeles Rams, but the Chiefs signed the swift runner the team needed for $400,000. "In the past we ground out yardage inch by inch. We moved by bus; now we travel by jet," said Stram. A crowd of 43,885, largest ever to see a sports event in Kansas City, turned out for the home opener against Buffalo. The Chiefs lost 29-14, but after the game, in the middle of the field, Stram and Bills' coach Joe Collier negotiated a trade. Kansas City got field goal kicker Mike Mercer for a fifth-round draft pick. The deal solidified the one weak link in the Chiefs' attack. Mercer proved his worth in a title-clinching 32-24 win over New York in late November, hitting from 32, 15, 47, and 33 yards. Garrett's lateral swiftness

Behind protection from Ed Budde (71) and E. J. Holub, Len Dawson passes over Ernie Ladd, 1968.

gave the Chiefs a genuine outside threat. Garrett was second in AFL rushing with 801 yards and his 5.45 yards per carry was the league's top average. Dawson led the league in passing, and Chris Burford tied for third in pass receiving. The Chiefs finished three games ahead of Oakland in the Western Division.

1967 Using a flashy I-formation offense and an assortment of defenses, the Chiefs confused and outplayed Buffalo to win the AFL championship 31-7 and gain a berth in the first Super Bowl. Kansas City went wild, with Chiefs' boosters mobbing the airport to greet the team upon its return. More than 6,300 fans purchased tickets for the trip to Los Angeles and the AFL-NFL World Championship Game, later renamed the Super Bowl. The Chiefs played Vince Lombardi's Green Bay Packers close for a half, trailing 14-10. But the Packers took charge in the final two periods for a 35-10 victory, January 15. The loss to Green Bay prompted an emphasis on defense in the Chiefs' 1967 draft. They got linebacking strength in Maxwell Trophy winner Jim Lynch from Notre Dame and Little All-America Willie Lanier from Morgan State. Specialists Jan Stenerud and Noland (Super Gnat) Smith also were selected. Interest in the team skyrocketed. Season ticket sales reached 22,000 in 1966. The figure went over 30,000 for 1967, and seating capacity for Municipal Stadium was increased from 40,000 to 47,000. In June, the voters in Jackson County approved a $43 million general obligation bond issue for construction of a sports complex that would feature both a football and baseball stadium. A two-thirds approval was required, and the bond carried with 67 percent of the vote. The Chiefs started well, but injuries to center Jon Gilliam and linebackers Holub and Lanier weakened the middle of the offensive and defensive lines. The team had to scramble for three consecutive wins at the end of the year, finishing second with a 9-5 mark. Stenerud, from Norway via Montana State, led the league in field goals with 21. Smith, a 5-foot 6-inch, 154-pound sprinter from Tennessee State, topped the AFL in kickoff return yardage.

1968 The Chiefs' offensive firepower was depleted early in the season by injuries to backs Garrett and Bert Coan, and receivers Taylor and Gloster Richardson. Kansas City's offense scored no touchdowns, all were by the defense, in a 20-19 loss to the Jets. Stram improvised, bringing quarterback Jacky Lee and running back Robert Holmes off the bench, and both were outstanding in a 34-2 win over Denver in the third game. Dawson returned the next week to direct a 48-3 bombing of Miami. The Chiefs ran the winning streak to six en route to a 12-2 finish and a tie with Oakland for the Western Division championship. But in the playoff game, the Raiders built a 21-0 lead in the first quarter and advanced to the championship with a 41-6 victory. All the Chiefs' scoring came in the second quarter, when they ran 10 plays inside the Raiders' 10-yard line and netted just two field goals.

1969 The Chiefs posted a 6-0 preseason mark and kept the string going with comfortable victories over San Diego and Boston at the outset of the regular schedule. But in the 31-0 drubbing of the Patriots, Dawson injured a knee and was replaced by Jacky Lee for game three against Cincinnati. The Chiefs lost the game 24-19, and lost Lee with a cracked bone in his ankle. Mike Livingston became the third quarterback in as many weeks, and helped turn things around in a 26-13 victory over Denver that began a seven-game winning streak. Two months into the season, Dawson returned to action. The Chiefs finished with an 11-3 record, second to Oakland's 12-1-1. But this was the first year of the new playoff system that pitted first- and second-place finishers in the opposite divisions against each other in the open-

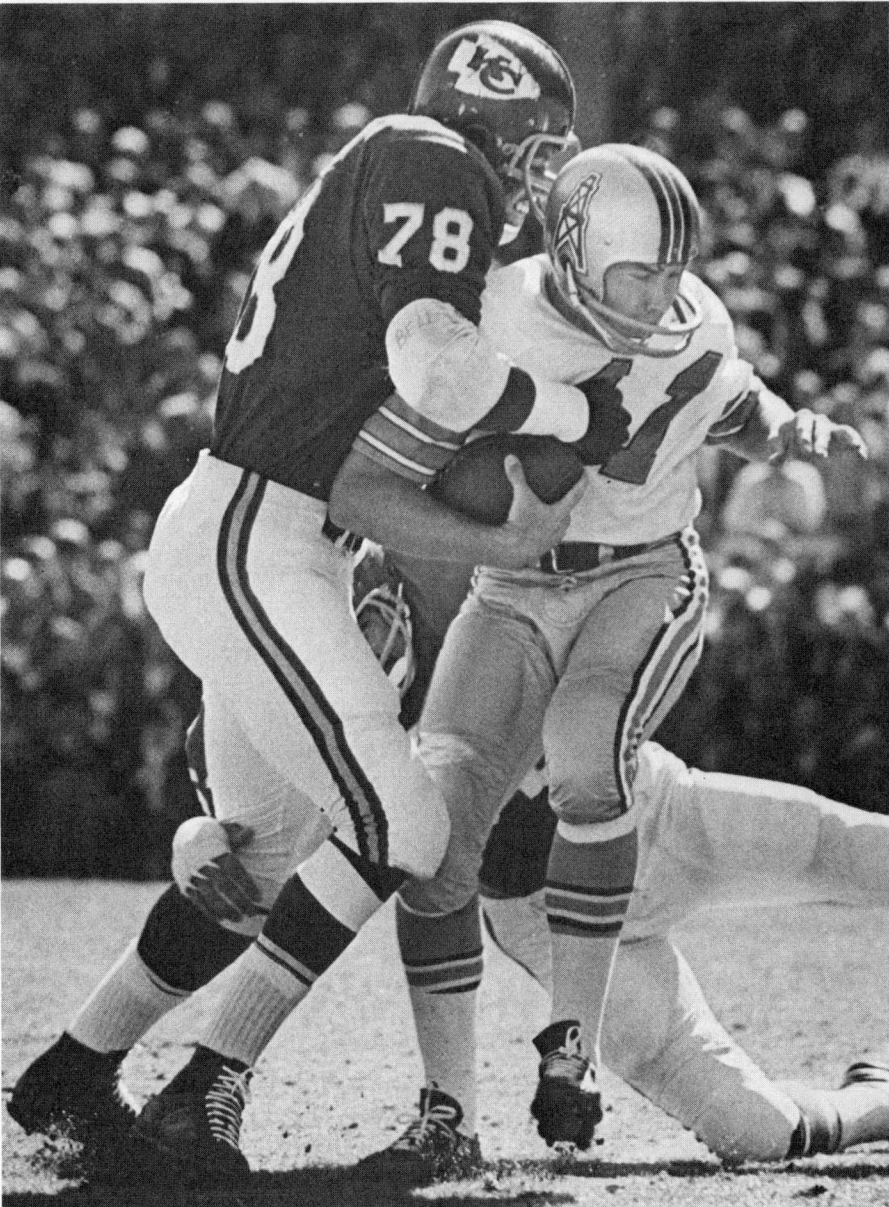

Linebacker Bobby Bell puts the clamps on Houston's Pete Beathard, 1969.

ing round. Kansas City relied on the strong defensive play, which had been the key to its season-long success, to turn back the defending Super Bowl champion New York Jets 13-6, while Oakland crushed Houston 56-7 in round one.

1970 The Chiefs, who had lost to Oakland twice in the regular season, rallied from an early 7-0 deficit to win 17-7 over the Raiders in the AFC Championship Game. Their opponents in Super Bowl IV in New Orleans were the Minnesota Vikings, and the Chiefs used the game as a crusade for the American Football League. They wore patches on their jerseys saying "AFL-10," which referred to the 10-year existence of the AFL, the league that would become extinct in the new NFL setup. Oddsmakers had established the Vikings two-touchdown favorites, but the Chiefs came out with three Stenerud field goals and a second quarter fumble recovery on the Minnesota 19-yard line that led to Mike Garrett's five-yard touchdown and a 16-0 halftime lead. A 46-yard pass from Dawson to Otis Taylor in the third quarter sealed Kansas City's first Super Bowl championship, 23-7. During the 1970 regular season, relations soured between

Stram and Garrett, and Garrett was traded to San Diego. Despite key injuries, the Chiefs' record after 12 games was 7-3-2. They traveled to Oakland and lost 20-6, then dropped the final game to San Diego 31-13 as Garrett haunted them with his best day of the year, 95 yards.

1971 Stram opened up the offense again with the help of receivers such as rookie Elmo Wright and Morris Stroud. Taylor emerged as one of the best pass catchers in football, leading the NFL in yards gained on receptions. Ed Podolak became the new running star, and the linebacking trio of Lanier, Bell, and Lynch was among the league's best. After an opening loss to San Diego, the Chiefs won five straight. In the next-to-last game with Oakland, a late field goal by Stenerud gave the Chiefs a 16-14 victory and the Western Division title. Stram awarded game balls to all 40 squad members. The team finished with a 10-3-1 record, one-and-a-half games ahead of Oakland in the Western Division. But in the AFC playoff against Eastern Division champion Miami, Kansas City dropped a 27-24 double-overtime decision to the Dolphins, December 25.

1972 All-star safety Johnny Robinson retired, but Dawson ended speculation that he would do the same by signing a two-year contract in April. Kansas City fans were introduced to their new, modernistic Arrowhead stadium, one of the most impressive facilities in pro football. With a seating capacity of 78,097, it was formally opened in a preseason game with the St. Louis Cardinals, August 12. The Chiefs opened the regular season with a loss to Miami but eventually rose to 5-3 with a 27-14 win over Oakland in the eighth week. Consecutive losses to Pittsburgh, San Diego, and Oakland put them out of contention, however, and they finished 8-6, second in the West. The future no longer looked bright—except in the stands.

1973 The defense continued to play with its customary vigor, but new holes began appearing in the Chiefs' offense. Dawson was hurt much of the time and had to give way to backup quarterback Pete Beathard, who had returned for his second tour of duty under Stram. Beathard could not get the club moving, so Mike Livingston got the next chance and generated some excitement by leading the club into first place in late November. But a 14-10 loss to Denver and a 37-7 loss to the division-leading Raiders took the Chiefs out of title contention.

1974 The Chiefs were 3-4 at the midway point of the season, but then lost consecutive games to the New York Giants and San Diego. The Chiefs' age was beginning to show. Dawson was 39. The offensive linemen were older, slower, and ready to be replaced. The defensive front four had to be overhauled. The result was the first losing record in Kansas City in 11 years. The Chiefs finished 5-9 and Stram, the only coach in the history of the franchise, was dismissed at the end of the season. Jack Steadman, the club's general manager, was appointed by Lamar Hunt to revamp the organization. Statistically, the highlight of the year was Emmitt Thomas's 12 interceptions, best in the NFL.

1975 Paul Wiggin, an assistant coach with the San Francisco 49ers, was named Chiefs' head coach. Wiggin directed his young, inexperienced club to four victories in five games at one point early in the season, including a 34-31 upset of Dallas on Monday night television. Injuries handicapped the Chiefs, and by the end of the year, they barely had enough able bodies. A 24-21 victory over the Detroit Lions was the only bright spot in the final six games, and Kansas City again finished 5-9 and third in the Western Division. After 19 memorable seasons, 14 with the Texans-Chiefs, quarterback Len Dawson announced his retirement.

1976 Continuing what he hoped was a rebuilding program, Wiggin suffered through four straight losses at the start of the season, before getting his club turned around. Livingston, who had seemed on the verge of becoming the regular quarterback several times in previous seasons, finally took over the position and improved noticeably as the season progressed. The team finished with two victories in its last three games, including an impressive 39-14 victory over Cleveland.

1977 The poorest season in the franchise's history cost both Wiggin and his successor, Tom Bettis, their jobs. Kansas City lost its first five games before winning on October 23. In that game, the Chiefs took advantage of San Diego fumbles to score twice in 31 seconds for a 21-16 win. The next week Cleveland defeated the Chiefs 44-7, and Wiggin was fired. Bettis was promoted to head coach. The Chiefs dedicated the next game to Wiggin and defeated Green Bay 20-10. But six straight losses closed out the season, and Bettis's contract was not renewed. The heart of the Chief's defense also departed, as 11-year veterans Jim Lynch and Willie Lanier retired after the season.

1978 Marv Levy, the former head coach of the Montreal Alouettes of the Canadian Football League, was named head coach. He drafted for defense, starting with defensive end Art Still in the first round. Levy installed the Wing-T as his offense. Although the Chiefs only passed for seven touchdowns, they had the second most productive ground game in the league: a record five backs ran for at least 100 yards in a game. The highlight of the season came in a 23-0 victory over the Chargers on November 26, when the Chiefs intercepted five San Diego passes.

1979 Quarterback Steve Fuller of Clemson was a first-round draft choice. Early in the season he replaced veteran Mike Livingston as the starter. With Fuller, the Chiefs improved from their 1-3 start to 7-9. Despite a gradual shift from the Wing-T, the running game remained effective. The passing game, however, was a disappointment, again producing only seven touchdowns. Late in the season, the Chiefs' defense began to make noticeable improvement, holding Baltimore to seven points and Tampa Bay to only a field goal.

1980 Despite injuries to some key starters, Kansas City continued to improve its record. It came back from an 0-4 start to finish 8-8. The defense came of age, with Gary Barbaro, Art Still, and Gary Green playing leading roles. When Fuller suffered a knee injury late in the season, Bill Kenney took over at quarterback and led the Chiefs to two victories in their last three games.

1981 With Kenney at quarterback, the Chiefs

Mike Garrett breaks through the New York Jets' line, 1969.

Chiefs defensive end Art Still, 1979.

Gary Barbaro

Buck Buchanan

Ed Budde

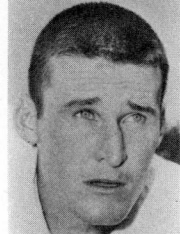
Chris Burford

Joe Delaney

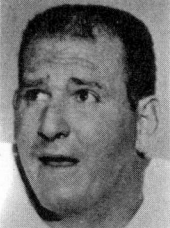
Sherrill Headrick

Robert Holmes

ignored their recent history of slow starts and came out winning. Linebacker Thomas Howard returned a fumble 65 yards for a touchdown with less than 2:00 remaining in the opener, and the Chiefs defeated the Steelers 37-33. On October 11, the Chiefs routed Oakland 27-0 on Kenney's 287 yards passing. Two weeks later the Chiefs defeated the Raiders again to take over first place in the AFC West with a 6-2 record. Two losses followed, but wins over Houston and Seattle put the Chiefs back in first place again. Three more losses eliminated the Chiefs from the playoffs, but a season-ending 10-6 victory over the Vikings guaranteed the Chiefs their first winning season since 1973. Rookie Joe Delaney rushed for 1,121 yards, a club record.

MEMBERS OF HALL OF FAME:
Lamar Hunt
CHIEFS RECORD, 1960-81

Year	Won	Lost	Tied	Pct.	Pts.	OP
Dallas Texans						
1960	8	6	0	.571	362	253
1961	6	8	0	.429	334	343
1962‡	11	3	0	.786	389	233
Kansas City Chiefs						
1963	5	7	2	.417	347	263
1964	7	7	0	.500	366	306
1965	7	5	2	.583	322	285
1966‡	11	2	1	.846	448	276
1967	9	5	0	.643	408	254
1968†	12	2	0	.857	371	170
1969*	11	3	0	.786	359	177
1970	7	5	2	.583	272	244
1971§	10	3	1	.769	302	208
1972	8	6	0	.571	287	254
1973	7	5	2	.571	231	192
1974	5	9	0	.357	233	293
1975	5	9	0	.357	282	341
1976	5	9	0	.357	290	376
1977	2	12	0	.143	225	349
1978	4	12	0	.250	243	327
1979	7	9	0	.438	238	262
1980	8	8	0	.500	319	336
1981	9	7	0	.563	343	290
22 Years	164	144	10	.531	6,971	6,032

‡AFL Champion
†AFL Western Division Co-Champion
*Super Bowl Champion
§AFC Western Division Champion

RECORD HOLDERS
Rushing (Yards)	Joe Delaney, 1981	1,121
Passing (Pct.)	Len Dawson, 1975	66.4
Passing (Yards)	Len Dawson, 1964	2,879
Passing (TDs)	Len Dawson, 1964	30
Receiving (No.)	Chris Burford, 1962	68
Receiving (Yards)	Otis Taylor, 1966	1,297
Interceptions (No.)	Emmitt Thomas, 1974	12
Punting (Avg.)	Jerrel Wilson, 1965	46.1
Punt Ret. (Avg.)	Abner Haynes, 1960	15.4
Kickoff Ret. (Avg.)	Dave Grayson, 1962	29.7
Touchdowns (Total)	Abner Haynes, 1962	19
Field Goals Made	Jan Stenerud, 1968, 1970	30
Points (No.)	Jan Stenerud, 1968	129

COACHING HISTORY
1960-74	Hank Stram	124-76-10
1975-77	Paul Wiggin*	11-24- 0
1977	Tom Bettis	1- 6- 0
1978-81	Marv Levy	28-36- 0

*Replaced after seven games in 1977

FIRST PLAYER SELECTED
1960	Don Meredith, QB, Southern Methodist
1961	E. J. Holub, C, Texas Tech
1962	Ronnie Bull, RB, Baylor
1963	Buck Buchanan, DT, Grambling
1964	Pete Beathard, QB, USC
1965	Gale Sayers, RB, Kansas
1966	Aaron Brown, DE, Minnesota
1967	Gene Trosch, DE-DT, Miami
1968	Mo Moorman, G, Texas A&M
1969	Jim Marsalis, CB, Tennessee State
1970	Sid Smith, T, USC
1971	Elmo Wright, WR, Houston
1972	Jeff Kinney, RB, Nebraska
1973	Gary Butler, TE (2), Rice
1974	Woody Green, RB, Arizona State
1975	Elmore Stephens, TE (2), Kentucky
1976	Rod Walters, G, Iowa
1977	Gary Green, CB, Baylor
1978	Art Still, DE, Kentucky
1979	Mike Bell, DE, Colorado State
1980	Brad Budde, G, USC
1981	Willie Scott, TE, South Carolina
1982	Anthony Hancock, WR, Tennessee

DALLAS TEXANS, 1960-62;
KANSAS CITY CHIEFS, 1963-81
Abell, Bud, LB, Missouri	1966-68
Adamle, Mike, RB, Northwestern	1971-72
Adams, Tony, QB, Utah State	1975-78
Agajanian, Ben, K, New Mexico	1961
Allen, Nate, CB, Texas Southern	1971-74
Anderson, Curtis, DE, Central State, Ohio	1979
Andrews, Billy, LB, Southeastern Louisiana	1976-77
Andrusyshyn, Zenon, P, UCLA	1978
Ane, Charlie, C, Michigan State	1975-80
Arbanas, Fred, TE, Michigan State	1962-70
Austin, Hise, CB, Prairie View	1975
Avery, Ken, LB, Southern Mississippi	1975

B
Bailey, Mark, RB, Long Beach State	1977-78
Barbaro, Gary, S, Nicholls State	1976-81
Barnes, Charley, E, Northeastern Louisiana	1961
Barton, Jim, C, Marshall	1960
Beathard, Pete, QB, USC	1964-67, 1973
Beckman, Ed, TE, Florida State	1977-81
Beisler, Randy, G, Indiana	1975
Bell, Bobby, LB, Minnesota	1963-74
Bell, Mike, DE, Colorado State	1979-81
Belton, Horace, RB, Southeastern Louisiana	1978-80
Besler, Ceasar, DB, Arkansas-Pine Bluff	1968-71
Bergey, Bruce, TE, UCLA	1971
Bernet, Ed, E, Southern Methodist	1960
Bernhardt, Roger, G, Kansas	1975
Best, Keith, LB, Kansas State	1972
Biodrowski, Dennis, G, Memphis State	1963-67
Bishop, Sonny, G, Fresno State	1962
Blanton, Jerry, LB, Kentucky	1979-81
Bledsoe, Curtis, RB, San Diego State	1981
Bookman, John, DB, Miami	1960
Boydston, Max, E, Oklahoma	1960-61
Branch, Mel, DE, Louisiana State	1960-65
Brannon, Solomon, DB, Morris Brown	1965-66
Briggs, Bob, DE, Heidelberg	1974
Brockington, John, RB, Ohio State	1977
Brooker, Tommy, TE-K, Alabama	1962-66
Brown, Aaron, DE, Minnesota	1966-72
Brown, Larry, T, Miami	1978-79
Brunson, Larry, WR, Colorado	1974-77
Bryant, Bob, E, Texas	1960
Buchanan, Buck, DT, Grambling	1963-75
Budde, Brad, G, USC	1980-81
Budde, Ed, G, Michigan State	1963-76
Burford, Chris, E, Stanford	1960-67
Burgmeier, Ted, S, Notre Dame	1978
Burks, Ray, LB, UCLA	1977
Burruss, Lloyd, S, Maryland	1981
Butler, Gary, TE, Rice	1973
Butler, Gerald, WR, Nicholls State	1977

C
Cadwell, John, G, Oregon State	1961
Cancik, Phil, LB, Northern Arizona	1981
Cannon, Billy, TE, Louisiana State	1970
Carlson, Dean, QB, Iowa State	1972-74
Carolan, Reg, E, Idaho	1964-68
Carson, Carlos, WR, Louisiana State	1980-81
Carter, M. L., CB, Cal State-Fullerton	1979-81
Case, Frank, DE, Penn State	1981

Cherry, Deron, S, Rutgers	1981
Christopher, Herb, S, Morris Brown	1979-81
Clark, Wayne, QB, U. S. International	1975
Clements, Tom, QB, Notre Dame	1980
Coan, Bert, RB, Kansas	1963-68
Collier, Tim, CB, East Texas State	1976-79
Collins, Ray, DT, Louisiana State	1960-61
Condon, Tom, G, Boston College	1974-81
Corey, Walt, LB, Miami	1960-66
Cornelison, Jerry, T, Southern Methodist	1960-65
Craig, Reggie, WR, Arkansas	1975-76
Culp, Curley, DT, Arizona State	1968-74

D
Daney, George, G, Texas-El Paso	1968-74
Daniels, Clem, RB, Prairie View	1960
Davidson, Cotton, QB, Baylor	1960-61
Davis, Dick, DE, Kansas	1962
Davis, Ricky, S, Alabama	1977
Dawson, Len, QB, Purdue	1962-75
DeBernardi, Fred, DE, Texas-El Paso	1974
Delaney, Joe, RB, Northwestern Louisiana	1981
Diamond, Charlie, T, Miami	1960-63
Dickinson, Bo, RB, Southern Mississippi	1960-61
DiMidio, Tony, T, West Chester State	1966-67
Dimmick, Tom, C, Houston	1960
Dirden, Johnnie, KR, Sam Houston State	1979
Dixon, Al, TE, Iowa State	1979-81
Dombroski, Paul, CB, Linfield	1980-81
Dorsey, Larry, WR, Tennessee State	1978
Dressler, Doug, RB, Chico State	1975
Drougas, Tom, T, Oregon	1974
Duncan, Randy, QB, Iowa	1961

E
Ellison, Willie, RB, Texas Southern	1973-74
Elrod, Jimbo, LB, Oklahoma	1976-78
Enis, Hunter, QB, Texas Christian	1960
Estes, Lawrence, DE, Alcorn State	1975-76

F
Farrier, Curt, DT, Montana State	1963-65
Flores, Tom, QB, Pacific	1969
Flynn, Don, DB, Houston	1960-61
Fournet, Sid, G, Louisiana State	1960-61
Fraser, Jim, LB, Wisconsin	1965
Frazier, Cliff, DT, UCLA	1977
Frazier, Wayne, C, Auburn	1966-67
Frazier, Willie, TE, Arkansas-Pine Bluff	1972
Frey, Dick, DE, Texas A&M	1960
Fuller, Steve, QB, Clemson	1979-81

G
Gagliano, Bob, QB, Utah State	1981
Gagner, Larry, G, Florida	1972
Gaines, Clark, RB, Wake Forest	1981
Gant, Earl, RB, Missouri	1979-80
Garcia, Bubba, WR, Texas-El Paso	1980-81
Garrett, Mike, RB, USC	1966-70
Gaunty, Steve, WR, Northern Colorado	1979
Gehrke, Jack, WR, Utah	
Getty, Charlie, T, Penn State	1974-81
Gilliam, Jon, C, East Texas State	1961-67
Golub, Chris, S, Kansas	1977
Gossett, Jeff, P, Eastern Illinois	1981
Graham, Tom, LB, Oregon	1974
Granderson, Rufus, T, Prairie View	1960
Gray, Tim, S, Texas A&M	1976-78
Grayson, Dave, DB, Oregon	1961-64
Green, Gary, CB, Baylor	1977-81
Green, Woody, RB, Arizona State	1974-76
Greene, Ted, LB, Tampa	1960-62
Greene, Tom, QB, Holy Cross	1961
Grupp, Bob, P, Duke	1979-81

H
Hadley, David, CB, Alcorn State	1970-72
Hadnot, James, RB, Texas Tech	1980-81
Hamilton, Andy, WR, Louisiana State	1973-74
Harris, Eric, CB, Memphis State	1980-81
Harris, Jimmy, DB, Oklahoma	1960
Harrison, Glynn, RB, Georgia	1976

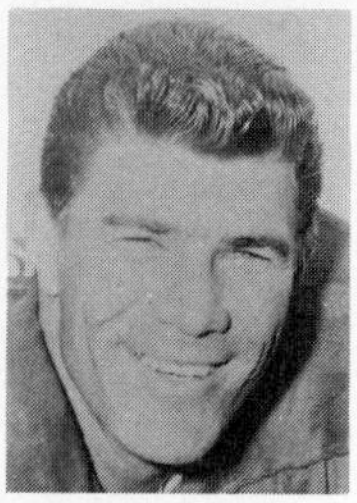

E. J. Holub

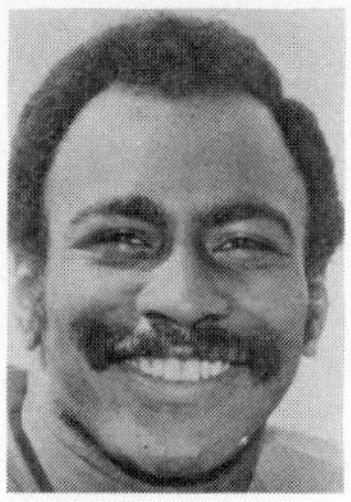

Willie Lanier

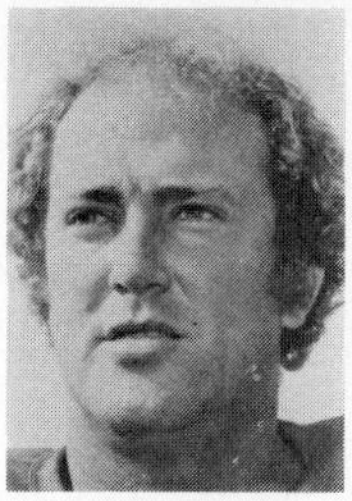

Mike Livingston

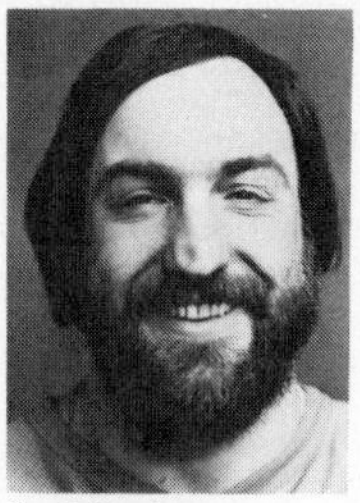

Jack Rudnay

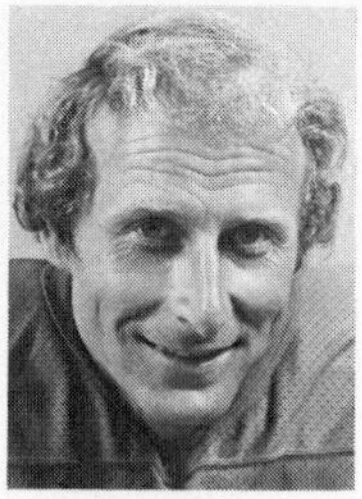

Jan Stenerud

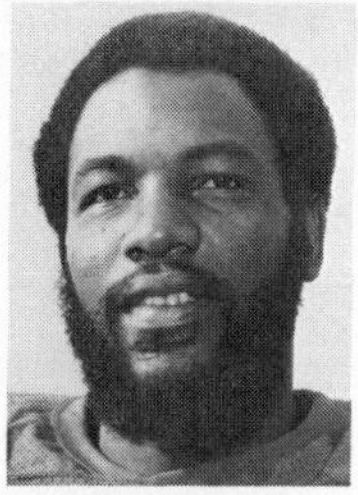

Otis Taylor

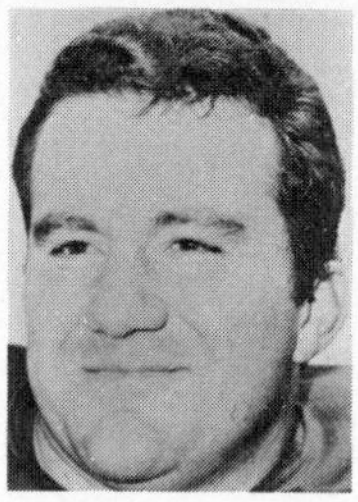

Jim Tyrer

Harvey, Marvin, TE, Southern Mississippi. 1981
Haslip, Wilbert, RB, Hawaii. 1979
Hayes, Wendell, RB, Humboldt State 1968-74
Haynes, Abner, RB, North Texas State 1960-65
Headrick, Sherrill, LB, Texas Christian 1960-67
Helton, Darius, G, North Carolina Central 1977
Herkenhoff, Matt, T, Minnesota. 1976-81
Hicks, Sylvester, DE, Tennessee State 1978-81
Hill, Dave, T, Auburn 1963-74
Hill, Jim, DB, Sam Houston State. 1966
Hill, Mack Lee, RB, Southern U. 1964-65
Hines, Jimmy, WR, Texas Southern 1970
Holmes, Pat, DE, Texas Tech 1973
Holmes, Robert, RB, Southern U. 1968-71
Holub, E. J., C-LB, Texas Tech 1961-70
Homan, Dennis, WR, Alabama 1971-72
Howard, Thomas, LB, Texas Tech 1977-81
Huarte, John, QB, Notre Dame. 1969-71
Hudock, Mike, C, Miami 1967
Hudson, Bob, LB, Clemson 1960
Hull, Bill, DE, Wake Forest. 1962
Humphrey, Tom, C, Abilene Christian 1974
Hunt, Bobby, DB, Auburn 1962-67
Hurston, Chuck, DE, Auburn. 1965-70

J

Jackson, Billy, RB, Alabama. 1981
Jackson, Charles, LB, Washington 1978-81
Jackson, Charlie, DB, Southern Methodist 1960
Jackson, Frank, WR, Southern Methodist. 1961-65
Jackson, Gerald, S, Mississippi State. 1979
Jankowski, Bruce, WR, Ohio State. 1971-72
Jaynes, David, QB, Kansas 1974
Jeralds, Luther, DE, North Carolina College 1961
Johnson, Curley, HB-P, Houston. 1960
Johnson, Dick, E, Minnesota 1963
Johnson, Jack, DB, Miami. 1961
Jones, Doug, DB, Cal State-Northridge 1973-74

K

Kearney, Jim, DB, Prairie View 1967-75
Kearney, Tim, LB, Northern MIchigan. 1975
Keating, Tom, DT, Michigan 1974-75
Kellar, Bill, WR, Stanford 1978
Kelley, Ed, DB, Texas. 1961
Kelly, Bobby, T, New Mexico State. 1967
Kenney, Bill, QB, Northern Colorado. 1979-81
Keyes, Leroy, RB, Purdue 1973
Kinney, Jeff, RB, Nebraska. 1972-76
Kirchbaum, Kelly, LB, Kentucky. 1980
Klug, Dave, LB, Concordia, Minnesota. 1981
Kratzer, Dan, WR, Missouri Valley 1973
Kremer, Ken, DE-NT, Ball State. 1979-81
Krisher, Bill, G, Oklahoma 1960-61

L

Ladd, Ernie, DT, Grambling 1967-68
LaGrand, Morris, RB, Tampa 1975
Lane, MacArthur, RB, Utah State. 1975-78
Lanier, Willie, LB, Morgan State 1967-77
Larpenter, Carl, G, Texas. 1962
Lee, Jacky, QB, Cincinnati 1967-69
Lee, Willie, DT, Bethune-Cookman 1976-77
Lewis, Will, KR, Millersville State 1981
Liggett, Bob, DT, Nebraska. 1970
Lindstrom, Dave, DE, Boston U. 1978-81
Livingston, Mike, QB, Southern Methodist 1968-79
Lloyd, Jeff, DT-NT, West Texas State. 1978
Lohmeyer, John, DE, Emporia State 1973, 1975-77
Longmire, Sam, DB, Purdue 1967-68
Lothamer, Ed, DT, Michigan State 1964-69, 1971-72
Lowe, Paul, RB, Oregon State 1968-69
Lowery, Nick, K, Dartmouth. 1980-81
Lynch, Jim, LB, Notre Dame. 1967-77

M

Maczuzak, John, DT, Pittsburgh. 1964
Maddox, Bob, DE, Frostburg State 1975-76
Mangiero, Dino, DT-NT, Rutgers. 1980-81
Manumaleuga, Frank, LB, San Jose State 1979-81
Marsalis, Jim, CB, Tennessee State. 1969-75
Marshall, Henry, WR, Missouri 1976-81
Marshall, Larry, DB-KR, Maryland. 1972-73, 1978
Martin, Dave, LB, Notre Dame 1968
Martin, Don, CB, Yale. 1975
Masters, Billy, TE, Louisiana State 1975-76
Matuszak, John, DT, Tampa 1974-75
Mays, Jerry, DT, Southern Methodist 1961-70
McCann, Jim, P, Arizona State 1975
McCarty, Mickey, TE, Texas Christian 1969
McClinton, Curtis, RB, Kansas. 1962-69
McKnight, Ted, RB, Minnesota-Duluth. 1977-81
McNeil, Pat, RB, Baylor 1976-77
McRae, Jerrold, WR, Tennessee State 1978
McVea, Warren, RB, Houston 1969-73
Mercer, Mike, K, Arizona State 1966
Merz, Curt, G, Iowa 1962-68
Meyers, Jerry, DE, Northern Illinois 1980
Miller, Bill, E, Miami 1962
Miller, Cleo, RB, Arkansas-Pine Bluff. 1974-75
Miller, Paul, DE, Louisiana State. 1960-61
Milo, Ray, S, New Mexico State 1978
Mitchell, Willie, DB, Tennessee State 1964-71
Moorman, Mo, G, Texas A&M. 1968-72
Morgado, Arnold, RB, Hawaii 1977-80
Morris, Donnie Joe, RB, North Texas State. 1974
Moser, Rick, RB, Rhode Island. 1981
Murphy, James, WR, Utah State. 1981

N

Napier, Walter (Buffalo), DT, Paul Quinn 1960-61
Nicholson, Jim, T, Michigan State 1974-79
Nix, Doyle, DB, Southern Methodist 1961
Nott, Mike, QB, Santa Clara 1976
Nunnery, R. B., DT, Louisiana State 1960

O

Oates, Brad, T, Brigham Young 1980
Odom, Ricky, S, USC. 1978
Olenchalk, John, LB, Stanford 1981
Olsen, Orrin, C-G, Brigham Young 1976
Oriard, Mike, C, Notre Dame. 1970-73
Osley, Willie, CB, Illinois 1974
Otis, Jim, RB, Ohio State. 1971-72

P

Palewicz, Al, LB, Miami 1973-75
Palmer, Gery, G, Kansas 1975
Parrish, Don, DT-NT, Pittsburgh 1978-81
Paul, Whitney, DE-LB, Colorado. 1976-81
Payton, Eddie, KR, Jackson State. 1978
Pearson, Barry, WR, Northwestern. 1974-76
Peay, Francis, T, Missouri 1973-74
Pennington, Durwood, K, Georgia. 1962
Perkins, Horace, CB, Colorado 1979
Peterson, Bill, LB, San Jose State 1975
Peterson, Cal, LB, UCLA. 1979-81
Pitts, Frank, WR, Southern U. 1965-71
Ply, Bobby, DB, Baylor 1962-67
Podolak, Ed, RB, Iowa 1969-77
Porter, Lewis, E, Southern U. 1970
Powers, Clyde, S, Oklahoma 1978
Pricer, Billy, RB, Oklahoma 1961
Prudhomme, Remi, G, Louisiana State 1968-69

R

Rasley, Rocky, G, Oregon State. 1975
Reamon, Tommy, RB, Missouri. 1976
Reardon, Kerry, CB, Iowa 1971-76
Reed, Tony, RB, Colorado 1977-80
Reese, Jerry, S, Oklahoma 1979-80
Reynolds, Al, G, Tarkio, Missouri 1960-67
Rice, Andy, DT, Texas Southern 1966
Richardson, Gloster, WR, Jackson State. 1967-70
Robinson, Johnny, S, Louisiana State 1960-71
Rochester, Paul, DT, Michigan State 1960-63
Rome, Stan, WR, Clemson 1979-81
Romeo, Tony, E, Florida State. 1961
Rosdahl, Harrison, DE, Penn State 1964-66
Rose, Donovan, CB, Hampton Institute 1980
Ross, Louis, DE, South Carolina State 1975
Rourke, Jim, G, Boston College. 1980-81
Rozumek, Dave, LB, New Hampshire 1976-79
Rudnay, Jack, C, Northwestern 1970-81

S

Samuels, Tony, TE, Bethune-Cookman 1977-80
Sanders, Clarence, LB, Cincinnati. 1978
Saxton, James, HB, Texas. 1962
Scott, Willie, TE, South Carolina 1981
Seals, George, DT, Missouri 1972-73
Sellers, Goldie, DB, Grambling 1968-69
Senisbaugh, Mike, S, Ohio State 1971-75
Shaw, Dennis, QB, San Diego State 1978
Simmons, Bob, G, Texas 1977-81
Simons, Keith, DT, Minnesota 1976-77
Smith, Dave, WR, Indiana, Pennsylvania 1973
Smith, Fletcher, DB, Tennessee State 1966-67
Smith, Franky, T, Alabama A&M 1980
Smith, J. T., WR, North Texas State 1978-81
Smith, Noland, KR, Tennessee State 1967-69
Smith, Sid, T, USC. 1970-72
Spani, Gary, LB, Kansas State 1978-81
Spikes, Jack, RB, Texas Christian 1960-64
Stein, Bob, LB, Minnesota. 1969-72
Stenerud, Jan, K, Montana State 1967-79
Still, Art, DE, Kentucky. 1978-81
Stone, Jack, T, Oregon 1960
Story, Bill, G, Southern Illinois 1975
Stover, Smokey, LB, Northeastern Louisiana 1960-66
Strada, John, TE, William Jewell 1974
Stroud, Morris, TE, Clark 1969-74
Swink, Jim, RB, Texas Christian 1960

T

Talton, Ken, RB, Cornell 1980
Taylor, Otis, WR, Prairie View 1965-75
Taylor, Roger, T, Oklahoma State 1981
Taylor, Steve, S, Kansas. 1976
Terrell, Marvin (Bo), G, Mississippi 1960-63
Thomas, Bill, RB, Boston College 1974
Thomas, Charlie, KR, Tennessee State. 1975
Thomas, Emmit, CB, Bishop 1966-78
Thomas, Gene, RB, Florida A&M 1966-67
Thomas, Todd, T-C, North Dakota 1981
Thornbladh, Bob, LB, Michigan 1974
Trosch, Gene, DE, Miami. 1967-69
Tyrer, Jim, T, Ohio State 1961-73

U

Upshaw, Marvin, DE, Trinity, Texas. 1970-75

V

Vitali, Mark, QB, Purdue 1977

W

Wade, Charlie, WR, Tennessee State 1977
Walker, Wayne, K, Northwestern Louisiana 1967
Walters, Rod, G, Iowa 1976, 1978-80
Walton, Wayne, G-T, Abilene Christian 1973-74
Warner, Charley, DB, Prairie View. 1963-64
Webster, Dave, DB, Prairie View. 1960-61
Werner, Clyde, LB, Washington 1970-74, 1976
Wesson, Ricky, CB, Southern Methodist. 1977
West, Robert, WR, San Diego State 1972-73
White, Walter, TE, Maryland. 1975-79
Wickert, Tom, G, Washington State 1977
Williams, Lawrence, KR-WR, Texas Tech 1976-77
Williams, Mike, RB-TE, New Mexico 1979-81
Williamson, Fred, DB, Northwestern 1965-67
Wilson, Eddie, QB, Arizona. 1962-64
Wilson, Jerrel, P, Southern Mississippi 1963-77
Wilson, Mike, G, Dayton 1975
Wolf, Jim, DT, Prairie View. 1976
Wood, Duane, DB, Oklahoma State. 1960-64
Wright, Elmo, WR, Houston 1971-74

Y

Young, Wilbur, DE, William Penn 1971-77

Z

Zaruba, Carroll, DB, Nebraska. 1960

LOS ANGELES RAMS

1937 The National Football League granted a Cleveland franchise to a syndicate headed by Homer Marshman, February 13. Hugo Bezdek was named the first head coach. The Rams had a 1-10 record.

1938 After losing four games in a row, Marshman fired Bezdek and hired assistant Art Lewis. The Rams won three of their remaining seven games, led by quarterback Bob Snyder and a sure-handed end from Arkansas, Jim Benton.

1939 Earl (Dutch) Clark, former star player for Portsmouth and Detroit replaced Lewis as head coach, but Lewis remained with the Rams as an assistant. The club made it to .500 for the first time, finishing 5-5-1. Parker Hall, a rookie tailback who was the team's first draft choice, won the Joe Carr trophy awarded to the NFL's official most valuable player, although he was not named to the official all-league team.

1940 The Rams got off to a fast start, winning their first game. But despite the emergence of Johnny Drake, a powerful new all-pro fullback from Purdue, the team slumped to a 4-6-1 record.

1941 Marshman and his associates sold the Rams to Daniel F. Reeves and Fred Levy, Jr., in June, 1941. The price was $100,000. Reeves, 29, whose older brother, Ed, had owned a part of the Washington Redskins, became the youngest owner in pro football. Billy Evans, former sports columnist, American Baseball League umpire, and Cleveland Indians general manager, was hired as the Rams' new general manager. The team won its first two games but lost its next nine to finish in last place.

1942 Billy Evans, general manager, resigned. Charles (Chile) Walsh replaced Art Lewis as an assistant coach under Clark. Lt. Reeves and Maj. Levy departed for the armed forces. The team climbed to a 5-6-0 record. Drake retired.

1943 Levy sold out to Reeves, who obtained league permission to suspend operations in 1943. Clark resigned and Chile Walsh was named head coach. The team did not play because of World War II.

1944 Walsh became general manager and appointed Aldo (Buff) Donelli, the former Pittsburgh Steelers and Duquesne University coach, as new head coach. The team, comprised mostly of pickup players, finished with a 4-6 record. UCLA quarterback Bob Waterfield was drafted as a "future."

1945 Donelli entered the service and was replaced by Chile Walsh's brother, Adam, who had been the center on the Notre Dame teams that featured the Four Horsemen. Adam Walsh inherited a team bursting with talent. Waterfield joined the club and immediately demonstrated he was a brilliant all-around player and consummate leader. He led the Rams to a 9-1-0 season to win the team's first division title. Then, on an icy field, Waterfield led the Rams to a 15-14 victory over the Washington Redskins for the NFL championship. Despite the championship, Reeves lost $50,000 for the season. Reeves, who long had been dreaming of a shift to the West Coast, had to get a place to play. He coveted the Los Angeles Memorial Coliseum, an amateur stronghold since the 1932 Olympic Games were held there. By making a deal with George Preston Marshall to play a preseason game with Marshall's Redskins for *Los Angeles Times* Charities, Reeves secured the 101,296-seat Coliseum for his home field.

1946 Reeves petitioned the other owners at the league meeting to move his franchise from Cleveland to Los Angeles. He was refused, and he vowed he would sell the club and get out of football. The other owners reconsidered. The All-America Football Conference began operation the same year, meaning the new Los Angeles Rams had to compete with the Los Angeles Dons. The Rams drafted Notre Dame's All-America runner, Emil Sitko, number one, but he signed with the AAFC. However, in their first year in Los Angeles, the Rams had Tom Harmon, the former Heisman Trophy winner from Michigan who had returned from the armed forces, Kenny Washington, the former UCLA All-America, and Woody Strode. Washington and Strode were the first black players in the NFL since 1933. They also had Fred Gehrke at halfback, Jim Hardy as a backup quarterback, and Fred Naumetz, a center and linebacker. Waterfield led the NFL passers with 127 completions in 251 attempts for 1,747 yards and 18 touchdowns. Benton led the league receivers with 63 catches for 981 yards. The Rams finished 6-4-1 but still lost money. Chile Walsh fired his brother, Adam, as head coach. Then Reeves fired Chile.

1947 Reeves assumed the duties of the general manager and hired Bob Snyder as head coach, with Joe Stydahar as an assistant. Financial losses mounted and Reeves decided he needed some partners. His former partner, Fred Levy; Ed Pauley and his brother Harold; and Hal Seley agreed to shoulder a proportionate share of the losses. In the process, they got one of the best bargains in sports history. For literally one dollar, Pauley bought 30 percent of the stock. The Rams drafted heralded St. Mary's All-America halfback Herman Wedemeyer, but he chose to play for the Dons. The preseason game with the Washington Redskins drew a pro football record 80,889 to the Coliseum. Washington provided a 92-yard touchdown run against the Cardinals, and Waterfield had an 86-yard punt against Green Bay, but the Rams lost both games. They beat Pittsburgh 48-7 and the title-bound Cardinals 27-7, but also were beaten 27-16 by the Boston Yanks. Harmon starred as a defensive back and Dick Huffman, a 250-pound tackle, was the defensive line standout in a 6-6 season.

1948 Snyder was fired and Clark Shaughnessy was named head coach, September 3. In the second game of the season, trailing the Eagles 28-0 with 16 minutes to play, Waterfield threw four touchdown passes and kicked four extra points for a 28-28 tie. The Rams lost four of their next five games before rebounding to win four of their last five. With Waterfield injured, Hardy gained a club record 406 yards passing against the Chicago Cardinals in a 27-24 loss. Hardy completed 28 of 53 attempts. The team finished 6-5-1. Benton retired. Rookie receiver Tom Fears led the league receivers with 51 catches for 698 yards. Linebacker Don Paul of UCLA was another prominent rookie. The Rams lost approximately $250,000. Only the new partners kept the franchise alive by helping to absorb the losses. The AAFC Dons were the top pro team in Los Angeles, averaging 41,096 spectators to less than 34,000 for the Rams in the Coliseum.

1949 Reeves's scouting system, one of the most innovative in pro sports, began to produce some of its best results, and players started turning up with degrees from tiny, little-known colleges. The rookie crop included quarterback Norm Van Brocklin from Oregon; Elroy (Crazylegs) Hirsch, an end and back from Wisconsin who had played three seasons for the Chicago Rockets of the AAFC; runners Verda (Vitamin T) Smith of Abilene Christian, Paul (Tank) Younger from then little-known Grambling; and defensive back Jerry Williams from Washington State. Shaughnessy molded them into an exciting, wide-open, winning team and they began with six straight victories. The acquisition of Van Brocklin, while it provided depth at quarterback, was to begin a great controversy—one which has raged in Los Angeles down through the years even though many different players have been involved—of which man should be number one. This first controversy involved Waterfield and Van Brocklin. Although the Rams slumped near season's end, winning two and losing two with two ties, they hung on to win their first Western Division title since moving from Cleveland. Fears repeated as the top pass catcher in the NFL with 77 for 1,013 yards and nine touchdowns. Philadelphia, long a jinx team for the Rams, beat Los Angeles again, 14-0 in a mud-covered championship game in Los Angeles. A heavy rainstorm which had ruined the field kept the crowd down to 27,980.

1950 The National Football League absorbed three members of the All-America Football Conference, and the Rams were left as the only pro team in Los Angeles. Shaughnessy was fired because of "internal friction" within the organization. Joe Stydahar, 39, became the new head coach. Stydahar appointed Hampton Pool, Mel Hein, and Howard (Red) Hickey as assistants. Another good group of rookies joined the Rams, players such as Bob Boyd, an end from Loyola of Los Angeles; Glenn Davis, half of the famed Army backfield combination of Davis and Blanchard; Woodley Lewis, a defensive back from Oregon; Deacon Dan Towler, a halfback from Washington & Jefferson, and Stan West, a middle guard from Oklahoma. In one game, the Rams ran up 70 points against Baltimore and 65 in another against Detroit. Against Green Bay, Fears caught 18 passes, an NFL single-game record. With a magnificent passing attack, the Rams ran up six straight victories and finished with a 9-3 record to tie the Chicago Bears for first place in the National Conference. They set 22 league records, scoring 466 points and 64 touchdowns. They gained 3,709 yards passing and 1,711 rushing. The Rams beat the Bears 24-14 in a playoff. In a classic league championship game, Cleveland used a field goal in the closing seconds to win 30-28 over Los Angeles in Cleveland. Davis, the former Heisman Trophy winner at Army, raced 82 yards to a touchdown on a pass from Waterfield on the Rams' first play from scrimmage. Dick Hoerner scored on three- and one-yard runs and defensive end Larry Brink rumbled six yards to score with a recovered fumble. Otto Graham threw four touchdown passes to lead Cleveland. Fears led NFL receivers for the third straight year with 84 catches for 1,116 yards and seven touchdowns. Van Brocklin led NFL passers with 127 completions in 223 attempts for a club record 2,061 yards and 18 touchdowns.

1951 Stydahar was given a three-year contract. With Stydahar keeping the players happy and Pool devising ways to tap the great offensive resources, the Rams continued to win. The team drafted Bud McFadin, a 245-pound tackle from Texas, number one, and also picked up Dick Daugherty, a linebacker from Oregon; Norb Hecker, a defensive back from Baldwin-Wallace; Andy Robustelli, a defensive end from Arnold College, and Charley Toogood, a tackle from Nebraska. A preseason game with the Redskins drew 95,985 to the Coliseum. Towler and Younger, two big, fast backs, joined Hoerner in what was known as the "Bull Elephant" backfield. Towler weighed 225 and Younger and Hoerner 220 each. Waterfield and Van Brocklin were still throwing passes to Hirsch and Fears. Van Brocklin passed for an NFL record 554 yards in a 54-14 win over the New York Yanks, September 28. Hirsch caught four from Van Brocklin against the Yanks for 41, 47, 26, and 1 yards. Later, against the Packers, he caught three scoring passes from Waterfield for 72, 37, and 19 yards. He led NFL receivers with 66 catches for 1,495 yards. Waterfield took over the NFL leadership from Van Brocklin with 88 completions in 176 attempts for 1,566 yards and 13 touchdowns. The Rams amassed more total yards, 5,506, than any club

Tank Younger, one of the Rams' "Bull Elephants," is on the loose against San Francisco, 1956.

in NFL history. The Rams won the division with an 8-4 record, finishing a half-game ahead of Detroit and San Francisco. In the NFL Championship Game, Los Angeles defeated Cleveland 24-17 on a pass from Van Brocklin to the double-teamed Fears which covered 73 yards. Hoerner and Towler also scored on one-yard bursts, and Waterfield kicked a 17-yard field goal. It was the Rams' first NFL championship in Los Angeles.

1952 Bill Wade, a quarterback from Vanderbilt, was the bonus draft choice. Guard Duane Putnam from College of the Pacific was another draft selection. Dick (Night Train) Lane was signed as a free agent. Skeet Quinlan, a back from San Diego State, was another promising rookie. The Rams traded 11 players to the Dallas Texans, including Hoerner, for linebacker Les Richter, who then entered the army for two years. A serious rift began to develop between Stydahar and his top assistant, Pool. After a season-opening loss to Cleveland, 37-7, Stydahar brought his problems with Pool to Reeves and when the dust had settled, Stydahar was gone and Pool, 37, was named new head coach. The Rams lost three of their first four games, but their lone victory in that stretch was a 30-28 win over Green Bay in the third game of the season. Trailing 28-6 in the last quarter, Waterfield rallied the Rams to 24 points for the victory, climaxing with a 92-yard drive in the last two min-

utes that took seven plays, including three Waterfield pass completions for gains of 20, 30, and 26 yards. Then the Rams won eight straight to tie the Detroit Lions for first place in the National Conference. The Rams lost 31-21 to Detroit in the playoff game. Van Brocklin took over the NFL passing leadership from Waterfield by completing 113 of 205 attempts for 1,736 yards and 14 touchdowns. Towler became the first Ram to lead the NFL in rushing when he gained 894 yards. Waterfield announced his retirement. He had led the team to four division titles and two NFL championships. Pete Rozelle, the sports information director at the University of San Francisco, was hired as a member of the Rams' public relations staff.

1953 Club co-owner Harold Pauley died. The number-one draft choice was Donn Moomaw, an All-America linebacker from UCLA, but he chose to go into the ministry instead of playing pro football. Rookies included Rudy Bukich, a quarterback from USC; Gene (Big Daddy) Lipscomb, a defensive tackle who had not attended college; and Harland Svare, a linebacker from Washington State. Los Angeles defeated Detroit twice, 31-19 and 37-24. The Rams finished 8-3-1, losing three games by a total of eight points. They placed third in the Western Conference.

1954 The Rams' bonus choice in the 1952 draft, Bill Wade, joined the team following military service.

Richter also joined the club from the army and moved in to start at linebacker. Amid rumors of dissension, the Rams were no longer as consistent on offense and the defense began to deteriorate. They skidded to fourth place at 6-5-1 and all of Pool's assistant coaches resigned. Van Brocklin won the NFL passing title for the third time in five years, by completing 139 of 260 passes for 2,637 yards, third best yardage figure in NFL history. Hirsch announced his retirement at the end of the season.

1955 Pool resigned. "Hamp had too many strikes against him," said Reeves. Then began a long, well-publicized search for a new Rams' coach. When the announcement finally came, January 26, many people were disappointed. Sid Gillman was the selection. Although he was well respected by football people and had been highly successful at the University of Cincinnati, the general Los Angeles public reaction was skeptical. Ron Waller from Maryland was drafted as a halfback. Other outstanding rookies were Don Burroughs, a defensive back from Colorado State University, and Larry Morris, a linebacker and the number-one draft choice from Georgia Tech. Hirsch was talked out of his retirement just before the start of the regular season. Linebacker Paul was traded to Cleveland. Gillman switched Waller to offense and the rookie had an outstanding season, rushing for 716 yards and was named to the all-pro team. The Rams lost two games to the Chicago Bears, but still finished a half game in front of Chicago in the Western Conference. In the league championship game before a record crowd of 85,693 in Los Angeles, the Rams were no match for the Cleveland Browns, losing 38-14. Cleveland intercepted seven Los Angeles passes—six by Van Brocklin. Some problems developed among the feuding Rams' owners. Reeves's old friend, Fred Levy, switched his vote and Reeves was relieved of the directorship of the team. Deacon Dan Towler retired with a club record 3,493 yards rushing, a career average of 5.2 yards per carry.

1956 Leon Clarke, an end from USC, and Tom Wilson, a running back with no college experience, were among the new additions to the club. The championship game loss to Cleveland convinced Gillman to make major changes. Veterans such as Robustelli and Hughes were traded. Lipscomb was picked up by Baltimore for the $100 waiver price. Gillman soon found he was not compatible with Van Brocklin. Wade began to get more playing time. Many veterans on the club were angered over Van Brocklin's bench-sitting. The fans split into Van Brocklin and Wade factions. Fears, Quinlan, and Toogood retired.

1957 McFadin, who was seriously wounded in an off-season shooting incident, retired. The Rams' owners signed a five-year operational contract and named Rozelle general manager. The club itself still was in the midst of a major rebuilding program. New faces included Jon Arnett, who was the number-one draft choice from USC; George Strugar, a hulking defensive tackle from Washington State; Jesse Wittenton, a defensive back from Texas Western; and Del Shofner, a defensive back and end from Baylor. The Rams made Shofner a first-round draft choice, obtained from the New York Giants in return for two players, Harland Svare and Andy Robustelli. In a game in the Coliseum, the Rams drew 102,368— a pro football record—to see a 37-24 victory over San Francisco. Hirsch retired again. A disgruntled Van Brocklin also announced his retirement.

1958 The top draft choice was Lou Michaels, a linebacker from Kentucky who was obtained in a trade with Washington. The Rams' other first round pick was Jim (Red) Phillips, an end from Auburn. Van Brocklin was traded to Philadelphia in the preseason for guard Buck Lansford and defensive back Jimmy Harris and a first-round draft pick that the Rams used to pick Dick Bass. That move made Wade the number-one quarterback for Los Angeles, but as a backup for Wade the Rams drafted Frank Ryan, the Rice University science major. Gillman made other moves to improve the Rams' offense. He put Jon Arnett in the starting backfield and shifted Del Shofner from defensive back to wide receiver. A crowd of 100,470 saw the Rams defeat the Chicago Bears 41-35 on Arnett's biggest day as a Ram. In 60 minutes, he ran a screen pass from Wade for 72 yards to the Chicago 3 to set up a touchdown; returned punts for 36 and 58 yards to set up touchdowns, and ran 52 yards from scrimmage to the Bears' 4 to set up another score. He finished the day with 298 total yards, yet never scored. A crowd of 100,202 showed up as the Rams defeated Baltimore's championship-bound Colts 30-28. Wade hit Shofner on a pass play covering 92 yards against the Bears, October 19. Wade and Red Phillips combined on a 93-yard pass play against Green Bay, November 16. Wade set several team passing records, including most yardage in a season—2,875 yards, just 63 yards short of the all-time NFL single-season record for yards gained passing, set by Sammy Baugh. Wade hit 181 of 341 passes for 18 touchdowns, and the Rams improved to an 8-4 record. Shofner caught 51 passes and averaged 21 yards a catch. Daugherty retired.

1959 Rozelle traded the rights to nine players to the Chicago Cardinals for running back Ollie Matson. Included in the Rams' package to the Cardinals were Frank Fuller, a defensive tackle, and Ken Panfil, another starting tackle. Later, Rozelle acquired defensive end Gene Brito from Washington. Halfback Dick Bass of College of the Pacific was drafted as a "future." Joe Marconi, a running back from West Virginia, was another draft choice, and another tough defensive back Ed Meador, who had been a running back at little Arkansas Tech. The New York Giants defeated the Rams 23-21 in the opening game. San Francisco shut the Rams out the next week 34-0. The Rams lost their last eight games to finish last in the Western Conference with a 2-10 record. Matson gained 837 yards in his first season. Reeves reportedly still had confidence in his head coach, but some of the other owners didn't. Gillman and his entire staff resigned on the last day of the season. Clarke retired. Burroughs was traded to Philadelphia.

1960 The Rams drafted Billy Cannon, the Heisman Trophy winning halfback from Louisiana State, number one. He also was picked number one by Houston of the new American Football League. His case went to court, which ruled he was property of the Houston club. Following the death of Commissioner Bert Bell in November, 1959 a search for a successor began—and Rozelle was the compromise selection of the owners. Reeves hired one of his all-time favorites, Hirsch, as the new general manager. Another all-time Ram, Waterfield, was named head coach; Waterfield chose his old coach, Pool, and former teammates Fears and Paul to be among his assistants. Bass, having graduated, joined the club and showed great promise as a rookie. He averaged nearly five yards per carry and gained 505 yards on rushing, pass receiving, and kick returning. The club improved on its 1959 record, going 4-7-1.

1961 The top draft choice was Marlin McKeever, an end from USC. The Rams also picked up Joe Scibelli, an offensive guard from Notre Dame, and Charlie Cowan, an offensive tackle from New Mexico Highlands. The Ram quarterback controversy combined with the rebuilding drive in a series of complicated trades on March 2. The Rams traded Wade to Chicago's Bears for defensive back Erich Barnes and quarterback Zeke Bratkowski. Then the Rams traded Barnes and linebacker John Guzick to the New York Giants for defensive back Lindon

Crow plus a first draft choice—which turned out to be North Carolina State's prized quarterback Roman Gabriel. Bass teamed with Arnett to give Los Angeles a dynamic, if little, running combination. But the defense, which boasted a promising rookie defensive end named David (Deacon) Jones, Meador, Lamar Lundy and others, had its problems and the Rams wound up only 4-10, ahead of only Minnesota, the expansion team.

1962 In a sealed-bid auction among Reeves, Pauley, Levy, Seley, and comedian Bob Hope, Reeves came up with the high bid of $7.1 million and reacquired control of the franchise. It cost Reeves $4.8 million to purchase the shares his partners had got for one dollar and a share of the liabilities just a few years earlier. A new corporation, the Los Angeles Rams Football Company, was headed by Reeves (51 percent), with 11 other minority partners. The Rams continued rebuilding through the draft. Besides Gabriel, Los Angeles also drafted defensive tackle Merlin Olsen from Utah State and Joe Carollo, a tackle from Notre Dame. Svare, 32, replaced Paul as defensive line coach. The new, promising rookies were unable to get the job done, however, and eight games into the season, Svare took over from Waterfield as head coach, and the Rams finished a dismal 1-12-1, the only victory a 28-14 victory over San Francisco. Bass became the first Ram to gain 1,000 yards rushing in a season, picking up 1,033 on 196 carries.

1963 Richter retired before the season. Defensive tackle Roosevelt Grier was obtained in a trade with the New York Giants. Torn by another quarterback controversy involving Bratkowski, Gabriel, and Terry Baker, the Heisman Trophy winner and number-one draft choice from Oregon State, the team lost its first five games. Svare installed Gabriel at quarterback and the team won five of its last nine games. A new defensive front four of Jones, Olsen, Lamar Lundy, and Grier began to make its presence felt. They became known as the Fearsome Foursome.

1964 The Rams signed a 10-year contract to play in the Coliseum's new, cut-down stadium—65,000 seats. Fourteen rookies made the team—including tight end Billy Truax from Louisiana State—but the team produced the same total of wins, five. And another quarterback Bill Munson of Utah State, entered the picture as the number-one draft choice. Munson took over when Gabriel was injured early.

1965 After the Coliseum installed theater-type seats, Reeves cracked, "We want to be sure our fans suffer in comfort." In a trade with Minnesota, the Rams picked up Notre Dame receiver Jack Snow, the Vikings' number-one choice, for Phillips and defensive tackle Gary Larsen. The Rams won only four games, but three came in the last four games—against Green Bay's NFL champions, St. Louis, and Cleveland—with Gabriel at quarterback after Munson injured his knee. Svare was fired as coach.

1966 The merger of the NFL and AFL was consummated, but no peace came to the Rams. It took a court battle to get Chicago Bears' assistant coach George Allen released from a contract with George Halas to become the Rams' new head coach. Allen had coached with the Rams as an assistant on Gillman's staff in 1957. The team's practice and coaching facilities were moved to Long Beach. The top draft choice was Tom Mack, a guard from Michigan. Bob Kelley, the radio voice of the Rams since 1937 and a vital force in their success in California, died. Allen made Gabriel the number-one quarterback. The team had a chance to finish second in the Western Conference until the final game, a 27-23 loss to champion Green Bay, and finished 8-6.

1967 After five years at Chapman College in Orange County, the club moved its training camp to California State-Fullerton. Allen, who put little faith in draft

picks, traded Los Angeles's number-one choice to Minnesota. Allen picked up Willie Ellison, a running back from Texas Southern, on the second round. With the defense now operating at optimum efficiency and the offense exhibiting a new ball control style, Los Angeles won eight in a row at season's end, including a 27-24 victory over Green Bay. Los Angeles was leading the Packers 17-10 when Green Bay's Travis Williams sprinted 104 yards with a kickoff to tie it. The Rams regained the lead on a Bruce Gossett field goal and seemed in control. Then Bass fumbled. Green Bay recovered and marched in for the go-ahead touchdown. With just 54 second left in the game, Tony Guillory blocked a Packers' punt and Claude Crabb picked up the ball and ran it to Green Bay's 5-yard line with 44 second to play. Ten seconds later, Gabriel threw a game-winning touchdown pass to Bernie Casey. The next week, the Rams beat Baltimore 34-10 to give Los Angeles an 11-1-2 record and its first division title since 1955. The year ended with a 28-7 loss to Green Bay in the Western Conference title game. Gabriel finished the year with a club record 25 touchdown passes, gaining 2,779 yards on 196 completions in 371 attempts.

1968 The Rams defeated Cleveland 30-6 in the Playoff Bowl, a game between conference runners-up, January 7. Los Angeles drafted Gary Beban, the All-America quarterback and Heisman Trophy winner from UCLA. Beban was traded to Washington for a number-one pick before the preseason games began. Los Angeles had another outstanding season (10-3-1), but Baltimore won 13 of 14 games to finish first in the Coastal Division. The Rams' defense set a 14-game record for fewest yards allowed, 3,118. A strong personality difference surfaced between Reeves and Allen, and Reeves fired the head coach, December 26. Rams players immediately raised an outcry in defense of Allen. A dozen players appeared with Allen in a televised press conference.

1969 Reeves called Allen and asked him to come back as coach, January 1. Allen did not give an answer immediately. Then, at a press conference, Reeves announced that Allen had been retained as coach, January 6. Hirsch left his job as assistant to Reeves to become athletic director at his alma mater, the University of Wisconsin. He was replaced by Jack Teele. John Sanders became assistant general manager. Los Angeles had three draft choices on the first round and they used them to pick running back Larry Smith from Florida, wide receiver Jim Seymour from Notre Dame, and tight end Bob Klein from USC. The Rams traded wide receiver Harold Jackson and defensive end John Zook for running back Izzy Lang. The team won its first 11 games. The streak ended at the Coliseum when Minnesota scored a 20-13 victory. Detroit shut out Los Angeles 28-0. Baltimore handed the Rams a 13-7 loss. Minnesota defeated the Rams 23-20 in the Western Conference title game in Bloomington, overcoming the Rams' 17-7 lead. Again, the Rams set new attendance records, drawing 1,307,989 to 22 games. Gabriel was named as the league's most valuable player. He completed 217 of 399 passes for 2,549 yards and 24 touchdowns. He set Rams' records for both attempts and completions. Bass retired with a career rushing record of 5,417 yards, tops in Rams' history.

1970 The Rams began their twenty-fifth anniversary year in Los Angeles with a 31-0 victory over Dallas in the Playoff Bowl in Miami. Los Angeles picked a linebacker, Jack Reynolds from Tennessee, number one in the draft. They also got center Rich Saul of Michigan State. The Rams compiled a 9-4-1 record, good for second place in the Western Division. The team drew a record 904,979 for 14 regular season games. At the end of the season, it was announced that George Allen's contract would not be renewed.

Allen had lasted five years, tying him with Sid Gillman for the Rams' longevity record. Allen's teams had won 49, lost 17, and tied 4.

1971 Tommy Prothro, head coach of UCLA, was named the new Rams' coach. Dan Reeves died of Hodgkin's disease in New York, April 15. William A. Barnes, Reeves's long-time friend and business associate, became president and general manager. Prothro made a trade with George Allen, who had taken the job coaching the Washington Redskins. Prothro sent linebackers Jack Pardee, Myron Pottios, and Maxie Baughan, and defensive tackle Diron Tal-

bert for linebacker Marlin McKeever and a host of draft choices. The Rams used one of the draft choices to choose Isiah Robertson, a linebacker from Southern University. The Rams also drafted Jack Youngblood, a defensive end from Florida, and Dave Elmendorf, a defensive back from Texas A&M. The Rams traded for Lance Rentzel, a controversial wide receiver from Dallas, and Travis Williams, a running back-kick returner from Green Bay. Faced with one of the toughest schedules in the league, the Rams went 8-5-1 and finished second to San Francisco in the NFC West. The Rams lost to George Allen and

the Redskins 38-24 in a Monday night game.

1972 Robert Irsay, a Chicago-based industrialist, purchased the Rams from the Reeves estate for $19 million. Irsay then traded the franchise to Carroll Rosenbloom in exchange for the Baltimore Colts and $3 to $4 million. Rosenbloom named Don Klosterman as executive vice president and general manager and moved the training camp from Fullerton to California State-Long Beach. The Rams drafted Jim Bertelsen, a running back from Texas, on the second round, and Lawrence McCutcheon, a running back from Colorado State University, on the third. Larry Brooks, a defensive tackle from Virginia State, came on the fourteenth round. Fred Dryer, a defensive end, was obtained in a trade with New England. The season was marred by injuries, particularly a mysterious ailment in Gabriel's right arm. The Rams were in contention in the first half of the season, then lost five of their last six and finished 6-7-1. Prothro and his coaching staff were dismissed.

1973 Chuck Knox, a Detroit Lions' assistant, was named head coach. The team returned to the colorful blue and gold uniforms of the 1950s after years of playing in blue and white. Klosterman traded defensive tackle Coy Bacon and running back Bob Thomas to San Diego for quarterback John Hadl. Ron Jaworski, a quick, strong-armed quarterback from Youngstown State, was drafted on the second round. Hadl moved in as the Rams' offensive leader and Gabriel asked to be traded. Gabriel was traded to Philadelphia for wide receiver Harold Jackson, plus first-round draft picks in 1974 and 1975 and a third-round choice in 1975. After a year in Long Beach, the team switched back to California State-Fullerton for training. The Rams won 12 of 14 games, the most victories in the team's history. Dallas upset the Rams 27-16 in the divisional playoffs. Hadl was named the NFC's most valuable player, and Knox was chosen coach of the year. McCutcheon gained 1,097 yards, becoming the third Ram in history to top 1,000 yards.

1974 Rosenbloom's son, Steve, was named assistant to the president. John Cappelletti, the Heisman Trophy winning running back from Penn State, was selected number one in the college draft. Hadl was traded to Green Bay after the Rams began the year with a 3-2 record and Los Angeles got five draft choices in return. Backup quarterback James Harris helped the Rams to a 10-4 record and another division title. Harris was the first black to quarterback a pro team to a championship. But the Rams were ousted once again in the playoffs. They beat Washington 19-10 in the divisional playoff, the Rams' first playoff victory since the 1951 championship. Then they lost 14-10 to Minnesota in the NFC title game at Minnesota. McCutcheon set a Rams' single-season rushing record by running for 1,109 yards on 236 carries. He added another 408 yards on 39 pass receptions and scored five touchdowns.

1975 The Rams had three first-round choices in the draft and they used them to select Mike Fanning, a defensive tackle from Notre Dame; Dennis Harrah, a guard from Miami; and Doug France, a tackle from Ohio State. The Rams lost 18-7 to Dallas in the opener. Los Angeles scored a 13-10 overtime victory over San Diego in the fourth week of the season. After a 24-23 loss to San Francisco, the Rams won six straight to close the regular season. Harris injured his shoulder in the third-to-last game against New Orleans and Ron Jaworski took over to lead victories over Green Bay and defending Super Bowl champion Pittsburgh. Led by the front four of Olsen, Youngblood, Larry Brooks (who was forced out with a knee injury the last six games), and Dryer, the Rams allowed the second fewest number of points, 135, in NFL history over a 14-game season. The Rams defeated St. Louis 35-23 in the divisional playoff game

The Rams' all-time leading rusher, running back Lawrence McCutcheon, 1975.

with Jaworski again filling in for Harris. McCutcheon broke an NFC playoff record with 202 yards on 37 carries. Dallas hammered the Rams 37-7 in the NFC Championship Game. Scibelli, Cowan, and Snow retired.

1976 Knox was given a new five-year contract by Rosenbloom, with a five-year mutual option. Then Knox was presented with that age-old problem for Rams head coaches: a quarterback controversy. Harris produced the Rams' best single-game passing performance in 25 years, completing 17 of 29 passes for 436 yards and two touchdowns in a 31-28 win over Miami. Shifting from Harris to Jaworski to first-year player Pat Haden, Knox finally settled on Haden for the last five games of the season. Haden, a poised, young Rhodes Scholar from USC who had played in the World Football League before coming to the Rams when the WFL folded, led the Rams to another Western Division championship. Los Angeles edged Dallas 14-12 in the first round of the playoffs. But there was frustration again in Minnesota. On their first drive in the NFC Championship Game, the Rams stalled inside the Vikings' 1-yard line on fourth down and elected to allow Tom Dempsey to try a field goal. It was blocked and returned for a 90-yard touchdown by the Vikings' Bobby Bryant. The Vikings went on to score a 24-13 victory. Olsen retired.

1977 Knox refuted rumors that he would accept the head coaching job in Detroit and announced his intention to remain in Los Angeles for the duration of his contract. Ron Jaworski, who had played out his option, was traded to Philadelphia for tight end Charle Young. An extraordinary draft reaped linebacker Bob Brudzinski, safety Nolan Cromwell, wide receiver Billy Waddy, running back Wendell Tyler, and quarterback Vince Ferragamo. On May 12, the club announced the signing of Joe Namath, the former New York Jets quarterback. Namath led the Rams to two wins in the first three weeks, but in a Monday night game against Chicago he completed only 16 of 40 passes with four interceptions before being forced out with injuries. The Rams lost 24-23. Pat Haden became the starter for the rest of the season. The club rolled to eight victories in the next nine weeks behind Haden and McCutcheon, who rushed for 1,238 yards to establish a team record of 5,523 yards in a career. A 20-14 victory over Oakland on December 4 clinched their fifth-straight NFC West title. On December 26, the Rams lost to Minnesota 14-7 in a NFC Divisional Playoff Game in a rare rain-and-mud game in the Coliseum.

1978 Knox resigned to become head coach of the Buffalo Bills. A coaching merry-go-round began when Rosenbloom hired George Allen to return to Los Angeles. After two preseason losses, Allen was released and replaced by Ray Malavasi, a Rams assistant coach since 1973. All-pro cornerback Monte Jackson, unhappy with the Rams, was traded to Oakland before the season. The Rams opened the year with seven consecutive victories, then slumped offensively in losses to New Orleans and Atlanta. But the team regrouped and won five of its last seven games for a 12-4 record and its sixth straight NFC West title. Haden, in his first full year as a starter, set team records for pass attempts (444), completions (229), and yardage (2,995). During the season, the club announced its move to Anaheim, scheduled to take place after the 1979 season. On December 31 in a divisional playoff game, the Rams trounced long-time nemesis Minnesota 34-10, outscoring the Vikings 24-0 in the second half.

1979 In the NFC Championship Game on January 7, the Rams lost to Dallas 28-0 after a scoreless tie at halftime. The Rams were hampered by the absence of McCutcheon and injuries to fullback John Cappelletti and Haden. On April 2, Rosenbloom drowned

while swimming off the Florida coast; his widow Georgia became majority owner of the team. Rosenbloom's son, Steve, was named executive vice-president in charge of day-to-day operations, but was soon replaced by Don Klosterman and left the organization. The club's administrative offices were moved to Rams Park in Anaheim. Guard Tom Mack, who played in eight AFC-NFC Pro Bowls, retired before the season. The team lost its opener to Oakland, then improved its record to 4-2. But a devastating string of injuries took its toll and the Rams lost four games in five weeks. Despite the injuries, the defense turned in a powerful performance on November 4, holding Seattle to minus seven yards in a 24-0 victory. Haden set a club record by completing 13 consecutive passes against the Seahawks, but was lost for the year with a broken finger. With Ferragamo at quarterback, the Rams won four straight to clinch their seventh-straight NFC West title with a 9-7 record. On December 30, Ferragamo threw three touchdown passes, the last with 2:06 left, and the Rams defeated the Cowboys in the divisional playoff game 21-19.

1980 In the NFC Championship Game January 6, the Rams earned their first trip to the Super Bowl with a 9-0 shutout of Tampa Bay. Jack Youngblood played

Defensive end Jack Youngblood, 1977.

with a broken leg, a feat he would duplicate in the Super Bowl and Pro Bowl. On January 20, the Rams lost to Pittsburgh 31-19 in Super Bowl XIV, as the Steelers came from behind in the fourth quarter. The Rams drafted two-time All-America defensive back Johnnie Johnson of Texas in the first round of the draft. Tyler injured his hip in an automobile accident in the offseason and missed 12 games. Larry Brooks, Brudzinski, Dennis Harrah, and Youngblood staged holdouts during training camp. The four players rejoined the team for the regular season, but Brudzinski walked out for good in midseason. Ferragamo led the offense, setting records for completions (240), yards (3,199), and touchdowns (30). He quarterbacked the Rams to an 11-5 record, good for second place in the NFC West. Cromwell was named the NFC's defensive player of the year by UPI. The season ended on a disappointing note as the Rams were routed 34-13 by the Cowboys in the wild card game on December 28.

1981 Brudzinski was traded to Miami, Jack Reynolds signed with San Francisco, and Fred Dyer was released. The offense also was hurt by the loss of Ferragamo, who signed with Montreal of the Canadian Football League. A four-game winning streak early in the season pushed the Rams into first place with a 4-2 record. A key figure was Jeff Rutledge, who

replaced Haden to lead victories over Green Bay and Atlanta. LeRoy Irvin also played a vital role in a 37-35 victory over the Falcons on October 11, when he returned two punts for touchdowns and set an NFL record for punt return yardage in a game (207). But injuries to Haden and Rutledge contributed to a collapse which resulted in seven losses in the next eight games, and the Rams ended the season with Dan Pastorini, a free agent acquisition, at quarterback. One of the few bright spots in the 6-10 season was Tyler, who came back from the previous season's injuries to lead the NFC with 17 touchdowns.

MEMBERS OF HALL OF FAME:
Tom Fears, Bill George, Elroy Hirsch, David (Deacon) Jones, Dick (Night Train) Lane, Ollie Matson, Merlin Olsen, Dan Reeves, Andy Robustelli, Norm Van Brocklin, Bob Waterfield

RAMS RECORD, 1937-81

Year	Won	Lost	Tied	Pct.	Pts.	OP
Cleveland Rams						
1937	1	10	0	.091	75	207
1938	4	7	0	.363	131	215
1939	5	5	1	.500	195	164
1940	4	6	1	.400	171	191
1941	2	9	0	.182	116	244
1942	5	6	0	.455	150	207
1943			The Rams suspended operations			
1944	4	6	0	.400	188	224
1945‡	9	1	0	.900	244	136
Los Angeles Rams						
1946	6	4	1	.600	277	257
1947	6	6	0	.500	259	214
1948	6	5	1	.545	327	269
1949§	8	2	2	.800	360	239
1950§	9	3	0	.750	466	309
1951‡	8	4	0	.667	392	261
1952	9	3	0	.750	349	234
1953	8	3	1	.727	366	236
1954	6	5	1	.545	314	285
1955§	8	3	1	.727	260	231
1956	4	8	0	.333	291	307
1957	6	6	0	.500	307	278
1958	8	4	0	.667	344	278
1959	2	10	0	.167	242	315
1960	4	7	1	.364	265	297
1961	4	10	0	.286	263	333
1962	1	12	1	.077	220	334
1963	5	9	0	.357	210	350
1964	5	7	2	.417	283	339
1965	4	10	0	.286	269	328
1966	8	6	0	.571	289	212
1967†	11	1	2	.917	398	196
1968	10	3	1	.769	312	200
1969†	11	3	0	.786	320	243
1970	9	4	1	.692	325	202
1971	8	5	1	.615	313	260
1972	6	7	1	.464	291	286
1973*	12	2	0	.857	388	178
1974*	10	4	0	.714	263	181
1975*	12	2	0	.857	312	135
1976*	10	3	1	.750	351	190
1977*	10	4	0	.714	302	146
1978*	12	4	0	.750	316	245
1979**	9	7	0	.563	323	309
1980***	11	5	0	.688	424	289
1981	6	10	0	.375	303	351
44 Years	306	241	20	.557	12,290	10,566

‡*NFL Champion*
§*NFL Western Conference Champion*
†*NFL Coastal Division Champion*
*NFC Western Division Champion
**NFC Champion
***NFC Wild Card Qualifier for Playoffs

RECORD HOLDERS

Rushing (Yards)	Lawrence McCutcheon, 1977	1,238
Passing (Pct.)	Vince Ferragamo, 1980	59.4
Passing (Yards)	Vince Ferragamo, 1980	3,199
Passing (TDs)	Vince Ferragamo, 1980	30
Receiving (No.)	Tom Fears, 1950	84
Receiving (Yards)	Elroy (Crazylegs) Hirsch, 1951	1,495
Interceptions (No.)	Dick (Night Train) Lane, 1951	14
Punting (Avg.)	Danny Villanueva, 1962	45.5
Punt Ret. (Avg.)	Woodley Lewis, 1952	18.5
Kickoff Ret. (Avg.)	Verda (Vitamin T.) Smith, 1950	33.7
Touchdowns (Total)	Elroy (Crazylegs) Hirsch, 1951	17
	Wendell Tyler, 1981	17
Field Goals Made	David Ray, 1973	30
Points (No.)	David Ray, 1973	130

COACHING HISTORY

1937-38	Hugo Bezdek*	1-13-0
1938	Art Lewis	4- 4-0
1939-42	Earl (Dutch) Clark	16-26-2
1943	The Rams suspended operations	
1944	Aldo (Buff) Donelli	4- 6-0

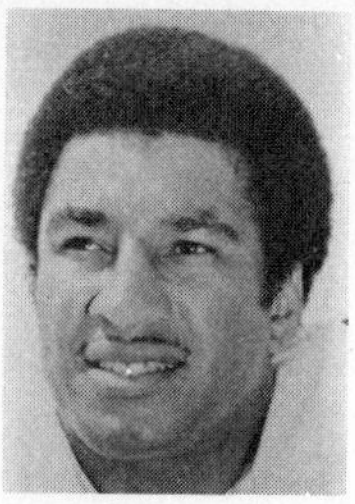
Dick Bass

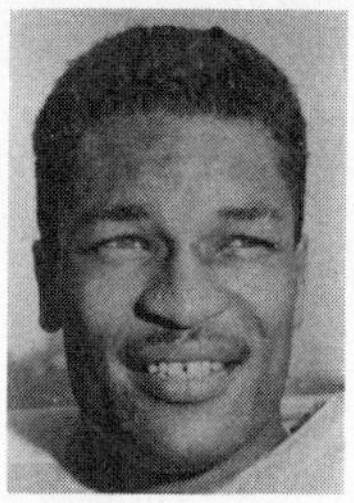
Bob Boyd

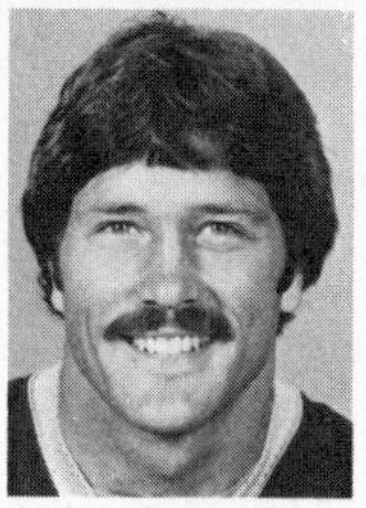
Nolan Cromwell

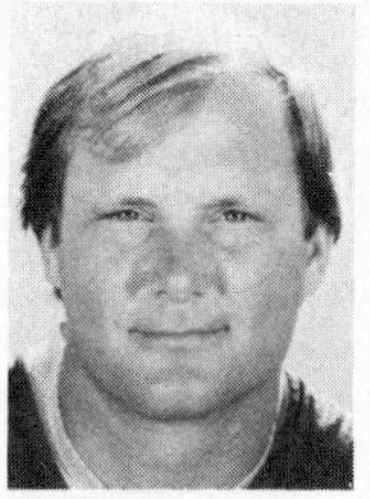
Pat Haden

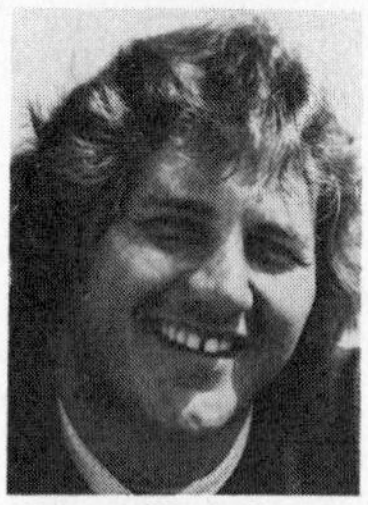
Dennis Harrah

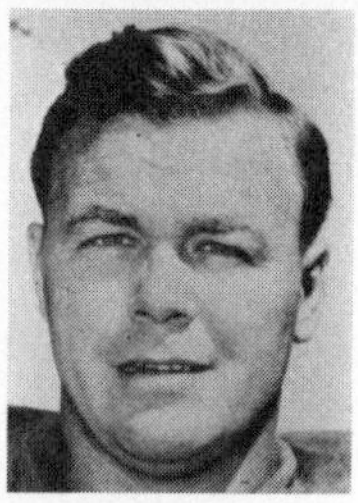
Dick Huffman

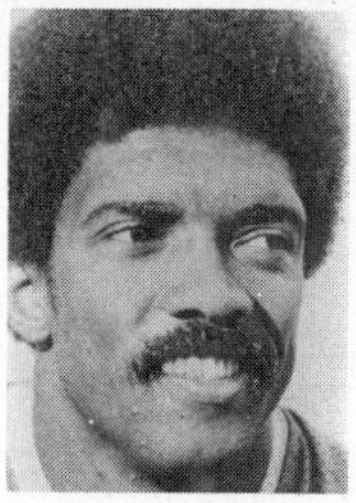
Harold Jackson

1945-46	Adam Walsh	15- 5-1
1947	Bob Snyder	6- 6-0
1948-49	Clark Shaughnessy	14- 7-3
1950-51	Joe Stydahar	17- 7-0
1952-54	Hampton Pool	23-11-2
1955-59	Sid Gillman	28-31-1
1960-62	Bob Waterfield**	9-24-1
1962-65	Harland Svare	14-31-3
1966-70	George Allen	49-17-4
1971-72	Tommy Prothro	14-12-2
1973-77	Chuck Knox	54-15-1
1978-81	Ray Malavasi	38-26-0

**Replaced after three games in 1938*
***Resigned after eight games in 1962*

FIRST PLAYER SELECTED

1937 Johnny Drake, B, Purdue
1938 Corbett Davis, B, Indiana
1939 Parker Hall, B, Mississippi
1940 Ollie Cordill, B, Rice
1941 Rudy Mucha, C, Washington
1942 Jack Wilson, B, Baylor
1943 Mike Holovak, B, Boston College
1944 Tony Butkovich, B, Illinois
1945 Elroy (Crazylegs) Hirsch, B, Wisconsin
1946 Emil Stiko, B, Notre Dame
1947 Herman Wedemeyer, B, St. Mary's, Cal.
1948 Tom Keane, B (2), West Virginia
1949 Bobby Thomason, B, Virginia Military
1950 Ralph Pasquariello, B, Villanova
1951 Bud McFadin, G, Texas
1952 Bill Wade, B, Vanderbilt
1953 Donn Moomaw, C, UCLA
1954 Ed Beatty, C, Cincinnati
1955 Larry Morris, C, Georgia Tech
1956 Joe Marconi, B, West Virginia
1957 Jon Arnett, B, USC
1958 Lou Michaels, T, Kentucky
1959 Dick Bass, B, Pacific
1960 Billy Cannon, RB, Louisiana State
1961 Marlin McKeever, E-LB, USC
1962 Roman Gabriel, QB, North Carolina
1963 Terry Baker, QB, Oregon State
1964 Bill Munson, QB, Utah State
1965 Clancy Williams, CB, Washington State
1966 Tom Mack, G, Michigan
1967 Willie Ellison, RB (2), Texas Southern
1968 Gary Beban, QB (2), UCLA
1969 Larry Smith, RB, Florida
1970 Jack Reynolds, LB, Tennessee
1971 Isiah Robertson, LB, Southern U.
1972 Jim Bertelsen, RB (2), Texas
1973 Cullen Bryant, DB (2), Colorado
1974 John Cappelletti, RB, Penn State
1975 Mike Fanning, DT, Notre Dame
1976 Kevin McLain, LB, Colorado State
1977 Bob Brudzinski, LB, Ohio State
1978 Elvis Peacock, RB, Oklahoma
1979 George Andrews, LB, Nebraska
1980 Johnnie Johnson, DB, Texas
1981 Mel Owens, LB, Michigan
1982 Barry Redden, RB, Richmond

CLEVELAND RAMS, 1937-45;
LOS ANGELES RAMS, 1946-81

Adams, Chet, T, Ohio U. 1939-42
Adams, John, TE, Cal State-Los Angeles 1963
Agajanian, Ben, K, New Mexico 1953
Agler, Bob, RB, Otterbein 1948-49
Alexander, Kermit, DB, UCLA 1970-71
Allen, Duane, E, Santa Ana JC 1961-64
Andersen, Stan, E, Stanford 1941
Anderson, Bruce, DE, Willamette 1966
Andrako, Steve, C, Ohio State 1941
Andrews, George, LB, Nebraska 1979-81
Armstrong, Graham, T, John Carroll 1941, 1945
Arnett, Jon, RB-KR, USC 1957-63
Arnold, Walt, TE, New Mexico 1980-81
Atkins, Pervis, RB, New Mexico State 1961-63
Atty, Alex, G, West Virginia 1939

B

Bacon, Coy, DT, Jackson State 1968-72
Bagarus, Steve, B, Notre Dame 1947
Bain, Bill, G, USC 1979-81
Baker, John, DT, North Carolina College 1958-61
Baker, Terry, QB-RB, Oregon State 1963-65
Baker, Tony, RB, Iowa State 1973-74
Banta, Jack, RB, USC 1946-48
Barber, Mark, B, South Dakota State 1937
Barle, Lou, B, Duluth 1939
Barry, Paul, RB, Tulsa 1950-52
Bass, Dick, RB, Pacific 1960-69
Battle, Ron, TE, North Texas State 1981
Baughan, Maxie, LB, Georgia Tech 1966-70
Beathard, Pete, QB, USC 1972
Benton, Jim, E, Arkansas 1938-42, 1944-47
Bernard, Dave, B, Mississippi 1944-45
Berry, Connie Mack, E, North Carolina State 1940
Bertelsen, Jim, RB, Texas 1972-76
Bettridge, John, B, Ohio State 1937
Bighead, Jack, E, Pepperdine 1955
Bleeker, Mel, RB, USC 1947
Boeke, Jim, T, Heidelberg 1960-63
Boone, Jack, B, Elon 1942
Bostick, Lew, G, Alabama 1939-42
Bouley, Gil, T, Boston College 1945-50
Bowers, Bill, DB, USC 1954
Boyd, Bob, E, Loyola, Cal. 1950-57
Braatz, Tom, E, Marquette 1958
Bradshaw, Charlie, T, Baylor 1958-60
Brahm, Larry, G, Temple 1942
Bratkowski, Zeke, QB, Georgia 1961-63
Bravo, Alex, DB, Cal Poly-San Luis Obispo 1957-58
Brazell, Carl, B, Baylor 1938
Breen, Gene, LB, Virginia Tech 1967-68
Brink, Larry, DE, Northern Illinois 1948-53
Brito, Gene, DE, Loyola, Cal. 1959-60
Britt, Charley, DB, Georgia 1960-63
Brooks, Larry, DT, Virginia State-Petersburg 1972-81
Brown, Bob, T, Nebraska 1969-70
Brown, Eddie, S-KR, Tennessee 1978-79
Brown, Fred, LB, Miami 1965
Brown, Roger, DT, Maryland-Eastern Shore 1967-69
Brown, Willie, WR-RB, USC 1964-65
Brudzinski, Bob, LB, Ohio State 1977-80
Bruney, Fred, DB, Ohio State 1958
Brumbaugh, Carl, B, Florida 1937
Bryant, Cullen, DB-RB, Colorado 1973-81
Buckley, Phil, E, Xavier 1937
Budka, Frank, DB, Notre Dame 1964
Bukich, Rudy, QB, USC 1953-56
Burke, Mike, P, Miami 1974
Burman, George, C-G, Northwestern 1967-70
Burmeister, Forrest, B, Purdue 1937
Burroughs, Don, DB, Colorado State 1955-59
Buzin, Rich, T, Penn State 1971
Byrd, Mac, LB, USC 1965

C

Cahill, Dave, DT, Northern Arizona 1967
Cappelletti, John, RB, Penn State 1974-78
Carey, Bob, E, Michigan State 1952, 1954, 1956
Carrell, Duane, P, Florida State 1975
Carollo, Joe, T, Notre Dame 1962-68, 1971
Carson, Howard, LB, Howard Payne 1981
Casey, Bernie, WR, Bowling Green 1967-68
Cash, Rick, DE, Northeast Missouri 1969-70
Casner, Ken, T, Baylor 1952
Cason, Jim, DB, Louisiana State 1955-56
Castete, Jesse, DB, McNeese State 1956-57
Cellotto, Mario, LB, USC 1981
Champagne, Ed, T, Louisiana State 1947-50
Chapple, Dave, P, UC Santa Barbara 1972-74
Cherundolo, Chuck, C, Penn State 1937-39
Chesbro, Marcel (Red), G, Colgate 1938
Childs, Henry, TE, Kansas City 1981
Chuy, Don, G, Clemson 1963-68
Clark, Al, CB, Eastern Michigan 1972-75
Clark, Ken, P, St. Mary's, Nova Scotia 1979
Clarke, Leon, E, USC 1956-59
Clay, Boyd, T, Tennessee 1940-42, 1944
Cobb, Bob, DE, Arizona 1981
Colella, Tommy, B, Canisius 1944-45
Collier, Bob, T, Southern Methodist 1951
Collins, Jim, LB, Syracuse 1981
Collins, Kirk, CB, Baylor 1981
Conkwright, Bill (Red), C, Oklahoma 1939-45
Conlee, Gerry, C, St. Mary's, Cal. 1938
Cooper, Bud, T, Penn State 1937
Corbo, Tom, G, Duquesne 1944
Cordileone, Lou, G, Clemson 1962
Cordill, Ollie, B, Rice 1940
Corn, Joe, RB, No college 1948
Corral, Frank, K-P, UCLA 1978-81
Cothren, Paige, K, Mississippi 1957-58
Cowan, Charlie, T, New Mexico Highlands 1961-75
Cowhig, Jerry, RB, Notre Dame 1947-49
Cowlings, Al, DE, USC 1975, 1977
Coyle, Ross, DB, Oklahoma 1961
Crabb, Claude, DB, Colorado 1966-68
Cromwell, Nolan, S, Kansas 1977-81
Cross, Bobby, T, Kilgore JC 1954-55
Cross, Irv, DB, Northwestern 1966-68
Crow, Lindon, DB, USC 1961-64
Crowder, Earl, B, Oklahoma 1940
Curran, Pat, TE-RB, Lakeland 1969-74
Currie, Dan, LB, Michigan State 1965-66
Curry, Bill, C, Georgia Tech 1974
Currivan, Don, E, Boston College 1948-49

D

Dahms, Tom, T, San Diego State 1951-54
Dale, Carroll, E, Virginia Tech 1960-64
Dalsasso, Chris, T, Indiana 1937
Daniel, Willie, DB, Mississippi State 1967-69
Daugherty, Dick, LB, Oregon 1951-58
David, Bob, G, Villanova 1947-48
Davis, Anthony, RB-KR, USC 1978
Davis, Corby, B, Indiana 1938-42
Davis, Glenn, RB, Army 1950-51
Davis, Roger, G, Syracuse 1964
Dean, Hal, G, Ohio State 1947-49
DeFruiter, Bob, DB, Nebraska 1948
Delaney, Jeff, S, Pittsburgh 1980
deLauer, Bob, C, USC 1945-46
DeMarco, Bob, C, Dayton 1975
Dempsey, Tom, K, Palomar JC 1975-76
Dennard, Preston, WR, New Mexico 1978-81
Dennis, Mike, RB, Mississippi 1968-69
Dickson, Paul, T, Baylor 1959
Doll, Don, DB, USC 1954
Doss, Reggie, DE, Hampton Institute 1978-81
Dougherty, Bob, LB, Kentucky 1957
Drake, Bill, DB, Oregon 1973-74
Drake, Johnny, B, Drake 1937-41
Dryer, Fred, DE, San Diego State 1972-81
DuBois, Phil, TE, San Diego State 1981
Dunstan, Bill, DT, Utah State 1979
Dunstan, Elwyn, T, Portland 1939-41
Dwyer, Jack, DB, Loyola, Cal. 1952-54
Dyer, Henry, RB, Grambling 1966-68

E

Eason, Roger, G, Oklahoma 1945-48
Ekern, Carl, LB, San Jose State 1976-78, 1980-81
Ellena, Jack, G, UCLA 1955-56
Ellersick, Don, DB, Washington State 1960
Ellis, Ken, CB, Southern U. 1979
Ellison, Willie, RB, Texas Southern 1967-72
Elmendorf, Dave, S, Texas A&M 1971-79
Elston, Art, C, South Carolina 1942
Emerick, Bob, T, Miami, Ohio 1937
Evey, Dick, DT, Tennessee 1970
Ezerins, Vilnis, RB, Whitewater State 1968

F

Fanning, Mike, DT, Notre Dame 1975-81
Fanning, Stan, DE, Idaho 1963
Farmer, Tom, RB, Iowa 1946
Fawcett, Jake, T, Southern Methodist 1942, 1944, 1946
Fears, Tom, E, UCLA 1948-56
Ferragamo, Vince, QB, Nebraska 1977-80
Ferris, Neil, DB, Loyola, Cal. 1953
Finch, Karl, E, Cal Poly-Pomona 1962
Finlay, Jack, G, UCLA 1947-51

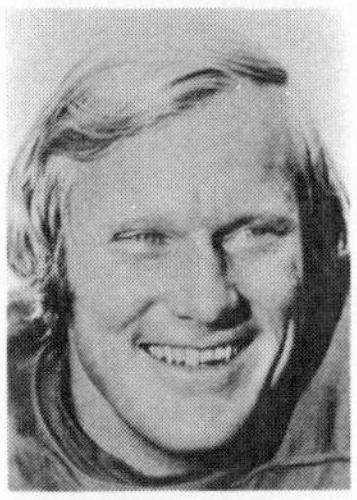
Les Josephson

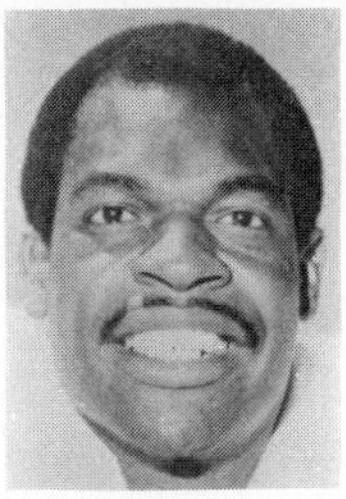
Lamar Lundy

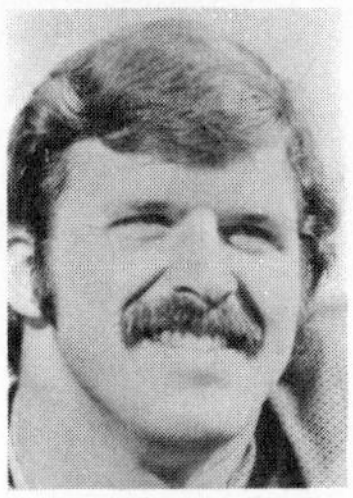
Tom Mack

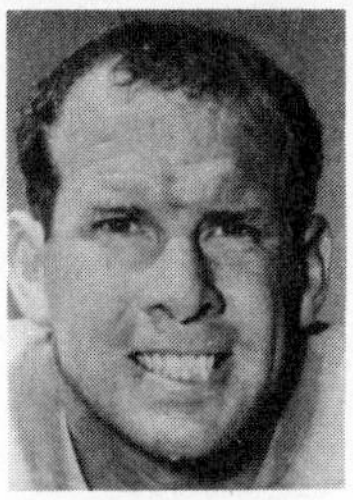
Leon McLaughlin

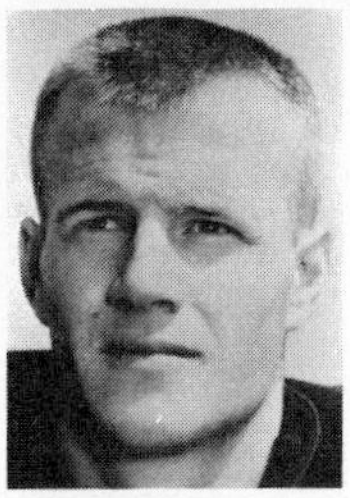
Eddie Meador

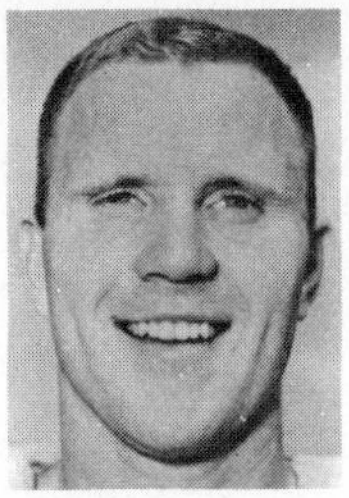
Jack Pardee

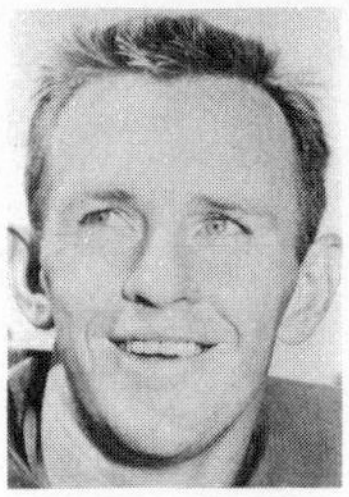
Jim (Red) Phillips

Fournet, Sid, DT, Louisiana State 1955-56
France, Doug, T, Ohio State 1975-81
Franckhauser, Tom, DB, Purdue 1959
Fry, Bob, T, Kentucky 1953-59
Fuller, Frank, DT, Kentucky 1953-58
Fulton, Ed, G, Maryland 1978

G

Gabriel, Roman, QB, North Carolina State 1962-72
Gallovich, Tony, B, Wake Forest 1941
Geddes, Ken, LB, Nebraska 1971-75
Gehrke, Fred, B, Utah 1940, 1945-49
George, Bill, LB, Wake Forest 1966
Geredine, Thomas, WR, Northeast Missouri State 1976
Giannoni, Jack, E, St. Mary's, Cal. 1938
Gibson, Billy Joe, C, Tulsa 1942, 1944
Gift, Wayne, B, Purdue 1937
Gilbert, Lewis, TE, Florida 1981
Goddard, Ed (Rip), B, Washington State 1937-38
Godfrey, Herb, E, Washington State 1942
Goodnight, Owen, B, Hardin-Simmons 1941
Goosby, Jim (Shag), C, Mississippi State 1940
Gordon, Dick, WR, Michigan State 1972-73
Gossett, Bruce, K, Richmond 1964-69
Gravelle, Gordon, T, Brigham Young 1979
Greenwood, Don, B, Missouri 1945
Gregory, John, G, Tennessee-Chattanooga 1941-42
Gremminger, Hank, DB, Baylor 1966
Grier, Rosey, DT, Penn State 1963-66
Griffin, Bob, C, Arkansas 1953-57
Griffin, John, DB, Memphis State 1963
Gudauskas, Peter, G, Murray State 1940
Guillory, Tony, LB, Lamar U. 1965, 1967-68
Guman, Mike, RB, Penn State 1980-81
Guzik, John, LB, Pittsburgh 1959-60

H

Haden, Pat, QB, USC 1976-81
Hadl, John, QB, Kansas 1973-74
Hall, Alvin, DB, No college 1961-63
Halleck, Paul, B, Ohio U. 1937
Halliday, Jack, DT, Southern Methodist 1951
Halverson, Dean, LB, Washington 1968, 1972
Haman, Jack C, Northwestern 1940-41
Hamilton, Ray, E, Arkansas 1938, 1944-47
Harding, Roger, C, California 1946
Hardy, Jim, QB, USC 1946-48
Harmon, Tom, RB, Michigan 1946-47
Harrah, Dennis, G, Miami 1975-81
Harris, James, QB, Grambling 1973-76
Harris, Jimmy, DB, Oklahoma 1958
Harris, Joe, LB, Georgia Tech 1979-81
Harris, Marv, LB, Stanford 1964
Hauser, Art, DT, Xavier 1954-57
Hayes, Larry, C, Vanderbilt 1962-63
Haymond, Alvin, DB, Southern U. 1969-71
Haynes, Hall, DB, Santa Clara 1954-56
Heckard, Steve, E, Davidson 1965-66
Hecker, Bob, DB, Baldwin-Wallace 1952
Hecker, Norb, DB, Baldwin-Wallace 1951-53
Hector, Willie, T, Pacific 1961
Heineman, Ken, B, Texas-El Paso 1940-41
Henry, Mike, LB, USC 1962-64
Henry, Urban, DT, Georgia Tech 1961
Hershey, Kirk, E, Cornell 1941
Hickey, Howard (Red), E, No college 1941, 1945-48
Hicks, Victor, TE, Oklahoma 1980
Hightower, Ben, E, Sam Houston State 1942
Hill, Drew, WR, Georgia Tech 1979-81
Hill, Eddie, RB, Memphis State 1979-80
Hill, Kent, T, Georgia Tech 1979-81
Hill, Winston, T, Texas Southern 1977
Hirsch, Elroy (Crazy Legs), E-RB, Wisconsin 1949-57
Hock, John, G, Santa Clara 1953-57
Hoerner, Dick, RB, Iowa 1947-51
Hoffman, Bob, RB, USC 1946-48
Holladay, Bob, RB, Tulsa 1956
Holovak, Mike, RB, Boston College 1946
Holtzman, Glenn, T, North Texas State 1955-58
Hord, Roy, G, Duke 1960-62
Horton, Greg, G, Colorado 1976-78, 1980
Horvath, Les, RB, Ohio State 1947-48
Houser, John, C-G, Redlands 1957-59
Howard, Gene, DB, Langston, Oklahoma 1971-72
Hubbell, Frank, DE-TE, Tennessee 1947-49
Huffman, Dick, T, Tennessee 1947-50
Huggins, Roy, B, Vanderbilt 1944
Hughes, Ed, DB, Tulsa 1954-55
Humphrey, Buddy, QB, Baylor 1959-60
Hunter, Art, C, Notre Dame 1960-64
Hupke, Tom, G, Alabama 1938-39

I

Iglehart, Floyd, DB, Wiley, Texas 1958
Iman, Ken, C, Southeast Missouri State 1965-74
Irvin, LeRoy, CB-KR, Kansas 1980-81
Isselhardt, Ralph, G, Franklin 1937

J

Jackson, Harold, WR, Jackson State 1968, 1973-77
Jackson, Monte, CB, San Diego State 1975-77
Jackson, Rusty, P, Louisiana State 1976
Jacobs, Jack, QB, Oklahoma 1942, 1945
Janerette, Charlie, G, Penn State 1960
Janiak, Len, B, Ohio U. 1940-42
Jaworski, Ron, QB, Youngstown State 1974-76
Jessie, Ron, WR, Kansas 1975-79
Jobko, Bill, LB, Ohio State 1958-62
Jodat, Jim, RB, Carthage 1977-79
Johns, Freeman, WR, Southern Methodist 1976-77
Johnson, Clyde, T, Kentucky 1946-47
Johnson, Don, C, Northwestern 1942
Johnson, Johnnie, S, Texas 1980-81
Johnson, Marvin, DB, San Jose State 1951-52
Johnson, Mitch, T, UCLA 1969-70
Jones, Cody, DT, San Jose State 1974-78, 1980-81
Jones, David (Deacon), DE, South Carolina State 1961-71
Jones, Harvey, B, Baylor 1944-45
Jones, Jimmy, RB, Washington 1958
Jordan, Jeff, RB, Washington 1970
Josephson, Les, RB, Augustana, South Dakota 1964-67, 1969-74
Justin, Sid, CB, Long Beach State 1979

K

Kabealo, Mike, B, Ohio State 1944
Kalmanir, Tom, RB, Nevada-Reno 1949-51
Karilivacz, Carl, DB, Syracuse 1959-60
Karras, Ted, G, Indiana 1966
Karrs, John, B, Duquesne 1944
Kay, Rick, LB, Colorado 1973, 1975-77
Keane, Tom, DB, West Virginia 1948-51
Keeble, Joe, B, UCLA 1937
Kemp, Jeff, QB, Dartmouth 1981
Kenerson, John, T, Kentucky State 1960
Kilgore, Jon, P, Auburn 1965-67
Kimbrough, Elbert, DB, Northwestern 1961
Kinek, Mike, E, Michigan State 1940
Kirk, Ken, C, Mississippi 1963
Klein, Bob, TE, USC 1969-76
Klosterman, Don, QB, Loyola, Cal. 1952
Koch, George, B, Baylor 1945
Konetsky, Floyd, E, Florida 1944-45
Kovatch, Johnny, E, Northwestern 1938
Krause, Bill, T, Baldwin-Wallace 1938
Ksionyzk, John, QB, St. Bonaventure 1947

L

LaHood, Mike, G, Wyoming 1969, 1971-72
Lamson, Chuck, DB, Wyoming 1965-67
Lane, Dick (Night Train), DB, Scottsbluff JC 1952-53
Lang, Izzy, RB, Tennessee State 1969
Lange, Bill, G, Dayton 1951-52
Lansford, Buck, G, Texas 1958-60
Larsen, Gary, DT, Concordia 1964
Latin, Jerry, RB-KR, Northern Illinois 1978
Lazetich, Milan, MG, Michigan 1945-50
Lazetich, Bill, B, Montana 1939, 1941-42
Lear, Les, G, Manitoba 1944-46
Lee, Bob, QB, Pacific 1979-80
Leggett, Earl, DT, Louisiana State 1966
Levy, Len, G, Minnesota 1945-46
Lewis, Art (Pappy), T, Ohio U. 1938-39
Lewis, Woodley, DB-E, Oregon 1950-55
Liles, Elvin (Sonny), G, Oklahoma State 1945
Lipscomb, Gene (Big Daddy), DT, No college 1953-55
Littlefield, Carl, B, Washington State 1938
Livingston, Cliff, LB, UCLA 1963-65
Long, Bob, LB, UCLA 1960-61
Long, Bob, WR, Wichita State 1970
Lothridge, Billy, P, Georgia Tech 1965
Love, John, WR, North Texas State 1972
LoVetere, John, DT, Compton JC 1959-62
Lundy, Lamar, DE-TE, Purdue 1957-69

M

Mack, Tom, G, Michigan 1966-78
Magnani, Dante, B, St. Mary's, Cal. 1940-42, 1947-48
Maher, Frank, B, Toledo 1941
Marchlewski, Frank, C, Minnesota 1965, 1968-69
Marconi, Joe, RB, West Virginia 1959-61
Markov, Vic, T, Washington 1938
Marshall, Larry, WR-KR, Maryland 1978
Martin, Aaron, DB, North Carolina College 1964-65
Martin, Jack, C, Navy 1947-49
Maslowski, Matt, WR, U. of San Diego 1971
Mason, Tommy, RB, Tulane 1967-70
Matheson, Riley, G, Texas-El Paso 1939-42, 1944-47
Matson, Ollie, RB-E, San Francisco 1959-62
Mattos, Harry, B, St. Mary's, Cal. 1937
Mayes, Carl, RB, Texas 1952
McCormick, Tom, RB, Pacific 1953-55
McCutcheon, Lawrence, RB, Colorado State 1972-79
McDonald, Tommy, WR, Oklahoma 1965-66
McFadin, Bud, DT-T, Texas 1952-56
McGarry, Barney, G, Utah 1939-42
McGee, Willie, WR, Alcorn State 1974-75
McGlasson, Ed, C, Youngstown State 1980
McIlhany, Dan, DB, Texas A&M 1965
McKeever, Marlin, LB-TE, USC 1961-66, 1971-72
McKinnely, Phil, T, UCLA 1981
McLain, Kevin, LB, Colorado State 1976-79
McLaughlin, Leon, C, UCLA 1951-55
McMillan, Eddie, CB, Florida State 1973-75
Meador, Ed, DB, Arkansas Tech 1959-70
Meisner, Greg, DT, Pittsburgh 1981
Mello, Jim, RB, Notre Dame 1948
Mergenthal, Art, G, Notre Dame 1945-46
Michaels, Lou, DE, Kentucky 1958-60
Miller, Charles (Ookie), C, Purdue 1937
Miller, Clark, DE, Utah State 1970
Miller, Paul, DE, Louisiana State 1954-57
Miller, Ralph (Primo), T, Rice 1937-38
Miller, Ron, E, USC 1956
Miller, Ron, QB, Wisconsin 1962
Miller, Willie, WR, Colorado State 1978-81
Mitchell, Lydell, RB, Penn State 1980
Moan, Emmett (Kelly), B, West Virginia 1937
Molden, Frank, DT, Jackson State 1965
Monaco, Ray, G, Holy Cross 1945
Mooney, Tex (see O. T. Schupbach), T, West Texas State 1941-42
Moore, Jeff, WR, Tennessee 1980-81
Moore, Tom, RB, Vanderbilt 1966
Morris, George, B, Baldwin-Wallace 1941-42
Morris, Jack, DB, Oregon 1958-60
Morris, Larry, LB, Georgia Tech 1955-57
Morrow, John, C, Michigan 1956-59
Mucha, Rudy, C-B, Washington 1941, 1945
Munson, Bill, QB, Utah State 1964-67
Murphy, Phil, DT, South Carolina State 1980-81
Myers, Brad, RB, Bucknell 1953-56
Myers, Jack (Moose), RB-DB, UCLA 1952

N

Namath, Joe, QB, Alabama 1977
Naumetz, Fred, LB-C, Boston College 1946-50
Neihaus, Ralph, T, Cincinnati 1939
Nelson, Bill, DT, Oregon State 1971-75
Nelson, Terry, TE, Arkansas-Pine Bluff 1973-80
Nemeth, Steve, B, Notre Dame 1945
Nettles, Jim, DB, Wisconsin 1969-72
Nichols, Bob, T, Stanford 1966-67
Nuzum, Rick, C, Kentucky 1977

O

Odom, Ricky, DB, USC 1979
Olsen, Merlin, DT, Utah State 1962-76

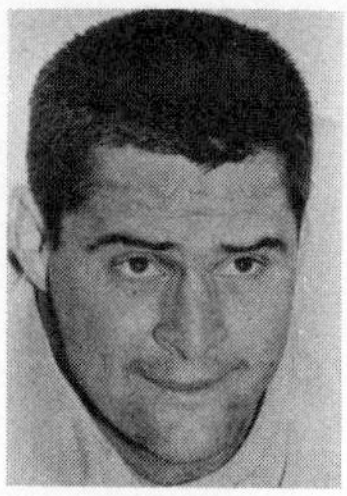

Duane Putnam

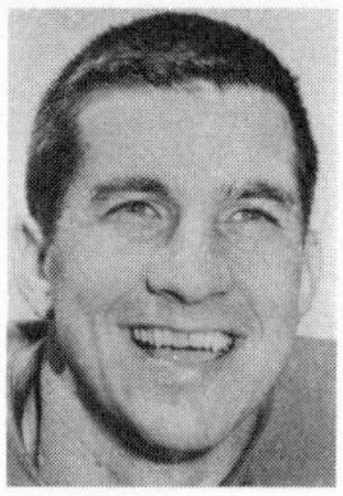

Les Richter

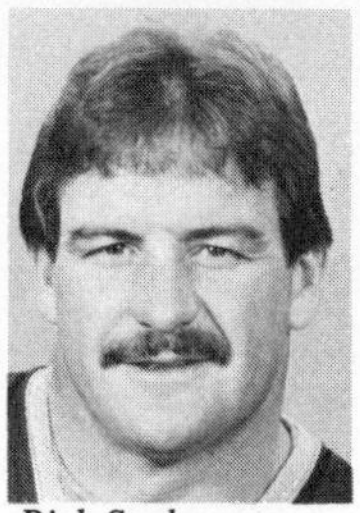

Rich Saul

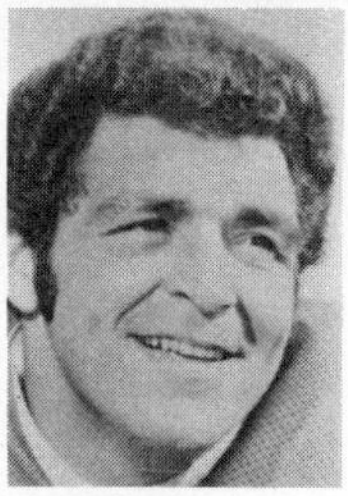

Joe Scibelli

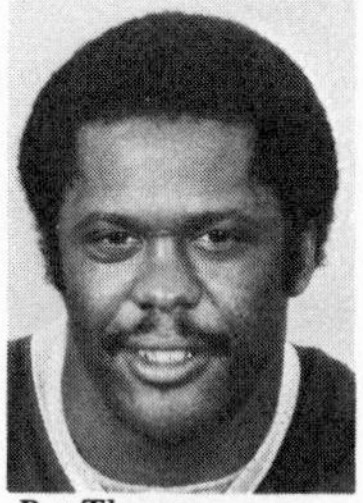

Pat Thomas

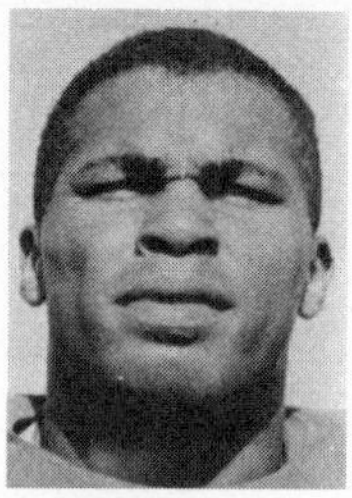

Dan Towler

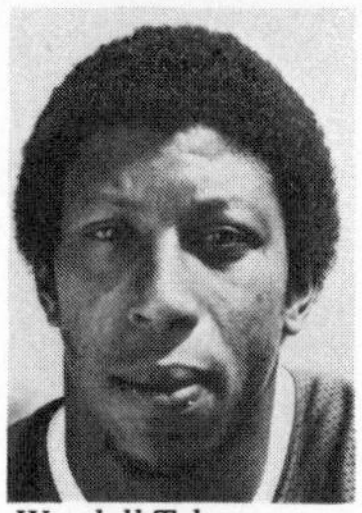

Wendell Tyler

Olsen, Norman, T, Alabama . . . 1944
Olsen, Phil, DT-DE, Utah State . . . 1971-74
O'Neill, Bill, B, Detroit . . . 1937
O'Steen, Dwayne, CB, San Jose State . . . 1978-79
Owens, Mel, LB, Michigan . . . 1981

P

Panfil, Ken, T, Purdue . . . 1956-58
Pankey, Irv, T, Penn State . . . 1980-81
Pardee, Jack, LB, Texas A&M . . . 1957-64, 1966-70
Parish, Don, LB, Stanford . . . 1971
Pasqua, Joe, T, Southern Methodist . . . 1942, 1946
Pasquariello, Ralph, RB, Villanova . . . 1950
Pastorini, Dan, QB, Santa Clara . . . 1981
Patt, Maurice (Babe), E, Carnegie Tech . . . 1939-42
Paul, Don, LB, UCLA . . . 1948-55
Peacock, Elvis, RB, Oklahoma . . . 1979-80
Penaranda, Jairo, RB, UCLA . . . 1981
Pergine, John, LB, Notre Dame . . . 1969-72
Perkins, Art, RB, North Texas State . . . 1962-63
Perry, Rod, CB, Colorado . . . 1975-81
Petchel, John, B, Duquesne . . . 1942, 1944
Peterson, Jim, LB, San Diego State . . . 1974-75
Peterson, Nelson, B, West Virginia Wesleyan . . . 1938
Petitbon, Richie, DB, Tulane . . . 1969-70
Phillips, George, B, UCLA . . . 1945
Phillips, Jim (Red), WR, Auburn . . . 1958-64
Phillips, Rod, RB, Jackson State . . . 1975-78
Pifferini, Bob, LB, UCLA . . . 1977
Pillath, Roger, T, Wisconsin . . . 1965
Pincura, Stan, B, Ohio State . . . 1937-38
Pitts, Elijah, RB, Philander Smith . . . 1970
Pitts, Hugh, LB, Texas Christian . . . 1956
Pivec, Dave, TE, Notre Dame . . . 1966-68
Platukas, George, E, Duquesne . . . 1941-42
Plum, Milt, QB, Penn State . . . 1968
Plummer, Tony, DB, Pacific . . . 1974
Plunkett, Warren, B, Minnesota . . . 1942
Pope, Bucky, WR, Catawba . . . 1964, 1966-67
Pottios, Myron, LB, Notre Dame . . . 1966-70
Powell, Tim, DE, Northwestern . . . 1965
Prather, Dale, E, George Washington . . . 1937-38
Preece, Steve, S, Oregon State . . . 1973-76
Pritchard, Bosh, B, Virginia Military . . . 1942
Pritko, Steve, DE, Villanova . . . 1946-47
Prochaska, Ray, E, Nebraska . . . 1941
Pudloski, Chet, T, Villanova . . . 1944
Purnell, Jim, LB, Wisconsin . . . 1969-72
Putnam, Duane, G, Pacific . . . 1952-59, 1962

Q

Quinlan, Skeet, RB, San Diego State . . . 1952-56

R

Ragazzo, Phil, T, Western Reserve . . . 1938-39
Rapp, Manny, B, St. Louis . . . 1941-42
Ray, David, K-WR, Alabama . . . 1969-74
Ream, Chuck, T, Ohio State . . . 1938
Reece, Geoff, C, Washington State . . . 1976
Reid, Joe, C, Louisiana State . . . 1951
Reinhard, Bob, T-DT, California . . . 1950
Reisz, Albie, B, Southeastern Louisiana . . . 1944-46
Rentzel, Lance, WR, Oklahoma . . . 1971-72, 1974
Repko, Joe, DT, Boston College . . . 1948-49
Reynolds, Jack, LB, Tennessee . . . 1970-80
Rhome, Jerry, QB, Tulsa . . . 1971
Rich, Herb, DB, Vanderbilt . . . 1951-53
Richardson, Jerry, DB, West Texas State . . . 1964-65
Richter, Les, LB, California . . . 1954-62
Rickards, Paul, B, Pittsburgh . . . 1948
Rieth, Bill, G, Carnegie Tech . . . 1941-42, 1944-45
Riffle, Charley, G, Notre Dame . . . 1944
Robertson, Isiah, LB, Southern U. . . . 1971-78
Robinson, Jack, T, Northeast Missouri . . . 1938
Robustelli, Andy, DE, Arnold . . . 1951-55
Rockwell, Hank, C, Arizona State . . . 1940-42
Rodak, Mike, G, Western Reserve . . . 1939-40
Rogers, Mel, LB, Florida A&M . . . 1976
Rosequist, Ted, T, Ohio State . . . 1937
Rucker, Conrad, G-T, Southern U. . . . 1980
Russell, Doug, B, Kansas State . . . 1939
Russell, Lloyd, B, Baylor . . . 1939
Ruthstrom, Ralph, RB, Southern Methodist . . . 1945-46
Rutledge, Jeff, QB, Alabama . . . 1979-81
Ryan, Frank, QB, Rice . . . 1958-61
Ryczek, Dan, C, Virginia . . . 1978-79

S

Saul, Rich, C-G, Michigan State . . . 1970-81
Savatsky, Ollie, E, Miami, Ohio . . . 1937
Scales, Dwight, WR, Grambling . . . 1976-78
Scarry, Mike, C, Waynesburg State . . . 1944-45
Schenker, Nate, T, Howard . . . 1939
Schultz, Eberle, T, Oregon State . . . 1946-47
Schuh, Harry, T, Memphis State . . . 1971-73
Schumacher, Gregg, DE, Illinois . . . 1967-68
Schupbach, O.T. (played as Tex Mooney), T, West Texas State 1941-42
Scibelli, Joe, G, Notre Dame . . . 1961-75
Scribner, Rob, RB, UCLA . . . 1973-76
Seabright, Charlie (Goose), B, West Virginia . . . 1941
Sebastian, Mike, B, Pittsburgh . . . 1937
Selawski, Gene, T, Purdue . . . 1959
Septien, Rafael, K, Southwestern Louisiana . . . 1977
Severson, Jeff, DB, Long Beach State . . . 1979
Sewell, Harley, G, Texas . . . 1963
Shannon, Carver, DB-RB, Southern Illinois . . . 1962-64
Shaw, Bob, E, Ohio State . . . 1945-49
Shaw, Glenn, RB, Kentucky . . . 1962
Shaw, Nate, DB, USC . . . 1969-70
Sherman, Rod, WR, USC . . . 1973
Sherman, Will, DB, St. Mary's, Cal. . . . 1954-60
Shirey, Fred, T, Nebraska . . . 1940-41
Shiver, Ray, DB, Miami . . . 1956
Shofner, Del, E, Baylor . . . 1957-60
Sikich, Rudy, T, Minnesota . . . 1945
Simensen, Don, T, St. Thomas . . . 1951-52
Simington, Milt, G, Arkansas . . . 1941
Simpson, Bill, S, Michigan State . . . 1974-78
Sims, George, DB, Baylor . . . 1949-50
Skoczen, Stan, B, Western Reserve . . . 1944
Skoronski, Ed, C, Purdue . . . 1937
Slater, Jackie, G-T, Jackson State . . . 1976-81
Slovak, Marty, B, Toledo . . . 1939-41
Smith, Billy Ray, DE, Arkansas . . . 1957
Smith, Bobby, DB, UCLA . . . 1962-65
Smith, Bruce, RB, Minnesota . . . 1948
Smith, Doug, C-G, Bowling Green . . . 1978-81
Smith, Gaylon, B, Southwestern . . . 1939-42
Smith, Larry, RB, Florida . . . 1969-73
Smith, Lucious, CB, Cal State-Fullerton . . . 1980-81
Smith, Ron, QB, Richmond . . . 1965
Smith, Ron, DB-KR, Wisconsin . . . 1968-69
Smith, Ron, WR, San Diego State . . . 1978-79
Smith, Verda (Vitamin T), RB, Abilene Christian . . . 1949-53
Smyth, Bill, T, Cincinnati . . . 1947-50
Snow, Jack, WR, Notre Dame . . . 1965-75
Snyder, Bob, B, Ohio U. . . . 1937-38
Spadaccini, Vic, T, Minnesota . . . 1938-40
Sparkman, Al, DT, Texas A&M . . . 1948-49
Stalcup, Jerry, LB, Wisconsin . . . 1960
Statuto, Art, C, Notre Dame . . . 1950
Stein, Bob, LB, Minnesota . . . 1973-74
Stephens, Johnny, E, Marshall . . . 1938
Stephens, Larry, DT, Texas . . . 1962
Stephenson, Dave (Trapper), G, West Virginia . . . 1950
Stevenson, Ralph, G, Oklahoma . . . 1940
Stiger, Jim, RB, Washington . . . 1965-67
Stokes, Tim, T, Oregon . . . 1974
Strode, Woody, E, UCLA . . . 1946
Strofolino, Mike, LB, Villanova . . . 1965
Strugar, George, DT, Washington . . . 1957-61
Stuart, Roy, G, Tulsa . . . 1942
Studstill, Pat, WR-P, Houston . . . 1968-71
Stukes, Charlie, CB, Maryland-Eastern Shore . . . 1973-74
Sucic, Steve, B, Illinois . . . 1946
Sully, Ivory, S, Delaware . . . 1979-81
Svare, Harland, LB, Washington State . . . 1953-54
Swain, Bill, LB, Oregon . . . 1963
Sweet, Joe, WR, Tennessee State . . . 1972-73
Sweetan, Karl, QB, Wake Forest . . . 1969-70

T

Talbert, Diron, DT, Texas . . . 1967-70
Tarbox, Bruce, G, Syracuse . . . 1961
Taylor, Cecil, RB, Kansas State . . . 1955-57
Teeuws, Len, T, Tulane . . . 1952-53
Thomas, Bob, RB, Arizona State . . . 1971-72
Thomas, Clendon, DB, Oklahoma . . . 1958-61
Thomas, Jewerl, RB, San Jose State . . . 1980-81
Thomas, Pat, CB, Texas A&M . . . 1976-81
Thomason, Bobby, QB, Virginia Military . . . 1949
Thompson, Harry, G, UCLA . . . 1950-54
Toogood, Charley, DT-T, Nebraska . . . 1951-56
Towler, Dan, RB, Washington & Jefferson . . . 1950-55
Truax, Billy, TE, Louisiana State . . . 1964-70
Tucker, Wendell, WR, South Carolina State . . . 1967-70
Tuckey, Dick, B, Manhattan . . . 1938
Turner, Jim, B, Oklahoma State . . . 1937
Tyler, Wendell, RB, UCLA . . . 1977-81

U

Underwood, Wayne, T, Davis & Elkins . . . 1937
Uzdavinis, Walter, E, Fordham . . . 1937

V

Valdez, Vernon, DB, U. of San Diego . . . 1960
Van Brocklin, Norm, QB-P, Oregon . . . 1949-57
Varrichione, Frank, T, Notre Dame . . . 1961-65
Vasicek, Vic, LB, Texas . . . 1950
Villanueva, Danny, P-K, New Mexico State . . . 1960-64
Von Sonn, Andy, LB, UCLA . . . 1964

W

Waddy, Billy, WR, Colorado . . . 1977-81
Wade, Bill, QB, Vanderbilt . . . 1954-60
Walker, Glen, P, USC . . . 1977-78
Wallace, Jackie, S, B, Arizona . . . 1977-79
Waller, Ron, RB, Maryland . . . 1955-58
Wardlow, Duane, DE, Washington . . . 1954-56
Washington, Kenny, B, UCLA . . . 1946-48
Waterfield, Bob, QB-DB-K-P, UCLA . . . 1945-52
Weisgerber, Dick, B, Willamette . . . 1938
Wendryhoski, Joe, C, Illinois . . . 1964-66
West, Pat, B, USC . . . 1944-48
West, Stan, G, Oklahoma . . . 1950-54
Westbrooks, Greg, LB, Colorado . . . 1979-80
White, Lee, RB, Weber State . . . 1971
Whitmyer, Nat, DB, Washington . . . 1963
Whittenton, Jess, DB, Texas-El Paso . . . 1956-57
Whittingham, Fred, LB, Cal Poly-San Luis Obispo . . . 1964
Wilbur, John, G, Stanford . . . 1970
Wilkins, Roy, LB, Georgia . . . 1958-59
Wilkinson, Jerry, DE, Oregon State . . . 1979
Williams, Charlie, WR, Prairie View . . . 1970
Williams, Clancy, DB, Washington State . . . 1965-72
Williams, Frank, RB, Pepperdine . . . 1961
Williams, Jeff, T, Rhode Island . . . 1977
Williams, Jerry, DB, Washington State . . . 1949-52
Williams, John, T, Minnesota . . . 1972-79
Williams, Roger, DB, Grambling . . . 1971-72
Williams, Sam, DE, Michigan State . . . 1959
Williams, Travis, RB, Arizona State . . . 1971
Wilson, Ben, RB, USC . . . 1963-65
Wilson, Jack, RB, Baylor . . . 1946-47
Wilson, Jim, T, Georgia . . . 1968
Wilson, Johnny, E, Western Reserve . . . 1939-42
Wilson, Tom, RB, No college . . . 1956-61
Winkler, Jim, DB, Texas A&M . . . 1951-52
Winkler, Joe, C, Purdue . . . 1945
Winston, Kelton, DB, Wiley . . . 1967-68
Wojcik, Greg, DT, USC . . . 1971
Woodlief, Doug, LB, Memphis State . . . 1965-69
Worden, Jim, B, Waynesburg . . . 1945

Y

Yagiello, Ray, G, Catawba . . . 1948-49
Young, Charle, TE, USC . . . 1977-79
Youngblood, George, DB, Cal State-Los Angeles . . . 1966
Youngblood, Jack, DE, Florida . . . 1971-81
Youngblood, Jim, LB, Tennessee Tech . . . 1973-81
Younger, Paul (Tank), RB-LB, Grambling . . . 1949-57

Z

Zilly, Jack, E, Notre Dame . . . 1947-51
Zirinsky, Walt, B, Lafayette . . . 1945
Zoll, Dick, G, Indiana . . . 1937-38

MIAMI DOLPHINS

1965 Joseph Robbie, a Minneapolis lawyer who owned a house in Miami, met AFL Commissioner Joe Foss in Washington, March 3. Robbie, a former classmate of Foss's at the University of South Dakota, was representing a friend who sought an AFL expansion franchise for Philadelphia. Foss rejected Philadelphia as a site, noting the Eagles had exclusive rights to Franklin Field. Foss suggested Robbie apply for the franchise in Miami. "With the population growth and climate, it'll be the best franchise in the league," Foss said. Seeking financial backing, Robbie went to entertainer Danny Thomas, a co-worker on the board of St. Jude's Hospital. Thomas, who earlier sought to buy the Chicago White Sox, agreed to become a partner. Thanks to the influence of then Vice President Hubert Humphrey, Robbie's friend from Minnesota, Miami Mayor Robert King High agreed to invite the AFL to Miami, with the assurance that the team could play in the Orange Bowl, May 6. The AFL awarded its first expansion franchise to Robbie and Thomas for $7.5 million, August 16. Joe Thomas of the Minnesota Vikings was named director of player personnel, September 21. Mrs. Robert Swanson of West Miami won two lifetime passes in a contest to pick a team nickname. Her suggestion, "Dolphins," was chosen from over 20,000 entries. In the first round of the AFL college draft, the Dolphins selected Kentucky quarterback Rick Norton and Illinois fullback Jim Grabowski, November 27.

1966 In the expansion draft, Miami picked 31 players from the eight AFL teams, 19 of them starters. The player selected fourteenth, offensive tackle Norm Evans of the Houston Oilers, was destined to be a 10-year regular with the Dolphins. George Wilson was hired as head coach, January 29. Wilson had coached the Detroit Lions for eight seasons and had spent one year as an assistant in Washington. The Dolphins opened their first training camp with 83 players in St. Petersburg, Florida, July 5. Grumbling began immediately as the players complained about the gravel practice field and the dormitory that was next to Sea World. "We couldn't sleep," Evans said. "The seals kept barking all night." The Dolphins left for their first game, a preseason test in San Diego, August 4. The flight, aboard an aged, propellor-driven aircraft, lasted 10 hours. Miami lost the game 30-10 and Wilson accused San Diego coach Sid Gillman of rolling up the score. Training camp was moved to Boca Raton, August 7. A crowd of 36,366 fans came to the Orange Bowl to see the Dolphins lose to Kansas City 33-0. The Dolphins opened the regular season at the Orange Bowl against Oakland, September 2. Joe Auer, a Buffalo castoff who owned a pet lion, thrilled the 26,776 fans by returning the opening kickoff 95 yards for a touchdown. The Raiders rallied to win 23-14. When injuries sidelined Norton and Dick Wood, Wilson installed his son, George, Jr., at quarterback. Wilson led the Dolphins to their first AFL victory, passing 67 yards to Billy Joe for a touchdown in a 24-7 win over Denver, October 16. The following week, Wilson injured his shoulder in a 20-13 win at Houston and his father signed John Stofa from a semipro league in Lakeland, Florida, to finish the season at quarterback. Stofa threw four touchdown passes, one to Auer with 38 seconds left, to give the Miami team its third win, a 29-28 surprise over Houston, December 18.

1967 It was a year of reorganization—on the field and in the front office. W.H. Keland of Racine, Wisconsin, purchased the interests of Martin Decker, George Hamid, Sr., and George Hamid, Jr., March

23. Robbie and Keland bought out Danny Thomas, June 1. In the first round of the first AFL-NFL draft, Miami drafted Purdue quarterback Bob Griese. Joe Thomas completed a seven-man trade, acquiring halfback Abner Haynes from Denver. In the regular season opener against Denver, Stofa broke his ankle, leaving Griese to run the offense. Griese played well and Haynes rushed for 151 yards in the 35-21 Miami win. Hard times followed as the Dolphins lost their next eight, scoring just seven touchdowns. They ended the losing streak by beating Buffalo 17-14 on a fourth down, 31-yard touchdown pass from Griese to Howard Twilley, November 26. The Dolphins defeated San Diego 41-24 and the Boston Patriots 41-32 to close out their home schedule. Cornerback Dick Westmoreland intercepted his tenth pass of the season against the Patriots. Griese finished the season fifth among NFL passers, so Thomas traded Stofa to Cincinnati for two high draft picks.

1968 The draft brought a fresh supply of talent to Miami. In the first five rounds, Thomas selected running backs Larry Csonka and Jim Kiick, offensive tackle Doug Crusan, and safety Dick Anderson. All were starters in 1968. The Dolphins won their first interleague victory, beating the Eagles 23-7 in a preseason game, August 17. Two weeks later, Griese's favorite receiver, Jack Clancy, suffered a broken leg in a 22-13 loss to Baltimore. In the regular season, Miami recovered from a 0-3 start to win five games. Griese set club passing records of 2,473 yards, 186 completions, and 21 touchdowns.

1969 Thomas continued to upgrade Miami's personnel, drafting defensive linemen Bill Stanfill and Bob Heinz, halfback Eugene (Mercury) Morris, and cornerback Lloyd Mumphord and trading for linebacker Nick Buoniconti and guard Larry Little. Griese passed for four touchdowns in a 34-31 loss to the New York Jets, November 2. One week later, Griese injured his right knee in a Boston downpour and missed the final five games. In all 20 players missed seven games or more due to injury. Robbie purchased the interest of W.H. Keland to become the club's majority owner. Racked by injuries, the Dolphins slipped back into last place (3-10-1) and Wilson was relieved of his coaching duties after the 1969 season.

1970 A new era began for the Dolphins when 40-year-old Don Shula left Baltimore to become head coach and vice president in Miami, February 18. Commissioner Pete Rozelle ordered Miami to give Baltimore its first-round draft pick in 1971 as compensation. "I'm not a miracle worker," Shula said. "I have no magic formulas. The only way I know is hard work." Shula put the Dolphins through a grueling training camp at Biscayne College in North Miami, starting every day with a 7 A.M. two-mile run followed by two 90-minute practices, followed by an evening walk-through. The regimen paid off as the Dolphins won four straight preseason games and four of their first five league games. On October 3, Miami beat Oakland for the first time, 20-

Linebacker Nick Buoniconti jolts Pittsburgh's John (Frenchy) Fuqua, 1971.

Larry Csonka takes a handoff from Earl Morrall and sweeps left behind the blocking of guard Bob Kuechenberg, 1972.

13, as newly acquired receiver Paul Warfield caught two touchdown passes. One week later, the Dolphins scored their first victory over the New York Jets, 20-6. The Dolphins went into a brief tailspin, losing three in a row, before closing the season with six consecutive wins. They avenged a 35-0 loss by beating Baltimore 34-17 as rookie safety Jake Scott scored on a 77-yard punt return, November 22. The Dolphins beat Buffalo 45-7 to clinch the AFC wild card spot, December 20. In Oakland's muddy Coliseum, the Dolphins lost their first playoff game to the Raiders 21-14.

1971 Miami got off to a slow start, tying Denver and losing to the New York Jets. Angered, Shula cracked down on his players and they responded. The Dolphins won eight in a row, including Miami's first shutout ever, a 34-0 romp over Buffalo, November 7. Griese had matured into a poised pro quarterback. In a 41-3 win over New England, Griese set a record by throwing three consecutive passes for touchdowns. He rallied Miami from a 21-3 deficit to a 24-21 victory over Pittsburgh, November 14. The Dolphins clinched first place in the AFC Eastern Division on

the final day of the season, beating Green Bay 27-6 before a record crowd of 74,215 at the Orange Bowl, December 19. Csonka became the club's first 1,000-yard rusher with 1,051 yards and placekicker Garo Yepremian led the NFL with 117 points. The Dolphins won the longest game in NFL history (82 minutes, 40 seconds) as Yepremian kicked a 37-yard field goal in the second overtime to beat Kansas City 27-24 in an AFC Divisional Playoff Game, December 25. Miami dethroned the Baltimore Colts, the defending world champions, in the AFC title game 21-0, January 2. It was the first shutout against the Colts in 97 games.

1972 The Dolphins fell to Dallas 24-3 in Super Bowl VI, January 16. "We'll be back," Robbie vowed. Joe Thomas left the Dolphins' front office. The Dolphins became the first team in NFL history to go through an entire season including postseason games, unbeaten and untied. They opened the year with a 20-10 win over Kansas City, September 17. Griese hit Jim Mandich with a last-minute touchdown pass to upset the Vikings in Minnesota 16-14, October 1. Two weeks later, Griese suffered a broken right leg and disclo-

cated ankle when he was hit by San Diego's Ron East. He was replaced by Earl Morrall, a 38-year-old backup quarterback who had been claimed on waivers from Baltimore in the spring. Yepremian kicked the longest field goal of his career (54 yards) to beat Buffalo 24-23 in the Orange Bowl, October 22. Shula became the first NFL coach to win 100 games in 10 seasons as Miami crushed New England with 501 yards 52-0, November 12. The Dolphins achieved the NFL's first 14-0 record by closing the regular season with a 16-0 win over Baltimore. Csonka and Morris both rushed for 1,000 yards as Miami set a league rushing record, 2,960 yards. Miami slipped past Cleveland 20-14 in an AFC divisional playoff, December 23. Griese came off the bench in the second half to spark the Dolphins to a 21-17 win over Pittsburgh in the AFC Championship Game, December 31.

1973 Miami capped its perfect season in Super Bowl VII at Los Angeles, defeating Washington for the world championship 14-7, January 14. As the 1973 season began, the Dolphins' hopes for another perfect season were dashed in the second week when they fell to Oakland 12-7, September 23. The Dolphins bounced back the following week to crush New England 44-23 as Morris scored three touchdowns and set a team record with 197 yards rushing. Miami shut out Baltimore for the fourth consecutive time 44-0 as cornerback Tim Foley returned two blocked punts for touchdowns, an NFL first, November 11. The next week, the Dolphins recorded their second consecutive shutout, beating Buffalo 17-0 to clinch their third successive AFC Eastern Division championship. Warfield caught four touchdown passes from Griese in the first half to pace a 34-7 rout of Detroit, December 15. The win concluded the regular season, giving Miami the best two-year record in NFL history, 26-2. Three days later, Shula signed a contract to coach the Dolphins through 1977. Miami defeated Cincinnati 34-16 in the AFC playoff, December 23. The Dolphins rushed for 266 yards to dominate Oakland 27-10 and win an unprecedented third straight AFC championship, December 30.

1974 Miami defeated Minnesota 24-7 in Super Bowl VIII at Houston's Rice Stadium, January 13. Csonka set Super Bowl records with 145 yards rushing on 33 carries. He scored two touchdowns and Kiick one as the Dolphins became only the second team to win back-to-back Super Bowls. The organization was jolted by an announcement that Csonka, Kiick, and Warfield had signed a $3.3 million package deal to play for the Toronto Northmen in the World Football League a season away in 1975, March 31. The season began dismally as the Dolphins lost the opener in New England 34-24, September 15; Miami had not lost to the Patriots since 1971. The Dolphins struggled through the next six weeks, winning five lackluster games and losing to Washington 20-17. The offense finally exploded in a 42-7 rout of Atlanta,

November 3. Two weeks later, Don Nottingham scored on a 23-yard run with 19 seconds left to beat Buffalo 35-28, the third time the Dolphins scored the winning points in the final minute. Csonka gained 123 yards in a 24-3 win over Cincinnati, the fifteenth time in his career he surpassed the 100-yard mark, December 2. Miami rallied from a 24-point deficit behind Morrall to beat New England 34-27 in the regular season finale, December 15. It was the Dolphins' thirty-first consecutive win at the Orange Bowl. A last-second desperation pass from Ken Stabler to Clarence Davis provided the winning touchdown as Oakland ended Miami's two-year domination of pro football with a dramatic 28-26 win in the playoffs, December 21.

1975 The departure of Csonka, Kiick, and Warfield weakened Miami. The Orange Bowl winning streak ended in the regular season opener as Oakland beat the Dolphins 31-21, despite three interceptions by safety Charlie Babb. The following week, the Dolphins rallied from a 14-0 halftime deficit to beat New England 22-14 and begin a seven-game winning streak. The Dolphins scored two touchdowns in the final two minutes to beat Buffalo 35-30 and reclaim first place in the AFC Eastern Division, October 26. Scott became the club's all-time interception leader with 34 when he picked off a Joe Namath pass, November 9. In a showdown for the division lead, Baltimore beat Miami 33-17 at the Orange Bowl, November 23. Griese tore tendons in his toe and was sidelined for the rest of the season. Morrall was lost with torn knee ligaments the following week, but Don Strock guided Miami to two straight wins. Baltimore beat the Dolphins 10-7 in overtime to knock the Dolphins out of the playoffs for the first time since 1970, December 14.

1976 Shula's contract was extended for five more years, July 9. Scott was suspended in a dispute with Shula, then traded to Washington, August 27. Miami was hampered by injuries that sidelined 18 players during the season. Bill Arnsparger, former assistant coach, rejoined the Dolphins at midseason after being released as head coach by the New York Giants; his return inspired the Dolphins' defense to its finest effort of the year, a 10-3 win over New England, October 31. Wide receiver Freddie Solomon had an electrifying game against Buffalo, scoring on a 79-yard punt return, a 59-yard run, and a 53-yard pass play, December 5. Shula suffered his first losing season in 14 years as an NFL head coach as the Dolphins fell to 6-8.

1977 Earl Morrall retired on May 2 after a 21-year NFL career. Griese, who took to wearing glasses on the field, led the league in passing, helping Miami bounce back to respectability in a strong but frustrating season. The Dolphins won their first three games and were 7-2 after nine games. But then they lost 23-17 to Cincinnati on November 20, when the Bengals scored on a triple-reverse in the last minute. The Dolphins came back on Thanksgiving to roll up 503 yards and beat St. Louis 55-14, as Griese threw a club record-tying six touchdown passes. A 17-6 victory over Baltimore put Miami in a three-way tie for first place with two weeks to go. Despite a closing victory over Buffalo, the Dolphins missed the playoffs on a tiebreaker.

1978 The Dolphins lost Griese in the preseason when he suffered torn ligaments in his left knee. The team didn't miss a beat with Don Strock at the controls, going 5-2. His best game was against Baltimore when he threw three touchdowns in a 42-0 victory. Griese returned for his first start of the season on October 22, but the Dolphins were defeated by the Patriots 33-24, knocking them out of first place. Miami came back to win three in a row but was defeated almost single-handedly by Houston's Earl

Quarterback Bob Griese sets up to pass against the New York Jets, 1979.

Jack Clancy

Vern Den Herder

Manny Fernandez

Tim Foley

Jim Kiick

Mike Kolen

Jim Langer

Campbell, who ran for 199 yards and four touchdowns, in a Monday night game 35-30. The Dolphins earned the right to host the wild card game with a 23-3 victory over New England on December 18. Miami's 11-5 record was its best since 1974. A big day by Houston's Dan Pastorini led to a 17-9 Oilers' win in the AFC Wild Card Game on December 24.

1979 Larry Csonka rejoined the Dolphins after four years on February 22. Miami opened with four straight wins, highlighted by Csonka's three touchdowns against the Bears in a 31-16 victory September 23. Consecutive losses to the Raiders and the Jets started Miami on a slump in which they went 3-5. With Griese benched in favor of Strock, the Dolphins defeated the Colts 28-24 on November 25. Two weeks later, Griese was back to complete 17 of 22 passes in a title clinching victory at Detroit. On December 30, the Dolphins were overwhelmed by Pittsburgh in the AFC Divisional Playoff Game 34-14.

1980 Two days before the season opener, Shula signed a new four-year contract. The Dolphins lost their 1980 debut, 17-7 to Buffalo. The loss ended the Dolphins' 20-game winning streak over the Bills. Miami played musical quarterbacks much of the season, with Griese, Strock, and rookie David Woodley all seeing action. Griese passed for 222 yards in the first half of a 30-17 loss to Baltimore on October 5, but suffered a shoulder injury that ended his career. Woodley finished the season as the starter, with his best day coming on November 9 when he ran for two touchdowns and threw for three more in a 35-14 win over Los Angeles.

1981 The offseason proved to be a tough time for the Dolphins. Little retired on February 5; Griese retired on June 25. Shula settled on Woodley at quarterback, and the second-year veteran got the Dolphins off to a 4-0 start before suffering a cracked rib against the Jets. Strock came in to salvage a 28-28 tie, but the Dolphins lost the next week to the Bills. With Woodley back in charge again, Miami got back on the winning track with a 13-10 victory over Washington. Coach Don Shula won his 200th game over New England November 8. The Dolphins lost back-to-back games but managed to remain in a first-place tie with the Jets. A four-game win streak ended the season with Miami in first place with an 11-4-1 record.

1982 The Dolphins were involved in another of the classic overtime confrontations in pro football playoff history. They lost to San Diego 41-38 in the 1981 divisional playoffs. The Chargers took advantage of Dolphins mistakes to take a 24-0 lead after the first quarter. By the half, the Dolphins had cut that lead to 24-17, and they went ahead in the fourth quarter 38-31. James Brooks's touchdown sent the game into overtime, and after each team had missed a field goal in the extra period, Rolf Benirschke won it with a 29-yarder after 13:52 of overtime.

MEMBERS OF HALL OF FAME:
None

DOLPHINS RECORD, 1966-81

Year	Won	Lost	Tied	Pct.	Pts.	OP
1966	3	11	0	.214	213	362
1967	4	10	0	.286	219	407
1968	5	8	1	.385	276	355
1969	3	10	1	.231	233	332
1970*	10	4	0	.714	297	228
1971‡	10	3	1	.769	315	174
1972**	14	0	0	1,000	385	171
1973**	12	2	0	.857	343	150
1974§	11	3	0	.786	327	216
1975	10	4	0	.714	357	222
1976	6	8	0	.429	263	264
1977	10	4	0	.714	313	197
1978*	11	5	0	.688	372	254
1979§	10	6	0	.625	341	257
1980	8	8	0	.500	266	305
1981§	11	4	1	.719	345	275
16 Years	138	90	4	.603	4,865	4,169

*AFC Wild Card Qualifier for Playoffs
‡AFC Champion
**Super Bowl Champion
§AFC Eastern Division Champion

RECORD HOLDERS

Rushing (Yards)	Delvin Williams, 1978	1,258
Passing (Pct.)	Bob Griese, 1978	63.0
Passing (Yards)	Bob Griese, 1978	2,473
Passing (TDs)	Bob Griese, 1977	22
Receiving (No.)	Jack Clancy, 1967	67
Receiving (Yards)	Paul Warfield, 1971	996
Interceptions (No.)	Dick Westmoreland, 1967	10
Punting (Avg.)	George Roberts, 1980	42.6
Punt Ret. (Avg.)	Freddie Solomon, 1975	12.3
Kickoff Ret. (Avg.)	Duriel Harris, 1976	32.9
Touchdowns (Total)	Nat Moore, 1977, and, Larry Csonka, 1979	13
Field Goals Made	Garo Yepremian, 1971	28
Points (No.)	Garo Yepremian, 1971	117

COACHING HISTORY

1966-69	George Wilson	15-39-2
1970-81	Don Shula	123-51-2

FIRST PLAYER SELECTED

1966	Rick Norton, QB, Kentucky	
1967	Bob Griese, QB, Purdue	
1968	Larry Csonka, RB, Syracuse	
1969	Bill Stanfill, DE, Georgia	
1970	Jim Mandich, TE (2), Michigan	
1971	Otto Stowe, WR (2), Iowa State	
1972	Mike Kadish, DT, Notre Dame	
1973	Chuck Bradley, T (2), Oregon	
1974	Don Reese, DE, Jackson State	
1975	Darryl Carlton, T, Tampa	
1976	Larry Gordon, LB, Arizona State	
1977	A. J. Duhe, DE, Louisiana State	
1978	Guy Benjamin, QB (2), Stanford	
1979	Jon Giesler, T, Michigan	
1980	Don McNeal, CB, Alabama	
1981	David Overstreet, RB, Oklahoma	
1982	Roy Foster, G, USC	

MIAMI DOLPHINS, 1966-81

Alexander, John, DE, Rutgers 1977-78
Allen, Jeff, CB, California-Davis 1980
Anderson, Dick, Colorado 1968-75, 1977
Anderson, Terry, WR, Bethune-Cookman 1977-78
Andrews, John, DE, Morgan State 1975-76
Auer, Joe, RB, Georgia Tech 1966-67

B

Babb, Charlie, S, Memphis State 1972-79
Bachman, Ted, CB, New Mexico State 1976
Bailey, Elmer, WR, Minnesota 1980-81
Baker, Mel, WR, Texas Southern 1974
Ball, Larry, LB, Louisville 1972-74, 1977-78
Bannon, Bruce, LB, Penn State 1973-74
Barber, Rudy, LB, Bethune-Cookman 1968
Barnett, Bill, DE, Nebraska 1980-81
Barisich, Carl, DT, Princeton 1977-80
Barnes, Rodrigo, LB, Rice 1975
Baumhower, Bob, Alabama 1977-81
Beaudoin, Doug, S, Minnesota 1980
Beier, Tom, S, Miami 1967, 1969
Benjamin, Guy, QB, Stanford 1978-79
Bennett, Woody, RB, Miami 1980-81
Berger, Ron, DE, Wayne State 1973
Bessillieu, Don, S, Georgia Tech 1979-81
Betters, Doug, DE, Nevada-Reno 1978-81

Blackwood, Glenn, S, Texas 1979-81
Blackwood, Lyle, S, Texas Christian 1981
Bokamper, Kim, DE-LB, San Jose State 1977-81
Bosarge, Wade, S, Tulsa 1977
Boutwell, Tom, QB, Southern Mississippi 1969
Boynton, John, T, Tennessee 1969
Bramlett, John (Bull), LB, Memphis State 1967-68
Branch, Mel, DE, Louisiana State 1966-68
Braxton, Jim, RB, West Virginia 1978
Briscoe, Marlin, WR, Nebraska-Omaha 1972-74
Brown, Dean, S, Valley State 1970
Brudzinski, Bob, LB, Ohio State 1981
Bruggers, Bob, LB, Minnesota 1966-68
Bulaich, Norm, RB, Texas Christian 1975-79
Buoniconti, Nick, LB, Notre Dame 1969-74, 1976

C

Canale, Whit, DE, Tennessee 1966
Carlton, Darryl, T, Tampa 1975-76
Carpenter, Preston, TE, Arkansas 1966
Casares, Rick, RB, Florida 1966
Cefalo, Jimmy, WR, Penn State 1978-81
Cesare, Billy, S, Miami 1980
Chambers, Rusty, LB, Tulane 1976-80
Chesser, George, RB, Delta State 1966-67
Clancy, Jack, WR, Michigan 1967-69
Clancy, Sean, LB, Amherst 1978
Cole, Terry, RB, Indiana 1971
Colzie, Neal, S, Ohio State 1979
Cooke, Ed, DE, Maryland 1966-67
Cornelius, Charles, CB, Bethune-Cookman 1977-78
Cornish, Frank, DT, Grambling 1970-71
Cox, Jim, TE, Miami 1968
Cronin, Bill, TE, Boston College 1966
Crowder, Randy, DT, Penn State 1974-76
Crusan, Doug, T, Indiana 1968-74
Csonka, Larry, RB, Syracuse 1968-74, 1979
Current, Mike, T, Ohio State 1967, 1977-79

D

Darnall, Bill, WR, North Carolina 1968-69
Davis, Gary, RB, Cal Poly-San Luis Obispo 1976-79
Davis, Ted, LB, Georgia Tech 1970
Del Gaizo, Jim, QB, Tampa 1972, 1975
DeMarco, Bob, C, Dayton 1970-71
Den Herder, Vern, DE, Central Iowa 1971-81
Dennard, Mark, C, Texas A&M 1979-81
Dennery Mike, LB, Southern Mississippi 1976

Bob Baumhower stops Houston's Tim Wilson, 1979.

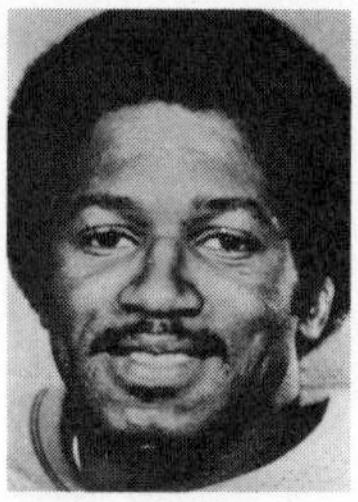

Mercury Morris

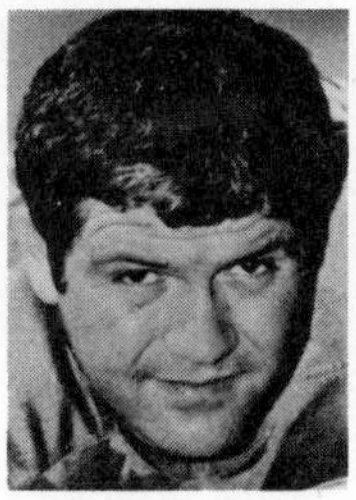

Billy Neighbors

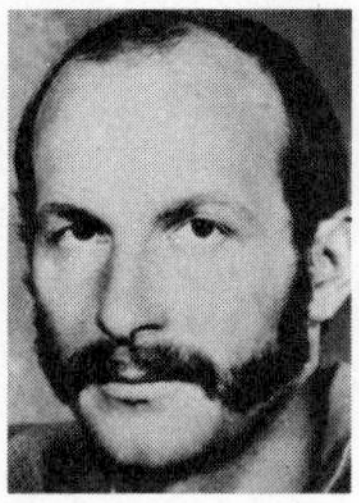

Jake Scott

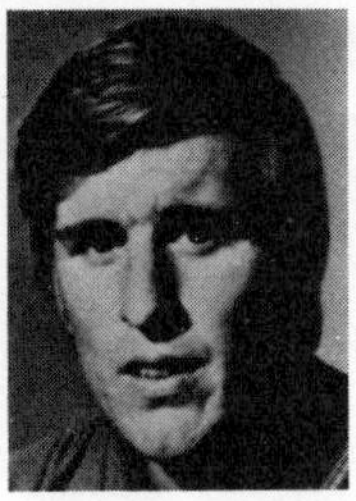

Larry Seiple

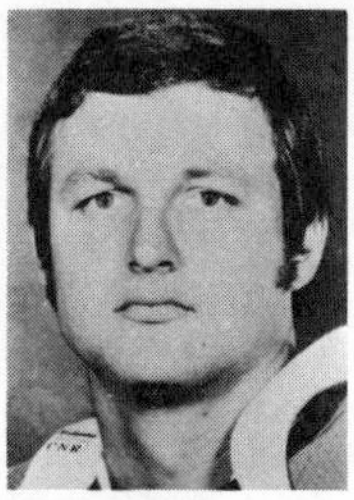

Bill Stanfill

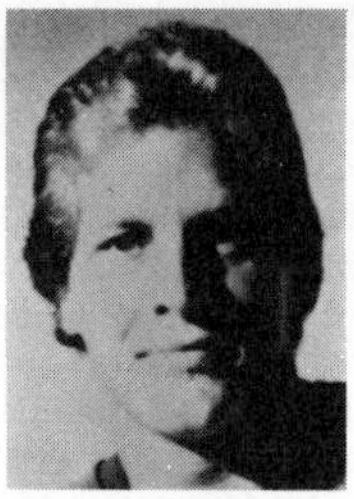

Steve Towle

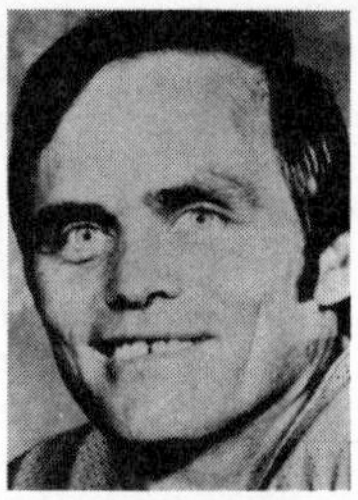

Howard Twilley

- Dornbrook, Thom, G, Kentucky ... 1980
- Dotson, Al, DT, Grambling ... 1966
- Drougas, Tom, T, Oregon ... 1975-76
- Duhe, A. J., DE, Louisiana State ... 1977-81
- Dunaway, Jim, DT, Mississippi ... 1972
- Dvorak, Rick, DE, Wichita State ... 1977

E

- Edmunds, Randall, LB, Georgia Tech ... 1969-69
- Elia, Bruce, LB, Ohio State ... 1975
- Ellis, Ken, CB, Southern U. ... 1976
- Emanuel, Frank, LB, Tennessee ... 1966-69
- Erlandson, Tom, LB, Washington State ... 1966-67
- Evans, Norm, T, Texas Christian ... 1966-75

F

- Faison, Earl, DE, Indiana ... 1966
- Farley, Dale, LB, West Virginia ... 1971
- Fernandez, Manny, DE, Utah ... 1968-75
- Fleming, Marv, TE, Utah ... 1970-74
- Foley, Tim, CB, Purdue ... 1970-80
- Fowler, Charlie, G, Houston ... 1967-68
- Franklin, Andra, RB, Nebraska ... 1981
- Fultz, Mike, DT-DE, Nebraska ... 1981
- Funchess, Tommy, T, Jackson State ... 1974

G

- Giaquinto, Nick, RB, Connecticut ... 1980-81
- Giesler, Jon, T, Michigan ... 1979-81
- Gilchrist, Cookie, RB, No college ... 1966
- Ginn, Hubert, RB, Florida A&M ... 1970-75
- Goode, Irv, C-G, Kentucky ... 1973-74
- Goode, Tom, C, Mississippi State ... 1966-69
- Gordon, Larry, LB, Arizona State ... 1976-81
- Grady, Garry, S, Eastern Michigan ... 1969
- Green, Cleveland, T, Southern U. ... 1979-81
- Griese, Bob, QB, Purdue ... 1967-80
- Groth, Jeff, WR, Bowling Green ... 1979

H

- Hammond, Kim, QB, Florida State ... 1968
- Hardy, Bruce, TE, Arizona State ... 1978-81
- Harper, Jack, RB, Florida ... 1967-68
- Harris, Duriel, WR, New Mexico State ... 1976-81
- Harris, Leroy, RB, Arkansas State ... 1977-78
- Haynes, Abner, RB, North Texas State ... 1967
- Heath, Clayton, RB, Wake Forest ... 1976
- Heinz, Bob, DT, Pacific ... 1969-74, 1976-77
- Higgins, Jim, G, Xavier ... 1966
- Hill, Barry, S, Iowa State ... 1975-76
- Hill, Eddie, RB, Memphis State ... 1981
- Hill, Ike, WR, Catawba ... 1976
- Hines, Jimmy, WR, Texas Southern ... 1969
- Holmes, John, DE, Florida A&M ... 1966
- Holmes, Mike, WR, Texas Southern ... 1976
- Hopkins, Jerry, LB, Texas A&M ... 1967-68
- Howell, Mike, DB, Grambling ... 1972
- Howell, Steve, RB, Baylor ... 1979-81
- Hudock, Mike, C, Miami ... 1966
- Hunter, Billy, RB, Syracuse ... 1966

J

- Jackson, Frank, WR, Southern Methodist ... 1966-67
- Jacobs, Ray, DT, Howard Payne ... 1967-68
- Jaquess, Pete, DB, Eastern New Mexico ... 1966-67
- Jenkins, Al, T, Tulsa ... 1972
- Jenkins, Ed, RB, Holy Cross ... 1972
- Jensen, Jim, QB, Boston University ... 1981
- Joe, Billy, RB, Villanova ... 1966
- Johnson, Curtis, CB, Toledo ... 1970-78
- Joswick, Bob, DE, Tulsa ... 1968-69

K

- Keating, Bill, DT, Michigan ... 1967
- Keyes, Jimmy, LB-K, Mississippi ... 1968-69
- Kiick, Jim, RB, Wyoming ... 1968-74
- Kindig, Howard, G-C, Cal State-Los Angeles ... 1972-73
- Kocourek, Dave, TE, Wisconsin ... 1966
- Kolen, Mike, LB, Auburn ... 1970-75, 1977
- Kozlowski, Mike, S, Colorado ... 1979, 1981
- Kremser, Karl, K, Tennessee ... 1969-70
- Kuechenberg, Bob, G, Notre Dame ... 1970-81

L

- Laakso, Eric, T, Tulane ... 1978-81
- Lamb, Mack, CB, Tennessee State ... 1967-68
- Land, Mel, LB, Michigan State ... 1979
- Langer, Jim, C, South Dakota State ... 1971-79
- Lawless, Burton, G, Florida ... 1981
- Lee, Ronnie, TE, Baylor ... 1979-81
- Leigh, Charles, RB, No college ... 1971-73
- Little, Larry, G, Bethune-Cookman ... 1969-80
- Lothridge, Billy, P, Georgia Tech ... 1972
- Lusteg, Booth, K, Connecticut ... 1967

M

- Malone, Benny, RB, Arizona State ... 1974-78
- Mandich, Jim, TE, Michigan ... 1970-77
- Mass, Wayne, T, Clemson ... 1971
- Matheson, Bob, LB, Duke ... 1971-79
- Matthews, Bo, RB, Colorado ... 1981
- Matthews, Wes, WR, Northeast Oklahoma ... 1966
- Mauck, Carl, C, Southern Illinois ... 1970
- McBride, Norm, DE, Utah ... 1969-70
- McCreary, Loaird, TE, Tennessee State ... 1976-78
- McCullers, Dale, LB, Florida State ... 1969
- McDaniel, Ed (Wahoo), LB, Oklahoma ... 1966-68
- McFarland, Jim, TE, Nebraska ... 1975
- McGeever, John, S, Auburn ... 1966
- McNeal, Don, CB, Alabama ... 1980-81
- Mertens, Jim, TE, Fairmont State ... 1969
- Michel, Mike, P-K, Stanford ... 1977
- Milton, Gene, WR, Florida A&M ... 1968-69
- Mingo, Gene, K, No college ... 1966-67
- Mira, George, QB, Miami ... 1971
- Mitchell, Melvin, G, Tennessee State ... 1976-78
- Mitchell, Stan, RB, Tennessee ... 1966-70
- Moore, Maulty, DT, Bethune-Cookman ... 1972-74
- Moore, Nat, WR, Florida ... 1974-81
- Moore, Wayne, T, Lamar U. ... 1970-78
- Moreau, Doug, TE, Louisiana State ... 1960-69
- Morrall, Earl, QB, Michigan State ... 1972-76
- Morris, Mercury, RB, West Texas State ... 1969-75
- Moser, Rick, RB, Rhode Island ... 1980
- Mumphord, Lloyd, CB, Texas Southern ... 1969-74

N

- Nathan, Tony, RB, Alabama ... 1979-81
- Neff, Bob, S, Stephen F. Austin ... 1966-68
- Neighbors, Billy, G, Alabama ... 1966-69
- Newman, Ed, G, Duke ... 1973-81
- Nomina, Tom, DT, Miami, Ohio ... 1966-68
- Noonan, Karl, WR, Iowa ... 1966-71
- Norton, Rick, QB, Kentucky ... 1966-69
- Nottingham, Don, RB, Kent State ... 1973-77

O

- Orosz, Tom, P, Ohio State ... 1981
- Ortega, Ralph, LB, Florida ... 1979-80
- Owens, Morris, WR, Arizona State ... 1975-76

P

- Palmer, Dick, LB, Kentucky ... 1970
- Park, Ernie, G, McMurry ... 1966
- Pearson, Willie, CB, North Carolina A&T ... 1969
- Pesuit, Wally, T, Kentucky ... 1977-78
- Petrella, Bob, S, Tennessee ... 1966-71
- Poole, Ken, DE, Northeastern Louisiana ... 1981
- Potter, Steve, LB, Virginia ... 1981
- Powell, Jesse, LB, West Texas State ... 1969-73
- Price, Sam, RB, Illinois ... 1966-68
- Pryor, Barry, RB, Boston U. ... 1969-70
- Pyburn, Jack, T, Texas A&M ... 1966-68

R

- Rather, Bo, WR, Michigan ... 1973, 1978
- Ray, Ricky, CB, Norfolk State ... 1981
- Reese, Don, DT, Jackson State ... 1974-76
- Rhone, Earnie, LB, Henderson, Arkansas ... 1975, 1977-81
- Rice, Ken, G, Auburn ... 1966-67
- Richardson, Jeff, T, Michigan State ... 1969
- Richardson, John, DT, UCLA ... 1967-71
- Richardson, Willie, WR, Jackson State ... 1970
- Riley, Jim, DE, Oklahoma ... 1967-71
- Roberson, Bo, WR, Cornell ... 1966
- Roberson, Vern, S, Grambling ... 1977
- Roberts, Archie, QB, Columbia ... 1967
- Roberts, George, P, Virginia Tech ... 1978-80
- Roberts, Guy, LB, Maryland ... 1977
- Robiskie, Terry, RB, Louisiana State ... 1980-81
- Roderick, John, WR, Southern Methodist ... 1966-67
- Rose, Joe, TE, California ... 1980-81
- Rudolph, Jack, LB, Georgia Tech ... 1966

S

- Salter, Bryant, S, Pittsburgh ... 1976
- Scott, Jake, S, Georgia ... 1970-75
- Seiple, Larry, P, Kentucky ... 1967-77
- Selfridge, Andy, LB, Virginia ... 1976
- Sellers, Ron, WR, Florida State ... 1973
- Shull, Steve, LB, William & Mary ... 1980-81
- Simpson, Bob, DE, Colorado ... 1978
- Small, Gerald, CB, San Jose State ... 1978-81
- Smith, Tom, RB, Miami ... 1973
- Solomon, Freddie, WR, Tampa ... 1975-77
- Speyrer, Cotton, WR, Texas ... 1975
- Stanfill, Bill, DE, Georgia ... 1969-76
- Stephenson, Dwight, C, Alabama ... 1980-81
- Stofa, John, QB, Buffalo ... 1966-67, 1969-70
- Stowe, Otto, WR, Iowa State ... 1971-72
- Strock, Don, QB, Virginia Tech ... 1974-81
- Stuckey, Henry, CB, Missouri ... 1972-74
- Swift, Doug, LB, Amherst ... 1970-75

T

- Taylor, Ed, CB, Memphis State ... 1979-81
- Testerman, Don, RB, Clemson ... 1980
- Thomas, Norris, CB, Southern Mississippi ... 1977-79
- Thomas, Rodell, LB, Alabama State ... 1981
- Thornton, Jack, LB, Auburn ... 1966
- Tillman, Andre, TE, Texas Tech ... 1975-78
- Toews, Jeff, G, Washington ... 1979-81
- Torczon, LaVerne, DE, Nebraska ... 1966
- Torrey, Bob, RB, Penn State ... 1979
- Towle, Steve, LB, Kansas ... 1975-80
- Tucker, Gary, RB, Tennessee-Chattanooga ... 1968
- Twilley, Howard, WR, Tulsa ... 1966-76

U

- Urbanek, Jim, DT, Mississippi ... 1968

V

- Vigorito, Tommy, RB, Virginia ... 1981
- Volk, Rick, S, Michigan ... 1977-78
- von Schamann, Uwe, K, Oklahoma ... 1979-81

W

- Wade, Charley, WR, Tennessee State ... 1973
- Walker, Fulton, CB, West Virginia ... 1981
- Walters, Rod, G, Iowa ... 1980
- Wantland, Hal, TE, Tennessee ... 1966
- Warfield, Paul, WR, Ohio State ... 1970-74
- Warren, Jimmy, CB, Illinois ... 1966-69
- Washington, Dick, DB, Bethune-Cookman ... 1968
- Weisacosky, Ed, LB, Miami ... 1968-70
- West, Willie, S, Oregon ... 1966-68
- Westmoreland, Dick, CB, North Carolina A&T ... 1966-69
- White, Jeris, CB, Hawaii ... 1974-76
- Wickert, Tom, T, Washington State ... 1974
- Williams, Delvin, RB, Kansas ... 1978-80
- Williams, Maxie, G-T, Southeastern Louisiana ... 1966-70
- Wilson, George Jr., QB, Xavier ... 1966
- Windauer, Bill, DT, Iowa ... 1975
- Winfrey, Stan, RB, Arkansas State ... 1975-77
- Wood, Dick, QB, Auburn ... 1966
- Woodley, David, QB, Louisiana State ... 1980-81
- Woods, Larry, DT, Tennessee State ... 1973
- Woodson, Fred, G, Florida A&M ... 1967-69

Y

- Yepremian, Garo, No college ... 1970-78
- Young, Steve, T, Colorado ... 1977
- Young, Willie, T, Alcorn State ... 1973

Z

- Zecher, Rich, DT, Utah State ... 1966-67

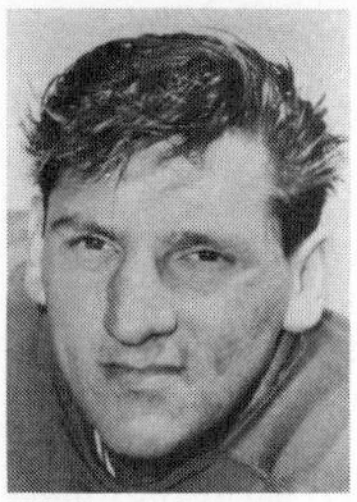
Ed Sharockman

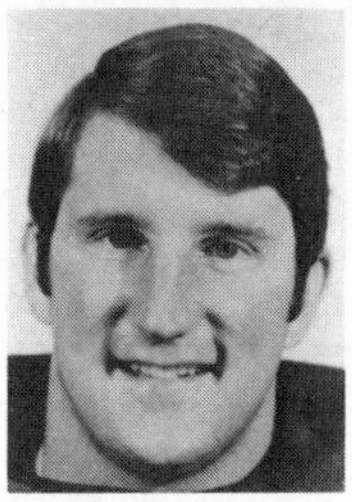
Jeff Siemon

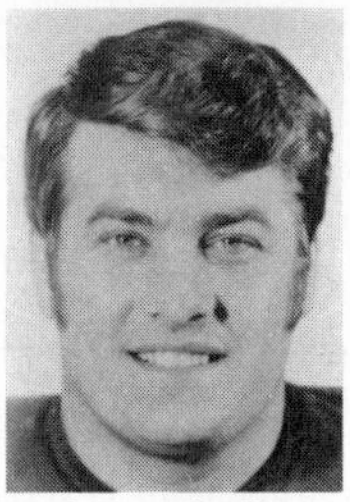
Mick Tingelhoff

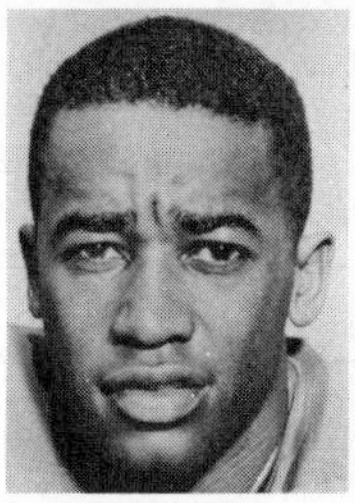
Gene Washington

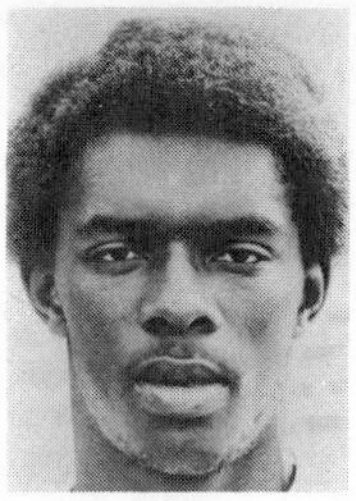
Sammy White

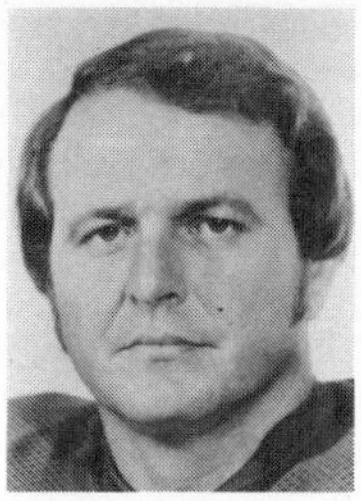
Roy Winston

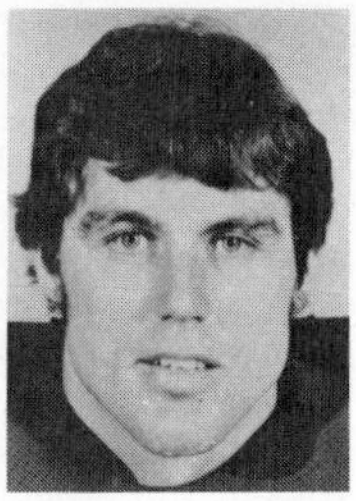
Ron Yary

H

Hackbart, Dale, DB, Wisconsin 1966-70
Haley, Dick, DB, Pittsburgh.......................... 1961
Hall, Tom, WR, Minnesota................ 1964-66, 1968-69
Hall, Windlan, CB, Arizona State 1976-77
Hamilton, Wes, G, Tulsa.......................... 1976-81
Hansen, Don, LB, Illinois.......................... 1966-67
Hannon, Tom, S, Michigan State 1977-81
Hargrove, Jim, LB, Howard Payne.................. 1967-70
Harrell, Sam, RB, East Carolina.......................... 1981
Harris, Bill, RB, Colorado.......................... 1969-70
Harris, Joe, LB, Georgia Tech 1979
Haslerig, Clint, WR, Michigan.......................... 1975
Hawkins, Rip, LB, North Carolina.................. 1961-65
Hayden, Leo, RB, Ohio State 1971
Hayes, Ray, RB, Central Oklahoma 1961
Henderson, John, WR, Michigan 1968-72
Hilgenberg, Wally, LB, Iowa 1968-79
Hill, Gary, DB, USC 1965
Hill, King, P-QB, Rice.......................... 1968
Hilton, John, TE, Richmond 1970
Holland, John, WR, Tennessee State 1974
Holloway, Randy, DE, Pittsburgh 1978-81
Hough, Jim, G, Utah State.......................... 1978-81
Huffman, David, T, Notre Dame 1979-81
Hultz, Don, DE, Southern Mississippi 1963
Huth, Gerry, G, Wake Forest 1961-63

I

Irwin, Tim, T, Tennessee 1981

J

Jackson, Joey, DT, New Mexico State.......................... 1977
Jenke, Noel, LB, Minnesota 1971
Jobko, Bill, LB, Ohio State.......................... 1963-65
Johnson, Dennis, LB, USC 1980-81
Johnson, Gene, DB, Cincinnati 1961
Johnson, Henry, LB, Georgia Tech.......................... 1980-81
Johnson, Sammy, RB, North Carolina 1976-78
Jones, Clint, RB, Michigan State 1967-72
Jordan, Jeff, DB, Tulsa.......................... 1965-67
Joyce, Don, DE, Tulane 1961

K

Kapp, Joe, QB, California.......................... 1967-69
Kassulke, Karl, DB, Drake.......................... 1963-72
Kellar, Mark, RB, Northern Illinois 1976-78
Keys, Brady, DB, Colorado State.......................... 1967
King, Phil, RB, Vanderbilt.......................... 1965-66
Kingsriter, Doug, TE, Minnesota.................. 1973-75
Kirby, John, LB, Nebraska.......................... 1964-68
Knoff, Kurt, S, Kansas 1979-81
Kosens, Terry, DB, Hofstra 1963
Kramer, Kent, TE, Minnesota.......................... 1969-70
Kramer, Tommy, QB, Rice 1977-81
Krause, Paul, S, Iowa.......................... 1968-79

L

Lacey, Bob, E, North Carolina 1964
Lamson, Chuck, DB, Wyoming.......................... 1962-63
Langer, Jim, C, South Dakota State.................. 1980-81
Lapham, Bill, C, Iowa.......................... 1961
Larsen, Gary, DT, Concordia.......................... 1965-74
Lash, Jim, WR, Northwestern 1973-76
Lawson, Steve, G, Kansas 1973-75
LeCount, Terry, WR, Florida.......................... 1979-81
Lee, Bob, QB, Pacific 1969-72, 1975-78
Leo, Jim, DE, Cincinnati 1961-62
Lester, Darrell, RB, McNeese.......................... 1964
Lewis, Leo, WR, Missouri 1981
Linden, Erroll, T, Houston 1962-65
Lindsey, Jim, RB, Arkansas.......................... 1966-72
Lingenfelter, Bob, T, Nebraska.......................... 1978
Livingston, Cliff, LB, UCLA 1962
Livingston, Mike, QB, Southern Methodist 1980
Luce, Derrel, LB, Baylor.......................... 1979-80
Lurtsema, Bob, DE, Western Michigan 1972-76

M

MacAfee, Ken, TE, Notre Dame.......................... 1981
Mackbee, Earsell, DB, Utah State 1965-69
Marinaro, Ed, RB, Cornell 1972-75
Marshall, Jim, DE, Ohio State.......................... 1961-79
Marshall, Larry, S, Maryland 1974
Martin, Amos, LB, Louisville 1972-77
Martin, Billy, TE, Georgia Tech 1968
Martin, Doug, DE, Washington 1980-81
Mason, Tommy, RB, Tulane 1961-66
Maurer, Andy, G, Oregon.......................... 1974-75
Mayberry, Doug, RB, Utah State 1961-62
McClanahan, Brent, RB, Arizona State 1973-1980
McCormick, John, QB, Massachusetts.......................... 1962
McCullum, Sam, WR, Montana State.................. 1974-75
McDole, Mardye, WR, Mississippi State.......................... 1981
McElhenny, Hugh, RB, Washington 1961-62
McGill, Mike, LB, Notre Dame 1968-70
McKeever, Marlin, TE, USC.......................... 1967
McNeill, Fred, LB, UCLA.......................... 1974-81
McNeill, Tom, P, Stephen F. Austin.......................... 1970
McWatters, Bill, RB, North Texas State 1964
Mercer, Mike, K, Northern Arizona.......................... 1961
Meylan, Wayne, LB, Nebraska.......................... 1970
Michel, Tom, RB, East Carolina 1964
Middleton, Dave, E, Auburn.......................... 1961
Miller, Kevin, WR, Louisville.......................... 1978-80
Miller, Robert, RB, Kansas.......................... 1975-80
Mitchell, Mel, G, Tennessee State 1980
Moore, Manfred, RB, USC.......................... 1977
Morris, Jack, DB, Oregon 1961
Mostardi, Rich, DB, Kent State.......................... 1961
Mullaney, Mark, DE, Colorado State 1975-81
Munsey, Nelson, CB, Wyoming 1978
Murphy, Fred, E, Georgia Tech.......................... 1961
Myers, Frank, T, Texas A&M 1978-80

N

Niehaus, Steve, DT, Notre Dame 1979
Nord, Keith, S, St. Cloud State 1979-81

O

O'Brien, Dave, G, Boston College 1963-64
Osborn, Dave, RB, North Dakota.................. 1965-75
Osborne, Clancy, LB, Arizona State 1961-62

P

Page, Alan, DT, Notre Dame.......................... 1967-78
Paschal, Doug, RB, North Carolina.......................... 1980
Patton, Jerry, DT, Nebraska.......................... 1971
Payton, Eddie, KR, Jackson State 1980-81
Perreault, Pete, G, Long Beach State.......................... 1971
Pesonen, Dick, DB, Minnesota-Duluth 1961
Peterson, Ken, C, Utah 1961
Phillips, Jim (Red), WR, Auburn.................. 1965-67
Poage, Ray, E, Texas 1963
Poltl, Randy, S, Stanford 1974
Porter, Ron, LB, Idaho 1973
Powers, John, TE, Notre Dame.......................... 1966
Prestel, Jim, DT, Idaho.......................... 1961-65
Provost, Ted, DB, Ohio State 1970
Pyle, Palmer, G, Michigan State.......................... 1964

R

Rabold, Mike, G, Indiana.......................... 1961-62
Randolph, Al, DB, Iowa 1973
Rashad, Ahmad, WR, Oregon 1976-81
Reaves, John, QB, Florida 1979
Redwine, Jarvis, RB, Nebraska 1981
Reed, Bob, RB, Pacific 1962-63
Reed, Oscar, RB, Colorado State.................. 1968-74
Reichow, Jerry, E, Iowa 1962-64
Reilly, Mike, LB, Iowa.......................... 1969
Rentzel, Lance, WR-E, Oklahoma 1965-66
Riley, Steve, T, USC 1974-81
Roller, Dave, DT, Kentucky 1979-80
Rose, George, CB, Auburn 1964-66
Rowland, Justin, DB, Texas Christian 1961
Rubke, Karl, LB, USC 1961
Russ, Pat, DT, Purdue 1963

S

Sanders, Ken, DE, Howard Payne 1980-81
Schmidt, Roy, G, Long Beach State 1970
Schmitz, Bob, LB, Montana State 1966
Schnelker, Bob, E, Bowling Green.......................... 1961
Sendlein, Robin, LB, Texas.......................... 1981
Senser, Joe, TE, West Chester State 1980-81
Sharockman, Ed, DB, Pittsburgh 1962-72
Shaw, George, QB, Oregon 1961
Shaw, Glenn, RB, Kentucky 1961
Shay, Jerry, DT, Purdue 1966-67
Sherman, Will, DB, St. Mary's, Cal.......................... 1961
Shields, Lebron, DE, Tennessee 1961
Siemon, Jeff, LB, Stanford.......................... 1972-81
Simkus, Arnie, DT, Michigan.......................... 1966
Simpson, Howard, T, Auburn 1964
Smith, Gordon, TE, Missouri 1961-65
Smith, Lyman, DT, Duke 1978
Smith, Steve, DE, Michigan.......................... 1968-70
Snead, Norman, QB, Wake Forest.......................... 1971
Spencer, Willie, RB, No college 1976
Steele, Robert, WR, North Alabama 1979
Stein, Bob, LB, Minnesota.......................... 1975
Stonebreaker, Steve, LB, Detroit.................. 1962-63
Studwell, Scott, LB, Illinois 1977-81
Sumner, Charley, DB, William & Mary 1961-62
Sunde, Milt, G, Minnesota 1964-74
Sutherland, Doug, DT, Superior State 1971-80
Sutton, Archie, T, Illinois 1965-67
Swain, Bill, LB, Oregon 1964
Swain, John, CB, Miami.......................... 1981
Swilley, Dennis, C, Texas A&M 1977-81

T

Tarkenton, Fran, QB, Georgia.............. 1961-66, 1972-78
Tatman, Pete, RB, Nebraska.......................... 1967
Teal, Willie, CB, Louisiana State.................. 1980-1981
Tilleman, Mike, DT, Montana.......................... 1966
Tingelhoff, Mick, C, Nebraska 1962-78
Tobey, Dave, LB, Oregon 1966
Triplett, Mel, RB, Toledo.......................... 1961-62
Tucker, Bob, TE, Bloomsburg State 1977-80
Turner, John, CB, Miami.......................... 1978-81

V

VanderKelen, Ron, QB, Wisconsin.................. 1963-67
Vargo, Larry, DB, Detroit 1964-65
Vella, John, T, USC.......................... 1980
Vellone, Jim, G, USC 1966-70
Voigt, Stu, TE, Wisconsin.......................... 1970-80

W

Walden, Bobby, P, Georgia 1964-67
Wallace, Jackie, CB, Arizona 1973-74
Ward, John, G-C, Oklahoma State.................. 1970-74
Warwick, Lonnie, LB, Tennessee Tech 1965-72
Washington, Gene, WR, Michigan State 1967-72
Washington, Harry, WR, Colorado State 1978
Wells, Mike, QB, Illinois 1973-74
West, Charlie, DB, Texas-El Paso.................. 1968-73
White, Ed, G, California 1969-77
White, James (Duck), DT, Oklahoma State.................. 1976-81
White, Sammy, WR, Grambling.................. 1976-81
Williams, A. D., E, Pacific 1961
Williams, Jeff, RB, Oklahoma State.......................... 1966
Williams, Walt, CB, New Mexico State 1981
Willis, Leonard, WR, Ohio State 1976
Wilson, Tom, RB, No college 1963
Wilson, Wade, QB-P, East Texas State 1981
Winfrey, Carl, LB, Wisconsin.......................... 1971
Winston, Roy, LB, Louisiana State 1962-76
Wise, Phil, S, Nebraska-Omaha 1977-79
Wright, Jeff, DB, Minnesota.......................... 1971-77
Wright, Nate, CB, San Diego State.................. 1971-80

Y

Yakavonis, Ray, DE, East Stroudsburg State 1981
Yary, Ron, T, USC 1968-81
Youso, Frank, T, Minnesota 1961-62
Young, Jim, RB, Queens, Ontario.......................... 1965-66
Young, Rickey, RB, Jackson State 1978-81

Z

Zaunbrecher, Godfrey, C, Louisiana State 1971-73

NEW ENGLAND PATRIOTS

1959 The American Football League's eighth franchise was awarded to Boston and William H. Sullivan, Jr. Mike Holovak, head coach at Boston College, was named director of player personnel. Ed McKeever was the club's first general manager. The team selected Northwestern running back Ron Burton as its first draft choice and Syracuse running back Gerhard Schwedes as its territorial pick.

1960 Lou Saban, little-known coach at Western Illinois University, was signed as the team's first head coach. "He's a Paul Brown with heart," said McKeever. A local newspaper held a contest to name the team. "Patriots," suggested by 74 people, was the winner. Sullivan's biggest problem was finding a facility where his team could play. Fenway Park was unavailable. So were the stadiums of Boston College and Harvard University. Boston University Field was chosen. Sullivan signed to play Patriots' games there for two years, with an option for a third. The Patriots became the first major league pro sports team in history to issue public stock, April 2. The club opened its first training camp at the University of Massachusetts in Amherst. Some 350 players showed up. One was Ed (Butch) Songin, a former Boston College star who had quit Canadian football and was working as a probation officer near Boston. It became evident early in camp that Songin would be the club's best passer. In the first pro sports event ever staged in Harvard Stadium, the Patriots lost a preseason game to the Dallas Texans 24-14, August 14. More importantly, the game had been played in one of the town's most influential settings. A crowd of 21,597 was present for the regular season opener at Boston University Field and welcomed pro football back to Boston after an 11-year absence, dating back to the 1949 Boston Yanks. But the Patriots lost the game to Denver 13-10. A week later, the Patriots defeated the New York Titans 28-24 for their first AFL victory. Financially, it was a rocky season for Sullivan. The team lost approximately $350,000, although the average home attendance of 16,500 provided some hope.

1961 In a five-player trade with Oakland, Boston acquired Babe Parilli, the experienced quarterback it felt it needed to build a winning team. A couple of second year men, wide receiver Gino Cappelletti and sprinter Larry Garron looked as if they would be of considerable help in the preseason. But Sullivan, who was hoping for 10,000 season ticket sales, sold barely a third that amount, and the team was not on solid footing as it began its second year. When the record fell to 2-3 and fan interest waned, Sullivan fired Saban and named Mike Holovak head coach, October 19. Holovak stressed defense and the turnaround was almost immediate. The Patriots were 7-1-1 with Holovak as coach, leading the division for awhile. Attendance improved, averaging more than 19,000. The club still lost money, but less than half the amount lost the previous year.

1962 Holovak was signed to a new two-year contract and made two acquisitions through the draft. Nick Buoniconti became the new middle linebacker and the key to the defense, and Billy Neighbors, an All-America blocker from Alabama, turned into the stabilizing force on the Patriots' offensive line. A victory over Houston 34-21 in the second game of the season stamped Boston as a strong contender. But in their next meeting later in the year, Parilli, now solidly entrenched as the quarterback, was hit just after throwing a second quarter pass. He broke his collarbone and was lost for the season. The Patriots lost the game and their chance at the championship, although finishing with a 9-4-1 record.

1963 The Patriots announced their new playing site of Fenway Park, home of the baseball Red Sox, with 38,000 seats. A severe spinal injury sidelined Burton and a pinched nerve inhibited Parilli. The team played erratically. In the highlight of what was probably Holovak's best coaching performance, Boston defeated Buffalo 26-8 in a snow-plagued playoff game dominated by Cappelletti's clutch field goal kicking. The collapse of Houston, the regrouping in New York, and a poor start by Buffalo kept the Patriots in the race, eventually allowing them to tie for first place in their division with a 7-6-1 record.

1964 In the AFL Championship Game with San Diego, the patched-up Patriots were no match for the Chargers. Keith Lincoln ran for 206 yards and San Diego scored an easy 51-10 victory. "They left nothing untouched," Holovak said afterward. The Patriots drafted Jack Concannon, the All-America quarterback from Boston College, number one. But after a wild bidding war, Concannon decided to sign with the Philadelphia Eagles. Although there was some criticism of Holovak's "old folks" roster, he managed to get a lot out of it, closing with a rush that fell just short of a repeat division championship. After setting a new attendance record of 199,707, the Patriots announced they had finished their first season in the black.

1965 Jim Nance, a powerful fullback from Syracuse, was drafted number 19 and signed. Joe Bellino, the former Heisman Trophy winner from Navy who spent four years in the service, also joined the team. Already weakened by age, the Patriots were further crippled by a series of injuries. Burton, Garron, and Cappelletti were a few of the top players who were injured. Parilli threw 26 interceptions.

1966 John Huarte, who originally signed with New York for a $200,000 bonus, was acquired from the Jets in a trade for Jim Colclough. Plans for a mammoth year-round sports complex, complete with a stadium that would feature a retractable roof, were revealed for downtown Boston. The price tag, however, was estimated at $80 million, and the method of financing such a project remained a major stumbling block. The key to the Patriots' season turned out to be Nance, who finished with 1,458 yards rushing, an AFL record. Nance's presence helped Parilli enjoy an excellent season. The Patriots battled Buffalo for first place all season, and a late 14-3 victory over the Bills had Boston fans thinking Super Bowl. But in the final game of the year, Joe Namath and the Jets knocked them out of the lead and cost them the title 38-28. Holovak was presented a new five-year contract with a substantial pay raise.

1967 Although Nance continued to gain big yardage, the Patriots slipped badly. Parilli showed signs of age, there was little outside speed, and the defense couldn't carry the team. The Patriots fell to last place in the Eastern Division. Nance still gained with 1,216 yards, tops in the league.

1968 In an attempt to trade some of the age for youth and enthusiasm, Holovak dealt Parilli to the New York Jets for quarterback Mike Taliaferro. But Taliaferro had his problems in Boston, eventually losing his job to rookie Tom Sherman. Few of the other Patriots responded with good seasons. Nance injured an ankle that limited his effectiveness. Bad knees knocked defensive end Larry Eisenhauer and middle linebacker Nick Buoniconti out of the lineup for a considerable time.

1969 Holovak was replaced as head coach by Clive Rush, who lost the first seven games of the season. Linebacker Buoniconti was traded to Miami. The Patriots rallied to win four of seven games. Key new contributors included running back Carl Garrett,

Jim Nance follows the block of center Jon Morris, 1967. Nance won the AFL rushing title.

NEW ORLEANS SAINTS

1966 The National Football League, long impressed by the support New Orleans fans displayed for preseason games at Tulane Stadium, awarded an expansion franchise to the Crescent City, November 1. John W. Mecom, Jr., a millionaire sportsman, was designated majority stockholder and president of the franchise, December 15. Among his limited partners was Al Hirt, the Bourbon Street trumpet player. Until he was granted an NFL team, Mecom's passion was auto racing and his family's entry, driven by the late Graham Hill, won the Indianapolis 500 in 1966.

1967 The team was named the "Saints," in honor of the Dixieland classic "When the Saints Go Marchin' In," which became the team's fight song. Mecom hired Tom Fears, former Hall of Fame end for Los Angeles and assistant coach for Green Bay under Vince Lombardi, as head coach, January 27. Fears chose to go with veteran players and assembled a cast of former NFL stars: Jim Taylor, Paul Hornung, Doug Atkins, Earl Leggett, and Lou Cordileone. The Saints traded their first draft choice to Baltimore for reserve quarterback Gary Cuozzo. New Orleans fans responded frantically to the Saints' arrival, purchasing 20,000 season tickets the day the box office opened. Fears played the preseason games to win, and the Saints finished the preseason with a 5-1 record, best ever for a first-year team. When rookie John Gilliam returned the opening kickoff 94 yards for a touchdown in their regular season debut against Los Angeles, the 80,789 fans in Tulane Stadium nearly went berserk. The Rams rallied to win 27-13 but the Saints made a strong first impression, September 17. New Orleans went winless through the first seven games before beating Philadelphia 31-24 at Tulane Stadium, November 5. Walter Roberts scored three touchdowns. The Saints' leading receiver was rookie Dan Abramowicz, who caught 50 passes. Taylor was the team's leading rusher with 390 yards.

1968 Vic Schwenk was promoted from head of player personnel to general manager, March 29. Fears improved his offense by signing end Dave Parks, who had played out his option in San Francisco, July 17. He had to pay a steep price, however, as Commissioner Pete Rozelle made New Orleans part with its top draft choice, defensive tackle Kevin Hardy of Notre Dame, and its number-one pick in the 1969 draft as compensation. Following a painful preseason, Taylor announced his retirement as a player, September 10. New Orleans played competitive football in every league game, beating Pittsburgh 24-14 in its final game to finish third in the Century Division. The Saints' two-year record of 7-20-1 was the best to date for an expansion team.

1969 Fears added several exciting offensive players, including running backs Andy Livingston and Tony Baker and placekicker Tom Dempsey. He also got surprising mileage out of quarterback Billy Kilmer, the quarterback San Francisco considered finished two years earlier. After an 0-6 start, the Saints rebounded. The turning point was a wild 51-42 win over St. Louis, November 2. Kilmer passed for 354 yards and six touchdowns in the victory. Dempsey set a club record with four field goals including one with 11 seconds left to pull out a 25-24 win over the New York Giants, November 16. The Saints closed the season with a 27-24 win over Pittsburgh and finished in third place at 5-9 in the Capitol Division. Abramowicz led the NFL with 73 pass receptions for 1,015 yards and seven touchdowns. Atkins, 39, retired after 17 seasons in the NFL.

1970 The Saints won only one of their first seven games. Mecom fired Fears and hired J.D. Roberts,

Archie Manning looks for an open receiver in a game in Los Angeles, 1977.

formerly of the Richmond, Virginia, team of the Atlantic Coast Football League, as head coach, November 3. In Roberts's first game, the Saints scored a memorable 19-17 upset of Detroit at Tulane Stadium, November 8. The winning points came on a record-setting, 63-yard field goal by Dempsey, the free agent kicker who was born without a right hand and without toes on his right foot.

1971 In the first round of the draft, the Saints selected Archie Manning, the All-America quarterback from the University of Mississippi, January 28. Manning, a long-time favorite with football fans in the South, received a hero's welcome in New Orleans. In his pro debut, Manning scored the winning touchdown on the last play of the game to upset Los Angeles 24-20 at Tulane Stadium. It was the Saints' first win ever over the Rams. Manning's fourth-quarter heroics also led to a 24-14 victory over Dallas. Foot and leg injuries sidelined Manning late in the season and New Orleans slipped to last place in the Western Division of the NFC. Jim Strong, acquired from the 49ers, led the Saints with 404 yards rushing.

1972 The Saints appointed former astronaut Richard F. Gordon, Jr., executive vice president, January 7. Gordon, who had piloted the Apollo XII moon mission in 1969, took over the club's front office operation. Gordon found exploring the galaxy easier than reversing the sinking fortunes of the Saints, who equaled their 1970 poorest season, 2-11-1. Manning netted more than 3,000 yards running and passing and accounted for 20 of the team's 26 touchdowns but took a terrible beating behind the Saints' porous offensive line.

1973 Mecom fired J.D. Roberts and appointed John North head coach, August 26. North, an ex-Marine, learned his football as an assistant under Blanton Collier at the University of Kentucky. After a scoreless first quarter, Atlanta erupted to embarrass New Orleans in the league opener 62-7 at Tulane Stadium, September 16. The following week, the Saints were humiliated 40-3 by Dallas at Texas Stadium. But the Saints won four of their next six games, including a 19-3 surprise of Washington, October 28. Bill McClard, acquired on waivers earlier in the week, kicked four field goals to beat the Redskins.

1974 The Saints snapped a 19-game winless streak on the road with a 13-3 decision over Atlanta, October 20. The Saints rushed for a club record 232 yards in the game and reserve quarterback Bobby Scott threw the first touchdown pass of his NFL career. New Orleans upset Philadelphia 14-10 the following week at Tulane Stadium. The Saints won their fifth game, equaling their best record, as rookie quarterback Larry Cipa, a fifteenth-round draft choice, defeated St. Louis 14-10, December 8.

1975 The Saints selected Larry Burton, a wide receiver from Purdue, as their first-round pick in the college draft. They traded defensive end Billy Newsome to New York for the Jets' first-round pick and selected Kurt Schumacher, an offensive tackle from Ohio State. The Saints moved into the world's largest indoor stadium, the Louisiana Superdome, to open the preseason against Houston, August 9. The move culminated years of controversy surrounding the construction of the gigantic arena, which had a football seating capacity of 72,000. Rich Szaro, a free agent from Harvard, kicked a 20-yard field goal to give the Saints a last-second, 20-19 victory over Green Bay, October 12. Following a 38-14 loss to Los Angeles, North was fired as head coach and replaced by Ernie Hefferle, the Saints' director of pro personnel, October 25. The Saints won their first game under Hefferle, 23-7 over Atlanta, but lost the last seven to finish 2-12.

1976 The Saints hired Hank Stram, the man who coached Kansas City to the Super Bowl IV championship, as their fifth head coach, January 20. Stram traded linebacker Rick Middleton to San Diego for quarterback Bobby Douglass and a third-round draft choice, April 2. The Saints first two draft choices were Chuck Muncie, All-America running back from California, and Tony Galbreath, running back from Missouri. The offense missed Manning, who sat out the entire season following surgery on his right arm. Stram's first victory was sweet revenge as his Saints defeated the Chiefs in Kansas City 27-17, September 26. In that game, Galbreath rushed for 146 and two touchdowns, Muncie for 126 yards. The Saints scored the most one-sided win in their history, a 30-0 rout of Atlanta, October 10. The Saints also beat Seattle 51-27, November 21.

1977 The Saints opened with two close losses, then

pounded Chicago 42-24, as Manning ran for three touchdowns and passed for a fourth. The defense proved unreliable during the season and gave up 336 points, the most in the NFC. New Orleans won only two more games the rest of the year and finished 3-11. One of those victories came against the Rams (27-26) on October 30 on a fake field goal-pass from Tom Blanchard to Elois Grooms. A low point occurred on December 11 when the Saints became the first team in the NFL to lose to Tampa Bay. The Buccaneers returned three interceptions for touchdowns in the 33-14 victory. Tight end Henry Childs was named the team's most valuable player after he caught 33 passes for nine touchdowns.

1978 All-pro guard Conrad Dobler and wide receiver Ike Harris were obtained from St. Louis. Dick Nolan was named to replace Hank Stram as head coach on February 6. Eddie Jones became the new executive vice president and Harry Hulmes was named vice president of player personnel. For only the second time in their 12-year history, the Saints won a season opener, defeating Minnesota 31-24. At 2-4 the Saints embarked on a three-game winning streak for the first time in their history, including a 10-3 victory over the Rams—the team's first win in the Los Angeles Coliseum. The Saints won only two more games, but both were landmarks. On December 3, a 24-13 victory over San Francisco made this the first Saints team to win six games in a season. In the season finale, the Saints gained revenge and a seventh victory with a 17-10 decision over Tampa Bay. The team's most valuable player was Manning, who completed 291 of 471 passes (62 percent) for 3,416 yards and 17 touchdowns. Manning also was named NFC player of the year.

1979 Russell Erxleben, an All-American kicker from Texas, was the Saints' first draft pick. On June 5 the Saints moved their administrative offices from

Lee Circle to the Superdome. New Orleans opened with three consecutive losses and was 2-4 after six weeks. But against Tampa Bay on October 14, the Saints enjoyed the biggest second half in club history with 42 points, resulting in a 42-14 victory. Consecutive wins over Detroit and Washington ignited a serious run at the NFC West title, and on six occasions in October and November the Saints were first or tied for first in the division as their record rose to 7-6. A loss to Oakland on December 3 crippled the team's title chances, and a week later San Diego eliminated the Saints from the division race. New Orleans closed out the season by defeating Los Angeles in the last game at the Los Angeles Coliseum. Finishing 8-8, the Saints ranked second in the NFC in points with 370. Chuck Muncie became the first Saint to top the 1,000-yard rushing total in a season with 1,198. On December 20, Steve Rosenbloom was named executive vice president and general manager.

1980 Muncie was named most valuable player in the Pro Bowl on January 27. Dick Steinberg, formerly with Los Angeles, was named vice president of player personnel on June 25. A disastrous season unfolded as the Saints lost their first 14 games and finished 1-15. Muncie was traded to San Diego after the fourth game. Nolan was relieved of his coaching duties November 25, the day after the club's twelfth loss. Dick Stanfel was appointed interim head coach. The Saints opened up a 35-7 lead at halftime over the 49ers on December 7, but still lost 38-35. A week later they finally won when Tony Galbreath scored on a one-yard run in the fourth quarter to beat the New York Jets 21-20. Ironically, Manning compiled the best statistics of his career: 309 completions, 3,716 yards, and 23 touchdowns. But the defense allowed a whopping 487 points.

1981 Rosenbloom and Steinberg resigned January 20. Two days later, O. A. (Bum) Phillips, formerly

Tommy Myers heads upfield with an interception against Cincinnati, 1981.

Dan Abramowicz   *Russell Erxleben*   *Joe Federspiel*   *Tony Galbreath*   *Ernie Jackson*   *Billy Kilmer*   *Earl Leggett*

with Houston, was named head coach. Fred Williams was appointed chief administrator. With the first choice in the draft, the Saints selected running back George Rogers, the Heisman Trophy winner from South Carolina. Galbreath was traded to Minnesota. After losing the opener to Atlanta, the Saints defeated Los Angeles 23-17, as Rogers rushed for 162 yards. Although they won only three more times, those included victories over AFC champion Cincinnati, a second win over the Rams, and a poignant 27-24 victory against Phillips's former team, the Oilers, at the Astrodome. Rogers set an NFL rookie rushing record, and led the league in rushing with 1,674 yards.

MEMBERS OF HALL OF FAME:
Doug Atkins, Jim Taylor

SAINTS RECORD, 1967-81

Year	Won	Lost	Tied	Pct.	Pts.	OP
1967	3	11	0	.214	233	379
1968	4	9	1	.308	246	327
1969	5	9	0	.357	311	393
1970	2	11	1	.154	172	347
1971	4	8	2	.333	266	347
1972	2	11	1	.179	215	361
1973	5	9	0	.357	163	312
1974	5	9	0	.357	166	263
1975	2	12	0	.143	165	360
1976	4	10	0	.286	253	346
1977	3	11	0	.214	232	336
1978	7	9	0	.438	281	298
1979	8	8	0	.500	370	360
1980	1	15	0	.063	291	487
1981	4	12	0	.250	207	378
15 Years	59	154	5	.282	3,571	5,294

RECORD HOLDERS
Rushing (Yards)	George Rogers, 1981	1,674
Passing (Pct.)	Archie Manning, 1978	61.8
Passing (Yards)	Archie Manning, 1980	3,716
Passing (TDs)	Archie Manning, 1980	23
Receiving (No.)	Tony Galbreath, 1978	74
Receiving (Yards)	Wes Chandler, 1979	1,069
Interceptions (No.)	Dave Whitsell, 1967	10
Punting (Avg.)	Tom McNeill, 1967	42.9
Punt Ret. (Avg.)	Gil Chapman, 1975	12.2
Kickoff Ret. (Avg.)	John Gilliam, 1967	30.1
Touchdowns (Total)	George Rogers, 1981	13
Field Goals Made	Tom Dempsey, 1969	22
Points (No.)	Tom Dempsey, 1969	99

COACHING HISTORY
1967-70	Tom Fears*	13-34-2
1970-72	J. D. Roberts	7-25-3
1973-75	John North**	11-23-0
1975	Ernie Hefferle	1- 7-0
1976-77	Hank Stram	7-21-0
1978-80	Dick Nolan***	15-29-0
1980	Dick Stanfel	1- 3-0
1981	Bum Phillips	4-12-0

*Replaced after seven games in 1970
**Replaced after six games in 1975
***Replaced after 12 games in 1980

FIRST PLAYER SELECTED
1967	Les Kelley, RB, Alabama
1968	Kevin Hardy, DE, Notre Dame
1969	John Shinners, G, Xavier
1970	Ken Burrough, WR, Texas Southern
1971	Archie Manning, QB, Mississippi
1972	Royce Smith, G, Georgia
1973	Derland Moore, DE (2), Oklahoma
1974	Rick Middleton, LB, Ohio State
1975	Larry Burton, WR, Purdue
1976	Chuck Muncie, RB, California
1977	Joe Campbell, DE, Maryland
1978	Wes Chandler, WR, Florida
1979	Russell Erxleben, P-K, Texas
1980	Stan Brock, T, Colorado
1981	George Rogers, RB, South Carolina
1982	Lindsay Scott, WR, Georgia

NEW ORLEANS SAINTS, 1967-81

Abramowicz, Dan, WR, Xavier ... 1967-73
Absher, Dick, LB, Maryland ... 1969-71
Adams, Sam, G, Prairie View ... 1981
Adkins, Margene, WR, Henderson JC ... 1972
Anderson, Dick, T, Ohio State ... 1967
Anderson, Gary, G, Stanford ... 1978
Askson, Burt, TE, Texas Southern ... 1973
Athas, Pete, S, Tennessee ... 1976
Atkins, Doug, DE, Tennessee ... 1967-69

B

Baker, Melvin, WR, Michigan ... 1975
Baker, Tony, RB, Iowa State ... 1968-71
Banks, Gordon, WR, Stanford ... 1980-81
Barrington, Tom, RB, Ohio State ... 1967-70
Baumgartner, Steve, DE, Purdue ... 1973-76
Beasley, John, TE, California ... 1973-74
Bell, Carlos, TE, Houston ... 1971
Benjamin, Guy, QB, Stanford ... 1980
Bennett, Barry, DT, Concordia ... 1978-81
Bennett, Monte, DT, Kansas State ... 1981
Blanchard, Tom, P, Oregon ... 1974-78
Boeke, Jim, T, Heidelberg ... 1968
Bordelon, Ken, LB, Louisiana State ... 1976-81
Bosarge, Wade, DB, Tulsa ... 1977
Boyarsky, Jerry, DT, Pittsburgh ... 1981
Boyd, Greg, S, Arizona ... 1974
Boykin, Greg, RB, Northwestern ... 1977
Brenner, Hoby, TE, USC ... 1981
Brewer, Johnny, LB, Mississippi ... 1968-70
Brock, Stan, T, Colorado ... 1980-81
Brown, Bob, TE, Alcorn State ... 1972-73
Brown, Charlie, RB, Missouri ... 1967-68
Brown, Ray, S, West Texas State ... 1978-80
Burchfield, Don, TE, Ball State ... 1971
Burke, Vern, TE, Oregon State ... 1967
Burkett, Jackie, LB, Auburn ... 1967, 1970
Burns, Ed, QB, Nebraska ... 1978-80
Burris, Bo, S, Houston ... 1967-69
Burrough, Ken, WR, Texas Southern ... 1970
Burton, Larry, WR, Purdue ... 1975-77
Butler, Bill, RB, Kansas State ... 1972-74
Butler, Skip, K, Texas-Arlington ... 1971

C

Campbell, Joe, DE, Maryland ... 1977-78
Carr, Tom, DE, Morgan State ... 1968
Cassady, Craig, DB, Ohio State ... 1976-77
Caster, Rich, TE, Jackson State ... 1981
Chambers, Rusty, LB, Tulane ... 1976
Chandler, Wes, WR, Florida ... 1978-81
Chapman, Clarence, CB, Eastern Michigan ... 1976-80
Chapman, Gil, WR, Michigan ... 1975
Childs, Henry, TE, Kansas State ... 1974-80
Cipa, Larry, QB, Michigan ... 1974-75
Cody, Bill, LB, Auburn ... 1967-70
Colchico, Dan, DE, San Jose State ... 1969
Coleman, Don, LB, Michigan ... 1974-75
Collins, Larry, RB, Texas A&I ... 1980
Colman, Wayne, LB, Temple ... 1969-76
Coombs, Larry, C, Idaho ... 1980
Cordileone, Lou, DT, Clemson ... 1967-68
Cordill, Ollie, P, Memphis State ... 1969
Cortez, Bruce, CB, Parsons ... 1967
Crangle, Mike, DE, Tennessee-Martin ... 1972
Creech, Bob, LB, Texas Christian ... 1973
Crist, Chuck, S, Penn State ... 1975-77
Croom, Sylvester, C, Alabama ... 1975
Crosby, Ron, LB, Penn State ... 1978
Cunningham, Carl, LB, Houston ... 1971
Cuozzo, Gary, QB, Virginia ... 1967

D

Dalton, Oakley, DT, No college ... 1977
Davis, Bob, QB, Virginia ... 1973
Davis, Dave, WR, Tennessee State ... 1974
Davis, Dick, RB, Nebraska ... 1970
Davis, Norman, G, Grambling ... 1969
Davis, Ted, LB, Georgia Tech ... 1967-69
DeGrenier, Jack, RB, Texas-Arlington ... 1974

Dempsey, Tom, K, Palomar JC ... 1969-70
Didion, John, LB-C, Oregon State ... 1971-74
Dodd, Al, WR, Northwestern Louisiana ... 1969-71
Donovan, Tom, WR, Penn State ... 1980
Dorris, Andy, DE, New Mexico State ... 1973-76
Douglas, John, CB, Texas Southern ... 1967-68
Douglass, Bobby, QB, Kansas ... 1976-77
Dunbar, Jubilee, WR, Southern U. ... 1973
Durkee, Charlie, K, Oklahoma State ... 1967-68, 1971-72
Dusenberry, Bill, RB, J. C. Smith ... 1970

E

Emanuel, Frank, LB, Tennessee ... 1970
Erxleben, Russell, P-K, Texas ... 1979-81
Estes, Lawrence, DE, Alcorn State ... 1970-71
Evans, Chuck, LB, Stanford ... 1980-81

F

Fagan, Julian, P, Mississippi ... 1970-72
Farasopolos, Chris, S, Brigham Young ... 1974
Farber, Hap, LB, Mississippi ... 1970
Federspiel, Joe, LB, Kentucky ... 1972-80
Feller, Happy, K, Texas ... 1972-73
Felton, Eric, CB, Texas Tech ... 1978-80
Fersen, Paul, T, Georgia ... 1973-74
Ferguson, Jim, LB, USC ... 1968
Fichtner, Ross, S, Purdue ... 1968
Fifer, Bill, G, West Texas State ... 1978
Fink, Mike, CB, Missouri ... 1973
Finnie, Roger, T, Florida A&M ... 1978
Ford, James, RB, Texas Southern ... 1971-72
Fraser, Jim, P, Wisconsin ... 1968
Fuller, Johnny, S, Lamar U. ... 1973-75
Fultz, Mike, DT, Nebraska ... 1977-80

G

Galbreath, Tony, RB, Missouri ... 1976-80
Garcia, Jim, DE, Purdue ... 1967
Garrett, Len, TE, New Mexico Highlands ... 1973-75
Gary, Russell, DB, Nebraska ... 1981
Gibbs, Donnie, P, Texas Christian ... 1974
Gilliam, John, WR, South Carolina State ... 1967-68, 1977
Granger, Hoyle, RB, Mississippi State ... 1971
Gray, David, CB, East Los Angeles JC ... 1979
Green, Arthur, RB, Albany State ... 1972
Green, Sammy, LB, Florida ... 1981
Gresham, Bob, RB, West Virginia ... 1971-72
Grooms, Elois, DE, Tennessee Tech ... 1975-81
Gros, Earl, RB, Louisiana State ... 1970
Gross, Lee, C, Auburn ... 1975-79
Groth, Jeff, WR-KR, Bowling Green ... 1981
Gwinn, Ross, G, Northwestern Louisiana ... 1968

H

Hall, Tom, WR, Minnesota ... 1967
Hall, Willie, LB, USC ... 1972-73
Hamilton, Andy, WR, Louisiana State ... 1975
Hardeman, Don, LB, Texas A&I ... 1981
Hardy, Larry, TE, Jackson State ... 1978-81
Hargett, Edd, QB, Texas A&M ... 1969-72
Harris, Bill, RB, Colorado ... 1971
Harris, Ike, WR, Iowa State ... 1978-81
Hart, Ben, S, Oklahoma ... 1967
Hart, Jeff, T, Oregon State ... 1976
Hart, Tommy, DE, Morris Brown ... 1979-80
Harvey, George, G, Kansas ... 1967
Havrilak, Sam, WR, Bucknell ... 1974
Hayes, Billie, CB, San Diego State ... 1972
Hazelton, Major, DB, Florida A&M ... 1970
Heidel, Jimmy, S, Mississippi ... 1967
Herrmann, Don, WR, Waynesburg ... 1975-77
Hester, Jim, TE, North Dakota ... 1967-69
Hester, Ray, LB, Tulane ... 1971-72
Hill, John, C, Lehigh ... 1975-81
Hines, Glen Ray, T, Arkansas ... 1971-72
Holden, Sam, T, Grambling ... 1971
Hollas, Hugo, S, Rice ... 1970-72
Holloway, Stan, LB, California ... 1980
Holmes, Jack, RB, Texas Southern ... 1978-81
Howard, Gene, CB, Langston, Oklahoma ... 1968-70
Howell, Delles, CB, Grambling ... 1970-72
Huard, John, LB, Maine ... 1971

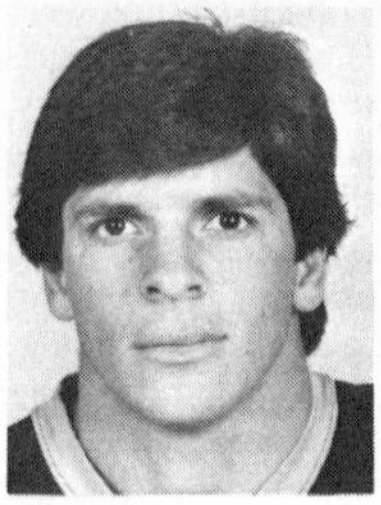
Rich Mauti

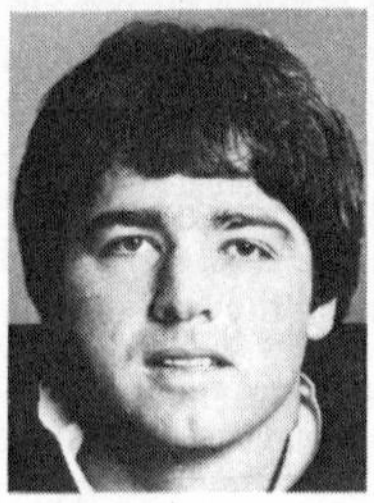
Derland Moore

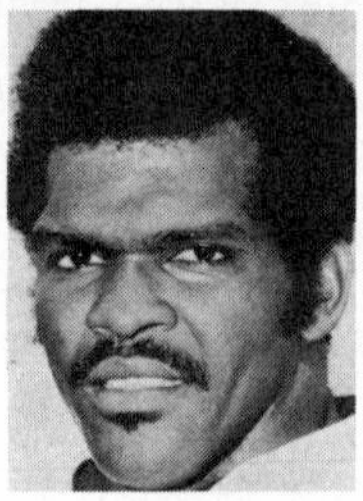
Bob Pollard

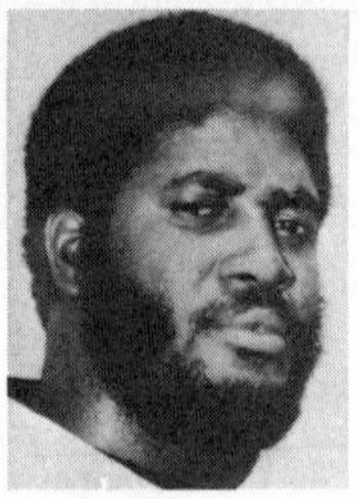
Elex Price

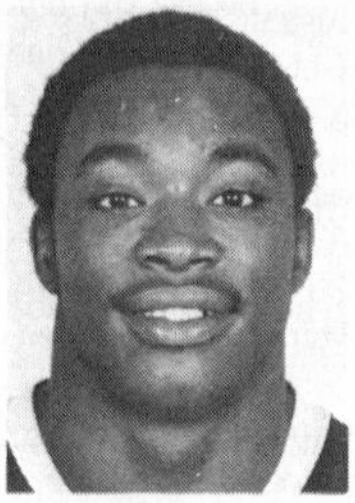
George Rogers

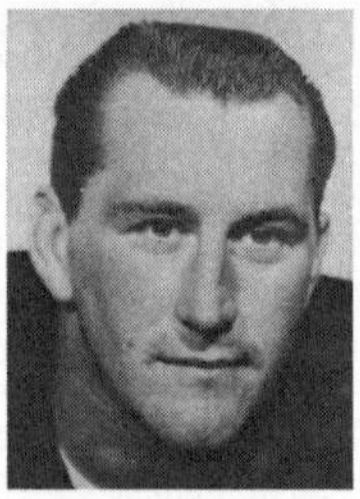
Steve Stonebreaker

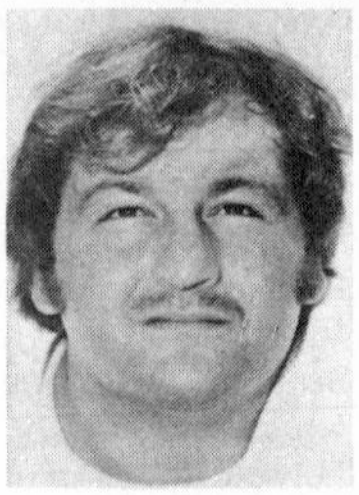
Del Williams

Hubbard, Dave, T, Brigham Young 1977
Hudson, Nat, G, Georgia 1981
Hughes, Pat, LB, Boston U. 1977-79
Hunt, Kevin, T, Doane 1978
Hyatt, Fred, WR, Auburn 1973

J

Jackson, Ernie, CB, Duke 1972-77
Jackson, Rickey, LB, Pittsburgh 1981
Jacobs, Harry, LB, Bradley 1970
Johnson, Bennie, CB, J. C. Smith 1976
Johnson, Carl, G, Nebraska 1972-73
Jones, Andrew, RB, Washington State 1975
Jones, Jerry, T, Bowling Green 1967-69
Jones, Kim, RB, Colorado State 1977-79
Jordan, Jimmy, RB, Florida 1967
Jurich, Tom, K, Northern Arizona 1978

K

Kearney, Jim, S, Prairie View 1976
Kelley, Les, LB, Alabama 1967-69
Kelly, Mike, TE, Davidson 1973
Kilmer, Billy, QB, UCLA 1967-70
Kimbrough, Elbert, S, Northwestern 1968
Kingrea, Rick, LB, Tulane 1973-77
Knowles, David, T, Indiana 1977
Kopay, Dave, RB, Washington 1971
Kovach, Jim, LB, Kentucky 1979-81
Kramer, Kent, TE, Minnesota 1967
Kupp, Jake, G, Washington 1967-75
Kuziel, Bob, C, Pittsburgh 1972

L

Lafary, Dave, T, Purdue 1977-81
LaGrande, Morris, RB, Tampa 1975
LaPorta, Phil, T, Penn State 1974-75
Lawson, Odell, RB, Langston, Oklahoma 1973-74
Lee, Bivian, CB, Prairie View 1971-75
Leggett, Earl, DT, Louisiana State 1967-68
Lemon, Mike, LB, Kansas 1975
Lewis, Gary, RB, Arizona State 1970
Leypoldt, John, K, No college 1978
Linden, Errol, T, Houston 1969-70
Linhart, Toni, K, Austria Tech 1972
Livingston, Andy, RB, Phoenix JC 1969-70
Logan, Obert, S, Trinity 1967
Long, Dave, DE, Iowa 1969-72
Looney, Joe Don, RB, Oklahoma 1969
Lorick, Tony, RB, Arizona State 1968-69
Lyons, Dick, S, Kentucky 1970

M

Manning, Archie, QB, Mississippi 1971-81
Marsalis, Jim, S, Tennessee State 1977
Marshall, James, CB, Jackson State 1980
Martin, D'Artagnan, CB, Kentucky State 1971-72
Martini, Rich, WR, California-Davis 1981
Mathis, Reggie, LB, Oklahoma 1979-80
Maurer, Andy, G, Oregon 1974
Mauti, Rich, WR, Penn State 1977-80
Maxson, Alvin, RB, Southern Methodist 1974-76
McCall, Don, RB, USC 1967-68, 1970
McClard, Bill, K, Arkansas 1973-75
McCormick, Dave, T, Louisiana State 1967-68
McCullouch, Earl, WR, USC 1974
McGill, Ralph, S, Tulsa 1978-79
McNeill, Rod, RB, USC 1974-75
McNeill, Tom, P, Stephen F. Austin 1967-69
McQuay, Leon, RB, Tampa 1976
Merkens, Guido, QB-DB-WR, Sam Houston State 1980-81
Merlo, Jim, LB, Stanford 1973-79
Meseroll, Mark, T, Florida State 1978
Middleton, Rick, LB, Ohio State 1974-76
Mike-Mayer, Steve, K, Maryland 1978
Minor, Lincoln, RB, New Mexico State 1973
Montgomery, Marv, T, USC 1976-77
Mooers, Doug, DE, Whittier 1971-72
Moore, Derland, DT, Oklahoma 1973-81
Moore, Jerry, S, Arkansas 1973-74
Moore, Reynaud, CB, UCLA 1971
Mooring, John, T, Tampa 1974
Morgan, Mike, LB, Louisiana State 1969-70
Morrison, Don, T, Texas-Arlington 1971-77
Muncie, Chuck, RB, California 1976-81
Myers, Tommy, S, Syracuse 1972-81

N

Nairne, Rob, LB, Oregon State 1981
Neal, Richard, DE, Southern U. 1969-72, 1978
Nevett, Elijah, CB, Clark 1967-70
Newland, Bob, WR, Oregon 1971-74
Newsome, Billy, DE, Grambling 1973-74
Ninowski, Jim, QB, Michigan State 1969
Nyval, Vic, RB, Northwestern Louisiana 1970

O

Ogden, Ray, WR, Alabama 1967
O'Neal, Steve, P, Texas A&M 1973
Otis, Jim, RB, Ohio State 1970
Owens, Artie, WR, West Virginia 1980
Owens, Joe, DE, Alcorn State 1971-75
Owens, Tinker, WR, Oklahoma 1976-80

P

Palmer, Dick, LB, Kentucky 1973
Parker, Joel, WR, Florida 1974-77
Parker, Steve, DE, Idaho 1980
Parks, Dave, TE, Texas Tech 1968-72
Partridge, Rick, P, Utah 1979-80
Pelluer, Scott, LB, Washington State 1981
Phillips, Jess, RB, Michigan State 1973-74
Pietrzak, Jim, C, Eastern Michigan 1979-81
Pitts, Elijah, RB, Philander Smith 1970
Poage, Ray, TE, Texas 1967-70
Poe, Johnnie, DB, Missouri 1981
Pollard, Bob, DE, Weber State 1971-77
Preece, Steve, DB, Oregon State 1969
Price, Elex, DT, Alcorn State 1973-80
Profit, Joe, RB, Northeastern Louisiana 1973
Prudhomme, Remi, G-C, Louisiana State 1971

R

Ramsey, Nate, S, Indiana 1973
Ramsey, Steve, QB, North Texas State 1970
Rasley, Rocky, G, Oregon State 1974
Ray, Ricky, CB, Norfolk State 1979-81
Reaves, Ken, CB, Norfolk State 1974
Rebowe, Rusty, LB, Nichols State 1978
Redd, Glen, LB, Brigham Young 1981
Reese, Don, DE, Jackson State 1978-80
Rengel, Mike, DT, Hawaii 1969
Ricardo, Benny, K, San Diego State 1980-81
Rice, Floyd, LB, Alcorn State 1978
Richey, Mike, T, North Carolina 1970
Riley, Preston, WR, Memphis State 1973
Rissmiller, Ray, T, Georgia 1967
Roberts, Walt, WR, San Jose State 1967
Robinson, Craig, T, Houston 1972-73
Robinson, Virgil, RB, Grambling 1971
Rogers, George, RB, South Carolina 1981
Rogers, Jimmy, RB, Oklahoma 1980-81
Rogers, Steve, RB, Louisiana State 1975
Rose, George, CB, Auburn 1967
Roussel, Tom, LB, Southern Mississippi 1971-72
Rowe, Dave, DT, Penn State 1967-70
Ryczek, Paul, C, Virginia 1981

S

Sandeman, Bill, T, Pacific 1967
Saul, Bill, LB, Penn State 1969
Scarpati, Joe, DB, North Carolina State 1970
Schmidt, Roy, G, Long Beach State 1967-68
Schmidt, Terry, CB, Ball State 1974-75
Schultz, Randy, RB, Iowa State Teachers 1967-68
Schumacher, Kurt, G, Ohio State 1975-77
Schwartz, Don, S, Washington State 1978-80
Schweda, Brian, DE, Kansas 1967-68
Scott, Bobby, QB, Tennessee 1973-81
Seal, Paul, TE, Michigan 1974-76
Shaw, Bob, WR, Winston-Salem 1970
Shinners, John, G, Xavier 1969-70
Shy, Don, RB, San Diego State 1969
Simmons, Dave, LB, Georgia Tech 1967
Simmons, Jerry, WR, Bethune-Cookman 1967
Smith, Royce, G, Georgia 1972-73
South, Ronny, CB, Arkansas 1968
Spencer, Maurice, CB, North Carolina 1974-78
Spivey, Mike, CB, Colorado 1980-81
Stauch, Scott, RB, UCLA 1981
Stevens, Howard, RB, Louisville 1973-74
Stewart, Jimmy, S, Tulsa 1977
Stickles, Monty, TE, Notre Dame 1968
Stieve, Terry, G, Wisconsin 1976-77
Stincic, Tom, LB, Michigan 1972
Stonebreaker, Steve, LB, Detroit 1967-68
Strachan, Mike, RB, Iowa State 1975-80
Strand, Eli, G, Iowa State 1967
Strong, Jim, RB, Houston 1971-72
Sturm, Jerry, T-C, Illinois 1967-70
Sturt, Fred, G, Bowling Green 1978-81
Sutherland, Doug, G, Wisconsin State 1970
Sweetan, Karl, QB, Wake Forest 1968
Swinney, Clovis, DT, Arkansas State 1970
Szaro, Rich, K, Harvard 1975-78
Szymakowski, Dave, WR, West Texas State 1968

T

Talbert, Don, T, Texas 1969-70
Taylor, James, T, Missouri 1978-81
Taylor, Jim, RB, Louisiana State 1967
Taylor, Mike, T, USC 1969-70
Thaxton, James, TE, Tennessee State 1976-77
Thomas, Charlie, KR, Tennessee State 1975
Thomas, Speedy, WR, Utah 1973-74
Thompson, Aundra, WR, East Texas State 1981
Thompson, Bobby, S, Arizona 1969
Thompson, Dave, T, Clemson 1974-75
Tilleman, Mike, DT, Montana 1967-70
Townes, Willie, DE, Tulsa 1970
Tyler, Toussaint, RB, Washington 1981

V

Vanderbundt, Skip, LB, Oregon State 1978
Vandersea, Phil, LB, Massachusetts 1967
Van Wagner, Jim, RB, Michigan Tech 1978

W

Walker, Mike, DE, Tulane 1971
Ward, Carl, S, Michigan 1969
Warren, Frank, DE, Auburn 1981
Washington, Dave, LB, Alcorn State 1980
Watson, John, T, Oklahoma 1977-79
Watson, Mike, T, Miami, Ohio 1977
Wattelet, Frank, S, Kansas 1981
Waymer, Dave, CB, Notre Dame 1980-81
Weatherspoon, Cephus, WR, Fort Lewis, Colorado 1972
Welch, Claxton, RB, Oregon 1970
Wendryhoski, Joe, C, Illinois 1967-68
Westbrooks, Greg, LB, Colorado 1975-77
Wheelwright, Ernie, RB, Southern Illinois 1967-70
Whitaker, Creston, WR, North Texas State 1972
Whitsell, Dave, S, Indiana 1967-69
Whittingham, Fred, LB, Cal Poly-San Luis Obispo .. 1967-68
Wickert, Tom, G, Washington State 1975-76
Wicks, Bob, WR, Utah State 1974
Wilks, Jim, DT, San Diego State 1981
Williams, Brooks, TE, North Carolina 1978-81
Williams, Del, G, Florida State 1967-73
Williams, Richard, WR, Abilene Christian 1974
Willis, Len, WR, Ohio State 1977
Wilson, Dave, QB, Illinois 1981
Wilson, Wayne, RB, Shepherd 1978-81
Winans, Jeff, DT, USC 1970
Winslow, Doug, WR, Drake 1973
Wood, Gary, QB, Cornell 1967
Woods, Robert, T, Tennessee State 1977-80
Woodson, Marv, S, Indiana 1969
Wyatt, Doug, S, Tulsa 1970-72

Y

Yepremian, Garo, K, No college 1979
Young, Bob, G, Howard Payne 1981
Youngblood, George, S, Cal State-Los Angeles 1967-68

Z

Zanders, Emanuel, G, Jackson State 1974-80

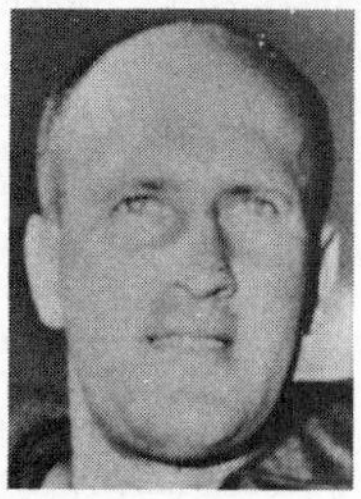

Al Dorow

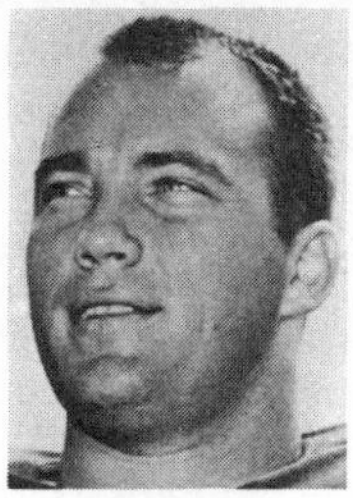

John Elliott

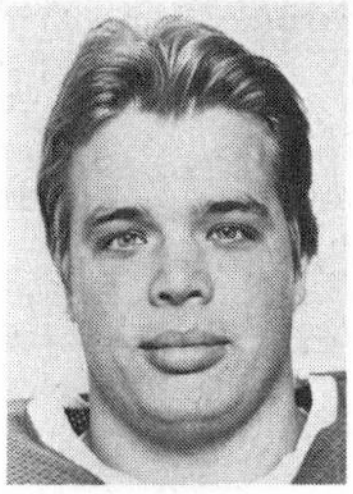

Joe Klecko

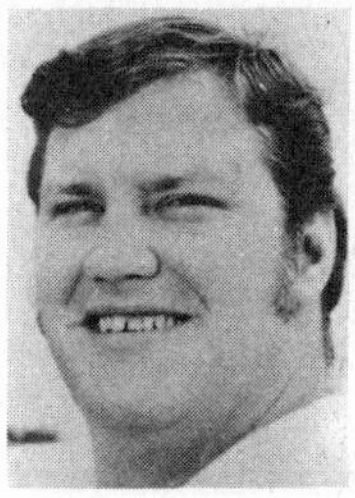

Pete Lammons

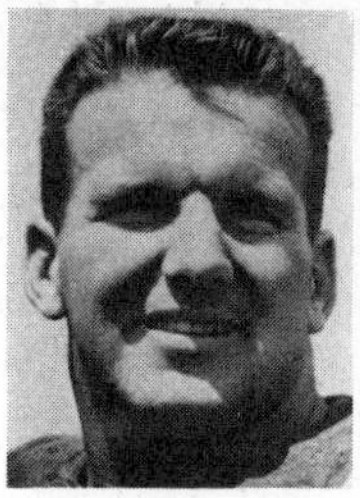

Bill Mathis

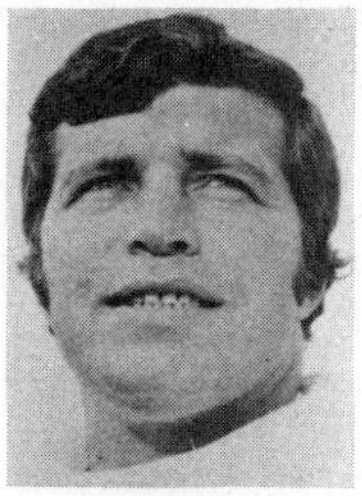

Gerry Philbin

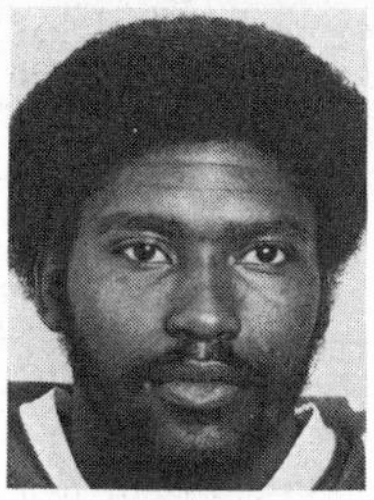

Wesley Walker

Klecko, Joe, DT-DE, Temple....................1977-81
Klotz, Jack, T, Widener....................1960-63
Knight, David, WR, William & Mary....................1973-77
Koegel, Warren, C, Penn State....................1974
Kovac, Ed, B, Cincinnati....................1962
Krevis, Al, T, Boston College....................1976
Kroll, Alex, C, Rutgers....................1962

L

Lamberti, Pat, LB, Richmond....................1961
Lammons, Pete, TE, Texas....................1966-71
Lawson, Al, WR, Delaware State....................1964
Leahy, Pat, K, St. Louis....................1974-81
Leonard, Cecil, DB, Tuskegee....................1969-70
Lester, Lance, E, No college....................1960
Lewis, Kenny, RB, Virginia Tech....................1980-81
Lewis, Richard, LB, Portland State....................1974-75
Lewis, Sherman, DB, Michigan State....................1966
Linhart, Toni, K, Austria Tech....................1979
Liske, Pete, QB-DB, Penn State....................1964
Little, John, DT-DE, Oklahoma State....................1970-74
Lomas, Mark, DT-DE, Northern Arizona....................1970-74
Long, Kevin, RB, South Carolina....................1977-81
Look, Dean, QB, Michigan State....................1962
Lusteg, Booth, K, No college....................1967
Lynn, Johnny, CB, UCLA....................1979-81
Lyons, Marty, DE, Alabama....................1979-81

M

Mabra, Ron, CB, Howard....................1977
Mackey, Dee, TE, East Texas State....................1963-65
Marinaro, Ed, RB, Cornell....................1976
Marques, Bob, C, Boston U....................1960
Marshall, Charles (Tank), DT, Texas A&M....................1977
Marshall, Ed, WR, Cameron State....................1976
Martin, Blanche, B, Michigan State....................1960
Martin, Bob, LB, Nebraska....................1976-79
Martin, Saladin, DB, San Diego State....................1980
Marvaso, Tommy, S-CB, Cincinnati....................1976-77
Mathis, Bill, RB, Clemson....................1960-69
Matlock, John, C, Miami....................1967
Maynard, Don, WR, Texas-El Paso....................1960-72
McAdams, Bob, DE, North Carolina College....................1963-64
McAdams, Carl, DT-LB, Oklahoma....................1967-69
McClain, Clifford, RB, South Carolina State....................1970-73
McCusker, Jim, T, Pittsburgh....................1964
McDaniel, Ed (Wahoo), LB, Oklahoma....................1964-65
McGlasson, Ed, C, Youngstown State....................1979
McKibben, Mike, LB, Kent State....................1979-80
McMullan, John, G, Notre Dame....................1960-62
McNeil, Freeman, RB, UCLA....................1981
Mehl, Lance, LB, Penn State....................1980-81
Mercein, Chuck, RB, Yale....................1970
Merrill, Mark, LB, Minnesota....................1978-79
Michaels, Walt, LB, Washington & Lee....................1963
Mischak, Bob, G, Army....................1960-62
Mock, Mike, LB, Texas Tech....................1978
Mooring, John, G, Tampa....................1971-73
Moreino, Joe, DE, Idaho State....................1978
Morelli, Fran, T, Colgate....................1962
Moresco, Tim, S, Syracuse....................1978-80
Mulligan, Wayne, C, Clemson....................1974-75
Mumley, Nick, DE, Purdue....................1960-62

N

Namath, Joe, QB, Alabama....................1965-76
Nance, Jim, RB, Syracuse....................1973
Neal, Richard, DT-DE, Southern U....................1973-77
Neidert, John, LB, Louisville....................1968-69
Neil, Kenny, DE-DT, Iowa State....................1981
Newsome, Billy, DE, Grambling....................1975-76
Newton, Tom, RB, California....................1977-81
Nock, George, RB, Morgan State....................1969-71

O

O'Mahoney, Jim, LB, Miami....................1965-66
O'Neal, Steve, P, Texas A&M....................1969-72
O'Neill, Bob, G, Notre Dame....................1961
Onkotz, Dennis, LB, Penn State....................1970
Osborne, Rich, TE, Texas A&M....................1976
Owens, Burgess, S, Miami....................1973-79
Owens, Marv, WR, San Diego State....................1974

P

Pagliei, Joe, B, Clemson....................1960
Palewicz, Al, LB, Miami....................1977
Palmer, Scott, DT, Texas....................1971
Parilli, Vito (Babe), QB, Kentucky....................1968-69
Parker, Artimus, S, USC....................1977
Pashe, Bill, DB, George Washington....................1964
Paulson, Dainard, DB, Oregon State....................1961-66
Pellegrini, Joe, DT, Idaho....................1978-79
Penrose, Craig, QB, San Diego State....................1980
Perkins, Bill, B, Iowa....................1963
Perreault, Pete, T-G, Boston U....................1963-67, 1969-70
Philbin, Gerry, DE, Buffalo....................1964-72
Piccone, Lou, WR-KR, West Liberty State....................1974-76
Pillers, Lawrence, DE, Alcorn State....................1976-80
Plunkett, Sherman, T, Maryland-Eastern Shore....................1963-67
Poole, Steve, LB, Tennessee....................1976
Powell, Art, WR, San Jose State....................1960-62
Powell, Darnell, RB, Tennessee-Chattanooga....................1978
Powell, Marvin, T, USC....................1977-81
Price, Jim, LB, Auburn....................1963
Prout, Bob, S, Knox....................1975
Puetz, Garry, G-T, Valparaiso....................1973-78

R

Raba, Bob, TE, Maryland....................1977-79
Rademacher, Bill, DB-WR, Northern Michigan....................1964-68
Ramsey, Chuck, P, Wake Forest....................1977-81
Randall, Dennis, DT, Oklahoma State....................1967
Rasmussen, Randy, G, Kearney State....................1967-81
Ray, Darrol, S, Oklahoma....................1980-81
Rechichar, Bert, DB, Tennessee....................1961
Reese, Steve, LB, Louisville....................1974-75
Reifsnyder, Bob, DE, Navy....................1960-61
Renn, Bobby, DB-WR, Florida State....................1961
Richards, Jim, S, Virginia Tech....................1968-69
Richards, Perry, WR Detroit....................1962
Richardson, Jeff, G, Michigan State....................1967-68
Riggins, John, RB, Kansas....................1971-75
Riley, Larry, CB, Salem, West Virginia....................1978
Riley, Lee, DB, Detroit....................1961-62
Rivers, Jamie, LB, Bowling Green....................1974-75
Roach, Travis, G, Texas....................1974
Roberts, Wesley, DE, Texas Christian....................1980
Robinson, Gregg, DE-DT, Dartmouth....................1978
Robinson, Jerry, WR, Grambling....................1965
Robinson, Matt, QB, Georgia....................1977-79
Robinson, Bill, B, Lincoln....................1960
Rochester, Paul, DT, Michigan State....................1963-69
Rogers, Steve, RB, Louisiana State....................1976
Roman, John, T, Idaho State....................1976-81
Rosecrans, Jim, LB, Penn State....................1976
Ross, Dave, E, Cal State-Los Angeles....................1960
Rowley, Bob, LB, Virginia....................1964
Rudolph, Ben, DT-DE, Long Beach State....................1981
Russ, Carl, LB, Michigan....................1976-77
Ryan, Joe, E, Villanova....................1960
Ryan, Pat, QB, Tennessee....................1978-81

S

Saidock, Tom, T, Michigan State....................1960-61
Salaam, Abdul, DT, Kent State....................1976-81
Sample, Johnny, CB, Maryland-Eastern Shore....................1966-68
Sapienza, Americo (Rick), B, Villanova....................1960
Satterwhite, Howard, WR, Sam Houston State....................1976
Sauer, George Jr., WR, Texas....................1965-70
Schmidt, Henry, DT, USC....................1966
Schmiesing, Joe, DT, New Mexico State....................1974
Schmitt, John, C, Hofstra....................1964-73
Schroy, Ken, S, Maryland....................1977-81
Schwedes, Ger, B, Syracuse....................1960
Schweickert, Bob, WR, Virginia Tech....................1965, 1967
Scrabis, Bob, QB, Penn State....................1960-62
Seiler, Paul, T-C, Notre Dame....................1967, 1969
Shockley, Bill, B-K, West Chester State....................1960-62
Shuler, Mickey, TE, Penn State....................1978-81
Simkus, Arnie, DT, Michigan....................1965
Smith, Allen, B, Findlay....................1966
Smolinski, Mark, RB-TE, Wyoming....................1963-68
Snell, Matt, RB, Ohio State....................1964-72
Sohn, Kurt, WR-KR, Fordham....................1981
Songin, Eddie (Butch), QB, Boston College....................1962
Sowells, Rich, DB, Alcorn State....................1971-76
Spicer, Rob, LB, Indiana....................1973
Springs, Kirk, DB, Miami, Ohio....................1981
Starks, Marshall, DB, Illinois....................1963-64
Stephens, Bruce, WR-KR, Columbia....................1978
Stephens, Harold (Hayseed), QB, Hardin-Simmons....................1962
Stephens, Steve, TE, Oklahoma State....................1981
Stewart, Wayne, TE, California....................1969-72
Stricker, Tony, DB, Colorado....................1963
Stromberg, Mike, LB, Temple....................1968
Strugar, George, DT, Washington....................1962-63
Studdard, Vern, WR-KR, Mississippi....................1971
Suggs, Shafer, DB, Ball State....................1976-80
Sullivan, John, LB, Illinois....................1979-80
Svihus, Bob, T, USC....................1971-72
Swinney, Clovis, DT, Arkansas State....................1971
Szaro, Rich, K, Harvard....................1979

T

Talamini, Bob, G, Kentucky....................1968
Taliaferro, Mike, QB, Illinois....................1964-67
Tannen, Steve, CB, Florida....................1970-74
Taylor, Billy, RB, Texas Tech....................1981
Taylor, Ed, CB, Memphis State....................1975-79
Taylor, Mike, LB, Michigan....................1972-73
Tharp, Corky, DB, Alabama....................1960
Thomas, Earlie, CB, Colorado State....................1970-74
Thompson, Steve, DT, Washington....................1968-70, 1972-73
Tiller, Jim, B, Purdue....................1962
Todd, Richard, QB, Alabama....................1976-81
Torczon, LaVerne, DE, Nebraska....................1962-65
Turk, Godwin, LB, Southern U....................1974-75
Turner, Rocky, WR-S, Tennessee-Chattanooga....................1972-73
Turner, Bake, WR, Texas Tech....................1963-69
Turner, Vince, DB, Missouri....................1964
Tyler, Maurice, CB, Morgan State....................1977

V

Van Galder, Tim, QB, Iowa State....................1973

W

Waldemore, Stan, C-G-T, Nebraska....................1978-81
Walker, Donnie, S, Central State, Ohio....................1975
Walker, Wesley, WR, California....................1977-81
Walsh, Ed, T, Widener....................1961
Walton, Sam, T, East Texas State....................1968-69
Ward, Chris, T, Ohio State....................1978-81
Washington, Al, LB, Ohio State....................1981
Washington, Clyde, DB, Purdue....................1963-65
Waskiewicz, Jim, LB, Wichita State....................1966-67
Watters, Bob, DE, Lincoln, Missouri....................1962-64
Wegert, Ted, B, No college....................1960
Weir, Sammy, WR, Arkansas State....................1966
Werl, Bob, DE, Miami....................1966
West, Dave, DB, Central State, Ohio....................1963
West, Mel, B, Missouri....................1961-63
West, Willie, DB, Oregon....................1964-65
Wetzel, Marty, LB, Tulane....................1981
White, Charlie, RB, Bethune-Cookman....................1977
White, Lee, RB, Weber State....................1968-70
Whitlatch, Blake, LB, Louisiana State....................1978
Wilder, Bert, DT, North Carolina State....................1964-67
Winkel, Bob, DT, Kentucky....................1979-80
Wise, Phil, S, Nebraska-Omaha....................1971-76
Wood, Bill, DB, West Virginia Wesleyan....................1963
Wood, Dick, QB, Auburn....................1963-64
Wood, Richard, LB, USC....................1975
Woodall, Al, QB, Duke....................1969-74
Woodring, John, LB, Brown....................1981
Woods, Larry, DT, Tennessee State....................1974-75
Woods, Robert, T, Tennessee State....................1973-77
Word, Roscoe, CB-KR, Jackson State....................1974-76
Wren, Lowe, DB, Missouri....................1961
Wright, Gordon, G, Delaware State....................1969

Y

Yearby, Bill, DT, Michigan....................1966
Yohn, John David, LB, Gettysburg....................1963
Youngelman, Sid, DE, Alabama....................1960-61

Z

Zapalac, Bill, DE-LB, Texas....................1971-73

OAKLAND RAIDERS

1959 The American Football League was organized, August 14. It held its first player draft, November 22, and another draft, completing 53 rounds in all, December 2.

1960 The Minnesota-St. Paul franchise of the AFL withdrew and elected to play in the National Football League instead. Barron Hilton, owner of the Los Angeles Chargers of the AFL, gave the league an ultimatum that unless it placed another franchise on the West Coast, he would withdraw from the AFL. Oakland became the eighth city to gain an AFL franchise, January 30. The franchise was owned by an eight-man syndicate headed by Y.C. (Chet) Soda and it included Ed McGah, Robert Osborne, and Wayne Valley. The AFL draft was past and the Oakland team got its first players by drafting from the rosters of the seven other clubs. "Dons," then "Senors," then "Raiders" was chosen as the team's name. Eddie Erdelatz of Navy was named the team's head coach. The regents of the University of California would not approve the use of its stadium for the Raiders' games, and they decided to play at Kezar Stadium in San Francisco, which also was the home of the rival 49ers of the NFL. Only 12,703 fans watched the Raiders lose to the Houston Oilers 37-22 in their first game. They had two good quarterbacks, Tom Flores and Babe Parilli, and center Jim Otto and guard Wayne Hawkins were solid players, but the Raiders had little else and finished their first season with a 6-8 record.

1961 The Raiders' home games were moved to Candlestick Park in San Francisco. McGah, Osborne, and Valley bought out their five partners, and McGah was named president of the club. The team lost its first two games to Houston 55-0 and San Diego 44-0. "I don't know what to do about it," Erdelatz said. He was fired as coach. Marty Feldman, one of Erdelatz's assistants, was given the job, but he didn't fare any better. The Raiders scored the fewest points in the league, allowed the most points, played before mostly empty seats, and won only two games. Osborne, discouraged by the turn of events, sold his interest in the club.

1962 Valley told Oakland city officials, "Either build us a stadium or we move." A much discussed Alameda County-Oakland Coliseum complex was still in the planning stages, so until further action could be taken on it, Frank Youell Field was designated for the Raiders. It was a small high school facility. Temporary stands were built and boosted its seating capacity to 20,000. It was still so small that even if the Raiders sold out every game, they would have lost money had it not been for the league's television contract. The team continued to struggle for victories, as well. Feldman was replaced by Bill (Red) Conkright after two games. On the final day of the season at Frank Youell Field, the Raiders finally won, beating Boston 20-0 for their only victory in 14 games.

1963 After refusing their offers on several occasions, Al Davis, an assistant coach for the San Diego Chargers, accepted a three-year contract as the Raiders' head coach and general manager. "What I want is enough time and money to build the Raiders into a professional football team," Davis told owners Valley and McGah. Davis immediately began reorganizing the entire franchise. He hired a new business manager, director of player personnel, and ticket manager. He signed split end Art Powell, who had played out his option with the New York Titans, got quarterback Tom Flores back from an extended illness, and coaxed several useful players away from other teams. Running back Clemon Daniels, a former tight end, rushed for 1,099 yards, an AFL record. The Oakland defense also prospered under Davis. After a 2-4 start, the Raiders rallied to win their last eight games and finish one game behind San Diego. The last three games, in particular, established Oakland and the AFL in its exciting, wide-open style. Trailing 27-10, the Raiders rallied in the fourth quarter to beat the Chargers 41-27. Then they edged Denver 35-31 and outscored Houston 52-49 in the highest scoring game in AFL history.

1964 Tony Lorick, the number-one draft choice from Arizona State, signed with Oakland. He also signed with Baltimore of the NFL and after a long hassle, wound up playing for the Colts. Davis's team slumped at the start, losing five straight, but came back to score four wins and a tie in the final five games, including victories over Buffalo and San Diego, the teams headed for the AFL title game. Two new acquisitions, 6-foot 7-inch, 265-pound end Ben Davidson and middle linebacker Dan Conners helped fortify Oakland's defense.

1965 Construction officially started on Oakland-Alameda County Coliseum. Davis continued to stockpile talent, acquiring such rookies as receiver Fred Biletnikoff, defensive back Kent McCloughan, linebacker Gus Otto, and tackles Harry Schuh and Bob Svihus. But an inability to beat Buffalo and San Diego—the Raiders lost all four of those games—killed the Raiders' title chances and they finished second to the Chargers in their division again.

1966 Davis was named commissioner of the American Football League, succeeding Joe Foss, in April. John Rauch was named Raiders' head coach. The AFL and NFL agreed to a merger, June 8. Davis resigned as AFL commissioner and returned to Oakland as managing general partner. Oakland-Alameda

Daryle Lamonica, the AFL's most valuable player in 1967 and 1969.

County Coliseum opened; the Kansas City Chiefs defeated the Raiders 32-10 before 50,746, September 18. The Raiders slipped to a 1-3 mark but late season victories over Kansas City, Houston, and San Diego helped produce an 8-5-1 season, good for second place in the Western Division.

1967 Davis traded quarterback Flores and wide receiver Powell to Buffalo for quarterback Daryle Lamonica and wide receiver Glenn Bass. The Raiders also acquired receiver Bill Miller from Buffalo, cornerback Willie Brown from Denver, and quarterback-kicker George Blanda, who had been released by Houston. Rookie guard Gene Upshaw from Texas A&I immediately established himself as one of the league's best blockers. The Raiders smashed Denver 51-0 in the season opener, and, after a 27-14 loss to New York in the fourth week, they won 10 straight games to capture the Western Division title with a 13-1 mark. Blanda won the AFL scoring championship with 20 field goals and 56 extra points for a total of 116. In the AFL Championship Game at Oakland, the Raiders stormed Houston 40-7 for the right to meet Green Bay in Super Bowl II. Lamonica was named AFL player of the year, having thrown for 3,228 yards and 30 touchdowns.

1968 The AFL champions met the Green Bay Packers in the second AFL-NFL World Championship Game. Oakland was too young and too inexperienced, and quarterback Bart Starr used up the clock with typical Packers' ball control to win 33-14. As the 1968 season began, the Raiders were hit with an unusual amount of regular season injuries, but found two new stars on offense, wide receiver Warren Wells and running back Charlie Smith. They played the New York Jets at Oakland and were trailing 32-29 with one minute, five seconds to play. The NBC television network switched from the game to begin the movie, "Heidi." The network's switchboard lit up with angry protests; the viewers never saw the Raiders come back with two late touchdowns to win what was later called the "Heidi Game," 43-32. Oakland rolled to a 12-2 record, but it wasn't enough for undisputed first place in the Western Division; they were tied with the Kansas City Chiefs. Oakland crushed the Chiefs 41-6 in a playoff. In the AFL title game in New York, the Raiders and Jets played a dramatic game with Joe Namath finally pulling it out for New York 27-23.

1969 Rauch became head coach of the Buffalo Bills. John Madden, a 32-year-old Raiders' assistant, replaced him, becoming the youngest head coach in pro football. Lamonica continued as one of the game's most effective passers. He threw six touchdown passes in the first half on the way to a 50-21 win over Buffalo, October 19. One week later, the Raiders beat San Diego to equal the AFL record for consecutive unbeaten games at 15. The streak ended the following week with a 31-17 loss to Cincinnati, but Oakland won its six remaining games and finished first in the Western Division with a 12-1-1 mark. Lamonica ended the season with 34 touchdown passes. Oakland routed Houston 56-7 in the first round of the playoffs.

1970 Kansas City, the second place team in the division, upset Oakland 17-7 in the AFC Championship Game at Oakland. The Raiders were placed in the AFC Western Division as realignment of pro football took place. The Raiders' season ticket sales hit a record high of 50,578 September 4. Blanda, 43, produced four victories and a tie in the final seconds of five consecutive games. Blanda threw two touchdown passes in a 31-14 victory over Pittsburgh. The following week he kicked a 48-yard field goal with three seconds remaining to tie Kansas City 17-17. A week later, again with three seconds left, he kicked a 52-yard field goal that gave the Raiders a 23-20 vic-

Ken Stabler rolls out and passes in a victory over San Dieo, 1974.

tory over Cleveland. In the next game, with Denver, Blanda came off the bench to ignite a late rally that beat the Broncos 24-19. Then he kicked a field goal with four seconds left to defeat San Diego 20-17. Thanks to Blanda, Oakland became the first AFC team to win four consecutive divisional championships. In the first round of the playoffs, the Raiders beat Miami 21-14 to advance to the championship game against Baltimore.

1971 In the AFC Championship Game with Baltimore, Blanda completed 17 of 32 passes for 271 yards, but the Colts made three key interceptions, Johnny Unitas staged a Cinderella passing exhibition of his own, and Baltimore advanced to the Super Bowl with a 27-17 victory. The Raiders lost to the New England Patriots 20-6 in the opening game of the regular season but went undefeated for the next

nine weeks. The team's two best running backs, Charlie Smith and Hewritt Dixon, both were sidelined with injuries. A 37-14 loss to Baltimore started a three-game losing streak, which included a 16-14 loss to Kansas City in the next to last game. Oakland finished with an 8-4-2 record. It was the first time in five years the Raiders failed to win the Western Division title.

1972 Marv Hubbard led all rushers in the Pro Bowl game, gaining 57 yards in the AFC's 26-13 win over the NFC. Davis and Madden continued to rebuild the Raiders and maintain the same remarkable winning percentage. Youngsters such as Horace Jones, Otis Sistrunk, Art Thoms, and Tony Cline were starting in the defensive line, and Phil Villapiano and Gerald Irons were new linebackers. Offensively, the flashy new addition was Clifford Branch, the world class sprinter from Colorado who was developing into a new deep threat. Branch caught a key 19-yard pass in a last-minute, 21-19 victory over San Diego. The win was the fourth in a six-game streak that closed out the Raiders' 10-3-1 season. After winning the Western Division title, Oakland traveled to Pittsburgh and was defeated 13-7 when Franco Harris scored the winning touchdown on a shoe-top catch of a deflected pass in the final seconds.

1973 The largest crowd ever to see a pro football game in the Bay Area, 74,121 at the University of California, watched Oakland end Miami's winning streak at 18 games with a 12-7 victory. After failing to score a touchdown in the first three games, Lamonica was benched in favor of Ken Stabler at quarterback. A mid-November slump cost the team a 17-9 loss to Pittsburgh and a 7-3 upset at the hands of Cleveland. The Raiders rallied for three consecutive victories, and entered the final game against Denver only a half-game in front of the vastly improved Broncos. The Raiders won 21-17, finishing at 9-4-1 for their sixth division championship in seven years. In the first round of the AFC playoffs, Oakland defeated Pittsburgh 33-14. Miami's defending Super Bowl champions were too strong in the AFC title game, however, and the Raiders fell 27-10.

1974 Madden and his staff coached the AFC to a 15-13 victory over the NFC in the Pro Bowl at Kansas City's Arrowhead stadium. A 27-7 victory over Kansas City began a nine-game winning streak for the Raiders, September 22. The following week, Oakland shut out Pittsburgh 17-0. The streak ended with a 20-17 loss to Denver in the eleventh game, but the Raiders won the next three and finished 12-2 for another Western Division championship. Against Miami in the first round of the AFC playoffs, Stabler took the Raiders on a pressure drive late in the fourth quarter, then threw a clutch touchdown pass to Clarence Davis in the final minutes for a 28-26 victory. Oakland's bid for the Super Bowl was shut off by Pittsburgh, 24-13, in the AFC title game at Oakland, December 29.

1975 Jim Otto, last of the original Raiders, retired after 15 years as the team's starting center. In a nationally televised Monday night game, Oakland opened the season with a 31-21 victory over Miami, ending the Dolphins' 31-game winning streak in the Orange Bowl. The Raiders won their next two games but were jolted 42-10 by Kansas City and lost to Cincinnati 14-10. They rebounded to win seven straight, clinching the division title with a 37-34 overtime victory over Atlanta, November 30. In the first round of the playoffs, the Raiders edged Cincinnati 31-28.

1976 In the AFC title game, Pittsburgh ended the Raiders' hopes again, hanging on for a 16-10 victory at snow-coated Three Rivers Stadium, January 4. Oakland trailed Pittsburgh 16-7 with 1:38 to play and the Steelers in possession on the Raiders' 36-yard line. But a fumble recovery, a 41-yard George Blanda field goal, and a recovered onside kick gave the Raiders a shot at the conference championship with seven seconds left. The game ended as Branch took a pass from Stabler and was tackled at the Pittsburgh 15-yard line. Blanda retired after 26 years in professional football. The Raiders opened the regular season with a turnabout, upending the Steelers 31-28 on Fred Steinfort's field goal with 18 seconds left. The following Monday night, Stabler completed 22 of 28 passing attempts in a 24-21 triumph over Kansas City. The Raiders got by Houston 14-13 on October 3. The following week their injury-riddled defense caved in and allowed New England seven touchdowns in a 48-17 loss. Oakland regrouped to win its last 10 games to finish 13-1 and claim another division championship. Stabler dived in for the winning touchdown with time running out as the Raiders beat

New England 24-21 in round one of the playoffs. In the AFC title game, Pittsburgh was weakened by the loss of injured Franco Harris and Rocky Bleier, its two best runners, December 26. Oakland took advantage of the situation, playing a conservative ground game to win 24-7 and earn a berth in Super Bowl XI.

1977 Oakland beat Minnesota decisively 32-14 in Super Bowl XI in Pasadena's Rose Bowl, January 9. Fred Biletnikoff was named the game's most valuable player after three clutch catches to set up Oakland touchdowns. The Raiders came into the regular season with a 13-game winning streak. They increased it to 17 before losing 30-7 to the Broncos, who intercepted Stabler seven times. Oakland bounced back with a 28-27 victory over the Jets, and then gave the Broncos their first defeat of the season, 24-14. On November 20, Stabler was injured in the first quarter and the Raiders lost to San Diego 12-7. The Raiders lost their third game of the season on December 4, 20-14 to Los Angeles. An 11-3 record earned a wild card spot in the playoffs. On December 24, Stabler threw three touchdowns to Dave Casper, the last after 15:43 of overtime, and the Raiders defeated the Colts 37-31 in the AFC Divisional Playoff Game.

1978 The Raiders lost to the Broncos 20-17 on January 1 in the 1977 AFC Championship Game. The 1978 season opened against the Broncos; the Broncos won 14-6. On September 10, Oakland evened its record at 1-1 when Stabler fumbled at his 24 on the last play of the game, Banaszak bobbled the ball forward, and Casper grabbed it in the end zone for the winning touchdown in a 21-20 victory over San Diego. Oakland was inconsistent throughout the season, with Stabler hitting 58 percent of his passes, but throwing 30 interceptions. The Raiders finished only 3-5 in the AFC West and 9-7 overall, missing the playoffs for the first time since 1971.

1979 After 10 years as head coach, Madden retired on January 4. One month later, former Oakland quarterback Tom Flores was named as Madden's successor. Injuries forced Flores to install a two-tight-end offense, and Dave Casper and Raymond Chester be-

came the first pair of tight ends from the same team to make the Pro Bowl. Although the passing game flourished, the running attack was a disappointment, finishing twenty-fourth in the league. The Raiders opened with a 24-17 victory over Los Angeles, then lost three games in a row. Battling back all year, the Raiders were still in the playoff picture until the last week of the season when a 29-24 Seattle victory gave Oakland its second straight 9-7 record and non-playoff season.

1980 Wanting a quarterback with better range, the Raiders traded Stabler to Houston for Dan Pastorini in the offseason. Mark van Eeghen broke the Raiders' career rushing yardage mark September 28 against Buffalo. After a 2-2 start, Pastorini was injured in a loss to Kansas City on October 5. Jim Plunkett, whose on-again, off-again career had him sitting on the Raiders' bench, took over and quarterbacked Oakland to six straight victories, a final record of 11-5, and into the AFC Wild Card Game. The defensive star for Oakland was Lester Hayes, who intercepted 13 passes, the second most in a single season in NFL history. On December 28, Plunkett threw two touchdown passes, Hayes returned an interception for a touchdown, and the Raiders defeated Houston in the AFC Wild Card Game 27-7.

1981 The defense won one, the offense won one, and they shared in the glory in the third, as the Raiders swept to a victory in the Super Bowl. In the AFC Divisional Playoff Game, the Raiders intercepted Cleveland's Brian Sipe three times, including a game-clincher in the end zone by safety Mike Davis in the fourth quarter, leading to a 14-12 victory. The next week, Plunkett passed for 261 yards and two touchdowns to help the Raiders defeat the Chargers 34-27 in the AFC Championship Game. Super Bowl XV was all Raiders, as they dominated the Eagles in a 27-10 victory. Plunkett was named the game's most valuable player. The Raiders' and the Los Angeles Coliseum Commission's antitrust suit against the NFL went to trial in Federal District Court in Los Angeles, May 11. The suit contended the league violated anti-monopoly statutes in blocking a proposed move by the Raiders from Oakland to the L.A. Coli-

Mark van Eeghen follows the blocking of Clarence Davis in the 1976 AFC Championship Game.

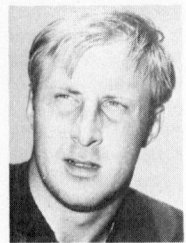
Fred Biletnikoff

Clifford Branch

Raymond Chester

Ben Davidson

Hewritt Dixon

Ray Guy

Marv Hubbard

seum to replace the Rams, who had moved to Anaheim Stadium. A mistrial was declared when the jury was unable to reach a verdict, August 13. The Cinderella season for Plunkett and the Raiders did not continue in 1981. Oakland fell to fourth place with a 7-9 record. The Raiders didn't win more than two games in a row at any point, and midway through the season Plunkett, center Dave Dalby, tight end Raymond Chester, and guard Gene Upshaw all were replaced by younger players. Van Eeghen and wide reciever Bobby Chandler spent most of the season on injured reserve.

MEMBERS OF HALL OF FAME:
George Blanda, Ron Mix, Jim Otto

RAIDERS RECORD, 1960-81

Year	Won	Lost	Tied	Pct.	Pts.	OP
1960	6	8	0	.429	319	388
1961	2	12	0	.143	237	458
1962	1	13	0	.071	213	370
1963	10	4	0	.714	363	288
1964	5	7	2	.417	303	350
1965	8	5	1	.615	298	239
1966	8	5	1	.615	315	288
1967‡	13	1	0	.929	468	233
1968§	12	2	0	.857	453	233
1969§	12	1	1	.923	377	242
1970†	8	4	2	.667	300	293
1971	8	4	2	.667	344	278
1972†	10	3	1	.750	365	248
1973†	9	4	1	.679	292	175
1974†	12	2	0	.857	355	228
1975†	11	3	0	.786	375	255
1976*	13	1	0	.929	350	237
1977**	11	3	0	.786	351	230
1978	9	7	0	.563	311	283
1979	9	7	0	.563	365	337
1980*	11	5	0	.688	364	306
1981	7	9	0	.438	273	343
22 Years	195	110	11	.634	7,391	6,302

‡*AFL Champion*
§*AFL Western Division Champion*
†*AFC Western Division Champion*
*Super Bowl Champion
**AFC Wild Card Qualifier for Playoffs

RECORD HOLDERS

Rushing (Yards)	Mark van Eeghen, 1977	1,273
Passing (Pct.)	Ken Stabler, 1976	66.7
Passing (Yards)	Ken Stabler, 1979	3,615
Passing (TDs)	Daryle Lamonica, 1969	34
Receiving (No.)	Art Powell, 1964	76
Receiving (Yards)	Art Powell, 1964	1,361
Interceptions (No.)	Lester Hayes, 1980	13
Punting (Avg.)	Ray Guy, 1973	45.3
Punt Ret. (Avg.)	Claude Gibson, 1964	14.4
Kickoff Ret. (Avg.)	Harold Hart, 1975	30.5
Touchdowns (Total)	Art Powell, 1963, and Pete Banaszak, 1975	16
Field Goals Made	George Blanda, 1973	23
Points (No.)	George Blanda, 1968	117

COACHING HISTORY

1960-61	Eddie Erdelatz*	6-10-0
1961-62	Marty Feldman**	2-15-0
1962	William (Red) Conkright	1- 8-0
1963-65	Al Davis	23-16-3
1966-68	John Rauch	33- 8-1
1969-78	John Madden	103-32-7
1979-81	Tom Flores	27-21-0

*Replaced after two games in 1961
**Replaced after two games in 1962

FIRST PLAYER SELECTED

1960	Dale Hackbart, CB, Wisconsin
1961	Joe Rutgens, DT, Illinois
1962	Roman Gabriel, QB, North Carolina State
1963	George Wilson, RB (6), Alabama
1964	Tony Lorick, RB, Arizona State
1965	Harry Schuh, T, Memphis State
1966	Rodger Bird, S, Kentucky
1967	Gene Upshaw, G, Texas A&I
1968	Eldridge Dickey, QB, Tennessee State
1969	Art Thoms, DT, Syracuse
1970	Raymond Chester, TE, Morgan State
1971	Jack Tatum, S, Ohio State
1972	Mike Siani, WR, Villanova
1973	Ray Guy, P-K, Southern Mississippi
1974	Henry Lawrence, T, Florida A&M
1975	Neal Colzie, DB, Ohio State
1976	Charles Philyaw, DT (2), Texas Southern
1977	Mike Davis, DB (2), Colorado
1978	Dave Browning, DE (2), Washington
1979	Willie Jones, DE (2), Florida State
1980	Marc Wilson, QB, Brigham Young
1981	Ted Watts, DB, Texas Tech
1982	Marcus Allen, RB, USC

OAKLAND RAIDERS, 1960-81

Agajanian, Ben, K, New Mexico	1962
Allen, Dalva, DE, Houston	1962-64
Allen, Jackie, DB, Baylor	1969
Archer, Dan, T, Oregon	1967
Armstrong, Ramon, T, Texas Christian	1960
Asad, Doug, TE, Northwestern	1960-61
Atkins, Pervis, RB-WR, New Mexico State	1965-66
Atkinson, George, DB, Morris Brown	1968-77

B

Bahr, Chris, K, Penn State	1980-81
Banaszak, Pete, RB, Miami	1966-78
Banks, Estes, RB, Colorado	1967
Bankston, Warren, RB, Tulane	1973-78
Bansavage, Al, LB, USC	1961
Barbee, Joe, T, Kent State	1960
Barnes, Jeff, LB, California	1977-81
Barnes, Larry, LB, Colorado State	1960
Barnes, Rodrigo, LB, Rice	1976
Barnwell, Malcolm, WR, Virginia Union	1981
Barrett, Jan, TE, Fresno State	1963-64
Bell, Joe, DE, Norfolk State	1979
Benson, Duane, LB, Hamline	1967-71
Bess, Rufus, DB, South Carolina State	1979
Biletnikoff, Fred, WR, Florida State	1965-78
Bird, Rodger, DB, Kentucky	1967-71
Birdwell, Dan, DT, Houston	1962-69
Bishop, Sonny, G, Fresno State	1963
Blanda, George, QB-K, Kentucky	1967-75
Blankenship, Greg, LB, Cal State-Hayward	1976
Bonness, Rik, LB, Nebraska	1976
Boydston, Max, TE, Oklahoma	1962
Boynton, George, DB, East Texas State	1962
Bracelin, Greg, LB, California	1981
Bradshaw, Morris, WR, Ohio State	1974-81
Branch, Cliff, WR, Colorado	1972-81
Bravo, Alex, DB, Cal Poly-San Luis Obispo	1960-61
Breech, Jim, K, California	1978-79
Brewington, Jim, T, North Carolina College	1961
Brown, Bob, T, Nebraska	1971-73
Brown, Charles, T, Houston	1962
Brown, Doug, DT, Fresno State	1964
Brown, Willie, DB, Grambling	1967-78
Browning, Dave, DE-DT, Washington	1978-81
Brunson, Larry, WR, Colorado	1978-79
Budness, Bill, LB, Boston U.	1964-70
Buehler, George, G, Stanford	1969-78
Buie, Drew, WR, Catawba	1969-71
Burch, Gerald, TE, Georgia Tech	1961

C

Campbell, Joe, DE, Maryland	1980-81
Campbell, Stan, G, Iowa State	1962
Cannavino, Joe, DB, Ohio State	1960-61
Cannon, Billy, TE, Louisiana State	1964-69
Carroll, Joe, LB, Pittsburgh	1972-73
Carter, Louis, RB, Maryland	1975
Casper, Dave, TE, Notre Dame	1974-80
Cavalli, Carmen, DE, Richmond	1960
Celotto, Mario, LB, USC	1980-81
Chandler, Bob, WR, USC	1980-81
Chester, Raymond, TE, Morgan State	1970-72, 1978-81
Christensen, Todd, RB-TE, Brigham Young	1979-81
Churchwell, Don, DT, Mississippi	1960

Cline, Tony, DE, Miami	1970-75
Colzie, Neal, DB, Ohio State	1975-78
Conners, Dan, LB, Miami	1964-74
Coolbaugh, Bob, WR, Richmond	1961
Costa, Dave, DT, Utah	1963-65
Craig, Dobie, WR, Howard Payne	1962-63
Crow, Wayne, RB-DB, California	1960-61

D

Dalby, Dave, C-G, UCLA	1972-81
Daniels, Clem, RB, Prairie View	1961-67
Daniels, Dave, DT, Florida A&M	1966
Davidson, Ben, DE, Washington	1964-71
Davidson, Cotton, QB, Baylor	1962-69
Davis, Bruce, T, UCLA	1979-81
Davis, Clarence, RB, USC	1971-78
Davis, Mike, DB, Colorado	1978-81
Dennery, Mike, LB, Southern Mississippi	1974-75
DePoyster, Jerry, K, Wyoming	1971-72
Deskins, Don, G, Michigan	1960
Dickey, Eldridge, WR, Tennessee State	1968-71
Dickinson, Bo, RB, Southern Mississippi	1964
Diehl, John, DT, Virginia	1965
Dittrich, John, G, Wisconsin	1960
Dixon, Hewritt, RB, Florida A&M	1966-70
Dorsey, Dick, WR, USC	1962
Dotson, Al, DT, Grambling	1968-70
Dougherty, Bob, LB, Kentucky	1960-63

E

Eason, John, TE, Florida A&M	1968
Edwards, Lloyd, TE, San Diego State	1969
Eischeid, Mike, P, Upper Iowa	1966-71
Ellison, Glenn, RB, Arkansas	1971
Enis, Hunter, QB, Texas Christian	1962
Enyart, Bill, LB, Oregon State	1971

F

Fairband, Bill, LB, Colorado	1967-68
Ficca, Dan, G, USC	1962
Fields, George, DT, Bakersfield JC	1960-61
Finnerman, Garry, DT, USC	1961
Fleming, George, RB, Washington	1961
Flores, Tom, QB, Pacific	1960-61, 1963-66
Fuller, Charley, RB, San Francisco State	1961-62

G

Gallegos, Chon, QB, San Jose State	1962
Garner, Bob, DB, Fresno State	1961-62
Garrett, Carl, RB, New Mexico Highlands	1976-77
Gibson, Claude, DB, North Carolina State	1963-65
Gillett, Fred, TE, Cal State-Los Angeles	1964
Ginn, Hubie, RB, Florida A&M	1976-78
Gipson, Tom, DT, Texas-El Paso	1971
Goldstein, Alan, WR, North Carolina	1960
Grayson, Dave, DB, Oregon	1965-70
Green, Charley, QB, Wittenberg	1966
Grossart, Kyle, QB, Oregon State	1980
Guy, Louie, DB, Mississippi	1964
Guy, Ray, P, Southern Mississippi	1973-81

H

Hagberg, Roger, RB, Minnesota	1965-69
Hall, Willie, LB, USC	1975-78
Hardman, Cedrick, DE, North Texas State	1980-81
Hardy, Charley, WR, San Jose State	1960-62
Harris, John, DB, Santa Monica JC	1960-61
Harrison, Dwight, DB, Texas A&I	1980
Hart, Harold, RB, Texas Southern	1974-75, 1978
Harvey, Jim, G, Mississippi	1966-71
Hawkins, Clarence, RB, Florida A&M	1979
Hawkins, Frank, RB, Nevada-Reno	1981
Hawkins, Wayne, G, Pacific	1960-70
Hayes, Lester, DB, Texas A&M	1977-81
Heinrich, Don, QB, Washington	1962
Hendricks, Ted, LB, Miami	1975-81
Hermann, Dick, LB, Florida State	1965
Herock, Ken, TE, West Virginia	1963-65, 1967
Highsmith, Don, RB, Michigan State	1970-72
Hill, Kenny, RS-S, Yale	1981
Hipp, I. M., RB, Nebraska	1980
Hoisington, Al, WR, Pasadena CC	1960

Kenny King

Rod Martin

Kent McCloughan

Art Shell

Charlie Smith

Phil Villapiano

Marc Wilson

Hopkins, Jerry, LB, Texas A&M 1968
Hubbard, Marv, RB, Colgate 1969-75
Huddleston, John, LB, Utah 1978-79
Hudson, Bob, RB, Northeastern Oklahoma 1973-74
Humm, David, QB, Nebraska 1975-79

I

Irons, Gerald, LB, Maryland-Eastern Shore 1970-75

J

Jackson, Bobby, RB, New Mexico State 1964
Jackson, Monte, QB, San Diego State 1978-81
Jackson, Rich, LB, Southern U. 1966
Jackson, Steve, DB, Louisiana State 1977
Jacobs, Proverb, T, California 1963-64
Jagielski, Harry, DT, Indiana 1961
Jakowenko, George, K, Syracuse 1974
Jelacic, Jon, DE, Minnesota 1961-64
Jennings, Rick, WR, Maryland 1976-77
Jensen, Derrick, RB, Texas-Arlington 1979-81
Johnson, Monte, LB, Nebraska 1973-80
Jones, Horace, DE, Louisville 1971-75
Jones, Jim, LB, Washington 1961
Jones, Willie, DE, Florida State 1979-81
Joyner, L. C., DB, Diablo Valley 1960

K

Keating, Tom, DT, Michigan 1966-72
Kent, Greg, T, Utah 1966
Keyes, Bob, RB, U. of San Diego 1960
King, Kenny, RB, Oklahoma 1980-81
Kinlaw, Reggie, DT, Oklahoma 1979-81
Klein, Dick, T, Iowa 1963-64
Kocourek, Dave, TE, Wisconsin 1967-68
Koegel, Warren, C, Penn State 1971
Korver, Kelvin, DT, Northwestern Iowa 1973-75
Kowalczyk, Walt, RB, Michigan State 1961
Koy, Ted, TE, Texas 1970
Krakoski, Joe, DB, Illinois 1963-66
Kruse, Bob, G, Wayne State 1967-68
Kunz, Terry, RB, Colorado 1976-77
Kwalick, Ted, TE, Penn State 1975-77

L

Lamonica, Daryle, QB, Notre Dame 1967-74
Larschied, Jack, RB, Pacific 1960-61
Larson, Paul, QB, California 1960
Laskey, Bill, LB, Michigan 1966-70
Lassiter, Isaac, DE, St. Augustine 1965-69
Lawrence, Henry, T, Florida A&M 1974-81
Lawrence, Larry, QB, Iowa 1974-75
Lewis, Hal, RB, Houston 1962
Liles, Alva, DT, Boise State 1980
Locklin, Billy Ray, G, New Mexico State 1960
Long, Howard, DT, Villanova 1981
Lott, Billy, RB, Mississippi 1960
Louderback, Tom, LB, San Jose State 1960-61

M

MacKinnon, Jacque, TE, Colgate 1970
Macon, Eddie, DB, Pacific 1960
Mann, Errol, K, North Dakota 1976-78
Manoukian, Don, G, Stanford 1960
Marinovich, Marv, G, USC 1965
Marsh, Curt, T, Washington 1981
Martin, Rod, LB, USC 1977-81
Martini, Rich, WR, California-Davis 1979-80
Marvin, Mickey, G, Tennessee 1977-81
Mason, Lindsey, T, Kansas 1978-81
Matsos, Archie, LB, Michigan State 1963-65
Matthews, Ira, RB-WR, Wisconsin 1979-81
Matuszak, John, DE, Tampa 1976-81
Maxwell, Tommy, DB, Texas A&M 1971-73
Mayberry, Doug, RB, Utah State 1963
McClanahan, Randy, LB, Southwestern Louisiana 1977-81
McCloughan, Kent, DB, Nebraska 1965-70
McCoy, Mike, DT, Notre Dame 1977-78
McFarlan, Nyle, DB, Brigham Young 1960
McKinney, Odis, DB, Colorado 1980-81
McMath, Herb, DT, Morningside 1976
McMillin, Jim, DB, Colorado State 1963-64
McMurtry, Chuck, DT, Whittier 1962-63
Medlin, Dan, G, North Carolina State 1974-76
Mendenhall, Terry, LB, San Diego State 1971-72
Mercer, Mike, K, Northern Arizona 1963-65
Millen, Matt, LB, Penn State 1980-81
Miller, Alan, RB, Boston College 1961, 1963-65
Miller, Bill, WR, Miami 1964, 1966-68
Mingo, Gene, K, No college 1964-65
Mirich, Rex, DT, Northern Arizona 1964-66
Mischak, Bob, TE-G, Army 1963-65
Mitchell, Tom, TE, Bucknell 1966
Mix, Ron, T, USC 1971
Montalbo, Mel, DB, Utah State 1962
Montgomery, Cleotha, KR, Abilene Christian 1981
Moody, Keith, DB, Syracuse 1980
Moore, Bob, TE, Stanford 1971-75
Moore, Manfred, RB, USC 1976
Morris, Riley, DE, Florida A&M 1960-62
Morrison, Dave, DB, Southwestern Texas State 1968
Morrow, Tom, DB, Southern Mississippi 1962-64
Mostardi, Rich, DB, Kent State 1962
Murdock, Jesse, RB, California Western 1963

N

Nelson, Bob, LB, Nebraska 1980
Nicklas, Pete, T, Baylor 1962
Norris, Jim, DT, Houston 1962-63
Novsek, Joe, DE, Tulsa 1962

O

Oats, Carleton, DT, Florida A&M 1965-72
Ogas, Dave, LB, San Diego State 1968
Oglesby, Paul, T, UCLA 1960
Oliver, Ralph (Chip), LB, USC 1968-69
Osborne, Clancy, LB, Arizona State 1963-64
O'Steen, Dwayne, DB, San Jose State 1980-81
Otto, Gus, LB, Missouri 1965-72
Otto, Jim, C, Miami 1960-74
Owens, Burgess, DB, Miami 1980-81

P

Papac, Nick, QB, Fresno State 1961
Parilli, Vito (Babe), QB, Kentucky 1960
Pastorini, Dan, QB, Santa Clara 1980
Pear, Dave, DT, Washington 1979-80
Peters, Volney, DT, USC 1961
Phillips, Charles, DB, USC 1975-80
Phillips, Jess, RB, Michigan State 1975
Philyaw, Charles, DE, Texas Southern 1976-79
Pitts, Frank, WR, Southern U. 1974
Plunkett, Jim, QB, Stanford 1978-81
Powell, Art, WR, San Jose State 1963-66
Powell, Charlie, DE, No college 1960-61
Powers, Warren, DB, Nebraska 1963-68
Prebola, Gene, TE, Boston U. 1960
Prout, Bob, DB, Knox 1974
Pyle, Palmer, G, Michigan State 1966

Q

Queen, Jeff, RB-TE, Morgan State 1973

R

Rae, Mike, QB, USC 1976-78
Ramsey, Derrick, TE, Kentucky 1978-81
Reinfeldt, Mike, DB, Wisconsin-Milwaukee 1976
Reynolds, Billy, QB, Pittsburgh 1960
Reynolds, M. C. (Mack), QB, Louisiana State 1961
Rice, Floyd, LB, Alcorn State 1976-77
Rice, Harold, DE, Tennessee State 1971
Rice, Ken, T, Auburn 1964-65
Rich, Randy, DB, New Mexico 1978
Ridlehuber, Preston, RB, Georgia 1968
Rieves, Charles, LB, Houston 1962-63
Rivera, Hank, DB, Oregon State 1962
Robertson, Bo, WR, Cornell 1962-65
Roberts, Cliff, DT, Illinois 1961
Robinson, Johnny, DT, Louisiana Tech 1981
Robiskie, Terry, RB, Louisiana State 1977-79
Roderick, John, WR, Southern Methodist 1968
Roedel, Herb, G, Marquette 1961
Rowe, Dave, DT, Penn State 1975-78
Rubke, Karl, DE, USC 1968
Russell, Booker, RB, Southwest Texas State 1978-79

S

Sabal, Ron, T, Purdue 1960-61
Schmautz, Ray, LB, San Diego State 1966
Schuh, Harry, T, Memphis State 1965-70
Seiler, Paul, T, Notre Dame 1971-73
Shaw, Glenn, RB, Kentucky 1963-64
Shell, Art, T, Maryland-Eastern Shore 1968-81
Sherman, Rod, WR, USC 1967, 1969-71
Shirkey, George, DT, Stephen F. Austin 1962
Siani, Mike, WR, Villanova 1972-77
Simpson, Jackie, LB, Mississippi 1962-64
Simpson, Willie, RB, San Francisco State 1962
Sistrunk, Otis, DE-DT, No college 1972-79
Sligh, Richard, T, North Carolina College 1967
Slough, Greg, LB, USC 1971-72
Smith, Bubba, DE, Michigan State 1973-74
Smith, Charlie, RB, Utah 1968-74
Smith, Hal, DT, UCLA 1961
Smith, James (Jetstream), RB, Compton JC 1960
Smith, Ron, DB-KR, Wisconsin 1974
Smith, Willie, RB, Michigan 1961
Sommer, Mike, RB, George Washington 1963
Spencer, Ollie, G, Kansas 1963
Spivey, Mike, DB, Colorado 1980
Stabler, Ken, QB, Alabama 1970-79
Steinfort, Fred, K, Boston College 1976
Stewart, Joe, WR, Missouri 1978-79
Stone, Jack, T, Oregon 1961-62
Streigel, Bill, LB, Pacific 1960
Svihus, Bob, T, USC 1965-70
Sweeney, Steve, WR, California 1973
Sylvester, Steve, C-G-T, Notre Dame 1975-81

T

Tatum, Jack, DB, Ohio State 1971-79
Teresa, Tony, RB, San Jose State 1960
Thomas, Skip, DB, USC 1972-78
Thoms, Art, DT, Syracuse 1969-76
Todd, Larry, RB, Arizona State 1965-70
Toomay, Pat, DE, Vanderbilt 1977-79
Trask, Orville, DT, Rice 1962
Truax, Dalton, DT, Tulane 1960
Tyson, Dick, G, Tulsa 1966

U

Upshaw, Gene, G, Texas A&I 1967-81
Urenda, Herman, WR, Pacific 1963

V

Valdez, Vernon, DB, U. of San Diego 1962
van Eeghen, Mark, RB, Colgate 1974-81
Vella, John, G-T, USC 1972-79
Villapiano, Phil, LB, Bowling Green 1971-79
Voight, Bob, DE, Cal State-Los Angeles 1961

W

Warren, Jimmy, DB, Illinois 1970-74, 1977
Warzeka, Ron, DE, Montana State 1960
Watts, Robert, LB, Boston College 1978
Watts, Ted, CB, Texas Tech 1981
Weathers, Carl, LB, San Diego State 1970-71
Weaver, Gary, LB, Fresno State 1973
Wells, Warren, WR, Texas Southern 1967-70
Westbrooks, Greg, LB, Colorado 1978-81
White, Gene, RB, Florida A&M 1962
Whittington, Arthur, RB, Southern Methodist 1978-81
Williams, Henry, DB, San Diego State 1979
Williams, Howie, DB, Howard 1964-69
Williams, Willie, DB, Grambling 1966
Williamson, Fred, DB, Northwestern 1961-64
Williamson, J. R., LB, Louisiana Tech 1964-67
Willis, Chester, RB, Auburn 1981
Wilson, Marc, QB, Brigham Young 1980-81
Wilson, Nemiah, DB, Grambling 1968-74
Winans, Jeff, G-DT, USC 1976
Wood, Dick, QB, Auburn 1965
Wyatt, Alvin, DB, Bethune-Cookman 1970

Y

Youso, Frank, T, Minnesota 1963-65

Z

Zecher, Rich, T, Utah State 1965

PHILADELPHIA EAGLES

1933 Knowing a state law banning sports on Sunday was about to be repealed, Bert Bell and Lud Wray formed a syndicate to purchase the Frankford Yellowjackets' NFL franchise. Bell and Wray bought the team for $2,500, July 9. Bell named the team in honor of the eagle, symbol of the National Recovery Administration of the New Deal. Bell was the team's general manager, Wray the coach. The Eagles opened with a 56-0 loss to the New York Giants. Remarkably, the rookie-laden Eagles regrouped and went four weeks without a loss. They even tied the powerful Chicago Bears 3-3 at Baker Bowl, November 12.

1934 The Eagles became known for their inconsistency in their second season. In one stretch, they lost four straight games while scoring just one touchdown. The following week, they blasted the Cincinnati Reds 64-0 at Baker Bowl. The Eagles' top player was Swede Hanson, a 6-foot 1-inch, 190-pound two-way halfback from Temple University. Hanson led the team with 805 yards rushing and was named second-team all-pro. Joe Carter, a receiver from Southern Methodist University, caught 16 passes for 238 yards and four touchdowns to lead the NFL.

1935 Realizing he was losing all the good college players to the top NFL teams, Bell proposed a draft, with the weakest clubs getting first shot at the All-America players. Bell's idea, considered the ideal way of balancing power in the league, was ratified by the owners, May 19. It didn't solve Bell's immediate problems, however. His Eagles continued to lose both games and money. The Eagles scored just two victories despite the addition of halfback Alabama Pitts, who learned to play football while serving time in Sing Sing.

1936 In the first three seasons, the Eagles had lost more than $80,000 and Bell's partners were losing interest in their investment. Bell purchased sole ownership for $4,000, disposed of Wray as head coach, and took the job himself. The first college draft was held and the Eagles, with the first pick, chose Jay Berwanger, the Heisman Trophy winning halfback from the University of Chicago. The Eagles traded the rights for him to the Chicago Bears, however, and he never played pro football. The Eagles' home games were moved from Baker Bowl to Municipal Stadium. They won their opener but then lost 11 straight games. They were shut out six times and their leading scorer was their center Hank Reese, who made nine points on three field goals.

1937 The Eagles improved but only slightly, winning two games. Bell traded his first draft choice, halfback Sam Francis, to the Chicago Bears for Bill Hewitt, a balding, veteran end with all-pro credentials. Hewitt led the team with 16 pass receptions, five for touchdowns. Bell uncovered an effective backfield pairing, Emmett Mortell of Wisconsin and Dave Smukler of Temple. Mortell led the Eagles with 312 yards rushing.

1938 Bell's blend of youth and experience finally jelled as the Eagles won five games and climbed past Pittsburgh into fourth place in the Eastern Division. The Eagles finished the year with wins over Pittsburgh and Detroit. The offensive star was Smukler, a versatile 6-foot 1-inch, 226-pounder with deceptive speed and agility. Smukler rushed for 313 yards, passed for 524 more, accounted for eight touchdowns and was six-for-six kicking extra points. The receivers, Carter and Hewitt, also had good seasons, catching 45 passes and scoring 11 touchdowns between them.

1939 Bell signed Davey O'Brien, the 5-foot 7-inch,

Davey O'Brien completes one of a then NFL record 33 passes against Washington, 1940.

150-pound quarterback from Texas Christian University. O'Brien signed for $12,000, plus a percentage of the gate. Bell had the tiny quarterback insured with Lloyds of London. The policy called for Lloyds to pay the Eagles $1,500 for every game O'Brien missed due to injury. O'Brien not only stayed intact but also set an NFL record for the most passing yardage in one season, 1,324. In a 27-14 loss to the Chicago Bears, O'Brien completed 21 of 36 passes for 247 yards. The Eagles finished with a 1-9-1 record.

1940 O'Brien was brilliant but he could not lift the Eagles out of the Eastern Division cellar. The Eagles switched their home field from Municipal Stadium to Shibe Park in North Philadelphia. The Eagles lost their first nine games before beating Pittsburgh 7-0. The following week, O'Brien and Washington's great Sammy Baugh hooked up in a spectacular passing exhibition. Inspired by playing against his Texas Christian predecessor, O'Brien threw a record 60 passes and completed 33 with no interceptions. He won his personal duel with Baugh, but the Eagles lost 13-6. Following the season, O'Brien retired to join the FBI. Don Looney, a rookie receiver also from Texas Christian, led the NFL with 58 catches.

1941 Bell gave up the Eagles in a complicated piece of front-office maneuvering. Bell sold half the franchise to Art Rooney, who had sold his Pittsburgh franchise to Alexis Thompson of New York. Before the teams took the field, Rooney and Bell swapped Thompson their Philadelphia franchise for his Pittsburgh franchise. Thompson hired Earle (Greasy) Neale to coach the Eagles, who were quarterbacked by Tommy Thompson, a Tulsa University graduate who was blind in one eye. Thompson was a deadly long passer and fit easily into Neale's offense. The Eagles adopted the T-formation.

1942 Most NFL teams lost their quarterbacks to the armed forces as World War II gained force. Not the Eagles, however, since Thompson was passed over due to his bad eye. The military depleted the Eagles in other key areas, however, taking the three top runners—Jim Castiglia, Dan DeSantis, and Terry Fox—as well as Bob Suffridge, Neale's best line-

man. The Eagles won their opener over Pittsburgh 24-14, but then lost eight straight.

1943 Faced with financial and manpower problems, the Eagles and Steelers joined forces. The hybrid team was called the "Phil-Pitt Steagles" and was coached jointly by Neale and Pittsburgh's Walt Kiesling. The Steagles uncovered surprising talent in the college ranks as rookie tackles Al Wistert from Michigan and Frank (Bucko) Kilroy from Temple excelled on the line. Free agent Jack Hinkle rushed for 571 yards and scored four touchdowns. Vic Sears, a second-year tackle from Oregon State, won a spot on the United Press all-pro team. Even end Bill Hewitt came out of retirement, wearing a helmet for the first time in his career. The Steagles won five games and finished just one game back in the Eastern Division.

1944 The Eagles and Steelers separated. The Eagles selected halfback Steve Van Buren of Louisiana State University in the first round of the college draft. The Eagles went unbeaten through seven games before losing to the Chicago Bears 28-7 at Shibe Park. Although they finished 7-1-2, their best record ever, the Eagles finished second behind the New York Giants in the Eastern Division. Van Buren, a 6-foot, 205-pound power runner with speed, bowled over the NFL's defenses. Van Buren and Hinkle teamed in a backfield that led the league with 1,661 yards rushing.

1945 The Eagles finished second to Washington with a 7-3 record. Van Buren led the NFL in rushing with 832 yards and scoring with 110 points (18 touchdowns, two extra points). Van Buren was the running game, carrying the ball 143 times. Van Buren scored on a 69-yard run against Detroit and returned a kickoff 98 yards for a touchdown against the New York Giants. The Eagles' top receiver was Jack Ferrante, a product of the Philadelphia sandlots who had never attended college. Ferrante caught 21 passes and scored seven touchdowns. Kilroy, a hard-hitting 6-foot 2-inch, 240 pounder, played middle guard in the defensive line.

1946 Neale added impressive talent to the Eagles' roster, trading for Alex Wojciechowicz, an outstanding center and linebacker, and Joe Muha, a rugged rookie fullback and punter. The Eagles also signed Bosh Pritchard, a quick, breakaway halfback who was just completing his military duty, and 5-foot 9-inch, 175-pound Russ Craft, a defensive back from the University of Alabama. An injury to Van Buren slowed the offense, however, and the Eagles' record slipped to 6-5. Van Buren rushed for 529 yards, third in the league.

1947 The last piece fit into Neale's offensive puzzle when the Eagles signed Pete Pihos, a 6-foot 1-inch, 215-pound rookie fullback from Indiana. The Eagles didn't need a fullback, so Neale made Pihos an end. Neale devised the Pihos screen, a short pass behind the line to Pihos. The threat of Pihos caused defenses to spread out, opening more holes for Van Buren and fullback Pritchard. Van Buren set a league record by rushing for 1,088 yards and 13 touchdowns. Thompson completed 53 percent of his passes. Meanwhile, Neale's Eagle defense caused havoc. He stacked the middle of his line with the likes of Kilroy and Sears and used his linebackers outside to hold up and intimidate the offensive ends. It was a 5-2-4 alignment, extremely physical, with the four deep backs playing up close. It was called the "Eagle" because the Eagles played it. They won their first Eastern Division title, beating Pittsburgh in a playoff 21-0, December 21. The Chicago Cardinals defeated the Eagles in the NFL Championship Game 28-21 at frozen Comiskey Park, December 28. The Eagles filed their cleats before the game to get better traction, but were discovered doing it and prohibited from wearing the sharpened cleats. Van Buren, slipping on the ice in flat-soled shoes, gained just 26 yards in 18 carries.

1948 The Eagles were winless in their first two games, losing 21-14 to the Chicago Cardinals and tying the Los Angeles Rams 28-28. They caught fire with back-to-back 45-0 victories over the New York Giants and Washington Redskins and Neale's team was unstoppable the rest of the year. Thompson ran the T-formation to perfection, completed 57 percent of his passes, and threw for 25 touchdowns. Van Buren led the league's rushers for the third time with 945 yards. Pritchard added seven touchdowns, four on runs, two on passes, and one on a punt return. Pihos caught 46 passes, 11 for touchdowns. Muha led the league with a 47.2-yard punting average. Neale even had the NFL's best kicker, Cliff (Automatic) Patton who converted 50 of 50 extra points and 8 of 12 field goal attempts. Captain Al Wistert, a tenacious 6-foot 1-inch, 215-pounder, was an all-pro tackle. The Eagles won their second Eastern Division title with a 9-2-1 record. They won their first world championship with a 7-0 victory over the Chicago Cardinals at Shibe Park, December 19. The game was played in a blinding snowstorm. Van Buren woke up that morning, saw the snow, and went back to bed, assuming the game was postponed. He was awakened by a phone call from Neale, rode to the stadium in a trolley car, and scored the game's only touchdown on a five-yard run.

1949 Thompson sold the Eagles to a syndicate of 100 local businessmen, organized by James P. Clark, for $250,000, January 15. Vince McNally was named general manager. In the first round of the draft, the Eagles selected Chuck Bednarik, All-America center-linebacker from the University of Pennsylvania. The Eagles rolled through the regular season, winning 11 games and losing only one. The Eagles won the Eastern Division for the third straight year. Van Buren set another league record, rushing for 1,146 yards. The Eagles' most impressive victory was a 38-14 trouncing of the previously unbeaten Los Angeles Rams at Shibe Park. The Rams and Eagles met again in the NFL Championship Game in Los Angeles Memorial Coliseum, December 18. A heavy rain turned

the field into a quagmire but it didn't slow the Eagles' punishing running attack, which rolled up 274 yards to the Rams' 21. Van Buren carried the ball 31 times for 196 yards to lead the Eagles' 14-0 championship triumph. The Eagles scored on Thompson's 31-yard pass to Pihos and a blocked punt by rookie end Leo Skladany.

1950 In the first week of the season, the defending NFL champion Eagles were matched against the Browns, the upstart newcomers from the All-America Football Conference, before a record 71,237 at Philadelphia's Municipal Stadium. The Browns pulled a stunning 35-10 upset foreshadowing the Eagles' decline. The Eagles won six of their next seven but Van Buren was sidelined with a foot injury and the team lacked the power to handle the top opponents. They lost their last four games to fall to third place in the Eastern Division. A feud between Neale and owner Clark erupted late in the season when the players had to pull Neale off Clark in the Polo Grounds' locker room. Neale was fired following the season.

1951 The Eagles named Alvin (Bo) McMillin head coach in February. McMillin, a successful college coach at Indiana, directed the Eagles to victories in their first two games but illness forced him to resign. Wayne Millner succeeded McMillin and the team sagged to 4-8. Van Buren played on the bad foot and gained just 327 yards on 112 carries. Adrian Burk succeeded the retired Thompson at quarterback and threw a league-high 23 interceptions. One bright note was the addition of Bobby Walston, a 6-foot, 190-pound end and placekicker from the University of Georgia. Walston caught 31 passes, scored eight touchdowns, and added 46 points kicking. He was named NFL rookie of the year.

1952 Former coach McMillin died of stomach cancer. Van Buren suffered a serious knee injury at training camp and retired. The club fired Millner and named Jim Trimble head coach, September 9. Trimble acquired Bobby Thomason from Green Bay and made him the starting quarterback. Trimble also moved Harry (Bud) Grant, the Eagles' top draft choice from Minnesota in 1951, ahead of Pihos at offensive end. Trimble felt Pihos would be more effective as a defensive end. The moves paid off as the Eagles won seven games and tied the New York Giants for second place. Grant caught 56 passes, seven for touchdowns, to rank second among NFL receivers. With Van Buren gone, most of the ball carrying was done by John Huzvar, a plodding 6-foot 4-inch, 240-pound fullback from North Carolina State.

1953 Clark retired as president and was named chairman of the board. Frank L. McNamee was elected club president. Trimble kept the Eagles in contention despite the loss of Grant, who jumped to the Canadian Football League. Trimble switched Pihos back to offense and he responded by catching 63 passes for 1,049 yards and 10 touchdowns to lead the NFL. Walston caught 41 passes as Thomason and Burk combined to pass for a league-high 3,089 yards. The Eagles had good balance in their running game with three backs—Don Johnson, Jerry Williams, and Frank Ziegler—totaling more than 1,100 yards. Rookie defensive back Tom Brookshier of Colorado led the club with eight interceptions. The highlight of the year came the final week, when the Eagles upset Cleveland 42-27 to spoil the Browns' hopes for a perfect season.

1954 The Eagles beat Cleveland 28-10 in the opener at Shibe Park, stirring hopes of a return to glory. The Eagles won their first four games, including a 49-21 rout of Washington, to take the early lead in the Eastern Division. The Eagles then lost four of five games, including a 6-0 rematch with the Browns. For the third straight year, the Eagles finished second

with seven wins. Pihos caught 60 passes to share the NFL receiving title with the 49ers' Billy Wilson. Walston caught 11 touchdown passes and led the league in scoring with 114 points.

1955 The Eagles overcame a 10-point deficit to defeat the New York Giants 27-17 in the league opener at Shibe Park, but the victory was costly. Bucko Kilroy, the all-pro tackle starting his one hundred and first consecutive game, tore ligaments in his knee and never played again. The defense recovered gradually as Norman (Wildman) Willey and Tom Scott developed into a pair of top-flight pass rushing ends. Young Jess Richardson, who played at Alabama, was groomed to replace Kilroy. Bednarik had another great season at linebacker. Pihos continued to show the way on offense, leading the NFL in pass receiving for the third straight year with 62 catches. The Eagles were plagued by an ineffective running game and suffered only their second losing season since 1951.

1956 Trimble was dismissed after four seasons as head coach. Hugh Devore, a Notre Dame graduate, was named to succeed him. The Eagles' veteran nucleus disappeared. Kilroy, Pihos, and defensive tackle Mike Jarmoluk all retired, leaving Devore with the weakest team in the Eastern Division. The Eagles' best runner was Ken Keller, a rookie from North Carolina, who gained 433 yards. The passing attack slipped badly due to the loss of Pihos. The strength of the team was a good defensive secondary, which included Brookshier, Ed (Bibbles) Bawel, Jerry Norton, and Eddie Bell.

1957 The Eagles had their best college draft, selecting Michigan State fullback Clarence Peaks, halfbacks Billy Ray Barnes of Wake Forest, and Tommy McDonald of Oklahoma, and quarterback Sonny Jurgensen of Duke. Assistant coach Charlie Gauer convinced Devore to use McDonald at wide receiver and against Washington the 5-foot 10-inch, 180-pound speedster caught two touchdown passes in a 21-12 win. Jurgensen split time with Thomason at quarterback and led the Eagles to a 17-7 upset of Cleveland. Barnes and Peaks combined for more than 1,000 yards rushing. The Eagles won only four games but they had promise for the future.

1958 Devore was fired and Buck Shaw hired as head coach. Shaw saw long-range potential in Jurgensen, but felt the Eagles needed an experienced quarterback to win in the next few years. He traded tackle Buck Lansford, defensive back Jim Harris, and a first-round draft choice to Los Angeles for 32-year-old Norm Van Brocklin. Shaw put together an exciting passing attack, employing McDonald at flanker and moving Pete Retzlaff, a 6-foot 1-inch, 210-pound fullback, to split end. Retzlaff, who was cut by Detroit in 1956, was a duplicate of Pihos with superb hands and an uncanny ability for running patterns. In his first year as a regular, Retzlaff caught 56 passes to tie Baltimore's Raymond Berry for the NFL receiving title. McDonald caught just 29 passes but nine went for touchdowns. Although the Eagles finished the year in last place (2-9-1), Van Brocklin predicted major improvement for next season. The Eagles also moved their home site from Connie Mack Stadium to the University of Pennsylvania's Franklin Field and attendance almost doubled.

1959 Led by Bednarik at center, the Eagles' offensive line gave Van Brocklin time to find his receivers. Given time, the Dutchman could pick apart almost any defense as he proved in a stunning 49-21 upset of the New York Giants, September 22. The win gave the younger Eagles confidence and they swept six of eight games to challenge New York and Cleveland for the Eastern Conference lead. McDonald was virtually unstoppable as he caught 47 passes and scored 11 touchdowns, one on an 81-yard punt return, the

Ron Jaworski passes during a 20-14 Thursday night win over Buffalo, 1981.

ries sweep of the Redskins since 1961. Following the season, Tose announced he would not renew McCormack's contract.

1976 Tose hired Dick Vermeil to become the Eagles' fifth head coach in nine years, February 8. Vermeil had gained national prominence a month earlier when his underdog UCLA team upset top-ranked Ohio State 23-10 in the Rose Bowl. Gabriel was slow recovering from offseason knee surgery and did not rejoin the team until mid-October. Given the starting spot, Boryla threw eight interceptions in the first three games. Vermeil won his first game as an NFL coach when the Eagles beat the New York Giants 20-7 at Veterans Stadium, September 19. Vermeil uncovered a potential star runner in rookie Mike Hogan, a ninth-round draft pick from Tennessee-Chattanooga. Hogan missed half the season with a dislocated shoulder and still led the team with 561 yards rushing. The Eagles went through a prolonged slump, losing eight of nine games, as the offense scored just two touchdowns in four weeks. The Eagles didn't score more than two touchdowns in the same game until the final week, when they trounced Seattle 27-10.

1977 Ron Jaworski was obtained from Los Angeles for tight end Charle Young. The club was without a draft choice for the first four rounds but selected Wilbert Montgomery, a running back from Abilene Christian, in the sixth round. Jaworski, a full time, starting quarterback for the first time in his career, led the club to a 13-3 victory over Tampa Bay in the season opener. However, the Eagles were haunted by a series of close defeats and lost 9 of the next 11 games. One bright spot was the defense, which recorded 47 sacks and 21 interceptions, while permitting just 207 points. With a 3-9 mark, the Eagles finished the season with back-to-back victories over the Giants and the Jets. In the season finale, Montgomery made his first start and rushed for 103 yards and two touchdowns. Jaworski finished the season with 18 touchdown passes.

1978 The season opened with a heartbreaking 16-14 loss to Los Angeles when the Rams scored on a 46-yard field goal with seven seconds left. Following another close loss to Washington, Montgomery rushed for 104 yards to key a 24-17 victory over New Orleans. But the club struggled to a 4-5 record after nine weeks. Then the newly installed 3-4 defense,

led by Bergey, asserted itself and helped deliver a four-game winning streak. With an 8-7 record, the Eagles entered the final contest against the Giants requiring a victory to make the playoffs for the first time since 1960. Montgomery rushed for 130 yards to lead a 20-3 win and clinch a winning record for the first time since 1966. In the wild card game on December 24, the Eagles jumped to a 13-0 lead over Atlanta midway through the fourth quarter, but Steve Bartkowski threw two touchdown passes, and the Falcons came back to win 14-13. Montgomery finished the season with 1,220 yards rushing to break a 29-year-old club record set by Steve Van Buren. Jaworski threw for 2,487 yards and 16 touchdowns, and Carmichael caught 55 passes for 1,072 yards.

1979 The Eagles used their first number-one draft choice since 1973 to select UCLA linebacker Jerry Robinson. They also chose linebacker Al Chesley and kicker Tony Franklin. Defensive end Claude Humphrey was obtained from Atlanta prior to the season. The Eagles opened the season by defeating the New York Giants, and had a 6-1 record after seven weeks. But a midseason slump produced three successive defeats. In one of those losses, a 24-19 defeat by Cleveland on November 4, Carmichael broke an NFL record by catching a pass in 106 consecutive games. The following week, the rest of the club awoke in a 31-21 victory over Dallas. The win launched a four-game winning streak, including a 44-7 romp over Detroit that insured a wild card berth in the playoffs. However, the Eagles lost a chance to win the NFC East when they were defeated by Dallas 24-17. Nonetheless, they finished with an 11-5 mark. Montgomery rushed for 1,512 yards to break his own club record. On December 23, a second-half rally led by Jaworski defeated Chicago in the wild card game 27-17. A week later the Eagles fell to Tampa Bay 24-17 in a divisional playoff game. Vermeil was chosen by his peers as the NFL coach of the year.

1980 Cornerback Roynell Young was the first draft pick. The Eagles got off to a fast start when they crushed Denver (27-6), Minnesota (42-7), and New York Giants (35-3). After a loss to St. Louis, they embarked on a new eight-game winning streak, including a 17-10 victory over Dallas on October 19. On November 23, the Eagles defeated Oakland 10-7, as the defense recorded eight sacks against their eventual opponent in the Super Bowl. Despite three

losses in four games to close out the season, the Eagles won the NFC East on tiebreaking procedures with a 12-4 record. The defense allowed fewer points (222) than any other team in the league, and held 10 opponents to under 100 yards rushing. The offense overcame the loss of Montgomery for part of the season, thanks to a big-play season by Jaworski, who passed for 3,529 yards and 27 touchdowns.

1981 The Eagles converted eight Minnesota turnovers into a 31-16 victory in a divisional playoff game on January 3. The defense then shut down Dallas to win the NFC Championship Game 20-7 on January 11. But the defense broke down and the offense sputtered in Super Bowl XV; the Raiders won 27-10. Injuries struck early in the 1981 season, as the Eagles lost both fullbacks, Leroy Harris and Perry Harrington, with broken legs. The team still raced to a 6-0 mark as the defense limited each opponent to 14 points or less. On November 1, the Eagles lost to the Cowboys 17-14 and fell into a first-place tie with Dallas at 7-2. Consecutive routs of St. Louis (52-10) and Baltimore (38-13) enabled Philadelphia to regain first place, but then the offense slumped and the Eagles suffered four successive defeats. The team ended the regular season with a 38-0 pounding of St. Louis, which gave the Eagles a 10-6 record, second place in the NFC East, and the home field in the wild card game. But on December 27, the other wild card team, the New York Giants, jumped to a 20-0 first-quarter lead and hung on to win 27-21. During the regular season, the Eagles could again point to their defense as one of the dominant forces in the NFL; it gave up only 221 points, the fewest in the league.

MEMBERS OF HALL OF FAME:
Chuck Bednarik, Bert Bell, Bill Hewitt, Ollie Matson, Earle (Greasy) Neale, Pete Pihos, Jim Ringo, Norm Van Brocklin, Steve Van Buren, Alex Wojciechowicz

EAGLES RECORD, 1933-81

Year	Won	Lost	Tied	Pct.	Pts.	OP
1933........	3	5	1	.375	77	158
1934........	4	7	0	.364	127	85
1935........	2	9	0	.182	60	179
1936........	1	11	0	.083	51	206
1937........	2	8	1	.200	86	177
1938........	5	6	0	.455	154	164
1939........	1	9	1	.100	105	200
1940........	1	10	0	.091	111	211
1941........	2	8	1	.200	119	218
1942........	2	9	0	.182	134	239
1943 (Phil-Pitt).	5	4	1	.556	225	230
1944........	7	1	2	.875	267	131
1945........	7	3	0	.700	272	133
1946........	6	5	0	.545	231	220
1947§.......	8	4	0	.667	308	242
1948‡.......	9	2	1	.818	376	156
1949‡.......	11	1	0	.917	364	134
1950........	6	6	0	.500	254	141
1951........	4	8	0	.333	234	264
1952........	7	5	0	.583	252	271
1953........	7	4	1	.636	352	215
1954........	7	4	1	.636	284	230
1955........	4	7	1	.364	248	231
1956........	3	8	1	.273	143	215
1957........	4	8	0	.333	173	230
1958........	2	9	1	.182	235	306
1959........	7	5	0	.583	268	278
1960‡.......	10	2	0	.833	321	246
1961........	10	4	0	.714	361	297
1962........	3	10	1	.231	282	356
1963........	2	10	2	.167	242	381
1964........	6	8	0	.429	312	313
1965........	5	9	0	.357	363	359
1966........	9	5	0	.643	326	340
1967........	6	7	1	.462	351	409
1968........	2	12	0	.143	202	351
1969........	4	9	1	.308	279	377
1970........	3	10	1	.231	241	332
1971........	6	7	1	.462	221	302
1972........	2	11	1	.179	145	352
1973........	5	8	1	.393	310	393
1974........	7	7	0	.500	242	217
1975........	4	10	0	.286	225	302
1976........	4	10	0	.286	165	286
1977........	5	9	0	.357	220	207
1978*.......	9	7	0	.563	270	250
1979*.......	11	5	0	.688	339	282
1980**......	12	4	0	.750	384	222

Neill Armstrong

Sam Baker

Billy Ray Barnes

Eddie Bell

Bill Bergey

Don Burroughs

Marion Campbell

1981*	10	6	0	.625	368	221
49 Years	262	336	22	.440	11,679	12,259

§*NFL Eastern Division Champion*
‡*NFL Champion*
*NFC Wild Card Qualifier for Playoffs
**NFC Champion

RECORD HOLDERS

Rushing (Yards)	Wilbert Montgomery, 1979	1,512
Passing (Pct.)	Roman Gabriel, 1973	58.7
Passing (Yards)	Sonny Jurgensen, 1961	3,723
Passing (TDs)	Sonny Jurgensen, 1961	32
Receiving (No.)	Harold Carmichael, 1973	67
Receiving (Yards)	Ben Hawkins, 1967	1,265
Interceptions (No.)	Bill Bradley, 1971	11
Punting (Avg.)	Joe Muha, 1948	47.2
Punt Ret. (Avg.)	Steve Van Buren, 1944	15.3
Kickoff Ret. (Avg.)	Al Nelson, 1972	29.1
Touchdowns (Total)	Steve Van Buren, 1945	18
Field Goals Made	Tom Dempsey, 1973	24
Points (No.)	Bobby Walston, 1954	114

COACHING HISTORY

1933-35	Lud Wray	9-21-1
1936-40	Bert Bell	10-44-2
1941-50	Earle (Greasy) Neale	63-43-5
1951	Alvin (Bo) McMillin*	2-0-0
1951	Wayne Millner	2-8-0
1952-55	Jim Trimble	25-20-3
1956-57	Hugh Devore	7-16-1
1958-60	Lawrence (Buck) Shaw	19-16-1
1961-63	Nick Skorich	15-24-3
1964-68	Joe Kuharich	28-41-1
1969-71	Jerry Williams**	7-22-2
1971-72	Ed Khayat	8-15-2
1973-75	Mike McCormack	16-25-1
1976-81	Dick Vermeil	51-41-0

*Retired after two games in 1951
**Replaced after three games in 1971

FIRST PLAYER SELECTED

1936	Jay Berwanger, B, Chicago
1937	Sam Francis, B, Nebraska
1938	Jim McDonald, B, Ohio State
1939	Davey O'Brien, B, Texas Christian
1940	George McAfee, B, Duke
1941	Art Jones, B (2), Richmond
1942	Pete Kmetovic, B, Stanford
1943	Joe Muha, B, Virginia Military
1944	Steve Van Buren, B, Louisiana State
1945	John Yonaker, E, Notre Dame
1946	Leo Riggs, B, USC
1947	Neill Armstrong, E, Oklahoma A&M
1948	Clyde (Smackover) Scott, B, Arkansas
1949	Chuck Bednarik, C, Pennsylvania
1950	Harry (Bud) Grant, E, Minnesota
1951	Ebert Van Buren, B, Louisiana State
1952	Johnny Bright, B, Drake
1953	Al Conway, B (2), Army
1954	Neil Worden, B, Notre Dame
1955	Dick Bielski, B, Maryland
1956	Bob Pellegrini, C, Maryland
1957	Clarence Peaks, B, Michigan State
1958	Walt Kowalczyk, B, Michigan State
1959	J. D. Smith, T (2), Rice
1960	Ron Burton, RB, Northwestern
1961	Art Baker, RB, Syracuse
1962	Pete Case, G (2), Georgia
1963	Ed Budde, G, Michigan State
1964	Bob Brown, T, Nebraska
1965	Ray Rissmiller, T (2), Georgia
1966	Randy Beisler, DE, Indiana
1967	Harry Jones, RB, Arkansas
1968	Tim Rossovich, DE, USC
1969	Leroy Keyes, RB, Purdue
1970	Steve Zabel, TE, Oklahoma
1971	Richard Harris, DE, Grambling
1972	John Reaves, QB, Florida
1973	Jerry Sisemore, T, Texas
1974	Mitch Sutton, DT (3), Kansas
1975	Bill Capraun, T (7), Miami
1976	Mike Smith, DE (4), Florida
1977	Skip Sharp, CB (5), Kansas
1978	Reggie Wilkes, LB (3), Georgia Tech

1979	Jerry Robinson, LB, UCLA
1980	Roynell Young, CB, Alcorn State
1981	Leonard Mitchell, DE, Houston
1982	Mike Quick, WR, North Carolina State

PHILADELPHIA EAGLES, 1933-81
The Eagles merged with the Pittsburgh Steelers in 1943.

Absher, Dick, LB, Maryland	1972
Adams, Gary, DB, Arkansas	1969
Agajanian, Ben, K, New Mexico	1945
Alexander, Kermit, DB, UCLA	1972-73
Allen, Chuck, LB, Washington	1972
Allen, Jackie, DB, Baylor	1972
Allison, Henry, G, San Diego State	1971-72
Amerson, Glen, B, Texas Tech	1961
Amundson, George, RB, Iowa State	1975
Andrews, Leroy, B, Pittsburg Teachers, Kansas	1934
Antwine, Houston, DT, Southern Illinois	1972
Armstrong, Neill, E, Oklahoma State	1947-51
Arnold, Jay, B, Texas	1937-40
Arrington, Rick, QB, Tulsa	1970-73
Aschbacher, Darrel, G, Oregon	1959
Atkins, Steve, RB, Maryland	1981
Auer, Howie, T, Michigan	1933

B

Bailey, Howard (Screeno), T, Tennessee	1935
Bailey, Tom, B, Florida State	1971-74
Baisi, Al, G, West Virginia	1947
Baker, John, E, North Carolina College	1962
Baker, Ron, G, Oklahoma State	1980-81
Baker, Sam, P-K, Oregon State	1964-69
Baker, Tony, RB, Iowa State	1971-72
Ballman, Gary, TE, Michigan State	1967-72
Banas, Steve, B, Notre Dame	1935
Banducci, Bruno, G, Stanford	1944-45
Banta, Jack, B, USC	1941, 1944-45
Barnes, Bill Ray, RB, Wake Forest	1957-61
Barnes, Larry, RB, Tennessee State	1978-79
Barnes, Walter (Piggy), G, Louisiana State	1948-51
Barnhart, Dan (Chief), B, Centenary	1934
Barni, Roy, B, San Francisco	1954-55
Barnum, Len, B, West Virginia Wesleyan	1940-42
Bartholomew, Sam, B, Tennessee	1941
Basca, Nick, B, Villanova	1941
Bassi, Dick, G, Santa Clara	1940
Bassman, Herman (Reds), B, Ursinus	1936
Baughan, Maxie, LB, Georgia Tech	1960-65
Bauman, Al, T, Northwestern	1947
Bausch, Frank, C, Kansas	1940-41
Bawel, Ed (Bibbles), B, Evansville	1952, 1955-56
Baze, Win, B, Texas Tech	1937
Beaver, Jim, G, Florida	1962
Bednarik, Chuck, C-LB, Pennsylvania	1949-62
Beisler, Randy, DE, Indiana	1966-68
Bell, Eddie, B, Pennsylvania	1955-58
Benson, Harry, G, Western Maryland	1935
Bergey, Bill, LB, Arkansas State	1974-80
Berry, Dan, B, California	1967
Berzinski, Willie, B, Wisconsin-LaCrosse	1956
Betterson, James, RB, North Carolina	1977-79
Bielski, Dick, B-E, Maryland	1955-59
Binotto, John, B, Duquesne	1942
Biorklund, Bob, C, Minnesota	1941
Blackmore, Richard, CB, Mississippi State	1979-81
Blaine, Ed, G, Missouri	1963-66
Bleamer, Jeff, T, Penn State	1975-76
Bleeker, Mel, B, USC	1944-46
Blue, Luther, WR, Iowa State	1980
Blye, Ron, RB, Notre Dame	1969
Boedecker, Bill, B, DePaul	1950
Bogren, Vince, E, New Mexico	1944
Boryla, Mike, QB, Stanford	1974-76
Bouggess, Lee, RB, Louisville	1970-73
Bova, Tony, E, St. Francis	1943
Bradley, Bill, S-P, Texas	1969-77
Bradley, Harold, G, Iowa	1958
Bredice, John, E, Boston U.	1956
Brennan, Leo, T, Holy Cross	1942
Brewer, John, B, Louisville	1952-53
Brian, Bill, T, Gonzaga	1935-36

Brodnicki, Chuck, C, Temple	1934
Brooks, Clifford, DB, Tennessee State	1975-76
Brookshier, Tom, B, Colorado	1953, 1956-61
Brown, Bob, T, Nebraska	1964-68
Brown, Fred, LB, Miami	1967-69
Brown, Gregory, DE, Kansas State	1981
Brown, Thomas, DE, Baylor	1980
Brown, Tim, RB, Ball State	1960-67
Brown, Willie, WR, USC	1966
Brumm, Don, DE, Purdue	1970-71
Brunski, Andy, C, Temple	1943
Bryant, Bill, CB, Grambling	1978
Budd, Frank, WR, Villanova	1962
Bukant, Joe, B, Washington, Missouri	1938-40
Bulaich, Norm, RB, Texas Christian	1973-74
Bull, Ronnie, RB, Baylor	1971
Bunting, John, LB, North Carolina	1972-81
Burk, Adrian, QB, Baylor	1951-56
Burke, Mark, DB, West Virginia	1976
Burnette, Tom, B, North Carolina	1938
Burnham, Lem, DE, U. S. International	1977-79
Burnine, Hank, E, Missouri	1956-57
Burroughs, Don, DB, Colorado State	1960-64
Bushby, Thomas, B, Kansas State	1935
Buss, Art, T, Michigan State	1936-37
Butler, Bob, G, Kentucky	1962
Butler, Johnny, B, Tennessee	1943, 1945
Byrne, Bill, G, Boston College	1963

C

Cabrelli, Larry, E, Colgate	1941-47
Caffey, Lee Roy, LB, Texas A&M	1963
Cagle, Jim, DT, Georgia	1974
Cahill, Dave, DT, Northern Arizona	1966
Calloway, Ernie, DT, Texas Southern	1969-72
Campbell, Glenn, E, Emporia Teachers	1935
Campbell, Marion, T, Georgia	1956-61
Campbell, Stan, G, Iowa State	1959-61
Campbell, Tommy, DB, Iowa State	1976
Campfield, Billy, RB, Kansas	1978-81
Campion, Tom, T, Southeastern Louisiana	1947
Canale, Rocco, G, Boston College	1943-45
Carmichael, Harold, WR, Southern U.	1971-81
Carollo, Joe, T, Notre Dame	1969-70
Carpe, Joe, T, Millikin	1933
Carr, Earl, RB, Florida	1979
Carr, Jimmy, B, Morris Harvey	1959-63
Carroccio, Russ, G, Virginia	1955
Carter, Joe, E, Southern Methodist	1933-40
Case, Pete, G, Georgia	1962-64
Cassady, Howard (Hopalong), B, Ohio State	1962
Castiglia, Jim, B, Georgetown	1941, 1945-46
Catlin, Tom, LB, Oklahoma	1959
Cemore, Tony, G, Creighton	1941
Ceppetelli, Gene, C, Villanova	1968-69
Cherundolo, Chuck, C, Penn State	1940
Chesley, Al, LB, Pittsburgh	1979-81
Chesson, West, WR, Duke	1973-74
Chuy, Don, G, Clemson	1969
Cifelli, Gus, T, Notre Dame	1954
Clark, Al, CB, Eastern Michigan	1976
Clark, Mike, K-E, Texas A&M	1963
Clark, Myers (Algy), B, Ohio State	1934
Clarke, Ken, NT, Syracuse	1978-81
Clayton, Don, T, No college	1936
Cody, Bill, LB, Auburn	1972
Colavito, Steve, LB, Wake Forest	1975
Cole, John (King), B, St. Joseph's	1938-40
Coleman, Al, DB, Tennessee State	1972
Colman, Wayne, DB, Temple	1968-69
Combs, Bill, E, Purdue	1942
Concannon, Jack, QB, Boston College	1964-66
Conjar, Larry, RB, Notre Dame	1968
Conti, Enio, B, Bucknell	1941-45
Cooke, Ed, E, Maryland	1958
Coston, Fred, C, Texas A&M	1939
Cothren, Paige, K, Mississippi	1959
Cowhig, Gerry, B, Notre Dame	1951
Crabb, Claude, DB, Colorado	1964-65
Craft, Russ, B, Alabama	1946-53
Creech, Bob, LB, Texas Christian	1971-72
Cronin, Bill, E, Boston College	1965

Harold Carmichael

Irv Cross

Ted Dean

Jack Ferrante

Charlie Johnson

Bucko Kilroy

Vic Lindskog

Cross, Irv, DB, Northwestern ... 1961-65, 1969
Crowe, Larry, RB, Texas Southern ... 1972
Cuba, Paul, T, Pittsburgh ... 1933-35
Culbreath, Jim, RB, Oklahoma ... 1980
Cullars, Willie, DE, Kansas State ... 1974
Cunningham, Dick, LB, Arkansas ... 1973
Cuppoletti, Bree, G, Oregon ... 1939-40
Curcio, Mike, LB, Temple ... 1981

D

D'Agostino, Frank, G, Auburn ... 1956
Davis, Al, B, Tennessee State ... 1971-72
Davis, Bob, B, Kentucky ... 1942
Davis, Norm, G, Grambling ... 1970
Davis, Stan, WR, Memphis State ... 1973
Davis, Sylvester (Red), B, Geneva ... 1933
Davis, Vern, DB, Western Michigan ... 1971
Dean, Ted, RB, Wichita State ... 1960-63
DeLucca, Jerry, T, Middle Tennessee State ... 1959
Demas, George, G, Washington & Jefferson ... 1933
Dempsey, Jack, T, Bucknell ... 1934, 1937
Dempsey, Tom, K, Palomar JC ... 1971-74
DeSantis, Dan, B, Niagra ... 1941
Dial, Benjy, B-QB, Eastern New Mexico ... 1967
DiFilippo, Dave, G, Villanova ... 1941
Dimmick, Tom, T, Houston ... 1956
Dirks, Mike, G, Wyoming ... 1968-71
Disend, Leo, T, Albright ... 1943
Ditka, Mike, TE, Pittsburgh ... 1967-68
Dixon, Zachary, RB, Temple ... 1980
Dobbins, Herb, T, San Diego State ... 1974
Dorow, Al, QB, Michigan State ... 1957
Doss, Noble, B, Texas ... 1947-48
Douglas, Merrill, RB, Utah ... 1962
Douglas, Otis, T, William & Mary ... 1946-69
Dow, Woody, B, West Texas State ... 1938-40
Dowda, Harry, B, Wake Forest ... 1954-55
Doyle, Ted, T, Nebraska ... 1943
Dudley, Paul, B, Arkansas ... 1963
Duncan, Rick, K, East Montana State ... 1968
Dunek, Ken, TE, Memphis State ... 1980
Dunstan, Bill, DT, Utah State ... 1973-76
Durko, John, E, Albright ... 1944

E

Edwards, Herman, DB, San Diego State ... 1977-81
Ehlers, Tom, LB, Kentucky ... 1975-77
Eibner, John, T, Kentucky ... 1941-42, 1946
Eiden, Ed, B, Scranton ... 1944
Ellis, Drew, T, Texas Christian ... 1938-40
Ellis, Ray, S, Ohio State ... 1981
Ellstrom, Marvin (Swede), B, Oklahoma City ... 1934
Emelianchik, Pete, E, Richmond ... 1967
Emmons, Frank, B, Oregon ... 1940
Engles, Rick, P, Tulsa ... 1978
Enke, Fred, QB, Arizona ... 1952
Erdlitz, Dick, B, Northwestern ... 1942, 1945
Estes, Larry, DE, Alcorn A&M ... 1972
Evans, Mike, C, Boston College ... 1968-73

F

Fagioli, Carl, G, No college ... 1944
Farragut, Ken, C, Mississippi ... 1951-54
Feather, Elvin (Tiny), B, Kansas State ... 1933
Felber, Fred, E, North Dakota ... 1933
Feller, Happy, K, Texas ... 1971
Fencl, Richard, E, Northwestern ... 1933
Ferko, John (Fritz), G, West Chester State ... 1937-38
Ferrante, Jack, E, No college ... 1941, 1944-50
Ferris, Neil, B, Loyola, Cal. ... 1952
Fiedler, William, G, Pennsylvania ... 1938
Field, Dick, G, No college ... 1939-40
Fitzgerald, Mickey, RB, Virginia Tech ... 1981
Fitzkee, Scott, WR, Penn State ... 1979-80
Folsom, Steve, TE, Utah ... 1981
Ford, Charlie, DB, Houston ... 1974
Fox, Terry, B, Miami ... 1941, 1945
Frahm, Herald (Dick), B, Nebraska ... 1935
Frank, Joe, T, Georgetown ... 1941, 1943
Franklin, Cleveland, RB, Baylor ... 1977-78
Franklin, Tony, K, Texas A&M ... 1979-81
Franks, Dennis, C, Michigan ... 1976-78
Freeman, Bobby, B, Auburn ... 1960-61
Frey, Glenn, B, Temple ... 1936-37
Friedlund, Bob, E, Michigan State ... 1946
Friedman, Bob, G, Washington ... 1944
Fritts, George, T, Clemson ... 1945
Fritz, Ralph, G, Michigan ... 1941
Fuller, Frank, T, Kentucky ... 1963

G

Gabriel, Roman, QB, North Carolina State ... 1973-77
Gambold, Bob, B, Washington State ... 1953
Gaona, Bob, T, Wake Forest ... 1957
Gauer, Charlie, E, Colgate ... 1943-45
Gay, Blenda, DE, Fayetteville State ... 1975-76
George, Ed, T, Wake Forest ... 1976-78
George, Ray, T, USC ... 1940
Gerber, Woody, G, Alabama ... 1941-42
Gersbach, Carl, LB, West Chester State ... 1970
Getchell, Gorham, E, Temple ... 1943
Ghecas, Lou, B, Georgetown ... 1941
Giammona, Louie, RB, Utah State ... 1978-81
Giancanelli, Harold (Skip), B, Loyola, Cal. ... 1953-56
Giannelli, Mario, G, Boston College ... 1948-51
Gibbs, Pat, DB, Lamar ... 1972
Gibron, Abe, G, Purdue ... 1956-57
Giddens, Frank, T, New Mexico ... 1981
Giddens, Herschel (Wimpy), T, Louisiana Tech ... 1938
Gilbert, Lewis, TE, Florida ... 1980
Gill, Roger, B, Texas Tech ... 1964-65
Ginney, Jerry, G, Santa Clara ... 1940
Glass, Glenn, B, Tennessee ... 1964-65
Gloden, Fred, B, Tulane ... 1941
Glover, Rich, DT, Nebraska ... 1975
Goldston, Ralph, B, Youngstown State ... 1952, 1954-55
Gollomb, Rudy, G, Carroll, Wisconsin ... 1936
Gonya, Robert, T, Northwestern ... 1933-34
Goode, Rob, B, Texas A&M ... 1955
Goodwin, Ronnie, E, Baylor ... 1963-68
Gossage, Gene, E, Northwestern ... 1960-62
Graham, Dave, T, Virginia ... 1963-69
Graham, Lyle, C, Richmond ... 1941
Graham, Tom, G, Temple ... 1935
Grant, Harry (Bud), E, Minnesota ... 1951-52
Graves, Ray, C, Tennessee ... 1942-43, 1946
Gray, Jim, B, Toledo ... 1967
Green, Donnie, T, Purdue ... 1977
Green, Johnny, E, Tulsa ... 1947-51
Gregory, Ken, E, Whittier ... 1962
Gros, Earl, B, Louisiana State ... 1964-66
Gudd, Len, E, Temple ... 1934
Gude, Henry, G, Vanderbilt ... 1946
Guglielmi, Ralph, QB, Notre Dame ... 1963
Guillory, Tony, LB, Lamar Tech ... 1969
Gunnels, Riley, T, Georgia ... 1960-64

H

Hackney, Elmer, B, Kansas State ... 1940-41
Hairston, Carl, DE, Maryland State ... 1976-81
Hajek, Chuck, C, Northwestern ... 1934
Hall, Irv, B, Brown ... 1942
Halverson, Dean, LB, Washington ... 1973-76
Halverson, William, T, Oregon State ... 1942
Hamilton, Ray, E, Arkansas ... 1940
Hampton, Dave, RB, Wyoming ... 1976
Hansen, Roscoe, T, North Carolina ... 1951
Hanson, Thomas (Swede), B, Temple ... 1933-37
Harding, Roger, C, California ... 1947
Harper, Maurice (Moose), C, Austin ... 1937-40
Harrington, Perry, RB, Jackson State ... 1980-81
Harris, Jimmy, B, Oklahoma ... 1957
Harris, Leroy, FB, Arkansas State ... 1979-80
Harris, Richard, DE, Grambling ... 1971-73
Harrison, Bob, LB, Oklahoma ... 1962-63
Harrison, Dennis, DE, Vanderbilt ... 1978-81
Harrison, Granville, E, Mississippi State ... 1941
Hart, Dick, G, No college ... 1967-71
Hartman, Fred, T, Rice ... 1948
Harvey, Richard, DB, Jackson State ... 1970
Hawkins, Ben, WR, Arizona State ... 1966-73
Hayden, Ken, C, Arkansas ... 1942
Hayes, Ed, DB, Morgan State ... 1970
Haymond, Alvin, DB, Southern U. ... 1968
Heath, Jo Jo, WR, Pittsburgh ... 1981
Heck, Ralph, LB, Colorado ... 1963-65
Henderson, Zac, S, Oklahoma ... 1980
Henry, Wally, WR-KR, UCLA ... 1977-81
Henson, Gary, E, Colorado ... 1963
Hershey, Kirk, E, Cornell ... 1941
Hertel, Rob, QB, USC ... 1980
Hewitt, Bill, E, Michigan ... 1936-39, 1943
Higgins, Tom, T, North Carolina ... 1954-55
Hill, Fred, WR, USC ... 1965-71
Hill, King, QB, Rice ... 1961-68
Hinkle, Jack, B, Syracuse ... 1941-47
Hix, Billy, E, Arkansas ... 1950
Hoague, Joe, B, Colgate ... 1943
Hobbs, Bill, LB, Texas A&M ... 1969-71
Hogan, Mike, RB, Tennessee-Chattanooga ... 1976-78; 1980
Holcomb, Bill (Tex), T, Texas Tech ... 1937
Hooks, Alvin, WR, Cal State-Northridge ... 1981
Hord, Roy, G, Duke ... 1962
Horrell, Bill, G, Michigan State ... 1952
Hoss, Clark, TE, Oregon State ... 1972
Howard, Bob, CB, San Diego State ... 1978-79
Howell, Lane, T, Grambling ... 1965-69
Hoyem, Lynn, G, Long Beach State ... 1964-67
Hrabetin, Frank, T, Loyola, Cal. ... 1942
Huarte, John, QB, Notre Dame ... 1968
Hudson, Bob, B, Clemson ... 1953-55, 1957-58
Hughes, Chuck, WR, Texas-El Paso ... 1967-69
Hughes, Bill (Hoss), C, Texas ... 1937-40
Hultz, Don, DT, Southern Mississippi ... 1964-73
Humbert, Dick, E, Richmond ... 1941, 1945-49
Humphrey, Claude, DE, Tennessee State ... 1979-81
Hunt, Calvin, C, Baylor ... 1970
Huth, Gerry, G, Wake Forest ... 1959-60
Huxhold, Ken, G, Wisconsin ... 1954-58
Huzvar, John, B, North Carolina State ... 1952

I

Ignatius, Jim, G, Holy Cross ... 1935
Illman, Ed, B, Montana ... 1933
Irvin, Willie, B, Florida A&M ... 1953

J

Jackson, Bobby, B, Alabama ... 1960
Jackson, Don, B, North Carolina ... 1936
Jackson, Harold, WR, Jackson State ... 1969-72
Jackson, Johnny, DE, Southern U. ... 1977
Jackson, Randy, RB, Wichita State ... 1974
Jackson, Trenton, WR, Illinois ... 1966
Jacobs, Proverb, T, California ... 1958
James, Ron (Po), RB, New Mexico State ... 1972-75
Janet, Ernie, T, Washington ... 1975
Jarmoluk, Mike, T, Temple ... 1949-55
Jarvi, Toimi, B, North Illinois ... 1944
Jaworski, Ron, QB, Youngstown State ... 1977-81
Jefferson, Billy, B, Mississippi State ... 1942
Johansson, Ove, K, Abilene Christian ... 1977
Johnson, Al, B, Hardin-Simmons ... 1948
Johnson, Bert, B, Kentucky ... 1942
Johnson, Charlie, DT-NT, Colorado ... 1977-81
Johnson, Don, B, California ... 1953-55
Johnson, Eric, DB, Washington State ... 1977-78
Johnson, Gene, B, Cincinnati ... 1959-60
Johnson, Jay, LB, East Texas State ... 1969
Jonas, Don, B, Penn State ... 1962
Jones, Don, B, Washington ... 1940
Jones, Harry, RB, Arkansas ... 1967-71
Jones, Joe, DE, Tennessee State ... 1974-75
Jones, Ray, DB, Southern U. ... 1970
Jones, Spike, P, Georgia ... 1975-77
Jorgenson, Carl, T, St. Mary's, Cal. ... 1935
Jurgensen, Sonny, QB, Duke ... 1957-63

K

Kane, Carl, B, St. Louis ... 1936
Kapele, John, T, Brigham Young ... 1962
Kaplan, Bernie, G, West Maryland ... 1942
Karnofsky, Sonny, B, Arizona ... 1945
Kasky, Ed, T, Villanova ... 1942
Kavel, George, B, Carnegie Tech ... 1934
Keeling, Ray, T, Texas ... 1938-39
Keen, Allen (Rabbit), B, Arkansas ... 1937-38

Tommy McDonald *Wilbert Montgomery* *Joe Muha* *Clarence Peaks* *Gary Pettigrew* *Bosh Pritchard* *Pete Retzlaff*

PIT

1933 A
player
$2,500.
Pittsbur
schedul
legal sr
professi
ed the p
free bo
was For
opener
compile
1934 R
and acq
but gift
was inj
Pirates
year. Tl
Heller
the tea
attempt
1935 R
his thirc
the succ
Philade
four gai
the rusl
linemar
255-pou
1936 B
helped t
the lead
Pirates
—Chic
left in t
beat the
Howeve
his tean
Coast. 1
Pittsbur
the big
lost 30
place.
1937 B
ing, anc
coach.
coach a
assistan
and enc
would v
show up
first gar
touchdc
and saic
The Pir
won th
Washin
ern Div
catches
1938 R
$15,80
date. W
Univers
postpon
White,
rushed
were in
Blood,
Washin
defense
their la:
1939 V

Kekeris, Jim, T, Missouri 1947
Keller, Ken, B, North Carolina. 1956-57
Kelley, Bob, C, West Texas State 1955-56
Kelley, Dwight (Ike), LB, Ohio State 1966-72
Kelly, Jim, E, Notre Dame 1965-67
Kenneally, George, E, St. Bonaventure 1933-35
Kenney, Steve, T, Clemson 1980-81
Kersey, Merritt, P, West Chester State 1974-75
Key, Wade, G-T, Southwest Texas State 1970-79
Keyes, Leroy, DB, Purdue 1969-72
Keys, Howard, T-C, Oklahoma State 1960-64
Khayat, Eddie, T, Tulane 1958-61, 1964-65
Kilroy, Frank (Bucko), T, Temple 1943-55
King, Don, T, Kentucky 1956
Kirkman, Roger (Reds), B, Washington & Jefferson . . . 1933-35
Kirksey, Roy, G, Maryland State 1973-74
Kish, Ben, B, Pittsburgh. 1942-49
Kloppenberg, Harry, T, Fordham 1936
Kmetovic, Pete, B, Stanford 1946
Knapper, Joe, B, Ottawa, Kansas 1934
Knox, Charlie, T, St. Edmunds 1937
Koeninger, Art, C, Tennessee-Chattanooga 1933
Kolberg, Elmer, B, Oregon State 1939-40
Koman, Bill, LB, North Carolina 1957-58
Konopka, John, B, Temple 1936
Kostos, Tony, E, Bucknell 1933
Kowalczyk, Walt, B, Michigan State 1958-59
Kramer, Kent, TE, Minnesota 1971-74
Krepfle, Keith, TE, Iowa State 1975-81
Kresky, Joe, G, Wisconsin 1933-35
Krieger, Bob, E, Dartmouth 1941, 1946
Kriel, Emmet, G, Baylor 1939
Kuczynski, Bert, E, Pennsylvania 1946
Kupcinet, Irv, B, North Dakota 1935
Kusko, John, B, Temple 1936-38

L

Laack, Galen, G, Pacific 1958
Lachman, Dick, B, No college 1933-35
Lainhart, Porter, B, Washington State 1933
Landsberg, Mort, B, Cornell 1941
Lang, Israel, RB, Tennessee State 1964-68
Lankas, Jim, B, St. Mary's, Texas 1942
Lansford, Buck, T, Texas 1955-57
Lapham, Bill, C, Iowa 1960
Larson, Bill, TE, Colorado State 1978
Latimer, Al, CB, Clemson 1979
Laux, Ted, B, St. Joseph's 1942-44
Lavender, Joe, DB, San Diego State 1973-75
Lawrence, Kent, WR, Georgia 1969
Lazetich, Pete, DT, Stanford 1976-77
Leathers, Milt, G, Georgia 1933
Ledbetter, Toy, B, Oklahoma State 1950, 1953-55
Lechthaler, Roy, G, Lebanon Valley 1933
Lee, Bernie, B, Villanova 1938
LeMaster, Frank, LB, Kentucky 1974-81
Leonard, Jim, B, Notre Dame 1934-37
Levanitis, Steve, T, Boston College 1942
Lewis, Joe, T, Compton JC 1962
Leyendecker, Charlie, T, Vanderbilt 1933
Lince, Dave, TE, North Dakota 1966-67
Lindskog, Vic, C, Stanford 1944-51
Lio, Augie, G, Georgetown 1946
Lipski, John (Bull), C, Temple 1933-34
Liske, Pete, QB, Penn State 1971-72
Lloyd, Dave, LB, Georgia 1963-70
Logan, Randy, DB, Michigan 1973-81
Looney, Don, E, Texas Christian 1940
Lou, Ron, C, Arizona State 1975
Louderback, Tom, LB, San Jose State 1958-59
Lucas, Dick, E, Boston College 1960-63
Lueck, Bill, G, Arizona 1975
Luft, Don, E, Indiana 1954
Luken, Tom, G, Purdue 1972-78
Lusk, Herb, RB, Long Beach State 1976-78

M

MacAfee, Ken, E, Alabama. 1959
MacDowell, Jay, E, Washington 1946-51
Macioszcyzk, Art, B, Western Michigan 1944-47
Mack, Bill (Red), E, Notre Dame 1964
Mackrides, Bill, B, Nevada-Reno 1947-51

MacMurdo, Jim, T, Pittsburgh 1934-37
Magee, John, G, Rice 1948-55
Mahalic, Drew, LB, Notre Dame 1976-78
Mallory, John, DB, West Virginia 1968
Malone, Art, RB, Arizona State 1975-76
Mandarino, Mike, G, La Salle 1944-45
Manning, Roosevelt, DT, Northeastern Oklahoma 1975
Mansfield, Ray, C, Washington 1963
Manske, Edgar (Eggs), E, Northwestern 1935-36
Manton, Taldon (Tillie), B, Texas Christian 1940
Manzini, Baptiste, C, St. Vincent's 1944-45, 1948
Marchi, Basilio, C, New York U. 1941-42
Marcus, Alex, E, Temple 1933
Maronic, Duke, G, No college 1944-50
Marshall, Larry, RB-KR, Maryland 1974-77
Martin, Aaron, DB, North Carolina College 1966-67
Mass, Wayne, T, Clemson 1972
Masters, Bob, B, Baylor 1937-38, 1941-43
Masters, Walt, B, Pennsylvania 1936
Matesic, Ed, B, Pittsburgh 1934-35
Matson, Ollie, B, San Francisco 1964-66
Mavraides, Menil (Minnie), G, Notre Dame 1954, 1957
Mayes, Rufus, T, Ohio State 1979
Maynard, Les, B, Rider 1933
Mazzanti, Jerry, DE, Arkansas 1963
McAfee, Wes, B, Duke 1941
McAlister, James, RB, UCLA 1975-76
McChesney, Bob, E, Hardin-Simmons 1950
McClellan, Mike, B, Oklahoma 1962-63
McCullough, Hugh, B, Oklahoma 1943
McCusker, Jim, T, Pittsburgh 1959-62
McDonald, Don (Flip), E, Oklahoma 1944-45
McDonald, Les, E, Nebraska 1940
McDonald, Tommy, WR, Oklahoma 1957-63
McDonough, Bob, G, Duke 1942-46
McHugh, Pat, B, Georgia Tech 1947-51
McKeever, Marlin, LB, USC 1973
McNeill, Tom, P, Stephen F. Austin 1971-73
McPherson, Forrest (Amy), T, Nebraska 1935-37
McRae, Jerrold, WR, Tennessee State 1979
Meadows, Ed, E, Duke 1958
Medved, Ron, DB, Washington 1966-70
Mellekas, John, T, Arizona 1963
Meyers, John, T, Washington 1964-67
Meyer, Fred, E, Stanford 1942, 1945
Michaels, Eddie, G, Villanova 1943-46
Michel, Mike, P-K, Stanford 1978
Michels, Johnny, G, Tennessee 1953
Middlebrook, Oren, WR, Arkansas State 1978
Mike-Mayer, Nick, K, Temple 1977-78
Milam, Barnes, C, Austin 1934
Miller, Don, B, Southern Methodist 1954
Miller, Tom, E, Hampton-Sydney 1942-44
Milling, Al, G, Richmond 1942
Mira, George, QB, Miami 1969
Mitcham, Gene, E, Arizona State 1958
Mitchell, Leonard, DE, Houston 1981
Mitchell, Martin, DB, Tulane 1977
Molden, Frank, T, Jackson State 1968
Monroe, Henry, CB, Mississippi State 1979
Montgomery, Wilbert, RB, Abilene Christian 1977-81
Morgan, Dennis, KR, Western Illinois 1975
Morgan, Mike, LB, Louisiana State 1964-67
Morriss, Guy, C, Texas Christian 1973-81
Mortell, Emmett, B, Wisconsin 1937-39
Moseley, Mark, K, Stephen F. Austin 1970
Moselle, Dom, B, Wisconsin-Superior 1954
Mrkonic, George, T, Kansas 1953
Muha, Joe, B, Virginia Military 1946-50
Muhlmann, Horst, K, No college 1975-77
Mulligan, George, E, Catholic U. 1936
Murley, Dick, T, Purdue 1956
Murray, Calvin, RB, Ohio State 1981
Murray, Franny, B, Pennsylvania 1939-40
Myers, Brad, B, Bucknell 1958
Myers, Jack (Moose), B, UCLA 1948-50

N

Nacrelli, Andy, E, Fordham 1958
Nelson, Al, DB, Cincinnati 1965-73
Nelson, Dennis, T, Illinois State 1976-77
Nettles, Jim, DB, Wisconsin 1965-68

Newton, Chuck, B, Washington 1939-40
Niland, John, G, Iowa 1975-76
Nipp, Maury, G, Loyola, Cal. 1952-53, 1956
Nocera, John, LB, Iowa 1959-62
Norby, Jack, B, Idaho 1934
Nordquist, Mark, G, Pacific 1968-74
Norton, Jerry, DB, Southern Methodist 1954-58
Norton, Jim, T, Washington 1968
Nowak, Walt, E, Villanova 1944

O

Oakes, Don, T, Virginia Tech 1961-62
O'Boyle, Harry, B, Notre Dame. 1933
O'Brien, Davey, B, Texas Christian 1939-40
Obst, Henry, G, Syracuse 1933
Olds, Bill, RB, Nebraska 1976
Oliver, Greg, RB, Trinity, Texas 1973-74
Oliver, Hubert, RB, Arizona 1981
Opperman, Jim, LB, Colorado State 1975
O'Quinn, John (Red), E, Wake Forest 1951
Ordway, Bill, B, North Dakota 1939
Oristaglio, Bob, E, Pennsylvania 1952
Ormsbee, Elliott, B, Bradley 1946
Osborn, Mike, LB, Kansas State 1978
Osborne, Richard, TE, Texas A&M. 1976-78
Outlaw, John, DB, Jackson State 1973-78
Overmyer, Bill, T, LB, Ashland 1972
Owens, Don, T, Southern Mississippi 1958-60

P

Padlow, Max, E, Ohio State 1935
Pagliei, Joe, B, Clemson 1959
Palmer, Les, B, North Carolina State 1948
Papale, Vince, WR, St. Joseph's 1976-78
Pape, Orrin, B, Iowa 1933
Parker, Artimus, DB, USC 1974-76
Parker, Rodney, WR, Tennessee State 1980-81
Parmer, Jim, B, Oklahoma State 1948-56
Paschka, Gordon, G, Minnesota 1943
Pate, Rupert, G, Wake Forest 1942
Patton, Cliff, G, Texas Christian 1946-50
Patton, Jerry, DT, Nebraska. 1974
Payne, Ken, WR, Langston, Oklahoma 1978
Peaks, Clarence, RB, Michigan State 1957-63
Pegg, Hal, C, Bucknell 1940
Pellegrini, Bob, LB, Maryland 1956, 1958-61
Peoples, Woody, G, Grambling 1978-
Perot, Petey, G, Northwestern Louisiana 1979-81
Peters, Floyd, T, San Francisco State 1964-69
Peters, Volney, T, USC 1958
Pettigrew, Gary, DT, Stanford 1966-74
Philbin, Gerry, DE, Buffalo 1973
Phillips, Ray, LB, Nebraska 1978-81
Piasecky, Al, E, Duke 1942
Picard, Bob, WR, Eastern Washington State 1973-76
Pihos, Pete, E, Indiana 1947-55
Pilconis, Joe, E, Temple 1934, 1936-37
Pinder, Cyril, RB, Illinois 1968-70
Piro, Hank, E, Syracuse 1941
Pisarcik, Joe, QB, New Mexico State 1980-81
Pitts, Alabama, B, No college 1935
Pivarnick, Joe, G, Notre Dame 1936
Poage, Ray, TE, Texas 1964-65
Pollard, Al, B, Army 1951-53
Pollock, Bill, B, Widener 1937, 1942-43
Porter, Ron, LB, Idaho 1969-72
Poth, Phil, G, Gonzaga 1934
Powell, Art, B, San Jose State 1959
Preece, Steve, DB, Oregon State 1970-72
Prescott, Harold (Ace), E, Hardin-Simmons 1947-49
Priestly, Bob, E, Brown 1942
Prisco, Nick, B, Rutgers 1933
Pritchard, Bosh, B, Virginia Military. 1942, 1946-51
Puetz, Garry, T, Valparaiso 1979
Pylman, Bob, T, South Dakota State 1938-39

Q

Quinlan, Billy, E, Michigan State 1963

R

Rado, George, E, Duquesne 1937-38

Cardinals tied Philadelphia for fifth place with a 2-9-1 record.

1959 The Cardinals rebuilt their offensive and defensive lines through trades. Night Train Lane was sent to Detroit for defensive end Perry Richards. Linebacker Bill Koman was acquired from Philadelphia for Chuck Weber. Then the Cardinals traded Matson to the Rams for the rights to nine players. The deal gave the Cardinals three players immediately, linemen Frank Fuller, Glen Holtzman, and Ken Panfil. They also got three draft choices. Two players, linemen Art Hauser and John Tracey, were added later, and so was another draft choice. The Cardinals finished last with a 2-10 record.

1960 Expansion studies done by the league office had found St. Louis to be a desirable city for an NFL franchise. All signs pointed to an expansion team locating there for the 1961 season. But at the same time, the new American Football League was making overtures to St. Louis. The NFL was in an expansion mood and did not want to lose such a promising bit of territory to the new league. The owners voted unanimously to allow the Chicago Cardinals to relocate in St. Louis, March 13. The Cardinals had to share 34,000-seat Busch Stadium with the baseball Cardinals. There was no regular place to practice, so the team worked out in an open field at a city park. Season ticket sales fell well below the 25,000 some city fathers had promised the league. The Cardinals quickly won over the town, however, when they beat the Rams in the season opener 43-21. They had their best year since 1956 and finished fourth with a 6-5-1 record. John David Crow broke Ollie Matson's season team rushing record by gaining 1,071 yards. Included were 203 yards gained in one game, against Pittsburgh the last week of the year.

1961 Ivy signed the Canadian Football League's leading passer for the last decade, Sam Etcheverry. Etcheverry had played college football at the University of Denver, but had been passed over by the NFL teams because of his size (5 foot 11 inches, 186 pounds). Ivy was so convinced of Etcheverry's ability that he traded away his best quarterback of the previous year, John Roach. In return, he got two starters from Cleveland, running back Prentice Gautt and tight end Taz Anderson. Etcheverry hurt his arm in training and never rebounded from the injury. Ivy traded quarterback George Izo, the club's number-one draft choice of 1960, to Washington for quarterback Ralph Guglielmi. Etcheverry and Guglielmi shared the position. Offensive lineman Ken Panfil dislocated a kneecap in the first preseason game, and Crow broke his ankle in the second one. Ivy resigned with two games left on the schedule. Assistant coaches Chuck Drulis, Ray Prochaska, and Ray Willsey took over for those games, and the Cardinals won them both to finish 7-7.

1962 Violet Bidwill Wolfner died, January 29. Under the terms of Mrs. Wolfner's will, all her property reverted to her sons upon death. She had owned 90 percent of the Cardinals, 10 percent having been bought by St. Louis beer magnate Joseph Griesedieck. Walter Wolfner contested the will, but a probate court in Chicago ruled it valid, March 28. With that, Charles and Bill Bidwill became legal owners of the Cardinals. The two men retained their titles of president (Charles or Stormy) and vice president (Bill), but each took a more active role in operations. Bill became the on-site director of activities. Charles kept his home and offices in Chicago, but planned to spend at least 40 percent of his time in St. Louis. The Bidwills selected Wally Lemm, who had been an assistant under both Ray Richards and Pop Ivy, as coach. Charley Johnson, who was selected in the tenth round of the 1960 draft as a future, became the starting quarterback in the fourth game. Lemm also switched running back Bobby Joe Conrad to flanker, and Conrad responded by catching 62 passes. Johnson completed 49 percent of his passes for over 2,400 yards.

1963 The Cardinals had an exceptional draft, selecting defensive end Don Brumm, end Billy Gambrell, linebacker Dave Meggyesy, offensive tackle Bob Reynolds, defensive tackle Sam Silas, tight end Jackie Smith, linebacker Larry Stallings, defensive back Jerry Stovall, and running backs Bill Thornton and Bob Paremore. Gautt was lost for the year with a knee injury in the first game. Crow was hobbled most of the year by injuries. Ground was broken for a new all-sports stadium in St. Louis. The Cardinals finished third in the Eastern Conference; the 9-5 record was their best since 1948. Bobby Joe Conrad caught 73 passes for 967 yards. Johnson set four club passing records—attempts (423), completions (222), yardage (3,280), and touchdowns (28). The day after the season ended, Lemm signed a new contract as coach.

1964 The completion date of 1965 for St. Louis's new stadium was obviously not going to be met. In July, a group from Atlanta approached the Bidwills about moving the team to that city. Atlanta was building a new stadium. The stadium authority in St. Louis matched Atlanta's terms; that plus renewed civic support for the team convinced the Bidwills to stay in St. Louis. The Cardinals had another successful year, stumbling only at midseason when they lost to Baltimore, Dallas, and New York. The team's 9-3-2 record was only one-half game behind Cleveland's 10-3-1. In two games against the Browns, the Cardinals got a tie and a victory. The Cardinals defeated

Jackie Smith, St. Louis's all-time leading receiver, in action against Philadelphia, 1973.

Green Bay 24-17 in the Playoff Bowl in Miami.

1965 The Cardinals drafted quarterback Joe Namath of Alabama in the first round but couldn't sign him. Crow was traded to the 49ers for kick returner Abe Woodson. The Cardinals won four of their first five games, but Johnson injured his shoulder in the fourth game and was not effective for the rest of the season. Both starting running backs, Gautt and Joe Childress, missed most of the season with injuries, and defensive backs Larry Wilson and Stovall were handicapped by injuries. The Cardinals lost eight of their last nine games and tied Philadelphia for fifth place in the Eastern Conference with a 5-9 record. Lemm announced after the last game that he would not return as coach.

1966 Charley Winner was named coach. The Cardinals moved into Busch Memorial Stadium, which seated 51,392. The Cardinals made their debut in Busch with a 20-10 preseason victory over the Atlanta Falcons, August 6. The team started fast under Winner, going 7-1-1 in its first nine games. Then Johnson was injured and lost for the year. A succession of injuries followed. Such key players as wide receiver Sonny Randle, cornerback Pat Fischer, and offensive linemen Bob DeMarco, Ken Gray, and Irv Goode were lost for varying lengths of time with injuries. The Cardinals scored only 52 points in their last five games. They lost four of them and finished fourth with an 8-5-1 record.

1967 After expanding to 16 teams, the NFL realigned its divisional setup. St. Louis was now in the Century Division of the Eastern Conference, along with Cleveland, New York, and Pittsburgh. Wide receiver Randle was traded to San Francisco. Johnson and Stallings were inducted into the army in August. Jim Hart, a free agent from Southern Illinois who had made the taxi squad in 1966, became the starting quarterback. Johnson and Stallings were available on some weekends. The Cardinals finished third in the four-team division with a 6-7-1 record.

1968 Linebackers Bill Koman and Dale Meinert and running back Prentice Gautt retired. Defensive end Joe Robb, cornerback Pat Fischer, and split end Billy Gambrell were traded. St. Louis beat Cleveland twice during the season. but had trouble with Coastal Division teams, losing to Los Angeles, Baltimore, and San Francisco. Hart passed for over 2,000 yards. The Cardinals accumulated a 9-4-1 record and finished second, one-half game behind the Browns in the Century Division.

1969 Injuries decimated the Cardinals as 11 members of the team underwent surgery. The defense was particularly affected. By mid-year Wilson was the only healthy veteran defensive back. The team became highly vulnerable to the pass, and it gave up an average of 27.7 points a game. Johnson returned from the army and won his quarterback job back in training camp from Hart. The Cardinals dropped to third place in the Century Division with a 4-9-1 record.

1970 The NFL officially merged with the AFL and in the realignment St. Louis was put in the Eastern Division of the NFC with Dallas, the New York Giants, Washington, and Philadelphia. Johnson was traded to Houston in a deal that brought quarterback Pete Beathard to St. Louis, January 21. Winner was re-signed to a one-year contract, February 20. The Cardinals lost to the Rams 34-13 in the season opener, but then won eight, lost one, and tied one. They went into the twelfth week of the season in first place with an 8-2-1 record. Then St. Louis collapsed, losing to Detroit, the Giants, and Washington in succession. That dropped them into third place in the Eastern Division. Winner was dismissed.

1971 The Cardinals drafted defensive back Norm Thompson, offensive lineman Dan Dierdorf, and

Ottis Anderson breaks into the open and scores on a 37-yard run against Philadelphia, 1980.

wide receiver Mel Gray. Bob Hollway, an assistant with the Minnesota Vikings, was named coach, February 14. Hart shared the quarterback job with Beathard. The team dropped to 4-9-1 and finished fourth in the Eastern Division.

1972 Bill Bidwill bought his brother Charles's share of the team, September 12. Assistant coach Chuck Drulis collapsed on the airplane carrying the team home from a preseason game in Houston; by the time the plane made an emergency landing in Little Rock, Arkansas, Drulis was dead of a heart attack. The Cardinals traded wide receiver John Gilliam to Minnesota for quarterback Gary Cuozzo. Tim Van Galder, who had been on the taxi squad since 1967, outplayed both Cuozzo and Hart in the preseason, and became the number-one quarterback. Van Galder was injured in the fourth game of the season, and the position became uncertain again. Two weeks before the season ended, Wilson announced the end of his 13-year playing career. For the second year in succession the Cardinals had a 4-9-1 record. After the last game, Hollway was fired as coach.

1973 Bidwill named Don Coryell, formerly of San Diego State, as the twenty-sixth head coach in the Cardinals' history, January 18. Joe Sullivan, assistant general manager under George Allen in Washington, was named the Cardinals' director of operations, February 23. Running back Terry Metcalf of Long Beach State was drafted. Training camp was moved to Illinois State University in Normal, Illinois. Coryell unequivocally named Hart as his starter at quarterback. The Cardinals finished 4-9-1 for the third season in a row.

1974 The Cardinals won their first seven games, then lost the next two before winning three of their last five. They clinched the Eastern Division title with a 26-14 win over the New York Giants in the last game of the season. St. Louis was involved in its first postseason championship competition of any kind since 1948. The Cardinals lost 30-14 to the Minnesota Vikings in a divisional playoff game.

1975 The Cardinals trained at Eastern Illinois University in Charleston, Illinois. They clinched their second consecutive Eastern Division title in the thirteenth week of the season when they beat the Chicago Bears 34-20. They finished with an 11-3 record,

their best since the 1948 team went 11-1. Fullback Jim Otis led the NFC in rushing with 1,076 yards. Metcalf set an NFL record for total yardage by gaining 2,462 with his running, receiving, and returning. The Cardinals met the Rams in Los Angeles in the first round of the playoffs. The Rams' Lawrence McCutcheon gained 202 yards on 37 carries and Los Angeles returned two interceptions of Hart passes for touchdowns in the first half. The Cardinals trailed 28-9 at halftime and lost 35-23.

1976 The training camp was moved to Lindenwood College in St. Charles, Missouri. The Cardinals lost 43-24 to San Diego in the third game and they never got above second place after that. After 11 weeks, Dallas was on top with a 9-2 record. St. Louis was second with 8-3, and Washington third at 7-4. However, Washington had beaten the Cardinals twice; in the event of a second-place tie, the Redskins would go to the playoffs as the wild card team. St. Louis lost to Dallas on Thanksgiving Day, and that dropped them into a tie with the Redskins. Both teams went on to win their last two games, but despite a 10-4 record the Cardinals failed to make the playoffs for the first time since Coryell's initial season.

1977 Held scoreless for the first time since 1974, the Cardinals lost their opener to Denver 7-0. A week later, Hart led the way to the first victory of the season by completing 12 consecutive passes, a club record, in a 16-13 win over Chicago. After two more losses, Hart got hot in a 21-17 victory over Philadelphia, and the Cardinals launched a six-game winning streak. Included in that streak was a 49-31 win over New Orleans on October 23, when Terry Metcalf accounted for 268 yards in offense. Against Dallas on November 14, Hart threw two touchdowns passes in the final quarter to beat the Cowboys 24-17. But the winning streak ended abruptly on November 24 when the Cardinals were demolished by Miami 55-14. The Cardinals never recovered and lost their final three games to fall out of playoff contention. The team finished 7-7, and a frustrated Don Coryell resigned as head coach after the season.

1978 After a 15-year absence from coaching, 62-year-old Bud Wilkinson, a legendary collegiate coach at Oklahoma, accepted the job as head coach of the Cardinals on March 2. He faced a rebuilding job with the offense, because Metcalf signed in the Canadian Football League and Ike Harris, the leading receiver in 1977, was traded to New Orleans along with all-pro guard Conrad Dobler. Steve Little, an All-America kicker from Arkansas, and Ken Greene, a defensive back from Washington State, each were selected in the first round of the draft. As the offense floundered, the Cardinals went winless through the first eight weeks of the season. Complicating matters was a shoulder injury to Hart. However, Hart regained his health and threw for 260 yards in a 16-10 win over Philadelphia on October 29. Wilkinson's first pro coaching victory was followed by three in succession and five in the final seven weeks, which gave the Cardinals a final record of 6-10. Hart enjoyed his most productive season: 240 completions for 3,121 yards and 16 touchdowns. Pat Tilley, with 62 receptions, had the best year of any St. Louis receiver since 1973. Following the season, kicker Jim Bakken retired after 17 years with the Cardinals.

1979 Tight end J. V. Cain, a former number-one draft choice, died of heart failure in training camp on July 22. The club's top draft choice in 1979 was Ottis Anderson of Miami, who rushed for 193 yards in an opening loss to Dallas and had the greatest season of any rookie running back in NFL history. Anderson rushed for 1,605 yards and had nine 100-yard games, both league records for a rookie. However, the Cardinals won only twice in the first nine weeks. In a 37-7 victory over Minnesota on November 4, Anderson ran for 164 yards to reach the 1,000-yard barrier in only 10 weeks. When the club plummeted to 3-10 following a loss to Cincinnati on November 25, Wilkinson was released as head coach. Former Cardinals safety Larry Wilson stepped in as interim coach. Steve Pisarkiewicz started at quarterback in a victory over San Francisco December 2, and the club won two of its final three games to end the year 5-11.

1980 Jim Hanifan, a former assistant coach for the Cardinals, was named head coach January 30. After an 0-3 start, the Cardinals upset Philadelphia 24-14, as Anderson rushed for 151 yards and two touchdowns. A 40-7 rout of New Orleans followed, but the Cardinals didn't win successive games again until the end of the season and finished the year at 5-11. Tilley enjoyed his best season with 68 catches for 966 yards. Mel Gray caught at least one pass in every game to keep alive his consecutive-game reception string at 105.

1981 E.J. Junior, a linebacker, and Neil Lomax, a quarterback, were selected in the first two rounds of the draft. The club lost its first two games, then defeated Washington 40-30 on September 20. The star of the Washington game was Roy Green, who doubled as a wide receiver and a safety and contributed a touchdown catch and a key interception. Green continued his double duty throughout the season and finished with 33 pass receptions and three interceptions. Despite victories over Dallas, when Neil O'Donoghue kicked a 37-yard field goal with 23 seconds left, and Minnesota, when Hart threw the two-hundredth touchdown pass of his career, the Cardinals fell to 3-7 after 10 weeks. On November 15, Lomax was given a start and he guided the Cardinals to a 24-0 victory over Buffalo. Lomax then started in consecutive victories over Baltimore, New England, and New Orleans that improved the Cardinals' record to 7-7 and moved them into contention for a wild card berth in the playoffs. But on December 13, the Cardinals lost to the New York Giants 20-10 to end their playoff hopes.

MEMBERS OF HALL OF FAME:

Charles Bidwill, Sr., Guy Chamberlin, Jimmy Conzelman, John (Paddy) Driscoll, Walt Kiesling, Earl (Curly) Lambeau, Dick (Night Train) Lane, Ollie Matson, Ernie Nevers, Jim Thorpe, Charley Trippi, Larry Wilson

CARDINALS RECORD, 1920-81

Year	Won	Lost	Tied	Pct.	Pts.	OP
Chicago Cardinals						
1920........	5	2	1	.714		
1921........	2	3	2	.400		
1922........	8	3	0	.727		
1923........	8	4	0	.667		
1924........	5	4	1	.556		
1925‡.......	11	2	1	.846		
1926........	5	6	1	.455		
1927........	3	7	1	.300		
1928........	1	5	0	.167		
1929........	6	6	1	.500		
1930........	5	6	2	.455		
1931........	5	4	0	.556		
1932........	2	6	2	.250		
1933........	1	9	1	.100	52	101
1934........	5	6	0	.455	80	84
1935........	6	4	2	.600	99	97
1936........	3	8	1	.273	74	143
1937........	5	5	1	.500	135	165
1938........	2	9	0	.182	111	168
1939........	1	10	0	.091	84	254
1940........	2	7	2	.222	139	222
1941........	3	7	1	.300	127	197
1942........	3	8	0	.273	98	209
1943........	0	10	0	.000	95	238
1944 (Card-Pitt)	0	10	0	.000	108	328
1945........	1	9	0	.100	98	228
1946........	6	5	0	.545	260	198
1947‡.......	9	3	0	.750	306	231
1948§.......	11	1	0	.917	395	226
1949........	6	5	1	.545	360	301
1950........	5	7	0	.417	233	287
1951........	3	9	0	.250	210	287
1952........	4	8	0	.333	172	221
1953........	1	10	1	.091	190	337
1954........	2	10	0	.167	183	347
1955........	4	7	1	.364	224	252
1956........	7	5	0	.583	240	182
1957........	3	9	0	.250	200	299
1958........	2	9	1	.182	261	356
1959........	2	10	0	.167	234	324
St. Louis Cardinals						
1960........	6	5	1	.545	288	230
1961........	7	7	0	.500	279	267
1962........	4	9	1	.308	287	361
1963........	9	5	0	.643	341	283
1964........	9	3	2	.750	357	331
1965........	5	9	0	.357	296	309
1966........	8	5	1	.615	264	265
1967........	6	7	1	.462	333	356
1968........	9	4	1	.692	325	289
1969........	4	9	1	.308	314	389
1970........	8	5	1	.615	325	228
1971........	4	9	1	.308	231	279
1972........	4	9	1	.308	193	303
1973........	4	9	1	.321	286	365
1974†.......	10	4	0	.714	285	218
1975†.......	11	3	0	.786	356	276
1976........	10	4	0	.714	309	267
1977........	7	7	0	.500	272	287
1978........	6	10	0	.375	248	296
1979........	5	11	0	.313	307	358
1980........	5	11	0	.313	299	350
1981........	7	9	0	.438	315	408
62 Years.....	311	410	36	.435		

‡NFL Champion
§NFL Western Division Champion
†NFC Eastern Division Champion

RECORD HOLDERS

Rushing (Yards)	Ottis Anderson, 1979	1,605
Passing (Pct.)	Jim Hart, 1976	56.2
Passing (Yards)	Charley Johnson, 1963	3,280
Passing (TDs)	Charley Johnson, 1963	28
Receiving (No.)	Bobby Joe Conrad, 1963	73
Receiving (Yards)	Jackie Smith, 1967	1,205
Interceptions (No.)	Bob Nussbaumer, 1949	12
Punting (Avg.)	Jerry Norton, 1960	45.6
Punt Ret. (Avg.)	John (Red) Cochran, 1949	20.9
Kickoff Ret. (Avg.)	Ollie Matson, 1958	35.5
Touchdowns (Total)	John David Crow, 1962	17
Field Goals Made	Jim Bakken, 1967	27
Points (No.)	Jim Bakken, 1967	117

COACHING HISTORY

1920	Marshall Smith	5- 2-1
1921-22	John (Paddy) Driscoll	10- 6-2
1923-24	Arnold Horween	13- 8-1
1925-26	Norman Barry	16- 8-2
1927	Fred Gillies	3- 7-1
1928	Guy Chamberlin	1- 5-0
1929-30	Ernie Nevers	11-12-3
1931	LeRoy Andrews*	0- 2-0
1931	Ernie Nevers	5- 2-0
1932	Jack Chevigny	2- 6-2
1933-34	Paul Schissler	6-15-1
1935-38	Milan Creighton	16-26-4
1939	Ernie Nevers	1-10-0
1940-42	Jimmy Conzelman	8-22-3
1943-45	Phil Handler**	1-29-0
1946-48	Jimmy Conzelman	26- 9-0
1949	Phil Handler, Raymond (Buddy) Parker***	6- 5-1
1950-51	Earl (Curly) Lambeau	8-16-0
1952	Joe Kuharich	4- 8-0
1953-54	Joe Stydahar	3-20-1
1955-57	Ray Richards	14-21-1
1958-61	Frank (Pop) Ivy	17-31-2
1962-65	Wally Lemm	27-26-3
1966-70	Charley Winner	35-30-5
1971-72	Bob Hollway	8-18-2
1973-77	Don Coryell	42-27-1
1978-79	Bud Wilkinson****	9-20-0
1979	Larry Wilson	2- 1-0
1980-81	Jim Hanifan	12-20-0

**Resigned after two games in 1931*
***Co-coach with Walt Kiesling of 1944 Chicago Cardinals-Pittsburgh merged team*
****Co-coaches*
*****Replaced after 13 games in 1979*

FIRST PLAYER SELECTED

1936	Jim Lawrence, B, Texas Christian
1937	Ray Buivid, B, Marquette
1938	Jack Robbins, B, Arkansas
1939	Charles (Ki) Aldrich, C, Texas Christian
1940	George Cafego, B, Tennessee
1941	John Kimbrough, B, Texas A&M
1942	Steve Lach, B, Duke
1943	Glenn Dobbs, B, Tulsa
1944	Pat Harder, B, Wisconsin
1945	Charley Trippi, B, Georgia
1946	Dub Jones, B, Louisiana State
1947	DeWitt (Tex) Coulter, T, Army
1948	Jim Spavital, B, Oklahoma A&M
1949	Bill Fischer, G, Notre Dame
1950	Jack Jennings, T (2), Ohio State
1951	Jerry Groom, C, Notre Dame
1952	Ollie Matson, B, San Francisco
1953	Johnny Olszewski, B, California
1954	Lamar McHan, B, Arkansas
1955	Max Boydston, E, Oklahoma
1956	Joe Childress, B, Auburn
1957	Jerry Tubbs, C, Oklahoma
1958	King Hill, B, Rice
1959	Billy Stacy, B, Mississippi State
1960	George Izo, QB, Notre Dame
1961	Ken Rice, T, Auburn
1962	Fate Echols, DT, Northwestern
1963	Jerry Stovall, S, Louisiana State
1964	Ken Kortas, DT, Louisville
1965	Joe Namath, QB, Alabama
1966	Carl McAdams, LB, Oklahoma
1967	Dave Williams, WR, Washington
1968	MacArthur Lane, RB, Utah State
1969	Roger Wehrli, CB, Missouri
1970	Larry Stegent RB, Texas A&M
1971	Norm Thompson, CB, Utah
1972	Bobby Moore, RB-WR, Oregon
1973	Dave Butz, DT, Purdue
1974	J. V. Cain, TE, Colorado
1975	Tim Gray, DB, Texas A&M
1976	Mike Dawson, DT, Arizona
1977	Steve Pisarkiewicz, QB, Missouri
1978	Steve Little, P-K, Arkansas
1979	Ottis Anderson, RB, Miami
1980	Curtis Greer, DE, Michigan
1981	E. J. Junior, LB, Alabama
1982	Luis Sharpe, T, UCLA

CHICAGO CARDINALS, 1920-59;
ST. LOUIS CARDINALS, 1960-81

The Cardinals merged with the Pittsburgh Steelers in 1944.

Acker, Bill, DT, Texas 1980-81
Adams, Henry, C, Pittsburgh 1939
Agee, Sam, B, Vanderbilt 1938-39
Ahrens, Dave, LB, Wisconsin 1981
Albert, Sergio, K, U.S. International.................. 1974
Albrecht, Art, T, Wisconsin 1943
Aldrich, Ki, C, Texas Christian 1939-40, 1943
Alford, Mike, C, Auburn............................ 1965
Allen, Carl, DB, Southern Mississippi 1977-81
Allen, Ed, E, Creighton 1928
Allen, Jeff, DB, Iowa State 1971
Allerman, Kurt, LB, Penn State.................... 1977-80
Allison, Henry, T, San Diego State 1975-76
Alton, Joe, T, Oklahoma 1942, 1944
Anderson, Charley, E, Louisiana Tech................. 1956
Anderson, Cliff, E, Indiana 1952-53
Anderson, Donny, RB, Texas Tech 1972-74
Anderson, Eddie, E, Notre Dame.................. 1922-25
Anderson, Ottis, RB, Miami....................... 1979-81
Anderson, Taz, TE, Georgia Tech.................. 1961-64
Anderson, Warren, WR, West Virginia State............ 1978
Andros, Plato, G, Oklahoma 1947-50
Angle, Bob, B, Iowa State 1950

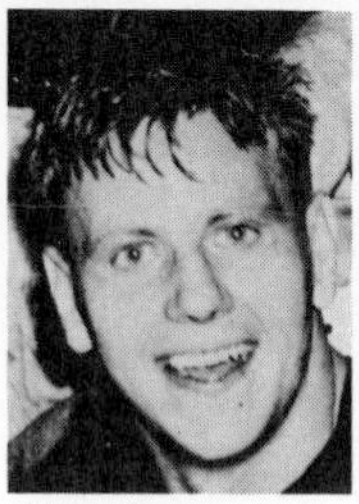
Elmer Angsman

Joe Childress

Bobby Joe Conrad

Dan Dierdorf

Bob Dove

Bill Fischer

Marshall Goldberg

Angsman, Elmer, B, Notre Dame ... 1946-52
Apolskis, Ray, T, Marquette ... 1941-42, 1945-50
Arms, Lloyd, G, Oklahoma State ... 1946-48
Arneson, Mark, LB, Arizona ... 1972-80
Arterburn, Elmer, B, Texas Tech ... 1954
Ashton, Josh, RB, Tulsa ... 1975
Atkins, Bob, DB, Grambling ... 1968-69
Audick, Dan, G, Hawaii ... 1977
Auer, Howie, T, Michigan ... 1933

B

Babartsky, Al, T, Fordham ... 1938-39, 1941-42
Badaczewski, John, G, Western Reserve ... 1948
Bagdon, Ed, G, Michigan State ... 1950-51
Baker, Charles, LB, New Mexico ... 1980-81
Bailey, Claron (Monk), DB, Utah ... 1964-65
Baker, Conway, T, Centenary ... 1936-43, 1945
Baker, Mel, WR, Texas Southern ... 1976
Baker, Roy (Bullet), B, USC ... 1929-30
Bakken, Jim, K, Wisconsin ... 1962-78
Balacz, Frank, B, Iowa ... 1941, 1945
Banks, Tom, C-G, Auburn ... 1971-80
Banonis, Vince, C, Detroit ... 1942, 1946-50
Barefield, John, LB, Texas A&I ... 1978-80
Barnes, Lawrence, RB, Tennessee State ... 1978
Barnes, Mike, DB, Texas-Arlington ... 1967-68
Barnes, Pete, LB, Southern U. ... 1973-75
Barni, Roy, DB, San Francisco ... 1952-53
Barry, Norm, B, Notre Dame ... 1921
Barry, Paul, B, Tulsa ... 1954
Bates, Ted, LB, Oregon State ... 1959-62
Bausch, Jim, B, Kansas ... 1934-36
Baynham, Craig, RB, Georgia Tech ... 1972
Beal, Norm, DB, Missouri ... 1962
Beathard, Pete, QB, USC ... 1970-71
Beatty, Charles, DB, North Texas State ... 1972
Beauchamp, Al, LB, Southern U. ... 1976
Beckman, Tom, DE, Michigan ... 1972
Beinor, Ed, E, Notre Dame ... 1940-41
Belden, Charles (Bunny), B, St. Mary's, Cal. ... 1929-31
Bell, Bob, DE, Cincinnati ... 1974-78
Bell, Gordon, RB, Michigan ... 1978-79
Bell, Mark, WR, Colorado State ... 1981
Belton, Willie, RB, Maryland-Eastern Shore ... 1973-74
Bennett, Chuck, B, Indiana ... 1933
Bergerson, Gil, T, Oregon State ... 1933
Bernardi, Frank, B, Colorado ... 1955-57
Berquist, Jay, G, Nebraska ... 1927
Berry, Gil, B, Illinois ... 1935
Bertagnolli, Libero, G, Washington, Missouri ... 1942, 1945
Bienermann, Tom, E, Drake ... 1951-56
Bilbo, Jon, T, Mississippi ... 1938-39
Birdsong, Carl, P, Southwest Oklahoma State ... 1981
Birlem, Keith, B, San Jose State ... 1939
Black, Tim, LB, Baylor ... 1977
Blackburn, Bill, C, Rice ... 1946-50
Blackwell, Hal, B, South Carolina ... 1945
Blazine, Tony, T, Illinois Wesleyan ... 1935-40
Bliss, Homer, G, Washington & Jefferson ... 1928
Blumenthal, Morris, B, Northwestern ... 1925
Blumer, Herb, E, Missouri ... 1925-30, 1933
Bock, Wayne, T, Illinois ... 1957
Bogue, George, B, Stanford ... 1930
Bohlmann, Frank, G, Marquette ... 1942
Bonelli, Ernie, B, Pittsburgh ... 1945
Booth, Clarence, T, Southern Methodist ... 1943
Bostic, Joe, T, Clemson ... 1979-81
Bova, Tony, E, St. Francis ... 1944
Boyd, Bill, B, Westminster, Missouri ... 1930-31
Boydston, Max, E, Oklahoma ... 1955-58
Boyette, Garland, LB, Grambling ... 1962-63
Braden, Dave, G, Marquette ... 1945
Bradley, Bill, DB, Texas ... 1977
Bradley, Dave, G, Penn State ... 1972
Bradley, Hal, E, Elon ... 1938-39
Brahaney, Tom, C, Oklahoma ... 1973-81
Braidwood, Chuck, E, Tennessee-Chattanooga ... 1932
Bredde, Bill, B, Oklahoma State ... 1954
Brennan, Willis, T, No college ... 1920-27
Brett, Ed, E, Washington State ... 1936
Brettschneider, Carl, LB, Iowa State ... 1956-59
Britton, Earl, B, Illinois ... 1929
Brooks, Jonathan, LB, Clemson ... 1980
Brooks, Leo, DE, Texas ... 1973-76
Brosky, Al, B, Illinois ... 1954
Brown, Bob, TE, Alcorn State ... 1969-70
Brown, Chuck, C-G, Houston ... 1979-80
Brown, Hardy, LB, Tulsa ... 1956
Brown, Rush, DT, Ball State ... 1980-81
Brown, Terry, DB, Oklahoma State ... 1969-70
Brown, Theotis, RB, UCLA ... 1979-81
Brubaker, Dick, E, Ohio State ... 1955, 1957
Bruckner, Les, B, Michigan State ... 1945
Brumm, Don, DE, Purdue ... 1963-69, 1972
Bryan, John, B, Chicago ... 1922
Bryant, Charlie, RB, Allen ... 1966-67
Bryant, Chuck, E, Ohio State ... 1962
Buckeye, Garland, T, No college ... 1920-24
Bucklin, Tom, B, Idaho ... 1927
Bukant, Joe, B, Washington, Missouri ... 1942-43
Bulger, Chet, T, Auburn ... 1942-43, 1945-49
Burkett, Jeff, E, Louisiana State ... 1947
Burl, Alex, B, Colorado State ... 1956
Burnett, Ray, B, No college ... 1938
Burns, Leon, RB, Long Beach State ... 1972
Burson, Jimmy, DB, Auburn ... 1963-67
Busler, Ray, T, Marquette ... 1940-41, 1945
Busse, Ellis, B, Chicago ... 1929
Butler, Jim (Cannonball), RB, Edward Waters ... 1972
Butler, Johnny, B, Tennessee ... 1944
Butts, Eddie, B, Chico State ... 1929
Butz, Dave, DE, Purdue ... 1973-74

C

Cahill, Ronnie, B, Holy Cross ... 1943
Cain, Jim, E, Alabama ... 1949
Cain, J. V., WR-TE, Colorado ... 1974-77
Campana, Al, B, Youngstown ... 1953
Campbell, Bill, G, Oklahoma ... 1945-49
Cantor, Leo, B, UCLA ... 1945
Carey, Joe, G, No college ... 1920
Carlson, Hal, G, DePaul ... 1937
Carpenter, Steve, S, Western Illinois ... 1981
Carr, Jimmy, B, Morris Harvey ... 1955, 1957
Carrell, Duane, P, Florida State ... 1977
Carter, Joe, E, Southern Methodist ... 1945
Carter, Ross, G, Oregon ... 1936-39
Carter, Willie, B, Tennessee State ... 1953
Caywood, Les, G, St. John, Minnesota ... 1931
Chamberlin, Guy, C, Nebraska ... 1927
Chandler, Al, TE, Oklahoma ... 1978-79
Charpier, Len, B, Illinois ... 1921
Cheatham, Lloyd, B, Auburn ... 1942
Cherry, Ed, B, Hardin-Simmons ... 1938-39
Chickillo, Nick, G, Miami ... 1953
Childress, Joe, RB, Auburn ... 1956-65
Childs, Jim, WR, Cal Poly-San Luis Obispo ... 1978-80
Chisick, Andy, C, Villanova ... 1940-41
Christiansen, Marty, B, Minnesota ... 1940
Christman, Paul, QB, Missouri ... 1945-49
Ciccone, Ben, C, Duquesne ... 1942
Clancy, Sean, LB, Amherst ... 1979-80
Clark, Beryl, B, Oklahoma ... 1940
Clark, Bill, G, No college ... 1920
Clark, Charlie, G, Harvard ... 1924
Clark, Ernie, LB, Michigan State ... 1968
Clark, Randy, C, Northern Illinois ... 1980-81
Clatt, Corwin, B, Notre Dame ... 1948-49
Claypool, Ralph, C, Purdue ... 1925-26, 1928
Clayton, Ralph, WR, Michigan ... 1981
Clement, Johnny (Zero), B, Southern Methodist ... 1941
Cobb, Tom, T, Arkansas ... 1931
Cochran, John (Red), B, Wake Forest ... 1947-50
Coder, Ron, G, Penn State ... 1980
Coffee, Pat, B, Louisiana State ... 1937-38
Colbert, Rondy, DB, Lamar U. ... 1977
Colhouer, Jake, G, Oklahoma State ... 1946-48
Collier, Tim, CB, East Texas State ... 1980-81
Collins, George, C, Georgia ... 1978-81
Collins, Paul, B, Missouri ... 1945
Combs, Chris, TE, New Mexico ... 1980-81
Compton, Ogden, QB, Hardin-Simmons ... 1955
Conley, Steve, LB, Kansas ... 1972
Conoly, Bill, G, Texas ... 1946
Conrad, Bobby Joe, WR, Texas A&M ... 1958-68
Cook, Dave, B, Illinois ... 1934-36
Cook, Ed, G, Notre Dame ... 1958-65
Coomer, Joe, T, Stephen F. Austin ... 1947-49
Coppage, Al, E, Oklahoma ... 1940-42
Cosner, Don, B, Montana State ... 1939
Cotton, Barney, G, Nebraska ... 1980-81
Cowhig, Jerry, B, Notre Dame ... 1950
Crangle, Jack, B, Illinois ... 1923
Crass, Bill, B, Louisiana State ... 1937
Creighton, Milan, E, Arkansas ... 1931-37
Crenshaw, Willis, RB, Kansas State ... 1964-69
Criswell, Kirby, DE, Kansas ... 1980-81
Crittendon, John, E, Wayne State ... 1954
Cross, Billy, B, West Texas State ... 1951-53
Cross, Bobby, T, Stephen F. Austin ... 1958-59
Crow, John David, RB, Texas A&M ... 1958-64
Crow, Lindon, DB, USC ... 1955-57
Crowder, Earl, B, Oklahoma ... 1939
Crum, Bob, DE, Arizona ... 1974
Crump, Dwayne, DB, Fresno State ... 1973-76
Cuff, Ward, B, Marquette ... 1946
Culpepper, Ed, G, Alabama ... 1958-60
Cunningham, Eric, G, Penn State ... 1980
Cuozzo, Gary, QB, Virginia ... 1972
Cuppoletti, Bree, G, Oregon ... 1934-38
Curcillo, Tony, B, Ohio State ... 1953
Curran, Harry, B, Boston College ... 1920-21
Currivan, Don, E, Boston College ... 1943
Curzon, Harry, B, No college ... 1928

D

Daanen, Jerry, WR, Miami ... 1968-70
Daddio, Bill, E-K, Pittsburgh ... 1941-42
Dahms, Tom, T, San Diego State ... 1956
Davidson, Joe, G, Colgate ... 1928
Davis, Bill, T, Texas Tech ... 1940-41
Davis, Charlie, DT, Texas Christian ... 1975-79
Davis, Jerry, B, Southeastern Louisiana ... 1948-51
Davis, Ray, E, Howard, Alabama ... 1935
Davis, Ron, DE, Virginia State ... 1973
Dawson, Mike, DT, Arizona ... 1976-81
Day, Tom, G, North Carolina A&T ... 1960
DeCorrevant, Bill, B, Northwestern ... 1947-48
Delevan, Burt, T, Pacific ... 1955-56
DeMarco, Bob, C, Dayton ... 1961-69
DesJardien, Paul (Shorty), G, Chicago ... 1920
Deskin, Versil, E, Drake ... 1935-39
DeStefano, Fred, B, Northwestern ... 1924-25
Detwiler, Chuck, S, Utah State ... 1973
Dewell, Bill, E, Southern Methodist ... 1940-41, 1945-49
Dickson, Paul, DT, Baylor ... 1971
Diehl, Charlie, G, Idaho ... 1930-31
Dierdorf, Dan, G, Michigan ... 1971-81
Dimancheff, Boris (Babe), B, Purdue ... 1947-50
Dittrich, John, G, Wisconsin ... 1956
Dobler, Conrad, G, Wyoming ... 1972-77
Donckers, Bill, QB, San Diego State ... 1976-77
Doolan, Jack, B, Georgetown ... 1947-48
Dorris, Andy, DE, New Mexico State ... 1973
Douds, Forrest (Jap), T, Washington & Jefferson ... 1932
Dougherty, Phil, C, Santa Clara ... 1938
Dove, Bob, E, Notre Dame ... 1948-53
Dowell, Gwyn (Mule), B, Texas Tech ... 1935-36
Dowling, Pat, E, DePaul ... 1929
Doyle, Ted, E, Nebraska ... 1944
Driscoll, John (Paddy), B, Northwestern ... 1920-25
Driskill, Joe, DB, Northeastern Louisiana ... 1960-61
Drulis, Al, B, Temple ... 1945-46
Dugan, Len, C, Wichita State ... 1937-39
Duggan, Gil, T, Oklahoma ... 1942-43, 1945
Duggins, George, E, Purdue ... 1934
Duncum, Bobby, T, West Texas State ... 1968
Dunn, Joe (Red), B, Marquette ... 1925-26
Dunstan, Elwyn, T, Portland State ... 1938-39
Duren, Clarence, S, California ... 1973-76
Durko, John, E, Albright ... 1945

E

Ebli, Ray, E, Notre Dame ... 1942
Echols, Fate, T, Northwestern ... 1962-63
Eckl, Bob, T, Wisconsin ... 1945

Mel Gray

Jerry Groom

Pat Harder

Jim Hart

Ed Henke

E.J. Junior

Bill Koman

Edwards, Cid, RB, Tennessee State 1968-71
Egan, Dick, E, Wilmington 1920-23
Eggers, Doug, LB, South Dakota State................. 1958
Eikenberg, Charley, QB, Rice 1948
Elkins, Fait, B, Haskell 1929
Ellis, Walt (Speed), T, Detroit 1926-27
Ellstrom, Marvin (Swede), B, Oklahoma 1936
Ellzey, Charley, C, Southern Mississippi 1960-61
Elwell, Jack, E, Purdue 1962
Embree, Mel, E, Pepperdine........................... 1954
Emerson, Vernon, T, Minnesota-Duluth 1969-71
Engebretsen, Paul, G, Northwestern.................... 1933
Enich, Steve, G, Marquette 1945
Erickson, Hal, B, Washington & Jefferson............ 1925-28
Erickson, Mickey, C, Northwestern.................. 1930-31
Esser, Clarence, E, Wisconsin 1947
Etcheverry, Sam, QB, Denver 1961-62
Evans, Dick, E, Iowa 1941-42
Evans, Earl (Buck), T, Harvard 1925

F

Failing, Fred, G, Central J.C., Kansas.................. 1930
Fanucchi, Ledio, T, Fresno State 1954
Farmer, Ted, RB, Oregon............................... 1978
Farr, Miller, CB, Wichita State 1970-72
Faust, George, B, Minnesota 1939
Favron, Calvin, LB, Southeastern Louisiana.......... 1979-81
Ferry, Lou, T, Villanova.............................. 1951
Field, Doak, LB, Baylor 1981
Field, Harry, T, Oregon State....................... 1934-36
Fife, Ralph, G, Pittsburgh....................... 1942, 1945
Finn, Bernie, B, Holy Cross........................... 1932
Finnie, Roger, T, Florida A&M 1973-78
Finnin, Tom, T, Detroit............................... 1957
Fischer, Bill, T, Notre Dame........................ 1949-53
Fischer, Pat, CB, Nebraska 1961-67
Fisher, Ev, B, Santa Clara.......................... 1938-39
Fisher, Mike, WR, Baylor 1981
Fiske, Max, B, DePaul 1937
Fitzgibbon, Paul, B, Creighton 1928
Flanagan, Latham, E, Carnegie Tech 1931
Flenniken, Max, B, Geneva............................ 1930
Florence, Paul, E, Loyola, Illinois 1920
Floyd, John, WR, Northeastern Louisiana 1981
Folz, Art, B, No college 1923-25
Foster, Ralph, T, Oklahoma State 1945-46
Francis, Gene, B, Chicago 1926
Fritsch, Ernie, C, Detroit 1960
Fugler, Dick, T, Tulane 1954
Fuller, Frank, T, Kentucky.......................... 1959-62

G

Gainor, Charlie, E, North Dakota 1939
Gambrell, Billy, WR, South Carolina................. 1963-67
Garlich, Chris, LB, Missouri 1979
Gasparella, Joe, B, Notre Dame 1951
Gautt, Prentice, RB, Oklahoma 1961-67
Gay, Billy, B, Notre Dame 1951-52
Gehrke, Fred, B, Utah 1950
George, Steve, DT, Houston 1974
Geri, Joe, B, Georgia 1952
German, Jimmy, B, Centre 1940
Gersbach, Carl, LB, West Chester State................. 1976
Ghersanich, Vern, G, Auburn 1943
Gibbons, Austin, C, DePaul 1929
Giblin, Robert, DB, Houston 1977
Gilchrist, George, T, Tennessee State 1953
Gill, Randy, LB, San Jose State 1978
Gillen, John, LB, Illinois.............................. 1981
Gillette, Walker, WR, Richmond 1972-73
Gilliam, John, WR, South Carolina State............. 1969-71
Gillies, Fred, T, Cornell 1920-28
Gillis, Don, C, Rice 1958-61
Glassgow, Bill, B, Iowa 1931
Glick, Fred, DB, Colorado State 1959-60
Goble, Les, B, Alfred 1954-55
Goldberg, Marshall (Biggie), B, Pittsburgh .. 1939-40, 1946-48
Goldman, Sam, E, Howard 1948
Goldsberry, John, T, Indiana........................ 1949-50
Goode, Irv, C, Kentucky............................ 1962-71
Goodman, Aubrey, T, Chicago 1927
Goodspeed, Mark, T, Nebraska......................... 1980

Gordon, Bob, B, Tennessee 1958
Gordon, Lou, T, Illinois............................ 1930-35
Graham, Al, G, No college 1932-33
Granger, Charley, G, Southern U. 1961
Grant, Hugh (Ducky), B, St. Mary's, Cal. 1928
Gray, Ken, G, Howard Payne 1958-69
Gray, Mel, WR, Missouri............................ 1971-81
Gray, Tim, DB, Texas A&M 1975
Green, Roy, DB-WR, Henderson State 1979-81
Greene, Ed, E, Loyola, Chicago..................... 1926-27
Greene, Doug, DB, Texas A&I 1978
Greene, Frank, B, Tulsa.............................. 1934
Greene, Ken, DB, Washington State 1978-81
Greer, Curtis, DE, Michigan 1980-81
Griffin, Bob, C, Arkansas............................. 1961
Griffin, Jeff, CB, Utah................................ 1981
Griffith, Homer, B, USC 1934
Grigas, John, B, Holy Cross 1943-44
Groome, Jerry, C, Notre Dame 1951-55
Grosvernor, George, B, Colorado.................... 1936-37
Guglielmi, Ralph, QB, Notre Dame 1961

H

Hackbart, Dale, S, Wisconsin 1971-72
Hall, John, B, Texas Christian 1940-41, 1943
Hall, Ken, RB, Texas A&M............................. 1961
Halstrom, Bernie, B, Illinois........................ 1920-21
Hammack, Mal, RB, Florida 1955, 1957-66
Hammond, Gary, WR, Southern Methodist............. 1973-76
Handler, Phil, G, Texas Christian 1930-36
Hanke, Carl, E, Minnesota............................ 1924
Hanlon, Bob, B, Loras 1948
Hansen, Cliff, B, Luther 1933
Hanson, Homer, G, Kansas State.................... 1935-36
Harder, Pat, B-K, Wisconsin 1946-50
Hardy, Jim, QB, USC 1949-51
Hargrove, Jim, LB, Howard Payne.................... 1971-72
Harmon, Ham, C, Tulsa 1937
Harrell, Willard, RB, Pacific........................ 1978-81
Harris, Ike, WR, Iowa State 1975-77
Harrison, Reggie, RB, Cincinnati 1974
Hart, Jim, QB, Southern Illinois 1966-81
Hartle, Greg, LB, Newberry.......................... 1974-76
Hartong, George, G, Chicago 1924
Hartshorn, Larry, G, Kansas State 1955
Hatley, John, G, Sul Ross State 1954-55
Hauser, Art, G, Xavier 1959
Hayden, Leo, RB, Ohio State 1972-73
Healy, Chip, LB, Vanderbilt 1959-70
Heater, Don, RB, Montana Tech........................ 1972
Heidel, Jimmy, DB, Mississippi 1966
Henke, Ed, DE, USC 1961-63
Hennessey, Jerry, E, Santa Clara 1950-51
Henry, Steve, DB, Emporia State 1979-80
Heron, Fred, DT, San Jose State 1966-72
Hickman, Larry, B, Baylor 1959
Higgins, John, G, Trinity, Texas........................ 1941
Higgins, Tom, T, North Carolina 1953
Hill, Don, B, Stanford 1929
Hill, Irv, B, Trinity, Texas 1931-32
Hill, Jimmy, DB, Sam Houston State 1955-57, 1960-64
Hill, King, QB, Rice 1958-60, 1969
Hillebrand, Jerry, LB, Colorado 1967
Hinchman, Hub, B, Butler 1933-34
Hock, John, T, Santa Clara 1950
Hoel, Bob, G, Pittsburgh 1937-38
Hoey, George, DB, Michigan 1971
Hoffman, John, DE, Hawaii............................ 1972
Hogan, Tom, T, Detroit............................... 1926
Hogland, Doug, G, Oregon State..................... 1956-58
Hogue, Murrell, T, Centenary 1929
Holm, Bernie, B, Alabama............................ 1932
Holmer, Walt, B, Northwestern 1931-32
Horstmann, Roy, B, Purdue........................... 1934
Horween, Arnold, B, Harvard 1921-24
Horween, Ralph, B, Harvard 1921-23
Houghton, Jerry, T, Washington State 1951
Houser, John, G, Redlands............................ 1963
Huffman, Frank, G, Marshall........................ 1939-41
Hughes, Bernie, C, Oregon.......................... 1934-36
Hultz, George, DT, Southern Mississippi 1962
Hummel, Arnie, B, Lombard........................... 1927

Humphrey, Buddy, QB, Baylor 1963-65
Hurlburt, John, G, Chicago 1924-25
Husmann, Ed, G, Nebraska.................. 1953, 1956-59
Hust, Al, E, Tennessee............................... 1946
Hutchison, Chuck, G, Ohio State 1970-72
Hyatt, Freddie, WR, Auburn 1968-72

I

Illman, Ed, B, Montana 1928
Imhof, Martin, DE, San Diego State.................... 1972
Isaacson, Ted, T, Washington 1934-35
Ivy, Frank (Pop), E, Oklahoma 1940-42, 1945-47
Izo, George, QB, Notre Dame 1960

J

Jackson, Charley, B, Southern Methodist............... 1958
Jackson, Roland, RB, Rice 1962
Jacobs, Marv, T, No college 1948
Jagielski, Harry, T, Indiana 1956
Jankovich, Keever, E, Pacific 1963
Jennings, Jack, T, Ohio State 1950-57
Johnson, Al, B, Kentucky........................... 1939-41
Johnson, Charles, CB, Grambling...................... 1981
Johnson, Charley, QB, New Mexico State............ 1961-69
Johnson, Jimmy, B, Washington........................ 1946
Johnson, Ray, B, Denver 1940
Jones, Ben, B, Grove City 1927-28
Jones, Steve, RB, Duke 1974-78
Joyce, Don, T, Tulane.............................. 1951-53
Joyce, Terry, TE, Southern State, Missouri 1976-77
Junior, E.J., LB, Alabama 1981

K

Karras, Johnny, B, Illinois 1952
Karwales, Jack, E, Michigan 1947
Kasperek, Dick, C, Iowa State 1966-68
Kassel, Chuck, E, Illinois........................... 1929-33
Keane, Tom, B, West Virginia 1955
Kearney, Tim, LB, Northern Michigan 1976-81
Kearns, Tom, T, Miami 1946
Keithley, Gary, QB, Texas-El Paso 1973-75
Kellogg, Bill, B, Syracuse 1926
Kellogg, Clarence, B, St. Mary's, Cal................... 1936
Kellum, Marv, LB, Wichita State 1977
Kenneally, George, G, St. Bonaventure 1930
Keys, Brady, DB, Colorado State....................... 1968
Kichefski, Walt, E, Miami............................. 1944
Kiesling, Walt, G, St. Thomas, Minnesota........... 1929-33
Kiley, Roger, E, Notre Dame 1923
Kindle, Greg, T, Tennessee State.................... 1974-76
Kinek, George, B, Tulane............................. 1954
King, Andy (Rip), B, West Virginia 1923-24
King, Emmett, B, No college 1954
Kingery, Ellsworth, B, Tulane.......................... 1954
Klimek, Tony, E, Illinois............................ 1951-52
Klumb, John, E, Washington State................... 1939-40
Knafelc, Gary, E, Colorado 1954
Knight, Charlie, C, No college 1920-21
Knolla, John, B, Creighton 1942, 1945
Kochel, Mike, G, Fordham............................ 1939
Koegel, Warren, G, Penn State......................... 1973
Koehler, Bob, G, Northwestern...................... 1921-26
Koken, Mike, B, Notre Dame 1933
Koman, Bill, LB, North Carolina..................... 1959-67
Konovsky, Bob, G, Wisconsin....................... 1956-58
Kortas, Ken, DT, Louisville 1964
Krejci, Joe, E, Peru State, Nebraska 1934
Krueger, Rolf, DE, Texas A&M...................... 1969-71
Kuharich, Joe, G, Notre Dame.............. 1940-41, 1945
Kutner, Mal, E, Texas 1946-50
Kuzman, John, T, Fordham............................ 1941

L

Lach, Steve, B, Duke 1942
Ladd, Jim, E, Bowling Green 1954
LaFleur, Greg, TE, Louisiana State 1981
LaHood, Mike, G, Wyoming 1970
Lainhart, Porter, B, Washington State 1933
Lamb, Roy, B, Lombard 1926-27, 1933
Lane, Dick (Night Train), CB, Scottsbluff J.C. 1954-59
Lane, MacArthur, RB, Utah State 1968-71
Lange, Bill, G, Dayton 1954-55
Lange, Jim, E, Montana State......................... 1929

Stan Mauldin

Ernie McMillan

Dale Meinert

Wayne Morris

Jim Otis

Buster Ramsay

Sonny Randle

LaRosa, Paul, E, No college 1920-21
Larson, Fred, C, Notre Dame 1929
Larson, Lou, B, No college 1929
Larson, Paul, QB, California 1957
Latin, Jerry, RB, Northern Illinois 1975-78
Latourette, Chuck, DB-P, Rice 1967-68, 1970-71
Lauro, Lindy, B, Pittsburgh 1951
Lawrence, Jim, B, Texas Christian 1936-39
Ledbetter, Homer (Doc), B, Arkansas 1932-33
Lee, Bob, E, Minnesota 1968
Lee, Jeff, WR, Nebraska 1980
Lee, Monte, LB, Texas 1961
Lee, Oudious, DT, Nebraska 1980
Leggett, Dave, B, Ohio State 1955
Leonard, John, T, Indiana 1922-23
LeVeck, Jack, LB, Ohio 1973-74
Lewis, Mac, T, Iowa 1959
Lewis, Woodley, B, Oregon 1956-59
Liebel, Frank, E, Norwich 1948
Lillard, Joe, B, Oregon State 1932-33
Lind, Al, C, Northwestern 1936
Lindow, Al, B, Washington, Missouri 1945
Lipinski, Jim, T, Fairmont State 1950
Lipostad, Ed, G, Wake Forest 1952
Lisch, Rusty, QB, Notre Dame 1980-81
Little, Steve, P-K, Arkansas 1978-80
Loepfe, Dick, T, Wisconsin 1948-49
Logan, Chuck, E, Northwestern 1965, 1967-68
Lokanc, Joe, G, Northwestern 1941
Lomax, Neil, QB, Portland State 1981
Long, Dave, DE, Iowa 1966-68
Longo, Tom, DB, Notre Dame 1971
Lott, Thomas, RB, Oklahoma 1979
Love, Randy, RB, Houston 1979-81
Loyd, Mike, QB, Southern State, Missouri 1979-80
Lunceford, Dave, T, Baylor 1957
Lunz, Gerry, G, Marquette 1925-26
Lyman, Jeff, LB, Brigham Young 1972
Lynch, Lynn, G, Illinois 1951

M

Madden, Lloyd, B, Colorado Mines 1940
Maddock, Bob, G, Notre Dame 1942, 1946
Maeda, Chet, B, Colorado State 1946
Magulick, George, B, St. Francis 1944
Mahoney, Ike, B, Creighton 1925-28, 1931
Mallouf, Ray, B, Southern Methodist 1941, 1946-48
Malloy, Les, B, Loyola, La. 1931-33
Manges, Mark, QB, Maryland 1978
Mann, Dave, B, Oregon State 1955-57
Maple, Howie, B, Oregon State 1930
Marchibroda, Ted, QB, Detroit 1957
Marcontell, Ed, G, Lamar U 1967
Marelli, Ray, G, Notre Dame 1928
Markham, Dale, T, North Dakota 1981
Marotti, Lou, G, Toledo 1943-45
Marquardt, John, E, Illinois 1921
Marsh, Doug, TE, Michigan 1980-81
Martin, Caleb, T, Louisiana Tech 1947
Martin, Glen, B, Southern Illinois 1932
Martin, John, B, Oklahoma 1941-44
Mason, Joel, E, Western Michigan 1939
Masters, Walt, B, Pennsylvania 1943-44
Matson, Ollie, RB, San Francisco 1952-58
Mauldin, Stan, T, Texas 1946-48
May, Bill, B, Louisiana State 1937-38
Maynard, Don, WR, Texas-El Paso 1973
Mays, Stafford, DE, Washington 1980-81
McBride, Charlie, B, Washington State 1936
McCarthy, John, B, St. Francis 1944
McCullough, Hugh, B, Oklahoma 1940-41
McCusker, Jim, T, Pittsburgh 1958
McDermott, Lloyd, T, Kentucky 1950-51
McDole, Ron, DE, Nebraska 1961
McDonald, Mike, LB, Catawba 1976
McDonnell, Mickey, B, No college 1925-30
McDonough, Coley, B, Dayton 1939, 1944
McDowell, John, T, St. John's, Minnesota 1966
McElwain, Bill, B, Northwestern 1924, 1926
McFarland, Jim, TE, Nebraska 1970-74
McGee, Bob, T, Santa Clara 1938
McGee, Mike, G, Duke 1960-62
McGill, Mike, LB, Notre Dame 1971-72
McGraw, Mike, LB, Wyoming 1976
McHan, Lamar, QB, Arkansas 1954-58
McInerny, Arnie, C, Notre Dame 1920-27
McInnis, Hugh, E, Southern Mississippi 1960-62
McIntyre, Jeff, LB, Arizona State 1980
McMahon, Byron, G, Cornell 1923
McMillan, Ernie, T, Illinois 1961-74
McNally, Frank, C, St. Mary's, Cal. 1931-34
McNulty, Paul, E, Notre Dame 1924-25
McPhee, Frank, E, Princeton 1955
McQuarters, Ed, DT, Oklahoma 1965
Meggyesy, Dave, LB, Syracuse 1963-69
Mehringer, Pete, T, Kansas 1934-36
Meillinger, Steve, E, Kentucky 1961
Meinert, Dale, LB, Oklahoma State 1958-67
Melinkovich, Mike, DE, Gray Harbor JC 1965-66
Memmelaar, Dave, G, Wyoming 1959-61
Mergen, Mike, T, San Francisco 1952
Merkovsky, Elmer, T, Pittsburgh 1944
Mestnik, Frank, RB, Marquette 1960-61
Metcalf, Terry, RB, Long Beach State 1973-77
Method, Russ, B, No college 1929
Mikulak, Mike, B, Oregon 1934-36
Miller, Milford (Dub), G, Chadron State, Nebraska 1936-37
Miller, Terry, LB, Illinois 1971-74
Mitchell, Stump, RB, Citadel 1981
Moe, Hal, B, Oregon State 1933
Mohardt, Johnny, B, Notre Dame 1922-23
Monahan, Regis, G, Ohio State 1939
Monfort, Avery, B, New Mexico 1941
Montgomery, Bill, B, Louisiana State 1946
Montgomery, Ralph (Sully), T, Centre 1923
Mooney, Jim, T, Georgetown 1935
Moore, Bill, B, Loyola, La. 1932
Moran, Francis (Hap), B, Grinnell 1927
Morgan, Bob, T, Maryland 1954
Moore, Bobby (later played as
Ahmad Rashad), WR, Oregon 1972-73
Morris, Wayne, RB, Southern Methodist 1976-81
Morrow, Bob, G, Illinois Wesleyan 1941-43
Morrow, John, G, Kearney State 1937-38
Moss, Eddie, RB, Southeastern Missouri 1973-76
Moynihan, Tim, C, Notre Dame 1932-33
Muellner, Bill, E, DePaul 1937
Mullen, Tom, G, Southwest Missouri 1978
Mullen, Verne, E, Illinois 1927
Mulleneaux, Lee, C, Arizona 1938
Mulligan, Wayne, C, Clemson 1969-73
Murphy, Bill, G, Washington, Missouri 1940-41
Murphy, Jim, B, St. Thomas, Minnesota 1928
Murphy, Tom, B, Arkansas 1934
Murrell, Bill, TE, Winston-Salem 1979

N

Nagel, Ray, QB, UCLA 1953
Nagel, Ross, T, St. Louis 1942
Nagler, Gern, E, Santa Clara 1953, 1955-58
Neacy, Clem, E, Colgate 1928
Neill, Jim, B, Texas Tech 1939
Neils, Steve, LB, Minnesota 1974-80
Nelson, Lee, S, Florida State 1976-81
Nesbitt, Dick, B, Drake 1933
Nevers, Ernie, B-K, Stanford 1929-31
Neuman, Bob, E, Illinois Wesleyan 1934-36
Nichelini, Al, B, St. Mary's, Cal. 1935-36
Nichols, Ham, G, Rice 1947-49
Nisbet, Dave, E, Washington 1933
Nofsinger, Terry, QB, Utah 1965-66
Nolan, Dick, B, Maryland 1958
Nolan, Earl, T, Arizona 1937-38
Norman, Bob, C, No college 1945
Norton, Jerry, DB-P, Southern Methodist 1959-61
Nussbaumer, Bob, DB, Michigan 1949-50

O

Oates, Brad, T, Brigham Young 1976-77, 1979-80
O'Brien, Dave, G, Boston College 1966-67
O'Connor, Dan, G, Georgetown 1920-24
O'Donoghue, Neil, K, Auburn 1980-81
Ogden, Ray, TE, Alabama 1965-66
Ogle, Rick, LB, Colorado 1971
Okoniewski, Steve, DT, Montana 1976
Olerich, Dave, LB, San Francisco 1969-70
Oliver, Clarence, CB, San Diego State 1973
Olson, Carl, T, UCLA 1942
Olszewski, Johnny, RB, California 1953-57
Osborne, Richard, TE, Texas A&M 1979
Otis, Jim, RB, Ohio State 1973-78
Owens, Don, DT, Southern Mississippi 1960-63
Owens, Luke, DT, Kent State 1958-65
Owens, Marv, WR, San Diego State 1973

P

Palmer, Scott, DT, Texas 1972
Panciera, Don, B, San Francisco 1952
Panfil, Ken, T, Purdue 1959-62
Pangle, Hal, B, Oregon State 1935-38
Pappio, Joe, B, Haskell 1930
Pardonner, Paul, B, Purdue 1934-35
Paremore, Bob, RB, Florida A&M 1963-64
Parish, Don, LB, Stanford 1970-72
Parker, Raymond (Buddy), B, Centenary 1937-43
Parker, Joe, E, Texas 1946-47
Parris, Gary, TE, Florida State 1979-80
Pasquariello, Ralph, B, Villanova 1951-52
Pasquesi, Tony, T, Notre Dame 1955-57
Patulski, Walt, DE, Notre Dame 1977
Paul, Don, DB, Washington State 1950-53
Pearson, Bert, C, Kansas State 1935-36
Pelfrey, Ray, E, Eastern Kentucky 1952
Perko, John, G, Minnesota 1944
Person, Ara, TE, Morgan State 1972
Perry, Gerry, K, California 1960-62
Peters, Forest (Frosty), B, Illinois 1932
Peters, Volney, T, USC 1952-53
Peterson, Ike, B, Gonzaga 1935
Petrovich, George, T, Texas 1949-50
Phillips, Rod, RB, Jackson State 1979-80
Philpott, Dean, B, Fresno State 1958
Pierce, Don, C, Kansas 1943
Pisarkiewicz, Steve, QB, Missouri 1977-79
Pittman, Charlie, RB, Penn State 1970
Plasman, Dick, E, Vanderbilt 1946-47
Plummer, Tony, DB, Pacific 1970
Plunkett, Art, T, Nevada-Las Vegas 1981
Pollard, Bob, DE, Weber State 1978-81
Polofsky, Gordon, G, Tennessee 1952-54
Polsfoot, Fran, E, Washington State 1950-52
Poole, Jim, E, Mississippi 1945
Popa, Eli, B, Illinois 1952
Popovich, John, B, St. Vincent 1944
Popovich, Milt, B, Montana 1938-42
Potteiger, Earl, B, Ursinus 1921
Provost, Ted, DB, Ohio State 1971
Psaltis, Jim, B, USC 1953, 1955
Puplis, Andy, B, Notre Dame 1943
Purdin, Cal, B, Tulsa 1943
Putman, Earl, C, Arizona State 1957

R

Rabold, Mike, G, Indiana 1960
Radford, Bruce, DE, Grambling 1981
Ramey, Jim, DE, Kentucky 1979
Ramsey, Garrard (Buster), G, William & Mary 1946-51
Ramsey, Knox, G, William & Mary 1950-51
Ramsey, Ray, B, Bradley 1950-53
Ramson, Eason, TE, Washington State 1978
Randle, Sonny, WR, Virginia 1959-66
Randolph, Clare, C, Indiana 1930
Rankin, Walt, B, Texas Tech 1941, 1943, 1945-47
Ranspot, Keith, E, Southern Methodist 1940
Rashad, Ahmad (played as
Bobby Moore), WR, Oregon 1972-73
Ravensburg, Bob, E, Indiana 1948-49
Reaves, Ken, S, Norfolk State 1974-77
Redmond, Tom, DE, Vanderbilt 1960-65
Reed, Joe, B, Louisiana State 1937, 1939
Rexer, Freeman, E, Tulane 1943, 1945
Reynolds, Bill, B, Mississippi 1945
Reynolds, Bob, T, Bowling Green 1963-71, 1973
Reynolds, John, C, Baylor 1937
Reynolds, M.C. (Mack), QB, Louisiana State 1958-59
Rhea, Floyd, G, Oregon 1943
Ribble, Loran (Babe), G, Hardin-Simmons 1933

Johnny Roland

Bob Rowe

Duke Slater

Larry Stallings

Don Stonesifer

Jerry Stovall

Roger Wehrli

Richards, Perry, E, Detroit 1959-60
Richardson, John, DT, UCLA 1972-73
Risk, Ed, B, Purdue 1932
Risvold, Ray, B, St. Edward's, Texas 1927-28
Rivers, Jamie, LB, Bowling Green 1968-73
Roach, John, QB, Southern Methodist 1956, 1959-60
Roach, Rollin, B, Texas Christian 1927
Robb, Joe, DE, Texas Christian 1961-67
Robbins, Jack, B, Arkansas 1938-39
Roberts, Hal, P, Houston 1974
Robinson, Jack, T, Northeastern Missouri 1936-37
Robl, Hal, B, Oshkosh State 1945
Robnett, Marshall, G, Texas A&M 1943, 1945
Rogers, Glynn, G, Texas Christian 1939
Rogge, George, E, Iowa 1931-33
Roland, Johnny, RB, Missouri 1966-72
Romanik, Steve, QB, Villanova 1953-54
Rooney, Bill, C, No college 1929
Rooney, Cobb, E, No college 1929-30
Root, Jim, QB, Miami, Ohio 1953, 1956
Rose, Gene, DB, Wisconsin 1929-32
Rosema, Rocky, LB, Michigan 1968-71
Rowe, Bob, DT, Western Michigan 1967-75
Roy, Frank, G, Utah 1966
Rozier, Bob, DE, California 1979
Rucinski, Eddie, E, Indiana 1943-46
Rudolph, Council, DE, Kentucky State 1973-75
Rundquist, Elmer, T, Illinois 1922
Rushing, Marion, LB, Southern Illinois 1959, 1962-65
Russell, Doug, B, Kansas State 1934-39
Ryan, Jim, B, Notre Dame 1924
Rydzewski, Frank, T, Notre Dame 1921

S

Sabados, Andy, G, Citadel 1939-40
Sachs, Len, E, Loyola, Chicago 1920-23, 1925
Sagely, Floyd, E, Arkansas 1957
Sanders, Lonnie, DB, Michigan State 1968-69
Sandifer, Dan, B, Louisiana State 1953
Sanford, Leo, C, Louisiana Tech 1951-57
Sarboe, Phil, B, Washington State 1934-36
Sarringhaus, Paul, B, Ohio State 1946
Sauls, Mac, DB, Southwest Texas State 1968-69
Scales, Hurles, DB, North Texas State 1974
Scanlon, John, B, DePaul 1921
Scardine, Carmen, B, No college 1932
Schleicher, Maury, LB, Penn State 1959
Schmidt, George, E, Lewis 1953
Schmiesing, Joe, DE, New Mexico State 1968-71
Schneider, Herman (Biff), B, Iowa 1940
Schultz, Eberle, G, Oregon State 1944
Schwall, Vic, B, Northwestern 1947-50
Schwartz, Don, S, Washington State 1981
Schwartz, Elmer, B, Washington State 1932
Schwenk, Wilson (Bud), B, Washington, Missouri 1942
Seabron, Thomas, LB, Michigan 1980
Sears, Jim, DB, USC 1954, 1957-58
Seibold, Champ, T, Wisconsin 1942
Self, Clarence, B, Wisconsin 1949
Semes, Bernie, B, Duquesne 1944
Seno, Frank, B, George Washington 1945-46
Sensibaugh, Mike, S, Ohio State 1976-78
Severson, Jeff, CB, Long Beach State 1976-77
Shaw, Bob, E, Ohio State 1950
Shaw, Dennis, QB, San Diego State 1974-75
Shaw, Jesse, G, USC 1931
Shelby, Willie, RB, Alabama 1978
Shelley, Dex, B, Texas 1932
Shenefelt, Paul, T, Manchester 1934-35
Shirk, John, E, Oklahoma 1940
Shivers, Roy, RB, Utah State 1966-72
Shook, Fred, C, Texas Christian 1941
Shy, Don, RB, San Diego State 1973
Sikora, Mike, G, Oregon 1952
Silas, Sam, DT, Southern Illinois 1963-67
Silvestri, Carl, DB, Wisconsin 1965
Simas, Bill, B, St. Mary's, Cal. 1932-33
Simmons, Dave, LB, Georgia Tech 1965-66
Simmons, Jack, C, Detroit 1951-56
Simons, Keith, DT, Minnesota 1978-79
Sitko, Emil, B, Notre Dame 1951-52
Siwek, Mike, DT, Western Michigan 1970
Slater, Fred (Duke), T, Iowa 1926-31
Sloan, Bonnie, DT, Austin Peay 1973
Sloan, Dwight, QB, Arkansas 1938
Smith, Bill, E-K, Washington 1934-39
Smith, Charlie, B, Georgia 1947
Smith, George (Locomotive), B, Villanova 1943
Smith, Jackie, TE, Northwestern Louisiana 1963-77
Smith, Perry, DB, Colorado State 1977-79
Smith, Russ, G, Illinois 1923
Smith, Wilfred, E, DePaul 1923-25
Snowden, Cal, DE, Indiana 1969-70
Sortun, Rick, G, Washington 1964-69
Southard, Tommy, WR, Furman 1978
Speegle, Cliff, C, Oklahoma 1945
Spence, Julian, B, Sam Houston State 1956
Spencer, Maurice, DB, North Carolina Central 1974
Spiller, Phil, DB, California State-Los Angeles 1967
Spinks, Jack, G, Alcorn State 1953
Springsteen, Bill, E, Lehigh 1927-28
Stacy, Billy, DB, Mississippi State 1959-63
Staggs, Jeff, LB, San Diego State 1972-73
Stallings, Larry, LB, Georgia Tech 1963-76
Stegent, Larry, RB, Texas A&M 1971
Steger, Pete, B, No college 1921
Stein, Bill, C, Fordham 1927-28
Steinbach, Larry, T, St. Thomas 1931-33
Stennett, Fred, B, St. Mary's, Cal. 1932
Stewart, Vaughan, C, Alabama 1943
Stief, Dave, WR, Portland State 1978-81
Stieve, Terry, G, Wisconsin 1981
Stokes, Lee (Dixie), Centenary 1943
Stone, Ken, DB, Vanderbilt 1977-80
Stonesifer, Don, E, Northwestern 1951-56
Stovall, Jerry, DB, Louisiana State 1963-71
Strader, Norman (Red), B, St. Mary's, Cal. 1927
Strausbaugh, Jim, B, Ohio State 1946
Stringer, Scott, DB, California 1974
Strofolino, Mike, LB, Villanova 1966-68
Stuessy, Mel, T, St. Edward's, Texas 1926
Sugar, Leo, DE, Purdue 1954-60
Suminski, Dave, G, Wisconsin 1953
Summerall, Pat, K-E, Arkansas 1953-57
Sutch, George, B, Temple 1946
Svoboda, Bill, LB, Tulane 1950-53
Swanson, Evar, E, Lombard 1925-27
Swider, Larry, P, Pittsburgh 1980
Swistowicz, Mike, B, Notre Dame 1950
Symank, John, DB, Florida 1963
Szot, Walt, T, Bucknell 1946-48

T

Taylor, Jim, LB, Baylor 1957-58
Taylor, Mike, T, USC 1973
Teeuws, Len, T, Tulane 1954-57
Thaxton, Jim, TE, Tennessee State 1978
Thomas, Earl, WR, Houston 1974-75
Thomas, Jim, G, Oklahoma 1939
Thomas, Ralph, E, San Francisco 1952
Thompson, Harry, G, UCLA 1955
Thompson, Norm, DB, Utah 1971-76
Thornton, Bill (Thunder), RB, Nebraska 1963-65, 1967
Thurbon, Bob, B, Pittsburgh 1944
Tilley, Pat, WR, Louisiana Tech 1976-81
Times, Ken, DT, Southern U. 1981
Tinsley, Gaynell, E, Louisiana State 1937-38, 1940
Tinsley, Jess, T, Louisiana State 1929-33
Tipton, Howard, B, USC 1933-37
Tolbert, Jim, S, Lincoln, Missouri 1973-75
Tonelli, Mario, B, Notre Dame 1940, 1945
Toogood, Charley, G, Nebraska 1957
Toscani, Frank (Bud), B, St. Mary's, Cal. 1932
Towns, Bobby, DB, Georgia 1960
Townsend, Curtis, LB, Arkansas 1978
Tracey, John, LB, Texas A&M 1959-60
Trays, Jim, B, Penn State 1925
Trippi, Charley, B, Georgia 1947-55
Triplett, Bill, RB, Miami, Ohio 1962-63, 1965-66
Triplett, Wally, B, Penn State 1952-53
Tripucka, Frank, QB, Notre Dame 1950-52
Tubbs, Jerry, LB, Oklahoma 1957-58
Turner, Herschel, G, Kentucky 1964-65
Tyler, Pete, B, Hardin-Simmons 1937-38

U

Ucovich, Mitch, T, San Jose State 1945
Ulrich, Chuck, T, Illinois 1954-58
Underwood, Jack, G, No college 1929
Upshaw, Marvin, DT, Trinity, Texas 1976

V

Van Galder, Tim, QB, Iowa State 1972
Vanzo, Fred, B, Northwestern 1941
Vaughan, Charles (Pug), B, Tennessee 1936
Vesser, John, E, Idaho 1927, 1930-31
Vodicka, Joe, B, No college 1945
Vokaty, Otto, B, Heidelberg 1933
Volok, Bill, G, Tulsa 1934-39

W

Wager, Clint, E, St. Mary's, Minnesota 1943, 1945
Wagstaff, Jim, B, Idaho State 1959
Waldron, Austin, G, Gonzaga 1927
Walker, Chuck, DE-DT, Duke 1964-72
Wallner, Fred, G, Notre Dame 1951-52, 1954-55
Washington, Eric, DB, Texas-El Paso 1972-73
Watford, Jerry, E, Alabama 1953-54
Watkins, Bobby, B, Ohio State 1958
Watt, Walt, B, Miami 1945
Weaver, Charles (Buck), G, Chicago 1930
Weber, Chuck, LB, West Chester State 1956-58
Wedel, Dick, G, Wake Forest 1948
Wehrli, Roger, CB, Missouri 1969-81
Weller, Ray (Bub), T, Nebraska 1926-27
Wendt, Ken, G, Marquette 1932
West, Jeff, P, Cincinnati 1975
West, Stan, G, Oklahoma 1956-57
West, Willie, DB, Oregon 1960-61
Whalen, Bill, T, No college 1920-24
Wham, Tom, E, Furman 1949-51
Wheeler, Ernie, B, North Dakota State 1939, 1942
Wheeler, Ted, G, West Texas State 1967-68
White, Paul, RB, Texas-El Paso 1970-71
White, Ray, LB, Syracuse 1975-77
Whitman, S.J., B, Tulsa 1951-53
Wicks, Bob, WR, Utah State 1972
Widerquist, Chet, T, Washington & Jefferson 1926-28
Willard, Ken, RB, North Carolina 1974
Williams, Bobby, DB, Central Oklahoma 1966-67
Williams, Clyde, T, Southern U. 1967-71
Williams, Dave, WR, Washington 1967-71
Williams, Eric, LB, USC 1977-81
Williams, Gerard, CB, Langston, Oklahoma 1980
Williams, Herb, S, Southern U. 1981
Williams, Jake, T, Texas Christian 1929-33
Williams, Rex, C, Texas Tech 1940
Willingham, Larry, DB, Auburn 1971-72, 1976
Wilson, Bill, E, Gonzaga 1935-37
Wilson, Gordon, C, Texas-El Paso 1942-43, 1945
Wilson, Larry, S, Utah 1960-72
Wilson, Mike, DB, Western Illinois 1969
Withrow, Cal, C, Kentucky 1974
Wood, Bob, T, Alabama 1940
Wood, Mike, P-K, Southeast Missouri 1978-79
Woodeschick, Tom, RB, West Virginia 1972
Woodruff, Jim, E, Pittsburgh 1926
Woodson, Abe, DB, Illinois 1965-66
Woolsey, Rolly, DB, Boise State 1978
Wortman, Keith, G, Nebraska 1976-81
Wright, Nate, DB, San Diego State 1969-70
Wright, Steve, T, Alabama 1972
Wutkis, Al, C, Duquesne 1944
Wyche, Sam, QB, Furman 1976

Y

Yablonski, Ventan, B, Columbia 1948-51
Yanowski, Ron, DE, Kansas State 1971-80
Yarr, Tom, C, Notre Dame 1933
Yeisley, Don, E, No college 1927-28
Young, Bob, G, Howard Payne 1972-79

Z

Zelencik, Frank, T, Oglethorpe 1939
Zimny, Bob, T, Indiana 1945-49
Zoia, Clyde, G, Notre Dame 1920-23
Zontini, Lou, B, Notre Dame 1940-41
Zook, John, DE, Kansas 1976-79

SAN DIEGO CHARGERS

1959 The Los Angeles Chargers were one of the original six teams as the American Football League was born August 14. Hotel magnate Barron Hilton formed the Chargers. Play was to begin in 1960, with the Chargers to use the Los Angeles Memorial Coliseum. Frank Leahy, legendary former coach of Notre Dame, signed to become general manager. Although Los Angeles already had one pro football team, the National Football League Rams, Hilton and his backers were confident the town could support another. Gerald Courtney won a trip to Mexico after submitting "Chargers" in a name-the-team contest.

1960 Sid Gillman, who coached the Rams for five years, was signed to a three-year contract as the first coach of the Chargers, January 7. A special tryout camp was conducted in Burbank, and 207 candidates showed up, April 9. General manager Leahy resigned due to ill health, July 1. Gillman took over the additional duties of general manager, July 9. In the team's first preseason game, Paul Lowe, who had called the club and offered his services, returned the opening kickoff 105 yards for a touchdown, August 6. The Chargers won the game 27-7 over the New York Titans, before 27,778 in the Coliseum. A few weeks later they edged Dallas 21-20 in the first league game, September 10. With Gillman choreographing a flashy, stylish offense, the Chargers won the Western Division championship. But only 9,928 people showed up to watch them defeat Denver 41-33 to clinch the title. Their final regular season record was 10-4.

1961 In the first AFL Championship Game, the Chargers were beaten 24-16 by the Houston Oilers and George Blanda in Houston, January 1. Those numbers weren't nearly as discouraging to Hilton as the team's financial statement. He found he had lost more than $900,000. At this point the city of San Diego, sensing Hilton's plight, rallied to form committees and sell tickets and boost enthusiasm for the AFL. Hilton was impressed. He applied for and was granted permission to move his team to San Diego, where it would play in an enlarged, 34,000-seat facility, Balboa Stadium, February 10. On a 93-degree August afternoon, the Chargers made their debut in their new home, beating Houston 27-14 before 12,304. The team logo, the lightning bolt seen on players' helmets, seemed to fit this club, with smooth quarterback Jack Kemp, the dangerous breakaway runner Lowe, and a solid collection of talent, particularly at the skilled positions. San Diego began to respond to the show. A crowd of 33,788 turned out to see the Chargers defeat the Dallas Texans 24-14 for their eleventh win of the season and their fifteenth straight overall. They won the Western Division title again, but again couldn't handle Houston in the AFL Championship Game, losing a tough, defensive struggle 10-3 before 29,556 in Balboa Stadium, December 24.

1962 Coached by Gillman, a West team featuring 11 Chargers, defeated the East 47-27 in the first AFL All-Star Game before 20,973 in Balboa Stadium. San Diego ends Dave Kocourek and Don Norton each caught touchdown passes. Perhaps the most important draft in the history of the franchise brought in two players who would have a profound effect on this team, wide receiver Lance Alworth from Arkansas and quarterback John Hadl from Kansas. Kemp, nursing an injured throwing hand, was placed on the waiver list and claimed by Buffalo for $100. Groping without an experienced leader and with 23 players who missed two or more games because of injuries, the Chargers finished their poorest season at 4-10.

1963 The West defeated the East 21-14 in the second AFL All-Star Game in Balboa Stadium. Chargers' defensive end Earl Faison was named player of the game. Gillman convinced Tobin Rote, the former National Football League quarterback with Green Bay and Detroit, to sign with the Chargers after he quit Toronto of the Canadian League. Hilton and his father, Conrad, decided to sell one-third interest in the team to San Diego businessmen John Mabee, George Pernicano, Kenneth Swanson, and James Copley, and M.L. Bengston of Los Angeles. Gillman moved the club's training camp to Rough Acres, a desert outpost 40 miles out of town. The Chargers came out of that camp fit and healthy, and, with Alworth and a devastating defensive line led by Faison and 315-pound Ernie Ladd, the team ran up an 11-3 record, topping it off with a 58-20 victory over Denver.

1964 The Chargers climaxed the best season in their history by burying Boston 51-10 before 30,127 in Balboa Stadium to win the AFL championship, January 5. Keith Lincoln, the exceptional all-around back from Washington State, rushed for 206 yards, including touchdown runs of 67 and 56 yards, caught six passes and accounted for 349 yards overall. He was voted the player of the game. Afterward, Otto Graham, the former Cleveland Browns' star and NFL coach, said, "If the Chargers could play the best in the NFL, I'd have to pick the Chargers. They have the linemen and everything to go with them." Lincoln capped his greatest year by winning the honor as the outstanding offensive player as the West defeated the East 27-24 in the AFL All-Star Game two weeks later. The Chargers opened the 1964 regular season with a win over Houston, then lost three straight. Rote had a sore arm, so Gillman moved Hadl in to start his first game in Boston. Hadl responded by completing 17 of 29 passes for 229 yards and three touchdowns in a 26-17 victory. The club established a San Diego attendance record when 34,865 saw the Chargers lose to Buffalo 27-24, November 26. A 38-3 rout of the New York Jets made it eight wins for the year and clinched a fourth Western Division championship. Alworth, who was considered the best pass receiver in pro football, was injured and missed the AFL title game in Buffalo. And after he sparked the first San Diego scoring drive in that game, Lincoln also went down. Without two of their most prominent weapons, the Chargers were beaten 20-7 by the Bills at War Memorial Stadium, December 26.

1965 Lincoln led the West to a 38-14 victory over the East in the AFL All-Star Game and again was voted the outstanding offensive player. Gillman suddenly began to have troubles at the bargaining table. Lincoln and linebacker Frank Buncom became stubborn holdouts. Faison and Ladd both announced their intentions of playing out their options. Ladd was fined, suspended, and finally reinstated. Construction of a $28 million San Diego Stadium in the heart of Mission Valley was authorized by a 73 percent "yes" vote in a special municipal election. Official groundbreaking ceremonies were held in Mission Valley to start work on the $28 million, 50,000-seat San Diego Stadium. Lowe and Alworth both had big years, finishing one-two in the balloting by AFL players for player of the year. The Chargers led the league from opening day, although Oakland and Kansas City made it interesting. A 9-2-3 record was enough, however, although Buffalo was there to spoil things again in the AFL title game, this time 23-0 at Balboa Stadium, December 26.

1966 Linebacker Buncom survived an early injury to become the most valuable defensive player as the AFL all-stars defeated Buffalo 30-19. Alworth scored two touchdowns on Joe Namath passes and Lowe ran for another. In the wake of the new merger

agreement between the NFL and AFL, the Chargers and Los Angeles Rams signed a three-year preseason contract for San Diego Stadium. A group of 21 business executives, headed by Eugene Klein and Sam Schulman of Beverly Hills, purchased the Chargers for $10 million. Klein and Schulman became general partners with Klein replacing Hilton as club president and Schulman taking over as chairman of the board. Barron and Conrad Hilton retained a substantial interest in the team. James Copley, San Diego newspaper publisher, and George Pernicano, restaurant owner, retained limited interests. Gillman was signed to a new five-year contract as coach and general manager. Hadl had his best season, throwing for 2,846 yards and 23 touchdowns, and Alworth made 73 receptions for 1,383 yards and 13 scores. The club finished 7-6-1, however, failing to win the Western Division for the first time since 1962.

1967 San Diego Stadium was dedicated as 45,988 fans looked on, August 20. Playing their first National Football League opponent that night, the Chargers were beaten 38-17 by Detroit in a preseason game. A week later, in their first confrontation with their southern California rivals, the Los Angeles Rams, the Chargers were whipped 50-7. San Diego opened the regular season with a flourish, however, going 5-0-1 and eventually ran its record to 8-1-1. But four straight losses dropped the Chargers to third place for the second year in a row.

1968 In a memorable preseason game, the Chargers beat the Rams 35-13 behind John Hadl's two touchdown passes and 302 yards, August 24. Getting off to another fast start, San Diego upset Oakland, the defending AFL champion, 23-14. Alworth caught nine passes for 182 yards to hand the Raiders their first loss at home in three years. Once again, an 8-2 start was spoiled by three losses in the final four games as the Chargers finished third in the AFL Western Division.

1969 The club moved its training camp facilities from Escondido to the University of California at Irvine, 90 miles north of San Diego. The Chargers opened the regular season with two losses on the road, but when they returned home a record crowd of 54,042 was in San Diego Stadium to see them play Joe Namath and the New York Jets. The Chargers won 34-27 as Gary Garrison caught 10 passes for 188 yards and two touchdowns. Gillman announced his retirement from coaching because of a stomach ulcer and chest hernia, November 10. He said he would continue as general manager. Offensive backfield coach Charlie Waller was appointed head coach and the team finished the year 8-6 and in third place for the fourth consecutive year. In the final week against Buffalo, Alworth caught a pass in his ninety-sixth consecutive game to break the pro record of Don Hutson, who was present in San Diego for congratulatory ceremonies. Alworth led the AFL in pass receptions with 68, and running back Dickie Post led the league in rushing with 873 yards.

1970 In the final American Football League All-Star Game, Hadl won the most valuable player award, helping the West beat the East 26-3 in Houston. The highlight of the Chargers' season was a 27-10 win over the Browns at Cleveland before 80,047, the largest crowd ever to see San Diego play, November 1. But the team struggled through its first losing season in eight years, although, once again, it finished third in its division. After the 5-6-3 finish, a reorganization was announced, with Gillman coming back as head coach and Waller staying on as offensive coach, December 20.

1971 Harland Svare was named general manager. Alworth was traded to Dallas for tight end Pettis Norman, defensive tackle Ron East, and tackle Tony Liscio. Klein announced Gillman's resignation "by mutual consent," November 22. Svare, who formerly coached the Rams, was named coach. A record San Diego Stadium crowd of 54,505 saw the Chargers upset Minnesota 30-14, then follow with a 45-17 rout of Denver. In the season's final game, however, San Diego lost to Houston 49-33.

1972 Svare began a series of major trades by dealing for defensive end David (Deacon) Jones of the Rams, in a transaction that involved three other players and three high draft choices. Svare changed the complexion of the club in a 12-hour trading session, acquiring running back Duane Thomas from Dallas, linebacker Tim Rossovich from Philadelphia, and defensive tackle Dave Costa from Denver, July 30. After much controversy, Thomas never played for the Chargers. Following a 2-1-1 start, the Chargers lost 8 of their last 10 games to finish 4-9-1 and in last place in the AFC Western Division. Mike Garrett gained 59 yards in the final game to finish with 1,031 yards and become the only pro player to gain 1,000 with two different teams. He had surpassed 1,000 with Kansas City in 1967.

1973 Heisman Trophy winner Johnny Rodgers was the Chargers' top draft choice, but the Nebraska running back decided to sign with Montreal of the Canadian Football League. Klein announced the acquisition of all-time great quarterback Johnny Unitas. "He's just the guy to run the offense we want here," said Svare. In the second part of that three-team deal, San Diego sent Hadl to Los Angeles for defensive lineman Coy Bacon and running back Bob Thomas. Unitas completed a 30-yard pass to Mike Garrett to go over 40,000 yards in his career. In Pittsburgh, in the fourth game of the year, a back injury that had plagued Unitas was aggravated and he was rendered almost immobile. The Steelers built a 38-0 halftime lead and rookie Dan Fouts took over at quarterback in the third quarter. Fouts remained there for most of the rest of the season, with Unitas playing in a total of five games and ending his long pro career. Offensive coordinator Bob Schnelker was fired in midseason. Svare announced his resignation as head coach but said he would remain as general manager, November 5. Ron Waller, special teams coach, was appointed interim head coach.

1974 Tommy Prothro, formerly of UCLA and the Los Angeles Rams, was appointed the Chargers' new coach. Prothro immediately began overhauling the team, trading Deacon Jones and Walt Sweeney to Washington to start the changes. Prothro's first Chargers' training camp at the new United States International University site was interrupted by picketing veterans who were striking as members of the NFL Players' Association. Unitas announced his retirement, July 24. A little known rookie, Don Woods, was picked up on waivers from Green Bay. Before the season was over, Woods established an NFL rookie rushing record, gaining 1,162 yards and winning rookie of the year honors in every poll.

1975 Johnny Sanders, a long-time Los Angeles Rams' executive, was named assistant to the president for player personnel, February 21. Paul (Tank) Younger, another ex-Rams player and scout, was appointed assistant general manager, June 17. The team struggled during the season, losing twice in overtime and dropping its first 11 games in a row, before rallying to win two of its final three games. A loss in Cincinnati on the last Sunday made the final record 2-12.

1976 Svare was released as general manager and replaced by Sanders, February 16. Joe Washington, the All-America runner from Oklahoma, was the team's top draft choice. The Chargers played the first NFL game outside of North America against the St. Louis Cardinals in Tokyo, August 16; St. Louis won 20-10. Washington injured a knee playing a preseason game in his old college stadium at Norman, Oklahoma,

Lance Alworth makes a catch in his ninety-sixth consecutive game, at the time, an NFL record, 1969.

John Hadl pitches to Dickie Post as Brad Hubbert moves up to block, 1967.

and had to undergo surgery. The club opened with its best record in years, 3-0, after beating St. Louis 43-24. But a porous pass defense finally caught up with San Diego and it finished the season 6-8, its best record in six years.

1977 Before the season began, the Chargers gained one quarterback and lost another. On July 12, they sent a draft choice to Los Angeles for James Harris. A 125-day retirement by Fouts made Harris the starter. Harris led the Chargers to three straight victories at one point, and on October 30 he rolled out and bulled his way into the end zone on the final play of the game for a 14-13 victory over Miami. An ankle injury ended his season on November 13 in a 17-14 loss to Denver, a game in which backup Bill Munson broke his leg. The next week rookie Cliff Olander, drafted primarily as a punter, was the quarterback in a 12-7 surprise of the Raiders. Fouts returned to lead the Chargers to two wins and two close losses in the last four games. San Diego's 7-7 record was its best since 1969.

1978 Lance Alworth became the first player from the AFL to be named to the Pro Football Hall of Fame on January 23. The season got off to a disappointing 1-3 start and Prothro resigned after four games. On September 25, former San Diego State and St. Louis Cardinals coach Don Coryell was named head coach. The team finished 7-1 for an overall record of 9-7. Fouts threw 24 touchdown passes, 13 to wide receiver John Jefferson, the first-round draft choice from Arizona State who was voted rookie of the year.

1979 The Chargers drafted tight end Kellen Winslow of Missouri on the first round. A record-setting passing attack led San Diego to the championship of the AFC West and a 12-4 record, the best since 1963. Fouts broke Joe Namath's single season passing record by throwing for 4,082 yards. On October 21, he passed for 326 yards and the Chargers beat upstate rival Los Angeles 40-16; Fouts tied an NFL record with his third consecutive 300-yard passing performance. San Diego completed its sweep of the teams that would play in the Super Bowl XIV with a 35-7 defeat of Pittsburgh that was highlighted by a 77-yard interception return by linebacker Woodrow Lowe. On December 17, San Diego won the division with a 17-7 victory over Denver. Houston's Vernon Perry intercepted four of Fouts's passes to help Houston to a 17-14 victory in the AFC Divisional Playoff Game.

1980 The Chargers won their second straight AFC West title with a passing attack that broke the records it set the year before. Fouts threw for an all-time high of 4,715 yards; Winslow, who returned to action after recovering from a broken leg he suffered his rookie year, led the league in receptions; and Winslow, Jefferson, and Charlie Joiner each had over 1,000 yards on receptions. The Chargers also improved their ground game with the acquisition of Chuck Muncie from New Orleans on September 29. The Chargers started off 4-0 and then after a slump finished 5-1 for an 11-5 record. On October 19, Fouts threw for a club record 444 yards in a 44-7 defeat of the New York Giants. A 26-17 victory over Pittsburgh in the season finale gave the Chargers the AFC West championship.

1981 Fouts hit Ron Smith with a 50-yard touchdown pass with 2:08 to go to lead the Chargers to a 20-14 victory over Buffalo in the 1980 AFC Divisional Playoff Game on January 3. A week later the Chargers couldn't overcome a 28-7 second-quarter deficit and lost 34-27 to the Raiders in the 1980 AFC Championship Game. A prolonged holdout by Jefferson from the start of training camp ended with his trade to Green Bay for draft choices and Aundra Thompson. The Chargers then obtained Wes Chandler from New Orleans for Thompson and draft choices. Fouts again broke his own single-season record by passing for

4,802 yards; Winslow again led the league in receiving; and Joiner and Chandler joined Winslow with over 1,000 yards receiving. Despite lapses by the defense, which allowed the second most points in the AFC, the Chargers were still very much in the playoff race late in the year. A 23-10 victory over Oakland in the final Monday night game, coupled with Denver's loss to Chicago the day before, gave the Chargers a 10-6 record and the AFC West championship for the third straight year.

1982 The Chargers-Dolphins matchup in the divisional playoffs on January 2 was a game to remember. The Chargers mounted a 24-0 first quarter lead. They then fell behind 38-31 in the fourth period, tied the score in the last minute, and finally won 41-38 after 13:52 of overtime on Rolf Benirschke's 29-yard field goal. Fouts passed for 433 yards. Winslow caught a postseason record 13 passes for 166 yards and blocked a Miami field goal attempt late in the fourth quarter. A week later, drained by the preceding game and facing sub-zero weather (minus 59 wind-chill factor) as well as a strong Cincinnati Bengals team, the Chargers lost in the AFC Championship Game 27-7. Fouts passed for only 173 yards, and the Chargers turned the ball over four times.

MEMBERS OF HALL OF FAME:
Lance Alworth, David (Deacon) Jones, Ron Mix, Johnny Unitas

CHARGERS RECORD, 1960-81

Year	Won	Lost	Tied	Pct.	Pts.	OP
Los Angeles Chargers						
1960§	10	4	0	.714	373	336
San Diego Chargers						
1961§	12	2	0	.857	396	219
1962	4	10	0	.286	314	392
1963‡	11	3	0	.786	399	256
1964§	8	5	1	.615	341	300
1965§	9	2	3	.818	340	227
1966	7	6	1	.538	335	284
1967	8	5	1	.615	360	352
1968	9	5	0	.643	382	310
1969	8	6	0	.571	288	276
1970	5	6	3	.455	282	278
1971	6	8	0	.429	311	341
1972	4	9	1	.321	264	344
1973	2	11	1	.179	188	386
1974	5	9	0	.357	212	285
1975	2	12	0	.143	189	345
1976	6	8	0	.429	248	285
1977	7	7	0	.500	222	205
1978	9	7	0	.563	355	309
1979†	12	4	0	.750	411	246
1980†	11	5	0	.688	418	327
1981†	10	6	0	.625	478	390
22 Years	165	140	11	.540	7,106	6,693

§*AFL Western Division Champion*
‡*AFL Champion*
†*AFC Western Division Champion*

Record-setting passer Dan Fouts against Los Angeles, 1979.

Chuck Allen

Rolf Benirschke

Earl Faison

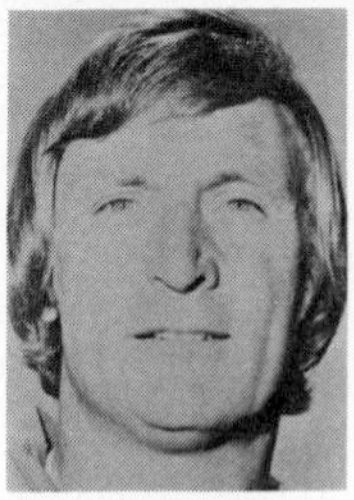
Gary Garrison

Sam Gruneisen

Gary Johnson

Louie Kelcher

RECORD HOLDERS

Rushing (Yards)	Don Woods, 1974	1,162
Passing (Pct.)	Dan Fouts, 1979	62.6
Passing (Yards)	Dan Fouts, 1981	4,802
Passing (TDs)	Dan Fouts, 1981	33
Receiving (No.)	Kellen Winslow, 1980	89
Receiving (Yards)	Lance Alworth, 1965	1,602
Interceptions (No.)	Charlie McNeal, 1961	9
Punting (Avg.)	Dennis Partee, 1969	44.6
Punt Ret. (Avg.)	Leslie (Speedy) Duncan, 1965	15.5
Kickoff Ret. (Avg.)	Keith Lincoln, 1962	28.4
Touchdowns (Total)	Chuck Muncie, 1981	19
Field Goals Made	Rolf Benirschke, 1980	24
Points (No.)	Rolf Benirschke, 1980	118

COACHING HISTORY

1960-69	Sid Gillman*	82-47-6
1969-70	Charlie Waller	9- 7-3
1971	Sid Gillman**	4- 6-0
1971-73	Harland Svare***	7-17-2
1973	Ron Waller	1- 5-0
1974-78	Tommy Prothro****	21-39-0
1978-81	Don Coryell	41-19-0

*Retired after nine games in 1969
**Replaced after 10 games in 1971
***Resigned after eight games in 1973
****Resigned after four games in 1978

FIRST PLAYER SELECTED

1960 Monty Stickles, E, Notre Dame
1961 Earl Faison, DE, Indiana
1962 Bob Ferguson, RB, Ohio State
1963 Walt Sweeney, G, Syracuse
1964 Ted Davis, LB, Georgia Tech
1965 Steve DeLong, DE, Tennessee
1966 Don Davis, DT, Cal State-Los Angeles
1967 Ron Billingsley, DE, Wyoming
1968 Russ Washington, DT, Missouri
1969 Marty Domres, QB, Columbia
1970 Walker Gillette, WR, Richmond
1971 Leon Burns, RB, Long Beach State
1972 Pete Lazetich, DE (2), Stanford
1973 Johnny Rodgers, RB, Nebraska
1974 Bo Matthews, RB, Colorado
1975 Gary Johnson, DT, Grambling
1976 Joe Washington, RB, Oklahoma
1977 Bob Rush, C, Memphis State
1978 John Jefferson, WR, Arizona State
1979 Kellen Winslow, TE, Missouri
1980 Ed Luther, QB (4), San Jose State
1981 James Brooks, RB, Auburn
1982 Hollis Hall, DB (7), Clemson

LOS ANGELES CHARGERS, 1960;
SAN DIEGO CHARGERS, 1961-81

Agajanian, Ben, K, New Mexico 1960-61, 1964
Aiu, Charlie, G, Hawaii 1976-78
Akin, Harold, T, Oklahoma State 1967-68
Aldridge, Lionel, DE, Utah State 1972-73
Allen, Chuck, LB, Washington 1961-69
Allison, Jim, RB, San Diego State 1965-68
Alworth, Lance, WR, Arkansas 1962-70
Anderson, Ralph, TE, Cal State-Los Angeles 1960
Anderson, Rickey, RB, South Carolina State 1978
Andrews, John, TE, Indiana 1972
Appleton, Scott, DT, Texas 1967-68
Audick, Dan, G, Hawaii 1978-80

B

Babich, Bob, LB, Miami, Ohio 1970-72
Baccaglio, Martin, DE, San Jose State 1968
Bacon, Coy, DE, Jackson State 1973-75
Baker, John, LB, Mississippi State 1967
Baker, Mel, WR, Texas Southern 1975
Bansavage, Al, G, USC 1960
Barnes, Ernie, G, North Carolina College 1960-62
Barnes, Lawrence, RB, Tennessee State 1977-78
Barnes, Pete, LB, Southern U. 1970-72
Barry, Al, G, USC 1960
Bauer, Hank, RB, California Lutheran 1977-81
Beauchamp, Joe, CB, Iowa State 1966-75
Beaudoin, Doug, S, Minnesota 1981
Beirne, Jim, WR, Purdue 1973-74
Bell, Eddie (the Flea), WR, Idaho State 1976
Belotti, George, G, USC 1961
Benirschke, Rolf, K, California-Davis 1977-81
Berry, Reggie, S, Long Beach State 1972-74
Bethune, Bobby, DB, Mississippi State 1962
Billingsley, Ron, DT, Wyoming 1967-70
Blair, George, DB-K, Mississippi 1961-64
Boatright, Bon, DT, Oklahoma State 1974
Bobo, Hubert, LB, Ohio State 1960
Botchan, Ron, LB, Occidental 1960
Bradley, Chuck, TE, Oregon 1975-76
Braxton, Hezekiah, RB, Virginia Union 1962
Breaux, Don, QB, McNeese State 1964-65
Briggs, Bob, DE, Heidelberg 1968-70
Briscoe, Marlin, WR, Nebraska-Omaha 1975
Brittenum, Jon, QB, Arkansas 1968
Brooks, Billy, WR, Oklahoma 1981
Brooks, James, RB, Auburn 1981
Brown, Bob, DT, Arkansas-Pine Bluff 1974
Brown, Booker, T, USC 1975-77
Brueckman, Charlie, LB, Pittsburgh 1960
Bruggers, Bob, LB, Minnesota 1968-71
Buchanon, Willie, DB, San Diego State 1979-81
Buncom, Frank, LB, USC 1962-67
Burns, Leon, RB, Long Beach State 1971
Burton, Larry, WR, Purdue 1978-79

C

Caffey, Lee Roy, LB, Texas A&M 1972
Campbell, Jim, LB, West Texas State 1969
Cappelletti, John, RB, Penn State 1980-81
Carolan, Reg, TE, Idaho 1962-63
Carr, Levert, T, North Central State, Illinois 1969
Carpenter, Ron, LB, Texas A&M 1964-65
Carter, Mike, WR, Sacramento State 1972
Carter, Virgil, QB, Brigham Young 1975
Chandler, Wes, WR, Florida 1981
Chorovich, Dick, DT, Miami, Ohio 1960
Clark, Howard, E, Tennessee-Chattanooga 1960-61
Clark, Wayne, QB, U.S. International 1970-72, 1976
Clatterbuck, Bobby, QB, Houston 1960
Claphan, Sam, T, Oklahoma 1981
Cline, Doug, LB, Clemson 1966
Coan, Bert, RB, Kansas 1962
Colbert, Danny, CB, Tulsa 1974-76
Cole, Fred, G, Maryland 1960
Cordill, Ollie, WR, Memphis State 1967
Costa, Dave, DT, Utah 1972-73
Cotton, Craig, TE, Youngstown State 1975
Curran, Pat, TE, Lakeland 1975-78

D

Davis, Harrison, WR, Virginia 1974
Day, Tom, DE, North Carolina A&T 1967
Dean, Fred, DE, Louisiana Tech 1975-81
Degan, Dick, LB, Long Beach State 1965-66
DeJurnett, Charles, DT, San Jose State 1976-80
DeLong, Steve, TE, Tennessee 1965-71
DeLuca, Sam, G, South Carolina 1960-61, 1963
Dennis, Al, G, Grambling 1973
Detwiler, Chuck, S, Utah State 1970-72
Dicus, Chuck, WR, Arkansas 1971-72
Domres, Marty, QB, Columbia 1969-71
Donnell, Ben, DE, Vanderbilt 1960
Dorsey, Larry, WR, Tennessee State 1976-77
Douglas, Jay, T, Memphis State 1973-74
Douglass, Bobby, QB, Kansas 1975
Dove, Jerome, DB, Colorado State 1977-80
Dragon, Oscar, RB, Arizona State 1972
Duncan, Frank, S, San Francisco State 1979-81
Duncan, Leslie (Speedy), DB, Jackson State 1964-70
Dunlap, Leonard, CB, North Texas State 1972-74
Duren, Clarence, S, California 1977
Dyer, Ken, DB, Arizona State 1968

E

East, Ron, DT, Montana State 1971-73
Eber, Rick, WR, Tulsa 1969
Edwards, Cid, RB, Tennessee State 1972-74
Edwards, Glen, S, Florida A&M 1978-81
Ellis, Allan, CB, UCLA 1981
Enis, Hunter, QB, Texas Christian 1961
Erickson, Bernard, LB, Abilene Christian 1967-68
Erlandson, Tom, LB, Washington State 1968
Estes, Don, G, Louisiana State 1966

F

Faison, Earl, DE, Indiana 1961-66
Farley, Dick, DB, Boston U. 1968-69
Farr, Miller, DB, Wichita State 1965-66
Farris, John, G, San Diego State 1965-66
Fenner, Lane, WR, Florida State 1968
Ferguson, Gene, T, Norfolk State 1969-70
Ferguson, Howie, RB, No college 1960
Ferguson, Keith, DE, Ohio State 1981
Ferrante, Orlando, G, USC 1960-61
Fetherston, Jim, LB, California 1968-69
Finneran, Gary, DT, USC 1960
Fitzkee, Scott, WR, Penn State 1981
Flanagan, Ed, C, Purdue 1975-76
Fletcher, Chris, S, Temple 1970-76
Flowers, Charlie, RB, Mississippi 1960-61
Floyd, John, WR, Northeastern Louisiana 1979-80
Ford, Fred, RB, Cal Poly-San Luis Obispo 1960
Forsberg, Fred, LB, Washington 1974
Foster, Gene, RB, Arizona State 1965-70
Fouts, Dan, QB, Oregon 1973-81
Frazier, Wayne, C, Auburn 1962
Frazier, Willie, TE, Arkansas-Pine Bluff 1966-70
Freitas, Jesse, QB, San Diego State 1974-75
Fritsch, Toni, K, No college 1976
Fuller, Mike, S, Auburn 1975-80

G

Garner, Bob, DB, Fresno State 1960
Garrett, Mike, RB, USC 1970-73
Garrison, Gary, WR, San Diego State 1966-76
Gay, Blenda, DE, Fayetteville State 1974
Gerela, Roy, K, New Mexico 1979
Gersbach, Carl, LB, West Chester State 1973-74
Gibson, Claude, DB, North Carolina State 1961-62
Gillett, Fred, LB, Cal State-Los Angeles 1962
Gillette, Walker, WR, Richmond 1970-71
Glick, Gary, DB, Colorado State 1963
Gob, Art, LB, Pittsburgh 1960
Good, Tom, LB, Marshall 1966
Goode, Don, LB, Kansas 1974-79
Gordon, Dick, WR, Michigan State 1974
Gordon, Ira, T, Kansas State 1970-75
Graham, Kenny, DB, Washington State 1964-69
Graham, Tom, LB, Oregon 1975-77
Grannell, Dave, TE, Arizona State 1974
Grant, Wes, DE, UCLA 1971
Greene, Tom, QB, Holy Cross 1961
Gregor, Bob, S, Washington State 1981
Griffin, Jim, DT, Grambling 1966-67
Gross, George, DT, Auburn 1963-67
Gruneisen, Sam, C, Villanova 1962-72

H

Hadl, John, QB, Kansas 1962-72
Hardaway, Milton, T, Oklahoma State 1978
Hardy, Kevin, DT, Notre Dame 1971-72
Harrington, LaRue, RB, Norfolk State 1980
Harris, Dick, DB, McNeese State 1960-65
Harris, James, QB, Grambling 1977-81
Hayes, Luther, WR, USC 1961
Hayes, Tom, CB, San Diego State 1976
Henderson, Wyatt, C, Fresno State 1981
Henning, Dan, QB, William & Mary 1966
Hill, Jim, S, Texas A&I 1969-71
Hoey, George, DB, Michigan 1974
Holliday, Ron, WR, Pittsburgh 1973
Holohan, Pete, TE, Notre Dame 1981
Holmes, Robert, RB, Southern U. 1973
Hoopes, Mitch, P, Arizona 1976
Horn, Bob, LB, Oregon State 1976-81
Horn, Don, QB, San Diego State 1974
Horton, Bob, LB, Boston U. 1964-65
Howard, Bob, CB, San Diego State 1967-74
Hubbert, Brad, RB, Arizona 1967-70
Hudson, Bill, DT, Clemson 1961-62
Hudson, Dick, T, Memphis State 1962
Huey, Gene, WR, Wyoming 1969
Hutcherson, Ken, LB, Livingston, Alabama 1975

Keith Lincoln

Paul Lowe

Dickie Post

Walt Sweeney

Dick Westmoreland

Doug Wilkerson

Mike Williams

J

Jackson, Bernard, DB, Washington State ... 1980
Jackson, Bobby, RB, New Mexico State ... 1962-63
Jefferson, John, WR, Arizona State ... 1978-80
Jeffrey, Neal, QB, Baylor ... 1976
Johnson, Gary, DT, Grambling ... 1975-81
Joiner, Charlie, WR, Grambling ... 1976-81
Jones, Clint, RB, Michigan State ... 1973
Jones, Curtis, G, Missouri ... 1968
Jones, David (Deacon), DE, South Carolina State ... 1972-73
Jones, Harris, G, Johnson C. Smith ... 1971
Jones, Leroy, DE, Norfolk State ... 1976-81
Jones, Ray, CB, Southern U. ... 1972

K

Karas, Emil, LB, Dayton ... 1960-64, 1966
Keckin, Val, QB, Southern Mississippi ... 1962
Kelcher, Louie, DT, Southern Methodist ... 1975-81
Kemp, Jack, QB, Occidental ... 1960-62
Kempinski, Charlie, G, Mississippi ... 1960
Kinderman, Keith, RB, Florida State ... 1963-64
Kindig, Howard, DE, Cal State-Los Angeles ... 1965-67
King, Linden, LB, Colorado State ... 1978-81
Kirner, Gary, T, USC ... 1964-69
Klein, Bob, TE, USC ... 1977-80
Klotz, Jack, DT, Widener ... 1962
Kocourek, Dave, TE, Wisconsin ... 1960-65
Kompara, John, DT, South Carolina ... 1960

L

Ladd, Ernie, DT, Grambling ... 1961-65
Lane, Bob, LB, Baylor ... 1963-64
Laraba, Bob, QB-LB, Texas Western ... 1960-61
Laslavic, Jim, LB, Penn State ... 1978, 1980-81
Latzke, Paul, C, Pacific ... 1966-68
Lazetich, Pete, LB, Stanford ... 1972-74
Lee, John, DT, Nebraska ... 1976-80
Lee, Mike, LB, Nevada-Las Vegas ... 1974
Lenkaitis, Bill, G, Penn State ... 1968-70
LeVias, Jerry, WR, Southern Methodist ... 1971-74
Lincoln, Keith, RB, Washington State ... 1961-66, 1968
Little, Larry, G, Bethune-Cookman ... 1967-68
Loewen, Chuck, G-T, South Dakota State ... 1980-81
London, Mike, LB, Wisconsin ... 1966
Longley, Clint, QB, Abilene Christian ... 1976
Loudd, Rommie, LB, UCLA ... 1960
Lowe, Paul, RB, Oregon State ... 1960-68
Lowe, Woodrow, LB, Alabama ... 1976-81
Luther, Ed, QB, San Jose State ... 1980-81

M

Macek, Don, G, Boston College ... 1976-81
Mackey, John, TE, Syracuse ... 1972
MacKinnon, Jacque, TE, Colgate ... 1961-69
Maguire, Paul, LB-P, Citadel ... 1960-63
Marsh, Frank, DB, Oregon State ... 1967
Martin, Blanche, RB, Michigan State ... 1960
Martin, Larry, DT, San Diego State ... 1966
Matsos, Archie, LB, Michigan State ... 1966
Matthews, Bo, RB, Colorado ... 1974-79
Mauck, Carl, C, Southern Illinois ... 1971-74
McCall, Ron, LB, Weber State ... 1967-68
McClard, Bill, K, Arkansas ... 1972
McCoy, Lloyd, G, San Diego State ... 1964
McCrary, Gregg, TE, Clark ... 1978-80
McDonald, Dwight, WR, San Diego State ... 1975-78
McDougall, Gerry, RB, UCLA ... 1962-64, 1968
McGee, Carl, LB, Duke ... 1980
McGee, Willie, CB, Alcorn State ... 1973
McNeil, Charlie, DB, Compton J.C. ... 1960-64
Mendez, Mario, WR, San Diego State ... 1964
Mercer, Mike, K, Northern Arizona ... 1970
Mialik, Larry, TE, Wisconsin ... 1976
Middleton, Rick, LB, Ohio State ... 1976-78
Mikolajewski, Pete, QB, Kent State ... 1969
Milks, Jack, LB, San Diego State ... 1966
Miller, Paul, DT, Louisiana State ... 1962
Mitchell, Ed, G, Southern U. ... 1965-66
Mitchell, Lydell, RB, Penn State ... 1978-79
Mitinger, Bob, LB, Penn State ... 1963-66, 1968
Mix, Ron, T, USC ... 1960-69
Montgomery, Mike, RB, Kansas State ... 1971
Moore, Fred, DT, Memphis State ... 1964-66
Morris, Mercury, RB, West Texas State ... 1976
Moss, Roland, TE, Toledo ... 1970
Muncie, Chuck, RB, California ... 1980-81
Myrtle, Chip, LB, Maryland ... 1974

N

Nery, Ron, DE, Kansas State ... 1960-62
Newell, Steve, WR, Long Beach State ... 1967
Nix, Doyle, DB, Southern Methodist ... 1960
Norman, Pettis, TE, Johnson C. Smith ... 1971-73
Norris, Trusse, WR, UCLA ... 1960
Norton, Don, WR, Iowa ... 1960-66
Nowak, Gary, T, Michigan State ... 1971

O

Olander, Cliff, QB, New Mexico State ... 1977-79
Owens, Artie, WR, West Virginia ... 1976-79
Owens, Joe, DE, Alcorn State ... 1970
Owens, Terry, T, Jacksonville State ... 1966-75

P

Park, Ernie, G, McMurry ... 1963-65
Parks, Billy, WR, Long Beach State ... 1971
Parris, Gary, TE, Florida State ... 1973-74
Partee, Dennis, P-K, Southern Methodist ... 1968-75
Partridge, Rick, P, Utah ... 1980
Perretta, Ralph, G, Purdue ... 1975-80
Perry, Scott, DB, Williams ... 1980
Peters, Volney, DT, USC ... 1960
Petrich, Bob, DE, West Texas State ... 1963-66
Phillips, Irvin, CB, Arkansas Tech ... 1981
Plump, Dave, WR, Fresno State ... 1966
Plunkett, Sherman, T, Maryland-Eastern Shore ... 1961-62
Post, Dickie, RB, Houston ... 1967-70
Preston, Ray, LB, Syracuse ... 1976-81
Print, Bob, LB, Dayton ... 1967-68
Protz, Jack, LB, Syracuse ... 1970

Q

Queen, Jeff, RB, Morgan State ... 1969-71

R

Ray, Eddie, RB, Louisiana State ... 1971
Redman, Rick, LB, Washington ... 1965-73
Reese, Don, DT, Jackson State ... 1981
Rentz, Larry, DB, Florida ... 1969
Rice, Andy, DT, Texas Southern ... 1970-71
Ridge, Houston, DT, San Diego State ... 1966-69
Roberson, Bo, WR, Cornell ... 1961
Roberts, George, P, Virginia Tech ... 1981
Robinson, Jerry, WR, Grambling ... 1962-64
Rodgers, Johnny, WR-RB, Nebraska ... 1977-78
Rogers, Don, C, South Carolina ... 1960-64
Rogers, Mel, LB, Florida A&M ... 1971, 1974
Rossovich, Tim, LB, USC ... 1972-73
Rote, Tobin, QB, Rice ... 1963-64
Rowe, Dave, DT, Penn State ... 1974-75
Rush, Bob, C, Memphis State ... 1977, 1979-81
Russell, Booker, RB, Southwest Texas State ... 1980

S

Salter, Bryant, S, Pittsburgh ... 1971-73
Sartin, Dan, C, Mississippi ... 1969
Sayers, Ron, RB, Nebraska-Omaha ... 1969
Scales, Dwight, WR, Grambling ... 1981
Scarber, Sam, RB, New Mexico ... 1975-76
Scarpitto, Bob, DB, Notre Dame ... 1961
Schleicher, Maury, DE, Penn State ... 1960-62
Schmedding, Jim, G, Weber State ... 1968-70
Schmidt, Henry, DT, USC ... 1961-64
Sears, Jim, DB, USC ... 1960
Selawski, Gene, T, Purdue ... 1961
Shaw, Pete, S, Northwestern ... 1977-81
Shea, Pat, G, USC ... 1962-65
Shields, Billy, T, Georgia Tech ... 1975-81
Sievers, Eric, TE, Maryland ... 1981
Singleton, Ron, T, Grambling ... 1976
Slater, Mark, C, Minnesota ... 1978
Smith, Charlie, RB, Utah ... 1975
Smith, Dave, RB, Utah ... 1970
Smith, Ron, S, Wisconsin ... 1973
Smith, Ron, WR, San Diego State ... 1980-81
Smith, Russ, RB, Miami ... 1967-70
Snowden, Cal, DE, Indiana ... 1972-73
Speights, Dick, WR, Wyoming ... 1968
Staggs, Jeff, LB, San Diego State ... 1966-71, 1974
Stein, Bob, LB, Minnesota ... 1975
Stephenson, Kay, QB, Florida ... 1967
Stewart, Wayne, TE, California ... 1974
Stratton, Mike, LB, Tennessee ... 1973
Stringert, Hal, CB, Hawaii ... 1975-80
Strozier, Art, TE, Kansas State ... 1970-71
Sweeney, Walt, G, Syracuse ... 1963-73
Sykes, John, RB, Morgan State ... 1972

T

Tanner, John, LB, Tennessee Tech ... 1971
Tate, Franklin, LB, North Carolina Central ... 1975
Taylor, Jessie, RB, Cincinnati ... 1972
Taylor, Sammie, WR, Grambling ... 1964
Tensi, Steve, QB, Florida State ... 1965-66
Thaxton, James, TE, Tennessee State ... 1973-74
Thomas, Bob, RB, Arizona State ... 1973-74
Thomas, Jesse, DB, Michigan State ... 1960
Thomas, Lee, DE, Jackson State ... 1971-72
Thomas, Mike, RB, Nevada-Las Vegas ... 1979-80
Thompson, Aundra, WR, East Texas State ... 1981
Thompson, Tommy, RB, Southern Illinois ... 1974
Thrift, Cliff, LB, East Central Oklahoma ... 1979-81
Tipton, Dave, DE, Stanford ... 1974-75
Tolbert, Jim, DB, Lincoln, Missouri ... 1966-71, 1976
Trapp, Richard, WR, Florida ... 1969
Travenio, Herb, K, Texas College ... 1965
Tuckett, Phil, WR, Weber State ... 1968

U

Unitas, Johnny, QB, Louisville ... 1973

V

Van Raaphorst, Dick, K, Ohio State ... 1966-67
Vertefeuille, Brian, G, Idaho State ... 1974

W

Wallace, Henry, DB, Pacific ... 1960
Waller, Ron, RB, Maryland ... 1960
Warren, Jimmy, DB, Illinois ... 1964-65
Washington, Joe, RB, Oklahoma ... 1976-77
Washington, Russ, T, Missouri ... 1968-81
Webb, Jimmy, DT, Mississippi State ... 1981
Wells, Robert, T, Johnson C. Smith ... 1968-70
Wenzel, Ralph, G, San Diego State ... 1972
Wersching, Ray, K, California ... 1973-76
West, Jeff, P, Cincinnati ... 1976-79
Westmoreland, Dick, DB, North Carolina A&T ... 1963-65
White, Andre, TE, Florida A&M ... 1968
White, Ed, G, California ... 1979-81
White, Lee, RB, Weber State ... 1972
White, Ray, LB, Syracuse ... 1971-73
Whitehead, Bud, DB, Florida State ... 1961-68
Whitmyer, Nat, DB, Washington ... 1966-67
Wilkerson, Doug, G, North Carolina Central ... 1971-81
Williams, Clarence, RB, South Carolina ... 1977-81
Williams, Dave, WR, Washington ... 1972
Williams, Jeff, G, Rhode Island ... 1981
Williams, Mike, CB, Louisiana State ... 1975-81
Williams, Sam, DB, California ... 1974-75
Williams, Tom, DT, California-Davis ... 1970-71
Winslow, Kellen, TE, Missouri ... 1979-81
Withrow, Cal, C, Kentucky ... 1970
Wojcik, Greg, DT, USC ... 1972-73
Womble, Royce, WR, North Texas State ... 1960
Wood, Dick, QB, Auburn ... 1962
Wood, Mike, P-K, Southwest Missouri ... 1979-80
Woodcock, John, DE-DT, Hawaii ... 1981
Woods, Don, RB, New Mexico ... 1974-80
Wright, Ernie, T, Ohio State ... 1960-67, 1972

Y

Young, Rickey, RB, Jackson State ... 1975-77
Young, Wilbur, DE, William Penn ... 1978-81

Z

Zeman, Bob, DB, Wisconsin ... 1960-61, 1965-66

SAN FRANCISCO 49ers

1946 Anthony J. (Tony) Morabito, a partner in a San Francisco lumber firm, formed the 49ers as a charter member of the All-America Football Conference. Morabito had tried but failed to get a franchise in the National Football League. One of Morabito's partners in Lumber Terminals of San Francisco, Allen E. Sorrell or E.J. Turre, selected the team's nickname; each has been given credit for it at one time or another. John Blackinger was named general manager of the 49ers. Their original emblem showed a booted prospector in a lumberjack's shirt and checkered pants, his hat blown off and his hair askew, his feet splayed apart, and in his hands two six-shooters firing. Morabito raided NFL teams, signing 12 of their players, and signed notable Bay Area college players such as quarterback Frankie Albert and fullback Norm Standlee of Stanford. Lawrence (Buck) Shaw of Santa Clara was named 49ers' head coach. The team rented Kezar Stadium for its games. It finished second to the Cleveland Browns in the AAFC's Western Division in its first season and won one of its two games against Cleveland, 34-20. Forty-Niners end Alyn Beals led the AAFC in pass receiving with 40 catches for 586 yards.

1947 The 49ers again finished second to the Browns in the Western Division. Morabito borrowed $100,000, bought out his original partners, and divided the ownership of the 49ers on a 75-25 basis with his brother Vic. "There's this nut with a hearing aid in San Francisco who is putting his own money into this damn team," said Harry Wismer, Washington Redskins broadcaster.

1948 The 49ers had a tremendous season but finished second in the division behind the Browns for the third time in a row. Albert, a 5-foot 9-inch, 175-pound quarterback, completed 29 touchdown passes. He and quarterback Otto Graham of Cleveland were named co-winners of the AAFC most valuable player award.

1949 San Francisco gave the Cleveland Browns the worst beating (56-28) in their history, as Albert threw

Two for the Hall of Fame: Joe Perry leads Hugh McElhenny (39) downfield against Green Bay, 1955.

five touchdown passes in a game at Kezar Stadium, October 9. The Browns, however, finished first in the AAFC for the fourth season. There was no division play and there was a playoff of the top four teams for the championship. A merger was arranged between the NFL and AAFC, and, by its terms, Cleveland, San Francisco, and the Baltimore Colts would enter the National Football League, December 9. The Browns and 49ers played for the AAFC championship in Cleveland and only 22,550 fans watched as Cleveland won 21-17. Shaw, coach of the 49ers, said, "Four years ago, I'd never even met Paul Brown [the Cleveland coach]. Now I scheme to beat him, dream of beating him, and wind up screaming because I haven't beaten him."

1950 The 49ers struggled through their first season in the NFL, winning only three games. A rival coach said they were "not big enough or tough enough." Tackle Leo Nomellini started his career with San Francisco, playing both offense and defense. Gordy Soltau was another star rookie.

1951 Quarterback Y.A. Tittle was acquired by the 49ers from the extinct 1950 Baltimore Colts franchise to play behind Albert. Albert, however, suffered a shoulder injury and Tittle was pressed into service immediately. The team became a contender, winning its last three games and finishing third in the NFL's National Conference. End Billy Wilson and linebacker Hardy Brown began their careers with the 49ers.

1952 Lou Spadia was named general manager of the 49ers. Standlee was stricken with polio and never played football again. Co-owner Tony Morabito suffered a heart attack. Rookie back Hugh McElhenny had a sensational season. Albert and back Johnny (Strike) Strykalski retired.

1953 Bob St. Clair, a 6-foot 9-inch, 260-pound tackle, joined the team. The 49ers had their best season to date in the NFL, losing only three games by a total of nine points. Tittle was absent during two of the three defeats with a severe facial injury. Back Joe Perry rushed for 1,018 yards and co-owner Tony Morabito gave Perry a bonus check for $5,090—$5 a yard. Soltau led the league in scoring for the second straight year.

1954 San Francisco acquired fullback John Henry Johnson from the Pittsburgh Steelers and he joined Tittle, Perry, and McElhenny in one of the best backfields in pro football history. It was broken up, however, when Tittle was sidelined with a broken hand early in the season and McElhenny went out with a shoulder separation in the sixth game; McElhenny had gained 515 yards in only 64 carries before his injury. Perry went on to gain 1,049 yards, becoming the first runner in history to gain 1,000 two years in a row.

1955 Shaw, the only coach the team had ever had, was fired and replaced by Norman (Red) Strader, a strict disciplinarian who was unpopular with the players. As a result, the team won only four games.

1956 Strader was replaced as coach by former 49ers' quarterback Frankie Albert. The team had a 1-6 record after seven games but righted itself and, with McElhenny and a little known back named Joe Arenas starring, won four games and tied one for the remainder of the season. The 49ers drew 522,339 fans for 12 games, an NFL record at the time.

1957 Tittle and 6-foot 5-inch rookie end R.C. Owens devised the Alley-Oop pass in which Tittle threw the ball in a high arc and Owens ran to the point of reception and outjumped the defensive backs for the ball. The 49ers were an exciting team that great crowds flocked to see wherever they played. Founder Tony Morabito suffered a fatal heart attack during a game against the Chicago Bears at Kezar Stadium. Albert told his players of Morabito's death during halftime,

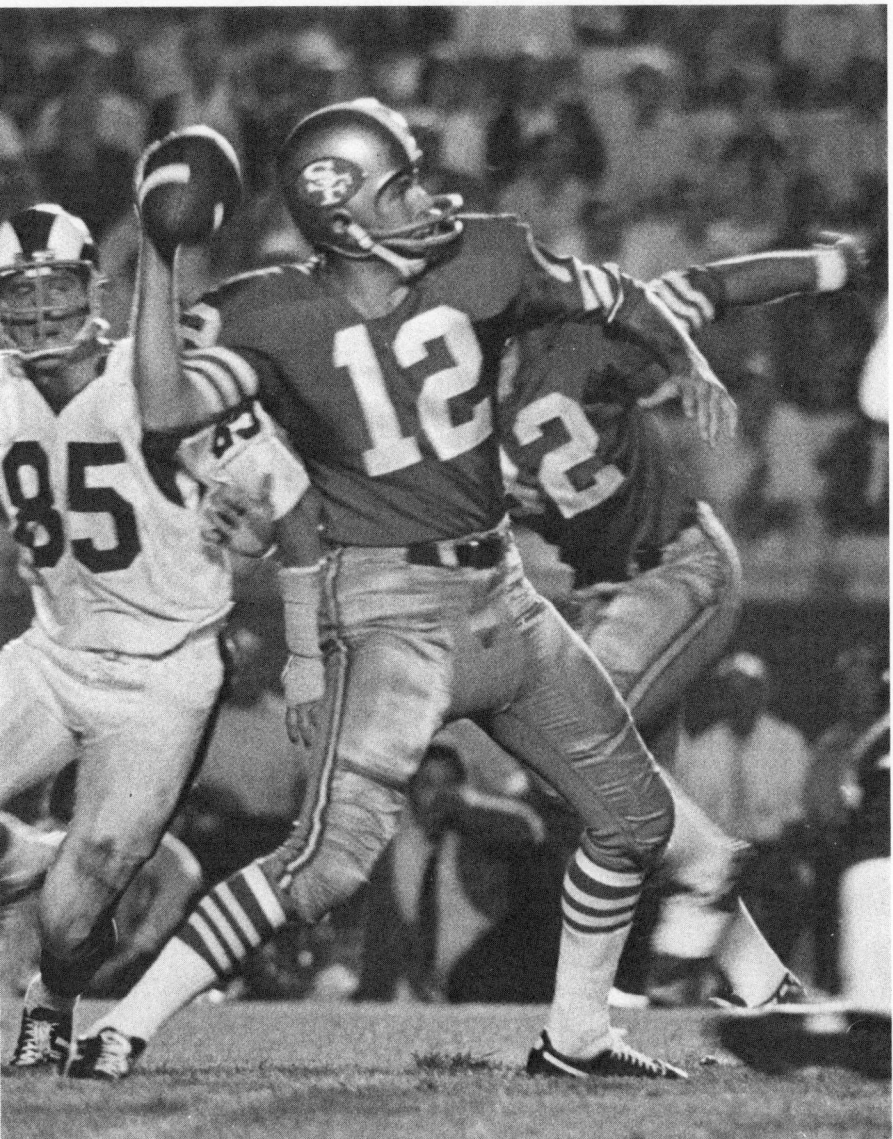

John Brodie passes against rush of Rams' defensive end Jack Youngblood, 1971.

and they made an emotional comeback to beat the Bears 21-17, October 27. Tittle suffered pulled muscles in both his legs in the next-to-last regular season game but rookie quarterback John Brodie came in and threw a touchdown pass to McElhenny as the 49ers defeated Baltimore 17-13. Tittle limped in the next week and the 49ers came from behind to defeat Green Bay 27-20 and tie the Detroit Lions for the Western Conference championship. The two teams met in a playoff and San Francisco took a 24-7 halftime lead, only to see Detroit come from behind and win 31-27 in one of the greatest comebacks in NFL history, December 22.

1958 Vic Morabito took over the team's operation. It had an up-and-down season and lost twice to Los Angeles by scores of 33-3 and 56-7. Albert resigned as coach.

1959 Assistant coach Howard (Red) Hickey was promoted to head coach. Brodie had a good season and so did running back J.D. Smith, who was a converted defensive back. Smith gained over 1,000 yards. Charlie Krueger was a rookie at defensive tackle.

1960 Hickey salvaged a frustrating season when he installed the Shotgun formation with the quarterback standing three to five yards back and taking a long snap from center, then passing or handing off. The 49ers won four of their last five games and tied for second place in the Western Conference.

1961 Tittle, who was better suited to the T-formation, was traded to the New York Giants for guard Lou Cordileone. There were still three 49ers' quarterbacks to operate the Shotgun formation—Brodie, Bobby Waters, and rookie Billy Kilmer, who had played tailback in the Single-wing formation at UCLA. San Francisco defeated Detroit 49-0 in the third week of the season. After five weeks the 49ers had a 4-1 record. The three quarterbacks alternated running the Shotgun. However, the Chicago Bears stopped the 49ers with middle linebacker Bill George playing on the line of scrimmage and often stunting and moving back into the backfield; Chicago won by a shocking 31-0 score. The 49ers went back to the T-formation but Hickey said he could have continued to play the Shotgun if his players had not lost confidence in it. San Francisco lost to Baltimore 27-24 on the final day of the season and missed a chance to finish in a tie for second place. Brodie had 2,588 yards passing for the season.

1962 The 49ers had their first losing season since 1956—6-8—and lost five out of seven games they played at home at Kezar Stadium.

1963 Hickey resigned as coach and assistant Jack Christiansen was named head coach. The 49ers defeated Chicago 20-14; the Bears went on to win the NFL championship. San Francisco had a disappointing 2-12 record, the poorest in its 18-year history. Defensive tackle Leo Nomellini retired from pro football holding the record for consecutive games played, 174.

1964 Owner Vic Morabito died of a heart attack at age 44; his brother, Tony, had been 47 when he died in 1957. Josephine and Jane Morabito, widows of the late brothers, kept control and gave Lou Spadia authority to run the team. End Dave Parks, quarterback George Mira, and linebacker Dave Wilcox had good rookie seasons.

1965 Running back John David Crow was acquired from the St. Louis Cardinals in a trade. San Francisco defeated Chicago 52-24 in the opening game, the most points ever scored against the Bears. Crow and rookie Ken Willard helped the 49ers' running game improve. Brodie had a good season at quarterback and Parks led the NFL with 80 pass receptions.

1966 San Francisco played another respectable but still disappointing season, 6-6-2. Parks had another good season and he and guard John Thomas were named to all-pro teams.

1967 The 49ers got off to a fast start, winning five out of six games. Hit by injuries, however, they then lost six straight. Mira came off the bench and led them to two victories at the end of the season. Christiansen was relieved as coach.

1968 Spadia took the title of president and Jack White was named general manager. Dallas Cowboys' assistant coach Dick Nolan was named 49ers' head coach. Nolan had a winning season in his first year. Brodie, Willard, and wide receiver Clifton McNeil starred on offense and defensive tackle Krueger, linebacker Wilcox, and cornerback Kermit Alexander on defense.

1969 Injuries hit the defensive line and the 49ers didn't win a game until the sixth week of the season, finishing 4-8-2. Jimmy Johnson emerged as an all-pro cornerback.

1970 The 49ers surged to a 10-3-1 record and the Western Division championship in the first year of realignment after the NFL-AFL merger. San Francisco and AFL rival Oakland were paired in the last game of the season and the 49ers won 38-7 for their tenth victory of the season. They then defeated the Minnesota Vikings 17-14 on two touchdown passes by quarterback Brodie in the fourth quarter, the last to wide receiver Dick Witcher with less than a minute to play in the game. The 49ers advanced to the NFC Championship Game and Nolan lost to his former teacher, Tom Landry, and the Dallas Cowboys 17-10. Nolan was named NFC coach of the year, Brodie player of the year, and cornerback Bruce Taylor rookie of the year. The NFC Western Division championship was the first title of any kind for the 49ers in their 25-year history.

1971 The 49ers left Kezar Stadium and moved their home games to Candlestick Park. They clinched their second consecutive division championship with a 31-27 victory over the Detroit Lions on the last day of the season. The score was the same as the one by which the Lions had upset the 49ers in their 1957 playoff. San Francisco defeated the Washington Redskins 24-20 but again faced Dallas in the championship game and again lost, this time 14-3. Brodie was intercepted three times in the game but defensive back Cedrick Hardman led a pass rush that sacked Dallas quarterback Roger Staubach six times. Wilcox, Johnson, and center Forrest Blue were named to all-pro teams.

1972 The Minnesota Vikings were the victims of another big San Francisco victory. This time it was the final game of the regular season and the 49ers won 20-17 on two fourth quarter touchdown passes by Brodie. His final pass again went to Witcher, this time with 19 seconds remaining. The victory gave the 49ers their third Western Division championship in a row, the first time since realignment that any team had won its division three straight seasons. The following week, San Francisco met its nemesis, Dallas, in the NFC divisional playoff and despite leading 28-13, lost 30-28 as Cowboys' quarterback Roger Staubach led a sensational comeback.

1973 The 49ers slumped to 5-9 after three consecutive Western Division titles. Despite the falloff and a number of key injuries, center Forrest Blue, linebacker Dave Wilcox, punter Tom Wittum, tight end Ted Kwalick, and guard Woody Peoples all made the Pro Bowl roster. John Brodie and Charlie Krueger retired at the end of the season.

1974 Quarterback Steve Spurrier was injured the week before the regular season began and was sidelined for most of the season. The 49ers used five different quarterbacks and lost a team record seven games in a row at one point. Dave Wilcox, outstanding linebacker for 11 years, retired.

1975 The 49ers' 24-23 victory at Los Angeles ended a string of 10 straight losses to the Rams in regular season games. The quarterback situation remained uncertain, but ends Cedrick Hardman and Tommy Hart were the leaders of a capable group of defensive players.

1976 Nolan was replaced as head coach by Miami Dolphins' assistant Monte Clark. Quarterback Jim Plunkett was acquired in a trade with the New England Patriots. San Francisco won six of its first seven games but lost a 23-20 sudden death overtime game at St. Louis, slumped, and finished second in the division behind Los Angeles. Hardman, Hart, Jimmy Webb, and Cleveland Elam became one of the best defensive lines in the league. The team's 8-6 record was its first winning season in four years.

1977 A new era began for the 49ers on March 31 when the team became the property of 31-year-old Edward J. DeBartolo, Jr., the youngest owner in the NFL. Joe Thomas was appointed vice president and general manager, and Ken Meyer, the former offensive coordinator with Los Angeles, became head coach. The 49ers went 0-5 to begin the season, including two losses by shutouts. On October 23, Jim Plunkett called his own plays for the first time all season, and the 49ers defeated Detroit 28-7. Then the defense took over and registered 22 sacks in consecutive victories over the Lions, Tampa Bay, Atlanta, and New Orleans, in which each opponent scored 10 points or less. On November 27, the 49ers defeated the Saints 20-17 to improve their record to 5-6. But the team was stunned the following week when Minnesota rallied from a 27-7 deficit in the fourth quarter to win 28-27. The erratic 49ers lost their final three games and finished 5-9. Delvin Williams and Wilbur Jackson combined for 1,711 yards rushing; Plunkett threw for 1,693 yards.

1978 Pete McCulley replaced Meyer as head coach. Thomas shuffled the team with a series of player personnel maneuvers: O. J. Simpson, after nine seasons with Buffalo, was obtained for draft choices; wide receiver Freddie Solomon was acquired from Miami for Williams; Tommy Hart was traded to Chicago; and Plunkett was released before the season. Steve DeBerg became the starting quarterback. The 49ers drafted linebacker Dan Bunz, but used their first choice on tight end Ken MacAfee, who never played regularly. San Francisco lost its first four games, then defeated Cincinnati 28-12. But the 49ers won only one more game in a disastrous season and finished 2-14, the worst record in club history. Simpson gained only 593 yards in nine games, then was lost for the

season with a shoulder injury. DeBerg completed only 45 percent of his passes and threw 22 interceptions. After a 1-8 start, McCulley was replaced by Fred O'Connor, who was released at the end of the season.

1979 Bill Walsh, the head coach at Stanford, was appointed head coach and general manager January 9; Thomas was released. Quarterback Joe Montana was selected in the third round of the draft and wide receiver Dwight Clark was chosen in the tenth round. The 49ers didn't win their first game until October 21 against Atlanta, 20-15, and again suffered a 2-14 season. But the offense displayed marked improvement by scoring 308 points, 89 more than the previous year. Walsh's innovative passing offense produced a big year, as DeBerg completed 347 of 578 passes for 3,652 yards and 17 touchdowns, and the 49ers ranked first in the NFC in passing offense. Simpson rushed for 460 yards, then retired after the season, ending his career with 11,236 yards, second best in NFL history.

1980 With two choices in the first round, the 49ers selected running back Earl Cooper and defensive end Jim Stuckey. The draft also produced linebackers Keena Turner and Craig Puki, punter Jim Miller, and safety Ricky Churchman. The 49ers won the season-opener over New Orleans 26-23 when Ray Wersching kicked a 37-yard field goal in the final seconds. They followed with consecutive victories over St. Louis and the New York Jets. DeBerg and Montana split playing time during most of the season, but Montana, favored by Walsh because of his mobility, started the last five games. After a 3-0 start, the 49ers lost their next eight games, and in a 59-14 loss to Dallas on October 12, running back Paul Hofer was lost for the year with a knee injury. On November 23, the 49ers blanked the New York Giants 12-0 and launched another three-game winning streak. Two weeks later, the 49ers overcame a 35-7 halftime deficit against New Orleans to win 38-35. The 49ers finished 6-10. Cooper led the NFC in receptions with 83; Clark was just behind with 82.

1981 A remarkable draft yielded Ronnie Lott, Eric Wright, and Carlton Williamson, all of whom earned starting positions in the defensive secondary. Jack Reynolds, released by the Rams, was signed and installed as an inside linebacker. DeBerg was traded to Denver before the season, allowing Montana to become the full-time starter. The club lost two of its first three games but then exploded for a seven-game winning streak to open up a three-game lead in the NFC West. Defensive end Fred Dean was obtained from San Diego before the Dallas game on October 11, and he became one of the leaders of the new defense. The 49ers routed the Cowboys 45-14, holding Dallas to 83 yards passing. After a loss to Cleveland on November 15, the 49ers won their final five games, and clinched the NFC West championship November 29 with a 17-10 victory over the New York Giants. San Francisco finished 13-3, the best record in the NFL. Montana threw for 3,565 yards and was the top-rated passer in the NFC. Clark led NFC receivers with 85 catches for 1,105 yards. The defense allowed just 250 points, the second lowest total in the conference.

1982 The 49ers opened the playoffs against the Giants in a divisional playoff game on January 3, and Montana passed for 304 yards and two touchdowns in a 38-24 victory. In the NFC Championship Game on January 10, Montana directed an 89-yard scoring drive in the closing minutes to defeat Dallas 28-27. Clark climaxed the drive with a leaping catch in the end zone for a six-yard touchdown. In Super Bowl XVI in Pontiac, Michigan, January 24, the 49ers defeated the Bengals 26-21 for San Francisco's first NFL championship.

49ERS RECORD, 1946-81

Year	Won	Lost	Tied	Pct.	Pts.	OP
1946	9	5	0	.643	307	189
1947	8	4	2	.667	327	264
1948	12	2	0	.857	495	248
1949	9	3	0	.750	416	227
1950	3	9	0	.250	213	300
1951	7	4	1	.636	255	205
1952	7	5	0	.583	285	221
1953	9	3	0	.750	372	237
1954	7	4	1	.636	313	251
1955	4	8	0	.333	216	298
1956	5	6	1	.455	233	284
1957	8	4	0	.667	260	264
1958	6	6	0	.500	257	324
1959	7	5	0	.583	255	237
1960	7	5	0	.583	208	205
1961	7	6	1	.538	346	272
1962	6	8	0	.429	282	331
1963	2	12	0	.143	198	391
1964	4	10	0	.286	236	330
1965	7	6	1	.538	421	402
1966	6	6	2	.500	320	325
1967	7	7	0	.500	273	337
1968	7	6	1	.538	303	310
1969	4	8	2	.333	277	319
1970§	10	3	1	.769	352	267
1971§	9	5	0	.643	300	216
1972§	8	5	1	.607	353	249
1973	5	9	0	.357	262	319
1974	6	8	0	.429	226	236
1975	5	9	0	.357	255	286
1976	8	6	0	.571	270	190
1977	5	9	0	.357	220	260
1978	2	14	0	.125	219	350
1979	2	14	0	.125	308	416
1980	6	10	0	.375	320	415
1981*	13	3	0	.813	357	250
32 NFL Years	199	223	12	.472	8,965	9,297

§NFC Western Division Champion
*Super Bowl Champion

RECORD HOLDERS

Rushing (Yards)	Delvin Williams, 1976	1,203
Passing (Pct.)	Joe Montana, 1980	64.5
Passing (Yards)	Steve DeBerg, 1979	3,652
Passing (TDs)	John Brodie, 1965	30
Receiving (No.)	Dwight Clark, 1981	85
Receiving (Yards)	Dave Parks, 1965	1,344
Interceptions (No.)	Dave Baker, 1960	10

Punting (Avg.)	Tommy Davis, 1965	45.8
Punt Ret. (Avg.)	Jim Cason, 1950	15.7
Kickoff Ret. (Avg.)	Joe Arenas, 1953	34.4
Touchdowns (Total)	Joe Perry, 1953	13
Field Goals Made	Bruce Gossett, 1973	26
Points (No.)	Gordy Soltau, 1953	114

COACHING HISTORY

1946-54	Lawrence (Buck) Shaw	71-39-6
		NFL only: 33-25-2
1955	Norman (Red) Strader	4- 8-0
1956-58	Frankie Albert	19-16-1
1959-63	Howard (Red) Hickey*	27-27-1
1963-67	Jack Christiansen	26-38-3
1968-75	Dick Nolan	54-53-5
1976	Monte Clark	8- 6-0
1977	Ken Meyer	5- 9-0
1978	Pete McCulley**	1- 8-0
1978	Fred O'Connor	1- 6-0
1979-81	Bill Walsh	21-27-0

*Resigned after three games in 1963
**Replaced after nine games in 1978

FIRST PLAYER SELECTED

1950	Leo Nomellini, T, Minnesota
1951	Y. A. Tittle, B, Louisiana State
1952	Hugh McElhenny, B, Washington
1953	Harry Babcock, E, Georgia
1954	Bernie Faloney, B, Maryland
1955	Dickie Moegle, B, Rice
1956	Earl Morrall, B, Michigan State
1957	John Brodie, B, Stanford
1958	Jim Pace, B, Michigan
1959	Dave Baker, B, Oklahoma
1960	Monty Stickles, E, Notre Dame
1961	Jimmy Johnson, CB, UCLA
1962	Lance Alworth, WR, Arkansas
1963	Kermit Alexander, CB, UCLA
1964	Dave Parks, WR, Texas Tech
1965	Ken Willard, RB, North Carolina
1966	Stan Hindman, DE, Mississippi
1967	Steve Spurrier, QB, Florida
1968	Forrest Blue, C, Auburn
1969	Ted Kwalick, TE, Penn State
1970	Cedrick Hardman, DE, North Texas State
1971	Tim Anderson, DB, Ohio State
1972	Terry Beasley, WR, Auburn
1973	Mike Holmes, DB, Texas Southern
1974	Wilbur Jackson, RB, Alabama
1975	Jimmy Webb, DT, Mississippi State
1976	Randy Cross, C (2), UCLA
1977	Elmo Boyd, WR (3), Eastern Kentucky
1978	Ken MacAfee, TE, Notre Dame
1979	James Owens, RB (2), UCLA

1980	Earl Cooper, RB, Rice
1981	Ronnie Lott, DB, USC
1982	Bubba Paris, T (2), Michigan

**SAN FRANCISCO 49ERS (AAFC), 1946-49;
SAN FRANCISCO 49ERS, 1950-81**

Abramowicz, Danny, WR, Xavier	1973-74
Albert, Frankie, QB-P, Stanford	1946-52
Aldridge, Ben, HB, Oklahoma State	1952
Aldridge, Jerry, B, Angelo State	1980
Alexander, Kermit, DB, UCLA	1963-69
Allen, Nate, CB, Texas Southern	1975
Anderson, Terry, WR, Bethune-Cookman	1980
Anderson, Tim, S, Ohio State	1975
Arenas, Joe, RB, Nebraska-Omaha	1951-57
Atkins, Billy, B, Auburn	1958-59
Atkins, Dave, RB, Texas-El Paso	1973
Audick, Dan, G, Hawaii	1981
Ayers, John, G, West Texas State	1977-81

B

Babb, Gene, RB, Austin	1957-58
Babcock, Harry, WR, Georgia	1953-55
Bahnsen, Ken, B, North Texas State	1953
Bahr, Matt, K, Penn State	1981
Baker, Dave, DB, Oklahoma	1959-61
Baker Wayne, DT, Brigham Young	1975
Balatti, Ed, E, No college	1946-47
Baldassin, Mike, LB, Washington	1977-78
Baldwin, Jack, C, No college	1947
Banaszek, Cas, T, Northwestern	1968-76
Banducci, Bruno, G, Stanford	1946-54
Barnes, Larry, B, Colorado	1957
Barrett, Jean, T, Tulsa	1973-80
Bassi, Dick, G, Santa Clara	1946-47
Beals, Alyn, E, Santa Clara	1946-51
Beard, Ed, LB, Tennessee	1965-72
Beasley, Terry, WR, Auburn	1972-75
Beatty, Ed, C, Mississippi	1955-56
Beisler, Randy, T, Indiana	1969-74
Belk, Bill, DE, Maryland-Eastern Shore	1968-74
Belser, Caesar, LB, Arkansas-Pine Bluff	1974
Benjamin, Guy, QB, Stanford	1981
Bentz, Roman, T, Tulane	1948
Berry, Rex, B, Brigham Young	1951-56
Bettiga, Mike, WR, Humboldt State	1973
Beverly, Ed, WR, Arizona State	1973
Black, Stan, DB, Mississippi State	1977
Blue, Forrest, C, Auburn	1968-74
Board, Dwaine, DE, North Carolina A&T	1979-81
Boone, J. R., B, Tulsa	1952
Bouza, Matt, WR, California	1981
Bosley, Bruce, G, West Virginia	1956-68
Bradley, Ed, LB, Wake Forest	1977-78
Bragonier, Dennis, DB, Stanford	1974
Bristor, John, S, Waynesburg State	1979
Britt, Charley, DB, Georgia State	1964
Brock, Clyde, T, Utah State	1963
Brodie, John, QB, Stanford	1957-73
Brown, Hardy (The Hatchet), LB, Tulsa	1951-56
Brown, Pete, C, Georgia Tech	1953-54
Bruce, Gail, E, Washington	1948-51
Bruer, Bob, TE, Mankato State	1979-80
Brumfield, Jack, E, Southern Mississippi	1954
Bruney, Fred, DB, Ohio State	1953, 1956
Bryant, Bob, T, Texas Tech	1946-49
Bull, Scott, QB, Arkansas	1976-78
Bungarda, Ken, T, Missouri	1980
Bunz, Dan, LB, Long Beach State	1978-81
Burke, Don, LB, USC	1950-54
Burke, Vern, WR, Oregon State	1965
Burns, Mike, DB, USC	1977

C

Calhoun, Mike, DT, Notre Dame	1980
Calvelli, Tony, C, Stanford	1949
Campbell, Carter, LB, Weber State	1970
Campbell, Marion, T, Georgia	1954-55
Campora, Don, T, Pacific	1950, 1952
Carapella, Al, T, Miami	1951-55
Carpenter, Jack, T, Michigan	1949
Carr, Earl, RB, Florida	1978
Carr, Eddie, B, No college	1947-49
Carr, Paul, LB, Houston	1955-58
Casanega, Ken, B, Santa Clara	1946, 1948
Casey, Bernie, WR, Bowling Green	1961-66
Cason, Jim, DB, Louisiana State	1948-52, 1954
Cassara, Frank, B, St. Mary's, Cal.	1954
Cathcart, Royal, B, California-Santa Barbara	1950
Cathcart, Sam, B, California-Santa Barbara	1949-50, 1952
Ceresino, Gordy, LB, Stanford	1979
Cerne, Joe, C, Northwestern	1965-67
Chapple, Jack, LB, Stanford	1965
Choma, John, G-C, Virginia	1981
Churchman, Ricky, S, Texas	1980-81
Clark, Don, G, USC	1948-49
Clark, Dwight, WR, Clemson	1979-81

Cornerback Ronnie Lott jars the ball from the grasp of Redskins' receiver Art Monk, 1981.

 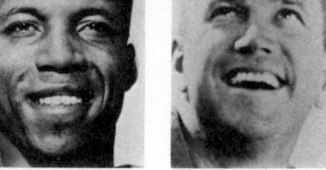 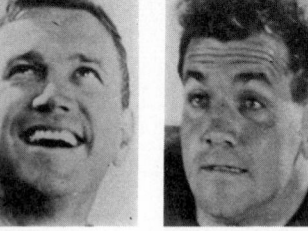    

Kermit Alexander	*Frankie Albert*	*Bruno Banducci*	*Bruce Bosley*	*Dwight Clark*	*Dan Colchico*	*Fred Dean*

Clark, Monte, T, USC 1959-61
Cline, Tony, DE, Miami 1976
Colchico, Dan, DE, San Jose State 1960-65
Collett, Elmer, G, San Francisco State 1967-72
Collier, Floyd, T, San Jose State 1948
Collins, Greg, LB, Notre Dame 1975
Collins, Ray, T, Louisiana State 1950-52
Conlee, Gerry, C, St. Mary's, Cal. 1946-47
Conner, Clyde, E, Pacific 1956-63
Connolly, Ted, G, Tulsa 1954, 1956-62
Cooke, Bill, DE, Massachusetts. 1976
Cooper, Bill, LB, Muskingum 1961-64
Cooper, Earl, RB, Rice 1980-81
Cordileone, Lou, G-LB, Clemson 1961
Cornelius, Charles, DB, Bethune-Cookman .. 1979-80
Cowlings, Al, DE, USC 1979
Cox, Jim, G, Stanford 1948
Cross, Bobby, T, Kilgore JC 1956-57
Cross, Randy, C, UCLA 1976-81
Crow, John David, RB, Texas A&M 1965-68
Crowe, Paul, B, St. Mary's, Cal. 1948
Crowell, Odis, T, Hardin-Simmons 1947
Cunningham, Doug, RB, Mississippi 1967-73

D

Dahms, Tom, T, San Diego State 1957
Daniels, Clem, RB, Prairie View 1968
Daughtery, Bob, B, Tulsa 1966-67
Davis, Johnny, RB, Alabama 1981
Davis, Kyle, C, Oklahoma 1978
Davis, Tommy, P-K, Louisiana State 1959-69
Dean, Floyd, LB, Florida 1963-64
Dean, Fred, DE, Louisiana Tech. 1981
DeBerg, Steve, QB, San Jose State 1977-80
Domres, Marty, QB, Columbia 1976
Donnelly, George, DB, Illinois 1965-67
Donohue, Leon, T, San Jose State 1962-64
Dove, Eddie, DB, Colorado State 1959-62
Dow, Harley, G, San Jose State 1950
Dowdle, Mike, LB, Texas 1963-65
Downing, Walt, G, Michigan 1978-81
Downs, Bob, G, USC 1951
Dugan, Fred, WR, Dayton 1958-59
Duncan, Maury, QB, San Francisco State ... 1954-55
Dungy, Tony, DB, Minnesota. 1979
Durdan, Don, B, Oregon State 1946-47

E

Easley, Walt, RB, West Virginia 1981
Edwards, Earl, DT, Wichita 1969-72
Elam, Cleveland, DE, Tennessee State 1976-78
Elia, Bruce, LB, Ohio State 1976-78
Elliott, Charlie, T, Oregon 1948
Elliott, Lenvil, RB, Northeastern Missouri .. 1979-81
Elston, Art, C, South Carolina 1946-48
Enderle, Dick, G, Minnesota. 1976
Enriss, Al, E, San Francisco State 1952
Eshmont, Len, B, Fordham 1946-49
Evans, Ray, G, Texas-El Paso 1949-50
Evansen, Paul, G, Oregon State. 1948

F

Fahnhorst, Keith, T, Minnesota 1974-81
Feher, Nick, G, Georgia 1951-54
Ferrell, Bob, RB, UCLA 1976-80
Fisk, Bill, E, USC 1946-47
Forrest, Ed, C, Santa Clara 1946-47
Francis, Phil, RB, Stanford. 1979-80
Franceschi, Pete, B, San Francisco. 1946
Freitas, Jesse, B, Santa Clara 1946
Fuller, Johnny, DB, Lamar U. 1968-72

G

Gaiters, Bob, B, New Mexico State 1962-63
Galiffa, Arnold, QB, Army 1954
Galigher, Ed, DT, UCLA 1977-79
Garlin, Don, B, USC 1949-50
Garrett, Len, TE, New Mexico Highlands 1975
Gavric, Momcilo, K, No college 1969
Gehrke, Fred, B, Utah 1950
Gervais, Rick, DB, Stanford 1981
Gilbert, Lewis, TE, Florida 1980

Goad, Paul, B, Abilene Christian 1956
Gonsoulin, Austin (Goose), DB, Baylor. 1967
Gonzaga, John, T, No college 1956-59
Gossett, Bruce, K, Richmond 1970-74
Gray, Tim, DB, Texas A&M 1979
Greenlee, Fritz, LB, Arizona 1969
Gregory, Garland, G, Louisiana Tech 1946-47
Grgich, Visco, G, Santa Clara 1946-52

H

Hall, Forrest, B, San Francisco. 1948
Hall, Parker, B, Mississippi 1946
Hall, Windlan, S, Arizona State 1972-75
Hanley, Dick, C, Fresno State 1947
Hantla, Bob, G, Kansas 1954-55
Hardman, Cedrick, DE, North Texas State .. 1970-79
Hardy, Carroll, B, Colorado. 1955
Hardy, Edgar, G, Jackson State 1973
Hardy, Kevin, DT, Notre Dame 1968
Harkey, Lem, B, Emporia State. 1955
Harper, Willie, LB, Nebraska. 1973-81
Harris, Joe, LB, Georgia Tech 1978
Harris, Tony, WR, Toledo 1971
Harrison, Bob, LB, Oklahoma 1959-61, 1965-67
Harrison, Kenny, WR, Southern Methodist .. 1976-78
Hart, Jeff, T, Oregon State. 1975
Hart, Tommy, DE, Morris Brown 1968-76
Harty, John, DT, Iowa 1981
Hayes, Bob, WR, Florida A&M 1975
Hays, Harold, LB, Southern Mississippi 1968-69
Hazeltine, Matt, LB, California 1955-68
Henderson, Thomas, LB, Langston, Oklahoma .. 1980
Henke, Ed, E, USC 1951-52, 1955-60
Herchman, Bill, T, Texas Tech 1956-59
Hettema, Dave, T, New Mexico 1967
Hicks, Dwight, S, Michigan 1979-81
Hilton, Scott, LB, No college. 1979-80
Hindman, Stan, DE, Mississippi. 1966-71, 1973-74
Hobbs, Homer, G, Georgia 1949-50
Hofer, Paul, RB, Mississippi 1976-81
Hogan, Mike, RB, Tennessee-Chattanooga ... 1979
Hogland, Doug, G, Oregon State 1953-55
Holladay, Bob, RB, Tulsa 1956-57
Hollas, Hugo, DB, Rice 1974
Holmes, Mike, DB, Texas Southern 1974-75
Holzer, Tom, DE, Louisville 1967
Horne, Dick, E, Oregon 1947
Hoskins, Bob, G, Wichita State. 1970-75
Howell, Clarence, E, Texas A&M 1948
Huff, Gary, QB, Florida State 1980
Huff, Marty, LB, Michigan 1972
Hughes, Ernie, G, Notre Dame 1978-80
Hull, Tom, LB, Penn State 1974
Hunt, Charlie, LB, Florida State 1973

I

Isenbarger, John, RB, Indiana 1970-73

J

Jackson, Jim, RB, Western Illinois 1966-67
Jackson, Randy, RB, Wichita 1973
Jackson, Wilbur, RB, Alabama 1974-79
Jennings, Rick, WR, Maryland 1977
Jessup, Bill, E, USC 1951-52, 1954-58
Johnson, Bill, C, Tyler JC 1948-56
Johnson, Charlie, DT, Louisville 1966-67
Johnson, Charles, DB, Grambling 1979-80
Johnson, Eric, S, Washington State 1979
Johnson, Jimmy, DB, UCLA 1961-76
Johnson, John Henry, RB, Arizona State. 1954-56
Johnson, Kermit, RB, UCLA 1975-76
Johnson, Leo, WR, Tennessee State 1969-70
Johnson, Rudy, RB, Nebraska 1964-65
Johnson, Sammy, RB, North Carolina 1974-76
Jones, Arrington, RB, Winston-Salem 1981
Jury, Bob, S, Pittsburgh 1978

K

Kammerer, Carl, LB, Pacific 1961-62
Kelley, Gordon, LB, Georgia 1960-61
Kennedy, Allan, T, Washington State. 1981
Kenny, Charlie, G, San Francisco 1947

Kilgore, Jon, P, Auburn 1969
Kilmer, Billy, QB, UCLA 1961-62, 1964, 1966
Kimbrough, Elbert, DB, Northwestern 1962-66
Knafelc, Gary, E, Colorado 1963
Knutson, Steve, G-T, USC 1978
Kopay, Dave, RB, Washington 1964-67
Kraemer, Eldred, G, Pittsburgh 1955
Krahl, Jim, DT, Texas Tech 1980
Kramer, Kent, TE, Minnesota 1966
Krueger, Charlie, E, Texas A&M 1959-73
Krueger, Rolf, DE, Texas A&M. 1972-74
Kugler, Pete, DT-DE, Penn State 1981
Kuzman, John, T, Fordham 1946
Kwalick, Ted, TE, Penn State 1969-74

L

Lakes, Roland, DT, Wichita 1961-70
Land, Fred, T, Louisiana State 1948
Land, Mel, DE, Michigan State. 1980
LaRose, Dan, DE, Missouri 1965
Larson, Bill, TE, Colorado State 1975
Lash, Jim, WR, Northwestern 1976
Latimer, Al, CB, Clemson 1980
Laughlin, Bud, B, Kansas 1955
Lawrence, Amos, RB, North Carolina 1981
Lawson, Steve, G, Kansas 1976
LeCount, Terry, WR, Florida. 1978
Ledyard, Hal, QB, Tennessee-Chattanooga. 1953
Lee, Dwight, RB, Michigan State 1968
Leonard, Tony, DB, Virginia Union 1976-78
Leopold, Bobby, LB, Notre Dame 1980-81
Lewis, Eddie, DB, Kansas 1976-79
Lewis, Gary, RB, Arizona State 1964-69
Lillywhite, Verl, B, USC 1948-51
Lind, Mike, RB, Notre Dame 1963-64
Lisbon, Don, RB, Bowling Green 1963-64
Livingston, Howie, B, Fullerton JC 1950
Looney, Jim, LB, Purdue 1981
Lopasky, Bill, G, West Virginia 1961
Lott, Ronnie, CB, USC 1981
Loyd, Alex, E, Oklahoma State. 1950
Luna, Bobby, B, Alabama 1955
Lyles, Lenny, B, Louisville 1959-60

M

MacAfee, Ken, TE, Notre Dame 1978-79
Mackey, Dee, TE, East Texas State 1960
Maderos, George, DB, Chico State 1955-56
Magac, Mike, G, Missouri 1960-64
Maloney, Norm, E, Purdue 1948-49
Manley, Joe, C-LB, Mississippi State. 1953
Martin, Bob, LB, Nebraska 1979
Martin, Saladin, DB, San Diego State 1981
Masini, Len, B, Fresno State 1947-48
Matheson, Riley, LB, Texas-El Paso 1948
Mathews, Ned, B, UCLA 1946-47
Matthews, Clay, E, Georgia Tech. 1950, 1953-55
Matuszak, Marv, LB, Tulsa 1957-58
Maurer, Andy, G, Oregon. 1976
McCann, Jim, P, Arizona State 1971-72
McColl, Milt, LB, Stanford 1981
McCormick, Dave, T, Louisiana State 1966
McCormick, Tom, B, Pacific 1956
McCormick, Walt, C, USC 1948
McCray, Willie, DE, Troy State 1978
McElhenny, Hugh, B, Washington 1952-60
McFarland, Kay, B, Colorado State 1962-68
McGee, Willie, WR, Alcorn State 1976
McGill, Ralph, CB, Tulsa 1972-76
McHan, Lamar, QB, Arkansas 1963
McIlheny, Don, RB, Southern Methodist 1961
McIntyre, Jeff, LB, Arizona State 1979
McKoy, Billy, LB, Purdue 1974
McNeil, Clifton, WR, Grambling 1968-69
Mellekas, John, C, Arizona 1962
Mellus, John, T, Villanova 1946
Melville, Dan, P, California 1979
Mertens, Jerry, DB, Drake 1958-65
Messer, Dale, RB-WR, Fresno State. 1961-65
Meyers, Bob, B, Stanford 1952
Michalik, Art, G, St. Ambrose 1953-54
Mike, Bob, T, UCLA 1948-49

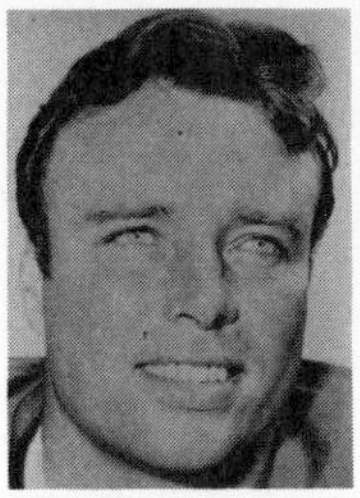
Matt Hazeltine

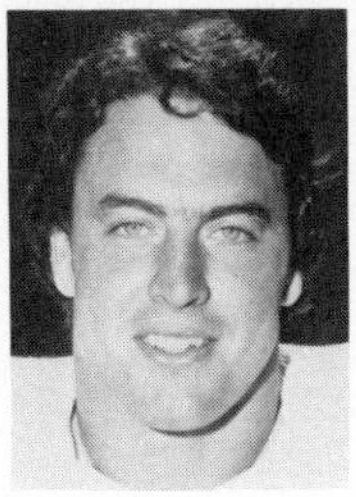
Paul Hofer

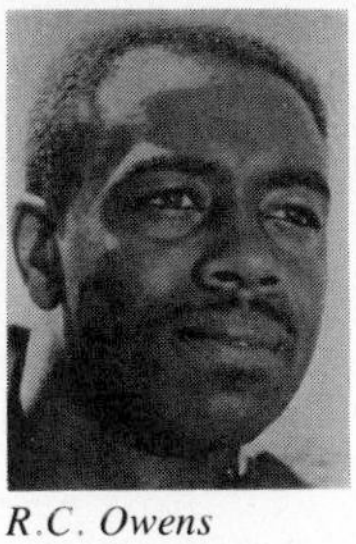
R.C. Owens

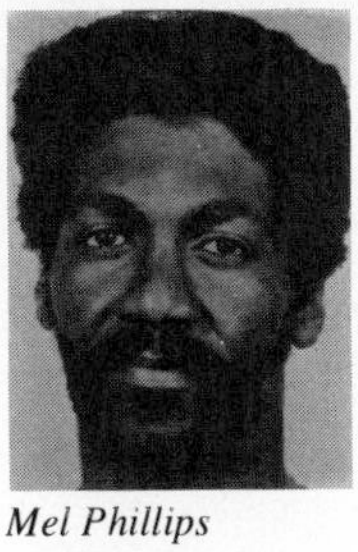
Mel Phillips

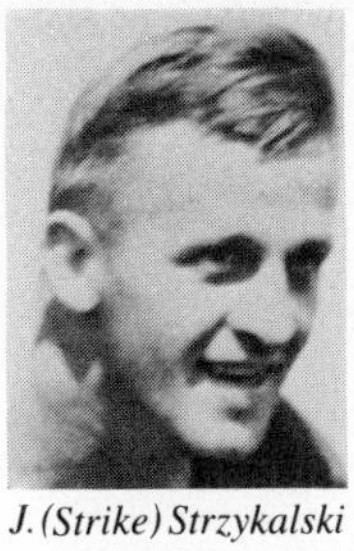
J. (Strike) Strzykalski

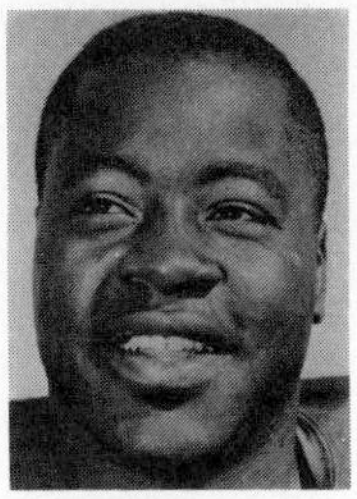
John Thomas

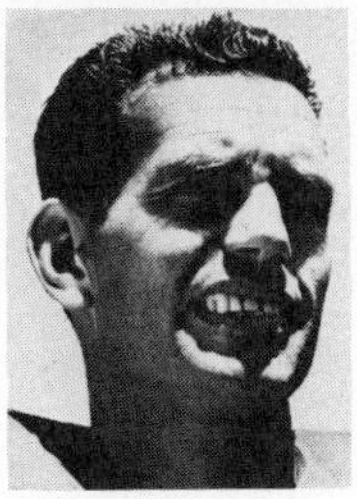
Billy Wilson

Mike-Mayer, Steve, K, Maryland 1975-76
Miles, Searcy, QB, San Jose State 1954-56
Miller, Clark, DE, Utah State 1962-68
Miller, Hal, T, Georgia Tech 1953
Miller, Jim, P, Mississippi 1980-81
Miller, Johnny, G, Livingston 1977-78
Mira, George, QB, Miami 1964-68
Mitchell, Dale, LB, USC 1976
Mitchell, Tom, TE, Bucknell 1974-77
Mixon, Billy, B, Georgia 1953-54
Moegle, Dicky, B, Rice 1955-59
Momsen, Bob, G, Ohio State 1952
Monachino, Jim, B, California 1951
Monds, Wonder, DB, Nebraska 1978
Montana, Joe, QB, Notre Dame 1979-81
Moore, Dean, LB, Iowa 1978
Moore, Eugene, RB, Occidental 1969
Moore, Manfred, RB, USC 1974-75
Morgan, Joe, T, Southern Mississippi 1949
Morgan, Melvin, DB, Mississippi Valley 1979-80
Morrall, Earl, QB, Michigan State 1956
Morris, Dennit, LB, Oklahoma 1958
Morris, George, C, Georgia Tech 1956
Morrison, Dennis, QB, Kansas State 1974
Morton, Dave, LB, UCLA 1979
Morton, John, LB, Texas Christian 1953
Morze, Frank, C, Boston College 1957-61
Mudd, Howard, G, Hillsdale 1964-69
Myers, Chip, WR, Northwestern Oklahoma 1967

N

Nichols, Mark, LB, Colorado State 1978
Nicholson, Jim, T, Michigan State 1981
Nix, Jack, E, USC 1950
Nomellini, Leo, T-DT, Minnesota 1950-63
Norberg, Hank, E, Stanford 1946-47
Nordquist, Mark, G, Pacific 1976
Norton, Jim, T, Washington 1965-66
Norton, Ray, RB, San Jose State 1960-61
Nunley, Frank, LB, Michigan 1967-76

O

Obradovich, Jim, TE, USC 1976
Odom, Ricky, DB, USC 1978
O'Donahue, Pat, E, Wisconsin 1952
Olerich, Dave, LB, San Francisco 1967-68, 1972-73
Olssen, Lance, T, Purdue 1968-69
Osborne, Clancy, LB, Arizona State 1959-60
Owens, Tom, QB, Wichita State 1974-75
Owens, James, WR, UCLA 1979-80
Owens, R. C., WR, College of Idaho 1957-61

P

Pace, Jim, B, Michigan 1958
Palatella, Lou, G, Pittsburgh 1955-58
Parker, Don, G, Virginia 1967
Parks, Dave, TE, Texas Tech 1964-67
Parsons, Earle, B, USC 1946-47
Patera, Dennis, K, Brigham Young 1968
Patton, Ricky, RB, Jackson State 1980-81
Pavlich, Chuck, G, No college 1946
Peets, Brian, TE, Pacific 1981
Penchlon, Bob, T, Alcorn State 1974-75
Peoples, Woody, G, Grambling 1968-76
Perry, Joe, RB, Compton JC 1948-60, 1963
Perry, Scott, S, Williams 1980
Phillips, Mel, DB, North Carolina A&T 1966-76
Pillers, Lawrence, DE, Alcorn State 1980-81
Pine, Eddie, LB, Utah 1962-64
Plunkett, Jim, QB, Stanford 1976-77
Poole, Bob, TE, Clemson 1964-65
Powell, Charley, E, No college 1952-53, 1955-57
Powers, Jim, QB, USC 1950-53
Puddy, Hal, T, Oregon 1948
Puki, Craig, LB, Tennessee 1980-81

Q

Quillan, Fred, C, Oregon 1978-81
Quilter, Chuck, T, Tyler JC 1949

R

Raines, Mike, DT, Alabama 1974
Ramson, Eason, TE, Washington State 1979-81
Randle, Sonny, WR, Virginia 1967
Randolph, Alvin, DB, Iowa 1966-70, 1974
Rasley, Rocky, G, Oregon State 1976
Reed, Joe, QB, Mississippi State 1972-74
Reese, Archie, DE, Grambling 1978-81
Reld, Bill, C, Stanford 1975
Remington, Bill, C, Washington State 1946
Renfro, Dick, B, Washington State 1946
Reynolds, Jack, LB, Tennessee 1981
Rhodes, Bruce, DB, San Francisco State 1976
Rhodes, Ray, CB, Tulsa 1980
Ridlon, Jim, DB, Syracuse 1957-62
Riley, Preston, WR, Memphis State 1970-72
Ring, Bill, RB, Brigham Young 1981
Rivera, Steve, WR, California 1976
Roberson, Vern, DB, Grambling 1978
Roberts, C. R., RB, USC 1959-62
Robinson, Jimmy, WR, Georgia Tech 1980
Robnett, Ed, B, Texas Tech 1947
Rock, Walter, T, Maryland 1963-67
Rohde, Len, T, Utah State 1960-74
Roskie, Ken, B, South Carolina 1946
Rubke, Karl, C, USC 1957-60, 1962-63, 1965
Rucka, Leo, C, Rice 1956

S

Sabuco, Tino, C, San Francisco 1949
Sagely, Floyd, E, Arkansas 1954-56
Salata, Paul, E, USC 1949-50
Sandifer, Bill, DT, UCLA 1974-76
Sandifer, Dan, B, Louisiana State 1950
Sardisco, Tony, G, Tulane 1956
Satterfield, Alf, T, Vanderbilt 1947
Saunders, John, DB, Toledo 1974-75
Schiechl, John, C, Santa Clara 1947
Schabarum, Pete, B, California 1951, 1953-54
Schmidt, Henry, T, USC 1959-60
Schreiber, Larry, RB, Tennessee Tech 1971-75
Scotti, Ben, B, Maryland 1964
Seabron, Thomas, LB, Michigan 1979-80
Seal, Paul, TE, Michigan 1977-79
Sharkey, Ed, G, Nevada-Reno 1955-56
Shaw, Charlie, G, Oklahoma State 1950
Sheriff, Stan, LB, Cal Poly-San Luis Obispo 1956-57
Shoener, Hal, E, Iowa 1948-50
Shumann, Mike, WR, Florida 1978-79, 1981
Sieminski, Chuck, T, Penn State 1963-65
Silas, Sam, DE, Southern Illinois 1969-70
Simpson, Mike, DB, Houston 1970-72
Simpson, O. J., RB, USC 1978-79
Singleton, Ron, T, Grambling 1977-80
Sitko, Emil, B, Notre Dame 1950
Smith, Charlie, E, Abilene Christian 1956
Smith, Ernie, B, Compton JC 1955-56
Smith, George, C, California 1947
Smith, J. D., B, North Carolina A&T 1956-64
Smith, Jerry, G, Wisconsin 1952-53
Smith, Noland, RB, Tennessee State 1969
Smith, Steve, E, Michigan 1966-67
Snead, Norman, QB, Wake Forest 1974-75
Sniadecki, Jim, LB, Indiana 1969-73
Solomon, Freddie, WR, Tampa 1979-81
Soltau, Gordy, E-K, Minnesota 1950-58
Sparks, Dave, G, South Carolina 1951
Spence, Julian, B, Sam Houston State 1957
Spurrier, Steve, QB-P, Florida 1967-75
Standlee, Norm, B-LB, Stanford 1946-52
St. Clair, Bob, T, Tulsa 1953-64
Steptoe, Jack, WR, Utah 1978
Stickles, Monty, TE, Notre Dame 1960-67
Stidham, Howard, LB, Tennessee Tech 1977
Stits, Bill, DB, UCLA 1957-58
Stolhandske, Tom, LB, Texas 1955
Strickland, Bishop, B, South Carolina 1951
Strong, Jim, RB, Houston 1970
Strzykalski, John (Strike), B, Marquette 1946-52
Stuckey, Jim, DE, Clemson 1980-81
Sullivan, Bob, B, Holy Cross 1948
Susoeff, Nick, E, Washington State 1946-49
Sutro, John, T, San Jose State 1962
Swinford, Wayne, DB, Georgia 1965-67

T

Tanner, Hamp, T, Georgia 1951
Tautolo, Terry, LB, UCLA 1980-81
Taylor, Bruce, CB, Boston U. 1970-76
Taylor, Roosevelt, S, Grambling 1969-71
Teresa, Tony, B, San Jose State 1958
Thomas, Aaron, E, Oregon State 1961
Thomas, Jimmy, RB, Texas-Arlington 1969-73
Thomas, John, T, Pacific 1958-67
Thomas, Lynn, DB, Pittsburgh 1981
Thornton, Rupe, G, Santa Clara 1946-47
Threadgill, Bruce, S, Mississippi State 1978
Tidwell, Billy, B, Texas A&M 1954
Times, Ken, DT, Southern U. 1980
Titchenal, Bob, E, San Jose State 1946
Tittle, Y. A., QB, Louisiana State 1951-60
Toneff, Bob, T, Notre Dame 1952, 1954-59
Trimble, Wayne, DB, Alabama 1967
Tubbs, Jerry, LB, Oklahoma 1958-59
Tucker, Bill, RB, Tennessee State 1967-70
Turner, Keena, LB, Purdue 1980-81

V

Vanderbundt, Skip, LB, Oregon State 1969-76
Van Doren, Bob, E, USC 1953
Vaughan, Ruben, DT, Colorado 1979
Vaught, Ted, E, Texas Christian 1955
Vetrano, Joe, B, Southern Mississippi 1946-49
Vincent, Ted, DT, Wichita State 1979-80
Visger, George, DT, Colorado 1980
Vollenwelder, Jim, FB, Miami 1962-63

W

Wagner, Lowell, B, USC 1949-53, 1955
Walker, Elliott, RB, Pittsburgh 1978
Walker, Val Joe, B, Southern Methodist 1957
Wallace, Bev, QB, Compton JC 1947-49
Washington, Dave, LB, Alcorn State 1975-76
Washington, Gene, WR, Stanford 1969-76
Washington, Vic, RB, Wyoming 1971-73
Waters, Bobby, QB, Presbyterian 1960-64
Watson, John, T, Oklahoma 1971-76
Webb, Jimmy, DT, Mississippi State 1975-80
Wersching, Ray, K, California 1977-81
West, Robert, WR, San Diego State 1974
White, Bob, B, Stanford 1951-52
Wilcox, Dave, LB, Oregon 1964-74
Wilkinson, Jerry, DE, Oregon State 1980
Willard, Ken, RB, North Carolina 1965-73
Williams, Dave, RB, Colorado 1977
Williams, Delvin, RB, Kansas 1974-76
Williams, Gerard, DB, Langston, Oklahoma 1979-80
Williams, Herb, CB, Southern U. 1980
Williams, Howie, B, Howard 1963
Williams, Joel, C, Texas 1948
Williams, Johnny, B, USC 1954
Williams, Roy, T, Pacific 1963
Williamson, Carlton, S, Pittsburgh 1981
Wilson, Billy, WR, San Jose State 1951-60
Wilson, Jerry, LB, Auburn 1960
Wilson, Jim, G, Georgia 1965-66
Wilson, Mike, WR, Washington State 1981
Windsor, Bob, TE, Kentucky 1967-71
Winston, Lloyd, B, USC 1962-63
Wismann, Pete, LB, St. Louis 1949-52, 1954
Witcher, Dick, WR, UCLA 1966-73
Wittenborn, John, G, Missouri State 1958-60
Wittum, Tom, P, Northern Illinois 1973-76
Woitt, John, DB, Mississippi State 1968-69
Wondolowski, Bill, WR, Eastern Montana 1969
Woods, Don, RB, New Mexico 1980
Woodson, Abe, DB, Illinois 1958-64
Woudenberg, John, T, Denver 1946-49
Wright, Eric, CB, Missouri 1981

Y

Yonamine, Wally, B, No college 1947
Young, Charle, TE, USC 1980-81
Youngelman, Sid, T, Alabama 1955
Yowarsky, Walt, C, Kentucky 1958

Z

Zamlynsky, Ziggie, B, Villanova 1946

SEATTLE SEAHAWKS

1972 Seattle Professional Football, Inc., a group of business and community leaders, announced its intention to bid for a National Football League franchise for the city of Seattle, June 15. Herman Sarkowsky, principal owner of the National Basketball Association's Portland Trail Blazers, was spokesman for the group. He was joined by D. E. (Ned) Skinner, Howard S. Wright, M. Lamont Bean, Lynn P. Himmelman, and Lloyd W. Nordstrom. In November, construction began on the $67 million Kingdome with a seating capacity of 65,000 for football.

1974 The National Football League awarded a franchise to Seattle Professional Football, Inc. for $16 million, December 5. The Nordstrom family was the majority owner, with Elmer Sarkowsky, Skinner, Himmelman, Wright, and Bean partners.

1975 John Thompson, executive director of the NFL Management Council, was named general manager of the Seattle franchise, March 6. In April, Mark Duncan was named assistant general manager and Dick Mansperger, director of player personnel with the Dallas Cowboys, was appointed to a similar post in Seattle. A contest to name the team drew 20,365 entries; "Seahawks" was selected, June 17. Season ticket applications were accepted and 24,168 requests arrived the first day, July 28. The season ticket sale closed 27 days later with 59,000 purchased. "We anticipated a good sale," Thompson said, "but no one in his right mind would have predicted this." They adopted blue, green, and silver as their official colors. The team signed a 20-year lease to play all home games in the Kingdome.

1976 Jack Patera, an assistant coach with the Minnesota Vikings, was named first head coach of the Seahawks, January 3. Lloyd Nordstrom, spokesman for the majority owners, died of a heart attack while vacationing in Mexico, January 20. The Seahawks selected 39 NFL veterans in the allocation draft, March 30. Among the top veterans chosen were tackle Norm Evans of Miami and linebacker Mike Curtis of Baltimore, both former members of Super Bowl champions and all-pro selections. The Seahawks selected 25 rookies in their first college draft, April 8. Steve Niehaus, a 6-foot 4-inch, 270-pound defensive tackle from Notre Dame, was the number one choice. In the second round, Seattle selected linebacker Sammy Green of Florida; Sherman Smith, a quarterback at Miami, Ohio; and wide receiver Steve Raible of Georgia Tech. The Seahawks won two games in their first season. In their league opener, they battled St. Louis furiously before losing 30-24 in the Kingdome, September 12. Jim Zorn, Seattle's left-handed rookie quarterback from Cal Poly-Pomona, passed for two touchdowns and ran for another. After losing five games, the Seahawks recorded their first victory, beating Tampa Bay 13-10, October 17. Seattle scored its first win over an established team as Sherman Smith, converted to running back, rushed for 124 yards and two touchdowns in a 30-13 rout of Atlanta, November 7. The following week, Zorn passed for two touchdowns and ran for a third as the Seahawks pushed Minnesota before losing 27-21. Smith led Seattle with 537 yards rushing. Steve Largent, a rookie wide receiver from Tulsa, caught 54 passes to rank third in the NFC. Zorn passed for 2,571 yards, the most ever by a first-year NFL quarterback.

1977 The Seahawks hosted the Pro Bowl on January 17. The crowd of 64,151 made for the first sellout in the 27-year history of the game. Seattle was permanently aligned in the AFC Western division. The Sea-

hawks traded their first-round draft choice to Dallas for the Cowboys' first-round pick and three second-round picks. The Cowboys chose Tony Dorsett; Seattle chose tackle Steve August on the first round. The Seahawks opened with four consecutive losses. Zorn was injured in the second game, a 42-20 loss to Cincinnati. On October 16, backup quarterback Steve Myer threw four touchdowns to lead Seattle to its first victory of the season, 30-23 over Tampa Bay. Two weeks later, Zorn made his first start in a month and threw for four touchdowns as Seattle set 15 club records in a 56-17 win over Buffalo. On November

13, the Seahawks registered their first shutout ever, 17-0 against the Jets. Victories in the last two games gave Seattle a 5-9 record, the best ever for a second-year expansion team.

1978 The Seahawks shed their expansion team tag. They finished 9-7 and only one game out of first place in the AFC West. The offense, led by Zorn, proved one of the most explosive in the NFL, but the defense lagged behind. On October 8, Efren Herrera kicked a 19-yard field goal on the final play of the game for a 29-28 victory over Minnesota. Two weeks later, the defense came alive and intercepted Ken Sta-

Seahawks' all-time leading receiver Steve Largent, 1981.

bler four times, leading to a 27-7 surprise of Oakland. An overtime loss to Denver was followed by four victories in five weeks. A 17-16 win in Oakland made the Seahawks the first team since 1965 to defeat the Raiders twice in the regular season. Although playoff hopes were dimmed by a loss to San Diego on December 10, the Seahawks closed out with a winning season in only their third year. David Sims finished with a league-leading 15 touchdowns, and Steve Largent made 71 receptions to lead the AFC.

1979 Jack Patera was named 1978 NFL coach of the year. On Janaury 29, Largent caught a record-equaling five passes as Seattle's first representative in the Pro Bowl. In a move to bolster the defense, Seattle made UCLA defensive tackle Manu Tuiasosopo its first choice in the draft. Sims was forced into early retirement with a neck injury in early season. The Seahawks started slowly, winning only twice in their first seven games. A 34-14 victory over the Oilers turned the season around and Seattle finished with a rush, going 7-2 and ending with wins over Denver and Oakland (their fourth straight against the Raiders). Zorn passed for a club record of 3,661 yards, and Largent, who was selected to his second straight AFC-NFC Pro Bowl, led the NFL with 1,237 yards receiving.

1980 The Seahawks were thinking playoffs after a 4-3 start that included a victory in Houston (26-7) and a 14-0 shutout of the Redskins in Washington. But the loss of Smith with a knee injury and the breakdown of the offensive line (which allowed 51 sacks) sent the Seahawks into a tailspin. They lost their last nine games and finished 4-12. Included in the disappointing record were eight straight losses in the Kingdome. Zorn again threw for over 3,000 yards (3,346) and Largent (66) and Sam McCullum (62) combined to catch 128 passes. The defense gave up 408 points, the most in the AFC.

1981 The Seahawks tried to shore up one of their weakest areas by drafting three-time UCLA All-America defensive back Kenny Easley. Seattle didn't get out of the cellar of the AFC West for one week in a disappointing season that saw the team start off 1-6. A strong finish brought the final record to 6-10, which included wins over Denver, San Diego, and the New York Jets. The Seahawks defeated the Jets twice, giving them victories in all six meetings between the clubs since Seattle entered the NFL. Largent was second in the AFC in receptions with a club record 75 and was chosen for his third AFC-NFC Pro Bowl appearance.

1982 Sarkowsky stepped down as managing general partner and was replaced by Nordstrom.

MEMBERS OF HALL OF FAME:
None

SEAHAWK'S RECORD, 1976-81

Year	Won	Lost	Tied	Pct.	Pts.	OP
1976	2	12	0	.143	229	429
1977	5	9	0	.357	282	373
1978	9	7	0	.563	345	358
1979	9	7	0	.563	378	372
1980	4	12	0	.250	291	408
1981	6	10	0	.375	322	388
6 Years	35	57	0	.380	1,847	2,328

RECORD HOLDERS

Rushing (Yards)	Sherman Smith, 1978	805
Passing (Pct.)	Jim Zorn, 1981	59.4
Passing (Yards)	Jim Zorn, 1979	3,661
Passing (TDs)	Jim Zorn, 1979	20
Receiving (No.)	Steve Largent, 1981	75
Receiving (Yards)	Steve Largent, 1979	1,237
Interceptions (No.)	John Harris, 1981	10
Punting (Avg.)	Herman Weaver, 1980	41.8
Punt Ret. (Avg.)	Paul Johns, 1981	11.1
Kickoff Ret. (Avg.)	Al Hunter, 1978	24.1
Touchdowns (Total)	David Sims, 1978, and Sherman Smith, 1979	15
Field Goals Made	Efren Herrera, 1980	20
Points (No.)	Efren Herrera, 1979	100

Safeties Kenny Easley (45) and John Harris (44) put the stops on Bengals' fullback Pete Johnson, 1981.

COACHING HISTORY

1976-81	Jack Patera	35-57-0

FIRST PLAYER SELECTED

1976	Steve Niehaus, DT, Notre Dame
1977	Steve August, G, Tulsa
1978	Keith Simpson, DB, Memphis State
1979	Manu Tuiasosopo, DT, UCLA
1980	Jacob Green, DE, Texas A&M
1981	Kenny Easley, DB, UCLA
1982	Jeff Bryant, DE, Clemson

SEATTLE SEAHAWKS, 1976-81

Adkins, Sam, QB, Wichita State 1977-81
Aiu, Charlie, G, Hawaii 1978
Alvarez, Wilson, K, Southeastern Louisiana 1981
Anderson, Fred, DE, Prairie View 1980-81
August, Steve, T, Tulsa 1977-81

B

Bachman, Ted, CB, New Mexico State 1976
Bailey, Edwin, G, South Carolina State 1981
Barisich, Carl, DT, Princeton 1976
Beamon, Autry, S, East Texas State 1977-79
Bebout, Nick, T, Wyoming 1976-79
Beeson, Terry, LB, Kansas 1977-81
Bell, Mark, TE, Colorado State 1979-80
Benjamin, Tony, RB, Duke 1977-79
Bitterlich, Don, K, Temple 1976
Blackwood, Lyle, S, Texas Christian 1976
Bolton, Andrew, RB, Fisk 1976
Boyd, Dennis, DT-DE, Oregon State 1977-79, 1981
Bradley, Ed, LB, Wake Forest 1976
Brinson, Larry, RB, Florida. 1980
Brown, Dave, CB, Michigan 1976-81
Brown, Theotis, RB, UCLA 1981
Bullard, Louis, T, Jackson State 1978-80
Butler, Keith, LB, Memphis State 1978-81

C

Clune, Don, WR, Pennsylvania 1976
Coder, Ron, G, Penn State 1976-77, 1979
Coffield, Randy, LB, Florida State 1976
Collins, Greg, LB, Notre Dame. 1976
Cooke, Bill, DT-DE, Massachusetts 1978-80
Cowlings, Al, DE, USC. 1976
Crawford, Rufus, RB, Virginia State 1978
Cronan, Peter, LB, Boston College 1977-79, 1981
Curtis, Mike, LB, Duke. 1976

D

Darby, Alvis, TE, Florida 1976
Demarie, John, G, Louisiana State 1976
Dion, Terry, DE, Oregon. 1980
Doornink, Dan, RB, Washington State 1979-81
Dorris, Andy, DE, New Mexico State 1977
Dufek, Don, S, Michigan 1976-77, 1979-81
Dugan, Bill, G, Penn State 1981

E

Easley, Kenny, S, UCLA 1981
East, Ron, DT, Montana State 1977
Eller, Carl, DE, Minnesota 1979
Engles, Rick, P, Tulsa 1976-77
Essink, Ron, T, Grand Valley State 1980-81
Evans, Norm, T, Texas Christian 1976-78

F

Fergerson, Duke, WR, San Diego State 1977-79
Fifer, Bill, T, West Texas State 1979
Flones, Brian, LB, Washington State 1981

G

Gaines, Greg, LB, Tennessee. 1981
Garcia, Frank, P, Arizona. 1981
Geddes, Ken, LB, Nebraska 1976-78
Graff, Neil, QB, Wisconsin. 1976
Green, Jacob, DE, Texas A&M 1980-81
Green, Jessie, WR, Tulsa 1979-80
Green, Sammy, LB, Florida 1976-79
Green, Tony, KR, Florida 1979
Gregory, Bill, DE-DT, Wisconsin 1978-80

H

Hansen, Don, LB, Illinois 1976
Hardy, Robert, DT, Jackson State. 1979-81
Harris, John, S, Arizona State 1978-81
Harris, Richard, DE-DT, Grambling 1976-77
Herrera, Efren, K, UCLA 1978-81
Hines, Andre, T, Stanford 1980
Hoaglin, Fred, C, Pittsburgh 1976
Howard, Ron, TE, Seattle 1976-78
Hughes, David, RB, Boise State 1981
Hunter, Al, RB, Notre Dame. 1977-80

J

Jackson, Michael, LB, Washington 1979-81
Jodat, Jim, FB, Carthage. 1980-81
Johns, Paul, WR, Tulsa 1981
Johnson, Greggory, S, Oklahoma State 1981
Jolley, Gordon, T-G, Utah 1976-77
Jones, Ernie, CB, Miami 1976
Jones, Horace, DE, Louisville 1977
Jones, Mike, LB, Jackson State 1977
Justin, Kerry, CB, Oregon State 1978-81

K

Kraayeveld, Dave, DE-DT, Milton 1978
Krieg, Dave, QB, Milton 1980-81
Kuehn, Art, C-G, UCLA 1976-81

L

Lane, Eric, RB, Brigham Young 1981
Largent, Steve, WR, Tulsa 1976-81
Lewis, Will, CB, Millersville State 1980-81
Leypoldt, John, K, No college 1976-78

Theotis Brown

Jacob Green

Efren Herrera

Michael Jackson

Jim Jodat

Sherman Smith

Manu Tuiasosopo

Long, Doug, S, Whitworth 1978
Lurtsema, Bob, DE-DT, Western Michigan 1976-77
Lynch, Tom, G, Boston College 1977-80

M

Marinaro, Ed, RB, Cornell 1977
Martin, Amos, LB, Louisville 1977
Matthews, Al, S, Texas A&I 1976
McCullum, Sam, WR, Montana State 1976-81
McCutcheon, Lawrence, RB, Colorado State 1980
McGrath, Mark, WR, Montana State 1981
McKinnis, Hugh, RB, Arizona State 1976
McMakin, John, TE, Clemson .1976
McMillan, Eddie, CB, Florida State 1976-77
McShane, Charles, LB, California Lutheran 1977-79
Miller, Terry, RB, Oklahoma State 1981
Minor, Vic, S, Northeastern Louisiana 1980-81
Moore, Jeff, RB, Jackson State 1979-81
Munson, Bill, QB, Utah State .1976
Myer, Steve, QB, New Mexico 1976-79

N

Nelson, Ralph, RB, No college .1976
Newton, Bob, G, Nebraska .1976-81
Niehaus, Steve, DT-DE, Notre Dame 1976-78
Norman, Joe, LB, Indiana 1979-81

O

O'Brien, Mike, S, California 1979
Olds, Bill, RB, Nebraska 1976

P

Packer, Walter, CB-KR, Mississippi State 1977
Peets, Brian, TE, Pacific 1978-79
Penchion, Bob, G, Alcorn State 1976
Polowski, Larry, LB, Boise State 1979
Preece, Steve, S, Oregon State 1977
Price, Ernie, DE, Texas A&I 1978-79

R

Raible, Steve, WR, Georgia Tech 1976-81
Rayhle, Fred, TE, Tennessee-Chattanooga 1977
Reece, Geoff, C, Washington State 1977
Rennaker, Terry, LB, Stanford 1980
Roche, Alden, DE, Southern U. 1977-78
Ross, Oliver, RB, Alabama A&M 1976

S

Sandifer, Bill, DT, UCLA 1977-78
Sawyer, John, TE, Southern Mississippi 1977-78, 1980-81
Sevy, Jeff, G-T, California 1979-80
Simonson, Dave, T, Minnesota 1976
Simpson, Keith, CB-S, Memphis State 1978-81
Sims, David, RB, Georgia Tech 1977-79

Smith, Sherman, RB, Miami, Ohio 1976-81
Sutherland, Doug, DT, Wisconsin-Superior 1981

T

Testerman, Don, RB, Clemson 1976-78
Thomas, Rodell, LB, Alabama State 1981
Tice, Mike, TE, Maryland 1981
Tipton, Dave, DE, Stanford 1976
Tuiasosopo, Manu, DT, UCLA 1979-81
Turner, Kevin, LB, Pacific 1981

W

Wagner, Vince, K, Northwestern, Minnesota 1981
Walker, Tim, LB, Savannah State 1980
Walsh, Jim, RB, San Jose State 1980
Weaver, Herman, P, Tennessee 1977-80
Webster, Cornell, CB, Tulsa 1977-80
West, Jeff, P, Cincinnati 1981
White, Jim, DE, Colorado State 1976
White, Mike, DE, Albany State 1981
Woods, Larry, DT, Tennessee State 1976
Woolsey, Rolly, CB, Boise State 1976

Y

Yarno, John, C, Idaho 1977-81

Z

Zorn, Jim, QB, Cal Poly-Pomona 1976-81

Southpaw quarterback Jim Zorn passes against San Diego, 1980.

Dave Brown eludes Mark Cotney of Tampa Bay, 1976.

TAMPA BAY BUCCANEERS

1974 Commissioner Pete Rozelle awarded a National Football League franchise to Tampa Bay in a press conference at New York's Drake Hotel, April 24. Rozelle said the league had long been impressed by Tampa Bay's strong support of NFL preseason games over the years. Overall, 13 preseason contests had been held at Tampa Stadium with an average attendance of 41,000. Philadelphia construction tycoon Tom McCloskey was awarded the franchise, October 30, but he withdrew from the project two weeks later. The franchise was awarded to Hugh F. Culverhouse, a Jacksonville attorney and real estate investor, for $16 million, December 5. Culverhouse had previously attempted to purchase the Los Angeles Rams.

1975 More than 400 nicknames for the team were submitted to an advisory board and Culverhouse selected "Buccaneers," February 15. The Tampa City Council voted to approve expansion of Tampa Stadium from 46,500 to 72,000 seats, making it the seventh largest stadium in the NFL. Ron Wolf, director of player personnel for the Oakland Raiders, was named vice president of operations, April 30. The Buccaneers adopted the colors of orange and white with red trim and approved the symbol of a swashbuckling buccaneer, June 15. Culverhouse signed John McKay to a five-year contract as head coach, October 31. While at USC, McKay won eight Pacific 8 titles, five Rose Bowls, and four national championships.

1976 Tampa Bay selected 39 players (20 defensive, 19 offensive) in the veteran allocation draft in New York, March 30. The Buccaneers made their first trade, sending two players and a draft choice to San Francisco for quarterback Steve Spurrier, the former Heisman Trophy winner from the University of Florida, April 2. A week later, Tampa Bay had the first pick in the college draft and selected Lee Roy Selmon, the All-America defensive tackle from Oklahoma. The Buccaneers drafted his brother, Dewey, a defensive tackle, on the second round. The Buccaneers became the first 0-14 team in NFL history, and the first team to go winless since the 1960 Dallas Cowboys. They failed to score a touchdown in their first three league games and were shut out five times. They opened with a 20-0 loss in Houston, September 12. While some of the defeats were one-sided, others were frustratingly close, such as a 23-20 final-minute setback to intrastate rival Miami on October 24. Tampa Bay's leading rusher was Louis Carter, who gained 521 yards. Spurrier, who alternated with rookie quarterback Parnell Dickinson, was the leading passer. Morris Owens was the leading receiver (30 catches) and scorer (36 points).

1977 With the first selection in the draft, the Buccaneers picked Ricky Bell, a running back from USC. McKay selected another of his former players, linebacker David Lewis, in the second round. The Buccaneers were realigned into the Central Division of the NFC. A unique schedule permitted the team to play one game against every team in its new conference. With McKay emphasizing defense, Tampa Bay ranked ninth in the NFC in defensive statistics. However, the offense scored a league-low 103 points and finished last in the NFL in every major offensive category. The troubles began in the preseason when quarterback Mike Boryla suffered a knee injury and was lost for the season. With Gary Huff also unavailable, the quarterbacking chores fell to untested Randy Hedberg and Jeb Blount. The Buccaneers lost their first 12 games of the season, including six by shutouts, and extended their winless streak to 26

games. But on December 11 in New Orleans, the defense became offensive and scored three touchdowns on interceptions, leading the Buccaneers to their first NFL victory 33-14. More than 8,000 fans were on hand to greet the team when it returned to Tampa. A week later, Tampa Bay made it two in a row with a 17-7 victory over St. Louis in Tampa.

1978 Tampa Bay traded the first choice in the draft to Houston for tight end Jimmie Giles and four draft choices. The Oilers selected Earl Campbell; the Buccaneers chose Doug Williams, a quarterback from Grambling. After two close losses to open the season, the Buccaneers defeated Minnesota 16-10. Lee Roy Selmon sparked the victory by recording three sacks. The team followed with a 14-9 victory over Atlanta on September 24. With an improving offense, the Buccaneers won three more games during the season and finished 5-11. Williams had his best game on October 8 when he threw for 226 yards in a 30-13 victory over Kansas City. In a loss to the New York Giants on October 15, Jimmy DuBose became the first Buccaneers running back to exceed 100 yards rushing in a game. The team scored 241 points, up 138 from the previous season.

1979 The Buccaneers opened the season with a convincing 31-16 victory over Detroit. A blossoming

All-pro defensive end Lee Roy Selmon smothers Chicago quarterback Bob Avellini, 1977.

Doug Williams looks for an open receiver against St. Louis, 1981.

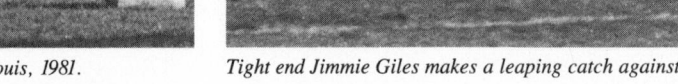

Tight end Jimmie Giles makes a leaping catch against Minnesota, 1979.

offense then sparked consecutive victories over Baltimore, Green Bay, and Los Angeles. On September 30, rookie Jerry Eckwood scored on the longest touchdown run in team history—61 yards—to spark the Buccaneers to a 17-13 win over Chicago. That victory preserved Tampa Bay's status as the lone unbeaten club in the NFL. Following a loss to the New York Giants, the team won four times in the next six weeks to move within one victory of clinching the divisional crown. On November 25, Bell rushed for 101 yards to become the first Tampa Bay runner to surpass the 1,000-yard mark in a season, but Minnesota blocked two extra points, a punt, and a field goal to win 23-22. The defeat was the first of three in a row for the Buccaneers, and forced a must-win situation in the season finale against Kansas City. Playing in a steady downpour, the Buccaneers won 3-0 on a 19-yard field goal in the fourth quarter. Tampa Bay finished 10-6 to tie Chicago in first place in the NFC Central. But the Buccaneers won the division on a tiebreaker. Selmon, with 11 sacks and 117 tackles, was named the NFC's defensive player of the year. Bell finished with 1,263 yards rushing, and Williams threw 18 touchdown passes. On December 29, the Buccaneers defeated Philadelphia in a divisional playoff game 24-17. With the victory, Tampa

Bay became the first expansion team to advance to a conference title game within its first four years of existence.

1980 In the NFC Championship Game on January 6, the Buccaneers were shut out by Los Angeles 9-0. McKay was given a five-year extension on his contract the next day. The draft brought in wide receiver Kevin House. The Buccaneers posted a 17-12 victory over Cincinnati in the season opener. On September 11, they avenged their loss in the title game by defeating Los Angeles 10-9. But Tampa Bay then stumbled to four losses and a tie in the next five games. Consecutive victories over San Francisco and the New York Giants improved their record to 4-4-1, but the Buccaneers won just one game in the final seven weeks and finished 5-10-1. The team's biggest failure was in its own division, where the Buccaneers were 1-6-1. Despite the decline, Williams had his best season, throwing for 3,396 yards and 20 touchdowns, both club records.

1981 Linebacker Hugh Green of Pittsburgh was Tampa Bay's top draft pick and became an immediate starter. Second-round pick James Wilder, a running back from Missouri, also started. James Owens was acquired from San Francisco. The Buccaneers opened the season with a 21-13 victory over Minne-

sota. With Williams on a tear, the club improved its record to 4-2 after consecutive victories over Detroit and Green Bay. But a midseason slump produced four defeats in five weeks, and Tampa Bay fell to 5-6. Trailing Minnesota by two games, on November 22 the offense jelled to lead a 37-3 rout of Green Bay. Owens rushed for 112 yards and a 35-yard touchdown. The Buccaneers followed with back-to-back victories over New Orleans and Atlanta and assumed first place in the division. But a loss to San Diego dropped the team into a first-place tie with Detroit, setting up a battle for the division championship with the Lions. In the season finale, the Buccaneers became the first visiting team in 1981 to win in the Pontiac Silverdome by defeating the Lions 20-17. David Logan, a nose tackle, scored the winning touchdown on a 21-yard run with a recovered fumble. Tampa Bay thus won the division with a 9-7 record. Williams threw for a career-high 3,563 yards and 19 touchdowns, and House caught 56 passes for 1,176 yards and nine touchdowns. The Buccaneers' revitalized defense was led by Cedric Brown's club-record nine interceptions, including two in the final win at Detroit.

1982 In a divisional playoff game in Dallas on January 2, the Buccaneers were beaten by the Cowboys

Ricky Bell

Mark Cotney

Hugh Green

Dave Pear

Danny Reece

Dave Stalls

Richard Wood

38-0. In separate moves linebackers David Lewis and Dewey Selmon, and running back Ricky Bell were traded to San Diego. Penn State guard Sean Farrell was drafted first.

MEMBERS OF HALL OF FAME:
None

BUCCANEER'S RECORD, 1976-81

Year	Won	Lost	Tied	Pct.	Pts.	OP
1976	0	14	0	.000	125	412
1977	2	12	0	.143	103	223
1978	5	11	0	.313	241	259
1979§	10	6	0	.625	273	237
1980	5	10	1	.344	271	341
1981§	9	7	0	.563	315	268
6 Years	31	60	1	.342	1,328	1,740

§NFC Central Division Champion

RECORD HOLDERS

Rushing (Yards)	Ricky Bell, 1979	1,263
Passing (Pct.)	Doug Williams, 1981	50.5
Passing (Yards)	Doug Williams, 1981	3,563
Passing (TDs)	Doug Williams, 1980	20
Receiving (No.)	Kevin House, 1981	56
Receiving (Yards)	Kevin House, 1981	1,176
Interceptions (No.)	Cedric Brown, 1981	9
Punting (Avg.)	Larry Swider, 1981	42.7
Punt Ret. (Avg.)	Danny Reece, 1978	8.9
Kickoff Ret. (Avg.)	Isaac Hagins, 1977	23.5
Touchdowns (Total)	Ricky Bell, 1979, and Kevin House, 1981	9
Field Goals Made	Garo Yepremian, 1980	16
Points (No.)	Garo Yepremian, 1980	79

COACHING HISTORY

1976-81 John McKay 31-60-1

FIRST PLAYER SELECTED

1976 Lee Roy Selmon, DE, Oklahoma
1977 Ricky Bell, RB, USC
1978 Doug Williams, QB, Grambling
1979 Greg Roberts, G (2), Oklahoma
1980 Ray Snell, G, Wisconsin
1981 Hugh Green, LB, Pittsburgh
1982 Sean Farrell, G, Penn State

TAMPA BAY BUCCANEERS, 1976-81

Alward, Tom, G, Nebraska ... 1976
Anderson, Jerry, DB, Oklahoma ... 1978
Austin, Darrell, G-C-T, South Carolina ... 1979-80

B

Ball, Larry, LB, Louisville ... 1976
Bell, Ricky, RB, USC ... 1977-81
Bell, Theo, WR, Arizona ... 1981
Berns, Rick, RB, Nebraska ... 1979-80
Blahak, Joe, DB, Nebraska ... 1976
Blanchard, Tom, P, Oregon ... 1979-81
Blount, Jeb, QB, Tulsa ... 1977
Bonness, Rik, LB, Nebraska ... 1977-79
Boryla, Mike, QB, Stanford ... 1978
Brantley, Scot, LB, Florida ... 1980-81
Brown, Aaron, LB, Ohio State ... 1978-80
Brown, Cedric, DB, Kent State ... 1976-81
Butler, Gary, TE, Rice ... 1977

C

Calhoun, Mike, DT-DE, Notre Dame ... 1980
Campbell, Joe, DE, Maryland ... 1981
Capece, Bill, K, Florida State ... 1981
Carlton, Daryl, T, Tampa ... 1977-79
Carter, Blanchard, G, Nevada-Las Vegas ... 1977
Carter, Gerald, WR, Texas A&M ... 1981
Carter, Louis, RB, Maryland ... 1976-78
Cesare, Billy, DB, Miami ... 1978-79, 1981
Chambers, Wally, DE, Eastern Kentucky ... 1978-79
Colzie, Neal, DB, Ohio State ... 1980-81
Cooper, Bert, LB, Florida State ... 1976
Cotney, Mark, DB, Cameron State ... 1976-80
Crowder, Randy, DT-DE, Penn State ... 1978-80
Current, Mike, T, Ohio State ... 1976

D

Darby, Alvis, TE, Florida ... 1978
Davis, Anthony, RB, USC ... 1977
Davis, Charlie, RB, Colorado ... 1976
Davis, Gary, RB, Cal Poly-San Luis Obispo ... 1980-81
Davis, Johnny, RB, Alabama ... 1978-80
Davis, Ricky, DB, Alabama ... 1976
Davis, Tony, RB, Nebraska ... 1979-81
Delaney, Jeff, S, Pittsburgh ... 1981
Dickinson, Parnell, QB, Mississippi Valley ... 1976
Douglas, Freddie, WR, Arkansas ... 1976
DuBose, Jimmy, RB, Florida ... 1976-78

E

Eckwood, Jerry, RB, Arkansas ... 1979-81

F

Farmer, Dave, RB, USC ... 1978
Farmer, Karl, WR, Pittsburgh ... 1978
Fest, Howard, G-T, Texas ... 1976-77
Ford, Mike, QB, Southern Methodist ... 1981
Franklin, Larry, WR, Jackson State ... 1978
Freitas, Rockne, T, Oregon State ... 1978
Fusina, Chuck, QB, Penn State ... 1979-81

G

Giles, Jimmie, TE, Alcorn State ... 1978-81
Gill, Randy, LB, San Jose State ... 1978
Grant, Frank, WR, Southern Colorado State ... 1978
Green, Dave, P, Ohio U. ... 1976-78
Green, Hugh, LB, Pittsburgh ... 1981
Gunn, Jimmy, LB, USC ... 1976

H

Hagins, Isaac, WR, Southern U. ... 1976-80
Hannah, Charley, T-DE, Alabama ... 1977-81
Hanratty, Terry, QB, Notre Dame ... 1976
Harris, Paul, LB, Alabama ... 1977-78
Hawkins, Andy, LB, Texas A&I ... 1980-81
Hedberg, Randy, QB, Minot State ... 1977
Holt, John, DB, West Texas State ... 1981
Horton, Greg, G, Colorado ... 1978-79
House, Kevin, WR, Southern Illinois ... 1980-81
Huff, Gary, QB, Florida State ... 1977-78
Hunt, Charles, LB, Florida State ... 1976
Hutchinson, Scott, DE, Florida ... 1981

I

Inmon, Earl, LB, Bethune-Cookman ... 1978

J

Jameson, Larry, DT, Indiana ... 1976
Johnson, Cecil, LB, Pittsburgh ... 1977-81
Johnson, Essex, RB, Grambling ... 1976
Johnson, Greg, DE, Florida State ... 1977
Johnson, Randy, C-G, Georgia ... 1977-78
Jones, Gordon, WR, Pittsburgh ... 1979-81
Jordan, Curtis, DB, Texas Tech ... 1976-80

K

Kendrick, Vince, RB, Florida ... 1976
Kollar, Bill, DE-DT, Montana State ... 1977-81

L

Lawrence, Larry, QB, Iowa ... 1976
Leavitt, Allan, K, Georgia ... 1977
Lemon, Mike, LB, Kansas ... 1976-77
Leonard, Jim, C, Santa Clara ... 1980-81
Levenseller, Mike, WR, Washington State ... 1978
Lewis, David, LB, USC ... 1977-81
Lewis, Reggie, DE, North Texas State ... 1979-80
Little, Everett, G-T, Houston ... 1976
Logan, David, DT, Pittsburgh ... 1979-81

M

Martin, Don, DB, Yale ... 1976
Maxson, Alvin, RB, Southern Methodist ... 1978
McAleney, Ed, DE, Massachusetts ... 1976
McGriff, Lee, WR, Florida ... 1976
McKay, John, WR, USC ... 1976-78
McNeill, Rod, RB, USC ... 1976
Medlin, Dan, G, North Carolina State ... 1977-78
Mitchell, Aaron, DB, Nevada-Las Vegas ... 1981
Moore, Bob, TE, Stanford ... 1976-77
Moore, Manfred, RB, USC ... 1976
Moore, Maulty, DT, Bethune-Cookman ... 1976
Moritz, Brett, G, Nebraska ... 1978
Mucker, Larry, WR, Arizona State ... 1977-80

N

Nafziger, Dana, LB-TE, Cal Poly-San Luis Obispo . 1977-79, 1981
Novak, Jack, TE, Wisconsin ... 1976-77

O

Obradovich, Jim, TE, USC ... 1978-81
O'Donoghue, Neil, K, Auburn ... 1978-79
Oliver, Frank, DB, Kentucky State ... 1976
Owens, James, RB, UCLA ... 1981
Owens, Morris, WR, Arizona State ... 1976-79

P

Packer, Walter, RB, Mississippi State ... 1977
Pagac, Fred, TE-LB, Ohio State ... 1976
Pear, Dave, DT, Washington ... 1976-78
Peterson, Calvin, LB, UCLA ... 1976
Peterson, Jim, LB, San Diego State ... 1976
Pierson, Reggie, DB, Oklahoma State ... 1976
Puetz, Garry, G-T, Valparaiso ... 1978

R

Radford, Bruce, DE-DT, Grambling ... 1980
Rae, Mike, QB, USC ... 1978-79
Ragsdale, George, RB-WR, North Carolina A&T ... 1977-79
Reavis, Dave, T, Arkansas ... 1976-81
Reece, Danny, DB-PR, USC ... 1976-80
Reese, Steve, LB, Louisville ... 1976
Roberts, Greg, G, Oklahoma ... 1979-81
Robinson, Glenn, DE, Oklahoma State ... 1976-77
Roder, Mirro, K, No college ... 1976
Rucker, Conrad, TE, Southern U. ... 1980
Rudolph, Council, DE, Kentucky State ... 1976-77
Ryczek, Dan, C, Virginia ... 1976-77

S

Samuels, Tony, TE, Bethune-Cookman ... 1980
Sanders, Gene, G-DT-DE, Texas A&M ... 1979-81
Schumacher, Kurt, G, Ohio State ... 1978
Selmon, Dewey, LB, Oklahoma ... 1976-80
Selmon, Lee Roy, DE, Oklahoma ... 1976-81
Short, Laval, DT, Colorado ... 1981
Shumann, Mike, WR, Florida State ... 1980
Sims, Jimmy, LB, USC ... 1976
Smith, Barry, WR, Florida State ... 1976
Snell, Ray, G, Wisconsin ... 1980-81
Spurrier, Steve, QB, Florida ... 1976
Stalls, Dave, DE, Northern Colorado ... 1980-81
Stone, Ken, DB, Vanderbilt ... 1976
Swider, Larry, P, Pittsburgh ... 1981

T

Thomas, Norris, DB, Southern Mississippi ... 1980-81
Toomay, Pat, DE, Vanderbilt ... 1976

W

Ward, John, C-G, Oklahoma State ... 1976
Washington, Mike, DB, Alabama ... 1976-81
Wender, Jack, RB, Fresno State ... 1977
White, Brad, DT, Tennessee ... 1981
White, Charlie, RB, Bethune-Cookman ... 1978
White, Jeris, DB, Hawaii ... 1977-79
Wilder, James, RB, Missouri ... 1981
Williams, Doug, QB, Grambling ... 1978-81
Williams, Ed, RB, Langston, Oklahoma ... 1976-77
Wilson, Steve, C-T-G, Georgia ... 1976-81
Winans, Jeff, T-G, USC ... 1977-78
Winfrey, Stan, RB, Arkansas State ... 1977
Wood, Richard, LB, USC ... 1976-81
Word, Roscoe, DB, Jackson State ... 1976

Y

Yarno, George, G-C, Washington State ... 1979-81
Yepremian, Garo, K, No college ... 1980-81
Young, Randy, T, Iowa State ... 1976
Young, Steve, T, Colorado ... 1976

WASHINGTON REDSKINS

1932 George Preston Marshall of Washington, D.C., headed a four-man syndicate that included Vincent Bendix, Jay O'Brien, and M. Dorland Doyle that bought the National Football League franchise for Boston. They contracted to play at Braves Field, home of the National League baseball team, and decided to call themselves the Braves, as well. Lud Wray was hired as the first coach. The team finished 4-4-2, lost $46,000 the first season, and all Marshall's partners gave up. Marshall stuck with it.

1933 Marshall moved the club to Fenway Park, home of baseball's American League Red Sox. He changed the name of the team to Redskins. Wray quit to coach Philadelphia. Marshall hired a full-blooded Indian as the team's coach, Will (Lone Star) Dietz. On opening day of practice, the entire club was lined up for the team picture in war paint, feathers, and full headdress. Dietz specialized in trick plays, although he had Jim Musick and Cliff Battles, who finished one-two in the league in rushing. The team stayed at .500 with a 5-5-2 record. Money was so tight that when the ball would go into the stands, Marshall would run to the spot and personally ask that it be returned. Glen (Turk) Edwards, a 250-pound tackle from Washington State, missed the first three minutes of the first game of the season and the last seven minutes of the last, but played every minute in between—710 out of a possible 720 minutes.

1934 The Redskins had a good crop of rookies and hoped to win their first championship, but only running backs Battles and Edwards played up to expectations. The team finished second—again at .500 with a 6-6 record. Marshall, however, was encouraged by the improved attendance and felt the franchise would soon turn into a money maker.

1935 In an attempt to draw more fans, Marshall dismissed Dietz and hired hometown hero Eddie Casey, former Harvard player, as his new coach. But Casey didn't make good and neither did Marshall's plan. The Redskins won only 2 of 11 games.

1936 Ray Flaherty was signed as the new head coach, and made his position clear from the outset. He insisted that Marshall stay off the field and in the stands. The team responded to Flaherty's leadership by winning the Eastern Division title with a 14-0 victory over the New York Giants in the final game of the season. When Boston failed to get excited enough for Marshall, he moved the championship game to New York, where nearly 30,000 people watched Green Bay beat the Redskins 21-6.

1937 The National Football League approved the transfer of the Boston Redskins' franchise to Washington, D.C. Marshall's showman instincts seemed to blossom in the nation's capital. He organized the Redskins' band and he produced elaborate halftime shows. The Redskins drafted Sammy Baugh, All-America tailback from Texas Christian University, then signed him for $8,000 a year. Baugh completed 11 of 16 passes his first game. Played in Griffith Stadium on a Thursday night, that first game drew 19,941 to see the Redskins beat the Giants 13-3. New York was the victim again in the game that decided the Eastern Division championship. The Redskins won 49-14 in a game that attracted 10,000 Washington fans to New York. Battles scored twice on runs of 75 and 76 yards. A week later, Baugh completed 17 of 33 passes for 335 yards and three touchdowns. His favorite receiver, Wayne Millner, caught nine passes for 160 yards, including touchdowns of 77 and 55 yards. And Washington won the world championship 28-21 over George Halas's Chicago Bears. Baugh completed 81 of 171 passes during the season for

1,127 yards and eight touchdowns. Battles gained 874 yards.

1938 The Redskins drafted Andy Farkas, a back from Detroit University, number one and also got Wee Willie Wilkin, a tackle from St. Mary's, California. Battles quit in a salary dispute after gaining more than 3,500 yards rushing in six years. Baugh separated his shoulder in the first game of the season. He came back sooner than expected, but then was injured again. Marshall signed Frank Filchock, a tailback from the University of Indiana, for $1,000—$200 less than Battles had sought. The Redskins used Filchock in a patched-up lineup and finished second to the New York Giants at 6-3-2.

1939 The Redskins trained at Cheyney, Washington. Flaherty, one of the most imaginative coaches in the league, designed a plan to try to keep the sometimes frail Baugh healthy. He alternated Filchock and Baugh at tailback, confusing opposing defenses, which didn't know whether to look for Filchock's runs or Baugh's passes. The Redskins played their first scoreless tie since 1935 against the Giants, October 1. Filchock and Farkas teamed on a record 99-yard touchdown pass play against Pittsburgh, October 15. The Eastern Division title came down to the final game—in fact, the final 45 seconds. But the Redskins' Bo Russell missed a disputed field goal attempt and New York won 9-7. Most of the players thought the kick was good, but the referee ruled the kick had sailed to the right of the goal post. On the train ride home, Marshall called Russell to his compartment and, before newsmen, signed him to a 1940 contract.

1940 The Redskins trained at Gonzaga University in Washington. Farkas was lost with a knee injury that required surgery three weeks before the start of the season. A healthy Baugh led the club to a 9-2 record and the Eastern Division championship, beating the Chicago Bears 7-3 along the way. The Bears complained about the officiating, and Marshall ripped them in the newspapers. "The Bears are front-runners," he said. "Quitters. They're not a second-half team, just a bunch of crybabies." Those remarks may have had something to do with what happened in the rematch with the Bears in the championship game. For the first time, an NFL game was broadcast coast-to-coast. Chicago, using the T-formation with man-in-motion, embarrassed the Redskins 73-0. Baugh was asked if an early Washington pass for a touchdown that was dropped would have made any difference. "Sure," drawled Baugh, "the game would have wound up 73-7." Baugh had his best season, completing 111 of 177 passes, a 62.7 completion percentage, for 1,367 yards and 12 touchdowns. Dick Todd led the Redskins' rushers with 408 yards.

1941 The draft produced ends Ed Cifers of Tennessee, Joe Aguirre of St. Mary's, California, and Al Krueger of USC, although blocking back Forest Evashevski of Michigan was drafted number one. The Redskins also picked up an all-pro caliber center from the Chicago Cardinals, Charles (Ki) Aldrich. The team trained at San Diego. The Redskins ran up a 5-1 record, then were hit by injuries and finished with only one win in the second half of the season. During a game on December 7, various high ranking government and military personnel were paged over the public address system as the Redskins beat Philadelphia 20-14, but it wasn't until after the game most of the fans learned that World War II had begun for the United States.

1942 Orban (Spec) Sanders, a back from Texas, was the top draft choice. In the second game of the season, the Giants failed to make one first down, gained only one yard rushing, and completed just one pass, but it was good for a touchdown. Another score on an interception gave New York a 14-7 victory, Septem-

ber 27. It was Washington's only loss en route to a 10-1 record. In Flaherty's last year as coach before entering the navy, he was able to avenge that 73-0 defeat to the Bears. To motivate the team, he simply wrote "73-0" in large figures on the blackboard in the Washington dressing room. That was enough as Baugh threw for one touchdown and Farkas ran for another in a 14-6 triumph that stopped the Bears' undefeated string at 18.

1943 The college draft produced Lou Rymkus, a tackle from Notre Dame, but Jack Jenkins, a back from Missouri, was the first pick. With Flaherty in the service, Arthur (Dutch) Bergman took over as coach. Because of the manpower shortage, Baugh was forced to play both offense and defense. The Redskins were unbeaten, with one tie, in their first seven games, but then lost twice to the New York Giants to finish the season tied with the Giants for the division title. Baugh had 23 touchdown passes and gained 1,754 yards on 133 completions in 239 attempts. In the division playoff, Baugh threw three touchdown passes and Washington defeated New York 28-0. Baugh was injured in the championship game against Chicago and the Bears won 41-21.

1944 Dudley DeGroot was the new head coach, and the new weapon in Washington was the T-formation. Marshall hired Clark Shaughnessy, who had been a voluntary assistant coach for the Bears, to teach it to Baugh and company. Baugh, who had always been a tailback, didn't care for it at first, but then slowly made the adjustment. Filchock, just out of the Coast Guard, split the passing with Baugh and led the league with 1,139 yards and 13 touchdowns. The Redskins finished 6-3-1.

1945 USC quarterback Jim Hardy was the number-one draft choice. Baugh, who had to do some running while operating the single- and double-wing, said he could "operate the T in tie and tails." He made it look almost that easy in a 24-14 win over the Giants in which he completed 20 of 24 passes for 265 yards and two touchdowns. The four misses were "throwaways," Baugh said. Baugh, now settled comfortably into the T, completed 70.3 percent of his passes to set an NFL record. The Redskins won the Eastern Division title, but lost the NFL Championship Game to the Cleveland Rams 15-14 in sub-zero weather when Baugh's pass hit the goal post for a safety and Bob Waterfield's try for a Rams' extra point hit the crossbar and bounced over for the margin of victory.

1946 Cal Rossi, a back from UCLA, was the top draftee but was lost when he was declared ineligible for the draft. Marshall refused to compete with the new All-America Football Conference, and lost some key players, such as Willie Wilkin, star end and placekicker Joe Aguirre, and even the coach, DeGroot. Turk Edwards took over as the new coach. Marshall traded Filchock to the New York Giants, a deal that backfired when Baugh was injured. Filchock led the Giants to the Eastern Division championship. The Redskins turned from near-champions to a 5-5-1 team.

1947 Cal Rossi was the number-one choice again. Rossi met with Marshall and Edwards, voiced his appreciation of their offer, and then returned to California to become a schoolteacher and small businessman. The Redskins lost 45-42 to Philadelphia on opening day and that set the tone for the season. Baugh had his biggest year, throwing for 11 touchdowns in a two-game stretch but it did little to advance the Redskins' cause in a 4-8 season. Washington scored plenty of points—295—but the opposition scored more—367. Baugh's best season included 210 completions in 354 attempts, for 2,938 yards and 25 touchdowns.

1948 Impressed with Alabama's Harry Gilmer, and worried about grooming a successor to Baugh, Marshall sold the draft rights to Mississippi quarterback Charlie Conerly and signed Gilmer as the top draft choice. Baugh proved there still was some life in his arm, however, as he passed for 446 yards in beating Boston 59-21. The Redskins' erratic defense kept them away from the championship and in second place with a 7-5 record. It was another big year for Baugh, who completed 185 of 315 passes for 2,599 yards and 22 touchdowns.

1949 Edwards was moved to the front office, and Admiral John (Billick) Whelchel, former Naval Academy coach, was brought in to take over as coach. He signed a five-year contract, but was gone three games before the end of the season and replaced by Herman Ball, a team scout. The team finished 4-7-1. There was considerable discontent in the media over Marshall's failure to sign black players.

1950 The Redskins became one of the first two pro teams to have all of their games televised; the other was Los Angeles in 1950. Young quarterback Gilmer and highly publicized running back Charlie (Choo Choo) Justice of North Carolina were disappointments. Baugh and his aging teammates could not stop the slide that resulted in eight straight losses and a 3-9-0 last place finish.

1951 Three games into the new season, Ball was fired and Marshall wanted to hire Heartley (Hunk) Anderson, a Bears' assistant coach. But George Halas wouldn't allow it unless the Redskins threw star tackle Paul Lipscomb into the deal. Marshall refused and decided instead to hire former Redskins' star Dick Todd as coach. The team responded by winning its first two games for Todd and finished third at 5-7. Rob Goode from Texas A&M became the closest thing the Redskins ever had to a 1,000-yard runner when he gained a club record 951 yards.

1952 Larry Isbell, a quarterback from Baylor, was the number-one draft pick. Todd signed for another year as coach, but resigned before September. He said he had to have respect to stay as coach, and, although he liked Marshall, he didn't "agree with the way he runs the Redskins." Earl (Curly) Lambeau, the first "name" coach hired by Marshall, took over. Baugh broke his hand in a preseason game and was limited to holding for kicks and teaching rookie Eddie LeBaron from College of the Pacific the nuances of quarterbacking in the pros. Gilmer backed up LeBaron. In the last game of the season, Baugh went in to hold for a placekick against the Philadelphia Eagles but the kick was blocked. Baugh's retirement from pro football after 16 years ended an era in Washington.

1953 The top draftee was quarterback Jack Scarbath of Maryland. LeBaron was the Redskins' starting quarterback. Gilmer was shifted to the defensive backfield, and Justice made a comeback in a year when Lambeau got the team winning again. The defense, featuring end Gene Brito from Loyola of Los Angeles, came on strong down the stretch. A 10-0 shutout of Philadelphia turned out to be Lambeau's 231st—and last—NFL victory.

1954 Lambeau's successor was Joe Kuharich. LeBaron and Brito jumped to the Canadian Football League. The Redskins never recovered in a 3-9-0 season. Tragedy struck near the end of the season when guard Dave Sparks died of a heart attack following a 34-14 loss to Cleveland.

1955 LeBaron and Brito returned from Canada and were joined on the new-look Redskins by Vic Janowicz, the All-America halfback from Ohio State who abandoned a professional baseball career to try the NFL. The Redskins scored 21 points in 137 seconds in a game with Philadelphia, October 1. Trailing 16-0 in the third quarter, Brito recovered a fumble on the Eagles' 32. LeBaron passed to Janowicz for a touchdown. Ralph Thomas recovered the kickoff in

the end zone for another touchdown. LaVern Torgeson recovered a fumble on the Eagles' 13. Janowicz scored immediately and the Redskins won 31-30. Janowicz wound up as the second leading scorer in the league, and the rejuvenated Redskins finished second in the Eastern Conference with an 8-4 record.

1956 In a tragic training camp accident, a car in which Janowicz was riding left the road. He was thrown from the car and against a tree, suffering brain damage. His football career was over. Sam Baker, a former star fullback at Oregon State, returned from a stint in the Canadian League and assumed Janowicz's punting and placekicking duties. Baker led the league with 17 field goals in 25 attempts and was the Redskins' top scorer with 67 points. But the team, demoralized by Janowicz's tragedy and injuries to quarterbacks LeBaron and Al Dorow, staggered to a 6-6-0 third place finish.

1957 Another training camp tragedy struck when de-fensive back Roy Barni was shot to death in a barroom brawl. The team struggled through most of the season. With three games left, the defense jelled and held Chicago, Philadelphia, and Pittsburgh to a combined total of 13 points. But the Redskins remained under .500 at 5-6-1.

1958 The club continued to have problems keeping pace with NFL contenders. And the pressure on Marshall to begin signing black players was building again. The Redskins had traded their number-one draft choice to Los Angeles for quarterback Rudy Bukich. They chose Mike Sommer, a back from George Washington, on the second round. Of the five previous first-round draft picks by Washington, only fullback Don Bosseler of Miami (1956) played regularly. The Redskins struggled through a 4-7-1 season. Kuharich was fired as coach.

1959 Don Allard of Boston College, a back, was the number-one draft pick. Assistant coach Mike Nixon

Johnny Olszewski eludes San Francisco linebacker Matt Hazeltine, 1959.

was promoted to the top job, but nothing changed. The Redskins still were losing almost all their games —eight of nine at one point. The highlight of the season was Sam Baker's 46-yard field goal that allowed Washington to upset the defending world champion Baltimore Colts 27-24, November 8. The club signed a 30-year lease to play in the proposed D.C. Stadium. Congress gave approval for construction of the stadium.

1960 Still seeking a quarterback after using four number-one choices in seven years in an attempt to solve the problem, the Redskins tried again with Richie Lucas of Penn State, who signed with Buffalo and played there. Ralph Guglielmi from Notre Dame kept the quarterback job, but he had to run for his life much of the season. The club scored 16 or fewer points in eight of its nine losses in a 1-9-2 season.

1961 Nixon was replaced by Bill McPeak, a rookie coach who opened with a rookie quarterback, Norm Snead of Wake Forest, the number-one draft choice. The pair suffered through a frightful season in their first year in new 55,004-seat D.C. Stadium, which opened October 1. The Redskins lost 12 straight before beating Dallas 34-24 in the final game to avert a winless season. Still, Snead passed for 2,337 yards and 11 touchdowns, the most passing yardage since Baugh's 2,599 in 1948. The running game was pitiful. Dick James led the rushers with just 374 yards.

1962 Marshall made history in Washington by drafting the Redskins' first black player, Heisman Trophy winner Ernie Davis from Syracuse. Then he traded Davis to Cleveland for Bobby Mitchell, a black runner-reciever from Illinois. John Nisby of Pacific, Leroy Jackson of Western Illinois, and Ron Hatcher of Michigan State, joined Mitchell as the first blacks on the Redskins' roster. McPeak's team showed immediate improvement. Mitchell became one of the league's most dangerous receivers, and Snead was developing into an effective quarterback, passing for 2,926 yards and 22 touchdowns. The record improved to 5-7-2. Mitchell's 72 receptions were the highest in the league and he gained 1,384 yards while scoring 11 touchdowns. Mitchell also returned a kickoff for one touchdown to lead the club in scoring with 72 points.

1963 The Redskins were exciting on offense, with Snead passing to Mitchell and an assortment of good receivers. Snead threw for a team record 3,043 yards on 175 completions in 363 attempts to top Baugh's 2,938 in 1947. But there was not much running attack. James gained just 384 yards to lead the team. And the defense still needed improvement. Mitchell again led the receivers with 69 catches for 1,436 yards and seven touchdowns.

1964 Snead was traded to Philadelphia for quarterback Sonny Jurgensen. Another controversial deal sent James to the Giants for Sam Huff, the celebrated middle linebacker. Charley Taylor, a wide receiver from Arizona State, was the number-one draft choice and he joined with Mitchell to inject speed into the Washington offense. Huff and rookie defensive back Paul Krause from Iowa put some muscle into the defense. The Redskins won five of their last eight games for a 6-8 record. All home games were sellouts. Jurgensen passed for 2,934 yards in his first season in Washington.

1965 Without a running game to balance it, the Washington offense slipped considerably and the team lost its first five games. But then the club played its greatest comeback game in history, rallying from a 21-point deficit for a 34-31 win over Dallas as Jurgensen passed for more than 400 yards and three touchdowns, November 28. The defense was better until cornerback Johnny Sample was suspended late in the season for insubordination.

1966 McPeak was released and Otto Graham, the

Charley Taylor makes one of his NFL record 649 career pass receptions, 1972.

former Cleveland Browns' all-pro quarterback, was named coach and general manager. Charley Gogolak, a kicker from Princeton, was the number-one draft choice. Graham emphasized the passing game even more than McPeak had. The offense improved. But Graham moved seven new players into the lineup on defense, and the best Washington could get was a 7-7 record. Jurgensen had his best season, throwing 436 times and completing 254 for 3,209 yards and 28 touchdowns. Gogolak kicked for 105 points.

1967 Jurgensen won the league passing title, setting league records for attempts, 508; completions, 288;

and yards, 3,747. He also passed for 31 touchdowns, a club record. Three Redskins' receivers were in the top four in NFL receiving, led by Taylor's 70—high in the league—for 990 yards and 9 touchdowns. But the running threat was still missing. Team leader A. D. Whitfield gained just 384 yards. The Washington kicking game also deteriorated and the team finished third in the four-team Capitol Division.

1968 Middle linebacker Sam Huff announced his retirement. Graham sent a future first-round draft pick to Los Angeles for Gary Beban, the Heisman Trophy winner from UCLA. Beban, after signing a lucrative contract, flopped in training camp, spent most of the year on the taxi squad, and was even tried unsuccessfully as a running back late in the season. Safety Paul Krause was traded to Minnesota. After a disappointing 5-9 season, Graham was fired at the end of the year. Jurgensen's passing yardage dipped to 1,980.

1969 The top draft pick was traded to San Francisco. Vince Lombardi left Green Bay to become part-owner, executive vice president, and head of the Redskins. Lombardi constructed what the other Washington coaches seemingly had ignored—a strong running game. Rookie halfback Larry Brown of Kansas State (888 yards) and fullback Charley Harraway (428 yards) formed a new backfield combination and the defense tightened considerably on the way to second place in the division. Jurgensen led the NFL in passing with 3,102 yards. Washington had its first winning season since 1955 with a 7-5-2 record.

1970 For the third straight year, the number-one draft choice was traded, this time to Los Angeles, but Washington picked up defensive end Bill Brundige of Colorado in the second round. Lombardi was missing when training camp opened. He was in the hospital, terminally ill. Two weeks before the start of the season, Lombardi died of cancer, September 3. Assistant coach Bill Austin took over, but the team didn't play with the same precision. Only Brown, coming into his own as an all-pro, had an outstanding year, becoming the first Redskin ever to gain 1,000 yards rushing. He ran for 1,125 on 237 carries, a 4.8 average. Jurgensen threw for 2,354 yards.

1971 Former Los Angeles Rams coach George Allen was named the new head coach and general manager of the Redskins. The top draft choice was traded away again, but Allen got Cotton Speyrer, a wide receiver from Texas, on the second round. Allen immediately implemented the plan he made so successful as Los Angeles coach. He started trading for as many veteran players as possible. They included quarterback Billy Kilmer, who came from New Orleans; wide receiver Roy Jefferson from Baltimore; defensive tackle Diron Talbert and linebacker Jack Pardee from Los Angeles; defensive end Ron McDole from Buffalo; defensive end Verlon Biggs from the New York Jets; and others, who became known as The Over-the-Hill-Gang. Construction began on Redskin Park, the team's new practice and training camp facility near Dulles Airport. Washington finished with a 9-4-1 record, the most Redskins' victories in 29 years, and got into its first playoff game in 26 years. Brown just missed 1,000 yards, gaining 948. Kilmer took over from Jurgensen and passed for 2,221 yards. After leading at halftime, the Redskins, who were the NFC wild card team, finally lost to San Francisco 24-20 in an NFC divisional playoff. Allen was named NFC coach of the year.

1972 Moses Denson, a running back from Maryland State, was Washington's top draftee after the first seven choices had been traded. Led by an outstanding defensive unit, the Redskins beat Dallas out of the division title for the first time since 1965. It was the Redskins' first championship in 30 years. Although Jurgensen was injured much of the time, the Washington offense operated efficiently, with Kilmer (1,648 yards and 19 touchdowns) and Brown maintaining ball control. Washington won a club record 11 games. Although he missed two games with injuries, Brown gained 1,216 yards to lead the conference in rushing and set a Redskins' record. In the first round of the playoffs, the Redskins defeated Green Bay 16-3. Then, in the championship game against their rivals from Dallas, the Redskins defeated the Cowboys 26-3 to gain their first Super Bowl.

1973 The Miami Dolphins, at the peak of their efficiency, downed the Redskins 14-7 in Super Bowl VII

in the Los Angeles Coliseum, January 14. The number-one draft choice was traded away again and some said Allen's old men couldn't come back. But they did. They were co-champions of the division, finishing with a 10-4 record, and made it as the wild card playoff team. Jurgensen and Kilmer shared playing time at quarterback. Kilmer passed for 1,656 yards and Jurgensen for 904. Brown and Harraway provided the running, with Brown gaining 860 yards and Harraway 452. In Minnesota, however, Washington was no match for the Super Bowl-bound Vikings and lost the playoff game 27-20.

1974 The number-one draft choice went to Los Angeles. The Over-the-Hill Gang proved it wasn't over the hill, again compiling another 10-4 season and making it to the playoffs for the fourth straight season. Jurgensen celebrated his fortieth birthday and led the NFC in passing. Brown was slowed with knee

Redskins' quarterback Sonny Jurgensen, 1973.

injuries, gaining only 430 yards. Some signs of age began to show up front in the Redskins' units. In the first round of the playoffs, the Redskins, again the wild card team, were beaten by the Los Angeles Rams 19-10.

1975 After 18 seasons in the league, 11 as a Redskin, Jurgensen retired. San Diego got the Redskins' number-one draft choice. Allen, who rarely employed first-year players, came up with an outstanding rookie in running back Mike Thomas of Nevada-Las Vegas. Thomas rushed for 919 yards to lead the team. Kilmer passed for 2,440 yards, but overall, the Redskins were sluggish on offense and played the poorest defense of the Allen years to miss the playoffs for the first time since he took over as coach. Charley Taylor became the NFL's all-time leading receiver when his career total reached 635. He caught 53 passes for the season.

1976 The number-one draft choice was traded to Miami for the rights to quarterback Joe Theismann, the eighth straight year the team had gone without a pick in the first round. Allen signed free agent running backs John Riggins and Calvin Hill. Again, the reports of the Redskins' collapse proved exaggerated. A new quarterback controversy developed between Kilmer and Theismann. The offense got 1,101 yards from Thomas. Dallas won the Eastern Division title, but Washington's 10-4 record was good for the wild card berth again. In the first round of the playoffs, the Redskins were beaten 35-20 by Minnesota.

1977 Cornerback Lemar Parrish and defensive end Coy Bacon were acquired in a trade with Cincinnati in June. Billy Kilmer opened the year as the starting quarterback, but later split time with Joe Theismann. The Redskins lost the opener when the Giants staged a late rally to win 20-17. The defeat was the first for an Allen-coached team in a season opener. Led by the defense, the Redskins rebounded with consecutive victories over Atlanta, St. Louis, and Tampa Bay. On October 16, running back John Riggins suffered a knee injury and was lost for the season, joining linebacker Chris Hanburger and cornerback Pat Fischer on injured reserve. Washington was defeated by Dallas 34-16, but then improved its record to 6-4 through the next five weeks. On November 27, the Redskins again lost to Dallas and apparently fell out of playoff contention. But the Redskins followed that loss with a shutout victory over Buffalo. On December 10, Kilmer made his first start in six weeks and guided the team to successive wins over St. Louis and Los Angeles. Despite a 9-5 record, the Redskins were edged out of the wild card spot for the playoffs by Chicago. The defense allowed only 189 points, a team record.

1978 Allen left to coach the Rams and was replaced by Jack Pardee, the former head coach of Chicago. Two 13-year veterans, tight end Jerry Smith and Charley Taylor, the NFL's all-time leading receiver, retired. Theismann won the job as starting quarterback and guided the team to six successive victories to open the season. The victory string included an offensive shootout with Philadelphia (35-30) and a defensive struggle with Dallas (9-5). The start was the club's best in 35 years. However, the offense settled into a prolonged slump and the Redskins won only two games in the final 10 weeks to drop to 8-8. Riggins bounced back from knee surgery to lead the team in rushing with 1,014 yards, but Mike Thomas, the club's leading rusher the previous three seasons, slipped to 534 yards.

1979 Thomas was traded to San Diego before the season. The Redskins opened the year with a narrow loss to Houston and then rolled to six wins in the next seven weeks. The defense posted one shutout in the streak and held four other opponents to nine points or less. The lone defeat, to Philadelphia, was avenged on October 21 with a 17-7 Redskins victory. Two more losses dropped the Redskins' record to 6-4, but then they won four games in the next five weeks. This time the spark was provided by the offense, which scored 30 or more points in all four games. Requiring a victory to advance to the playoffs, the Redskins ended the season with a divisional showdown in Dallas. Despite building a 34-21 lead, the Redskins couldn't stop Roger Staubach, who passed for two late touchdowns and a 35-34 Dallas victory. The Redskins finished 10-6, and Theismann ended the season with 2,797 yards passing and 20 touchdowns. The defense finished with 47 sacks, 26 interceptions, and 34 fumble recoveries. Pardee was named NFL coach of the year by the *Associated Press*.

1980 With its first number-one draft choice since 1968, Washington selected Art Monk, a wide receiver from Syracuse. Monk proceeded to lead the team in pass receptions with 58 for 797 yards. But the offense was hurt when Riggins sat out the season due to a contract dispute. The Redskins won their first game on September 14 with a 23-21 victory over the Giants, but won only twice more in the next 11 weeks. On December 7, the Redskins shut off San Diego's passing attack and defeated the Chargers 40-17. The victory preceded season-closing victories over the Giants and St. Louis for a 6-10 final record. Despite the losing record, the Redskins' pass defense was rated best in the NFL, permitting an average of only 135.7 yards per game and a completion rate of 47 percent by opposing quarterbacks. Theismann threw for a personal high 2,962 yards. Safety Ken Houston retired after the season.

1981 Pardee was released as head coach and replaced on January 13 by Joe Gibbs, the San Diego Chargers' offensive coordinator. The offense received an apparent boost when Riggins rejoined the team, Joe Washington was acquired from Baltimore, and Terry Metcalf was acquired from St. Louis. Still, the Redskins opened the year with five straight losses, as the offense was slow to get untracked. Washington won its first game on October 11 with a 24-7 victory over Chicago. Two weeks later, Theismann converted a broken play into a one-yard touchdown run and a 24-22 victory over New England. The victory sparked the dormant offense and was the first of four in a row, including a 42-21 win over St. Louis on November 1 in which Riggins ran for three touchdowns. Following two losses, the Redskins closed out their season by defeating Philadelphia, Baltimore, and Los Angeles to finish 8-8.

1982 Former Redskins linebacker Sam Huff was inducted into the Pro Football Hall of Fame.

MEMBERS OF HALL OF FAME:
Cliff Battles, Sammy Baugh, Bill Dudley, Glen (Turk) Edwards, Ray Flaherty, Otto Graham, Sam Huff, David (Deacon) Jones, Earl (Curly) Lambeau, Vince Lombardi, George Preston Marshall, Wayne Millner

REDSKINS' RECORD, 1932-81

Year	Won	Lost	Tied	Pct.	Pts.	OP
Boston Braves						
1932	4	4	2	.500	55	79
Boston Redskins						
1933	5	5	2	.500	103	97
1934	6	6	0	.500	107	94
1935	2	8	1	.200	65	123
1936§	7	5	0	.583	149	110
Washington Redskins						
1937‡	8	3	0	.727	195	120
1938	6	3	2	.667	148	154
1939	8	2	1	.800	242	94
1940§	9	2	0	.818	245	142
1941	6	5	0	.545	176	174
1942‡	10	1	0	.909	227	102
1943§	6	3	1	.667	229	137
1944	6	3	1	.667	169	180
1945§	8	2	0	.800	209	121
1946	5	5	1	.500	171	191
1947	4	8	0	.333	295	367
1948	7	5	0	.583	291	287
1949	4	7	1	.364	268	339
1950	3	9	0	.250	232	326
1951	5	7	0	.417	183	296
1952	4	8	0	.333	240	287
1953	6	5	1	.545	208	215
1954	3	9	0	.250	207	432
1955	8	4	0	.667	246	222
1956	6	6	0	.500	183	225
1957	5	6	1	.455	251	230
1958	4	7	1	.364	214	268
1959	3	9	0	.250	185	350
1960	1	9	2	.100	178	309
1961	1	12	1	.077	174	392
1962	5	7	2	.417	305	376
1963	3	11	0	.214	279	398
1964	6	8	0	.429	307	305
1965	6	8	0	.429	257	301
1966	7	7	0	.500	351	355
1967	5	6	3	.455	347	353
1968	5	9	0	.357	249	358
1969	7	5	2	.583	307	319
1970	6	8	0	.429	297	314
1971*	9	4	1	.692	276	190
1972†	11	3	0	.786	336	218
1973*	10	4	0	.714	325	198
1974*	10	4	0	.714	320	196
1975	8	6	0	.571	325	276
1976*	10	4	0	.714	291	217
1977	9	5	0	.643	196	189
1978	8	8	0	.500	273	283
1979	10	6	0	.625	348	295
1980	6	10	0	.375	261	293
1981	8	8	0	.500	347	349
50 Years	309	299	26	.508	11,842	12,246

§*NFL Eastern Division Championship*
‡*NFL Champion*
**NFC Wild Card Qualifier for Playoffs*
†*NFC Champion*

RECORD HOLDERS

Rushing (Yards)	Larry Brown, 1972	1,216
Passing (Pct.)	Sammy Baugh, 1945	70.3
Passing (Yards)	Sonny Jurgensen, 1967	3,747
Passing (TDs)	Sonny Jurgensen, 1967	31
Receiving (No.)	Bobby Mitchell, 1962, and Charley Taylor, 1966	72
Receiving (Yards)	Bobby Mitchell, 1963	1,436
Interceptions (No.)	Don Sandifer, 1948	13
Punting (Avg.)	Sammy Baugh, 1940	51.4
Punt Ret. (Avg.)	Dick Todd, 1941	17.0
Kickoff Ret. (Avg.)	Mike Nelms, 1981	29.7
Touchdowns (Total)	Charley Taylor, 1966	15
Field Goals Made	Curt Knight, 1971	29
Points (No.)	Curt Knight, 1971	114

COACHING HISTORY

1932	Lud Wray	4- 4-2
1933-34	William (Lone Star) Dietz	11-11-2
1935	Eddie Casey	2- 8-1
1936-42	Ray Flaherty	54-21-3
1943	Arthur (Dutch) Bergman	6- 3-1
1944-45	Dudley DeGroot	14- 5-1
1946-48	Glen (Turk) Edwards	16-18-1
1949	John Whelchel*	2- 4-1
1949-51	Herman Ball**	5-15-0
1951	Dick Todd	5- 4-0
1952-53	Earl (Curly) Lambeau	10-13-1
1954-58	Joe Kuharich	26-32-2
1959-60	Mike Nixon	4-18-2
1961-65	Bill McPeak	21-46-3
1966-68	Otto Graham	17-22-3
1969	Vince Lombardi	7- 5-2
1970	Bill Austin	6- 8-0
1971-77	George Allen	67-30-1
1978-80	Jack Pardee	24-24-0
1981	Joe Gibbs	8- 8-0

Replaced after seven games in 1949
**Replaced after three games in 1951*

FIRST PLAYER SELECTED

1936	Riley Smith, B, Alabama
1937	Sammy Baugh, B, Texas Christian
1938	Andy Farkas, B, Detroit
1939	I. B. Hale, T, Texas Christian
1940	Ed Boell, B, New York U.
1941	Forest Evashevski, B, Michigan
1942	Orban (Spec) Sanders, B, Texas
1943	Jack Jenkins, B, Missouri
1944	Mike Micka, B, Colgate
1945	Jim Hardy, B, USC
1946	Cal Rossi, B, UCLA*
1947	Cal Rossi, B, UCLA
1948	Harry Gilmer, B, Alabama
1949	Rob Goode, B, Texas A&M
1950	George Thomas, B, Oklahoma
1951	Leon Heath, B, Oklahoma
1952	Larry Isbell, B, Baylor
1953	Jack Scarbath, B, Maryland
1954	Steve Meilinger, E. Kentucky
1955	Ralph Guglielmi, B, Notre Dame
1956	Ed Vereb, B, Maryland
1957	Don Bosseler, B, Miami
1958	Mike Sommer, B (2), George Washington
1959	Don Allard, B, Boston College
1960	Richie Lucas, QB, Penn State
1961	Norman Snead, QB, Wake Forest
1962	Leroy Jackson, WR, Illinois Central
1963	Pat Richter, TE, Wisconsin
1964	Charley Taylor, RB-WR, Arizona State
1965	Bob Breitenstein, T (2), Tulsa
1966	Charlie Gogolak, K, Princeton
1967	Ray McDonald, RB, Idaho
1968	Jim Smith, DB, Oregon
1969	Eugene Epps, DB (2), Texas-El Paso
1970	Bill Brundige, DT (2), Colorado
1971	Cotton Speyrer, WR (2), Texas
1972	Moses Denson, RB (8), Maryland State
1973	Charles Cantrell, G (5), Lamar Tech
1974	Jon Keyworth, TE (6), Colorado
1975	Mike Thomas, RB (5), Nevada-Las Vegas
1976	Mike Hughes, G (5), Baylor
1977	Duncan McColl, DE (4), Stanford
1978	Tony Green, RB (6), Florida
1979	Don Warren, TE (4), San Diego State
1980	Art Monk, WR, Syracuse
1981	Mark May, T, Pittsburgh
1982	Vernon Dean, DB (2), San Diego State

Choice lost due to ineligibility

BOSTON BRAVES, 1932;
BOSTON REDSKINS, 1932-36;
WASHINGTON REDSKINS, 1937-81

Absher, Dick, LB, Maryland	1967
Adams, John (Tree), T, Notre Dame	1945-49
Adams, Willie, LB, New Mexico State	1965-66
Aducci, Nick, B, Nebraska	1954-55
Aguirre, Joe, E-K, St. Mary's, Cal.	1941, 1943-45
Akins, Frank, B, Washington State	1943-46
Alban, Dick, B, Northwestern	1952-55
Aldrich, Ki, C, Texas Christian	1941-42, 1945-47
Alford, Bruce, K, Texas Christian	1967
Allen, Gerry, RB, Nebraska-Omaha	1967-69
Allen, John, C, Purdue	1955-58
Alston, Mack, TE, Maryland-Eastern Shore	1970-72
Ananis, Vito, B, Boston College	1945
Anderson, Bill, E, Tennessee	1958-63
Anderson, Bob, RB, Colorado	1975
Anderson, Bruce, DE, Willamette	1970
Anderson, Gary, G, Stanford	1980
Anderson, Terry, WR, Bethune-Cookman	1978
Andrako, Steve, C, Ohio State	1940
Arenz, Arnie, B, St. Louis	1934
Arneson, Jim, G, Arizona	1975
Artman, Corman (Tarzan), T, Stanford	1932
Atkeson, Dale, B, No college	1954-56
Audet, Earl, T, USC	1945
Aveni, John, K, Indiana	1961
Avery, Don, T, USC	1946-47
Avery, Jim, E, Northern Illinois	1966

B

Bacon, Coy, DE, Jackson State	1978-81
Badaczewski, John, G, Western Reserve	1949-51
Bagarus, Steve, B, Notre Dame	1945-46, 1948
Bagdon, Ed, G, Michigan State	1952
Baker, Sam, P-K, Oregon State	1953, 1956-59
Baltzell, Vic, B, Southwest Kansas	1935
Bandy, Don, G, Tulsa	1967-68
Barber, Ernie, C, San Francisco	1945
Barber, Jim, T, San Francisco	1935-41
Barefoot, Ken, DE, Virginia Tech	1968
Barfield, Ken, T, Mississippi	1954
Barker, Ed, E, Washington State	1954
Barnes, Billy Ray, RB, Wake Forest	1962-63
Barnes, Walter, DT, Nebraska	1966-68
Barnett, Steve, T, Oregon	1964
Barni, Roy, B, San Francisco	1955-56
Barrington, Tom, RB, Ohio State	1966
Barry, Paul, B, Tulsa	1953
Bartos, Hank, B, North Carolina	1938
Bartos, Joe, B, Navy	1950
Bass, Mike, CB, Michigan	1969-75
Bassi, Dick, G, Santa Clara	1937
Battles, Cliff, B, West Virginia Wesleyan	1932-37
Baugh, Sammy, HB-QB-P, Texas Christian	1937-52
Baughan, Maxie, LB, Georgia Tech	1971, 1974
Bausch, Frank, C, Kansas	1934-36
Beatty, Ed, C, Mississippi	1961
Beban, Gary, QB-WR, UCLA	1968-69
Bedore, Tom, G, No college	1944
Beinor, Ed, T, Notre Dame	1941-42
Berrang, Ed, E, Villanova	1949-52
Berschet, Marv, G, Illinois	1954-55
Biggs, Verlon, DE, Jackson State	1971-75
Birlem, Keith, E, San Jose State	1939
Boensch, Fred, G, Stanford	1947-48
Boll, Don, T, Nebraska	1953-59
Bond, Chuck, T, Washington	1937-38
Bond, Randall (Rink), B, Washington	1938
Bosch, Frank, DT, Colorado	1968-69
Bosseler, Don, B, Miami	1957-64
Bostic, Jeff, C, Clemson	1980-81
Boswell, Ben, T, Texas Christian	1934
Braatz, Tom, B, Marquette	1957-59
Bradley, Hal, E, Elon	1938-39
Bragg, Mike, P, Richmond	1968-79
Breding, Ed, LB, Texas A&M	1967-68
Breedlove, Rod, LB, Maryland	1960-64
Brewer, Billy, B, Mississippi	1960
Briggs, Bill, DE, Iowa	1966-67
Briggs, Bob, B, Central State, Oklahoma	1965
Brito, Gene, DE, Loyola, Cal.	1951-53, 1955-58
Britt, Ed, B, Holy Cross	1936-37
Britt, Oscar, B, Mississippi	1946
Brooks, Perry, DT, Southern U.	1978-81
Brown, Bill (Buddy), G, Arkansas	1951-52
Brown, Dan, E, Villanova	1950
Brown, Eddie, S, Tennessee	1975-77
Brown, Hardy, LB, Tulsa	1950
Brown, Larry, RB, Kansas State	1969-76
Brown, Tom, RB, Maryland	1969

Charles (Ki) Aldrich

Steve Bagarus

Don Bosseler

Al DeMao

Harry Gilmer

Rob Goode

Len Hauss

Brueckman, Charlie, C, Pittsburgh 1958
Brundige, Bill, DE, Colorado 1970-77
Brunet, Bob, RB, Louisiana Tech 1968, 1970-77
Bryant, Trent, CB, Arkansas 1981
Budd, Frank, WR, Villanova 1963
Buggs, Danny, WR, West Virginia 1976-79
Bukich, Rudy, QB, USC 1957-58
Buksar, George, B, Purdue 1951-52
Burman, George, C, Northwestern 1971-72
Burrell, John, WR, Rice 1966-67
Busich, Sam, E, Ohio State 1936
Butkus, Carl, T, George Washington 1948
Butsko, Harry, LB, Maryland 1963
Butz, Dave, DE, Purdue 1975-81

C

Cafego, George, B, Tennessee 1943
Campiglio, Bob, B, West Liberty State 1933
Campora, Don, T, Pacific 1953
Carpenter, Preston, E, Arkansas 1964-66
Carr, Jimmy, LB, Morris Harvey 1964-65
Carroll, Jim, LB, Notre Dame 1966-68
Carroll, Leo, DE, San Diego State 1969-70
Carroll, Vic, T, Nevada 1936-42
Carson, Johnny, E, Georgia 1954-59
Casares, Rick, RB, Florida 1965
Caster, Richard, TE, Jackson State 1981
Castiglia, Jim, B, Georgetown 1947-48
Cherne, Hal, T, DePaul 1933
Cheroke, George, B, Ohio State 1946
Christensen, Erik, E, Richmond 1956
Churchwell, Don, T, Mississippi 1959
Cichowski, Gene, B, Indiana 1958-59
Cifers, Ed, E, Tennessee 1941-42, 1946
Clair, Frank, E, Ohio State 1941
Claitt, Rickey, RB, Bethune-Cookman 1980-81
Clark, Calvin, DE, Purdue 1981
Clark, Jim, G, Oregon State 1952-53
Clark, Mike, DE, Florida 1981
Clark, Myers (Algy), B, Ohio State 1932
Clay, Billie, B, Mississippi 1966
Clay, Ozzie, B, Iowa State 1964
Cloud, Jack, B, William & Mary 1952-53
Cochran, Tom, B, Auburn 1949
Coia, Angelo, WR, USC 1964-65
Coleman, Monte, LB, Central Arkansas 1979-81
Collier, Jim, E, Arkansas 1963
Collins, Paul (Rip), E, Pittsburgh 1932-35
Concannon, Ernie, G, New York U. 1934-36
Condit, Merlyn, B, Carnegie Tech 1945
Conkright, Bill (Red), C, Oklahoma 1943
Connell, Mike, P, Cincinnati 1980-81
Corbitt, Don, C, Arizona 1948
Couppee, Al, B, Iowa 1946
Cox, Billy, B, Duke 1951-52, 1955
Crabb, Claude, DB, Colorado 1962-63
Crane, Dennis, DT, USC 1968-69
Crisler, Hal, E, San Jose State 1948-49
Crissy, Cris, WR, Princeton 1981
Croftcheck, Don, G, Indiana 1965-66
Cronan, Pete, LB, Boston College 1981
Cronin, Gene, DE, Pacific 1961-62
Crossan, Dave, C, Maryland 1965-69
Crotty, Jim, B, Notre Dame 1960-61
Crow, Orien, C, Haskell 1933-34
Cudzik, Walt, C, Purdue 1954
Cunningham, Doug, RB, Mississippi 1974
Cunningham, Jim, B, Pittsburgh 1961-63
Curtis, Mike, LB, Duke 1977-78
Cvercko, Andy, G, Northwestern 1963

D

Dale, Roland, E, Mississippi 1950
Darre, Bernie, G, Tulane 1961
Daum, Mike, T, Cal Poly-San Luis Obispo 1981
Davidson, Ben, DT, Washington 1962-63
Davis, Andy, B, George Washington 1952
Davis, Fred, T, Alabama 1941-42, 1945
Davlin, Mike, T, San Francisco 1955
Day, Eagle, QB, Mississippi 1959-60
Deal, Rufus, B, Auburn 1942
Dean, Fred, G, Texas Southern 1978-80
DeCarlo, Art, B, Georgia 1956-57
DeCorrevant, Bill, B, Northwestern 1945
Dee, Bob, E, Holy Cross 1957-58
Deeks, Don, T, Washington 1947
DeFrance, Chris, WR, Arizona State 1979
DeFruiter, Bob, B, Nebraska 1945-47
Dekker, Paul, E, Michigan State 1953
Deloplaine, Jack, RB, Salem 1978
DeMao, Al, C, Duquesne 1945-53
Denson, Moses, RB, Maryland-East Shore 1974-75
Dess, Darrell, G, North Carolina State 1965-66
Didion, John, LB, Oregon State 1969
Doll, Don, DB, USC 1953
Doolan, Jack, B, Georgetown 1945
Dorow, Al, QB, Michigan State 1954-56
Dow, Ken, B, Oregon State 1941
Dowda, Harry, B, Wake Forest 1949-53
Dowler, Boyd, WR, Colorado 1971
Drazenovich, Chuck, LB, Penn State 1950-59
Dubinetz, Greg, G, Yale 1979
DuBois, Phil, TE, San Diego State 1979-80
Duckworth, Joe, E, Colgate 1947
Dudley, Bill, B, Virginia 1950-51, 1953
Dugan, Fred, E, Dayton 1961-63
Duich, Steve, G, San Diego State 1969
Duncan, Leslie (Speedy), DB, Jackson State 1971-73
Dunn, Coye, B, USC 1943
Dusek, Brad, LB, Texas A&M 1974-81
Dwyer, Jack, B, Loyola, Cal. 1951
Dye, Les, E, Syracuse 1944-45
Dyer, Henry, RB, Grambling 1969-70

E

Ecker, Ed, T, John Carroll 1952
Edwards, Glen (Turk), T, Washington State 1932-40
Edwards, Weldon, T, Texas Christian 1948
Ellstrom, Marvin (Swede), B, Oklahoma 1934
Elmore, Doug, B, Mississippi 1962
Elter, Leo, B, Duquesne 1955-57
Erickson, Carl (Bud), C, Washington 1938-39
Erickson, Mickey, C, Northwestern 1932
Evans, Charlie, RB, USC 1974

F

Fanucci, Mike, DE, Arizona State 1972
Farkas, Andy, B, Detroit 1938-44
Farman, Dick, G, Washington State 1939-43
Farmer, Tom, B, Iowa 1947-48
Feagin, Tom, G, Houston 1963
Felber, Fred (Nip), E, North Dakota 1932
Felton, Ralph, B, Maryland 1954-60
Ferris, Neil, B, Loyola, Cal. 1951-52
Filchock, Frank, B, Indiana 1938-41, 1944-45
Fiorentino, Al, G, Boston College 1943-44
Fischer, Pat, CB, Nebraska 1968-77
Fisher, Bob, T, USC 1940
Flick, Tom, QB, Washington 1981
Foltz, Vern, C, St. Vincent 1944
Forte, Ike, RB, Arkansas 1978
Francis, Dave, B, Ohio State 1963
Frankian, Ike, E, St. Mary's, Cal. 1933
Freeman, Bobby, B, Auburn 1962
Fritsch, Ted, C, St. Norbert 1976-79
Fryer, Brian, WR, Alberta 1976-77
Fugett, Jean, TE, Amherst 1976-79
Fulcher, Bill, LB, Georgia Tech 1956-58
Fuller, Larry, B, No college 1944-45

G

Gaffney, Jim, B, Tennessee 1945-46
Garrett, Alvin, WR, Angelo State 1981
Garzoni, Mike, G, USC 1947
Gentry, Lee, B, Tulsa 1941
German, Jimmy, B, Centre 1939
Giaquinto, Nick, RB, Connecticut 1981
Gibson, Joe, B, Tulsa 1943
Gilmer, Harry, QB, Alabama 1948-52, 1954
Glick, Gary, DB, Colorado State 1959-61
Gob, Art, E, Pittsburgh 1959-60
Gogolak, Charley, K, Princeton 1966-68
Goode, Rob, B, Texas A&M 1949-51, 1954-55
Goodnight, Clyde, E, Tulsa 1949-50
Goodyear, John, B, Marquette 1942
Goosby, Tom, G, Baldwin-Wallace 1966
Graf, Dave, LB, Penn State 1981
Grant, Bob, LB, Wake Forest 1971
Grant, Darryl, G, Rice 1981
Grant, Frank, WR, South Colorado State 1973-78
Gray, Bill, G, Oregon State 1947-48
Green, Tony, RB, Florida 1978
Grimm, Dan, C, Colorado 1969
Grimm, Russ, C-G, Pittsburgh 1981
Guglielmi, Ralph, QB, Notre Dame 1955, 1958-60

H

Hackbart, Dale, DB, Wisconsin 1961-63
Hageman, Fred, C, Kansas 1961-64
Haines, Kris, WR, Notre Dame 1979
Haley, Dick, B, Pittsburgh 1959-60
Hall, Galen, QB, Penn State 1962
Hall, Windlan, DB, Arizona State 1977
Hamlin, Gene, C, Western Michigan 1970
Hammond, Bobby, RB, Morgan State 1979-80
Hanburger, Chris, LB, North Carolina 1965-78
Hancock, Mike, TE, Idaho State 1973-75
Hanna, Elzaphan (Zip), G, South Carolina 1945
Hansen, Ron, G, Minnesota 1954
Hardeman, Buddy, RB, Iowa State 1979-80
Hare, Cecil, B, Gonzaga 1941-42, 1945
Hare, Ray, B, Gonzaga 1940-43
Harlan, Jim, T, Howard Payne 1978
Harmon, Clarence, RB, Mississippi State 1977-81
Harold, George, DB, Allen 1968
Harraway, Charley, RB, San Jose State 1969-73
Harris, Don, S, Rutgers 1978-79
Harris, Hank, G, Texas 1947-48
Harris, Jim, DB, Howard Payne 1970
Harris, Joe, LB, Georgia Tech 1977
Harris, Rickie, DB, Arizona 1962-65, 1970
Harrison, Kenny, WR, Southern Methodist 1980
Hartley, Howard, B, Duke 1948
Hartman, Bill, B, Georgia 1938
Hatcher, Ron, B, Michigan State 1962
Hauss, Len, C, Georgia 1964-77
Hayden, Ken, C, Arkansas 1943
Haymond, Alvin, DB, Southern U. 1972
Haynes, Hall, B, Santa Clara 1950-55
Haynes, Reggie, TE, Nevada-Las Vegas 1978
Hazelwood, Ted, T, North Carolina 1953
Heath, Leon, B, Oklahoma 1951-53
Hecker, Norb, DB, Baldwin-Wallace 1955-57
Heenan, Pat, E, Notre Dame 1960
Hegarty, Bill, T, Villanova 1953
Heinz, Bob, DT, Pacific 1978
Hendershot, Larry, LB, Arizona State 1967
Henderson, Jon, WR, Colorado State 1970
Hendren, Bob, T, USC 1949-51
Hennessey, Jerry, E, Santa Clara 1952-53
Hermeling, Terry, T, Nevada-Reno 1970-80
Hernandez, Joe, E, Arizona 1964
Hickman, Dallas, DE, California 1976-81
Hickman, Donnie, G, USC 1978
Hill, Calvin, RB, Yale 1976-77
Hodgson, Pat, TE, Georgia 1966
Hoffman, Bob, B, USC 1940-41
Hoffman, John, E, Hawaii 1969-70
Hokuf, Steve, B, Nebraska 1933-35
Hollar, John, B, Appalachian State 1948-49
Holman, Willie, DE, South Carolina State 1973
Holmer, Walt, B, Northwestern 1933
Horner, Sam, DB, Virginia Military 1960-61
Horstmann, Roy, B, Purdue 1933
Houghton, Jerry, T, Washington State 1950
Houston, Ken, S, Prairie View 1973-80
Houston, Walt, G, Purdue 1955
Hover, Don, LB, Washington State 1978-79
Howell, Millard (Dixie), B, Alabama 1937
Hudson, Bob, LB, Clemson 1959
Huff, Sam, LB, West Virginia 1964-67, 1969
Hughes, Henry, B, Oregon State 1932
Hughley, George, B, Central State, Oklahoma 1965
Hull, Mike, RB, USC 1971-74
Hunter, Bill, DB, Syracuse 1965
Hurley, George, B, Washington State 1932-33

Dick James

Ron McDole

Bobby Mitchell

Mark Moseley

Brig Owens

John Paluck

Jim Podoley

Hyatt, Fred, WR, Auburn ... 1973

I

Imhof, Martin, DE, San Diego State ... 1974
Intriere, Marne, G, Loyola, Maryland ... 1933-34
Irwin, Don, B, Colgate ... 1936-39
Izo, George, QB, Notre Dame ... 1961-64

J

Jackson, Leroy, B, Western Illinois ... 1962-63
Jackson, Steve, LB, Texas-Arlington ... 1966-67
Jackson, Trenton, RB, Illinois ... 1967
Jackson, Wilbur, RB, Alabama ... 1980-81
Jacobs, Jack, B, Oklahoma ... 1946
Jacoby, Joe, T, Louisville ... 1981
Jaffurs, Johnny, B, Penn State ... 1946
Jagielski, Harry, T, Indiana ... 1956
James, Dick, B, Oregon ... 1956-63
Janowicz, Vic, B, Ohio State ... 1954-55
Jacqua, Jon, DB, Lewis & Clark ... 1970-72
Jefferson, Roy, WR, Utah ... 1971-76
Jencks, Bob, K-E, Miami, Ohio ... 1965
Jenkins, Jacque, B, Vanderbilt ... 1943, 1946-47
Johnson, Dennis, DT, Delaware ... 1974-77
Johnson, Larry, C, Haskell ... 1933-35, 1944
Johnson, Mitch, T, UCLA ... 1966-68, 1972
Johnson, Randy, QB, Texas A&I ... 1975-76
Johnston, Jimmy, B, Washington ... 1939-40
Jones, Chuck, E, George Washington ... 1955
Jones, David (Deacon), DE, South Carolina State ... 1974
Jones, Harvey, B, Baylor ... 1947
Jones, Jimmie, DE, Wichita State ... 1971-73
Jones, Joe, DE, Tennessee State ... 1979-80
Jones, Larry, WR, Northeast Missouri ... 1974-77
Jones, Melvin, G, Houston ... 1981
Jones, Stan, T, Maryland ... 1966
Jordan, Curtis, DB, Texas Tech ... 1981
Jordan, Jeff, RB, Washington ... 1971-72
Justice, Charlie (Choo Choo), B, North Carolina 1950, 1952-54
Justice, Ed, B, Gonzaga ... 1936-42
Junker, Steve, E, Xavier ... 1961-62
Jurgensen, Sonny, QB, Duke ... 1964-74
Juzwik, Steve, B, Notre Dame ... 1942

K

Kahn, Eddie, G, North Carolina ... 1935-37
Kammerer, Carl, DE, Pacific ... 1963-69
Kamp, Jim, T, Oklahoma City ... 1933
Kantor, Joe, B, Notre Dame ... 1966
Karamatic, George (Automatic) B, Gonzaga ... 1938
Karcher, Jim, G, Ohio State ... 1936-39
Karras, Lou, T, Purdue ... 1950-51
Katrishen, Mike, T, Southern Mississippi ... 1948-49
Kaufman, Mel, LB, Cal Poly-San Luis Obispo ... 1981
Keenan, Jack, G, South Carolina ... 1944-45
Kelley, Gordon, LB, Georgia ... 1962-63
Kelly, John, T, Florida A&M ... 1966-67
Kenneally, George, E, St. Bonaventure ... 1929-32
Kerr, Jim, DB, Penn State ... 1961-62
Khayat, Bob, K, Mississippi ... 1960, 1962-63
Khayat, Eddie, DT, Tulane ... 1957, 1962-63
Kiick, Jim, RB, Wyoming ... 1977
Kilmer, Billy, QB, UCLA ... 1971-78
Kimmel, J. D., T, Houston ... 1955-56
Kincaid, Jim, B, South Carolina ... 1954
Knight, Curt, K, Coast Guard ... 1969-73
Koniszewski, John, T, George Washington ... 1945-46, 1948
Kopay, Dave, RB, Washington ... 1969-70
Kovatch, Johnny, E, Notre Dame ... 1942, 1946
Krakoski, Joe, B, Illinois ... 1961
Krause, Max, B, Gonzaga ... 1937-40
Krause, Paul, DB, Iowa ... 1964-67
Krause, Henry (Red), C, St. Louis ... 1937-40
Kresky, Joe, G, Wisconsin ... 1932
Krueger, Al, E, USC ... 1941-42
Kruczek, Mike, QB, Boston College ... 1980
Kuchta, Frank, C, Notre Dame ... 1958-59
Kupp, Jake, G, Washington ... 1966
Kuziel, Bob, C, Pittsburgh ... 1975-80

L

Laaveg, Paul, G, Iowa ... 1970-75
Lapka, Ted, E, St. Ambrose ... 1943-44, 1946
Larson, Bill, TE, Colorado State ... 1977
Larson, Pete, RB, Cornell ... 1967-68
Lasse, Dick, LB, Syracuse ... 1960-61
Lavender, Joe, DB, San Diego State ... 1976-81
Law, Dennis, WR, East Tennessee State ... 1979
Lawrence, Don, T, Notre Dame ... 1959-61
LeBaron, Eddie, QB, Pacific ... 1952-53, 1955-59
Lemek, Ray, T, Notre Dame ... 1957-61
Lennan, Reid, G, No college ... 1945
Leon, Tony, G, Alabama ... 1943
Lewis, Dan, B, Wisconsin ... 1965
Lipscomb, Paul, T, Tennessee ... 1950-54
Livingston, Howie, B, Fullerton JC ... 1948-50
Lockett, J. W., B, Central State-Oklahoma ... 1964
Lolotai, Al, G, Weber State ... 1945
Long, Bob, WR, Wichita ... 1969
Lookabaugh, John, E, Maryland ... 1946-47
Looney, Joe Don, RB, Oklahoma ... 1966-67
Lorch, Karl, DT, USC ... 1976-81
Love, John, WR, North Texas State ... 1967
Lowe, Gary, B, Michigan State ... 1956-57
Lowry, Quentin, LB, Youngstown State ... 1981
Luce, Lew, B, Penn State ... 1961
Lynch, Dick, DB, Notre Dame ... 1958

M

MacAfee, Ken, E, Alabama ... 1959
Macioszczyk, Art, B, Western Michigan ... 1948
MacMurdo, Jim, T, Pittsburgh ... 1932-33
Madarik, Elmer (Tippy), B, Detroit ... 1948
Malinchak, Bill, WR, Indiana ... 1970-74, 1976
Malone, Benny, RB, Arizona State ... 1978-79
Malone, Charley, E, Texas A&M ... 1934-40, 1942
Manley, Dexter, DE, Oklahoma State ... 1981
Manton, Taldon (Tillie), B, Texas Christian ... 1938
Marciniak, Ron, G, Kansas State ... 1955
Marcus, Pete, E, Kentucky ... 1944
Marshall, Rich, T, Stephen F. Austin ... 1966
Martin, Aaron, DB, North Carolina College ... 1968
Martin, Jim, K, Notre Dame ... 1964
Mason, Tommy, RB, Tulane ... 1971-72
Masterson, Bob, E, Miami ... 1938-43
Mattson, Riley, T, Oregon ... 1961-64
May, Mark, T, Pittsburgh ... 1981
Mazurek, Fred, B, Pittsburgh ... 1965-66
McCabe, Richie, B, Pittsburgh ... 1959
McChesney, Bob, E, UCLA ... 1936-42
McCrary, Greg, TE, Clark ... 1978, 1981
McDaniel, John, WR, Lincoln ... 1978-80
McDaniel, LeCharles, S, Cal Poly-San Luis Obispo ... 1981
McDole, Ron, DE, Nebraska ... 1971-78
McDonald, Ray, RB, Idaho ... 1967-68
McKee, Paul, E, Syracuse ... 1947-48
McKeever, Marlin, LB, USC ... 1968-70
McKinney, Zion, WR, South Carolina ... 1980
McLinton, Harold, LB, Southern U. ... 1969-78
McNamara, Bob, E, New York U. ... 1934
McNeil, Clifton, WR, Grambling ... 1971-72
McPhail, Hal, B, Xavier ... 1934-35
McQuilken, Kim, QB, Lehigh ... 1978-80
Meade, Jim, B, Maryland ... 1939-40
Meadows, Ed, DE, Duke ... 1959
Meilinger, Steve, E, Kentucky ... 1956-57
Mendenhall, Mat, DE, Brigham Young ... 1981
Mercein, Chuck, RB, Yale ... 1969
Merkle, Ed, G, Oklahoma State ... 1944
Metcalf, Terry, RB, Long Beach State ... 1981
Michaels, Eddie, G, Villanova ... 1937
Micka, Mike, B, Colgate ... 1944-45
Miller, Allen, LB, Ohio U. ... 1962-63
Miller, Clark, E, Utah State ... 1969
Miller, Fred, T, Pacific ... 1955
Miller, Johnny, T, Boston College ... 1956, 1958-59
Miller, Tom, B, Hampton-Sydney ... 1945
Millner, Wayne, E, Notre Dame ... 1936-41, 1945
Milot, Rich, LB, Penn State ... 1979-81
Mingo, Gene, K, No college ... 1967
Mitchell, Bobby, HB-WR, Illinois ... 1962-68
Modzelewski, Dick, DT, Maryland ... 1953-54
Momsen, Tony, C, Michigan ... 1952
Monachino, Jim, RB, California ... 1955
Monaco, Ray, G, Holy Cross ... 1944
Monasco, Don, B, Texas ... 1954
Monk, Art, WR, Syracuse ... 1980-81
Mont, Tommy, QB, Maryland ... 1947-49
Moore, Chuck, G, Arkansas ... 1962
Moore, Wilbur, B, Minnesota ... 1939-46
Moran, Jim, G, Holy Cross ... 1935-36
Morgan, Bob, DT, Maryland ... 1954
Morgan, Boyd, B, USC ... 1939-40
Morgan, Mike, LB, Louisiana State ... 1968
Morley, Sam, E, Stanford ... 1954
Mortensen, Fred, QB, Arizona State ... 1979
Moseley, Mark, K, Stephen F. Austin ... 1974-81
Moss, Eddie, RB, Southeast Missouri ... 1977
Moss, Joe, T, Maryland ... 1952
Mul-Key, Herb, RB, No college ... 1972-74
Murphy, Mark, S, Colgate ... 1977-81
Musgrove, Spain, DT, Utah State ... 1967-69

N

Natowich, Andy, B, Holy Cross ... 1944
Nelms, Mike, S-KR, Baylor ... 1980-81
Nelson, Ralph, RB, No college ... 1975
Niemi, Laurie, T, Washington State ... 1949-53
Ninowski, Jim, QB, Michigan State ... 1967-68
Nisby, John, G, Pacific ... 1962-64
Nix, Doyle, B, Southern Methodist ... 1958-59
Nobile, Leo, G, Penn State ... 1947
Nock, George, RB, Morgan State ... 1972
Norman, Jim, T, No college ... 1955
Norris, Hal, B, California ... 1955-56
North, Jim, T, Central Washington ... 1944
Norton, Jim, T, Washington ... 1968
Nott, Doug, B, Detroit ... 1935
Nugent, Dan, G, Auburn ... 1976-78, 1980
Nussbaumer, Bob, E, Michigan ... 1947-48

O

O'Brien, Fran, T, Michigan State ... 1960-66
O'Brien, Gail, T, Nebraska ... 1934-36
O'Dell, Stu, LB, Indiana ... 1974-76
Oden, Olaf (Curley), B, Brown ... 1932
Ogrin, Pat, DE, Wyoming ... 1981
Olkewicz, Neal, LB, Maryland ... 1979-81
Olsson, Les, G, Mercer ... 1934-38
Olszewski, Johnny, RB, California ... 1958-60
Osborne, Tom, E, Hastings, Nebraska ... 1960-61
Ostrowski, Chet, E, Notre Dame ... 1954-59
Owens, Brig, DB, Cincinnati ... 1966-77
Owens, Don, T, Southern Mississippi ... 1957

P

Paluck, John, DE, Pittsburgh ... 1956, 1959-65
Pape, Oran, B, Iowa ... 1932
Papit, Johnny, B, Virginia ... 1951-53
Pardee, Jack, LB, Texas A&M ... 1971-72
Parks, Ed (Mickey), C, Oklahoma ... 1938-40
Parrish, Lemar, CB, Lincoln, Missouri ... 1978-81
Pasqua, Joe, T, Southern Methodist ... 1943
Paternoster, Angelo, G, Georgetown ... 1943
Peebles, Jim, E, Vanderbilt ... 1946-49, 1951
Peiffer, Dan, C, Southeast Missouri ... 1980
Pellegrini, Bob, LB, Maryland ... 1962-65
Pepper, Gene, G, Missouri ... 1950-53
Pergine, John, LB, Notre Dame ... 1973-75
Perrin, Lonnie, RB, Illinois ... 1979
Peters, Floyd, T, San Francisco State ... 1970
Peters, Tony, S, Oklahoma ... 1979-81
Peters, Volney, T, USC ... 1954-57
Peterson, Russ, T, Montana ... 1932
Petitbon, Richie, S, Tulane ... 1971-73
Piasecky, Al, E, Duke ... 1943-45
Pierce, Dan, RB, Memphis State ... 1970
Pinckert, Erny, B, USC ... 1932-40
Plansky, Tony, B, Georgetown ... 1932
Planutis, Jerry, B, Michigan State ... 1956
Podoley, Jim, RB, Central Michigan ... 1957-60
Poillon, Dick, B, Canisius ... 1942, 1946-49
Polsfoot, Fran, E, Washington State ... 1953
Pottios, Myron, LB, Notre Dame ... 1971-73
Pressley, Lee, C, Oklahoma ... 1945
Prestel, Jim, T, Idaho ... 1967

Myron Pottios

Vince Promuto

Ray Schoenke

Diron Talbert

Hugh (Bones) Taylor

Joe Theismann

LaVern Torgeson

Promuto, Vince, G, Holy Cross 1960-70

Q

Quinlan, Billy, DE, Michigan State 1965
Quirk, Ed, B, Missouri 1948-51

R

Raba, Bob, TE, Maryland 1981
Rae, Mike, QB, USC 1981
Ramsey, Knox, G, William & Mary 1952-53
Rector, Ron, B, Northwestern 1966
Reed, Alvin, TE, Prairie View 1973-75
Reed, Bob, G, Tennessee State 1965
Reger, John, LB, Pittsburgh 1964-66
Rehnquist, Milt, C, Bethany, Kansas 1932
Renfro, Will, T, Memphis State 1957-59
Rentner, Ernest (Pug), B, Northwestern 1934-36
Reynolds, M. C. (Mack), QB, Louisiana State 1960
Ribar, Frank, G, Duke 1943
Ricca, Jim, G, Georgetown 1951-54
Richardson, Grady, TE, Cal State-Fullerton 1979-80
Richter, Pat, TE, Wisconsin 1963-70
Riggins, John, RB, Kansas 1976-79, 1981
Riley, Jack, T, Northwestern 1933
Roberts, John, B, Georgia 1932
Roberts, Walter, WR, San Jose State 1969-70
Robinson, Dave, LB, Penn State 1973-74
Rock, Walter, T, Maryland 1968-73
Rosato, Sal, B, Villanova 1945-47
Rosso, George, B, Ohio State 1954
Roussel, Tom, LB, Southern Mississippi 1968-70
Roussos, Mike, T, Pittsburgh 1948-49
Runnels, Tom, B, North Texas State 1956-57
Russell, Torrance (Bo), T, Auburn 1939-40
Rust, Reggie, B, Oregon State 1932
Rutgens, Joe, DT, Illinois 1961-69
Ruthstrom, Ralph, B, Southern Methodist 1947
Ryan, Frank, QB, Rice 1969-70
Ryczek, Dan, C, Virginia 1973-75
Rykovich, Julie, B, Illinois 1952-53
Rymkus, Lou, T, Notre Dame 1943
Rzempoluch, Ted, T, Virginia 1963

S

Saenz, Eddie, B, USC 1946-51
Salem, Ed, B, Alabama 1951
Salter, Bryant, S, Pittsburgh 1974-75
Sample, Johnny, DB, Maryland State 1963-65
Sanchez, John, T, San Francisco 1947-49
Sanders, Lonnie, DB, Michigan State 1963-67
Sandifer, Dan, T, Louisiana State 1948-49
Sanford, Haywood (Sandy), E, Alabama 1940
Sarboe, Phil, B, Washington State 1934
Saul, Ron, G, Michigan State 1976-81
Sardisco, Tony, G, Tulane 1956
Scafide, John, T, Tulane 1933
Scanlan, Jerry, T, Hawaii 1980-81
Scarbath, Jack, QB, Maryland 1953-54
Schick, Doyle, LB, Kansas 1961
Schilling, Ralph, E, Oklahoma City 1946
Schmidt, Kermit (Dutch), E, Cal Poly-San Luis Obispo . . . 1932
Schoenke, Ray, G, Southern Methodist 1966-75
Schrader, Jim, C, Notre Dame 1954, 1956-61
Schuette, Paul, G, Wisconsin 1932
Scott, Jake, S, Georgia 1976-78
Scotti, Ben, DB, Maryland 1959-61
Scudero, Joe, B, San Francisco 1954-58
Seals, George, G, Missouri 1964
Seay, Virgil, WR, Troy State 1981
Sebastian, Mike, B, Pittsburgh 1935
Sebek, Nick, B, Indiana 1950
Seedborg, John, K, Arizona State 1965
Seno, Frank, B, George Washington 1943-44, 1949
Severson, Jeff, DB, Long Beach State 1972
Seymour, Bob, B, Oklahoma 1940-45
Sharp, Ev, T, Cal Poly-San Luis Obispo 1944-45
Shepherd, Bill, B, West Maryland 1935
Shiner, Dick, QB, Maryland 1964-66
Shoener, Herb, E, Iowa 1948-49
Shorter, Jim, DB, Detroit 1964-67
Shugart, Clyde, G, Iowa State 1939-44
Shula, Don, DB, John Carroll 1957
Siano, Tony, C, Fordham 1932
Siegert, Herb, G, Illinois 1949-51
Siemering, Larry, C, San Francisco 1935-36
Sinko, Steve, T, Duquesne 1934-36
Sistrunk, Manny, DT, Arkansas-Pine Bluff 1970-75
Slivinski, Steve, G, Washington 1939-43
Smith, Ben, E, Alabama 1937
Smith, Dick, DB, Northwestern 1967-68
Smith, Ed, B, New York U 1936
Smith, George, C, California 1937, 1941-43
Smith, Hugh, E, Kansas 1962
Smith, Jerry, TE, Arizona State 1965-77
Smith, Jim (Yazoo), DB, Oregon 1968
Smith, Jack, E, Stanford 1943
Smith, John, WR, North Texas State 1978
Smith, Larry, RB, Florida 1974
Smith, Paul, DE, New Mexico 1979-80
Smith, Riley, B, Alabama 1936-38
Snead, Norman, QB, Wake Forest 1961-63
Sneddon, Bob, B, St. Mary's, Cal 1964
Snidow, Ron, DE, Oregon 1963-67
Snowden, Jim, T, Notre Dame 1965-72
Sobolenski, Joe, G, Michigan 1949
Sommer, Mike, B, George Washington 1958-59, 1961
Sommers, Jack, C, UCLA 1947
Spaniel, Frank, B, Notre Dame 1950
Sparks, Dave, G, South Carolina 1954
Spellman, John, E, Brown 1932
Spirida, Jon, E, St. Anselm's 1939
Stacco, Ed, T, Colgate 1948
Stallings, Don, E, North Carolina 1960
Stanfel, Dick, G, San Francisco 1956-58
Starke, George, T, Columbia 1973-81
Stasica, Leo, B, Colorado 1943
Steber, John, G, Georgia Tech 1946-50
Steffen, Jim, DB, UCLA 1961-65
Stenn, Paul (Stenko), T, Villanova 1946
Stephens, Lou (Red), G, San Francisco 1955-60
Steponovich, Mike, G, St. Mary's, Cal 1933
Stits, Bill, DB, UCLA 1959
Stokes, Tim, T, Oregon 1975-77
Stone, Ken, S, Vanderbilt 1973-75
Stout, Pete, B, Texas Christian 1949-50
Stovall, Dick, C, Abilene Christian 1949
Stralka, Clem, G, Georgetown 1938-42, 1945-46
Stuart, Jim, T, Oregon 1941
Sturt, Fred, G, Bowling Green 1974
Stynchula, Andy, DT, Penn State 1960-63
Suminski, Dave, G, Wisconsin 1953
Sutton, Eddie, B, North Carolina 1957-59
Sweeney, Walt, G, Syracuse 1974-75
Sykes, Bob, B, San Jose State 1952
Szafaryn, Len, T, North Carolina 1949

T

Talbert, Diron, DT, Texas 1971-80
Taylor, Charley, WR, Arizona State 1964-77
Taylor, Hugh (Bones), E, Oklahoma City 1947-54
Taylor, Mike, T, USC 1971
Taylor, Roosevelt, DB, Grambling 1972
Temple, Mark, B, Oregon 1936
Tereshinski, Joe, E, Georgia 1947-54
Theismann, Joe, QB, Notre Dame 1974-81
Theofiledes, Harry, QB, Waynesburg State 1968
Thomas, Duane, RB, West Texas State 1973-74
Thomas, George, B, Oklahoma 1950-51
Thomas, Mike, RB, Nevada-Las Vegas 1975-78
Thomas, Ralph, E, San Francisco 1955-56
Thomas, Spencer, S, Washburn 1975
Thompson, Ricky, WR, Baylor 1978-81
Thurlow, Steve, RB, Stanford 1966-68
Tillman, Rusty, LB, Northern Arizona 1970-77
Titchenal, Bob, E, San Jose State 1940-42
Todd, Dick, B, Texas A&M 1939-42, 1945-48
Toneff, Bob, DT, Notre Dame 1959-64
Torgeson, LaVern, LB, Washington State 1955-57
Tosi, Flavio, E, Boston College 1934-36
Tracy, Tom, RB, Tennessee 1963-64
Tucker, Tuckey, B, Manhattan 1938
Turley, Doug, E, Scranton 1944-48
Turner, Jay, B, George Washington 1938-39
Turner, Kevin, LB, Pacific 1981
Tyrer, Jim, T, Ohio State 1974

U

Ucovich, Mitch, T, San Jose State 1944
Uhrinyak, Steve, G, Marshall 1939
Ulinski, Harry, C, Kentucky 1950-51, 1953-56
Ungerer, Joe, T, Fordham 1944-45

V

Vactor, Ted, DB, Nebraska 1969-74
Varty, Mike, LB, Northwestern 1974
Venuto, Sam, B, Guilford 1952
Vereb, Ed, RB, Maryland 1960
Voytek, Ed, G, Purdue 1957-58

W

Waddy, Ray, CB, Texas A&I 1979-80
Wade, Bob, DB, Morgan State 1969
Walker, Rick, TE, UCLA 1980-81
Walters, Tom, DB, Southern Mississippi 1964-67
Walton, Frank (Tiger), G, Pittsburgh 1934-35
Walton, Joe, E, Pittsburgh 1957-60
Ward, Bill, G, Washington State 1946-47
Ward, Dave, G, New Mexico 1933
Warren, Don, TE, San Diego State 1979-81
Washington, Fred, T, North Texas State 1968
Washington, Joe, RB, Oklahoma 1981
Waters, Dale, E, Florida 1932-33
Watson, Jim, C, Pacific 1945
Watson, Sid, B, Northeastern 1958
Watts, George, B, Appalachian State 1942
Weatherall, Jim, T, Oklahoma 1958
Weaver, Charlie, LB, USC 1981
Weisenbaugh, Henry, B, Pittsburgh 1935-36
Weldon, Larry, B, Presbyterian 1944-45
Weller, Lou (Rabbit), B, Haskell 1933
Wells, Billy, B, Michigan State 1954, 1956-57
Westfall, Ed, B, Ohio Wesleyan 1932-33
White, Jeris, CB, Hawaii 1980-81
Whited, Marv, G, Oklahoma 1942, 1945
Whitfield, A. D., RB, North Texas State 1966-68
Whitlow, Bob, C, Arizona 1960-61
Wilbur, John, G, Stanford 1971-73
Wilde, George, B, Texas A&M 1947
Wilkin, Wilbur (Wee Willie), T, St. Mary's, Cal 1938-43
Wilkins, Roy, C, Georgia 1960-61
Williams, Fred, T, Arkansas 1964-65
Williams, Gerard, DB, Langston, Oklahoma 1976-78
Williams, Jeff, T, Rhode Island 1978-80
Williams, John, B, USC 1952-53
Williams, Sid, LB, Southern U 1967
Williamson, Ernie, T, North Carolina 1947
Willis, Larry, S, Texas-El Paso 1973
Wingate, Heath, C, Bowling Green 1967
Winslow, Doug, WR, Drake 1976-77
Witucki, Casimir (Slug), G, Indiana 1950-51, 1953-56
Wonsley, Otis, RB, Alcorn State 1981
Woodruff, Lee (Cowboy), B, Mississippi 1932
Woods, Robert, T, Tennessee State 1981
Woodward, Dick, C, Iowa 1952
Wooten, John, G, Colorado 1968
Wright, Steve, T, Alabama 1970
Wright, Ted, B, North Texas State 1934-35
Wulff, Jim, B, Michigan State 1960-61
Wyant, Fred, QB, West Virginia 1956
Wyche, Sam, QB, Furman 1971-73
Wycoff, Doug, B, Georgia Tech 1934
Wynn, Will, DE, Tennessee State 1977
Wysocki, Pete, LB, Western Michigan 1975-80

Y

Yonaker, John, E, Notre Dame 1952
Youel, Jim, B, Iowa 1946-48
Young, Bill, T, Alabama 1937-42, 1946
Young, Roy, T, Texas A&M 1938
Young, Wilbur, DE, William Penn 1981
Yowarsky, Walt, E, Kentucky 1951-54

Z

Zagers, Bert, B, Michigan State 1955, 1957-58
Zeno, Joe, G, Holy Cross 1942-44
Zimmerman, Leroy, B, San Jose State 1940-42

All-Time Team vs. Team

This is the record of games won and lost and points scored by National Football League and 1960-69 American Football League teams since 1933.

The sites of each game are abbreviated and in parentheses.

"OT" means overtime game.

Philadelphia and Pittsburgh merged in 1943 and the Chicago Cardinals and Pittsburgh merged in 1944. The scores of Phil-Pitt are under Philadelphia and Pittsburgh, and the scores of Card-Pitt are under the St. Louis Cardinals and Pittsburgh.

Six teams moved from one city to another. Two of the six changed their names. The Portsmouth, Ohio, Spartans became the Detroit Lions in 1934. The Boston Redskins became the Washington Redskins in 1937. The Cleveland Rams became the Los Angeles Rams in 1946. The Chicago Cardinals became the St. Louis Cardinals in 1960. The Los Angeles Chargers became the San Diego Chargers in 1961. The Dallas Texans became the Kansas City Chiefs in 1963. There was another team called the Dallas Texans and it played in the NFL in 1952.

ATLANTA vs. BALTIMORE
Colts lead series, 8-0
1966—Colts, 19-7 (A)
1967—Colts, 38-31 (B)
Colts, 49-7 (A)
1968—Colts, 28-20 (A)
Colts, 44-0 (B)
1969—Colts, 21-14 (A)
Colts, 13-6 (B)
1974—Colts, 17-7 (A)
(Points—Colts 229, Falcons 92)
ATLANTA vs. BUFFALO
Bills lead series, 2-1
1973—Bills, 17-6 (A)
1977—Bills, 3-0 (B)
1980—Falcons, 30-14 (B)
(Points—Falcons 36, Bills 34)
ATLANTA vs. CHICAGO
Falcons lead series, 8-4
1966—Bears, 23-6 (C)
1967—Bears, 23-14 (A)
1968—Falcons, 16-13 (C)
1969—Falcons, 48-31 (A)
1970—Bears, 23-14 (A)
1972—Falcons, 37-21 (C)
1973—Falcons, 46-6 (A)
1974—Falcons, 13-10 (A)
1976—Falcons, 10-0 (A)
1977—Falcons, 16-10 (C)
1978—Bears, 13-7 (C)
1980—Falcons, 28-17 (A)
(Points—Falcons 255, Bears 190)
ATLANTA vs. CINCINNATI
Bengals lead series, 3-1
1971—Falcons, 9-6 (C)
1975—Bengals, 21-14 (A)
1978—Bengals, 37-7 (C)
1981—Bengals, 30-28 (A)
(Points—Bengals 94, Falcons 58)
ATLANTA vs. CLEVELAND
Browns lead series, 5-1
1966—Browns, 49-17 (A)
1968—Browns, 30-7 (C)
1971—Falcons, 31-14 (C)
1976—Browns, 20-17 (A)
1978—Browns, 24-16 (A)
1981—Browns, 28-17 (C)
(Points—Browns 165, Falcons 105)
ATLANTA vs. DALLAS
Cowboys lead series, 7-1
1966—Cowboys, 47-14 (A)
1967—Cowboys, 37-7 (D)
1969—Cowboys, 24-17 (A)
1970—Cowboys, 13-0 (D)
1974—Cowboys, 24-0 (A)
1976—Falcons, 17-10 (A)
1978—*Cowboys, 27-20 (D)
1980—*Cowboys, 30-27 (A)
(Points—Cowboys 212, Falcons 102)
*NFC Divisional Playoff
ATLANTA vs. DENVER
Series tied, 2-2
1970—Broncos, 24-10 (D)
1972—Falcons, 23-20 (A)
1975—Falcons, 35-21 (A)
1979—Broncos, 20-17 (A) OT
(Points—Falcons 85, Broncos 85)
ATLANTA vs. DETROIT
Lions lead series, 10-3
1966—Lions, 28-10 (D)
1967—Lions, 24-3 (A)
1968—Lions, 24-7 (A)
1969—Lions, 27-21 (D)

1971—Lions, 41-38 (D)
1972—Lions, 26-23 (A)
1973—Lions, 31-6 (D)
1975—Lions, 17-14 (A)
1976—Lions, 24-10 (D)
1977—Falcons, 17-6 (A)
1978—Falcons, 14-0 (A)
1979—Lions, 24-23 (D)
1980—Falcons, 43-28 (A)
(Points—Lions 300, Falcons 229)
ATLANTA vs. GREEN BAY
Packers lead series, 7-5
1966—Packers, 56-3 (Mil)
1967—Packers, 23-0 (Mil)
1968—Packers, 38-7 (A)
1969—Packers, 28-10 (GB)
1970—Packers, 27-24 (GB)
1971—Falcons, 28-21 (A)
1972—Falcons, 10-9 (Mil)
1974—Falcons, 10-3 (A)
1975—Packers, 22-13 (GB)
1976—Packers, 24-20 (A)
1979—Falcons, 25-7 (A)
1981—Falcons, 31-17 (GB)
(Points—Packers 275, Falcons 181)
ATLANTA vs. HOUSTON
Falcons lead series, 3-1
1972—Falcons, 20-10 (A)
1976—Oilers, 20-14 (H)
1978—Falcons, 20-14 (A)
1981—Falcons, 31-27 (H)
(Points—Falcons 85, Oilers 71)
ATLANTA vs. KANSAS CITY
Chiefs lead series, 1-0
1972—Chiefs, 17-14 (A)
ATLANTA vs. LOS ANGELES
Rams lead series, 24-5-2
1966—Rams, 19-14 (A)
1967—Rams, 31-3 (A)
Rams, 20-3 (LA)
1968—Rams, 27-14 (LA)
Rams, 17-10 (A)
1969—Rams, 17-7 (LA)
Rams, 38-6 (A)
1970—Tie, 10-10 (LA)
Rams, 17-7 (A)
1971—Tie, 20-20 (LA)
Rams, 24-16 (A)
1972—Falcons, 31-3 (A)
Rams, 20-7 (LA)
1973—Rams, 31-0 (LA)
Falcons, 15-13 (A)
1974—Rams, 21-0 (LA)
Rams, 30-7 (A)
1975—Rams, 22-7 (LA)
Rams, 16-7 (A)
1976—Rams, 30-14 (A)
Rams, 59-0 (LA)
1977—Falcons, 17-6 (A)
Rams, 23-7 (LA)
1978—Rams, 10-0 (LA)
Falcons, 15-7 (A)
1979—Rams, 20-14 (LA)
Rams, 34-13 (A)
1980—Falcons, 13-10 (A)
Rams, 20-17 (LA) OT
1981—Rams, 37-35 (A)
Rams, 21-16 (LA)
(Points—Rams 673, Falcons 345)
ATLANTA vs. MIAMI
Dolphins lead series, 3-0
1970—Dolphins, 20-7 (A)
1974—Dolphins, 42-7 (M)

1980—Dolphins, 20-17 (A)
(Points—Dolphins 82, Falcons 31)
ATLANTA vs. MINNESOTA
Vikings lead series, 7-5
1966—Falcons, 20-13 (M)
1967—Falcons, 21-20 (A)
1968—Vikings, 47-7 (A)
1969—Falcons, 10-3 (A)
1970—Vikings, 37-7 (A)
1971—Vikings, 24-7 (M)
1973—Falcons, 20-14 (A)
1974—Vikings, 23-10 (M)
1975—Vikings, 38-0 (M)
1977—Vikings, 14-7 (A)
1980—Vikings, 24-23 (M)
1981—Falcons, 31-30 (A)
(Points—Vikings 287, Falcons 163)
ATLANTA vs. NEW ENGLAND
Patriots lead series, 2-1
1972—Patriots, 21-20 (NE)
1977—Patriots, 16-10 (A)
1980—Falcons, 37-21 (NE)
(Points—Falcons 67, Patriots 58)
ATLANTA vs. NEW ORLEANS
Falcons lead series, 19-7
1967—Saints, 27-24 (NO)
1969—Falcons, 45-17 (A)
1970—Falcons, 14-3 (NO)
Falcons, 32-14 (A)
1971—Falcons, 28-6 (A)
Falcons, 24-20 (NO)
1972—Falcons, 21-14 (NO)
Falcons, 36-20 (A)
1973—Falcons, 62-7 (NO)
Falcons, 14-10 (A)
1974—Saints, 14-13 (NO)
Saints, 13-3 (A)
1975—Falcons, 14-7 (A)
Saints, 23-7 (NO)
1976—Saints, 30-0 (NO)
Falcons, 23-20 (A)
1977—Falcons, 21-20 (NO)
Falcons, 35-7 (A)
1978—Falcons, 20-17 (NO)
Falcons, 20-17 (A)
1979—Falcons, 40-34 (NO) OT
Saints, 37-6 (A)
1980—Falcons, 41-14 (NO)
Falcons, 31-13 (A)
1981—Falcons, 27-0 (A)
Falcons, 41-10 (NO)
(Points—Falcons 641, Saints 415)
ATLANTA vs. N.Y. GIANTS
Falcons lead series, 5-3
1966—Falcons, 27-16 (NY)
1968—Falcons, 24-21 (A)
1971—Giants, 21-17 (A)
1974—Falcons, 14-7 (New Haven)
1977—Falcons, 17-3 (A)
1978—Falcons, 23-20 (A)
1979—Giants 24-3 (NY)
1981—Giants, 27-24 (A) OT
(Points—Falcons 149, Giants 139)
ATLANTA vs. N.Y. JETS
Series tied, 1-1
1973—Falcons, 28-20 (NY)
1980—Jets, 14-7 (A)
(Points—Falcons 35, Jets 34)
ATLANTA vs. OAKLAND
Raiders lead series, 2-1
1971—Falcons, 24-13 (A)
1975—Raiders, 37-34 (O) OT
1979—Raiders, 50-19 (O)
(Points—Raiders 100, Falcons 77)
ATLANTA vs. PHILADELPHIA
Falcons lead series, 5-4-1
1966—Eagles, 23-10 (P)
1967—Falcons, 38-7 (A)
1969—Falcons, 27-3 (P)
1970—Tie, 13-13 (P)
1973—Falcons, 44-27 (P)
1976—Eagles, 14-13 (A)
1978—*Falcons, 14-13 (A)
1979—Falcons, 14-10 (P)
1980—Falcons, 20-17 (P)
1981—Eagles, 16-13 (P)
(Points—Falcons 175, Eagles 174)
*NFC First Round Playoff
ATLANTA vs. PITTSBURGH
Steelers lead series, 5-1
1966—Steelers, 57-33 (A)
1968—Steelers, 41-21 (A)
1970—Falcons, 27-16 (A)
1974—Steelers, 24-17 (A)
1978—Steelers, 31-7 (P)
1981—Steelers, 34-20 (A)
(Points—Steelers 203, Falcons 125)
ATLANTA vs. ST. LOUIS

Cardinals lead series, 5-3
1966—Falcons, 16-10 (A)
1968—Cardinals, 17-12 (StL)
1971—Cardinals, 26-9 (A)
1973—Cardinals, 32-10 (A)
1975—Cardinals, 23-20 (StL)
1978—Cardinals, 42-21 (StL)
1980—Falcons, 33-27 (StL) OT
1981—Falcons, 41-20 (A)
(Points—Cardinals 197, Falcons 162)
ATLANTA vs. SAN DIEGO
Falcons lead series, 2-0
1973—Falcons, 41-0 (SD)
1979—Falcons, 28-26 (SD)
(Points—Falcons 69, Chargers 26)
ATLANTA vs. SAN FRANCISCO
49ers lead series, 16-15
1966—49ers, 44-7 (A)
1967—49ers, 38-7 (SF)
49ers, 34-28 (A)
1968—49ers, 28-13 (SF)
49ers, 14-12 (A)
1969—Falcons, 24-12 (A)
Falcons, 21-7 (SF)
1970—Falcons, 21-20 (A)
49ers, 24-20 (SF)
1971—Falcons, 20-17 (A)
49ers, 24-3 (SF)
1972—49ers, 49-14 (A)
49ers, 20-0 (SF)
1973—49ers, 13-9 (A)
Falcons, 17-3 (SF)
1974—49ers, 16-10 (A)
49ers, 27-0 (SF)
1975—Falcons, 17-3 (SF)
Falcons, 31-9 (A)
1976—49ers, 15-0 (SF)
Falcons, 21-16 (A)
1977—Falcons, 7-0 (SF)
49ers, 10-3 (A)
1978—Falcons, 20-17 (SF)
Falcons, 21-10 (A)
1979—49ers, 20-15 (SF)
Falcons, 31-21 (A)
1980—Falcons, 20-17 (SF)
Falcons, 35-10 (A)
1981—Falcons, 34-17 (A)
49ers, 17-14 (SF)
(Points—49ers 572, Falcons 495)
ATLANTA vs. SEATTLE
Seahawks lead series, 2-0
1976—Seahawks, 30-13 (S)
1979—Seahawks, 31-28 (A)
(Points—Seahawks 61, Falcons 41)
ATLANTA vs. TAMPA BAY
Series tied, 2-2
1977—Falcons, 17-0 (TB)
1978—Buccaneers, 14-9 (TB)
1979—Falcons, 17-14 (A)
1981—Buccaneers, 24-23 (TB)
(Points—Falcons 66, Buccaneers 52)
ATLANTA vs. WASHINGTON
Redskins lead series, 6-2-1
1966—Redskins, 33-20 (W)
1967—Tie, 20-20 (A)
1969—Redskins, 27-20 (W)
1972—Redskins, 24-13 (W)
1975—Redskins, 30-27 (A)
1977—Redskins, 10-6 (W)
1978—Falcons, 20-17 (A)
1979—Redskins, 16-7 (A)
1980—Falcons, 10-6 (A)
(Points—Redskins 183, Falcons 143)

*1950 BALTIMORE vs. **CHI. CARDINALS
Cardinals won series, 1-0
1950—Cardinals 55-13
*Extinct team
**Franchise moved to St. Louis in 1960
*1950 BALTIMORE vs. CLEVELAND
Browns won series, 1-0
1950—Browns, 31-0
*Extinct team
*1950 BALTIMORE vs. DETROIT
Lions won series, 1-0
1950—Lions, 45-21
*1950 BALTIMORE vs. GREEN BAY
Colts won series, 1-0
1950—Colts, 41-21
*Extinct team
*1950 BALTIMORE vs. LOS ANGELES
Rams won series, 1-0
1950—Rams, 70-27
*Extinct team

*1950 BALTIMORE vs. N.Y. GIANTS
Giants won series, 1-0
1950—Giants, 55-20
*Extinct team
*1950 BALTIMORE vs. *N.Y. YANKS
Yanks won series, 1-0
1950—Yanks, 51-14
*Both extinct teams
*1950 BALTIMORE vs. PHILADELPHIA
Eagles won series, 1-0
1950—Eagles, 24-14
*Extinct team
*1950 BALTIMORE vs. PITTSBURGH
Steelers won series, 1-0
1950—Steelers, 17-7
*Extinct team
*1950 BALTIMORE vs. SAN FRANCISCO
49ers won series, 1-0
1950—49ers, 17-14
*Extinct team
*1950 BALTIMORE vs. WASHINGTON
Redskins won series, 2-0
1950—Redskins, 38-14
Redskins, 38-28
(Points—Redskins 76, Colts 42)
*Extinct team

BALTIMORE vs. ATLANTA
Colts lead series, 8-0;
See Atlanta vs. Baltimore
BALTIMORE vs. BUFFALO
Colts lead series, 13-10-1
1970—Tie, 17-17 (Balt)
Colts, 20-14 (Buff)
1971—Colts, 43-0 (Buff)
Colts, 24-0 (Balt)
1972—Colts, 17-0 (Buff)
Colts, 35-7 (Balt)
1973—Bills, 31-13 (Buff)
Bills, 24-17 (Balt)
1974—Bills, 27-14 (Balt)
Bills, 6-0 (Buff)
1975—Bills, 38-31 (Balt)
Colts, 42-35 (Buff)
1976—Colts, 31-13 (Buff)
Colts, 58-20 (Balt)
1977—Colts, 17-14 (Balt)
Colts, 31-13 (Buff)
1978—Bills, 24-17 (Balt)
Bills, 21-14 (Balt)
1979—Bills, 31-13 (Balt)
Colts, 14-13 (Buff)
1980—Colts, 17-12 (Buff)
Colts, 28-24 (Balt)
1981—Bills, 35-3 (Balt)
Bills, 23-17 (Buff)
(Points—Colts 533, Bills 442)
BALTIMORE vs. CHICAGO
Colts lead series, 20-13
1953—Colts, 13-9 (B)
Colts, 16-14 (C)
1954—Bears, 28-9 (C)
Bears, 28-13 (B)
1955—Colts, 23-17 (B)
Bears, 38-10 (C)
1956—Colts, 28-21 (B)
Bears, 58-27 (C)
1957—Colts, 21-10 (B)
Colts, 29-14 (C)
1958—Colts, 51-38 (B)
Colts, 17-0 (C)
1959—Bears, 26-21 (B)
Colts, 21-7 (C)
1960—Colts, 42-7 (B)
Colts, 24-20 (C)
1961—Bears, 24-10 (C)
Bears, 21-20 (B)
1962—Bears, 35-15 (C)
Bears, 57-0 (B)
1963—Bears, 10-3 (C)
Bears, 17-7 (B)
1964—Colts, 52-0 (B)
Colts, 40-24 (C)
1965—Colts, 26-21 (C)
Bears, 13-0 (B)
1966—Bears, 27-17 (C)
Colts, 21-16 (B)
1967—Colts, 24-3 (C)
1968—Colts, 28-7 (B)
1969—Colts, 24-21 (C)
1970—Colts, 21-20 (B)
1975—Colts, 35-7 (C)

(Points—Colts 708, Bears 658)

BALTIMORE vs. CINCINNATI
Colts lead series, 4-3
1970—*Colts, 17-0 (B)
1972—Colts, 20-19 (C)
1974—Bengals, 24-14 (B)
1976—Colts 28-27 (B)
1979—Colts, 38-28 (B)
1980—Bengals, 34-33 (C)
1981—Bengals, 41-19 (B)
(Points—Bengals 173, Colts 169)
*AFC Divisional Playoff

BALTIMORE vs. CLEVELAND
Browns lead series, 9-5
1956—Colts, 21-7 (C)
1959—Browns, 38-31 (B)
1962—Colts, 36-14 (C)
1964—*Browns, 27-0 (C)
1968—Browns, 30-20 (B)
    *Colts, 34-0 (C)
1971—Browns, 14-13 (B)
    **Colts, 20-3 (C)
1973—Browns, 24-14 (C)
1975—Colts, 21-7 (B)
1978—Browns, 45-24 (B)
1979—Browns, 13-10 (C)
1980—Browns, 28-27 (B)
1981—Browns, 42-28 (C)
(Points—Colts 299, Browns 292)
*NFL Championship
**AFC Divisional Playoff

BALTIMORE vs. DALLAS
Cowboys lead series, 5-3
1960—Colts, 45-7 (D)
1967—Colts, 23-17 (B)
1969—Cowboys, 27-10 (D)
1970—*Colts, 16-13 (Miami)
1972—Cowboys, 21-0 (B)
1976—Cowboys, 30-27 (D)
1978—Cowboys, 38-0 (D)
1981—Cowboys, 37-13 (B)
(Points—Cowboys 190, Colts 134)
*Super Bowl V

BALTIMORE vs. DENVER
Broncos lead series, 3-1
1974—Broncos, 17-6 (B)
1977—Broncos, 27-13 (D)
1978—Colts, 7-6 (B)
1981—Broncos, 28-10 (D)
(Points—Broncos 78, Colts 36)

BALTIMORE vs. DETROIT
Series tied, 16-16-2
1953—Lions, 27-17 (B)
    Lions, 17-7 (D)
1954—Lions, 35-0 (D)
    Lions, 27-3 (B)
1955—Colts, 28-13 (B)
    Lions, 24-14 (D)
1956—Colts, 31-14 (B)
    Lions 27-3 (D)
1957—Colts, 34-14 (B)
    Lions, 31-27 (D)
1958—Colts, 28-15 (B)
    Colts, 40-14 (D)
1959—Colts, 21-9 (B)
    Colts, 31-24 (D)
1960—Lions, 30-17 (B)
    Lions, 20-15 (D)
1961—Lions, 16-15 (B)
    Colts, 17-14 (D)
1962—Lions, 29-20 (B)
    Lions, 21-14 (D)
1963—Colts, 25-21 (D)
    Colts, 24-21 (B)
1964—Colts, 34-0 (D)
    Lions, 31-14 (B)
1965—Colts, 31-7 (B)
    Tie, 24-24 (D)
1966—Colts, 45-14 (B)
    Lions, 20-14 (D)
1967—Colts, 41-7 (B)
1968—Colts, 27-10 (D)
1969—Tie, 17-17 (B)
1973—Colts, 29-27 (D)
1977—Lions, 13-10 (B)
1980—Colts, 10-9 (D)
(Points—Colts 710, Lions 659)

BALTIMORE vs. GREEN BAY
Packers lead series, 18-16
1953—Packers, 37-14 (GB)
    Packers, 35-24 (B)
1954—Packers, 7-6 (B)
    Packers, 24-13 (Mil)
1955—Colts, 24-20 (Mil)
    Colts, 14-10 (B)
1956—Packers, 38-33 (Mil)
    Colts, 28-21 (B)
1957—Colts, 45-17 (Mil)
    Packers, 24-21 (B)
1958—Colts, 24-17 (Mil)
    Colts, 56-0 (B)
1959—Colts, 38-21 (B)
    Colts, 28-24 (B)
1960—Packers, 35-21 (GB)
    Colts, 38-24 (B)
1961—Packers, 45-7 (GB)
    Colts, 45-21 (B)
1962—Packers, 17-6 (B)
    Packers, 17-13 (GB)
1963—Packers, 31-20 (GB)
    Packers, 34-20 (B)
1964—Colts, 21-20 (GB)
    Colts, 24-21 (B)
1965—Packers, 20-17 (Mil)
    Packers, 42-27 (B)
    *Packers, 13-10 (GB) OT
1966—Packers, 24-3 (Mil)
    Packers, 14-10 (B)
1967—Colts, 13-10 (B)
1968—Colts, 16-3 (GB)
1969—Colts, 14-6 (B)
1970—Colts, 13-10 (GB)
1974—Packers, 20-13 (B)
(Points—Packers 722, Colts 719)
*Conference Playoff

BALTIMORE vs. HOUSTON
Oilers lead series, 3-2
1970—Colts, 24-20 (H)
1973—Oilers, 31-27 (B)
1976—Colts, 38-14 (B)
1979—Oilers, 28-16 (B)
1980—Oilers, 21-16 (H)
(Points—Colts 121, Oilers 114)

BALTIMORE vs. KANSAS CITY
Chiefs lead series, 5-3
1970—Chiefs, 44-24 (B)
1972—Chiefs, 24-10 (KC)
1975—Colts, 28-14 (B)
1977—Colts, 17-6 (KC)
1979—Colts, 14-0 (KC)
    Chiefs, 10-7 (B)
1980—Chiefs, 31-24 (KC)
    Chiefs, 38-28 (B)
(Points—Chiefs 174, Colts 145)

BALTIMORE vs. LOS ANGELES
Colts lead series, 20-14-2
1953—Rams, 21-13 (B)
    Rams, 45-2 (LA)
1954—Rams, 48-0 (B)
    Colts, 22-21 (LA)
1955—Tie, 17-17 (B)
    Rams, 20-14 (LA)
1956—Colts, 56-21 (B)
    Rams, 31-7 (LA)
1957—Colts, 31-14 (B)
    Rams, 37-21 (LA)
1958—Colts, 34-7 (B)
    Rams, 30-28 (LA)
1959—Colts, 35-21 (B)
    Colts, 45-26 (LA)
1960—Colts, 31-17 (B)
    Rams, 10-3 (LA)
1961—Colts, 27-24 (B)
    Rams, 34-17 (LA)
1962—Colts, 30-27 (B)
    Colts, 14-2 (LA)
1963—Rams, 17-16 (LA)
    Colts, 19-16 (B)
1964—Colts, 35-20 (B)
    Colts, 24-7 (LA)
1965—Colts, 35-20 (B)
    Colts, 20-17 (LA)
1966—Colts, 17-3 (LA)
    Rams, 23-7 (B)
1967—Tie, 24-24 (B)
    Rams, 34-10 (LA)
1968—Colts, 27-10 (B)
    Colts, 28-24 (LA)
1969—Rams, 27-20 (B)
    Colts, 13-7 (LA)
1971—Colts, 24-17 (B)
1975—Rams, 24-13 (LA)
(Points—Colts 779, Rams 763)

BALTIMORE vs. MIAMI
Dolphins lead series, 16-9
1970—Colts, 35-0 (B)
    Dolphins, 34-17 (M)
1971—Dolphins, 17-14 (M)
    Colts, 14-3 (B)
    *Dolphins, 21-0 (M)
1972—Dolphins, 23-0 (B)
    Dolphins, 16-0 (M)
1973—Dolphins, 44-0 (M)
    Colts, 16-3 (B)
1974—Dolphins, 17-7 (M)
    Dolphins, 17-16 (B)
1975—Colts, 33-17 (M)
    Colts, 10-7 (B) OT
1976—Colts, 28-14 (B)
    Colts, 17-16 (M)
1977—Colts, 45-28 (B)
    Dolphins, 17-6 (M)
1978—Dolphins, 42-0 (B)
    Dolphins, 26-8 (M)
1979—Dolphins, 19-0 (M)
    Dolphins, 28-24 (B)
1980—Colts, 30-17 (M)
    Dolphins, 24-14 (B)
1981—Dolphins, 31-28 (B)
    Dolphins, 27-10 (M)
(Points—Dolphins 508, Colts 372)
*AFC Championship

BALTIMORE vs. MINNESOTA
Colts lead series, 12-4-1
1961—Colts, 34-33 (B)
    Vikings, 28-20 (M)
1962—Colts, 34-7 (M)
    Colts, 42-17 (B)
1963—Colts, 37-34 (M)
    Colts, 41-10 (B)
1964—Vikings, 34-24 (M)
    Colts, 17-14 (B)
1965—Colts, 35-16 (B)
    Colts, 41-21 (M)
1966—Colts, 38-23 (M)
    Colts, 20-17 (B)
1967—Tie, 20-20 (M)
1968—Colts, 21-9 (B)
    *Colts, 24-14 (B)
1969—Vikings, 52-14 (M)
1971—Vikings, 10-3 (M)
(Points—Colts 465, Vikings 359)
*Conference Championship

BALTIMORE vs. *NEW ENGLAND
Colts lead series, 13-11
1970—Colts, 14-6 (Bos)
    Colts, 27-3 (Balt)
1971—Colts, 23-3 (NE)
    Patriots, 21-17 (Balt)
1972—Colts, 24-17 (NE)
    Colts, 31-0 (Balt)
1973—Patriots, 24-16 (NE)
    Colts, 18-13 (Balt)
1974—Patriots, 42-3 (NE)
    Patriots, 27-17 (Balt)
1975—Patriots, 21-10 (NE)
    Colts, 34-21 (Balt)
1976—Colts, 27-13 (NE)
    Patriots, 21-14 (Balt)
1977—Patriots, 17-3 (NE)
    Colts, 30-24 (Balt)
1978—Colts, 34-27 (NE)
    Patriots, 35-14 (Balt)
1979—Colts, 31-26 (Balt)
    Patriots, 50-21 (NE)
1980—Patriots, 37-21 (Balt)
    Patriots, 47-21 (NE)
1981—Colts, 29-28 (NE)
    Colts, 23-21 (Balt)
(Points—Patriots 544, Colts 502)
*Franchise in Boston prior to 1971

BALTIMORE vs. NEW ORLEANS
Colts lead series, 3-0
1967—Colts, 30-10 (B)
1969—Colts, 30-10 (NO)
1973—Colts, 14-10 (B)
(Points—Colts 74, Saints 30)

BALTIMORE vs. N.Y. GIANTS
Colts lead series, 7-3
1954—Colts, 20-14 (B)
1955—Giants, 17-7 (NY)
1958—Giants, 24-21 (NY)
    *Colts, 23-17 (NY) OT
1959—*Colts, 31-16 (B)
1963—Giants, 37-28 (B)
1968—Colts, 26-0 (B)
1971—Colts, 31-7 (NY)
1975—Colts, 21-0 (NY)
1979—Colts, 31-7 (NY)
(Points—Colts 239, Giants 139)
*NFL Championship

BALTIMORE vs. N.Y. JETS
Colts lead series, 14-11
1968—*Jets, 16-7 (Miami)
1970—Colts, 29-22 (NY)
    Colts, 35-20 (B)
1971—Colts, 22-0 (B)
    Colts, 14-13 (NY)
1972—Jets, 44-34 (B)
    Jets, 24-20 (NY)
1973—Jets, 34-10 (B)
    Jets, 20-17 (NY)
1974—Colts, 35-20 (NY)
    Jets, 45-38 (B)
1975—Colts, 45-28 (NY)
    Colts, 52-19 (B)
1976—Colts, 20-0 (NY)
    Colts, 33-16 (B)
1977—Colts, 20-12 (NY)
    Colts, 33-12 (B)
1978—Jets, 33-10 (B)
    Jets, 24-16 (NY)
1979—Colts, 10-8 (B)
    Jets, 30-17 (NY)
1980—Colts, 17-14 (NY)
    Colts, 35-21 (B)
1981—Jets, 41-14 (B)
    Jets, 25-0 (NY)
(Points—Colts 583, Jets 541)
*Super Bowl III

BALTIMORE vs. OAKLAND
Raiders lead series, 3-2
1970—*Colts, 27-17 (B)
1971—Colts, 37-14 (O)
1973—Raiders, 34-21 (B)
1975—Raiders, 31-20 (B)
1977—**Raiders, 37-31 (B) OT
(Points—Colts 136, Raiders 133)
*AFC Championship
**AFC Divisional Playoff

BALTIMORE vs. PHILADELPHIA
Series tied, 4-4
1953—Eagles, 45-14 (P)
1965—Colts, 34-24 (B)
1967—Colts, 38-6 (P)
1969—Colts, 24-20 (B)
1970—Colts, 29-10 (B)
1974—Eagles, 30-10 (P)
1978—Eagles, 17-14 (B)
1981—Eagles, 38-13 (P)
(Points—Eagles 190, Colts 176)

BALTIMORE vs. PITTSBURGH
Steelers lead series, 7-3
1957—Steelers, 19-13 (B)
1968—Colts, 41-7 (P)
1971—Colts, 34-21 (B)
1974—Steelers, 30-0 (B)
1975—*Steelers, 28-10 (P)
1976—Steelers, 40-14 (B)
1977—Colts, 31-21 (B)
1978—Steelers, 35-13 (P)
1979—Steelers, 17-13 (P)
1980—Steelers, 20-17 (B)
(Points—Steelers 238, Colts 186)
*AFC Divisional Playoff

BALTIMORE vs. ST. LOUIS
Series tied, 4-4
1961—Colts, 16-0 (B)
1964—Colts, 47-27 (B)
1968—Colts, 27-0 (B)
1972—Cardinals, 10-3 (B)
1976—Cardinals, 24-17 (StL)
1978—Colts, 30-17 (StL)
1980—Cardinals, 17-10 (B)
1981—Cardinals, 35-24 (B)
(Points—Colts 174, Cardinals 130)

BALTIMORE vs. SAN DIEGO
Series tied, 2-2
1970—Colts, 16-14 (SD)
1972—Chargers, 23-20 (B)
1976—Colts, 37-21 (SD)
1981—Chargers, 43-14 (B)
(Points—Chargers 101, Colts 87)

BALTIMORE vs. SAN FRANCISCO
Colts lead series, 21-14
1953—49ers, 38-21 (B)
    49ers, 45-14 (SF)
1954—Colts, 20-13 (B)
    49ers, 10-7 (SF)
1955—Colts, 26-14 (B)
    49ers, 35-24 (SF)
1956—49ers, 20-17 (B)
    49ers, 30-17 (SF)
1957—Colts, 27-21 (B)
    49ers, 17-13 (SF)
1958—Colts, 35-27 (B)
    49ers, 21-12 (SF)
1959—Colts, 45-14 (B)
    Colts, 34-14 (SF)
1960—49ers, 30-22 (B)
    49ers, 34-10 (SF)
1961—Colts, 20-17 (B)
    Colts, 27-24 (SF)
1962—49ers, 21-13 (B)
    Colts, 22-3 (SF)
1963—Colts, 20-14 (B)
    Colts, 20-3 (SF)
1964—Colts, 37-7 (B)
    Colts, 14-3 (SF)
1965—Colts, 27-24 (B)
    Colts, 34-28 (SF)
1966—Colts, 36-14 (B)
    Colts, 30-14 (SF)
1967—Colts, 41-7 (B)
    Colts, 26-9 (SF)
1968—Colts, 27-10 (B)
    Colts, 42-14 (SF)
1969—49ers, 24-21 (B)
    49ers, 20-17 (SF)
1972—49ers, 24-21 (SF)
(Points—Colts 836, 49ers 663)

BALTIMORE vs. SEATTLE
Colts lead series, 2-0
1977—Colts, 29-14 (S)
1978—Colts, 17-14 (S)
(Points—Colts 46, Seahawks 28)

BALTIMORE vs. TAMPA BAY
Series tied, 1-1
1976—Colts, 42-17 (B)
1979—Buccaneers, 29-26 (B) OT
(Points—Colts 68, Buccaneers 46)

BALTIMORE vs. WASHINGTON
Colts lead series, 15-5
1953—Colts, 27-17 (B)
1954—Redskins, 24-21 (W)
1955—Redskins, 14-13 (B)
1956—Colts, 19-17 (B)
1957—Colts, 21-17 (W)
1958—Colts, 35-10 (B)
1959—Redskins, 27-24 (W)
1960—Colts, 20-0 (B)
1961—Colts, 27-6 (W)
1962—Colts, 34-21 (B)
1963—Colts, 36-20 (W)
1964—Colts, 45-17 (B)
1965—Colts, 38-7 (W)
1966—Colts, 37-10 (B)
1967—Colts, 17-13 (W)
1969—Colts, 41-17 (B)
1973—Redskins, 22-14 (W)
1977—Colts, 10-3 (B)
1978—Colts, 21-17 (B)
1981—Redskins, 38-14 (W)
(Points—Colts 514, Redskins 317)

---

*BOS. YANKS vs. *BROOKLYN DODGERS
Yanks won series, 2-0
1944—Yanks 17-14
    Yanks 13-6
(Points—Yanks 30, Dodgers 20)
*Extinct team

*BOS. YANKS vs. CHI. BEARS
Bears won series, 3-0
1944—Bears, 21-7
1947—Bears, 28-24
1948—Bears, 51-17
(Points—Bears 100, Yanks 48)
*Extinct team

*BOS. YANKS vs. **CHI. CARDINALS
Cardinals won series, 3-0
1946—Cardinals, 28-14
1947—Cardinals, 27-7
1948—Cardinals, 49-27
(Points—Cardinals 104, Yanks 48)
*Extinct team
**Franchise moved to St. Louis in 1960

*BOS. YANKS vs. DETROIT
Lions won series, 3-2
1944—Lions, 38-7
1945—Lions, 10-9
1946—Yanks, 34-10
1947—Lions, 21-7
1948—Yanks, 17-14
(Points—Lions 93, Yanks 74)
*Extinct team

*BOS. YANKS vs. GREEN BAY
Packers won series, 2-0
1945—Packers, 38-14
    Packers, 28-0
(Points—Packers 66, Yanks 14)
*Extinct team

*BOS. YANKS vs. **LOS ANGELES
Yanks won series, 2-1
1945—Rams, 20-7
1946—Yanks, 40-21
1947—Yanks, 27-16
(Points—Yanks 74, Rams 57)
*Extinct team
**Franchise in Cleveland prior to 1946

*BOS. YANKS vs. N.Y. GIANTS
Giants won series, 5-1-3
1944—Giants, 22-10
    Giants, 31-0
1945—Tie, 13-13
1946—Giants, 17-0

Tie, 28-28
1947—Tie, 7-7
　　　Yanks, 14-0
1948—Giants, 27-7
　　　Giants, 28-14
(Points—Giants 173, Yanks 93)
*Extinct team

*BOS. YANKS vs. PHILADELPHIA
Eagles won series, 7-2
1944—Eagles, 28-7
　　　Eagles, 38-0
1945—Eagles, 35-7
1946—Eagles, 49-25
　　　Eagles, 40-14
1947—Eagles, 32-0
　　　Yanks, 21-14
1948—Eagles, 45-0
　　　Yanks, 37-14
(Points—Eagles 295, Yanks 111)
*Extinct team

*BOS. YANKS vs. PITTSBURGH
Steelers won series, 5-3
1945—Yanks, 28-7
　　　Yanks, 10-6
1946—Steelers, 16-7
　　　Steelers, 33-7
1947—Steelers, 30-14
　　　Steelers, 17-7
1948—Steelers, 24-14
　　　Yanks, 13-7
(Points—Steelers 140, Yanks 100)
*Extinct team

*BOS. YANKS vs. WASHINGTON
Redskins won series, 8-2
1944—Redskins, 21-14
　　　Redskins, 14-7
1945—Yanks, 28-20
　　　Redskins, 34-7
1946—Redskins, 14-6
　　　Redskins, 17-14
1947—Yanks, 27-24
　　　Redskins, 40-13
1948—Redskins, 59-21
　　　Redskins, 23-7
(Points—Redskins 266, Yanks 144)

*BROOKLYN DODGERS vs. *BOS. YANKS
Yanks won series, 2-0
See *Boston Yanks vs. *Brooklyn
Dodgers
*Extinct team

*BROOKLYN DODGERS vs. CHI. BEARS
Bears won series, 11-0
1931—Bears, 26-0
1932—Bears, 13-0
　　　Bears, 20-0
1933—Bears, 10-0
1934—Bears, 21-7
1935—Bears, 24-14
1937—Bears, 29-7
1938—Bears, 24-6
1940—Bears, 16-7
1942—Bears, 35-0
1943—Bears, 33-21
(Points—Bears 251, Dodgers 62)
*Extinct team

*BROOKLYN DODGERS vs. **CHI. CARDINALS
Dodgers won series, 7-4
1931—Cardinals, 14-7
1932—Cardinals, 27-7
　　　Dodgers, 3-0
1933—Dodgers, 7-0
　　　Dodgers, 3-0
1934—Cardinals, 21-0
1936—Dodgers, 9-0
1938—Dodgers, 13-0
1940—Dodgers, 14-9
1941—Cardinals, 20-6
1943—Dodgers, 7-0
(Points—Cardinals 91, Dodgers 76)
　*Extinct team
**Franchise moved to St. Louis in
1960

*BROOKLYN DODGERS vs. *CINCINNATI REDS
Series tied, 1-1
1933—Dodgers, 27-0
　　　Reds, 10-0
(Points—Dodgers 27, Reds 10)
*Extinct team

*BROOKLYN DODGERS vs. **CLEVELAND RAMS
Dodgers won series, 3-1
1937—Dodgers, 9-7
1939—Dodgers, 23-12

1940—Dodgers, 29-14
1942—Rams, 17-0
(Points—Dodgers 61, Rams 50)
　*Extinct team
**Franchise moved to Los Angeles
in 1946

*BROOKLYN DODGERS vs. **DETROIT
Lions won series, 11-3
1930—Spartans, 14-0
1931—Spartans, 19-0
1932—Spartans, 17-7
1934—Lions, 28-0
1935—Dodgers, 12-10
　　　Lions, 28-0
1936—Lions, 14-7
　　　Lions, 14-6
1937—Lions, 30-0
1939—Lions, 27-7
1941—Dodgers, 14-7
1942—Dodgers, 28-7
1943—Lions, 27-0
1944—Lions, 19-14
(Points—Lions 261, Dodgers 95)
　*Extinct team
**Franchise in Portsmouth prior to
1934 and known as the Spartans.

*BROOKLYN DODGERS vs. GREEN BAY
Packers won series, 8-0
1931—Packers, 7-0
1932—Packers, 7-0
1936—Packers, 38-7
1938—Packers, 35-7
1939—Packers, 28-0
1941—Packers, 30-7
1943—Packers, 31-7
1944—Packers, 14-7
(Points—Packers 190, Dodgers 35)
*Extinct Team

*BROOKLYN DODGERS vs. N.Y. GIANTS
Giants won series, 24-5-3
1926—Giants, 17-0
　　　Giants, 27-0
1930—Dodgers, 7-6
　　　Giants, 13-0
1931—Giants, 27-0
　　　Giants, 19-6
1932—Giants, 20-12
　　　Giants, 13-7
1933—Giants, 21-7
　　　Giants, 10-0
1934—Giants, 14-0
　　　Giants, 27-0
1935—Giants, 10-7
　　　Giants, 21-0
1936—Tie, 10-10
　　　Giants, 14-0
1937—Giants, 21-0
　　　Tie, 13-13
1938—Giants, 28-14
　　　Tie, 7-7
1939—Giants, 7-6
　　　Giants, 28-7
1940—Giants, 10-7
　　　Dodgers, 14-6
1941—Dodgers, 16-13
　　　Dodgers, 21-7
1942—Dodgers, 17-7
　　　Giants, 10-0
1943—Giants, 20-0
　　　Giants, 24-7
1944—Giants, 14-7
　　　Giants, 7-0
(Points—Giants 491, Dodgers 192)
*Extinct team

*BROOKLYN DODGERS vs. PHILADELPHIA
Dodgers won series, 14-5-1
1934—Dodgers, 10-7
　　　Eagles, 13-0
1935—Dodgers, 17-6
　　　Dodgers, 3-0
1936—Dodgers, 18-0
　　　Dodgers, 13-7
1937—Dodgers, 13-7
　　　Eagles, 14-10
1938—Dodgers, 10-7
　　　Dodgers, 32-14
1939—Tie, 0-0
　　　Dodgers, 23-14
1940—Dodgers, 30-17
　　　Dodgers, 21-7
1941—Dodgers, 24-13
　　　Dodgers, 15-6
1942—Dodgers, 35-14
　　　Eagles, 14-7

1944—Eagles, 21-7
　　　Eagles, 34-0
(Points—Dodgers 288, Eagles 215)
*Extinct team

*BROOKLYN DODGERS vs. PITTSBURGH
Dodgers won series, 11-8-1
1933—Tie, 3-3
　　　Dodgers, 32-0
1934—Dodgers, 21-3
　　　Dodgers, 10-0
1935—Dodgers, 13-7
　　　Steelers, 16-7
1936—Steelers, 10-6
　　　Steelers, 10-7
1937—Steelers, 21-0
　　　Dodgers, 23-0
1938—Steelers, 17-3
　　　Dodgers, 17-7
1939—Dodgers, 12-7
　　　Dodgers, 17-13
1940—Dodgers, 10-3
　　　Dodgers, 21-0
1941—Steelers, 14-7
　　　Dodgers, 35-7
1942—Dodgers, 7-0
　　　Steelers, 13-0
(Points—Dodgers 244, Steelers 158)
*Extinct team

*BROOKLYN DODGERS vs. **WASHINGTON REDSKINS
Redskins won series, 17-5-3
1932—Dodgers, 14-0
　　　Redskins, 7-0
1933—Dodgers, 14-0
1934—Dodgers, 10-6
　　　Redskins, 13-3
1935—Redskins, 7-0
　　　Tie, 0-0
1936—Redskins, 14-3
　　　Redskins, 30-3
1937—Redskins, 11-7
　　　Redskins, 21-0
1938—Tie, 16-16
　　　Tie, 6-6
1939—Redskins, 41-13
　　　Redskins, 42-0
1940—Redskins, 24-17
　　　Dodgers, 16-14
1941—Redskins, 3-0
　　　Dodgers, 13-7
1942—Redskins, 21-10
　　　Redskins, 23-3
1943—Redskins, 27-0
　　　Redskins, 48-10
1944—Redskins, 17-14
　　　Redskins, 10-0
(Points—Redskins 408, Dodgers 175)
　*Extinct team
**Franchise in Boston prior to 1937

BUFFALO vs. ATLANTA
Bills lead series, 2-1;
See Atlanta vs. Buffalo
BUFFALO vs. BALTIMORE
Colts lead series, 13-10-1
See Baltimore vs. Buffalo
BUFFALO vs. CHICAGO
Bears lead series, 2-1
1970—Bears, 31-13 (C)
1974—Bills, 16-6 (B)
1979—Bears, 7-0 (B)
(Points—Bears 44, Bills 29)
BUFFALO vs. CINCINNATI
Bengals lead series, 6-4
1968—Bengals, 34-23 (C)
1969—Bills, 16-13 (B)
1970—Bengals, 43-14 (B)
1973—Bengals, 16-13 (B)
1975—Bengals, 33-24 (C)
1978—Bills, 5-0 (B)
1979—Bills, 51-24 (B)
1980—Bills, 14-0 (C)
1981—Bengals, 27-24 (C) OT
　　　*Bengals, 28-21 (C)
(Points—Bengals 218, Bills 205)
*AFC Divisional Playoff
BUFFALO vs. CLEVELAND
Browns lead series, 3-2
1972—Browns, 27-10 (C)
1974—Bills, 15-10 (C)
1977—Browns, 27-16 (B)
1978—Browns, 41-20 (C)
1981—Bills, 22-13 (B)
(Points—Browns 118, Bills 83)
BUFFALO vs. DALLAS
Cowboys lead series, 3-0

1971—Cowboys, 49-37 (B)
1978—Cowboys, 17-10 (D)
1981—Cowboys, 27-14 (D)
(Points—Cowboys 93, Bills 61)
BUFFALO vs. DENVER
Bills lead series, 13-8-1
1960—Broncos, 27-21 (B)
　　　Tie, 38-38 (D)
1961—Broncos, 22-10 (B)
　　　Bills, 23-10 (D)
1962—Broncos, 23-20 (B)
　　　Bills, 45-38 (D)
1963—Bills, 30-28 (D)
　　　Bills, 27-17 (B)
1964—Bills, 30-13 (D)
　　　Bills, 30-19 (B)
1965—Bills, 30-15 (D)
　　　Bills, 31-13 (B)
1966—Bills, 38-21 (B)
1967—Bills, 17-16 (D)
　　　Broncos, 21-20 (B)
1968—Broncos, 34-32 (D)
1969—Bills, 41-28 (B)
1970—Broncos, 25-10 (B)
1975—Bills, 38-14 (B)
1977—Broncos, 26-6 (D)
1979—Broncos, 19-16 (B)
1981—Bills, 9-7 (B)
(Points—Bills 562, Broncos 474)
BUFFALO vs. DETROIT
Series tied, 1-1-1
1972—Tie, 21-21 (B)
1976—Lions, 27-14 (D)
1979—Bills, 20-17 (D)
(Points—Lions 65, Bills 55)
BUFFALO vs. GREEN BAY
Bills lead series, 2-0
1974—Bills, 27-7 (GB)
1979—Bills, 19-12 (B)
(Points—Bills 46, Packers 19)
BUFFALO vs. HOUSTON
Oilers lead series, 17-7
1960—Bills, 25-24 (B)
　　　Oilers, 31-23 (H)
1961—Bills, 22-12 (H)
　　　Oilers, 28-16 (B)
1962—Oilers, 28-23 (B)
　　　Oilers, 17-14 (H)
1963—Oilers, 31-20 (B)
　　　Oilers, 28-14 (H)
1964—Bills, 48-17 (H)
　　　Bills, 24-10 (B)
1965—Oilers, 19-17 (B)
　　　Bills, 29-18 (H)
1966—Bills, 27-20 (B)
　　　Bills, 42-20 (H)
1967—Oilers, 20-3 (B)
　　　Oilers, 10-3 (H)
1968—Oilers, 30-7 (B)
　　　Oilers, 35-6 (H)
1969—Oilers, 17-3 (B)
　　　Oilers, 28-14 (H)
1971—Oilers, 20-14 (B)
1974—Oilers, 21-9 (B)
1976—Oilers, 13-3 (B)
1978—Oilers, 17-10 (H)
(Points—Oilers 514, Bills 416)
BUFFALO vs. *KANSAS CITY
Bills lead series, 12-11-1
1960—Texans, 45-28 (B)
　　　Texans, 24-7 (D)
1961—Bills, 27-24 (B)
　　　Bills, 30-20 (D)
1962—Texans, 41-21 (D)
　　　Bills, 23-14 (B)
1963—Tie, 27-27 (B)
　　　Bills, 35-26 (KC)
1964—Bills, 34-17 (B)
　　　Bills, 35-22 (KC)
1965—Bills, 23-7 (KC)
　　　Bills, 34-25 (B)
1966—Chiefs, 42-20 (B)
　　　Bills, 29-14 (KC)
　　　**Chiefs, 31-7 (B)
1967—Chiefs, 23-13 (KC)
1968—Chiefs, 18-7 (B)
1969—Chiefs, 29-7 (B)
　　　Chiefs, 22-19 (KC)
1971—Chiefs, 22-9 (KC)
1973—Bills, 23-14 (B)
1976—Bills, 50-17 (B)
1978—Bills, 28-13 (B)
　　　Chiefs, 14-10 (KC)
(Points—Chiefs 551, Bills 546)
*Franchise in Dallas prior to 1963
and known as Texans
**AFL Championship
BUFFALO vs. LOS ANGELES

Rams lead series, 2-1
1970—Rams, 19-0 (B)
1974—Rams, 19-14 (LA)
1980—Bills, 10-7 (B) OT
(Points—Rams 45, Bills 24)
BUFFALO vs. MIAMI
Dolphins lead series, 25-6-1
1966—Bills, 58-24 (B)
　　　Bills, 29-0 (M)
1967—Bills, 35-13 (B)
　　　Dolphins, 17-14 (M)
1968—Tie, 14-14 (M)
　　　Dolphins, 21-17 (B)
1969—Dolphins, 24-6 (M)
　　　Bills, 28-3 (B)
1970—Dolphins, 33-14 (B)
　　　Dolphins, 45-7 (M)
1971—Dolphins, 29-14 (B)
　　　Dolphins, 34-0 (M)
1972—Dolphins, 24-23 (M)
　　　Dolphins, 30-16 (B)
1973—Dolphins, 27-6 (M)
　　　Dolphins, 17-0 (B)
1974—Dolphins, 24-16 (B)
　　　Dolphins, 35-28 (M)
1975—Dolphins, 35-30 (B)
　　　Dolphins, 31-21 (M)
1976—Dolphins, 30-21 (B)
　　　Dolphins, 45-27 (M)
1977—Dolphins, 13-0 (B)
　　　Dolphins, 31-14 (M)
1978—Dolphins, 31-24 (M)
　　　Dolphins, 25-24 (B)
1979—Dolphins, 9-7 (B)
　　　Dolphins, 17-7 (M)
1980—Bills, 17-7 (B)
　　　Dolphins, 17-14 (M)
1981—Bills, 31-21 (B)
　　　Dolphins, 16-6 (M)
(Points—Dolphins 742, Bills 568)
BUFFALO vs. MINNESOTA
Vikings lead series, 3-0
1971—Vikings, 19-0 (M)
1975—Vikings, 35-13 (B)
1979—Vikings, 10-3 (M)
(Points—Vikings 64, Bills 16)
BUFFALO vs. *NEW ENGLAND
Bills lead series, 23-21-1
1960—Bills, 13-0 (B)
　　　Bills, 38-14 (Bu)
1961—Patriots, 23-21 (B)
　　　Patriots, 52-21 (B)
1962—Tie, 28-28 (Bu)
　　　Patriots, 21-10 (B)
1963—Bills, 28-21 (Bu)
　　　Patriots, 17-7 (B)
　　　**Patriots, 26-8 (Bu)
1964—Patriots, 36-28 (Bu)
　　　Bills, 24-14 (B)
1965—Bills, 24-7 (Bu)
　　　Bills, 23-7 (B)
1966—Patriots, 20-10 (Bu)
　　　Patriots, 14-3 (B)
1967—Patriots, 23-0 (Bu)
　　　Bills, 44-16 (B)
1968—Patriots, 16-7 (Bu)
　　　Patriots, 23-6 (B)
1969—Bills, 23-16 (Bu)
　　　Patriots, 35-21 (B)
1970—Bills, 45-10 (B)
　　　Patriots, 14-10 (Bu)
1971—Patriots, 38-33 (NE)
　　　Bills, 27-20 (Bu)
1972—Bills, 38-14 (Bu)
　　　Bills, 27-24 (NE)
1973—Bills, 31-13 (NE)
　　　Bills, 37-13 (Bu)
1974—Bills, 30-28 (Bu)
　　　Bills, 29-28 (NE)
1975—Bills, 45-31 (Bu)
　　　Bills, 34-14 (NE)
1976—Patriots, 26-22 (Bu)
　　　Patriots, 20-10 (NE)
1977—Bills, 24-14 (NE)
　　　Patriots, 20-7 (Bu)
1978—Patriots, 14-10 (Bu)
　　　Patriots, 26-24 (NE)
1979—Patriots, 26-6 (Bu)
　　　Bills, 16-13 (NE) OT
1980—Bills, 31-13 (NE)
　　　Patriots, 24-2 (NE)
1981—Bills, 20-17 (Bu)
　　　Bills, 19-10 (NE)
(Points—Bills 964, Patriots 899)
*Franchise in Boston prior to 1971
**Division Playoff
BUFFALO vs. NEW ORLEANS
Series tied, 1-1

1973—Saints, 13-0 (NO)
1980—Bills, 35-26 (NO)
(Points—Saints 39, Bills 35)

BUFFALO vs. N.Y. GIANTS
Giants lead series, 2-1
1970—Giants, 20-6 (NY)
1975—Giants, 17-14 (B)
1978—Bills, 41-17 (B)
(Points—Bills 61, Giants 54)

BUFFALO vs. *N.Y. JETS
Bills lead series, 25-20
1960—Titans, 27-3 (NY)
　　　Titans, 17-13 (B)
1961—Bills, 41-31 (B)
　　　Titans, 21-14 (NY)
1962—Titans, 17-6 (B)
　　　Bills, 20-3 (NY)
1963—Bills, 45-14 (B)
　　　Bills, 19-10 (NY)
1964—Bills, 34-24 (B)
　　　Bills, 20-7 (NY)
1965—Bills, 33-21 (B)
　　　Jets, 14-12 (NY)
1966—Bills, 33-23 (NY)
　　　Bills, 14-3 (B)
1967—Bills, 20-17 (B)
　　　Jets, 20-10 (NY)
1968—Bills, 37-35 (B)
　　　Jets, 25-21 (NY)
1969—Jets, 33-19 (B)
　　　Jets, 16-6 (NY)
1970—Bills, 34-31 (B)
　　　Bills, 10-6 (NY)
1971—Jets, 28-17 (B)
　　　Jets, 20-7 (B)
1972—Jets, 41-24 (B)
　　　Jets, 41-3 (NY)
1973—Bills, 9-7 (B)
　　　Bills, 34-14 (NY)
1974—Bills, 16-12 (B)
　　　Jets, 20-10 (NY)
1975—Bills, 42-14 (B)
　　　Bills, 24-23 (NY)
1976—Bills, 17-14 (NY)
　　　Jets, 19-14 (B)
1977—Jets, 24-19 (B)
　　　Bills, 14-10 (NY)
1978—Jets, 21-20 (B)
　　　Jets, 45-14 (NY)
1979—Bills, 46-31 (B)
　　　Bills, 14-12 (NY)
1980—Bills, 20-10 (B)
　　　Bills, 31-24 (NY)
1981—Bills, 31-0 (B)
　　　Jets, 33-14 (NY)
　　　**Bills, 31-27 (NY)
(Points—Bills 932, Jets 908)
*Jets known as Titans prior to 1963
**AFC First Round Playoff

BUFFALO vs. OAKLAND
Series tied, 11-11
1960—Bills, 38-9 (B)
　　　Raiders, 20-7 (O)
1961—Raiders, 31-22 (B)
　　　Bills, 26-21 (O)
1962—Bills, 14-6 (B)
　　　Bills, 10-6 (O)
1963—Raiders, 35-17 (O)
　　　Bills, 12-0 (B)
1964—Bills, 23-20 (B)
　　　Raiders, 16-13 (O)
1965—Bills, 17-12 (B)
　　　Bills, 17-14 (O)
1966—Bills, 31-10 (O)
1967—Raiders, 24-20 (B)
　　　Raiders, 28-21 (O)
1968—Raiders, 48-6 (B)
　　　Raiders, 13-10 (O)
1969—Raiders, 50-21 (O)
1972—Raiders, 28-16 (O)
1974—Bills, 21-20 (B)
1977—Raiders, 34-13 (O)
1980—Bills, 24-7 (B)
(Points—Raiders 452, Bills 399)

BUFFALO vs. PHILADELPHIA
Series tied, 1-1.
1973—Bills, 27-26 (B)
1981—Eagles, 20-14 (B)
(Points—Eagles 46, Bills 41)

BUFFALO vs. PITTSBURGH
Steelers lead series, 5-2
1970—Steelers, 23-10 (P)
1972—Steelers, 38-21 (B)
1974—*Steelers, 32-14 (P)
1975—Bills, 30-21 (P)
1978—Steelers, 28-17 (B)
1979—Steelers, 28-0 (P)
1980—Bills, 28-13 (B)

(Points—Steelers 183, Bills 120)
*AFC Divisional Playoff

BUFFALO vs. ST. LOUIS
Cardinals lead series, 2-1
1971—Cardinals, 28-23 (B)
1975—Bills, 32-14 (StL)
1981—Cardinals, 24-0 (StL)
(Points—Cardinals 66, Bills 55)

BUFFALO vs. *SAN DIEGO
Chargers lead series, 15-9-2
1960—Chargers, 24-10 (B)
　　　Bills, 32-3 (LA)
1961—Chargers, 19-11 (B)
　　　Chargers, 28-10 (SD)
1962—Bills, 35-10 (B)
　　　Bills, 40-20 (SD)
1963—Chargers, 14-10 (SD)
　　　Chargers, 23-13 (B)
1964—Bills, 30-3 (B)
　　　Bills, 27-24 (SD)
　　　**Bills, 20-7 (B)
1965—Chargers, 34-3 (B)
　　　Tie, 20-20 (SD)
　　　**Bills, 23-0 (SD)
1966—Chargers, 27-7 (SD)
　　　Tie, 17-17 (B)
1967—Chargers, 37-17 (B)
1968—Chargers, 21-6 (B)
1969—Chargers, 45-6 (SD)
1971—Chargers, 20-3 (SD)
1973—Chargers, 34-7 (SD)
1976—Chargers, 34-13 (B)
1979—Chargers, 27-19 (SD)
1980—Bills, 26-24 (SD)
　　　***Chargers, 20-14 (SD)
1981—Bills, 28-27 (SD)
(Points—Chargers 562, Bills 447)
*Franchise in Los Angeles prior to
1961
**AFL Championship
***AFC Divisional Playoff

BUFFALO vs. SAN FRANCISCO
Bills lead series, 2-0
1972—Bills, 27-20 (B)
1980—Bills, 18-13 (SF)
(Points—Bills 45, 49ers 33)

BUFFALO vs. SEATTLE
Seahawks lead series, 1-0
1977—Seahawks, 56-17 (S)

BUFFALO vs. TAMPA BAY
Series tied, 1-1
1976—Bills, 14-9 (TB)
1978—Buccaneers, 31-10 (TB)
(Points—Buccaneers 40, Bills 24)

BUFFALO vs. WASHINGTON
Bills lead series, 2-1
1972—Bills, 24-17 (W)
1977—Redskins, 10-0 (B)
1981—Bills, 21-14 (B)
(Points—Bills 45, Redskins 41)

CHICAGO vs. ATLANTA
Falcons lead series, 8-4;
See Atlanta vs. Chicago

CHICAGO vs. BALTIMORE
Colts lead series, 20-13;
See Baltimore vs. Chicago

CHICAGO vs. *BOS. YANKS
Bears won series 3-0
See *Boston Yanks vs. Chicago
*Extinct team

**CHICAGO vs. *BROOKLYN
DODGERS**
Bears won series 11-0
See *Brooklyn Dodgers vs. Chicago
*Extinct team

CHICAGO vs. BUFFALO
Bears lead series, 2-1;
See Buffalo vs. Chicago

CHICAGO vs. CINCINNATI
Bengals lead series, 2-0;
1972—Bengals, 13-3 (Chi)
1980—Bengals, 17-14 (Chi) OT
(Points—Bengals 30, Bears 17)

CHICAGO vs. *CINCINNATI REDS
Bears won series 2-0
1934—Bears, 21-3
　　　Bears, 41-7
(Points—Bears 62, Reds 10)
*Extinct team

CHICAGO vs. CLEVELAND
Browns lead series, 6-2
1951—Browns, 42-21 (Cle)
1954—Browns, 39-10 (Chi)
1960—Browns, 42-0 (Cle)
1961—Bears, 17-14 (Chi)
1967—Browns, 24-0 (Cle)
1969—Browns, 28-24 (Chi)

1972—Bears, 17-0 (Cle)
1980—Browns, 27-21 (Cle)
(Points—Browns 216, Bears 110)

CHICAGO vs. DALLAS
Cowboys lead series, 7-3
1960—Bears, 17-7 (D)
1962—Bears, 34-33 (D)
1964—Cowboys, 24-10 (C)
1968—Cowboys, 34-3 (C)
1971—Bears, 23-19 (C)
1973—Cowboys, 20-17 (C)
1976—Cowboys, 31-21 (D)
1977—*Cowboys, 37-7 (D)
1979—Cowboys, 24-20 (D)
1981—Cowboys, 10-9 (D)
(Points—Cowboys 239, Bears 161)
*NFC Divisional Playoff

CHICAGO vs. *DALLAS TEXANS
Series tied 1-1
1952—Bears, 38-20
　　　Texans 27-23
(Points—Bears 61, Texans 47)
*Extinct team

CHICAGO vs. DENVER
Broncos lead series, 3-2
1971—Broncos, 6-3 (D)
1973—Bears, 33-14 (D)
1976—Broncos, 28-14 (C)
1978—Broncos, 16-7 (D)
1981—Bears, 35-24 (C)
(Points—Bears 92, Broncos 88)

CHICAGO vs. *DETROIT
Bears lead series, 59-41-5
1930—Spartans, 7-6 (P)
　　　Bears, 14-6 (C)
1931—Bears, 9-6 (C)
　　　Spartans, 3-0 (P)
1932—Tie, 13-13 (C)
　　　Tie, 7-7 (P)
　　　**Bears, 9-0 (C)
1933—Bears, 17-14 (C)
　　　Bears, 17-7 (P)
1934—Bears, 19-16 (D)
　　　Bears, 10-7 (C)
1935—Tie, 20-20 (C)
　　　Lions, 14-2 (D)
1936—Bears, 12-10 (C)
　　　Lions, 13-7 (D)
1937—Bears, 28-20 (C)
　　　Bears, 13-0 (D)
1938—Lions, 13-7 (C)
　　　Lions, 14-7 (D)
1939—Lions, 10-0 (C)
　　　Bears, 23-13 (D)
1940—Bears, 7-0 (C)
　　　Lions, 17-14 (D)
1941—Bears, 49-0 (C)
　　　Bears, 24-7 (D)
1942—Bears, 16-0 (C)
　　　Bears, 42-0 (D)
1943—Bears, 27-21 (C)
　　　Bears, 35-14 (D)
1944—Tie, 21-21 (C)
　　　Lions, 41-21 (D)
1945—Lions, 16-10 (C)
　　　Lions, 35-28 (C)
1946—Bears, 42-6 (C)
　　　Bears, 45-24 (D)
1947—Bears, 33-24 (D)
　　　Bears, 34-14 (D)
1948—Bears, 28-0 (C)
　　　Bears, 42-14 (D)
1949—Bears, 27-24 (C)
　　　Bears, 28-7 (D)
1950—Bears, 35-21 (D)
　　　Bears, 6-3 (C)
1951—Bears, 28-23 (C)
　　　Lions, 41-28 (C)
1952—Lions, 24-23 (C)
　　　Lions, 45-21 (D)
1953—Lions, 20-16 (C)
　　　Lions, 13-7 (D)
1954—Lions, 48-23 (C)
　　　Bears, 28-24 (C)
1955—Bears, 24-14 (D)
　　　Bears, 21-20 (C)
1956—Lions, 42-10 (D)
　　　Bears, 38-21 (C)
1957—Bears, 27-7 (D)
　　　Lions, 21-13 (C)
1958—Bears, 20-7 (D)
　　　Bears, 21-16 (C)
1959—Bears, 24-14 (D)
　　　Bears, 25-14 (C)
1960—Bears, 28-7 (C)
　　　Lions, 36-0 (D)
1961—Bears, 31-17 (D)
　　　Lions, 16-15 (C)

1962—Lions, 11-3 (D)
　　　Bears, 3-0 (C)
1963—Bears, 37-21 (D)
　　　Bears, 24-14 (C)
1964—Lions, 10-0 (C)
　　　Bears, 27-24 (D)
1965—Bears, 38-10 (C)
　　　Bears, 17-10 (D)
1966—Lions, 14-3 (D)
　　　Tie, 10-10 (C)
1967—Bears, 14-3 (C)
　　　Bears, 27-13 (D)
1968—Lions, 42-0 (D)
　　　Bears, 28-10 (C)
1969—Lions, 13-7 (C)
　　　Lions, 20-3 (C)
1970—Lions, 28-14 (D)
　　　Lions, 16-10 (C)
1971—Bears, 28-23 (D)
　　　Lions, 28-3 (C)
1972—Lions, 38-24 (D)
　　　Lions, 14-0 (C)
1973—Lions, 30-7 (C)
　　　Lions, 40-7 (D)
1974—Bears, 17-9 (C)
　　　Lions, 34-17 (D)
1975—Lions, 27-7 (D)
　　　Bears, 25-21 (C)
1976—Bears, 10-3 (C)
　　　Lions, 14-10 (D)
1977—Bears, 30-20 (C)
　　　Bears, 31-14 (D)
1978—Bears, 19-0 (C)
　　　Lions, 21-17 (C)
1979—Bears, 35-7 (C)
　　　Lions, 20-0 (D)
1980—Bears, 24-7 (C)
　　　Bears, 23-17 (D) OT
1981—Lions, 48-17 (D)
　　　Lions, 23-7 (C)
(Points—Bears 1,931, Lions 1,756)
*Franchise in Portsmouth prior to 1934
and known as the Spartans
**Championship

CHICAGO vs. GREEN BAY
Bears lead series, 66-53-6
1921—Staleys, 20-0 (C)
1923—Bears, 3-0 (GB)
1924—Bears, 3-0 (C)
1925—Packers, 14-10 (GB)
　　　Bears, 21-0 (C)
1926—Tie 6-6 (GB)
　　　Bears, 19-13 (C)
　　　Tie, 3-3 (C)
1927—Bears, 7-6 (GB)
　　　Bears, 14-6 (C)
1928—Tie, 12-12 (GB)
　　　Packers, 16-6 (C)
　　　Packers, 6-0 (C)
1929—Packers, 23-0 (GB)
　　　Packers, 14-0 (C)
　　　Packers, 25-0 (C)
1930—Packers, 7-0 (GB)
　　　Packers, 13-12 (C)
　　　Bears, 21-0 (C)
1931—Packers, 7-0 (GB)
　　　Packers, 6-2 (C)
　　　Bears, 7-6 (C)
1932—Tie, 0-0 (GB)
　　　Packers, 2-0 (C)
　　　Bears, 9-0 (C)
1933—Bears, 14-7 (GB)
　　　Bears, 10-7 (C)
　　　Bears, 7-6 (C)
1934—Bears, 24-10 (GB)
　　　Bears, 27-14 (C)
1935—Packers, 7-0 (GB)
　　　Packers, 17-14 (C)
1936—Bears, 30-3 (GB)
　　　Packers, 21-10 (C)
1937—Bears, 14-2 (GB)
　　　Packers, 24-14 (C)
1938—Bears, 2-0 (GB)
　　　Packers, 24-17 (C)
1939—Packers, 21-16 (GB)
　　　Bears, 30-27 (C)
1940—Bears, 41-10 (GB)
　　　Bears, 14-7 (C)
1941—Bears, 25-17 (GB)
　　　Packers, 16-14 (C)
　　　**Bears, 33-14 (C)
1942—Bears, 44-28 (GB)
　　　Bears, 38-7 (C)
1943—Tie, 21-21 (GB)
　　　Bears, 21-7 (C)
1944—Packers, 42-28 (GB)
　　　Bears, 21-0 (C)
1945—Packers, 31-21 (GB)

Bears, 28-24 (C)
1946—Bears, 30-7 (GB)
　　　Bears, 10-7 (C)
1947—Packers, 29-20 (GB)
　　　Bears, 20-17 (C)
1948—Bears, 45-7 (GB)
　　　Bears, 7-6 (C)
1949—Bears, 17-0 (GB)
　　　Bears, 24-3 (C)
1950—Packers, 31-21 (GB)
　　　Bears, 28-14 (C)
1951—Bears, 31-20 (GB)
　　　Bears, 24-13 (C)
1952—Packers, 24-14 (GB)
　　　Packers, 41-28 (C)
1953—Bears, 17-13 (GB)
　　　Tie, 21-21 (C)
1954—Bears, 10-3 (GB)
　　　Bears, 28-23 (C)
1955—Packers, 24-3 (GB)
　　　Bears, 52-31 (C)
1956—Bears, 37-21 (GB)
　　　Bears, 38-14 (C)
1957—Packers, 21-17 (GB)
　　　Bears, 21-14 (C)
1958—Bears, 34-20 (GB)
　　　Bears, 24-10 (C)
1959—Packers, 9-6 (GB)
　　　Bears, 28-17 (C)
1960—Bears, 17-14 (GB)
　　　Packers, 41-13 (C)
1961—Packers, 24-0 (GB)
　　　Packers, 31-28 (C)
1962—Packers, 49-0 (GB)
　　　Packers, 38-7 (C)
1963—Bears, 10-3 (GB)
　　　Bears, 26-7 (C)
1964—Packers, 23-12 (GB)
　　　Packers, 17-3 (C)
1965—Packers, 23-14 (GB)
　　　Bears, 31-10 (C)
1966—Packers, 17-0 (GB)
　　　Packers, 13-6 (C)
1967—Packers, 13-10 (GB)
　　　Packers, 17-13 (C)
1968—Bears, 13-10 (GB)
　　　Packers, 28-27 (C)
1969—Packers, 17-0 (GB)
　　　Packers, 21-3 (C)
1970—Packers, 20-19 (GB)
　　　Bears, 35-17 (C)
1971—Packers, 17-14 (GB)
　　　Packers, 31-10 (C)
1972—Packers, 20-17 (GB)
　　　Packers, 23-17 (C)
1973—Packers, 31-17 (GB)
　　　Packers, 21-0 (C)
1974—Bears, 10-9 (C)
　　　Packers, 20-3 (Mil)
1975—Packers, 27-14 (C)
　　　Packers, 28-7 (GB)
1976—Bears, 24-13 (C)
　　　Bears, 16-10 (GB)
1977—Bears, 26-0 (C)
　　　Packers, 21-10 (C)
1978—Packers, 24-14 (GB)
　　　Bears, 14-0 (C)
1979—Bears, 6-3 (C)
　　　Bears, 15-14 (GB)
1980—Packers, 12-6 (GB) OT
　　　Bears, 61-7 (C)
1981—Packers, 16-9 (C)
　　　Packers, 27-17 (GB)
(Points—Bears 2,070, Packers 1,832)
*Bears known as Staleys prior to 1922
**Division Playoff

CHICAGO vs. HOUSTON
Oilers lead series, 2-1
1973—Bears, 35-14 (C)
1977—Oilers, 47-0 (H)
1980—Oilers, 10-6 (C)
(Points—Oilers 71, Bears 41)

CHICAGO vs. KANSAS CITY
Bears lead series, 2-1
1973—Chiefs, 19-7 (KC)
1977—Bears, 28-27 (C)
1981—Bears, 16-13 (KC) OT
(Points—Chiefs 59, Bears 51)

CHICAGO vs. *LOS ANGELES
Bears lead series, 41-25-3
1937—Bears, 20-2 (Clev)
　　　Bears, 15-7 (C)
1938—Rams, 14-7 (C)
　　　Rams, 23-21 (Clev)
1939—Bears, 30-21 (Clev)
　　　Bears, 35-21 (C)
1940—Bears, 21-14 (Clev)
　　　Bears, 47-25 (C)

303

1941—Bears, 48-21 (Clev)
    Bears, 31-13 (C)
1942—Bears, 21-7 (Clev)
    Bears, 47-0 (C)
1944—Rams, 19-7 (Clev)
    Bears, 28-21 (C)
1945—Rams, 17-0 (Clev)
    Rams, 41-21 (C)
1946—Tie, 28-28 (C)
    Bears, 27-21 (LA)
1947—Bears, 41-21 (LA)
    Rams, 17-14 (C)
1948—Bears, 42-21 (C)
    Bears, 21-6 (LA)
1949—Rams, 31-16 (C)
    Rams, 27-24 (LA)
1950—Rams, 24-20 (LA)
    Bears, 24-14 (C)
    **Rams, 24-14 (LA)
1951—Rams, 42-17 (C)
1952—Rams, 31-7 (LA)
    Rams, 40-24 (C)
1953—Bears, 38-24 (LA)
    Bears, 24-21 (C)
1954—Rams, 42-38 (LA)
    Bears, 24-13 (C)
1955—Bears, 31-20 (LA)
    Bears, 24-3 (C)
1956—Bears, 35-24 (LA)
    Bears, 30-21 (C)
1957—Bears, 34-26 (C)
    Bears, 16-10 (LA)
1958—Bears, 31-10 (C)
    Rams, 41-35 (LA)
1959—Bears, 28-21 (C)
    Bears, 26-21 (LA)
1960—Bears, 34-27 (C)
    Tie, 24-24 (LA)
1961—Bears, 21-17 (LA)
    Bears, 28-24 (C)
1962—Bears, 27-23 (LA)
    Bears, 30-14 (C)
1963—Bears, 52-14 (LA)
    Bears, 6-0 (C)
1964—Bears, 38-17 (C)
    Bears, 34-24 (LA)
1965—Rams, 30-28 (LA)
    Bears, 31-6 (C)
1966—Rams, 31-17 (LA)
    Bears, 17-10 (C)
1967—Bears, 28-17 (C)
1968—Bears, 17-16 (LA)
1969—Rams, 9-7 (C)
1971—Rams, 17-3 (LA)
1972—Tie, 13-13 (C)
1973—Rams, 26-0 (C)
1975—Rams, 38-10 (LA)
1976—Rams, 20-12 (LA)
1977—Bears, 24-23 (C)
1979—Bears, 27-23 (C)
1981—Rams, 24-7 (C)
(Points—Bears 1,639, Rams 1,425)
*Franchise in Cleveland prior to 1946
**Conference Playoff

CHICAGO vs. MIAMI
Dolphins lead series, 3-0
1971—Dolphins, 34-3 (M)
1975—Dolphins, 46-13 (C)
1979—Dolphins, 31-16 (M)
(Points—Dolphins 111, Bears 32)

CHICAGO vs. MINNESOTA
Vikings lead series, 23-17-2
1961—Vikings, 37-13 (M)
    Bears, 52-35 (C)
1962—Bears, 13-0 (M)
    Bears, 31-30 (C)
1963—Bears, 28-7 (M)
    Tie, 17-17 (C)
1964—Bears, 34-28 (M)
    Vikings, 41-14 (C)
1965—Bears, 45-37 (M)
    Vikings, 24-17 (C)
1966—Bears, 13-10 (M)
    Bears, 41-28 (C)
1967—Bears, 17-7 (M)
    Tie, 10-10 (C)
1968—Bears, 27-17 (M)
    Bears, 26-24 (C)
1969—Vikings, 31-0 (C)
    Vikings, 31-14 (M)
1970—Vikings, 24-0 (C)
    Vikings, 16-13 (M)
1971—Bears, 20-17 (M)
    Vikings, 27-10 (C)
1972—Bears, 13-10 (C)
    Vikings, 23-10 (M)
1973—Vikings, 22-13 (C)
    Vikings, 31-13 (M)

1974—Vikings, 11-7 (M)
    Vikings, 17-0 (C)
1975—Vikings, 28-3 (M)
    Vikings, 13-9 (C)
1976—Vikings, 20-19 (M)
    Bears, 14-13 (C)
1977—Vikings, 22-16 (M) OT
    Bears, 10-7 (C)
1978—Vikings, 24-20 (M)
    Vikings, 17-14 (M)
1979—Bears, 26-7 (C)
    Vikings, 30-27 (M)
1980—Vikings, 34-14 (C)
    Vikings, 13-7 (M)
1981—Vikings, 24-21 (M)
    Bears, 10-9 (C)
(Points—Vikings 873, Bears 721)

CHICAGO vs. NEW ENGLAND
Patriots lead series, 2-0
1973—Patriots, 13-10 (C)
1979—Patriots, 27-7 (C)
(Points—Patriots 40, Bears 17)

CHICAGO vs. NEW ORLEANS
Bears lead series, 6-2
1968—Bears, 23-17 (NO)
1970—Bears, 24-3 (NO)
1971—Bears, 35-14 (C)
1973—Saints, 21-16 (NO)
1974—Bears, 24-10 (C)
1975—Bears, 42-17 (NO)
1977—Saints, 42-24 (C)
1980—Bears, 22-3 (C)
(Points—Bears 210, Saints 127)

CHICAGO vs. N.Y. GIANTS
Bears lead series, 26-16-2
1925—Bears, 19-7 (NY)
    Giants, 9-0 (C)
1926—Bears, 7-0 (C)
1927—Giants, 13-7 (NY)
1928—Bears, 13-0 (C)
1929—Giants, 26-14 (C)
    Giants, 34-0 (NY)
    Giants, 14-9 (C)
1930—Giants, 12-0 (C)
    Bears, 12-0 (NY)
1931—Bears, 6-0 (C)
    Bears, 12-6 (NY)
    Giants, 25-6 (C)
1932—Bears, 28-8 (NY)
    Bears, 6-0 (C)
1933—Bears, 14-10 (C)
    Giants, 3-0 (NY)
    *Bears, 23-21 (C)
1934—Bears, 27-7 (C)
    Bears, 10-9 (NY)
    *Giants, 30-13 (NY)
1935—Bears, 20-3 (NY)
    Giants, 3-0 (C)
1936—Bears, 25-7 (NY)
1937—Tie, 3-3 (NY)
1939—Giants, 16-13 (NY)
1940—Bears, 37-21 (NY)
1941—*Bears, 37-9 (C)
1942—Bears, 26-7 (NY)
1943—Bears, 56-7 (NY)
1946—Giants, 14-0 (NY)
    *Bears, 24-14 (NY)
1948—Bears, 35-14 (C)
1949—Giants, 35-28 (NY)
1956—Tie, 17-17 (NY)
    *Giants, 47-7 (NY)
1962—Giants, 26-24 (C)
1963—*Bears, 14-10 (C)
1965—Bears, 35-14 (NY)
1967—Bears, 34-7 (C)
1969—Giants, 28-24 (NY)
1970—Bears, 24-16 (NY)
1974—Bears, 16-13 (C)
1977—Bears, 12-9 (NY) OT
(Points—Bears 737, Giants 574)
*NFL Championship

CHICAGO vs. N.Y. JETS
Series tied, 1-1
1974—Jets, 23-21 (C)
1979—Bears, 23-13 (C)
(Points—Bears 44, Jets 36)

CHICAGO vs. *N.Y. YANKS
Bears won series, 3-1
1950—Yanks, 38-27
    Bears, 28-20
1951—Bears, 24-21
    Bears, 45-21
(Points—Bears 124, Yanks 100)
*Extinct team

CHICAGO vs. OAKLAND
Raiders lead series, 3-1
1972—Raiders, 28-21 (O)
1976—Raiders, 28-27 (C)

1978—Raiders, 25-19 (C) OT
1981—Bears, 23-6 (O)
(Points—Bears 90, Raiders 87)

CHICAGO vs. PHILADELPHIA
Bears lead series, 17-4-1
1933—Tie, 3-3 (P)
1935—Bears, 39-0 (P)
1936—Bears, 17-0 (P)
    Bears, 28-7 (P)
1938—Bears, 28-6 (P)
1939—Bears, 27-14 (C)
1941—Bears, 49-14 (P)
1942—Bears, 45-14 (C)
1944—Bears, 28-7 (P)
1946—Bears, 21-14 (C)
1947—Bears, 40-7 (C)
1948—Eagles, 12-7 (P)
1949—Bears, 38-21 (C)
1955—Bears, 17-10 (C)
1961—Eagles, 16-14 (P)
1963—Bears, 16-7 (C)
1968—Bears, 29-16 (P)
1970—Bears, 20-16 (C)
1972—Bears, 21-12 (P)
1975—Bears, 15-13 (C)
1979—*Eagles, 27-17 (P)
1980—Eagles, 17-14 (P)
(Points—Bears 533, Eagles 253)
*NFC First Round Playoff

CHICAGO vs. *PITTSBURGH
Bears lead series, 13-4-1
1934—Bears, 28-0 (P)
1935—Bears, 23-7 (P)
1936—Bears, 27-9 (P)
    Bears, 26-6 (C)
1937—Bears, 7-0 (P)
1939—Bears, 32-0 (P)
1941—Bears, 34-7 (C)
1945—Bears, 28-7 (P)
1947—Bears, 49-7 (C)
1949—Bears, 30-21 (C)
1958—Steelers, 24-10 (P)
1959—Bears, 27-21 (C)
1963—Tie, 17-17 (P)
1967—Steelers, 41-13 (P)
1969—Bears, 38-7 (C)
1971—Bears, 17-15 (C)
1975—Steelers, 34-3 (P)
1980—Steelers, 38-3 (P)
(Points—Bears 412, Steelers 261)
*Steelers known as Pirates prior to 1941

***CHICAGO vs. **ST. LOUIS**
Bears lead series, 50-23-6
(NP denotes Normal Park;
Wr denotes Wrigley Field;
Co denotes Comiskey Park;
So denotes Soldier Field;
all Chicago)
1920—Cardinals, 7-6 (NP)
    Staleys, 10-0 (Wr)
1921—Tie, 0-0 (Wr)
1922—Cardinals, 6-0 (Co)
    Cardinals, 9-0 (Co)
1923—Bears, 3-0 (Wr)
1924—Bears, 6-0 (Wr)
    Bears, 21-0 (Co)
1925—Cardinals, 9-0 (Co)
    Tie, 0-0 (Wr)
1926—Bears, 16-0 (Wr)
    Bears, 10-0 (So)
    Tie, 0-0 (Wr)
1927—Bears, 9-0 (NP)
    Cardinals, 3-0 (Wr)
1928—Bears, 15-0 (NP)
    Bears, 34-0 (Wr)
1929—Tie, 0-0 (Wr)
    Cardinals, 40-6 (Co)
1930—Bears, 32-6 (Co)
    Bears, 6-0 (Wr)
1931—Bears, 26-13 (Wr)
    Bears, 18-7 (Wr)
1932—Tie, 0-0 (Wr)
    Bears, 34-0 (Wr)
1933—Bears, 12-9 (Wr)
    Bears, 22-6 (Wr)
1934—Bears, 20-0 (Wr)
    Bears, 17-6 (Wr)
1935—Tie, 7-7 (Wr)
    Bears, 13-0 (Wr)
1936—Bears, 7-3 (Wr)
    Cardinals, 14-7 (Wr)
1937—Bears, 16-7 (Wr)
    Bears, 42-28 (Wr)
1938—Bears, 16-13 (So)
    Bears, 34-28 (Wr)
1939—Bears, 44-7 (Wr)
    Bears, 48-7 (Co)

1940—Cardinals, 21-7 (Co)
    Bears, 31-23 (Wr)
1941—Bears, 53-7 (Wr)
    Bears, 34-24 (Co)
1942—Bears, 41-14 (Wr)
    Bears, 21-7 (Co)
1943—Bears, 20-0 (Wr)
    Bears, 35-24 (Co)
1945—Cardinals, 16-7 (Wr)
    Bears, 28-20 (Co)
1946—Bears, 34-17 (Co)
    Cardinals, 35-28 (Wr)
1947—Cardinals, 31-7 (Co)
    Cardinals, 30-21 (Wr)
1948—Bears, 28-17 (Co)
    Cardinals, 24-21 (Wr)
1949—Bears, 17-7 (Co)
    Bears, 52-21 (Wr)
1950—Bears, 27-6 (Wr)
    Cardinals, 20-10 (Co)
1951—Cardinals, 28-14 (Co)
    Cardinals, 24-14 (Wr)
1952—Cardinals, 21-10 (Co)
    Bears, 10-7 (Wr)
1953—Cardinals, 24-17 (Wr)
    Bears, 29-7 (Co)
1954—Cardinals, 53-14 (Co)
1955—Cardinals, 53-14 (Co)
1956—Bears, 10-3 (Wr)
1957—Bears, 14-6 (Co)
1958—Bears, 30-14 (Wr)
1959—Bears, 31-7 (So)
1965—Bears, 34-13 (Wr)
1966—Cardinals, 24-17 (StL)
1967—Bears, 30-3 (Wr)
1969—Cardinals, 20-17 (StL)
1972—Bears, 27-10 (StL)
1975—Cardinals, 34-20 (So)
1977—Cardinals, 16-13 (StL)
1978—Bears, 17-10 (So)
1979—Cardinals, 42-6 (So)
(Points—Bears 1,489, Cardinals 929)
*Franchise in Decatur prior to 1921;
Bears known as Staleys prior to 1922
**Franchise in Chicago prior to 1960

CHICAGO vs. SAN DIEGO
Chargers lead series, 3-1
1970—Chargers, 20-7 (C)
1974—Chargers, 28-21 (SD)
1978—Chargers, 40-7 (SD)
1981—Bears, 20-17 (C) OT
(Points—Chargers 105, Bears 55)

CHICAGO vs. SAN FRANCISCO
Series tied, 22-22-1
1950—Bears, 32-20 (SF)
    Bears, 17-0 (C)
1951—Bears, 13-7 (C)
1952—49ers, 40-16 (C)
    Bears, 20-17 (SF)
1953—49ers, 35-28 (C)
    49ers, 24-14 (SF)
1954—49ers, 31-24 (C)
    Bears, 31-27 (SF)
1955—Bears, 20-19 (C)
    Bears, 34-23 (SF)
1956—Bears, 31-7 (C)
    Bears, 38-21 (SF)
1957—49ers, 21-17 (C)
    49ers, 21-17 (SF)
1958—Bears, 28-6 (C)
    Bears, 27-14 (SF)
1959—49ers, 20-17 (SF)
    Bears, 14-3 (C)
1960—Bears, 27-10 (C)
    49ers, 25-7 (SF)
1961—Bears, 31-0 (C)
    49ers, 41-31 (SF)
1962—Bears, 30-14 (SF)
    49ers, 34-27 (C)
1963—49ers, 20-14 (SF)
    Bears, 27-7 (C)
1964—49ers, 31-21 (SF)
    Bears, 23-21 (C)
1965—49ers, 52-24 (SF)
    Bears, 61-20 (C)
1966—Tie, 30-30 (C)
    49ers, 41-14 (SF)
1967—Bears, 28-14 (SF)
1968—Bears, 27-19 (C)
1969—49ers, 42-21 (SF)
1970—49ers, 37-16 (C)
1971—49ers, 13-0 (SF)
1972—49ers, 34-21 (C)
1974—49ers, 34-0 (C)
1975—49ers, 31-3 (SF)
1976—49ers, 19-12 (SF)
1978—Bears, 16-13 (SF)
1979—Bears, 28-27 (SF)
1981—Bears, 28-17 (SF)

(Points—49ers 1,007, Bears 1,000)
CHICAGO vs. SEATTLE
Series tied, 1-1
1976—Bears, 34-7 (S)
1978—Seahawks, 31-29 (C)
(Points—Bears 63, Seahawks 38)

CHICAGO vs. TAMPA BAY
Bears lead series, 6-3
1977—Bears, 10-0 (TB)
1978—Buccaneers, 33-19 (TB)
    Bears, 14-3 (C)
1979—Buccaneers, 17-13 (C)
    Bears, 14-0 (TB)
1980—Bears, 23-0 (C)
    Bears, 14-13 (TB)
1981—Bears, 28-17 (C)
    Buccaneers, 20-10 (TB)
(Points—Bears 145, Buccaneers 103)

CHICAGO vs. *WASHINGTON
Bears lead series, 18-11-1
1932—Tie, 7-7 (B)
1933—Bears, 7-0 (C)
    Redskins, 10-0 (B)
1934—Bears, 21-0 (B)
1935—Bears, 30-14 (B)
1936—Bears, 26-0 (B)
1937—**Redskins, 28-21 (C)
1938—Bears, 31-7 (C)
1940—Redskins, 7-3 (W)
    **Bears, 73-0 (W)
1941—Bears, 35-21 (C)
1942—**Redskins, 14-6 (W)
1943—Redskins, 21-7 (W)
    **Bears, 41-21 (C)
1945—Redskins, 28-21 (W)
1946—Bears, 24-20 (C)
1947—Bears, 56-20 (W)
1948—Bears, 48-13 (C)
1949—Bears, 31-21 (W)
1951—Bears, 27-0 (W)
1953—Bears, 27-24 (W)
1957—Redskins, 14-3 (C)
1964—Redskins, 27-20 (W)
1968—Bears, 38-28 (W)
1971—Bears, 16-15 (C)
1974—Redskins, 42-0 (C)
1976—Bears, 33-7 (C)
1978—Bears, 14-10 (W)
1980—Bears, 35-21 (C)
1981—Redskins, 24-7 (C)
(Points—Bears 698, Redskins 474)
*Franchise in Boston prior to 1937
and known as Braves prior to 1933
**NFL Championship

CINCINNATI vs. ATLANTA
Bengals lead series, 3-1;
See Atlanta vs. Cincinnati
CINCINNATI vs. BALTIMORE
Colts lead series, 4-3;
See Baltimore vs. Cincinnati
CINCINNATI vs. BUFFALO
Bengals lead series, 6-4;
See Buffalo vs. Cincinnati
CINCINNATI vs. CHICAGO
Bengals lead series, 2-0;
See Chicago vs. Cincinnati
CINCINNATI vs. CLEVELAND
Browns lead series, 13-11
1970—Browns, 30-27 (Cle)
    Bengals, 14-10 (Cin)
1971—Browns, 27-24 (Cin)
    Browns, 31-27 (Cle)
1972—Browns, 27-6 (Cle)
    Browns, 27-24 (Cin)
1973—Browns, 17-10 (Cle)
    Bengals, 34-17 (Cin)
1974—Bengals, 33-7 (Cin)
    Bengals, 34-24 (Cle)
1975—Bengals, 24-17 (Cin)
    Browns, 35-23 (Cle)
1976—Bengals, 45-24 (Cle)
    Bengals, 21-6 (Cle)
1977—Browns, 13-3 (Cin)
    Bengals, 10-7 (Cle)
1978—Browns, 13-10 (Cle) OT
    Bengals, 48-16 (Cin)
1979—Browns, 28-27 (Cle)
    Bengals, 16-12 (Cin)
1980—Browns, 31-7 (Cle)
    Browns, 27-24 (Cin)
1981—Browns, 20-17 (Cin)
    Bengals, 41-21 (Cle)
(Points—Bengals 549, Browns 487)
CINCINNATI vs. DALLAS
Cowboys lead series, 2-0
1973—Cowboys, 38-10 (D)
1979—Cowboys, 38-13 (D)

(Points—Cowboys 76, Bengals 23)
CINCINNATI vs. DENVER
Series tied, 6-6
1968—Bengals, 24-10 (C)
Broncos, 10-7 (D)
1969—Broncos, 30-23 (C)
Broncos, 27-16 (D)
1971—Bengals, 24-10 (D)
1972—Bengals, 21-10 (C)
1973—Broncos, 28-10 (D)
1975—Bengals, 17-16 (D)
1976—Bengals, 17-7 (C)
1977—Broncos, 24-13 (C)
1979—Broncos, 10-0 (D)
1981—Bengals, 38-21 (C)
(Points—Bengals 210, Broncos 203)
CINCINNATI vs. DETROIT
Lions lead series, 2-0
1970—Lions, 38-3 (D)
1974—Lions, 23-19 (C)
(Points—Lions 61, Bengals 22)
CINCINNATI vs. GREEN BAY
Series tied, 2-2
1971—Packers, 20-17 (GB)
1976—Bengals, 28-7 (C)
1977—Bengals, 17-7 (Mil)
1980—Packers, 14-9 (GB)
(Points—Bengals 71, Packers 48)
CINCINNATI vs. HOUSTON
Bengals lead series, 13-12-1
1968—Oilers, 27-17 (C)
1969—Tie, 31-31 (H)
1970—Oilers, 20-13 (C)
Bengals, 30-20 (H)
1971—Oilers, 10-6 (H)
Bengals, 28-13 (C)
1972—Bengals, 30-7 (C)
Bengals, 61-17 (H)
1973—Bengals, 24-10 (C)
Bengals, 27-24 (H)
1974—Oilers, 34-21 (C)
Oilers, 20-3 (H)
1975—Bengals, 21-19 (H)
Bengals, 23-19 (C)
1976—Bengals, 27-7 (H)
Bengals, 31-27 (C)
1977—Bengals, 13-10 (C) OT
Oilers, 21-16 (H)
1978—Bengals, 28-13 (C)
Oilers, 17-10 (H)
1979—Oilers, 30-27 (C) OT
Oilers, 42-21 (H)
1980—Oilers, 13-10 (C)
Oilers, 23-3 (H)
1981—Oilers, 17-10 (H)
Bengals, 34-21 (C)
(Points—Bengals 565, Oilers 512)
CINCINNATI vs. KANSAS CITY
Bengals lead series, 7-6
1968—Chiefs, 13-3 (KC)
Chiefs, 16-9 (C)
1969—Bengals, 24-19 (C)
Chiefs, 42-22 (KC)
1970—Chiefs, 27-19 (C)
1972—Bengals, 23-16 (KC)
1973—Bengals, 14-6 (C)
1974—Bengals, 33-6 (C)
1976—Bengals, 27-24 (KC)
1977—Bengals, 27-7 (KC)
1978—Chiefs, 24-23 (C)
1979—Chiefs, 10-7 (C)
1980—Bengals, 20-6 (KC)
(Points—Bengals 251, Chiefs 216)
CINCINNATI vs. LOS ANGELES
Bengals lead series, 3-1
1972—Rams, 15-12 (LA)
1976—Bengals, 20-12 (C)
1978—Bengals, 20-19 (LA)
1981—Bengals, 24-10 (C)
(Points—Bengals 76, Rams 56)
CINCINNATI vs. MIAMI
Dolphins lead series, 6-3
1968—Dolphins, 24-22 (C)
Bengals, 38-21 (M)
1969—Bengals, 27-21 (C)
1971—Dolphins, 23-13 (C)
1973—*Dolphins, 34-16 (M)
1974—Dolphins, 24-3 (M)
1977—Bengals, 23-17 (C)
1978—Dolphins, 21-0 (M)
1980—Dolphins, 17-16 (M)
(Points—Dolphins 202, Bengals 158)
**AFC Divisional Playoff*
CINCINNATI vs. MINNESOTA
Bengals lead series, 2-1
1973—Bengals, 27-0 (C)
1977—Vikings, 42-10 (M)
1980—Bengals, 14-0 (C)
(Points—Bengals 51, Vikings 42)
CINCINNATI vs. *NEW ENGLAND
Patriots lead series, 4-3
1968—Patriots, 33-14 (B)
1969—Patriots, 25-14 (C)
1970—Bengals, 45-7 (C)
1972—Bengals, 31-7 (NE)
1975—Bengals, 27-10 (C)
1978—Patriots, 10-3 (C)
1979—Patriots, 20-14 (C)
(Points—Bengals 148, Patriots 112)
**Franchise in Boston prior to 1971*
CINCINNATI vs. NEW ORLEANS
Series tied, 2-2
1970—Bengals, 26-6 (C)
1975—Bengals, 21-0 (NO)
1978—Saints, 20-18 (C)
1981—Saints, 17-7 (NO)
(Points—Bengals 72, Saints 43)
CINCINNATI vs. N. Y. GIANTS
Bengals lead series, 2-0
1972—Bengals, 13-10 (C)
1977—Bengals, 30-13 (C)
(Points—Bengals 43, Giants 23)
CINCINNATI vs. N. Y. JETS
Jets lead series, 4-3
1968—Jets, 27-14 (NY)
1969—Jets, 21-7 (C)
Jets, 40-7 (NY)
1971—Jets, 35-21 (NY)
1973—Bengals, 20-14 (C)
1976—Bengals, 42-3 (NY)
1981—Bengals, 31-30 (NY)
(Points—Jets 170, Bengals 142)
CINCINNATI vs. OAKLAND
Raiders lead series, 10-3
1968—Raiders, 31-10 (O)
Raiders, 34-0 (C)
1969—Bengals, 31-17 (C)
Raiders, 37-17 (O)
1970—Bengals, 31-21 (C)
1971—Raiders, 31-27 (O)
1972—Raiders, 20-14 (C)
1974—Raiders, 30-27 (O)
1975—Bengals, 14-10 (C)
*Raiders, 31-28 (O)
1976—Raiders, 35-20 (O)
1978—Raiders, 34-21 (C)
1980—Raiders, 28-17 (O)
(Points—Raiders 359, Bengals 257)
**AFC Divisional Playoff*
CINCINNATI vs. PHILADELPHIA
Bengals lead series, 3-0
1971—Bengals, 37-14 (C)
1975—Bengals, 31-0 (P)
1979—Bengals, 37-13 (C)
(Points—Bengals 105, Eagles 27)
CINCINNATI vs. PITTSBURGH
Steelers lead series, 14-10
1970—Steelers, 21-10 (P)
Bengals, 34-7 (C)
1971—Steelers, 21-10 (P)
Steelers, 21-13 (C)
1972—Bengals, 15-10 (C)
Steelers, 40-17 (P)
1973—Bengals, 19-7 (C)
Steelers, 20-13 (P)
1974—Bengals, 17-10 (C)
Steelers, 27-3 (P)
1975—Steelers, 30-24 (C)
Steelers, 35-14 (P)
1976—Steelers, 23-6 (P)
Steelers, 7-3 (C)
1977—Steelers, 20-14 (P)
Bengals, 17-10 (C)
1978—Steelers, 28-3 (C)
Steelers, 7-6 (P)
1979—Bengals, 34-10 (C)
Steelers, 37-17 (P)
1980—Bengals, 30-28 (C)
Bengals, 17-16 (P)
1981—Bengals, 34-7 (C)
Bengals, 17-10 (P)
(Points—Steelers 452, Bengals 387)
CINCINNATI vs. ST. LOUIS
Bengals lead series, 2-0
1973—Bengals, 42-24 (C)
1979—Bengals, 34-28 (C)
(Points—Bengals 76, Cardinals 52)
CINCINNATI vs. SAN DIEGO
Chargers lead series, 8-7
1968—Chargers, 29-13 (SD)
Chargers, 31-10 (C)
1969—Bengals, 34-20 (C)
Chargers, 21-14 (SD)
1970—Bengals, 17-14 (SD)
1971—Bengals, 31-0 (C)
1973—Bengals, 20-13 (SD)
1974—Chargers, 20-17 (C)
1975—Bengals, 47-17 (C)
1977—Chargers, 24-3 (SD)
1978—Chargers, 22-13 (SD)
1979—Chargers, 26-24 (C)
1980—Chargers, 31-14 (C)
1981—Bengals, 40-17 (SD)
*Bengals, 27-7 (C)
(Points—Bengals 324, Chargers 292)
**AFC Championship*
CINCINNATI vs. SAN FRANCISCO
49ers lead series, 3-1
1974—Bengals, 21-3 (SF)
1978—49ers, 28-12 (SF)
1981—49ers, 21-3 (C)
*49ers, 26-21 (Detroit)
(Points—49ers 78, Bengals 57)
**Super Bowl XVI*
CINCINNATI vs. SEATTLE
Bengals lead series, 2-0
1977—Bengals, 42-20 (C)
1981—Bengals, 27-21 (C)
(Points—Bengals 69, Seahawks 41)
CINCINNATI vs. TAMPA BAY
Series tied, 1-1
1976—Bengals, 21-0 (C)
1980—Buccaneers, 17-12 (C)
(Points—Bengals 33, Buccaneers 17)
CINCINNATI vs. WASHINGTON
Redskins lead series, 2-1
1970—Redskins, 20-0 (W)
1974—Bengals, 28-17 (C)
1979—Redskins, 28-14 (W)
(Points—Redskins 65, Bengals 42)
***CINCINNATI REDS vs. *BROOKLYN DODGERS**
Series tied, 1-1; See Brooklyn Dodgers vs. Cincinnati Reds
**Extinct teams*
***CINCINNATI REDS vs. CHICAGO**
Bears won series, 2-0
See Chicago vs. *Cincinnati Reds
**Extinct team*
***CINCINNATI REDS vs. **CHICAGO CARDINALS**
Cardinals won series, 3-1
1933—Cardinals, 3-0
Reds, 12-9
1934—Cardinals, 9-0
Cardinals, 16-0
(Points—Cardinals 37, Reds 12)
**Extinct team*
***Franchise moved to St. Louis in 1960*
***CINCINNATI REDS vs. **DETROIT**
Lions won series, 2-1
1933—Spartans, 21-0
Reds, 10-7
1934—Lions, 38-0
(Points—Spartans-Lions 66, Reds 10)
**Extinct team*
***Franchise in Portsmouth prior to 1934 and known as the Spartans*
***CINCINNATI REDS vs. GREEN BAY**
Packers won series, 1-0
1934—Packers, 41-0
**Extinct team*
***CINCINNATI REDS vs. PHILADELPHIA**
Eagles won series, 3-0
1933—Eagles, 6-0
Eagles, 20-3
1934—Eagles, 64-0
(Points—Eagles 26, Reds 3)
**Extinct team*
***CINCINNATI REDS vs. PITTSBURGH**
Steelers won series, 2-0-1
1933—Steelers, 17-3
Tie, 0-0
1934—Steelers, 13-0
(Points—Steelers 30, Reds 3)
**Extinct team*

CLEVELAND vs. ATLANTA
Browns lead series, 5-1;
See Atlanta vs. Cleveland
CLEVELAND vs. BALTIMORE
Browns lead series, 9-5;
See Baltimore vs. Cleveland
CLEVELAND vs. *1950 BALTIMORE
Browns won series, 1-0
See *Baltimore vs. Cleveland
**Extinct team*
CLEVELAND vs. BUFFALO
Browns lead series, 3-2;
See Buffalo vs. Cleveland
CLEVELAND vs. CHICAGO
Browns lead series, 6-2;
See Chicago vs. Cleveland
CLEVELAND vs. CINCINNATI
Browns lead series, 13-11;
See Cincinnati vs. Cleveland
CLEVELAND vs. DALLAS
Browns lead series, 15-7
1960—Browns, 48-7 (D)
1961—Browns, 25-7 (C)
Browns, 38-17 (D)
1962—Browns, 19-10 (C)
Cowboys, 45-21 (D)
1963—Browns, 41-24 (D)
Browns, 27-17 (C)
1964—Browns, 27-6 (C)
Browns, 20-16 (D)
1965—Browns, 23-17 (C)
Browns, 24-17 (D)
1966—Browns, 30-21 (C)
Cowboys, 26-14 (D)
1967—Cowboys, 21-14 (C)
*Cowboys, 52-14 (D)
1968—Cowboys, 28-7 (C)
*Browns, 31-20 (C)
1969—Browns, 42-10 (C)
*Browns, 38-14 (D)
1970—Cowboys, 6-2 (C)
1974—Cowboys, 41-17 (D)
1979—Browns, 26-7 (C)
(Points—Browns 548, Cowboys 429)
**Conference Championship*
CLEVELAND vs. DENVER
Broncos lead series, 6-3
1970—Browns, 27-13 (D)
1971—Broncos, 27-0 (C)
1972—Browns, 27-20 (D)
1974—Browns, 23-21 (C)
1975—Broncos, 16-15 (D)
1976—Broncos, 44-13 (D)
1978—Broncos, 19-7 (C)
1980—Broncos, 19-16 (C)
1981—Broncos, 23-20 (D) OT
(Points—Broncos 202, Browns 148)
CLEVELAND vs. DETROIT
Lions lead series, 12-2
1952—Lions, 17-6 (D)
*Lions, 17-7 (C)
1953—*Lions, 17-16 (D)
1954—Lions, 14-10 (C)
*Browns, 56-10 (C)
1957—Lions, 20-7 (D)
*Lions, 59-14 (D)
1958—Lions, 30-10 (C)
1963—Lions, 38-10 (D)
1964—Browns, 37-21 (C)
1967—Lions, 31-14 (D)
1969—Lions, 28-21 (C)
1970—Lions, 41-24 (C)
1975—Lions, 21-10 (D)
(Points—Lions 364, Browns 242)
**NFL Championship*
CLEVELAND vs. GREEN BAY
Packers lead series, 6-5
1953—Browns, 27-0 (Mil)
1955—Browns, 41-10 (C)
1956—Browns, 24-7 (Mil)
1961—Packers, 49-17 (C)
1964—Packers, 28-21 (Mil)
1965—*Packers, 23-12 (GB)
1966—Packers, 21-20 (C)
1967—Packers, 55-7 (Mil)
1969—Browns, 20-7 (C)
1972—Packers, 26-10 (C)
1980—Browns, 26-21 (C)
(Points—Packers 247, Browns 225)
**NFL Championship*
CLEVELAND vs. HOUSTON
Browns lead series, 14-10
1970—Browns, 28-14 (C)
Browns, 21-10 (H)
1971—Browns, 31-0 (C)
Browns, 37-24 (H)
1972—Browns, 23-17 (H)
Browns, 20-0 (C)
1973—Browns, 42-13 (C)
Browns, 23-13 (H)
1974—Browns, 20-7 (C)
Oilers, 28-24 (H)
1975—Oilers, 40-10 (C)
Oilers, 21-10 (H)
1976—Browns, 21-7 (H)
Browns, 13-10 (C)
1977—Browns, 24-23 (H)
Oilers, 19-15 (C)
1978—Oilers, 16-13 (C)
Oilers, 14-10 (H)
1979—Oilers, 31-10 (H)
Browns, 14-7 (C)
1980—Oilers, 16-7 (C)
Browns, 17-14 (H)
1981—Oilers, 9-3 (C)
Oilers, 17-13 (H)
(Points—Browns 449, Oilers 370)
CLEVELAND vs. KANSAS CITY
Series tied, 4-4-1
1971—Chiefs, 13-7 (KC)
1972—Chiefs, 31-7 (C)
1973—Tie, 20-20 (KC)
1975—Browns, 40-14 (C)
1976—Chiefs, 39-14 (KC)
1977—Browns, 44-7 (C)
1978—Chiefs, 17-3 (KC)
1979—Browns, 27-24 (KC)
1980—Browns, 20-13 (C)
(Points—Browns 182, Chiefs 178)
CLEVELAND vs. LOS ANGELES
Browns lead series, 8-6
1950—*Browns, 30-28 (C)
1951—Browns, 38-23 (LA)
*Rams, 24-17 (LA)
1952—Browns, 37-7 (C)
1955—*Browns, 38-14 (LA)
1957—Browns, 45-31 (C)
1958—Browns, 30-27 (LA)
1963—Browns, 20-6 (C)
1965—Rams, 42-7 (LA)
1968—Rams, 24-6 (C)
1973—Rams, 30-17 (LA)
1977—Rams, 9-0 (C)
1978—Browns, 30-19 (C)
1981—Rams, 27-16 (LA)
(Points—Browns 331, Rams 311)
**NFL Championship*
CLEVELAND vs. MIAMI
Browns lead series, 3-2
1970—Browns, 28-0 (M)
1972—*Dolphins, 20-14 (M)
1973—Dolphins, 17-9 (C)
1976—Browns, 17-13 (C)
1979—Browns, 30-24 (C) OT
(Points—Browns 98, Dolphins 74)
**AFC Divisional Playoff*
CLEVELAND vs. MINNESOTA
Vikings lead series, 6-1
1965—Vikings, 27-17 (C)
1967—Browns, 14-10 (C)
1969—Vikings, 51-3 (M)
*Vikings, 27-7 (M)
1973—Vikings, 26-3 (M)
1975—Vikings, 42-10 (C)
1980—Vikings, 28-23 (M)
(Points—Vikings 211, Browns 77)
**NFL Championship*
CLEVELAND vs. NEW ENGLAND
Browns lead series, 3-1
1971—Browns, 27-7 (C)
1974—Browns, 21-14 (NE)
1977—Browns, 30-27 (C) OT
1980—Patriots, 34-17 (NE)
(Points—Browns 95, Patriots 82)
CLEVELAND vs. NEW ORLEANS
Browns lead series, 8-0
1967—Browns, 42-7 (NO)
1968—Browns, 24-10 (NO)
Browns, 35-17 (C)
1969—Browns, 27-17 (NO)
1971—Browns, 21-17 (NO)
1975—Browns, 17-16 (C)
1978—Browns, 24-16 (NO)
1981—Browns, 20-17 (C)
(Points—Browns 210, Saints 117)
CLEVELAND vs. N. Y. GIANTS
Browns lead series, 25-16-2
1950—Giants, 6-0 (C)
Giants, 17-13 (NY)
*Browns, 8-3 (C)
1951—Browns, 14-13 (C)
Browns, 10-0 (NY)
1952—Giants, 17-9 (C)
Giants, 37-34 (NY)
1953—Browns, 7-0 (NY)
Browns, 62-14 (C)
1954—Browns, 24-14 (C)
Browns, 16-7 (NY)
1955—Browns, 24-14 (C)
Tie, 35-35 (NY)
1956—Giants, 21-9 (C)
Browns, 24-7 (NY)
1957—Browns, 6-3 (C)
Browns, 34-28 (NY)
1958—Giants, 21-17 (C)
Giants, 13-10 (NY)

*Giants, 10-0 (NY)
1959—Giants, 10-6 (C)
    Giants, 48-7 (NY)
1960—Giants, 17-13 (C)
    Browns, 48-34 (NY)
1961—Giants, 37-21 (C)
    Tie, 7-7 (NY)
1962—Browns, 17-7 (C)
    Giants, 17-13 (NY)
1963—Browns, 35-24 (NY)
    Giants, 33-6 (C)
1964—Browns, 42-20 (C)
    Browns, 52-20 (NY)
1965—Browns, 38-14 (NY)
    Browns, 34-21 (C)
1966—Browns, 28-7 (NY)
    Browns, 49-40 (C)
1967—Giants, 38-34 (NY)
    Browns, 24-14 (C)
1968—Browns, 45-10 (C)
1969—Browns, 28-17 (C)
    Giants, 27-14 (NY)
1973—Browns, 12-10 (C)
1977—Browns, 21-7 (NY)
(Points—Browns 950, Giants 759)
*Conference Playoff

CLEVELAND vs. N. Y. JETS
Browns lead series, 6-1
1970—Browns, 31-21 (C)
1972—Browns, 26-10 (NY)
1976—Browns, 38-17 (C)
1978—Browns, 37-34 (C) OT
1979—Browns, 25-22 (NY) OT
1980—Browns, 17-14 (C)
1981—Jets, 14-13 (C)
(Points—Browns 187, Jets 132)

CLEVELAND vs. OAKLAND
Raiders lead series, 7-1
1970—Raiders, 23-20 (C)
1971—Raiders, 34-20 (C)
1973—Browns, 7-3 (O)
1974—Raiders, 40-24 (C)
1975—Raiders, 38-17 (O)
1977—Raiders, 26-10 (C)
1979—Raiders, 19-14 (C)
1980—*Raiders, 14-12 (C)
(Points—Raiders 197, Browns 124)
*AFC Divisional Playoff

CLEVELAND vs. PHILADELPHIA
Browns lead series, 29-10-1
1950—Browns, 35-10 (P)
    Browns, 13-7 (C)
1951—Browns, 20-17 (C)
    Browns, 24-9 (NY)
1952—Browns, 49-7 (C)
    Eagles, 28-20 (C)
1953—Browns, 37-13 (C)
    Eagles, 42-27 (P)
1954—Eagles, 28-10 (P)
    Browns, 6-0 (C)
1955—Browns, 21-17 (C)
    Eagles, 33-17 (P)
1956—Browns, 16-0 (P)
    Browns, 17-14 (C)
1957—Browns, 24-7 (C)
    Eagles, 17-7 (P)
1958—Browns, 28-14 (C)
    Browns, 21-14 (P)
1959—Browns, 28-7 (C)
    Browns, 28-21 (P)
1960—Browns, 41-24 (P)
    Eagles, 31-29 (C)
1961—Eagles, 27-20 (P)
    Browns, 45-24 (C)
1962—Eagles, 35-7 (P)
    Tie, 14-14 (C)
1963—Browns, 37-7 (C)
    Browns, 23-17 (P)
1964—Browns, 28-20 (P)
    Browns, 38-24 (C)
1965—Browns, 35-17 (P)
    Browns, 38-34 (C)
1966—Browns, 27-7 (C)
    Eagles, 33-21 (P)
1967—Eagles, 28-24 (P)
1968—Browns, 47-13 (C)
1969—Browns, 27-20 (P)
1972—Browns, 27-17 (C)
1976—Browns, 24-3 (C)
1979—Browns, 24-19 (P)
(Points—Browns 1,024, Eagles 719)

CLEVELAND vs. PITTSBURGH
Browns lead series, 37-27
1950—Browns, 30-17 (P)
    Browns, 45-7 (C)
1951—Browns, 17-0 (C)
    Browns, 28-0 (P)
1952—Browns, 21-20 (P)

Browns, 29-28 (C)
1953—Browns, 34-16 (C)
    Browns, 20-16 (P)
1954—Steelers, 55-27 (P)
    Browns, 42-7 (C)
1955—Browns, 41-14 (C)
    Browns, 30-7 (P)
1956—Browns, 14-10 (P)
    Steelers, 24-16 (C)
1957—Browns, 23-12 (P)
    Browns, 24-0 (C)
1958—Browns, 45-12 (P)
    Browns, 27-10 (C)
1959—Steelers, 17-7 (P)
    Steelers, 21-20 (C)
1960—Steelers, 28-20 (C)
    Steelers, 14-10 (P)
1961—Browns, 30-28 (P)
    Steelers, 17-13 (C)
1962—Browns, 41-14 (P)
    Browns, 35-14 (C)
1963—Browns, 35-23 (C)
    Steelers, 9-7 (P)
1964—Steelers, 23-7 (C)
    Browns, 30-17 (P)
1965—Browns, 24-19 (C)
    Browns, 42-21 (P)
1966—Browns, 41-10 (C)
    Steelers, 16-6 (P)
1967—Browns, 21-10 (C)
    Browns, 34-14 (P)
1968—Browns, 31-24 (C)
    Browns, 45-24 (P)
1969—Browns, 42-31 (C)
    Browns, 24-3 (P)
1970—Browns, 15-7 (C)
    Steelers, 28-9 (P)
1971—Browns, 27-17 (C)
    Steelers, 26-9 (P)
1972—Browns, 26-24 (C)
    Steelers, 30-0 (P)
1973—Browns, 33-6 (P)
    Browns, 21-16 (C)
1974—Steelers, 20-16 (P)
    Steelers, 26-16 (C)
1975—Steelers, 42-6 (C)
    Browns, 31-17 (P)
1976—Steelers, 31-14 (P)
    Browns, 18-16 (C)
1977—Steelers, 28-14 (C)
    Steelers, 35-31 (P)
1978—Steelers, 15-9 (P) OT
    Steelers, 34-14 (C)
1979—Steelers, 51-35 (C)
    Steelers, 33-30 (P) OT
1980—Browns, 27-26 (C)
    Steelers, 16-13 (P)
1981—Steelers, 13-7 (C)
    Steelers, 32-10 (C)
(Points—Browns 1,476, Steelers 1,274)

CLEVELAND vs. *ST. LOUIS
Browns lead series, 30-9-3
1950—Browns, 34-24 (Cle)
    Browns, 10-7 (Chi)
1951—Browns, 34-17 (Chi)
    Browns, 49-28 (Cle)
1952—Browns, 28-13 (Cle)
    Browns, 10-0 (Chi)
1953—Browns, 27-7 (Chi)
    Browns, 27-16 (Cle)
1954—Browns, 31-7 (Cle)
    Browns, 35-3 (Chi)
1955—Browns, 26-20 (Chi)
    Browns, 35-24 (Cle)
1956—Cardinals, 9-7 (Chi)
    Cardinals, 24-7 (Cle)
1957—Browns, 17-7 (Chi)
    Browns, 31-0 (Cle)
1958—Browns, 35-28 (Cle)
    Browns, 38-24 (Chi)
1959—Browns, 34-7 (Chi)
    Browns, 17-7 (Cle)
1960—Browns, 28-27 (Cle)
    Tie, 17-17 (StL)
1961—Browns, 20-17 (C)
    Browns, 21-10 (StL)
1962—Browns, 34-7 (StL)
    Browns, 38-14 (C)
1963—Cardinals, 20-14 (C)
    Browns, 24-10 (StL)
1964—Tie, 33-33 (C)
    Cardinals, 28-19 (StL)
1965—Cardinals, 49-13 (C)
    Browns, 27-24 (StL)
1966—Cardinals, 34-28 (C)
    Browns, 38-10 (StL)
1967—Browns, 20-16 (C)

Browns, 20-16 (StL)
1968—Cardinals, 27-21 (C)
    Cardinals, 27-16 (StL)
1969—Tie, 21-21 (C)
    Browns, 27-21 (StL)
1974—Cardinals, 29-7 (StL)
1979—Browns, 38-20 (StL)
(Points—Browns 1,056, Cardinals 749)
*Franchise in Chicago (Chi) prior to 1960

CLEVELAND vs. SAN DIEGO
Chargers lead series, 4-2-1
1970—Chargers, 27-10 (C)
1972—Browns, 21-17 (SD)
1973—Tie, 16-16 (C)
1974—Chargers, 36-35 (SD)
1976—Browns, 21-17 (C)
1977—Chargers, 37-14 (SD)
1981—Chargers, 44-14 (C)
(Points—Chargers 194, Browns 131)

CLEVELAND vs. SAN FRANCISCO
Browns lead series, 8-3
1950—Browns, 34-14 (C)
1951—49ers, 24-10 (SF)
1953—Browns, 23-21 (C)
1955—Browns, 38-3 (SF)
1959—49ers, 21-20 (C)
1962—Browns, 13-10 (SF)
1968—Browns, 33-21 (SF)
1970—49ers, 34-31 (SF)
1974—Browns, 7-0 (C)
1978—Browns, 24-7 (C)
1981—Browns, 15-12 (SF)
(Points—Browns 248, 49ers 167)

CLEVELAND vs. SEATTLE
Seahawks lead series, 4-1
1977—Seahawks, 20-19 (S)
1978—Seahawks, 47-24 (S)
1979—Seahawks, 29-24 (S)
1980—Browns, 27-3 (S)
1981—Seahawks, 42-21 (S)
(Points—Seahawks 141, Browns 115)

CLEVELAND vs. TAMPA BAY
Browns lead series, 2-0
1976—Browns, 24-7 (TB)
1980—Browns, 34-27 (TB)
(Points—Browns 58, Buccaneers 34)

CLEVELAND vs. WASHINGTON
Browns lead series, 31-7-1
1950—Browns, 20-14 (C)
    Browns, 45-21 (W)
1951—Browns, 45-0 (C)
1952—Browns, 19-15 (C)
    Browns, 48-24 (W)
1953—Browns, 30-14 (W)
    Browns, 27-3 (C)
1954—Browns, 62-3 (C)
    Browns, 34-14 (W)
1955—Redskins, 27-17 (C)
    Browns, 24-14 (W)
1956—Redskins, 20-9 (W)
    Redskins, 20-17 (C)
1957—Browns, 21-17 (C)
    Tie, 30-30 (W)
1958—Browns, 20-10 (W)
    Browns, 21-14 (C)
1959—Browns, 34-7 (C)
    Browns, 31-17 (W)
1960—Browns, 31-10 (W)
    Browns, 27-16 (C)
1961—Browns, 31-7 (C)
    Browns, 17-6 (W)
1962—Redskins, 17-16 (C)
    Redskins, 17-9 (W)
1963—Browns, 37-14 (C)
    Browns, 27-20 (W)
1964—Browns, 27-13 (W)
    Browns, 34-24 (C)
1965—Browns, 17-7 (W)
    Browns, 24-16 (C)
1966—Browns, 38-14 (W)
    Browns, 14-3 (C)
1967—Browns, 42-37 (C)
1968—Browns, 24-21 (W)
1969—Browns, 27-23 (C)
1971—Browns, 20-13 (W)
1975—Redskins, 23-7 (C)
1979—Redskins, 13-9 (C)
(Points—Browns 1,032, Redskins 598)

DALLAS vs. ATLANTA
Cowboys lead series, 7-1;
See Atlanta vs. Dallas

DALLAS vs. BALTIMORE
Cowboys lead series, 5-3;
See Baltimore vs. Dallas

DALLAS vs. BUFFALO
Cowboys lead series, 3-0;
See Buffalo vs. Dallas

DALLAS vs. CHICAGO
Cowboys lead series, 7-3;
See Chicago vs. Dallas

DALLAS vs. CINCINNATI
Cowboys lead series, 2-0;
See Cincinnati vs. Dallas

DALLAS vs. CLEVELAND
Browns lead series, 15-7;
See Cleveland vs. Dallas

DALLAS vs. DENVER
Cowboys lead series, 3-1
1973—Cowboys, 22-10 (Den)
1977—Cowboys, 14-6 (Dal)
    *Cowboys, 27-10 (New Orleans)
1980—Broncos, 41-20 (Den)
(Points—Cowboys 83, Broncos 67)
*Super Bowl XII

DALLAS vs. DETROIT
Cowboys lead series, 6-2
1960—Lions, 23-14 (Det)
1963—Cowboys, 17-14 (Dal)
1968—Cowboys, 59-13 (Dal)
1970—*Cowboys, 5-0 (Dal)
1972—Cowboys, 28-24 (Dal)
1975—Cowboys, 36-10 (Det)
1977—Cowboys, 37-0 (Dal)
1981—Lions, 27-24 (Det)
(Points—Cowboys 220, Lions 111)
*NFC Divisional Playoff

DALLAS vs. GREEN BAY
Packers lead series, 8-3
1960—Packers, 41-7 (GB)
1964—Packers, 45-21 (D)
1965—Packers, 13-3 (Mil)
1966—*Packers, 34-27 (D)
1967—*Packers, 21-17 (GB)
1968—Packers, 28-17 (D)
1970—Cowboys, 16-3 (D)
1972—Packers, 16-13 (Mil)
1975—Cowboys, 19-17 (D)
1978—Cowboys, 42-14 (Mil)
1980—Cowboys, 28-7 (Mil)
(Points—Packers 241, Cowboys 208)
*NFL Championship

DALLAS vs. HOUSTON
Cowboys lead series, 2-1
1970—Cowboys, 52-10 (D)
1974—Cowboys, 10-0 (H)
1979—Oilers, 30-24 (D)
(Points—Cowboys 86, Oilers 40)

DALLAS vs. KANSAS CITY
Series tied, 1-1
1970—Cowboys, 27-16 (KC)
1975—Chiefs, 34-31 (D)
(Points—Cowboys 58, Chiefs 50)

DALLAS vs. LOS ANGELES
Cowboys lead series, 9-8
1960—Rams, 38-13 (D)
1962—Cowboys, 27-17 (LA)
1967—Rams, 35-13 (D)
1969—Rams, 24-23 (LA)
1971—Cowboys, 28-21 (D)
1973—Rams, 37-31 (LA)
    *Cowboys, 27-16 (D)
1975—Cowboys, 18-7 (D)
    **Cowboys, 37-7 (LA)
1976—*Rams, 14-12 (D)
1978—Rams, 27-14 (LA)
    **Cowboys, 28-0 (LA)
1979—Cowboys, 30-6 (D)
    *Rams, 21-19 (D)
1980—Rams, 38-14 (LA)
    ***Cowboys, 34-13 (D)
1981—Cowboys, 29-17 (D)
(Points—Cowboys 397, Rams 338)
*NFC Divisional Playoff
**NFC Championship
***NFC First Round Playoff

DALLAS vs. MIAMI
Series tied, 2-2
1971—*Cowboys, 24-3 (New Orleans)
1973—Dolphins, 14-7 (D)
1978—Dolphins, 23-16 (M)
1981—Cowboys, 28-27 (D)
(Points—Cowboys 75, Dolphins 67)
*Super Bowl VI

DALLAS vs. MINNESOTA
Cowboys lead series, 9-4
1961—Cowboys, 21-7 (D)
    Cowboys, 28-0 (M)
1966—Cowboys, 28-17 (D)
1968—Cowboys, 20-7 (M)
1970—Vikings, 54-13 (M)

1971—*Cowboys, 20-12 (M)
1973—**Vikings, 27-10 (D)
1974—Vikings, 23-21 (D)
1975—*Cowboys, 17-14 (M)
1977—Cowboys, 16-10 (M) OT
    **Cowboys, 23-6 (D)
1978—Vikings, 21-10 (D)
1979—Cowboys, 36-20 (M)
(Points—Cowboys 263, Vikings 218)
*NFC Divisional Playoff
**NFC Championship

DALLAS vs. NEW ENGLAND
Cowboys lead series, 4-0
1971—Cowboys, 44-21 (D)
1975—Cowboys, 34-31 (NE)
1978—Cowboys, 17-10 (D)
1981—Cowboys, 35-21 (NE)
(Points—Cowboys 130, Patriots 83)

DALLAS vs. NEW ORLEANS
Cowboys lead series, 8-1
1967—Cowboys, 14-10 (D)
    Cowboys, 27-10 (NO)
1968—Cowboys, 17-3 (NO)
1969—Cowboys, 21-17 (NO)
    Cowboys, 33-17 (D)
1971—Saints, 24-14 (NO)
1973—Cowboys, 40-3 (D)
1976—Cowboys, 24-6 (NO)
1978—Cowboys, 27-7 (D)
(Points—Cowboys 217, Saints 97)

DALLAS vs. N.Y. GIANTS
Cowboys lead series, 28-11-2
1960—Tie, 31-31 (NY)
1961—Giants, 31-10 (D)
    Cowboys, 17-16 (NY)
1962—Giants, 41-10 (D)
    Giants, 41-31 (NY)
1963—Giants, 37-21 (NY)
    Giants, 34-27 (D)
1964—Tie, 13-13 (D)
    Cowboys, 31-21 (NY)
1965—Cowboys, 31-2 (D)
    Cowboys, 38-20 (NY)
1966—Cowboys, 52-7 (D)
    Cowboys, 17-7 (NY)
1967—Cowboys, 38-24 (D)
1968—Giants, 27-21 (D)
    Cowboys, 28-10 (NY)
1969—Cowboys, 25-3 (D)
1970—Cowboys, 28-10 (D)
    Giants, 23-20 (NY)
1971—Cowboys, 20-13 (D)
    Cowboys, 42-14 (NY)
1972—Cowboys, 23-14 (NY)
    Giants, 23-3 (D)
1973—Cowboys, 45-28 (D)
    Cowboys, 23-10 (New Haven)
1974—Giants, 14-6 (D)
    Cowboys, 21-7 (New Haven)
1975—Cowboys, 13-7 (NY)
    Cowboys, 14-3 (D)
1976—Cowboys, 24-14 (NY)
    Cowboys, 9-3 (D)
1977—Cowboys, 41-21 (D)
    Cowboys, 24-10 (NY)
1978—Cowboys, 34-24 (NY)
    Cowboys, 24-3 (D)
1979—Cowboys, 16-14 (NY)
    Cowboys, 28-7 (D)
1980—Cowboys, 24-3 (D)
    Giants, 38-35 (NY)
1981—Cowboys, 18-10 (D)
    Giants, 13-10 (NY) OT
(Points—Cowboys 986, Giants 691)

DALLAS vs. N.Y. JETS
Cowboys lead series, 3-0
1971—Cowboys, 52-10 (D)
1975—Cowboys, 31-21 (NY)
1978—Cowboys, 30-7 (D)
(Points—Cowboys 113, Jets 38)

DALLAS vs. OAKLAND
Series tied, 1-1
1974—Raiders, 27-23 (O)
1980—Cowboys, 19-13 (O)
(Points—Cowboys 42, Raiders 40)

DALLAS vs. PHILADELPHIA
Cowboys lead series, 29-15
1960—Eagles, 27-25 (D)
1961—Cowboys, 43-7 (D)
    Eagles, 35-13 (P)
1962—Cowboys, 41-19 (D)
    Eagles, 28-14 (P)
1963—Cowboys, 24-21 (P)
    Cowboys, 27-20 (D)
1964—Eagles, 17-14 (P)
    Eagles, 24-14 (P)
1965—Eagles, 35-24 (D)
    Cowboys, 21-19 (P)

1966—Cowboys, 56-7 (D)
Eagles, 24-23 (P)
1967—Eagles, 21-14 (P)
Cowboys, 38-17 (D)
1968—Cowboys, 45-13 (P)
Cowboys, 34-14 (D)
1969—Cowboys, 38-7 (P)
Cowboys, 49-14 (D)
1970—Cowboys, 17-7 (P)
Cowboys, 21-17 (D)
1971—Cowboys, 42-7 (P)
Cowboys, 20-7 (D)
1972—Cowboys, 28-6 (D)
Cowboys, 28-7 (P)
1973—Eagles, 30-16 (P)
Cowboys, 31-10 (D)
1974—Eagles, 13-10 (P)
Cowboys, 31-24 (D)
1975—Cowboys, 20-17 (P)
Cowboys, 27-17 (D)
1976—Cowboys, 27-7 (D)
Cowboys, 26-7 (P)
1977—Cowboys, 16-10 (P)
Cowboys, 24-14 (D)
1978—Cowboys, 14-7 (D)
Cowboys, 31-13 (P)
1979—Eagles, 31-21 (D)
Cowboys, 24-17 (P)
1980—Eagles, 17-10 (P)
Cowboys, 35-27 (D)
*Eagles, 20-7 (P)
1981—Cowboys, 17-14 (P)
Cowboys, 21-10 (D)
(Points—Cowboys 1,082, Eagles 764)
*NFC Championship
DALLAS vs. PITTSBURGH
Steelers lead series, 11-10
1960—Steelers, 35-28 (D)
1961—Cowboys, 27-24 (D)
Steelers, 37-7 (D)
1962—Steelers, 30-28 (D)
Cowboys, 42-27 (P)
1963—Steelers, 27-21 (P)
Steelers, 24-19 (D)
1964—Steelers, 23-17 (P)
Cowboys, 17-14 (D)
1965—Steelers, 22-13 (P)
Cowboys, 24-17 (D)
1966—Cowboys, 52-21 (D)
Cowboys, 20-7 (P)
1967—Cowboys, 24-21 (P)
1968—Cowboys, 28-7 (D)
1969—Cowboys, 10-7 (P)
1972—Cowboys, 17-13 (D)
1975—*Steelers, 21-17 (Miami)
1977—Steelers, 28-13 (P)
1978—**Steelers, 35-31 (Miami)
1979—Steelers, 14-3 (P)
(Points—Cowboys 458, Steelers 454)
*Super Bowl X
**Super Bowl XIII
DALLAS vs. ST. LOUIS
Cowboys lead series, 24-15-1
1960—Cardinals, 12-10 (StL)
1961—Cardinals, 31-17 (D)
Cardinals, 31-13 (StL)
1962—Cardinals, 28-24 (D)
Cardinals, 52-20 (StL)
1963—Cardinals, 34-7 (D)
Cowboys, 28-24 (StL)
1964—Cardinals, 16-6 (D)
Cowboys, 31-13 (StL)
1965—Cardinals, 20-13 (StL)
Cowboys, 27-13 (D)
1966—Tie, 10-10 (StL)
Cowboys, 31-17 (D)
1967—Cowboys, 46-21 (D)
1968—Cowboys, 27-10 (StL)
1969—Cowboys, 24-3 (D)
1970—Cardinals, 20-7 (StL)
Cardinals, 38-0 (D)
1971—Cowboys, 16-13 (StL)
Cowboys, 31-12 (D)
1972—Cowboys, 33-24 (D)
Cowboys, 27-6 (StL)
1973—Cowboys, 45-10 (D)
Cowboys, 30-3 (StL)
1974—Cardinals, 31-28 (StL)
Cowboys, 17-14 (D)
1975—Cowboys, 37-31 (D) OT
Cardinals, 31-17 (StL)
1976—Cardinals, 21-17 (StL)
Cowboys, 19-14 (D)
1977—Cowboys, 30-24 (StL)
Cardinals, 24-17 (D)
1978—Cowboys, 21-12 (D)
Cowboys, 24-21 (StL) OT
1979—Cowboys, 22-21 (StL)

Cowboys, 22-13 (D)
1980—Cowboys, 27-24 (StL)
Cowboys, 31-21 (D)
1981—Cowboys, 30-17 (D)
Cardinals, 20-17 (StL)
(Points—Cowboys 899, Cardinals 800)
DALLAS vs. SAN DIEGO
Cowboys lead series, 2-0
1972—Cowboys, 34-28 (SD)
1980—Cowboys, 42-31 (D)
(Points—Cowboys 76, Chargers 59)
DALLAS vs. SAN FRANCISCO
Cowboys lead series, 8-6-1
1960—49ers, 26-14 (D)
1963—49ers, 31-24 (SF)
1965—Cowboys, 39-31 (D)
1967—49ers, 24-16 (SF)
1969—Tie, 24-24 (D)
1970—*Cowboys, 17-10 (SF)
1971—*Cowboys, 14-3 (D)
1972—49ers, 31-10 (D)
**Cowboys, 30-28 (SF)
1974—Cowboys, 20-14 (D)
1977—Cowboys, 42-35 (SF)
1979—Cowboys, 21-13 (SF)
1980—Cowboys, 59-14 (D)
1981—49ers, 45-14 (SF)
*49ers, 28-27 (SF)
(Points—Cowboys 371, 49ers 357)
*NFC Championship
**NFC Divisional Playoff
DALLAS vs. SEATTLE
Cowboys lead series, 2-0
1976—Cowboys, 28-13 (S)
1980—Cowboys, 51-7 (D)
(Points—Cowboys 79, Seahawks 20)
DALLAS vs. TAMPA BAY
Cowboys lead series, 3-0
1977—Cowboys, 23-7 (D)
1980—Cowboys, 28-17 (D)
1981—*Cowboys, 38-0 (D)
(Points—Cowboys 89, Buccaneers 24)
*NFC Divisional Playoff
DALLAS vs. WASHINGTON
Cowboys lead series, 26-16-2
1960—Redskins, 26-14 (W)
1961—Tie, 28-28 (D)
Redskins, 34-24 (W)
1962—Tie, 35-35 (D)
Cowboys, 38-10 (W)
1963—Redskins, 21-17 (W)
Cowboys, 35-20 (D)
1964—Cowboys, 24-18 (D)
Redskins, 28-16 (W)
1965—Cowboys, 27-7 (D)
Redskins, 34-31 (W)
1966—Cowboys, 31-30 (W)
Redskins, 34-31 (D)
1967—Cowboys, 17-14 (W)
Cowboys, 27-20 (D)
1968—Cowboys, 44-24 (W)
Cowboys, 29-20 (D)
1969—Cowboys, 41-28 (W)
Cowboys, 20-10 (D)
1970—Cowboys, 45-21 (W)
Cowboys, 34-0 (D)
1971—Redskins, 20-16 (D)
Cowboys, 13-0 (W)
1972—Redskins, 24-20 (W)
Cowboys, 34-24 (D)
*Redskins, 26-3 (W)
1973—Redskins, 14-7 (W)
Cowboys, 27-7 (D)
1974—Redskins, 28-21 (W)
Cowboys, 24-23 (D)
1975—Redskins, 30-24 (W) OT
Cowboys, 31-10 (D)
1976—Cowboys, 20-7 (W)
Redskins, 27-14 (D)
1977—Cowboys, 34-16 (D)
Cowboys, 14-7 (W)
1978—Redskins, 9-5 (W)
Cowboys, 37-10 (D)
1979—Redskins, 34-20 (W)
Cowboys, 35-34 (D)
1980—Cowboys, 17-3 (W)
Cowboys, 14-10 (D)
1981—Cowboys, 26-10 (W)
Cowboys, 24-10 (D)
(Points—Cowboys 1,081, Redskins 852)
*NFC Championship
***DALLAS TEXANS vs. CHICAGO**
Series tied, 1-1
See Chicago vs. *Dallas Texans
*Extinct team

***DALLAS TEXANS vs. DETROIT**
Lions won series, 2-0
1952—Lions, 43-13
Lions, 41-6
(Points—Lions 84, Texans 19)
*Extinct team
***DALLAS TEXANS vs. GREEN BAY**
Packers won series, 2-0
1952—Packers, 24-14
Packers, 42-14
(Points—Packers 66, Texans 28)
*Extinct team
***DALLAS TEXANS vs. LOS ANGELES**
Rams won series, 2-0
1952—Rams, 42-20
Rams, 27-6
(Points—Rams 69, Texans 26)
*Extinct team
***DALLAS TEXANS vs. N.Y. GIANTS**
Giants won series, 1-0
1952—Giants, 24-6
*Extinct team
***DALLAS TEXANS vs. PHILADELPHIA**
Eagles won series, 1-0
1952—Eagles, 38-21
*Extinct team
***DALLAS TEXANS vs. SAN FRANCISCO**
49ers won series, 2-0
1952—49ers, 37-14
49ers, 48-21
(Points—49ers 85, Texans 35)
*Extinct team

DENVER vs. ATLANTA
Series tied, 2-2
See Atlanta vs. Denver
DENVER vs. BALTIMORE
Broncos lead series, 3-1;
See Baltimore vs. Denver
DENVER vs. BUFFALO
Bills lead series, 13-8-1
See Buffalo vs. Denver
DENVER vs. CHICAGO
Broncos lead series, 3-2;
See Chicago vs. Denver
DENVER vs. CINCINNATI
Series tied, 6-6;
See Cincinnati vs. Denver
DENVER vs. CLEVELAND
Broncos lead series, 6-3;
See Cleveland vs. Denver
DENVER vs. DALLAS
Cowboys lead series, 3-1;
See Dallas vs. Denver
DENVER vs. DETROIT
Series tied, 2-2
1971—Lions, 24-20 (Den)
1974—Broncos, 31-27 (Det)
1978—Lions, 17-14 (Det)
1981—Broncos, 27-21 (Den)
(Points—Broncos 92, Lions 89)
DENVER vs. GREEN BAY
Broncos lead series, 2-1
1971—Packers, 34-13 (Mil)
1975—Broncos, 23-13 (D)
1978—Broncos, 16-3 (D)
(Points—Broncos 52, Packers 50)
DENVER vs. HOUSTON
Oilers lead series, 18-8-1
1960—Oilers, 45-25 (D)
Oilers, 20-10 (H)
1961—Oilers, 55-14 (D)
Oilers, 45-14 (H)
1962—Broncos, 20-10 (D)
Oilers, 34-17 (H)
1963—Oilers, 20-14 (H)
Oilers, 33-24 (D)
1964—Oilers, 38-17 (D)
Oilers, 34-15 (H)
1965—Broncos, 28-17 (D)
Broncos, 31-21 (H)
1966—Oilers, 45-7 (D)
Broncos, 40-38 (D)
1967—Oilers, 10-6 (H)
Oilers, 20-18 (D)
1968—Oilers, 38-17 (H)
1969—Oilers, 24-21 (H)
Tie, 20-20 (D)
1970—Oilers, 31-21 (H)
1972—Broncos, 30-17 (D)
1973—Broncos, 48-20 (H)
1974—Broncos, 37-14 (D)
1976—Oilers, 17-3 (H)

1977—Broncos, 24-14 (H)
1979—*Oilers, 13-7 (H)
1980—Oilers, 20-16 (D)
(Points—Oilers 713, Broncos 544)
*AFC First Round Playoff
DENVER vs. *KANSAS CITY
Chiefs lead series, 30-14
1960—Texans, 17-14 (D)
Texans, 34-7 (Da)
1961—Texans, 19-12 (D)
Texans, 49-21 (Da)
1962—Texans, 24-3 (D)
Texans, 17-10 (Da)
1963—Chiefs, 59-7 (D)
Chiefs, 52-21 (KC)
1964—Broncos, 33-27 (D)
Chiefs, 49-39 (KC)
1965—Chiefs, 31-23 (D)
Chiefs, 45-35 (KC)
1966—Chiefs, 37-10 (D)
Chiefs, 56-10 (D)
1967—Chiefs, 52-9 (KC)
Chiefs, 38-24 (D)
1968—Chiefs, 34-2 (KC)
Chiefs, 30-7 (D)
1969—Chiefs, 26-13 (D)
Chiefs, 31-17 (KC)
1970—Broncos, 26-13 (D)
Chiefs, 16-0 (KC)
1971—Chiefs, 16-3 (D)
Chiefs, 28-10 (KC)
1972—Chiefs, 45-24 (D)
Chiefs, 24-21 (KC)
1973—Chiefs, 16-14 (KC)
Broncos, 14-10 (D)
1974—Broncos, 17-14 (KC)
Chiefs, 42-34 (D)
1975—Broncos, 37-33 (D)
Chiefs, 26-13 (KC)
1976—Broncos, 35-26 (KC)
Broncos, 17-16 (D)
1977—Broncos, 23-7 (D)
Broncos, 14-7 (KC)
1978—Broncos, 23-17 (KC) OT
Broncos, 24-3 (D)
1979—Broncos, 24-10 (KC)
Broncos, 20-3 (D)
1980—Chiefs, 23-17 (D)
Chiefs, 31-14 (KC)
1981—Chiefs, 28-14 (KC)
Broncos, 16-13 (D)
(Points—Chiefs 1,194, Broncos 771)
*Franchise in Dallas prior to 1963 and known as Texans
DENVER vs. LOS ANGELES
Rams lead series, 2-1
1972—Broncos, 16-10 (LA)
1974—Rams, 17-10 (D)
1979—Rams, 13-9 (D)
(Points—Rams 40, Broncos 35)
DENVER vs. MIAMI
Dolphins lead series, 4-2-1
1966—Dolphins, 24-7 (M)
Broncos, 17-7 (D)
1967—Dolphins, 35-21 (M)
1968—Dolphins, 21-14 (D)
1969—Dolphins, 27-24 (M)
1971—Tie, 10-10 (D)
1975—Dolphins, 14-13 (M)
(Points—Dolphins 131, Broncos 113)
DENVER vs. MINNESOTA
Vikings lead series, 2-1
1972—Vikings, 23-20 (D)
1978—Vikings, 12-9 (M) OT
1981—Broncos, 19-17 (D)
(Points—Vikings 52, Broncos 48)
DENVER vs. *NEW ENGLAND
Patriots lead series, 12-10
1960—Broncos, 13-10 (D)
Broncos, 31-24 (D)
1961—Patriots, 45-17 (B)
Patriots, 28-24 (D)
1962—Patriots, 41-16 (B)
Patriots, 33-29 (D)
1963—Broncos, 14-10 (D)
Patriots, 40-21 (B)
1964—Patriots, 39-10 (D)
Patriots, 12-7 (B)
1965—Broncos, 27-10 (B)
Patriots, 28-20 (D)
1966—Patriots, 24-10 (D)
Broncos, 17-10 (B)
1967—Broncos, 26-21 (B)
1968—Patriots, 20-17 (D)
Broncos, 35-14 (B)
1969—Broncos, 35-7 (D)
1972—Broncos, 45-21 (D)
1976—Patriots, 38-14 (NE)

1979—Broncos, 45-10 (D)
1980—Patriots, 23-14 (NE)
(Points—Patriots 508, Broncos 487)
*Franchise in Boston prior to 1971
DENVER vs. NEW ORLEANS
Broncos lead series, 3-0
1970—Broncos, 31-6 (NO)
1974—Broncos, 33-17 (D)
1979—Broncos, 10-3 (D)
(Points—Broncos 74, Saints 26)
DENVER vs. N. Y. GIANTS
Broncos lead series, 2-1
1972—Giants, 29-17 (NY)
1976—Broncos, 14-13 (D)
1980—Broncos, 14-9 (NY)
(Points—Giants 51, Broncos 45)
DENVER vs. *N. Y. JETS
Series tied, 10-10-1
1960—Titans, 28-24 (NY)
Titans, 30-27 (NY)
1961—Titans, 35-28 (NY)
Broncos, 27-10 (D)
1962—Broncos, 32-10 (NY)
Titans, 46-45 (D)
1963—Tie, 35-35 (NY)
Jets, 14-9 (D)
1964—Jets, 30-6 (NY)
Broncos, 20-16 (D)
1965—Broncos, 16-13 (D)
Jets, 45-10 (NY)
1966—Jets, 16-7 (D)
1967—Jets, 38-24 (D)
Broncos, 33-24 (NY)
1968—Broncos, 21-13 (NY)
1969—Jets, 21-19 (D)
1973—Jets, 40-28 (NY)
1976—Broncos, 46-3 (D)
1978—Jets, 31-28 (D)
1980—Broncos, 31-24 (NY)
(Points—Broncos 530, Jets 508)
*Jets known as Titans prior to 1963
DENVER vs. OAKLAND
Raiders lead series, 31-12-2
1960—Broncos, 31-14 (D)
Raiders, 48-10 (O)
1961—Raiders, 33-19 (D)
Raiders, 27-24 (O)
1962—Broncos, 44-7 (D)
Raiders, 23-6 (O)
1963—Raiders, 26-10 (O)
Raiders, 35-31 (O)
1964—Raiders, 40-7 (O)
Tie, 20-20 (D)
1965—Raiders, 28-20 (O)
Raiders, 24-13 (O)
1966—Raiders, 17-3 (D)
Raiders, 28-10 (O)
1967—Raiders, 51-0 (O)
Raiders, 21-17 (O)
1968—Raiders, 43-7 (D)
Raiders, 33-27 (O)
1969—Raiders, 24-14 (D)
Raiders, 41-10 (O)
1970—Raiders, 35-23 (O)
Raiders, 24-19 (D)
1971—Raiders, 27-16 (O)
Raiders, 21-13 (O)
1972—Broncos, 30-23 (O)
Raiders, 37-20 (O)
1973—Tie, 23-23 (D)
Raiders, 21-17 (O)
1974—Raiders, 28-17 (D)
Broncos, 20-17 (O)
1975—Raiders, 42-17 (O)
Raiders, 17-10 (D)
1976—Raiders, 17-10 (D)
Raiders, 19-6 (O)
1977—Broncos, 30-7 (O)
Raiders, 24-14 (D)
*Broncos, 20-17 (D)
1978—Broncos, 14-6 (O)
Broncos, 21-6 (D)
1979—Raiders, 27-3 (O)
Raiders, 14-10 (D)
1980—Broncos, 9-3 (D)
Raiders, 24-21 (D)
1981—Broncos, 9-7 (D)
Broncos, 17-0 (O)
(Points—Raiders 1,055, Broncos 746)
*AFC Championship
DENVER vs. PHILADELPHIA
Eagles lead series, 2-1
1971—Eagles, 17-16 (P)
1975—Broncos, 25-10 (D)
1980—Eagles, 27-6 (P)
(Points—Eagles 54, Broncos 47)
DENVER vs. PITTSBURGH
Broncos lead series, 5-4-1

1970—Broncos, 16-13 (D)
1971—Broncos, 22-10 (P)
1973—Broncos, 23-13 (P)
1974—Tie, 35-35 (D) OT
1975—Steelers, 20-9 (D)
1977—Broncos, 21-7 (D)
　　　*Broncos, 34-21 (D)
1978—Steelers, 21-17 (D)
　　　*Steelers, 33-10 (P)
1979—Steelers, 42-7 (P)
(Points—Steelers 215, Broncos 194)
*AFC Divisional Playoff
DENVER vs. ST. LOUIS
Broncos lead series, 1-0-1
1973—Tie, 17-17 (StL)
1977—Broncos, 7-0 (D)
(Points—Broncos 24, Cardinals 17)
DENVER vs. *SAN DIEGO
Chargers lead series, 23-20-1
1960—Chargers, 23-19 (D)
　　　Chargers, 41-33 (LA)
1961—Chargers, 37-0 (SD)
　　　Chargers, 19-16 (D)
1962—Broncos, 30-21 (D)
　　　Broncos, 23-20 (SD)
1963—Broncos, 50-34 (D)
　　　Chargers, 58-20 (SD)
1964—Chargers, 42-14 (D)
　　　Chargers, 31-20 (D)
1965—Chargers, 34-31 (SD)
　　　Chargers, 33-21 (D)
1966—Chargers, 24-17 (SD)
　　　Broncos, 20-17 (D)
1967—Chargers, 38-21 (D)
　　　Chargers, 24-20 (SD)
1968—Chargers, 55-24 (SD)
　　　Chargers, 47-23 (D)
1969—Broncos, 13-0 (D)
　　　Chargers, 45-24 (SD)
1970—Chargers, 24-21 (SD)
　　　Tie, 17-17 (D)
1971—Broncos, 20-16 (D)
　　　Chargers, 45-17 (SD)
1972—Chargers, 37-14 (SD)
　　　Broncos, 38-13 (D)
1973—Chargers, 30-19 (D)
　　　Broncos, 42-28 (SD)
1974—Broncos, 27-7 (D)
　　　Chargers, 17-0 (SD)
1975—Broncos, 27-17 (SD)
　　　Broncos, 13-10 (D) OT
1976—Broncos, 26-0 (D)
　　　Broncos, 17-0 (SD)
1977—Broncos, 17-14 (SD)
　　　Broncos, 17-9 (D)
1978—Broncos, 27-14 (D)
　　　Chargers, 23-0 (SD)
1979—Broncos, 7-0 (D)
　　　Chargers, 17-7 (SD)
1980—Chargers, 30-13 (D)
　　　Broncos, 20-13 (SD)
1981—Broncos, 42-24 (D)
　　　Chargers, 34-17 (SD)
(Points—Chargers 1,071, Broncos 915)
*Franchise in Los Angeles prior to 1961
DENVER vs. SAN FRANCISCO
49ers lead series, 2-1
1970—49ers, 19-14 (SF)
1973—49ers, 36-34 (D)
1979—Broncos, 38-28 (SF)
(Points—Broncos 86, 49ers 83)
DENVER vs. SEATTLE
Broncos lead series, 7-2
1977—Broncos, 24-13 (S)
1978—Broncos, 28-7 (D)
　　　Broncos, 20-17 (S) OT
1979—Broncos, 37-34 (D)
　　　Seahawks, 28-23 (S)
1980—Broncos, 36-20 (D)
　　　Broncos, 25-17 (S)
1981—Seahawks, 13-10 (S)
　　　Broncos, 23-13 (D)
(Points—Broncos 226, Seahawks 162)
DENVER vs. TAMPA BAY
Broncos lead series, 2-0
1976—Broncos, 48-13 (D)
1981—Broncos, 24-7 (TB)
(Points—Broncos 72, Buccaneers 20)
DENVER vs. WASHINGTON
Redskins lead series, 2-1
1970—Redskins, 19-3 (D)
1974—Redskins, 30-3 (W)
1980—Broncos, 20-17 (D)
(Points—Redskins 66, Broncos 26)

DETROIT vs. ATLANTA
Lions lead series, 10-3;
See Atlanta vs. Detroit
DETROIT vs. *1950 BALTIMORE
Lions won series, 1-0
See *Baltimore vs. Detroit
*Extinct team
DETROIT vs. BALTIMORE
Series tied, 16-16-2;
See Baltimore vs. Detroit
DETROIT vs. *BOSTON YANKS
Lions won series, 3-2
See *Boston Yanks vs. Detroit
*Extinct team
DETROIT vs. *BROOKLYN DODGERS
Lions won series, 11-3
See *Brooklyn Dodgers vs. Detroit
*Extinct team
DETROIT vs. BUFFALO
Series tied, 1-1-1;
See Buffalo vs. Detroit
DETROIT vs. CHICAGO
Bears lead series, 59-41-5;
See Chicago vs. Detroit
DETROIT vs. CINCINNATI
Lions lead series, 2-0;
See Cincinnati vs. Detroit
DETROIT vs. *CINCINNATI REDS
Lions won series, 2-1
See *Cincinnati Reds vs. Detroit
*Extinct team
DETROIT vs. CLEVELAND
Lions lead series, 12-2;
See Cleveland vs. Detroit
DETROIT vs. DALLAS
Cowboys lead series, 6-2;
See Dallas vs. Detroit
DETROIT vs. *DALLAS TEXANS
Lions won series, 2-0
See *Dallas Texans vs. Detroit
*Extinct team
DETROIT vs. DENVER
Series tied, 2-2;
See Denver vs. Detroit
***DETROIT vs. GREEN BAY**
Packers lead series, 54-42-7
1930—Packers, 47-13 (GB)
　　　Tie, 6-6 (P)
1932—Packers, 15-10 (GB)
　　　Spartans, 19-0 (P)
1933—Packers, 17-0 (GB)
　　　Spartans, 7-0 (P)
1934—Lions, 3-0 (GB)
　　　Packers, 3-0 (D)
1935—Packers, 13-9 (GB)
　　　Packers, 31-7 (GB)
　　　Lions, 20-10 (D)
1936—Packers, 20-18 (GB)
　　　Packers, 26-17 (D)
1937—Packers, 26-6 (GB)
　　　Packers, 14-13 (D)
1938—Lions, 17-7 (GB)
　　　Packers, 28-7 (D)
1939—Packers, 26-7 (GB)
　　　Packers, 12-7 (D)
1940—Lions, 23-14 (GB)
　　　Packers, 50-7 (D)
1941—Packers, 23-0 (GB)
　　　Packers, 24-7 (D)
1942—Packers, 38-7 (Mil)
　　　Packers, 28-7 (D)
1943—Packers, 35-14 (GB)
　　　Packers, 27-6 (D)
1944—Packers, 27-6 (GB)
　　　Packers, 14-0 (D)
1945—Packers, 57-21 (Mil)
　　　Lions, 14-3 (D)
1946—Packers, 10-7 (Mil)
　　　Packers, 9-0 (D)
1947—Packers, 34-17 (GB)
　　　Packers, 35-14 (GB)
1948—Packers, 33-21 (GB)
　　　Lions, 24-20 (D)
1949—Packers, 16-14 (GB)
　　　Lions, 21-7 (D)
1950—Packers, 45-7 (GB)
　　　Lions, 24-21 (D)
1951—Lions, 24-17 (GB)
　　　Lions, 52-35 (D)
1952—Lions, 52-17 (GB)
　　　Lions, 48-24 (D)
1953—Lions, 14-7 (GB)
　　　Lions, 34-15 (D)
1954—Lions, 21-17 (GB)
　　　Lions, 28-24 (D)
1955—Packers, 20-17 (GB)

Lions, 24-10 (D)
1956—Lions, 20-16 (GB)
　　　Packers, 24-20 (D)
1957—Lions, 24-14 (GB)
　　　Lions, 18-6 (D)
1958—Tie, 13-13 (GB)
　　　Lions, 24-14 (D)
1959—Packers, 28-10 (GB)
　　　Packers, 24-17 (D)
1960—Packers, 28-9 (GB)
　　　Lions, 23-10 (D)
1961—Lions, 17-13 (Mil)
　　　Packers, 17-9 (D)
1962—Packers, 9-7 (GB)
　　　Lions, 26-14 (D)
1963—Packers, 31-10 (Mil)
　　　Tie, 13-13 (D)
1964—Packers, 14-10 (D)
　　　Packers, 30-7 (GB)
1965—Packers, 31-21 (D)
　　　Lions, 12-7 (GB)
1966—Packers, 23-14 (GB)
　　　Packers, 31-7 (D)
1967—Tie, 17-17 (GB)
　　　Packers, 27-17 (D)
1968—Lions, 23-17 (GB)
　　　Tie, 14-14 (D)
1969—Packers, 28-17 (D)
　　　Lions, 16-10 (GB)
1970—Lions, 40-0 (D)
　　　Lions, 20-0 (GB)
1971—Lions, 31-28 (D)
　　　Tie, 14-14 (Mil)
1972—Packers, 24-23 (D)
　　　Packers, 33-7 (GB)
1973—Tie, 13-13 (GB)
　　　Lions, 34-0 (D)
1974—Packers, 21-19 (Mil)
　　　Lions, 19-17 (D)
1975—Lions, 30-16 (Mil)
　　　Lions, 13-10 (D)
1976—Packers, 24-14 (GB)
　　　Lions, 27-6 (D)
1977—Lions, 10-6 (D)
　　　Packers, 10-9 (GB)
1978—Packers, 13-7 (D)
　　　Packers, 35-14 (Mil)
1979—Packers, 24-16 (Mil)
　　　Packers, 18-13 (D)
1980—Lions, 29-7 (Mil)
　　　Lions, 24-3 (D)
1981—Lions, 31-27 (D)
　　　Packers, 31-17 (GB)
(Points—Packers 1,922, Lions 1,708)
*Franchise in Portsmouth prior to 1934 and known as the Spartans
DETROIT vs. HOUSTON
Series tied, 1-1
1971—Lions, 31-7 (H)
1975—Oilers, 24-8 (H)
(Points—Lions 39, Oilers 31)
DETROIT vs. KANSAS CITY
Series tied, 2-2
1971—Lions, 32-21 (D)
1975—Chiefs, 24-21 (KC) OT
1980—Chiefs, 20-17 (KC)
1981—Lions, 27-10 (D)
(Points—Lions 97, Chiefs 75)
DETROIT vs. *LOS ANGELES
Rams lead series, 35-33-1
1937—Lions, 28-0 (C)
　　　Lions, 27-7 (D)
1938—Rams, 21-17 (C)
　　　Lions, 6-0 (D)
1939—Lions, 15-7 (D)
　　　Rams, 14-3 (C)
1940—Lions, 6-0 (D)
　　　Rams, 24-0 (C)
1941—Lions, 17-7 (D)
　　　Lions, 14-0 (C)
1942—Lions, 14-0 (D)
　　　Rams, 27-7 (C)
1944—Rams, 20-17 (D)
　　　Lions, 26-14 (C)
1945—Rams, 28-21 (D)
1946—Rams, 35-14 (LA)
　　　Rams, 41-20 (D)
1947—Rams, 27-13 (D)
　　　Rams, 28-17 (LA)
1948—Rams, 44-7 (LA)
　　　Rams, 34-27 (D)
1949—Rams, 27-24 (LA)
　　　Rams, 21-10 (D)
1950—Rams, 30-28 (D)
　　　Rams, 65-24 (LA)
1951—Rams, 27-21 (D)
　　　Lions, 24-22 (LA)
1952—Lions, 17-14 (LA)

Lions, 24-16 (D)
**Lions, 31-21 (D)
1953—Rams, 31-19 (D)
　　　Rams, 37-24 (LA)
1954—Lions, 21-3 (D)
　　　Lions, 27-24 (LA)
1955—Rams, 17-10 (D)
　　　Rams, 24-13 (LA)
1956—Lions, 24-21 (D)
　　　Lions, 16-7 (LA)
1957—Lions, 10-7 (D)
　　　Rams, 35-17 (LA)
1958—Rams, 42-28 (D)
　　　Lions, 41-24 (LA)
1959—Lions, 17-7 (LA)
　　　Lions, 23-17 (D)
1960—Rams, 48-35 (LA)
　　　Lions, 12-10 (D)
1961—Lions, 14-13 (D)
　　　Lions, 28-10 (LA)
1962—Lions, 13-10 (D)
　　　Lions, 12-3 (LA)
1963—Lions, 23-2 (LA)
　　　Rams, 28-21 (D)
1964—Tie, 17-17 (LA)
　　　Lions, 37-17 (D)
1965—Lions, 20-0 (D)
　　　Lions, 31-7 (LA)
1966—Rams, 14-7 (D)
　　　Rams, 23-3 (LA)
1967—Rams, 31-7 (D)
1968—Rams, 10-7 (LA)
1969—Rams, 28-0 (D)
1970—Lions, 28-23 (LA)
1971—Rams, 21-13 (D)
1972—Rams, 34-17 (LA)
1974—Rams, 16-13 (LA)
1975—Rams, 20-0 (LA)
1976—Rams, 20-17 (D)
1980—Lions, 41-20 (LA)
1981—Rams, 20-13 (LA)
(Points—Rams 1,331, Lions 1,269)
*Franchise in Cleveland prior to 1946
**Conference Playoff
DETROIT vs. MIAMI
Dolphins lead series, 2-0
1973—Dolphins, 34-7 (M)
1979—Dolphins, 28-10 (D)
(Points—Dolphins 62, Lions 17)
DETROIT vs. MINNESOTA
Vikings lead series, 26-14-2
1961—Lions, 37-10 (M)
　　　Lions, 13-7 (D)
1962—Lions, 17-6 (M)
　　　Lions, 37-23 (D)
1963—Lions, 28-10 (D)
　　　Vikings, 34-31 (M)
1964—Lions, 24-20 (M)
　　　Tie, 23-23 (D)
1965—Lions, 31-29 (M)
　　　Vikings, 29-7 (D)
1966—Lions, 32-31 (M)
　　　Vikings, 28-16 (D)
1967—Tie, 10-10 (M)
　　　Lions, 14-3 (D)
1968—Vikings, 24-10 (M)
　　　Vikings, 13-6 (D)
1969—Vikings, 24-10 (M)
　　　Vikings, 27-0 (D)
1970—Vikings, 30-17 (D)
　　　Vikings, 24-20 (M)
1971—Vikings, 16-13 (D)
　　　Vikings, 29-10 (M)
1972—Vikings, 34-10 (D)
　　　Vikings, 16-14 (M)
1973—Vikings, 23-9 (D)
　　　Vikings, 28-7 (M)
1974—Vikings, 7-6 (D)
　　　Lions, 20-16 (M)
1975—Vikings, 25-19 (M)
　　　Lions, 17-10 (D)
1976—Vikings, 10-9 (D)
　　　Vikings, 31-23 (M)
1977—Vikings, 14-7 (M)
　　　Vikings, 30-21 (D)
1978—Vikings, 17-7 (M)
　　　Lions, 45-14 (D)
1979—Vikings, 13-10 (D)
　　　Vikings, 14-7 (M)
1980—Lions, 27-7 (D)
　　　Vikings, 34-0 (M)
1981—Vikings, 26-24 (M)
　　　Lions, 45-7 (D)
(Points—Vikings 826, Lions 733)
DETROIT vs. NEW ENGLAND
Lions lead series, 2-1
1971—Lions, 34-7 (NE)
1976—Lions, 30-10 (D)

1979—Patriots, 24-17 (NE)
(Points—Lions 81, Patriots 41)
DETROIT vs. NEW ORLEANS
Series tied, 4-4-1
1968—Tie, 20-20 (D)
1970—Saints, 19-17 (NO)
1972—Lions, 27-14 (D)
1973—Saints, 20-13 (NO)
1974—Lions, 19-14 (D)
1976—Saints, 17-16 (NO)
1977—Lions, 23-19 (D)
1979—Saints, 17-7 (NO)
1980—Lions, 24-13 (D)
(Points—Lions 166, Saints 153)
DETROIT vs. *N.Y. BULLDOGS
Lions won series, 1-0
1949—Lions, 28-27 (D)
*Extinct team
***DETROIT vs. N. Y. GIANTS**
Lions lead series, 17-10-1
1930—Giants, 19-6 (P)
1931—Spartans, 14-6 (P)
　　　Giants, 14-0 (NY)
1932—Spartans, 7-0 (P)
　　　Spartans, 6-0 (NY)
1933—Spartans, 17-7 (P)
　　　Giants, 13-10 (NY)
1934—Lions, 9-0 (D)
1935—**Lions, 26-7 (D)
1936—Giants, 14-7 (NY)
　　　Lions, 38-0 (D)
1937—Lions, 17-0 (NY)
1939—Lions, 18-14 (D)
1941—Giants, 20-13 (NY)
1943—Tie, 0-0 (D)
1945—Giants, 35-14 (NY)
1947—Giants, 35-7 (D)
1949—Lions, 45-21 (NY)
1953—Lions, 27-16 (NY)
1955—Giants, 24-19 (D)
1958—Giants, 19-17 (D)
1962—Giants, 17-14 (NY)
1964—Lions, 26-3 (D)
1967—Lions, 30-7 (NY)
1969—Lions, 24-0 (D)
1972—Lions, 30-16 (D)
1974—Lions, 20-19 (D)
1976—Lions, 24-10 (NY)
(Points—Lions 499, Giants 322)
*Franchise in Portsmouth prior to 1934 and known as the Spartans
**NFL Championship
DETROIT vs. N. Y. JETS
Series tied, 1-1
1972—Lions, 37-20 (D)
1979—Jets, 31-10 (NY)
(Points—Jets 51, Lions 47)
DETROIT vs. *N.Y. YANKS
Lions won series, 2-1-1
1950—Yanks, 44-21
　　　Lions, 49-14
1951—Lions, 37-10
　　　Tie, 24-24
(Points—Lions 131, Yanks 92)
*Extinct team
DETROIT vs. OAKLAND
Series tied, 2-2
1970—Lions, 28-14 (D)
1974—Raiders, 35-13 (O)
1978—Raiders, 29-17 (O)
1981—Lions, 16-0 (D)
(Points—Raiders 78, Lions 74)
***DETROIT vs. PHILADELPHIA**
Lions lead series, 11-9-1
1933—Spartans, 25-0 (P)
1934—Lions, 10-0 (D)
1935—Lions, 35-0 (D)
1936—Lions, 23-0 (P)
1938—Eagles, 21-7 (D)
1940—Lions, 21-0 (P)
1941—Lions, 21-17 (D)
1945—Lions, 28-24 (D)
1948—Eagles, 45-21 (P)
1949—Eagles, 22-14 (D)
1951—Lions, 28-10 (P)
1954—Tie, 13-13 (D)
1957—Lions, 27-16 (P)
1960—Eagles, 28-10 (P)
1961—Eagles, 27-24 (D)
1965—Lions, 35-28 (P)
1968—Eagles, 12-0 (D)
1971—Eagles, 23-20 (D)
1974—Eagles, 28-17 (P)
1977—Lions, 17-13 (D)
1979—Eagles, 44-7 (P)
(Points—Lions 403, Eagles 371)
*Franchise in Portsmouth prior to 1934 and known as the Spartans

DETROIT vs. *PITTSBURGH
Lions lead series, 12-8-1
1934—Lions, 40-7 (D)
1936—Lions, 28-3 (D)
1937—Lions, 7-3 (D)
1938—Lions, 16-7 (D)
1940—Pirates, 10-7 (D)
1942—Steelers, 35-7 (D)
1946—Lions, 17-7 (D)
1947—Steelers, 17-10 (P)
1948—Lions, 17-14 (D)
1949—Steelers, 14-7 (P)
1950—Lions, 10-7 (D)
1952—Lions, 31-6 (P)
1953—Lions, 38-21 (D)
1955—Lions, 31-28 (D)
1956—Lions, 45-7 (D)
1959—Tie, 10-10 (P)
1962—Lions, 45-7 (D)
1966—Steelers, 17-3 (P)
1967—Steelers, 24-14 (D)
1969—Steelers, 16-13 (P)
1973—Steelers, 24-10 (D)
(Points—Lions 406, Steelers 284)
Steelers known as Pirates prior to 1941
*DETROIT vs. **ST. LOUIS
Lions lead series, 25-15-5
1930—Tie, 0-0 (P)
    Cardinals, 23-0 (C)
1931—Cardinals, 20-19 (C)
1932—Tie, 7-7 (P)
1933—Spartans, 7-6 (P)
1934—Lions, 6-0 (D)
    Lions, 17-13 (C)
1935—Tie, 10-10 (D)
    Lions, 7-6 (C)
1936—Lions, 39-0 (D)
    Lions, 14-7 (C)
1937—Lions, 16-7 (D)
    Lions, 16-7 (D)
1938—Lions, 10-0 (D)
    Lions, 7-3 (C)
1939—Lions, 21-3 (D)
    Lions, 17-3 (C)
1940—Tie, 0-0 (Buffalo)
    Lions, 43-14 (C)
1941—Tie, 14-14 (D)
    Lions, 21-3 (D)
1942—Cardinals, 13-0 (C)
    Cardinals, 7-0 (D)
1943—Lions, 35-17 (D)
    Lions, 7-0 (C)
1945—Lions, 10-0 (C)
    Lions, 26-0 (D)
1946—Cardinals, 34-14 (C)
    Cardinals, 36-14 (D)
1947—Cardinals, 45-21 (C)
    Lions, 17-7 (D)
1948—Cardinals, 56-20 (C)
    Cardinals, 28-14 (D)
1949—Lions, 24-7 (C)
    Cardinals, 42-19 (D)
1959—Lions, 45-21 (D)
1961—Lions, 45-14 (StL)
1967—Cardinals, 38-28 (StL)
1969—Lions, 20-0 (D)
1970—Lions, 16-3 (D)
1973—Lions, 20-16 (StL)
1975—Cardinals, 24-13 (D)
1978—Cardinals, 21-14 (StL)
1980—Lions, 20-7 (D)
    Cardinals, 24-23 (StL)
(Points—Lions 746, Cardinals 626)
Franchise in Portsmouth prior to 1934 and known as the Spartans
**Franchise in Chicago prior to 1960*
DETROIT vs. *ST. LOUIS GUNNERS
Lions won series, 1-0
1934—Lions, 40-7
Extinct team
DETROIT vs. SAN DIEGO
Lions lead series, 3-1
1972—Lions, 34-20 (D)
1977—Lions, 20-0 (D)
1978—Lions, 31-14 (D)
1981—Chargers, 28-23 (SD)
(Points—Lions 108, Chargers 62)
DETROIT vs. SAN FRANCISCO
Lions lead series, 25-21-1
1950—Lions, 24-7 (D)
    49ers, 28-27 (SF)
1951—49ers, 20-10 (D)
    49ers, 21-17 (SF)
1952—49ers, 17-3 (SF)
    49ers, 28-0 (D)
1953—Lions, 24-21 (D)

Lions, 14-10 (SF)
1954—49ers, 37-31 (SF)
    Lions, 48-7 (D)
1955—49ers, 27-24 (D)
    49ers, 38-21 (SF)
1956—Lions, 20-17 (D)
    Lions, 17-13 (SF)
1957—49ers, 35-31 (SF)
    Lions, 31-10 (D)
    *Lions, 31-27 (SF)
1958—49ers, 24-21 (SF)
    Lions, 35-21 (D)
1959—49ers, 34-13 (D)
    49ers, 33-7 (SF)
1960—49ers, 14-10 (D)
    Lions, 24-0 (SF)
1961—49ers, 49-0 (D)
    Tie, 20-20 (SF)
1962—Lions, 45-24 (D)
    Lions, 38-24 (SF)
1963—Lions, 26-3 (D)
    Lions, 45-7 (SF)
1964—Lions, 26-17 (SF)
    Lions, 24-7 (D)
1965—49ers, 27-21 (D)
    49ers, 17-14 (SF)
1966—49ers, 27-24 (SF)
    49ers, 41-14 (D)
1967—Lions, 45-3 (SF)
1968—49ers, 14-7 (D)
1969—Lions, 26-14 (SF)
1970—Lions, 28-7 (D)
1971—49ers, 31-27 (SF)
1973—Lions, 30-20 (D)
1974—Lions, 17-13 (D)
1975—Lions, 28-17 (SF)
1977—49ers, 28-7 (SF)
1978—Lions, 33-14 (D)
1980—Lions, 17-13 (D)
1981—Lions, 24-17 (D)
(Points—Lions 1,069, 49ers 943)
Conference Playoff
DETROIT vs. SEATTLE
Series tied, 1-1
1976—Lions, 41-14 (S)
1978—Seahawks, 28-16 (S)
(Points—Lions 57, Seahawks 42)
DETROIT vs. TAMPA BAY
Lions lead series, 5-4
1977—Lions, 16-7 (D)
1978—Lions, 15-7 (TB)
    Lions, 34-23 (D)
1979—Buccaneers, 31-16 (TB)
    Buccaneers, 16-14 (D)
1980—Lions, 24-10 (TB)
    Lions, 27-14 (D)
1981—Buccaneers, 28-10 (TB)
    Buccaneers, 20-17 (D)
(Points—Lions 173, Buccaneers 156)
*DETROIT vs. **WASHINGTON
Redskins lead series, 15-8
1932—Spartans, 10-0 (P)
1933—Spartans, 13-0 (B)
1934—Lions, 24-0 (D)
1935—Lions, 17-7 (B)
    Lions, 14-0 (D)
1938—Redskins, 7-5 (D)
1939—Redskins, 31-7 (W)
1940—Redskins, 20-14 (D)
1942—Redskins, 15-3 (D)
1943—Redskins, 42-20 (W)
1946—Redskins, 17-16 (W)
1947—Lions, 38-21 (D)
1948—Redskins, 46-21 (W)
1951—Lions, 35-17 (D)
1956—Redskins, 18-17 (D)
1965—Lions, 14-10 (D)
1968—Redskins, 14-3 (W)
1970—Redskins, 31-10 (W)
1973—Redskins, 20-0 (D)
1976—Redskins, 20-7 (W)
1978—Redskins, 21-19 (D)
1979—Redskins, 27-24 (D)
1981—Redskins, 33-31 (W)
(Points—Redskins 417, Lions 362)
Franchise in Portsmouth prior to 1934 and known as the Spartans.
**Franchise in Boston prior to 1937*

GREEN BAY vs. ATLANTA
Packers lead series, 7-5;
See Atlanta vs. Green Bay
GREEN BAY vs. BALTIMORE
Packers lead series, 18-16;
See Baltimore vs. Green Bay
GREEN BAY vs. *1950 BALTIMORE
Colts won series, 1-0

See *Baltimore vs. Green Bay
Extinct team
GREEN BAY vs. *BOSTON YANKS
Packers won series, 2-0
See *Boston Yanks vs. Green Bay
Extinct team
GREEN BAY vs. *BROOKLYN DODGERS
Packers won series, 8-0
See *Brooklyn Dodgers vs. Green Bay
Extinct team
GREEN BAY vs. BUFFALO
Bills lead series, 2-0;
See Buffalo vs. Green Bay
GREEN BAY vs. CHICAGO
Bears lead series, 66-53-6;
See Chicago vs. Green Bay
GREEN BAY vs. CINCINNATI
Series tied, 2-2;
See Cincinnati vs. Green Bay
GREEN BAY vs. *CINCINNATI REDS
Packers won series, 1-0
See *Cincinnati Reds vs. Green Bay
Extinct Team
GREEN BAY vs. CLEVELAND
Packers lead series, 6-5;
See Cleveland vs. Green Bay
GREEN BAY vs. DALLAS
Packers lead series, 8-3;
See Dallas vs. Green Bay
GREEN BAY vs. *DALLAS TEXANS
Packers won series, 2-0
See *Dallas Texans vs. Green Bay
Extinct team
GREEN BAY vs. DENVER
Broncos lead series, 2-1;
See Denver vs. Green Bay
GREEN BAY vs. DETROIT
Packers lead series, 54-42-7;
See Detroit vs. Green Bay
GREEN BAY vs. HOUSTON
Oilers lead series, 2-1
1972—Packers, 23-10 (H)
1977—Oilers, 16-10 (GB)
1980—Oilers, 22-3 (GB)
(Points—Oilers 48, Packers 36)
GREEN BAY vs. KANSAS CITY
Series tied, 1-1-1
1966—*Packers, 35-10 (Los Angeles)
1973—Tie, 10-10 (Mil)
1977—Chiefs, 20-10 (KC)
(Points—Packers 55, Chiefs 40)
Super Bowl I
GREEN BAY vs. *LOS ANGELES
Rams lead series, 38-31-2
1937—Packers, 35-10 (C)
    Packers, 35-7 (GB)
1938—Packers, 26-17 (GB)
    Packers, 28-7 (C)
1939—Rams, 27-24 (GB)
    Packers, 7-6 (C)
1940—Packers, 31-14 (GB)
    Tie, 13-13 (C)
1941—Packers, 24-7 (Mil)
    Packers, 17-14 (C)
1942—Packers, 45-28 (GB)
    Packers, 30-12 (C)
1944—Packers, 30-21 (GB)
    Packers, 42-7 (C)
1945—Rams, 27-14 (GB)
    Rams, 20-7 (C)
1946—Rams, 21-17 (Mil)
    Rams, 38-17 (LA)
1947—Packers, 17-14 (Mil)
    Packers, 30-10 (LA)
1948—Packers, 16-0 (GB)
    Rams, 24-10 (LA)
1949—Rams, 48-7 (GB)
    Rams, 35-7 (LA)
1950—Rams, 45-14 (Mil)
    Rams, 51-14 (LA)
1951—Rams, 28-0 (Mil)
    Rams, 42-14 (LA)
1952—Rams, 30-28 (Mil)
    Rams, 45-27 (LA)
1953—Rams, 38-20 (Mil)
    Rams, 33-17 (LA)
1954—Packers, 35-17 (Mil)
    Rams, 35-27 (LA)
1955—Packers, 30-28 (Mil)
    Rams, 31-17 (LA)
1956—Packers, 42-17 (Mil)
    Rams, 49-21 (LA)
1957—Rams, 31-27 (Mil)
    Rams, 42-17 (LA)
1958—Rams, 20-7 (GB)
    Rams, 34-20 (LA)

1959—Rams, 45-6 (Mil)
    Packers, 38-20 (LA)
1960—Rams, 33-31 (Mil)
    Packers, 35-21 (LA)
1961—Packers, 35-17 (GB)
    Packers, 24-17 (LA)
1962—Packers, 41-10 (Mil)
    Packers, 20-17 (LA)
1963—Packers, 42-10 (GB)
    Packers, 31-14 (LA)
1964—Rams, 27-17 (Mil)
    Tie, 24-24 (LA)
1965—Packers, 6-3 (Mil)
    Rams, 21-10 (LA)
1966—Packers, 24-13 (GB)
    Packers, 27-23 (LA)
1967—Rams, 27-24 (LA)
    **Packers, 28-7 (Mil)
1968—Rams, 16-14 (Mil)
1969—Rams, 34-21 (LA)
1970—Rams, 31-21 (GB)
1971—Rams, 30-13 (LA)
1973—Rams, 24-7 (LA)
1974—Packers, 17-6 (Mil)
1975—Rams, 22-5 (LA)
1977—Rams, 24-6 (Mil)
1978—Rams, 31-14 (LA)
1980—Rams, 51-21 (LA)
1981—Rams, 35-23 (LA)
(Points—Rams 1,696, Packers 1,531)
Franchise in Cleveland prior to 1946
**Conference Championship*
GREEN BAY vs. MIAMI
Dolphins lead series, 3-0
1971—Dolphins, 27-6 (Mia)
1975—Dolphins, 31-7 (GB)
1979—Dolphins, 27-7 (Mia)
(Points—Dolphins 85, Packers 20)
GREEN BAY vs. MINNESOTA
Vikings lead series, 23-18-1
1961—Packers, 33-7 (Minn)
    Packers, 28-10 (Mil)
1962—Packers, 34-7 (GB)
    Packers, 48-21 (Minn)
1963—Packers, 37-28 (Minn)
    Packers, 28-7 (GB)
1964—Vikings, 24-23 (GB)
    Packers, 42-13 (Minn)
1965—Packers, 38-13 (Minn)
    Packers, 24-19 (GB)
1966—Vikings, 20-17 (GB)
    Packers, 28-16 (Minn)
1967—Vikings, 10-7 (Mil)
    Packers, 30-27 (Minn)
1968—Vikings, 26-13 (Mil)
    Vikings, 14-10 (Minn)
1969—Vikings, 19-7 (Mil)
    Vikings, 9-7 (Mil)
1970—Packers, 13-10 (Mil)
    Vikings, 10-3 (Minn)
1971—Vikings, 24-13 (Mil)
    Vikings, 3-0 (Minn)
1972—Vikings, 27-13 (GB)
    Packers, 23-7 (Mil)
1973—Vikings, 11-3 (Minn)
    Vikings, 31-7 (GB)
1974—Vikings, 32-17 (Mil)
    Packers, 19-7 (Minn)
1975—Vikings, 28-17 (GB)
    Vikings, 24-3 (Minn)
1976—Vikings, 17-10 (Mil)
    Vikings, 20-9 (Minn)
1977—Vikings, 19-7 (Minn)
    Vikings, 13-6 (GB)
1978—Vikings, 21-7 (Minn)
    Tie, 10-10 (GB) OT
1979—Vikings, 27-21 (Minn) OT
    Packers, 19-7 (GB)
1980—Packers, 16-3 (GB)
    Vikings, 25-13 (Minn)
1981—Vikings, 30-13 (Mil)
    Packers, 35-23 (Minn)
(Points—Packers 763, Vikings 707)
GREEN BAY vs. NEW ENGLAND
Series tied, 1-1
1973—Patriots, 33-24 (NE)
1979—Packers, 27-14 (GB)
(Points—Packers 51, Patriots 47)
GREEN BAY vs. NEW ORLEANS
Packers lead series, 8-2
1968—Packers, 29-7 (GB)
1971—Saints, 29-21 (Mil)
1972—Packers, 30-20 (NO)
1973—Packers, 30-10 (GB)
1975—Saints, 20-19 (NO)
1976—Packers, 32-27 (GB)
1977—Packers, 24-20 (NO)
1978—Packers, 28-17 (Mil)

1979—Packers, 28-19 (Mil)
1981—Packers, 35-7 (NO)
(Points—Packers 276, Saints 176)
GREEN BAY vs. *N.Y. BULLDOGS
Packers won series, 1-0
1949—Packers, 19-0
Extinct team
GREEN BAY vs. N.Y. GIANTS
Packers lead series, 23-17-2
1928—Giants, 6-0 (GB)
    Packers, 7-0 (NY)
1929—Packers, 20-6 (NY)
1930—Packers, 14-7 (GB)
    Giants, 13-6 (NY)
1931—Packers, 27-7 (GB)
    Packers, 14-10 (NY)
1932—Packers, 13-0 (GB)
    Giants, 6-0 (NY)
1933—Giants, 10-7 (GB)
    Giants, 17-6 (NY)
1934—Packers, 20-6 (Mil)
    Giants, 17-3 (NY)
1935—Packers, 16-7 (GB)
1936—Packers, 26-14 (NY)
1937—Packers, 10-0 (NY)
1938—Packers, 15-3 (NY)
    *Giants, 23-17 (NY)
1939—*Packers, 27-0 (Mil)
1940—Packers, 7-3 (NY)
1942—Tie, 21-21 (NY)
1943—Packers, 35-21 (NY)
1944—*Giants, 24-0 (NY)
    *Packers, 14-7 (NY)
1945—Packers, 23-14 (NY)
1947—Tie, 24-24 (NY)
1948—Giants, 49-3 (Mil)
1949—Giants, 30-10 (GB)
1952—Packers, 17-3 (NY)
1957—Giants, 31-17 (GB)
1959—Giants, 20-3 (NY)
1961—Packers, 20-17 (Mil)
    *Packers, 37-0 (GB)
1962—*Packers, 16-7 (NY)
1967—Packers, 48-21 (NY)
1969—Packers, 20-10 (Mil)
1971—Giants, 42-40 (GB)
1973—Packers, 16-14 (New Haven)
1975—Packers, 40-14 (Mil)
1980—Giants, 27-21 (NY)
1981—Packers, 27-14 (NY)
    Packers, 26-24 (Mil)
(Points—Packers 707, Giants 615)
NFL Championship
GREEN BAY vs. N.Y. JETS
Jets lead series, 2-1
1973—Packers, 23-7 (Mil)
1979—Jets, 27-22 (GB)
1981—Jets, 28-3 (NY)
(Points—Jets 62, Packers 48)
GREEN BAY vs. *N.Y. YANKS
Yanks won series, 3-1
1950—Yanks, 44-31
    Yanks, 35-17
1951—Packers, 29-27
    Yanks, 31-28
(Points—Yanks 137, Packers 105)
Extinct team
GREEN BAY vs. OAKLAND
Raiders lead series, 3-1
1967—*Packers, 33-14 (Miami)
1972—Raiders, 20-14 (GB)
1976—Raiders, 18-14 (O)
1978—Raiders, 28-3 (GB)
(Points—Raiders 80, Packers 64)
Super Bowl II
GREEN BAY vs. PHILADELPHIA
Packers lead series, 17-5
1933—Packers, 35-9 (GB)
    Packers, 10-0 (P)
1934—Packers, 19-6 (GB)
1935—Packers, 13-6 (P)
1937—Packers, 37-7 (Mil)
1939—Packers, 23-16 (P)
1940—Packers, 27-20 (GB)
1942—Packers, 7-0 (P)
1946—Packers, 19-7 (P)
1947—Eagles, 28-14 (P)
1951—Packers, 37-24 (GB)
1952—Packers, 12-10 (Mil)
1954—Packers, 37-14 (P)
1958—Packers, 38-35 (GB)
1960—*Eagles, 17-13 (P)
1962—Packers, 49-0 (P)
1968—Packers, 30-13 (GB)
1970—Packers, 30-17 (Mil)
1974—Eagles, 36-14 (P)
1976—Packers, 28-13 (GB)
1978—Eagles, 10-3 (P)

1979—Eagles, 21-10 (GB)
(Points—Packers 505, Eagles 309)
*NFL Championship
GREEN BAY vs. *PITTSBURGH
Packers lead series, 16-9
1933—Packers, 47-0 (GB)
1935—Packers, 27-0 (GB)
　　　　Packers, 34-14 (P)
1936—Packers, 42-10 (Mil)
1938—Packers, 20-0 (GB)
1940—Packers, 24-3 (Mil)
1941—Packers, 54-7 (P)
1942—Packers, 24-21 (Mil)
1946—Packers, 17-7 (GB)
1947—Steelers, 18-17 (Mil)
1948—Steelers, 38-7 (P)
1949—Steelers, 30-7 (Mil)
1951—Packers, 35-33 (Mil)
　　　　Steelers, 28-7 (P)
1953—Steelers, 31-14 (P)
1954—Steelers, 21-20 (GB)
1957—Packers, 27-10 (P)
1960—Packers, 19-13 (P)
1963—Packers, 33-14 (Mil)
1965—Packers, 41-9 (P)
1967—Steelers, 24-17 (GB)
1969—Packers, 38-34 (P)
1970—Packers, 20-12 (P)
1975—Steelers, 16-13 (Mil)
1980—Packers, 22-20 (P)
(Points—Packers 624, Steelers 415)
*Steelers known as Pirates prior to 1941
GREEN BAY vs. *ST. LOUIS
Packers lead series, 36-20-4
1921—Tie, 3-3 (C)
1922—Cardinals, 16-3 (C)
1924—Cardinals, 3-0 (C)
1925—Cardinals, 9-6 (C)
1926—Cardinals, 13-7 (GB)
　　　　Packers, 3-0 (C)
1927—Packers, 13-0 (GB)
　　　　Tie, 6-6 (C)
1928—Packers, 20-0 (GB)
1929—Packers, 9-2 (GB)
　　　　Packers, 7-6 (C)
　　　　Packers, 12-0 (C)
1930—Packers, 14-0 (GB)
　　　　Cardinals, 13-6 (C)
1931—Packers, 26-7 (GB)
　　　　Cardinals, 21-13 (C)
1932—Packers, 15-7 (GB)
　　　　Packers, 19-9 (C)
1933—Packers, 14-6 (C)
1934—Packers, 15-0 (GB)
　　　　Cardinals, 9-0 (Mil)
　　　　Cardinals, 6-0 (C)
1935—Cardinals, 7-6 (GB)
　　　　Packers, 3-0 (Mil)
　　　　Cardinals, 9-7 (C)
1936—Packers, 10-7 (GB)
　　　　Packers, 24-0 (Mil)
　　　　Tie, 0-0 (C)
1937—Cardinals, 14-7 (GB)
　　　　Packers, 34-13 (Mil)
1938—Packers, 28-7 (Mil)
　　　　Packers, 24-22 (Buffalo)
1939—Packers, 14-10 (GB)
　　　　Packers, 27-20 (Mil)
1940—Packers, 31-6 (Mil)
　　　　Packers, 28-7 (C)
1941—Packers, 14-13 (Mil)
　　　　Packers, 17-9 (C)
1942—Packers, 17-13 (C)
　　　　Packers, 55-24 (GB)
1943—Packers, 28-7 (C)
　　　　Packers, 35-14 (Mil)
1945—Packers, 33-14 (GB)
1946—Packers, 19-7 (C)
　　　　Cardinals, 24-6 (GB)
1947—Cardinals, 14-10 (GB)
　　　　Cardinals, 21-20 (C)
1948—Cardinals, 17-7 (Mil)
　　　　Cardinals, 42-7 (C)
1949—Cardinals, 39-17 (Mil)
　　　　Cardinals, 41-21 (C)
1955—Packers, 31-14 (GB)
1956—Packers, 24-21 (C)
1962—Packers, 17-0 (Mil)
1963—Packers, 30-7 (StL)
1967—Packers, 31-23 (StL)
1969—Packers, 45-28 (GB)
1971—Tie, 16-16 (StL)
1973—Packers, 25-21 (GB)
1976—Cardinals, 29-0 (StL)
(Points—Packers 976, Cardinals 719)
*Franchise in Chicago prior to 1960

GREEN BAY vs. *ST. LOUIS GUNNERS
Packers won series, 1-0
1934—Packers, 21-14
*Extinct team
GREEN BAY vs. SAN DIEGO
Packers lead series, 3-0
1970—Packers, 22-20 (SD)
1974—Packers, 34-0 (GB)
1978—Packers, 24-3 (SD)
(Points—Packers 80, Chargers 23)
GREEN BAY vs. SAN FRANCISCO
49ers lead series, 22-20-1
1950—Packers, 25-21 (GB)
　　　　49ers, 30-14 (SF)
1951—49ers, 31-19 (SF)
1952—49ers, 24-14 (SF)
1953—49ers, 37-7 (Mil)
　　　　49ers, 48-14 (SF)
1954—49ers, 23-17 (Mil)
　　　　49ers, 35-0 (SF)
1955—Packers, 27-21 (Mil)
　　　　Packers, 28-7 (SF)
1956—49ers, 17-16 (GB)
　　　　49ers, 38-20 (SF)
1957—49ers, 24-14 (Mil)
　　　　49ers, 27-20 (SF)
1958—49ers, 33-12 (Mil)
　　　　49ers, 48-21 (SF)
1959—Packers, 21-20 (GB)
　　　　Packers, 36-14 (SF)
1960—Packers, 41-14 (Mil)
　　　　Packers, 13-0 (SF)
1961—Packers, 30-10 (Mil)
　　　　49ers, 22-21 (SF)
1962—Packers, 31-13 (Mil)
　　　　Packers, 31-21 (SF)
1963—Packers, 28-10 (Mil)
　　　　Packers 21-17 (SF)
1964—Packers, 24-14 (Mil)
　　　　49ers, 24-14 (SF)
1965—Packers, 27-10 (GB)
　　　　Tie, 24-24 (SF)
1966—49ers, 21-20 (SF)
　　　　Packers, 20-7 (Mil)
1967—49ers, 13-0 (GB)
1968—49ers, 27-20 (SF)
1969—49ers, 14-7 (Mil)
1970—49ers, 26-10 (SF)
1972—Packers, 34-24 (Mil)
1973—49ers, 20-6 (SF)
1974—49ers, 7-6 (SF)
1976—Packers, 26-14 (GB)
1977—Packers, 16-14 (Mil)
1980—Packers, 23-16 (Mil)
1981—49ers, 13-3 (Mil)
(Points—49ers 885, Packers 829)
GREEN BAY vs. SEATTLE
Packers lead series, 3-0
1976—Packers, 27-20 (Mil)
1978—Packers, 45-28 (Mil)
1981—Packers, 34-24 (GB)
(Points—Packers 106, Seahawks 72)
GREEN BAY vs. TAMPA BAY
Buccaneers lead series, 5-3-1
1977—Packers, 13-0 (TB)
1978—Packers, 9-7 (GB)
　　　　Packers, 17-7 (TB)
1979—Buccaneers, 21-10 (GB)
　　　　Buccaneers, 21-3 (TB)
1980—Tie, 14-14 (TB) OT
　　　　Buccaneers, 20-17 (Mil)
1981—Buccaneers, 21-10 (GB)
　　　　Buccaneers, 37-3 (TB)
(Points—Buccaneers 148, Packers 96)
GREEN BAY vs. *WASHINGTON
Packers lead series, 13-11-1
1932—Packers, 21-0 (B)
1933—Tie, 7-7 (GB)
　　　　Redskins, 20-7 (B)
1934—Packers, 10-0 (B)
1936—Packers, 31-2 (GB)
　　　　Packers, 7-3 (B)
　　　　**Packers, 21-6 (New York)
1937—Redskins, 14-6 (W)
1939—Packers, 24-14 (Mil)
1941—Packers, 22-17 (W)
1943—Redskins, 33-7 (Mil)
1946—Packers, 20-7 (W)
1947—Packers, 27-10 (Mil)
1948—Redskins, 23-7 (Mil)
1949—Redskins, 30-0 (W)
1950—Packers, 35-21 (Mil)
1952—Packers, 35-20 (Mil)
1958—Redskins, 37-21 (W)
1959—Packers, 21-0 (GB)
1968—Packers, 27-7 (W)

1972—Redskins, 21-16 (W)
　　　　***Redskins, 16-3 (W)
1974—Redskins, 17-6 (GB)
1977—Redskins, 10-9 (W)
1979—Redskins, 38-21 (W)
(Points—Packers 411, Redskins 373)
*Franchise in Boston prior to 1937 and known as Braves prior to 1933
**NFL Championship
***NFC Divisional Playoff

HOUSTON vs. ATLANTA
Falcons lead series, 3-1;
See Atlanta vs. Houston
HOUSTON vs. BALTIMORE
Oilers lead series, 3-2;
See Baltimore vs. Houston
HOUSTON vs. BUFFALO
Oilers lead series, 17-7;
See Buffalo vs. Houston
HOUSTON vs. CHICAGO
Oilers lead series, 2-1;
See Chicago vs. Houston
HOUSTON vs. CINCINNATI
Bengals lead series, 13-12-1;
See Cincinnati vs. Houston
HOUSTON vs. CLEVELAND
Browns lead series, 14-10;
See Cleveland vs. Houston
HOUSTON vs. DALLAS
Cowboys lead series, 2-1;
See Dallas vs. Houston
HOUSTON vs. DENVER
Oilers lead series, 18-8-1;
See Denver vs. Houston
HOUSTON vs. DETROIT
Series tied, 1-1;
See Detroit vs. Houston
HOUSTON vs. GREEN BAY
Oilers lead series, 2-1;
See Green Bay vs. Houston
HOUSTON vs. *KANSAS CITY
Chiefs lead series, 19-10
1960—Oilers, 20-10 (H)
　　　　Texans, 24-0 (D)
1961—Texans, 26-21 (D)
　　　　Oilers, 38-7 (H)
1962—Texans, 31-7 (H)
　　　　Oilers, 14-6 (D)
　　　　**Texans, 20-17 (H) OT
1963—Chiefs, 28-7 (KC)
　　　　Oilers, 28-7 (H)
1964—Chiefs, 28-7 (KC)
　　　　Chiefs, 28-19 (H)
1965—Chiefs, 52-21 (KC)
　　　　Oilers, 38-36 (H)
1966—Chiefs, 48-23 (KC)
　　　　Chiefs, 24-19 (H)
1967—Chiefs, 25-20 (H)
　　　　Oilers, 24-19 (KC)
1968—Chiefs, 24-10 (H)
　　　　Chiefs, 24-10 (KC)
1969—Chiefs, 24-0 (KC)
1970—Chiefs, 24-9 (KC)
1971—Oilers, 20-16 (H)
1973—Chiefs, 38-14 (KC)
1974—Chiefs, 17-7 (H)
1975—Oilers, 17-13 (KC)
1977—Oilers, 34-20 (H)
1978—Oilers, 20-17 (KC)
1979—Oilers, 20-6 (H)
1980—Chiefs, 21-20 (KC)
1981—Chiefs, 23-10 (KC)
(Points—Chiefs 668, Oilers 502)
*Franchise in Dallas prior to 1963 and known as Texans
**AFL Championship
HOUSTON vs. LOS ANGELES
Rams lead series, 2-1
1973—Rams, 31-26 (H)
1978—Rams, 10-6 (H)
1981—Oilers, 27-20 (LA)
(Points—Rams 61, Oilers 59)
HOUSTON vs. MIAMI
Oilers lead series, 9-7
1966—Dolphins, 20-13 (H)
　　　　Dolphins, 29-28 (M)
1967—Oilers, 17-14 (H)
　　　　Oilers, 41-10 (M)
1968—Oilers, 24-10 (M)
　　　　Dolphins, 24-7 (H)
1969—Oilers, 22-10 (H)
　　　　Oilers, 32-7 (M)
1970—Dolphins, 20-10 (H)
1972—Dolphins, 34-13 (M)
1975—Oilers, 20-19 (H)
1977—Dolphins, 27-7 (M)
1978—Oilers, 35-30 (H)
　　　　*Oilers, 17-9 (M)

1979—Oilers, 9-6 (M)
1981—Dolphins, 16-10 (H)
(Points—Oilers 305, Dolphins 285)
*AFC First Round Playoff
HOUSTON vs. MINNESOTA
Series tied, 1-1
1974—Vikings, 51-10 (M)
1980—Oilers, 20-16 (H)
(Points—Vikings 67, Oilers 30)
HOUSTON vs. *NEW ENGLAND
Series tied, 13-13-1
1960—Oilers, 24-10 (B)
　　　　Oilers, 37-21 (H)
1961—Tie, 31-31 (B)
　　　　Oilers, 27-15 (H)
1962—Patriots, 34-21 (B)
　　　　Oilers, 21-17 (H)
1963—Patriots, 45-3 (B)
　　　　Patriots, 46-28 (H)
1964—Patriots, 25-24 (B)
　　　　Patriots, 34-17 (H)
1965—Oilers, 31-10 (H)
　　　　Patriots, 42-14 (B)
1966—Patriots, 27-21 (B)
　　　　Patriots, 38-14 (H)
1967—Patriots, 18-7 (B)
　　　　Oilers, 27-6 (H)
1968—Oilers, 16-0 (B)
　　　　Oilers, 45-17 (H)
1969—Oilers, 24-0 (B)
　　　　Oilers, 27-23 (H)
1971—Patriots, 28-20 (NE)
1973—Patriots, 32-0 (H)
1975—Oilers, 7-0 (NE)
1978—Oilers, 26-23 (NE)
　　　　**Oilers, 31-14 (NE)
1980—Oilers, 38-34 (H)
1981—Patriots, 38-10 (NE)
(Points—Patriots 652, Oilers 567)
*Franchise in Boston prior to 1971
**AFC Divisional Playoff
HOUSTON vs. NEW ORLEANS
Oilers lead series, 2-1-1
1971—Tie, 13-13 (H)
1976—Oilers, 31-26 (NO)
1978—Oilers, 17-12 (NO)
1981—Saints, 27-24 (H)
(Points—Oilers 85, Saints 78)
HOUSTON vs. N.Y. GIANTS
Giants lead series, 1-0
1973—Giants, 34-14 (NY)
HOUSTON vs. *N.Y. JETS
Oilers lead series, 14-10-1
1960—Oilers, 27-21 (H)
　　　　Oilers, 42-28 (NY)
1961—Oilers, 49-13 (H)
　　　　Oilers, 48-21 (NY)
1962—Oilers, 56-17 (H)
　　　　Oilers, 44-10 (NY)
1963—Jets, 24-17 (NY)
　　　　Oilers, 31-27 (H)
1964—Jets, 24-21(NY)
　　　　Oilers, 33-17 (H)
1965—Oilers, 27-21 (H)
　　　　Jets, 41-14 (NY)
1966—Oilers, 52-13 (NY)
　　　　Oilers, 24-0 (H)
1967—Tie, 28-28 (NY)
1968—Oilers, 20-14 (H)
　　　　Jets, 26-7 (NY)
1969—Jets, 26-17 (NY)
　　　　Jets, 34-26 (H)
1972—Oilers, 26-20 (H)
1974—Oilers, 27-22 (NY)
1977—Oilers, 20-0 (H)
1979—Oilers, 27-24 (H) OT
1980—Jets, 31-28 (NY) OT
1981—Jets, 33-17 (NY)
(Points—Oilers 683, Jets 580)
*Jets known as Titans prior to 1963
HOUSTON vs. OAKLAND
Raiders lead series, 19-10
1960—Oilers, 37-22 (O)
　　　　Raiders, 14-13 (H)
1961—Oilers, 55-0 (H)
　　　　Oilers, 47-16 (O)
1962—Oilers, 28-20 (O)
　　　　Oilers, 32-17 (H)
1963—Raiders, 24-13 (H)
　　　　Raiders, 52-49 (O)
1964—Oilers, 42-28 (H)
　　　　Oilers, 20-10 (O)
1965—Raiders, 21-17 (O)
　　　　Raiders, 33-21 (H)
1966—Oilers, 31-0 (H)
　　　　Raiders, 38-23 (O)
1967—Raiders, 19-7 (H)
　　　　*Raiders, 40-7 (O)

1968—Raiders, 24-15 (H)
1969—Raiders, 21-17 (O)
　　　　**Raiders, 56-7 (O)
1971—Raiders, 41-21 (O)
1972—Raiders, 34-0 (H)
1973—Raiders, 17-6 (H)
1975—Raiders, 27-26 (O)
1976—Raiders, 14-13 (H)
1977—Raiders, 34-29 (O)
1978—Raiders, 21-17 (O)
1979—Oilers, 31-17 (H)
1980—***Raiders, 27-7 (O)
1981—Raiders, 17-16 (H)
(Points—Raiders 712, Oilers 639)
*AFL Championship
**Inter-Divisional Playoff
***AFC First Round Playoff
HOUSTON vs. PHILADELPHIA
Eagles lead series, 2-0
1972—Eagles, 18-17 (H)
1979—Eagles, 26-20 (H)
(Points—Eagles 44, Oilers 37)
HOUSTON vs. PITTSBURGH
Steelers lead series, 18-8
1970—Oilers, 19-7 (H)
　　　　Steelers, 7-3 (H)
1971—Steelers, 23-16 (H)
　　　　Oilers, 29-3 (H)
1972—Steelers, 24-7 (P)
　　　　Steelers, 9-3 (H)
1973—Steelers, 36-7 (H)
　　　　Steelers, 33-7 (P)
1974—Steelers, 13-7 (H)
　　　　Oilers, 13-10 (P)
1975—Steelers, 24-17 (H)
　　　　Steelers, 32-9 (H)
1976—Steelers, 32-16 (H)
　　　　Steelers, 21-0 (H)
1977—Oilers, 27-10 (H)
　　　　Steelers, 27-10 (P)
1978—Oilers, 24-17 (P)
　　　　Steelers, 13-3 (H)
　　　　*Steelers, 34-5 (P)
1979—Steelers, 38-7 (P)
　　　　Oilers, 20-17 (H)
　　　　*Steelers, 27-13 (P)
1980—Steelers, 31-17 (P)
　　　　Oilers, 6-0 (H)
1981—Steelers, 26-13 (P)
　　　　Oilers, 21-20 (H)
(Points—Steelers 534, Oilers 319)
*AFC Championship
HOUSTON vs. ST. LOUIS
Cardinals lead series, 3-0
1970—Cardinals, 44-0 (StL)
1974—Cardinals, 31-27 (H)
1979—Cardinals, 24-17 (H)
(Points—Cardinals 99, Oilers 44)
HOUSTON vs. *SAN DIEGO
Chargers lead series, 15-11-1
1960—Oilers, 38-28 (H)
　　　　Chargers, 24-21 (LA)
　　　　**Oilers, 24-16 (H)
1961—Chargers, 34-24 (SD)
　　　　Oilers, 33-13 (H)
　　　　**Oilers, 10-3 (SD)
1962—Chargers, 42-17 (SD)
　　　　Oilers, 33-27 (H)
1963—Chargers, 27-0 (SD)
　　　　Chargers 20-14 (H)
1964—Chargers, 27-21 (SD)
　　　　Chargers, 20-17 (H)
1965—Chargers, 31-14 (SD)
　　　　Chargers, 37-26 (H)
1966—Chargers, 28-22 (H)
　　　　Chargers, 13-3 (SD)
1967—Chargers, 13-3 (SD)
　　　　Oilers, 24-17 (H)
1968—Chargers, 30-14 (SD)
1969—Chargers, 21-17 (H)
1970—Tie, 31-31 (SD)
1971—Oilers, 49-33 (H)
1972—Chargers, 34-20 (SD)
1974—Oilers, 21-14 (H)
1975—Oilers, 33-17 (H)
1976—Chargers, 30-27 (SD)
1978—Chargers, 45-24 (H)
1979—***Oilers, 17-14 (SD)
(Points—Chargers 651, Oilers 619)
*Franchise in Los Angeles prior to 1961
**AFL Championship
***AFC Divisional Playoff
HOUSTON vs. SAN FRANCISCO
Series tied, 2-2
1970—49ers, 30-20 (H)
1975—Oilers, 27-13 (SF)
1978—Oilers, 20-19 (H)
1981—49ers, 28-6 (SF)

(Points—49ers 90, Oilers 73)
HOUSTON vs. SEATTLE
Series tied, 2-2
1977—Oilers, 22-10 (S)
1979—Seahawks, 34-14 (S)
1980—Seahawks, 26-7 (H)
1981—Oilers, 35-17 (H)
(Points—Seahawks 87, Oilers 78)
HOUSTON vs. TAMPA BAY
Oilers lead series, 2-0
1976—Oilers, 20-0 (H)
1980—Oilers, 20-14 (H)
(Points—Oilers 40, Buccaneers 14)
HOUSTON vs. WASHINGTON
Oilers lead series, 2-1
1971—Redskins, 22-13 (W)
1975—Oilers, 13-10 (H)
1979—Oilers, 29-27 (W)
(Points—Redskins 59, Oilers 55)

KANSAS CITY vs. ATLANTA
Chiefs lead series, 1-0;
See Atlanta vs. Kansas City
KANSAS CITY vs. BALTIMORE
Chiefs lead series, 5-3;
See Baltimore vs. Kansas City
KANSAS CITY vs. BUFFALO
Bills lead series, 12-11-1;
See Buffalo vs. Kansas City
KANSAS CITY vs. CHICAGO
Bears lead series, 2-1;
See Chicago vs. Kansas City
KANSAS CITY vs. CINCINNATI
Bengals lead series, 7-6;
See Cincinnati vs. Kansas City
KANSAS CITY vs. CLEVELAND
Series tied, 4-4-1;
See Cleveland vs. Kansas City
KANSAS CITY vs. DALLAS
Series tied, 1-1;
See Dallas vs. Kansas City
KANSAS CITY vs. DENVER
Chiefs lead series, 30-14;
See Denver vs. Kansas City
KANSAS CITY vs. DETROIT
Series tied, 2-2;
See Detroit vs. Kansas City
KANSAS CITY vs. GREEN BAY
Series tied, 1-1-1;
See Green Bay vs. Kansas City
KANSAS CITY vs. HOUSTON
Chiefs lead series, 19-10;
See Houston vs. Kansas City
KANSAS CITY vs. LOS ANGELES
Rams lead series, 1-0
1973—Rams, 23-13 (KC)
KANSAS CITY vs. MIAMI
Chiefs lead series, 7-4
1966—Chiefs, 34-16 (KC)
Chiefs, 19-18 (M)
1967—Chiefs, 24-0 (M)
Chiefs, 41-0 (KC)
1968—Chiefs, 48-3 (M)
1969—Chiefs, 17-10 (KC)
1971—*Dolphins, 27-24 (KC) OT
1972—Dolphins, 20-10 (KC)
1974—Dolphins, 9-3 (M)
1976—Chiefs, 20-17 (M) OT
1981—Dolphins, 17-7 (KC)
(Points—Chiefs 247, Dolphins 137)
**AFC Divisional Playoff*
KANSAS CITY vs. MINNESOTA
Series tied, 2-2
1969—*Chiefs, 23-7 (New Orleans)
1970—Vikings, 27-10 (M)
1974—Vikings, 35-15 (KC)
1981—Chiefs, 10-6 (M)
(Points—Vikings 75, Chiefs 58)
**Super Bowl IV*
***KANSAS CITY vs.**
****NEW ENGLAND**
Chiefs lead series, 11-7-3
1960—Patriots, 42-14 (B)
Texans, 34-0 (D)
1961—Patriots, 18-17 (D)
Patriots, 28-21 (B)
1962—Texans, 42-28 (D)
Texans, 27-7 (B)
1963—Tie, 24-24 (B)
Chiefs, 35-3 (KC)
1964—Patriots, 24-7 (B)
Patriots, 31-24 (KC)
1965—Chiefs, 27-17 (KC)
Tie, 10-10 (B)
1966—Chiefs, 43-24 (B)
Tie, 27-27 (KC)
1967—Chiefs, 33-10 (B)
1968—Chiefs, 31-17 (KC)
1969—Chiefs, 31-0 (B)
1970—Chiefs, 23-10 (KC)
1973—Chiefs, 10-7 (NE)
1977—Patriots, 21-17 (NE)
1981—Patriots, 33-17 (NE)
(Points—Chiefs 514, Patriots 381)
**Franchise located in Dallas prior to 1963 and known as Texans*
***Franchise in Boston prior to 1971*
KANSAS CITY vs. NEW ORLEANS
Series tied, 1-1
1972—Chiefs, 20-17 (NO)
1976—Saints, 27-17 (KC)
(Points—Saints 44, Chiefs 37)
KANSAS CITY vs. N. Y. GIANTS
Giants lead series, 3-0
1974—Giants, 33-27 (KC)
1978—Giants, 26-10 (NY)
1979—Giants, 21-17 (KC)
(Points—Giants 80, Chiefs 54)
***KANSAS CITY vs. **N. Y. JETS**
Chiefs lead series, 12-9
1960—Titans, 37-35 (D)
Titans, 41-35 (NY)
1961—Titans, 28-7 (NY)
Texans, 35-24 (D)
1962—Texans, 20-17 (D)
Texans, 52-31 (NY)
1963—Jets, 17-0 (NY)
Chiefs, 48-0 (KC)
1964—Jets, 27-14 (NY)
Chiefs, 24-7 (KC)
1965—Chiefs, 14-10 (NY)
Jets, 13-10 (KC)
1966—Chiefs, 32-24 (NY)
1967—Chiefs, 42-18 (KC)
Chiefs, 21-7 (NY)
1968—Jets, 20-19 (KC)
1969—Chiefs, 34-16 (NY)
***Chiefs, 13-6 (NY)
1971—Jets, 13-10 (NY)
1974—Chiefs, 24-16 (KC)
1975—Jets, 30-24 (KC)
(Points—Chiefs 513, Jets 402)
**Franchise in Dallas prior to 1963 and known as Texans*
***Jets known as Titans prior to 1963*
****Inter-Divisional Playoff*
***KANSAS CITY vs. OAKLAND**
Raiders lead series, 24-20-2
1960—Texans, 34-16 (O)
Raiders, 20-19 (D)
1961—Texans, 42-35 (O)
Texans, 43-11 (D)
1962—Texans, 26-16 (O)
Texans, 35-7 (D)
1963—Raiders, 10-7 (O)
Raiders, 22-7 (KC)
1964—Chiefs, 21-9 (O)
Chiefs, 42-7 (KC)
1965—Raiders, 37-10 (O)
Chiefs, 14-7 (KC)
1966—Chiefs, 32-10 (O)
Raiders, 34-13 (KC)
1967—Raiders, 23-21 (O)
Raiders, 44-22 (KC)
1968—Chiefs, 24-10 (KC)
Raiders, 38-21 (O)
**Raiders, 41-6 (O)
1969—Raiders, 27-24 (KC)
Raiders, 10-6 (O)
***Chiefs, 17-7 (O)
1970—Tie, 17-17 (KC)
Raiders, 20-6 (O)
1971—Tie, 20-20 (O)
Chiefs, 16-14 (KC)
1972—Chiefs, 27-14 (KC)
Raiders, 26-3 (O)
1973—Chiefs, 16-3 (KC)
Raiders, 37-7 (O)
1974—Raiders, 27-7 (O)
Raiders, 7-6 (KC)
1975—Chiefs, 42-10 (KC)
Raiders, 28-20 (O)
1976—Raiders, 24-21 (KC)
Raiders, 21-10 (O)
1977—Raiders, 37-28 (KC)
Raiders, 21-20 (O)
1978—Raiders, 28-6 (O)
Raiders, 20-10 (KC)
1979—Chiefs, 35-7 (KC)
Chiefs, 24-21 (O)
1980—Raiders, 27-14 (KC)
Chiefs, 31-17 (O)
1981—Chiefs, 27-0 (KC)
Chiefs, 28-17 (O)
(Points—Chiefs 927, Raiders 904)
**Franchise in Dallas prior to 1963 and known as Texans*
***Division Playoff*
****AFL Championship*
KANSAS CITY vs. PHILADELPHIA
Eagles lead series, 1-0
1972—Eagles, 21-20 (KC)
KANSAS CITY vs. PITTSBURGH
Steelers lead series, 7-3
1970—Chiefs, 31-14 (P)
1971—Chiefs, 38-16 (KC)
1972—Steelers, 16-7 (P)
1974—Steelers, 34-24 (KC)
1975—Steelers, 28-3 (P)
1976—Steelers, 45-0 (KC)
1978—Steelers, 27-24 (P)
1979—Steelers, 30-3 (KC)
1980—Steelers, 21-16 (P)
1981—Chiefs, 37-33 (P)
(Points—Steelers 264, Chiefs 183)
KANSAS CITY vs. ST. LOUIS
Chiefs lead series, 2-0-1
1970—Tie, 6-6 (KC)
1974—Chiefs, 17-13 (StL)
1980—Chiefs, 21-13 (StL)
(Points—Chiefs 44, Cardinals 32)
***KANSAS CITY vs. **SAN DIEGO**
Chargers lead series, 23-20-1
1960—Chargers, 21-20 (LA)
Texans, 17-0 (D)
1961—Chargers, 26-10 (D)
Chargers, 24-14 (SD)
1962—Chargers, 32-28 (SD)
Texans, 26-17 (D)
1963—Chargers, 24-10 (SD)
Chargers, 38-17 (KC)
1964—Chargers, 28-14 (KC)
Chiefs, 49-6 (SD)
1965—Tie, 10-10 (SD)
Chiefs, 31-7 (KC)
1966—Chiefs, 24-14 (KC)
Chiefs, 27-17 (SD)
1967—Chargers, 45-31 (SD)
Chargers, 17-16 (KC)
1968—Chiefs, 27-20 (KC)
Chiefs, 40-3 (SD)
1969—Chiefs, 27-9 (SD)
Chiefs, 27-3 (KC)
1970—Chiefs, 26-14 (KC)
Chargers, 31-13 (SD)
1971—Chargers, 21-14 (SD)
Chiefs, 31-10 (KC)
1972—Chiefs, 26-14 (SD)
Chargers, 27-17 (KC)
1973—Chiefs, 19-0 (SD)
Chiefs, 33-6 (KC)
1974—Chiefs, 24-14 (SD)
Chargers, 14-7 (KC)
1975—Chiefs, 12-10 (SD)
Chargers, 28-20 (KC)
1976—Chargers, 30-16 (KC)
Chiefs, 23-20 (SD)
1977—Chargers, 23-7 (KC)
Chiefs, 21-16 (SD)
1978—Chargers, 29-23 (SD) OT
Chiefs, 23-0 (KC)
1979—Chargers, 20-14 (KC)
Chargers, 28-7 (SD)
1980—Chargers, 24-7 (KC)
Chargers, 20-7 (SD)
1981—Chargers, 42-31 (KC)
Chargers, 22-20 (SD)
(Points—Chiefs 906, Chargers 824)
**Franchise in Dallas prior to 1963 and known as Texans*
***Franchise in Los Angeles prior to 1961*
KANSAS CITY vs.
SAN FRANCISCO
Series tied, 1-1
1971—Chiefs, 26-17 (SF)
1975—49ers, 20-3 (KC)
(Points—49ers 37, Chiefs 29)
KANSAS CITY vs. SEATTLE
Chiefs lead series, 5-4
1977—Seahawks, 34-31 (KC)
1978—Seahawks, 13-10 (KC)
Seahawks, 23-19 (S)
1979—Chiefs, 24-6 (S)
Chiefs, 37-21 (KC)
1980—Seahawks, 17-16 (KC)
Chiefs, 31-30 (S)
1981—Chiefs, 20-14 (S)
Chiefs, 40-13 (KC)
(Points—Chiefs 228, Seahawks 171)
KANSAS CITY vs. TAMPA BAY
Series tied, 2-2
1976—Chiefs, 28-19 (TB)
1978—Buccaneers, 30-13 (KC)
1979—Buccaneers, 3-0 (TB)
1981—Chiefs, 19-10 (KC)
(Points—Buccaneers 62, Chiefs 60)
KANSAS CITY vs. WASHINGTON
Chiefs lead series, 2-0
1971—Chiefs, 27-20 (KC)
1976—Chiefs, 33-30 (W)
(Points—Chiefs 60, Redskins 50)

LOS ANGELES vs. ATLANTA
Rams lead series, 24-5-2;
See Atlanta vs. Los Angeles
LOS ANGELES vs. *1950 BALTIMORE
Rams won series, 1-0
See *Baltimore vs. Los Angeles
**Extinct team*
LOS ANGELES vs. BALTIMORE
Colts lead series, 20-14-2;
See Baltimore vs. Los Angeles
LOS ANGELES vs. *BOSTON YANKS
Yanks won series, 2-1
See *Boston Yanks vs. Los Angeles
**Extinct team*
LOS ANGELES vs. *BROOKLYN DODGERS
Dodgers won series, 3-1
See *Brooklyn Dodgers vs. Cleveland Rams
**Extinct team*
LOS ANGELES vs. BUFFALO
Rams lead series, 2-1;
See Buffalo vs. Los Angeles
LOS ANGELES vs. CHICAGO
Bears lead series, 41-25-3;
See Chicago vs. Los Angeles
LOS ANGELES vs. CINCINNATI
Bengals lead series, 3-1;
See Cincinnati vs. Los Angeles
LOS ANGELES vs. CLEVELAND
Browns lead series, 8-6;
See Cleveland vs. Los Angeles
LOS ANGELES vs. DALLAS
Cowboys lead series, 9-8;
See Dallas vs. Los Angeles
LOS ANGELES vs. *DALLAS TEXANS
Rams won series, 2-0
See *Dallas Texas vs. Los Angeles
**Extinct team*
LOS ANGELES vs. DENVER
Rams lead series, 2-1;
See Denver vs. Los Angeles
LOS ANGELES vs. DETROIT
Rams lead series, 35-33-1;
See Detroit vs. Los Angeles
LOS ANGELES vs. GREEN BAY
Rams lead series, 38-31-2;
See Green Bay vs. Los Angeles
LOS ANGELES vs. HOUSTON
Rams lead series, 2-1;
See Houston vs. Los Angeles
LOS ANGELES vs. KANSAS CITY
Rams lead series, 1-0;
See Kansas City vs. Los Angeles
LOS ANGELES vs. MIAMI
Dolphins lead series, 2-1
1971—Dolphins, 20-14 (LA)
1976—Rams, 31-28 (M)
1980—Dolphins, 35-14 (LA)
(Points—Dolphins 83, Rams 59)
LOS ANGELES vs. MINNESOTA
Vikings lead series, 15-11-2
1961—Rams, 31-17 (LA)
Vikings, 42-21 (M)
1962—Vikings, 38-14 (LA)
Tie, 24-24 (M)
1963—Rams, 27-24 (LA)
Vikings, 21-13 (M)
1964—Rams, 22-13 (LA)
Vikings, 34-13 (M)
1965—Vikings, 38-35 (LA)
Vikings, 24-13 (M)
1966—Vikings, 35-7 (M)
Rams, 21-6 (LA)
1967—Rams, 39-3 (LA)
1968—Rams, 31-3 (M)
1969—Vikings, 20-13 (LA)
*Vikings, 23-20 (M)
1970—Vikings, 13-3 (M)
1972—Vikings, 45-41 (LA)
1973—Vikings, 10-9 (M)
1974—Rams, 20-17 (LA)
**Vikings, 14-10 (M)
1976—Tie, 10-10 (M) OT
**Vikings, 24-13 (M)
1977—Rams, 35-3 (LA)
***Vikings, 14-7 (LA)
1978—Rams, 34-17 (M)
***Rams, 34-10 (LA)
1979—Rams, 27-21 (LA) OT
(Points—Rams 587, Vikings 563)
**Conference Championship*
***NFC Championship*
****NFC Divisional Playoff*
LOS ANGELES vs. NEW ENGLAND
Series tied, 1-1
1974—Patriots, 20-14 (NE)
1980—Rams, 17-14 (NE)
(Points—Patriots 34, Rams 31)
LOS ANGELES vs. NEW ORLEANS
Rams lead series, 18-8
1967—Rams 27-13 (NO)
1969—Rams, 36-17 (LA)
1970—Rams, 30-17 (NO)
Rams, 34-16 (LA)
1971—Saints, 24-20 (NO)
Rams, 45-28 (LA)
1972—Rams, 34-14 (LA)
Saints, 19-16 (NO)
1973—Rams, 29-7 (LA)
Rams, 24-13 (NO)
1974—Rams, 24-0 (LA)
Saints, 20-7 (NO)
1975—Rams, 38-14 (LA)
Rams, 14-7 (NO)
1976—Rams, 16-10 (NO)
Rams, 33-14 (LA)
1977—Rams, 14-7 (LA)
Saints, 27-26 (NO)
1978—Rams, 26-20 (NO)
Saints, 10-3 (LA)
1979—Rams, 35-17 (NO)
Saints, 29-14 (LA)
1980—Rams, 45-31 (LA)
Rams, 27-7 (NO)
1981—Saints, 23-17 (NO)
Saints, 21-13 (LA)
(Points—Rams 647, Saints 425)
LOS ANGELES vs. *N.Y. BULLDOGS
Rams won series, 1-0
1949—Rams, 42-20
**Extinct team*
***LOS ANGELES vs. N.Y. GIANTS**
Rams lead series, 14-6
1938—Giants, 28-0 (NY)
1940—Rams, 13-0 (NY)
1941—Giants, 49-14 (NY)
1945—Rams, 21-17 (NY)
1946—Rams, 31-21 (NY)
1947—Rams, 34-10 (LA)
1948—Rams, 52-37 (NY)
1953—Rams, 21-7 (LA)
1954—Rams, 17-16 (NY)
1959—Giants, 23-21 (LA)
1961—Giants, 24-14 (NY)
1966—Rams, 55-14 (LA)
1968—Rams, 24-21 (LA)
1970—Rams, 31-3 (NY)
1973—Rams, 40-6 (LA)
1976—Rams, 24-10 (LA)
1978—Rams, 20-17 (NY)
1979—Giants, 20-14 (LA)
1980—Rams, 28-7 (NY)
1981—Giants, 10-7 (NY)
(Points—Rams 481, Giants 340)
**Franchise in Cleveland prior to 1946*
LOS ANGELES vs. N.Y. JETS
Rams lead series, 2-1
1970—Jets, 31-20 (LA)
1974—Rams, 20-13 (NY)
1980—Rams, 38-13 (LA)
(Points—Rams 78, Jets 57)
LOS ANGELES vs. *N.Y. YANKS
Rams won series, 4-0
1950—Rams, 45-28
Rams, 43-35
1951—Rams, 54-14
Rams, 48-21
(Points—Rams 190, Yanks 98)
LOS ANGELES vs. OAKLAND
Raiders lead series, 2-1
1972—Raiders, 45-17 (O)
1977—Rams, 20-14 (LA)
1979—Raiders, 24-17 (LA)
(Points—Raiders 83, Rams 54)
***LOS ANGELES vs. PHILADELPHIA**
Rams lead series, 14-8-1
1937—Rams, 21-3 (P)
1939—Rams, 35-13
(Colorado Springs)
1940—Rams, 21-13 (C)
1942—Rams, 24-14 (Akron)

1944—Eagles, 26-13 (P)
1945—Eagles, 28-14 (P)
1946—Eagles, 25-14 (LA)
1947—Eagles, 14-7 (P)
1948—Tie, 28-28 (LA)
1949—Eagles, 38-14 (P)
  **Eagles, 14-0 (LA)
1950—Eagles, 56-20 (P)
1955—Rams, 23-21 (P)
1956—Rams, 27-7 (LA)
1957—Rams, 17-13 (LA)
1959—Eagles, 23-20 (P)
1964—Rams, 20-10 (LA)
1967—Rams, 33-17 (LA)
1969—Rams, 23-17 (P)
1972—Rams, 34-3 (P)
1975—Rams, 42-3 (P)
1977—Rams, 20-0 (LA)
1978—Rams, 16-14 (P)
(Points—Rams 486, Eagles 400)
*Franchise in Cleveland prior to 1946
**NFL Championship
LOS ANGELES vs. **PITTSBURGH
Rams lead series, 12-3-2
1938—Rams, 13-7 (New Orleans)
1939—Tie, 14-14 (C)
1941—Rams, 17-14 (Akron)
1947—Rams, 48-7 (P)
1948—Rams, 31-14 (LA)
1949—Tie, 7-7 (P)
1952—Rams, 28-14 (LA)
1955—Rams, 27-26 (LA)
1956—Steelers, 30-13 (P)
1961—Rams, 24-14 (LA)
1964—Rams, 26-14 (P)
1968—Rams, 45-10 (LA)
1971—Rams, 23-14 (P)
1975—Rams, 10-3 (LA)
1978—Rams, 10-7 (LA)
1979—***Steelers, 31-19 (Pasadena)
1981—Steelers, 24-0 (LA)
(Points—Rams 355, Steelers 250)
*Franchise in Cleveland prior to 1946
**Steelers known as Pirates prior to 1941
***Super Bowl XIV
LOS ANGELES vs. **ST. LOUIS
Rams lead series, 18-15-2
1937—Cardinals, 13-7 (Clev)
  Cardinals, 13-7 (Chi)
1938—Cardinals, 7-6 (Clev)
  Cardinals, 31-17 (Chi)
1939—Rams, 24-0 (Clev)
  Rams, 14-0 (Clev)
1940—Rams, 26-14 (Clev)
  Cardinals, 17-7 (Chi)
1941—Rams, 10-6 (Clev)
  Cardinals, 7-0 (Chi)
1942—Cardinals, 7-0 (Clev)
  Rams, 7-3 (Clev)
1945—Rams, 21-0 (Clev)
  Rams, 35-21 (Chi)
1946—Cardinals, 34-10 (Chi)
  Rams, 17-14 (LA)
1947—Rams, 27-7 (LA)
  Cardinals, 17-10 (Chi)
1948—Cardinals, 27-22 (LA)
  Cardinals, 27-24 (Chi)
1949—Tie, 28-28 (Chi)
  Cardinals, 31-27 (LA)
1951—Rams, 45-21 (LA)
1953—Tie, 24-24 (Chi)
1954—Rams, 28-17 (LA)
1958—Rams, 20-14 (Chi)
1960—Cardinals, 43-21 (LA)
1965—Rams, 27-3 (StL)
1968—Rams, 24-13 (LA)
1970—Rams, 34-13 (LA)
1972—Cardinals, 24-14 (StL)
1975—***Rams, 35-23 (LA)
1976—Cardinals, 30-28 (LA)
1979—Rams, 21-0 (LA)
1980—Rams, 21-13 (StL)
(Points—Rams 681, Cardinals 555)
*Franchise in Cleveland prior to 1946
**Franchise in Chicago prior to 1960
***NFC Divisional Playoff
LOS ANGELES vs. SAN DIEGO
Rams lead series, 2-1
1970—Rams, 37-10 (LA)
1975—Rams, 13-10 (SD) OT
1979—Chargers, 40-16 (LA)
(Points—Rams 66, Chargers 60)
LOS ANGELES vs. SAN FRANCISCO
Rams lead series, 41-21-2
1950—Rams, 35-14 (SF)
  Rams, 28-21 (LA)

1951—49ers, 44-17 (SF)
  Rams, 23-16 (LA)
1952—Rams, 35-9 (LA)
  Rams, 34-21 (SF)
1953—49ers, 31-30 (SF)
  49ers, 31-27 (SF)
1954—Tie, 24-24 (LA)
  Rams, 42-34 (SF)
1955—Rams, 23-14 (SF)
  Rams, 27-14 (LA)
1956—49ers, 33-30 (SF)
  Rams, 30-6 (LA)
1957—49ers, 23-20 (LA)
  Rams, 37-24 (LA)
1958—Rams, 33-3 (SF)
  Rams, 56-7 (LA)
1959—49ers, 34-0 (SF)
  49ers, 24-16 (LA)
1960—49ers, 13-9 (SF)
  Rams, 23-7 (LA)
1961—49ers, 35-0 (SF)
  Rams, 17-7 (LA)
1962—Rams, 28-14 (SF)
  49ers, 24-17 (LA)
1963—Rams, 28-21 (LA)
  Rams, 21-17 (SF)
1964—Rams, 42-14 (LA)
  49ers, 28-7 (SF)
1965—49ers, 45-21 (LA)
  49ers, 30-27 (SF)
1966—Rams, 34-3 (LA)
  49ers, 21-13 (SF)
1967—49ers, 27-24 (LA)
  Rams, 17-7 (SF)
1968—Rams, 24-10 (LA)
  Tie, 20-20 (SF)
1969—Rams, 27-21 (SF)
  Rams, 41-30 (LA)
1970—49ers, 20-6 (LA)
  Rams, 30-13 (SF)
1971—Rams, 20-13 (LA)
  Rams, 17-6 (LA)
1972—Rams, 31-7 (LA)
  Rams, 26-16 (SF)
1973—Rams, 40-20 (SF)
  Rams, 31-13 (LA)
1974—Rams, 37-14 (LA)
  Rams, 15-13 (SF)
1975—Rams, 23-14 (SF)
  49ers, 24-23 (LA)
1976—49ers, 16-0 (LA)
  Rams, 23-3 (SF)
1977—Rams, 34-14 (LA)
  Rams, 23-10 (SF)
1978—Rams, 27-10 (LA)
  Rams, 31-28 (SF)
1979—Rams, 27-24 (LA)
  Rams, 26-20 (SF)
1980—Rams, 48-26 (LA)
  Rams, 31-17 (SF)
1981—Rams, 20-17 (SF)
  49ers, 33-31 (LA)
(Points—Rams 1,608, 49ers 1,231)
LOS ANGELES vs. SEATTLE
Rams lead series, 2-0
1976—Rams, 45-6 (LA)
1979—Rams, 24-0 (S)
(Points—Rams 69, Seahawks 6)
LOS ANGELES vs. TAMPA BAY
Rams lead series, 3-2
1977—Rams, 31-0 (LA)
1978—Rams, 26-23 (LA)
1979—Buccaneers, 21-6 (TB)
  *Rams, 9-0 (TB)
1980—Buccaneers, 10-9 (TB)
(Points—Rams 81, Buccaneers 54)
*NFC Championship
LOS ANGELES vs. WASHINGTON
Redskins lead series, 12-5-1
1937—Redskins, 16-7 (C)
1938—Redskins, 37-13 (W)
1941—Redskins, 17-13 (W)
1942—Redskins, 33-14 (W)
1944—Redskins, 14-10 (W)
1945—**Redskins, 15-14 (C)
1948—Rams, 41-13 (W)
1949—Rams, 53-27 (LA)
1951—Redskins, 31-21 (W)
1962—Redskins, 20-14 (LA)
1963—Redskins, 37-14 (LA)
1967—Tie, 28-28 (LA)
1969—Rams, 24-13 (W)
1971—Redskins, 38-24 (LA)
1974—Redskins, 23-17 (LA)
  ***Rams, 19-10 (LA)
1977—Redskins, 17-14 (W)
1981—Redskins, 30-7 (LA)
(Points—Redskins 418, Rams 348)

*Franchise in Cleveland prior to 1946
**NFL Championship
***NFC Championship

MIAMI vs. ATLANTA
Dolphins lead series, 3-0;
See Atlanta vs. Miami
MIAMI vs. BALTIMORE
Dolphins lead series, 16-9;
See Baltimore vs. Miami
MIAMI vs. BUFFALO
Dolphins lead series, 25-6-1;
See Buffalo vs. Miami
MIAMI vs. CHICAGO
Dolphins lead series, 3-0;
See Chicago vs. Miami
MIAMI vs. CINCINNATI
Dolphins lead series, 6-3;
See Cincinnati vs. Miami
MIAMI vs. CLEVELAND
Browns lead series, 3-2;
See Cleveland vs. Miami
MIAMI vs. DALLAS
Series tied, 2-2;
See Dallas vs. Miami
MIAMI vs. DENVER
Dolphins lead series, 4-2-1;
See Denver vs. Miami
MIAMI vs. DETROIT
Dolphins lead series, 2-0;
See Detroit vs. Miami
MIAMI vs. GREEN BAY
Dolphins lead series, 3-0;
See Green Bay vs. Miami
MIAMI vs. HOUSTON
Oilers lead series, 9-7;
See Houston vs. Miami
MIAMI vs. KANSAS CITY
Chiefs lead series, 7-4;
See Kansas City vs. Miami
MIAMI vs. LOS ANGELES
Dolphins lead series, 2-1;
See Los Angeles vs. Miami
MIAMI vs. MINNESOTA
Dolphins lead series, 3-1
1972—Dolphins, 16-14 (Minn)
1973—*Dolphins, 24-7 (Houston)
1976—Vikings, 29-7 (Mia)
1979—Dolphins, 27-12 (Minn)
(Points—Dolphins 74, Vikings 62)
*Super Bowl VIII
MIAMI vs. *NEW ENGLAND
Dolphins lead series, 20-11
1966—Patriots, 20-14 (M)
1967—Patriots, 41-10 (B)
  Dolphins, 41-32 (M)
1968—Dolphins, 34-10 (B)
  Dolphins, 38-7 (M)
1969—Dolphins, 17-16 (B)
  Patriots, 38-23 (Tampa)
1970—Patriots, 27-14 (B)
  Dolphins, 37-20 (M)
1971—Dolphins, 41-3 (M)
  Patriots, 34-13 (NE)
1972—Dolphins, 52-0 (M)
  Dolphins, 37-21 (NE)
1973—Dolphins, 44-23 (M)
  Dolphins, 30-14 (NE)
1974—Patriots, 34-24 (NE)
  Dolphins, 34-27 (M)
1975—Dolphins, 22-14 (NE)
  Dolphins, 20-7 (M)
1976—Patriots, 30-14 (NE)
  Dolphins, 10-3 (M)
1977—Dolphins, 17-5 (M)
  Patriots, 14-10 (NE)
1978—Patriots, 33-24 (NE)
  Dolphins, 23-3 (M)
1979—Patriots, 28-13 (NE)
  Dolphins, 39-24 (M)
1980—Patriots, 34-0 (NE)
  Dolphins, 16-13 (M) OT
1981—Dolphins, 30-27 (NE) OT
  Dolphins, 24-14 (M)
(Points—Dolphins 765, Patriots 616)
*Franchise in Boston prior to 1971
MIAMI vs. NEW ORLEANS
Dolphins lead series, 3-0
1970—Dolphins, 21-10 (M)
1974—Dolphins, 21-0 (NO)
1980—Dolphins, 21-16 (M)
(Points—Dolphins 63, Saints 26)
MIAMI vs. N.Y. GIANTS
Dolphins lead series, 1-0
1972—Dolphins, 23-13 (NY)
MIAMI vs. N.Y. JETS
Jets lead series, 17-14-1
1966—Jets, 19-14 (M)

  Jets, 30-13 (NY)
1967—Jets, 29-7 (NY)
  Jets, 33-14 (M)
1968—Jets, 35-17 (NY)
  Jets, 31-7 (M)
1969—Jets, 34-31 (NY)
  Jets, 27-9 (NY)
1970—Dolphins, 20-6 (NY)
  Dolphins, 16-10 (M)
1971—Jets, 14-10 (M)
  Dolphins, 30-14 (NY)
1972—Dolphins, 27-17 (NY)
  Dolphins, 28-24 (M)
1973—Dolphins, 31-3 (M)
  Dolphins, 24-14 (NY)
1974—Dolphins, 21-17 (M)
  Jets, 17-14 (NY)
1975—Dolphins, 43-0 (NY)
  Dolphins, 27-7 (M)
1976—Dolphins, 16-0 (M)
  Dolphins, 27-7 (NY)
1977—Dolphins, 21-17 (M)
  Dolphins, 14-10 (NY)
1978—Jets, 33-20 (NY)
  Jets, 24-13 (M)
1979—Jets, 33-27 (NY)
  Dolphins, 27-24 (M)
1980—Jets, 17-14 (NY)
  Jets, 24-17 (M)
1981—Tie, 28-28 (M) OT
  Jets, 16-15 (NY)
(Points—Dolphins 639, Jets 617)
MIAMI vs. OAKLAND
Raiders lead series, 12-3-1
1966—Raiders, 23-14 (M)
  Raiders, 21-10 (O)
1967—Raiders, 31-17 (O)
1968—Raiders, 47-21 (M)
1969—Raiders, 20-17 (O)
  Tie, 20-20 (M)
1970—Dolphins, 20-13 (M)
1973—*Raiders, 21-14 (O)
  **Dolphins, 27-10 (M)
1974—*Raiders, 28-26 (O)
1975—Dolphins, 31-21 (M)
1978—Dolphins, 23-6 (M)
1979—Raiders, 13-3 (O)
1980—Raiders, 16-10 (O)
1981—Raiders, 33-17 (M)
(Points—Raiders 345, Dolphins 267)
*AFC Divisional Playoff
**AFC Championship
MIAMI vs. PHILADELPHIA
Series tied, 2-2
1970—Eagles, 24-17 (P)
1975—Dolphins, 24-16 (M)
1978—Eagles, 17-3 (P)
1981—Dolphins, 13-10 (M)
(Points—Eagles 67, Dolphins 57)
MIAMI vs. PITTSBURGH
Dolphins lead series, 4-3
1971—Dolphins, 24-21 (M)
1972—*Dolphins, 21-17 (P)
1973—Dolphins, 30-26 (M)
1976—Steelers, 14-3 (P)
1979—**Steelers, 34-14 (P)
1980—Steelers, 23-10 (P)
1981—Dolphins, 30-10 (M)
(Points—Steelers 145, Dolphins 132)
*AFC Championship
**AFC Divisional Playoff
MIAMI vs. ST. LOUIS
Dolphins lead series, 4-0
1972—Dolphins, 31-10 (M)
1977—Dolphins, 55-14 (StL)
1978—Dolphins, 24-10 (M)
1981—Dolphins, 20-7 (StL)
(Points—Dolphins 130, Cardinals 41)
MIAMI vs. SAN DIEGO
Chargers lead series, 7-4
1966—Chargers, 44-10 (SD)
1967—Chargers, 24-0 (SD)
  Dolphins, 41-24 (M)
1968—Chargers, 34-28 (SD)
1969—Chargers, 21-14 (M)
1972—Dolphins, 24-10 (M)
1974—Dolphins, 28-21 (SD)
1977—Chargers, 14-13 (M)
1978—Dolphins, 28-21 (SD)
1980—Chargers, 27-24 (M) OT
1981—*Chargers, 41-38 (M) OT
(Points—Chargers 281, Dolphins 248)
*AFC Divisional Playoff
MIAMI vs. SAN FRANCISCO
Dolphins lead series, 3-0
1973—Dolphins, 21-13 (M)

1977—Dolphins, 19-15 (SF)
1980—Dolphins, 17-13 (M)
(Points—Dolphins 57, 49ers 41)
MIAMI vs. SEATTLE
Dolphins lead series, 2-0
1977—Dolphins, 31-13 (M)
1979—Dolphins, 19-10 (M)
(Points—Dolphins 50, Seahawks 23)
MIAMI vs. TAMPA BAY
Dolphins lead series, 1-0
1976—Dolphins, 23-20 (TB)
MIAMI vs. WASHINGTON
Dolphins lead series, 3-1
1972—*Dolphins, 14-7 (Los Angeles)
1974—Redskins, 20-17 (W)
1978—Dolphins, 16-0 (W)
1981—Dolphins, 13-10 (M)
(Points—Dolphins 60, Redskins 37)
*Super Bowl VII

MINNESOTA vs. ATLANTA
Vikings lead series, 7-5;
See Atlanta vs. Minnesota
MINNESOTA vs. BALTIMORE
Colts lead series, 12-4-1;
See Baltimore vs. Minnesota
MINNESOTA vs. BUFFALO
Vikings lead series, 3-0;
See Buffalo vs. Minnesota
MINNESOTA vs. CHICAGO
Vikings lead series, 23-17-2;
See Chicago vs. Minnesota
MINNESOTA vs. CINCINNATI
Bengals lead series, 2-1;
See Cincinnati vs. Minnesota
MINNESOTA vs. CLEVELAND
Vikings lead series, 6-1;
See Cleveland vs. Minnesota
MINNESOTA vs. DALLAS
Cowboys lead series, 9-4;
See Dallas vs. Minnesota
MINNESOTA vs. DENVER
Vikings lead series, 4-1;
See Denver vs. Minnesota
MINNESOTA vs. DETROIT
Vikings lead series, 26-14-2;
See Detroit vs. Minnesota
MINNESOTA vs. GREEN BAY
Vikings lead series, 23-18-1
See Green Bay vs. Minnesota
MINNESOTA vs. HOUSTON
Series tied, 1-1;
See Houston vs. Minnesota
MINNESOTA vs. KANSAS CITY
Series tied, 2-2;
See Kansas City vs. Minnesota
MINNESOTA vs. LOS ANGELES
Vikings lead series, 15-11-2;
See Los Angeles vs. Minnesota
MINNESOTA vs. MIAMI
Dolphins lead series, 3-1;
See Miami vs. Minnesota
MINNESOTA vs. *NEW ENGLAND
Patriots lead series, 2-1
1970—Vikings, 35-14 (B)
1974—Patriots, 17-14 (M)
1979—Patriots, 27-23 (NE)
(Points—Vikings 72, Patriots 58)
*Franchise in Boston prior to 1971
MINNESOTA vs. NEW ORLEANS
Vikings lead series, 8-2
1968—Saints, 20-17 (NO)
1970—Vikings, 26-0 (M)
1971—Vikings, 23-10 (NO)
1972—Vikings, 37-6 (M)
1974—Vikings, 29-9 (M)
1975—Vikings, 20-7 (NO)
1976—Vikings, 40-9 (NO)
1978—Saints, 31-24 (NO)
1980—Vikings, 23-20 (NO)
1981—Vikings, 20-10 (M)
(Points—Vikings 259, Saints 122)
MINNESOTA vs. N.Y. GIANTS
Vikings lead series, 6-1
1964—Vikings, 30-21 (M)
1965—Vikings, 40-14 (M)
1967—Vikings, 27-24 (M)
1969—Giants, 24-23 (NY)
1971—Vikings, 17-10 (NY)
1973—Vikings, 31-7 (New Haven)
1976—Vikings, 24-7 (M)
(Points—Vikings 192, Giants 107)
MINNESOTA vs. N.Y. JETS
Jets lead series, 2-1
1970—Jets, 20-10 (NY)
1975—Vikings, 29-21 (M)
1979—Jets, 14-7 (NY)
(Points—Jets 55, Vikings 46)

MINNESOTA vs. OAKLAND
Raiders lead series, 4-1
1973—Vikings, 24-16 (M)
1976—*Raiders 32-14 (Pasadena)
1977—Raiders, 35-13 (O)
1978—Raiders, 27-20 (O)
1981—Raiders, 36-10 (M)
(Points—Raiders 146, Vikings 81)
Super Bowl XI
MINNESOTA vs. PHILADELPHIA
Vikings lead series, 8-2
1962—Vikings, 31-21 (M)
1963—Vikings, 34-13 (P)
1968—Vikings, 24-17 (P)
1971—Vikings, 13-0 (P)
1973—Vikings, 28-21 (M)
1976—Vikings, 31-12 (P)
1978—Vikings, 28-27 (M)
1980—Eagles, 42-7 (M)
*Eagles, 31-16 (P)
1981—Vikings, 35-23 (M)
(Points—Vikings 247, Eagles 207)
NFC Divisional Playoff
MINNESOTA vs. PITTSBURGH
Series tied, 4-4
1962—Steelers, 39-31 (P)
1964—Vikings, 30-10 (M)
1967—Vikings, 41-27 (P)
1969—Vikings, 52-14 (M)
1972—Steelers, 23-10 (P)
1974—*Steelers, 16-6 (New Orleans)
1976—Vikings, 17-6 (M)
1980—Steelers, 23-17 (M)
(Points—Vikings 204, Steelers 158)
Super Bowl IX
MINNESOTA vs. ST. LOUIS
Cardinals lead series, 6-3
1963—Cardinals, 56-14 (M)
1967—Cardinals, 34-24 (M)
1969—Vikings, 27-10 (StL)
1972—Cardinals, 19-17 (M)
1974—Vikings, 28-24 (StL)
*Vikings, 30-14 (M)
1977—Cardinals, 27-7 (M)
1979—Cardinals, 37-7 (StL)
1981—Cardinals, 30-17 (StL)
(Points—Cardinals 251, Vikings 171)
NFC Divisional Playoff
MINNESOTA vs. SAN DIEGO
Series tied, 2-2
1971—Chargers, 30-14 (SD)
1975—Vikings, 28-13 (M)
1978—Chargers, 13-7 (M)
1981—Vikings, 33-31 (SD)
(Points—Chargers 87, Vikings 82)
MINNESOTA vs. SAN FRANCISCO
Vikings lead series, 12-10-1
1961—49ers, 38-24 (M)
49ers, 38-28 (SF)
1962—49ers, 21-7 (SF)
49ers, 35-12 (M)
1963—Vikings, 24-20 (SF)
Vikings, 45-14 (M)
1964—Vikings, 27-22 (SF)
Vikings, 24-7 (M)
1965—Vikings, 42-41 (SF)
49ers, 45-24 (M)
1966—Tie, 20-20 (SF)
Vikings, 28-3 (SF)
1967—49ers, 27-21 (M)
1968—Vikings, 30-20 (SF)
1969—Vikings, 10-7 (M)
1970—*49ers, 17-14 (M)
1971—49ers, 13-9 (M)
1972—49ers, 20-17 (SF)
1973—Vikings, 17-13 (SF)
1975—Vikings, 27-17 (M)
1976—49ers, 20-16 (SF)
1977—Vikings, 28-27 (M)
1979—Vikings, 28-22 (M)
(Points—Vikings 522, 49ers 507)
NFC Divisional Playoff
MINNESOTA vs. SEATTLE
Series tied, 1-1
1976—Vikings, 27-21 (M)
1978—Seahawks, 29-28 (S)
(Points—Vikings 55, Seahawks 50)
MINNESOTA vs. TAMPA BAY
Vikings lead series, 6-3
1977—Vikings, 9-3 (TB)
1978—Buccaneers, 16-10 (M)
Vikings, 24-7 (TB)
1979—Buccaneers, 12-10 (M)
Vikings, 23-22 (TB)
1980—Vikings, 38-30 (M)
Vikings, 21-10 (TB)
1981—Buccaneers, 21-13 (TB)
Vikings, 25-10 (M)
(Points—Vikings 173, Buccaneers 131)
MINNESOTA vs. WASHINGTON
Vikings lead series, 5-2
1968—Vikings, 27-14 (M)
1970—Vikings, 19-10 (W)
1972—Redskins, 24-21 (M)
1973—*Vikings, 27-20 (M)
1975—Redskins, 31-30 (W)
1976—*Vikings 35-20 (M)
1980—Vikings, 39-14 (W)
(Points—Vikings 198, Redskins 133)
NFC Divisional Playoff

NEW ENGLAND vs. ATLANTA
Patriots lead series, 2-1;
See Atlanta vs. New England
NEW ENGLAND vs. BALTIMORE
Colts lead series, 13-11;
See Baltimore vs. New England
NEW ENGLAND vs. BUFFALO
Bills lead series, 23-21-1;
See Buffalo vs. New England
NEW ENGLAND vs. CHICAGO
Patriots lead series, 2-0;
See Chicago vs. New England
NEW ENGLAND vs. CINCINNATI
Patriots lead series, 4-3;
See Cincinnati vs. New England
NEW ENGLAND vs. CLEVELAND
Browns lead series, 3-1;
See Cleveland vs. New England
NEW ENGLAND vs. DALLAS
Cowboys lead series, 4-0;
See Dallas vs. New England
NEW ENGLAND vs. DENVER
Patriots lead series, 12-10;
See Denver vs. New England
NEW ENGLAND vs. DETROIT
Lions lead series, 2-1;
See Detroit vs. New England
NEW ENGLAND vs. GREEN BAY
Series tied, 1-1;
See Green Bay vs. New England
NEW ENGLAND vs. HOUSTON
Series tied, 13-13-1;
See Houston vs. New England
NEW ENGLAND vs. KANSAS CITY
Chiefs lead series, 11-7-3;
See Kansas City vs. New England
NEW ENGLAND vs. LOS ANGELES
Series tied, 1-1;
See Los Angeles vs. New England
NEW ENGLAND vs. MIAMI
Dolphins lead series, 20-11;
See Miami vs. New England
NEW ENGLAND vs. MINNESOTA
Patriots lead series, 2-1;
See Minnesota vs. New England
NEW ENGLAND vs. NEW ORLEANS
Patriots lead series, 3-0
1972—Patriots, 17-10 (NO)
1976—Patriots, 27-6 (NE)
1980—Patriots, 38-27 (NO)
(Points—Patriots 82, Saints 43)
***NEW ENGLAND vs. N. Y. GIANTS**
Series tied, 1-1
1970—Giants, 16-0 (B)
1974—Patriots, 28-20 (New Haven)
(Points—Giants 36, Patriots 28)
**Franchise in Boston prior to 1971*
***NEW ENGLAND vs. **N. Y. JETS**
Jets lead series, 26-17-1
1960—Patriots, 28-24 (NY)
Patriots, 38-21 (B)
1961—Titans, 21-20 (B)
Titans, 37-30 (NY)
1962—Patriots, 43-14 (NY)
Patriots, 24-17 (B)
1963—Patriots, 38-14 (B)
Jets, 31-24 (NY)
1964—Patriots, 26-10 (B)
Jets, 35-14 (NY)
1965—Jets, 30-20 (B)
Patriots, 27-23 (NY)
1966—Tie, 24-24 (B)
Jets, 38-28 (NY)
1967—Jets, 30-23 (NY)
Jets, 29-24 (B)
1968—Jets, 47-31 (Birmingham)
Jets, 48-14 (NY)
1969—Jets, 23-14 (B)
Jets, 23-17 (NY)
1970—Jets, 31-21 (B)
Jets, 17-3 (NY)
1971—Patriots, 20-0 (NE)
Jets, 13-6 (NY)
1972—Jets, 41-13 (NE)
Jets, 34-10 (NY)
1973—Jets, 9-7 (NE)
Jets, 33-13 (NY)
1974—Patriots, 24-0 (NY)
Jets, 21-16 (NE)
1975—Jets, 36-7 (NY)
Jets, 30-28 (NE)
1976—Patriots, 41-7 (NE)
Patriots, 38-24 (NY)
1977—Jets, 30-27 (NY)
Patriots, 24-13 (NE)
1978—Patriots, 55-21 (NE)
Patriots, 19-17 (NY)
1979—Patriots, 56-3 (NE)
Jets, 27-26 (NY)
1980—Patriots, 21-11 (NY)
Patriots, 34-21 (NE)
1981—Jets, 28-24 (NY)
Jets, 17-6 (NE)
(Points—Patriots 1,046, Jets 1,023)
**Franchise in Boston prior to 1971*
***Jets known as Titans prior to 1963*
***NEW ENGLAND vs. OAKLAND**
Series tied, 11-11-1
1960—Raiders, 27-14 (O)
Patriots, 34-28 (B)
1961—Patriots, 20-17 (B)
Patriots, 35-21 (O)
1962—Patriots, 26-16 (B)
Raiders, 20-0 (O)
1963—Patriots, 20-14 (O)
Patriots, 20-14 (B)
1964—Patriots, 17-14 (O)
Tie, 43-43 (B)
1965—Raiders, 24-10 (B)
Raiders, 30-21 (O)
1966—Patriots, 24-21 (B)
1967—Raiders, 35-7 (O)
Raiders, 48-14 (B)
1968—Raiders, 41-10 (O)
1969—Raiders, 38-23 (B)
1971—Patriots, 20-6 (NE)
1974—Raiders, 41-26 (O)
1976—Patriots, 48-17 (NE)
**Raiders, 24-21 (O)
1978—Patriots, 21-14 (O)
1981—Raiders, 27-17 (O)
(Points—Raiders 580, Patriots 491)
**Franchise in Boston prior to 1971*
***AFC Divisional Playoff*
NEW ENGLAND vs. PHILADELPHIA
Series tied, 2-2
1973—Eagles, 24-23 (P)
1977—Patriots, 14-6 (NE)
1978—Patriots, 24-14 (NE)
1981—Eagles, 13-3 (P)
(Points—Patriots 64, Eagles 57)
NEW ENGLAND vs. PITTSBURGH
Steelers lead series, 4-1
1972—Steelers, 33-3 (P)
1974—Steelers, 21-17 (NE)
1976—Patriots, 30-27 (P)
1979—Steelers, 16-13 (NE) OT
1981—Steelers, 27-21 (P) OT
(Points—Steelers 124, Patriots 84)
***NEW ENGLAND vs. ST. LOUIS**
Cardinals lead series, 3-1
1970—Cardinals, 31-0 (StL)
1975—Cardinals, 24-17 (StL)
1978—Patriots, 16-6 (StL)
1981—Cardinals, 27-20 (NE)
(Points—Cardinals 88, Patriots 53)
**Franchise in Boston prior to 1971*
***NEW ENGLAND vs. **SAN DIEGO**
Series tied, 12-12-2
1960—Patriots, 35-0 (LA)
Chargers, 45-16 (B)
1961—Chargers, 38-27 (B)
Patriots, 41-0 (SD)
1962—Patriots, 24-20 (B)
Patriots, 20-14 (SD)
1963—Chargers, 17-13 (SD)
Chargers, 7-6 (B)
***Chargers, 51-10 (SD)
1964—Patriots, 33-28 (SD)
Chargers, 26-17 (B)
1965—Tie, 10-10 (B)
Patriots, 22-6 (SD)
1966—Chargers, 24-0 (SD)
Patriots, 35-17 (B)
1967—Chargers, 28-14 (SD)
Tie, 31-31 (SD)
1968—Chargers, 27-17 (B)
1969—Chargers, 13-10 (B)
Chargers, 28-18 (SD)
1970—Chargers, 16-14 (B)
1973—Patriots, 30-14 (NE)
1975—Patriots, 33-19 (SD)
1977—Patriots, 24-20 (SD)
1978—Patriots, 28-23 (NE)
1979—Patriots, 27-21 (NE)
(Points—Patriots 555, Chargers 543)
**Franchise in Boston prior to 1971*
***Franchise in Los Angeles prior to 1961*
****AFL Championship*
NEW ENGLAND vs. SAN FRANCISCO
49ers lead series, 2-1
1971—49ers, 27-10 (SF)
1975—Patriots, 24-16 (NE)
1980—49ers, 21-17 (SF)
(Points—49ers 64, Patriots 51)
NEW ENGLAND vs. SEATTLE
Patriots lead series, 2-0
1977—Patriots, 31-0 (NE)
1980—Patriots, 37-31 (S)
(Points—Patriots 68, Seahawks 31)
NEW ENGLAND vs. TAMPA BAY
Patriots lead series, 1-0
1976—Patriots, 31-14 (TB)
NEW ENGLAND vs. WASHINGTON
Redskins lead series, 2-1
1972—Patriots, 24-23 (NE)
1978—Redskins, 16-14 (NE)
1981—Redskins, 24-22 (W)
(Points—Redskins 63, Patriots 60)

NEW ORLEANS vs. ATLANTA
Falcons lead series, 19-7;
See Atlanta vs. New Orleans
NEW ORLEANS vs. BALTIMORE
Colts lead series, 3-0;
See Baltimore vs. New Orleans
NEW ORLEANS vs. BUFFALO
Series tied, 1-1;
See Buffalo vs. New Orleans
NEW ORLEANS vs. CHICAGO
Bears lead series, 6-2;
See Chicago vs. New Orleans
NEW ORLEANS vs. CINCINNATI
Series tied, 2-2;
See Cincinnati vs. New Orleans
NEW ORLEANS vs. CLEVELAND
Browns lead series, 8-0;
See Cleveland vs. New Orleans
NEW ORLEANS vs. DALLAS
Cowboys lead series, 8-1;
See Dallas vs. New Orleans
NEW ORLEANS vs. DENVER
Broncos lead series, 3-0;
See Denver vs. New Orleans
NEW ORLEANS vs. DETROIT
Series tied, 4-4-1;
See Detroit vs. New Orleans
NEW ORLEANS vs. GREEN BAY
Packers lead series, 8-2;
See Green Bay vs. New Orleans
NEW ORLEANS vs. HOUSTON
Oilers lead series, 2-1-1;
See Houston vs. New Orleans
NEW ORLEANS vs. KANSAS CITY
Series tied, 1-1;
See Kansas City vs. New Orleans
NEW ORLEANS vs. LOS ANGELES
Rams lead series, 18-8;
See Los Angeles vs. New Orleans
NEW ORLEANS vs. MIAMI
Dolphins lead series, 3-0;
See Miami vs. New Orleans
NEW ORLEANS vs. MINNESOTA
Vikings lead series, 8-2;
See Minnesota vs. New Orleans
NEW ORLEANS vs. NEW ENGLAND
Patriots lead series, 3-0;
See New England vs. New Orleans
NEW ORLEANS vs. N. Y. GIANTS
Giants lead series, 5-4
1967—Giants, 27-21 (NY)
1968—Giants, 38-21 (NY)
1969—Saints, 25-24 (NY)
1970—Saints, 14-10 (NO)
1972—Giants, 45-21 (NY)
1975—Giants, 28-14 (NY)
1978—Saints, 28-17 (NO)
1979—Saints, 24-14 (NO)
1981—Giants, 20-7 (NY)
(Points—Giants 223, Saints 175)
NEW ORLEANS vs. N. Y. JETS
Jets lead series, 2-1
1972—Jets, 18-17 (NY)
1977—Jets, 16-13 (NO)
1980—Saints, 21-20 (NY)
(Points—Jets 54, Saints 51)
NEW ORLEANS vs. OAKLAND
Raiders lead series, 2-0-1
1971—Tie, 21-21 (NO)
1975—Raiders, 48-10 (O)
1979—Raiders, 42-35 (NO)
(Points—Raiders 111, Saints 66)
NEW ORLEANS vs. PHILADELPHIA
Eagles lead series, 8-4
1967—Saints, 31-24 (NO)
Eagles, 48-21 (P)
1968—Eagles, 29-17 (P)
1969—Eagles, 13-10 (P)
Saints, 26-17 (NO)
1972—Saints, 21-3 (NO)
1974—Saints, 14-10 (NO)
1977—Eagles, 28-7 (P)
1978—Eagles, 24-17 (NO)
1979—Eagles, 26-14 (NO)
1980—Eagles, 34-21 (NO)
1981—Eagles, 31-14 (NO)
(Points—Eagles 287, Saints 213)
NEW ORLEANS vs. PITTSBURGH
Steelers lead series, 4-3
1967—Steelers, 14-10 (NO)
1968—Saints, 16-12 (P)
Saints, 24-14 (NO)
1969—Saints, 27-24 (NO)
1974—Steelers, 28-7 (NO)
1978—Steelers, 20-14 (P)
1981—Steelers, 20-6 (NO)
(Points—Steelers 132, Saints 104)
NEW ORLEANS vs. ST. LOUIS
Cardinals lead series, 7-2
1967—Cardinals, 31-20 (StL)
1968—Cardinals, 21-20 (NO)
Cardinals, 31-17 (StL)
1969—Saints, 51-42 (StL)
1970—Cardinals, 24-17 (StL)
1974—Saints, 14-0 (NO)
1977—Cardinals, 49-31 (StL)
1980—Cardinals, 40-7 (NO)
1981—Cardinals, 30-3 (StL)
(Points—Cardinals 268, Saints 180)
NEW ORLEANS vs. SAN DIEGO
Chargers lead series, 3-0
1973—Chargers, 17-14 (SD)
1977—Chargers, 14-0 (NO)
1979—Chargers, 35-0 (NO)
(Points—Chargers 66, Saints 14)
NEW ORLEANS vs. SAN FRANCISCO
49ers lead series, 17-7-2
1967—49ers, 27-13 (SF)
1969—Saints, 43-38 (NO)
1970—Tie, 20-20 (SF)
49ers, 38-27 (NO)
1971—49ers, 38-20 (NO)
Saints, 26-20 (SF)
1972—49ers, 37-2 (NO)
Tie, 20-20 (SF)
1973—49ers, 40-0 (SF)
Saints, 16-10 (NO)
1974—49ers, 17-13 (NO)
49ers, 35-21 (SF)
1975—49ers, 35-21 (SF)
49ers, 16-6 (NO)
1976—49ers, 33-3 (SF)
49ers, 27-7 (NO)
1977—49ers, 10-7 (NO) OT
49ers, 20-17 (SF)
1978—Saints, 14-7 (SF)
Saints, 24-13 (NO)
1979—Saints, 30-21 (SF)
Saints, 31-20 (NO)
1980—49ers, 26-23 (NO)
49ers, 38-35 (SF) OT
1981—49ers, 21-14 (SF)
49ers, 21-17 (NO)
(Points—49ers 648, Saints 470)
NEW ORLEANS vs. SEATTLE
Series tied, 1-1
1976—Saints, 51-27 (S)
1979—Seahawks, 38-24 (S)
(Points—Saints 75, Seahawks 65)
NEW ORLEANS vs. TAMPA BAY
Series tied, 2-2
1977—Buccaneers, 33-14 (NO)
1978—Saints, 17-10 (TB)
1979—Saints, 42-14 (TB)
1981—Buccaneers, 31-14 (NO)
(Points—Buccaneers 88, Saints 87)
NEW ORLEANS vs. WASHINGTON
Redskins lead series, 6-4
1967—Redskins, 30-10 (NO)
Saints, 30-14 (W)
1968—Saints, 37-17 (NO)
1969—Redskins, 26-20 (NO)
Redskins, 17-14 (W)
1971—Redskins, 24-14 (W)

1973—Saints, 19-3 (NO)
1975—Redskins, 41-3 (W)
1979—Saints, 14-10 (W)
1980—Redskins, 22-14 (W)
(Points—Redskins 204, Saints 175)
*N.Y. BULLDOGS vs. **CHICAGO CARDINALS
Cardinals won series, 1-0
1949—Cardinals, 65-20
*Extinct team
**Franchise moved to St. Louis in 1960
*N.Y. BULLDOGS vs. DETROIT
Lions won series, 1-0
See Detroit vs. N.Y. Bulldogs
*Extinct team
*N.Y. BULLDOGS vs. GREEN BAY
Packers won series, 1-0
See Green Bay vs. N.Y. Bulldogs
*Extinct team
*N.Y. BULLDOGS vs. LOS ANGELES
Rams won series, 1-0
See Los Angeles vs. N.Y. Bulldogs
*Extinct team
*N.Y. BULLDOGS vs. N.Y. GIANTS
Series tied, 1-1
1949—Giants, 38-14
Bulldogs, 31-24
(Points—Giants 62, Bulldogs 45)
*Extinct team
*N.Y. BULLDOGS vs. PHILADELPHIA
Eagles won series, 2-0
1949—Eagles, 7-0
Eagles, 42-0
(Points—Eagles 49, Bulldogs 0)
*Extinct team
*N.Y. BULLDOGS vs. PITTSBURGH
Steelers won series, 2-0
1949—Steelers, 24-13
Steelers, 27-0
(Points—Steelers 51, Bulldogs 13)
*Extinct team
*N.Y. BULLDOGS vs. WASHINGTON
Redskins won series, 1-0-1
1949—Redskins, 38-14
Tie, 14-14
*Extinct team

N.Y. GIANTS vs. ATLANTA
Falcons lead series, 5-3;
See Atlanta vs. N.Y. Giants
N.Y. GIANTS vs. *1950 BALTIMORE
Giants won series, 1-0
See *Baltimore vs. N.Y. Giants
*Extinct team
N.Y. GIANTS vs. BALTIMORE
Colts lead series, 7-3;
See Baltimore vs. N.Y. Giants
N.Y. GIANTS vs. *BOSTON YANKS
Giants won series, 5-1-3;
See *Boston Yanks vs. N.Y. Giants
*Extinct team
N.Y. GIANTS vs. *BROOKLYN DODGERS
Giants won series, 24-5-3;
See *Brooklyn Dodgers vs. N.Y. Giants
*Extinct team
N.Y. GIANTS vs. BUFFALO
Giants lead series, 2-1;
See Buffalo vs. N.Y. Giants
N.Y. GIANTS vs. CHICAGO
Bears lead series, 26-16-2;
See Chicago vs. N.Y. Giants
N.Y. GIANTS vs. CINCINNATI
Bengals lead series, 2-0;
See Cincinnati vs. N.Y. Giants
N.Y. GIANTS vs. CLEVELAND
Browns lead series, 25-16-2;
See Cleveland vs. N.Y. Giants
N.Y. GIANTS vs. DALLAS
Cowboys lead series, 28-11-2;
See Dallas vs. N.Y. Giants
N.Y. GIANTS vs. *DALLAS TEXANS
Giants won series, 1-0;
See *Dallas Texans vs. N.Y. Giants
*Extinct team
N.Y. GIANTS vs. DENVER
Broncos lead series, 2-1;
See Denver vs. N.Y. Giants
N.Y. GIANTS VS. DETROIT
Lions lead series, 17-10-1;

See Detroit vs. N.Y. Giants
N.Y. GIANTS vs. GREEN BAY
Packers lead series, 23-17-2;
See Green Bay vs. N.Y. Giants
N.Y. GIANTS vs. HOUSTON
Giants lead series, 1-0;
See Houston vs. N.Y. Giants
N.Y. GIANTS vs. KANSAS CITY
Giants lead series, 3-0;
See Kansas City vs. N.Y. Giants
N.Y. GIANTS vs. LOS ANGELES
Rams lead series, 14-6;
See Los Angeles vs. N.Y. Giants
N.Y. GIANTS vs. MIAMI
Dolphins lead series, 1-0;
See Miami vs. N.Y. Giants
N.Y. GIANTS vs. MINNESOTA
Vikings lead series, 6-1;
See Minnesota vs. N.Y. Giants
N.Y. GIANTS vs. NEW ENGLAND
Series tied, 1-1;
See New England vs. N.Y. Giants
N.Y. GIANTS vs. NEW ORLEANS
Giants lead series, 5-4;
See New Orleans vs. N.Y. Giants
N.Y. GIANTS vs. N.Y. JETS
Jets lead series, 2-1
1970—Giants, 22-10 (NYJ)
1974—Jets, 26-20 (New Haven) OT
1981—Jets, 26-7 (NYG)
(Points—Jets 62, Giants 49)
N.Y. GIANTS vs. *N.Y. YANKS
Giants won series, 3-0
1950—Giants, 51-7
1951—Giants, 37-31
Giants, 27-17
(Points—Giants 115, Yanks 55)
*Extinct team
N.Y. GIANTS vs. OAKLAND
Raiders lead series, 2-0
1973—Raiders, 42-0 (O)
1980—Raiders, 33-17 (NY)
(Points—Raiders 75, Giants 17)
N.Y. GIANTS vs. PHILADELPHIA
Giants lead series, 50-43-2
1933—Giants, 56-0 (NY)
Giants, 20-14 (P)
1934—Giants, 17-0 (NY)
Eagles, 6-0 (P)
1935—Giants, 10-0 (NY)
Giants, 21-14 (P)
1936—Eagles, 10-7 (NY)
Giants, 21-17 (NY)
1937—Giants, 16-7 (P)
Giants, 21-0 (NY)
1938—Eagles, 14-10 (P)
Giants, 17-7 (NY)
1939—Giants, 13-3 (P)
Giants, 27-10 (NY)
1940—Giants, 20-14 (P)
Giants, 17-7 (NY)
1941—Giants, 24-0 (P)
Giants, 16-0 (NY)
1942—Giants, 35-17 (NY)
Giants, 14-0 (P)
1944—Eagles, 24-17 (NY)
Tie, 21-21 (P)
1945—Eagles, 38-17 (NY)
Giants, 28-21 (NY)
1946—Eagles, 24-14 (P)
Giants, 45-17 (NY)
1947—Eagles, 23-0 (P)
Eagles, 41-24 (NY)
1948—Eagles, 45-0 (NY)
Giants, 35-14 (NY)
1949—Eagles, 24-3 (NY)
Eagles, 17-3 (P)
1950—Giants, 7-3 (NY)
Giants, 9-7 (P)
1951—Giants, 26-24 (NY)
Giants, 23-7 (P)
1952—Giants, 31-7 (P)
Eagles, 14-10 (NY)
1953—Giants, 30-7 (P)
Giants, 37-28 (NY)
1954—Giants, 27-14 (NY)
Eagles, 29-14 (P)
1955—Eagles, 27-17 (P)
Giants, 31-7 (NY)
1956—Giants, 20-3 (NY)
Giants, 21-7 (P)
1957—Giants, 24-20 (P)
Giants, 13-0 (NY)
1958—Eagles, 27-24 (P)
Giants, 24-10 (NY)
1959—Eagles, 49-21 (P)
Giants, 24-7 (NY)
1960—Eagles, 17-10 (NY)

Eagles, 31-23 (P)
1961—Giants, 38-21 (NY)
Giants, 28-24 (P)
1962—Giants, 29-13 (P)
Giants, 19-14 (NY)
1963—Giants, 37-14 (P)
Giants, 42-14 (NY)
1964—Eagles, 38-7 (P)
Eagles, 23-17 (NY)
1965—Giants, 16-14 (P)
Giants, 35-27 (NY)
1966—Eagles, 35-17 (P)
Eagles, 31-3 (NY)
1967—Eagles, 44-7 (NY)
Giants, 7-6 (P)
1968—Giants, 34-25 (P)
Giants, 7-6 (NY)
1969—Eagles, 23-20 (NY)
1970—Giants, 30-23 (NY)
Eagles, 23-20 (P)
1971—Eagles, 23-7 (P)
Eagles, 41-28 (NY)
1972—Giants, 27-12 (P)
Giants, 62-10 (NY)
1973—Tie, 23-23 (NY)
Eagles, 20-16 (P)
1974—Eagles, 35-7 (P)
Eagles, 20-7 (New Haven)
1975—Giants, 23-14 (P)
Eagles, 13-10 (NY)
1976—Eagles, 20-7 (P)
Eagles, 10-0 (NY)
1977—Eagles, 28-10 (NY)
Eagles, 17-14 (P)
1978—Eagles, 19-17 (NY)
Eagles, 20-3 (P)
1979—Eagles, 23-17 (P)
Eagles, 17-13 (NY)
1980—Eagles, 35-3 (P)
Eagles, 31-16 (NY)
1981—Eagles, 24-10 (NY)
Giants, 20-10 (P)
*Giants, 27-21 (P)
(Points—Giants 1,821, Eagles 1,699)
*NFC First Round Playoff
N.Y. GIANTS vs. *PITTSBURGH
Giants lead series, 40-26-3
1933—Giants, 23-2 (P)
Giants, 27-3 (NY)
1934—Giants, 14-12 (P)
Giants, 17-7 (NY)
1935—Giants, 42-7 (P)
Giants, 13-0 (NY)
1936—Pirates, 10-7 (P)
1937—Giants, 10-7 (P)
Giants, 17-0 (NY)
1938—Giants, 27-14 (P)
Pirates, 13-10 (NY)
1939—Giants, 14-7 (P)
Giants, 23-7 (NY)
1940—Tie, 10-10 (P)
Giants, 12-0 (NY)
1941—Giants, 37-10 (P)
Giants, 28-7 (NY)
1942—Steelers, 13-10 (P)
Steelers, 17-9 (NY)
1945—Giants, 34-6 (P)
Steelers, 21-7 (NY)
1946—Giants, 17-14 (P)
Giants, 7-0 (NY)
1947—Steelers, 38-21 (NY)
Steelers, 24-7 (P)
1948—Giants, 34-27 (NY)
Steelers, 38-28 (P)
1949—Steelers, 28-7 (P)
Steelers, 21-17 (NY)
1950—Giants, 18-7 (P)
Steelers, 17-6 (NY)
1951—Tie, 13-13 (P)
Giants, 14-0 (NY)
1952—Steelers, 63-7 (P)
1953—Giants, 24-14 (NY)
Steelers, 14-10 (NY)
1954—Giants, 30-6 (P)
Giants, 24-3 (NY)
1955—Steelers, 30-23 (P)
Steelers, 19-17 (NY)
1956—Giants, 38-10 (NY)
Giants, 17-14 (P)
1957—Giants, 35-0 (NY)
Steelers, 21-10 (P)
1958—Giants, 17-6 (NY)
Steelers, 31-10 (P)
1959—Giants, 21-16 (P)
Steelers, 14-9 (NY)
1960—Giants, 19-17 (P)
Giants, 27-24 (NY)
1961—Giants, 17-14 (NY)
Giants, 42-21 (NY)

1962—Giants, 31-27 (P)
Steelers, 20-17 (NY)
1963—Steelers, 31-0 (P)
Giants, 33-17 (NY)
1964—Steelers, 27-24 (P)
Steelers, 44-17 (NY)
1965—Giants, 23-13 (P)
Giants, 35-10 (NY)
1966—Tie, 34-34 (P)
Steelers, 47-28 (NY)
1967—Giants, 27-24 (P)
Giants, 28-20 (NY)
1968—Giants, 34-20 (P)
Giants, 10-7 (NY)
1969—Giants, 21-17 (P)
1971—Steelers, 17-13 (P)
1976—Steelers, 27-0 (NY)
(Points—Giants 1,342, Steelers 1,149)
*Steelers known as Pirates prior to 1941
N.Y. GIANTS vs. *ST. LOUIS
Giants lead series, 50-28-1
1926—Giants, 20-0 (NY)
1927—Giants, 28-7 (NY)
1929—Giants, 24-21 (NY)
1930—Giants, 25-12 (NY)
Giants, 13-7 (C)
1935—Cardinals, 14-13 (NY)
1936—Giants, 14-6 (NY)
1938—Giants, 6-0 (NY)
1939—Giants, 17-7 (NY)
1941—Cardinals, 10-7 (NY)
1942—Giants, 21-7 (NY)
1943—Giants, 24-13 (NY)
1946—Giants, 28-24 (NY)
1947—Cardinals, 35-31 (NY)
1948—Cardinals, 63-35 (NY)
1949—Giants, 41-38 (C)
1950—Cardinals, 17-3 (C)
Giants, 51-21 (NY)
1951—Giants, 28-17 (NY)
Giants, 10-0 (C)
1952—Cardinals, 24-23 (NY)
Giants, 28-6 (C)
1953—Giants, 21-7 (NY)
Giants, 23-20 (C)
1954—Cardinals, 41-10 (C)
Giants, 31-17 (NY)
1955—Cardinals, 28-17 (C)
Giants, 10-0 (NY)
1956—Cardinals, 35-27 (C)
Giants, 23-10 (NY)
1957—Giants, 27-14 (NY)
Giants, 28-21 (C)
1958—Giants, 37-7 (Buffalo)
Cardinals, 23-6 (NY)
1959—Giants, 9-3 (NY)
Giants, 30-20 (Minn)
1960—Giants, 35-14 (StL)
Cardinals, 20-13 (NY)
1961—Cardinals, 21-10 (NY)
Giants, 24-9 (StL)
1962—Giants, 31-14 (NY)
Giants, 31-28 (StL)
1963—Giants, 38-21 (StL)
Cardinals, 24-17 (NY)
1964—Giants, 34-17 (StL)
Tie, 10-10 (NY)
1965—Giants, 14-10 (NY)
Giants, 28-15 (StL)
1966—Cardinals, 24-19 (StL)
Cardinals, 20-17 (NY)
1967—Giants, 37-20 (StL)
Giants, 37-14 (NY)
1968—Cardinals, 28-21 (NY)
Cardinals, 42-17 (StL)
1969—Giants, 49-6 (NY)
1970—Giants, 35-17 (NY)
Giants, 34-17 (StL)
1971—Giants, 21-20 (StL)
Cardinals, 24-7 (NY)
1972—Giants, 27-21 (NY)
Giants, 13-7 (StL)
1973—Cardinals, 35-27 (StL)
Giants, 24-13 (New Haven)
1974—Cardinals, 23-21 (New Haven)
Cardinals, 26-14 (StL)
1975—Cardinals, 26-14 (StL)
Cardinals, 20-13 (NY)
1976—Cardinals, 27-21 (StL)
Cardinals, 17-14 (NY)
1977—Cardinals, 28-0 (StL)
Giants, 27-7 (NY)
1978—Cardinals, 20-10 (StL)
Giants, 17-0 (NY)
1979—Cardinals, 27-14 (NY)
Cardinals, 29-20 (StL)

1980—Giants, 41-35 (StL)
Cardinals, 23-7 (NY)
1981—Giants, 34-14 (NY)
Giants, 20-10 (StL)
(Points—Giants 1,781, Cardinals 1,403)
*Franchise in Chicago prior to 1960
N.Y. GIANTS vs. SAN DIEGO
Giants lead series, 2-1
1971—Giants, 35-17 (NY)
1975—Giants, 35-24 (NY)
1980—Chargers, 44-7 (SD)
(Points—Chargers 85, Giants 77)
N.Y. GIANTS vs. SAN FRANCISCO
Giants lead series, 9-5
1952—Giants, 23-14 (NY)
1956—Giants, 38-21 (SF)
1957—49ers, 27-17 (NY)
1960—Giants, 21-19 (SF)
1963—Giants, 48-14 (NY)
1968—49ers, 26-10 (NY)
1972—Giants, 23-17 (SF)
1975—Giants, 26-23 (SF)
1977—Giants, 20-17 (NY)
1978—Giants, 27-10 (SF)
1979—Giants, 32-16 (NY)
1980—49ers, 12-0 (SF)
1981—49ers, 17-10 (SF)
*49ers, 38-24 (SF)
(Points—Giants 319, 49ers 271)
*NFC Divisional Playoff
N.Y. GIANTS vs. SEATTLE
Giants lead series, 3-0
1976—Giants, 28-16 (NY)
1980—Giants, 27-21 (S)
1981—Giants, 32-0 (S)
(Points—Giants 87, Seahawks 37)
N.Y. GIANTS vs. TAMPA BAY
Giants lead series, 4-2
1977—Giants, 10-0 (TB)
1978—Giants, 19-13 (TB)
Giants, 17-14 (NY)
1979—Giants, 17-14 (NY)
Buccaneers, 31-3 (TB)
1980—Buccaneers, 30-13 (TB)
(Points—Buccaneers 102, Giants 79)
N.Y. GIANTS vs. *WASHINGTON
Giants lead series, 56-40-3
1932—Braves, 14-6 (B)
Tie, 0-0 (B)
1933—Redskins, 21-20 (B)
Giants, 7-0 (B)
1934—Giants, 16-13 (B)
Giants, 3-0 (NY)
1935—Giants, 20-12 (B)
Giants, 17-6 (NY)
1936—Giants, 7-0 (B)
Redskins, 14-0 (NY)
1937—Redskins, 13-3 (W)
Redskins, 49-14 (NY)
1938—Giants, 10-7 (W)
Giants, 36-0 (NY)
1939—Tie, 0-0 (W)
Giants, 9-7 (NY)
1940—Redskins, 21-7 (W)
Giants, 21-7 (NY)
1941—Giants, 17-10 (W)
Giants, 20-13 (NY)
1942—Giants, 14-7 (W)
Redskins, 14-7 (NY)
1943—Giants, 14-10 (NY)
Giants, 31-7 (W)
**Redskins, 28-0 (NY)
1944—Giants, 16-13 (NY)
Giants, 31-0 (W)
1945—Redskins, 24-14 (NY)
Redskins, 17-0 (W)
1946—Redskins, 24-14 (W)
Giants, 31-0 (NY)
1947—Redskins, 28-20 (W)
Giants, 35-10 (NY)
1948—Redskins, 41-10 (W)
Redskins, 28-21 (NY)
1949—Giants, 45-35 (W)
Giants, 23-7 (NY)
1950—Giants, 21-17 (W)
Giants, 24-21 (NY)
1951—Giants, 35-14 (NY)
Giants, 28-14 (W)
1952—Giants, 14-10 (NY)
Redskins, 27-17 (NY)
1953—Redskins, 13-9 (W)
Redskins, 24-21 (NY)
1954—Giants, 51-21 (W)
Giants, 24-7 (NY)
1955—Giants, 35-7 (NY)
Giants, 27-20 (W)
1956—Redskins, 33-7 (W)

Giants, 28-14 (NY)
1957—Giants, 24-20 (W)
Redskins, 31-14 (NY)
1958—Giants, 21-14 (W)
Giants, 30-0 (NY)
1959—Giants, 45-14 (NY)
Giants, 24-10 (W)
1960—Tie, 24-24 (NY)
Giants, 17-3 (W)
1961—Giants, 24-21 (W)
Giants, 53-0 (NY)
1962—Giants, 49-34 (NY)
Giants, 42-24 (NY)
1963—Giants, 24-14 (W)
Giants, 44-14 (NY)
1964—Giants, 13-10 (NY)
Redskins, 36-21 (W)
1965—Redskins, 23-7 (NY)
Giants, 27-10 (W)
1966—Giants, 13-10 (NY)
Redskins, 72-41 (W)
1967—Redskins, 38-34 (W)
Giants, 48-21 (W)
1968—Giants, 13-10 (W)
1969—Redskins, 20-14 (W)
1970—Giants, 35-33 (NY)
Giants, 27-24 (W)
1971—Redskins, 30-3 (NY)
Redskins, 23-7 (W)
1972—Redskins, 23-16 (NY)
Redskins, 27-13 (W)
1973—Redskins, 21-3 (New Haven)
Redskins, 27-24 (W)
1974—Redskins, 13-10 (New Haven)
Redskins, 24-3 (W)
1975—Redskins, 49-13 (W)
Redskins, 21-13 (NY)
1976—Redskins, 19-17 (W)
Giants, 12-9 (NY)
1977—Giants, 20-17 (NY)
Giants, 17-6 (W)
1978—Giants, 17-6 (NY)
Redskins, 16-13 (W) OT
1979—Redskins, 27-0 (W)
Giants, 14-6 (NY)
1980—Redskins, 23-21 (NY)
Redskins, 16-13 (W)
1981—Giants, 17-7 (W)
Redskins, 30-27 (NY) OT
(Points—Giants 1,921, Redskins 1,712)

*Franchise in Boston prior to 1937 and known as Braves prior to 1933
**Division Playoff

N. Y. JETS vs. ATLANTA
Series tied, 1-1;
See Atlanta vs. N. Y. Jets
N. Y. JETS vs. BALTIMORE
Colts lead series, 14-11;
See Baltimore vs. N. Y. Jets
N. Y. JETS vs. BUFFALO
Bills lead series, 25-20;
See Buffalo vs. N. Y. Jets
N. Y. JETS vs. CHICAGO
Series tied, 1-1;
See Chicago vs. N. Y. Jets
N. Y. JETS vs. CINCINNATI
Jets lead series, 4-3;
See Cincinnati vs. N. Y. Jets
N. Y. JETS vs. CLEVELAND
Browns lead series, 6-1;
See Cleveland vs. N. Y. Jets
N. Y. JETS vs. DALLAS
Cowboys lead series, 3-0;
See Dallas vs. N. Y. Jets
N. Y. JETS vs. DENVER
Series tied, 10-10-1;
See Denver vs. N. Y. Jets
N. Y. JETS vs. DETROIT
Series tied, 1-1;
See Detroit vs. N. Y. Jets
N. Y. JETS vs. GREEN BAY
Jets lead series, 2-1;
See Green Bay vs. N. Y. Jets
N. Y. JETS vs. HOUSTON
Oilers lead series, 14-10-1;
See Houston vs. N. Y. Jets
N. Y. JETS vs. KANSAS CITY
Chiefs lead series, 12-9;
See Kansas City vs. N. Y. Jets
N. Y. JETS vs. LOS ANGELES
Rams lead series, 2-1;
See Los Angeles vs. N. Y. Jets
N. Y. JETS vs. MIAMI
Jets lead series, 17-14-1;
See Miami vs. N. Y. Jets
N. Y. JETS vs. MINNESOTA

Jets lead series, 2-1;
See Minnesota vs. N. Y. Jets
N. Y. JETS vs. NEW ENGLAND
Jets lead series, 26-17-1;
See New England vs. N. Y. Jets
N. Y. JETS vs. NEW ORLEANS
Jets lead series, 2-1;
See New Orleans vs. N. Y. Jets
N. Y. JETS vs. N. Y. GIANTS
Jets lead series, 2-1;
See N. Y. Giants vs. N. Y. Jets
***N. Y. JETS vs. OAKLAND**
Raiders lead series, 11-10-2
1960—Raiders, 28-27 (NY)
Titans, 31-28 (O)
1961—Titans, 14-6 (O)
Titans, 23-12 (NY)
1962—Titans, 28-17 (O)
Titans, 31-21 (NY)
1963—Jets, 10-7 (NY)
Raiders, 49-26 (O)
1964—Jets, 35-13 (NY)
Raiders, 35-26 (O)
1965—Tie, 24-24 (NY)
Raiders, 24-14 (O)
1966—Raiders, 24-21 (NY)
Tie, 28-28 (O)
1967—Jets, 27-14 (NY)
Raiders, 38-29 (O)
1968—Raiders, 43-32 (O)
**Jets, 27-23 (NY)
1969—Raiders, 27-14 (NY)
1970—Raiders, 14-13 (NY)
1972—Raiders, 24-16 (O)
1977—Raiders, 28-27 (NY)
1979—Jets, 28-19 (NY)
(Points—Jets 551, Raiders 546)
*Jets known as Titans prior to 1963
**AFL Championship
N. Y. JETS vs. PHILADELPHIA
Eagles lead series, 3-0
1973—Eagles, 24-23 (P)
1977—Eagles, 27-6 (P)
1978—Eagles, 17-9 (P)
(Points—Eagles 68, Jets 32)
N. Y. JETS vs. PITTSBURGH
Steelers lead series, 6-0
1970—Steelers, 21-17 (P)
1973—Steelers, 26-14 (P)
1975—Steelers, 20-7 (NY)
1977—Steelers, 23-20 (NY)
1978—Steelers, 28-17 (NY)
1981—Steelers, 38-10 (P)
(Points—Steelers 156, Jets 85)
N. Y. JETS vs. ST. LOUIS
Cardinals lead series, 2-1
1971—Cardinals, 17-10 (StL)
1975—Cardinals 37-6 (NY)
1978—Jets, 23-10 (NY)
(Points—Cardinals 64, Jets 39)
***N. Y. JETS vs. **SAN DIEGO**
Chargers lead series, 14-6-1
1960—Chargers, 21-7 (NY)
Chargers, 50-43 (LA)
1961—Chargers, 25-10 (NY)
Chargers, 48-13 (SD)
1962—Chargers, 40-14 (SD)
Titans, 23-3 (NY)
1963—Chargers, 24-20 (SD)
Chargers, 53-7 (NY)
1964—Tie, 17-17 (NY)
Chargers, 38-3 (SD)
1965—Chargers, 34-9 (NY)
Chargers, 38-7 (SD)
1966—Jets, 17-16 (NY)
Chargers, 42-27 (SD)
1967—Jets, 42-31 (SD)
1968—Jets, 23-20 (NY)
Jets, 37-15 (SD)
1969—Chargers, 34-27 (SD)
1971—Chargers, 49-21 (SD)
1974—Jets, 27-14 (NY)
1975—Chargers, 24-16 (SD)
(Points—Chargers 636, Jets 410)
*Jets known as Titans prior to 1963
**Franchise in Los Angeles prior to 1961
N. Y. JETS vs. SAN FRANCISCO
49ers lead series, 3-0
1971—49ers, 24-21 (NY)
1976—49ers, 17-6 (SF)
1980—49ers, 37-27 (NY)
(Points—49ers 78, Jets 54)
N. Y. JETS vs. SEATTLE
Seahawks lead series, 6-0
1977—Seahawks, 17-0 (NY)
1978—Seahawks, 24-17 (NY)
1979—Seahawks, 30-7 (S)

1980—Seahawks, 27-17 (NY)
1981—Seahawks, 19-3 (NY)
Seahawks, 27-23 (S)
(Points—Seahawks 144, Jets 67)
N. Y. JETS vs. TAMPA BAY
Jets lead series, 1-0
1976—Jets, 34-0 (NY)
N. Y. JETS vs. WASHINGTON
Redskins lead series, 3-0
1972—Redskins, 35-17 (NY)
1976—Redskins, 37-16 (NY)
1978—Redskins, 23-3 (W)
(Points—Redskins 95, Jets 36)
***N.Y. YANKS vs. *1950 BALTIMORE**
Yanks won series, 1-0;
See *Baltimore vs. *N.Y. Yanks
*Extinct team
***N.Y. YANKS vs. CHICAGO**
Bears won series, 3-0;
See Chicago vs. *N.Y. Yanks
*Extinct team
***N.Y. YANKS vs. DETROIT**
Lions won series, 2-1-1;
See Detroit vs. *N.Y. Yanks
*Extinct team
***N.Y. YANKS vs. GREEN BAY**
Yanks won series, 3-1;
See Green Bay vs. *N.Y. Yanks
*Extinct team
***N.Y. YANKS vs. LOS ANGELES**
Rams won series, 4-0;
See Los Angeles vs. *N.Y. Yanks
*Extinct team
***N.Y. YANKS vs. N.Y. GIANTS**
Giants won series, 3-0;
See *N.Y. Yanks vs. N.Y. Giants
*Extinct team
***N.Y. YANKS vs. SAN FRANCISCO**
Yanks won series, 2-1-1
1950—Yanks, 21-17
Yanks, 29-24
1951—49ers, 19-14
Tie, 10-10
(Points—Yanks 74, 49ers 70)
*Extinct team

OAKLAND vs. ATLANTA
Raiders lead series, 2-1;
See Atlanta vs. Oakland
OAKLAND vs. BALTIMORE
Raiders lead series, 3-2;
See Baltimore vs. Oakland
OAKLAND vs. BUFFALO
Series tied, 11-11;
See Buffalo vs. Oakland
OAKLAND vs. CHICAGO
Raiders lead series, 3-1;
See Chicago vs. Oakland
OAKLAND vs. CINCINNATI
Raiders lead series, 10-3;
See Cincinnati vs. Oakland
OAKLAND vs. CLEVELAND
Raiders lead series, 7-1;
See Cleveland vs. Oakland
OAKLAND vs. DALLAS
Series tied, 1-1;
See Dallas vs. Oakland
OAKLAND vs. DENVER
Raiders lead series, 31-12-2;
See Denver vs. Oakland
OAKLAND vs. DETROIT
Series tied, 2-2;
See Detroit vs. Oakland
OAKLAND vs. GREEN BAY
Raiders lead series, 3-1;
See Green Bay vs. Oakland
OAKLAND vs. HOUSTON
Raiders lead series, 19-10;
See Houston vs. Oakland
OAKLAND vs. KANSAS CITY
Raiders lead series, 24-20-2;
See Kansas City vs. Oakland
OAKLAND vs. LOS ANGELES
Raiders lead series, 2-1;
See Los Angeles vs. Oakland
OAKLAND vs. MIAMI
Raiders lead series, 12-3-1;
See Miami vs. Oakland
OAKLAND vs. MINNESOTA
Raiders lead series, 4-1;
See Minnesota vs. Oakland
OAKLAND vs. NEW ENGLAND
Series tied, 11-11-1;
See New England vs. Oakland
OAKLAND vs. NEW ORLEANS
Raiders lead series, 2-0-1;
See New Orleans vs. Oakland
OAKLAND vs. N.Y. GIANTS

Raiders lead series, 2-0;
See N.Y. Giants vs. Oakland
OAKLAND vs. N.Y. JETS
Raiders lead series, 11-10-2;
See N.Y. Jets vs. Oakland
OAKLAND vs. PHILADELPHIA
Raiders lead series, 3-1
1971—Raiders, 34-10 (O)
1976—Raiders, 26-7 (P)
1980—Eagles, 10-7 (P)
*Raiders, 27-10 (NO)
(Points—Raiders 94, Eagles 37)
*Super Bowl XV
OAKLAND vs. PITTSBURGH
Raiders lead series, 8-5
1970—Raiders, 31-14 (O)
1972—Steelers, 34-28 (P)
*Steelers, 13-7 (P)
1973—Steelers, 17-9 (O)
*Raiders, 33-14 (O)
1974—Raiders, 17-0 (P)
**Steelers, 24-13 (O)
1975—**Steelers, 16-10 (P)
1976—Raiders, 31-28 (O)
**Raiders, 24-7 (O)
1977—Raiders, 16-7 (P)
1980—Raiders, 45-34 (P)
1981—Raiders, 30-27 (O)
(Points—Raiders 294, Steelers 235)
*AFC Divisional Playoff
**AFC Championship
OAKLAND vs. ST. LOUIS
Raiders lead series, 1-0
1973—Raiders, 17-10 (StL)
***OAKLAND vs. *SAN DIEGO**
Raiders lead series, 26-17-2
1960—Chargers, 52-28 (LA)
Chargers, 41-17 (O)
1961—Chargers, 44-0 (SD)
Chargers, 41-10 (O)
1962—Chargers, 42-33 (O)
Chargers, 31-21 (SD)
1963—Raiders, 34-33 (SD)
Raiders, 41-27 (O)
1964—Chargers, 31-17 (O)
Raiders, 21-20 (SD)
1965—Chargers, 17-6 (O)
Chargers, 24-14 (SD)
1966—Chargers, 29-20 (O)
Raiders, 41-19 (SD)
1967—Raiders, 51-10 (O)
Raiders, 41-21 (SD)
1968—Chargers, 23-14 (O)
Raiders, 34-27 (SD)
1969—Chargers, 24-12 (SD)
Raiders, 21-16 (O)
1970—Tie, 27-27 (SD)
Raiders, 20-17 (O)
1971—Raiders, 34-0 (O)
Raiders, 34-33 (O)
1972—Tie, 17-17 (O)
Raiders, 21-19 (SD)
1973—Raiders, 27-17 (SD)
Raiders, 31-3 (O)
1974—Raiders, 14-10 (SD)
Raiders, 17-10 (O)
1975—Raiders, 6-0 (SD)
Raiders, 25-0 (O)
1976—Raiders, 27-17 (SD)
Raiders, 24-0 (O)
1977—Raiders, 24-0 (O)
Chargers, 12-7 (SD)
1978—Raiders, 21-20 (SD)
Chargers, 27-23 (O)
1979—Chargers, 30-10 (SD)
Raiders, 45-22 (O)
1980—Chargers, 30-24 (SD) OT
Raiders, 38-24 (O)
**Raiders, 34-27 (SD)
1981—Chargers, 55-21 (O)
Chargers, 23-10 (SD)
(Points—Raiders 1,069, Chargers 1,000)
*Franchise in Los Angeles prior to 1961
**AFC Championship
OAKLAND vs. SAN FRANCISCO
Raiders lead series, 2-1
1970—49ers, 38-7 (O)
1974—Raiders, 35-24 (SF)
1979—Raiders, 23-10 (O)
(Points—49ers 72, Raiders 65)
OAKLAND vs. SEATTLE
Raiders lead series, 5-4
1977—Raiders, 44-7 (O)
1978—Seahawks, 27-7 (S)
Seahawks, 17-16 (O)
1979—Seahawks, 27-10 (S)

Seahawks, 29-24 (O)
1980—Raiders, 33-14 (O)
Raiders, 19-17 (S)
1981—Raiders, 20-10 (O)
Raiders, 32-31 (S)
(Points—Raiders 205, Seahawks 179)
OAKLAND vs. TAMPA BAY
Raiders lead series, 2-0
1976—Raiders, 49-16 (O)
1981—Raiders, 18-16 (O)
(Points—Raiders 67, Buccaneers 32)
OAKLAND vs. WASHINGTON
Raiders lead series, 3-0
1970—Raiders, 34-20 (O)
1975—Raiders, 26-23 (W) OT
1980—Raiders, 24-21 (O)
(Points—Raiders 84, Redskins 64)

PHILADELPHIA vs. ATLANTA
Falcons lead series, 5-4-1;
See Atlanta vs. Philadelphia
PHILADELPHIA vs. *1950 BALTIMORE
Eagles won series, 1-0;
See *Baltimore vs. Philadelphia
*Extinct team
PHILADELPHIA vs. BALTIMORE
Series tied, 4-4;
See Baltimore vs. Philadelphia
PHILADELPHIA vs. *BOSTON YANKS
Eagles won series, 7-2;
See *Boston Yanks vs. Philadelphia
*Extinct team
PHILADELPHIA vs. *BROOKLYN DODGERS
Dodgers won series, 14-5-1;
See *Brooklyn Dodgers vs. Philadelphia
*Extinct team
PHILADELPHIA vs. BUFFALO
Series tied, 1-1;
See Buffalo vs. Philadelphia
PHILADELPHIA vs. CHICAGO
Bears lead series, 17-4-1;
See Chicago vs. Philadelphia
PHILADELPHIA vs. CINCINNATI
Bengals lead series, 3-0;
See Cincinnati vs. Philadelphia
PHILADELPHIA vs. *CINCINNATI REDS
Eagles won series, 2-1;
See *Cincinnati Reds vs. Philadelphia
*Extinct team
PHILADELPHIA vs. CLEVELAND
Browns lead series, 29-10-1;
See Cleveland vs. Philadelphia
PHILADELPHIA vs. DALLAS
Cowboys lead series, 29-15;
See Dallas vs. Philadelphia
PHILADELPHIA vs. *DALLAS TEXANS
Eagles won series, 1-0;
See *Dallas Texans vs. Philadelphia
*Extinct team
PHILADELPHIA vs. DENVER
Eagles lead series, 2-1;
See Denver vs. Philadelphia
PHILADELPHIA vs. DETROIT
Lions lead series, 12-9-1;
See Detroit vs. Philadelphia
PHILADELPHIA vs. GREEN BAY
Packers lead series, 17-5;
See Green Bay vs. Philadelphia
PHILADELPHIA vs. HOUSTON
Eagles lead series, 2-0;
See Houston vs. Philadelphia
PHILADELPHIA vs. KANSAS CITY
Eagles lead series, 1-0;
See Kansas City vs. Philadelphia
PHILADELPHIA vs. LOS ANGELES
Rams lead series, 14-8-1;
See Los Angeles vs. Philadelphia
PHILADELPHIA vs. MIAMI
Series tied, 2-2;
See Miami vs. Philadelphia
PHILADELPHIA vs. MINNESOTA
Vikings lead series, 8-2;
See Minnesota vs. Philadelphia
PHILADELPHIA vs. NEW ENGLAND
Series tied, 2-2;
See New England vs. Philadelphia
PHILADELPHIA vs. NEW ORLEANS
Eagles lead series, 8-4;
See New Orleans vs. Philadelphia
PHILADELPHIA vs. *N.Y. BULLDOGS
Eagles won series, 2-0;

See *N.Y. Bulldogs vs. Philadelphia
*Extinct team
PHILADELPHIA vs. N.Y. GIANTS
Giants lead series, 50-43-2;
See N.Y. Giants vs. Philadelphia
PHILADELPHIA vs. N.Y. JETS
Eagles lead series, 3-0;
See N.Y. Jets vs. Philadelphia
PHILADELPHIA vs. OAKLAND
Raiders lead series, 3-1;
See Oakland vs. Philadelphia
PHILADELPHIA vs. *PITTSBURGH
Eagles lead series, 42-25-3
1933—Eagles, 25-6 (Phila)
1934—Eagles, 17-0 (Pitt)
Pirates, 9-7 (Phila)
1935—Pirates, 17-7 (Phila)
Eagles, 17-6 (Pitt)
1936—Pirates, 17-0 (Pitt)
Pirates, 6-0 (Johnstown, Pa.)
1937—Pirates, 27-14 (Pitt)
Pirates, 16-7 (Pitt)
1938—Eagles, 27-7 (Buffalo)
Eagles, 14-7
(Charleston, W. Va)
1939—Eagles, 17-14 (Phila)
Pirates, 24-12 (Pitt)
1940—Pirates, 7-3 (Pitt)
Eagles, 7-0 (Phila)
1941—Eagles, 10-7 (Pitt)
Tie, 7-7 (Phila)
1942—Eagles, 24-14 (Pitt)
Steelers, 14-0 (Phila)
1945—Eagles, 45-3 (Pitt)
Eagles, 30-6 (Phila)
1946—Steelers, 10-7 (Pitt)
Eagles, 10-7 (Phila)
1947—Steelers, 35-24 (Pitt)
Eagles, 21-0 (Phila)
**Eagles, 21-0 (Pitt)
1948—Eagles, 34-7 (Pitt)
Eagles, 17-0 (Phila)
1949—Eagles, 38-7 (Pitt)
Eagles, 34-17 (Phila)
1950—Eagles, 17-10 (Pitt)
Steelers, 9-7 (Phila)
1951—Eagles, 34-13 (Pitt)
Steelers, 17-13 (Phila)
1952—Eagles, 31-25 (Pitt)
Eagles, 26-21 (Phila)
1953—Eagles, 23-17 (Phila)
Eagles, 35-7 (Pitt)
1954—Eagles, 24-22 (Phila)
Steelers, 17-7 (Pitt)
1955—Steelers, 13-7 (Pitt)
Eagles, 24-0 (Phila)
1956—Eagles, 35-21 (Pitt)
Eagles, 14-7 (Phila)
1957—Steelers, 6-0 (Pitt)
Eagles, 7-6 (Phila)
1958—Steelers, 24-3 (Pitt)
Steelers, 31-24 (Phila)
1959—Eagles, 28-24 (Phila)
Steelers, 31-0 (Pitt)
1960—Eagles, 34-7 (Phila)
Steelers, 27-21 (Pitt)
1961—Eagles, 21-16 (Phila)
Eagles, 35-24 (Pitt)
1962—Steelers, 13-7 (Pitt)
Steelers, 26-17 (Phila)
1963—Tie, 21-21 (Phila)
Tie, 20-20 (Pitt)
1964—Eagles, 21-7 (Phila)
Eagles, 34-10 (Pitt)
1965—Steelers, 20-14 (Phila)
Eagles, 47-13 (Pitt)
1966—Eagles, 31-14 (Pitt)
Eagles, 27-23 (Phila)
1967—Eagles, 34-24 (Phila)
1968—Steelers, 6-3 (Pitt)
1969—Eagles, 41-27 (Phila)
1970—Eagles, 30-20 (Phila)
1974—Steelers, 27-0 (Pitt)
1979—Eagles, 17-14 (Phila)
(Points—Eagles 1,330, Steelers 967)
*Steelers known as Pirates prior to 1941
**Division Playoff
***PHILADELPHIA vs. *ST. LOUIS**
Cardinals lead series, 35-32-4
1935—Cardinals, 12-3 (C)
1936—Cardinals, 13-0 (C)
1937—Tie, 6-6 (P)
1938—Eagles, 7-0 (Erie, Pa.)
1941—Eagles, 21-14 (P)
1945—Eagles, 21-6 (P)
1947—Cardinals, 45-21 (P)
**Cardinals, 28-21 (C)
1948—Cardinals, 21-14 (C)
**Eagles, 7-0 (P)
1949—Eagles, 28-3 (P)
1950—Eagles, 45-7 (C)
Cardinals, 14-10 (P)
1951—Eagles, 17-14 (C)
1952—Eagles, 10-7 (P)
Cardinals, 28-22 (C)
1953—Eagles, 56-17 (C)
Eagles, 38-0 (P)
1954—Eagles, 35-16 (C)
Eagles, 30-14 (P)
1955—Tie, 24-24 (C)
Eagles, 27-3 (P)
1956—Cardinals, 20-6 (P)
Cardinals, 28-17 (C)
1957—Eagles, 38-21 (C)
Cardinals, 31-27 (P)
1958—Tie, 21-21 (C)
Eagles, 49-21 (P)
1959—Eagles, 28-24 (Minn)
Eagles, 27-17 (P)
1960—Eagles, 31-27 (P)
Eagles, 20-6 (StL)
1961—Cardinals, 30-27 (P)
Eagles, 20-7 (StL)
1962—Cardinals, 27-21 (P)
Cardinals, 45-35 (StL)
1963—Cardinals, 28-24 (P)
Cardinals, 38-14 (StL)
1964—Cardinals, 38-13 (P)
Cardinals, 36-34 (StL)
1965—Eagles, 34-27 (P)
Eagles, 28-24 (StL)
1966—Cardinals, 16-13 (StL)
Cardinals, 41-10 (P)
1967—Cardinals, 48-14 (StL)
1968—Cardinals, 45-17 (P)
1969—Eagles, 34-30 (StL)
1970—Cardinals, 35-20 (P)
Cardinals, 23-14 (StL)
1971—Eagles, 37-20 (StL)
Eagles, 19-7 (P)
1972—Tie, 6-6 (P)
Cardinals, 24-23 (StL)
1973—Cardinals, 34-23 (P)
Eagles, 27-24 (StL)
1974—Cardinals, 7-3 (StL)
Cardinals, 13-3 (P)
1975—Cardinals, 31-20 (StL)
Cardinals, 24-23 (P)
1976—Cardinals, 33-14 (StL)
Cardinals, 17-14 (P)
1977—Cardinals, 21-17 (P)
Cardinals, 21-16 (StL)
1978—Cardinals, 16-10 (P)
Eagles, 14-10 (StL)
1979—Eagles, 24-20 (StL)
Eagles, 16-13 (P)
1980—Cardinals, 24-14 (StL)
Eagles, 17-3 (P)
1981—Eagles, 52-10 (StL)
Eagles, 38-0 (P)
(Points—Eagles 1,529, Cardinals 1,424)
*Franchise in Chicago prior to 1960
**NFL Championship
PHILADELPHIA vs. SAN DIEGO
Series tied, 1-1
1974—Eagles, 13-7 (SD)
1980—Chargers, 22-21 (SD)
(Points—Eagles 34, Chargers 29)
PHILADELPHIA vs. SAN FRANCISCO
49ers lead series, 8-3-1
1951—Eagles, 21-14 (P)
1953—49ers, 31-21 (SF)
1956—Tie, 10-10 (P)
1958—49ers, 30-24 (P)
1959—49ers, 24-14 (SF)
1964—49ers, 28-24 (P)
1966—Eagles, 35-34 (SF)
1967—49ers, 28-27 (P)
1969—49ers, 14-13 (SF)
1971—49ers, 31-3 (P)
1973—49ers, 38-28 (SF)
1975—Eagles, 27-17 (P)
(Points—49ers 299, Eagles 247)
PHILADELPHIA vs. SEATTLE
Eagles lead series, 2-0
1976—Eagles, 27-10 (P)
1980—Eagles, 27-20 (S)
(Points—Eagles 54, Seahawks 30)
PHILADELPHIA vs. TAMPA BAY
Eagles lead series, 2-1
1977—Eagles, 13-3 (P)
1979—*Buccaneers, 24-17 (TB)
1981—Eagles, 20-10 (P)
(Points—Eagles 50, Buccaneers 37)
*NFC Divisional Playoff
PHILADELPHIA vs. *WASHINGTON
Redskins lead series, 51-37-5
1934—Redskins 6-0 (B)
Redskins 14-7 (P)
1935—Eagles 7-6 (B)
1936—Redskins 26-3 (P)
Redskins 17-7 (B)
1937—Eagles, 14-0 (W)
Redskins, 10-7 (P)
1938—Redskins, 26-23 (P)
Redskins, 20-14 (W)
1939—Redskins, 7-0 (P)
Redskins, 7-6 (W)
1940—Redskins, 34-17 (P)
Redskins, 13-6 (W)
1941—Redskins, 21-17 (P)
Redskins, 20-14 (W)
1942—Redskins, 14-10 (P)
Redskins, 30-27 (W)
1944—Tie, 31-31 (P)
Eagles, 37-7 (W)
1945—Redskins, 24-14 (W)
Eagles, 16-0 (P)
1946—Eagles, 28-24 (W)
Redskins, 27-10 (P)
1947—Eagles, 45-42 (P)
Eagles, 38-14 (W)
1948—Eagles, 45-0 (W)
Eagles, 42-21 (P)
1949—Eagles, 49-14 (P)
Eagles, 44-21 (W)
1950—Eagles, 35-3 (P)
Eagles, 33-0 (W)
1951—Redskins, 27-23 (P)
Eagles, 35-21 (W)
1952—Eagles, 38-20 (P)
Redskins, 27-21 (W)
1953—Tie, 21-21 (P)
Redskins, 10-0 (W)
1954—Eagles, 49-21 (W)
Eagles, 41-33 (P)
1955—Redskins, 31-30 (P)
Redskins, 34-21 (W)
1956—Eagles, 13-9 (P)
Redskins, 19-17 (W)
1957—Eagles, 21-12 (P)
Redskins, 42-7 (W)
1958—Redskins, 24-14 (P)
Redskins, 20-0 (W)
1959—Eagles, 30-23 (P)
Eagles, 34-14 (W)
1960—Eagles, 19-13 (P)
Eagles, 38-28 (W)
1961—Eagles, 14-7 (P)
Eagles, 27-24 (W)
1962—Redskins, 27-21 (P)
Eagles, 37-14 (W)
1963—Eagles, 37-24 (W)
Redskins, 13-10 (P)
1964—Redskins, 35-20 (W)
Redskins, 21-10 (P)
1965—Redskins, 23-21 (W)
Eagles, 21-14 (P)
1966—Redskins, 27-13 (P)
Eagles, 37-28 (W)
1967—Eagles, 35-24 (P)
Tie, 35-35 (W)
1968—Redskins, 17-14 (W)
Redskins, 16-10 (P)
1969—Tie, 28-28 (W)
Redskins, 34-29 (P)
1970—Redskins, 33-21 (P)
Redskins, 24-6 (W)
1971—Tie, 7-7 (W)
Redskins, 20-13 (P)
1972—Redskins, 14-0 (W)
Redskins, 23-7 (P)
1973—Redskins, 28-7 (P)
Redskins, 38-20 (W)
1974—Redskins, 27-20 (P)
Redskins, 26-7 (W)
1975—Eagles, 26-10 (P)
Eagles, 26-3 (W)
1976—Redskins, 20-17 (P) OT
Redskins, 24-0 (W)
1977—Redskins, 23-17 (W)
Redskins, 17-14 (P)
1978—Redskins, 35-30 (W)
Eagles, 17-10 (P)
1979—Eagles, 28-17 (P)
Redskins, 17-7 (W)
1980—Eagles, 24-14 (P)
Eagles, 24-0 (W)
1981—Eagles, 36-13 (P)
Redskins, 15-13 (W)
(Points—Eagles 1,924, Redskins 1,817)
*Franchise in Boston prior to 1937

PITTSBURGH vs. ATLANTA
Steelers lead series, 5-1;
See Atlanta vs. Pittsburgh
PITTSBURGH vs. *1950 BALTIMORE
Steelers won series, 1-0
See *1950 Baltimore vs. Pittsburgh
*Extinct team
PITTSBURGH vs. BALTIMORE
Steelers lead series, 7-3;
See Baltimore vs. Pittsburgh
PITTSBURGH vs. *BOSTON YANKS
Steelers won series, 5-3
See *Boston Yanks vs. Pittsburgh
*Extinct team
PITTSBURGH vs. *BROOKLYN DODGERS
Dodgers won series, 11-8-1;
See *Brooklyn Dodgers vs. Pittsburgh
*Extinct team
PITTSBURGH vs. BUFFALO
Steelers lead series, 5-2;
See Buffalo vs. Pittsburgh
PITTSBURGH vs. CHICAGO
Bears lead series, 13-4-1;
See Chicago vs. Pittsburgh
PITTSBURGH vs. CINCINNATI
Steelers lead series, 14-10;
See Cincinnati vs. Pittsburgh
PITTSBURGH vs. *CINCINNATI REDS
Steelers won series, 2-0-1;
See *Cincinnati Reds vs. Pittsburgh
*Extinct team
PITTSBURGH vs. CLEVELAND
Browns lead series, 37-27;
See Cleveland vs. Pittsburgh
PITTSBURGH vs. DALLAS
Steelers lead series, 11-10;
See Dallas vs. Pittsburgh
PITTSBURGH vs. DENVER
Broncos lead series, 5-4-1;
See Denver vs. Pittsburgh
PITTSBURGH vs. DETROIT
Lions lead series, 12-8-1;
See Detroit vs. Pittsburgh
PITTSBURGH vs. GREEN BAY
Packers lead series, 16-9;
See Green Bay vs. Pittsburgh
PITTSBURGH vs. HOUSTON
Steelers lead series, 18-8;
See Houston vs. Pittsburgh
PITTSBURGH vs. KANSAS CITY
Steelers lead series, 7-3;
See Kansas City vs. Pittsburgh
PITTSBURGH vs. LOS ANGELES
Rams lead series, 12-3-2;
See Los Angeles vs. Pittsburgh
PITTSBURGH vs. MIAMI
Dolphins lead series, 4-3;
See Miami vs. Pittsburgh
PITTSBURGH vs. MINNESOTA
Series tied, 4-4;
See Minnesota vs. Pittsburgh
PITTSBURGH vs. NEW ENGLAND
Steelers lead series, 4-1;
See New England vs. Pittsburgh
PITTSBURGH vs. NEW ORLEANS
Steelers lead series, 4-3;
See New Orleans vs. Pittsburgh
PITTSBURGH vs. *N.Y. BULLDOGS
Steelers won series, 2-0;
See *N.Y. Bulldogs vs. Pittsburgh
*Extinct team
PITTSBURGH vs. N.Y. GIANTS
Giants lead series, 40-26-3;
See N.Y. Giants vs. Pittsburgh
PITTSBURGH vs. N.Y. JETS
Steelers lead series, 6-0;
See N.Y. Jets vs. Pittsburgh
PITTSBURGH vs. OAKLAND
Raiders lead series, 8-5;
See Oakland vs. Pittsburgh
PITTSBURGH vs. PHILADELPHIA
Eagles lead series, 42-25-3;
See Philadelphia vs. Pittsburgh
***PITTSBURGH vs. **ST. LOUIS**
Steelers lead series, 28-20-3
1933—Pirates, 14-13 (C)
1935—Pirates, 17-13 (P)
1936—Cardinals, 14-6 (C)
1937—Cardinals, 13-7 (P)
1939—Cardinals, 10-0 (P)
1940—Tie, 7-7 (P)
1942—Steelers, 19-3 (P)
1945—Steelers, 23-0 (P)
1946—Steelers, 14-7 (P)
1948—Cardinals 24-7 (P)
1950—Steelers, 28-17 (C)
Steelers, 28-7 (P)
1951—Steelers, 28-14 (C)
1952—Steelers, 34-28 (C)
Steelers, 17-14 (P)
1953—Steelers, 31-28 (P)
Steelers, 21-17 (C)
1954—Cardinals 17-14 (C)
Steelers, 20-17 (P)
1955—Steelers, 14-7 (P)
Cardinals 27-13 (C)
1956—Steelers, 14-7 (P)
Cardinals, 38-27 (C)
1957—Steelers, 29-20 (P)
Steelers, 27-2 (C)
1958—Steelers, 27-20 (C)
Steelers, 38-21 (P)
1959—Cardinals, 45-24 (C)
Steelers, 35-20 (P)
1960—Steelers, 27-14 (P)
Cardinals, 38-7 (StL)
1961—Steelers, 30-27 (P)
Cardinals, 20-0 (StL)
1962—Steelers, 26-17 (StL)
Steelers, 19-7 (P)
1963—Steelers, 23-10 (P)
Cardinals, 24-23 (StL)
1964—Cardinals, 34-30 (StL)
Cardinals, 21-20 (P)
1965—Cardinals, 20-7 (P)
Cardinals, 21-17 (P)
1966—Steelers, 30-9 (P)
Cardinals, 6-3 (StL)
1967—Cardinals, 28-14 (P)
Tie, 14-14 (StL)
1968—Tie, 28-28 (StL)
Cardinals, 20-10 (P)
1969—Cardinals, 27-14 (P)
Cardinals, 47-10 (StL)
1972—Steelers, 25-19 (StL)
1979—Steelers, 24-21 (StL)
(Points — Steelers 984, Cardinals 942)
*Steelers known as Pirates prior to 1941
**Franchise in Chicago prior to 1960
PITTSBURGH vs. *ST. LOUIS GUNNERS
Gunners won series, 1-0
1934—Gunners, 6-0
*Extinct team
PITTSBURGH vs. SAN DIEGO
Steelers lead series, 6-2
1971—Steelers, 21-17 (P)
1972—Steelers, 24-2 (SD)
1973—Steelers, 38-21 (P)
1975—Steelers, 37-0 (SD)
1976—Steelers, 23-0 (P)
1977—Steelers, 10-9 (SD)
1979—Chargers, 35-7 (SD)
1980—Chargers, 26-17 (SD)
(Points—Steelers 177, Chargers 110)
PITTSBURGH vs. SAN FRANCISCO
49ers lead series, 6-5
1951—49ers, 28-24 (P)
1952—Steelers, 24-7 (SF)
1954—49ers, 31-3 (SF)
1958—49ers, 23-20 (SF)
1961—Steelers, 20-10 (P)
1965—49ers, 27-17 (SF)
1968—49ers, 45-28 (P)
1973—Steelers, 37-14 (SF)
1977—Steelers, 27-0 (P)
1978—Steelers, 24-7 (SF)
1981—49ers, 17-14 (P)
(Points—Steelers 238, 49ers 209)
PITTSBURGH vs. SEATTLE
Steelers lead series, 2-1
1977—Steelers, 30-20 (P)
1978—Steelers, 21-10 (P)
1981—Seahawks, 24-21 (S)
(Points—Steelers 72, Seahawks 54)
PITTSBURGH vs. TAMPA BAY
Steelers lead series, 2-0
1976—Steelers, 42-0 (P)
1980—Steelers, 24-21 (TB)
(Points—Steelers 66, Buccaneers 21)
***PITTSBURGH vs. **WASHINGTON**
Redskins lead series, 39-27-3
1933—Redskins, 21-6 (P)
Pirates, 16-14 (B)

1934—Redskins, 7-0 (P)
Redskins, 39-0 (B)
1935—Pirates, 6-0 (P)
Redskins, 13-3 (B)
1936—Pirates, 10-0 (P)
Redskins, 30-0 (B)
1937—Redskins, 34-20 (W)
Pirates, 21-13 (P)
1938—Redskins, 7-0 (P)
Redskins, 15-0 (W)
1939—Redskins, 44-14 (W)
Redskins, 21-14 (P)
1940—Redskins, 40-10 (P)
Redskins, 37-10 (W)
1941—Redskins, 24-20 (P)
Redskins, 23-3 (W)
1942—Redskins, 28-14 (W)
Redskins, 14-0 (P)
1945—Redskins, 14-0 (P)
Redskins, 24-0 (W)
1946—Tie, 14-14 (W)
Steelers, 14-7 (P)
1947—Redskins, 27-26 (W)
Steelers, 21-14 (P)
1948—Redskins, 17-14 (W)
Steelers, 10-7 (P)
1949—Redskins, 27-14 (P)
Redskins, 27-14 (W)
1950—Steelers, 26-7 (W)
Redskins, 24-7 (P)
1951—Redskins, 22-7 (P)
Steelers, 20-10 (W)
1952—Redskins, 28-24 (P)
Steelers, 24-23 (W)
1953—Redskins, 17-9 (P)
Steelers, 14-13 (W)
1954—Steelers, 37-7 (P)
Redskins, 17-14 (W)
1955—Redskins, 23-14 (P)
Redskins, 28-17 (W)
1956—Steelers, 30-13 (P)
Steelers, 23-0 (W)
1957—Steelers, 28-7 (P)
Redskins, 10-3 (W)
1958—Steelers, 24-16 (P)
Tie, 14-14 (W)
1959—Redskins, 23-17 (P)
Steelers, 27-6 (W)
1960—Tie, 27-27 (W)
Steelers, 22-10 (P)
1961—Steelers, 20-0 (P)
Steelers, 30-14 (P)
1962—Steelers, 23-21 (P)
Steelers, 27-24 (W)
1963—Steelers, 38-27 (P)
Steelers, 34-28 (W)
1964—Redskins, 30-0 (P)
Steelers, 14-7 (W)
1965—Redskins, 31-3 (P)
Redskins, 35-14 (W)
1966—Redskins, 33-27 (P)
Redskins, 24-10 (W)
1967—Redskins, 15-10 (P)
1968—Redskins, 16-13 (W)
1969—Redskins, 14-7 (P)
1973—Steelers, 21-16 (P)
1979—Steelers, 38-7 (P)
(Points—Redskins 1,289, Steelers 1,051)
Steelers known as Pirates prior to 1941
***Franchise in Boston prior to 1937*

ST. LOUIS vs. ATLANTA
Cardinals lead series, 5-3;
See Atlanta vs. St. Louis
ST. LOUIS vs. *1950 BALTIMORE
Cardinals won series, 1-0
See *Baltimore vs. Chicago Cardinals
*Extinct team
ST. LOUIS vs. BALTIMORE
Series tied, 4-4;
See Baltimore vs. St. Louis
ST. LOUIS vs. *BOSTON YANKS
Cardinals won series, 3-0;
See *Boston Yanks vs. Chicago Cardinals
*Extinct team
ST. LOUIS vs. *BROOKLYN DODGERS
Dodgers won series, 7-4;
See *Brooklyn Dodgers vs. Chicago Cardinals
*Extinct team
ST. LOUIS vs BUFFALO
Cardinals lead series, 2-1;
See Buffalo vs. St. Louis
ST. LOUIS vs. CHICAGO
Bears lead series, 50-23-6;
See Chicago vs. St. Louis
ST. LOUIS vs. CINCINNATI
Bengals lead series, 2-0;
See Cincinnati vs. St. Louis
ST. LOUIS vs. *CINCINNATI REDS
Cardinals won series, 3-1;
See *Cincinnati Reds vs. Chicago Cardinals
*Extinct team
ST. LOUIS vs. CLEVELAND
Browns lead series, 30-9-3;
See Cleveland vs. St. Louis
ST. LOUIS vs. DALLAS
Cowboys lead series, 24-15-1;
See Dallas vs. St. Louis
ST. LOUIS vs. DENVER
Broncos lead series, 1-0-1;
See Denver vs. St. Louis
ST. LOUIS vs. DETROIT
Lions lead series, 25-15-5;
See Detroit vs. St. Louis
ST. LOUIS vs. GREEN BAY
Packers lead series 36-20-4;
See Green Bay vs. St. Louis
ST. LOUIS vs. HOUSTON
Cardinals lead series, 3-0;
See Houston vs. St. Louis
ST. LOUIS vs. KANSAS CITY
Chiefs lead series, 2-0-1;
See Kansas City vs. St. Louis
ST. LOUIS vs. LOS ANGELES
Rams lead series, 18-15-2;
See Los Angeles vs. St. Louis
ST. LOUIS vs. MIAMI
Dolphins lead series, 4-0;
See Miami vs. St. Louis
ST. LOUIS vs. MINNESOTA
Cardinals lead series, 6-3;
See Minnesota vs. St. Louis
ST. LOUIS vs. NEW ENGLAND
Cardinals lead series, 3-1;
See New England vs. St. Louis
ST. LOUIS vs. NEW ORLEANS
Cardinals lead series, 7-2;
See New Orleans vs. St. Louis
ST. LOUIS vs. *N.Y. BULLDOGS
Cardinals won series, 1-0;
See *N.Y. Bulldogs vs. St. Louis
*Extinct team
ST. LOUIS vs. N.Y. GIANTS
Giants lead series, 50-28-1;
See N.Y. Giants vs. St. Louis
ST. LOUIS vs. N.Y. JETS
Cardinals lead series, 2-1;
See N.Y. Jets vs. St. Louis
ST. LOUIS vs. OAKLAND
Raiders lead series, 1-0;
See Oakland vs. St. Louis
ST. LOUIS vs. PHILADELPHIA
Cardinals lead series, 35-32-4;
See Philadelphia vs. St. Louis
ST. LOUIS vs. PITTSBURGH
Steelers lead series, 28-20-3;
See Pittsburgh vs. St. Louis
ST. LOUIS vs. SAN DIEGO
Chargers lead series, 2-0;
1971—Chargers, 20-17 (SD)
1976—Chargers, 43-24 (SD)
(Points—Chargers 63, Cardinals 41)
***ST. LOUIS vs. SAN FRANCISCO**
Cardinals lead series, 7-4
1951—Cardinals, 27-21 (SF)
1957—Cardinals, 20-10 (SF)
1962—49ers, 24-17 (StL)
1964—Cardinals, 23-13 (SF)
1968—49ers, 35-17 (SF)
1971—49ers, 26-14 (StL)
1974—Cardinals, 34-9 (SF)
1976—Cardinals, 23-20 (StL) OT
1978—Cardinals, 16-10 (SF)
1979—Cardinals, 13-10 (StL)
1980—49ers, 24-21 (SF) OT
(Points—Cardinals 225, 49ers 202)
*Team in Chicago prior to 1960
ST. LOUIS vs. SEATTLE
Cardinals lead series, 1-0
1976—Cardinals, 30-24 (S)
ST. LOUIS vs. TAMPA BAY
Buccaneers lead series, 2-0
1977—Buccaneers, 17-7 (TB)
1981—Buccaneers, 20-10 (TB)
(Points—Buccaneers 37, Cardinals 17)
***ST. LOUIS vs. **WASHINGTON**
Redskins lead series, 42-31-2
1932—Cardinals, 9-0 (B)
Braves, 8-6 (C)
1933—Redskins, 10-0 (C)
Tie, 0-0 (B)
1934—Redskins, 9-0 (B)
1935—Cardinals, 6-0 (B)
1936—Redskins, 13-10 (B)
1937—Cardinals, 21-14 (W)
1939—Redskins, 28-7 (W)
1940—Redskins, 28-21 (W)
1942—Redskins, 28-0 (W)
1943—Redskins, 13-7 (W)
1945—Redskins, 24-21 (W)
1947—Redskins, 45-21 (W)
1949—Cardinals, 38-7 (C)
1950—Cardinals, 38-28 (W)
1951—Redskins, 7-3 (C)
Redskins, 20-17 (W)
1952—Redskins, 23-7 (C)
Cardinals, 17-6 (W)
1953—Redskins, 24-13 (C)
Redskins, 28-17 (W)
1954—Cardinals, 38-16 (C)
Redskins, 37-20 (W)
1955—Cardinals, 24-10 (W)
Redskins, 31-0 (C)
1956—Cardinals, 31-3 (W)
Redskins, 17-14 (C)
1957—Redskins, 37-14 (C)
Cardinals, 44-14 (W)
1958—Cardinals, 37-10 (C)
Redskins, 45-31 (W)
1959—Cardinals, 49-21 (C)
Redskins, 23-14 (W)
1960—Cardinals, 44-7 (StL)
Cardinals, 26-14 (W)
1961—Cardinals, 24-0 (W)
Cardinals, 38-24 (StL)
1962—Redskins, 24-14 (W)
Tie, 17-17 (StL)
1963—Cardinals, 21-7 (W)
Cardinals, 24-20 (StL)
1964—Cardinals, 23-17 (W)
Cardinals, 38-24 (StL)
1965—Cardinals, 37-16 (W)
Redskins, 24-20 (StL)
1966—Cardinals, 23-7 (StL)
Redskins, 26-20 (W)
1967—Cardinals, 27-21 (W)
1968—Cardinals, 41-14 (StL)
1969—Redskins, 33-17 (W)
1970—Cardinals, 27-17 (StL)
Redskins, 28-27 (W)
1971—Redskins, 24-17 (StL)
Redskins, 20-0 (W)
1972—Redskins, 24-10 (W)
Redskins, 33-3 (StL)
1973—Cardinals, 34-27 (StL)
Redskins, 31-13 (W)
1974—Cardinals, 17-10 (W)
Cardinals, 23-20 (StL)
1975—Redskins, 27-17 (W)
Cardinals, 20-17 (StL) OT
1976—Redskins, 20-10 (W)
Redskins, 16-10 (StL)
1977—Redskins, 24-14 (W)
Redskins, 26-20 (StL)
1978—Redskins, 28-10 (StL)
Cardinals, 27-17 (W)
1979—Redskins, 17-7 (StL)
Redskins, 30-28 (W)
1980—Redskins, 23-0 (W)
Redskins, 31-7 (StL)
1981—Cardinals, 40-30 (StL)
Redskins, 42-21 (W)
(Points—Redskins 1,504, Cardinals 1,451)
Team in Chicago prior to 1960
***Team in Boston prior to 1937 and known as Braves prior to 1933*

***ST. LOUIS GUNNERS vs. DETROIT**
Lions won series, 1-0;
See Detroit vs. *St. Louis Gunners
*Extinct team
***ST. LOUIS GUNNERS vs. GREEN BAY**
Packers won series, 1-0;
See Green Bay vs. *St. Louis Gunners
*Extinct team
***ST. LOUIS GUNNERS vs. PITTSBURGH**
Gunners won series, 1-0;
See Pittsburgh vs. *St. Louis Gunners
*Extinct team
SAN DIEGO vs. ATLANTA
Falcons lead series, 2-0;
See Atlanta vs. San Diego
SAN DIEGO vs. BALTIMORE
Series tied, 2-2;
See Baltimore vs. San Diego
SAN DIEGO vs. BUFFALO
Chargers lead series, 15-9-2;
See Buffalo vs. San Diego
SAN DIEGO vs. CHICAGO
Chargers lead series, 3-1;
See Chicago vs. San Diego
SAN DIEGO vs. CINCINNATI
Chargers lead series, 8-7;
See Cincinnati vs. San Diego
SAN DIEGO vs. CLEVELAND
Chargers lead series, 4-2-1;
See Cleveland vs. San Diego
SAN DIEGO vs. DALLAS
Cowboys lead series, 2-0;
See Dallas vs. San Diego
SAN DIEGO vs. DENVER
Chargers lead series, 23-20-1;
See Denver vs. San Diego
SAN DIEGO vs. DETROIT
Lions lead series, 3-1;
See Detroit vs. San Diego
SAN DIEGO vs. GREEN BAY
Packers lead series, 3-0;
See Green Bay vs. San Diego
SAN DIEGO vs. HOUSTON
Chargers lead series, 15-11-1;
See Houston vs. San Diego
SAN DIEGO vs. KANSAS CITY
Chargers lead series, 23-20-1;
See Kansas City vs. San Diego
SAN DIEGO vs. LOS ANGELES
Rams lead series, 2-1;
See Los Angeles vs. San Diego
SAN DIEGO vs. MIAMI
Chargers lead series, 7-4;
See Miami vs. San Diego
SAN DIEGO vs. MINNESOTA
Series tied, 2-2;
See Minnesota vs. San Diego
SAN DIEGO vs. NEW ENGLAND
Series tied, 12-12-2;
See New England vs. San Diego
SAN DIEGO vs. NEW ORLEANS
Chargers lead series, 3-0;
See New Orleans vs. San Diego
SAN DIEGO vs. N.Y. GIANTS
Giants lead series, 2-1;
See N.Y. Giants vs. San Diego
SAN DIEGO vs. N.Y. JETS
Chargers lead series, 14-6-1;
See N.Y. Jets vs. San Diego
SAN DIEGO vs. OAKLAND
Raiders lead series, 26-17-2;
See Oakland vs. San Diego
SAN DIEGO vs. PHILADELPHIA
Series tied, 1-1;
See Philadelphia vs. San Diego
SAN DIEGO vs. PITTSBURGH
Steelers lead series, 6-2;
See Pittsburgh vs. San Diego
SAN DIEGO vs. ST. LOUIS
Chargers lead series, 2-0;
See St. Louis vs. San Diego
SAN DIEGO vs. SAN FRANCISCO
Chargers lead series, 2-1
1972—49ers, 34-3 (SF)
1976—Chargers, 13-7 (SD) OT
1979—Chargers, 31-9 (SD)
(Points—49ers 50, Chargers 47)
SAN DIEGO vs. SEATTLE
Chargers lead series, 8-1
1977—Chargers, 30-28 (S)
1978—Chargers, 24-20 (S)
Chargers, 37-10 (SD)
1979—Chargers, 33-16 (S)
Chargers, 20-10 (SD)
1980—Chargers, 34-13 (S)
Chargers, 21-14 (SD)
1981—Chargers, 24-10 (SD)
Seahawks, 44-23 (S)
(Points—Chargers 246, Seahawks 165)
SAN DIEGO vs. TAMPA BAY
Chargers lead series, 2-0
1976—Chargers, 23-0 (TB)
1981—Chargers, 24-23 (TB)
(Points—Chargers 47, Buccaneers 23)
SAN DIEGO vs. WASHINGTON
Redskins lead series, 2-0
1973—Redskins, 38-0 (W)
1980—Redskins, 40-17 (W)
(Points—Redskins 78, Chargers 17)

SAN FRANCISCO vs. ATLANTA
49ers lead series, 16-15;
See Atlanta vs. San Francisco
SAN FRANCISCO vs. *1950 BALTIMORE
49ers won series, 1-0;
See *Baltimore vs. San Francisco
*Extinct team
SAN FRANCISCO vs. BALTIMORE
Colts lead series, 21-14;
See Baltimore vs. San Francisco
SAN FRANCISCO vs. BUFFALO
Bills lead series, 2-0;
See Buffalo vs. San Francisco
SAN FRANCISCO vs. CHICAGO
Series tied, 22-22-1;
See Chicago vs. San Francisco
SAN FRANCISCO vs. CINCINNATI
49ers lead series, 3-1;
See Cincinnati vs. San Francisco
SAN FRANCISCO vs. CLEVELAND
Browns lead series, 8-3;
See Cleveland vs. San Francisco
SAN FRANCISCO vs. DALLAS
Cowboys lead series, 8-6-1;
See Dallas vs. San Francisco
SAN FRANCISCO vs. *DALLAS TEXANS
49ers won series, 2-0;
See *Dallas Texans vs. San Francisco
*Extinct team
SAN FRANCISCO vs. DENVER
49ers lead series, 2-1;
See Denver vs. San Francisco
SAN FRANCISCO vs. DETROIT
Lions lead series, 25-21-1;
See Detroit vs. San Francisco
SAN FRANCISCO vs. GREEN BAY
49ers lead series, 22-20-1;
See Green Bay vs. San Francisco
SAN FRANCISCO vs. HOUSTON
Series tied, 2-2;
See Houston vs. San Francisco
SAN FRANCISCO vs. KANSAS CITY
Series tied, 1-1;
See Kansas City vs. San Francisco
SAN FRANCISCO vs. LOS ANGELES
Rams lead series, 41-21-2;
See Los Angeles vs. San Francisco
SAN FRANCISCO vs. MIAMI
Dolphins lead series, 3-0;
See Miami vs. San Francisco
SAN FRANCISCO vs. MINNESOTA
Vikings lead series, 12-10-1;
See Minnesota vs. San Francisco
SAN FRANCISCO vs. NEW ENGLAND
49ers lead series, 2-1;
See New England vs. San Francisco
SAN FRANCISCO vs. NEW ORLEANS
49ers lead series, 17-7-2;
See New Orleans vs. San Francisco
SAN FRANCISCO vs. N.Y. GIANTS
Giants lead series, 9-5;
See N.Y. Giants vs. San Francisco
SAN FRANCISCO vs. N.Y. JETS
49ers lead series, 3-0;
See N.Y. Jets vs. San Francisco
SAN FRANCISCO vs. *N.Y. YANKS
Yanks won series, 2-1-1;
See *N.Y. Yanks vs. San Francisco
*Extinct team
SAN FRANCISCO vs. OAKLAND
Raiders lead series, 2-1;
See Oakland vs. San Francisco
SAN FRANCISCO vs. PHILADELPHIA
49ers lead series, 8-3-1;
See Philadelphia vs. San Francisco
SAN FRANCISCO vs. PITTSBURGH
49ers lead series, 6-5;
See Pittsburgh vs. San Francisco
SAN FRANCISCO vs. ST. LOUIS
Cardinals lead series, 7-4;
See St. Louis vs. San Francisco
SAN FRANCISCO vs. SAN DIEGO
Chargers lead series, 2-1;
See San Diego vs. San Francisco
SAN FRANCISCO vs. SEATTLE
Series tied, 1-1
1976—49ers, 37-21 (S)

1979—Seahawks, 35-24 (SF)
(Points—49ers 61, Seahawks 56)
SAN FRANCISCO vs. TAMPA BAY
49ers lead series, 3-1
1977—49ers, 20-10 (SF)
1978—49ers, 6-3 (SF)
1979—49ers, 23-7 (SF)
1980—Buccaneers, 24-23 (SF)
(Points—49ers 72, Buccaneers 44)
**SAN FRANCISCO vs.
WASHINGTON**
49ers lead series, 6-5-1
1952—49ers, 23-17 (W)
1954—49ers, 41-7 (SF)
1955—Redskins, 7-0 (W)
1961—49ers, 35-3 (SF)
1967—Redskins, 31-28 (W)
1969—Tie, 17-17 (SF)
1970—49ers, 26-17 (SF)
1971—*49ers, 24-20 (SF)
1973—Redskins, 33-9 (W)
1976—Redskins, 24-21 (SF)
1978—Redskins, 38-20 (W)
1981—49ers, 30-17 (W)
(Points—49ers 274, Redskins 231)
*NFC Divisional Playoff

SEATTLE vs. ATLANTA
Seahawks lead series, 2-0;
See Atlanta vs. Seattle
SEATTLE vs. BALTIMORE
Colts lead series, 2-0;
See Baltimore vs. Seattle
SEATTLE vs. BUFFALO
Seahawks lead series, 1-0;
See Buffalo vs. Seattle
SEATTLE vs. CHICAGO
Series tied, 1-1;
See Chicago vs. Seattle
SEATTLE vs. CINCINNATI
Bengals lead series, 2-0;
See Cincinnati vs. Seattle
SEATTLE vs. CLEVELAND
Seahawks lead series, 4-1;
See Cleveland vs. Seattle
SEATTLE vs. DALLAS
Cowboys lead series, 2-0;
See Dallas vs. Seattle
SEATTLE vs. DENVER
Broncos lead series, 7-2;
See Denver vs. Seattle
SEATTLE vs. DETROIT
Series tied, 1-1;
See Detroit vs. Seattle
SEATTLE vs. GREEN BAY
Packers lead series, 3-0;
See Green Bay vs. Seattle
SEATTLE vs. HOUSTON
Series tied, 2-2;
See Houston vs. Seattle
SEATTLE vs. KANSAS CITY
Chiefs lead series, 5-4;
See Kansas City vs. Seattle
SEATTLE vs. LOS ANGELES
Rams lead series, 2-0;
See Los Angeles vs. Seattle
SEATTLE vs. MIAMI
Dolphins lead series, 2-0;
See Miami vs. Seattle
SEATTLE vs. MINNESOTA
Series tied, 1-1;
See Minnesota vs. Seattle
SEATTLE vs. NEW ENGLAND
Patriots lead series, 2-0;
See New England vs. Seattle
SEATTLE vs. NEW ORLEANS
Series tied, 1-1;
See New Orleans vs. Seattle
SEATTLE vs. N.Y. GIANTS
Giants lead series, 3-0;
See N.Y. Giants vs. Seattle
SEATTLE vs. N.Y. JETS
Seahawks lead series, 6-0;
See N.Y. Jets vs. Seattle
SEATTLE vs. OAKLAND
Raiders lead series, 5-4;
See Oakland vs. Seattle
SEATTLE vs. PHILADELPHIA
Eagles lead series, 2-0;
See Philadelphia vs. Seattle
SEATTLE vs. PITTSBURGH
Steelers lead series, 2-1;
See Pittsburgh vs. Seattle
SEATTLE vs. ST. LOUIS
Cardinals lead series, 1-0;
See St. Louis vs. Seattle
SEATTLE vs. SAN DIEGO
Chargers lead series, 8-1;

See San Diego vs. Seattle
SEATTLE vs. SAN FRANCISCO
Series tied, 1-1;
See San Francisco vs. Seattle
SEATTLE vs. TAMPA BAY
Seahawks lead series, 2-0
1976—Seahawks, 13-10 (TB)
1977—Seahawks, 30-23 (S)
(Points—Seahawks 43, Buccaneers 33)
SEATTLE vs. WASHINGTON
Series tied, 1-1
1976—Redskins, 31-7 (W)
1980—Seahawks, 14-0 (W)
(Points—Redskins 31, Seahawks 21)

TAMPA BAY vs. ATLANTA
Series tied, 2-2;
See Atlanta vs. Tampa Bay
TAMPA BAY vs. BALTIMORE
Series tied, 1-1;
See Baltimore vs. Tampa Bay
TAMPA BAY vs. BUFFALO
Series tied, 1-1;
See Buffalo vs. Tampa Bay
TAMPA BAY vs. CHICAGO
Bears lead series, 6-3;
See Chicago vs. Tampa Bay
TAMPA BAY vs. CINCINNATI
Series tied, 1-1;
See Cincinnati vs. Tampa Bay
TAMPA BAY vs. CLEVELAND
Browns lead series, 2-0;
See Cleveland vs. Tampa Bay
TAMPA BAY vs. DALLAS
Cowboys lead series, 3-0;
See Dallas vs. Tampa Bay
TAMPA BAY vs. DENVER
Broncos lead series, 2-0;
See Denver vs. Tampa Bay
TAMPA BAY vs. DETROIT
Lions lead series, 5-4;
See Detroit vs. Tampa Bay
TAMPA BAY vs. GREEN BAY
Buccaneers lead series, 5-3-1;
See Green Bay vs. Tampa Bay
TAMPA BAY vs. HOUSTON
Oilers lead series, 2-0;
See Houston vs. Tampa Bay
TAMPA BAY vs. KANSAS CITY
Series tied, 2-2;
See Kansas City vs. Tampa Bay
TAMPA BAY vs. LOS ANGELES
Rams lead series, 3-2;
See Los Angeles vs. Tampa Bay
TAMPA BAY vs. MIAMI
Dolphins lead series, 1-0;
See Miami vs. Tampa Bay
TAMPA BAY vs. MINNESOTA
Vikings lead series, 6-3;
See Minnesota vs. Tampa Bay
TAMPA BAY vs. NEW ENGLAND
Patriots lead series, 1-0;
See New England vs. Tampa Bay
TAMPA BAY vs. NEW ORLEANS
Series tied, 2-2;
See New Orleans vs. Tampa Bay
TAMPA BAY vs. N.Y. GIANTS
Giants lead series, 4-2;
See N.Y. Giants vs. Tampa Bay
TAMPA BAY vs. N.Y. JETS
Jets lead series, 1-0;
See N.Y. Jets vs. Tampa Bay
TAMPA BAY vs. OAKLAND
Raiders lead series, 2-0;
See Oakland vs. Tampa Bay
TAMPA BAY vs. PHILADELPHIA
Eagles lead series, 2-1;
See Philadelphia vs. Tampa Bay
TAMPA BAY vs. PITTSBURGH
Steelers lead series, 2-0;
See Pittsburgh vs. Tampa Bay
TAMPA BAY vs. ST. LOUIS
Buccaneers lead series, 2-0;
See St. Louis vs. Tampa Bay
TAMPA BAY vs. SAN DIEGO
Chargers lead series, 2-0;
See San Diego vs. Tampa Bay
**TAMPA BAY vs.
SAN FRANCISCO**
49ers lead series, 3-1;
See San Francisco vs. Tampa Bay
TAMPA BAY vs. SEATTLE
Seahawks lead series, 2-0;
See Seattle vs. Tampa Bay
TAMPA BAY vs. WASHINGTON
Redskins lead series, 1-0
1977—Redskins, 10-0 (TB)

WASHINGTON vs. ATLANTA
Redskins lead series, 6-2-1;
See Atlanta vs. Washington
**WASHINGTON vs. *1950
BALTIMORE**
Redskins won series, 2-0;
See *Baltimore vs. Washington
*Extinct team
WASHINGTON vs. BALTIMORE
Colts lead series, 15-5;
See Baltimore vs. Washington
**WASHINGTON vs. *BOSTON
YANKS**
Redskins won series, 8-2;
See *Boston Yanks vs. Washington
*Extinct team
**WASHINGTON vs. *BROOKLYN
DODGERS**
Redskins won series, 17-5-3;
See *Brooklyn Dodgers vs.
Washington
*Extinct team
WASHINGTON vs. BUFFALO
Bills lead series, 2-1;
See Buffalo vs. Washington
WASHINGTON vs. CHICAGO
Bears lead series, 18-11-1;
See Chicago vs. Washington
WASHINGTON vs. CINCINNATI
Redskins lead series, 2-1;
See Cincinnati vs. Washington
WASHINGTON vs. CLEVELAND
Browns lead series, 31-7-1;
See Cleveland vs. Washington
WASHINGTON vs. DALLAS
Cowboys lead series, 26-16-2;
See Dallas vs. Washington
WASHINGTON vs. DENVER
Redskins lead series, 2-1;
See Denver vs. Washington
WASHINGTON vs. DETROIT
Redskins lead series, 15-8;
See Detroit vs. Washington
WASHINGTON vs. GREEN BAY
Packers lead series, 13-11-1;
See Green Bay vs. Washington
WASHINGTON vs. HOUSTON
Oilers lead series, 2-1;
See Houston vs. Washington
WASHINGTON vs. KANSAS CITY
Chiefs lead series, 2-0;
See Kansas City vs. Washington
WASHINGTON vs. LOS ANGELES
Redskins lead series, 12-5-1;
See Los Angeles vs. Washington
WASHINGTON vs. MIAMI
Dolphins lead series, 3-1;
See Miami vs. Washington
WASHINGTON vs. MINNESOTA
Vikings lead series, 5-2;
See Minnesota vs. Washington
WASHINGTON vs. NEW ENGLAND
Redskins lead series, 2-1;
See New England vs. Washington
WASHINGTON vs. NEW ORLEANS
Redskins lead series, 6-4;
See New Orleans vs. Washington
WASHINGTON vs. N.Y. GIANTS
Giants lead series, 56-40-3;
See N.Y. Giants vs. Washington
WASHINGTON vs. N.Y. JETS
Redskins lead series, 3-0;
See N.Y. Jets vs. Washington
**WASHINGTON vs. *N.Y.
BULLDOGS**
Redskins won series, 1-0-1;
See *N.Y. Bulldogs vs. Washington
*Extinct team
WASHINGTON vs. OAKLAND
Raiders lead series, 3-0;
See Oakland vs. Washington
WASHINGTON vs. PHILADELPHIA
Redskins lead series, 51-37-5;
See Philadelphia vs. Washington
WASHINGTON vs. PITTSBURGH
Redskins lead series, 39-27-3;
See Pittsburgh vs. Washington
WASHINGTON vs. ST. LOUIS
Redskins lead series, 42-31-2;
See St. Louis vs. Washington
WASHINGTON vs. SAN DIEGO
Redskins lead series, 2-0;
See San Diego vs. Washington
**WASHINGTON vs.
SAN FRANCISCO**
49ers lead series, 6-5-1;
See San Francisco vs. Washington

WASHINGTON vs. SEATTLE
Series tied, 1-1;
See Seattle vs. Washington
WASHINGTON vs. TAMPA BAY
Redskins lead series, 1-0;
See Tampa Bay vs. Washington

ALL-TIME WINNING PERCENTAGE

Team	Years	Won	Lost	Tied	Pctg.
Detroit Wolverines, 1928	1	7	2	1	.750
Canton Bulldogs/Cleveland Bulldogs, 1921-24	6	37	17	10	.656
Los Angeles Buccaneers, 1926	1	6	3	1	.650
Oakland Raiders, 1960-1981	22	195	110	11	.635
Dallas Cowboys, 1960-1981	22	196	112	6	.634
Cleveland Browns, 1950-1981	32	268	157	9	.628
Buffalo All-Americans/Buffalo Bisons, 1921-24	4	23	13	6	.619
Miami Dolphins, 1966-1981	16	138	90	4	.603
Decatur Staleys/Chicago Staleys/ Chicago Bears, 1920-1981	62	461	298	41	.602
Frankford Yellowjackets, 1924-1931	8	69	46	14	.589
Rock Island, Ill., Independents, 1921-25	5	22	14	10	.587
Detroit Panthers, 1925-26	2	12	8	4	.583
Pottsville, Pa., Maroons, 1925-28	4	27	20	1	.573
Providence Steamroller, 1925-1931	7	44	32	10	.570
Minnesota Vikings, 1960-1981	22	167	126	9	.568
Green Bay Packers, 1921-1981	61	418	320	35	.563
Toledo Maroons, 1922-23	2	7	5	4	.562
Cleveland Rams/Los Angeles Rams, 1937-1942, 1944-1981	44	306	241	20	.557
Baltimore Colts, 1953-1981	29	215	177	6	.548
New York Giants, 1925-1981	57	387	319	31	.546
Los Angeles Chargers/ San Diego Chargers, 1960-1981	22	165	140	11	.540
Dallas Texans/ Kansas City Chiefs, 1960-1981	22	164	142	10	.535
Cleveland Bulldogs, 1925, 1927	2	13	12	2	.519
Portsmouth Spartans/ Detroit Lions, 1930-1981	52	325	304	32	.516
Boston Braves/Boston Redskins/ Washington Redskins, 1932-1981	50	309	299	26	.508
Buffalo Rangers, 1926	1	4	4	2	.500
Boston Bulldogs, 1929	1	4	4	0	.500
Cincinnati Bengals, 1968-1981	14	99	104	1	.488
Racine, Wis., Legion, 1922-24, 1926	4	14	15	6	.486
Houston Oilers, 1960-1981	22	148	162	6	.478
Boston Patriots/ New England Patriots, 1960-1981	22	141	166	9	.460
Pittsburgh Pirates/ Pittsburgh Steelers, 1933-1981	49	276	327	20	.459
New York Titans/ New York Jets, 1960-1981	22	136	163	7	.456
Orange, N.J., Tornadoes, 1929	1	3	4	4	.455
Kansas City Cowboys, 1924-26	3	12	15	2	.448
Duluth Kelleys/Duluth Eskimos, 1923-27	5	16	20	2	.447
Buffalo Bills, 1960-1981	22	137	171	8	.446
Philadelphia Eagles, 1933-1981	49	262	336	22	.440
Chicago Cardinals/ St. Louis Cardinals, 1920-1981	62	311	410	36	.435
Cleveland Indians, 1921, 1923	2	5	7	3	.433
Denver Broncos, 1960-1981	22	132	175	9	.432
Akron Pros/Akron Indians, 1921-26	6	17	24	8	.429
New York Yanks, 1927-28	2	11	16	2	.414
Stapleton Stapes, 1929-1932	4	14	22	9	.411
Atlanta Falcons, 1966-1981	16	91	137	4	.401
Milwaukee Badgers, 1922-26	5	16	27	6	.388
Brooklyn Dodgers/Brooklyn Tigers, 1930-1944	15	60	100	9	.382
Seattle Seahawks, 1976-1981	6	35	57	0	.380
Tampa Bay Buccaneers, 1976-1981	6	31	60	1	.342
Hartford Blues, 1926	1	3	7	0	.300
St. Louis All-Stars, 1923	1	1	4	2	.286
New Orleans Saints, 1967-1981	15	59	154	5	.282
Brooklyn Lions, 1926	1	3	8	0	.273
Boston Yanks/New York Bulldogs/ New York Yanks/Dallas Texans, 1944-1952	9	24	73	6	.262
Dayton Triangles, 1921-29	9	13	49	6	.235
Columbus Panhandles/Columbus Tigers, 1921-26	6	10	36	1	.223
Hammond, Ind., Pros, 1921-26	5	4	18	3	.220
Cincinnati Reds/St. Louis Gunners, 1933-34	2	4	16	1	.214
Minneapolis Marines, 1922-24	3	3	14	2	.211
Cleveland Indians, 1931	1	2	8	0	.200
Detroit Heralds, 1921	1	1	7	1	.167
Oorang Indians, Marion, Ohio, 1922-23	2	3	16	0	.158
Buffalo Bisons, 1927, 1929	3	2	18	3	.152
Minneapolis Red Jackets, 1929-1930	2	2	16	1	.132
Newark Tornadoes, 1930	1	1	10	1	.125
Rochester Jeffersons, 1921-25	5	2	24	2	.107
Kenosha, Wis., Maroons, 1924	1	0	5	1	.100
Baltimore Colts, 1950	1	1	11	0	.090
Evansville Crimson Giants, 1922	1	0	2	0	.000
Louisville Colonels, 1926	1	0	4	0	.000
Louisville Brecks, 1922-23	2	0	6	0	.000
Cincinnati Celts, 1921	1	0	8	0	.000

The Super Bowl

SUPER BOWL I

GREEN BAY 35, KANSAS CITY 10

The Green Bay Packers, leading 14–10 at halftime, scored two third-quarter touchdowns and advanced to a 35–10 victory over the Kansas City Chiefs in the first Super Bowl, officially designated as the AFL-NFL World Championship Game.

The Super Bowl was the result of a 1966 merger between the American Football League and National Football League. The game matched champions from each league in the Los Angeles Memorial Coliseum. Green Bay of the NFL was a 13½-point favorite but the game was in doubt after Kansas City of the AFL outgained the Packers 181–164 and led 11–9 in first downs in the first half.

Green Bay was the first team to score after nine minutes of the first quarter. The Packers marched 43 yards in five plays to the Chiefs' 37-yard line after an exchange of punts. On the sixth play, quarterback Bart Starr froze the Chiefs' secondary with a play-action fake at the line of scrimmage, then passed to end Max McGee. The ball was thrown slightly behind McGee, who caught the pass with one hand, balanced the ball on his hip, and outran the Chiefs the remaining 19 yards to the end zone.

The 34-year old McGee, who caught four passes for 91 yards and one touchdown during the regular season, replaced Boyd Dowler on the second play of the game. Dowler reinjured a shoulder blocking linebacker E.J. Holub on a sweep to the left side of the field by Elijah Pitts.

Kansas City tied the score 7–7 in the second quarter with a six-play, 66-yard drive. Quarterback Len Dawson threw a lead pass from the 7-yard line to fullback Curtis McClinton, who caught the ball in the end zone. The Packers went ahead 14–7 on their next possession. A 64-yard pass play, Starr to Carroll Dale, that went for a touchdown was called back because left tackle Bob Skoronski was in motion before the snap of the ball. The Packers recovered from the setback to score 11 plays later. Fullback Jim Taylor, behind blocks from guards Fred (Fuzzy) Thurston and Jerry Kramer, swept left end for 14 yards, concluding a 73-yard drive that took 14 plays. The Packers kept the drive going by converting four third downs into first downs.

The Chiefs started from their 26 on the next series. After Dawson was dropped for an eight-yard loss on first down, Kansas City moved 50 yards in five plays. On third and 10 from Green Bay's 32, Dawson connected with running back Mike Garrett for an eight-yard gain. Mike Mercer then kicked a 31-yard field goal with 54 seconds remaining in the half, cutting the Packers' lead to 14–10.

The Chiefs marched 20 yards in three plays after taking the kickoff for the third quarter. On third down and five yards from Kansas City's 49, Dawson received a heavy rush from tackle Henry Jordan and end Willie Davis. Jordan hit Dawson's arm as he followed through on a pass and Willie Wood intercepted. Wood returned the ball 50 yards to the Chiefs' 5-yard line. Elijah Pitts went through left tackle on the next play for a touchdown that made it 21–10.

The Chiefs did not threaten again. They had the ball for six more series and punted each time—from the 50-yard line and their 18, 2, 39, 40, and 16.

Packers coach Vince Lombardi, whose team converted 10 of 14 third-down situations into first downs, was asked to compare the Chiefs with teams of the NFL, a question many sports fans had been asking.

"In my opinion, the Chiefs don't rate with the top names in the NFL," he said. "They are a good football team with fine speed, but I'd have to say NFL football is better. Dallas is a better team and so are several others. That's what you wanted me to say, wasn't it?"

Green Bay's McGee makes one of his seven catches between Kansas City's Headrick (69) and Robinson.

Participants—Green Bay Packers, champions of the National Football League, and Kansas City Chiefs, champions of the American Football League
Date—January 15, 1967
Site—Los Angeles Memorial Coliseum
Time—1:05 P.M. PST
Conditions—72 degrees, sunny
Playing Surface—Grass
Television and Radio—National Broadcasting Company (NBC) and Columbia Broadcasting System (CBS)
Regular Season Records—Green Bay, 12-2; Kansas City, 11-2-1
League Championships—Green Bay defeated the Dallas Cowboys 34-27 for the NFL title; Kansas City defeated the Buffalo Bills 31-7 for the AFL title
Players' Shares—$15,000 to each member of the winning team; $7,500 to each member of the losing team
Attendance—61,946
Gross Receipts—$2,768,211.64
Officials—Referee, Norm Schacter, NFL; umpire, George Young, AFL; line judge, Al Sabato, AFL; head linesman, Bernie Ulman, NFL; back judge, Jack Reader, AFL; field judge, Mike Lisetski, NFL
Coaches—Vince Lombardi, Green Bay; Hank Stram, Kansas City

| Kansas City | ...... | 0 | 10 | 0 | 0 | — | 10 |
| Green Bay | .... | 7 | 7 | 14 | 7 | — | 35 |

GB—McGee 37 pass from Starr (Chandler kick)
KC—McClinton 7 pass from Dawson (Mercer kick)
GB—Taylor 14 run (Chandler kick)
KC—FG Mercer 31
GB—Pitts 5 run (Chandler kick)
GB—McGee 13 pass from Starr (Chandler kick)
GB—Pitts 1 run (Chandler kick)

TEAM STATISTICS	KC	GB
First downs	17	21
Rushing	4	10
Passing	12	11
By penalty	1	0
Total yardage	239	358
Net rushing yardage	72	130
Net passing yardage	167	228
Passes att.-comp.-had int.	32-17-1	24-16-1

RUSHING
Kansas City—Dawson, 3 for 24; Garrett, 6 for 17; McClinton, 6 for 16; Beathard, 1 for 14; Coan, 3 for 1.
Green Bay—J. Taylor, 16 for 53; 1 TD; Pitts, 11 for 45, 2 TDs; D. Anderson, 4 for 30; Grabowski, 2 for 2.

PASSING
Kansas City—Dawson, 16 of 27 for 211, 1 TD, 1 int.; Beathard, 1 of 5 for 17.
Green Bay—Starr, 16 of 23 for 250, 2 TDs, 1 int.; Bratkowski, 0 of 1.

RECEIVING
Kansas City—Burford, 4 for 67; O. Taylor, 4 for 57; Garrett, 3 for 28; McClinton, 2 for 34, 1 TD; Arbanas, 2 for 30; Carolan, 1 for 7; Coan, 1 for 5.
Green Bay—McGee, 7 for 138, 2 TDs; Dale, 4 for 59; Pitts, 2 for 32; Fleming, 2 for 22; J. Taylor, 1 for −1.

PUNTING
Kansas City—Wilson, 7 for 317, 45.3 average.
Green Bay—Chandler, 3 for 130, 43.3 average; D. Anderson, 1 for 43.

PUNT RETURNS
Kansas City—Garrett, 2 for 17; E. Thomas, 1 for 2.
Green Bay—D. Anderson, 3 for 25; Wood, 1 for −2, 1 fair catch.

KICKOFF RETURNS
Kansas City—Coan, 4 for 87; Garrett, 2 for 23.
Green Bay—Adderley, 2 for 40; D. Anderson, 1 for 25.

INTERCEPTIONS
Kansas City—Mitchell, 1 for 0.
Green Bay—Wood, 1 for 50.

Kansas City	Starters, Offense	Green Bay
Chris Burford	LE	Carroll Dale
Jim Tyrer	LT	Bob Skoronski
Ed Budde	LG	Fred (Fuzzy) Thurston
Wayne Frazier	C	Bill Curry
Curt Merz	RG	Jerry Kramer
Dave Hill	RT	Forrest Gregg
Fred Arbanas	RE	Marv Fleming
Len Dawson	QB	Bart Starr
Otis Taylor	FL	Boyd Dowler
Mike Garrett	RB	Elijah Pitts
Curtis McClinton	RB	Jim Taylor
	Starters, Defense	
Jerry Mays	LE	Willie Davis
Andy Rice	LT	Ron Kostelnik
Buck Buchanan	RT	Henry Jordan
Chuck Hurston	RE	Lionel Aldridge
Bobby Bell	LLB	Dave Robinson
Sherrill Headrick	MLB	Ray Nitschke
E. J. Holub	RLB	Lee Roy Caffey
Fred Williamson	LHB	Herb Adderley
Willie Mitchell	RHB	Bob Jeter
Bobby Hunt	LS	Tom Brown
Johnny Robinson	RS	Willie Wood

Dawson looks for a receiver as Green Bay's Davis closes in.

GREEN BAY PACKERS

No.	Name	Pos.	Ht.	Wt.	Age	Year	College
26	Adderley, Herb	DB	6-0	210	27	6	Michigan State
82	Aldridge, Lionel	DE	6-4	245	25	4	Utah State
88	Anderson, Bill	E	6-3	216	30	8	Tennessee
44	Anderson, Donny	RB	6-2	210	22	1	Texas Tech
57	Bowman, Ken	C	6-3	230	23	3	Wisconsin
12	Bratkowski, Zeke	QB	6-3	200	34	11	Georgia
78	Brown, Bob	DE	6-5	270	25	1	Arkansas -Pine Bluff
40	Brown, Tom	DB	6-1	190	25	3	Maryland
60	Caffey, Lee Roy	LB	6-3	250	25	4	Texas A&M
34	Chandler, Don	P-K	6-2	210	32	11	Florida
56	Crutcher, Tommy	LB	6-3	230	24	3	Texas Christian
50	Curry, Bill	C	6-2	235	24	2	Georgia Tech
84	Dale, Carroll	FL	6-2	200	28	7	Virginia Tech
87	Davis, Willie	DE	6-3	245	32	9	Grambling
86	Dowler, Boyd	E	6-5	225	28	8	Colorado
81	Fleming, Marv	TE	6-4	235	24	4	Utah
68	Gillingham, Gale	G	6-3	250	22	1	Minnesota
33	Grabowski, Jim	RB	6-2	215	21	1	Illinois
75	Gregg, Forrest	T	6-4	250	32	10	Southern Methodist
43	Hart, Doug	DB	6-0	190	27	3	Texas-Arlington
45	Hathcock, Dave	DB	6-0	190	23	1	Memphis State
5	Hornung, Paul	RB	6-2	215	30	9	Notre Dame
21	Jeter, Bob	DB	6-1	205	29	4	Iowa
74	Jordan, Henry	DT	6-3	250	31	10	Virginia
77	Kostelnik, Ron	DT	6-4	260	26	6	Cincinnati
64	Kramer, Jerry	G	6-3	245	30	9	Idaho
80	Long, Bob	FL	6-3	190	24	3	Wichita State
27	Mack, Bill (Red)	FL	5-10	185	29	6	Notre Dame
85	McGee, Max	E	6-3	205	34	11	Tulane
66	Nitschke, Ray	LB	6-3	240	29	9	Illinois
22	Pitts, Elijah	RB	6-1	205	27	6	Philander Smith
89	Robinson, Dave	LB	6-3	245	25	4	Penn State
76	Skoronski, Bob	DT	6-3	250	32	9	Indiana
15	Starr, Bart	QB	6-1	200	32	11	Alabama
31	Taylor, Jim	RB	6-0	215	30	9	Louisiana State
63	Thurston, Fred (Fuzzy)	G	6-1	245	32	9	Valparaiso
37	Vandersea, Phil	RB	6-2	225	23	1	Massachusetts
73	Weatherwax, Jim	DT	6-7	275	23	1	Cal. State-L.A.
24	Wood, Willie	DB	5-10	190	29	7	USC
72	Wright, Steve	T	6-6	250	24	3	Alabama

Head coach—Vince Lombardi. **Assistants**—Phil Bengtson, Jerry Burns, John (Red) Cochran, Dave Hanner, Bob Schnelker, Ray Witecha.

KANSAS CITY CHIEFS

No.	Name	Pos.	Ht.	Wt.	Age	Year	College
52	Abell, Bud	LB	6-3	220	25	4	Missouri
84	Arbanas, Fred	TE	6-3	240	27	5	Michigan State
10	Beathard, Pete	QB	6-2	210	24	3	USC
78	Bell, Bobby	LB	6-4	228	26	4	Minnesota
61	Biodrowski, Denny	G	6-1	225	26	4	Memphis State
87	Brown, Aaron	DE	6-5	265	22	1	Minnesota
86	Buchanan, Buck	DT	6-7	287	26	4	Grambling
71	Budde, Ed	G	6-5	260	65	4	Michigan State
88	Burford, Chris	E	6-3	220	28	7	Stanford
80	Carolan, Reg	TE	6-6	238	25	5	Idaho
23	Coan, Bert	RB	6-4	220	26	5	Kansas
56	Corey, Walt	LB	6-1	233	28	6	Miami
16	Dawson, Len	QB	6-0	190	31	10	Purdue
72	DiMidio, Tony	T	6-3	250	25	1	West Chester State
66	Frazier, Wayne	C	6-3	245	25	3	Auburn
21	Garrett, Mike	RB	5-9	195	22	1	USC
69	Headrick, Sherrill	LB	6-2	240	29	8	Texas Christian
73	Hill, Dave	T	6-5	264	25	4	Auburn
55	Holub, E. J.	LB	6-4	236	28	6	Texas Tech
20	Hunt, Bobby	DB	6-1	193	24	5	Auburn
85	Hurston, Chuck	DE	6-6	240	24	2	Auburn
75	Mays, Jerry	DE	6-4	252	26	6	Southern Methodist
32	McClinton, Curtis	RB	6-3	227	27	5	Kansas
15	Mercer, Mike	K	6-0	210	28	6	Arizona State
64	Merz, Curt	G	6-4	267	27	7	Iowa
22	Mitchell, Willie	DB	6-1	185	24	3	Tennessee State
25	Pitts, Frank	FL	6-2	190	22	2	Southern U.
14	Ply, Bobby	DB	6-1	196	25	5	Baylor
60	Reynolds, Al	G	6-3	250	28	7	Tarkio, Mo.
58	Rice, Andy	DT	6-2	260	24	1	Texas Southern
42	Robinson, Johnny	DB	6-1	205	27	7	Louisiana State
17	Smith, Fletcher	DB	6-2	188	22	1	Tennessee State
35	Stover, Stewart (Smokey)	LB	6-0	227	27	7	N.E. Louisiana
89	Taylor, Otis	FL	6-2	211	23	2	Prairie View
18	Thomas, Emmitt	DB	6-2	189	22	1	Bishop
45	Thomas, Gene	RB	6-1	210	23	1	Florida A&M
77	Tyrer, Jim	T	6-6	292	27	6	Ohio State
24	Williamson, Fred	DB	6-3	209	28	7	Northwestern
44	Wilson, Jerrel	P	6-4	222	24	4	Southern Mississippi

Head coach—Hank Stram. **Assistants**—Tom Bettis, Darrell (Pete) Brewster, Chuck Mills, Tom Pratt, Bill Walsh.

Kansas City's Mitchell is too late as Pitts scores the Packers' final touchdown.

SUPER BOWL II

GREEN BAY 33, OAKLAND 14

The Green Bay Packers, 14-point favorites at the start of the game, defeated the Oakland Raiders 33–14 for their second straight Super Bowl victory. Packers quarterback Bart Starr completed 13 of 24 passes for 202 yards and one touchdown and helped the Packers convert 6 of 11 third-down situations into first downs.

The Packers moved 34 yards in 10 plays the first time they had the ball. On fourth down and 11 yards for a first down at Oakland's 32, Don Chandler kicked a 39-yard field goal, his first of four. The Packers held the ball for 8:40 during their second possession, moving 84 yards, from their 3 to the Raiders' 13, in 17 plays. Chandler kicked a 20-yard field goal on fourth down for a 6–0 lead.

Green Bay increased its lead to 13–0 in the second quarter. On the first play from the Packers' 38-yard line after a punt, Starr passed to Boyd Dowler, a 6-foot 5-inch end who ran inside of cornerback Kent McCloughan and was beyond the last defender when he caught the ball and completed a 62-yard touchdown. "I just bulled by McCloughan," Dowler explained. "He was playing me tight and bumped me and I ran through him. There was no one left to stop me." Carroll Dale had been the primary receiver, but when the Raiders blitzed, Starr sensed that Dowler would be open and changed direction.

Oakland closed to 13–7 on the following series. The Raiders moved 78 yards in nine plays, scoring on Daryle Lamonica's 23-yard pass to end Bill Miller. The drive took 1:54 as Lamonica completed four of five passes for 58 yards. Miller got behind defensive backs Herb Adderley and Tom Brown in the end zone. "I was supposed to take Miller deep, but I played him too 'soft,'" said Brown. "Linebacker Dave Robinson dropped back with him as far as he could and I should have taken him, but I didn't."

Green Bay led 16–7 at halftime after Oakland's Rodger Bird fumbled a fair catch on a punt at the Raiders' 45-yard line. Dick Capp, who had been activated by Green Bay the day before, made the recovery. Starr completed a pass to Dowler for a nine-yard gain to the 36 with six seconds left in the half. Chandler then kicked a 43-yard field goal.

The Packers broke open the game in the third quarter, just as they had done in defeating the Kansas City Chiefs 35–10 in Super Bowl I. They went 82 yards in 11 plays on their second possession. Donny Anderson scored a touchdown from the 2-yard line to make the score 23–7. Starr converted two third-down situations during that drive, once passing to Max McGee for a 25-yard gain on third and one and passing 11 yards to Dale on third and nine.

Chandler's 31-yard field goal gave Green Bay a 26–7 lead at the end of the quarter. Early in the fourth period, defensive back Herb Adderley intercepted a pass by Lamonica and ran 60 yards for Green Bay's final touchdown. "Lamonica was trying to hit Fred Biletnikoff on a slant-in," said Adderley. "I played the ball and cut in front of him. It was no gamble."

Oakland scored the final touchdown with 9:13 remaining in the game. The Raiders went 74 yards in four plays, Lamonica throwing to Miller again for 23 yards and the touchdown. Miller beat Brown once more after a pass play from Lamonica to Pete Banaszak covered 41 yards and set up the play.

"It wasn't our best," said Packers coach Vince Lombardi of his team's effort. "All year it seemed like as soon as we got a couple touchdowns ahead we let up. Maybe that's the sign of a veteran team, such as ours. I don't know."

Several days after the game Lombardi announced that he was retiring as the Packers' coach to devote full time to his job as general manager.

Green Bay's Brown watches as Miller pulls in his second touchdown pass for Oakland.

Participants—Green Bay Packers, champions of the National Football League, and Oakland Raiders, champions of the American Football League
Date—January 14, 1968
Site—Orange Bowl, Miami
Time—3:05 P.M. EST
Conditions—86 degrees, partly cloudy
Playing Surface—Grass
Television and Radio—Columbia Broadcasting System (CBS)
Regular Season Records—Green Bay, 9-4-1, Oakland, 13-1
League Championships—Green Bay defeated the Dallas Cowboys 21-17 for the NFL title; Oakland defeated the Houston Oilers 40-7 for the AFL title
Players' Shares—$15,000 to each member of the winning team; $7,500 to each member of the losing team
Attendance—75,546
Gross Receipts—$3,349,106.89
Officials—Referee, Jack Vest, AFL; umpire, Ralph Morcroft, NFL; line judge, Bruce Alford, NFL; head linesman, Tony Veteri, AFL; back judge, Stan Javie, NFL; field judge, Bob Bauer, AFL
Coaches—Vince Lombardi, Green Bay; John Rauch, Oakland

Green Bay	Starters, Offense	Oakland
Boyd Dowler	LE	Bill Miller
Bob Skoronski	LT	Bob Svihus
Gale Gillingham	LG	Gene Upshaw
Ken Bowman	C	Jim Otto
Jerry Kramer	RG	Wayne Hawkins
Forrest Gregg	RT	Harry Schuh
Marv Fleming	RE	Billy Cannon
Carroll Dale	FL	Fred Biletnikoff
Bart Starr	QB	Daryle Lamonica
Donny Anderson	RB	Pete Banaszak
Ben Wilson	RB	Hewritt Dixon
	Starters, Defense	
Willie Davis	LE	Isaac Lassiter
Ron Kostelnik	LT	Dan Birdwell
Henry Jordan	RT	Tom Keating
Lionel Aldridge	RE	Ben Davidson
Dave Robinson	LLB	Bill Laskey
Ray Nitschke	MLB	Dan Conners
Lee Roy Caffey	RLB	Gus Otto
Herb Adderley	LHB	Kent McCloughan
Bob Jeter	RHB	Willie Brown
Tom Brown	LS	Warren Powers
Willie Wood	RS	Howie Williams

Green Bay	3	13	10	7	— 33
Oakland	0	7	0	7	— 14

GB —FG Chandler 39
GB —FG Chandler 20
GB —Dowler 62 pass from Starr (Chandler kick)
Oak—Miller 23 pass from Lamonica (Blanda kick)
GB —FG Chandler 43
GB —Anderson 2 run (Chandler kick)
GB —FG Chandler 31
GB —Adderley 60 interception (Chandler kick)
Oak—Miller 23 pass from Lamonica (Blanda kick)

TEAM STATISTICS	GB	Oak
First downs	19	16
Rushing	11	5
Passing	7	10
By penalty	1	1
Total yardage	322	293
Net rushing yardage	160	107
Net passing yardage	162	186
Passes att.-comp.-had int.	24-13-0	34-15-1

RUSHING
Green Bay—Wilson, 17 for 62; Anderson, 14 for 48, 1 TD; Williams, 8 for 36; Starr, 1 for 14; Mercein, 1 for 0.
Oakland—Dixon, 12 for 54; Todd, 2 for 37; Banaszak, 6 for 16.

PASSING
Green Bay—Starr, 13 of 24 for 202, 1 TD.
Oakland—Lamonica, 15 of 34 for 208, 2 TDs, 1 int.

RECEIVING
Green Bay—Dale, 4 for 43; Fleming, 4 for 35; Anderson, 2 for 18; Dowler, 2 for 71, 1 TD; McGee, 1 for 35.
Oakland—Miller, 5 for 84, 2 TDs; Banaszak, 4 for 69; Cannon, 2 for 25; Biletnikoff, 2 for 10; Wells, 1 for 17; Dixon, 1 for 3.

PUNTING
Green Bay—Anderson, 6 for 234, 39.0 average.
Oakland—Eischeid, 6 for 264, 44.0 average.

PUNT RETURNS
Green Bay—Wood, 5 for 35.
Oakland—Bird, 2 for 12, 1 fair catch.

KICKOFF RETURNS
Green Bay—Adderley, 1 for 24; Williams, 1 for 18; Crutcher, 1 for 7.
Oakland—Todd, 3 for 63; Grayson, 2 for 61; Hawkins, 1 for 3; Kocourek, 1 for 0, Kocourek lateraled to Grayson, who returned 11 yards.

INTERCEPTIONS
Green Bay—Adderley, 1 for 60, 1 TD.
Oakland—None.

Adderley steps in front of Biletnikoff to intercept; he went 60 yards to score.

Starr lofts a pass for Green Bay over the onrushing Birdwell.

GREEN BAY PACKERS

No.	Name	Pos.	Ht.	Wt.	Age	Year	College
26	Adderley, Herb	DB	6-0	200	28	7	Michigan State
82	Aldridge, Lionel	DE	6-4	245	26	5	Utah State
44	Anderson, Donny	RB-P	6-3	210	24	2	Texas Tech
57	Bowman, Ken	C	6-3	230	24	4	Wisconsin
12	Bratkowski, Zeke	QB	6-3	210	34	12	Georgia
83	Brown, Allen	TE	6-5	235	24	2	Mississippi
78	Brown, Bob	DE	6-5	260	26	2	Arkansas-Pine Bluff
40	Brown, Tom	DB	6-1	195	26	4	Maryland
60	Caffey, Lee Roy	LB	6-3	250	26	5	Texas A&M
88	Capp, Dick	TE	6-3	235	23	1	Boston College
34	Chandler, Don	K	6-2	210	33	12	Florida
56	Crutcher, Tommy	LB	6-3	230	25	4	Texas Christian
84	Dale, Carroll	E	6-2	200	28	8	Virginia Tech
87	Davis, Willie	DE	6-3	245	32	10	Grambling
86	Dowler, Boyd	E	6-5	225	29	9	Colorado
55	Flanigan, Jim	LB	6-3	240	21	1	Pittsburgh
81	Fleming, Marv	TE	6-4	235	25	5	Utah
68	Gillingham, Gale	G	6-3	255	23	2	Minnesota
33	Grabowski, Jim	RB	6-2	220	23	2	Illinois
75	Gregg, Forrest	T	6-4	250	33	11	Southern Methodist
43	Hart, Doug	DB	6-0	190	28	4	Texas-Arlington
13	Horn, Don	QB	6-2	195	22	1	San Diego State
50	Hyland, Bob	C-G	6-5	250	21	1	Boston College
21	Jeter, Bob	DB	6-1	205	30	5	Iowa
74	Jordan, Henry	DT	6-3	250	32	11	Virginia
77	Kostelnik, Ron	DT	6-4	260	27	7	Cincinnati
64	Kramer, Jerry	G	6-3	245	31	10	Idaho
80	Long, Bob	FL	6-3	205	24	4	Wichita State
85	McGee, Max	E	6-3	210	35	12	Tulane
30	Mercein, Chuck	RB	6-2	225	24	4	Yale
66	Nitschke, Ray	LB	6-3	235	30	10	Illinois
89	Robinson, Dave	LB	6-3	240	26	5	Penn State
45	Rowser, John	DB	6-1	180	22	1	Michigan
76	Skoronski, Bob	T	6-3	245	33	10	Indiana
15	Starr, Bart	QB	6-1	190	33	12	Alabama
63	Thurston, Fred (Fuzzy)	G	6-1	245	33	10	Valparaiso
73	Weatherwax, Jim	DT	6-7	260	24	2	Cal. State-L.A.
23	Williams, Travis	RB	6-1	210	21	1	Arizona State
36	Wilson, Ben	RB	6-1	230	27	4	USC
24	Wood, Willie	DB	5-10	190	30	8	USC
72	Wright, Steve	T	6-6	250	25	4	Alabama

Head coach—Vince Lombardi. **Assistants**—Phil Bengtson, Jerry Burns, Dave Hanner, Tom McCormick, Bob Schnelker, Ray Witecha.

OAKLAND RAIDERS

No.	Name	Pos.	Ht.	Wt.	Age	Year	College
78	Archer, Dan	G-T	6-5	245	22	1	Oregon
40	Banaszak, Pete	RB	5-11	200	23	2	Miami
50	Benson, Duane	LB	6-2	215	21	1	Hamline
25	Biletnikoff, Fred	FL	6-1	190	24	3	Florida State
21	Bird, Rodger	DB	5-11	195	23	2	Kentucky
53	Birdwell, Dan	DT	6-4	250	29	6	Houston
16	Blanda, George	K-QB	6-3	215	40	18	Kentucky
24	Brown, Willie	DB	6-1	190	27	5	Grambling
48	Budness, Bill	LB	6-2	215	24	4	Boston U.
33	Cannon, Billy	TE	6-1	215	30	8	Louisiana State
55	Conners, Dan	LB	6-1	230	25	4	Miami
83	Davidson, Ben	DE	6-7	265	28	7	Washington
35	Dixon, Hewritt	RB	6-1	220	26	5	Florida A&M
11	Eischeid, Mike	P	6-0	190	26	2	Upper Iowa
45	Grayson, Dave	DB	5-10	185	28	7	Oregon
30	Hagberg, Roger	RB	6-1	215	28	6	Minnesota
70	Harvey, Jim	G	6-5	245	23	2	Mississippi
65	Hawkins, Wayne	G	6-0	240	29	8	Pacific
84	Herock, Ken	E	6-2	230	26	4	West Virginia
74	Keating, Tom	DT	6-2	247	25	4	Michigan
88	Kocourek, Dave	TE	6-5	240	29	9	Wisconsin
62	Kruse, Bob	G	6-2	250	22	1	Wayne State
3	Lamonica, Daryle	QB	6-3	215	25	5	Notre Dame
42	Laskey, Bill	LB	6-3	235	25	3	Michigan
77	Lassiter, Isaac	DE	6-5	270	26	6	St. Augustine, N.C.
47	McCloughan, Kent	DB	6-1	190	23	3	Nebraska
89	Miller, Bill	E	6-0	190	28	6	Miami
85	Oats, Carleton	DE	6-2	235	24	3	Florida A&M
34	Otto, Gus	LB	6-2	220	24	3	Missouri
00	Otto, Jim	C	6-2	240	28	8	Miami
20	Powers, Warren	DB	6-0	190	26	5	Nebraska
79	Schuh, Harry	T	6-2	260	24	3	Memphis State
23	Sherman, Rod	FL	6-0	190	21	1	USC
73	Sligh, Richard	DT-DE	7-0	300	22	1	North Carolina College
76	Svihus, Bob	T	6-4	245	24	3	USC
22	Todd, Larry	RB	6-1	185	24	3	Arizona State
63	Upshaw, Gene	G	6-5	255	22	1	Texas A&I
81	Wells, Warren	E	6-1	190	24	2	Texas Southern
29	Williams, Howie	DB	6-1	186	28	6	Howard
52	Williamson, John	LB	6-2	220	25	4	Louisiana Tech

Head coach—John Rauch. **Assistants**—Tom Dahms, John Madden, John Polonchek, Ollie Spencer, Charlie Sumner.

SUPER BOWL VIII

MIAMI 24, MINNESOTA 7

The Miami Dolphins defeated the Minnesota Vikings 24–7 in Super Bowl VIII, a game in which the Dolphins took control on the first series of offensive plays.

Miami moved 62 yards in 10 plays, scoring on Larry Csonka's five-yard run after accepting the opening kickoff. After Minnesota ran three plays and punted, Miami marched 56 yards in 10 plays, scoring on Jim Kiick's one-yard run.

At the end of the first quarter, Miami had run 20 plays and gained 118 yards. Minnesota had run six plays and gained 16 yards. The Dolphins had eight first downs, the Vikings none.

The Dolphins marched 44 yards in seven plays to Yepremian's 28-yard field goal that made the score 17–0 with 6:02 left in the half. The Vikings had run 12 plays and gained 27 yards at this point. Miami had run 31 plays that had gained 153 yards. Minnesota took the following kickoff and drove 74 yards to the Dolphins' 6-yard line. On fourth down and one yard for a first down, Oscar Reed fumbled when hit by Nick Buoniconti and Miami's Jake Scott recovered on the 6.

Minnesota lost a chance to get back into the game at the beginning of the third quarter. John Gilliam returned Garo Yepremian's kickoff 65 yards to Miami's 34-yard line, but Minnesota's Stu Voigt was penalized for clipping and the ball was returned to the Vikings' 11-yard line. The Vikings punted four plays later and Miami began from Minnesota's 43. In eight plays the Dolphins scored on Larry Csonka's two-yard run.

Csonka was confused on the play on which he scored his second touchdown, which punctuated a performance in which he set Super Bowl records with 33 carries and 145 yards rushing. Quarterback Bob Griese forgot the number on which the ball was supposed to be snapped by center Jim Langer. "What's the count?" Griese asked Csonka. The running back thought for a moment. "What's the count?" Griese demanded. "It's on two, isn't it?" said Csonka. "No, no...it's on one," said Jim Kiick, the other running back. Griese finally agreed with Csonka. But Langer snapped the ball to the startled quarterback on one; Griese juggled the ball and handed off to Csonka, who followed Kiick, Langer, guard Larry Little, and tackle Norm Evans into the end zone.

"Bob had that wide-eyed look when he gave me the ball," said Csonka. "I'm just happy I didn't cause him to drop the ball."

Minnesota scored its touchdown after a drive that began on the Vikings' 43-yard line with 1:34 left in the third quarter and concluded with quarterback Fran Tarkenton's four-yard touchdown run 1:35 into the final quarter.

The Vikings moved from their 3-yard line to Miami's 32 later in the quarter but Tarkenton's pass to Jim Lash was intercepted on the goal line by Curtis Johnson. Miami took possession with 6:24 remaining in the game and moved 61 yards in 13 plays before the clock ran out and the game ended.

The victory was Miami's second in a row in the Super Bowl, equalling Green Bay's achievement in Super Bowls I and II. Csonka was asked if he thought Miami was stronger than the Packers' teams.

"I don't know about legends or statistics," said Csonka. "Football is a 'now' game; that's all that matters."

Miami also set a record by making its third appearance in the game. Minnesota set a record by losing for the second time.

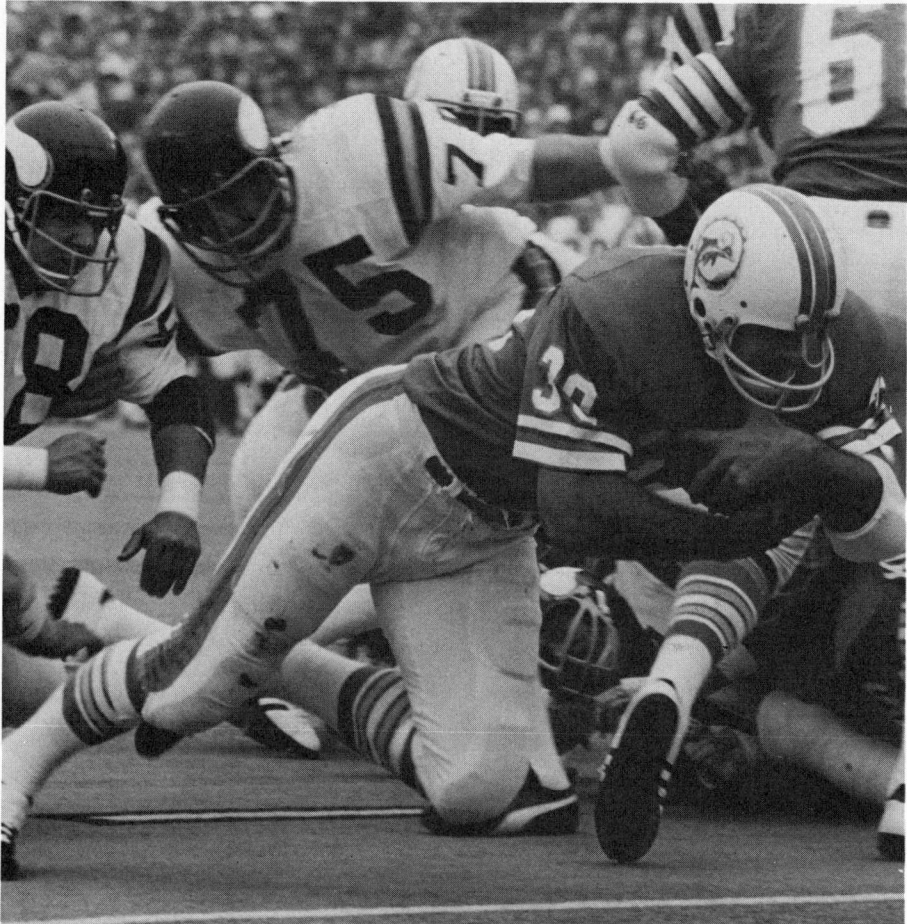

The Dolphins take control and Csonka scores the first touchdown 10 plays after the opening kickoff.

Participants—Miami Dolphins, champions of the American Football Conference, and Minnesota Vikings, champions of the National Football Conference
Date—January 13, 1974
Site—Rice Stadium, Houston
Time—2:30 P.M. CST
Conditions—50 degrees, overcast
Playing Surface—AstroTurf
Television and Radio—Columbia Broadcasting System (CBS)
Regular Season Records—Miami, 12-2; Minnesota, 12-2
Conference Championships—Miami defeated the Oakland Raiders 27-10 for the AFC title; Minnesota defeated the Dallas Cowboys 27-10 for the NFC title
Players' Shares—$15,000 to each member of the winning team; $7,500 to each member of the losing team
Attendance—68,142
Gross Receipts—$3,953,641.22
Officials—Referee, Ben Dreith; umpire, Ralph Morcroft; line judge, Jack Fette; head linesman, Leo Miles; back judge, Stan Javie; field judge, Fritz Graf
Coaches—Don Shula, Miami; Bud Grant, Minnesota

Minnesota	0	0	0	7	—	7
Miami	14	3	7	0	—	24

Mia —Csonka 5 run (Yepremian kick)
Mia —Kiick 1 run (Yepremian kick)
Mia —FG Yepremian 28
Mia —Csonka 2 run (Yepremian kick)
Minn—Tarkenton 4 run (Cox kick)

TEAM STATISTICS	Minn	Mia
First downs	14	21
Rushing	5	13
Passing	8	4
By penalty	1	4
Total yardage	238	259
Net rushing yardage	72	196
Net passing yardage	166	63
Passes att.-comp.-had int.	28-18-1	7-6-0

RUSHING
Minnesota—Reed, 11 for 32; Foreman, 7 for 18; Tarkenton, 4 for 17, 1 TD; Marinaro, 1 for 3; B. Brown, 1 for 2.
Miami—Csonka, 33 for 145, 2 TDs; Morris, 11 for 34; Kiick, 7 for 10, 1 TD; Griese, 2 for 7.

PASSING
Minnesota—Tarkenton, 18 of 28 for 182, 1 int.
Miami—Griese, 6 of 7 for 73.

RECEIVING
Minnesota—Foreman, 5 for 27; Gilliam, 4 for 44; Voigt, 3 for 46; Marinaro, 2 for 39; B. Brown, 1 for 9; Kingsriter, 1 for 9; Lash, 1 for 9; Reed, 1 for -1.
Miami—Warfield, 2 for 33; Mandich, 2 for 21; Briscoe, 2 for 19.

PUNTING
Minnesota—Eischeid, 5 for 211, 42.2 average.
Miami—Seiple, 3 for 119, 39.7 average.

PUNT RETURNS
Minnesota—Bryant, 1 fair catch.
Miami—Scott, 3 for 20, 1 fair catch.

KICKOFF RETURNS
Minnesota—Gilliam, 2 for 41; West, 2 for 28.
Miami—Scott, 2 for 47.

INTERCEPTIONS
Minnesota—None.
Miami—Johnson, 1 for 10.

Minnesota	Starters, Offense	Miami
Carroll Dale	WR	Paul Warfield
Grady Alderman	LT	Wayne Moore
Ed White	LG	Bob Kuechenberg
Mick Tingelhoff	C	Jim Langer
Frank Gallagher	RG	Larry Little
Ron Yary	RT	Norm Evans
Stu Voigt	TE	Jim Mandich
John Gilliam	WR	Marlin Briscoe
Fran Tarkenton	QB	Bob Griese
Chuck Foreman	RB	Eugene (Mercury) Morris
Oscar Reed	RB	Larry Csonka
	Starters, Defense	
Carl Eller	LE	Vern Den Herder
Gary Larsen	LT	Manny Fernandez
Alan Page	RT	Bob Heinz
Jim Marshall	RE	Bill Stanfill
Roy Winston	LLB	Doug Swift
Jeff Siemon	MLB	Nick Buoniconti
Wally Hilgenberg	RLB	Mike Kolen
Nate Wright	LCB	Lloyd Mumphord
Bob Bryant	RCB	Curtis Johnson
Jeff Wright	LS	Dick Anderson
Paul Krause	RS	Jake Scott

Tarkenton sneaks over for a Vikings' touchdown in the fourth quarter.

Defenders Stanfill (84), Kolen (57), and Matheson (53) stop the Vikings' Reed.

MINNESOTA VIKINGS

No.	Name	Pos.	Ht.	Wt.	Age	Year	College
67	Alderman, Grady	T	6-2	247	34	14	Detroit
85	Ballman, Gary	TE	6-1	215	33	12	Michigan State
17	Berry, Bob	QB	5-11	185	31	9	Oregon
30	Brown, Bill	RB	5-11	222	35	13	Illinois
24	Brown, Terry	S	6-2	205	26	4	Oklahoma State
20	Bryant, Bob	CB	6-1	170	29	6	South Carolina
14	Cox, Fred	K	5-10	200	34	11	Pittsburgh
84	Dale, Carroll	WR	6-2	200	35	14	Virginia Tech
86	Dawson, Rhett	WR	6-1	182	24	2	Florida State
11	Eischeid, Mike	P	6-0	190	31	7	Upper Iowa
81	Eller, Carl	DE	6-6	247	31	10	Minnesota
44	Foreman, Chuck	RB	6-2	216	23	1	Miami
66	Gallagher, Frank	G	6-2	245	30	7	North Carolina
42	Gilliam, John	WR	6-1	195	28	7	South Carolina State
68	Goodrum, Charles	T-G	6-2	256	23	1	Florida A&M
58	Hilgenberg, Wally	LB	6-3	229	31	10	Iowa
89	Kingsriter, Doug	TE	6-2	222	23	1	Minnesota
22	Krause, Paul	S	6-3	200	31	10	Iowa
77	Larsen, Gary	DT	6-5	255	33	10	Concordia, Minn.
82	Lash, Jim	WR	6-2	199	22	1	Northwestern
65	Lawson, Steve	G	6-3	265	24	3	Kansas
75	Lurtsema, Bob	DT-DE	6-6	250	31	7	Western Michigan
49	Marinaro, Ed	RB	6-2	212	23	2	Cornell
70	Marshall, Jim	DE	6-4	240	35	14	Ohio State
55	Martin, Amos	LB	6-3	228	24	2	Louisville
33	McClanahan, Brent	RB	5-10	202	22	1	Arizona State
41	Osborn, Dave	RB	6-0	208	30	9	North Dakota
88	Page, Alan	DT	6-4	245	28	7	Notre Dame
52	Porter, Ron	LB	6-3	232	28	7	Idaho
34	Randolph, Al	S	6-2	205	29	7	Iowa
32	Reed, Oscar	RB	6-0	222	29	6	Colorado State
50	Siemon, Jeff	LB	6-2	230	23	2	Stanford
74	Smiley, Larry	DT	6-5	248	23	1	Texas Southern
64	Sunde, Milt	G	6-2	250	31	10	Minnesota
69	Sutherland, Doug	DT	6-3	250	25	4	Wisconsin-Superior
10	Tarkenton, Fran	QB	6-0	190	33	13	Georgia
53	Tingelhoff, Mick	C	6-2	237	33	12	Nebraska
83	Voigt, Stu	TE	6-1	225	25	4	Wisconsin
25	Wallace, Jackie	CB	6-2	203	22	1	Arizona
15	Wells, Mike	QB	6-5	229	22	1	Illinois
40	West, Charlie	CB	6-1	197	26	6	Texas-El Paso
62	White, Ed	G	6-3	262	25	5	California
60	Winston, Roy	LB	5-11	222	33	12	Louisiana State
23	Wright, Jeff	S	5-11	190	24	3	Minnesota
43	Wright, Nate	CB	5-11	180	26	5	San Diego State
73	Yary, Ron	T	6-6	255	27	6	USC
51	Zaunbrecher, Godfrey	C	6-2	240	25	3	Louisiana State

Head coach—Bud Grant. **Assistants**—Neill Armstrong, Jerry Burns, Bus Mertes, John Michels, Jocko Nelson, Jack Patera.

MIAMI DOLPHINS

No.	Name	Pos.	Ht.	Wt.	Age	Year	College
40	Anderson, Dick	S	6-2	196	27	6	Colorado
49	Babb, Charles	S	6-0	190	23	2	Memphis State
51	Ball, Larry	LB	6-6	235	24	2	Louisville
58	Bannon, Bruce	LB	6-3	225	22	1	Penn State
86	Briscoe, Marlin	WR	5-11	175	27	6	Nebraska-Omaha
85	Buoniconti, Nick	LB	5-11	220	32	12	Notre Dame
77	Crusan, Doug	T	6-4	250	27	6	Indiana
39	Csonka, Larry	RB	6-2	237	26	6	Syracuse
83	Den Herder, Vern	DE	6-6	252	24	3	Central Iowa
73	Evans, Norm	T	6-5	250	30	9	Texas Christian
75	Fernandez, Manny	DT	6-2	250	27	6	Utah
80	Fleming, Marv	TE	6-4	230	31	11	Utah
25	Foley, Tim	CB	6-0	194	24	4	Purdue
55	Goode, Irv	C-G	6-5	262	32	11	Kentucky
12	Griese, Bob	QB	6-1	190	28	7	Purdue
72	Heinz, Bob	DT-DE	6-6	265	26	5	Pacific
45	Johnson, Curtis	CB	6-1	196	25	4	Toledo
21	Kiick, Jim	RB	5-11	214	27	6	Wyoming
57	Kolen, Mike	LB	6-2	222	25	4	Auburn
67	Kuechenberg, Bob	G	6-2	252	25	4	Notre Dame
62	Langer, Jim	C	6-2	253	25	4	South Dakota State
23	Leigh, Charles	RB	5-11	206	27	5	No college
66	Little, Larry	G	6-1	265	27	7	Bethune-Cookman
88	Mandich, Jim	TE	6-2	224	25	4	Michigan
53	Matheson, Bob	LB	6-4	235	28	7	Duke
65	Moore, Maulty	DT	6-5	265	27	2	Bethune-Cookman
79	Moore, Wayne	T	6-6	265	27	4	Lamar U.
15	Morrall, Earl	QB	6-2	210	39	18	Michigan State
22	Morris, Eugene (Mercury)	RB	5-10	192	26	5	West Texas State
26	Mumphord, Lloyd	CB	5-11	176	26	5	Texas Southern
64	Newman, Ed	G	6-2	245	22	1	Duke
36	Nottingham, Don	RB	5-10	210	24	3	Kent State
82	Rather, David (Bo)	WR	6-1	182	22	1	Michigan
13	Scott, Jake	S	6-0	188	28	4	Georgia
20	Seiple, Larry	P-TE	6-0	214	28	7	Kentucky
34	Sellers, Ron	WR	6-4	204	26	5	Florida State
29	Smith, Tom	RB	6-1	218	23	1	Miami
84	Stanfill, Bill	DE	6-5	252	26	5	Georgia
10	Strock, Don	QB	6-5	216	22	1	Virginia Tech
48	Stuckey, Henry	CB	6-1	180	24	1	Missouri
59	Swift, Doug	LB	6-3	226	25	4	Amherst
81	Twilley, Howard	WR	5-10	185	29	8	Tulsa
89	Wade, Charley	WR	5-10	170	23	1	Tennessee State
42	Warfield, Paul	WR	6-0	188	30	10	Ohio State
70	Woods, Larry	DT	6-6	260	25	3	Tennessee State
1	Yepremian, Garo	K	5-8	175	29	7	No college
76	Young, Willie	T	6-5	262	26	4	Alcorn State

Head coach—Don Shula. **Assistants**—Bill Arnsparger, Monte Clark, Tom Keane, Bill McPeak, Mike Scarry, Carl Taseff.

SUPER BOWL IX

PITTSBURGH 16, MINNESOTA 6

Fullback Franco Harris set Super Bowl records by rushing 34 times for 158 yards, and the Pittsburgh Steelers outrushed the Minnesota Vikings 249-17 and won Super Bowl IX 16–6, the club's first championship in its 42-year history. The loss was the Vikings' third without a victory in the Super Bowl.

The Steelers led 2–0 at halftime. With 6:11 left in the second quarter Minnesota quarterback Fran Tarkenton fumbled a pitchout to running back Dave Osborn. Attempting to regain possession of the ball, Tarkenton slid into the end zone where he was downed by Dwight White for a safety.

Harris, who gained 97 yards in 22 carries in the second half, scored on a nine-yard run to increase Pittsburgh's lead to 9–0 after just 1:35 of the third quarter. The Steelers moved 30 yards in four plays to the score after Marv Kellum recovered a fumble on the kickoff by Minnesota's Bill Brown.

The score remained 9–0 until early in the fourth quarter. Bobby Walden was in punt formation for the Steelers on fourth down at Pittsburgh's 15-yard line. Linebacker Matt Blair blocked the punt and the ball was recovered in the end zone by the Vikings' Terry Brown for a touchdown with 10:33 remaining in the game. Fred Cox's extra point hit the left upright and the score was 9–6.

The Steelers began their next series on the 34-yard line. At the 42, quarterback Terry Bradshaw faced third down and two yards for a first down. Disdaining the run and a short pass, Bradshaw threw a 30-yard completion to tight end Larry Brown. After Harris and Rocky Bleier carried the ball from the Vikings' 28 to the 5, Bradshaw faced another third down situation. He rolled to his right, searched for a receiver, and found Brown for a touchdown that resulted in a 16–6 lead.

"I looked first to pass to the halfback [Rocky Bleier]," said Bradshaw. "It depended on what their cornerbacks did. If they had come up, I would have passed; if they had laid back I would have run. They laid back, so I started to run, but I knew I couldn't run the ball in for a touchdown."

Bradshaw said Brown made a smart move. "He stopped after running toward the corner of the end zone, then started again. That made the middle linebacker [Jeff Siemon] commit himself, and I drilled the ball to Larry." The Steelers had driven 66 yards in 12 plays and controlled the ball for seven minutes and two seconds.

Minnesota took over on its 9-yard line with 3:20 remaining. Tarkenton threw a pass intended for John Gilliam, who was running down the middle of the field on first down. Free safety Mike Wagner intercepted the pass on Pittsburgh's 33 and returned the ball 26 yards to Minnesota's 41. Pittsburgh held possession for seven more plays, surrendering the ball on downs to the Vikings at their 23 with 41 seconds left.

The Steelers appeared to confuse the Vikings with misdirection running plays as they outgained Minnesota 333-119 in total offense. Harris and Bleier repeatedly found holes in the defense that were opened when Vikings linemen followed the flow of pulling Steelers linemen. On defense, the Steelers put a man directly over center Mick Tingelhoff. Tackle Ernie Holmes sometimes would attack Tingelhoff directly after the snap of the ball; sometimes Holmes would loop around Joe Greene to the outside and participate in double-teaming action with Greene. Tarkenton was the objective. He completed just 11 of 26 passes for 102 yards with three interceptions. Four attempts were deflected and many others were thrown under severe pressure.

Bleier cuts down the Vikings' Marshall as Harris sweeps left end behind guard Clack.

Participants—Pittsburgh Steelers, champions of the American Football Conference, and Minnesota Vikings, champions of the National Football Conference
Date—January 12, 1975
Site—Tulane Stadium, New Orleans
Time—2:00 P.M. CST
Conditions—46 degrees, cloudy
Playing Surface—Poly-Turf
Television and Radio—National Broadcasting Company (NBC)
Regular Season Records—Pittsburgh, 10-3-1; Minnesota, 10-4
Conference Championships—Pittsburgh defeated the Oakland Raiders 24-13 for the AFC title; Minnesota defeated the Los Angeles Rams 14-10 for the NFC title
Players' Shares—$15,000 to each member of the winning team; $7,500 to each member of the losing team
Attendance—80,997
Gross Receipts—$5,259,766.90
Officials—Referee, Bernie Ulman; umpire, Al Conway; line judge, Bruce Alford; head linesman, Ed Marion; back judge, Ray Douglas; field judge, Dick Dolack
Coaches—Chuck Noll, Pittsburgh; Bud Grant, Minnesota

Pittsburgh	Starters, Offense	Minnesota
Frank Lewis	WR	Jim Lash
Jon Kolb	LT	Charles Goodrum
Jim Clack	LG	Andy Maurer
Ray Mansfield	C	Mick Tingelhoff
Gerry Mullins	RG	Ed White
Gordon Gravelle	RT	Ron Yary
Larry Brown	TE	Stu Voigt
Ron Shanklin	WR	John Gilliam
Terry Bradshaw	QB	Fran Tarkenton
Rocky Bleier	RB	Chuck Foreman
Franco Harris	RB	Dave Osborn
	Starters, Defense	
L. C. Greenwood	LE	Carl Eller
Joe Greene	LT	Doug Sutherland
Ernie Holmes	RT	Alan Page
Dwight White	RE	Jim Marshall
Jack Ham	LLB	Roy Winston
Jack Lambert	MLB	Jeff Siemon
Andy Russell	RLB	Wally Hilgenberg
J. T. Thomas	LCB	Nate Wright
Mel Blount	RCB	Jackie Wallace
Mike Wagner	LS	Jeff Wright
Glen Edwards	RS	Paul Krause

Pittsburgh	0	2	7	7	— 16
Minnesota	0	0	0	6	— 6

Pitt —Safety, White downed Tarkenton in end zone
Pitt —Harris 12 run (Gerela kick)
Minn—T. Brown recovered blocked punt in end zone (kick failed)
Pitt —L. Brown 4 pass from Bradshaw (Gerela kick)

TEAM STATISTICS	Pitt	Minn
First downs	17	9
Rushing	11	2
Passing	5	5
By penalty	1	2
Total yardage	333	119
Net rushing yardage	249	17
Net passing yardage	84	102
Passes att.-comp.-had int.	14-9-0	26-11-3

RUSHING
Pittsburgh—Harris, 34 for 158, 1 TD; Bleier, 17 for 65; Bradshaw, 5 for 33; Swann, 1 for -7.
Minnesota—Foreman, 12 for 18; Tarkenton, 1 for 0; Osborn, 8 for -1.
PASSING
Pittsburgh—Bradshaw, 9 of 14 for 97, 1 TD.
Minnesota—Tarkenton, 11 of 26 for 102, 3 int.
RECEIVING
Pittsburgh—Brown, 3 for 49, 1 TD; Stallworth, 3 for 24; Bleier, 2 for 11; Lewis, 1 for 12.
Minnesota—Foreman, 5 for 50; Voigt, 2 for 31; Osborn, 2 for 7; Gilliam, 1 for 16; Reed, 1 for -2.
PUNTING
Pittsburgh—Walden, 7 for 243, 34.7 average.
Eischeid, 6 for 223, 37.2 average.
PUNT RETURNS
Pittsburgh—Swann, 3 for 34; Edwards, 2 for 2.
Minnesota—McCullum, 3 for 11; N. Wright, 1 for 1; Wallace, 1 fair catch.
KICKOFF RETURNS
Pittsburgh—Harrison, 2 for 17; Pearson, 1 for 15.
Minnesota—McCullum, 1 for 26; McClanahan, 1 for 22; B. Brown, 1 for 2.
INTERCEPTIONS
Pittsburgh—Wagner, 1 for 26; Blount, 1 for 10; Greene, 1 for 10.
Minnesota—None.

White (78), Holmes (63), and Lambert (58) rack up Osborn of the Vikings.

Blair blocks Walden's punt; Terry Brown recovered in end zone for touchdown.

PITTSBURGH STEELERS

No.	Name	Pos.	Ht.	Wt.	Age	Year	College
45	Allen, Jim	CB	6-2	194	22	R	UCLA
20	Bleier, Rocky	RB	5-11	210	28	6	Notre Dame
47	Blount, Mel	CB	6-3	205	26	5	Southern U.
38	Bradley, Ed	LB	6-2	239	24	3	Wake Forest
12	Bradshaw, Terry	QB	6-3	218	26	5	Louisiana Tech
87	Brown, Larry	TE	6-4	229	25	4	Kansas
50	Clack, Jim	G-C	6-3	250	27	4	Wake Forest
22	Conn, Richard	S	6-0	185	23	R	Georgia
77	Davis, Charlie	DT	6-1	265	23	R	Texas Christian
57	Davis, Sam	G	6-1	255	30	8	Allen
35	Davis, Steve	RB	6-1	218	25	3	Delaware State
73	Druschel, Rick	G-T	6-2	248	22	R	North Carolina State
27	Edwards, Glen	S	6-0	185	27	4	Florida A&M
64	Furness, Steve	DT-DE	6-4	255	24	3	Rhode Island
86	Garrett, Reggie	WR	6-1	172	23	R	Eastern Michigan
10	Gerela, Roy	K	5-10	185	26	6	New Mexico State
17	Gilliam, Joe	QB	6-2	187	23	3	Tennessee State
71	Gravelle, Gordon	G-T	6-5	250	25	3	Brigham Young
75	Greene, Joe	DT	6-4	275	28	6	North Texas State
68	Greenwood, L. C.	DE	6-6	245	28	6	Arkansas-Pine Bluff
84	Grossman, Randy	TE	6-1	215	21	R	Temple
59	Ham, Jack	LB	6-1	225	25	4	Penn State
5	Hanratty, Terry	QB	6-1	210	26	6	Notre Dame
32	Harris, Franco	RB	6-2	230	24	3	Penn State
46	Harrison, Reggie	RB	5-11	215	24	R	Cincinnati
63	Holmes, Ernie	DT	6-3	260	26	3	Texas Southern
54	Kellum, Marv	LB	6-2	225	22	R	Wichita State
55	Kolb, Jon	T	6-3	262	27	6	Oklahoma State
58	Lambert, Jack	LB	6-4	215	22	R	Kent State
43	Lewis, Frank	WR	6-1	196	27	4	Grambling
56	Mansfield, Ray	C	6-3	260	33	12	Washington
89	McMakin, John	TE	6-3	232	24	3	Clemson
72	Mullins, Gerry	G-T	6-3	244	25	4	USC
26	Pearson, Preston	RB	6-1	205	29	8	Illinois
74	Reavis, Dave	T	6-5	250	24	1	Arkansas
34	Russell, Andy	LB	6-2	225	33	10	Missouri
25	Shanklin, Ron	WR	6-1	190	26	5	North Texas State
31	Shell, Donnie	S-CB	5-11	190	22	R	South Carolina State
82	Stallworth, John	WR	6-2	183	22	R	Alabama A&M
88	Swann, Lynn	WR	5-10	178	22	R	USC
24	Thomas, J. T.	CB	6-2	196	23	2	Florida State
51	Toews, Loren	LB	6-3	212	23	2	California
23	Wagner, Mike	S	6-1	210	25	4	Western Illinois
39	Walden, Bobby	P	6-0	190	36	11	Georgia
52	Webster, Mike	C-G	6-1	232	22	R	Wisconsin
78	White, Dwight	DE	6-4	255	25	4	East Texas State
62	Wolf, Jim	DE	6-2	230	22	R	Prairie View

Head coach—Chuck Noll. **Assistants**—Bud Carson, Dick Hoak, George Perles, Dan Radakovich, Lionel Taylor, Woody Widenhofer.

MINNESOTA VIKINGS

No.	Name	Pos.	Ht.	Wt.	Age	Year	College
67	Alderman, Grady	T	6-2	247	36	15	Detroit
56	Anderson, Scott	C	6-4	234	23	R	Missouri
17	Berry, Bob	QB	5-11	185	32	10	Oregon
21	Blahak, Joe	CB-S	5-10	188	24	2	Nebraska
59	Blair, Matt	LB	6-5	229	23	R	Iowa State
71	Boone, Dave	DE	6-3	248	23	R	Eastern Michigan
30	Brown, Bill	RB	5-11	222	36	14	Illinois
24	Brown, Terry	S	6-2	205	27	5	Oklahoma State
14	Cox, Fred	K	5-10	200	36	12	Pittsburgh
84	Craig, Steve	TE	6-3	231	23	R	Northwestern
11	Eischeid, Mike	P	6-0	190	34	8	Upper Iowa
81	Eller, Carl	DE	6-6	247	32	11	Minnesota
44	Foreman, Chuck	RB	6-2	207	24	2	Miami
42	Gilliam, John	WR	6-1	195	29	8	South Carolina State
68	Goodrum, Charles	T-G	6-3	256	25	2	Florida A&M
58	Hilgenberg, Wally	LB	6-3	229	32	11	Iowa
85	Holland, John	WR	6-0	190	24	R	Tennessee State
89	Kingsriter, Doug	TE	6-2	222	24	2	Minnesota
22	Krause, Paul	S	6-3	200	34	11	Iowa
77	Larsen, Gary	DT	6-5	255	34	11	Concordia, Minn.
82	Lash, Jim	WR	6-2	199	23	2	Northwestern
65	Lawson, Steve	G	6-3	265	26	4	Kansas
75	Lurtsema, Bob	DE-DT	6-6	250	32	8	Western Michigan
49	Marinaro, Ed	RB	6-2	212	24	3	Cornell
70	Marshall, Jim	DE	6-4	240	37	15	Ohio State
55	Martin, Amos	LB	6-3	228	25	3	Louisville
66	Maurer, Andy	G	6-3	247	26	5	Oregon
33	McClanahan, Brent	RB	5-10	202	24	2	Arizona State
80	McCullum, Sam	WR	6-2	203	22	R	Montana State
54	McNeill, Fred	LB	6-2	229	24	R	UCLA
41	Osborn, Dave	RB	6-0	208	31	10	North Dakota
88	Page, Alan	DT	6-4	245	29	8	Notre Dame
29	Poltl, Randy	CB	6-3	190	24	R	Stanford
32	Reed, Oscar	RB	6-0	222	30	7	Colorado State
78	Riley, Steve	T	6-6	258	22	R	USC
50	Siemon, Jeff	LB	6-2	230	24	3	Stanford
64	Sunde, Milt	G	6-2	250	32	11	Minnesota
69	Sutherland, Doug	DT	6-3	250	26	5	Wisconsin-Superior
10	Tarkenton, Fran	QB	6-0	190	34	14	Georgia
53	Tingelhoff, Mick	C	6-2	240	34	13	Nebraska
83	Voigt, Stu	TE	6-1	225	26	5	Wisconsin
25	Wallace, Jackie	CB	6-3	197	23	1	Arizona
62	White, Ed	G	6-2	268	27	6	California
60	Winston, Roy	LB	5-11	222	34	13	Louisiana State
23	Wright, Jeff	S	5-11	190	25	4	Minnesota
43	Wright, Nate	CB	5-11	180	27	6	San Diego State
73	Yary, Ron	T	6-6	255	28	7	USC

Head coach—Bud Grant. **Assistants**—Neill Armstrong, Jerry Burns, Bus Mertes, John Michels, Jocko Nelson, Jack Patera.

SUPER BOWL X

PITTSBURGH 21, DALLAS 17

Quarterback Terry Bradshaw threw a pass that covered 59 yards to wide receiver Lynn Swann, who carried the ball the final five yards for a 64-yard touchdown that proved to be the crucial points in the Steelers' 21–17 victory over the Dallas Cowboys in Super Bowl X. Bradshaw was knocked unconscious when he was hit by safety Cliff Harris and did not see Swann make the catch.

The touchdown gave Pittsburgh a 21–10 lead with 3:02 remaining in the game. Dallas took over on its 20-yard line with 2:54 remaining and went 80 yards in five plays, scoring with 1:48 remaining on Roger Staubach's 34-yard pass to Percy Howard.

Pittsburgh began the next series of plays on Dallas's 42 after guard Gerry Mullins of Pittsburgh recovered Toni Fritsch's onside kick. On fourth down and nine at the Cowboys' 41, the Steelers did not punt and running back Rocky Bleier was stopped after a two-yard gain. Dallas moved to the Steelers' 38-yard line before Staubach's pass to Drew Pearson was intercepted by Glen Edwards in the end zone. Edwards returned the ball 30 yards as the game came to an end.

In a game that generally was acclaimed the best and most exciting of the Super Bowl series, the Steelers outgained Dallas 339-270 but did not take the lead until the fourth quarter.

Pittsburgh's Bobby Walden was in punt formation at the end of the Steelers' first offensive series. Walden bobbled the snap from center and recovered at his 29-yard line, where he was tackled by Billy Joe DuPree.

Staubach then threw a pass to Drew Pearson, who was alone on a crossing pattern in the middle of the field at the 15-yard line; Pearson scored the game's first touchdown after 4:36 of play.

The Steelers answered on the next series, moving 67 yards in eight plays and scoring on a seven-yard pass from Bradshaw to tight end Randy Grossman. Dallas went ahead 10–7 on the next series by marching 46 yards in 11 plays to Fritsch's 36-yard field goal.

Dallas held its three-point lead for the rest of the second quarter, all of the third quarter, and for the first 3:32 of the fourth quarter, a total of 33 minutes, 17 seconds. At that point, Pittsburgh's Reggie Harrison blocked a punt by Mitch Hoopes and the ball rolled out of the end zone for a safety and two points for the Steelers.

After Hoopes punted on the ensuing free kick, the Steelers moved 25 yards in six plays to position Roy Gerela for a 36-yard field goal. Pittsburgh led 12–10 with 8:14 left. Mike Wagner of the Steelers intercepted a pass from Staubach that was intended for Drew Pearson who ran the same pattern on which he scored in the first quarter. Wagner's 19-yard return set up an 18-yard field goal by Gerela that came on fourth down and goal to go at the Cowboys' 1. Pittsburgh led 15–10 with 6:37 remaining.

Pittsburgh took over again with 4:25 left in the game. On third down and four yards at the Steelers' 36, Bradshaw called for a play that is known as "60 Flanker Post" in the Steelers' nomenclature. The flanker, Swann, is supposed to run a diagonal pattern to the goal posts. Bradshaw took the snap from center and backpedaled. Swann headed toward the goal posts, cornerback Mark Washington matching him stride for stride. Harris blitzed and arrived at Bradshaw at about the same time as tackle Larry Cole. Bradshaw unloaded his pass and immediately was hit by Harris. Swann got a step on Washington as the pass hurtled out of the late-afternoon sky.

Bradshaw was helped to the dressing room a few moments later. It was there that someone told him that his pass to Swann had gone for a touchdown.

Wagner (23) can't close in fast enough to stop Drew Pearson on Dallas's first touchdown of the game.

Participants—Pittsburgh Steelers, champions of the American Football Conference, and Dallas Cowboys, champions of the National Football Conference
Date—January 18, 1976
Site—Orange Bowl, Miami
Time—2:00 P.M. EST
Conditions—57 degrees, clear
Playing Surface—Poly-Turf
Television and Radio—Columbia Broadcasting System (CBS)
Regular Season Records—Pittsburgh, 12-2; Dallas, 10-4
Conference Championships—Pittsburgh defeated the Oakland Raiders 16-10 for the AFC title; Dallas defeated the Los Angeles Rams 37-7 for the NFC title
Players' Shares—$15,000 to each member of the winning team; $7,500 to each member of the losing team
Attendance—80,187
Gross Receipts—$5,242,641.25
Officials—Referee, Norm Schachter; umpire, Joe Connell; line judge, Jack Fette; head linesman, Leo Miles; back judge, Stan Javie; field judge, Bill O'Brien
Coaches—Chuck Noll, Pittsburgh; Tom Landry, Dallas

Dallas	Starters, Offense	Pittsburgh
Golden Richards	WR	John Stallworth
Ralph Neely	LT	Jon Kolb
Burton Lawless	LG	Jim Clack
John Fitzgerald	C	Ray Mansfield
Blaine Nye	RG	Gerry Mullins
Rayfield Wright	RT	Gordon Gravelle
Jean Fugett	TE	Larry Brown
Drew Pearson	WR	Lynn Swann
Roger Staubach	QB	Terry Bradshaw
Preston Pearson	RB	Rocky Bleier
Robert Newhouse	RB	Franco Harris
	Starters, Defense	
Ed Jones	LE	L. C. Greenwood
Jethro Pugh	LT	Joe Greene
Larry Cole	RT	Ernie Holmes
Harvey Martin	RE	Dwight White
Dave Edwards	LLB	Jack Ham
Lee Roy Jordan	MLB	Jack Lambert
D. D. Lewis	RLB	Andy Russell
Mark Washington	LCB	J. T. Thomas
Mel Renfro	RCB	Mel Blount
Charlie Waters	LS	Mike Wagner
Cliff Harris	RS	Glen Edwards

Dallas	7	3	0	7	— 17
Pittsburgh	7	0	0	14	— 21

Dall—D. Pearson 29 pass from Staubach (Fritsch kick)
Pitt—Grossman 7 pass from Bradshaw (Gerela kick)
Dall—FG Fritsch 36
Pitt—Safety, Harrison blocked Hoopes' punt through end zone
Pitt—FG Gerela 36
Pitt—FG Gerela 18
Pitt—Swann 64 pass from Bradshaw (kick failed)
Dall—P. Howard 34 pass from Staubach (Fritsch kick)

TEAM STATISTICS	Dall	Pitt
First downs	14	13
Rushing	6	7
Passing	8	6
By penalty	0	0
Total yardage	270	339
Net rushing yardage	108	149
Net passing yardage	162	190
Passes att.-comp.-had int.	24-15-3	19-9-0

RUSHING
Dallas—Newhouse, 16 for 56; Staubach, 5 for 22; Dennison, 5 for 16; P. Pearson, 5 for 14.
Pittsburgh—Harris, 27 for 82; Bleier, 15 for 51; Bradshaw, 4 for 16.
PASSING
Dallas—Staubach, 15 of 24 for 204, 2 TDs, 3 int.
Pittsburgh—Bradshaw, 9 for 19 for 209, 2 TDs.
RECEIVING
Dallas—P. Pearson, 5 for 53; Young, 3 for 31; D. Pearson, 2 for 59, 1 TD; Newhouse, 2 for 12; P. Howard, 1 for 34, 1 TD; Fugett, 1 for 9; Dennison, 1 for 6.
Pittsburgh—Swann, 4 for 161, 1 TD; Stallworth, 2 for 8; Harris, 1 for 26; Grossman, 1 for 7; L. Brown, 1 for 7.
PUNTING
Dallas—Hoopes, 7 for 245, 35.0 average.
Walden, 4 for 159, 39.8 average.
PUNT RETURNS
Dallas—Richards, 1 for 5, 3 fair catches.
Pittsburgh—D. Brown, 3 for 14; Edwards, 2 for 17.
KICKOFF RETURNS
Dallas—T. Henderson, 48 after a lateral; P. Pearson, 4 for 48.
Pittsburgh—Blount, 3 for 64; Collier, 1 for 25.
INTERCEPTIONS
Dallas—None.
Pittsburgh—Edwards, 1 for 35; Thomas, 1 for 35; Wagner, 1 for 19.

Harrison blocks Hoopes's punt; the ball rolled out of the end zone for a safety.

Far downfield at 10-yard line, Swann takes Bradshaw's long bomb and scores.

DALLAS COWBOYS

No.	Name	Pos.	Ht.	Wt.	Age	Year	College
31	Barnes, Benny	CB	6-1	185	24	4	Stanford
53	Breunig, Bob	LB	6-2	227	22	R	Arizona State
59	Capone, Warren	LB	6-1	218	24	1	Louisiana State
63	Cole, Larry	DT	6-5	250	29	8	Hawaii
57	Davis, Kyle	C	6-4	240	23	R	Oklahoma
21	Dennison, Doug	RB	6-0	195	24	2	Kutztown State
67	Donovan, Pat	T	6-4	250	22	R	Stanford
89	DuPree, Billy Joe	TE	6-4	228	25	3	Michigan State
52	Edwards, Dave	LB	6-1	225	36	13	Auburn
62	Fitzgerald, John	C	6-5	255	27	5	Boston College
15	Fritsch, Toni	K	5-7	195	30	4	No college
84	Fugett, Jean	TE-WR	6-3	226	24	4	Amherst
77	Gregory, Bill	DT	6-5	252	26	5	Wisconsin
43	Harris, Cliff	S	6-1	190	27	6	Ouachita
56	Henderson, Thomas	LB	6-2	220	22	R	Langston, Okla.
9	Hoopes, Mitch	P	6-1	210	22	R	Arizona
81	Howard, Percy	WR	6-4	210	23	R	Austin Peay
87	Howard, Ron	TE	6-4	225	24	2	Seattle
42	Hughes, Randy	S	6-4	200	22	R	Oklahoma
72	Jones, Ed	DE	6-9	260	24	2	Tennessee State
55	Jordan, Lee Roy	LB	6-1	221	34	13	Alabama
66	Lawless, Burton	G	6-4	250	22	R	Florida
50	Lewis, D.D.	LB	6-1	218	30	7	Mississippi
19	Longley, Clint	QB	6-1	193	23	2	Abilene Christian
79	Martin, Harvey	DE	6-5	250	25	3	East Texas State
73	Neely, Ralph	T	6-6	260	32	11	Oklahoma
44	Newhouse, Robert	RB	5-10	200	26	4	Houston
61	Nye, Blaine	G	6-4	255	29	8	Stanford
88	Pearson, Drew	WR	6-0	180	25	3	Tulsa
26	Pearson, Preston	RB	6-1	205	31	9	Illinois
58	Peterson, Calvin	LB	6-3	220	23	2	UCLA
75	Pugh, Jethro	DT	6-6	250	31	11	Elizabeth City State
20	Renfro, Mel	CB	6-0	190	34	12	Oregon
83	Richards, Golden	WR	6-0	183	25	3	Hawaii
68	Scott, Herbert	G	6-2	250	23	R	Virginia Union
12	Staubach, Roger	QB	6-3	197	33	7	Navy
78	Walton, Bruce	T	6-6	252	24	3	UCLA
46	Washington, Mark	CB	5-11	186	28	6	Morgan State
41	Waters, Charlie	S	6-2	193	27	6	Clemson
54	White, Randy	LB	6-4	245	23	R	Maryland
45	Woolsey, Roland	DB	6-1	182	22	R	Boise State
70	Wright, Rayfield	T	6-6	260	30	9	Fort Valley State
30	Young, Charles	RB	6-1	210	23	2	North Carolina State

Head coach—Tom Landry. **Assistants**—Ermal Allen, Mike Ditka, Ed Hughes, Jim Myers, Dan Reeves, Gene Stallings, Ernie Stautner, Jerry Tubbs.

PITTSBURGH STEELERS

No.	Name	Pos.	Ht.	Wt.	Age	Year	College
45	Allen, Jim	DB	6-2	194	23	2	UCLA
76	Banaszak, John	DE	6-3	232	25	R	Eastern Michigan
20	Bleier, Rocky	RB	5-11	210	29	7	Notre Dame
47	Blount, Mel	CB	6-3	200	27	6	Southern U.
38	Bradley, Ed	LB	6-2	232	25	4	Wake Forest
12	Bradshaw, Terry	QB	6-3	210	27	6	Louisiana Tech
36	Brown, Dave	DB	6-1	200	23	R	Michigan
87	Brown, Larry	TE	6-4	230	26	5	Kansas
50	Clack, Jim	G	6-3	250	28	5	Wake Forest
44	Collier, Mike	RB	5-11	200	22	R	Morgan State
57	Davis, Sam	G	6-1	250	31	9	Allen
27	Edwards, Glen	S	6-0	185	28	5	Florida A&M
33	Fuqua, John	RB	5-11	200	29	7	Morgan State
64	Furness, Steve	DT	6-4	255	25	4	Rhode Island
86	Garrett, Reggie	WR	6-1	175	24	2	Eastern Michigan
10	Gerela, Roy	K	5-10	190	27	7	New Mexico State
17	Gilliam, Joe	QB	6-2	187	25	4	Tennessee State
71	Gravelle, Gordon	T	6-5	255	26	4	Brigham Young
75	Greene, Joe	DT	6-4	275	29	7	North Texas State
68	Greenwood, L.C.	DE	6-6	245	29	7	Arkansas-Pine Bluff
84	Grossman, Randy	TE	6-1	215	22	2	Temple
59	Ham, Jack	LB	6-1	225	27	5	Penn State
5	Hanratty, Terry	QB	6-1	205	27	7	Notre Dame
32	Harris, Franco	RB	6-2	230	25	4	Penn State
46	Harrison, Reggie	RB	5-11	215	26	2	Cincinnati
63	Holmes, Ernie	DT	6-3	260	27	4	Texas Southern
54	Kellum, Marv	LB	6-2	225	23	2	Wichita State
55	Kolb, Jon	T	6-3	262	28	7	Oklahoma State
58	Lambert, Jack	LB	6-4	220	23	2	Kent State
43	Lewis, Frank	WR	6-1	196	28	5	Grambling
56	Mansfield, Ray	C	6-3	260	34	13	Washington
72	Mullins, Gerry	G-T	6-3	240	26	5	USC
74	Reavis, Dave	T	6-5	254	25	2	Arkansas
34	Russell, Andy	LB	6-2	220	34	11	Missouri
31	Shell, Donnie	DB	5-11	195	23	2	South Carolina State
82	Stallworth, John	WR	6-2	185	23	2	Alabama A&M
88	Swann, Lynn	WR	6-0	180	23	2	USC
24	Thomas, J.T.	CB	6-2	196	24	3	Florida State
51	Toews, Loren	LB	6-3	222	24	3	California
23	Wagner, Mike	S	6-1	210	26	5	Western Illinois
39	Walden, Bobby	P	6-0	197	37	12	Georgia
52	Webster, Mike	C	6-1	245	23	2	Wisconsin
78	White, Dwight	DE	6-4	255	26	5	East Texas State

Head coach—Chuck Noll. **Assistants**—Bud Carson, Dick Hoak, George Perles, Dan Radakovich, Lionel Taylor, Woody Widenhofer.

SUPER BOWL XI

OAKLAND 32, MINNESOTA 14

The Oakland Raiders, making their first appearance in the Super Bowl in nine years, defeated the Minnesota Vikings 32–14 to score the most decisive victory in the series since Dallas beat Miami by 21 points in Super Bowl VI. Minnesota lost in the Super Bowl for the fourth time in four appearances.

Oakland took the ball after the opening kickoff and went from its 34 to the Vikings' 11 in eight plays. On fourth down, Errol Mann attempted a 29-yard field goal but the ball hit the left upright. Raiders quarterback Ken Stabler summed up the confidence of his team when he conferred with head coach John Madden after the missed field goal. "Don't worry," said Stabler. "There's more where that came from."

Oakland's Ray Guy sustained the first blocked punt of his four-season NFL career late in the first quarter. Minnesota's Fred McNeill blocked the ball at Oakland's 28. Guy finally tackled McNeill at the 3 after a wild scramble for the ball. But the Vikings' Brent McClanahan fumbled on the second play after the recovery and Oakland's Willie Hall recovered. Using the last 4:35 of the first quarter and the first 48 seconds of the second quarter, the Raiders then drove 90 yards in 12 plays. Mann's 24-yard field goal put Oakland on top 3–0.

Minnesota gave up the ball without gaining a first down on its next possession. Beginning at its 36, Oakland moved 64 yards in 10 plays, scoring on Stabler's one-yard pass to Dave Casper, who was alone in the end zone. The Vikings could not gain a first down on their next series and, after a 25-yard punt return by Neal Colzie, Oakland went 35 yards in five plays, Pete Banaszak getting the touchdown that supplied a 16–0 halftime lead.

After 30 minutes of play, Oakland had gained 288 yards, Minnesota 86. Oakland had 16 first downs, Minnesota 4. Clarence Davis of Oakland had gained 86 yards in 11 carries (his game total 137 yards, in 16 carries, represented a high for his six-year pro career).

The Raiders, who were directing most of their attack over the left side of their line—behind tackle Art Shell and guard Gene Upshaw—moved 31 yards in five plays to Mann's 40-yard field goal from the 23-yard line and a 19–0 lead with 5:16 left in the third quarter.

Minnesota scored on the next series. Fran Tarkenton's eight-yard pass to Sammy White with 47 seconds remaining in the quarter concluded a 12-play, 68-yard advance.

Tarkenton had the Vikings on the move in the fourth period. They went from their 22 to Oakland's 37, but Tarkenton's pass intended for Chuck Foreman at the 30 was intercepted by Hall, who brought the ball back 16 yards. That served as the catalyst for a 54-yard march that ended with Banaszak scoring from the 2. The big play of the series was a 48-yard pass from Stabler to Fred Biletnikoff. Oakland led 26–7 with 7:21 remaining.

The Vikings' next thrust reached the Minnesota 47. On first down, Tarkenton threw a sideline pass to White. Willie Brown intercepted at the 25 and outraced Tarkenton, the final defender, on a 75-yard touchdown return that made it 32–7.

Minnesota scored the final touchdown on a nine-play, 86-yard drive that culminated with an eight-yard pass from Bob Lee, who had replaced Tarkenton, to Stu Voigt. Twenty-five seconds remained in the game.

"When you've got the horses, you ride them," said Stabler, referring to Shell and Upshaw. "We're not a fancy team. We just line up and try to knock you out of there. Nobody's better at it than those two guys."

Tight end Casper of the Raiders is all alone in the end zone, scoring the first touchdown.

Participants—Oakland Raiders, champions of the American Football Conference, and Minnesota Vikings, champions of the National Football Conference
Date—January 9, 1977
Site—Rose Bowl, Pasadena
Time—12:30 P.M. PST
Conditions—58 degrees, clear and sunny
Playing Surface—Grass
Television and Radio—National Broadcasting Company (NBC)
Regular Season Records—Oakland, 13–1; Minnesota, 11–2–1
Conference Championships—Oakland defeated the Pittsburgh Steelers 24–7 for the AFC title; Minnesota defeated the Los Angeles Rams 24–13 for the NFC title
Players' Shares—$15,000 to each member of the winning team; $7,500 to each member of the losing team
Attendance—100,421
Gross Receipts—$5,768,772.73
Officials—Referee, Jim Tunney; umpire, Lou Palazzi; line judge, Bill Swanson; head linesman, Ed Marion; back judge, Tom Kelleher; field judge, Armen Terzian
Coaches—John Madden, Oakland; Bud Grant, Minnesota

Oakland	Starters, Offense	Minnesota
Clifford Branch	WR	Ahmad Rashad
Art Shell	LT	Steve Riley
Gene Upshaw	LG	Charles Goodrum
Dave Dalby	C	Mick Tingelhoff
George Buehler	RG	Ed White
John Vella	RT	Ron Yary
Dave Casper	TE	Stu Voigt
Fred Biletnikoff	WR	Sammy White
Ken Stabler	QB	Fran Tarkenton
Mark van Eeghen	RB	Chuck Foreman
Clarence Davis	RB	Brent McClanahan
	Starters, Defense	
John Matuszak	LE	Carl Eller
Dave Rowe	NT-LT	Doug Sutherland
Otis Sistrunk	RE-RT	Alan Page
Phil Villapiano	LOLB-RE	Jim Marshall
Monte Johnson	LILB-LLB	Matt Blair
Willie Hall	RILB-MLB	Jeff Siemon
Ted Hendricks	ROLB-RLB	Wally Hilgenberg
Alonzo (Skip) Thomas	LCB	Nate Wright
Willie Brown	RCB	Bobby Bryant
George Atkinson	LS	Jeff Wright
Jack Tatum	RS	Paul Krause

Oakland	0	16	3	13	— 32
Minnesota	0	0	7	7	— 14

Oak —FG Mann 24
Oak —Casper 1 pass from Stabler (Mann kick)
Oak —Banaszak 1 run (kick failed)
Oak —FG Mann 40
Minn—S. White 8 pass from Tarkenton (Cox kick)
Oak —Banaszak 2 run (Mann kick)
Oak —Brown 75 interception return (kick failed)
Minn—Voigt 13 pass from Lee (Cox kick)

TEAM STATISTICS

	Oak	Minn
First downs	21	20
Rushing	13	2
Passing	8	15
By penalty	0	3
Total yardage	429	353
Net rushing yardage	266	71
Net passing yardage	163	282
Passes att.-comp.-had int.	19-12-0	44-24-2

RUSHING
Oakland—Davis, 16, for 137; van Eeghen, 18 for 73; Garrett, 4 for 19; Banaszak, 10 for 19, 2 TDs; Ginn, 2 for 9; Rae, 2 for 9.
Minnesota—Foreman, 17 for 44; Johnson, 2 for 9; S. White, 1 for 7; Lee, 1 for 4; Miller, 2 for 4; McClanahan, 3 for 3.
PASSING
Oakland—Stabler, 12 of 19 for 180, 1 TD.
Minnesota—Tarkenton, 17 of 35 for 205, 1 TD, 2 int.; Lee, 7 of 9 for 81, 1 TD.
RECEIVING
Oakland—Biletnikoff, 4 for 79; Casper, 4 for 70, 1 TD; Branch, 3 for 20; Garrett, 1 for 11.
Minnesota—S. White, 5 for 77, 1 TD; Foreman, 5 for 62; Voigt, 4 for 49, 1 TD; Miller, 4 for 19; Rashad, 3 for 53; Johnson, 3 for 26.
PUNTING
Oakland—Guy, 4 for 162, 40.5 average.
Minnesota—Clabo, 7 for 265, 37.9 average.
PUNT RETURNS
Oakland—Colzie, 4 for 43.
Minnesota—Willis, 3 for 57.
KICKOFF RETURNS
Oakland—Garrett, 2 for 47; Siani, 1 for 0.
Minnesota—Willis, 3 for 57; S. White, 4 for 79.
INTERCEPTIONS
Oakland—Brown, 1 for 75, 1 TD; Hall, 1 for 16.
Minnesota—None.

Biletnikoff rambles 48 yards to set up Oakland's first fourth-period touchdown.

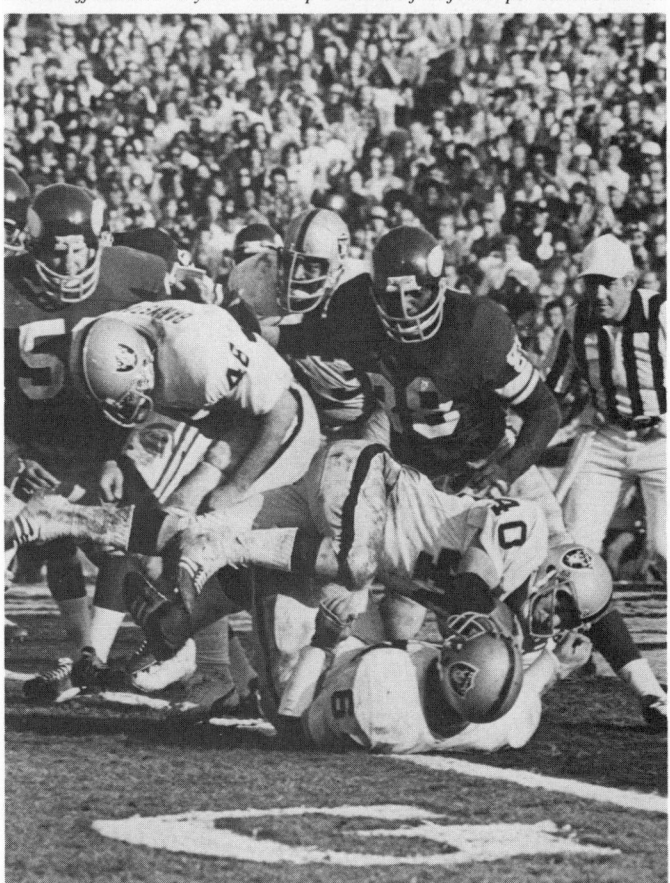

Bankston (46), Buehler (on ground) block as Banaszak scores second time.

OAKLAND RAIDERS

No.	Name	Pos.	Ht.	Wt.	Age	Year	College
43	Atkinson, George	S	6-0	185	30	9	Morris Brown
40	Banaszak, Pete	RB	6-0	210	32	11	Miami
46	Bankston, Warren	RB-TE	6-4	235	29	8	Tulane
51	Barnes, Rodrigo	LB	6-1	215	26	4	Rice
25	Biletnikoff, Fred	WR	6-1	190	33	12	Florida State
54	Bonness, Rik	LB	6-3	220	22	R	Nebraska
81	Bradshaw, Morris	WR	6-1	195	24	3	Ohio State
21	Branch, Clifford	WR	5-11	170	28	5	Colorado
24	Brown, Willie	CB	6-1	210	36	14	Grambling
64	Buehler, George	G	6-2	270	29	8	Stanford
87	Casper, Dave	TE	6-4	228	25	3	Notre Dame
20	Colzie, Neal	CB	6-2	205	23	2	Ohio State
50	Dalby, Dave	C	6-3	250	26	5	UCLA
28	Davis, Clarence	RB	5-10	195	27	6	USC
31	Garrett, Carl	RB	5-10	205	29	8	New Mexico Highlands
29	Ginn, Hubert	RB	5-9	185	30	7	Florida A&M
8	Guy, Ray	P	6-3	195	27	4	Southern Mississippi
39	Hall, Willie	LB	6-2	225	27	4	USC
83	Hendricks, Ted	LB	6-7	220	29	8	Miami
11	Humm, David	QB	6-2	184	24	2	Nebraska
58	Johnson, Monte	LB	6-5	240	25	4	Nebraska
70	Lawrence, Henry	T	6-4	273	25	3	Florida A&M
14	Mann, Errol	K	6-0	205	35	9	North Dakota
72	Matuszak, John	DE	6-7	270	26	4	Tampa
61	McMath, Herb	DE	6-4	245	22	R	Morningside
79	Medlin, Dan	G	6-4	252	27	3	North Carolina State
36	Moore, Manfred	RB	6-0	200	26	3	USC
47	Phillips, Charles	S	6-2	215	24	2	USC
77	Philyaw, Charles	DE	6-9	270	22	R	Texas Southern
15	Rae, Mike	QB	6-1	190	25	R	USC
52	Rice, Floyd	LB	6-3	225	27	6	Alcorn State
74	Rowe, Dave	NT	6-7	271	31	10	Penn State
78	Shell, Art	T	6-5	265	30	9	Maryland-Eastern Shore
49	Siani, Mike	WR	6-2	195	26	5	Villanova
60	Sistrunk, Otis	DE	6-3	273	29	5	No college
12	Stabler, Ken	QB	6-3	215	31	7	Alabama
66	Sylvester, Steve	C	6-4	262	23	2	Notre Dame
32	Tatum, Jack	S	5-11	206	28	5	Ohio State
26	Thomas, Alonzo (Skip)	CB	6-1	205	26	5	USC
63	Upshaw, Gene	G	6-5	255	31	10	Texas A&I
30	van Eeghen, Mark	RB	6-2	225	24	3	Colgate
75	Vella, John	T	6-4	260	26	5	USC
41	Villapiano, Phil	LB	6-2	225	27	6	Bowling Green

Head coach—John Madden. **Assistants**—Tom Dahms, Lew Erber, Tom Flores, Joe Scannella, Don Shinnick, Ollie Spencer, Bob Zeman.

MINNESOTA VIKINGS

No.	Name	Pos.	Ht.	Wt.	Age	Year	College
20	Allen, Nate	CB	5-11	174	26	6	Texas Southern
27	Beamon, Autry	S	6-1	190	23	2	East Texas State
17	Berry, Bob	QB	5-11	185	34	12	Oregon
59	Blair, Matt	LB	6-5	229	25	3	Iowa State
20	Bryant, Bobby	CB	6-1	170	32	8	South Carolina
74	Buetow, Bart	T	6-5	250	26	3	Minnesota
12	Clabo, Neil	P	6-2	200	24	2	Tennessee
14	Cox, Fred	K	5-10	200	38	14	Pittsburgh
84	Craig, Steve	TE	6-3	231	25	3	Northwestern
57	Dumler, Doug	C	6-3	245	26	4	Nebraska
81	Eller, Carl	DE	6-6	247	34	13	Minnesota
44	Foreman, Chuck	RB	6-2	207	26	4	Miami
68	Goodrum, Charles	T	6-3	256	27	4	Florida A&M
26	Grim, Bob	WR	6-0	188	31	10	Oregon State
47	Groce, Ron	RB	6-2	211	22	R	Macalester
40	Hall, Windlan	S	5-11	175	26	5	Arizona State
61	Hamilton, Wes	G	6-3	255	23	R	Tulsa
58	Hilgenberg, Wally	LB	6-3	229	34	13	Iowa
48	Johnson, Sammy	RB	6-1	226	24	3	North Carolina
22	Krause, Paul	S	6-3	200	34	13	Iowa
19	Lee, Bob	QB	6-2	195	31	8	Pacific
70	Marshall, Jim	DE	6-4	240	39	17	Ohio State
55	Martin, Amos	LB	6-3	228	27	5	Louisville
33	McClanahan, Brent	RB	5-10	202	26	4	Arizona State
54	McNeill, Fred	LB	6-2	229	24	3	UCLA
35	Miller, Robert	RB	5-11	204	24	2	Kansas
77	Mullaney, Mark	DE	6-6	242	23	2	Colorado State
88	Page, Alan	DT	6-4	245	31	10	Notre Dame
28	Rashad, Ahmad	WR	6-2	200	27	4	Oregon
78	Riley, Steve	T	6-5	258	24	5	USC
50	Siemon, Jeff	LB	6-3	237	26	5	Stanford
69	Sutherland, Doug	DT	6-3	250	28	7	Wisconsin-Superior
10	Tarkenton, Fran	QB	6-0	190	36	16	Georgia
53	Tingelhoff, Mick	C	6-2	240	36	15	Nebraska
83	Voigt, Stu	TE	6-1	225	28	7	Wisconsin
62	White, Ed	G	6-2	270	29	8	California
72	White, James	DT	6-3	263	23	R	Oklahoma State
85	White, Sammy	WR	5-11	189	22	R	Grambling
80	Willis, Leonard	WR	5-10	180	23	R	Ohio State
60	Winston, Roy	LB	5-11	222	36	15	Louisiana State
23	Wright, Jeff	S	5-11	190	27	6	Minnesota
42	Wright, Nate	CB	5-11	180	29	8	San Diego State
73	Yary, Ron	T	6-5	255	30	9	USC

Head coach—Bud Grant. **Assistants**—Neill Armstrong, Jerry Burns, Bus Mertes, John Michels, Jocko Nelson, Buddy Ryan.

SUPER BOWL XII

DALLAS 27, DENVER 10

The Dallas Cowboys' defense totally controlled the first half of the game, intercepting four passes and recovering three fumbles. The Cowboys converted two of the interceptions into 10 points on the way to building a 13-0 halftime lead and went on to even their Super Bowl record at 2-2 with a 27-10 victory.

The game started slowly; there were three punts—two by the Cowboys—in the first 7:35. Midway through the first quarter, with Denver on its own 29-yard line, Dallas safety Randy Hughes intercepted a pass by Craig Morton to set the Cowboys up at the Broncos' 25. Five plays later Tony Dorsett scored from three yards out.

Denver's John Schultz returned the ensuing Dallas kickoff to the Broncos' 40. Two plays later Aaron Kyle intercepted Morton again and returned the ball to the Denver 35. Two Dallas runs gave the Cowboys a first-and-goal at the Denver 8. The Broncos' defense stiffened and the Cowboys were forced to settle for a 35-yard field goal by Efren Herrera.

Denver punted to start the second quarter. The Cowboys drove 32 yards to set up a 43-yard field goal by Herrera, which gave Dallas a 13-0 lead.

The last five times the Broncos had possession of the ball in the second quarter, they turned it over to the Cowboys. The Cowboys came up empty, however. Denver linebacker Tom Jackson recovered Billy Joe DuPree's fumble and Herrera missed three field goals.

Denver drove 35 yards to set up Jim Turner's field goal to start the second half. After an exchange of punts, the Cowboys marched 58 yards in only six plays to take a 20-3 lead. On third-and-10, Roger Staubach threw a 45-yard touchdown pass to Butch Johnson, who made a spectacular diving catch in the end zone.

Denver gained some momentum with a 67-yard kickoff return to the Dallas 26 by Rick Upchurch. After his first pass was almost intercepted, Morton was relieved at quarterback by Norris Weese. Four plays later, Weese sent Rob Lytle off the left side of the line for a one-yard touchdown that cut the Cowboys' lead to 20-10.

With less than eight minutes remaining, the Cowboys' defense set up the final touchdown of the game. Weese fumbled while trying to pass and defensive end Harvey Martin recovered on the Denver 29. On the next play, running back Robert Newhouse took a hand-off, went wide left, stopped, and threw a pass to wide receiver Golden Richards, who was alone in the end zone. It was the first touchdown pass Newhouse had thrown since the regular season of 1975.

The Broncos only had one more possession, which ended on the Dallas 24 when Weese's fourth-down pass went through Upchurch's hands. The Cowboys ran off the last three minutes of the game, helped by a roughing the kicker penalty.

The Cowboys dominated the statistics as well as the score, running up 325 yards to 156 for the Broncos. Staubach completed 17 of 25 for 183 yards and one touchdown. The Cowboys' defense held Morton to 19 net yards passing and intercepted four passes in all. Weese didn't fare much better than Morton; he ended with 16 net yards passing.

"They played the kind of game we usually play," said Morton. "The beat us at our own game—taking turnovers. So many times this season other teams gave us all those turnovers. Today it was just our turn."

Martin and defensive tackle Randy White were named the game's co-most valuable players.

Dorsett leaves Broncos in his wake as he scores on a three-yard run.

Participants—Denver Broncos, champions of the American Football Conference, and Dallas Cowboys, champions of the National Football Conference
Date—January 15, 1978
Site—Louisiana Superdome, New Orleans
Time—5:15 P.M. CST
Conditions—70 degrees, indoors
Playing Surface—AstroTurf
Television and Radio—Columbia Broadcasting System (CBS)
Regular Season Records—Denver, 12-2; Dallas, 12-2
Conference Championships—Denver defeated the Oakland Raiders 20-17 for the AFC title; Dallas defeated the Minnesota Vikings 23-6 for the NFC title
Players' Shares—$18,000 to each member of the winning team; $9,000 to each member of the losing team
Attendance—75,583
Gross Receipts—$6,923,141.50
Officials—Referee, Jim Tunney; umpire, Joe Connell; line judge, Art Holst; head linesman, Tony Veteri; back judge, Ray Douglas; field judge, Bob Wortman
Coaches—Red Miller, Denver; Tom Landry, Dallas

Dallas	Starters, Offense	Denver
Butch Johnson	WR	Jack Dolbin
Ralph Neely	LT	Andy Maurer
Herbert Scott	LG	Tom Glassic
John Fitzgerald	C	Mike Montler
Tom Rafferty	RG	Paul Howard
Pat Donovan	RT	Claudie Minor
Billy Joe DuPree	TE	Riley Odoms
Drew Pearson	WR	Haven Moses
Roger Staubach	QB	Craig Morton
Robert Newhouse	RB	Jon Keyworth
Tony Dorsett	RB	Otis Armstrong
	Starters, Defense	
Ed Jones	LE	Barney Chavous
Jethro Pugh	LT-NT	Rubin Carter
Randy White	RT-RE	Lyle Alzado
Harvey Martin	RE-LOLB	Bob Swenson
Thomas Henderson	LLB-LILB	Joe Rizzo
Bob Breunig	MLB-RILB	Randy Gradishar
D. D. Lewis	RLB-ROLB	Tom Jackson
Benny Barnes	LCB	Louis Wright
Aaron Kyle	RCB	Steve Foley
Charlie Waters	SS	Billy Thompson
Cliff Harris	FS	Bernard Jackson

Dallas	10	3	7	7	— 27
Denver	0	0	10	0	— 10

Dall—Dorsett 3 run (Herrera kick)
Dall—FG Herrera 35
Dall—FG Herrera 43
Den—FG Turner 47
Dall—Johnson 45 pass from Staubach (Herrera kick)
Den—Lytle 1 run (Turner kick)
Dall—Richards 29 pass from Newhouse (Herrera kick)

TEAM STATISTICS	Dall	Den
First downs	17	11
Rushing	8	8
Passing	8	1
By penalty	1	2
Total yardage	325	156
Net rushing yardage	143	121
Net passing yardage	182	35
Passes att.-comp.-had int.	28-19-0	25-8-4

RUSHING
Dallas—Dorsett, 15 for 66, 1 TD; Newhouse, 14 for 55; White, 1 for 13; P. Pearson, 3 for 11; Staubach, 3 for 6; Laidlaw, 1 for 1; Johnson, 1 for -9.
Denver—Lytle, 10 for 35, 1 TD; Armstrong, 7 for 27; Weese, 3 for 26; Jensen, 1 for 16; Keyworth, 5 for 9; Perrin, 3 for 8.
PASSING
Dallas—Staubach, 17 of 25 for 183, 1 TD; Newhouse, 1 of 1 for 29, 1 TD; White, 1 of 2 for 5.
Denver—Morton, 4 of 15 for 39, 4 int.; Weese, 4 of 10 for 22.
RECEIVING
Dallas—P. Pearson, 5 for 37; DuPree, 4 for 66; Newhouse, 3 for -1; Johnson, 2 for 53, 1 TD; Richards, 2 for 38, 1 TD; Dorsett, 2 for 11; D. Pearson, 1 for 13.
Denver—Dolbin, 2 for 24; Odoms, 2 for 9; Moses, 1 for 21; Upchurch, 1 for 9; Jensen, 1 for 5; Perrin, 1 for -7.
PUNTING
Dallas—White, 5 for 208, 41.6 average.
Denver—Dilts, 4 for 153, 38.2 average.
PUNT RETURNS
Dallas—Hill, 1 for 1.
Denver—Upchurch, 3 for 22; Schultz, 1 for 0.
KICKOFF RETURNS
Dallas—Johnson, 2 for 29; Brinson, 1 for 22.
Denver—Upchurch, 3 for 94; Schultz, 2 for 62; Jensen, 1 for 17.
INTERCEPTIONS
Dallas—Washington, 1 for 27; Kyle, 1 for 19; Barnes, 1 for 0; Hughes, 1 for 0.
Denver—None.

Johnson's fingertip catch gives the Cowboys a 20-10 lead.

Co-most valuable player Randy White forces Morton into errant pass.

DALLAS COWBOYS

No.	Name	Pos.	Ht.	Wt.	Age	Year	College
31	Barnes, Benny	CB	6-1	195	26	6	Stanford
53	Breunig, Bob	LB	6-2	227	24	3	Arizona State
36	Brinson, Larry	RB	6-0	214	23	R	Florida
59	Brown, Guy	LB	6-4	215	22	R	Houston
18	Carano, Glenn	QB	6-3	195	22	R	Nevada-Las Vegas
63	Cole, Larry	DT	6-5	260	31	10	Hawaii
61	Cooper, Jim	T-G	6-5	252	22	R	Temple
21	Dennison, Doug	RB	6-0	204	26	4	Kutztown State
67	Donovan, Pat	T	6-4	255	24	3	Stanford
33	Dorsett, Tony	RB	5-11	192	23	R	Pittsburgh
89	DuPree, Billy Joe	TE	6-4	226	27	5	Michigan State
62	Fitzgerald, John	C	6-5	260	29	7	Boston College
71	Frederick, Andy	T	6-6	241	23	R	New Mexico
77	Gregory, Bill	DT	6-5	260	28	7	Wisconsin
43	Harris, Cliff	S	6-1	192	29	8	Ouachita Baptist
58	Hegman, Mike	LB	6-1	225	24	2	Tennessee State
56	Henderson, Thomas	LB	6-2	220	24	3	Langston
1	Herrera, Efren	K	5-9	190	26	3	UCLA
80	Hill, Tony	WR	6-2	196	21	R	Stanford
42	Hughes, Randy	S	6-4	208	24	3	Oklahoma
57	Huther, Bruce	LB	6-1	217	23	R	New Hampshire
86	Johnson, Butch	WR	6-1	191	23	2	California-Riverside
72	Jones, Ed	DE	6-9	265	26	4	Tennessee State
25	Kyle, Aaron	CB	5-10	185	23	2	Wyoming
35	Laidlaw, Scott	RB	6-0	205	24	3	Stanford
66	Lawless, Burton	G	6-4	250	24	3	Florida
50	Lewis, D. D.	LB	6-1	215	32	9	Mississippi State
79	Martin, Harvey	DE	6-5	252	27	5	East Texas State
73	Neely, Ralph	T	6-6	255	34	13	Oklahoma
44	Newhouse, Robert	RB	5-10	205	28	6	Houston
88	Pearson, Drew	WR	6-0	183	27	5	Tulsa
26	Pearson, Preston	RB	6-1	206	32	11	Illinois
75	Pugh, Jethro	DT	6-6	250	33	13	Elizabeth City State
64	Rafferty, Tom	G-C	6-3	250	23	2	Penn State
20	Renfro, Mel	CB	6-0	192	36	14	Oregon
83	Richards, Golden	WR	6-0	180	27	5	Hawaii
87	Saldi, Jay	TE	6-3	224	23	2	South Carolina
68	Scott, Herbert	G	6-2	250	24	3	Virginia Union
65	Stalls, David	DT	6-4	236	22	R	Northern Colorado
12	Staubach, Roger	QB	6-3	202	35	9	Navy
46	Washington, Mark	CB	5-11	187	30	8	Morgan State
41	Waters, Charlie	S	6-2	198	29	8	Clemson
11	White, Danny	QB-P	6-2	192	25	3	Arizona State
54	White, Randy	DT	6-4	245	25	3	Maryland
70	Wright, Rayfield	T	6-6	260	32	11	Fort Valley State

Head coach—Tom Landry. **Assistants**—Ermal Allen, Mike Ditka, Jim Myers, Dan Reeves, Gene Stallings, Ernie Stautner, Jerry Tubbs, Bob Ward.

DENVER BRONCOS

No.	Name	Pos.	Ht.	Wt.	Age	Year	College
77	Alzado, Lyle	DE	6-3	250	28	7	Yankton
73	Allison, Henry	T	6-3	263	30	5	San Diego State
24	Armstrong, Otis	RB	5-10	197	27	5	Purdue
68	Carter, Rubin	NT	6-0	254	25	3	Miami
79	Chavous, Barney	DE	6-3	250	26	5	South Carolina State
10	Dilts, Bucky	P	5-9	190	24	R	Georgia
82	Dolbin, Jack	WR	5-10	183	29	3	Wake Forest
85	Egloff, Ron	TE	6-5	227	22	R	Wisconsin
56	Evans, Larry	LB	6-2	218	24	2	Mississippi College
43	Foley, Steve	CB	6-2	190	24	2	Tulane
62	Glassic, Tom	G	6-4	248	23	2	Virginia
53	Gradishar, Randy	LB	6-3	231	25	4	Ohio State
63	Grant, John	NT	6-3	246	27	5	USC
60	Howard, Paul	G	6-3	260	27	4	Brigham Young
65	Hyde, Glenn	T	6-3	255	26	4	Pittsburgh
29	Jackson, Bernard	S	6-0	181	27	6	Washington State
57	Jackson, Tom	LB	5-11	224	26	5	Louisville
30	Jensen, Jim	RB	6-3	240	24	2	Iowa
32	Keyworth, Jon	RB	6-3	234	27	4	Colorado
41	Lytle, Rob	RB	6-1	198	23	R	Michigan
66	Manor, Brison	DE	6-4	247	25	1	Arkansas
50	Maples, Bobby	C	6-3	250	35	13	Baylor
74	Maurer, Andy	T	6-3	265	29	8	Oregon
71	Minor, Claudie	T	6-4	280	26	4	San Diego State
52	Montler, Mike	C	6-4	250	34	9	Colorado
7	Morton, Craig	QB	6-4	213	34	13	California
25	Moses, Haven	WR	6-2	200	31	10	San Diego State
58	Nairne, Rob	LB	6-4	220	23	R	Oregon State
88	Odoms, Riley	TE	6-4	232	27	6	Houston
12	Penrose, Craig	QB	6-3	205	24	2	San Diego State
35	Perrin, Lonnie	RB	6-1	224	25	2	Illinois
21	Poltl, Randy	S	6-3	188	25	4	Stanford
40	Rich, Randy	S	5-10	181	24	R	New Mexico
26	Riley, Larry	CB	5-10	189	23	R	Salem
59	Rizzo, Joe	LB	6-1	223	27	4	Merchant Marine Academy
67	Schindler, Steve	G	6-3	252	23	R	Boston College
86	Schultz, John	WR-KR	5-10	183	24	2	Maryland
70	Smith, Paul	NT	6-3	250	32	10	New Mexico
51	Swenson, Bob	LB	6-3	225	24	3	California
36	Thompson, Billy	S	6-1	200	31	9	Maryland State
55	Turk, Godwin	LB	6-3	230	27	4	Southern U.
15	Turner, Jim	K	6-2	212	36	14	Utah State
80	Upchurch, Rick	WR-KR	5-10	180	23	3	Minnesota
14	Weese, Norris	QB	6-1	193	26	2	Mississippi
20	Wright, Louis	CB	6-2	195	24	3	San Jose State

Head coach—Red Miller. **Assistants**—Marv Braden, Joe Collier, Bob Gambold, Ken Gray, Stan Jones, Myrel Moore, Babe Parilli, Fran Polsfoot, Paul Roach.

SUPER BOWL XIII

PITTSBURGH 35, DALLAS 31

In the first Super Bowl rematch, Pittsburgh quarter-back Terry Bradshaw threw four touchdown passes to lead the Steelers to a 35-31 victory over the Dallas Cowboys. The Steelers became the first team to win three Super Bowls.

In the highest-scoring Super Bowl of all, Bradshaw threw for a personal high 318 yards. He broke Bart Starr's passing yardage record by halftime, throwing for 253 yards and touchdowns on his 11 first-half completions. He was voted the game's most valuable player.

Pittsburgh opened the scoring on its first possession. Bradshaw capped a 53-yard drive with a 28-yard pass to John Stallworth.

The Cowboys scored on the last play of the first quarter to tie the score at 7-7. Roger Staubach found Tony Hill alone on the 26, and Hill ran in for the touchdown to complete a 39-yard play.

Dallas took its only lead of the game when line-backer Mike Hegmen wrestled the ball away from Bradshaw early in the second quarter and ran 37 yards for a touchdown. Three plays later the score was tied again. Bradshaw threw a 75-yard touchdown pass to Stallworth, who caught it on the Dallas 35 and eluded Aaron Kyle en route to the end zone.

Pittsburgh's final score of the first half came with only 26 seconds left. With the Cowboys deep in Steelers territory, Mel Blount intercepted Staubach and returned it to the Pittsburgh 29. A personal foul penalty against Dallas took the ball to the 44. Bradshaw passed to Swann for 29 yards, to Swann again for 21, and then to Rocky Bleier for 7 yards and a touchdown.

Dallas cut the Pittsburgh margin to only four points midway through the third quarter, but Rafael Septien's 27-yard field goal represented a moral victory for the Steelers. A short punt and a 12-yard return by Butch Johnson had set the Cowboys up on the Pittsburgh 42. With a third-and-three at the 10, Staubach passed to tight end Jackie Smith, who was alone in the end zone—and dropped the pass. Dallas settled for the field goal and the Steelers seemed in control thereafter.

Another major play occurred in the fourth quarter. Dallas cornerback Benny Barnes was called for pass interference on Swann, setting up the Steelers on the Dallas 23 after the 33-yard penalty. Three plays later, Franco Harris scored on a 22-yard run. The Steelers scored again following a fumble recovery on the ensuing kickoff. Bradshaw threw an 18-yard touchdown pass to Swann for the second Pittsburgh touchdown within 19 seconds.

Staubach got the Cowboys on the move late in the game. With only 2:23 left in the game, he passed for a seven-yard touchdown to Billy Joe DuPree, capping an eight-play, 89-yard drive. Dennis Thurman recovered Septien's onside kick at the Dallas 48, and Staubach led the Cowboys to another score. Passing on every down, Staubach completed a nine-play, 52-yard drive with a four-yard touchdown to Johnson with only 22 seconds left. A second onside kickoff attempt was recovered by Bleier to seal the victory.

"We were coming back until the Smith play," said Dallas coach Tom Landry. "That play really swung the momentum. You can tell how much it hurt us by looking at the difference in the score. Then at the end of the game there was just too much to make up in too little time—our offense couldn't quite do it."

The Dallas offense had nothing to be ashamed of—it netted 330 yards, only 27 less than the Steelers. The defenses each came up with big plays; there were six turnovers and nine sacks in the game.

Stallworth's 26-yard reception opens Super Bowl XIII's touchdown parade.

Participants—Pittsburgh Steelers, champions of the American Football Conference, and Dallas Cowboys, champions of the National Football Conference
Date—January 21, 1979
Site—Orange Bowl, Miami
Time—4:15 P.M. EST
Conditions—71 degrees, cloudy
Playing surface—Grass
Television—National Broadcasting Company (NBC)
Radio—Columbia Broadcasting System (CBS)
Regular Season Records—Pittsburgh, 14-2; Dallas, 12-4
Conference Championships—Pittsburgh defeated the Houston Oilers 34-5 for the AFC title; Dallas defeated the Los Angeles Rams 28-0 for the NFC title
Players' Shares—$18,000 to each member of the winning team; $9,000 to each member of the losing team
Attendance—79,484
Gross Receipts—$8,833,185.26
Officials—Referee, Pat Haggerty; umpire, Art Demmas; line judge, Jack Fette; head linesman, Jerry Bergman; back judge, Pat Knight; side judge, Dean Look; field judge, Fred Swearingen
Coaches—Chuck Noll, Pittsburgh; Tom Landry, Dallas

Pittsburgh	Starters, Offense	Dallas
John Stallworth	WR	Tony Hill
Jon Kolb	LT	Pat Donovan
Sam Davis	LG	Herbert Scott
Mike Webster	C	John Fitzgerald
Gerry Mullins	RG	Tom Rafferty
Ray Pinney	RT	Rayfield Wright
Randy Grossman	TE	Billy Joe DuPree
Lynn Swann	WR	Drew Pearson
Terry Bradshaw	QB	Roger Staubach
Rocky Bleier	RB	Robert Newhouse
Franco Harris	RB	Tony Dorsett
	Starters, Defense	
L. C. Greenwood	LE	Ed Jones
Joe Greene	LT	Larry Cole
Steve Furness	RT	Randy White
John Banaszak	RE	Harvey Martin
Jack Ham	LLB	Thomas Henderson
Jack Lambert	MLB	Bob Breunig
Loren Toews	RLB	D. D. Lewis
Ron Johnson	LCB	Benny Barnes
Mel Blount	RCB	Aaron Kyle
Donnie Shell	SS	Charlie Waters
Mike Wagner	FS	Cliff Harris

Pittsburgh	7	14	0	14	— 35
Dallas	7	7	3	14	— 31

Pitt —Stallworth 28 pass from Bradshaw (Gerela kick)
Dall—Hill 39 pass from Staubach (Septien kick)
Dall—Hegman 37 fumble recovery return (Septien kick)
Pitt —Stallworth 75 pass from Bradshaw (Gerela kick)
Pitt —Bleier 7 pass from Bradshaw (Gerela kick)
Dall—FG Septien 27
Pitt —Harris 22 run (Gerela kick)
Pitt —Swann 18 pass from Bradshaw (Gerela kick)
Dall—DuPree 7 pass from Staubach (Septien kick)
Dall—Johnson 4 pass from Staubach (Septien kick)

TEAM STATISTICS	Pitt	Dall
First downs	19	21
Rushing	2	6
Passing	15	13
By penalty	2	2
Total yardage	357	330
Net rushing yardage	66	154
Net passing yardage	291	176
Passes att.-comp.-had int.	30-17-1	30-17-1

RUSHING
Pittsburgh—Harris, 20 for 68, 1 TD; Bleier, 2 for 3; Bradshaw, 2 for -5.
Dallas—Dorsett, 16 for 96; Staubach, 4 for 37; Laidlaw, 3 for 12; P. Pearson, 1 for 6; Newhouse, 8 for 3.
PASSING
Pittsburgh—Bradshaw, 17 of 30 for 318, 4 TDs, 1 int.
Dallas—Staubach, 17 of 30 for 228, 3 TDs, 1 int.
RECEIVING
Pittsburgh—Swann, 7 for 124, 1 TD; Stallworth, 3 for 115, 2 TDs; Grossman, 3 for 29; Bell, 2 for 21; Harris, 1 for 22; Bleier, 1 for 7, 1 TD.
Dallas—Dorsett, 5 for 44; D. Pearson, 4 for 73; Hill, 2 for 49, 1 TD; Johnson, 2 for 30, 1 TD; DuPree, 2 for 17, 1 TD; P. Pearson, 2 for 15.
PUNTING
Pittsburgh—Colquitt, 3 for 129, 43.0 average.
Dallas—D. White, 5 for 198, 39.6 average.
PUNT RETURNS
Pittsburgh—Bell, 4 for 27.
Dallas—Johnson, 2 for 33.
KICKOFF RETURNS
Pittsburgh—L. Anderson, 3 for 45.
Dallas—Johnson, 3 for 63; Brinson, 2 for 41; R. White, 1 for 0.
INTERCEPTIONS
Pittsburgh—Blount, 1 for 13.
Dallas—Lewis, 1 for 21.

Harris runs 22 yards up the middle for fourth-quarter score.

Swann eludes Cowboys' secondary for game-deciding touchdown.

PITTSBURGH STEELERS

No.	Name	Pos.	Ht.	Wt.	Age	Year	College
69	Anderson, Fred	DE-DT	6-5	235	24	R	Prairie View
30	Anderson, Larry	CB-KR	5-11	177	22	R	Louisiana Tech
76	Banaszak, John	DT-DE	6-3	244	28	4	Eastern Michigan
65	Beasley, Tom	DT	6-5	253	24	1	Virginia Tech
83	Bell, Theo	WR-KR	6-0	180	25	2	Arizona
20	Bleier, Rocky	RB	5-11	210	32	10	Notre Dame
47	Blount, Mel	CB	6-3	205	30	9	Southern U.
12	Bradshaw, Terry	QB	6-3	215	30	9	Louisiana Tech
79	Brown, Larry	T	6-4	245	29	8	Kansas
56	Cole, Robin	LB	6-2	220	23	2	New Mexico
5	Colquitt, Craig	P	6-2	182	24	R	Tennessee
77	Courson, Steve	G	6-1	260	23	1	South Carolina
89	Cunningham, Bennie	TE	6-5	247	24	3	Clemson
57	Davis, Sam	G	6-1	255	34	12	Allen
35	Deloplaine, Jack	RB-KR	5-10	205	24	3	Salem
21	Dungy, Tony	S	6-0	190	23	2	Minnesota
67	Dunn, Gary	DT	6-3	247	25	2	Miami
64	Furness, Steve	DT-DE	6-4	255	28	7	Rhode Island
10	Gerela, Roy	K	5-10	185	30	10	New Mexico State
75	Greene, Joe	DT	6-4	260	32	10	North Texas State
68	Greenwood, L.C.	DE	6-7	250	32	10	Arkansas-Pine Bluff
84	Grossman, Randy	TE	6-1	215	26	5	Temple
59	Ham, Jack	LB	6-1	225	30	8	Penn State
32	Harris, Franco	RB	6-2	225	28	7	Penn State
29	Johnson, Ron	CB	5-10	200	22	R	Eastern Michigan
55	Kolb, Jon	T	6-2	262	31	10	Oklahoma State
15	Kruczek, Mike	QB	6-1	205	25	3	Boston College
58	Lambert, Jack	LB	6-4	220	26	5	Kent State
87	Mandich, Jim	TE	6-2	214	30	8	Michigan
39	Moser, Rick	RB-KR	6-0	218	22	R	Rhode Island
72	Mullins, Gerry	G	6-3	244	29	8	USC
25	Oldham, Ray	S	5-11	192	27	6	Middle Tennessee State
66	Petersen, Ted	C-T	6-5	244	23	2	Eastern Illinois
74	Pinney, Ray	T-C	6-4	240	24	3	Washington
31	Shell, Donnie	S	5-11	190	26	5	South Carolina State
86	Smith, Jim	WR-KR	6-2	205	23	2	Michigan
82	Stallworth, John	WR	6-2	183	26	5	Alabama A&M
18	Stoudt, Cliff	QB	6-4	210	23	2	Youngstown State
88	Swann, Lynn	WR	6-0	180	26	5	USC
38	Thornton, Sidney	RB	5-11	230	24	2	Northwestern Louisiana
51	Toews, Loren	LB	6-3	222	27	6	California
23	Wagner, Mike	S	6-2	200	30	8	Western Illinois
52	Webster, Mike	C	6-2	250	26	5	Wisconsin
78	White, Dwight	DE	6-4	255	30	8	East Texas State
53	Winston, Dennis	LB	6-0	228	23	2	Arkansas

Head coach—Chuck Noll. **Assistants**—Rollie Dotsch, Dick Hoak, Tom Moore, George Perles, Lou Riecke, Paul Uram, Dick Walker, Woody Widenhofer.

DALLAS COWBOYS

No.	Name	Pos.	Ht.	Wt.	Age	Year	College
31	Barnes, Benny	CB	6-1	195	27	7	Stanford
76	Bethea, Larry	DT	6-5	254	22	R	Michigan State
24	Blackwell, Alois	RB	5-10	195	24	R	Houston
53	Breunig, Bob	LB	6-2	225	25	4	Arizona State
36	Brinson, Larry	RB	6-0	214	24	2	Florida
59	Brown, Guy	LB	6-4	228	23	2	Houston
18	Carano, Glenn	QB	6-3	202	23	2	Nevada-Las Vegas
63	Cole, Larry	DT	6-5	252	32	11	Hawaii
61	Cooper, Jim	C-G-T	6-5	260	23	2	Temple
67	Donovan, Pat	T	6-4	250	25	4	Stanford
33	Dorsett, Tony	RB	5-11	190	24	2	Pittsburgh
89	DuPree, Billy Joe	TE	6-4	229	28	6	Michigan State
62	Fitzgerald, John	C	6-5	260	30	8	Boston College
71	Frederick, Andy	T	6-6	255	24	2	New Mexico
43	Harris, Cliff	S	6-1	192	30	9	Ouachita Baptist
58	Hegman, Mike	LB	6-1	225	26	3	Tennessee State
56	Henderson, Thomas	LB	6-2	220	25	4	Langston
80	Hill, Tony	WR	6-2	198	22	2	Stanford
42	Hughes, Randy	S	6-4	207	25	4	Oklahoma
57	Huther, Bruce	LB	6-1	220	24	2	New Hampshire
86	Johnson, Butch	WR	6-1	192	24	3	California-Riverside
72	Jones, Ed	DE	6-9	270	27	5	Tennessee State
25	Kyle, Aaron	CB	5-10	185	24	3	Wyoming
35	Laidlaw, Scott	RB	6-0	205	25	4	Stanford
66	Lawless, Burton	G	6-4	255	25	4	Florida
50	Lewis, D. D.	LB	6-1	215	33	10	Mississippi State
79	Martin, Harvey	DE	6-5	250	28	6	East Texas State
44	Newhouse, Robert	RB	5-10	215	29	7	Houston
88	Pearson, Drew	WR	6-0	183	28	6	Tulsa
26	Pearson, Preston	RB	6-1	206	34	12	Illinois
75	Pugh, Jethro	DT	6-6	255	34	14	Elizabeth City State
64	Rafferty, Tom	G	6-3	250	24	3	Penn State
60	Randall, Tom	G	6-5	245	22	R	Iowa State
68	Scott, Herbert	G	6-2	252	26	4	Virginia Union
1	Septien, Rafael	K	5-9	171	25	2	Southwestern Louisiana
81	Smith, Jackie	TE	6-4	230	38	16	Northwestern Louisiana
65	Stalls, Dave	DT-DE	6-4	245	23	2	Northern Colorado
12	Staubach, Roger	QB	6-3	202	36	10	Navy
82	Steele, Robert	WR	6-4	196	22	R	North Alabama
32	Thurman, Dennis	CB	5-11	170	22	R	USC
46	Washington, Mark	CB	5-11	187	31	9	Morgan State
41	Waters, Charlie	S	6-2	200	30	9	Clemson
11	White, Danny	QB-P	6-2	192	26	3	Arizona State
54	White, Randy	DT	6-4	250	26	4	Maryland
70	Wright, Rayfield	T	6-6	260	33	12	Fort Valley State

Head coach—Tom Landry. **Assistants**—Ermal Allen, Mike Ditka, Jim Myers, Dan Reeves, Gene Stallings, Ernie Stautner, Jerry Tubbs, Bob Ward.

SUPER BOWL XIV

PITTSBURGH 31, LOS ANGELES 19

Quarterback Terry Bradshaw threw a 73-yard touchdown pass to John Stallworth to bring the Pittsburgh Steelers from behind early in the fourth quarter, and then hit Stallworth again, with a 45-yard pass, to set up an insurance touchdown, as the Steelers won their fourth Super Bowl in as many appearances, a 31-19 victory over the Los Angeles Rams.

The first of the two long passes came with 2:56 gone in the fourth quarter and the Steelers trailing 19-17. On third-and-eight at the Pittsburgh 27, Bradshaw called a "60 Prevent Slot Hook and Go." Stallworth got behind Rams defensive backs Rod Perry and Dave Elmendorf, took the pass in stride at the Rams' 32-yard line, and ran in for the score.

Two series later, Stallworth ran the same pattern and Bradshaw found him for a first down at the Rams' 22. Franco Harris scored four plays later after a pass interference penalty on Pat Thomas gave the Steelers the ball on the 1-yard line.

In a game that ranks as one of the most exciting Super Bowls, the Rams' defense stopped the Steelers running game, but was exploited by the poised Bradshaw. He overcame three interceptions to complete 14 of 21 passes for 309 yards and two touchdowns, and be voted the most valuable player.

The Steelers scored first, driving 55 yards the first time they had the ball to set up a 41-yard field goal by rookie Matt Bahr. Harris and Rocky Bleier ran the ball on 8 of the 10 plays in the drive.

A short kickoff gave the ball to the Rams at their 41. From there, they went 59 yards in eight plays to take the lead 7-3. After a short Vince Ferragamo to Wendell Tyler pass, the Rams ran on seven straight plays, culminating in a one-yard run by fullback Cullen Bryant for the score.

A 45-yard kickoff return by Larry Anderson set Pittsburgh up on their own 47. Nine plays later Harris scored his first touchdown of the day on a one-yard run. Bradshaw passed twice on first down during the drive, picking up 12 yards to wide receiver Lynn Swann and 13 to tight end Bennie Cunningham.

Again, the Rams came back to score immediately. They drove 67 yards to the Pittsburgh 14, before settling for a 31-yard Frank Corral field goal that tied the game 10-10.

Two series later, Elmendorf intercepted Bradshaw and returned it to the Pittsburgh 39. Eight plays netted only 12 yards, and with 14 seconds left in the half Corral kicked a 45-yard field goal to send the Rams to the locker room with a 13-10 lead.

The statistics were close at halftime. The Rams led in total yards 130 to 127, each team had nine first downs, and the only turnover was Elmendorf's interception.

The Steelers wasted little time in the second half getting back on top. A 37-yard kickoff return by Anderson put them on their own 39, and, five plays later, Bradshaw threw a 47-yard touchdown pass to Swann.

But the Rams again matched the Steelers' score, this time in only four plays. A 50-yard pass from Ferragamo to Billy Waddy put the Rams on the 24. On the next play Ferragamo handed off to halfback Lawrence McCutcheon, who swept right, stopped, and threw a 24-yard touchdown pass to Ron Smith, who had eluded defensive back Ron Johnson downfield.

The Rams still led 19-17 after Corral missed the extra point, but Bradshaw's two long passes put the Steelers ahead. Linebacker Jack Lambert intercepted Ferragamo at the Pittsburgh 14 to end one Rams' threat, and the Steelers held on downs to stop the last Los Angeles drive late in the game.

Tyler runs out of Lambert's (58) grasp and turns upfield.

Participants—Pittsburgh Steelers, champions of the American Football Conference, and the Los Angeles Rams, champions of the National Football Conference
Date—January 20, 1980
Site—Rose Bowl, Pasadena
Time—3:15 P.M. PST
Conditions—67 degrees, sunny
Playing surface—Grass
Television and Radio—Columbia Broadcasting System (CBS)
Regular Season Records—Pittsburgh, 12-4; Los Angeles 9-7
Conference Championships—Pittsburgh defeated the Houston Oilers 27-13 for the AFC title; Los Angeles defeated the Tampa Bay Buccaneers 9-0 for the NFC title
Players' Shares—$18,000 to each member of the winning team; $9,000 to each member of the losing team
Attendance—103,985
Gross Receipts—$9,489,274.00
Officials—Referee, Fred Silva; umpire, Al Conway; line judge, Bob Beeks; head linesman, Burl Toler; back judge, Stan Javie; side judge, Ben Tompkins; field judge, Charley Musser
Coaches—Chuck Noll, Pittsburgh; Ray Malavasi, Los Angeles

Los Angeles	Starters, Offense	Pittsburgh
Billy Waddy	WR	John Stallworth
Doug France	LT	Jon Kolb
Kent Hill	LG	Sam Davis
Rich Saul	C	Mike Webster
Dennis Harrah	RG	Gerry Mullins
Jackie Slater	RT	Larry Brown
Terry Nelson	TE	Bennie Cunningham
Preston Dennard	WR	Lynn Swann
Vince Ferragamo	QB	Terry Bradshaw
Cullen Bryant	RB	Rocky Bleier
Wendell Tyler	RB	Franco Harris
	Starters, Defense	
Jack Youngblood	LE	L. C. Greenwood
Mike Fanning	LT	Joe Greene
Larry Brooks	RT	Gary Dunn
Fred Dryer	RE	John Banaszak
Jim Youngblood	LLB	Dennis Winston
Jack Reynolds	MLB	Jack Lambert
Bob Brudzinski	RLB	Robin Cole
Pat Thomas	LCB	Ron Johnson
Rod Perry	RCB	Mel Blount
Dave Elmendorf	SS	Donnie Shell
Nolan Cromwell	FS	J. T. Thomas

Los Angeles......	7	6	6	0	— 19
Pittsburgh	3	7	7	14	— 31

Pitt—FG Bahr 41
LA—Bryant 1 run (Corral kick)
Pitt—Harris 1 run (Bahr kick)
LA—FG Corral 31
LA—FG Corral 45
Pitt—Swann 47 pass from Bradshaw (Bahr kick)
LA—R. Smith 24 pass from McCutcheon (kick failed)
Pitt—Stallworth 73 pass from Bradshaw (Bahr kick)
Pitt—Harris 1 run (Bahr kick)

TEAM STATISTICS	LA	Pitt
First downs	16	19
Rushing	6	8
Passing	9	10
By penalty	1	1
Total yardage	301	393
Net rushing yardage	107	84
Net passing yardage	194	309
Passes att.-comp.-had int.	26-16-1	21-14-3

RUSHING
Los Angeles—Tyler, 17 for 60; Bryant, 6 for 30, 1 TD; McCutcheon, 5 for 10; Ferragamo, 1 for 7.
Pittsburgh—Harris, 20 for 46, 2 TDs; Bleier, 10 for 25; Bradshaw, 3 for 9; Thornton, 4 for 4.
PASSING
Los Angeles—Ferragamo, 15 of 25 for 212, 1 int.; McCutcheon, 1 of 1 for 24, 1 TD.
Pittsburgh—Bradshaw, 14 of 21 for 309, 2 TDs, 3 int.
RECEIVING
Los Angeles—Waddy, 3 for 75; Bryant, 3 for 21; Tyler, 3 for 20; Dennard, 2 for 32; Nelson, 2 for 20; D. Hill, 1 for 28; Smith, 1 for 24, 1 TD; McCutcheon, 1 for 16.
Pittsburgh—Swann, 5 for 79, 1 TD; Stallworth, 3 for 121, 1 TD; Harris, 3 for 66; Cunningham, 2 for 21; Thornton, 1 for 22.
PUNTING
Los Angeles—Clark, 5 for 220, 44.0 average.
Pittsburgh—Colquitt, 2 for 85, 42.5 average.
PUNT RETURNS
Los Angeles—Brown, 1 for 4.
Pittsburgh—Bell, 2 for 17; Smith, 2 for 14.
KICKOFF RETURNS
Los Angeles—E. Hill, 3 for 47; Jodat, 2 for 32; Andrews, 1 for 0.
Pittsburgh—L. Anderson, 5 for 162.
INTERCEPTIONS
Los Angeles—Elmendorf, 1 for 10; Brown, 1 for 6; Perry, 1 for 1-1; Thomas, 0 for 6.
Pittsburgh—Lambert, 1 for 16.

McCutcheon throws touchdown pass to Smith (84) over Lambert (58).

Stallworth beats Perry for touchdown that seals Rams fate.

LOS ANGELES RAMS

No.	Name	Pos.	Ht.	Wt.	Age	Year	College
52	Andrews, George	LB	6-3	226	24	R	Nebraska
62	Bain, Bill	G	6-4	270	27	5	USC
90	Brooks, Larry	DT	6-3	254	29	8	Virginia State-Petersburg
25	Brown, Eddie	S-KR	5-11	190	27	5	Tennessee
59	Brudzinski, Bob	LB	6-4	231	25	3	Ohio State
32	Bryant, Cullen	RB	6-1	234	28	7	Colorado
13	Clark, Ken	P	6-2	197	31	1	St. Mary's, Nova Scotia
3	Corral, Frank	K	6-2	220	24	2	UCLA
21	Cromwell, Nolan	S	6-1	197	24	3	Kansas
88	Dennard, Preston	WR	6-1	185	24	2	New Mexico
71	Doss, Reggie	DE	6-4	267	23	2	Hampton Institute
89	Dryer, Fred	DE	6-6	230	33	11	San Diego State
28	Ellis, Ken	CB	5-11	180	32	10	Southern U.
42	Elmendorf, Dave	S	6-1	196	30	9	Texas A&M
79	Fanning, Mike	DT	6-6	248	26	5	Notre Dame
15	Ferragamo, Vince	QB	6-3	207	25	3	Nebraska
77	France, Doug	T	6-5	268	26	5	Ohio State
73	Gravelle, Gordon	T	6-5	252	30	8	Brigham Young
60	Harrah, Dennis	G	6-5	251	26	5	Miami
51	Harris, Joe	LB	6-1	225	27	3	Georgia Tech
87	Hill, Drew	WR-KR	5-9	170	23	R	Georgia Tech
24	Hill, Eddie	RB-KR	6-2	197	22	R	Memphis State
72	Hill, Kent	G	6-5	260	22	R	Georgia Tech
43	Jodat, Jim	RB	5-11	207	25	3	Carthage
19	Lee, Bob	QB	6-2	195	33	11	Pacific
30	McCutcheon, Lawrence	RB	6-1	205	29	7	Colorado State
83	Nelson, Terry	TE	6-2	241	28	6	Arkansas-Pine Bluff
33	O'Steen, Dwayne	CB	6-1	190	25	2	San Jose State
49	Perry, Rod	CB	5-9	177	26	5	Colorado
64	Reynolds, Jack	LB	6-1	231	32	10	Tennessee
8	Rutledge, Jeff	QB	6-2	200	22	R	Alabama
54	Ryczek, Dan	C-G	6-3	245	30	7	Virginia
61	Saul, Rich	C	6-3	243	31	10	Michigan State
78	Slater, Jackie	T	6-4	269	25	4	Jackson State
84	Smith, Ron	WR	6-0	185	23	2	San Diego State
37	Sully, Ivory	S-CB	6-0	193	22	R	Delaware
27	Thomas, Pat	CB	5-9	184	25	4	Texas A&M
26	Tyler, Wendell	RB	5-10	188	24	2	UCLA
80	Waddy, Billy	WR	5-11	180	25	3	Colorado
20	Wallace, Jackie	S	6-3	196	28	6	Arizona
57	Westbrooks, Greg	LB	6-3	215	26	5	Colorado
70	Wilkinson, Jerry	DE	6-9	255	23	R	Oregon State
86	Young, Charle	TE	6-4	234	28	7	USC
85	Youngblood, Jack	DE	6-4	243	29	9	Florida
53	Youngblood, Jim	LB	6-3	231	29	7	Tennessee Tech

Head coach—Ray Malavasi. **Assistants**—Bud Carson, Clyde Evans, Jack Faulkner, Bill Hickman, Paul Lanham, Frank Lauterbur, Dan Radkovich, Lionel Taylor, LaVern Torgeson.

PITTSBURGH STEELERS

No.	Name	Pos.	Ht.	Wt.	Age	Year	College
33	Anderson, Anthony	RB	6-0	197	23	R	Temple
30	Anderson, Larry	CB-KR	5-11	177	23	2	Louisiana Tech
9	Bahr, Matt	K	5-10	165	23	R	Penn State
76	Banaszak, John	DE-DT	6-3	244	29	5	Eastern Michigan
65	Beasley, Tom	DT	6-5	253	25	2	Virginia Tech
83	Bell, Theo	WR-KR	6-0	180	26	3	Arizona
20	Bleier, Rocky	RB	5-11	210	33	11	Notre Dame
47	Blount, Mel	CB	6-3	205	31	10	Southern U.
12	Bradshaw, Terry	QB	6-3	215	31	10	Louisiana Tech
79	Brown, Larry	T	6-4	255	30	9	Kansas
56	Cole, Robin	LB	6-2	220	24	3	New Mexico
5	Colquitt, Craig	P	6-2	182	25	2	Tennessee
77	Courson, Steve	G	6-1	260	24	2	South Carolina
89	Cunningham, Bennie	TE	6-5	247	25	4	Clemson
57	Davis, Sam	G	6-1	255	35	13	Allen
63	Dornbrook, Thom	C-G	6-2	240	23	1	Kentucky
67	Dunn, Gary	DT	6-3	247	26	3	Miami
64	Furness, Steve	DT-DE	6-4	255	29	8	Rhode Island
50	Graves, Tom	LB	6-3	228	24	R	Michigan State
75	Greene, Joe	DT	6-4	260	33	11	North Texas State
68	Greenwood, L. C.	DE	6-7	250	33	11	Arkansas-Pine Bluff
84	Grossman, Randy	TE	6-1	215	27	6	Temple
59	Ham, Jack	LB	6-1	225	31	9	Penn State
32	Harris, Franco	RB	6-2	225	29	8	Penn State
27	Hawthorne, Greg	RB	6-3	225	23	R	Baylor
29	Johnson, Ron	CB	5-10	200	23	2	Eastern Michigan
55	Kolb, Jon	T	6-2	262	32	11	Oklahoma State
15	Kruczek, Mike	QB	6-1	205	26	4	Boston College
58	Lambert, Jack	LB	6-4	220	27	6	Kent State
39	Moser, Rick	RB	6-0	210	23	2	Rhode Island
72	Mullins, Gerry	G	6-3	244	30	9	USC
66	Petersen, Ted	T-C	6-5	244	24	3	Eastern Illinois
31	Shell, Donnie	S	5-11	190	27	6	South Carolina State
86	Smith, Jim	WR-KR	6-2	205	24	3	Michigan
82	Stallworth, John	WR	6-2	183	27	6	Alabama A&M
18	Stoudt, Cliff	QB	6-4	218	24	3	Youngstown State
88	Swann, Lynn	WR	6-0	180	27	6	USC
24	Thomas, J. T.	S	6-2	196	28	6	Florida State
38	Thornton, Sidney	RB	5-11	230	25	3	Northwestern Louisiana
51	Toews, Loren	LB	6-3	222	28	7	California
54	Valentine, Zack	LB	6-2	220	22	R	East Carolina
52	Webster, Mike	C	6-2	250	27	6	Wisconsin
78	White, Dwight	DE	6-4	255	30	9	East Texas State
53	Winston, Dennis	LB	6-0	228	24	3	Arkansas
22	Woodruff, Dwayne	CB	5-11	189	22	R	Louisville

Head coach—Chuck Noll. **Assistants**—Rollie Dotsch, Dick Hoak, Tom Moore, George Perles, Lou Riecke, Paul Uram, Dick Walker, Woody Widenhofer.

SUPER BOWL XV

OAKLAND 27, PHILADELPHIA 10

The Oakland Raiders' defense, led by linebacker Rod Martin's game-record three interceptions, set up 10 points and controlled the tempo of the game as the Raiders defeated the Philadelphia Eagles 27-10. The win was the second in three Super Bowl appearances for the Raiders and marked the first time that a wild card team had won a Super Bowl.

Oakland took control of the game early. On the third play of the game, Martin intercepted Ron Jaworski's pass on the Philadelphia 47-yard line and returned it to the 30. Seven plays later, Raiders quarterback Jim Plunkett threw the first of his three touchdown passes on the day, a two-yarder to Clifford Branch.

The Eagles could gain only two first downs on the next two series, but after their second punt, the Raiders were pinned back on their own 14-yard line. With a third-and-four from the Oakland 20-yard line, Plunkett passed to running back Kenny King, who gathered the ball in at the Oakland 39 and raced down the left sideline 61 yards, completing an 80-yard touchdown, the longest play in Super Bowl history.

The Eagles sustained a drive to score as the second quarter opened. Jaworski hit John Spagnola for 22 yards on the left side, and then came back to halfback Wilbert Montgomery for 25 yards over the middle to move the Eagles inside the Oakland 20. The Raiders held, and Philadelphia settled for a 30-yard field goal by Tony Franklin.

Neither team could score for the rest of the half. Raiders kicker Chris Bahr missed on a 45-yard field goal attempt with less than four minutes in the half. Then, after the Eagles drove 62 yards to the Oakland 11-yard line with less than a minute in the half, Franklin's short field goal attempt was blocked by linebacker Ted Hendricks and recovered by rookie linebacker Matt Millen.

After 30 minutes of play, each team had netted 164 yards, but the Raiders had dominated play and the scoreboard. Jaworski had completed only 9 of 22 passes and had the one big interception.

Behind Plunkett's passing, the Raiders applied the knockout punch to the Eagles early in the third quarter. Plunkett passed to King for 13 yards and a first down, to Bob Chandler for 32 yards and another first down, and to Branch for 29 yards and a touchdown. The scoring drive covered 76 yards in only five plays and took only 2:36 off the clock.

When the Eagles tried to get back into the game on Jaworski's arm, Martin intercepted his second pass of the game, setting up a 46-yard field goal by Bahr, which increased the Oakland lead to 24-3.

Jaworski led the Eagles to their only touchdown of the day to start the fourth quarter. He capped a 12-play, 88-yard drive with an eight-yard pass to tight end Keith Krepfle for the touchdown.

Any comeback hopes the Eagles had died when Oakland took the ensuing kickoff and marched 72 yards to Bahr's 35-yard field goal.

The last two Philadelphia thrusts each reached Oakland territory, but Willie Jones recovered Jaworski's fumble on the Oakland 42, and Martin intercepted his third pass of the day at the Raiders' 37. Oakland ran out the clock deep in the Eagles' territory.

"All Jim [Plunkett] needed was for someone to believe in him," said Raiders coach Tom Flores of his quarterback who was voted the most valuable player in the game, after completing 13 of 21 for 261 yards and three touchdowns. "Out there today he could accomplish almost anything he wanted. He was the key for us the whole way."

With Chandler (85) as an escort, King takes Plunkett's pass 80 yards for a score.

Participants—Oakland Raiders, champions of the American Football Conference, and Philadelphia Eagles, champions of the National Football Conference
Date—January 25, 1981
Site—Louisiana Superdome, New Orleans
Time—5:15 P.M. CST
Conditions—72 degrees, indoors
Playing surface—AstroTurf
Television—National Broadcasting Company (NBC)
Radio—Columbia Broadcasting System (CBS)
Regular Season Records—Oakland, 11-5; Philadelphia, 12-4
Conference Championships—Oakland defeated the San Diego Chargers 34-27 for the AFC title; Philadelphia defeated the Dallas Cowboys 20-7 for the NFC title
Players' Shares—$18,000 to each member of the winning team; $9,000 to each member of the losing team
Attendance—76,135
Gross Receipts—$10,328,664.57
Officials—Referee, Ben Dreith; umpire, Frank Sinkovitz; line judge, Tom Dooley; head linesman, Tony Veteri; back judge, Tom Kelleher; side judge, Dean Look; field judge, Fritz Graf
Coaches—Tom Flores, Oakland; Dick Vermeil, Philadelphia

Oakland	Starters, Offense	Philadelphia
Clifford Branch	WR	Harold Carmichael
Art Shell	LT	Stan Walters
Gene Upshaw	LG	Petey Perot
Dave Dalby	C	Guy Morriss
Mickey Marvin	RG	Woody Peoples
Henry Lawrence	RT	Jerry Sisemore
Raymond Chester	TE	Keith Krepfle
Bob Chandler	WR-TE	John Spagnola
Jim Plunkett	QB	Ron Jaworski
Mark van Eeghen	RB	Leroy Harris
Kenny King	RB	Wilbert Montgomery
	Starters, Defense	
John Matuszak	LE	Dennis Harrison
Reggie Kinlaw	NT	Charlie Johnson
Dave Browning	RE	Carl Hairston
Ted Hendricks	LOLB	John Bunting
Matt Millen	LILB	Bill Bergey
Bob Nelson	RILB	Frank LeMaster
Rod Martin	ROLB	Jerry Robinson
Lester Hayes	LCB	Roynell Young
Dwayne O'Steen	RCB	Herman Edwards
Mike Davis	SS	Randy Logan
Burgess Owens	FS	Brenard Wilson

Oakland	14	0	10	3	—	27
Philadelphia	0	3	0	7	—	10

Oak—Branch 2 pass from Plunkett (Bahr kick)
Oak—King 80 pass from Plunkett (Bahr kick)
Phil—FG Franklin 30
Oak—Branch 29 pass from Plunkett (Bahr kick)
Oak—FG Bahr 46
Phil—Krepfle 8 pass from Jaworski (Franklin kick)
Oak—FG Bahr 35

TEAM STATISTICS	Oak	Phil
First downs	17	19
Rushing	6	3
Passing	10	14
By penalty	1	2
Total yardage	377	360
Net rushing yardage	117	69
Net passing yardage	260	291
Passes att.-comp.-had int.	21-13-0	38-18-3

RUSHING
Oakland—van Eeghen, 19 for 80; King, 6 for 18; Jensen, 3 for 12; Plunkett, 3 for 9; Whittington, 3 for – 2.
Philadelphia—Montgomery, 16 for 44; Harris, 7 for 14; Giammona, 1 for 7; Harrington, 1 for 4; Jaworski, 1 for 0.

PASSING
Oakland—Plunkett, 13 of 21 for 261, 3 TDs.
Philadelphia—Jaworski, 18 of 38 for 291, 1 TD, 3 int.

RECEIVING
Oakland—Branch, 5 for 67, 2 TDs; Chandler, 4 for 77; King, 2 for 93, 1 TD; Chester, 2 for 24.
Philadelphia—Montgomery, 6 for 91; Carmichael, 5 for 83; Smith, 2 for 59; Krepfle, 2 for 16, 1 TD; Spagnola, 1 for 22; Parker, 1 for 19; Harris, 1 for 1.

PUNTING
Oakland—Guy, 3 for 126, 42.0 average.
Philadelphia—Runager, 3 for 110, 36.7 average.

PUNT RETURNS
Oakland—Matthews, 2 for 1.
Philadelphia—Sciarra, 2 for 18; Henry, 1 for 2.

KICKOFF RETURNS
Oakland—Matthews, 2 for 29; Moody, 1 for 19.
Philadelphia—Campfield, 5 for 87; Harrington, 1 for 0.

INTERCEPTIONS
Oakland—Martin, 3 for 44.
Philadelphia—none.

Martin (53) returns one his three interceptions of Jaworski (7).

Hendricks (center) goes high to reject Franklin's second quarter field goal.

OAKLAND RAIDERS

No.	Name	Pos.	Ht.	Wt.	Age	Year	College
10	Bahr, Chris.	K	5-10	175	27	5	Penn State
56	Barnes, Jeff.	LB	6-2	215	25	4	California
81	Bradshaw, Morris	WR	6-1	195	28	7	Ohio State
21	Branch, Clifford.	WR	5-11	170	32	9	Colorado
73	Browning, Dave	DE	6-5	245	24	3	Washington
77	Campbell, Joe	DE-NT	6-6	250	25	4	Maryland
52	Celotto, Mario	LB	6-3	225	24	2	USC
85	Chandler, Bob	WR	6-1	180	31	10	USC
88	Chester, Raymond	TE	6-4	235	32	11	Morgan State
46	Christensen, Todd	TE-RB	6-3	230	24	2	Brigham Young
50	Dalby, Dave.	C	6-3	250	30	9	UCLA
79	Davis, Bruce	G-T	6-6	280	24	2	UCLA
36	Davis, Mike	S	6-2	200	24	3	Colorado
8	Guy, Ray	P	6-3	190	31	8	Southern Mississippi
86	Hardman, Cedrick	DE	6-4	245	32	11	North Texas State
37	Hayes, Lester	CB	6-0	195	25	4	Texas A & M
83	Hendricks, Ted	LB	6-7	225	33	12	Miami
42	Jackson, Monte	CB	5-11	200	27	6	San Diego State
31	Jensen, Derrick	RB	6-1	225	24	2	Texas-Arlington
90	Jones, Willie	DE	6-4	245	23	2	Florida State
33	King, Kenny	RB	5-11	205	23	2	Oklahoma
62	Kinlaw, Reggie	NT	6-2	240	24	2	Oklahoma
70	Lawrence, Henry	T	6-4	270	29	7	Florida A & M
53	Martin, Rod	LB	6-2	210	26	4	USC
89	Martini, Rich	WR	6-2	185	25	2	California-Davis
65	Marvin, Mickey	G	6-4	270	25	4	Tennessee
71	Mason, Lindsey	T-G	6-5	265	25	2	Kansas
43	Matthews, Ira	KR-WR-RB	5-8	175	23	2	Wisconsin
72	Matuszak, John	DE	6-8	280	30	8	Tampa
57	McClanahan, Randy	LB	6-5	225	26	3	Southwestern Louisiana
23	McKinney, Odis	CB	6-2	190	23	3	Colorado
55	Millen, Matt	LB	6-2	260	22	R	Penn State
26	Moody, Keith	CB-KR	5-11	175	27	5	Syracuse
51	Nelson, Bob	LB	6-4	230	27	5	Nebraska
35	O'Steen, Dwayne	CB	6-1	195	26	3	San Jose State
44	Owens, Burgess	S	6-2	200	29	8	Miami
74	Pear, Dave.	NT	6-2	250	27	6	Washington
16	Plunkett, Jim	QB	6-2	205	33	10	Stanford
84	Ramsey, Derrick	TE	6-4	225	24	3	Kentucky
78	Shell, Art	T	6-5	280	34	13	Maryland-Eastern Shore
66	Sylvester, Steve	G-C	6-4	260	27	6	Notre Dame
63	Upshaw, Gene	G	6-5	255	35	14	Texas A & I
30	van Eeghen, Mark	RB	6-2	225	28	7	Colgate
22	Whittington, Arthur	RB	5-11	180	25	3	Southern Methodist
6	Wilson, Marc	QB	6-5	205	23	R	Brigham Young

Head coach—Tom Flores. **Assistants**—Sam Boghosian, Willie Brown, Lew Erber, Chet Franklin, Earl Leggett, Joe Madro, Bob Mischak, Steve Ortmayer, Charlie Sumner, Ray Willsey.

PHILADELPHIA EAGLES

No.	Name	Pos.	Ht.	Wt.	Age	Year	College
63	Baker, Ron.	G	6-4	250	26	3	Oklahoma State
66	Bergey, Bill	LB	6-3	245	35	12	Arkansas State
27	Blackmore, Richard	CB	5-10	174	24	2	Mississippi State
97	Brown, Thomas	DE	6-4	240	23	R	Baylor
95	Bunting, John	LB	6-1	220	30	9	North Carolina
37	Campfield, Billy	RB	6-0	205	24	3	Kansas
17	Carmichael, Harold	WR	6-8	225	31	10	Southern U.
59	Chesley, Al	LB	6-3	240	23	2	Pittsburgh
71	Clarke, Ken	NT	6-2	255	24	3	Syracuse
46	Edwards, Herman	CB	6-0	190	26	4	San Diego State
1	Franklin, Tony	K	5-8	182	24	2	Texas A & M
33	Giammona, Louie	RB-KR	5-9	180	27	4	Utah State
78	Hairston, Carl	DE	6-3	260	28	5	Maryland State
35	Harrington, Perry	RB	5-11	210	22	R	Jackson State
20	Harris, Leroy	RB	5-9	230	26	4	Arkansas State
68	Harrison, Dennis	DE	6-8	275	24	3	Vanderbilt
24	Henderson, Zac	S	6-1	190	25	R	Oklahoma
89	Henry, Wally	WR-KR	5-8	170	26	4	UCLA
16	Hertel, Rob	QB	6-2	198	25	2	USC
87	Humphrey, Claude.	DE	6-5	258	36	13	Tennessee State
7	Jaworski, Ron.	QB	6-2	196	29	6	Youngstown State
65	Johnson, Charlie	NT	6-3	262	29	4	Colorado
73	Kenney, Steve	T	6-4	262	25	1	Clemson
84	Krepfle, Keith	TE	6-3	230	28	6	Iowa State
55	LeMaster, Frank	LB	6-2	238	28	7	Kentucky
41	Logan, Randy	S	6-1	195	29	8	Michigan
31	Montgomery, Wilbert	RB	5-10	195	26	4	Abilene Christian
50	Morriss, Guy	C	6-4	255	29	8	Texas Christian
83	Parker, Rodney	WR	6-1	190	27	1	Tennessee State
69	Peoples, Woody	G	6-2	260	37	12	Grambling
62	Perot, Petey	G	6-2	261	23	2	Northwestern Louisiana
52	Phillips, Ray	LB	6-4	230	26	4	Nebraska
9	Pisarcik, Joe	QB	6-4	220	28	4	New Mexico State
56	Robinson, Jerry	LB	6-2	218	24	2	UCLA
4	Runager, Max	P	6-1	189	24	2	South Carolina
21	Sciarra, John.	S-KR	5-11	185	26	3	UCLA
76	Sisemore, Jerry	T	6-4	265	29	8	Texas
61	Slater, Mark.	C	6-2	257	25	3	Minnesota
85	Smith, Charles.	WR	6-1	185	30	7	Grambling
88	Spagnola, John	TE	6-4	240	23	2	Yale
39	Torrey, Bob	RB	6-2	232	23	3	Penn State
75	Walters, Stan	T	6-6	275	32	9	Syracuse
51	Wilkes, Reggie	LB	6-4	230	24	3	Georgia Tech
22	Wilson, Brenard	S	6-0	175	25	2	Vanderbilt
43	Young, Roynell	CB	6-1	181	23	R	Alcorn State

Head coach—Dick Vermeil. **Assistants**—Chuck Bednarik, Fred Bruney, Marion Campbell, Chuck Clausen, Dick Coury, Sid Gillman, George Hill, Ken Iman, Billy Joe, Lynn Stiles, Jerry Wampfler.

SUPER BOWL XVI

SAN FRANCISCO 26, CINCINNATI 21

The San Francisco defense came up with big plays throughout the game, including a four-play goal-line stand late in the third quarter, to stave off Cincinnati's explosive offense and record a 26-21 victory in Super Bowl XVI at the Pontiac Silverdome.

The 49ers' defense set the tone of the game early in the first quarter. Amos Lawrence fumbled the opening kickoff and the Bengals recovered at the 49ers' 26-yard line. Six plays later, free safety Dwight Hicks intercepted Ken Anderson's pass, which was intended for Isaac Curtis, at the 5-yard line and returned it 27 yards.

The 49ers then drove 68 yards on 11 plays for a touchdown. The key play in the drive was a 14-yard "gadget" pass from Joe Montana to tight end Charle Young on third-and-one at the Cincinnati 47. On the play, Montana handed off to Ricky Patton, who gave the ball to Freddie Solomon, who pitched back to Montana, who threw to Young. The drive culminated in a one-yard run by Montana that gave San Francisco a 7-0 lead.

Early in the second quarter the 49ers defense thwarted another Cincinnati drive when Eric Wright stripped the ball loose from Cris Collinsworth at the San Francisco 8. Lynn Thomas recovered for the 49ers. Twelve plays and 92 yards later, Montana threw an 11-yard touchdown pass to running back Earl Cooper to complete the longest drive in Super Bowl history.

David Verser's fumble of the ensuing kickoff and a penalty for an illegal block pinned the Bengals at their 2. Six plays later, they were forced to punt.

Ray Wersching's 22-yard field goal with 15 seconds left in the half was followed 13 seconds later by three more points, set up by a San Francisco recovery of Archie Griffin's fumbled kickoff return.

Cincinnati marched to a touchdown to start the third quarter, driving 83 yards in nine plays. Anderson scored on a five-yard run.

An exchange of punts—one by the Bengals, two by the 49ers—gave Cincinnati the ball at midfield with 6:53 left in the quarter. Two big plays in the drive—a 49-yard pass from Anderson to Collinsworth on third-and-23 and Pete Johnson's two-yard run on fourth-and-one at the San Francisco 5—put the Bengals in a first-and-goal situation at the 3. Johnson gained two on first down, but the 49ers rose to the occasion and stopped three successive plays from the 1 and took over with 1:17 left in the period.

The Cincinnati defense forced a punt, giving the Bengals possession at their 47. Eight plays later, Anderson threw a four-yard touchdown pass to tight end Dan Ross, cutting the 49ers' lead to 20-14 with 10:06 left in the game.

Montana then moved the 49ers 50 yards on a drive that ended in a 40-yard field goal by Wersching. Moments later, Anderson was intercepted by Wright, who returned it to the Cincinnati 22. Wersching kicked his fourth field goal, tying the Super Bowl record, with 1:57 left in the game.

Cincinnati took over at its own 26, and Anderson threw six consecutive completions, the last a three-yard touchdown pass to Ross with 16 seconds left. The Bengals' onside kick attempt was recovered by the 49ers, who ran out the clock.

Despite the 49ers victory, the Bengals dominated the statistics, holding a 356-275 yardage edge. Anderson completed a record 25 (of 34) passes for 300 yards and two touchdowns, both to Ross, who set a Super Bowl mark with 11 receptions. Montana, the game's most valuable player, threw for 157 yards and one touchdown, completing 14 of 22 passes.

Bunz (57) stops Alexander on the third play of the 49ers' goal line stand.

Participants—Cincinnati Bengals, champions of the American Football Conference, and San Francisco 49ers, champions of the National Football Conference
Date—January 24, 1982
Site—Pontiac Silverdome, Pontiac, Michigan
Time—4:00 P.M. EST
Conditions—70 degrees, indoors
Playing Surface—AstroTurf
Television and Radio—Columbia Broadcasting System (CBS)
Regular Season Records—Cincinnati, 12-4; San Francisco, 13-3
Conference Championships—Cincinnati defeated the San Diego Chargers 27-7 for the AFC title; San Francisco defeated the Dallas Cowboys 28-27 for the NFC title
Players' Shares—$18,000 to each member of the winning team; $9,000 to each member of the losing team
Attendance—81,270
Gross Receipts—$10,641,034.83
Officials—Referee, Pat Haggerty; umpire, Al Conway; line judge, Bob Beeks; head linesman, Jerry Bergman; back judge, Bill Swanson; side judge, Bob Rice; field judge, Don Hakes
Coaches—Forrest Gregg, Cincinnati; Bill Walsh, San Francisco

San Francisco	Starters, Offense	Cincinnati
Dwight Clark	WR	Cris Collinsworth
Dan Audick	LT	Anthony Munoz
John Ayers	LG	Dave Lapham
Fred Quillan	C	Blair Bush
Randy Cross	RG	Max Montoya
Keith Fahnhorst	RT	Mike Wilson
Charle Young	TE	Dan Ross
Freddie Solomon	WR	Isaac Curtis
Joe Montana	QB	Ken Anderson
Ricky Patton	RB	Pete Johnson
Earl Cooper	RB	Charles Alexander
	Starters, Defense	
Jim Stuckey	LE	Eddie Edwards
Archie Reese	NT	Wilson Whitley
Dwaine Board	RE	Ross Browner
Willie Harper	LOLB	Bo Harris
Jack Reynolds	LILB	Jim LeClair
Craig Puki	RILB	Glenn Cameron
Keena Turner	ROLB	Reggie Williams
Ronnie Lott	LCB	Louis Breeden
Eric Wright	RCB	Ken Riley
Carlton Williamson	SS	Bobby Kemp
Dwight Hicks	FS	Bryan Hicks

San Francisco....	7	13	0	6	— 26
Cincinnati........	0	0	7	14	— 21

SF —Montana 1 run (Wersching kick)
SF —Cooper 11 pass from Montana (Wersching kick)
SF —FG Wersching 22
SF —FG Wersching 26
Cin—Anderson 5 run (Breech kick)
Cin—Ross 4 pass from Anderson (Breech kick)
SF —FG Wersching 40
SF —FG Wersching 23
Cin—Ross 3 pass from Anderson (Breech kick)

TEAM STATISTICS	SF	Cin
First downs	20	24
Rushing	9	7
Passing	9	13
By penalty	2	4
Total yardage	275	356
Net rushing yardage	127	72
Net passing yardage	148	284
Passes att.-comp.-had int	22-14-0	34-25-2

RUSHING
San Francisco—Patton, 17 for 55; Cooper, 9 for 34; Montana, 6 for 18, 1 TD; Ring, 5 for 17; Davis, 2 for 5; Clark, 1 for −2.
Cincinnati—Johnson, 14 for 36; Alexander, 5 for 17; Anderson, 4 for 15, 1 TD; A. Griffin, 1 for 4.
PASSING
San Francisco—Montana, 14 of 22 for 157, 1 TD.
Cincinnati—Anderson, 25 of 34 for 300, 2 TDs, 2 int.
RECEIVING
San Francisco—Solomon, 4 for 52; Clark, 4 for 45; Cooper, 2 for 15, 1 TD; Wilson, 1 for 22; Young, 1 for 14; Patton, 1 for 6; Ring, 1 for 3.
Cincinnati—Ross, 11 for 104, 2 TDs; Collinsworth, 5 for 107; Curtis, 3 for 42; Kreider, 2 for 36; Johnson, 2 for 8; Alexander, 2 for 3.
PUNTING
San Francisco—Miller, 4 for 185, 46.3 average.
Cincinnati—McInally, 3 for 131, 43.7 average.
PUNT RETURNS
San Francisco—Hicks, 1 for 6.
Cincinnati—Fuller, 4 for 35.
KICKOFF RETURNS
San Francisco—Hicks, 1 for 23; Lawrence, 1 for 17; Clark, 1 for 0.
Cincinnati—Verser, 5 for 52; A. Griffin, 1 for 0; Frazier, 1 for 0.
INTERCEPTIONS
San Francisco—Hicks, 1 for 27; Wright, 1 for 25.
Cincinnati—None.

Ross—a record 11 catches for 104 yards and two scores—was a star in defeat.

Montana leads the 49ers drive for their final field goal.

SAN FRANCISCO 49ERS

No.	Name	Pos.	Ht.	Wt.	Age	Year	College
61	Audick, Dan	T	6-3	253	27	4	Hawaii
68	Ayers, John	G	6-5	260	28	5	West Texas State
7	Benjamin, Guy	QB	6-3	210	26	4	Stanford
76	Board, Dwaine	DE	6-5	250	25	3	North Carolina A & T
57	Bunz, Dan	LB	6-4	225	26	4	Long Beach State
60	Choma, John	G-T	6-6	261	26	1	Virginia
87	Clark, Dwight	WR	6-4	210	25	3	Clemson
49	Cooper, Earl	RB	6-2	227	24	2	Rice
51	Cross, Randy	G	6-3	250	27	6	UCLA
38	Davis, Johnny	RB	6-1	235	25	4	Alabama
74	Dean, Fred	DE	6-2	230	29	7	Louisiana Tech
62	Downing, Walt	C-G	6-3	254	25	4	Michigan
31	Easley, Walt	RB	6-1	226	24	R	West Virginia
35	Elliott, Lenvil	RB	6-0	210	30	9	Northeast Missouri State
71	Fahnhorst, Keith	T	6-6	263	29	8	Minnesota
24	Gervais, Rick	S	5-11	190	22	R	Stanford
59	Harper, Willie	LB	6-2	215	31	8	Nebraska
75	Harty, John	NT	6-4	253	23	R	Iowa
22	Hicks, Dwight	S	6-1	189	25	3	Michigan
66	Kennedy, Allan	T	6-7	245	24	R	Washington State
20	Lawrence, Amos	RB	5-10	179	24	R	North Carolina
52	Leopold, Bobby	LB	6-1	215	24	2	Notre Dame
42	Lott, Ronnie	CB	6-0	199	22	R	USC
29	Martin, Saladin	CB	6-1	180	26	2	San Diego State
53	McColl, Milt	LB	6-6	220	22	R	Stanford
3	Miller, Jim	P	5-11	183	24	2	Mississippi
16	Montana, Joe	QB	6-2	200	25	3	Notre Dame
32	Patton, Ricky	RB	5-11	192	27	4	Jackson State
65	Pillers, Lawrence	DE	6-4	260	29	6	Alcorn State
54	Puki, Craig	LB	6-1	231	25	2	Tennessee
56	Quillan, Fred	C	6-5	260	25	4	Oregon
80	Ramson, Eason	TE	6-2	234	25	3	Washington State
78	Reese, Archie	NT	6-3	262	25	4	Clemson
64	Reynolds, Jack	LB	6-1	232	34	12	Tennessee
30	Ring, Bill	RB-KR	5-10	215	25	1	Brigham Young
84	Shumann, Mike	WR	6-0	175	26	4	Florida State
88	Solomon, Freddie	WR-KR	5-11	185	29	7	Tampa
79	Stuckey, Jim	DE	6-4	251	23	2	Clemson
28	Thomas, Lynn	CB	5-11	181	22	R	Pittsburgh
58	Turner, Keena	LB	6-2	219	23	2	Purdue
14	Wersching, Ray	K	5-11	210	31	9	California
27	Williamson, Carlton	S	6-0	204	23	R	Pittsburgh
85	Wilson, Mike	WR	6-3	210	23	R	Washington State
21	Wright, Eric	CB	6-1	180	22	R	Missouri
86	Young, Charle	TE	6-4	234	30	9	USC

Head coach—Bill Walsh. **Assistants**—Cas Banaszek, Norb Hecker, Milt Jackson, Billie Matthews, Bobb McKittrick, Bill McPherson, George Seifert, Chuck Studley, Al Vermeil, Sam Wyche.

CINCINNATI BENGALS

No.	Name	Pos.	Ht.	Wt.	Age	Year	College
40	Alexander, Charles	RB	6-1	221	24	3	Louisiana State
14	Anderson, Ken	QB	6-3	212	32	11	Augustana, Illinois
84	Bass, Don	WR-TE	6-2	220	25	4	Houston
10	Breech, Jim	K	5-6	161	25	3	California
34	Breeden, Louis	CB	5-11	185	28	4	North Carolina Central
79	Browner, Ross	DE	6-3	261	27	4	Notre Dame
74	Bujnoch, Glenn	G	6-5	258	28	6	Texas A&M
67	Burley, Gary	DE	6-3	274	29	6	Pittsburgh
58	Bush, Blair	C	6-3	252	25	4	Washington
50	Cameron, Glenn	LB	6-2	228	28	7	Florida
80	Collinsworth, Cris	WR	6-5	192	22	R	Florida
85	Curtis, Isaac	WR	6-1	192	31	9	San Diego State
21	Davis, Oliver	S	6-1	205	27	5	Tennessee
52	Dinkel, Tom	LB	6-3	237	25	4	Kansas
73	Edwards, Eddie	DE	6-5	256	27	5	Miami
49	Frazier, Guy	LB	6-2	215	22	R	Wyoming
42	Fuller, Mike	S	5-10	182	28	7	Auburn
45	Griffin, Archie	RB	5-9	184	27	6	Ohio State
44	Griffin, Ray	CB	5-10	186	25	4	Ohio State
36	Hargrove, Jim	RB	6-2	228	24	R	Wake Forest
53	Harris, Bo	LB	6-3	226	29	7	Louisiana State
83	Harris, M. L.	TE	6-5	238	28	2	Kansas State
27	Hicks, Bryan	S	6-0	192	25	2	McNeese State
71	Horn, Rod	NT	6-4	268	25	2	Nebraska
46	Johnson, Pete	RB	6-0	249	27	5	Ohio State
26	Kemp, Bobby	S	6-0	186	22	R	Cal State-Fullerton
86	Kreider, Steve	WR	6-3	192	23	3	Lehigh
62	Lapham, Dave	G	6-4	262	29	8	Syracuse
55	LeClair, Jim	LB	6-3	234	31	10	North Dakota
87	McInally, Pat	P-WR	6-6	212	28	6	Harvard
65	Montoya, Max	G	6-5	275	25	3	UCLA
60	Moore, Blake	C-T	6-5	267	23	2	Wooster
78	Munoz, Anthony	T	6-6	278	23	2	USC
68	Obrovac, Mike	G	6-6	275	26	R	Bowling Green
51	Razzano, Rick	LB	5-11	227	26	2	Virginia Tech
13	Riley, Ken	CB	6-0	183	34	13	Florida A&M
89	Ross, Dan	TE	6-4	235	24	3	Northeastern
72	St. Clair, Mike	DE	6-5	254	28	6	Grambling
15	Schonert, Turk	QB	6-1	185	25	2	Stanford
25	Simmons, John	CB	5-11	192	23	R	Southern Methodist
12	Thompson, Jack	QB	6-3	217	25	3	Washington State
81	Verser, David	WR-KR	6-1	200	23	R	Kansas
75	Whitley, Wilson	NT	6-3	265	26	5	Houston
57	Williams, Reggie	LB	6-0	228	25	6	Dartmouth
77	Wilson, Mike	T	6-5	271	26	4	Georgia

Head coach—Forrest Gregg. **Assistants**—Hank Bullough, Bruce Coslet, Lindy Infante, Dick LeBeau, Jim McNally, Dick Modzelewski, George Sefcik, Kim Wood.

SUPER BOWL HISTORY

Date	Game	Result	Winning League or Conference	Site (attendance)
Jan. 15, 1967	I	Green Bay 35, Kansas City 10	NFL	Los Angeles Memorial Coliseum (61,946)
Jan. 14, 1968	II	Green Bay 33, Oakland 14	NFL	Orange Bowl, Miami (75,546)
Jan. 12, 1969	III	N.Y. Jets 16, Baltimore 7	AFL	Orange Bowl, Miami (75,389)
Jan. 11, 1970	IV	Kansas City 23, Minnesota 7	AFL	Tulane Stadium, New Orleans (80,562)
Jan. 17, 1971	V	Baltimore 16, Dallas 13	AFC	Orange Bowl, Miami (79,204)
Jan. 16, 1972	VI	Dallas 24, Miami 3	NFC	Tulane Stadium, New Orleans (81,023)
Jan. 14, 1973	VII	Miami 14, Washington 7	AFC	Los Angeles Memorial Coliseum (90,182)
Jan. 13, 1974	VIII	Miami 24, Minnesota 7	AFC	Rice Stadium, Houston (71,882)
Jan. 12, 1975	IX	Pittsburgh 16, Minnesota 6	AFC	Tulane Stadium, New Orleans (80,997)
Jan. 18, 1976	X	Pittsburgh 21, Dallas 17	AFC	Orange Bowl, Miami (80,187)
Jan. 9, 1977	XI	Oakland 32, Minnesota 14	AFC	Rose Bowl, Pasadena (100,421)
Jan. 15, 1978	XII	Dallas 27, Denver 10	NFC	Louisiana Superdome, New Orleans (75,583)
Jan. 21, 1979	XIII	Pittsburgh 35, Dallas 31	AFC	Orange Bowl, Miami (79,484)
Jan. 20, 1980	XIV	Pittsburgh 31, Los Angeles 19	AFC	Rose Bowl, Pasadena (103,985)
Jan. 25, 1981	XV	Oakland 27, Philadelphia 10	AFC	Louisiana Superdome, New Orleans (76,135)
Jan. 24, 1982	XVI	San Francisco 26, Cincinnati 21	NFC	Silverdome, Pontiac (81,270)

Championship Games

1933

CHI. BEARS 23, N.Y. GIANTS 21

Karr (22) catches Hewitt lateral, scores TD.

The Chicago Bears came from behind in the final three minutes to defeat the New York Giants 23–21.

The Bears, trailing 7–6 at the half, 14–9 in the third quarter, and 21–16 in the fourth quarter, went ahead for the last time after the Giants' Ken Strong punted eight yards and Chicago took over on New York's 46 yard line. Keith Molesworth passed nine yards to Carl Brumbaugh. Bronko Nagurski, the Bears' leading rusher with 65 yards in 14 carries, gained four yards to the 33. On the next play, Nagurski threw a jump pass to Bill Hewitt. Hewitt gained 14 yards and lateraled to Bill Karr. Karr covered the remaining 19 yards for the winning score.

Fog hung over Wrigley Field and it was misting in the first half, when the Giants took a 7–6 lead on Harry Newman's 29-yard pass to Morris (Red) Badgro.

Newman, who completed 12 of 17 passes for 201 yards and two touchdowns, figured in the game's most exciting play on the first play of the fourth quarter. After the Bears went in front 16–14, Newman began moving the Giants from their 26 yard line. Five successive pass completions put the ball on the Bears' 8. Strong took a handoff on the next play but became trapped near the sideline. He lateraled to the surprised Newman, who scrambled until he was trapped at the 15. Newman then threw a desperation pass to Strong, who had slipped free in the corner of the end zone and caught the ball for a touchdown.

December 17, at Chicago

N.Y. Giants	Starting Lineups	Chi. Bears
Morris (Red) Badgro	LE	Bill Hewitt
Len Grant	LT	Roy (Link) Lyman
Denver (Butch) Gibson	LG	Jules Carlson
Mel Hein	C	Charles (Ookie) Miller
Tom (Pottsville) Jones	RG	Joe Kopcha
Steve Owen	RT	George Musso
Ray Flaherty	RE	Bill Karr
Harry Newman	QB	Carl Brumbaugh
Ken Strong	LH	Keith Molesworth
Dale Burnett	RH	Gene Ronzani
John (Bo) Molenda	FB	Bronko Nagurski

N.Y. Giants	0	7	7	7	— 21
Chi. Bears	3	10	7	—	23

Chi —FG Manders 16
Chi —FG Manders 40
NYG—Badgro 29 pass from Newman (Strong kick)
Chi —FG Manders 28
NYG—Krause 1 run (Strong kick)
Chi —Karr 8 pass from Nagurski (Manders kick)
NYG—Strong 8 pass from Newman (Strong kick)
Chi —Karr 19 lateral from Hewitt, who caught 14 pass from Nagurski (Brumbaugh kick)
Attendance—26,000

TEAM STATISTICS	NYG	Chi
First downs	13	12
Rushing	4	9
Passing	8	3
By penalty	1	0
Total yardage	307	311
Net rushing yardage	99	161
Net passing yardage	208	150
Passes att.-comp.-had int.	20-14-1	16-7-1

1934

N.Y. GIANTS 30, CHI. BEARS 13

Strong's 38-yard field goal gives Giants a 3-0 lead.

The New York Giants rallied for 27 points to overcome a 13–3 Chicago lead and score a 30–13 victory in the "sneakers game." The Giants switched from football shoes to basketball shoes on a frozen field in the Polo Grounds.

Giants' president John V. Mara inspected the playing field the morning of the game and reported the condition to head coach Steve Owen. The temperature was nine degrees. Owen and team captain Ray Flaherty discussed the idea of wearing basketball shoes. Some of the Giants' players were asked to bring their own sneakers to the game. Abe Cohen, a clubhouse equipment aide, made a trip to Manhattan College for additional pairs. There were no sporting goods stores open.

The Giants did not put on the rubber-soled shoes until the start of the third quarter. They trailed 10–3 at the half and fell behind 13–3 in the third quarter. The comeback did not begin until well into the final period. Rookie Ed Danowski, who replaced the injured Harry Newman at tailback in the Giants' single-wing formation in midseason, threw a 28-yard touchdown pass to Malcolm (Ike) Frankian to make the score 13–10. The Bears did not advance on their next possession and, after a 20-yard punt, the Giants took over on Chicago's 42. Ken Strong, behind blocking from tackle Bill Morgan, fullback John (Bo) Molenda, and Danowski ran straight up the field for a touchdown to give New York a 17–13 lead.

December 9, at New York

Chi. Bears	Starting Lineups	N.Y. Giants
Bill Hewitt	LE	Malcolm (Ike) Frankian
Roy (Link) Lyman	LT	Bill Morgan
Bert Pearson	LG	Denver (Butch) Gibson
Ed Kawal	C	Mel Hein
Jules Carlson	RG	Tom (Pottsville) Jones
George Musso	RT	Cecil (Tex) Irvin
Bill Karr	RE	Ray Flaherty
Carl Brumbaugh	QB	Ed Danowski
Gene Ronzani	LH	Dale Burnett
Keith Molesworth	RH	Ken Strong
Bronko Nagurski	FB	John (Bo) Molenda

Chi. Bears	0	10	3	0	— 13
N.Y. Giants	3	0	0	27	— 30

NYG—FG Strong 38
Chi —Nagurski 1 run (Manders kick)
Chi —FG Manders 17
Chi —FG Manders 24
NYG—Frankian 28 pass from Danowski (Strong kick)
NYG—Strong 42 run (Strong kick)
NYG—Strong 11 run (kick failed)
NYG—Danowski 9 run (Molenda kick)
Attendance—35,059

TEAM STATISTICS	Chi	NYG
First downs	10	12
Rushing	7	7
Passing	3	5
By penalty	0	0
Total yardage	165	276
Net rushing yardage	89	173
Net passing yardage	76	103
Passes att.-comp.-had int.	15-6-3	12-7-2

1935

DETROIT 26, N.Y. GIANTS 7

Gutowsky's two-yard run puts Lions ahead 6-0.

The Detroit Lions took the opening kickoff and marched 61 yards to a touchdown and never trailed the New York Giants on a day when wind, rain, sleet, and snow turned the University of Detroit field into a swamp. The Lions' 26–7 victory marked their first NFL championship and it came two months after the baseball Tigers had won their first World Series.

Ace Gutowsky ran two yards for Detroit's first score. Earl (Dutch) Clark increased the Lions' lead to 13–0 in the first period with a twisting run of 40 yards. The Giants did not score until midway in the second quarter, when Ed Danowski threw a pass to Ken Strong. Gutowsky, who was defending on the play, deflected the pass with his fingertips but Strong gained control of the ball and ran 31 yards to complete a 42-yard play.

With three minutes left in the game Danowski tried a quick-kick, but the kick was low and hit the back of one of the Giants' blockers. Detroit's George Christiansen recovered on New York's 26 yard line. The Lions ran five plays into the line. On the sixth, from the 4 yard line, Clark faked into the middle and Ernie Caddel swept around the drawn-in defense for a touchdown.

Harry Newman returned the kickoff to the Giants' 32 yard line, then replaced Danowski as New York lined up in a T-formation. Raymond (Buddy) Parker intercepted Newman's flat pass on first down and ran 22 yards to the 10. Caddel ran four yards and Parker two before Parker scored from the 4 yard line in the final seconds.

December 15, at Detroit

N.Y. Giants	Starting Lineups	Detroit
Malcolm (Ike) Frankian	LE	Ed Klewicki
Bill Morgan	LT	John Johnson
Tom (Pottsville) Jones	LG	Regis Monahan
Mel Hein	C	Clare Randolph
Bill Owen	RG	Grover (Ox) Emerson
Len Grant	RT	George Christiansen
Charles (Tod) Goodwin	RE	John Schneller
Ed Danowski	QB	Glenn Presnell
Elvin (Kink) Richards	LH	Frank Christiansen
Ken Strong	RH	Ernie Caddel
Les (Red) Corzine	FB	Leroy (Ace) Gutowsky

N.Y. Giants	0	7	0	0	— 7
Detroit	13	0	0	13	— 26

Det —Gutowsky 2 run (Presnell kick)
Det —Clark 40 run (kick failed)
NYG—Strong 42 pass from Danowski (Strong kick)
Det —Caddel 4 run (kick failed)
Det —Parker 4 run (Clark kick)
Attendance—15,000

TEAM STATISTICS	NYG	Det
First downs	9	16
Rushing	4	14
Passing	3	2
By penalty	2	0
Total yardage	194	298
Net rushing yardage	106	246
Net passing yardage	88	52
Passes att.-comp.-had int.	13-4-2	5-2-0

1936

GREEN BAY 21, BOSTON REDSKINS 6

Hinkle (41) gains 10 yards for Packers.

The Polo Grounds was the site of the championship game, although the participating teams were Western champion Green Bay and Eastern champion Boston. George Preston Marshall, owner of the Redskins, moved the game from Boston to New York, because the Redskins were going to transfer to another city, most likely Washington. Green Bay won 21–6.

For the first time in the four-year history of the championship game, the weather was not severe. The temperature was 36 degrees and the sun was shining.

Boston's all-league halfback Cliff Battles, who gained 18 yards in his first two carries, was injured on the tenth play of the game. On that play, teammate Riley Smith fumbled Battles's lateral and Lou Gordon recovered for Green Bay on the Packers' 46-yard line. Three plays later Arnie Herber completed a touchdown pass to Don Hutson on a long side line pattern. The play covered 50 yards and put Green Bay ahead 7–0 after Ernie Smith's conversion kick.

Ernest (Pug) Rentner, Battles's replacement, scored Boston's only touchdown in the second quarter. Rentner gained 13 yards in five carries and completed two passes for 41 yards in a 10-play, 78-yard drive that ended with Rentner's scoring the 2.

Green Bay increased its lead to 14–6 in the third quarter on Herber's five-yard pass to Milt Gantenbein. A 55-yard pass play—Herber to Johnny Blood (McNally)—set up the score. Boston's Riley Smith was in punt formation from the Redskins' 22 yard line in the fourth quarter when his kick was blocked by Lon Evans and recovered on the 3 yard line by Clarke Hinkle. Bob Monnett, who was in the game for Herber, scored on the second play from the 3.

December 13, at New York

Green Bay	Starting Lineups	Boston
Milt Gantenbein	LE	Wayne Millner
Ernie Smith	LT	Glen (Turk) Edwards
Paul Engebretsen	LG	Les Olsson
George Svendsen	C	Frank Bausch
Lon Evans	RG	Jim Karcher
Lou Gordon	RT	Jim Barber
Don Hutson	RE	Charley Malone
Hank Bruder	QB	Riley Smith
George Sauer	LH	Cliff Battles
Arnie Herber	RH	Ed Justice
Clarke Hinkle	FB	Don Irwin

Green Bay	7	0	7	7	—	21
Boston	0	6	0	0	—	6

GB —Hutson 50 pass from Herber (E. Smith kick)
Bos—Rentner 2 run (kick failed)
GB —Gantenbein 5 pass from Herber (E. Smith kick)
GB —Monnett 3 run (Engebretsen kick)
Attendance—29,545

TEAM STATISTICS	GB	Bos
First downs	7	8
Rushing	2	4
Passing	4	3
By penalty	1	1
Total yardage	220	130
Net rushing yardage	67	39
Net passing yardage	153	91
Passes att.-comp.-had int.	23-9-2	26-7-1

1937

WASHINGTON 28, CHI. BEARS 21

Baugh throws for one of three TDs.

Sammy Baugh completed 18 of 33 passes for 335 yards and three touchdowns, including scoring passes of 78 and 35 yards in the fourth quarter as the Washington Redskins came from behind to defeat the Chicago Bears 28–21. Baugh's performance was achieved on an icy field in 15-degree weather.

Baugh, a rookie from Texas Christian University, established the Redskins' intentions on their first play from scrimmage. Passing from his own end zone, Baugh hit fullback Cliff Battles, who advanced the ball to Washington's 49, a gain of 42 yards. The Redskins were forced to punt, but the next time they had possession Baugh moved them 53 yards in 10 plays to a touchdown.

The Bears contained the Redskins for the remainder of the half and led 14–7 in the third quarter. Washington tied the score when Baugh passed to Wayne Millner, who ran a crossing pattern, caught the ball at Chicago's 35 yard line, and outran Bernie Masterson to complete a 55-yard play.

After Chicago went back in front 21–14 with a touchdown that concluded a 13-play, 73-yard advance, the Redskins struck for their two last-quarter touchdowns. They took the kickoff on their 22-yard line with 9:04 remaining in the game. On the first play, Baugh threw a 28-yard pass to Millner, who ran 50 yards, with Jack Manders and Bronko Nagurski in pursuit, to score on a 78-yard play. After the Bears punted following the next kickoff, Washington went 80 yards in 11 plays, Baugh combining with Ed Justice on a 35-yard scoring pass.

December 12, at Chicago

Washington	Starting Lineups	Chi. Bears
Wayne Millner	LE	Edgar (Eggs) Manske
Glen (Turk) Edwards	LT	Joe Stydahar
Les Olsson	LG	Danny Fortmann
Ed Kawal	C	Frank Bausch
Jim Karcher	RG	George Musso
Jim Barber	RT	Del Bjork
Charley Malone	RE	George Wilson
Riley Smith	QB	Bernie Masterson
Sammy Baugh	LH	Ray Nolting
Erny Pinckert	RH	Jack Manders
Cliff Battles	FB	Bronko Nagurski

Washington	7	0	21	0	—	28
Chi. Bears	14	0	7	0	—	21

Wash—Battles 7 run (R. Smith kick)
Chi —Manders 10 run (Manders kick)
Chi —Manders 37 pass from Masterson (Manders kick)
Wash—Millner 55 pass from Baugh (R. Smith kick)
Chi —Manske 3 pass from Masterson (Manders kick)
Wash—Millner 78 pass from Baugh (R. Smith kick)
Wash—Justice 35 pass from Baugh (R. Smith kick)
Attendance—15,870

TEAM STATISTICS	Wash	Chi
First downs	18	11
Rushing	8	7
Passing	10	4
By penalty	0	0
Total yardage	441	335
Net rushing yardage	70	128
Net passing yardage	371	207
Passes att.-comp.-had int.	40-22-3	31-8-3

1938

N.Y. GIANTS 23, GREEN BAY 17

Giants' blockers clear Leemans for 14-yard gain.

The Green Bay Packers outgained the New York Giants 379-212 in total yardage, but the Giants' defense blocked two punts that led to nine points and a 23–17 victory. The crowd of 48,120 on a 31-degree afternoon in the Polo Grounds set a record.

Clarke Hinkle was in punt formation on his goal line with third down and 11 yards for a first down during the Packers' second possession in the first quarter. The Giants' Jim Lee Howell blocked Hinkle's kick and Leland Shaffer recovered for New York on the 7 yard line. Ward Cuff kicked a 14-yard field goal on fourth down for a 3–0 lead.

Cecil Isbell's punt was blocked by Jim Poole with Howell recovering on Green Bay's 28 during the Packers' next possession. Alphonse (Tuffy) Leemans ran six yards for a touchdown four plays later. After John Gildea missed the extra point, the Packers replaced their entire team except for guard Charles (Buckets) Goldenberg.

Green Bay took a 17–16 lead in the third quarter when it marched 53 yards to Paul Engebretsen's 15-yard field goal. The Giants began the following series on their 39-yard line. Halfback Hank Soar carried the ball on five of the next six plays. He threw an incomplete pass on the seventh, then caught a pass for nine yards from quarterback Ed Danowski, and ran three yards to put the ball on Green Bay's 23 yard line. Danowski lofted a 17-yard pass. Soar and Poole leaped for the ball with two defenders. Soar made the catch and dragged a Packers defensive back the last six yards for the winning touchdown.

December 11, at New York

Green Bay	Starting Lineups	N.Y. Giants
Wayland Becker	LE	Jim Poole
Champ Seibold	LT	Ed Widseth
Russ Letlow	LG	John Dell Isola
Lee Mulleneaux	C	Mel Hein
Charles Goldenberg	RG	Orville Tuttle
Bill Lee	RT	Owen (Ox) Parry
Milt Gantenbein	RE	Jim Lee Howell
Herman Schneidman	QB	Ed Danowski
Cecil Isbell	LH	Hank Soar
Joe Laws	RH	Ward Cuff
Clarke Hinkle	FB	Leland Shaffer

Green Bay	0	14	3	0	—	17
N.Y. Giants	9	7	7	0	—	23

NYG—FG Cuff 14
NYG—Leemans 6 run (kick failed)
GB —C. Mulleneaux 40 pass from Herber (Engebretsen kick)
NYG—Barnard 21 pass from Danowski (Cuff kick)
GB —Hinkle 1 run (Engebretsen kick)
GB —FG Engebretsen 15
NYG—Soar 23 pass from Danowski (Cuff kick)
Attendance—48,120

TEAM STATISTICS	GB	NYG
First downs	14	10
Rushing	9	6
Passing	4	2
By penalty	1	2
Total yardage	378	212
Net rushing yardage	164	118
Net passing yardage	214	94
Passes att.-comp.-had int.	19-8-1	15-8-1

1939

GREEN BAY 27, N.Y. GIANTS 0

Giants' Falaschi (left) recovers blocked punt.

Winds blowing across the Wisconsin flatlands through the open ends of Milwaukee's State Fair Park were measured in gusts up to 35 miles per hour. The Green Bay Packers' passers, Arnie Herber and Cecil Isbell, were intercepted three times, but they completed 7 of 10 attempts for 96 yards and two touchdowns. Giants passers completed 9 of 26 passes for 98 yards and had 6 intercepted as the Packers scored a 27–0 victory.

The Packers scored on a 54-yard drive in the first quarter when Herber passed seven yards to Milt Gantenbein, who was open between the goal posts in the end zone after the Giants assigned double coverage to Don Hutson. The score was 7–0 at the half. New York had three scoring opportunities, but Ward Cuff missed field goal attempts of 42 and 41 yards, and Lem Barnum missed from 47.

Paul Engebretsen put the Packers in front 10–0 with a 23-yard field goal in the third quarter. Joe Laws returned a punt 30 yards to his 45 and the Packers moved 32 yards in seven plays to position Engebretsen. The score became 17–0 in the third quarter after Gantenbein intercepted a pass by Ed Danowski at the Giants' 33. Cecil Isbell threw a 25-yard pass on second down to Laws, who caught the ball on the 6 yard line and scored to complete a 31-yard play.

Ernie Smith's 42-yard field goal and Ed Jankowski's one-yard run finished the scoring in the fourth quarter. The Giants were on the 3-yard line when the game ended. Their deepest penetration had been the 16 in the third quarter, when the score was 17–0.

December 10, at Milwaukee

N.Y. Giants	Starting Lineups	Green Bay
Jim Poole	LE	Don Hutson
Frank Cope	LT	Buford (Baby) Ray
John Dell Isola	LG	Russ Letlow
Mel Hein	C	Earl Svendsen
Orville Tuttle	RG	Charles Goldenberg
John Mellus	RT	Bill Lee
Jim Lee Howell	RE	Milt Gantenbein
Ed Danowski	QB	Larry Craig
Elvin (Kink) Richards	LH	Cecil Isbell
Ward Cuff	RH	Joe Laws
Nello Falaschi	FB	Clarke Hinkle

N.Y. Giants	0	0	0	0	— 0
Green Bay	7	0	10	10	— 27

GB—Gantenbein 7 pass from Herber (Engebretsen kick)
GB—FG Engebretsen 23
GB—Laws 31 pass from Isbell (Engebretsen kick)
GB—FG E. Smith 42
GB—Jankowski 1 run (E. Smith kick)
Attendance—32,279

TEAM STATISTICS	NYG	GB
First downs	9	10
Rushing	5	6
Passing	3	2
By penalty	1	2
Total yardage	168	230
Net rushing yardage	70	131
Net passing yardage	98	99
Passes att.-comp.-had int.	26-9-6	10-7-3

1940

CHI. BEARS 73, WASHINGTON 0

Osmanski turns corner on 68-yard run for score.

Fullback Bill Osmanski of the Chicago Bears ran around left end for 68 yards and a touchdown on the second play of the game. The next time the Bears were on offense they held possession of the ball for 17 plays, marching 79 yards and two feet before scoring on quarterback Sid Luckman's one-foot plunge. The third time Chicago had the ball, fullback Joe Maniaci swept end for 42 yards and a touchdown on the first play. The Bears scored three touchdowns in the first 12 minutes, 40 seconds of the game; they rushed for 382 yards overall, amassed 501 total yards, intercepted eight passes, and won their second NFL championship, 73–0 over the Washington Redskins, the team that had beaten them 7–3 three weeks before in the ninth game of the season.

The Bears led 28–0 at the half after Luckman's 30-yard touchdown pass to Ken Kavanaugh. Luckman did not play the second half; quarterbacks Bernie Masterson, Bob Snyder, and Saul Sherman directed the team on four more scoring drives. The defense returned three passes for touchdowns. Redskins fans in Griffith Stadium began hooting in derision whenever the home team did something positive.

The Bears' T-formation with man-in-motion was awesome. Stanford University also had the T in 1940. It became the game's most popular formation.

December 8, at Washington

Chi. Bears	Starting Lineups	Washington
Bob Nowaskey	LE	Bob Masterson
Joe Stydahar	LT	Willie Wilkin
Danny Fortmann	LG	Dick Farman
Clyde (Bulldog) Turner	C	Bob Titchenal
George Musso	RG	Steve Slivinski
Lee Artoe	RT	Jim Barber
George Wilson	RE	Charley Malone
Sid Luckman	QB	Max Krause
Ray Nolting	LH	Sammy Baugh
George McAfee	RH	Ed Justice
Bill Osmanski	FB	Jim Johnston

Chi. Bears	21	7	26	19	— 73
Washington	0	0	0	0	— 0

Chi—Osmanski 68 run (Manders kick)
Chi—Luckman 1 run (Snyder kick)
Chi—Maniaci 42 run (Martinovich kick)
Chi—Kavanaugh 30 pass from Luckman (Snyder kick)
Chi—Pool 15 interception return (Plasman kick)
Chi—Nolting 23 run (kick failed)
Chi—McAfee 34 interception return (Stydahar kick)
Chi—Turner 24 interception return (kick failed)
Chi—Clark 44 run (kick failed)
Chi—Famiglietti 2 run (Maniaci, pass from Sherman)
Chi—Clark 1 run (pass failed)
Attendance—36,034

TEAM STATISTICS	Chi	Wash
First downs	17	17
Rushing	13	4
Passing	3	10
By penalty	1	3
Total yardage	501	245
Net rushing yardage	382	22
Net passing yardage	119	223
Passes att.-comp.-had int.	10-7-0	51-20-8

1941

CHI. BEARS 37, N.Y. GIANTS 9

Bears' Standlee (22) stops Leemans.

The Chicago Bears won their third championship and became the first team to win two in a row when they broke a 9–9 tie in the third quarter and defeated the New York Giants 37–9. The Wrigley Field crowd of 13,341 persons was the smallest in playoff history, coming one week after the Bears defeated Green Bay 33–14 for the Western Conference championship in a divisional playoff before 43,425.

The Bears trailed 6–3 at the end of the first quarter. They led 9–6 at the half after having possession of the ball 53 plays to the Giants' 10. Chicago controlled the ball for the first 10:34 of the first quarter, scoring on Bob Snyder's 14-yard field goal. This followed a series of penalties against Chicago and a blocked field goal that hit New York's Ken (Kayo) Lunday in the face but was recovered by the Bears. New York scored its only touchdown after the field goal. It marched 59 yards in four plays, scoring on Alphonse (Tuffy) Leemans's 31-yard pass to George Franck.

The Bears, who had a total yardage edge of 389–157, began pulling away from the Giants after Ward Cuff's 16-yard field goal tied the score in the first three minutes of the third quarter. The Bears went 71, 66, and 54 yards for touchdowns. Their last score came in the final nine seconds of the game. The Giants' Hank Soar lateraled to Andy Marefos, who attempted to throw a pass on a halfback option. Marefos was hit by several Bears defenders and fumbled. Ken Kavanaugh picked up the ball and ran 42 yards.

December 21, at Chicago

N.Y. Giants	Starting Lineups	Chicago Bears
Jim Poole	LE	Dick Plasman
John Mellus	LT	Ed Kolman
Ken (Kayo) Lunday	LG	Danny Fortmann
Mel Hein	C	Clyde (Bulldog) Turner
Len Younce	RG	Ray Bray
Bill Edwards	RT	Lee Artoe
Jim Lee Howell	RE	John Siegal
Nello Falaschi	QB	Sid Luckman
George Franck	LH	Ray Nolting
Ward Cuff	RH	Hugh Gallarneau
Alphonse (Tuffy) Leemans	FB	Norm Standlee

N.Y. Giants	6	0	3	0	— 9
Chi. Bears	3	6	14	14	— 37

Chi —FG Snyder 14
NYG—Franck 31 pass from Leemans (kick failed)
Chi —FG Snyder 39
Chi —FG Snyder 37
NYG—FG Cuff 16
Chi —Standlee 2 run (Snyder kick)
Chi —Standlee 7 run (Maniaci kick)
Chi —McAfee 5 run (Artoe kick)
Chi —Kavanaugh 42 fumble return (McLean kick)
Attendance—13,341

TEAM STATISTICS	NYG	Chi
First downs	8	20
Rushing	4	14
Passing	2	5
By penalty	2	1
Total yardage	157	389
Net rushing yardage	84	207
Net passing yardage	73	182
Passes att.-comp.-had int.	15-3-3	19-11-0

1942

WASHINGTON 14, CHI. BEARS 6

Bears (striped jerseys) surround Farkas.

The Washington Redskins defeated the Chicago Bears 14–6 in a game in which the Bears were favored by 22 points. Chicago had won 24 games in a row, including postseason and exhibition contests, and 39 of its previous 40 games. The Bears had not been beaten since a 16–14 loss to Green Bay November 2, 1941.

Chicago took a 6–0 lead in the second quarter when Lee Artoe, a 230-pound tackle, ran 50 yards for a touchdown with a recovered fumble. The fumble resulted when Chicago's George Wilson tackled Dick Todd. The Redskins returned the following kickoff to the Bears' 42 yard line and scored in three plays, Sammy Baugh passing 38 yards to Wilbur Moore for the touchdown. Andy Farkas's one-yard run in the third quarter completed the scoring.

Baugh, who completed 5 of 13 passes for 66 yards, made one of the game's biggest defensive plays when he stopped a Bears' drive that had reached Washington's 12 yard line by intercepting a pass in the end zone. The Bears marched to the Redskins' 27 and 28 yard lines in the first period but came up empty when Artoe missed a 46-yard field goal the first time and they fumbled the second time. Chicago went 79 yards from its 20 to Washington's 1 in the fourth quarter. Halfback Hugh Gallarneau scored on the next play, but the Bears were penalized for backfield in motion. They surrendered the ball on downs and the Redskins controlled possession the last three minutes.

Washington and Chicago each finished the season with 11–1 records, including the championship playoff. The Redskins' loss was 14–7 to New York, which was beaten 26–7 by Chicago.

December 13, at Washington

Chi. Bears	Starting Lineups	Washington
Bob Nowaskey	LE	Bob Masterson
Ed Kolman	LT	Willie Wilkin
Danny Fortmann	LG	Dick Farman
Clyde (Bulldog) Turner	C	Charles (Ki) Aldrich
Ray Bray	RG	Steve Slivinski
Lee Artoe	RT	Bill Young
George Wilson	RE	Ed Cifers
Sid Luckman	QB	Ray Hare
Ray Nolting	LH	Sammy Baugh
Hugh Gallarneau	RH	Ed Justice
Gary Famiglietti	FB	Andy Farkas

Chi. Bears	0	6	0	0	—	6
Washington	0	7	7	0	—	14

Chi —Artoe 50 fumble return (kick failed)
Wash—Moore 38 pass from Baugh (Masterson kick)
Wash—Farkas 1 run (Masterson kick)
Attendance—36,006

TEAM STATISTICS	Chi	Wash
First downs	10	9
Rushing	4	5
Passing	5	2
By penalty	1	2
Total yardage	199	166
Net rushing yardage	69	101
Net passing yardage	130	65
Passes att.-comp.-had int.	20-10-3	13-5-2

1943

CHI. BEARS 41, WASHINGTON 21

Moore skirts Bears' defense.

Quarterback Sid Luckman completed 14 of 26 passes for 276 yards and five touchdowns and rushed for 64 yards in eight carries as the Chicago Bears defeated Washington 41–21.

The Bears, who were idle for 29 days after clinching the NFL West championship with a victory over the Chicago Cardinals, gained a total of 455 yards to the Redskins' 249 but trailed 7–0 after Andy Farkas concluded a 60-yard Redskins drive with a one-yard run in the second quarter. The Bears went 67 and 55 yards for touchdowns after the Washington score to take a 14–7 lead.

Redskins quarterback Sammy Baugh left the game after one play of the first quarter and sat on the bench weeping for the remainder of the half as physicians tried to determine the severity of a concussion he sustained on the opening kickoff. Baugh returned in the second half and completed 7 of 11 passes for 106 yards and two touchdowns. His replacement, George Cafego, completed 3 of 11 for 76 yards.

The championship game was the third in four years between the Bears and Washington. Typical of the rivalry between them was an incident in the first half when Redskins owner George Preston Marshall was ejected from the playing field after attempting to gain access to the Redskins' bench. Bears general manager Ralph Brizzolara ordered police to remove Marshall, who returned later and termed the Bears' action "a first-class, bush league trick."

December 26, at Chicago

Washington	Starting Lineups	Chicago Bears
Bob Masterson	LE	Jim Benton
Lou Rymkus	LT	Dominic Sigillo
Clyde Shugart	LG	Danny Fortmann
George Smith	C	Clyde (Bulldog) Turner
Steve Slivinski	RG	George Musso
Joe Pasqua	RT	Al Hoptowit
Joe Aguirre	RE	George Wilson
Ray Hare	QB	Bob Snyder
Frank Seno	LH	Harry Clark
George Cafego	RH	Dante Magnani
Andy Farkas	FB	Bob Masters

Washington	0	7	7	7	—	21
Chi. Bears	0	14	13	14	—	41

Wash—Farkas 1 run (Masterson kick)
Chi —Nagurski 3 run (Snyder kick)
Chi —Clark 31 pass from Luckman (Snyder kick)
Chi —Magnani 36 pass from Luckman (Snyder kick)
Chi —Magnani 66 pass from Luckman (kick failed)
Wash—Farkas 17 pass from Baugh (Masterson kick)
Chi —Benton 26 pass from Luckman (Snyder kick)
Chi —Clark 16 pass from Luckman (Snyder kick)
Wash—Aguirre 25 pass from Baugh (Aguirre kick)
Attendance—34,320

TEAM STATISTICS	Wash	Chi
First downs	11	14
Rushing	4	8
Passing	6	6
By penalty	1	0
Total yardage	249	455
Net rushing yardage	50	169
Net passing yardage	199	286
Passes att.-comp.-had int.	24-11-4	27-15-0

1944

GREEN BAY 14, N.Y. GIANTS 7

Laws gains 72 yards in 13 carries for the Packers.

The Green Bay Packers won their third NFL championship and first in five years when they scored a 14–7 victory over the New York Giants, who were losers for the fifth time in seven championship games. The Packers, who outgained the Giants 235-187 in total yards, scored both of their touchdowns in the second quarter on plays involving fullback Ted Fritsch.

Fritsch scored on a one-yard run early in the quarter, following a block by left guard Charles (Buckets) Goldenberg, the Packers' 33-year-old, 12-year veteran. The touchdown came on fourth down after the Giants had held the Packers without a gain for three downs.

Fritsch scored again on a 26-yard pass from Irv Comp. Don Hutson, the Packers' all-league end, figured prominently in the play. After Hutson gained 24 yards on a pass from Comp that put the ball on the 30, Hutson served as a decoy on the next play. Hutson ran a crossing pattern from his left end position, drawing the Giants' secondary with him. Fritsch looped out of the backfield and caught Comp's pass on the 5. There wasn't a defender within 10 yards.

New York, which did not advance beyond its 35 yard line in the first half, scored on Ward Cuff's one-yard run in the fourth quarter. Cuff, who had played wingback in the Giants' single-wing formation for his entire eight-season career, scored from the tailback position. The touchdown was set up by a 41-yard pass from Arnie Herber to Frank Liebel. Herber, who had been out of pro football four years before joining the Giants in 1944, played with the Packers from 1930 through 1940.

December 17, at New York

Green Bay	Starting Lineups	N.Y. Giants
Don Hutson	LE	O'Neal Adams
Buford (Baby) Ray	LT	Frank Cope
Bill Kuusisto	LG	Len Younce
Charles Brock	C	Mel Hein
Charles Goldenberg	RG	Jim Sivell
Paul Berezney	RT	Vic Carroll
Harry Jacunski	RE	Frank Liebel
Irv Comp	QB	Len Calligaro
Irv Comp	LH	Arnie Herber
Joe Laws	RH	Ward Cuff
Ted Fritsch	FB	Howie Livingston

Green Bay	0	14	0	0	—	14
N.Y. Giants	0	0	0	7	—	7

GB —Fritsch 1 run (Hutson kick)
GB —Fritsch 26 pass from Comp (Hutson kick)
NYG—Cuff 1 run (Strong kick)
Attendance—46,016

TEAM STATISTICS	GB	NYG
First downs	11	10
Rushing	9	5
Passing	2	4
By penalty	0	1
Total yardage	235	187
Net rushing yardage	162	70
Net passing yardage	73	117
Passes att.-comp.-had int.	11-3-3	22-8-4

1945

CLEVELAND 15, WASHINGTON 14

When Baugh passes, ball hits goal post for safety.

Rookie quarterback Bob Waterfield completed 14 of 27 passes for 192 yards and two touchdowns; halfback Jim Gillette gained 101 yards in 17 carries and scored once, and end Jim Benton caught nine passes for 125 yards and a touchdown as the Cleveland Rams defeated the Washington Redskins 15–14. The difference between a victory and a defeat for Cleveland was a hurriedly thrown pass by Redskins quarterback Sammy Baugh in the first quarter. Baugh's pass from Washington's end zone struck the goal post and fell into the end zone for a safety.

Baugh, who had been injured in the Redskins' victory over the New York Giants the week before, was taken out of the game in the first quarter and returned only to hold the ball on extra points. Frank Filchock, Baugh's replacement, completed 8 of 14 passes for 178 yards and two touchdowns. Filchock helped put the Redskins ahead 7–2 with 9:09 left in the first half when he combined with halfback Steve Bagarus on a 38-yard pass play.

Waterfield's 38-yard pass to Benton put Cleveland back in front with three minutes remaining in the half. Waterfield's extra point was partially blocked and struck the goal post crossbar, teetered for a moment, and dropped into the end zone, giving Cleveland a 9–7 lead. The Rams increased their advantage to 15–7 in the third quarter, when Waterfield threw a 35-yard pass to Gillette, who caught the ball and ran nine yards to complete a 44-yard play.

The game was played in six-degree weather. The Memorial Stadium side line was piled with snow after workers arrived early to clear the playing area.

December 16, at Cleveland

Washington	Starting Lineups	Cleveland
Wayne Millner	LE	Floyd Konetsky
Fred Davis	LT	Eberle Schultz
Al Lolotai	LG	Riley Matheson
Charles (Ki) Aldrich	C	Mike Scarry
Marvin Whited	RG	Milan Lazetich
Earl Audet	RT	Gil Bouley
Doug Turley	RE	Steve Pritko
Sammy Baugh	QB	Steve Nemeth
Dick Todd	LH	Fred Gehrke
Merlyn Condit	RH	Jim Gillette
Frank Akins	FB	Pat West

Washington	0	7	7	0	—	14
Cleveland	2	7	6	0	—	15

Cle —Safety, Baugh's pass hit goal post
Wash—Bagarus 38 pass from Filchock (Aguirre kick)
Cle —Benton 38 pass from Waterfield (Waterfield kick)
Cle —Gillette 44 pass from Waterfield (kick failed)
Wash—Seymour 8 pass from Filchock (Aguirre kick)
Attendance—32,178

TEAM STATISTICS	Wash	Cle
First downs	8	14
Rushing	3	9
Passing	4	4
By penalty	1	1
Total yardage	214	372
Net rushing yardage	35	180
Net passing yardage	179	192
Passes att.-comp.-had int.	20–9–2	27–14–2

1946

CHI. BEARS 24, N.Y. GIANTS 14

Luckman surprises the Giants with 19-yard TD run.

The Chicago Bears won their fifth NFL championship playoff in 14 years when they scored a 24–14 victory over the New York Giants. A crowd of 58,346 persons in the Polo Grounds set a playoff record. The Giants overcame a 14–0 Bears lead, but with the score tied 14–14 early in the fourth quarter, Bears quarterback Sid Luckman crossed up the Giants' defense and scored the winning touchdown. The play was called "ninety-seven bingo, keep it" in the Bears' nomenclature. From the Giants' 19 yard line, Luckman looked over the defense and then called time out for a conference with coach George Halas. "Now?" Luckman inquired of the coach about a specially designed trap play. "Now," said Halas. Luckman faked a handoff to halfback George McAfee, hid the ball on his hip and ran to his right while the Giants' defense followed the Bears' line, which pulled to the left. Luckman scored his only touchdown of 1946 after shaking off a tackler at the 10 yard line and picking up blocks from center Clyde (Bulldog) Turner and guard Ray Bray.

Luckman's run made the score 21–14. He contributed to one other touchdown, throwing a 21-yard pass to Ken Kavanaugh that gave the Bears a 7–0 lead. Luckman completed 9 of 22 passes for 144 yards and a touchdown.

The Giants tied the score in the third quarter. End Jim Lee Howell recovered Joe Osmanski's fumble on Chicago's 20. A roughing penalty put the ball on the 10. Three plays later Frank Filchock passed five yards to Steve Filipowicz.

December 15, at New York

Chi. Bears	Starting Lineups	N.Y. Giants
Ken Kavanaugh	LE	Jim Poole
Fred Davis	LT	DeWitt (Tex) Coulter
Rudy Mucha	LG	Bob Dobelstein
Clyde (Bulldog) Turner	C	Chet Gladchuk
Ray Bray	RG	Len Younce
Mike Jarmoluk	RT	Jim White
George Wilson	RE	Jim Lee Howell
Joe Osmanski	QB	Steve Filipowicz
Dante Magnani	LH	Dave Brown
Hugh Gallarneau	RH	Howie Livingston
Bill Osmanski	FB	Ken Strong

Chi. Bears	14	0	0	10	—	24
N.Y. Giants	7	0	7	0	—	14

Chi —Kavanaugh 21 pass from Luckman (Maznicki kick)
Chi —Magnani 19 pass interception (Maznicki kick)
NYG—Liebel 38 pass from Filchock (Strong kick)
NYG—Filipowicz 5 pass from Filchock (Strong kick)
Chi —Luckman 19 run (Maznicki kick)
Chi —FG Maznicki 26
Attendance—58,346

TEAM STATISTICS	Chi	NYG
First downs	10	13
Rushing	5	6
Passing	4	4
By penalty	1	3
Total yardage	245	248
Net rushing yardage	101	120
Net passing yardage	144	128
Passes att.-comp.-had int.	23–9–2	26–9–5

1947

CHI. CARDINALS 28, PHILADELPHIA 21

Trippi (62) was one of Cardinal's heroes.

A frozen field in Comiskey Park did not prevent an offensive game as the Chicago Cardinals defeated the Philadelphia Eagles 28–21 in their first NFL championship playoff. The Cardinals' Elmer Angsman set a record by rushing for 159 yards in 10 carries, scoring twice on 70-yard runs. Philadelphia's Tommy Thompson set a record with 27 pass completions in 44 attempts. Thompson accounted for 297 yards and one touchdown. The Cardinals' Charley Trippi ran 44 yards from scrimmage for one touchdown and returned a kickoff 75 yards for another. Chicago held Steve Van Buren, the NFL's leading ground gainer with 945 yards, to 26 yards in 18 carries.

The Cardinals started the game wearing basketball shoes. The Eagles followed suit a few minutes later but Philadelphia was penalized for wearing illegal equipment. Some of the Eagles' players had wrapped tape around their shoes. At this point, the Cardinals held a 7–0 lead after Trippi's 44-yard touchdown run with 8:38 left in the first quarter. It was 14–0 before the Eagles scored on Thompson's pass to William (Pat) McHugh, who caught a 36-yard pass on Chicago's 17 and completed a 53-yard play.

Philadelphia never got closer than one touchdown as the Cardinals held leads of 21–7 and 28–14 in the second half. Philadelphia led 357–336 in total offense, partly because Paul Christman of the Cardinals completed 3 of 14 passes for 54 yards. The Eagles' eight-man defensive line succeeded in pressuring Christman into hurried passes but it could not stop the Cardinals' running attack.

December 28, at Chicago

Philadelphia	Starting Lineups	Chi. Cardinals
Jack Ferrante	LE	Bill Blackburn
Vic Sears	LT	Dick Plasman
Cliff Patton	LG	Lloyd Arms
Alex Wojiechowicz	C	Vince Banonis
Frank (Bucko) Kilroy	RG	Hamilton Nichols
Al Wistert	RT	Stan Mauldin
Pete Pihos	RE	John Doolan
William (Pat) McHugh	QB	Bill Campbell
Steve Van Buren	LH	John (Red) Cochran
Bosh Pritchard	RH	Marshall Goldberg
Joe Muha	FB	Walt Rankin

Philadelphia	0	7	7	7	—	21
Chi. Cardinals	7	7	7	7	—	28

Chi —Trippi 44 run (Harder kick)
Chi —Angsman 70 run (Harder kick)
Phil—McHugh 53 pass from Thompson (Patton kick)
Chi —Trippi 75 punt return (Harder kick)
Phil—Van Buren 1 run (Patton kick)
Chi —Angsman 70 run (Harder kick)
Phil—Craft 1 run (Patton kick)
Attendance—30,759

TEAM STATISTICS	Phil	Chi
First downs	22	11
Rushing	10	8
Passing	11	2
By penalty	1	1
Total yardage	357	336
Net rushing yardage	60	282
Net passing yardage	297	54
Passes att.-comp.-had int.	44–27–3	14–3–2

1948

PHILADELPHIA 7, CHI. CARDINALS 0

The Eagles on offense in seven inches of snow.

A protective tarpaulin was not removed from the playing field in Shibe Park until 30 minutes before the kickoff, but snow blanketed the entire field by game time. Of the 36,309 persons who bought tickets and assured a sellout, a total of 28,664 were on hand as the Philadelphia Eagles defeated the Chicago Cardinals 7–0 in a rematch of the teams that played for the NFL championship in 1947.

The Eagles scored the only touchdown at the end of a sequence that began near the conclusion of the third quarter. The Cardinals' Elmer Angsman fumbled a handoff on his 17 yard line and Philadelphia's Frank (Bucko) Kilroy recovered. Three plays into the fourth quarter, Steve Van Buren scored on a five-yard run.

Conditions were so adverse that the stadium lights cast eerie shadows on the piles of snow along the side and on the field. NFL commissioner Bert Bell decreed that while the 10-yard first-down chain would be used there would be no measuring; the referee would be the final judge of all first downs. The sidelines were marked by ropes tied to stakes carried by officials. Each time a field goal was tried, players from the kicking team would kneel and clear the snow with their hands to get a firmer footing.

The first time the Eagles had possession of the ball quarterback Tommy Thompson combined with end Jack Ferrante on a 65-yard pass play for a "touchdown." An official's white penalty flag was thrown but it was invisible in the snow. When the Eagles realized the play would be called back because of an offside violation, Ferrante asked the official who had moved across the line of scrimmage before the snap of the ball. "You," said the official.

December 19, at Philadelphia

Chi. Cardinals	Starting Lineups	Philadelphia
John (Red) Cochran	LE	John Green
Bob Zimny	LT	Jay MacDowell
Garrard (Buster) Ramsey	LG	Duke Maronic
Vince Banonis	C	Vic Lindskog
Plato Andros	RG	Frank (Bucko) Kilroy
Chet Bulger	RT	Al Wistert
Corwin Clatt	RE	Neill Armstrong
Jerry Davis	QB	Tommy Thompson
Charley Trippi	LH	Ernie Steele
Elmer Angsman	RH	Russ Craft
Pat Harder	FB	Joe Muha

Chi. Cardinals	0	0	0	0	—	0
Philadelphia	0	0	0	7	—	7

Phil—Van Buren 5 run (Patton kick)
Attendance—28,864

TEAM STATISTICS	Chi	Phil
First downs	6	16
Rushing	3	15
Passing	3	0
By penalty	0	1
Total yardage	131	232
Net rushing yardage	96	225
Net passing yardage	35	7
Passes att.-comp.-had int.	11-3-1	12-2-2

1949

PHILADELPHIA 14, LOS ANGELES 0

Van Buren sets records for yards, number of carries.

The NFL was finishing its thirtieth season and the Philadelphia Eagles defeated the Los Angeles Rams 14–0 in the seventeenth championship playoff as fullback Steve Van Buren set records with 31 carries and 196 yards gained. Van Buren achieved the record after a storm that began 24 hours before kickoff dropped almost two inches of rain in Los Angeles. A crowd of more than 60,000, which would have set a playoff record, was expected before the storm. A total of 22,245 of the 27,980 persons who purchased tickets attended the game, which was played on a muddy field.

With Van Buren carrying the ball, the Eagles were able to control possession for 70 plays, compared to the Rams' 51. Philadelphia rushed for 274 yards, compared to 21 for Los Angeles. The Rams did not advance the ball further than the Eagles' 26 yard line. Philadelphia scored one of its touchdowns, the first of the game, in the second quarter, on a 31-yard pass, quarterback Tommy Thompson to end Pete Pihos. It was Pihos's seventh touchdown in five games against Los Angeles.

The Eagles' other score came in the third quarter. Defensive end Len Skladany blocked Bob Waterfield's punt from the 5 yard line. The snap of the ball from center Don Paul was high and Waterfield had no chance to get the kick away. Skladany picked up the bouncing ball on the 2 yard line and scored.

The victory was Philadelphia's second in a row and it marked the Eagles' third straight appearance in the championship playoff, climaxing the rise that began when Earle (Greasy) Neale was hired as coach in 1941.

December 18, at Los Angeles

Philadelphia	Starting Lineups	Los Angeles
Jack Ferrante	LE	Tom Fears
Vic Sears	LT	Dick Huffman
Cliff Patton	LG	Hal Dean
Vic Lindskog	C	John Martin
Frank (Bucko) Kilroy	RG	Ray Yagiello
Al Wistert	RT	Gil Bouley
Pete Pihos	RE	Bill Smyth
Tommy Thompson	QB	Bob Waterfield
Steve Van Buren	LH	Tom Kalmanir
Clyde (Smackover) Scott	RH	Verda (Vitamin T.) Smith
John Myers	FB	Dick Hoerner

Philadelphia	0	7	7	0	—	14
Los Angeles	0	0	0	0	—	0

Phil—Pihos 31 pass from Thompson (Patton kick)
Phil—Skladany 2 blocked punt return (Patton kick)
Attendance—22,245

TEAM STATISTICS	Phil	LA
First downs	17	7
Rushing	12	0
Passing	4	6
By penalty	1	1
Total yardage	342	119
Net rushing yardage	274	21
Net passing yardage	68	98
Passes att.-comp.-had int.	9-5-1	27-10-2

1950

CLEVELAND 30, LOS ANGELES 28

All eyes are on Groza's winning field goal.

The Cleveland Browns, who joined the NFL in 1950 after winning four consecutive All-America Football Conference championships, defeated the Los Angeles Rams 30–28 on Lou Groza's 16-yard field goal with 20 seconds left in the game. Although the game was played on a frozen field amid snow flurries in 27-degree weather, Groza's kick was the final offensive thrust on an afternoon in which 832 yards were amassed, 418 by the Rams, 414 by Cleveland. Los Angeles quarterback Bob Waterfield threw for 312 yards and one touchdown but had four passes intercepted. Cleveland's Otto Graham threw for 298 yards and four touchdowns and had one interception.

The Rams led 14–13 at halftime but the Browns took a 20–14 lead on a 39-yard pass play involving Graham and Dante Lavelli, who caught 11 passes for 128 yards and two touchdowns. The Rams went back in front 28–20 at the end of the third quarter. Cleveland closed to 28–27 with 4:35 left in the game after a 65-yard, 14-play drive. Graham completed nine passes during the march, including five in a row to Lavelli. Two minutes remained when the Browns took a Rams punt on their 32. They moved to the 11 to position Groza's field goal.

The Rams succeeded in stopping Marion Motley, the Browns fullback who led the NFL with 810 yards rushing. Motley gained nine yards in six attempts, but Graham gained 99 in 12 carries when he was unable to find open receivers.

December 24, at Cleveland

Los Angeles	Starting Lineups	Cleveland
Tom Fears	LE	Mac Speedie
Dick Huffman	LT	Lou Groza
John Finlay	LG	Weldon Humble
Fred Naumetz	C	Frank Gatski
Harry Thompson	RG	Lin Houston
Bob Reinhard	RT	Lou Rymkus
Jack Zilly	RE	Dante Lavelli
Bob Waterfield	QB	Otto Graham
Glenn Davis	LH	Rex Bumgardner
Verda (Vitamin T.) Smith	RH	Dub Jones
Dick Hoerner	FB	Marion Motley

Los Angeles	14	0	14	0	—	28
Cleveland	7	6	7	10	—	30

LA —Davis 82 pass from Waterfield (Waterfield kick)
Cle—Jones 32 pass from Graham (Groza kick)
LA —Hoerner 3 run (Waterfield kick)
Cle—Lavelli 35 pass from Graham (kick failed)
Cle—Lavelli 39 pass from Graham (Groza kick)
LA —Hoerner 1 run (Waterfield kick)
LA —Brink 6 fumble return (Waterfield kick)
Cle—Bumgardner 14 pass from Graham (Groza kick)
Cle—FG Groza 16
Attendance—29,751

TEAM STATISTICS	LA	Cle
First downs	22	22
Rushing	9	8
Passing	12	13
By penalty	1	1
Total yardage	418	414
Net rushing yardage	106	116
Net passing yardage	312	298
Passes att.-comp.-had int.	32-18-5	33-22-1

1951

LOS ANGELES 24, CLEVELAND 17

Hoerner (31) scores the Ram's first touchdown.

The Los Angeles Rams won their first NFL championship since moving from Cleveland in 1946. The Rams defeated the Cleveland Browns 24–17 with the winning play a 73-yard pass and run involving quarterback Norm Van Brocklin and end Tom Fears. On third down and three yards for a first down from the 27 yard line, Van Brocklin threw a 23-yard pass to Fears. Fears ran between defenders Cliff Lewis and Tom James, caught the ball at the 50 yard line, and ran to the end zone with 7:25 remaining in the game.

The Rams took a 7–0 lead in the second quarter on Dick Hoerner's one-yard run but they trailed 10–7 at the half after Lou Groza set a playoff record with a 52-yard field goal and Otto Graham threw a 17-yard touchdown pass to Dub Jones. The Rams assumed a 17–10 lead early in the fourth quarter after a one-yard run by Dan Towler and a 17-yard field goal by Bob Waterfield. The Browns tied the score on a 70-yard, eight-play drive that featured a 52-yard pass gain, Graham to Mac Speedie.

Fears described Van Brocklin's effort as "the best thrown pass I've ever caught. He laid it right in there full stride." Browns coach Paul Brown thought the play would not have worked if Lewis and James had not collided trying to cover Fears.

The Browns had a 372–334 edge in total offense, outpassing the Rams 280–253 and outrushing them 92–81. Fears caught four passes for 146 yards in his best game of the season; he had been troubled with a sore knee.

December 23, at Los Angeles

Cleveland	Starting Lineups	Los Angeles
Mac Speedie	LE	Tom Fears
Lou Groza	LT	Don Simensen
Abe Gibron	LG	Dick Daugherty
Frank Gatski	C	Leon McLaughlin
Bob Gaudio	RG	Bill Lange
Lou Rymkus	RT	Tom Dahms
Dante Lavelli	RE	Elroy (Crazylegs) Hirsch
Otto Graham	QB	Bob Waterfield
Ken Carpenter	LH	Dan Towler
Dub Jones	RH	Paul (Tank) Younger
Marion Motley	FB	Dick Hoerner

Cleveland	0	10	0	7	— 17
Los Angeles	0	7	7	10	— 24

LA—Hoerner 1 run (Waterfield kick)
Cle—FG Groza 52
Cle—Jones 17 pass from Graham (Groza kick)
LA—Towler 1 run (Waterfield kick)
LA—FG Waterfield 17
Cle—Carpenter 2 run (Groza kick)
LA—Fears 73 pass from Van Brocklin (Waterfield kick)
Attendance—57,522

TEAM STATISTICS	Cle	LA
First downs	22	20
Rushing	6	9
Passing	16	9
By penalty	0	2
Total yardage	372	334
Net rushing yardage	92	81
Net passing yardage	280	253
Passes att.-comp.-had int.	41-19-3	30-13-2

1952

DETROIT 17, CLEVELAND 7

The Lions open big hole, Layne scores.

The Cleveland Browns outgained the Detroit Lions 384–258 and had 22 first downs to 10, but the Lions stopped Cleveland on their 21, 21, 24, 5, and 8 yard lines and scored a 17–7 victory for their first NFL championship since 1935. The Lions' most important defensive stand came in the fourth quarter when the score was 14–7. Cleveland fullback Marion Motley ran 43 yards to the Lions' 5. Motley was thrown for a five-yard loss on the next play. Quarterback Otto Graham was thrown for a 12-yard loss attempting to pass on the next play. The Browns gained a yard on third down and Graham threw an incomplete pass to Motley on fourth down.

Detroit went ahead early in the second quarter when quarterback Bobby Layne scored on a two-yard run at the end of a 50-yard drive. The score became 14–0 in the third quarter when halfback Doak Walker ran 67 yards for a touchdown. Walker, who had been injured most of the season, had not scored a touchdown coming into the game. The Browns scored their touchdown on the following series, marching 67 yards in 11 plays. Fullback Harry (Chick) Jagade scored on a seven-yard run.

Pat Harder's 36-yard field goal in the fourth quarter clinched the victory for Detroit. The Lions had been forced to punt but the Browns' Ken Carpenter fumbled Bob Smith's kick and Jim Martin recovered for Detroit on the 23. Following Harder's placement, the Browns moved from their 15 yard line to Detroit's 8 in the final minutes. Graham passed to Ray Renfro in the end zone but Renfro deflected the ball to Darrell (Pete) Brewster. It was an illegal catch—two offensive players made contact before a defensive player.

December 28, at Cleveland

Detroit	Starting Lineups	Cleveland
Cloyce Box	LE	Darrell (Pete) Brewster
Bob Miller	LT	Lou Groza
Lou Creekmur	LG	Abe Gibron
Vince Banonis	C	Frank Gatski
Jim Martin	RG	Joe Skibinski
Gus Cifelli	RT	John Sandusky
Leon Hart	RE	Dante Lavelli
Bobby Layne	QB	Otto Graham
Doak Walker	LH	Ken Carpenter
Bob Hoernschemeyer	RH	Rex Bumgardner
Pat Harder	FB	Harry (Chick) Jagade

Detroit	0	7	7	3	— 17
Cleveland	0	0	7	0	— 7

Det—Layne 2 run (Harder kick)
Det—Walker 67 run (Harder kick)
Cle—Jagade 7 run (Groza kick)
Det—FG Harder 36
Attendance—50,934

TEAM STATISTICS	Det	Cle
First downs	10	22
Rushing	8	15
Passing	2	7
By penalty	0	0
Total yardage	258	384
Net rushing yardage	199	227
Net passing yardage	59	157
Passes att.-comp.-had int.	10-7-0	36-20-1

1953

DETROIT 17, CLEVELAND 16

Layne scrambles around Browns' Bill Willis.

The Detroit Lions marched 80 yards to a touchdown late in the game to defeat the Cleveland Browns 17–16 in Briggs Stadium for their second straight NFL championship.

After Lou Groza kicked a 43-yard field goal to put the Browns ahead 16–10, the Lions took the kickoff on their 20-yard line with 4:10 remaining. Quarterback Bobby Layne passed 18 yards to Jim Doran on the first play. Two more passes were incomplete, but on third down Layne passed 18 yards to Doran for a first down on Cleveland's 44. Layne then passed nine yards to Cloyce Box, but Bob Hoernschemeyer was stopped for no gain. On third down and one, Layne dived over center for a first down at Cleveland's 33. Layne then called a time out and discussed strategy with Lions coach Raymond (Buddy) Parker, who had been informed by coaches in the press box that the rush of Cleveland defensive end Len Ford created the possibility of the Lions succeeding on a screen pass to one of their running backs.

When Layne returned to the huddle he decided on another play. "Doran had been begging me to throw deep all day," said Layne. "Doran said he could get a step on Warren Lahr. The Lions' receiver was behind Lahr when he caught the ball on the 10 yard line. Doran, who was in the game because of an injury to starter Leon Hart, scored with 2:08 remaining; Doak Walker's extra point provided the final score.

The Lions led 10–3 at the half, but the Browns went ahead on a touchdown by Harry (Chick) Jagade and two field goals by Groza.

December 27, at Detroit

Detroit	Starting Lineups	Cleveland
Dorne Dibble	LE	Darrell (Pete) Brewster
Lou Creekmur	LT	Lou Groza
Harley Sewell	LG	Abe Gibron
Vince Banonis	C	Frank Gatski
Dick Stanfel	RG	Chuck Noll
Ollie Spencer	RT	John Sandusky
Leon Hart	RE	Dante Lavelli
Bobby Layne	QB	Otto Graham
Doak Walker	LH	Ken Carpenter
Gene Gedman	RH	Billy Reynolds
Bob Hoernschemeyer	FB	Harry (Chick) Jagade

Cleveland	0	3	7	6	— 16
Detroit	7	3	0	7	— 17

Det—Walker 1 run (Walker kick)
Cle—FG Groza 13
Det—FG Walker 23
Cle—Jagade 9 run (Groza kick)
Cle—FG Groza 15
Cle—FG Groza 43
Det—Doran 33 pass from Layne (Walker kick)
Attendance—54,577

TEAM STATISTICS	Cle	Det
First downs	11	18
Rushing	9	10
Passing	1	7
By penalty	1	1
Total yardage	191	293
Net rushing yardage	182	129
Net passing yardage	9	164
Passes att.-comp.-had int.	16-3-2	25-12-2

<table>
<tr><th>1954</th><th>1955</th><th>1956</th></tr>
</table>

1954

CLEVELAND 56, DETROIT 10

Renfro beats Lions for TD pass from Graham.

Otto Graham completed 9 of 12 passes for 163 yards and three touchdowns and scored on runs of one, five, and one yard as the Cleveland Browns defeated the Detroit Lions 56–10.

The Browns had lost seven games in a row to the Lions, including a 14–10 defeat in the final minute of the last regular season game the week before. Cleveland had lost its league opener 28–10 to Philadelphia and had been beaten 55–27 by Pittsburgh in the third game. Although they had appeared in championship games every year since 1946, when they were members of the All-America Football Conference, the Browns had not won an NFL title since 1950, their first year in the league.

The Browns converted six Detroit fumbles and interceptions into touchdowns. A penalty on Gil Mains for roughing kicker Horace Gillom set up another. That came on a 35-yard pass, Graham to Ray Renfro, that gave Cleveland a 7–3 lead.

Renfro caught two passes and scored two touchdowns. The Browns had noticed that Bill Stits played close to the line when Cleveland was in a straight T-formation with no pass receiving flanker in the loss to Detroit the previous week. The Browns decided to send Renfro out of the backfield on passes and they engaged the Lions' safeties by sending their ends on crossing patterns. Stits did not have support and was unable to cover Renfro himself.

December 26, at Cleveland

Detroit	Starting Lineups	Cleveland
Dorne Dibble	LE	Darrell (Pete) Brewster
Lou Creekmur	LT	Lou Groza
Harley Sewell	LG	Abe Gibron
Andy Miketa	C	Frank Gatski
Jim Martin	RG	Chuck Noll
Charlie Ane	RT	John Sandusky
Earl (Jug) Girard	RE	Dante Lavelli
Bobby Layne	QB	Otto Graham
Doak Walker	LH	Ray Renfro
Lew Carpenter	RH	Billy Reynolds
Bill Bowman	FB	Maurice Bassett

Detroit	3	7	0	0	—	10
Cleveland	14	21	14	7	—	56

Det—FG Walker 36
Cle—Renfro 35 pass from Graham (Groza kick)
Cle—Brewster 10 pass from Graham (Groza kick)
Cle—Graham 1 run (Groza kick)
Det—Bowman 5 run (Walker kick)
Cle—Graham 5 run (Groza kick)
Cle—Renfro 31 pass from Graham (Groza kick)
Cle—Graham 1 run (Groza kick)
Cle—Morrison 12 run (Groza kick)
Cle—Hanulak 10 run (Groza kick)
Attendance—43,827

TEAM STATISTICS	Det	Cle
First downs	16	17
Rushing	5	8
Passing	9	6
By penalty	2	2
Total yardage	331	303
Net rushing yardage	136	140
Net passing yardage	195	163
Passes att.-comp.-had int.	44-19-6	12-9-2

1955

CLEVELAND 38, LOS ANGELES 14

Cleveland's Paul (right) races 65 yards.

Quarterback Otto Graham ended a 10-year professional football career by completing 14 of 25 passes for 209 yards and two touchdowns and scoring on runs of 1 and 15 yards as the Cleveland Browns defeated the Los Angeles Rams 38–14 before a record championship playoff crowd of 85,693 persons. Graham announced his retirement after the game. In 10 seasons with the Browns, Graham was the quarterback in 10 championship games.

Graham had three passes intercepted, but the Rams were unable to convert. The Browns intercepted six of Los Angeles quarterback Norm Van Brocklin's passes. They converted four of the interceptions into a total of 24 points—the margin of difference.

The Rams moved from their 20 to Cleveland's 24 in the first quarter. Ken Konz intercepted Van Brocklin on first down and the Browns marched to Lou Groza's 26-yard field goal. In the second quarter, Van Brocklin was intercepted by Don Paul, who set a playoff record with a 65-yard return for a touchdown. After another interception by Tom James, Graham passed 50 yards to Dante Lavelli for a touchdown that made the score 17–7 at the half. An interception by Sam Palumbo set in motion a drive that ended with Graham's one-yard touchdown and a 31–7 Browns' lead in the third quarter.

The Rams scored on a 67-yard pass play, Van Brocklin to Volney (Skeet) Quinlan, in the second quarter and on a four-yard run by Ron Waller in the fourth quarter.

December 26, at Los Angeles

Cleveland	Starting Lineups	Los Angeles
Darrell (Pete) Brewster	LE	Tom Fears
Lou Groza	LT	Bob Cross
Abe Gibron	LG	Duane Putnam
Frank Gatski	C	Leon McLaughlin
Harold Bradley	RG	John Hock
Mike McCormack	RT	Charley Toogood
Dante Lavelli	RE	Elroy (Crazylegs) Hirsch
Otto Graham	QB	Norm Van Brocklin
Ray Renfro	LH	Ron Waller
Fred (Curly) Morrison	RH	Volney (Skeet) Quinlan
Ed Modzelewski	FB	Dan Towler

Cleveland	3	14	14	7	—	38
Los Angeles	0	7	0	7	—	14

Cle—FG Groza 26
Cle—Paul 65 interception return (Groza kick)
LA—Quinlan 67 pass from Van Brocklin (Richter kick)
Cle—Lavelli 50 pass from Graham (Groza kick)
Cle—Graham 15 run (Groza kick)
Cle—Graham 1 run (Groza kick)
Cle—Renfro 35 pass from Graham (Groza kick)
LA—Waller 4 run (Richter kick)
Attendance—85,693

TEAM STATISTICS	Cle	LA
First downs	17	17
Rushing	7	8
Passing	10	8
By penalty	0	1
Total yardage	371	259
Net rushing yardage	202	143
Net passing yardage	169	116
Passes att.-comp.-had int.	25-14-3	28-11-7

1956

N.Y. GIANTS 47, CHI. BEARS 7

Webster scores to give the Giants a 27-7 lead.

Gene Filipski returned George Blanda's opening kickoff 53 yards to the Chicago Bears' 39 yard line. The New York Giants scored four plays later on Mel Triplett's 17-yard run, signaling a 34-point first half en route to a 47–7 victory. The championship was the Giants' first since 1938 and was reminiscent of their victory over the Bears in the 1934 title game.

In 1934, the Giants beat the Bears 30–13 in the Polo Grounds in 9-degree weather on a frozen field after they switched from football cleats to basketball shoes in the second half. Before the 1956 game, which was played in 20-degree weather in Yankee Stadium, Giants' coach Jim Lee Howell sent Filipski and defensive back Ed Hughes to test the field. Hughes, who was wearing football shoes, slipped and fell after taking a few steps. Filipski maneuvered without trouble in basketball shoes. "Everyone wear sneakers," Howell announced to the team.

The Bears also wore rubber-soled shoes but they fell behind 20–0 before scoring a touchdown and trailed 34–7 at the half. It was 13–0 at the end of the first quarter, when Charlie Conerly replaced Don Heinrich at quarterback for New York. Conerly directed three second-period touchdown drives and threw two touchdown passes in the second half. Conerly completed 7 of 10 passes for 195 yards. Frank Gifford caught four for 131 and one touchdown and Alex Webster five for 76.

December 30, at New York

N.Y. Giants	Starting Lineups	Chi. Bears
Kyle Rote	LE	Harlon Hill
Roosevelt Brown	LT	Bill Wightkin
Bill Austin	LG	Herman Clark
Ray Wietecha	C	Larry Strickland
Jack Stroud	RG	Stan Jones
Dick Yelvington	RT	Kline Gilbert
Ken MacAfee	RE	Bill McColl
Don Heinrich	QB	George Blanda
Frank Gifford	LH	Bob Watkins
Alex Webster	RH	John Hoffman
Mel Triplett	FB	Rick Casares

Chi. Bears	0	7	0	0	—	7
N.Y. Giants	13	21	6	7	—	47

NYG—Triplett 17 run (Agajanian kick)
NYG—FG Agajanian 17
NYG—FG Agajanian 43
NYG—Webster 3 run (Agajanian kick)
Chi—Casares 9 run (Blanda kick)
NYG—Webster 1 run (Agajanian kick)
NYG—Moore blocked punt recovery in end zone (Agajanian kick)
NYG—Rote 9 pass from Conerly (kick failed)
NYG—Gifford 14 pass from Conerly (Agajanian kick)
Attendance—56,836

TEAM STATISTICS	Chi	NYG
First downs	19	16
Rushing	8	8
Passing	10	8
By penalty	1	0
Total yardage	280	348
Net rushing yardage	67	126
Net passing yardage	213	222
Passes att.-comp.-had int.	47-20-2	20-11-0

1957

DETROIT 59, CLEVELAND 14

Gedman (fourth from left) scores for Lions.

The Detroit Lions defeated the Cleveland Browns 59–14 for their third NFL championship in six seasons, and four months and 19 days after coach Raymond (Buddy) Parker resigned at a "Meet the Lions" banquet at which Parker said, "This team is dead." After winning three of their first six games, the Lions captured five of their last six to tie for the NFL West championship, then defeated San Francisco in a playoff for the right to meet Cleveland.

Quarterback Tobin Rote, acquired from Green Bay at the start of training camp and the Lions' regular since Bobby Layne was hurt late in the season's eleventh game against Cleveland, completed 12 of 19 passes for 280 yards and four touchdowns. One of Rote's most important passes came in the second quarter. Fullback Jim Brown had run 29 yards for a touchdown to end a Browns drive of 78 yards that made the score 17–7 in favor of Detroit. The Lions moved to Cleveland's 26 on their next possession and apparently were going to attempt a field goal on fourth down. Rote kneeled to accept the snap from center and place the ball for kicker Jim Martin. But instead of acting as Martin's holder, Rote straightened up, moved to his right, and threw a 26-yard pass to Steve Junker that made the score 24–7.

The Browns never got closer than 31–14, which was the score after Lew Carpenter ran five yards in the third quarter.

December 29, at Detroit

Cleveland	Starting Lineups	Detroit
Darrel (Pete) Brewster	LE	Jim Doran
Lou Groza	LT	Lou Creekmur
Herschel Forester	LG	Harley Sewell
Art Hunter	C	Frank Gatski
Fred Robinson	RG	Stan Campbell
Mike McCormack	RT	Ken Russell
Preston Carpenter	RE	Steve Junker
Tommy O'Connell	QB	Tobin Rote
Ray Renfro	LH	Gene Gedman
Lew Carpenter	RH	Howard (Hopalong) Cassady
Jim Brown	FB	John Henry Johnson

Cleveland	0	7	7	0	—	14
Detroit	17	14	14	14	—	59

Det—FG Martin 31
Det—Rote 1 run (Martin kick)
Det—Gedman 1 run (Martin kick)
Cle—Brown 29 run (Groza kick)
Det—Junker 26 pass from Rote (Martin kick)
Det—Barr 19 interception return (Martin kick)
Cle—Carpenter 5 run (Groza kick)
Det—Doran 78 pass from Rote (Martin kick)
Det—Junker 23 pass from Rote (Martin kick)
Det—Middleton 32 pass from Rote (Martin kick)
Det—Cassady 16 pass from Reichow (Martin kick)
Attendance—55,263

TEAM STATISTICS	Cle	Det
First downs	17	22
Rushing	11	9
Passing	5	10
By penalty	1	3
Total yardage	313	433
Net rushing yardage	218	137
Net passing yardage	95	296
Passes att.-comp.-had int.	21-9-4	21-13-0

1958

BALTIMORE 23, N.Y. GIANTS 17

Unitas throws for 349 yards.

The Baltimore Colts, who tied the game 17–17 on Steve Myhra's 20-yard field goal with seven seconds to play, defeated the New York Giants 23–17 in the first championship playoff to be decided in sudden death overtime. The Colts marched 80 yards in 13 plays after taking a Giants punt in the extra period and scored on Alan Ameche's one-yard run with 8:15 elapsed. Quarterback Johnny Unitas completed four passes during the drive, including two for 33 yards to end Raymond Berry. The key play in the march was a 23-yard run by Ameche that put the ball on the Giants' 20. Ameche profited from guard Art Spinney's trap block on tackle Dick Modzelewski. Tackle George Preas of the Colts then cut off Giants middle linebacker Sam Huff.

Unitas completed 26 of 40 passes for 349 yards and one touchdown. Berry set playoff records with 12 catches for 178 yards. Unitas's 15-yard pass to Berry gave Baltimore a 14–3 lead at halftime. After the Giants stopped a 58-yard Colts drive on the 5 yard line in the third quarter, they marched 95 yards to a touchdown. The big play was a pass play involving Charlie Conerly and Kyle Rote that covered 62 yards. When Rote fumbled at Baltimore's 24, Alex Webster picked up the ball and ran to the 1.

The Giants took a 17–14 lead in the first minute of the fourth quarter after an 81-yard drive. Conerly threw to end Bob Schnelker for gains of 17 and 46 yards, then connected with halfback Frank Gifford from the 15 yard line for the touchdown.

December 28, at New York

Baltimore	Starting Lineups	N.Y. Giants
Raymond Berry	LE	Kyle Rote
Jim Parker	LT	Roosevelt Brown
Art Spinney	LG	Al Barry
Madison (Buzz) Nutter	C	Ray Wietecha
Alex Sandusky	RG	Bob Mischak
George Preas	RT	Frank Youso
Jim Mutscheller	RE	Bob Schnelker
Johnny Unitas	QB	Don Heinrich
L. G. Dupre	LH	Frank Gifford
Lenny Moore	RH	Alex Webster
Alan Ameche	FB	Mel Triplett

Baltimore	0	14	0	3	6	—	23
N.Y. Giants	3	0	7	7	0	—	17

NYG—FG Summerall 36
Balt—Ameche 2 run (Myhra kick)
Balt—Berry 15 pass from Unitas (Myhra kick)
NYG—Triplett 1 run (Summerall kick)
NYG—Gifford 15 pass from Conerly (Summerall kick)
Balt—FG Myhra 20
Balt—Ameche 1 run (no extra point attempted)
Attendance—64,185

TEAM STATISTICS	Balt	NYG
First downs	27	10
Rushing	9	3
Passing	17	7
By penalty	1	0
Total yardage	460	266
Net rushing yardage	138	88
Net passing yardage	322	178
Passes att.-comp.-had int.	40-26-1	18-12-0

1959

BALTIMORE 31, N.Y. GIANTS 16

Colts' fans tear down goal posts after victory.

Trailing 9–7 as the third quarter was coming to an end, the Baltimore Colts began a 55-yard drive that concluded with a touchdown and was the start of 24 straight points that buried the New York Giants and gave the Colts a 31–16 victory.

Field goals of 23, 37, and 22 yards by the Giants' Pat Summerall had overcome an early Baltimore lead of 7–0 that had materialized the first time the Colts had the ball. Baltimore moved 80 yards in six plays, scoring on a 59-yard pass play, Johnny Unitas to Lenny Moore. After Summerall's third kick, which concluded a 71-yard advance, the Colts moved back in front on Unitas's four-yard run, which came on the heels of a 36-yard Unitas-to-Moore pass that moved the ball to New York's 13.

Andy Nelson intercepted a pass by Charlie Conerly and returned the ball 17 yards to New York's 14 to set up Baltimore's next touchdown, a 12-yard pass from Unitas to Gerry Richardson. The Colts moved in front 28–9 when Johnny Sample intercepted a Conerly pass, ran 42 yards for a score. Sample intercepted another Conerly pass and his 24-yard return set up a 25-yard field goal by Steve Myhra.

Trailing 31–9, the Giants moved 70 yards, scoring with 32 seconds left in the game on Conerly's 32-yard pass to Bob Schnelker. The pass gave New York a final total yardage advantage of 323–280 over the Colts, who were outrushed 118–73 and led only 207–205 in passing yardage.

December 27, at Baltimore

N.Y. Giants	Starting Lineups	Baltimore
Kyle Rote	LE	Raymond Berry
Roosevelt Brown	LT	Jim Parker
Darrell Dess	LG	Art Spinney
Ray Wietecha	C	Madison (Buzz) Nutter
Jack Stroud	RG	Alex Sandusky
Frank Youso	RT	George Preas
Bob Schnelker	RE	Jim Mutscheller
Charlie Conerly	QB	Johnny Unitas
Frank Gifford	LH	Mike Sommer
Alex Webster	RH	Lenny Moore
Mel Triplett	FB	Alan Ameche

N.Y. Giants	3	3	3	7	—	16
Baltimore	7	0	0	24	—	31

Balt—Moore 59 pass from Unitas (Myrha kick)
NYG—FG Summerall 23
NYG—FG Summerall 37
NYG—FG Summerall 22
Balt—Unitas 4 run (Myhra kick)
Balt—Richardson 12 pass from Unitas (Myhra kick)
Balt—Sample 42 interception return (Myrha kick)
Balt—FG Myrha 25
NYG—Schnelker 32 pass from Conerly (Summerall kick)
Attendance—57,545

TEAM STATISTICS	NYG	Balt
First downs	16	13
Rushing	4	3
Passing	11	10
By penalty	1	0
Total yardage	323	280
Net rushing yardage	118	73
Net passing yardage	205	207
Passes att.-comp.-had int.	38-17-3	29-18-0

1960 NFL

PHILADELPHIA 17, GREEN BAY 13

Dean struggles until key kickoff return.

The Philadelphia Eagles overcame leads of 6–0 and 13–10 by the Green Bay Packers to score a 17–13 victory for their first NFL championship in 11 years and in the final game for head coach Lawrence (Buck) Shaw and quarterback Norm Van Brocklin, who announced their retirements. Concluding a 12-year career, Van Brocklin passed for 197 yards and one touchdown. Rookie halfback Ted Dean rushed for 54 yards in 13 carries and scored once.

Bill Quinlan intercepted Van Brocklin's first pass on the second play of the game. The Packers gave up the ball on downs at the 5, but they regained possession when Dean fumbled on the 22. Five plays later Paul Hornung kicked a 20-yard field goal. Hornung's 22-yard field goal increased Green Bay's lead to 6–0 in the second quarter. Philadelphia got on the scoreboard with a two-play, 57-yard drive. Van Brocklin passed 22 yards to Tommy McDonald, then teamed with McDonald on a 35-yard TD pass.

It was 10–6 at the half after Bobby Walston's 15-yard field goal for Philadelphia, but Green Bay took a 13–10 lead in the first two minutes of the fourth quarter. Bart Starr's seven-yard pass to Max McGee marked the Packers' only touchdown. Dean returned Hornung's ensuing kickoff 58 yards to the Packers' 39. A holding penalty moved the Eagles to the 32. Dean made six yards and Billy Barnes followed with six for a first down on the 20. Van Brocklin was thrown for a loss of seven, but he recovered with a 13-yard pass to Barnes. Dean and Barnes carried the ball in for the score from there.

December 26, at Philadelphia

Green Bay	Starting Lineups	Philadelphia
Max McGee	LE	Pete Retzlaff
Bob Skoronski	LT	Jim McCusker
Fred (Fuzzy) Thurston	LG	Gerry Huth
Jim Ringo	C	Chuck Bednarik
Jerry Kramer	RG	Stan Campbell
Forrest Gregg	RT	J.D. Smith
Gary Knafelc	RE	Bobby Walston
Bart Starr	QB	Norm Van Brocklin
Paul Hornung	LH	Billy Barnes
Boyd Dowler	RH	Tommy McDonald
Jim Taylor	FB	Ted Dean

Green Bay	3	3	0	7	— 13
Philadelphia	0	10	0	7	— 17

GB —FG Hornung 20
GB —FG Hornung 22
Phil—McDonald 35 pass from Van Brocklin (Walston kick)
Phil—FG Walston 15
GB —McGee 7 pass from Starr (Hornung kick)
Phil—Dean 5 run (Walston kick)
Attendance—67,325

TEAM STATISTICS	GB	Phil
First downs	22	13
Rushing	14	5
Passing	8	6
By penalty	0	2
Total yardage	401	296
Net rushing yardage	223	99
Net passing yardage	178	197
Passes att.-comp.-had int.	35-21-0	20-9-0

1960 AFL

HOUSTON 24, LOS ANGELES 16

Houston's Smith scores on pass from Blanda.

The Houston Oilers defeated the Los Angeles Chargers 24–16 in the American Football League's first championship game, which was played in 50-degree weather on New Year's Day, 1961, in Jeppesen Stadium on the University of Houston campus. The rivalry between the teams, who divided two hotly contested regular season games, was so intense that Los Angeles's Maury Schleicher and Houston's Julian Spence and Hogan Wharton were thrown out of the game for fighting.

Houston led 17–16 in the fourth quarter but was on its 12-yard line. Quarterback George Blanda then threw a medium-deep sideline pass to Billy Cannon, who caught the ball, broke a tackle, and outran the Chargers' secondary to complete an 88-yard touchdown. Los Angeles moved to Houston's 22 in the final minute but was stopped on fourth down. Had Los Angeles scored a touchdown it would have tried for a two-point conversion that could have tied the game and created a sudden death overtime.

January 1, at Houston

Los Angeles	Starters, Offense	Houston
Don Norton	LE	Bill Groman
Ernie Wright	LT	Al Jamison
Orlando Ferrante	LG	Bob Talamini
Don Rogers	C	George Belotti
Fred Cole	RG	Hogan Wharton
Ron Mix	RT	John Simerson
Dave Kocourek	RE	John Carson
Jack Kemp	QB	George Blanda
Paul Lowe	LH	Billy Cannon
Royce Womble	RH	Charley Hennigan
Howie Ferguson	FB	Dave Smith
	Starters, Defense	
Maury Schleicher	LE	Dalva Allen
Volney Peters	LT	Orville Trask
Garry Finneran	RT	George Shirkey
Ron Nery	RE	Dan Lanphear
Ron Botchan	LLB	Al Witcher
Emil Karas	MLB	Dennit Morris
Rommie Loudd	RLB	Mike Dukes
Charlie McNeil	LCB	Jim Norton
Dick Harris	RCB	Mark Johnston
Jim Sears	LS	Julian Spence
Bob Zeman	RS	Bobby Gordon

Los Angeles	6	3	7	0	— 16
Houston	0	10	7	7	— 24

LA —FG Agajanian 38
LA —FG Agajanian 22
Hou—Smith 17 pass from Blanda (Blanda kick)
Hou—FG Blanda 18
LA —FG Agajanian 27
Hou—Groman 7 pass from Blanda (Blanda kick)
LA —Lowe 2 run (Agajanian kick)
Hou—Cannon 88 pass from Blanda (Blanda kick)
Attendance—32,183

TEAM STATISTICS	LA	Hou
First downs	21	17
Rushing	11	4
Passing	9	13
By penalty	1	0
Total yardage	333	401
Net rushing yardage	162	100
Net passing yardage	171	301
Passes att.-comp.-had int.	41-21-2	32-16-0

1961 AFL

HOUSTON 10, SAN DIEGO 3

Tolar leads rushers with 52 yards in 16 carries.

The Houston Oilers defeated the San Diego Chargers 10-3 for the AFL championship in the fifth game between the teams that season. The two teams also played for the 1960 title, when the Chargers were representing Los Angeles. The Chargers defeated the Oilers twice in the 1961 preseason and the teams divided two regular season games, the Oilers winning the last meeting 33-13 to snap the Chargers' 11-game winning streak.

Houston led 3-0 after a 46-yard field goal by George Blanda in the second quarter. On third and five yards at San Diego's 35 in the third quarter, Blanda was forced to leave the passing pocket when his receivers were covered. Running to his right, Blanda threw an 18-yard pass to Billy Cannon, who was running to his left and jumped to catch the ball. As Cannon came down, he shook off a tackler at the 17 and ran for a touchdown and 10-0 lead. The Chargers' only score came with 12 seconds elapsed in the fourth quarter when George Blair kicked a 12-yard field goal. There were 10 interceptions in the game, six by San Diego.

December 24, at San Diego

Houston	Starters, Offense	San Diego
Bill Groman	LE	Don Norton
Al Jamison	LT	Ernie Wright
Bob Talamini	LG	Ernie Barnes
Bob Schmidt	C	Don Rogers
Hogan Wharton	RG	Ron Mix
Rich Michael	RT	Sherman Plunkett
Willard Dewveall	RE	Dave Kocourek
George Blanda	QB	Jack Kemp
Billy Cannon	LH	Paul Lowe
Charley Hennigan	RH	Bob Scarpitto
Charlie Tolar	FB	Keith Lincoln
	Starters, Defense	
Dalva Allen	LE	Earl Faison
George Shirkey	LT	Henry Schmidt
Ed Husmann	RT	Bill Hudson
Don Floyd	RE	Ron Nery
Doug Cline	LLB	Maury Schleicher
Dennit Morris	MLB	Emil Karas
Mike Dukes	RLB	Bob Laraba
Tony Banfield	LCB	Claude Gibson
Mark Johnston	RCB	Dick Harris
Jim Norton	LS	Charlie McNeil
Fred Glick	RS	Bob Zeman

Houston	0	3	7	0	— 10
San Diego	0	0	0	3	— 3

Hou—FG Blanda 46
Hou—Cannon 35 pass from Blanda (Blanda kick)
SD —FG Blair 12
Attendance—29,556

TEAM STATISTICS	Hou	SD
First downs	18	15
Rushing	6	6
Passing	8	8
By penalty	4	1
Total yardage	256	256
Net rushing yardage	96	79
Net passing yardage	160	177
Passes att.-comp.-had int.	41-18-6	32-17-4

1961 NFL

GREEN BAY 37, N.Y. GIANTS 0

Kramer (88) scores to give Green Bay a 21-0 lead.

Pvt. Paul Hornung, on leave from the U.S. Army, rushed for 89 yards in 20 carries and scored a record total of 19 points as the Green Bay Packers won their first championship in 17 years, defeating the New York Giants 37–0 in 21-degree weather at Lambeau Field. In their last appearance in a championship game, the Packers scored a 14–7 victory over the Giants in 1944.

Despite the cold, the field was in good condition. Fifty stadium workers had begun removing 14 inches of snow that covered 20 tons of hay at 6 A.M. the morning of the game. The bench areas of both teams were warmed by large infra-red heating units.

The Packers, who outgained New York 345-130 in total yardage, scored 24 points to break open the game in the second quarter following a scoreless first period. Hornung's six-yard run four seconds into the second quarter was followed by touchdown passes of 13 and 14 yards from Bart Starr to Boyd Dowler and Ron Kramer and a 17-yard field goal by Hornung just before halftime.

December 31, at Green Bay

N.Y. Giants	Starters, Offense	Green Bay
Del Shofner	LE	Max McGee
Roosevelt Brown	LT	Bob Skoronski
Darrell Dess	LG	Fred (Fuzzy) Thurston
Ray Wietecha	C	Jim Ringo
Jack Stroud	RG	Forrest Gregg
Greg Larson	RT	Norm Masters
Joe Walton	RE	Ron Kramer
Y.A. Tittle	QB	Bart Starr
Joel Wells	LH	Paul Hornung
Kyle Rote	RH	Boyd Dowler
Alex Webster	FB	Jim Taylor
	Starters, Defense	
Jim Katcavage	LE	Willie Davis
Dick Modzelewski	LT	Dave Hanner
Roosevelt Grier	RT	Henry Jordan
Andy Robustelli	RE	Bill Quinlan
Cliff Livingston	LLB	Dan Currie
Sam Huff	MLB	Ray Nitschke
Tom Scott	RLB	Bill Forester
Erich Barnes	LCB	Hank Gremminger
Dick Lynch	RCB	Jesse Whittenton
Joe Morrison	LS	John Symank
Jim Patton	RS	Willie Wood

N.Y. Giants	0	0	0	0	—	0
Green Bay	0	24	10	3	—	37

GB—Hornung 6 run (Hornung kick)
GB—Dowler 13 pass from Starr (Hornung kick)
GB—R. Kramer 14 pass from Starr (Hornung kick)
GB—FG Hornung 17
GB—FG Hornung 22
GB—R. Kramer 13 pass from Starr (Hornung kick)
GB—FG Hornung 19
Attendance—39,029

TEAM STATISTICS	NYG	GB
First downs	6	19
Rushing	1	10
Passing	4	8
By penalty	1	1
Total yardage	130	345
Net rushing yardage	31	181
Net passing yardage	99	164
Passes att.-comp.-had int.	29-10-4	19-10-0

1962 AFL

DALLAS 20, HOUSTON 17

Blanda (16) passes to Tolar for eight-yard gain.

The Dallas Texans won the longest game in the history of professional football (to that point) on Tommy Brooker's 25-yard field goal at 2:54 of the sixth quarter—after 17:54 of sudden death overtime. Brooker's kick gave the Texans a 20–17 victory over the Houston Oilers before a record AFL championship crowd of 37,981 in Jeppesen Stadium.

The kick also saved Abner Haynes, Dallas's all-league halfback and captain, from being an embarrassing footnote to history. When Haynes went to the center of the field to participate in the coin toss at the start of the fifth quarter, he put the Texans in jeopardy. Haynes won the toss and inadvertently said the Texans "would kick to the clock," not only giving the Oilers possession of the ball, but with the wind at their backs. Houston was not able to capitalize on either advantage, although the Oilers got to Dallas's 35 yard line. On second down, a George Blanda pass was intercepted by Texans defensive end Bill Hull, who ran 23 yards to midfield. Dallas then started its winning drive.

December 23, at Houston

Dallas	Starters, Offense	Houston
Tommy Brooker	LE	Willard Dewveall
Jim Tyrer	LT	Al Jamison
Marvin Terrell	LG	Bob Talamini
Jon Gilliam	C	Bob Schmidt
Al Reynolds	RG	Hogan Wharton
Jerry Cornelison	RT	Rich Michael
Fred Arbanas	RE	Bob McLeod
Len Dawson	QB	George Blanda
Abner Haynes	LH	Billy Cannon
Frank Jackson	RH	Charley Hennigan
Curtis McClinton	FB	Charlie Tolar
	Starters, Defense	
Curt Merz	LE	Gary Cutsinger
Paul Rochester	LT	Ed Culpepper
Jerry Mays	RT	Ed Husmann
Mel Branch	RE	Don Floyd
E.J. Holub	LLB	Doug Cline
Sherrill Headrick	MLB	Gene Babb
Walt Corey	RLB	Mike Dukes
Duane Wood	LCB	Tony Banfield
Dave Grayson	RCB	Bobby Jancik
Bobby Hunt	LS	Jim Norton
Bobby Ply	RS	Fred Glick

Dallas Texans	3	14	0	0	0	3	—	20
Houston	0	0	7	10	0	0	—	17

Dall —FG Brooker 16
Dall —Haynes 28 pass from Dawson (Brooker kick)
Dall —Haynes 2 run (Brooker kick)
Hou —Dewveall 15 pass from Blanda (Blanda kick)
Hou —FB Blanda 31
Hou —Tolar 1 run (Blanda kick)
Dall —FG Brooker 25
Attendance—37,981

TEAM STATISTICS	Dall	Hou
First downs	19	21
Rushing	10	6
Passing	5	15
By penalty	4	0
Total yardage	237	359
Net rushing yardage	199	98
Net passing yardage	38	261
Passes att.-comp.-had int.	14-9-0	46-23-5

1962 NFL

GREEN BAY 16, N.Y. GIANTS 7

Green Bay's Nitschke (66)—the defensive star.

The Green Bay Packers fought off the New York Giants in 13-degree cold and winds that gusted up to 40 miles per hour in Yankee Stadium to score a 16–7 victory for their fifth NFL championship and second in a row. The Giants lost in the championship playoff for the fourth time in five years and the tenth time in thirteen appearances. Offensive backfield coach Kyle Rote, who retired as a Giants player after the 1961 season, remarked, "I never before saw a team that tried so hard and lost."

The Giants concentrated most of their efforts on fullback Jim Taylor, who tied a record with 31 carries. Taylor gained 85 yards, scored on a seven-yard touchdown run in the second quarter, and maintained a constant exchange with Giants defenders, challenging them to "hit me harder."

Although they outgained Green Bay 291–244 in total yards, the Giants never led. Their only touchdown came when the score was 10-0 in the third quarter. Erich Barnes blocked Max McGee's punt and Jim Collier recovered in the end zone for a touchdown.

December 30, at New York

Green Bay	Starters, Offense	N.Y. Giants
Max McGee	LE	Del Shofner
Norm Masters	LT	Roosevelt Brown
Fred (Fuzzy) Thurston	LG	Darrell Dess
Jim Ringo	C	Ray Wietecha
Jerry Kramer	RG	Greg Larson
Forrest Gregg	RT	Jack Stroud
Ron Kramer	RE	Joe Walton
Bart Starr	QB	Y.A. Tittle
Paul Hornung	LH	Phil King
Boyd Dowler	RH	Frank Gifford
Jim Taylor	FB	Alex Webster
	Starters, Defense	
Willie Davis	LE	Jim Katcavage
Dave Hanner	LT	Dick Modzelewski
Henry Jordan	RT	Roosevelt Grier
Bill Quinlan	RE	Andy Robustelli
Dan Currie	LLB	Bill Winter
Ray Nitschke	MLB	Sam Huff
Bill Forester	RLB	Tom Scott
Herb Adderley	LCB	Erich Barnes
Jesse Whittenton	RCB	Dick Lynch
Hank Gremminger	LS	Alan Webb
Willie Wood	RS	Jim Patton

Green Bay	3	7	3	3	—	16
N.Y. Giants	0	0	7	0	—	7

GB —FG J. Kramer 26
GB —Taylor 7 run (J. Kramer kick)
NYG—Collier blocked punt recovery in end zone
    (Chandler kick)
GB —FG J. Kramer 29
GB —FG J. Kramer 30
Attendance—64,892

TEAM STATISTICS	GB	NYG
First downs	18	18
Rushing	11	5
Passing	6	11
By penalty	1	2
Total yardage	244	291
Net rushing yardage	148	94
Net passing yardage	96	197
Passes att.-comp.-had int.	22-10-0	41-18-1

1963 NFL

CHICAGO 14, N.Y. GIANTS 10

Tittle is injured when tackled by Morris.

The sun was shining but the temperature was 11 degrees in Wrigley Field, where the Chicago Bears intercepted five passes by New York Giants quarterback Y.A. Tittle, two of them setting up touchdowns in a 14–10 victory. Tittle played the second half with a severely strained knee, the result of a second-quarter tackle by Larry Morris.

The Bears scored their first touchdown after linebacker Morris intercepted a screen pass intended for Phil King and returned the ball 61 yards to New York's 5-yard line. Quarterback Bill Wade scored on a two-yard run. The second touchdown followed an interception of another screen pass, this by defensive end Ed O'Bradovich, who returned the ball 10 yards to the Giants' 14. Wade scored five plays later from the 1.

The Giants led 7–0 after Tittle's 14-yard pass to Frank Gifford in the first quarter and 10–7 after Don Chandler's 13-yard field goal in the second quarter. The Giants' defeat was their fifth in a row in the championship playoff. Their overall record was 3-11 since they lost to the Bears 23–21 in Wrigley Field in the NFL's first playoff game in 1933.

December 29, at Chicago

N.Y. Giants	Starters, Offense	Chicago
Del Shofner	LE	John Farrington
Roosevelt Brown	LT	Herman Lee
Darrell Dess	LG	Ted Karras
Greg Larson	C	Mike Pyle
Treva (Bookie) Bolin	RG	Roger Davis
Jack Stroud	RT	Bob Wetoska
Joe Walton	RE	Mike Ditka
Y.A. Tittle	QB	Bill Wade
Frank Gifford	FL	Johnny Morris
Phil King	HB	Willie Galimore
Joe Morrison	FB	Joe Marconi
	Starters, Defense	
Jim Katcavage	LE	Ed O'Bradovich
Dick Modzelewski	LT	Stan Jones
John LoVetere	RT	Fred Williams
Andy Robustelli	RE	Doug Atkins
Jerry Hillebrand	LLB	Joe Fortunato
Sam Huff	MLB	Bill George
Tom Scott	RLB	Larry Morris
Erich Barnes	LCB	Bennie McRae
Dick Lynch	RCB	Dave Whitsell
Dick Pesonen	LS	Richie Petitbon
Jim Patton	RS	Roosevelt Taylor

N.Y. Giants	7	3	0	0	—	10
Chicago	7	0	7	0	—	14

NYG—Gifford 14 pass from Tittle (Chandler kick)
Chi —Wade 2 run (Jencks kick)
NYG—FG Chandler 13
Chi —Wade 1 run (Jencks kick)
Attendance—45,801

TEAM STATISTICS	NYG	Chi
First downs	17	14
Rushing	8	6
Passing	9	7
By penalty	0	1
Total yardage	268	222
Net rushing yardage	128	93
Net passing yardage	140	129
Passes att.-comp.-had int.	30-11-5	28-10-0

1963 AFL

SAN DIEGO 51, BOSTON 10

Boston can't defense the Chargers Lincoln.

Fullback Keith Lincoln of San Diego outgained the Boston Patriots 334-261 in total offense and led the Chargers to a 51–10 victory. Chargers coach Sid Gillman, pointing to the rival NFL, said after the game, "We're the champions of the world. If anyone wants to debate it, let them play us."

Lincoln gained 206 yards in 13 carries and scored on a 67-yard run. He caught seven passes for 128 yards and scored on a 25-yard pass from John Hadl. The Chargers, who led 21–7 at the end of the first quarter and 31–10 at halftime, rushed for 318 yards and passed for 292—a total offense of 610 yards. The Chargers' running attack averaged almost 10 yards for each attempt. Halfback Paul Lowe backed up Lincoln with 94 yards in 12 carries and scored on a 58-yard run. Flanker Lance Alworth caught four passes for 77 yards.

"I didn't think it would ever go like this . . . not like this," said Patriots coach Mike Holovak.

January 5, at San Diego

Boston	Starters, Offense	San Diego
Gino Cappelletti	LE	Don Norton
Don Oakes	LT	Ernie Wright
Charlie Long	LG	Sam DeLuca
Walt Cudzik	C	Don Rogers
Billy Neighbors	RG	Pat Shea
Milt Graham	RT	Ron Mix
Tony Romeo	RE	Dave Kocourek
Babe Parilli	QB	Tobin Rote
Ron Burton	LH	Paul Lowe
Jim Colclough	RH	Lance Alworth
Larry Garron	FB	Keith Lincoln
	Starters, Defense	
Larry Eisenhauer	LE	Earl Faison
Jesse Richardson	LT	Henry Schmidt
Houston Antwine	RT	George Gross
Bob Dee	RE	Bob Petrich
Tom Addison	LLB	Emil Karas
Nick Buoniconti	MLB	Chuck Allen
Jack Rudolph	RLB	Paul Maguire
Dick Felt	LCB	Bud Whitehead
Bob Suci	RCB	Dick Harris
Ron Hall	LS	George Blair
Ross O'Hanley	RS	Gary Glick

Boston	7	3	0	0	—	10
San Diego	21	10	7	13	—	51

SD —Rote 2 run (Blair kick)
SD —Lincoln 67 run (Blair kick)
Bos—Garron 7 run (Cappelletti kick)
SD —Lowe 58 run (Blair kick)
SD —FG Blair 11
Bos—FG Cappelletti 15
SD —Norton 14 pass from Rote (Blair kick)
SD —Alworth 48 pass from Rote (Blair kick)
SD —Lincoln 25 pass from Hadl (pass failed)
SD —Hadl 1 run (Blair kick)
Attendance—30,127

TEAM STATISTICS	Bos	SD
First downs	14	21
Rushing	6	11
Passing	8	9
By penalty	0	1
Total yardage	261	610
Net rushing yardage	75	318
Net passing yardage	186	292
Passes att.-comp.-had int.	37-17-2	26-17-0

1964 AFL

BUFFALO 20, SAN DIEGO 7

Gilchrist sheds San Diego defense.

The San Diego Chargers scored on a 26-yard pass from quarterback Tobin Rote to end Dave Kocourek and were driving again in the first quarter when Rote threw an 11-yard pass to fullback Keith Lincoln, who had swung out of the backfield. Bills linebacker Mike Stratton came up to make the tackle and hit Lincoln with such force that the San Diego star suffered a broken rib and had to be carried off the field. Lincoln, who also had rushed for 47 yards in three carries, did not return. The Chargers struggled without him and dropped a 20–7 decision to the Buffalo Bills.

An AFL championship game record crowd of 40,242 persons in War Memorial Stadium saw the Bills take a 13–7 halftime lead on field goals of 12 and 17 yards by Pete Gogolak, sandwiched around a four-yard run by Wray Carlton. Quarterback Jack Kemp and end Glenn Bass combined on a 48-yard pass play in the fourth quarter to set up the Bills' final score. Kemp went over from the 1 yard line two plays later.

Kemp completed 10 of 20 passes for 188 yards. Fullback Cookie Gilchrist gained 122 yards in 16 carries and Carlton added 70 in 18.

December 26, at Buffalo

San Diego	Starters, Offense	Buffalo
Don Norton	LE	Glenn Bass
Ernie Wright	LT	Stew Barber
Pat Shea	LG	Billy Shaw
Don Rogers	C	Walt Cudzik
Walt Sweeney	RG	Al Bemiller
Ron Mix	RT	Dick Hudson
Dave Kocurek	RE	Ernie Warlick
Tobin Rote	QB	Jack Kemp
Paul Lowe	LHB	Wray Carlton
Jerry Robinson	RHB	Elbert Dubenion
Keith Lincoln	FB	Cookie Gilchrist
	Starters, Defense	
Earl Faison	LE	Ron McDole
George Gross	LT	Jim Dunaway
Ernie Ladd	RT	Tom Sestak
Bob Petrich	RE	Tom Day
Ron Carpenter	LLB	John Tracey
Chuck Allen	MLB	Harry Jacobs
Frank Buncom	RLB	Mike Stratton
Jim Warren	LCB	Charlie Warner
Dick Westmoreland	RCB	George (Butch) Byrd
Kenny Graham	LS	Gene Sykes
Bud Whitehead	RS	George Saimes

San Diego	7	0	0	0	—	7
Buffalo	3	10	0	7	—	20

SD —Kocourek 26 pass from Rote (Lincoln kick)
Buff—FG Gogolak 12
Buff—Carlton 4 run (Gogolak kick)
Buff—FG Gogolak 17
Buff—Kemp 1 run (Gogolak kick)
Attendance—40,242

TEAM STATISTICS	SD	Buff
First downs	15	21
Rushing	7	12
Passing	7	8
By penalty	1	1
Total yardage	259	387
Net rushing yardage	124	219
Net passing yardage	135	168
Passes att.-comp.-had int.	36-13-3	20-10-0

1964 NFL

CLEVELAND 27, BALTIMORE 0

Ryan throws for three touchdowns to Collins.

Forty-year-old Lou Groza, playing in the twelfth championship game of his 18-year career in professional football, kicked two field goals, including a 43-yard attempt that began the Cleveland Browns' 27–0 victory over the Baltimore Colts. Browns quarterback Frank Ryan completed 11 of 18 passes for 197 yards and three touchdowns to Gary Collins; fullback Jim Brown rushed for 114 yards in 27 carries, and the Browns' defense restricted the Colts to 92 yards passing and 89 yards rushing. The Colts gained only 54 yards in 22 offensive plays in the second half.

After a scoreless first half, the Browns scored 17 points in the third quarter, benefitting partly from a blustery wind at their backs. Groza's first field goal was followed by an 18-yard touchdown pass from Ryan to flanker Collins. The play was set up by a 46-yard run by Jim Brown. Collins, who caught five passes for 130 yards, scored again on a 42-yard pass play in the third quarter and on a 51-yard pass play in the fourth quarter.

Ryan's performance climaxed a strong personal finish to the season. He threw five touchdown passes the week before in the last regular season game.

December 27, at Cleveland

Baltimore	Starters, Offense	Cleveland
Raymond Berry	LE	Paul Warfield
Bob Vogel	LT	Dick Schafrath
Jim Parker	LG	John Wooten
Dick Szymanski	C	John Morrow
Alex Sandusky	RG	Gene Hickerson
George Preas	RT	Monte Clark
John Mackey	RE	John Brewer
Johnny Unitas	QB	Frank Ryan
Jimmy Orr	FL	Gary Collins
Lenny Moore	HB	Ernie Green
Jerry Hill	FB	Jim Brown
	Starters, Defense	
Gino Marchetti	LE	Paul Wiggin
Guy Reese	LT	Dick Modzelewski
Fred Miller	RT	Jim Kanicki
Ordell Braase	RE	Bill Glass
Steve Stonebreaker	LLB	Jim Houston
Bill Pellington	MLB	Vince Costello
Don Shinnick	RLB	Galen Fiss
Bobby Boyd	LCB	Bernie Parrish
Lenny Lyles	RCB	Walter Beach
Jerry Logan	LS	Larry Benz
Jim Welch	RS	Ross Fitchner

Baltimore	0	0	0	0	—	0
Cleveland	0	0	17	10	—	27

Cle—FG Groza 43
Cle—Collins 18 pass from Ryan (Groza kick)
Cle—Collins 42 pass from Ryan (Groza kick)
Cle—FG Groza 10
Cle—Collins 51 pass from Ryan (Groza kick)
Attendance—79,544

TEAM STATISTICS	Balt	Cle
First downs	11	20
Rushing	5	8
Passing	4	9
By penalty	2	3
Total yardage	181	339
Net rushing yardage	92	142
Net passing yardage	89	197
Passes att.-comp.-had int.	20-12-2	18-11-1

1965 AFL

BUFFALO 23, SAN DIEGO 0

Clarke blocks Harris, frees Byrd on return.

Mixing their defensive alignments, the Buffalo Bills used a three-man line with an end dropping off to cover passes and a safety blitz to confuse the San Diego Chargers' offense. They also assigned double coverage to pass receiver Lance Alworth, in addition to using two tight ends on offense. The result was a 23–0 victory over a team that had outgained them 816-381 in total offense in two regular season games. San Diego had won one of those games 34–3; the other was a 20–20 tie.

The Chargers never penetrated beyond Buffalo's 24-yard line. Buffalo scored first-half touchdowns on an 18-yard pass from quarterback Jack Kemp to tight end Ernie Warlick and on a 74-yard punt return by George (Butch) Byrd. Pete Gogolak kicked field goals of 11 and 39 yards in the third quarter and 32 yards in the fourth quarter.

Paul Lowe, whose 1,121 yards rushing during the regular season had set an AFL record and was 28 yards more than nine Bills runners netted all year, gained 57 yards in 12 carries. Forty-seven of Lowe's yards came on one carry.

December 26, at San Diego

Buffalo	Starters, Offense	San Diego
Charlie Ferguson	LE	Don Norton
Stew Barber	LT	Ernie Wright
George Flint	LG	Ernest Park
Al Bemiller	C	Sam Gruneisen
Joe O'Donnell	RG	Walt Sweeney
Dick Hudson	RT	Ron Mix
Paul Costa	RE	Dave Kocourek
Jack Kemp	QB	John Hadl
Billy Joe	LH	Paul Lowe
Irwin (Bo) Roberson	FL	Lance Alworth
Wray Carlton	FB	Gene Foster
	Starters, Defense	
Ron McDole	LE	Earl Faison
Jim Dunaway	LT	George Gross
Tom Sestak	RT	Ernie Ladd
Tom Day	RE	Bob Petrich
John Tracey	LLB	Dick Degen
Harry Jacobs	MLB	Chuck Allen
Mike Stratton	RLB	Frank Buncom
Booker Edgerson	LCB	Jim Warren
George (Butch) Byrd	RCB	Leslie (Speedy) Duncan
Hagood Clarke	LS	Kenny Graham
George Saimes	RS	Bud Whitehead

Buffalo	0	14	6	3	—	23
San Diego	0	0	0	0	—	0

Buff—Warlick 18 pass from Kemp (Gogolak kick)
Buff—Byrd 74 interception return (Gogolak kick)
Buff—FG Gogolak 11
Buff—FG Gogolak 39
Buff—FG Gogolak 32
Attendance—30,361

TEAM STATISTICS	Buff	SD
First downs	23	12
Rushing	13	5
Passing	9	7
By penalty	1	0
Total yardage	260	229
Net rushing yardage	108	119
Net passing yardage	152	110
Passes att.-comp.-had int.	20-9-1	25-12-2

1965 NFL

GREEN BAY 23, CLEVELAND 12

Taylor (31) battles Browns with tough running.

Lambeau Field was cleared of four inches of snow but a freezing rain turned the field into mud as the Green Bay Packers defeated the Cleveland Browns 23–12 and held fullback Jim Brown to 50 yards in 12 carries. Brown had led the NFL with 1,544 yards rushing during the season. Packers runners Paul Hornung and Jim Taylor met with more success.

Taylor never gained more than eight yards on a single attempt, but when the Packers controlled the ball for almost 14 minutes during two second-half drives to a touchdown and field goal, he was given the ball 12 times in 24 plays.

The Packers led 13–12 at the half; they pulled away in the third quarter on a 13-yard run by Hornung and on Don Chandler's 29-yard field goal in the fourth quarter.

"The snow and mud were our allies," said Packers coach Vince Lombardi. "When you have conditions like these, it's best to be basic, not fancy. And we're the most basic offensive team there is."

January 2, at Green Bay

Cleveland	Starters, Offense	Green Bay
Paul Warfield	LE	Boyd Dowler
John Brown	LT	Bob Skoronski
John Wooten	LG	Fred (Fuzzy) Thurston
Gene Hickerson	C	Ken Bowman
Monte Clark	RG	Jerry Kramer
John Morrow	RT	Forrest Gregg
John Brewer	RE	Bill Anderson
Frank Ryan	QB	Bart Starr
Gary Collins	FL	Carroll Dale
Ernie Green	HB	Paul Hornung
Jim Brown	FB	Jim Taylor
	Starters, Defense	
Paul Wiggin	LE	Willie Davis
Dick Modzelewski	LT	Ron Kostelnik
Jim Kanicki	RT	Henry Jordan
Bill Glass	RE	Lionel Aldridge
Jim Houston	LLB	Dave Robinson
Vince Costello	MLB	Ray Nitschke
Galen Fiss	RLB	Lee Roy Caffey
Bernie Parrish	LCB	Herb Adderley
Walter Beach	RCB	Doug Hart
Ross Fichtner	LS	Tom Brown
Larry Benz	RS	Willie Wood

Cleveland	9	3	0	0	—	12
Green Bay	7	6	7	3	—	23

GB—Dale 47 pass from Starr (Chandler kick)
Cle—Collins 17 pass from Ryan (kick failed)
Cle—FG Groza 24
GB—FG Chandler 15
GB—FG Chandler 23
Cle—FG Groza 28
GB—Hornung 13 run (Chandler kick)
GB—FG Chandler 29
Attendance—50,777

TEAM STATISTICS	Cle	GB
First downs	8	21
Rushing	2	10
Passing	5	9
By penalty	1	2
Total yardage	161	332
Net rushing yardage	64	204
Net passing yardage	97	128
Passes att.-comp.-had int.	18-8-2	19-10-1

1966 AFL

KANSAS CITY 31, BUFFALO 7

Buffalo has no solution for Dawson's passing.

The Kansas City Chiefs qualified as the AFL's first representative in the Super Bowl when they defeated the Buffalo Bills 31–7. The Chiefs, who won the 1962 AFL title as the Dallas Texans, had a total yardage advantage of 277-255; their defense was responsible for the game's biggest play.

Trailing 14–7 near the end of the first half, Buffalo had the ball on the Chiefs' 10 yard line. Quarterback Jack Kemp passed to Bobby Crockett, but Chiefs safety Johnny Robinson intercepted the ball and ran 72 yards. The Chiefs converted the interception into Mike Mercer's 32-yard field goal and led 17–7 at halftime. Instead of a possible tie with Kansas City, the Bills trailed by 10 points at the start of the second half.

The Chiefs' Mike Garrett scored on runs of 1 and 18 yards in the fourth quarter. Quarterback Len Dawson, who completed 16 of 24 passes for 227 yards, passed 29 yards each to tight end Fred Arbanas and flanker Otis Taylor to produce touchdowns in the first half. Buffalo scored on a 69-yard pass play, Kemp to Elbert Dubenion.

January 1, at Buffalo

Kansas City	Starters, Offense	Buffalo
Chris Burford	LE	Bobby Crockett
Jim Tyrer	LT	Stew Barber
Ed Budde	LG	Billy Shaw
Wayne Frazier	C	Al Bemiller
Curt Merz	RG	Joe O'Donnell
Dave Hill	RT	Dick Hudson
Fred Arbanas	RE	Paul Costa
Len Dawson	QB	Jack Kemp
Mike Garrett	LH	Bob Burnett
Otis Taylor	FL	Elbert Dubenion
Curtis McClinton	FB	Wray Carlton
	Starters, Defense	
Jerry Mays	LE	Ron McDole
Ed Lothamer	LT	Jim Dunaway
Buck Buchanan	RT	Tom Sestak
Chuck Hurston	RE	Tom Day
Bobby Bell	LLB	John Tracey
Sherrill Headrick	MLB	Harry Jacobs
E.J. Holub	RLB	Mike Stratton
Fred Williamson	LCB	Tom Janik
Willie Mitchell	RCB	George (Butch) Byrd
Bobby Hunt	LS	Hagood Clarke
Johnny Robinson	RS	George Saimes

Kansas City	7	10	0	14	—	31
Buffalo	7	0	0	0	—	7

KC —Arbanas 29 pass from Dawson (Mercer kick)
Buff—Dubenion 69 pass from Kemp (Lusteg kick)
KC —Taylor 29 pass from Dawson (Mercer kick)
KC —FG Mercer 32
KC —Garrett 1 run (Mercer kick)
KC —Garrett 18 run (Mercer kick)
Attendance—42,080

TEAM STATISTICS	KC	Buff
First downs	14	9
Rushing	6	2
Passing	8	7
By penalty	0	0
Total yardage	277	255
Net rushing yardage	113	40
Net passing yardage	164	215
Passes att.-comp.-had int.	24-16-0	27-12-2

1966 NFL

GREEN BAY 34, DALLAS 27

Packers' Dale beats Green on a 51-yard pass play.

With less than two minutes remaining in the game, the Dallas Cowboys had a first down on the Green Bay Packers' 2-yard line, but they failed to score and the Packers won 34–27 in the Cotton Bowl.

Packers quarterback Bart Starr, who completed 19 of 28 passes for 304 yards and four touchdowns, passed 28 yards to end Max McGee to put Green Bay ahead 34–20 with 5:20 left in the game. Don Chandler's extra-point attempt was blocked by Bob Lilly. Dallas scored on a 68-yard pass play, Don Meredith to Frank Clarke. With 4:09 left the score was 34–27. The Packers' next possession ended with a 16-yard punt by Chandler. Dallas took over on Green Bay's 47. On second down from the 22, Green Bay's Tom Brown was called for pass interference on Clarke in the end zone. That put the ball on the 2-yard line with 1:52 left. On fourth down, Meredith threw a pass that was intercepted by Brown in the end zone with 28 seconds remaining.

January 1, at Dallas

Green Bay	Starters, Offense	Dallas
Carroll Dale	LE	Bob Hayes
Bob Skoronski	LT	Jim Boeke
Fred (Fuzzy) Thurston	LG	Tony Liscio
Bill Curry	C	Dave Manders
Jerry Kramer	RG	Leon Donohue
Forrest Gregg	RT	Ralph Neely
Marv Fleming	RE	Pettis Norman
Bart Starr	QB	Don Meredith
Boyd Dowler	FL	Pete Gent
Elijah Pitts	HB	Dan Reeves
Jim Taylor	FB	Don Perkins
	Starters, Defense	
Willie Davis	LE	Willie Townes
Ron Kostelnik	LT	Jim Colvin
Henry Jordan	RT	Bob Lilly
Lionel Aldridge	RE	George Andrie
Dave Robinson	LLB	Chuck Howley
Ray Nitschke	MLB	Lee Roy Jordan
Lee Roy Caffey	RLB	Dave Edwards
Herb Adderley	LCB	Cornell Green
Bob Jeter	RCB	Warren Livingston
Tom Brown	LS	Mike Gaechter
Willie Wood	RS	Mel Renfro

Green Bay	14	7	7	6	—	34
Dallas	14	3	3	7	—	27

GB —Pitts 17 pass from Starr (Chandler kick)
GB —Grabowski 18 fumble return (Chandler kick)
Dall—Reeves 3 run (Villanueva kick)
Dall—Perkins 23 run (Villanueva kick)
GB —Dale 51 pass from Starr (Chandler kick)
Dall—FG Villanueva 11
Dall—FG Villanueva 32
GB —Dowler 16 pass from Starr (Chandler kick)
GB —McGee 28 pass from Starr (kick blocked)
Dall—Clarke 68 pass from Meredith (Villanueva kick)
Attendance—74,152

TEAM STATISTICS	GB	Dall
First downs	19	23
Rushing	3	12
Passing	14	10
By penalty	2	1
Total yardage	367	418
Net rushing yardage	102	187
Net passing yardage	265	231
Passes att.-comp.-had int.	28-19-0	31-15-1

1967 AFL

OAKLAND 40, HOUSTON 7

Lamonica passes for two touchdowns.

The Oakland Raiders scored a touchdown on a fake field goal with 18 seconds remaining in the half and went on to defeat the Houston Oilers 40–7 for their first AFL championship. With the score 10-0, Oakland quarterback Daryle Lamonica took the snap from center for an apparent field goal attempt by George Blanda from the Oilers' 17 yard line. Instead, Lamonica ran to his right and passed to end Dave Kocourek, who was open at the 10 yard line and scored to give Oakland a 17–0 lead at the half.

The Raiders had built a 10–0 lead on a 37-yard field goal by Blanda and a 69-yard run by fullback Hewritt Dixon. They increased their advantage to 30–0 in the fourth quarter before Houston scored on Pete Beathard's five-yard pass to Charlie Frazier.

Dixon carried the ball 21 times for 144 yards, two yards less than the Oilers' total offense. Pete Banaszak rushed for 116 yards in 15 carries. Lamonica completed 10 of 24 passes for 111 yards and two touchdowns.

December 31, at Oakland

Houston	Starters, Offense	Oakland
Lionel Taylor	LE	Bill Miller
Walt Suggs	LT	Bob Svihus
Bob Talamini	LG	Gene Upshaw
Bobby Maples	C	Jim Otto
Erwin (Sonny) Bishop	RG	Wayne Hawkins
Glen Ray Hines	RT	Harry Schuh
Alvin Reed	TE	Billy Cannon
Pete Beathard	QB	Daryle Lamonica
Ode Burrell	FL	Fred Biletnikoff
Woody Campbell	RB	Pete Banaszak
Hoyle Granger	RB	Hewritt Dixon
	Starters, Defense	
Pat Holmes	LE	Isaac Lassiter
Willie Parker	LT	Dan Birdwell
George Rice	RT	Tom Keating
Richard Marshall	RE	Ben Davidson
George Webster	LLB	Bill Laskey
Garland Boyette	MLB	Dan Conners
Olen Underwood	RLB	Gus Otto
Miller Farr	LCB	Kent McCloughan
W. K. Hicks	RCB	Willie Brown
Ken Houston	LS	Warren Powers
Jim Norton	RS	Dave Grayson

Houston	0	0	0	7	—	7
Oakland	3	14	10	13	—	40

Oak —FG Blanda 37
Oak —Dixon 69 run (Blanda kick)
Oak —Kocourek 17 pass from Lamonica (Blanda kick)
Oak —Lamonica 1 run (Blanda kick)
Oak —FG Blanda 40
Oak —FG Blanda 42
Hous—Frazier 5 pass from Beathard (Wittenborn kick)
Oak —FG Blanda 36
Oak —Miller 12 pass from Lamonica (Blanda kick)
Attendance—53,330

TEAM STATISTICS	Hou	Oak
First downs	11	18
Rushing	4	11
Passing	6	6
By penalty	1	1
Total yardage	146	364
Net rushing yardage	38	263
Net passing yardage	108	101
Passes att.-comp.-had int.	35-15-1	26-10-0

1967 NFL

GREEN BAY 21, DALLAS 17

Starr (15) scores, climaxing winning drive.

No professional football playoff ever took place in conditions to match the 13-below temperature and 15-miles-per-hour winds that enveloped Lambeau Field. Breathing steam and spitting ice, the Green Bay Packers and Dallas Cowboys came to the final 13 seconds, when Packers quarterback Bart Starr scored a touchdown and gave Green Bay a 21–17 victory—their third consecutive NFL championship, a record, and fifth title in seven years.

Starr slid across the goal line between blocks by center Ken Bowman and right guard Jerry Kramer on third down after Green Bay had taken its final time out. The score climaxed a 12-play, 68-yard drive that began after Dallas had gone ahead 17–14 on a 50-yard pass play, halfback Dan Reeves to flanker Lance Rentzel, eight seconds into the final quarter. The big play in the winning drive for the Packers, who led 14–0 in the first half, came with two minutes left. Starr threw a short pass to halfback Chuck Mercein, who ran 19 yards to the Dallas 11. Mercein then gained eight yards to the 3. Starr scored three plays later.

December 31, at Green Bay

Dallas	Starters, Offense	Green Bay
Bob Hayes	LE	Boyd Dowler
Tony Liscio	LT	Bob Skoronski
John Niland	LG	Gale Gillingham
Mike Connelly	C	Ken Bowman
Leon Donohue	RG	Jerry Kramer
Ralph Neely	RT	Forrest Gregg
Pettis Norman	TE	Marv Fleming
Don Meredith	QB	Bart Starr
Lance Rentzel	FL	Carroll Dale
Dan Reeves	RB	Donny Anderson
Don Perkins	RB	Chuck Mercein
	Starters, Defense	
Willie Townes	LE	Willie Davis
Jethro Pugh	LT	Ron Kostelnik
Bob Lilly	RT	Henry Jordan
George Andrie	RE	Lionel Aldridge
Chuck Howley	LLB	Dave Robinson
Lee Roy Jordan	MLB	Ray Nitschke
Dave Edwards	RLB	Lee Roy Caffey
Cornell Green	LCB	Herb Adderley
Mike Johnson	RCB	Bob Jeter
Mike Gaechter	LS	Tom Brown
Mel Renfro	RS	Willie Wood

Dallas	0	10	0	7	—	17
Green Bay	7	7	0	7	—	21

GB —Dowler 8 pass from Starr (Chandler kick)
GB —Dowler 46 pass from Starr (Chandler kick)
Dall—Andrie 7 fumble return (Villanueva kick)
Dall—FG Villanueva 21
Dall—Rentzel 50 pass from Reeves (Villanueva kick)
GB —Starr 1 run (Chandler kick)
Attendance—50,861

TEAM STATISTICS	Dall	GB
First downs	11	18
Rushing	4	5
Passing	6	10
By penalty	1	3
Total yardage	192	195
Net rushing yardage	92	80
Net passing yardage	100	115
Passes att.-comp.-had int.	26-11-1	24-14-1

1968 AFL

N.Y. JETS 27, OAKLAND 23

Jets' Snell leads rushers with 71 yards in 19 carries.

The Oakland Raiders had the ball on the New York Jets' 24-yard line in the final two minutes of the game; rookie halfback Charlie Smith fumbled a lateral from quarterback Daryle Lamonica and linebacker Ralph Baker of the Jets picked up the free ball to save a 27–23 victory for New York and its first AFL championship before a record AFL playoff crowd of 62,627 persons.

Despite icy winds and a hard playing surface in Shea Stadium, the Jets and Raiders raced up and down the field, piling up a combined total of 843 yards offense. Namath and Lamonica filled the air with 96 passes. Lamonica completed 20 of 47 for 401 yards and one touchdown. Namath completed 19 of 49 for 266 yards and three touchdowns.

The Jets led 10–0 at the end of the first quarter; the Raiders caught them at 13–13 in the third period, fell behind 20–13, then went ahead 23–20. The Jets moved back in front 27–23 in the final period.

December 29, at New York

Oakland	Starters, Offense	N.Y. Jets
Warren Wells	LE	George Sauer
Bob Svihus	LT	Winston Hill
Gene Upshaw	LG	Bob Talamini
Jim Otto	C	John Schmitt
Jim Harvey	RG	Randy Rasmussen
Harry Schuh	RT	Dave Herman
Billy Cannon	TE	Pete Lammons
Daryle Lamonica	QB	Joe Namath
Fred Biletnikoff	FL	Don Maynard
Charlie Smith	RB	Emerson Boozer
Hewritt Dixon	RB	Matt Snell
	Starters, Defense	
Isaac Lassiter	LE	Gerry Philbin
Dan Birdwell	LT	Paul Rochester
Carleton Oats	RT	John Elliott
Ben Davidson	RE	Verlon Biggs
Ralph (Chip) Oliver	LLB	Ralph Baker
Dan Conners	MLB	Al Atkinson
Gus Otto	RLB	Larry Grantham
George Atkinson	LCB	Johnny Sample
Willie Brown	RCB	Randy Beverly
Rodger Bird	LS	Jim Hudson
Dave Grayson	RS	Bill Baird

Oakland	0	10	3	10	—	23
N.Y. Jets	10	3	7	7	—	27

NYJ—Maynard 14 pass from Namath (J. Turner kick)
NYJ—FG J. Turner 33
Oak—Biletnikoff 29 pass from Lamonica (Blanda kick)
NYJ—FG J. Turner 36
Oak—FG Blanda 26
Oak—FG Blanda 9
NYJ—Lammons 20 pass from Namath (J. Turner kick)
Oak—FG Blanda 20
Oak—Banaszak 5 run (Blanda kick)
NYJ—Maynard 6 pass from Namath (J. Turner kick)
Attendance—62,627

TEAM STATISTICS	Oak	NYJ
First downs	18	25
Rushing	3	9
Passing	14	15
By penalty	1	1
Total yardage	443	400
Net rushing yardage	50	144
Net passing yardage	393	256
Passes att.-comp.-had int.	47-20-0	49-19-1

1968 NFL

BALTIMORE 34, CLEVELAND 0

Browns' Ryan (13) watches ball bounce away.

The Baltimore Colts were hailed as one of the greatest teams in NFL history after winning their fifteenth game against one loss by blanking the Cleveland Browns 34–0 for their first championship since 1959. The shutout was only the second in the Browns' 24-year history.

The Colts broke the game open with 17 points in the second quarter, beginning with a 28-yard field goal by Lou Michaels. Halfback Tom Matte scored touchdowns on runs of 1 and 12 yards, then tied a record with his third touchdown, on a two-yard run, in the third quarter.

Baltimore finished the Browns in the fourth quarter on Michaels's 10-yard field goal and Timmy Brown's four-yard run.

The Colts outgained the Browns 353-173 in total offense and had 22 first downs to 12. Baltimore held a 184-56 rushing advantage as Matte gained 88 yards in 17 carries and fullback Jerry Hill 60 in 11. Cleveland's Leroy Kelly, who led professional football in 1968 with 1,239 yards rushing, was held to 28 yards in 13 carries.

December 29, at Cleveland

Baltimore	Starters, Offense	Cleveland
Jimmy Orr	LE	Paul Warfield
Bob Vogel	LT	Dick Schafrath
Glenn Ressler	LG	John Demarie
Bill Curry	C	Fred Hoaglin
Dan Sullivan	RG	Gene Hickerson
Sam Ball	RT	Monte Clark
John Mackey	TE	Milt Morin
Earl Morrall	QB	Bill Nelsen
Willie Richardson	FL	Gary Collins
Tom Matte	RB	Leroy Kelly
Jerry Hill	RB	Charley Harraway
	Starters, Defense	
Charles (Bubba) Smith	LE	Ron Snidow
Billy Ray Smith	LT	Jim Kanicki
Fred Miller	RT	Walter Johnson
Ordell Braase	RE	Jack Gregory
Mike Curtis	LLB	Jim Houston
Dennis Gaubatz	MLB	Bob Matheson
Don Shinnick	RLB	Dale Lindsey
Bobby Boyd	LCB	Erich Barnes
Lenny Lyles	RCB	Ben Davis
Jerry Logan	LS	Ernie Kellermann
Rick Volk	RS	Mike Howell

Baltimore	0	17	7	10	—	34
Cleveland	0	0	0	0	—	0

Balt—FG Michaels 28
Balt—Matte 1 run (Michaels kick)
Balt—Matte 12 run (Michaels kick)
Balt—Matte 2 run (Michaels kick)
Balt—FG Michaels 10
Balt—Brown 4 run (Michaels kick)
Attendance—78,410

TEAM STATISTICS	Balt	Cle
First downs	22	12
Rushing	13	2
Passing	8	8
By penalty	1	2
Total yardage	353	173
Net rushing yardage	184	56
Net passing yardage	169	117
Passes att.-comp.-had int.	25-11-1	32-13-2

1969 AFL

KANSAS CITY 17, OAKLAND 7

Chiefs' Arbanas blocks for Garrett.

The Kansas City Chiefs won the last championship of the AFL when they defeated the Oakland Raiders 17–7 after losing to that team twice in the regular season. The Chiefs turned the ball over three times inside their 30-yard line in the fourth quarter, but they intercepted three of Raiders quarterback Daryle Lamonica's passes during that time. Kansas City won two other titles in 1962 as the Dallas Texans and in 1966, during the 10-year history of the AFL.

The Chiefs broke a 7–7 tie midway in the third quarter. Faced with a third-and-14 situation on his 2 yard line, quarterback Len Dawson scrambled out of trouble in his end zone and completed a 35-yard pass to Otis Taylor. That play began a 98-yard march to the touchdown that made the score 14–7. The Raiders' first opportunity to tie came when Lamonica, who had returned to the game after jamming his throwing hand against the helmet of Kansas City's Aaron Brown early in the quarter, moved Oakland from its 6 yard line to Kansas City's 39. Jim Kearney intercepted for Kansas City at the 24. Two series later Emmitt Thomas intercepted Lamonica and the Chiefs went 62 yards to Jan Stenerud's 22-yard field goal.

January 4, at Oakland

Kansas City	Starters, Offense	Oakland
Frank Pitts	WR	Rod Sherman
Jim Tyrer	LT	Bob Svihus
Ed Budde	LG	Gene Upshaw
E.J. Holub	C	Jim Otto
Mo Moorman	RG	Jim Harvey
Dave Hill	RT	Harry Schuh
Fred Arbanas	TE	Billy Cannon
Otis Taylor	WR	Fred Biletnikoff
Len Dawson	QB	Daryle Lamonica
Mike Garrett	RB	Charlie Smith
Robert Holmes	RB	Hewritt Dixon
	Starters, Defense	
Jerry Mays	LE	Isaac Lassiter
Curley Culp	LT	Carleton Oats
Buck Buchanan	RT	Tom Keating
Aaron Brown	RE	Ben Davidson
Bobby Bell	LLB	Ralph (Chip) Oliver
Willie Lanier	MLB	Dan Conners
Jim Lynch	RLB	Gus Otto
Jim Marsalis	LCB	Nemiah Wilson
Emmitt Thomas	RCB	Willie Brown
Jim Kearney	LS	George Atkinson
Johnny Robinson	RS	Dave Grayson

Kansas City	0	7	7	3	—	17
Oakland	7	0	0	0	—	7

Oak—Smith 3 run (Blanda kick)
KC—Hayes 1 run (Stenerud kick)
KC—Holmes 5 run (Stenerud kick)
KC—FG Stenerud 22
Attendance—53,564

TEAM STATISTICS	KC	Oak
First downs	13	18
Rushing	5	6
Passing	6	10
By penalty	2	2
Total yardage	207	233
Net rushing yardage	86	79
Net passing yardage	121	154
Passes att.-comp.-had int.	17-7-0	45-17-4

1969 NFL

MINNESOTA 27, CLEVELAND 7

Three Browns can't stop Kapp.

Snow was stacked along the sidelines and the temperature was eight degrees in Metropolitan Stadium as the Minnesota Vikings became the first expansion team to win the NFL championship when they defeated the Cleveland Browns 27–7. The 50-year-old NFL, led by a team that was completing its ninth season of play, was scheduled to merge with the 10-year-old AFL the following year.

The Vikings scored the first two times they had the ball. Quarterback Joe Kapp, who joined them in 1967 after playing eight seasons in the Canadian Football League, scored on a seven-yard run and teamed with Gene Washington on a 75-yard touchdown pass. Washington caught three passes for 120 yards and a touchdown and Kapp completed 7 of 13 passes for 169 yards and a touchdown.

Fred Cox kicked a 30-yard field goal for a 17–0 lead in the second quarter and Dave Osborn, who led all rushers with 108 yards in 18 carries, made the score 24–0 at halftime with a 20-yard run. It was 27–0 in the third quarter after Cox's 32-yard field goal.

January 4, at Bloomington, Minnesota

Cleveland	Starters, Offense	Minnesota
Paul Warfield	WR	Gene Washington
Dick Schafrath	LT	Grady Alderman
John Demarie	LG	Jim Vellone
Fred Hoaglin	C	Mick Tingelhoff
Gene Hickerson	RG	Milt Sunde
Monte Clark	RT	Ron Yary
Milt Morin	TE	John Beasley
Gary Collins	WR	John Henderson
Bill Nelsen	QB	Joe Kapp
Leroy Kelly	RB	Dave Osborn
Robert (Bo) Scott	RB	Bill Brown
	Starters, Defense	
Ron Snidow	LE	Carl Eller
Walter Johnson	LT	Gary Larsen
Jim Kanicki	RT	Alan Page
Jack Gregory	RE	Jim Marshall
Jim Houston	LLB	Roy Winston
Dale Lindsey	MLB	Lonnie Warwick
John Garlington	RLB	Wally Hillgenberg
Erich Barnes	LCB	Earsell Mackbee
Walt Sumner	RCB	Ed Sharockman
Ernie Kellermann	LS	Karl Kassulke
Mike Howell	RS	Paul Krause

Cleveland	0	0	0	7	—	7
Minnesota	14	10	3	0	—	27

Minn—Kapp 7 run (Cox kick)
Minn—Washington 75 pass from Kapp (Cox kick)
Minn—FG Cox 30
Minn—Osborn 20 run (Cox kick)
Minn—FG Cox 32
Cle—Collins 3 pass from Nelsen (Cockroft kick)
Attendance—46,503

TEAM STATISTICS	Cle	Minn
First downs	14	18
Rushing	4	13
Passing	10	5
By penalty	0	0
Total yardage	268	383
Net rushing yardage	97	222
Net passing yardage	171	161
Passes att.-comp.-had int.	33-17-2	13-7-0

1970 AFC

BALTIMORE 27, OAKLAND 17

Colts' Bubba Smith harrasses Blanda.

The Baltimore Colts became the first champion of the American Football Conference when they defeated the Oakland Raiders 27–17. The Raiders were an original AFL squad but the Colts joined the AFC with Pittsburgh and Cleveland from the NFL after the two leagues merged in 1970.

Running back Norm Bulaich and quarterback Johnny Unitas provided the offensive impetus for the Colts. George Blanda, who replaced Daryle Lamonica in the second quarter for Oakland, set a record for being the oldest quarterback to perform in a championship game. The 42-year-old Blanda threw for two touchdowns and completed 17 of 32 passes for 271 yards.

Bulaich gained 71 yards in 22 carries and scored twice. His 11-yard run in the third quarter gave the Colts a 20–10 lead. After Oakland closed to 20–17 on a 15-yard, Blanda-to-Warren Wells pass, the Colts put the game away on a 68-yard pass play, Unitas to Ray Perkins. Perkins got behind Oakland's Nemiah Wilson, who fell trying to cover Perkins.

January 3, at Baltimore

Oakland	Starters, Offense	Baltimore
Warren Wells	WR	Eddie Hinton
Art Shell	LT	Bob Vogel
Gene Upshaw	LG	Glenn Ressler
Jim Otto	C	Dan Curry
Jim Harvey	RG	John Williams
Harry Schuh	RT	Dan Sullivan
Raymond Chester	TE	John Mackey
Fred Biletnikoff	WR	Roy Jefferson
Daryle Lamonica	QB	Johnny Unitas
Charlie Smith	RB	Norm Bulaich
Hewritt Dixon	RB	Tom Nowatzke
	Starters, Defense	
Tony Cline	LE	Charles (Bubba) Smith
Carleton Oats	LT	Billy Ray Smith
Tom Keating	RT	Fred Miller
Ben Davidson	RE	Roy Hilton
Bill Laskey	LLB	Ray May
Dan Conners	MLB	Mike Curtis
Gus Otto	RLB	Ted Hendricks
Kent McCloughan	LCB	Charlie Stukes
Willie Brown	RCB	Jim Duncan
George Atkinson	LS	Jerry Logan
Dave Grayson	RS	Rick Volk

Oakland	0	3	7	7	—	17
Baltimore	3	7	10	7	—	27

Balt—FG O'Brien 16
Balt—Bulaich 2 run (O'Brien kick)
Oak—FG Blanda 48
Oak—Biletnikoff 38 pass from Blanda (Blanda kick)
Balt—FG O'Brien 23
Balt—Bulaich 11 run (O'Brien kick)
Oak—Wells 15 pass from Blanda (Blanda kick)
Balt—Perkins 68 pass from Unitas (O'Brien kick)
Attendance—54,799

TEAM STATISTICS	Oak	Balt
First downs	16	18
Rushing	5	7
Passing	10	11
By penalty	1	0
Total yardage	336	363
Net rushing yardage	107	126
Net passing yardage	229	237
Passes att.-comp.-had int.	36-18-3	30-11-0

1970 NFC

DALLAS 17, SAN FRANCISCO 10

Victorious Cowboys surround coach Landry.

Rookie running back Duane Thomas rushed for 143 yards in 27 carries and scored on a 13-yard run as the Dallas Cowboys defeated the San Francisco 49ers 17–10 and won their first conference championship after losses in the playoffs four consecutive years.

Middle linebacker Lee Roy Jordan of the Cowboys intercepted a pass by John Brodie to set up Thomas's touchdown run that broke a 3–3 tie in the third quarter. Another interception by cornerback Mel Renfro paved the way for the clinching touchdown, a five-yard pass from quarterback Craig Morton to running back Walt Garrison in the third quarter.

Trailing 17-3, the 49ers scored in the third quarter on a 26-yard pass from Brodie to wide receiver Dick Witcher. Brodie completed 19 of 40 passes for 262 yards and a touchdown with two interceptions. The game marked the 49ers' final appearance in Kezar Stadium, their home since they began play in the All-America Football Conference in 1946. They were scheduled to move into Candlestick Park in 1971.

January 3, at San Francisco

Dallas	Starters, Offense	San Francisco
Bob Hayes	WR	Dick Witcher
Ralph Neely	LT	Len Rohde
John Niland	LG	Randy Beisler
Dave Manders	C	Forrest Blue
Blaine Nye	RG	Woody Peoples
Rayfield Wright	RT	Cas Banaszek
Pettis Norman	TE	Bob Windsor
Reggie Rucker	WR	Gene Washington
Craig Morton	QB	John Brodie
Duane Thomas	RB	Ken Willard
Walt Garrison	RB	Doug Cunningham
	Starters, Defense	
Larry Cole	LE	Tommy Hart
Jethro Pugh	LT	Charlie Krueger
Bob Lilly	RT	Roland Lakes
George Andrie	RE	Bill Belk
Dave Edwards	LLB	Dave Wilcox
Lee Roy Jordan	MLB	Frank Nunley
Chuck Howley	RLB	Jim Sniadecki
Herb Adderley	LCB	Jimmy Johnson
Mel Renfro	RCB	Bruce Taylor
Cornell Green	LS	Mel Phillips
Charlie Waters	RS	Roosevelt Taylor

Dallas	0	3	14	0	—	17
San Francisco	3	0	7	0	—	10

SF —FG Gossett 16
Dall—FG Clark 21
Dall—Thomas 13 run (Clark kick)
Dall—Garrison 5 pass from Morton (Clark kick)
SF —Witcher 26 pass from Brodie (Gossett kick)
Attendance—59,364

TEAM STATISTICS	Dall	SF
First downs	22	15
Rushing	16	2
Passing	5	12
By penalty	1	1
Total yardage	319	307
Net rushing yardage	229	61
Net passing yardage	90	246
Passes att.-comp.-had int.	22-7-0	40-19-2

1971 AFC

MIAMI 21, BALTIMORE 0

Anderson cuts to sideline on touchdown return.

The Miami Dolphins led the Baltimore Colts 7–0 in the third quarter at the Orange Bowl. After repeatedly throwing hook passes to wide receiver Eddie Hinton, Baltimore quarterback Johnny Unitas had Hinton open deep. But the ball was thrown short, and Hinton tipped it away from Miami's Curtis Johnson. The Dolphins' Dick Anderson intercepted, setting off a chain reaction. One by one, six Baltimore players were knocked down in the open field by Miami blockers as Anderson weaved 62 yards to a touchdown. The Dolphins went on to win 21-0.

Anderson's convoy included safety Jake Scott, cornerback Tim Foley, linebackers Doug Swift and Mike Kolen, defensive end Bill Stanfill, and defensive tackle Bob Heinz, who flattened Unitas, the last Colt in Anderson's way. Miami scored again in the fourth quarter on Larry Csonka's five-yard run.

Miami had taken the lead in the first quarter. Dolphins quarterback Bob Griese faked Csonka into the line; the fake froze Baltimore safety Rick Volk. When Volk retreated to cover wide receiver Paul Warfield, he was too late to stop Griese's perfect pass—one that resulted in a 75-yard touchdown.

January 2, at Miami

Baltimore	Starters, Offense	Miami
Eddie Hinton	WR	Paul Warfield
Bob Vogel	LT	Doug Crusan
Glenn Ressler	LG	Bob Kuechenberg
Bill Curry	C	Bob DeMarco
John Williams	RG	Larry Little
Dan Sullivan	RT	Norm Evans
Tom Mitchell	TE	Marv Fleming
Ray Perkins	WR	Howard Twilley
Johnny Unitas	QB	Bob Griese
Don McCauley	RB	Jim Kiick
Don Nottingham	RB	Larry Csonka
	Starters, Defense	
Charles (Bubba) Smith	LE	Jim Riley
Billy Newsome	LT	Manny Fernandez
Fred Miller	RT	Bob Heinz
Roy Hilton	RE	Bill Stanfill
Ray May	LLB	Doug Swift
Mike Curtis	MLB	Nick Buoniconti
Ted Hendricks	RLB	Mike Kolen
Charlie Stukes	LCB	Tim Foley
Rex Kern	RCB	Curtis Johnson
Jerry Logan	LS	Dick Anderson
Rick Volk	RS	Jake Scott

Baltimore	0	0	0	0	—	0
Miami	7	0	7	7	—	21

Mia—Warfield 75 pass from Griese (Yepremian kick)
Mia—Anderson 62 interception return (Yepremian kick)
Mia—Csonka 5 run (Yepremian kick)
Attendance—76,622

TEAM STATISTICS	Balt	Mia
First downs	16	13
Rushing	6	8
Passing	10	4
By penalty	0	1
Total yardage	302	286
Net rushing yardage	93	144
Net passing yardage	209	142
Passes att.-comp.-had int.	36-20-3	8-4-1

1971 NFC

DALLAS 14, SAN FRANCISCO 3

Touchdown by Thomas (33) wraps up victory.

The Dallas Cowboys broke a scoreless tie in the second quarter when defensive end George Andrie, hidden by San Francisco tackle Len Rohde, emerged to intercept John Brodie's screen pass to running back Ken Willard and ran the ball eight yards to the 49ers' 2 yard line. Calvin Hill scored from the one and the touchdown was sufficient as Dallas won its second straight NFC championship over San Francisco, 14–3.

Dallas led 7–3 in the fourth quarter when strong safety Mel Phillips of San Francisco went out with an ankle injury. Reacting immediately on third and two at the 49ers' 12, Dallas coach Tom Landry sent in a pass play to tight end Mike Ditka. Ditka caught a five-yard pass that set up a two-yard touchdown run by Duane Thomas two plays later.

Dallas converted 8 of 14 third downs into first downs, including 4 on the 80-yard, 14-play drive that led to the final score. San Francisco converted 1 of 11 third down situations.

January 2, at Irving, Texas

San Francisco	Starters, Offense	Dallas
Dick Witcher	WR	Bob Hayes
Len Rohde	LT	Tony Liscio
Randy Beisler	LG	John Niland
Forrest Blue	C	Dave Manders
Woody Peoples	RG	Blaine Nye
Cas Banaszek	RT	Rayfield Wright
Ted Kwalick	TE	Mike Ditka
Gene Washington	WR	Lance Alworth
John Brodie	QB	Roger Staubach
Ken Willard	RB	Calvin Hill
Vic Washington	RB	Duane Thomas
	Starters, Defense	
Tommy Hart	LE	Larry Cole
Charlie Krueger	LT	Jethro Pugh
Earl Edwards	RT	Bob Lilly
Cedrick Hardman	RE	George Andrie
Dave Wilcox	LLB	Dave Edwards
Frank Nunley	MLB	Lee Roy Jordan
William (Skip) Vanderbundt	RLB	Chuck Howley
Jimmy Johnson	LCB	Herb Adderley
Bruce Taylor	RCB	Mel Renfro
Mel Phillips	LS	Cornell Green
Roosevelt Taylor	RS	Cliff Harris

San Francisco	0	0	3	0	—	3
Dallas	0	7	0	7	—	14

Dall—Hill 1 run (Clark kick)
SF —FG Gossett 28
Dall—Thomas 2 run (Clark kick)
Attendance—63,409

TEAM STATISTICS	SF	Dall
First downs	9	16
Rushing	2	9
Passing	7	7
By penalty	0	0
Total yardage	239	244
Net rushing yardage	61	172
Net passing yardage	178	72
Passes att.-comp.-had int.	30-14-3	18-9-0

1972 AFC

MIAMI 21, PITTSBURGH 17

Seiple fools Steelers with run from punt formation.

Quarterback Bob Griese, sidelined since the fifth game of the season with a broken ankle, came off the bench at the start of the second half and directed touchdown marches of 80 and 49 yards that broke a 7–7 tie and led the Miami Dolphins to a 21–17 victory over the Pittsburgh Steelers. The victory was Miami's second in a row in the AFC championship and their sixteenth of the season without defeat.

Pittsburgh took a 7–0 lead in the first quarter after quarterback Terry Bradshaw fumbled in the Miami end zone and the fumble was recovered by teammate Gerry Mullins. In the second quarter, Miami's Larry Seiple was in punt formation at Pittsburgh's 49 when he noticed that the defense had retreated to set up a punt return. Seiple ran instead of punting, gaining 37 yards to the 12 and set up Miami's first touchdown. That came on a nine-yard pass from quarterback Earl Morrall to running back Larry Csonka.

The running of Csonka (68 yards in 24 carries) and Mercury Morris (76 in 16) helped Miami control the ball. The Dolphins had 65 plays to Pittsburgh's 48 and led in total offense 314–250.

December 31, at Pittsburgh

Miami	Starters, Offense	Pittsburgh
Paul Warfield	WR	Al Young
Wayne Moore	LT	Jon Kolb
Bob Kuechenberg	LG	Sam Davis
Jim Langer	C	Ray Mansfield
Larry Little	RG	Bruce Van Dyke
Norm Evans	RT	Gerry Mullins
Marv Fleming	TE	John McMakin
Howard Twilley	WR	Ron Shanklin
Earl Morrall	QB	Terry Bradshaw
Eugene (Mercury) Morris	RB	Franco Harris
Larry Csonka	RB	John Fuqua
	Starters, Defense	
Vern Den Herder	LE	L. C. Greenwood
Manny Fernandez	LT	Joe Greene
Bob Heinz	RT	Ben McGee
Bill Stanfill	RE	Dwight White
Doug Swift	LLB	Jack Ham
Nick Buoniconti	MLB	Henry Davis
Mike Kolen	RLB	Andy Russell
Tim Foley	LCB	John Rowser
Curtis Johnson	RCB	Mel Blount
Jake Scott	LS	Glen Edwards
Dick Anderson	RS	Mike Wagner

Miami	0	7	7	7	— 21
Pittsburgh	7	0	3	7	— 17

Pitt—Mullins fumble recovery in end zone (Gerela kick)
Mia—Csonka 9 pass from Griese (Yepremian kick)
Pitt—FG Gerela 14
Mia—Kiick 2 run (Yepremian kick)
Mia—Kiick 3 run (Yepremian kick)
Pitt—Young 12 pass from Bradshaw (Gerela kick)
Attendance—50,845

TEAM STATISTICS	Mia	Pitt
First downs	19	13
Rushing	11	6
Passing	6	6
By penalty	2	1
Total yardage	314	250
Net rushing yardage	193	128
Net passing yardage	121	122
Passes att.-comp.-had int.	16–10–1	20–10–2

1972 NFC

WASHINGTON 26, DALLAS 3

Taylor scores on 45-yard pass for 16-3 lead.

Quarterback Billy Kilmer threw touchdown passes of 15 and 45 yards to wide receiver Charley Taylor and the Washington Redskins did not allow Dallas to move beyond its 30 yard line in the third quarter and not beyond midfield in the second half. The Redskins scored a 26–3 victory for their first championship since 1942. Kilmer completed 14 of 18 passes for 194 yards and two touchdowns and Taylor caught 7 passes for 146 yards and two touchdowns.

Taylor's first scoring catch gave Washington a 10–0 lead in the second quarter. His second provided a 17–3 advantage in the fourth quarter. The Redskins scored first on Curt Knight's 18-yard field goal, which came at the end of a 16-play, 62-yard drive that consumed nine and one-half minutes of the first quarter.

Knight kicked four field goals without a miss, giving him seven in a row in the playoffs. The Redskins controlled the ball for 62 plays to Dallas's 45. They outgained the Cowboys 316-169.

December 31, at Washington

Dallas	Starters, Offense	Washington
Ron Sellers	WR	Charley Taylor
Ralph Neely	LT	Terry Hermeling
John Niland	LG	Paul Laaveg
Dave Manders	C	Len Hauss
Blaine Nye	RG	John Wilbur
Rayfield Wright	RT	Walter Rock
Mike Ditka	TE	Jerry Smith
Lance Alworth	WR	Roy Jefferson
Roger Staubach	QB	Billy Kilmer
Calvin Hill	RB	Larry Brown
Walt Garrison	RB	Charley Harraway
	Starters, Defense	
Larry Cole	LE	Ron McDole
Jethro Pugh	LT	Manny Sistrunk
Bob Lilly	RT	Diron Talbert
Pat Toomay	RE	Verlon Biggs
Dave Edwards	LLB	Jack Pardee
Lee Roy Jordan	MLB	Myron Pottios
D.D. Lewis	RLB	Chris Hanburger
Charlie Waters	LCB	Pat Fischer
Mel Renfro	RCB	Mike Bass
Cornell Green	LS	Brig Owens
Cliff Harris	RS	Roosevelt Taylor

Dallas	0	3	0	0	— 3
Washington	0	10	0	16	— 26

Wash—FG Knight 18
Wash—Taylor 15 pass from Kilmer (Knight kick)
Dall—FG Fritsch 35
Wash—Taylor 45 pass from Kilmer (Knight kick)
Wash—FG Knight 39
Wash—FG Knight 46
Wash—FG Knight 45
Attendance—53,129

TEAM STATISTICS	Dall	Wash
First downs	8	16
Rushing	3	4
Passing	3	11
By penalty	2	1
Total yardage	169	316
Net rushing yardage	96	122
Net passing yardage	73	194
Passes att.-comp.-had int.	21–9–0	18–14–0

1973 AFC

MIAMI 27, OAKLAND 10

Miami defense causes fourth-quarter fumble.

The Miami Dolphins scored a touchdown the first time they had the ball, marched 63 yards to another score in the closing seconds of the first half, and went on to a 27–10 victory over the Oakland Raiders for their third straight AFC championship. Dolphins quarterback Bob Griese, who scrambled 27 yards to the Raiders' 11 on the play before running back Larry Csonka scored Miami's first touchdown, threw six passes as the Dolphins rushed for 266 yards.

The Raiders scored on George Blanda's 21-yard field goal that cut the score to 14–3 in the third quarter, but that was balanced on the next series by a 42-yard field goal by Garo Yepremian after Miami's Charlie Leigh returned the kickoff 52 yards. The Raiders made it 17–10 near the end of the quarter on a 25-yard pass from quarterback Ken Stabler to wide receiver Mike Siani, but the Dolphins put it away on Yepremian's second field goal and Csonka's third touchdown.

December 30, at Miami

Oakland	Starters, Offense	Miami
Mike Siani	WR	Paul Warfield
Art Shell	LT	Wayne Moore
Gene Upshaw	LG	Bob Kuechenberg
Jim Otto	C	Jim Langer
George Buehler	RG	Larry Little
John Vella	RT	Norm Evans
Bob Moore	TE	Jim Mandich
Fred Biletnikoff	WR	Marlin Briscoe
Ken Stabler	QB	Bob Griese
Charlie Smith	RB	Eugene (Mercury) Morris
Marv Hubbard	RB	Larry Csonka
	Starters, Defense	
Tony Cline	LE	Vern Den Herder
Otis Sistrunk	LT	Manny Fernandez
Art Thoms	RT	Bob Heinz
Horace Jones	RE	Bill Stanfill
Phil Villapiano	LLB	Doug Swift
Dan Conners	MLB	Nick Buoniconti
Gerald Irons	RLB	Mike Kolen
Nemiah Wilson	LCB	Lloyd Mumphord
Willie Brown	RCB	Curtis Johnson
George Atkinson	LS	Jake Scott
Jack Tatum	RS	Dick Anderson

Oakland	0	0	10	0	— 10
Miami	7	7	3	10	— 27

Mia—Csonka 11 run (Yepremian kick)
Mia—Csonka 2 run (Yepremian kick)
Oak—FG Blanda 21
Mia—FG Yepremian 42
Oak—Siani 25 pass from Stabler (Blanda kick)
Mia—FG Yepremian 26
Mia—Csonka 2 run (Yepremian kick)
Attendance—74,384

TEAM STATISTICS	Oak	Mia
First downs	15	21
Rushing	4	18
Passing	9	2
By penalty	2	1
Total yardage	236	292
Net rushing yardage	107	266
Net passing yardage	129	26
Passes att.-comp.-had int.	23–15–1	6–3–1

1973 NFC

MINNESOTA 27, DALLAS 10

Foreman gains 76 yards, scores once for Vikings.

The Minnesota Vikings outgained the Dallas Cowboys 306-153 in total yardage, had 20 first downs to 9, and ran 72 plays to the Cowboys' 49 to score a 27–10 victory in Texas Stadium for the NFC championship.

The Vikings led 10–0 at the end of the first half after a 55-yard field goal by Fred Cox and a five-yard run by Chuck Foreman that concluded an 86-yard drive. Dallas, which did not score an offensive touchdown, cut the lead to 10–7 in the third quarter on a 63-yard punt return by Golden Richards. But three plays later Vikings quarterback Fran Tarkenton combined with wide receiver John Gilliam, who had gotten a step behind cornerback Mel Renfro, on a 54-yard pass that restored Minnesota's 10-point lead.

When Dallas was behind 24–10 in the fourth quarter, Cowboys quarterback Roger Staubach threw to wide receiver Drew Pearson. Cornerback Nate Wright of Minnesota deflected the ball to free safety Jeff Wright, whose interception set up another Cox field goal.

December 30, At Irving, Texas

Minnesota	Starters, Offense	Dallas
Carroll Dale	WR	Bob Hayes
Grady Alderman	LT	Ralph Neely
Ed White	LG	John Niland
Mick Tingelhoff	C	John Fitzgerald
Milt Sunde	RG	Blaine Nye
Ron Yary	RT	Rayfield Wright
Stu Voigt	TE	Billy Joe DuPree
John Gilliam	WR	Drew Pearson
Fran Tarkenton	QB	Roger Staubach
Chuck Foreman	RB	Robert Newhouse
Oscar Reed	RB	Walt Garrison
	Starters, Defense	
Carl Eller	LE	Larry Cole
Gary Larsen	LT	Jethro Pugh
Alan Page	RT	Bill Gregory
Jim Marshall	RE	Pat Toomay
Roy Winston	LLB	Dave Edwards
Jeff Siemon	MLB	Lee Roy Jordan
Wally Hilgenberg	RLB	D.D. Lewis
Nate Wright	LCB	Charlie Waters
Bobby Bryant	RCB	Mel Renfro
Jeff Wright	LS	Cornell Green
Paul Krause	RS	Cliff Harris

Minnesota	3	7	7	10	—	27
Dallas	0	0	10	0	—	10

Minn—FG Cox 44
Minn—Foreman 5 run (Cox kick)
Dall —Richards 63 punt return (Fritsch kick)
Minn—Gilliam 54 pass from Tarkenton (Cox kick)
Dall —FG Fritsch 17
Minn—Bryant 63 interception return (Cox kick)
Minn—FG Cox 34
Attendance—59,688

TEAM STATISTICS	Minn	Dall
First downs	20	9
Rushing	14	3
Passing	6	5
By penalty	0	1
Total yardage	306	153
Net rushing yardage	203	90
Net passing yardage	103	63
Passes att.-comp.-had int.	21-10-1	21-10-4

1974 AFC

PITTSBURGH 24, OAKLAND 13

Swann beats Thomas; Bradshaw (12) watches.

A 21-point final quarter gave the Pittsburgh Steelers a 24–13 victory over the Oakland Raiders.

The Steelers trailed 10–3 at the end of the third quarter, but tied the score on Franco Harris's eight-yard run. Steelers linebacker Jack Ham intercepted a pass by Oakland quarterback Ken Stabler on the next series and Pittsburgh converted Ham's play into a six-yard touchdown pass from quarterback Terry Bradshaw to wide receiver Lynn Swann.

Oakland had an opportunity to tie the score, but on third down and six yards for a first down at the Steelers' 12, Stabler had to throw the ball away under a heavy pass rush. The Raiders settled for a 24-yard field goal by George Blanda.

Pittsburgh controlled the ball and the scoreboard clock late in the game when Bradshaw fumbled at Oakland's 46. Raiders linebacker Gerald Irons could not get to the ball, and Rocky Bleier recovered for Pittsburgh, which gained a first down on the next play. The Steelers then drove to the clinching touchdown, a 21-yard run by Harris.

December 29, at Oakland

Pittsburgh	Starters, Offense	Oakland
Frank Lewis	WR	Clifford Branch
Jon Kolb	LT	Art Shell
Jim Clack	LG	Gene Upshaw
Ray Mansfield	C	Jim Otto
Gerry Mullins	RG	George Buehler
Gordon Gravelle	RT	John Vella
Larry Brown	TE	Bob Moore
Ron Shanklin	WR	Fred Biletnikoff
Terry Bradshaw	QB	Ken Stabler
Rocky Bleier	RB	Clarence Davis
Franco Harris	RB	Marv Hubbard
	Starters, Defense	
L.C. Greenwood	LE	Charles (Bubba) Smith
Joe Greene	LT	Otis Sistrunk
Ernie Holmes	RT	Art Thoms
Dwight White	RE	Horace Jones
Jack Ham	LLB	Phil Villapiano
Jack Lambert	MLB	Dan Conners
Andy Russell	RLB	Gerald Irons
J.T. Thomas	LCB	Alonzo (Skip) Thomas
Mel Blount	RCB	Nemiah Wilson
Mike Wagner	LS	George Atkinson
Glen Edwards	RS	Jack Tatum

Pittsburgh	0	3	0	21	—	24
Oakland	3	0	7	3	—	13

Oak—FG Blanda 40
Pitt —FG Gerela 23
Oak—Branch 38 pass from Stabler (Blanda kick)
Pitt —Harris 8 run (Gerela kick)
Pitt —Swann 6 pass from Bradshaw (Gerela kick)
Oak—Blanda 24
Pitt —Harris 21 run (Gerela kick)
Attendance—53,023

TEAM STATISTICS	Pitt	Oak
First downs	20	15
Rushing	11	0
Passing	7	13
By penalty	2	2
Total yardage	305	278
Net rushing yardage	210	29
Net passing yardage	95	249
Passes att.-comp.-had int.	17-8-1	36-19-3

1974 NFC

MINNESOTA 14, LOS ANGELES 10

Hilgenberg's interception in end zone hurts Rams.

Minnesota was in the midst of a winter heat wave. It was 31 degrees and the sun was blinding as the Minnesota Vikings defeated the Los Angeles Rams 14–10 in the Rams' first appearance in a championship game since 1955 and the Vikings' third appearance in six years.

The Rams outgained the Vikings 340–269, a total that included a 98-yard drive in the third quarter in which Los Angeles did not score. The big play was a 73-yard pass and run involving quarterback James Harris and wide receiver Harold Jackson. Safety Jeff Wright knocked Jackson out of bounds on the 2. On second down at the 1, Rams guard Tom Mack was called for illegal motion, moving the ball back to the 6. Harris ran for four yards on third down, but his fourth-down pass to tight end Pat Curran was deflected by cornerback Jackie Wallace and caught in the end zone for a touchback by linebacker Wally Hilgenberg. Minnesota still led 7–3.

The Vikings increased their lead to 14–3 on Dave Osborn's one-yard run in the fourth quarter.

December 29, at Bloomington, Minnesota

Los Angeles	Starters, Offense	Minnesota
Harold Jackson	WR	Jim Lash
Charlie Cowan	LT	Charles Goodrum
Tom Mack	LG	Andy Maurer
Ken Iman	C	Mick Tingelhoff
Joe Scibelli	RG	Ed White
John Williams	RT	Ron Yary
Bob Klein	TE	Stu Voigt
Jack Snow	WR	John Gilliam
James Harris	QB	Fran Tarkenton
Jim Bertelsen	RB	Chuck Foreman
Lawrence McCutcheon	RB	Dave Osborn
	Starters, Defense	
Jack Youngblood	LE	Carl Eller
Merlin Olsen	LT	Doug Sutherland
Larry Brooks	RT	Alan Page
Fred Dryer	RE	Jim Marshall
Ken Geddes	LLB	Roy Winston
Jack Reynolds	MLB	Jeff Siemon
Isiah Robertson	RLB	Wally Hilgenberg
Charlie Stukes	LCB	Nate Wright
Al Clark	RCB	Jackie Wallace
Dave Elmendorf	LS	Jeff Wright
Bill Simpson	RS	Paul Krause

Los Angeles	0	3	0	7	—	10
Minnesota	0	7	0	7	—	14

Minn—Lash 29 pass from Tarkenton (Cox kick)
LA —FG Ray 27
Minn—Osborn 4 run (Cox kick)
LA —Jackson 44 pass from Harris (Ray kick)
Attendance—48,444

TEAM STATISTICS	LA	Minn
First downs	15	18
Rushing	5	9
Passing	10	7
By penalty	0	2
Total yardage	340	269
Net rushing yardage	121	164
Net passing yardage	219	105
Passes att.-comp.-had int.	23-13-2	20-10-1

<table>
<tr><td>

1975 AFC
PITTSBURGH 16, OAKLAND 10

Harris shakes off Colzie on icy touchdown run.

With snow in the 18-degree air and ice on the Three Rivers Stadium playing field, the Pittsburgh Steelers held off a late charge by the Oakland Raiders to win 16–10 for their second straight AFC championship.

With 17 seconds left in the game, Oakland trailed 16–7. On third down and two yards at Pittsburgh's 24 yard line, Oakland's 48-year-old George Blanda kicked his longest field goal of the year, 41 yards. The Raiders attempted an onside kick on the ensuing kickoff. Marv Hubbard recovered the ball when Pittsburgh's Reggie Garrett fumbled. Seven seconds remained in the game. Quarterback Ken Stabler of Oakland threw a 37-yard pass to Cliff Branch, who caught the ball on the Steelers' 15. Time ran out before Branch could get out of bounds.

There were eight fumbles and five pass interceptions. Jack Lambert's recovery of Clarence Davis's fumble at Pittsburgh's 30 late in the third quarter started the Steelers on a 70-yard drive to their first touchdown. Franco Harris, running brilliantly on the icy turf, scored the touchdown on a 25-yard end sweep to give the Steelers a 10–0 lead.

January 4, at Pittsburgh

Oakland	Starters, Offense	Pittsburgh
Clifford Branch	WR	Frank Lewis
Art Shell	LT	Jon Kolb
Gene Upshaw	LG	Jim Clack
Dave Dalby	C	Ray Mansfield
George Buehler	RG	Gerry Mullins
John Vella	RT	Gordon Gravelle
Bob Moore	TE	Larry Brown
Mike Siani	WR	Lynn Swann
Ken Stabler	QB	Terry Bradshaw
Clarence Davis	RB	Rocky Bleier
Marv Hubbard	RB	Franco Harris
	Starters, Defense	
Otis Sistrunk	LE	L.C. Greenwood
Art Thoms	NT-LT	Joe Greene
Horace Jones	RE-RT	Ernie Holmes
Phil Villapiano	LOLB-RE	Dwight White
Monte Johnson	LILB-LLB	Jack Ham
Gerald Irons	RILB-MLB	Jack Lambert
Ted Hendricks	ROLB-RLB	Andy Russell
Alonzo (Skip) Thomas	LCB	J. T. Thomas
Neal Colzie	RCB	Mel Blount
George Atkinson	LS	Mike Wagner
Jack Tatum	RS	Glen Edwards

Oakland	0	0	0	10	—	10
Pittsburgh	0	3	0	13	—	16

Pitt —FG Gerela 36
Pitt —Harris 25 run (Gerela kick)
Oak—Siani 14 pass from Stabler (Blanda kick)
Pitt —Stallworth 20 pass from Bradshaw (kick failed)
Oak—FG Blanda 41
Attendance—50,609

TEAM STATISTICS	Oak	Pitt
First downs	18	16
Rushing	3	5
Passing	13	10
By penalty	2	1
Total yardage	321	332
Net rushing yardage	93	117
Net passing yardage	228	215
Passes att.-comp.-had int.	42-18-2	25-15-3

</td><td>

1975 NFC
DALLAS 37, LOS ANGELES 7

Preston Pearson's first score puts Dallas in front.

Running back Preston Pearson, waived by Pittsburgh at the end of the preseason and signed as a free agent by Dallas, caught seven passes for 123 yards and three touchdowns as the Cowboys defeated the Los Angeles Rams 37–7.

Pearson took a short pass from quarterback Roger Staubach and scissored through the Rams' defense for 18 yards and Dallas's first touchdown after linebacker D.D. Lewis intercepted Rams quarterback James Harris's first pass of the game. Staubach, who threw four touchdown passes, kept the Rams' defense off balance by leaving his passing pocket and scrambling seven times for 54 yards. The Cowboys averaged a gain of 5.7 yards for each of their 78 offensive plays; the Rams averaged 2.6 for each of their 45 plays.

Los Angeles trailed 7–0 in the first quarter when Tom Dempsey lined up for a 34-yard field goal. Rookie linebacker Thomas Henderson blocked the kick.

January 4, at Los Angeles

Dallas	Starters, Offense	Los Angeles
Golden Richards	WR	Harold Jackson
Ralph Neely	LT	Charlie Cowan
Burton Lawless	LG	Tom Mack
John Fitzgerald	C	Rich Saul
Blaine Nye	RG	Joe Scibelli
Rayfield Wright	RT	John Williams
Jean Fugett	TE	Terry Nelson
Drew Pearson	WR	Ron Jessie
Roger Staubach	QB	James Harris
Preston Pearson	RB	Lawrence McCutcheon
Robert Newhouse	RB	Cullen Bryant
	Starters, Defense	
Ed (Too Tall) Jones	LE	Jack Youngblood
Jethro Pugh	LT	Merlin Olsen
Larry Cole	RT	Cody Jones
Harvey Martin	RE	Fred Dryer
Dave Edwards	LLB	Ken Geddes
Lee Roy Jordan	MLB	Jack Reynolds
D. D. Lewis	RLB	Isiah Robertson
Mark Washington	LCB	Eddie McMillan
Mel Renfro	RCB	Monte Jackson
Charlie Waters	LS	Bill Simpson
Cliff Harris	RS	Dave Elmendorf

Dallas	7	14	13	3	—	37
Los Angeles	0	0	0	7	—	7

Dall—P. Pearson 18 pass from Staubach (Fritsch kick)
Dall—Richards 4 pass from Staubach (Fritsch kick)
Dall—P. Pearson 15 pass from Staubach (Fritsch kick)
Dall—P. Pearson 19 pass from Staubach (Fritsch kick)
Dall—FG Fritsch 40
Dall—FG Fritsch 26
LA —Cappelletti 1 run (Dempsey kick)
Dall—FG Fritsch 26
Attendance—88,919

TEAM STATISTICS	Dall	LA
First downs	24	9
Rushing	8	1
Passing	15	7
By penalty	1	1
Total yardage	441	118
Net rushing yardage	195	22
Net passing yardage	246	96
Passes att.-comp.-had int.	28-18-1	24-11-3

</td><td>

1976 AFC
OAKLAND 24, PITTSBURGH 7

Bankston is alone, catches pass in end zone.

After losses in the playoffs in seven of the eight previous years, the Oakland Raiders defeated the Pittsburgh Steelers 24–7 for their first conference championship since 1967.

Quarterback Ken Stabler completed 10 of 16 passes for 88 yards and two touchdowns as the Raiders broke to a 10–0 lead and put an important touchdown on the scoreboard in the last 19 seconds of the first half. With a first down on the Steelers' 4 yard line, the Raiders lined up with three tight ends as if to run. Pittsburgh braced with an eight-man line. Oakland quarterback Ken Stabler called for a fake run to the right side as tight end Warren Bankston slipped free to the left side and caught Stabler's pass for a 17–7 halftime lead.

Pittsburgh played without running backs Franco Harris and Rocky Bleier and started the game using a three-tight-end offense. Harris, who gained 1,128 yards during the regular season, had sore ribs. Bleier, who gained 1,036 yards, had a bruised big toe. Their replacements for most of the game were John (Frenchy) Fuqua and Reggie Harrison.

December 26, at Oakland

Pittsburgh	Starters, Offense	Oakland
Larry Brown	WR	Fred Biletnikoff
Jon Kolb	LT	Art Shell
Sam Davis	LG	Gene Upshaw
Mike Webster	C	Dave Dalby
Jim Clack	RG	George Buehler
Gerry Mullins	RT	John Vella
Bennie Cunningham	TE	Dave Casper
Lynn Swann	WR	Clifford Branch
Terry Bradshaw	QB	Ken Stabler
Randy Grossman	RB	Clarence Davis
Reggie Harrison	RB	Mark van Eeghen
	Starters, Defense	
L.C. Greenwood	LE	John Matuszak
Joe Greene	LT-NT	Dave Rowe
Ernie Holmes	RT-RE	Otis Sistrunk
Dwight White	RE-LOLB	Phil Villapiano
Jack Ham	LLB-LILB	Monte Johnson
Jack Lambert	MLB-RILB	Willie Hall
Andy Russell	RLB-ROLB	Ted Hendricks
J.T. Thomas	LCB	Alonzo (Skip) Thomas
Mel Blount	RCB	Willie Brown
Glen Edwards	LS	George Atkinson
Mike Wagner	RS	Jack Tatum

Pittsburgh	0	7	0	0	—	7
Oakland	3	14	7	0	—	24

Oak—FG Mann 39
Oak—Davis 1 run (Mann kick)
Pitt —Harrison 3 run (Mansfield kick)
Oak—Bankston 4 pass from Stabler (Mann kick)
Oak—Banaszak 5 pass from Stabler (Mann kick)
Attendance—53,739

TEAM STATISTICS	Pitt	Oak
First downs	13	15
Rushing	3	7
Passing	8	7
By penalty	2	1
Total yardage	237	228
Net rushing yardage	72	157
Net passing yardage	165	71
Passes att.-comp.-had int.	34-14-1	16-10-0

</td></tr>
</table>

1976 NFC

MINNESOTA 24, LOS ANGELES 13

Foreman dodges three Rams for 57-yard gain.

The Minnesota Vikings became the first team to qualify for four Super Bowl appearances when they defeated the Los Angeles Rams 24–13 on a day when the temperature was 12 degrees under a bright sun and the wind-chill factor was 12 below.

Running back Chuck Foreman gained 118 yards in 15 carries and caught five passes for 81 yards. With the Vikings leading 10–0 and in possession of the ball on the first series of the third quarter, Foreman broke through the Rams' right side, faked safety Bill Simpson, and ran 62 yards to the 2-yard line. Foreman scored two plays later.

The Vikings led 17–13 in the fourth quarter when Foreman turned a short pass from quarterback Fran Tarkenton into a 57-yard gain that put the ball on the Rams' 12 with 1:57 remaining. Sammy Johnson scored to put the game out of reach.

Los Angeles' Lawrence McCutcheon was the game's leading ground gainer with 128 yards in 26 carries and one touchdown. The Rams outgained the Vikings 336–267 in total offense and had 21 first downs to 13.

December 26, at Bloomington, Minnesota

Los Angeles	Starters, Offense	Minnesota
Harold Jackson	WR	Ahmad Rashad
Doug France	LT	Steve Riley
Tom Mack	LG	Charles Goodrum
Rich Saul	C	Mick Tingelhoff
Dennis Harrah	RG	Ed White
John Williams	RT	Ron Yary
Bob Klein	TE	Stu Voigt
Ron Jessie	WR	Sammy White
Pat Haden	QB	Fran Tarkenton
John Cappelletti	RB	Brent McClanahan
Lawrence McCutcheon	RB	Chuck Foreman
	Starters, Defense	
Jack Youngblood	LE	Carl Eller
Merlin Olsen	LT	Doug Sutherland
Larry Brooks	RT	Alan Page
Fred Dryer	RE	Jim Marshall
Jim Youngblood	LLB	Matt Blair
Jack Reynolds	MLB	Amos Martin
Isiah Robertson	RLB	Wally Hilgenberg
Rod Perry	LCB	Nate Wright
Monte Jackson	RCB	Bobby Bryant
Dave Elmendorf	LS	Jeff Wright
Bill Simpson	RS	Paul Krause

Los Angeles	0	0	13	0	—	13
Minnesota	7	3	7	7	—	24

Minn—Bryant 90 blocked field goal return (Cox kick)
Minn—FG Cox 25
Minn—Foreman 2 run (Cox kick)
LA —McCutcheon 10 run (kick failed)
LA —H. Jackson 5 pass from Haden (Dempsey kick)
Minn—Johnson 12 run (Cox kick)
Attendance—47,191

TEAM STATISTICS	LA	Minn
First downs	21	13
Rushing	14	6
Passing	7	7
By penalty	0	0
Total yardage	336	267
Net rushing yardage	193	158
Net passing yardage	143	109
Passes att.-comp.-had int.	22-9-2	27-12-1

1977 AFC

DENVER 20, OAKLAND 17

Davis's fumble is recovered by Manor.

Playing in a championship game for the first time in the history of the franchise, the Broncos used three big plays to defeat the Raiders 20-17. The teams had met twice during the regular season, each winning once.

After the Raiders had gone ahead 3-0 on their initial drive, the Broncos needed only two plays to take a 7-3 lead. Craig Morton passed to Haven Moses 35 yards downfield and Moses outraced the Oakland defenders to the end zone, completing a 74-yard play.

The Broncos increased their advantage to 14-3 in the third period on a one-yard run by Jon Keyworth. Brison Manor's recovery of Clarence Davis's fumble at the Raiders' 17 set up the touchdown. After the Raiders scored early in the fourth quarter, the Broncos came up with their third big play to clinch the game. Bob Swenson intercepted Ken Stabler's pass and returned it to the Oakland 17, setting up a Morton-to-Moses touchdown pass three plays later.

Morton finished the day with 224 yards passing, including five completions to Moses for 168 yards and two touchdowns.

January 1, 1978 at Denver

Oakland	Starters, Offense	Denver
Clifford Branch	WR	Jack Dolbin
Art Shell	LT	Andy Maurer
Gene Upshaw	LG	Tom Glassic
Dave Dalby	C	Mike Montler
George Buehler	RG	Paul Howard
Henry Lawrence	RT	Claudie Minor
Dave Casper	TE	Riley Odoms
Fred Biletnikoff	WR	Haven Moses
Ken Stabler	QB	Craig Morton
Mark van Eeghen	RB	Jon Keyworth
Clarence Davis	RB	Rob Lytle
	Starters, Defense	
Jonn Matuszak	LE	Barney Chavous
Dave Rowe	NT	Rubin Carter
Otis Sistrunk	RE	Lyle Alzado
Floyd Rice	LOLB	Bob Swenson
Monte Jackson	LILB	Joe Rizzo
Willie Hall	RILB	Randy Gradishar
Ted Hendricks	ROLB	Tom Jackson
Lester Hayes	LCB	Louis Wright
Willie Brown	RCB	Steve Foley
Skip Thomas	SS	Bill Thompson
Jack Tatum	FS	Bernard Jackson

Oakland	3	0	0	14	—	17
Denver	7	0	7	6	—	20

Oak—FG Mann 20
Den—Moses 74 pass from Morton (Turner kick)
Den—Keyworth 1 run (Turner kick)
Oak—Casper 7 pass from Stabler (Mann kick)
Den—Moses 12 pass from Morton (pass failed)
Oak—Casper 17 pass from Stabler (Mann kick)
Attendance—74,982

TEAM STATISTICS	Oak	Den
First downs	20	16
Rushing	6	6
Passing	11	8
By penalty	3	2
Total yardage	298	308
Net rushing yardage	94	91
Net passing yardage	204	217
Passes att.-comp.-had int.	35-17-1	20-10-1

1977 NFC

DALLAS 23, MINNESOTA 6

Newhouse powers for a sizeable gain.

It was 30 degrees in Irving, but the Cowboys' defense was as hot as the day was cold. Led by defensive ends Harvey Martin and Ed (Too Tall) Jones, Dallas stopped the Vikings 23-6 and advanced to an NFL record-tying fourth Super Bowl appearance.

Dallas gained an early lead after Martin recovered Robert Miller's fumble on Minnesota's 39-yard line. Two plays later, Roger Staubach threw a 32-yard touchdown pass to Golden Richards.

The Cowboys increased their lead to 13-0 with a five-yard touchdown run by Robert Newhouse. The score climaxed a 46-yard drive that had been kept alive by Danny White's 14-yard run out of punt formation.

With a 16-6 halftime lead, the Cowboys' defense took over, limiting the Vikings to 22 yards rushing in the second half. For the game, Jones made 12 tackles and Martin recovered two of the three fumbles the Vikings lost.

For the Cowboys, Staubach passed for 165 yards. Newhouse (81) and Tony Dorsett (71) combined to rush for 152 yards.

January 1, 1978 at Irving, Texas

Minnesota	Starters, Offense	Dallas
Ahmad Rashad	WR-TE	Jay Saldi
Steve Riley	LT	Ralph Neely
Charles Goodrum	LG	Herbert Scott
Mick Tingelhoff	C	John Fitzgerald
Ed White	RG	Tom Rafferty
Ron Yary	RT	Pat Donovan
Stu Voigt	TE	Billy Joe Dupree
Sammy White	WR	Drew Pearson
Bob Lee	QB	Roger Staubach
Robert Miller	RB	Robert Newhouse
Chuck Foreman	RB	Tony Dorsett
	Starters, Defense	
Carl Eller	LE	Ed Jones
Doug Sutherland	LT	Jethro Pugh
Alan Page	RT	Randy White
Jim Marshall	RE	Harvey Martin
Matt Blair	LLB	Thomas Henderson
Jeff Siemon	MLB	Bob Breunig
Fred McNeill	RLB	D. D.Lewis
Nate Wright	LCB	Benny Barnes
Bobby Bryant	RCB	Aaron Kyle
Jeff Wright	SS	Charlie Waters
Paul Krause	FS	Cliff Harris

Minnesota	0	6	0	0	—	6
Dallas	6	10	0	7	—	23

Dall —Richards 32 pass from Staubach (kick blocked)
Dall —Newhouse 5 run (Herrera kick)
Minn—FG Cox 33
Minn—FG Cox 37
Dall —FG Herrera 21
Dall —Dorsett 11 run (Herrera kick)
Attendance—61,968

TEAM STATISTICS	Min	Dall
First downs	12	16
Rushing	4	7
Passing	6	7
By penalty	2	2
Total yardage	214	328
Net rushing yardage	66	170
Net passing yardage	148	158
Passes att.-comp.-had int.	31-14-1	23-12-1

1978 AFC

PITTSBURGH 34, HOUSTON 5

Harris's seven yarder gets Steelers off right.

A freezing rain, a smothering defense that came up with nine turnovers, and a 17-point outburst in a 48-second span were part of the Steelers' 34-5 rout of the Oilers, who were appearing in their first championship game since 1967.

The Steelers led the entire way, but broke the game open in the last minute of the first half. Touchdown runs by Franco Harris and Rocky Bleier had resulted in a 14-3 Steelers' lead, and then Houston's Ronnie Coleman fumbled with 1:23 to go in the half. Moments later Terry Bradshaw passed 29 yards to Lynn Swann for a touchdown. Johnny Dirden fumbled the ensuing kickoff and the Steelers recoverd at the Oilers' 17. Two plays later Bradshaw passed to John Stallworth for another touchdown. And after the Oilers took the next kickoff, Coleman fumbled on the first play from scrimmage, setting up Roy Gerela's field goal with four seconds left in the half.

Defense dominated the second half. The Steelers intercepted Dan Pastorini five times, and limited Earl Campbell to 62 yards rushing for the game.

January 7, 1979 at Pittsburgh

Houston	Starters, Offense	Pittsburgh
Ken Burrough	WR	John Stallworth
Greg Sampson	LT	Jon Kolb
George Reihner	LG	Sam Davis
Carl Mauck	C	Mike Webster
Ed Fisher	RG	Ray Pinney
Conway Hayman	RT	Larry Brown
Mike Barber	TE	Randy Grossman
Rich Caster	WR	Lynn Swann
Dan Pastorini	QB	Terry Bradshaw
Tim Wilson	RB	Rocky Bleier
Earl Campbell	RB	Franco Harris
	Starters, Defense	
James Young	LE	L. C. Greenwood
Curly Culp	NT-LT	Joe Greene
Elvin Bethea	RE-RT	Steve Furness
Robert Brazile	LOLB-RE	John Banaszak
Steve Kiner	LILB-LLB	Jack Ham
Gregg Bingham	RILB-MLB	Jack Lambert
Ted Washington	ROLB-RLB	Robin Cole
Willie Alexander	LCB	Ron Johnson
Greg Stemrick	RCB	Mel Blount
Bill Currier	SS	Donnie Shell
Mike Reinfeldt	FS	Mike Wagner

Houston	0	3	2	0	—	5
Pittsburgh	14	17	3	0	—	34

Pitt —Harris 7 run (Gerela kick)
Pitt —Bleier 15 run (Gerela kick)
Hou —FG Fritsch 19
Pitt —Swann 29 pass from Bradshaw (Gerela kick)
Pitt —Stallworth 17 pass from Bradshaw (Gerela kick)
Pitt —FG Gerela 37
Pitt —FG Gerela 22
Hou —Safety, Washington tackled Bleier in end zone
Attendance—49,417

TEAM STATISTICS	Hou	Pitt
First downs	10	21
Rushing	5	8
Passing	3	11
By penalty	2	2
Total yardage	142	379
Net rushing yardage	72	179
Net passing yardage	70	200
Passes att.-comp.-had int.	26-12-5	19-11-2

1978 NFC

DALLAS 28, LOS ANGELES 0

Dorsett's five-yard run breaks open scoreless game.

An opportunistic Cowboys defense came up with five second-half turnovers, three of which set up touchdowns to break open a scoreless game, and the Cowboys defeated the Rams 28-0.

Both teams had scoring opportunities in the first half, but came up empty due to turnovers and missed field goals.

With 1:52 to go in the third quarter, Dallas strong safety Charlie Waters intercepted Pat Haden's pass and returned it to the Rams' 10-yard line. Five plays later Tony Dorsett, who rushed for a game-high 101 yards, scored from five yards out. Shortly before the end of the quarter, Waters intercepted another pass to set up a touchdown toss from Roger Staubach to Scott Laidlaw.

After the Dallas defense held the Rams on fourth-and-one, Staubach culminated a Dallas drive with a touchdown pass to Billy Joe DuPree. The final Dallas score came with 1:19 remaining when linebacker Thomas Henderson intercepted a pass from Rams quarterback Vince Ferragamo and returned it 68 yards down the left sideline.

For the most part the statistics were close: Dallas led only 16-15 in first downs.

January 7, 1979 at Los Angeles

Dallas	Starters, Offense	Los Angeles
Tony Hill	WR	Willie Miller
Pat Donovan	LT	Doug France
Herbert Scott	LG	Tom Mack
John Fitzgerald	C	Rich Saul
Tom Rafferty	RG	Dennis Harrah
Rayfield Wright	RT	John Williams
Billy Joe DuPree	TE	Terry Nelson
Drew Pearson	WR	Ron Jessie
Roger Staubach	QB	Pat Haden
Scott Laidlaw	RB	John Cappelletti
Tony Dorsett	RB	Cullen Bryant
	Starters, Defense	
Ed Jones	LE	Jack Youngblood
Larry Cole	LT	Cody Jones
Randy White	RT	Mike Fanning
Harvey Martin	RE	Fred Dryer
Thomas Henderson	LLB	Jim Youngblood
Bob Breunig	MLB	Jack Reynolds
D. D. Lewis	RLB	Bob Brudzinski
Benny Barnes	LCB	Pat Thomas
Aaron Kyle	RCB	Rod Perry
Charlie Waters	SS	Dave Elmendorf
Cliff Harris	FS	Bill Simpson

Dallas	0	0	7	21	—	28
Los Angeles	0	0	0	0	—	0

Dall—Dorsett 5 run (Septien kick)
Dall—Laidlaw 4 pass from Staubach (Septien kick)
Dall—DuPree 11 pass from Staubach (Septien kick)
Dall—Henderson 68 interception return (Septien kick)
Attendance—67,470

TEAM STATISTICS	Dall	LA
First downs	16	15
Rushing	7	3
Passing	7	11
By penalty	2	1
Total yardage	235	277
Net rushing yardage	126	81
Net passing yardage	109	196
Passes att.-comp.-had int.	25-13-2	35-14-5

1979 AFC

PITTSBURGH 27, HOUSTON 13

Shell unloads on Renfro, causing first-half fumble.

The Steelers set an AFC Championship Game record by holding the Oilers to only 24 yards rushing, but had to withstand a brilliant passing attack to win the right to go their fourth Super Bowl.

The Oilers jumped into an early lead when rookie strong safety Vernon Perry intercepted Terry Bradshaw and returned his pass 75 yards for a touchdown. Bradshaw bounced back to throw touchdown passes to Bennie Cunningham and John Stallworth to give the Steelers a 17-10 halftime lead.

After the Oilers cut the Steelers' lead to four points on a fourth-quarter field goal by Toni Fritsch, the Steelers drove 78 yards to Matt Bahr's field goal. Pittsburgh clinched the game on a four-yard touchdown run by Rocky Bleier, after Donnie Shell recovered an Oilers fumble on the Houston 45.

The Steelers held the NFL's leading rusher, Earl Campbell, to only 15 yards on 17 carries, to offset Dan Pastorini's 19 completions in 28 attempts for 203 yards.

January 6, 1980 at Pittsburgh

Houston	Starters, Offense	Pittsburgh
Ken Burrough	WR	John Stallworth
Leon Gray	LT	Ted Peterson
David Carter	LG	Sam Davis
Carl Mauck	C	Mike Webster
Ed Fisher	RG	Steve Courson
Conway Hayman	RT	Larry Brown
Mike Barber	TE	Bennie Cunningham
Rich Caster	WR	Lynn Swann
Dan Pastorini	QB	Terry Bradshaw
Tim Wilson	RB	Rocky Bleier
Earl Campbell	RB	Franco Harris
	Starters, Defense	
Andy Dorris	LE	L. C. Greenwood
Curley Culp	NT-LT	Joe Greene
Elvin Bethea	RE-RT	Gary Dunn
Ted Washington	LOLB-RE	John Banaszak
Gregg Bingham	LILB-LLB	Dennis Winston
Art Stringer	RILB-MLB	Jack Lambert
Robert Brazile	ROLB-RLB	Robin Cole
J. C. Wilson	LCB	Ron Johnson
Greg Stemrick	RCB	Mel Blount
Vernon Perry	SS	Donnie Shell
Mike Reinfeldt	FS	J. T. Thomas

Houston	7	3	0	3	—	13
Pittsburgh	3	14	0	10	—	27

Hou—Perry 75 interception return (Fritsch kick)
Pitt —FG Bahr 21
Hou—FG Fritsch 27
Pitt —Cunningham 16 pass from Bradshaw (Bahr kick)
Pitt —Stallworth 20 pass from Bradshaw (Bahr kick)
Hou—FG Fritsch 23
Pitt —FG Bahr 39
Pitt —Bleier 4 run (Bahr kick)
Attendance—50,475

TEAM STATISTICS	Hou	Pitt
First downs	11	22
Rushing	2	9
Passing	7	13
By penalty	2	0
Total yardage	227	358
Net rushing yardage	24	161
Net passing yardage	203	197
Passes att.-comp.-had int.	29-20-1	30-18-1

1979 NFC

LOS ANGELES 9, TAMPA BAY 0

Corral's field goals give Rams NFC championship.

After four losses in the last five championship games, the Rams qualified for their first Super Bowl by defeating the Buccaneers 9-0 in the first title game in which no touchdowns were scored.

Frank Corral accounted for all the points in the game. The Rams were able to move the ball well, but couldn't get into the end zone. Corral kicked two short field goals after Los Angeles drives stalled within the Tampa Bay 5-yard line in the second quarter. He added the final score on a 23-yarder with only 8:09 left in the game.

The Rams dominated the game with a punishing ground attack and a swarming defense. Cullen Bryant ran for 108 yards and Wendell Tyler added 86. Vince Ferragamo completed 12 of 23 passes for 163 yards.

The Rams' defense held the Buccaneers to only 13 yards in the first quarter and did not allow a first down until 7:55 remained in the second quarter. Ricky Bell gained 59 yards on 20 carries just one week after he set a playoff record with 38 carries (for 142 yards). Tampa Bay's quarterbacks completed only 4 of 26 passes for 54 yards and netted only 43 yards.

January 6, 1980 at Tampa

Los Angeles	Starters, Offense	Tampa Bay
Billy Waddy	WR	Isaac Hagins
Doug France	LT	Dave Reavis
Kent Hill	LG	Greg Horton
Rich Saul	C	Steve Wilson
Dennis Harrah	RG	Greg Roberts
Jackie Slater	RT	Charley Hannah
Terry Nelson	TE	Jimmie Giles
Preston Dennard	WR	Larry Mucker
Vince Ferragamo	QB	Doug Williams
Cullen Bryant	RB	Ricky Bell
Wendell Tyler	RB-TE	Jim Obradovich
	Starters, Defense	
Jack Youngblood	LE	Wally Chambers
Mike Fanning	LT-NT	Randy Crowder
Larry Brooks	RT-RE	Lee Roy Selmon
Fred Dryer	RE-LOLB	David Lewis
Jim Youngblood	LLB-LILB	Dewey Selmon
Jack Reynolds	MLB-RILB	Richard Wood
Bob Brudzinski	RLB-ROLB	Cecil Johnson
Pat Thomas	LCB	Jeris White
Rod Perry	RCB	Mike Washington
Dave Elmendorf	SS	Mark Cotney
Nolan Cromwell	FS	Cedric Brown

Los Angeles	0	6	0	3	—	9
Tampa Bay	0	0	0	0	—	0

LA—FG Corral 19
LA—FG Corral 21
LA—FG Corral 23
Attendance—72,033

TEAM STATISTICS	LA	TB
First downs	23	7
Rushing	13	3
Passing	8	4
By penalty	2	0
Total yardage	369	177
Net rushing yardage	216	92
Net passing yardage	153	85
Passes att.-comp.-had int.	23-12-0	27-5-1

1980 AFC

OAKLAND 34, SAN DIEGO 27

Chester eludes Fuller and scores 65-yard touchdown.

The Raiders jumped to a 28-7 lead and held on to defeat the Chargers 34-27 in a game matching two Western Division teams with identical records.

Jim Plunkett completed 14 of 18 passes for 261 yards and accounted for the three first quarter scores for the Raiders. He threw a 65-yard touchdown pass to Raymond Chester, ran for a five-yard touchdown, and passed 21 yards to halfback Kenny King as Oakland built a 21-7 margin.

Chargers quarterback Dan Fouts and wide receiver Charlie Joiner connected for their second touchdown pass of the game 1:05 before the half to cut the Raiders' lead to 28-14. The Chargers closed to 28-24 in the third quarter, but two field goals by Chris Bahr clinched the game for Oakland.

San Diego rolled up 351 yards passing, 434 total yards, and 26 first downs. The Chargers also fumbled five times, and Fouts threw two interceptions.

January 11, 1981 at San Diego

Oakland	Starters, Offense	San Diego
Clifford Branch	WR	Charlie Joiner
Art Shell	LT	Billy Shields
Gene Upshaw	LG	Doug Wilkerson
Dave Dalby	C	Don Macek
Mickey Marvin	RG	Ed White
Henry Lawrence	RT	Dan Audick
Raymond Chester	TE	Kellen Winslow
Bob Chandler	WR	John Jefferson
Jim Plunkett	QB	Dan Fouts
Mark van Eeghen	RB	Chuck Muncie
Kenny King	RB-WR	Ron Smith
	Starters, Defense	
John Matuszak	LE	Leroy Jones
Reggie Kinlaw	NT-LT	Louie Kelcher
Dave Browning	RE-RT	Gary Johnson
Ted Hendricks	LOLB-RE	Fred Dean
Matt Millen	LILB-LLB	Ray Preston
Bob Nelson	RILB-MLB	Bob Horn
Rod Martin	ROLB-RLB	Woodrow Lowe
Lester Hayes	LCB	Willie Buchanon
Dwayne O'Steen	RCB	Mike Williams
Mike Davis	SS	Mike Fuller
Burgess Owens	FS	Glen Edwards

Oakland	21	7	3	3	—	34
San Diego	7	7	10	3	—	27

Oak—Chester 65 pass from Plunkett (Bahr kick)
SD—Joiner 48 pass from Fouts (Benirschke kick)
Oak—Plunkett 5 run (Bahr kick)
Oak—King 21 pass from Plunkett (Bahr kick)
Oak—van Eeghen 3 run (Bahr kick)
SD—Joiner 8 pass from Fouts (Benirschke kick)
SD—FG Benirschke 26
SD—Muncie 6 run (Benirschke kick)
Oak—FG Bahr 27
Oak—FG Bahr 33
SD—FG Benirschke 27
Attendance—52,428

TEAM STATISTICS	Oak	SD
First downs	21	26
Rushing	8	6
Passing	12	17
By penalty	1	3
Total yardage	362	434
Net rushing yardage	138	83
Net passing yardage	224	351
Passes att.-comp.-had int.	18-14-0	46-23-2

1980 NFC

PHILADELPHIA 20, DALLAS 7

Montgomery gives Eagles 7-0 lead on 42-yard run.

With a 14-mile-per-hour wind and 16-degree temperature helping stall both teams' passing attacks, Wilbert Montgomery accounted for most of the offense as the Eagles advanced to their first Super Bowl with a 20-7 victory over the Cowboys.

Montgomery ran for 194 yards, only 2 short of the championship game record. He scored the Eagles' first touchdown on a 42-yard run through the Cowboys' defense after only 2:11 of play.

The Cowboys tied the score before the half on a three-yard touchdown run by Tony Dorsett, but didn't get past the Eagles' 39-yard line the rest of the game.

While the Eagles' defense controlled the Cowboys in the second half, the offense took advantage of two Dallas turnovers, which set up 10 third quarter Philadelphia points. Tony Franklin kicked a 26-yard field goal after Danny White lost a fumble, and Leroy Harris scored on a nine-yard run after Jerry Robinson recovered Dorsett's fumble. The Eagles held Dorsett to only 41 yards rushing on 13 attempts, and Danny White to only 12 completions in 31 attempts for 127 yards.

January 11, 1981 at Philadelphia

Dallas	Starters, Offense	Philadelphia
Butch Johnson	WR	Harold Carmichael
Pat Donovan	LT	Stan Walters
Herbert Scott	LG	Pete Perot
Robert Shaw	C	Guy Morriss
Tom Rafferty	RG	Woody Peoples
Jim Cooper	RT	Jerry Sisemore
Billy Joe DuPree	TE	Keith Krepfle
Drew Pearson	WR	Rodney Parker
Danny White	QB	Ron Jaworski
Robert Newhouse	RB	Leroy Harris
Tony Dorsett	RB	Wilbert Montgomery
	Starters, Defense	
Ed Jones	LE	Dennis Harrison
Larry Cole	LT-NT	Charlie Johnson
Randy White	RT-RE	Carl Hairston
Harvey Martin	RE-LOLB	John Bunting
Guy Brown	LLB-LILB	Bill Bergey
Bob Breunig	MLB-RILB	Frank LeMaster
D. D. Lewis	RLB-ROLB	Jerry Robinson
Benny Barnes	LCB	Roynell Young
Aaron Mitchell	RCB	Herman Edwards
Charlie Waters	SS	Randy Logan
Dennis Thurman	FS	Brenard Wilson

Dallas	0	7	0	0	—	7
Philadelphia	7	0	10	3	—	20

Phil—Montgomery 42 run (Franklin kick)
Dall—Dorsett 3 run (Septien kick)
Phil—FG Franklin 26
Phil—Harris 9 run (Franklin kick)
Phil—FG Franklin 20
Attendance—70,696

TEAM STATISTICS	Dall	Phil
First downs	11	19
Rushing	5	13
Passing	6	5
By penalty	0	1
Total yardage	206	340
Net rushing yardage	90	263
Net passing yardage	116	77
Passes att.-comp.-had int.	32-12-1	29-9-2

1981 AFC

CINCINNATI 27, SAN DIEGO 7

Bengals defense—and weather—blunts the Chargers.

Amidst a temperature of nine degrees below zero and a 35-mile-per-hour wind that created a wind chill factor of minus 59, the Bengals dominated the Chargers to win their first AFC Championship Game 27-7.

Dan Fouts had averaged over 300 yards passing per game in the regular season, but the cruel weather helped limit the record-setting San Diego passing attack to only 173 net yards. Bengals quarterback Ken Anderson threw 14 completions in 22 attempts for 161 yards and two touchdowns.

The Bengals scored first on a 31-yard field goal by Jim Breech. When James Brooks fumbled the ensuing kickoff, the Bengals recovered and drove in for a 10-0 lead on an eight-yard touchdown pass from Anderson to tight end M. L. Harris.

The Chargers cut the lead to 10-7 on a 33-yard pass from Fouts to Kellen Winslow, but Cincinnati increased its lead to 17-7 at halftime on Pete Johnson's touchdown run from one yard out.

The Bengals' defense owned the second half. It shut out the Chargers and set up one score with a fumble recovery.

January 10, 1982 at Cincinnati

San Diego	Starters, Offense	Cincinnati
Charlie Joiner	WR	Cris Collinsworth
Billy Shields	LT	Anthony Munoz
Doug Wilkerson	LG	Dave Lapham
Don Macek	C	Blair Bush
Ed White	RG	Max Montoya
Russ Washington	RT	Mike Wilson
Kellen Winslow	TE	Dan Ross
Wes Chandler	WR	Isaac Curtis
Dan Fouts	QB	Ken Anderson
James Brooks	RB	Charles Alexander
Chuck Muncie	RB	Pete Johnson
	Starters, Defense	
Leroy Jones	LE	Eddie Edwards
Louie Kelcher	LT-NT	Wilson Whitley
Gary Johnson	RT-RE	Ross Browner
John Woodcock	RE-LOLB	Bo Harris
Linden King	LLB-LILB	Jim LeClair
Bob Horn	MLB-RILB	Glenn Cameron
Woodrow Lowe	RLB-ROLB	Reggie Williams
Willie Buchanon	LCB	Louis Breeden
Allan Ellis	RCB	Ken Riley
Pete Shaw	SS	Bobby Kemp
Glen Edwards	FS	Bryan Hicks

San Diego	0	7	0	0	—	7
Cincinnati	10	7	3	7	—	27

Cin—FG Breech 31
Cin—M. L. Harris 8 pass from Anderson (Breech kick)
SD—Winslow 33 pass from Fouts (Benirschke kick)
Cin—Johnson 1 run (Breech kick)
Cin—FG Breech 38
Cin—Bass 3 pass from Anderson (Breech kick)
Attendance—46,302

TEAM STATISTICS	SD	Cin
First downs	18	19
Rushing	11	8
Passing	7	11
By penalty	0	0
Total yardage	301	318
Net rushing yardage	128	143
Net passing yardage	173	175
Passes att.-comp.-had int.	28-15-2	23-15-0

1981 NFC

SAN FRANCISCO 28, DALLAS 27

Clark's catch puts 49ers in Super Bowl XVI.

Joe Montana climaxed an 89-yard drive with a six-yard touchdown pass to Dwight Clark with 51 seconds left in the game, and the 49ers edged the Cowboys 28-27 in a see-saw battle to win the NFC championship.

The 49ers led early on a Montana-to-Freddie Solomon touchdown pass, but the Cowboys seized a 10-7 lead at the end of the first quarter.

Montana threw 20 yards to Clark for a 14-10 lead, but Dallas rebounded with a five-yard touchdown run by Tony Dorsett for a 17-14 halftime lead.

The 49ers scored next for a 21-17 lead, but a 21-yard pass from Danny White to Doug Cosbie gave the Cowboys a 27-21 lead in the fourth quarter.

With 4:54 left in the game the 49ers gained possession on their own 11-yard line and drove 89 yards in 13 plays. On third down, Montana threw a high pass to the back of the end zone and Clark made a leaping catch for the winning score.

Montana finished with 286 yards and three touchdowns passing.

January 10, 1982 at San Francisco

Dallas	Starters, Offense	San Francisco
Tony Hill	WR	Mike Wilson
Pat Donovan	LT	Dan Audick
Herbert Scott	LG	John Ayers
Tom Rafferty	C	Fred Quillan
Kurt Peterson	RG	Randy Cross
Jim Cooper	RT	Keith Fahnhorst
Billy Joe DuPree	TE	Charle Young
Drew Pearson	WR	Mike Shumann
Danny White	QB	Joe Montana
Tony Dorsett	RB	Earl Cooper
Ron Springs	RB	Lenvil Elliott
	Starters, Defense	
Ed Jones	LE	Jim Stuckey
Larry Bethea	LT-NT	Archie Reese
Randy White	RT-RE	Dwaine Board
Harvey Martin	RE-LOLB	Willie Harper
Mike Hegman	LLB-LILB	Jack Reynolds
Bob Breunig	MLB-RILB	Craig Puki
D. D. Lewis	RLB-ROLB	Keena Turner
Everson Walls	LCB	Ronnie Lott
Dennis Thurman	RCB	Eric Wright
Charlie Waters	SS	Carlton Williamson
Michael Downs	FS	Dwight Hicks

Dallas	10	7	0	10	—	27
San Francisco	7	7	7	7	—	28

SF —Solomon 8 pass from Montana (Wersching kick)
Dall—FG Septien 44
Dall—Hill 26 pass from D. White (Septien kick)
SF —Clark 20 pass from Montana (Wersching kick)
Dall—Dorsett 5 run (Septien kick)
SF —Davis 2 run (Wersching kick)
Dall—FG Septien 22
Dall—Cosbie 21 pass from D. White (Septien kick)
SF —Clark 6 pass from Montana (Wersching kick)
Attendance—60,525

TEAM STATISTICS	Dall	SF
First downs	16	26
Rushing	5	6
Passing	9	17
By penalty	2	3
Total yardage	250	393
Net rushing yardage	115	127
Net passing yardage	135	266
Passes att.-comp.-had int.	24-16-1	35-22-3

CHAMPIONSHIP HISTORY

Date	League or Conference	Result	Site (attendance)
Dec. 17, 1933	NFL	Chi. Bears 23, N.Y. Giants 21	Wrigley Field, Chicago (26,000)
Dec. 9, 1934	NFL	N.Y. Giants 30, Chi. Bears 13	Polo Grounds, New York (35,059)
Dec. 15, 1935	NFL	Detroit 26, N.Y. Giants 7	University of Detroit Stadium (15,000)
Dec. 13, 1936	NFL	Green Bay 21, Boston Redskins 6	Polo Grounds, New York (29,545)
Dec. 12, 1937	NFL	Washington 28, Chi. Bears 21	Wrigley Field, Chicago (15,870)
Dec. 11, 1938	NFL	N.Y. Giants 23, Green Bay 17	Polo Grounds, New York (48,120)
Dec. 10, 1939	NFL	Green Bay 27, N.Y. Giants 0	State Fair Park, Milwaukee (32,279)
Dec. 8, 1940	NFL	Chi. Bears 73, Washington 0	Griffith Stadium, Washington (36,034)
Dec. 21, 1941	NFL	Chi. Bears 37, N.Y. Giants 9	Wrigley Field, Chicago (13,341)
Dec. 13, 1942	NFL	Washington 14, Chi. Bears 6	Griffith Stadium, Washington (36,006)
Dec. 26, 1943	NFL	Chi. Bears 41, Washington 21	Wrigley Field, Chicago (34,320)
Dec. 17, 1944	NFL	Green Bay 14, N.Y. Giants 7	Polo Grounds, New York (46,016)
Dec. 16, 1945	NFL	Cleveland Rams 15, Washington 14	Municipal Stadium, Cleveland (32,178)
Dec. 15, 1946	NFL	Chi. Bears 24, N.Y. Giants 14	Polo Grounds, New York (58,346)
Dec. 28, 1947	NFL	Chi. Cardinals 28, Philadelphia 21	Comiskey Park, Chicago (30,759)
Dec. 19, 1948	NFL	Philadelphia 7, Chi. Cardinals 0	Shibe Park, Philadelphia (28,664)
Dec. 18, 1949	NFL	Philadelphia 14, Los Angeles 0	Los Angeles Memorial Coliseum (22,245)
Dec. 24, 1950	NFL	Cleveland 30, Los Angeles 28	Municipal Stadium, Cleveland (29,751)
Dec. 23, 1951	NFL	Los Angeles 24, Cleveland 17	Los Angeles Memorial Coliseum (57,522)
Dec. 28, 1952	NFL	Detroit 17, Cleveland 7	Memorial Stadium, Cleveland (50,934)
Dec. 27, 1953	NFL	Detroit 17, Cleveland 16	Briggs Stadium, Detroit (54,577)
Dec. 26, 1954	NFL	Cleveland 56, Detroit 10	Municipal Stadium, Cleveland (43,827)
Dec. 26, 1955	NFL	Cleveland 38, Los Angeles 14	Los Angeles Memorial Coliseum (85,693)
Dec. 30, 1956	NFL	N.Y. Giants 47, Chi. Bears 7	Yankee Stadium, New York (56,836)
Dec. 29, 1957	NFL	Detroit 59, Cleveland 14	Briggs Stadium, Detroit (55,263)
Dec. 28, 1958	NFL	Baltimore 23, N.Y. Giants 17	Yankee Stadium, New York (64,185)
Dec. 27, 1959	NFL	Baltimore 31, N.Y. Giants 16	Memorial Stadium, Baltimore (57,545)
Dec. 26, 1960	NFL	Philadelphia 17, Green Bay 13	Franklin Field, Philadelphia (67,235)
Jan. 1, 1961	AFL	Houston 24, Los Angeles Chargers 16	Jeppesen Stadium, Houston (32,183)
Dec. 24, 1961	AFL	Houston 10, San Diego 3	Balboa Stadium, San Diego (29,556)
Dec. 31, 1961	NFL	Green Bay 37, N.Y. Giants 0	Lambeau Field, Green Bay (39,029)
Dec. 23, 1962	AFL	Dallas Texans 20, Houston 17	Jeppesen Stadium, Houston (37,981)
Dec. 30, 1962	NFL	Green Bay 16, N.Y. Giants 7	Yankee Stadium, New York (64,892)
Dec. 29, 1963	NFL	Chicago 14, N.Y. Giants 10	Wrigley Field, Chicago (45,801)
Jan. 5, 1964	AFL	San Diego 51, Boston 10	Balboa Stadium, San Diego (30,127)
Dec. 26, 1964	AFL	Buffalo 20, San Diego 7	War Memorial Stadium, Buffalo (40,242)
Dec. 27, 1964	NFL	Cleveland 27, Baltimore 0	Municipal Stadium, Cleveland (79,544)
Dec. 26, 1965	AFL	Buffalo 23, San Diego 0	Balboa Stadium, San Diego (30,361)
Jan. 2, 1966	NFL	Green Bay 23, Cleveland 12	Lambeau Field, Green Bay (50,777)
Jan. 1, 1967	AFL	Kansas City 31, Buffalo 7	War Memorial Stadium, Buffalo (42,080)
Jan. 1, 1967	NFL	Green Bay 34, Dallas 27	Cotton Bowl, Dallas (74,152)
Dec. 31, 1967	AFL	Oakland 40, Houston 7	Oakland Coliseum (53,330)
Dec. 31, 1967	NFL	Green Bay 21, Dallas 17	Lambeau Field, Green Bay (50,861)
Dec. 29, 1968	AFL	N.Y. Jets 27, Oakland 23	Shea Stadium, New York (62,627)
Dec. 29, 1968	NFL	Baltimore 34, Cleveland 0	Memorial Stadium, Cleveland (78,410)
Jan. 4, 1969	AFL	Kansas City 17, Oakland 7	Oakland Coliseum (53,564)
Jan. 4, 1969	NFL	Minnesota 27, Cleveland 7	Metropolitan Stadium, Bloomington (46,503)
Jan. 3, 1970	AFC	Baltimore 27, Oakland 17	Memorial Stadium, Baltimore (54,799)
Jan. 3, 1970	NFC	Dallas 17, San Francisco 10	Candlestick Park, San Francisco (59,364)
Jan. 2, 1971	AFC	Miami 21, Baltimore 0	Orange Bowl, Miami (76,622)
Jan. 2, 1971	NFC	Dallas 14, San Francisco 3	Texas Stadium, Irving (63,409)
Dec. 31, 1972	AFC	Miami 21, Pittsburgh 17	Three Rivers Stadium, Pittsburgh (50,845)
Dec. 31, 1972	NFC	Washington 26, Dallas 3	RFK Stadium, Washington (53,129)
Dec. 30, 1973	AFC	Miami 27, Oakland 10	Orange Bowl, Miami (79,325)
Dec. 30, 1973	NFC	Minnesota 27, Dallas 10	Texas Stadium, Irving (64,222)
Dec. 29, 1974	AFC	Pittsburgh 24, Oakland 13	Oakland Coliseum (53,800)
Dec. 29, 1974	NFC	Minnesota 14, Los Angeles 10	Metropolitan Stadium, Bloomington (48,444)
Jan. 4, 1976	AFC	Pittsburgh 16, Oakland 10	Three Rivers Stadium, Pittsburgh (50,609)
Jan. 4, 1976	NFC	Dallas 37, Los Angeles 7	Los Angeles Memorial Coliseum (88,919)
Dec. 26, 1976	AFC	Oakland 24, Pittsburgh 7	Oakland Coliseum (53,739)
Dec. 26, 1976	NFC	Minnesota 24, Los Angeles 13	Metropolitan Stadium, Bloomington (47,191)
Jan. 1, 1978	AFC	Denver 20, Oakland 17	Mile High Stadium, Denver (74,982)
Jan. 1, 1978	NFC	Dallas 23, Minnesota 6	Texas Stadium, Irving (61,968)
Jan. 7, 1979	AFC	Pittsburgh 34, Houston 5	Three Rivers Stadium, Pittsburgh (49,417)
Jan. 7, 1979	NFC	Dallas 28, Los Angeles 0	Los Angeles Memorial Coliseum (67,470)
Jan. 6, 1980	AFC	Pittsburgh 27, Houston 13	Three Rivers Stadium, Pittsburgh (50,475)
Jan. 6, 1980	NFC	Los Angeles 9, Tampa Bay 0	Tampa Stadium (72,033)
Jan. 11, 1981	AFC	Oakland 34, San Diego 27	San Diego Jack Murphy Stadium (52,428)
Jan. 11, 1981	NFC	Philadelphia 20, Dallas 7	Veterans Stadium, Philadelphia (70,696)
Jan. 10, 1982	AFC	Cincinnati 27, San Diego 7	Riverfront Stadium, Cincinnati (46,302)
Jan. 10, 1982	NFC	San Francisco 28, Dallas 27	Candlestick Park, San Francisco (60,525)

Divisional
Playoff
Games

1941

CHI. BEARS 33, GREEN BAY 14

A brilliant sun couldn't melt the snow that framed the playing area on a 16-degree day at Wrigley Field, where Hugh Gallarneau's 81-yard punt return for a touchdown in the first quarter signaled 30 unanswered points for Chicago. Gallarneau had fumbled the opening kickoff, setting up a five-play, 18-yard touchdown drive that put the Packers ahead 7–0.

Green Bay and Chicago tied for first with 10–1 records in the NFL's Western Division, necessitating the playoff, which was conducted with rules allowing for sudden death overtime periods.

Chicago outrushed Green Bay 267–35 as George McAfee ran for 119 yards; Norm Standlee gained 79.

December 14, at Chicago

Green Bay	Starting Lineups	Chi. Bears
Don Hutson	LE	Dick Plasman
Buford (Baby) Ray	LT	Ed Kolman
C. (Buckets) Goldenberg	LG	Danny Fortmann
George Svendsen	C	Clyde (Bulldog) Turner
Lee McLaughlin	RG	Ray Bray
Charlie Schultz	RT	Lee Artoe
Ray Riddick	RE	John Siegal
Larry Craig	QB	Sid Luckman
Cecil Isbell	LH	Ray Nolting
Herman Rohrig	RH	Hugh Gallarneau
Clarke Hinkle	FB	Norm Standlee

Green Bay	7	0	7	0	—	14
Chi. Bears	6	24	0	3	—	33

GB—Hinkle 1 run (Hutson kick)
Chi—Gallarneau 81 punt return (kick blocked)
Chi—FG Snyder 24
Chi—Standlee 3 run (Stydahar kick)
Chi—Standlee 2 run (Stydahar kick)
Chi—Swisher 9 run (Stydahar kick)
GB—Van Every 10 pass from Isbell (Hutson kick)
Chi—FG Snyder 26
Attendance—43,425

1943

WASHINGTON 28, N.Y. GIANTS 0

Washington's Sammy Baugh roamed the Polo Grounds completing 16 of 21 passes for 199 yards and one touchdown and intercepting two passes, returning one 28 yards to set up another score. Baugh also punted four times for a 40-yard average as the Redskins snapped a two-game losing streak to the Giants, who had beaten them 14–0 and 31–7 the previous two Sundays in the final games of the regular season.

Fullback Andy Farkas scored touchdowns on runs of 2, 2, and 1 yard; all of them came behind blocks from right guard Steve Slivinski.

The Redskins outgained the Giants 296–98 in total offense and threw New York's Alphonse (Tuffy) Leemans for 25 yards in rushing losses. The Giants crossed midfield twice. Their deepest penetration was Washington's 32-yard line on a 42-yard pass, Leemans to Ward Cuff.

December 19, at New York

Washington	Starting Lineups	N.Y. Giants
Bob Masterson	LE	Frank Liebel
Lou Rymkus	LT	Frank Cope
Clyde Shugart	LG	Len Younce
George Smith	C	Mel Hein
Steve Slivinski	RG	Vic Carroll
Joe Pasqua	RT	Al Blozis
Joe Aguirre	RE	Steve Pritko
Ray Hare	QB	Leland Shaffer
George Cafego	LH	Ward Cuff
Frank Seno	RH	Dave Brown
Andy Farkas	FB	Hank Soar

Washington	0	14	0	14	—	28
N.Y. Giants	0	0	0	0	—	0

Wash—Farkas 2 run (Masterson kick)
Wash—Farkas 2 run (Masterson kick)
Wash—Farkas 1 run (Masterson kick)
Wash—Lapka 11 pass from Baugh (Masterson kick)
Attendance—42,800

1947

PHILADELPHIA 21, PITTSBURGH 0

End Pete Pihos blocked Bob Cifers's punt in the first quarter, setting up the Philadelphia Eagles' first touchdown in a 21–0 victory over Pittsburgh at Forbes Field. Two plays after the blocked punt, quarterback Tommy Thompson passed 15 yards to Steve Van Buren.

Pittsburgh and Philadelphia had divided their regular season games and tied for first in the Eastern Division with 8–4 records.

Thompson threw for one other touchdown, 28 yards to Jack Ferrante in the second quarter, and completed 11 of 18 passes for 131 yards. Van Buren, who in 1947 became the second man in the NFL's 28-season history to rush for 1,000 yards, gained 47 yards in 18 carries. Ferrante caught 5 passes for 73.

The 1947 Steelers coached by Dr. Jock Sutherland were the last single-wing team to reach the NFL playoffs. Sutherland died of a stroke in 1948.

December 21, at Pittsburgh

Philadelphia	Starting Lineups	Pittsburgh
Jack Ferrante	LE	Charles Mehelich
Jay MacDowell	LT	Jack Wiley
Cliff Patton	LG	Bill Moore
Alex Wojciechowicz	C	Chuck Cherundolo
Frank (Bucko) Kilroy	RG	John Mastrangelo
Al Wistert	RT	Frank Wydo
Pete Pihos	RE	Bob Davis
Tommy Thompson	QB	Charlie Seabright
Steve Van Buren	LH	Walter Slater
Bosh Pritchard	RH	Bob Cifers
Joe Muha	FB	Tony Compagno

Philadelphia	7	7	7	0	—	21
Pittsburgh	0	0	0	0	—	0

Phil—Van Buren 15 pass from Thompson (Patton kick)
Phil—Ferrante 28 pass from Thompson (Patton kick)
Phil—Pritchard 79 punt return (Patton kick)
Attendance—35,729

1950

CLEVELAND 8, N.Y. GIANTS 3

Lou Groza's 28-yard field goal with 58 seconds left in the game broke a 3–3 tie as the Cleveland Browns beat the New York Giants 8–3 in 17-degree weather.

Trailing 3–0 in the fourth quarter, the Giants had a first down on Cleveland's 4-yard line after Gene Roberts ran 32 yards on a reverse. On third down from the 3, Charlie Conerly passed to Bob McChesney in the end zone, but the Giants were penalized for being offside. On fourth down Conerly's pass was intercepted by Tom James, but Cleveland was penalized for holding. The Giants were penalized for being in motion before the snap of the ball on the next play and moved back to the 9. On the sixth play of the sequence, New York's Joe Scott collided with his blocker, Joe Sulaitis, and went down at the 13. Randy Clay then kicked a 20-yard field goal that tied the score.

December 17, at Cleveland

N.Y. Giants	Starting Lineups	Cleveland
Ellery Williams	LE	Mac Speedie
Arnie Weinmeister	LT	Lou Groza
Bill Milner	LG	Weldon Humble
John Rapacz	C	Frank Gatski
Bill Austin	RG	Lin Houston
Al DeRogatis	RT	Lou Rymkus
Bob McChesney	RE	Dante Lavelli
Travis Tidwell	QB	Otto Graham
Charlie Conerly	LH	Rex Bumgardner
Joe Scott	RH	Dub Jones
Eddie Price	FB	Marion Motley

N.Y. Giants	0	0	0	3	—	3
Cleveland	3	0	0	5	—	8

Cle —FG Groza 11
NYG—FG Clay 20
Cle —FG Groza 28
Cle —Safety, Willis tackled Conerly in end zone
Attendance—33,754

1950

LOS ANGELES 24, CHI. BEARS 14

Quarterback Bob Waterfield, unable to practice all week because of an attack of the flu, came off the bench late in the first quarter and threw three touchdown passes to Tom Fears, on an 84-degree afternoon, as the Rams defeated the Chicago Bears 24-14.

Waterfield completed 14 of 21 passes for 280 yards and Fears caught 7 for 198 after Waterfield replaced starter Norm Van Brocklin, who completed 2 of 10 passes for 17 yards. With the Bears leading 7–3 in the second quarter, Waterfield and Fears combined on 43- and 68-yard touchdown plays to put Los Angeles ahead 17–7 at the half. A 27-yard Waterfield-to-Fears pass made the score 24–7 in the third quarter.

The Bears led the Rams 229–74 in rushing yardage and 422–371 in total yardage.

December 17, at Los Angeles

Chi. Bears	Starting Lineups	Los Angeles
Bill Wightkin	LE	Tom Fears
George Connor	LT	Dick Huffman
Dick Barwegan	LG	John Finlay
Clyde (Bulldog) Turner	C	Art Statuto
Ray Bray	RG	Dave Stephenson
Paul Stenn	RT	Bob Reinhard
Ed Sprinkle	RE	Elroy (Crazylegs) Hirsch
Johnny Lujack	QB	Norm Van Brocklin
George Gulyanics	LH	Glenn Davis
Julie Rykovich	RH	Verda (Vitamin T.) Smith
Fred (Curly) Morrison	FB	Dick Hoerner

Chi. Bears	0	7	0	7	—	14
Los Angeles	3	14	7	0	—	24

LA —FG Waterfield 43
Chi—Campana 23 run (Lujack kick)
LA —Fears 43 pass from Waterfield (Waterfield kick)
LA —Fears 68 pass from Waterfield (Waterfield kick)
LA —Fears 27 pass from Waterfield (Waterfield kick)
Chi—Morrison 4 run (Lujack kick)
Attendance—83,501

1952

DETROIT 31, LOS ANGELES 21

Detroit's Pat Harder was an elusive figure in the dense fog and 37-degree weather of Briggs Stadium. He rushed for 72 yards in eight carries, scored two touchdowns and four extra points, and kicked a 43-yard field goal in the Lions' 31–21 victory over Los Angeles.

Harder's third-quarter field goal gave the Lions a 24–7 lead. The Rams rallied for two fourth-quarter touchdowns to close the margin to 24–21. LaVern Torgeson intercepted a pass by the Rams' Bob Waterfield in the final minute of play, setting up Bob Hoernschmeyer's nine-yard touchdown run with 30 seconds left. Detroit's Leon Hart caught 5 passes for 86 yards and one touchdown.

December 21, at Detroit

Los Angeles	Starting Lineups	Detroit
Tom Fears	LE	Cloyce Box
Don Simensen	LT	Lou Creekmur
Dick Daugherty	LG	Jim Martin
Leon McLaughlin	C	Vince Banonis
Harry Thompson	RG	Dick Stanfel
Tom Dahms	RT	Gus Cifelli
Elroy (Crazylegs) Hirsch	RE	Leon Hart
Norm Van Brocklin	QB	Bobby Layne
(Deacon) Dan Towler	LH	Doak Walker
Verda (Vitamin T.) Smith	RH	Byron Bailey
Paul (Tank) Younger	FB	Pat Harder

Los Angeles	0	7	0	14	—	21
Detroit	7	7	10	7	—	31

Det—Harder 12 run (Harder kick)
Det—Harder 4 run (Harder kick)
LA —Fears 14 pass from Van Brocklin (Waterfield kick)
Det—Hart 24 pass from Walker (Harder kick)
Det—FG Harder 43
LA —Towler 5 run (Waterfield kick)
LA —Smith 56 punt return (Harder kick)
Det—Hoernschmeyer 9 run (Harder kick)
Attendance—47,645

1957

DETROIT 31, SAN FRANCISCO 27

Tom Tracy, a seldom-used fullback, replaced the injured John Henry Johnson in the third quarter and scored two touchdowns in the span of 89 seconds as the Detroit Lions overcame a 20-point deficit to defeat the San Francisco 49ers 31-27.

The 49ers led 27-7 when quarterback Y.A. Tittle fumbled and Bob Long recovered on Detroit's 27. The Lions marched 73 yards to Tracy's one-yard touchdown run. After a San Francisco punt, Tracy ran 58 yards on Detroit's first play for a touchdown. Three minutes later Gene Gedman scored to put Detroit in front.

December 22, at San Francisco

Detroit	Starting Lineups	San Francisco
Jim Doran	LE	Clyde Conner
Lou Creekmur	LT	Bob Cross
Harley Sewell	LG	Bruce Bosley
Frank Gatski	C	Frank Morze
Stan Campbell	RG	Lou Palatella
Charlie Ane	RT	Bob St. Clair
Steve Junker	RE	Billy Wilson
Tobin Rote	QB	Y.A. Tittle
Howard (Hopalong) Cassady	LH	Hugh McElhenny
Dave Middleton	RH	R.C. Owens
John Henry Johnson	FB	Joe Perry

Detroit	0	7	14	10	—	31
San Francisco	14	10	3	0	—	27

SF —Owens 34 pass from Tittle (Soltau kick)
SF —McElhenny 47 pass from Tittle (Soltau kick)
Det—Junker 4 pass from Rote (Martin kick)
SF —Wilson 12 pass from Tittle (Soltau kick)
SF —FG Soltau 25
SF —FG Soltau 10
Det—Tracy 1 run (Martin kick)
Det—Tracy 58 run (Martin kick)
Det—Gedman 2 run (Martin kick)
Det—FG Martin 13
Attendance—60,118

1958

N.Y. GIANTS 10, CLEVELAND 0

The New York Giants scored on a play they had first worked on in practice the week of the game to defeat the Cleveland Browns 10-0. Alex Webster took a handoff from quarterback Charlie Conerly, then handed off to Frank Gifford on a double reverse. Gifford ran eight yards to the Browns' 10 and lateraled to Conerly, who was trailing the play. Conerly ran for the touchdown. "The lateral was optional," said Conerly. "I was there if Gifford needed me."

Cleveland's Jim Brown, who set an NFL record with 1,527 yards rushing during the season, was held to 8 yards in 7 carries; the Browns totaled 86 yards, 24 rushing and 62 passing. Cleveland moved to New York's 6-yard line early in the fourth quarter, but Sam Huff intercepted Milt Plum's pass and the Giants controlled the ball for 10 of the last 11 minutes.

Gifford led all rushers with 95 yards in 23 carries.

December 21, at New York

Cleveland	Starting Lineups	N.Y. Giants
Darrell (Pete) Brewster	LE	Kyle Rote
Lou Groza	LT	Roosevelt Brown
Jim Ray Smith	LG	Al Barry
Art Hunter	C	Ray Wietecha
Chuck Noll	RG	Jack Stroud
Willie McClung	RT	Frank Youso
Preston Carpenter	RE	Bob Schnelker
Milt Plum	QB	Don Heinrich
Ray Renfro	LH	Frank Gifford
Bobby Mitchell	RH	Alex Webster
Jim Brown	FB	Mel Triplett

Cleveland	0	0	0	0	—	0
N.Y. Giants	7	3	0	0	—	10

NYG—Conerly 10 lateral from Gifford, who had run 8 (Summerall kick)
NYG—FG Summerall 26
Attendance—61,274

1963 AFL

BOSTON 26, BUFFALO 8

Fullback Larry Garron turned short pass receptions from Babe Parilli into 59- and 17- yard touchdowns as the Boston Patriots beat the Buffalo Bills in 20-degree weather in War Memorial Stadium.

December 28, at Buffalo

Boston	Starters, Offense	Buffalo
Gino Cappelletti	LE	Bill Miller
Don Oakes	LT	Stew Barber
Chuck Long	LG	Tom Day
Walt Cudzik	C	Al Bemiller
Billy Neighbors	RG	Billy Shaw
Milt Graham	RT	Ken Rice
Tony Romeo	RE	Ernie Warlick
Babe Parilli	QB	Jack Kemp
Ron Burton	LH	Elbert Dubenion
Jim Colclough	RH	Glenn Bass
Larry Garron	FB	Cookie Gilchrist
Starters, Defense		
Bob Dee	LE	Ron McDole
Houston Antwine	LT	Tom Sestak
Jesse Richardson	RT	Jim Dunaway
Jim Hunt	RE	Mack Yoho
Tom Addison	LLB	John Tracey
Nick Buoniconti	MLB	Harry Jacobs
Jack Rudolph	RLB	Mike Stratton
Dick Felt	LCB	Willie West
Bob Suci	RCB	Booker Edgerson
Ron Hall	LS	George Saimes
Ross O'Hanley	RS	Ray Abruzzese

Boston	10	6	0	10	—	26
Buffalo	0	0	8	0	—	8

Bos—FG Cappelletti 28
Bos—Garron 59 pass from Parilli (Cappelletti kick)
Bos—FG Cappelletti 12
Bos—FG Cappelletti 33
Buff—Dubenion 93 pass from Lamonica (Tracey pass from Lamonica)
Bos—Garron 17 pass from Parilli (Cappelletti kick)
Bos—FG Cappelletti 36
Attendance—33,044

1965 NFL

GREEN BAY 13, BALTIMORE 10

Don Chandler's field goal at 13:39 of sudden death overtime won the game. Baltimore led for more than 58 minutes, although quarterbacks Johnny Unitas and Gary Cuozzo were injured and Ed Brown had been acquired too late for postseason play. Halfback Tom Matte taped the game plan to his wrist and played quarterback in 1965 for the first time since 1960.

December 26, at Green Bay

Baltimore	Starters, Offense	Green Bay
Raymond Berry	LE	Boyd Dowler
Bob Vogel	LT	Bob Skoronski
Jim Parker	LT	Fred (Fuzzy) Thurston
Dick Szymanski	C	Ken Bowman
Alex Sandusky	RG	Jerry Kramer
George Preas	RT	Forrest Gregg
John Mackey	RE	Bill Anderson
Tom Matte	QB	Bart Starr
Lenny Moore	LH	Paul Hornung
Jimmy Orr	RH	Carroll Dale
Jerry Hill	FB	Jim Taylor
Starters, Defense		
Lou Michaels	LE	Willie Davis
Fred Miller	LT	Ron Kostelnik
Billy Ray Smith	RT	Henry Jordan
Ordell Braase	RE	Lionel Aldridge
Steve Stonebreaker	LLB	Dave Robinson
Dennis Gaubatz	MLB	Ray Nitschke
Don Shinnick	RLB	Lee Roy Caffey
Bobby Boyd	LCB	Herb Adderley
Lenny Lyles	RCB	Doug Hart
Jerry Logan	LS	Tom Brown
Wendell Harris	RS	Willie Wood

Baltimore	7	3	0	0	0	—	10
Green Bay	0	0	7	3	3	—	13

Balt—Shinnick 25 fumble return (Michaels kick)
Balt—FG Michaels 15
GB—Hornung 1 run (Chandler kick)
GB—FG Chandler 27
GB—FG Chandler 25
Attendance—50,484

1967 NFL

GREEN BAY 28, LOS ANGELES 7

After losing to Los Angeles 27-24 two weeks before, Green Bay yielded a first-quarter touchdown to the Rams, then went on to win 28-7.

Rookie running back Travis Williams rushed for 88 yards and scored on runs of 46 and 2 yards. Quarterback Bart Starr completed 17 of 23 passes for 222 yards.

December 23, at Milwaukee

Los Angeles	Starters, Offense	Green Bay
Jack Snow	LE	Boyd Dowler
Joe Carollo	LT	Bob Skoronski
Tom Mack	LG	Gale Gillingham
Ken Iman	C	Ken Bowman
Joe Scibelli	RG	Jerry Kramer
Charlie Cowan	RT	Forrest Gregg
Billy Truax	RE	Marv Fleming
Roman Gabriel	QB	Bart Starr
Les Josephson	LH	Donny Anderson
Bernie Casey	RH	Carroll Dale
Dick Bass	FB	Chuck Mercein
Starters, Defense		
David (Deacon) Jones	LE	Willie Davis
Merlin Olsen	LT	Ron Kostelnik
Roger Brown	RT	Henry Jordan
Lamar Lundy	RE	Lionel Aldridge
Jack Pardee	LLB	Dave Robinson
Myron Pottios	MLB	Ray Nitschke
Maxie Baughan	RLB	Lee Roy Caffey
Clancy Williams	LCB	Herb Adderley
Irv Cross	RCB	Bob Jeter
Chuck Lamson	LS	Tom Brown
Ed Meador	RS	Willie Wood

Los Angeles	7	0	0	0	—	7
Green Bay	0	14	7	7	—	28

LA—Casey 29 pass from Gabriel (Gossett kick)
GB—Williams 46 run (Chandler kick)
GB—Dale 17 pass from Starr (Chandler kick)
GB—Mercein 6 run (Chandler kick)
GB—Williams 2 run (Chandler kick)
Attendance—49,861

1967 NFL

DALLAS 52, CLEVELAND 14

End Bob Hayes teamed with quarterback Don Meredith on an 86-yard touchdown pass play and set up two other scores on punt returns of 68 and 64 yards.

December 24, at Dallas

Cleveland	Starters, Offense	Dallas
Paul Warfield	LE	Bob Hayes
Dick Schafrath	LT	Tony Liscio
John Wooten	LG	John Niland
Fred Hoaglin	C	Mike Connelly
Gene Hickerson	RG	Leon Donohue
Monte Clark	RT	Ralph Neely
Ralph Smith	RE	Pettis Norman
Frank Ryan	QB	Don Meredith
Leroy Kelly	LH	Dan Reeves
Gary Collins	RH	Lance Rentzel
Ernie Green	FB	Don Perkins
Starters, Defense		
Paul Wiggin	LE	Willie Townes
Walter Johnson	LT	Jethro Pugh
Jim Kanicki	RT	Bob Lilly
Bill Glass	RE	George Andrie
Jim Houston	LLB	Chuck Howley
Dale Lindsey	MLB	Lee Roy Jordan
John Brewer	RLB	Dave Edwards
Erich Barnes	LCB	Cornell Green
Mike Howell	RCB	Mike Johnson
Ernie Kellerman	LS	Mel Renfro
Ross Fichtner	RS	Phil Clark

Cleveland	0	7	0	7	—	14
Dallas	14	10	21	7	—	52

Dall—Baynham 3 pass from Meredith (Villanueva kick)
Dall—Perkins 4 run (Villanueva kick)
Dall—Hayes 86 pass from Meredith (Villanueva kick)
Dall—FG Villanueva 10
Cle—Morin 13 pass from Ryan (Groza kick)
Dall—Baynham 1 run (Villanueva kick)
Dall—Perkins 1 run (Villanueva kick)
Dall—Green 60 interception return (Villanueva kick)
Dall—Baynham 1 run (Villanueva kick)
Cle—Warfield 75 pass from Ryan (Groza kick)
Attendance—70,786

1968 AFL

OAKLAND 41, KANSAS CITY 6

Quarterback Daryle Lamonica threw for 347 yards and five touchdowns and the Kansas City Chiefs went without a touchdown for the first time since 1963 as the Raiders scored a 41–6 victory.

December 22, at Oakland

Kansas City	Starters, Offense	Oakland
Frank Pitts	LE	Warren Wells
Jim Tyrer	LT	Bob Svihus
Ed Budde	LG	Gene Upshaw
E. J. Holub	C	Jim Otto
Mo Moorman	RG	Jim Harvey
Dave Hill	RT	Harry Schuh
Fred Arbanas	TE	Billy Cannon
Len Dawson	QB	Daryle Lamonica
Mike Garrett	LH	Charlie Smith
Otis Taylor	RH	Fred Biletnikoff
Robert Holmes	FB	Hewritt Dixon
	Starters, Defense	
Jerry Mays	LE	Isaac Lassiter
Ed Lothamer	LT	Dan Birdwell
Buck Buchanan	RT	Carleton Oats
Aaron Brown	RE	Ben Davidson
Bobby Bell	LLB	Ralph (Chip) Oliver
Willie Lanier	MLB	Dan Conners
Jim Lynch	RLB	Gus Otto
Goldie Sellers	LCB	George Atkinson
Emmitt Thomas	RCB	Willie Brown
Jim Kearney	LS	Rodger Bird
Johnny Robinson	RS	Dave Grayson

Kansas City	0	6	0	0	—	6
Oakland	21	7	0	13	—	41

Oak—Biletnikoff 24 pass from Lamonica (Blanda kick)
Oak—Wells 23 pass from Lamonica (Blanda kick)
Oak—Biletnikoff 44 pass from Lamonica (Blanda kick)
KC —FG Stenerud 10
KC —FG Stenerud 8
Oak—Biletnikoff 54 pass from Lamonica (Blanda kick)
Oak—Wells 35 pass from Lamonica (Blanda kick)
Oak—FG Blanda 41
Oak—FG Blanda 40
Attendance—53,605

1968 NFL

CLEVELAND 31, DALLAS 20

The Cleveland Browns scored three touchdowns in a three-and-a-half-minute period at the conclusion of the first half and start of the second half and went on to defeat the Dallas Cowboys 31–20.

December 21, at Cleveland

Dallas	Starters, Offense	Cleveland
Bob Hayes	WR	Paul Warfield
Tony Liscio	LT	Dick Schafrath
John Niland	LG	John Demarie
Malcolm Walker	C	Fred Hoaglin
John Wilbur	RG	Gene Hickerson
Ralph Neely	RT	Monte Clark
Pettis Norman	TE	Milt Morin
Don Meredith	QB	Bill Nelsen
Lance Rentzel	WR	Gary Collins
Don Perkins	RB	Leroy Kelly
Craig Baynham	RB	Charley Harraway
	Starters, Defense	
Larry Cole	LE	Ron Snidow
Jethro Pugh	LT	Walter Johnson
Bob Lilly	RT	Jim Kanicki
George Andrie	RE	Jack Gregory
Chuck Howley	LLB	Jim Houston
Lee Roy Jordan	MLB	Bob Matheson
Dave Edwards	RLB	Dale Lindsey
Cornell Green	LCB	Erich Barnes
Mel Renfro	RCB	Ben Davis
Mike Gaechter	LS	Ernie Kellerman
Dick Daniels	RS	Mike Howell

Dallas	7	3	3	7	—	20
Cleveland	3	7	14	7	—	31

Cle —FG Cockroft 38
Dall—Howley 44 fumble return (Clark kick)
Dall—FG Clark 16
Cle —Kelly 45 pass from Nelsen (Cockroft kick)
Cle —Lindsey 27 interception return (Cockroft kick)
Cle —Kelly 35 run (Cockroft kick)
Dall—FG Clark 47
Cle —Green 2 run (Cockroft kick)
Dall—Garrison 2 pass from Morton (Clark kick)
Attendance—81,497

1968 NFL

BALTIMORE 24, MINNESOTA 14

Touchdown passes from Earl Morrall to Tom Mitchell and John Mackey and a 60-yard touchdown run with a fumble by Mike Curtis gave the Baltimore Colts a 21–0 lead through three quarters in a game they went on to win 24–14. The game was played in a steady downpour.

December 22, at Baltimore

Minnesota	Starters, Offense	Baltimore
Gene Washington	WR	Jimmy Orr
Grady Alderman	LT	Bob Vogel
Jim Vellone	LG	Glenn Ressler
Mick Tingelhoff	C	Bill Curry
Milt Sunde	RG	Dan Sullivan
Doug Davis	RT	Sam Ball
John Beasley	TE	John Mackey
Joe Kapp	QB	Earl Morrall
John Henderson	WR	Willie Richardson
Bill Brown	RB	Tom Matte
Dave Osborn	RB	Preston Pearson
	Starters, Defense	
Carl Eller	LE	Charles (Bubba) Smith
Alan Page	LT	Billy Ray Smith
Gary Larsen	RT	Fred Miller
Jim Marshall	RE	Ordell Braase
Roy Winston	LLB	Mike Curtis
Lonnie Warwick	MLB	Dennis Gaubatz
Wally Hilgenberg	RLB	Don Shinnick
Earsell Mackbee	LCB	Bobby Boyd
Ed Sharockman	RCB	Lenny Lyles
Karl Kassulke	LS	Jerry Logan
Paul Krause	RS	Rick Volk

Minnesota	0	0	0	14	—	14
Baltimore	0	7	14	3	—	24

Balt —Mitchell 3 pass from Morrall (Michaels kick)
Balt —Mackey 49 pass from Morrall (Michaels kick)
Balt —Curtis 60 fumble return (Michaels kick)
Minn—Martin 1 pass from Kapp (Cox kick)
Balt —FG Michaels 33
Minn—Brown 7 pass from Kapp (Cox kick)
Attendance—60,238

1969 AFL

KANSAS CITY 13, N.Y. JETS 6

The Kansas City Chiefs moved 80 yards in two plays early in the fourth quarter, scoring on Len Dawson's 19-yard pass to Gloster Richardson, and defeated the New York Jets 13–6.

The Jets had a first down on the Chiefs' 1-yard line late in the third quarter but settled for a field goal by Jim Turner that tied the score 6–6.

December 20, at New York

Kansas City	Starters, Offense	N.Y. Jets
Frank Pitts	WR	George Sauer
Jim Tyrer	LT	Winston Hill
Ed Budde	LG	Randy Rasmussen
E. J. Holub	C	John Schmitt
Mo Moorman	RG	Dave Herman
Dave Hill	RT	Roger Finnie
Fred Arbanas	TE	Pete Lammons
Otis Taylor	WR	Robert (Bake) Turner
Len Dawson	QB	Joe Namath
Mike Garrett	RB	Emerson Boozer
Robert Holmes	RB	Matt Snell
	Starters, Defense	
Jerry Mays	LE	Gerry Philbin
Curley Culp	LT	Steve Thompson
Buck Buchanan	RT	John Elliott
Aaron Brown	RE	Verlon Biggs
Bobby Bell	LLB	Ralph Baker
Willie Lanier	MLB	Al Atkinson
Jim Lynch	RLB	Larry Grantham
Jim Marsalis	LCB	Cornell Gordon
Emmitt Thomas	RCB	Randy Beverly
Johnny Robinson	LS	Bill Baird
Jim Kearney	RS	Jim Richards

Kansas City	0	3	3	7	—	13
N.Y. Jets	3	0	0	3	—	6

NYJ—FG J. Turner 27
KC —FG Stenerud 23
KC —FG Stenerud 25
NYJ—FG J. Turner 7
KC —Richardson 19 pass from Dawson (Stenerud kick)
Attendance—62,977

1969 AFL

OAKLAND 56, HOUSTON 7

The Oakland Raiders scored four touchdowns within a span of 4:22 and led 28–0 after the first eight minutes of play after capitalizing on two fumbles and a pass interception, then coasted to a 56–7 victory.

December 21, at Oakland

Houston	Starters, Offense	Oakland
Jim Beirne	WR	Rod Sherman
Walt Suggs	LT	Bob Svihus
Tom Regner	LG	Gene Upshaw
Bobby Maples	C	Jim Otto
Erwin (Sonny) Bishop	RG	Jim Harvey
Glen Ray Hines	RT	Harry Schuh
Alvin Reed	TE	Billy Cannon
Jerry LeVias	WR	Fred Biletnikoff
Pete Beathard	QB	Daryle Lamonica
Woody Campbell	RB	Charlie Smith
Hoyle Granger	RB	Hewritt Dixon
	Starters, Defense	
Pat Holmes	LE	Isaac Lassiter
Carel Stith	LT	Carleton Oats
Tom Domres	RT	Tom Keating
Elvin Bethea	RE	Ben Davidson
George Webster	LLB	Ralph (Chip) Oliver
Garland Boyette	MLB	Dan Conners
Olen Underwood	RLB	Gus Otto
Miller Farr	LCB	Nemiah Wilson
Zeke Moore	RCB	Willie Brown
Ken Houston	LS	George Atkinson
Johnny Peacock	RS	Dave Grayson

Houston	0	0	0	7	—	7
Oakland	28	7	14	7	—	56

Oak—Biletnikoff 13 pass from Lamonica (Blanda kick)
Oak—Atkinson 57 interception return (Blanda kick)
Oak—Sherman 24 pass from Lamonica (Blanda kick)
Oak—Biletnikoff 31 pass from Lamonica (Blanda kick)
Oak—Smith 60 pass from Lamonica (Blanda kick)
Oak—Sherman 23 pass from Lamonica (Blanda kick)
Oak—Cannon 3 pass from Lamonica (Blanda kick)
Hou—Reed 8 pass from Beathard (Gerela kick)
Oak—Hubbard 4 run (Blanda kick)
Attendance—53,539

1969 NFL

MINNESOTA 23, LOS ANGELES 20

The Minnesota Vikings drove 65 yards to a fourth quarter touchdown and added a safety 35 seconds later. Joe Kapp completed three passes for 40 yards and ran the final two yards in the touchdown march.

December 27, at Bloomington, Minnesota

Los Angeles	Starters, Offense	Minnesota
Jack Snow	WR	Gene Washington
Charlie Cowan	LT	Grady Alderman
Tom Mack	RG	Jim Vellone
Ken Iman	C	Mick Tingelhoff
Mike LaHood	RG	Milt Sunde
Bob Brown	RT	Ron Yary
Billy Truax	TE	John Beasley
Wendell Tucker	WR	John Henderson
Roman Gabriel	QB	Joe Kapp
Larry Smith	RB	Dave Osborn
Les Josephson	RB	Bill Brown
	Starters, Defense	
David (Deacon) Jones	LE	Carl Eller
Merlin Olsen	LT	Gary Larsen
Coy Bacon	RT	Alan Page
Diron Talbert	RE	Jim Marshall
Jack Pardee	LLB	Roy Winston
Doug Woodlief	MLB	Lonnie Warwick
Maxie Baughan	RLB	Wally Hilgenberg
Clancy Williams	LCB	Earsell Mackbee
Jim Nettles	RCB	Ed Sharockman
Richie Petitbon	LS	Karl Kassulke
Ed Meador	RS	Paul Krause

Los Angeles	7	10	0	3	—	20
Minnesota	7	0	7	9	—	23

LA —Klein 3 pass from Gabriel (Gossett kick)
Minn—Osborn 1 run (Cox kick)
LA —FG Gossett 20
LA —Truax 2 pass from Gabriel (Gossett kick)
Minn—Osborn 1 run (Cox kick)
LA —FG Gossett 27
Minn—Kapp 2 run (Cox kick)
Minn—Safety, Eller tackled Gabriel in end zone
Attendance—47,900

1969 NFL

CLEVELAND 38, DALLAS 14

Bill Nelsen completed 15 of 22 passes for 184 yards and one touchdown as the Cleveland Browns took a 17-0 halftime lead and went on to a 38-14 victory over the Dallas Cowboys.

December 28, at Dallas

Cleveland	Starters, Offense	Dallas
Paul Warfield	WR	Bob Hayes
Dick Schafrath	LT	Tony Liscio
John Demarie	LG	John Niland
Fred Hoaglin	C	Malcolm Walker
Gene Hickerson	RG	John Wilbur
Monte Clark	RT	Ralph Neely
Milt Morin	TE	Pettis Norman
Gary Collins	WR	Lance Rentzel
Bill Nelsen	QB	Craig Morton
Leroy Kelly	RB	Calvin Hill
Robert (Bo) Scott	RB	Walt Garrison
	Starters, Defense	
Ron Snidow	LE	Larry Cole
Walter Johnson	LT	Jethro Pugh
Jim Kanicki	RT	Bob Lilly
Jack Gregory	RE	George Andrie
Jim Houston	LLB	Dave Edwards
Dale Lindsey	MLB	Lee Roy Jordan
John Garlington	RLB	Chuck Howley
Erich Barnes	LCB	Cornell Green
Walt Sumner	RCB	Otto Brown
Ernie Kellerman	LS	Mike Gaechter
Mike Howell	RS	Mel Renfro

Cleveland	7	10	7	14	—	38
Dallas	0	0	7	7	—	14

Cle —Scott 2 run (Cockroft kick)
Cle —Morin 6 pass from Nelsen (Cockroft kick)
Cle —FG Cockroft 29
Cle —Scott 2 run (Cockroft kick)
Dall—Morton 2 run (Clark kick)
Cle —Kelly 1 run (Cockroft kick)
Cle —Sumner 88 interception return (Cockroft kick)
Dall—Rentzel 5 pass from Staubach (Clark kick)
Attendance—69,321

1970 AFC

BALTIMORE 17, CINCINNATI 0

Fifteen-year veteran Johnny Unitas threw touchdown passes of 45 and 53 yards to Roy Jefferson and Eddie Hinton to lead the Baltimore Colts to a 17-0 victory over the Cincinnati Bengals.

The Bengals had won their last seven games to finish the regular season with an 8-6 record and gain the playoffs in their third year. No expansion team had been able to achieve that level in that period.

December 26, at Baltimore

Cincinnati	Starters, Offense	Baltimore
Philip (Chip) Myers	WR	Eddie Hinton
Ernie Wright	LT	Bob Vogel
Rufus Mayes	LG	Glenn Ressler
Bob Johnson	C	Bill Curry
Pat Matson	RG	John Williams
Howard Fest	RT	Dan Sullivan
Bob Trumpy	TE	John Mackey
Louis (Speedy) Thomas	WR	Roy Jefferson
Virgil Carter	QB	Johnny Unitas
Paul Robinson	RB	Norm Bulaich
Jess Phillips	RB	Tom Nowatzke
	Starters, Defense	
Royce Berry	LE	Charles (Bubba) Smith
Mike Reid	LT	Billy Ray Smith
Steve Chomyszak	RT	Fred Miller
Ron Carpenter	RE	Roy Hilton
Al Beauchamp	LLB	Ray May
Bill Bergey	MLB	Mike Curtis
Ken Avery	RLB	Ted Hendricks
Lemar Parrish	LCB	Charlie Stukes
Ken Riley	RCB	Jim Duncan
Fletcher Smith	LS	Jerry Logan
Ken Dyer	RS	Rick Volk

Cincinnati	0	0	0	0	—	0
Baltimore	7	3	0	7	—	17

Balt—Jefferson 45 pass from Unitas (O'Brien kick)
Balt—FG O'Brien 44
Balt—Hinton 53 pass from Unitas (O'Brien kick)
Attendance—51,127

1970 AFC

OAKLAND 21, MIAMI 14

An 82-yard pass play from quarterback Daryle Lamonica to wide receiver Rod Sherman with 9:34 remaining was the difference as the Oakland Raiders defeated Miami on a field slowed by heavy rain.

Lamonica threw a 37-yard pass to Sherman, who caught the ball on the sideline over Curtis Johnson, trying for an interception.

December 27, at Oakland

Miami	Starters, Offense	Oakland
Paul Warfield	WR	Warren Wells
Doug Crusan	LT	Art Shell
Bob Kuechenberg	LG	Gene Upshaw
Carl Mauck	C	Jim Otto
Larry Little	RG	Jim Harvey
Norm Evans	RT	Harry Schuh
Marv Fleming	TE	Raymond Chester
Howard Twilley	WR	Fred Biletnikoff
Bob Griese	QB	Daryle Lamonica
Jim Kiick	RB	Charlie Smith
Larry Csonka	RB	Hewritt Dixon
	Starters, Defense	
Jim Riley	LE	Tony Cline
Frank Cornish	LT	Carleton Oats
John Richardson	RT	Tom Keating
Bill Stanfill	RE	Ben Davidson
Doug Swift	LLB	Bill Laskey
Nick Buoniconti	MLB	Dan Conners
Mike Kolen	RLB	Gus Otto
Curtis Johnson	LCB	Kent McCloughan
Lloyd Mumphord	RCB	Willie Brown
Dick Anderson	LS	George Atkinson
Jake Scott	RS	Dave Grayson

Miami	0	7	0	7	—	14
Oakland	0	7	7	7	—	21

Mia —Warfield 16 pass from Griese (Yepremian kick)
Oak—Biletnikoff 22 pass from Lamonica (Blanda kick)
Oak—Brown 50 interception return (Blanda kick)
Oak—Sherman 82 pass from Lamonica (Blanda kick)
Mia —W. Richardson 7 pass from Griese (Yepremian kick)
Attendance—54,401

1970 NFC

DALLAS 5, DETROIT 0

Rookie running back Duane Thomas gained 135 yards in 30 carries, including 104 in 22 in the second half, but the Dallas Cowboys used a field goal and safety to produce a 5-0 victory.

The Cowboys controlled the ball for seven minutes on a 15-play, 77-yard drive that ended at Detroit's 1-yard line in the fourth quarter. Three plays later, George Andrie trapped Lions quarterback Greg Landry in the end zone for a safety.

December 26, at Dallas

Detroit	Starters, Offense	Dallas
Earl McCullouch	WR	Bob Hayes
Roger Shoals	LT	Ralph Neely
Chuck Walton	LG	John Niland
Ed Flanagan	C	Dave Manders
Frank Gallagher	RG	Blaine Nye
Rockne (Rocky) Freitas	RT	Rayfield Wright
Charlie Sanders	TE	Pettis Norman
Larry Walton	WR	Reggie Rucker
Greg Landry	QB	Craig Morton
Mel Farr	RB	Duane Thomas
Altie Taylor	RB	Walt Garrison
	Starters, Defense	
Jim Mitchell	LE	Larry Cole
Alex Karras	LT	Jethro Pugh
Jerry Rush	RT	Bob Lilly
Larry Hand	RE	George Andrie
Paul Naumoff	LLB	Dave Edwards
Mike Lucci	MLB	Lee Roy Jordan
Wayne Walker	RLB	Chuck Howley
Lem Barney	LCB	Herb Adderley
Dick LeBeau	RCB	Mel Renfro
Mike Weger	LS	Cornell Green
Tom Vaughn	RS	Charlie Waters

Detroit	0	0	0	0	—	0
Dallas	3	0	0	2	—	5

Dall—FG Clark 26
Dall—Safety, Andrie tackled Landry in end zone
Attendance—73,167

1970 NFC

SAN FRANCISCO 17, MINNESOTA 14

Quarterback John Brodie scored on a 1-yard run with 1:20 left in the game, giving San Francisco a 17-7 lead en route to a 17-14 victory.

On a day when the temperature fluctuated between 5 and 11 degrees and winds gusted at 15 miles an hour, the 49ers overcame a 7-0 Vikings lead in the first quarter.

December 27, at Bloomington, Minnesota

San Francisco	Starters, Offense	Minnesota
Gene Washington	WR	Gene Washington
Len Rohde	LT	Grady Alderman
Randy Beisler	LG	Jim Vellone
Forrest Blue	C	Mick Tingelhoff
Woody Peoples	RG	Milt Sunde
Cas Banaszek	RT	Ron Yary
Bob Windsor	TE	John Beasley
Dick Witcher	WR	John Henderson
John Brodie	QB	Gary Cuozzo
Ken Willard	RB	Clinton Jones
Bill Tucker	RB	Dave Osborn
	Starters, Defense	
Tommy Hart	LE	Carl Eller
Charlie Krueger	LT	Gary Larsen
Roland Lakes	RT	Alan Page
Bill Belk	RE	Jim Marshall
Dave Wilcox	LLB	Roy Winston
Frank Nunley	MLB	Lonnie Warwick
Jim Sniadecki	RLB	Wally Hilgenberg
Jimmy Johnson	LCB	Bobby Bryant
Bruce Taylor	RCB	Ed Sharockman
Roosevelt Taylor	LS	Karl Kassulke
Mel Phillips	RS	Paul Krause

San Francisco	7	3	0	7	—	17
Minnesota	7	0	0	7	—	14

Minn—Krause 22 fumble return (Cox kick)
SF —Witcher 26 pass from Brodie (Gossett kick)
SF —FG Gossett 40
SF —Brodie 1 run (Gossett kick)
Minn—Washington 24 pass from Cuozzo (Cox kick)
Attendance—45,103

1971 AFC

MIAMI 27, KANSAS CITY 24

Garo Yepremian kicked a 37-yard field goal after 7:40 of the sixth quarter to give the Miami Dolphins a 27–24 victory over the Kansas City Chiefs in the longest professional football game in history.

December 25, at Kansas City

Miami	Starters, Offense	Kansas City
Paul Warfield	WR	Elmo Wright
Doug Crusan	LT	Jim Tyrer
Bob Kuechenberg	LG	Ed Budde
Bob DeMarco	C	Jack Rudnay
Larry Little	RG	Mo Moorman
Norm Evans	RT	Dave Hill
Marv Fleming	TE	Morris Stroud
Howard Twilley	WR	Otis Taylor
Bob Griese	QB	Len Dawson
Jim Kiick	RB	Wendell Hayes
Larry Csonka	RB	Ed Podolak
	Starters, Defense	
Jim Riley	LE	Marvin Upshaw
Manny Fernandez	LT	Curley Culp
Bob Heinz	RT	Buck Buchanan
Bill Stanfill	RE	Aaron Brown
Doug Swift	LLB	Bobby Bell
Nick Buoniconti	MLB	Willie Lanier
Bob Matheson	RLB	Jim Lynch
Tim Foley	LCB	Jim Marsalis
Curtis Johnson	RCB	Emmitt Thomas
Jake Scott	LS	Jim Kearney
Dick Anderson	RS	Johnny Robinson

Miami	0	10	7	7	0	3	—	27
Kansas City	10	0	7	7	0	0	—	24

KC —FG Stenerud 24
KC —Podolak 7 pass from Dawson (Stenerud kick)
Mia—Csonka 1 run (Yepremian kick)
Mia—FG Yepremian 14
KC —Otis 1 run (Stenerud kick)
Mia—Kiick 1 run (Yepremian kick)
KC —Podolak 3 run (Stenerud kick)
Mia—Fleming 5 pass from Griese (Yepremian kick)
Mia—FG Yepremian 37
Attendance—50,374

1971 AFC

BALTIMORE 20, CLEVELAND 3

Rookie running back Don Nottingham, a replacement for injured Norm Bulaich rushed for 92 yards and scored Baltimore's first two touchdowns.

Nottingham's runs of one and seven yards gave the Colts a 14–0 halftime lead. Cleveland scored on Don Cockroft's 14-yard field goal. Charles (Bubba) Smith blocked two other field goal attempts.

December 26, at Cleveland

Baltimore	Starters, Offense	Cleveland
Eddie Hinton	WR	Fair Hooker
Bob Vogel	LT	Doug Dieken
Glenn Ressler	LG	John Demarie
Bill Curry	C	Jim Copeland
John Williams	RG	Gene Hickerson
Dan Sullivan	RT	Bob McKay
Tom Mitchell	TE	Milt Morin
Ray Perkins	WR	Frank Pitts
Johnny Unitas	QB	Bill Nelsen
Tom Matte	RB	Leroy Kelly
Don Nottingham	RB	Robert (Bo) Scott
	Starters, Defense	
Charles (Bubba) Smith	LE	Ron Snidow
Billy Newsome	LT	Walter Johnson
Fred Miller	RT	Jerry Sherk
Roy Hilton	RE	Jack Gregory
Ray May	LLB	John Garlington
Mike Curtis	MLB	Jim Houston
Ted Hendricks	LLB	Bill Andrews
Charlie Stukes	LCB	Clarence Scott
Rex Kern	RCB	Ben Davis
Jerry Logan	LS	Walt Sumner
Rick Volk	RS	Mike Howell

Baltimore	0	14	3	3	—	20
Cleveland	0	0	3	0	—	3

Balt—Nottingham 1 run (O'Brien kick)
Balt—Nottingham 7 run (O'Brien kick)
Cle—FG Cockroft 14
Balt—FG O'Brien 42
Balt—FG O'Brien 15
Attendance—74,082

1971 NFC

DALLAS 20, MINNESOTA 12

Safety Cliff Harris intercepted a pass by Bob Lee to set up a 13-yard touchdown by Duane Thomas that gave the Dallas Cowboys a 13–3 lead in the third quarter en route to a 20–12 victory over the Minnesota Vikings.

December 25, at Bloomington, Minnesota

Dallas	Starters, Offense	Minnesota
Bob Hayes	WR	Gene Washington
Tony Liscio	LT	Grady Alderman
John Niland	LG	Ed White
Dave Manders	C	Mick Tingelhoff
Blaine Nye	RG	Milt Sunde
Rayfield Wright	RT	Ron Yary
Mike Ditka	TE	Bob Brown
Lance Alworth	WR	Bob Grim
Roger Staubach	QB	Bob Lee
Calvin Hill	RB	Clinton Jones
Duane Thomas	RB	Dave Osborn
	Starters, Defense	
Larry Cole	LE	Carl Eller
Jethro Pugh	LT	Gary Larsen
Bob Lilly	RT	Alan Page
George Andrie	RE	Jim Marshall
Dave Edwards	LLB	Carl Winfrey
Lee Roy Jordan	MLB	Lonnie Warwick
Chuck Howley	RLB	Wally Hilgenberg
Herb Adderley	LCB	Bobby Bryant
Mel Renfro	RCB	Ed Sharockman
Cornell Green	LS	Charlie West
Cliff Harris	RS	Paul Krause

Dallas	3	3	14	0	—	20
Minnesota	0	3	0	9	—	12

Dall—FG Clark 26
Minn—FG Cox 27
Dall—FG Clark 44
Dall—D. Thomas 13 run (Clark kick)
Dall—Hayes 9 pass from Staubach (Clark kick)
Minn—Safety, Page tackled Staubach in end zone
Minn—Voight 6 pass from Cuozzo (Cox kick)
Attendance—49,100

1971 NFC

SAN FRANCISCO 24, WASHINGTON 20

With the San Francisco 49ers leading 17–13 early in the fourth quarter, Washington punter Mike Bragg had a poor snap from center roll through his legs. The 49ers' Bob Hoskins recovered in the end zone.

December 26, at San Francisco

Washington	Starters, Offense	San Francisco
Clifton McNeil	WR	Dick Witcher
Jim Snowden	LT	Len Rohde
Ray Schoenke	LG	Randy Beisler
Len Hauss	C	Forrest Blue
John Wilbur	RG	Woody Peoples
Walter Rock	RT	Cas Banaszek
Jerry Smith	TE	Ted Kwalick
Roy Jefferson	WR	Gene Washington
Billy Kilmer	QB	John Brodie
Larry Brown	RB	Vic Washington
Charley Harraway	RB	Ken Willard
	Starters, Defense	
Ron McDole	LE	Tommy Hart
Manny Sistrunk	LT	Charlie Krueger
Diron Talbert	RT	Earl Edwards
Verlon Biggs	RE	Cedrick Hardman
Jack Pardee	LLB	Dave Wilcox
Myron Pottios	MLB	Frank Nunley
Chris Hanburger	RLB	Skip Vanderbundt
Pat Fischer	LCB	Jimmy Johnson
Mike Bass	RCB	Bruce Taylor
Richie Petitbon	LS	Mel Phillips
Brig Owens	RS	Roosevelt Taylor

Washington	7	3	3	7	—	20
San Francisco	0	3	14	7	—	24

Wash—Smith 5 pass from Kilmer (Knight kick)
SF —FG Gossett 23
Wash—FG Knight 40
SF —G. Washington 78 pass from Brodie (Gossett kick)
SF —Windsor 2 pass from Brodie (Gossett kick)
Wash—FG Knight 36
SF —Hoskins, fumble recovery in end zone (Gossett kick)
Wash—Brown 16 pass from Kilmer (Knight kick)
Attendance—45,364

1972 AFC

PITTSBURGH 13, OAKLAND 7

Pittsburgh came from behind to defeat the Oakland Raiders 13–7 when Terry Bradshaw's fourth down pass in the final 22 seconds ricocheted off Oakland's Jack Tatum and was picked off at the shoetops on the Raiders' 42 by Franco Harris, who scored on a 60-yard touchdown play with five seconds left.

Ken Stabler scrambled 30 yards with 1:13 left for Oakland's touchdown and a 7–6 lead.

December 23, at Pittsburgh

Oakland	Starters, Offense	Pittsburgh
Mike Siani	WR	Al Young
Art Shell	LT	Jon Kolb
Gene Upshaw	LG	Sam Davis
Jim Otto	C	Ray Mansfield
George Buehler	RG	Bruce Van Dyke
Bob Brown	RT	Gerry Mullins
Raymond Chester	TE	John McMakin
Fred Biletnikoff	WR	Ron Shanklin
Daryle Lamonica	QB	Terry Bradshaw
Charlie Smith	RB	Franco Harris
Marv Hubbard	RB	John Fuqua
	Starters, Defense	
Tony Cline	LE	L. C. Greenwood
Otis Sistrunk	LT	Joe Greene
Art Thoms	RT	Ben McGee
Horace Jones	RE	Dwight White
Phil Villapiano	LLB	Jack Ham
Dan Conners	MLB	Henry Davis
Gerald Irons	RLB	Andy Russell
Nemiah Wilson	LCB	John Rowser
Willie Brown	RCB	Mel Blount
George Atkinson	LS	Glen Edwards
Jack Tatum	RS	Mike Wagner

Oakland	0	0	0	7	—	7
Pittsburgh	0	0	3	10	—	13

Pitt —FG Gerela 18
Pitt —FG Gerela 29
Oak—Stabler 30 run (Blanda kick)
Pitt —Harris 60 pass from Bradshaw (Gerela kick)
Attendance—50,350

1972 AFC

MIAMI 20, CLEVELAND 14

Miami marched 80 yards to a fourth-quarter touchdown that overcame a 14–13 lead. Bob Griese passed 15 and 35 yards to Paul Warfield. Warfield was fouled by Bill Andrews on a 10-yard pass. That put the ball on the 8; Jim Kiick scored the next play.

December 24, at Miami

Cleveland	Starters, Offense	Miami
Fair Hooker	WR	Paul Warfield
Doug Dieken	LT	Wayne Moore
Gene Hickerson	LG	Bob Kuechenberg
Bob DeMarco	C	Jim Langer
John Demarie	RG	Larry Little
Bob McKay	RT	Norm Evans
Milt Morin	TE	Marv Fleming
Frank Pitts	WR	Howard Twilley
Mike Phipps	QB	Bob Griese
Leroy Kelly	RB	Jim Kiick
Robert (Bo) Scott	RB	Larry Csonka
	Starters, Defense	
Nick Roman	LE	Vern Den Herder
Walter Johnson	LT	Manny Fernandez
Jerry Sherk	RT	Bob Heinz
Bob Briggs	RE	Bill Stanfill
Charlie Hall	LLB	Doug Swift
Dale Lindsey	MLB	Nick Buoniconti
Bill Andrews	RLB	Mike Kolen
Clarence Scott	LCB	Tom Foley
Ben Davis	RCB	Curtis Johnson
Thom Darden	LS	Jake Scott
Walt Sumner	RS	Dick Anderson

Cleveland	0	0	7	7	—	14
Miami	10	0	0	10	—	20

Mia—Babb 5 blocked punt return (Yepremian kick)
Mia—FG Yepremian 40
Cle—Phipps 5 run (Cockroft kick)
Mia—FG Yepremian 46
Cle—Hooker 27 pass from Phipps (Cockroft kick)
Mia—Kiick 8 run (Yepremian kick)
Attendance—80,010

1972 NFC

WASHINGTON 16, GREEN BAY 3

A five-man defensive line helped the Washington Redskins contain the Green Bay Packers' running attack in a 16–3 victory. Rookie John Brockington, who rushed for 1,027 yards for Green Bay during the season, was limited to 13 yards in nine carries.

The Redskins led 10–3 at halftime and held off Green Bay in the second half with two field goals.

December 24, at Washington

Green Bay	Starters, Offense	Washington
Leland Glass	WR	Charley Taylor
Bill Hayhoe	LT	Terry Hermeling
Bill Lueck	LG	Paul Laaveg
Ken Bowman	C	Len Hauss
Malcolm Snider	RG	Ray Schoenke
Dick Himes	RT	Walter Rock
Len Garrett	TE	Mack Alston
Carroll Dale	WR	Roy Jefferson
Scott Hunter	QB	Billy Kilmer
MacArthur Lane	RB	Larry Brown
John Brockington	RB	Charley Harraway
	Starters, Defense	
Clarence Williams	LE	Ron McDole
Mike McCoy	LT	Bill Brundige
Bob Brown	RT	Diron Talbert
Alden Roche	RE	Verlon Biggs
Dave Robinson	LLB	Jack Pardee
Jim Carter	MLB	Myron Pottios
Fred Carr	RLB	Chris Hanburger
Willie Buchanon	LCB	Pat Fischer
Ken Ellis	RCB	Mike Bass
Al Matthews	LS	Brig Owens
Jim Hill	RS	Roosevelt Taylor

Green Bay	0	3	0	0	—	3
Washington	0	10	0	6	—	16

GB —FG Marcol 17
Wash—Jefferson 32 pass from Kilmer (Knight kick)
Wash—FG Knight 42
Wash—FG Knight 35
Wash—FG Knight 46
Attendance—53,140

1972 NFC

DALLAS 30, SAN FRANCISCO 28

Roger Staubach came off the bench late in the third quarter to pass for 174 yards and two touchdowns as Dallas overcame a 28-13 fourth-quarter deficit.

December 23 at San Francisco

Dallas	Starters, Offense	San Francisco
Ron Sellers	WR	Gene Washington
Ralph Neely	LT	Len Rohde
John Niland	LG	Randy Beisler
Dave Manders	C	Forrest Blue
Blaine Nye	RG	Woody Peoples
Rayfield Wright	RT	Cas Banaszek
Mike Ditka	TE	Ted Kwalick
Lance Alworth	WR	Preston Riley
Craig Morton	QB	John Brodie
Calvin Hill	RB	Vic Washington
Walt Garrison	RB	Larry Schreiber
	Starters, Defense	
Larry Cole	LE	Tommy Hart
Jethro Pugh	LT	Charlie Krueger
Bob Lilly	RT	Earl Edwards
Pat Toomay	RE	Cedrick Hardman
Dave Edwards	LLB	Dave Wilcox
Lee Roy Jordan	MLB	Ed Beard
D.D. Lewis	RLB	Skip Vanderbundt
Charlie Waters	LCB	Jimmy Johnson
Mel Renfro	RCB	Bruce Taylor
Cornell Green	LS	Windlan Hall
Cliff Harris	RS	Mike Simpson

Dallas	3	10	0	17	—	30
San Francisco	7	14	7	0	—	28

SF —V. Washington 97 kickoff return (Gossett kick)
Dall—FG Fritsch 37
SF —Schreiber 1 run (Gossett kick)
SF —Schreiber 1 run (Gossett kick)
Dall—FG Fritsch 45
Dall—Alworth 28 pass from Morton (Fritsch kick)
SF —Schreiber 1 run (Gossett kick)
Dall—FG Fritsch 27
Dall—Parks 20 pass from Staubach (Fritsch kick)
Dall—Sellers 10 pass from Staubach (Fritsch kick)
Attendance—61,214

1973 AFC

OAKLAND 33, PITTSBURGH 14

The Oakland Raiders moved 82 yards in 16 plays after the opening kickoff to score with 4:51 to play in the first quarter on their way to a 33–14 victory over the Pittsburgh Steelers.

December 22, at Oakland

Pittsburgh	Starters, Offense	Oakland
Frank Lewis	WR	Mike Siani
Jon Kolb	LT	Art Shell
Sam Davis	LG	Gene Upshaw
Ray Mansfield	C	Jim Otto
Bruce Van Dyke	RG	George Buehler
Glen Ray Hines	RT	John Vella
John McMakin	TE	Bob Moore
Barry Pearson	WR	Fred Biletnikoff
Terry Bradshaw	QB	Ken Stabler
Preston Pearson	RB	Charlie Smith
Franco Harris	RB	Marv Hubbard
	Starters, Defense	
L. C. Greenwood	LE	Tony Cline
Joe Greene	LT	Otis Sistrunk
Tom Keating	RT	Art Thoms
Dwight White	RE	Horace Jones
Jack Ham	LLB	Phil Villapiano
Henry Davis	MLB	Dan Conners
Andy Russell	RLB	Gerald Irons
John Rowser	LCB	Nemiah Wilson
Mel Blount	RCB	Willie Brown
Mike Wagner	LS	George Atkinson
Glen Edwards	RS	Jack Tatum

Pittsburgh	0	7	0	7	—	14
Oakland	7	3	13	10	—	33

Oak—Hubbard 1 run (Blanda kick)
Oak—FG Blanda 25
Pitt—B. Pearson 4 pass from Bradshaw (Gerela kick)
Oak—FG Blanda 31
Oak—FG Blanda 22
Oak—W. Brown 54 interception return (Blanda kick)
Oak—FG Blanda 10
Pitt—Lewis 26 pass from Bradshaw (Gerela kick)
Oak—Hubbard 1 run (Blanda kick)
Attendance—51,110

1973 AFC

MIAMI 34, CINCINNATI 16

The Miami Dolphins put together touchdown drives of 80, 80, and 75 yards, rolling up 400 yards offense and setting a playoff record with 27 first downs.

December 23, at Miami

Cincinnati	Starters, Offense	Miami
Charlie Joiner	WR	Paul Warfield
Rufus Mayes	LT	Wayne Moore
Howard Fest	LG	Bob Kuechenberg
Bob Johnson	C	Jim Langer
Pat Matson	RG	Larry Little
Vernon Holland	RT	Norm Evans
Bob Trumpy	TE	Jim Mandich
Isaac Curtis	WR	Marlin Briscoe
Ken Anderson	QB	Bob Griese
Essex Johnson	RB	Eugene (Mercury) Morris
Charles (Boobie) Clark	RB	Larry Csonka
	Starters, Defense	
Royce Berry	LE	Vern Den Herder
Mike Reid	LT	Maulty Moore
Ron Carpenter	RT	Bob Heinz
Sherman White	RE	Bill Stanfill
Al Beauchamp	LLB	Doug Swift
Bill Bergey	MLB	Nick Buoniconti
Ken Avery	RLB	Mike Kolen
Lemar Parrish	LCB	Lloyd Mumphord
Ken Riley	RCB	Curtis Johnson
Neal Craig	LS	Jake Scott
Tommy Casanova	RS	Dick Anderson

Cincinnati	3	13	0	0	—	16
Miami	14	7	10	3	—	34

Mia —Warfield 13 pass from Griese (Yepremian kick)
Cin —FG Muhlmann 24
Mia —Csonka 1 run (Yepremian kick)
Mia —Morris 4 run (Yepremian kick)
Cin —Craig 45 interception return (Muhlmann kick)
Cin —FG Muhlmann 46
Cin —FG Muhlmann 10
Mia —Mandich 7 pass from Griese (Yepremian kick)
Mia —FG Yepremian 50
Mia —FG Yepremian 46
Attendance—74,770

1973 NFC

MINNESOTA 27, WASHINGTON 20

Quarterback Fran Tarkenton threw touchdown passes of 28 and 8 yards to John Gilliam within a period of 1:05 of the fourth quarter as the Minnesota Vikings overcame a 13-10 deficit.

December 22, at Bloomington, Minnesota

Washington	Starters, Offense	Minnesota
Charley Taylor	WR	Carroll Dale
Terry Hermeling	LT	Grady Alderman
Paul Laaveg	LG	Ed White
Len Hauss	C	Mick Tingelhoff
John Wilbur	RG	Milt Sunde
George Starke	RT	Ron Yary
Jerry Smith	TE	Stu Voight
Roy Jefferson	WR	John Gilliam
Billy Kilmer	QB	Fran Tarkenton
Larry Brown	RB	Chuck Foreman
Charley Harraway	RB	Oscar Reed
	Starters, Defense	
Ron McDole	LE	Carl Eller
Bill Brundige	LT	Gary Larsen
Diron Talbert	RT	Alan Page
Verlon Biggs	RE	Jim Marshall
Dave Robinson	LLB	Roy Winston
Myron Pottios	MLB	Jeff Siemon
Chris Hanburger	RLB	Wally Hilgenberg
Pat Fischer	LCB	Nate Wright
Mike Bass	RCB	Bobby Bryant
Ken Houston	LS	Jeff Wright
Brig Owens	RS	Paul Krause

Washington	0	7	3	10	—	20
Minnesota	0	3	7	17	—	27

Minn —FG Cox 19
Wash—Brown 2 run (Knight kick)
Minn —B. Brown 2 run (Cox kick)
Wash—FG Knight 52
Wash—FG Knight 42
Minn —Gilliam 28 pass from Tarkenton (Cox kick)
Minn —Gilliam 8 pass from Tarkenton (Cox kick)
Wash—Jefferson 28 pass from Kilmer (Knight kick)
Minn —FG Cox 30
Attendance—45,475

1973 NFC

DALLAS 27, LOS ANGELES 16

Drew Pearson caught a 34-yard pass between Steve Preece and Eddie McMillan and ran 49 yards to an 83-yard touchdown in the Cowboys' victory.

December 23, at Irving, Texas

Los Angeles	Starters, Offense	Dallas
Harold Jackson	WR	Bob Hayes
Charlie Cowan	LT	Ralph Neely
Tom Mack	LG	John Niland
Ken Iman	C	John Fitzgerald
Joe Scibelli	RG	Blaine Nye
John Williams	RT	Rayfield Wright
Bob Klein	TE	Billy Joe DuPree
Jack Snow	WR	Drew Pearson
John Hadl	QB	Roger Staubach
Jim Bertelsen	RB	Calvin Hill
Lawrence McCutcheon	RB	Walt Garrison
	Starters, Defense	
Jack Youngblood	LE	Larry Cole
Merlin Olsen	LT	Jethro Pugh
Larry Brooks	RT	Bob Lilly
Fred Dryer	RE	Pat Toomay
Ken Geddes	LLB	Dave Edwards
Jack Reynolds	MLB	Lee Roy Jordan
Isiah Robertson	RLB	D. D. Lewis
Charlie Stukes	LCB	Charlie Waters
Eddie McMillan	RCB	Mel Renfro
Dave Elmendorf	LS	Cornell Green
Steve Preece	RS	Cliff Harris

Los Angeles	0	6	0	10	—	16
Dallas	14	3	0	10	—	27

Dall—Hill 3 run (Fritsch kick)
Dall—Pearson 4 pass from Staubach (Fritsch kick)
Dall—FG Fritsch 39
LA —FG Ray 33
LA —FG Ray 37
LA —FG Ray 40
LA —Baker 5 run (Ray kick)
Dall—Pearson 83 pass from Staubach (Fritsch kick)
Dall—FG Fritsch 12
Attendance—64,291

1974 AFC

OAKLAND 28, MIAMI 26

As he was being tackled, Ken Stabler threw an eight-yard touchdown pass to Clarence Davis with 26 seconds left. The Raiders had driven 68 yards after Miami went ahead with 2:08 remaining.

December 21, at Oakland

Miami	Starters, Offense	Oakland
Paul Warfield	WR	Clifford Branch
Wayne Moore	LT	Art Shell
Bob Kuechenberg	LG	Gene Upshaw
Jim Langer	C	Jim Otto
Larry Little	RG	George Buehler
Norm Evans	RT	John Vella
Marv Fleming	TE	Bob Moore
Nat Moore	WR	Fred Biletnikoff
Bob Griese	QB	Ken Stabler
Benny Malone	RB	Clarence Davis
Larry Csonka	RB	Marv Hubbard
	Starters, Defense	
Vern Den Herder	LE	Charles (Bubba) Smith
Manny Fernandez	LT	Otis Sistrunk
Bob Heinz	RT	Art Thoms
Bill Stanfill	RE	Horace Jones
Bob Matheson	LLB	Phil Villapiano
Nick Buoniconti	MLB	Dan Conners
Mike Kolen	RLB	Gerald Irons
Tim Foley	LCB	Alonzo (Skip) Thomas
Curtis Johnson	RCB	Nemiah Wilson
Dick Anderson	LS	George Atkinson
Jake Scott	RS	Jack Tatum

Miami	7	3	6	10	—	26
Oakland	0	7	7	14	—	28

Mia—N. Moore 89 kickoff return (Yepremian kick)
Oak—C. Smith 31 pass from Stabler (Blanda kick)
Mia—FG Yepremian 33
Oak—Biletnikoff 13 pass from Stabler (Blanda kick)
Mia—Warfield 16 pass from Griese (kick failed)
Mia—FG Yepremian 46
Oak—Branch 72 pass from Stabler (Blanda kick)
Mia—Malone 23 run (Yepremian kick)
Oak—Davis 8 pass from Stabler (Blanda kick)
Attendance—52,817

1974 AFC

PITTSBURGH 32, BUFFALO 14

Franco Harris scored three touchdowns within a 4-minute, 52-second stretch of the second quarter as the Pittsburgh Steelers scored a total of 26 points in the quarter and coasted to a 32–14 victory.

December 22, at Pittsburgh

Buffalo	Starters, Offense	Pittsburgh
J. D. Hill	WR	Frank Lewis
Dave Foley	LT	Jon Kolb
Reggie McKenzie	LG	Jim Clack
Mike Montler	C	Ray Mansfield
Joe DeLamielleure	RG	Gerry Mullins
Donnie Green	RT	Gordon Gravelle
Paul Seymour	TE	Larry Brown
Ahmad Rashad	WR	Ron Shanklin
Joe Ferguson	QB	Terry Bradshaw
O. J. Simpson	RB	Rocky Bleier
Jim Braxton	RB	Franco Harris
	Starters, Defense	
Walt Patulski	LE	L. C. Greenwood
Mike Kadish	NT-LT	Joe Greene
Earl Edwards	RE-RT	Ernie Holmes
Dave Washington	LOLB-RE	Dwight White
Jim Cheyunski	LILB-LLB	Jack Ham
Doug Allen	RILB-MLB	Jack Lambert
Bo Cornell	ROLB-RLB	Andy Russell
Robert James	LCB	J. T. Thomas
Dwight Harrison	RCB	Mel Blount
Neal Craig	LS	Mike Wagner
Rex Kern	RS	Glen Edwards

Buffalo	7	0	7	0	—	14
Pittsburgh	3	26	0	3	—	32

Pitt—FG Gerela 21
Buff—Seymour 22 pass from Ferguson (Leypoldt kick)
Pitt—Bleier 27 pass from Bradshaw (kick blocked)
Pitt—Harris 1 run (Gerela kick)
Pitt—Harris 4 run (kick blocked)
Pitt—Harris 1 run (Gerela kick)
Buff—Simpson 3 pass from Ferguson (Leypoldt kick)
Pitt—FG Gerela 22
Attendance—48,321

1974 NFC

MINNESOTA 30, ST. LOUIS 14

With the score 7–7 in the third quarter, the Minnesota Vikings' Jeff Wright intercepted a pass by Jim Hart to set up a field goal by Fred Cox. One minute later, Nate Wright picked up a fumble by Terry Metcalf and ran 20 yards to give Minnesota a 17–7 lead.

December 21, at Bloomington, Minnesota

St. Louis	Starters, Offense	Minnesota
Earl Thomas	WR	Jim Lash
Roger Finnie	LT	Charles Goodrum
Bob Young	LG	Andy Maurer
Tom Brahaney	C	Mick Tingelhoff
Conrad Dobler	RG	Ed White
Dan Dierdorf	RT	Ron Yary
Jackie Smith	TE	Stu Voigt
Mel Gray	WR	John Gilliam
Jim Hart	QB	Fran Tarkenton
Terry Metcalf	RB	Chuck Foreman
Jim Otis	RB	Dave Osborn
	Starters, Defense	
Council Rudolph	LE	Carl Eller
Leo Brooks	LT	Doug Sutherland
Bob Rowe	RT	Alan Page
Ron Yankowski	RE	Jim Marshall
Larry Stallings	LLB	Roy Winston
Mark Arneson	MLB	Jeff Siemon
Pete Barnes	RLB	Wally Hilgenberg
Norm Thompson	LCB	Nate Wright
Roger Wehrli	RCB	Jackie Wallace
Jim Tolbert	LS	Jeff Wright
Clarence Duren	RS	Paul Krause

St. Louis	0	7	0	7	—	14
Minnesota	0	7	16	7	—	30

StL—Thomas 13 pass from Hart (Bakken kick)
Minn—Gilliam 16 pass from Tarkenton (Cox kick)
Minn—FG Cox 37
Minn—N. Wright 20 fumble return (Cox kick)
Minn—Gilliam 38 pass from Tarkenton (kick failed)
Minn—Foreman 4 run (Cox kick)
StL—Metcalf 11 run (Bakken kick)
Attendance—44,626

1974 NFC

LOS ANGELES 19, WASHINGTON 10

The temperature was 61 degrees with the wind blowing at 25 miles per hour in Los Angeles as the Rams turned two fumble recoveries into field goals to take a 13–10 lead at the beginning of the fourth quarter and go on to a 19–10 victory over the Washington Redskins.

December 22, at Los Angeles

Washington	Offense	Los Angeles
Charley Taylor	WR	Harold Jackson
Ray Schoenke	LT	Charlie Cowan
Paul Laaveg	LG	Tom Mack
Len Hauss	C	Ken Iman
Walt Sweeney	RG	Joe Scibelli
George Starke	RT	John Williams
Jerry Smith	TE	Bob Klein
Roy Jefferson	WR	Jack Snow
Billy Kilmer	QB	James Harris
Larry Brown	RB	Jim Bertelsen
Moses Denson	RB	Lawrence McCutcheon
	Starters, Defense	
Ron McDole	LE	Jack Youngblood
Bill Brundige	LT	Merlin Olsen
Diron Talbert	RT	Larry Brooks
Verlon Biggs	RE	Fred Dryer
Dave Robinson	LLB	Ken Geddes
Rusty Tillman	MLB	Jack Reynolds
Chris Hanburger	RLB	Isiah Robertson
Pat Fischer	LCB	Charlie Stukes
Mike Bass	RCB	Al Clark
Ken Houston	LS	Dave Elmendorf
Brig Owens	RS	Bill Simpson

Washington	3	7	0	0	—	10
Los Angeles	7	0	3	9	—	19

LA—Klein 10 pass from Harris (Ray kick)
Wash—FG Bragg 35
Wash—Denson 1 run (Bragg kick)
LA—FG Ray 37
LA—FG Ray 26
LA—Robertson 59 interception return (pass failed)
Attendance—80,118

1975 AFC

PITTSBURGH 28, BALTIMORE 10

The Pittsburgh Steelers' Franco Harris set a divisional playoff record by rushing for 153 yards in 27 carries, in a 28–10 victory.

The Steelers scored three second-half touchdowns to overcome a 10–7 lead by the Colts, who were limited to 154 yards—82 rushing, 72 passing.

December 27, at Pittsburgh

Baltimore	Starters, Offense	Pittsburgh
Roger Carr	WR	Frank Lewis
David Taylor	LT	Jon Kolb
Robert Pratt	LG	Jim Clack
Ken Mendenhall	C	Ray Mansfield
Elmer Collett	RG	Gerry Mullins
George Kunz	RT	Gordon Gravelle
Raymond Chester	TE	Larry Brown
Glenn Doughty	WR	Lynn Swann
Bert Jones	QB	Terry Bradshaw
Lydell Mitchell	RB	Rocky Bleier
Bill Olds	RB	Franco Harris
	Starters, Defense	
Fred Cook	LE	L.C. Greenwood
Mike Barnes	LT	Steve Furness
Joe Erhmann	RT	Ernie Holmes
John Dutton	RE	Dwight White
Tom MacLeod	LLB	Jack Ham
Jim Cheyunski	MLB	Jack Lambert
Stan White	RLB	Andy Russell
Lloyd Mumphord	LCB	J.T. Thomas
Nelson Munsey	RCB	Mel Blount
Bruce Laird	LS	Mike Wagner
Jackie Wallace	RS	Glen Edwards

Baltimore	0	7	3	0	—	10
Pittsburgh	7	0	7	14	—	28

Pitt—Harris 8 run (Gerela kick)
Balt—Doughty 5 pass from Domres (Linhart kick)
Balt—FG Linhart 21
Pitt—Bleier 7 run (Gerela kick)
Pitt—Bradshaw 2 run (Gerela kick)
Pitt—Russell 93 fumble return (Gerela kick)
Attendance—49,053

1975 AFC

OAKLAND 31, CINCINNATI 28

Quarterback Ken Stabler completed 17 of 23 passes for 199 yards and three touchdowns as the Oakland Raiders built a 31–14 lead early in the fourth quarter, then held off the Cincinnati Bengals 31–28.

December 28, at Oakland

Cincinnati	Starters, Offense	Oakland
Isaac Curtis	WR	Clifford Branch
Rufus Mayes	LT	Art Shell
Howard Fest	LG	Gene Upshaw
Bob Johnson	C	Dave Dalby
John Shinners	RG	George Buehler
Vernon Holland	RT	John Vella
Bob Trumpy	TE	Bob Moore
Charlie Joiner	WR	Mike Siani
Ken Anderson	QB	Ken Stabler
Stan Fritts	RB	Clarence Davis
Charles (Boobie) Clark	RB	Marv Hubbard
	Starters, Defense	
Ken Johnson	LE	Otis Sistrunk
Bob Brown	LT-NT	Art Thoms
Ron Carpenter	RT-RE	Horace Jones
Sherman White	RE-LOLB	Ted Hendricks
Al Beauchamp	LLB-LILB	Phil Villapiano
Jim LeClair	MLB-RILB	Monte Jackson
Ron Pritchard	RLB-ROLB	Gerald Irons
Lemar Parrish	LCB	Alonzo (Skip) Thomas
Ken Riley	RCB	Neal Colzie
Tommy Casanova	LS	George Atkinson
Bernard Jackson	RS	Jack Tatum

Cincinnati	0	7	7	14	—	28
Oakland	3	14	7	7	—	31

Oak—FG Blanda 27
Oak—Siani 9 pass from Stabler (Blanda kick)
Cin—Fritts 1 run (Green kick)
Oak—Moore 8 pass from Stabler (Blanda kick)
Oak—Banaszak 6 run (Blanda kick)
Cin—Elliott 6 run (Green kick)
Oak—Casper 2 pass from Stabler (Blanda kick)
Cin—Joiner 25 pass from Anderson (Green kick)
Cin—Curtis 14 pass from Anderson (Green kick)
Attendance—53,039

1975 NFC

LOS ANGELES 35, ST. LOUIS 23

Los Angeles and St. Louis accounted for 803 yards offense—440 for Los Angeles, 363 for St. Louis. The Rams Lawrence McCutcheon set NFC post-season records, 202 yards rushing and 37 carries.

December 27, at Los Angeles

St. Louis	Starters, Offense	Los Angeles
Mel Gray	WR	Harold Jackson
Roger Finnie	LT	Doug France
Bob Young	LG	Tom Mack
Tom Banks	C	Rich Saul
Conrad Dobler	RG	Joe Scibelli
Dan Dierdorf	RT	John Williams
Jackie Smith	TE	Terry Nelson
J.V. Cain	WR	Ron Jessie
Jim Hart	QB	Ron Jaworski
Terry Metcalf	RB	Lawrence McCutcheon
Jim Otis	RB	Cullen Bryant
	Starters, Defense	
Bob Bell	LE	Jack Youngblood
Charlie Davis	LT	Merlin Olsen
Bob Rowe	RT	Cody Jones
Ron Yankowski	RE	Fred Dryer
Larry Stallings	LLB	Ken Geddes
Greg Hartle	MLB	Jack Reynolds
Pete Barnes	RLB	Isiah Robertson
Norm Thompson	LCB	Eddie McMillan
Roger Wehrli	RCB	Monte Jackson
Ken Reaves	LS	Dave Elmendorf
Clarence Duren	RS	Bill Simpson

St. Louis	0	9	7	7	—	23
Los Angeles	14	14	0	7	—	35

LA —Jaworski 5 run (Dempsey kick)
LA —Jack Youngblood 47 interception return (Dempsey kick)
LA —Simpson 65 interception return (Dempsey kick)
StL—Otis 3 run (kick blocked)
LA —H. Jackson 66 pass from Jaworski (Dempsey kick)
StL—FG Bakken 39
StL—Gray 11 pass from Hart (Bakken kick)
LA —Jessie 2 fumble return (Dempsey kick)
StL—Jones 3 run (Bakken kick)
Attendance—72,650

1975 NFC

DALLAS 17, MINNESOTA 14

The Dallas Cowboys marched 85 yards in the game's last two minutes to upend the Minnesota Vikings 17–14. The winning touchdown came on Roger Staubach's pass to Drew Pearson, who ran the final 5 yards to complete a 50-yard play with 24 seconds left.

Staubach completed other passes of 9, 7, and 25 yards to Pearson during the eight-play drive.

December 28, at Bloomington, Minnesota

Dallas	Starters, Offense	Minnesota
Golden Richards	WR	Jim Lash
Ralph Neely	LT	Steve Riley
Burton Lawless	LG	Andy Maurer
John Fitzgerald	C	Mick Tingelhoff
Blaine Nye	RG	Ed White
Rayfield Wright	RT	Ron Yary
Jean Fugett	TE	Stu Voigt
Drew Pearson	WR	John Gilliam
Roger Staubach	QB	Fran Tarkenton
Preston Pearson	RB	Chuck Foreman
Robert Newhouse	RB	Ed Marinaro
	Starters, Defense	
Ed (Too Tall) Jones	LE	Carl Eller
Jethro Pugh	LT	Doug Sutherland
Larry Cole	RT	Alan Page
Harvey Martin	RE	Jim Marshall
Dave Edwards	LLB	Fred McNeill
Lee Roy Jordan	MLB	Jeff Siemon
D.D. Lewis	RLB	Wally Hilgenberg
Mark Washington	LCB	Nate Wright
Mel Renfro	RCB	Bobby Bryant
Charlie Waters	LS	Terry Brown
Cliff Harris	RS	Paul Krause

Dallas	0	0	7	10	—	17
Minnesota	0	7	0	7	—	14

Minn—Foreman 1 run (Cox kick)
Dall—Dennison 4 run (Fritsch kick)
Dall—FG Fritsch 24
Minn—McClanahan 1 run (Cox kick)
Dall—D. Pearson 50 pass from Staubach (Fritsch kick)
Attendance—46,425

1976 AFC

OAKLAND 24, NEW ENGLAND 21

Ken Stabler's one-yard run with 10 seconds left gave Oakland a 24–21 victory. The Raiders marched 73 yards after New England's John Smith was short on a 50-yard field goal with 4:30 remaining. A penalty stalled the Patriots on Oakland's 27-yard line.

December 18, at Oakland

New England	Starters, Offense	Oakland
Randy Vataha	WR	Clifford Branch
Leon Gray	LT	Art Shell
John Hannah	LG	Gene Upshaw
Bill Lenkaitis	C	Dave Dalby
Sam Adams	RG	George Buehler
Bob McKay	RT	John Vella
Russ Francis	TE	Dave Casper
Darryl Stingley	WR	Fred Biletnikoff
Steve Grogan	QB	Ken Stabler
Andy Johnson	RB	Clarence Davis
Sam Cunningham	RB	Mark van Eeghen
	Starters, Defense	
Mel Lunsford	LE	John Matuszak
Ray Hamilton	NT	Dave Rowe
Julius Adams	RE	Otis Sistrunk
Steve Zabel	LOLB	Phil Villapiano
Sam Hunt	LILB	Monte Johnson
Steve Nelson	RILB	Willie Hall
Pete Barnes	ROLB	Ted Hendricks
Bob Howard	LCB	Alonzo (Skip) Thomas
Mike Haynes	RCB	Willie Brown
Prentice McCray	LS	George Atkinson
Tim Fox	RS	Jack Tatum

New England	7	0	14	0	—	21
Oakland	3	7	0	14	—	24

NE —Johnson 1 run (Smith kick)
Oak—FG Mann 40
Oak—Biletnikoff 31 pass from Stabler (Mann kick)
NE —Francis 26 pass from Grogan (Smith kick)
NE —Phillips 3 run (Smith kick)
Oak—van Eeghen 1 run (Mann kick)
Oak—Stabler 1 run (Mann kick)
Attendance—53,045

1976 AFC

PITTSBURGH 40, BALTIMORE 14

Terry Bradshaw, who had missed six starting assignments because of injuries, completed 14 of 18 passes for 264 yards and three touchdowns as Pittsburgh, favored by three points, beat Baltimore by 26.

December 19, at Baltimore

Pittsburgh	Starters, Offense	Baltimore
Lynn Swann	WR	Roger Carr
Jon Kolb	LT	David Taylor
Sam Davis	LG	Robert Pratt
Mike Webster	C	Ken Mendenhall
Jim Clack	RG	Elmer Collett
Gerry Mullins	RT	George Kunz
Larry Brown	TE	Raymond Chester
Frank Lewis	WR	Glenn Doughty
Terry Bradshaw	QB	Bert Jones
Franco Harris	RB	Lydell Mitchell
Rocky Bleier	RB	Roosevelt Leaks
	Starters, Defense	
L.C. Greenwood	LE	Fred Cook
Joe Greene	LT	Mike Barnes
Ernie Holmes	RT	Joe Ehrmann
Dwight White	RE	John Dutton
Jack Ham	LLB	Derrel Luce
Jack Lambert	MLB	Jim Cheyunski
Andy Russell	RLB	Stan White
J.T. Thomas	LCB	Lloyd Mumphord
Mel Blount	RCB	Ray Oldham
Mike Wagner	LS	Bruce Laird
Glen Edwards	RS	Jackie Wallace

Pittsburgh	9	17	0	14	—	40
Baltimore	7	0	0	7	—	14

Pitt —Lewis 76 pass from Bradshaw (kick failed)
Pitt —FG Gerela 45
Balt—Carr 17 pass from Jones (Linhart kick)
Pitt —Harrison 1 run (Gerela kick)
Pitt —Swann 29 pass from Bradshaw (Gerela kick)
Pitt —FG Gerela 25
Pitt —Swann 11 pass from Bradshaw (Gerela kick)
Balt—Leaks 1 run (Linhart kick)
Pitt —Harrison 9 run (Mansfield kick)
Attendance—60,020

1976 NFC

MINNESOTA 35, WASHINGTON 20

Tight end Stu Voigt, left guard Charles Goodrum, and running back Chuck Foreman blocked right on Minnesota's first play and Brent McClanahan ran left 41 yards to set up the Vikings' first touchdown.

December 18, at Bloomington, Minnesota

Washington	Starters, Offense	Minnesota
Frank Grant	WR	Ahmad Rashad
Tim Stokes	LT	Steve Riley
Ron Saul	LG	Charles Goodrum
Len Hauss	C	Mick Tingelhoff
Terry Hermeling	RG	Ed White
George Starke	RT	Ron Yary
Jean Fugett	TE	Stu Voigt
Roy Jefferson	WR	Sammy White
Billy Kilmer	QB	Fran Tarkenton
Mike Thomas	RB	Chuck Foreman
John Riggins	RB	Brent McClanahan
	Starters, Defense	
Ron McDole	LE	Carl Eller
Dave Butz	LT	Doug Sutherland
Diron Talbert	RT	Alan Page
Dennis Johnson	RE	Jim Marshall
Brad Dusek	LLB	Matt Blair
Harold McLinton	MLB	Jeff Siemon
Chris Hanburger	RLB	Wally Hilgenberg
Pat Fischer	LCB	Nate Wright
Joe Lavender	RCB	Bobby Bryant
Ken Houston	LS	Jeff Wright
Jake Scott	RS	Paul Krause

Washington	3	0	3	14	—	20
Minnesota	14	7	14	0	—	35

Minn—Voigt 18 pass from Tarkenton (Cox kick)
Wash—FG Moseley 47
Minn—White 27 pass from Tarkenton (Cox kick)
Minn—Foreman 2 run (Cox kick)
Minn—Foreman 30 run (Cox kick)
Wash—FG Moseley 35
Minn—White 9 pass from Tarkenton (Cox kick)
Wash—Grant 12 pass from Kilmer (Moseley kick)
Wash—Jefferson 3 pass from Kilmer (Moseley kick)
Attendance—47,221

1976 NFC

LOS ANGELES 14, DALLAS 12

With four seconds left in the game, Los Angeles punter Rusty Jackson took the snap from center in his end zone and ran out of the end zone as the game ended, giving Dallas a two-point safety but clinching the Rams' 14–12 victory. Dallas's Charlie Waters had blocked two of Jackson's punts earlier in the game, one setting up a Cowboys field goal.

December 19, Irving, Texas

Los Angeles	Starters, Offense	Dallas
Harold Jackson	WR	Golden Richards
Doug France	LT	Ralph Neely
Tom Mack	LG	Herbert Scott
Rich Saul	C	John Fitzgerald
Dennis Harrah	RG	Blaine Nye
John Williams	RT	Rayfield Wright
Bob Klein	TE	Billy Joe DuPree
Ron Jessie	WR	Drew Pearson
Pat Haden	QB	Roger Staubach
Lawrence McCutcheon	RB	Preston Pearson
John Cappelletti	RB	Robert Newhouse
	Starters, Defense	
Jack Youngblood	LE	Ed (Too Tall) Jones
Merlin Olsen	LT	Jethro Pugh
Larry Brooks	RT	Larry Cole
Fred Dryer	RE	Harvey Martin
Jim Youngblood	LLB	Bob Breunig
Jack Reynolds	MLB	Lee Roy Jordan
Isiah Robertson	RLB	D.D. Lewis
Rod Perry	LCB	Benny Barnes
Monte Jackson	RCB	Mark Washington
Dave Elmendorf	LS	Charlie Waters
Bill Simpson	RS	Cliff Harris

Los Angeles	0	7	0	7	—	14
Dallas	3	7	0	2	—	12

Dall—FG Herrera 44
LA —Haden 4 run (Dempsey kick)
Dall—Laidlaw 1 run (Herrera kick)
LA —McCutcheon 1 run (Dempsey kick)
Dall—Safety, R. Jackson ran out of end zone
Attendance—62,436

1977 AFC

OAKLAND 37, BALTIMORE 31

The Raiders won the third-longest game in history.

December 24, at Baltimore

Oakland	Starters, Offense	Baltimore
Clifford Branch	WR	Freddie Scott
Art Shell	LT	David Taylor
Gene Upshaw	LG	Robert Pratt
Dave Dalby	C	Ken Mendenhall
George Buehler	RG	Ken Huff
Henry Lawrence	RT	George Kunz
Dave Casper	TE	Raymond Chester
Fred Biletnikoff	WR	Glenn Doughty
Ken Stabler	QB	Bert Jones
Mark van Eeghen	RB	Roosevelt Leaks
Clarence Davis	RB	Lydell Mitchell
	Starters, Defense	
John Matuszak	LE	Fred Cook
Dave Rowe	NT-LT	Mike Barnes
Otis Sistrunk	RE-RT	Joe Ehrmann
Floyd Rice	LOLB-RE	John Dutton
Monte Johnson	LILB-LLB	Tom MacLeod
Willie Hall	RILB-MLB	Ed Simonini
Ted Hendricks	ROLB-RLB	Stan White
Lester Hayes	LCB	Norm Thompson
Willie Brown	RCB	Nelson Muncey
Skip Thomas	SS	Bruce Laird
Jack Tatum	FS	Lyle Blackwood

Oakland	7	0	14	10	0	6	—	37
Baltimore	0	10	7	14	0	0	—	31

Oak—Davis 30 run (Mann kick)
Balt—Laird 61 interception return (Linhart kick)
Balt—FG Linhart 36
Oak—Casper 8 pass from Stabler (Mann kick)
Balt—Johnson 87 kickoff return (Linhart kick)
Oak—Casper 10 pass from Stabler (Mann kick)
Balt—R. Lee 1 run (Linhart kick)
Oak—Banaszak 1 run (Mann kick)
Balt—R. Lee 13 run (Linhart kick)
Oak—FG Mann 22
Oak—Casper 10 pass from Stabler (no kick) (0:43 of second extra period)
Attendance—59,925

1977 AFC

DENVER 34, PITTSBURGH 21

Two fourth-quarter interceptions by Denver linebacker Tom Jackson set up scores that broke open a close game in the Broncos' first playoff appearance.

December 24, at Denver

Pittsburgh	Starters, Offense	Denver
John Stallworth	WR	Haven Moses
Jon Kolb	LT	Andy Maurer
Sam Davis	LG	Tom Glassic
Mike Webster	C	Mike Montler
Jim Clack	RG	Paul Howard
Ray Pinney	RT	Claudie Minor
Larry Brown	TE	Riley Odoms
Lynn Swann	WR	Jack Dolbin
Terry Bradshaw	QB	Craig Morton
Rocky Bleier	RB	Jon Keyworth
Franco Harris	RB	Rob Lytle
	Starters, Defense	
Steve Furness	LE	Barney Chavous
Joe Greene	LT-NT	Rubin Carter
Ernie Holmes	RT-RT	Lyle Alzado
Dwight White	RE-LOLB	Bob Swenson
Jack Ham	LLB-LILB	Randy Gradishar
Jack Lambert	MLB-RILB	Tom Jackson
Loren Toews	RLB-ROLB	Joe Rizzo
J. T. Thomas	LCB	Louis Wright
Jimmy Allen	RCB	Steve Foley
Donnie Shell	SS	Billy Thompson
Glen Edwards	FS	Bernard Jackson

Pittsburgh	0	14	0	7	—	21
Denver	7	7	7	13	—	34

Den—Lytle 7 run (Turner kick)
Pitt—Bradshaw 1 run (Gerela kick)
Den—Armstrong 10 run (Turner kick)
Pitt—Harris 1 run (Gerela kick)
Den—Odoms 30 pass from Morton (Turner kick)
Pitt—Brown 1 pass from Bradshaw (Gerela kick)
Den—FG Turner 44
Den—FG Turner 25
Den—Dolbin 34 pass from Morton (Turner kick)
Attendance—75,059

1977 NFC

DALLAS 37, CHICAGO 7

Dallas safety Charlie Waters set a divisional playoff record by intercepting three passes, and the Cowboys held the Bears scoreless until late in the fourth quarter on the way to an easy 37-7 victory.

December 26, at Irving, Texas

Chicago	Starters, Offense	Dallas
Bo Rather	WR	Golden Richards
Ted Albrecht	LT	Ralph Neely
Noah Jackson	LG	Herbert Scott
Dan Peiffer	C	John Fitzgerald
Revie Sorey	RG	Tom Rafferty
Dennis Lick	RT	Pat Donovan
Greg Latta	TE	Billy Joe DuPree
James Scott	WR	Drew Pearson
Bob Avellini	QB	Roger Staubach
Roland Harper	RB	Robert Newhouse
Walter Payton	RB	Tony Dorsett
	Starters, Defense	
Mike Hartenstine	LE	Ed Jones
Jim Osborne	LT	Jethro Pugh
Ron Rydalch	RT	Randy White
Billy Newsome	RE	Harvey Martin
Doug Buffone	LLB	Thomas Henderson
Tom Hicks	MLB	Bob Breunig
Waymond Bryant	RLB	D. D. Lewis
Allan Ellis	LCB	Benny Barnes
Virgil Livers	RCB	Aaron Kyle
Gary Fencik	SS	Charlie Waters
Doug Plank	FS	Cliff Harris

Chicago	0	0	0	7	—	7
Dallas	7	10	17	3	—	37

Dall—Dennison 2 run (Herrera kick)
Dall—DuPree 28 pass from Staubach (Herrera kick)
Dall—FG Herrera 21
Dall—Dorsett 23 run (Herrera kick)
Dall—FG Herrera 31
Dall—Dorsett 7 run (Herrera kick)
Dall—FG Herrera 27
Chi—Schubert 34 pass from Avellini (Thomas kick)
Attendance—63,260

1977 NFC

MINNESOTA 14, LOS ANGELES 7

Chuck Foreman ran for 101 yards on 31 carries in a heavy rain to lead the Vikings to their fourth consecutive playoff victory over the Rams, 14-7. Quarterback Bob Lee, playing for the injured Fran Tarkenton, called 28 consecutive running plays in the third and fourth quarters, after the Vikings got an early lead on Foreman's five-yard touchdown run in the first quarter.

December 26, at Los Angeles

Minnesota	Starters, Offense	Los Angeles
Ahmad Rashad	WR	Harold Jackson
Steve Riley	LT	Doug France
Charles Goodrum	LG	Tom Mack
Mick Tingelhoff	C	Rich Saul
Ed White	RG	Greg Horton
Ron Yary	RT	John Williams
Stu Voigt	TE	Terry Nelson
Sammy White	WR	Billy Waddy
Bob Lee	QB	Pat Haden
Robert Miller	RB	Lawrence McCutcheon
Chuck Foreman	RB	John Cappelletti
	Starters, Defense	
Carl Eller	LE	Jack Youngblood
Doug Sutherland	LT	Cody Jones
Alan Page	RT	Larry Brooks
Jim Marshall	RE	Fred Dryer
Matt Blair	LLB	Jim Youngblood
Jeff Siemon	MLB	Jack Reynolds
Fred McNeill	RLB	Isiah Robertson
Nate Wright	LCB	Pat Thomas
Bobby Bryant	RCB	Monte Jackson
Jeff Wright	SS	Dave Elmendorf
Paul Krause	FS	Nolan Cromwell

Minnesota	7	0	0	7	—	14
Los Angeles	0	0	0	7	—	7

Minn—Foreman 5 run (Cox kick)
Minn—S. Johnson 1 run (Cox kick)
LA —H. Jackson 1 pass from Haden (Septien kick)
Attendance—70,203

1978 AFC

PITTSBURGH 33, DENVER 10

The Steelers broke open a close game with two long touchdown passes from Terry Bradshaw in a span of 14 seconds in the fourth quarter. Franco Harris ran for 105 yards and the first two Steelers touchdowns.

December 30, at Pittsburgh

Denver	Starters, Offense	Pittsburgh
Jack Dolbin	WR	John Stallworth
Claudie Minor	LT	Jon Kolb
Tom Glassic	LG	Sam Davis
Bill Bryan	C	Mike Webster
Paul Howard	RG	Ray Pinney
Tom Neville	RT	Larry Brown
Riley Odoms	TE	Randy Grossman
Haven Moses	WR	Lynn Swann
Craig Morton	QB	Terry Bradshaw
Jon Keyworth	RB	Rocky Bleier
Rob Lytle	RB	Franco Harris
	Starters, Defense	
Barney Chavous	LE	L. C. Greenwood
Rubin Carter	NT-LT	Joe Greene
Lyle Alzado	RE-RT	Steve Furness
Bob Swenson	LOLB-RE	John Banaszak
Joe Rizzo	LILB-LLB	Jack Ham
Randy Gradishar	RILB-MLB	Jack Lambert
Tom Jackson	ROLB-RLB	Robin Cole
Louis Wright	LCB	Ron Johnson
Steve Foley	RCB	Mel Blount
Billy Thompson	SS	Donnie Shell
Bernard Jackson	FS	Mike Wagner

Denver	3	7	0	0	—	10
Pittsburgh	6	13	0	14	—	33

Den—FG Turner 37
Pitt —Harris 1 run (kick failed)
Pitt —Harris 18 run (Gerela kick)
Pitt —FG Gerela 24
Den—Preston 3 run (Turner kick)
Pitt —FG Gerela 27
Pitt —Stallworth 45 pass from Bradshaw (Gerela kick)
Pitt —Swann 38 pass from Bradshaw (Gerela kick)
Attendance—50,230

1978 AFC

HOUSTON 31, NEW ENGLAND 14

Dan Pastorini threw three touchdown passes in the second quarter as Houston jumped to a 21-0 halftime lead and coasted to a 31-14 victory. Pastorini completed 12 of 15 passes for 200 yards and Earl Campbell ran for 118 yards for the Oilers.

December 31, at Foxboro, Massachusetts

Houston	Starters, Offense	New England
Ken Burrough	WR	Stanley Morgan
Greg Sampson	LT	Leon Gray
George Reihner	LG	John Hannah
Carl Mauck	C	Bill Lenkaitis
Ed Fisher	RG	Sam Adams
Conway Hayman	RT	Shelby Jordan
Mike Barber	TE	Russ Francis
Richard Caster	WR	Harold Jackson
Dan Pastorini	QB	Steve Grogan
Tim Wilson	RB	Sam Cunningham
Earl Campbell	RB	Andy Johnson
	Starters, Defense	
James Young	LE	Mel Lunsford
Curley Culp	NT	Ray Hamilton
Elvin Bethea	RE	Richard Bishop
Robert Brazile	LOLB	Steve Zabel
Gregg Bingham	LILB	Steve Nelson
Steve Kiner	RILB	Sam Hunt
Ted Washington	ROLB	Rod Shoate
Willie Alexander	LCB	Raymond Clayborn
Greg Stemrick	RCB	Mike Haynes
Bill Currier	SS	Doug Beaudoin
Mike Reinfeldt	FS	Tim Fox

Houston	0	21	3	7	—	31
New England	0	0	7	7	—	14

Hou—Burrough 71 pass from Pastorini (Fritsch kick)
Hou—Barber 19 pass from Pastorini (Fritsch kick)
Hou—Barber 13 pass from Pastorini (Fritsch kick)
Hou—FG Fritsch 30
NE —Jackson 24 pass from Johnson (Posey kick)
NE —Francis 14 pass from Owens (Posey kick)
Hou—Campbell 2 run (Fritsch kick)
Attendance—60,735

1978 NFC

DALLAS 27, ATLANTA 20

Backup quarterback Danny White led the Cowboys to two second-half touchdowns and a 27-20 come-from-behind victory.

December 30, at Irving, Texas

Atlanta	Starters, Offense	Dallas
Wallace Francis	WR	Tony Hill
Mike Kenn	LT	Pat Donovan
Dave Scott	LG	Herbert Scott
Jeff Van Note	C	John Fitzgerald
R. C. Thielemann	RG	Tom Rafferty
Phil McKinnely	RT	Rayfield Wright
Jim Mitchell	TE	Billy Joe DuPree
Billy Ryckman	WR	Drew Pearson
Steve Bartkowski	QB	Roger Staubach
Bubba Bean	RB	Tony Dorsett
Haskel Stanback	RB	Scott Laidlaw
	Starters, Defense	
Jeff Yeates	LE	Ed Jones
Jim Bailey	LT	Larry Cole
Mike Lewis	RT	Randy White
Jeff Merrow	RE	Harvey Martin
Fulton Kuykendall	LLB	Thomas Henderson
Robert Pennywell	MLB	Bob Breunig
Greg Brezina	RLB	D. D. Lewis
Rolland Lawrence	LCB	Benny Barnes
Rick Byas	RCB	Aaron Kyle
Frank Reed	SS	Charlie Waters
Tom Pridemore	FS	Cliff Harris

Atlanta	7	13	0	0	—	20
Dallas	10	3	7	7	—	27

Dall—FG Septien 34
Atl —Bean 14 run (Mazzetti kick)
Dall—Laidlaw 13 run (Septien kick)
Atl —FG Mazzetti 42
Dall—FG Septien 48
Atl —Francis 17 pass from Bartkowski (Mazzetti kick)
Atl —FG Mazzetti 22
Dall—Smith 2 pass from D. White (Septien kick)
Dall—Laidlaw 1 run (Septien kick)
Attendance—63,406

1978 NFC

LOS ANGELES 34, MINNESOTA 10

Quarterback Pat Haden threw for 209 yards and two touchdowns as the Rams broke a four-game losing streak against the Vikings in the playoffs. Los Angeles scored 24 second-half points.

December 31, at Los Angeles

Minnesota	Starters, Offense	Los Angeles
Ahmad Rashad	WR	Willie Miller
Frank Myers	LT	Doug France
Charles Goodrum	LG	Tom Mack
Mick Tingelhoff	C	Rich Saul
Wes Hamilton	RG	Dennis Harrah
Ron Yary	RT	John Williams
Bob Tucker	TE	Terry Nelson
Sammy White	WR	Ron Jessie
Fran Tarkenton	QB	Pat Haden
Rickey Young	RB	Cullen Bryant
Chuck Foreman	RB	John Cappelletti
	Starters, Defense	
Mark Mullaney	LE	Jack Youngblood
Doug Sutherland	LT	Cody Jones
James White	RT	Larry Brooks
Jim Marshall	RE	Fred Dryer
Matt Blair	LLB	Jim Youngblood
Jeff Siemon	MLB	Jack Reynolds
Fred McNeill	RLB	Bob Brudzinski
John Turner	LCB	Pat Thomas
Bobby Bryant	RCB	Rod Perry
Phil Wise	SS	Dave Elmendorf
Tom Hannon	FS	Bill Simpson

Minnesota	3	7	0	0	—	10
Los Angeles	0	10	14	10	—	34

Minn—FG Danmeier 42
LA —Miller 9 pass from Haden (Corral kick)
LA —FG Corral 43
Minn—Rashad 1 pass from Tarkenton (Danmeier kick)
LA —Bryant 3 run (Corral kick)
LA —Jessie 27 pass from Haden (Corral kick)
LA —FG Corral 28
LA —Jodat 3 run (Corral kick)
Attendance—70,436

1979 AFC

HOUSTON 17, SAN DIEGO 14

Rookie strong safety Vernon Perry set a postseason game record by making four interceptions, and also returned a blocked field goal 57 yards, as Houston defeated the Chargers 17-14 despite the absence of Earl Campbell and Dan Pastorini. Backup quarterback Gifford Nielsen threw the winning touchdown pass with 2:05 left in the third quarter.

December 29, at San Diego

Houston	Starters, Offense	San Diego
Mike Renfro	WR	John Jefferson
Leon Gray	LT	Billy Shields
David Carter	LG	Doug Wilkerson
Carl Mauck	C	Bob Rush
Ed Fisher	RG	Ed White
Conway Hayman	RT	Russ Washington
Mike Barber	TE	Bob Klein
Richard Caster	WR	Charlie Joiner
Gifford Nielsen	QB	Dan Fouts
Tim Wilson	RB	Clarence Williams
Rob Carpenter	RB	Lydell Mitchell
	Starters, Defense	
Andy Dorris	LE	Leroy Jones
Curley Culp	NT-LT	Wilbur Young
Elvin Bethea	RE-RT	Gary Johnson
Ted Washington	LOLB-RE	Fred Dean
Gregg Bingham	LILB-LLB	Ray Preston
Art Stringer	RILB-MLB	Bob Horn
Robert Brazile	ROLB-RLB	Woodrow Lowe
J. C. Wilson	LCB	Willie Buchanon
Greg Stemrick	RCB	Mike Williams
Vernon Perry	SS	Mike Fuller
Mike Reinfeldt	FS	Pete Shaw

Houston	0	10	7	0	—	17
San Diego	7	0	7	0	—	14

SD —C. Williams 1 run (Wood kick)
Hou—FG Fritsch 26
Hou—Clark 1 run (Fritsch kick)
SD —Mitchell 8 run (Wood kick)
Hou—Renfro 47 pass from Nielsen (Fritsch kick)
Attendance—51,192

1979 AFC

PITTSBURGH 34, MIAMI 14

The Steelers' offense scored on its first three possessions and then turned the game over to the "Steel Curtain," which had led the AFC in total defense. The Steelers held Miami to 25 yards rushing as they won their fifteenth consecutive home game.

December 30, at Pittsburgh

Miami	Starters, Offense	Pittsburgh
Duriel Harris	WR	John Stallworth
Bob Kuechenberg	LT	Ted Peterson
Ed Newman	LG	Sam Davis
Mark Dennard	C	Mike Webster
Larry Little	RG	Steve Courson
Mike Current	RT	Larry Brown
Bruce Hardy	TE	Bennie Cunningham
Nat Moore	WR	Lynn Swann
Bob Griese	QB	Terry Bradshaw
Larry Csonka	RB	Sidney Thornton
Delvin Williams	RB	Franco Harris
	Starters, Defense	
Vern Den Herder	LE	L. C. Greenwood
Bob Baumhower	NT-LT	Joe Greene
A. J. Duhe	RE-RT	Gary Dunn
Kim Bokamper	LOLB-RE	John Banaszak
Steve Towle	LILB-LLB	Dennis Winston
Rusty Chambers	RILB-MLB	Jack Lambert
Larry Gordon	ROLB-RLB	Robin Cole
Norris Thomas	LCB	Ron Johnson
Gerald Small	RCB	Mel Blount
Tim Foley	SS	Donnie Shell
Neal Colzie	FS	J. T. Thomas

Miami	0	0	7	7	—	14
Pittsburgh	20	0	7	7	—	34

Pitt —Thornton 1 run (Bahr kick)
Pitt —Stallworth 17 pass from Bradshaw (kick blocked)
Pitt —Swann 20 pass from Bradshaw (Bahr kick)
Mia—D. Harris 7 pass from Griese (von Schamann kick)
Pitt —Bleier 1 run (Bahr kick)
Pitt —F. Harris 5 run (Bahr kick)
Mia—Csonka 1 run (von Schamann kick)
Attendance—50,214

1979 NFC

TAMPA BAY 24, PHILADELPHIA 17

Ricky Bell ran for 142 yards and two touchdowns on a divisional playoff-record 38 carries to power Tampa Bay to a 24-17 victory. The Buccaneers' defense limited the Eagles' Wilbert Montgomery to only 35 yards.

December 29, at Tampa

Philadelphia	Starters, Offense	Tampa Bay
Harold Carmichael	WR-TE	Jim Obradovich
Stan Walters	LT	Dave Reavis
Wade Key	LG	Greg Horton
Guy Morriss	C	Steve Wilson
Woody Peoples	RG	Greg Roberts
Jerry Sisemore	RT	Darryl Carlton
Keith Krepfle	TE	Jimmie Giles
Charles Smith	WR	Larry Mucker
Ron Jaworski	QB	Doug Williams
Leroy Harris	RB	Jerry Eckwood
Wilbert Montgomery	RB	Ricky Bell
	Starters, Defense	
Claude Humphrey	LE	Wally Chambers
Charlie Johnson	NT	Randy Crowder
Carl Hairston	RE	Lee Roy Selmon
John Bunting	LOLB	David Lewis
Jerry Robinson	LILB	Dewey Selmon
Frank LeMaster	RILB	Richard Wood
Reggie Wilkes	ROLB	Cecil Johnson
Bobby Howard	LCB	Jeris White
Herman Edwards	RCB	Mike Washington
Randy Logan	SS	Mark Cotney
John Sciarra	FS	Cedric Brown

Philadelphia	0	7	3	7	—	17
Tampa Bay	7	10	0	7	—	24

TB —Bell 4 run (O'Donoghue kick)
TB —FG O'Donoghue 40
TB —Bell 1 run (O'Donoghue kick)
Phil—Smith 11 pass from Jaworski (Franklin kick)
Phil—FG Franklin 42
TB —Giles 9 pass from Williams (O'Donoghue kick)
Phil—Carmichael 37 pass from Jaworski (Franklin kick)
Attendance—71,402

1979 NFC

LOS ANGELES 21, DALLAS 19

Vince Ferragamo's third touchdown pass of the game, a 50-yarder to Billy Waddy with 2:06 remaining, lifted Los Angeles to a 21-19 victory over Dallas. In the first half Ferragamo had given the Rams a 14-5 lead with a 43-yard touchdown pass to Ron Smith.

December 30, at Irving, Texas

Los Angeles	Starters, Offense	Dallas
Billy Waddy	WR	Tony Hill
Doug France	LT	Pat Donovan
Kent Hill	LG	Herbert Scott
Rich Saul	C	John Fitzgerald
Dennis Harrah	RG	Tom Rafferty
Jackie Slater	RT	Rayfield Wright
Terry Nelson	TE	Billy Joe DuPree
Preston Dennard	WR	Drew Pearson
Vince Ferragamo	QB	Roger Staubach
Cullen Bryant	RB-TE	Doug Cosbie
Wendell Tyler	RB	Tony Dorsett
	Starters, Defense	
Jack Youngblood	LE	John Dutton
Mike Fanning	LT	Larry Cole
Larry Brooks	RT	Randy White
Fred Dryer	RE	Harvey Martin
Jim Youngblood	LLB	Mike Hegman
Jack Reynolds	MLB	Bob Breunig
Bob Brudzinski	RLB	D. D. Lewis
Dwayne O'Steen	LCB	Benny Barnes
Rod Perry	RCB	Aaron Kyle
Dave Elmendorf	SS	Randy Hughes
Nolan Cromwell	FS	Cliff Harris

Los Angeles	0	14	0	7	—	21
Dallas	2	3	7	7	—	19

Dall—Safety, R. White tackled Ferragamo in end zone
LA —Tyler 32 pass from Ferragamo (Corral kick)
Dall—FG Septien 33
LA —R. Smith 43 pass from Ferragamo (Corral kick)
Dall—Springs 1 run (Septien kick)
Dall—Saldi 2 pass from Staubach (Septien kick)
LA —Waddy 50 pass from Ferragamo (Corral kick)
Attendance—64,792

1980 AFC

SAN DIEGO 20, BUFFALO 14

Dan Fouts threw a 50-yard touchdown pass to Ron Smith with only 2:08 left in the game as San Diego came from behind to win 20-14. The Bills led 14-3 at halftime, but in the second half the Chargers intercepted three of Joe Ferguson's passes, and Fouts threw two touchdown passes.

January 3, 1981 at San Diego

Buffalo	Starters, Offense	San Diego
Jerry Butler	WR	Charlie Joiner
Ken Jones	LT	Billy Shields
Reggie McKenzie	LG	Doug Wilkerson
Will Grant	C	Don Macek
Conrad Dobler	RG	Ed White
Joe Devlin	RT	Dan Audick
Mark Brammer	TE	Kellen Winslow
Frank Lewis	WR	John Jefferson
Joe Ferguson	QB	Dan Fouts
Curtis Brown	RB-TE	Gregg McCrary
Joe Cribbs	RB	Chuck Muncie
	Starters, Defense	
Ben Williams	LE	Leroy Jones
Fred Smerlas	NT-LT	Louie Kelcher
Sherman White	RE-RT	Gary Johnson
Lucius Sanford	LOLB-RE	Charles DeJurnett
Jim Haslett	LILB-LLB	Ray Preston
Shane Nelson	RILB-MLB	Bob Horn
Isiah Robertson	ROLB-RLB	Woodrow Lowe
Mario Clark	LCB	Willie Buchanon
Charles Romes	RCB	Mike Williams
Steve Freeman	SS	Mike Fuller
Bill Simpson	FS	Glen Edwards

Buffalo	0	14	0	0	—	14
San Diego	3	0	7	10	—	20

SD —FG Benirschke 22
Buff—Leaks 1 run (Mike-Mayer kick)
Buff—Lewis 9 pass from Ferguson (Mike-Mayer kick)
SD —Joiner 9 pass from Fouts (Benirschke kick)
SD —FG Benirschke 22
SD —Smith 50 pass from Fouts (Benirschke kick)
Attendance—52,253

1980 AFC

OAKLAND 14, CLEVELAND 12

Oakland strong safety Mike Davis intercepted Brian Sipe's pass in the end zone with 41 seconds remaining to preserve Oakland's victory. Cleveland had marched from its own 14 to the Raiders' 13 in the last two minutes of the game. Mark van Eeghen had scored on a one-yard run in the fourth quarter to give the Raiders their winning margin.

January 4, 1981 at Cleveland

Oakland	Starters, Offense	Cleveland
Clifford Branch	WR	Dave Logan
Art Shell	LT	Doug Dieken
Gene Upshaw	LG	Henry Sheppard
Dave Dalby	C	Tom DeLeone
Mickey Marvin	RG	Joe DeLamielleure
Henry Lawrence	RT	Cody Risien
Raymond Chester	TE	Ozzie Newsome
Bob Chandler	WR	Reggie Rucker
Jim Plunkett	QB	Brian Sipe
Mark van Eeghen	RB	Calvin Hill
Kenny King	RB	Mike Pruitt
	Starters, Defense	
John Matuszak	LE	Marshall Harris
Reggie Kinlaw	NT	Henry Bradley
Dave Browning	RE	Lyle Alzado
Ted Hendricks	LOLB	Charlie Hall
Matt Millen	LILB	R. L. Jackson
Bob Nelson	RILB	Dick Ambrose
Rod Martin	ROLB	Clay Matthews
Lester Hayes	LCB	Ron Bolton
Dwayne O'Steen	RCB	Clinton Burrell
Mike Davis	SS	Clarence Scott
Burgess Owens	FS	Thom Darden

Oakland	0	7	0	7	—	14
Cleveland	0	6	6	0	—	12

Çle —Bolton 42 interception return (kick blocked)
Oak—van Eeghen 1 run (Bahr kick)
Cle —FG Cockroft 30
Cle —FG Cockroft 30
Oak—van Eeghen 1 run (Bahr kick)
Attendance—78,245

1980 NFC

PHILADELPHIA 31, MINNESOTA 16

The Eagles turned a game in which they were trailing at halftime into a rout in the second half with the help of eight Minnesota turnovers, including five interceptions, in the final two periods.

January 3, 1981 at Philadelphia

Minnesota	Starters, Offense	Philadelphia
Ahmad Rashad	WR	Harold Carmichael
Steve Riley	LT	Stan Walters
Brent Boyd	LG	Petey Perot
Dennis Swilley	C	Guy Morriss
Wes Hamilton	RG	Woody Peoples
Ron Yary	RT	Jerry Sisemore
Bob Tucker	TE	Keith Krepfle
Sammy White	WR	Scott Fitzkee
Tommy Kramer	QB	Ron Jaworski
Rickey Young	RB	Leroy Harris
Ted Brown	RB	Wilbert Montgomery
	Starters, Defense	
Mark Mullaney	LE	Dennis Harrison
James White	LT-NT	Charlie Johnson
Doug Sutherland	RT-RE	Carl Hairston
Doug Martin	RE-LOLB	John Bunting
Matt Blair	LLB-LILB	Bill Bergey
Scott Studwell	MLB-RILB	Frank LeMaster
Fred McNeill	RLB-ROLB	Jerry Robinson
John Turner	LCB	Roynell Young
Bobby Bryant	RCB	Herman Edwards
Tom Hannon	SS	Randy Logan
Kurt Knoff	FS	Brenard Wilson

Minnesota	7	7	2	0	—	16
Philadelphia	0	7	14	10	—	31

Minn—S. White 30 pass from Kramer (Danmeier kick)
Minn—Brown 1 run (Danmeier kick)
Phil —Carmichael 9 pass from Jaworski (Franklin kick)
Phil —Montgomery 8 run (Franklin kick)
Minn—Safety, Jaworski tackled in end zone by Martin and Blair
Phil —Montgomery 5 run (Franklin kick)
Phil —FG Franklin 33
Phil —Harrington 2 run (Franklin kick)
Attendance—70,178

1980 NFC

DALLAS 30, ATLANTA 27

The Dallas Cowboys scored three fourth-quarter touchdowns to come from behind and defeat the Falcons.

January 4, 1981 at Atlanta

Dallas	Starters, Offense	Atlanta
Tony Hill	WR	Wallace Francis
Pat Donovan	LT	Mike Kenn
Herbert Scott	LG	Dave Scott
Robert Shaw	C	Jeff Van Note
Tom Rafferty	RG	R. C. Thielemann
Jim Cooper	RT	Warren Bryant
Billy Joe DuPree	TE	Junior Miller
Drew Pearson	WR	Alfred Jenkins
Danny White	QB	Steve Bartkowski
Robert Newhouse	RB	Lynn Cain
Tony Dorsett	RB	William Andrews
	Starters, Defense	
Ed Jones	LE	Jeff Yeates
Larry Cole	LT-NT	Don Smith
Randy White	RT-RE	Jeff Merrow
Harvey Martin	RE-LOLB	Al Richardson
Guy Brown	LLB-LILB	Fulton Kuykendall
Bob Breunig	MLB-RILB	Buddy Curry
D. D. Lewis	RLB-ROLB	Joel Williams
Benny Barnes	LCB	Rolland Lawrence
Aaron Mitchell	RCB	Kenny Johnson
Charlie Waters	SS	Bob Glazebrook
Dennis Thurman	FS	Tom Pridemore

Dallas	3	7	0	20	—	30
Atlanta	10	7	7	3	—	27

Atl —FG Mazzetti 38
Atl —Jenkins 60 pass from Bartkowski (Mazzetti kick)
Dall—FG Septien 38
Dall—DuPree 5 pass from White (Septien kick)
Atl —Cain 1 run (Mazzetti kick)
Atl —Andrews 12 pass from Bartkowski (Mazzetti kick)
Dall—Newhouse 1 run (Septien kick)
Atl —FG Mazzetti 34
Dall—D. Pearson 14 pass from White (Septien kick)
Dall—D. Pearson 23 pass from White (Septien kick)
Attendance—59,793

1981 AFC

SAN DIEGO 41, MIAMI 38

January 2, 1982 at Miami

San Diego	Starters, Offense	Miami
Charlie Joiner	WR	Jimmy Cefalo
Billy Shields	LT	Jon Giesler
Doug Wilkerson	LG	Bob Kuechenberg
Don Macek	C	Mark Dennard
Ed White	RG	Ed Newman
Russ Washington	RT	Eric Laasko
Kellen Winslow	TE	Ronnie Lee
Wes Chandler	WR	Nat Moore
Dan Fouts	QB	David Woodley
John Cappelletti	RB	Andra Franklin
Chuck Muncie	RB-TE	Bruce Hardy
	Starters, Defense	
Leroy Jones	LE	Doug Betters
Louie Kelcher	LT-NT	Bob Baumhower
Gary Johnson	RT-RE	Vern Den Herder
John Woodcock	RE-LOLB	Bob Brudzinski
Linden King	LLB-LILB	Earnest Rhone
Bob Horn	MLB-RILB	A. J. Duhe
Woodrow Lowe	RLB-ROLB	Larry Gordon
Willie Buchanon	LCB	Fulton Walker
Mike Williams	RCB	Gerald Small
Pete Shaw	SS	Glenn Blackwood
Glen Edwards	FS	Lyle Blackwood

San Diego	24	0	7	7	3	—	41
Miami	0	17	14	7	0	—	38

SD —FG Benirschke 32
SD —Chandler 56 punt return (Benirschke kick)
SD —Muncie 1 run (Benirschke kick)
SD —Brooks 8 run (Benirschke kick)
Mia —FG von Schamann 34
Mia —Rose 1 pass from Strock (von Schamann kick)
Mia —Nathan 25 lateral from Harris after pass from Strock (von Schamann kick)
SD —Winslow 25 pass from Fouts (Benirschke kick)
Mia —Rose 15 pass from Strock (von Schamann kick)
Mia —Hardy 50 pass from Strock (von Schamann kick)
Mia —Nathan 12 run (von Schamann kick)
SD —Brooks 9 pass from Fouts (Benirschke kick)
SD —FG Benirschke 29
Attendance—73,735

1981 AFC

CINCINNATI 28, BUFFALO 21

Buffalo was driving for the possible tying touchdown late in the fourth quarter, but suffered a costly delay of game penalty on fourth down at the Bengals' 21. The Bills didn't make their first down and the Bengals ran out the clock.

January 3, 1982 at Cincinnati

Buffalo	Starters, Offense	Cincinnati
Jerry Butler	WR	Cris Collinsworth
Ken Jones	LT	Anthony Munoz
Jon Borchardt	LG	Dave Lapham
Will Grant	C	Blair Bush
Tom Lynch	RG	Max Montoya
Joe Devlin	RT	Mike Wilson
Mark Brammer	TE	Dan Ross
Frank Lewis	WR	Isaac Curtis
Joe Ferguson	QB	Ken Anderson
Roosevelt Leaks	RB	Pete Johnson
Joe Cribbs	RB	Charles Alexander
	Starters, Defense	
Ben Williams	LE	Eddie Edwards
Fred Smerlas	NT	Wilson Whitley
Sherman White	RE	Ross Browner
Lucius Sanford	LOLB	Bo Harris
Jim Haslett	LILB	Jim LeClair
Phil Villapiano	RILB	Glenn Cameron
Isiah Robertson	ROLB	Reggie Williams
Mario Clark	LCB	Louis Breeden
Charles Romes	RCB	Ken Riley
Steve Freeman	SS	Bobby Kemp
Bill Simpson	FS	Bryan Hicks

Buffalo	0	7	7	7	—	21
Cincinnati	14	0	7	7	—	28

Cin —Alexander 4 run (Breech kick)
Cin —Johnson 1 run (Breech kick)
Buff—Cribbs 1 run (Mike-Mayer kick)
Buff—Cribbs 44 run (Mike-Mayer kick)
Cin —Alexander 10 run (Breech kick)
Buff—Butler 21 pass from Ferguson (Mike-Mayer kick)
Cin —Collinsworth 16 pass from Anderson (Breech kick)
Attendance—55,420

1981 NFC

DALLAS 38, TAMPA BAY 0

The Dallas defensive line dominated the game, holding Tampa Bay to 74 yards rushing, sacking Doug Williams four times, and pressuring him into four interceptions. The Cowboys rushed for 212 yards and four touchdowns, netted 345 total yards, and did not have a turnover.

January 2, 1982 at Irving, Texas

Tampa Bay	Starters, Offense	Dallas
Theo Bell	WR	Tony Hill
Gene Sanders	LT	Pat Donovan
Ray Snell	LG	Herbert Scott
Steve Wilson	C	Tom Rafferty
Greg Roberts	RG	Kurt Petersen
Charley Hannah	RT	Jim Cooper
Jimmie Giles	TE	Billy Joe DuPree
Kevin House	WR	Butch Johnson
Doug Williams	QB	Danny White
James Wilder	RB	Ron Springs
James Owens	RB	Tony Dorsett
	Starters, Defense	
Dave Stalls	LE	Ed Jones
David Logan	NT-LT	John Dutton
Lee Roy Selmon	RE-RT	Randy White
Andy Hawkins	LOLB-RE	Harvey Martin
Cecil Johnson	LILB-LLB	Mike Hegman
Richard Wood	RILB-MLB	Bob Breunig
Hugh Green	ROLB-RLB	D. D. Lewis
Norris Thomas	LCB	Everson Walls
Mike Washington	RCB	Dennis Thurman
Neal Colzie	SS	Charlie Waters
Cedric Brown	FS	Michael Downs

Tampa Bay	0	0	0	0	—	0
Miami	0	10	21	7	—	38

Dall—Hill 9 pass from White (Septien kick)
Dall—FG Septien 32
Dall—Springs 1 run (Septien kick)
Dall—Dorsett 5 run (Septien kick)
Dall—Jones 5 run (Septien kick)
Dall—Newsome 1 run (Septien kick)
Attendance—64,848

1981 NFC

SAN FRANCISCO 38, N. Y. GIANTS 24

Joe Montana passed for 304 yards and two touchdowns. Ronnie Lott scored for the 49ers in the fourth quarter on a 20-yard return of an interception.

January 3, 1982 at San Francisco

N. Y. Giants	Starters, Offense	San Francisco
Earnest Gray	WR	Mike Shumann
Jeff Weston	LT	Dan Audick
Billy Ard	LG	John Ayers
Jim Clack	C	Fred Quillan
J. T. Turner	RG	Randy Cross
Gordon King	RT	Keith Fahnhorst
Tom Mullady	TE	Charle Young
Johnny Perkins	WR	Mike Wilson
Scott Brunner	QB	Joe Montana
Leon Perry	RB	Ricky Patton
Rob Carpenter	RB	Earl Cooper
	Starters, Defense	
George Martin	LE	Jim Stuckey
Bill Neill	NT	Archie Reese
Gary Jeter	RE	Dwaine Board
Byron Hunt	LOLB	Willie Harper
Brian Kelley	LILB	Jack Reynolds
Harry Carson	RILB	Craig Puki
Lawrence Taylor	ROLB	Kenna Turner
Mark Haynes	LCB	Ronnie Lott
Terry Jackson	RCB	Eric Wright
Bill Currier	SS	Carlton Williamson
Larry Flowers	FS	Dwight Hicks

N. Y. Giants	7	3	7	7	—	24
San Francisco	7	17	0	14	—	38

SF —Young 8 pass from Montana (Wersching kick)
NYG—Gray 72 pass from Brunner (Danelo kick)
SF —FG Wersching 22
SF —Solomon 58 pass from Montana (Wersching kick)
SF —Patton 25 run (Wersching kick)
NYG—FG Danelo 48
NYG—Perkins 59 pass from Brunner (Danelo kick)
SF —Ring 3 run (Wersching kick)
SF —Lott 20 interception return (Wersching kick)
NYG—Perkins 17 pass from Brunner (Danelo kick)
Attendance—58,360

DIVISIONAL PLAYOFF HISTORY

Date	Playoff	Result	Site (attendance)
Dec. 14, 1941	NFL Western Division	Chi. Bears 33, Green Bay 14	Wrigley Field, Chicago (43,425)
Dec. 19, 1943	NFL Eastern Division	Washington 28, N.Y. Giants 0	Polo Grounds, New York (42,800)
Dec. 21, 1947	NFL Eastern Division	Philadelphia 21, Pittsburgh 0	Forbes Field, Pittsburgh (35,729)
Dec. 17, 1950	NFL American Conference	Cleveland 8, N.Y. Giants 3	Memorial Stadium, Cleveland (33,754)
Dec. 17, 1950	NFL National Conference	Los Angeles 24, Chi. Bears 14	Los Angeles Memorial Coliseum (83,501)
Dec. 21, 1952	NFL National Conference	Detroit 31, Los Angeles 21	Briggs Stadium, Detroit (47,645)
Dec. 22, 1957	NFL Western Conference	Detroit 31, San Francisco 27	Kezar Stadium, San Francisco (60,118)
Dec. 21, 1958	NFL Eastern Conference	N.Y. Giants 10, Cleveland 0	Yankee Stadium, New York (61,274)
Dec. 28, 1963	AFL Eastern Division	Boston 26, Buffalo 8	War Memorial Stadium, Buffalo (33,044)
Dec. 26, 1965	NFL Western Conference	Green Bay, 13, Baltimore 10	Lambeau Field, Green Bay (50,484)
Dec. 23, 1967	NFL Western Conference	Green Bay 28, Los Angeles 7	Milwaukee County Stadium (49,861)
Dec. 24, 1967	NFL Eastern Conference	Dallas 52, Cleveland 14	Cotton Bowl, Dallas (70,786)
Dec. 21, 1968	NFL Eastern Conference	Cleveland 31, Dallas 20	Memorial Stadium, Cleveland (81,497)
Dec. 22, 1968	AFL Western Division	Oakland 41, Kansas City 6	Oakland Coliseum (53,605)
Dec. 22, 1968	NFL Western Conference	Baltimore 24, Minnesota 14	Memorial Stadium, Baltimore (60,238)
Dec. 20, 1969	AFL Inter-Divisional	Kansas City 13, N.Y. Jets 6	Shea Stadium, New York (62,977)
Dec. 21, 1969	AFL Inter-Divisional	Oakland 56, Houston 7	Oakland Coliseum (53,539)
Dec. 27, 1969	NFL Western Conference	Minnesota 23, Los Angeles 20	Metropolitan Stadium, Bloomington (47,900)
Dec. 28, 1969	NFL Eastern Conference	Cleveland 38, Dallas 14	Cotton Bowl, Dallas (69,321)
Dec. 26, 1970	AFC First Round	Baltimore 17, Cincinnati 0	Memorial Stadium, Baltimore (51,127)
Dec. 27, 1970	AFC First Round	Oakland 21, Miami 14	Oakland Coliseum (54,401)
Dec. 26, 1970	NFC First Round	Dallas 5, Detroit 0	Cotton Bowl, Dallas (73,167)
Dec. 27, 1970	NFC First Round	San Francisco 17, Minnesota 14	Metropolitan Stadium, Bloomington (45,103)
Dec. 25, 1971	AFC First Round	Miami 27, Kansas City 24	Memorial Stadium, Kansas City (50,374)
Dec. 26, 1971	AFC First Round	Baltimore 20, Cleveland 3	Memorial Stadium, Cleveland (74,082)
Dec. 25, 1971	NFC First Round	Dallas 20, Minnesota 12	Metropolitan Stadium, Bloomington (49,100)
Dec. 26, 1971	NFC First Round	San Francisco 24, Washington 20	Candlestick Park, San Francisco (45,364)
Dec. 23, 1972	AFC First Round	Pittsburgh 13, Oakland 7	Three Rivers Stadium, Pittsburgh (50,350)
Dec. 24, 1972	AFC First Round	Miami 20, Cleveland 14	Orange Bowl, Miami (80,010)
Dec. 23, 1972	NFC First Round	Dallas 30, San Francisco 28	Candlestick Park, San Francisco (61,214)
Dec. 24, 1972	NFC First Round	Washington 16, Green Bay 3	RFK Stadium, Washington (53,140)
Dec. 23, 1973	AFC First Round	Oakland 33, Pittsburgh 14	Oakland Coliseum (51,110)
Dec. 23, 1973	AFC First Round	Miami 34, Cincinnati 16	Orange Bowl, Miami (74,770)
Dec. 22, 1973	NFC First Round	Minnesota 27, Washington 20	Metropolitan Stadium, Bloomington (45,475)
Dec. 23, 1973	NFC First Round	Dallas 27, Los Angeles 16	Texas Stadium, Irving (64,291)
Dec. 21, 1974	AFC First Round	Oakland 28, Miami 26	Oakland Coliseum (52,817)
Dec. 22, 1974	AFC First Round	Pittsburgh 32, Buffalo 14	Three Rivers Stadium, Pittsburgh (48,321)
Dec. 21, 1974	NFC First Round	Minnesota 30, St. Louis 14	Metropolitan Stadium, Bloomington (44,626)
Dec. 22, 1974	NFC First Round	Los Angeles 19, Washington 10	Los Angeles Memorial Coliseum (80,118)
Dec. 27, 1975	AFC First Round	Pittsburgh 28, Baltimore 10	Three Rivers Stadium, Pittsburgh (49,053)
Dec. 27, 1975	AFC First Round	Oakland 31, Cincinnati 28	Oakland Coliseum (53,039)
Dec. 28, 1975	NFC First Round	Los Angeles 35, St. Louis 23	Los Angeles Memorial Coliseum (72,650)
Dec. 28, 1975	NFC First Round	Dallas 17, Minnesota 14	Metropolitan Stadium, Bloomington (46,425)
Dec. 18, 1976	AFC First Round	Oakland 24, New England 21	Oakland Coliseum (53,045)
Dec. 19, 1976	AFC First Round	Pittsburgh 40, Baltimore 14	Memorial Stadium, Baltimore (60,020)
Dec. 18, 1976	NFC First Round	Minnesota 35, Washington 20	Metropolitan Stadium, Bloomington (47,221)
Dec. 19, 1976	NFC First Round	Los Angeles 14, Dallas 12	Texas Stadium, Irving (62,436)
Dec. 24, 1977	AFC Divisional Playoff	Oakland 37, Baltimore 31 (2OT)	Memorial Stadium, Baltimore (59,925)
Dec. 24, 1977	AFC Divisional Playoff	Denver 34, Pittsburgh 21	Mile High Stadium, Denver (75,059)
Dec. 26, 1977	NFC Divisional Playoff	Dallas 37, Chicago 7	Texas Stadium, Irving (63,260)
Dec. 26, 1977	NFC Divisional Playoff	Minnesota 14, Los Angeles 7	Los Angeles Memorial Coliseum (70,203)
Dec. 30, 1978	AFC Divisional Playoff	Pittsburgh 33, Denver 10	Three Rivers Stadium, Pittsburgh (50,230)
Dec. 31, 1978	AFC Divisional Playoff	Houston 31, New England 14	Schaefer Stadium, Foxboro (60,735)
Dec. 30, 1978	NFC Divisional Playoff	Dallas 27, Atlanta 20	Texas Stadium, Irving (63,406)
Dec. 31, 1978	NFC Divisional Playoff	Los Angeles 34, Minnesota 10	Los Angeles Memorial Coliseum (70,436)
Dec. 29, 1979	AFC Divisional Playoff	Houston 17, San Diego 14	San Diego Stadium (51,192)
Dec. 30, 1979	AFC Divisional Playoff	Pittsburgh 34, Miami 14	Three Rivers Stadium, Pittsburgh (50,214)
Dec. 29, 1979	NFC Divisional Playoff	Tampa Bay 24, Philadelphia 17	Tampa Stadium (71,402)
Dec. 30, 1979	NFC Divisional Playoff	Los Angeles 21, Dallas 19	Texas Stadium (64,792)
Jan. 3, 1981	AFC Divisional Playoff	San Diego 20, Buffalo 14	San Diego Stadium (52,253)
Jan. 4, 1981	AFC Divisional Playoff	Oakland 14, Cleveland 12	Cleveland Stadium (78,245)
Jan. 3, 1981	NFC Divisional Playoff	Philadelphia 31, Minnesota 16	Philadelphia Veterans Stadium (70,178)
Jan. 4, 1981	NFC Divisional Playoff	Dallas 30, Atlanta 27	Atlanta-Fulton County Stadium (59,793)
Jan. 2, 1982	AFC Divisional Playoff	San Diego 41, Miami 38	Orange Bowl, Miami (73,735)
Jan. 3, 1982	AFC Divisional Playoff	Cincinnati 28, Buffalo 21	Riverfront Stadium, Cincinnati (55,420)
Jan. 2, 1982	NFC Divisional Playoff	Dallas 38, Tampa Bay 0	Texas Stadium, Irving (64,848)
Jan. 3, 1982	NFC Divisional Playoff	San Francisco 38, N. Y. Giants 24	Candlestick Park, San Francisco (58,360)

Wild Card Games

1978 AFC

HOUSTON 17, MIAMI 9

Houston quarterback Dan Pastorini completed 20 of 29 passes for 306 yards and one touchdown. With the score tied 7-7 midway through the fourth quarter, Pastorini completed four consecutive passes to set up Tony Fritsch's 35-yard field goal, and moments later the Oilers clinched the game on Earl Campbell's one-yard touchdown run.

December 24, at Miami

Houston	Starters, Offense	Miami
Ken Burrough	WR	Nat Moore
Greg Sampson	LT	Wayne Moore
Conway Hayman	LG	Bob Kuechenberg
Carl Mauck	C	Jim Langer
Ed Fisher	RG	Eric Laakso
Morris Towns	RT	Mike Current
Mike Barber	TE	Andre Tillman
Guido Merkins	WR	Duriel Harris
Dan Pastorini	QB	Bob Griese
Tim Wilson	RB	Leroy Harris
Earl Campbell	RB	Delvin Williams
	Starters, Defense	
Jim Young	LE	Vern Den Herder
Curley Culp	NT	Bob Baumhower
Elvin Bethea	RE	A. J. Duhe
Robert Brazile	LOLB	Kim Bokamper
Gregg Bingham	LILB	Steve Towle
Steve Kiner	RILB	Rusty Chambers
Ted Washington	ROLB	Larry Gordon
Willie Alexander	LCB	Norris Thomas
Greg Stemrick	RCB	Gerald Small
Bill Currier	SS	Tim Foley
Mike Reinfeldt	FS	Charlie Babb

Houston	7	0	0	10	—	17
Miami	7	0	0	2	—	9

Mia—Tillman 13 pass from Griese (Yepremian kick)
Hou—T. Wilson 13 pass from Pastorini (Fritsch kick)
Hou—FG Fritsch 35
Hou—Campbell 1 run (Fritsch kick)
Mia—Safety, Pastorini ran out of end zone
Attendance—72,445

1978 NFC

ATLANTA 14, PHILADELPHIA 13

Quarterback Steve Bartkowski threw two touchdown passes in the final five minutes of the game to bring the Falcons back from a 13-0 deficit.

The Eagles had a chance to win with 13 seconds left, but Mike Michel's 34-yard field goal attempt sailed wide to the right. Michel earlier missed a 42-yard field goal attempt and an extra point.

December 24, at Atlanta

Philadelphia	Starters, Offense	Atlanta
Harold Carmichael	WR	Wallace Francis
Stan Walters	LT	Mike Kenn
Wade Key	LG	Dave Scott
Guy Morriss	C	Jeff Van Note
Woody Peoples	RG	R. C. Thielemann
Jerry Sisemore	RT	Phil McKinnely
Richard Osborne	TE	Jim Mitchell
Bill Larson	TE-WR	Billy Ryckman
Ron Jaworski	QB	Steve Bartkowski
Mike Hogan	RB	Bubba Bean
Wilbert Montgomery	RB	Haskel Stanback
	Starters, Defense	
Dennis Harrison	LE	Jeff Yeates
Charlie Johnson	NT-LT	Jim Bailey
Carl Hairston	RE-RT	Mike Lewis
Reggie Wilkes	LOLB-RE	Jeff Merrow
Bill Bergey	LILB-LLB	Fulton Kuykendall
Frank LeMaster	RILB-MLB	Robert Pennywell
Ray Phillips	ROLB-RLB	Greg Brezina
Bobby Howard	LCB	Rolland Lawrence
Herman Edwards	RCB	Rick Byas
Randy Logan	SS	Frank Reed
John Sanders	FS	Tom Pridemore

Philadelphia	6	0	7	0	—	13
Atlanta	0	0	0	14	—	14

Phil—Carmichael 13 pass from Jaworski (kick failed)
Phil—Montgomery 1 run (Michel kick)
Atl—Mitchell 20 pass from Bartkowski (Mazzetti kick)
Atl—Francis 37 pass from Bartkowski (Mazzetti kick)
Attendance—59,403

1979 AFC

HOUSTON 13, DENVER 7

The Oilers' defense shut down the Broncos, and Houston won 13-7 despite the loss of Earl Campbell and Dan Pastorini for the second half due to injuries.

Campbell scored on a three-yard run shortly before the half to give the Oilers a 10-7 lead. The defense took over from there, with Gregg Bingham's interception setting up the final points.

December 23, at Houston

Denver	Starters, Offense	Houston
Rick Upchurch	WR	Ken Burrough
Dave Studdard	LT	Leon Gray
Tom Glassic	LG	David Carter
Bill Bryan	C	Carl Mauck
Paul Howard	RG	Ed Fisher
Claudie Minor	RT	Conway Hayman
Riley Odoms	TE	Mike Barber
Haven Moses	WR	Richard Caster
Craig Morton	QB	Dan Pastorini
Jon Keyworth	RB	Tim Wilson
Otis Armstrong	RB	Earl Campbell
	Starters, Defense	
Barney Chavous	LE	Andy Dorris
Rubin Carter	NT	Curley Culp
Brison Manor	RE	Elvin Bethea
Bob Swenson	LOLB	Ted Washington
Joe Rizzo	LILB	Gregg Bingham
Randy Gradishar	RILB	Art Stringer
Tom Jackson	ROLB	Robert Brazile
Louis Wright	LCB	J. C. Wilson
Steve Foley	RCB	Greg Stemrick
Billy Thompson	SS	Vernon Perry
Bernard Jackson	FS	Mike Reinfeldt

Denver	7	0	0	0	—	7
Houston	3	7	0	3	—	13

Hou—FG Fritsch 31
Den—Preston 7 pass from Morton (Turner kick)
Hou—Campbell 3 run (Fritsch kick)
Hou—FG Fritsch 20
Attendance—48,776

1979 NFC

PHILADELPHIA 27, CHICAGO 17

Quarterback Ron Jaworski threw three touchdown passes, including two in a second-half comeback, as the Eagles overcame a 17-10 halftime deficit to win their first postseason game in 19 years.

December 23, at Philadelphia

Chicago	Starters, Offense	Philadelphia
Rickey Watts	WR	Harold Carmichael
Ted Albrecht	LT	Stan Walters
Noah Jackson	LG	Wade Key
Dan Neal	C	Guy Morriss
Revie Sorey	RG	Woody Peoples
Dennis Lick	RT	Jerry Sisemore
Mike Cobb	TE	Keith Krepfle
Brian Baschnagel	WR	Charles Smith
Mike Phipps	QB	Ron Jaworski
Dave Williams	RB	Leroy Harris
Walter Payton	RB	Wilbert Montgomery
	Starters, Defense	
Dan Hampton	LE	Claude Humphrey
Jim Osborne	LT-NT	Charlie Johnson
Alan Page	RT-RE	Carl Hairston
Mike Hartenstine	RE-LOLB	John Bunting
Jerry Muckensturm	LLB-LILB	Jerry Robinson
Tom Hicks	MLB-RILB	Frank LeMaster
Gary Campbell	RLB-ROLB	Reggie Wilkes
Terry Schmidt	LCB	Bobby Howard
Allan Ellis	RCB	Herman Edwards
Gary Fencik	SS	Randy Logan
Doug Plank	FS	John Sciarra

Chicago	7	10	0	0	—	17
Philadelphia	7	3	10	7	—	27

Phil—Carmichael 17 pass from Jaworski (Franklin kick)
Chi—Payton 2 run (Thomas kick)
Phil—FG Franklin 29
Chi—Payton 1 run (Thomas kick)
Chi—FG Thomas 30
Phil—Carmichael 29 pass from Jaworski (Franklin kick)
Phil—Campfield 63 pass from Jaworski (Franklin kick)
Phil—FG Franklin 34
Attendance—69,397

1980 AFC

OAKLAND 27, HOUSTON 7

The Raiders scored 17 points in the fourth quarter to break open a low-scoring game and defeat the Oilers 27-7. Oakland cornerback Lester Hayes sacked quarterback Ken Stabler twice and intercepted two passes, one in the Oakland end zone and one that he ran back for a touchdown.

December 28, at Oakland

Houston	Starter, Offense	Oakland
Dave Casper	TE-WR	Clifford Branch
Angelo Fields	LT	Art Shell
Bob Young	LG	Gene Upshaw
Carl Mauck	C	Dave Dalby
Ed Fisher	RG	Mickey Marvin
Morris Towns	RT	Henry Lawrence
Mike Barber	TE	Raymond Chester
Mike Renfro	WR	Bob Chandler
Ken Stabler	QB	Jim Plunkett
Tim Wilson	RB	Mark van Eeghen
Earl Campbell	RB	Kenny King
	Starters, Defense	
Andy Dorris	LE	John Matuszak
Ken Kennard	NT	Reggie Kinlaw
Elvin Bethea	RE	Dave Browning
Ted Washington	LOLB	Ted Hendricks
Daryl Hunt	LILB	Matt Millen
Gregg Bingham	RILB	Bob Nelson
Robert Brazile	ROLB	Rod Martin
J. C. Wilson	LCB	Lester Hayes
Greg Stemrick	RCB	Dwayne O'Steen
Vernon Perry	SS	Mike Davis
Mike Reinfeldt	FS	Burgess Owens

Houston	7	0	0	0	—	7
Oakland	3	7	0	17	—	27

Oak—FG Bahr 47
Hou—Campbell 1 run (Fritsch kick)
Oak—Christensen 1 pass from Plunkett (Bahr kick)
Oak—Whittington 44 pass from Plunkett (Bahr kick)
Oak—FG Bahr 37
Oak—Hayes 20 interception return (Bahr kick)
Attendance—53,333

1980 NFC

DALLAS 34, LOS ANGELES 13

Dallas quarterback Danny White threw touchdown passes in each of the Cowboys' first three possessions of the second half to break open a 13-13 tie. Tony Dorsett rushed for 160 yards for Dallas.

December 28, at Irving, Texas

Los Angeles	Starters, Offense	Dallas
Preston Dennard	WR	Tony Hill
Doug France	LT	Pat Donovan
Kent Hill	LG	Herbert Scott
Rich Saul	C	Robert Shaw
Dennis Harrah	RG	Tom Rafferty
Jackie Slater	RT	Jim Cooper
Victor Hicks	TE	Billy Joe DuPree
Billy Waddy	WR	Drew Pearson
Vince Ferragamo	QB	Danny White
Cullen Bryant	RB	Robert Newhouse
Jewerl Thomas	RB	Tony Dorsett
	Starters, Defense	
Jack Youngblood	LE	Ed Jones
Cody Jones	LT	Larry Cole
Larry Brooks	RT	Randy White
Fred Dryer	RE	Harvey Martin
Jim Youngblood	LLB	Mike Hegman
Jack Reynolds	MLB	Bob Breunig
George Andrews	RLB	D. D. Lewis
LeRoy Irvin	LCB	Benny Barnes
Rod Perry	RCB	Aaron Mitchell
Johnnie Johnson	SS	Charlie Waters
Nolan Cromwell	FS	Randy Hughes

Los Angeles	6	7	0	0	—	13
Dallas	3	10	14	7	—	34

Dall—FG Septien 28
LA—Thomas 1 run (kick blocked)
Dall—FG Septien 29
LA—Dennard 21 pass from Ferragamo (Corral kick)
Dall—Dorsett 12 run (Septien kick)
Dall—Dorsett 10 pass from White (Septien kick)
Dall—Johnson 35 pass from White (Septien kick)
Dall—D. Pearson 11 pass from White (Septien kick)
Attendance—63,052

1981 AFC

BUFFALO 31, N.Y. JETS 27

Richard Todd threw for 377 yards to bring the Jets back from a 24-0 deficit, but Bill Simpson intercepted Todd's pass on the 2-yard line to kill the Jets' last rally.

December 27, at New York

Buffalo	Starters, Offense	N.Y. Jets
Jerry Butler	WR	Wesley Walker
Ken Jones	LT	Chris Ward
Tom Lynch	LG	Randy Rasmussen
Will Grant	C	Joe Fields
Jon Borchardt	RG	Dan Alexander
Joe Devlin	RT	Marvin Powell
Mark Brammer	TE	Jerome Barkum
Frank Lewis	WR	Derrick Gaffney
Joe Ferguson	QB	Richard Todd
Roosevelt Leaks	RB	Freeman McNeil
Joe Cribbs	RB	Tom Newton
	Starters, Defense	
Ben Williams	LE	Mark Gastineau
Fred Smerlas	NT-LT	Abdul Salaam
Sherman White	RE-RT	Marty Lyons
Lucius Sanford	LOLB-RE	Joe Klecko
Jim Haslett	LILB-LLB	Greg Buttle
Phil Villapiano	RILB-MLB	Stan Blinka
Isiah Robertson	ROLB-RLB	Lance Mehl
Mario Clark	LCB	Donald Dykes
Charles Romes	RCB	Jerry Holmes
Steve Freeman	SS	Ken Schroy
Bill Simpson	FS	Darrol Ray

Buffalo	17	7	0	7	—	31
N.Y. Jets	0	10	3	14	—	27

Buff—Romes 26 fumble recovery return (Mike-Mayer kick)
Buff—Lewis 50 pass from Ferguson (Mike-Mayer kick)
Buff—FG Mike-Mayer 29
Buff—Lewis 26 pass from Ferguson (Mike-Mayer kick)
NYJ—Shuler 30 pass from Todd (Leahy kick)
NYJ—FG Leahy 26
NYJ—FG Leahy 19
Buff—Cribbs 45 run (Mike-Mayer kick)
NYJ—B. Jones 30 pass from Todd (Leahy kick)
NYJ—Long 1 run (Leahy kick)
Attendance—57,050

1981 NFC

N.Y. GIANTS 27, PHILADELPHIA 21

The Giants built a 20-0 first-quarter lead and then withstood a late Philadelphia rally to defeat the Eagles 27-21. Kick returner Wally Henry's fumbles set up two of the Giants' scores. New York's Rob Carpenter rushed for 161 yards.

December 27, at Philadelphia

N.Y. Giants	Starters, Offense	Philadelphia
Earnest Gray	WR	Harold Carmichael
Jeff Weston	LT	Stan Walters
Billy Ard	LG	Steve Kenney
Jim Clack	C	Guy Morriss
J. T. Turner	RG	Ron Baker
Gordon King	RT	Jerry Sisemore
Gary Shirk	TE	Keith Krepfle
Johnny Perkins	WR-RB	Booker Russell
Scott Brunner	QB	Ron Jaworski
Leon Perry	RB	Hubert Oliver
Rob Carpenter	RB	Wilbert Montgomery
	Starters, Defense	
George Martin	LE	Dennis Harrison
Bill Neill	NT	Charlie Johnson
Gary Jeter	RE	Carl Hairston
Byron Hunt	LOLB	John Bunting
Brian Kelley	LILB	Al Chesley
Harry Carson	RILB	Frank LeMaster
Lawrence Taylor	ROLB	Jerry Robinson
Mark Haynes	LCB	Roynell Young
Terry Jackson	RCB	Herman Edwards
Bill Currier	SS	Randy Logan
Beasley Reece	FS	Brenard Wilson

N.Y. Giants	20	7	0	0	—	27
Philadelphia	0	7	7	7	—	21

NYG—Bright 9 pass from Brunner (kick failed)
NYG—Mistler 10 pass from Brunner (Danelo kick)
NYG—Haynes recovered fumble in end zone (Danelo kick)
Phil —Carmichael 15 pass from Jaworski (Franklin kick)
NYG—Mullady 22 pass from Brunner (Danelo kick)
Phil —Montgomery 6 run (Franklin kick)
Phil —Montgomery 1 run (Franklin kick)
Attendance—71,611

WILD CARD HISTORY

Date	Conf	Result	Site (attendance)
Dec. 24, 1978	AFC	Houston 17, Miami 9	Orange Bowl, Miami (72,445)
Dec. 24, 1978	NFC	Atlanta 14, Philadelphia 13	Atlanta-Fulton County Stadium (59,403)
Dec. 23, 1979	AFC	Houston 13, Denver 7	Astrodome, Houston (48,776)
Dec. 23, 1979	NFC	Philadelphia, 27, Chicago 17	Philadelphia Veterans Stadium (69,397)
Dec. 28, 1980	AFC	Oakland 27, Houston 7	Oakland-Alameda County Coliseum (53,333)
Dec. 28, 1980	NFC	Dallas 34, Los Angeles 13	Texas Stadium, Irving (63,052)
Dec. 27, 1981	AFC	Buffalo 31, N.Y. Jets 27	Shea Stadium, New York (57,050)
Dec. 27, 1981	NFC	N.Y. Giants 27, Philadelphia 21	Philadelphia Veterans Stadium (71,611)

Pro Bowl Games

1939

N.Y. GIANTS 13, PRO ALL-STARS 10

Ward Cuff's 18-yard field goal with five minutes remaining in the game provided the New York Giants, 1938 NFL champions, with a 13–10 victory over the Pro All-Stars, comprised of players from other NFL teams and members of the Los Angeles Bulldogs, an independent professional team.

A crowd estimated at 20,000 persons watched in Wrigley Field, a baseball stadium in Los Angeles. Game officials predicted that 30,000 persons would attend and said the lower turnout was the result of a heavy fog that covered the Los Angeles basin.

The Giants trailed 10–3 entering the fourth quarter and tied the score on a 22-yard touchdown pass from Ed Danowski to Chuck Gelatka.

January 15, at Los Angeles

N.Y. Giants	Starting Lineups		Pro All-Stars
Jim Lee Howell		LE	G. Tinsley (Chi. Cardinals)
Ed Widseth		LT	Joe Stydahar (Chi. Bears)
Orville Tuttle		LG	Byron Gentry (Pittsburgh)
Mel Hein		C	John Wiatrak (Detroit)
Ken (Kayo) Lunday		RG	P. Mehringer (L.A. Bulldogs)
Owen (Ox) Parry		RT	F. (Bruiser) Kinard (Bkn)
Jim Poole		RE	Perry Schwartz (Brooklyn)
Nello Falaschi		QB	Erny Pinckert (Washington)
Hank Soar		LH	Lloyd Cardwell (Detroit)
Ward Cuff		RH	S. Baugh (Washington)
Ed Danowski		FB	Clarke Hinkle (Green Bay)

Head coaches—Steve Owen, N.Y. Giants; Ray Flaherty (Washington), and Elmer (Gus) Henderson (Detroit), Pro All-Stars

N.Y. Giants	0	3	0	10	—	13
Pro All-Stars	0	3	7	0	—	10

NYG —FG Barnum 18
All-Stars —FG E. Smith 25
All-Stars —Cardwell 71 pass from Baugh (Stydahar kick)
NYG —Gelatka 22 pass from Danowski (Cuff kick)
NYG —FG Cuff 18
Attendance—20,000

JANUARY, 1940

GREEN BAY 16, PRO ALL-STARS 7

Cecil Isbell and Don Hutson combined to produce a 92-yard touchdown as the Green Bay Packers, winners of the 1939 NFL championship, defeated selected players from other NFL teams 16–7.

The Packers were leading 6–0 in the second quarter and had the ball on their 8-yard line. Isbell took the snap from center, faked a running play, and hurled a 61-yard pass to Hutson, sprinting free at the All-Stars' 31-yard line.

The game had been postponed a week because of threatening weather and rains that soaked the playing field in Gilmore Stadium, home field for the Hollywood Bears of the Pacific Coast League and a stadium built for football.

January 14, at Los Angeles

Green Bay	Starting Lineups		Pro All-Stars
Don Hutson		LE	Jim Poole (N.Y. Giants)
Buford (Baby) Ray		LT	Joe Stydahar (Chi. Bears)
Paul Engebretsen		LG	Byron Gentry (Pittsburgh)
Tom Greenfield		C	Mel Hein (N.Y. Giants)
C. (Buckets) Goldenberg		RG	F. (Bruiser) Kinard (Bkn)
Bill Lee		RT	Ray George (Detroit)
Milt Gantenbein		RE	Perry Schwartz (Brooklyn)
Larry Craig		QB	Fred Vanzo (Detroit)
Cecil Isbell		LH	Parker Hall (Cleveland)
Arnie Herber		RH	Erny Pinckert (Washington)
Clarke Hinkle		FB	Johnny Drake (Cleveland)

Head coaches—Earl (Curly) Lambeau, Green Bay; Steve Owen (N.Y. Giants), Pro All-Stars

Green Bay	3	10	0	3	—	16
Pro All-Stars	0	0	7	0	—	7

GB —FG Hinkle 45
GB —FG Smith 15
GB —Hutson 92 pass from Isbell (Smith kick)
All-Stars —Carter 4 pass from O'Brien (Cuff kick)
GB —FG Smith 7
Attendance—18,000

DECEMBER, 1940

CHI. BEARS 28, PRO ALL-STARS 14

Dick Plasman intercepted a pass by Sammy Baugh and ran 26 yards to the 5-yard line, setting up the touchdown that broke a 14–14 tie and helped the Chicago Bears to a 28–14 victory over the Pro All-Stars before an overflow crowd of 21,624 persons in Gilmore Stadium.

Bears quarterback Sid Luckman scored from the 1-yard line three plays after Plasman's interception to give Chicago a 21–14 lead. Plasman also figured in the Bears' first touchdown. He caught a short pass from Luckman at midfield, advanced two yards, then lateraled to Hampton Pool, who ran 48 yards to a touchdown.

December 29, at Los Angeles

Chi. Bears	Starting Lineups		Pro All-Stars
Dick Plasman		LE	C. Mulleneaux (Green Bay)
Joe Stydahar		LT	Jim Barber (Washington)
Danny Fortmann		LG	D. Oldershaw (N.Y. Giants)
Clyde (Bulldog) Turner		C	Mel Hein (N.Y. Giants)
George Musso		RG	Dick Bassi (Philadelphia)
Lee Artoe		RT	F. (Bruiser) Kinard (Bkn)
Hampton Pool		RE	Jim Poole (N.Y. Giants)
Sid Luckman		QB	C. (Pug) Manders (Bkn)
Ray Nolting		LH	Merlyn Condit (Pittsburgh)
Gary Famiglietti		RH	Sammy Baugh (Wash.)
Bill Osmanski		FB	Johnny Drake (Cleveland)

Head coaches—George Halas, Chi. Bears; Ray Flaherty (Washington), Pro All-Stars

Chi. Bears	7	7	7	7	—	28
Pro All-Stars	0	14	0	0	—	14

Chi —Pool 48 lateral from Plasman, who caught 9 pass from Luckman (Martinovich kick)
All-Stars —Livingston 10 interception return (Hinkle kick)
Chi —Clark 65 pass from Luckman (Martinovich kick)
All-Stars —Looney 3 pass from Baugh (Hutson kick)
Chi —Luckman 1 run (Snyder kick)
Chi —Maniachi 3 run (Maniachi kick)
Attendance—21,624

JANUARY, 1942

CHI. BEARS 35, PRO ALL-STARS 24

The Chicago Bears scored three touchdowns in the second quarter and turned back an All-Stars threat in the third quarter to score a 35–24 victory. The game was moved to the Polo Grounds in New York because of the danger inherent in large gatherings in cities on the West Coast, which was protecting against the possibility of a Japanese attack not long after the bombing of Pearl Harbor in Hawaii.

The Bears drove 53 yards to George McAfee's one-yard touchdown run for their first score. McAfee gave them a 14–3 lead with a 68-yard punt return.

January 4, at New York

Chi. Bears	Starting Lineups		Pro All-Stars
Dick Plasman		LE	Perry Schwartz (Brooklyn)
Ed Kolman		LT	Willie Wilkin (Washington)
Danny Fortmann		LG	Jim Sivell (Brooklyn)
Clyde (Bulldog) Turner		C	Mel Hein (N.Y. Giants)
Ray Bray		RG	J. Kuharich (Chi. Cardinals)
Lee Artoe		RT	F. (Bruiser) Kinard (Bkn)
John Siegal		RE	B. Dewell (Chi. Cardinals)
Sid Luckman		QB	N. Falaschi (N.Y. Giants)
Ray Nolting		LH	F. Filchock (Washington)
Hugh Gallarneau		RH	Ward Cuff (N.Y. Giants)
Norm Standlee		FB	C. (Pug) Manders (Bkn)

Head coaches—George Halas, Chi. Bears; Steve Owen (N.Y. Giants), Pro All-Stars

Chi. Bears	0	21	7	7	—	35
Pro All-Stars	3	0	14	7	—	24

All-Stars —FG Cuff 19
Chi —McAfee 1 run (Snyder kick)
Chi —McAfee 68 punt return (Artoe kick)
Chi —Swisher 6 run (Stydahar kick)
All-Stars —Schwartz 15 pass from Baugh (Cuff kick)
All-Stars —Dewell 24 pass from Baugh (Cuff kick)
Chi —McLean 5 pass from Luckman (Stydahar kick)
Chi —Kavanaugh 7 pass from Bussey (Stydahar kick)
All-Stars —Schwartz 26 pass from Baugh (Cuff kick)
Attendance—17,725

DECEMBER, 1942

PRO ALL-STARS 17, WASHINGTON 14

The Washington Redskins lost to the All-Stars in Philadelphia without star player Sammy Baugh.

Baugh explained that an automobile was supposed to have been provided by Redskins management to take him from Sweetwater, Texas (30 miles from his ranch in Rotan), to the airport in Dallas for an 11:50 P.M. flight the Friday before the Sunday game. Baugh said the car was not there, so he had the Sweetwater police call the airport in nearby Abilene. The police were told the last flight already had left Abilene at 6 P.M. Baugh said he then tried to get a taxi from Sweetwater to Dallas (230 miles away), "but the taxi driver was in a movie and when he got out it was too late. So I came home."

December 27, at Philadelphia

Washington	Starting Lineups		Pro All-Stars
Bob Masterson		LE	Perry Schwartz (Brooklyn)
Fred Davis		LT	Chet Adams (Cleveland)
Dick Farman		LG	Augie Lio (Detroit)
Charles (Ki) Aldrich		C	C. Cherundolo (Pittsburgh)
Steve Slivinski		RG	Enio Conti (Philadelphia)
Bill Young		RT	J. Woudenberg (Pittsburgh)
Ed Cifers		RE	Eddie Rucinski (Brooklyn)
Ray Hare		QB	T. Thompson (Philadelphia)
Roy Zimmerman		LH	Bill Dudley (Pittsburgh)
Ed Justice		RH	Merlyn Condit (Brooklyn)
Andy Farkas		FB	Harry Hopp (Detroit)

Head coaches—Ray Flaherty, Washington; Heartley (Hunk) Anderson (Chi. Bears), Pro All-Stars

Washington	7	0	7	0	—	14
Pro All-Stars	0	0	14	3	—	17

Wash —Aldrich 30 punt return (Masterson kick)
All-Stars —Dudley 97 interception return (Maznicki kick)
All-Stars —Petty 2 run (Maznicki kick)
Wash —Seymour 14 pass from Zimmerman (Masterson kick)
All-Stars —FG Artoe 43
Attendance—18,671

1951

AMERICAN 28, NATIONAL 27

Quarterback Otto Graham of the Cleveland Browns was named player of the game after scoring touchdowns on runs of 6 and 10 yards in the third quarter as the American Conference All-Stars overcame a 27–14 National Conference lead to win the first Pro Bowl in the game's revival in Memorial Coliseum, Los Angeles. Graham also completed 19 of 27 passes.

Quarterbacks Bob Waterfield and Norm Van Brocklin of the Los Angeles Rams combined to complete 21 of 44 passes for 294 yards and three touchdowns for the National Conference.

January 14, at Los Angeles

American Conf.	Starting Lineups		National Conf.
Pete Pihos (Philadelphia)		LE	Tom Fears (Los Angeles)
Lou Groza (Cleveland)		LT	Dick Huffman (Los Angeles)
Weldon Humble (Cleveland)		LG	Dick Barwegan (Chicago)
Bill Walsh (Pittsburgh)		C	Brad Ecklund (N.Y. Yanks)
Bill Willis (Cleveland)		RG	Lou Creekmur (Detroit)
Al Wistert (Philadelphia)		RT	Thurman McGraw (Detroit)
Bob Shaw (Chi. Cardinals)		RE	Dan Edwards (N.Y. Yanks)
Otto Graham (Cleveland)		QB	B. Waterfield (Los Angeles)
Gene Roberts (N.Y. Giants)		LH	Glenn Davis (Los Angeles)
E. Angsman (Chi. Card.)		RH	Billy Grimes (Green Bay)
Marion Motley (Cleveland)		FB	Dick Hoerner (Los Angeles)

Head coaches—Paul Brown (Cleveland), American Conference; Joe Stydahar (Los Angeles), National Conference

American Conf.	7	7	14	0	—	28
National Conf.	7	13	7	0	—	27

National —Fears 22 pass from Waterfield (Waterfield kick)
American —Dudley 47 punt return (Groza kick)
National —FG Waterfield 30
American —Shaw 47 pass from Graham (Groza kick)
National —FG Waterfield 27
National —Fears 5 pass from Van Brocklin (Waterfield kick)
National —Edwards 65 pass from Waterfield (Waterfield kick)
American —Graham 6 run (Harder kick)
American —Graham 10 run (Harder kick)
Attendance—53,678

1952

NATIONAL 30, AMERICAN 13

The National Conference All-Stars capitalized on two fourth-quarter fumbles by American Conference quarterback Sammy Baugh to score two touchdowns in a 20-point period in which they overcame a 13–10 American Conference lead to win 30–13. Baugh, playing in the fourth quarter, fumbled four times in a driving rain and had his only pass intercepted.

With the Nationals leading 16–13, Baugh fumbled on the Americans' 24. Defensive tackle Leo Nomellini picked up the ball on the 20 and ran for a touchdown that put the National team ahead 23–13.

January 12, at Los Angeles

National Conf.	Starting Lineups	American Conf.
G. Soltau (San Francisco)	LE	F. Polsfoot (Chi. Cardinals)
George Connor (Chi Bears)	LT	Lou Groza (Cleveland)
Lou Creekmur (Detroit)	LG	B. Fischer (Chi. Cardinals)
Brad Ecklund (N.Y. Yanks)	C	Bill Walsh (Pittsburgh)
Dick Barwegan (Chi. Bears)	RG	George Hughes (Pittsburgh)
M. McCormack (N.Y. Yanks)	RT	D. (Tex) Coulter (N.Y. G.)
E. (Crazylegs) Hirsch (L.A.)	RE	Dante Lavelli (Cleveland)
B. Waterfield (Los Angeles)	QB	Otto Graham (Cleveland)
Dan Towler (Los Angeles)	LH	Ken Carpenter (Cleveland)
P. (Tank) Younger (L.A.)	RH	Dub Jones (Cleveland)
John Dottley (Chi. Bears)	FB	Eddie Price (N.Y. Giants)

Head coaches—Paul Brown (Cleveland), American Conference; Raymond (Buddy) Parker (Detroit), National Conference

National Conf.	3	7	0	20	—	30
American Conf.	7	6	0	0	—	13

American—Jones 44 pass from Graham (Graham kick)
National —FG Waterfield 30
American—FG Groza 45
American—FG Groza 11
National —Soltau 1 pass from Van Brocklin (Waterfield kick)
National —Dottley 2 run (kick failed)
National —Nomellini 20 fumble return (Waterfield kick)
National —Hirsch 7 pass from Walker (Lujack kick)
Attendance—19,400

1953

NATIONAL 27, AMERICAN 7

Fullback Dan Towler took a handoff from quarterback Bobby Layne and threw a 13-yard pass to Hugh McElhenny for the game's first score in a 27–7 National Conference victory. The pass was the first Towler had thrown in three seasons as a professional.

Towler's Los Angeles Rams teammate, Norm Van Brocklin, replaced Layne at quarterback on the next offensive series. On Van Brocklin's first play, he threw a 39-yard pass to Green Bay's Bill Howton, who caught the ball on the American Conference's 35-yard line and ran for a touchdown that completed a 74-yard play.

Van Brocklin completed 5 of 15 passes.

January 10, at Los Angeles

National Conf.	Starting Lineups	American Conf.
Cloyce Box (Detroit)	LE	H. (Bones) Taylor (Wash.)
Lou Creekmur (Detroit)	LT	Lou Groza (Cleveland)
Dick Barwegan (Chi. Bears)	LG	Abe Gibron (Cleveland)
B. Johnson (San Francisco)	C	D. (Tex) Coulter (N.Y.G.)
John Wozniak (Dallas)	RG	B. Fischer (Chi. Cardinals)
Fred Williams (Chi. Bears)	RT	F. (Bucko) Kilroy (Phil.)
E. (Crazylegs) Hirsch (L.A.)	RE	Elbie Nickel (Pittsburgh)
Bobby Layne (Detroit)	QB	Otto Graham (Cleveland)
B. Hoernschemeyer (Detroit)	LH	Ray Mathews (Pittsburgh)
Billy Howton (Green Bay)	RH	L. Chandnois (Pittsburgh)
Dan Towler (Los Angeles)	FB	O. Matson (Chi. Cardinals)

Head coaches—Paul Brown (Cleveland), American Conference; Raymond (Buddy) Parker (Detroit), National Conference

National Conf.	14	0	3	10	—	27
American Conf.	0	0	7	0	—	7

National —McElhenny 13 pass from Towler (Harder kick)
National —Howton 74 pass from Van Brocklin (Harder kick)
National —FG Harder 23
American—Graham 1 run (Groza kick)
National —FG Harder 13
National —McElhenny 7 pass from Van Brocklin (Harder kick)
Attendance—34,208

1954

EAST 20, WEST 9

Linebacker Chuck Bednarik of the Philadelphia Eagles returned an intercepted pass for a touchdown, recovered a fumble that led to a field goal, punted five times for a 43-yard average, and was named player of the game as the East scored a 20–9 victory.

The East took a 3–0 lead in the first quarter on an 11-yard field goal by Lou Groza that followed a fumble by Joe Perry which was recovered by Emlen Tunnel. Don Kindt tackled East quarterback Otto Graham in the end zone for a safety that made the score 3-2 at halftime.

West halfback Hugh McElhenny had 74 yards in 10 carries. Perry had 60 yards in 12 carries.

January 17, at Los Angeles

East	Starting Lineups	West
Pete Pihos (Philadelphia)	LE	G. Soltau (San Francisco)
Lou Groza (Cleveland)	LT	Lou Creekmur (Detroit)
Abe Gibron (Cleveland)	LG	Dick Barwegan (Baltimore)
K. Farragut (Philadelphia)	C	B. Johnson (San Francisco)
George Hughes (Pittsburgh)	RG	Dick Stanfel (Detroit)
Ken Snyder (Philadelphia)	RT	L. Nomellini (San Francisco)
Dante Lavelli (Cleveland)	RE	E. (Crazylegs) Hirsch (L.A.)
Otto Graham (Cleveland)	QB	Bobby Layne (Detroit)
Ray Renfro (Cleveland)	LH	Doak Walker (Detroit)
L. Chandnois (Pittsburgh)	RH	P. (Tank) Younger (L.A.)
H. (Chick) Jagade (Cle.)	FB	Joe Perry (San Francisco)

Head coaches—Paul Brown (Cleveland), East; Raymond (Buddy) Parker (Detroit), West

East	3	0	10	7	—	20
West	0	2	0	7	—	9

East —FG Groza 11
West —Safety, Kindt tackled Graham in end zone
East —FG Groza 25
East —Bednarik 24 interception return (Groza kick)
West —Perry 16 run (Walker kick)
East —Renfro 25 run (Groza kick)
Attendance—44,214

1955

WEST 26, EAST 19

Player-of-the-game Billy Wilson caught 11 passes for 157 yards and one touchdown as the West overcame a 19–3 East lead in the second quarter to score a 26–19 victory.

Doak Walker's 30-yard field goal tied the game 19–19 with 11:31 remaining in the fourth quarter. On the East's next possession, quarterback Adrian Burk's pass was intercepted by LaVern Torgeson, who returned the ball 37 yards to the East's 4-yard line. Fullback Joe Perry gained three yards on the first play and scored from the 1 on the next play.

Y. A. Tittle completed 16 of 26 passes for the West.

January 16, at Los Angeles

West	Starting Lineups	East
Harlon Hill (Chi. Bears)	LE	Pete Pihos (Philadelphia)
Lou Creekmur (Detroit)	LT	Lou Groza (Cleveland)
B. Banducci (S. F.)	LG	Bill Austin (N.Y. Giants)
L. McLaughlin (L.A.)	C	Frank Gatski (Cleveland)
D. Putnam (Los Angeles)	RG	Abe Gibron (Cleveland)
Bill Bishop (Chi. Bears)	RT	K. Snyder (Philadelphia)
Billy Wilson (S.F.)	RE	Dante Lavelli (Cleveland)
Y.A. Tittle (S.F.)	QB	Otto Graham (Cleveland)
J.H. Johnson (S.F.)	LH	O. Matson (Chi. Cardinals)
Doak Walker (Detroit)	RH	Kyle Rote (N.Y. Giants)
Joe Perry (San Francisco)	FB	Eddie Price (N.Y. Giants)

Head coaches—Joe Kuharich (Washington), East; Lawrence (Buck) Shaw (San Francisco), West

West	3	6	7	10	—	26
East	13	6	0	0	—	19

East —Matson 6 pass from Graham (Groza kick)
East —Willey 5 fumble return (kick failed)
West —FG Walker 35
East —Taylor 33 pass from Burk (kick failed)
West —Wilson 14 pass from Tittle (kick failed)
West —Hill 42 pass from Tittle (Walker kick)
West —FG Walker 30
West —Perry 1 run (Walker kick)
Attendance—43,972

1956

EAST 31, WEST 30

The West's Jack Christensen returned the opening kickoff 103 yards for a touchdown. The East's Ollie Matson returned the second half kickoff 91 yards.

After moving from its 24 to the West's 44 in nine plays, the East came to fourth down and three yards for a first down. Lou Groza put the East ahead 24–23 with a 50-yard field goal.

Matson was named player of the game. He gained 83 yards in 11 carries and scored one touchdown, caught three passes for 9 yards, returned two punts 57 yards, and two kickoffs 137 yards, scoring once.

January 15, at Los Angeles

West	Starting Lineups	East
Harlon Hill (Chi. Bears)	LE	C. Massey (Cleveland)
Lou Creekmur (Detroit)	LT	Lou Groza (Cleveland)
Duane Putnam (L.A.)	LG	Abe Gibron (Cleveland)
D. Szymanski (Baltimore)	C	H. Ulinski (Washington)
Stan Jones (Chi. Bears)	RG	Jack Stroud (N.Y. Giants)
Bill Wightkin (Chi. Bears)	RT	F. Varrichone (Pittsburgh)
Billy Wilson (S.F.)	RE	Pete Pihos (Philadelphia)
Norm Van Brocklin (L.A.)	QB	Adrian Burk (Philadelphia)
Ron Waller (Los Angeles)	LH	F. Gifford (N.Y. Giants)
Doak Walker (Detroit)	RH	Ray Mathews (Pittsburgh)
H. Ferguson (Green Bay)	FB	F. (Curly) Morrison (Cle.)

Head coaches—Joe Kuharich (Washington), East; Sid Gillman (Los Angeles), West

West	7	7	9	7	—	30
East	7	0	14	10	—	31

West—Christensen 103 kickoff return (Richter kick)
East—Pihos 12 pass from LeBaron (Groza kick)
West—Howton 73 pass from Brown (Richter kick)
East—Matson 91 kickoff return (Groza kick)
West—Ferguson 1 run (kick blocked)
East—Matson 15 run (Groza kick)
West—FG Rechichar 46
East—FG Groza 50
East—Mathews 20 pass from LeBaron
West—Waller 3 run (Richter kick)
Attendance—37,867

1957

WEST 19, EAST 10

In a game in which the total offense of both teams was 229 yards, the West's Bert Rechichar provided the difference with field goals of 41, 44, 44, and 52 yards in a 19–10 victory by the West.

Pittsburgh's Ernie Stautner blocked Rechichar's first field goal attempt, from 47 yards in the first quarter. The East then marched 40 yards in 10 plays to score its only touchdown. Frank Gifford ran three yards to the 1-yard line and fumbled. Kyle Rote recovered in the end zone for the touchdown.

The West scored its touchdown after Joe Schmidt recovered Ollie Matson's fumble on the East's 12-yard line.

January 13, at Los Angeles

West	Starting Lineups	East
Harlon Hill (Chi. Bears)	LE	D. Brewster (Cleveland)
Lou Creekmur (Detroit)	LT	R. Brown (N.Y. Giants)
Stan Jones (Chi. Bears)	LG	B. Lansford (Philadelphia)
Charlie Ane (Detroit)	C	J. Simmons (Chi. Cardinals)
Bill George (Chi. Bears)	RG	Dick Stanfel (Washington)
B. St. Clair (San Francisco)	RT	M. McCormack (Cleveland)
Billy Howton (Green Bay)	RE	Elbie Nickel (Pittsburgh)
Ed Brown (Chi. Bears)	QB	C. Conerly (N.Y. Giants)
H. McElhenny (S.F.)	LH	F. Gifford (N.Y. Giants)
B. Wilson (San Francisco)	RH	O. Matson (Chi. Cardinals)
Rick Casares (Chi. Bears)	FB	Fran Rogel (Pittsburgh)

Head coaches—Jim Lee Howell (N.Y. Giants), East; John (Paddy) Driscoll (Chi. Bears), West

West	7	3	3	6	—	19
East	0	7	3	0	—	10

West—Brown 1 run (Layne kick)
East—Rote fumble recovery in end zone (Baker kick)
West—FG Rechichar 41
East—FG Baker 52
West—FG Rechichar 44
West—FG Rechichar 44
West—FG Rechichar 52
Attendance—44,177

1958

WEST 26, EAST 7

The West trailed 7–6 after Earl Morrall's 39-yard touchdown pass to Ray Renfro in the second quarter. Bert Rechichar's nine-yard field goal with 38 seconds left in the half put the West back in front 9–7 and it never trailed again, scoring a 26–7 victory before a record crowd of 66,634 persons.

West quarterback Y.A. Tittle and Johnny Unitas completed 15 of 25 passes for 159 yards and one touchdown. East quarterbacks Morrall and Eddie LeBaron completed 5 of 20 for 75 yards.

The West had a 17–7 advantage in first downs and outgained the East 340-149. Alan Ameche was the West's leading ground gainer with 85 yards in nine carries.

January 12, at Los Angeles

West	Starting Lineups	East
Billy Howton (Green Bay)	LE	L. Sanford (Chi. Cardinals)
Lou Creekmur (Detroit)	LT	M. McCormack (Cleveland)
D. Putnam (Los Angeles)	LG	Bob Gain (Cleveland)
Jim Ringo (Green Bay)	C	C. Bednarik (Philadelphia)
Harley Sewell (Detroit)	RG	E. Stautner (Pittsburgh)
Kline Gilbert (Chi. Bears)	RT	R. Brown (N.Y. Giants)
B. Wilson (San Francisco)	RE	Walt Michaels (Cleveland)
Y.A. Tittle (San Francisco)	QB	E. LeBaron (Washington)
Jon Arnett (Los Angeles)	LH	E. Tunnell (N.Y. Giants)
H. McElhenny (S.F.)	RH	J. Norton (Philadelphia)
Alan Ameche (Baltimore)	FB	B.R. Barnes (Philadelphia)

Head coaches—Raymond (Buddy) Parker (Pittsburgh), East; George Wilson (Detroit), West

West	6	3	10	7	—	26
East	0	7	0	0	—	7

West—Dillon 39 interception return (kick blocked)
East—Renfro 39 pass from Morrall (Groza kick)
West—FG Rechichar 9
West—FG Rechichar 23
West—T. Wilson 10 run (Rechichar kick)
West—Ameche 8 pass from Tittle (Rechichar kick)
Attendance—66,634

1959

EAST 28, WEST 21

Frank Gifford, voted the game's outstanding back, gained 12 yards in six carries, caught three passes for 54 yards, and completed three of four passes for 75 yards and a touchdown.

Trailing 21–16 at the end of three quarters, the East scored a touchdown, field goal, and a safety in the fourth quarter to win 28–21 before a record crowd of 72,250 persons.

Each of the East's passers—Gifford, Eddie LeBaron, and Norm Van Brocklin—threw for a touchdown. They completed 16 of 34 passes for 214 yards.

January 11, at Los Angeles

East	Starting Lineups	West
P. Retzlaff (Philadelphia)	LE	Raymond Berry (Baltimore)
R. Brown (N.Y. Giants)	LT	Jim Parker (Baltimore)
Jim Ray Smith (Cleveland)	LG	D. Putnam (Los Angeles)
Jim Schrader (Washington)	C	Jim Ringo (Green Bay)
Dick Stanfel (Washington)	RG	Harley Sewell (Detroit)
F. Varrichione (Pittsburgh)	RT	B. St. Clair (San Francisco)
Bob Schnelker (N.Y. Giants)	RE	B. Wilson (San Francisco)
N. Van Brocklin (Phil.)	QB	Johnny Unitas (Baltimore)
F. Gifford (N.Y. Giants)	LH	Jon Arnett (Los Angeles)
Alex Webster (N.Y. Giants)	RH	Lenny Moore (Baltimore)
Jim Brown (Cleveland)	FB	Alan Ameche (Baltimore)

Head coaches—Jim Lee Howell (N.Y. Giants), East; Weeb Ewbank (Baltimore), West

East	9	7	0	12	—	28
West	7	7	0	0	—	21

West—Ameche 1 run (Richter kick)
East—FG Groza 25
East—Webster 40 pass from Gifford (kick blocked)
West—McElhenny 20 pass from Wade (Richter kick)
East—Nagler 7 pass from LeBaron (Groza kick)
West—Wade 10 run (Richter kick)
East—FG Groza 25
East—Retzlaff 15 pass from Van Brocklin (Groza kick)
East—Safety, Scott tackled McElhenny in end zone
Attendance—72,250

1960

WEST 38, EAST 21

Johnny Unitas and Y.A. Tittle combined to complete 27 of 40 passes for 365 yards and four touchdowns for the West, which led 31-14 at the half enroute to a 38–21 victory. Unitas completed 14 of 22 passes for 187 yards and three touchdowns, ran for 43 yards in six carries, and was selected the outstanding back.

Unitas and Tittle threw to eight different receivers. Unitas's Baltimore Colts teammate, Lenny Moore, caught five for 103 yards and two touchdowns, and Del Shofner of the Los Angeles Rams caught six for 88. The West's Jon Arnett led rushers with 61 yards in 11 carries.

January 17, at Los Angeles

East	Starting Lineups	West
B. Anderson (Washington)	LE	Del Shofner (Los Angeles)
R. Brown (N.Y. Giants)	LT	Jim Parker (Baltimore)
E. Stautner (Pittsburgh)	LG	Art Spinney (Baltimore)
Jim Schrader (Washington)	C	Jim Ringo (Green Bay)
John Nisby (Pittsburgh)	RG	Stan Jones (Chi. Bears)
K. Panfil (Chi. Cardinals)	RT	B. St. Clair (San Francisco)
B. Schnelker (N.Y. Giants)	RE	Raymond Berry (Baltimore)
Bobby Layne (Pittsburgh)	QB	Johnny Unitas (Baltimore)
F. Gifford (N.Y. Giants)	LH	Jon Arnett (Los Angeles)
T. McDonald (Philadelphia)	RH	Lenny Moore (Baltimore)
Jim Brown (Cleveland)	FB	J.D. Smith (San Francisco)

Head coaches—Lawrence (Buck) Shaw (Philadelphia), East; Howard (Red) Hickey (San Francisco), West

East	7	7	0	7	—	21
West	10	21	0	7	—	38

East—Patton 23 interception return (Groza kick)
West—Berry 22 pass from Unitas (Hornung kick)
West—FG Hornung 16
East—McDonald 63 pass from Layne (Groza kick)
West—Moore 13 pass from Tittle (Hornung kick)
West—Moore 65 pass from Unitas (Hornung kick)
West—Smith 6 pass from Unitas (Hornung kick)
East—J. Brown 2 pass from Layne (Groza kick)
West—Hornung 2 run (Hornung kick)
Attendance—56,876

1961

WEST 35, EAST 31

The West and East divided eight touchdowns in the last three quarters, with the difference in the West's 35–31 victory coming in the first quarter, when it scored a touchdown on Jim Taylor's two-yard run and the East's Bobby Walston kicked a field goal.

Taylor scored three touchdowns and Sonny Randle scored two touchdowns for the East. West quarterback Johnny Unitas was voted the outstanding back after completing 10 of 18 passes for 218 yards and a touchdown and directing each of his team's five touchdown drives.

January 15, at Los Angeles

East	Starting Lineups	West
Bill Anderson (Washington)	LE	Gail Cogdill (Detroit)
R. Brown (N.Y. Giants)	LT	Jim Parker (Baltimore)
Jim Ray Smith (Cleveland)	LG	B. Bosley (San Francisco)
Ray Wietecha (N.Y. Giants)	C	Jim Ringo (Green Bay)
Jack Stroud (N.Y. Giants)	RG	Stan Jones (Chicago)
Mike McCormack (Cleve.)	RT	B. St. Clair (San Francisco)
Sonny Randle (St. Louis)	RE	Jim (Red) Phillips (L.A.)
N. Van Brocklin (Phil.)	QB	Johnny Unitas (Baltimore)
J. David Crow (St. Louis)	LH	Paul Hornung (Green Bay)
T. McDonald (Philadelphia)	RH	Lenny Moore (Baltimore)
Jim Brown (Cleveland)	FB	Jim Taylor (Green Bay)

Head coaches—Lawrence (Buck) Shaw (Philadelphia), East; Vince Lombardi (Green Bay), West

East	3	14	7	7	—	31
West	7	14	7	7	—	35

West—Taylor 2 run (Hornung kick)
East—FG Walston 22
West—Taylor 1 run (Hornung kick)
East—Randle 51 pass from Plum (Waltson kick)
East—McDonald 46 pass from Van Brocklin (Walston kick)
West—Moore 44 pass from Unitas (Hornung kick)
West—Taylor 1 run (Hornung kick)
East—Retzlaff 43 pass from Van Brocklin (Walston kick)
West—Arnett 20 run (Hornung kick)
East—Randle 36 pass from Van Brocklin (Walston kick)
Attendance—62,971

1962 AFL

WEST 47, EAST 27

January 7, at San Diego

East	Starters, Offense	West
Gino Cappelletti (Boston)	LE	Don Norton (San Diego)
Al Jamison (Houston)	LT	Ernie Wright (San Diego)
Chuck Leo (Boston)	LG	Ken Adamson (Denver)
Bob Schmidt (Houston)	C	Jim Otto (Oakland)
Bob Mischak (N.Y. Titans)	RG	Bill Krisher (Dallas)
Ken Rice (Buffalo)	RT	Ron Mix (San Diego)
Bob McLeod (Houston)	RE	Dave Kocourek (San Diego)
George Blanda (Houston)	QB	Jack Kemp (San Diego)
Billy Cannon (Houston)	LH	Abner Haynes (Dallas)
C. Hennigan (Houston)	RH	Lionel Taylor (Denver)
Bill Mathis (N.Y. Titans)	FB	Alan Miller (Oakland)

Starters, Defense

East		West
LaVerne Torczon (Buffalo)	LE	Earl Faison (San Diego)
Chuck McMurtry (Buffalo)	LT	Bud McFadin (Denver)
Jim Hunt (Boston)	RT	Paul Rochester (Dallas)
Don Floyd (Houston)	RE	Mel Branch (San Diego)
Tom Addison (Boston)	LLB	Emil Karas (San Diego)
Archie Matsos (Buffalo)	MLB	Sherrill Headrick (Dallas)
Dennit Morris (Houston)	RLB	E.J. Holub (Dallas)
Tony Banfield (Houston)	LCB	Fred Williamson (Oakland)
Dick Felt (N.Y. Titans)	RCB	Dave Webster (Dallas)
Bill Atkins (Buffalo)	LS	Austin Gonsoulin (Denver)
Fred Bruney (Boston)	RS	Charlie McNeil (San Diego)

Head coaches—Wally Lemm (Houston), East; Sid Gillman (San Diego), West

East	5	7	7	8	—	27
West	0	21	14	12	—	47

East—FG Blanda 32
East—Safety, Haynes tackled in end zone
West—Stone 45 pass from Davidson (Blair kick)
East—Cannon 34 pass from Blanda (Blanda kick)
West—Haynes 12 run (Blair kick)
West—Kocourek 24 pass from Davidson (Blair kick)
West—Haynes 66 punt return (Blair kick)
West—Norton 10 pass from Davidson (Blair kick)
East—Cappelletti 5 pass from Blanda (Blanda kick)
West—Williamson 53 interception return (kick failed)
East—Hennigan 2 pass from Dorow (Dorow run)
West—Stone 15 run (pass failed)
Attendance—20,973

1962 NFL

WEST 31, EAST 30

Jon Arnett scored and the West won a narrow 31–30 victory.

January 14, at Los Angeles

East	Starters, Offense	West
Del Shofner (N.Y. Giants)	LE	Raymond Berry (Baltimore)
Ray Lemek (Washington)	LT	Jim Parker (Baltimore)
John Nisby (Pittsburgh)	LG	Stan Jones (Chicago)
John Morrow (Cleveland)	C	Jim Ringo (Green Bay)
Jim Ray Smith (Cleveland)	RG	T. Connolly (San Francisco)
M. McCormack (Cleveland)	RT	B. St. Clair (San Francisco)
B. Walston (Philadelphia)	RE	Jim (Red) Phillips (L.A.)
Y.A. Tittle (N.Y. Giants)	QB	Bart Starr (Green Bay)
Don Perkins (Dallas)	LH	Jon Arnett (Los Angeles)
T. McDonald (Philadelphia)	RH	Lenny Moore (Baltimore)
Jim Brown (Cleveland)	FB	Jim Taylor (Green Bay)

Starters, Defense

East		West
Jim Katcavage (N.Y. Giants)	LE	Doug Atkins (Chicago)
Bob Gain (Cleveland)	LT	Henry Jordan (Green Bay)
Bob Toneff (Washington)	RT	Alex Karras (Detroit)
Ernie Stautner (Pittsburgh)	RE	Gino Marchetti (Baltimore)
John Reger (Pittsburgh)	LLB	Bill Forester (Green Bay)
Sam Huff (N.Y. Giants)	MLB	Joe Schmidt (Detroit)
M. Baughan (Philadelphia)	RLB	Bill George (Chicago)
Erich Barnes (N.Y. Giants)	LHB	D. (Night Train) Lane (Det.)
Jimmy Hill (St. Louis)	RHB	J. Whittenton (Green Bay)
Jerry Norton (St. Louis)	LS	A. Woodson (San Francisco)
Jim Patton (N.Y. Giants)	RS	Eddie Dove (San Francisco)

Head coaches—Allie Sherman (N.Y. Giants), East; Norm Van Brocklin (Minnesota), West

East	3	7	6	14	—	30
West	14	3	7	7	—	31

East—FG Walston 33
West—Berry 16 pass from Unitas (Martin kick)
West—Lane 42 pass interception (Martin kick)
East—Bielski 10 pass from Tittle (Walston kick)
West—FG Martin 27
West—McElhenny 10 pass from Starr (Martin kick)
East—Walston 12 pass from Plum (kick blocked)
East—Webster 2 pass from Tittle (Walston kick)
East—Brown 70 run (Walston kick)
West—Arnett 12 pass from Unitas (Martin kick)
Attendance—57,409

1963 AFL

WEST 21, EAST 14

Denver Broncos teammates Frank Tripucka and Lionel Taylor combined on a 20-yard pass with 8:56 remaining in the game for the touchdown that provided the West a 21-14 victory. Tripucka replaced Dallas's Len Dawson.

January 13, at San Diego

West	Starters, Offense	East
Reg Carolan (San Diego)	LE	Ernie Warlick (Buffalo)
Jim Tyrer (Dallas)	LT	Al Jamison (Houston)
Marvin Terrell (Dallas)	LG	Bob Talamini (Houston)
Jim Otto (Oakland)	C	Bob Schmidt (Houston)
Ron Mix (San Diego)	RG	Bob Mischak (N.Y. Titans)
Jerry Cornelison (Dallas)	RT	Rich Michael (Houston)
Dave Kocourek (San Diego)	RE	Willard Dewveal (Houston)
Len Dawson (Dallas)	QB	George Blanda (Houston)
Abner Haynes (Dallas)	LH	Dick Christy (N.Y. Titans)
Lionel Taylor (Denver)	RH	C. Hennigan (Houston)
Curtis McClinton (Dallas)	FB	Cookie Gilchrist (Buffalo)
	Starters, Defense	
Earl Faison (San Diego)	LE	Don Floyd (Houston)
Bud McFadin (Denver)	LT	Ed Husmann (Houston)
Ernie Ladd (San Diego)	RT	Tom Sestak (Buffalo)
Mel Branch (Dallas)	RE	Dick Klein (Boston)
Emil Karas (San Diego)	LLB	Tom Addison (Boston)
Sherrill Headrick (Dallas)	MLB	Arche Matsos (Buffalo)
Jim Fraser (Denver)	RLB	Marv Matuszak (Buffalo)
Fred Williamson (Oakland)	LCB	Tony Banfield (Houston)
Bob Zeman (Denver)	RCB	Fred Bruney (Boston)
A. Gonsoulin (Denver)	LS	Jim Norton (Houston)
Dave Grayson (Dallas)	RS	Fred Glick (Houston)

Head coaches—Frank (Pop) Ivy (Houston), East; Hank Stram (Dallas), West

West	7	7	0	7	—	21
East	0	0	14	0	—	14

West—McClinton 64 run (Mingo kick)
West—Kocourek 11 pass from Dawson (Mingo kick)
East—Hennigan 8 pass from Blanda (Blanda kick)
East—Grantham 32 interception return (Blanda kick)
West—Taylor 20 pass from Tripucka (Mingo kick)
Attendance—27,641

1963 NFL

EAST 30, WEST 20

Jim Brown gained 144 yards and scored twice to give the East a 30-20 victory despite Johnny Unitas's 210 yards passing.

January 13, at Los Angeles

East	Starters, Offense	West
Del Shofner (N.Y. Giants)	LE	Gail Cogdill (Detroit)
R. Brown, (N.Y. Giants)	LT	Jim Parker (Baltimore)
Jim Ray Smith (Cleveland)	LG	Harley Sewell (Detroit)
Ray Wietecha (N.Y. Giants)	C	Jim Ringo (Green Bay)
John Nisby (Washington)	RG	Jerry Kramer (Green Bay)
M. McCormack (Cleveland)	RT	Forrest Gregg (Green Bay)
P. Carpenter (Pittsburgh)	RE	Mike Ditka (Chicago)
Y. A. Tittle (N.Y. Giants)	QB	Johnny Unitas (Baltimore)
J. David Crow (St. Louis)	LH	Dick Bass (Los Angeles)
T. McDonald (Philadelphia)	RH	Lenny Moore (Baltimore)
Jim Brown (Cleveland)	FB	J.D. Smith (San Francisco)
	Starters, Defense	
Lou Michaels (Pittsburgh)	LE	Doug Atkins (Chicago)
Bob Gain (Cleveland)	LT	Alex Karras (Detroit)
Big Daddy Lipscomb (Pitt.)	RT	Roger Brown (Detroit)
J. Katcavage (N.Y. Giants)	RE	Gino Marchetti (Baltimore)
Galen Fiss (Cleveland)	LLB	Joe Fortunato (Chicago)
Jerry Tubbs (Dallas)	MLB	Joe Schmidt (Detroit)
R. Breedlove (Washington)	RLB	Bill Forester (Green Bay)
Erich Barnes (N.Y. Giants)	LHB	D. (Night Train) Lane (Det.)
Jimmy Hill (St. Louis)	RHB	Abe Woodson (S.F.)
Jimmy Patton (N.Y. Giants)	LS	W. Wood (Green Bay)
Larry Wilson (St. Louis)	RS	Yale Lary (Detroit)

Head coaches—Allie Sherman (N.Y. Giants), East; Vince Lombardi (Green Bay), West

East	13	0	0	17	—	30
West	0	3	17	0	—	20

East—J. Brown 1 run (Michaels kick)
East—J. Brown 50 run (kick failed)
West—FG Davis 49
West—Bass 1 run (Davis kick)
West—FG Davis 32
West—Ditka 6 pass from Unitas (Davis kick)
East—Carpenter 19 pass from Tittle (Gain kick)
East—FG Michaels 27
East—Bishop 20 fumble return (Michaels kick)
Attendance—61,374

1964 NFL

WEST 31, EAST 17

The West broke open the game with two quick touchdowns in the third quarter and won 31-17 over the East.

January 12, at Los Angeles

East	Starters, Offense	West
Del Shofner (N.Y. Giants)	LE	Raymond Berry (Baltimore)
Dick Schafrath (Cleveland)	LT	G. Alderman (Minnesota)
Darrell Dess (N.Y. Giants)	LG	John Gordy (Detroit)
Bob DeMarco (St. Louis)	C	Jim Ringo (Green Bay)
Ken Gray (St. Louis)	RG	Jerry Kramer (Green Bay)
C. Bradshaw (Pittsburgh)	RT	Forrest Gregg (Green Bay)
Pete Retzlaff (Philadelphia)	RE	Mike Ditka (Chicago)
C. Johnson (St. Louis)	QB	Johnny Unitas (Baltimore)
B. Mitchell (Washington)	FL	Terry Barr (Detroit)
Timmy Brown (Philadelphia)	HB	Tommy Mason (Minnesota)
Jim Brown (Cleveland)	FB	Jim Taylor (Green Bay)
	Starters, Defense	
Bill Glass (Cleveland)	LE	Doug Atkins (Chicago)
J. LoVetere (N.Y. Giants)	LT	Merlin Olsen (Los Angeles)
Joe Krupa (Pittsburgh)	RT	Roger Brown (Detroit)
J. Katcavage (N.Y. Giants)	RE	Gino Marchetti (Baltimore)
Myron Pottios (Pittsburgh)	LLB	Wayne Walker (Detroit)
Galen Fiss (Cleveland)	MLB	Joe Fortunato (Chicago)
Dale Meinert (St. Louis)	RLB	Rip Hawkins (Minnesota)
Erich Barnes (N.Y. Giants)	LHB	Herb Adderley (Green Bay)
Dick Lynch (N.Y. Giants)	RHB	J. Whittenton (Green Bay)
C. Thomas (Pittsburgh)	LS	Richie Petitbon (Chicago)
Larry Wilson (St. Louis)	RS	Roosevelt Taylor (Chicago)

Head coaches—Allie Sherman (N.Y. Giants), East; George Halas (Chicago), West

East	3	0	0	14	—	17
West	7	7	14	3	—	31

East—FG Baker 30
West—Taylor 37 run (T. Davis kick)
West—Berry 4 pass from Unitas (T. Davis kick)
West—Whittenton 26 interception return (T. Davis kick)
West—Cogdill 5 pass from Unitas (T. Davis kick)
East—J. Brown 8 run (Baker kick)
West—FG T. Davis 38
East—J. Brown 3 run (Baker kick)
Attendance—67,242

1964 AFL

WEST 27, EAST 24

Cotton Davidson threw a 25-yard pass to Oakland teammate Art Powell in the final 43 seconds for a 27-24 West victory.

January 19, at San Diego

West	Starters, Offense	East
Art Powell (Oakland)	LE	Gino Cappelletti (Boston)
Jim Tyrer (Kansas City)	LT	Stew Barber (Buffalo)
Wayne Hawkins (Oakland)	LG	Billy Shaw (Buffalo)
Jim Otto (Oakland)	C	Bob Schmidt (Houston)
Ed Budde (Kansas City)	RG	Chuck Long (Boston)
Ron Mix (San Diego)	RT	Rich Micheal (Houston)
Dave Kocourek (San Diego)	RE	Ernie Warlick (Buffalo)
Tobin Rote (San Diego)	QB	Babe Parilli (Boston)
Clem Daniels (Oakland)	LH	Larry Garron (Boston)
Lance Alworth (San Diego)	RH	C. Hennigan (Houston)
Keith Lincoln (San Diego)	FB	Cookie Gilchrist (Buffalo)
	Starters, Defense	
Earl Faison (San Diego)	LE	Bob Dee (Boston)
Dave Costa (Oakland)	LT	Ed Husmann (Houston)
Ernie Ladd (San Diego)	RT	Tom Sestak (Buffalo)
Mel Branch (Kansas City)	RE	Larry Eisenhauer (Boston)
Emil Karas (San Diego)	LLB	Nick Buoniconti (Boston)
Archie Matsos (Buffalo)	MLB	Tom Addison (Boston)
Jim Fraser (Denver)	RLB	Larry Grantham (N.Y. Jets)
Fred Williamson (Oakland)	LCB	Galen Hall (N.Y. Jets)
A. Gonsoulin (Denver)	RCB	Tony Banfield (Houston)
J. Robinson (Kansas City)	LS	Jim Norton (Houston)
Dave Grayson (Kansas City)	RS	Fred Glick (Houston)

Head coaches—Mike Holovak (Boston), East; Sid Gillman (San Diego), West

West	0	3	14	10	—	27
East	10	14	0	0	—	24

East—Gilchrist 1 run (Cappelletti kick)
East—FG Cappelletti 35
West—FG Fraser 19
East—Garron 12 pass from Parilli (Cappelletti kick)
East—Mathis 3 pass from Parilli (Cappelletti kick)
West—Lincoln 64 run (Fraser kick)
West—Lowe 5 run (Fraser kick)
West—FG Fraser 7
West—Powell 25 pass from Davidson (Fraser kick)
Attendance—20,016

1965 NFL

WEST 34, EAST 14

The West outgained the East 300-47 in the first half and led 17-7 on a 15-yard field goal by Wayne Walker and two touchdowns by Bill Brown.

January 10, at Los Angeles

West	Starters, Offense	East
Raymond Berry (Baltimore)	LE	Paul Warfield (Cleveland)
Bob Vogel (Baltimore)	LT	Dick Schafrath (Cleveland)
John Gordy (Detroit)	LG	Vince Promuto (Washington)
Dick Szymanski (Baltimore)	C	Jim Ringo (Philadelphia)
Jim Parker (Baltimore)	RG	Ken Gray (St. Louis)
Forrest Gregg (Green Bay)	RT	C. Bradshaw (Pittsburgh)
Mike Ditka (Chicago)	RE	P. Retzlaff (Philadelphia)
Johnny Unitas (Baltimore)	QB	Frank Ryan (Cleveland)
Terry Barr (Detroit)	FL	Bobby Mitchell (Cleveland)
Lenny Moore (Baltimore)	HB	C. Taylor (Washington)
Jim Taylor (Green Bay)	FB	Jim Brown (Cleveland)
	Starters, Defense	
Willie Davis (Green Bay)	LE	Bill Glass (Cleveland)
Merlin Olsen (Los Angeles)	LT	Bob Lilly (Dallas)
Roger Brown (Detroit)	RT	F. Peters (Philadelphia)
Gino Marchetti (Baltimore)	RE	John Paluck (Washington)
Wayne Walker (Detroit)	LLB	M. Baughan (Philadelphia)
Ray Nitschke (Green Bay)	MLB	Myron Pottios (Pittsburgh)
Joe Fortunato (Chicago)	RLB	Jim Houston (Cleveland)
Bobby Boyd (Baltimore)	LHB	Pat Fischer (St. Louis)
Dick LeBeau (Detroit)	RHB	Irv Cross (Philadelphia)
Willie Wood (Green Bay)	LS	Mel Renfro (Dallas)
Ed Meador (Los Angeles)	RS	Paul Krause (Washington)

Head coaches—Blanton Collier (Cleveland), East; Don Shula (Baltimore), West

West	3	14	10	7	—	34
East	0	7	0	7	—	14

West—FG Walker 15
West—B. Brown 2 run (Walker kick)
East—Renfro 47 interception return (Baker kick)
West—B. Brown 2 pass from Tarkenton (Walker kick)
West—Nitschke 42 interception return (Walker kick)
West—FG Walker 28
West—Moore 2 run (Walker kick)
East—J. Brown 27 pass from Jurgensen (Baker kick)
Attendance—60,598

1965 AFL

WEST 38, EAST 14

The All-Star game was scheduled to be played in New Orleans but was moved the week of the game to Houston's Jeppesen Stadium. The West won its fourth consecutive game 38-14.

January 16, at Houston

West	Starters, Offense	East
Art Powell (Oakland)	LE	G. Cappeletti (Boston)
Jim Tyrer (Kansas City)	LT	Stew Barber (Buffalo)
Wayne Hawkins (Oakland)	LG	Billy Shaw (Buffalo)
Jim Otto (Oakland)	C	Jon Morris (Boston)
W. Sweeney (San Diego)	RG	Bob Talamini (Houston)
Ron Mix (San Diego)	RT	S. Plunkett (N.Y. Jets)
D. Kocourek (San Diego)	RE	E. Warlick (Buffalo)
Len Dawson (Kansas City)	QB	Babe Parilli (Boston)
C. Daniels (Oakland)	LH	Larry Garron (Boston)
Lance Alworth (San Diego)	RH	C. Hennigan (Houston)
K. Lincoln (San Diego)	FB	Sid Blanks (Houston)
	Starters, Defense	
B. Bell (Kansas City)	LE	Bob Dee (Boston)
J. Mays (Kansas City)	LT	Tom Sestak (Buffalo)
Ernie Ladd (San Diego)	RT	H. Antwine (Boston)
E. Faison (San Diego)	RE	L. Eisenhauer (Boston)
Jim Fraser (Denver)	LLB	Tom Addison (Boston)
C. Allen (San Diego)	MLB	N. Buoniconti (Boston)
F. Buncom (San Diego)	RLB	L. Grantham (N.Y. Jets)
D. Grayson (Kansas City)	LCB	Pete Jaquess (Houston)
W. Brown (Denver)	RCB	G. (Butch) Byrd (Buff.)
A. Gonsoulin (Denver)	LS	Fred Glick (Houston)
B. Hunt (Kansas City)	RS	G. Saimes (Buffalo)

Head coaches—Lou Saban (Buffalo), East; Sid Gillman (San Diego), West

West	7	10	14	7	—	38
East	0	14	0	0	—	14

West—Lincoln 73 pass from Dawson (Brooker kick)
West—Daniels 5 pass from Hadl (Brooker kick)
East—Blanks 5 run (Cappelletti kick)
West—FG Brooker 46
East—Buoniconti 17 fumble return (Cappelletti kick)
West—Lincoln 80 run (Brooker kick)
West—Alworth 7 pass from Hadl (Brooker kick)
West—Powell 17 pass from Hadl (Brooker kick)
Attendance—15,446

1966 AFL

AFL ALL-STARS 30, BUFFALO 19

A team of AFL All-Stars defeated the champion Bills.

January 15, at Houston

Buffalo	**Starters, Offense**	**All-Stars**
Paul Costa	LE	Art Powell (Oakland)
Stew Barber	LT	E. Danenhauer (Denver)
Billy Shaw	LG	B. Talamini (Houston)
Al Bemiller	C	Jim Otto (Oakland)
George Flint	RG	W. Hawkins (Oakland)
Dick Hudson	RT	J. Tyrer (Kansas City)
Ernie Warlick	RE	W. Frazier (Houston)
Jack Kemp	QB	John Hadl (San Diego)
Bob Smith	LH	Paul Lowe (S.D.)
Ed Rutowski	RH	C. Hennigan (Houston)
Billy Joe	FB	C. Gilchrist (Buffalo)
	Starters, Defense	
Tom Day	LE	J. Mays (Kansas City)
Cecil (Dud) Meredith	LT	E. Ladd (San Diego)
Jim Dunaway	RT	H. Antwine (Boston)
Ron McDole	RE	Earl Faison (San Diego)
Mike Stratton	LLB	S. Headrick (Kansas City)
Harry Jacobs	MLB	N. Buoniconti (Boston)
John Tracey	RLB	Bobby Bell (Kansas City)
Booker Edgerson	LCB	W. Brown (Denver)
George (Butch) Byrd	RCB	Dave Grayson (Oakland)
Hagood Clark	LS	K. Graham (San Diego)
George Saimes	RS	J. Robinson (Kansas City)

Head coaches—Sid Gillman (San Diego), AFL All-Stars; Lou Saban, Buffalo

Buffalo	10	3	0	6	—	19
AFL All-Stars	0	6	17	7	—	30

Buff —FG Gogolak 20
Buff —Saimes 61 fumble return (Gogolak kick)
All-Stars—FG Cappelletti 46
Buff —FG Gogolak 11
All-Stars—FG Cappelletti 14
All-Stars—FG Cappelletti 32
All-Stars—Lowe 1 run (Cappelletti kick)
All-Stars—Alworth 43 pass from Namath (Cappelletti kick)
All-Stars—Alworth 10 pass from Namath (Cappelletti kick)
Buff —Carlton 34 pass from Lamonica (run failed)
Attendance—35,572

1966 NFL

EAST 36, WEST 7

Fullback Jim Brown scored on three short runs in the first half as the East built a 23–0 lead. Brown was in his ninth Pro Bowl and his final NFL game.

January 16, at Los Angeles

East	**Starters, Offense**	**West**
S. Randle (St. Louis)	LE	D. Parks (San Francisco)
R. Brown (N.Y. Giants)	LT	Bob Vogel (Baltimore)
J. Wooten (Cleveland)	LG	Jim Parker (Baltimore)
Jim Ringo (Philadelphia)	C	B. Bosley (San Francisco)
G. Hickerson (Cle.)	RG	John Gordy (Detroit)
B. Brown (Philadelphia)	RT	W. Rock (San Francisco)
P. Retzlaff (Philadelphia)	RE	J. Mackey (Baltimore)
Frank Ryan (Cleveland)	QB	J. Brodie (San Francisco)
G. Collins (Cleveland)	FL	T. McDonald (Los Angeles)
T. Brown (Philadelphia)	HB	Gale Sayers (Chicago)
Jim Brown (Cleveland)	FB	K. Willard (San Francisco)
	Starters, Defense	
P. Wiggin (Cleveland)	LE	W. Davis (Green Bay)
S. Silas (St. Louis)	LT	M. Olsen (Los Angeles)
Bob Lilly (Dallas)	RT	Roger Brown (Detroit)
G. Andrie (Dallas)	RE	Doug Atkins (Chicago)
Jim Houston (Cleveland)	LLB	Joe Fortunato (Chicago)
D. Meinert (St. Louis)	MLB	Dick Butkus (Chicago)
M. Baughan (Phil.)	RLB	L. Roy Caffey (Green Bay)
P. Fischer (St. Louis)	LHB	H. Adderley (Green Bay)
I. Cross (Philadelphia)	RHB	Dick LeBeau (Detroit)
Mel Renfro (Dallas)	LS	E. Meador (Los Angeles)
P. Krause (Washington)	RS	W. Wood (Green Bay)

Head coaches—Blanton Collier (Cleveland), East; Vince Lombardi (Green Bay), West

East	10	13	3	10	—	36
West	0	0	0	7	—	7

East —FG Bakken 41
East —J. Brown 2 run (Bakken kick)
East —J. Brown 2 run (Bakken kick)
East —J. Brown 1 run (kick failed)
East —FG Bakken 36
East —FG Bakken 42
East —Renfro 20 interception return (Bakken kick)
West—McDonald 31 pass from Brodie (Walker kick)
Attendance — 60,124

1967 AFL

EAST 30, WEST 23

The East-West format was restored. Torrential rains flooded Oakland as the East rallied for a 30–23 win.

January 21, at Oakland

East	**Starters, Offense**	**West**
George Sauer (N.Y. Jets)	SE	Art Powell (Oakland)
Stew Barber (Buffalo)	LT	Jim Tyrer (Kansas City)
Billy Shaw (Buffalo)	LG	Wayne Hawkins (Oakland)
Jon Morris (Boston)	C	Jim Otto (Oakland)
Bob Talamini (Houston)	RG	Ed Budde (Kansas City)
S. Plunkett (N.Y. Jets)	RT	Ron Mix (San Diego)
Paul Costa (Buffalo)	TE	J. MacKinnon (San Diego)
Jack Kemp (Buffalo)	QB	Len Dawson (Kansas City)
Charley Frazier (Houston)	FL	Lance Alworth (San Diego)
Bobby Burnett (Buffalo)	HB	Clem Daniels (Oakland)
Matt Snell (N.Y. Jets)	FB	C. McClinton (Kansas City)
	Starters, Defense	
Larry Eisenhauer (Boston)	LE	Jerry Mays (Kansas City)
Jim Dunaway (Buffalo)	LT	Tom Keating (Oakland)
Houston Antwine (Boston)	RT	B. Buchanan (Kansas City)
Verlon Biggs (N.Y. Jets)	RE	Ben Davidson (Oakland)
Mike Stratton (Buffalo)	LLB	Bobby Bell (Kansas City)
Nick Buoniconti (Boston)	MLB	S. Headrick (Kansas City)
Larry Grantham (N.Y. Jets)	RLB	E.J. Holub (Kansas City)
W. K. Hicks (Houston)	LCB	K. McCloughan (Oakland)
G. (Butch) Byrd (Buffalo)	RCB	Dave Grayson (Oakland)
Willie West (Miami)	LS	A. Gonsoulin (Denver)
George Saimes (Buffalo)	RS	J. Robinson (Kansas City)

Head coaches—Mike Holovak (Boston), East; John Rauch (Oakland), West

East	0	0	16	14	—	30
West	9	7	7	0	—	23

West—McClinton 31 pass from Dawson (Van Raaphorst kick)
West—Safety, center snap out of end zone
West—Dixon 17 pass from Flores (Van Raaphorst kick)
East —Safety, Dawson tackled in end zone
West—Buchanan 39 fumble return (Van Raaphorst kick)
East —Biggs 50 interception return (Cappelletti kick)
East —Carlton 3 pass from Parilli (Cappelletti kick)
East —Burnett 12 run (Cappelletti kick)
East —Frazier 17 pass from Parilli (Cappelletti kick)
Attendance—18,876

1967 NFL

EAST 20, WEST 10

The East scored a 20–10 victory, although Gale Sayers of the West was named outstanding back after gaining 110 yards in 11 carries, breaking runs of 52 and 42 yards on a muddy field slowed by heavy rains.

Penalties spoiled 80- and 55-yard plays by Sayers.

January 22, at Los Angeles

West	**Starters, Offense**	**East**
Dave Parks (S.F.)	LE	Bob Hayes (Dallas)
G. Alderman (Minnesota)	LT	Dick Schafrath (Cleveland)
Howard Mudd (S.F.)	LG	John Wooten (Cleveland)
M. Tingelhoff (Minnesota)	C	Dave Manders (Dallas)
Milt Sunde (Minnesota)	RG	G. Hickerson (Cleveland)
Forrest Gregg (Green Bay)	RT	Bob Brown (Philadelphia)
John Mackey (Baltimore)	RE	Jackie Smith (St. Louis)
Johnny Unitas (Baltimore)	QB	Don Meredith (Dallas)
Pat Studstill (Detroit)	FL	Gary Collins (Cleveland)
Gale Sayers (Chicago)	HB	Leroy Kelly (Cleveland)
Dick Bass (Los Angeles)	FB	Don Perkins (Dallas)
	Starters, Defense	
D. (Deacon) Jones (L.A.)	LE	Joe Robb (St. Louis)
Merlin Olsen (Los Angeles)	LT	F. Peters (Philadelphia)
Roger Brown (Detroit)	RT	Bob Lilly (Dallas)
Willie Davis (Green Bay)	RE	George Andrie (Dallas)
Dave Robinson (Green Bay)	LLB	Chuck Howley (Dallas)
Dick Butkus (Chicago)	MLB	Tommy Nobis (Atlanta)
M. Baughan (Los Angeles)	RLB	John Brewer (Cleveland)
Herb Adderley (Green Bay)	LH	Cornell Green (Dallas)
Dick LeBeau (Detroit)	RH	Brady Keys (Pittsburgh)
Willie Wood (Green Bay)	LS	Mel Renfro (Dallas)
Richie Petitbon (Chicago)	RS	Larry Wilson (St. Louis)

Head coaches—Tom Landry (Dallas), East; George Allen (Los Angeles), West

West	0	0	3	7	—	10
East	6	14	0	0	—	20

East —FG Clark 18
East —FG Clark 17
East —Roland 1 run (Clark kick)
East —Collins 18 pass from Ryan (Clark kick)
West—FG Gossett 27
West—Willard 51 pass from Starr (Gossett kick)
Attendance—15,062

1968 AFL

EAST 25, WEST 24

A record AFL All-Star game crowd of 40,103 in the Gator Bowl in Jacksonville, Florida, saw the East win 25–24.

January 21, at Jacksonville, Florida

East	**Starters, Offense**	**West**
George Sauer (N.Y. Jets)	LE	Lance Alworth (San Diego)
Walt Suggs (Houston)	LT	Ron Mix (San Diego)
Bob Talamini (Houston)	LG	Walt Sweeney (San Diego)
Jon Morris (Boston)	C	Jim Otto (Oakland)
Billy Shaw (Buffalo)	RG	Wayne Hawkins (Oakland)
Don Oakes (Boston)	RT	Harry Schuh (Oakland)
Pete Lammons (N.Y. Jets)	TE	Fred Arbanas (Kansas City)
Joe Namath (N.Y. Jets)	QB	Daryle Lamonica (Oakland)
Don Maynard (N.Y. Jets)	FL	Al Denson (Denver)
Keith Lincoln (Buffalo)	RB	Mike Garrett (Kansas City)
Jim Nance (Boston)	RB	Hewritt Dixon (Oakland)
	Starters, Defense	
Ron McDole (Buffalo)	LE	Jerry Mays (Kansas City)
Jim Hunt (Boston)	LT	Tom Keating (Oakland)
Jim Dunaway (Buffalo)	RT	B. Buchanan (Kansas City)
Verlon Biggs (N.Y. Jets)	RE	Ben Davidson (Oakland)
Larry Grantham (N.Y. Jets)	LLB	Bobby Bell (Kansas City)
Nick Buoniconti (Boston)	MLB	Dan Conners (Oakland)
Mike Stratton (Buffalo)	RLB	Frank Buncom (San Diego)
Miller Farr (Houston)	LCB	Willie Brown (Oakland)
Dick Westmoreland (Miami)	RCB	L. (Speedy) Duncan (S.D.)
George Saimes (Buffalo)	LS	Kenny Graham (San Diego)
Jim Norton (Houston)	RS	J. Robinson (Kansas City)

Head coaches—Joe Collier (Buffalo), East; Lou Saban (Denver), West

East	3	10	0	12	—	25
West	7	14	0	3	—	24

East —FG Mercer 10
West—Duncan 90 punt return (Blanda kick)
West—Frazier 3 pass from Lamonica (Blanda kick)
East —Lammons 35 pass from Namath (Mercer kick)
West—Alworth 9 pass from Lamonica (Blanda kick)
East —FG Mercer 33
West—FG Blanda 28
East —Maynard 24 pass from Namath (pass failed)
East —Namath 1 run (run failed)
Attendance—40,103

1968 NFL

WEST 38, EAST 20

The West rallied for 21 points and beat the East 38–20.

January 21, at Los Angeles

East	**Starters, Offense**	**West**
Bob Hayes (Dallas)	LE	B. Dowler (Green Bay)
D. Schafrath (Clev.)	LT	B. Vogel (Baltimore)
Ken Gray (St. Louis)	LG	J. Kramer (Green Bay)
Jim Ringo (Philadelphia)	C	M. Tingelhoff (Minn.)
G. Hickerson (Clev.)	RG	Tom Mack (Los Angeles)
R. Neely (Dallas)	RT	F. Gregg (Green Bay)
J. Smith (Washington)	TE	John Mackey (Baltimore)
Don Meredith (Dallas)	QB	Johnny Unitas (Baltimore)
H. Jones (N.Y. Giants)	FL	W. Richardson (Balt.)
Leroy Kelly (Cleveland)	RB	Gale Sayers (Chicago)
Don Perkins (Dallas)	RB	Bill Brown (Minnesota)
	Starters, Defense	
Paul Wiggin (Cleveland)	LE	D. (Deacon) Jones (L.A.)
F. Peters (Philadelphia)	LT	M. Olsen (Los Angeles)
Bob Lilly (Dallas)	RT	Roger Brown (Los Angeles)
G. Andrie (Dallas)	RE	W. Davis, (Green Bay)
Chuck Howley (Dallas)	LLB	D. Robinson (Green Bay)
D. Meinert (St. Louis)	MLB	Dick Butkus (Chicago)
C. Hanburger (Washington)	RLB	M. Baughan (Los Angeles)
Cornell Green (Dallas)	LHB	H. Adderley (Green Bay)
D. Whitsell (New Orleans)	RHB	Bob Jeter (Green Bay)
J. Stovall (St. Louis)	LS	R. Petitbon (Chicago)
L. Wilson (St. Louis)	RS	Willie Wood (Green Bay)

Head coaches—Otto Graham (Washington), East; Don Shula (Baltimore), West

East	0	13	7	0	—	20
West	10	7	0	21	—	38

West—FG Chandler 26
West—Josephson 4 run (Chandler kick)
East —FG Bakken 45
East —FG Bakken 25
West—Farr 39 pass from Gabriel (Chandler kick)
East —Kelly 1 run (Bakken kick)
East —Taylor 9 pass from Meredith (Bakken kick)
West—Sayers 3 run (Chandler kick)
West—Petitbon 70 interception return (Chandler kick)
West—B. Brown 19 run (Chandler kick)
Attendance—53,289

1969 AFL

WEST 38, EAST 25

January 19, at Jacksonville, Florida

East	Starters, Offense	West
G. Sauer (N.Y. Jets)	LE	W. Wells (Oakland)
W. Hill (N.Y. Jets)	LT	Jim Tyrer (K.C.)
Billy Shaw (Buffalo)	LG	Ed Budde (Kansas City)
Jon Morris (Boston)	C	Jim Otto (Oakland)
D. Herman (N.Y. Jets)	RG	W. Sweeney (San Diego)
G.R. Hines (Houston)	RT	Ron Mix (San Diego)
Alvin Reed (Houston)	TE	J. MacKinnon (San Diego)
Joe Namath (N.Y. Jets)	QB	John Hadl (San Diego)
D. Maynard (N.Y. Jets)	FL	Lance Alworth (San Diego)
Jim Kiick (Miami)	RB	Paul Robinson (Cin.)
H. Granger (Houston)	RB	H. Dixon (Oakland)
	Starters, Defense	
G. Philbin (N.Y. Jets)	LE	J. Mays (Kansas City)
J. Dunaway (Buffalo)	LT	Dan Birdwell (Oakland)
H. Antwine (Boston)	RT	B. Buchanan (Kansas City)
V. Biggs (N.Y. Jets)	RE	Ben Davidson (Oakland)
G. Webster (Houston)	LLB	Bobby Bell (K.C.)
G. Boyette (Houston)	MLB	D. Conners (Oakland)
M. Stratton (Buffalo)	RLB	Jim Lynch (Kansas City)
M. Farr (Houston)	LCB	G. Atkinson (Oakland)
G. (Butch) Byrd (Buffalo)	RCB	W. Brown (Oakland)
Ken Houston (Houston)	LS	K. Graham (San Diego)
G. Saimes (Buffalo)	RS	J. Robinson (Kansas City)

Head coaches—George Wilson (Miami), East; Lou Saban (Denver), West

West	3	0	10	25	— 38
East	3	16	3	3	— 25

East—FG Turner 27
West—FG Stenerud 51
East—Kiick 2 run (Turner kick)
East—FG Turner 16
East—FG Turner 19
East—FG Turner 13
West—Trumpy 6 pass from Dawson (Stenerud kick)
East—FG Turner 18
West—FG Stenerud 30
East—FG Turner 21
West—Dixon 1 run (Stenerud kick)
West—Robinson 1 run (Robinson run)
West—Robinson 1 run (Stenerud kick)
West—FG Stenerud 32
Attendance—41,058

1969 NFL

WEST 10, EAST 7

The Los Angeles Rams' delegation played the major role in the West's 10–7 victory. George Allen was head coach, quarterback Roman Gabriel the outstanding back, and defensive tackle Merlin Olsen the outstanding lineman.

With 3:52 remaining in the game, Gabriel started the West on a march to the winning touchdown.

January 19, at Los Angeles

East	Starters, Offense	West
H. Jones (N.Y. Giants)	LE	C. McNeil (San Francisco)
Bob Reynolds (St. Louis)	LT	C. Cowan (Los Angeles)
John Niland (Dallas)	LG	Tom Mack (Los Angeles)
Len Hauss (Washington)	C	M. Tingelhoff (Minn.)
G. Hickerson (Cleveland)	RG	H. Mudd (San Francisco)
Bob Brown (Philadelphia)	RT	F. Gregg (Green Bay)
J. Smith (St. Louis)	TE	J. Mackey (Baltimore)
Don Meredith (Dallas)	QB	E. Morrall (Baltimore)
P. Warfield (Cleveland)	FL	W. Richardson (Baltimore)
Leroy Kelly (Cleveland)	RB	Tom Matte (Baltimore)
Don Perkins (Dallas)	RB	Ken Willard (San Francisco)
	Starters, Defense	
Don Brumm (St. Louis)	LE	D. (Deacon) Jones (L.A.)
W. Johnson (Cleveland)	LT	M. Olsen (Los Angeles)
Bob Lilly (Dallas)	RT	Alan Page (Minnesota)
George Andrie (Dallas)	RE	Jim Marshall (Minnesota)
C. Howley (Dallas)	LLB	Mike Curtis (Baltimore)
L.R. Jordan (Dallas)	MLB	Dick Butkus (Chicago)
C. Hanburger (Washington)	RLB	M. Baughan (Los Angeles)
E. Barnes (Cleveland)	LHB	Lem Barney (Detroit)
Mel Renfro (Dallas)	RHB	K. Alexander (San Fran.)
E. Kellerman (Cleveland)	LS	W. Wood (Green Bay)
L. Wilson (St. Louis)	RS	R. Taylor (Chicago)

Head coaches—Tom Landry (Dallas), East; George Allen (Los Angeles), West

East	0	0	7	0	— 7
West	0	3	0	7	— 10

West—FG Gossett 20
East—Warfield 3 pass from Meredith (Baker kick)
West—Brown 1 run (Gossett kick)
Attendance—32,050

1970 AFL

WEST 26, EAST 3

The Houston Astrodome was the site of the final AFL All-Star game. John Hadl completed 18 of 26 passes for 224 yards and one touchdown in the West's 26–3 victory.

January 17, at Houston

East	Starters, Offense	West
G. Sauer (N.Y. Jets)	WR	F. Biletnikoff (Oakland)
W. Hill (N.Y. Jets)	LT	J. Tyrer (Kansas City)
Billy Shaw (Buffalo)	LG	Ed Budde (Kansas City)
Jon Morris (Boston)	C	Jim Otto (Oakland)
Dave Herman (N.Y. Jets)	RG	Walt Sweeney (San Diego)
G.R. Hines (Houston)	RT	Harry Schuh (Oakland)
Alvin Reed (Houston)	TE	Billy Cannon (Oakland)
Ron Sellers (Boston)	WR	Lance Alworth (San Diego)
M. Talliaferro (Boston)	QB	John Hadl (San Diego)
Carl Garrett (Boston)	RB	Dickie Post (San Diego)
Matt Snell (N.Y. Jets)	RB	R. Holmes (Kansas City)
	Starters, Defense	
G. Philbin (N.Y. Jets)	LE	Rich Jackson (Denver)
Jim Hunt (Boston)	LT	Curley Culp (Kansas City)
J. Elliott (N.Y. Jets)	RT	B. Buchanan (Kansas City)
Elvin Bethea (Houston)	RE	Steve DeLong (San Diego)
G. Boyette (Houston)	LLB	Bobby Bell (Kansas City)
N. Buoniconti (Miami)	MLB	W. Lanier (Kansas City)
L. Grantham (N.Y. Jets)	RLB	Gus Otto (Oakland)
Miller Farr (Houston)	LCB	J. Marsalis (Kansas City)
G. (Butch) Byrd (Buffalo)	RCB	Willie Brown (Oakland)
Ken Houston (Houston)	LS	Kenny Graham (San Diego)
Don Webb (Boston)	RS	Dave Grayson (Oakland)

Head coaches—George Wilson (Miami), East; Lou Saban (Denver), West

East	0	0	3	0	— 3
West	13	0	3	10	— 26

West—Post 1 run (kick failed)
West—Alworth 21 pass from Hadl (Stenerud kick)
West—FG Stenerud 38
East—FG Turner 44
West—FG Stenerud 30
West—Livingston 11 run (Stenerud kick)
Attendance—30,170

1970 NFL

WEST 16, EAST 13

Almost replaying the final minutes of the 1969 game, Los Angeles Rams quarterback Roman Gabriel marched the West 55 yards to the winning touchdown, overcoming a 13–9 East lead.

January 18, at Los Angeles

East	Starters, Offense	West
P. Warfield (Cleveland)	WR	G. Washington (Minn.)
Bob Reynolds (St. Louis)	LT	G. Alderman (Minnesota)
John Niland (Dallas)	LG	Tom Mack (Los Angeles)
Len Hauss (Washington)	C	M. Tingelhoff (Minnesota)
G. Hickerson (Cleveland)	RG	G. Gillingham (Green Bay)
Ralph Neely (Dallas)	RT	C. Cowan (Los Angeles)
J. Smith (Washington)	TE	C. Sanders (Detroit)
R. Jefferson (Pitt.)	WR	C. Dale (Green Bay)
Bill Nelsen (Cleveland)	QB	R. Gabriel (Los Angeles)
L. Brown (Washington)	RB	Gale Sayers (Chicago)
Leroy Kelly (Cleveland)	RB	Tom Matte (Baltimore)
	Starters, Defense	
T. Rossovich (Phil.)	LE	Carl Eller (Minnesota)
W. Johnson (Cleveland)	LT	M. Olsen (Los Angeles)
Bob Lilly (Dallas)	RT	Alan Page (Minnesota)
G. Andrie (Dallas)	RE	J. Marshall (Minnesota)
C. Hanburger (Washington)	LLB	D. Robinson (Green Bay)
Dave Lloyd (Philadelphia)	MLB	Dick Butkus (Chicago)
Chuck Howley (Dallas)	RLB	D. Wilcox (S.F.)
Pat Fischer (Wash.)	LCB	Lem Barney (Detroit)
Mel Renfro (Dallas)	RCB	Bob Jeter (Green Bay)
J. Stovall (St. Louis)	LS	Rick Volk (Baltimore)
L. Wilson (St. Louis)	RS	P. Krause (Minnesota)

Head coaches—Tom Fears (New Orleans), East; Norm Van Brocklin (Atlanta), West

East	7	6	0	0	— 13
West	0	7	0	9	— 16

East—Kelly 10 run (Dempsey kick)
East—FG Dempsey 46
West—Gabriel 1 run (Etter kick)
East—FG Dempsey 27
West—Safety, Brezina tackled Walden in end zone
West—Dale 28 pass from Gabriel (Etter kick)
Attendance—57,786

1971

NFC 27, AFC 6

Dallas's Mel Renfro broke open the first game between the all-stars of the American Football Conference and National Football Conference when he returned punts 82 and 56 yards for touchdowns.

January 24, at Los Angeles

AFC	Starters, Offense	NFC
Warren Wells (Oakland)	WR	G. Washington (S.F.)
Jim Tyrer (Kansas City)	LT	C. Cowan (Los Angeles)
Ed Budde (Kansas City)	LG	Tom Mack (Los Angeles)
Jim Otto (Oakland)	C	Ed Flanagan (Detroit)
Walt Sweeney (San Diego)	RG	G. Gillingham (Green Bay)
Harry Schuh (Oakland)	RT	Ernie McMillan (St. Louis)
R. Chester (Oakland)	TE	Charlie Sanders (Detroit)
Marlin Briscoe (Buffalo)	WR	G. Washington (Minnesota)
Daryle Lamonica (Oakland)	QB	J. Brodie (San Francisco)
Leroy Kelly (Cleveland)	RB	Larry Brown (Washington)
Hewritt Dixon (Oakland)	RB	MacArthur Lane (St. Louis)
	Starters, Defense	
C. (Bubba) Smith (Balt.)	LE	D. (Deacon) Jones (L.A.)
Joe Greene (Pittsburgh)	LT	Alan Page (Minnesota)
B. Buchanan (Kansas City)	RT	Bob Lilly (Dallas)
Rich Jackson (Denver)	RE	Carl Eller (Minnesota)
Bobby Bell (Kansas City)	LLB	L. Stallings (St. Louis)
W. Lanier (Kansas City)	MLB	Dick Butkus (Chicago)
Andy Russell (Pittsburgh)	RLB	Fred Carr (Green Bay)
Jim Marsalis (Kansas City)	LCB	J. Johnson (San Francisco)
Willie Brown (Oakland)	RCB	Mel Renfro (Dallas)
Ken Houston (Houston)	LS	Willie Wood (Green Bay)
J. Robinson (Kansas City)	RS	Larry Wilson (St. Louis)

Head coaches—John Madden (Oakland), AFC; Dick Nolan (San Francisco), NFC

AFC	0	3	3	0	— 6
NFC	0	3	10	14	— 27

AFC—FG Stenerud 37
NFC—FG Cox 13
NFC—Osborn 23 pass from Brodie (Cox kick)
NFC—FG Cox 35
AFC—FG Stenerud 16
NFC—Renfro 82 punt return (Cox kick)
NFC—Renfro 56 punt return (Cox kick)
Attendance—48,222

1972

AFC 26, NFC 13

Len Dawson entered the game as quarterback in the third quarter and directed the AFC to two touchdowns and three field goals for a 26–13 victory.

January 23, at Los Angeles

NFC	Starters, Offense	AFC
G. Washington (S.F.)	WR	Fred Biletnikoff (Oakland)
Ron Yary (Minnesota)	LT	Jim Tyrer (Kansas City)
John Niland (Dallas)	LG	Ed Budde (Kansas City)
F. Blue (San Francisco)	C	Bill Curry (Baltimore)
G. Gillingham (Green Bay)	RG	Walt Sweeney (San Diego)
George Kunz (Atlanta)	RT	Winston Hill (N.Y. Jets)
T. Kwalick (San Francisco)	TE	R. Chester (Oakland)
Dick Gordon (Chicago)	WR	Paul Warfield (Miami)
Roger Staubach (Dallas)	QB	Bob Griese (Miami)
Larry Brown (Washington)	RB	Larry Csonka (Miami)
Steve Owens (Detroit)	RB	Floyd Little (Denver)
	Starters, Defense	
Claude Humphrey (Atlanta)	LE	C. (Bubba) Smith (Balt.)
Alan Page (Minnesota)	LT	Joe Greene (Pittsburgh)
Bob Lilly (Dallas)	RT	B. Buchanan (Kansas City)
C. Hardman (S. F.)	RE	Elvin Bethea (Houston)
D. Wilcox (San Francisco)	LLB	Ted Hendricks (Baltimore)
Dick Butkus (Chicago)	MLB	Mike Curtis (Baltimore)
Chuck Howley (Dallas)	RLB	Bobby Bell (Kansas City)
J. Johnson (San Francisco)	LCB	E. Thomas (Kansas City)
Roger Wehrli (St. Louis)	RCB	Willie Brown (Oakland)
Cornell Green (Dallas)	LS	Ken Houston (Houston)
Mel Renfro (Dallas)	RS	Rick Volk (Baltimore)

Head coaches—Don McCafferty (Baltimore), AFC; Dick Nolan (San Francisco), NFC

NFC	0	6	0	7	— 13
AFC	0	3	13	10	— 26

NFC—Grim 50 pass from Landry (kick failed)
AFC—FG Stenerud 25
AFC—FG Stenerud 23
AFC—FG Stenerud 48
AFC—Morin 5 pass from Dawson (Stenerud kick)
AFC—FG Stenerud 42
NFC—V. Washington 2 run (Knight kick)
AFC—F. Little 6 run (Stenerud kick)
Attendance—53,647

1973

AFC 33, NFC 28

The Pro Bowl left Los Angeles after 22 years.

January 21, at Irving, Texas

AFC	Starters, Offense	NFC
Otis Taylor (Kansas City)	WR	Gene Washington (S.F.)
Art Shell (Oakland)	LT	Ron Yary (Minnesota)
Gene Upshaw (Oakland)	LG	John Niland (Dallas)
Jim Otto (Oakland)	C	Forrest Blue (S.F.)
Larry Little (Miami)	RG	Tom Mack (Los Angeles)
Winston Hill (N.Y. Jets)	RT	Rayfield Wright (Dallas)
Raymond Chester (Oakland)	TE	Ted Kwalick (S.F.)
Gary Garrison (San Diego)	WR	John Gilliam (Minnesota)
Daryle Lamonica (Oakland)	QB	Billy Kilmer (Washington)
O. J. Simpson (Buffalo)	RB	Ron Johnson (N.Y. Giants)
Franco Harris (Pittsburgh)	RB	John Brockington (G.B.)
	Starters, Defense	
Deacon Jones (San Diego)	LE	Claude Humphrey (Atlanta)
Joe Greene (Pittsburgh)	LT	Merlin Olsen (Los Angeles)
Mike Reid (Cincinnati)	RT	Bob Brown (Green Bay)
Elvin Bethea (Houston)	RE	Coy Bacon (Los Angeles)
Ted Hendricks (Baltimore)	LLB	Dave Wilcox (S.F.)
Willie Lanier (Kansas City)	MLB	Tommy Nobis (Atlanta)
Andy Russell (Pittsburgh)	RLB	Chris Hanburger (Wash.)
Robert James (Buffalo)	LCB	Jimmy Johnson (S.F.)
Willie Brown (Oakland)	RCB	Lem Barney (Detroit)
Ken Houston (Houston)	LS	Cornell Green (Dallas)
Jake Scott (Miami)	RS	Bill Bradley (Philadelphia)

Head coaches—Chuck Noll (Pittsburgh), AFC; Tom Landry (Dallas), NFC

AFC	0	10	10	13	—	33
NFC	14	0	0	14	—	28

NFC—Brockington 1 run (Marcol kick)
NFC—Brockington 3 pass from Kilmer (Marcol kick)
AFC—Simpson 7 run (Gerela kick)
AFC—FG Gerela 18
AFC—FG Gerela 22
AFC—Hubbard 11 run (Gerela kick)
AFC—Taylor 5 pass from Lamonica (kick failed)
AFC—Bell 12 interception return (Gerela kick)
NFC—Brockington 1 run (Marcol kick)
NFC—Kwalick 12 pass from Snead (Marcol kick)
Attendance—47,879

1974

AFC 15, NFC 13

Garo Yepremian kicked five field goals in five attempts, the last with 21 seconds remaining, for all of the AFC's points in a 15-13 victory.

January 20, at Kansas City

NFC	Starters, Offense	AFC
Charley Taylor (Washington)	WR	Isaac Curtis (Cincinnati)
Ron Yary (Minnesota)	LT	Art Shell (Oakland)
Tom Mack (Los Angeles)	LG	Gene Upshaw (Oakland)
Forrest Blue (S.F.)	C	Jim Langer (Miami)
John Niland (Dallas)	RG	Larry Little (Miami)
Rayfield Wright (Dallas)	RT	Winston Hill (N.Y. Jets)
Ted Kwalick (S.F.)	TE	Riley Odoms (Denver)
Harold Jackson (L.A.)	WR	Fred Biletnikoff (Oakland)
John Hadl (Los Angeles)	QB	Ken Stabler (Oakland)
Chuck Foreman (Minn.)	RB	O. J. Simpson (Buffalo)
John Brockington (G.B.)	RB	Marv Hubbard (Oakland)
	Starters, Defense	
John Zook (Atlanta)	LE	L. C. Greenwood (Pitt.)
Merlin Olsen (Los Angeles)	LT	Joe Greene (Pittsburgh)
Alan Page (Minnesota)	RT	Paul Smith (Denver)
Claude Humphrey (Atlanta)	RE	Elvin Bethea (Houston)
Dave Wilcox (S.F.)	LLB	Ted Hendricks (Baltimore)
Jeff Siemon (Minnesota)	MLB	Willie Lanier (Kansas City)
Chris Hanburger (Wash.)	RLB	Andy Russell (Pittsburgh)
Lem Barney (Detroit)	LCB	Clarence Scott (Cleveland)
Mel Renfro (Dallas)	RCB	Willie Brown (Oakland)
Ken Houston (Washington)	LS	Dick Anderson (Miami)
Paul Krause (Minnesota)	RS	Jake Scott (Miami)

Head coach—John Madden (Oakland), AFC; Tom Landry (Dallas), NFC

NFC	0	10	0	3	—	13
AFC	3	3	3	6	—	15

AFC—FG Yepremian 16
NFC—FG Mike-Mayer 27
NFC—McCutcheon 14 pass from Gabriel (Mike-Mayer kick)
AFC—FG Yepremian 37
AFC—FG Yepremian 27
AFC—FG Yepremian 41
NFC—FG Mike-Mayer 21
AFC—FG Yepremian 42
Attendance—51,484

1975

NFC 17, AFC 10

James Harris, a pregame roster replacement for the injured Fran Tarkenton, and a second-quarter quarterback substitute for the injured Jim Hart, threw two eight-yard touchdown passes in the fourth quarter and the NFC won the first nighttime Pro Bowl game.

January 20, at Miami

NFC	Starters, Offense	AFC
Charley Taylor (Washington)	WR	Cliff Branch (Oakland)
Ron Yary (Minnesota)	LT	Art Shell (Oakland)
Tom Mack (Los Angeles)	LG	Gene Upshaw (Oakland)
Jeff Van Note (Atlanta)	C	Jim Langer (Miami)
Gale Gillingham (G.B.)	RG	Larry Little (Miami)
Rayfield Wright (Dallas)	RT	Russ Washington (S.D.)
Charle Young (Philadelphia)	TE	Riley Odoms (Denver)
Drew Pearson (Dallas)	WR	Isaac Curtis (Cincinnati)
Jim Hart (St. Louis)	QB	Ken Stabler (Oakland)
Chuck Foreman (Minnesota)	RB	O. J. Simpson (Buffalo)
L. McCutcheon (L.A.)	RB	Otis Armstrong (Denver)
	Starters, Defense	
Carl Eller (Minnesota)	LE	L. C. Greenwood (Pitt.)
Merlin Olsen (Los Angeles)	LT	Joe Greene (Pittsburgh)
Alan Page (Minnesota)	RT	Jerry Sherk (Cleveland)
Claude Humphrey (Atlanta)	RE	Bill Stanfill (Miami)
Ted Hendricks (Green Bay)	LLB	Jack Ham (Pittsburgh)
Bill Bergey (Philadelphia)	MLB	Mike Curtis (Baltimore)
Chris Hanburger (Wash.)	RLB	Andy Russell (Pittsburgh)
Willie Buchanan (G.B.)	LCB	Robert James (Buffalo)
Roger Wehrli (St. Louis)	RCB	Emmitt Thomas (K.C.)
Ken Houston (Washington)	LS	Dick Anderson (Miami)
Paul Krause (Minnesota)	RS	Jack Tatum (Oakland)

Head coaches—John Madden (Oakland), AFC; Chuck Knox (Los Angeles), NFC

NFC	0	3	0	14	—	17
AFC	0	0	10	0	—	10

NFC—FG Marcol 33
AFC—Warfield 32 pass from Griese (Gerela kick)
AFC—FG Gerela 33
NFC—Gray 8 pass from James Harris (Marcol kick)
NFC—Taylor 8 pass from James Harris (Marcol kick)
Attendance—26,484

1976

NFC 23, AFC 20

Quarterback replacement Mike Boryla threw two touchdown passes for a 23-20 NFC victory. Billy Johnson had 233 yards in kick returns for the AFC.

January 26, at New Orleans

AFC	Starters, Offense	NFC
Isaac Curtis (Cincinnati)	WR	Mel Gray (St. Louis)
Art Shell (Oakland)	LT	Ron Yary (Minnesota)
Gene Upshaw (Oakland)	LG	Ed White (Minnesota)
Jim Langer (Miami)	C	Tom Banks (St. Louis)
Bob Kuechenberg (Miami)	RG	Conrad Dobler (St. Louis)
George Kunz (Baltimore)	RT	Dan Dierdorf (St. Louis)
Riley Odoms (Denver)	TE	Charle Young (Philadelphia)
Lynn Swann (Pittsburgh)	WR	John Gilliam (Minnesota)
Ken Anderson (Cincinnati)	QB	Jim Hart (St. Louis)
O. J. Simpson (Buffalo)	RB	Terry Metcalf (St. Louis)
Franco Harris (Pittsburgh)	RB	Chuck Foreman (Minnesota)
	Starters, Defense	
L. C. Greenwood (Pitt.)	LE	Jack Youngblood (L.A.)
Joe Greene (Pittsburgh)	LT	Merlin Olsen (Los Angeles)
Jerry Sherk (Cleveland)	RT	Alan Page (Minnesota)
John Dutton (Baltimore)	RE	Cedrick Hardman (S.F.)
Jack Ham (Pittsburgh)	LLB	Isiah Robertson (L.A.)
Jack Lambert (Pittsburgh)	MLB	Jeff Siemon (Minnesota)
Andy Russell (Pittsburgh)	RLB	Chris Hanburger (Wash.)
Lemar Parrish (Cincinnati	LCB	Lem Barney (Detroit)
Mel Blount (Pittsburgh)	RCB	Roger Wehrli (St. Louis)
Mike Wagner (Pittsburgh)	LS	Ken Houston (Washington)
Jake Scott (Miami)	RS	Cliff Harris (Dallas)

Head coaches—John Madden (Oakland), AFC; Chuck Knox (Los Angeles), NFC

AFC	0	13	0	7	—	20
NFC	0	0	9	14	—	23

AFC—FG Stenerud 20
AFC—FG Stenerud 35
AFC—Burrough 64 pass from Pastorini (Stenerud kick)
NFC—FG Bakken 42
NFC—Foreman 4 pass from Hart (kick blocked)
AFC—Johnson 90 punt return (Stenerud kick)
NFC—Metcalf 14 pass from Boryla (Bakken kick)
NFC—Gray 8 pass from Boryla (Bakken kick)
Attendance—32,108

1977

AFC 24, NFC 14

The AFC intercepted six passes—five by members of the Pittsburgh Steelers, including two by cornerback Mel Blount—in a 24-4 victory. The crowd of 63,214 was the largest since 67,242 in 1964.

January 17, at Seattle

NFC	Starters, Offense	AFC
Mel Gray (St. Louis)	WR	Cliff Branch (Oakland)
Ron Yary (Minnesota)	LT	Art Shell (Oakland)
Ed White (Minnesota)	LG	John Hannah (New England)
Tom Banks (St. Louis)	C	Jim Langer (Miami)
Conrad Dobler (St. Louis)	RG	Joe DeLamielleure (Buffalo)
Dan Dierdorf (St. Louis)	RT	George Kunz (Baltimore)
Billy Joe DuPree (Dallas)	TE	Dave Casper (Oakland)
Drew Pearson (Dallas)	WR	Isaac Curtis (Cincinnati)
Roger Staubach (Dallas)	QB	Bert Jones (Baltimore)
Walter Payton (Chicago)	RB	O. J. Simpson (Buffalo)
Delvin Williams (S.F.)	RB	Lydell Mitchell (Baltimore)
	Starters, Defense	
Tommy Hart (San Francisco)	LE	Coy Bacon (Cincinnati)
Cleveland Elam (S.F.)	LT	Curley Culp (Houston)
Wally Chambers (Chicago)	RT	Jerry Sherk (Cleveland)
Jack Youngblood (L.A.)	RE	John Dutton (Baltimore)
Isiah Robertson (L.A.)	LLB	Jack Ham (Pittsburgh)
Bill Bergey (Philadelphia)	MLB	Jack Lambert (Pittsburgh)
Brad Van Pelt (N.Y. Giants)	RLB	Robert Brazile (Houston)
Monte Jackson (L.A.)	LCB	Lemar Parrish (Cincinnati)
Roger Wehrli (St. Louis)	RCB	Mel Blount (Pittsburgh)
Ken Houston (Washington)	LS	Tom Casanova (Cincinnati)
Cliff Harris (Dallas)	RS	Glen Edwards (Pittsburgh)

Coaches—John Madden (Oakland), AFC; Chuck Knox (Los Angeles), NFC.

NFC	0	14	0	0	—	14
AFC	10	7	0	7	—	24

AFC—Simpson 3 run (Linhart kick)
AFC—FG Linhart 31
NFC—Thomas 15 run (Bakken kick)
AFC—Joiner 12 pass from Anderson (Linhart kick)
NFC—McCutcheon 1 run (Bakken kick)
AFC—Branch 27 pass from Anderson (Linhart kick)
Attendance—63,214

1978

NFC 14, AFC 13

Quarterback Jim Hart replaced starter Pat Haden in the fourth quarter and completed five of six passes in a 63-yard drive that led to the winning touchdown. Player of the game Walter Payton gained 77 yards and scored the winning touchdown.

January 23, at Tampa

AFC	Starters, Offense	NFC
Lynn Swann (Pittsburgh)	WR	Sammy White (Minnesota)
Art Shell (Oakland)	LT	Dan Dierdorf (St. Louis)
Gene Upshaw (Oakland)	LG	Ed White (Minnesota)
Jim Langer (Miami)	C	Tom Banks (St. Louis)
Joe DeLamielleure (Buffalo)	RG	Conrad Dobler (St. Louis)
George Kunz (Baltimore)	RT	Ron Yary (Minnesota)
Dave Casper (Oakland)	TE	Billy Joe DuPree (Dallas)
Nat Moore (Miami)	WR	Drew Pearson (Dallas)
Bob Griese (Miami)	QB	Pat Haden (Los Angeles)
Franco Harris (Pittsburgh)	RB	L. McCutcheon (L.A.)
Lydell Mitchell (Baltimore)	RB	Walter Payton (Chicago)
	Starters, Defense	
John Dutton (Baltimore)	LE	Jack Youngblood (L.A.)
Mike Barnes (Baltimore)	LT	Cleveland Elam (San Fran.)
Curley Culp (Houston)	RT	Larry Brooks (Los Angeles)
Lyle Alzado (Denver)	RE	Harvey Martin (Dallas)
Jack Ham (Pittsburgh)	LLB	Brad Van Pelt (N.Y. Giants)
Randy Gradishar (Denver)	MLB	Bill Bergey (Philadelphia)
Robert Brazile (Houston)	RLB	Isiah Robertson (L.A.)
Lemar Parrish (Cincinnati)	LCB	Rolland Lawrence (Atlanta)
Mike Haynes (New England)	RCB	Roger Wehrli (St. Louis)
Billy Thompson (Denver)	LS	Charlie Waters (Dallas)
Tom Casanova (Cincinnati)	RS	Cliff Harris (Dallas)

Coaches—Ted Marchibroda (Baltimore), AFC; Chuck Knox (Los Angeles), NFC

AFC	3	10	0	0	—	13
NFC	0	0	7	7	—	14

AFC—FG Linhart 21
AFC—Branch 10 pass from Stabler (Linhart kick)
AFC—FG Linhart 39
NFC—Metcalf 4 pass from Haden (Herrera kick)
NFC—Payton 1 run (Herrera kick)
Attendance—51,337

1979

NFC 13, AFC 7

Quarterback Roger Staubach completed 9 of 15 passes for 125 yards, including one for the winning touchdown to Dallas Cowboys teammate Tony Hill in the third quarter. Ahmad Rashad tied a Pro Bowl record by catching five passes. The victory gave the NFC a 5-4 advantage in AFC-NFC Pro Bowl games.

January 29, at Los Angeles

NFC	Starters, Offense		AFC
Harold Carmichael (Phil.)	WR		Lynn Swann (Pittsburgh)
Doug France (Los Angeles)	LT		Leon Gray (New England)
Bob Young (St. Louis)	LG		John Hannah (New England)
Tom Banks (St. Louis)	C		Mike Webster (Pittsburgh)
Dennis Harrah (Los Angeles)	RG		Joe DeLamielleure (Buffalo)
Dan Dierdorf (St. Louis)	RT		Russ Washington (S.D.)
Billy Joe DuPree (Dallas)	TE		Dave Casper (Oakland)
Ahmad Rashad (Minnesota)	WR		Wesley Walker (N.Y. Jets)
Roger Staubach (Dallas)	QB		Terry Bradshaw (Pittsburgh)
Tony Dorsett (Dallas)	RB		Earl Campbell (Houston)
Walter Payton (Chicago)	RB		Delvin Williams (Miami)
	Starters, Defense		
Jack Youngblood (L.A.)	LE		Lyle Alzado (Denver)
Doug English (Detroit)	LT		Joe Greene (Pittsburgh)
Dave Pear (Tampa Bay)	RT		Louie Kelcher (San Diego)
Al Baker (Detroit)	RE		Elvin Bethea (Houston)
Matt Blair (Minnesota)	LLB		Robert Brazile (Houston)
Bill Bergey (Philadelphia)	MLB		Randy Gradishar (Denver)
Brad Van Pelt (N.Y. Giants)	RLB		Jack Ham (Pittsburgh)
Willie Buchanon (Green Bay)	LCB		Louis Wright (Denver)
Pat Thomas (Los Angeles)	RCB		Mike Haynes (New England)
Charlie Waters (Dallas)	LS		Billy Thompson (Denver)
Cliff Harris (Dallas)	RS		Thom Darden (Cleveland)

Coaches—Chuck Fairbanks (New England), AFC; Bud Grant (Minnesota), NFC

NFC	0	6	7	0	—	13
AFC	0	7	0	0	—	7

NFC—Montgomery 2 run (kick failed)
AFC—Largent 8 pass from Griese (Yepremian kick)
NFC—T. Hill 19 pass from Staubach (Corral kick)
Attendance—46,281

1980

NFC 37, AFC 27

The game was the first played in a non-NFL city.

January 27, at Honolulu

AFC	Starters, Offense		NFC
John Stallworth (Pittsburgh)	WR		Ahmad Rashad (Minnesota)
Leon Gray (Houston)	LT		Stan Walters (Philadelphia)
John Hannah (New England)	LG		Bob Young (St. Louis)
Mike Webster (Pittsburgh)	C		Rich Saul (Los Angeles)
Joe DeLamielleure (Buffalo)	RG		Dennis Harrah (Los Angeles)
Russ Washington (S.D.)	RT		Pat Donovan (Dallas)
Dave Casper (Oakland)	TE		Henry Childs (New Orleans)
John Jefferson (San Diego)	WR		Harold Carmichael (Phil.)
Dan Fouts (San Diego)	QB		Roger Staubach (Dallas)
Earl Campbell (Houston)	RB		Ottis Anderson (St. Louis)
Franco Harris (Pittsburgh)	RB		Walter Payton (Chicago)
	Starters, Defense		
L. C. Greenwood (Pittsburgh)	LE		Jack Youngblood (L.A.)
Joe Greene (Pittsburgh)	LT		Charlie Johnson (Phil.)
Bob Baumhower (Miami)	RT		Randy White (Dallas)
Fred Dean (San Diego)	RE		Harvey Martin (Dallas)
Kim Bokamper (Miami)	LLB		Brad Van Pelt (N.Y. Giants)
Jack Lambert (Pittsburgh)	MLB		Harry Carson (N.Y. Giants)
Robert Brazile (Houston)	RLB		Jim Youngblood (L.A.)
Louis Wright (Denver)	LCB		Lemar Parrish (Washington)
Mike Haynes (New England)	RCB		Roger Wehrli (St. Louis)
Donnie Shell (Pittsburgh)	LS		Randy Logan (Philadelphia)
Mike Reinfeldt (Houston)	RS		Tom Myers (New Orleans)

Coaches—Don Coryell (San Diego), AFC; Tom Landry (Dallas), NFC

AFC	3	7	10	7	—	27
NFC	3	20	7	7	—	37

NFC—FG Moseley 37
AFC—FG Fritsch 19
NFC—Muncie 1 run (Moseley kick)
AFC—Pruitt 1 pass from Bradshaw (Fritsch kick)
NFC—David Hill 13 pass from Manning (kick failed)
NFC—Tony Hill 25 pass from Muncie (Moseley kick)
NFC—Henry 86 punt return (Moseley kick)
AFC—Campbell 2 run (Fritsch kick)
AFC—FG Fritsch 29
NFC—Muncie 11 run (Moseley kick)
AFC—Campbell 1 run (Fritsch kick)
Attendance—48,060

1981

NFC 21, AFC 7

Ed Murray kicked four field goals, and Steve Bartkowski threw a 55-yard touchdown pass to Alfred Jenkins in the fourth quarter.

February 1, at Honolulu

NFC	Starters, Offense		AFC
Harold Carmichael (Phil.)	WR		Stanley Morgan (N.E.)
Mike Kenn (Atlanta)	LT		Doug Dieken (Cleveland)
Herbert Scott (Dallas)	LG		John Hannah (New England)
Rich Saul (Los Angeles)	C		Mike Webster (Pittsburgh)
Kent Hill (Los Angeles)	RG		Joe DeLamielleure (Cleve.)
Dan Dierdorf (St. Louis)	RT		Marvin Powell (N.Y. Jets)
Jimmie Giles (Tampa Bay)	TE		Kellen Winslow (San Diego)
James Lofton (Green Bay)	WR		John Jefferson (San Diego)
Steve Bartkowski (Atlanta)	QB		Brian Sipe (Cleveland)
Walter Payton (Chicago)	RB		Earl Campbell (Houston)
Ottis Anderson (St. Louis)	RB		Mike Pruitt (Cleveland)
	Starters, Defense		
Al Baker (Detroit)	LE		Art Still (Kansas City)
Charlie Johnson (Phil.)	LT		Louie Kelcher (San Diego)
Randy White (Dallas)	RT		Gary Johnson (San Diego)
Lee Roy Selmon (T.B.)	RE		Fred Dean (San Diego)
Brad Van Pelt (N.Y. Giants)	LLB		Ted Hendricks (Oakland)
Bob Breunig (Dallas)	MLB		Jack Lambert (Pittsburgh)
Matt Blair (Minnesota)	RLB		Robert Brazile (Houston)
Lemar Parrish (Washington)	LCB		Lester Hayes (Oakland)
Rod Perry (Los Angeles)	RCB		Mike Haynes (New England)
Randy Logan (Philadelphia)	LS		Donnie Shell (Pittsburgh)
Nolan Cromwell (L.A.)	RS		Gary Barbaro (Kansas City)

Coaches—Sam Rutigliano (Cleveland), AFC; Leeman Bennett (Atlanta), NFC

NFC	3	6	0	12	—	21
AFC	0	7	0	0	—	7

NFC—FG Murray 31
AFC—Morgan 9 pass from Sipe (J. Smith kick)
NFC—FG Murray 31
NFC—FG Murray 34
NFC—Jenkins 55 pass from Bartkowski (Murray kick)
NFC—FG Murray 36
NFC—Safety, AFC holding in end zone
Attendance—50,360

1982

AFC 16, NFC 13

Nick Lowery kicked a 23-yard field goal with three seconds left in the game to give the AFC its first Pro Bowl victory in five years, 16-13. The NFC had tied the game just over two-and-a-half minutes earlier when Tony Dorsett scored on a four-yard run.

January 31, at Honolulu

AFC	Starters, Offense		NFC
Cris Collinsworth (Cin.)	WR		James Lofton (Green Bay)
Anthony Munoz (Cincinnati)	LT		Pat Donovan (Dallas)
Doug Wilkerson (San Diego)	LG		Herbert Scott (Dallas)
Mike Webster (Pittsburgh)	C		Rich Saul (Los Angeles)
John Hannah (New England)	RG		Randy Cross (S.F.)
Marvin Powell (N.Y. Jets)	RT		Mike Kenn (Atlanta)
Kellen Winslow (San Diego)	TE		Jimmie Giles (Tampa Bay)
Frank Lewis (Buffalo)	WR		Alfred Jenkins (Atlanta)
Ken Anderson (Cincinnati)	QB		Joe Montana (S.F.)
Pete Johnson (Cincinnati)	RB		Tony Dorsett (Dallas)
Joe Delaney (Kansas City)	RB		Billy Sims (Detroit)
	Starters, Defense		
Mark Gastineau (N.Y. Jets)	LE		Ed Jones (Dallas)
Bob Baumhower (Miami)	LT		Doug English (Detroit)
Gary Johnson (San Diego)	RT		Randy White (Dallas)
Joe Klecko (New York Jets)	RE		Lee Roy Selmon (T.B.)
Ted Hendricks (Oakland)	LLB		Lawrence Taylor (N.Y.G.)
Jack Lambert (Pittsburgh)	MLB		Harry Carson (N.Y. Giants)
Robert Brazile (Houston)	RLB		Matt Blair (Minnesota)
Lester Hayes (Oakland)	LCB		Roynell Young (Phil.)
Mel Blount (Pittsburgh)	RCB		Ronnie Lott (San Francisco)
Donnie Shell (Pittsburgh)	LS		Gary Fencik (Chicago)
Gary Barbaro (Kansas City)	RS		Nolan Cromwell (L.A.)

Coaches—Don Shula (Miami), AFC; John McKay (Tampa Bay), NFC

AFC	0	0	13	3	—	16
NFC	0	6	0	7	—	13

NFC—Giles 4 pass from Montana (kick blocked)
AFC—Muncie 2 run (kick failed)
AFC—Campbell 1 run (Lowery kick)
NFC—Dorsett 4 run (Septien kick)
AFC—FG Lowery 23
Attendance—50,402

George Andrie   *Fred Arbanas*   *Jon Arnett*   *Maxie Baughan*   *Elvin Bethea*   *Mel Blount*   *Ordell Braase*

PRO BOWL SELECTIONS

The year shown refers to the year the game was played, not the season it followed. Twice, in 1940 and again in 1942, there were two games. The January games represented the 1939 and 1941 seasons, respectively. The December games represented the 1940 and 1942 seasons.

A

Adamle, Tony, RB, Cleveland (2) 1951-52
Adams, Chet, T, Cleveland Rams (2) Jan. 1942, Dec. 1942
Adams, Julius, DE, New England (1) 1981
Adamson, Ken, G, Denver (1) 1962
Adderley, Herb, DB, Green Bay (5) 1964-68
Addison, Tom, LB, Boston Patriots (4) 1962-65
Alban, Dick, RB, Washington (1) 1955
Albert, Frankie, QB, San Francisco (1) 1951
Alderman, Grady, T, Minnesota (6) 1964-68, 1970
Aldrich, Charles (Ki), C (2) Chicago Cardinals, 1940; Washington, 1942
Alexander, Kermit, S, San Francisco (1) 1969
Allen, Chuck, LB, San Diego (2) 1964-65
Alworth, Lance, WR, San Diego (7) 1964-70
Alzado, Lyle, DE, Denver (2) 1978-79
Ameche, Alan, RB, Baltimore (4) 1956-59
Anderson, Bill, E, Washington (2) 1960-61
Anderson, Dick, S, Miami (3) 1973-75
Anderson, Ken, QB, Cincinnati (3) 1976-77, 1982
Anderson, Ottis, RB, St. Louis (2) 1980-81
Andrews, William, RB, Atlanta (2) 1981-82
Andrie, George, DE, Dallas (5) 1966-70
Ane, Charley, T, Detroit (2) 1957, 1959
Angsman, Elmer, RB, Chicago Cardinals (1) 1951
Antwine, Houston, DT, Boston Patriots (6) 1964*, 1965-69
Apolskis, Ray, C, Chicago Cardinals (1) Jan. 1942
Arbanas, Fred, TE (5) Dallas Texans, 1963; Kansas City, 1964*, 1965*, 1966, 1968
Armstrong, Otis, RB, Denver (2) 1975, 1977
Arnett, Jon, RB, Los Angeles (5) 1958-62
Artoe, Lee, T, Chicago Bears (3) Dec. 1940, Jan.1942, Dec. 1942
Atkins, Bill, DB, Buffalo (1) 1962
Atkins, Doug, DE, Chicago Bears (8) 1958-64, 1966
Atkinson, Al, LB, New York Jets (1) 1969
Atkinson, George, S, Oakland (2) 1969-70
Austin, Bill, G, New York Giants (1) 1955

B

Bacon, Coy, DE (3) Los Angeles, 1973; Cincinnati, 1977-78
Baisi, Al, G, Chicago Bears (2) Dec. 1940, Jan. 1942
Baker, Al, DE, Detroit (3) 1979-81
Baker, Dave, S, San Francisco (1) 1960
Baker, Jon, G, New York Giants (2) 1952-53
Baker, Sam, K (4) Washington, 1957; Dallas, 1964; Philadelphia, 1965, 1969
Baker, Tony, RB, New Orleans (1) 1970*
Bakken, Jim, K, St. Louis (4) 1966, 1968, 1976-77
Balaz, Frank, G, Green Bay (1) Jan. 1940
Ballman, Gary, WR, Pittsburgh (2) 1965-66
Banducci, Bruno, G, San Francisco (1) 1955
Banfield, Tony, DB, Houston (3) 1962-64
Banks, Tom, C, St. Louis (4) 1976-79
Barbaro, Gary, S, Kansas City (2) 1981-82
Barber, Stew, T, Buffalo (5) 1964-68
Barkum, Jerome, WR, New York Jets (1) 1974
Barnard, Hap, E, New York Giants (1) 1939
Barnes, Billy Ray, RB, Philadelphia (3) 1958-60
Barnes, Erich, DB (6) Chicago, 1960; New York Giants, 1962-65; Cleveland, 1969
Barnes, Mike, DT, Baltimore (1) 1978
Barnes, Walt, G, Philadelphia (1) 1953
Barney, Lem, CB, Detroit (7) 1968-70, 1973-74, 1976-77
Barnum, Len (Feets), B, New York Giants (1) 1939
Barr, Terry, WR, Detroit (2) 1964-65
Bartkowski, Steve, QB, Atlanta (2) 1981-82
Barwegan, Dick, G (4) Chicago Bears, 1951-53; Baltimore, 1954
Bass, Dick, RB, Los Angeles (3) 1963-64, 1967

Bassi, Dick, G, Philadelphia (1) Dec. 1940
Baugh, Sammy, QB, Washington (5) 1939, Dec. 1940, Jan. 1942, Dec. 1942*, 1952
Baughan, Maxie, LB (9) Philadelphia, 1961-62, 1964-66; Los Angeles, 1967-69, 1970*
Baumhower, Bob, DT, Miami (2) 1980, 1982
Bausch, Frank, C, Chicago Bears (1) Dec. 1940
Bednarik, Chuck, LB, Philadelphia (8) 1951-55, 1957-58, 1961
Behrman, Dave, LB, Buffalo (1) 1966
Beinor, Ed, T, Washington (1) Dec. 1942
Bell, Bobby, LB, Kansas City (7) 1965-68, 1971-73
Bemiller, Al, G, Buffalo (1) 1966
Benton, Jim, E, Cleveland Rams (1) Jan. 1940
Bergey, Bill, LB, Philadelphia, (4) 1975, 1977-79
Berry, Bob, QB, Atlanta (1) 1970
Berry, Raymond, WR, Baltimore (5) 1959-60, 1962, 1964-65
Bertelsen, Jim, RB, Los Angeles (1) 1974
Bethea, Elvin, DE, Houston (7) 1972-76, 1979-80
Bielski, Dick, E, Dallas (1) 1962
Biggs, Verlon, DE, New York Jets (3) 1967-69
Biletnikoff, Fred, WR, Oakland (6) 1968, 1970-72, 1974-75
Bingaman, Les, G, Detroit (2) 1952, 1954
Birdwell, Dan, DE, Oakland (1) 1969
Bishop, Bill, T, Chicago Bears (1) 1955
Bishop, Don, DB, Dallas (1) 1963
Bishop, Sonny, G, Houston (1) 1969
Bjork, Del, T, Chicago Bears (1) 1939
Blair, George, DB, San Diego (1) 1962
Blair, Matt, LB, Minnesota (5) 1978-82
Blanda, George, QB-K, (4) Houston, 1962-64; Oakland, 1968
Blanks, Sid, RB, Houston (1) 1965
Blazine, Tony, T, Chicago Cardinals (1) Jan. 1940
Blount, Mel, CB, Pittsburgh (5) 1976-77, 1979-80, 1982
Blozis, Al, T, New York Giants (1) Dec. 1942
Blue, Forrest, C, San Francisco (4) 1972-75
Bokamper, Kim, LB, Miami (1) 1980
Boozer, Emerson, RB, New York Jets (2) 1967, 1969
Boryla, Mike, QB, Philadelphia (1) 1976
Bosley, Bruce, C, San Francisco (4) 1961, 1966-68
Bosseler, Don, RB, Washington (1) 1960
Boyd, Bob, E, Los Angeles (1) 1955
Boyd, Bobby, DB, Baltimore (2) 1965, 1969
Boyette, Garland, LB, Houston (2) 1969-70
Box, Cloyce, E, Detroit (2) 1951, 1953
Braase, Ordell, DE, Baltimore (2) 1967-68
Bradley, Bill, S, Philadelphia (3) 1972-74
Bradshaw, Charlie, T, Pittsburgh (2) 1964-65
Bradshaw, Terry, QB, Pittsburgh (3) 1976*, 1979-80
Bramlett, John, LB (2) Denver, 1967; Miami, 1968
Branch, Clifford, WR, Oakland (4) 1975-78
Branch, Mel, DE (3) Dallas Texans, 1962-63; Kansas City, 1964
Bray, Ray, G, Chicago Bears (4) Dec. 1940, Jan. 1942, 1951-52
Brazile, Robert, LB, Houston (6) 1977-82
Breedlove, Rod, LB, Washington (1) 1963
Breunig, Bob, LB, Dallas (2) 1980-81
Brewer, John, LB, Cleveland (1) 1967
Brewster, Darrell (Pete), E, Cleveland (2) 1956-57
Brezina, Greg, LB, Atlanta (1) 1970
Brink, Larry, DE, Los Angeles (2) 1951-52
Briscoe, Marlin, WR, Buffalo (1) 1971
Brito, Gene, DE, Washington (5) 1954, 1956-59
Brock, Charles, C, Green Bay (3) Jan. 1940, Dec. 1940, Dec. 1942
Brockington, John, RB, Green Bay (3) 1972-74
Brodie, John, QB, San Francisco (2) 1966, 1971
Brooker, Tommy, K, Kansas City (1) 1965
Brooks, Larry, DT, Los Angeles (4) 1978, 1979*, 1980-81
Brooks, Leo, DT, St. Louis (1) 1977
Brookshier, Tom, DB, Philadelphia (2) 1960-61
Brown, Bill, RB, Minnesota (4) 1965-66, 1968-69
Brown, Bob, T (6) Philadelphia, 1966-67, 1969; Los Angeles, 1970*, 1971*; Oakland 1972*
Brown, Bob, DT, Green Bay (1) 1973
Brown, Ed, QB, Chicago Bears (2) 1956-57
Brown, Eddie, KR, Washington (2) 1977-78
Brown, Hardy, LB, San Francisco (1) 1953
Brown, Jim, RB, Cleveland (9) 1958-66
Brown, Larry, RB, Washington (4) 1970-72, 1973*
Brown, Roger, DT (6) Detroit, 1963-66; Los Angeles, 1967-68
Brown, Roosevelt, T, New York Giants (9) 1956-61, 1963, 1965-66
Brown, Timmy, RB, Philadelphia (3) 1963-64, 1966
Brown, Willie, CB (9) Denver, 1965-66; Oakland, 1968-74
Bruder, Henry, B, Green Bay (1) Jan. 1940

Brumm, Don, DE, St. Louis (1) 1969
Bruney, Fred, DB, Boston Patriots (2) 1962-63
Bryant, Bobby, CB, Minnesota (2) 1976-77
Buchanan, Buck, DT, Kansas City (8) 1965-72
Buchanon, Willie, CB, Green Bay (2) 1974-75
Budde, Ed, G, Kansas City (7) 1964, 1967-72
Buhler, Larry, B, Green Bay (1) Jan. 1940
Bulaich, Norm, RB, Baltimore (1) 1972*
Buncom, Frank, LB, San Diego (3) 1965-66, 1968
Buoniconti, Nick, LB (8) Boston Patriots, 1964-68; Miami, 1970, 1973*, 1974
Burford, Chris, E, Dallas Texans (1) 1962
Burk, Adrian, QB, Philadelphia (2) 1955-56
Burnett, Bob, RB, Buffalo (1) 1967
Burnett, Dale, B, New York Giants (1) 1939
Burrell, Ode, WR, Houston (1) 1966
Burrough, Ken, WR, Houston (2) 1976, 1978
Bussey, Young, B, Chicago Bears (1) Jan. 1942
Butkus, Dick, LB, Chicago (8) 1966-73
Butler, Jack, DB, Pittsburgh (4) 1956-59
Butler, Jerry, WR, Buffalo (1) 1981
Butler, Jim, RB, Atlanta (1) 1970
Byrd, George (Butch), CB, Buffalo (5) 1965-67, 1969-70

C

Caffey, Lee Roy, LB, Green Bay (1) 1966
Campbell, Earl, RB, Houston (4) 1979-82
Campbell, Marion, DT, Philadelphia (2) 1960-61
Campbell, Woodie, RB, Houston (1) 1968*
Cannady, John, C, New York Giants (2) 1951, 1953
Cannon, Billy, RB-TE (2) Houston, 1962; Oakland, 1970
Cappelletti, Gino, WR-K, Boston Patriots (5) 1962, 1964-67
Carapella, Al, T, San Francisco (1) 1955
Carlton, Wray, RB, Buffalo (2) 1966-67
Cardwell, Lloyd, B, Detroit (1) 1939
Carmichael, Harold, WR, Philadelphia (4) 1974, 1979-81
Carolan, Reg, E, Dallas Texans (1) 1963
Caroline, J.C., B, Chicago Bears (1) 1957
Carpenter, Ken, B, Cleveland (1) 1952
Carpenter, Preston, E, Pittsburgh (1) 1963
Carr, Fred, LB, Green Bay (3) 1971, 1973, 1976
Carr, Roger, WR, Baltimore (1) 1977
Carroll, Vic, G, Washington (1) Dec. 1942
Carson, Harry, LB, New York Giants (3) 1979*, 1980, 1982
Carson, John, E, Washington (1) 1958
Carter, Jim, LB, Green Bay (1) 1974
Carter, Joe, E, Philadelphia (2) 1939, Jan. 1940
Casanova, Tommy, S, Cincinnati (3) 1975, 1977-78
Casares, Rick, RB, Chicago (5) 1956-60
Casey, Bernie, WR, Los Angeles (1) 1968
Cason, Jim, B, San Francisco (2) 1952, 1955
Casper, Dave, TE (5) Oakland, 1977-80; Houston, 1981
Caster, Rich, TE, New York Jets (3) 1973, 1975-76
Chambers, Wally, DT, Chicago (3) 1974, 1976-77
Chandler, Don, K, Green Bay (1) 1968
Chandler, Wes, WR, New Orleans (1) 1980
Chandnois, Lynn, B, Pittsburgh (2) 1953-54
Chapple, Dave, P, Los Angeles (1) 1973
Cherundolo, Chuck, C, Pittsburgh (2) Jan. 1942, Dec. 1942
Chesney, Chester, C, Chicago Bears (1) Dec. 1940
Chester, Raymond, TE, Oakland (4) 1971-73, 1980
Childs, Henry, TE, New Orleans (1) 1980
Christiansen, Jack, S, Detroit (5) 1954-58
Christy, Dick, RB, New York Jets (1) 1963
Cifers, Ed, E, Washington (1) Dec. 1942
Clancy, Jack, WR, Miami (1) 1968
Clark, Dwight, WR, San Francisco (1) 1982
Clark, Harry, B, Chicago Bears (2) Dec. 1940, Jan. 1942
Clark, Mike, T, Pittsburgh (1) 1967
Clarke, Hagood, DB, Buffalo (1) 1966
Clarke, Leon, E, Los Angeles (2) 1956-57
Cogdill, Gail, WR, Detroit (3) 1961, 1963-64
Colclough, Jim, E, Boston Patriots (1) 1963*
Cole, Pete, G, New York Giants (1) 1939
Collett, Elmer, G, San Francisco (1) 1970
Collins, Gary, WR, Cleveland (2) 1966-67
Collinsworth, Cris, WR, Cincinnati (1) 1982
Colo, Don, T, Cleveland (3) 1955-56, 1959
Condit, Merlyn, B (2) Pittsburgh, Dec. 1940; Brooklyn Dodgers, Dec. 1942
Conerly, Charlie, QB, New York Giants (2) 1951, 1957
Connolly, Ted, G, San Francisco (1) 1962

Willie Brown

Nick Buoniconti

Fred Carr

John David Crow

Isaac Curtis

Carroll Dale

Conrad Dobler

Connor, George, T, Chicago Bears (4) 1951-54
Connors, Dan, LB, Oakland (3) 1967-69
Conrad, Bobby Joe, WR, St. Louis (1) 1955
Conti, Enio, G, Philadelphia (1) Dec. 1942
Cooke, Ed, DE, Miami (1) 1967
Coomer, Joe, T, Pittsburgh (1) Jan. 1942
Cope, Frank, T, New York Giants (2) 1939, Dec. 1940
Cordell, Ollie, B, Cleveland Rams (1) Dec. 1940
Corey, Walt, LB, Kansas City (1) 1964
Cornelison, Jerry, T, Dallas Texans (1) 1963
Corral, Frank, K, Los Angeles (1) 1979
Costa, Dave, DT (5) Oakland, 1964; Buffalo, 1967; Denver, 1968-70
Costa, Paul, TE, Buffalo (1) 1966
Coulter, DeWitt (Tex), T, New York Giants (2) 1952-53
Cowan, Charlie, T, Los Angeles (3) 1969-71
Cox, Fred, K, Minnesota (1) 1971
Craft, Russ, B, Philadelphia (2) 1952-53
Craig, Larry, QB, Green Bay (3) Jan. 1940, Jan. 1942, Dec. 1942
Creekmur, Lou, T, Detroit (8) 1951-58
Cribbs, Joe, RB, Buffalo (2) 1981, 1982*
Cromwell, Nolan, S, Los Angeles (2) 1981-82
Cross, Irv, DB, Philadelphia (2) 1965-66
Cross, Randy, G, San Francisco (1) 1982
Crow, John David, RB (4) St. Louis, 1960-61, 1963; San Francisco, 1966
Crow, Lindon, DB (3) St. Louis, 1957-58; New York Giants, 1960
Csonka, Larry, RB, Miami, (5) 1971-72, 1973*, 1974*, 1975
Cuff, Ward, B, New York Giants (3) 1939, Jan. 1940, Jan. 1942
Culp, Curley, DT (6) Kansas City, 1970, 1972; Houston, 1976-79
Cunningham, Sam, RB, New England (1) 1979
Current, Mike, T, Denver (1) 1970
Currie, Dan, LB, Green Bay (1) 1961
Curry, Bill, C, Baltimore (2) 1972-73
Curtis, Isaac, WR, Cincinnati (4) 1974-77
Curtis, Mike, LB, Baltimore (4) 1969, 1971-72, 1975

D

Dalby, Dave, C, Oakland (1) 1978
Dale, Carroll, WR, Green Bay (3) 1969-71
Danenhauer, Eldon, T, Denver (2) 1963, 1966
Daniels, Clem, RB, Oakland (4) 1964-67
Danowski, Ed, B, New York Giants (1) 1939
Darden, Thom, S, Cleveland (1) 1979
Daughtery, Dick, LB, Los Angeles (1) 1958
David, Jim, DB, Detroit (6) 1955-60
Davidson, Ben, DE, Oakland (3) 1967-69
Davidson, Cotton, QB (2) Dallas Texans, 1962; Oakland, 1964
Davis, Ben, CB, Cleveland (1) 1973
Davis, Fred, T (2) Washington, Dec. 1942; Chicago Bears, 1951
Davis, Glenn, B, Los Angeles (1) 1951
Davis, Tommy, K, San Francisco (2) 1963-64
Davis, Willie, DE, Green Bay (5) 1964-68
Dawson, Len, QB (7) Dallas Texans, 1963; Kansas City, 1965, 1967-69, 1970*, 1972
Day, Tom, DE, Buffalo (1) 1966
Deal, Rufus, B, Washington (1) Dec. 1942
Dean, Fred, DE (3) San Diego, 1980-81; San Francisco, 1982
Dean, Ted, RB, Philadelphia (1) 1962
Dee, Bob, DE, Boston Patriots (4) 1962, 1964-66
Delaney, Joe, RB, Kansas City (1) 1982
DeLamielleure, Joe, G (6) Buffalo, 1976-80; Cleveland, 1981
DeLeone, Tom, C, Cleveland (2) 1980-81
DeLong, Steve, DE, San Diego (1) 1970
DeMarco, Bob, C, St. Louis (3) 1964, 1966, 1968*
Dempsey, Tom, K, New Orleans (1) 1970
Denson, Al, WR, Denver (2) 1968, 1970
Derby, Dean, B, Pittsburgh (1) 1960
DeRogatis, Al, T, New York Giants (2) 1951-52
Dess, Darrell, G, New York Giants (2) 1963-64
Dewell, Bill, E, Chicago Cardinals (1) Jan. 1942
Dewveall, Willard, E, Houston (1) 1963
Dial, Buddy, WR, Pittsburgh (1) 1962
Dieken, Doug, T, Cleveland (1) 1981
Dierdorf, Dan, T, St. Louis (6) 1975-79, 1981
Dillon, Bobby, B, Green Bay (4) 1956-59
Ditka, Mike, TE, Chicago (5) 1962-66
Dixon, Hewritt, RB, Oakland (4) 1967-69, 1971
Dobler, Conrad, G, St. Louis (3) 1976-78
Dodrill, Dale, G, Pittsburgh (4) 1954-56, 1958

Doll, Don, DB (4) Detroit 1951-53; Washington, 1954
Donovan, Art, DT, Baltimore (5) 1954-58
Donovan, Pat, T, Dallas (3) 1980-82
Doran, Jim, E, Dallas (1) 1961
Dorow, Al, QB (2) Washington, 1957; New York Titans, 1962
Dorsett, Tony, RB, Dallas (2) 1979, 1982
Dottley, John, B, Chicago Bears (1) 1952
Dougherty, Phil, C, Chicago Cardinals (1) 1939
Dove, Bob, E, Chicago Cardinals (1) 1951
Dove, Eddie, DB, San Francisco (1) 1962
Dowler, Boyd, WR, Green Bay (2) 1966, 1968
Drake, Johnny, B, Cleveland Rams (3) 1939, Jan. 1940, Dec. 1940
Drazenovich, Chuck, LB, Washington (4) 1956-59
Drulis, Chuck, G, Chicago Bears (1) Dec. 1942
Dryer, Fred, DE, Los Angeles (1) 1976
Dubenion, Elbert, WR, Buffalo (1) 1965
Dudley, Bill, B (3) Pittsburgh, Dec. 1942; Washington, 1951-52
Dunaway, Jim, DT, Buffalo (4) 1966-1969
Duncan, Leslie (Speedy), DB (4) San Diego, 1966-68; Washington, 1972
DuPree, Billy Joe, TE, Dallas (3) 1977-79
Dutton, John, DE, Baltimore (2) 1976-77

E

Ecklund, Brad, C, New York Yanks (2) 1951-52
Edgerson, Booker, DB, Buffalo (1) 1966
Edwards, Dan, E, New York Giants (1) 1951
Edwards, Glen (Turk), T, Washington (1) Jan. 1940
Edwards, Glen, S, Pittsburgh (2) 1976-77
Eisenhauer, Larry, DE, Boston Patriots (4) 1963-65, 1967
Elam, Cleveland, DT, San Francisco (2) 1977-78
Eller, Carl, DE, Minnesota (6) 1969-72, 1974*, 1975
Elliott, John, DT, New York Jets (3) 1969-71
Ellis, Allan, CB, Chicago (1) 1978
Ellis, Ken, CB, Green Bay (2) 1974-75
Ellison, Willie, RB, Los Angeles (1) 1972*
Elter, Leo, B, Washington (1) 1957
Engebretsen, Paul, G, Green Bay (1) Jan. 1940
English, Doug, DT, Detroit (2) 1979, 1982
Erlandson, Tom, LB, Miami (1) 1967
Etter, Bob, K, Atlanta (1) 1970
Evans, Norm, T, Miami (2) 1973, 1975

F

Faison, Earl, DE, San Diego (5) 1962-66
Falaschi, Nello, B, New York Giants (2) 1939, Jan. 1942
Famiglietti, Gary, B, Chicago Bears (3) Dec. 1940, Jan. 1942, Dec. 1942
Farkas, Andy, B, Washington (2) Jan. 1940, Dec. 1942
Farman, Dick, G, Washington (1) Dec. 1942
Farr, Mel, RB, Detroit (2) 1968, 1971
Farragut, Ken, C, Philadelphia (1) 1954
Fears, Tom, E, Los Angeles (1) 1951
Federovich, John, T, Chicago Bears (1) Jan. 1942
Felt, Dick, DB (2) New York Titans, 1962; Boston Patriots, 1963
Fencik, Gary, S, Chicago (2) 1981-82
Ferguson, Charley, E, Buffalo (1) 1966
Ferguson, Howie, RB, Green Bay (1) 1956
Fields, Joe, C, New York Jets (1) 1982
Filchock, Frank, B, Washington (2) Jan. 1940, Jan. 1942
Finks, Jim, QB, Pittsburgh (1) 1953
Fischer, Bill, G, Chicago Cardinals (3) 1951-53
Fischer, Pat, CB (3) St. Louis, 1965-66; Washington, 1970
Fiss, Galen, LB, Cleveland (2) 1963-64
Flanagan, Ed, C, Detroit (4) 1970-72, 1974
Flatley, Paul, WR, Minnesota (1) 1967
Flint, George, G, Buffalo (1) 1966
Flores, Tom, QB, Oakland (1) 1967
Floyd, Don, DE, Houston (2) 1962-63
Foley, Dave, T, Buffalo (1) 1974
Foley, Tim, S, Miami (1) 1980
Folkins, Lee, TE, Dallas (1) 1964
Ford, Len, DE, Cleveland (4) 1952-55
Foreman, Chuck, RB, Minnesota (5) 1974-76, 1977*, 1978
Forester, Bill, LB, Green Bay (4) 1960-63
Forte, Aldo, G, Chicago Bears (2) Dec. 1940, Jan. 1942
Fortmann, Danny, G, Chicago Bears (3) Dec. 1940, Jan. 1942, Dec. 1942
Fortunato, Joe, LB, Chicago Bears (5) 1959, 1963-66
Fouts, Dan, QB, San Diego (3) 1980-82
Fox, Tim, S, New England (1) 1981
France, Doug, T, Los Angeles (2) 1978-79

Francis, Russ, TE, New England (3) 1977-79
Fraser, Jim, LB (3) Denver, 1963; Kansas City, 1964-65
Frazier, Charlie, TE, Houston (1) 1967
Frazier, Willie, TE, San Diego (3) 1966, 1968, 1970
Frederickson, Tucker, RB, New York Giants (1) 1966
Freitas, Rockne (Rocky), T, Detroit (1) 1973*
Fritsch, Toni, K, Houston (1) 1980
Fugett, Jean, TE, Washington (1) 1978
Fuller, Frank, T, St. Louis (1) 1960

G

Gabriel, Roman, QB (4) Los Angeles, 1968-70; Philadelphia, 1974
Gain, Bob, DT, Cleveland (5) 1958-60, 1962-63
Galazin, Stan, C, New York Giants (1) 1939
Galimore, Willie, RB, Chicago Bears (1) 1959
Gallarneau, Hugh, B, Chicago Bears (1) Jan. 1942
Gantenbein, Milt, E, Green Bay (1) 1942
Garrett, Carl, RB, Boston Patriots (1) 1970
Garrett, Mike, RB, Kansas City (2) 1967-68
Garrison, Gary, WR, San Diego (4) 1969, 1971*, 1972-73
Garrison, Walt, RB, Dallas (1) 1973
Garron, Larry, RB, Boston Patriots (3) 1962, 1964-65
Gastineau, Mark, DE, New York Jets (1) 1982
Gatski, Frank, C, Cleveland (1) 1955
Gelatka, Chuck, E, New York Giants (1) 1939
Gentry, Byron, G, Pittsburgh (2) 1939, Jan. 1940
George, Bill, LB, Chicago Bears (8) 1955-1962
George, Ray, T, Detroit (1) Jan. 1940
Gerela, Roy, K, Pittsburgh (2) 1973, 1975
Geri, Joe, B, Pittsburgh (2) 1951-52
Gibbons, Jim, TE, Detroit (3) 1961-62, 1965
Gibron, Abe, G, Cleveland (4) 1953-56
Gifford, Frank, RB, New York Giants (7) 1954-57, 1959-60, 1964
Gilbert, Kline, T, Chicago Bears (1) 1958
Gilchirst, Cookie, RB (4) Buffalo 1963-65; Denver, 1966
Gildea, John, B, New York Giants (1) 1939
Giles, Jimmie, TE, Tampa Bay (2) 1981-82
Gilliam, John, WR, Minnesota (4) 1973-76
Gilliam, Jon, C, Dallas Texans (1) 1962
Gillingham, Gale, G, Green Bay (5) 1970-72, 1974*, 1975
Gillom, Horace, E-P, Cleveland (1) 1953
Gilmer, Harry, QB, Washington (2) 1951, 1953
Glass, Bill, DE, Cleveland (4) 1963-65, 1968
Glick, Fred, DB, Houston (3) 1963-65
Goddard, Ed, B, Cleveland Rams (1) 1939
Goeddeke, George, G, Denver (1) 1970
Gogolak, Pete, K, Buffalo (1) 1966
Goldenberg, Charles (Buckets), G, Green Bay (1) Jan. 1940
Gonsoulin, Austin (Goose), DB, Denver (5) 1962-65, 1967
Goode, Rob, RB, Washington (2) 1952, 1955
Goode, Irv, G, St. Louis (2) 1965, 1968
Goode, Tom, C, Miami (1) 1970
Gordon, Dick, WR, Chicago (2) 1971*, 1972
Gordy, John, G, Detroit (3) 1964-66
Gossett, Bruce, K, Los Angeles (2) 1967, 1969
Gradishar, Randy, LB, Denver (5) 1976, 1978-80, 1982
Graham, Kenny, DB, San Diego (4) 1966, 1968-70
Graham, Otto, QB, Cleveland (5) 1951-55
Granger, Hoyle, RB, Houston (2) 1968-69
Grantham, Larry, LB, New York Jets (5) 1963-65, 1967, 1970
Gray, Ken, G, St. Louis (6) 1962, 1964-65, 1967-69
Gray, Leon, T (4) New England 1977, 1979; Houston, 1980, 1982
Gray, Mel, WR, St. Louis (4) 1975-78
Grayson, Dave, DB (6) Dallas Texans, 1963; Kansas City, 1964-65; Oakland, 1966-67, 1970
Green, Bobby Joe, P, Chicago (1) 1971
Green, Cornell, DB, Dallas (5) 1966-68, 1972-73
Green, Ernie, RB, Cleveland (2) 1967-68
Green, Gary, CB, Kansas City (1) 1982
Green, John, E, Philadelphia (1) 1951
Green, Tony, KR, Washington (1) 1979
Greene, Joe, DT, Pittsburgh (10) 1970-77, 1979-80
Greene, Tony, S, Buffalo (1) 1978
Greenfield, Tom, C, Green Bay (1) Jan. 1940
Greenwood, L.C., DE, Pittsburgh (6) 1974-77, 1979-80
Gregg, Forrest, T, Green Bay (9) 1960-65, 1967-69
Gregory, Jack, DE (2) Cleveland, 1970; New York Giants, 1973
Grgich, Visco, G, San Francisco (1) 1951

*Selected but did not play

Norm Evans *Tucker Frederickson* *John Gilliam* *Ken Gray* *John Hadl* *Winston Hill* *Mike Kenn*

Grier, Roosevelt, DT, New York Giants (3) 1954, 1957, 1961
Griese, Bob, QB, Miami (8) 1968-69, 1971-72, 1974-75, 1978-79
Grim, Bob, WR, Minnesota (1) 1972
Grimes, Billy, B, Green Bay (2) 1951-52
Groom, Jerry, T, Chicago Cardinals (1) 1955
Groza, Lou, T-K, Cleveland (9) 1951-56, 1958-60
Grupp, Bob, P, Kansas City (1) 1980
Guy, Ray, P, Oakland (7) 1974-79, 1981

H

Haden, Jack, T, New York Giants (1) 1939
Haden, Pat, QB, Los Angeles (1) 1978
Hadl, John, QB (6) San Diego, 1965-66, 1969-70, 1973; Los Angeles, 1974
Hall, Parker, B, Cleveland Rams (1) Jan. 1940
Hall, Ron, DB, Boston Patriots (1) 1964
Ham, Jack, LB, Pittsburgh (8) 1974*, 1975-79, 1980*, 1981
Hampton, Dan, DE, Chicago (1) 1981
Hanburger, Chris, LB, Washington (9) 1967-70, 1973-76, 1977*
Hanken, Ray, E, New York Giants (1) 1939
Hannah, John, G, New England (5) 1977, 1979-82
Hanner, Dave, DT, Green Bay (2) 1954-55
Harder, Pat, B, Chicago Cardinals (2) 1951, 1953
Hardman, Cedrick, DE, San Francisco (2) 1972, 1976
Hardy, Jim, QB, Chicago Cardinals (1) 1951
Hare, Cecil, B, Washington (2) Jan. 1942, Dec. 1942
Hare, Ray, B, Washington (1) Dec. 1942
Harrah, Dennis, G, Los Angeles (3) 1979-81
Harris, Cliff, S, Dallas (5) 1975-76, 1978-80
Harris, Dick, DB, San Diego (1) 1962
Harris, Franco, RB, Pittsburgh (8) 1973-76, 1977*, 1978-80
Harris, James, QB, Los Angeles (1) 1975
Hart, Jim, QB, St. Louis (4) 1975-78
Hart, Leon, E, Detroit (1) 1952
Hart, Tommy, DE, San Francisco (1) 1977
Hauss, Len, C, Washington (5) 1967, 1969-71, 1973
Hawkins, Rip, LB, Minnesota (1) 1964
Hawkins, Wayne, G, Oakland (5) 1964-68
Hayes, Bob, WR, Dallas (3) 1966-68
Hayes, Lester, CB, Oakland (2) 1981-82
Haynes, Abner, RB (3) Dallas Texans, 1962-63; Kansas City, 1965
Haynes, Mike, CB, New England (5) 1977*, 1978-81
Hazeltine, Matt, LB, San Francisco (2) 1963, 1965
Headrick, Sherrill, LB (4) Dallas Texans, 1962-63; Kansas City, 1966-67
Hein, Mel, C, New York Giants (4) 1939, Jan. 1940, Dec. 1940, Jan. 1942
Henderson, Thomas, LB, Dallas (1) 1979
Hendricks, Ted, LB (6) Baltimore, 1972-74; Green Bay, 1975; Oakland, 1981-82
Henke, Ed, E, San Francisco (1) 1953
Hennigan, Charley, WR, Houston (5) 1962-66
Henry, Wally, KR, Philadelphia (1) 1980
Herber, Arnie, B, Green Bay (1) Jan. 1940
Herman, Dave, G, New York Jets (2) 1969-70
Herrera, Efren, K, Dallas (1) 1978
Hickerson, Gene, G, Cleveland (6) 1966-71
Hicks, Dwight, S, San Francisco (1) 1982
Hicks, W.K., DB, Houston (1) 1967
Hill, Calvin, RB, Dallas (4) 1970*, 1973, 1974*, 1975
Hill, David, TE, Detroit (2) 1979-80
Hill, Harlon, E, Chicago Bears (3) 1955-57
Hill, J.D., WR, Buffalo (1) 1973
Hill, Jimmy, DB, St. Louis (3) 1961-63
Hill, Kent, G, Los Angeles (1) 1981
Hill, Mack Lee, RB, Kansas City (1) 1965
Hill, Tony, WR, Dallas (2) 1979-80
Hill, Winston, T, New York Jets (8) 1965, 1968-74
Hines, Glen Ray, T, Houston (2) 1969-70
Hinkle, Clarke, B, Green Bay (3) 1939, Jan. 1940, Dec. 1940
Hirsch, Elroy (Crazylegs), E, Los Angeles (3) 1952-54
Hoaglin, Fred, C, Cleveland (1) 1970
Hoak, Dick, RB, Pittsburgh (1) 1969
Hock, John, G, Los Angeles (1) 1957
Hoerner, Dick, RB, Los Angeles (1) 1951
Hoernschemeyer, Bob (Hunchy), B, Detroit (2) 1952-53
Hoffman, John, B-E, Chicago Bears (2) 1954, 1956
Holmes, Robert, RB, Kansas City (1) 1970
Holmes, Pat, DE, Houston (2) 1968-69
Holub, E.J., LB (5) Dallas Texans, 1962, 1963*; Kansas City 1965*, 1966-67

Hopp, Harry, B, Detroit (1) Dec. 1942
Hornung, Paul, RB, Green Bay (2) 1960-61
Houston, Jim, LB, Cleveland (4) 1965-66, 1970-71
Houston, Ken, S (12) Houston, 1969-73; Washington, 1974-79, 1980*
Howell, Jim Lee, E, New York Giants (1) 1939
Howley, Chuck, LB, Dallas (6) 1966-70, 1972
Howton, Bill, E, Green Bay (4) 1953, 1956-58
Hubbard, Marv, RB, Oakland (3) 1972-74
Hubbert, Brad, RB, San Diego (1) 1968
Hudson, Bill, DT, San Diego (1) 1962
Hudson, Dick, T, Buffalo (1) 1966
Huff, Sam, LB (5) New York Giants, 1959-62; Washington, 1965
Huffman, Dick, T, Los Angeles (1) 1951
Hughes, Bill, C, Chicago Bears (1) Jan. 1942
Hughes, George, G, Pittsburgh (2) 1952, 1954
Humbert, Dick, E, Philadelphia (1) Jan. 1942
Humble, Weldon, G, Cleveland (1) 1951
Humphrey, Claude, DE, Atlanta (6) 1971-75, 1978
Hunt, Bobby, DB, Kansas City (1) 1965
Hunt, Jim, DT, Boston Patriots (3) 1967-68, 1970
Hunter, Art, C, Cleveland (1) 1960
Husmann, Ed, DT, Houston (3) 1962-64
Hutson, Don, E, Green Bay (4) Jan. 1940, Dec. 1940, Jan. 1942, Dec. 1942

I

Isbell, Cecil, B, Green Bay (4) 1939, Jan. 1940, Jan. 1942, Dec. 1942
Ivy, Frank (Pop), E, Chicago Cardinals (1) Dec. 1942

J

Jackson, Frank, WR, Kansas City (1) 1966
Jackson, Harold, WR (5) Philadelphia, 1970, 1973; Los Angeles, 1974, 1976, 1978
Jackson, Monte, CB, Los Angeles (2) 1977, 1978*
Jackson, Rich, DE, Denver (3) 1969-71
Jackson, Tom, LB, Denver (3) 1978-80
Jacobs, Harry, LB, Buffalo (2) 1966, 1970
Jacunski, Harry, E, Green Bay (1) Jan. 1940
Jagade, Harry (Chick), B, Cleveland (1) 1954
James, Dick, RB, Washington (1) 1962
James, John, P, Atlanta (3) 1976-78
James, Robert, CB, Buffalo (3) 1973-75
James, Tommy, B, Cleveland (1) 1954
Jamison, Al, T, Houston (2) 1962-63
Janik, Tom, DB, Buffalo (2) 1966, 1968
Jankowski, Ed, B, Green Bay (1) Jan. 1940
Jaquess, Lindel (Pete), DB, Houston (1) 1965
Jarmoluk, Mike, T, Philadelphia (1) 1952
Jauron, Dick, KR, Detroit (1) 1975
Jaworski, Ron, QB, Philadelphia (1) 1981
Jefferson, John, WR, San Diego (3) 1979-81
Jefferson, Roy, WR (3) Pittsburgh, 1969-70; Washington, 1972
Jenkins, Alfred, WR, Atlanta (2) 1981-82
Jennings, Dave, P, New York Giants (3) 1979-81
Jessie, Ron, WR, Los Angeles (1) 1977
Jeter, Bob, DB, Green Bay (2) 1968, 1970
Joe, Billy, RB, Buffalo (1) 1966
Johnson, Bill, C, San Francisco (2) 1953-54
Johnson, Billy, KR, Houston (2) 1976, 1978
Johnson, Bob, C, Cincinnati (1) 1969
Johnson, Charley, QB, St. Louis (1) 1964
Johnson, Charlie, DT, Philadelphia (3) 1980-82
Johnson, Curley, P, New York Jets (1) 1966
Johnson, Ezra, DE, Green Bay (1) 1979
Johnson, Gary, DT, San Diego (3) 1980-82
Johnson, Jimmy, CB, San Francisco (5) 1970*, 1971-73, 1975*
Johnson, John, T, Detroit (1) Jan. 1940
Johnson, John Henry, RB (4) San Francisco, 1955; Pittsburgh, 1963-65
Johnson, Larry, C, New York Giants (1) 1939
Johnson, Pete, RB, Cincinnati (1) 1982
Johnson, Ron, RB, New York Giants (2) 1971, 1973
Johnson, Walter, DT, Cleveland (3) 1968-70
Johnston, Mark, DB, Houston (1) 1962
Joiner, Charlie, WR, San Diego (3) 1977, 1980-81
Jones, Art, B, Pittsburgh (1) Jan. 1942
Jones, Bert, QB, Baltimore (1) 1977
Jones, Cody, DT, Los Angeles (1) 1979
Jones, David (Deacon), DE (8) Los Angeles, 1965-71; San Diego, 1973

Jones, Dub, B, Cleveland (1) 1951-52
Jones, Ed, DE, Dallas (1) 1982
Jones, Homer, WR, New York Giants (2) 1968-69
Jones, Stan, G, Chicago Bears (7) 1956-62
Jordan, Henry, DT, Green Bay (4) 1961-62, 1964, 1967
Jordan, Lee Roy, LB, Dallas (5) 1968-69, 1970*, 1974*, 1975
Josephson, Les, RB, Los Angeles (1) 1968
Joyce, Don, DE, Baltimore (1) 1959
Jurgensen, Sonny, QB (5) Philadelphia, 1962*; Washington, 1965, 1967*, 1968*, 1970*
Justice, Ed, B, Washington (1) Dec. 1942

K

Kaminski, Larry, C, Denver (1) 1968
Kapp, Joe, QB, Minnesota (1) 1970*
Karas, Emil, LB, San Diego (3) 1962-64
Karcis, John, B, New York Giants (1) 1939
Karras, Alex, DT, Detroit (4) 1961-63, 1966
Kassulke, Karl, S, Minnesota (1) 1971
Katcavage, Jim, DE, New York Giants (3) 1962-64
Kavanaugh, Ken, E, Chicago Bears (2) Dec. 1940, Jan. 1942
Keane, Tom, DB, Baltimore (1) 1954
Keating, Tom, DT, Oakland (2) 1967-68
Kelcher, Louie, DT, San Diego (3) 1978-79, 1981
Kell, Paul, T, Green Bay (1) Jan. 1940
Kellerman, Ernie, DB, Cleveland (1) 1969
Kelly, Leroy, RB, Cleveland (6) 1967-72
Kemp, Jack, QB (7) San Diego, 1962; Buffalo, 1963, 1964*, 1965-67, 1970
Kenn, Mike, T, Atlanta (2) 1981-82
Keys, Brady, DB, Pittsburgh (1) 1967
Khayat, Bobby, G, Washington (1) 1961
Kilick, Jim, RB, Miami (2) 1969-70
Kilmer, Billy, QB, Washington (1) 1973
Kilroy, Frank (Bucko), G, Philadelphia (3) 1953-55
Kinard, Frank (Bruiser), T, Brooklyn Dodgers (5) 1939, Jan. 1940, Dec. 1940, Jan. 1942, Dec. 1942
Kindt, Don, B, Chicago Bears (1) 1954
King, Kenny, RB, Oakland (1) 1981
Klecko, Joe, DE, New York Jets (1) 1982
Klein, Dick, T, Boston Patriots (1) 1963
Knight, Curt, K, Washington (1) 1972
Kocourek, Dave, TE, San Diego (4) 1962-65
Kolman, Ed, T, Chicago Bears (3) Dec. 1940, Jan. 1942, Dec. 1942
Koman, Bill, DE, St. Louis (2) 1963, 1965
Konz, Ken, DB, Cleveland (1) 1956
Koy, Ernie, RB, New York Giants (1) 1968
Kramer, Jerry, G, Green Bay (3) 1962-64, 1968
Kramer, Ron, TE, Green Bay (1) 1963
Krause, Paul, S (8) Washington, 1965-66; Minnesota, 1970, 1972-76
Krisher, Bill, G, Dallas Texans (1) 1962
Krouse, Ray, T, New York Giants (1) 1955
Krueger, Al, E, Washington (1) Dec. 1942
Krueger, Charlie, DT, San Francisco (2) 1961, 1965
Kuechenberg, Bob, G, Miami (4) 1975-76, 1978-79
Kuharich, Joe, G, Chicago Cardinals (1) Jan. 1940
Kunz, George, T (8) Atlanta, 1970, 1972-74; Baltimore 1975-78
Kupp, Jake, G, New Orleans (1) 1970
Kwalick, Ted, TE, San Francisco (3) 1972-74

L

Ladd, Ernie, DT, San Diego (4) 1963-66
Lahar, Harold, G, Chicago Bears (1) Jan. 1942
Laird, Bruce, KR, Baltimore (1) 1973
Lambert, Jack, LB, Pittsburgh (7) 1976-82
Lammons, Pete, TE, New York Jets (1) 1968
Lamonica, Daryle, QB (4) Buffalo, 1966; Oakland, 1968, 1971, 1973
Landry, Greg, QB, Detroit (1) 1972
Landry, Tom, DB, New York Giants (1) 1955
Lane, Dick (Night Train), DB (7) Chicago Cardinals, 1955-57, 1959; Detroit, 1961-63
Lane, MacArthur, RB, St. Louis (1) 1971
Langer, Jim, C, Miami (6) 1974-79
Lanier, Willie, LB, Kansas City (8) 1969-75, 1976*
Lansford, Buck, G, Philadelphia (1) 1957
Largent, Steve, WR, Seattle (3) 1979-80, 1982
Larsen, Gary, DT, Minnesota (2) 1970-71
Larson, Greg, C, New York Giants (1) 1969
Lary, Yale, S, Detroit (9) 1954, 1957-63, 1965

George Kunz

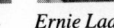
Ernie Ladd

Eddie LeBaron

John Mackey

Chester Marcol

Dave Parks

Floyd Peters

Laskey, Bill, LB, Buffalo (1) 1966
Lassiter, Isaac, DE, Oakland (1) 1967
Lattner, Johnny, B, Pittsburgh (1) 1955
Lavelli, Dante, E, Cleveland (3) 1952, 1954-55
Lavender, Joe, CB, Washington (1) 1980
Lawrence, James, B, Green Bay (1) Jan. 1940
Lawrence, Rolland, CB, Atlanta (1) 1978
Laws, Joe, B, Green Bay (1) Jan. 1940
Layne, Bobby, QB (5) Detroit, 1952-54, 1957; Pittsburgh, 1960
LeBaron, Eddie, QB (4) Washington, 1956, 1958-59; Dallas, 1963
LeBeau, Dick, DB, Detroit (3) 1965-67
LeClair, Jim, LB, Cincinnati (1) 1977
Lee, Bill, T, Green Bay (1) Jan. 1940
Leemans, Alphonse (Tuffy), B, New York Giants (2) 1939, Jan. 1942
LeMaster, Frank, LB, Philadelphia (1) 1982
Lemek, Ray, T, Washington (1) 1962
Leo, Charles, G, Boston Patriots (1) 1962
Letlow, Russ, G, Green Bay (2) 1939, Jan. 1940
LeVias, Jerry, WR, Houston (1) 1970*
Lewis, David, LB, Tampa Bay (1) 1981
Lewis, Frank, WR, Buffalo (1) 1982
Lewis, Woodley, DB, Los Angeles (1) 1951
Lilly, Bob, DT, Dallas (11)1963,1965-72, 1973*, 1974*
Lincoln, Keith, RB (5) San Diego, 1963-66; Buffalo, 1968
Linhart, Toni, K, Baltimore (2) 1977-78
Lio, Augie, G, Detroit (2) Jan. 1942, Dec. 1942
Lipscomb, Gene (Big Daddy), DT (3) Baltimore, 1959-60; Pittsburgh, 1963
Lipscomb, Paul, T, Washington (4) 1951-54
Little, Floyd, RB, Denver (5) 1969-72, 1974
Little, Larry, G, Miami (5) 1970, 1972-75
Livingston, Andy, RB, New Orleans (1) 1970
Livingston, Mike, QB, Kansas City (1) 1970
Livingston, Ted, G, Cleveland Rams (1) Dec. 1940
Lloyd, Dave, LB, Philadelphia (1) 1970
Lockhart, Carl (Spider), DB, New York Giants (2) 1967, 1969
Lofton, James, WR, Green Bay (3) 1979, 1981-82
Logan, Jerry, S, Baltimore (3) 1966, 1971-72
Logan, Randy, S, Philadelphia (2) 1980-81
Long, Charley, G, Boston Patriots (2) 1963-64
Looney, Don, E, Philadelphia (1) Dec. 1940
Lott, Ronnie, CB, San Francisco (1) 1982
LoVetere, John, DT, New York Giants (1) 1964
Lowe, Paul, RB, San Diego (2) 1964, 1966
Lowery, Nick, K, Kansas City (1) 1982
Lucci, Mike, LB, Detroit (1) 1972
Luckman, Sid, QB, Chicago Bears (3) Dec. 1940, Jan. 1942, Dec. 1942
Lujack, Johnny, QB, Chicago Bears (2) 1951-52
Lunday, Ken (Kayo), G, New York Giants (1) 1939
Lundy, Lamar, DE, Los Angeles (1) 1960
Lyles, Lenny, DB, Baltimore (1) 1967
Lynch, Dick, DB, New York Giants (1)1964
Lynch, Jim, LB, Kansas City (1) 1969

M

Mack, Tom, G, Los Angeles (11) 1968-76, 1978-79
Mackey, John, TE, Baltimore (5) 1964, 1966-69
MacKinnon, Jacques, TE, San Diego (2) 1967, 1969
Magnani, Dante, B, Cleveland Rams (1) Dec. 1942
Maguire, Paul, LB (2) San Diego, 1963; Buffalo, 1966
Malone, Charley, E, Washington (1) Dec. 1942
Manders, Dave, C, Dallas (1) 1967
Manders, Clarence (Pug), B, Brooklyn Dodgers (3) Jan. 1940, Dec. 1940, Jan. 1942
Maniaci, Joe, B, Chicago Bears (2) Dec. 1940, Jan. 1942
Manning, Archie, QB, New Orleans (2) 1979-80
Manske, Edgar (Eggs) E, Chicago Bears (1) Dec. 1940
Maples, Bobby, C, Houston (1) 1969
Marchetti, Gino, DE, Baltimore (10) 1955-58, 1960-65
Marcol, Chester, K, Green Bay (2) 1973, 1975
Marconi, Joe, RB, Chicago (1) 1964
Marsalis, Jim, CB, Kansas City (2) 1970-71
Marshall, Jim, DE, Minnesota (2) 1969-70
Martin, Harvey, DE, Dallas (4) 1977-78, 1979*, 1980
Martin, Jim, K, Detroit (1) 1962
Marinkovic, John, E, Green Bay (2) 1954, 1956
Marinovich, Phil, G, Chicago Bears (1) Dec. 1940
Mason, Tommy, RB, Minnesota (3) 1963-65
Massey, Carlton, E, Cleveland (1) 1956

Masterson, Bernie, QB, Chicago Bears (1) Dec. 1940
Masterson, Bob, E, Washington (1) Dec. 1942
Mathews, Ray, B, Pittsburgh (2) 1953, 1956
Mathis, Bill, RB (2) New York Titans, 1962: New York Jets, 1964
Matson, Ollie, RB, Chicago Cardinals (5) 1953, 1955-58
Matsos, Archie, LB (3) Buffalo, 1962-63; Oakland, 1964
Matte, Tom, RB, Baltimore (2) 1969-70
Matuszak, Marv, LB (3) Pittsburgh, 1954; San Francisco, 1958; Buffalo 1963
Matuza, Al, C, Chicago Bears (1) Jan. 1942
Maynard, Don, WR, New York Jets (3) 1966, 1968, 1970*
Mays, Jerry, DE (7) Dallas Texans, 1963; Kansas City, 1965-69, 1971
Maznicki, Frank, B, Chicago Bears (1) Dec. 1942
McAfee, George, B, Chicago Bears (1) Jan. 1942
McChesney, Bob, E, Washington (2) 1939, Dec. 1942
McClairen, Jack, E, Pittsburgh (1) 1958
McClinton, Curtis, RB (3) Dallas Texans, 1963; Kansas City, 1967-68
McCloughan, Kent, CB, Oakland (2) 1967, 1968*
McCord, Darris, DE, Detroit (1) 1958
McCormack, Mike, T (6) New York Yanks, 1951; Cleveland, 1957-58, 1961-63
McCutcheon, Lawrence, RB, Los Angeles (5) 1974-78
McDole, Ron, DE, Buffalo (2) 1966, 1968
McDonald, Tommy, WR (6) Philadelphia, 1959-63; Los Angeles, 1966
McElhenny, Hugh, RB (6) San Francisco, 1953-54, 1957-59; Minnesota, 1962
McFadin, Bud, T (5) Los Angeles, 1956-57; Denver, 1962-64
McGee, Ben, DE, Pittsburgh (2) 1967, 1969
McGee, Max, E, Green Bay (1) 1962
McGraw, Thurman, T, Detroit (1) 1951
McInally, Pat, P, Cincinnati (1) 1982
McKeever, Marlin, DE, Los Angeles (1) 1967
McLaughlin, Leon, C, Los Angeles (1) 1955
McLean, Ray (Scooter), B, Chicago Bears (2) Dec. 1940, Jan. 1942
McLeod, Bob, E, Houston (1) 1962
McMillan, Ernie, T, St. Louis (4) 1966, 1968, 1970-71
McMurty, Chuck, DT, Buffalo (1) 1962
McNeil, Charles, DB, San Diego (1) 1962
McNeil, Clifton, WR, San Francisco (1) 1969
McPeak, Bill, E, Pittsburgh (3) 1953-54, 1957
Meador, Eddie, DB, Los Angeles (5) 1961, 1965-67, 1969
Meinert, Dale, LB, St. Louis (3) 1964, 1966, 1968
Mellus, John, T, New York Giants (2) 1939, Jan. 1942
Mercer, Mike, K, Buffalo (1) 1968
Meredith, Don, QB, Dallas (3) 1967-69
Meredith, Dudley, DT, Buffalo (1) 1966
Mertens, Jerry, B, San Francisco (1) 1959
Metcalf, Terry, RB, St. Louis (3) 1975-76, 1978
Michael, Rich, T, Houston (2) 1963-64
Michaels, Lou, K-DE, Pittsburgh (2) 1963-64
Michaels, Walt, LB, Cleveland (5) 1956-60
Michalik, Art, G, San Francisco (1) 1954
Middleton, Terdell, RB, Green Bay (1) 1979
Mihal, Joe, T, Chicago Bears (2) Dec. 1940, Jan. 1942
Mike-Mayer, Nick, K, Atlanta (1) 1974
Miller, Alan, RB, Oakland (1) 1962
Miller, Fred, DT, Baltimore (3) 1968-69, 1970*
Miller, Junior, TE, Atlanta (2) 1981-82
Miller, Paul, DE, Los Angeles (2) 1956-57
Mills, Pete, DE, Buffalo (1) 1966
Mingo, Gene, K-RB, Denver (1) 1963
Mischak, Bob, G (2) New York Titans, 1962; New York Jets, 1963
Mitchell, Bobby, RB (4) Cleveland, 1961; Washington 1963-65
Mitchell, Jim, TE, Atlanta (2) 1970, 1973
Mitchell, Leroy, DB, Boston Patriots (1) 1969
Mitchell, Lydell, RB, Baltimore (3) 1976-78
Mix, Ron, T, San Diego (8) 1962-69
Modzelewski, Dick, DT, Cleveland (1) 1965
Moegle, Dickie, RB, San Francisco (1) 1956
Montana, Joe, QB, San Francisco (1) 1982
Montgomery, Wilbert, RB, Philadelphia (2) 1979-80
Moore, Al, E, Green Bay (1) Jan. 1940
Moore, Lenny, RB, Baltimore (7) 1957, 1959-63, 1965
Moore, Nat, WR, Miami (1) 1978
Moore, Tom, RB, Green Bay (1) 1963
Moore, Wayne, T, Miami (1) 1974*
Moore, Wilbur, B, Washington (1) Dec. 1942
Moore, Zeke, CB, Houston (2) 1970-71

Morin, Milt, TE, Cleveland (2) 1969, 1972
Morgan, Stanley, WR, New England (2) 1980-81
Morrall, Earl, QB (2) Pittsburgh, 1958; Baltimore, 1969
Morris, Dennit, LB, Houston (1) 1962
Morris, Johnny, B, Chicago (1) 1961
Morris, Jon, C, Boston/New England Patriots (7) 1965-71
Morris, Eugene (Mercury), RB, Miami (3) 1972-73, 1974*
Morrison, Fred, (Curley), B, Cleveland (1) 1956
Morrow, John, C, Cleveland (2) 1962, 1964
Moseley, Mark, K, Washington (1) 1980
Moses, Haven, WR, Denver (1) 1974
Motley, Marion, B, Cleveland (1) 1951
Mudd, Howard, G, San Francisco (3) 1967-69
Mul-Key, Herb, KR, Washington (1) 1974
Mulleneaux, Carl, E, Green Bay (2) Jan. 1940, Dec. 1940
Muncie, Chuck, RB (2) New Orleans, 1980; San Diego, 1982
Murray, Ed, K, Detroit (1) 1981
Musso, George, G, Chicago Bears (3) Jan. 1940, Dec. 1940, Jan. 1942
Mutscheller, Jim, E, Baltimore (1) 1958
Myers, Philip (Chip), WR, Cincinnati (1) 1973
Myers, Tommy, S, New Orleans (1) 1981

N

Nagler, Gern, E, Chicago Cardinals (1) 1959
Namath, Joe, QB, New York Jets (5) 1966, 1968-69, 1970*, 1973*
Nance, Jim, RB, Boston Patriots (2) 1967*, 1968
Naumoff, Paul, LB, Detroit (1) 1971
Neal, Ed, C, Green Bay (1) 1951
Neely, Ralph, T, Dallas (2) 1968, 1970
Neighbors, Billy, G, Boston Patriots (1) 1964
Nelms, Mike, KR, Washington (2) 1981-82
Nelsen, Bill, QB, Cleveland (1) 1970
Nelson, Andy, S, Baltimore (1) 1961
Nelson, Steve, LB, New England (1) 1981
Neville, Tom, T, Boston Patriots (1) 1967
Newman, Ed, G, Miami (1) 1982
Newsome, Ozzie, TE, Cleveland (1) 1982
Nickel, Elbie, E, Pittsburgh (3) 1953-54, 1957
Niemi, Laurie, T, Washington (2) 1952-53
Niland, John, G, Dallas (6) 1969-74
Nisby, John, G, Pittsburgh (3) 1960, 1962-63
Nitschke, Ray, LB, Green Bay (1) 1965
Nobis, Tommy, LB, Atlanta (5) 1967-69, 1971, 1973
Nolting, Ray, B, Chicago Bears (2) Dec. 1940, Jan. 1942
Nomellini, Leo, DT, San Francisco (10) 1951-54, 1957-62
Noonan, Karl, WR, Miami (1) 1969
Norton, Don, E, San Diego (2) 1962, 1963*
Norton, Jerry, S (5) Philadelphia, 1958-59; St. Louis, 1960-62
Norton, Jim, DB, Houston (3) 1963-64, 1968
Nowaskey, Bob, E, Chicago Bears (2) Dec. 1940, Jan. 1942
Nutter, Madison (Buzz), C, Pittsburgh (1) 1963
Nye, Blaine, G, Dallas (2) 1975, 1977

O

Oakes, Don, T, Boston Patriots (1) 1968
O'Brien, Davey, B, Philadelphia (1), Jan. 1940
Odom, Steve, KR, Green Bay (1) 1976
Odoms, Riley, TE, Denver (3) 1974-76
O'Donnell, Joe, T, Buffalo (1) 1966
Oldershaw, Doug, G, New York Giants (1) Dec. 1940
Olsen, Merlin, DT, Los Angeles (14) 1963-70, 1971*, 1972-76
Olson, Harold, T, Buffalo (1) 1962
Olszewski, Johnny, B, Chicago Cardinals (2) 1954, 1956
Orr, Jimmy, WR (2) Pittsburgh, 1960; Baltimore, 1966
Osborn, Dave, RB, Minnesota (1) 1971
Osmanski, Bill, B, Chicago Bears (2) Dec. 1940, Jan. 1942
Otis, Jim, RB, St. Louis (1) 1976
Otto, Gus, LB, Oakland (1) 1970
Otto, Jim, C, Oakland (12) 1962-73
Owens, Steve, RB, Detroit (1) 1972

P

Page, Alan, DT, Minnesota (9) 1969-76, 1977*
Paluck, John, DE, Washington (1) 1965
Panfil, Ken, T, St. Louis (1) 1960
Pardee, Jack, LB, Los Angeles (1) 1964
Parilli, Babe, QB, Boston Patriots (2) 1964-65
Parker, Jim, T, Baltimore (8) 1959-66
Parks, Dave, WR, San Francisco (2) 1965, 1967

*Selected but did not play

Jack Rudnay   *Bob St. Clair*   *Jake Scott*   *Jerry Sherk*   *Jerry Smith*   *Matt Snell*   *Gordy Soltau*

Parrish, Bernie, DB, Cleveland (2) 1961, 1964
Parrish, Lemar, CB-KR (8) Cincinnati, 1971-72, 1975-78; Washington, 1980-81
Parry, Owen (Ox), T, New York Giants (1) 1939
Pastorini, Dan, QB, Houston (1) 1976
Patton, Jim, S, New York Giants (5) 1959 -63
Paul, Don, S (4) Chicago Cardinals, 1954; Cleveland, 1957-59
Paul, Don, LB, Los Angeles (3) 1952-54
Paulson, Dainard, DB, New York Jets (2) 1965-66
Payton, Walter, RB, Chicago (5) 1977-81
Pear, Dave, DT, Tampa Bay (1) 1979
Pearson, Drew, WR, Dallas (3) 1975, 1977-78
Peoples, Woody, G, San Francisco (2) 1973-74
Perkins, Don, RB, Dallas (6) 1962-64, 1967-69
Perry, Joe, RB, San Francisco (3) 1953-55
Perry, Rod, CB, Los Angeles (2) 1979, 1981
Peters, Floyd, DT, Philadelphia (3) 1965, 1967-68
Peters, Volney, T, Washington (1) 1956
Petitbon, Richie, DB, Chicago (4) 1963-64, 1967-68
Petty, John, B, Chicago Bears (1) Dec. 1942
Philbin, Gerry, DE, New York Jets (2) 1969-70
Phillips, Jim, WR, Los Angeles (3) 1961-63
Pietrosante, Nick, RB, Detroit (2) 1961-62
Pihos, Pete, E, Philadelphia (6) 1951-56
Pinckert, Erny, B, Washington (2) 1939, Jan. 1940
Plasman, Dick, E, Chicago Bears (2) Dec. 1940, Jan. 1942
Plum, Milt, QB, Cleveland (2) 1961-62
Plunkett, Sherman, T, New York Jets (2) 1965, 1967
Podoley, Jim, B, Washington (1) 1958
Poillon, Dick, B, Washington (1) Dec. 1942
Polsfoot, Fran, E, Chicago Cardinals (1) 1952
Pool, Hampton, E, Chicago Bears (2) Dec. 1940, Jan. 1942
Poole, Jim, E, New York Giants (3) 1939, Jan. 1940, Dec. 1940
Post, Dickie, RB, San Diego (2) 1968*, 1970
Pottios, Myron, LB, Pittsburgh (3) 1962, 1964-65
Powell, Art, E, Oakland (4) 1964-67
Powell, Marvin, T, New York Jets (3) 1980-82
Price, Cotton, B, Detroit (1) Dec. 1940
Price, Eddie, RB, New York Giants (3) 1952-53, 1955
Pritchard, Bosh, B, Philadelphia (1) Dec. 1942
Promuto, Vince, G, Washington (2) 1964-65
Pruitt, Greg, KR-RB, Cleveland (4) 1974-75, 1977-78
Pruitt, Mike, RB, Cleveland (2) 1980-81
Putnam, Duane, G, Los Angeles (4) 1955-56, 1958-59
Pyle, Mike, C, Chicago (1) 1964

Q

Quinlan, Volney (Skeet), B, Los Angeles (1) 1955

R

Radovich, Bill, G, Detroit (1) 1939
Randle, Sonny, WR, St. Louis (4) 1961-63, 1966
Rashad, Ahmad, WR, Minnesota (4) 1979-82
Ray, Buford (Baby), T, Green Bay (1) Jan. 1940
Reaves, Ken, CB, Atlanta (1) 1970
Rechichar, Bert, B-K, Baltimore (3) 1956-58
Redman, Rick, LB, San Diego (1) 1968
Reed, Alvin, TE, Houston (2) 1969-70
Reger, John, LB, Pittsburgh (3) 1960-62
Reichow, Jerry, E, Minnesota (1) 1962
Reid, Mike, DT, Cincinnati (2) 1973, 1974*
Reinfeldt, Mike, S, Houston (1) 1980
Renfro, Mel, DB, Dallas (10) 1965-72, 1973*, 1974
Renfro, Ray, B, Cleveland (3) 1954, 1958, 1961
Retzlaff, Pete, E, Philadelphia (5) 1959, 1961, 1964-66
Reynolds, Bob, T, St. Louis (3) 1967, 1969-70
Reynolds, Jack, LB, Los Angeles (2) 1976, 1981
Rice, Ken, T, Buffalo (1) 1962
Richards, Elvin, B, New York Giants (2) 1939, Dec. 1940
Richardson, Jesse, T, Philadelphia (1) 1960
Richardson, Willie, WR, Baltimore (2) 1968-69
Richter, Les, LB, Los Angeles (8) 1955-62
Riffle, Dick, B, Pittsburgh (1) Jan. 1942
Riggins, John, RB, New York Jets (1) 1976
Ringo, Jim, C (10) Green Bay, 1958-64; Philadelphia, 1965-66, 1968
Roaches, Carl, KR, Houston (1) 1982
Robb, Joe, DE, St. Louis (1) 1967
Roberson, Irwin (Bo), WR, Buffalo (1) 1966
Roberts, Gene, B, New York Giants (1) 1951
Robertson, Isiah, LB, Los Angeles (6) 1972, 1974-78
Robinson, Dave, LB, Green Bay (3) 1967-68, 1970

Robinson, Jerry, LB, Philadelphia (1) 1982
Robinson, Johnny, S, Kansas City (7) 1964, 1965*, 1966-69, 1971
Robinson, Paul, RB, Cincinnati (2) 1969-70
Robinson, Wayne, LB, Philadelphia (2) 1955-56
Robustelli, Andy, DE (7) Los Angeles, 1954, 1956; New York Giants, 1957-58, 1960-62
Rochester, Paul, DT, Dallas Texans (1) 1962
Rock, Walter, T, San Francisco (1) 1966
Rogel, Fran, B, Pittsburgh (1) 1957
Rogers, George, RB, New Orleans (1) 1982
Rohde, Len, T, San Francisco (1) 1971
Roland, Johnny, RB, St. Louis (2) 1967, 1968*
Rossovich, Tim, LB, Philadelphia (1) 1970
Rote, Kyle, E, New York Giants (4) 1954*, 1955-57
Rote, Tobin, QB (2) Green Bay, 1957; San Diego, 1964
Rowe, Bob, DE, St. Louis (1) 1969
Rucinski, Eddie, S, Brooklyn Dodgers (1) Dec. 1942
Rudnay, Jack, C, Kansas City (4) 1974-77
Russell, Andy, LB, Pittsburgh (7) 1969, 1971-76
Rutgens, Joe, DT, Washington (2) 1964, 1966
Rutkowski, Ed, WR, Buffalo (1) 1966
Ryan, Frank, QB, Cleveland (3) 1965-67

S

Saimes, George, CB, Buffalo (5) 1965-69
Sanders, Charlie, TE, Detroit (7) 1969-72, 1975-77
Sanders, Orban (Spec), B, New York Yanks (1) 1951
Sandusky, Mike, G, Pittsburgh (1) 1961
Sanford, Leo, C, Chicago Cardinals (2) 1957-58
Sauer, George, WR, New York Jets (4) 1967-70
Saul, Rich, C, Los Angeles (6) 1977-82
Sayers, Gale, RB, Chicago (4) 1966-68, 1970
Scarpitto, Bob, WR, Denver (1) 1967
Schafrath, Dick, T, Cleveland (6) 1964-69
Schmidt, Bob, C, Houston (3) 1962-64
Schmidt, Henry, DT, Buffalo (1) 1966
Schmidt, Joe, LB, Detroit (9) 1955-63
Schnelker, Bob, E, New York Giants (2) 1959-60
Schnellbacher, Otto, DB, New York Giants (2) 1951-52
Schottenheimer, Marty, LB, Buffalo (1) 1966
Schrader, Jim, C, Washington (3) 1959-60, 1962
Schroeder, Gene, E, Chicago Bears (1) 1953
Schuh, Harry, T, Oakland (3) 1968, 1970-71
Schultz, Charles, T, Green Bay (1) Jan. 1940
Schwartz, Perry, E, Brooklyn Dodgers (4) 1939, Jan. 1940, Jan. 1942, Dec. 1942
Scott, Clarence, CB, Cleveland (1) 1974
Scott, Herbert, G, Dallas (3) 1980-82
Scott, Jake, S, Miami (5) 1972*, 1973-74, 1975*, 1976
Scott, Tom, E, Philadelphia (2) 1958-59
Scudero, Joe, B, Washington (1) 1956
Sellers, Ron, WR, Boston Patriots (1) 1970
Selmon, Lee Roy, DE, Tampa Bay (3) 1980-82
Senser, Joe, TE, Minnesota (1) 1982*
Septien, Rafael, K, Dallas (1) 1982
Sestak, Tom, T, Buffalo (4) 1963-65, 1966*
Sewell, Harley, G, Detroit (4) 1958-60, 1963
Seymour, Bob, B, Washington (1) Dec. 1942
Shaffer, Leland, B, New York Giants (1) 1939
Shanklin, Ron, WR, Pittsburgh (1) 1974*
Shaw, Billy, G, Buffalo (8) 1963-70
Shaw, Bob, E, Chicago Cardinals (1) 1951
Shell, Art, T, Oakland (8) 1973-79, 1981
Shell, Donnie, S, Pittsburgh (4) 1979-82
Sherk, Jerry, DT, Cleveland (4) 1974-77
Sherman, Saul, QB, Chicago Bears (1) Dec. 1940
Sherman, Will, S, Los Angeles (2) 1956, 1959
Shipkey, Jerry, B, Pittsburgh (3) 1951-53
Shirk, John, E, Chicago Cardinals (1) Dec. 1940
Shofner, Del, WR (5) Los Angeles, 1959-60; New York Giants, 1962-64
Shonta, Chuck, DB, Boston Patriots (1) 1967
Shugart, Clyde, G, Washington (2) Jan. 1942, Dec. 1942
Siegal, John, E, Chicago Bears (3) Dec. 1940, Jan. 1942, Dec. 1942
Siemon, Jeff, LB, Minnesota (4) 1974, 1976-78
Silas, Sam, DT, St. Louis (1) 1966
Simington, Milt, G, Pittsburgh (1) Dec. 1942
Simmons, Jack, C, Chicago Cardinals (1) 1956
Simpson, O.J., RB, Buffalo (6) 1970, 1973-77
Sims, Billy, RB, Detroit (2) 1981-82
Sipe, Brian, QB, Cleveland (1) 1981

Sisemore, Jerry, T, Philadelphia (2) 1980, 1982
Sistrunk, Otis, DT, Oakland (1) 1975
Sivell, Jim, G, Brooklyn Dodgers (1) Jan. 1942
Skladany, Tom, P, Detroit (1) 1982
Skoronski, Bob, T, Green Bay (1) 1967
Slivinski, Steve, G, Washington (1) Jan. 1942
Smerlas, Fred, DT, Buffalo (2) 1981-82
Smith, Bill, E, Chicago Cardinals (1) Jan. 1940
Smith, Bob, RB, Buffalo (1) 1966
Smith, Bob, B, Detroit (1) 1953
Smith, Charles (Bubba), DE, Baltimore (2) 1971-72
Smith, Ernie, T, Green Bay (1) Jan. 1940
Smith, George, C, Washington (1) Dec. 1942
Smith, Harry, G, Detroit (1) Dec. 1940
Smith, Jackie, TE, St. Louis (5) 1967-71
Smith, J.D., T, Philadelphia (1) 1962*
Smith, J.D., RB, San Francisco (2) 1960, 1963
Smith, Jerry, TE, Washington (2) 1968, 1970
Smith, Jim Ray, G, Cleveland (5) 1959-63
Smith, John, K, New England (1) 1981
Smith, J.T., KR, Kansas City (1) 1981
Smith, Paul, DT, Denver (2) 1973-74
Smith, Ron, KR, Chicago (1) 1973
Smith, Stu, B, Pittsburgh (1) 1939
Snead, Norm, QB (3) Washington, 1964; Philadelphia, 1966; New York Giants, 1973
Snell, Matt, RB, New York Jets (3) 1965*, 1967, 1970
Snow, Jack, WR, Los Angeles (1) 1968*
Snyder, Bob, B, Chicago Bears (2) Dec. 1940, Jan. 1942
Snyder, Ken, T, Philadelphia (2) 1954-55
Soar, Hank, B, New York Giants (1) 1939
Soltau, Gordy, E, San Francisco (3) 1952-54
Spadaccini, Vic, QB, Cleveland Rams (1) 1940
Speedie, Mac, E, Cleveland (1) 1951
Spinney, Art, G, Baltimore (2) 1960-61
Sprinkle, Ed, DE, Chicago Bears (4) 1951-53, 1955
Stabler, Ken, QB, Oakland (4) 1974-75, 1977*, 1978
Stacy, Bill, DB, St. Louis (1) 1962
Stallings, Larry, LB, St. Louis (1) 1971
Stallworth, John, WR, Pittsburgh (1) 1980
Standlee, Norm, B (2) Chicago Bears, Jan. 1942; San Francisco 1951
Stanfel, Dick, G (5) Detroit, 1954; Washington, 1956-59
Stanfill, Bill, DE, Miami (5) 1970, 1972, 1973*, 1974*, 1975
Starr, Bart, QB, Green Bay (4) 1961-63, 1967
Staubach, Roger, QB, Dallas (5) 1972, 1977, 1978*, 1979-80
Stautner, Ernie, DE, Pittsburgh (9) 1953-54, 1956-62
St. Clair, Bob, T, San Francisco (3) 1957, 1959-62
Stemrick, Greg, CB, Houston (1) 1981
Stenerud, Jan, K, Kansas City (5) 1969-72, 1976
Still, Art, DE, Kansas City (2) 1981-82
Stits, Bill, B, Detroit (1) 1955
St. Jean, Len, G, Boston Patriots (1) 1967
Stone, Donnie, RB, Denver (1) 1962
Stovall, Jerry DB, St. Louis (3) 1967-68, 1970
Stralka, Clem, G, Washington (1) Dec. 1942
Stratton, Mike, LB, Buffalo (6) 1964-69
Strickland, Larry, C, Chicago Bears (1) 1957
Stroud, Jack, G, New York Giants (3) 1956, 1958, 1961
Stryzkalski, John (Strike), B, San Francisco (1) 1951
Studstill, Pat, WR, Detroit (2) 1966-67
Sturm, Jerry, C, Denver (2) 1965, 1967
Stydahar, Joe, T, Chicago Bears (4) 1939, Jan. 1940, Dec. 1940, Jan. 1942
Sugar, Leo, DE, St. Louis (2) 1959, 1961
Suggs, Walt, T, Houston (2) 1968-69
Sunde, Milt, G, Minnesota (1) 1967
Swendsen, Bud, C, Green Bay (1) Jan. 1940
Swoboda, Bill, B, Chicago Cardinals (1) 1954
Swann, Lynn, WR, Pittsburgh (3) 1976, 1978-79
Sweeney, Walt, G, San Diego (9) 1965-73
Swenson, Bob, LB, Denver (1) 1982
Swisher, Bob, B, Chicago Bears (2) Dec. 1940, Jan. 1942
Szymanski, Dick, C, Baltimore (3) 1956, 1963, 1965

T

Talamini, Bob, G, Houston (6) 1963-68
Talbert, Diron, DT, Washington (1) 1975
Taliaferro, George, B (3) New York Yanks, 1952; Dallas Texans, 1953; Baltimore 1954
Taliaferro, Mike, QB, Boston Patriots (1) 1970
Tarkenton, Fran, QB (9) Minnesota, 1965-66, 1975*, 1976*,

Otis Taylor   *Gene Upshaw*   *Gene Washington*   *Russ Washington*   *Mike Webster*   *Randy White*   *Jack Youngblood*

1977*, New York Giants, 1968-71
Tatum, Jack, S, Oakland (3) 1974-75, 1976*
Taylor, Bruce, CB, San Francisco (1) 1972*
Taylor, Charley, WR, Washington (8) 1965-68, 1973-76
Taylor, Hugh (Bones), E, Washington (2) 1953, 1955
Taylor, Jim, RB, Green Bay (4) 1961-62, 1964-65
Taylor, Lawrence, LB, New York Giants (1) 1982
Taylor, Lionel, E, Denver (3) 1962-63, 1966*
Taylor, Otis, WR, Kansas City (2) 1972-73
Taylor, Roosevelt, DB, Chicago (2) 1964, 1969
Terrell, Marvin, G, Dallas Texans (1) 1963
Teteak, Deral, G, Green Bay (1) 1953
Thielemann, R.C., G, Atlanta (1) 1982
Thomas, Aaron, WR, New York Giants (1) 1965
Thomas, Clendon, DB, Pittsburgh (1) 1964
Thomas, Emmitt, CB, Kansas City (5) 1969, 1972-73, 1975-76
Thomas, John, G, San Francisco (1) 1967
Thomas, Pat, CB, Los Angeles (2) 1979, 1981
Thomason, Bobby, QB, Philadelphia (3) 1954, 1956-57
Thompson, Billy, S, Denver (3) 1978-79, 1982
Thompson, Tommy, QB, Philadelphia (1) Dec. 1942
Tilley, Pat, WR, St. Louis (1) 1981
Tingelhoff, Mick, C, Minnesota (6) 1965-70
Tinsley, Gaynell, E, Chicago Cardinals (1) 1939
Tinsley, Pete, G, Green Bay (1) Jan. 1940
Titchenal, Bob, C, Washington (1) Dec. 1942
Tittle, Y.A., QB (6) San Francisco, 1954-55, 1958, 1960; New York Giants, 1962-63
Todd, Dick, B, Washington (2) Dec. 1940, Dec. 1942
Tolar, Charlie, RB, Houston (2) 1962-63
Toneff, Bob, DT (4) San Francisco, 1956; Washington, 1960-62
Tonnemaker, Clayton, LB, Green Bay (1) 1954
Torczon, LaVerne, DE, Buffalo (1) 1962
Torgeson, LaVern, LB (3) Detroit, 1955; Washington, 1956-57
Torrance, Jack, T, Chicago Bears (1) Dec. 1940
Toth, Zollie, B, New York Yanks (1) 1951
Towler, Dan, RB, Los Angeles (4) 1952-55
Tracey, John, LB, Buffalo (2) 1966-67
Tracy, Tom, RB, Pittsburgh (2) 1959, 1961
Trippi, Charley, B, Chicago Cardinals (2) 1953-54
Tripson, John, T, Detroit (1) Jan. 1942
Tripucka, Frank, QB, Denver (1) 1963
Trumpy, Bob, TE, Cincinnati (4) 1969, 1970*, 1971, 1974
Tubbs, Jerry, LB, Dallas (1) 1963
Tunnell, Emlen, S (9) New York Giants, 1951-58; Green Bay, 1960
Turner, Robert (Bake), WR, New York Jets (1) 1964
Turner, Cecil, KR, Chicago (1) 1971
Turner, Clyde (Bulldog), C, Chicago Bears (4) Dec. 1941, Jan. 1942, 1951-52
Turner, Jim, K, New York Jets (2) 1969-70
Tuttle, Orville, G, New York Giants (2) 1939, Jan. 1940
Tyrer, Jim, T (9) Dallas Texans, 1963; Kansas City, 1964-67 1969-72

U

Ulinski, Harry, C, Washington (1) 1956
Unitas, Johnny, QB, Baltimore (10) 1958-65, 1967-68
Upchurch, Rick, KR, Denver (3) 1977, 1979-80
Upshaw, Gene, G, Oakland (7) 1969, 1973-78
Uram, Andy, B, Green Bay (1) Jan. 1940

V

Van Brocklin, Norm, QB (9) Los Angeles, 1951-56; Philadelphia, 1959-61
Van Dyke, Bruce, G, Pittsburgh (1) 1974

van Eeghen, Mark, RB, Oakland (1) 1978
Van Note, Jeff, C, Atlanta (4) 1975-76, 1981-82
Van Pelt, Brad, LB, New York Giants (5) 1977-81
Van Raaphorst, Dick, K, San Diego (1) 1967
Vanzo, Fred, B, Detroit (1) Jan. 1940
Varrichione, Frank, T (5) Pittsburgh, 1956, 1958-59, 1961; Los Angeles, 1963
Villapiano, Phil, LB, Oakland (4) 1974-77
Vogel, Bob, T, Baltimore (4) 1965-66, 1968, 1972
Volk, Rick, DB, Baltimore (3) 1968, 1970, 1972

W

Wade, Bill, QB (2) Los Angeles, 1959; Chicago, 1964
Wagner, Mike, S, Pittsburgh (2) 1976-77
Walden, Bobby, P, Pittsburgh (1) 1970
Walker, Chuck, DT, St. Louis (1) 1967
Walker, Doak, B, Detroit (5) 1951-52, 1954-56
Walker, Wayne, LB-K, Detroit (3) 1964-66
Walker, Wesley, WR, New York Jets (1) 1979
Waller, Ron, B, Los Angeles (1) 1956
Wallner, Fred, G, Chicago Cardinals (1) 1956
Walls, Everson, CB, Dallas (1) 1982
Walsh, Bill, C, Pittsburgh (2) 1951-52
Walston, Bobby, E-K, Philadelphia (2) 1961-62
Walters, Stan, T, Philadelphia (2) 1979-80
Warfield, Paul, WR (8) Cleveland, 1965, 1969-70; Miami, 1971-72, 1973*, 1974*, 1975
Warlick, Ernie, E, Buffalo (4) 1963-66
Warner, Charles, DB, Buffalo (1) 1966
Warren, Jim, DB, Miami (1) 1967
Washington, Gene, WR, Minnesota (2) 1970-71
Washington, Gene, WR, San Francisco (4) 1970-73
Washington, Joe, RB, Baltimore (1) 1980
Washington, Russ, T, San Diego (5) 1975-76, 1978-80
Washington, Vic, RB, San Francisco (1) 1972
Waterfield, Bob, QB, Los Angeles (2) 1951-52
Waters, Charlie, S, Dallas (4) 1977-79
Watson, Steve, WR, Denver (1) 1982
Watts, George, T, Washington (1) Dec. 1942
Weatherall, Jim, T, Philadelphia (2) 1956-57
Webb, Don, CB, Boston Patriots (1) 1970
Webster, Alex, RB, New York Giants (2) 1959, 1962
Webster, David, DB, Dallas Texans (1) 1962
Webster, George, LB, Houston (3) 1968*, 1969, 1970*
Webster, Mike, C, Pittsburgh (4) 1979-82
Wehrli, Roger, CB, St. Louis (6) 1971, 1975-78, 1980
Weinmeister, Arnie, T, New York Giants (4) 1951-54
Weisgerber, Dick, B, Green Bay (1) Jan. 1940
Wells, Billy, B, Washington (1) 1955
Wells, Warren, WR, Oakland (2) 1969, 1971
West, Stan, G, Los Angeles (2) 1952-53
West, Willie, DB (2) Buffalo, 1964; Miami, 1967
Westmoreland, Dick, DB, Miami (1) 1968
Wham, Tom, E, Chicago Cardinals (1) 1952
White, Arthur (Tarzan), G, New York Giants (1) 1939
White, Dwight, DE, Pittsburgh (2) 1973-74
White, Ed, G (4) Minnesota, 1976-78, San Diego, 1980
White, Randy, DT, Dallas (5) 1978-82
White, Sammy, WR, Minnesota (2) 1977-78
Whited, Marvin, B, Washington (1) Dec. 1942
Whitsell, Dave, DB, New Orleans (1) 1968
Whitenton, Jesse, DB, Green Bay (2) 1962, 1964
Wiatrak, John, C, Cleveland Rams (1) 1939
Widby, Ron, P, Dallas (1) 1972

Widseth, Ed, T, New York Giants (1) 1939
Wietecha, Ray, C, New York Giants (4) 1958-59, 1961, 1963
Wiggin, Paul, DE, Cleveland (2) 1966, 1968
Wightkin, Bill, T, Chicago Bears (1) 1956
Wilcox, Dave, LB, San Francisco (7) 1967, 1969-70, 1971*, 1972-74
Wildung, Dick, T, Green Bay (1) 1952
Wilkerson, Doug, G, San Diego (2) 1981-82
Wilkin, Willie, T, Washington (3) Dec. 1940, Jan. 1942, Dec. 1942
Willard, Ken, RB, San Francisco (4) 1966-67, 1969-70
Willey, Norm, E, Philadelphia (2) 1955-56
Williams, Delvin, RB (2) San Francisco, 1977; Miami, 1979
Williams, Fred, T, Chicago Bears (4) 1953-54, 1959-60
Williams, Johnny, B, Washington (1) 1953
Williams, Willie, DB, New York Giants (1) 1970
Williamson, Fred, DB, Oakland (3) 1962-64
Willis, Bill, G, Cleveland (3) 1951-53
Wilson, Billy, E, San Francisco (6) 1955-60
Wilson, George, E, Chicago Bears (3) Dec. 1940, Jan. 1942, Dec. 1942
Wilson, Jerrel, P, Kansas City (3) 1971-73
Wilson, Larry, S, St. Louis (8) 1963-64, 1966-71
Wilson, Nemiah, DB, Oakland (1) 1968
Wilson, Tom, B, Los Angeles (1) 1958
Wimberly, Abner, E, Green Bay (1) 1953
Winkler, Jim, T, Los Angeles (1) 1953
Winslow, Kellen, TE, San Diego (2) 1981-82
Wistert, Al, T, Philadelphia (1) 1951
Wittum, Tom, P, San Francisco (2) 1974-75
Wood, Duane, DB, Kansas City (1) 1964
Wood, Willie, S, Green Bay (8) 1963, 1965-71
Woodeshick, Tom, RB, Philadelphia (1) 1969
Woodson, Abe, B, San Francisco (5) 1960-64
Woodson, Marv, DB, Pittsburgh (1) 1968
Wooten, John, G, Cleveland (2) 1966-67
Woudenberg, John, T, Pittsburgh (1) Dec. 1942
Wozniak, John, G, Dallas Texans (1) 1953
Wright, Ernie, T, San Diego (3) 1962, 1964, 1966
Wright, Louis, CB, Denver (3) 1978-80
Wright, Rayfield, T, Dallas (6) 1972-77

Y

Yary, Ron, T, Minnesota (7) 1972-78
Yepremian, Garo, K, Miami (2) 1974, 1979
Young, Bill, T, Washington (1) Dec. 1942
Young, Bob, G, St. Louis (2) 1979-80
Young, Buddy, B, Baltimore (1) 1955
Young, Charle, TE, Philadelphia (3) 1974-76
Young, Roynell, CB, Philadelphia (1) 1982
Youngblood, Jack, DE, Los Angeles (7) 1974-80
Youngblood, Jim, LB, Los Angeles (1) 1980
Younger, Paul (Tank), RB, Los Angeles (4) 1952-54, 1956*

Z

Zarnas, Gus, G, Green Bay (1) Jan. 1940
Zatkoff, Roger, LB, Green Bay (3) 1955-57
Zeman, Bob, DB, Denver (1) 1963
Zeno, Joe, G, Washington (1) Dec. 1942
Zimmerman, Roy, B, Washington (1) Dec. 1942
Zook, John, DE, Atlanta (1) 1974

*Selected but did not play

PRO BOWL HISTORY

Date	Result	Site (attendance)	Honored players
Jan. 15, 1939	New York Giants 13, Pro All-Stars 10	Wrigley Field, Los Angeles (20,000)	
Jan. 14, 1940	Green Bay 16, Pro All-Stars 7	Gilmore Stadium, Los Angeles (18,000)	
Dec. 29, 1940	Chicago Bears 28, Pro All-Stars 14	Gilmore Stadium, Los Angeles (21,624)	
Jan. 4, 1942	Chicago Bears 35, Pro All-Stars 24	Polo Grounds, New York (17,725)	
Dec. 27, 1942	Pro All-Stars 17, Washington 14	Shibe Park, Philadelphia (18,671)	
Jan. 14, 1951	American Conf. 28, National Conf. 27	Los Angeles Memorial Coliseum (53,676)	Otto Graham, Cleveland, player of the game
Jan. 12, 1952	National Conf. 30, American Conf. 13	Los Angeles Memorial Coliseum (19,400)	Dan Towler, Los Angeles, player of the game
Jan. 10, 1953	National Conf. 27, American Conf. 7	Los Angeles Memorial Coliseum (34,208)	Don Doll, Detroit, player of the game
Jan. 17, 1954	East 20, West 9	Los Angeles Memorial Coliseum (44,214)	Chuck Bednarik, Philadelphia, player of the game
Jan. 1, 1955	West 26, East 19	Los Angeles Memorial Coliseum (43,972)	Billy Wilson, San Francisco, player of the game
Jan. 15, 1956	East 31, West 30	Los Angeles Memorial Coliseum (37,867)	Ollie Matson, Chi. Cardinals, player of the game
Jan. 13, 1957	West 19, East 10	Los Angeles Memorial Coliseum (44,177)	Bert Rechichar, Baltimore, outstanding back Ernie Stautner, Pittsburgh, outstanding lineman
Jan. 12, 1958	West 26, East 7	Los Angeles Memorial Coliseum (66,634)	Hugh McElhenny, San Francisco, outstanding back Gene Brito, Washington, outstanding lineman
Jan. 11, 1959	East 28, West 21	Los Angeles Memorial Coliseum (72,250)	Frank Gifford, N.Y. Giants, outstanding back Doug Atkins, Chi. Bears, outstanding lineman
Jan. 17, 1960	West 38, East 21	Los Angeles Memorial Coliseum (56,876)	Johnny Unitas, Baltimore, outstanding back Gene (Big Daddy) Lipscomb, Baltimore, outstanding lineman
Jan. 15, 1961	West 35, East 31	Los Angeles Memorial Coliseum (62,971)	Johnny Unitas, Baltimore, outstanding back Sam Huff, N.Y. Giants, outstanding lineman
Jan. 7, 1962	AFL West 47, East 27	Balboa Stadium, San Diego (20,973)	Cotton Davidson, Dallas Texans, player of the game
Jan. 14, 1962	NFL West 31, East 30	Los Angeles Memorial Coliseum (57,409)	Jim Brown, Cleveland, outstanding back Henry Jordan, Green Bay, outstanding lineman
Jan. 13, 1963	AFL West 21, East 14	Balboa Stadium, San Diego (27,641)	Curtis McClinton, Dallas Texans, outstanding offensive player Earl Faison, San Diego, outstanding defensive player
Jan. 13, 1963	NFL East 30, West 20	Los Angeles Memorial Coliseum (61,374)	Jim Brown, Cleveland, player of the game Gene (Big Daddy) Lipscomb, Pittsburgh, outstanding lineman
Jan. 12, 1964	NFL West 31, East 17	Los Angeles Memorial Coliseum (67,242)	Johnny Unitas, Baltimore, player of the game Gino Marchetti, Baltimore, outstanding lineman
Jan. 19, 1964	AFL West 27, East 24	Balboa Stadium, San Diego (20,016)	Keith Lincoln, San Diego, outstanding offensive player Archie Matsos, Oakland, outstanding defensive player
Jan. 10, 1965	NFL West 34, East 14	Los Angeles Memorial Coliseum (60,598)	Fran Tarkenton, Minnesota, outstanding back Terry Barr, Detroit, outstanding lineman
Jan. 16, 1965	AFL West 38, East 14	Jeppesen Stadium, Houston (15,446)	Keith Lincoln, San Diego, outstanding offensive player Willie Brown, Denver, outstanding defensive player
Jan. 15, 1966	AFL All-Stars 30, Buffalo 19	Rice Stadium, Houston (35,572)	Joe Namath, N.Y. Jets, most valuable player, offense Frank Buncom, San Diego, most valuable player, defense
Jan. 15, 1966	NFL East 36, West 7	Los Angeles Memorial Coliseum (60,124)	Jim Brown, Cleveland, outstanding back Dale Meinert, St. Louis, outstanding lineman
Jan. 21, 1967	AFL East 30, West 23	Oakland Coliseum (18,876)	Babe Parilli, Boston, outstanding offensive player Verlon Biggs, N.Y. Jets, outstanding defensive player
Jan. 22, 1967	NFL East 20, West 10	Los Angeles Memorial Coliseum (15,062)	Gale Sayers, Chicago, outstanding back Floyd Peters, Philadelphia, outstanding lineman
Jan. 21, 1968	AFL East 25, West 24	Gator Bowl, Jacksonville, Fla. (40,103)	Joe Namath and Don Maynard, N.Y. Jets, out. off. players Leslie (Speedy) Duncan, San Diego, out. def. player
Jan. 21, 1968	NFL West 38, East 20	Los Angeles Memorial Coliseum (53,289)	Gale Sayers, Chicago, outstanding back Dave Robinson, Green Bay, outstanding lineman
Jan. 19, 1969	AFL West 38, East 25	Gator Bowl, Jacksonville, Fla. (41,058)	Len Dawson, Kansas City, outstanding offensive player George Webster, Houston, outstanding defensive player
Jan. 19, 1969	NFL West 10, East 7	Los Angeles Memorial Coliseum (32,050)	Roman Gabriel, Los Angeles, outstanding back Merlin Olsen, Los Angeles, outstanding lineman
Jan. 17, 1970	AFL West 26, East 3	Astrodome, Houston (30,170)	John Hadl, San Diego, player of the game
Jan. 18, 1970	NFL West 16, East 13	Los Angeles Memorial Coliseum (57,486)	Gale Sayers, Chicago, outstanding back George Andrie, Dallas, outstanding lineman
Jan. 24, 1971	NFC 27, AFC 6	Los Angeles Memorial Coliseum (48,222)	Mel Renfro, Dallas, outstanding back Fred Carr, Green Bay, outstanding lineman
Jan. 23, 1972	AFC 26, NFC 13	Los Angeles Memorial Coliseum (53,647)	Jan Stenerud, Kansas City, outstanding offensive player Willie Lanier, Kansas City, outstanding defensive player
Jan. 21, 1973	AFC 33, NFC 28	Texas Stadium, Irving (47,879)	O. J. Simpson, Buffalo, player of the game
Jan. 20, 1974	AFC 15, NFC 13	Arrowhead, Kansas City (51,484)	Garo Yepremian, Miami, player of the game
Jan. 20, 1975	NFC 17, AFC 10	Orange Bowl, Miami (26,484)	James Harris, Los Angeles, player of the game
Jan. 26, 1976	NFC 23, AFC 20	Louisiana Superdome, New Orleans (32,108)	Billy Johnson, Houston, player of the game
Jan. 17, 1977	AFC 24, NFC 14	Kingdome, Seattle (63,214)	Mel Blount, Pittsburgh, player of the game
Jan. 23, 1978	NFC 14, AFC 13	Tampa Stadium (51,337)	Walter Payton, Chicago, player of the game
Jan. 29, 1979	NFC 13, AFC 7	Los Angeles Memorial Coliseum (46,281)	Ahmad Rashad, Minnesota, player of the game
Jan. 27, 1980	NFC 37, AFC 27	Aloha Stadium, Honolulu (48,060)	Chuck Muncie, New Orleans, player of the game
Feb. 1, 1981	NFC 21, AFC 7	Aloha Stadium, Honolulu (50,360)	Ed Murray, Detroit, player of the game
Jan. 31, 1982	AFC 16, NFC 13	Aloha Stadium, Honolulu (50,402)	Kellen Winslow, San Diego, and Lee Roy Selmon, Tampa Bay, players of the game

Chicago All-Star Games

1934

CHI. BEARS 0, ALL-STARS 0

The first Chicago All-Star game ended in a scoreless tie, punctuated by 12 punts by the Chicago Bears and 11 by the College All-Stars. The All-Stars outgained the Bears 143–123 and had six first downs to the Bears' three.

Chicago moved to the collegians' 9-yard line in the second quarter, but end Bill Hewitt fumbled on a reverse and Ed (Moose) Krause of Notre Dame recovered on the 19-yard line. The All-Stars' Bill Smith attempted a 41-yard field goal on the last play of the game, but it was blocked and recovered by Chicago's Carl Brumbaugh. Smith also missed a 32-yard attempt.

The game matched the 1933 champions of the National Football League and graduated college seniors who were selected in a poll conducted by the sponsoring *Chicago Tribune* and 105 associated newspapers throughout the United States. A crowd of 79,432 was in attendance.

August 31, at Soldier Field

Chi. Bears	Starting Lineups	College All-Stars
Bill Hewitt	LE	E. (Eggs) Manske (N'wstn.)
Roy (Link) Lyman	LT	Ed Krause (Notre Dame)
Jules Carlson	LG	Frank Walton (Pittsburgh)
Charles (Ookie) Miller	C	Chuck Bernard (Michigan)
Joe Zeller	RG	Bob Jones (Indiana)
George Musso	RT	A. Schwammel (Oregon St.)
Luke Johnsos	RE	Joe Skladany (Pittsburgh)
Carl Brumbaugh	QB	Homer Griffith (USC)
Gene Ronzani	LH	Beattie Feathers (Tenn.)
George Corbett	RH	Joe Laws (Iowa)
Bronko Nagurski	FB	Mike Mikulak (Oregon)

Head coaches—George Halas, Chi. Bears; Nobel Kizer (Purdue), College All-Stars

Chi. Bears	0	0	0	0	—	0
College All-Stars	0	0	0	0	—	0

Attendance—79,432

1935

CHI. BEARS 5, ALL-STARS 0

The Chicago Bears, runners-up to the New York Giants for the 1934 NFL championship, combined a field goal and a safety to defeat the College All-Stars in a game that was finished in a driving rainstorm.

The Bears' Jack Manders kicked a 27-yard field goal in the first quarter. All-Stars punter Bill Shepherd of Western Maryland fumbled a snap from center in the fourth quarter and recovered in the end zone, where he was downed for a safety.

The All-Stars had a first down on the Bears' 8-yard line in the fourth quarter, but gave up possession on downs without gaining a yard.

Chicago led 168–62 in total yardage and had nine first downs to five. The punting game dominated the contest. Each team punted 14 times, the Bears averaging 43.2 yards a kick, the All-Stars 37.1.

August 29, at Soldier Field

Chi. Bears	Starting Lineups	College All-Stars
Bill Hewitt	LE	Don Hutson (Alabama)
Art Buss	LT	Tony Blazine (Illinois)
Ray Richards	LG	Regis Monahan (Ohio State)
Ed Kawal	C	George Shotwell (Pitt.)
Joe Kopcha	RG	Billy Bevan (Minnesota)
George Musso	RT	Jim Barber (San Francisco)
Bill Karr	RE	Ray Fuqua (SMU)
Bernie Masterson	QB	Miller Munjas (Pittsburgh)
Beattie Feathers	LH	Bill Shepherd (W. Maryland)
John Sisk	RH	Al Nichelini (St. Mary's)
Jack Manders	FB	Stan Kostka (Minnesota)

Head coaches—George Halas, Chi. Bears; Frank Thomas (Alabama), College All-Stars

Chi. Bears	3	0	0	2	—	5
College All-Stars	0	0	0	0	—	0

Chi—FG Manders 27
Chi—Safety, Shepherd downed in end zone after fumbled center snap
Attendance—77,450

1936

DETROIT 7, ALL-STARS 7

Fullback Sheldon Beise and tailback Vernal (Babe) LeVoir, teammates on the University of Minnesota's 1934-35 national collegiate champion teams, combined their efforts to score the first touchdown of the three-year-old series as the All-Stars battled the Detroit Lions, 1935 NFL champions, to a 7-7 tie.

On fourth down and eight yards for a first down on the Lions' 17-yard line in the second quarter, Beise faked a plunge into the line, then pitched the ball back to LeVoir, who cut over tackle behind good blocking and scored, ending a five-play, 61-yard drive.

Detroit's touchdown came with slightly more than two minutes remaining in the game. Ernie Caddel ran eight yards on fourth down and one.

The game was delayed 24 hours because of rain. The All-Stars led in total yardage 184–128 and had nine first downs to the Lions' six.

September 2, at Soldier Field

Detroit	Starting Lineups	All-Stars
Ed Klewicki	LE	Wayne Millner (Notre Dame)
John Johnson	LT	Dick Smith (Minnesota)
Frank Knox	LG	Paul Tangora (N'wstn.)
Clare Randolph	C	Gomer Jones (Ohio State)
Grover (Ox) Emerson	RG	Vernon Oech (Minnesota)
George Christensen	RT	Truman Spain (SMU)
John Schneller	RE	Keith Topping (Stanford)
Earl (Dutch) Clark	QB	Riley Smith (Alabama)
Ernie Caddel	LH	Jay Berwanger (Chicago)
Frank Christensen	RH	B. Shakespeare (N'tre D'me)
Raymond (Buddy) Parker	FB	Sheldon Beise (Minnesota)

Head coaches—George (Potsy) Clark, Detroit; Bernie Bierman (Minnesota), College All-Stars

Detroit	0	0	0	7	—	7
College All-Stars	0	7	0	0	—	7

All-Stars—LeVoir 17 run (Fromhart kick)
Det—Caddel 8 run (Clark dropkick)
Attendance—76,361

1937

ALL-STARS 6, GREEN BAY 0

Quarterback Sammy Baugh of Texas Christian University completed 7 of 13 passes for 115 yards and one touchdown and intercepted two passes as the College All-Stars defeated the Green Bay Packers 6–0.

After replacing Pittsburgh's Bobby LaRue on the second play of the game, Baugh teamed with Gaynell Tinsley on a first-quarter touchdown pass play that covered 47 yards. The All-Stars threatened three other times but two field goal attempts by Nebraska's Sam Francis and one by Minnesota's Bud Wilkinson failed.

Green Bay, which outgained the collegians 298–180 in total offense and led 17–8 in first downs, moved from its 24-yard line to the All-Stars' 3 in the fourth quarter. On fourth down, Arnie Herber passed in the flat to Don Hutson, who was tackled for no gain by Johnny Drake of Purdue. Herber completed 14 of 38 passes for 202 yards.

September 1, at Soldier Field

Green Bay	Starting Lineups	College All-Stars
Don Hutson	LE	Gaynell Tinsley (LSU)
Ernie Smith	LT	Ed Widseth (Minnesota)
Paul Engebretsen	LG	Max Starcevich (Wash.)
George Svendsen	C	Earl Svendsen (Minnesota)
Lon Evans	RG	Steve Reid (Northwestern)
Lou Gordon	RT	Averell Daniell (Pitt.)
Milt Gantenbein	RE	Merle Wendt (Ohio State)
Hank Bruder	QB	Vern Huffman (Indiana)
Paul Miller	LH	Bobby LaRue (Pittsburgh)
Arnie Herber	RH	Johnny Drake (Purdue)
Clarke Hinkle	FB	Sam Francis (Nebraska)

Head coaches—Earl (Curly) Lambeau, Green Bay; Charles (Gus) Dorais (Detroit), College All-Stars

Green Bay	0	0	0	0	—	0
College All-Stars	6	0	0	0	—	6

All-Stars—Tinsley 47 pass from Baugh (kick failed)
Attendance—84,560

1938

ALL-STARS 28, WASHINGTON 16

Cecil Isbell of Purdue threw a 39-yard touchdown pass to Northwestern's John Kovatch and Bill Daugherty of Santa Clara intercepted a pass by George Karamatic and ran 40 yards for a touchdown as the College All-Stars scored four touchdowns in the second half to defeat the Washington Redskins 28–16.

Isbell was named the most valuable player after completing 7 of 14 passes for 159 yards and a touchdown. The All-Stars trailed 10–3 at halftime after a two-yard touchdown run by Washington's Max Krause and a 30-yard field goal by Riley Smith.

August 31, at Soldier Field

Washington	Starting Lineups	College All-Stars
Wayne Millner	LE	Perry Schwartz (California)
Glen (Turk) Edwards	LT	Fred Shirey (Nebraska)
Les Olsson	LG	Joe Routt (Texas A&M)
Vic Carroll	C	Ralph Wolf (Ohio State)
Jim Karcher	RG	Leroy Monsky (Alabama)
Jim Barber	RT	Vic Markov (Washington)
Charley Malone	RE	C. Sweeney (Notre Dame)
Riley Smith	QB	Andy Puplis (Notre Dame)
Sammy Baugh	LH	Cecil Isbell (Purdue)
George Karamatic	RH	Andy Uram (Minnesota)
Max Krause	FB	Frank Patrick (Pittsburgh)

Head coaches—Ray Flaherty, Washington; Alvin (Bo) McMillin (Indiana), College All-Stars

Washington	7	3	0	6	—	16
College All-Stars	3	0	12	13	—	28

All-Stars—FG McDonald 15
Wash—Krause 2 run (Smith kick)
Wash—FG Smith 30
All-Stars—Kovatch 39 pass from Isbell (kick failed)
All-Stars—Daugherty 40 interception return (kick failed)
All-Stars—Davis 1 run (kick blocked)
Wash—Karamatic 2 run (kick blocked)
All-Stars—Uram 35 interception return (Patrick kick)
Attendance—74,250

1939

N.Y. GIANTS 9, ALL-STARS 0

Field goals of 34 yards by Ward Cuff and 22 and 41 yards by Ken Strong elevated the New York Giants to a 9–0 victory over the College All-Stars.

The game marked Strong's first appearance in a Giants' uniform since the 1935 season. He played for the New York Yankees of the American Football League in 1936–37 and for the Jersey City Giants of the American Professional Football Association in 1938. The APFL was a minor professional football league.

The All-Stars advanced to the Giants' 34-yard line in the second quarter and gave up the ball on downs. Len Barnum's intercepted pass stopped a collegiate drive at New York's 31 in the fourth quarter, and John Mellus's interception at the 22 stopped the All-Stars as the game ended.

August 30, at Soldier Field

N.Y. Giants	Starting Lineups	College All-Stars
Jim Poole	LE	Bowden Wyatt (Tennessee)
Frank Cope	LT	Joe Mihal (Purdue)
John Dell Isola	LG	Francis Twedell (Minn.)
Mel Hein	C	Charlie Brock (Nebraska)
Orville Tuttle	RG	Ralph Heikkinen (Michigan)
John Mellus	RT	Bob Haak (Indiana)
Jim Lee Howell	RE	Earl Brown (Notre Dame)
Ed Danowski	QB	Davey O'Brien (TCU)
Ward Cuff	LH	Marshall Goldberg (Pitt.)
Leland Shaffer	RH	Bob MacLeod (Dartmouth)
John Karcis	FB	Howard Weiss (Wisconsin)

Head coaches—Steve Owen, N.Y. Giants; Elmer Layden (Notre Dame), College All-Stars

N.Y. Giants	3	3	0	3	—	9
College All-Stars	0	0	0	0	—	0

NYG—FG Cuff 34
NYG—FG Strong 22
NYG—FG Strong 41
Attendance—81,456

1940

GREEN BAY 45, ALL-STARS 28

Cecil Isbell and Arnie Herber combined to complete 11 of 20 passes for 306 yards and five touchdowns as the Green Bay Packers outscored the All-Stars.

Ambrose Schindler of USC put the All-Stars ahead with a six-yard run in the first quarter. The score was tied 14–14 in the second quarter and the All-Stars still were within reach of the Packers at 35–28 in the fourth. Isbell threw for three touchdowns, 81 and 35 yards to Don Hutson and 26 yards to Carl Mulleneaux.

August 29, at Soldier Field

Green Bay	Starting Lineups	College All-Stars
Don Hutson	LE	Bill Fisk (USC)
Buford (Baby) Ray	LT	Nick Cutlich (Northwestern)
Russ Letlow	LG	Jim Logan (Indiana)
George Svendsen	C	C. Turner (Hardin-Simmons)
C. (Buckets) Goldenberg	RG	Harry Smith (USC)
Bill Lee	RT	Tad Harvey (Notre Dame)
Milt Gantenbein	RE	Esco Sarkinen (Ohio State)
Larry Craig	QB	Ambrose Schindler (USC)
Cecil Isbell	LH	Nile Kinnick (Iowa)
Joe Laws	RH	Lou Brock (Purdue)
Clarke Hinkle	FB	Joe Thesing (Notre Dame)

Head coaches—Earl (Curly) Lambeau, Green Bay; Eddie Anderson (Iowa), College All-Stars

Green Bay	14	14	7	10	—	45
College All-Stars	7	14	0	7	—	28

All-Stars—Schindler 6 run (Kinnick dropkick)
GB —Hutson 81 pass from Isbell (Smith kick)
GB —Mulleneaux 26 pass from Isbell (Smith kick)
All-Stars—Washington 1 run (Kellogg kick)
GB —Uram 60 pass from Herber (Engebretsen kick)
GB —Hutson 35 pass from Isbell (Smith kick)
All-Stars—McFadden 56 pass from Kinnick (Kinnick dropkick)
GB —Hutson 29 pass from Herber (Smith kick)
All-Stars—Schindler 1 run (Kinnick dropkick)
GB —FG Smith 34
GB —Isbell 4 run (Hutson kick)
Attendance—84,567

1941

CHI. BEARS 37, ALL-STARS 13

The Chicago Bears marched 45, 71, and 82 yards for touchdowns in the final 12 minutes of play to defeat the College All-Stars 37–13.

The All-Stars trailed 16–6 at the end of the third quarter and closed the score to 16–13 early in the fourth quarter when Charlie O'Rourke of Boston College passed to Jackie Robinson of UCLA.

Harry Clark scored from the one on the Bears' next possession to give Chicago a 23–13 lead. Quarterback Sid Luckman passed to George McAfee in the flat and McAfee scored on a 25-yard play to increase Chicago's advantage to 30–13.

August 28, at Soldier Field

Chi. Bears	Starting Lineups	College All-Stars
Dick Plasman	LE	Dave Rankin (Purdue)
Joe Stydahar	LT	Ernest Plannell (Texas A&M)
Danny Fortmann	LG	Augie Lio (Georgetown)
Clyde (Bulldog) Turner	C	Rudy Mucha (Washington)
George Musso	RG	Tommy O'Boyle (Tulane)
Lee Artoe	RT	Nick Drahos (Cornell)
George Wilson	RE	Ed Rucinski (Indiana)
Sid Luckman	QB	Forrest Evashevski (Mich.)
Ray Nolting	LH	Tom Harmon (Michigan)
George McAfee	RH	George Franck (Minn.)
Bill Osmanski	FB	G. Paskvan (Wisconsin)

Head coaches—George Halas, Chi. Bears; Carl Snavely (Cornell), College All-Stars

Chi. Bears	6	7	3	21	—	37
College All-Stars	6	0	0	7	—	13

Chi —Kavanaugh 34 pass from Luckman (kick blocked)
All-Stars—Franck 22 pass from Harmon (kick blocked)
Chi —Clark 1 run (Manders kick)
Chi —FG Artoe 46
All-Stars—Robinson 46 pass from O'Rourke (Lio kick)
Chi —Clark 1 run (Manders kick)
Chi —McAfee 25 pass from Luckman (Manders kick)
Chi —Nowaskey 9 pass from Bussey (Manders kick)
Attendance—98,203

1942

CHI. BEARS 21, ALL-STARS 0

The Chicago Bears' dominance of the College All-Stars was more apparent than the final score of 21–0. The Bears outrushed the collegians 268–36 and outpassed them 203–77 for a total yardage advantage of 471–113.

The Bears' first touchdown was scored by Hugh Gallarneau on a four-yard run on fourth down after 8:40 of the first quarter. In the first quarter, Steve Juzwick of Notre Dame ran 91 yards from the All-Stars' 3-yard line to the Bears' 6. But the All-Stars did not score, giving up the ball on downs.

Juzwik's fumble at the collegians' 23 in the second period set up Chicago's second touchdown, a 21-yard pass, Young Bussey to Hampton Pool. Gallarneau scored Chicago's final touchdown in the third quarter on an eight-yard run.

August 28, at Soldier Field

Chi. Bears	Starting Lineups	College All-Stars
John Siegal	LE	Mal Kutner (Texas)
Ed Kolman	LT	Jim Daniell (Ohio State)
Danny Fortmann	LG	Rob Jeffries (Missouri)
Clyde (Bulldog) Turner	C	Vince Banonis (Detroit)
Ray Bray	RG	B. Crimmins (Notre Dame)
Lee Artoe	RT	Al Blozis (Georgetown)
Hampton Pool	RE	Judd Ringer (Minnesota)
Sid Luckman	QB	Dick Erdlitz (Northwestern)
Ray Nolting	LH	Bruce Smith (Minnesota)
Hugh Gallarneau	RH	Steve Juzwik (Notre Dame)
Bill Osmanski	FB	Jack Graf (Ohio State)

Head coaches—George Halas, Chi. Bears; Bob Zuppke (Illinois), College All-Stars

Chi. Bears	7	7	7	0	—	21
College All-Stars	0	0	0	0	—	0

Chi—Gallarneau 4 run (Stydahar kick)
Chi—Pool 21 pass from Bussey (Stydahar kick)
Chi—Gallarneau 8 run (Stydahar kick)
Attendance—101,100

1943

ALL-STARS 27, WASHINGTON 7

The College All-Stars defeated the Washington Redskins 27–7 for their first victory in five years over an NFL champion. The All-Stars' roster was selected by team coaches instead of by a nationwide newspaper poll. The site of the game was switched to Dyche Stadium on the Northwestern University campus.

The All-Stars scored first when Missouri's Bob Steuber returned a punt 50 yards down the sideline for a touchdown.

The All-Stars began pulling away on a 37-yard touchdown pass play, Glenn Dobbs to Pat Harder, who ran the final 20 yards. Washington moved from its 43 to the All-Stars' 18 in the third quarter; Otto Graham, intercepted a pass on the 3 and returned the ball 97 yards for a touchdown.

August 25, at Evanston, Illinois

Washington	Starting Lineups	College All-Stars
Bob Masterson	LE	Pete Pihos (Indiana)
Willie Wilkin	LT	Al Wistert (Michigan)
Dick Farman	LG	Felix Bucek (Texas A&M)
George Smith	C	Vic Lindskog (Stanford)
Steve Slivinski	RG	Buster Ramsey (Wm. & M.)
Clyde Shugart	RT	Dick Wildung (Minnesota)
Bob McChesney	RE	Bill Huber (Notre Dame)
Ray Hare	QB	D. Renfro (Washington St.)
Sammy Baugh	LH	Otto Graham (Northwestern)
Wilbur Moore	RH	Bob Steuber (Missouri)
Bob Seymour	FB	Pat Harder (Wisconsin)

Head coaches—Arthur (Dutch) Bergman, Washington; Harry Stuhldreher (Wisconsin), College All-Stars

Washington	0	7	0	0	—	7
College All-Stars	7	7	6	7	—	27

All-Stars—Steuber 50 punt return (Harder kick)
Wash —Aguirre 6 pass from Baugh (Masterson kick)
All-Stars—Harder 37 pass from Dobbs (Harder kick)
All-Stars—O. Graham 97 interception return (kick blocked)
All-Stars—Harder 33 run (Graham kick)
Attendance—48,471

1944

CHI. BEARS 24, ALL-STARS 21

Pete Gudauskas's 13-yard field goal with 10:42 left in the game gave the Chicago Bears a 24–21 victory.

Tulsa University's Glenn Dobbs, making his second appearance in the game as a collegian under wartime eligibility rules, threw a four-yard pass to Notre Dame's Creighton Miller for the All-Stars' first touchdown. That concluded a 33-yard drive after a short Bears' punt. The All-Stars went ahead 14–0 later in the first quarter when Dobbs, unable to find a pass receiver, scrambled 12 yards to the Bears' 1. Dobbs fumbled at that point and teammate John Tavener of Indiana recovered in the end zone.

August 30, at Evanston, Illinois

Chi. Bears	Starting Lineups	College All-Stars
Jim Benton	LE	John Dugger (Ohio State)
Dominic Sigillo	LT	Bill Willis (Ohio State)
Pete Gudauskas	LG	Dick Barwegan (Purdue)
Clyde (Bulldog) Turner	C	John Tavener (Indiana)
George Zorich	RG	Lin Houston (Ohio State)
Al Hoptowit	RT	Bob Zimny (Indiana)
George Wilson	RE	John Yonakor (Notre Dame)
John Long	QB	Lou Saban (Indiana)
Ray Nolting	LH	Glenn Dobbs (Tulsa)
Doug McEnulty	RH	Charley Trippi (Georgia)
Gary Famiglietti	FB	C. Miller (Notre Dame)

Head coaches—Heartley (Hunk) Anderson and Luke Johnsos, Chi. Bears; Lynn (Pappy) Waldorf (Northwestern), College All-Stars

Chi. Bears	0	14	7	3	—	24
College All-Stars	14	0	7	0	—	21

All-Stars—Miller 4 pass from Dobbs (Saban kick)
All-Stars—Tavener fumble recovery in end zone (Saban kick)
Chi —Famiglietti 3 run (Gudauskas kick)
Chi —Benton 12 pass from Luckman (Gudauskas kick)
All-Stars—Saban 1 run (Saban kick)
Chi —McLean 19 run (Gudauskas kick)
Chi —FG Gudauskas 13
Attendance—48,769

1945

GREEN BAY 19, ALL-STARS 7

Don Hutson intercepted a pass by Perry Moss of Tulsa in the first minute of the fourth quarter and ran 85 yards for the final touchdown in the Green Bay Packers' 19–7 victory over the College All-Stars. The game was returned to Soldier Field.

Hutson also kicked a 20-yard field goal and two extra points. The All-Stars scored in the second quarter on a 62-yard pass play, Bob Kennedy of Washington State to Nick Scollard of St. Joseph's, Indiana.

The collegians advanced to the Packers' 24-yard line in the second quarter, but Michigan's Tom Harmon fumbled after a 46-yard run. Georgia's Charley Trippi ran to Green Bay's 2-yard line in the fourth quarter, but a penalty set the collegians back to the 7 and they fumbled on the next play.

August 30, at Soldier Field

Green Bay	Starting Lineups	College All-Stars
Don Hutson	LE	Ted Cook (Alabama)
Buford (Baby) Ray	LT	Bob Zimny (Indiana)
Bill Kuusisto	LG	Damon Tassos (Texas A&M)
Charlie Brock	C	Tex Warrington (Auburn)
C. (Buckets) Goldenberg	RG	Glen Burgeis (Tulsa)
Paul Berezney	RT	R. Foster (Oklahoma St.)
Joel Mason	RE	Bill Huber (Notre Dame)
Larry Craig	QB	Charles Mitchell (Tulsa)
Irv Comp	LH	Charley Trippi (Georgia)
Lou Brock	RH	Don Greenwood (Illinois)
Ted Fritsch	FB	B. Kennedy (Washington St.)

Head coaches—Earl (Curly) Lambeau, Green Bay; Bernie Bierman (Minnesota), College All-Stars

Green Bay	3	9	0	7	—	19
College All-Stars	0	7	0	0	—	7

GB —FG Hutson 20
GB —Safety, Kennedy stepped into end zone
GB —McKay 20 pass from Rohrig (Hutson kick)
All-Stars—Scollard 68 pass from Kennedy (Harmon kick)
GB —Hutson 85 interception return (Hutson kick)
Attendance—92,753

1946

ALL-STARS 16, LOS ANGELES 0

Elroy (Crazylegs) Hirsch of the University of Wisconsin ran 68 yards for a first-quarter touchdown and turned a 32-yard pass from Northwestern's Otto Graham into a 62-yard touchdown in the third quarter of the College All-Stars' 16–0 victory over the Los Angeles Rams.

The Rams, representing Los Angeles for the first time since moving from Cleveland after the 1945 season, had the ball on the collegians' 19, 29, 18, 10, and 36 in the first half, but could not score. The All-Stars fumbled seven times in the game and the Rams recovered four.

Because they had played as underclassmen during World War II eligibility rules, some of the players on the college roster were making their second and third appearances in the game.

August 23, at Soldier Field

Los Angeles	Starting Lineups	College All-Stars
Howard (Red) Hickey	LE	Jack Russell (Baylor)
Eberle Schultz	LT	Martin Ruby (Texas A&M)
Riley Matheson	LG	Visco Grgich (Santa Clara)
Bob DeLauer	C	Bill Godwin (Georgia)
Milan Lazetich	RG	Buster Ramsey (Wm. & M.)
Gil Bouley	RT	Derrell Palmer (TCU)
Steve Pritko	RE	Ralph Heywood (USC)
Bob Waterfield	QB	Otto Graham (Northwestern)
Fred Gehrke	LH	Billy Hillenbrand (Indiana)
Jim Gillette	RH	Dub Jones (Tulane)
Pat West	FB	Pat Harder (Wisconsin)

Head coaches—Adam Walsh, Los Angeles; Alvin (Bo) McMillin (Indiana), College All-Stars

Los Angeles	0	0	0	0	— 0
College All-Stars	7	0	7	2	— 16

All-Stars—Hirsch 68 run (Harder kick)
All-Stars—Hirsch 62 pass from Graham (Harder kick)
All-Stars—Safety, Walker tackled Washington in end zone
Attendance—97,380

1947

ALL-STARS 16, CHI. BEARS 0

A record crowd of 105,840 persons, attracted partly by the presence of the hometown Bears and an All-Stars team coached by Notre Dame University's Frank Leahy, saw the collegians score a 16–0 victory, their second shutout in a row by that margin.

The All-Stars used a T-formation offense for the first time in the series. It was an offense made famous by the Bears earlier in the decade. The collegians outgained the professionals 340–116 in total yards and outrushed them 189–35.

The All-Stars went 82 yards in 11 plays the first time they had the ball and 87 in two plays on their second series. Illinois's Claude (Buddy) Young set up both touchdowns by running 31 yards on one play in the first drive and moving 41 yards with a flat pass in the second drive.

August 22, at Soldier Field

Chi. Bears	Starting Lineups	College All-Stars
Ken Kavanaugh	LE	Horace Gillom (Nevada)
Fred Davis	LT	Dick Barwegan (Purdue)
Chuck Drulis	LG	Alex Agase (Illinois)
Clyde (Bulldog) Turner	C	Paul Duke (Georgia Tech)
Ray Bray	RG	Weldon Humble (Rice)
Walt Stickel	RT	J. Mastrangelo (Notre Dame)
Ed Sprinkle	RE	Joe Tereschinski (Georgia)
Sid Luckman	QB	G. Ratterman (Notre Dame)
Ray (Scooter) McLean	LH	Buddy Young (Illinois)
Hugh Gallarneau	RH	Vic Schwall (Northwestern)
Joe Osmanski	FB	Jim Mello (Notre Dame)

Head coaches—George Halas, Chi. Bears; Frank Leahy (Notre Dame), College All-Stars

Chi. Bears	0	0	0	0	— 0
College All-Stars	13	0	3	0	— 16

All-Stars—Mello 6 run (kick blocked)
All-Stars—Zilly 46 pass from Ratterman (Case kick)
All-Stars—FG Case 21
Attendance—105,840

1948

CHI. CARDINALS 28, ALL-STARS 0

The Chicago Cardinals moved 80 yards to a touchdown the second time they had possession of the ball and went on to a 28–0 victory over the College All-Stars. Charley Trippi, who scored the Cardinals' final touchdown on a 13-yard pass from Ray Mallouf, set a record by appearing in his fifth All-Star game, his first as a professional.

The Cardinals outgained the All-Stars 333–235. The All-Stars marched 84 yards and two feet to the Cardinals' 1-foot line in the third quarter, when the score was 14–0, but Floyd Simmons of Notre Dame was stopped by Marshall Goldberg on fourth down.

Vince Banonis intercepted a pass by Perry Moss of Illinois and ran 31 yards for a touchdown to give Chicago a 21–0 lead in the fourth quarter.

August 20, at Soldier Field

Chi. Cardinals	Starting Lineups	College All-Stars
Bill Dewell	LE	Paul Cleary (USC)
Chet Bulger	LT	G. Connor (Notre Dame)
Lloyd Arms	LG	Arnie Weinmeister (Wash.)
Vince Banonis	C	Dick Scott (Navy)
Garrard (Buster) Ramsey	RG	Howard Brown (Indiana)
Stan Mauldin	RT	Z. Czarobski (Notre Dame)
Mal Kutner	RE	Len Ford (Michigan)
Paul Christman	QB	J. Lujack (Notre Dame)
Charley Trippi	LH	Bob Chappuis (Michigan)
Marshall Goldberg	RH	Charlie Conerly (Miss.)
Pat Harder	FB	C. (Bump) Elliott (Michigan)

Head coaches—Jimmy Conzelman, Chi. Cardinals; Frank Leahy (Notre Dame), College All-Stars

Chi. Cardinals	7	7	0	14	— 28
College All-Stars	0	0	0	0	— 0

Chi—Angsman 2 run (Harder kick)
Chi—Schwall 14 run (Harder kick)
Chi—Banonis 31 interception return (Harder kick)
Chi—Trippi 13 pass from Mallouf (Harder kick)
Attendance—101,220

1949

PHILADELPHIA 38, ALL-STARS 0

The day before the game with the Philadelphia Eagles, Bud Wilkinson, coach of the College All-Stars, said, "We haven't got a chance . . . and I'm not kidding.'' The Eagles shut down the All-Stars' passing game for three yards in losses, outrushed the collegians 228–116 for a 358–113 total yardage advantage, and won 38–0.

The Eagles defensed the collegians' split T formation with an eight-man line. Their three-man secondary also was close to the line. The professionals penetrated so quickly the All-Stars were unable to set up a passing attack.

Philadelphia broke a scoreless tie in the second quarter by marching 71 yards to a touchdown.

August 12, at Soldier Field

Philadelphia	Starting Lineups	College All-Stars
Jack Ferrante	LE	Barney Poole (Mississippi)
Vic Sears	LT	George Petrovich (Texas)
Cliff Patton	LG	Marty Wendell (Notre Dame)
Vic Lindskog	C	Chuck Bednarik (Penn.)
Frank (Bucko) Kilroy	RG	Bill Fischer (Notre Dame)
Al Wistert	RT	Al DeRogatis (Duke)
Pete Pihos	RE	Mel Sheehan (Missouri)
Tommy Thompson	QB	Jack Mitchell (Oklahoma)
Steve Van Buren	LH	George Taliaferro (Indiana)
Bosh Pritchard	RH	Jerry Williams (Wash. St.)
Joe Muha	FB	Joe Geri (Georgia)

Head coaches—Earle (Greasy) Neale, Philadelphia; Bud Wilkinson (Oklahoma), College All-Stars

Philadelphia	0	17	7	14	— 38
College All-Stars	0	0	0	0	— 0

Phil—Van Buren 1 run (Patton kick)
Phil—FG Patton 14
Phil—Craft 4 run (Patton kick)
Phil—Pihos 7 pass from Thompson (Patton kick)
Phil—Doss 4 run (Patton kick)
Phil—Armstrong 13 pass from Mackrides (Patton kick)
Attendance—93,780

1950

ALL-STARS 17, PHILADELPHIA 7

Halfback Charlie (Choo Choo) Justice of North Carolina gained 133 yards in nine carries and scored on a 35-yard pass from quarterback Eddie LeBaron of College of Pacific as the College All-Stars defeated the Philadelphia Eagles 17–7. The game was televised nationally for the first time on a 29-station network.

Justice gained 31 and 12 yards as the All-Stars marched 54 yards in six plays to a touchdown on their second series. They led 14–0 at the half after Santa Clara's Hall Haynes recovered a fumble by Clyde (Smackover) Scott at the Eagles' 35; LeBaron scrambled away from a strong rush and dumped the ball to Justice, who caught LeBaron's pass at the line of scrimmage and weaved his way to a touchdown.

August 11, at Soldier Field

Philadelphia	Starting Lineups	College All-Stars
Jack Ferrante	LE	Art Weiner (North Carolina)
Vic Sears	LT	D. (Tiny) Campora (Pacific)
Cliff Patton	LG	Porter Payne (Georgia)
Vic Lindskog	C	Clayton Tonnemaker (Minn.)
Frank (Bucko) Kilroy	RG	George Hughes (Wm. & M.)
Al Wistert	RT	Bill Manley (Oklahoma)
Pete Pihos	RE	Jim Martin (Notre Dame)
Tommy Thompson	QB	Travis Tidwell (Auburn)
Steve Van Buren	LH	Doak Walker (SMU)
Clyde (Smackover) Scott	RH	Hall Haynes (Santa Clara)
Joe Muha	F. (Curly) Morrison (Ohio St.)	

Head coaches—Earle (Greasy) Neale, Philadelphia; Eddie Anderson (Holy Cross), College All-Stars

Philadelphia	0	0	0	7	— 7
College All-Stars	7	7	0	3	— 17

All-Stars—Pasquariello 1 run (Soltau kick)
All-Stars—Justice 35 pass from LeBaron (Soltau kick)
Phil—Van Buren 1 run (Soltau kick)
All-Stars—FG Soltau 23
Attendance—88,885

1951

CLEVELAND 33, ALL-STARS 0

Halfback Dub Jones rushed for 105 yards and two touchdowns and quarterback Otto Graham completed 16 of 30 passes for 263 yards and two touchdowns as the Cleveland Browns outgained the College All-Stars 425–126 and posted a 33–0 victory.

The All-Stars made only five first downs; their longest gain was a 23-yard run by Southern Methodist's Kyle Rote, who led the collegians with 45 yards in eight carries.

The Browns took a 2–0 lead in the first quarter when Rote fumbled a handoff from Notre Dame quarterback Bob Williams, who recovered the ball in the end zone but was downed by Len Ford for a safety. The score was 12–0 at halftime.

August 17, at Soldier Field

Cleveland	Starting Lineups	College All-Stars
Mac Speedie	LE	Don Stonesifer (N'wstn.)
Lou Groza	LT	Bob Gain (Kentucky)
Abe Gibron	LG	Bud McFadin (Texas)
Frank Gatski	C	Jerry Groom (Notre Dame)
Lin Houston	RG	Lynn Lynch (Illinois)
Lou Rymkus	RT	Mike McCormack (Kansas)
Dante Lavelli	RE	Bob Wilkinson (UCLA)
Otto Graham	QB	Bob Williams (Notre Dame)
Rex Bumgardner	LH	Wilford White (Arizona St.)
Dub Jones	RH	Kyle Rote (SMU)
Emerson Cole	FB	Dan Dufek (Michigan)

Head coaches—Paul Brown, Cleveland; Herman Hickman (Yale), College All-Stars

Cleveland	2	10	7	14	— 33
College All-Stars	0	0	0	0	— 0

Cle—Safety, Ford downed Williams in end zone
Cle—Jones 2 run (Groza kick)
Cle—FG Groza 17
Cle—Jones 3 run (Groza kick)
Cle—Lavelli 14 pass from Graham (Groza kick)
Cle—Cole 8 pass from Graham (Groza kick)
Attendance—92,180

1952

LOS ANGELES 10, ALL-STARS 7

The Los Angeles Rams drove 51 yards midway in the fourth quarter to position Bob Waterfield for a 24-yard field goal that gave the Rams a 10–7 victory.

The All-Stars led 7–0 going into the final quarter after a 69-yard touchdown drive that ended with Ohio State's Vic Janowicz running three yards in the second quarter. Quarterback Babe Parilli, who gained 68 yards in seven carries, contributed a 41-yard run to the march.

The professionals tied the score in the early minutes of the fourth period on a three-yard pass, Norm Van Brocklin to Paul (Tank) Younger. The score was set up by a penalty against San Francisco's Ollie Matson, who drew pass interference defending a Van Brocklin pass to Volney (Skeet) Quinlan that put the ball on the 7-yard line.

August 15, at Soldier Field

Los Angeles	Starting Lineups	College All-Stars
Tom Fears	LE	Leo Sugar (Purdue)
Don Simensen	LT	Harold Mitchell (UCLA)
Dick Daugherty	LG	Don Coleman (Michigan St.)
Leon McLaughlin	C	Doug Mosley (Kentucky)
Bill Lange	RG	Bob Ward (Maryland)
Tom Dahms	RT	Bill Pearman (Tennessee)
Elroy (Crazylegs) Hirsch	RE	Billy Howton (Rice)
Bob Waterfield	QB	Babe Parilli (Kentucky)
Dan Towler	LH	Vic Janowicz (Ohio State)
Verda (Vitamin T.) Smith	RH	Hugh McElhenny (Wash.)
John Myers	FB	Ed Modzelewski (Maryland)

Head coaches—Joe Stydahar, Los Angeles; Bobby Dodd (Georgia Tech), College All-Stars

Los Angeles	0	0	0	10	— 10
College All-Stars	0	7	0	0	— 7

All-Stars—Janowicz 3 run (Janowicz kick)
LA —Younger 3 pass from Van Brocklin (Waterfield kick)
LA —FG Waterfield 24
Attendance—88,316

1953

DETROIT 24, ALL-STARS 10

Detroit's Bobby Layne set a record by completing 21 of 31 passes for 323 yards and one touchdown as the Lions rolled up a record 21 first downs and outgained the College All-Stars 473–187 in a 24–10 victory.

Layne's primary receivers were ends Leon Hart, who caught seven passes for 106 yards, and Cloyce Box, five for 108, and halfback Doak Walker, eight for 97. Three All-Star quarterbacks completed only 9 of 27 passes for 81 yards.

The Lions' first touchdown was typical of their free-wheeling attack. They drove 80 yards, with the big play a Layne-to-Hart pass with a lateral from Hart to Walker that covered 47 yards, setting up Bob Hoernschemeyer's five-yard scoring run.

August 14, at Soldier Field

Detroit	Starting Lineups	College All-Stars
Cloyce Box	LE	Bernie Flowers (Purdue)
Lou Creekmur	LT	Kline Gilbert (Mississippi)
Jim Martin	LG	Donn Moomaw (UCLA)
Vince Banonis	C	G. Morris (Georgia Tech)
Dick Stanfel	RG	Harley Sewell (Texas)
Gus Cifelli	RT	J.D. Kimmel (Houston)
Leon Hart	RE	Tom Scott (Virginia)
Bobby Layne	QB	Jack Scarbath (Maryland)
Doak Walker	LH	Fred Bruney (Ohio State)
Bob Hoernschemeyer	RH	Jim Sears (USC)
Pat Harder	FB	Buck McPhail (Okla.)

Head coaches—Raymond (Buddy) Parker, Detroit; Bobby Dodd (Georgia Tech), College All-Stars

Detroit	7	3	7	7	— 24
College All-Stars	0	3	0	7	— 10

Det —Hoernschemeyer 5 run (Harder kick)
Det —FG Walker 10
All-Stars—FG Dawson 23
Det —Box 8 pass from Layne (Harder kick)
Det —Hoernschemeyer 2 run (Harder kick)
All-Stars—Dawson 17 run (Samuels kick)
Attendance—93,818

1954

DETROIT 31, ALL-STARS 6

The Detroit Lions played without starting quarterback Bobby Layne, but reserve quarterback Tom Dublinski completed 10 of 15 passes for 103 yards as the Lions outgained the College All-Stars 361–144 in total yardage and won 31–6.

Layne did not play because the Lions feared he would be injured by also participating on defense. The game was conducted under collegiate rules as stipulated in the contract between the sponsoring *Chicago Tribune* and NFL. Colleges played one-platoon football in 1953. The Lions and other professional teams played with two platoons. It was the first time in 10 years the All-Star game was played with limited substitution.

August 13, at Soldier Field

Detroit	Starting Lineups	College All-Stars
Dorne Dibble	LE	Carlton Massey (Texas)
Lou Creekmur	LT	Bob Morgan (Maryland)
Jim Martin	LG	Jerry Hilgenberg (Iowa)
LaVern Torgeson	C	Ed Beatty (Mississippi)
Harley Sewell	RG	M. Mavraides (Notre Dame)
Charlie Ane	RT	Stan Jones (Maryland)
Leon Hart	RE	Dick Deitrick (Pittsburgh)
Tom Dublinski	QB	Zeke Bratkowski (Georgia)
Doak Walker	LH	Chet Hanulak (Maryland)
Jack Christiansen	RH	Johnny Lattner (Notre Dame)
Lew Carpenter	FB	Neil Worden (Notre Dame)

Head coaches—Raymond (Buddy) Parker, Detroit; Jim Tatum (Maryland), College All-Stars

Detroit	17	0	7	7	— 31
College All-Stars	0	0	6	0	— 6

Det —FG Martin 46
Det —Walker 5 run (Walker kick)
Det —Carpenter 4 run (Girard kick)
All-Stars—Lattner 4 run (kick blocked)
Det —Carpenter 1 run (Martin kick)
Det —Doran 37 fumble return (Walker kick)
Attendance—93,470

1955

ALL-STARS 30, CLEVELAND 27

The College All-Stars broke a string of four straight victories by the NFL champion and improved their record in the series to 8 victories against 13 losses and 1 tie with a 30–27 win over the Cleveland Browns.

Tad Weed, a 5-foot 6-inch, 146-pound kicker from Ohio State, made field goals of 21, 19, and 41 yards, the last giving the Collegians a 30–20 lead with six minutes remaining.

The Browns were ahead for the final time 20–17 with 19 seconds remaining in the half after a 25-yard pass from George Ratterman to Ray Renfro.

August 12, at Soldier Field

Cleveland	Starting Lineups	College All-Stars
Darrell (Pete) Brewster	LE	Max Boydston (Oklahoma)
Lou Groza	LT	Jim Ray Smith (Baylor)
Abe Gibron	LG	H. Bullough (Michigan St.)
Frank Gatski	C	D. Szymanski (Notre Dame)
Harold Bradley	RG	Bud Brooks (Arkansas)
Mike McCormack	RT	F. Varrichione (Notre Dame)
Dante Lavelli	RE	Henry Hair (Georgia Tech)
George Ratterman	QB	R. Guglielmi (Notre Dame)
Ray Renfro	LH	Dickie Moegle (Rice)
Dub Jones	RH	Dave Middleton (Auburn)
Maurice Bassett	FB	Alan Ameche (Wisconsin)

Head coaches—Paul Brown, Cleveland; Earl (Curly) Lambeau, College All-Stars

Cleveland	7	13	0	7	— 27
College All-Stars	3	14	3	10	— 30

All-Stars—FG Weed 21
Cle —Ratterman 1 run (Groza kick)
All-Stars—Eidom 2 run (Weed kick)
Cle —Renfro 18 run (Groza kick)
All-Stars—FG Weed 19
Cle —Renfro 25 pass from Ratterman (kick blocked)
All-Stars—FG Weed 19
All-Stars—Triplett 1 run (Leggett run)
All-Stars—FG Weed 41
Cle —Morrison 5 run (Groza kick)
Attendance—75,000

1956

CLEVELAND 26, ALL-STARS 0

The Cleveland Browns drove 80 yards in 12 plays the first time they had the ball and won 26–0.

On the first series of plays, Michigan State quarterback Earl Morrall passed 11 yards to Navy's Ron Beagle, ran 10 yards himself, and handed off to Ohio State's Howard (Hopalong) Cassady for a nine-yard gain, moving the All-Stars to Cleveland's 34. Morrall was shaken up, however, on the play involving Cassady, and Jerry Reichow of Iowa replaced him. Reichow threw a pass on his first play and the Browns' Warren Lahr intercepted in the end zone. Cleveland took over on its 20 and moved to the first touchdown. Groza kicked field goals of 45, 37, 24, and 27 yards.

August 10, at Soldier Field

Cleveland	Starting Lineups	College All-Stars
Darrel (Pete) Brewster	LE	Ron Beagle (Navy)
Lou Groza	LT	Frank D'Agostino (Auburn)
Abe Gibron	LG	Hugh Pitts (TCU)
Frank Gatski	C	Bob Pellegrini (Maryland)
Herschel Forester	RG	Sam Huff (West Virginia)
Mike McCormack	RT	Bob Skoronski (Indiana)
Dante Lavelli	RE	Don Holleder (Army)
George Ratterman	QB	Earl Morrall (Michigan St.)
Fred (Curly) Morrison	LH	Hopalong Cassady (Ohio St.)
Ray Renfro	RH	Don McIlhenny (SMU)
Ed Modzelewski	FB	Don Schaefer (Notre Dame)

Head coaches—Paul Brown, Cleveland; Earl (Curly) Lambeau, College All-Stars

Cleveland	7	6	6	7	— 26
College All-Stars	0	0	0	0	— 0

Cle—Morrison 13 pass from Ratterman (Groza kick)
Cle—FG 45 Groza
Cle—FG 37 Groza
Cle—FG 24 Groza
Cle—FG 27 Groza
Cle—Filipski 3 run (Groza kick)
Attendance—75,000

1957

N.Y. GIANTS 22, ALL-STARS 12

Quarterback Charlie Conerly and end Ken McAfee combined on touchdown pass plays of 38 and 10 yards as the New York Giants overcame an early lead to score a 22–12 victory.

Wake Forest's Billy Barnes ran two yards for a touchdown to end a 55-yard drive that began when Illinois's Wayne Bock recovered a fumble by Alex Webster on the collegians' 45-yard line.

A fumble by Barnes later in the first quarter was recovered by Charlie Toogood and the Giants converted the turnover into a 33-yard field goal by Ben Agajanian.

August 9, at Soldier Field

N.Y. Giants	Starting Lineups	College All-Stars
Kyle Rote	LE	Ron Kramer (Michigan)
Roosevelt Brown	LT	Carl Vereen (Georgia Tech)
Gerald Huth	LG	Dalton Truax (Tulane)
Ray Wietecha	C	Joe Amstutz (Indiana)
Jack Stroud	RG	Mike Sandusky (Maryland)
Dick Yelvington	RT	Earl Leggett (LSU)
Ken McAfee	RE	Tom Maentz (Michigan)
Don Heinrich	QB	John Brodie (Stanford)
Frank Gifford	LH	Jon Arnett (USC)
Alex Webster	RH	Abe Woodson (Illinois)
Mel Triplett	FB	Don Bosseler (Miami)

Head coaches—Jim Lee Howell, N.Y. Giants; Earl (Curly) Lambeau, College All-Stars

N.Y. Giants	3	7	7	5	— 22
College All-Stars	6	3	0	3	— 12

All-Stars—Barnes 2 run (kick failed)
NYG —FG Agajanian 33
NYG —McAfee 38 pass from Conerly (Agajanian kick)
All-Stars—FG Cothren 17
NYG —McAfee 10 pass from Conerly (Agajanian kick)
NYG —FG Agajanian 45
All-Stars—FG Cothren 25
NYG —Safety, Nolan tackled Woodson in end zone
Attendance—75,000

1958

ALL-STARS 35, DETROIT 19

The Detroit Lions outrushed the College All-Stars 179–3 and had 22 first downs to 11, but the collegians struck for 20 points in the second quarter.

The Lions led 7–0 at the end of the first quarter after a 24-yard pass, Tobin Rote to Jim Doran. On second down at the All-Stars' 40 after a Lions' punt, Jim Pace of Michigan caught a pass from King Hill of Rice at the line of scrimmage and ran 57 yards to Detroit's 3, setting up a 19-yard field goal by Texas A&M's Bobby Joe Conrad.

The Lions led 7–0 at the end of the first quarter...

August 15, at Soldier Field

Detroit	Starting Lineups	College All-Stars
Jim Doran	LE	C. Krueger (Texas A&M)
Lou Creekmur	LT	Lou Michaels (Kentucky)
Harley Sewell	LG	Jerry Kramer (Idaho)
Charlie Ane	C	Dan Currie (Michigan State)
Stan Campbell	RG	Bill Krisher (Oklahoma)
Ken Russell	RT	G. Hickerson (Mississippi)
Steve Junker	RE	Jim Gibbons (Iowa)
Tobin Rote	QB	King Hill (Rice)
Gene Gedman	LH	Jim Pace (Michigan)
H. (Hopalong) Cassady	RH	B. Joe Conrad (Texas A&M)
John Henry Johnson	FB	W. Kowalczyk (Michigan St.)

Head coaches—George Wilson, Detroit; Otto Graham, College All-Stars

Detroit	7	0	6	6	—	19
College All-Stars	0	20	2	13	—	35

Det —Doran 24 pass from Rote (Layne kick)
All-Stars—FG Conrad 19
All-Stars—Mitchell 84 pass from Ninowski (Conrad kick)
All-Stars—Mitchell 18 pass from Ninowski (Conrad kick)
All-Stars—FG Conrad 33
All-Stars—Safety, Jobko tackled Rote in end zone
Det —Gedman 9 run (kick blocked)
All-Stars—FG Conrad 24
All-Stars—FG Conrad 24
All-Stars—Howley 29 interception return (Conrad kick)
Det —Pfeifer 1 run (kick blocked)
Attendance—70,000

1959

BALTIMORE 29, ALL-STARS 0

The College All-Stars had a 19–18 edge in first downs, but the Baltimore Colts converted three turnovers into touchdowns and scored all of their points in the first half en route to a 29–0 victory.

Center Dan James of Ohio State snapped the ball over the head of Southern Methodist punter Dave Scherer and the ball went out of the end zone for a safety. The Colts' Carl Taseff returned the ensuing free kick 42 yards. Johnny Unitas passed 33 yards to Jim Mutscheller and three yards to Raymond Berry for a touchdown and an 8-0 lead.

Bill Stacy of Mississippi State fumbled a punt in the second quarter and Baltimore's Tom Addison recovered, setting up a 29-yard pass, Unitas to Mutscheller.

August 14, at Soldier Field

Baltimore	Starting Lineups	College All-Stars
Raymond Berry	LE	Buddy Dial (Rice)
Jim Parker	LT	Gene Selawski (Purdue)
Art Spinney	LG	Mike Rabold (Indiana)
Madison (Buzz) Nutter	C	Dan James (Ohio State)
Alex Sandusky	RG	A. Cvercko (Northwestern)
George Preas	RT	Fran O'Brien (Michigan St.)
Jim Mutscheller	RE	Dave Sherer (SMU)
Johnny Unitas	QB	Lee Grosscup (Utah)
L.G. Dupre	LH	Don Brown (Houston)
Lenny Moore	RH	Dick Haley (Pittsburgh)
Alan Ameche	FB	N. Pietrosante (Notre Dame)

Head coaches—Weeb Ewbank, Baltimore; Otto Graham (Coast Guard), College All-Stars

Baltimore	8	21	0	0	—	29
College All-Stars	0	0	0	0	—	0

Balt—Safety, James centered ball out of end zone
Balt—Berry 3 pass from Unitas (kick failed)
Balt—Mutscheller 29 pass from Unitas (Rechichar kick)
Balt—Dupre 13 pass from Unitas (Rechichar kick)
Balt—Davis 36 interception return (Rechichar kick)
Attendance—70,000

1960

BALTIMORE 32, ALL-STARS 7

Quarterback Johnny Unitas completed 22 of 42 passes for 281 yards and three touchdowns, and the Baltimore Colts outgained the College All-Stars 416-120 in total offense and posted a 32-7 victory.

Baltimore moved 69 yards in seven plays the second time it had the ball to take a 7–0 lead. The All-Stars moved to the Colts' 5-yard line in the second quarter, but quarterback Don Meredith of Southern Methodist fumbled. The Colts' Gino Marchetti recovered, and Baltimore marched 95 yards to a touchdown.

August 12, at Soldier Field

Baltimore	Starting Lineups	College All-Stars
Raymond Berry	LE	Carroll Dale (Virginia Tech)
George Preas	LT	B. Denton (Pacific)
Art Spinney	LG	C. Janerette (Penn State)
Madison (Buzz) Nutter	C	Bill Lapham (Iowa)
Alex Sandusky	RG	Mike McGee (Duke)
Jim Parker	RT	G. Gossage (Northwestern)
Jim Mutscheller	RE	H. McInnis (So. Mississippi)
Johnny Unitas	QB	George Izo (Notre Dame)
Lenny Moore	LH	Prentice Gautt (Oklahoma)
Alan Ameche	RH	Tom Moore (Vanderbilt)
L.G. Dupre	FB	Frank Mestnik (Marquette)

Head coaches—Weeb Ewbank, Baltimore; Otto Graham (Coast Guard), College All-Stars

Baltimore	7	17	5	3	—	32
College All-Stars	0	0	0	7	—	7

Balt —Moore 4 pass from Unitas (Myhra kick)
Balt —Moore 3 pass from Unitas (Myhra kick)
Balt —FG Myhra 38
Balt —Moore 14 pass from Unitas (Myhra kick)
Balt —Safety, Lipscomb and Joyce tackled Izo in end zone
Balt —FG Myhra 27
All-Stars—Gautt 60 pass from Meredith (Khayat kick)
Balt —FG Myhra 26
Attendance—70,000

1961

PHILADELPHIA 28, ALL-STARS 14

Trapped behind the line of scrimmage, quarterback Sonny Jurgensen improvised with a behind-the-back pass to Pete Retzlaff for a first down that sustained the first of four touchdown drives in the Philadelphia Eagles' 28–14 victory over the College All-Stars.

August 4, at Soldier Field

Philadelphia	Starters, Offense	College All-Stars
Pete Retzlaff	LE	A. Thomas (Oregon State)
Jim McCusker	LT	Roland Lakes (Wichita St.)
John Wittenborn	LG	Billy Shaw (Georgia Tech)
Chuck Bednarik	C	Greg Larson (Minnesota)
Stan Campbell	RG	H. Antwine (So. Illinois)
J.D. Smith	RT	Jim Tyrer (Ohio State)
Bobby Walston	RE	Mike Ditka (Pittsburgh)
Sonny Jurgensen	QB	Norm Snead (Wake Forest)
Billy Barnes	LH	P. Atkins (New Mexico St.)
Tommy McDonald	RH	B. Casey (Bowling Green)
Clarence Peaks	FB	Bill Brown (Illinois)
Starters, Defense		
Leo Sugar	LE	Earl Faison (Indiana)
Jess Richardson	LT	Joe Rutgens (Illinois)
Ed Khayat	RT	Ernie Ladd (Grambling)
Marion Campbell	RE	Bill Lilly (Texas Christian)
John Nocera	LLB	Frank Visted (Navy)
Chuck Weber	MLB	E.J. Holub (Texas Tech)
Maxie Baughan	RLB	Fred Hageman (Kansas)
Jim Carr	LHB	Ed Sharockman (Pittsburgh)
Tom Brookshier	RHB	C. Gibson (No. Caro. St.)
Bob Freeman	LS	Tom Matte (Ohio State)
Don Burroughs	RS	Joe Krakoski (Illinois)

Head coaches—Nick Skorich, Philadelphia; Otto Graham (Coast Guard), College All-Stars

Philadelphia	14	7	0	7	—	28
College All-Stars	0	0	0	14	—	14

Phil —McDonald 27 pass from Jurgensen (Walston kick)
Phil —Retzlaff 25 pass from Jurgensen (Walston kick)
Phil —McDonald 24 pass from Hill (Walston kick)
Phil —McDonald 24 pass from Jurgensen (Walston kick)
All-Stars—Gregory 18 pass from Kilmer (Fleming kick)
All-Stars—Grecni 57 interception return (Fleming kick)
Attendance—66,000

1962

GREEN BAY 42, ALL-STARS 20

Quarterback Bart Starr completed 13 of 22 passes for 255 yards and a record five touchdowns.

August 3, at Soldier Field

Green Bay	Starters, Offense	College All-Stars
Max McGee	LE	Reg Carolan (Idaho)
Bob Skoronski	LT	Fate Echols (Northwestern)
Fred (Fuzzy) Thurston	LG	B. Hudson (Memphis State)
Jim Ringo	C	Wayne Frazier (Auburn)
Jerry Kramer	RG	R. Winston (Louisiana State)
Forrest Gregg	RT	Joe Carollo (Notre Dame)
Ron Kramer	RE	Charles Bryant (Ohio State)
Bart Starr	QB	John Hadl (Kansas)
Paul Hornung	LH	Curtis McClinton (Kansas)
Boyd Dowler	RH	Lance Alworth (Arkansas)
Jim Taylor	FB	Earl Gros (Louisiana State)
Starters, Defense		
Willie Davis	LE	Frank Parker (Okla. State)
Dave Hanner	LT	Merlin Olsen (Utah State)
Henry Jordan	RT	John Meyers (Washington)
Bill Quinlan	RE	Clark Miller (Utah State)
Dan Currie	LLB	Bill Saul (Penn State)
Ray Nitschke	MLB	Larry Onesti (Northwestern)
Bill Forester	RLB	Frank Buncom (USC)
Hank Gremminger	LHB	James Saxton (Texas)
Jesse Whittenton	RHB	W. Harris (Louisiana State)
John Symank	LS	T. Dellinger (No. Caro. St.)
Willie Wood	RS	A. Dabiero (Notre Dame)

Head coaches—Vince Lombardi, Green Bay; Otto Graham (Coast Guard), College All-Stars

Green Bay	7	7	7	21	—	42
College All-Stars	3	10	0	7	—	20

All-Stars—Gros 1 run (Mather kick)
GB —Dowler 22 pass from Starr (Hornung kick)
All-Stars—FG Mather 26
GB —R. Kramer 4 pass from Starr (Hornung kick)
All-Stars—Bryant 21 pass from Hadl (Mather kick)
GB —Dowler 22 pass from Starr (Hornung kick)
All-Stars—FG Mather 15
GB —McGee 20 pass from Starr (Hornung kick)
GB —McGee 36 pass from Starr (Hornung kick)
GB —Pitts 3 run (Hornung kick)
Attendance—65,000

1963

ALL-STARS 20, GREEN BAY 17

A third-down pass from quarterback Ron Vander-Kelen to Pat Richter, VanderKelen's University of Wisconsin teammate, resulted in the All-Stars' first victory in the series since 1958.

August 2, at Soldier Field

Green Bay	Starters, Offense	College All-Stars
Max McGee	LE	Pat Richter (Wisconsin)
Bob Skoronski	LT	Bob Vogel (Ohio State)
Fred (Fuzzy) Thurston	LG	Ed Budde (Michigan State)
Jim Ringo	C	D. Behrman (Michigan State)
Jerry Kramer	RG	Don Chuy (Clemson)
Forrest Gregg	RT	Daryl Sanders (Ohio State)
Ron Kramer	RE	Bob Jencks (Miami, Ohio)
Bart Starr	QB	Ron VanderKelen (Wis.)
Boyd Dowler	FL	Paul Flatley (Northwestern)
Tom Moore	HB	Larry Ferguson (Iowa)
Jim Taylor	FB	Bill Thornton (Nebraska)
Starters, Defense		
Willie Davis	LE	Fred Miller (Louisiana State)
Dave Hanner	LT	Charles Sieminski (Penn St.)
Henry Jordan	RT	Jim Dunaway (Mississippi)
Urban Henry	RE	Don Brumm (Purdue)
Dan Currie	LLB	Dave Robinson (Penn State)
Ken Iman	MLB	Lee Roy Jordan (Alabama)
Bill Forester	RLB	Bobby Bell (Minnesota)
Herb Adderley	LHB	Tom Janik (Texas A&I)
Jesse Whittenton	RHB	Larry Glueck (Villanova)
Hank Gremminger	LS	L. Sanders (Michigan St.)
Willie Wood	RS	Kermit Alexander (UCLA)

Head coaches—Vince Lombardi, Green Bay; Otto Graham (Coast Guard), College All Stars

Green Bay	7	3	0	7	—	17
College All-Stars	3	7	10	0	—	20

GB —Taylor 2 run (J. Kramer kick)
All-Stars—FG Jencks 20
All-Stars—Ferguson 6 run (Jencks kick)
GB —FG Kramer 21
All-Stars—FG Jencks 33
All-Stars—Richter 73 pass from VanderKelen (Jencks kick)
GB —Taylor 1 run (J. Kramer kick)
Attendance—65,000

1964

CHICAGO 28, ALL-STARS 17

The Chicago Bears overcame the College All-Stars' 10-7 halftime lead with three consecutive touchdowns in the third and fourth quarters on their way to a 28–17 victory.

August 7, at Soldier Field

Chicago	Starters, Offense	College All-Stars
Gary Barnes	LE	C. Logan (Northwestern)
Herman Lee	LT	Lloyd Voss (Nebraska)
Ted Karras	LG	Harrison Rosdahl (Penn St.)
Mike Pyle	C	Ray Kubala (Texas A&M)
Jim Cadile	RG	Dick Evey (Tennessee)
Bob Wetoska	RT	Ernie Borghetti (Pittsburgh)
Mike Ditka	RE	Ted Davis (Georgia Tech)
Bill Wade	QB	Pete Beathard (USC)
Johnny Morris	FL	Paul Warfield (Ohio State)
Ron Bull	HB	Tony Lorick (Arizona State)
Joe Marconi	FB	W. Crenshaw (Kansas St.)
	Starters, Defense	
Ed O'Bradovich	LE	George Seals (Missouri)
Stan Jones	LT	Tom Keating (Michigan)
Earl Leggett	RT	Geo. Bednar (Notre Dame)
Doug Atkins	RE	Ed Lothamer (Michigan)
Joe Fortunato	LLB	Wally Hilgenberg (Iowa)
Bill George	MLB	Mike Reilly (Iowa)
Larry Morris	RLB	Dave Wilcox (Oregon)
Bennie McRae	LHB	George Rose (Auburn)
Dave Whitsell	RHB	J. Richardson (W. Texas St.)
Richie Petitbon	LS	Perry Lee Dunn (Miss.)
Roosevelt Taylor	RS	Mel Renfro (Oregon)

Head coaches—George Halas, Chicago; Otto Graham (Coast Guard), College All-Stars

Chicago	0	7	14	7	—	28
College All-Stars	0	10	0	7	—	17

All-Stars—FG Van Raaphorst 14
Chi —Ditka 13 pass from Wade (Jencks kick)
All-Stars—Davis 14 pass from Taylor (Van Raaphorst kick)
Chi —Wade 1 run (Jencks kick)
Chi —Barnes 20 pass from Wade (Jencks kick)
Chi —Bivins 30 pass from Bukich (Jencks kick)
All-Stars—Taylor 5 pass from Mira (Van Raaphorst kick)
Attendance—65,000

1965

CLEVELAND 24, ALL-STARS 16

Cleveland's Jamie Caleb blocked a punt by Mississippi's Frank Lambert when the College All-Stars had 10 men on the field in the second quarter and Stan Sczurek recovered the ball in the end zone.

August 6, at Soldier Field

Cleveland	Starters, Offense	College All-Stars
Paul Warfield	LE	Bob Hayes (Florida, A&M)
Dick Schafrath	LT	Ralph Neely (Oklahoma)
John Wooten	LG	Bob Breitenstein (Tulsa)
John Morrow	C	Bill Curry (Georgia Tech)
Gene Hickerson	RG	Jim Wilson (Georgia)
Monte Clark	RT	Harry Schuh (Memphis St.)
Johnny Brewer	RE	Fred Brown (Miami)
Frank Ryan	QB	Roger Staubach (Navy)
Gary Collins	FL	Fred Biletnikoff (Florida St.)
Ernie Green	HB	Pat Donnelly (Navy)
Jim Brown	FB	Ken Willard (North Carolina)
	Starters, Defense	
Paul Wiggin	LE	Jim Garcia (Purdue)
Dick Modzelewski	LT	J. Szczecko (N'western)
Jim Kanicki	RT	Jim Norton (Washington)
Bill Glass	RE	Verlon Biggs (Jackson St.)
Jim Houston	LLB	Don Croftcheck (Indiana)
Vince Costello	MLB	Dick Butkus (Illinois)
Galen Fiss	RLB	Marty Schottenheimer (Pitt.)
Bernie Parrish	LHB	C. Williams (Washington St.)
Walter Beach	RHB	Roy Jefferson (Utah)
Ross Fichtner	LS	Al Nelson (Cincinnati)
Larry Benz	RS	George Donnelly (Illinois)

Head coaches—Blanton Collier, Cleveland; Otto Graham (Coast Guard), College All-Stars

Cleveland	7	10	7	0	—	24
College All-Stars	0	3	6	7	—	16

Cle —Brown 7 run (Groza kick)
All-Stars—FG Mercein 36
Cle —Sczurek, blocked punt recovery in end zone
Cle —FG Groza 30
Cle —Collins 10 pass from Ryan (Groza kick)
All-Stars—Mercein 5 pass from Huarte (kick failed)
All-Stars—Rentzel 5 pass from Huarte (Mercein kick)
Attendance—68,000

1966

GREEN BAY 38, ALL-STARS 0

Quarterback Steve Sloan of Alabama fumbled on the game's first play from scrimmage, and Green Bay's Lionel Aldridge recovered on the College All-Stars' 33-yard line. Five plays later the Packers scored.

August 5, at Soldier Field

Green Bay	Starters, Offense	College All-Stars
Carroll Dale	LE	G. Garrison (San Diego St.)
Bob Skoronski	LT	D. McCormick (LSU)
Fred (Fuzzy) Thurston	LG	John Niland (Iowa)
Ken Bowman	C	Pat Killorin (Syracuse)
Jerry Kramer	RG	Tom Mack (Michigan)
Forrest Gregg	RT	Francis Peay (Missouri)
Bill Anderson	RE	Milt Morin (Massachusetts)
Bart Starr	QB	Steve Sloan (Alabama)
Boyd Dowler	FL	D. Anderson (Texas Tech)
Paul Hornung	HB	Roy Shivers (Utah State)
Jim Taylor	FB	Johnny Roland (Missouri)
	Starters, Defense	
Willie Davis	LE	Stan Hindman (Mississippi)
Ron Kostelnik	LT	Jerry Shay (Purdue)
Henry Jordan	RT	George Rice (Louisiana St.)
Lionel Aldridge	RE	Aaron Brown (Minnesota)
Dave Robinson	LLB	Doug Buffone (Louisville)
Ray Nitschke	MLB	Tommy Nobis (Texas)
Lee Roy Caffey	RLB	Don Hansen (Illinois)
Herb Adderley	LHB	S. Quintana (New Mexico)
Bob Jeter	RHB	Charlie King (Purdue)
Willie Wood	LS	Doug McFalls (Georgia)
Tom Brown	RS	Nick Rassas (Notre Dame)

Head coaches—Vince Lombardi, Green Bay; John Sauer, College All-Stars

Green Bay	7	21	10	0	—	38
College All-Stars	0	0	0	0	—	0

GB—Dowler 10 pass from Starr (Chandler kick)
GB—B. Anderson 13 pass from Starr (Chandler kick)
GB—Taylor 1 run (Chandler kick)
GB—Adderley 36 interception return (Chandler kick)
GB—FG Chandler 17
GB—Taylor 13 run (Chandler kick)
Attendance—72,000

1967

GREEN BAY 27, ALL-STARS 0

Quarterback Bart Starr completed 15 of 21 passes for 212 yards and two touchdowns and turned nine third-down situations into six first downs before leaving the game at the end of the half with the Green Bay Packers leading the College All-Stars 20–0.

August 4, at Soldier Field

Green Bay	Starters, Offense	College All-Stars
Boyd Dowler	LE	G. Washington (Michigan St.)
Bob Skoronski	LT	Gene Upshaw (Texas A&I)
Gale Gillingham	LG	Tom Regner (Notre Dame)
Ken Bowman	C	B. Hyland (Boston College)
Jerry Kramer	RG	Norman Davis (Grambling)
Forrest Gregg	RT	Mike Current (Ohio State)
Allen Brown	TE	Tom Beer (Houston)
Bart Starr	QB	Steve Spurrier (Florida)
Carroll Dale	FL	Dave Williams (Wash.)
Elijah Pitts	RB	Floyd Little (Syracuse)
Ben Wilson	RB	Mel Farr (UCLA)
	Starters, Defense	
Willie Davis	LE	Leo Carroll (San Diego St.)
Ron Kostelnik	LT	Bubba Smith (Michigan St.)
Henry Jordan	RT	Dave Rowe (Penn State)
Lionel Aldridge	RE	Alan Page (Notre Dame)
Dave Robinson	LLB	G. Webster (Michigan St.)
Ray Nitschke	MLB	Jim Lynch (Notre Dame)
Lee Roy Caffey	RLB	Paul Naumoff (Tennessee)
Herb Adderley	LHB	Bob Grim (Oregon State)
Bob Jeter	RHB	Phil Clark (Northwestern)
Tom Brown	LS	Rick Volk (Michigan)
Willie Wood	RS	Henry King (Utah State)

Head coaches—Vince Lombardi, Green Bay; John Sauer, College All-Stars

Green Bay	6	14	0	7	—	27
College All-Stars	0	0	0	0	—	0

GB—FG Chandler 13
GB—FG Chandler 13
GB—Dowler 11 pass from Starr (Chandler kick)
GB—Long 22 pass from Starr (Chandler kick)
GB—Grabowski 22 run (Chandler kick)
Attendance—70,934

1968

GREEN BAY 34, ALL-STARS 17

Quarterback Bart Starr completed 17 of 23 passes for 288 yards and three touchdowns.

August 2, at Soldier Field

Green Bay	Starters, Offense	College All-Stars
Boyd Dowler	LE	B. Wallace (Texas-El Paso)
Bob Skoronski	LT	Mo Moorman (Texas A&M)
Gale Gillingham	LG	Bill Leuck (Arizona)
Ken Bowman	C	Bob Johnson (Tennessee)
Jerry Kramer	RG	John Williams (Minnesota)
Forrest Gregg	RT	Ron Yary (USC)
Marv Fleming	TE	C. Sanders (Minnesota)
Bart Starr	QB	Gary Beban (UCLA)
Carroll Dale	FL	Dennis Homan (Alabama)
Elijah Pitts	RB	MacArthur Lane (Utah St.)
Jim Grabowski	RB	Larry Csonka (Syracuse)
	Starters, Defense	
Willie Davis	LE	C. Humphrey (Tenn. St.)
Ron Kostelnik	LT	Curley Culp (Arizona State)
Henry Jordan	RT	Bill Staley (Utah State)
Lionel Aldridge	RE	M. Upshaw (Trinity, Tex.)
Dave Robinson	LLB	Fred Carr (Texas-El Paso)
Ray Nitschke	MLB	Mike McGill (Notre Dame)
Lee Roy Caffey	RLB	Adrian Young (USC)
Herb Adderley	LHB	J. Henderson (Colorado St.)
Bob Jeter	RHB	Jim Smith (Oregon)
Tom Brown	LS	M. Hazelton (Florida A&M)
Willie Wood	RS	Bob Atkins (Grambling)

Head coaches—Phil Bengtson, Green Bay; Norm Van Brocklin, College All-Stars

Green Bay	7	17	0	10	—	34
College All-Stars	0	3	7	7	—	17

GB —Anderson 1 run (Kramer kick)
GB —Dale 20 pass from Starr (Kramer kick)
GB —Dale 36 pass from Starr (Kramer kick)
All-Stars—FG DePoyster 22
GB —FG Traynham 30
All-Stars—McCullouch 7 pass from Beban (DePoyster kick)
GB —Dale 23 pass from Starr (Kramer kick)
GB —FG Kramer 47
All-Stars—McCullouch 24 pass from Landry (DePoyster kick)
Attendance—69,917

1969

N.Y. JETS 26, ALL-STARS 24

The New York Jets scored a 26-24 victory.

August 1, at Soldier Field

N.Y. Jets	Starters, Offense	College All-Stars
George Sauer	WR	Jim Seymour (Notre Dame)
Winston Hill	LT	Dave Foley (Ohio State)
Randy Rasmussen	LG	Mike Montler (Colorado)
John Schmitt	C	Jon Kolb (Oklahoma State)
Dave Herman	RG	John Shinners (Xavier)
Sam Walton	RT	George Kunz (Notre Dame)
Pete Lammons	TE	Bob Klein (USC)
Don Maynard	WR	Jerry LeVias (SMU)
Joe Namath	QB	Terry Hanratty (Notre Dame)
Emerson Boozer	RB	Altie Taylor (Utah State)
Matt Snell	RB	Paul Gipson (Houston)
	Starters, Defense	
Gerry Philbin	LE	Bill Stanfill (Georgia)
Paul Rochester	LT	Rich Moore (Villanova)
John Elliott	RT	Rolf Krueger (Texas A&M)
Verlon Biggs	RE	Fred Dryer (San Diego St.)
John Neidert	LLB	Ron Pritchard (Arizona St.)
Al Atkinson	MLB	Bill Bergey (Arkansas State)
Ralph Baker	RLB	Bob Babich (Miami, Ohio)
Johnny Sample	LCB	J. Marsalis (Tennessee St.)
Randy Beverly	RCB	B. Thompson (Maryland St.)
Bill Baird	LS	Gene Epps (Texas-El Paso)
Jim Hudson	RS	Roger Wehrli (Missouri)

Head coaches—Weeb Ewbank, N.Y. Jets; Otto Graham, College All-Stars

N.Y. Jets	6	7	10	3	—	26
College All-Stars	0	0	17	7	—	24

NYJ —FG J. Turner 43
NYJ —FG J. Turner 16
NYJ —Snell 3 run (J. Turner kick)
NYJ —FG J. Turner 42
All-Stars—Washington 17 pass from Cook (Gerela kick)
All-Stars—FG Gerela 28
NYJ —Snell 35 run (J. Turner kick)
All-Stars—Klein 12 pass from Cook (Gerela kick)
NYJ —FG J. Turner 18
All-Stars—LeVias 19 pass from Cook (Gerela kick)
Attendance—74,208

1970

KANSAS CITY 24, ALL-STARS 3

Len Dawson was successful on 17 of 21 passes, including 12 of 14 for 117 yards and one touchdown in the first half, as the Kansas City Chiefs defeated the College All-Stars 24–3.

Dawson's 36-yard pass to Frank Pitts put Kansas City ahead 7–0 the first time it had the ball.

July 31, at Soldier Field

Kansas City	Starters, Offense	College All-Stars
Frank Pitts	WR	Jerry Hendren (Idaho)
Jim Tyrer	LT	Bob McKay (Texas)
Ed Budde	LG	D. Wilkerson (No. Car. Cent.)
E. J. Holub	C	Sid Smith (USC)
Mo Moorman	RG	C. Hutchison (Ohio State)
Dave Hill	RT	Bob Asher (Vanderbilt)
Fred Arbanas	TE	R. Caster (Jackson State)
Otis Taylor	WR	Ron Shanklin (No. Texas St.)
Len Dawson	QB	D. Shaw (San Diego State)
Mike Garrett	RB	Bob Anderson (Colorado)
Robert Holmes	RB	Art Malone (Arizona State)
	Starters, Defense	
Jerry Mays	LE	Al Cowlings (USC)
Curley Culp	LT	Mike McCoy (Notre Dame)
Buck Buchanan	RT	Mike Reid (Penn State)
Aaron Brown	RE	C. Hardman (No. Texas St.)
Bobby Bell	LLB	John Small (The Citadel)
Willie Lanier	MLB	Steve Zabel (Oklahoma)
Jim Lynch	RLB	Jim Files (Oklahoma)
Jim Marsalis	LCB	Bruce Taylor (Boston U.)
Emmitt Thomas	RCB	Al Mathews (Texas A&I)
Jim Kearney	LS	Steve Tannen (Florida)
Johnny Robinson	RS	Charlie Waters (Clemson)

Head coaches–Hank Stram, Kansas City; Otto Graham, College All-Stars

Kansas City	10	14	0	0	—	24
College All-Stars	0	0	3	0	—	3

KC —Pitts 36 pass from Dawson (Stenerud kick)
KC —FG Stenerud 43
KC —McVea 3 run (Stenerud kick)
KC —Kearney 65 interception return (Stenerud kick)
All-Stars—FG Delaney 26
Attendance—69,940

1971

BALTIMORE 24, ALL-STARS 17

The Baltimore Colts' 24–17 victory over the College All-Stars was the professionals' eighth in a row and gave them a record of 27 victories, 10 losses, and 1 tie in the series.

July 30, at Soldier Field

Baltimore	Starters, Offense	College All-Stars
Eddie Hinton	WR	J. D. Hill (Arizona State)
Bob Vogel	LT	Marv Montgomery (USC)
Glenn Ressler	LG	Steve Lawson (Kansas)
Bill Curry	C	Warren Koegel (Penn State)
John Williams	RG	H. Allison (San Diego St.)
Dan Sullivan	RT	Vern Holland (Tenn. State)
John Mackey	TE	Bob Moore (Stanford)
Ray Perkins	WR	E. Jennings (Air Force)
Earl Morrall	QB	Jim Plunkett (Stanford)
Tom Matte	RB	J. Brockington (Ohio State)
Norm Bulaich	RB	M. Adamle (Northwestern)
	Starters, Defense	
Charles (Bubba) Smith	LE	Jack Youngblood (Florida)
Jim Bailey	LT	J. Adams (Texas Southern)
Billy Newsome	RT	Tony McGee (Bishop)
Roy Hilton	RE	Richard Harris (Grambling)
Ray May	LLB	Ron Hornsby (SE Louisiana)
Mike Curtis	MLB	I. Robertson (Southern U.)
Ted Hendricks	RLB	Jack Ham (Penn State)
Charlie Stukes	LCB	C. Scott (Kansas State)
Jim Duncan	RCB	Ike Thomas (Bishop)
Jerry Logan	LS	Charles Hall (Pittsburgh)
Rick Volk	RS	Jack Tatum (Ohio State)

Head coaches—Don McCafferty, Baltimore; Blanton Collier, College All-Stars

Baltimore	7	7	3	7	—	24
College All-Stars	0	10	0	7	—	17

Balt —Perkins 24 pass from Morrall (O'Brien kick)
All-Stars—Brockington 1 run (Pastorini kick)
Balt —Matte 15 pass from Morrall (O'Brien kick)
All-Stars—FG Jacobs 40
Balt —FG O'Brien 22
Balt —Mitchell 44 pass from Morrall (O'Brien kick)
All-Stars—Ham 47 fumble return (Jacobs kick)
Attendance—52,289

1972

DALLAS 20, ALL-STARS 7

The Dallas Cowboys converted a pass interception and recovered fumble into 10 points.

Mel Renfro intercepted a pass by Jerry Tagge at the All-Stars' 30 in the first quarter; the Cowboys turned the mistake into Mike Clark's 31-yard field goal.

July 28, at Soldier Field

Dallas	Starters, Offense	College All-Stars
Bob Hayes	WR	Mike Siani (Villanova)
Ralph Neely	LT	Lionel Antoine (So. Illinois)
John Niland	LG	R. McKenzie (Michigan)
Dave Manders	C	Bob Kuziel (Pittsburgh)
Blaine Nye	RG	S. Okoniewski (Montana)
Rayfield Wright	RT	Dan Yockum (Syracuse)
Mike Ditka	TE	Riley Odoms (Houston)
Lance Alworth	WR	Glenn Doughty (Michigan)
Roger Staubach	QB	Jerry Tagge (Nebraska)
Duane Thomas	RB	Jeff Kinney (Nebraska)
Walt Garrison	RB	Franco Harris (Penn State)
	Starters, Defense	
Larry Cole	LE	Walt Patulski (Notre Dame)
Jethro Pugh	LT	J. Mendenhall (Grambling)
Bob Lilly	RT	Pete Lazetich (Stanford)
George Andrie	RE	Sherman White (California)
Dave Edwards	LLB	Willie Hall (USC)
Lee Roy Jordan	MLB	Jeff Siemon (Stanford)
Chuck Howley	RLB	Mike Taylor (Michigan)
Herb Adderley	LCB	W. Buchanon (San Diego St.)
Mel Renfro	RCB	Tommy Casanova (LSU)
Cornell Green	LS	Thom Darden (Michigan)
Cliff Harris	RS	Craig Clemons (Iowa)

Head coaches–Tom Landry, Dallas; Bob Devaney (Nebraska), College All-Stars

Dallas	3	7	7	3	—	20
College All-Stars	0	0	0	7	—	7

Dall —FG Clark 31
Dall —Sellers 18 pass from Morton (Clark kick)
Dall —Hayes 24 pass from Morton (Fritsch kick)
Dall —FG Fritsch 33
All-Stars—Newhouse 1 run (Marcol kick)
Attendance—54,162

1973

MIAMI 14, ALL-STARS 3

The Miami Dolphins marched 66 yards to Larry Csonka's three-yard touchdown run the first time they had the ball and went on to defeat the College All-Stars 14–3.

Csonka gained 76 yards in 17 carries as the professionals outgained the collegians 251–143 in total offense.

July 27, at Soldier Field

Miami	Starters, Offense	College All-Stars
Paul Warfield	WR	Barry Smith (Florida State)
Wayne Moore	LT	Paul Seymour (Michigan)
Bob Kuechenberg	LG	Pete Adams (USC)
Jim Langer	C	Dave Brown (USC)
Larry Little	RG	John Hannah (Alabama)
Norm Evans	RT	Jerry Sisemore (Texas)
Marv Fleming	TE	Charles Young (USC)
Howard Twilley	WR	Steve Holden (Arizona St.)
Bob Griese	QB	Bert Jones (Louisiana State)
Jim Kiick	RB	T. Metcalf (Long Beach St.)
Larry Csonka	RB	Chuck Foreman (Miami)
	Starters, Defense	
Vern Den Herder	LE	W. Chambers (E. Kentucky)
Manny Fernandez	LT	John Grant (USC)
Bob Heinz	RT	Richard Glover (Nebraska)
Bill Stanfill	RE	John Matuszak (Tampa)
Doug Swift	LLB	Jim Merlo (Stanford)
Nick Buoniconti	MLB	J. Youngblood (Tenn. Tech)
Bob Matheson	RLB	Gary Weaver (Fresno State)
Tim Foley	LCB	Burgess Owens (Miami)
Curtis Johnson	RCB	M. Holmes (Texas Southern)
Charlie Babb	LS	J. T. Thomas (Florida State)
Dick Anderson	RS	Jackie Wallace (Arizona)

Head coaches–Don Shula (Miami); John McKay (USC), College All-Stars

Miami	7	0	0	7	—	14
College All-Stars	0	3	0	0	—	3

Mia —Csonka 3 run (Yepremian kick)
All-Stars—FG Guy 10
Mia —Csonka 7 run (Yepremian kick)
Attendance—54,103

1974

NO GAME

The forty-first Chicago All-Star game was canceled by the sponsoring *Chicago Tribune* after the NFL Players' Association said it would not give full sanction to the game between the College All-Stars and Miami Dolphins.

The Players' Association and NFL owners were involved in a collective bargaining dispute that had resulted in some of the Association's members striking their summer training camps. The All-Stars voted not to continue preparation for the contest unless the players and owners settled their dispute.

1975

PITTSBURGH 21, ALL-STARS 14

Trailing 14–7 at the half, the Pittsburgh Steelers rallied for a 21–14 victory over the College All-Stars behind quarterback Joe Gilliam, who passed for two touchdowns in the fourth quarter.

Gilliam replaced starter Terry Bradshaw.

August 1, at Soldier Field

Pittsburgh	Starters, Offense	College All-Stars
Frank Lewis	WR	Pat McInally (Harvard)
Jon Kolb	LT	Dennis Harrah (Miami)
Jim Clack	LG	Ken Huff (North Carolina)
Ray Mansfield	C	Kyle Davis (Oklahoma)
Gerry Mullins	RG	L. Boden (South Dakota St.)
Gordon Gravelle	RT	Kurt Schumacher (Ohio St.)
Larry Brown	TE	Russ Francis (Oregon)
Ron Shanklin	WR	Emmett Edwards (Kansas)
Terry Bradshaw	QB	S. Bartkowski (California)
Rocky Bleier	RB	Walter Payton (Jackson St.)
Franco Harris	RB	Stan Winfrey (Arkansas St.)
	Starters, Defense	
L. C. Greenwood	LE	Mike Fanning (Notre Dame)
Joe Greene	LT	Mike Hartenstine (Penn St.)
Ernie Holmes	RT	Randy White (Maryland)
Dwight White	RE	Robert Brazile (Jackson St.)
Jack Ham	LLB	Glenn Cameron (Florida)
Jack Lambert	MLB	Ralph Ortega (Florida)
Andy Russell	RLB	Richard Wood (USC)
J. T. Thomas	LCB	Neal Colzie (Ohio State)
Mel Blount	RCB	Louis Wright (San Jose St.)
Mike Wagner	LS	Charles Phillips (USC)
Glen Edwards	RS	Marvin Cobb (USC)

Head coaches—Chuck Noll, Pittsburgh; John McKay (USC), College All-Stars

Pittsburgh	0	7	0	14	—	21
College All-Stars	7	7	0	0	—	14

All-Stars—McInally 26 pass from Bartkowski (Mike-Mayer kick)
Pitt —Grossman 2 pass from Bradshaw (Gerela kick)
All-Stars—Livers 86 punt return (Mike-Mayer kick)
Pitt —Bleier 6 pass from Gilliam (Gerela kick)
Pitt —Lewis 21 pass from Gilliam (Gerela kick)
Attendance–54,103

1976

PITTSBURGH 24, ALL-STARS 0

The Pittsburgh Steelers won 24–0 in the last Chicago All-Star Game. It was called with 1:22 left in the third quarter. A thunderstorm flooded the field and 12 minutes later game officials agreed with NFL Commissioner Pete Rozelle to suspend play.

July 23, at Soldier Field

Pittsburgh	Starters, Offense	College All-Stars
Frank Lewis	WR	D. Harris (New Mexico St.)
Jon Kolb	LT	Mark Koncar (Colorado)
Jim Clack	LG	Tom Glassic (Virginia)
Mike Webster	C	Pete Brock (Colorado)
Gerry Mullins	RG	Jackie Slater (Jackson St.)
Gordon Gravelle	RT	Dennis Lick (Wisconsin)
Larry Brown	TE	B. Cunningham (Clemson)
Lynn Swann	WR	Brian Baschnagel (Ohio St.)
Terry Bradshaw	QB	M. Kruczek (Boston Coll.)
Rocky Bleier	RB	Joe Washington (Oklahoma)
Franco Harris	RB	Tony Galbreath (Missouri)
Starters, Defense		
L. C. Greenwood	LE	Troy Archer (Colorado)
Joe Greene	LT	L. Roy Selmon (Oklahoma)
Ernie Holmes	RT	Dewey Selmon (Oklahoma)
Dwight White	RE	James White (Oklahoma St.)
Jack Ham	LLB	Kevin McLain (Colorado St.)
Jack Lambert	MLB	Ed Simonini (Texas A&M)
Andy Russell	RLB	Larry Gordon (Arizona St.)
J. T. Thomas	LCB	Aaron Kyle (Wyoming)
Mel Blount	RCB	Mario Clark (Oregon)
Mike Wagner	LS	Shafer Suggs (Ball State)
Glen Edwards	RS	Ed Lewis (Kansas)

Head coaches–Chuck Noll, Pittsburgh; Ara Parseghian, College All-Stars

Pittsburgh	3	6	15	—	24
College All-Stars	0	0	0	—	0

Pitt—FG Gerela 29
Pitt—FG Gerela 32
Pitt—FG Gerela 23
Pitt—Safety, Pinney centered ball out of end zone
Pitt—Harris 21 run (Gerela kick)
Pitt—Reamon 2 run (kick failed)
Attendance—52,895

CHICAGO ALL-STAR GAME HISTORY

Date	Result	Site (attendance)
Aug. 31, 1934	Chi. Bears 0, College All-Stars 0	Soldier Field, Chicago (79,432)
Aug. 29, 1935	Chi. Bears 5, College All-Stars 0	Soldier Field, Chicago (77,450)
Sept. 3, 1936	College All-Stars 7, Detroit Lions 0	Soldier Field, Chicago (76,000)
Sept. 1, 1937	College All-Stars 6, Green Bay Packers 0	Soldier Field, Chicago (84,560)
Aug. 31, 1938	College All-Stars 28, Washington 16	Soldier Field, Chicago (74,250)
Aug. 30, 1939	N.Y. Giants 9, College All-Stars 0	Soldier Field, Chicago (81,456)
Aug. 29, 1940	Green Bay 45, College All-Stars 28	Soldier Field, Chicago (84,567)
Aug. 28, 1941	Chi Bears 37, College All-Stars 13	Soldier Field, Chicago (98,203)
Aug. 28, 1942	Chi. Bears 21, College All-Stars 0	Soldier Field, Chicago (101,100)
Aug. 25, 1943	College All-Stars 27, Washington 7	Dyche Stadium, Evanston (48,471)
Aug. 30, 1944	Chi. Bears 24, College All-Stars 21	Dyche Stadium, Evanston (48,769)
Aug. 30, 1945	Green Bay 19, College All-Stars 7	Soldier Field, Chicago (92,753)
Aug. 23, 1946	College All-Stars 16, Los Angeles 0	Soldier Field, Chicago (97,380)
Aug. 22, 1947	College All-Stars 16, Chi. Bears 0	Soldier Field, Chicago (105,840)
Aug. 20, 1948	Chi. Cardinals 28, College All-Stars 0	Soldier Field, Chicago (101,220)
Aug. 12, 1949	Philadelphia 38, College All-Stars 0	Soldier Field, Chicago (93,780)
Aug. 11, 1950	College All-Stars 17, Philadelphia 7	Soldier Field, Chicago (88,885)
Aug. 17, 1951	Cleveland 33, College All-Stars 0	Soldier Field, Chicago (92,180)
Aug. 15, 1952	Los Angeles 10, College All-Stars 7	Soldier Field, Chicago (88,316)
Aug. 14, 1953	Detroit 24, College All-Stars 10	Soldier Field, Chicago (93,818)
Aug. 13, 1954	Detroit 31, College All-Stars 6	Soldier Field, Chicago (93,470)
Aug. 12, 1955	College All-Stars 30, Cleveland 27	Soldier Field, Chicago (75,000)
Aug. 10, 1956	Cleveland 26, College All-Stars 0	Soldier Field, Chicago (75,000)
Aug. 9, 1957	N.Y. Giants 22, College All-Stars 12	Soldier Field, Chicago (75,000)
Aug. 15, 1958	College All-Stars 35, Detroit 19	Soldier Field, Chicago (70,000)
Aug. 14, 1959	Baltimore 29, College All-Stars 0	Soldier Field, Chicago (70,000)
Aug. 12, 1960	Baltimore 32, College All-Stars 7	Soldier Field, Chicago (70,000)
Aug. 4, 1961	Philadelphia 28, College All-Stars 14	Soldier Field, Chicago (66,000)
Aug. 3, 1962	Green Bay 42, College All-Stars 20	Soldier Field, Chicago (65,000)
Aug. 2, 1963	College All-Stars 20, Green Bay 17	Soldier Field, Chicago (65,000)
Aug. 7, 1964	Chicago 28, College All-Stars 17	Soldier Field, Chicago (65,000)
Aug. 6, 1965	Cleveland 24, College All-Stars 16	Soldier Field, Chicago (68,000)
Aug. 5, 1966	Green Bay 38, College All-Stars 0	Soldier Field, Chicago (72,000)
Aug. 4, 1967	Green Bay 27, College All-Stars 0	Soldier Field, Chicago (70,934)
Aug. 2, 1968	Green Bay 34, College All-Stars 17	Soldier Field, Chicago (69,917)
Aug. 1, 1969	N.Y. Jets 26, College All-Stars 24	Soldier Field, Chicago (74,208)
July 31, 1970	Kansas City 24, College All-Stars 3	Soldier Field, Chicago (69,940)
July 30, 1971	Baltimore 24, College All-Stars 17	Soldier Field, Chicago (52,289)
July 28, 1972	Dallas 20, College All-Stars 7	Soldier Field, Chicago (54,162)
July 27, 1973	Miami 14, College All-Stars 3	Soldier Field, Chicago (54,103)
July 26, 1974	No game was played because of NFL players-owners dispute	
Aug. 1, 1975	Pittsburgh 21, College All-Stars 14	Soldier Field, Chicago (54,103)
July 23, 1976	Pittsburgh 24, College All-Stars 0	Soldier Field, Chicago (52,895)

Professional teams, 31 victories; College All-Stars 10 victories; 1 tie

All-Pros

Red Badgro

Ernie Caddel

Gaynell Tinsley

Willie Wilkin

Al Wistert

Johnny Lujack

Lou Creekmur

The first official all-pro team was picked by the NFL in 1931. The practice continued until 1943, the first year of the news service teams. *Associated Press* (AP) and *United Press* (UP; UPI since 1958) picked the all-pro teams until 1960. From 1961-68, AP, UPI, and *Newspaper Enterprise Association* (NEA) picked the all-pro teams for the NFL.

The AFL all-pro teams were picked by the players in 1960 and from 1962-66; the coaches picked the team in 1961. In 1964, AP and UPI started picking AFL all-pro teams, joining the players from 1964-66. In 1967, the players stopped their picks and the wire services were the only AFL all-pro teams in 1967 and 1968.

In 1969, the first combined NFL-AFL all-pro team was picked by the Pro Football Hall of Fame. In 1970-71 the official team was chosen by the Professional Football Writers Association (PFWA). From 1972-75, both the PFWA and the NEA picked all-pro teams. Since 1976, the PFWA, NEA, and AP have picked teams.

1931
Lavern Dilweg, Green Bay . . . E
Morris (Red) Badgro, N.Y. Giants . . . E
Cal Hubbard, Green Bay . . . T
George Christensen, Portsmouth . . . T
Mike Michalske, Green Bay . . . G
Denver (Butch) Gibson, N.Y. Giants . . . G
Frank McNally, Chicago Cardinals . . . C
Earl (Dutch) Clark, Portsmouth . . . QB
Harold (Red) Grange, Chicago Bears . . . HB
Johnny Blood (McNally), Green Bay . . . HB
Ernie Nevers, Chicago Cardinals . . . FB

1932
Ray Flaherty, N.Y. Giants . . . E
Luke Johnsos, Chicago Bears . . . E
Cal Hubbard, Green Bay . . . T
Glen (Turk) Edwards, Boston Redskins . . . T
Jules Carlson, Chicago Bears . . . G
Walt Kiesling, Chicago Cardinals . . . G
Nate Barrager, Green Bay . . . C
Earl (Dutch) Clark, Portsmouth . . . QB
Arnie Herber, Green Bay . . . HB
Roy Lumpkin, Portsmouth . . . HB
Bronko Nagurski, Chicago Bears . . . FB

1933
Bill Hewitt, Chicago Bears . . . E
Morris (Red) Badgro, N.Y. Giants . . . E
Cal Hubbard, Green Bay . . . T
Glen (Turk) Edwards, Boston Redskins . . . T
Herman Hickman, Brooklyn . . . G
Joe Kopcha, Chicago Bears . . . G
Mel Hein, N.Y. Giants . . . C
Harry Newman, N.Y. Giants . . . QB
Glenn Presnell, Portsmouth . . . HB
Cliff Battles, Boston Redskins . . . HB
Bronko Nagurski, Chicago Bears . . . FB

1934
Bill Hewitt, Chicago Bears . . . E
Morris (Red) Badgro, N.Y. Giants . . . E
George Christensen, Detroit . . . T
Bill Morgan, N.Y. Giants . . . T
Denver (Butch) Gibson, N.Y. Giants . . . G
Joe Kopcha, Chicago Bears . . . G
Mel Hein, N.Y. Giants . . . C
Earl (Dutch) Clark, Detroit . . . QB
Beattie Feathers, Chicago Bears . . . HB
Ken Strong, N.Y. Giants . . . HB
Bronko Nagurski, Chicago Bears . . . FB

1935
Bill Smith, Chicago Cardinals . . . E
Bill Karr, Chicago Bears . . . E
Bill Morgan, N.Y. Giants . . . T
George Musso, Chicago Bears . . . T
Joe Kopcha, Chicago Bears . . . G
Mike Michalske, Green Bay . . . G
Mel Hein, N.Y. Giants . . . C
Earl (Dutch) Clark, Detroit . . . QB
Ed Danowski, N.Y. Giants . . . HB
Ernie Caddel, Detroit . . . HB
Mike Mikulak, Chicago Cardinals . . . FB

1936
Bill Hewitt, Chicago Bears - Philadelphia . . . E
Don Hutson, Green Bay . . . E
Glen (Turk) Edwards, Boston Redskins . . . T
Ernie Smith, Green Bay . . . T
Lon Evans, Green Bay . . . G
Grover (Ox) Emerson, Detroit . . . G
Mel Hein, N.Y. Giants . . . C
Earl (Dutch) Clark, Detroit . . . QB
Cliff Battles, Boston Redskins . . . HB
Alphonse (Tuffy) Leemans, N.Y. Giants . . . HB
Clarke Hinkle, Green Bay . . . FB

1937
Bill Hewitt, Philadelphia . . . E
Gaynell Tinsley, Chicago Cardinals . . . E
Joe Stydahar, Chicago Bears . . . T
Glen (Turk) Edwards, Washington . . . T
Lon Evans, Green Bay . . . G
George Musso, Chicago Bears . . . G
Mel Hein, N.Y. Giants . . . C
Earl (Dutch) Clark, Detroit . . . QB
Cliff Battles, Washington . . . HB
Sammy Baugh, Washington . . . HB
Clarke Hinkle, Green Bay . . . FB

1938
Don Hutson, Green Bay . . . E
Gaynell Tinsley, Chicago Cardinals . . . E
Ed Widseth, N.Y. Giants . . . T
Joe Stydahar, Chicago Bears . . . T
Danny Fortmann, Chicago Bears . . . G
Russ Letlow, Green Bay . . . G
Mel Hein, N.Y. Giants . . . C
Clarence (Ace) Parker, Brooklyn . . . QB
Ed Danowski, N.Y. Giants . . . HB
Lloyd Cardwell, Detroit . . . HB
Clarke Hinkle, Green Bay . . . FB

1939
Don Hutson, Green Bay . . . E
Jim Poole, N.Y. Giants . . . E
Joe Stydahar, Chicago Bears . . . T
Jim Barber, Washington . . . T
Danny Fortmann, Chicago Bears . . . G
John Dell Isola, N.Y. Giants . . . G
Mel Hein, N.Y. Giants . . . C
Davey O'Brien, Philadelphia . . . QB
Alphonse (Tuffy) Leemans, N.Y. Giants . . . HB
Andy Farkas, Washington . . . HB
Bill Osmanski, Chicago Bears . . . FB

1940
Don Hutson, Green Bay . . . E
Perry Schwartz, Brooklyn . . . E
Joe Stydahar, Chicago Bears . . . T
Frank (Bruiser) Kinard, Brooklyn . . . T
Danny Fortmann, Chicago Bears . . . G
John Wiethe, Detroit . . . G
Mel Hein, N.Y. Giants . . . C
Clarence (Ace) Parker, Brooklyn . . . QB
Sammy Baugh, Washington . . . HB
Byron (Whizzer) White, Detroit . . . HB
Johnny Drake, Cleveland Rams . . . FB

1941
Don Hutson, Green Bay . . . E
Perry Schwartz, Brooklyn . . . E
Frank (Bruiser) Kinard, Brooklyn . . . T
Willie Wilkin, Washington . . . T
Danny Fortmann, Chicago Bears . . . G
Joe Kuharich, Chicago Cardinals . . . G
Clyde (Bulldog) Turner, Chicago Bears . . . C
Sid Luckman, Chicago Bears . . . QB
Cecil Isbell, Green Bay . . . HB
George McAfee, Chicago Bears . . . HB
Clarke Hinkle, Green Bay . . . FB

1942
Don Hutson, Green Bay . . . E
Bob Masterson, Washington . . . E
Willie Wilkin, Washington . . . T
Lee Artoe, Chicago Bears . . . T
Danny Fortmann, Chicago Bears . . . G
Bill Edwards, N.Y. Giants . . . G
Clyde (Bulldog) Turner, Chicago Bears . . . C
Sid Luckman, Chicago Bears . . . QB
Cecil Isbell, Green Bay . . . HB
Bill Dudley, Pittsburgh . . . HB
Gary Famiglietti, Chicago Bears . . . FB

1943
Don Hutson, Green Bay (AP, UP) . . . E
Ed Rucinzki, Chicago Cardinals (AP, UP) . . . E
Albert Blozis, N.Y. Giants (AP, UP) . . . T
Frank (Bruiser) Kinard, Brooklyn (AP) . . . T
Vic Sears, Philadelphia-Pittsburgh (UP) . . . T
Danny Fortmann, Chicago Bears (AP, UP) . . . G
Richard Farman, Washington (AP, UP) . . . G
Clyde (Bulldog) Turner, Chicago Bears (AP, UP) . . . C
Sid Luckman, Chicago Bears (AP, UP) . . . QB
Sammy Baugh, Washington (AP, UP) . . . HB
Harry Clark, Chicago Bears (AP, UP) . . . HB
Tony Canadeo, Green Bay (AP) . . . FB
Ward Cuff, N.Y. Giants (UP) . . . FB

1944
Don Hutson, Green Bay (AP, UP) . . . E
Joe Aguirre, Washington (AP, UP) . . . E
Al Wistert, Philadelphia (AP, UP) . . . T
Frank (Bruiser) Kinard, Brooklyn (AP) . . . T
Frank Cope, N.Y. Giants (UP) . . . T
Len Younce, N.Y. Giants (AP, UP) . . . G
Riley Matheson, Cleveland Rams (AP, UP) . . . G
Clyde (Bulldog) Turner, Chicago Bears (AP, UP) . . . C
Sid Luckman, Chicago Bears (AP) . . . QB
Leroy Zimmerman, Philadelphia (UP) . . . QB
Frank Sinkwich, Detroit (AP, UP) . . . HB
Steve Van Buren, Philadelphia (AP) . . . HB
Ward Cuff, N.Y. Giants (UP) . . . HB
Bill Paschal, N.Y. Giants (AP, UP) . . . FB

1945
Don Hutson, Green Bay (AP, UP) . . . E
Jim Benton, Cleveland Rams (AP) . . . E
Steve Pritko, Cleveland Rams (UP) . . . E
Al Wistert, Philadelphia (AP, UP) . . . T
Frank Cope, N.Y. Giants (AP) . . . T
Emil Uremovich, Detroit (UP) . . . T
Riley Matheson, Cleveland Rams (AP, UP) . . . G
Bill Radovich, Detroit (AP, UP) . . . G
Charley Brock, Green Bay (AP, UP) . . . C
Bob Waterfield, Cleveland Rams (AP) . . . QB
Sammy Baugh, Washington (UP) . . . QB
Steve Van Buren, Philadelphia (AP, UP) . . . HB
Steve Bagarus, Washington (AP) . . . HB
Bob Waterfield, Cleveland Rams (UP) . . . HB
Bob Westfall, Detroit (AP) . . . FB
Ted Fritsch, Green Bay (UP) . . . FB

1946
Jim Benton, Los Angeles (AP, UP) . . . E
Jim Poole, N.Y. Giants (AP) . . . E
Ken Kavanaugh, Chicago Bears (UP) . . . E
Al Wistert, Philadelphia (AP, UP) . . . T
Jim White, N.Y. Giants (AP, UP) . . . T
Riley Matheson, Los Angeles (AP, UP) . . . G
Len Younce, N.Y. Giants (AP) . . . G
Augie Lio, Philadelphia (UP) . . . G
Clyde (Bulldog) Turner, Chicago Bears (AP, UP) . . . C
Bob Waterfield, Los Angeles (AP, UP) . . . QB
Bill Dudley, Pittsburgh (AP, UP) . . . HB
Sid Luckman, Chicago Bears (AP) . . . HB
Frank Filchock, N.Y. Giants (UP) . . . HB
Ted Fritsch, Green Bay (AP, UP) . . . FB

1947
Ken Kavanaugh, Chicago Bears (AP, UP) . . . E
Mal Kutner, Chicago Cardinals (AP, UP) . . . E
Al Wistert, Philadelphia (AP, UP) . . . T
Dick Huffman, Los Angeles (AP) . . . T
Fred Davis, Chicago Bears (UP) . . . T
Riley Matheson, Los Angeles (AP) . . . G
Garrard (Buster) Ramsey, Chicago Cardinals (AP) . . . G
Len Younce, N.Y. Giants (UP) . . . G
Bill Moore, Pittsburgh (UP) . . . G
Clyde (Bulldog) Turner, Chicago Bears (AP) . . . C
Vince Banonis, Chicago Cardinals (UP) . . . C

Arnie Weinmeister

Mac Speedie

Dale Dodrill

Don Paul

Billy Wilson

Gene Brito

Billy Howton

Sid Luckman, Chicago Bears (AP, UP) QB
Steve Van Buren, Philadelphia (AP, UP) HB
Sammy Baugh, Washington (AP, UP) HB
John Clement, Pittsburgh (AP) FB
Pat Harder, Chicago Cardinals (UP) FB

1948

Pete Pihos, Philadelphia (AP, UP) E
Mal Kutner, Chicago Cardinals (AP, UP) E
Dick Huffman, Los Angeles (AP, UP) T
Fred Davis, Chicago Bears (AP) T
Al Wistert, Philadelphia (UP) T
Garrard (Buster) Ramsey, Chicago Cardinals (AP, UP) G
Charley Drulis, Chicago Bears (AP) G
Ray Bray, Chicago Bears (UP) G
Clyde (Bulldog) Turner, Chicago Bears (AP) C
Fred Naumetz, Los Angeles (UP) C
Sammy Baugh, Washington (AP, UP) QB
Steve Van Buren, Philadelphia (AP, UP) HB
Charley Trippi, Chicago Cardinals (AP, UP) HB
Tommy Thompson, Philadelphia (AP) FB
Pat Harder, Chicago Cardinals (UP) FB

1949

Pete Pihos, Philadelphia (AP, UP) E
Tom Fears, Los Angeles (AP, UP) E
Dick Huffman, Los Angeles (AP, UP) T
George Connor, Chicago Bears (AP) T
Vic Sears, Philadelphia (UP) T
Ray Bray, Chicago Bears (AP, UP) G
Garrard (Buster) Ramsey, Chicago Cardinals (AP, UP) G
Fred Naumetz, Los Angeles (AP, UP) C
Bob Waterfield, Los Angeles (AP, UP) QB
Steve Van Buren, Philadelphia (AP, UP) HB
Tony Canadeo, Green Bay (AP, UP) HB
Elmer Angsman, Chicago Cardinals (AP) FB
Pat Harder, Chicago Cardinals (UP) FB

1950

Tom Fears, Los Angeles (AP, UP) E
Dan Edwards, N.Y. Yanks (AP) E
Mac Speedie, Cleveland (UP) E
George Connor, Chicago Bears (AP, UP) T
Arnie Weinmeister, N.Y. Giants (AP, UP) T
Dick Barwegan, Chicago Bears (AP, UP) G
Joe Signaigo, N.Y. Yanks (AP) G
Bill Willis, Cleveland (UP) G
Chuck Bednarik, Philadelphia (AP) C
Clayton Tonnemaker, Green Bay (UP) C
Johnny Lujack, Chicago Bears (AP, UP) QB
Doak Walker, Detroit (AP, UP) HB
Joe Geri, Pittsburgh (AP, UP) HB
Marion Motley, Cleveland (AP, UP) FB

1951

Offense

Elroy (Crazylegs) Hirsch, Los Angeles (AP, UP) E
Leon Hart, Detroit (AP) E
Dante Lavelli, Cleveland (UP) E
George Connor, Chicago Bears (AP) T
Lou Groza, Cleveland (UP) T
Leo Nomellini, San Francisco (AP) T
DeWitt (Tex) Coulter, N.Y. Giants (UP) T
Lou Creekmur, Detroit (AP, UP) G
Dick Barwegan, Chicago Bears (AP, UP) G
Vic Lindskog, Philadelphia (AP) C
Frank Gatski, Cleveland (UP) C
Otto Graham, Cleveland (AP, UP) QB
Doak Walker, Detroit (AP, UP) HB
Dub Jones, Cleveland (AP, UP) HB
Eddie Price, N.Y. Giants (AP) FB
(Deacon) Dan Towler, Los Angeles (UP) FB

Defense

Len Ford, Cleveland (AP, UP) DE
Larry Brink, Los Angeles (AP) DE
Leon Hart, Detroit (UP) DE
Arnie Weinmeister, N.Y. Giants (AP, UP) DT
Al DeRogatis, N.Y. Giants (AP) DT
George Connor, Chicago Bears (UP) DT
Bill Willis, Cleveland (AP, UP) MG
Les Bingaman, Detroit (AP) MG
Jon Baker, N.Y. Giants (UP) MG
Chuck Bednarik, Philadelphia (AP, UP) LB
Paul (Tank) Younger, Los Angeles (AP) LB
Tony Adamle, Cleveland (UP) LB
Otto Schnellbacher, N.Y. Giants (AP, UP) DB
Jerry Shipkey, Pittsburgh (AP) DB
Warren Lahr, Cleveland (UP) DB
Emlen Tunnell, N.Y. Giants (AP, UP) DB

1952

Offense

Gordy Soltau, San Francisco (AP, UP) E
Cloyce Box, Detroit (AP) E
Mac Speedie, Cleveland (UP) E
Leo Nomellini, San Francisco (AP, UP) T
George Connor, Chicago Bears (AP) T
Lou Groza, Cleveland (UP) T
Lou Creekmur, Detroit (AP, UP) G
Lou Groza, Cleveland (AP) G
Bill Fischer, Chicago Cardinals (UP) G
Frank Gatski, Cleveland (AP) C
Bill Walsh, Pittsburgh (UP) C
Bobby Layne, Detroit (AP) QB
Otto Graham, Cleveland (UP) QB
Hugh McElhenny, San Francisco (AP, UP) HB
(Deacon) Dan Towler, Los Angeles (AP, UP) HB
Eddie Price, N.Y. Giants (AP, UP) FB

Defense

Len Ford, Cleveland (AP, UP) DE
Larry Brink, Los Angeles (UP) DE
Pete Pihos, Philadephia (AP) DE
Arnie Weinmeister, N.Y. Giants (AP, UP) DT
Thurman McGraw, Detroit (AP, UP) DT
Stan West, Los Angeles (AP, UP) MG
Bill Willis, Cleveland (AP) MG
Les Bingaman, Detroit (UP) MG
Chuck Bednarik, Philadelphia (AP, UP) LB
Jerry Shipkey, Pittsburgh (AP) LB
George Connor, Chicago Bears (UP) LB
Jack Christiansen, Detroit (AP) DB
Ollie Matson, Chicago Cardinals (AP) DB
Bob Smith, Detroit (UP) DB
Herb Rich, Los Angeles (UP) DB
Emlen Tunnell, N.Y. Giants (AP, UP) DB

1953

Offense

Pete Pihos, Philadelphia (AP, UP) E
Dante Lavelli, Cleveland (UP) E
Elroy (Crazylegs) Hirsch, Los Angeles (AP) E
George Connor, Chicago Bears (AP) T
Lou Groza, Cleveland (AP, UP) T
Lou Creekmur, Detroit (UP) T
Dick Stanfel, Detroit (AP, UP) G
Lou Creekmur, Detroit (AP) G
Bruno Banducci, San Francisco (UP) G
Frank Gatski, Cleveland (AP, UP) C
Otto Graham, Cleveland (AP, UP) QB
Hugh McElhenny, San Francisco (AP, UP) HB
Doak Walker, Detroit (AP) HB
(Deacon) Dan Towler, Los Angeles (UP) HB
Joe Perry, San Francisco (AP, UP) FB

Defense

Len Ford, Cleveland (AP, UP) DE
Andy Robustelli, Los Angeles (AP) DE
Norm Willey, Philadelphia (UP) DE
Arnie Weinmeister, N.Y. Giants (AP, UP) DT
Leo Nomellini, San Francisco (AP, UP) DT
Les Bingaman, Detroit (AP, UP) MG
Bill Willis, Cleveland (AP) MG
Dale Dodrill, Pittsburgh (UP) MG
Chuck Bednarik, Philadelphia (AP) LB
Don Paul, Los Angeles (AP) LB
Tommy Thompson, Cleveland (UP) LB
George Connor, Chicago Bears (UP) LB
Tom Keane, Baltimore (AP, UP) DB
Tommy Thompson, Cleveland (AP) DB
Jack Christiansen, Detroit (AP, UP) DB
Ken Gorgal, Cleveland (UP) DB

1954

Offense

Pete Pihos, Philadelphia (AP, UP) E
Bob Boyd, Los Angeles (AP) E
Harlon Hill, Chicago Bears (UP) E
Lou Creekmur, Detroit (AP, UP) T
Lou Groza, Cleveland (AP, UP) T
Dick Stanfel, Detroit (AP, UP) G
Bruno Banducci, San Francisco (AP, UP) G
Bill Walsh, Pittsburgh (AP, UP) C
Otto Graham, Cleveland (AP, UP) QB
Doak Walker, Detroit (AP, UP) HB
Ollie Matson, Chicago Cardinals (AP, UP) HB
Joe Perry, San Francisco (AP, UP) FB

Defense

Len Ford, Cleveland (AP, UP) DE
Norm Willey, Philadelphia (AP, UP) DE
Leo Nomellini, San Francisco (AP, UP) DT
Art Donovan, Baltimore (AP, UP) DT
Les Bingaman, Detroit (AP, UP) MG
Dale Dodrill, Pittsburgh (AP) MG
Frank (Bucko) Kilroy, Philadelphia (UP) MG
Chuck Bednarik, Philadelphia (AP, UP) LB
Joe Schmidt, Detroit (AP) LB
Roger Zatkoff, Green Bay (UP) LB
Tom Landry, N.Y. Giants (AP, UP) DB
Bobby Dillon, Green Bay (AP) DB
Jim David, Detroit (UP) DB
Jack Christiansen, Detroit (AP, UP) DB

1955

Offense

Harlon Hill, Chicago Bears (AP, UP) E
Billy Wilson, San Francisco (UP) E
Pete Pihos, Philadelphia (AP) E
Lou Groza, Cleveland (AP, UP) T
Bill Wightkin, Chicago Bears (AP) T
Bob St. Clair, San Francisco (UP) T
Stan Jones, Chicago Bears (AP) G
Duane Putnam, Los Angeles (AP) G
Abe Gibron, Cleveland (UP) G
Bill Austin, N.Y. Giants (UP) G
Frank Gatski, Cleveland (AP, UP) C
Otto Graham, Cleveland (AP, UP) QB
Ollie Matson, Chicago Cardinals (AP, UP) HB
Frank Gifford, N.Y. Giants (AP) HB
Ron Waller, Los Angeles (UP) HB
Alan Ameche, Baltimore (AP, UP) FB

Defense

Gene Brito, Washington (AP, UP) DE
Andy Robustelli, Los Angeles (AP) DE
Len Ford, Cleveland (UP) DE
Art Donovan, Baltimore (AP, UP) DT
Bob Toneff, San Francisco (AP) DT
Don Colo, Cleveland (UP) DT
Bill George, Chicago Bears (AP) MG
Dale Dodrill, Pittsburgh (UP) MG
Chuck Bednarik, Philadelphia (UP) LB
George Connor, Chicago Bears (UP) LB
Roger Zatkoff, Green Bay (AP) LB
Joe Schmidt, Detroit (AP) LB
Bobby Dillon, Green Bay (AP, UP) DB
Will Sherman, Los Angeles (AP, UP) DB
Jack Christiansen, Detroit (AP, UP) DB
Emlen Tunnell, N.Y. Giants (AP) DB
Don Paul, Cleveland (UP) DB

1956

Offense

Harlon Hill, Chicago Bears (AP, UP) E
Billy Howton, Green Bay (AP, UP) E
Lou Creekmur, Detroit (AP, UP) T
Roosevelt Brown, N.Y. Giants (AP, UP) T
Stan Jones, Chicago Bears (AP, UP) G
Dick Stanfel, Washington (AP, UP) G
Larry Strickland, Chicago Bears (AP) C
Charlie Ane, Detroit (UP) C
Bobby Layne, Detroit (AP, UP) QB
Frank Gifford, N.Y. Giants (AP, UP) HB
Ollie Matson, Chicago Cardinals (AP, UP) HB
Rick Casares, Chicago Bears (AP, UP) FB

Defense

Andy Robustelli, N.Y. Giants (AP, UP) DE
Gene Brito, Washington (AP, UP) DE
Rosey Grier, N.Y. Giants (AP, UP) DT
Art Donovan, Baltimore (AP) DT
Ernie Stautner, Pittsburgh (UP) DT
Bill George, Chicago Bears (AP, UP) MG
Joe Schmidt, Detroit (AP, UP) LB
Les Richter, Los Angeles (AP) LB
Chuck Bednarik, Philadelphia (UP) LB
Dick (Night Train) Lane, Chicago Cardinals (AP, UP) DB
Emlen Tunnell, N.Y. Giants (AP, UP) DB
Jack Christiansen, Detroit (AP, UP) DB

Del Shofner

Jim Ringo

Jim Otto

Abner Haynes

Ron Mix

Cookie Gilchrist

Larry Wilson

Yale Lary, Detroit (AP) ... DB
Bobby Dillon, Green Bay (UP) ... DB

1957

Offense

Billy Wilson, San Francisco (AP, UP) ... E
Billy Howton, Green Bay (AP, UP) ... E
Roosevelt Brown, N.Y. Giants (AP, UP) ... T
Lou Creekmur, Detroit (AP) ... T
Lou Groza, Cleveland (UP) ... T
Duane Putnam, Los Angeles (AP, UP) ... G
Dick Stanfel, Washington (AP, UP) ... G
Jim Ringo, Green Bay (AP) ... C
Larry Strickland, Chicago Bears (UP) ... C
Y. A. Tittle, San Francisco (AP, UP) ... QB
Frank Gifford, N.Y. Giants (AP, UP) ... HB
Ollie Matson, Chicago Cardinals (AP, UP) ... HB
Jim Brown, Cleveland (AP, UP) ... FB

Defense

Gino Marchetti, Baltimore (AP, UP) ... DE
Andy Robustelli, N.Y. Giants (UP) ... DE
Gene Brito, Washington (AP) ... DE
Leo Nomellini, San Francisco (AP, UP) ... DT
Art Donovan, Baltimore (AP, UP) ... DT
Joe Schmidt, Detroit (AP, UP) ... LB
Marv Matuszak, San Francisco (AP, UP) ... LB
Bill George, Chicago Bears (AP, UP) ... LB
Jack Christiansen, Detroit (AP, UP) ... DB
Bobby Dillon, Green Bay (AP, UP) ... DB
Jack Butler, Pittsburgh (AP, UP) ... DB
Yale Lary, Detroit (UP) ... DB
Milt Davis, Baltimore (AP) ... DB

1958

Offense

Raymond Berry, Baltimore (AP, UPI) ... E
Del Shofner, Los Angeles (AP, UPI) ... E
Roosevelt Brown, N.Y. Giants (AP, UPI) ... T
Jim Parker, Baltimore (AP, UPI) ... T
Dick Stanfel, Washington (AP, UPI) ... G
Duane Putnam, Los Angeles (AP, UPI) ... G
Ray Wietecha, N.Y. Giants (AP, UPI) ... C
Johnny Unitas, Baltimore (AP, UPI) ... QB
Lenny Moore, Baltimore (AP, UPI) ... HB
Jon Arnett, Los Angeles (AP, UPI) ... HB
Jim Brown, Cleveland (AP, UPI) ... FB

Defense

Gino Marchetti, Baltimore (AP, UPI) ... DE
Andy Robustelli, N.Y. Giants (AP) ... DE
Gene Brito, Washington (UPI) ... DE
Gene (Big Daddy) Lipscomb, Baltimore (AP, UPI) ... DT
Ernie Stautner, Pittsburgh (AP, UPI) ... DT
Joe Schmidt, Detroit (AP, UPI) ... LB
Sam Huff, N.Y. Giants (AP, UPI) ... LB
Bill George, Chicago Bears (AP, UPI) ... LB
Jack Butler, Pittsburgh (AP, UPI) ... DB
Yale Lary, Detroit (AP, UPI) ... DB
Jim Patton, N.Y. Giants (AP, UPI) ... DB
Bobby Dillon, Green Bay (AP, UPI) ... DB

1959

Offense

Raymond Berry, Baltimore (AP, UPI) ... E
Del Shofner, Los Angeles (AP, UPI) ... E
Roosevelt Brown, N.Y. Giants (AP, UPI) ... T
Jim Parker, Baltimore (AP, UPI) ... T
Jim Ray Smith, Cleveland (AP, UPI) ... G
Stan Jones, Chicago Bears (AP) ... G
Art Spinney, Baltimore (UP) ... G
Jim Ringo, Green Bay (AP, UPI) ... C
Johnny Unitas, Baltimore (AP, UPI) ... QB
Frank Gifford, N.Y. Giants (AP, UPI) ... HB
Lenny Moore, Baltimore (AP) ... HB
J. D. Smith, San Francisco (UPI) ... HB
Jim Brown, Cleveland (AP, UPI) ... FB

Defense

Gino Marchetti, Baltimore (AP, UPI) ... DE
Andy Robustelli, N.Y. Giants (AP, UPI) ... DE
Gene (Big Daddy) Lipscomb, Baltimore (AP, UPI) ... DT
Leo Nomellini, San Francisco (AP, UPI) ... DT
Joe Schmidt, Detroit (AP, UPI) ... LB
Sam Huff, N.Y. Giants (AP, UPI) ... LB
Bill George, Chicago Bears (AP, UPI) ... LB
Abe Woodson, San Francisco (AP, UPI) ... DB
Jack Butler, Pittsburgh (AP, UPI) ... DB
Jim Patton, N.Y. Giants (AP, UPI) ... DB
Dean Derby, Pittsburgh (UPI) ... DB
Andy Nelson, Baltimore (AP) ... DB

1960 NFL

Offense

Raymond Berry, Baltimore (AP, UPI) ... E
Sonny Randle, St. Louis (AP, UPI) ... E
Jim Parker, Baltimore (AP, UPI) ... T
Forrest Gregg, Green Bay (AP) ... T
Roosevelt Brown, N.Y. Giants (UPI) ... T
Jim Ray Smith, Cleveland (AP, UPI) ... G
Stan Jones, Chicago (UPI) ... G
Jerry Kramer, Green Bay (AP) ... G
Jim Ringo, Green Bay (AP, UPI) ... C
Norm Van Brocklin, Philadelphia (AP, UPI) ... QB
Paul Hornung, Green Bay (AP, UPI) ... HB
Lenny Moore, Baltimore (AP, UPI) ... HB
Jim Brown, Cleveland (AP, UPI) ... FB

Defense

Gino Marchetti, Baltimore (AP, UPI) ... DE
Andy Robustelli, N.Y. Giants (AP) ... DE
Doug Atkins, Chicago (UPI) ... DE
Henry Jordan, Green Bay (AP, UPI) ... DT
Alex Karras, Detroit (AP, UPI) ... DT
Chuck Bednarik, Philadelphia (AP, UPI) ... LB
Bill Forester, Green Bay (AP, UPI) ... LB
Bill George, Chicago (AP, UPI) ... LB
Tom Brookshier, Philadelphia (AP, UPI) ... DB
Abe Woodson, San Francisco (AP) ... DB
Dick (Night Train) Lane, Detroit (UPI) ... DB
Jerry Norton, St. Louis (AP, UPI) ... DB
Jim Patton, N.Y. Giants (AP, UPI) ... DB

1960 AFL

Offense

Bill Groman, Houston ... E
Lionel Taylor, Denver ... E
Rich Michael, Houston ... T
Ron Mix, Los Angeles Chargers ... T
Bill Krisher, Dallas Texans ... G
Bob Mischak, N.Y. Titans ... G
Jim Otto, Oakland ... C
Jack Kemp, Los Angeles Chargers ... QB
Abner Haynes, Dallas Texans ... HB
Paul Lowe, Los Angeles Chargers ... HB
Dave Smith, Houston ... FB

Defense

LaVerne Torczon, Buffalo ... DE
Mel Branch, Dallas Texans ... DE
Bud McFadin, Denver ... DT
Volney Peters, Los Angeles Chargers ... DT
Archie Matsos, Buffalo ... LB
Sherrill Headrick, Dallas Texans ... LB
Tom Addison, Boston Patriots ... LB
Richie McCabe, Buffalo ... DB
Dick Harris, Los Angeles Chargers ... DB
Ross O'Hanley, Boston Patriots ... DB
Austin (Goose) Gonsoulin, Denver ... DB

1961 NFL

Offense

Del Shofner, N.Y. Giants (AP, UPI, NEA) ... E
Jim (Red) Phillips, Los Angeles (AP, UPI) ... E
Mike Ditka, Chicago (NEA) ... E
Roosevelt Brown, N.Y. Giants (AP, UPI, NEA) ... T
Jim Parker, Baltimore (AP, NEA) ... T
Forrest Gregg, Green Bay (UPI) ... T
Jim Ray Smith, Cleveland (AP, UPI, NEA) ... G
Fred (Fuzzy) Thurston, Green Bay (AP, UPI, NEA) ... G
Jim Ringo, Green Bay (AP, UPI, NEA) ... C
Sonny Jurgensen, Philadelphia (AP, UPI) ... QB
Y. A. Tittle, N.Y. Giants (NEA) ... QB
Lenny Moore, Baltimore (AP, UPI, NEA) ... HB
Paul Hornung, Green Bay (AP, UPI) ... HB
Jim Taylor, Green Bay (NEA) ... HB
Jim Brown, Cleveland (AP, UPI, NEA) ... FB

Defense

Gino Marchetti, Baltimore (AP, UPI, NEA) ... DE
Jim Katcavage, N.Y. Giants (AP, UPI) ... DE
Doug Atkins, Chicago (NEA) ... DE
Henry Jordan, Green Bay (AP, UPI, NEA) ... DT
Alex Karras, Detroit (AP, UPI) ... DT
Gene (Big Daddy) Lipscomb, Pittsburgh (NEA) ... DT
Joe Schmidt, Detroit (AP, UPI, NEA) ... LB
Dan Currie, Green Bay (UPI, NEA) ... LB
Bill George, Chicago (AP, NEA) ... LB
Bill Forester, Green Bay (AP, UPI) ... LB
Dick (Night Train) Lane, Detroit (AP, NEA) ... DB
Jesse Whittenton, Green Bay (AP, UPI) ... DB
Erich Barnes, N.Y. Giants (AP, UPI) ... DB
Jimmy Hill, St. Louis (NEA) ... DB
Jim Patton, N.Y. Giants (AP, UPI, NEA) ... DB
Johnny Sample, Pittsburgh (UPI) ... DB
Jerry Norton, St. Louis (NEA) ... DB

1961 AFL

Offense

Lionel Taylor, Denver ... E
Charley Hennigan, Houston ... E
Ron Mix, San Diego ... T
Al Jamison, Houston ... T
Bob Mischak, N.Y. Titans ... G
Chuck Leo, Boston Patriots ... G
Jim Otto, Oakland ... C
George Blanda, Houston ... QB
Abner Haynes, Dallas Texans ... HB
Billy Cannon, Houston ... HB
Billy Mathis, N.Y. Titans ... FB

Defense

Earl Faison, San Diego ... DE
Don Floyd, Houston ... DE
Bud McFadin, Denver ... DT
Chuck McMurtry, Buffalo ... DT
Sherril Headrick, Dallas Texans ... LB
Archie Matsos, Buffalo ... LB
Chuck Allen, San Diego ... LB
Tony Banfield, Houston ... DB
Dick Harris, San Diego ... DB
Dave Webster, Dallas Texans ... DB
Charlie McNeil, San Diego ... DB

1962 NFL

Offense

Del Shofner, N.Y. Giants (AP, UPI, NEA) ... SE
Mike Ditka, Chicago (UPI, NEA) ... TE
Ron Kramer, Green Bay (AP) ... TE
Bobby Mitchell, Washington (AP, UPI, NEA) ... FL
Forrest Gregg, Green Bay (AP, UPI, NEA) ... T
Roosevelt Brown, N.Y. Giants (AP, UPI) ... T
Jim Parker, Baltimore (NEA) ... T
Jerry Kramer, Green Bay (AP, UPI, NEA) ... G
Jim Parker, Baltimore (AP) ... G
Jim Ray Smith, Cleveland (NEA) ... G
Fred (Fuzzy) Thurston, Green Bay (UPI) ... G
Jim Ringo, Green Bay (AP, UPI, NEA) ... C
Y. A. Tittle, N.Y. Giants (AP, UPI, NEA) ... QB
Jim Taylor, Green Bay (AP, UPI, NEA) ... RB
Don Perkins, Dallas Cowboys (AP, NEA) ... RB
Dick Bass, Los Angeles (UPI) ... RB

Defense

Gino Marchetti, Baltimore (AP, UPI, NEA) ... DE
Jim Katcavage, N.Y. Giants (UPI, NEA) ... DE
Willie Davis, Green Bay (AP) ... DE
Roger Brown, Detroit (AP, UPI, NEA) ... DT
Alex Karras, Detroit (UPI, NEA) ... DT
Henry Jordan, Green Bay (AP) ... DT
Joe Schmidt, Detroit (AP, UPI, NEA) ... MLB
Dan Currie, Green Bay (AP, UPI, NEA) ... LB
Bill Forester, Green Bay (AP, UPI, NEA) ... LB
Dick (Night Train) Lane, Detroit (AP, UPI, NEA) ... CB
Herb Adderly, Green Bay (AP, UPI) ... CB
Abe Woodson, San Francisco (NEA) ... CB
Yale Lary, Detroit (AP, UPI, NEA) ... S
Jim Patton, N.Y. Giants (AP, UPI, NEA) ... S

1962 AFL

Offense

Charley Hennigan, Houston ... SE
Dave Kocourek, San Diego ... TE
Chris Burford, Dallas Texans ... FL
Eldon Danenhauer, Denver ... T
Jim Tyrer, Dallas Texans ... T
Bob Talamini, Houston ... G
Ron Mix, San Diego ... G
Jim Otto, Oakland ... C
Len Dawson, Dallas Texans ... QB
Abner Haynes, Dallas Texans ... RB
Cookie Gilchrist, Buffalo ... RB

Clem Daniels

Merlin Olsen

Larry Grantham

Bobby Bell

Cornell Green

Dick Butkus

Tommy Nobis

Defense
Don Floyd, Houston . . . DE
Mel Branch, Dallas Texans . . . DE
Bud McFadin, Denver . . . DT
Jerry Mays, Dallas Texans . . . DT
Sherrill Headrick, Dallas Texans . . . MLB
Larry Grantham, N.Y. Titans . . . LB
E.J. Holub, Dallas Texans . . . LB
Tony Banfield, Houston . . . CB
Fred Williamson, Oakland . . . CB
Austin (Goose) Gonsoulin, Denver . . . S
Bob Zeman, Denver . . . S

1963 NFL
Offense
Del Shofner, N.Y. Giants (AP, UPI, NEA) . . . SE
Mike Ditka, Chicago (AP, UPI, NEA) . . . TE
Bobby Joe Conrad, St. Louis (AP, UPI) . . . FL
Bobby Mitchell, Washington (NEA) . . . FL
Forrest Gregg, Green Bay (AP, UPI, NEA) . . . T
Roosevelt Brown, N.Y. Giants (UPI, NEA) . . . T
Dick Schafrath, Cleveland (AP) . . . T
Jerry Kramer, Green Bay (AP, UPI, NEA) . . . G
Jim Parker, Baltimore (AP, NEA) . . . G
Ken Gray, St. Louis (UPI) . . . G
Jim Ringo, Green Bay (AP, UPI, NEA) . . . C
Y.A. Tittle, N.Y. Giants (AP, UPI, NEA) . . . QB
Tommy Mason, Minnesota (AP, UPI, NEA) . . . RB
Jim Brown, Cleveland (AP, UPI, NEA) . . . RB
Defense
Doug Atkins, Chicago (AP, UPI, NEA) . . . DE
Jim Katcavage, N.Y. Giants (AP, UPI) . . . DE
Gino Marchetti, Baltimore (NEA) . . . DE
Henry Jordan, Green Bay (AP, UPI, NEA) . . . DT
Roger Brown, Detroit (AP, UPI, NEA) . . . DT
Bill George, Chicago (AP, UPI) . . . MLB
Joe Schmidt, Detroit (NEA) . . . MLB
Joe Fortunato, Chicago (AP, UPI, NEA) . . . LB
Jack Pardee, Los Angeles (AP) . . . LB
Myron Pottios, Pittsburgh (NEA) . . . LB
Bill Forester, Green Bay (UPI) . . . LB
Dick Lynch, N.Y. Giants (AP, UPI, NEA) . . . CB
Herb Adderley, Green Bay (AP) . . . CB
Abe Woodson, San Francisco (NEA) . . . CB
Dick (Night Train) Lane, Detroit (UPI) . . . CB
Roosevelt Taylor, Chicago (AP, NEA) . . . S
Richie Petitbon, Chicago (AP, UPI) . . . S
Willie Wood, Green Bay (NEA) . . . S
Larry Wilson, St. Louis (UPI) . . . S

1963 AFL
Offense
Art Powell, Oakland . . . SE
Fred Arbanas, Kansas City . . . TE
Lance Alworth, San Diego . . . FL
Ron Mix, San Diego . . . T
Jim Tyrer, Kansas City . . . T
Billy Shaw, Buffalo . . . G
Bob Talamini, Houston . . . G
Jim Otto, Oakland . . . C
Tobin Rote, San Diego . . . QB
Clem Daniels, Oakland . . . RB
Keith Lincoln, San Diego . . . RB
Defense
Larry Eisenhauer, Boston Patriots . . . DE
Earl Faison, San Diego . . . DE
Tom Sestak, Buffalo . . . DT
Houston Antwine, Boston Patriots . . . DT
Archie Matsos, Oakland . . . MLB
E.J. Holub, Kansas City . . . LB
Tom Addison, Boston Patriots . . . LB
Dave Grayson, Kansas City . . . CB
Fred Williamson, Oakland . . . CB
Fred Glick, Houston . . . S
Austin (Goose) Gonsoulin, Denver . . . S

1964 NFL
Offense
Frank Clarke, Dallas (AP) . . . SE
Paul Warfield, Cleveland (NEA) . . . SE
Bobby Mitchell, Washington (UPI) . . . SE
Mike Ditka, Chicago (AP, UPI, NEA) . . . TE
Johnny Morris, Chicago (AP, UPI, NEA) . . . FL
Forrest Gregg, Green Bay (AP, UPI, NEA) . . . T
Dick Schfrath, Cleveland (AP, UPI) . . . T
Bob Vogel, Baltimore (NEA) . . . T
Jim Parker, Baltimore (AP, UPI, NEA) . . . G
Ken Gray, St. Louis (AP, UPI) . . . G
John Gordy, Detroit (NEA) . . . G
Mick Tingelhoff, Minnesota (AP, UPI) . . . C
Bob DeMarco, St. Louis (NEA) . . . C
Johnny Unitas, Baltimore (AP, UPI, NEA) . . . QB
Lenny Moore, Baltimore (AP, UPI, NEA) . . . RB
Jim Brown, Cleveland (AP, UPI, NEA) . . . RB
Defense
Willie Davis, Green Bay (AP, UPI, NEA) . . . DE
Gino Marchetti, Baltimore (AP, UPI, NEA) . . . DE
Bob Lilly, Dallas (AP, UPI, NEA) . . . DT
Henry Jordan, Green Bay (AP, UPI) . . . DT
Merlin Olsen, Los Angeles (NEA) . . . DT
Ray Nitschke, Green Bay (AP, UPI) . . . MLB
Dale Meinert, St. Louis (NEA) . . . MLB
Joe Fortunato, Chicago (AP, UPI, NEA) . . . LB
Maxie Baughan, Philadelphia (AP) . . . LB
Jim Houston, Cleveland (NEA) . . . LB
Wayne Walker, Detroit (UPI) . . . LB
Pat Fischer, St. Louis (AP, UPI, NEA) . . . CB
Bobby Boyd, Baltimore (AP, UPI) . . . CB
Erich Barnes, N.Y. Giants (NEA) . . . CB
Paul Krause, Washington (AP, UPI, NEA) . . . S
Willie Wood, Green Bay (AP, UPI, NEA) . . . S

1964 AFL
Offense
Charley Hennigan, Houston (AP, UPI) . . . SE
Art Powell, Oakland (PL) . . . SE
Fred Arbanas, Kansas City (AP, UPI, PL) . . . TE
Lance Alworth, San Diego (AP, UPI, PL) . . . FL
Ron Mix, San Diego (AP, UPI, PL) . . . T
Stew Barber, Buffalo (AP, UPI) . . . T
Jim Tyrer, Kansas City (PL) . . . T
Billy Shaw, Buffalo (AP,UPI, PL) . . . G
Billy Neighbors, Boston Patriots (AP, UPI) . . . G
Bob Talamini, Houston (PL) . . . G
Jim Otto, Oakland (AP, UPI, PL) . . . C
Babe Parilli, Boston Patriots (AP, UPI, PL) . . . QB
Keith Lincoln, San Diego (AP, UPI, PL) . . . RB
Cookie Gilchrist, Buffalo (AP, UPI, PL) . . . RB
Defense
Earl Faison, San Diego (AP, UPI, PL) . . . DE
Larry Eisenhauer, Boston Patriots (AP, PL) . . . DE
Bobby Bell, Kansas City (UPI) . . . DE
Tom Sestak, Buffalo (AP, UPI, PL) . . . DT
Ernie Ladd, San Diego (AP, UPI) . . . DT
Jerry Mays, Kansas City (PL) . . . DT
Nick Buoniconti, Boston Patriots (AP, UPI, PL) . . . MLB
Larry Grantham, N.Y. Jets (AP, UPI, PL) . . . LB
Mike Stratton, Buffalo (AP, UPI) . . . LB
Tom Addison, Boston Patriots (PL) . . . LB
Willie Brown, Denver (AP, UPI, PL) . . . CB
Dave Grayson, Kansas City (AP, PL) . . . CB
Fred Williamson, Kansas City (UPI) . . . CB
Ron Hall, Boston Patriots (AP, UPI) . . . S
Dainard Paulson, N.Y. Jets (UPI, PL) . . . S
Fred Glick, Houston (PL) . . . S
George Saimes, Buffalo (AP) . . . S

1965 NFL
Offense
Dave Parks, San Francisco (AP, UPI, NEA) . . . SE
Pete Retzlaff, Philadelphia (AP, UPI, NEA) . . . TE
Jimmy Orr, Baltimore (AP, NEA) . . . FL
Gary Collins, Cleveland (UPI) . . . FL
Bob Brown, Philadelphia (AP, NEA) . . . T
Dick Schafrath, Cleveland (AP, UPI) . . . T
Forrest Gregg, Green Bay (UPI) . . . T
Bob Vogel, Baltimore (NEA) . . . T
Jim Parker, Baltimore (AP, UPI, NEA) . . . G
John Gordy, Detroit (NEA) . . . G
Ken Gray, St. Louis (UPI) . . . G
Forrest Gregg, Green Bay (AP) . . . G
Mick Tingelhoff, Minnesota (AP, UPI, NEA) . . . C
Johnny Unitas, Baltimore (AP, UPI, NEA) . . . QB
Gale Sayers, Chicago (AP, UPI, NEA) . . . RB
Jim Brown, Cleveland (AP, UPI, NEA) . . . RB
Defense
Willie Davis, Green Bay (AP, UPI, NEA) . . . DE
David (Deacon) Jones, Los Angeles (AP, UPI, NEA) . . . DE
Alex Karras, Detroit (AP, UPI, NEA) . . . DT
Bob Lilly, Dallas (AP, UPI, NEA) . . . DT
Dick Butkus, Chicago (AP, NEA) . . . MLB
Ray Nitschke, Green Bay (UPI) . . . MLB
Wayne Walker, Detroit (AP, UPI, NEA) . . . LB
Joe Fortunato, Chicago (AP, NEA) . . . LB
Jim Houston, Cleveland (UPI) . . . LB
Bobby Boyd, Baltimore (AP, UPI, NEA) . . . CB
Herb Adderley, Green Bay (AP, UPI, NEA) . . . CB
Willie Wood, Green Bay (AP, UPI, NEA) . . . S
Paul Krause, Washington (AP, UPI) . . . S
Mel Renfro, Dallas (NEA) . . . S

1965 AFL
Offense
Lionel Taylor, Denver (AP, UPI, PL) . . . SE
Art Powell, Oakland (PL) . . . SE
Willie Frazier, Houston (AP, UPI, PL) . . . TE
Lance Alworth, San Diego (AP, UPI, PL) . . . FL
Jim Tyrer, Kansas City (AP, UPI, PL) . . . T
Ron Mix, San Diego (AP, UPI) . . . T
Eldon Danenhauer, Denver (PL) . . . T
Billy Shaw, Buffalo (AP, UPI, PL) . . . G
Bob Talamini, Houston (AP, UPI, PL) . . . G
Jim Otto, Oakland (AP, UPI, PL) . . . C
Jack Kemp, Buffalo (AP, UPI, PL) . . . QB
Paul Lowe, San Diego (AP, UPI, PL) . . . RB
Cookie Gilchrist, Denver (AP, UPI, PL) . . . RB
Pete Gogolak, Buffalo (PL) . . . K
Defense
Earl Faison, San Diego (AP, UPI, PL) . . . DE
Jerry Mays, Kansas City (AP, PL) . . . DE
Ron McDole, Buffalo (UPI) . . . DE
Tom Sestak, Buffalo (AP, UPI, PL) . . . DT
Ernie Ladd, San Diego (AP, UPI, PL) . . . DT
Nick Buoniconti, Boston Patriots (AP, UPI, PL) . . . MLB
Mike Stratton, Buffalo (PL) . . . LB
Bobby Bell, Kansas City (AP, UPI, PL) . . . LB
Dave Grayson, Oakland (AP, UPI, PL) . . . CB
George (Butch) Byrd, Buffalo (AP, PL) . . . CB
Fred Williamson, Kansas City (UPI) . . . CB
George Saimes, Buffalo (AP, UPI, PL) . . . S
Johnny Robinson, Kansas City (AP, PL) . . . S
Dainard Paulson, N.Y. Jets (UPI) . . . S
Curley Johnson, N.Y. Jets (PL) . . . P

1966 NFL
Offense
Bob Hayes, Dallas (AP, UPI, NEA) . . . SE-FL
Dave Parks, San Francisco (NEA) . . . SE
John Mackey, Baltimore (AP, UPI, NEA) . . . TE
Pat Studstill, Detroit (AP, UPI) . . . FL
Bob Brown, Philadelphia (AP, UPI, NEA) . . . T
Forrest Gregg, Green Bay (AP, UPI, NEA) . . . T
Jerry Kramer, Green Bay (AP, UPI) . . . G
John Thomas, San Francisco (AP, NEA) . . . G
John Gordy, Detroit (UPI) . . . G
Gene Hickerson, Cleveland (NEA) . . . G
Mick Tingelhoff, Minnesota (AP, UPI, NEA) . . . C
Bart Starr, Green Bay (AP, UPI, NEA) . . . QB
Leroy Kelly, Cleveland (AP, UPI, NEA) . . . RB
Gale Sayers, Chicago (AP, UPI, NEA) . . . RB
Defense
Willie Davis, Green Bay (AP, UPI, NEA) . . . DE
David (Deacon) Jones, Los Angeles (AP, UPI, NEA) . . . DE
Bob Lilly, Dallas (AP, UPI, NEA) . . . DT
Merlin Olsen, Los Angeles (AP, UPI, NEA) . . . DT
Ray Nitschke, Green Bay (AP, UPI, NEA) . . . MLB
Chuck Howley, Dallas (AP, UPI, NEA) . . . LB
Lee Roy Caffey, Green Bay (AP, UPI) . . . LB
Maxie Baughan, Los Angeles (NEA) . . . LB
Herb Adderley, Green Bay (AP, UPI, NEA) . . . CB
Cornell Green, Dallas (AP, NEA) . . . CB
Bobby Boyd, Baltimore (UPI) . . . CB
Larry Wilson, St. Louis (AP, UPI, NEA) . . . S
Willie Wood, Green Bay (AP, UPI, NEA) . . . S

1966 AFL
Offense
Otis Taylor, Kansas City (AP, UPI) . . . SE
Art Powell, Oakland (PL) . . . SE
Fred Arbanas, Kansas City (AP, UPI, PL) . . . TE
Lance Alworth, San Diego (AP, UPI, PL) . . . FL
Jim Tyrer, Kansas City (AP, UPI, PL) . . . T
Ron Mix, San Diego (AP, UPI) . . . T
Sherman Plunkett, N.Y. Jets (PL) . . . T

Dave Wilcox *Alan Page* *Larry Little* *Bob Griese* *Joe Greene* *Riley Odoms* *Curley Culp*

Billy Shaw, Buffalo (AP, UPI, PL)............G
Bob Talamini, Houston (PL)............G
Ed Budde, Kansas City (AP)............G
Wayne Hawkins, Oakland (UPI)............G
Jon Morris, Boston Patriots (AP)............C
Jim Otto, Oakland (UPI, PL)............C
Len Dawson, Kansas City (AP, UPI, PL)............QB
Clem Daniels, Oakland (AP, UPI, PL)............RB
Jim Nance, Boston Patriots (AP, UPI, PL)............RB
Gino Cappelletti, Boston Patriots (PL)............K

Defense

Jerry Mays, Kansas City (AP, UPI, PL)............DE
Larry Eisenhauer, Boston Patriots (PL)............DE
Ron McDole, Buffalo (AP)............DE
Verlon Biggs, N.Y. Jets (UPI)............DE
Buck Buchanan, Kansas City (AP, UPI, PL)............DT
Jim Dunaway, Buffalo (AP)............DT
Houston Antwine, Boston Patriots (UPI, PL)............DT
Nick Buoniconti, Boston Patriots (AP, UPI, PL)............MLB
Mike Stratton, Buffalo (AP, UPI, PL)............LB
Bobby Bell, Kansas City (AP, UPI, PL)............LB
George (Butch) Byrd, Buffalo (AP, UPI, PL)............CB
Dave Grayson, Oakland (PL)............CB
Kent McCloughan, Oakland (AP, UPI)............CB
Johnny Robinson, Kansas City (AP, UPI, PL)............S
Kenny Graham, San Diego (AP, UPI)............S
George Saimes, Buffalo (PL)............S
Bob Scarpitto, Denver (PL)............P

1967 NFL
Offense

Charley Taylor, Washington (AP, UPI, NEA)............WR
Homer Jones, N.Y. Giants (UPI, NEA)............WR
Willie Richardson, Baltimore (AP)............WR
John Mackey, Baltimore (AP, NEA)............TE
Jackie Smith, St. Louis (UPI)............TE
Ralph Neely, Dallas (AP, UPI)............T
Forrest Gregg, Green Bay (AP, UPI)............T
Ernie McMillan, St. Louis (NEA)............T
Bob Vogel, Baltimore (NEA)............T
Gene Hickerson, Cleveland (AP, UPI, NEA)............G
Jerry Kramer, Green Bay (AP, UPI)............G
Howard Mudd, San Francisco (NEA)............G
Mick Tingelhoff, Minnesota (UPI, NEA)............C
Bob DeMarco, St. Louis (AP)............C
Johnny Unitas, Baltimore (AP, UPI, NEA)............QB
Leroy Kelly, Cleveland (AP, UPI, NEA)............RB
Gale Sayers, Chicago (AP, UPI, NEA)............RB

Defense

Willie Davis, Green Bay (AP, UPI, NEA)............DE
David (Deacon) Jones, Los Angeles (AP, UPI, NEA)............DE
Bob Lilly, Dallas (AP, UPI, NEA)............DT
Merlin Olsen, Los Angeles (AP, UPI, NEA)............DT
Dick Butkus, Chicago (UPI, NEA)............MLB
Tommy Nobis, Atlanta (AP)............MLB
Dave Robinson, Green Bay (AP, UPI, NEA)............LB
Chuck Howley, Dallas (AP)............LB
Maxie Baughan, Los Angeles (UPI)............LB
Dave Wilcox, San Francisco (NEA)............LB
Bob Jeter, Green Bay (AP, UPI, NEA)............CB
Cornell Green, Dallas (AP, UPI, NEA)............CB
Willie Wood, Green Bay (AP, UPI)............S
Eddie Meador, Los Angeles (UPI, NEA)............S
Larry Wilson, St. Louis (AP, NEA)............S

1967 AFL
Offense

George Sauer, N.Y. Jets (AP, UPI)............WR
Lance Alworth, San Diego (AP, UPI)............WR
Billy Cannon, Oakland (AP, UPI)............TE
Ron Mix, San Diego (AP, UPI)............T
Jim Tyrer, Kansas City (AP)............T
Harry Schuh, Oakland (UPI)............T
Bob Talamini, Houston (UPI)............G
Walt Sweeney, San Diego (AP, UPI)............G
Jim Otto, Oakland (AP, UPI)............C
Daryle Lamonica, Oakland (AP, UPI)............QB
Mike Garrett, Kansas City (AP, UPI)............RB
Jim Nance, Boston Patriots (AP, UPI)............RB

Defense

Ben Davidson, Oakland (AP, UPI)............DE
Pat Holmes, Houston (AP, UPI)............DE
Buck Buchanan, Kansas City (AP, UPI)............DT
Tom Keating, Oakland (AP, UPI)............DT

Nick Buoniconti, Boston Patriots (AP, UPI)............MLB
George Webster, Houston (AP, UPI)............LB
Bobby Bell, Kansas City (AP, UPI)............LB
Miller Farr, Houston (AP, UPI)............CB
Kent McCloughan, Oakland (AP, UPI)............CB
George Saimes, Buffalo (AP, UPI)............S
Johnny Robinson, Kansas City (AP, UPI)............S

1968 NFL
Offense

Clifton McNeil, San Francisco (AP, UPI, NEA)............WR
Paul Warfield, Cleveland (UPI, NEA)............WR
Bob Hayes, Dallas (AP)............WR
John Mackey, Baltimore (AP, UPI, NEA)............TE
Ralph Neely, Dallas (AP, UPI, NEA)............T
Bob Brown, Philadelphia (AP, NEA)............T
Bob Vogel, Baltimore (UPI)............T
Gene Hickerson, Cleveland (AP, UPI, NEA)............G
Howard Mudd, San Francisco (AP, UPI, NEA)............G
Mick Tingelhoff, Minnesota (AP, UPI, NEA)............C
Earl Morrall, Baltimore (AP, UPI, NEA)............QB
Leroy Kelly, Cleveland (AP, UPI, NEA)............RB
Gale Sayers, Chicago (AP, UPI, NEA)............RB

Defense

David (Deacon) Jones, Los Angeles (AP, UPI, NEA)............DE
Carl Eller, Minnesota (AP, UPI, NEA)............DE
Merlin Olsen, Los Angeles (AP, UPI, NEA)............DT
Bob Lilly, Dallas (AP, UPI, NEA)............DT
Dick Butkus, Chicago (AP, UPI, NEA)............MLB
Mike Curtis, Baltimore (AP, UPI)............LB
Chuck Howley, Dallas (AP, NEA)............LB
Dave Robinson, Green Bay (UPI, NEA)............LB
Lem Barney, Detroit (AP, UPI, NEA)............CB
Bobby Boyd, Baltimore (AP, UPI)............CB
Cornell Green, Dallas (NEA)............CB
Larry Wilson, St. Louis (AP, UPI, NEA)............S
Eddie Meador, Los Angeles (AP)............S
Willie Wood, Green Bay (UPI)............S
Rick Volk, Baltimore (NEA)............S

1968 AFL
Offense

Lance Alworth, San Diego (AP, UPI)............WR
George Sauer, N.Y. Jets (AP, UPI)............WR
Jim Whalen, Boston Patriots (AP, UPI)............TE
Ron Mix, San Diego (AP)............T
Jim Tyrer, Kansas City (AP, UPI)............T
Walt Sweeney, San Diego (AP, UPI)............G
Gene Upshaw, Oakland (AP, UPI)............G
Jim Otto, Oakland (AP, UPI)............C
Joe Namath, N.Y. Jets (AP, UPI)............QB
Paul Robinson, Cincinnati (AP, UPI)............RB
Hewritt Dixon, Oakland (AP, UPI)............RB

Defense

Gerry Philbin, N.Y. Jets (AP, UPI)............DE
Rich Jackson, Denver (AP, UPI)............DE
Buck Buchanan, Kansas City (AP, UPI)............DT
Dan Birdwell, Oakland (AP, UPI)............DT
Willie Lanier, Kansas City (AP)............MLB
Dan Conners, Oakland (UPI)............MLB
George Webster, Houston (AP, UPI)............LB
Bobby Bell, Kansas City (AP, UPI)............LB
Miller Farr, Houston (AP, UPI)............CB
Willie Brown, Oakland (AP, UPI)............CB
Dave Grayson, Oakland (AP, UPI)............S
Johnny Robinson, Kansas City (AP, UPI)............S

1969
Offense

Lance Alworth, San Diego............WR
Paul Warfield, Cleveland............WR
Bob Trumpy, Cincinnati............TE
Bob Brown, Los Angeles............T
Jim Tyrer, Kansas City............T
Tom Mack, Los Angeles............G
Gene Hickerson, Cleveland............G
Mick Tingelhoff, Minnesota............C
Roman Gabriel, Los Angeles............QB
Gale Sayers, Chicago............RB
Calvin Hill, Dallas............RB
Jan Stenerud, Kansas City............K

Defense

David (Deacon) Jones, Los Angeles............DE
Carl Eller, Minnesota............DE
Merlin Olsen, Los Angeles............DT

Bob Lilly, Dallas............DT
Dick Butkus, Chicago............MLB
Bobby Bell, Kansas City............LB
Chuck Howley, Dallas............LB
Lem Barney, Detroit............CB
Willie Brown, Oakland............CB
Larry Wilson, St. Louis............S
Johnny Robinson, Kansas City............S
David Lee, Baltimore............P

1970
Offense

Gene Washington, San Francisco............WR
Dick Gordon, Chicago............WR
Charlie Sanders, Detroit............TE
Jim Tyrer, Kansas City............T
Bob Brown, Los Angeles............T
Gene Upshaw, Oakland............G
Gene Hickerson, Cleveland............G
Mick Tingelhoff, Minnesota............C
John Brodie, San Francisco............QB
Larry Brown, Washington............RB
Ron Johnson, N.Y. Giants............RB
Jan Stenerud, Kansas City............K

Defense

Carl Eller, Minnesota............DE
Rich Jackson, Denver............DE
Alan Page, Minnesota............DT
Merlin Olsen, Los Angeles............DT
Dick Butkus, Chicago............MLB
Bobby Bell, Kansas City............LB
Chuck Howley, Dallas............LB
Willie Brown, Oakland............CB
Jimmy Johnson, San Francisco............CB
Johnny Robinson, Kansas City............S
Larry Wilson, St. Louis............S
Dave Lewis, Cincinnati............P

1971
Offense

Otis Taylor, Kansas City............WR
Paul Warfield, Miami............WR
Charlie Sanders, Detroit............TE
Ron Yary, Minnesota............T
Rayfield Wright, Dallas............T
Larry Little, Miami............G
John Niland, Dallas............G
Forrest Blue, San Francisco............C
Bob Griese, Miami............QB
John Brockington, Green Bay............RB
Larry Csonka, Miami............RB
Garo Yepremian, Miami............K
Jan Stenerud, Kansas City............K

Defense

Carl Eller, Minnesota............DE
Charles (Bubba) Smith, Baltimore............DE
Bob Lilly, Dallas............DT
Alan Page, Minnesota............DT
Willie Lanier, Kansas City............MLB
Ted Hendricks, Baltimore............LB
Dave Wilcox, San Francisco............LB
Jimmy Johnson, San Francisco............CB
Willie Brown, Oakland............CB
Rick Volk, Baltimore............S
Bill Bradley, Philadelphia............S
Jerrel Wilson, Kansas City............P

1972
Offense

Gene Washington, San Francisco (PFWA)............WR
Otis Taylor, Kansas City (PFWA)............WR
Fred Biletnikoff, Oakland (NEA)............WR
Paul Warfield, Miami (NEA)............WR
Bob Tucker, N.Y. Giants (PFWA)............TE
Ted Kwalick, San Francisco (NEA)............TE
Rayfield Wright, Dallas (PFWA, NEA)............T
Bob Brown, Oakland (PFWA)............T
George Kunz, Atlanta (NEA)............T
Larry Little, Miami (PFWA, NEA)............G
Gene Upshaw, Oakland (PFWA)............G
Blaine Nye, Dallas (NEA)............G
Forrest Blue, San Francisco (PFWA)............C
Len Hauss, Washington (NEA)............C
Joe Namath, N.Y. Jets (PFWA, NEA)............QB
Larry Brown, Washington (PFWA, NEA)............RB

Fran Tarkenton

John Hannah

Larry Brooks

Louis Wright

Earl Campbell

Al Baker

Marvin Powell

O.J. Simpson, Buffalo (PFWA, NEA) ... RB
Chester Marcol, Green Bay (PFWA, NEA) ... K

Defense

Claude Humphrey, Atlanta (PFWA, NEA) ... DE
Jack Gregory, N.Y. Giants (PFWA, NEA) ... DE
Joe Greene, Pittsburgh (PFWA, NEA) ... DT
Mike Reid, Cincinnati (PFWA, NEA) ... DT
Dick Butkus, Chicago (PFWA, NEA) ... MLB
Dave Wilcox, San Francisco (PFWA, NEA) ... LB
Chris Hanburger, Washington (PFWA, NEA) ... LB
Willie Brown, Oakland (PFWA, NEA) ... CB
Jimmy Johnson, San Francisco (PFWA, NEA) ... CB
Dick Anderson, Miami (PFWA, NEA) ... S
Bill Bradley, Philadelphia (PFWA, NEA) ... S
Jerrel Wilson, Kansas City (PFWA) ... P
Don Cockroft, Cleveland (NEA) ... P

1973

Offense

Harold Jackson, Los Angeles (PFWA, NEA) ... WR
Harold Carmichael, Philadelphia (PFWA) ... WR
John Gilliam, Minnesota (NEA) ... WR
Charles Young, Philadelphia (PFWA) ... TE
Riley Odoms, Denver (NEA) ... TE
Ron Yary, Minnesota (PFWA) ... T
Rayfield Wright, Dallas (PFWA) ... T
Art Shell, Oakland (NEA) ... T
George Kunz, Atlanta (NEA) ... T
Larry Little, Miami (PFWA, NEA) ... G
Reggie McKenzie, Buffalo (PFWA) ... G
Joe Scibelli, Los Angeles (NEA) ... G
Forrest Blue, San Francisco (PFWA) ... C
Bob Johnson, Cincinnati (NEA) ... C
John Hadl, Los Angeles (PFWA) ... QB
Fran Tarkenton, Minnesota (NEA) ... QB
O.J. Simpson, Buffalo (PFWA, NEA) ... RB
Calvin Hill, Dallas (PFWA) ... RB
John Brockington, Green Bay (NEA) ... RB
Garo Yepremian, Miami (PFWA, NEA) ... K

Defense

Bill Stanfill, Miami (PFWA, NEA) ... DE
Claude Humphrey, Atlanta (PFWA) ... DE
Alan Page, Minnesota (NEA) ... DE
Joe Greene (PFWA, NEA) ... DT
Alan Page, Minnesota (PFWA) ... DT
Mike Reid, Cincinnati (NEA) ... DT
Lee Roy Jordan, Dallas (PFWA, NEA) ... MLB
Dave Wilcox, San Francisco (PFWA, NEA) ... LB
Isiah Robertson, Los Angeles (PFWA) ... LB
Chris Hanburger, Washington (NEA) ... LB
Willie Brown, Oakland (PFWA, NEA) ... CB
Mel Renfro, Dallas (PFWA, NEA) ... CB
Dick Anderson, Miami (PFWA, NEA) ... S
Jake Scott, Miami (PFWA) ... S
Bill Bradley, Philadelphia (NEA) ... S
Ray Guy, Oakland (PFWA, NEA) ... P

1974

Offense

Clifford Branch, Oakland (PFWA, NEA) ... WR
Drew Pearson, Dallas (PFWA) ... WR
Mel Gray, St. Louis (NEA) ... WR
Riley Odoms, Denver (PFWA, NEA) ... TE
Ron Yary, Minnesota (PFWA, NEA) ... T
Art Shell, Oakland (PFWA, NEA) ... T
Tom Mack, Los Angeles (PFWA) ... G
Larry Little, Miami (PFWA) ... G
Ed White, Minnesota (NEA) ... G
Gale Gillingham, Green Bay (NEA) ... G
Jim Langer, Miami (PFWA, NEA) ... C
Ken Stabler, Oakland (PFWA, NEA) ... QB
O.J. Simpson, Buffalo (PFWA, NEA) ... RB
Otis Armstrong, Denver (PFWA) ... RB
Lawrence McCutcheon, Los Angeles (NEA) ... RB
Chester Marcol, Green Bay (PFWA) ... K
Jan Stenerud, Kansas City (NEA) ... K

Defense

Jack Youngblood, Los Angeles (PFWA) ... DE
L.C. Greenwood, Pittsburgh (PFWA) ... DE
Claude Humphrey, Atlanta (NEA) ... DE
Fred Dryer, Los Angeles (NEA) ... DE
Joe Greene, Pittsburgh (PFWA, NEA) ... DT
Alan Page, Minnesota (PFWA, NEA) ... DT
Bill Bergey, Philadelphia (PFWA) ... MLB
Willie Lanier, Kansas City (NEA) ... MLB
Jack Ham, Pittsburgh (PFWA, NEA) ... LB
Ted Hendricks, Green Bay (PFWA, NEA) ... LB
Robert James, Buffalo (PFWA, NEA) ... CB
Emmitt Thomas, Kansas City (PFWA) ... CB
Roger Wehrli, St. Louis (NEA) ... CB
Tony Greene, Buffalo (PFWA, NEA) ... S
Ken Houston, Washington (PFWA) ... S
Dick Anderson, Miami (NEA) ... S
Ray Guy, Oakland (PFWA, NEA) ... P

1975

Offense

Lynn Swann, Pittsburgh (PFWA) ... WR
Mel Gray, St. Louis (PFWA) ... WR
Clifford Branch, Oakland (NEA) ... WR
Isaac Curtis, Cincinnati (NEA) ... WR
Charles Young, Philadelphia (PFWA, NEA) ... TE
Ron Yary, Minnesota (PFWA, NEA) ... T
Dan Dierdorf, St. Louis (PFWA) ... T
Rayfield Wright, Dallas (NEA) ... T
Larry Little, Miami (PFWA) ... G
Joe DeLamielleure, Buffalo (PFWA) ... G
Bob Kuechenberg, Miami (NEA) ... G
Ed White, Minnesota (NEA) ... G
Jim Langer, Miami (PFWA, NEA) ... C
Fran Tarkenton, Minnesota (PFWA, NEA) ... QB
O.J. Simpson, Buffalo (PFWA, NEA) ... RB
Chuck Foreman, Minnesota (PFWA, NEA) ... RB
Jim Bakken, St. Louis (PFWA, NEA) ... K

Defense

Jack Youngblood, Los Angeles (PFWA, NEA) ... DE
L.C. Greenwood, Pittsburgh (PFWA, NEA) ... DE
Curley Culp, Houston (PFWA, NEA) ... DT
Alan Page, Minnesota (PFWA) ... DT
Wally Chambers, Chicago (NEA) ... DT
Jack Lambert, Pittsburgh (PFWA) ... MLB
Willie Lanier, Kansas City (NEA) ... MLB
Jack Ham, Pittsburgh (PFWA, NEA) ... LB
Andy Russell, Pittsburgh (PFWA) ... LB
Isiah Robertson, Los Angeles (NEA) ... LB
Mel Blount, Pittsburgh (PFWA, NEA) ... CB
Rogert Wehrli, St. Louis (PFWA) ... CB
Emmitt Thomas, Kansas City (NEA) ... CB
Ken Houston, Washington (PFWA, NEA) ... S
Paul Krause, Minnesota (PFWA) ... S
Cliff Harris, Dallas (NEA) ... S
Ray Guy, Oakland (PFWA, NEA) ... P

1976

Offense

Clifford Branch, Oakland (PFWA, NEA, AP) ... WR
Drew Pearson, Dallas (PFWA, AP) ... WR
Isaac Curtis, Cincinnati (NEA) ... WR
Dave Casper, Oakland (PFWA, NEA, AP) ... TE
Dan Dierdorf, St. Louis (PFWA, NEA, AP) ... T
Ron Yary, Minnesota (PFWA, NEA, AP) ... T
Joe DeLamiellure, Buffalo (PFWA, NEA, AP) ... G
John Hannah, New England (PFWA, AP) ... G
Conrad Dobler, St. Louis (NEA) ... G
Jim Langer, Miami (PFWA, NEA) ... C
Tom Banks, St. Louis (AP) ... C
Bert Jones, Baltimore (PFWA, NEA, AP) ... QB
O.J. Simpson, Buffalo (PFWA, NEA, AP) ... RB
Walter Payton, Chicago (PFWA, AP) ... RB
Chuck Foreman, Minnesota (NEA) ... RB
Jim Bakken, St. Louis (PFWA, NEA, AP) ... K
Rick Upchurch, Denver (AP) ... KR

Defense

Jack Youngblood, Los Angeles (PFWA, NEA, AP) ... DE
Tommy Hart, San Francisco (PFWA, NEA) ... DE
John Dutton, Baltimore (AP) ... DE
Wally Chambers, Chicago (PFWA, NEA, AP) ... DT
Jerry Sherk, Cleveland (PFWA, NEA, AP) ... DT
Jack Lambert, Pittsburgh (PFWA, NEA, AP) ... MLB
Jack Ham, Pittsburgh (PFWA, NEA, AP) ... LB
Robert Brazile, Houston (PFWA) ... LB
Chris Hanburger, Washington (NEA) ... LB
Isiah Robertson, Los Angeles (AP) ... LB
Monte Jackson, Los Angeles (PFWA, NEA, AP) ... CB
Roger Wehrli, St. Louis (PFWA, AP) ... CB
Lemar Parrish, Cincinnati (NEA) ... CB
Cliff Harris, Dallas (PFWA, NEA, AP) ... S
Ken Houston, Washington (PFWA, NEA) ... S
Tommy Casanova, Cincinnati (AP) ... S
Ray Guy, Oakland (PFWA, NEA, AP) ... P

1977

Offense

Drew Pearson, Dallas (AP, NEA, PFWA) ... WR
Nat Moore, Miami (AP, PFWA) ... WR
Clifford Branch, Oakland (NEA) ... WR
Dave Casper, Oakland (AP, NEA, PFWA) ... TE
Dan Dierdorf, St. Louis (AP, NEA, PFWA) ... T
Art Shell, Oakland (AP, NEA, PFWA) ... T
Joe DeLamielleure, Buffalo (AP, NEA, PFWA) ... G
Gene Upshaw, Oakland (AP, PFWA) ... G
Larry Little, Miami (PFWA) ... G
John Hannah, New England (NEA) ... G
Jim Langer, Miami (AP, NEA, PFWA) ... C
Bob Griese, Miami (AP, NEA, PFWA) ... QB
Franco Harris, Pittsburgh (AP, NEA, PFWA) ... RB
Walter Payton, Chicago (AP, NEA, PFWA) ... RB
Efren Herrera, Dallas (AP, NEA, PFWA) ... K
Billy Johnson, Houston (AP, PFWA) ... KR

Defense

Harvey Martin, Dallas (AP, NEA, PFWA) ... DE
Lyle Alzado, Denver (AP, PFWA) ... DE
Claude Humphrey, Atlanta (NEA) ... DE
Cleveland Elam, San Francisco (AP, NEA, PFWA) ... DT
Louie Kelcher, San Diego (NEA) ... DT
Larry Brooks, Los Angeles (PFWA) ... DT
Joe Greene, Pittsburgh (AP) ... DT
Bill Bergey, Philadelphia (NEA, PFWA) ... MLB
Randy Gradishar, Denver (AP) ... MLB
Jack Ham, Pittsburgh (AP, NEA, PFWA) ... LB
Tom Jackson, Denver (AP, PFWA) ... LB
Robert Brazile, Houston (NEA) ... LB
Rolland Lawrence, Atlanta (AP, PFWA) ... CB
Roger Wehrli, St. Louis (AP, NEA) ... CB
Monte Jackson, Los Angeles (PFWA) ... CB
Mel Blount, Pittsburgh (NEA) ... CB
Cliff Harris, Dallas (AP, NEA, PFWA) ... S
Ken Houston, Washington (NEA) ... S
Bill Thompson, Denver (AP) ... S
Charlie Waters, Dallas (PFWA) ... S
Ray Guy, Oakland (AP, NEA, PFWA) ... P

1978

Offense

Lynn Swann, Pittsburgh (AP, NEA, PFWA) ... WR
Wesley Walker, N.Y. Jets (AP, NEA, PFWA) ... WR
Dave Casper, Oakland (AP, NEA, PFWA) ... TE
Dan Dierdorf, St. Louis (AP, NEA, PFWA) ... T
Leon Gray, New England (AP, PFWA) ... T
Russ Washington, San Diego (NEA) ... T
John Hannah, New England (AP, NEA, PFWA) ... G
Joe DeLamielleure, Buffalo (NEA, PFWA) ... G
Bob Kuechenberg, Miami (AP) ... G
Mike Webster, Pittsburgh (AP, NEA, PFWA) ... C
Terry Bradshaw, Pittsburgh (AP, PFWA) ... QB
Jim Zorn, Seattle (NEA) ... QB
Earl Campbell, Houston (AP, NEA, PFWA) ... RB
Walter Payton, Chicago (NEA, PFWA) ... RB
Delvin Williams, Miami (AP) ... RB
Frank Corral, Los Angeles (NEA, PFWA) ... K
Pat Leahy, N.Y. Jets (AP) ... K
Rick Upchurch, Denver (AP, PFWA) ... KR

Defense

Al Baker, Detroit (AP, NEA, PFWA) ... DE
Jack Youngblood, Los Angeles (AP, NEA, PFWA) ... DE
Randy White, Dallas (AP, NEA, PFWA) ... DT
Louie Kelcher, San Diego (AP, NEA, PFWA) ... DT
Randy Gradishar, Denver (AP, NEA, PFWA) ... MLB
Jack Ham, Pittsburgh (AP, NEA, PFWA) ... LB
Robert Brazile, Houston (AP, NEA, PFWA) ... LB
Louis Wright, Denver (AP, NEA, PFWA) ... CB
Willie Buchanon, Green Bay (AP, PFWA)* ... CB
Mike Haynes, New England (NEA, PFWA)* ... CB
Charlie Waters, Dallas (NEA, PFWA) ... S
Thom Darden, Cleveland (NEA, PFWA)† ... S
Cliff Harris, Dallas (AP, PFWA)† ... S
Ken Houston, Washington (AP) ... S
Ray Guy, Oakland (AP, NEA, PFWA) ... P

**Haynes and Buchanon tied in PFWA BALLOTING.*
†Darden and Harris tied in PFWA BALLOTING.

Mike Reinfeldt *James Lofton* *Matt Blair* *Lester Hayes* *Kellen Winslow* *Doug English* *Ronnie Lott*

1979

Offense

John Jefferson, San Diego (AP, NEA, PFWA)	WR
John Stallworth, Pittsburgh (AP, NEA, PFWA)	WR
Dave Casper, Oakland (AP)	TE
Raymond Chester, Oakland (NEA)	TE
Ozzie Newsome, Cleveland (PFWA)	TE
Leon Gray, Houston (AP, NEA, PFWA)	T
Marvin Powell, N.Y. Jets (AP, PFWA)	T
Jon Kolb, Pittsburgh (NEA)	T
John Hannah, New England (AP, NEA, PFWA)	G
Joe DeLamielleure, Buffalo (NEA, PFWA)	G
Bob Young, St. Louis (AP)	G
Mike Webster, Pittsburgh (AP, NEA, PFWA)	C
Dan Fouts, San Diego (AP, NEA, PFWA)	QB
Earl Campbell, Houston (AP, NEA, PFWA)	RB
Ottis Anderson, St. Louis (AP, PFWA)	RB
Walter Payton, Chicago (NEA)	RB
Toni Fritsch, Houston (AP, NEA, PFWA)	K
Tony Nathan, Miami (AP)	KR
Rick Upchurch, Denver (PFWA)	KR
J.T. Smith, Kansas City (PFWA)	PR

Defense

Lee Roy Selmon, Tampa Bay (AP, NEA, PFWA)	DE
Jack Youngblood, Los Angeles (AP, NEA, PFWA)	DE
Randy White, Dallas (AP, NEA, PFWA)	DT
Larry Brooks, Los Angeles (AP)	DT
Joe Greene, Pittsburgh (PFWA)	DT
Charlie Johnson, Philadelphia (NEA)	DT
Jack Lambert, Pittsburgh (AP, NEA)	MLB
Randy Gradishar, Denver (PFWA)	MLB
Robert Brazile, Houston (AP, NEA, PFWA)	LB
Jack Ham, Pittsburgh (AP, NEA, PFWA)	LB
Lemar Parrish, Washington (AP, NEA, PFWA)	CB
Louis Wright, Denver (AP, NEA, PFWA)	CB
Mike Reinfeldt, Houston (AP, NEA, PFWA)	S
Donnie Shell, Pittsburgh (AP, NEA)	S
Gary Fencik, Chicago (PFWA)	S
Bob Grupp, Kansas City (NEA, PFWA)	P
Dave Jennings, N.Y. Giants (AP)	P

1980

Offense

John Jefferson, San Diego (AP, NEA, PFWA)	WR
James Lofton, Green Bay (NEA, PFWA)	WR
Charlie Joiner, San Diego (AP)	WR
Kellen Winslow, San Diego (AP, NEA, PFWA)	TE
Mike Kenn, Atlanta (AP, NEA, PFWA)	T
Leon Gray, Houston (AP, PFWA)	T
Dan Dierdorf, St. Louis (NEA)	T
John Hannah, New England (AP, NEA, PFWA)	G
Herbert Scott, Dallas (AP, NEA)	G
Joe DeLamielleure, Cleveland (PFWA)	G
Mike Webster, Pittsburgh (AP, NEA, PFWA)	C
Brian Sipe, Cleveland (AP, NEA, PFWA)	QB
Earl Campbell, Houston (AP, NEA, PFWA)	RB
Walter Payton, Chicago (AP, NEA, PFWA)	RB
Ed Murray, Detroit (AP, NEA, PFWA)	K
Horace Ivory, New England (PFWA)	KR
J.T. Smith, Kansas City (AP, PFWA)	PR

Defense

Lee Roy Selmon, Tampa Bay (NEA, PFWA)	DE
Art Still, Kansas City (NEA, PFWA)	DE
Lyle Alzado, Cleveland (AP)	DE
Fred Dean, San Diego (AP)	DE
Gary Johnson, San Diego (AP, NEA, PFWA)	DT
Randy White, Dallas (NEA, PFWA)	DT
Charlie Johnson, Philadelphia (AP)	DT
Jack Lambert, Pittsburgh (AP, NEA, PFWA)	MLB
Ted Hendricks, Oakland (AP, NEA, PFWA)	LB
Robert Brazile, Houston (NEA, PFWA)	LB
Matt Blair, Minnesota (AP)	LB
Lester Hayes, Oakland (AP, NEA, PFWA)	CB
Lemar Parrish, Washington (NEA, PFWA)	CB
Pat Thomas, Los Angeles (AP)	CB
Nolan Cromwell, Los Angeles (AP, NEA, PFWA)	S
Donnie Shell, Pittsburgh (AP, NEA, PFWA)	S
Dave Jennings, N.Y. Giants (AP, NEA, PFWA)	P

1981

Offense

James Lofton, Green Bay (AP, NEA, PFWA)	WR
Alfred Jenkins, Atlanta (AP, NEA, PFWA)	WR
Kellen Winslow, San Diego (AP, NEA, PFWA)	TE
Anthony Munoz, Cincinnati (AP, NEA, PFWA)	T
Marvin Powell, N.Y. Jets (AP, NEA, PFWA)	T
John Hannah, New England (AP, NEA, PFWA)	G
Randy Cross, San Francisco (NEA, PFWA)	G
Herbert Scott, Dallas (AP)	G
Mike Webster, Pittsburgh (AP, NEA, PFWA)	C
Ken Anderson, Cincinnati (AP, NEA, PFWA)	QB
Tony Dorsett, Dallas (AP, NEA, PFWA)	RB
Billy Sims, Detroit (NEA, PFWA)	RB
George Rogers, New Orleans (AP)	RB
Rafael Septien, Dallas (AP, PFWA)	K
Nick Lowery, Kansas City (NEA)	K
LeRoy Irvin, Los Angeles (AP, PFWA)	KR
Mike Nelms, Washington (PFWA)	PR

Defense

Joe Klecko, N.Y. Jets (AP, NEA, PFWA)	DE
Fred Dean, San Francisco (AP, PFWA)	DE
Ed Jones, Dallas (NEA)	DE
Randy White, Dallas (AP, NEA, PFWA)	DT
Gary Johnson, San Diego (AP, PFWA)	DT
Doug English, Detroit (NEA)	DT
Charlie Johnson, Philadelphia (AP)	NT
Jack Lambert, Pittsburgh (AP, NEA, PFWA)	MLB
Lawrence Taylor, N.Y. Giants (AP, NEA, PFWA)	LB
Bob Swenson, Denver (AP, NEA)	LB
Jerry Robinson, Philadelphia (PFWA)	LB
Ronnie Lott, San Francisco (AP, NEA, PFWA)	CB
Mel Blount, Pittsburgh (AP, PFWA)	CB
Mark Haynes, N.Y. Giants (NEA)	CB
Nolan Cromwell, Los Angeles (AP, NEA, PFWA)	S
Gary Barbaro, Kansas City (NEA, PFWA)	S
Gary Fencik, Chicago (AP)	S
Pat McInally, Cincinnati (AP, PFWA)	P
Tom Skladany, Detroit (NEA)	P

Three all-pros—St. Louis's Bob Young and Ottis Anderson and Dallas's Cliff Harris—converge, 1979.

ALL-PRO SQUAD OF THE 1920s

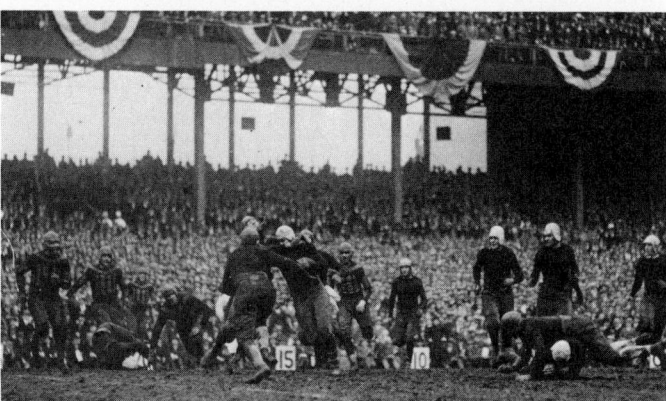

The New York Giants with ball vs. Chicago Bears and Red Grange, 1925.

The roster chosen by the Hall of Fame Selection Committee

Name	Pos.	Ht.	Wt.	Teams
Guy Chamberlin	End	6-2	210	1920 Decatur Staleys, 1921 Chicago Staleys, 1922-23 Canton Bulldogs, 1924 Cleveland Bulldogs, 1925-26 Frankford Yellowjackets, 1927 Chicago Cardinals
Lavern Dilweg	End	6-3	203	1926 Milwaukee Badgers, 1927-34 Green Bay Packers
George Halas	End	6-1	180	1920 Decatur Staleys, 1921 Chicago Staleys, 1922-29 Chicago Bears
Ed Healey	Tackle	6-3	220	1920-22 Rock Island Independents, 1922-27 Chicago Bears
Wilbur (Pete) Henry	Tackle	6-0	250	1920-23, 1925-26 Canton Bulldogs, 1927 New York Giants, 1927-28 Pottsville Maroons
Cal Hubbard	Tackle	6-5	250	1927-28 New York Giants, 1929-1933, 1935 Green Bay Packers, 1936 New York Giants, 1936 Pittsburgh Pirates
Steve Owen	Tackle	6-2	235	1924-25 Kansas City Cowboys, 1926-1931, 1933 New York Giants
Heartley (Hunk) Anderson	Guard	5-11	195	1922-25 Chicago Bears
Walt Kiesling	Guard	6-2	245	1926-27 Duluth Eskimos, 1928 Pottsville Maroons, 1929-1933 Chicago Cardinals, 1934 Chicago Bears, 1935-36 Green Bay Packers, 1937-38 Pittsburgh Pirates
Mike Michalske	Guard	6-0	209	1926 New York Yankees (AFL), 1927-28 New York Yankees (NFL), 1929-1935, 1937 Green Bay Packers
George Trafton	Center	6-2	235	1920 Decatur Staleys, 1921 Chicago Staleys, 1922-1932 Chicago Bears
Jimmy Conzelman	Quarterback	6-0	180	1920 Decatur Staleys, 1921-22 Rock Island Independents, 1923-24 Milwaukee Badgers, 1925-26 Detroit Panthers, 1927-29 Providence Steamrollers
John (Paddy) Driscoll	Quarterback	5-11	160	1920 Decatur Staleys, 1920-25 Chicago Cardinals, 1926-29 Chicago Bears
Harold (Red) Grange	Halfback	6-0	185	1925 Chicago Bears, 1926 New York Yankees (AFL), 1927 New York Yankees (NFL), 1929-1934 Chicago Bears
Joe Guyon	Halfback	6-1	180	1920 Canton Bulldogs, 1921 Cleveland Indians, 1922-23 Oorang Indians, 1924 Rock Island Independents, 1924-25 Kansas City Cowboys, 1927 New York Giants
Earl (Curly) Lambeau	Halfback	6-0	195	1921-29 Green Bay Packers
Jim Thorpe	Halfback	6-1	190	1920 Canton Bulldogs, 1921 Cleveland Indians, 1922-23 Oorang Indians, 1923 Toledo Maroons, 1924 Rock Island Independents, 1925 New York Giants, 1926 Canton Bulldogs, 1928 Chicago Cardinals
Ernie Nevers	Fullback	6-1	205	1926-27 Duluth Eskimos, 1929-1931 Chicago Cardinals

ALL-PRO SQUAD OF THE 1930s

Bill Hewitt (56, with no helmet) and the Eagles vs. Green Bay Packers, 1937.

The roster chosen by the Hall of Fame Selection Committee

Name	Pos.	Ht.	Wt.	Teams
Bill Hewitt	End	5-11	191	1932-36 Chicago Bears, 1937-39 Philadelphia Eagles, 1943 Phil-Pitt
Don Hutson	End	6-1	180	1935-1945 Green Bay Packers
Wayne Millner	End	6-0	191	1936 Boston Redskins, 1937-1941, 1945 Washington Redskins
Gaynell Tinsley	End	6-1	200	1937-38, 1940 Chicago Cardinals
George Christensen	Tackle	6-2	238	1931-33 Portsmouth Spartans, 1934-38 Detroit Lions
Frank Cope	Tackle	6-3	234	1938-1947 New York Giants
Glen (Turk) Edwards	Tackle	6-2	260	1932 Boston Braves, 1933-36 Boston Redskins, 1937-1940 Washington Redskins
Bill Lee	Tackle	6-2	235	1935-37 Brooklyn Dodgers, 1937-1942, 1946 Green Bay Packers
Joe Stydahar	Tackle	6-4	230	1936-1942, 1945-46 Chicago Bears
Grover (Ox) Emerson	Guard	6-0	190	1931-33 Portsmouth Spartans, 1934-37 Detroit Lions, 1938 Brooklyn Dodgers
Danny Fortmann	Guard	6-0	207	1936-1943 Chicago Bears
Charles (Buckets) Goldenberg	Guard	5-10	222	1933-1945 Green Bay Packers
Ross Letlow	Guard	6-0	212	1936-1942, 1946 Green Bay Packers
Mel Hein	Center	6-2	225	1931-1945 New York Giants
George Svendsen	Center	6-4	240	1935-37, 1940-41 Green Bay Packers
Earl (Dutch) Clark	Quarterback	6-0	185	1931-32 Portsmouth Spartans, 1934-38 Detroit Lions
Arnie Herber	Quarterback	6-1	200	1930-1940 Green Bay Packers, 1944-45 New York Giants
Cecil Isbell	Quarterback	6-0	190	1938-1942 Green Bay Packers
Cliff Battles	Halfback	6-1	201	1932 Boston Braves, 1933-36 Boston Redskins, 1937 Washington Redskins
Beattie Feathers	Halfback	5-11	177	1934-37 Chicago Bears, 1938-39 Brooklyn Dodgers, 1940 Green Bay Packers
Alphonse (Tuffy) Leemans	Halfback	6-0	200	1936-1943 New York Giants
Johnny Blood (McNally)	Halfback	6-0	185	1925-26 Milwaukee Badgers, 1926-27 Duluth Eskimos, 1928 Pottsville Maroons, 1929-1933 Green Bay Packers, 1934 Pittsburgh Pirates, 1935-36 Green Bay Packers, 1937-38 Pittsburgh Pirates, 1939 Pittsburgh Steelers
Ken Strong	Halfback	5-11	210	1929-1932 Stapleton Stapes, 1933-35 New York Giants, 1936-37 New York Yanks (AFL), 1939, 1944-47 New York Giants
Clarke Hinkle	Fullback	5-11	191	1932-1941 Green Bay Packers
Bronko Nagurski	Fullback	6-2	225	1930-37, 1943 Chicago Bears

ALL-PRO SQUAD OF THE 1940s

Steve Van Buren of Philadelphia running against Washington, late 1940s.

The roster chosen by the Hall of Fame Selection Committee

Name	Pos.	Ht.	Wt.	Teams
Jim Benton	End	6-3	210	1938-1940, 1942, 1944-45 Cleveland Rams, 1943 Chicago Bears, 1946-47 Los Angeles Rams
Jack Ferrante	End	6-1	205	1941, 1944-50 Philadelphia Eagles
Ken Kavanaugh	End	6-3	205	1940-41, 1945-50 Chicago Bears
Dante Lavelli	End	6-0	192	1946-49 Cleveland Browns (AAFC), 1950-56 Cleveland Browns
Pete Pihos	End	6-1	210	1947-1955 Philadelphia Eagles
Mac Speedie	End	6-3	205	1946-49 Cleveland Browns (AAFC), 1950-52 Cleveland Browns
Ed Sprinkle	End	6-1	207	1944-1955 Chicago Bears
Al Blozis	Tackle	6-7	250	1942-44 New York Giants
George Connor	Tackle	6-3	240	1948-1955 Chicago Bears
Frank (Bucko) Kilroy	Tackle	6-2	244	1943 Phil-Pitt, 1944-1955 Philadelphia Eagles
Buford (Baby) Ray	Tackle	6-6	250	1938-1948 Green Bay Packers
Vic Sears	Tackle	6-3	236	1941-42 Philadelphia Eagles, 1943 Phil-Pitt, 1945-1953 Philadelphia Eagles
Al Wistert	Tackle	6-1	214	1943 Phil-Pitt, 1944-1951 Philadelphia Eagles
Bruno Banducci	Guard	5-11	220	1944-45 Philadelphia Eagles, 1946-49 San Francisco 49ers (AAFC), 1950-54 San Francisco 49ers
Bill Edwards	Guard	6-3	218	1940-42, 1946 New York Giants
Garrard (Buster) Ramsey	Guard	6-1	220	1946-1951 Chicago Cardinals
Bill Willis	Guard	6-2	215	1946-49 Cleveland Browns (AAFC), 1950-53 Cleveland Browns
Len Younce	Guard	6-1	210	1941, 1943-44, 1946-48 New York Giants
Charles Brock	Center	6-2	210	1939-1947 Green Bay Packers
Clyde (Bulldog) Turner	Center	6-2	235	1940-1952 Chicago Bears
Alex Wojciechowicz	Center	6-0	235	1938-1946 Detroit Lions, 1946-1950 Philadelphia Eagles
Sammy Baugh	Quarterback	6-2	180	1937-1952 Washington Redskins
Sid Luckman	Quarterback	6-0	195	1939-1950 Chicago Bears
Bob Waterfield	Quarterback	6-2	200	1945 Cleveland Rams, 1946-1952 Los Angeles Rams
Tony Canadeo	Halfback	5-11	195	1941-44, 1946-1952 Green Bay Packers
Bill Dudley	Halfback	5-10	176	1942,1945-46 Pittsburgh Steelers, 1947-49 Detroit Lions, 1950-51, 1953 Washington Redskins
George McAfee	Halfback	6-0	177	1940-41, 1945-1950 Chicago Bears
Charley Trippi	Halfback	6-0	185	1947-1955 Chicago Cardinals
Steve Van Buren	Halfback	6-1	200	1944-1951 Philadelphia Eagles
Byron (Whizzer) White	Halfback	6-1	188	1938 Pittsburgh Pirates, 1940-41 Detroit Lions
Pat Harder	Fullback	5-11	205	1946-1950 Chicago Cardinals, 1951-53 Detroit Lions
Marion Motley	Fullback	6-1	238	1946-49 Cleveland Browns (AAFC), 1950-53 Cleveland Browns, 1955 Pittsburgh Steelers
Bill Osmanski	Fullback	5-11	200	1939-1943, 1946-47 Chicago Bears

ALL-PRO SQUAD OF THE 1950s

Hugh McElhenny of San Francisco looking for opening against Rams, 1954.

The roster chosen by the Hall of Fame Selection Committee

OFFENSE

Name	Pos.	Ht.	Wt.	Teams
Raymond Berry	End	6-2	187	1955-1967 Baltimore Colts
Tom Fears	End	6-2	215	1948-1956 Los Angeles Rams
Bobby Walston	End	6-0	195	1951-1962 Philadelphia Eagles
Elroy (Crazylegs) Hirsch	Halfback-End	6-2	190	1946-48 Chicago Rockets (AAFC), 1949-1957 Los Angeles Rams
Roosevelt Brown	Tackle	6-3	255	1953-1965 New York Giants
Bob St. Clair	Tackle	6-9	265	1953-1963 San Francisco 49ers
Dick Barwegan	Guard	6-1	228	1947 New York Yankees (AAFC), 1948-49 Baltimore Colts (AAFC), 1950-52 Chicago Bears, 1953-54 Baltimore Colts
Jim Parker	Guard	6-3	273	1957-1967 Baltimore Colts
Dick Stanfel	Guard	6-3	240	1952-55 Detroit Lions, 1956-58 Washington Redskins
Chuck Bednarik	Center	6-3	230	1949-1962 Philadelphia Eagles
Otto Graham	Quarterback	6-1	195	1946-49 Cleveland Browns (AAFC), 1950-55 Cleveland Browns
Bobby Layne	Quarterback	6-2	190	1948 Chicago Bears, 1949 New York Bulldogs, 1950-58 Detroit Lions, 1958-1962 Pitt. Steelers
Norm Van Brocklin	Quarterback	6-1	190	1949-1957 Los Angeles Rams, 1958-1960 Philadelphia Eagles
Frank Gifford	Halfback	6-1	200	1952-1960, 1962-64 New York Giants
Ollie Matson	Halfback	6-2	220	1952, 1954-58 Chicago Cardinals, 1959-1962 Los Angeles Rams, 1963 Detroit Lions, 1964-66 Philadelphia Eagles
Hugh McElhenny	Halfback	6-1	198	1952-1960 San Francisco 49ers, 1961-62 Minnesota Vikings, 1963 New York Giants, 1964 Detroit Lions
Lenny Moore	Halfback	6-1	190	1956-1967 Baltimore Colts
Alan Ameche	Fullback	6-1	220	1955-1960 Baltimore Colts
Joe Perry	Fullback	6-0	200	1948-49 San Francisco 49ers (AAFC), 1950-1960 San Francisco 49ers, 1961-62 Baltimore Colts, 1963 San Francisco 49ers
Lou Groza	Kicker	6-3	250	1946-49 Cleveland Browns (AAFC), 1950-59, 1961-67 Cleveland Browns

DEFENSE

Name	Pos.	Ht.	Wt.	Teams
Len Ford	End	6-5	248	1948-49 Los Angeles Dons (AAFC), 1950-57 Cleveland Browns, 1958 Green Bay Packers
Gino Marchetti	End	6-4	245	1952 Dallas Texans, 1953-1964, 1966 Baltimore Colts
Art Donovan	Tackle	6-3	265	1950 Baltimore Colts, 1951 New York Yanks, 1952 Dallas Texans, 1953-1961 Baltimore Colts
Leo Nomellini	Tackle	6-3	264	1950-1963 San Francisco 49ers
Ernie Stautner	Tackle	6-2	235	1950-1963 Pittsburgh Steelers
Joe Fortunato	Linebacker	6-1	225	1955-1966 Chicago Bears
Bill George	Linebacker	6-2	230	1952-1965 Chicago Bears, 1966 Los Angeles Rams
Sam Huff	Linebacker	6-1	230	1956-1963 New York Giants, 1964-67, 1969 Washington Redskins
Joe Schmidt	Linebacker	6-0	222	1953-1965 Detroit Lions
Jack Butler	Halfback	6-1	193	1951-59 Pittsburgh Steelers
Dick (Night Train) Lane	Halfback	6-2	210	1952-53 Los Angeles Rams, 1954-59 Chicago Cardinals, 1960-65 Detroit Lions
Jack Christiansen	Safety	6-1	185	1951-58 Detroit Lions
Yale Lary	Safety	5-11	190	1952-53, 1956-1964 Detroit Lions
Emlen Tunnell	Safety	6-1	200	1948-1958 New York Giants, 1959-1961 Green Bay Packers

ALL-PRO SQUAD OF THE 1960s

Jim Brown of Cleveland after taking a handoff from Frank Ryan, 1964.

The roster chosen by the Hall of Fame Selection Committee

OFFENSE

Name	Pos.	Ht.	Wt.	Teams
Del Shofner	Split End	6-3	190	1957-1960 Los Angeles Rams, 1961-67 New York Giants
Charley Taylor	Split End	6-3	210	1964-1977 Washington Redskins
Gary Collins	Flanker	6-4	215	1962-1967 Cleveland Browns
Boyd Dowler	Flanker	6-5	225	1959-1969 Green Bay Packers, 1971 Washington Redskins
John Mackey	Tight End	6-2	224	1963-1971 Baltimore Colts, 1972 San Diego Chargers
Bob Brown	Tackle	6-4	295	1964-68 Philadelphia Eagles, 1969-1970 Los Angeles Rams, 1971-73 Oakland Raiders
Forrest Gregg	Tackle	6-4	250	1956, 1958-1970 Green Bay Packers, 1971 Dallas Cowboys
Ralph Neely	Tackle	6-6	265	1965-1977 Dallas Cowboys
Gene Hickerson	Guard	6-3	260	1958-1960, 1962-1973 Cleveland Browns
Jerry Kramer	Guard	6-3	254	1958-1968 Green Bay Packers
Howard Mudd	Guard	6-2	254	1964-69 San Francisco 49ers, 1969-1970 Chicago Bears
Jim Ringo	Center	6-2	230	1953-1963 Green Bay Packers, 1964-67 Philadelphia Eagles
Sonny Jurgensen	Quarterback	6-0	203	1957-1963 Philadelphia Eagles, 1964-1974 Washington Redskins
Bart Starr	Quarterback	6-1	190	1956-1971 Green Bay Packers
Johnny Unitas	Quarterback	6-1	196	1956-1972 Baltimore Colts, 1973 San Diego Chargers
John David Crow	Halfback	6-2	224	1958-59 Chicago Cardinals, 1960-64 St. Louis Cardinals, 1965-68 San Francisco 49ers
Paul Hornung	Halfback	6-2	215	1957-1962, 1964-66 Green Bay Packers
Leroy Kelly	Halfback	6-0	200	1964-1973 Cleveland Browns
Gale Sayers	Halfback	6-0	198	1965-1971 Chicago Bears
Jim Brown	Fullback	6-2	232	1957-1965 Cleveland Browns
Jim Taylor	Fullback	6-0	215	1958-1966 Green Bay Packers, 1967 New Orleans Saints
Jim Bakken	Kicker	6-0	200	1962- St. Louis Cardinals

DEFENSE

Name	Pos.	Ht.	Wt.	Teams
Doug Atkins	End	6-8	270	1953-54 Cleveland Browns, 1955-1966 Chicago Bears, 1967-69 New Orleans Saints
Willie Davis	End	6-3	245	1958-59 Cleveland Browns, 1960-69 Green Bay Packers
David (Deacon) Jones	End	6-5	260	1961-71 Los Angeles Rams, 1972-73 San Diego Chargers, 1974 Washington Redskins
Alex Karras	Tackle	6-2	245	1958-62, 1964-1970 Detroit Lions
Bob Lilly	Tackle	6-5	260	1961-1974 Dallas Cowboys
Merlin Olsen	Tackle	6-5	270	1962-1976 Los Angeles Rams
Dick Butkus	Linebacker	6-3	245	1965-1973 Chicago Bears
Larry Morris	Linebacker	6-2	220	1955-57 Los Angeles Rams, 1959-1965 Chicago Bears, 1966 Atlanta Falcons
Ray Nitschke	Linebacker	6-3	240	1958-1972 Green Bay Packers
Tommy Nobis	Linebacker	6-2	235	1966-1976 Atlanta Falcons
Dave Robinson	Linebacker	6-3	240	1963-1972 Green Bay Packers, 1973-74 Washington Redskins
Herb Adderley	Cornerback	6-0	200	1961-69 Green Bay Packers, 1970-72 Dallas Cowboys
Lem Barney	Cornerback	6-0	202	1967-1977 Detroit Lions
Bobby Boyd	Cornerback	5-10	192	1960-68 Baltimore Colts
Eddie Meador	Safety	5-11	199	1959-1970 Los Angeles Rams
Larry Wilson	Safety	6-0	190	1960-1972 St. Louis Cardinals
Willie Wood	Safety	5-10	160	1960-1971 Green Bay Packers
Don Chandler	Punter	6-2	210	1956-1964 New York Giants, 1965-67 Green Bay Packers

ALL-TIME ALL-PROS

Gale Sayers looks for running room against the 49ers, 1967.

The roster chosen by the Hall of Fame Selection Committee in 1969 in honor of the 50th anniversary of the NFL

OFFENSE

Name	Pos.	Ht.	Wt.	Teams
Don Hutson	Split End	6-1	180	1935-1945 Green Bay Packers
John Mackey	Tight End	6-2	224	1963-1971 Baltimore Colts, 1972 San Diego Chargers
Cal Hubbard	Tackle	6-5	250	1927-28, 1936 New York Giants, 1929-1933, 1935 Green Bay Packers, 1936 Pittsburgh Pirates
Jerry Kramer	Guard	6-3	254	1958-1968 Green Bay Packers
Chuck Bednarik	Center	6-3	230	1949-1962 Philadelphia Eagles
Elroy (Crazylegs) Hirsch	Flanker	6-2	190	1946-48 Chicago Rockets (AAFC), 1949-1957 Los Angeles Rams
Johnny Unitas	Quarterback	6-1	196	1956-1972 Baltimore Colts, 1973 San Diego Chargers
Jim Thorpe	Halfback	6-1	190	1920 Canton Bulldogs, 1921 Cleveland Indians, 1922-23 Oorang Indians, 1923 Toledo Maroons, 1924 Rock Island Independents, 1925 New York Giants, 1926 Canton Bulldogs, 1928 Chicago Cardinals
Gale Sayers	Halfback	6-0	198	1965-1971 Chicago Bears
Jim Brown	Fullback	6-2	232	1957-1965 Cleveland Browns
Lou Groza	Kicker	6-3	250	1946-49 Cleveland Browns (AAFC), 1950-59, 1961-67 Cleveland Browns

DEFENSE

Name	Pos.	Ht.	Wt.	Teams
Gino Marchetti	End	6-4	245	1952 Dallas Texans, 1953-1964, 1966 Baltimore Colts
Leo Nomellini	Tackle	6-3	264	1950-1963 San Francisco 49ers
Ray Nitschke	Linebacker	6-3	240	1958-1972 Green Bay Packers
Dick (Night Train) Lane	Cornerback	6-2	210	1952-53 Los Angeles Rams, 1954-59 Chicago Cardinals, 1960-65 Detroit Lions
Emlen Tunnell	Safety	6-1	200	1949-1958 New York Giants, 1959-1961 Green Bay Packers

ALL-TIME AFL TEAM

Joe Namath of the New York Jets throws a jump pass to Matt Snell, 1965.

Chosen by AFL members of the Hall of Fame Selection Committee

OFFENSE

Name	Pos.	Ht.	Wt.	Teams
Lance Alworth	Flanker	6-0	180	1962-1970 San Diego Chargers, 1971-72 Dallas Cowboys
Don Maynard	End	6-1	179	1958 New York Giants, 1960-62 New York Titans, 1963-1972 New York Jets
Fred Arbanas	Tight End	6-3	240	1962 Dallas Texans, 1963-1970 Kansas City Chiefs
Ron Mix	Tackle	6-4	250	1960 Los Angeles Chargers, 1961-69 San Diego Chargers, 1971 Oakland Raiders
Jim Tyrer	Tackle	6-6	274	1961-62 Dallas Texans, 1963-1973 Kansas City Chiefs, 1974 Washington Redskins
Ed Budde	Guard	6-5	265	1963-1976 Kansas City Chiefs
Billy Shaw	Guard	6-2	258	1961-69 Buffalo Bills
Jim Otto	Center	6-2	248	1960-1974 Oakland Raiders
Joe Namath	Quarterback	6-2	195	1965-1976 New York Jets, 1977 Los Angeles Rams
Clem Daniels	Running Back	6-1	220	1960 Dallas Texans, 1961-67 Oakland Raiders, 1968 San Francisco 49ers
Paul Lowe	Running Back	6-0	205	1960 Los Angeles Chargers, 1961, 1963-68 San Diego Chargers, 1968-69 Kansas City Chiefs
George Blanda	Kicker	6-2	215	1949-1958 Chicago Bears, 1960-66 Houston Oilers, 1967-1975 Oakland Raiders

DEFENSE

Name	Pos.	Ht.	Wt.	Teams
Jerry Mays	End	6-4	252	1961-62 Dallas Texans, 1963-1970 Kansas City Chiefs
Gerry Philbin	End	6-2	245	1964-1972 New York Jets, 1973 Philadelphia Eagles
Houston Antwine	Tackle	6-1	270	1961-1970 Boston Patriots, 1971 New England Patriots
Tom Sestak	Tackle	6-4	260	1962-68 Buffalo Bills
Bobby Bell	Linebacker	6-4	228	1963-1974 Kansas City Chiefs
George Webster	Linebacker	6-4	223	1967-1972 Houston Oilers, 1972-73 Pittsburgh Steelers, 1974-76 New England Patriots
Nick Buoniconti	Linebacker	5-11	220	1962-68 Boston Patriots, 1969- Miami Dolphins
Willie Brown	Cornerback	6-1	190	1963-66 Denver Broncos, 1967- Oakland Raiders
Dave Grayson	Cornerback	5-10	187	1961-62 Dallas Texans, 1963-64 Kansas City Chiefs, 1965-1970 Oakland Raiders
Johnny Robinson	Safety	6-1	205	1960-62 Dallas Texans, 1963-1971 Kansas City Chiefs
George Saimes	Safety	5-11	186	1963-69 Buffalo Bills, 1970-72 Denver Broncos
Jerrel Wilson	Punter	6-2	222	1963-1977 Kansas City Chiefs, 1978 New England Patriots

ALL-PRO SQUAD OF THE 1970s

O.J. Simpson of Buffalo on his way through the Detroit Lions, 1976.

The roster chosen by the Hall of Fame Selection Committee

OFFENSE

Name	Pos.	Ht.	Wt.	Teams
Harold Carmichael	Wide Receiver	6-8	225	1971- Philadelphia Eagles
Drew Pearson	Wide Receiver	6-0	183	1973- Dallas Cowboys
Lynn Swann	Wide Receiver	6-0	180	1974- Pittsburgh Steelers
Paul Warfield	Wide Receiver	6-0	188	1964-1969, 1976-77 Cleveland Browns, 1970-74 Miami Dolphins 1975 Memphis (WFL)
Dave Casper	Tight End	6-4	230	1974-1980 Oakland Raiders, 1980- Houston Oilers
Charlie Sanders	Tight End	6-4	230	1966-1977 Detroit Lions
Dan Dierdorf	Tackle	6-3	288	1971- St. Louis Cardinals
Art Shell	Tackle	6-5	286	1968- Oakland Raiders
Rayfield Wright	Tackle	6-6	260	1967-1979 Dallas Cowboys
Ron Yary	Tackle	6-6	255	1968- Minnesota Vikings
Joe DeLamielleure	Guard	6-3	245	1973-79 Buffalo Bills, 1980- Cleveland Browns
John Hannah	Guard	6-2	265	1973- New England Patriots
Larry Little	Guard	6-1	265	1967-68 San Diego Chargers, 1969-1980 Miami Dolphins
Gene Upshaw	Guard	6-5	255	1967- Oakland Raiders
Jim Langer	Center	6-2	257	1970-1980 Miami Dolphins 1980- Minnesota Vikings
Mike Webster	Center	6-2	255	1974- Pittsburgh Steelers
Terry Bradshaw	Quarterback	6-3	215	1970- Pittsburgh Steelers
Ken Stabler	Quarterback	6-3	215	1970-79 Oakland Raiders, 1980- Houston Oilers
Roger Staubach	Quarterback	6-3	197	1969-1979 Dallas Cowboys
Earl Campbell	Running Back	5-11	224	1978- Houston Oilers
Franco Harris	Running Back	6-3	230	1972- Pittsburgh Steelers
Walter Payton	Running Back	5-10	202	1975- Chicago Bears
O.J. Simpson	Running Back	6-1	216	1969-1977 Buffalo Bills, 1978-79 San Francisco 49ers
Garo Yepremian	Kicker	5-8	175	1966-67 Detroit Lions, 1970-78 Miami Dolphins, 1979 New Orleans Saints, 1980-81 Tampa Bay Buccaneers

DEFENSE

Name	Pos.	Ht.	Wt.	Teams
Carl Eller	End	6-6	247	1964-1978 Minnesota Vikings, 1979 Seattle Seahawks
L.C. Greenwood	End	6-6	245	1969- Pittsburgh Steelers
Harvey Martin	End	6-5	250	1973- Dallas Cowboys
Jack Youngblood	End	6-4	244	1971- Los Angeles Rams
Joe Greene	Tackle	6-4	275	1969-1981 Pittsburgh Steelers
Bob Lilly	Tackle	6-5	260	1961-1974 Dallas Cowboys
Merlin Olsen	Tackle	6-5	270	1962-1978 Los Angeles Rams
Alan Page	Tackle	6-4	245	1967-1978 Minnesota Vikings, 1978-1981 Chicago Bears
Bobby Bell	Linebacker	6-4	228	1963-1974 Kansas City Chiefs
Robert Brazile	Linebacker	6-4	238	1975- Houston Oilers
Dick Butkus	Linebacker	6-3	245	1965-1973 Chicago Bears
Jack Ham	Linebacker	6-1	225	1969-1973 Baltimore Colts
Ted Hendricks	Linebacker	6-7	225	1969-1973 Baltimore Colts, 1974 Green Bay Packers, 1975- Oakland Raiders
Jack Lambert	Linebacker	6-4	220	1974- Pittsburgh Steelers
Willie Brown	Cornerback	6-1	190	1963-66 Denver Broncos, 1967-1978 Oakland Raiders
Jimmy Johnson	Cornerback	6-2	185	1961-1976 San Francisco 49ers
Roger Wehrli	Cornerback	6-0	190	1969- St. Louis Cardinals
Louis Wright	Cornerback	6-2	200	1975- Denver Broncos
Dick Anderson	Safety	6-2	196	1968-1977 Miami Dolphins
Cliff Harris	Safety	6-1	192	1970-79 Dallas Cowboys
Ken Houston	Safety	6-3	198	1967-1972 Houston Oilers, 1973-1980 Washington Redskins
Larry Wilson	Safety	6-0	190	1960-1973 St. Louis Cardinals
Ray Guy	Punter	6-3	195	1973- Oakland Raiders

The Hall of Fame

The Pro Football Hall of Fame in Canton, Ohio.

Herb Adderley

Cornerback. 6-1, 200. Born in Philadelphia, Pennsylvania, June 8, 1939. Michigan State. Inducted in 1980. 1961-69 Green Bay Packers, 1970-72 Dallas Cowboys.

Herb Adderley came out of Michigan State in 1961 as a first-round draft choice with a reputation as an offensive performer. Though he was switched to defense in the NFL, Adderley did compile some impressive offensive figures for a cornerback. Of his six interceptions in 1965, he returned three for touchdowns, which stood as an NFL single-season record until 1971. Counting kickoff returns and interceptions, Adderley scored nine touchdowns. He played in five consecutive Pro Bowls (1963-67) and was named all-pro four times. While with the Packers he played in Super Bowls I and II. He announced his retirement following the 1969 season, a year in which he led the NFL in interception return yardage, but decided to continue playing after he was traded to the Dallas Cowboys. He played three years with Dallas and appeared in Super Bowls V and VI.

INTERCEPTIONS

Year	Team	No.	Yards	Avg.	Long	TD
1961	Green Bay	1	9	9.0	9	0
1962	Green Bay	7	132	18.9	50t	1
1963	Green Bay	5	86	17.2	39	0
1964	Green Bay	4	56	14.0	35	0
1965	Green Bay	6	175	29.2	44	3
1966	Green Bay	4	125	31.3	68t	1
1967	Green Bay	4	16	4.0	12t	1
1968	Green Bay	3	27	9.0	17	0
1969	Green Bay	5	169	33.8	80t	1
1970	Dallas	3	69	23.0	30	0
1971	Dallas	6	182	30.3	46	0
1972	Dallas	0	0	0.0	0	0
Totals		48	1,066	22.2	80t	7

KICKOFF RETURNS

120, 3,080 Yards, 25.7 Avg., 103 Long, 2 TD

Doug Atkins

Defensive end. 6-8, 275. Born in Humboldt, Tennessee, May 8, 1930. Tennessee. Inducted in 1982. 1953-54 Cleveland Browns, 1955-1966 Chicago Bears, 1967-69 New Orleans Saints.

Only one lineman (Jim Marshall, 1960-1979) in the history of the NFL played more than the 17 seasons completed by Doug Atkins. Few played as well. One of only a handful of stars of the 1950s and 1960s who wouldn't be undersize by today's standards, he combined strength, size, skill, agility, and aggressiveness. Atkins was a relentless pass rusher, often hurdling blockers to get to the quarterback. He was equally as strong against the running game. Atkins, who originally attended college on a basketball scholarship, was an all-pro in 1960, 1961, and 1963 (the last year the Bears won the NFL championship). He was named to the Pro Bowl eight times in a nine-year span (1958-1966) and was selected as the outstanding lineman of the 1959 game. Thought to be near the end of his career when traded to the expansion New Orleans Saints in 1967, Atkins turned in three strong seasons before retiring. At that time, his 205 games were second only to kicker-tackle Lou Groza's 216 in the NFL length of service record column.

Lance Alworth

Flanker. 6-0, 184. Born in Houston, Texas, August 3, 1940. Arkansas. Inducted in 1978. 1962-1970 San Diego Chargers, 1971-72 Dallas Cowboys.

Lance Alworth was the first American Football League player to be inducted into the Hall of Fame. An All-America halfback at Arkansas, he was drafted by the Oakland Raiders in 1962 and immediately traded to the Chargers for three players. Alworth, nicknamed "Bambi" because of his boyish looks, speed, grace, and leaping ability, owns an NFL record for gaining more than 1,000 yards receiving in seven consecutive seasons. He was the AFL's leading receiver three times (1966, 1968-69). With San Diego (from 1962-69) he caught passes in 96 consecutive games, surpassing Hall of Fame member Don Hutson's NFL record of 95 games (the record has since been broken). In nine years with the Chargers he played on one AFL championship team (1963) and two Western Division titlists (1964-65). With Dallas, he played in Super Bowl VI, which Dallas won 24-3 against Miami.

RECEIVING

Year	Team	No.	Yards	Avg.	Long	TD
1962	San Diego	10	226	22.6	67	3
1963	San Diego	61	1,205	19.8	85	11
1964	San Diego	61	1,235	20.2	82	13
1965	San Diego	69	1,602	23.2	85	14
1966	San Diego	73	1,383	18.9	78	13
1967	San Diego	52	1,010	19.4	71t	9
1968	San Diego	68	1,312	19.3	80t	10
1969	San Diego	64	1,003	15.7	76t	4
1970	San Diego	35	608	17.4	80t	4
1971	Dallas	34	487	14.3	26	2
1972	Dallas	15	195	13.0	30	2
Totals		542	10,266	18.9	85	85

RUSHING

24 Att., 129 Yards, 5.4 Avg., 35 Long, 2 TD

Morris (Red) Badgro

End. 6-0, 190. Born in Orilla, Washington, December 1, 1902. USC. Inducted in 1981. 1927 New York Yankees, 1930-35 New York Giants, 1936 Brooklyn Dodgers.

NFL players in Red Badgro's era were sixty-minute men. They played on offense, defense, and special teams. Their statistics wouldn't elicit a second look in most cases today, but there were those who were a cut above in the league's pioneer days. Badgro was one of them. Badgro was a versatile athlete, to be sure. He went to USC on a basketball scholarship. His pro football career began in 1927 with the New York Yankees and was renewed with the Giants in 1930 after two years in professional baseball. A two-way performer who also was a rugged blocker, Badgro played his way into the record books as a receiver. He scored the first touchdown in the first official NFL Championship Game (1933). Badgro tied for the league lead in receptions in 1934 with 16, a respectable total for the era. He was on the all-pro teams in 1930-31 and 1933-34.

Cliff Battles

Halfback. 6-1, 201. Born in Akron, Ohio, May 1, 1910. Died April 27, 1981. West Virginia Wesleyan. Inducted in 1968. 1932 Boston Braves, 1933-36 Boston Redskins, 1937 Washington Redskins.

Cliff Battles played only six seasons in the NFL but he gained 3,542 yards for the Braves and Redskins. Big and fast, he was the first NFL runner to gain more than 200 yards in a game. A Phi Beta Kappa scholar, he was one of the first professional stars to come from a small college, West Virginia Wesleyan. His final season, 1937, was a memorable one in which he gained 874 yards, won his second rushing title, and earned all-pro honors for the third time in six years.

RUSHING

Year	Team	Att.	Yards	Avg.	TD
1932	Boston Braves	148	576	3.9	3
1933	Boston Redskins	136	737	5.0	3
1934	Boston Redskins	96	511	5.0	6
1935	Boston Redskins	67	230	3.4	1
1936	Boston Redskins	176	614	3.5	5
1937	Washington	216	874	4.0	5
Totals		839	3,542	4.2	23

SCORING

31 TD, 1 FG, 1 PAT, 190 Points

Sammy Baugh

Quarterback. 6-2, 180. Born in Temple, Texas, March 17, 1914. Texas Christian. Inducted in 1963. 1937-1952 Washington Redskins.

In his 16-year career in the pros, Sammy Baugh led the league in passing six times. His passing effi-ciency percentage of 70.33 in 1945 is an NFL record. He held virtually every passing record when he re-tired. All of that is even more remarkable when you consider that he came to pro football from Texas Christian as a single-wing tailback and had to make a transition to T-formation quarterback halfway through his career. Baugh set the NFL record for ca-reer punting average, 45.1, made 28 interceptions while playing safety in the one-platoon era, and in 1943 led the league in passing, punting, and interceptions.

PASSING

Year	Team	Att.	Comp.	Yards	TD	Int.
1937	Washington.	171	81	1,127	8	14
1938	Washington.	128	63	853	5	11
1939	Washington.	96	53	518	6	9
1940	Washington.	177	111	1,367	12	10
1941	Washington.	193	106	1,236	10	19
1942	Washington.	225	132	1,524	16	11
1943	Washington.	239	133	1,754	23	19
1944	Washington.	146	82	849	4	8
1945	Washington.	182	128	1,669	11	4
1946	Washington.	161	87	1,163	8	17
1947	Washington.	354	210	2,938	25	15
1948	Washington.	315	185	2,599	22	23
1949	Washington.	255	145	1,903	18	14
1950	Washington.	166	90	1,130	11	11
1951	Washington.	154	67	1,104	7	17
1952	Washington.	33	20	152	2	1
Totals	. . . .	2,995	1,693	21,886	187	203

PUNTING

Year	Team	No.	Yards	Avg.	Long	Blk.
1937	Washington.					
1938	Washington.					
1939	Washington.	26		38.0	69	
1940	Washington.	35		51.3	85	
1941	Washington.	30		48.7	75	0
1942	Washington.	37		46.6	74	0
1943	Washington.	50		45.9	81	3
1944	Washington.	44		40.6	76	1
1945	Washington.	33		43.3	57	0
1946	Washington.	33		45.1	60	0
1947	Washington.	35		43.7	67	2
1948	Washington.	0	0	0.0	0	0
1949	Washington.	1	53	53.0	53	0
1950	Washington.	9		39.1	58	1
1951	Washington.	4		55.3	58	0
1952	Washington.	1	48	48.0	48	0
Totals	. . . .	338	15,245	45.1	85	7

RUSHING
324 Att., 325 Yards, 1.0 Avg., 41 Long, 9 TD
INTERCEPTIONS
28, 407 Yards, 14.5 Avg., 74 Long, 0 TD
PUNT RETURNS
11, 99 Yards, 9.0 Avg., 20 Long, 0 TD
SCORING
9 TD, 1 PAT, 55 Points

Chuck Bednarik

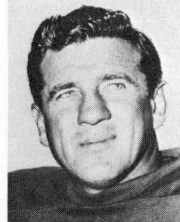

Center-linebacker. 6-3, 230. Born in Bethlehem, Pennsylvania, May 1, 1925. Pennsylvania. Inducted in 1967. 1949-1962 Philadel-phia Eagles.

Pro football was a highly specialized game by 1960 but Chuck Bednarik, at 35, played both offensively and defensively in a string of key games that helped the Eagles into the NFL title game, where he played over 50 minutes. His tackle of Jim Taylor, nine yards short of the goal line, preserved Philadelphia's win over Green Bay, on the game's final play. In 14 sea-sons, the durable Bednarik missed only three games. He won all-pro honors both as a center and a line-backer. A two-time All-America at Pennsylvania, Bednarik was the NFL's "bonus" draft choice in 1949. He played in eight Pro Bowls, and was hon-ored as player of the game in the 1954 game.

Bert Bell

Commissioner. Team own-er. Born in Philadelphia, Pennsylvania, February 25, 1895. Died October 11, 1959. Pennsylvania. Induct-ed in 1963. 1933-1940 Phila-delphia Eagles, 1941-46 Pittsburgh Steelers.

Bert Bell, who was elect-ed Commissioner in 1946, saw the NFL through a bitter and costly power strug-gle with the rival All-America Football Conference. Bell provided strong leadership until his death in the grandstands at an Eagles-Steelers game in 1959. He was a football man most of his life, having played at Pennsylvania and later coaching there and at other schools. Bell, who took charge of the newly formed Philadelphia Eagles in 1933, sought to increase com-petitive balance in the NFL by proposing the college player draft in 1935. After serving the Eagles as gen-eral manager, ticket manager, publicity director, and head coach, he joined the Steelers as co-owner and head coach in 1941. In later work as Commissioner he laid down strong anti-gambling policies and insti-tuted the home television "blackout" of NFL games.

Raymond Berry

End. 6-2. 187. Born in Cor-pus Christi, Texas, February 27, 1933. Southern Meth-odist. Inducted in 1973. 1955-1967 Baltimore Colts.

Raymond Berry proved that dedication, concen-tration, and long hours of practice can compensate for limited physical skills. Berry worked with quarterback Johnny Unitas at Bal-timore to form a remarkable passing combination. When he retired he was the leading receiver in NFL history. His 12 receptions in the memorable 1958 sud-den death Championship Game are still a record. He used gadgets such as tinted goggles to gain an advan-tage over his opponents and he practiced long after regular sessions were over; he had average size and speed. His play was much more than average, how-ever. He and Unitas perfected the sideline pass. In 13 seasons he fumbled only once. A twentieth-round draft choice, he was on all-pro teams three times and played in five Pro Bowls.

RECEIVING

Year	Team	No.	Yards	Avg.	Long	TD
1955	Baltimore	13	205	15.8	45	0
1956	Baltimore	37	601	16.2	54	2
1957	Baltimore	47	800	17.0	67t	6
1958	Baltimore	56	794	14.2	54	9
1959	Baltimore	66	959	14.5	55t	14
1960	Baltimore	74	1,298	17.5	70t	10
1961	Baltimore	75	873	11.6	44	0
1962	Baltimore	51	687	13.5	37	3
1963	Baltimore	44	703	16.0	64t	3
1964	Baltimore	43	663	15.4	46	6
1965	Baltimore	58	739	12.7	40	7
1966	Baltimore	56	786	14.0	40t	7
1967	Baltimore	11	167	15.2	40	1
Totals	. . . .	631	9,275	14.7	70t	68

SCORING
68 TD, 408 Points

Charles W. Bidwill, Sr.

Team owner. Born in Chi-cago, Illinois, September 16, 1895. Died April 19, 1947. Loyola of Chicago. Inducted in 1967. 1933-1947 Chicago Cardinals.

Charles Bidwill's interest in pro football preceded his ownership of the Chicago Cardinals by some years. His financial support enabled George Halas to retain ownership of the Chicago Bears during the early days of the Depression. Bidwill took over the Cardinals in 1933. The team lost games but he kept his faith in the sport. After World War II, Bidwill signed Charley Trippi to a $100,000 contract to complete a "dream backfield" that also included Paul Christman, Mar-shall Goldberg, and Pat Harder. But Bidwill wasn't around to see his team win the NFL championship in 1947. He died in April of that year. The ownership of the team passed to his wife, Violet, and eventually to his sons, Charles, Jr., and Bill. A non-conformist, Bidwill was often called "Blue Shirt" Bidwill be-cause he spurned traditional white shirts and busi-nessmen's shoes in favor of blue shirts and high boots.

George Blanda

Quarterback-kicker. 6-2, 215. Born in Youngwood, Pennsylvania, September 17, 1927. Kentucky. Inducted in 1981. 1949-1958 Chicago Bears, 1950 Baltimore Colts, 1960-66 Houston Oilers, 1967-1976 Oakland Raiders.

George Blanda became a folk hero even before his selection into the Hall of Fame. At age 43 (1970), he passed or kicked the Oakland Raiders to a final-second tie and four last-minute victories in five successive weeks. He went on to play five more seasons, becoming the oldest player in NFL history. Blanda's career lasted 26 seasons, an all-time NFL service record. After sitting out the 1959 season, Blanda signed with Houston for the AFL's first season and led the Oilers to the 1960 and 1961 championships. He was later traded to Oakland and kicked 201 consecutive extra points between 1967-1971.

SCORING

Year	Team	TD	FG	PAT	Points
1949	Chi. Bears	1	7-15	0-0	27
1950	Baltimore	0	0-0	0-0	0
	Chi. Bears	0	6-15	0-0	18
1951	Chi. Bears	0	6-17	26-26	44
1952	Chi. Bears	1	6-25	30-30	54
1953	Chi. Bears	0	7-20	27-27	48
1954	Chi. Bears	0	8-16	23-23	47
1955	Chi. Bears	2	11-16	37-37	82
1956	Chi. Bears	0	12-28	45-47	81
1957	Chi. Bears	1	14-26	23-23	71
1958	Chi. Bears	0	11-23	36-37	69
1959	Did not play pro football				
1960	Houston	4	15-34	46-47	115
1961	Houston	0	16-26	64-65	112
1962	Houston	0	11-26	48-49	81
1963	Houston	0	9-22	39-39	66
1964	Houston	0	13-29	37-38	76
1965	Houston	0	11-21	28-28	61
1966	Houston	0	16-30	39-40	87
1967	Oakland	0	20-30	56-57	116
1968	Oakland	0	21-34	54-54	117
1969	Oakland	0	20-37	45-45	105
1970	Oakland	0	16-29	36-36	84
1971	Oakland	0	15-22	41-42	86
1972	Oakland	0	17-26	44-44	95
1973	Oakland	0	23-33	31-31	100
1974	Oakland	0	11-17	44-46	77
1975	Oakland	0	13-21	44-48	83
Totals		9	335-638	943-959	2,002

PASSING

Year	Team	Att.	Comp.	Yards	TD	Int.
1949	Chi. Bears	21	9	197	0	5
1950	Baltimore	0	0	0	0	0
	Chi. Bears	0	0	0	0	0
1951	Chi. Bears	0	0	0	0	0
1952	Chi. Bears	131	47	664	8	11
1953	Chi. Bears	362	169	2,164	14	23
1954	Chi. Bears	281	131	1,929	15	17
1955	Chi. Bears	97	42	459	4	7
1956	Chi. Bears	69	37	439	7	4
1957	Chi. Bears	19	8	65	0	3
1958	Chi. Bears	7	2	19	0	0
1959	Did not play pro football					
1960	Houston	363	169	2,413	24	22
1961	Houston	362	187	3,330	36	22
1962	Houston	418	197	2,810	27	42
1963	Houston	423	224	3,003	24	25
1964	Houston	505	262	3,287	17	27
1965	Houston	442	186	2,542	20	30
1966	Houston	271	122	1,764	17	21
1967	Oakland	38	15	285	3	3
1968	Oakland	49	30	522	6	2
1969	Oakland	13	6	73	2	1
1970	Oakland	55	29	461	6	5
1971	Oakland	58	32	378	4	6
1972	Oakland	15	5	77	1	0
1973	Oakland	0	0	0	0	0
1974	Oakland	4	1	28	1	0
1975	Oakland	3	1	11	0	1
Totals		4,007	1,911	26,920	236	277

RUSHING
135 Att., 344 Yards, 2.5 Avg., 19 Long, 9 TD

PUNTING
20, 39.3 Avg., Long 57, 0 Blk.

Jim Brown

Fullback. 6-2, 232. Born in St. Simons, Georgia, February 17, 1936. Syracuse. Inducted in 1971. 1957-1965 Cleveland Browns.

The amazingly durable Jim Brown never missed a game in nine years of NFL play, during which he gained a record 12,312 yards. A player who had the perfect combination of size, speed, and power, Brown is considered by many the finest runner ever in football. He led the NFL in rushing in eight of his nine seasons, made an all-pro team eight times, and played in nine straight Pro Bowls. He scored 756 points, the highest NFL total by a non-kicker. And only twice did he fail to go over the 1,000-yard rushing mark, his first season and 1962, when he played with a severely sprained wrist. The former Syracuse fullback rushed for more than 100 yards a game 58 times, almost half his pro starts. He retired at the top of his game, prior to the 1966 season, to pursue an acting career.

RUSHING

Year	Team	Att.	Yards	Avg.	Long	TD
1957	Cleveland	202	942	4.7	69t	9
1958	Cleveland	257	1,527	5.9	65t	17
1959	Cleveland	290	1,329	4.6	70t	14
1960	Cleveland	215	1,257	5.8	71t	9
1961	Cleveland	305	1,408	4.6	38	8
1962	Cleveland	230	996	4.3	31	13
1963	Cleveland	291	1,863	6.4	80t	12
1964	Cleveland	280	1,446	5.2	71	7
1965	Cleveland	289	1,544	5.3	67	17
Totals		2,359	12,312	5.2	80t	106

RECEIVING

Year	Team	No.	Yards	Avg.	Long	TD
1957	Cleveland	16	55	3.4	12	1
1958	Cleveland	16	138	8.6	46	1
1959	Cleveland	24	190	7.9	25	0
1960	Cleveland	19	204	10.7	37t	2
1961	Cleveland	46	459	10.0	77t	2
1962	Cleveland	47	517	11.0	53t	5
1963	Cleveland	24	268	11.2	83t	3
1964	Cleveland	36	340	9.4	40t	2
1965	Cleveland	34	328	9.6	32t	4
Totals		262	2,499	9.5	83t	20

SCORING
126 TD, 756 Points

Paul Brown

Coach. Born in Norwalk, Ohio, September 7, 1908. Miami, Ohio. Inducted in 1967. 1946-49 Cleveland Browns (AAFC), 1950-1962 Cleveland Browns, 1968-1975 Cincinnati Bengals.

Many of the things that are part of pro football today—full-time coaching staffs, calling plays via messengers, precise pass routes—were either Paul Brown innovations or were raised to a higher level of efficiency by him. Brown was hired by the Cleveland Browns of the newly organized All-America Football Conference in 1945, when he was still coaching at Great Lakes Naval Training Station. He took over in Cleveland in 1946 and the Browns won league championships all four seasons of the AAFC's existence. In 1950, after the AAFC merged with the NFL, Brown and the Browns again won the championship, and they were in the title game the next five seasons. Brown's Cleveland teams won three NFL titles and seven divisional championships in 13 seasons. Only once—the year after Otto Graham retired—did a Paul Brown Cleveland team finish below .500. Brown began a second successful coaching career with the Cincinnati Bengals in 1968, a year after his induction into the Hall of Fame, and retired as a coach after the 1975 season.

Roosevelt Brown

Offensive tackle. 6-3, 255. Born in Charlottesville, Virginia, October 20, 1932. Morgan State. Inducted in 1975. 1953-1965 New York Giants.

Almost any biography of Roosevelt (Rosey) Brown mentions him as one of the NFL's most notable "sleeper" draft choices. He was picked on the twenty-seventh round in 1953. He became a starter his first season and remained so for 13 years. From 1956 through 1963, Brown was an all-pro tackle and played in nine Pro Bowl games. The Giants made excellent use of Brown's outstanding speed by designing special plays that used him as a pulling blocker from his tackle position. Prior to this, pulling was done mainly by offensive guards. Brown was also used defensively on goal-line stands. Phlebitis forced his retirement in 1966.

Dick Butkus

Linebacker. 6-3, 245. Born in Chicago, Illinois, December 9, 1942. Illinois. Inducted in 1979. 1965-1973 Chicago Bears.

When he was 10 years old, Dick Butkus decided on his future occupation—pro football player. He pursued his goal through an all-state scholastic career and an All-America collegiate career at Illinois. Butkus joined the Bears as a first-round draft choice in 1965—the same season that Gale Sayers, also a member of the Hall of Fame, was another Bears first-round selection. Butkus played in eight Pro Bowl games in his nine-year career, which was shortened considerably by injuries. He also was named to the all-pro team six times. Butkus is considered by many to have been the game's premier middle linebacker and most intimidating player. The 25 opponents' fumbles Butkus recovered during his career is the second-highest total in league history.

Tony Canadeo

Halfback. 5-11, 195. Born in Chicago, Illinois, May 5, 1919. Gonzaga. Inducted in 1974. 1941-44, 1946-1952 Green Bay Packers.

Tony Canadeo was a versatile, two-way performer. He ran, passed, punted, returned punts and kickoffs, caught passes, and played defense. He was adept at all of them. Taking all categories into account, Canadeo averaged 75 yards a game over his 11 seasons. Before entering the service, he was the Packers' leading passer. Upon his return, he was their heavy-duty runner. In 1949, he became only the third man in NFL history to rush for more than 1,000 yards in a season; he rushed for 4,197 yards in his career. A fiery competitor, Canadeo refused to let tacklers help him to his feet. Art Daley, a Green Bay writer, said Canadeo even thumbed his nose at opponents.

RUSHING

Year	Team	Att.	Yards	Avg.	Long	TD
1941	Green Bay	43	137	3.2	16	3
1942	Green Bay	89	272	3.1	50	3
1943	Green Bay	94	489	5.2	35	3
1944	Green Bay	31	149	4.8	34	0
1945	Military service					
1946	Green Bay	122	476	3.9	27	0
1947	Green Bay	103	464	4.5	35	2
1948	Green Bay	123	589	4.8	49	4
1949	Green Bay	208	1,052	5.1	54	4
1950	Green Bay	93	247	2.6	15	4
1951	Green Bay	54	131	2.4	15	1
1952	Green Bay	65	191	2.9	35	2
Totals		1,025	4,197	4.1	54	26

PASSING
268 Att., 108 Comp., 1,642 Yards, 16 TD, 20 Int.
RECEIVING
69, 579 Yards, 8.4 Avg., 46 Long, 5 TD
INTERCEPTIONS
9, 129 Yards, 14.3 Avg., 35 Long, 0 TD
PUNTING
45, 1,669 Yards, 37.1 Avg., 62 Long, 0 Blk.
PUNT RETURNS
46, 513 Yards, 11.2 Avg., 26 Long, 0 TD
KICKOFF RETURNS
75, 1,736 Yards, 23.1 Avg., 55 Long, 0 TD
SCORING
31 TD, 186 Points

Tony Canadeo eludes Ken McAfee in Green Bay's 29-20 victory over Chicago, 1947.

Joe Carr

NFL President. Born in Columbus, Ohio, October 22, 1880. Died May 20, 1939. Did not attend college. Inducted in 1963. President, 1921-1939 National Football League.

A sports promoter and sportswriter, Joe Carr was involved in pro football long before there was an NFL. He founded the Columbus Panhandles in 1904. The Panhandles later featured the six legendary Nesser brothers. Carr was also a pro basketball and minor league baseball executive. In 1921 he became president of the American Professional Football Association, which changed its name to the National Football League in 1922. During his tenure, the league moved from sandlots and rickety ballparks to the nation's largest stadiums. Carr was a pioneer in other areas, too. He introduced the standard player contract and barred collegiate players from signing with NFL teams until their class graduated. As president, he set down guidelines followed in later years by other NFL leaders. His administration, regarded as strict but fair, ended with his death in 1939.

Guy Chamberlin

End. Coach. 6-2, 210. Born in Blue Springs, Nebraska, January 16, 1894. Died April 4, 1967. Nebraska. Inducted in 1965. 1920 Decatur Staleys, 1921 Chicago Staleys, 1922-23 Canton Bulldogs, 1924 Cleveland Bulldogs, 1925-26 Frankford Yellowjackets, 1927-28 Chicago Cardinals.

Wherever Guy Chamberlin went, victories seemed to follow. He established a reputation as a fine pass-catcher at a time when passing wasn't commonplace. And he also turned end-around plays into long gainers. It was said he was never hurt, as a collegian or pro. In 1920 and 1921 Chamberlin was paired with another of football's biggest names —George Halas—at end for the Decatur and Chicago Staleys. The ex-Nebraska All-America served as a part-time player as well as a coach from 1922-26, when he helped win four NFL championships with three different teams—Canton, Cleveland, and Frankford. At Cleveland in 1924, Chamberlin was one of the first coaches to institute planned, daily practices. His coaching record was 56-14-5. Chamberlin was named as an end on the all-decade team of the 1920s.

Jack Christiansen

Defensive Back. 6-1, 185. Born in Sublette, Kansas, December 20, 1928. Colorado State. Inducted in 1970. 1951-58 Detroit Lions.

As a rookie in 1951, Jack Christiansen set an NFL record by returning four punts for touchdowns. The record stood alone until Denver's Rick Upchurch tied it in 1976. Christiansen's two touchdowns in a single game on punt returns in 1951 set another record that has since been tied. In eight years, Christiansen scored a record eight times on punt returns. He led the NFL in interceptions in 1953 and 1957 on the way to a career total of 46. The Lions' secondary was called "Chris's Crew" after him. He was one of the first defensive specialists to become a dangerous weapon. Opponents passed and punted the ball away from him.

INTERCEPTIONS

Year	Team	No.	Yards	Avg.	Long	TD
1951	Detroit	2	53	26.5	53	0
1952	Detroit	2	47	23.5	32	0
1953	Detroit	12	238	19.8	92t	1
1954	Detroit	8	84	10.5	30t	1
1955	Detroit	3	49	16.3	29	0
1956	Detroit	8	109	13.6	33	0
1957	Detroit	10	137	13.7	52	1
1958	Detroit	1	0	0.0	0	0
Totals		46	717	15.6	92t	3

PUNT RETURNS

Year	Team	No.	Yards	Avg.	Long	TD
1951	Detroit	18	343	19.1	89t	4
1952	Detroit	15	322	21.5	79t	2
1953	Detroit	8	22	2.8	10	0
1954	Detroit	23	225	9.8	61t	1
1955	Detroit	12	87	7.3	42	0
1956	Detroit	6	73	12.2	66t	1
1957	Detroit	3	12	4.0	8	0
1958	Detroit	0	0	0.0	0	0
Totals		85	1,084	12.8	89t	8

KICKOFF RETURNS
59, 1,329 Yards, 22.5 Avg., 46 Long, 0 TD

Earl (Dutch) Clark

Quarterback. 6-0, 185. Born in Fowler, Colorado, October 11, 1906. Died August 5, 1978. Colorado College. Inducted in 1963. 1931-32 Portsmouth Spartans, 1934-38 Detroit Lions.

Earl (Dutch) Clark was a scoring threat from anywhere, in any manner. As a tailback in the single-wing, he was a legitimate triple-threat. He scored by running, passing, and kicking. He was the last of the NFL's dropkickers. He was the Lions' player-coach in 1937 and 1938. Clark, the only All-America ever produced at Colorado College, made an all-pro team in six of his seven seasons. He led NFL scorers three times—in 1932, 1935, and 1936.

RUSHING

Year	Team	Att.	Yards	Avg.	TD
1931	Portsmouth Spartans				
1932	Portsmouth Spartans	111	461	4.2	2
1933	Did not play football				
1934	Detroit	123	763	6.2	6
1935	Detroit	120	412	3.4	4
1936	Detroit	123	628	5.1	6
1937	Detroit	96	468	4.9	5
1938	Detroit	7	25	3.6	0
Totals		580	2,757	4.8	23

PASSING
197 Att., 97 Comp., 1,235 Yards, 8 TD, 14 Int.

SCORING
42 TD, 15 FG, 72 PAT, 369 Points

Jack Christiansen (24) and Joe Schmidt move in on Pete Pihos, 1953.

George Connor

Tackle-linebacker. 6-3, 240. Born in Chicago, Illinois, January 1, 1925. Holy Cross, Notre Dame. Inducted in 1975. 1948-1955 Chicago Bears.

George Connor was an All-America at both Holy Cross and Notre Dame. He was all-pro at three positions: offensive tackle, defensive tackle, and linebacker. Connor, a native of Chicago, played for Holy Cross in 1942-43 and for Notre Dame in 1946-47. He was drafted by the New York Giants in 1946, when his original Holy Cross class graduated. The rights to him were traded by the Giants in 1948 to the Boston Yanks for quarterback Paul Governali, and the Yanks in turn traded the rights to Connor to the Bears for end-tackle Mike Yarmaluk. Connor joined the Bears as a two-way tackle. But in 1949 the Bears moved him to linebacker, where he became one of the prototypes for the big, fast, agile, and aggressive men who play that position in today's NFL. He was strong enough to meet and stop the power plays smaller linebackers couldn't handle, and he also was an intelligent player who was good at reading plays. In two years, he made all-pro teams on both offense and defense, and he played in four Pro Bowls. A leg injury ended his career at age 30.

Jimmy Conzelman

Quarterback. Coach. Team owner. 6-0, 180. Born in St. Louis, Missouri, March 6, 1898. Died July 31, 1970. Washington, Mo. Inducted in 1964. 1920 Decatur Staleys, 1921-22 Rock Island Independents, 1923-24 Milwaukee Badgers; owner-coach, 1925-26 Detroit Panthers; coach, 1927-28 Detroit Panthers; coach, 1929-1930 Providence Steamroller; coach, 1940-42, 1946-48 Chicago Cardinals.

As a collegian Jimmy Conzelman played in the 1919 Rose Bowl. He then was a teammate of George Halas at Great Lakes Naval Training Station. As a two-way professional player, he starred with five teams, including Halas's 1920 Decatur Staleys, before a knee injury ended his playing career in 1928. That season, as player-coach, he led Providence to an NFL championship. He owned and coached the Detroit Panthers in the mid-1920s. As a non-playing coach, he took a floundering Chicago Cardinals team and won two divisional titles, and in 1947, an NFL championship. He was also an actor, author, executive, songwriter, and orator.

Willie Davis

Defensive end. 6-3, 245. Born in Lisbon, Louisiana, July 24, 1934. Grambling. Inducted in 1981. 1958-59 Cleveland Browns, 1960-69 Green Bay Packers.

The early part of Willie Davis's career showed no indication of eventual enshrinement in the Hall of Fame. He was drafted on the fifteenth round by Cleveland in 1956 as a guard out of Grambling. After three weeks in training camp he was drafted again, this time by the U.S. Army. After two years in the service, Davis returned to the Browns and played two seasons as a defensive end; he also played at offensive tackle. In 1960, he was traded to the Packers and started his march to the Hall. He played 10 years at one position—defensive end—as the Packers became the NFL's dominant team. Davis earned all-pro honors five times (1962, 1964-67) in a six-year span and was selected to play in five consecutive Pro Bowls (1964-68).

Art Donovan

Defensive tackle. 6-3, 265. Born in Bronx, New York, June 5, 1925. Boston College. Inducted in 1968. 1950 Baltimore Colts, 1951 New York Yanks, 1952 Dallas Texans, 1953-1961 Baltimore Colts.

Art Donovan didn't come into the NFL until he was 25, because of Marine Corps service. After playing on mediocre teams his first three seasons he became a star on the Colts' championship teams. He was a complete defensive lineman, outstanding against both the run and the pass. Donovan was on all-pro teams four times and appeared in five Pro Bowls. His father was a boxing referee and his grandfather was a middleweight boxing champion.

John (Paddy) Driscoll

Quarterback. 5-11, 160. Born in Evanston, Illinois, January 11, 1896. Died June 29, 1968. Northwestern. Inducted in 1965. 1920 Decatur Staleys, 1920-25 Chicago Cardinals, 1926-29 Chicago Bears.

Paddy Driscoll was a teammate of George Halas at Great Lakes Naval Training Station during World War I and joined Halas on the Decatur Staleys in 1920. Driscoll then switched to the Chicago Cardinals, where he became a fine all-around player, particularly adept at kicking. He was an accurate dropkicker and placekicker who was booed for punting away from Red Grange in Grange's first appearance as a pro. He also was a slick broken-field runner and an accurate passer throwing the large football of his day. Driscoll's contract was sold to the Bears in 1926. He took over as coach of the Bears in 1956 and 1957, winning a divisional championship his first year. He stayed with the team in various jobs until his death in 1968.

Bill Dudley

Halfback. 5-10, 176. Born in Bluefield, Virginia, December 24, 1921. Virginia. Inducted in 1966. 1942, 1945-46 Pittsburgh Steelers, 1947-49 Detroit Lions, 1950-51, 1953 Washington Redskins.

"Bullet Bill" Dudley threw sidearm passes. He got most of his rushing yardage through effective use of blockers rather than his own speed. He didn't use any approach steps as a placekicker. He simply stood where the ball was to be placed down, swung his right leg back, and then forward as he kicked. Dudley led the NFL in rushing, interceptions, and punt returns in 1946. Dudley was the NFL's first draft choice in 1942 after an All-America career at Virginia, and he rushed for a league-leading 696 yards his first season. Dudley divided his nine-year pro career into three segments with Pittsburgh, Detroit, and Washington, and he remains among the most popular players ever to perform in those cities. He gained 8,147 combined yards on rushing, receiving, and returns.

RUSHING

Year	Team	Att.	Yards	Avg.	Long	TD
1942	Pittsburgh	162	696	4.3	66	5
1943	Military service					
1944	Military service					
1945	Pittsburgh	57	204	3.5	32	3
1946	Pittsburgh	146	604	4.1	41	3
1947	Detroit	80	302	3.8	28	2
1948	Detroit	33	97	2.9	11	0
1949	Detroit	125	402	3.2	26	3
1950	Washington	66	339	5.1	27	1
1951	Washington	91	398	4.4	40	2
1952	Did not play football					
1953	Washington	5	15	3.0	7	0
Totals		765	3,057	4.0	66	19

PUNT RETURNS

Year	Team	No.	Yards	Avg.	Long	TD
1942	Pittsburgh	20	271	13.5	47	0
1943	Military service					
1944	Military service					
1945	Pittsburgh	5	20	4.0	6	0
1946	Pittsburgh	27	385	14.2	52	0
1947	Detroit	11	182	16.5	84t	1
1948	Detroit	8	67	8.4	18	0
1949	Detroit	11	199	18.1	67t	1
1950	Washington	12	185	15.4	96t	1
1951	Washington	22	172	7.8	27	0
1952	Did not play football					
1953	Washington	8	34	4.3	16	0
Totals		124	1,515	12.2	96t	3

PASSING
222 Att., 81 Comp., 985 Yards, 6 TD, 17 Int.
RECEIVING
123, 1,383 Yards, 11.2 Avg., 18 TD
INTERCEPTIONS
23, 459 Yards, 20.0 Avg., 80 Long, 2 TD
PUNTING
191, 38.2 Avg., 4 Blk.
KICKOFF RETURNS
78, 1,743 Yards, 22.3 Avg., 1 TD
SCORING
44 TD, 33 FG, 121 PAT, 484 Points

Glen (Turk) Edwards

Tackle, 6-2, 260. Born in Mold, Washington, September 28, 1907. Died January 10, 1973. Washington State. Inducted in 1969. 1932 Boston Braves, 1933-36 Boston Redskins, 1937-1940 Washington Redskins.

At 260 pounds Glen (Turk) Edwards was bigger than most linemen of his time. He made all-pro teams in 1932, 1933, 1936, and 1937. Edwards was outstanding both as an offensive blocker and as a defender, largely because of his unusual quickness and agility. An All-America and Rose Bowl star at Washington State, Edwards played for $150 a game when he joined the Boston Braves in 1932. His career ended in a strange way. After meeting Mel Hein—his former Washington State teammate and the New York Giants' center and captain—at the center of the field for a pregame coin toss, Edwards turned to go back to the bench. But his knee collapsed and he never played again.

Weeb Ewbank

Coach. Born in Richmond, Indiana, May 6, 1907. Miami, Ohio. Inducted in 1978. 1954-1962 Baltimore Colts, 1963-73 New York Jets.

Weeb Ewbank is the only head coach to win world championships in both the National Football League and the American Football League. His title teams were the 1958 and 1959 Baltimore Colts and the 1968 New York Jets, who defeated the Colts in Super Bowl III. Ewbank, one of many NFL coaches from Miami, Ohio's "Cradle of Coaches," began his career with the Cleveland Browns in 1949 as an assistant under Paul Brown. He took part in the development of two of the game's most renowned quarterbacks, Johnny Unitas and Joe Namath. Although his overall record was only one game above .500 (130-129-7), Ewbank undertook and completed successful rebuilding projects with both franchises.

Tom Fears

End. 6-2, 215. Born in Los Angeles, California, December 3, 1923. Santa Clara, UCLA. Inducted in 1970. 1948-1956 Los Angeles Rams.

Tom Fears came into pro football projected as a defensive specialist, but in each of his first three seasons, he led the NFL in pass receiving. In 1950, Fears caught 84 passes, a record that stood for a decade. His 18 catches in one game against the Packers that season is still a record. In his career, Fears, who was not only big and fast but ran precise patterns, caught 400 passes for 5,397 yards and 38 touchdowns. He made three touchdown catches as the Rams won a divisional playoff game in 1950, and in 1951 he scored on a 73-yard pass-and-run play as Los Angeles beat the Cleveland Browns and won its only NFL title.

RECEIVING

Year	Team	No.	Yards	Avg.	Long	TD
1948	Los Angeles	51	698	13.7	80t	4
1949	Los Angeles	77	1,013	13.2	51t	9
1950	Los Angeles	84	1,116	13.3	53t	7
1951	Los Angeles	32	528	16.5	54	3
1952	Los Angeles	48	600	12.5	36	6
1953	Los Angeles	23	278	12.1	31	4
1954	Los Angeles	36	546	15.2	43	3
1955	Los Angeles	44	569	12.9	31	2
1956	Los Angeles	5	49	9.8	18	0
Totals		400	5,397	13.5	80t	38

SCORING
39 TD, 1 FG, 12 PAT, 249 Points

Ray Flaherty

Coach. Born in Spokane, Washington, September 1, 1904. Gonzaga. Inducted in 1976. 1926 Los Angeles Wildcats (AFL), 1927 New York Yankees, 1928-29, 1931-35 New York Giants. Coach, 1936 Boston Redskins, 1937-1942 Washington Redskins, 1946-48 New York Yankees (AAFC), 1949 Chicago Hornets (AAFC).

Ray Flaherty was an all-pro end with the New York Giants in 1928 and 1932, leading the NFL in pass receptions in 1932, the first season official statistics were kept. He was captain of the Giants and later an assistant coach with New York before taking over the Redskins as head coach in 1936. Flaherty won four Eastern Division titles and two world championships with the Redskins and his record overall was 80-37-5. His All-America Football Conference New York Yankees won divisional titles in 1946 and 1947 but lost the title game to the Cleveland Browns in both years. It was Flaherty who suggested the use of sneakers in the 1934 NFL Championship Game won by the Giants over the Bears. In college at Gonzaga a heel bruise forced him to wear tennis shoes in practice one day and he found they gave him excellent traction on frozen fields.

Len Ford

End. 6-5, 260. Born in Washington, D.C., February 18, 1926. Died March 14, 1972. Michigan. Inducted in 1976. 1948-49 Los Angeles Dons (AAFC), 1950-57 Cleveland Browns, 1958 Green Bay Packers.

Len Ford entered professional football as a two-way end and caught 67 passes for the Los Angeles Dons of the All-America Football Conference in 1948 and 1949. But when the Dons and their league folded, Ford was acquired by Cleveland and used exclusively as a defensive end. He made all-pro teams five consecutive years, 1951-55, and played in the Pro Bowl four times. Ford was one of the first defensive ends to be known for his all-out pass rush—he often leaped over blockers to get to the quarterback. Ford recovered 20 fumbles during his career. After missing much of the 1950 season because of severe facial injuries, he wore a special mask and played an outstanding game in the Browns' 1950 championship victory over the Rams.

Danny Fortmann

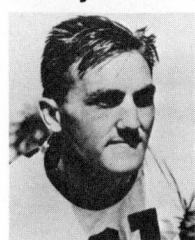

Guard. 6-0, 207. Born in Pearl River, New York, April 11, 1916. Colgate. Inducted in 1965. 1936-1943 Chicago Bears.

George Halas of the Chicago Bears reportedly chose Danny Fortmann of Colgate as he was making the last selection of the 1936 college player draft because he liked the sound of his name. Fortmann was small for a lineman even for that day, and his football career also appeared unpromising because he wanted to become a doctor. But he played eight years. He became one of the best linemen of all time, making all-pro six consecutive years, 1938-1943, playing offensively and defensively. A Phi Beta Kappa student in college, Fortmann was one of a group whose members attended medical or dental school while playing for Chicago. Fortmann was a practicing physician before he retired as a Bears player in 1943. He later served the Los Angeles Rams as team doctor.

Bill George

Linebacker. 6-2, 230. Born in Waynesburg, Pennsylvania, October 27, 1930. Wake Forest. Inducted in 1974. 1952-1965 Chicago Bears, 1966 Los Angeles Rams.

The Chicago Bears thought so highly of Bill George they selected him on the second round of the 1951 draft, when he still had a year of eligibility left. He reported in 1952 and went on to play 14 years. He played middle linebacker and called defensive signals. He recovered 16 fumbles and had 18 interceptions. George played in eight Pro Bowl games and made all-pro as many times. Early in his career he placekicked, scoring 26 points on four field goals and 14 extra points.

Frank Gifford

Halfback. 6-1, 195. Born in Santa Monica, California, August 16, 1930. USC. Inducted in 1977. 1952-1960, 1962-64 New York Giants.

The New York Giants made the NFL title game five times with Frank Gifford on the team. In 1956, the season they won the NFL championship 47-7 over the Bears, Gifford was one of the top players in the league. Gifford, who had been a college star at USC, played running back, flanker, and—early in his career—defensive back for the Giants. He was all-pro in 1955, 1956, 1957, and 1959. He had a spectacular year in 1956, rushing for 819 yards and catching 51 passes for 603 yards. He also caught a pass for a touchdown from Charlie Conerly in the championship game.

RUSHING

Year	Team	Att.	Yards	Avg.	Long	TD
1952	N.Y. Giants	38	116	3.1	15	0
1953	N.Y. Giants	50	157	3.1	15	2
1954	N.Y. Giants	66	368	5.6	30	2
1955	N.Y. Giants	86	351	4.1	49	3
1956	N.Y. Giants	159	819	5.2	69	5
1957	N.Y. Giants	136	528	3.9	41	5
1958	N.Y. Giants	115	468	4.1	33	8
1959	N.Y. Giants	106	540	5.1	79	3
1960	N.Y. Giants	77	232	3.0	13	4
1961	Did not play football					
1962	N.Y. Giants	2	18	9.0	12	1
1963	N.Y. Giants	4	10	2.5	12	0
1964	N.Y. Giants	1	2	2.0	2t	1
Totals		840	3,609	4.3	79	34

RECEIVING

Year	Team	No.	Yards	Avg.	Long	TD
1952	N.Y. Giants	5	36	7.2	11	0
1953	N.Y. Giants	18	292	16.2	49t	4
1954	N.Y. Giants	14	154	11.0	35t	1
1955	N.Y. Giants	33	437	13.2	54	4
1956	N.Y. Giants	51	603	11.8	48	4
1957	N.Y. Giants	41	588	14.3	63	4
1958	N.Y. Giants	29	330	11.4	41	2
1959	N.Y. Giants	42	768	18.3	77t	4
1960	N.Y. Giants	24	344	14.3	44t	3
1961	Did not play football					
1962	N.Y. Giants	39	796	20.4	63t	7
1963	N.Y. Giants	42	657	15.6	64	7
1964	N.Y. Giants	29	429	14.8	40t	3
Totals		367	5,434	14.8	77t	43

PASSING
63 Att., 29 Comp. 823 Yards, 14 TD, 6 Int.

INTERCEPTIONS
2, 112 Yards, 56.0 Avg., 1 TD

PUNT RETURNS
24, 118 Yards, 4.9 Avg., 0 TD

KICKOFF RETURNS
18, 480 Yards, 26.7 Avg., 0 TD

SCORING
78 TD, 2 FG, 10 PAT, 484 Points

Otto Graham

Quarterback. 6-1, 195. Born in Waukegan, Illinois, December 6, 1921. Northwestern. Inducted in 1965. 1946-49 Cleveland Browns (AAFC), 1950-55 Cleveland Browns.

Otto Graham was converted from a college single-wing tailback to a T-formation quarterback in pro football. Graham became the top-ranked passer of his time. In 10 seasons with the Browns, he led them into 10 championship games. He led the All-America Football Conference in passing each of his four years in that league, and the NFL twice. In the 1950 NFL Championship Game, Graham threw for four touchdowns. In the 1954 title game, he threw for three and ran for three. In addition to becoming a star football player at Northwestern, Graham was a basketball All-America.

PASSING

Year	Team	Att.	Comp.	Yards	TD	Int.
1946	Cleveland (AAFC)	174	95	1,834	17	5
1947	Cleveland (AAFC)	269	163	2,753	25	11
1948	Cleveland (AAFC)	333	173	2,713	25	15
1949	Cleveland (AAFC)	285	161	2,785	19	10
1950	Cleveland	253	137	1,943	14	20
1951	Cleveland	265	147	2,205	17	16
1952	Cleveland	364	181	2,816	20	24
1953	Cleveland	258	167	2,722	11	9
1954	Cleveland	240	142	2,092	11	17
1955	Cleveland	185	98	1,721	15	8
NFL Totals		1,565	872	13,499	88	94

RUSHING

306 Att., 682 Yards, 2.2 Avg., 36 Long, 33 TD

Red Grange

Halfback, 6-0, 185. Born in Forksville, Pennsylvania, June 13, 1903. Illinois. Inducted in 1963. 1925 Chicago Bears, 1926 New York Yankees (AFL), 1927 New York Yankees, 1929-1934 Chicago Bears.

Red Grange's reputation as a runner was already established when he joined the Chicago Bears on Thanksgiving Day in 1925. The man nicknamed "the Galloping Ghost" had been one of the most famous college players ever, and his name brought the first huge crowds to pro football, perhaps assuring a successful future of the sport. Grange and the Bears went on an 18-game coast-to-coast tour after the 1925 season, giving the game an audience it had never had. Grange and his personal manager, C. C. (Cash and Carry) Pyle, established the first American Football League in 1926. It folded after one season and Grange and other players joined the NFL. A knee injury caused Grange to miss all of the 1928 season and robbed him of much elusiveness, but he remained a fine defensive player and a big box-office attraction.

Forrest Gregg

Tackle. 6-4, 250. Born in Sulphur Springs, Texas, October 18, 1933. Southern Methodist. Inducted in 1977. 1956, 1958-1970 Green Bay Packers, 1971 Dallas Cowboys.

Forrest Gregg joined Green Bay in 1956, and his career was interrupted by 21 months of military service. Gregg came back in 1958, Vince Lombardi became Packers' coach in 1959, and they made one of the most dramatic turn-arounds in NFL history. Gregg was a key player at tackle and guard, and was named to the Pro Bowl seven out of eight years, nine times in all. He played on three Super Bowl-winning teams, two in Green Bay and one in Dallas, his last season as an active player.

Lou Groza

Tackle-Kicker. 6-3, 250. Born in Martin's Ferry, Ohio, January 25, 1924. Ohio State. Inducted in 1974. 1946-49 Cleveland Browns (AAFC), 1950-59 Cleveland Browns, 1961-67 Cleveland Browns.

Lou (the Toe) Groza was one of the greatest kickers in NFL history. He scored 1,349 points in the NFL. His last-second field goal won the 1950 NFL Championship Game 30-28 for the Browns over the Rams. Altogether, he played in 13 championship games, four in the All-America Football Conference, nine in the NFL. He played in nine Pro Bowls. And he was more than just a kicker. He was also an excellent tackle, six times all-pro, pass blocking for Otto Graham and opening holes for Marion Motley, Dub Jones, Bobby Mitchell, and Jim Brown. A back injury forced him to retire in 1960 but he came back in 1961 and played strictly as a kicker for seven more years.

SCORING

Year	Team	FG	PAT	Points
1946	Cleveland (AAFC)	13-29	45-47	84
1947	Cleveland (AAFC)	7-21	39-42	60
1948	Cleveland (AAFC)	8-19	51-52	75
1949	Cleveland (AAFC)	2- 7	34-35	40
1950	Cleveland	13-19	29-29	*74
1951	Cleveland	10-23	43-43	73
1952	Cleveland	19-33	32-32	89
1953	Cleveland	23-26	39-40	108
1954	Cleveland	16-24	37-38	85
1955	Cleveland	11-22	44-45	77
1956	Cleveland	11-20	18-18	51
1957	Cleveland	15-22	32-32	77
1958	Cleveland	8-19	36-38	60
1959	Cleveland	5-16	33-37	48
1960	Retired from football			
1961	Cleveland	16-23	37-38	85
1962	Cleveland	14-31	33-35	75
1963	Cleveland	15-23	40-43	85
1964	Cleveland	22-33	49-49	115
1965	Cleveland	16-25	45-45	93
1966	Cleveland	9-23	51-52	78
1967	Cleveland	11-23	43-43	76
NFL Totals		234-405	641-657	*1,349

*Includes a touchdown.

Joe Guyon

Halfback. 6-1, 180. Born in Mahnomen, Minnesota, November 26, 1892. Died November 27, 1971. Carlisle, Georgia Tech. Inducted in 1966. 1920 Canton Bulldogs, 1921 Cleveland Indians, 1922-23 Oorang Indians, 1924 Rock Island Independents, 1924-25 Kansas City Cowboys, 1927 New York Giants.

The career of Joe Guyon, a Chippewa Indian from Minnesota, roughly paralleled that of Jim Thorpe. Guyon played with Thorpe at Carlisle Indian School. Then Guyon was an All-America tackle at Georgia Tech. He was a triple-threat halfback in the pros. He played on four different teams with Thorpe. In 1927, a touchdown pass by Guyon gave the New York Giants a victory over the Chicago Bears and won the NFL championship for the Giants. Guyon didn't confine his athletic activity to football. He played minor league baseball in the summers—when football started later and the baseball season was shorter. A baseball injury in 1928 ended Guyon's pro football career.

George Halas

End. Coach. Team Owner. Born in Chicago, Illinois, February 2, 1895. Illinois. Inducted in 1963. 1920 Decatur Staleys, 1921 Chicago Staleys, 1922-29 Chicago Bears; coach 1933-1942, 1946-1955, 1958-67 Chicago Bears. Chairman of the Board of the Bears.

George Halas's career parallels the history of the National Football League. Just out of college at Illinois, Halas was in Canton, Ohio, on September 17, 1920 when the NFL's organizational meeting was held. He remained active in the administration of the Chicago Bears—the only man in the NFL in 1982 to have been associated with it since its inception. Halas, known as "Papa Bear," coached the Chicago team for 40 seasons and his 325 NFL victories are the most by any coach. Before settling into coaching and administration, Halas was a top two-way end for 11 seasons. In 1923, he picked up a Jim Thorpe fumble and ran it back 98 yards for a touchdown, an NFL record for a fumble return until it was broken in 1972. He coached the Bears to eight divisional titles and six NFL championships.

Ed Healey

Tackle. 6-3, 220. Born in Indian Orchard, Massachusetts, December 28, 1894. Died December 9, 1978. Dartmouth. Inducted in 1964. 1920-22 Rock Island Independents, 1922-27 Chicago Bears.

After playing at Dartmouth, Ed Healey went into coaching—until he decided to try out in the new professional league at Rock Island, Illinois, in 1920 and made the team. While playing for the Rock Island Independents in 1922, Healey impressed George Halas and the Chicago coach made one of the first player deals to get him. Healey's contract was transferred to the Bears for $100. Halas later called Healey "the most versatile tackle ever." Healey's teammate, Red Grange, said, "He loved to come downfield under a punt. He was an absolutely vicious player." Healey was outstanding in the Bears' long barnstorming tour after the 1925 season. The tour was set up to showcase Grange, but it turned Healey into a star, too.

Mel Hein

Center. 6-2, 225. Born in Redding, California, August 22, 1909. Washington State. Inducted in 1963. 1931-1945 New York Giants.

Mel Hein was outstanding as a center, guard, and tackle at Washington State, but he had to write to three NFL teams offering his services before he was signed by the New York Giants for $150 a game. He became the Giants' regular center and started there and at linebacker for 15 seasons. He never missed a game and he rarely played less than the full 60 minutes. He was a strong blocker despite having to deliver accurate long snaps before blocking opposing linemen. On defense, he covered passes and tackled as well as any player in the league. He was all-pro for eight consecutive seasons, 1933-1940.

Wilbur (Pete) Henry

Tackle. 6-0, 250. Born in Mansfield, Ohio, October 31, 1897. Died February 7, 1952. Washington & Jefferson. Inducted in 1963. 1920-23, 1925-26 Canton Bulldogs, 1927 New York Giants, 1927-28 Pottsville Maroons.

Wilbur Henry was a hefty player nicknamed "Fats." But he was a quick and powerful man who did many things well. He played tackle, but sometimes he was used as a power ball carrier, or as the receiver on a tackle-eligible pass play. He was called the best kick-blocker of his time. He also kicked, sharing the record for the longest dropkick field goal (50 yards) with fellow Hall of Famer Paddy Driscoll. His 94-yard punt was an NFL record for nearly half a century. A three-time college All-America at Washington & Jefferson, Henry signed with the Canton Bulldogs the day the NFL was organized in that Ohio town, and he was an offensive and defensive standout as the team won consecutive NFL titles in 1922 and 1923.

Arnie Herber

Quarterback. 6-1, 200. Born in Green Bay, Wisconsin, April 2, 1910. Died October 14, 1969. Wisconsin, Regis College. Inducted in 1966. 1930-1940 Green Bay Packers, 1944-45 New York Giants.

Pro football's first heralded passing combination was quarterback Arnie Herber of the Green Bay Packers to receiver Don Hutson in the 1930s. Herber predated Hutson by five seasons, and had built a reputation as a star by the time Hutson arrived. In the days when the forward pass was mostly a desperation play, Herber and the Packers used it anytime and anywhere with great success. He was especially effective throwing long. Herber led the Packers to four NFL championships and was the league's top passer three seasons—1932, 1934, and 1936. He retired in 1940, but came back in 1944 with the New York Giants and led them to the Eastern Division title. His lifetime statistics show 8,033 yards passing and 79 touchdown passes, despite the fact he had small fingers and had to pass a melon-shaped ball the first three seasons of his career.

PASSING

Year	Team	Att.	Comp.	Yards	TD	Int.
1930	Green Bay					
1931	Green Bay					
1932	Green Bay	101	37	639	9	9
1933	Green Bay	126	56	656	4	12
1934	Green Bay	115	42	799	8	12
1935	Green Bay	106	40	729	8	6
1936	Green Bay	173	77	1,239	11	13
1937	Green Bay	104	47	676	7	10
1938	Green Bay	55	22	336	4	4
1939	Green Bay	139	57	1,107	8	9
1940	Green Bay	89	38	560	5	7
1941	Retired from football					
1942	Retired from football					
1943	Retired from football					
1944	N.Y. Giants	86	36	651	6	8
1945	N.Y. Giants	80	35	641	9	8
Totals		1,174	487	8,033	79	98

Bill Hewitt

End. 5-11, 191. Born in Bay City, Michigan, October 8, 1909. Died January 14, 1947. Michigan. Inducted in 1971. 1932-36 Chicago Bears, 1937-39 Philadelphia Eagles, 1943 Phil-Pitt Steagles.

Bill Hewitt was not especially big but he was an intense player. His initial charge was so quick that opponents often claimed he was offside. Hewitt played without a helmet from 1932-39 and his return to the league from retirement in 1943 may have prompted the rules change making the wearing of helmets mandatory. He was one of the first linemen to pursue all over the field. He made an all-pro team with two different clubs, the Chicago Bears in 1933 and 1934 and the Philadelphia Eagles in 1937. In 1936, Hewitt made all-pro even though he was traded from the Bears to the Eagles midway through the season. He had perhaps his finest game in the NFL when he led the Bears to victory in the 1933 Championship Game against the New York Giants. He was killed in an automobile accident in Pennsylvania in January, 1947.

RECEIVING

Year	Team	No.	Yards	Avg.	TD
1932	Chi. Bears				
1933	Chi. Bears	16	274	17.1	2
1934	Chi. Bears	10	151	15.1	5
1935	Chi. Bears	5	80	16.0	0
1936	Chi. Bears-Philadelphia	15	358	23.9	6
1937	Philadelphia	16	197	12.3	5
1938	Philadelphia	18	237	13.2	4
1939	Philadelphia	15	243	16.2	1
1940	Retired from football				
1941	Retired from football				
1942	Retired from football				
1943	Phil-Pitt	2	22	11.0	0
Totals		97	1,562	16.1	22

Clarke Hinkle

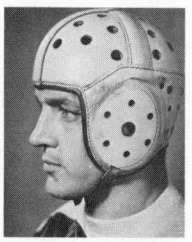

Fullback. 5-11, 201. Born in Toronto, Ohio, April 10, 1912. Bucknell. Inducted in 1964. 1932-1941 Green Bay Packers.

Hinkle has been called the fiercest competitor ever in football. He had stirring personal duels with Bronko Nagurski of the Bears. Hinkle was a battering-ram runner and a hard-tackling linebacker but he also passed, punted, placekicked, caught passes and defended against them. An all-pro choice four times, he was the NFL's all-time leading ground gainer when he retired, with 3,860 yards. He had a 43.4-yard punting average. Hinkle also led the NFL in scoring in 1938 and in field goals in 1940 and 1941.

RUSHING

Year	Team	Att.	Yards	Avg.	Long	TD
1932	Green Bay	95	331	3.4	27	3
1933	Green Bay	139	413	2.9	33	4
1934	Green Bay	144	359	2.4	32	1
1935	Green Bay	77	273	3.5	17	2
1936	Green Bay	100	476	4.7	57	5
1937	Green Bay	129	552	4.2	41	5
1938	Green Bay	114	299	2.6	46	3
1939	Green Bay	135	381	2.7	29	5
1940	Green Bay	109	383	3.5	31	2
1941	Green Bay	129	393	3.0	20	5
Totals		1,171	3,860	3.2	57	35

RECEIVING
49, 537 Yards, 11.0 Avg., 9 TD

SCORING
44 TD, 26 FG, 28 PAT, 370 Points

Elroy (Crazylegs) Hirsch

Halfback-End. 6-2, 190. Born in Wausau, Wisconsin, June 17, 1923. Wisconsin, Michigan. Inducted in 1968. 1946-48 Chicago Rockets (AAFC), 1949-1957 Los Angeles Rams.

Elroy Hirsch is remembered mostly as one of the most spectacular pass receivers ever to play in the NFL but he got his nickname—Crazylegs—because of his unusual running style. He was one of the first backs to be moved out wide and made a flanker, with the Los Angeles Rams in 1950. A star with the Chicago Rockets of the All-America Football Conference before coming to the NFL, Hirsch teamed with fellow Hall of Famers Tom Fears, Bob Waterfield, and Norm Van Brocklin to set scoring records that still stand. In 1951, Hirsch caught 66 passes for 1,495 yards and 17 touchdowns. He was honored as the flanker on the all-time NFL team in 1969. He ended his career in 1957 with 343 catches for 6,299 yards and 53 touchdowns. He played the title role in his film biography and starred in two other movies.

RECEIVING

Year	Team	No.	Yards	Avg.	Long	TD
1946	Chi. Rockets (AAFC)	27	347	12.9		3
1947	Chi. Rockets (AAFC)	10	282	28.2		3
1948	Chi. Rockets (AAFC)	7	101	14.4		1
1949	Los Angeles	22	326	14.8	48t	4
1950	Los Angeles	42	687	16.4	58t	7
1951	Los Angeles	66	1,495	22.7	91t	17
1952	Los Angeles	25	590	23.6	84t	4
1953	Los Angeles	61	941	15.4	70	4
1954	Los Angeles	35	720	20.6	66	3
1955	Los Angeles	25	460	18.4	72t	2
1956	Los Angeles	35	603	17.2	76t	6
1957	Los Angeles	32	477	14.9	45	6
NFL Totals		343	6,299	18.4	91t	53

RUSHING
74 Att., 317 Yards, 4.3 Avg., 51 Long, 2 TD

Cal Hubbard

Tackle. 6-5, 250. Born in Keytesville, Missouri, October 11, 1900. Died October 17, 1977. Centenary, Geneva. Inducted in 1963. 1927-28 New York Giants, 1929-1933, 1935 Green Bay Packers, 1936 New York Giants, 1936 Pittsburgh Pirates.

Cal Hubbard is the only man to be enshrined in both the Pro Football Hall of Fame and the Baseball Hall of Fame. He was the most feared lineman of his era and one of the few early pros who was as large as today's players. As a rookie in 1927, he was a keystone in the New York Giants' championship defense, which limited opponents to 20 points for the season. A powerful blocker, he stood out on offense, too. He was selected as a tackle on the NFL's all-time team, chosen in 1969. After retiring from football, Hubbard was a respected American League baseball umpire and became umpire-in-chief.

Sam Huff

Linebacker. 6-1, 230. Born in Morgantown, West Virginia, October 4, 1934. West Virginia. Inducted in 1982. 1956-1963 New York Giants, 1964-67, 1969 Washington Redskins.

In the 1950s, Sam Huff was the first defensive player to attain the type of notoriety previously reserved for offensive players. As an integral part of a strong Giants defense, Huff helped defenders, and more particularly linebackers, gain public recognition; a half-hour television special in 1961, "The Violent World of Sam Huff," also helped. So did the fact that the Giants won a world championship (1956) and six division titles. Huff came to the Giants as a third-round choice in the 1956 draft. He played in five Pro Bowls (1959-1962, 1965) and was named outstanding lineman of the 1961 game. Huff was traded to the Redskins in 1964, where he played through 1967. After a one-year retirement, Huff came back in 1969 as a player-coach under Vince Lombardi. During Huff's early career, Lombardi was a Giants assistant.

Lamar Hunt

Team Owner. Born in El Dorado, Arkansas, August 2, 1932. Southern Methodist. Inducted in 1972. 1960-62 Dallas Texans, 1963-1982 Kansas City Chiefs.

Lamar Hunt failed several times in a bid to gain an NFL franchise for his home state of Texas in the 1950s. He formed the American Football League in 1959, and it began play in 1960. Hunt was owner and founder of the Dallas Texans. After a difficult struggle the league merged with the NFL in 1966. Hunt moved the Dallas franchise to Kansas City in 1963, and it became one of football's strongest organizations, winning Super Bowl IV in 1970. Hunt once played football behind Raymond Berry at Southern Methodist. When he was elected to the Hall of Fame, he said it was a triumph symbolic of all the officials, coaches, and players of the AFL.

Sam Huff stops Jim Brown cold in a 48-7 Giants win against the Browns, 1959.

Don Hutson

End. 6-1, 180. Born in Pine Bluff, Arkansas, January 31, 1913. Alabama. Inducted in 1963. 1935-1945 Green Bay Packers.

Don Hutson entered the NFL in the mid-1930s, but he was similar to today's receivers in his style of play. He dominated the NFL. He was an all-pro nine times, and he led the NFL in receptions eight times. Five times he topped the league's scorers. He caught at least one pass in 95 consecutive games from 1937 through 1945, a record that lasted almost a quarter century. During his 11-year career. Hutson caught 488 passes, 99 of them for touchdowns. Early in his career he was a two-way end, and he was named to the NFL's all-time team at that position in 1969. He later played defensive safety. Hutson also kicked extra points and field goals, scoring 823 lifetime points.

RECEIVING

Year	Team	No.	Yards	Avg.	Long	TD
1935	Green Bay	18	420	23.3	83	6
1936	Green Bay	34	536	15.8	87	8
1937	Green Bay	41	552	13.5	78	7
1938	Green Bay	32	548	17.1	54	9
1939	Green Bay	34	846	24.9	92	6
1940	Green Bay	45	664	14.8	36	7
1941	Green Bay	58	738	12.7	45	10
1942	Green Bay	74	1,211	16.4	73	17
1943	Green Bay	47	776	16.5	79	11
1944	Green Bay	58	866	14.9	55t	9
1945	Green Bay	47	834	17.7	75t	9
Totals		488	7,991	16.4	92	99

SCORING

Year	Team	TD	FG	PAT	Points
1935	Green Bay	7	0-	1-	43
1936	Green Bay	9	0-	0-	54
1937	Green Bay	7	0-	0-	42
1938	Green Bay	9	0-	3-	57
1939	Green Bay	6	0-0	2-	38
1940	Green Bay	7	0-0	15-	57
1941	Green Bay	12	1-2	20-24	95
1942	Green Bay	17	1-4	33-34	138
1943	Green Bay	12	3-5	36-36	117
1944	Green Bay	9	0-3	31-33	85
1945	Green Bay	10	2-4	31-35	97
Totals		105	7-	172-	823

RUSHING
62 Att., 284 Yards, 4.6 Avg., 27 Long, 3 TD

INTERCEPTIONS
30, 389 Yards, 13.0 Avg., 84 Long, 1 TD

David (Deacon) Jones

Defensive end. 6-5, 250. Born in Eatonville, Florida, December 9, 1938. South Carolina State, Mississippi Vocational. Inducted in 1980. 1961-1971 Los Angeles Rams, 1972-73 San Diego Chargers, 1974 Washington Redskins.

When David Jones arrived in Los Angeles as a fourteenth-round draft choice he found 10 pages of Joneses in the telephone book, and about 20 David Joneses. To establish an identity he nicknamed himself "Deacon." Later he was called the "Secretary of Defense." Credited with coining the term "sack," Jones elevated pass rushing technique to the point where the fan could see and appreciate them. Anchored by Jones and fellow Hall of Fame member Merlin Olsen, the Rams' defensive line of the 1960s was known as the Fearsome Foursome. Jones was traded to the San Diego Chargers for the 1972 season, and finished his career with the Washington Redskins in 1974. In Washington he was reunited with George Allen, who had coached him for much of his career in Los Angeles. Jones was named all-pro five times (in 11 seasons with Los Angeles) and played in eight Pro Bowls.

Walt Kiesling

Guard. Coach. 6-2, 245. Born in St. Paul, Minnesota, March 27, 1903. Died March 2, 1962. St. Thomas (Minnesota). Inducted in 1966. 1926-27 Duluth Eskimos, 1928 Pottsville Maroons, 1929-1933 Chicago Cardinals, 1934 Chicago Bears, 1935-36 Green Bay Packers, 1937-38 Pittsburgh Pirates; Coach 1939-1940 Pittsburgh Pirates, 1941-42 Pittsburgh Steelers; Co-coach 1943 Phil-Pitt, 1944 Card-Pitt.; Coach 1954-56 Pittsburgh Steelers.

As a player and coach, Walt Kiesling was in the NFL 34 years. He spent 13 of those years as a guard for six different teams. As a coach, he spent most of his time as a Steelers assistant, but also was head coach of the team twice. And during World War II, he was co-head coach of the 1943 Phil-Pitt and 1944 Card-Pitt merged teams. Kiesling helped give perennial loser Pittsburgh its first winning season in 1942. As a player he had a tackle's size but was used at guard offensively because of his quickness in pulling to lead plays. Defensively, he was one of the league's best. His finest playing years were with the Cardinals in 1929-1933 when he made all-pro teams almost every season, and 1934, when he starred for an unbeaten Chicago Bears team.

Deacon Jones (75), Lamar Lundy (85), and Merlin Olsen (74) break up Len Dawson's pass attempt, 1968.

Emlen Tunnell

Safety. 6-1, 200. Born in Bryn Mawr, Pennsylvania, March 29, 1925. Died July 23, 1975. Toledo, Iowa. Inducted in 1967. 1948-1958 New York Giants, 1959-1961 Green Bay Packers.

Like Dick (Night Train) Lane, Emlen Tunnell walked into a team office and asked for a pro tryout. He soon became a key in the New York Giants' "Umbrella" defense. He was the team's "offense on defense" because of his yardage totals on punt returns and interceptions. His lifetime interceptions (79 for 1,282 yards) and punt return yards (2,209) set NFL records. Tunnell played in nine Pro Bowls and was all-pro four times. During much of Tunnell's time with the Giants, Vince Lombardi was one of the Giants' assistant coaches. Lombardi took Tunnell with him to Green Bay, where he finished his career.

INTERCEPTIONS

Year	Team	No.	Yards	Avg.	Long	TD
1948	N.Y. Giants	7	116	16.6	43t	1
1949	N.Y. Giants	10	251	25.1	55t	2
1950	N.Y. Giants	7	167	23.9	35	0
1951	N.Y. Giants	9	74	8.2	30	0
1952	N.Y. Giants	7	149	21.3	40	0
1953	N.Y. Giants	6	117	19.5	44	0
1954	N.Y. Giants	8	108	13.5	43	0
1955	N.Y. Giants	7	76	10.9	26	0
1956	N.Y. Giants	6	87	14.5	23	0
1957	N.Y. Giants	6	87	14.5	52t	1
1958	N.Y. Giants	1	8	8.0	8	0
1959	Green Bay	2	20	10.0	18	0
1960	Green Bay	3	22	7.3	22	0
1961	Green Bay	0	0	0.0	0	0
	Totals	79	1,282	16.2	55t	4

PUNT RETURNS

Year	Team	No.	Yards	Avg.	Long	TD
1948	N.Y. Giants	12	115	9.6	25	0
1949	N.Y. Giants	26	315	12.1	67t	1
1950	N.Y. Giants	31	305	9.8	43	0
1951	N.Y. Giants	34	489	14.4	81t	3
1952	N.Y. Giants	30	411	13.7	60	0
1953	N.Y. Giants	38	223	5.9	37	0
1954	N.Y. Giants	21	70	3.3	12	0
1955	N.Y. Giants	25	98	3.9	66t	1
1956	N.Y. Giants	22	120	5.5	14	0
1957	N.Y. Giants	12	60	5.0	23	0
1958	N.Y. Giants	6	0	0.0	0	0
1959	Green Bay	1	3	3.0	3	0
1960	Green Bay	0	0	0.0	0	0
1961	Green Bay	0	0	0.0	0	0
	Totals	258	2,209	8.6	81t	5

KICKOFF RETURNS

46, 1,265 Yards, 27.5 Avg., 100 Long, 1 TD

Clyde (Bulldog) Turner

Center. 6-2, 235. Born in Sweetwater, Texas, November 10, 1919. Hardin-Simmons. Inducted in 1966. 1940-1952 Chicago Bears.

Long before other teams in the NFL began doing it, the Chicago Bears picked players from obscure colleges and developed them into all-stars. Clyde (Bulldog) Turner was one of the best examples. His college was Hardin-Simmons, but Turner was a first-round choice by the Bears. He became an all-pro six times. Turner was a student of football; his grasp of the Bears' T-formation was on a par with that of quarterback Sid Luckman. He was effective both as an offensive blocker and as a linebacker. In 1942, he led the league in interceptions. Turner played on four NFL championship teams, and in the five title games in which he participated, he made four interceptions.

Johnny Unitas

Quarterback. 6-1, 195. Born in Pittsburgh, Pennsylvania, May 7, 1933. Louisville. Inducted in 1979. 1956-1972 Baltimore Colts, 1973 San Diego Chargers.

The Cinderella story of Johnny Unitas is well-documented: A small college career at Louisville; drafted and waived by the Pittsburgh Steelers; earned $6.00 a game with the Bloomfield (a section of Pittsburgh) Rams; offered a $7,000 contract with the Baltimore Colts on a 65¢ telephone call. Unitas, considered by many to be the premier quarterback in NFL history, retired after the 1973 season holding nearly every meaningful career passing record: most attempts, most completions, most yardage, most 300-yard games, and most touchdown passes. From 1956 to 1960 he set a record by throwing at least one touchdown pass in 47 consecutive games. What do not show in Mr. Quarterback's statistics were the coolness and poise he exhibited under pressure. His tying and winning drives in the 1958 NFL title game remain textbook examples of the two-minute drill.

PASSING

Year	Team	Att.	Comp.	Yards	TD	Int.
1956	Baltimore	198	110	1,498	9	10
1957	Baltimore	301	172	2,550	24	17
1958	Baltimore	263	136	2,007	19	7
1959	Baltimore	367	193	2,899	32	14
1960	Baltimore	378	190	3,099	25	24
1961	Baltimore	420	229	2,990	16	24
1962	Baltimore	389	222	2,967	23	23
1963	Baltimore	410	237	3,481	20	12
1964	Baltimore	305	158	2,824	19	6
1965	Baltimore	282	164	2,530	23	12
1966	Baltimore	348	195	2,748	22	24
1967	Baltimore	436	255	3,428	20	16
1968	Baltimore	32	11	139	2	4
1969	Baltimore	327	178	2,342	12	20
1970	Baltimore	321	166	2,213	14	18
1971	Baltimore	176	92	942	3	9
1972	Baltimore	157	88	1,111	4	6
1973	San Diego	76	34	471	3	7
	Totals	5,186	2,830	40,239	290	253

RUSHING

450 Att., 1,777 Yards, 3.9 Avg., 34 Long, 13 TD

Norm Van Brocklin

Quarterback. 6-1, 190. Born in Eagle Butte, South Dakota, March 15, 1926. Oregon. Inducted in 1971. 1949-1957 Los Angeles Rams, 1958-1960 Philadelphia Eagles.

Norm Van Brocklin divided playing time during most of his career with two other Los Angeles Rams quarterbacks—first Hall of Famer Bob Waterfield, then Bill Wade. It wasn't until he joined the Philadelphia Eagles in 1958 that he had the position to himself. But he always starred. In the 1951 title game, his pass to Tom Fears helped win the NFL championship for the Rams. In the 1960 title game, his passing was the key as the Eagles beat the Green Bay Packers in Vince Lombardi's only defeat in a championship game. Van Brocklin led the NFL's passers three different years; he also led the league in punting twice. His mark of 554 yards passing in a game in 1951 set a record. He had 23,611 yards passing and 173 touchdowns. He played in eight Pro Bowls.

PASSING

Year	Team	Att.	Comp.	Yards	TD	Int.
1949	Los Angeles	58	32	601	6	2
1950	Los Angeles	233	127	2,061	18	14
1951	Los Angeles	194	100	1,725	13	11
1952	Los Angeles	205	113	1,736	14	17
1953	Los Angeles	286	156	2,393	19	14
1954	Los Angeles	260	139	2,637	13	21
1955	Los Angeles	272	144	1,890	8	15
1956	Los Angeles	124	68	966	7	12
1957	Los Angeles	265	132	1,105	20	21
1958	Philadelphia	374	198	2,409	15	20
1959	Philadelphia	340	191	2,617	16	14
1960	Philadelphia	284	153	2,471	24	17
	Totals	2,895	1,553	23,611	173	178

PUNTING

Year	Team	No.	Avg.	Long	Blk.
1949	Los Angeles	2	45.5	46	0
1950	Los Angeles	11	42.4	51	0
1951	Los Angeles	48	41.5	62	1
1952	Los Angeles	29	43.1	66	0
1953	Los Angeles	60	42.2	57	0
1954	Los Angeles	44	42.6	61	0
1955	Los Angeles	60	44.6	61	0
1956	Los Angeles	48	43.1	72	0
1957	Los Angeles	54	44.3	71	0
1958	Philadelphia	54	41.2	58	1
1959	Philadelphia	53	42.7	59	1
1960	Philadelphia	60	43.1	70	0
	Totals	523	42.9	72	3

RUSHING

102 Att., 40 Yards, 0.4 Avg., 16 Long, 11 TD

Steve Van Buren

Halfback. 6-1, 200. Born in La Ceiba, Honduras, December 28, 1920. Louisiana State. Inducted in 1965. 1944-1951 Philadelphia Eagles.

Steve Van Buren was a runner who combined speed, power, and elusiveness. He had halfback speed and fullback size. In 1947, he became only the second man in NFL history to gain more than 1,000 yards. He led the NFL's rushers four times in his eight-year pro career. Three were consecutive, (1947-49) and he went over 1,000 yards twice. He finished his career with 5,860 yards. As a rookie in 1944, Van Buren led the league in punt returns; he set the pace in kickoff returns the following year. He was a blocking back in college for baseball star Alvin Dark. As a professional, he doubled as a defensive back much of his career.

RUSHING

Year	Team	Att.	Yards	Avg.	Long	TD
1944	Philadelphia	80	444	5.5	70t	5
1945	Philadelphia	143	832	5.8	69t	15
1946	Philadelphia	116	529	4.6	58	5
1947	Philadelphia	217	1,008	4.6	45	13
1948	Philadelphia	201	945	4.7	29	10
1949	Philadelphia	263	1,146	4.4	41	11
1950	Philadelphia	188	629	3.3	41	4
1951	Philadelphia	112	327	2.9	17	6
	Totals	1,320	5,860	4.4	70t	69

RECEIVING
45, 523 Yards, 11.6 Avg., 50 Long, 3 TD
PUNT RETURNS
34, 473 Yards, 13.9 Avg., 55 Long, 2 TD
KICKOFF RETURNS
76, 2,030 Yards, 26.7 Avg., 98 Long, 3 TD
SCORING
77 TD, 2 PAT, 464 Points

Bob Waterfield

Quarterback. 6-2, 200. Born in Elmira, New York, July 26, 1920. UCLA. Inducted in 1965. 1945 Cleveland Rams, 1946-1952 Los Angeles Rams.

Bob Waterfield led his team to an NFL championship in his first pro season. His two touchdown passes provided the victory in the 1945 title game. A cool, gifted performer in all phases of athletics, Waterfield passed well enough to lead the league in 1946 and 1951. He made 315 extra points and 60 field goals. His punting average was 42.4 yards. On defense, he made 20 interceptions. He was one of the first quarterbacks to throw the long pass consistently on third down.

PASSING

Year	Team	Att.	Comp.	Yards	TD	Int.
1945	Cleveland Rams	171	89	1,609	14	17
1946	Los Angeles	251	127	1,747	17	17
1947	Los Angeles	221	96	1,210	8	18
1948	Los Angeles	180	87	1,354	14	18
1949	Los Angeles	296	154	2,168	17	24
1950	Los Angeles	213	122	1,540	11	13
1951	Los Angeles	176	88	1,566	13	10
1952	Los Angeles	109	51	655	3	11
	Totals	1,617	814	11,849	97	128

PUNTING

Year	Team	No.	Yards	Avg.	Long	Blk.
1945	Cleveland Rams	39	1,588	40.7	68	1
1946	Los Angeles	39	1,745	44.6	65	0
1947	Los Angeles	59	2,500	42.4	86	1
1948	Los Angeles	43	1,843	42.6	88	0
1949	Los Angeles	49	2,177	44.4	61	1
1950	Los Angeles	52	2,087	40.1	61	2
1951	Los Angeles	4	166	41.5	52	0
1952	Los Angeles	30	1,276	42.5	88	0
	Totals	315	13,382	42.4	88	5

INTERCEPTIONS
20, 228 Yards, 11.4 Avg., 35 Long, 0 TD
SCORING
13 TD, 60 FG, 315 PAT, 573 Points

Bill Willis

Guard. 6-2, 215. Born in Columbus, Ohio, October 5, 1921. Ohio State. Inducted in 1977. 1946-49 Cleveland Browns (AAFC), 1950-53 Cleveland Browns.

Bill Willis was one of the two black players signed by Paul Brown of the Cleveland Browns in 1946 (Marion Motley was the other) when the color line was broken in the All-America Football Conference. The Los Angeles Rams had recently broken the 12-year-old color line in the NFL with the signing of Kenny Washington and Woody Strode. Willis, a smallish lineman out of Ohio State, excelled for four seasons as the Browns won four straight AAFC titles, and was with them four more years when they moved to the NFL. An all-star in the AAFC, Willis was all-pro all four years in the NFL.

Larry Wilson

Safety. 6-0, 190. Born in Rigby, Idaho, March 24, 1938. Utah. Inducted in 1978. 1960-1972 St. Louis Cardinals.

One way or another, Larry Wilson left a lasting impression on nearly every quarterback he faced in his 13-year NFL career. If he wasn't smothering them in their own backfield with a safety blitz, he was intercepting their passes downfield. He compiled impressive offensive statistics during a career at Utah as a two-way halfback, but defense was his forte. He got his chance to play safety in the final preseason game of 1960, his rookie year, and became a fixture at the position. Of Wilson's 52 career interceptions, perhaps the most dramatic was one he made against the Pittsburgh Steelers in 1965; he had casts on both hands, which were broken. Bobby Layne once called Wilson "pound-for-pound, the toughest player in the NFL."

INTERCEPTIONS

Year	Team	No.	Yards	Avg.	Long	TD
1960	St. Louis	2	4	2.0	4	0
1961	St. Louis	3	36	12.0	25	0
1962	St. Louis	2	59	29.5	57t	1
1963	St. Louis	4	67	16.8	36	0
1964	St. Louis	3	44	14.7	42t	1
1965	St. Louis	6	153	25.5	96t	1
1966	St. Louis	10	180	18.0	91t	2
1967	St. Louis	4	75	18.8	44	0
1968	St. Louis	4	14	3.5	8	0
1969	St. Louis	2	15	7.5	15	0
1970	St. Louis	5	72	14.4	22	0
1971	St. Louis	4	46	11.5	23	0
1972	St. Louis	3	35	11.7	24	0
	Totals	52	800	15.4	96t	5

Alex Wojciechowicz

Center. 6-0, 235. Born in South River, New Jersey, August 12, 1915. Fordham. Inducted in 1968. 1938-1946 Detroit Lions, 1946-1950 Philadelphia Eagles.

His name was hard to pronounce, and equally hard to spell but he was a great player. He came into pro football with much expected of him. He was a two-time All-America at Fordham and, with Vince Lombardi, one of the "Seven Blocks of Granite" in that school's line. The Detroit Lions made him their number-one draft pick. Even though the team was not a contender in his era, he was a top-flight, two-way center. Midway through his eighth season in the league, he was acquired by the Eagles and Earle (Greasy) Neale made him a full-time linebacker. Wojciechowicz excelled at the role. He was solid against running plays, but he was also noted for his play against the pass. He was the NFL's best at chucking receivers. As a center, he was known for his unusually wide stance over the ball.

HALL OF FAME CLASSES

1963
Charter members
September 7, 1963 at Canton, Ohio
Sammy Baugh
Bert Bell
Joe Carr
Earl (Dutch) Clark
Red Grange
George Halas
Mel Hein
Wilbur (Pete) Henry
Cal Hubbard
Don Hutson
Earl (Curly) Lambeau
Tim Mara
George Preston Marshall
Johnny Blood (McNally)
Bronko Nagurski
Ernie Nevers
Jim Thorpe
1964
September 6, 1964 at Canton, Ohio
Jimmy Conzelman
Ed Healey
Clarke Hinkle
Roy (Link) Lyman
Mike Michalske
Art Rooney, Sr.
George Trafton
1965
September 12, 1965 at Canton, Ohio
Guy Chamberlin
John (Paddy) Driscoll
Danny Fortmann
Otto Graham
Sid Luckman
Steve Van Buren
Bob Waterfield
1966
September 17, 1966 at Canton, Ohio
Bill Dudley
Joe Guyon
Arnie Herber
Walt Kiesling
George McAfee
Steve Owen
Hugh (Shorty) Ray
Clyde (Bulldog) Turner
1967
August 5, 1967 at Canton, Ohio
Chuck Bednarik
Charles W. Bidwill, Sr.
Paul Brown
Bobby Layne
Daniel F. Reeves
Ken Strong
Joe Stydahar
Emlen Tunnell
1968
August 3, 1968 at Canton, Ohio
Cliff Battles
Art Donovan
Elroy (Crazylegs) Hirsch
Wayne Millner
Marion Motley
Charley Trippi
Alex Wojciechowicz
1969
September 13, 1969 at Canton, Ohio
Glen (Turk) Edwards
Earle (Greasy) Neale
Leo Nomellini
Joe Perry
Ernie Stautner
1970
August 8, 1970 at Canton, Ohio
Jack Christiansen
Tom Fears
Hugh McElhenny
Pete Pihos
1971
July 31, 1971 at Canton, Ohio
Jim Brown
Bill Hewitt
Frank (Bruiser) Kinard
Vince Lombardi
Andy Robustelli
Y. A. Tittle
Norm Van Brocklin
1972
July 29, 1972 at Canton, Ohio
Lamar Hunt
Gino Marchetti
Ollie Matson
Clarence (Ace) Parker

1973
July 28, 1973 at Canton, Ohio
Raymond Berry
Jim Parker
Joe Schmidt
1974
July 27, 1974 at Canton, Ohio
Tony Canadeo
Bill George
Lou Groza
Dick (Night Train) Lane
1975
August 2, 1975 at Canton, Ohio
Roosevelt Brown
George Connor
Dante Lavelli
Lenny Moore
1976
July 24, 1976 at Canton, Ohio
Ray Flaherty
Len Ford
Jim Taylor
1977
July 30, 1977 at Canton, Ohio
Frank Gifford
Forrest Gregg
Gale Sayers
Bart Starr
Bill Willis
1978
July 29, 1978 at Canton, Ohio
Lance Alworth
Weeb Ewbank
Alphonse (Tuffy) Leemans
Ray Nitschke
Larry Wilson
1979
July 28, 1979 at Canton, Ohio
Dick Butkus
Yale Lary
Ron Mix
Johnny Unitas
1980
August 2, 1980 at Canton, Ohio
Herb Adderley
David (Deacon) Jones
Bob Lilly
Jim Otto
1981
August 1, 1981 at Canton, Ohio
Morris (Red) Badgro
George Blanda
Willie Davis
Jim Ringo
1982
August 7, 1982 at Canton, Ohio
Doug Atkins
Sam Huff
George Musso
Merlin Olsen

PRESENTERS

Presenters make the speeches of presentation for inductees at the annual ceremonies at the Hall of Fame during "Football's Greatest Weekend" in Canton, Ohio. At first presenters were appointed by the Hall of Fame but later the policy was changed allowing each Hall of Fame nominee to choose the person who would present him for induction.

Inductee	Presenter
Herb Adderley	Willie Davis
Lance Alworth	Al Davis
Doug Atkins	Ed McCaskey
Morris (Red) Badgro	Mel Hein
Cliff Battles	Edward Bennett Williams
Sammy Baugh	Harry Stuhldreher
Chuck Bednarik	Earle (Greasy) Neale
Bert Bell	David McDonald
Art Rooney accepted for the late Bell	
Raymond Berry	Weeb Ewbank
Charles W. Bidwill, Sr.	Art Rooney, Sr.
Charles W. (Stormy) Bidwill, Jr. accepted for his late father	
George Blanda	Al Davis
Jim Brown	Ken Malloy
Paul Brown	Otto Graham
Roosevelt Brown	Talmadge Hill
Dick Butkus	George Halas
Tony Canadeo	Dick Bourguignon
Joe Carr	Earl Schreiber
Dan Tehan accepted for the late Carr	
Guy Chamberlin	Wallace (Doc) Elliott
Jack Christiansen	Raymond (Buddy) Parker
Earl (Dutch) Clark	Senator Philip A. Hart
George Connor	George S. Halas
Jimmy Conzelman	Justice William O. Douglas
Willie Davis	E. G. (Eddie) Robinson
Art Donovan	Jim Mutscheller
John (Paddy) Driscoll	Jimmy Conzelman
Bill Dudley	Bob Waterfield
Glen (Turk) Edwards	Mel Hein

Weeb Ewbank	Paul Brown
Tom Fears	Hal Dean
Ray Flaherty	Jim Barber
Len Ford	Ted McIntyre
Debbie Ford accepted for her late father	
Danny Fortmann	Andy Kerr
Bill George	Ed McCaskey
Frank Gifford	Wellington Mara
Otto Graham	Paul Brown
Red Grange	Jimmy Conzelman
Forrest Gregg	Marie Lombardi
Lou Groza	Paul Brown
Joe Guyon	Jimmy Conzelman
George Halas	David L. Lawrence
Ed Healey	Harry Stuhldreher
Mel Hein	Frank T. Bow
Wilbur (Pete) Henry	E. E. (Rip) Miller
Harry Robb accepted for the late Henry	
Arnie Herber	Clarke Hinkle
Bill Hewitt	Upton Bell
Mrs. Mary Ellen Concozza, daughter of the late Hewitt, accepted for him	
Clarke Hinkle	Bronko Nagurski
Elroy (Crazylegs) Hirsch	Hampton Pool
Cal Hubbard	Paul Kerr
Sam Huff	Tom Landry
Lamar Hunt	William H. Sullivan, Jr.
Don Hutson	Dante Lavelli
David (Deacon) Jones	George Allen
Walt Kiesling	Justice Byron R. White
Johnny Blood (McNally) accepted for the late Kiesling	
Frank (Bruiser) Kinard	Jack White
Earl (Curley) Lambeau	Jim Crowley
Dick (Night Train) Lane	W. E. Pigford
Yale Lary	Buster Ramsey
Dante Lavelli	Paul Brown
Bobby Layne	Raymond (Buddy) Parker
Alphonse (Tuffy) Leemans	Peter Guzy
Bob Lilly	Tom Landry
Vince Lombardi	Wellington Mara
Vince Lombardi, Jr. accepted for his late father	
Sid Luckman	Lou Little
Roy (Link) Lyman	William E. Umstattd
Tim Mara	Arthur Daley
Jack Mara accepted for his late father	
Gino Marchetti	Carroll Rosenbloom
George Preston Marshall	Maj. Gen. Harry W. Abendroth
Milton King accepted for Marshall, who was ill	
Ollie Matson	Joe Kuharich
George McAfee	Dick Gallagher
Hugh McElhenny	Lou Spadia
Johnny Blood (McNally)	Justice Byron R. White
Mike Michalske	L. C. Timm
Wayne Millner	Ray Flaherty
Ron Mix	Joe Madro
Lenny Moore	Andy Stopper
Marion Motley	Bill Willis
George Musso	George Halas
Bronko Nagurski	Don Miller
Earle (Greasy) Neale	Chuck Bednarik
Ernie Nevers	Elmer Layden
Ray Nitschke	Phil Bengtson
Leo Nomellini	Mrs. Victor Morabito
Merlin Olsen	Tony Knap
Jim Otto	Al Davis
Steve Owen	Mel Hein
Jim Lee Howell accepted for the late Owen	
Clarence (Ace) Parker	Jack White
Jim Parker	Woody Hayes
Joe Perry	Mrs. Tony Morabito
Pete Pihos	Howard Brown
Hugh (Shorty) Ray	Dan Tehan
Hugh L. Ray, Jr. accepted for his late father	
Daniel F. Reeves	Bob Waterfield
Jim Ringo	Willard (Whiz) Rinehart
Andy Robustelli	J. Walter Kennedy
Art Rooney, Sr.	David L. Lawrence
Gale Sayers	George Halas
Joe Schmidt	William Clay Ford
Bart Starr	Bill Moseley
Ernie Stautner	Art Rooney
Ken Strong	Chick Meehan
Joe Stydahar	Dr. Danny Fortmann
Jim Taylor	Marie Lombardi
Jim Thorpe	Henry A. Roemer
Pete Calac accepted for the late Thorpe	
Y. A. Tittle	Wellington Mara
George Trafton	Ernie Nevers
Charley Trippi	Paul Shebby
Emlen Tunnell	Father Benedict Dudley, O.F.M.
Clyde (Bulldog) Turner	Ed Healey
Johnny Unitas	Frank Gitschier
Norm Van Brocklin	Rankin Smith
Steve Van Buren	Clarke Hinkle
Bob Waterfield	Pat O'Brien
Bill Willis	Paul Brown
Larry Wilson	Jack Curtis
Alex Wojciechowicz	Earle (Greasy) Neale

All-Time Records

Earl Morrall

Gino Cappelletti

Paul Hornung

Jim Bakken

Curt Knight

Dub Jones

Charlie Gogolak

INDIVIDUAL RECORDS

SERVICE

Most Seasons
- 26 George Blanda, Chi. Bears, 1949, 1950-58; Baltimore, 1950; Houston, 1960-66; Oakland, 1967-75
- 21 Earl Morrall, San Francisco, 1956; Pittsburgh, 1957-58; Detroit, 1958-64; N.Y. Giants, 1965-67; Baltimore, 1968-71; Miami, 1972-76
- 20 Jim Marshall, Cleveland, 1960; Minnesota, 1961-79

Most Seasons, One Club
- 19 Jim Marshall, Minnesota, 1961-79
- 17 Lou Groza, Cleveland, 1950-59, 1961-67
  Johnny Unitas, Baltimore, 1956-72
  John Brodie, San Francisco, 1957-73
  Jim Bakken, St. Louis, 1962-78
  Mick Tingelhoff, Minnesota, 1962-78
- 16 Sammy Baugh, Washington, 1937-52
  Bart Starr, Green Bay, 1956-71
  Jimmy Johnson, San Francisco, 1961-76
  Jim Hart, St. Louis, 1966-81

Most Games Played, Career
- 340 George Blanda, Chi. Bears, 1949, 1950-58; Baltimore, 1950; Houston, 1960-66; Oakland, 1967-75
- 282 Jim Marshall, Cleveland, 1960; Minnesota, 1961-79
- 255 Earl Morrall, San Francisco, 1958; Pittsburgh, 1957-58; Detroit, 1958-64; N.Y. Giants, 1965-67; Baltimore, 1968-71; Miami, 1972-76

Most Consecutive Games Played, Career
- 282 Jim Marshall, Cleveland, 1960; Minnesota, 1961-79
- 240 Mick Tingelhoff, Minnesota, 1962-78
- 234 Jim Bakken, St. Louis, 1962-78

Most Seasons, Coach
- 40 George Halas, Chi. Bears, 1920-29, 1933-42, 1946-55, 1958-67
- 33 Earl (Curly) Lambeau, Green Bay, 1921-49; Chi. Cardinals, 1950-51; Washington, 1952-53
- 23 Steve Owen, N.Y. Giants, 1931-53

SCORING

Most Seasons Leading League
- 5 Don Hutson, Green Bay, 1940-44
  Gino Cappelletti, Boston, 1961, 1963-66
- 3 Earl (Dutch) Clark, Portsmouth, 1932; Detroit, 1935-36
  Pat Harder, Chi. Cardinals, 1947-49
  Paul Hornung, Green Bay, 1959-61
- 2 Jack Manders, Chi. Bears, 1934, 1937
  Gordy Soltau, San Francisco, 1952-53
  Doak Walker, Detroit, 1950, 1955
  Gene Mingo, Denver, 1960, 1962
  Jim Turner, N.Y. Jets, 1968-69
  Fred Cox, Minnesota, 1969-70
  Chester Marcol, Green Bay, 1972, 1974
  John Smith, New England, 1979-80

Most Consecutive Seasons Leading League
- 5 Don Hutson, Green Bay, 1940-44
- 4 Gino Cappelletti, Boston, 1963-66
- 3 Pat Harder, Chi. Cardinals, 1947-49
  Paul Hornung, Green Bay, 1959-61

POINTS

Most Points, Career
- 2,002 George Blanda, Chi. Bears, 1949, 1950-58; Baltimore, 1950; Houston, 1960-66; Oakland, 1967-75 (9-td, 943-pat, 335-fg)
- 1,439 Jim Turner, N.Y. Jets, 1964-70; Denver, 1971-79 (1-td, 521-pat, 304-fg)
- 1,380 Jim Bakken, St. Louis, 1962-78 (534-pat, 282-fg)

Most Points, Season
- 176 Paul Hornung, Green Bay, 1960 (15-td, 41-pat, 15-fg)
- 155 Gino Cappelletti, Boston, 1964 (7-td, 38-pat, 25-fg)
- 147 Gino Cappelletti, Boston, 1961 (8-td, 48-pat, 17-fg)

Most Seasons, 100 or More Points
- 6 Gino Cappelletti, Boston, 1961-66
  George Blanda, Houston, 1960-61; Oakland, 1967-69, 1973
  Bruce Gossett, Los Angeles, 1966-67, 1969; San Francisco, 1970-71, 1973
  Jan Stenerud, Kansas City, 1967-71; Green Bay, 1981
- 5 Lou Michaels, Pittsburgh, 1962; Baltimore, 1964-65, 1967-68
- 4 Fred Cox, Minnesota, 1964-65, 1969-70

Most Points, Rookie, Season
- 132 Gale Sayers, Chicago, 1965 (22-td)
- 128 Doak Walker, Detroit, 1950 (11-td, 38-pat, 8-fg)
  Cookie Gilchrist, Buffalo, 1962 (15-td, 14-pat, 8-fg)
  Chester Marcol, Green Bay, 1972 (29-pat, 33-fg)
- 123 Gene Mingo, Denver, 1960 (6-td, 33-pat, 18-fg)

Most Points, Game
- 40 Ernie Nevers, Chi. Cardinals vs. Chi. Bears, Nov. 28, 1929 (6-td, 4-pat)
- 36 Dub Jones, Cleveland vs. Chi. Bears, Nov. 25, 1951 (6-td)
  Gale Sayers, Chicago vs. San Francisco, Dec. 12, 1965 (6-td)
- 33 Paul Hornung, Green Bay vs. Baltimore, Oct. 8, 1961 (4-td, 6-pat, 1-fg)

Most Consecutive Games Scoring
- 151 Fred Cox, Minnesota, 1963-73
- 133 Garo Yepremian, Miami, 1970-78; New Orleans, 1979
- 118 Jim Turner, N.Y. Jets, 1966-70; Denver, 1971-74

TOUCHDOWNS

Most Seasons Leading League
- 8 Don Hutson, Green Bay, 1935-38, 1941-44
- 3 Jim Brown, Cleveland, 1958-59, 1963
  Lance Alworth, San Diego, 1964-66
- 2 By many players

Most Consecutive Seasons Leading League
- 4 Don Hutson, Green Bay, 1935-38, 1941-44
- 3 Lance Alworth, San Diego, 1964-66
- 2 By many players

Most Touchdowns, Career
- 126 Jim Brown, Cleveland, 1957-65 (106-r, 20-p)
- 113 Lenny Moore, Baltimore, 1956-67 (63-r, 48-p, 2-ret)
- 105 Don Hutson, Green Bay, 1935-45 (3-r, 99-p, 3-ret)

Most Touchdowns, Season
- 23 O.J. Simpson, Buffalo, 1975 (16-r, 7-p)
- 22 Gale Sayers, Chicago, 1965 (14-r, 6-p, 2-ret)
  Chuck Foreman, Minnesota, 1975 (13-r, 9-p)
- 21 Jim Brown, Cleveland, 1965 (17-r, 4-p)

Most Touchdowns, Rookie, Season
- 22 Gale Sayers, Chicago, 1965 (14-r, 6-p, 2-ret)
- 16 Billy Sims, Detroit, 1980 (13-r, 3-p)
- 15 Cookie Gilchrist, Buffalo, 1962 (13-r, 2-p)

Most Touchdowns, Game
- 6 Ernie Nevers, Chi. Cardinals vs. Chi. Bears, Nov. 28, 1929 (6-r)
  Dub Jones, Cleveland vs. Chi. Bears, Nov. 25, 1951 (4-r, 2-p)
  Gale Sayers, Chicago vs. San Francisco, Dec. 12, 1965 (4-r, 1-p, 1-ret)
- 5 Bob Shaw, Chi. Cardinals vs. Baltimore, Oct. 2, 1950 (5-p)
  Jim Brown, Cleveland vs. Baltimore, Nov. 1, 1959 (5-r)
  Abner Haynes, Dall. Texans vs. Oakland, Nov. 26, 1961 (4-r, 1-p)
  Billy Cannon, Houston vs. N.Y. Titans, Dec. 10, 1961 (3-r, 2-p)
  Cookie Gilchrist, Buffalo vs. N.Y. Jets, Dec. 8, 1963 (5-r)
  Paul Hornung, Green Bay vs. Baltimore, Dec. 12, 1965 (3-r, 2-p)
  Kellen Winslow, San Diego vs. Oakland, Nov. 22, 1981 (5-p)
- 4 By many players

Most Consecutive Games Scoring Touchdowns
- 18 Lenny Moore, Baltimore, 1963-65
- 14 O.J. Simpson, Buffalo, 1975
- 11 Elroy (Crazylegs) Hirsch, Los Angeles, 1950-51
  Buddy Dial, Pittsburgh, 1959-60

POINTS AFTER TOUCHDOWN

Most Seasons Leading League
- 8 George Blanda, Chi. Bears, 1956; Houston, 1961-62; Oakland, 1967-69, 1972, 1974
- 4 Bob Waterfield, Cleveland, 1945; Los Angeles, 1946, 1950, 1952
- 3 Earl (Dutch) Clark, Portsmouth, 1932; Detroit, 1935-36
  Jack Manders, Chi. Bears, 1933-35
  Don Hutson, Green Bay, 1941-42, 1945

Most Points After Touchdown Attempted, Career
- 959 George Blanda, Chi. Bears, 1949, 1950-58; Baltimore, 1950; Houston, 1960-66; Oakland, 1967-75
- 657 Lou Groza, Cleveland, 1950-59, 1961-67
- 553 Jim Bakken, St. Louis, 1962-78

Most Points After Touchdown Attempted, Season
- 65 George Blanda, Houston, 1961
- 61 Rolf Benirschke, San Diego, 1981
- 60 Rafael Septien, Dallas, 1980

Most Points After Touchdown Attempted, Game
- 10 Charlie Gogolak, Washington vs. N.Y. Giants, Nov. 27, 1966
- 9 Pat Harder, Chi. Cardinals vs. N.Y. Giants, Oct. 17, 1948; vs. N.Y. Bulldogs, Nov. 13, 1949
  Bob Waterfield, Los Angeles vs. Baltimore, Oct. 22, 1950
  Bob Thomas, Chicago vs. Green Bay, Dec. 7, 1980
- 8 By many players

Most Points After Touchdown, Career
- 943 George Blanda, Chi. Bears, 1949, 1950-58; Baltimore, 1950; Houston, 1960-66; Oakland, 1967-75
- 641 Lou Groza, Cleveland, 1950-59, 1961-67
- 534 Jim Bakken, St. Louis, 1962-78

Tommy Davis *Danny Villanueva* *Bruce Gossett* *Garo Yepremian* *Tom Dempsey* *Tony Franklin* *Fred Dryer*

Most Points After Touchdown, Season
64 George Blanda, Houston, 1961
59 Rafael Septien, Dallas, 1980
56 Danny Villanueva, Dallas, 1966
George Blanda, Oakland, 1967

Most Points After Touchdown, Game
9 Pat Harder, Chi. Cardinals vs. N.Y. Giants, Oct. 17, 1948
Bob Waterfield, Los Angeles vs. Baltimore, Oct. 22, 1950
Charlie Gogolak, Washington vs. N.Y. Giants, Nov. 27, 1966
8 By many players

Most Consecutive Points After Touchdown
234 Tommy Davis, San Francisco, 1959-65
221 Jim Turner, N.Y. Jets, 1967-70; Denver, 1971-74
201 George Blanda, Oakland, 1967-75

Highest Points After Touchdown Percentage, Career (200 points after touchdown)
99.43 Tommy Davis, San Francisco, 1959-69 (350-348)
98.33 George Blanda, Chi. Bears, 1949, 1950-58; Baltimore, 1950; Houston, 1960-66; Oakland, 1967-75 (959-943)
97.93 Danny Villanueva, L.A. Rams, 1960-64; Dallas, 1965-67 (241-236)

Most Points After Touchdown, No Misses, Season
56 Danny Villanueva, Dallas, 1966
54 Mike Clark, Dallas, 1968
George Blanda, Oakland, 1968
53 Pat Harder, Chi. Cardinals, 1948

Most Points After Touchdown, No Misses, Game
9 Pat Harder, Chi. Cardinals vs. N.Y. Giants, Oct. 17, 1948
Bob Waterfield, Los Angeles vs. Baltimore, Oct. 22, 1950
8 By many players

FIELD GOALS
Most Seasons Leading League
5 Lou Groza, Cleveland, 1950, 1952-54, 1957
4 Jack Manders, Chi. Bears, 1933-34, 1936-37
Ward Cuff, N.Y. Giants, 1938-39, 1943; Green Bay, 1947
3 Bob Waterfield, Los Angeles, 1947, 1949, 1951
Gino Cappelletti, Boston, 1961, 1963-64
Fred Cox, Minnesota, 1965, 1969-70
Jan Stenerud, Kansas City, 1967, 1970, 1975
Mark Moseley, Washington, 1976-77, 1979

Most Consecutive Seasons Leading League
3 Lou Groza, Cleveland, 1952-54
2 By many players

Most Field Goals Attempted, Career
638 George Blanda, Chi. Bears, 1949, 1950-58; Baltimore, 1950; Houston, 1960-66; Oakland, 1967-75
488 Jim Turner, N.Y. Jets, 1964-70; Denver, 1971-79
465 Jan Stenerud, Kansas City, 1967-79; Green Bay, 1980-81

Most Field Goals Attempted, Season
49 Bruce Gossett, Los Angeles, 1966
Curt Knight, Washington, 1971
48 Chester Marcol, Green Bay, 1972
47 Jim Turner, N.Y. Jets, 1969
David Ray, Los Angeles, 1973

Most Field Goals Attempted, Game
9 Jim Bakken, St. Louis vs. Pittsburgh, Sept. 24, 1967
8 Lou Michaels, Pittsburgh vs. St. Louis, Dec. 2, 1962
Garo Yepremian, Detroit vs. Minnesota, Nov. 13, 1966
Jim Turner, N.Y. Jets vs. Buffalo, Nov. 3, 1968
7 By many players

Most Field Goals, Career
335 George Blanda, Chi. Bears, 1949, 1950-58; Baltimore, 1950; Houston, 1960-66; Oakland, 1967-75
304 Jim Turner, N.Y. Jets, 1964-70; Denver, 1971-79
Jan Stenerud, Kansas City, 1967-79; Green Bay, 1980-81
282 Fred Cox, Minnesota, 1963-77
Jim Bakken, St. Louis, 1962-78

Most Field Goals, Season
34 Jim Turner, N.Y. Jets, 1968
33 Chester Marcol, Green Bay, 1972
32 Jim Turner, N.Y. Jets, 1969

Most Field Goals, Rookie, Season
33 Chester Marcol, Green Bay, 1972
29 Frank Corral, Los Angeles, 1978
27 Ed Murray, Detroit, 1980

Most Field Goals, Game
7 Jim Bakken, St. Louis vs. Pittsburgh, Sept. 24, 1967
6 Gino Cappelletti, Boston vs. Denver, Oct. 4, 1964
Garo Yepremian, Detroit vs. Minnesota, Nov. 13, 1966
Jim Turner, N.Y. Jets vs. Buffalo, Nov. 3, 1968
Tom Dempsey, Philadelphia vs. Houston, Nov. 12, 1972
Bobby Howfield, N.Y. Jets vs. New Orleans, Dec. 3, 1972
Jim Bakken, St. Louis vs. Atlanta, Dec. 9, 1973
Joe Danelo, N.Y. Giants vs. Seattle, Oct. 18, 1981
5 By many players

Most Field Goals, One Quarter
4 Garo Yepremian, Detroit vs. Minnesota, Nov. 13, 1966 (second quarter)
Curt Knight, Washington vs. N.Y. Giants, Nov. 15, 1970 (second quarter)
3 By many players

Most Consecutive Games Scoring Field Goals
31 Fred Cox, Minnesota, 1968-70
28 Jim Turner, N.Y. Jets, 1970; Denver, 1971-72
21 Bruce Gossett, San Francisco, 1970-72

Most Consecutive Field Goals
20 Garo Yepremian, Miami, 1978; New Orleans, 1979
16 Jan Stenerud, Kansas City, 1969
Don Cockroft, Cleveland, 1974-75
Rolf Benirschke, San Diego, 1978-80
14 Toni Fritsch, Houston, 1979-80

Longest Field Goal
63 Tom Dempsey, New Orleans vs. Detroit, Nov. 8, 1970
59 Tony Franklin, Philadelphia vs. Dallas, Nov. 12, 1979
57 Don Cockroft, Cleveland vs. Denver, Oct. 29, 1972
Nick Lowery, Kansas City vs. Seattle, Sept. 14, 1980
Fred Steinfort, Denver vs. Washington, Oct. 13, 1980

Highest Field Goal Percentage, Career (100 field goals)
68.79 Efren Herrera, Dallas, 1974, 1976-77; Seattle, 1978-81 (157-108)
68.30 Toni Fritsch, Dallas, 1971-73, 1975; San Diego, 1976; Houston, 1977-81 (224-153)
67.80 John Smith, New England, 1974-81 (177-120)

Highest Field Goal Percentage, Season (14 attempts)
91.67 Jan Stenerud, Green Bay, 1981 (24-22)
88.46 Lou Groza, Cleveland, 1953 (26-23)
87.50 Don Cockroft, Cleveland, 1974 (16-14)

Most Field Goals, No Misses, Game
6 Gino Cappelletti, Boston vs. Denver, Oct. 4, 1964
Joe Danelo, N.Y. Giants vs. Seattle, Oct. 18, 1981
5 Roger LeClerc, Chicago vs. Detroit, Dec. 3, 1961
Lou Michaels, Baltimore vs. San Francisco, Sept. 25, 1966
Mac Percival, Chicago vs. Philadelphia, Oct. 20, 1968
Roy Gerela, Houston vs. Miami, Sept. 28, 1969
Jan Stenerud, Kansas City vs. Buffalo, Nov. 2, 1969; vs. Buffalo, Dec. 7, 1969
Horst Muhlmann, Cincinnati vs. Buffalo, Nov. 8, 1970; vs. Pittsburgh, Sept. 24, 1972
Bruce Gossett, San Francisco vs. Denver, Sept. 23, 1973
Nick Mike-Mayer, Atlanta vs. Los Angeles, Nov. 4, 1973
Curt Knight, Washington vs. Baltimore, Nov. 18, 1973
Tim Mazzetti, Atlanta vs. Los Angeles, Oct. 30, 1978
Ed Murray, Detroit vs. Green Bay, Sept. 14, 1980

SAFETIES
Most Safeties, Career
4 Ted Hendricks, Baltimore, 1969-73; Green Bay, 1974; Oakland, 1975-81
3 Bill McPeak, Pittsburgh, 1949-57
Charlie Krueger, San Francisco, 1959-73
Ernie Stautner, Pittsburgh, 1950-63
Jim Katcavage, N.Y. Giants, 1956-68
Roger Brown, Detroit, 1960-66; Los Angeles, 1967-69
Bruce Maher, Detroit, 1960-67; N.Y. Giants, 1968-69
Ron McDole, St. Louis, 1961; Houston, 1962; Buffalo, 1963-70; Washington, 1971-78
Alan Page, Minnesota, 1967-78; Chicago, 1979-81
2 By many players

Most Safeties, Season
2 Tom Nash, Green Bay, 1932
Roger Brown, Detroit, 1962
Ron McDole, Buffalo, 1964
Alan Page, Minnesota, 1971
Fred Dryer, Los Angeles, 1973
Benny Barnes, Dallas, 1973
James Young, Houston, 1977
Tom Hannon, Minnesota, 1981

Most Safeties, Game
2 Fred Dryer, Los Angeles vs. Green Bay, Oct. 21, 1973

| O. J. Simpson | Earl Campbell | Lydell Mitchell | Andy Uram | Bob Gage | Bobby Douglass | Beattie Feathers |

RUSHING

Most Seasons Leading League
- 8 Jim Brown, Cleveland, 1957-61, 1963-65
- 4 Steve Van Buren, Philadelphia, 1945, 1947-49
  - O.J. Simpson, Buffalo, 1972-73, 1975-76
- 3 Earl Campbell, Houston, 1978-80

Most Consecutive Seasons Leading League
- 5 Jim Brown, Cleveland, 1957-61
- 3 Steve Van Buren, Philadelphia, 1947-49
  - Jim Brown, Cleveland, 1963-65
  - Earl Campbell, Houston, 1978-80
- 2 Bill Paschal, N.Y. Giants, 1943-44
  - Joe Perry, San Francisco, 1953-54
  - Jim Nance, Boston, 1966-67
  - Leroy Kelly, Cleveland, 1967-68
  - O.J. Simpson, Buffalo, 1972-73; 1975-76

ATTEMPTS

Most Seasons Leading League
- 6 Jim Brown, Cleveland, 1958-59, 1961, 1963-65
- 4 Steve Van Buren, Philadelphia, 1947-50
  - Walter Payton, Chicago, 1976-79
- 3 Cookie Gilchrist, Buffalo, 1963-64; Denver, 1965
  - Jim Nance, Boston, 1966-67, 1969
  - O. J. Simpson, Buffalo, 1973-75

Most Consecutive Seasons Leading League
- 4 Steve Van Buren, Philadelphia, 1947-50
  - Walter Payton,Chicago, 1976-79
- 3 Jim Brown, Cleveland, 1963-65
  - Cookie Gilchrist, Buffalo, 1963-64; Denver, 1965
  - O. J. Simpson, Buffalo, 1973-75
- 2 By many players

Most Attempts, Career
- 2,462 Franco Harris, Pittsburgh, 1972-81
- 2,404 O.J. Simpson, Buffalo, 1969-77; San Francisco, 1978-79
- 2,359 Jim Brown, Cleveland, 1957-65

Most Attempts, Season
- 378 George Rogers, New Orleans, 1981
- 373 Earl Campbell, Houston, 1980
- 369 Walter Payton, Chicago, 1979

Most Attempts, Rookie, Season
- 378 George Rogers, New Orleans, 1981
- 331 Ottis Anderson, St. Louis, 1979
- 306 Joe Cribbs, Buffalo, 1980

Most Attempts, Game
- 41 Franco Harris, Pittsburgh vs. Cincinnati, Oct. 17, 1976
- 40 Lydell Mitchell, Baltimore vs. N.Y. Jets, Oct. 20, 1974
  - Walter Payton, Chicago vs. Minnesota, Nov. 20, 1977
- 39 O.J. Simpson, Buffalo vs. Kansas City, Oct. 29, 1973
  - Terdell Middleton, Green Bay vs. Minnesota, Nov. 26, 1978 (OT)
  - Walter Payton, Chicago vs. Buffalo, Oct. 7, 1979
  - Ricky Bell, Tampa Bay vs. Kansas City, Dec. 16, 1979
  - Earl Campbell, Houston vs. Seattle, Oct. 11, 1981

YARDS GAINED

Most Yards Gained, Career
- 12,312 Jim Brown, Cleveland, 1957-65
- 11,236 O.J. Simpson, Buffalo, 1969-77; San Francisco, 1978-79
- 10,339 Franco Harris, Pittsburgh, 1972-81

Most Seasons, 1,000 or More Yards Rushing
- 7 Jim Brown, Cleveland, 1958-61, 1963-65
  - Franco Harris, Pittsburgh, 1972, 1974-79
- 6 Walter Payton, Chicago, 1976-81
- 5 Jim Taylor, Green Bay, 1960-64
  - O.J. Simpson, Buffalo, 1972-76
  - Tony Dorsett, Dallas, 1977-81

Most Yards Gained, Season
- 2,003 O.J. Simpson, Buffalo, 1973
- 1,934 Earl Campbell, Houston, 1980
- 1,863 Jim Brown, Cleveland, 1963

Most Yards Gained, Rookie, Season
- 1,674 George Rogers, New Orleans, 1981
- 1,605 Ottis Anderson, St. Louis, 1979
- 1,450 Earl Campbell, Houston, 1978

Most Yards Gained, Game
- 275 Walter Payton, Chicago vs. Minnesota, Nov. 20, 1977
- 273 O.J. Simpson, Buffalo vs. Detroit, Nov. 25, 1976
- 250 O.J. Simpson, Buffalo vs. New England, Sept. 16, 1973

Most Games, 200 or More Yards Rushing, Career
- 6 O.J. Simpson, Buffalo, 1969-77; San Francisco, 1978-79
- 4 Jim Brown,Cleveland, 1957-65
  - Earl Campbell, Houston, 1978-81
- 2 Walter Payton, Chicago, 1975-81

Most Games, 200 or More Yards Rushing, Season
- 4 Earl Campbell, Houston, 1980
- 3 O.J. Simpson, Buffalo, 1973
- 2 Jim Brown, Cleveland, 1963
  - O.J. Simpson, Buffalo, 1976
  - Walter Payton, Chicago, 1977

Most Consecutive Games, 200 or More Yards Rushing
- 2 O.J. Simpson, Buffalo, 1973, 1976
  - Earl Campbell, Houston, 1980

Most Games, 100 or More Yards Rushing, Career
- 58 Jim Brown, Cleveland, 1957-65
- 46 Walter Payton, Chicago, 1975-81
- 42 O.J. Simpson, Buffalo, 1969-77; San Francisco, 1978-79

Most Games, 100 or More Yards Rushing, Season
- 11 O.J. Simpson, Buffalo, 1973
  - Earl Campbell, Houston, 1979
- 10 Walter Payton, Chicago, 1977
  - Earl Campbell, Houston, 1980
- 9 Jim Brown, Cleveland, 1958, 1963
  - Ottis Anderson, St. Louis, 1979
  - Tony Dorsett, Dallas, 1981
  - George Rogers. New Orleans, 1981

Most Consecutive Games, 100 or More Yards Rushing
- 7 O.J. Simpson, Buffalo, 1972-73
  - Earl Campbell, Houston, 1979
- 6 Jim Brown, Cleveland, 1958
  - Franco Harris, Pittsburgh, 1972
  - Earl Campbell, Houston, 1980
- 5 Rob Goode, Washington, 1951
  - Jim Brown, Cleveland, 1961
  - Jim Nance, Boston, 1966
  - O.J. Simpson, Buffalo, 1973, 1975
  - Walter Payton, Chicago, 1977

Longest Run From Scrimmage
- 97 Andy Uram, Green Bay vs. Chi. Cardinals, Oct. 8, 1939 (TD)
  - Bob Gage, Pittsburgh vs. Chi. Bears, Dec. 4, 1949 (TD)
- 96 Jim Spavital, Baltimore vs. Green Bay, Nov. 5, 1950 (TD)
  - Bob Hoernschemeyer, Detroit vs. N.Y. Yanks, Nov. 23, 1950 (TD)
- 94 O.J. Simpson, Buffalo vs. Pittsburgh, Oct. 29, 1972 (TD)

AVERAGE GAIN

Highest Average Gain, Career (700 attempts)
- 5.22 Jim Brown, Cleveland, 1957-65 (2,359-12,312)
- 5.14 Eugene (Mercury) Morris, Miami, 1969-75; San Diego, 1976 (804-4,133)
- 5.00 Gale Sayers, Chicago, 1965-71 (991-4,956)

Highest Average Gain, Season (Qualifiers)
- 9.94 Beattie Feathers, Chi. Bears, 1934 (101-1,004)
- 6.87 Bobby Douglass, Chicago, 1972 (141-968)
- 6.78 Dan Towler, Los Angeles, 1951 (126-854)

Highest Average Gain, Game (10 attempts)
- 17.09 Marion Motley, Cleveland vs. Pittsburgh, Oct. 29, 1950 (11-188)
- 16.70 Bill Grimes, Green Bay vs. N.Y. Yanks, Oct. 8, 1950 (10-167)
- 16.57 Bobby Mitchell, Cleveland vs. Washington, Nov. 15, 1959 (14-232)

TOUCHDOWNS

Most Seasons Leading League
- 5 Jim Brown, Cleveland, 1957-59, 1963, 1965
- 4 Steve Van Buren, Philadelphia, 1945, 1947-49
- 3 Abner Haynes, Dall. Texans, 1960-62
  - Cookie Gilchrist, Buffalo, 1962-64
  - Paul Lowe, L.A. Chargers, 1960; San Diego, 1961, 1965
  - Leroy Kelly, Cleveland, 1966-68

Most Consecutive Seasons Leading League
- 3 Steve Van Buren, Philadelphia, 1947-49
  - Jim Brown, Cleveland, 1957-59
  - Abner Haynes, Dall. Texans, 1960-62
  - Cookie Gilchrist, Buffalo, 1962-64
  - Leroy Kelly, Cleveland, 1966-68

Most Touchdowns, Career
- 106 Jim Brown, Cleveland, 1957-65
- 84 Franco Harris, Pittsburgh, 1972-81
- 83 Jim Taylor, Green Bay, 1958-66; New Orleans, 1967

Chuck Muncie *Pete Banaszak* *Cecil Isbell* *Jim Hart* *Jim Zorn* *Steve Dils* *Richard Todd*

Most Touchdowns, Season
- 19 Jim Taylor, Green Bay, 1962
    Earl Campbell, Houston, 1979
    Chuck Muncie, San Diego, 1981
- 17 Jim Brown, Cleveland, 1958, 1965
- 16 Lenny Moore, Baltimore, 1964
    Leroy Kelly, Cleveland, 1968
    Pete Banaszak, Oakland, 1975
    O.J. Simpson, Buffalo, 1975

Most Touchdowns, Rookie, Season
- 14 Gale Sayers, Chicago, 1965
- 13 Cookie Gilchrist, Buffalo, 1962
    Earl Campbell, Houston, 1978
    Billy Sims, Detroit, 1980
    George Rogers, New Orleans, 1981
- 12 Tony Dorsett, Dallas, 1977

Most Touchdowns, Game
- 6 Ernie Nevers, Chi. Cardinals vs. Chi. Bears, Nov. 28, 1929
- 5 Jim Brown, Cleveland vs. Baltimore, Nov. 1, 1959
    Cookie Gilchrist, Buffalo vs. N.Y. Jets, Dec. 8, 1963
- 4 By many players

Most Consecutive Games Rushing for Touchdowns
- 11 Lenny Moore, Baltimore, 1963-64
- 9 Leroy Kelly, Cleveland, 1968
- 8 Steve Van Buren, Philadelphia, 1947

PASSING

Most Seasons Leading League
- 6 Sammy Baugh, Washington, 1937, 1940, 1943, 1945, 1947, 1949
- 4 Len Dawson, Dall. Texans; 1962; Kansas City, 1964, 1966, 1968
    Roger Staubach, Dallas, 1971, 1973, 1978-79
- 3 Arnie Herber, Green Bay, 1932, 1934, 1936
    Norm Van Brocklin, Los Angeles, 1950, 1952, 1954
    Bart Starr, Green Bay, 1962, 1964, 1966
    Ken Anderson, Cincinnati, 1974-75, 1981

Most Consecutive Seasons Leading League
- 2 Cecil Isbell, Green Bay, 1941-42
    Milt Plum, Cleveland, 1960-61
    Ken Anderson, Cincinnati, 1974-75
    Roger Staubach, Dallas, 1978-79

ATTEMPTS

Most Seasons Leading League
- 4 Sammy Baugh, Washington, 1937, 1943, 1947-48
    Johnny Unitas, Baltimore, 1957, 1959-61
    George Blanda, Chi. Bears, 1953; Houston, 1963-65
- 3 Arnie Herber, Green Bay, 1932, 1934, 1936
    Sonny Jurgensen, Washington, 1966-67, 1969
- 2 By many players

Most Consecutive Seasons Leading League
- 3 Johnny Unitas, Baltimore, 1959-61
    George Blanda, Houston, 1963-65
- 2 By many players

Most Passes Attempted, Career
- 6,467 Fran Tarkenton, Minnesota, 1961-66, 1972-78; N.Y. Giants, 1967-71
- 5,186 Johnny Unitas, Baltimore, 1956-72; San Diego, 1973
- 4,945 Jim Hart, St. Louis, 1966-81

Most Passes Attempted, Season
- 609 Dan Fouts, San Diego, 1981
- 593 Tommy Kramer, Minnesota, 1981
- 589 Dan Fouts, San Diego, 1980

Most Passes Attempted, Rookie, Season
- 439 Jim Zorn, Seattle, 1976
- 392 Butch Songin, Boston, 1960
- 375 Norm Snead, Washington, 1961

Most Passes Attempted, Game
- 68 George Blanda, Houston vs. Buffalo, Nov. 1, 1964
- 62 Joe Namath, N.Y. Jets vs. Baltimore, Oct. 18, 1970
    Steve Dils, Minnesota vs. Tampa Bay, Sept. 5, 1981
- 61 Tommy Kramer, Minnesota vs. Buffalo, Dec. 16, 1979

COMPLETIONS

Most Seasons Leading League
- 5 Sammy Baugh, Washington, 1937, 1943, 1945, 1947-48
- 4 George Blanda, Chi. Bears, 1953; Houston, 1963-65
    Sonny Jurgensen, Philadephia, 1961; Washington, 1966-67, 1969
- 3 Arnie Herber, Green Bay, 1932, 1934, 1936
    Johnny Unitas, Baltimore, 1959-60, 1963
    John Brodie, San Francisco, 1965, 1968, 1970
    Fran Tarkenton, Minnesota, 1975-76, 1978

Most Consecutive Seasons Leading League
- 3 George Blanda, Houston, 1963-65
- 2 By many players

Most Passes Completed, Career
- 3,686 Fran Tarkenton, Minnesota, 1961-66, 1972-78; N.Y. Giants, 1967-71
- 2,830 Johnny Unitas, Baltimore, 1956-72; San Diego, 1973
- 2,521 Jim Hart, St. Louis, 1966-81

Most Passes Completed, Season
- 360 Dan Fouts, San Diego, 1981
- 348 Dan Fouts, San Diego, 1980
- 347 Steve DeBerg, San Francisco, 1979

Most Passes Completed, Rookie, Season
- 208 Jim Zorn, Seattle, 1976
- 187 Butch Songin, Boston, 1960
- 183 Jeff Komlo, Detroit, 1979

Most Passes Completed, Game
- 42 Richard Todd, N.Y. Jets vs. San Francisco, Sept. 21, 1980
- 38 Tommy Kramer, Minnesota vs. Cleveland, Dec. 14, 1980
    Tommy Kramer, Minnesota vs. Green Bay, Nov. 29, 1981
- 37 George Blanda, Houston vs. Buffalo, Nov. 1, 1964
    Steve Dils, Minnesota vs. Tampa Bay, Sept. 5, 1981

Most Consecutive Passes Completed
- 17 Bert Jones, Baltimore vs. N.Y. Jets, Dec. 15, 1974
- 16 Ken Anderson, Cincinnati vs. Baltimore (8), Nov. 3; vs. Pittsburgh (8), Nov. 10, 1974
    Craig Morton, Denver vs. Kansas City, Dec. 10, 1978
    Tommy Kramer, Minnesota vs. Green Bay, Nov. 11, 1979
- 15 Len Dawson, Kansas City vs. Houston, Sept. 9, 1967
    Joe Namath, N.Y. Jets vs. Miami (12), Oct. 22; vs. Boston (3), Oct. 29, 1967
    Archie Manning, New Orleans vs. Tampa Bay (8), Oct. 14; vs. Detroit (7), Oct. 21, 1979
    Lynn Dickey, Green Bay vs. San Francisco, Nov. 9, 1980
    Dan Fouts, San Diego vs. Cleveland, Sept. 7, 1981

COMPLETION PERCENTAGE

Most Seasons Leading League
- 8 Len Dawson, Dall. Texans, 1962; Kansas City, 1964-69, 1975
- 7 Sammy Baugh, Washington, 1940, 1942-43, 1945, 1947-49
- 4 Bart Starr, Green Bay, 1962, 1966, 1968-69

Most Consecutive Seasons Leading League
- 6 Len Dawson, Kansas City, 1964-69
- 3 Sammy Baugh, Washington, 1947-49
    Otto Graham, Cleveland, 1953-55
    Milt Plum, Cleveland, 1959-61
- 2 By many players

Highest Completion Percentage, Career (1,500 attempts)
- 60.32 Ken Stabler, Oakland, 1970-79; Houston, 1980-81 (3,223-1,944)
- 57.73 Dan Fouts, San Diego, 1973-81 (3,203-1,849)
- 57.53 Ken Anderson, Cincinnati, 1971-81 (3,539-2,036)

Highest Completion Percentage, Season (Qualifiers)
- 70.33 Sammy Baugh, Washington, 1945 (182-128)
- 66.67 Ken Stabler, Oakland, 1976 (291-194)
- 66.43 Len Dawson, Kansas City, 1975 (140-93)

Highest Completion Percentage, Rookie, Season (Qualifiers)
- 56.07 Fran Tarkenton, Minnesota, 1961 (280-157)
- 55.56 Johnny Unitas, Baltimore, 1956 (198-110)
- 55.45 Dennis Shaw, Buffalo, 1970 (321-178)

Highest Completion Percentage, Game (20 attempts)
- 90.91 Ken Anderson, Cincinnati vs. Pittsburgh, Nov. 10, 1974 (22-20)
- 90.48 Lynn Dickey, Green Bay vs. New Orleans, Dec. 13, 1981 (21-19)
- 86.36 Craig Morton, Denver vs. Kansas City, Dec. 10, 1978 (22-19)

YARDS GAINED

Most Seasons Leading League
- 5 Sonny Jurgensen, Philadelphia, 1961-62; Washington, 1966-67, 1969
- 4 Sammy Baugh, Washington, 1937, 1940, 1947-48
    Johnny Unitas, Baltimore, 1957, 1959-60, 1963
- 3 Arnie Herber, Green Bay, 1932, 1934, 1936
    Sid Luckman, Chi. Bears, 1943, 1945-46
    John Brodie, San Francisco, 1965, 1968, 1970
    John Hadl, San Diego, 1965, 1968, 1971
    Joe Namath, N.Y. Jets, 1966-67, 1972
    Dan Fouts, San Diego, 1979-81

Most Consecutive Seasons Leading League
- 3 Dan Fouts, San Diego, 1979-81
- 2 By many players

Most Yards Gained, Career
- 47,003 Fran Tarkenton, Minnesota, 1961-66, 1972-78; N.Y. Giants, 1967-71
- 40,239 Johnny Unitas, Baltimore, 1956-72; San Diego, 1973
- 33,848 Jim Hart, St. Louis, 1966-81

  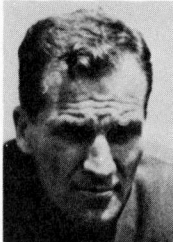  

Sonny Jurgensen   *Brian Sipe*   *Dennis Shaw*   *Butch Songin*   *Daryle Lamonica*   *Joe Kapp*   *Adrian Burk*

PASSING Continued

Most Seasons, 3,000 or More Yards Passing
5	Sonny Jurgensen, Philadelphia, 1961-62; Washington, 1966-67, 1969
3	Johnny Unitas, Baltimore, 1960, 1963, 1967
	George Blanda, Houston, 1961, 1963-64
	Joe Namath, N.Y. Jets, 1966-68
	Daryle Lamonica, Oakland, 1967-69
	John Hadl, San Diego, 1967-68, 1971
	Bert Jones, Baltimore, 1976, 1980-81
	Archie Manning, New Orleans, 1978-80
	Jim Zorn, Seattle, 1978-80
	Dan Fouts, San Diego, 1979-81
	Tommy Kramer, Minnesota, 1979-81
	Brian Sipe, Cleveland, 1979-81
2	By many players

Most Yards Gained, Season
4,802	Dan Fouts, San Diego, 1981
4,715	Dan Fouts, San Diego, 1980
4,132	Brian Sipe, Cleveland, 1980

Most Yards Gained, Rookie, Season
2,571	Jim Zorn, Seattle, 1976
2,507	Dennis Shaw, Buffalo, 1970
2,476	Butch Songin, Boston, 1960

Most Yards Gained, Game
554	Norm Van Brocklin, Los Angeles vs. N.Y. Yanks, Sept. 28, 1951
505	Y.A. Tittle, N.Y. Giants vs. Washington, Oct. 28, 1962
496	Joe Namath, N.Y. Jets vs. Baltimore, Sept. 24, 1972

Most Games, 300 or More Yards Passing, Career
26	Johnny Unitas, Baltimore, 1956-72; San Diego, 1973
25	Sonny Jurgensen, Philadelphia, 1957-63; Washington, 1964-74
25	Dan Fouts, San Diego, 1973-81
	Joe Namath, N.Y. Jets, 1965-76; Los Angeles, 1977

Most Games, 300 or More Yards Passing, Season
8	Dan Fouts, San Diego, 1980
7	Dan Fouts, San Diego, 1981
6	Joe Namath, N.Y. Jets, 1967
	Dan Fouts, San Diego, 1979
	Archie Manning, New Orleans, 1980
	Brian Sipe, Cleveland, 1980

Most Consecutive Games, 300 or More Yards, Passing, Season
4	Dan Fouts, San Diego, 1979
3	Frank Tripucka, Denver, 1960
	Johnny Unitas, Baltimore, 1963
	George Blanda, Houston, 1964
	Cotton Davidson, Oakland, 1964
	John Hadl, San Diego, 1967
	Sonny Jurgensen, Washington, 1967
	Dan Fouts, San Diego, 1980
2	By many players

Longest Pass Completion (All TDs except as noted)
99	Frank Filchock (to Farkas), Washington vs. Pittsburgh, Oct. 15, 1939
	George Izo (to Mitchell), Washington vs. Cleveland, Sept. 15, 1963
	Karl Sweetan (to Studstill), Detroit vs. Baltimore, Oct. 16, 1966
	Sonny Jurgensen (to Allen), Washington vs. Chicago, Sept. 15, 1968
98	Doug Russell (to Tinsley), Chi. Cardinals vs. Cleveland, Nov. 27, 1938
	Ogden Compton (to Lane), Chi. Cardinals vs. Green Bay, Nov. 13, 1955
	Bill Wade (to Farrington), Chicago Bears vs. Detroit, Oct. 8, 1961
	Jacky Lee (to Dewveall), Houston vs. San Diego, Nov. 25, 1962
	Earl Morrall (to Jones), N.Y. Giants vs. Pittsburgh, Sept. 11, 1966
	Jim Hart (to Moore), St. Louis vs. Los Angeles, Dec. 10, 1972 (no TD)
97	Pat Coffee (to Tinsley), Chi. Cardinals vs. Chi. Bears, Dec. 5, 1937
	Bobby Layne (to Box), Detroit vs. Green Bay, Nov. 26, 1953
	George Shaw (to Tarr), Denver vs. Boston, Sept. 21, 1962

AVERAGE GAIN

Most Seasons Leading League
7	Sid Luckman, Chi. Bears, 1939-43, 1946-47
3	Arnie Herber, Green Bay, 1932, 1934, 1936
	Norm Van Brocklin, Los Angeles, 1950, 1952, 1954
	Len Dawson, Dall. Texans, 1962; Kansas City, 1966, 1968
	Bart Starr, Green Bay, 1966-68

Most Consecutive Seasons Leading League
5	Sid Luckman, Chi. Bears, 1939-43
3	Bart Starr, Green Bay, 1966-68
2	Bernie Masterson, Chi. Bears, 1937-38
	Sid Luckman, Chi. Bears, 1946-47
	Johnny Unitas, Baltimore, 1964-65
	Terry Bradshaw, Pittsburgh, 1977-78
	Steve Grogan, New England, 1980-81

Highest Average Gain, Career (1,500 attempts)
8.63	Otto Graham, Cleveland, 1950-55 (1,565-13,499)
8.42	Sid Luckman, Chi. Bears, 1939-50 (1,744-14,686)
8.16	Norm Van Brocklin, Los Angeles, 1949-57; Philadelphia, 1958-60 (2,895- 23,611)

Highest Average Gain, Season (Qualifiers)
11.17	Tommy O'Connell, Cleveland, 1957 (110-1,229)
10.86	Sid Luckman, Chi. Bears, 1943 (202-2,194)
10.55	Otto Graham, Cleveland, 1953 (258-2,722)

Highest Average Gain, Rookie, Season (Qualifiers)
9.411	Greg Cook Cincinnati, 1969 (197-1,854)
9.409	Bob Waterfield, Cleveland, 1945 (171-1,609)
8.36	Zeke Bratkowski, Chi. Bears, 1954 (130-1,087)

Highest Average Gain, Game (20 attempts)
18.58	Sammy Baugh, Washington vs. Boston, Oct. 31, 1948 (24-446)
18.50	Johnny Unitas, Baltimore vs. Atlanta, Nov. 12, 1967 (20-370)
17.71	Joe Namath, N.Y. Jets vs. Baltimore, Sept. 24, 1972 (28-496)

TOUCHDOWNS

Most Seasons Leading League
4	Johnny Unitas, Baltimore, 1957-60
	Len Dawson, Dall. Texans, 1962; Kansas City, 1963, 1965-66
3	Arnie Herber, Green Bay, 1932, 1934, 1936
	Sid Luckman, Chi. Bears, 1943, 1945-46
	Y.A. Tittle, San Francisco, 1955; N.Y. Giants, 1962-63
2	By many players

Most Consecutive Seasons Leading League
4	Johnny Unitas, Baltimore, 1957-60
2	By many players

Most Touchdown Passes, Career
342	Fran Tarkenton, Minnesota, 1961-66, 1972-78; N.Y. Giants, 1967-71
290	Johnny Unitas, Baltimore, 1956-72; San Diego, 1973
255	Sonny Jurgensen, Philadelphia, 1957-63; Washington, 1964-74

Most Touchdown Passes, Season
36	George Blanda, Houston, 1961
	Y.A. Tittle, N.Y. Giants, 1963
34	Daryle Lamonica, Oakland, 1969
33	Y.A. Tittle, N.Y. Giants, 1962
	Dan Fouts, San Diego, 1981

Most Touchdown Passes, Rookie, Season
22	Charlie Conerly, N.Y. Giants, 1948
	Butch Songin, Boston, 1960
19	Jim Plunkett, New England, 1971
18	Fran Tarkenton, Minnesota, 1961
	Joe Namath, N.Y. Jets, 1965

Most Touchdown Passes, Game
7	Sid Luckman, Chi. Bears vs. N.Y. Giants, Nov. 14, 1943
	Adrian Burk, Philadelphia vs. Washington, Oct. 17, 1954
	George Blanda, Houston vs. N.Y. Titans, Nov. 19, 1961
	Y.A. Tittle, N.Y. Giants vs. Washington, Oct. 28, 1962
	Joe Kapp, Minnesota vs. Baltimore, Sept. 28, 1969
6	By many players. Last time: Dan Fouts, San Diego vs. Oakland, Nov. 22, 1981

Most Consecutive Games, Touchdown Passes
47	Johnny Unitas, Baltimore, 1956-60
25	Daryle Lamonica, Oakland, 1968-70
23	Frank Ryan, Cleveland, 1965-67
	Sonny Jurgensen, Washington, 1966-68

HAD INTERCEPTED

Fewest Passes Had Intercepted, Season (Qualifiers)
1	Joe Ferguson, Buffalo, 1976
3	Gary Wood, N.Y. Giants, 1964
	Bart Starr, Green Bay, 1966
4	Sammy Baugh, Washington, 1945
	Harry Gilmer, Detroit, 1955
	Charlie Conerly, N.Y. Giants, 1959
	Bart Starr, Green Bay, 1964
	Roger Staubach, Dallas, 1971
	Len Dawson, Kansas City, 1975

Most Consecutive Passes Attempted, None Intercepted
294	Bart Starr, Green Bay, 1964-65
208	Milt Plum, Cleveland, 1959-60
206	Roman Gabriel, Los Angeles, 1968-69

Most Passes Had Intercepted, Career
277	George Blanda, Chi. Bears, 1949, 1950-58; Baltimore, 1950; Houston, 1960-66; Oakland, 1967-75
268	John Hadl, San Diego, 1962-72; Los Angeles, 1973-74; Green Bay, 1974-75; Houston, 1976-77
266	Fran Tarkenton, Minnesota, 1961-66, 1972-78; N.Y. Giants, 1967-71

Lionel Taylor

Charley Taylor

Art Powell

Charley Hennigan

Bill Groman

Charlie Joiner

Jim Benton

Most Passes Had Intercepted, Season
42 George Blanda, Houston, 1962
34 Frank Tripucka, Denver, 1960
32 John Hadl, San Diego, 1968
Fran Tarkenton, Minnesota, 1978

Most Passes Had Intercepted, Game
8 Jim Hardy, Chi. Cardinals vs. Philadelphia, Sept. 24, 1950
7 Parker Hall, Cleveland vs. Green Bay, Nov. 8, 1942
Frank Sinkwich, Detroit vs. Green Bay, Oct. 24, 1943
Bob Waterfield, Los Angeles vs. Green Bay, Oct. 17, 1948
Zeke Bratkowski, Chicago vs. Baltimore, Oct. 2, 1960
Tommy Wade, Pittsburgh vs. Philadelphia, Dec. 12, 1965
Ken Stabler, Oakland vs. Denver, Oct. 16, 1977
6 By many players

LOWEST PERCENTAGE, PASSES HAD INTERCEPTED
Most Seasons Leading League, Lowest Percentage, Passes Had Intercepted
5 Sammy Baugh, Washington, 1940, 1942, 1944-45, 1947
3 Charlie Conerly, N.Y. Giants, 1950, 1956, 1959
Bart Starr, Green Bay, 1962, 1964, 1966
Roger Staubach, Dallas, 1971, 1977, 1979
2 By many players

Lowest Percentage, Passes Had Intercepted, Career (1,500 attempts)
3.31 Roman Gabriel, Los Angeles, 1962-72; Philadelphia, 1973-77 (4,498-149)
3.50 Ken Anderson, Cincinnati, 1971-81 (3,539-124)
3.68 Roger Staubach, Dallas, 1969-79 (2,958-109)

Lowest Percentage, Passes Had Intercepted, Season (Qualifiers)
0.66 Joe Ferguson, Buffalo, 1976 (151-1)
1.20 Bart Starr, Green Bay, 1966 (251-3)
1.47 Bart Starr, Green Bay, 1964 (272-4)

Lowest Percentage, Passes Had Intercepted, Rookie, Season (Qualifiers)
2.10 Gary Wood, N.Y. Giants, 1964 (143-3)
3.83 Butch Songin, Boston, 1960 (392-15)
4.12 Doug Williams. Tampa Bay, 1978 (194-8)

PASS RECEIVING
Most Seasons Leading League
8 Don Hutson, Green Bay, 1936-37, 1939, 1941-45
5 Lionel Taylor, Denver, 1960-63, 1965
3 Tom Fears, Los Angeles, 1948-50
Pete Pihos, Philadelphia, 1953-55
Billy Wilson, San Francisco, 1954, 1956-57
Raymond Berry, Baltimore, 1958-60
Lance Alworth, San Diego, 1966, 1968-69

Most Consecutive Seasons Leading League
5 Don Hutson, Green Bay, 1941-45
4 Lionel Taylor, Denver, 1960-63
3 Tom Fears, Los Angeles, 1948-50
Pete Pihos, Philadelphia, 1953-55
Raymond Berry, Baltimore, 1958-60

Most Pass Receptions, Career
649 Charley Taylor, Washington, 1964-75, 1977
633 Don Maynard, N.Y. Giants, 1958; N.Y. Jets, 1960-72; St. Louis, 1973
631 Raymond Berry, Baltimore, 1955-67

Most Seasons, 50 or More Pass Receptions
7 Raymond Berry, Baltimore, 1958-62, 1965-66
Art Powell, N.Y. Titans, 1960-62; Oakland, 1963-66
Lance Alworth, San Diego, 1963-69
Charley Taylor, Washington, 1964, 1966-67, 1969, 1973-75
6 Lionel Taylor, Denver, 1960-65
Bobby Mitchell, Washington, 1962-67
Ahmad Rashad, Minnesota, 1976-81
5 Billy Wilson, San Francisco, 1953-57
Pete Retzlaff, Philadelphia, 1958, 1961, 1963-65
Bernie Casey, San Francisco, 1962, 1964-66; Los Angeles, 1967
Don Maynard, N.Y. Jets, 1960, 1962, 1965, 1967-68
Lydell Mitchell, Baltimore, 1974-77; San Diego, 1978
Harold Carmichael, Philadelphia, 1973-74, 1978-79, 1981
Steve Largent, Seattle, 1976, 1978-81

Most Pass Receptions, Season
101 Charley Hennigan, Houston, 1964
100 Lionel Taylor, Denver, 1961
93 Johnny Morris, Chicago, 1964

Most Pass Receptions, Rookie, Season
83 Earl Cooper, San Francisco, 1980
72 Bill Groman, Houston, 1960
67 Jack Clancy, Miami, 1967
Cris Collinsworth, Cincinnati, 1981

Most Pass Receptions, Game
18 Tom Fears, Los Angeles vs. Green Bay, Dec. 3, 1950
17 Clark Gaines, N.Y. Jets vs. San Francisco, Sept. 21, 1980
16 Sonny Randle, St. Louis vs. N.Y. Giants, Nov. 4, 1962

Most Consecutive Games, Pass Receptions
127 Harold Carmichael, Philadelphia, 1972-80
117 Mel Gray, St. Louis, 1973-81 (current)
105 Dan Abramowicz, New Orleans, 1967-73; San Francisco, 1973-74

YARDS GAINED
Most Seasons Leading League
7 Don Hutson, Green Bay, 1936, 1938-39, 1941-44
3 Raymond Berry, Baltimore, 1957, 1959-60
Lance Alworth, San Diego, 1965-66, 1968
2 By many players

Most Consecutive Seasons Leading League
4 Don Hutson, Green Bay, 1941-44
2 By many players

Most Yards Gained, Career
11,834 Don Maynard, N.Y. Giants, 1958; N.Y. Jets, 1960-72; St. Louis, 1973
10,266 Lance Alworth, San Diego, 1962-70; Dallas, 1971-72
10,246 Harold Jackson, Los Angeles, 1968, 1973-77; Philadelphia, 1969-72; New England, 1978-81

Most Seasons, 1,000 or More Yards, Pass Receiving
7 Lance Alworth, San Diego, 1963-69
5 Art Powell, N.Y. Titans, 1960, 1962; Oakland, 1963-64, 1966
Don Maynard, N.Y. Jets, 1960, 1962, 1965, 1967-68
4 Del Shofner, Los Angeles, 1958; N.Y. Giants, 1961-63
Lionel Taylor, Denver, 1960-61, 1963, 1965
Charlie Joiner, San Diego, 1976, 1979-81
Steve Largent, Seattle, 1978-81

Most Yards Gained, Season
1,746 Charley Hennigan, Houston, 1961
1,602 Lance Alworth, San Diego, 1965
1,546 Charley Hennigan, Houston, 1964

Most Yards Gained, Rookie, Season
1,473 Bill Groman, Houston, 1960
1,231 Bill Howton, Green Bay, 1952
1,124 Harlon Hill, Chi. Bears, 1954

Most Yards Gained, Game
303 Jim Benton, Cleveland vs. Detroit, Nov. 22, 1945
302 Cloyce Box, Detroit vs. Baltimore, Dec. 3, 1950
272 Charley Hennigan, Houston vs. Boston, Oct. 13, 1961

Most Games, 100 or More Yards Pass Receiving, Career
50 Don Maynard, N.Y. Giants, 1958; N.Y. Jets, 1960-72; St. Louis, 1973
41 Lance Alworth, San Diego, 1962-70; Dallas, 1971-72
31 Art Powell, Philadelphia, 1959; N.Y. Titans, 1960-62; Oakland, 1963-66; Buffalo, 1967; Minnesota, 1968

Most Games, 100 or More Yards Pass Receiving, Season
10 Charley Hennigan, Houston, 1961
9 Elroy (Crazylegs) Hirsch, Los Angeles, 1951
Bill Groman, Houston, 1960
Lance Alworth, San Diego, 1965
Don Maynard, N.Y. Jets, 1967
8 Charley Hennigan, Houston, 1964
Lance Alworth, San Diego, 1967

Most Consecutive Games, 100 or More Yards Pass Receiving
7 Charley Hennigan, Houston, 1961
Bill Groman, Houston, 1961
6 Raymond Berry, Baltimore, 1960
Pat Studstill, Detroit, 1966
5 Elroy (Crazylegs) Hirsch, Los Angeles, 1951
Bob Boyd, Los Angeles, 1954
Terry Barr, Detroit, 1963
Lance Alworth, San Diego, 1966

Longest Pass Reception (All TDs except as noted)
99 Andy Farkas (from Filchock), Washington vs. Pittsburgh, Oct. 15, 1939
Bobby Mitchell (from Izo), Washington vs. Cleveland, Sept. 15, 1963
Pat Studstill (from Sweetan), Detroit vs. Baltimore, Oct. 16, 1966
Gerry Allen (from Jurgensen), Washington vs. Chicago, Sept. 15, 1968
98 Gaynell Tinsley (from Russell), Chi. Cardinals vs. Cleveland, Nov. 17, 1938
Dick (Night Train) Lane (from Compton), Chi. Cardinals vs. Green Bay, Nov. 13, 1955
John Farrington (from Wade), Chicago vs. Detroit, Oct. 8, 1961
Willard Dewveall (from Lee), Houston vs. San Diego, Nov. 25, 1962
Homer Jones (from Morrall), N.Y. Giants vs. Pittsburgh, Sept. 11, 1966
Bobby Moore (from Hart), St. Louis vs. Los Angeles, Dec. 10, 1972 (no TD)
97 Gaynell Tinsley (from Coffee), Chi. Cardinals vs. Chi. Bears, Dec. 5, 1937
Cloyce Box (from Layne), Detroit vs. Green Bay, Nov. 26, 1953
Jerry Tarr (from Shaw), Denver vs. Boston, Sept. 21, 1962

John Jefferson

Johnny Robinson

Bill Bradley

Paul Krause

Bobby Dillon

Charley McNeil

Ken Houston

PASS RECEIVING Continued

TOUCHDOWNS

Most Seasons Leading League
- 9   Don Hutson, Green Bay, 1935-38, 1940-44
- 3   Lance Alworth, San Diego, 1964-66
- 2   By many players

Most Consecutive Seasons Leading League
- 5   Don Hutson, Green Bay, 1940-44
- 4   Don Hutson, Green Bay, 1935-38
- 3   Lance Alworth, San Diego, 1964-66

Most Touchdowns, Career
- 99   Don Hutson, Green Bay, 1935-45
- 88   Don Maynard, N.Y. Giants, 1958; N.Y. Jets, 1960-72; St. Louis, 1973
- 85   Lance Alworth, San Diego, 1962-70; Dallas, 1971-72
-      Paul Warfield, Cleveland, 1964-69; 1976-77; Miami, 1970-74

Most Touchdowns, Season
- 17   Don Hutson, Green Bay, 1942
-      Elroy (Crazylegs) Hirsch, Los Angeles, 1951
-      Bill Groman, Houston, 1961
- 16   Art Powell, Oakland, 1963
- 15   Cloyce Box, Detroit, 1952
-      Sonny Randle, St. Louis, 1960

Most Touchdowns, Rookie, Season
- 13   Bill Howton, Green Bay, 1952
-      John Jefferson, San Diego, 1979
- 12   Harlon Hill, Chi. Bears, 1954
-      Bill Groman, Houston, 1960
-      Mike Ditka, Chicago, 1961
-      Bob Hayes, Dallas, 1965
- 10   Bill Swiacki, N.Y. Giants, 1948
-      Bucky Pope, Los Angeles, 1964
-      Sammy White, Minnesota, 1976

Most Touchdowns, Game
- 5   Bob Shaw, Chi. Cardinals vs. Baltimore, Oct. 2, 1950
-     Kellen Winslow, San Diego vs. Oakland, Nov. 22, 1981
- 4   By many players

Most Consecutive Games, Touchdowns
- 11   Elroy (Crazylegs) Hirsch, Los Angeles, 1950-51
-      Buddy Dial, Pittsburgh, 1959-60
- 9   Lance Alworth, San Diego, 1963
- 8   Bill Groman, Houston, 1961
-     Dave Parks, San Francisco, 1965

INTERCEPTIONS BY

Most Seasons Leading League
- 2   Dick (Night Train) Lane, Los Angeles, 1952; Chi. Cardinals, 1954
-     Jack Christiansen, Detroit, 1953, 1957
-     Milt Davis, Baltimore, 1957, 1959
-     Dick Lynch, N.Y. Giants, 1961, 1963
-     Johnny Robinson, Kansas City, 1966, 1970
-     Bill Bradley, Philadelphia, 1971-72
-     Emmitt Thomas, Kansas City, 1969, 1974

Most Interceptions By, Career
- 81   Paul Krause, Washington, 1964-67; Minnesota, 1968-79
- 79   Emlen Tunnell, N.Y. Giants, 1948-58; Green Bay, 1959-61
- 68   Dick (Night Train) Lane, Los Angeles, 1952-53; Chi. Cardinals, 1954-59; Detroit, 1960-65

Most Interceptions By, Season
- 14   Dick (Night Train) Lane, Los Angeles, 1952
- 13   Dan Sandifer, Washington, 1948
-      Orban (Spec) Sanders, N.Y. Yanks, 1950
-      Lester Hayes, Oakland, 1980
- 12   By nine players

Most Interceptions By, Rookie, Season
- 14   Dick (Night Train) Lane, Los Angeles, 1952
- 13   Dan Sandifer, Washington, 1948
- 12   Woodley Lewis, Los Angeles, 1950
-      Paul Krause, Washington, 1964

Most Interceptions By, Game
- 4   Sammy Baugh, Washington vs. Detroit, Nov. 14, 1943
-     Dan Sandifer, Washington vs. Boston, Oct. 31, 1948
-     Don Doll, Detroit vs. Chi. Cardinals, Oct. 23, 1949
-     Bob Nussbaumer, Chi. Cardinals vs. N.Y. Bulldogs, Nov. 13, 1949
-     Russ Craft, Philadelphia vs. Chi. Cardinals, Sept. 24, 1950
-     Bobby Dillon, Green Bay vs. Detroit, Nov. 26, 1953
-     Jack Butler, Pittsburgh vs. Washington, Dec. 13, 1953
-     Austin (Goose) Gonsoulin, Denver vs. Buffalo, Sept. 18, 1960
-     Jerry Norton, St. Louis vs. Washington, Nov. 20, 1960; vs. Pittsburgh, Nov. 26, 1961
-     Dave Baker, San Francisco vs. L.A. Rams, Dec. 4, 1960
-     Bobby Ply, Dall. Texans vs. San Diego, Dec. 16, 1962
-     Bobby Hunt, Kansas City vs. Houston, Oct. 4, 1964
-     Willie Brown, Denver vs. N.Y. Jets, Nov. 15, 1964
-     Dick Anderson, Miami vs. Pittsburgh, Dec. 3, 1973
-     Willie Buchanon, Green Bay vs. San Diego, Sept. 24, 1978

Most Consecutive Games, Passes Intercepted By
- 8   Tom Morrow, Oakland, 1962-63
- 7   Paul Krause, Washington, 1964
-     Larry Wilson, St. Louis, 1966
-     Ben Davis, Cleveland, 1968
- 6   Dick (Night Train) Lane, Chi. Cardinals, 1954-55
-     Will Sherman, Los Angeles, 1954-55
-     Jim Shofner, Cleveland, 1960
-     Paul Krause, Minnesota, 1968
-     Willie Williams, N.Y. Giants, 1968
-     Kermit Alexander, San Francisco, 1968-69
-     Eric Harris, Kansas City, 1980
-     Lester Hayes, Oakland, 1980

YARDS GAINED

Most Seasons Leading League
- 2   Dick (Night Train) Lane, Los Angeles, 1952; Chi. Cardinals, 1954
-     Herb Adderley, Green Bay, 1965, 1969
-     Dick Anderson, Miami, 1968, 1970

Most Yards Gained, Career
- 1,282   Emlen Tunnell, N.Y. Giants, 1948-58; Green Bay, 1959-61
- 1,207   Dick (Night Train) Lane, Los Angeles, 1952-53; Chi. Cardinals, 1954-59; Detroit, 1960-65
- 1,185   Paul Krause, Washington, 1964-67; Minnesota, 1968-79

Most Yards Gained, Season
- 349   Charley McNeil, San Diego, 1961
- 301   Don Doll, Detroit, 1949
- 298   Dick (Night Train) Lane, Los Angeles, 1952

Most Yards Gained, Rookie, Season
- 301   Don Doll, Detroit, 1949
- 298   Dick (Night Train) Lane, Los Angeles, 1952
- 275   Woodley Lewis, Los Angeles, 1950

Most Yards Gained, Game
- 177   Charley McNeil, San Diego vs. Houston, Sept. 24, 1961
- 167   Dick Jauron, Detroit vs. Chicago, Nov. 18, 1973
- 151   Tom Myers, New Orleans vs. Minnesota, Sept. 3, 1978

Longest Return (All TDs)
- 102   Bob Smith, Detroit vs. Chi. Bears, Nov. 24, 1949
-      Erich Barnes, N.Y. Giants vs. Dall. Cowboys, Oct. 22, 1961
-      Gary Barbaro, Kansas City vs. Seattle, Dec. 11, 1977
-      Louis Breeden, Cincinnati vs. San Diego, Nov. 8, 1981
- 101   Richie Petitbon, Chicago vs Los Angeles, Dec. 9, 1962
-      Henry Carr, N.Y. Giants vs. Los Angeles, Nov. 13, 1966
-      Tony Greene, Buffalo vs. Kansas City, Oct. 3, 1976
-      Tom Pridemore, Atlanta vs. San Francisco, Sept. 20, 1981
- 100   Vern Huffman, Detroit vs. Brooklyn, Oct. 17, 1937
-      Mike Gaechter, Dall. Cowboys vs. Philadelphia, Oct. 14, 1962
-      Les (Speedy) Duncan, San Diego vs. Kansas City, Oct. 15, 1967
-      Tom Janik, Buffalo vs. N.Y. Jets, Sept. 29, 1968
-      Tim Collier, Kansas City vs. Oakland, Dec. 18, 1977

TOUCHDOWNS

Most Touchdowns, Career
- 9   Ken Houston, Houston, 1967-72; Washington, 1973-80
- 7   Herb Adderley, Green Bay, 1961-69; Dallas, 1970-72
-     Erich Barnes, Chi. Bears, 1958-60; N.Y. Giants, 1961-64; Cleveland, 1965-70
-     Lem Barney, Detroit, 1967-77
- 6   Tom Janik, Denver, 1963-64; Buffalo, 1965-68; Boston, 1969-70; New England, 1971
-     Miller Farr, Denver, 1965; San Diego, 1965-66; Houston, 1967-69; St. Louis, 1970-72; Detroit, 1973
-     Bobby Bell, Kansas City, 1963-74

Jerrel Wilson

Steve O'Neal

Bob Cifers

Speedy Duncan

Billy Johnson

James Jones
Alvin Haymond

Most Touchdowns, Season
- 4 Ken Houston, Houston, 1971
   Jim Kearney, Kansas City, 1972
- 3 Dick Harris, San Diego, 1961
   Dick Lynch, N.Y. Giants, 1963
   Herb Adderley, Green Bay, 1965
   Lem Barney, Detroit, 1967
   Miller Farr, Houston, 1967
   Monte Jackson, Los Angeles, 1976
   Rod Perry, Los Angeles, 1978
   Ronnie Lott, San Francisco, 1981
- 2 By many players

Most Touchdowns, Rookie, Season
- 3 Lem Barney, Detroit, 1967
   Ronnie Lott, San Francisco, 1981
- 2 By many players

Most Touchdowns, Game
- 2 Bill Blackburn, Chi. Cardinals vs. Boston, Oct. 24, 1948
   Dan Sandifer, Washington vs. Boston, Oct. 31, 1948
   Bob Franklin, Cleveland vs. Chicago, Dec. 11, 1960
   Bill Stacy, St. Louis vs. Dall. Cowboys, Nov. 5, 1961
   Jerry Norton, St. Louis vs. Pittsburgh, Nov. 26, 1961
   Miller Farr, Houston vs. Buffalo, Dec. 7, 1968
   Ken Houston, Houston vs. San Diego, Dec. 19, 1971
   Jim Kearney, Kansas City vs. Denver, Oct. 1, 1972
   Lemar Parrish, Cincinnati vs. Houston, Dec. 17, 1972
   Dick Anderson, Miami vs. Pittsburgh, Dec. 3, 1973
   Prentice McCray, New England vs. N.Y. Jets, Nov. 21, 1976

PUNTING
Most Seasons Leading League
- 4 Sammy Baugh, Washington, 1940-43
   Jerrel Wilson, Kansas City, 1965, 1968, 1972-73
- 3 Yale Lary, Detroit, 1959, 1961, 1963
   Jim Fraser, Denver, 1962-64
   Ray Guy, Oakland, 1974-75, 1977
- 2 By many players

Most Consecutive Seasons Leading League
- 4 Sammy Baugh, Washington, 1940-43
- 3 Jim Fraser, Denver, 1962-64
- 2 By many players

PUNTS
Most Punts, Career
- 1,072 Jerrel Wilson, Kansas City, 1963-77; New England, 1978
- 978 Mike Bragg, Washington, 1968-79; Baltimore, 1980
- 974 Bobby Walden, Minnesota, 1964-67; Pittsburgh, 1968-76

Most Punts, Season
- 114 Bob Parsons, Chicago, 1981
- 109 John James, Atlanta, 1978
- 106 David Beverly, Green Bay, 1978

Most Punts, Rookie, Season
- 96 Mike Connell, San Francisco, 1978
- 93 Wilbur Summers, Detroit, 1977
   Ken Clark, Los Angeles, 1979
- 90 Bucky Dilts, Denver, 1977

Most Punts, Game
- 14 Dick Nesbitt, Chi. Cardinals vs. Chi. Bears, Nov. 30, 1933
   Keith Molesworth, Chi. Bears vs. Green Bay, Dec. 10, 1933
   Sammy Baugh, Washington vs. Philadelphia, Nov. 5, 1939
   Carl Kinscherf, N.Y. Giants vs. Detroit, Nov. 7, 1943
   George Taliaferro, N.Y. Yanks vs. Los Angeles, Sept. 28, 1951
- 12 Parker Hall, Cleveland vs. Green Bay, Nov. 26, 1939
   Beryl Clark, Chi. Cardinals vs. Detroit, Sept. 15, 1940
   Len Barnum, Philadelphia vs. Washington, Oct. 4, 1942
   Horace Gillom, Cleveland vs. Philadelphia, Dec. 3, 1950
   Adrian Burk, Philadelphia vs. Green Bay, Nov. 2, 1952; vs. N.Y. Giants, Dec. 12, 1954
   Bob Scarpitto, Denver vs. Oakland, Sept. 10, 1967
   Bill Van Heusen, Denver vs. Cincinnati, Oct. 6, 1968
   Tom Blanchard, New Orleans vs. Minnesota, Nov. 16, 1975
   Rusty Jackson, Los Angeles vs. San Francisco, Nov. 21, 1976
   Wilbur Summers, Detroit vs. San Francisco, Oct. 23, 1977
   John James, Atlanta vs. Washington, Dec. 10, 1978
   Luke Prestridge, Denver vs. Buffalo, Oct. 25, 1981
- 11 By many players

Longest Punt
- 98 Steve O'Neal, N.Y. Jets vs. Denver, Sept. 21, 1969
- 94 Joe Lintzenich, Chi. Bears vs. N.Y. Giants, Nov. 16, 1931
- 90 Don Chandler, Green Bay vs. San Francisco, Oct. 10, 1965

AVERAGE YARDAGE
Highest Average, Punting, Career (300 punts)
- 45.10 Sammy Baugh, Washington, 1937-52
- 44.68 Tommy Davis, San Francisco, 1959-69
- 44.29 Yale Lary, Detroit, 1952-53, 1956-64

Highest Average, Punting, Season (Qualifiers)
- 51.40 Sammy Baugh, Washington, 1940
- 48.94 Yale Lary, Detroit, 1963
- 48.73 Sammy Baugh, Washington, 1941

Highest Average, Punting, Rookie, Season (Qualifiers)
- 46.40 Bobby Walden, Minnesota, 1964
- 46.22 Dave Lewis, Cincinnati, 1970
- 45.92 Frank Sinkwich, Detroit, 1943

Highest Average, Punting, Game (4 punts)
- 61.75 Bob Cifers, Detroit vs. Chi. Bears, Nov. 24, 1946
- 61.60 Roy McKay, Green Bay vs. Chi. Cardinals, Oct. 28, 1945
- 59.40 Sammy Baugh, Washington vs. Detroit, Oct. 27, 1940

PUNT RETURNS
Most Seasons Leading League
- 3 Les (Speedy) Duncan, San Diego, 1965-66; Washington, 1971
- 2 Dick Christy, N.Y. Titans, 1961-62
   Claude Gibson, Oakland, 1963-64
   Billy Johnson, Houston, 1975, 1977
   Rick Upchurch, Denver, 1976, 1978

PUNT RETURNS
Most Punt Returns, Career
- 258 Emlen Tunnell, N.Y. Giants, 1948-58; Green Bay, 1959-61
- 253 Alvin Haymond, Baltimore, 1964-67; Philadelphia, 1968; Los Angeles, 1969-71; Washington, 1972; Houston, 1973
- 235 Ron Smith, Chicago, 1965, 1970-72; Atlanta, 1966-67; Los Angeles, 1968-69; San Diego, 1973; Oakland, 1974
   Mike Fuller, San Diego, 1975-80; Cincinnati, 1981

Most Punt Returns, Season
- 70 Danny Reece, Tampa Bay, 1979
- 58 J. T. Smith, Kansas City, 1979
- 57 Eddie Brown, Washington, 1977
   Danny Reece, Tampa Bay, 1980

Most Punt Returns, Rookie, Season
- 54 James Jones, Dallas, 1980
- 52 Leon Bright, N.Y. Giants, 1981
   Robbie Martin, Detroit, 1981
- 48 Neal Colzie, Oakland, 1975
   Kevin Miller, Minnesota, 1978
   Mike Nelms, Washington, 1980

Most Punt Returns, Game
- 11 Eddie Brown, Washington vs. Tampa Bay, Oct. 9, 1977
- 10 Theo Bell, Pittsburgh vs. Buffalo, Dec. 16, 1979
- 9 Rodger Bird, Oakland vs. Denver, Sept. 10, 1967
   Ralph McGill, San Francisco vs. Atlanta, Oct. 29, 1972
   Ed Podolak, Kansas City vs. San Diego, Nov. 10, 1974
   Anthony Leonard, San Francisco vs. New Orleans, Oct. 17, 1976
   Butch Johnson, Dallas vs. Buffalo, Nov. 15, 1976
   Larry Marshall, Philadelphia vs. Tampa Bay, Sept. 18, 1977
   Nesby Glasgow, Baltimore vs. Kansas City, Sept. 2, 1979
   Mike Nelms, Washington vs. St. Louis, Dec. 21, 1980

FAIR CATCHES
Most Fair Catches, Season
- 24 Ken Graham, San Diego, 1969
- 22 Lem Barney, Detroit, 1976
- 21 Ed Podolak, Kansas City, 1970
   Steve Schubert, Chicago, 1978
   Stanley Morgan, New England, 1979

Most Fair Catches, Game
- 7 Lem Barney, Detroit vs. Chicago, Nov. 21, 1976
- 6 Jake Scott, Miami vs. Buffalo, Dec. 20, 1970
- 5 By many players

YARDS GAINED
Most Seasons Leading League
- 3 Alvin Haymond, Baltimore, 1965-66; Los Angeles, 1969
- 2 Bill Dudley, Pittsburgh, 1942, 1946
   Emlen Tunnell, N.Y. Giants, 1951-52
   Dick Christy, N.Y. Titans, 1961-62
   Claude Gibson, Oakland, 1963-64
   Rodger Bird, Oakland, 1966-67
   J. T. Smith, Kansas City, 1979-80

| *LeRoy Irvin* | *Drew Hill* | *Bruce Harper* | *Bobby Jancik* | *Al Carmichael* | *Travis Williams* | *Timmy Brown* |

PUNT RETURNS Continued

Most Yards Gained, Career
- 2,714   Rick Upchurch, Denver, 1975-81
- 2,565   Mike Fuller, San Diego, 1975-80; Cincinnati, 1981
- 2,209   Emlen Tunnell, N.Y. Giants, 1948-58; Green Bay, 1959-61

Most Yards Gained, Season
- 655   Neal Colzie, Oakland, 1975
- 653   Rick Upchurch, Denver, 1977
- 646   Eddie Brown, Washington, 1976

Most Yards Gained, Rookie, Season
- 655   Neal Colzie, Oakland, 1975
- 608   Mike Haynes, New England, 1976
- 577   Lynn Swann, Pittsburgh, 1974

Most Yards Gained, Game
- 207   LeRoy Irvin, Los Angeles vs. Atlanta, Oct. 11, 1981
- 205   George Atkinson, Oakland vs. Buffalo, Sept. 15, 1968
- 184   Tom Watkins, Detroit vs. San Francisco, Oct. 6, 1963

Longest Punt Return (All TDs)
- 98   Gil LeFebvre, Cincinnati vs. Brooklyn, Dec. 3, 1933
-      Charlie West, Minnesota vs. Washington, Nov. 3, 1968
-      Dennis Morgan, Dallas vs. St. Louis, Oct. 13, 1974
- 96   Bill Dudley, Washington vs. Pittsburgh, Dec. 3, 1950
- 95   Frank Bernardi, Chi. Cardinals vs. Washington, Oct. 14, 1956
-      Les (Speedy) Duncan, San Diego vs. N.Y. Jets, Nov. 24, 1968
-      Steve Odom, Green Bay vs. Chicago, Nov. 10, 1974

AVERAGE YARDAGE

Highest Average, Career (75 returns)
- 13.16   Billy Johnson, Houston, 1974-80
- 12.78   George McAfee, Chi. Bears, 1940-41, 1945-50
- 12.75   Jack Christiansen, Detroit, 1951-58

Highest Average, Season (Qualifiers)
- 23.00   Herb Rich, Baltimore, 1950
- 21.47   Jack Christiansen, Detroit, 1952
- 21.28   Dick Christy, N.Y. Titans, 1961

Highest Average, Rookie, Season (Qualifiers)
- 23.00   Herb Rich, Baltimore, 1950
- 20.88   Jerry Davis, Chi. Cardinals, 1948
- 20.73   Frank Sinkwich, Detroit, 1943

Highest Average, Game (3 returns)
- 47.67   Chuck Latourette, St. Louis vs. New Orleans, Sept. 29, 1968
- 47.33   Johnny Roland, St. Louis vs. Philadelphia, Oct. 2, 1966
- 45.67   Dick Christy, N.Y. Titans vs. Denver, Sept. 24, 1961

TOUCHDOWNS

Most Touchdowns, Career
- 8   Jack Christiansen, Detroit, 1951-58
- 6   Rick Upchurch, Denver, 1975-81
- 5   Emlen Tunnell, N.Y. Giants, 1948-58; Green Bay, 1959-61
-    Billy Johnson, Houston, 1974-80

Most Touchdowns, Season
- 4   Jack Christiansen, Detroit, 1951
-    Rick Upchurch, Denver, 1976
- 3   Emlen Tunnell, N.Y. Giants, 1951
-    Billy Johnson, Houston, 1975
-    LeRoy Irvin, Los Angeles, 1981
- 2   By many players

Most Touchdowns, Rookie, Season
- 4   Jack Christiansen, Detroit, 1951
- 2   By five players

Most Touchdowns, Game
- 2   Jack Christiansen, Detroit vs. Los Angeles, Oct. 14, 1951; vs. Green Bay, Nov. 22, 1951
-    Dick Christy, N.Y. Titans vs. Denver, Sept. 24, 1961
-    Rick Upchurch, Denver vs. Cleveland, Sept. 26, 1976
-    LeRoy Irvin, Los Angeles vs. Atlanta, Oct. 11, 1981

KICKOFF RETURNS

Most Seasons Leading League
- 3   Abe Woodson, San Francisco, 1959, 1962-63
- 2   Lynn Chandnois, Pittsburgh, 1951-52
-    Bobby Jancik, Houston, 1962-63
-    Travis Williams, Green Bay, 1967; Los Angeles, 1971

KICKOFF RETURNS

Most Kickoff Returns, Career
- 275   Ron Smith, Chicago, 1965, 1970-72; Atlanta, 1966-67; Los Angeles, 1968-69; San Diego, 1973; Oakland, 1974
- 224   Bruce Harper, N.Y. Jets, 1977-81
- 193   Abe Woodson, San Francisco, 1958-64; St. Louis, 1965-66

Most Kickoff Returns, Season
- 60   Drew Hill, Los Angeles, 1981
- 55   Bruce Harper, N.Y. Jets, 1978, 1979
-    David Turner, Cincinnati, 1979
-    Stump Mitchell, St. Louis, 1981
- 53   Eddie Payton, Minnesota, 1980

Most Kickoff Returns, Rookie, Season
- 55   Stump Mitchell, St. Louis, 1981
- 50   Nesby Glasgow, Baltimore, 1979
-    Dino Hall, Cleveland, 1979
- 47   Odell Barry, Denver, 1964

Most Kickoff Returns, Game
- 9   Noland Smith, Kansas City vs. Oakland, Nov. 23, 1967
-    Dino Hall, Cleveland vs. Pittsburgh, Oct. 7, 1979
- 8   George Taliaferro, N.Y. Yanks vs. N.Y. Giants, Dec. 3, 1950
-    Bobby Jancik, Houston vs. Boston, Dec. 8, 1963; vs. Oakland, Dec. 22, 1963
-    Mel Renfro, Dallas vs. Green Bay, Nov. 29, 1964
-    Willie Porter, Boston vs. N.Y. Jets, Sept. 22, 1968
-    Keith Moody, Buffalo vs. Seattle, Oct. 30, 1977
-    Brian Baschnagel, Chicago vs. Houston, Nov. 6, 1977
-    Bruce Harper, N.Y. Jets vs. New England, Oct. 29, 1978; vs. New England, Sept. 9, 1979
-    Terry Metcalf, Washington vs. St. Louis, Sept. 20, 1981
- 7   By many players

YARDS GAINED

Most Seasons Leading League
- 3   Bruce Harper, N.Y. Jets, 1977-79
- 2   Marshall Goldberg, Chi. Cardinals, 1941-42
-    Woodley Lewis, Los Angeles, 1953-54
-    Al Carmichael, Green Bay, 1956-57
-    Timmy Brown, Philadelphia, 1961, 1963
-    Bobby Jancik, Houston, 1963, 1966
-    Ron Smith, Atlanta, 1966-67

Most Yards Gained, Career
- 6,922   Ron Smith, Chicago, 1965, 1970-72; Atlanta, 1966-67; Los Angeles, 1968-69; San Diego, 1973; Oakland, 1974
- 5,538   Abe Woodson, San Francisco, 1958-64; St. Louis, 1965-66
- 5,023   Bruce Harper, N.Y. Jets, 1977-81

Most Yards Gained, Season
- 1,317   Bobby Jancik, Houston, 1963
- 1,314   Dave Hampton, Green Bay, 1971
- 1,292   Stump Mitchell, St. Louis, 1981

Most Yards Gained, Rookie, Season
- 1,292   Stump Mitchell, St. Louis, 1981
- 1,245   Odell Barry, Denver, 1964
- 1,148   Noland Smith, Kansas City, 1967

Most Yards Gained, Game
- 294   Wally Triplett, Detroit vs. Los Angeles, Oct. 29, 1950
- 247   Timmy Brown, Philadelphia vs. Dallas, Nov. 6, 1966
- 244   Noland Smith, Kansas City vs. San Diego, Oct. 15, 1967

Longest Kickoff Return (All TDs)
- 106   Al Carmichael, Green Bay vs. Chi. Bears, Oct. 7, 1956
-      Noland Smith, Kansas City vs. Denver, Dec. 17, 1967
-      Roy Green, St. Louis vs. Dallas, Oct. 21, 1979
- 105   Frank Seno, Chi. Cardinals vs. N.Y. Giants, Oct. 20, 1946
-      Ollie Matson, Chi. Cardinals vs. Washington, Oct. 14, 1956
-      Abe Woodson, San Francisco vs. Los Angeles, Nov. 8, 1959
-      Timmy Brown, Philadelphia vs. Cleveland, Sept. 17, 1961
-      Jon Arnett, Los Angeles vs. Detroit, Oct. 29, 1961
-      Eugene (Mercury) Morris, Miami vs. Cincinnati, Sept. 14, 1969
-      Travis Williams, Los Angeles vs. New Orleans, Dec. 5, 1971
- 104   By many players

AVERAGE YARDAGE

Highest Average, Career (75 returns)
- 30.56   Gale Sayers, Chicago, 1965-71
- 29.57   Lynn Chandnois, Pittsburgh, 1950-56
- 28.69   Abe Woodson, San Francisco, 1958-64; St. Louis, 1965-66

Highest Average, Season (Qualifiers)
- 41.06   Travis Williams, Green Bay, 1967
- 37.69   Gale Sayers, Chicago, 1967
- 35.50   Ollie Matson, Chi. Cardinals, 1958

Highest Average, Rookie, Season (Qualifiers)
- 41.06   Travis Williams, Green Bay, 1967
- 33.08   Tom Moore, Green Bay, 1960
- 32.88   Duriel Harris, Miami, 1976

Highest Average, Game (3 returns)
- 73.50   Wally Triplett, Detroit vs. Los Angeles, Oct. 29, 1950
- 67.33   Lenny Lyles, San Francisco vs. Baltimore, Dec. 18, 1960
- 65.33   Ken Hall, Houston vs. N.Y. Titans, Oct. 23, 1960

Ron Smith *Stump Mitchell* *Mike Nelms* *Rick Upchurch* *Eddie Payton* *Nesby Glasgow* *Roman Gabriel*

TOUCHDOWNS
Most Touchdowns, Career
- 6 Ollie Matson, Chi. Cardinals, 1952, 1954-58; L.A. Rams, 1959-62; Detroit, 1963; Philadelphia, 1964
   Gale Sayers, Chicago, 1965-71
   Travis Williams, Green Bay, 1967-70; Los Angeles, 1971
- 5 Bobby Mitchell, Cleveland, 1958-61; Washington, 1962-68
   Abe Woodson, San Francisco, 1958-64; St. Louis, 1965-66
   Timmy Brown, Green Bay, 1959; Philadelphia, 1960-67; Baltimore, 1968
- 4 Cecil Turner, Chicago, 1968-73

Most Touchdowns, Season
- 4 Travis Williams, Green Bay, 1967
   Cecil Turner, Chicago, 1970
- 3 Verda (Vitamin T) Smith, Los Angeles, 1950
   Abe Woodson, San Francisco, 1963
   Gale Sayers, Chicago, 1967
   Raymond Clayborn, New England, 1977
- 2 By many players

Most Touchdowns, Rookie, Season
- 4 Travis Williams, Green Bay, 1967
- 3 Raymond Clayborn, New England, 1977
- 2 By six players

Most Touchdowns, Game
- 2 Timmy Brown, Philadelphia vs. Dallas, Nov. 6, 1966
   Travis Williams, Green Bay vs. Cleveland, Nov. 12, 1967

COMBINED KICK RETURNS
Most Combined Kick Returns, Career
- 510 Ron Smith, Chicago, 1965, 1970-72; Atlanta, 1966-67; Los Angeles, 1968-69; San Diego, 1973; Oakland, 1974 (p-235, k-275)
- 423 Alvin Haymond, Baltimore, 1964-67; Philadelphia, 1968; Los Angeles, 1969-71; Washington, 1972; Houston, 1973 (p-253, k-170)
- 384 Bruce Harper, N.Y. Jets, 1977-81 (p-160, k-224)

Most Combined Kick Returns, Season
- 100 Larry Jones, Washington, 1975 (p-53, k-47)
- 97 Stump Mitchell, St. Louis, 1981 (p-42, k-55)
- 94 Nesby Glasgow, Baltimore, 1979 (k-50, p-44)

Most Combined Kick Returns, Game
- 13 Stump Mitchell, St. Louis vs. Atlanta, Oct. 18, 1981 (p-6, k-7)
- 12 Mel Renfro, Dallas vs. Green Bay, Nov. 29, 1964 (p-4, k-8)
   Larry Jones, Washington vs. Dallas, Dec. 13, 1975 (p-6, k-6)
   Eddie Brown, Washington vs. Tampa Bay, Oct. 9, 1977 (p-11, k-1)
   Nesby Glasgow, Baltimore vs. Denver, Sept. 2, 1979 (p-9, k-3)
- 11 Noland Smith, Kansas City vs. Oakland, Nov. 23, 1967 (p-2, k-9)
   Larry Jones, Washington vs. Oakland, Nov. 23, 1975 (p-6, k-5)
   Rolland Lawrence, Atlanta vs. New Orleans, Oct. 10, 1976 (p-6, k-5)
   Butch Johnson, Dallas vs. Buffalo, Nov. 15, 1976 (p-9, k-2)
   Larry Marshall, Philadelphia vs. Tampa Bay, Sept. 18, 1977 (p-9, k-2)
   Dino Hall, Cleveland vs. Pittsburgh, Oct. 7, 1979 (k-9, p-2)

YARDS GAINED
Most Yards Returned, Career
- 8,710 Ron Smith, Chicago, 1965, 1970-72; Atlanta, 1966-67; Los Angeles, 1968-69; San Diego, 1973; Oakland, 1974 (p-1,788, k-6,922)
- 6,740 Les (Speedy) Duncan, San Diego, 1964-70; Washington, 1971-74 (p-2,201, k-4,539)
- 6,623 Bruce Harper, N.Y. Jets, 1977-81 (p-1,600, k-5,023)

Most Yards Returned, Season
- 1,737 Stump Mitchell, St. Louis, 1981 (p-445, k-1,292)
- 1,658 Bruce Harper, N.Y. Jets, 1978 (p-378, k-1,280)
- 1,591 Mike Nelms, Washington, 1981 (p-492, k-1,099)

Most Yards Returned, Game
- 294 Wally Triplett, Detroit vs. Los Angeles, Oct. 29, 1950 (k-294)
   Woodley Lewis, Los Angeles vs. Detroit, Oct. 18, 1953 (p-120, k-174)
- 289 Eddie Payton, Detroit vs. Minnesota, Dec. 17, 1977 (p-105, k-184)
- 282 Les (Speedy) Duncan, San Diego vs. N.Y. Jets, Nov. 24, 1968 (p-102, k-180)

TOUCHDOWNS
Most Touchdowns, Career
- 9 Ollie Matson, Chi. Cardinals, 1952, 1954-58; Los Angeles, 1959-62; Detroit, 1963; Philadelphia, 1964-66 (p-3, k-6)
- 8 Jack Christiansen, Detroit, 1951-58 (p-8)
   Bobby Mitchell, Cleveland, 1958-61; Washington, 1962-68 (p-3, k-5)
   Gale Sayers, Chicago, 1965-71 (p-2, k-6)
- 7 Abe Woodson, San Francisco, 1958-64; St. Louis, 1965-66 (p-2, k-5)
   Billy Johnson, Houston, 1974-80 (p-5, k-2)

Most Touchdowns, Season
- 4 Jack Christiansen, Detroit, 1951 (p-4)
   Emlen Tunnell, N.Y. Giants, 1951 (p-3, k-1)
   Gale Sayers, Chicago, 1967 (p-1, k-3)
   Travis Williams, Green Bay, 1967 (k-4)
   Cecil Turner, Chicago, 1970 (k-4)
   Billy Johnson, Houston, 1975 (p-3, k-1)
   Rick Upchurch, Denver, 1976 (p-4)
- 3 Verda (Vitamin T) Smith, Los Angeles, 1950 (k-3)
   Abe Woodson, San Francisco, 1963 (k-3)
   Raymond Clayborn, New England, 1977 (k-3)
   Billy Johnson, Houston, 1977 (p-2, k-1)
   LeRoy Irvin, Los Angeles, 1981 (p-3)
- 2 By many players

Most Touchdowns, Game
- 2 Jack Christiansen, Detroit vs. Los Angeles, Oct. 14, 1951 (p-2); vs. Green Bay, Nov. 22, 1951 (p-2)
   Jim Patton, N.Y. Giants vs. Washington, Oct. 30, 1955 (p-1, k-1)
   Bobby Mitchell, Cleveland vs. Philadelphia, Nov. 23, 1958 (p-1, k-1)
   Dick Christy, N.Y. Titans vs. Denver, Sept. 24, 1961 (p-2)
   Al Frazier, Denver vs. Boston, Dec. 3, 1961 (p-1, k-1)
   Timmy Brown, Philadelphia vs. Dallas, Nov. 6, 1966 (k-2)
   Travis Williams, Green Bay vs. Cleveland, Nov. 12, 1967 (k-2); vs. Pittsburgh, Nov. 2, 1969 (p-1, k-1)
   Gale Sayers, Chicago vs. San Francisco, Dec. 3, 1967 (p-1, k-1)
   Rick Upchurch, Denver vs. Cleveland, Sept. 26, 1976 (p-2)
   Eddie Payton, Detroit vs. Minnesota, Dec. 17, 1977 (p-1, k-1)
   LeRoy Irvin, Los Angeles vs. Atlanta, Oct. 11, 1981 (p-2)

FUMBLES
Most Fumbles, Career
- 105 Roman Gabriel, Los Angeles, 1962-72; Philadelphia, 1973-77
- 95 Johnny Unitas, Baltimore, 1956-72; San Diego, 1973
- 84 Len Dawson, Pittsburgh, 1957-59; Cleveland, 1960-61; Dall. Texans, 1962; Kansas City, 1963-75
   Fran Tarkenton, Minnesota, 1961-66, 1972-78; N.Y. Giants, 1967-71

Most Fumbles, Season
- 17 Dan Pastorini, Houston, 1973
- 16 Don Meredith, Dallas, 1964
   Joe Cribbs, Buffalo, 1980
   Steve Fuller, Kansas City, 1980
- 15 Paul Christman, Chi. Cardinals, 1946
   Sammy Baugh, Washington, 1947
   Sam Etcheverry, St. Louis, 1961
   Len Dawson, Kansas City, 1964
   Terry Metcalf, St. Louis, 1976

Most Fumbles, Game
- 7 Len Dawson, Kansas City vs. San Diego, Nov. 15, 1964
- 6 Sam Etcheverry, St. Louis vs. N.Y. Giants, Sept. 17, 1961
- 5 Paul Christman, Chi. Cardinals vs. Green Bay, Nov. 10, 1946
   Charlie Conerly, N.Y. Giants vs. San Francisco, Dec. 1, 1957
   Jack Kemp, Buffalo vs. Houston, Oct. 29, 1967
   Roman Gabriel, Philadelphia vs. Oakland, Nov. 21, 1976

FUMBLES RECOVERED
Most Fumbles Recovered, Career, Own and Opponents'
- 43 Fran Tarkenton, Minnesota, 1961-66, 1972-78; N.Y. Giants, 1967-71 (43 own)
- 38 Jack Kemp, Pittsburgh, 1957; L.A. Chargers, 1960; San Diego, 1961-62; Buffalo, 1962-67, 1969 (38 own)
- 37 Roman Gabriel, Los Angeles, 1962-72; Philadelphia, 1973-77 (37 own)

Most Fumbles Recovered, Season, Own and Opponents'
- 9 Don Hultz, Minnesota, 1963 (9 opp)
- 8 Paul Christman, Chi. Cardinals, 1945 (8 own)
   Joe Schmidt, Detroit, 1955 (8 opp)
   Bill Butler, Minnesota, 1963 (8 own)
   Kermit Alexander, San Francisco, 1965 (4 own, 4 opp)
   Jack Lambert, Pittsburgh, 1976 (1 own, 7 opp)
   Danny White, Dallas, 1981 (8 own)
- 7 By many players

Most Fumbles Recovered, Game, Own and Opponents'
- 4 Otto Graham, Cleveland vs. N.Y. Giants, Oct. 25, 1953 (4 own)
   Sam Etcheverry, St. Louis vs. N.Y. Giants, Sept. 17, 1961 (4 own)
   Roman Gabriel, Los Angeles vs. San Francisco, Oct. 12, 1969 (4 own)
   Joe Ferguson, Buffalo vs. Miami, Sept. 18, 1977 (4 own)
- 3 By many players

OWN FUMBLES RECOVERED
Most Own Fumbles Recovered, Career
- 43 Fran Tarkenton, Minnesota, 1961-66, 1972-78; N.Y. Giants, 1967-71
- 38 Jack Kemp, Pittsburgh, 1957; L.A. Chargers, 1960; San Diego, 1961-62; Buffalo, 1962-67, 1969
- 37 Roman Gabriel, Los Angeles, 1962-72; Philadelphia, 1973-77

Jack Tatum *Chuck Howley* *Chris Hanburger* *George Martin* *Brad Dusek* *Terry Metcalf* *Mack Herron*

FUMBLES Continued

Most Own Fumbles Recovered, Season
- 8 Paul Christman, Chi. Cardinals, 1945
  Bill Butler, Minnesota, 1963
  Danny White, Dallas, 1981
- 7 Sammy Baugh, Washington, 1947
  Tommy Thompson, Philadelphia, 1947
  John Roach, St. Louis, 1960
  Jack Larscheid, Oakland, 1960
  Gary Huff, Chicago, 1974
  Terry Metcalf, St. Louis, 1974
  Joe Ferguson, Buffalo, 1977
  Fran Tarkenton, Minnesota, 1978
- 6 By many players

Most Own Fumbles Recovered, Game
- 4 Otto Graham, Cleveland vs. N.Y. Giants, Oct. 25, 1953
  Sam Etcheverry, St. Louis vs. N.Y. Giants, Sept. 17, 1961
  Roman Gabriel, Los Angeles vs. San Francisco, Oct. 12, 1969
  Joe Ferguson, Buffalo vs. Miami, Sept. 18, 1977
- 3 By many players

OPPONENTS' FUMBLES RECOVERED

Most Opponents' Fumbles Recovered, Career
- 29 Jim Marshall, Cleveland, 1960; Minnesota, 1961-79
- 25 Dick Butkus, Chicago, 1965-73
- 23 Carl Eller, Minnesota, 1964-78; Seattle, 1979

Most Opponents' Fumbles Recovered, Season
- 9 Don Hultz, Minnesota, 1963
- 8 Joe Schmidt, Detroit, 1955
- 7 Alan Page, Minnesota, 1970
  Jack Lambert, Pittsburgh, 1976

Most Opponents' Fumbles Recovered, Game
- 3 Corwin Clatt, Chi. Cardinals vs. Detroit, Nov. 6, 1949
  Vic Sears, Philadelphia vs. Green Bay, Nov. 2, 1952
  Ed Beatty, San Francisco vs. Los Angeles, Oct. 7, 1956
  Ron Carroll, Houston vs. Cincinnati, Oct. 27, 1974
  Maurice Spencer, New Orleans vs. Atlanta, Oct. 10, 1976
  Steve Nelson, New England vs. Philadelphia, Oct. 8, 1978
  Charles Jackson, Kansas City vs. Pittsburgh, Sept. 6, 1981
  Willie Buchanon, San Diego vs. Denver, Sept. 27, 1981
- 2 By many players

YARDS RETURNING FUMBLES

Longest Fumble Run (All TDs)
- 104 Jack Tatum, Oakland vs. Green Bay, Sept. 24, 1972 (opp)
- 98 George Halas, Chi. Bears vs. Oorang Indians, Marion, Ohio, Nov. 4, 1923 (opp)
- 97 Chuck Howley, Dallas vs. Atlanta, Oct. 2, 1966 (opp)

TOUCHDOWNS

Most Touchdowns, Career (Total)
- 4 Bill Thompson, Denver, 1969-81
- 3 Ralph Heywood, Detroit, 1947-48; Boston, 1948; N.Y. Bulldogs, 1949
  Leo Sugar, Chi. Cardinals, 1954-59; St. Louis, 1960; Philadelphia, 1961; Detroit, 1962
  Bud McFadin, Los Angeles, 1952-56; Denver, 1960-63; Houston, 1964-65
  Doug Cline, Houston, 1960-66; San Diego, 1966
  Bob Lilly, Dall. Cowboys, 1961-74
  Chris Hanburger, Washington, 1965-78
  Lemar Parrish, Cincinnati, 1970-77; Washington, 1978-81
  Paul Krause, Washington, 1964-67; Minnesota, 1968-79
  Brad Dusek, Washington, 1974-81
- 2 By many players

Most Touchdowns, Season (Total)
- 2 Harold McPhail, Boston, 1934
  Harry Ebding, Detroit, 1937
  John Morelli, Boston, 1944
  Frank Maznicki, Boston, 1947
  Fred (Dippy) Evans, Chi. Bears, 1948
  Ralph Heywood, Boston, 1948
  Art Tait, N.Y. Yanks, 1951
  John Dwyer, Los Angeles, 1952
  Leo Sugar, Chi. Cardinals, 1957
  Doug Cline, Houston, 1961
  Jim Bradshaw, Pittsburgh, 1964
  Royce Berry, Cincinnati, 1970
  Ahmad Rashad, Buffalo, 1974
  Tim Gray, Kansas City, 1977
  Charles Phillips, Oakland, 1978
  Kenny Johnson, Atlanta, 1981
  George Martin, N.Y. Giants, 1981

Most Touchdowns, Career (Own recovered)
- 2 Ken Kavanaugh, Chi. Bears, 1940-41, 1945-50
  Mike Ditka, Chicago, 1961-66; Philadelphia, 1967-68; Dallas, 1969-72
  Gail Cogdill, Detroit, 1960-68; Baltimore, 1968; Atlanta, 1969-70`
  Ahmad Rashad, St. Louis, 1972-73; Buffalo, 1974; Minnesota, 1976-81
  Jim Mitchell, Atlanta, 1969-79
  Drew Pearson, Dallas, 1973-81

Most Touchdowns, Season (Own recovered)
- 2 Ahmad Rashad, Buffalo, 1974
- 1 By many players

Most Touchdowns, Career (Opponents' recovered)
- 3 Leo Sugar, Chi. Cardinals, 1954-59; St. Louis, 1960; Philadelphia, 1961; Detroit, 1962
  Doug Cline, Houston, 1960-66; San Diego, 1966
  Bud McFadin, Los Angeles, 1952-56; Denver, 1960-63; Houston, 1964-65
  Bob Lilly, Dall. Cowboys, 1961-74
  Chris Hanburger, Washington, 1965-78
  Paul Krause, Washington, 1964-67; Minnesota, 1968-79
  Lemar Parrish, Cincinnati, 1970-77; Washington, 1978-81
  Bill Thompson, Denver, 1969-81
  Brad Dusek, Washington, 1974-81
- 2 By many players

Most Touchdowns, Season (Opponents' recovered)
- 2 Harold McPhail, Boston, 1934
  Harry Ebding, Detroit, 1937
  John Morelli, Boston, 1944
  Frank Maznicki, Boston, 1947
  Fred Evans, Chi. Bears, 1948
  Ralph Heywood, Boston, 1948
  Art Tait, N.Y. Yanks, 1951
  John Dwyer, Los Angeles, 1952
  Leo Sugar, Chi. Cardinals, 1957
  Doug Cline, Houston, 1961
  Jim Bradshaw, Pittsburgh, 1964
  Royce Berry, Cincinnati, 1970
  Tim Gray, Kansas City, 1977
  Charles Phillips, Oakland, 1978
  Kenny Johnson, Atlanta, 1981
  George Martin, N.Y. Giants, 1981

Most Touchdowns, Game (Opponents' recovered)
- 2 Fred (Dippy) Evans, Chi. Bears vs. Washington, Nov. 28, 1948

COMBINED NET YARDS GAINED

Rushing, receiving, interception returns, punt returns, kickoff returns, and fumble returns

Most Seasons Leading League
- 5 Jim Brown, Cleveland, 1958-61, 1964
- 3 Cliff Battles, Boston, 1932-33; Washington, 1937
  Gale Sayers, Chicago, 1965-67
- 2 By many players

Most Consecutive Seasons Leading League
- 4 Jim Brown, Cleveland, 1958-61
- 3 Gale Sayers, Chicago, 1965-67
- 2 Cliff Battles, Boston, 1932-33
  Charley Trippi, Chi. Cardinals, 1948-49
  Timmy Brown, Philadelphia, 1962-63
  Floyd Little, Denver, 1967-68

ATTEMPTS

Most Attempts, Career
- 2,728 Franco Harris, Pittsburgh, 1972-81
- 2,658 Jim Brown, Cleveland, 1957-65
- 2,648 O.J. Simpson, Buffalo, 1969-77; San Francisco, 1978-79

Most Attempts, Season
- 402 Walter Payton, Chicago, 1979
- 399 Earl Campbell, Houston, 1981
- 395 George Rogers, New Orleans, 1981

Most Attempts, Rookie, Season
- 395 George Rogers, New Orleans, 1981
- 390 Joe Cribbs, Buffalo, 1980
- 373 Ottis Anderson, St. Louis, 1979

Most Attempts, Game
- 43 Lydell Mitchell, Baltimore vs. N.Y. Jets, Oct. 20, 1974
- 42 Walter Payton, Chicago vs. Minnesota, Nov. 20, 1977
  Earl Campbell, Houston vs. Seattle, Oct. 11, 1981
- 41 Ron Johnson, N.Y. Giants vs. Philadelphia, Oct. 2, 1972
  Franco Harris, Pittsburgh vs. Cincinnati, Oct. 17, 1976
  Terdell Middleton, Green Bay vs. Minnesota, Nov. 26, 1978 (OT)
  Walter Payton, Chicago vs. Buffalo, Oct. 7, 1979
  Franco Harris, Pittsburgh vs. Cleveland, Nov. 25, 1979 (OT)

YARDS GAINED
Most Yards Gained, Career
  15,459 Jim Brown, Cleveland, 1957-65
  14,368 O.J. Simpson, Buffalo, 1969-77; San Francisco, 1978-79
  14,078 Bobby Mitchell, Cleveland, 1958-61; Washington, 1962-68
Most Yards Gained, Season
  2,462 Terry Metcalf, St. Louis, 1975
  2,444 Mack Herron, New England, 1974
  2,440 Gale Sayers, Chicago, 1966
Most Yards Gained, Rookie, Season
  2,272 Gale Sayers, Chicago, 1965
  2,100 Abner Haynes, Dall. Texans, 1960
  2,093 James Brooks, San Diego, 1981
Most Yards Gained, Game
  373 Billy Cannon, Houston vs. N.Y. Titans, Dec. 10, 1961
  341 Timmy Brown, Philadelphia vs. St. Louis, Dec. 16, 1962
  339 Gale Sayers, Chicago vs. Minnesota, Dec. 18, 1966

MISCELLANEOUS
Longest Return of Missed Field Goal (All TDs)
  101 Al Nelson, Philadelphia vs. Dallas, Sept. 26, 1971
  100 Al Nelson, Philadelphia vs. Cleveland, Dec. 11, 1966
        Ken Ellis, Green Bay vs. N.Y. Giants, Sept. 19, 1971
   99 Jerry Williams, Los Angeles vs. Green Bay, Dec. 16, 1951
        Carl Taseff, Baltimore vs. Los Angeles, Dec. 12, 1959
        Timmy Brown, Philadelphia vs. St. Louis, Sept. 16, 1962

TEAM RECORDS

CHAMPIONSHIPS
Most Seasons League Champion
  11 Green Bay, 1929-31, 1936, 1939, 1944, 1961-62, 1965-67
   8 Chi. Bears, 1921, 1932-33, 1940-41, 1943, 1946, 1963
   4 N.Y. Giants, 1927, 1934, 1938, 1956
      Detroit, 1935, 1952-53, 1957
      Clev. Browns, 1950, 1954-55, 1964
      Baltimore, 1958-59, 1968, 1970
      Pittsburgh, 1974-75, 1978-79
Most Consecutive Seasons League Champion
   3 Green Bay, 1929-31, 1965-67
   2 Canton, 1922-23
      Chi. Bears, 1932-33, 1940-41
      Philadelphia, 1948-49
      Detroit, 1952-53
      Cleveland, 1954-55
      Baltimore, 1958-59
      Houston, 1960-61
      Green Bay, 1961-62
      Buffalo, 1964-65
      Miami, 1972-73
      Pittsburgh, 1974-75, 1978-79
Most Times Finishing First, Regular Season (Since 1933)
  14 N.Y. Giants, 1933-35, 1938-39, 1941, 1944, 1946, 1956, 1958-59, 1961-63
      Clev./L.A. Rams, 1945, 1949-51, 1955, 1967, 1969, 1973-79
      Clev. Browns, 1950-55, 1957, 1964-65, 1967-69, 1971, 1980
  12 Dallas, 1966-71, 1973, 1976-79, 1981
  11 Green Bay, 1936, 1938-39, 1944, 1960-62, 1965-67, 1972
      Minnesota, 1968-71, 1973-78, 1980
Most Consecutive Times Finishing First, Regular Season (Since 1933)
   7 Los Angeles, 1973-79
   6 Cleveland, 1950-55
      Dallas, 1966-71
      Minnesota, 1973-78
      Pittsburgh, 1974-79
   5 Oakland, 1972-76

GAMES WON
Most Consecutive Games Won (Incl. postseason games)
  18 Chi. Bears, 1933-34, 1941-42
      Miami, 1972-73
  17 Oakland, 1976-77
  14 Washington, 1942-43
Most Consecutive Games Won (Regular season)
  17 Chi. Bears, 1933-34
  16 Chi. Bears, 1941-42
      Miami, 1971-73
  15 L.A. Chargers/San Diego, 1960-61
Most Consecutive Games Without Defeat (Incl. postseason games)
  24 Canton, 1922-23 (won 21, tied 3)
  23 Green Bay, 1928-30 (won 21, tied 2)
  18 Chi. Bears, 1933-34 (won 18); 1941-42 (won 18)
      Miami, 1972-73 (won 18)
Most Consecutive Games Without Defeat (Regular season)
  24 Canton, 1922-23 (won 21, tied 3)
      Chi. Bears, 1941-43 (won 23, tied 1)
  23 Green Bay, 1928-30 (won 21, tied 2)
  17 Chi. Bears, 1933-34 (won 17)

Most Games Won, One Season (Incl. postseason games)
  17 Miami, 1972
      Pittsburgh, 1978
  16 Oakland, 1976
      San Francisco, 1981
  15 Miami, 1973
      Baltimore, 1968
      Pittsburgh, 1975, 1979
      Dallas, 1977
      Oakland, 1980
Most Games Won, Season (Since 1932)
  14 Miami, 1972
      Pittsburgh, 1978
  13 Chi. Bears, 1934
      Green Bay, 1962
      Oakland, 1967, 1976
      Baltimore, 1968
      San Francisco, 1981
  12 By many teams
Most Consecutive Games Won, One Season (Incl. postseason games)
  17 Miami, 1972
  13 Chi. Bears, 1934
      Oakland, 1976
  12 Minnesota, 1969
Most Consecutive Games Won, One Season
  14 Miami, 1972
  13 Chi. Bears, 1934
  12 Minnesota, 1969
Most Consecutive Games Won, Start of Season
  14 Miami, 1972, entire season
  13 Chi. Bears, 1934, entire season
  11 Chi. Bears, 1942, entire season
      Cleveland, 1953
      San Diego, 1961
      Los Angeles, 1969
Most Consecutive Games Won, End of Season
  14 Miami, 1972, entire season
  13 Chi. Bears, 1934, entire season
  11 Chi. Bears, 1942, entire season
      Cleveland, 1951
Most Consecutive Games Without Defeat, One Season (Incl. postseason games)
  17 Miami, 1972
  13 Chi. Bears, 1926, 1934
      Green Bay, 1929
      Baltimore, 1967
      Oakland, 1976
  12 Canton, 1922, 1923
      Minnesota, 1969
Most Consecutive Games Without Defeat, One Season
  14 Miami, 1972
  13 Chi. Bears, 1926, 1934
      Green Bay, 1929
      Baltimore, 1967
  12 Canton, 1922, 1923
      Minnesota, 1969
Most Consecutive Games Without Defeat, Start of Season
  14 Miami, 1972, entire season
  13 Chi. Bears, 1926; 1934, entire season
      Green Bay, 1929, entire season
      Baltimore, 1967
  12 Canton, 1922, 1923, entire seasons
Most Consecutive Games Without Defeat, End of Season
  14 Miami, 1972, entire season
  13 Green Bay, 1929, entire season
      Chi. Bears, 1934, entire season
  12 Canton, 1922, 1923, entire seasons
Most Consecutive Home Games Won
  26 Miami, 1971-74
  20 Green Bay, 1929-32
  18 Oakland, 1968-70
      Dallas, 1979-81 (current)
Most Consecutive Home Games Without Defeat
  30 Green Bay, 1928-33 (won 27, tied 3)
  26 Miami, 1971-74 (won 26)
  18 Chi. Bears, 1932-35 (won 17, tied 1); 1941-44 (won 17, tied 1)
      Oakland, 1968-70 (won 18)
      Dallas, 1979-81 (won 18) (current)
Most Consecutive Road Games Won
  11 L.A. Chargers/San Diego, 1960-61
  10 Chi. Bears, 1941-42
      Dallas, 1968-69
   9 Chi. Bears, 1933-34
      Kansas City, 1966-67
      Oakland, 1967-68, 1974-75, 1976-77
      Pittsburgh, 1974-75
Most Consecutive Road Games Without Defeat
  13 Chi. Bears, 1941-43 (won 12, tied 1)
  12 Green Bay, 1928-30 (won 10, tied 2)
  11 L.A. Chargers/San Diego, 1960-61 (won 11)
      Los Angeles, 1966-68 (won 10, tied 1)
Most Shutout Games Won or Tied, Season (Since 1932)
   7 Chi. Bears, 1932 (won 4, tied 3)
      Green Bay, 1932 (won 6, tied 1)
      Detroit, 1934 (won 7)
   5 Chi. Cardinals, 1934 (won 5)
      N.Y. Giants, 1944 (won 5)
      Pittsburgh, 1976 (won 5)
   4 By many teams

GAMES WON Continued

Most Consecutive Shutout Games Won or Tied (Since 1932)
- 7 Detroit, 1934 (won 7)
- 3 Chi. Bears, 1932 (tied 3)
  - Green Bay, 1932 (won 3)
  - New York, 1935 (won 3)
  - St. Louis, 1970 (won 3)
  - Pittsburgh, 1976 (won 3)
- 2 By many teams

GAMES LOST

Most Consecutive Games Lost
- 26 Tampa Bay, 1976-77
- 19 Chi. Cardinals, 1942-43, 1945
  - Oakland, 1961-62
- 18 Houston, 1972-73

Most Consecutive Games Without Victory
- 26 Tampa Bay, 1976-77 (lost 26)
- 23 Washington, 1960-61 (lost 20, tied 3)

Most Games Lost, Season (Since 1932)
- 15 New Orleans, 1980
- 14 Tampa Bay, 1976
  - San Francisco, 1978, 1979
  - Detroit, 1979
  - Baltimore, 1981
  - New England, 1981
- 13 Oakland, 1962
  - Chicago, 1969
  - Pittsburgh, 1969
  - Buffalo, 1971
  - Houston, 1972, 1973

Most Consecutive Games Lost, One Season
- 14 Tampa Bay, 1976
  - New Orleans, 1980
  - Baltimore, 1981
- 13 Oakland, 1962
- 12 Tampa Bay, 1977

Most Consecutive Games Lost, Start of Season
- 14 Tampa Bay, 1976, entire season
  - New Orleans, 1980
- 13 Oakland, 1962
- 12 Tampa Bay, 1977

Most Consecutive Games Lost, End of Season
- 14 Tampa Bay, 1976, entire season
- 13 Pittsburgh, 1969
- 11 Philadelphia, 1936
  - Detroit, 1942, entire season
  - Houston, 1972

Most Consecutive Games Without Victory, One Season
- 14 Tampa Bay, 1976, entire season
  - New Orleans, 1980
  - Baltimore, 1981
- 13 Washington, 1961
  - Oakland, 1962
- 12 Dall. Cowboys, 1960, entire season
  - Tampa Bay, 1977

Most Consecutive Games Without Victory, Start of Season
- 14 Tampa Bay, 1976, entire season
  - New Orleans, 1980
- 13 Washington, 1961
  - Oakland, 1962
- 12 Dall. Cowboys, 1960, entire season
  - Tampa Bay, 1977

Most Consecutive Games Without Victory, End of Season
- 14 Tampa Bay, 1976, entire season
- 13 Pittsburgh, 1969
- 12 Dall. Cowboys, 1960, entire season

Most Consecutive Home Games Lost
- 13 Houston, 1972-73
  - Tampa Bay, 1976-77
- 11 Oakland, 1961-62
  - Los Angeles, 1961-63
- 10 Pittsburgh, 1937-39, 1943-45
  - Washington, 1960-61
  - N.Y. Giants, 1973-75
  - New Orleans, 1979-80

Most Consecutive Home Games Without Victory
- 13 Houston, 1972-73 (lost 13)
  - Tampa Bay, 1976-77 (lost 13)
- 12 Philadelphia, 1936-38 (lost 11, tied 1)
- 11 Washington, 1960-61 (lost 10, tied 1)
  - Oakland, 1961-62 (lost 11)
  - Los Angeles, 1961-63 (lost 11)

Most Consecutive Road Games Lost
- 18 San Francisco, 1977-79
- 16 Chicago, 1973-75
- 14 Brooklyn, 1942-44
  - Chi. Cardinals, 1942-45
  - New Orleans, 1972-74

Most Consecutive Road Games Without Victory
- 18 Washington, 1959-62 (lost 15, tied 3)
  - New Orleans, 1971-74 (lost 17, tied 1)
  - San Francisco, 1977-79 (lost 18)
- 17 Denver, 1962-65 (lost 16, tied 1)
- 16 Chicago, 1973-75 (lost 16)

Most Shutout Games Lost or Tied, Season (Since 1932)
- 6 Cincinnati, 1934 (lost 6)
  - Pittsburgh, 1934 (lost 6)
  - Philadelphia, 1936 (lost 6)
  - Tampa Bay, 1977 (lost 6)
- 5 Boston, 1932 (lost 4, tied 1), 1933 (lost 4, tied 1)
  - N.Y. Giants, 1932 (lost 4, tied 1)
  - Cincinnati, 1933 (lost 4, tied 1)
  - Brooklyn, 1934 (lost 5), 1942 (lost 5)
  - Detroit, 1942 (lost 5)
  - Tampa Bay, 1976 (lost 5)
- 4 By many teams

Most Consecutive Shutout Games Lost or Tied (Since 1932)
- 6 Brooklyn, 1942-43 (lost 6)
- 4 Chi. Bears, 1932 (lost 1, tied 3)
  - Philadelphia, 1936 (lost 4)
- 3 Chi. Cardinals, 1934 (lost 3), 1938 (lost 3)
  - Brooklyn, 1935 (lost 3), 1937 (lost 3)
  - Oakland, 1981 (lost 3)

TIE GAMES

Most Tie Games, Season
- 6 Chi. Bears, 1932
- 5 Frankford, 1929
- 4 Chi. Bears, 1924
  - Orange, 1929
  - Portsmouth, 1929

Most Consecutive Tie Games
- 3 Chi. Bears, 1932
- 2 By many teams

SCORING

Most Seasons Leading League
- 9 Chi. Bears, 1934-35, 1939, 1941-43, 1946-47, 1956
- 6 Green Bay, 1932, 1936-38, 1961-62
  - L.A. Rams, 1950-52, 1957, 1967, 1973
- 5 Oakland, 1967-69, 1974, 1977
  - Dall. Cowboys, 1966, 1968, 1971, 1978, 1980

Most Consecutive Seasons Leading League
- 3 Green Bay, 1936-38
  - Chi. Bears, 1941-43
  - Los Angeles, 1950-52
  - Oakland, 1967-69

POINTS

Most Points, Season
- 513 Houston, 1961
- 478 San Diego, 1981
- 468 Oakland, 1967

Fewest Points, Season (Since 1932)
- 37 Cincinnati/St. Louis, 1934
- 38 Cincinnati, 1933
  - Detroit, 1942
- 51 Pittsburgh, 1934
  - Philadelphia, 1936

Most Points, Game
- 72 Washington vs. N.Y. Giants, Nov. 27, 1966
- 70 Los Angeles vs. Baltimore, Oct. 22, 1950
- 65 Chi. Cardinals vs. N.Y. Bulldogs, Nov. 13, 1949
  - Los Angeles vs. Detroit, Oct. 29, 1950

Most Points, Both Teams, Game
- 113 Washington (72) vs. N.Y. Giants (41), Nov. 27, 1966
- 101 Oakland (52) vs. Houston (49), Dec. 22, 1963
- 98 Chi. Cardinals (63) vs. N.Y. Giants (35), Oct. 17, 1948

Fewest Points, Both Teams, Game
- 0 In many games. Last time: N.Y. Giants vs. Detroit, Nov. 7, 1943

Most Points, Shutout Victory, Game
- 64 Philadelphia vs. Cincinnati, Nov. 6, 1934
- 59 Los Angeles vs. Atlanta, Dec. 4, 1976
- 57 Chicago vs. Baltimore, Nov. 25, 1962

Fewest Points, Shutout Victory, Game
- 2 Green Bay vs. Chi. Bears, Oct. 16, 1932
  - Chi. Bears vs. Green Bay, Sept. 18, 1938

Most Points Overcome to Win Game
- 28 San Francisco vs. New Orleans, Dec. 7, 1980 (OT) (trailed 7-35, won 38-35)
- 24 Philadelphia vs. Washington, Oct. 27, 1946 (trailed 0-24, won 28-24)
  - Denver vs. Boston, Oct. 23, 1960 (trailed 0-24, won 31-24)
  - Miami vs. New England, Dec. 15, 1974 (trailed 0-24, won 34-27)
  - Minnesota vs. San Francisco, Dec. 4, 1977 (trailed 0-24, won 28-27)
  - Denver vs. Seattle, Sept. 23, 1979) (trailed 10-34, won 37-34)

Most Points Overcome to Tie Game
- 31 Denver vs. Buffalo, Nov. 27, 1960 (trailed 7-38, tied 38-38)
- 28 Los Angeles vs. Philadelphia, Oct. 3, 1948 (trailed 0-28, tied 28-28)

Most Points, Each Half
- 1st: 45 Green Bay vs. Cleveland, Nov. 12, 1967
- 2nd: 48 Chi. Cardinals vs. Baltimore, Oct. 2, 1950
  - N.Y. Giants vs. Baltimore, Nov. 19, 1950

Most Points, Both Teams, Each Half
- 1st: 70 Houston (35) vs. Oakland (35), Dec. 22, 1963
- 2nd: 65 Washington (38) vs. N.Y. Giants (27), Nov. 27, 1966

Most Points, One Quarter
- 41 Green Bay vs. Detroit, Oct. 7, 1945 (second quarter)
  - Los Angeles vs. Detroit, Oct. 29, 1950 (third quarter)
- 37 Los Angeles vs. Green Bay, Sept. 21, 1980 (second quarter)
- 35 Chi. Cardinals vs. Boston, Oct. 24, 1948 (third quarter)
  - Green Bay vs. Cleveland, Nov. 12, 1967 (first quarter)

Most Points, Both Teams, One Quarter
- 49 Oakland (28) vs. Houston (21), Dec. 22, 1963 (second quarter)
- 48 Green Bay (41) vs. Detroit (7), Oct. 7, 1945 (second quarter)
  Los Angeles (41) vs. Detroit (7), Oct. 29, 1950 (third quarter)
- 47 St. Louis (27) vs. Philadelphia (20), Dec. 13, 1964 (second quarter)

Most Points, Each Quarter
- 1st: 35 Green Bay vs. Cleveland, Nov. 12, 1967
- 2nd: 41 Green Bay vs. Detroit, Oct. 7, 1945
- 3rd: 41 Los Angeles vs. Detroit, Oct. 29, 1950
- 4th: 31 Oakland vs. Denver, Dec. 17, 1960; vs. San Diego, Dec. 8, 1963
  Atlanta vs. Green Bay, Sept. 13, 1981

Most Points, Both Teams, Each Quarter
- 1st: 42 Green Bay (35) vs. Cleveland (7), Nov. 12, 1967
- 2nd: 49 Oakland (28) vs. Houston (21), Dec. 22, 1963
- 3rd: 48 Los Angeles (41) vs. Detroit (7), Oct. 29, 1950
- 4th: 42 Chi. Cardinals (28) vs. Philadelphia (14), Dec. 7, 1947
  Green Bay (28) vs. Chi. Bears (14), Nov. 6, 1955
  N.Y. Jets (28) vs. Boston (14), Oct. 27, 1968
  Pittsburgh (21) vs. Cleveland (21), Oct. 18, 1969

GAMES
Most Consecutive Games Scoring
- 274 Cleveland, 1950-71
- 217 Oakland, 1966-81
- 179 Kansas City, 1963-76

TOUCHDOWNS
Most Seasons Leading League, Touchdowns
- 13 Chi. Bears, 1932, 1934-35, 1939, 1941-44, 1946-48, 1956, 1965
- 7 Dall. Cowboys, 1966, 1968, 1971, 1973, 1977-78, 1980
- 6 Oakland, 1967-69, 1972, 1974, 1977

Most Consecutive Seasons Leading League, Touchdowns
- 4 Chi. Bears, 1941-44
  Los Angeles, 1949-52
- 3 Chi. Bears, 1946-48
  Baltimore, 1957-59
  Oakland, 1967-69

Most Touchdowns, Season
- 66 Houston, 1961
- 64 Los Angeles, 1950
- 61 San Diego, 1981

Fewest Touchdowns, Season (Since 1932)
- 3 Cincinnati, 1933
- 4 Cincinnati/St. Louis, 1934
- 5 Detroit, 1942

Most Touchdowns, Game
- 10 Philadelphia vs. Cincinnati, Nov. 6, 1934
  Los Angeles vs. Baltimore, Oct. 22, 1950
  Washington vs. N.Y. Giants, Nov. 27, 1966
- 9 Chi. Cardinals vs. Rochester, Oct. 7, 1923; vs. N.Y. Giants, Oct. 17, 1948; vs. N.Y. Bulldogs, Nov. 13, 1949
  Los Angeles vs. Detroit, Oct. 29, 1950
  Pittsburgh vs. N.Y. Giants, Nov. 30, 1952
  Chicago vs. San Francisco, Dec. 12, 1965; vs. Green Bay, Dec. 7, 1980
- 8 By many teams.

Most Touchdowns, Both Teams, Game
- 16 Washington (10) vs. N.Y. Giants (6), Nov. 27, 1966
- 14 Chi. Cardinals (9) vs. N.Y. Giants (5), Oct. 17, 1948
  Los Angeles (10) vs. Baltimore (4), Oct. 22, 1950
  Houston (7) vs. Oakland (7), Dec. 22, 1963
- 13 New Orleans (7) vs. St. Louis (6), Nov. 2, 1969

Most Consecutive Games Scoring Touchdowns
- 166 Cleveland, 1957-69
- 97 Oakland, 1966-73
- 96 Kansas City, 1963-70

POINTS AFTER TOUCHDOWN
Most Points After Touchdown, Season
- 65 Houston, 1961
- 59 Los Angeles, 1950
  Dallas, 1980
- 56 Dallas, 1966
  Oakland, 1967

Fewest Points After Touchdown, Season
- 2 Chi. Cardinals, 1933
- 3 Cincinnati, 1933
  Pittsburgh, 1934
- 4 Cincinnati/St. Louis, 1934

Most Points After Touchdown, Game
- 10 Los Angeles vs. Baltimore, Oct. 22, 1950
- 9 Chi. Cardinals vs. N.Y. Giants, Oct. 17, 1948
  Pittsburgh vs. N.Y. Giants, Nov. 30, 1952
  Washington vs. N.Y. Giants, Nov. 27, 1966
- 8 By many teams

Most Points After Touchdown, Both Teams, Game
- 14 Chi. Cardinals (9) vs. N.Y. Giants (5), Oct. 17, 1948
  Houston (7) vs. Oakland (7), Dec. 22, 1963
  Washington (9) vs. N.Y. Giants (5), Nov. 27, 1966
- 13 Los Angeles (10) vs. Baltimore (3), Oct. 22, 1950
- 12 In many games

FIELD GOALS
Most Seasons Leading League, Field Goals
- 11 Green Bay, 1935-36, 1940-43, 1946-47, 1955, 1972, 1974
- 6 N.Y. Giants, 1933, 1937, 1939, 1941, 1944, 1959
  Washington, 1945, 1956, 1971, 1976-77, 1979
- 5 Clev. Browns, 1950, 1952-54, 1957
  L.A. Rams, 1949, 1951, 1958, 1966, 1973
  Portsmouth/Detroit, 1932-33, 1937-38, 1980

Most Consecutive Seasons Leading League, Field Goals
- 4 Green Bay, 1940-43
- 3 Cleveland, 1952-54
- 2 By many teams

Most Field Goals Attempted, Season
- 49 Los Angeles, 1966
  Washington, 1971
- 48 Green Bay, 1972
- 47 N.Y. Jets, 1969
  Los Angeles, 1973

Fewest Field Goals Attempted, Season (Since 1938)
- 0 Chi. Bears, 1944
- 2 Cleveland, 1939
  Card-Pitt, 1944
  Boston, 1946
  Chi. Bears, 1947
- 3 Chi. Bears, 1945
  Cleveland, 1945

Most Field Goals Attempted, Game
- 9 St. Louis vs. Pittsburgh, Sept. 24, 1967
- 8 Pittsburgh vs. St. Louis, Dec. 2, 1962
  Detroit vs. Minnesota, Nov. 13, 1966
  N.Y. Jets vs. Buffalo, Nov. 3, 1968
- 7 By many teams

Most Field Goals Attempted, Both Teams, Game
- 11 St. Louis (6) vs. Pittsburgh (5), Nov. 13, 1966
  Washington (6) vs. Chicago (5), Nov. 14, 1971
  Green Bay (6) vs. Detroit (5), Sept. 29, 1974
  Washington (6) vs. N.Y. Giants (5), Nov. 14, 1976
- 10 Denver (5) vs. Boston (5), Nov. 11, 1962
  Boston (7) vs. San Diego (3), Sept. 20, 1964
  Buffalo (7) vs. Houston (3), Dec. 5, 1965
  St. Louis (7) vs. Atlanta (3), Dec. 11, 1966
  Boston (7) vs. Buffalo (3), Sept. 24, 1967
  Detroit (7) vs. Minnesota (3), Sept. 20, 1971
  Washington (7) vs. Houston (3), Oct. 10, 1971
  Green Bay (5) vs. St. Louis (5), Dec. 5, 1971
  Kansas City (7) vs. Buffalo (3), Dec. 19, 1971
  Kansas City (5) vs. San Diego (5), Oct. 29, 1972
  Minnesota (6) vs. Chicago (4), Sept. 23, 1973
  Cleveland (7) vs. Denver (3), Oct. 19, 1975
  Cleveland (5) vs. Denver (5), Oct. 5, 1980
- 9 In many games

Most Field Goals, Season
- 34 N.Y. Jets, 1968
- 33 Green Bay, 1972
- 32 N.Y. Jets, 1969

Fewest Field Goats, Season (Since 1932)
- 0 Boston, 1932, 1935
  Chi. Cardinals, 1932, 1945
  Green Bay, 1932, 1944
  New York, 1932
  Brooklyn, 1944
  Card-Pitt, 1944
  Chi. Bears, 1944, 1947
  Boston, 1946
  Baltimore, 1950
  Dallas, 1952

Most Field Goals, Game
- 7 St. Louis vs. Pittsburgh, Sept. 24, 1967
- 6 Boston vs. Denver, Oct. 4, 1964
  Detroit vs. Minnesota, Nov. 13, 1966
  N.Y. Jets vs. Buffalo, Nov. 3, 1968; vs. New Orleans, Dec. 3, 1972
  Philadelphia vs. Houston, Nov. 12, 1972
  St. Louis vs. Atlanta, Dec. 9, 1973
  N.Y. Giants vs. Seattle, Oct. 18, 1981
- 5 By many teams

Most Field Goals, Both Teams, Game
- 8 Cleveland (4) vs. St. Louis (4), Sept. 20, 1964
  Chicago (5) vs. Philadelphia (3), Oct. 20, 1968
  Washington (5) vs. Chicago (3), Nov. 14, 1971
  Kansas City (5) vs. Buffalo (3), Dec. 19, 1971
  Detroit (4) vs. Green Bay (4), Sept. 29, 1974
  Cleveland (5) vs. Denver (3), Oct. 19, 1975
  New England (4) vs. San Diego (4), Nov. 9, 1975
- 7 In many games

Most Consecutive Games Scoring Field Goals
- 31 Minnesota, 1968-70
- 21 San Francisco, 1970-72
- 20 Los Angeles, 1970-71
  Miami, 1970-72

SCORING Continued

SAFETIES

Most Safeties, Season
- 4 Detroit, 1962
- 3 Green Bay, 1932, 1975
  - Pittsburgh, 1947
  - N.Y. Yanks, 1950
  - Detroit, 1960
  - St. Louis, 1960
  - Buffalo, 1964
  - Minnesota, 1965, 1981
  - Cleveland, 1970
  - Los Angeles, 1973
  - Houston, 1977
  - Dallas, 1981
  - Oakland, 1981
- 2 By many teams

Most Safeties, Game
- 2 Cincinnati vs. Chi. Cardinals, Nov. 19, 1933
  - Detroit vs. Brooklyn, Dec. 1, 1935
  - N.Y. Giants vs. Pittsburgh, Sept. 17, 1950; vs. Washington, Nov. 5, 1961
  - Chicago vs. Pittsburgh, Nov. 9, 1969
  - Dallas vs. Philadelphia, Nov. 19, 1972
  - Los Angeles vs. Green Bay, Oct. 21, 1973
  - Oakland vs. San Diego, Oct. 26, 1975

Most Safeties, Both Teams, Game
- 2 Chi. Bears (1) vs. San Francisco (1), Oct. 19, 1952
  - Cincinnati (1) vs. Los Angeles (1), Oct. 22, 1972
  - Atlanta (1) vs. Detroit (1), Oct. 5, 1980
  - (Also see previous record)

FIRST DOWNS

Most Seasons Leading League
- 9 Chi. Bears, 1935, 1939, 1941, 1943, 1945, 1947-49, 1955
- 6 L.A. Rams, 1946, 1950-51, 1954, 1957, 1973
- 5 Green Bay, 1940, 1942, 1944, 1960, 1962

Most Consecutive Seasons Leading League
- 3 Chi. Bears, 1947-49
- 2 By many teams

Most First Downs, Season
- 379 San Diego, 1981
- 372 San Diego, 1980
- 364 Cleveland, 1981

Fewest First Downs, Season
- 51 Cincinnati, 1933
- 64 Pittsburgh, 1935
- 67 Philadelphia, 1937

Most First Downs, Game
- 38 Los Angeles vs. N.Y. Giants, Nov. 13, 1966
- 37 Green Bay vs. Philadelphia, Nov. 11, 1962
- 36 Pittsburgh vs. Cleveland, Nov. 25, 1979 (OT)

Fewest First Downs, Game
- 0 N.Y. Giants vs. Green Bay, Oct. 1, 1933; vs. Washington, Sept. 27, 1942
  - Pittsburgh vs. Boston, Oct. 29, 1933
  - Philadelphia vs. Detroit, Sept. 20, 1935
  - Denver vs. Houston, Sept. 3, 1966

Most First Downs, Both Teams, Game
- 58 Los Angeles (30) vs. Chi. Bears (28), Oct. 24, 1954
  - Denver (34) vs. Kansas City (24), Nov. 18, 1974
  - Atlanta (35) vs. New Orleans (23), Sept. 2, 1979 (OT)
  - Pittsburgh (36) vs. Cleveland (22), Nov. 25, 1979 (OT)
- 57 Los Angeles (32) vs. N.Y. Yanks (25), Nov. 19, 1950
  - Baltimore (33) vs. N.Y. Jets (24), Dec. 15, 1974
- 56 Buffalo (28) vs. Cincinnati (28), Oct. 29, 1978

Fewest First Downs, Both Teams, Game
- 5 N.Y. Giants (0) vs. Green Bay (5), Oct. 1, 1933

Most First Downs, Rushing, Season
- 181 New England, 1978
- 177 Los Angeles, 1973
- 170 Miami, 1972

Fewest First Downs, Rushing, Season
- 36 Cleveland, 1942
  - Boston, 1944
- 39 Brooklyn, 1943
- 40 Philadelphia, 1940
  - Detroit, 1945

Most First Downs, Rushing, Game
- 25 Philadelphia vs. Washington, Dec. 2, 1951
- 21 Cleveland vs. Philadelphia, Dec. 13, 1959
  - Los Angeles vs. New Orleans, Nov. 25, 1973
  - Pittsburgh vs. Kansas City, Nov. 7, 1976
  - New England vs. Denver, Nov. 28, 1976
  - Oakland vs. Green Bay, Sept. 17, 1978
- 20 By eight teams

Fewest First Downs, Rushing, Game
- 0 By many teams

Most First Downs, Passing, Season
- 244 San Diego, 1980
- 224 San Diego, 1981
- 217 Minnesota, 1981

Fewest First Downs, Passing, Season
- 18 Pittsburgh, 1941
- 23 Brooklyn, 1942
  - N.Y. Giants, 1944
- 24 N.Y. Giants, 1943

Most First Downs, Passing, Game
- 25 Denver vs. Kansas City, Nov. 18, 1974
  - N.Y. Jets vs. San Francisco, Sept. 21, 1980
- 24 Houston vs. Buffalo, Nov. 1, 1964
  - Minnesota vs. Baltimore, Sept. 28, 1969
- 23 Dallas vs. San Francisco, Nov. 10, 1963
  - Denver vs. Houston, Dec. 20, 1964
  - San Diego vs. N.Y. Giants, Oct. 19, 1980

Fewest First Downs, Passing, Game
- 0 By many teams

Most First Downs, Penalty, Season
- 39 Seattle, 1978
- 37 Cleveland, 1981
- 36 Baltimore, 1979
  - Cleveland, 1979

Fewest First Downs, Penalty, Season
- 2 Brooklyn, 1940
- 4 Chi. Cardinals, 1940
  - N.Y. Giants, 1942, 1944
  - Washington, 1944
  - Cleveland, 1952
  - Kansas City, 1969
- 5 Brooklyn, 1939
  - Chi. Bears, 1939
  - Detroit, 1953
  - Los Angeles, 1953

Most First Downs, Penalty, Game
- 9 Chi. Bears vs. Cleveland, Nov. 25, 1951
  - Baltimore vs. Pittsburgh, Oct. 30, 1977
- 8 Philadelphia vs. Detroit, Dec. 2, 1979
- 7 Boston vs. Houston, Sept. 19, 1965
  - Baltimore vs. Detroit, Nov. 19, 1967; vs. Buffalo, Dec. 17, 1978; vs. Pittsburgh, Sept. 14, 1980
  - Oakland vs. Boston, Oct. 6, 1968
  - Cleveland vs. Buffalo, Oct. 23, 1977; vs. Pittsburgh, Sept. 24, 1978; vs. Atlanta, Sept. 27, 1981
  - Buffalo vs. Cleveland, Oct. 29, 1978
  - Cincinnati vs. Oakland, Nov. 9, 1980

Fewest First Downs, Penalty, Game
- 0 By many teams

NET YARDS GAINED RUSHING AND PASSING

Most Seasons Leading League
- 12 Chi. Bears, 1932, 1934-35, 1939, 1941-44, 1947, 1949, 1955-56
- 6 L.A. Rams, 1946, 1950-51, 1954, 1957, 1973
  - Baltimore, 1958-60, 1964, 1967, 1976
  - Dall. Cowboys, 1966, 1968-69, 1971, 1974, 1977
- 4 San Diego, 1963, 1965, 1980-81

Most Consecutive Seasons Leading League
- 4 Chi. Bears, 1941-44
- 3 Baltimore, 1958-60
  - Houston, 1960-62
  - Oakland, 1968-70
- 2 By many teams

Most Yards Gained, Season
- 6,744 San Diego, 1981
- 6,410 San Diego, 1980
- 6,288 Houston, 1961

Fewest Yards Gained, Season
- 1,150 Cincinnati, 1933
- 1,443 Chi. Cardinals, 1934
- 1,486 Chi. Cardinals, 1933

Most Yards Gained, Game
- 735 Los Angeles vs. N.Y. Yanks, Sept. 28, 1951
- 683 Pittsburgh vs. Chi. Cardinals, Dec. 13, 1958
- 682 Chi. Bears vs. N.Y. Giants, Nov. 14, 1943

Fewest Yards Gained, Game
- −7 Seattle vs. Los Angeles, Nov. 4, 1979
- −5 Denver vs. Oakland, Sept. 10, 1967
- 14 Chi. Cardinals vs. Detroit, Sept. 15, 1940

Most Yards Gained, Both Teams, Game
- 1,133 Los Angeles (636) vs. N.Y. Yanks (497), Nov. 19, 1950
- 1,087 St. Louis (589) vs. Philadelphia (498), Dec. 16, 1962
- 1,064 Atlanta (552) vs. New Orleans (512), Sept. 2, 1979 (OT)

Fewest Yards Gained, Both Teams, Game
- 30 Chi. Cardinals (14) vs. Detroit (16), Sept. 15, 1940

Most Consecutive Games, 400 or More Yards Gained
- 6 Houston, 1961-62
  - San Diego, 1981
- 5 Chi. Bears, 1947, 1955
  - Los Angeles, 1950
  - Philadelphia, 1953
  - Oakland, 1968
  - New England, 1981
- 4 Chi. Cardinals, 1948
  - Los Angeles, 1954
  - Houston, 1961
  - Oakland, 1967, 1975
  - Dallas, 1976
  - Kansas City, 1976
  - Baltimore, 1976
  - Cleveland, 1980

Most Consecutive Games, 300 or More Yards Gained
- 29 Los Angeles, 1949-51
- 20 Chi. Bears, 1948-50
- 19 Cleveland, 1978-79

RUSHING

Most Seasons Leading League
- 11 Chi. Bears, 1932, 1934-35, 1939-42, 1951, 1955-56, 1968, 1977
- 6 Clev. Browns, 1958-59, 1963, 1965-67
- 4 Green Bay, 1946; 1961-62, 1964
  Dall. Texans/Kansas City, 1961, 1966, 1968-69
  Buffalo, 1962, 1964, 1973, 1975
  Detroit, 1936-38, 1981

Most Consecutive Seasons Leading League
- 4 Chi. Bears, 1939-42
- 3 Detroit, 1936-38
  San Francisco, 1952-54
  Cleveland, 1965-67
- 2 By many teams

Most Rushing Attempts, Season
- 681 Oakland, 1977
- 671 New England, 1978
- 659 Los Angeles, 1973

Fewest Rushing Attempts, Season
- 274 Detroit, 1946
- 285 Philadelphia, 1937
- 294 Detroit, 1943

Most Rushing Attempts, Game
- 72 Chi. Bears vs. Brooklyn, Oct. 20, 1935
- 70 Chi. Cardinals vs. Green Bay, Nov. 25, 1951
- 69 Chi. Cardinals vs. Green Bay, Dec. 6, 1936
  Kansas City vs. Cincinnati, Sept. 3, 1978

Fewest Rushing Attempts, Game
- 6 Chi. Cardinals vs. Boston, Oct. 29, 1933
- 7 Oakland vs. Buffalo, Oct. 15, 1963
- 8 Denver vs. Oakland, Dec. 17, 1960

Most Rushing Attempts, Both Teams, Game
- 108 Chi. Cardinals (70) vs. Green Bay (38), Dec. 5, 1948
- 105 Oakland (62) vs. Atlanta (43), Nov. 30, 1975 (OT)
- 103 Kansas City (53) vs. San Diego (50), Nov. 12, 1978 (OT)

Fewest Rushing Attempts, Both Teams, Game
- 36 Cincinnati (16) vs. Chi. Bears (20), Sept. 30, 1934
- 38 N.Y. Jets (13) vs. Buffalo (25), Nov. 8, 1964
- 39 Denver (16) vs. N.Y. Titans (23), Sept. 24, 1961
  Denver (14) vs. Boston (25), Sept. 21, 1962
  Denver (14) vs. Houston (25), Dec. 2, 1962

YARDS GAINED

Most Yards Gained Rushing, Season
- 3,165 New England, 1978
- 3,088 Buffalo, 1973
- 2,986 Kansas City, 1978

Fewest Yards Gained Rushing, Season
- 298 Philadelphia, 1940
- 467 Detroit, 1946
- 471 Boston, 1944

Most Yards Gained Rushing, Game
- 426 Detroit vs. Pittsburgh, Nov. 4, 1934
- 423 N.Y. Giants vs. Baltimore, Nov. 19, 1950
- 420 Boston vs. N.Y. Giants, Oct. 8, 1933

Fewest Yards Gained Rushing, Game
- −53 Detroit vs. Chi. Cardinals, Oct. 17, 1943
- −36 Philadelphia vs. Chi. Bears, Nov. 19, 1939
- −33 Phil-Pitt vs. Brooklyn, Oct. 2, 1943

Most Yards Gained Rushing, Both Teams, Game
- 595 Los Angeles (371) vs. N.Y. Yanks (224), Nov. 18, 1951
- 574 Chi. Bears (396) vs. Pittsburgh (178), Oct. 10, 1934
- 557 Chi. Bears (406) vs. Green Bay (151), Nov. 6, 1955

Fewest Yards Gained Rushing, Both Teams, Game
- −15 Detroit (−53) vs. Chi. Cardinals (38), Oct. 17, 1943
- 4 Detroit (−10) vs. Chi. Cardinals (14), Sept. 15, 1940
- 63 Chi. Cardinals (−1) vs. N.Y. Giants (64), Oct. 18, 1953

AVERAGE GAIN

Highest Average Gain, Rushing, Season
- 5.74 Cleveland, 1963
- 5.65 San Francisco, 1954
- 5.56 San Diego, 1963

Lowest Average Gain, Rushing, Season
- 0.94 Philadelphia, 1940
- 1.45 Boston, 1944
- 1.55 Pittsburgh, 1935

TOUCHDOWNS

Most Touchdowns, Rushing, Season
- 36 Green Bay, 1962
- 33 Pittsburgh, 1976
- 30 Chi. Bears, 1941
  New England, 1978

Fewest Touchdowns, Rushing, Season
- 1 Brooklyn, 1934
- 2 Chi. Cardinals, 1933
  Cincinnati, 1933
  Pittsburgh, 1934, 1940
  Philadelphia, 1935, 1936, 1937, 1938, 1972
- 3 By eight teams

Most Touchdowns, Rushing, Game
- 7 Los Angeles vs. Atlanta, Dec. 4, 1976
- 6 By many teams

Most Touchdowns, Rushing, Both Teams, Game
- 8 Los Angeles (6) vs. N.Y. Yanks (2), Nov. 18, 1951
  Cleveland (6) vs. Los Angeles (2), Nov. 24, 1957
- 7 In many games

PASSING

Most Seasons Leading League
- 10 Washington, 1937, 1939-40, 1942-45, 1947, 1967, 1974
- 9 N.Y. Giants, 1932, 1934-35, 1938, 1948, 1959, 1962-63, 1972
- 6 L.A. Rams, 1946, 1949-51, 1954, 1973

ATTEMPTS

Most Passes Attempted, Season
- 709 Minnesota, 1981
- 629 San Diego, 1981
- 624 Cleveland, 1981

Fewest Passes Attempted, Season
- 102 Cincinnati, 1933
- 106 Boston, 1933
- 120 Detroit, 1937

Most Passes Attempted, Game
- 68 Houston vs. Buffalo, Nov 1, 1964
- 63 Minnesota vs. Tampa Bay, Sept. 5, 1981
- 62 N.Y. Jets vs. Denver, Dec. 3, 1967; vs Baltimore, Oct. 18, 1970

Fewest Passes Attempted, Game
- 0 Green Bay vs. Portsmouth, Oct. 8, 1933; vs. Chi. Bears, Sept. 25, 1949
  Detroit vs. Cleveland, Sept. 10, 1937
  Pittsburgh vs. Brooklyn, Nov. 16, 1941; vs. Los Angeles, Nov. 13, 1949
  Cleveland vs. Philadelphia, Dec. 3, 1950

Most Passes Attempted, Both Teams, Game
- 98 Minnesota (56) vs. Baltimore (42), Sept. 28, 1969
- 97 Denver (53) vs. Houston (44), Dec. 2, 1962
- 96 Tampa Bay (56) vs. Minnesota (40), Nov. 16, 1980

Fewest Passes Attempted, Both Teams, Game
- 4 Chi. Cardinals (1) vs. Detroit (3), Nov. 3, 1935
  Detroit (0) vs. Cleveland (4), Sept. 10, 1937
- 6 Chi. Cardinals (2) vs. Detroit (4), Sept 15, 1940
- 8 Brooklyn (2) vs. Philadelphia (6), Oct. 1, 1939

COMPLETIONS

Most Passes Completed, Season
- 382 Minnesota, 1981
- 368 San Diego, 1981
- 363 San Francisco, 1980

Fewest Passes Completed, Season
- 25 Cincinnati, 1933
- 33 Boston, 1933
- 34 Chi. Cardinals, 1934
  Detroit, 1934

Most Passes Completed, Game
- 42 N.Y. Jets vs. San Francisco, Sept. 21, 1980
- 38 Minnesota vs. Cleveland, Dec. 14, 1980; vs. Green Bay, Nov. 29, 1981
- 37 Houston vs. Buffalo, Nov. 1, 1964
  Minnesota vs. Tampa Bay, Sept. 5, 1981

Most Passes Completed, Both Teams, Game
- 63 N.Y. Jets (42) vs. San Francisco (21), Sept. 21, 1980
- 58 Minnesota (38) vs. Cleveland (20), Dec. 14, 1980
- 56 Minnesota (36) vs. Baltimore (20), Sept. 28, 1969
  Minnesota (38) vs. Green Bay (18), Nov. 29, 1981

Fewest Passes Completed, Both Teams, Game
- 1 Chi. Cardinals (0) vs. Philadelphia (1), Nov. 8, 1936
  Detroit (0) vs. Cleveland (1), Sept. 10, 1937
  Chi. Cardinals (0) vs. Detroit (1), Sept. 15, 1940
  Pittsburgh (0) vs. Pittsburgh (1), Nov. 29, 1942
- 2 Chi. Cardinals (0) vs. Detroit (2), Nov. 3, 1935
  Buffalo (0) vs. N.Y. Jets (2), Sept. 29, 1974
- 3 Brooklyn (1) vs. Philadelphia (2), Oct. 1, 1939

YARDS GAINED

Most Seasons Leading League, Passing Yardage
- 8 Chi. Bears, 1932, 1939, 1941, 1943, 1945, 1949, 1954, 1964
- 7 Washington, 1938, 1940, 1944, 1947-48, 1967, 1974
  San Diego, 1965, 1968, 1971, 1978-81
- 5 Green Bay, 1934-37, 1942
  Philadelphia, 1953, 1955, 1961-62, 1973
  Baltimore, 1957, 1959-60, 1963, 1976

Most Consecutive Seasons Leading League, Passing Yardage
- 4 Green Bay, 1934-37
  San Diego, 1978-81
- 2 By many teams

Most Yards Gained, Passing, Season
- 4,739 San Diego, 1981
- 4,531 San Diego, 1980
- 4,392 Houston, 1961

Fewest Yards Gained, Passing, Season
- 302 Chi. Cardinals, 1934
- 357 Cincinnati, 1933
- 459 Boston, 1934

Most Yards Gained, Passing, Game
- 554 Los Angeles vs. N.Y. Yanks, Sept. 28, 1951
- 530 Minnesota vs. Baltimore, Sept. 28, 1969
- 505 N.Y. Giants vs. Washington, Oct. 28, 1962

Fewest Yards Gained, Passing, Game
- −53 Denver vs. Oakland, Sept. 10, 1967
- −52 Cincinnati vs. Houston, Oct. 31, 1971
- −39 Atlanta vs. San Francisco, Oct. 23, 1976

Most Yards Gained, Passing, Both Teams, Game
- 834 Philadelphia (419) vs. St. Louis (415), Dec. 16, 1962
- 822 N.Y. Jets (490) vs. Baltimore (332), Sept. 24, 1972
- 821 N.Y. Giants (505) vs. Washington (316), Oct. 28, 1962

PASSING Continued

Fewest Yards Gained, Passing, Both Teams, Game
- −11   Green Bay (−10) vs. Dallas (−1), Oct. 24, 1965
- 1   Chi. Cardinals (0) vs. Philadelphia (1), Nov. 8, 1936
- 7   Brooklyn (0) vs. Pittsburgh (7), Nov. 29, 1942

TACKLED ATTEMPTING PASSES

Most Times Tackled, Attempting Passes, Season
- 70   Atlanta, 1968
- 68   Dallas, 1964
- 67   Detroit, 1976

Fewest Times Tackled, Attempting Passes, Season
- 8   San Francisco, 1970
  St. Louis, 1975
- 9   N.Y. Jets, 1966
- 10   N.Y. Giants, 1972

Most Times Tackled, Attempting Passes, Game
- 12   Pittsburgh vs. Dallas, Nov. 20, 1966
  Baltimore vs. St. Louis, Oct. 26, 1980
- 11   St. Louis vs. N.Y. Giants, Nov. 1, 1964
  Los Angeles vs. Baltimore, Nov. 22, 1964
  Denver vs. Buffalo, Dec. 13, 1964; vs. Oakland, Nov. 5, 1967
  Green Bay vs. Detroit, Nov. 7, 1965
  Buffalo vs. Oakland, Oct. 15, 1967
  Atlanta vs. St. Louis, Nov. 24, 1968
  Detroit vs. Dallas, Oct. 6, 1975
- 10   By many teams. Last time: N.Y. Giants vs. San Francisco, Nov. 23, 1980

Most Times Tackled, Attempting Passes, Both Teams, Game
- 18   Green Bay (10) vs. San Diego (8), Sept. 24, 1978
- 17   Buffalo (10) vs. N.Y. Titans (7), Nov. 23, 1961
  Pittsburgh (12) vs. Dallas (5), Nov. 20, 1966
- 16   Los Angeles (11) vs. Baltimore (5), Nov. 22, 1964
  Buffalo (11) vs. Oakland (5), Oct. 15, 1967

COMPLETION PERCENTAGE

Most Seasons Leading League, Completion Percentage
- 11   Washington, 1937, 1939-40, 1942-45, 1947-48, 1969-70
- 7   Green Bay, 1936, 1941, 1961-62, 1964, 1966, 1968
- 6   Clev. Browns, 1951, 1953-55, 1959-60
  Dall. Texans/Kansas City, 1962, 1964, 1966-69

Most Consecutive Seasons Leading League, Completion Percentage
- 4   Washington, 1942-45
  Kansas City, 1966-69
- 3   Cleveland, 1953-55
- 2   By many teams

Highest Completion Percentage, Season
- 64.3   Oakland, 1976
- 64.0   Washington, 1945
- 63.9   Houston, 1980

Lowest Completion Percentage, Season
- 22.9   Philadelphia, 1936
- 24.5   Cincinnati, 1933
- 25.0   Pittsburgh, 1941

TOUCHDOWNS

Most Touchdowns, Passing, Season
- 48   Houston, 1961
- 39   N.Y. Giants, 1963
- 36   Oakland, 1969

Fewest Touchdowns, Passing, Season
- 0   Cincinnati, 1933
  Pittsburgh, 1945
- 1   Boston, 1932, 1933
  Chi. Cardinals, 1934
  Cincinnati/St. Louis, 1934
  Detroit, 1942
- 2   Chi. Cardinals, 1932, 1935
  Stapleton, 1932
  Brooklyn, 1936
  Pittsburgh, 1942

Most Touchdowns, Passing, Game
- 7   Chi. Bears vs. N.Y. Giants, Nov. 14, 1943
  Philadelphia vs. Washington, Oct. 17, 1954
  Houston vs. N.Y. Titans, Nov. 19, 1961; vs. N.Y. Titans, Oct. 14, 1962
  N.Y. Giants vs. Washington, Oct. 28, 1962
  Minnesota vs. Baltimore, Sept. 28, 1969
  San Diego vs. Oakland, Nov. 22, 1981
- 6   By many teams.

Most Touchdowns, Passing, Both Teams, Game
- 12   New Orleans (6) vs. St. Louis (6), Nov. 2, 1969
- 11   N.Y. Giants (7) vs. Washington (4), Oct. 28, 1962
  Oakland (6) vs. Houston (5), Dec. 22, 1963
- 9   In many games

PASSES HAD INTERCEPTED

Most Passes Had Intercepted, Season
- 48   Houston, 1962
- 45   Denver, 1961
- 41   Card-Pitt, 1944

Fewest Passes Had Intercepted, Season
- 5   Cleveland, 1960
  Green Bay, 1966
- 6   Green Bay, 1964
- 7   Los Angeles, 1969

Most Passes Had Intercepted, Game
- 9   Detroit vs. Green Bay, Oct. 24, 1943
  Pittsburgh vs. Philadelphia, Dec. 12, 1965
- 8   Green Bay vs. N.Y. Giants, Nov. 21, 1948
  Chi. Cardinals vs. Philadelphia, Sept. 24, 1950
  N.Y. Yanks vs. N.Y. Giants, Dec. 16, 1951
  Denver vs. Houston, Dec. 2, 1962
  Chi. Bears vs. Detroit, Sept. 22, 1968
  Baltimore vs. N.Y. Jets, Sept. 23, 1973
- 7   By many teams

Most Passes Had Intercepted, Both Teams, Game
- 13   Denver (8) vs. Houston (5), Dec. 2, 1962
- 11   Philadelphia (7) vs. Boston (4), Nov. 3, 1935
  Boston (6) vs. Pittsburgh (5), Dec. 1, 1935
  Cleveland (7) vs. Green Bay (4), Oct. 30, 1938
  Green Bay (7) vs. Detroit (4), Oct. 20, 1940
  Detroit (7) vs. Chi. Bears (4), Nov. 22, 1942
  Detroit (7) vs. Cleveland (4), Nov. 26, 1944
  Chi. Cardinals (8) vs. Philadelphia (3), Sept. 24, 1950
  Washington (7) vs. N.Y. Giants (4), Dec. 8, 1963
  Pittsburgh (9) vs. Philadelphia (2), Dec 12, 1965
- 10   In many games

PUNTING

Most Seasons Leading League (Average distance)
- 6   Washington, 1940-43, 1945, 1958
- 5   Denver, 1962-64, 1966-67
  Kansas City, 1968, 1971-73, 1979
- 4   L.A. Rams, 1946, 1949, 1955-56

Most Consecutive Seasons Leading League (Average Distance)
- 4   Washington, 1940-43
- 3   Cleveland, 1950-52
  Denver, 1962-64
  Kansas City, 1971-73

Most Punts, Season
- 114   Chicago, 1981
- 113   Boston, 1934
  Brooklyn, 1934
- 112   Boston, 1935

Fewest Punts, Season
- 32   Chi. Bears, 1941
- 33   Washington, 1945
- 38   Chi. Bears, 1947

Most Punts, Game
- 17   Chi. Bears vs. Green Bay, Oct. 22, 1933
  Cincinnati vs. Pittsburgh, Oct. 22, 1933
- 16   Cincinnati vs. Portsmouth, Sept. 17, 1933
  Chi. Cardinals vs. Chi. Bears, Nov. 30, 1933; vs. Detroit, Sept. 15, 1940

Fewest Punts, Game
- 0   By many teams. Last time: Tampa Bay vs. Green Bay, Nov. 22, 1981

Most Punts, Both Teams, Game
- 31   Chi. Bears (17) vs. Green Bay (14), Oct. 22, 1933
  Cincinnati (17), vs. Pittsburgh (14), Oct. 22, 1933
- 29   Chi. Cardinals (15) vs. Cincinnati (14), Nov. 12, 1933
  Chi. Cardinals (16) vs. Chi. Bears (13), Nov. 30, 1933
  Chi. Cardinals (16) vs. Detroit (13), Sept. 15, 1940

Fewest Punts, Both Teams, Game
- 1   Dall. Cowboys (0) vs. Cleveland (1), Dec. 3, 1961
  Chicago (0) vs. Detroit (1), Oct. 1, 1972
  San Francisco (0) vs. N.Y. Giants (1), Oct. 15, 1972
- 2   Philadelphia (0) vs. Cleveland (2), Sept. 25, 1960
  Philadelphia (0) vs. Dall. Cowboys (2), Oct. 22, 1961
  Detroit (0) vs. Kansas City (2), Nov. 25, 1971
  N.Y. Giants (1) vs. Philadelphia (1), Nov. 25, 1973
  Buffalo (0) vs. New England (2), Nov. 3, 1974
  San Diego (0) vs. Cleveland (2), Dec. 4, 1977
  Miami (0) vs. Chicago (2), Sept. 23, 1979
  Oakland (0) vs. Seattle (2), Dec. 16, 1979
  Kansas City (1) vs. New England (1), Oct. 4, 1981
- 3   In many games

AVERAGE YARDAGE

Highest Average Distance, Punting, Season
- 47.6   Detroit, 1961
- 47.0   Pittsburgh, 1961
- 46.9   Pittsburgh, 1953

Lowest Average Distance, Punting, Season
- 32.7   Card-Pitt, 1944
- 33.9   Detroit, 1969
- 34.4   Phil-Pitt, 1943

PUNT RETURNS

Most Seasons Leading League (Average return)
- 8   Detroit, 1943-45, 1951-52, 1962, 1966, 1969
- 5   Chi. Cardinals, 1948-49, 1955-56, 1959
  Clev. Browns, 1958, 1960, 1964-65, 1967
  Green Bay, 1950, 1953-54, 1961, 1972
  Dall. Texans/Kansas City, 1960, 1968, 1970, 1979-80
- 3   Denver, 1963, 1967, 1969
  San Diego, 1965-66, 1973
  Washington, 1957, 1963, 1976
  N.Y. Jets, 1961-62, 1978

Most Consecutive Seasons Leading League (Average Return)
- 3   Detroit, 1943-45
- 2   By many teams

Most Punt Returns, Season
  71 Pittsburgh, 1976
      Tampa Bay, 1979
  67 Pittsburgh, 1974
      Los Angeles, 1978
  65 San Francisco, 1976
Fewest Punt Returns, Season
  12 Baltimore, 1981
  14 Los Angeles, 1961
      Philadelphia, 1962
  15 Houston, 1960
      Washington, 1960
      Oakland, 1961
      N.Y. Giants, 1969
      Philadelphia, 1973
Most Punt Returns, Game
  12 Philadelphia vs. Cleveland, Dec. 3, 1950
  11 Chi. Bears vs. Chi. Cardinals, Oct. 8, 1950
      Washington vs. Tampa Bay, Oct. 9, 1977
  10 Philadelphia vs. N.Y. Giants, Nov. 26, 1950
      Philadelphia vs. Tampa Bay, Sept. 18, 1977
      Pittsburgh vs. Buffalo, Dec. 16, 1979
Most Punt Returns, Both Teams, Game
  17 Philadelphia (12) vs. Cleveland (5), Dec. 3, 1950
  16 N.Y. Giants (9) vs. Philadelphia (7), Dec. 12, 1954
      Washington (11) vs. Tampa Bay (5), Oct. 9, 1977
  15 Detroit (8) vs. Cleveland (7), Sept. 27, 1942
      Los Angeles (8) vs. Baltimore (7), Nov. 27, 1966
      Pittsburgh (8) vs. Houston (7), Dec. 1, 1974
      Philadelphia (10) vs. Tampa Bay (5), Sept. 18, 1977
      Baltimore (9) vs. Kansas City (6), Sept. 2, 1979

FAIR CATCHES
Most Fair Catches, Season
  34 Baltimore, 1971
  32 San Diego, 1969
  30 St. Louis, 1967
      Minnesota, 1971
Fewest Fair Catches, Season
   0 San Diego, 1975
      New England, 1976
      Tampa Bay, 1976
      Pittsburgh, 1977
   1 Cleveland, 1974
      San Francisco, 1975
      Kansas City, 1976
      St. Louis, 1976
      San Diego, 1976
   2 By many teams
Most Fair Catches, Game
   7 Minnesota vs. Dallas, Sept. 25, 1966
      Detroit vs. Chicago, Nov. 21, 1976
   6 Minnesota vs. Baltimore, Nov. 17, 1963; vs. Atlanta, Nov. 28, 1971
      Chicago vs. St. Louis, Oct. 31, 1966; vs. Minnesota, Dec. 10, 1967
      Cleveland vs. St. Louis, Dec. 17, 1966
      San Francisco vs. Baltimore, Oct. 13, 1968
      Miami vs. Buffalo, Dec. 20, 1970
      Cincinnati vs. Pittsburgh, Sept. 26, 1971
      N.Y. Giants vs. Minnesota, Oct. 31, 1971
      Baltimore vs. N.Y. Jets, Nov. 14, 1971
      Green Bay vs. Chicago, Dec. 16, 1973
      San Diego vs. Chicago, Dec. 4, 1978
   5 By many teams

YARDS GAINED
Most Yards, Punt Returns, Season
  781 Chi. Bears, 1948
  774 Pittsburgh, 1974
  729 Green Bay, 1950
Fewest Yards, Punt Returns, Season
   27 St. Louis, 1965
   35 N.Y. Giants, 1965
   37 New England, 1972
Most Yards, Punt Returns, Game
  231 Detroit vs. San Francisco, Oct. 6, 1963
  225 Oakland vs. Buffalo, Sept. 15, 1968
  219 Los Angeles vs. Atlanta, Oct. 11, 1981
Most Yards, Punt Returns, Both Teams, Game
  282 Los Angeles (219) vs. Atlanta (63), Oct. 11, 1981
  245 Detroit (231) vs. San Francisco (14), Oct. 6, 1963
  244 Oakland (225) vs. Buffalo (19), Sept. 15, 1968

AVERAGE YARDS RETURNING PUNTS
Highest Average, Punt Returns, Season
  20.2 Chi. Bears, 1941
  19.1 Chi. Cardinals, 1948
  18.2 Chi. Cardinals, 1949
Lowest Average, Punt Returns, Season
   1.2 St. Louis, 1965
   1.5 N.Y. Giants, 1965
   1.7 Washington, 1970

TOUCHDOWNS RETURNING PUNTS
Most Touchdowns, Punt Returns, Season
   5 Chi. Cardinals, 1959
   4 Chi. Cardinals, 1948
      Detroit, 1951
      N.Y. Giants, 1951
      Denver, 1976
   3 Washington, 1941
      Detroit, 1952
      Pittsburgh, 1952
      Houston, 1975
      Los Angeles, 1981
Most Touchdowns, Punt Returns, Game
   2 Detroit vs. Los Angeles, Oct. 14, 1951; vs. Green Bay, Nov. 22, 1951
      Chi. Cardinals vs. Pittsburgh, Nov. 1, 1959; vs. N.Y. Giants, Nov. 22, 1959
      N.Y. Titans vs. Denver, Sept. 24, 1961
      Denver vs. Cleveland, Sept. 26, 1976
      Los Angeles vs. Atlanta, Oct. 11, 1981
Most Touchdowns, Punt Returns, Both Teams, Game
   2 Philadelphia (1) vs. Washington (1), Nov. 9, 1952
      Kansas City (1) vs. Buffalo (1), Sept. 11, 1966
      Baltimore (1) vs. New England (1), Nov. 18, 1979
      (Also see previous record)

KICKOFF RETURNS
Most Seasons Leading League (Average return)
   7 Washington, 1942, 1947, 1962-63, 1973-74, 1981
   5 N.Y. Giants, 1944, 1946, 1949, 1951, 1953
      Chi. Bears, 1943, 1948, 1958, 1966, 1972
   4 Houston, 1960, 1962-63, 1968
Most Consecutive Seasons Leading League (Average return)
   3 Denver, 1965-67
   2 By many teams
Most Kickoff Returns, Season
  88 New Orleans, 1980
  84 Balitmore, 1981
  82 Atlanta, 1966
Fewest Kickoff Returns, Season
  17 N.Y. Giants, 1944
  20 N.Y. Giants, 1941
      Chi. Bears, 1942
      N.Y. Giants, 1943
  23 Washington, 1942
Most Kickoff Returns, Game
  12 N.Y. Giants vs. Washington, Nov. 27, 1966
  10 By many teams
Most Kickoff Returns, Both Teams, Game
  19 N.Y. Giants (12) vs. Washington (7), Nov. 27, 1966
  18 Houston (10) vs. Oakland (8), Dec. 22, 1963
  16 N.Y. Giants (10) vs. Chi. Cardinals (6), Oct. 17, 1948
      N.Y. Titans (10) vs. L.A. Chargers (6), Dec. 18, 1960
      Cleveland (8) vs. St. Louis (8), Sept. 20, 1964
      Cleveland (8) vs. N.Y. Giants (8), Dec. 4, 1966

YARDS GAINED
Most Yards, Kickoff Returns, Season
  1,973 New Orleans, 1980
  1,824 Houston, 1963
  1,801 Denver, 1963
Fewest Yards, Kickoff Returns, Season
   282 N.Y. Giants, 1940
   381 Green Bay, 1940
   424 Chicago, 1963
Most Yards, Kickoff Returns, Game
   362 Detroit vs. Los Angeles, Oct. 29, 1950
   304 Chi. Bears vs. Green Bay, Nov. 9, 1952
   295 Denver vs. Boston, Oct. 4, 1964
Most Yards, Kickoff Returns, Both Teams, Game
   560 Detroit (362) vs. Los Angeles (198), Oct. 29, 1950
   453 Washington (236) vs. Philadelphia (217), Sept. 28, 1947
   447 N.Y. Giants (236) vs. Cleveland (211), Dec. 4, 1966

AVERAGE YARDAGE
Highest Average, Kickoff Returns, Season
  29.4 Chicago, 1972
  28.9 Pittsburgh, 1952
  28.2 Washington, 1962
Lowest Average, Kickoff Returns, Season
  16.3 Chicago, 1963
  16.5 San Diego, 1961
  16.7 Chi. Cardinals, 1947

TOUCHDOWNS
Most Touchdowns, Kickoff Returns, Season
   4 Green Bay, 1967
      Chicago, 1970
   3 Los Angeles, 1950
      Chi. Cardinals, 1954
      San Francisco, 1963
      Denver, 1966
      Chicago, 1967
      New England, 1977
   2 By many teams

KICKOFF RETURNS Continued

Most Touchdowns, Kickoff Returns, Game

  2 Chi. Bears vs. Green Bay, Sept. 22, 1940; vs. Green Bay, Nov. 9, 1952
     Philadelphia vs. Dallas, Nov. 6, 1966
     Green Bay vs. Cleveland, Nov. 12, 1967

Most Touchdowns, Kickoff Returns, Both Teams, Game

  2 Washington (1) vs. Philadelphia (1), Nov. 1, 1942
     Washington (1) vs. Philadelphia (1), Sept. 28, 1947
     Los Angeles (1) vs. Detroit (1), Oct. 29, 1950
     N.Y. Yanks (1) vs. N.Y. Giants (1), Nov. 4, 1951 (consecutive)
     Baltimore (1) vs. Chi. Bears (1), Oct. 4, 1958
     Buffalo (1) vs. Boston (1), Nov. 3, 1962
     Pittsburgh (1) vs. Dallas (1), Oct. 30, 1966
     St. Louis (1) vs. Washington (1), Sept. 23, 1973 (consecutive)
     (Also see previous record)

FUMBLES

Most Fumbles, Season

 56 Chi. Bears, 1938
     San Francisco, 1978
 54 Philadelphia, 1946
 51 New England, 1973

Fewest Fumbles, Season

  8 Cleveland, 1959
 11 Green Bay, 1944
 12 Brooklyn, 1934
     Detroit, 1943

Most Fumbles, Game

 10 Phil-Pitt vs. New York, Oct. 9, 1943
     Detroit vs. Minnesota, Nov. 12, 1967
     Kansas City vs. Houston, Oct. 12, 1969
     San Francisco vs. Detroit, Dec. 17, 1978
  9 Philadelphia vs. Green Bay, Oct. 13, 1946
     Kansas City vs. San Diego, Nov. 15, 1964
     N.Y. Giants vs. Buffalo, Oct. 20, 1975
     St. Louis vs. Washington, Oct. 25, 1976
     San Diego vs. Green Bay, Sept. 24, 1978
     Pittsburgh vs. Cincinnati, Oct. 14, 1979
     Cleveland vs. Seattle, Dec. 20, 1981
  8 By many teams

Most Fumbles, Both Teams, Game

 14 Chi. Bears (7) vs. Cleveland (7), Nov. 24, 1940
     St. Louis (8) vs. N.Y. Giants (6), Sept. 17, 1961
     Kansas City (10) vs. Houston (4), Oct. 12, 1969
 13 Washington (8) vs. Pittsburgh (5), Nov. 14, 1937
     Philadelphia (7) vs. Boston (6), Dec. 8, 1946
     N.Y. Giants (7) vs. Washington (6), Nov. 5, 1950
     Kansas City (9) vs. San Diego (4), Nov. 15, 1964
     Buffalo (7) vs. Denver (6), Dec. 13, 1964
     N.Y. Jets (7) vs. Houston (6), Sept. 12, 1965
     Houston (8) vs. Pittsburgh (5), Dec. 9, 1973
     St. Louis (9) vs. Washington (4), Oct. 25, 1976
     Cleveland (9) vs. Seattle (4), Dec. 20, 1981
 12 In many games

FUMBLES LOST

Most Fumbles Lost, Season

 36 Chi. Cardinals, 1959
 29 Chi. Cardinals, 1946
 28 Pittsburgh, 1977

Fewest Fumbles Lost, Season

  3 Philadelphia, 1938
     Minnesota, 1980
  4 San Francisco, 1960
  5 Chi. Cardinals, 1943
     Detroit, 1943
     N.Y. Giants, 1943
     Cleveland, 1959

Most Fumbles Lost, Game

  8 St. Louis vs. Washington, Oct. 25, 1976
  7 Cincinnati vs. Buffalo, Nov. 30, 1969
     Cleveland vs. Seattle, Dec. 20, 1981
  6 By many teams

FUMBLES RECOVERED

Most Fumbles Recovered, Season, Own and Opponents'

 58 Minnesota, 1963 (27 own, 31 opp)
 51 Chi. Bears, 1938 (37 own, 14 opp)
     San Francisco, 1978 (24 own, 27 opp)
 47 Atlanta, 1978 (22 own, 25 opp)

Fewest Fumbles Recovered, Season, Own and Opponents'

 13 Baltimore, 1967 (5 own, 8 opp)
     N.Y. Jets, 1967 (7 own, 6 opp)
     Philadelphia, 1968 (6 own, 7 opp)
     Miami, 1973 (5 own, 8 opp)
 14 Cleveland, 1956 (6 own, 8 opp)
     Kansas City, 1966 (5 own, 9 opp)
 15 Chi. Bears, 1943 (9 own, 6 opp)
     San Francisco, 1951 (6 own, 9 opp)
     Cleveland, 1959 (3 own, 12 opp)
     Kansas City, 1971 (9 own, 6 opp)

Most Fumbles Recovered, Game, Own and Opponents'

 10 Denver vs. Buffalo, Dec. 13, 1964 (5 own, 5 opp)
     Pittsburgh vs. Houston, Dec. 9, 1973 (5 own, 5 opp)
     Washington vs. St. Louis, Oct. 25, 1976 (2 own, 8 opp)
  9 St. Louis vs. N.Y. Giants, Sept. 17, 1961 (6 own, 3 opp)
     Houston vs. Cincinnati, Oct. 27, 1974 (4 own, 5 opp)
     Kansas City vs. Dallas, Nov. 10, 1975 (4 own, 5 opp)
  8 By many teams

Most Own Fumbles Recovered, Season

 37 Chi. Bears, 1938
 27 Philadelphia, 1946
     Minnesota, 1963
 26 Washington, 1940
     Pittsburgh, 1948

Fewest Own Fumbles Recovered, Season

  2 Washington, 1958
  3 Detroit, 1956
     Cleveland, 1959
  4 By many teams

Most Opponents' Fumbles Recovered, Season

 31 Minnesota, 1963
 29 Cleveland, 1951
 28 Green Bay, 1946
     Houston, 1977

Fewest Opponents' Fumbles Recovered, Season

  3 Los Angeles, 1974
  4 Philadelphia, 1944
  6 Brooklyn, 1939
     Chi. Bears, 1943, 1945
     Washington, 1945
     N.Y. Jets, 1967
     San Diego, 1969
     Kansas City, 1971
     Oakland, 1975

Most Opponents' Fumbles Recovered, Game

  8 Washington vs. St. Louis, Oct. 25, 1976
  7 Buffalo vs. Cincinnati, Nov. 30, 1969
     Seattle vs. Cleveland, Dec. 20, 1981
  6 By many teams

TOUCHDOWNS

Most Touchdowns, Fumbles Recovered, Season, Own and Opponents'

  5 Chi. Bears, 1942 (1 own, 4 opp)
     Los Angeles, 1952 (1 own, 4 opp)
     San Francisco, 1965 (1 own, 4 opp)
     Oakland, 1978 (2 own, 3 opp)
  4 Chi. Bears, 1948 (1 own, 3 opp)
     Boston, 1948 (4 opp)
     Denver, 1979 (1 own, 3 opp)
     Atlanta, 1981 (1 own, 3 opp)
  3 By many teams

Most Touchdowns, Own Fumbles Recovered, Season

  2 Chi. Bears, 1953
     New England, 1973
     Buffalo, 1974
     Denver, 1975
     Oakland, 1978

Most Touchdowns, Opponents' Fumbles Recovered, Season

  4 Detroit, 1937
     Chi. Bears, 1942
     Boston, 1948
     Los Angeles, 1952
     San Francisco, 1965
  3 By many teams

Most Touchdowns, Fumbles Recovered, Game, Own and Opponents'

  2 Detroit vs. Cleveland, Nov. 7, 1937 (2 opp); vs. Los Angeles, Sept. 17, 1950
       (1 own, 1 opp); vs. Chi. Cardinals, Dec. 6, 1959 (1 own, 1 opp);
       vs. Minnesota, Dec. 9, 1962 (1 own, 1 opp)
     Philadelphia vs. New York, Sept. 25, 1938 (2 opp) vs. St. Louis, Nov. 21, 1971
       (1 own, 1 opp)
     Chi. Bears vs. Washington, Nov. 28, 1948 (2 opp)
     N.Y. Giants vs. Pittsburgh, Sept. 17, 1950 (2 opp); vs. Green Bay, Sept. 19,
       1971 (2 opp)
     Cleveland vs. Dall. Cowboys, Dec. 3, 1961 (2 opp); vs. N.Y. Giants, Oct. 25,
       1964 (2 opp)
     Green Bay vs. Dallas, Nov. 26, 1964 (2 opp)
     San Francisco vs. Detroit, Nov. 14, 1965 (2 opp)
     Oakland vs. Buffalo, Dec. 24, 1967 (2 opp)
     Washington vs. San Diego, Sept. 16, 1973 (2 opp)
     New Orleans vs. San Francisco, Oct 19, 1975 (2 opp)
     Cincinnati vs. Pittsburgh, Oct. 14, 1979 (2 opp)
     Atlanta vs. Detroit, Oct. 5, 1980 (2 opp)
     Kansas City vs. Oakland, Oct. 5, 1980 (2 opp)
     New England vs. Baltimore, Nov. 23, 1980 (2 opp)

Most Touchdowns, Own Fumbles Recovered, Game

  1 By many teams

Most Touchdowns, Opponents' Fumbles Recovered, Game
- 2   Detroit vs. Cleveland, Nov. 7, 1937
    Philadelphia vs. N.Y. Giants, Sept. 25, 1938
    Chi. Bears vs. Washington, Nov. 28, 1948
    N.Y. Giants vs. Pittsburgh, Sept. 17, 1950; vs. Green Bay, Sept. 19, 1971
    Cleveland vs. Dall. Cowboys, Dec. 3, 1961; vs. N.Y. Giants, Oct. 25, 1964
    Green Bay vs. Dallas, Nov. 26, 1964
    San Francisco vs. Detroit, Nov. 14, 1965
    Oakland vs. Buffalo, Dec. 24, 1967
    Washington vs. San Diego, Sept. 16, 1973
    New Orleans vs. San Francisco, Oct. 19, 1975
    Cincinnati vs. Pittsburgh, Oct. 14, 1979
    Atlanta vs. Detroit, Oct. 5, 1980
    Kansas City vs. Oakland, Oct. 5, 1980
    New England vs. Baltimore, Nov. 23, 1980

TURNOVERS
(Number of times losing the ball on interceptions and fumbles.)
Most Turnovers, Season
- 63   San Francisco, 1978
- 58   Chi. Bears, 1947
    Pittsburgh, 1950
- 57   Green Bay, 1950
    Houston, 1962, 1963
    Pittsburgh, 1965

Fewest Turnovers, Season
- 14   N.Y. Giants, 1943
    Cleveland, 1959
- 16   San Francisco, 1960
- 17   N.Y. Giants, 1939
    St. Louis, 1974

Most Turnovers, Game
- 12   Detroit vs. Chi. Bears, Nov. 22, 1942
    Chi. Cardinals vs. Philadelphia, Sept. 24, 1950
    Pittsburgh vs. Philadelphia, Dec. 12, 1965
- 11   San Diego vs. Green Bay, Sept. 24, 1978
- 10   Washington vs. N.Y. Giants, Dec. 4, 1938; vs. N.Y. Giants, Dec. 8, 1963
    Pittsburgh vs. Green Bay, Nov. 23, 1941
    Detroit vs. Green Bay, Oct. 24, 1943
    Chi. Cardinals vs. Green Bay, Nov. 10, 1946; vs. N.Y. Giants, Nov. 2, 1952
    Minnesota vs. Detroit, Dec. 9, 1962
    Houston vs. Oakland, Sept. 7, 1963
    Chicago vs. Detroit, Sept. 22, 1968
    St. Louis vs. Washington, Oct. 25, 1976
    N.Y. Jets vs. New England, Nov. 21, 1976
    San Francisco vs. Dallas, Oct. 12, 1980
    Cleveland vs. Seattle, Dec. 20, 1981

Most Turnovers, Both Teams, Game
- 17   Detroit (12) vs. Chi. Bears (5), Nov. 22, 1942
    Boston (9) vs. Philadelphia (8), Dec. 8, 1946
- 16   Chi. Cardinals (12) vs. Philadelphia (4), Sept. 24, 1950
    Chi. Cardinals (8) vs. Chi. Bears (8), Dec. 7, 1958
    Minnesota (10) vs. Detroit (6), Dec. 9, 1962
    Houston (9) vs. Kansas City (7), Oct. 12, 1969
- 15   Philadelphia (8) vs. Chi. Cardinals (7), Oct. 3, 1954
    Denver (9) vs. Houston (6), Dec. 2, 1962
    Washington (10) vs. N.Y. Giants (5), Dec. 8, 1963

PENALTIES
Most Seasons Leading League, Fewest Penalties
- 9   Pittsburgh, 1946-47, 1950-52, 1954, 1963, 1965, 1968
- 7   Miami, 1968, 1976-81
- 5   Green Bay, 1955-56, 1966-67, 1974

Most Consecutive Seasons Leading League, Fewest Penalties
- 6   Miami, 1976-81
- 3   Pittsburgh, 1950-52
- 2   By many teams

Most Seasons Leading League, Most Penalties
- 16   Chi. Bears, 1941-44, 1946-49, 1951, 1959-61, 1963, 1965, 1968, 1976
- 6   L.A. Rams, 1950, 1952, 1962, 1969, 1978, 1980
- 5   Oakland, 1963, 1966, 1968-69, 1975

Most Consecutive Seasons Leading League, Most Penalties
- 4   Chi. Bears, 1941-44, 1946-49
- 3   Chi. Cardinals, 1954-56
    Chi. Bears, 1959-61

Fewest Penalties, Season
- 19   Detroit, 1937
- 21   Boston, 1935
- 24   Philadelphia, 1936

Most Penalties, Season
- 137   Baltimore, 1979
- 133   Los Angeles, 1978
- 132   Denver, 1978

Fewest Penalties, Game
- 0   By many teams. Last time: Dallas vs. Washington, Nov. 23, 1980

Most Penalties, Game
- 22   Brooklyn vs. Green Bay, Sept. 17, 1944
    Chi. Bears vs. Philadelphia, Nov. 26, 1944
- 21   Cleveland vs. Chi. Bears, Nov. 25, 1951
- 20   Tampa Bay vs. Seattle, Oct. 17, 1976

Fewest Penalties, Both Teams, Game
- 0   Brooklyn vs. Pittsburgh, Oct. 28, 1934
    Brooklyn vs. Boston, Sept. 28, 1936
    Cleveland vs. Chi. Bears, Oct. 9, 1938
    Pittsburgh vs. Philadelphia, Nov. 10, 1940

Most Penalties, Both Teams, Game
- 37   Cleveland (21) vs. Chi. Bears (16), Nov. 25, 1951
- 35   Tampa Bay (20) vs. Seattle (15), Oct. 17, 1976
- 33   Brooklyn (22) vs. Green Bay (11), Sept. 17, 1944

YARDS PENALIZED
Most Seasons Leading League, Fewest Yards Penalized
- 8   Miami, 1967-68, 1973, 1977-81
- 7   Pittsburgh, 1946-47, 1950, 1952, 1962, 1965, 1968
    Boston/Washington, 1935, 1953-54, 1956-58, 1970
- 4   Philadelphia, 1936, 1940, 1951, 1964
    Boston, 1962, 1964-66

Most Consecutive Seasons Leading League, Fewest Yards Penalized
- 5   Miami, 1977-81
- 3   Washington, 1956-58
    Boston, 1964-66
- 2   By many teams

Most Seasons Leading League, Most Yards Penalized
- 15   Chi. Bears, 1935, 1937, 1939-44, 1946-47, 1949, 1951, 1961-62, 1968
- 5   Oakland, 1963-64, 1968-69, 1975
    Cleveland, 1965, 1976-78, 1980
    Buffalo, 1962, 1967, 1970, 1972, 1981
- 4   Baltimore, 1957, 1959, 1963, 1979

Most Consecutive Seasons Leading League, Most Yards Penalized
- 6   Chi. Bears, 1939-44
- 3   Cleveland, 1976-78
- 2   By many teams

Fewest Yards Penalized, Season
- 139   Detroit, 1937
- 146   Philadelphia, 1937
- 159   Philadelphia, 1936

Most Yards Penalized, Season
- 1,274   Oakland, 1969
- 1,239   Baltimore, 1979
- 1,194   Chicago, 1968

Fewest Yards Penalized, Game
- 0   By many teams. Last time: Dallas vs. Washington, Nov. 23, 1980

Most Yards Penalized, Game
- 209   Cleveland vs. Chi. Bears, Nov. 25, 1951
- 190   Tampa Bay vs. Seattle, Oct. 17, 1976
- 189   Houston vs. Buffalo, Oct. 31, 1965

Fewest Yards Penalized, Both Teams, Game
- 0   Brooklyn vs. Pittsburgh, Oct. 28, 1934
    Brooklyn vs. Boston, Sept. 28, 1936
    Cleveland vs. Chi. Bears, Oct. 9, 1938
    Pittsburgh vs. Philadelphia, Nov. 10, 1940

Most Yards Penalized, Both Teams, Game
- 374   Cleveland (209) vs. Chi. Bears (165), Nov. 25, 1951
- 310   Tampa Bay (190) vs. Seattle (120), Oct. 17, 1976
- 309   Green Bay (184) vs. Boston (125), Oct. 21, 1945

Paul Krause, career interception leader.

SPECIAL ACHIEVEMENTS

1922 Wilbur (Pete) Henry, Canton Bulldogs, drop-kicked a 50-yard field goal vs. Toledo Maroons, November 13.

John (Paddy) Driscoll, Chicago Cardinals, drop-kicked three field goals (30, 23, and 12 yards) vs. Chicago Bears, December 10.

1923 John (Paddy) Driscoll, Chicago Cardinals, scored 27 points (four touchdowns, three extra points) vs. Rochester Jeffersons, October 7.

George Halas, Chicago Bears, recovered a fumble and returned it 98 yards for a touchdown vs. Oorang Indians, Marion, Ohio, November 4.

1924 John (Paddy) Driscoll, Chicago Cardinals, drop-kicked a 50-yard field goal vs. Milwaukee Badgers, September 28.

John (Paddy) Driscoll, Chicago Cardinals, drop-kicked four field goals (23, 18, 50, and 35 yards) vs. Columbus Tigers, October 11.

John (Paddy) Driscoll, Chicago Cardinals, drop-kicked 11 field goals in a season (14 games).

1929 Ernie Nevers, Chicago Cardinals, scored 40 points (six touchdowns rushing, four extra points) vs. Chicago Bears, November 28.

1933 Martin Kottler, Pittsburgh Pirates, intercepted a pass and returned it 99 yards vs. Chicago Cardinals, September 27.

Cliff Battles, Boston Redskins, gained 215 yards rushing (16 attempts) vs. New York Giants, October 8.

Jack McBride, New York Giants, kicked five extra points vs. Philadelphia Eagles, October 15.

Gil Lefebvre, Cincinnati Reds, returned a punt 98 yards vs. Brooklyn Dodgers, December 3.

Harry Newman, New York Giants, attempted 136 passes, completed 53 for 973 yards passing in a season.

1934 Doug Russell, Chicago Cardinals, returned a kickoff 102 yards vs. Cincinnati Reds, September 24.

Glenn Presnell, Detroit Lions, kicked a 54-yard field goal vs. Green Bay Packers, October 7.

Harry Newman, New York Giants, carried the ball 39 times vs. Green Bay Packers, November 11.

Beattie Feathers, Chicago Bears, gained 1,004 yards rushing (101 attempts) in a season and averaged 9.94 yards per carry.

Jack Manders, Chicago Bears, scored 76 points (three touchdowns, 10 field goals, 28 extra points) in a season.

1936 Alphonse (Tuffy) Leemans, New York Giants, carried the ball 206 times in a season (12 games).

Arnie Herber, Green Bay Packers, attempted 173 passes, completed 77 for 1,239 yards passing in a season (12 games).

Don Hutson, Green Bay Packers, caught 34 passes for 536 yards and eight touchdowns in a season (12 games).

1937 Vern Huffman, Detroit Lions, intercepted a pass and returned it 100 yards vs. Brooklyn Dodgers, October 17.

Ray Buivid, Chicago Bears, threw five touchdown passes vs. Chicago Cardinals, December 5.

Pat Coffee and Gaynell Tinsley, Chicago Cardinals, combined for a 97-yard touchdown pass vs. Chicago Bears, December 5.

Riley Smith, Washington Redskins, kicked seven extra points vs. New York Giants, December 5.

Cliff Battles, Washington Redskins, carried the ball 216 times in a season (11 games).

Sammy Baugh, Washington Redskins, attempted 171 passes, completed 81 for 1,127 yards passing in a season (11 games).

Don Hutson, Green Bay Packers, caught 41 passes in a season (11 games).

1938 Doug Russell and Gaynell Tinsley, Chicago Cardinals, combined for a 98-yard touchdown pass vs. Cleveland Rams, November 27.

1939 Andy Uram, Green Bay Packers, had a 97-yard run from scrimmage vs. Chicago Cardinals, October 8.

Frank Filchock and Andy Farkas, Washington Redskins, combined for a 99-yard touchdown pass vs. Pittsburgh Pirates, October 15.

Parker Hall, Cleveland Rams, completed 106 passes (208 attempts) in a season (11 games).

Don Hutson, Green Bay Packers, had 846 yards (34 receptions) pass receiving in a season (11 games).

1940 Lee Artoe, Chicago Bears, kicked a 52-yard field goal vs. New York Giants, October 27.

Sammy Baugh, Washington Redskins, had a 59.4 punting average (five punts) vs. Detroit Lions, October 27.

Davey O'Brien, Philadelphia Eagles, completed 33 of 60 passes for 316 yards vs. Washington Redskins, December 1.

Don Looney, Philadelphia Eagles, caught 14 passes for 180 yards vs. Washington Redskins, December 1.

Davey O'Brien, Philadelphia Eagles, attempted 277 passes (124 completions) in a season (11 games).

Don Looney, Philadelphia Eagles, caught 58 passes in a season (11 games).

1941 Cecil Isbell, Green Bay Packers, completed 117 passes (206 attempts) for 1,479 yards passing and 15 touchdowns in a season (11 games).

Don Hutson, Green Bay Packers, scored 95 points (12 touchdowns, one field goal, 20 extra points) in a season (11 games).

1942 Don Hutson, Green Bay Packers, caught 13 passes for 209 yards pass receiving vs. Cleveland Rams, October 18.

Cecil Isbell, Green Bay Packers, had 333 yards passing (10 completions) vs. Chicago Cardinals, November 1.

Cecil Isbell, Green Bay Packers, completed 146 of 268 passes for 2,021 yards passing and 24 touchdowns in a season (11 games).

Cecil Isbell, Green Bay Packers, completed a string in which he threw at least one touchdown pass in 23 consecutive games in 1941 and 1942.

Wilson Schwenk, Chicago Cardinals, attempted 295 passes (126 completions) in a season (11 games).

Don Hutson, Green Bay Packers, caught 74 passes for 1,211 yards pass receiving and 17 touchdowns in a season (11 games).

Clyde (Bulldog) Turner, Chicago Bears, intercepted eight passes in a season (11 games).

Don Hutson, Green Bay Packers, scored 138 points (17 touchdowns, one field goal, 33 extra points) in a season (11 games).

1943 Sammy Baugh, Washington Redskins, had 376 yards passing (28 attempts, 16 completions) for six touchdowns vs. Brooklyn Dodgers, October 31.

Wilbur Moore, Washington Redskins, had 213 yards pass receiving (seven receptions) vs. Brooklyn Dodgers, October 31.

Sid Luckman, Chicago Bears, completed 21 of 32 passes for 433 yards passing and seven touchdowns vs. New York Giants, November 14.

Don Hutson, Green Bay Packers, had 237 yards pass receiving (eight receptions) vs. Brooklyn Dodgers, November 21.

Sid Luckman, Chicago Bears, attempted 202 passes, completed 110 for 2,194 yards passing and 28 touchdowns in a season (10 games).

Sammy Baugh, Washington Redskins, intercepted 11 passes in a season (10 games).

Bob Snyder, Chicago Bears, kicked 39 extra points in a season (10 games).

1944 Don Hutson, Green Bay Packers, completed a string in which he scored in 41 consecutive games.

1945 Don Hutson, Green Bay Packers, caught four touchdown passes and scored 29 points in one quarter, 31 in the game (four touchdowns, seven extra points) vs. Detroit Lions, October 7.

Jim Benton, Cleveland Rams, had 303 yards pass receiving (10 receptions) vs. Detroit Lions, November 22.

Sammy Baugh, Washington Redskins, had a 70.3 completion percentage in passing (182 attempts, 128 completions) for a season and only four of his passes were intercepted (10 games).

Don Hutson, Green Bay Packers, retired from football with a string of 95 consecutive games in which he caught at least one pass.

Steve Van Buren, Philadelphia Eagles, scored 18 touchdowns, 15 of them rushing, in a season (10 games).

1946 Frank Seno, Chicago Cardinals, returned a kickoff 105 yards vs. New York Giants, October 20.

1947 Steve Van Buren, Philadelphia Eagles, gained 1,008 yards rushing (217 attempts) in a season (12 games).

Sammy Baugh, Washington Redskins, attempted 354 passes, completed 210 for 2,938 yards passing in a season (12 games).

1948 Pat Harder, Chicago Cardinals, kicked nine extra points vs. New York Giants, October 17.

Bob Waterfield, Los Angeles Rams, made an 88-yard punt vs. Green Bay Packers, October 17.

Sammy Baugh, Washington Redskins, had 446 yards passing (17 completions) vs. Boston Yanks, October 31.

Dick Poillon, Washington Redskins, intercepted a lateral and returned it 93 yards for a touchdown vs. Philadelphia Eagles, November 21.

Fred (Dippy) Evans, Chicago Bears, scored two touchdowns on fumble recoveries vs. Washington Redskins, November 28.

Charlie Conerly, New York Giants, completed 36 passes (53 attempts) vs. Pittsburgh Steelers, December 5.

Dan Sandifer, Washington Redskins, intercepted 13 passes and had 258 yards in interception returns in a season.

Pat Harder, Chicago Cardinals, kicked 53 extra points without a miss.

Jim Hardy, Los Angeles Rams, threw 114 passes without an interception.

1949 Jim Keane, Chicago Bears, caught 14 passes (193 yards) vs. New York Giants, October 23.

Bob Smith, Detroit Lions, intercepted a pass and returned it 102 yards for a touchdown vs. Chicago Bears, November 24.

Ralph Heywood, New York Bulldogs, caught 14 passes (151 yards) vs. Detroit Lions, December 4.

Bob Gage, Pittsburgh Steelers, ran 97 yards from scrimmage vs. Chicago Bears, December 4.

Johnny Lujack, Chicago Bears, had 468 yards passing (24 completions) vs. Chicago Cardinals, December 11.

Bob Shaw, Los Angeles Rams, caught four touchdown passes vs. Washington Redskins, December 11.

Tom Fears, Los Angeles Rams, caught 77 passes in a season (12 games).

Cliff Patton, Philadelphia Eagles, completed a string in which he made 84 consecutive extra points between 1947 and 1949.

1950 Bob Shaw, Chicago Cardinals, caught five touchdown passes vs. Baltimore Colts, October 2.

Norm Van Brocklin, Los Angeles Rams, completed 11 consecutive passes vs. Detroit Lions (10), October 15, and Baltimore Colts (1), October 22.

Marion Motley, Cleveland Browns, averaged 17.09 yards per rushing attempt (11 for 188 yards) vs. Pittsburgh Steelers, October 29.

Wally Triplett, Detroit Lions, returned four kickoffs for 294 yards, a 73.5-yard average, vs. Los Angeles Rams, October 29.

Gene Roberts, New York Giants, gained 218 yards rushing (26 attempts) vs. Chicago Cardinals, November 12.

George Buskar and Ernie Zalejski, Baltimore Colts, combined for a 99-yard return of an intercepted lateral (18 yards by Buksar, 81 by Zalejski) vs. Washington Redskins, November 26.

Tom Fears, Los Angeles Rams, caught 18 passes (189 yards) vs. Green Bay, December 3.

Cloyce Box, Detroit Lions, had 302 yards pass receiving (12 receptions) vs. Baltimore Colts, December 3.

Doak Walker, Detroit Lions, scored 128 points in his rookie season (11 touchdowns, eight field goals, 38 extra points).

Orban (Spec) Sanders, New York Yanks, intercepted 13 passes in a season (12 games).

Tom Fears, Los Angeles Rams, caught 84 passes (1,116 yards) in a season (12 games).

1951 Norm Van Brocklin, Los Angeles Rams, had 554 yards passing (41 attempts, 27 completions) vs. N. Y. Yanks, September 28.

Jack Christiansen, Detroit Lions, returned punts twice for touchdowns, in two different games, vs. Los Angeles Rams, October 14, and vs. Green Bay Packers, November 22. He had 175 yards in punt returns (four returns, 43.8 average) vs. Green Bay.

Dub Jones, Cleveland Browns, scored six touchdowns (four rushing, two pass receiving) vs. Chicago Bears, November 25.

Bob Waterfield, Los Angeles Rams, kicked five field goals (17, 40, 25, 20, and 39 yards) vs. Detroit Lions, December 9.

Jerry Williams, Los Angeles Rams, returned a missed field goal 99 yards for a touchdown vs. Green Bay Packers, December 16.

Eddie Price, New York Giants, carried the ball 271 times (971 yards) in a season (12 games).

Elroy (Crazylegs) Hirsch, Los Angeles Rams, had 1,495 yards in pass receiving (66 receptions) and scored 17 touchdowns pass receiving in a season (12 games).

1952 Otto Graham, Cleveland Browns, attempted 364 passes (181 completions) in a season (12 games).

Dick (Night Train) Lane, Los Angeles Rams, intercepted 14 passes (298 yards) in a season (12 games).

Lou Groza, Cleveland Browns, kicked 19 field goals (33 attempts) in a season (12 games).

1953 Bert Rechichar, Baltimore Colts, kicked a 56-yard field goal vs. Chicago Bears, September 27

Lou Groza, Cleveland Browns, kicked 23 field goals (26 attempts) in a season (12 games).

Lou Groza, Cleveland Browns, completed a string of 109 consecutive extra points and another of scoring in 45 consecutive regular season games between 1950 and 1953.

1954 Adrian Burk, Philadelphia Eagles, threw seven touchdown passes vs. Washington Redskins, October 17.

Tobin Rote, Green Bay Packers, attempted 382 passes (180 completions) in a season.

1956 George Ratterman, Cleveland Browns, completed 11 consecutive passes vs. Pittsburgh Steelers, October 6.

Al Carmichael, Green Bay Packers, returned a kickoff 106 yards for a touchdown vs. Chicago Bears, October 7.

Tommy Wilson, Los Angeles Rams, gained 223 yards rushing (23 attempts) vs. Green Bay Packers, December 16.

George Blanda, Chicago Bears, completed a string in which he made 156 consecutive extra points between 1951 and 1956.

1957 Jim Brown, Cleveland Browns, gained 237 yards rushing (31 attempts) vs. Los Angeles Rams, November 24.

1958 Jim Brown, Cleveland Browns, gained 1,527 yards rushing (257 attempts) in a season (12 games), and had 100 yards or more in a game nine times.

Jim Brown, Cleveland Browns, scored 18 touchdowns (17 rushing, 1 pass receiving) in a season (12 games).

1959 Carl Taseff, Baltimore Colts, returned a missed field goal 99 yards for a touchdown vs. Los Angeles Rams, December 12.

Johnny Unitas, Baltimore Colts, threw 32 touchdown passes in a season (12 games).

Jim Brown, Cleveland Browns, carried the ball 290 times (1,329 yards) in a season (12 games).

1960 Milt Plum, Cleveland Browns, completed 11 consecutive passes vs. Washington Redskins, October 30.

George Blanda, Houston Oilers, attempted 55 passes (31 completions) vs. Los Angeles Chargers, November 13.

Frank Tripucka, Denver Broncos, attempted 478 passes in a season (14 games).

Milt Plum, Cleveland Browns, completed a string in which he threw 208 consecutive passes without an interception in 1959 and 1960.

Johnny Unitas, Baltimore Colts, had 3,099 yards passing (190 completions) and threw 25 touchdown passes.

Johnny Unitas, Baltimore Colts, completed a string in which he threw a touchdown pass in 47 consecutive regular season games between 1956 and 1960.

Lionel Taylor, Denver Broncos, caught 92 passes (1,235 yards) in a season (14 games).

Paul Hornung, Green Bay Packers, scored 176 points (15 touchdowns, 13 rushing, 2 pass receiving; 15 field goals; and 41 extra points) in a season (12 games).

1961 Paul Hornung, Green Bay Packers, scored 33 points (four touchdowns, one field goal, six extra points) vs. Baltimore Colts, October 8.

Erich Barnes, New York Giants, intercepted a pass and returned it 102 yards for a touchdown vs. Dallas Cowboys, October 22.

George Blanda, Houston Oilers, threw seven touchdown

passes vs. New York Titans, November 19.
Jim Brown, Cleveland Browns, gained 237 yards rushing (34 attempts) vs. Philadelphia Eagles, November 19.
Roger Leclerc, Chicago Bears, kicked five field goals (12, 30, 12, 32, and 15 yards) vs. Detroit Lions, December 3.
Fran Tarkenton, Minnesota Vikings, completed 13 consecutive passes vs. Los Angeles Rams, December 3.
Jim Brown, Cleveland Browns, carried the ball 305 times (1,408 yards) in a season (14 games).
Johnny Unitas, Baltimore Colts, attempted 420 passes (229 completions) in a season (14 games).
George Blanda, Houston Oilers, threw 36 touchdown passes in a season (14 games).
Sonny Jurgensen, Philadelphia Eagles, completed 235 passes (416 attempts) for 3,723 yards and 32 touchdowns in a season (14 games).
Lionel Taylor, Denver Broncos, caught 100 passes (1,176 yards) in a season (14 games).
Charley Hennigan, Houston Oilers, had 1,746 yards pass receiving (82 receptions) in a season (14 games).
Bill Groman, Houston Oilers, caught 17 touchdown passes in a season (14 games).
George Blanda, Houston Oilers, kicked 64 out of 65 extra point attempts in a season (14 games).
1962 Timmy Brown, Philadelphia Eagles, returned a missed field goal 99 yards for a touchdown vs. St. Louis Cardinals, September 15.
Frank Tripucka, Denver Broncos, attempted 56 passes (29 completions) vs. Buffalo Bills, September 15.
Y. A. Tittle, New York Giants, threw seven touchdown passes and had 505 yards passing (39 attempts, 27 completions) vs. Washington Redskins, October 28.
Sonny Randle, St. Louis Cardinals, caught 16 passes and had 256 yards pass receiving vs. New York Giants, November 4.
Abner Hayes, Dallas Texans, scored 19 touchdowns (13 rushing, 6 pass receiving) in a season (14 games).
Jim Taylor, Green Bay Packers, scored 19 touchdowns (all rushing) in a season (14 games).
Cookie Gilchrist, Buffalo Bills, scored touchdowns rushing in seven consecutive games.
Lou Michaels, Pittsburgh Steelers, made 26 field goals (42 attempts) in a season (14 games).
Roger Brown, Detroit Lions, scored two safeties in a season (14 games).
1963 George Izo and Bobby Mitchell, Washington Redskins, combined for a 99-yard touchdown pass vs. Cleveland Browns, September 15.
Tom Watkins, Detroit Lions, gained 184 yards on punt returns (five returns) vs. San Francisco 49ers, October 6.
Cookie Gilchrist, Buffalo Bills, gained 243 yards rushing (36 attempts) vs. New York Jets, December 8.
Jim Brown, Cleveland Browns, gained 1,863 yards rushing (291 attempts), had 200 or more in a game two times. Altogether he gained 100 or more yards in a game nine times.
Charley Johnson, St. Louis Cardinals, attempted 423 passes (222 completions) in a season (14 games).
Johnny Unitas, Baltimore Colts, completed 237 passes (410 attempts) in a season (14 games).
Y. A. Tittle, New York Giants, threw 36 touchdown passes in a season (14 games).
Tommy Morrow, Oakland Raiders, completed a string in which he intercepted passes in eight consecutive games in 1962 and 1963.
1964 Gino Cappelletti, Boston Patriots, kicked six field goals in six attempts vs. Denver Broncos, October 4.
George Blanda, Houston Oilers, attempted 68 passes (37 completions) vs. Buffalo Bills, November 1.
Rudy Bukich, Chicago Bears, completed 13 consecutive passes vs. San Francisco 49ers (6), November 22, and Detroit Lions (7), November 26.
George Blanda, Houston Oilers, attempted 505 passes and completed 262 in a season (14 games).
Charley Hennigan, Houston Oilers, caught 101 passes in a season (14 games).
Johnny Morris, Chicago Bears, caught 93 passes in a season (14 games).
Paul Krause, Washington Redskins, intercepted passes in seven consecutive games.
Lenny Moore, Baltimore Colts, scored 20 touchdowns (16 rushing, 3 pass receiving, 1 fumble return) in a season (14 games).
Lance Alworth, San Diego Chargers, scored touchdowns in nine consecutive games.
1965 Gale Sayers, Chicago Bears, scored six touchdowns (four rushing, 1 pass receiving, 1 punt return) vs. San Francisco 49ers, December 12.
John Brodie, San Francisco 49ers, completed 242 passes (391 attempts) in a season (14 games).
Bart Starr, Green Bay Packers, completed a string in which he threw 294 consecutive passes without an interception between 1964 and 1965.
Gale Sayers, Chicago Bears, scored a record 22 touchdowns in his rookie season (14 rushing, 6 pass receiving, 1 punt return, 1 kickoff return) for 132 points.
Lenny Moore, Baltimore Colts, completed a string in which he scored touchdowns in 18 consecutive games between 1963 and 1965.
Tommy Davis, San Francisco 49ers, completed a string in which he kicked 234 consecutive extra points between 1959 and 1965.
1966 Karl Sweetan and Pat Studstill, Detroit Lions, combined for a 99-yard touchdown pass vs. Baltimore Colts, October 16.
Garo Yepremian, Detroit Lions, kicked four field goals in one quarter (the second) and six in the game vs. Minnesota Vikings, November 13.
Charlie Gogolak, Washington Redskins, kicked nine extra points in 10 attempts vs. New York Giants, November 27.
Timmy Brown, Philadelphia Eagles, returned two kickoffs for touchdowns vs. Dallas Cowboys, November 6.
Al Nelson, Philadelphia Eagles, returned a missed field goal 100 yards for a touchdown vs. Cleveland Browns, December 11.
Larry Wilson, St. Louis Cardinals, intercepted passes in seven consecutive games.
Bruce Gossett, Los Angeles Rams, kicked 28 field goals (49 attempts) in a season (14 games).
Tommy Brooker, Kansas City Chiefs, completed a string in which he scored in 45 consecutive games and another in which he kicked 149 consecutive extra points between 1962 and 1966.
Danny Villanueva, Dallas Cowboys, kicked 56 extra points without a miss.
1967 Len Dawson, Kansas City Chiefs, completed 15 consecutive passes vs. Houston Oilers, September 9.
Bill Nelsen, Pittsburgh Steelers, completed a string in which he completed 13 consecutive passes vs. Atlanta Falcons (11), December 18, 1966, and Chi. Bears (2), September 17, 1967.
Jim Bakken, St. Louis Cardinals, kicked seven field goals (nine attempts) vs. Pittsburgh Steelers, September 24.
Joe Namath, New York Jets, completed 15 consecutive passes vs. Miami Dolphins (12), October 22, and Boston Patriots (3), October 29.
Travis Williams, Green Bay Packers, returned two kickoffs for touchdowns vs. Cleveland Browns, November 12.
Billy Kilmer and Walter Roberts, New Orleans Saints, combined for a 96-yard pass, not a touchdown, vs. Philadelphia Eagles, November 19.
Noland Smith, Kansas City Chiefs, returned a kickoff 106 yards for a touchdown vs. Denver Broncos, December 17.
Joe Namath, New York Jets, had 4,007 yards passing in a season (14 games).
Sonny Jurgensen, Washington Redskins, completed 288 of 508 passes for 3,747 yards passing in a season (14 games).
Travis Williams, Green Bay Packers, had 739 yards in kickoff returns, a 41.1 average, and four kickoff returns for touchdowns in a season (14 games).
Jim Turner, New York Jets, completed a string in which he kicked field goals in 18 consecutive games in 1966 and 1967.
1968 George Atkinson, Oakland Raiders, had 205 yards in punt returns (five returns) vs. Buffalo Bills, September 15.
Sonny Jurgensen and Gerry Allen, Washington Redskins, combined for a 99-yard touchdown pass vs. Chicago Bears, September 15.
Charley West, Minnesota Vikings, returned a punt 98 yards for a touchdown vs. Washington Redskins, November 3.
Jim Turner, New York Jets, kicked 34 field goals in a season (14 games).
Dennis Partee, San Diego Chargers, kicked 10 consecutive field goals, November 3 through December 15.
1969 Steve O'Neal, New York Jets, made a 98-yard punt vs. Denver Broncos, September 21.
Joe Kapp, Minnesota Vikings, threw seven touchdown passes vs. Baltimore Colts, September 28.
Lance Alworth, San Diego Chargers, completed a string in which he caught at least one pass in 96 consecutive games.
Jan Stenerud, Kansas City Chiefs, kicked 16 consecutive field goals.
1970 Tom Dempsey, New Orleans Saints, kicked a 63-yard field goal vs. Detroit Lions, November 8.
Curt Knight, Washington Redskins, kicked four field goals in one quarter (the second) vs. New York Giants, November 15.
Ken Houston, Houston Oilers, returned two interceptions for touchdowns vs. San Diego Chargers, December 19.
John Brockington, Green Bay Packers, gained 1,105 yards rushing (216 attempts) in his rookie season.
Bob Tucker, New York Giants, caught 59 passes.
Ken Houston, Houston Oilers, returned four interceptions for touchdowns in a season (14 games).
Cecil Turner, Chicago Bears, returned four kickoffs for touchdowns in a season (14 games).
Fred Cox, Minnesota Vikings, completed a string in which he made at least one field goal in 31 consecutive games between 1968 and 1970.
1971 Ken Ellis, Green Bay Packers, returned a missed field goal 100 yards vs. New York Giants, September 19.
Al Nelson, Philadelphia Eagles, returned a missed field goal 101 yards vs. Dallas Cowboys, September 26.
Willie Ellison, Los Angeles Rams, gained 247 yards rushing (26 attempts) vs. New Orleans Saints, December 5.
1972 Jack Tatum, Oakland Raiders, recovered a fumble and returned it 104 yards vs. Green Bay Packers, September 24.
Jim Hart and Bobby Moore (later named Ahmad Rashad), St. Louis Cardinals, combined for a 98-yard pass, not a touchdown, vs. Los Angeles Rams, December 10.
Bobby Douglass, quarterback for the Chicago Bears, gained 968 yards rushing (141 attempts) in a season (14 games).
Jim Kearney, Kansas City Chiefs, returned four interceptions for touchdowns in a season (14 games).
1973 O. J. Simpson, Buffalo Bills, gained 250 yards rushing and carried the ball 29 times vs. New England Patriots, September 16.
Fred Dryer, Los Angeles Rams, made two safeties vs. Green Bay Packers, October 21.
O. J. Simpson, Buffalo Bills, gained 2,003 yards rushing (332 attempts) had 200 or more in a game three times, and 100 or more in a game 11 times.
1974 Dennis Morgan, Dallas Cowboys, returned a punt 98 yards for a touchdown vs. St. Louis Cardinals, October 13.
Lydell Mitchell, Baltimore Colts, made 40 rushing attempts vs. New York Jets, October 20.
Bert Jones, Baltimore Colts, completed 17 consecutive passes vs. New York Jets, December 15.
Dan Abramowicz, San Francisco 49ers, completed a string in which he caught at least one pass in 105 consecutive games between 1967 and 1973.
1975 O. J. Simpson, Buffalo Bills, scored 23 touchdowns (16 rushing, 7 pass receiving) in a season (14 games).
Don Cockroft, Cleveland Browns, completed a string in which he kicked 16 consecutive field goals in 1974 and 1975.
1976 Rick Upchurch, Denver Broncos, returned two punts for touchdowns vs. Cleveland Browns, September 26.
Franco Harris, Pittsburgh Steelers, made 41 rushing attempts vs. Cincinnati Bengals, October 17.
O. J. Simpson, Buffalo Bills, gained 273 yards rushing (29 attempts) vs. Detroit Lions, November 25.
Rick Upchurch, Denver Broncos, returned four punts for touchdowns in a season (14 games).
1977 Walter Payton, Chicago Bears, gained 275 yards rushing on 40 carries vs. Minnesota Vikings, November 20.
Gary Barbaro, Kansas City Chiefs, returned an interception 102 yards for a touchdown vs. Seattle Seahawks, December 11.
James Young, Houston Oilers, recorded two safeties in a season.
1978 Willie Buchanon, Green Bay Packers, intercepted four passes vs. San Diego Chargers, September 24.
Fran Tarkenton, Minnesota Vikings, completed 345 of 572 passes in a season (16 games).
Rickey Young, a running back for the Minnesota Vikings, caught 88 passes.
Earl Campbell, Houston Oilers, set a rookie rushing record of 1,450 yards.
1979 Roy Green, St. Louis Cardinals, returned a kickoff 106 yards for a touchdown vs. Dallas Cowboys, October 21.
Tony Franklin, Philadelphia Eagles, kicked a 59-yard field goal vs. Dallas Cowboys, November 12.
Garo Yepremian, New Orleans Saints, kicked 20 consecutive field goals with the Miami Dolphins (1978) and Saints (1979) and completed a string of 133 consecutive games in which he scored for the Dolphins (1970-78) or the Saints (1979).
Earl Campbell, Houston Oilers, rushed for 19 touchdowns and had 11 100-yard games, including 7 in a row.
Steve DeBerg, San Francisco 49ers, completed 347 of 578 passes in a season (16 games).
Dan Fouts, San Diego Chargers, passed for 4,082 yards in a season (16 games), including four straight 300-yard games.
Jim Marshall, Minnesota Vikings, completed a string in which he played 282 consecutive games with the Cleveland Browns (1960) and the Vikings (1961-1979).
Ottis Anderson, St. Louis Cardinals, set an NFL rookie rushing record of 1,605 yards.
1980 Billy Thompson, Denver Broncos, made his fourth fumble recovery for a touchdown vs. Dallas Cowboys, September 14.
Richard Todd, New York Jets, completed 42 passes vs. San Francisco 49ers, September 21.
Harold Carmichael, Philadelphia Eagles, completed a string in which he caught at least one pass in 127 consecutive games between 1972 and 1980.
Earl Campbell, Houston Oilers, rushed for 1,934 yards, and had 10 100-yard games and 4 200-yard games, including 2 consecutive 200-yard games.
Dan Fouts, San Diego Chargers, completed 348 of 589 passes for 4,715 yards in a season (16 games).
Lester Hayes, Oakland Raiders, intercepted 13 passes in a season (16 games).
Kellen Winslow, a tight end for the San Diego Chargers, caught 89 passes in a season (16 games).
1981 Steve Dils, Minnesota Vikings, completed 37 of 62 passes vs. Tampa Bay Buccaneers, September 5.
LeRoy Irvin, Los Angeles Rams, returned two punts for touchdowns and totaled 207 yards in punt returns vs. Atlanta Falcons, October 11.
Louis Breeden, Cincinnati Bengals, returned an intercepted pass 102 yards for a touchdown vs. San Diego Chargers, November 8.
Mel Gray, St. Louis Cardinals, continued a string in which he had caught at least one pass in 117 consecutive games between 1973 and 1981.
Dan Fouts, San Diego Chargers, completed 360 of 609 passes for 4,802 yards in a season (16 games).
Chuck Muncie, San Diego Chargers, rushed for 19 touchdowns in a season (16 games).
George Rogers, New Orleans Saints, carried the ball 378 times in a season (16 games) and set a rookie rushing record with 1,674 yards.
Tony Dorsett, Dallas Cowboys, became the first NFL player to rush for at least 1,000 yards in each of his first five seasons.

1,000 YARDS RUSHING IN A SEASON

Year	Player, Team	Att.	Yards	Avg.	Long	TD
1934	**Beattie Feathers, Chi. Bears**	101	1,004	9.9	82	8
1947	Steve Van Buren, Philadelphia	217	1,008	4.6	45	13
1949	Steve Van Buren, Philadelphia$_2$	263	1,146	4.4	41	11
	Tony Canadeo, Green Bay	208	1,052	5.1	54	4
1953	Joe Perry, San Francisco	192	1,018	5.3	51	10
1954	Joe Perry, San Francisco$_2$	173	1,049	6.1	58	8
1956	Rick Casares, Chi. Bears	234	1,126	4.8	68	12
1958	Jim Brown, Cleveland	257	1,527	5.9	65	17
1959	Jim Brown, Cleveland$_2$	290	1,329	4.6	70	14
	J. D. Smith, San Francisco	207	1,036	5.0	73	10
1960	Jim Brown, Cleveland$_3$	215	1,257	5.8	71	9
	Jim Taylor, Green Bay	230	1,101	4.8	32	11
	John David Crow, St. Louis	183	1,071	5.9	57	6
1961	Jim Brown, Cleveland$_4$	305	1,408	4.6	38	8
	Jim Taylor, Green Bay$_2$	243	1,307	5.4	53	15
1962	Jim Taylor, Green Bay$_3$	272	1,474	5.4	51	19
	John Henry Johnson, Pittsburgh	251	1,141	4.5	40	7
	Cookie Gilchrist, Buffalo	214	1,096	5.1	44	13
	Abner Haynes, Dallas Texans	221	1,049	4.7	71	13
	Dick Bass, Los Angeles	196	1,033	5.3	57	6
	Charlie Tolar, Houston	244	1,012	4.1	25	7
1963	Jim Brown, Cleveland$_5$	291	1,863	6.4	80	12
	Clem Daniels, Oakland	215	1,099	5.1	74	3
	Jim Taylor, Green Bay$_4$	248	1,018	4.1	40	9
	Paul Lowe, San Diego	177	1,010	5.7	66	8
1964	Jim Brown, Cleveland$_6$	280	1,446	5.2	71	7
	Jim Taylor, Green Bay$_5$	235	1,169	5.0	84	12
	John Henry Johnson, Pittsburgh$_2$	235	1,048	4.5	45	7
1965	Jim Brown, Cleveland$_7$	289	1,544	5.3	67	17
	Paul Lowe, San Diego$_2$	222	1,121	5.0	59	7
1966	Jim Nance, Boston	299	1,458	4.9	65	11
	Gale Sayers, Chicago	229	1,231	5.4	58	8
	Leroy Kelly, Cleveland	209	1,141	5.5	70	15
	Dick Bass, Los Angeles$_2$	248	1,090	4.4	50	8
1967	Jim Nance, Boston$_2$	269	1,216	4.5	53	7
	Leroy Kelly, Cleveland$_2$	235	1,205	5.1	42	11
	Hoyle Granger, Houston	236	1,194	5.1	67	6
	Mike Garrett, Kansas City	236	1,087	4.6	58	9
1968	Leroy Kelly, Cleveland$_3$	248	1,239	5.0	65	16
	Paul Robinson, Cincinnati	238	1,023	4.3	87	8
1969	Gale Sayers, Chicago$_2$	236	1,032	4.4	28	8
1970	Larry Brown, Washington	237	1,125	4.7	75	5
	Ron Johnson, N.Y. Giants	263	1,027	3.9	68	8
1971	Floyd Little, Denver	284	1,133	4.0	40	6
	John Brockington, Green Bay	216	1,105	5.1	52	4
	Larry Csonka, Miami	195	1,051	5.4	28	7
	Steve Owens, Detroit	246	1,035	4.2	23	8
	Willie Ellison, Los Angeles	211	1,000	4.7	80	4
1972	O.J. Simpson, Buffalo	292	1,251	4.3	94	6
	Larry Brown, Washington$_2$	285	1,216	4.3	38	8
	Ron Johnson, N.Y. Giants$_2$	298	1,182	4.0	35	9
	Larry Csonka, Miami$_2$	213	1,117	5.2	45	6
	Marv Hubbard, Oakland	219	1,100	5.0	39	4
	Franco Harris, Pittsburgh	188	1,055	5.6	75	10
	Calvin Hill, Dallas	245	1,036	4.2	26	6
	Mike Garrett, San Diego$_2$	272	1,031	3.8	41	6
	John Brockington, Green Bay$_2$	274	1,027	3.7	30	8
	Eugene (Mercury) Morris, Miami	190	1,000	5.3	33	12
1973	O.J. Simpson, Buffalo$_2$	332	2,003	6.0	80	12
	John Brockington, Green Bay$_3$	265	1,144	4.3	53	3
	Calvin Hill, Dallas$_2$	273	1,142	4.2	21	6
	Lawrence McCutcheon, Los Angeles	210	1,097	5.2	37	2
	Larry Csonka, Miami$_3$	219	1,003	4.6	25	5
1974	Otis Armstrong, Denver	263	1,407	5.3	43	9
	Don Woods, San Diego	227	1,162	5.1	56	7
	O.J. Simpson, Buffalo$_3$	270	1,125	4.2	41	3
	Lawrence McCutcheon, Los Angeles$_2$	236	1,109	4.7	23	3
	Franco Harris, Pittsburgh$_2$	208	1,006	4.8	54	5
1975	O.J. Simpson, Buffalo$_4$	329	1,817	5.5	88	16
	Franco Harris, Pittsburgh$_3$	262	1,246	4.8	36	10
	Lydell Mitchell, Baltimore	289	1,193	4.1	70	11
	Jim Otis, St. Louis	269	1,076	4.0	30	5
	Chuck Foreman, Minnesota	280	1,070	3.8	31	13
	Greg Pruitt, Cleveland	217	1,067	4.9	50	8
	John Riggins, N.Y. Jets	238	1,005	4.2	42	8
	Dave Hampton, Atlanta	250	1,002	4.0	22	5
1976	O.J. Simpson, Buffalo$_5$	290	1,503	5.2	75	8
	Walter Payton, Chicago	311	1,390	4.5	60	13
	Delvin Williams, San Francisco	248	1,203	4.9	80	7
	Lydell Mitchell, Baltimore$_2$	289	1,200	4.2	43	5
	Lawrence McCutcheon, Los Angeles$_3$	291	1,168	4.0	40	9
	Chuck Foreman, Minnesota$_2$	278	1,155	4.2	46	13
	Franco Harris, Pittsburgh$_4$	289	1,128	3.9	30	14
	Mike Thomas, Washington	254	1,101	4.3	28	5
	Rocky Bleier, Pittsburgh	220	1,036	4.7	28	5
	Mark van Eeghen, Oakland	233	1,012	4.3	21	3
	Otis Armstrong, Denver$_2$	247	1,008	4.1	31	5
	Greg Pruitt, Cleveland$_2$	209	1,000	4.8	64	4

Bold face—first year in the league.

Rick Casares, Chicago Bears.

Year	Player, Team	Att.	Yards	Avg.	Long	TD
1977	Walter Payton, Chicago$_2$	339	1,852	5.5	73	14
	Mark van Eeghen, Oakland$_2$	324	1,273	3.9	27	7
	Lawrence McCutcheon, Los Angeles$_4$	294	1,238	4.2	48	7
	Franco Harris, Pittsburgh$_5$	300	1,162	3.9	61	11
	Lydell Mitchell, Baltimore$_3$	301	1,159	3.9	64	3
	Chuck Foreman, Minnesota$_3$	270	1,112	4.1	51	6
	Greg Pruitt, Cleveland$_3$	236	1,086	4.6	78	3
	Sam Cunningham, New England	270	1,015	3.8	31	4
	Tony Dorsett, Dallas	208	1,007	4.8	84	12
1978	**Earl Campbell, Houston**	302	1,450	4.8	81	13
	Walter Payton, Chicago$_3$	333	1,395	4.2	76	11
	Tony Dorsett, Dallas$_2$	290	1,325	4.6	63	7
	Delvin Williams, Miami$_2$	272	1,258	4.6	58	8
	Wilbert Montgomery, Philadelphia	259	1,220	4.7	47	9
	Terdell Middleton, Green Bay	284	1,116	3.9	76	11
	Franco Harris, Pittsburgh$_6$	310	1,082	3.5	37	8
	Mark van Eeghen, Oakland$_3$	270	1,080	4.0	34	9
	Terry Miller, Buffalo	238	1,060	4.5	60	7
	Tony Reed, Kansas City	206	1,053	5.1	62	5
	John Riggins, Washington$_2$	248	1,014	4.1	31	5
1979	Earl Campbell, Houston$_2$	368	1,697	4.6	61	19
	Walter Payton, Chicago$_4$	369	1,610	4.4	43	14
	Ottis Anderson, St. Louis	331	1,605	4.8	76	8
	Wilbert Montgomery, Philadelphia$_2$	338	1,512	4.5	62	9
	Mike Pruitt, Cleveland	264	1,294	4.9	77	9
	Ricky Bell, Tampa Bay	283	1,263	4.5	49	7
	Chuck Muncie, New Orleans	238	1,198	5.0	69	11
	Franco Harris, Pittsburgh$_7$	267	1,186	4.4	71	11
	John Riggins, Washington$_3$	260	1,153	4.4	66	9
	Wendell Tyler, Los Angeles	218	1,109	5.1	63	9
	Tony Dorsett, Dallas$_3$	250	1,107	4.4	41	6
	William Andrews, Atlanta	239	1,023	4.3	23	3
1980	Earl Campbell, Houston$_3$	373	1,934	5.2	55	13
	Walter Payton, Chicago$_5$	317	1,460	4.6	69	6
	Ottis Anderson, St. Louis$_2$	301	1,352	4.5	52	9
	William Andrews, Atlanta$_2$	265	1,308	4.9	33	4
	Billy Sims, Detroit	313	1,303	4.2	52	13
	Tony Dorsett, Dallas$_4$	278	1,185	4.3	56	11
	Joe Cribbs, Buffalo	306	1,185	3.9	48	11
	Mike Pruitt, Cleveland$_2$	249	1,034	4.2	56	6
1981	**George Rogers, New Orleans**	378	1,674	4.4	79	13
	Tony Dorsett, Dallas$_5$	342	1,646	4.8	75	4
	Billy Sims, Detroit$_2$	296	1,437	4.9	51	13
	Wilbert Montgomery, Philadelphia$_3$	286	1,402	4.9	41	8
	Ottis Anderson, St. Louis$_3$	328	1,376	4.2	28	9
	Earl Campbell, Houston$_4$	361	1,376	3.8	43	10
	William Andrews, Atlanta$_3$	289	1,301	4.5	29	10
	Walter Payton, Chicago$_6$	339	1,222	3.6	39	6
	Chuck Muncie, San Diego$_2$	251	1,144	4.6	73	19
	Joe Delaney, Kansas City	234	1,121	4.8	82	3
	Mike Pruitt, Cleveland$_3$	247	1,103	4.5	21	7
	Joe Cribbs, Buffalo$_2$	257	1,097	4.3	35	3
	Pete Johnson, Cincinnati	274	1,077	3.9	39	12
	Wendell Tyler, Los Angeles$_2$	260	1,074	4.1	69	12
	Ted Brown, Minnesota	274	1,063	3.9	34	6

200 YARDS RUSHING IN A GAME

Date	Player, Team, Opponent	Att.	Yards	TD
Oct. 8, 1933	Cliff Battles, Bos. Redskins vs. N.Y. Giants..........	16	215	1
Nov. 27, 1949	Steve Van Buren, Philadelphia vs. Pittsburgh	27	205	0
Nov. 12, 1950	Gene Roberts, N.Y. Giants vs. Chi. Cardinals..........	26	218	2
Nov. 22, 1953	Dan Towler, Los Angeles vs. Baltimore ...	14	205	1
Dec. 16, 1956	Tom Wilson, Los Angeles vs. Green Bay............	23	223	0
Nov. 24, 1957	Jim Brown, Cleveland vs. Los Angeles	31	237	4
Nov. 15, 1959	Bobby Mitchell, Cleveland vs. Washington	14	232	3
Dec. 18, 1960	John David Crow, St. Louis vs. Pittsburgh	24	203	0
Nov. 19, 1961	Jim Brown, Cleveland vs. Philadelphia	34	237	4
Dec. 10, 1961	Billy Cannon, Houston vs. N.Y. Titans	25	216	3
Sept. 22, 1963	Jim Brown, Cleveland vs. Dallas	20	232	2
Oct. 20, 1963	Clem Daniels, Oakland vs. N.Y. Jets	27	200	2
Nov. 3, 1963	Jim Brown, Cleveland vs. Philadelphia	28	223	1
Dec. 8, 1963	Cookie Gilchrist, Buffalo vs. N.Y. Jets	36	243	5
Oct. 10, 1964	John Henry Johnson, Pittsburgh vs. Cleveland	30	200	3
Oct. 30, 1966	Jim Nance, Boston vs. Oakland	38	208	2
Nov. 3, 1968	Gale Sayers, Chicago vs. Green Bay...........	24	205	0
Dec. 20, 1970	John (Frenchy) Fuqua, Pittsburgh vs. Philadelphia ...	20	218	2
Dec. 5, 1971	Willie Ellison, Los Angeles vs. New Orleans	26	247	1
Sept. 16, 1973	O. J. Simpson, Buffalo vs. New England	29	250	2
Dec. 9, 1973	O. J. Simpson, Buffalo vs. New England	22	219	1
Dec. 16, 1973	O. J. Simpson, Buffalo vs. N.Y. Jets	34	200	1
Sept. 28, 1975	O. J. Simpson, Buffalo vs. Pittsburgh..........	28	227	1
Dec. 14, 1975	Greg Pruitt, Cleveland vs. Kansas City	26	214	3
Oct. 24, 1976	Chuck Foreman, Minnesota vs. Philadelphia	28	200	2
Nov. 25, 1976	O. J. Simpson, Buffalo vs. Detroit	29	273	2
Dec. 5, 1976	O. J. Simpson, Buffalo vs. Miami	24	203	1
Oct. 30, 1977	Walter Payton, Chicago vs. Green Bay	23	205	2
Nov. 20, 1977	Walter Payton, Chicago vs. Minnesota.........	40	275	1
Dec. 4, 1977	Tony Dorsett, Dallas vs. Philadelphia..........	23	206	2
Nov. 26, 1978	Terry Miller, Buffalo vs. N.Y. Giants..........	21	208	2
Oct. 19, 1980	Earl Campbell, Houston vs. Tampa Bay	33	203	0
Oct. 26, 1980	Earl Campbell, Houston vs. Cincinnati	27	202	2
Nov. 16, 1980	Earl Campbell, Houston vs. Chicago	31	206	0
Dec. 21, 1980	Earl Campbell, Houston vs. Minnesota	29	203	1

400 YARDS PASSING IN A GAME

Date	Player, Team, Opponent	Att.	Comp.	Yards	TD
Nov. 14, 1943	Sid Luckman, Chi. Bears vs. N.Y. Giants	32	21	433	7
Oct. 31, 1948	Sammy Baugh, Washington vs. Boston Yanks.........	24	17	446	4
Oct. 31, 1948	Jim Hardy, Los Angeles vs. Chi. Cardinals.........	53	28	406	3
Dec. 11, 1949	Johnny Lujack, Chi. Bears vs. Chi. Cardinals........	39	24	468	6
Sept. 28, 1951	Norm Van Brocklin, Los Angeles vs. N.Y. Yanks	41	27	554	5
Oct. 4, 1952	Otto Graham, Cleveland vs. Pittsburgh	49	21	401	3
Nov. 8, 1953	Bobby Thomason, Philadelphia vs. N.Y. Giants.......	44	22	437	4
Dec. 13, 1958	Bobby Layne, Pittsburgh vs. Chi. Cardinals	49	23	409	2
Oct. 13, 1961	Jacky Lee, Houston vs. Boston	41	27	457	2
Oct. 29, 1961	George Blanda, Houston vs. Buffalo.............	32	18	464	4
Oct. 29, 1961	Sonny Jurgensen, Philadelphia vs. Washington	41	27	436	3
Nov. 19, 1961	George Blanda, Houston vs. N.Y. Titans..........	32	20	418	7
Dec. 17, 1961	Sonny Jurgensen, Philadelphia vs. Detroit.........	42	27	403	3
Sept. 15, 1962	Frank Tripucka, Denver vs. Buffalo	56	29	447	2
Oct. 28, 1962	Y. A. Tittle, N.Y. Giants vs. Washington..........	39	27	505	7
Nov. 18, 1962	Bill Wade, Chicago vs. Dallas................	46	28	466	2
Dec. 16, 1962	Sonny Jurgensen, Philadelphia vs. St. Louis	34	15	419	5
Oct. 13, 1963	Charley Johnson, St. Louis vs. Pittsburgh	41	20	428	2
Nov. 10, 1963	Don Meredith, Dallas vs. San Francisco..........	48	30	460	3
Nov. 17, 1963	Norm Snead, Washington vs. Pittsburgh..........	40	23	424	2
Dec. 22, 1963	Tom Flores, Oakland vs. Houston	29	17	407	6
Oct. 16, 1964	Babe Parilli, Boston vs. Oakland	47	25	422	4
Oct. 25, 1964	Cotton Davidson, Oakland vs. Denver	36	23	427	5
Nov. 1, 1964	Len Dawson, Kansas City vs. Denver	38	23	435	6
Oct. 24, 1965	Fran Tarkenton, Minnesota vs. San Francisco	35	21	407	3
Nov. 28, 1965	Sonny Jurgensen, Washington vs. Dallas..........	43	26	411	3
Nov. 13, 1966	Don Meredith, Dallas vs. Washington	29	21	406	2
Sept. 17, 1967	Johnny Unitas, Baltimore vs. Atlanta	32	22	401	2
Oct. 1, 1967	Joe Namath, N.Y. Jets vs. Miami	39	23	415	3
Nov. 26, 1967	Sonny Jurgensen, Washington vs. Cleveland	50	32	418	3
Sept. 9, 1968	Pete Beathard, Houston vs. Kansas City	48	23	413	2
Sept. 28, 1969	Joe Kapp, Minnesota vs. Baltimore............	43	28	449	7
Dec. 21, 1969	Don Horn, Green Bay vs. St. Louis	31	22	410	5
Sept. 24, 1972	Joe Namath, N.Y. Jets vs. Baltimore	28	15	496	6
Dec. 11, 1972	Joe Namath, N.Y. Jets vs. Oakland	46	25	403	1
Nov. 18, 1974	Charley Johnson, Denver vs. Kansas City	42	28	445	2
Nov. 17, 1975	Ken Anderson, Cincinnati vs. Buffalo	46	30	447	2
Oct. 3, 1976	James Harris, Los Angeles vs. Miami	29	17	436	2
Sept. 21, 1980	Richard Todd, N.Y. Jets vs. San Francisco........	60	42	447	3
Oct. 12, 1980	Lynn Dickey, Green Bay vs. Tampa Bay...........	51	35	418	1
Oct. 19, 1980	Dan Fouts, San Diego vs. N.Y. Giants...........	41	26	444	3
Nov. 16, 1980	Doug Williams, Tampa Bay vs. Minnesota	55	30	486	4
Dec. 14, 1980	Tommy Kramer, Minnesota vs. Cleveland	49	38	456	4
Oct. 11, 1981	Tommy Kramer, Minnesota vs. San Diego	43	27	444	4
Oct. 25, 1981	Brian Sipe, Cleveland vs. Baltimore	41	30	444	4
Oct. 25, 1981	David Woodley, Miami vs. Dallas..............	37	21	408	3
Nov. 15, 1981	Steve Bartkowski, Atlanta vs. Pittsburgh..........	50	33	416	2

Clem Daniels, Oakland Raiders.

Charley Johnson, St. Louis Cardinals.

1,200 YARDS RECEIVING IN A SEASON

Year	Player, Team	No.	Yards	Avg.	Long	TD
1942	Don Hutson, Green Bay	74	1,211	16.4	73	17
1951	Elroy (Crazylegs) Hirsch, Los Angeles	66	1,495	22.7	91	17
1952	**Billy Howton, Green Bay**	53	1,231	23.2	90	13
1954	Bob Boyd, Los Angeles	53	1,212	22.9	80	6
1960	**Bill Groman, Houston**	72	1,473	20.5	92	12
	Raymond Berry, Baltimore	74	1,298	17.5	70	10
	Don Maynard, N.Y. Titans	72	1,265	17.6	65	6
	Lionel Taylor, Denver	92	1,235	13.4	80	12
1961	Charley Hennigan, Houston	82	1,746	21.3	80	12
1962	Bobby Mitchell, Washington	72	1,384	19.2	81	11
1963	Bobby Mitchell, Washington	69	1,436	20.8	99	7
	Art Powell, Oakland	73	1,304	17.9	85	16
	Buddy Dial, Pittsburgh	60	1,295	21.6	83	9
	Lance Alworth, San Diego	61	1,205	19.8	85	11
1964	Charley Hennigan, Houston	101	1,546	15.3	53	8
	Art Powell, Oakland	76	1,361	17.9	77	11
	Lance Alworth, San Diego	61	1,235	20.2	82	13
	Johnny Morris, Chicago	93	1,200	12.9	63	10
1965	Lance Alworth, San Diego	69	1,602	23.2	85	14
	Dave Parks, San Francisco	80	1,344	16.8	53	12
	Don Maynard, N.Y. Jets	68	1,218	17.9	56	14
1966	Lance Alworth, San Diego	73	1,383	18.9	78	13
	Otis Taylor, Kansas City	58	1,297	22.4	89	8
	Pat Studstill, Detroit	67	1,266	18.9	99	5
	Bob Hayes, Dallas	64	1,232	19.3	95	13
1967	Don Maynard, N.Y. Jets	71	1,434	20.2	75	10
	Ben Hawkins, Philadelphia	59	1,265	21.4	87	10
	Homer Jones, N.Y. Giants	49	1,209	24.7	70	13
	Jackie Smith, St. Louis	56	1,205	21.5	76	9
1968	Lance Alworth, San Diego	68	1,312	19.3	80	10
	Don Maynard, N.Y. Jets	57	1,297	22.8	87	10
1969	Warren Wells, Oakland	47	1,260	26.8	80	14
1979	Steve Largent, Seattle	66	1,237	18.7	55	9
1980	John Jefferson, San Diego	82	1,340	16.3	58	13
	Kellen Winslow, San Diego	89	1,290	14.5	65	9
	James Lofton, Green Bay	71	1,226	17.3	47	4
1981	Alfred Jenkins, Atlanta	70	1,358	19.4	67	13
	James Lofton, Green Bay	71	1,294	18.2	75	8
	Frank Lewis, Buffalo	70	1,244	17.8	33	4
	Steve Watson, Denver	60	1,244	20.7	95	13
	Steve Largent, Seattle	75	1,224	16.3	57	9

Bold face—first year in the league.

250 YARDS RECEIVING IN A GAME

Date	Player, Team, Opponent	No.	Yards	TD
Nov. 22, 1945	Jim Benton, Cleveland vs. Detroit	10	303	1
Dec. 3, 1950	Cloyce Box, Detroit vs. Baltimore	12	302	4
Oct. 21, 1956	Billy Howton, Green Bay vs. Los Angeles	7	257	2
Oct. 13, 1961	Charley Hennigan, Houston vs. Boston	13	272	1
Oct. 28, 1962	Del Shofner, N.Y. Giants vs. Washington	11	269	1
Nov. 4, 1962	Sonny Randle, St. Louis vs. N.Y. Giants	16	256	1
Sept. 23, 1979	Jerry Butler, Buffalo vs. N.Y. Jets	10	255	4

Johnny Robinson, Kansas City Chiefs.

Bobby Mitchell, Washington Redskins.

Abe Woodson, San Francisco 49ers.

TOP 10 SCORERS

Player	Years	TD	FG	PAT	TP
George Blanda	26	9	335	943	2,002
Jim Turner	16	1	304	521	1,439
Jim Bakken	17	0	282	534	1,380
Fred Cox	15	0	282	519	1,365
Lou Groza	17	1	234	641	1,349
Jan Stenerud	15	0	304	432	1,344
Gino Cappelletti	11	42	176	350	1,130
Don Cockroft	13	0	216	432	1,080
Garo Yepremian	14	0	210	444	1,074
Bruce Gossett	11	0	219	374	1,031

Cappelletti's total includes four two-point conversions.

TOP 10 TOUCHDOWN SCORERS

Player	Years	Rush	Pass Rec.	Returns	Total TD
Jim Brown	9	106	20	0	126
Lenny Moore	12	63	48	2	113
Don Hutson	11	3	99	3	105
Jim Taylor	10	83	10	0	93
Franco Harris	10	84	7	0	91
Bobby Mitchell	11	18	65	8	91
Leroy Kelly	10	74	13	3	90
Charley Taylor	13	11	79	0	90
Don Maynard	15	0	88	0	88
Lance Alworth	11	2	85	0	87

TOP 10 RUSHERS

Player	Years	Att.	Yards	Avg.	Long	TD
Jim Brown	9	2,359	12,312	5.2	80	106
O. J. Simpson	11	2,404	11,236	4.7	94	61
Franco Harris	10	2,462	10,339	4.2	75	84
Walter Payton	7	2,204	9,608	4.4	76	71
Jim Taylor	10	1,941	8,597	4.4	84	83
Joe Perry	14	1,737	8,378	4.8	78	53
Larry Csonka	11	1,891	8,081	4.3	54	64
John Riggins	10	1,861	7,536	4.0	66	55
Leroy Kelly	10	1,727	7,274	4.2	70	74
John Henry Johnson	13	1,571	6,803	4.3	87	48

TOP 10 PASSERS

Player	Years	Att.	Comp.	Pct. Comp.	Yards	TD	Pct. TD	Int.	Pct. Int.	Avg. Gain	Rating
Roger Staubach	11	2,958	1,685	57.0	22,700	153	5.2	109	3.7	7.67	83.5
Sonny Jurgensen	18	4,262	2,433	57.1	32,224	255	6.0	189	4.4	7.56	82.8
Len Dawson	19	3,741	2,136	57.1	28,711	239	6.4	183	4.9	7.67	82.6
Ken Anderson	11	3,539	2,036	57.5	25,562	160	4.5	124	3.5	7.22	80.5
Fran Tarkenton	18	6,467	3,686	57.0	47,003	342	5.3	266	4.1	7.27	80.5
Bart Starr	16	3,149	1,808	57.4	24,718	152	4.8	138	4.4	7.85	80.3
Bert Jones	9	2,464	1,382	56.1	17,663	122	5.0	97	3.9	7.17	79.1
Dan Fouts	9	3,203	1,849	57.7	24,256	145	4.5	142	4.4	7.57	78.4
Johnny Unitas	18	5,186	2,830	54.6	40,239	290	5.6	253	4.9	7.76	78.2
Otto Graham	6	1,565	872	55.7	13,499	88	5.6	94	6.0	8.63	78.1

1,500 or more attempts. The passing ratings are based on performance standards established for completion percentage, interception percentage, touchdown percentage, and average gain. Passers are allocated points according to how their marks compare with those standards.

TOP 10 PASS RECEIVERS

Player	Years	No.	Yards	Avg.	Long	TD
Charley Taylor	13	649	9,110	14.0	88	79
Don Maynard	15	633	11,834	18.7	87	88
Raymond Berry	13	631	9,275	14.7	70	68
Fred Biletnikoff	14	589	8,974	15.2	82	76
Harold Jackson	14	571	10,246	17.9	79	75
Lionel Taylor	10	567	7,195	12.7	80	45
Lance Alworth	11	542	10,266	18.9	85	85
Bobby Mitchell	11	521	7,954	15.3	99	65
Harold Carmichael	11	516	7,923	15.4	85	72
Billy Howton	12	503	8,459	16.8	90	61

TOP 10 INTERCEPTORS

Player	Years	No.	Yards	Avg.	Long	TD
Paul Krause	16	81	1,185	14.6	81	3
Emlen Tunnell	14	79	1,282	16.2	55	4
Dick (Night Train) Lane	14	68	1,207	17.8	80	5
Dick LeBeau	13	62	762	12.3	70	3
Emmitt Thomas	13	58	937	16.2	73	5
Bobby Boyd	9	57	994	17.4	74	4
Johnny Robinson	12	57	741	13.0	57	1
Lem Barney	11	56	1,077	19.2	71	7
Pat Fischer	17	56	941	16.8	69	4
Willie Brown	16	54	472	8.7	45	2

TOP 10 PUNTERS

Player	Years	No.	Yards	Avg.	Long	Blk.
Sammy Baugh	16	338	15,245	45.1	85	9
Tommy Davis	11	511	22,833	44.7	82	2
Yale Lary	11	503	22,279	44.3	74	4
Horace Gillom	7	385	16,872	43.8	80	5
Jerry Norton	11	358	15,671	43.8	78	2
Don Chandler	12	660	28,678	43.5	90	4
Ray Guy	9	654	28,262	43.2	74	3
Jerrel Wilson	16	1,072	46,139	43.0	72	12
Norm Van Brocklin	12	523	22,413	42.9	72	3
Danny Villanueva	8	488	20,862	42.8	68	2

300 or more punts.

TOP 10 PUNT RETURNERS

Player	Years	No.	Yards	Avg.	Long	TD
Billy Johnson	7	155	2,040	13.2	87	5
George McAfee	8	112	1,431	12.8	74	2
Jack Christiansen	8	85	1,084	12.8	89	8
Claude Gibson	5	110	1,381	12.6	85	3
Bill Dudley	9	124	1,515	12.2	96	3
Rick Upchurch	7	229	2,714	11.9	92	6
Mack Herron	3	84	982	11.7	66	0
Bill Thompson	13	157	1,814	11.6	60	0
J. T. Smith	4	152	1,754	11.5	88	4
Roger Bird	3	94	1,063	11.3	78	0

75 or more returns.

TOP 10 KICKOFF RETURNERS

Player	Years	No.	Yards	Avg.	Long	TD
Gale Sayers	7	91	2,781	30.6	103	6
Lynn Chandnois	7	92	2,720	29.6	93	3
Abe Woodson	9	193	5,538	28.7	105	5
Claude (Buddy) Young	6	90	2,514	27.9	104	2
Travis Williams	5	102	2,801	27.5	105	6
Joe Arenas	7	139	3,798	27.3	96	1
Clarence Davis	8	79	2,140	27.1	76	0
Steve Van Buren	8	76	2,030	26.7	98	3
Lenny Lyles	12	81	2,161	26.7	103	3
Eugene (Mercury) Morris	8	111	2,947	26.5	105	3

75 or more returns.

Leroy Kelly, Cleveland Browns.

Larry Brown, Washington Redskins.

Greg Cook, Cincinnati Bengals.

ANNUAL RUSHING LEADERS

Year	Player, Team	Att.	Yards	Avg.	TD
1932	**Cliff Battles, Boston Braves**	148	576	3.9	3
1933	Jim Musick, Boston Redskins	173	809	4.7	5
1934	**Beattie Feathers, Chi. Bears**	101	1,044	9.9	8
1935	Doug Russell, Chi. Cardinals	140	499	3.6	0
1936	**Alphonse (Tuffy) Leemans, N.Y. Giants**	206	830	4.0	2
1937	Cliff Battles, Washington	216	874	4.0	5
1938	**Byron (Whizzer) White, Pittsburgh**	152	567	3.7	4
1939	**Bill Osmanski, Chi. Bears**	121	699	5.8	7
1940	Byron (Whizzer) White, Detroit	146	514	3.5	5
1941	Clarence (Pug) Manders, Brooklyn	111	486	4.4	5
1942	**Bill Dudley, Pittsburgh**	162	696	4.3	5
1943	**Bill Paschal, N.Y. Giants**	147	572	3.9	10
1944	Bill Paschal, N.Y. Giants	196	737	3.8	9
1945	Steve Van Buren, Philadelphia	143	832	5.8	15
1946	Bill Dudley, Pittsburgh	146	604	4.1	3
1947	Steve Van Buren, Philadelphia	217	1,008	4.6	13
1948	Steve Van Buren, Philadelphia	201	945	4.7	10
1949	Steve Van Buren, Philadelphia	263	1,146	4.4	11
1950	**Marion Motley, Cleveland**	140	810	5.8	3
1951	Eddie Price, N.Y. Giants	271	971	3.6	7
1952	Dan Towler, Los Angeles	156	894	5.7	10
1953	Joe Perry, San Francisco	192	1,018	5.3	10
1954	Joe Perry, San Francisco	173	1,049	6.1	8
1955	**Alan Ameche, Baltimore**	213	961	4.5	9
1956	Rick Casares, Chi. Bears	234	1,126	4.8	12
1957	**Jim Brown, Cleveland**	202	942	4.7	9
1958	Jim Brown, Cleveland	257	1,527	5.9	17
1959	Jim Brown, Cleveland	290	1,329	4.6	14
1960	Jim Brown, Cleveland, NFL	215	1,257	5.8	9
	Abner Haynes, Dallas Texans, AFL	157	875	5.6	9
1961	Jim Brown, Cleveland, NFL	305	1,408	4.6	8
	Billy Cannon, Houston, AFL	200	948	4.7	6
1962	Jim Taylor, Green Bay, NFL	272	1,474	5.4	19
	Cookie Gilchrist, Buffalo, AFL	214	1,096	5.1	13
1963	Jim Brown, Cleveland, NFL	291	1,863	6.4	12
	Clem Daniels, Oakland, AFL	215	1,099	5.1	3
1964	Jim Brown, Cleveland, NFL	280	1,446	5.1	7
	Cookie Gilchrist, Buffalo, AFL	230	981	4.3	6
1965	Jim Brown, Cleveland, NFL	289	1,544	5.3	17
	Paul Lowe, San Diego, AFL	222	1,121	5.0	7
1966	Jim Nance, Boston, AFL	299	1,458	4.9	11
	Gale Sayers, Chicago, NFL	229	1,231	5.4	8
1967	Jim Nance, Boston, AFL	269	1,216	4.5	7
	Leroy Kelly, Cleveland, NFL	235	1,205	5.1	11
1968	Leroy Kelly, Cleveland, NFL	248	1,239	5.0	16
	Paul Robinson, Cincinnati, AFL	238	1,023	4.3	8
1969	Gale Sayers, Chicago, NFL	236	1,032	4.4	8
	Dickie Post, San Diego, AFL	182	873	4.8	6
1970	Larry Brown, Washington, NFC	237	1,125	4.7	5
	Floyd Little, Denver, AFC	209	901	4.3	3
1971	Floyd Little, Denver, AFC	284	1,133	4.0	6
	John Brockington, Green Bay, NFC	216	1,105	5.1	4
1972	O.J. Simpson, Buffalo, AFC	292	1,251	4.3	6
	Larry Brown, Washington, NFC	285	1,216	4.3	8
1973	O.J. Simpson, Buffalo, AFC	332	2,003	6.0	12
	John Brockington, Green Bay, NFC	265	1,144	4.3	3
1974	Otis Armstrong, Denver, AFC	263	1,407	5.3	9
	Lawrence McCutcheon, Los Angeles, NFC	236	1,109	4.7	3
1975	O.J. Simpson, Buffalo, AFC	329	1,817	5.5	16
	Jim Otis, St. Louis, NFC	269	1,076	4.0	5
1976	O.J. Simpson, Buffalo, AFC	290	1,503	5.2	8
	Walter Payton, Chicago, NFC	311	1,390	4.5	13
1977	Walter Payton, Chicago, NFC	339	1,852	5.5	14
	Mark van Eeghen, Oakland, AFC	324	1,273	3.9	7
1978	**Earl Campbell, Houston, AFC**	302	1,450	4.8	13
	Walter Payton, Chicago, NFC	333	1,395	4.2	11
1979	Earl Campbell, Houston, AFC	368	1,697	4.6	19
	Walter Payton, Chicago, NFC	369	1,610	4.4	14
1980	Earl Campbell, Houston, AFC	373	1,934	5.2	13
	Walter Payton, Chicago, NFC	317	1,460	4.6	6
1981	**George Rogers, New Orleans, NFC**	378	1,674	4.4	13
	Earl Campbell, Houston, AFC	361	1,376	3.9	10

Bold face—first year in the league.

PASSING

Year	Player, Team	Att.	Comp.	Yards	TD	Int.
1932	Arnie Herber, Green Bay	101	37	639	9	9
1933	**Harry Newman, N.Y. Giants**	136	53	973	11	17
1934	Arnie Herber, Green Bay	115	42	799	8	12
1935	Ed Danowski, N.Y. Giants	113	57	794	10	9
1936	Arnie Herber, Green Bay	173	77	1,239	11	13
1937	**Sammy Baugh, Washington**	171	81	1,127	8	14
1938	Ed Danowski, N.Y. Giants	129	70	848	7	8
1939	**Parker Hall, Cleveland Rams**	208	106	1,227	9	13
1940	Sammy Baugh, Washington	177	111	1,367	12	10
1941	Cecil Isbell, Green Bay	206	117	1,479	15	11
1942	Cecil Isbell, Green Bay	268	146	2,021	24	14
1943	Sammy Baugh, Washington	239	133	1,754	23	19
1944	Frank Filchock, Washington	147	84	1,139	13	9
1945	Sammy Baugh, Washington	182	128	1,669	11	4
	Sid Luckman, Chi. Bears	217	117	1,725	14	10
1946	Bob Waterfield, Los Angeles	251	127	1,747	18	17
1947	Sammy Baugh, Washington	354	210	2,938	25	15
1948	Tommy Thompson, Philadelphia	246	141	1,965	25	11
1949	Sammy Baugh, Washington	255	145	1,903	18	14
1950	Norm Van Brocklin, Los Angeles	233	127	2,061	18	14
1951	Bob Waterfield, Los Angeles	176	88	1,566	13	10
1952	Norm Van Brocklin, Los Angeles	205	113	1,736	14	17
1953	Otto Graham, Cleveland	258	167	2,722	11	9
1954	Norm Van Brocklin, Los Angeles	260	139	2,637	13	21
1955	Otto Graham, Cleveland	185	98	1,721	15	8
1956	Ed Brown, Chi. Bears	168	96	1,667	11	12
1957	Tommy O'Connell, Cleveland	110	63	1,229	9	8
1958	Eddie LeBaron, Washington	145	79	1,365	11	10
1959	Charlie Conerly, N.Y. Giants	194	113	1,706	14	4
1960	Milt Plum, Cleveland, NFL	250	151	2,297	21	5
	Jack Kemp, L.A. Chargers, AFL	406	211	3,018	20	25
1961	George Blanda, Houston, AFL	362	187	3,330	36	22
	Milt Plum, Cleveland, NFL	302	177	2,416	18	10
1962	Len Dawson, Dallas, AFL	310	189	2,759	29	17
	Bart Starr, Green Bay, NFL	285	178	2,438	12	9
1963	Y.A. Tittle, N.Y. Giants, NFL	367	221	3,145	36	14
	Tobin Rote, San Diego, AFL	286	170	2,510	20	17
1964	Len Dawson, Kansas City, AFL	354	199	2,879	30	18
	Bart Starr, Green Bay, NFL	272	163	2,144	15	4
1965	Rudy Bukich, Chicago, NFL	312	176	2,641	20	9
	John Hadl, San Diego, AFL	348	174	2,798	20	21
1966	Bart Starr, Green Bay, NFL	251	156	2,257	14	3
	Len Dawson, Kansas City, AFL	284	159	2,527	26	10
1967	Sonny Jurgensen, Washington, NFL	508	288	3,747	31	16
	Daryle Lamonica, Oakland, AFL	425	220	3,228	30	20
1968	Len Dawson, Kansas City, AFL	224	131	2,109	17	9
	Earl Morrall, Baltimore, NFL	317	182	2,909	26	17
1969	Sonny Jurgensen, Washington, NFL	442	274	3,102	22	15
	Greg Cook, Cincinnati, AFL	197	106	1,854	15	11
1970	John Brodie, San Francisco, NFC	378	223	2,941	24	10
	Daryle Lamonica, Oakland, AFC	356	179	2,516	22	15
1971	Roger Staubach, Dallas, NFC	211	126	1,882	15	4
	Bob Griese, Miami, AFC	263	145	2,089	19	9
1972	Norm Snead, N.Y. Giants, NFC	325	196	2,307	17	12
	Earl Morrall, Miami, AFC	150	83	1,360	11	7
1973	Roger Staubach, Dallas, NFC	286	179	2,428	23	15
	Ken Stabler, Oakland, AFC	260	163	1,997	14	10
1974	Ken Anderson, Cincinnati, AFC	328	213	2,667	18	10
	Sonny Jurgensen, Washington, NFC	167	107	1,185	11	5
1975	Ken Anderson, Cincinnati, AFC	377	228	3,169	21	11
	Fran Tarkenton, Minnesota, NFC	425	273	2,994	25	13
1976	Ken Stabler, Oakland, AFC	291	194	2,737	27	17
	James Harris, Los Angeles, NFC	158	91	1,460	8	6
1977	Bob Griese, Miami, AFC	307	180	2,252	22	13
	Roger Staubach, Dallas, NFC	361	210	2,620	18	9
1978	Roger Staubach, Dallas, NFC	413	231	3,190	25	16
	Terry Bradshaw, Pittsburgh, AFC	368	207	2,915	28	20
1979	Roger Staubach, Dallas, NFC	461	267	3,586	27	11
	Dan Fouts, San Diego, AFC	530	332	4,082	24	24
1980	Brian Sipe, Cleveland, AFC	554	337	4,132	30	14
	Ron Jaworski, Philadelphia, NFC	451	257	3,529	27	12
1981	Ken Anderson, Cincinnati, AFC	479	300	3,753	29	10
	Joe Montana, San Francisco, NFC	488	311	3,565	19	12

Bold face—first year in the league.

PASS RECEIVING

Year	Player, Team	No.	Yards	Avg.	TD
1932	Ray Flaherty, N.Y. Giants	21	350	16.7	3
1933	John (Shipwreck) Kelly, Brooklyn	22	246	11.2	3
1934	Joe Carter, Philadelphia	16	238	14.9	4
	Morris (Red) Badgro, N.Y. Giants	16	206	12.9	1
1935	**Tod Goodwin, N.Y. Giants**	26	432	16.6	4
1936	Don Hutson, Green Bay	34	536	15.8	8
1937	Don Hutson, Green Bay	41	552	13.5	7
1938	Gaynell Tinsley, Chi. Cardinals	41	516	12.6	1
1939	Don Hutson, Green Bay	34	846	24.9	6
1940	**Don Looney, Philadelphia**	58	707	12.2	4
1941	Don Hutson, Green Bay	58	738	12.7	10
1942	Don Hutson, Green Bay	74	1,211	16.4	17
1943	Don Hutson, Green Bay	47	776	16.5	11
1944	Don Hutson, Green Bay	58	866	14.9	9
1945	Don Hutson, Green Bay	47	834	17.7	9
1946	Jim Benton, Los Angeles	63	981	15.6	6
1947	Jim Keane, Chi. Bears	64	910	14.2	10
1948	**Tom Fears, Los Angeles**	51	698	13.7	4
1949	Tom Fears, Los Angeles	77	1,013	13.2	9
1950	Tom Fears, Los Angeles	84	1,116	13.3	7
1951	Elroy (Crazylegs) Hirsch, Los Angeles	66	1,495	22.7	17
1952	Mac Speedie, Cleveland	62	911	14.7	5
1953	Pete Pihos, Philadelphia	63	1,049	16.7	10
1954	Pete Pihos, Philadelphia	60	872	14.5	10
	Billy Wilson, San Francisco	60	830	13.8	5
1955	Pete Pihos, Philadelphia	62	864	13.9	7
1956	Billy Wilson, San Francisco	60	889	14.8	5
1957	Billy Wilson, San Francisco	52	757	14.6	6
1958	Raymond Berry, Baltimore	56	794	14.2	9
	Pete Retzlaff, Philadelphia	56	766	13.7	2
1959	Raymond Berry, Baltimore	66	959	14.5	14
1960	Lionel Taylor, Denver, AFL	92	1,235	13.4	12
	Raymond Berry, Baltimore, NFL	74	1,298	17.5	10
1961	Lionel Taylor, Denver, AFL	100	1,176	11.8	4
	Jim (Red) Phillips, Los Angeles, NFL	78	1,092	14.0	5
1962	Lionel Taylor, Denver, AFL	77	908	11.8	4
	Bobby Mitchell, Washington, NFL	72	1,384	19.2	11
1963	Lionel Taylor, Denver, AFL	78	1,101	14.1	10
	Bobby Joe Conrad, St. Louis, NFL	73	967	13.2	10
1964	Charley Hennigan, Houston, AFL	101	1,546	15.3	8
	Johnny Morris, Chicago, NFL	93	1,200	12.9	10
1965	Lionel Taylor, Denver, AFL	85	1,131	13.3	6
	Dave Parks, San Francisco, NFL	80	1,344	16.8	12
1966	Lance Alworth, San Diego, AFL	73	1,383	18.9	13
	Charley Taylor, Washington, NFL	72	1,119	15.5	12
1967	George Sauer, N.Y. Jets, AFL	75	1,189	15.9	6
	Charley Taylor, Washington, NFL	70	990	14.1	9
1968	Clifton McNeil, San Francisco, NFL	71	994	14.0	7
	Lance Alworth, San Diego, AFL	68	1,312	19.3	10
1969	Dan Abramowicz, New Orleans, NFL	73	1,015	13.9	7
	Lance Alworth, San Diego, AFL	64	1,003	15.7	4
1970	Dick Gordon, Chicago, NFC	71	1,026	14.5	13
	Marlin Briscoe, Buffalo, AFC	57	1,036	18.2	8
1971	Fred Biletnikoff, Oakland, AFC	61	929	15.2	9
	Bob Tucker, N.Y. Giants, NFC	59	791	13.4	4
1972	Harold Jackson, Philadelphia, NFC	62	1,048	16.9	4
	Fred Biletnikoff, Oakland, AFC	58	802	13.8	7
1973	Harold Carmichael, Philadelphia, NFC	67	1,116	16.7	9
	Fred Willis, Houston, AFC	57	371	6.5	1
1974	Lydell Mitchell, Baltimore, AFC	72	544	7.6	2
	Charle Young, Philadelphia, NFC	63	696	11.0	3
1975	Chuck Foreman, Minnesota, NFC	73	691	9.5	9
	Reggie Rucker, Cleveland, AFC	60	770	12.8	3
1976	MacArthur Lane, Kansas City, AFC	66	686	10.4	1
	Drew Pearson, Dallas, NFC	58	806	13.9	6
1977	Lydell Mitchell, Baltimore, AFC	71	620	8.7	4
	Ahmad Rashad, Minnesota, NFC	51	681	13.4	2
1978	Rickey Young, Minnesota, NFC	88	704	8.0	5
	Steve Largent, Seattle, AFC	71	1,168	16.5	8
1979	Joe Washington, Baltimore, AFC	82	750	9.1	3
	Ahmad Rashad, Minnesota, NFC	80	1,156	14.5	9
1980	Kellen Winslow, San Diego, AFC	89	1,290	14.5	9
	Earl Cooper, San Francisco, NFC	83	567	6.8	4
1981	Kellen Winslow, San Diego, AFC	88	1,075	12.2	10
	Dwight Clark, San Francisco, NFC	85	1,105	13.0	4

Bold face—first year in the league.

INTERCEPTIONS

Year	Player, Team	No.	Yards	TD
1940	Clarence (Ace) Parker, Brooklyn	6	146	1
	Kent Ryan, Detroit	6	65	0
	Don Hutson, Green Bay	6	24	0
1941	Marshall Goldberg, Chi. Cardinals	7	54	0
	Art Jones, Pittsburgh	7	35	0
1942	**Clyde (Bulldog) Turner, Chi. Bears**	8	96	1
1943	Sammy Baugh, Washington	11	112	0
1944	**Howard Livingston, N.Y. Giants**	9	172	1
1945	Roy Zimmerman, Philadelphia	7	90	0
1946	Bill Dudley, Pittsburgh	10	242	1
1947	Frank Reagan, N.Y. Giants	10	203	0
	Frank Seno, Boston Yanks	10	100	0
1948	**Dan Sandifer, Washington**	13	258	2
1949	Bob Nussbaumer, Chi. Cardinals	12	157	0
1950	**Orban (Spec) Sanders, N.Y. Yanks**	13	199	0
1951	Otto Schnellbacher, N.Y. Giants	11	194	2
1952	**Dick (Night Train) Lane, Los Angeles**	14	298	2
1953	Jack Christiansen, Detroit	12	238	1
1954	Dick (Night Train) Lane, Chi. Cardinals	10	181	0
1955	Will Sherman, Los Angeles	11	101	0
1956	Lindon Crow, Chi. Cardinals	11	170	0
1957	**Milt Davis, Baltimore**	10	219	2
	Jack Christiansen, Detroit	10	137	1
	Jack Butler, Pittsburgh	10	85	0
1958	Jim Patton, N.Y. Giants	11	183	0
1959	Dean Derby, Pittsburgh	7	127	0
	Milt Davis, Baltimore	7	119	1
	Don Shinnick, Baltimore	7	70	0
1960	**Austin (Goose) Gonsoulin, Denver, AFL**	11	98	0
	Dave Baker, San Francisco, NFL	10	96	0
	Jerry Norton, St. Louis, NFL	10	96	0
1961	Billy Atkins, Buffalo, AFL	10	158	0
	Dick Lynch, N.Y. Giants, NFL	9	60	0
1962	Lee Riley, N.Y. Titans, AFL	11	122	0
	Willie Wood, Green Bay, NFL	9	132	0
1963	Fred Glick, Houston, AFL	12	180	1
	Dick Lynch, N.Y. Giants, NFL	9	251	3
	Roosevelt Taylor, Chicago, NFL	9	172	1
1964	Dainard Paulson, N.Y. Jets, AFL	12	157	1
	Paul Krause, Washington, NFL	12	140	1
1965	W.K. Hicks, Houston, AFL	9	156	0
	Bob Boyd, Baltimore, NFL	9	78	1
1966	Larry Wilson, St. Louis, NFL	10	180	2
	Johnny Robinson, Kansas City, AFL	10	136	1
	Bobby Hunt, Kansas City, AFL	10	113	0
1967	Miller Farr, Houston, AFL	10	264	3
	Lem Barney, Detroit, NFL	10	232	3
	Tom Janik, Buffalo AFL	10	222	2
	Dave Whitsell, New Orleans, NFL	10	178	2
	Dick Westmoreland, Miami, AFL	10	127	1
1968	Dave Grayson, Oakland, AFL	10	195	1
	Willie Williams, N.Y. Giants, NFL	10	103	0
1969	Mel Renfro, Dallas, NFL	10	118	0
	Emmitt Thomas, Kansas City, AFL	9	146	1
1970	Johnny Robinson, Kansas City, AFC	10	155	0
	Dick LeBeau, Detroit, NFC	9	96	0
1971	Bill Bradley, Philadelphia, NFC	11	248	0
	Ken Houston, Houston, AFC	9	220	4
1972	Bill Bradley, Philadelphia, NFC	9	73	0
	Mike Sensibaugh, Kansas City, AFC	8	65	0
1973	Dick Anderson, Miami, AFC	8	163	2
	Mike Wagner, Pittsburgh, AFC	8	134	0
	Bobby Bryant, Minnesota, NFC	7	105	1
1974	Emmitt Thomas, Kansas City, AFC	12	214	2
	Ray Brown, Atlanta, NFC	8	164	1
1975	Mel Blount, Pittsburgh, AFC	11	121	0
	Paul Krause, Minnesota, NFC	10	201	0
1976	Monte Jackson, Los Angeles, NFC	10	173	3
	Ken Riley, Cincinnati, AFC	9	141	1
1977	Lyle Blackwood, Baltimore, AFC	10	163	0
	Rolland Lawrence, Atlanta, NFC	7	138	0
1978	Thom Darden, Cleveland, AFC	10	200	0
	Ken Stone, St. Louis, NFC	9	139	0
	Willie Buchanon, Green Bay, NFC	9	93	1
1979	Mike Reinfeldt, Houston, AFC	12	205	0
	Lemar Parrish, Washington, NFC	9	65	0
1980	Lester Hayes, Oakland, AFC	13	273	1
	Nolan Cromwell, Los Angeles, NFC	8	140	1
1981	**Everson Walls, Dallas, NFC**	11	133	0
	John Harris, Seattle, AFC	10	155	2

Bold face—first year in the league.

Ray Guy, Oakland Raiders.

Bob Hayes, Dallas Cowboys.

PUNTING

Year	Player, Team	No.	Avg.	Long
1939	**Parker Hall, Cleveland Rams**	58	40.8	80
1940	Sammy Baugh, Washington	35	51.4	85
1941	Sammy Baugh, Washington	30	48.7	75
1942	Sammy Baugh, Washington	37	48.2	74
1943	Sammy Baugh, Washington	50	45.9	81
1944	Frank Sinkwich, Detroit	45	41.0	73
1945	Roy McKay, Green Bay	44	41.2	73
1946	Roy McKay, Green Bay	64	42.7	64
1947	Jack Jacobs, Green Bay	57	43.5	74
1948	Joe Muha, Philadelphia	57	47.3	82
1949	Mike Boyda, N.Y. Bulldogs	56	44.2	61
1950	**Fred (Curly) Morrison, Chi. Bears**	57	43.3	65
1951	Horace Gillom, Cleveland	73	45.5	66
1952	Horace Gillom, Cleveland	61	45.7	73
1953	Pat Brady, Pittsburgh	80	46.9	64
1954	Pat Brady, Pittsburgh	66	43.2	72
1955	Norm Van Brocklin, Los Angeles	60	44.6	61
1956	Norm Van Brocklin, Los Angeles	48	43.1	72
1957	Don Chandler, N.Y. Giants	60	44.6	61
1958	Sam Baker, Washington	48	45.4	64
1959	Yale Lary, Detroit	45	47.1	67
1960	Jerry Norton, St. Louis, NFL	39	45.6	62
	Paul Maguire, Los Angeles, AFL	43	40.5	61
1961	Yale Lary, Detroit, NFL	52	48.4	71
	Billy Atkins, Buffalo, AFL	85	44.5	70
1962	Tommy Davis, San Francisco, NFL	48	45.6	82
	Jim Fraser, Denver, AFL	55	43.6	75
1963	Yale Lary, Detroit, NFL	35	48.9	73
	Jim Fraser, Denver, AFL	81	44.4	66
1964	**Bobby Walden, Minnesota, NFL**	72	46.4	73
	Jim Fraser, Denver, AFL	73	44.2	67
1965	Gary Collins, Cleveland, NFL	65	46.7	71
	Jerrel Wilson, Kansas City, AFL	68	46.1	64
1966	Bob Scarpitto, Denver, AFL	76	45.8	70
	David Lee, Baltimore, NFL	49	45.6	64
1967	Bob Scarpitto, Denver, AFL	105	44.9	73
	Billy Lothridge, Atlanta, NFL	87	43.7	62
1968	Jerrel Wilson, Kansas City, AFL	63	45.1	70
	Billy Lothridge, Atlanta, NFL	75	44.3	70
1969	David Lee, Baltimore, NFL	57	45.3	66
	Dennis Partee, San Diego, AFL	71	44.6	62
1970	**Dave Lewis, Cincinnati, AFC**	79	46.2	63
	Julian Fagan, New Orleans, NFC	77	42.5	64
1971	Dave Lewis, Cincinnati, AFC	72	44.8	56
	Tom McNeill, Philadelphia, NFC	73	42.0	64
1972	Jerrel Wilson, Kansas City, AFC	66	44.8	69
	Dave Chapple, Los Angeles, NFC	53	44.2	70
1973	Jerrel Wilson, Kansas City, AFC	80	45.5	68
	Tom Wittum, San Francisco, NFC	79	43.7	62
1974	Ray Guy, Oakland, AFC	74	42.2	66
	Tom Blanchard, New Orleans, NFC	88	42.1	71
1975	Ray Guy, Oakland, AFC	68	43.8	64
	Herman Weaver, Detroit, NFC	80	42.0	61
1976	Marv Bateman, Buffalo, AFC	86	42.8	78
	John James, Atlanta, NFC	101	42.1	67
1977	Ray Guy, Oakland, AFC	59	43.3	74
	Tom Blanchard, New Orleans, NFC	82	42.4	66
1978	Pat McInally, Cincinnati, AFC	91	43.1	65
	Tom Skladany, Detroit, NFC	86	42.5	63
1979	**Bob Grupp, Kansas City, AFC**	89	43.6	74
	Dave Jennings, N.Y. Giants, NFC	104	42.7	72
1980	Dave Jennings, N.Y. Giants, NFC	94	44.8	63
	Luke Prestridge, Denver, AFC	70	43.9	57
1981	Pat McInally, Cincinnati, AFC	72	45.4	62
	Tom Skladany, Detroit, NFC	64	43.5	74

Bold face—first year in the league.

PUNT RETURNS

Year	Player, Team	No.	Yards	Avg.	Long	TD
1941	Byron (Whizzer) White, Detroit	19	262	13.8	64	0
1942	Merlyn Condit, Brooklyn	21	210	10.0	23	0
1943	Andy Farkas, Washington	15	168	11.2	33	0
1944	**Steve Van Buren, Philadelphia**	15	230	15.3	55	1
1945	**Dave Ryan, Detroit**	15	220	14.7	56	0
1946	Bill Dudley, Pittsburgh	27	385	14.2	52	0
1947	**Walt Slater, Pittsburgh**	28	435	15.5	33	0
1948	George McAfee, Chi. Bears	30	417	13.9	60	1
1949	Verda (Vitamin T) Smith, Los Angeles	27	427	15.8	85	1
1950	**Herb Rich, Baltimore**	12	276	23.0	86	1
1951	Claude (Buddy) Young, N.Y. Yanks	12	231	19.3	79	1
1952	Jack Christiansen, Detroit	15	322	21.5	79	2
1953	Charley Trippi, Chi. Cardinals	21	239	11.4	38	0
1954	**Veryl Switzer, Green Bay**	24	306	12.8	93	1
1955	Ollie Matson, Chi. Cardinals	13	245	18.8	78	2
1956	Ken Konz, Cleveland	13	187	14.4	65	1
1957	Bert Zagers, Washington	14	217	15.5	76	2
1958	Jon Arnett, Los Angeles	18	223	12.4	58	0
1959	Johnny Morris, Chi. Bears	14	171	12.2	78	1
1960	**Abner Haynes, Dallas Texans, AFL**	14	215	15.4	46	0
	Abe Woodson, San Francisco, NFL	13	174	13.4	48	0
1961	Dick Christy, N.Y. Titans, AFL	18	383	21.3	70	2
	Willie Wood, Green Bay, NFL	14	225	16.1	72	2
1962	Dick Christy, N.Y. Titans, AFL	15	250	16.7	73	2
	Pat Studstill, Detroit, NFL	29	457	15.8	44	0
1963	Dick James, Washington, NFL	16	214	13.4	39	0
	Claude Gibson, Oakland, AFL	26	307	11.8	85	2
1964	Bobby Jancik, Houston, AFL	12	220	18.3	82	1
	Tommy Watkins, Detroit, NFL	16	238	14.9	68	2
1965	Leroy Kelly, Cleveland, NFL	17	265	15.6	67	2
	Leslie (Speedy) Duncan, San Diego, AFL	30	464	15.5	66	2
1966	Leslie (Speedy) Duncan, San Diego, AFL	18	238	13.2	81	1
	Johnny Roland, St. Louis, NFL	20	221	11.1	86	1
1967	Floyd Little, Denver, AFL	16	270	16.9	72	1
	Ben Davis, Cleveland, NFL	18	229	12.7	52	1
1968	Bob Hayes, Dallas, NFL	15	312	20.8	90	2
	Noland Smith, Kansas City, AFL	18	270	15.0	80	1
1969	Alvin Haymond, Los Angeles, NFL	33	435	13.2	52	0
	Billy Thompson, Denver, AFL	25	288	11.5	40	0
1970	Ed Podolak, Kansas City, AFC	23	311	13.5	60	0
	Bruce Taylor, San Francisco, NFC	43	516	12.0	76	0
1971	Leslie (Speedy) Duncan, Washington, NFC	22	233	10.6	33	0
	Leroy Kelly, Cleveland, AFC	30	292	9.7	74	0
1972	**Ken Ellis, Green Bay, NFC**	14	215	15.4	80	1
	Chris Farasopoulos, N.Y. Jets, AFC	17	179	10.5	65	1
1973	Bruce Taylor, San Francisco, NFC	15	207	13.8	61	0
	Ron Smith, San Diego, AFC	27	352	13.0	84	2
1974	Lemar Parrish, Cincinnati, AFC	18	338	18.8	90	2
	Dick Jauron, Detroit, NFC	17	286	16.8	58	0
1975	Billy Johnson, Houston, AFC	40	612	15.3	83	3
	Terry Metcalf, St. Louis, NFC	23	285	12.4	69	1
1976	Rick Upchurch, Denver, AFC	39	536	13.7	92	4
	Eddie Brown, Washington, NFC	48	646	13.5	71	1
1977	Billy Johnson, Houston, AFC	35	539	15.4	87	2
	Larry Marshall, Philadelphia, NFC	46	489	10.6	48	0
1978	Rick Upchurch, Denver, AFC	36	493	13.7	75	1
	Jackie Wallace, Los Angeles, NFC	52	618	11.9	58	0
1979	John Sciarra, Philadelphia, NFC	16	182	11.4	38	0
	Tony Nathan, Miami, AFC	28	306	10.9	86	1
1980	J. T. Smith, Kansas City, AFC	40	581	14.5	75	2
	Kenny Johnson, Atlanta, NFC	23	281	12.2	56	0
1981	LeRoy Irvin, Los Angeles, NFC	46	615	13.4	84	3
	James Brooks, San Diego, AFC	22	290	13.2	42	0

Bold face—first year in the league.

Travis Williams, Green Bay Packers.

KICKOFF RETURNS

Year	Player, Team	No.	Yards	Avg.	Long	TD
1941	Marshall Goldberg, Chi. Cardinals	12	290	24.2	41	0
1942	Marshall Goldberg, Chi. Cardinals	15	393	26.2	95	1
1943	Ken Heineman, Brooklyn	16	444	27.8	69	0
1944	Bob Thurbon, Card-Pitt	12	291	24.3	55	0
1945	Steve Van Buren, Philadelphia	13	373	28.7	98	1
1946	Abe Karnofsky, Boston Yanks	21	599	28.5	97	1
1947	Ed Saenz, Washington	29	797	27.4	94	2
1948	**Joe Scott, N.Y. Giants**	20	569	28.5	99	1
1949	**Don Doll, Detroit**	21	536	25.5	56	0
1950	Verda (Vitamin T) Smith, Los Angeles	22	724	33.7	97	3
1951	Lynn Chandnois, Pittsburgh	12	390	32.5	55	0
1952	Lynn Chandnois, Pittsburgh	17	599	35.2	93	2
1953	Joe Arenas, San Francisco	16	551	34.4	82	0
1954	Billy Reynolds, Cleveland	14	413	29.5	51	0
1955	Al Carmichael, Green Bay	14	418	29.9	100	1
1956	**Tom Wilson, Los Angeles**	15	477	31.8	103	1
1957	**Jon Arnett, Los Angeles**	18	504	28.0	98	1
1958	Ollie Matson, Chi. Cardinals	14	497	35.5	101	2
1959	Abe Woodson, San Francisco	13	382	29.4	105	1
1960	**Tom Moore, Green Bay, NFL**	12	397	33.1	84	0
	Ken Hall, Houston, AFL	19	594	31.3	104	1
1961	Dick Bass, Los Angeles, NFL	23	698	30.3	64	0
	Dave Grayson, Dallas Texans, AFL	16	453	28.3	73	0
1962	Abe Woodson, San Francisco, NFL	37	1,157	31.3	79	0
	Bobby Jancik, Houston, AFL	24	726	30.3	61	0
1963	Abe Woodson, San Francisco, NFL	29	935	32.2	103	3
	Bobby Jancik, Houston, AFL	45	1,317	29.3	53	0
1964	**Clarence Childs, N.Y. Giants, NFL**	34	987	29.0	100	1
	Erwin (Bo) Roberson, Oakland, AFL	36	975	27.1	59	0
1965	Tommy Watkins, Detroit NFL	17	584	34.4	94	0
	Abner Haynes, Denver, AFL	34	901	26.5	60	0
1966	Gale Sayers, Chicago, NFL	23	718	31.2	93	2
	Goldie Sellers, Denver, AFL	19	541	28.5	100	2
1967	**Travis Williams, Green Bay, NFL**	18	739	41.1	104	4
	Zeke Moore, Houston, AFL	14	405	28.9	92	1
1968	Preston Pearson, Baltimore, NFL	15	527	35.1	102	2
	George Atkinson, Oakland, AFL	32	802	25.1	60	0
1969	Bobby Williams, Detroit, NFL	17	563	33.1	96	1
	Billy Thompson, Denver, AFL	18	513	28.5	63	0
1970	Jim Duncan, Baltimore, AFC	20	707	35.4	99	1
	Cecil Turner, Chicago, NFC	23	752	32.7	96	4
1971	Travis Williams, Los Angeles, NFC	25	743	29.7	105	1
	Eugene (Mercury) Morris, Miami, AFC	15	423	28.2	94	1
1972	Ron Smith, Chicago, NFC	30	924	30.8	94	1
	Bruce Laird, Baltimore, AFC	29	843	29.1	73	0
1973	Carl Garrett, Chicago, NFC	16	486	30.4	67	0
	Wallace Francis, Buffalo, AFC	23	687	29.9	101	2
1974	Terry Metcalf, St. Louis, NFC	20	623	31.2	94	1
	Greg Pruitt, Cleveland, AFC	22	606	27.5	88	1
1975	**Walter Payton, Chicago, NFC**	14	444	31.7	70	0
	Harold Hart, Oakland, AFC	17	518	30.5	102	1
1976	**Duriel Harris, Miami, AFC**	17	559	32.9	69	0
	Cullen Bryant, Los Angeles, NFC	16	459	28.7	90	1
1977	**Raymond Clayborn, New England, AFC**	28	869	31.0	101	3
	Wilbert Montgomery, Philadelphia, NFC	23	619	26.9	99	1
1978	Steve Odom, Green Bay, NFC	25	677	27.1	95	1
	Keith Wright, Cleveland, AFC	30	789	26.3	86	0
1979	Larry Brunson, Oakland, AFC	17	441	25.9	89	0
	Jimmy Edwards, Minnesota, NFC	44	1,103	25.1	83	0
1980	Horace Ivory, New England, AFC	36	992	27.6	98	1
	Rich Mauti, New Orleans, NFC	31	798	25.7	52	0
1981	Mike Nelms, Washington, NFC	37	1,099	29.7	84	0
	Carl Roaches, Houston, AFC	28	769	27.5	96	1

Bold face—first year in the league.

SCORING

Year	Player, Team	TD	FG	PAT	TP
1932	Earl (Dutch) Clark, Portsmouth	6	3	10	55
1933	Ken Strong, N.Y. Giants	6	5	13	64
	Glenn Presnell, Portsmouth	6	6	10	64
1934	Jack Manders, Chi. Bears	3	10	28	76
1935	Earl (Dutch) Clark, Detroit	6	1	16	55
1936	Earl (Dutch) Clark, Detroit	7	4	19	73
1937	Jack Manders, Chi. Bears	5	8	15	69
1938	Clarke Hinkle, Green Bay	7	3	7	58
1939	Andy Farkas, Washington	11	0	2	68
1940	Don Hutson, Green Bay	7	0	15	57
1941	Don Hutson, Green Bay	12	1	20	95
1942	Don Hutson, Green Bay	17	1	33	138
1943	Don Hutson, Green Bay	12	3	36	117
1944	Don Hutson, Green Bay	9	0	31	85
1945	Steve Van Buren, Philadelphia	18	0	2	110
1946	Ted Fritsch, Green Bay	10	9	13	100
1947	Pat Harder, Chi. Cardinals	7	7	39	102
1948	Pat Harder, Chi. Cardinals	6	7	53	110
1949	Pat Harder, Chi. Cardinals	8	3	45	102
	Gene Roberts, N.Y. Giants	17	0	0	102
1950	**Doak Walker, Detroit**	11	8	38	128
1951	Elroy (Crazylegs) Hirsch, Los Angeles	17	0	0	102
1952	Gordy Soltau, San Francisco	7	6	34	94
1953	Gordy Soltau, San Francisco	6	10	48	114
1954	Bobby Walston, Philadelphia	11	4	36	114
1955	Doak Walker, Detroit	7	9	27	96
1956	Bobby Layne, Detroit	5	12	33	99
1957	Sam Baker, Washington	1	14	29	77
	Lou Groza, Cleveland	0	15	32	77
1958	Jim Brown, Cleveland	18	0	0	108
1959	Paul Hornung, Green Bay	7	7	31	94
1960	Paul Hornung, Green Bay, NFL	15	15	41	176
	Gene Mingo, Denver, AFL	6	18	33	123
1961	Gino Cappelletti, Boston, AFL	8	17	48	147
	Paul Hornung, Green Bay, NFL	10	15	41	146
1962	Gene Mingo, Denver, AFL	4	27	32	137
	Jim Taylor, Green Bay, NFL	19	0	0	114
1963	Gino Cappelletti, Boston, AFL	2	22	35	113
	Don Chandler, N.Y. Giants, NFL	0	18	52	106
1964	Gino Cappelletti, Boston, AFL	7	25	36	155
	Lenny Moore, Baltimore, NFL	20	0	0	120
1965	**Gale Sayers, Chicago, NFL**	22	0	0	132
	Gino Cappelletti, Boston, AFL	0	17	27	132
1966	Gino Cappelletti, Boston, AFL	6	16	35	119
	Bruce Gossett, Los Angeles, NFL	0	28	29	113
1967	Jim Bakken St. Louis, NFL	0	27	36	117
	George Blanda, Oakland, AFL	0	20	56	116
1968	Jim Turner, N.Y. Jets, AFL	0	34	43	145
	Leroy Kelly, Cleveland, NFL	20	0	0	120
1969	Jim Turner, N.Y. Jets, AFL	0	32	33	129
	Fred Cox, Minnesota, NFL	0	26	43	121
1970	Fred Cox, Minnesota, NFC	0	30	35	125
	Jan Stenerud, Kansas City, AFC	0	30	26	116
1971	Garo Yepremian, Miami, AFC	0	28	33	117
	Curt Knight, Washington, NFC	0	29	27	114
1972	**Chester Marcol, Green Bay, NFC**	0	33	29	128
	Bobby Howfield, N.Y. Jets, AFC	0	27	40	121
1973	David Ray, Los Angeles, NFC	0	30	40	130
	Roy Gerela, Pittsburgh, AFC	0	29	36	123
1974	Chester Marcol, Green Bay, NFC	0	25	19	94
	Roy Gerela, Pittsburgh, AFC	0	20	33	93
1975	O.J. Simpson, Buffalo, AFC	23	0	0	138
	Franco Harris, Pittsburgh, AFC	14	0	0	84
1976	Chuck Foreman, Minnesota, NFC	14	0	0	84
	Chuck Foreman, Minnesota, NFC	22	0	0	132
1977	Errol Mann, Oakland, AFC	0	20	39	99
	Walter Payton, Chicago, NFC	16	0	0	96
1978	**Frank Corral, Los Angeles, NFC**	0	29	31	118
	Pat Leahy, N.Y. Jets, AFC	0	22	41	107
1979	John Smith, New England, AFC	0	23	46	115
	Mark Moseley, Washington, NFC	0	25	39	114
1980	John Smith, New England, AFC	0	26	51	129
	Ed Murray, Detroit, NFC	0	27	35	116
1981	Ed Murray, Detroit, NFC	0	25	46	121
	Rafael Septien, Dallas, NFC	0	27	40	121
	Jim Breech, Cincinnati, AFC	0	22	49	115
	Nick Lowery, Kansas City, AFC	0	26	37	115

Bold face—first year in the league.

FIELD GOALS

Year	Player, Team	Attempts	Made	Pct.
1932	Earl (Dutch) Clark, Portsmouth		3	
1933	**Jack Manders, Chi. Bears**		6	
	Glenn Presnell, Portsmouth		6	
1934	Jack Manders, Chi. Bears		10	
1935	Armand Niccolai, Pittsburgh		6	
	Bill Smith, Chi. Cardinals		6	
1936	Jack Manders, Chi. Bears		7	
	Armand Niccolai, Pittsburgh		7	
1937	Jack Manders, Chi. Bears		8	
1938	Ward Cuff, N.Y. Giants	9	5	55.6
	Ralph Kercheval, Brooklyn	13	5	38.5
1939	Ward Cuff, N.Y. Giants	16	7	43.8
1940	Clarke Hinkle, Green Bay	14	9	64.3
1941	Clarke Hinkle, Green Bay	14	6	42.9
1942	Bill Daddio, Chi. Cardinals	10	5	50.0
1943	Ward Cuff, N.Y. Giants	9	3	33.3
	Don Hutson, Green Bay	5	3	60.0
1944	Ken Strong, N.Y. Giants	12	6	50.0
1945	Joe Aguirre, Washington	13	7	53.8
1946	Ted Fritsch, Green Bay	17	9	52.9
1947	Ward Cuff, Green Bay	16	7	43.8
	Pat Harder, Chi. Cardinals	10	7	70.0
	Bob Waterfield, Los Angeles	16	7	43.8
1948	Cliff Patton, Philadelphia	12	8	66.7
1949	Cliff Patton, Philadelphia	18	9	50.0
	Bob Waterfield, Los Angeles	16	9	56.3
1950	**Lou Groza, Cleveland**	19	13	68.4
1951	Bob Waterfield, Los Angeles	23	13	56.5
1952	Lou Groza, Cleveland	33	19	57.6
1953	Lou Groza, Cleveland	26	23	88.5
1954	Lou Groza, Cleveland	24	16	66.7
1955	Fred Cone, Green Bay	24	16	66.7
1956	Sam Baker, Washington	25	17	68.0
1957	Lou Groza, Cleveland	22	15	68.2
1958	Paige Cothren, Los Angeles	25	14	56.0
	Tom Miner, Pittsburgh	28	14	50.0
1959	Pat Summerall, N.Y. Giants	29	20	69.0
1960	Tommy Davis, San Francisco, NFL	32	19	59.4
	Gene Mingo, Denver, AFL	28	18	64.3
1961	Steve Myhra, Baltimore, NFL	39	21	53.8
	Gino Cappelletti, Boston, AFL	32	17	53.1
1962	Gene Mingo, Denver, AFL	39	27	69.2
	Lou Michaels, Pittsburgh, NFL	42	26	61.9
1963	Jim Martin, Baltimore, NFL	39	24	61.5
	Gino Cappelletti, Boston, AFL	39	22	57.9
1964	Jim Bakken, St. Louis, NFL	38	25	65.8
	Gino Cappelletti, Boston, AFL	39	25	64.1
1965	Pete Gogolak, Buffalo, AFL	46	28	60.9
	Fred Cox, Minnesota, NFL	35	23	65.7
1966	Bruce Gossett, Los Angeles, NFL	49	28	57.1
	Mike Mercer, Oakland-Kansas City, AFL	30	21	70.0
1967	Jim Bakken, St. Louis, NFL	39	27	69.2
	Jan Stenerud, Kansas City, AFL	36	21	58.3
1968	Jim Turner, N.Y. Jets, AFL	46	34	73.9
	Mac Percival, Chicago, NFL	36	25	69.4
1969	Jim Turner, N.Y. Jets, AFL	47	32	68.1
	Fred Cox, Minnesota, NFL	37	26	70.3
1970	Fred Cox, Minnesota, NFC	46	30	65.2
	Jan Stenerud, Kansas City, AFC	42	30	71.4
1971	Curt Knight, Washington, NFC	49	29	59.2
	Garo Yepremian, Miami, AFC	40	28	70.0
1972	**Chester Marcol, Green Bay, NFC**	48	33	68.8
	Roy Gerela, Pittsburgh, AFC	41	28	68.3
1973	David Ray, Los Angeles, NFC	47	30	63.8
	Roy Gerela, Pittsburgh, AFC	43	29	67.4
1974	Chester Marcol, Green Bay, NFC	39	25	64.1
	Roy Gerela, Pittsburgh, AFC	29	20	69.0
1975	Jan Stenerud, Kansas City, AFC	32	22	68.8
	Toni Fritsch, Dallas, NFC	35	22	62.9
1976	Mark Moseley, Washington, NFC	34	22	64.7
	Jan Stenerud, Kansas City, AFC	38	21	55.3
1977	Mark Moseley, Washington, NFC	37	21	56.8
	Errol Mann, Oakland, AFC	28	20	71.4
1978	**Frank Corral, Los Angeles, NFC**	43	29	67.4
	Pat Leahy, N.Y. Jets, AFC	30	22	73.3
1979	Mark Moseley, Washington, NFC	33	25	75.8
	John Smith, New England, AFC	33	23	69.7
1980	**Ed Murray, Detroit, NFC**	42	27	64.3
	John Smith, New England, AFC	34	26	76.5
	Fred Steinfort, Denver, AFC	34	26	76.5
1981	Rafael Septien, Dallas, NFC	35	27	77.1
	Nick Lowery, Kansas City, AFC	36	26	72.2

Bold face—first year in the league.

WINNINGEST COACHES

Coaches with 60 or more National Football League and 1960-69 American Football League regular season victories.

Rank	Yrs.	W	L	T
1. George Halas, 1920-29 Chicago Bears (85-30-18); 1933-1942 Chicago Bears (85-22-4); 1946-1955 Chicago Bears (75-42-2); 1958-1967 Chicago Bears (75-53-6)	40	320	147	30
2. Earl (Curly) Lambeau, 1921-1949 Green Bay Packers (213-104-22); 1950-51 Chicago Cardinals (8-16-0); 1952-53 Washington Redskins (10-13-1)	33	231	133	23
3. Tom Landry, 1960-1981 Dallas Cowboys (196-112-6)	22	196	112	6
4. Don Shula, 1963-69 Baltimore Colts (71-23-4); 1970-1981 Miami Dolphins (123-50-5)	19	194	74	6
5. Paul Brown, 1950-1962 Cleveland Browns (111-44-5); 1968-1975 Cincinnati Bengals (55-56-1)	21	166	100	6
6. Steve Owen, 1931-1953 New York Giants (151-100-17)	23	151	100	17
7. Bud Grant, 1967-1981 Minnesota Vikings (138-75-5)	15	138	75	5
8. Hank Stram, 1960-62 Dallas Texans (25-17-0); 1963-1974 Kansas City Chiefs (99-49-10); 1976-77 New Orleans Saints (7-21-0)	17	131	97	10
9. Weeb Ewbank, 1954-1962 Baltimore Colts (59-52-1); 1963-1973 New York Jets (71-77-6)	20	130	129	7
10. Sid Gillman, 1955-59 Los Angeles Rams (28-31-1); 1960 Los Angeles Chargers (10-4-0); 1961-69 San Diego Chargers (72-43-6); 1971 San Diego Chargers (4-6-0); 1973-74 Houston Oilers (8-15-0)	18	122	99	7
11. Chuck Noll, 1969-1981 Pittsburgh Steelers (117-72-1)	13	117	72	1
12. George Allen, 1966-1970 Los Angeles Rams (49-17-4); 1971-77 Washington Redskins (67-30-1)	12	116	47	5
13. Raymond (Buddy) Parker, 1949 Chicago Cardinals (6-5-1); 1951-56 Detroit Lions (47-23-2); 1957-1964 Pittsburgh Steelers (51-47-6)	15	104	75	9
14. John Madden, 1969-1978 Oakland Raiders (103-32-7)	10	103	32	7
15. Vince Lombardi, 1959-1967 Green Bay Packers (89-29-4); 1969 Washington Redskins (7-5-2)	10	96	34	6
16. Lou Saban, 1960-61 Boston Patriots (7-12-0); 1962-65 Buffalo Bills (36-17-3); 1967-1971 Denver Broncos (20-42-3); 1972-76 Buffalo Bills (32-28-1)	16	95	99	7
17. Chuck Knox, 1973-77 Los Angeles Rams (54-15-1); 1978-1981 Buffalo Bills (33-31-0)	9	87	46	1
18. Don Coryell, 1973-77 St. Louis Cardinals (42-27-1); 1978-1981 San Diego Chargers (41-19-0)	9	83	46	1
19. Blanton Collier, 1963-1970 Cleveland Browns (76-34-2)	8	76	34	2
20. George (Potsy) Clark, 1930-33 Portsmouth Spartans (28-16-7); 1934-36 Detroit Lions (25-10-2); 1937-39 Brooklyn Dodgers (11-17-5); 1940 Detroit Lions (5-5-1)	11	69	48	15
21. Dick Nolan, 1968-1975 San Francisco 49ers (54-53-5); 1978-1980 New Orleans Saints (15-29-0)	11	69	82	5
22. George Wilson, 1957-1964 Detroit Lions (53-45-6); 1966-69 Miami Dolphins (15-39-2)	12	68	84	8
23. Norm Van Brocklin, 1961-66 Minnesota Vikings (29-51-4); 1968-1974 Atlanta Falcons (37-49-3)	13	66	100	7
24. Wally Lemm, 1961 Houston Oilers (9-0-0); 1962-65 St. Louis Cardinals (27-26-3); 1966-1970 Houston Oilers (28-38-4)	11	64	64	7
25. Earle (Greasy) Neale, 1941-1950 Philadelphia Eagles (63-43-5)	10	63	43	5

Top 10 winning percentages—John Madden, .750; Vince Lombardi, .728; Don Shula, .718; Blanton Collier, .687; George Halas, .674; Chuck Knox, .653; Bud Grant, .644; Don Coryell, .642; Tom Landry, .634; Earl (Curly) Lambeau, .627.

The Draft

The advent of a draft of college football players by teams of the National Football League, beginning in 1936, brought needed order to the process of acquiring new players and helped the league achieve more competitive balance by allowing the team with the poorest won-lost record each year to make the first draft choice.

The National and American Football Leagues held separate drafts from 1960 through 1966. Their first joint action after their agreement to merge was the combined draft of college players March 14 and 15, 1967. Defensive tackle Bubba Smith of Michigan State was the number-one selection, by Baltimore.

Another interesting era in the history of the draft was the 12-year period of the bonus choice, from 1947 to 1958. The first selection each year was awarded to each team on a rotating basis. The bonus choices were Bob Fenimore, Harry Gilmer, Chuck Bednarik, Leon Hart, Kyle Rote, Bill Wade, Harry Babcock, Bobby Garrett, George Shaw, Gary Glick, Paul Hornung, and King Hill.

The table lists only the first players selected by each team. If the player was not a first round choice, his team having traded a choice or choices, the player's actual round is in parentheses. Bold face indicates the first draft choice of the entire league for the year.

1936
Boston Redskins, Riley Smith, B .... Alabama
Brooklyn Dodgers, Dick Crayne, B .... Iowa
Chi. Bears, Joe Stydahar, T .... West Virginia
Chi. Cardinals, Jim Lawrence, B .... TCU
Detroit, Sid Wagner, G .... Michigan State
Green Bay, Russ Letlow, G .... San Francisco
N.Y. Giants, Art Lewis, T .... Ohio U.
Philadelphia, Jay Berwanger, B .... Chicago
Pittsburgh, Bill Shakespeare, B .... Notre Dame
1937
Boston Redskins, Sammy Baugh, B .... TCU
Brooklyn Dodgers, Ed Goddard, B .... Washington State
Chi. Bears, Les McDonald, E .... Nebraska
Chi. Cardinals, Ray Buivid, B .... Marquette
Detroit, Lloyd Cardwell, B .... Nebraska
Green Bay, Ed Jankowski, B .... Wisconsin
N.Y. Giants, Ed Widseth, T .... Minnesota
Philadelphia, Sam Francis, B .... Nebraska
Pittsburgh, Mike Basrak, C .... Duquesne
John Drake, B* .... Purdue
*Awarded to the league's new franchise, which became the Cleveland Rams.
1938
Brooklyn Dodgers, Boyd Brumbaugh, B .... Duquesne
Chi. Bears, Joe Gray, B .... Oregon State
Chi. Cardinals, Jack Robbins, B .... Arkansas
Cleveland Rams, Corby Davis, B .... Indiana
Detroit, Alex Wojciechowicz, C .... Fordham
Green Bay, Cecil Isbell, B .... Purdue
N.Y. Giants, George Karamatic, B .... Gonzaga
Philadelphia, Jim McDonald, B .... Ohio State
Pittsburgh, Byron (Whizzer) White, B .... Colorado
Washington, Andy Farkas, B .... Detroit
1939
Brooklyn Dodgers, Bob MacLeod, B .... Dartmouth
Chi. Bears, Sid Luckman, B .... Columbia
Chi. Cardinals, Charles (Ki) Aldrich, C .... TCU
Cleveland Rams, Parker Hall, B .... Mississippi
Detroit, John Pingel, B .... Michigan State
Green Bay, Larry Buhler, B .... Minnesota
N.Y. Giants, Walt Nielson, B .... Arizona
Philadelphia, Davey O'Brien, B .... TCU
Pittsburgh, Clarence (Pug) Manders, B(2) .... Drake
Washington, I.B. Hale, T .... TCU
1940
Brooklyn Dodgers, Banks McFadden, B .... Clemson
Chi. Bears, Clyde (Bulldog) Turner, C .... Hardin-Simmons
Chi. Cardinals, George Cafego, B .... Tennessee
Cleveland Rams, Ollie Cordill, B .... Rice
Detroit, Doyle Nave, B .... USC
Green Bay, Hal Van Every, B .... Marquette
N.Y. Giants, Grenny Lansdell, B .... USC
Philadelphia, George McAfee, B .... Duke
Pittsburgh, Kay Eakin, B .... Arkansas
Washington, Ed Boell, B .... New York U.
1941
Brooklyn Dodgers, Dean McAdams, B .... Washington
Chi. Bears, Tom Harmon, B .... Michigan
Chi. Cardinals, John Kimbrough, B .... Texas A&M
Cleveland Rams, Rudy Mucha, C .... Washington
Detroit, Jim Thomason, B .... Texas A&M
Green Bay, George Paskvan, B .... Wisconsin
N.Y. Giants, George Franck, B .... Minnesota
Philadelphia, Art Jones, B(2) .... Richmond
Pittsburgh, Chet Gladchuk, C(2) .... Boston College
Washington, Forest Evashevski, B .... Michigan
1942
Brooklyn Dodgers, Bob Robertson, B .... USC
Chi. Bears, Frankie Albert, B .... Stanford
Chi. Cardinals, Steve Lach, B .... Duke
Cleveland Rams, Jack Wilson, B .... Baylor
Detroit, Bob Westfall, B .... Michigan
Green Bay, Urban Odson, T .... Minnesota
N.Y. Giants, Merle Hapes, B .... Mississippi
Philadelphia, Pete Kmetovic, B .... Stanford
Pittsburgh, Bill Dudley, B .... Virginia
Washington, Orban (Spec) Sanders, B .... Texas
1943
Brooklyn Dodgers, Paul Governali, B .... Columbia
Chi. Bears, Bob Steuber, B .... Missouri
Chi. Cardinals, Glenn Dobbs, B .... Tulsa
Cleveland Rams, Mike Holovak, B .... Boston College
Detroit, Frank Sinkwich, B .... Georgia
Green Bay, Dick Wildung, T .... Minnesota
N.Y. Giants, Steve Filipowicz, B .... Fordham
Philadelphia, Joe Muha, B .... VMI
Pittsburgh, Bill Daley, B .... Minnesota
Washington, Jack Jenkins, B .... Missouri
1944
Boston Yanks, Angelo Bertelli, B .... Notre Dame
Brooklyn Dodgers, Creigton Miller, B .... Notre Dame
Chi. Bears, Ray Evans, B .... Kansas
Chi. Cardinals, Pat Harder, B .... Wisconsin
Cleveland Rams, Tony Butkovich, B .... Illinois
Detroit, Otto Graham, B .... Northwestern
Green Bay, Merv Pregulman, G .... Michigan
N.Y. Giants, Billy Hillenbrand, B .... Indiana
Philadelphia, Steve Van Buren, B .... LSU
Pittsburgh, Johnny Podesto, B .... St. Mary's, Calif.
Washington, Mike Micka, B .... Colgate
1945
Boston Yanks, Eddie Prokop, B .... Georgia Tech
Brooklyn Dodgers, Joe Renfroe, B .... Tulane
Chi. Bears, Don Lund, B .... Michigan
Chi. Cardinals, Charley Trippi, B .... Georgia
Cleveland Rams, Elroy (Crazylegs) Hirsch, B .... Wisconsin
Detroit, Frank Szymanski, C .... Notre Dame
Green Bay, Walt Schlinkman, B .... Texas Tech
N.Y. Giants, Elmer Barbour, B .... Wake Forest
Philadelphia, John Yonakor, E .... Notre Dame
Pittsburgh, Paul Duhart, B* .... Florida
Washington, Jim Hardy, B .... USC
*Duhart played for Green Bay in 1944. Under wartime eligibility rules, he was subject to the 1945 NFL draft and was selected by Pittsburgh.
1946
Boston Yanks, Frank Dancewicz, B .... Notre Dame
Chi. Bears, Johnny Lujack, B .... Notre Dame
Chi. Cardinals, Dub Jones, B .... LSU
Detroit, Bill Dellastatious, B .... Missouri
Green Bay, Johnny Strzykalski, B .... Marquette
Los Angeles, Emil Sitko, B .... Notre Dame
N.Y. Giants, George Connor, T .... Notre Dame
Philadelphia, Leo Riggs, B .... USC
Pittsburgh, Felix (Doc) Blanchard, B .... Army
Washington, Cal Rossi, B* .... UCLA
*Choice lost due to ineligibility.
1947
Boston Yanks, Fritz Barzilauskas, G .... Yale
Chi. Bears, Bob Fenimore, B* .... Oklahoma A&M
Chi. Cardinals, DeWitt (Tex) Coulter, T** .... Army
Detroit, Glenn Davis, B .... Army
Green Bay, Ernie Case, B .... UCLA
Los Angeles, Herman Wedemeyer, B .... St. Mary's, Calif.
N.Y. Giants, Vic Schwall, B .... Northwestern
Philadelphia, Neill Armstrong, E .... Oklahoma A&M
Pittsburgh, Hub Bechtol, E .... Texas
Washington, Cal Rossi, B .... UCLA
*Bonus choice
**Coulter was eligible for the 1947 draft although he played for New York in 1946.
1948
Boston Yanks, Vaughan Mancha, C .... Alabama
Chi. Bears, Bobby Layne, B* .... Texas
Chi. Cardinals, Jim Spavital, B .... Oklahoma A&M
Detroit, Y. A. Tittle, B .... LSU
Green Bay, Earl (Jug) Girard, B .... Wisconsin
Los Angeles, Tom Keane, B(2) .... West Virginia
N.Y. Giants, Tony Minisi, B .... Pennsylvania
Philadelphia, Clyde (Smackover) Scott, B .... Arkansas
Pittsburgh, Dan Edwards, E .... Georgia
Washington, Harry Gilmer, B** .... Alabama
*The choice used to select Layne was traded by Pittsburgh through Detroit to the Chicago Bears.
**Bonus choice
1949
Boston Yanks, Doak Walker, B .... Southern Methodist
Chi. Bears, Dick Harris, C .... Texas
Chi. Cardinals, Bill Fischer, G .... Notre Dame
Detroit, John Rauch, B .... Georgia
Green Bay, Stan Heath, B .... Nevada
Los Angeles, Bobby Thomason, B .... VMI
N.Y. Giants, Paul Page, B .... Southern Methodist
Philadelphia, Chuck Bednarik, C* .... Pennsylvania
Pittsburgh, Bobby Gage, B .... Clemson
Washington, Rob Goode, B .... Texas A&M
*Bonus choice
1950
Baltimore, Adrian Burk, B .... Baylor
Chi. Bears, Chuck Hunsinger, B .... Florida
Chi. Cardinals, Jack Jennings, T (2) .... Ohio State
Cleveland, Ken Carpenter, B .... Oregon State
Detroit, Leon Hart, E* .... Notre Dame
Green Bay, Clayton Tonnemaker, C .... Minnesota
Los Angeles, Ralph Pasquariello, B .... Villanova
N.Y. Yanks, Art Weiner, E (2) .... North Carolina
N.Y. Giants, Travis Tidwell, B .... Auburn
Philadelphia, Harry (Bud) Grant, E .... Minnesota
Pittsburgh, Lynn Chandnois, B .... Michigan State
San Francisco, Leo Nomellini, T .... Minnesota
Washington, George Thomas, B .... Oklahoma
*Bonus choice.
1951
Chi. Bears, Bob Williams, B .... Notre Dame
Chi. Cardinals, Jerry Groom, C .... Notre Dame
Cleveland, Ken Konz, B .... LSU
Detroit, Dick Stanfel, G (2) .... San Francisco
Green Bay, Bob Gain, T .... Kentucky
Los Angeles, Bud McFadin, G .... Texas
N.Y. Giants, Kyle Rote, B* .... Southern Methodist
N.Y. Yanks, Ken Jackson, T .... Texas
Philadelphia, Ebert Van Buren, B .... LSU
Pittsburgh, Butch Avinger, B .... Alabama
San Francisco, Y.A. Tittle, B** .... LSU
Washington, Leon Heath, B .... Oklahoma
*Bonus choice.
**Players of the extinct Baltimore team were eligible for the draft.
1952
Chi. Bears, Jim Dooley, B .... Miami
Chi. Cardinals, Ollie Matson, B .... San Francisco
Cleveland, Bert Rechichar, B .... Tennessee
Dallas Texans, Les Richter, G .... California
Detroit, Yale Lary, B (3) .... Texas A&M
Green Bay, Babe Parilli, B .... Kentucky
Los Angeles, Bill Wade, QB* .... Vanderbilt
N.Y. Giants, Frank Gifford, B .... USC
Philadelphia. Johnny Bright, B .... Drake
Pittsburgh, Ed Modzelewski, B .... Maryland
San Francisco, Hugh McElhenny, B .... Washington
Washington, Larry Isbell, B .... Baylor
*Bonus choice.
1953
Baltimore. Billy Vessels, B .... Oklahoma
Chi. Bears, Billy Anderson, B .... Compton J.C.
Chi. Cardinals, Johnny Olszewski, B .... California
Cleveland, Doug Atkins, T .... Tennessee
Detroit, Harley Sewell, G .... Texas
Green Bay, Al Carmichael, B .... USC
Los Angeles, Donn Moomaw, C .... UCLA
N.Y. Giants, Bobby Marlow, B .... Alabama
Philadelphia, Al Conway, B(2) .... Army
Pittsburgh, Ted Marchibroda, B .... St. Bonaventure
San Francisco, Harry Babcock, E* .... Georgia
Washington, Jack Scarbath, B .... Maryland
*Bonus choice.
1954
Baltimore, Cotton Davidson, B .... Baylor
Chi. Bears, Stan Wallace, B .... Illinois
Chi. Cardinals, Lamar McHan, B .... Arkansas
Cleveland, Bobby Garrett, QB* .... Stanford
Detroit, Dick Chapman, T .... Rice
Green Bay, Art Hunter, T .... Notre Dame
Los Angeles, Ed Beatty, C .... Mississippi
N.Y. Giants, Ken Buck, E .... Pacific
Philadelphia, Neil Worden, B .... Notre Dame
Pittsburgh, Johnny Lattner, B .... Notre Dame
San Francisco, Bernie Faloney, B .... Maryland
Washington, Steve Meilinger, E .... Kentucky
*Bonus choice.
1955
Baltimore, George Shaw, QB* .... Oregon
Chi. Bears, Ron Drzewiecki, B .... Marquette
Chi. Cardinals, Max Boydston, E .... Oklahoma
Cleveland, Kurt Burris, C .... Oklahoma
Detroit, Dave Middleton, B .... Auburn
Green Bay, Tom Bettis, G .... Purdue
Los Angeles, Larry Morris, C .... Georgia Tech
N.Y. Giants, Joe Heap, B .... Notre Dame
Philadelphia, Dick Bielski, B .... Maryland
Pittsburgh, Frank Varrichione, T .... Notre Dame
San Francisco, Dickie Moegle, B .... Rice
Washington, Ralph Guglielmi, B .... Notre Dame
*Bonus choice.
1956
Baltimore, Lenny Moore, B .... Penn State
Chi. Bears, Menan (Tex) Schriewer, E .... Texas
Chi. Cardinals, Joe Childress, B .... Auburn
Cleveland, Preston Carpenter, B .... Arkansas
Detroit, Howard (Hopalong) Cassady, B .... Ohio State

Frankie Albert

Kyle Rote

Jim Brown

Marlin McKeever

Lee Roy Jordan

Calvin Hill

Lee Roy Selmon

Green Bay, Jack Losch, B ... Miami
Los Angeles, Joe Marconi, B ... West Virginia
N.Y. Giants, Henry Moore, B ... Arkansas
Philadelphia, Bob Pellegrini, C ... Maryland
Pittsburgh, Gary Glick, B* ... Colorado A&M
San Francisco, Earl Morrall, B ... Michigan State
Washington, Ed Vereb, B ... Maryland
*Bonus choice.

1957
Baltimore, Jim Parker, G ... Ohio State
Chi. Bears, Earl Leggett, T ... LSU
Chi. Cardinals, Jerry Tubbs, C ... Oklahoma
Cleveland, Jim Brown, B ... Syracuse
Detroit, Bill Glass, G ... Baylor
Green Bay, Paul Hornung, B* ... Notre Dame
Los Angeles, Jon Arnett, B ... USC
N.Y. Giants, Sam DeLuca, T(2) ... South Carolina
Philadelphia, Clarence Peaks, B ... Michigan State
Pittsburgh, Len Dawson, B ... Purdue
San Francisco, John Brodie, B ... Stanford
Washington, Don Bosseler, B ... Miami
*Bonus choice.

1958
Baltimore, Lenny Lyles, B ... Louisville
Chi. Bears, Chuck Howley, G ... West Virginia
Chi. Cardinals, King Hill, B* ... Rice
Cleveland, Jim Shofner, B ... TCU
Detroit, Alex Karras, T ... Iowa
Green Bay, Dan Currie, C ... Michigan State
Los Angeles, Lou Michaels, T ... Kentucky
N.Y. Giants, Phil King, B ... Vanderbilt
Philadelphia, Walt Kowalczyk, B ... Michigan State
Pittsburgh, Larry Krutko, B ... West Virginia
San Francisco, Jim Pace, B ... Michigan
Washington, Mike Sommer, B ... George Washington
*Bonus choice.

1959
Baltimore, Jackie Burkett, C ... Auburn
Chi. Bears, Don Clark, B ... Ohio State
Chi. Cardinals, Billy Stacy, B ... Mississippi State
Cleveland, Rich Kreitling, E ... Illinois
Detroit, Nick Pietrosante, B ... Notre Dame
Green Bay, Randy Duncan, B ... Iowa
Los Angeles, Dick Bass, B ... Pacific
N.Y. Giants, Lee Grosscup, B ... Utah
Philadelphia, J. D. Smith, T(2) ... Rice
Pittsburgh, Tom Barnett, B(8) ... Purdue
San Francisco, Dave Baker, B ... Oklahoma
Washington, Don Allard, B ... Boston College

1960 NFL
Baltimore, Ron Mix, T ... USC
Chicago, Roger Davis, G ... Syracuse
Cleveland, Jim Houston, E ... Ohio State
Detroit, Johnny Robinson, B ... LSU
Green Bay, Tom Moore, B ... Vanderbilt
Los Angeles, Billy Cannon, B ... LSU
N.Y. Giants, Lou Cordileone, T ... Clemson
Philadelphia, Ron Burton, B ... Northwestern
Pittsburgh, Jack Spikes, B ... TCU
San Francisco, Monty Stickles, E ... Notre Dame
St. Louis, George Izo, B ... Notre Dame
Washington, Richie Lucas, QB ... Penn State

1960 AFL
Boston Patriots, Gerhard Schwedes, B ... Syracuse
Buffalo, Richie Lucas, QB ... Penn State
Dallas Texans, Don Meredith, QB ... Southern Methodist
Denver, Roger LeClerc, C ... Trinity, Conn.
Houston, Billy Cannon, B ... LSU
Los Angeles Chargers, Monty Stickles, E ... Notre Dame
Minneapolis, Dale Hackbart, B* ... Wisconsin
N.Y. Titans, George Izo, B ... Notre Dame
*Minneapolis became the Minnesota NFL franchise. The Minneapolis AFL draft list was turned over to Oakland.

1961 NFL
Baltimore, Tom Matte, B ... Ohio State
Chicago, Mike Ditka, E ... Pittsburgh
Cleveland, Bobby Crespino, B ... Mississippi
Dallas, Bob Lilly, T ... TCU
Detroit, Danny LaRose, T(2) ... Missouri
Green Bay, Herb Adderley, B ... Michigan State
Los Angeles, Marlin McKeever, E ... USC
Minnesota, Tommy Mason, B ... Tulane
N.Y. Giants, Bruce Tarbox, G(2) ... Syracuse
Philadelphia, Art Baker, B ... Syracuse
Pittsburgh, Myron Pottios, G(2) ... Notre Dame
St. Louis, Ken Rice, T ... Auburn
San Francisco, Jimmy Johnson, B ... UCLA
Washington, Norman Snead, B ... Wake Forest

1961 AFL
Boston Patriots, Tommy Mason, B ... Tulane
Buffalo, Ken Rice, T ... Auburn
Dallas Texans, E.J. Holub, LB ... Texas Tech
Denver, Bob Gaiters, B ... New Mexico State
Houston, Mike Ditka, E. ... Pittsburgh
N.Y. Titans, Tom Brown, G ... Minnesota
Oakland, Joe Rutgens, T ... Illinois
San Diego, Earl Faison, E ... Indiana

1962 NFL
Baltimore, Wendell Harris, B ... LSU
Chicago, Ronnie Bull, B ... Baylor
Cleveland, Gary Collins, E ... Maryland
Dallas, Sonny Gibbs, QB(2) ... TCU
Detroit, John Hadl, QB ... Kansas
Green Bay, Earl Gros, B ... LSU
Los Angeles, Roman Gabriel, QB ... N. Carolina State
Minnesota, Bill Miller, E(2) ... Miami
N.Y. Giants, Jerry Hillebrand, E ... Colorado
Philadelphia, Pete Case, T(2) ... Georgia
Pittsburgh, Bob Ferguson, B ... Ohio State
St. Louis, Fate Echols, T ... Northwestern
San Francisco, Lance Alworth, B ... Arkansas
Washington, Ernie Davis, B ... Syracuse

1962 AFL
Boston Patriots, Gary Collins, E ... Maryland
Buffalo, Ernie Davis, B ... Syracuse
Dallas Texans, Ronnie Bull, B ... Baylor
Denver, Merlin Olsen, T ... Utah State
Houston, Ray Jacobs, T ... Howard Payne
N.Y. Titans, Sandy Stephens, B ... Minnesota
Oakland, Roman Gabriel, QB ... N. Carolina State
San Diego, Bob Ferguson, B ... Ohio State

1963 NFL
Baltimore, Bob Vogel, T ... Ohio State
Chicago, Dave Behrman, C ... Michigan State
Cleveland, Tom Hutchinson, E ... Kentucky
Dallas, Lee Roy Jordan, C ... Alabama
Detroit, Daryl Sanders, T ... Ohio State
Green Bay, Dave Robinson, E ... Penn State
Los Angeles, Terry Baker, QB ... Oregon State
Minnesota, Jim Dunaway, T ... Mississippi
N.Y. Giants, Frank Lasky, T(2) ... Florida
Philadelphia, Ed Budde, T ... Michigan State
Pittsburgh, Frank Atkinson, T(8) ... Stanford
St. Louis, Jerry Stovall, B ... LSU
San Francisco, Kermit Alexander, B ... UCLA
Washington, Pat Richter, E ... Wisconsin

1963 AFL
Boston Patriots, Art Graham, E ... Boston College
Buffalo, Dave Behrman, C ... Michigan State
Denver, Kermit Alexander, B ... UCLA
Houston, Danny Brabham, B ... Arkansas
Kansas City, Buck Buchanan, T ... Grambling
N.Y. Jets, Jerry Stovall, B ... LSU
Oakland, Butch Wilson, B(6) ... Alabama
San Diego, Walt Sweeney, E ... Syracuse

1964 NFL
Baltimore, Marv Woodson, B ... Indiana
Chicago, Dick Evey, T ... Tennessee
Cleveland, Paul Warfield, B ... Ohio State
Dallas, Scott Appleton, T ... Texas
Detroit, Pete Beathard, QB ... USC
Green Bay, Lloyd Voss, T ... Nebraska
Los Angeles, Bill Munson, QB ... Utah State
Minnesota, Carl Eller, T ... Minnesota
N.Y. Giants, Joe Don Looney, B. ... Oklahoma
Philadelphia, Bob Brown, G ... Nebraska
Pittsburgh, Paul Martha, B ... Pittsburgh
St. Louis, Ken Kortas, T ... Louisville
San Francisco, Dave Parks, E ... Texas Tech
Washington, Charley Taylor, B ... Arizona State

1964 AFL
Boston Patriots, Jack Concannon, QB ... Boston College
Buffalo, Carl Eller, T ... Minnesota
Denver, Bob Brown, G ... Nebraska
Houston, Scott Appleton, T ... Texas
Kansas City, Pete Beathard, QB ... USC
N.Y. Jets, Matt Snell, B ... Ohio State
Oakland, Tony Lorick, B ... Arizona State
San Diego, Ted Davis, E ... Georgia Tech

1965 NFL
Baltimore, Mike Curtis, B ... Duke
Chicago, Dick Butkus, C ... Illinois
Cleveland, Jim Garcia, T(2) ... Purdue
Dallas, Craig Morton, QB ... California
Detroit, Tom Nowatzke, B ... Indiana
Green Bay, Donny Anderson, B ... Texas Tech
Los Angeles, Clancy Williams, B ... Washington State
Minnesota, Jack Snow, E ... Notre Dame
N.Y. Giants, Tucker Frederickson, B ... Auburn
Philadelphia, Ray Rissmiller, T(2) ... Georgia
Pittsburgh, Roy Jefferson, B(2) ... Utah
St. Louis, Joe Namath, QB ... Alabama
San Francisco, Ken Willard, B ... North Carolina
Washington, Bob Breitenstein, T(2) ... Tulsa

1965 AFL
Boston Patriots, Jerry Rush, T ... Michigan State
Buffalo, Jim Davidson, T ... Ohio State
Denver, Dick Butkus, C(2) ... Illinois
Houston, Lawrence Elkins, E ... Baylor
Kansas City, Gale Sayers, B ... Kansas
N.Y. Jets, Joe Namath, QB ... Alabama
Oakland, Harry Schuh, T ... Memphis State
San Diego, Steve DeLong, G ... Tennessee

1966 NFL
Atlanta, Tommy Nobis, LB ... Texas
Baltimore, Sam Ball, T ... Kentucky
Chicago, George Rice, T ... LSU
Cleveland, Milt Morin, E ... Massachusetts
Dallas, John Niland G ... Iowa
Detroit, Nick Eddy, B(2) ... Notre Dame
Green Bay, Jim Grabowski, B ... Illinois
Los Angeles, Tom Mack, T ... Michigan
Minnesota, Jerry Shay, T ... Purdue
N.Y. Giants, Francis Peay, T ... Missouri
Philadelphia, Randy Beisler, E ... Indiana
Pittsburgh, Dick Leftridge, B ... West Virginia
St. Louis, Carl McAdams, C ... Oklahoma
San Francisco, Stan Hindman, T ... Mississippi
Washington, Charley Gogolak, K ... Princeton

1966 AFL
Boston Patriots, Karl Singer, T ... Purdue
Buffalo, Mike Dennis, B ... Mississippi
Denver, Jerry Shay, T ... Purdue
Houston, Tommy Nobis, G ... Texas
Kansas City, Aaron Brown, E ... Minnesota
Miami, Jim Grabowski, B ... Illinois
N.Y. Jets, Bill Yearby, T ... Michigan
Oakland, Rodger Bird, B ... Kentucky
San Diego, Don Davis, T ... Cal. State-L.A.

1967
Combined Draft
Atlanta, Leo Carroll, DE(2) ... San Diego State
Baltimore, Bubba Smith, DT ... Michigan State
Boston Patriots, John Charles, DB ... Purdue
Buffalo, John Pitts, WR ... Arizona State
Chicago, Loyd Phillips, DE ... Arkansas
Cleveland, Bob Matheson, LB ... Duke
Dallas, Phil Clark, DB(3) ... Northwestern
Denver, Floyd Little, RB ... Syracuse
Detroit, Mel Farr, RB ... UCLA
Green Bay, Bob Hyland, G ... Boston College
Houston, George Webster, LB ... Michigan State
Kansas City, Gene Trosch, DT ... Miami
Los Angeles, Willie Ellison, RB(2) ... Texas Southern
Miami, Bob Griese, QB ... Purdue
Minnesota, Clint Jones, RB ... Michigan State
N.Y. Giants, Lou Thompson, DT(2) ... Alabama
N.Y. Jets, Paul Seiler, G ... Notre Dame
New Orleans, Les Kelley, RB ... Alabama
Oakland, Gene Upshaw, G ... Texas A&I
Philadelphia, Harry Jones, RB ... Arkansas
Pittsburgh, Don Shy, RB(2) ... San Diego State
St. Louis, Dave Williams, WR ... Washington
San Diego, Ron Billingsley, DT ... Wyoming
San Francisco, Steve Spurrier, QB ... Florida
Washington, Ray McDonald, RB ... Idaho

1968
Atlanta, Claude Humphrey, DE ... Tennessee State
Baltimore, John Williams, T ... Minnesota

Stanley Morgan

Wes Chandler

Ted Brown

Jerry Robinson

Johnnie Johnson

Lawrence Taylor

Kenneth Sims

Boston Patriots, Dennis Byrd, T ... N. Carolina State
Buffalo, Haven Moses, WR ... San Diego State
Chicago, Mike Hull, RB ... USC
Cleveland, Marvin Upshaw, DE ... Trinity, Tex.
Cincinnati, Bob Johnson, C ... Tennessee
Dallas, Dennis Homan, WR ... Alabama
Denver, Curley Culp, DE(2) ... Arizona State
Detroit, Greg Landry, QB ... Massachusetts
Green Bay, Fred Carr, LB ... Texas-El Paso
Houston, Mac Haik, WR(2) ... Mississippi
Kansas City, Mo Moorman, G ... Texas A&M
Los Angeles, Gary Beban, QB(2) ... UCLA
Miami, Larry Csonka, RB ... Syracuse
Minnesota, Ron Yary, T ... USC
New Orleans, Kevin Hardy, DE ... Notre Dame
N.Y. Giants, Rich Buzin, T(2) ... Penn State
N.Y. Jets, Lee White, RB ... Weber State
Oakland, Eldridge Dickey, QB ... Tennessee State
Philadelphia, Tim Rossovich, DE ... USC
Pittsburgh, Mike Taylor, T ... USC
St. Louis, MacArthur Lane, RB ... Utah State
San Diego, Russ Washington, T ... Missouri
San Francisco, Forrest Blue, C ... Auburn
Washington, Jim Smith, DB ... Oregon

1969

Atlanta, George Kunz, T ... Notre Dame
Baltimore, Eddie Hinton, WR ... Oklahoma
Boston Patriots, Ron Sellers, WR ... Florida State
Buffalo, O.J. Simpson, RB ... USC
Chicago, Rufus Mayes, T ... Ohio State
Cincinnati, Greg Cook, QB ... Cincinnati
Cleveland, Ron Johnson, RB ... Michigan
Dallas, Calvin Hill, RB ... Yale
Denver, Grady Cavness, DB(2) ... Texas-El Paso
Detroit, Altie Taylor, RB(2) ... Utah State
Green Bay, Rich Moore, DT ... Villanova
Houston, Ron Pritchard, LB ... Arizona State
Kansas City, Jim Marsalis, DB ... Tennessee State
Los Angeles, Larry Smith, RB ... Florida
Miami, Bill Stanfill, DE ... Georgia
Minnesota, Ed White, G(2) ... California
New Orleans, John Shinners, G ... Xavier
N.Y. Giants, Fred Dryer, DE ... San Diego State
N.Y. Jets, Dave Foley, T ... Ohio State
Oakland, Art Thoms, DT ... Syracuse
Philadelphia, Leroy Keyes, RB ... Purdue
Pittsburgh, Joe Greene, DT ... N. Texas State
St. Louis, Roger Wehrli, DB ... Missouri
San Diego, Marty Domres, QB ... Columbia
San Francisco, Ted Kwalick, TE ... Penn State
Washington, Eugene Epps, DB(2) ... Texas-El Paso

1970

Atlanta, John Small, LB ... The Citadel
Baltimore, Norm Bulaich, RB ... TCU
Boston Patriots, Phil Olsen, DT ... Utah State
Buffalo, Al Cowlings, DE ... USC
Chicago, George Farmer, WR(3) ... UCLA
Cincinnati, Mike Reid, DT ... Penn State
Cleveland, Mike Phipps, QB ... Purdue
Dallas, Duane Thomas, RB ... W. Texas State
Denver, Bobby Anderson, RB ... Colorado
Detroit, Steve Owens, RB ... Oklahoma
Green Bay, Mike McCoy, DT ... Notre Dame
Houston, Doug Wilkerson, G ... N. Carolina Central
Kansas City, Sid Smith, T ... USC
Los Angeles, Jack Reynolds, LB ... Tennessee
Miami, Jim Mandich, TE(2) ... Michigan
Minnesota, John Ward, T ... Oklahoma State
New Orleans, Ken Burrough, WR ... Texas Southern
N.Y. Giants, Jim Files, LB ... Oklahoma
N.Y. Jets, Steve Tannen, DB ... Florida
Oakland, Raymond Chester, TE ... Morgan State
Philadelphia, Steve Zabel, TE ... Oklahoma
Pittsburgh, Terry Bradshaw, QB ... Louisiana Tech
St. Louis, Larry Stegent, RB ... Texas A&M
San Diego, Walker Gillette, WR ... Richmond
San Francisco, Cedrick Hardman, DE ... N. Texas State
Washington, Bill Brundige, DE(2) ... Colorado

1971

Atlanta, Joe Profit, RB ... N.E. Louisiana
Baltimore, Don McCauley, RB ... North Carolina
Buffalo, J. D. Hill, WR ... Arizona State
Chicago, Joe Moore, RB ... Missouri
Cincinnati, Vernon Holland, T ... Tennessee State
Cleveland, Clarence Scott, DB ... Kansas State
Dallas, Tody Smith, DE ... USC
Denver, Marv Montgomery, T ... USC
Detroit, Bob Bell, DT ... Cincinnati
Green Bay, John Brockington, RB ... Ohio State
Houston, Dan Pastorini, QB ... Santa Clara
Kansas City, Elmo Wright, WR ... Houston
Los Angeles, Isiah Robertson, LB ... Southern U.
Miami, Otto Stowe, WR(2) ... Iowa State
Minnesota, Leo Hayden, RB ... Ohio State
New England, Jim Plunkett, QB ... Stanford
New Orleans, Archie Manning, QB ... Mississippi
N.Y. Giants, Rocky Thompson, WR ... W. Texas State
N.Y. Jets, John Riggins, RB ... Kansas
Oakland, Jack Tatum, DB ... Ohio State
Philadelphia, Richard Harris, DE ... Grambling
Pittsburgh, Frank Lewis, WR ... Grambling
St. Louis, Norm Thompson, DB ... Utah
San Diego, Leon Burns, RB ... Cal. State-Long Beach
San Francisco, Tim Anderson, DB ... Ohio State
Washington, Cotton Speyrer, WR(2) ... Texas

1972

Atlanta, Clarence Ellis, DB ... Notre Dame
Baltimore, Tom Drougas, T ... Oregon
Buffalo, Walt Patulski, DE ... Notre Dame
Chicago, Lionel Antoine, T ... Southern Illinois
Cincinnati, Sherman White, DE ... California
Cleveland, Thom Darden, DB ... Michigan
Dallas, Bill Thomas, RB ... Boston College
Denver, Riley Odoms, TE ... Houston
Detroit, Herb Orvis, DE ... Colorado
Green Bay, Willie Buchanon, DB ... San Diego State
Houston, Greg Sampson, DE ... Stanford
Kansas City, Jeff Kinney, RB ... Nebraska
Los Angeles, Jim Bertelsen, RB(2) ... Texas
Miami, Mike Kadish, DT ... Notre Dame
Minnesota, Jeff Siemon, LB ... Stanford
New England, Tom Reynolds, WR(2) ... San Diego State
New Orleans, Royce Smith, G ... Georgia
N.Y. Giants, Eldridge Small, DB ... Texas A&I
N.Y. Jets, Jerome Barkum, WR ... Jackson State
Oakland, Mike Siani, WR ... Villanova
Philadelphia, John Reaves, QB ... Florida
Pittsburgh, Franco Harris, RB ... Penn State
St. Louis, Bobby Moore, WR ... Oregon
San Diego, Pete Lazetich, DE(2) ... Stanford
San Francisco, Terry Beasley, WR ... Auburn
Washington, Moses Denson, RB(8) ... Maryland State

1973

Atlanta, Greg Marx, DT(2) ... Notre Dame
Baltimore, Bert Jones, QB ... LSU
Buffalo, Paul Seymour, T ... Michigan
Chicago, Wally Chambers, DE ... Eastern Kentucky
Cincinnati, Isaac Curtis, WR ... San Diego State
Cleveland, Steve Holden, WR ... Arizona State
Dallas, Billy Joe DuPree, TE ... Michigan State
Denver, Otis Armstrong, RB ... Purdue
Detroit, Ernie Price, DE ... Texas A&I
Green Bay, Barry Smith, WR ... Florida State
Houston, John Matuszak, DE ... Tampa
Kansas City, Gary Butler, TE(2) ... Rice
Los Angeles, Cullen Bryant, DB(2) ... Colorado
Miami, Chuck Bradley, T(2) ... Oregon
Minnesota, Chuck Foreman, RB ... Miami
New England, John Hannah, G ... Alabama
New Orleans, Derland Moore, DE(2) ... Oklahoma
N.Y. Giants, Brad Van Pelt, LB ... Michigan State
N.Y. Jets, Burgess Owens, DB ... Miami
Oakland, Ray Guy, P-K ... So. Mississippi
Philadelphia, Jerry Sisemore, T ... Texas
Pittsburgh, James Thomas, CB ... Florida State
St. Louis, Dave Butz, DT ... Purdue
San Diego, Johnny Rodgers, WR ... Nebraska
San Francisco, Mike Holmes, DB ... Texas Southern
Washington, Charles Cantrell, G(5) ... Lamar Tech

1974

Atlanta, Gerald Tinker, WR(2) ... Kent State
Baltimore, John Dutton, DE ... Nebraska
Buffalo, Reuben Gant, TE ... Oklahoma State
Chicago, Waymond Bryant, LB ... Tennessee State
Cincinnati, Bill Kollar, DT ... Montana State
Cleveland, Billy Corbett, T(2) ... Johnson C. Smith
Dallas, Ed Jones, DE ... Tennessee State
Denver, Randy Gradishar, LB ... Ohio State
Detroit, Ed O'Neil, LB ... Penn State
Green Bay, Barty Smith, RB ... Richmond
Houston, Steve Manstedt, LB(4) ... Nebraska
Kansas City, Woody Green, RB ... Arizona State
Los Angeles, John Cappelletti, RB ... Penn State
Miami, Don Reese, DE ... Jackson State
Minnesota, Fred McNeill, LB ... UCLA
New England, Steve Corbett, G(2) ... Boston College
New Orleans, Rick Middleton, LB ... Ohio State
N.Y. Giants, John Hicks, G ... Ohio State
N.Y. Jets, Carl Barzilauskas, DT ... Indiana
Oakland, Henry Lawrence, T ... Florida A&M
Philadelphia, Mitch Sutton, DT(3) ... Kansas
Pittsburgh, Lynn Swann, WR ... USC
St. Louis, J. V. Cain, TE ... Colorado
San Diego, Bo Matthews, RB ... Colorado
San Francisco, Wilbur Jackson, RB ... Alabama
Washington, Jon Keyworth, RB(6) ... Colorado

1975

Atlanta, Steve Bartkowski, QB ... California
Baltimore, Ken Huff, G ... North Carolina
Buffalo, Tom Ruud, LB ... Nebraska
Chicago, Walter Payton, RB ... Jackson State
Cincinnati, Glenn Cameron, LB ... Florida
Cleveland, Mack Mitchell, DE ... Houston
Dallas, Randy White, LB ... Maryland
Denver, Louis Wright, DB ... San Jose State
Detroit, Lynn Boden, G ... S. Dakota State
Green Bay, Bill Bain, G(2) ... USC
Houston, Robert Brazile, LB ... Jackson State
Kansas City, Elmore Stephens, TE(2) ... Kentucky
Los Angeles, Mike Fanning, DT ... Notre Dame
Miami, Darryl Carlton, T ... Tampa
Minnesota, Mark Mullaney, DE ... Colorado State
New England, Russ Francis, TE ... Oregon
New Orleans, Larry Burton, WR ... Purdue
N.Y. Giants, Al Simpson, T(2) ... Colorado State
N.Y. Jets, Anthony Davis, RB(2) ... USC
Oakland, Neal Colzie, DB ... Ohio State
Philadelphia, Bill Capraun, T(7) ... Miami
Pittsburgh, Dave Brown, DB ... Michigan
St. Louis, Tim Gray, DB ... Texas A&M
San Diego, Gary Johnson, DT ... Grambling
San Francisco, Jimmy Webb, DT ... Mississippi State
Washington, Mike Thomas, RB(5) ... Nevada-Las Vegas

1976

Atlanta, Bubba Bean, RB ... Texas A&M
Baltimore, Ken Novak, DT ... Purdue
Buffalo, Mario Clark, DB ... Oregon
Chicago, Dennis Lick, T ... Wisconsin
Cincinnati, Billy Brooks, WR ... Oklahoma
Cleveland, Mike Pruitt, RB ... Purdue
Dallas, Aaron Kyle, DB ... Wyoming
Denver, Tom Glassic, G ... Virginia
Detroit, James Hunter, DB ... Grambling
Green Bay, Mark Koncar, T ... Colorado
Houston, Mike Barber, TE(2) ... Louisiana Tech
Kansas City, Rod Walters, G ... Iowa
Los Angeles, Kevin McLain, LB ... Colorado State
Miami, Larry Gordon, LB ... Arizona State
Minnesota, James White, DT ... Oklahoma State
New England, Mike Haynes, DB ... Arizona State
New Orleans, Chuck Muncie, RB ... California
N.Y. Giants, Troy Archer, DE ... Colorado
N.Y. Jets, Richard Todd, QB ... Alabama
Oakland, Charles Philyaw, DT(2) ... Texas Southern
Philadelphia, Mike Smith, DE(4) ... Florida
Pittsburgh, Bennie Cunningham, TE ... Clemson
St. Louis, Mike Dawson, DT ... Arizona
San Diego, Joe Washington, RB ... Oklahoma
San Francisco, Randy Cross, C(2) ... UCLA
Seattle, Steve Niehaus, DT ... Notre Dame
Tampa Bay, Lee Roy Selmon, DE ... Oklahoma
Washington, Mike Hughes, G(5) ... Baylor

1977

Atlanta, Warren Bryant, T ... Kentucky
Baltimore, Randy Burke, WR ... Kentucky
Buffalo, Phil Dokes, DT(2) ... Oklahoma State

502 THE DRAFT

Chicago, Ted Albrecht, T . . . . California
Cincinnati, Eddie Edwards, DT . . . . Miami
Cleveland, Robert L. Jackson, LB . . . . Texas A&M
Dallas, Tony Dorsett, RB . . . . Pittsburgh
Denver, Steve Schindler, G . . . . Boston College
Detroit, Walt Williams, DB(2) . . . . New Mexico State
Green Bay, Mike Butler, DE . . . . Kansas
Houston, Morris Towns, T . . . . Missouri
Kansas City, Gary Green, DB . . . . Baylor
Los Angeles, Bob Brudzinski, LB . . . . Ohio State
Miami, A. J. Duhe, DT . . . . Louisiana State
Minnesota, Tommy Kramer, QB . . . . Rice
New England, Raymond Clayborn, DB . . . . Texas
New Orleans, Joe Campbell, DE . . . . Maryland
N.Y. Giants, Gary Jeter, DT . . . . USC
N.Y. Jets, Marvin Powell, T . . . . USC
Oakland, Mike Davis, DB(2) . . . . Colorado
Philadelphia, Skip Sharp, DB(5) . . . . Kansas
Pittsburgh, Robin Cole, LB . . . . New Mexico
St. Louis, Steve Pisarkiewicz, QB . . . . Missouri
San Diego, Bob Rush, C . . . . Memphis State
San Francisco, Elmo Boyd, WR(3) . . . . Eastern Kentucky
Seattle, Steve August, G . . . . Tulsa
Tampa Bay, Ricky Bell, RB . . . . USC
Washington, Duncan McColl, DE(4) . . . . Stanford
1978
Atlanta, Mike Kenn, T . . . . Michigan
Baltimore, Reese McCall, TE . . . . Auburn
Buffalo, Terry Miller, RB . . . . Oklahoma State
Chicago, Brad Shearer, DT(3) . . . . Texas
Cincinnati, Ross Browner, DE . . . . Notre Dame
Cleveland, Clay Matthews, LB . . . . USC
Dallas, Larry Bethea, DE . . . . Michigan State
Denver, Don Latimer, DT . . . . Miami
Detroit, Luther Bradley, DB . . . . Notre Dame
Green Bay, James Lofton, WR . . . . Stanford
Houston, Earl Campbell, RB . . . . Texas
Kansas City, Art Still, DE . . . . Kentucky
Los Angeles, Elvis Peacock, RB . . . . Oklahoma
Miami, Guy Benjamin, QB(2) . . . . Stanford
Minnesota, Randy Holloway, DE . . . . Pittsburgh
New England, Bob Cryder, G . . . . Alabama
New Orleans, Wes Chandler, WR . . . . Florida
N.Y. Giants, Gordon King, T . . . . Stanford
N.Y. Jets, Chris Ward, T . . . . Ohio State
Oakland, Dave Browning, DE(2) . . . . Washington
Philadelphia, Reggie Wilkes, LB(3) . . . . Georgia Tech
Pittsburgh, Ron Johnson, DB . . . . Eastern Michigan
St. Louis, Steve Little, K . . . . Arkansas
San Diego, John Jefferson, WR . . . . Arizona State
San Francisco, Ken McAfee, TE . . . . Notre Dame
Seattle, Keith Simpson, DB . . . . Memphis State
Tampa Bay, Doug Williams, QB . . . . Grambling
Washington, Tony Green, RB(6) . . . . Florida
1979
Atlanta, Don Smith, DE . . . . Miami
Baltimore, Barry Krauss, LB . . . . Alabama
Buffalo, Tom Cousineau, LB . . . . Ohio State
Chicago, Dan Hampton, DT . . . . Arkansas
Cincinnati, Jack Thompson, QB . . . . Washington State
Cleveland, Willis Adams, WR . . . . Houston
Dallas, Robert Shaw, C . . . . Tennessee
Denver, Kelvin Clark, T . . . . Nebraska
Detroit, Keith Dorney, T . . . . Penn State
Green Bay, Eddie Lee Ivery, RB . . . . Georgia Tech
Houston, Mike Stensrud, DE(2) . . . . Iowa State
Kansas City, Mike Bell, DE . . . . Colorado State
Los Angeles, George Andrews, LB . . . . Nebraska
Miami, Jon Giesler, T . . . . Michigan
Minnesota, Ted Brown, RB . . . . North Carolina State
New England, Rick Sanford, DB . . . . South Carolina
New Orleans, Russell Erxleben, K . . . . Texas
N.Y. Giants, Phil Simms, QB . . . . Morehead State
N.Y. Jets, Marty Lyons, DE . . . . Alabama
Oakland, Willie Jones, DE(2) . . . . Florida State
Philadelphia, Jerry Robinson, LB . . . . UCLA
Pittsburgh, Greg Hawthorne, RB . . . . Baylor
St. Louis, Ottis Anderson, RB . . . . Miami
San Diego, Kellen Winslow, TE . . . . Missouri
San Francisco, James Owens, WR(2) . . . . UCLA
Seattle, Manu Tuiasosopo, DT . . . . UCLA
Tampa Bay, Greg Roberts, G(2) . . . . Oklahoma
Washington, Don Warren, TE(4) . . . . San Diego State
1980
Atlanta, Junior Miller, TE . . . . Nebraska
Baltimore, Curtis Dickey, RB . . . . Texas A&M
Buffalo, Jim Ritcher, C . . . . North Carolina State
Chicago, Otis Wilson, LB . . . . Louisville
Cincinnati, Anthony Munoz, T . . . . USC
Cleveland, Charles White, RB . . . . USC
Dallas, Bill Roe, LB(3) . . . . Colorado
Denver, Rulon Jones, DE(2) . . . . Utah State
Detroit, Billy Sims, RB . . . . Oklahoma
Green Bay, Bruce Clark, DE . . . . Penn State
Houston, Angelo Fields, T(2) . . . . Michigan State
Kansas City, Brad Budde, G . . . . USC
Los Angeles, Johnnie Johnson, DB . . . . Texas
Miami, Don McNeal, DB . . . . Alabama

Minnesota, Doug Martin, DT . . . . Washington
New England, Roland James, DB . . . . Tennessee
New Orleans, Stan Brock, T . . . . Colorado
N.Y. Giants, Mark Haynes, DB . . . . Colorado
N.Y. Jets, Johnny (Lam) Jones, WR . . . . Texas
Oakland, Marc Wilson, QB . . . . Brigham Young
Philadelphia, Roynell Young, DB . . . . Alcorn State
Pittsburgh, Mark Malone, QB . . . . Arizona State
St. Louis, Curtis Greer, DE . . . . Michigan
San Diego, Ed Luther, QB(4) . . . . San Jose State
San Francisco, Earl Cooper, RB . . . . Rice
Seattle, Jacob Green, DE . . . . Texas A&M
Tampa Bay, Ray Snell, G . . . . Wisconsin
Washington, Art Monk, WR . . . . Syracuse
1981
Atlanta, Bobby Butler, DB . . . . Florida State
Baltimore, Randy McMillan, RB . . . . Pittsburgh
Buffalo, Booker Moore, RB . . . . Penn State
Chicago, Keith Van Horne, T . . . . USC
Cincinnati, David Verser, WR . . . . Kansas
Cleveland, Hanford Dixon, DB . . . . Southern Mississippi
Dallas, Howard Richards, T . . . . Missouri
Denver, Dennis Smith, DB . . . . USC
Detroit, Mark Nichols, WR . . . . San Jose State
Green Bay, Rich Campbell, QB . . . . California
Houston, Michael Holston, WR(3) . . . . Morgan State
Kansas City, Willie Scott, TE . . . . South Carolina
Los Angeles, Mel Owens, LB . . . . Michigan
Miami, David Overstreet, RB . . . . Oklahoma
Minnesota, Mardye McDole, WR(2) . . . . . Mississippi State
New England, Brian Holloway, T . . . . Stanford
New Orleans, George Rogers, RB . . . . South Carolina
N.Y. Giants, Lawrence Taylor, LB . . . . North Carolina
N.Y. Jets, Freeman McNeil, RB . . . . UCLA
Oakland, Ted Watts, DB . . . . Texas Tech
Philadelphia, Leonard Mitchell, DE . . . . Houston
Pittsburgh, Keith Gary, DE . . . . Oklahoma
St. Louis, E. J. Junior, LB . . . . Alabama
San Diego, James Brooks, RB . . . . Auburn
San Francisco, Ronnie Lott, DB . . . . USC
Seattle, Ken Easley, DB . . . . UCLA
Tampa Bay, Hugh Green, LB . . . . Pittsburgh
Washington, Mark May, T . . . . Pittsburgh
1982
Atlanta, Gerald Riggs, RB . . . . Arizona State
Baltimore, Johnie Cooks, LB . . . . Mississippi State
Buffalo, Perry Tuttle, WR . . . . Clemson
Chicago, Jim McMahon, QB . . . . Brigham Young
Cincinnati, Glen Collins, DE . . . . Mississippi State
Cleveland, Chip Banks, LB . . . . USC
Dallas, Rod Hill, DB . . . . Kentucky State
Denver, Gerald Willhite, RB . . . . San Jose State
Detroit, Jimmy Williams, LB . . . . Nebraska
Green Bay, Ron Hallstrom, G . . . . Iowa
Houston, Mike Munchak, G . . . . Penn State
Kansas City, Anthony Hancock, WR . . . . Tennessee
Los Angeles, Barry Redden, RB . . . . Richmond
Miami, Roy Foster, G . . . . USC
Minnesota, Darrin Nelson, RB . . . . Stanford
New England, Kenneth Sims, DT . . . . Texas
New Orleans, Lindsay Scott, WR . . . . Georgia
N.Y. Giants, Butch Woolfolk, RB . . . . Michigan
N.Y. Jets, Bob Crable, LB . . . . Notre Dame
Oakland, Marcus Allen, RB . . . . USC
Philadelphia, Mike Quick, WR . . . . North Carolina State
Pittsburgh, Walter Abercrombie, RB . . . . Baylor
St. Louis, Luis Sharpe, T . . . . UCLA
San Diego, Hollis Hall, CB(7) . . . . Clemson
San Francisco, Bubba Paris, T(2) . . . . Michigan
Seattle, Jeff Bryant, DE . . . . Clemson
Tampa Bay, Sean Farrell, G . . . . Penn State
Washington, Vernon Dean, DB(2) . . . . San Diego State

A Diagram History of Pro Football

AMOS ALONZO STAGG
Stagg was the most innovative coach in history. Responsible historians credit him with having invented two-dozen or more football techniques, plays, and strategies. He coached at the University of Chicago for 41 years. He lived to be 102 years old; he was born during the Civil War and died in 1965.

Football diagrams are little utopias. Any play can appear devastating in a diagram. The following plays and formations and strategies were successful often enough that they have survived where perhaps several hundred thousand others over the last 100 years have not.

1 Wedge

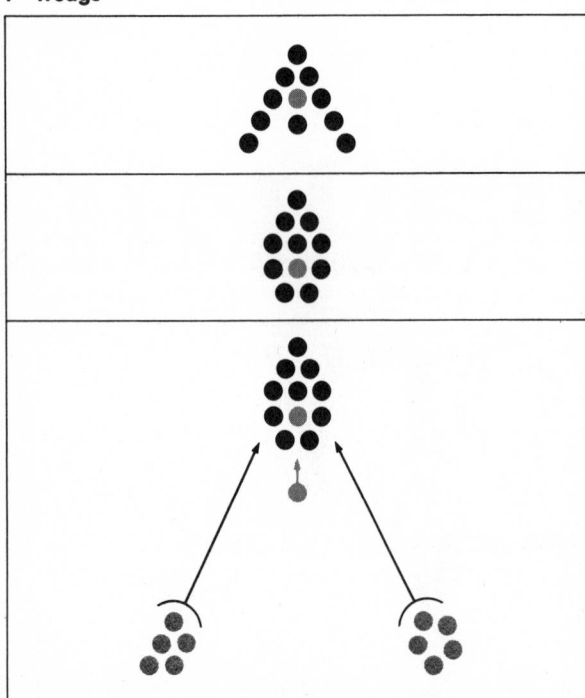

Historian Alexander Weyand wrote that the Princeton wedge of 1884 (top) was "the first great tactical weapon to make its appearance in American football." The ball wasn't kicked off or centered; rather, play began when the wedge moved forward. The person behind the ball carrier pushed him. The wedge was fearsome but Walter (Pudge) Heffelfinger found a solution to it. According to one historian, Heffelfinger "rushed at the mighty engine, leaped high in the air, completely cleared its forward ramparts, and came down on top of the men on the inside of the wedge, whom he flattened to the ground, and among whom was the carrier of the ball." Walter Camp of Yale adopted the wedge for scrimmage play and modified it, making the "shoving wedge" (center). Harvard then contributed the most frightening formation of all in the "mass play" era, the "flying wedge" (below). Two groups of five players each started from 25 yards back, converged around the ball carrier at full speed, and they smashed into the opposition.

2 T Formation

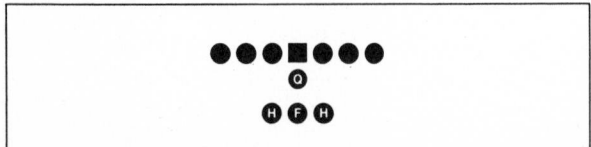

Football players who took the brunt of the wedges actually died on the playing field. "Mass play" led to the reforms requiring seven men on the line of scrimmage when the ball was centered—another innovation. The first T formation resulted.

3 Tackles Back

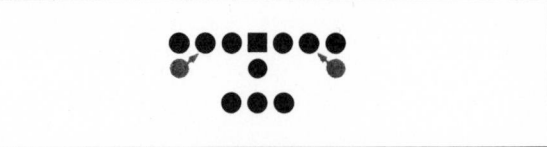

Tackles back, ends back, and guards back conformed to the regulation but tried to restore the momentum of the wedge by shifting linemen up to the line on the snap. This strategy led to the multiple shifts that followed. The tackles back formation shown here was copied from the 1920 book of plays of the Decatur Staleys coached by George Halas.

4 Minnesota Shift

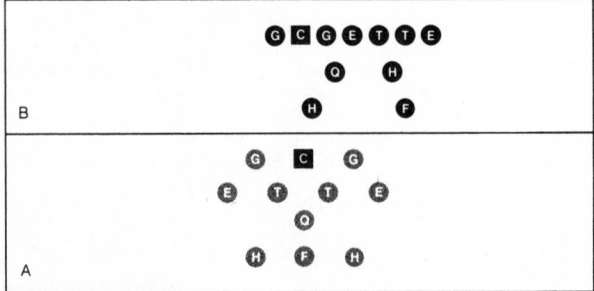

A brilliant coach at the University of Minnesota named Dr. Henry Williams introduced this shift in 1910, according to Alexander Weyand. The original position of the players is shown in diagram A, their eventual position in B.

5 Heisman Shift

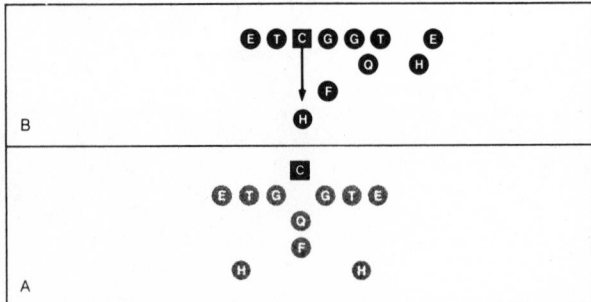

Another popular shift was this one invented by John Heisman, coach of Georgia Tech. He was later the person for whom the Heisman Trophy, given each year to the outstanding college player, was named.

6 Single Wing

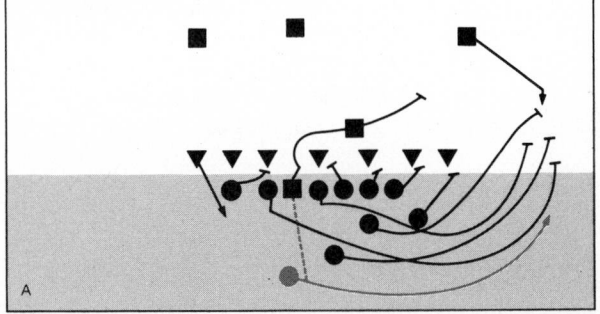

6 continued

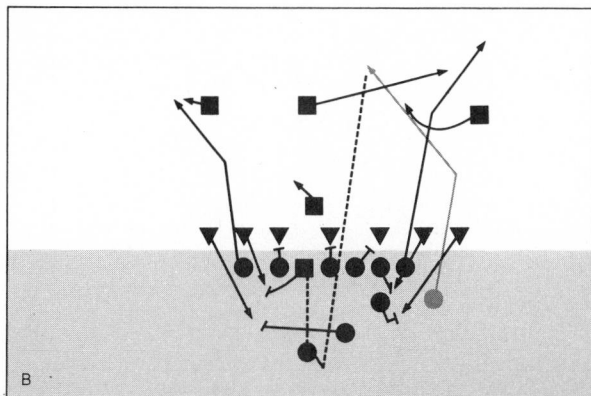

B

Invented by Glenn (Pop) Warner about 1906, it was one of the most successful formations ever and the typical running play (A) was, as Warner himself said, "one of the strongest plays ever developed." It still is today—The Green Bay sweep. A Princeton single wing tailback, Dick Kazmaier, won the Heisman Trophy in 1951 and the formation was still being played in 1954 by UCLA, Arkansas, and the Pittsburgh Steelers. A typical single wing pass is shown above.

7 Short Punt

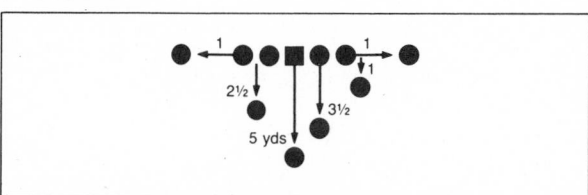

Punting played so large a part in strategy that it was not uncommon for teams to line up in punt formation all the time, hence this popular alignment of the twenties and thirties.

8 Rockne Shift

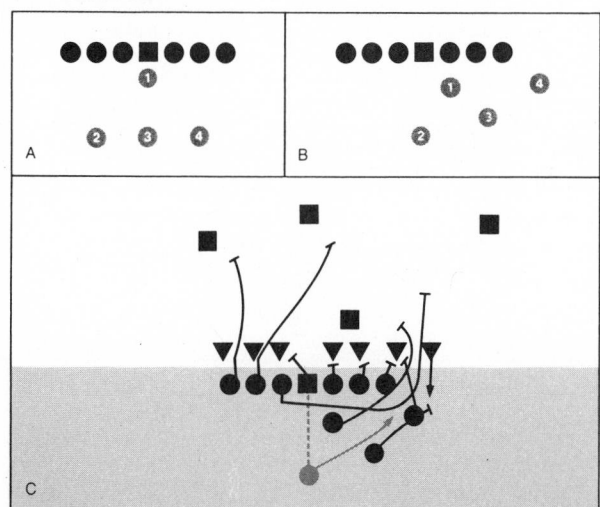

In the Notre Dame system devised by coach Knute Rockne about 1920, the Fighting Irish shifted from the T-formation (A) into their "box"

GLENN (POP) WARNER

Warner was the second most innovative coach after Stagg and he was also second to Stagg in most victories in college football at the time. Warner pioneered the single wing formation that Jim Thorpe brought into pro football with Canton in 1916, and the double wing that Sammy Baugh played with the Washington Redskins.

(B) and were then off on a devastating end run, practically all in one motion. The rules were eventually changed to require that all players be still a full second before the snap. Rockne's annual games against Howard Jones of USC displayed the best football to be seen anywhere and coaches flocked to the games, Braven Dyer of the *Los Angeles Times* wrote, "as young doctors would to the Mayo Clinic, to see the masters at work."

9 Double Wing

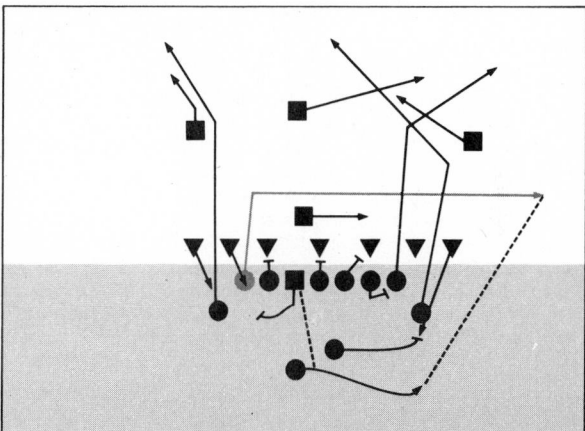

While Rockne was having a poor season in 1928, Glenn (Pop) Warner brought his Stanford University team to New York City to play Army. Warner had had the double wingback formation in his system perhaps as early as 1911, when he was at Carlisle, but did not play it on a regular basis until he moved to Stanford in the twenties. His team beat Army easily and the system was widely adopted while imitation of Rockne waned. Double wing laid the foundation for spread formations such as shotguns that would still be firing in the seventies and eighties.

10 Early Man-in-Motion

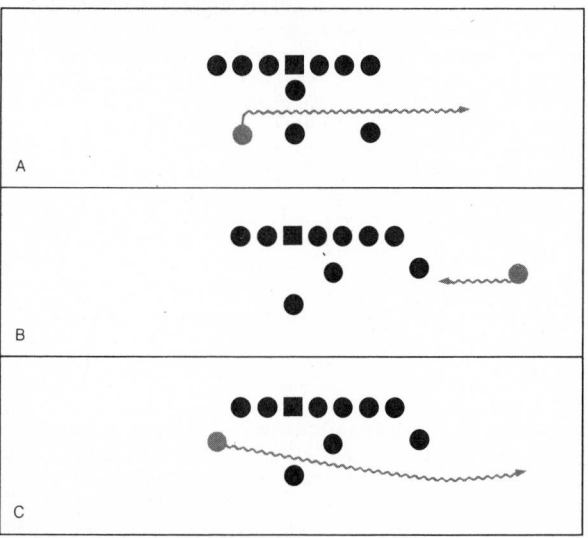

The element that the Chicago Bears would add to the ancient T formation in 1930 had actually been around a long time (A) in the turn-of-the-century T of Amos Alonzo Stagg at the University of Chicago, (B) in the single wing, and (C) in the double wing.

11 Bears' T With Man-in-Motion

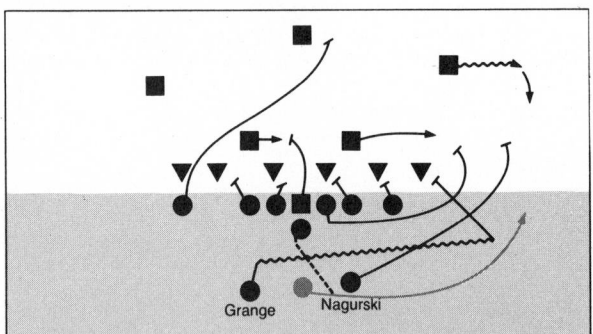

In 1932, two years after the Bears first used this formation, they played six ties, three of them scoreless, and Ralph Jones, the T-with-motion father, quit as coach. But this formation spread the defense, then light years behind in development; put little, fast men out wide where they could get running room or get downfield for passes; and reinstated a quarterback under the center. The play shown is a lateral to Bronko Nagurski with Red Grange, the man-in-motion, making a crackback block on the defensive end.

12 Invention of Inbounds Lines

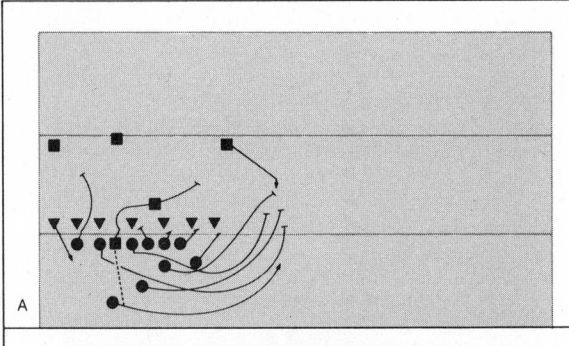

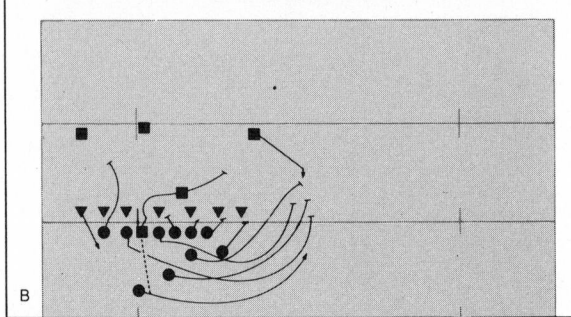

The Inbounds lines, or hashmarks, limed onto the dirt floor of the Chicago Stadium in 1932 for the Bears-Spartans playoff, turned coaches into strategists who studied not only power, speed, and deception, but also geography. Plays that ended near the sideline or with the runner going out of bounds had started at the sideline (A); they now began 10 yards in from the sideline (B). Also, the field now had a "short" side and "wide" side of predictable breadth; the side most favored by a team in its running game could be studied by scouts. And hashmarks set up points of reference for players taking their stances or running pass routes, and defenders mapping out the territorial zones they would cover.

13 The Five-Three Defense

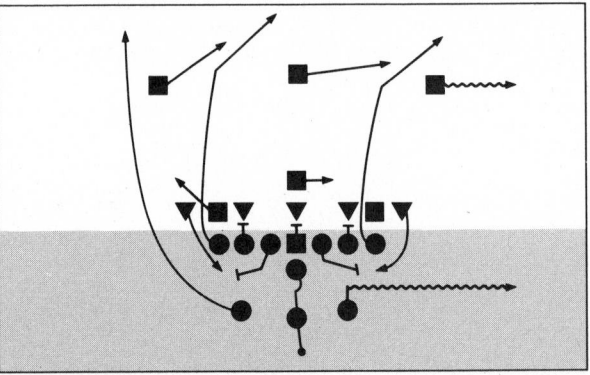

Defenses had previously placed nine, eight, seven, or six men on the line of scrimmage. To reduce that number to five, in order to get more men back in pass protection, was a brazen step. It was probably first taken at Temple in 1930 by a line coach named John (Ox) DaGrosa. The New York Giants copied it in 1934. This became the standard NFL defense for a decade. The five-three had a middle linebacker—30 years before Bill George, Sam Huff, Les Richter, and Joe Schmidt.

14 Don Hutson's First Play in the NFL

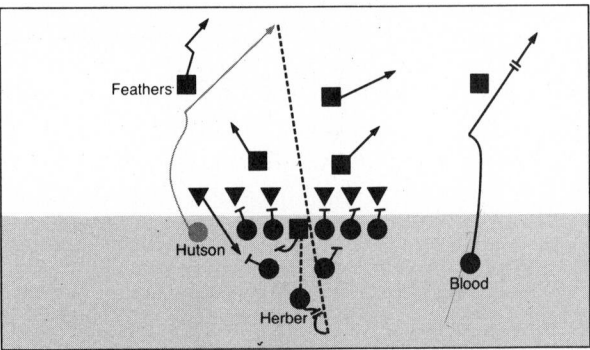

Don Hutson, the Green Bay Packers' great end, scored an 83-yard touchdown on his first play from scrimmage in the NFL. Chicago Bears safety Beattie Feathers stole a look at Arnie Herber's fake to Johnny Blood, and at that moment Hutson, who had been loping along, went into high gear and left Feathers far behind. *True Sport* said, "Herber's pass, counting his retreat, as checked on motion pictures, went 66 yards in the air."

15 Dutch Meyer Spreads

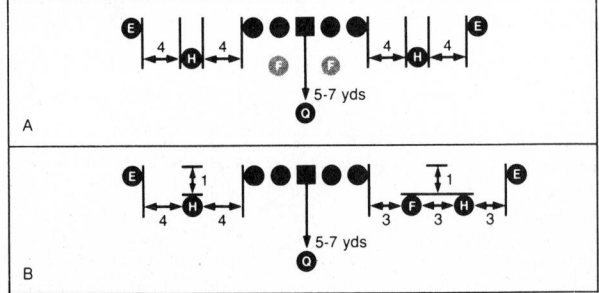

It is wrong to say that Clark Shaughnessy or anyone else in pro football invented the "three-end offense." Three represented a modest number

EARLE (GREASY) NEALE

Neale was the second NFL coach after George Halas to adopt the T formation. Neale built a power offense around Steve Van Buren that grew stronger each year in the forties and eventually won NFL championships in 1948 and 1949. He also devised the Eagle defense, which was one of the forerunners of the four-three.

15 continued

of ends in the spread formations played by Dutch Meyer at Texas Christian University in the thirties. These were the formations played by TCU quarterbacks, or tailbacks, Sammy Baugh and Davey O'Brien.

16 A Typical Sammy Baugh Pass

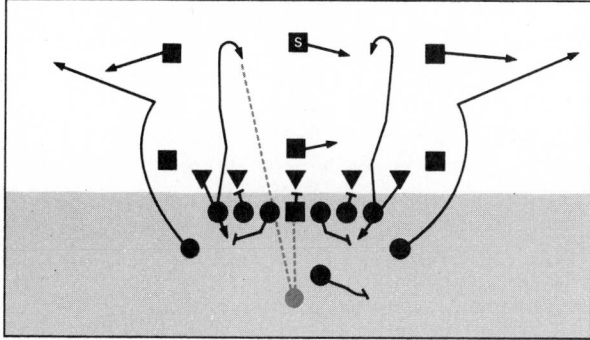

Baugh picked apart the five-three defenses of the NFL as a rookie with the Washington Redskins in 1937. He passed for 335 yards in the championship game against the Bears.

17 Steve Owen's A Formation

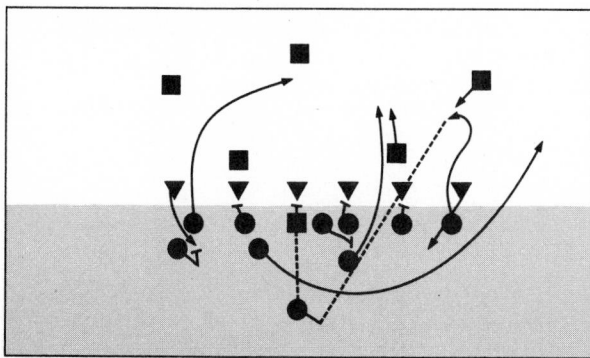

The A formation of coach Steve Owen of the New York Giants had unusual line splits, a line strong to one side and a backfield strong to the other, and a direct snap to the left halfback instead of a T-quarterback. Owen played it and other formations from 1937 to 1952. As a stunt, he once had his team run three plays from three different formations.

18 Oklahoma Defense

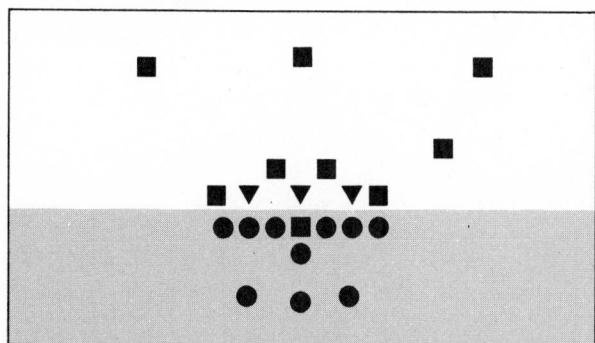

Begun at the University of Oklahoma by coach Bud Wilkinson, probably in 1947, it strongly influenced the new pro defenses that sprouted

immediately afterward. It became the dominant defense in college football for the next 20 years but was scoffed at by the pros until Miami adopted it in 1972 and had a 17-0 season. It is alternately dismissed as weak against the run. However, the pros have refined it immensely; today it is known as the 3-4.

19 Eagle Defense

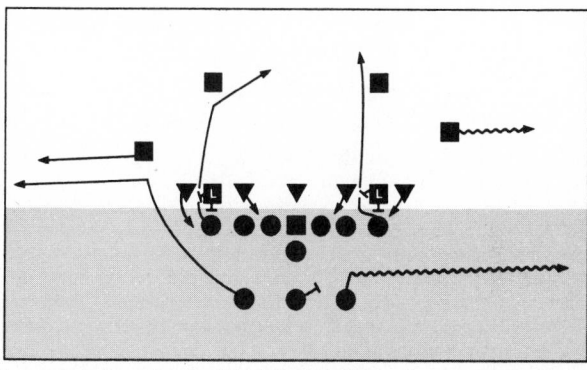

It was first played by the Philadelphia Eagles and coach Greasy Neale about 1948. It evolved out of the five-three and it had the first four-deep secondary, but no middle linebacker. The outside linebackers no longer had to try to cover deep passes but instead harassed and delayed receivers and covered short passes.

20 Steps Taken Against the Eagle

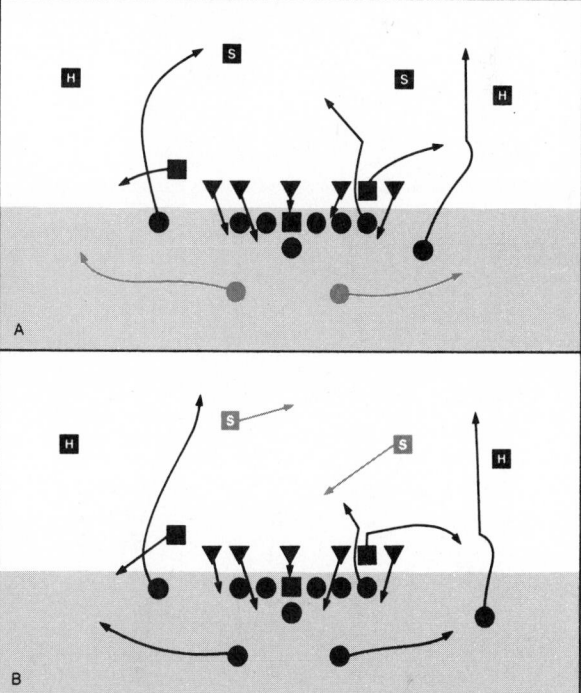

It was woefully weak over the middle. The offenses simply sent their backs to the flat areas to lure the linebackers away, and get an end free in the middle (A). The defense reacted by having one safety fill that area; the other covered behind him if the end went deep, perhaps the start of "combination" pass defense in the NFL (B).

STEVE OWEN

The development of the Eagle defense of Neale and the "umbrella" defense of Owen coincided with the advent of unlimited free substitution in pro football. These three factors combined to bring about the style of defense in the NFL in the 1950s and 1960s. Owen coached the New York Giants from 1931 until 1953.

21 Otto Graham Passes

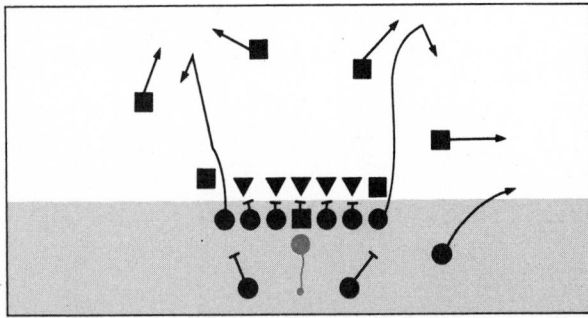

The Eagle was very important as a defense that offenses exploited and out of which much of modern football evolved. Its next challenge was quarterback Otto Graham and the Cleveland Browns, who met Philadelphia for the first time in 1950. Cleveland won 35-10 and its ends, Mac Speedie and Dante Lavelli, were the first to run "comeback" patterns—17 yards downfield, then turning back for the ball at 15 yards. The Eagles had not seen such pass routes before.

22 Umbrella Defense

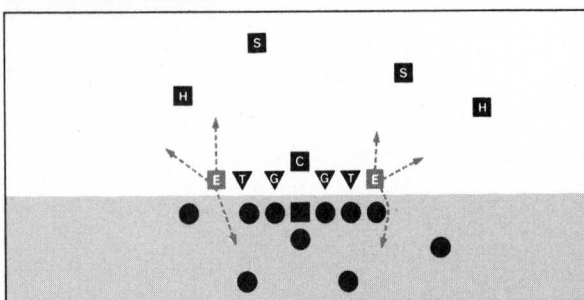

Steve Owen of the New York Giants devised it for the Browns in 1950 and shut them out once and also won a second game. The Giants' deep backs threw a figurative "umbrella" over the passing game, and their ends sometimes rushed and sometimes dropped off to cover passes, in the manner of later outside linebackers.

23 A Rams' Bomb to Hirsch

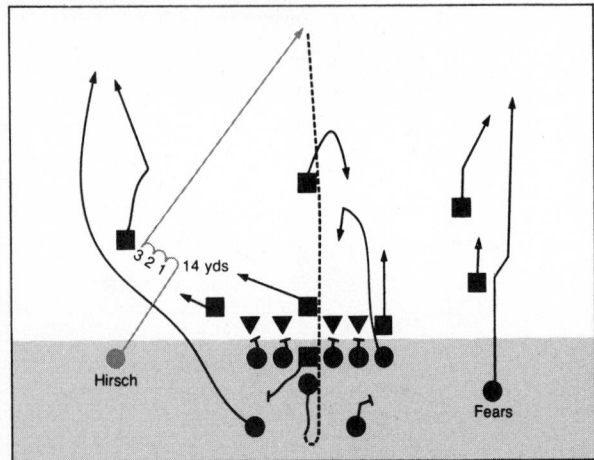

For all its offensive brilliance, Cleveland still played the outdated five-

three defense in the early fifties. Its three-deep secondary was no match for Los Angeles's great end Elroy Hirsch. He scored 17 touchowns during the 1951 season and Los Angeles won the championship from Cleveland. This pass route was Hirsch's favorite during his career.

24 Split T and the Belly Series

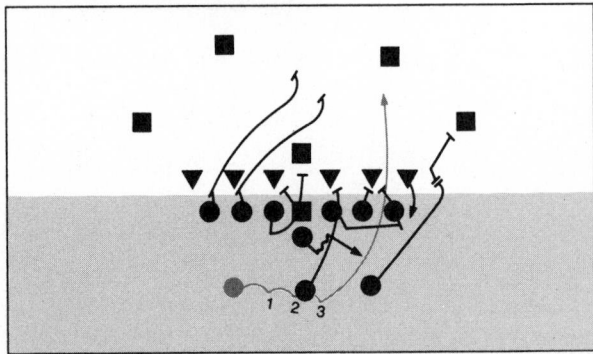

Innovative changes in the T formation had taken place at Missouri, Oklahoma, Maryland, College of the Pacific, and other institutions where football teams were using the split T formation and belly series. The quarterback slid down the line of scrimmage riding the ball in the belly of a back and left it there, kept it, handed off again, pitched, or ran with it. The collegiate triple option, wishbone, and veer systems of later years evolved out of the split T.

25 Continuing Changes in the Eagle

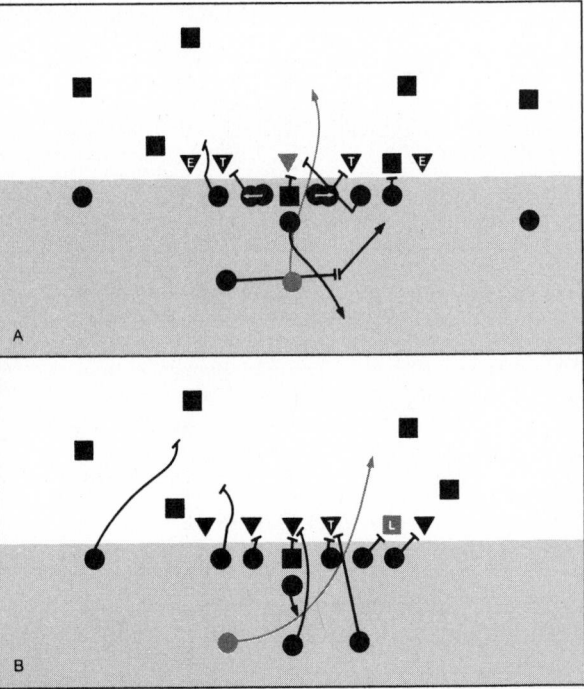

It was put to rest at last by the big line splits that the pros adopted as a result of the popularity of split T. These splits moved the offensive tackles out so far that the defensive middle guard found himself isolated, forced to try to stop the inside running plays alone (A). If his defensive tackles closed in to help, that isolated the outside linebacker (B).

PAUL BROWN

Brown is the professional coach most responsible for an important attitude of coaches of the 1960s and 1970s: that no aspect of organization can be ignored if the coach is to be successful. The careful filming and grading of plays and players and the dominance of the game from the side line are the results of Brown's influence.

26 Four-Three Defense

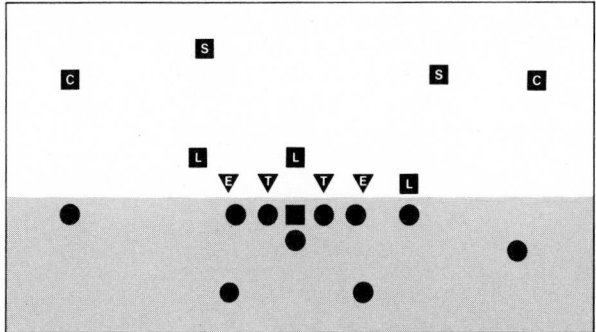

Teams playing the Eagle in the mid-fifties decided to drop their middle guard off and make him a middle linebacker. If their middle guard was unsuited for the new position, they found a player who was. This evolution in the Eagle was as much responsible for the adoption of the modern four-three defense as was the New York umbrella. The distinctive identity of each position in the four-three also crystallized as the result of free substitution, since it was now possible to send an entirely different team into the game to play defense.

27 Slot-T

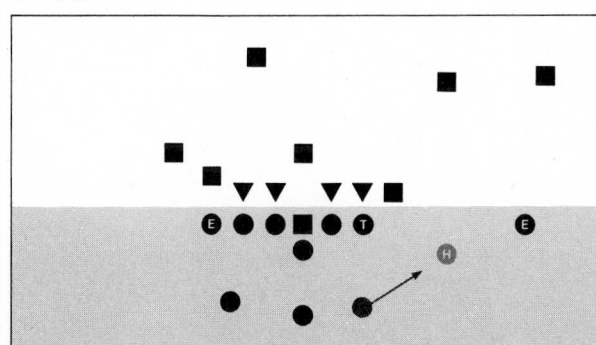

Two decades before, the Chicago Bears had removed one man from the offensive formation by putting him in motion. By the late forties, that player was being permanently stationed out wide, rather than going in motion into that position. He was the "flanker." An alignment placing him in a slot between the spread end and tackle was popular in the NFL throughout the fifties.

28 Three-End Offense

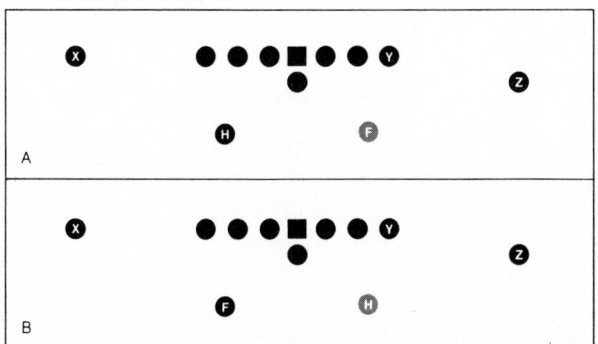

28 continued

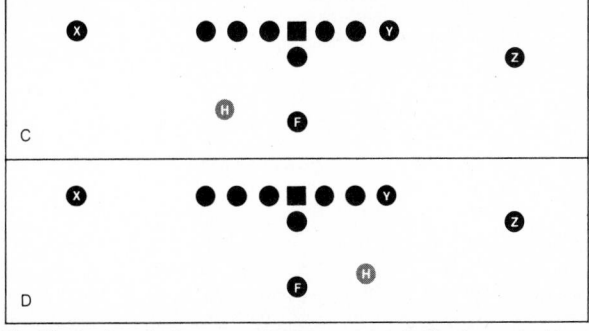

The "flanker" gradually came to be seen not as a halfback removed from the backfield but instead as a third end. Later, the terms "wide receiver" and "tight end" were adopted to name the three ends. Here are four of the most important three-end formations and the names given them in the various systems of language spoken by pro teams: (A) full, split right, or red; (B) half, split left, or green; (C) far, opposite, or brown; and (D) near, wing, or blue.

29 Pass Rush and Linebacker Blitz

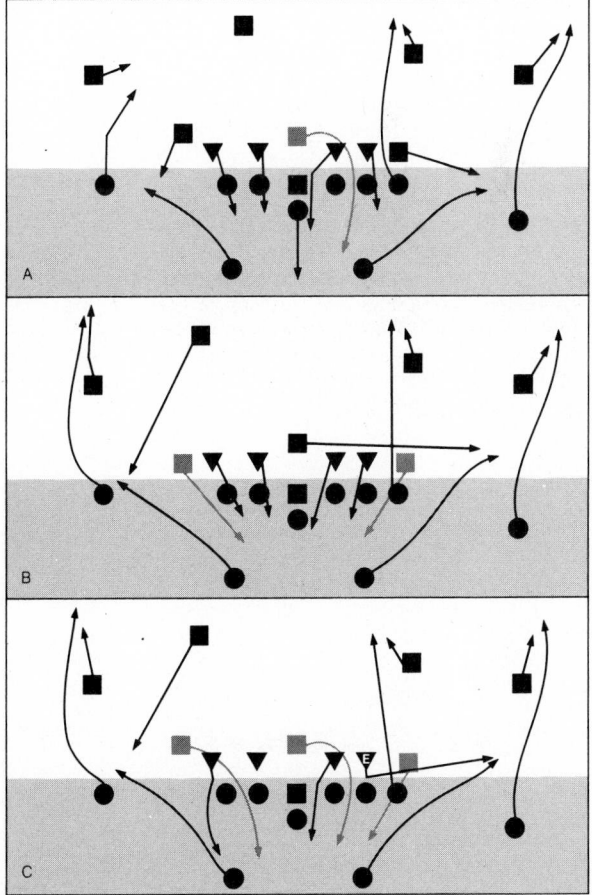

The offense had spread itself wider than ever and was increasingly

dependent on the pass. The defense now mounted such methods of rushing the passer as these: (A) the four linemen and the middle linebacker; (B) the line and the outside linebackers; and (C) actual "blitz," the line and all three linebackers.

30 Man-for-Man Coverage

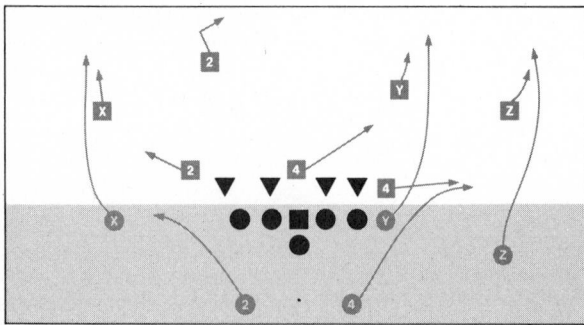

This is man-for-man defense at its simplest and in a form played widely in the fifties in the NFL. The numerals 2 and 4 are the offensive backs and the coaching symbols X, Y, and Z stand for the wide receivers and tight end. Corresponding symbols on defensive players name who is responsible for each.

31 Zone Defense

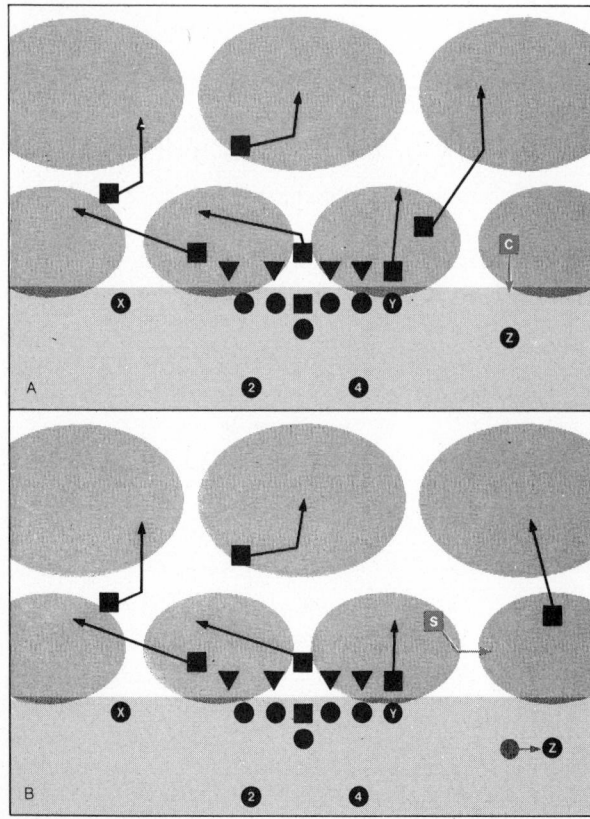

The most basic type of zone defense is "rotation," and was played expertly by the Detroit Lions in the fifties. The defense has "rotated" to the side of the tight end and flanker and there are four zones (oval areas) up

close and three deep. In diagram B, the flanker has taken a position so wide that if it were a running play he could block down on the cornerback. Seeing this, the defense has changed its zone so the safety not the cornerback is up close. It is this swapping of coverage areas among cornerbacks, safeties, and linebackers that has made zones grow in complexity and produce great problems for young quarterbacks.

32 Green Bay Sweep

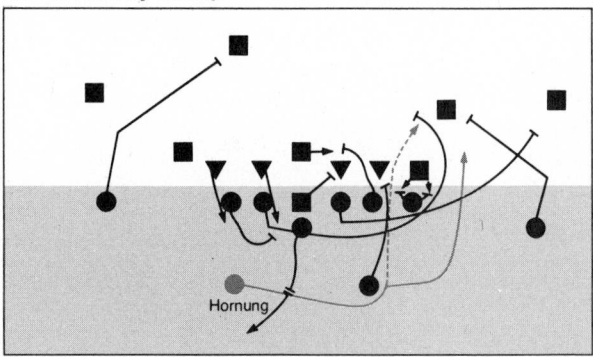

When Vince Lombardi became coach of the Green Bay Packers in 1959, he was convinced that defenses had become so sophisticated that it was time for the offense to go back to the basics—to avoid frills and to carry out fundamentals well. These principles were borne out in his Green Bay sweep, with Paul Hornung carrying the ball. Hornung followed pulling guards Fuzzy Thurston and Jerry Kramer and fullback Jim Taylor in a devastating end run. It is interesting to compare the play with those of Warner and Rockne in diagrams 6A and 8C.

33 Weakside Slant and Its Companion Play

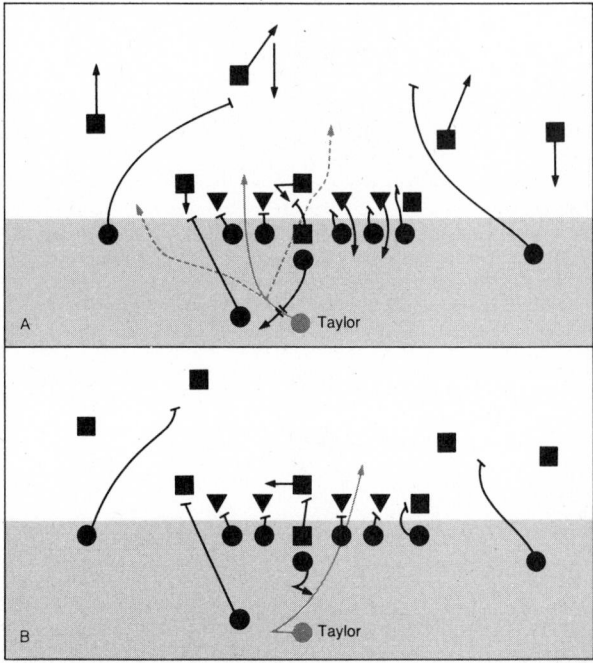

The weakside slant (A) and the companion play it set up (B) became the heart of the Packers' offense after defenses found ways to stop the sweep. Jim Taylor "ran to daylight" where he found it. Jim Brown of Cleve-

VINCE LOMBARDI

Lombardi reinstated the simple verities of football in the NFL and reversed the trend to a more and more complicated sport. He took the Green Bay Packers and the entire game back to the basics and won by running the same plays over and over—strongside sweeps with Paul Hornung and weakside slants with Jim Taylor.

33 continued

land, Taylor's contemporary, also ran the weakside slant among other plays, and the play is the most basic one in pro football today.

34 Shotgun

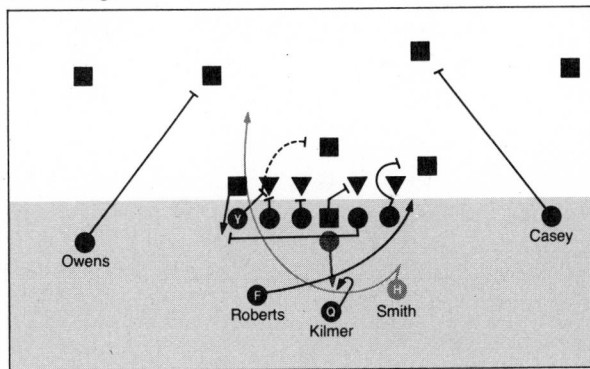

The patterns of play in the four-three defense and three-end offense had grown rather stereotyped by 1960. That was one reason why coach Red Hickey of San Francisco created what he called the shotgun formation. The quarterback stood back from the center as in the formations of old. San Francisco played it with success for part of 1960 and 1961, until it was stopped by Chicago and Pittsburgh and 49ers' players lost confidence in it. Bill Kilmer, John Brodie, and Bobby Waters alternated at quarterback in the system. The play shown here is a shovel pass to halfback J. D. Smith, a play that was also a favorite of the Dallas Cowboys when they revived the shotgun in 1975 and played it part of the time while winning the NFC Championship.

35 Shotgun-inspired Spreads

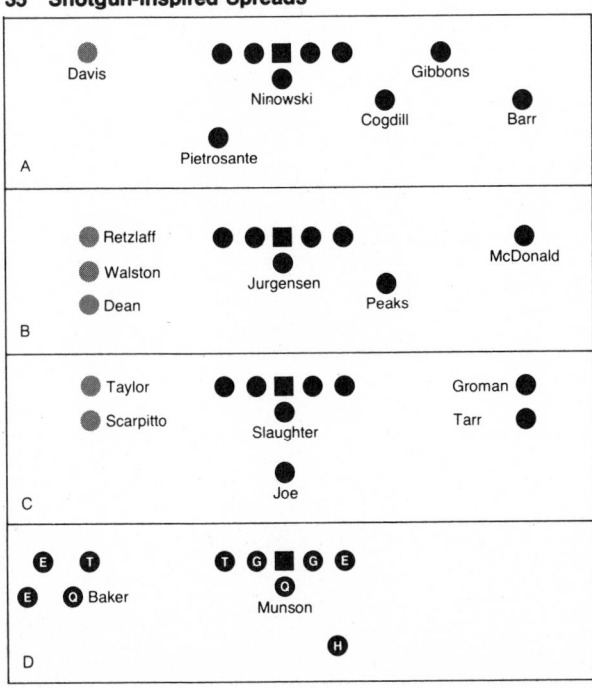

A variety of formations that, like the shotgun, spread receivers and running backs across the field but unlike the shotgun kept the quarterback under

center, sprang up around the league. Examples shown here are (A) Detroit's "Zephyr" formation of 1961, an attempt to exploit the speed of former Olympic sprinter Glenn Davis, "the Zephyr"; (B) Philadelphia's "stacked deck" of the same season, designed for the Eagles' young quarterback Sonny Jurgensen; (C) Denver's "double stack" in the American Football League; and (D) Los Angeles's "outpost and settlement" of 1964. In the latter, the group of players around the ball and quarterback Bill Munson was the "settlement" and the group around a second quarterback, Terry Baker, was the "outpost."

36 Two That Endured—T Double Wing and Triple Wing

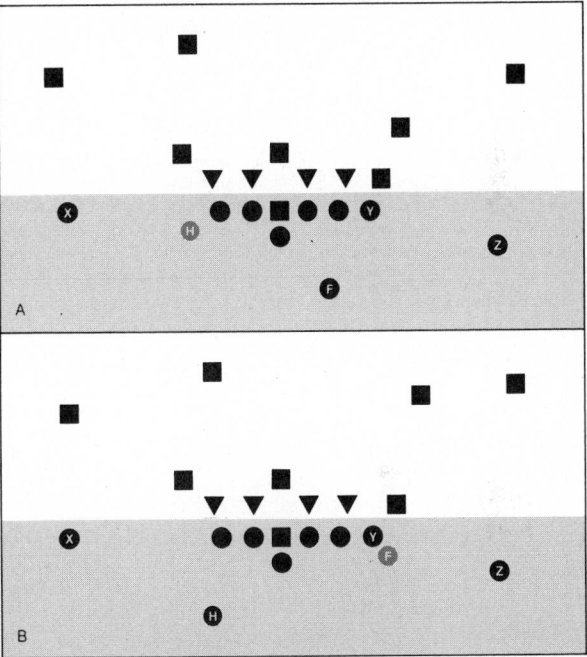

The double wing and triple wing survive today from the era of the original shotgun and its imitations. Triple wing is also called "trips." In double wing (A), the halfback is up close to the line, and in triple wing (B) it is the fullback who is up close to release quickly for a pass. The names for each of them lack real literal meaning, having been plagiarized from the past and Pop Warner.

37 I and Its Varieties

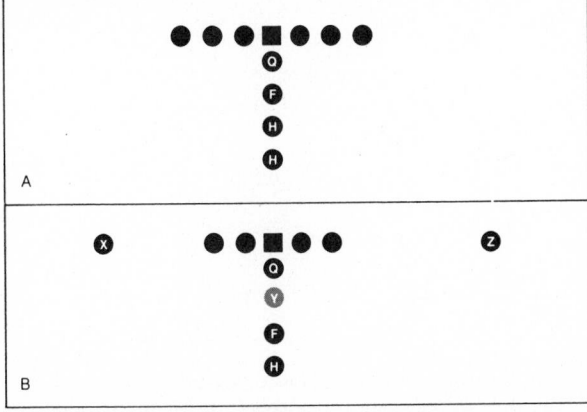

513

TOM LANDRY

Landry became the antithesis of Lombardi and his great rival for preeminence among coaches in pro football in the sixties. Lombardi was fundamental, Landry complex and computer-oriented. Landry experimented with multiple offense, flexed and gapping defenses, and motion and shifts to delay tipping the strength of formations.

37 continued

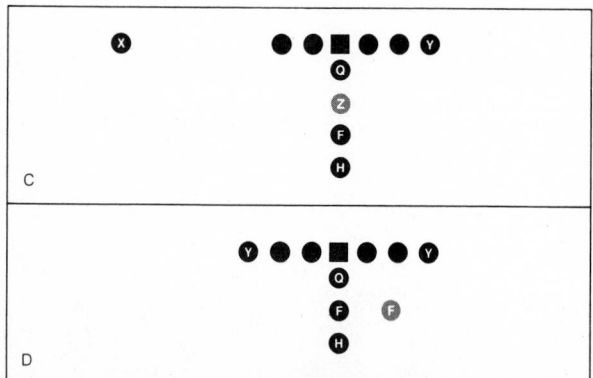

The I formation popular in the NFL today was invented by an obscure college coach named Tom Nugent in the fifties. Hank Stram of the Kansas City Chiefs was the first to place his tight end in the I (B). The Dallas Cowboys frequently have lined up their flanker in the I (C) before shifting. The power I (D) that John McKay perfected at USC is seen in the NFL in short-yardage situations.

38 Wishbone

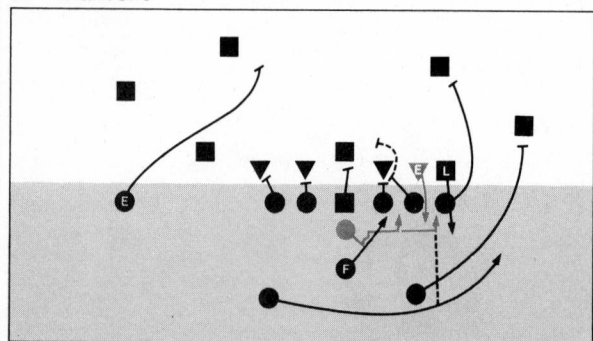

The wishbone reinstated balance in college football and made it more exciting after introduction of the offense by the University of Texas in 1968. But it is a grind-it-out, ball-control offense with only one spread end compared to at least two, and often more, in professional formations.

39 Relocated Hashmarks

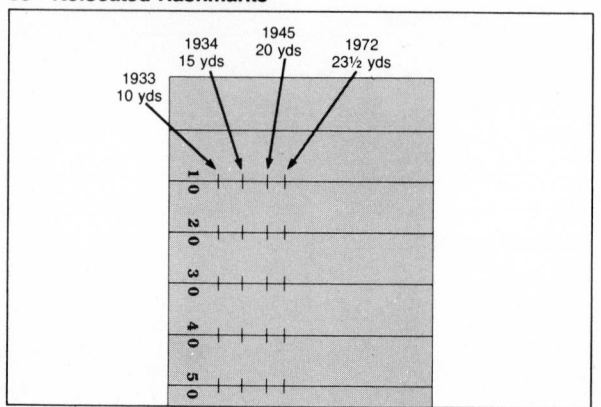

Moving NFL hashmarks in 1972 helped the offense. The defense previously had an advantage on any run or pass to the narrow side of the field.

The 1972 move was actually the third by the NFL since 1933. Hashmarks on college fields remain at a point about 17½ yards from the sideline.

40 Evolution of a Cowboys' Play

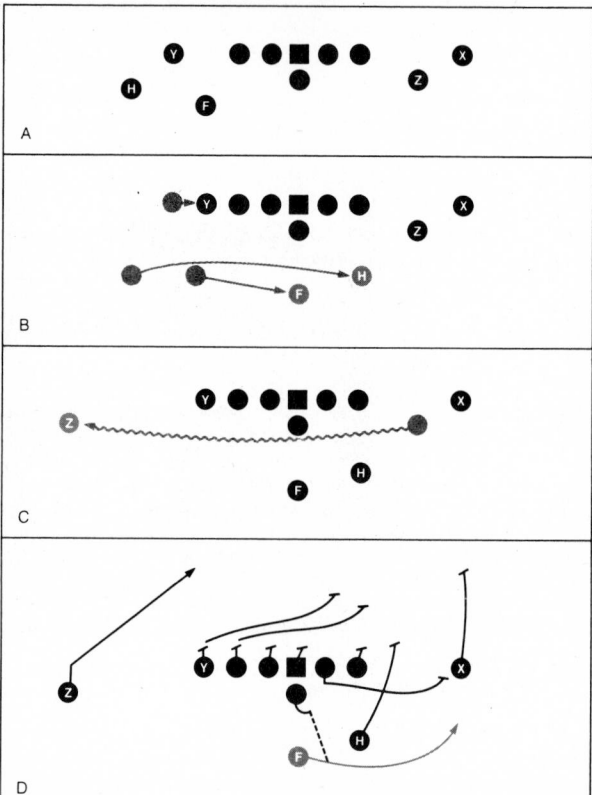

Man-in-motion, which A. A. Stagg used, and shifts, which Dr. Henry Williams popularized, are part of the "preshift" used today by the Dallas Cowboys. It is one of the most unique strategies now being played. Here is an example of how it works: (A) the backs and receivers leave the huddle and line up this way; (B) the backs shift as shown; (C) the flanker goes in motion; and (D) the Cowboys are now in their brown left formation, ready to run their play.

Pro Football Language

Pro football teams have their own language. It is different from the language of the sports page or the television booth. It is strange, even bizarre. And it may be the single most complex aspect of the sport.

The following terms are authentic. Coaches and players actually speak them to each other. Terms such as these and others that teams adopt for a season make up the jargon they speak—the secret language of their meetings, practices, and games. But if coaches and players can understand pro football language, others can, too. In doing so, it is possible to gain greater insight into the true nature of the game and how its people think.

A 1. The halfback on the left side. 2. The onside guard pulling and blocking a cornerback or safety.

ace A formation with two wide receivers on one side, a third wide receiver or back on the other side out wide, and one back in the backfield.

alley The area between the hashmarks and the field numbers, from the line of scrimmage to 15 yards downfield.

audible A call changing the offensive and defensive plan at the line of scrimmage.

away The remaining back going away from the point of attack.

ax Knocking down a receiver.

B The back on the right side.

back A call by Mac to change the defense from a called front to a four-three front.

backer A linebacker.

Ben A block by a back on a defensive end.

blast Pass rush by defensive tackles.

blitz Jill or Sam dogging.

blue A formation with the fullback behind the quarterback and the halfback on the strongside; same as near, strong, two left, and wing.

Bob A block by a back on a backer.

bomb A long pass intended to be a touchdown.

bomber Force by a backer; same as bronco.

bootleg The quarterback moving with the ball away from the flow.

boss A block by the near back on the first defensive back to show.

both near A formation with both X and Z one to three yards from the offensive tackles.

bronco Force by a backer; same as bomber.

brown A formation with the fullback behind the quarterback and the halfback on the weakside; same as far, four right, and opposite.

Buck The backside or weakside linebacker; same as Wanda and Willie.

Buck ax Buck knocking down a receiver.

Buck I Buck dogging.

buzz A linebacker covering passes; same as drop.

call A command.

check with me A call by the quarterback in the huddle telling the team he will audible a play at the line of scrimmage.

Cleo 1. Force by a cornerback; same as cloud and crash. 2. A block by a wide receiver on a cornerback.

close The alignment of a slot receiver in tight less than three yards from the tackle.

cloud Force by a cornerback; same as Cleo and crash.

club A block by a tackle on a middle linebacker.

combo Combination pass coverage by Jill and Sam on Y and the strongside linebacker.

corner The deep outside zone of the field.

counter A play in which one or more backs move away from the point of attack.

crackback A block by a wide receiver on a linebacker. Illegal.

crash Force by a cornerback; same as Cleo and cloud.

cross A call alerting the defense that a receiver is crossing shallow.

cutback Maintaining inside position on a running back and tackling him when he turns inside; same as fill.

deep middle The middle one-third of the field from 15 yards from the line of scrimmage to the goal line; same as post.

delayed sweep A sweep with backfield deception and which develops late.

dog Pass rush by defensive players other than linemen.

double wing A formation with two wide receivers on each side and only the halfback in the backfield behind the quarterback; same as dual, deuce, and duce.

down A block by the tight end and tackle one man farther in than usual, the tight end now blocking the defensive end and the tackle blocking the defensive tackle.

draw A running play with a delayed handoff and delayed blocking off an initial action that shows pass.

drop A linebacker covering passes; same as buzz.

dual Same as double wing.

duce Same as double wing and dual.

eat A double team block by a tight end and tackle on a defensive end.

even 1. A defensive front with tackles head on the offensive guards and ends head on the offensive tackles. 2. Ordinary run blocking with each lineman responsible for the defender in front of him. 3. A block by the onside guard pulling and blocking a cornerback or safety, with the tackle going through on the middle linebacker and the center cut-blocks.

F 1. A series or family of running plays in which the fullback hits over the onside guard as a blocker, faker, or ball carrier. 2. A replacement block by a back on a defensive tackle.

fan The areas of the field between the flats and the corners.

far 1. A formation with the fullback behind the quarterback and the halfback on the weakside; same as brown, four right, and opposite. 2. A position of the weakside back more than three yards from the tackle.

fill Maintaining inside position on a running back and tackling him when he turns inside; same as cutback.

fire A call by a defensive player as soon as he has made an interception; same as oskie.

five-three A defense with five linemen and three linebackers.

flanker Z.

flare action The coordinated movement of running backs to block dogging linebackers, or if there are none, to go out for passes.

flat The area of the field from the line of scrimmage to a point eight yards downfield and, horizontally, from two yards outside the field numbers on each side of the side lines.

flex 1. A defense with the linemen staggered on and off the line of scrimmage. 2. The alignment of X only three to six yards from the tackle.

flip 1. A quick lateral pass to a back in the two or four position. 2. A series or family of plays built around that play. 3. A block by the onside tackle on the cornerback or safety.

float Alignment of Z three to six yards from Y; same as X in flex.

flood Putting more than one receiver in a zone so the defender playing that zone can't cover them all.

flop Change sides.

flow 1. The direction of play. 2. Movement of the remaining back or backs to the side of the point of attack. 3. A series or family of plays with the backs moving toward the same side.

flux A formation with X flexed and Z floating.

fly A back in motion to the weakside.

fold A combination block by the center and a guard against an even front, the center blocking on the de-

fensive tackle and the guard pulling through and blocking the middle linebacker.

force Turning a running play inside; same as support.

four position Behind the right offensive tackle.

four I A formation with the tight end and the two running backs in a line behind the quarterback.

four right Early name for formation in which the back in the four position moves out to become the flanker; same as brown, far, and opposite.

four-three A defense with four linemen and three linebackers.

front The defensive line and linebackers.

full 1. A formation with the running backs behind the tackles and the fullback in the four position; same as red and split right. 2. A series or family of plays in which attack as a blocker, faker, or ball carrier. 3. A block by a back or a defensive tackle or linebacker after the guard has pulled.

G A block by the onside guard, pulling and blocking the outside man on the line of scrimmage, usually the outside linebacker.

gadget A trick play.

gap 1. The space between two offensive linemen. 2. A defense with a man in every gap.

gap over A defense with the weakside defensive tackle moving into the weakside guard-center gap.

gap under A defense with the strongside defensive tackle moving into the strongside guard-center gap.

gas A double-team block by the center and a guard on a defensive tackle.

go A back in motion to the strongside.

gob A block by a guard on a backer; same as G.

gone A defense without a middle linebacker.

green A formation with the running backs behind the tackles and the halfback in the four position; same as half and split left.

gut A cross block by the onside guard and tackle, the guard going first.

half A formation with the running backs behind the tackles and the halfback in the four position; same as green and split left.

half zoom Z in motion toward the ball and the ball snapped before he reaches the tight end.

hole The area of the field between the hooks.

hook 1. A block by a tight end on a linebacker, preventing him from going outside. 2. The area of the field extending from the Y position to points 15 to 18 yards upfield.

I 1. A formation with two running backs in a line behind the quarterback. 2. A series or family of plays from the I formation.

I man A defensive tackle.

influence Deception by the offensive line, denying keys to the defense and leading it away from the play.

isolation block A block by a back on a defensive lineman who has been influenced.

Jack A combination block with the guard blocking the middle linebacker

Jerry A charge by a defensive tackle to the inside gap.

Jill The weakside or free safety.

jumbo A defense with six or more linemen.

key An alignment or movement telling a defensive player where the ball is going or what blocks to expect.

lead A block by a running back, preceding the other running back into the line and blocking the first defender in his path.

Les The left safety, who could be Jill or Sam.

Lex A stunt by Lon and Lin, crossing at the snap of the ball.

Lin The left I man or defensive tackle.

Linda Zone rotation left.

Link The left linebacker, who might be Stub or Buck.

Linki Link inside his normal position.

Numbering Positions and Plays

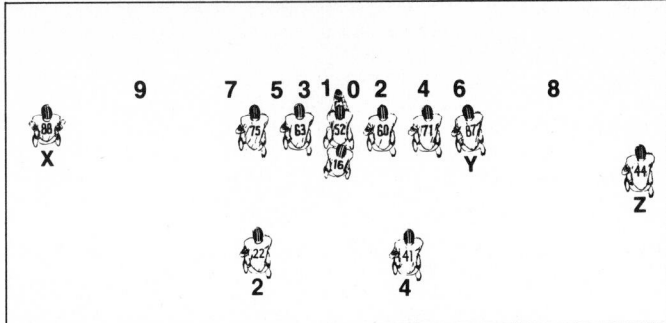

The play is the back plus the hole; 26 is the 2 back in the 6 hole.

Formations

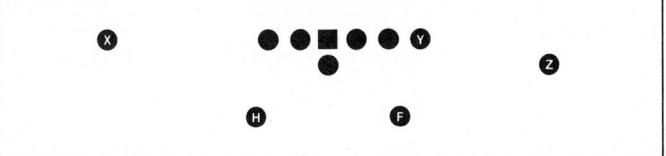

Full, red, or split right.

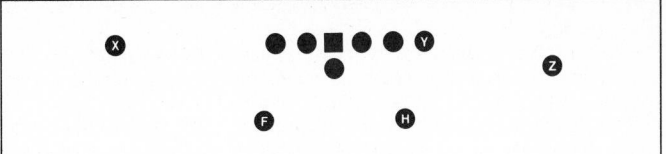

Half, green, or split right.

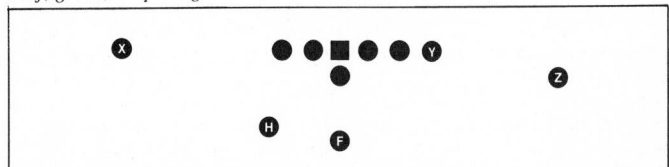

Far, brown, or opposite right.

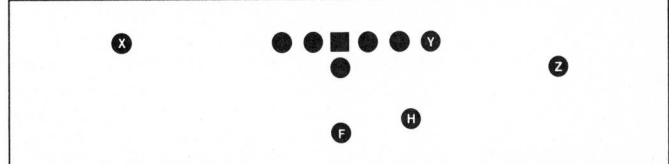

Near, blue, or strong right.

Types of Back Action

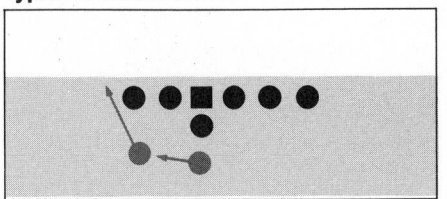

Flow action: both backs to the same side.

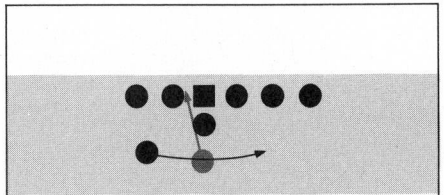

Full action: fullback over guard away from p.o.a.

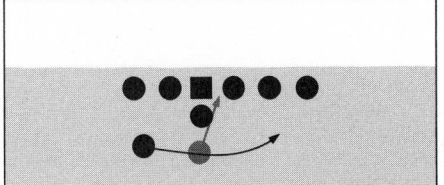

F action: fullback over guard on side of p.o.a.

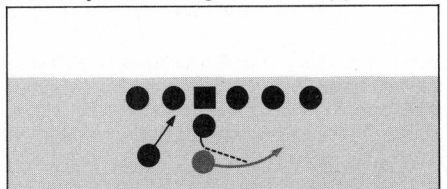

Toss action: toss to one back, other hits into line.

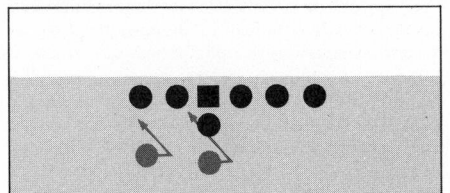

Counter action: one or more backs step away from point of attack, then counter.

Blocks

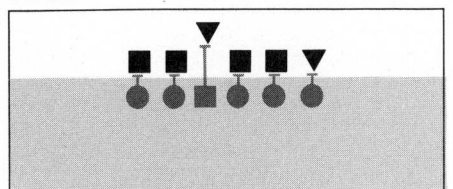

Man: ordinary man-for-man blocking.

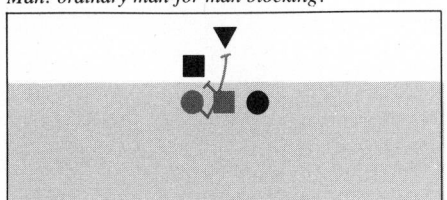

Scissors: cross-blocking.

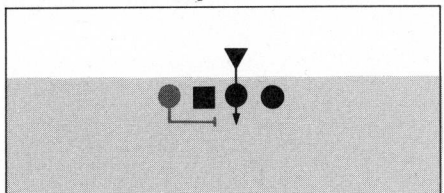

Trap: the off guard to the onside.

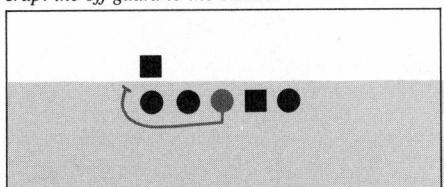

Gob: A guard on a backer.

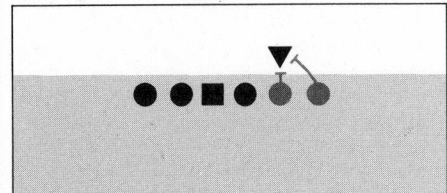

Double team: two men block one.

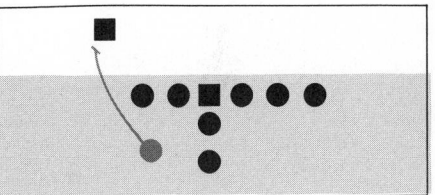

Bob: a back on a backer.

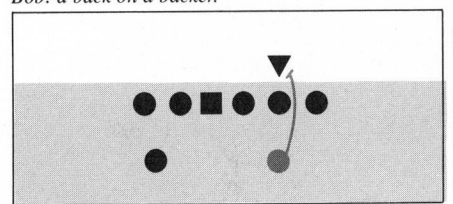

Ben: a back on an end.

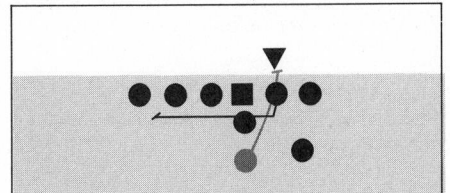

Replacement: a back on a tackle.

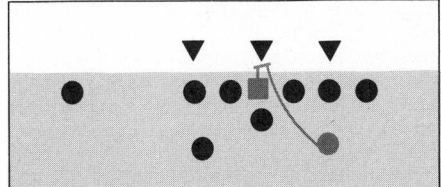

Wham: double team on nose tackle in 3-4.

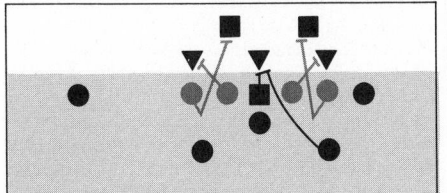

Double scissors: cross blocking against 3-4.

517

Pass Patterns

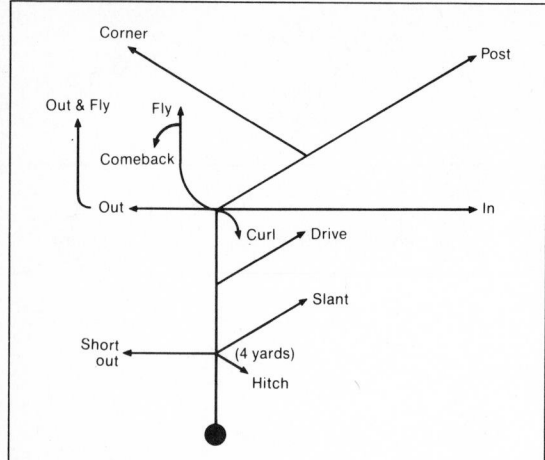

The "tree" of possible pass routes by a wide receiver.

Back Routes

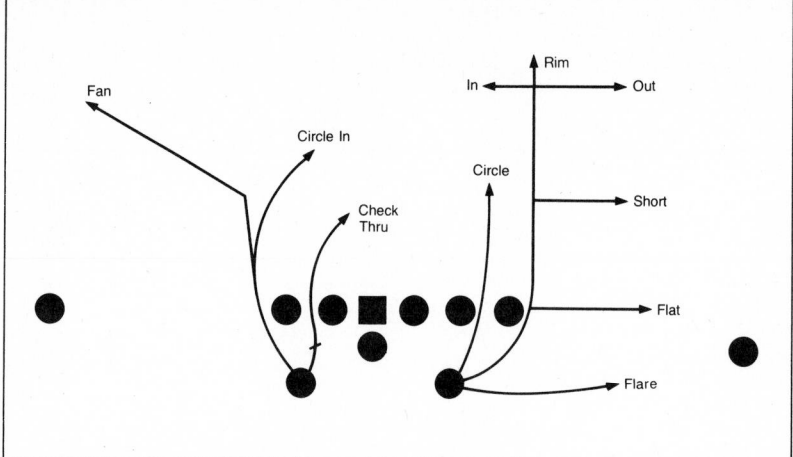

The "tree" of possible routes by a running back.

Types of Flare Action

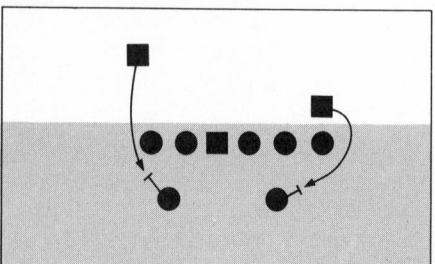

Both backs stay in to block.

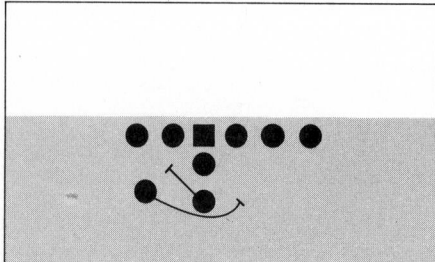

They cross, then block.

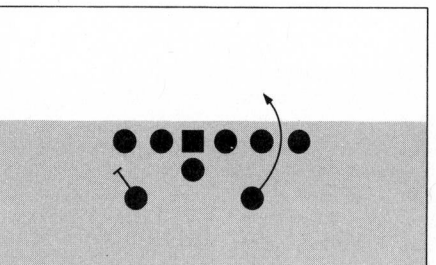

One blocks, the other runs a circle.

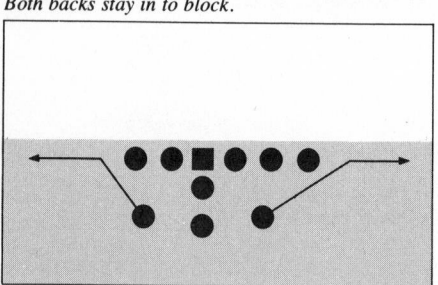

Both run to the flats.

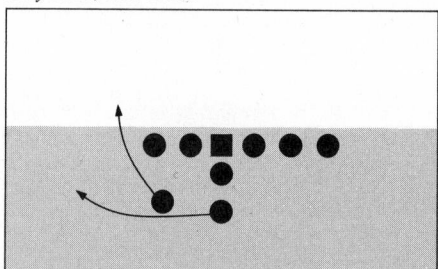

Both run to the weakside.

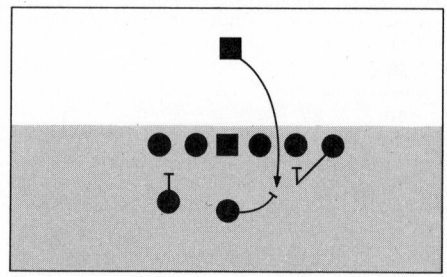

Seeing a dog coming, backs and Y stay home.

Linko Link outside his normal position.

lion A slant by both defensive tackles to the left.

log A block by pulling linemen, hooking the defender to the inside.

Lon The left O man or defensive end.

Lou The left cornerback.

Mac The middle linebacker.

Mac I Mac dogging.

mad dog Mac, Stub, and Buck dogging.

man-for-man Pass coverage in which each defender is assigned to a specific receiver for the entire play.

Mike A nose tackle.

misdirection Deception by the offensive backfield, denying keys to the defense and leading it away from the play.

mix A stunt by Mac and a defensive tackle.

mombo Combination pass coverage by Mac and the outside linebacker on Y and the first back out of the backfield.

near 1. A formation with the fullback behind the quarterback and the halfback on the strongside; same as blue, strong, two left, and wing. 2. Alignment of X only one to three yards from the tackle.

nickel A defense with five defensive backs.

nose tackle A lineman head on the center.

O A block by the offside guard, pulling to the onside and leading the back through the hole.

odd A defense that is not even, i.e., an over or under.

offside The side away from the play.

Okie A three-four defense.

O man A defensive end.

onside The side to which the play goes.

opposite A formation with the fullback behind the quarterback and the halfback on the weakside; same as brown, far, and four right.

option 1. Running without predetermining the hole in the line where the ball carrier must go, allowing him to run wherever he sees open space; same as running to daylight. 2. A running play in which the quarterback moves down the line and has the option to hand off, pitch, or run. 3. A play in which the runner has the option to run or pass. 4. Blocking in which the lineman carries the defender in the direction his own momentum is taking him rather than in a predetermined direction.

oskie A call by a defensive player as soon as he has made an interception; same as fire.

over A defense with the weakside defensive tackle head on the center and Mac head on the weakside guard.

peel A dogging linebacker or defensive back stopping his rush and covering an offensive back who releases for a pass.

pick A screen by a receiver on a defensive back to take him out of coverage.

pinch A charge by the defensive linemen to the inside.

pix Y when he is the only receiver on his side.

play action Plays in which the quarterback fakes a handoff and passes; same as play pass.

play pass Same as play action.

poc Alignment of Y one to three yards from the tackle.

port Early name for left defensive halfback.

post 1. The middle one-third of the field from a point 15 yards from the line of scrimmage to the goal line; same as deep middle. 2. The outside receiver on the two-receiver side of a slot formation. 3. A call by defenders to teammates that a receiver has broken for the deep middle.

power 1. Any formation with three running backs in the backfield. 2. Double-team blocking at the point of attack.

prevent Any defense designed specifically to stop long passes.

pro A four-three defense.

queen A combination block with the tackle blocking the middle linebacker.

Rat A right linebacker farther in than Ripi.

read See a key and interpret it.

red A formation with the running backs behind the tackles and the fullback in the four position; same as full and split right.

red dog Stub and Buck dogging.

replacement block A back filling the space left when a lineman pulls, blocking the defender in that gap.

Rex A stunt by Ric and Roy, crossing at the snap of the ball.

Ric The right I man or defensive tackle.

Rip 1. The right linebacker, who could be Stub or Buck. 2. A charge by Mike to the right.

Ripi Rip inside his normal position.

Ripo Rip outside his normal position.

Roger Zone rotation right.

Rose The right cornerback.

rotation Shifting zone coverage left or right.

Roy The right O man or defensive end.

rule blocking The coordinated action by which offensive linemen know substitute blocking assignments if the defense changes its alignment.

run to daylight Running without predetermining the hole in the line where the ball carrier must go, allowing him to run wherever he sees open space; same as option running.

Russ The right safety, who could be Jill or Sam.

Sam The strongside safety.

Sara The strongside linebacker; same as Stub.

scissors Cross-blocking.

scoop A block by an offside lineman toward the onside, usually against an odd front.

scramble screen A screen pass in which the tackles pass protect and the guards and center fake a roll or cut-block and scramble to set up a blocking wall left or right.

scrape Charge by a linebacker off the position of a defensive lineman.

screen A pass that develops behind the line of scrimmage, in which the rushers are allowed to penetrate while the offensive linemen fake blocks and then set up a wall for the receiver.

shield A block by a wide receiver on a cornerback.

shotgun A red formation with the quarterback seven to nine yards behind and taking a long snap from center.

shovel pass A pass behind the line of scrimmage to a receiver who then runs in a designated hole.

Sid The middle safety of a three-deep defense.

sky 1. Force by a safety; same as stone. 2. A block by a wide receiver on a safety.

slam The strongside defensive end charging to the inside.

slant 1. A planned charge by a defensive lineman to the left or right instead of straight ahead. 2. A running play hitting sharply off guard or tackle. 3. A series or family of plays built around that play.

slash A shield block by a wide receiver on a linebacker.

slot 1. A formation with both wide receivers on the same side; same as twin. 2. The inside receiver on that side. 3. The area between X and his tackle and, on the other side, between Z and Y, to points eight yards downfield.

split left A formation with the running backs behind the tackles and the halfback in the four position; same as green and half.

split right A formation with the running backs behind the tackles and the fullback in the four position; same as full and red.

split end X.

spread A formation with no running backs at all in the backfield with the quarterback.

Defensive Positions

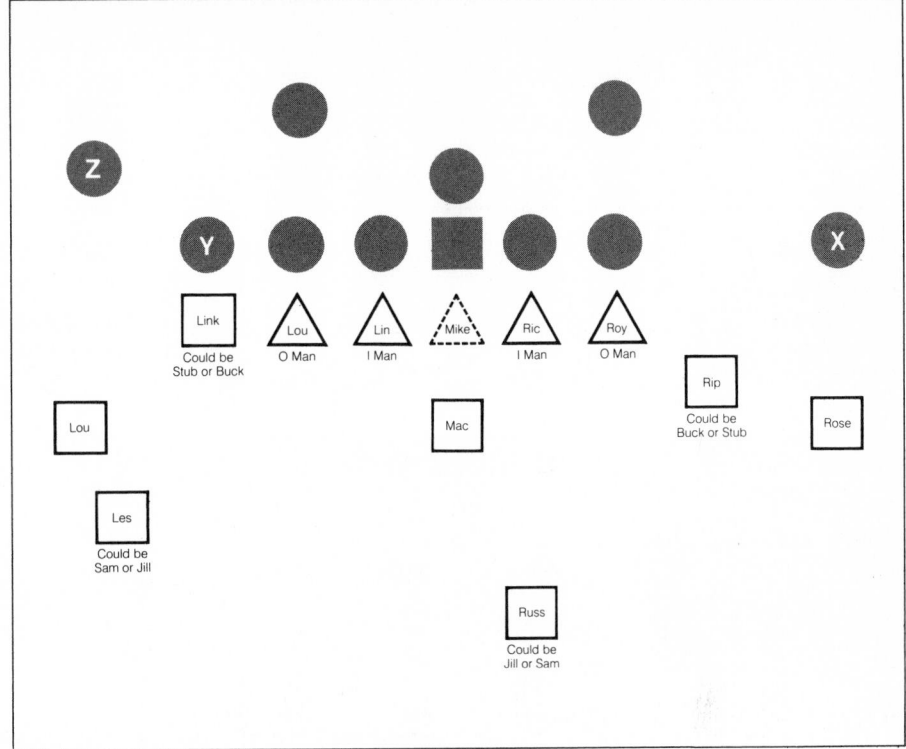

An example of pro football jargon for the 11 defensive positions.

Stunts

Lex: a stunt on the left side.

Rex: a stunt on the right side.

Tex: Lex and Rex at the same time.

Types of Forces

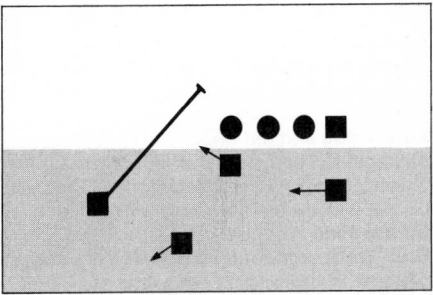

Crash: by the cornerback.

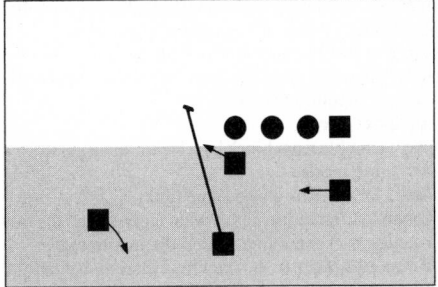

Sky: by the safety.

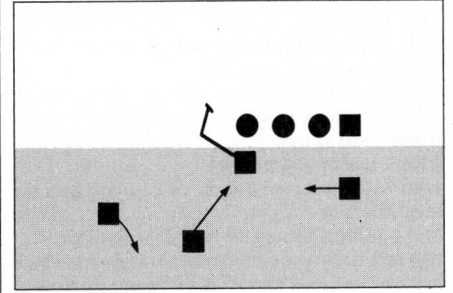

Bomber: by the backer.

ATLANTA FALCONS

Atlanta-Fulton County Stadium

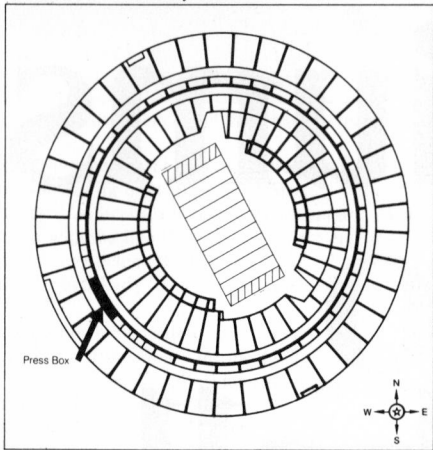

Press Box

Address: 521 Capitol Avenue, S.W., Atlanta, Georgia 30312.
Architects: Finch-Heery, Architects and Engineers.
Contractors: Thompson and Street, Inc.
Cost: $14.2 million.
Year Opened: 1965.
Origin of Stadium Name: For the city and county.
Owners: Atlanta and Fulton County.
Manager: Fulton County Recreation Authority.
Recent Improvements: None.
Planned Improvements: None.
Special Seating Facilities: Five private suites.
Miscellaneous Facts: None.
Playing Surface: Grass.
Scoreboard Manufacturer: General Indicator Corporation.
Scoreboard Features: Scores, messages.
Parking Lot Capacity: 4,000.
Tenants: Falcons and Atlanta Braves baseball team.
Football Seating Capacity: 60,763.
Falcons' Attendance Record: 60,022, January 5, 1981 vs. Dallas Cowboys in NFC Divisional Playoff Game.

BALTIMORE COLTS

Memorial Stadium

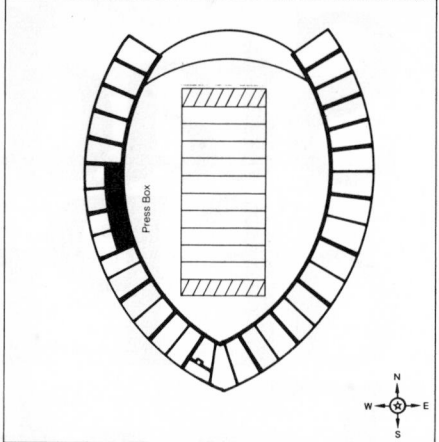

Press Box

Address: 1000 East 33rd Street, Baltimore, Maryland 21218.
Architects: Hall, Border, Donaldson–Architects.
Contractors: Joseph F. Hughes and Company, Inc.
Cost: $6 million.
Year Opened: 1954.
Origin of Stadium Name: In honor of the men and women who served in American wars.
Owner: Baltimore.
Manager: Baltimore Division of Recreation and Parks Department.
Recent Improvements: Fixed seats were replaced with new aluminum benches beginning in 1975.
Planned Improvements: Installation of moveable stands in right and left field.
Special Seating Facilities: None.
Miscellaneous Facts: None.
Playing Surface: Grass
Scoreboard Manufacturer: General Indicator Corporation.
Scoreboard Features: Scores, messages.
Parking Lot Capacity: 5,400.
Tenants: Colts and Baltimore Orioles baseball team.
Football Seating Capacity: 60,714.
Colts' Attendance Record: 60,763, December 24, 1977 vs. Oakland Raiders in AFC Divisional Play-off Game.

BUFFALO BILLS

Rich Stadium

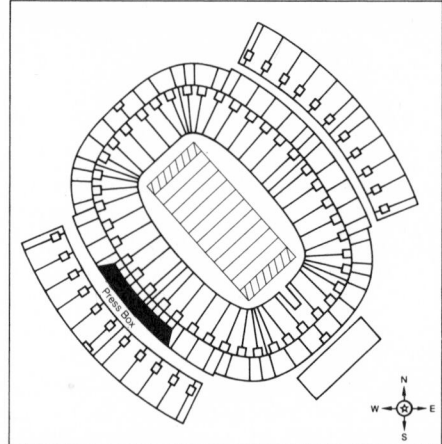

Press Box

Address: One Bills Drive, Orchard Park, New York 14127.
Architects: Finch-Heery, Architects and Engineers.
Contractors: Cowper Construction Company.
Cost: $22 million.
Year Opened: 1973.
Origin of Stadium Name: The stadium name was purchased by Rich Products Corporation at the time the stadium was built.
Owner: Erie County.
Manager: The Bills have an exclusive 25-year tenancy and are responsible for maintenance and operation costs.
Recent Improvements: The Bills spent $3 million on private suites, the scoreboard, landscaping, and office improvements.
Planned Improvements: None.
Special Seating Facilities: 34 private suites, each seating 25, leased on an annual basis.
Miscellaneous Facts: The playing field is 50 feet below ground level.
Playing Surface: AstroTurf.
Scoreboard Manufacturer: Conrac Corporation.
Scoreboard Features: Scores, messages; the scoreboard is 30 feet high and 105 feet wide and has message and instant replay capabilities.
Parking Lot Capacity: 14,000.
Tenants: Bills.
Football Seating Capacity: 80,020.
Bills' Attendance Record: 80,020, many times.

CHICAGO BEARS

Soldier Field

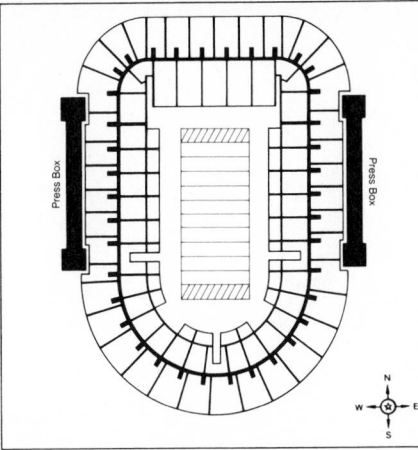

Address: 425 McFetridge Place, Chicago, Illinois 60605.
Architects: Holabird and Roche–Architects.
Contractors: Many during four periods of construction—1922, 1929, 1940, 1979-1982.
Cost: Approximately $10 million.
Year Opened: 1926.
Origin of Stadium Name: In honor of men and women who served in American wars.
Owner: Chicago.
Manager: Chicago Park District.
Recent Improvements: Over a four-year period (1979-1982) the stadium was completely remodeled.
Planned Improvements: A major renovation is under consideration.
Special Seating Facilities: 60 skyboxes.
Playing Surface: AstroTurf.
Scoreboard Manufacturer: White Way Sign.
Scoreboard Features: Scores, messages, cartoons.
Parking Lot Capacity: 8,000.
Tenants: Bears and Chicago Sting soccer team.
Football Seating Capacity: 64,519.
Bears' Attendance Record: 67,343, September 9, 1951 vs. Cleveland Browns; Soldier Field's football attendance record of 111,000 was set at its dedication date, November 27, 1926 at the twenty-ninth Army-Navy game.

CINCINNATI BENGALS

Riverfront Stadium

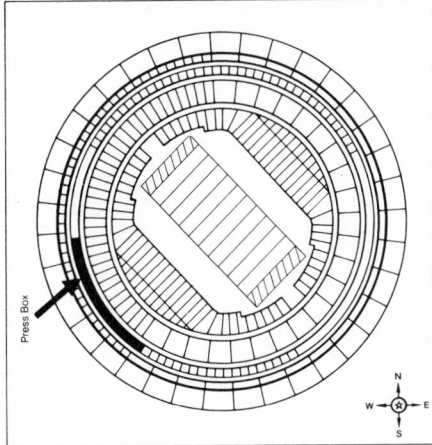

Address: 200 East Second Street, Cincinnati, Ohio 45202.
Architects: Heery and Heery–Architects.
Contractors: Huber, Hunt, and Nichols, Inc.
Cost: $45 million.
Year Opened: 1970.
Origin of Stadium Name: The stadium was renamed Charles P. Taft Riverfront Stadium in January, 1977 in honor of a former member of the city council for 30 years, and for its location on the Ohio River.
Owner: Hamilton County.
Manager: City of Cincinnati.
Recent Improvements: None.
Planned Improvements: None.
Special Seating Facilities: 20 private boxes.
Miscellaneous Facts: It encompasses more than eight acres; one section of the grandstand has moveable stands.
Playing Surface: AstroTurf.
Scoreboard Manufacturer: American Sign Indicator Corporation.
Scoreboard Features: Scores, messages, and animation through a computer; the scoreboard is 20 feet high and 180 feet wide.
Parking Lot Capacity: 4,500; 20,000 cars can be parked within a 12-block radius of the stadium.
Tenants: Bengals and Cincinnati Reds baseball team.
Football Seating Capacity: 59,754.
Bengals' Attendance Record: 60,284, October 17, 1971 vs. Cleveland Browns.

CLEVELAND BROWNS

Cleveland Stadium

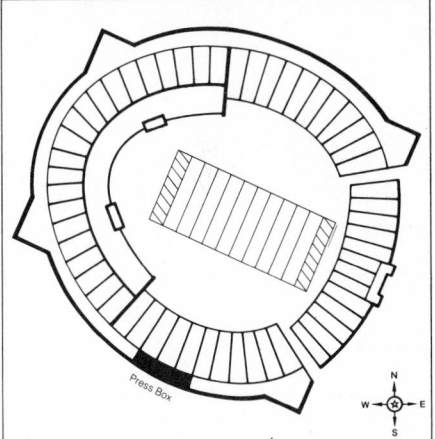

Address: West Third Street, Cleveland, Ohio, 44114.
Architects: Osborn Engineering Company.
Contractors: Osborn Engineering Company.
Cost: Original construction, $3.5 million; 1973-77 renovation, $7 million.
Year Opened: 1932.
Origin of Stadium Name: For the city.
Owner: Cleveland.
Manager: Cleveland Stadium Corporation.
Recent Improvements: A new scoreboard was installed in 1977.
Planned Improvements: None.
Special Seating Facilities: 108 private loges, each with a suite, seating 8 to 10 people.
Miscellaneous Facts: None.
Playing Surface: Grass.
Scoreboard Manufacturer: Cleveland Stadium Corporation, formed by the Browns to gather the component parts and construct a new scoreboard in 1977.
Scoreboard Features: Scores, messages, and a computerized game-in-progress capacity.
Parking Lot Capacity: 4,000.
Tenants: Browns and Cleveland Indians baseball team.
Football Seating Capacity: 80,322.
Browns' Attendance Record: 85,703, September 21, 1971 vs. New York Jets.

DALLAS COWBOYS

Texas Stadium

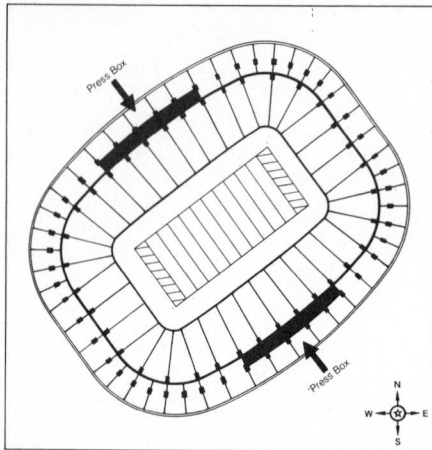

Address: Irving, Texas 75062.
Architect: A. Warren Morey and Associates.
Contractors: J. W. Bateson and Co., Inc.
Cost: $29.5 million.
Year Opened: 1971.
Origin of Stadium Name: For the state.
Owner: Irving, Texas.
Manager: Texas Stadium Corporation.
Recent Improvements: Installation of new playing surface in 1981.
Planned Improvements: None.
Special Seating Facilities: 178 private suites, each seating 12; each suite investment $50,000, with payment covering all years until 2008. Purchaser receives $60,000 return for $50,000 investment no later than 2008.
Miscellaneous Facts: A seven-and-three-quarter acre roof covers all seats. There is a two-and-one-quarter acre opening in the middle of the roof.
Playing Surface: Texas Turf.
Scoreboard Manufacturer: Conrac Corporation.
Scoreboard Features: Computer operated. Matrix message portion measures 18 feet by 70 feet.
Parking Lot Capacity: 15,000.
Tenants: Cowboys and Southern Methodist University.
Football Seating Capacity: 65,101.
Cowboys' Attendance Record: 65,101, many times.

DENVER BRONCOS

Denver Mile High Stadium

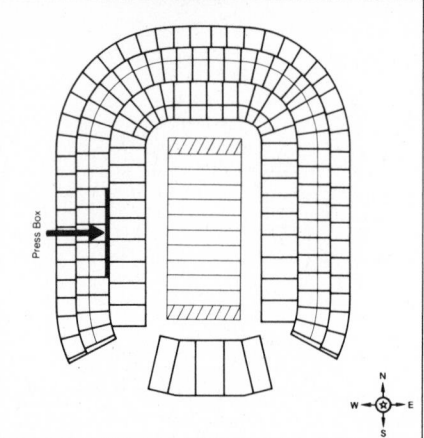

Address: 1900 West Eliot, Denver, Colorado 80204.
Architects: 1976-77 expansion, DMJM Phillips-Reister.
Contractors: Gerald H. Phipps Construction Co.; 1971 and 1976-77 expansion, Nick Petry Construction Co.
Cost: 1976-77 expansion, $25 million.
Year Opened: 1948.
Origin of Stadium Name: Indicative of the city and its elevation, it was adopted in 1967; the earlier name was "Bears Stadium," for its baseball team.
Owners: Denver and Denver County.
Managers: Denver and Denver County.
Recent Improvements: Expansion in 1976-77 increased the stadium's capacity by 12,500 and added a new scoreboard and other features.
Planned Improvements: None.
Special Seating Facilities: 54 private suites.
Miscellaneous Facts: None.
Playing Surface: Prescription Athletic Turf.
Scoreboard Manufacturer: Electric Division, Stewart-Warner Corporation.
Scoreboard Features: Scores, messages, instant replays, photograph reproductions.
Parking Lot Capacity: 7,000.
Tenants: Broncos and Denver Bears minor league baseball team.
Football Seating Capacity: 75,103.
Broncos' Attendance Record: 75,103, many times.

DETROIT LIONS

Pontiac Silverdome

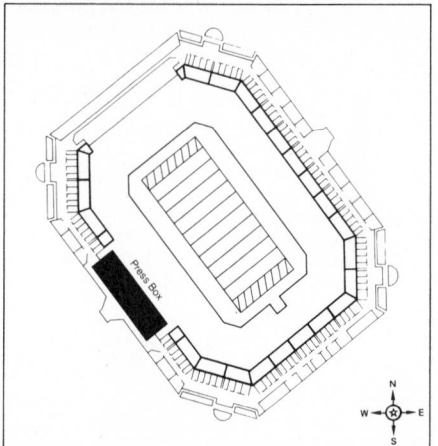

Address: 1200 Featherstone Road, Box 4200, Pontiac, Michigan 48057.
Architects: O'Dell/Hewlett and Luckenbach, Inc.
Contractors: Barton-Malow Company.
Cost: $55 million.
Year Opened: 1975.
Origin of Stadium Name: Inspired by the stadium's unique appearance. It was adopted in 1976. The facility was originally called Pontiac Metropolitan Stadium, or Ponmet.
Owner: Pontiac, Michigan.
Manager: Pontiac Stadium Building Authority.
Recent Improvements: None.
Planned Improvements: None.
Special Seating Facilities: 102 private suites, each featuring closed-circuit color television.
Miscellaneous Facts: It is the only domed stadium that has a Fiberglas roof, which is kept inflated by 25 blowers during events; two blowers do the job at other times. The roof cost $4.5 million. The Silverdome was the site of Super Bowl XVI, the first Super Bowl to be played in the north.
Playing Surface: AstroTurf.
Scoreboard Manufacturer: American Sign Company.
Scoreboard Features: Scores, messages, instant replays.
Parking Lot Capacity: 9,900.
Tenants: Lions and Detroit Pistons basketball team.
Football Seating Capacity: 80,638.
Lions' Attendance Record: 80,291, September 28, 1980 vs. Minnesota Vikings.

GREEN BAY PACKERS

Lambeau Field

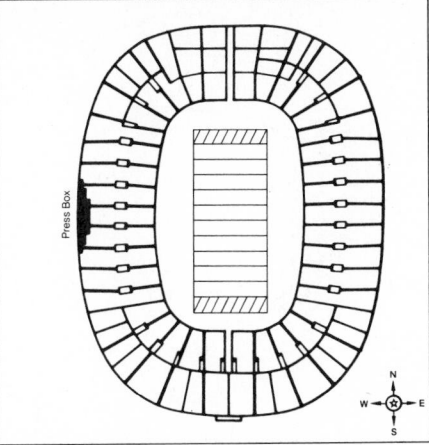

Address: 1265 Lombardi Avenue, Green Bay, Wisconsin 54303.
Architects: John E. Somerville Associates, Inc.
Contractors: George M. Hougard and Sons.
Cost: Renovations between 1961 and 1970, $3,778,000.
Year Opened: 1957.
Origin of Stadium Name: For the late Earl (Curly) Lambeau, founder, player, and coach of the team.
Owner: Green Bay.
Manager: Stadium Commission.
Recent Improvements: Renovations between 1961 and 1970 have increased the stadium to its present seating capacity.
Planned Improvements: None.
Special Seating Facilities: None.
Miscellaneous Facts: The field has electric heating coils, which are installed to provide proper footing despite the elements. No seat in the oval bowl is more than 250 feet from the playing surface.
Playing Surface: Grass.
Scoreboard Manufacturer: American Sign Company.
Scoreboard Features: Scores, messages.
Parking Lot Capacity: 7,000.
Tenants: Packers and Green Bay high school teams.
Football Seating Capacity: 56,267.
Packers' Attendance Record in Green Bay: 56,267, many times. All league games sold out since 1959.

GREEN BAY PACKERS

Milwaukee County Stadium

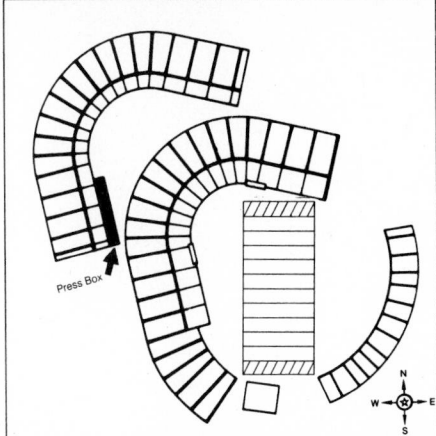

Address: 201 South 46th Street, Milwaukee, Wisconsin 53214.
Architects: Osborn Engineering Company.
Contractors: Huntzinger Construction Company—General Contractors.
Cost: $6 million.
Year Opened: 1953.
Origin of Stadium Name: For the county.
Owner: Milwaukee County.
Manager: County of Milwaukee Park Commission.
Recent Improvements: The capacity was increased from 47,823 to its present amount.
Planned Improvements: None.
Special Seating Facilities: None.
Miscellaneous Facts: None.
Playing Surface: Grass.
Scoreboard Manufacturer: General Indicator Corporation.
Scoreboard Features: Scores, messages.
Parking Lot Capacity: 11,500.
Tenants: Packers and Milwaukee Brewers baseball team.
Football Seating Capacity: 55,896.
Packers' Attendance Record in Milwaukee: 55,896, three times in 1976.

HOUSTON OILERS

Astrodome

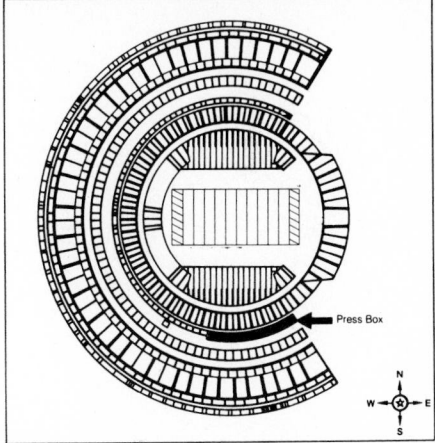

Address: Loop 610 South at Kirby Drive, Houston, Texas 77202.
Architects: Lloyd and Morgan, and Wilson, Morris, Crain and Anderson.
Contractors: H. A. Lott, Inc.
Cost: $38 million.
Year Opened: 1965.
Origin of Stadium Name: In recognition of Houston's NASA space center, the stadium's status as the first domed stadium, and for the Houston Astros baseball team.
Owner: Harris County.
Manager: Astrodome-Astrohall Stadium Corp.
Recent Improvements: The original roof was replaced with an all-aluminum one in 1975.
Planned Improvements: None.
Special Seating Facilities: 52 private suites and two private clubs.
Miscellaneous Facts: The Astrodome was the first domed stadium.
Playing Surface: AstroTurf.
Scoreboard Manufacturers: Fair Play Scoreboard Company and Federal Sign and Signal Corp.
Scoreboard Features: Scores, messages, animated sequences. The scoreboard is four stories high and 474 feet wide.
Parking Lot Capacity: 30,000.
Tenants: Oilers, Houston Astros baseball team, Astro-Bluebonnet Bowl, University of Houston, and Texas Southern University.
Football Seating Capacity: 50,452.
Oilers' Attendance Record: 55,452, November 30, 1980 vs. Cleveland Browns; December 4, 1980 vs. Pittsburgh Steelers.

KANSAS CITY CHIEFS

Arrowhead

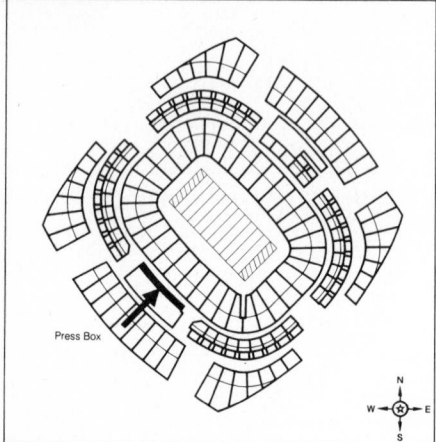

Press Box

Address: One Arrowhead Drive, Kansas City, Missouri 64129.

Architects: Kivett-Myers and Associates.

Contractors: Sharp-Kidde-Webb.

Cost: Dual stadium complex, which includes the adjacent Royals Stadium, $73 million.

Year Opened: 1972.

Origin of Stadium Name: In recognition of the arrowhead emblem worn on the Chiefs' helmet.

Owner: Jackson County Sports Authority.

Manager: Kansas City Chiefs.

Recent Improvements: None.

Planned Improvements: None.

Special Seating Facilities: 83 private suites.

Miscellaneous Facts: Arrowhead is a complete bowl, with all seats facing toward the center of the field. It is exclusively designed for football.

Playing Surface: Tartan Turf.

Scoreboard Manufacturer: Stewart-Warner Company.

Scoreboard Features: Scores, messages, instant replays, and animation.

Parking Lot Capacity: 20,000.

Tenant: Chiefs.

Football Seating Capacity: 78,096.

Chiefs' Attendance Record: 82,094, November 5, 1972 vs. Oakland Raiders.

LOS ANGELES RAMS

Anaheim Stadium

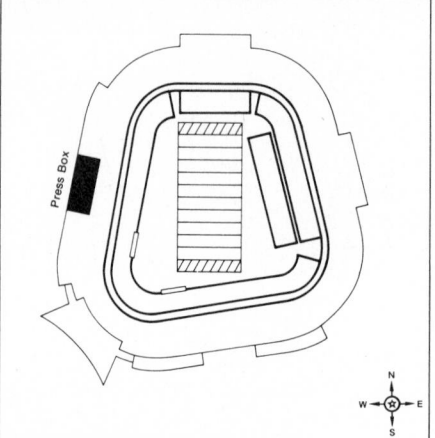

Press Box

Address: 2000 South State College Boulevard, Anaheim, California 92806.

Architects: Skidmore, Owings & Merrill.

Contractors: Continental Heller Corporation.

Cost: Original construction, $20 million; 1979-1980 expansion construction, $29 million.

Year Opened: 1966.

Origin of Stadium Name: For the city.

Owner: Anaheim Stadium, Inc.

Manager: Tom Leigler.

Recent Improvements: Expansion to present capacity and new scoreboard.

Planned Improvements: None.

Special Seating Facilities: 108 private suites, each featuring closed-circuit color television. Two wheelchair sections.

Miscellaneous Facts: None.

Playing Surface: Grass.

Scoreboard Manufacturer: Stewart-Warner Corporation.

Scoreboard Features: The largest electronic video matrix board designed for a major sports facility. Television style pictures.

Parking Lot Capacity: 12,500.

Tenants: Rams and California Angels baseball team.

Football Seating Capacity: 69,006.

Rams' Attendance Record: 65,154, December 15, 1981 vs. Dallas Cowboys.

MIAMI DOLPHINS

Orange Bowl

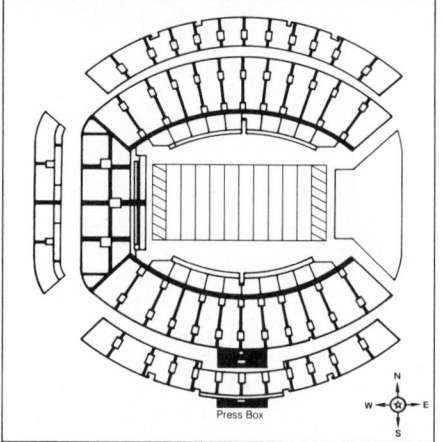

Press Box

Address: 1500 Northwest Third Street, Miami, Florida 33125.

Architects: 1938-1959, City of Miami public works engineers; 1960-1970, Kunde & Associates.

Contractors: Original construction, Works Progress Administration.

Cost: Original construction, $325,000; 1945 addition, $88,500; 1947, $300,000; 1949-1950, $196,000; 1950-51, $21,000; 1954, $13,250; 1955-56, $532,737; 1959-60, $350,000.

Year Opened: 1938.

Origin of Stadium Name: For the college bowl classic.

Owner: Miami.

Manager: Miami.

Recent Improvements: Renovations increased the stadium's capacity from its original figure of 22,000 in 1938 to its present amount.

Planned Improvements: A new scoreboard.

Special Seating Facilities: None.

Miscellaneous Facts: None.

Playing Surface: Prescription Athletic Turf.

Scoreboard Manufacturer: Fair Play Scoreboard Company.

Scoreboard Features: Game in progress information.

Parking Lot Capacity: 3,600.

Tenants: Dolphins, University of Miami, Orange Bowl.

Football Seating Capacity: 75,449.

Dolphins' Attendance Record: 78,914, November 19, 1972 vs. New York Jets. The Orange Bowl's football attendance record of 80,699 was set in the 1971 Orange Bowl when Nebraska played Louisiana State University.

MINNESOTA VIKINGS

Hubert H. Humphrey Metrodome

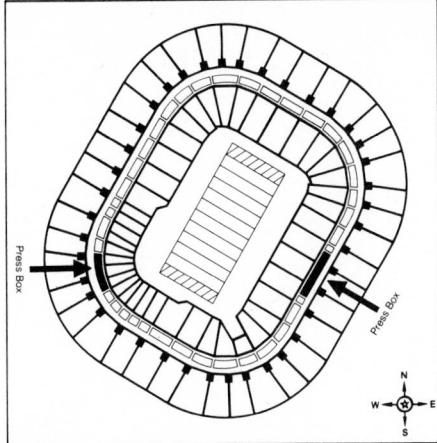

Address: 900 South 5th St., Minneapolis, Minnesota 55415.

Architects: Skidmore, Owings & Merrill.

Contractors: Barton-Mallow/Construction Management Services, Inc.

Cost: $52.7 million.

Year Opened: 1982.

Origin of Stadium Name: For the late Vice President of the United States.

Owner: Metropolitan Sports Facilities Commission.

Manager: Metropolitan Sports Facilities Commission.

Recent Improvements: Stadium recently completed.

Planned Improvements: None.

Special Seating Facilities: 115 private suites.

Miscellaneous Facts: None.

Playing Surface: Super Turf.

Scoreboard Manufacturer: American Sign and Indicator Company.

Scoreboard Features: Scores, messages.

Parking Lot Capacity: 20,000 in immediate area.

Tenants: Vikings and Minnesota Twins baseball team.

Football Seating Capacity: 63,000.

Vikings' Attendance Record: At Metropolitan Stadium: 47,708, October 16, 1977 vs. Chicago Bears.

NEW ENGLAND PATRIOTS

Schaefer Stadium

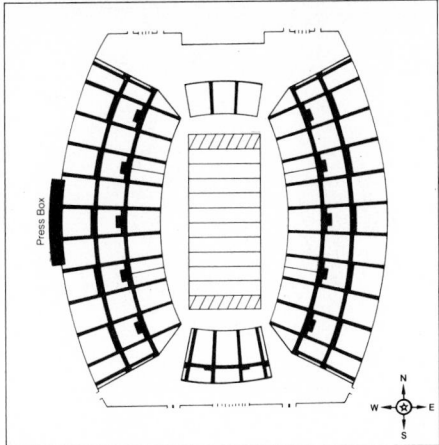

Address: Route One, Foxboro, Massachusetts 02035.

Architects: David M. Berg Incorporated, structural engineer; Finch-Heery-Architects and Engineers, consulting architects.

Contractors: J. F. White Construction Company.

Cost: $6.7 million.

Year Opened: 1971.

Origin of Stadium Name: For Schaefer Brewing Company, which purchased $1,000,000 worth of stock.

Owner: Charles Sullivan.

Manager: Billy Sullivan, III.

Recent Improvements: Redesigned and expanded press box; installation of luxury boxes; and addition of new adminstrative and practice facilities.

Planned Improvements: Installation of a new artificial playing surface.

Special Seating Facilities: Handicapped seating area.

Miscellaneous Facts: The stadium is part of a sports complex in suburban Boston that includes the adjoining New England Harness Raceway.

Playing Surface: Super Turf.

Scoreboard Manufacturer: Diamond Vision by Mitsubishi.

Scoreboard Features: Scores, messages.

Parking Lot Capacity: 16,000.

Tenant: Patriots.

Football Seating Capacity: 61,297.

Patriots' Attendance Record: 61,457, December 5, 1971 vs. Miami Dolphins.

NEW ORLEANS SAINTS

Louisiana Superdome

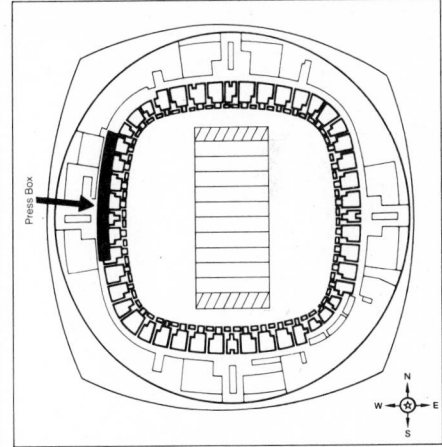

Address: 1500 Poydras Street, New Orleans, Louisiana 70112.

Prime Architects: Curtis & Davis–Architects & Planners, Inc.

Contractors: Huber, Hunt, and Nichols, Inc., and Blount Brothers, Inc.

Cost: $163 million.

Year Opened: 1975.

Origin of Stadium Name: For the state and the size and the type of building.

Owner: State of Louisiana.

Manager: H.M.C. Management Corporation.

Recent Improvements: None.

Planned Improvements: None.

Special Seating Facilities: 64 private suites, seating up to 29.

Miscellaneous Facts: The dome rises 273 feet, more than twice as high as the U.S. Capitol in Washington.

Playing Surface: AstroTurf (Mardi Grass).

Scoreboard Manufacturer: Ad Art Incorporated of California.

Scoreboard Features: Four scoreboards feature scores, messages; six giant television screens show instant replays and advertising.

Parking Lot Capacity: 5,000.

Tenants: Saints, Tulane University, and Sugar Bowl.

Football Seating Capacity: 71,330. Expanded Football Capacity, 76,791.

Saints' Attendance Record: 72,434, August 9, 1975 vs. Houston Oilers.

NEW YORK GIANTS

Giants Stadium

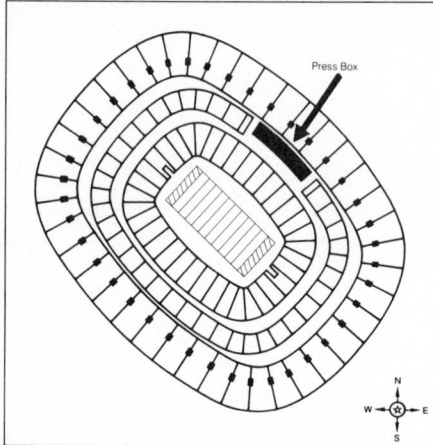

Address: East Rutherford, New Jersey 07073.
Architects: Ewing, Cole, Erdman, Ewbank, Clauss and Nolan–Architects, Engineers, and Planners.
Contractors: George A. Fuller Company. Frank Briscoe Company.
Cost: $71,071,000.
Year Opened: 1976.
Origin of Stadium Name: For the team.
Owner: Privately financed.
Manager: New Jersey Sports and Exposition Authority.
Recent Improvements: Additional locker and office space.
Planned Improvements: None.
Special Seating Facilities: 72 private suites, each seating 16, and a private stadium club seating 1,400.
Miscellaneous Facts: Giants Stadium is part of the New Jersey Sports & Exposition Complex that includes the adjacent Meadowlands Racetrack.
Playing Surface: AstroTurf.
Scoreboard Manufacturer: Stewart-Warner Company.
Scoreboard Features: Scores, messages, full-color instant replays.
Parking Lot Capacity: 24,000.
Tenants: Giants and New York Cosmos soccer team.
Football Seating Capacity: 76,891.
Giants Attendance Record: 76,490, November 4, 1979 vs. Dallas Cowboys.

NEW YORK JETS

Shea Stadium

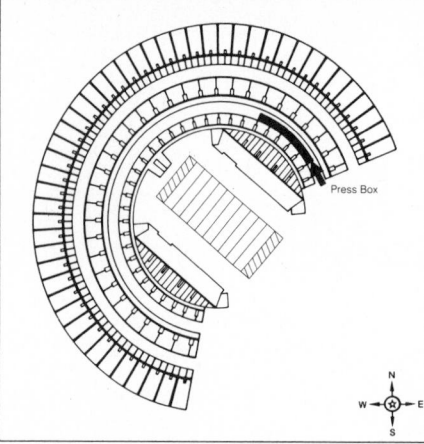

Address: Flushing, New York 11368.
Architects: Praeger-Kavanagh-Waterbury, Engineers-Architects.
Contractors: P. J. Carlin Construction Co., Thomas Crimmins Contracting Co.
Cost: $26 million.
Year Opened: 1964.
Origin of Stadium Name: For William Shea, attorney and a member of the Mayor's Commission for Sports.
Owner: City of New York.
Manager: New York Department of Parks.
Recent Improvements: Installation of an auxiliary scoreboard, new locker room facilities, and new seats in parts of the stadium.
Planned Improvements: None.
Special Seating Facilities: None.
Miscellaneous Facts: When the stadium is converted to football, two blocks containing over 10,000 seats are electrically powered on tracks to parallel the sidelines of the field.
Playing Surface: Grass.
Scoreboard Manufacturer: General Indicator Corporation; Diamond Vision by Mitsubishi.
Scoreboard Features: Scores, messages.
Parking Lot Capacity: 7,500.
Tenants: Jets and New York Mets baseball team.
Football Seating Capacity: 60,372.
Jets' Attendance Record: 63,962, November 5, 1972 vs. Washington Redskins.

OAKLAND RAIDERS

Oakland-Alameda County Coliseum

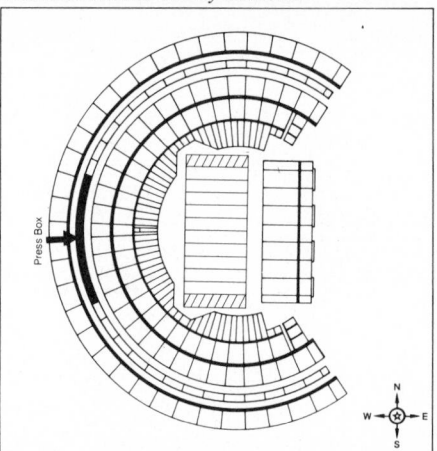

Address: Hegenberger Road and Nimitz Freeway, Oakland, California 94621.
Architects: Skidmore, Owings and Merrill–Architects.
Contractors: Guy F. Atkinson Company.
Cost: $30 million.
Year Opened: 1966.
Origin of Stadium Name: For the city and county.
Owners: Oakland and Alameda County.
Manager: Oakland-Alameda County Coliseum, Inc.
Recent Improvements: None.
Planned Improvements: None.
Special Seating Facilities: None.
Miscellaneous Facts: The Coliseum is part of a complex that also includes an adjacent arena, which is the home of the Golden State Warriors basketball team.
Playing Surface: Grass.
Scoreboard Manufacturer: Conrac Corporation.
Scoreboard Features: Scores, messages.
Parking Lot Capacity: 10,000.
Tenants: Raiders and Oakland Athletics baseball team.
Football Seating Capacity: 54,616.
Raiders' Attendance Record: 54,999, December 17, 1978 vs. Minnesota Vikings.

PHILADELPHIA EAGLES

Philadelphia Veterans Stadium

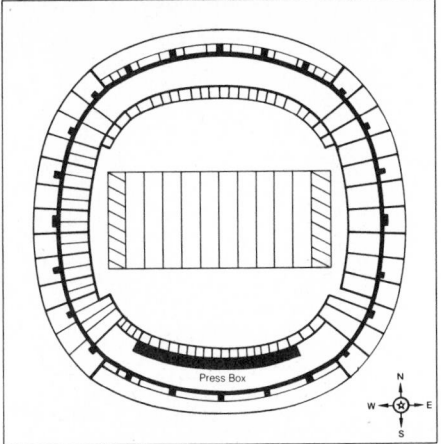

Address: Broad Steet and Pattison Avenue, Philadelphia, Pennsylvania 19148.

Architects: Ewing, Stonorov and Haws, General Contractors.

Contractors: McCloskey and Company.

Cost: $48 million.

Year Opened: 1971.

Origin of Stadium Name: In honor of veterans of American wars.

Owner: Philadelphia.

Manager: Philadelphia.

Recent Improvements: Replacement of the the AstroTurf and installation of a new baseball warning track.

Planned Improvements: None.

Special Seating Facilities: 23 suites and a stadium restaurant that seats 500.

Miscellaneous Facts: None.

Playing Surface: AstroTurf.

Scoreboard Manufacturer: Artkraft Strauss Sign Corporation.

Scoreboard Features: Scores, messages, animation.

Parking Lot Capacity: 6,000 and another 6,000 in surrounding lots.

Tenants: Eagles and Philadelphia Phillies baseball team.

Football Seating Capacity: 72,204.

Eagles' Attendance Record: 71,488, October 5, 1981 vs. Atlanta Falcons.

PITTSBURGH STEELERS

Three Rivers Stadium

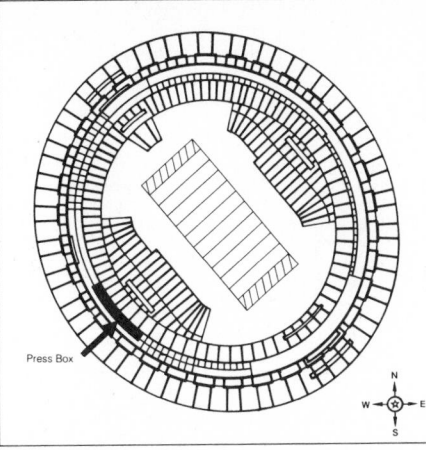

Press Box

Address: 300 Stadium Circle, Pittsburgh, Pennsylvania 15212.

Architects: Deeter, Richey, Sipple, Architects.

Contractors: Hubert, Hunt and Nichols–Architects.

Cost: $45 million.

Year Opened: 1970.

Origin of Stadium Name: Because of its location, the point at which the Allegheny and Monongahela Rivers join to form the Ohio River.

Owner: Stadium Authority, City of Pittsburgh.

Manager: Three Rivers Management Corporation.

Recent Improvements: Addition of 3,700 seats in 1980.

Planned Improvements: None.

Special Seating Facilities: 62 private suites and a private stadium club that has 1,200 members.

Miscellaneous Facts: Moveable stands are used to convert the stadium from baseball configuration to football.

Playing Surface: Tartan Turf.

Scoreboard Manufacturer: Stewart-Warner Corporation.

Scoreboard Features: Scores, messages, animation. The scoreboard is 30 feet high and 274 feet wide.

Parking Lot Capacity: 8,000 within a 12-block radius.

Tenants: Steelers and Pittsburgh Pirates baseball team.

Football Seating Capacity: 54,000.

Steelers' Attendance Record: 54,000, many times.

ST. LOUIS CARDINALS

Busch Memorial Stadium

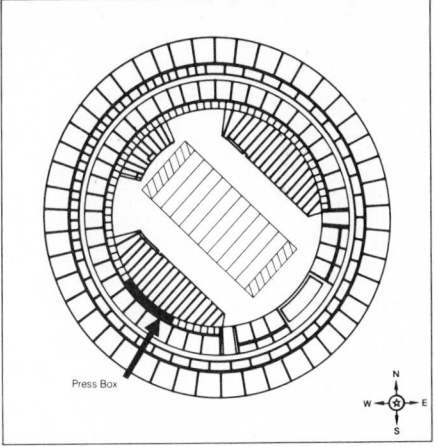

Press Box

Address: 300 Stadium Plaza, St. Louis, Missouri 63102.

Architects: Sverdrup and Parcel and Associates, Inc.; Schwarz and Van Hofen; and design collaborator Edward Durrell Stone.

Contractors: Fruin-Colnon, Millstone-General Contractors.

Cost: $27 million.

Year Opened: 1966.

Origin of Stadium Name: As a memorial to the family of August A. Busch, Jr., retired chairman of the board of Anheuser-Busch.

Owner: Privately financed.

Manager: Civic Center Redevelopment Corporation.

Recent Improvements: A new sound system was installed in 1972.

Planned Improvements: None.

Special Seating Facilities: 39 suites. A stadium restaurant overlooks the field.

Miscellaneous Facts: Moveable stands in right and left field convert the stadium from baseball configuration to football or soccer in less than two hours.

Playing Surface: AstroTurf.

Scoreboard Manufacturer: Fair Play Scoreboard Company.

Scoreboard Features: Scores, messages.

Parking Lot Capacity: 6,982.

Tenants: Cardinals and St. Louis Cardinals baseball team.

Football Seating Capacity: 51,392.

Cardinals' Football Attendance Record: 50,701, November 2, 1980 vs. Dallas Cowboys.

SAN DIEGO CHARGERS

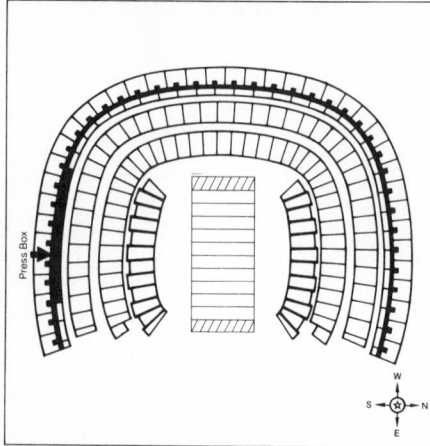

San Diego Jack Murphy Stadium

Address: 9449 Friars Road, San Diego, California 92120.

Architects: Frank L. Hope and Associates of San Diego.

Contractors: Robertson-Larsen-Donovan—Contractors.

Cost: $27.7 million.

Year Opened: 1967.

Origin of Stadium Name: For the city and the late sports editor of the *San Diego Union*.

Owners: City of San Diego and San Diego County.

Manager: City of San Diego.

Recent Improvements: The baseball infield was renovated in 1981.

Planned Improvements: None.

Special Seating Facilities: None.

Miscellaneous Facts: Moveable stands convert the stadium from baseball configuration to football.

Playing Surface: Grass.

Scoreboard Manufacturer: American Sign and Indicator Company.

Scoreboard Features: Scores and messages.

Parking Lot Capacity: 17,000.

Tenants: Chargers, San Diego Padres baseball team, San Diego Sockers soccer team, and San Diego State.

Football Seating Capacity: 52,675.

Chargers' Attendance Record: 54,611, December 3, 1972 vs. Oakland Raiders.

SAN FRANCISCO 49ERS

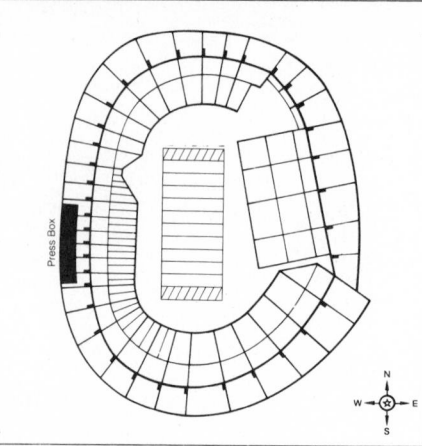

Candlestick Park

Address: San Francisco, California 94124.

Architect: John Bolles.

Contractors: Original construction, Charles Harney, General Contractors; 1971 improvements, Williams and Burrough, General Contractors.

Cost: Original construction, $11 million; 1971 improvements, $15 million.

Year Opened: 1958.

Origin of Stadium Name: For its location on Candlestick Point on San Francisco Bay.

Owner: San Francisco.

Manager: City Parks and Recreation Department.

Recent Improvements: A major renovation in 1971 added more than 16,000 seats to the original 45,000 capacity. The renovation also enclosed the stadium, cutting off the winds off San Francisco Bay, and included the construction of a football press box.

Planned Improvements: None.

Special Seating Facilities: None.

Miscellaneous Facts: Moveable stands convert the stadium from baseball configuration to football.

Playing Surface: Grass.

Scoreboard Manufacturer: Conrac Corporation.

Scoreboard Features: Scores, messages.

Parking Lot Capacity: 14,400.

Tenants: 49ers and San Francisco Giants baseball team.

Football Seating Capacity: 61,201.

49ers' Attendance Record: 60,525, January 10, 1982 vs. Dallas Cowboys, NFC Championship Game.

SEATTLE SEAHAWKS

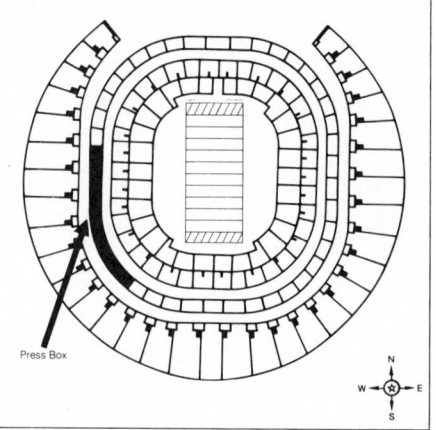

Kingdome

Address: 201 South King Street, Seattle, Washington 98104.

Architect: Naramore, Skilling and Praeger, Architects.

Contractors: Donald M. Drake Company; Peter Kiewit and Sons.

Cost: $67 million.

Year Opened: 1976.

Origin of Stadium Name: For the county and the kind of building.

Owner: King County.

Manager: E. O. (Ted) Bowsfield.

Recent Improvements: New video display system.

Planned Improvements: None.

Special Seating Facilities: None.

Miscellaneous Facts: Retractable and removeable stands permit the conversion of the field for various sports and functions. The walls of the dome anchor the world's largest self-supporting concrete roof.

Playing Surface: AstroTurf.

Scoreboard Manufacturer: "Diamond Vision" by Mitsubishi.

Scoreboard Features: Scores, messages, instant replays.

Parking Lot Capacity: 2,200; 15,000 within a nine-block radius.

Tenants: Seahawks, Seattle Mariners baseball team, Seattle Sounders soccer team, and Seattle Supersonics basketball team.

Football Seating Capacity: 64,757.

Seahawks' Attendance Record: 63,235, August 17, 1978 vs. Los Angeles Rams, a preseason game.

TAMPA BAY BUCCANEERS

Tampa Stadium

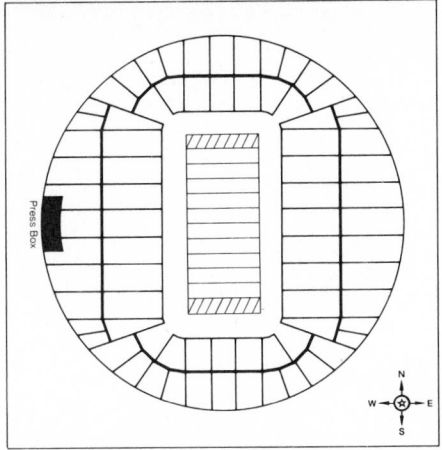

Address: 4201 North Dale Mabry Highway, Tampa, Florida 33607.

Architect: Watson and Company.

Contractors: Original construction, Jones-Mahoney Corporation; 1976 expansion, J. A. Jones Company.

Cost: Original construction, $4.6 million; 1976 expansion, $10.5 million.

Year Opened: 1967.

Origin of Stadium Name: For the city.

Owner: Tampa Sports Authority.

Manager: Tampa Sports Authority.

Recent Improvements: Expansion in 1976 added nearly 25,000 seats to the stadium's original 46,500 capacity.

Planned Improvements: Additional lounge boxes.

Special Seating Facilities: 22 private lounge boxes, each featuring closed-circuit television.

Miscellaneous Facts: None.

Playing Surface: Grass.

Scoreboard Manufacturer: American Sign and Indicator Corporation.

Scoreboard Features: Scores, messages, animation.

Parking Lot Capacity: 10,000.

Tenants: Buccaneers and Tampa Bay Rowdies soccer team.

Football Seating Capacity: 71,128.

Buccaneers' Attendance Record: 72,033, January 6, 1980 vs. Los Angeles Rams, NFC Championship Game.

WASHINGTON REDSKINS

RFK Memorial Stadium

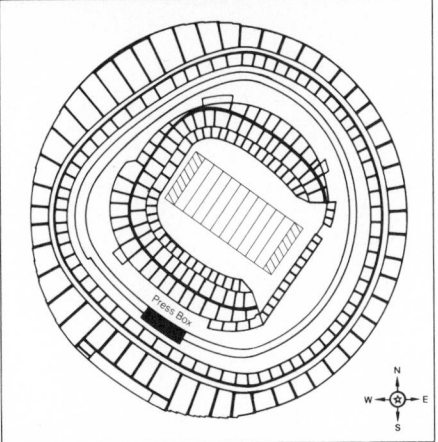

Address: 22nd and East Capitol Streets N.W., Washington, D.C. 20003.

Architects: George L. Dahl; Osborn Company.

Contractors: McCloskey and Company.

Cost: $22 million.

Year Opened: 1961.

Origin of Stadium Name: For the late Robert F. Kennedy in 1968. The original name was District of Columbia Stadium.

Owner: District of Columbia Armory Board.

Manager: District of Columbia Armory Board.

Recent Improvements: A new playing surface was installed in 1975.

Planned Improvements: None.

Special Seating Facilities: None.

Miscellaneous Facts: Moveable stands permit the conversion of the field for various sports and functions.

Playing Surface: Prescription Athletic Turf.

Scoreboard Manufacturer: Spencer Sign Company.

Scoreboard Features: Scores, messages.

Parking Lot Capacity: 10,000.

Tenants: Redskins.

Football Seating Capacity: 55,045.

Redskins' Attendance Record: 55,045, September 8, 1980, vs. Dallas Cowboys.

Rules of
the Game

DIGEST OF NFL RULES

RULE 1   THE FIELD

It is 360 feet long and 160 feet wide. The end zones are 30 feet or 10 yards deep. The hashmarks or in-bounds lines are 70 feet 9 inches from each side line. The lines used for tries-for-point are two yards from each goal line.

Sidelines and end lines are out of bounds. The goal line is in the end zone. A player with the ball in his possession scores when the ball is on, above, or over the goal line.

Goal posts must be the single standard type, offset from the end line and painted bright gold. The actual goal is the plane extending indefinitely above the crossbar between the outer edges of the posts. Goal posts must be 18 feet 6 inches wide and the top face of the crossbar 10 feet above the ground. The post must extend at least 30 feet above the crossbar.

Decorations in the end zone and at the 50-yard line must be approved by the commissioner to avoid confusing where the goal lines, sidelines, and end lines are.

RULE 2   THE BALL

The ball must be a Wilson ball bearing the signature of Commissioner Pete Rozelle.

It shall be made of an inflated rubber bladder enclosed in a pebble-grained leather case of natural tan color without corrugations of any kind. It shall have the form of a prolate spheroid. It shall be inflated to 12½ to 13½ pounds.

The home team must have 24 balls available for testing by the referee one hour before each game.

RULE 3   DEFINITIONS

Chucking is warding off an opponent who is in front of a defender by contacting him with a quick extension of the arm or arms, followed by the return of the arm or arms to a flexed position, thereby breaking the original contact.

Clipping is throwing the body across the back of an opponent's leg or hitting him from the back while moving up from behind unless the opponent is a runner or the action is in close line play.

Close line play is the the area between the positions normally occupied by the offensive tackles, extending three yards on each side of the line of scrimmage.

A dead ball is a ball not in play.

A double foul is a foul by each team during the same down.

A down is the period of action that starts when the ball is put in play and ends when it is dead.

Encroachment occurs when a player moves across the neutral zone and makes contact with an opponent before the ball is snapped.

A fair catch is an unhindered catch of a kick by a member of the receiving team who must raise one arm at full length above his head while the kick is in flight.

A foul is any violation of a playing rule.

A free kick is a kickoff, a kick after safety, or a kick after a fair catch. It may be a placekick, a dropkick, or punt, except a punt may not be used on a kickoff.

A fumble is the loss of possession of the ball.

Impetus is the action of a player that gives momentum to the ball.

A live ball is a ball legally free kicked or snapped and it continues in play until the down ends.

A loose ball is a live ball not in the possession of any player.

A muff is the touching of a loose ball by a player in an unsuccessful attempt to obtain possession.

The neutral zone is the space the length of the ball between the two scrimmage lines.

Offside means a player has any part of his body beyond his scrimmage or free kick line when the ball is snapped.

Possession of a pass is when a player controls the ball throughout the act of clearly touching both feet, or any other part of his body other than the hand(s), to the ground inbounds.

A punt is a kick made when a player drops the ball and kicks it while it is in flight.

A safety is when the ball is dead on or behind a team's own goal if the impetus comes from a player of that team. Two points are scored for the opposing team.

A shift is the movement of two or more offensive players at the same time before the snap.

Sudden death is the continuation of a tied game into sudden death overtime in which the team scoring first by safety, field goal, or touchdown wins.

A touchback is when a ball is dead on or behind a team's own goal line and the impetus came from a player on the opposing team and the play was not a touchdown or missed field goal.

A touchdown is when any part of the ball, legally in possession of a player inbounds, is on, above, or over the opponent's goal line, provided it is not a touchback.

Unsportsmanlike conduct is any act contrary to the generally understood principles of sportsmanship.

RULE 4   HOW THE GAME IS STARTED, CONDUCTED, AND TIMED

A game is 60 minutes long, divided into four periods of 15 minutes each. Halftime is 15 minutes long.

The stadium electric clock keeps the official time. The line judge supervises the timing. The clock operator starts and stops the clock upon the signal of any official.

The toss of the coin takes place three minutes before the kickoff. The visiting captain calls the toss. The winner of the toss makes one of two choices, whether his team will receive or kick or secondly, the goal his team will defend. The loser of the toss gets the other choice. For the second half, the loser of the toss has the first choice of the two privileges.

The teams change goals at the end of the first and third periods.

The clock operator starts the clock when the ball is kicked off to start the game and thereafter following any time out the clock starts when the ball is snapped or free kicked.

Three charged team time outs are allowed each team during each half.

Time outs last one minute 30 seconds.

The referee may allow two minutes for an injured player and three minutes for repair of equipment.

The offense has 30 seconds to put the ball in play.

The clock starts when the ball is snapped following a change of possession.

In the last two minutes of each half the clock does not start on a kickoff until the ball has been legally touched by a player of either team in the field of play.

A team cannot get an extra time out and take a penalty in the last two minutes of each half. But a fourth time out is allowed without a penalty for an injured player who must be removed immediately. A fifth time out or more is allowed for an injury and a five-yard penalty is assessed if the clock was running. In addition, if the clock is running and the score is tied or the team in possession is losing, the ball cannot be put in play for at least 10 seconds on the fourth or more time out. The half or game can end while those 10 seconds are being run off the clock.

The down is replayed on a foul by the defense on the last play of the half or game if the penalty is accepted by the offense.

The down is not replayed on a foul by the offense on the last play of the half or game, and the play in which the foul was committed is nullified. Exceptions are fair catch interference, a foul following a change of possession, and illegal touching. No score by the offense counts.

The down is replayed when a double foul occurs on the last play of the half or game.

RULE 5   THE PLAYERS, SUBSTITUTES, AND THEIR EQUIPMENT

Each team is permitted 11 men on the field at the snap.

All players must be numbered according to their positions as follows: quarterbacks and kickers, 1-19; all backs, running and defensive, 20-49; centers and linebackers, 50-59; defensive linemen and interior offensive linemen, including centers, 60-79; further, defensive linemen also may be numbered 90-99; wide receivers and tight ends, 80-89. All players who had been in the NFL in 1972 may use their old numbers. Otherwise, any and all players entering the league must be numbered in accordance with the preceding rules.

Substitutes may not enter the field while the ball is in play. They may enter at any time while the ball is dead, provided the players they replace have cleared the field on their own side between the end lines prior to the snap or free kick. Players who have been substituted for may not linger on the field. If they do it is unsportsmanlike conduct.

A substitute is not to report to any official. He becomes a player when he informs a teammate he is replacing him; a teammate voluntarily withdraws upon his entering; he participates in at least one play after communicating with a teammate; or, in the absence of any of these, he is on the field at the time of the snap or free kick.

No player can wear equipment that, in the opinion of the officials, endangers other players.

RULE 6   THE FREE KICK

A free kick called a kickoff puts the ball in play at the start of each half, after a try for point, and after a successful field goal.

The free kick line is the 35.

The kicker may use a tee up to three inches high on a kickoff.

A kickoff is illegal unless it travels 10 yards or is touched by the receiving team. It is a free ball once it is touched by the receiving team. The receiving team may recover and advance it. The kicking team may recover but not advance it unless it was first possessed and lost by the receiving team. If it recovers it in the end zone it is a touchdown.

If a kickoff goes through the opponent's goal posts it is not a field goal.

When a kickoff goes out of bounds between the goal lines without being touched by the receiving team it must be kicked again and there is a five-yard penalty against the kicking team.

A kick after a safety and a kick after a fair catch are also free kicks. In each case a dropkick, placekick, or punt may be used. A punt may not be used on a kickoff.

On a kick after a fair catch the receiving team has the option to put the ball in play by a punt, dropkick, or placekick without a tee, or by a snap. If the team dropkicks or placekicks and the ball goes between the uprights of the opponent's goal it is a field goal.

RULE 7   THE SCRIMMAGE

The offensive team must have at least seven players on the line of scrimmage at the snap.

Offensive players not on the line of scrimmage, except for the player who takes the snap, must be at least one yard back.

No player of either team may enter the neutral zone before the snap.

All offensive players must be stationary at the snap, except that one back may be in motion parallel to the line of scrimmage or backward from it. No interior linemen may move after taking or simulating a three-point stance. No offensive player may charge or move after assuming a set position in such a manner as to lead the defense to believe that the play has started when it has not.

A quarterback can be called for a false start penalty if his action is judged to be an obvious attempt to draw an opponent offside.

Linemen may lock legs only with the snapper.

After a shift all offensive players must come to an absolute stop for at least one second before the snap.

RULE 8 FORWARD AND BACKWARD PASS AND FUMBLE

The offense may make only one forward pass each play.

The passer must be behind his line of scrimmage.

A forward pass may be touched or caught only by an eligible player—an offensive player on either end of the line or at least one yard behind the line at the snap, except for the T-formation quarterback, or any defensive player.

If a forward pass is touched by a defensive player before, at the same time as, or after touching by an eligible offensive player, all offensive players then become eligible.

If a forward pass is caught simultaneously by eligible players of both teams it goes to the passing team.

A pass is incomplete and the ball is dead if the pass hits the ground or goes out of bounds, hits the goal post or the crossbar of either team, is caught by an offensive player after touching an ineligible receiver, or is caught by the passer.

If a pass is touched by one offensive player and touched or caught by a second eligible offensive player, the pass completion is legal.

A forward pass is complete when a receiver has possession of the ball and touches the ground with both feet inbounds. If he is carried out of bounds by an opponent while in possession in the air, the pass is complete where he went out of bounds.

If a pass is incomplete on fourth down on a play that starts inside the opponent's 20-yard line, the defense gets the ball at the line of scrimmage, not the 20-yard line.

It is intentional grounding when the ball strikes the ground after the passer throws, tosses, or lobs it to prevent loss of yards by his team.

No defensive player may run into a passer of a legal forward pass after the ball has left the passer's hands. The referee must determine whether the opponent had a reasonable chance to stop his momentum during an attempt to block the pass or tackle the passer while he still had the ball.

A pass begins when the passer starts to bring his hand forward. If the ball then hits the ground it is an incomplete pass. If the passer loses control of it before he brings his hand forward it is a fumble.

The restriction against pass interference begins for the passing team at the snap. The restriction begins for the defensive team when the ball leaves the passer's hand. The restrictions end for both when the ball is touched by anyone.

If there is defensive pass interference in the end zone, it is first down for the offense on the defense's 1-yard line.

It is not interference when two or more eligible players make a simultaneous and bona fide attempt to catch or bat the ball, each playing the ball and making contact unavoidable and incidental to the act of trying to catch or bat the ball. Defensive players have as

much right to the path of the ball as eligible receivers.

Any pass that is not a forward pass is a backward pass, or lateral.

A runner may pass backward at any time.

Any player on either team may catch the backward pass or recover the ball after it touches the ground. The offense can recover and advance it but the defense can only recover it, unless it is in the air, and in that case the defense can both recover and advance it.

A fumble may be advanced by any player on either team regardless of whether it is recovered before or after the ball hits the ground.

If an offensive player fumbles anywhere on the field during a fourth-down play, or if a player fumbles on any down after the two-minute warning, only the fumbling player is permitted to recover and/or advance the ball. If the ball is recovered by any other offensive player, the ball is dead at the spot of the fumble unless it is recovered behind the spot of the fumble. Any defensive player may recover and/or advance any fumble. The fourth-down fumble rule does not apply if any player touches, but does not possess a direct snap from center.

RULE 9 THE SCRIMMAGE KICK

Scrimmage kicks are punts, dropkicks, and placekicks.

During a scrimmage kick only the end men on the line of scrimmage at the snap may go beyond the line before the ball is kicked. If there is an eligible receiver aligned or in motion behind the line and more than one yard outside the end man on his side, clearly making him the outside receiver, he may replace the end man as the player eligible to go downfield before the snap.

Any punt that is blocked and does not cross the line of scrimmage may be recovered and advanced by either team. If the offensive team recovers after the ball has been touched by the defensive team, the offensive team must make the yardage necessary for its first down, if it is fourth down, to retain possession of the ball.

The kicking team may never advance its own kick beyond the line of scrimmage.

No player on the receiving team may run into or rough the kicker.

The penalty for running into the kicker is 5 yards and for roughing the kicker it is 15. If the roughing the kicker penalty is flagrant it is disqualification.

It is legal for a player on the receiving team to run into or rough the kicker if the contact is incidental to and after the receiving team player has touched the ball in flight; the contact is caused by the kicker's own motions; or, the contact occurs during a quick kick or a kick made after a run or when the kicker recovers a loose ball. It is a loose ball when the kicker muffs the snap or the snap hits the ground.

If a member of the kicking team who is attempting to down the ball on or inside the opponent's 5-yard line carries it into the end zone, it is a touchback.

Any member of the punting team may down the ball anywhere in the field of play.

If the receiving team commits a foul before gaining possession and the ball is still in the air or rolling on the ground after a punt or field goal attempt, the receiving team will retain possession of the ball and be penalized for its foul.

The defensive team may advance all kicks from scrimmage, including missed field goals, whether the ball crosses the defensive team's goal line or not.

It is illegal for a defensive player to stand on, jump on, or be picked up by a teammate or use a hand or hands on a teammate to gain additional height in an attempt to block a kick.

When a field goal is missed and the line of scrimmage is beyond the 20, the defensive team gets the

ball at the line of scrimmage. When a field goal is missed inside the 20, the ball reverts to the 20.

RULE 10 THE FAIR CATCH

It is a legal fair catch signal when one arm is raised at full length above the head while the ball is in flight.

No opponent may interfere with the fair catcher, the ball, or his path to the ball.

The fair catcher is not required to catch the ball.

After signaling he cannot block or initiate contact with any opponent until the ball touches someone.

The fair catch signal is off if the ball is touched by a member of the kicking team while it is in flight, or it hits the ground.

It is delay of game and a five-yard penalty if the fair catcher unduly advances the ball. The ball is dead at the spot of the catch.

If time expires while the ball is in play and a fair catch is awarded, the receiving team may choose to extend the period with one free-kick down.

RULE 11 SCORING

The team that scores the most points in the game is the winner.

A touchdown counts six points, a field goal three, a safety two, and a successful try for point one.

The ball is automatically dead at the instant of legal player possession on, above, or behind the opponent's goal line.

The referee may award a touchdown when the offended team is deprived of one by a palpably unfair act, such as the act of a player coming off the bench and tackling a runner apparently en route to a touchdown.

The ball may be spotted for a try for point anywhere between the inbounds lines, two or more yards from the goal line.

A successful conversion counts one point whether it is by run, pass, or kick.

The defensive team can never score on a try for point.

RULE 12 CONDUCT OF PLAYERS

A runner may ward off opponents with his hands and arms but no other player on offense may use his hands or arms to obstruct an opponent by grasping with the hands or pushing or encircling any part of his body during a block.

No offensive player may assist the runner except by blocking for him. There can be no interlocking interference.

Any offensive player who pretends to possess the ball or to whom a teammate pretends to give the ball may be tackled provided he is crossing his scrimmage line between the ends of a normal tight offensive line.

An offensive player who lines up more than two yards outside his own tackle and who moves toward the ball in an area within three yards on either side of the line may not contact an opponent below the waist—a crackback block.

Pass blocking is the obstruction of an opponent by the use of that part of the body above the knees. During a legal block, hands (open or closed) must be inside the blocker's elbows and can be thrust forward to contact an opponent as long as the contact is inside the frame. Hands cannot be thrust forward above the frame to contact an opponent on the neck, face, or head. The blocker cannot use his hands or arms to push from behind, hand onto, or encircle an opponent in a manner that restricts his movements as the play develops. The blocker may ward off an opponent's attempt to grasp his jersey or arms and prevent legal contact to the head.

A defensive player may not tackle or hold an

opponent other than the runner.

A defensive player may use his hands and arms only to ward off an obstructing opponent, to push or pull an opponent out of the way on the line of scrimmage, in an actual attempt to get at or tackle the runner, to push or pull an opponent out of the way in a legal attempt to recover a loose ball, during a legal block on an opponent who is not an eligible pass receiver; and when legally blocking an eligible pass receiver above the waist.

A defensive player must not contact an opponent above the shoulders with the palm of his hand—head slap—except during his initial charge or to ward him off the line. It cannot be a repeated act against the same opponent during any one contact.

A defensive player may use his hands or arms to contact an eligible receiver only to a point five yards beyond the line of scrimmage. Beyond this limitation, a defender may use his hands or arms only to defend or protect himself against impending contact caused by a receiver.

A defensive player may block an eligible receiver below the waist—roll block him—provided the receiver is within three yards of the line of scrimmage and lined up within two yards of the tackle.

A player may bat or punch a loose ball in the field of play but not toward the opponent's goal line. In either end zone, he may not bat or punch a loose ball in any direction.

A player may not bat or punch a ball while it is in player possession.

A player may not kick at a ball except as a punt, dropkick, or placekick.

A player may not strike with the fists, kick, knee, or strike on the head, neck, or face with the heel, back, or side of the hand, wrist, forearm, elbow, or clasped hands.

A player may not grasp the face mask of an opponent.

There shall be no piling on, unnecessary roughness, clipping, crawling, or any form of unsportsmanlike conduct.

Clipping is legal in close line play, in an area extending laterally to the positions originally occupied by the offensive tackles and longitudinally three yards on either side of the line of scrimmage.

RULE 13   CONDUCT OF NON-PLAYERS

There shall be no unsportsmanlike conduct by a substitute, coach, attendants, or any other non-player.

Loudspeaker coaching from the sideline is not permitted.

Coaches may move in an area extending 18 yards in both directions from the middle of the team's bench.

Each team may have no more than 15 non-players in its bench area.

RULE 14   ENFORCEMENT PENALTIES

Penalties are enforced from four spots: (1) the previous spot is where the ball was put in play; (2) the spot of the foul is where it occurred; (3) the spot of the snap, pass, fumble, return kick, or free kick is where one of those things occurred; (4) the succeeding spot is where the ball would be put in play if no distance penalty were to be enforced.

Fouls by the offense behind the line of scrimmage and on the field of play are penalized from the previous spot.

If there is a double foul during a down in which there is a change of possession, the team last gaining possession may keep the ball unless its foul was committed prior to the change of possession.

If there is a double foul after a change of possession the defensive team retains the ball at the spot it gained possession.

If one of the fouls of a double foul involves disqualification the player must be removed but no penalty yardage is assessed.

The penalty is assessed on the following kickoff when a team scores and either team commits a personal foul, unsportsmanlike conduct, or any obviously unfair act.

RULE 15   OFFICIALS DUTIES

They are the referee, umpire, head linesman, line judge, back judge, side judge, and field judge.

If one of them is absent, the crew is to be arranged on the most feasible basis.

All officials are to wear the uniform prescribed by the league.

All officials have concurrent jurisdiction over any foul.

The referee has general oversight and control of the game. He is the final authority for the score and number of the down. He sees that the ball is properly put in play. He notifies the coach and captain when a team has used its three time outs and he notifies both coaches when two minutes remain in a half.

The umpire has primary jurisdiction over the equipment of the players and the conduct and action of the players on the line of scrimmage.

The head linesman is primarily responsible for offside, encroaching, any actions pertaining to the scrimmage line prior to the snap, and the work of the chain crew.

The line judge times the game and in case the stadium clock becomes inoperative takes over the timing on the field. He works on the side of the field opposite the head linesman and is primarily responsible for watching illegal motion behind the line at the snap and illegal shifts. He fires a pistol signaling that time has expired at the end of a period.

The back judge works on the same side of the field as the line judge, 17 yards deep. He is responsible for watching all eligible receivers on his side of the field. After receivers have cleared the line of scrimmage, he concentrates on action in the area between the umpire and the field judge.

The field judge is in the defensive secondary 25 yards deep and watches forward passes, kicks from scrimmage, loose balls out of the range of the umpire, back judge, or head linesman, times the 30 seconds the offensive team has to put the ball in play, and checks for illegal substitutions.

The side judge works on the same side of the field as the head linesman, 17 yards deep. He is responsible for all eligible receivers on his side of the field. After the receivers have cleared the line of scrimmage, the side judge concentrates on action in the area between the umpire and field judge. The side judge also is responsible for counting the number of players on the field at the time of the snap.

RULE 16   SUDDEN DEATH

Sudden death prevails for all games, but preseason and regular season games have a maximum of one 15-minute period of overtime.

The team scoring first during overtime play is the winner of the game.

RULE 17   HANDLING AN EMERGENCY

If any non-player enters the field or end zones and in the judgment of an official interferes with play, the referee, after consulting with the crew, shall enforce any such penalty or score as the interference warrants.

If in the opinion of the referee the game cannot continue, he shall declare a time out, note the down, distance to be gained, position of the ball on the field, and time remaining, and then instruct the home team to clear the field and restore order. When that is done, the game is to continue. It must be completed.

MAJOR RULES CHANGES

The rules of football had already gone through a half-century of development before the league that became the NFL arrived in 1920.

College football was by then a major part of American life. And just as millions followed the sport in the huge arenas where it was played or through newspaper accounts of the game's heroes, the way it was played and governed was also of great interest. The decisions reached at the annual meeting of the rules committee were reported and studied and argued over.

By the time of the NFL, this annual process had been going on for a long time. The colleges had already established the major rules that laid the foundation for the game: the field 100 by 53 yards (1876); 11 players on a side (1880); three downs to make five yards (1881), later settling at four downs to make 10 yards (1912); seven men required on the offensive line at the snap (1895); the ball a prolate spheroid (1897); a neutral zone between the lines (1906); three points for a field goal (1909) and six for a touchdown (1912); and a four-man officials' crew of referee, umpire, field judge, and head linesman (1907).

The rule books used today in professional, college, and high school football resemble very much the single rule book used in the nineteenth century in its headings and the way it was organized. A chapter in a rule book is a "rule." The headings in today's books resemble those in the book of 1900—"Rule 1, The Field; Rule 2, The Ball; Rule 3, Players and Substitutes, etc."

The subdivisions of today's rule books are the same as those in the book used at the turn of the century by men of property such as Walter Camp and Walter Okeson who also dabbled in football and set up the rules in the language of a legal covenant—rule, section, article. Just as any legal document has a chapter on the definitions of the agreement, so does a football rule book, only in this case what it defines are fair catches, field goals, huddles, and the line of scrimmage.

No one in pro football "wrote the rule book." Building on the original book of Camp and others, the governing bodies of professional, college, and high school football made committees that wrote changes to meet their needs. The NFL made no major changes in the rules for 13 years—until the league meetings of 1933 and 1934, when it invented hashmarks or inbounds lines, moved the goal posts to the goal line (a rules change it would find necessary to undo in the seventies), and allowed forward passes from anywhere behind the line of scrimmage.

The payment of adults to play football was once considered heresy. "Professionalism" was a tainted word. How could a game played by pros be anything more than tedium? How could there be any real incentive for football players away from pennant-waving crowds, raccoon coats, coeds, and Saturday's Big Game?

The NFL was compelled, therefore, to open up its game and make it exciting and irresistible. Its decision to do so underlies the whole history of its rules changes. It got the game off the sideline through its invention of hashmarks and ended wasted downs that were necessary to move the ball to the middle of the field for genuine attempts to make yardage. It passed rules favoring forward passes at a time when many dismissed them as the lazy man's way to touchdowns. The NFL more readily accepted free substitution, opening the way to specialization. And it consistently moved against tied games, finally adopting sudden death for all games (preseason and regular season games were given a maximum of one 15-minute overtime period).

One of the persons who had the greatest influence on the NFL rules and how they are enforced was Hugh (Shorty) Ray, the league's "technical advisor" from 1938 until 1956. So great were Ray's contributions that he was elected to the Hall of Fame in 1966.

Ray advised the NFL owners on rules changes to be considered each year. Ray selected, tested, graded, and supervised the work of NFL officials. He improved the way officials work, made the game safer, and made it move faster.

A small (5 feet 6 inches), squeaky-voiced mechanical drawing instructor at Harrison High School in Chicago, Ray was one of the best game officials in the Big Ten Conference when George Halas of the Chicago Bears recommended that the NFL hire him. Ray became technical advisor and rule book associate editor for the National Federation of State High School Associations at the same time he was also employed by the NFL. For that reason, the rules of high school and professional football were similar in Ray's years and immediately thereafter.

Ray constantly pushed NFL officials to be the best in the sport. He held clinics for them, made them take tests, mailed them open-book examinations to take and return to him for grading, and mailed them a steady stream of announcements, approved rules, and the annual "play situation book," forerunner of the present-day "case books."

"He pounded the rules into his officials so they could average ninety-five percent on a test on even the most difficult problems," George Halas recalled.

During games, Ray and his part-time assistants watched officials from the press box or grandstands with watches, clipboards, and pencils at the ready, timing every move. If Ray did not get an eyewitness report on a game, he studied movies of the game with his time and motion movie projector. When the season ended, he presented his conclusions to league meetings in voluminous ring binders packed with data on every NFL game played, every down, every play situation.

As a result, NFL officials learned to work efficiently and at high speed because they knew they were being watched and graded every play. The pros began to run off more plays and their games ended sooner.

In addition, Ray changed officials mechanics on long incomplete passes and out-of-bounds plays. Previously, the receiver or the field judge ran back to the line of scrimmage returning the football or, after a play went out-of-bounds, an official ran back with the ball. That took too much time, Ray reasoned. He ordered that in those instances a second football be passed to the referee at the previous spot or at the hashmark, to be spotted there immediately by the referee and play resumed.

A summary of the important year-by-year changes in the NFL rules follows.

1929 A fourth official, the line judge, is added.

1933 The ball will be moved in 10 yards to the hashmarks or inbounds lines whenever it is in play within ten yards of the side lines.

The clipping penalty is increased to 25 yards. The goal posts are moved to the goal lines.

1934 A player entering the game may communicate with his teammates immediately instead of waiting until one play is completed.

Officials must notify the coach when a team has exhausted its three legal time outs in each half.

A forward pass made hand-to-hand behind the line of scrimmage that becomes incomplete is a fumble and may be advanced by either team.

Within 10 yards of the goal, a defensive team can be penalized only half the distance for offside violations.

The second incomplete pass over the goal line in the same series or a fourth down incompletion in the

end zone results in a touchback.

Forward passing is legalized from any spot behind the line of scrimmage.

A runner who falls to the ground, or who is tackled, may advance unless a defender continues to hold him on the ground.

Flying blocks and flying tackles are permitted.

Players of the receiving team may be stationed at any place on the field, so long as they do not advance within 10 yards of the ball before it is kicked.

The ball may be kicked off from a dirt tee.

A fumbled ball, except fumbles resulting from lateral passes, may be advanced by either team, no matter whether the ball strikes the ground or not. If the defense recovers a fumbled lateral, the ball is dead; if the offense recovers a fumbled lateral, it may advance.

When a team completes a legal forward pass, which is in turn followed by a second forward pass, the penalty will be loss of five yards from the point of the second and illegal forward pass.

1935 All penalties will be enforced from the point where the ball was put in play and not from the point where the foul occurred.

A pass thrown beyond the line of scrimmage intended as a lateral but going forward will be declared downed at the point of throwing.

The ball, when fumbled, is free except when kicked or thrown.

A fourth down incomplete pass, or a second incomplete pass in the same series that goes into the end zone, is returned to the point where the ball was put in play, except when the previous play originated inside the 20 yard line.

The hashmarks or inbounds lines are moved for the second time: a ball out of bounds will be brought in 15 yards.

1936 When the goal posts interfere with the play of the team that is in possession of the ball, it will have the privilege of moving the ball five yards to either side of the goal posts without penalty.

1937 No changes.

1938 After a kickoff goes out of bounds, the ball will be put in play on the receiving team's 45 yard line.

Any two players withdrawn from a game during fourth quarter may re-enter once.

All penalties against the defense within the 10 yard line will be half the distance to the goal line.

The referee may penalize 15 yards for deliberate roughing of a passer after the ball has left his hand.

The penalty for a second forward pass behind the line of scrimmage is loss of down instead of loss of down and five yards.

If a kickoff goes out of bounds between the goal lines, the opponents will have the option of putting it in play by a scrimmage anywhere on their 45 yard line or at a point 15 yards in from where the ball crossed the side line. If the ball is last touched by the receivers, the ball will be put in play at the inbounds spot.

1939 During the last two minutes of the second half, additional time outs by the offense after its third legal one are not allowed unless it is for a designated injured player who is to be removed. A fourth time out under these conditions is not penalized, but additional time outs are treated as excess time outs.

During a kickoff, the kicking team may use only a natural tee made of the soil in the immediate vicinity of the kick and it must not be more than three inches in height.

The penalty for a forward pass touching an ineligible player on or behind his line of scrimmage is loss of down and 15 yards from the previous spot, and this penalty may not be declined.

The penalty for a forward pass striking an ineligible player beyond the line of scrimmage will be loss of the ball at the previous spot.

Before a forward pass is thrown from behind the

line of scrimmage, ineligible players may not legally cross that line except in an initial line charge while blocking an opponent. The penalty is loss of down and 15 yards.

1940 The clipping penalty is reduced to 15 yards.

The defense has the choice of loss of down and 15 yards from the previous spot or a touchback for pass interference by the offense behind the defense's goal line.

The penalty for a forward pass not from scrimmage is five yards.

A penalty enforced in the field of play cannot carry the ball more than one half the distance to the offenders' goal line.

The penalty for a foul prior to a kick or pass from behind the line is enforced from the previous spot or behind that spot if the offensive team commits a foul behind the previous spot.

1941 The penalty for an illegal shift is five yards.

A kick from scrimmage or a return kick crossing the receivers' goal line from the impetus of the kick is a touchback.

The penalty for a personal foul by the opponents of the scoring team is enforced on the kickoff.

Illegal touching of a kicked ball is not an offset foul and the ball is dead when illegally recovered.

The penalty for a disqualifying foul is 15 yards.

The penalty for an illegal bat or kick is 15 yards.

The umpire is to time the game and the head linesman and field judge are to supervise substitutions.

1942 The snapper is not offside unless some portion of his body is ahead of the defense's line.

A free kick cannot be made in a side zone.

A detachable kicking toe is illegal.

Pass interference by the offense in the defense's end zone is a touchback during any down.

A forward pass that has touched a second eligible or an ineligible player may be intercepted.

The coach's area is to extend 10 yards in both directions from the center of his team's bench.

1943 Free substitution is permitted.

The time out rule applies at the end of both halves.

Players must wear helmets.

The offense may intercept and advance the defense's illegal pass from end zone.

1944 A substitute is not required to report to an official and he becomes a player when he informs a teammate that he is replacing him or when he communicates with any teammate.

All enforcements for fouls during a free kick, except fair catch interference, are from the previous spot.

Communication between players and their coach is legal provided the coach is in his prescribed area and it does not cause delay.

Offensive pass interference in the end zone is not a touchback.

A designated center, guard, or tackle or one shifted to an end or back position may return to any position if he is withdrawn for one play.

1945 The hashmarks or inbounds lines are moved a third time, to a point 20 yards from the side line.

It is mandatory to enforce a penalty for encroachment if the defensive signal caller is beyond his line after the neutral zone is established.

A player under the center who extends his hands must receive the snap.

When the snap in flight is muffed by the receiver and then touches the ground, the defense may recover and advance.

The ball is dead when any receiver catches after a fair catch signal unless the kick is touched in flight by the members of the kicking team.

It is first and 10 for the offense when it recovers a kick from scrimmage anywhere in the field of play after it has first been touched by the defense beyond the line.

A player in blocking may not strike an opponent below the shoulders with elbows by pivoting or turning his trunk at the waist.

Players must wear long stockings in league games.

During a try, the snap may be made two or more yards from the goal line.

The referee is to designate an offending player when known.

A rule regarding attempts to consume or conserve time at the end of the second and fourth periods is extended to also include the first and third periods.

On a personal foul prior to a completion or an interception of a legal pass by the offended team, it will have the choice of the usual penalty or 15 yards from the spot of the dead ball.

1946 An offensive player is on his line provided one hand is touching the ground and it is on or within one foot of his line.

When a forward pass from behind the line touches either team's goal post or crossbar it is incomplete.

The toss of the coin must be held before the teams leave the field at the conclusion of pregame warmups.

The captains are to meet at the center of the field at the usual three minutes before game time, but only the receivers and their goal are to be indicated.

The penalty for an invalid fair catch signal is five yards from the spot of the signal.

The penalty for illegal equipment is five yards for delay and suspension for at least one down.

Substitution is limited to no more than three men at one time.

The receiving team is permitted to run punts and unsuccessful field goal attempts out from behind the goal line.

1947 The officials automatically will re-spot the ball on the nearest inbounds line when the spot of the snap is between the inbounds lines and inside the offense's 10 yard line.

When a team has less than 11 players on the field prior to the snap or free kick, officials are not to inform them.

During a try, if the kick is not successful, the ball becomes dead as soon as the failure is evident.

When a scrimmage or return kick crosses the receivers' goal line from the impetus of the kick, it is a touchback.

The kicker loses his usual protection if he kicks after recovering a loose ball on the ground.

A fifth official, the back judge, is added.

During a forward pass if the spot of a pass violation is behind the offense's goal line, the penalty is enforced from previous spot.

The field judge may use his whistle to assist the referee or other officials in declaring the ball dead.

Sudden death is adopted for divisional playoffs and championship games.

1948 Officials notifying each team that there are five minutes before the start of the second half must notify the head coach personally.

If an intended pass is downed behind the line, it is a referee's time out until any players who have gone downfield for a pass have had a reasonable time to return.

Plastic helmets are prohibited and coaches are to assume primary responsibility for the use of equipment that endangers their own or opponents' players.

A flexible artificial tee may be used at the kickoff.

If a foul occurs beyond the line during a backward pass or a fumble from scrimmage, the basic spot of enforcement is the spot of the pass or fumble.

It is illegal to bat or punch a ball in any direction while it is in player's possession.

When a player is disqualified, the referee must notify his coach.

1949 Any number of substitutes may enter while the ball is dead during time in.

Eligible pass receivers of a given team may wear different color helmets than their teammates. All the receivers must wear the same color.

Both the players' benches may be located on the same side of the field.

Plastic helmets are permitted.

1950 Free substitution is readopted.

A backward pass going out of bounds between the goal lines belongs to the team last in possession.

1951 Aluminum shoe cleats are illegal.

A center, guard, or tackle is not eligible to touch a forward pass from scrimmage even when he is on the end of the line.

An illegal-touching violation by a member of the kicking team does not offset a foul by the receivers.

1952 All players must be numbered according to their position "except as provided for nationally known players."

A player is not considered to be illegally in motion provided he is not going forward at the snap.

The penalty for offensive pass interference is 15 yards from the previous spot and not loss of down.

1953 Withdrawn players and substitutes do not have to participate for at least one play or down.

A foul between downs must occur after the play has definitely ended.

Rules regarding hurdling cover only the act of a runner.

Players must be moving forward to be considered illegally in motion.

1954 The referee is the sole judge of and must pressure gauge all game balls on the field prior to the start of a game.

In case of rain or a wet or slippery field, playable balls can be requested at any time by the offensive team, and are to be furnished by the home team attendant from the side lines.

There will be a referee's time out for at least 10 seconds during change of possession, longer when required.

The use of a tee for a free kick after a fair catch is prohibited.

Illegal "kicking" of ball must be with the foot to be considered a foul.

1955 The ball is put in play at the spot of the interception when intercepting momentum causes the ball to be declared dead in the end zone possession.

Ten seconds may be run off the clock for the team in possession during the last two minutes of a half if it is behind in the score or the game is tied.

If a player touches the ground with any part of his body, except his hands or feet, while in the grasp of an opponent and irrespective of the grasp being broken, the ball is declared dead immediately.

A player on the kicking team who has been out of bounds may not touch, recover, or advance a scrimmage kick beyond the line.

1956 When a runner is contacted by a defensive player and he touches the ground with any part of his body except his hands or feet, the ball shall be declared dead immediately.

A brown ball with white stripes will be used for night games.

No artificial material shall be permitted to assist in the execution of a field goal or try-for-point.

Halftime will be 20 minutes long.

It is illegal to grab or grasp face guards, except the ball carrier's.

Loudspeaker coaching from sidelines is not permitted.

When an interior lineman takes a three-point stance and moves after taking that stance, he must be ruled offside or illegally in motion.

1957 On all requested time outs the referee will not sound his whistle for play to start until 60 seconds have elapsed.

Head linesmen will use a clamp on the chains when measuring for a first down.

1958 The back judge will be the official timer of the game.

On all requested time outs, the referee will not signify that the ball will be put in play prior to one minute and 30 seconds of elapsed time.

1959 No changes.

1960 American Football League permits one- or two-point conversion.

The official time is kept on the scoreboard clock in the AFL.

1961 No changes.

1962 No player shall grasp the face mask of an opponent. A flagrant offender will be disqualified.

The sudden death rule applies to the Pro Bowl game.

1963 When the spot of the snap is inside the offense's 15 yard line and between the inbounds lines, the ball is spotted at the nearest inbound line.

1964 No changes.

1965 The color of the officials' flags will be bright gold.

A sixth official, the line judge, is added.

A shift will begin after players assume a set position instead of when they come out of the huddle.

1966 Goal posts will be offset from the goal line and the uprights will extend a minimum of 20 feet above the crossbar and will be painted bright gold in color.

1967 A player who signals for a fair catch may not block or initiate contact with one of the kickers until the ball touches a player.

Goal posts will be single standard.

Fields will be rimmed by a white border, six feet wide.

1968 No changes.

1969 Kicking shoes will be of standard production and not subsequently modified in any manner.

The referee can charge a team time out when it is apparent an injured player cannot leave the field under his own power. The referee does not have to wait until the captain requests the team time out.

The kicker as well as the holder may be beyond the line when a placekick is made.

1970 The official time will be kept on the scoreboard clock.

1971 A team will not be charged a time out for an injured player unless the injury occurs in the last two minutes of either half.

The defense may advance on unsuccessful field goal attempt after it crosses the defense's goal line.

Holding, illegal use of hands, and clipping fouls committed by the offensive team behind the line of scrimmage during forward passes will be penalized from the previous spot.

If there is a double foul during a down in which there is a change of possession, the team last gaining possession may keep the ball after enforcement for its foul, provided its foul was not prior to the final change of possession—the "clean hands" rule.

A new pass blocking definition is added. Pass blocking is the obstruction of an opponent by the use of that part of the blocker's body above his knees. During a legal block, the hands must be cupped or closed and remain inside the blocker's elbows and must remain inside the frame of the opponent as well as the blocker's body. The arms must be in a flexed position, but cannot be fully extended to create a push. By use of up and down action of flexed arms, the blocker is permitted to ward off the opponent's attempt to grasp his jersey or arms and prevent legal contact to his head. The blocker is not permitted to push, clamp down on, hang on to, or encircle the opponent.

A passer can be penalized when he throws, tosses, or lobs the ball away with a deliberate attempt to prevent a loss of yardage by his team.

1972 The inbounds lines or hashmarks are moved to

70 feet, 9 inches from the side lines.

When it is fourth down for the offense at or inside its 15 yard line, the ball will be spotted 20 yards from the side line.

The penalty for an illegal receiver accidentally going out of bounds and returning to touch a pass is reduced from 15 yards and loss of down to loss of down.

The penalty for grasping a face mask, unless flagrantly, is reduced to five yards.

The commissioner will notify teams when a brown ball with white stripes will be used for a late-starting game.

A kick from scrimmage that crosses the goal line may be advanced by the defensive team into the field of play.

All fouls by the offense behind the line of scrimmage in the field of play will be penalized from the previous spot.

Disqualified players may not re-enter during overtime periods.

1973 The clock will start on the snap following all changes of team possession.

Periods can be extended if there is a change of team possession after there is a foul by the offense.

All players are to be numbered according to their positions.

Close line play is defined as the area ordinarily occupied by offensive tackles and longitudinally three yards on either side of the line of scrimmage.

A defensive player who jumps or stands on a teammate or who is picked up by a teammate cannot attempt to block a kick.

If the receiving team commits a foul during a kick from scrimmage after the ball is kicked, it will not lose the ball as part of its penalty.

1974 The goal posts are moved from the goal line to the end line.

Kickoffs will be made from the 35 not the 40 yard line.

During a kick from scrimmage, only the end men are permitted to go beyond the line of scrimmage before the ball is kicked.

Field goals attempted and missed from the scrimmage line beyond the 20 yard line will result in the defensive team taking possession of the ball at the line of scrimmage. Field goals attempted and missed from the line of scrimmage inside the 20 yard line will result in the defensive team taking possession at the 20 yard line.

When the spot of enforcement for holding, illegal use of hands, arms, or body on offense as well as tripping fouls is not in the field of play at or behind the line of scrimmage or no deeper than three yards beyond the line of scrimmage, the penalty will be 10 yards.

Eligible pass receivers can only be chucked once by any defender after the receiver has gone three yards beyond the line of scrimmage.

Eligible receivers who line up in a position within two yards of a tackle may be legally blocked below the waist at the line of scrimmage.

Eligible receivers who line up more than two yards from a tackle may not be blocked below the waist at or behind the line of scrimmage.

It is illegal for an offensive player to block an opponent below the waist within an area three yards on either side of the line of scrimmage if the blocker is aligned in a position more than two yards outside his tackle and is moving in toward the position of the ball, either at the snap or after it is made—an illegal crackback.

The sudden death system of determining the winner when the score is tied at end of regulation playing time is in effect for preseason and regular season games except that the playing time will be limited to a maximum of one 15-minute period.

A broken limit line is to encompass the entire field two feet outside the white border except in the coaching areas.

1975 End zone markings and club identification at the 50 yard line must be approved by the commissioner.

Pylons not flags will be used for goal line and end line markings.

There will be standard side line markers and chain crews will be uniformly attired.

Ball boys will be clearly identifiable.

Unsportsmanlike conduct includes lingering on the field when being substituted for.

A team may use a double shift on or inside the opponent's 20 yard line after showing it at least three times previously in the game.

A fourth down pass that is incomplete in or through the end zone when the line of scrimmage is inside the 20 will result in the opponent taking possession at the previous line of scrimmage.

If there are penalties on each team on the same play and one results in disqualification, the penalties will be offsetting, but the disqualification will stand.

The penalty for an ineligible player downfield on a forward pass is reduced from 15 to 10 yards.

The penalty for offensive pass interference is reduced from 15 to 10 yards.

Penalties for defensive holding or illegal use of hands will be assessed from the previous line of scrimmage rather than from the spot where the ball is blown dead if that spot is behind the line of scrimmage.

1976 There will be 24 not 12 footballs available each game.

Footballs with stripes will no longer be used.

The toss of the coin will be held three minutes before the kickoff, not 30 minutes before.

A delay of game penalty will no longer be enforced when a runner carries the ball in a manner clearly designed to consume playing time.

Any foul committed by the defense which prevents the try-for-point from being attempted will result in the down being replayed and the kicking team having the option as to when the yardage penalty will be assessed—on the next try or on the ensuing kickoff. Any foul committed by the defense on a successful try will result in a distance penalty being assessed on the following kickoff.

It is illegal for a defender to use a hand or hands on a teammate to gain additional height in an attempt to block a kick.

Each team may not have more than 15 persons in addition to its uniformed players on each side line.

When spectators enter the playing field before the game is over, the field must be cleared in order to allow completion of the game.

Two 30-second clocks visible to players, officials, and fans will be displayed, noting the official time between the ready-for-play signal and the snap of the ball.

A ribbon 2 inches by 36 inches long will be attached to the top of each goal post to assist in determining wind direction.

A player who reports a change in his eligibility, prior to a touchdown, can legally return to his original position for a try-for-point attempt without having to leave the field for one play.

A defender is not permitted to rough a ball carrier who falls to the ground untouched by running or diving into him.

Whenever a disqualified player is banished from a game, he must leave the entire playing field area.

1977 It is illegal for a defensive lineman to strike an opponent above the shoulders or to make a head slap.

The coin toss may be held at any time within three minutes of kickoff.

It is illegal for a back who lines up inside a tight end to move to the outside and then back inside again to crack back on a defender below the waist.

An offensive lineman who takes a two point stance must have some part of his body within one foot of his end of the ball to be legally on the line of scrimmage.

Any shoe worn by a player with an artificial limb must have its kicking surface conform to that of a normal kicking toe.

If the kicking team fouls during a punt before possession changes and the receiving team fouls after possession changes, the penalties will offset and the down will be replayed.

A defender will be permitted to make contact with an eligible receiver either in the three-yard zone beyond the line of scrimmage or once beyond that zone, but not both.

A team will lose its coin toss option and sustain a 15-yard penalty if it does not arrive on the field for warmup at least 15 minutes before the scheduled kickoff.

It is illegal for a wide receiver to clip an opponent anywhere, including in the legal clipping zone.

Kicking a loose ball is a foul only if the act is deliberate.

1978 Extended arms and open hands are permissible in pass blocking.

During the last two minutes of a half, it is the responsibility of the defensive team to line up properly when the referee signals ready for play.

The officials have the right to not stop the clock or to run 10 seconds off a stopped clock when a team deliberately attempts to conserve time in the last two minutes of a half.

When the ball is carried across the line of scrimmage, no legal forward pass can be thrown.

A double touch of a forward pass is legal, but batting a pass in flight toward an opponent's goal line is illegal.

The penalty for intentional grounding in the field of play is reduced from a loss of down and 15 yards to a loss of down and 10 yards. It is a safety when a passer illegally grounds a ball in the end zone.

Defenders are permitted to maintain contact with receivers in a five-yard zone beyond the line of scrimmage, but contact is restricted beyond that point.

Hurdling is no longer a foul.

Taunting or baiting opponents is an unsportsmanlike conduct penalty.

A 15-yard penalty will be assessed during a down involving a double foul without change of possession when one foul carries a 15-yard penalty and the other only 5 yards.

There will be seven game officials instead of six. A side judge was added.

All 15-yard penalties are reduced to 10 yards except those involving unnecessary roughness, unsportsmanlike conduct, personal fouls, disqualification, or palpably unfair acts.

If there is a defensive foul behind the line of scrimmage during a play in which a runner is downed behind the line, the offensive team will be awarded sufficient penalty yardage to advance the ball to at least the former line of scrimmage and a first down.

1979 The captain who lost the pregame coin toss can delay his second-half choice until immediately before the start of the second half.

A team whose player is injured by a personal foul committed during the last two minutes of a half will not be charged with a time out if the player is disabled after the penalty has been assessed.

There will be a consistent length of time for the clock to be stopped before it is restarted again whenever a quarterback is sacked behind the line of scrimmage.

Defensive linemen can wear numbers in the nineties.

Any time a player leaves the field on the wrong side of the field or over the end line of the end zone, his team will be penalized five yards from the previous spot of the ball, whether the violation is discovered during the down or at the end of the down.

If an offensive player fumbles anywhere on the field during a fourth-down play, or if a player fumbles on any down after the two-minute warning in a half, only the fumbling player can recover and/or advance the ball.

If a member of the receiving team touches a scrimmage kick in the field of play or in the end zone, and a member of the kicking team legally recovers the ball in the end zone, the kicking team will retain possession either at the spot the ball was first touched by the receiving team or at the 1-yard line.

No player on the receiving team can block opponents below the waist during a kickoff, punt, or field goal attempt.

The prohibited crackback zone on either side of the line of scrimmage is extended from three yards to five.

Officials are to blow the play dead as soon as the quarterback is clearly in the grasp and control of any tackler.

A player will be penalized for unsportsmanlike conduct when he commits a non-contact act such as throwing a punch or a forearm or kicking at an opponent.

It is illegal for a player to use his helmet to butt or ram an opponent, or to use the crown of the helmet unnecessarily (spearing).

A period can be extended to permit a team whose opportunity to catch a scrimmage kick has been interfered with on the last play. The offended team can run one play from scrimmage, attempt a field goal, or attempt a free kick.

1980 Members of both teams may talk to their respective coaches during any injury time out.

A time out for injury will not be charged to a team if any foul committed by an opponent in the last two minutes of a half caused the injury.

It is illegal for a player to strike, swing, or club an opponent in the head, neck, or face even if the initial contact is below the head.

It is mandatory for the official to run the clock for 10 seconds before permitting the ball to be put in play when officials rule that a team has used illegal efforts to conserve time during the last two minutes of a half.

1981 It is illegal for players to use any form of adhesive substance while participating in a game.

A player will be credited with a catch if he controls the ball when his second foot clearly lands on the ground inbounds.

Players who change their eligibility by virtue of a change of position must report such change to the referee before the start of each play.

An intentional grounding penalty will result in a loss of down and the ball will be put in play at the spot of the foul if that spot was more than 10 yards behind the line of scrimmage.

When an ineligible receiver touches a forward pass on or behind the line of scrimmage, the penalty will be loss of down. When an ineligible receiver is touched beyond the line of scrimmage, the penalty will be a loss of 10 yards.

The penalty for offensive blocking from behind above the waist is 10 yards.

The penalty for defensive fouls committed behind the line when the runner or intended passer is tackled behind the line will be enforced from the spot of the foul, or the spot where the ball becomes dead.

Eliminated the spot where possession was lost as a potential spot of enforcement for a personal foul committed prior to a completion or interception of a pass. The penalty will be assessed from the previous spot and the offended team will retain possession of the ball.

The fourth-down fumble rule will no longer apply when a player touches, but does not possess, a snap from center, unless there is a hand-to-hand exchange.

1982 There will be no automatic first down if the defense is penalized for incidental grasping of the face mask.

The player possession rule was altered to read: A player other than an eligible receiver is in possession when he has held the ball firmly in his grasp long enough to have established control. In order for an eligible receiver of a forward pass to be in possession, he must control the ball throughout the act of clearly touching both feet, or any other part of his body other than his hand(s), to the ground inbounds. If the player is hit, causing the ball to come loose simultaneously while clearly touching both feet or any other part of his body except the hand(s) inbounds, there is no possession.

Illegal uniform items now include hard or soft hip pads that are not covered by the outer uniform.

Rules covering the showing of a double shift inside the opponent's 20 yard line and the shortening of the length of the game were eliminated.

The penalties for illegal batting or punching the ball, and illegal kicking of the ball with the foot or leg are 10 yards (instead of 15). Neither is a personal foul.

PENALTIES

FIVE YARDS

1. Crawling.
2. Defensive holding or illegal use of the hands (automatic first down).
3. Delay of game (15 yards if at the start of the half).
4. Encroachment.
5. Too many time outs.
6. False start.
7. Illegal formation.
8. Illegal shift.
9. Illegal motion.
10. Illegal substitution.
11. Kickoff out of bounds between the goal lines and not touched.
12. Invalid fair catch signal.
13. More than 11 players on the field at the snap for either team.
14. Less than seven men on the offensive line at the snap.
15. Offside.
16. Failure to pause one second after a shift or huddle.
17. Running into the kicker (automatic first down).
18. More than one man in motion at the snap.
19. Grasping the face mask of opponent.
20. Player out of bounds at the snap.
21. Ineligible member(s) of the kicking team going beyond the line of scrimmage before the ball is kicked.
22. Illegal return.
23. Failure to report change of eligibility.

FIVE YARDS AND LOSS OF DOWN

1. Forward pass thrown from beyond the line of scrimmage.

SUSPENSION FROM GAME

1. Illegal equipment; the player may return after one down when he is legally equipped.

10 YARDS

1. Offensive pass interference.
2. Ineligible player downfield during a passing down.

3. Holding, illegal use of hands, arms, or body by the offense.
4. Tripping by a member of either team.
5. Helping the runner.
6. Illegal batting or punching a loose ball.
7. Deliberately kicking a loose ball.

10 YARDS AND LOSS OF DOWN

1. Intentional grounding of a forward pass; it is a safety if the passer is in his own end zone.

15 YARDS

1. Clipping below the waist.
2. Fair catch interference.
3. Illegal crackback block by the offense.
4. Piling on (automatic first down).
5. Roughing the kicker (automatic first down).
6. Roughing the passer (automatic first down).
7. Twisting, turning, or pulling an opponent by the face mask.
8. Unnecessary roughness.
9. Unsportsmanlike conduct.
10. Delay of the game at the start of either half.
11. Illegal blocking below the waist.
12. A tackler using his helmet to butt, spear, or ram an opponent.
13. Any player using the top of his helmet unnecessarily.
14. A team's late arrival on the field prior to the scheduled kickoff (includes loss of coin toss option).

15 YARDS AND DISQUALIFICATION IF FLAGRANT

1. Striking an opponent with a fist.
2. Kicking or kneeing an opponent.
3. Striking an opponent on the head or neck with a forearm, elbow, or hands.
4. Roughing the kicker.
5. Roughing the passer.
6. Malicious unnecessary roughness.
7. Unsportsmanlike conduct.
8. Palpably unfair act.

LOSS OF DOWN—NO YARDAGE

1. Second forward pass behind the line.
2. Forward pass striking the ground, goal post, or crossbar.
3. Forward pass going out of bounds.
4. Forward pass first touched by an eligible receiver who has gone out of bounds and returned.
5. Forward pass touched or caught by an ineligible receiver on or behind the line of scrimmage.
6. Forward pass thrown from behind the line of scrimmage after the ball has crossed the line.

AUTOMATIC FIRST DOWN

1. All defensive fouls except offside, encroachment, delay of game, illegal substitution, excessive time outs, and incidental grasp of the face mask.

A TOUCHDOWN AWARDED

1. When the referee determines that a palpably unfair act deprives a team of a touchdown, such as the act of a player coming off the bench and tackling a runner apparently en route to a touchdown.

WHERE OFFICIALS STAND

DURING A KICKOFF

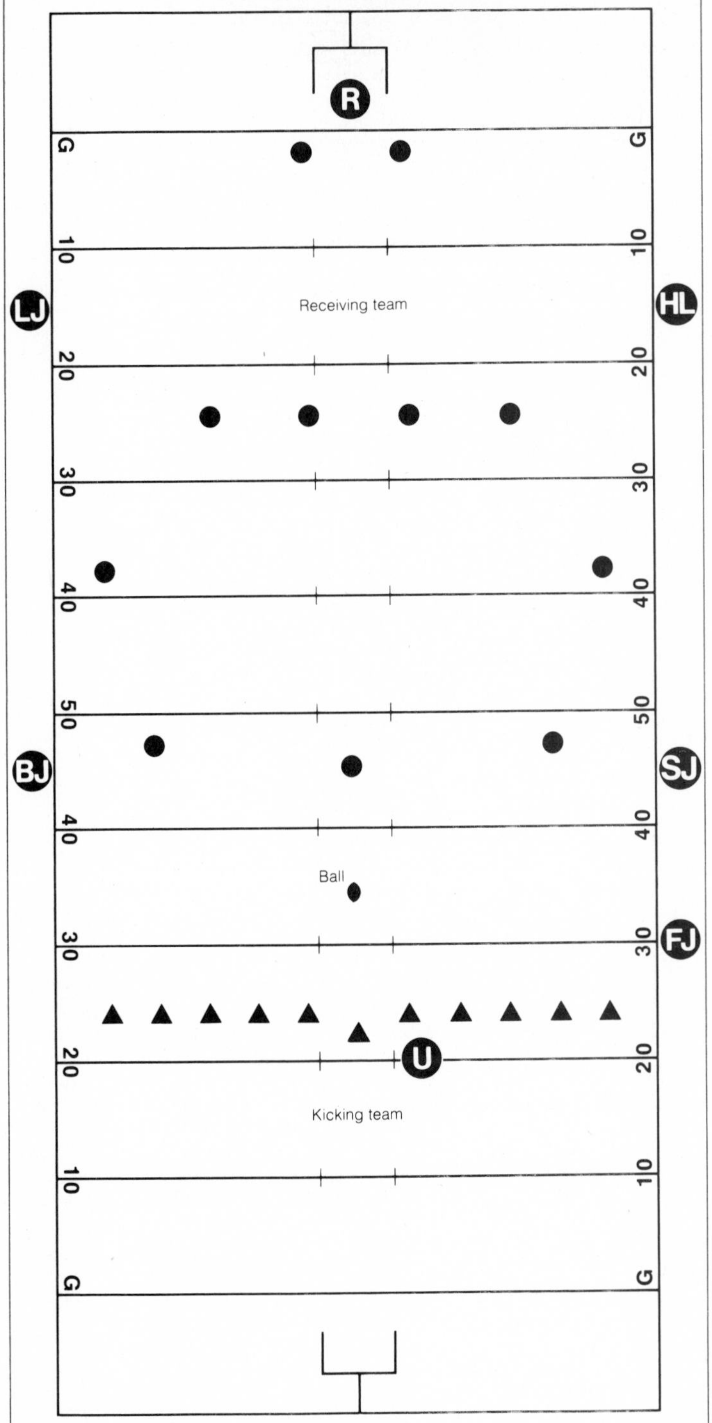

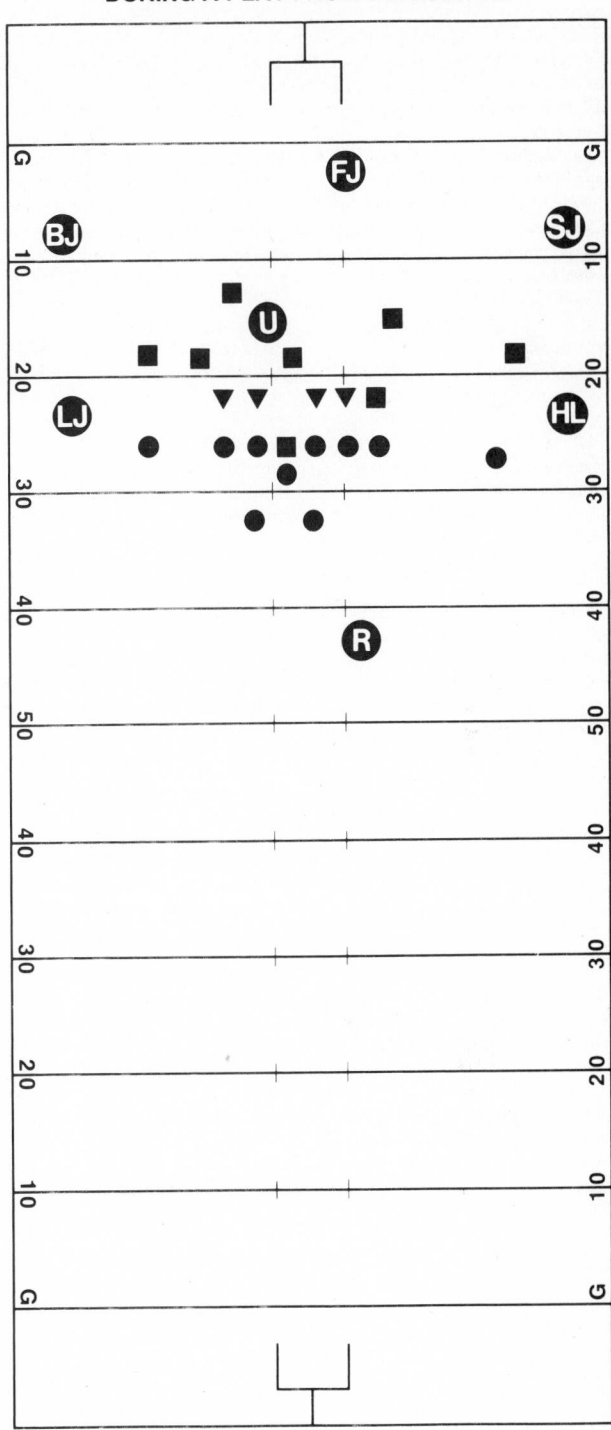

DURING A PLAY FROM SCRIMMAGE

Legend
R   Referee
U   Umpire
LJ Line Judge
HL Head Linesman
BJ Back Judge
SJ Side Judge
FJ Field Judge

AFTER A PASS IS THROWN

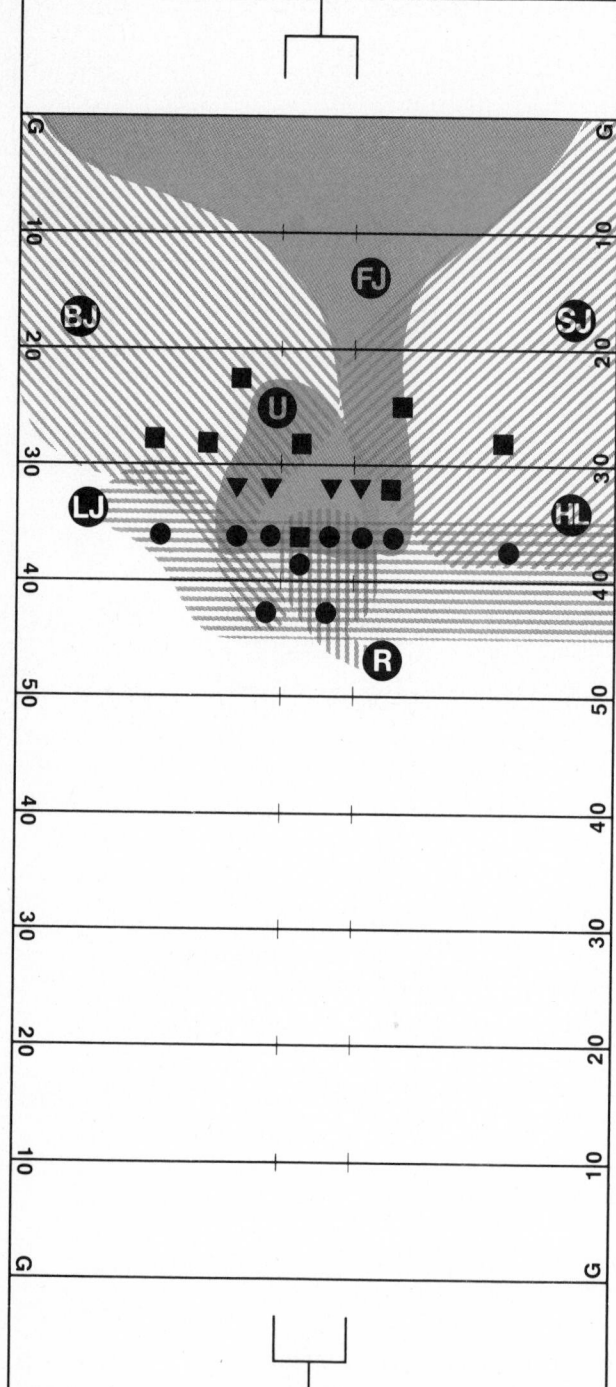

DURING A FIELD GOAL ATTEMPT

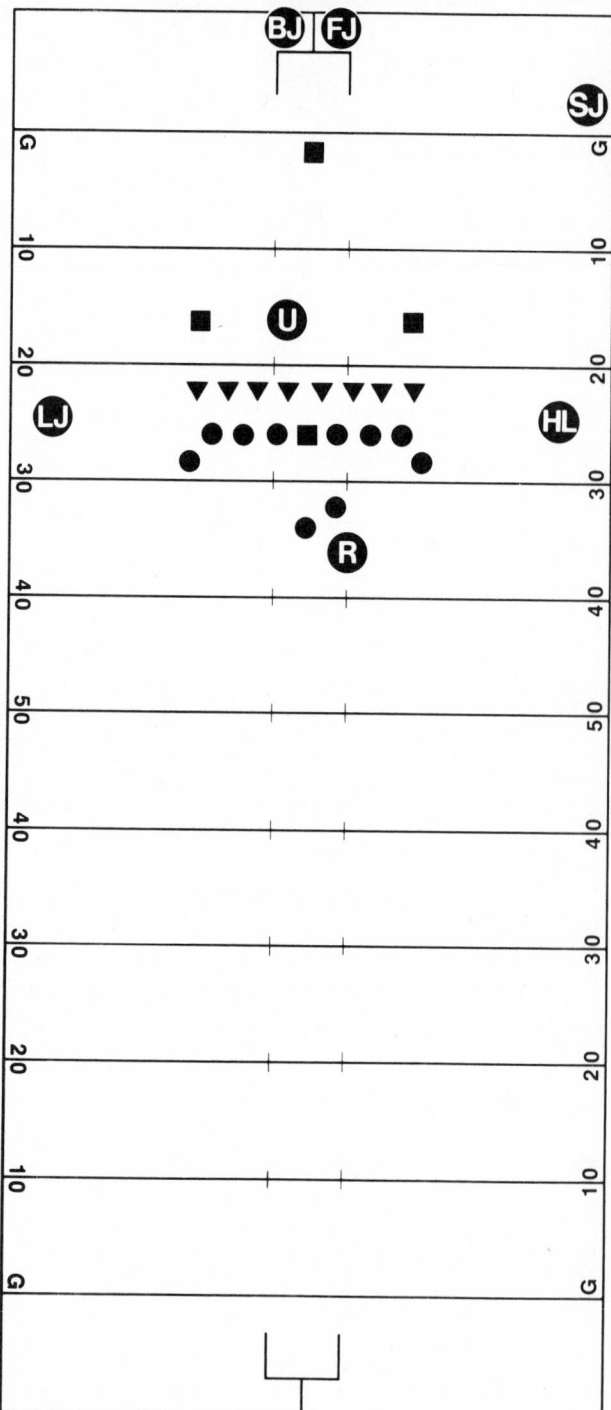

DURING A PUNT

G   G

FJ

BJ   SJ

10   10

■   ■

20   20

30   30

40   40

50   50

40   40

■   U   ■

LJ   ▼ ▼ ▼ ▼ ▼ ▼   HL
● ● ● ● ● ● ●
● ●
●
●

R

G   G

TOOLS OF NFL OFFICIALS

UNIFORM Uniforms—especially striped shirts—are the trademarks of officials. The distinctive long-sleeved shirts worn in the NFL, with two-inch vertical stripes throughout, an abbreviation for the position along with the number on the breast pocket, and the official's position and number on the back, are made for the league by Bug Sporting Goods Company; no other model is allowed. A new official hired by the NFL gets two shirts. He also is issued a new pair of knickers, or pants, standard black stockings with horizontal white stripes, and two penalty flags. He provides his own cap (black with white piping for the referee, white for the other six officials), belt, shoes, and other items. Measures are taken to ensure standard appearance. There is no rule for how and where the knickers are tucked under at the knee, but the black stockings must be worn on the outside, with cotton socks and sanitary hose underneath. Belts and shoes must be solid black. In inclement weather, officials wear black and plastic rain jackets with vertical stripes. When it is very cold they may wear thermal underwear or rubberized sweatwear under their uniforms. They are encouraged not to put on pair after pair of extra socks that may make them slow afoot; instead, ordinary grocery store Baggies on each foot have been found to serve extremely well as an insulator. A ski headband and gloves are acceptable, too, in cold weather, but they must be black or white in color. The late Jack Vest once wore blue gloves during a chilly Monday night television game and the letters received later at NFL headquarters making light of Vest's blue gloves have never been forgotten.

BALL It is manufactured by the Wilson Sporting Goods Company of Ada, Ohio, and sold at a retail price of $40.00. The home team in every game must provide 24 of them to the referee and it is his responsibility before the game to make sure they are properly inflated and, using a wet towel, to wipe away the gloss that may still be on the ball from the factory.

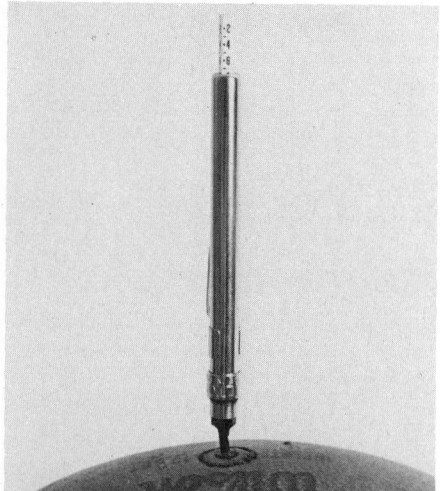

PRESSURE GAUGE It is provided by the league to all its referees and it is the tool they use to insure that the 36 balls used in each game are properly inflated to 12½ to 13½ pounds of air.

COIN The referee tosses it to determine which team wins the right to choose whether to receive or kick off. It is not league issue; referees provide it from their own pockets. Silver dollars are used more than any other coins and referees like to use a coin with sentimental value, for example one that has been in their family for a long time. Because regular and postseason games may go into sudden death and another coin toss is necessary to start it, the coin must be carried in the pocket for the entire game instead of being stored in a bag.

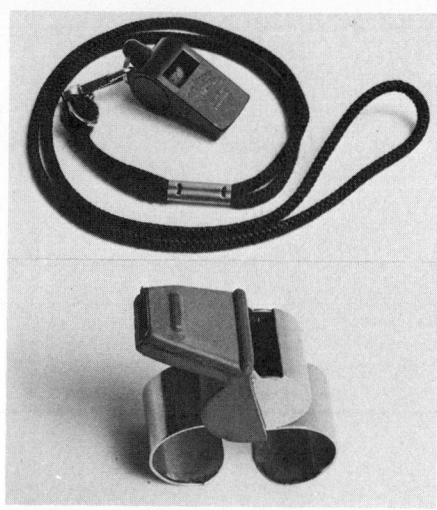

WHISTLES Officials signal to start and end plays hundreds of times during a game. They need a strong pair of lungs and a good whistle. It is estimated that 60 percent of the NFL officials prefer to wear their whistles around their necks, on a necklace of cord, leather, or ordinary hobby shop lanyard. The whistle rests on the end of the necklace or is carried in the lips and blown at the proper time. The other 40 percent of the officials favor the finger whistle; they argue that, carried on the finger, the whistle must be brought to the lips before it can be blown and therefore there is no chance for a "quick whistle."

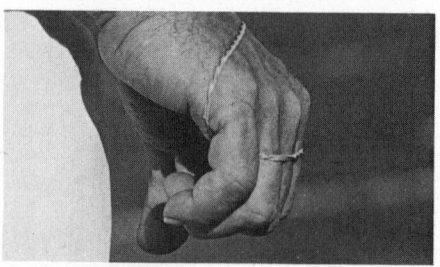

RUBBER BAND Improvisation is the hallmark of any good official and ordinary office supply rubber bands serve an important function. Two of them are knotted together and, worn round a wrist and the correct fingers, keep the official informed of the down in progress. One finger, first down; two fingers, second down; and so on.

PENALTY FLAG It is the instrument with which NFL games are policed. Flying through the air, it is the sight coaches and players like to see least. It can end drives, break hearts, and shorten careers . . . and there would be no league without it. The league issues it to the official but he must sew some object into a corner of it—a fishing lead or a nut, bolt, or washer—that will weight it and make it land accurately near the point of the infraction. When not in use it is tucked away in the official's back pocket.

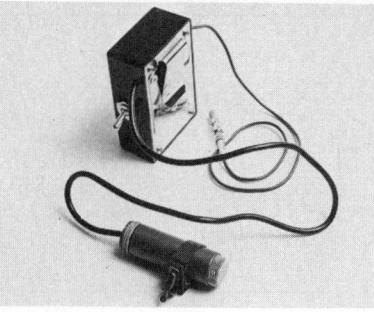

MICROPHONE The referee is the only official equipped with a microphone and he uses it to announce penalties. He wears a Vega transmitter with a four-inch antenna on his belt behind him. The transmitter has a nine-volt battery, a frequency of 150 megacycles, and a power output of 20 milowatts. A cord connects the transmitter to a microphone worn clipped to the official's striped shirt at the chest. Only announcements are heard because he has an on-and-off switch on his transmitter. The radio unit, which is built exclusively for stadium use to prevent receiving other signals on the business band, is connected to the public address system.

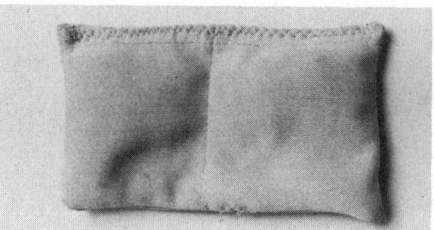

BEANBAG Rarely used, it marks the spot of the change of possession—where the interception was made, where the fumble was picked up. Its role can be vital when a foul occurs after such a change of possession. The deep officials on kicks—head linesmen and line judge on kickoffs, back, side, and field judges on punts—also assist statisticians by marking the spot where the kickoff or punt was caught. The statistician in the press box can then determine the length of the kick and return, especially if the kickoff is fielded in the end zone, where there are no yard lines. Beanbags once were yellow but everyone kept confusing them with penalty flags. They changed to green but then no one could see them. They then changed to blue.

HEAD LINESMAN'S CLIP This important tool is used when first down measurements are made. The chain must be moved from the sideline to the hashmarks and so its location must be carefully noted before it is moved. The head linesman marks it with this clip at the nearest major yard line and adjusts the disc attached to the clip to indicate the yard line. Moved to the hashmarks for the measurement, the chain is then put down and stretched from the identical forward edge of the same yard line for the measurement.

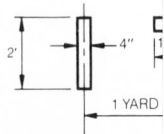

NUMBERS It woul[d]
game—and impossi[ble]
game film of it—with[out]
feet high, large enoug[h]
the farthest seat in th[e]
the official detail spe[cifies]
making their field nu[mbers]
approximating a face
but highly readable.

HASHMARKS Thi[s]
tion given NFL te[ams]
hashmarks. When th[e]
hashmarks, it is retur[ned]
next play. Since ther[e]
yards, hashmarks the

SIDELINE YARD
yard line marker use[d]
fabric cover over a p[ole]
players or others strik[e]
the corners to keep it
wind is blowing. This
are made for the NFL
of El Reno, Oklahom[a]

PYLON A pylon ma[rks]
It is a 4″ × 4″ × 18″
ground. It will bend
upright position after
safer than the flag and
each corner of the en[d]
receivers cut toward t[he]
This should be chang[ed]
patterns," but it is hig[h]
pen.

STOPWATCH Electronics has taken over the job of timing pro football games but there are still two officials equipped with stopwatches in case the machines fail. Backing up the clock operator who is on the sideline or in the press box, the line judge times the game with a Swiss Heuer Game Master stopwatch, worth approximately $110, worn on his wrist. The reset button on the base of the watch can be screwed tight so the line judge can continue to start and stop the watch using the other buttons, free of worry about hitting the reset button and losing track of time. The field judge also is equipped with a stopwatch. He backs up the 30-second clock operator in timing the offense putting the ball in play. He wears a $200 Longines Chronograph for this job.

GAME DATA CARD It is the referee's report to the league of every call made by his crew during the game. Each crew member charts his calls and other important information during the game and it is then placed on a single card by the referee and mailed to the NFL headquarters immediately after the game.

PISTOL The field judge carries a .22 caliber pistol and fires it to signal the end of each quarter. The pistol fires blanks. It was once carried from game to game by the field judge but the era of hijackings of airplanes, and the resultant tightened security measures, ended that. Now each team's equipment manager stores a pistol in the locker room and turns it over to the field judge before each game.

FIELD AND STADIUM HARDWARE

FIELD This is the official NFL diagram for a football field. It is distributed to each team and must be followed explicitly. The field is 160 feet wide and, including the end zones, 360 feet long. It is surrounded by a six-foot wide white border that appears in black on the diagram; this border assists officials in making sideline calls, improves fan vantage, and restrains and protects photographers. The numbers are 36 feet, or 12 yards, from each sideline; the hashmarks 70 feet 9 inches, or about 23 yards from each sideline.

STADIUM CLOCK It is the official timekeeper for the game and is operated by an experienced and knowledgeable football official who is appointed by the Commissioner. That is his only job. The additional functions of electronic message and scoreboards are done by other people. Their jobs are unrelated to the all-important timing of the game.

30-SECOND CLOCK Another official appointed by the Commisioner operates the 30-second clock. It was used for the first time in 1976 and is manufactured by the General Indicator Company. It is four feet high and six feet wide and is raised at least five feet off the ground so it can be seen clearly by fans, quarterback, the referee, and the field judge. There is a 30-second clock at each end of the field. The offense has 30 seconds to put the ball in play from the time the referee signals ready for play. If it does not, it incurs a five-yard delay of game penalty.

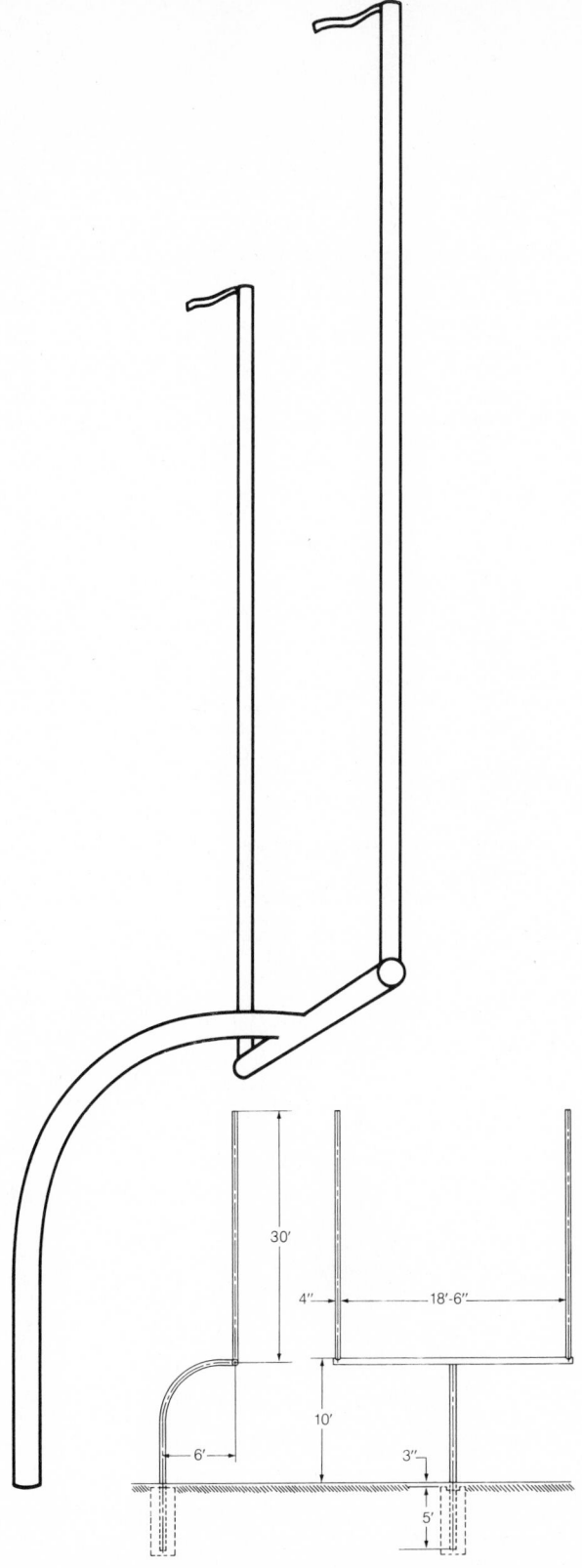

GOAL POSTS The bright gold single standard offset Triman Tele-Goal is used in every NFL stadium. It was invented by Jim Trimble, who is now director of pro personnel for the New York Giants and at the time was a Canadian Football League coach, and Joel Rottman, a Canadian engineer and football fan. It weighs 240 pounds. The crossbar is 10 feet above the end line and the uprights soar 30 feet above the crossbar, a full 20 feet higher than those in high school and college. This eliminates a large share of the arguments that occur when placekicks go above, not between, the uprights. Ribbons 4″x 36″ were added in 1976 to assist kickers in determining wind direction.

FIELD AND STADIUM HARDWARE

STOPWATCH Electronics has taken over the job of timing pro football games but there are still two officials equipped with stopwatches in case the machines fail. Backing up the clock operator who is on the sideline or in the press box, the line judge times the game with a Swiss Heuer Game Master stopwatch, worth approximately $110, worn on his wrist. The reset button on the base of the watch can be screwed tight so the line judge can continue to start and stop the watch using the other buttons, free of worry about hitting the reset button and losing track of time. The field judge also is equipped with a stopwatch. He backs up the 30-second clock operator in timing the offense putting the ball in play. He wears a $200 Longines Chronograph for this job.

GAME DATA CARD It is the referee's report to the league of every call made by his crew during the game. Each crew member charts his calls and other important information during the game and it is then placed on a single card by the referee and mailed to the NFL headquarters immediately after the game.

PISTOL The field judge carries a .22 caliber pistol and fires it to signal the end of each quarter. The pistol fires blanks. It was once carried from game to game by the field judge but the era of hijackings of airplanes, and the resultant tightened security measures, ended that. Now each team's equipment manager stores a pistol in the locker room and turns it over to the field judge before each game.

FIELD This is the official NFL diagram for a football field. It is distributed to each team and must be followed explicitly. The field is 160 feet wide and, including the end zones, 360 feet long. It is surrounded by a six-foot wide white border that appears in black on the diagram; this border assists officials in making sideline calls, improves fan vantage, and restrains and protects photographers. The numbers are 36 feet, or 12 yards, from each sideline; the hashmarks 70 feet 9 inches, or about 23 yards from each sideline.

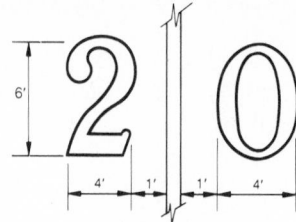

NUMBERS It would be aggravating to watch a game—and impossible to broadcast it or study a game film of it—without field numbers. They are six feet high, large enough so that they can be seen from the farthest seat in the largest NFL stadiums. This is the official detail specification given NFL teams for making their field numbers. The type face, roughly approximating a face called Caslon, is old-fashioned but highly readable.

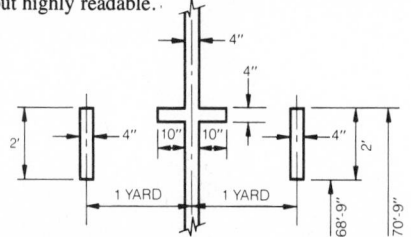

HASHMARKS This is the official detail specification given NFL teams for making their field hashmarks. When the ball is carried outside the hashmarks, it is returned to them for the start of the next play. Since there are yard lines only every five yards, hashmarks themselves are yard lines.

SIDELINE YARD MARKER Each sideline yard line marker used in NFL games is an A-frame fabric cover over a polyfoam pad, for safety in case players or others strike it, and it has lead imbedded in the corners to keep it from being carried away if the wind is blowing. This and all the following products are made for the NFL by the 5-K Products Company of El Reno, Oklahoma.

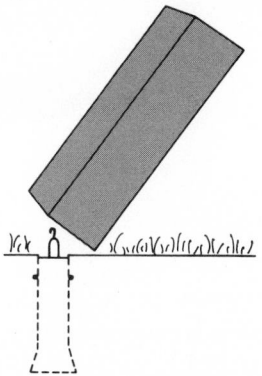

PYLON A pylon marks the corner of each end zone. It is a 4″ × 4″ × 18″ polyfoam pad anchored in the ground. It will bend on contact and snap back to an upright position after it has been struck. It is much safer than the flag and metal flagstaff that was used in each corner of the end zone before 1975. When pass receivers cut toward the flag they ran "flag patterns." This should be changed in NFL playbooks to "pylon patterns," but it is highly unlikely that will ever happen.

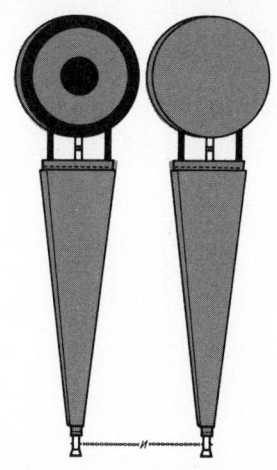

CHAIN UNIT In an age of synthetics the simple metal chain remains the best way to measure the 10 yards of a football field the offense must cover to make a first down. Chain is still best because it does not stretch or tear. The shafts or poles at each end are bright orange for visibility and padded for safety.

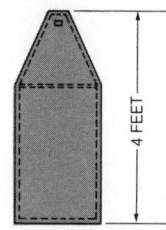

FIRST DOWN GROUND SPOTTER A furious sweep or off-tackle play coming hard for the side line can send even the most well-meaning chain crew member scrambling for safety. When that happens, the sticks are left unattended and their place may be lost, and, in addition, the ball carrier who is driving earnestly for the forward stick to make a first down has lost his target when the stick is thrown to the ground and the chain crew dashes away. In such a situation the first down ground spotter saves the day. Four feet long and bright red in color, it remains in place on the ground even when the sticks are taken away.

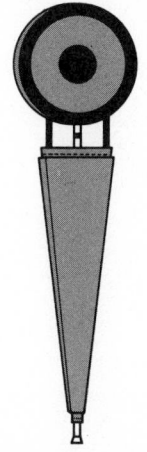

OPPOSITE SIDE BULLSEYE The chain unit is used on one side of the field for the first half and on the other half of the field for the second half. Therefore, on any plays going in the direction away from the chain unit it would be impossible for the runner, receiver, and quarterback to determine the point they must reach to make a first down without the opposite side bullseye. The "bullseye" name and design correctly reflect the exclamation of these players—and their coach—when they reach it.

INDICATOR It indicates the down. The carrier flips over a new card to indicate a new down.

DRIVE START MARKER This is the only tool of NFL officials that has virtually nothing to do with the policing of the game and instead is there entirely for the benefit of the fans and press. It marks the start of a drive made by the offense and is not moved until a score is made or the ball changes hands. It resembles a railroad crossing traffic sign and, at the end of a long drive, the lonely member of the chain crew standing at the far end of the field with the drive start marker shows everyone in the stadium just how far the offense traveled.

OFFICIAL SIGNALS

TOUCHDOWN, FIELD GOAL, or SUCCESSFUL TRY
Both arms extended above head.

UNSPORTSMANLIKE CONDUCT (Non-contact fouls)
Arms outstretched, palms down. (Same signal means continuous action fouls are disregarded.)

DEAD BALL or NEUTRAL ZONE ESTABLISHED
One arm above head with an open hand. With fist closed: **Fourth Down.**

ILLEGAL CONTACT
One open hand extended forward.

FALSE START, ILLEGAL SHIFT, ILLEGAL PROCEDURE, ILLEGAL FORMATION, or KICKOFF OR SAFETY KICK OUT OF BOUNDS
Forearms rotated over and over in front of body.

PLAYER DISQUALIFIED
Ejection signal.

ILLEGAL USE OF HANDS, ARMS, OR BODY
Grasping one wrist, the hand open and facing forward, in front of chest.

ILLEGAL FORWARD PASS
One hand waved behind back followed by loss of down signal.

BALL ILLEGALLY TOUCHED, KICKED, OR BATTED
Fingertips tap both shoulders.

INTENTIONAL GROUNDING OF PASS
Parallel arms waved in a diagonal plane across body.

PASS JUGGLED INBOUNDS AND CAUGHT OUT OF BOUNDS
Hands up and down in front of chest (following incomplete pass signal).

NO TIME OUT or TIME IN WITH WHISTLE
Full arm circled to simulate moving clock.

PERSONAL FOUL
One wrist striking the other above head.
Same signal followed by swinging leg: **Running Into or Roughing Kicker.**
Same signal followed by raised arm swinging forward: **Running Into or Roughing Passer.**
Same signal followed by hand striking back of calf: **Clipping.**

PENALTY REFUSED, INCOMPLETE PASS, PLAY OVER, OR MISSED GOAL
Hands shifted in horizontal plane.

TOUCHING A FORWARD PASS OR SCRIMMAGE KICK
Diagonal motion of one hand across another.

LOSS OF DOWN
Both hands held behind head.

ILLEGAL CUT OR BLOCKING BELOW THE WAIST
Hand striking front of thigh.

CRAWLING, INTERLOCKING INTERFERENCE, PUSHING, OR HELPING RUNNER
Pushing movement of hands to front with arms downward.

TIME OUT
Hands crisscrossed above head.
Same signal followed by placing one hand on top of cap: **Referee's Time Out.**
Same signal followed by arm swung at side: **Touchback.**

SAFETY
Palms together above head.

INVALID FAIR CATCH SIGNAL
One hand waved above head.

FIRST DOWN
Arms pointed toward defensive team's goal.

**INELIGIBLE RECEIVER
or INELIGIBLE
MEMBER OF KICKING
TEAM DOWNFIELD**
Right hand touching top of cap.

**DELAY OF GAME or
EXCESS TIME OUT**
Folded arms.

ILLEGAL MOTION AT SNAP
Horizontal arc with one hand.

OFFSIDE or ENCROACHING
Hands on hips.

TRIPPING
Repeated action of right foot
in back of left heel.

ILLEGAL CRACKBACK
Strike of an open right hand
against the right mid thigh.

**INTERFERENCE WITH FORWARD
PASS or FAIR CATCH**
Hands open
and extended forward from
shoulders with hands vertical.

HOLDING
Grasping one wrist,
the fist clenched,
in front of chest.

A History of Football Equipment

There is an old saying that, "Clothes make the man." And there is an enduring conviction in the sport of football that new equipment—a change of uniforms—can help transform a losing team into a winner. It is the first impulse of any new coach, about to embark on a campaign to build a juggernaut upon the rubble of long years of poor won-and-lost records, to march earnestly to the office of the general manager or athletic director and persuade him that, hang the expense, the team must order new uniforms right away.

George (Potsy) Clark left the Detroit Lions in 1937 to become the coach of the Brooklyn Dodgers. An enterprising and imaginative man, he had steered the Lions to the NFL championship in 1934 and, in 1935, authored *Football by Potsy Clark,* one of the first magazines about professional football. He now planned to stand the league on its ear by dressing the Dodgers in scintillating new uniforms. They were going to be so grand, the *Brooklyn Eagle* said, "that Solomon in all his glory would look like Mahatma Gandhi.

"One of the things that may have been the matter with the Dodgers last year was their drab and lifeless uniform," the newspaper continued. "No athlete with any aesthetic sensibility could be expected to gain ground wearing the hideous green and white combination in which they were clothed.

"It has been proven time and again that gorgeous uniforms make soldiers brave. A man might be able to fight just as well in a two-pants suit or a pair of overalls, but he wouldn't have the inspiration that makes heroes."

To tackle the problem, Clark called in Wilford A. Lindberg, color engineer of the Chrysler Corporation. "He has a laboratory that the late Thomas A. Edison would have envied," the *Eagle* wrote. "He polished up his instruments, whirled his discs, started his machines, and got down his big black books. When everything had been added up and measured and divided up and so on, the answer was 'Toreador Red.'

"That would be the dominant motif for Brooklyn's football team. It will be the color of their jerseys. Their trousers, helmets, and even their shoelaces, meanwhile, will be silver. These colors suggest action and energy. The red falls between the Lithum lines of 6708 and 6104 Angstrom units and is very high intensity, calculated to create interest on the part of the spectators.

"It is easy to see what the psychological effect of these costumes will be. Potsy likes for his players to come out of the huddle as if shot from guns. In these new suits they will look like a burst of flame as they jump to their positions."

The other teams in the NFL, unfortunately, kept from being charred by the Dodgers. In fact, Brooklyn won only 11 games and lost 17 during the next three years with Clark as their coach and Toreador Red as their motif. Wilford A. Lindberg was never consulted again by any football team but he continued to design the color combinations for Chrysler automobiles until 1945. The Dodgers became a winning team for a time under another coach, Dr. John B. (Jock) Sutherland, but went out of business in 1945.

Equipment may or may not be able to turn losers into winners, but it definitely performs a larger function: It protects players and prevents injuries. It is an obvious fact, however, that football players still get injured. That is why manufacturers keep devising better equipment and teams and leagues keep insisting that they do so.

The soccer game Princeton and Rutgers played in 1869, called the first college football game in America, involved no equipment at all other than the ball. The players merely "laid aside their hats, coats, and vests," according to Allison Danzig. "Neither team was in uniform, although some Rutgers players wore scarlet stocking-caps."

When Harvard played McGill University of Montreal in 1874, the Harvard players wore sweaters and handkerchiefs around their heads, and the McGill players wore white trousers, striped jerseys, and turbans, according to Rawlings Sporting Goods. Princeton or Yale in 1876 may have been the first to wear a complete uniform in its games. Football gradually became an overwhelmingly popular college sport. Its rules were still rather amorphous and the combatants played the Princeton wedge, shoving wedge, and flying wedge with great gusto. There were 18 deaths from playing football in 1905, according to Amos Alonzo Stagg. Public outcries about football violence almost brought about its extinction. It was saved when reforms were made in its rules in 1906, 1907, and 1909. There remained a great demand for enough equipment to supply all the teams playing football, and for quality equipment that would make the game safer.

A. G. Spalding & Company Sporting Goods was the first manufacturer of athletic equipment. Others sprang up rapidly and played an important role in the growth of the game of football. Spalding was notable not only as a manufacturer but as a publisher as well. It published the *Official Football Guide,* for college football, from 1895 until 1940, when it was taken over by the National Collegiate Athletic Association. The book was edited by Walter Camp each year until his death in 1925. Spalding also issued the *Official National Football League Guide* from 1935 until 1940, when it was taken over by the NFL. These pocket books were only part of *Spalding's Athletic Library* of record books and instructional manuals.

A man named Ed Thorp had a great influence on the sport. Thorp was the referee of the 1925 Rose Bowl game between the Notre Dame team that had the "Four Horsemen" in the backfield and the Stanford team that had Ernie Nevers at fullback. Thorp refereed other important games, became well known in college and pro football, and formed Thorp Sporting Goods. It is not clear how it happened, but the trademark for a football called "The Duke" was sold by Thorp to Wilson Sporting Goods and became the trademark on the official ball of the NFL. Wilson was the manufacturer but it was stamped "Thorp Sporting Goods," and elsewhere, "The Duke." After his death, sometime in the 1930s, the NFL began awarding the Ed Thorp Memorial Trophy to the winner of the title game, and it was called not the "NFL championship" but the "Ed Thorp Memorial Championship Game."

There was a time when it appeared that manufacturers of football equipment would become extinct, and equipment would become unnecessary. "The roughness of the game has been practically eliminated by the new rules," the 1909 *Spalding Guide* said. "Still, shin guards and shoulder pads are sometimes needed."

That report proved optimistic. Football players did not begin to wear fewer pads but in fact became covered with them. And the rules organizations for high school, college, and—after 1920—professional football went right on changing the game and writing strict rules about equipment.

The first major rules change the NFL made having to do with equipment was the seemingly long-overdue requirement in 1943 that players wear helmets; "head protectors" was the language used. Elmer Layden, commissioner of the NFL in 1941–46, believed genuinely that many of the players in the league had rather bad-looking legs and he considered it one of the momentous acts of his administration that he pushed through a rule in 1945 requiring them to wear long stockings.

Plastic helmets were banned in 1948 and permitted in 1949; they went on to become standard throughout the sport. It was all right to grab a face mask in 1956 provided it was the ball carrier's; the grabbing of any face mask was prohibited in 1962.

White footballs with black stripes were made illegal in 1956, in favor of a brown ball with white stripes. In 1972, the commissioner was made the judge of when teams could use a brown ball with white stripes for late-starting games. In 1976, they were outlawed altogether.

Beginning in 1970, the members of the league required themselves—not in their rules, but in their by-laws—to give the commissioner a year's notice before changing their uniform.

Injuries are a regrettable by-product of football. They have concerned football leagues and teams as long as the game has existed. In 1974, the NFL commissioned a study of injuries by the Stanford Research Institute in Menlo Park, California. It was actually the third such report prepared by that organization for the NFL. Its findings were exhaustive, covering every facet of football injuries. Among them: There were 1,169 injuries in the NFL in 1974; 1,044 in 1973; and 1,157 in 1972. There are more knee injuries than any other. A kickoff is the most dangerous play. Running back and cornerback are the most hazardous positions. Offensive players get more injuries than defensive players, but neither are injured as often as special teams players. And shoulder pads cause more injuries than helmets.

Teams understandably spare no expense to get the best equipment possible. The Los Angeles Rams said in 1982 they spend an estimated $90,000 a year on equipment. They own enough of it to completely outfit 100 football players, which they must do every year because that is the average number of players reporting at the start of training camp. When they take a trip, the Rams said, they load 4,000 pounds of equipment on the airplane; if they expect foul weather, more gear such as heavy parkas swells the load to 6,500 pounds. Thus, the equipment taken on on one road trip by an NFL team in the eighties probably equals the combined weight of all the players who took part in that famous game between Princeton and Rutgers back in 1869.

I. THE BALL

Dr. Glenn Seaborg, Nobel Prize winner and former chairman of the Atomic Energy Commission, was seen crossing the campus of the University of California carrying an official NFL football. Since he was not a member of Cal's football team, there had to be another reason why this eminent physicist was carrying a football across the campus. There was. He was on his way to teach the university's large freshman chemistry class, College Chemistry I, and was going to use a football to demonstrate the shape of the nucleus of the uranium atom—a prolate spheroid.

The unusual shape of a football, which Dr. Seaborg used to advantage, contributes immeasurably to the variety of the sport played with it and the fascination others have for it. Not being round, it bounces oddly. Being elliptical, it is aerodynamically superior to a round ball, so it passes better. It can be handed off and carried more easily than a round ball of the same size.

The word prolate is from the Latin *prolatus,* meaning stretched out. The polar axis of a prolate spheroid is longer than its equatorial diameter. Most of the sports balls in the world are round or oblate, not prolate. Of all the sports shown in a 1974 book, *Rules of the Game,* only four used prolate balls. They were rugby and American, Australian, and Canadian football.

Rugby began in England in 1823. Players could run with or lateral the ball as well as kick it; rugby balls became prolate. Soccer frowned on all that and remained a kicking game; soccer balls stayed round.

The game between Princeton and Rutgers in 1869

Peck & Snyder "Foot Ball Inflator," 1886.

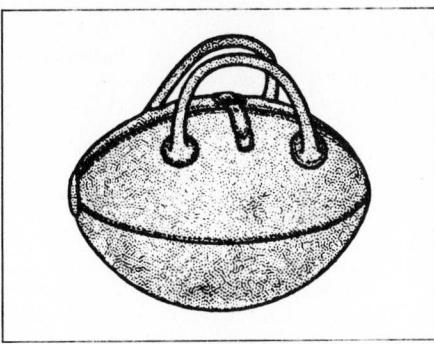

For team that has everything, "Football Carrier," 1925.

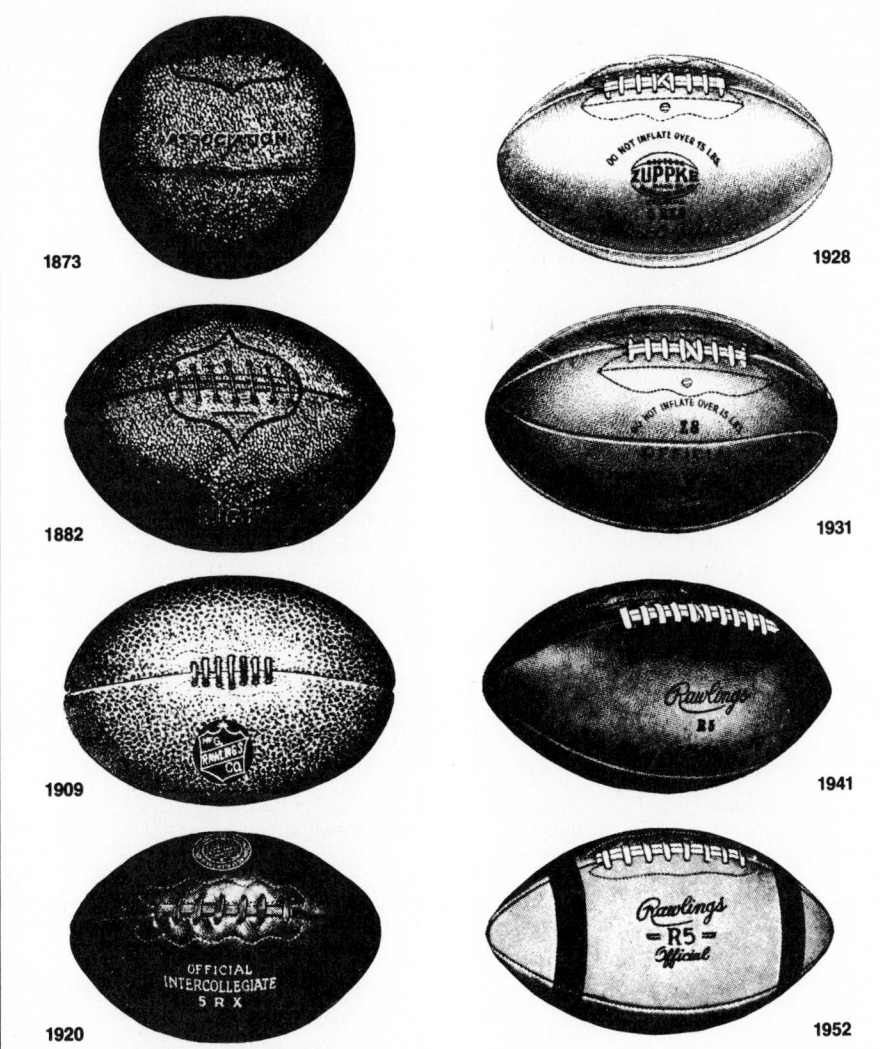

1873

1882

1909

1920

1928

1931

1941

1952

Footballs made by Rawlings Sporting Goods through the years.

The 1960s Wilson ball for the NFL, left, and Spalding's for the AFL.

was played with a round English soccer ball. Rugby gained the upper hand, however, when McGill University of Montreal put it on display in games against Harvard in 1874. Rugby football went on to become, simply, football. The hopes of the exponents of a round ball for the sport went flat, and prolate spheroids became the rule.

As its name implies, football was originally played only with the feet. Everything man had learned to do with his hands since the thumb became independent of the four fingers was left out of the game. Rugby brought the hands into play in 1823. The ball could be picked up and passed. Nearly another century went by, however, before it could be passed *forward*.

Traditions die hard. The rule permitting the forward pass in 1906 was virtually ignored until well-known teams—for example, the 1913 Notre Dame team with Gus Dorais at tailback and Knute Rockne at end—began using the forward pass. Changes in the ball's specifications were ordered. It became slimmer, lighter, and easier to pass. It changed dramatically; pumpkins, watermelons, and other fruits suffered in the public eye as writers used them for comparisons to describe what the football had been, in contrast to its new, sleek shape.

Five rules were made—all by college and not professional football—affecting the football's shape. Its weight was set at 14 to 15 ounces in 1912. Its long axis became 28″ to 28½″ the same year. Its short axis—around the middle—went from 22½″ to 23″ in 1912, to 22″ to 22½″ in 1929, to 21¼″ to 21½″ in 1934. Its length became 11 to 11¼″ in 1931. And the amount of air that can be pumped into it was set at 12½ to 13½ pounds in 1934.

Manufacturers met those specifications in varying degrees. The Pro Football Hall of Fame has on display a half-moon templet used before games in the early days of football. The ball was lowered into it to determine whether it had the proper shape and amount of inflation. A similar operation is performed before games today; the referee personally checks every football, 24 in all, to make sure each has 12½ to 13½ pounds of air pressure in it.

The rules changes affecting the shape of the football ended in 1934. That roughly coincided with the NFL's rules changes of 1933 and 1934, the first significant ones it ever made, creating inbounds lines or hashmarks to which the ball had to be returned for the start of a new play whenever it was carried near or over the sideline, and allowing forward passes from anywhere behind the line of scrimmage. The colleges had been responsible for slimming the football. The pros were responsible for removing puritanical strictures limiting the amount of passing in a game, and moving the ball nearer the center of the field, opening the way for rollout, bootleg, and sprint-out passing.

Footballs are not "pigskins." Yet that term persisted for years. Why? This explanation is usually offered: "The earliest footballs generally were inflated animal bladders, often those of pigs, which led to the term 'pigskin.'"

But do sports terms endure so long as that? Surely it has been centuries since any civilized person actually ripped the bladder from some poor slain hog—and it would have had to have been a large one to have a bladder big enough to become part of a game of football—and gone off kicking it around. Furthermore, a pig's skin and the membrane covering one of its internal organs, its bladder, are two different things; are we to believe the person who supposedly coined the phrase confused the two? A more likely explanation is that he was woefully uninformed, and his error was repeated by others who were equally uninformed, of the simple fact that footballs are made of steerhide.

Rubber gained a foothold in 1951. "There was wild rejoicing among the bovine population throughout

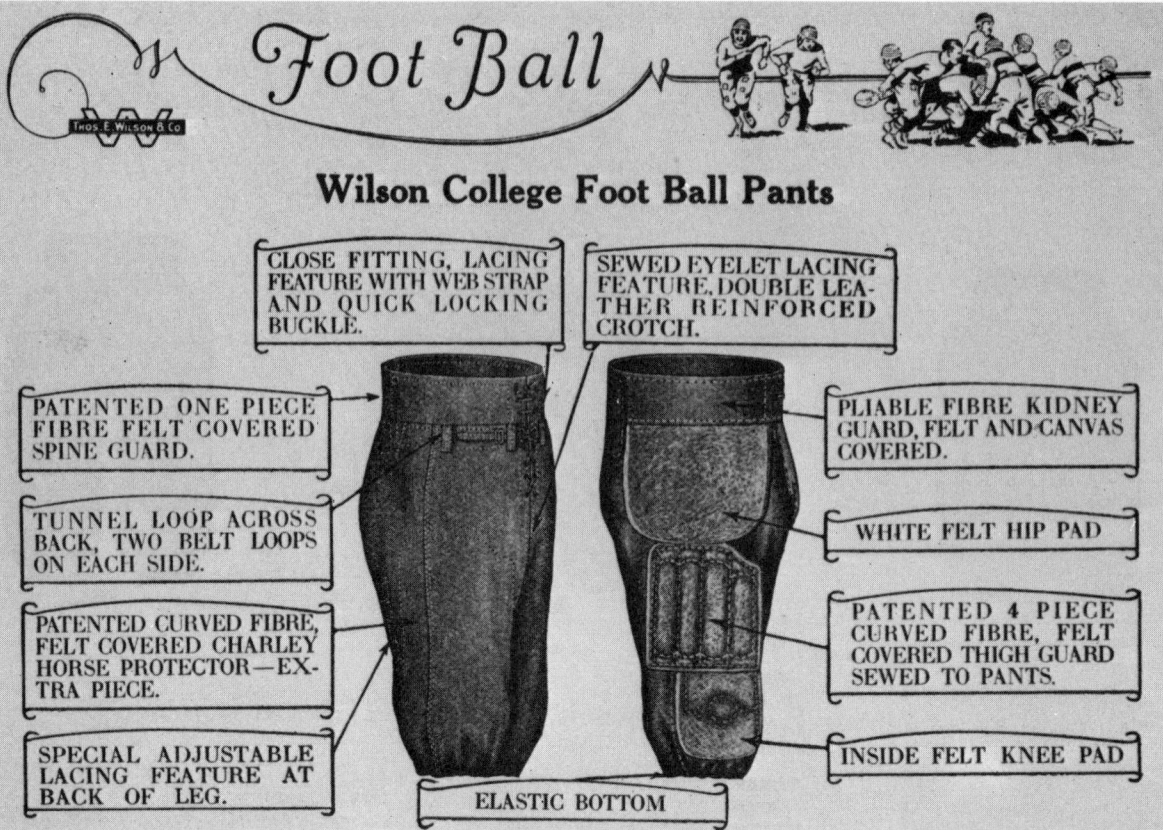

Foot Ball

Wilson College Foot Ball Pants

CLOSE FITTING, LACING FEATURE WITH WEB STRAP AND QUICK LOCKING BUCKLE.

SEWED EYELET LACING FEATURE. DOUBLE LEATHER REINFORCED CROTCH.

PATENTED ONE PIECE FIBRE FELT COVERED SPINE GUARD.

PLIABLE FIBRE KIDNEY GUARD, FELT AND CANVAS COVERED.

TUNNEL LOOP ACROSS BACK, TWO BELT LOOPS ON EACH SIDE.

WHITE FELT HIP PAD

PATENTED CURVED FIBRE, FELT COVERED CHARLEY HORSE PROTECTOR—EXTRA PIECE.

PATENTED 4 PIECE CURVED FIBRE, FELT COVERED THIGH GUARD SEWED TO PANTS.

SPECIAL ADJUSTABLE LACING FEATURE AT BACK OF LEG.

INSIDE FELT KNEE PAD

ELASTIC BOTTOM

B905. Wilson Football Pants made of khaki colored 8 oz. duck; double stitched, reinforced crotch; tunnel loops; flexible hip pad of heavy white felt; pliable fibre kidney guard protected by felt and covered with canvas; one piece fibre spine guard, patented curved fibre thigh guards and Charley Horse pad covered with white felt. Special adjustable lacing feature at back of leg. Inside white felt knee pad; elastic bottoms..............Per Pair, $10.00

There were even "Charley Horse pads" in these "College Foot Ball Pants" offered by Wilson Sporting Goods, 1925.

the land," *Pro Football Illustrated* wrote. The victory was short-lived. Steerhide remained the preferred material for quality footballs. Cowhide is second best. The next alternative is bullhide but it is never used; bulls escape the auctioneer's gavel and remain in the pasture to father new offspring.

The bladder in a football has nothing to do with pigs and it is made of rubber. Inflating it and keeping it inflated was a problem that plagued the sport for 50 years. The ball in the second game in 1869 between Rutgers and Princeton, according to Allison Danzig, kept losing its shape and "several times during the game play had to be stopped, and a little key was brought out from the sideline to unlock the small nozzle tucked into the ball. The players took turns blowing the ball up."

In 1886, the Peck & Snyder Sporting Goods catalog advertised a device resembling a syringe called "The New Patent Foot Ball Inflator." It was "far superior, in every respect, to the old style large brass pumps. With it the largest ball can be inflated to its fullest capacity in five minutes time while the old way took half an hour."

"It is not advisable to inflate Foot Balls with the breath, as the moisture that collects in them soon rots the bladder."

Stem valves that protruded from the ball and had to be tucked in during play gave way to metal valves such as those on automobile tires. They were considered unsafe and so rubber valves were developed for footballs. The final step in making an efficient ball was prelacing; it developed about 1920 and after that

the ball no longer had to unlaced to be inflated.

White footballs were used for a time, too. In 1956, the NFL okayed the use of white footballs in night games. For the next 20 years, there were "night footballs" with white stripes around each end. They were prohibited in 1976 because the paint made the balls slick. The rules continued to call for a ball that is "...a pebble grained, leather case of natural tan color."

The Spalding J5-V was the official NFL ball from 1920 until 1940, and it was used in the AFL between 1960 and 1969. Spalding named the ball "The Duke" apparently during the 1930s. "The Duke" was the boyhood nickname of Wellington Mara of the New York Giants. Thorp Sporting Goods began making a ball called "The Duke," and sold the registered name to Spalding. Wilson Sporting Goods took it over when it became the manufacturer of official NFL footballs in 1941. "The Duke" was retired in 1969 and Wilson's ball was renamed, simply, "NFL."

The leather Wilson uses comes primarily from the Horween Leather Company, which is owned and operated by Arnold Horween, Sr., who was the coach at Harvard University from 1926-30. He tans hides and sells them to Wilson. It uses only full grain steerhide, the full thickness of the hide, in NFL footballs. The four panels for the ball are cut in such a way that any blemishes on the hide are avoided. The panels are skived to a specified thickness and then weighed to make sure they meet specifications, and checked to make sure their appearance is uniform.

Linings for each panel and reinforcements for the

bladder opening and the valve ring are added. The panels are sewn together inside out. The ball is then turned through the lace opening using an iron post, in an operation that requires strength and dexterity. The bladder is inserted and the ball is laced. It is inflated to 80 pounds, 65 above the required amount of pressure, so it can be examined for appearance, stitching, and shape. If it meets every requirement, it is stamped "NFL," deflated, and delivered. It is then used in an NFL game—preseason, regular season, and postseason. It becomes the object of all the blocking and tackling, blitzing and red dogs, bombs and bump-and-runs, the only truly essential piece of equipment in the game.

II. PANTS AND JERSEYS

The first football pants and jerseys, in the 1870s, were made of canvas. They were knee-length togs or breeches and long- or short-sleeved jackets that laced in the front. Canvas is sturdy and durable; it is good for making tents. After a long, hot game in which the players had perspired freely, football uniforms made of canvas must not have needed folding; they probably would have stood up by themselves.

Moleskin, "a heavy-napped cotton twill fabric," replaced canvas in football pants. The tolerance for canvas jerseys must have waned, too; in the 1890s, according to a Rawlings Sporting Goods publication, "No player was seen without his turtle neck sweater."

The most significant thing that happened to pants and jerseys, however, was that they were sewn together to make one unit, an all-purpose football-playing suit of canvas, moleskin, or leather into which a player gradually inserted himself, laced it up all around, and went out to scrimmage. The Smock football suit, the varsity union suit, and "Whitley's Football Armor" were examples of this medieval contraption. It became a museum piece about the turn of the century, and pants and jerseys went back to being worn separately.

The wedge play and the flying tackle were the rule in football. It was a furious sport and manufacturers took steps to make equipment safer. New types of pads appeared to protect the knees, thighs, hips, kidneys, and ribs. The best way to hold them in place, it seemed, was to lace them to or hang them from the player's pants. Experiments began to find the right way to connect pads and pants, and went on for the next 25 years.

Strips of cane sewn into the lining for thigh pads appeared in the advertisements in the *Spalding Guide* in 1906; these hard strips must have been a bell-ringer for a head-on tackler. The next step was laces around each leg, permitting the thigh pads to be raised and lowered. Tunnel belt-loops and a reinforced crotch arrived. There was a period of time in which manufacturers came to see the pants as merely a "shell" on which all manner of pads were to be hung. In 1915, Spalding offered a "complete padded harness with heavy felt hip pad connected with wide elastic belt at back, fiber thigh guards laced in special canvas and webbing reinforced pockets all securely mounted on simple but strong skeleton pants form." It must have taken a long time to dress for football in those days.

At last, a simpler pair of pants emerged. They had pockets on the inside for the player to insert his thigh and knee pads; all other pads were strapped on independent of the pants.

Beginning with canvas, moleskin, and leather, a great variety of fabrics have been used in football pants. Khaki cloth or drill, fustian cloth, and duck-cloth were first used about 1910. According to Rawling Sporting Goods, "Duck became the primary pants material for over 30 years."

Spalding's "Intercollegiate" pants in 1931 were made of Army duck. But in 1933 its "College Speed Pants," the top of the Spalding line, were made of "Skookum Cloth, the strongest, lighest fabric suitable for football pants."

There was, however, a family of new synthetic fibers that would make Skookum Cloth, whatever it may have been, obsolete for football pants. Knits first appeared in 1934, according to Rawling Sporting Goods. "The first all-knit shell was introduced in 1936 and the first half-fabric, half-knit model made its bow in 1937. Many different combinations of knit materials have been developed through the years, with the latest knit incorporating the highly-popular Spandex, a stretch polyurethane material."

Spandex was the principal fiber in the most expensive model pants displayed in the catalogs of Rawlings and two other major manufacturers. It actually is the general term for all fibers that resemble rubber in that they have a high extensibility and highly retractive forces that derive from their chemical nature, according to chemist R. W. Moncrieff. Its special properties make it very good for football pants and a far cry from the canvas, moleskin, and leather of the 1900s.

One final characteristic of football pants remains to be explored. A coach talks about it often with his players, especially when they're going up against a really tough opponent. It appears they don't have a prayer. But, as the coach points out, trying to encourage them, "The other team puts its pants on one leg at a time."

Jerseys have a somewhat more limited history. Canvas was the first fabric used in them; before the

A canvas football jacket, 1886.

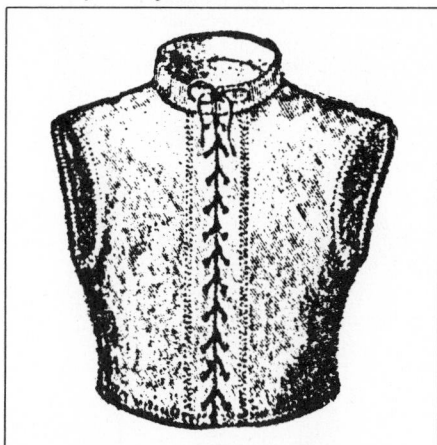
Sleeveless vest of a "canvasback," 1906.

Jersey with "grip-sure cloth," 1928.

Full-block lettering, left, and "NCAA."

turn of the century, players were sometimes called "canvasbacks" because of the sleeveless canvas vests they wore over their turtlenecks.

The first real football jerseys were made of cotton and wool and those fabrics prevailed for 40 years, until the arrival of synthetics in jerseys in about 1950. They were, according to Rawlings Sporting Goods, rayon-durene, nylon-durene, rayon-cotton, and nylon-cotton. Nylon-mesh jerseys arrived and were even lighter and more comfortable that the rest; even the NFL teams in the coolest climates favored them, wearing them on cold days over thermal underwear.

Among the innovations in jerseys that did not succeed were Rawlings's 1928-29 model, which featured "grip-sure cloth, sewn to the jersey front to aid in holding onto the ball," and "tear-away jerseys," which allowed a runner to rip free from the grasp of a tackler holding onto his shirt, but which threatened to bankrupt the teams that used them as they struggled to keep their running backs in jerseys game after game.

Decorations on jerseys go back at least as far as 1876, when each Princeton player wore a "P" on his sweater in a game against Pennsylvania. Either Amos Alonzo Stagg or Glenn (Pop) Warner invented jersey numbers about 1905. Manufacturers arrayed the numbers and stripes on jerseys on a great variety that knew little restraint. The Canton Bulldogs of 1921 wore horizontal stripes around their middles, which only accentuated the considerable girth of their star tackle, Fats Henry. The St. Louis Gunners of 1934 wore jerseys with a cannon superimposed on a patriotic shield. They left history a photograph of one of their players wearing this creation; the player was Homer Reynolds, "The Human Cannon." His uniform and those of countless other football players over the last 100 years have at times reflected the willingness of manufacturers to offer any fashion or style, no matter how unorthodox and even silly, as long as there were coaches who would buy them.

Football pants and jerseys are the largest parts of the uniform; they cover the player from his knees to his neck. They are very important to the game and sometimes they can be a very personal thing, as they were for star tackle George Christiansen of the 1932 Portsmouth Spartans. As the local newspaper reported, "The Spartans were stumped about an easy way to inform Chris that his last year's pants had seen plenty service and would not harmonize with the new ones the team will use. Before anyone could say a word, Chris began bemoaning the fact that he lost his pants and would have to buy a new pair. 'What a break!' his buddies chorused gleefully."

III. THE HELMET

Jerseys and pants identify players. Helmets and pads protect them. The one event that more than any other was responsible for making these articles of protection necessary took place in 1888. The annual rules convention for the emerging sport of college football passed a rule permitting tackling below the waist. Football changed dramatically. Teams no longer arrayed themselves across the entire breadth of the field (such "spread" formations a half-century later would be termed radical breakthroughs in strategy, and coaches who used them great innovators). Teams bunched themselves around the runner to block for him. The wedge and "mass play" arrived. Football became, for a time, a savage sport full of fights, brawling, even fatalities.

Grudgingly, football players accepted the wearing of protective equipment. Step-by-step, courageous figures whose names are lost to history braved being called sissies to wear pads of various types that in just a few years would be considered essential.

The article they accepted last of all was the helmet.

The banal head harnesses and then the leather helmets that emerged were always disdained by a macho few. Even Glenn (Pop) Warner, the famous coach, counseled his Carlisle players against them in 1912. "Playing without helmets gives players more confidence, saves their heads from many hard jolts, and keeps their ears from becoming torn or sore," he said. "I do not encourage their use. . . I have never seen an accident to the head which was serious, but I have many times seen cases when hard bumps on the head so dazed the player receiving them that he lost his memory for a time and had to be removed from the game."

Gerald Ford, who later became President of the United States, played center for the University of Michigan in 1932-34 without a helmet. It was not a required article of equipment in college football until 1939.

The National Football League did not require the wearing of helmets until 1943, although the great majority of professional players had long since taken to wearing them. Through the imperfect method of examining all the available photographs, it has been determined that the last NFL player to play in a game without a helmet was probably end Dick Plasman of the Chicago Bears in 1940. There is a photo of him without one, taken during the 1940 championship game in which Chicago crushed the Washington Redskins 73-0.

End Bill Hewitt of the Bears and Philadelphia Eagles was another player who took the field without anything covering his head, and he was eventually elected to the Hall of Fame, making him far better known than Plasman. Hewitt, however, retired in 1939. He came back for one season during World War II, 1943, but by then the rules required him to put on a helmet.

Ivy League teams played in the first games, wrote the first rules, and formed the first college football association. In 1889, Princeton players adopted the practice of growing their hair long to protect themselves against head injuries. According to researcher Paul Quam, "this fad swept the country, and football players with their unsightly mops of hair became the delight of cartoonists."

Yale's powerful team, led by Camp, took up the practice. Their flowing locks became their trademark for a time, and they dominated their rivals. "Interlopers invited to play in the sacrosanct New Haven precincts were supposed to succumb with grace and speed to the horrendous longhairs who wore the Blue," wrote Stanley Woodward.

Wearing long hair while playing football went out of fashion, according to Quam, "when a championship Yale team appeared with close-cropped heads in 1895." (The crew-cut became *de rigueur* and remained in fashion for nearly 70 years.) The next phase in the development of the helmet began with the appearance of the head harness. Its name had a little of the livery stable in it, and that is not surprising since the age of the automobile in America was just beginning.

Quam found a reference to a head harness being used in 1893. In *Gang Way for Navy* in 1951, Admiral Joseph Mason Reeves explained how he had invented a football headgear and wore it for the first time in the 1893 Army game. The young cadet had had it made, he said, "after a Navy doctor warned him that another kick in the head most likely would mean insanity."

A somewhat less colorful claim is made for halfback George Barclay of Lafayette College in 1896. He "designed a headgear which had three thick leather straps forming a tight fit around his head, and had it made by a harness maker. It was only logical that it became known as a head harness."

Contraptions made of an assortment of straps and pads turned into leather caps. They acquired ear flaps and then the flaps acquired ear holes, which must have improved communication greatly. There is no way these things could have provided anything more than rudimentary protection to the portion of the football-playing population (the percentage of which is uncertain) that wore them.

"Nose protectors" were an interesting by-product of the head harness era. Edgar Allen Poe was one of six sons of a nephew of the famous poet who played football for Princeton. He used a nose guard against Yale in 1890. Other players started using it. A hard leather proboscis hung from a strap around the forehead, fit over the nose, and had an extension at the bottom that the wearer clenched in his teeth to hold the device in place. They interfered with good vision and that even more important requisite of a person going through strenuous activity—the ability to breathe easily. "No player should wear a nose protector unless he has a sore nose," said Pop Warner in 1912. One of the oddest creations in the history of football equipment soon went out of style.

The head harness began to take the shape and appearance we would recognize today as a football

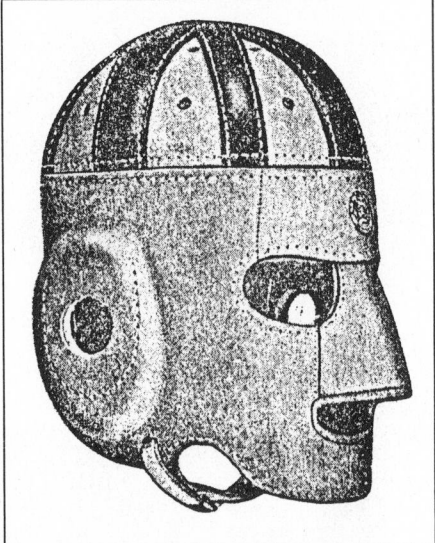

A "nose protector helmet," 1931.

helmet. That became its name, instead of "head harness." But it still had a serious deficiency. As long as it sat right down on the skull, it was only pretending to protect the wearer. Then suspension appeared, probably in 1917, to cradle the skull away from the leather shell. Straps of fabric formed a pattern inside the helmet. They absorbed and distributed the impact better, and they allowed for ventilation. It was a tremendous breakthrough in helmet-making. Rawlings introduced the Zuppke helmet, designed by the Illinois coach, and Spalding introduced the first of what would become a well-known line, its "ZH" helmets, in 1925.

An innovation 14 years later, however, dwarfed all that had gone before. Gerry E. Morgan and other employees of the John T. Riddell Company in Chicago, manufacturers of sporting goods, invented and patented a plastic football helmet in 1939. It was a single molded shell. It was a stronger, more durable, and lighter than leather helmets, and it wouldn't rot or mildew the way they did if it became damp. It had a revolutionary web suspension inside it.

In 1940, Riddell devised the first chinstrap worn on the chin and not the Adam's apple, and the first plastic face mask.

A Concise Guide to Plastics defines them as materials "that contain as an essential ingredient an organic substance or large molecular weight, is solid in its finished state, and at some stage in its manufacture or in its processing into finished articles, can be shaped by flow." Most plastics are synthetic. They are derived from petroleum, coal, salt, air, and water. They are light in weight, "but for their weight they are prodigiously strong." Thermoplastics are one type; the name means they are remeltable. Among the 15 or more types of thermoplastics are acrylonitrile-butadiene-styrene (ABS) and polycarbonate. Their features are "excellent toughness" and "high impact strength." They are the plastics used in football helmets.

From 1939 through 1940, Chicago was a sports hotbed and a sports laboratory. The All-Star Game, which was founded by *Chicago Tribune* sports editor Arch Ward, was drawing crowds of 80,000 or more annually. Clark Shaughnessy was advising the Chicago Bears' coaches and they were creating the blocking and ball-handling wizardry and original play-calling language of their T-formation with man-in-motion, which would alter the course of football.

Riddell made its plastic helmets and they were worn for the first time in a game by some of the players on the College All-Star team of 1939. The company also had another first. Founder John T. Riddell, Sr. and owner-coach George Halas of the Bears devised low-cut football shoes and the 1940 Bears became the first team ever to wear such shoes. National attention was focused on the Bears when they smashed the Washington Redskins 73-0 in the NFL Championship Game.

Riddell's plastic helmet emerged in such an atmosphere. It was "a little flat on top" at first but it gradually changed to its characteristic teardrop shape, which allowed the impact of a blow to slide to one side or the other rather than be met head-on. Its web suspension could be raised or lowered to fit the head of whatever person pulled it on proudly, expanding the frontiers of football science.

The eve of a world war, however, is not the best time to come up with a new sports invention. Football is not exactly an essential industry and Riddell could not get plastic. The full-fledged assault on the leather helmet would have to wait until the war ended.

That does not mean Riddell did not turn a profit immediately as a result of its invention. It did. Inventing the plastic helmet at the start of World War II proved one of the master strokes of timing in the history of American business. The army had a problem in that it was impractical to manufacture steel helmets in sizes, it was both too expensive and impractical. The army purchased Riddell's patent rights and ordered the manufacturing of millions of M-1 helmet liners in sizes, to be worn by soldiers under what they called their "steel pots." G.I.s at Corregidor, Anzio, and Omaha Beach went into battle wearing on their heads the practical wartime application of an invention created for the sport of football.

Military use of first the plastic and later the fiberglass helmet expanded with the arrival of jet airplanes, and the extra protection required in high-speed escape, after World War II. Pilots of fighters, bombers, and helicopters adopted such helmets. Civilian use of them was made by cyclists, race drivers, and speedboat racers.

The fact that the United States Military Academy football team of 1944 became the first to ever wear plastic helmets may have resulted from the army being privy to Riddell's research, or it may have been because Army was coached by a bright, innovative, and far-thinking man, Earl (Red) Blaik. He won national collegiate championship in 1944, and